The PLANT FINDER

Devised & Compiled by Chris Philip

Edited by Tony Lord

Produced by:
Headmain Ltd for the Hardy Plant Society

British Library Cataloguing in Publication Data.

Philip, Chris *1928-*
The Plant Finder. - 5th. ed.
1. Great Britain. Gardens. Hardy plants
I. Title II. Lord, Tony *1949-*
635.9

ISBN 0-9512161-3-9
ISSN 0961-2599

First edition April 1987
Second edition April 1988
Reprinted August 1988
Third edition April 1989
Reprinted September 1989
Fourth edition April 1990
Fifth edition April 1991

Produced and Computer typeset by:
Headmain Ltd.
Lakeside
Whitbourne
Worcs. WR6 5RD

Agents for the book trade:
Moorlands Publishing Co Ltd.
Moor Farm Road West
Airfield Estate
Ashbourne DE6 1HD

Maps by:
à la carte
13 Lloyd Street
Llandudno
Gwynedd LL30 2UU

Printed by:
Benham & Co.
Sheepen Place
Colchester
Essex CO3 3LH

Cover:
Meconopsis x *sheldonii* 'Branklyn'
Marijke Heuff - *The Garden Picture Library*

TABLE OF CONTENTS

SYMBOLS AND ABBREVIATIONS

PLANT DIRECTORY

*	Name not validated. Not listed in the appropriate International Registration Authority checklist nor in works cited in the Bibliography. For fuller discussion see NOMENCLATURE chapter.
¶	New plant entry in this year's Edition, (or reinstated from list of previously deleted plants)
®	Registered Trade Mark or Selling name
♦	New or amended synonym or cross-reference included for the first time this year
§	Plant listed elsewhere in the PLANT DIRECTORY under a synonym
†	A National Council for the Conservation of Plants and Gardens (NCCPG) Collection exists for all or part of this GENUS.
C	Culinary (for Fruit)
cv(s)	Cultivar(s)
D	Dessert (for Fruit)
d	Double flowered
g	Grex
gr.	Group
(g.&cl.)	Grex and Clone (Rhododendron)
I	Invalid name. See International Code of Nomenclature for Cultivated Plants 1980. For fuller discussion see NOMENCLATURE chapter.
F	Fruit
N	Refer to NOMENCLATURE NOTES on page 17
S	Shrubby
sp.	Species

NURSERY INDEX

SO	Export of Seed only
BO	Export of Bulbs only

For **COLLECTOR'S REFERENCES** see page 30

For abbreviations relating to individual genera see
CLASSIFICATION OF GENERA page 25

IMPORTANT NOTE TO USERS

This, the Fifth Edition of **THE PLANT FINDER**, contains over 50,000 plant names and details of the nurseries which list them. The Directory is not necessarily compiled from individual catalogues but sometimes from lists specially prepared for us by the nurseries. As a result there may be some differences between our listing and that of a nursery's current catalogue.

No nursery, by the very nature of its business, will be able to provide everything in its list at all times. This is, of course, particularly true of plants which are rare, seldom asked for, or difficult to propagate. To avoid disappointment, we suggest that you always:

CHECK WITH THE NURSERY BEFORE VISITING OR ORDERING

THE PLANT FINDER exists to put gardeners in touch with nurserymen. It does *not* offer value judgements on the nurseries or the plants it lists nor intend any reflection on any other nursery or plant not listed.

In addition, **THE PLANT FINDER** tries to cross-reference plant names as used by nurseries to their correct *valid* name, although in some cases it is all too easy to understand why British nurserymen have preferred a more immediately comprehensible one!

It is, clearly, the nursery's responsibility to ensure that its stock is accurately named both in its catalogue and on the plant when it is sold. *Caveat Emptor*.

The Compiler and Editor of **THE PLANT FINDER** have taken every care, in the time available, to check all the information supplied to them by the nurseries concerned. Nevertheless, in a work of this kind, containing as it does, almost half-a-million separate computer encodings, errors and omissions will, inevitably, occur. Neither The Hardy Plant Society nor the Compiler or Editor can accept responsibility for any consequences that may arise from such errors.

If you find mistakes in **THE PLANT FINDER** we hope that you will firstly, forgive the Compiler and secondly, let him know so that the matter can be corrected in the next edition.

INTRODUCTION - 1991/92 EDITION

We have made a number of changes and improvements to **THE PLANT FINDER** since the last Edition which are detailed below.

Seed Suppliers

The main addition this year is that of a Directory of **SEED** suppliers, many of whom can also supply vegetables and Seed Potatoes. As a result of this addition the only plants that are not now covered in the Plant Directory are Cacti & Orchids.

Plant nomenclature changes

Major changes have occurred since the last edition to the following genera:- Cotoneaster, Gaultheria/Pernettya, Lobelia/Pratia, Lavandula, shrubby Potentilla and Bamboos. References to these changes can be found in the appropriate section of the Bibliography. (Page 652).

Sorting order of subspecies and cultivars

Although it is botanically correct to sort cultivars after subspecies, it can become very difficult to find an individual item for those species that have a large number of both subspecies and cultivars. We have therefore arranged this year to sort all subspecies and cultivars in one alphabetical order and not two as previously.

Reversed order of listing of species and cultivars

In order to help users locate plants within a large Genus where they might be unsure of the species to which a cultivar belongs, we have reversed the names so that the cultivar is listed first and the species follows in brackets e.g. CAMELLIA 'Debbie' (x *williamsii*). This approach has also been adopted for ASTILBE, HOSTA, SAXIFRAGA and VITIS.

ICBN recommendations

From time to time the International Committee on Botanical Nomenclature publish 'Recommendations' concerning the way that plants should be named or alterations effected. Because they are not 'Mandatory' this can cause conflict between those who follow these recommendations and those who would prefer not to make a change. Some, of course, will sit on the fence and do a bit of both! For example, some Cultivar Registrars have retained the abbreviation of 'Doctor' to 'Dr' or 'Saint' to 'St' and other have not.

Cultivar names

One of the problems frequently encountered is that of the nursery which, seeing a plant, described in another catalogue as apparently being identical to one in their own, nevertheless finds it has been given a different name and possibly the claim that it is a 'New Introduction'.

It appears that, at present, there is no easy solution to this problem which, inevitably, means that there are similar, or even identical, cultivars in circulation with differing names.

If the Genus in question has its own International Registration Authority, the person or organisation breeding a new cultivar should contact the appropriate IRA and register the name that they propose for their new introduction. It is then the Registrar's duty to check his Register to ensure that the name has not previously been used and is legal so far as the rules of the ICBN are concerned. It is *not* his duty to test the distinctness or value of the plant submitted for registration. Some IRA's do attempt to assist in this particular matter but, without examining flowering specimens side-by-side, this is not really practicable.

The matter is complicated by what is meant by distinctness. What, to many gardeners, may appear to be no more than the variations in habit and colour that they normally experience in the cultivation of a plant, might nevertheless appear to the expert to be distinctive differences meriting a new name.

The possibility of further duplication may also arise because the ICBN Code permits one or more legitimate 'Commercial Synonyms' which may be used instead of the plant's correct name if, for instance, the original name is 'unacceptable' in a particular country. A good example is Penstemon 'Garnet'. Its original name of 'Andenken an Friedrich Hahn' would prove less than commercially viable outside Germany!

There are several genera in which differently named cultivars might well appear to be identical when viewed side-by-side. For example, these include some of the Argyranthemum and Penstemons. Would-be purchasers should therefore satisfy themselves, either by examination of flowering specimens, or by a catalogue description, that they are distinctly different.

For a fuller discussion of this matter see Dr Alan Leslie's article in *The Garden* for May 1990.

New cross-references

Major new cross-references and synonyms have been marked with a ♦. This sign has only been used when the genus, species or cultivar name has been altered, but not where there have been merely minor typographic or orthographic changes.

New nursery entries

Nurseries that are appearing in **THE PLANT FINDER**, for the first time are printed in **bold type** in the Nursery-Code Index starting on page 553.

Deleted plants

The DELETED INDEX contains some 5000 plant names that were listed in one of the previous editions of **THE PLANT FINDER**, but which are now no longer represented. As a result there are a few instances where a Genus exists in the main Plant Index but with no apparent entries for either species or cultivars. These will be found in the DELETED INDEX. It is also possible that some of the cross-references may not apparently refer to an entry in the main Directory. Again this is because the plant in question had a supplier or suppliers but is now in the DELETED INDEX. These references are deliberately kept in order to provide an historic record of synonyms and plant availability.

Great care should be taken in making any judgement concerning these deletions. They arise, not only because the nursery that supplied the plants may have gone out of business, but also because a few nurseries who were included previously have not responded to our latest questionnaire and have thus had to be deleted. This particularly applies to several Fuchsia, Dahlia and Chrysanthemum (Dendranthema) nurseries, thus resulting in a large number of these cultivars no longer appearing in the Directory. Such plants may well be still available but we have no current knowledge of their whereabouts. Furthermore, some items may have been misnamed by nurseries in previous editions, but now appear under their correct name.

New plant entries

Plants that are new to this Edition (or were listed in previous Editions as having been deleted) have been marked with a ¶.

International Plant Finders

Since the first Edition of **THE PLANT FINDER** was published in 1987 there have been a number of other similar directories published in Canada, Germany and the United States, as well as an international on-line computer database of plant availability, primarily designed to help American amenity organisations and landscape architects. Details of these other reference sources have been added to the Bibliography at the end of this volume, page 652. We would be very pleased to hear of any other similar publications.

'Widely available' plants

In order to prevent **THE PLANT FINDER** becoming too large the number of nurseries offering commonly available plants has been restricted to 25. There are about 1000 such plants which are therefore entered as 'Widely available' and, in general, these plants can easily be obtained from local nurseries or Garden Centres. However, if any readers have difficulty in finding such plants, we will be pleased to send them a full list of all the nurseries that we have listed and this could include anything from 26 to a maximum of 50. Please write to:

THE PLANT FINDER, Lakeside, Whitbourne, Worcester WR6 5RD

All such enquiries **MUST** included the full name of the plant being sought, as shown in **THE PLANT FINDER**, together with a STAMPED ADDRESSED ENVELOPE.

HOW TO USE THE DIRECTORY

1. Look up the Plant you require in the alphabetical PLANT DIRECTORY. Against each plant you will find a four-letter Code, or Codes, for example 'CBre SHil', each code representing one nursery offering that plant. The first letter of each Code indicates the main area of the country in which the nursery is situated like this:

   C = South West England

   Avon, Devon, Dorset, Channel Isles, Cornwall, Isles of Scilly, Somerset & Wiltshire.

   E = Eastern England

   Cambridge, Essex, Lincoln, Norfolk & Suffolk.

   G = Scotland

   Borders, Central, Dumfries & Galloway, Fife, Grampian, Highlands, Inverness, Strathclyde.

   I = Northern Ireland & Eire.

   L = London area

   Bedford, Berkshire, Buckinghamshire, Hertfordshire, London, Middlesex, Surrey.

   M = Midlands

   Cheshire, Derbyshire, Greater Manchester, Isle of Man, Leicestershire, Northamptonshire, Nottinghamshire, Oxfordshire, Staffordshire, Warwickshire, West Midlands.

   N = Northern England

   Cleveland, Cumbria, Durham, East Yorkshire, Humberside, Lancashire, Merseyside, Northumberland, North Yorkshire, South Yorkshire, Tyne & Wear, West Yorkshire.

   S = Southern England

   East Sussex, Hampshire, Isle of Wight, Kent, West Sussex.

   W = Wales & Western England

   Dyfed, Clywd, Glamorganshire, Gloucestershire, Gwent, Gwynedd, Herefordshire & Worcestershire, Powys, Shropshire.

2. Turn to the CODE-NURSERY INDEX on page 559 where, in alphabetical order of CODES, you will find details of each nursery which offers the plant in question. If you wish to visit any of these nurseries you can find its *approximate* location on one of the maps at the back. Those few nurseries which sell ONLY by Mail Order are not shown on the maps. Always check that the nursery you select has the plant in stock before you set out.

3. If more than 25 nurseries offer any plant the Directory gives no Code and the plant is listed as 'Widely available'. This has been done to prevent **THE PLANT FINDER** becoming too bulky. In this Edition there are just over 1000 plants listed as 'Widely available' and you should have little difficulty in finding these in local nurseries or Garden Centres. We can however provide a list of nurseries that we have recorded as having these 'Widely available' plants; for details see page 7.

4. For convenience, a reverse NURSERY-CODE INDEX is also included on page 553. This gives the NAMES of the nurseries listed in the PLANT DIRECTORY in alphabetical order together with their relevant Codes.

5. There is also an ADDITIONAL NURSERY INDEX, on page 610, containing brief details of other nurseries that have not been included in the PLANT DIRECTORY. They may be listed in this Index for a number of reasons, for example, their stock is small and changes too quickly for them to be able to issue a viable catalogue, or the major part of their stock would have to be listed as 'Widely available', or simply because their latest Catalogue was not received in time for inclusion. Again, their catalogues may either give mainly English names, (and this particularly applies to Herb nurseries) or Latin names which do not provide sufficient information to establish easily the genus or species of the plant concerned.

If you cannot immediately find the plant you seek in the PLANT DIRECTORY, look through the various species of the genus. You may be using an incomplete name. The problem is most likely to arise in very large genera such as PHLOX where there are a number of possible Species, each with a large number of cultivars. A search through the whole genus may well bring success.

If the plant you seek is not listed in the PLANT DIRECTORY, it is possible that a nursery in the ADDITIONAL NURSERY INDEX which specialises in similar plants may be able to offer it.

In addition to the plants listed in their catalogues, many nurseries are often able to supply other plants of the same general type that they specialise in. They may not list them if they only have a few available. In some cases they can arrange to propagate special items from their stock plants.

INTRODUCTION

The 1991/92 Edition of **THE PLANT FINDER** is, with over 50,000 plant listings more than double the size of the First Edition. **THE PLANT FINDER** now includes every type of plant with the exception of Cacti and Orchids.

It lists over 3,200 synonyms that have been used recently in nursery catalogues, but it is very encouraging to discover that some nurseries have brought their lists up-to-date. Many more, however, still cling to old names that are obsolete, obsolescent or, worse still, figments of their imagination. There are far too many plants on sale under confusing and inaccurate names. Although we shall continue to check and, where necessary, cross-reference every inaccuracy we find, the task is enormous and we do not pretend to have corrected every name or eliminated every duplication. For further details and an explanation of some of the problems involved with particular Genera please read the section on NOMENCLATURE (page 14) and NOMENCLATURE NOTES on page 17.

Some nurseries have only made a few additions and deletions to their latest Catalogues; some have entirely revised them, so users should not rely on previous editions of **THE PLANT FINDER**.

Wholesalers.

Those who are known to have a retail outlet have been included but, as they do not always publish a catalogue they have been listed in the Additional Nursery Index. Those who ONLY have a wholesale business have not been included.

Garden Centres.

A large number of these do not publish a regular catalogue and many of their plants may be bought in. There are, however, some that do propagate a lot of their own material and can sometimes offer uncommon items. A few of these have been included but we would like to hear from others who feel that they can offer an unusual or a specialised range of plants.

The general exclusion of Garden Centres has created a slightly anomalous situation as regards very common plants some of which only appear in **THE PLANT FINDER** to have a few suppliers. The reason is that these items are normally only propagated in large quantities by Wholesale Nurseries and then 'bought-in' by Garden Centres. They are, therefore, by definition, 'widely available'.

National Couuncil for the Conservation of Plants & Gardens

Over 450 Genera have National Collections devoted to all or part of them, supervised by the NCCPG. These Genera are marked with a † and full details are given in the *National Plant Collection Directory 1991* obtainable for £2.00 (incl. p&p) from the General Secretary:

R A W Lowe
The Pines
c/o Wisley Gardens
Woking,
Surrey GU23 6QB .

Suggested new introductions

The enterprising nurseryman could use **THE PLANT FINDER** and the list of 'Deleted Plants' to determine which marketable plants are not readily available. A great many first-rate plants are offered by only one or two nurseries and many more seem not to be available from any British nursery known to us.

The following is a random selection of plants which surely deserve to be more widely grown.

Acanthus 'Lady Moore'
Aconitum cvs. eg 'Gletschereis'
Agapanthus cvs. eg 'Loch Hope', 'Alice Gloucester'
Agapanthus inapertus forms
Alternanthera cvs.
Anemonella thalictroides 'Arnold Schoaf'
Angelica atropurpurea & *A. triquinata*

Astilbe rivularis
Berberis 'Cheal's Scarlet'
Callisia spp.
Catalpa x *Chiliopsis*
Ceanothus x *delileanus* 'Gloire des Plantières'
Ceanothus x *delileanus* 'Charles Détriché'
Cheiranthus 'Miss Massey'
Chrysopsis mariana, C. villosa & C. v. 'Golden Sunshine'
Clerodenron philippinum
Coccoloba spp.
Cortaderia selloana 'Monstrosa'
Crataegus azarolus
Dianthus Malmaison carnations
Dombeya spp.
Echinops ritro ruthenicus
Erythrina x *bidwillii*
Gerbera cvs. Gladiolus Professor Barnard's hybrids
Gymnocladus dioica 'Variegata'
Hepatica double cvs.
Hibiscus acetosella
Iberis semperflorens
Iresine cvs.
Ixora cvs.
Lithospermum canescens & L. carolinense
Lonicera acuminata
Lupinus ornatus
Megacarpaea polyandra
Nepeta 'Blauknirps'
Nerine cvs
Paeonia suffruticosa 'Joseph Rock'
Pamianthe peruviana
Papaver orientale 'May Queen'
Philadelphus ' 'Norma, 'Voie Lactée'
Phlox paniculata 'Antoine Mercier' &'Sepιemberschnee'
Prunus x *blireana* 'Moseri'
Pyrus 'Barland' (Perry)
Ranunculus aconitifolius 'Luteus Plenus'
Ranunculus 'Essex'
Rosa 'Madge'
Rubus biflorus
Ruta graveolens 'Blue Beauty' & *R. g.* 'Blue Mound'
Salvia 'Purple Majesty'
Saxifraga fortunei 'Windsor'
Scabiosa caucasica 'Goldingensis'
Symphytum officinale 'Variegatum'
Syringa vulgaris 'Lavaliensis' & 'Angel White'
Thalictrum aquilegiifolium 'White Cloud'
Tulipa Old English florists cultivars
Wisteria sinensis 'Showa-beni'

THE PLANT FINDER makes commercially viable the plantsman's plants by bringing them to the attention of a wide gardening public. It is hoped that nurseries will cultivate many more rare plants, not just those listed above but, for instance, those which appear in the NCCPG 'Pink Sheets' of endangered plants. This is the most certain way of ensuring the survival of old and gardenworthy varieties.

New Nurseries

We are well aware that there are a number of nurseries that have not been included simply because we do not know about them. If they wish to be considered for inclusion in the next edition of **THE PLANT FINDER** they should write, with a catalogue to:

The Plant Finder
c/o Lakeside
Gaines Road
Whitbourne
Worcs WR6 5RD

We are always grateful for suggestions for new inclusions but it should however be realised, that if your favourite nursery has not been included, it may be that it has specifically asked that we should not do so or that it may not have responded to our repeated requests for information.

COMPILER'S NOTES

Please read carefully.

Nurseries

The details given for each nursery (listed in the Indices at the back) have been compiled from information supplied to us in answer to a questionnaire. In some cases, because of constraints of space, the entries have been slightly abbreviated and blanks have been left where no information has been provided.

Opening Times

The word 'Daily' implies every day including Sunday and Bank Holidays. Although opening times have been given as provided and where applicable, it is *always* advisable, especially if travelling a long distance, to check with the nursery first.

Mail Order

Many nurseries provide a Mail Order service and this is indicated. Where it is shown that there is no minimum charge it should be realised that to send even one plant may involve the nursery in substantial postage and packing costs.

Catalogue Cost

Some nurseries offer their catalogue free, or for a few stamps (the odd value quoted can usually be made up from a combination of first or second class stamps), but a ***large*** stamped addressed envelope is always appreciated as well.

Wholesale Or Retail

The main trading method is indicated, but it should be stressed that some wholesalers do have retail outlets and many retailers also have a wholesale trade and would frequently be prepared to offer discounts for large single orders.

Export

The Hardy Plant Society has a large number of overseas members and many copies of **THE PLANT FINDER** go to overseas customers, nurseries and botanic gardens. These are often eager to purchase plants from the UK which, in many instances, may be the only source of supply available in the world. In order to assist these potential customers we have asked which UK nurseries are prepared to accept orders from overseas. As a result several nurseries have indicated that they are prepared to accept such orders. However because of the very high cost of obtaining the necessary phytosanitary certificates together with other customs, currency conversion and freight charges, most nurseries that are prepared to accept export orders impose a MINIMUM plant charge of £50 plus the other costs involved. It is most unfortunate that the excessive charges imposed by EEC Regulations makes the exportation of plants a very expensive undertaking for the small specialist nursery.

Even though a nursery may be listed as being prepared to export, nevertheless, in some instances the particular requirements of an individual country may make compliance with regulations virtually impossible. Indeed some of them require methods of sterilisation that would be more likely to kill the plant than eliminate any possible disease!

Because of these difficulties some nurseries are only prepared to export Bulbs or Seeds. (These are marked BO or SO respectively).

NOMENCLATURE

"The question of nomenclature is always a vexed one. The only thing certain is, that it is impossible to please everyone." W J Bean - Preface to First Edition of Trees & Shrubs Hardy in the British Isles'.

As in previous editions, we remain committed to the use of plant names which are as correct as possible and agree with the current opinions of botanists. Of course, gardeners and nurserymen are still at liberty to use old and well-loved names if they wish but to adopt any middle course for **THE PLANT FINDER** work, keeping some old (but wrong) names and introducing some new ones, would be a recipe for chaos and confusion. Such a course would ultimately result in botanists and gardeners speaking different, mutually incomprehensible languages and we would all be the poorer.

However, this does not mean that we will change a name the moment we hear that one botanist considers it to be wrong; name changes, once they are considered correct by the great majority of experts are likely to become permanent and to be used by gardeners and botanists alike. Only then do we accept new names and we do not inflict them on gardeners or nurseries purely out of perversity.

Verification of names

Although we find that many nurseries have greatly improved the accuracy of their plant naming, plants which are new entries often appear under a bewildering variety of wrong names and misspellings. This is partly a reflection on the rarity of the plants and nurserymen are not to be blamed for not finding correct names for plants which do not appear in recent authoritative garden literature. Some plants are simply too new for valid names and descriptions yet to have appeared in print.

we try to verify every name which appears in these pages, but the amount of time which can be allotted to checking each of over 50,000 entries must be limited. There is always a proportion which do not appear in any of the reference sources used, (ie.. those listed in the Bibliography) and those unverified names for which there may be scope for error are marked with an asterisk. Such errors may occur with species we cannot find listed, (possibly synonyms for more recent and better known names), or may include misspellings, (particularly of names transliterated from Japanese or Chinese, or commemorating a person). We are especially circumspect about names not known to the International Registrar for a particular genus. We are always grateful to receive information about the naming and origin of any asterisked plant and once we feel reassured about the plant's pedigree, the asterisk will be removed. Of course, many such names will prove to be absolutely correct and buyers can be reassured if they know that the selling nursery takes great care with the naming of its plants.

Rules of Nomenclature

Throughout **THE PLANT FINDER** we try to follow the rules of nomenclature set out in the *International Code of Nomenclature for Cultivated Plants* 1980. Cultivar names which are clearly not permissible under this Code and for which there seems to be no valid alternative are marked with an 'I' (for invalid). The commonest sorts of invalid names seem to be those that are wholly or partly in Latin (not permissible since 1959, eg 'Pixie Alba', 'Superba', 'Variegata') and those which use Latin generic names as a cultivar name (eg *Rosa* 'Corylus', *Viola* 'Gazania'). If no prior valid name exists, an enterprising nurseryman may publish a new valid name for any such plant. This would be considered validly published if it appeared in a dated catalogue with a clear description of the plant; the originator, if still alive, must accept the new name.

Apart from being discourteous to the plants' originators and their countries, the translating of foreign plant names into English is a bad and insular practice that is likely to cause confusion; it may be years yet before we make sense of the host of German names and apparent English translations for a genus such as Coreopsis, many of which must be synonyms. Throughout **THE PLANT FINDER**, we have tried to give preference to the original name in every case, although English names are also given.

The substitution of slick selling names by nurseries which do not like, or have not bothered to find out, the correct names of the plants they sell is sharp practice; it is also a probable breach of the Trades Description Act.

The recent ruling on orthography, that is retention, in commemorative names, of a person's name in its original form, is discussed in the supplement to Bean's *Trees and Shrubs Hardy in the British Isles* (1988). The gist of this is, that, except for full-scale latinisation of names (eg *brunonius* for Brown, thus *Rosa brunonii*), the name of the person commemorated must remain in its original form. Some names falling into this category were corrected in our previous two edition and further corrections will be found this year: for instance T S Brandegee, frequently deprived of one or even both of his last e's. is given both of them back in numerous *brandegeei's* and *brandegeeanum's*. Lady Dalhousie has also had her termination restored, most noticeably for *Rhododendron dalhousieae*. There are many similar examples, although in a few cases there is debate about whether the specific names constitute full-scale latinisation or not. Names ending in -er (eg Solander, Faber) may become *solandri* as in pure Latin, (because -er is a usual Latin termination) or *solanderi*, if the specific name was originally spelt this way.

International Registration Authorities

International Registration Authorities (IRAs) have been a great help and although it is perhaps invidious to single out any for special mention, the International Registrars acting for the Royal Horticultural Society have all been exceptionally helpful and have shown just how valuable such schemes can be when well organised with up-to-date and complete records. We have had much help from other Registrars mentioned in the acknowledgments and have followed their ruling implicitly in almost every case.

Recent nomenclature changes

For this edition, we have received a great deal of help from botanists, gardeners and nurserymen who have made comments about plant names. Perhaps most startling and least popular will be some of the name changes brought to our attention by Douglas Kent: *Silene maritima* becomes *S. uniflora*, *Rhus typhina* changes to *R. hirta* and rhubarb (*Rheum* x *cultorum)* is now *R.* x *hybridum*. The reasons for these changes seem sound and unlikely to be overturned, nor in any of these cases, in Mr Kent's opinion, are the better-known names likely to be conserved.

Pelargoniums and roses, whose species and cultivars alike give taxonomists nightmares, have received considerable attention and research, both in their names and their classifications. The help provided by Mrs Hazel Key has been invaluable in correcting and standardising pelargonium names.

Shrubby potentillas have all been assigned to *P. fruticosa* following the recent paper in the *Canadian Journal of Botany*. (See Bibliography).

In this edition, *Pernettya* and *Gaultheria* have been united under *Gaultheria* for the reasons set out in David Middleton's article in *The Plantsman*. For the same reasons, it is not satisfactory to separate *Lobelia* and *Pratia* and we have followed Mabberley's *Plant-Book* in uniting them under *Lobelia*.

Lavenders have always been taxonomically difficult because of the varying degrees of hybridity of their cultivars; the paper by Hensen and Tucker (see Bibliography) has provided a helpful basis for ascribing most of them either to *L. angustifolia* or *L* x *intermedia*.

We have great sympathy for gardeners who want to find a particular cultivar but are not sure to which species it belongs. The problem is acute for Juniperus and readers must search through all the entries to find their plant; nurseries also seem uncertain of the species of 'Skyrocket'.

Plant Gender

Latin adjectival names, whether for species, subspecies, cultivar etc., must agree in gender with the genus, not with the specific name if the latter is a noun, (as for *Phyllitis scolopendrium*, *Rhamnus alaternus* etc.). Thus azaleas have to agree with Rhododendron, their true genus (neuter), rather than Azalea with whatever is being described: for roses, this is almost always *la rose* (feminine) but on rare occasions *le rosier* (when describing vegetative characteristics such as climbing forms). *l'oeillet* or *le pompon* (all masculine).

NOMENCLATURE

It is often the case that gardeners consider two plants to be distinct, but botanists, who know of a whole range of intermediates linking the two, consider them to be the same species. The most notable example is for the rhododendrons; many species of which were 'sunk' in Cullen and Chamberlain's recent revision. In such cases we have always tried to provide names that retain important horticultural entities, even if not botanically distinct, often by giving the sunk species a group name, such as *Rhododendron rubiginosum* Desquamatum group. Rhododendrons and orchids are also blessed with grex names for swarms of hybrids with the same parentage such as *R.* Polar Bear or *Pleione* Shantung. Such names are not enclosed in quotes but, particularly for rhododendrons, a single clone from the grex may be given the same cultivar name, ie 'Polar Bear'. In many cases nursery catalogues do not specify whether the named clone is being offered or other selections from the hybrid swarm and entries are therefore given as eg *Rhododendron* Polar Bear (g.&cl.), ie. grex and clone.

There are a few cases in which it is difficult to tell whether a sunk species remains horticulturally distinct enough to merit a group name,; we would be grateful if users would let us know of any plants that we have 'sunk' in synonymy but still need to be distinguished by separate names. In many cases, the plants gardeners grow will be the most extreme variants of a species; although one 'end' of the species will seem to be quite different from the other 'end', the botanist will see them as the outer limits of a continuous range of variation and will give them the same species name. We often hear gardeners complain "How can these two plants have the same name? They are DIFFERENT!"; in such cases, although the botanist may have to 'lump' them under the same name, we will always try to provide an acceptable name to distinguish an important horticultural entity, even if it is not botanically distinct.

THE PLANT FINDER is useful not only as a directory of plant sources but as a 'menu' of plants grown by British gardeners. Such a list is of great value not only to private gardeners, landscapers can use it to check the range of plants they can incorporate in designs; botanists can discover the species grown in Britain, some of them from recorded natural sources; nurserymen can use it to select for propagation first-rate plants that are still not readily available: horticultural authors, who often only want to write about plants the public are able to buy, will find it invaluable. For all such users, **THE PLANT FINDER** is offered as a source of standard, up-to-date and reliable nomenclature.

Chris Philip and Tony Lord
March 1991

NOMENCLATURE NOTES

These notes refer to plants in the main PLANT DIRECTORY that are marked with a 'N'.

'Bean Supplement' refers to W J Bean *Trees & Shrubs Hardy in the British Isles* (Supplement to the 8th edition) edited by D L Clarke 1988.

ACER *grosseri*
See note in Bean Supplement, p 42.

ACER *palmatum coreanum*
See note in Bean Supplement, p 51.

ACER *palmatum* 'Sango-kaku'
See note in Bean Supplement, p 52.

ACER *palmatum* 'Senkaki'
See note in Bean Supplement, p 52.

ACONITUM *autumnale*
This name is a synonym both of A. *napellus* and A. *carmichaelii wilsonii.*

ADENOPHORA *latifolia*
Plants under this name may be A. *pereskiifolia.*

ALLIUM *aflatunense*
Plants sold under this name are probably A. *stipitatum*, although several other closely related species may be involved.

ALLIUM *beesianum*
Plants sold under this name are often A. *cyaneum.*

ALLIUM *narcissiflorum*
Plants sold under this name are usually A. *insubricum.*

ALLIUM *pyrenaicum*
Plants are often A. *angulosum.*

ALOPECURUS *pratensis* 'Aureus'
This name applies only to plants with all gold leaves, not with green & gold striped forms.

ANEMONE x *hybrida* 'Alba'
A number of white-flowered forms are grown under this name especially 'Honorine Jobert'. The true cultivar is considerably taller than 'H.J.'.

ANEMONE *magellanica*
According to *European Garden Flora* this is a form of the very variable A. *multifida.*

ANEMONE *nemorosa* 'Alba Plena'
This name is used for several double white forms including A. *n.* 'Flore Pleno' and A. *n.* 'Vestal'.

ARUM *italicum marmoratum*
This is the correct name for the plant formerly know as *A. i. pictum* which is distinct from the species *A. pictum.*

ARUM *italicum pictum*
See note above.

ARUM *pictum*
See note above.

ASTER *amellus* 'Violet Queen'
It is probable that more than one cultivar is sold under this name.

ASTER *dumosus*
Many of the Asters listed under *A. novi-belgii* contain varying amounts of A. *dumosus* blood in their parentage. It is not possible to allocate these to one species or the other and they are therfore listed under A. *novi-belgii.*

ASTER x *frikartii* 'Mönch'
The true plant of this name is very rare in British gardens. Most plants are another for of A. x *frikartii* usually 'Wunder von Stafa'.

ASTER *novi-belgii* 'Ada Ballard'
See note under A. *dumosus.*

AUBRIETA *deltoidea* 'Variegata'
This name may refer to any of the variegated cultivars of Aubrieta.

BERBERIS *aristata*
See note in Bean Vol. I.

BERBERIS x *ottawensis* 'Purpurea'
See note in Bean Supplement, p 109.

BERBERIS x *ottawensis* 'Superba'
See note in Bean Supplement, p 109.

BERGENIA Ballawley Hybrids
The name 'Ballawley' refers only to plants vegetatively propagated from ther original clone. Seed raised plants, which may differ considerably, should be called Ballawley Hybrids.

BETULA *alba*
This is a synonym of both B. *pendula* and B. *pubescens*

BETULA *costata*
Plants sold under this name are sometimes B. *ermanii.*

BETULA *pendula* 'Dalecarlica'
See note in Bean Supplement, p 118.

BETULA *utilis jacquemontii*
Plants sold under this name are often the clone 'Inverleith' which may or may not be a form of B. *utilis.*

BRACHYSCOME
Originally published as BRACHYCOME by Cassini who later revised his spelling to BRACHYSCOME. In spite of the priority, the more recent spelling has been internationally adopted.

BRACHYGLOTTIS *greyi* and *laxifolia*
Both these species are extremely rare in cultivation. Plants under these names usually being B. 'Sunshine'.

BUDDLEJA *davidii* Petite Indigo ®, Petite Plum ® 'Nanho Blue', 'Nanho Purple'
These cultivars or hybrids of B. *d. nanhoensis* are claimed by some to be synonyms while others claim the 'Nanho' plants were raised in Holland and the 'Petite' plants in the USA. We are not yet certain whether these names are synonyms and if so which have priority.

BUDDLEJA *fallowiana*
Many plants in cultivation are not the true species but the hybrid 'West Hill'.

CALLUNA *vulgaris* 'Terrick's Orange'
This may be a misnomer for C. *v.* 'Prostrate Orange'.

CAMELLIA 'Campbellii'
This name is used for five cvs. including 'Margherita Coleoni'.

CAMELLIA 'Cleopatra'
There are three cultivars with this name.

CAMPANULA *persicifolia*
Plants under 'cup and saucer white' are not definately ascribed to a particular cultivar. 'White Cup and Saucer' is a cultivar named by Margery Fish.

CAREX *conica* 'Hime-kan-suge'/ 'Hino-kansuge' / 'Variegata'
This variegated sedge is listed under over a dozen variants of the above names, none of which is legitimate. Dr Alan Leslie has proposed the cultivar name 'Snowline' for this plant.

CASSIA *corymbosa*
See note in Bean Supplement, p 148.

CASSIA *obtusa*
This name is used for two species, C. *obtusa* (Roxb.) Wight (1844) and for C. *obtusa* Clos (1847). The latter, often confused with C. *cormbosa*, is correctly called C. *candolleana.*

CEDRUS *deodara* 'Prostrata'
The true plant is extremely rare if not lost to cultivation. Most plants under this name are in fact C. *d.* 'Pendula'.

CHAMAECYPARIS *lawsoniana* 'Smithii'
Plants under this name may include some which are C. *l.* 'Darleyensis'.

CHAMAECYPARIS *pisifera* 'Aurea Nana'
Probably should be called C. *p.* 'Strathmore'.

CHEIRANTHUS *cheiri* 'Baden Powell'
Plant of uncertain origin differing from C. *c.* 'Harpur Crewe' only in its shorter stature.

CISTUS *crispus*
C. *pulverulentus* is sometimes offered under this name.

CISTUS *hirsutus* and C. *h. psilosepalus*
These do not appear to be distinct in cultivation.

CISTUS *ladanifer*
C. x *cyprius* is sometimes offered under this name.

CISTUS x *loretii*
C. x *lusitanicus* is sometimes offered under this name.

CISTUS *parviflorus*
Most plants offered under this name are hybrids, usually C. 'Grayswood Pink'.

CISTUS x *purpureus*
Most plants in cultivation may be the cultivar 'Betty Taudevin'

CLEMATIS *chrysocoma*
The true C. *chrysocoma* is a non-climbing erect plant with dense yellow down on the young growth, still uncommon in cultivation.

CLEMATIS *heracleifolia* 'Campanile'
May be *C.*x *bonstedtii* 'C'.

CLEMATIS *heracleifolia* 'Cote d'Azur'
May be C. x *bonstedtii* 'C. d'A.'

CLEMATIS *montana*
This name should refer to the white-flowered form only. Pink-flowered forms should be known as C. *m. rubens*.

COLCHICUM 'Autumn Queen'
Entries here may refer to the slightly different *C*. 'Prinses Astrid'.

CORNUS 'Norman Hadden'
See note in Bean Supplement. p 184.

COTINUS *coggygria* 'Notcutt's Variety'
See note in Bean Supplement, p 190.

COTINUS *coggygria rubrifolius*
See note in Bean Supplement, p 190.

COTONEASTER *dammeri*
Plants sold under this name are usually C. *d.*'Major'.

CRATAEGUS *crus-galli*
See note in Bean Supplement, p 194.

CROCOSMIA 'Citronella'
The true plant of this name has a dark eye and grows at Wisley. The plant usually offered may be more correctly *C*. 'Golden Fleece'.

CROCOSMIA 'Honey Angels'
Also wrongly referred to as 'Citronella'. May be correctly 'Golden Fleece'.

CROCOSMIA 'Solfaterre'
This the original and therefore correct spelling.

NOMENCLATURE NOTES

CROCUS *cartwrightianus albus*
The plant offered is the true form and not C. *hadriaticus*.

CUPHEA *platycentra*
Plants under this name are usually C. *ignea*, otherwise C. *microphylla*.

CYTISUS x *praecox* 'Warminster'
See note in Bean Supplement, p 205.

DIANTHUS 'Musgrave's Pink' (p)
This is the registered name of this white-flowered cultivar.

DRYOPTERIS *affinis polydactyla*
This name covers at least three different clones.

ELYMUS *magellanicus*
Although this is a valid name Mr Roger Grounds has suggested that many plants might belong to a different, perhaps unnamed species.

ERIGERON *salsuginosus*
Is a synonym of ASTER *sibiricus* but plants in cultivation under this name may be E. *peregrinus callianthemus*

ERODIUM *cheilanthifolium*
Most plants under this name are hybrids.

ERODIUM *glandulosum*
Plants under this name are often hybrids.

ERODIUM *guttatum*
Doubtfully in commerce, plants under this name are usually E. *heteradenum*, E. *cheilanthifolium* or hybrids.

ERODIUM *petraeum*
Many plants under this name are hybrids, often E. 'Merstham Pink'.

ERYSIMUM 'Variegatum'
This name may refer to any of the variegated cultivars of *Erysimum*.

EUCRYPHIA x *hillieri* 'Penwith'
The cultivar name 'Penwith' was origianlly given to a hybrid of E. *cordifolia* x E. *lucida*, not E. x *hillieri*.

EUPHORBIA *longifolia*
E. *cornigera* is sometimes offered under this name.

EUPHORBIA *wallichii*
Many plants grown under this name are E. *longifolia* or E. *cornigera*.

FAGUS *sylvatica* 'Pendula'
This name refers to the Knap Hill clone, the most common weeping form in English gardens. Other clones occur, particularly in Ireland.

FORSYTHIA 'Beatrix Farrand'
The true plant may not be in cultivation.

FRAGARIA *chiloensis* 'Variegata'
Most, possibly all, plants under this name are F. x *ananassa* 'Variegata'.

FREESIA *refracta alba*
Plants under this name may be F. *lactea* or F. *sparrmannii*.

FUCHSIA
All names marked N refer to more than one cultivar or species.

GALANTHUS *reginae-olgae* Corcyrensis group
This name is used for late autumn flowering forms which flower with their leaves as opposed to typical G. *r-o* which flowers in mid-Autumn before its leaves appear.

GENISTA
All names marked N refer to prostrate forms of uncertain identity, probably belonging to G. *tinctoria*.

GERANIUM *eriostemon*
Entries under this name may refer to *G. sinense*.

HEBE 'Amy'
May include entries which refer to H. 'Purple Queen'.

HEBE *anomala*
Most plants grown under this name are the hybrid 'Imposter'.

HEBE 'C P Raffill'
See note in Bean Supplement, p 265.

HEBE 'Carl Teschner'
See note in Bean Supplement, p 264.

HEBE 'Glaucophylla'
This plant is a green reversion of the hybrid H. 'Glaucophylla Variegata'.

HEBE 'Purple Tips'/'Tricolor'
New Zealand authorities consider these to be identical, but Mr Graham Hutchins consider that, in cultivation in Britain, they appear to be distinct.

HEDERA *helix* 'Caenwoodiana'/'Pedata'
Some authorities consider these to be distinct cultivars whilst others think them different morphological forms of the same unstable clone.

HEDYOTIS *caerulea*
Plants in cultivation may be H. *michauxii* (syn. HOUSTONIA *serpyllifolia*).

HEMEROCALLIS *fulva* 'Kwanso', 'Kwanso Variegata', 'Flore Pleno' and 'Green Kwanso'
For a discussion of these plants see *The Plantsman* (Vol. 7 Pt. II).

HEUCHERA *micrantha* 'Palace Purple'
This cultivar name refers only to plants with deep purple-red foliage. Seed-raised plants of inferior colouring should not be offered under this name.

HOSTA 'Marginata Alba'
This name is wrongly used both for H. *crispula* and, more commonly, for H. *fortunei* 'Albomarginata'.

HOSTA *montana*
This name refers only to plants long grown in Europe, which differ from H. *elata*.

HOSTA 'Venusta Variegated'
In spite of its name this plant is not a form of H. *venusta*.

HYPERICUM *henryi*
See note in Bean Supplement. p 281.

HYPERICUM *fragile*
The true H. *fragile* is probably not available from British nurseries.

ILEX x *altaclerensis*
The argument for this correct spelling is given by Susyn Andrews (*The Plantsman* Vol.5, Pt.II) and is not superceded by the more recent but erroneous comments in the Supplement to Bean's *Trees and Shrubs*.

IRIS *bucharica*
Entries under this name may be *I. orchioides*.

IRIS *pallida* 'Variegata'
The white-variegated I. *p.* 'Argentea Variegata' is sometimes wrongly supplied under this name, which refers only to the gold-variegated form.

KALMIA *polifolia*
See note in Bean Supplement, p 296.

KNIPHOFIA *galpinii*
Most plants are not the true species but are K. *triangularis triangularis*.

LAMIUM *maculatum* 'Chequers'
This name refers to two plants; the first, validly named, is a large and vigorous form of L. *maculatum* with a stripe down the centre of the leaf; the second is silver-leaved and very similar to L. *m.* 'Beacon Silver'.

LAVATERA *olbia*
Although L. *olbia* is usually shrubby and L. *thuringiaca* usually herbaceous, both species are very variable. Cultivars formally ascribed to one species or the other are quite possibly hybrids and are listed by cultivar name alone pending the results of further research.

LEPTOSPERMUM *flavescens*
This name is usually applied to plants correctly named L. *glaucescens*.

LOBELIA
PRATIA (fruit a berry) and LOBELIA (fruit a capsule) are here united because L. *angulata* has fruits that are intermediate between a berry and a capsule (cf. PERNETTYA and GAULTHERIA). The two genera cannot therefore satisfactorily be separated.

LONICERA x *americana*
Probably all, plants under this name are correctly L. x *italica*.. See *The Plantsman* (Vol. 12 Pt. II).

LONICERA *periclymenum* 'Belgica'
See note in Bean Supplement, p 315.

LONICERA *periclymenum* 'Serotina'
See note in Bean Supplement, p 315.

MACLEYA *cordata*
Most, if not all plants offered under this name are M. x *kewensis*.

MAGNOLIA x *highdownensis*
Believed to fall within the range of variation of M. *wilsonii*.

MAGNOLIA *obovata*
This name refers to either M. *hypoleuca* or M. *officinalis*. The former is more common in culivation.

MAGNOLIA x *soulangeana* 'Burgundy'
See note in Bean Supplement, p 330.

MAHONIA *pinnata*
Plants in cultivation under this name are believed to belong to M. x *wagneri* 'Pinnacle'.

MALUS *domestica* 'Dumeller's Seedling'
The phonetic spelling 'Dumelow's Seedling' contravenes the ICBN recommendations on orthography, i.e. that commemorative names should retain the original spelling of the person's name.

PAPAVER *orientale 'Trkenlouis'/'Turkish Delight'*
These name are definitely synonymous. However, other wrongly named cultivars are often sold as 'Turkish Delight'.

PAULOWNIA *fargesii*
Plants under this name are often P. *lilacina*.

PELARGONIUM 'Beauty of Eastbourne'
This should not be confused with P. 'Eastbourne Beauty', a different cultivar.

PELARGONIUM 'Lass o'Gowrie'
The American plant of this name has pointed, not rounded leaf lobes.

PELARGONIUM *quercifolium*
Plants under this name are mainly hybrid. The true species has pointed, not rounded leaf lobes.

PERNETTYA
Botanists now consider that PERNETTYA (fruit a berry) is not separable from GAULTHERIA (fruit a capsule) because in some species the fruit is intermediate bewteen a berry and a capsule. For a fuller explanation see D. Middleton *The Plantsman*. 1991 (Vol 12 Pt. III).

PICEA *pungens* 'Glauca Pendula'
This name may be one of several blue cultivars.

PINUS *aristata*
May include plants referrable to P. *longaeva*.

PINUS *nigra* 'Cebennensis Nana'
A doubtful and illegitimate name, probably a synonym for P. *n*. 'Nana'.

PODOCARPUS *alpinus*
See note in Bean Supplement, p 386.

POLYGONATUM *odoratum* 'Variegatum'
Plants under this name be P. x *falcatum* 'Variegatum.

POLYSTICHUM *setiferum* 'Wollaston'
Incomplete name which may refer to either of two cultivars.

POPULUS *nigra italica*
See note in Bean Supplement, p 393.

PRATIA
See Note under LOBELIA.

PRUNUS *cerasifera* 'Nigra'
Plants under this name may be referrable to P. *c.* 'Woodii'.

PRUNUS 'Kanzan'
See note in Bean Supplement, p 400

PRUNUS *laurocerasus* 'Castlewellan'
We are grateful to Dr Charles Nelson for informing us that the name 'Marbled White' is not valid because although it has priority of publication it does not have the approval of the originator who asked for it to be called 'Castlewellan'

PRUNUS *laurocerasus* 'Variegata'
The true 'Variegata' dates from 1811 but this name is also used for the relatively recent cultivar P. *l.* 'Castewellan'.

PRUNUS *serrulata pubescens*
See note in Bean Supplement, p 398.

PYRACANTHA 'Orange Charmer'
See note in Bean Supplement, p 404.

RAOULIA *australis*
Plants under this name are usually R. *hookeri.*

RHEUM x *cultorum*
The name R. x *cultorum was published without adequate description and must be abandoned in favour of the validly published R. -hybridum.*

RHODODENDRON Azalea
All names marked N refer to more than one cultivar.

RHODODENRON Hybrid Loderi/Kewense
The grex name Kewense has priority of 13 years over the name Loderi for hybrids of R. *griffithianum* x *fortunei* ssp. *fortunei* and would, under normal circumstances be considered correct. However, the RHS as IRA for Rhododendrons has declared Loderi as a name to be conserved.

RHODODENDRON *tubiforme*
See note in Bean Supplement, p 445.

RHUS *typhina*
Linnaeus published both R. *typhina* and R. *hirta* as names for the same species but R. *hirta* has priority and should be used in preference to the newer name.

ROBINIA *hispida* 'Rosea'
This name is applied to R. *hispida*, (young shoots with bristles), R. *elliottii*, (young shoots with grey down) and R. *boyntonii*, (young shoot with neither bristles nor down).

ROSA
New cultivar names, the first three letters of which normally derive from the name of the breeder, are not given for ROSA. These are usually sold under Registered Trade Marks '®'. Roses often known by common names, eg. Rosa Mundi, Hume's Blush are referred to botanical names as given in Bean.

ROSA 'Gros Choux de Hollande' (Bb)
It is doubtful if this name is correctly applied.

ROSA 'Maiden's Blush'
R. 'Great Maiden's Blush' may be supplied under this name.

ROSA Sweetheart ®
This is not the same as the Sweetheart Rose, a common name for R. 'Cécile Brunner'.

SALIX *alba* 'Tristis'
This cultivar should not be confused with S. *tristis*, which is now correctly S. *humilis*.

SALIX *caprea pendula*
Entries cover both the male form 'Kilmarnock' and the female form 'Weeping Sally'.

SALIX *japonica*
This name is sometimes used for S. *babylonica* 'Lavallei'.

SALIX *rosmarinifolia*
This name is used for two plants, S. *r.* Host = S. *elaegnos angustifolia* and S. *r.* Linnaeus.

SALIX x *smithiana*
See note in Bean Supplement, p 486.

SALVIA *officinalis* 'Aurea'
S. *o. aurea* is a rare form of the common sage with leaves entirely of gold. It is represented in cultivation by the cultivar 'Kew Gold'. The plant usually offered as S. *o.* 'Aurea' is the gold variegated sage S. *o.* 'Icterina'.

SAMBUCUS *nigra* 'Aurea'
Plants under this name are usually S. *canadensis* 'Aurea'.

SEDUM *nevii*
The true species is not in cultivation. Plants under this name are usually either S. *glaucophyllum*, occasionally S. *beyrichianum*.

SEDUM *spathulifolium* 'Cape Blanco'
This is the correct spelling.

SEMPERVIVUM *arachnoideum tomentosum*
Entries here may include plants classified as *S.* 'Hookeri'.

SISYRINCHIUM
All the names with '*' have been used to refer to more than one species.

SKIMMIA *japonica* 'Foremanii'
The true cultivar, which belong to S. *japonica* Rogersii group, is believed to be lost to cultivation. Plants offered under this name are usually S. *japonica* 'Veitchii'.

SOPHORA *prostrata*
Plants under this name may be the hybrid S. 'Little Baby'.

STEWARTIA *ovata grandiflora.*
Most, possibly all, plants available from British nurseries under this name are not true to name but are derived from the improved Nymans form.

TEUCRIUM *chamaedrys*
Most plants grown under this name are the hybrid T. x *lucidrys*.

THYMUS x *citriodorus* 'Silver Posie'
The cultivar name 'Silver Posie' is applied to several different plants, not all of them x *citriodorus*.

TRICYRTIS Hototogisu
This is the common name applied generally to all Japanese Tricyrtis and specifically to T. *hirta*.

TRICYRTIS *macropoda*
This name has been used for at least five different species.

UNCINIA *rubra*
This name is loosely applied to UU. *egmontiana* and *unciniata*.

VERBENA 'Kemerton'
Origin unknown, not from Kemerton.

VIBURNUM *opulus* 'Fructu-luteo'
See note below.

VIBURNUM *opulus* 'Xanthocarpum'
Entries here include the closely similar V. *o.* 'Fructu-luteo'.

VIBURNUM *plicatum*
Entries under this name may include the "Snowball" form, V. *plicatum* 'Sterile'.

CLASSIFICATION OF GENERA

CHRYSANTHEMUM
(Now correctly DENDRANTHEMA)

(By the Floral Committee of the National Chrysanthemum Society)

Indoor Cultivars

Section 1 LARGE EXHIBITION

Section 2 MEDIUM EXHIBITION

Section 3 INCURVED
- (a) Large-flowered
- (b) Medium-flowered
- (c) Small-flowered

Section 4 REFLEXED
- (a) Large-flowered
- (b) Medium-flowered
- (c) Small-flowered

Section 5 INTERMEDIATE
- (a) Large-flowered
- (b) Medium-flowered
- (c) Small-flowered

Section 6 ANEMONES
- (a) Large-flowered
- (b) Medium-flowered
- (c) Small-flowered

Section 7 SINGLES
- (a) Large-flowered
- (b) Medium-flowered
- (c) Small-flowered

Section 8 POMPONS
- (a) True Poms
- (b) Semi-Poms

Section 9 SPRAYS
- (a) Anemones
- (b) Pompons
- (c) Reflexed
- (d) Singles
- (e) Intermediate
- (f) Spider, Quills, Spoons and any other type

Section 10
- (a) Spiders
- (b) Quills
- (c) Spoons

Section 11 ANY OTHER TYPES

Section 12
- (a) Charms
- (b) Cascades

October-flowered Chrysanthemums

Section 13 INCURVED
- (a) Large-flowered
- (b) Medium-flowered
- (c) Small-flowered

Section 14 REFLEXED
- (a) Large-flowered
- (b) Medium-flowered
- (c) Small-flowered

Section 15 INTERMEDIATE
- (a) Large-flowered
- (b) Medium-flowered
- (c) Small-flowered

Section 16 LARGE OCTOBER FLOWERING

Section 17 SINGLES
- (a) Large-flowered
- (b) Medium-flowered
- (c) Small-flowered

Section 18 POMPONS
- (a) True Poms
- (b) Semi-poms

Section 19 SPRAYS
- (a) Anemones
- (b) Pompons
- (c) Reflexed
- (d) Singles
- (e) Intermediate
- (f) Spider, Quills, Spoons and any other type

Section 20 ANY OTHER TYPES

Early-flowering Chrysanthemums

Outdoor Cultivars

Section 23 INCURVED
- (a) Large-flowered
- (b) Medium-flowered
- (c) Small-flowered

Section 24 REFLEXED
- (a) Large-flowered
- (b) Medium-flowered

(c)	Small-flowered

Section 25 INTERMEDIATE

(a)	Large-flowered
(b)	Medium-flowered
(c)	Small-flowered

Section 26 ANEMONE

(a)	Large-flowered
(b)	Medium-flowered

Section 27 SINGLES

(a)	Large-flowered
(b)	Medium-flowered

Section 28 POMPONS

(a)	True Poms
(b)	Semi-poms

Section 29 SPRAYS

(a)	Anemones
(b)	Pompons
(c)	Reflexed
(d)	Singles
(e)	Intermediate
(f)	Spider, Quills, Spoons and any other type
K	Korean
Rub	Rubellum

Section 30 ANY OTHER TYPE

BEGONIA

C	Cane
R	Rex
S	Semperflorens
T	x tuberhybrida (Tuberous)

CLEMATIS

(T)	Texensis hybrids
(V)	Viticella hybrids

DAHLIAS

(By The National Dahlia Society)

1	Single	Sin
2	Anemone-flowered	Anem
3	Collerette	Col
4B	Waterlily, large	LWL
4C	Waterlily, medium	MWL
4D	Waterlily, small	SWL
4E	Waterlily, miniature	MinWL
5A	Decorative, giant	GD
5B	Decorative, large	LD
5C	Decorative, medium	MD
5D	Decorative, small	SD
5E	Decorative, miniature	MinD
6A	Small ball	SBa
6B	Miniature ball	MinBa
7	Pompon	Pom
8A	Cactus, giant	GC
8B	Cactus, large	LC
8C	Cactus, medium	MC
8D	Cactus, small	SC
8E	Cactus, miniature	MinC
9A	Semi-cactus, giant	GSC
9B	Semi-cactus, large	LSC
9C	Semi-cactus, medium	MSC
9D	Semi-cactus, small	SSC
9E	Semi-cactus, miniature	MinSC
10	Miscellaneous	Misc
-	Orchid flowering	O
-	Botanical	B
-	Dwarf bedding	DwB
-	Fimbriated	Fim
	Lilliput	Lil

DIANTHUS

(p)	Pinks
(p,a)	Annual pinks
(pf)	Perpetual flowering
(b)	Border
(m)	Malmaison

GLADIOLUS

(B)	Butterfly
(Colv)	Colvillei
(G)	Giant
(L)	Large
(M)	Medium
(Min)	Miniature
(N)	Nanus
(P)	Primulinus
(S)	Small

HYDRANGEA macrophylla

H	Hortensia
L	Lacecap

IRIS

(AB)	Arilbred
(BB)	Border Bearded
(CH)	Californian Hybrid
(DB)	Dwarf Bearded
(Dut)	Dutch
(IB)	Intermediate Bearded
(MDB)	Miniature Dwarf Bearded
(MTB)	Miniature Tall Bearded
(SDB)	Standard Dwarf Bearded
(Sp)	Spuria
(TB)	Tall Bearded

LILIUM

'International Lily Register' (Third Edition)
The Royal Horticultural Society 1982

I	Hybrids derived from LL.*lancifolium cernuum, davidii, leichtlinii, x maculatum, x hollandicum, amabile, pumilum, concolor, & bulbiferum*
I(a)	Early flowering with upright flowers, single or in an umbel
I(b)	Outward facing flowers
I(c)	Pendant flowers
II	Hybrids of Martagon type, one parent having been a form of LL. *martagon* or *hansonii*
III	Hybrids from LL. *candidum, chalcedonicum* and other related European species (ex. L. *martagon*)
IV	Hybrids of American species
V	Hybrids derived from LL. *longiflorum & formosanum*
VI	Hybrid Trumpet Lilies & Aurelian Hybrids from Asiatic species, incl. L. *henryi* but excluding those from LL. *auratum, speciosum, japonicum & rubellum*
VI(a)	with trumpet-shaped flowers
VI(b)	with bowl-shaped & outward-facing
VI(c)	with pendant flowers
VI(d)	with flat, star-shaped flowers
VII	Hybrids of Far Eastern species as, LL *auratum, speciosum, rubellum, & japonicum*
VII(a)	with trumper-shape flowers
VII(b)	with bowl-shaped flowers
VII(c)	with flat flowers
VII(d)	with recurved flowers
VIII	All Hybrids not in another division
IX	All species & their varieties & forms

NARCISSUS

Classification by The Royal Horticultural Society (Revised 1977)

Division 1	Trumpet
Division 2	Large-cupped
Division 3	Small-cupped
Division 4	Double
Division 5	Triandrus
Division 6	Cyclamineus
Division 7	Jonquilla
Division 8	Tazetta
Division 9	Poeticus
Division 10	Species and wild forms & hybrids
Division 11	Split-corona
Division 12	Miscellaneous

PELARGONIUM

A	Angel
C	Coloured foliage (in combination)
Ca	Cactus (in combination)
D	Double (in combination)
Dec	Decorative
Dw	Dwarf
DwI	Dwarf Ivy-leaved
Fr	Frutetorum
I	Ivy-leaved
Min	Miniature or Dwarf
MinI	Miniature Ivy-leaved
R	Regal
Sc	Scented
St	Stellar (in combination)
T	Tulip (in combination)
U	Unique
V	Variegated (in combination)
Z	Zonal

PRIMULA

(1)	Amethystina
(2)	Auricula
(3)	Bullatae
(4)	Candelabra
(5)	Capitatae
(6)	Carolinella
(7)	Cortusoides
(8)	Cuneifolia
(9)	Denticulata
(10)	Dryadifolia
(11)	Farinosae
(12)	Floribundae
(13)	Grandis
(14)	Malacoides
(15)	Malvacea
(16)	Minutissimae
(17)	Muscarioides
(18)	Nivales
(19)	Obconica
(20)	Parryi
(21)	Petiolares
(22)	Pinnatae
(23)	Pycnoloba
(24)	Reinii
(25)	Rotundifolia
(26)	Sikkimensis
(27)	Sinenses
(28)	Soldenelloideae
(29)	Souliei
(30)	Vernales
(A)	Alpine Auricula
(B)	Border Auricula
(D)	Double

(Poly)	Polyanthus
(Prim)	Primrose
(S)	Show Auricula

RHODODENDRON (Azalea)

(E)	Evergreen
(G)	Ghent
(K)	Knaphill or Exbury
(M)	Mollis
(O)	Occidentalis
(R)	Rustica
(V)	Viscosa

ROSA

(A)	Alba
(Bb)	Bourbon
(Bs)	Boursault
(Ce)	Centifolia
(Ch)	China
(Cl)	Climbing
(Co)	Compacta
(D)	Damask
(DPo)	Damask Portland
(F)	Floribunda or Cluster-flowered
(G)	Gallica
(Ga)	Garnette
(GC)	Ground Cover
(HScB)	Hybrid Scots Briar
(HSwB)	Hybrid Sweet Briar
(HM)	Hybrid Musk
(HP)	Hybrid Perpetual
(HT)	Hybrid Tea or Large-flowered
(Min)	Miniature
(Mo)	Moss
(N)	Noisette
(Patio)	Patio or Miniature Floribunda
(Poly)	Polyanthus
(Ra)	Rambler
(Ru)	Rugosa
(S)	Shrub
(T)	Tea

SAXIFRAGA

1	Micranthes
2	Hirculus
3	Gymnopera
4	Diptera
5	Trachyphyllum
6	Xanthizoon
7	Aizoonia
8	Porophyllum
9	Porophyrion
10	Miscopetalum
11	Saxifraga
12	Trachyphylloides
13	Cymbalaria
14	Discogyne

TULIPA

'Revised Classification of Tulips' by Koninklijke Algemeene Vereening voor Bloembollenculture 1981

Early Flowering

1	Single Early
2	Double Early

Mid-Season

3	Triumph
4	Darwin hybrid

Late Flowering

5	Single Late (incl. Darwin)
6	Lily-Flowered
7	Fringed
8	Viridiflora
9	Rembrandt
10	Parrot
11	Double Late

Species and their Hybrids

12	Kaufmanniana
13	Fosteriana
14	Greigii

VIOLA

(C)	Cornuta hybrid
(DVt)	Double Violet
(ExV)	Exhibition Viola
(FP)	Fancy Pansy
(SP)	Show Pansy
(T)	Tricolor
(V)	Viola
(Vt)	Violet
(Vtta)	Violetta

VITIS

B	Black
G	Glasshouse
O	Outdoor
R	Red
W	White

ACKNOWLEDGEMENTS

The compilers of THE PLANT FINDER are very grateful to all the numerous people who have given advice and devoted much time and effort in checking and correcting the nomenclature in both the previous editions and this edition. For the compilation of this edition, we are particularly indebted to Messrs P J Chappell, H Gardner, G Hutchins, J Irons, D Kent, A C Leslie, E C Nelson, M Parr, R Poulett, J Sharman, P Trehane, P Whittaker, Miss E Strangeman and Sandra Bond for many helpful general comments on plant nomenclature. Many others have assisted with the checking of specific genera or groups. Particularly:

Alchemilla	Professor S M Walters ('90)
Australian Plants	G Butler, Registrar, Australian Cultivar Registration Authority. ('89)
Bamboos	D McClintock ('90 & '91)
Bulbs	Ing. J R Stuurman, Royal General Bulbgrowers Society, Holland. ('89)
Camellia	T J Savige, The International Registrar, New South Wales & J Gallagher, International Camellia Society, Dorset ('90)
Campanula	Mrs M Lynch, The Hardy Plant Society ('88)
Conifers	J Lewis, The International Registrar, RHS, Wisley. ('90) H J Welch, World Conifer Data Pool, Devon. ('90 & '91)
Corydalis	R Cooper ('88)
Cotoneaster	Jeanette Fryer, NCCPG National Collection holder. ('91)
Dahlia	D Pycraft, The International Registrar, Royal Horticultural Soc.('90 & '91)
Delphinium	Dr A C Leslie, The International Registrar, Royal Horticultural Society ('90 & '91)
Dianthus	Dr A C Leslie, The International Registrar, Royal Horticultural Society ('90 & '91)
Dicentra	R Cooper ('88)
Erodium	J Ross. ('90)
Euphorbia	R Turner. ('91)
Ferns	P Barnes, Royal Horticultural Society. ('89)
Fuchsia	Mrs D A Logan, The International Registrar, American Fuchsia Society. ('91)
Gesneriaceae	J D Dates, The International Registrar, American Gloxinia and Gesneriad Society. ('91)
Heathers	D McClintock ('88)
Hebe	G Scoble, The Hebe Society ('88)
Hedera	P Q Rose & Mrs H Key. ('91)
Helianthemum	H Gardner, formerly of Hilliers Arboretum ('88 -'91)
Hosta	Mrs Diana Grenfell ('88)
Hoya	D Kent. ('91)
Ilex	Susyn Andrews ('91)
Jovibarba & Sempervivum	P J Mitchell, The International Registrar, The Sempervivum Society. ('91)
Kalmia	R A Jaynes, The International Registrar, Broken Arrow Nursery, Connecticut, USA. ('89)
Narcissus	Mrs Sally Kington, The International Registrar, RHS Wisley ('90 & '91)
Mentha	Dr R Harley, The Royal Botanic Gardens, Kew. ('91)
Oleaceae	P S Green, Royal Botanic Gardens, Kew. ('89)
Paeonia	R Cooper ('88)
Passiflora	D Kent. ('91)
Pelargonium	Mrs H Key. ('91)
Pelargonium (Balcon)	Dr A Hamilton
Phormium	L J Metcalf, The International Registrar, New Zealand. (1990/91)
Polygonum (Persicaria)	D H Kent. ('90)
Rhododendron	Dr A C Leslie, The International Registrar, RHS Wisley. ('90 & '91)

To all these, as well as the many readers and nurseries who have also made comments and suggestions, we are, once again, sincerely grateful.

COLLECTORS' REFERENCES

A C&H	Apold, Cox & Hutchinson. 1962 expedition to NE Turkey
AC&W	Albury, Cheese & Watson
A&L	Ala & Lancaster expedition to N Iran 1972
B	Len Beer
BC&W	Beckett, Cheese & Watson
BL&M	Beer, Lancaster & Morris
BH	Brian Halliwell
B&L	Brickell & Leslie, China
BL&M	Beer, Lancaster & Morris. 1971 NE Nepal
BM	Brian Mathew
BM&W	Binns, Mason & Wright
BSBE	Bowles Scholarship Botanical Expedition
C&H	Cox & Hutchinson. 1965 expediton to Assam, NE Frontier & N Bengal
CC	Chris Chadwell
C&W	Cheese & Watson
C&R	Christian & Roderick. (California, Oregon, Washington).
DF	Derek Fox
EGM	E G Millais
EM	East Malling Research Station. Clonal selection scheme
EMR	E Martyn Rix
F	George Forrest (1873-1932)
Farrer	Reginald Farrer (1880-1920)
G	Gardner
G&K	Gardner & Knees
GS	George Sherriff (1898-1967)
Guiz	Guizhou Expedition 1985
H	Paul Huggins
HM&S	Halliwell, Mathew & Smallcombe
JCA	J C Archibald
JR	J Russell
KR	Keith Rushforth
KW	Frank Kingdon-Ward (1885-1958)
L	Roy Lancaster
LA	Long Ashton Research Station. Clonal Selection scheme.
LS	Ludlow (1885-1972) & G Sherriff
LS&E	Ludlow, Sherriff & Elliott
LS&H	Ludlow, Sherriff & Hicks, 1949 to Bhutan
LS&T	Ludlow Sherriff & Taylor. 1938 to SE Tibet
Mac&W	MacPhail & Watson
McB	Ron McBeath
PD	Peter Davis
PF	Paul Furse
PJC	P J Christian
PS&W	Polunin, Sykes & Williams. 1952/4 Nepal
R	J F C Rock (1884-1962)
RV	Richard Valder
SBEC	Sino-British expedition to SWChina (1981)
Sch	A D Schilling
SEP	Swedish expedition to Pakistan
SS&W	Stainton, Sykes & Williams
T	Nigel Taylor
T&K	Taylor & Knees
TSS	T Spring-Smyth
VH	Professor Vernon Heywood
W	E H Wilson, (1876-1930)
W A	E H Wilson, for Arnold Arboretum - (1906-1919)
Wr	David & Anke Wraight
W V	E H Wilson, for Veitch - (1899-1905)

NOTE: Collectors' numbers which do not appear to relate to the species listed are given an asterisk after the number. For the Collections of Joseph Rock, a number of nurseries quote United States Department of Agriculture numbers rather than Rock's own collection number. We have tried to make clear which of the two numbers is quoted and to give Rock's own numbers wherever possible.

PLANT DIRECTORY

ABELIA † (Caprifoliaceae)

chinensis	CB&S CGre MCot MRav SHil SLon SPer WHCG WSHC WWat
'Edward Goucher'	CB&S CBot CBow CCla CFis CSco ELan MGos SBla SHil SPla SSta WOld WPat WSHC WWeb
'Engleriana'	CMal WWat
floribunda	CB&S CBot CChu CGle CHan CLan CPle CSco CTrw ELan IOrc ISea SHil SPer SSpi SSta WAbe WBod WWat
graebneriana	CHan
§ x ***grandiflora***	Widely available
♦– 'Aurea'	See A. x *g.* 'Goldsport'
– 'Francis Mason'	Widely available
♦– 'Gold Strike'	See A. x *g.* 'Goldsport'
§– 'Goldsport'	CB&S CCla IOrc MPla SCro WPat WWat
– 'Prostrata'	CBot WHCG
– 'Variegata'	CLan WWat WWin
rupestris	See A. x ***grandiflora***
schumannii	CB&S CBot CBow CBra CChu CCla CFis CGle CLan CMHG CSam CSco ENot SDry SHil SLon SPer SPla SReu SSta WAbe WHCG WOld WPat
triflora	CBot CHan ECtt SHil SPla SSta WWat

ABELIOPHYLLUM (Oleaceae)

distichum	CB&S CBot CBow CBrd CChu CCor ELan ENot LSav MBri MWal SBra SHil SPer SPla SReu SSpi SSta SSus WBod WPat WSHC WWat
– ***roseum***	CSam EBre ECro ELan ERav LSav MPla SSpi WEas

ABELMOSCHUS (Malvaceae)

¶ ***moschatus*** 'Mischief'	SMrm WPer
¶– 'Mischief Soft Pink'	SMrm

ABIES † (Pinaceae)

alba	CDoC EHul ISea MBar WCon
– 'Compacta'	CKen
¶ ***amabilis***	WFro
– 'Spreading Star'	SHil WCon
x ***arnoldiana***	NHol
balsamea balsamea	EHar NWea WCoo
– ***hudsonia***	CDoC CKen CMac EHar EHul ENHC EPla GDra IOrc LLin MBal MBar MGos MPla NHol SHil SIng SPla WAbe WCon
– 'Nana'	CKen EBre EHul IDai IJoh MBri MPla WAbe WCon
bornmuelleriana	LSav
brachyphylla dwarf form	See A. ***homolepis*** 'Prostrata'
bracteata	ISea SHil WCoo
cephalonica	CBow EHar NWea SHil
§– 'Meyer's Dwarf'	EBre EHar MBar
I – 'Nana'	See A. x *c.* 'Meyer's Dwarf'
concolor	CBow CDoC EHar GRei IJoh IOrc ISea LSav MBal MBar NWea SHil SPer WCon WCoo
– 'Archer's Dwarf'	CKen
¶– 'Argentea'	SHil WAbe
– 'Candicans'	See A. *c.* 'Argentea'
§– 'Compacta'	CBra CKen LLin MBal MBar MGos NHol SHil SSta WCon
– 'Fagerhult'	CKen
– 'Gable's Weeping'	CKen
– 'Glauca'	See A. *c.* 'Violacea'
– 'Glauca Compacta'	See A. *c.* 'Compacta'
– ***lowiana***	NWea
– 'Masonic Broom'	CKen
– 'Piggelmee'	CKen
§– 'Violacea'	CBra LSav MBar MBri SSta WCon
– 'Wattezii'	CKen LLin SHil
§ ***delavayi delavayi***	CMCN IBar IOrc
§ ***delavayi delavayi*** Fabri group	CMCN WCoo
fabri	See A. ***delavayi delavayi*** Fabri group
§ ***fargesii***	SHil
– ***faxoniana***	CMCN LSav
forrestii	SHil
fraseri 'Klein's Nest'	CKen
grandis	CB&S EHar ENot GRei IOrc MBar NWea SHil SMad WCon WCoo WMou
– 'Compacta'	CKen
holophylla	CMCN WCoo
homolepis	LSav MBlu NWea WCoo
§– 'Prostrata'	CKen
koreana	Widely available
– 'Aurea'	See A. *k.* 'Flava'
– 'Compact Dwarf'	MGos SSta WAbe
§– 'Flava'	CDoC MBar MBri NHol WCon
¶– 'Nisbet'	CKen
– 'Piccolo'	CKen MBar NHol
– 'Silberlocke'	CBra CKen EBre IOrc MBri MGos NHol SGar SHil SSta
¶– 'Starker's Dwarf'	CKen
*– 'Violacea Prostrata'	NHol
lasiocarpa	LSav WCon WCoo
– ***arizonica***	LSav SHil SSta
– 'Compacta'	CDoC CKen CMac CSco EHar IOrc LLin MBar MBri MGos NHol SHil SSta WAbe WCon
– 'Glauca'	See A. ***concolor*** 'Violacea'
– 'Globe'	CKen
– 'Green Globe'	CKen
– 'Kenwith Blue'	CKen
magnifica	EHar LSav SHil WCoo
– 'Glauca'	SHil
minensis	See A. ***delavayi delavayi***
nephrolepis	CMCN
nobilis	See A. ***procera***
nordmanniana	CDoC EHar EHul IJoh LBuc LSav MBal MBar MBri MGos NWea SHil WCon
– 'Golden Spreader'	CKen MBar NHol SHil SSta
¶ ***numidica***	LPan
– 'Pendula'	CKen
pindrow	EHal SHil
pinsapo	EHar MBar SHil
– 'Aurea'	CKen NHol
– 'Glauca'	CDoC EHar ELan IOrc LPan MBar MBlu MBri NHol SHil WCon

– 'Hamondii'	CKen
I – 'Horstmann'	CKen EBre
§ *procera*	CDoC EHul GRei IDai ISea MBal MBar NWea SHil WCon WCoo WMou
¶ – 'Blaue Hexe'	CKen
– 'Glauca'	CDoC CMac EHar IOrc LPan MBar MBri WCon
– 'Glauca Prostrata'	EBre ENHC IOrc LPan MBal MBar MGos NHol SHil SSta
sachalinensis	NWea SHil
sibirica	NWea
spectabilis	SHil WCoo
squamata	CMCN SHil
sutchuenensis	See A. ***fargesii***
veitchii	GRei IJoh IOrc MBar NWea SHil WCon WMou
¶ – 'Hedergott'	CKen

ABROMEITIELLA (Bromeliaceae)

ABROTANELLA (Compositae)

ABUTILON † (Malvaceae)

'Amsterdam'	ERea
'Ashford Red'	CB&S CBot CTre IBlr IJoh IOrc LGre SHil SLMG WOMN WOld WWeb
'Boule de Neige'	CBot CGre ERea LRHS MBri
'Canary Bird'	CB&S CBot CGre CPle CSun CTre ERea LGre LHop MBri SLMG WWeb
'Cannington Carol'	CSun ERea
'Cannington Peter'	CGre
¶ 'Cannington Sonia'	CGre
'Cerise Queen'	CB&S
'Cynthia Pike'	CGre LHop
'Fireball'	LHop
globosum	See A. × ***hybridum***
'Hinton Seedling'	CBow CTre LHop SLMG SSus
§ × ***hybridum***	CB&S MBri MNew
– 'Golden Fleece'	CKni ERea IBlr SLMG
– 'Master Michael'	CKni ERea
– 'Savitzii'	CB&S CBot ERea IReg
'Kentish Belle'	CB&S CBot CBra CChu CLan CMHG CPle CSco CTre EBre ECtt ENot IOrc ISea SBra SHil SLMG SPer
'Louise Marignac'	CB&S CSun LHop WWeb
megapotamicum	Widely available
– 'Variegatum'	CB&S CBot CBow CCla CLan CSun ECtt ELan GWic IBar IBlr IOrc MBri SAxl SBra SHil SLMG SLon SMad WPat
– 'Wisley Red'	CTre
× ***milleri***	CB&S CBot CChu CCla CGre CSun ELan ERea IBar SBra WSHC
– 'Variegatum'	CB&S CKni CSun NRar SLMG
'Nabob'	CGre CSun CTre ERea LHop LRHS MBri SLMG WOld
ochsenii	SHil
¶ 'Orange Glow'	CGre
'Orange King'	CB&S
'Patrick Synge'	CChu CGre CMHG CSun ERav ERea LGre SLMG SSpi SSus
§ ***pictum***	ERea MBri SLMG
– 'Thompsonii'	CBot CSun EFol ERea ESim IBlr IOrc ISea LHil SLMG
'Pink Lady'	CGre
sellowianum mamoratum	ERea SLMG
'Souvenir de Bonn'	CGre CSun ERea IBlr LHop WWeb
♦ ***striatum***	See A. ***pictum***
× ***suntense***	CB&S CBow CCla CGle CHEx CMHG CPle CSco CTrw EBre ELan ERav IJoh LAbb MBal NRed SLMG SPer SSta WPat WSHC
– 'Gorer's White'	SSpi
– 'Jermyns'	CBot CBra ECtt ISea LGre LSav MGos MUlv SHil WSHC WWat WWeb
– ***violaceum***	SSpi
– 'White Charm'	SHil
'Violetta'	CBot SBla SPer
vitifolium	CB&S CBot CCla CFis CGle IOrc LHop MBal MNew SFis SPer WWat WWin
– ***album***	CB&S CBot CBow CCla CFis CGle CMHG CSco CTrw ELan ERav LHop MBal NRar NRed NTow SPer SSpi WHal WWat
– 'Tennant's White'	CBot CCla CGre LGre SHil
– 'Veronica Tennant'	CGle ERav ISea LGre SHil SSpi WKif

ACACIA † (Leguminosae)

armata	CHan ERea IOrc MBri
§ – ***angustifolia***	CSun
§ ***baileyana***	CB&S CBow CSun ERea SHil WCel
§ – 'Purpurea'	CB&S CBow CGre SMad SSpi
¶ ***cultriformis***	IOrc
§ ***dealbata***	Widely available
– 'Mirandole'	ERea
§ – ***subalpina***	SArc WCel
decurrens	CSun
Exeter hybrid	CGre ERea
¶ ***farnesiana***	CPle
filicifolia	SArc WCel
frigescens	SArc WCel
genistifolia	CSun
julibrissin	See ALBIZIA ***j.***
juniperina	CGre CPle
kybeanensis	WCel
longifolia	CB&S CHEx IOrc
– ***floribunda*** 'Lisette'	ERea
§ ***mearnsii***	WCel
§ ***melanoxylon***	IBar IOrc LRHS MNew WCel
mucronata	CB&S CGre SHil
obliquinervia	WCel
paradoxa	See ACACIA ***armata angustifolia***
pendula	MBri
§ ***podalyriifolia***	CMHG CPle
§ ***pravissima***	CB&S CChu CHEx CHan CMHG CPle CSun ERea LHop MBal SArc SSpi WCel WNor WSHC
rhetinodes	CB&S CGre ERea LHol MNew
§ ***riceana***	CB&S SMad WCel
¶ ***rubida***	SArc
¶ ***saligna***	IOrc
sentis	See A. ***victoriae***
¶ ***verticillata***	CB&S
victoriae	ERea SLMG

ACAENA (Rosaceae)

§ ***adscendens***	CHoe CRiv CRow ECha ECro ECtt EMon LHil MWgw NNor SDix STre WWin
– 'Glauca'	LHop NBir NNor

affinis	See A. ***adscendens***
§ *anserinifolia*	CGle CLew EBar ECha GCHN LHil NCat NHol NRar NRed WEas WHil WWin
argentea	SBla
§ 'Blue Haze'	Widely available
buchananii	CRiv CRow CShe CTom EPar MBar MBri MCas MMth MWgw NKay NNor SIng SSmi STre WCla WHea WHil WHoo
caerulea	See A. ***caesiiglauca***
§ *caesiiglauca*	CMer CRiv ECro ESis GGar MWat NCat NHol NNor SCro SIng WEas WPer
fissistipula	GGar
glaucophylla	See A. ***magellanica***
inermis	CCor CGle CLew CMer CSun EBre ECha ELan EPar MMth MWat NNrd SIng SSmi WHil
§ – 'Kupferteppich' ('Copper Carpet')	CHar CHoe CRiv CRow EBre ECro GGar IBar MBri MRav NCat NHar NVic SIng WHea WPat
§ *magellanica*	ECro GWic SIng
microphylla	CHad CMer CSun ECro ESis GGar MBri MRav MWat NGre NRed SIng SLHN SSmi WCla WHal WHoo WPer
– 'Glauca'	See A. ***caesiiglauca***
– 'Pallidolivacea'	CRow
– 'Pulchella'	CTom EBre GAbr MRav NHol SFir SLHN
¶ *myriophylla*	
novae-zelandiae	CRiv CRow ECro NRed SDix SIng WPer
ovalifolia	CRow CTom MFir NCat NRed
'Pewter'	See A. 'Blue Haze'
'Purple Carpet'	See A. ***inermis*** 'Kupferteppich'
saccaticupula	CSun
sanguisorbae	See A. ***anserinifolia***

ACALYPHA (Euphorbiaceae)

hispida	MBri
wilkesiana	MBri
– 'Can-Can'	MBri
– 'Gold Cant'	MBri
– *pudsiana*	MBri

ACANTHOLIMON (Plumbaginaceae)

androsaceum	EPot
glumaceum	EBre GLoc MDHE MHig WPer
ulicinum Mac&W 5887	SOkd

ACANTHOPANAX See **ELEUTHEROCOCCUS**

ACANTHUS † (Acanthaceae)

§ *balcanicus*	CBow CHan GWic MFir SBla SDix SPer
¶ *caroli-alexandri*	EMon
dioscoridis perringii	LGre MCab SBla
hirsutus	EMon LGre
hungaricus	CCla EMon
longifolius	See A. ***balcanicus***
mollis	Widely available
– Latifolius group	CHan CSco ECro EFou EGol ERou LHil MCot MRav MWgw NHol SChu SPer SSpi WWat
spinosus	Widely available
¶ – 'Lady Moore'	IFer
– Spinosissimus group	CGle CHad ECha LGre NOak SBla

ACCA (Myrtaceae)

F 'Coolidge'	ERea
§ *sellowiana*	CB&S CBow CBra CChu CCla CHan CMHG CPle CSam ELan ERea ESim LAbb LHop SBor SGar SHil SLon SSpi WBod WPat WSHC
F – 'Apollo'	ERea ESim
F – 'Mammoth'	ERea
F – 'Triumph'	ERea ESim
§ – 'Variegata'	CGre SHil

ACER † (Aceraceae)

acuminatum	CMCN WNor
albopurpurescens	CMCN
amplum	CMCN
argutum	CMCN LSav SSpi WCoo WNor
barbinerve	CMCN
buergerianum	CB&S CMCN EHar IJoh LSav MUlv SPer SSpi STre WCoo WMou WNor
– 'Goshiki-kaede'	SSpi
caesium	CMCN LSav
campbellii	CB&S CMCN WNor
– *yunnanense*	CMCN
campestre	CBra CKin CLnd CMCN CPer CSco ENot GRei IOrc LBuc MBar MBri MGos NWea SHil SPer STre WCoo WMou WNor
– 'Elsrijk'	CLnd SSpi
– 'Postelense'	CMCN LMer SHil
– 'Pulverulentum'	CMCN SHil
¶ – 'Royal Ruby'	MBri
– 'Schwerinii'	CMCN SHil
capillipes	Widely available
cappadocicum	CMCN SExT SHil WCoo WNor WPat
– 'Aureum'	CLnd CMCN CSco EHar ELan ENot IOrc LNet MBri SExT SHil SMad SPer SSpi WMou
– *mono*	See A. ***mono***
– 'Rubrum'	CLnd CMCN EHar ENot IHos IOrc LHop MBlu MUlv SExT SHil SPer SSpi SSta WMou
– *sinicum*	CMCN
carpinifolium	CCor CMCN MBri SHil SSpi WCoo
§ *caudatifolium*	CMCN WCoo
cinerascens	CMCN
cinnamomifolium	CMCN
circinatum	CBow CChu CCla CMCN ECtt EHar IBar IJoh LNet LSav NBar SHil SMad SReu SSpi SSta WCoo WNor WWat
– 'Little Gem'	CMCN
– 'Monroe'	CMCN LNet
x *cissifolium*	CMCN SSpi WCoo
§ *cordatum*	CMCN
coriaceifolium	See A. ***cinnamomifolium***
x *coriaceum*	CMCN
crataegifolium	CMCN SSpi WCoo
– 'Veitchii'	CMCN LNet
creticum	See A. ***sempervirens***
dasycarpum	See A. ***saccharinum***
davidii	CB&S CBow CCla CMCN CMHG CSco EHar ENot IBar IOrc LSav MBal MBar MBri MGos MRav NBar SExT SMad SPer SPla SSta WFro WNor

Plant	Suppliers
– 'Ernest Wilson'	CB&S CMCN ELan SSpi WNor
– 'George Forrest'	CMCN ELan SHil SSpi
– 'Karmen'	MBri
– 'Rosalie'	MBri
– 'Serpentine'	ELan MBri SPer
diabolicum	CMCN
x ***dieckii***	CMCN
distylum	CMCN SHil
divergens	CMCN
elegantulum	CMCN
erianthum	CMCN LSav SSpi WNor
fabri	CMCN
flabellatum	CMCN
forrestii	CMCN SHil SSpi WCoo WNor
– 'Alice'	CB&S LNet MBri SSpi
franchetii	CMCN
fulvescens	See A. ***longipes***
ginnala	See A. ***tataricum ginnala***
giraldii	CMCN
glabrum	CMCN WNor
– ***douglasii***	CMCN
globosum	See A. ***platanoides*** 'Globosum'
grandidentatum	CMCN
griseum	Widely available
N***grosseri***	CMCN
– ***hersii***	CBra CGre CLnd CTre ECtt EHar ELan ENot MBal MBri MRav NWea SExT SHil SMad SPer SSpi SSta WNor WWat
heldreichii	CLnd CMCN LSav SSpi WCoo
henryi	CMCN ENot LNet SSpi WNor
x ***hillieri***	CMCN
hookeri	CMCN
§ ***hyrcanum***	CMCN
japonicum	CMCN LNet LSav MBal MBar SSta WAbe WNor
§ – ***aconitifolium***	CBra CMCN CSco CShe EHar ELan ENot GRei IHos IJoh IOrc LNet LSav MBar MBri MGos NJap SExT SHil SPer SReu SSpi SSta WNor
♦– ***aureum***	See A. ***shirasawanum aureum***
– 'Ezono-momiji'	CMCN
– 'Filicifolium'	IDai
– 'Green Cascade'	CFor CMCN
– 'Laciniatum'	See A. ***j. aconitifolium***
– ***microphyllum***	CMCN
– 'Ogurayama'	LNet
– 'O-isami'	CMCN
– 'Vitifolium'	CMCN ELan IOrc LNet LSav SExT SHil SPer SSpi SSta
kawakamii	See A. ***caudatifolium***
laevigatum	CMCN
lanceolatum	CMCN
laxiflorum	CB&S CMCN SSpi
lobelii	CMCN EHar ENot NWea SExT SHil SSpi WNor
§ ***longipes***	CMCN
macrophyllum	CMCN EHar IOrc ISea SHil SSpi WCoo
– 'Kimballae'	CMCN
– 'Seattle Sentinel'	CMCN
§ ***maximowiczianum***	CFor CMCN EHar ELan IOrc MBri SHil SPer SSpi SSta WNor WCoo
¶ – ***morifolium***	CMCN IBar LSav SHil WNor
maximowiczii	CMCN SSpi WCoo WNor
micranthum	CMCN WNor
miyabei	CMCN LSav MBri
§ ***mono***	

Plant	Suppliers
– 'Hoshiyadori'	CMCN
– 'Shuhu-nishiki'	CMCN
– ***tricuspis***	CMCN
monspessulanum	CMCN LSav
morrisonense	See A. ***caudatifolium***
negundo	CLnd CMCN ELan ENot ISea NBar SHil WNor
– 'Argenteovariegatum'	See A. ***n.*** 'Variegatum'
– 'Auratum'	CMCN MBri SHil SPer SSpi
– 'Aureovariegatum'	CB&S ELan IJoh MBar NJap
– 'Elegans'	CBow CLnd CMCN CSco EBre ENot LHop NJap NKay SExT SHil SPer SReu SSpi
– 'Elegantissimum'	CBra ELan
– 'Flamingo'	Widely available
– 'Kelly's Gold'	SGar
§ – 'Variegatum'	CB&S CBra CHoe CLnd CSco EGol ENot IDai ISea MGos SHil SPer
– ***violaceum***	CMCN ELan SHil
nigrum	CMCN
nikoense	See A. ***maximowiczianum***
nipponicum	CMCN
oblongum	CMCN
obtusifolium	CMCN LRHS
okamotoanum	CMCN
oliverianum	CMCN SSpi WNor
opalus	CMCN WNor
orientale	See A. ***sempervirens***
palmatum	CBow CLan CMCN CMHG ENot LNet LSav MBal MBar SHil SPer SPla SSta STre WAbe WCoo WNor
– 'Aka-shigitatsu-sawa'	CMCN LNet NJap SSpi
– 'Akegarasu'	CMCN
– 'Aoyagi'	CMCN LNet NJap SSpi
– 'Ao-shime-no-uchi'	See A. ***p.*** 'Shino-buga-oka'
– 'Asahi-zuru'	CMCN LNet SHil SSpi SSta
– ***atropurpureum***	Widely available
§ – 'Atropurpureum Superbum'	CMCN MBri
– 'Aureum'	CMCN CSco LNet MBri SReu SSpi SSta
– Autumn Glory group	CFor SSpi
– 'Awa-kawa'	CMCN
– 'Azuma-murasaki'	CMCN
– 'Beni-kagami'	CMCN LNet MBri NJap
– 'Beni-komachi'	CMCN LNet
– 'Beni-maiko'	CMCN LNet SHil
– 'Beni-schichihenge'	CMCN LNet MBri SHil SSta
– 'Beni-shidare Variegated'	CMCN LNet
– 'Beni-tsukasa'	CFor LNet NJap SSpi
– 'Bloodgood'	CB&S CCla CMCN CSam EHar ELan ENot IBar LNet LSav MBar MBri MGos MR&S NJap SHil SPer SReu SSpi SSta WBod
– 'Brocade'	CMCN
– 'Burgundy Lace'	CMCN IOrc LNet MBri MGos NJap SHil SSpi
– 'Butterfly'	CB&S CMCN ELan IBar IOrc LNet LSav MBar MBri MGos NJap SHil SPer SReu SSpi SSta WPat
– 'Chirimen-nishiki'	CMCN LNet
§ – 'Chishio'	CB&S CMCN LHyd LNet NJap SGar SPer SSpi
– 'Chishio Improved'	See A. ***p.*** 'Improved Chishio'
– 'Chitoseyama'	CCla CMCN LNet LSav MBri SHil SSpi SSta

– 'Coonara Pygmy'	CMCN LNet
– 'Corallinum'	CFor CMCN SHil
N– ***coreanum***	CMCN NJap SHil SSpi WNor
– 'Crimson Queen'	CMCN CSco ENot IOrc LNet LSav MBri MGos MR&S NJap SHil SPer SReu SSpi WPat
– 'Crippsii'	SGar
– 'Deshojo'	CMCN SGar SHil
– ***dissectum***	CBra CShe ENot IJoh IOrc ISea LHyd LSav MBar MBri MGos NWea SHil SReu WNor WPat WWat
– 'Dissectum Atropurpureum'	CB&S CBra CHoe CSco CShe ELan ENot IBar IDai IJoh LHyd LNet MBal MBar MGos MR&S NWea SHil SPer SReu SSta WBod WWat
– 'Dissectum Flavescens'	CMCN
♦– 'Dissectum Nigrum'	See A. ***p.*** 'Ever Red'
– 'Dissectum Ornatum'	ELan IJoh SHil
– 'Dissectum Palmatifidum'	LNet NBar
– 'Dissectum Variegatum'	ELan LNet SGar SSpi SSta
– ***dissectum viride***	CB&S CBra CCla CFor CMCN CSco ELan GRei IDai LNet MR&S NJap NKay SPer SPla SSta WBod
*– 'Eddisbury'	SSta
*– 'Efegi'	CSco
§– 'Ever Red'	CFor LNet MR&S SHil SPer SSpi WBod
– 'Filigree'	CMCN EHar LNet MGos NJap SHil SMad SSpi
*– 'Fireglow'	MBri
– 'Frederici Guglielmi'	See A. ***p.*** 'Dissectum Variegatum'
– 'Garnet'	CBra CCla CMCN CSam ECtt EHar ELan IHos LSav MBar MBri MR&S NJap SMad SPer SSpi SSta WPat WWat
– 'Goshiki-kotohime'	CMCN
– 'Goshiki-shidare'	CMCN LNet
§– 'Hagoromo'	LNet
– 'Hanami-nishiki'	CMCN
– 'Harusame'	LNet
– 'Hazeroino'	CMCN
– ***heptalobum***	CMCN
§– 'Heptalobum Elegans'	CMCN SHil SPer SReu SSpi
– 'Heptalobum Elegans Purpureum'	See A. ***p.*** 'Hessei'
– 'Heptalobum Lutescens'	SPer SSpi
§– 'Hessei'	CMCN CSco LNet MBri SHil SReu
– 'Higasayama'	CB&S CMCN IBar LNet NJap SSpi
– 'Hogyoku'	CMCN NJap
– 'Ichigyoji'	NJap
§– 'Improved Chishio'	LNet MGos NJap SHil WPat
– 'Inaba-shidare'	CSam CSco GRei LNet MBar MBri MGos NJap SExT SHil SPer SReu SSta
– 'Inazuma'	CMCN NJap SSpi
– 'Jiro-shidare'	SSpi
§– 'Kagiri-nishiki'	CB&S CBra CMCN COtt CSco LNet MBri MGos NJap SHil SSpi SSta
– 'Kamagata'	CMCN SSpi SSta
– 'Karaori-nishiki'	LNet NJap
– 'Karasugawa'	CMCN SHil
– 'Kasagiyama'	CMCN LRHS NJap SHil SSpi
– 'Kashima'	CMCN NJap
– 'Katsura'	CB&S CFor CMCN ELan LNet MBri NJap SGar SPer SSta
– 'Kinran'	CMCN LNet SSpi
– 'Kinshii'	CMCN LRHS SSpi SSta
– 'Kiyohime'	CMCN
– 'Ki-hachijo'	CMCN NJap
– 'Kotohime'	CMCN
– 'Kurui-jishi'	LNet
– 'Linearilobum'	CFor CMCN LHyd LNet NJap SHil SPer SSpi
– 'Linearilobum Atropurpureum'	CFor SHil SReu SSpi SSta
– 'Little Princess'	ELan LRHS MBri WWat
– 'Maimori'	SSta
– 'Mapi-no-machihime'	SSta
– 'Matsukaze'	COtt MBri NJap SSpi
– 'Mirte'	LNet
– 'Moonfire'	CMCN LNet NJap
– 'Mure-hibari'	CMCN
– 'Murogawa'	CMCN
– 'Nicholsonii'	CMCN
– 'Nigrum'	CMCN SGar
– 'Nishiki-gawa'	See A. ***p.*** 'Pine Bark Maple'
– 'Nomurishidare'	LRHS SSpi
– 'Nuresagi'	CMCN LNet
– 'Okushimo'	CMCN LNet SSpi SSta
– 'Omurayama'	LNet LRHS NJap SSta
– 'Orido-nishiki'	CMCN LNet MGos
– 'Ornatum'	MBri NJap SPer
– 'Osakazuki'	Widely available
– 'Oshio-beni'	CMCN SHil
– 'Oshu-shidare'	CMCN
– 'O-kagami'	COtt LNet
– 'Pendulum Julian'	CMCN
§– 'Pine Bark Maple'	CMCN
– 'Red Dragon'	MBri SGar SPer
– 'Red Pygmy'	CB&S CFor CMCN COtt CSco LNet MBri MGos NJap SHil SSpi SSta
– 'Reticulatum'	See A. ***p.*** 'Shigitatsu-sawa'
– 'Ribesifolium'	See A. ***p.*** 'Shishigashira'
♦– 'Roseomarginatum'	See A. ***p.*** 'Kagiri-nishiki'
– 'Rough Bark Maple'	CMCN
– 'Rubrum'	CMCN MBal NJap SHil SSpi
– 'Rufescens'	CMCN
– 'Sagara-nishiki'	CMCN
– 'Samidare'	CMCN NJap
N– 'Sango-kaku'	CFor CMCN CSam CSco CShe ELan ENot LNet MBal MBar MBri MGos NJap SHil SPer SReu SSpi SSta WPat
– 'Saoshika'	CMCN
– 'Sazanami'	CMCN NJap
– 'Seiryu'	CB&S CFor CMCN EHar ELan LNet LSav MBri MGos NJap SGar SHil SPer SSpi SSta SSus WAbe
N– 'Senkaki'	CB&S CBow EHar ELan IBar IHos IOrc LHyd LNet MR&S MRav NHol SExT SPer SPla WBod WPat WWat
– 'Septemlobum Elegans'	See A. ***p.*** 'Heptalobum Elegans'
– 'Septemlobum Purpureum'	See A. ***p.*** 'Hessei'
– 'Sessilifolium'	See A. ***p.*** 'Hagoromo'
– 'Sherwood Flame'	CMCN LNet MBri MGos NJap

§ – 'Shigitatsu-sawa' CMCN SHil
– 'Shime-no-uchi' CMCN LNet
– 'Shindeshojo' CMCN ELan LNet LSav MBri NJap SPer SSta
– 'Shinonome' CMCN COtt CSco
§ – 'Shino-buga-oka' CMCN LNet
§ – 'Shishigashira' CMCN EHar MBri SHil SSta
– 'Shishio' See A. ***p.*** 'Chishio'
– 'Shishio Improved' See A. ***p.*** 'Improved Chishio'
– 'Shojo-nomura' COtt
¶ – 'Stella Rossa' MBri
– 'Suminagashi' CMCN LNet
– 'Takinogawa' LRHS SSpi SSta
– 'Tamahime' NJap
– 'Tamukeyama' CMCN
– 'Tana' CMCN NJap
– 'Trompenburg' CMCN COtt LNet MBri NJap SHil SSpi SSta
– 'Tsukubane' CMCN
– 'Tsuma-beni' CMCN SSta
– 'Tsuma-gaki' CMCN
– 'Ukigumo' CB&S LNet MGos NJap SHil SPer SSpi SSta
– 'Ukon' CMCN NJap SSta
– 'Umegae' CMCN
– 'Utsu-semi' CMCN SSpi
– 'Versicolor' LNet NJap
– 'Villa Taranto' CMCN LNet MBlu MGos NJap SSpi SSta
– 'Volubile' CMCN
– 'Wabito' CMCN
– 'Wada's Flame' SSta
– 'Waterfall' CMCN LNet MGos NJap
– 'Wou-nishiki' CMCN LNet MBri NJap
papilio CMCN
paxii CMCN
pectinatum CMCN
– 'Sirene' MBri
pensylvanicum CBow CCla CMCN IJoh LSav MBri MGos MRav NBar NWea SHil SMad SPer SReu SSpi WCoo WNor WWeb
– 'Erythrocladum' CFor CMCN LNet MBlu SHil SSpi
pentaphyllum CMCN SHil
§ ***pentapotamicum*** CMCN
pictum See A. ***mono***
platanoides CBra CKin CLan CLnd CMCN CPer ELan ENot GRei IDai IJoh ISea LBuc MBri MGos NWea SHil SPer WAbe WMou WNor
– 'Cleveland' CB&S ENot SExT
– 'Columnare' CMCN ENot IOrc NWea SExT SHil
– 'Crimson King' CB&S CBow CBra CCla CMCN CSam CSco ECtt ELan GRei IDai IJoh LNet MBar MR&S NBar NWea SExT SHil SMad SPer SReu SSta WAbe
– 'Crimson Sentry' IHos LNet MBri SExT SHil
– 'Deborah' SExT SHil
– 'Drummondii' CB&S CBra CCla CLnd CMCN CSco ELan ENot GRei IDai IJoh LNet MBar MBri MGos MR&S NWea SExT SHil SPer SReu SSta WAbe WJas
– 'Emerald Queen' ENot SExT SHil
– 'Erectum' CMCN
§ – 'Globosum' CLnd CMCN ENot SExT SHil
– 'Goldsworth Purple' CFis CLnd MGos WAbe
– 'Laciniatum' CMCN ENot SExT
– 'Lorbergii' See A. ***p.*** 'Palmatifidum'
– 'Olmstead' ENot LNet
– 'Royal Red' ENot MBri SExT SPer
– 'Schwedleri' CBra CLnd CSco ENot GRei MGos SExT SPer
– 'Summershade' SExT
pseudoplatanus CB&S CKin CLnd CMCN CPer ELan ENot GRei IDai IJoh LBuc MBar MBri MGos NWea SHil SPla WMou
§ – 'Atropurpureum' CLnd ENot IJoh IOrc NWea SHil
– 'Brilliantissimum' Widely available
– 'Corstorphinense' CMCN
– 'Erectum' ENot SExT SHil
– 'Leopoldii' CB&S CBra CFis CLnd CMCN CSco ELan ENot IOrc MBar MBri SExT SHil SPer
– 'Negenia' SExT
– 'Nizetii' EHar ENot SHil
– 'Prinz Handjery' CB&S CFor CMCN CSco EHar LNet MBar NJap SHil SSpi
– 'Simon-Louis Frères' CBra CLnd LNet MBri MGos NJap SExT
– 'Spaethii' See A. ***p.*** 'Atropurpureum'
– 'Worleei' CB&S CBra CLnd CMCN CSco ECtt EHar ENot GRei IOrc NWea SExT SHil SPer WAbe WMou
pseudo-sieboldianum CMCN WNor
pycnanthum CMCN SSpi
regelii See A. ***pentapotamicum***
rubescens SSpi
rubrum CB&S CBow CBra CLan CLnd CMCN LSav NBar NWea SExT SHil SPer WAbe WBod WNor
– 'Columnare' SExT
– 'October Glory' CFor CMCN CMHG CSam EHar IOrc MBlu MUlv SHil SSpi SSta WWeb
– 'Red Sunset' CMCN MBri
– 'Scanlon' CMCN SExT SHil
– 'Schlesingeri' CMCN SExT SHil
– 'Tridens' CMCN
rufinerve CB&S CLnd CMCN EHar ENot IOrc LSav MBri MR&S NBar NWea SExT SHil SPer SReu WNor
– 'Albomarginatum' See A. ***r.*** 'Hatsuyuki'
§ – 'Hatsuyuki' CMCN MBri SSpi
§ ***saccharinum*** CB&S CLnd CMCN EHar ENot MGos MR&S NWea SExT SHil SPer SSpi SSta STre WMou
– 'Elegans' CMCN
– 'Fastigiatum' See A. ***s.*** 'Pyramidale'
– ***laciniatum*** CMCN EHar ENot MBlu MGos SHil SPer
– 'Lutescens' CBow CMCN EHar ENot SPer WMou
§ – 'Pyramidale' CLnd CMCN EHar ENot IOrc SExT SHil SPer
– 'Wieri' CLnd SExT
saccharum CBra CMCN EHar STre WMou WNor
*– 'Aureum' IOrc
– 'Newton Sentry' CMCN
– 'Temple's Upright' CMCN
§ ***sempervirens*** CMCN
serrulatum CMCN
shirasawanum CMCN SSpi WNor
§ – ***aureum*** Widely available
– 'Microphyllum' LNet
– 'Palmatifolium' CMCN MGos

sieboldianum	CMCN EHar SSpi SSta WNor
– 'Sode-no-uchi'	CMCN
'Silver Vein'	CMCN LRHS MBri SHil
sinense	CMCN
sinopurpurascens	CMCN
spicatum	CB&S CMCN SSpi WCoo WNor
♦*stachyophyllum*	See A. ***tetramerum***
§ *sterculiaceum*	CMCN
syriacum	CMCN
takesimense	CMCN WCoo
taronense	CMCN
§ *tataricum ginnala*	CCla CLnd CMCN CMHG ENot IOrc MBal MBri MFir MGos NJap SChu SExT SHil SPer SSta WCoo WMou WNor WWat
*– – 'Fire'	LNet
– – 'Flame'	CMCN
– – *semenowii*	CMCN
tegmentosum	CMCN WCoo
tegmentosum glaucorufinerve 'Albolimbatum'	See A. ***rufinerve*** 'Hatsuyuki'
tenuifolium	CMCN
§ *tetramerum*	CMCN SSpi
thomsonii	CMCN
trautvetteri	CMCN SSpi WNor
triflorum	CMCN SHil SSpi
truncatum	CMCN LSav WNor
– 'Akikaze-nishiki'	LNet
tschonoskii	CMCN MBri
turkestanicum	CMCN
ukurunduense	CMCN WNor
velutinum	CMCN
villosum	See A. ***sterculiaceum***
wilsonii	CMCN SHil
x *zoeschense*	CMCN SHil
¶ – 'Annae'	IOrc

ACERIPHYLLUM (Saxifragaceae)

rossii	See MUKDENIA ***rossii***

ACHILLEA † (Compositae)

abrotanoides	ELan EMon
ageratifolia	CLew ECha EFol GAbr MHig MTho NHol NNor SSmi WWin
§ – *aizoon*	NKay WPer
'Apfelblüte' ('Appleblossom')	CHar CSco CSun EBre ECha EFol EFou ELan EOrc ERou LHop MBri NHol SPer
argentea	See A. ***clavennae***, Tanacetum ***argenteum***
aurea 'Grandiflora'	See A. ***chrysocoma*** 'G.'
borealis	MSal
cartilaginea	EFou LHop
chrysocoma	CMer ELan ESis GAbr MCas MWat NKay NTow SSmi
§ – 'Grandiflora'	CFis CHad SIng
§ *clavennae*	CGle CHar CSev CShe CTom GCHN MCas MHig MPla MWat NNor NRoo SBla SIng WHil WOld
– *integrifolia*	NHol WDav
'Coronation Gold'	CBre CKel CSco CShe EFou ELan ENot ERou IDai MBri MWat NBar NKay SPer WEas
¶ 'Credo'	EMon
'Croftway'	SCro
decolorans	CArn Effi GPoy LHol MChe MSal SIde WSto
– 'W B Child'	CChu CHar ECha EFou ELan EMon ERou WEas
erba-rotta rupestris	CLew ESis GAbr MHig NKay SIng
'Fanal'	CBre CHar COtt CSco CSev CSun ELan EMon EOrc ERou LHop MTho NCat NHol SCro SPer WWin
filipendulina	MFir MWat WWin
– 'Cloth of Gold'	EBar ECtt EPad LAbb LHil MBri MPit MWgw NNor NRoo WHoo
– 'Gold Plate'	CB&S CGle CSco CShe CTom ECha EFou ELan ERou MBri MCot MWgw NKay NOrc SCro SPer WEas WHil
¶ – 'Parker's Variety'	NOak
'Forncett Beauty'	EFou
'Forncett Candy'	EFou
'Forncett Fletton'	EFou
¶ 'Forncett Ivory'	EFou
'Forncett Tapestry'	EFou
grandifolia	CHan EMon EPad
'Great Expectations'	See A. 'Hoffnung'
'Hartington White'	EMon LRHS
§ 'Hoffnung'	CBre CHar COtt CSco CSev CSun EBre ECha ECtt EFou EOrc ERou LHop NHol SPer WWin
x *huteri*	CLew CMHG CSam CSev CShe ECtt ELan EPot ESis GLoc MBro MCas MHig MMth MPlt NCat NHol NNor NNrd NTow SIng SSmi WEas WPer
x *jaborneggii*	GCHN NKay
x *kellereri*	MBro MCas MHig SSmi
x *kolbiana*	EOrc EPad LHop MHig MWat NHol NNrd NRoo SSmi WDav WPat WWin
§ – 'Weston'	CMHG NRoo NTow
'Lachsschönheit' ('Salmon Beauty')	CBre CHad CHar COtt CSco CSev CSun EBar ECha EFol EFou ELan EMon ERou LHop NBar NHol SAxl SChu SCro SPer WHal WWin
§ x *lewisii* 'King Edward'	CKel CSam EBre ECha EFol EFou ESis GLoc MRav MTho NKay NNrd NRoo NTow NVic SBla SIng SSmi
¶ 'Martina'	EMon
millefolium	CArn CGle CSFH EEls EJud Effi GPoy LHol NLan NSel SIde WOak WSto
– 'Burgundy'	EOrc
– 'Cerise Queen'	CB&S CBow CGle CHar CKel CSco CShe EBre ELan ERou GCHN GPla MFir MPit MWat NHol NKay NNor NOrc SPer WEas WHil WOld WPer
– 'Fire King'	CSco
¶ – 'Kelwayi'	LHil
– 'Lansdorferglut'	NBar
– 'Lavender Beauty'	See A. ***m.*** 'Lilac Beauty'
§ – 'Lilac Beauty'	CB&S CBre CTom ECha EFol EFou EOrc ERou
– 'Paprika'	EBar MBri NBar
– 'Red Beauty'	MBri NBar
– *rosea*	CHar EJud MBal NRoo
¶ – 'Rougham Beauty'	ERou
– 'Sammetriese'	ELan EMon
– 'Wesersandstein'	EMon MBri
'Moonbeam'	EBre ECha EOrc
'Moonshine'	Widely available

nana	WHil WPer
¶ *nobilis neilreichii*	LHil WCot
'Peter Davis'	See TANACETUM *herderi*
ptarmica	CKin LHol MChe MCot MSal NSel SPer WSto
*– 'Ballerina'	EFou
§ – 'Boule de Neige'	CB&S CBre CElw CGle CKel CSco CShe EBre ECha EFou ELan ERou GCHN IDai LHop MFir MWat MWgw NKay NNor NSti SPer WEas WOld
– 'Nana Compacta'	ECha ECro
– 'Perry's White'	CBos EMon GWic MBri MUlv NBar WCot
– 'The Pearl'	See A. *p.* 'Boule de Neige'
– 'Unschuld' ('Innocence')	NBir NRoo
¶ 'Rougham Salmon'	ERou
'Salmon Beauty'	See A. 'Lachsschönheit'
'Schwefelblüte' ('Flowers of Sulphur')	CSco ELan EMon WCot
'Schwellenburg'	CSev EFou SCro
sibirica	CLew CSun
¶ Summer Pastels	WHen WHil WPer
'Taygetea'	EBre ECha ELan EOrc ERou MBri MWat SChu SDix SPer WKif WRus WSHC
'The Beacon'	See A. 'Fanal'
tomentosa	CGle CMer CTom EBre ECha ECtt ELan IDai LHop MBal MPit NKay NNor NNrd NRoo WHil
§ – 'Aurea'	CLew ECtt EFou EMon LHol MBar MPit MSal NHol NSti SCro SIde WHen WWin
– 'Maynard's Gold'	See A. *t.* 'Aurea'
umbellata	IDai WPer
– 'Weston'	See A. x *kolbiana* 'W.'
x *wilczekii*	NHol

X ACHIMENANTHA (Gesneriaceae)

♦ 'Cerulean Mink'	See X SMITHICODONIA 'C.M'
'Dutch Treat'	NMos
'Ginger Peachy'	NMos
'Inferno'	NMos
'Rose Bouquet'	NMos
'Royal'	NMos

ACHIMENES (Gesneriaceae)

'Adelaide'	NMos
'Adèle Delahaute'	LTow NMos
'Admiration'	LAma
'Adonis Blue'	LTow NMos
'Almandine'	LTow NMos
'Ambleside'	NMos
'Ambroise Verschaffelt'	LAma LTow NMos
'Ami Van Houtte'	LTow NMos
'Ann Marie'	NMos
antirrhina	LTow
– 'Redcap'	LTow
'Apricot Glow'	LTow NMos
'Aquamarine'	LTow NMos
'Ballerina'	LTow
'Bassenthwaite'	NMos
'Bea'	NMos
♦ *bella*	See EUCODONIA *verticillata*
'Bernice'	LTow NMos
'Blauer Planet'	NMos
'Bloodstone'	NMos
'Blue Gown'	LTow NMos
¶ 'Blue John'	LTow
'Bright Jewel'	LTow
'Brilliant'	LTow NMos
'Butterfield Bronze'	NMos
'Buttermere'	NMos
'Camberwell Beauty'	LTow NMos
¶ 'Cameo Lilac'	LTow
'Cameo Rose'	LTow NMos
'Cameo Triumph'	LTow NMos
'Camille Brozzoni'	NMos
'Camille Pink'	LTow
candida	NMos
'Carmencita'	LTow
'Carmine Queen'	LTow NMos
'Carnelian'	LTow
'Cascade Cockade'	LTow NMos
'Cascade Evening Glow'	LTow NMos
'Cascade Fairy Pink'	NMos
'Cascade Fashionable Pink'	LTow NMos
'Cascade Rosy Red'	LTow NMos
'Cascade Violet Night'	LTow NMos
'Cattleya'	LAma LTow NMos
cettoana	LTow
– 'Tiny Blue'	LTow
'Chalkhill Blue'	LTow NMos
'Charm'	LAma LTow NMos
'Clouded Yellow'	LTow NMos
'Compact Great Rosy Red'	NMos
'Coniston Water'	LTow NMos
'Copeland Boy'	NMos
'Copeland Girl'	NMos
'Coral Cameo'	LTow
'Coral Sunset'	LTow NMos
'Cornell Favourite 'A''	NMos
'Cornell Favourite 'B''	NMos
'Crimson Beauty'	NMos
'Crimson Glory'	NMos
'Crimson Tiger'	NMos
'Crummock Water'	LTow NMos
'Crystal'	LTow
'Cupido'	LTow NMos
'Dentoniana'	LTow NMos
'Derwentwater'	NMos
'Diadem'	LTow
'Dorothy'	NMos
'Dot'	LTow NMos
dulcis	LTow NMos
'Early Arnold'	LTow NMos
♦	See EUCODONIA *e.*
'Elke Michelssen'	NMos
'English Waltz'	LTow NMos
erecta	LTow
– 'Mexican Dwarf'	LTow
¶ – *rosea*	LTow
'Erlkönig'	LTow
'Escheriana'	LTow NMos
¶ 'Fascination'	LTow
'Flamboyant'	LTow
'Flamenco'	LTow NMos
'Flamingo'	LTow SW&B
flava	LTow NMos
'Fritz Michelssen'	NMos
'Gary John'	LTow NMos

'Gary/Jennifer'	NMos
'Germanica'	LAma
'Glacier'	LTow
grandiflora	LTow
'Grape Wine'	NMos
'Grasmere'	NMos
'Harry Williams'	LAma
§ 'Harveyi'	LTow NMos
'Haweswater'	NMos
'Hilda Michelssen'	LTow NMos
'Honey Gold'	LTow NMos
'Ida Michelssen'	NMos
'India'	LTow NMos
¶ 'Indian Hybrid'	LTow
§ 'Jaureguia Maxima'	LTow NMos
'Jennifer Goode'	LTow NMos
'Jewel Glow'	LTow
'Jewell Blue'	NMos
'Johanna Michelssen'	NMos
'Jubilee Gem'	LTow NMos
'Lady Lyttelton'	LTow
'Lake City'	LAma
'Lakeland Lady'	NMos
'Lavender Fancy'	NMos
'Lavender Jade'	LTow
¶ 'Leonora'	LTow
'Little Beauty'	LAma LTow NMos
'Little Red Tiger'	NMos
longiflora	LAma LTow NMos
♦– 'Alba'	See A. 'Jaureguia Maxima'
– 'Major'	LTow NMos
'Madame Gehune'	LTow
'Magnificent'	LTow NMos
'Mair's White'	LTow
'Margaret White'	LAma
'Margarita'	LTow
'Marie'	NMos
'Master Ingram'	LAma
'Masterpiece'	LTow NMos
¶ 'Mauve Delight'	LTow
'Mauve Queen'	LAma LTow
'Maxima'	LAma
'Menuett '80'	LTow NMos
mexicana	LTow
'Milton'	LTow NMos
'Miniata'	LTow
'Minute'	LAma
misera	LTow NMos
'Miss Blue'	LAma
'Moonstone'	LTow NMos
'National Velvet'	LTow
'Nessida'	LAma
'Old Rose Pink'	LAma NMos
¶ 'Opal'	LTow
'Orange Queen'	LTow NMos
¶ 'Painted Lady'	LTow
'Pally'	NMos
'Panic Pink'	NMos
'Patens Major'	LAma NMos
'Patricia'	NMos
'Paul Arnold'	LAma LTow NMos SW&B
'Peach Blossom'	LAma LTow NMos SW&B
'Peach Glow'	LTow NMos
'Peacock'	LTow NMos
'Pearly Grey'	LTow
'Pearly Queen'	LTow NMos
pedunculata	LTow
'Pendant Blue'	LTow NMos
'Pendant Purple'	LTow NMos
'Petticoat Pink'	NMos
'Pink Beauty'	LTow NMos
'Pinocchio'	LTow NMos
'Prima Donna'	LAma LTow NMos
'Pulcherrima'	LAma
'Purple King'	LAma LTow NMos
'Purple Queen'	LTow
'Purple Triumph'	LTow
'Queen of Sheba'	LTow NMos
'Quickstep'	NMos
'Rachael'	LTow NMos
'Red Admiral'	LTow NMos
'Red Giant'	LTow NMos
'Red Imp'	NMos
'Red Riding Hood'	LTow
'Red Top Hybrid'	NMos
'Robin'	NMos
'Rosenelfe'	NMos
'Rosy Doll'	NMos
'Rosy Frost'	NMos
'Ruby'	LAma LTow
'Rydal Water'	LTow NMos
'Scafell'	NMos
¶ 'Schneewittchen' ('Snow White')	LTow
'Shirley Dwarf White'	NMos
'Shirley Fireglow'	See A. 'Harveyi'
'Show-Off'	LTow NMos
'Silver Wedding'	NMos
skinneri	LTow
'Snow Princess'	SW&B
'Sparkle'	LTow NMos
'Stan's Delight'	LTow NMos
'Sue'	NMos
'Sunburst'	LTow
'Tango'	LTow NMos
'Tantivvy'	NMos
'Tarantella'	LTow NMos
'Teresa'	LTow NMos
¶ 'Tetra Blauer Planet'	LTow
¶ 'Tetra Orange Star'	LTow
¶ 'Tetra Purple Elfe'	LTow
¶ 'Tetra Rosa Queen'	LTow
¶ 'Tetra Verschaffelt'	LTow
¶ 'Tetra Weinrote Elfe'	LTow
¶ 'The Monarch'	LTow
¶ 'Tiger Eye'	LTow
'Tiny Blue'	NMos
¶ 'Topaz'	LTow
'Topsy'	LAma NMos
¶ 'Tresco'	LTow
'Troutbeck'	LTow NMos
'Ullswater'	NMos
'Vanessa'	LTow NMos
'Viola Michelssen'	LTow NMos
'Violacea Semiplena'	LTow NMos
'Violetta'	LAma
¶ ***virginata***	LTow
'Vivid'	LAma LTow NMos
'Warren'	NMos
warscewicziana	LTow
'Wastwater'	NMos
'Wetterflow's Triumph'	LAma LTow NMos
'White Admiral'	NMos
'White Giant'	LTow
'White Knight'	LTow
'White Marvel'	LAma
'White Rajah'	LTow NMos
'Wilma'	NMos

'Windermere'	NMos
'Yellow Beauty'	LTow

ACHNATHERUM See STIPA

ACIDANTHERA See GLADIOLUS

ACINOS (Labiatae)

§ *alpinus*	CLew CShe CSun GLoc LGre MHig MWat NNrd WPer
– meridionalis	NHol
♦*arvensis*	See CLINOPODIUM *acinos*
§ *corsicus*	EBre EPot GLoc ITim LGre SCro SLHN WPat WWin

ACIPHYLLA (Umbelliferae)

aurea	MBal SPou
crenulata	MBal
glaucescens	GDra GLoc MBal SArc WDav
hectorii	GArf GDra
monroi	GDra MBal WHal
pinnatifida	MBal
scott-thomsonii	ECou
squarrosa	EBul

ACNISTUS (Solanaceae)

¶ *australis* blue	CSun WCar
– white	CSun

ACONITUM (Ranunculaceae)

anglicum	See A. *napellus* Anglicum group
¶ *anthora*	ECro
N*autumnale*	NBir
'Blue Sceptre'	CHar CSco EBre NOak NRoo WEas
'Bressingham Spire'	CCla CKel CSco CShe EBre EFou ELan ERou GAbr MBri MCot MWat MWgw NKay NRoo SChu SPer
x *cammarum* 'Bicolor'	CGle CHad CRow CSev EBre EFou EGol ELan EOrc ERou GDra GWic MBri MRav NBar NHol NRoo NSti SChu SPer WEas
– 'Grandiflorum Album'	CHar ELan ERou SPer
§ *carmichaelii*	CBot CBre CGle CHad ECro EFou ELan GAbr MBro MPar MRav NRar NRoo SAxl WHoo WRus
– 'Arendsii'	CCla CHar EBre ECha EOrc ERou MBri MCot NBar NRoo SChu SFis SPer WEas
– 'Barker's Variety'	CElw CRow CSco MBri NHol NSti
– 'Kelmscott'	EFou ELan ERou MCot SBla
– 'Kelmscott Variegated'	SBla
– wilsonii	CHan GGar NHol
cilicicum	See ERANTHIS *hyemalis* Cilicicus group
elwesii	GGar
**falconeri*	ECro
fischeri	See A. *carmichaelii*
§ *hemsleyanum*	CArn CBot CChu CGle CRow CSun ERav LHol MFir MPar MTho MWgw NHol NSti NTow SAxl SBla SPou WEas WOMN
hyemalis	See ERANTHIS *hyemalis*
'Ivorine'	Widely available
¶ *kirinense*	EMon
lamarckii	See A. *lycoctonum neapolitanum*
§ *lycoctonum lycoctonum*	ECro MSal
§ *– vulparia*	CArn CFis CGle CRow CTom ECha ECro EFou GPoy LHol LSav NHol NRoo
napellus	CArn CRow CShe CTom ECro ECtt GAbr GPoy LHol MBro MPit MWat NNor NSel SIde WHoo WOld
– 'Albidum'	EFou GWic MBri NRoo SMrm
§ – Anglicum group	CBre CKin CRow NSti SIng
– carneum	EFou ELan ERou GWic NRoo SChu
neapolensis	See A. *lycoctonum neapolitanum*
'Newry Blue'	CHar ECro ELan MBri MFir MPit NKay
orientale	See A. *lycoctonum vulparia*
septentrionale	See A. *lycoctonum lycoctonum*
**smithii*	CBrd
'Spark's Variety'	CHan CSco ELan EOrc ERou MBri MRav NKay NRoo NSti SCro SDix SMad
x *tubergenii*	See ERANTHIS *hyemalis* Tubergenii group
volubile	See A. *hemsleyanum*
vulparia	See A. *lycoctonum v.*

ACONOGONUM See POLYGONUM

ACORUS (Araceae)

calamus	CArn CRow EHon EWav Effi GPoy LMay MSal MSta SHig
¶ – 'Purpureus'	CBot
– 'Variegatus'	CHan CRow CWGN ECha EGol EHon EWav GWic LMay MSta SHig SLon
gramineus	CRow EFou LMay SApp
♦– 'Oborozuki'	See A. *g.* 'Ogon'
§ – 'Ogon'	CHoe EGol EHal EPla GWic SApp SSus WRus
– 'Pusillus'	CRiv SIng
– 'Variegatus'	CBrd CChu CCla CElw CHan CHoe CRiv CRow CWGN EJud ELan EPar GPla GWic LMay LSav MBal MCot MFir MSta NSti SApp SIng WRus

ACRADENIA (Rutaceae)

frankliniae	CChu CPle CTre IBar IBlr SArc SBor SSpi WBod

ACTAEA (Ranunculaceae)

§ *alba*	CBrd CChu CCla CHan CRow ECha ECro EPar GPoy IBlr MBri MUlv NHol NSti SMad SWas WOMN WRus WWat
§ *erythrocarpa*	CHan EBre ECro GDra GLoc GPoy MUlv NHol SDix WEas WOMN WWat WWin
pachypoda	See A. *alba*
rubra	CBro CCla CHad CHan CMHG CRow ECha ECro ELan GWic IBlr MBri NSti SAxl
¶ *– arguta*	WDav
– neglecta	CHan WRus
spicata	CLew ECro GPoy NHol NSti WPer
– alba	See A. *spicata*
– rubra	See A. *erythrocarpa*

ACTINELLA (Compositae)
scaposa See HYMENOXYS *scaposa*

ACTINIDIA † (Actinidaceae)
arguta CB&S CCla CSco SReu
– (m) CB&S ESim
F – 'Ananasnaja' (f) ESim
F – 'Meader No 2' (f) ESim
F – 'Stamford' (f) ESim
chinensis See A. *deliciosa*
§ *deliciosa* CCla CLan CMac CSco CTre ELan ENot ISea LHol MGos MWat NBar SReu SSpi WSHC
F – (f) EMui IJoh SHil SPer WHig WWeb
– (m) EMui IJoh SHil SPer WHig WWeb
– 'Atlas' MBri
F – 'Hayward' (f) CB&S CMac ELan ERea IOrc MBri MGos MWat NPal SBra SDea WWeb
F – hermaphrodite SSpi
¶ – 'Jenny' (s-p) LBuc MRea
– 'Tomuri' (m) CB&S CMac EBar ELan ERea IOrc MWat NPal SBra WWeb
giraldii SSta
kolomikta Widely available
* *pilulosa* GWic
polygama WSHC

ACTINOTUS (Umbelliferae)
helianthi CSun

ADELOCARYUM (Boraginaceae)
anchusoides CHan GWic WCru
¶ – short form GWic

ADENOPHORA (Campanulaceae)
bulleyana CHan CSev ECro IBlr
¶ *forrestii* LHil
himalayana CSam CSun NCat NRed WHil
khasiana CHan GWic
N *latifolia* WHCG WHil
liliifolia ECro ELan EMon EPad MTho NHol NSti WHCG WHoo WPer
¶ *nikoensis* WPer
pereskiifolia NRed
polyantha CHan
potaninii CHan EPad
– *alba* CHan
sp. AGSJ 227 GArf
¶ *takedae* WPer
tashiroi CChu CTom ECro EPad ITim MBro NWCA SIgm WHoo WOld

ADIANTUM † (Adiantaceae)
capillus-veneris CHEx NMar SSpi
– 'Banksianum' NMar
– 'Mairisii' See A. x *mairisii*
– 'Pointonii' NMar
concinnum NMar
cuneatum See A. *raddianum*
diaphanum NMar
edgeworthii NMar
formosum NMar
¶ *henslowianum* NMar
§ x *mairisii* NMar
¶ *monochlamys* NKay
* *monocolor* MBri
pedatum CHEx EBre ECha EFou ELan LSav MBal MBri NHol NKay SBar SMad SSpi
– *aleuticum* See A. *p. subpumilum*
§ – Asiatic form CWGN MBri NKay SApp SSpi WFib
– 'Imbricatum' NMar SBla WFib
– *japonicum* See A. *p.* Asiatic form
– 'Laciniatum' NKay
– *minus* EBre SPou
– 'Miss Sharples' NMar
* – *roseum* ELan
§ – *subpumilum* ELan IOrc LSav MBri NHol NKay SBla SMad SSpi SWas
– *subpumilum minimum* NMar
peruvianum MBri
pubescens MBri NMar
§ *raddianum* NMar SSpi
– 'Brilliantelse' MBri NMar WFib
– 'Crested Majus' NMar
– 'Crested Micropinnulum' NMar
– 'Deflexum' NMar
– *elegans* NMar
– 'Elegans' WFib
– 'Feltham Beauty' WFib
– 'Fragrans' See A. *r.* 'Fragrantissimum'
§ – 'Fragrantissimum' MBri NMar
– 'Fritz Luthi' MBri NMar WFib
– 'Gracilis' See A. *r.* 'Gracillimum'
§ – 'Gracillimum' NMar WFib
– 'Kensington Gem' NMar WFib
– 'Lady Geneva' WFib
– 'Legrand Morgan' NMar
– 'Legrandii' NMar
– 'Micropinnulum' NMar WFib
– 'Micropinnulum Mist' NMar
– 'Pacific Maid' NMar WFib
– 'Pacottii' NMar
– 'Triumph' NMar
– 'Tuffy Tips' NMar
¶ – 'Variegated Tesselate' NMar
– 'Victoria's Elegans' NMar
– 'Weigandii' NMar
tenerum 'Scutum Roseum' WFib
trapeziforme NMar
venustum CFor EBre ECha EPot LHop MBal MPar NKay NMar NNrd SApp SBla SDix SSpi SWas WEas WFib WOMN

ADLUMIA (Fumariaceae)
fungosa WCot WCru WMar

ADONIS (Ranunculaceae)
amurensis EBre EPar EPot LAma MRav MUlv NHol WCot
– 'Fukujukai' ECro
– 'Plena' COtt EBre EGol EPar MBri MUlv NNrd SPer
¶ *brevistyla* GArf
¶ *chrysocyathus* SIng WDav
vernalis ECro MSal

ADOXA (Adoxaceae)
moschatellina CArn CKin MTho

AECHMEA † (Bromeliaceae)

caerulea	See A. ***lueddemanniana***
chantinii	MBri
fasciata	MBri
– 'Romeo'	MBri
'Foster's Favorite'	SLMG
'Grand Prix'	MBri
'Romero'	MBri
**serventensis*	MBri

AEGLE (Rutaceae)

sepiaria	See PONCIRUS ***trifoliata***

AEGOPODIUM (Umbelliferae)

podagraria 'Variegatum'	Widely available

AEONIUM (Crassulaceae)

arboreum	CHEx SLMG
¶ – 'Albovariegatum'	NRar
– *atropurpureum*	CHEx ERea IBlr MBri SLMG WEas
¶ *balsamiferum*	CHEx NRar
¶ *canariense*	CHEx
¶ *cuneatum*	CHEx
x *domesticum*	See AICHRYSON x ***d.***
¶ *haworthii*	CHEx
holochrysum	IBlr
¶ *nobile*	CHEx
percarneum	SLMG
¶ *rubrolineatum*	NRar
¶ *simsii*	CHEx
tabuliforme	CHEx
¶ *undulatum*	CHEx
'Zwartkop'	CHEx CTre

AESCHYNANTHUS (Gesneriaceae)

'Big Apple'	WEfe
¶ 'Greensleeves'	WEfe
hildebrandii	SLMG WEfe
lobbianus	See A. ***parvifolius***
longicaulis	MBri
'Mira'	MBri
'Mona'	MBri
§ *parvifolius*	MBri
'Pullobia'	MBri
'Purple Star'	MBri
radicans lobbianus	EBak
'Rigel'	MBri
**rigidus*	SLMG
speciosus	LAbb
– *rubens*	MBri
'Topaz'	MBri WEfe

AESCULUS † (Hippocastanaceae)

x *arnoldiana*	CMCN
californica	CTrw LSav SHil SSpi WWat
x *carnea*	GRei MBal MBar SExT
¶ – 'Aureomarginata'	EMon
– 'Briotii'	CBra CLnd CSco EHar ELan ENot IHos IJoh IOrc MBri MGos NWea SHil SPer SSta
§ *flava*	CCla CMCN CSco EHar ENot LSav MBri SExT SHil SPer SSpi SSta WCoo
§ *georgiana*	SHil SSpi
glabra	CMCN EHar
hippocastanum	CB&S CBra CKin CLnd CPer CSco ELan ENot GRei IDai IJoh ISea LBuc MBal MBar MBri NWea SHil SPer WCoo WMou
§ – 'Baumannii'	CBow CLnd CSco ENot MBri MGos SExT SHil SPer
– 'Flore Pleno'	See A. ***h.*** 'Baumannii'
– 'Hampton Court Gold'	WMou
– 'Pyramidalis'	EHar
indica	CCla CHEx CLnd CSam CSco CTrw ENot IHos IJoh IOrc ISea LSav MBri SExT SHil SPer SSpi SSta WMou
– 'Sydney Pearce'	CMCN EHar MBri MMea SHil
x *mutabilis* 'Induta'	MBlu SHil
x *neglecta*	SExT
– 'Erythroblastos'	CMCN EHar MBlu SHil SSpi WMou
– *georgiana*	See A. ***georgiana***
octandra	See A. ***flava***
parviflora	CB&S CCla CHad CMCN CSco EHar ELan ENot ERav ISea LNet LSav MBal MBlu MBri SExT SHil SMad SPer SSpi WWat
§ *pavia*	CChu CCla CMCN EHar ISea SHil SMad SSpi
– 'Atrosanguinea'	MBri SHil SSpi
– 'Rosea Nana'	CMCN SSpi
'Plantierensis'	ENot SExT
splendens	See A. ***pavia***
turbinata	CMCN ISea LSav MBri SBor SHil SSpi WCoo

AETHIONEMA (Cruciferae)

armenum	CLew CSam ECro EPot MPlt NHol WHil
¶ – 'Warley Ruber'	MHig
coridifolium	WPer
graecum	See A. ***saxatile***
grandiflorum	CShe CSun LHil MHig NNor NRya NTow SBla SLHN SWas WHal WHil WPer
– Pulchellum group	CGle CLew EPot LHop MCas NHol NKay SIng WHoo WWin
iberideum	MWat NKay WPat
§ *oppositifolium*	EPot MBro MWat NHol NKay SIng WAbe WDav WHoo WPat WPer
§ *saxatile*	NTow WOMN
schistosum	CSun GLoc NGre NRya WCla WHil WPer
'Warley Rose'	Widely available

AGAPANTHUS † (Liliaceae/Alliaceae)

africanus	IBlr NRog SLMG WPer
– *albus*	CB&S
– 'Sapphire'	CB&S
Ardernei hybrid	CBot IBlr
'Blue Giant'	EBre
'Blue Moon'	CBro ECha
'Blue Star'	ERav MUlv NSti
'Blue Triumphator'	LBow WCot
'Bressingham Blue'	EBre MBri MRav
'Bressingham White'	EBre LGre MBri MRav NRoo SSus
'Buckingham Palace'	SSpi
§ *campanulatus*	CB&S CGle CHad CKel ELan ERav IDai ISea SApp SCro SHig
– *albovittatus*	CRow LGre
– *albus*	CB&S CCla CSco EBre ECha EFou ELan GWic IDai ISea MPlt NHol NRoo NVic SPer SWas
– bright blue	GWic
– cobalt blue	ECha GWic

- 'Isis' CBro CRow ECha MUlv SPer
- pale form GWic
- *patens* LHil SHig SPer WWat
- 'Profusion' ECha MUlv
- 'Ultramarine' CKel
¶ - variegated form ECha
'Castle of Mey' LHyd SApp
Giant hybrids ERav LHop
§ Headbourne hybrids Widely available
- - 'Golden Rule' CRow ELan LHop
'Hydon Mist' LHyd
'Kingston Blue' SWas
'Lady Moore' MPar
'Lilliput' COtt CRow ECtt LGre MRav MTho NRoo SBla SSus
'Marjorie' SBla
'Midnight Blue' CGle ERav GWic IBlr LGre MUlv
'Midnight Star' ERav
'Norman Hadden' EBul
Palmer's hybrids See A. Heabourne hybrids
* 'Penelope Palmer' WCot
'Peter Pan' EFou GWic MTho
praecox orientalis CHEx ERea NPal WWat
- *orientalis albus* LBow NPal
- *praecox* SLHN
- 'Variegatus' SLHN
'Sky Star' ERav MUlv
'Torbay' MUlv SApp SBla
umbellatus See AA. ***campanulatus, africanus, praecox orientalis***
'White Star' ERav MUlv
'White Starlet' ERav MUlv
'Windsor Castle' SSpi
'Zella Thomas' LHyd

AGAPETES (Ericaceae)
'Ludgvan Cross' CGre MBal
§ *serpens* CGre CSun MBal
¶ - 'Nepal Cream' CGre
- 'Scarlet Elf' CB&S

AGARISTA (Ericaceae)
§ *populifolia* SSta

AGASTACHE (Labiatae)
anethiodora See A. ***foeniculum***
anisata See A. ***foeniculum***
barberi CSun LGre WDav
*- 'Tutti-Frutti' CSun
§ *foeniculum* Widely available
§ - 'Alabaster' ECro EFou EMon SAxl
♦- 'Alba' See A. ***f.*** 'Alabaster'
mexicana CFis CHan CRow ECro ELan EMon GWic IBrk LHop SFis WHer
*- 'Firebird' CSun
nepetoides MSal
pallidiflora GWic LGre WDav
rugosa CArn CSev ECro GPoy MSal WPer
¶ *urticifolia* 'Alba' CBre EGol WPer

AGATHAEA (Compositae)
coelestis See FELICIA ***amelloides***

AGATHIS (Araucariaceae)
australis MBal SHil

AGAVE (Agavaceae)
affinis See A. ***sobria sobria***
americana CB&S CHEx IBlr LHil LPal SArc SLMG
- 'Marginata' IBlr LHop SMad SSus
- 'Mediopicta' CHEx SArc SLMG SSus
- 'Variegata' CB&S CHEx MBri NRar SArc SLMG SSpi
avellanidens See A. ***sebastiana***
¶ *celsii* CHEx SArc
cerulata cerulata CMal
coarctata See A. ***mitriiformis***
colorata CMal
¶ *ellemeetiana* CHEx
ferdinandi-regis CMal
¶ *ferox* CHEx
¶ *filifera* CHEx
franzosinii SArc
funkiana CMal
gigantensis CMal
hoveyi CMal
§ *mitriiformis* CMal
parryi CHEx SArc SIgm SSpi
- *couesii* See A. ***p. parryi***
- *parryi* SArc
potatorum verschaffeltii CMal
¶ *schottii* SIgm
sebastiana CMal
sobria sobria SLMG
* *striata rubra* SIgm
toumeyana CMal
- *bella* CMal
utahensis SArc SIgm
- *discreta* SArc
- *eborispina* CMal
- *kaibabensis* SArc
- *nevadensis* SArc
victoriae-reginae SLMG WMar
¶ *weberi* CHEx
¶ *xylonacantha* CHEx

AGLAONEMA (Araceae)
crispum MBri
*- 'Marie' MBri
'Malay Beauty' MBri
roebelinii See A. ***crispum***
'Silver King' MBri
'Silver Queen' MBri

AGRIMONIA (Rosaceae)
eupatoria CArn CKin EHfi GPoy LHol MChe NLan NSel SIde WCla WOak
odorata See A. ***repens***
repens MSal

AGROPYRON (Gramineae)
glaucum See ELYMUS ***hispidus***
magellanicum See ELYMUS ***magellanicus***
pubiflorum See ELYMUS ***magellanicus***
* *scabrum* CHoe

AGROSTEMMA (Carophyllaceae)
coronaria See LYCHNIS ***coronaria***
githago CNat MSal SFir WCla WOak

AGROSTIS (Gramineae)
canina 'Silver Needles' CElw CHoe SApp

AGROSTOCRINUM (Liliaceae)
**scabrum* CSun

AICHRYSON (Crassulaceae)
§ x *domesticum* CHEx SLMG
– 'Variegatum' EBak SLMG

AILANTHUS (Simaroubaceae)
§ *altissima* CB&S CBot CBra CChu CHEx CLnd CSco ECtt ELan ENot IOrc SExT SHil SLHN SPer WCoo WNor
glandulosa See A. ***altissima***

AJUGA † (Labiatae)
¶ *chamaepitys* WHil
genevensis 'Tottenham' MBri
*'Jumbo' EMon
metallica See A. ***pyramidalis***
*'Pink Surprise' EMon LRHS
§ *pyramidalis* CKel CRow EBre ECha EGol ERou MRav NOak SCro WHer
– 'Metallica Crispa' CLew CMHG CRow CShe EFou NNrd WThu
reptans CFis CHan CKin CRow CSFH ECtt GPoy LHol LMay MPla NOrc WSto
– 'Alba' CArn CBre CHan CRow CTom ECha EFou EGol GPla GWic NOak NSti WBon WPer
§ – 'Atropurpurea' Widely available
– 'Braunherz' CElw CHad CHoe CRow EBar EBre ECro EFol EGol GAbr LHop MBri MRav NOak SPer WHea WHen
– 'Burgundy Glow' Widely available
I – 'Burgundy Metallica' ECro
*– 'Burgundy Red' GDra
– 'Catlin's Giant' ECha ECtt EFol EGol EMon ERou LHop NSti SMad
*– 'Cristata' SPer
– 'Delight' EFou ELan EMon EPot IBar MBri NNrd WEas
– 'Jungle Beauty' CCor CGle CHad CHan CMHG CRow EGol EOrc EPar GWic SAxl SSpi
*– *macrophylla* ELan
– 'Multicolor'/ 'Rainbow'/ 'Tricolor' Widely available
– 'Pink Elf' CRow CSun EBre ECha EFol NOak NSti SIng WBon WPer
– 'Purple Torch' ECha EFou ESis LHop MBri WEas
– 'Purpurea' See A. *r.* 'Atropurpurea'
¶ – 'Silver Shadow' EMon
– 'Tortoiseshell' CGle
– 'Variegata' ('Argentea') Widely available

AKEBIA (Lardizabalaceae)
x *pentaphylla* ERea SBra SSta SSus WSHC
quinata Widely available
trifoliata CB&S CChu MUlv SBra SHil SSpi WSHC

ALANGIUM (Alangiaceae)
platanifolium CBot CCla CLan
– *macrophyllum* CCla

ALBIZIA (Leguminosae)
§ *distachya* CHEx CHil WNor
§ *julibrissin* CB&S CBot CHil EHal ELan ISea SArc SExT SGar SIgm SPer WFro WPat
– 'Rosea' CGre CHEx IOrc SArc SHil SLHN SMad WNor WSHC WWeb
♦ *lophantha* See A. ***distachya***

ALBUCA (Liliaceae/Hyacinthaceae)
¶ *canadensis* WPer
humilis CAvo EPot GLoc MHig NHol NNrd SIng SSpi
nelsonii CAvo
**setosa* CHan

ALCEA (Malvaceae)
ficifolia CGle
rosea CGle CHad MFir MWgw WEas
– 'Chater's Double' ECtt ELan ERou MBri MFir NNor
– 'Majorette' ECtt EFol
– 'Nigra' CArn CGle CHad EFou MFir MWgw NNor SFir SMad WRus
– 'Powder Puff' ELan
rugosa CGle CHad CHan CSun ELan LHop SDix WCar WCot WOMN WOld WRus

ALCHEMILLA † (Rosaceae)
abyssinica CRiv CRow SIng
**affinis venosa* EPla
alpina Widely available
*– 'Nana' WWat
arvensis See APHANES ***a.***
¶ *bulgarica* EPad
conjuncta CBot CBre CHan ECha ECro EFou EGol ELun LHop MWgw NHol NOak SWas WEas WRus WSto
¶ *elizabethae* EMon EPad
ellenbeckii CElw CLew CMHG EBre ECro ELan ESis GCHN GHig MHig MPlt MRav MTho NNor NNrd NOrc NRoo NRya SLHN WEas WHoo WPer
erythropoda Widely available
faeroensis GLoc MDHE WRus
**hookeri* EOrc
¶ *lapeyrousei* CHad SIng
mollis Widely available
*– 'Grandiflora' GWic MUlv
*– 'Robusta' ECro WHal
'Mr Poland's Variety' SPer WWat
¶ *plicatula* EMon EPad
splendens CArn CCla CHar CMer CRiv EBre ECro EOrc LGan NHol NRoo
♦ *vulgaris* See A. ***xanthochlora***
§ *xanthochlora* EGol Effi GGar GPoy MSal WOak WSto

ALECTRYON (Sapindaceae)
excelsus WCoo

ALETRIS (Liliaceae)
farinosa MSal

ALISMA (Alismataceae)
parviflorum CWGN LMay MSta SHig

plantago-aquatica	CKin CRow CWGN EHon LMay MSta SHig

ALKANNA (Boraginaceae)

¶ ***orientalis***	WCru
tinctoria	MChe MSal

ALLAMANDA (Apocynaceae)

cathartica	MBri WCar
– 'Birthe'	MBri
neriifolia	CSun

ALLIARIA (Cruciferae)

petiolata	CArn CKin WCla

ALLIUM † (Liliaceae/Alliaceae)

acuminatum	GCHN LGre NBir NHol WChr WCot
N***aflatunense***	CBro CGle ECam ECha ECtt EFou EPar ETub LAma LBow MBri SIng SMad WPer
– 'Purple Sensation'	CAvo CBro EFou EMon EPot ETub LAma LBow MBri
akaka	ECam EPot LAma
albidum	SIng
albopilosum	See A. ***christophii***
amabile	See A. ***mairei a.***
ampeloprasum	ECha
– ***babingtonii***	CCor
amplectens	WChr
¶ ***angulosum***	WCot
atropurpureum	EMon EPar ETub LBow LRoo NHol
azureum	See A. ***caeruleum***
barszczewskii	ECam
N***beesianum***	CGle EPot MBal MPar NHol NRya NWCA SPou
bucharicum	ECam
bulgaricum	See NECTAROSCORDUM ***siculum bulgaricum***
§ ***caeruleum***	CAvo CBro CGle ECam ELan EPar ETub LAma LBlo LBow LRoo MBri NSti SSpi WPer
caesium	ECam SPou
callimischon	CBro EPot MHig WEas
– ***haemostictum***	MPar SIng SPou
¶ ***canadense***	WCot
§ ***carinatum pulchellum***	CArn CAvo CBro CCor CGle CHan EBul ECam ECha EFou EPar ITim LAma LBow LHop MBal MPar MWat NHar NHol NNor NTow SPou WPer
– – ***album***	CAvo CBro CHan ECha EMon EPot ETub MBal MBro MPar NTow SIng SPou
carolinianum CHA 322	WDav
cepa Aggregatum group	MPlt WHil
– 'Perutile'	CArn EJud GPoy
– Proliferum group	CArn CSev EJud GPoy MChe MFir SIde
cernuum	Widely available
– ***neo-mexicanum***	EBul
§ ***christophii***	CAvo CBro CGle ECam ECha EFou ELan EOrc EPar EPot ERav ETub LAma LBlo LBow MBri NSel SChu SIng SSpi WChr WEas WKif WOMN
cirrhosum	See A. ***carinatum pulchellum***
cowanii	See A. ***neapolitanum***
cyaneum	CBro CTom EBre EFol ELan EPot GEdr GLoc MCas NHol NNrd NRya SPou WEas WOMN WRus WWin
– ***album***	SPou
cyathophorum	CArn NWCA
– ***farreri***	CArn CAvo CBro CRiv CSun GLoc MBal NHol SIng WAbe WEas WHil WRus WThu
dichlamydeum	CBro SPou WChr
drummondii	WBon
elatum	See A. ***macleanii***
¶ ***falcifolium***	WChr
¶ ***fimbriatum purdyi***	WChr
fistulosum	CArn CSFH EJud ELan GPoy LHil MChe MFir SIde WPer
flavum	CArn CAvo CBro CTom ECam ECha ELan EPar ETub GPla LBow LRoo MHig MPar MWat NHol SIng SPou WCla WHil WPer WRus
– forms	SPou
*– ***glaucum***	EPot SBar
– ***minus***	ECam ELan GLoc NHol NWCA WHil
– ***tauricum***	SIng
geyeri	WChr
giganteum	CArn CBot ELan EPar ETub LAma LBlo LBow LRoo MBri MRav NNor NSel SIng WPer
'Gladiator'	LAma
glaucum	See A. ***senescens montanum***
'Globus'	EPot
heldreichii	SPou
insubricum forms	NBir NWCA SPou SWas
kansuense	See A. ***sikkimense***
karataviense	Widely available
kharputense	LAma
* 'Laxton Sunset'	GLoc
'Lucy Ball'	LAma
§ ***macleanii***	EMon EPar LAma LBow
macranthum	GCHN GLoc MBro MPar NHol NSti SWas WDav
macrochaetum	LAma
mairei	CRiv EPot GCHN MCas MTho WAbe WOMN
§ – ***amabile***	CMal GEdr GLoc MBal MHig MPar NHol NNrd NTow
§ – ***amabile*** pink form	GLoc SPou
moly	CAvo CBro CGle CHad CRiv ECam ELan EPar ETub LAma LBlo LBow LRoo MBri MBro NHol NNrd NRya SIng WCla WEas WHil WPer WThu
– 'Jeannine'	CBro
multibulbosum	See A. ***nigrum***
murrayanum	See A. ***unifolium***
N***narcissiflorum***	CLew EPot GLoc ITim MHig MPar MTho NSti WAbe WEas WPer
– pink form	MS&S
§ ***neapolitanum***	CArn CBro CGle CLew EBul ECam ELan EPar LAma LRoo MBri NHol SIng WEas WHil WPer
– ***grandiflorum***	ETub
§ ***nigrum***	EFou LAma LRoo MPar
nuttallii	See A. ***drummondii***
obliquum	CAvo ECam ECha WPer
odorum	See A. ***ramosum***
olympicum	SPou

- ACW 2372 GLoc
§ *oreophilum* CAvo CBro CCla ECam ECha ECtt EPar GHig GLoc LAma LBlo LBow MBri MBro MHig NHol SIng WCla WOMN WPer
- 'Zwanenburg' CBro EPot ETub WDav
orientale LAma
ostrowskianum See A. *oreophilum*
pallens CBre LGre MTho
paniculatum SChu
¶ - CDB SPou
paradoxum SPou
pedemontanum See A. *narcissiflorum*
peninsulare SPou WChr
polyastrum GCHN
pskemense SPou
pulchellum See A. *carinatum p.*
N *pyrenaicum* CAvo ELan SSus
§ *ramosum* WPer
'Rien Poortvliet' LAma
rosenbachianum CBro EPar EPot ETub LAma LBow
- W 4865 LRHS WChr
- *album* CBro EPar LAma SIng
roseum CAvo ECtt EMon ETub LAma SIng WPer WWin
*- 'Grandiflorum' MPlt
sativum CArn EEls EJud GPoy MBri NSel SIde
schoenoprasum CArn CSFH CSev GPoy LHol MBal MBri MBro MChe MFir MPit NCat NHol NNor NSel SIde WEas WHil WPer WThu
- 'Forescate' CCla EBre ECha LHol MBri MUlv NHol SSus
- *roseum* GPoy
- 'Shepherds Crooks' WThu
- *sibiricum* GGar GPoy MBri NSel SIde
- white form SApp
schubertii CAvo CBro EPar ETub LAma LBow
scorodoprasum jajlae CSun NHol
senescens CArn EBre ECam ECro ELan EPla GCHN SSpi WHil
§ - *glaucum* CTom ECha GCHN GLoc NHol WEas WHal
§ - *montanum* CCor CLew EBul ELan EPot ERav MCas MHig SDix SIng SLHN WChr WDav WHil WThu
siculum See NECTAROSCORDUM *siculum*
§ *sikkimense* CSun GDra MBro MPar NHol NNrd NTow SPou WAbe WCla WDav WHil WOMN
sphaerocephalon CArn CAvo CHad ECam ELan EPar ETub LAma LBlo LBow LHop LRoo NLan NSti SIng SLHN SMrm WEas WPer
splendens See A. *stellerianum*
stellerianum GCHN WHal WPer
- *kurilense* CAvo SPou WThu
stipitatum LAma LBow WCot
- *album* EMon ETub LAma LBow MBro
subhirsutum EFou ETub WPer
tanguticum GCHN
thunbergii GLoc NBir NHol SOkd SWas
tibeticum EPot NHol NWCA WDav WEas
triquetrum CAvo ETub GGar IBlr LAma NLan SIng WPer WSto WWin
tuberosum CArn CAvo CLew CSFH CSev EBul ECha EFou EJud GPoy LHol MBri MChe NSel SIde WHal WHil WPer
unifolium CBro EBar EBul ETub LAma LBlo LBow LRoo MBri SDix SSpi WChr WCla WRus
ursinum CArn CAvo CKin CSFH ETub GPoy LAma LHol LRoo MSal SIde WHen
¶ *victorialis* WPer
vineale CArn CKin
* *violaceum* GCHN
¶ *virgunculae* WChr
wallichianum B 445 EMon NBir WDav
zebdanense ETub LAma NHol WCla WPer

ALLOCASUARINA (Casuarinaceae)

distyla ISea
¶ *verticillata* SDry

ALMOND See PRUNUS *dulcis*

ALNUS † (Betulaceae)

cordata CKin CLnd CPer CSco CSto EHar ELan ENot GRei IJoh IOrc LBuc LSav MBri MR&S SHil SMad SPer SSta WMou
- wild origin CSto
cremastogyne CMCN
¶ *firma* EPla MBlu
- *multinervis* See A. *pendula*
- *sieboldiana* See A. *sieboldiana*
glutinosa CB&S CBra CKin CLnd CPer CSto ENot GRei IDai IOrc LBuc MBar MBri MGos MR&S NWea SExT SHil SPer WMou
- 'Aurea' WMou
- 'Imperialis' CLnd CSco EGol EHar ELan ENot LSav SExT SHil SPer SSpi WMou WWat
- *incisa* ELan MR&S
- 'Laciniata' CSco IOrc MBlu SExT WMou
hirsuta CMCN CSto
incana CKin CLnd CSto ENot GRei IOrc LBuc MBar MBri MR&S NWea SExT SHil WMou
- 'Aurea' CB&S CBow CCla CLnd COtt CSco EHar ELan ENot IOrc MBar MBlu MBri MR&S SExT SGar SHil SPer WMou
- 'Laciniata' EHar ENot SSpi WMou
- 'Pendula' SHil WMou
japonica CSto
maximowiczii CCor CSto
oregona See A. *rubra*
pendula CSto
* *pinnatisecta* EHar
rhombifolia CSto
§ *rubra* CKin CLnd CSto ELan ENot GRei IOrc WMou
§ *rugosa* CMCN CSto
serrulata See A. *rugosa*
sieboldiana CSto
x *spaethii* SHil WMou
subcordata WMou
viridis CSto NWea WMou

ALOCASIA (Araceae)

x *amazonica* MBri
sanderiana MBri

ALONSOA (Scrophulariaceae)
acutifolia coral form — ERea
warscewiczii — CHad CHan CRiv CSun EFol ERav ERea IBlr LHil SAxl SChu SMrm WEas WOMN WPer
– pale form — See A. *w.* 'Peachy-Keen'
§ – 'Peachy-Keen' — EMon LHop SAxl SMrm WPer

ALOPECURUS (Gramineae)
alpinus — CElw CHoe
lanatus — NHol SIng
pratensis
'Aureovariegatus' — CHoe ECro EHal EMon ERou GWic IBlr SPer WRus
N– 'Aureus' — CElw CRiv ECha EFou EPar EPot MBal MBri MCot MPar NHol NSti SApp SSpi WWin

ALOYSIA (Verbenaceae)
citriodora — See A. *triphylla*
§ *triphylla* — Widely available

ALOË (Liliaceae/Aloeaceae)
¶ *arborescens* — CHEx
aristata — CHEx MBri SArc SCro
barbadensis — See A. *vera*
¶ *brevifolia* — CHEx
camperi 'Maculata' — MBri
ciliaris — CHEx ERea
¶ *ferox* — CHEx
humilis — IBlr
¶ *mitriformis* — CHEx
saponaria — SLMG
sp. yellow flowered — IBlr
¶ *striata* — CHEx
vera — GPoy SLMG
* 'Walmsley's Blue' — MBri

ALPINIA (Zingiberaceae)
speciosa — See A. *zerumbet*
zerumbet — MNew

ALSOBIA (Gesneriaceae)
§ *dianthiflora* — CSun MBri MNew WEfe
* 'Iris August' — MBri
* 'San Miguel' — MBri WEfe

ALSTROEMERIA (Liliaceae/Alstroemeriaceae)
aurantiaca — See A. *aurea*
§ *aurea* — CB&S CGle ELan LHil MUlv NCat SPer WHil
– 'Dover Orange' — CB&S CGle SFis SMrm SPer SPla
– 'Orange King' — CKel
Beatrix ® / 'Stadoran' — LCha
brasiliensis — CChu CFor
Butterfly hybrids — CB&S
Diana ® — See A. Mona Lisa ®
Frederika ® / 'Stabronza' — LCha
'Furie' — MLin
Grace ® — See A. King Cardinal ®
hookeri — SWas WOMN
Ileana ® — See A. 'Rita'
'Jolicoeur' — MLin
§ King Cardinal ® / 'Starodo' — LCha
Ligtu hybrids — CAvo CB&S CGle CKel CShe ECha EFou ELan ERav ERou LHop MBri MFir MWgw SDix SPer SW&B WRus
Margaret ® / 'Stakova' — LCha
Marie-Louise ® — See A. Manon ®
¶ 'Ohio' — MBri
'Orange King' — MBri
pelegrina — LHil MTho
§ *psittacina* — CAvo CChu CFor CGle CHad CSun ELan EPar ERav GWic LGre LHil LHop SAxl SLHN SLMG WRus WSHC
¶ – *variegata* — ELan
pulchella — See A. *psittacina*
pulchra BC&W 4762 — SBla
'Purple Joy' — COtt MLin
pygmaea — MTho WDav
Rosello ® / 'Stalrobu' — LCha
'Rosy Wings' — COtt MBri MLin
Sarah ® / 'Stalicamp' — LCha
'Saxony' — MBri
Sophia ® — See A. Yellow King ®
'Sovereign' — COtt MBri MLin
* 'Striped Bird' — COtt
* 'Sunny Way' — COtt MLin
'Sunrise' — MBri
'Sweetheart' — MLin
'Vanitas' — MBri
Victoria ® / 'Regina' — LCha
Walter Fleming ® — MLin
Yellow King ® / 'Stajello' — LCha

ALTHAEA (Malvaceae)
armeniaca — CCor
cannabina — EMon GWic LRHS WHoo WRus
officinalis — CArn CHan CKin CSev ELan EMon Effi GPoy LHol LHop MChe NSel SIde WOak WSto

ALYOGYNE (Malvaceae)
hakeifolia — CSun LHop
huegelii — CSun
– 'Santa Cruz' — CHil ERea LHop

ALYSSOIDES (Cruciferae)
utriculata — CCor CLew CTom EBar ELan GAbr LHop NGre SAxl WHil WOld WPer
– *graeca* — NHol SIng

ALYSSUM (Cruciferae)
argenteum — WHoo
cuneifolium — WAbe
*– *pyreneum* — MHig
idaeum — MCas MWat
moellendorfianum — EPad EPot
montanum — CLew CRiv CShe EBre ECha EFou EMNN MPit MPla SChu SIng
– 'Berggold' ('Mountain Gold') — CB&S LAbb MCas MRav NNrd NRoo NVic WHil
¶ *repens* — NGre
saxatile — CB&S CShe GDra IDai MBal MBar MPla NKay SIng WWin
*– 'Argenteum' — EFou
– *citrinum* — CShe EBre ECha EFou MBal MCot MPar MWat SDix
– 'Compactum' — CHar CKel EBre ECtt ENot MFir NNor WCla WHil WHoo
– 'Dudley Neville' — CRiv CShe ECha EFol EFou GLoc MBal MCas MPla MWat NRar SBla SChu

– 'Dudley Neville Variegated' — EBre ECha ERav GLoc MCas MPla NRar NRoo NSti WOld WPer
– 'Flore Pleno' — CLew ECha MBal NRoo NSti SBla WEas WHil
– 'Gold Dust' — ECtt LGro NGre
– 'Golden Queen' — ECtt NNrd
– 'Goldkugel' ('Gold Ball') — ELan EMNN MPit NVic
– 'Nelly Reuben' — CMal
– 'Silver Queen' — ELan NKay NRoo WEas
– 'Variegatum' — CLew SBla WHil
scardicum — WPer
serpyllifolium — CLew GLoc MBro MHig NHol NKay NTow WPat WPer
spinosum — See PTILOTRICHUM ***spinosum***
stribrnyi — CLew LRHS MHig NTow WPer
tortuosum — ESis NGre NTow WAbe WCla WDav WPer
wulfenianum — CCor CMHG CSun GLoc MHig WHil

AMANA (Liliaceae)
edulis — See TULIPA ***edulis***

X AMARINE (Liliaceae/Amaryllidaceae)
* 'Monta Rosa' — MFir
§ *tubergenii* — ETub LBow
– 'Zwanenburg' — CAvo LBow

X AMARYGIA (Liliaceae/Amaryllidaceae)
parkeri — LBow
§ – 'Alba' — CAvo LBow

AMARYLLIS (Liliaceae/Amaryllidaceae)
amethystina — LAma
belladonna — CB&S CBro CFor CHEx IHos LAma LHop LSav MBri MUlv SIng SLHN SMad SW&B WThu
– 'Bloemfontein' — CAvo
– 'Hathor' — LSav
– 'Johannesburg' — CAvo LAma LBow
– 'Kimberley' — CAvo LAma LBow
– 'Major' — CAvo
– 'Parkeri Alba' — See X AMARYGIA ***parkeri*** 'Alba'
– 'Purpurea' — SApp
– 'Windhoek' — CAvo

AMELANCHIER † (Rosaceae)
alnifolia — ESim
asiatica — SHil
'Ballerina' — CB&S CCla CSco EBre EHar ELan ESim LNet MBri MGos SHil SMad SPer SPla SReu SSpi SSta SSus WPat WWat
canadensis — Widely available
– *micropetala* — LSav NHol
florida — WCoo
x *grandiflora* 'Rubescens' — SHil SSpi SSta
laevis — CBot CChu CCla CSco CShe MBal NNor SHil SPer
lamarckii — CB&S CBow CChu CCla CSco EGol ELan ENot IHos IOrc LBuc LSav MBri MGos MR&S NHol NKay SHil SPer SReu
pumila — LHop MBal MGos NTow SIng WDav WNor WThu

AMICIA (Leguminosae)
zygomeris — CBrd CHEx GWic WSHC

AMOMUM (Zingiberaceae)
cardamomum — See A. ***compactum***
§ *compactum* — MNew

AMOMYRTUS (Myrtaceae)
luma — See MYRCEUGENIA ***exserta***

AMORPHA (Leguminosae)
canescens — CB&S CBow CPle ELan NSti SLHN
fruticosa — CB&S CBot CBow CCla CPle EHal IOrc WCoo

AMORPHOPHALLUS (Araceae)
rivierei — EPot

AMPELOPSIS † (Vitaceae)
glandulosa brevipedunculata — CBra CHan SAxl SPer SPla
§ – *brevipedunculata* 'Elegans' — CChu CCla CHad CHan CMac EFou EHar ELan IJoh LHop LNet MBal MBar MR&S NBar NRog SBra SHig SHil SMad SPer SSta WSHC
♦ – *brevipedunculata* 'Tricolor' — See A. ***g. b.*** 'Elegans'
– *citrulloides* — SHil
henryana — See PARTHENOCISSUS ***h.***
megalophylla — CBot ELan GWic ISea LGre SHil
♦ *sempervirens* — See CISSUS ***striata***
tricuspidata 'Veitchii' — See PARTHENOCISSUS ***t.*** 'V.'

AMPHICOME See **INCARVILLEA**

AMSONIA (Apocynaceae)
¶ *ciliata* — WPer
illustris — EBre
tabernaemontana — CHan ELan SIng SWas
– *salicifolia* — CLew CShe ECha ECro WPer

AMYGDALUS See **PRUNUS**

ANACYCLUS (Compositae)
pyrethrum — CSam GPoy MSal
– *depressus* — CGle CHoe CLew CSam CSun EBre EFou ELan EOrc ESis GEdr GLoc MBro MCas MHig MRav NHol NNor SBla SIng WEas WHoo WOMN WPer
* – *depressus* 'Golden Gnome' — EHal WHil

ANAGALLIS (Primulaceae)
* *alternifolia repens* — ECou EPot ITim
arvensis — GPoy MSal WEas WPer
– *caerulea* — WOMN
– *latifolia* — CRiv NRed
foemina — MSal
linifolia — See A. ***monelli***
§ *monelli* — CElw CRiv EBar ELan GLoc LGre MMth SBla SIng WCla WEas WWin

– 'Caerulea'	SLHN
– 'Sunrise'	CHar CRiv GLoc WOMN
tenella	WCla
– 'Studland'	EPot GEdr MTho NGre NNrd NTow SIng SLHN SOkd WAbe WMar WOMN

ANANAS (Bromeliaceae)

comosus 'Variegatus'	MBri

ANAPHALIS (Compositae)

alpicola	EPot
§ *cinnamomea*	CGle CHad CHan CKel CLew CSco ECha EFou EJud ELan EPar ERav NHol NKay NRar SCro SDix WEas WHil
margaritacea	CBre CLew CSco ECtt EFou EJud EPad GCHN MBri MPlt NKay NSti WHal WSto
– 'Neuschnee' ('New Snow')	CCla EGol IBrk NHol NRoo SFis SPla WPer
♦ *nepalensis*	See A. ***triplinervis monocephala***
nubigena	CB&S CGle CHad ELan EMon ERav MBri MCot MWat NSti SChu
sinica morii	EPla LRHS SBar SChu
§ *subrigida*	ECou
§ *trinerve*	ECou
triplinervis	CBre CElw CFis CGle CHoe CKel CSco CShe EFol EFou EGol ELan IDai MBri MCot MWgw NHol NKay NNor WEas WHoo WOld WRus WWin
§ – *monocephala* B&L 12606	EMon
¶ – *monocephala* C&R 366	ITim
– 'Sommerschnee' ('Summer Snow')	CCla CHar CKel EBre ECha EOrc ERou MBri MWgw NNor SPer
yedoensis	See A. ***cinnamomea***

ANARRHINUM (Scrophulariaceae)

¶ *bellidifolium*	WPer

ANCHUSA (Boraginaceae)

angustissima	See A. ***leptophylla incana***
¶ *arvensis*	CKin MSal
§ *azurea*	NOrc WEas WHal WHil
¶ – 'Blue Ball'	ERou
– 'Dropmore'	CBow EBar WHer
– 'Feltham Pride'	CHar ECtt IBrk MBro NRoo NVic SFis WHoo WPer
– 'Little John'	CHad CSco EFou ERou GWic MBri NRoo
– 'Loddon Royalist'	CB&S CKel CSco CSev CShe EFou ELan EMon ERou IDai LHop MWat MWgw NBar NRoo
– 'Morning Glory'	CKel CSco SFis
– 'Opal'	CHad CSco CSev EMon GWic LHop MWat
caespitosa	EBre ELan EPad EPot GLoc ITim LHop MTho NNrd
¶ *capensis*	CHan WHil
italica	See A. ***azurea***
§ *leptophylla incana*	MPlt SCro WCru
myosotidiflora	See BRUNNERA ***macrophylla***
officinalis	CArn CSFH EJud LHol MSal SIde WOak
sempervirens	See PENTAGLOTTIS ***sempervirens***

ANDROMEDA (Ericaceae)

glaucophylla	IOrc MBar
polifolia	CBow CRiv EGol IOrc NBar NCat NHar NLan SLHN SLon SReu WBod
– 'Alba'	ELan MBal MBar MHig SBar SMrm SPer SSta WAbe WDav WSHC WThu
– 'Compacta'	ELan EMNN EPot MBal MBar MBlu MBri MGos MMth MPla NHar NHol SHil SIng SPer SReu WSHC WWin
– 'Grandiflora'	ITim MBal NNrd SPer WThu
– 'Kirikamina'	MBal SSta WAbe
– 'Macrophylla'	EPot GDra ITim MBal MHig NHar SSta WAbe WThu
– 'Major'	MBal SHil
– 'Minima'	GLoc MBal
– 'Nana'	ELan EPot GAbr LNet NRya SMrm WDav WPat WWat WWeb
– 'Nikko'	IJoh MBal MBar MHig SPer
– 'Shibutsu'	GArf SPer SSta

ANDROPOGON (Gramineae)

scoparius	CHoe EMon GWic

ANDROSACE (Primulaceae)

albana	NHol NNrd NRed NWCA
carnea	EMNN EPot MTho WCla WDav WEas WHal WHil
– *alba*	CSun MBro NGre NHol NNrd NRya WDav WThu
– *brigantiaca*	EMNN GEdr GLoc MCas MHig NHol NKay NRed NRya NTow WAbe
¶ – *brigantiaca* 'Myer's form'	NHol
– *halleri*	See A. ***c. rosea***
– *laggeri*	EMNN EPot GDra GEdr NNrd NRya
§ – *rosea*	GDra GEdr GHig GLoc MBro MCas NGre NHar NHol NNrd NRya NTow WCla WHea
– *rosea* x *laggeri*	GDra NHol NNrd
– x *pyrenaica*	CSun EPot GDra MHig NHol WDav
chamaejasme	GLoc WWin
ciliata	EPot ITim MCas NNrd NTow
cylindrica	EPot GDra MTho NGre NHar NHol NNrd NRed NTow WDav
– x *hirtella*	EPot GDra GLoc MHig NGre NHol NRed WAbe
delavayi	EPot GEdr ITim MHig NNrd
¶ *elongata*	EBar
foliosa	SIng
geraniifolia	SWas
globifera	EPot
hedraeantha	GDra GEdr ITim MHig NGre NHol NNrd NRya WAbe WDav
x *heeri* 'Alba'	ITim
hirtella	EPot MBro MCas MTho NHol NNrd NTow WDav
jacquemontii	See A. ***villosa jacquemontii***
lactea	MCas NGre NNrd
lanuginosa	CLew CRiv CShe CSun GLoc LHil LHop MBro MHig MWat NHol NKay WAbe WDav WHoo WPat WWin
– 'Leichtlinii'	WThu

limprichtii — See A. ***sarmentosa watkinsii***
mathildae — CSun GLoc NHol NTow SIng WDav WHoo
microphylla — See A. ***mucronifolia***
§ *mollis* — EPot MBro NNrd NTow SBar SOkd WDav WHil
§ *mucronifolia* — GEdr ITim NGre NHar NWCA
muscoidea — MHig
primuloides — GLoc MBal NCat NNrd
– 'Salmon's Variety' — See A. ***sarmentosa*** 'S.V.'
pubescens — CSun EPot GDra GLoc NHol NNrd NTow SIng
pyrenaica — CSun EPot GDra GLoc ITim MCas MHig NGre NHar NHol NNrd NTow SIng WAbe WDav WEas
rotundifolia — CLew GCHN GEdr MCas NGre NHol
salicifolia — See A. ***lactiflora***
sarmentosa — CHar CLew CSun ELan EPar ITim LHil MBro MHig MWat NGre NNrd SChu SSmi WAbe WEas WHal WHil WHoo
– *chumbyi* — CRiv CSun MBro NHol NKayI NTow SBla WDav WPat WThu
§ – 'Salmon's Variety' — MCas
– 'Sherriff's' — CShe EPot GCHN MBro NHol SBla WDav WHal WPat WThu
§ – *watkinsii* — EPot MBro NHar NHol NNrd WDav WThu
– *yunnanensis* — See A. ***mollis***
sempervivoides — Widely available
– 'Brilliant' — ELan
– dark form — NHol
septentrionalis puberulenta — WHil
strigillosa — EPad GEdr ITim NHar NWCA SIng
¶ *uliginosa* — WOMN
vandellii — EPot MHig NGre NHar NHol NRed NTow SIng WAbe WDav
§ *villosa* — MHig NTow
§ – *jacquemontii* — EPot GLoc MBro MHig NHar NRya WAbe WDav WThu
– *jacquemontii* pink form — EPot NHol WDav
– 'Superba' — EPot
vitaliana — See VITALIANA ***primuliflora***
watkinsii — See A. ***sarmentosa watkinsii***

ANDRYALA (Compositae)

agardhii — ESis GAbr LHil MPar NHol SIng WDav
lanata — See HIERACIUM ***lanatum***

ANEMIA (Schizaeaceae)

phyllitidis — NMar

ANEMONE † (Ranunculaceae)

altaica — CFor EPot
apennina — CBro EPar ETub LAma MBri NTow SCro WEas
– CEH 538 — LRHS
– *albiflora* — EPar LAma
– 'Petrovac' — WChr
baldensis — CGle ECro MBro NNrd NWCA
blanda — CSam ECam EFou EOrc GLoc LAma LBow LHop MBri MBro MHig MPlt NHol NNrd SChu SMad WOMN WPat
– 'Atrocaerulea' — ELan EPar LAma MBal SIng SW&B
– blue — CAvo CBro CRiv ELan EPot ETub LAma LRoo MBri WHil
– 'Blue Mist' — LBlo NNor
– 'Charmer' — CAvo CBro CCla EPar EPot ETub NHol NNrd SIng WPat
– 'Pink Star' — CRiv EPot LAma LBlo LBow LRoo MBri NHol NNor
– 'Radar' — CAvo CBro ELan EPar EPot ETub LAma LBlo LBow NHol WChr
– *rosea* — EFou ELan ETub LAma NHol WPat
– 'Violet Star' — CBro EPot
– 'White Splendour' — CAvo CBro CCla EFou ELan EOrc EPar EPot ETub LAma LBlo LBow LRoo MCot MHig NHol SChu SIng WEas WHil WPat
¶ *bucharica* — WChr
canadensis — CCla SIng
caroliniana — CGle ESis GLoc
caucasica — ECam EPot
coronaria 'De Caen' 'Excelsior' — LRoo
– – forms — ECam
– – 'group '! — CKel ETub LAma LRoo MBri
¶ – – 'His Excellency' — NHol
– – 'Hollandia' — ETub
– – 'Mister Fokker' — LAma LRoo
– – 'Mount Everest' — ETub NHol
– – 'Saint Brigid' — CKel CSut ETub LAma LBlo LRoo MBri SW&B
– – 'The Admiral' — LRoo
– – 'The Governor' — LRoo
cylindrica — CAvo CHar CLew NHol
drummondii — CHar GEdr MHig NWCA SIng WHil
eranthoides — ECam LAma WChr
flaccida — EPot
× *fulgens* — EPar LAma LRoo
– 'Annulata Grandiflora' — CBro LBlo
– 'Multipetala' — CBro
– Saint Bavo group — CBro ETub LAma SIng
globosa — See A. ***multifida***
¶ *heldreichiana* — SWas
hepatica transsilvanica — See HEPATICA ***transsilvanica***
hupehensis — CBos WCot
§ – 'Bowles' Pink' — MPar MWat
– 'Eugenie' — CGle
– 'Hadspen Abundance' — CHad ECha ECtt ELun EMon GWic LGre NSti NTow SAxl WAbb
– *praecox* — MBri
– 'Rosenschale' — GWic
– 'September Charm' — CCla CKel EBre EFol EFou EGol ELan EOrc ERou MBri NBar NSti SChu SCro SDix SMad SPer
– *splendens* — CCla EFou
hupehensis japonica — CHan EMon GWic LGro NNor SAxl SMad WEas WRus
§ – – 'Bressingham Glow' — CB&S CSco CShe EBre EFou EGol ELan ELun EOrc ERou LHop MBri MPit MRav NBar NHol NRoo NVic SPer SSpi

§ – – 'Prinz Heinrich'	CCla CHad CHan ECha EFou LGre LHop MBri NJap SPla SSpi WHoo
§ x ***hybrida***	CAvo CHad CKel EFou EPar IHos MBro MFir MWgw NBar NOak SChu SMad SWas WAbe WOld
N– 'Alba'	MPar
¶ – 'Alba Dura'	WCot
– 'Bowles' Pink'	See A. ***hupehensis*** 'B.P.'
– 'Bresssingham Glow'	See A. ***hupehensis japonica*** 'B.G.'
– 'Coupe d'Argent'	CSco
– 'Elegans'	EFou
§ – 'Géante des Blanches'	CKel EBre ECro ECtt EFou ERou NNor NRoo SApp SPer
– 'Honorine Jobert'	Widely available
– 'Königin Charlotte'	CCla CGle CHad CHar CKel CSco EBre ECha EFou EGol ELan ERou MBri MPit NBar NBir NHol SBla SPer SSpi WRus
– 'Kriemhilde'	NJap
♦– 'Lady Gilmour'	See A. x ***h.*** 'Margarete'
– 'Loreley'	MWat NHol WCot
– 'Luise Uhink'	CBos CKel CSco ENot NBir SSpi WEas
§ – 'Margarete'	CCla CHad CKel EBre EFou EGol ELan EOrc ERou MBri MCot MPar MRav NBar NJap SPer
– 'Max Vogel'	CSco
– 'Monterosa'	EOrc ERou GWic MBal MRav NBar
– 'Pamina'	GWic
– 'Prinz Heinrich' ('Prince Henry')	See A. ***hupehensis japonica*** 'P.H.'
– 'Profusion'	SPla WHoo WRus
– 'Richard Ahrens'	MBri SAxl
§ – 'Superba'	CSco SBla WKif
– 'Whirlwind' ('Wirbelwind')	EFou EGol ELan EOrc LHop MBri MRav NBar NHol NJap NRoo NSti SCro WHoo WRus
– 'White Queen'	See A. x ***h.*** 'Géante des Blanches'
japonica	See A. x ***hybrida***
x ***lesseri***	Widely available
§ x ***lipsiensis***	CAvo CBro ECha EPar EPot GEdr GLoc LGre MPar MTho NHol NTow SOkd SPou SWas WChr WThu
¶ – forms	SPou
– 'Pallida'	GEdr SPou
N ***magellanica***	See A. ***multifida***
§ ***multifida***	Widely available
– 'Major'	CHar NKay SBla SWas WBon WHil
narcissiflora	ECro SFis
nemorosa	CArn CAvo CBre CBro CKin EPar EPot LAma LBow MBal MSal NHol NLan SIng SSpi WBon
N– 'Alba Plena'	CAvo CBro CChu CFor ECha EPot MHig SBla SIng WAbb WEas WHil WMar WRus
– 'Allenii'	CAvo CBos CBro ECha EPot GEdr MBal MCas NTow SIng SSpi WChr
– 'Atrocaerulea'	CFor EPot GEdr NHol
– 'Blue Beauty'	EPot GEdr GLoc MBal NHol NNrd
– 'Blue Bonnet'	CChu
– 'Blue Queen'	EPot
– 'Bowles' Purple'	GEdr NTow WChr
– 'Bracteata Plena'	EPot LHop MBal
– ***coerulea***	EPot
– 'Currie's Pink'	GEdr
– 'Danica'	MBal
– 'Flore Pleno'	CTre GEdr MBal MTho SBla
¶ – forms	SPou
¶ – 'Green Fingers'	WChr
– 'Hannah Gubbay'	GEdr MBal SIng
– 'Hilda'	EPot GEdr MBal WChr
– 'Lady Doneraile'	MPar
– 'Leeds' Variety'	EPot WChr
– 'Lychette'	EPot GEdr MBal
– ***monstrosa***	EPot
– 'Pentre Pink'	WChr
– 'Purity'	LBlo
– 'Robinsoniana'	CBro CChu CHad EPot GEdr LGre MBal MCas MHig MTho NTow SIng
– 'Rosea'	EPot GEdr LAma NHol WChr
– 'Royal Blue'	CBro EPot GEdr LAma NHol
– 'Vestal'	CGle GEdr MPar SBar
– 'Virescens'	GEdr
¶ – 'Viridiflora'	WChr
– 'Wilks' White'	EPot GEdr MBal
– x ***ranunculoides***	See A. x ***lipsiensis***
obtusiloba	EPot GDra
– ***alba***	GDra NHar NHol
palmata	NRed
parviflora	NHol
patens	See PULSATILLA ***p.***
pavonina	NBir SIng SLHN SWas WPer
petiolulosa	ECam EPot WChr
polyanthes	MBro WEas
pseudoaltaica	EPot
pulsatilla	See PULSATILLA ***vulgaris***
ranunculoides	CAvo CBro EPar EPot GEdr LAma MHig NHol NKay NNrd SIng SPou WChr WHil WOMN
– 'Flore Pleno'	EPot GEdr MPar WChr WMar
rivularis	Widely available
'Saint Piran'	SW&B
x ***seemannii***	See A. x ***lipsiensis***
sulphurea	See PULSATILLA ***alpina apiifolia***
superba 'Pink'	See A. x ***hybrida*** 'Superba'
sylvestris	CCla CGle CHan CHar CLew EPar GWic MBri MPar MSal MWgw NHol NRoo NSel NSti SAxl SBla SIng SSpi WEas WHal WRus WWin
¶ – ***macrantha***	EMon SWas
tetrasepala	MBro
tomentosa	ECha NHol NSti SMad WEas
§ – 'Robustissima'	CSco EFou EGol GWic LHop MBri MBro NOrc SHig WRus
trifolia	GEdr GLoc MBal SWas WChr WPat
trullifolia SBEC 797	NHar NHol
¶ – ***alba***	NHar
tschernjaewii	EPot MBro
vernalis	See PULSATILLA ***vernalis***
¶ ***virginiana***	WHoo
vitifolia	ECro GGar MPar
– 'Robustissima'	See A. ***tomentosa*** 'R.'

ANEMONELLA (Ranunculaceae)
thalictroides LAma LBow NHar SSpi
– pink form SOkd
– semi-double white form SOkd

ANEMONOPSIS (Ranunculaceae)
macrophylla CFor ECha ECro LGre MUlv NHol NTow SAxl SBla SOkd SWas WEas WOld

ANETHUM (Umbelliferae)
graveolens CArn EJud GPoy LHol MChe MPit NSel SIde WPer WSto

ANGELICA (Umbelliferae)
archangelica CArn CFis CGle CSFH CSco CSev ECha EEls ELan ERav Effi GPoy LHol MBri MChe MCot NRoo NSel SBla SChu SIde SIng WEas WOak
♦ *curtisii* See A. ***triquinata***
gigas CBre CFor ECha SAxl
montana ECou LHop
sylvestris CArn CKin MSal WHer
§ *triquinata* MSal

ANIGOZANTHOS (Haemodoraceae)
bicolor CSun
flavidus CSun MBri MCab SLMG WTay
– green form ERav
– grey form CSun
– orange form CSun
– red form CSun ERav LHil LHop
¶ – yellow form LHil
gabrielae CSun
manglesii CB&S WPer
preissii CSun
viridis CSun

ANISODONTEA (Malvaceae)
capensis CB&S CHad CHil ERea IBlr LHop SAxl SBar SChu SMrm WEas WWin
§ *hypomadarum* CChu CElw CHan CMHG CSev CSun CTre EOrc MPla NPer NTow WHal WOMN WOld WPer WRus
¶ *malvastroides* GWic
scabrosa SCro SLon

ANISOTOME (Umbelliferae)
flexuosa NSti
haastii NHol

ANODA (Malvaceae)
cristata 'Opal Cup' EMon LHil LRHS WRus

ANOIGANTHUS See **CYRTANTHUS**

ANOMATHECA (Iridaceae)
cruenta See A. ***laxa***
§ *laxa* CAvo CBro CElw ECha ELan EPot GCHN GLoc LGre LHop MTho SAxl SChu SDix SLHN SPou SSpi WAbe WHal WOMN WPat WWin
– *alba* CAvo CElw ELan EPot GLoc LGre MPit NWCA SChu SPou WAbe WOMN WThu
¶ – *alba maculata* SPou
viridis CAvo GLoc LBow LHop SSad

ANOPTERUS (Grossulariaceae)
glandulosus CHEx IBlr

ANREDERA (Basellaceae)
cordifolia LHop NHex

ANTENNARIA (Compositae)
¶ *alpina* ITim
aprica See A. ***parvifolia***
dioica CHar CRiv ECro ELan GCHN GPoy LHil LHol MSal NLan SIng WCla WHal WHil WHoo
– 'Aprica' See A. ***parvifolia***
§ – *hyperborea* CLew LGro SSmi WAbe
– *minima* CGle CHar CLew EPot GDra GLoc MHig MPla MWat NHar NHol
– 'Nyewoods Variety' GDra GHig MHig MTho NHol NTow WDav
– *rosea* CGle CLew CMHG CRiv EMNN IDai MBar MCas MPla MPlt MTho NHol NKay NNor NNrd SIng SSmi WHal WPer WWin
– 'Rosea Plena' CGle NHar NKay
– *rubra* CHar CKel ECha NHol NKay SBla SSmi WAbe
– *tomentosa* See A. ***d. hyperborea***
macrophylla WEas WOMN
neglecta gaspensis SIng
§ *parvifolia* EMNN ESis GCHN GDra GLoc MBar MPla NHol NNrd NSti SIng WCla WEas WHil WWin

ANTHEMIS (Compositae)
aizoon See ACHILLEA ***ageratifolia a.***
biebersteinii See A. ***marschalliana***
cretica carpatica LGre
¶ – – 'Karpatenschnee' EFou
'Eva' LGan WEas
frutescens See ARGYRANTHEMUM ***frutescens***
§ *marschalliana* CGle CHan CKel CShe EBre ECha EPot ESis GAbr GDra GHig GLoc LHop NKay NNor NNrd NOak SSmi WEas WPer WWin
nobilis See CHAMAEMELUM ***nobile***
punctata cupaniana Widely available
– *cupaniana nana* NPer
rudolphiana See A. ***marschalliana***
sancti-johannis CGle CLew CSco EBar EFou ERou MBri NCat NOak NPer WHil WPer
tinctoria CArn CGle CHad EJud ELan EMon GPoy LHol MChe MPit NKay NPer NSel SIde WAbe WOak WWin
– 'Alba' EFou EMon NPer
– 'E C Buxton' Widely available
– 'Grallach Gold' CGle ECha EMon EPad GAbr IDai LRHS MUlv MWat NCat NHol NPer SCro WEas
– 'Kelwayi' CGle CHad CHar CRiv EBar ECtt ERou GAbr GCHN GWic LAbb LHop MFir NPer SLHN WHen WPer
¶ – 'Pride of Grallach' GWic

– 'Sauce Hollandaise' EFou EMon LRHS NPer
– 'Wargrave Variety' CBre CElw CGle ECha EFol EFou EMon GAbr GWic MUlv MWat NPer NRar SAxl SChu SDix
tuberculata ESis LHop MCas SBla SIng WEas

ANTHERICUM † (Liliaceae/Anthericaceae)
algeriense See A. ***liliago major***
liliago CBro CChu CSun EBar ELan GDra GLoc GWic LHop MBro SPer WCla WDav WPer WWat
§ – ***major*** EBre ECha GDra IBlr LGre SPer WOld
ramosum EBul ECha ECro MBro NHol NNrd SIng WCla WPer
– JCA 166.300 CAvo WDav
– ***plumosum*** CBro
¶ ***tibeticum*** WDav

ANTHOCERCIS (Solanaceae)
littorea CPle

ANTHOLYZA (Iridaceae)
coccinea See CROCOSMIA ***paniculata***
paniculata See CROCOSMIA ***paniculata***

ANTHOXANTHUM (Gramineae)
odoratum CSFH GPoy WHer

ANTHRISCUS (Umbelliferae)
cerefolium CArn CSFH CSev EJud GPoy LHol MChe NSel SIde WOak WPer WSto
sylvestris 'Ravenswing' CElw EMon ERav LRHS
¶ – ***roseus*** LSav

ANTHURIUM (Araceae)
* ***amazone*** MBri
andreanum MBri
– 'Rose' See A. x ***ferrierense*** 'Roseum'
clarinervium MBri
cordatum See A. ***leuconeurum***
x ***ferrierense*** 'Roseum' MBri
scherzerianum MBri
– 'Rosemarie' MBri

ANTHYLLIS (Leguminosae)
hermanniae CMHG CSam CSun MCas SHil SIng WAbe WEas WSHC
– 'Minor' EPot
montana CLew ELan LHil MPlt WPer
– ***rubra*** EPot GLoc MHig NKay NNrd SIng WThu WWin
vulneraria CKin MChe MSal NKay NLan SFir WCla WHil WPer
– ***coccinea*** GAbr GDra GEdr MTho NHol NNrd NTow WHil

ANTIGONON (Polygonaceae)
leptopus CPle MNew

ANTIRRHINUM (Scrophulariaceae)
asarina See ASARINA ***procumbens***
'Black Prince' CCor
braun-blanquetii CSun GGar LHop SFis
glutinosum roseum See ASARINA ***hispanicum hispanicum roseum***
hispanicum GWic WOMN
¶ ***majus*** ECro
– ***linkianum*** WOMN
– 'Taff's White' MTho WRus
molle CHar CLew CSpe CSun LHop MCot MHig MTho NPer NTow SIng WHil WPer
pulverulentum LGre LHop SMrm WEas WHea WPer
sempervirens EPad MTho WOMN

APHANES (Rosaceae)
arvensis GPoy MSal NHex

APHELANDRA (Acanthaceae)
* ***alexandra*** SLMG
squarrosa MBri
– 'Dania' MBri

APHYLLANTHES (Liliaceae/Aphyllanthaceae)
monspeliensis CLew SPou WDav WOMN

APIOS (Leguminosae)
§ ***americana*** WSHC
tuberosa See A. ***americana***

APIUM (Umbelliferae)
graveolens EJud GPoy MSal WOak

APOCYNUM (Apocynaceae)
androsaemifolium MSal
cannabinum CArn GPoy MSal

APONOGETON (Aponogetonaceae)
distachyos CBWG CHEx CRow CWGN EHon ELan EWav LMay MBal MSta SHig SLon
krausseanus See A. ***desertorum***

APPLE See **MALUS** ***domestica***

APPLE, Crab See **MALUS**

APRICOT See **PRUNUS** ***armeniaca***

APTENIA (Aizoaceae)
cordifolia CHEx CSev
¶ – 'Variegata' CHEx LHil

AQUILEGIA † (Ranunculaceae)
akitensis See A. ***flabellata pumila***
* ***alba*** CSco
alpina CHad CRow CShe ECtt EDra EFou ELan ESis GCHN LHil MCas MCot MWgw NHol NNrd WCla WHen WPer WWin
– 'Hensol Harebell' See A. 'H.H.'
'Alpine Blue' CSco SIde
amaliae See A. ***ottonis a.***
§ ***atrata*** CArn CRow EDra GAbr GCHN GLoc MBro MWat NOak NSti SIng WCar WDav WHer WPer
* – 'Carl Ziepke' GWic
aurea EDra
baicalensis baicalensis See A. ***vulgaris*** Baicalensis group
barnebyi EDra

¶ – JCA 11410	WDav
bertolonii	CGle CHad CHar CLew CRiv EDra EFou GAbr GEdr MBal MBro MCas MPla NHol NRoo SBla SSmi SSpi SWas WAbe WDav WHoo
– 'Blue Berry'	MBro MPla WCla WHoo
'Betty Barton'	MFir
'Biedermeier'	EDra WHil
'Blue Spurs'	EDra
brevistyla	EDra WDav
buergeriana	EDra GGar NKay WCla
caerulea	EDra EPad GCHN GDra SIng WCar WHer
– ***ochroleuca***	GCHN LGre NHol
canadensis	CCla CGle CHan EBre EDra ELan GAbr GEdr LHop MBal MHig MSal NGre NOak NSti WEas WHer WPer
– 'Nana'	CSam EDra
cazorlensis	EDra GCHN
'Celestial Blue'	CRow ELan LGre NSti
chrysantha	EBar EDra ELan EPad GWic LGre LRHS WDav
– ***chaplinei***	CBot EDra GWic LGre NBir WDav
– ***hinckleyana***	EDra
¶ – 'Yellow Queen'	GWic NHol
* ***coronata***	EDra
'Crimson Star'	CCla CKel EBre EDra ELan SPer WRus
* ***desertorum***	EDra LGre WDav
* ***dinarica***	EDra
discolor	CHar CLew CRiv EDra GDra MBro MPla NGre NKay NRoo NTow SIng WAbe WDav WOMN WPat WThu
'Dragonfly'	CB&S CBow GAbr LSav MBri MPit MRav NOak NVic WPer
'Eastgrove'	WEas
ecalcarata	See SEMIAQUILEGIA ***ecalcarata***
einseleana	CBot EDra NHol NWCA
* ***elegantissima***	CHad GDra NNrd
elegantula	LGre WDav WOMN
eximia	EDra WCar
flabellata	CGle CHad ECha EDra EFou EMNN GAbr GCHN MPlt NHol WHal WHil WPat WPer
§ – ***alba***	CBot ELan EMNN GCHN GGar NHol NWCA SBla WDav WEas
* – 'Kudo'	WAbe
– 'Mini Star'	EBar EDra ESis LHop NOak NRoo SIng WHil WHoo WPer WWin
– ***nana***	See A. ***f. pumila***
– 'Nana Alba'	CBot CGle EBre EDra EMon GEdr GWic MCas MTho NRoo NRya SIng WAbe WWin
– Reban form	NRed SOkd WDav
* – 'White Angel'	EFou
§ ***flabellata pumila***	Widely available
– – ***alba***	ECha EDra GDra ITim MBal NHol SBla WDav
– – ***kurilensis***	GDra NKay WCla
flavescens	EDra
formosa	CBot CFor CHan CSun ECha EDra EFol ELan GAbr GCHN GGar GWic MWgw NHol NRoo NRya SBla WCar WDav WHal
¶ – ***nana***	CLew
– ***truncata***	NHol
– x ***longissima***	EDra
fragrans	CArn CFor CHad CHan EDra GPla LGre MBro MPar MTho NHar NOak SBla SLHN WCar WDav WEas WHer WHoo WPer
– KBE 48	NHol
glandulosa	CSam EDra GDra GEdr ITim NHol WDav WEas WPer
– ***jucunda***	EDra
§ ***glauca***	EDra SBla SWas
grata	CHar CSun EDra LGre WCar
¶ – JCA 173.700	NHol
Harbutt's hybrids	ERou
'Hensol Harebell'	CGle CHan EDra GAbr MBro MWgw NHol NKay SPer WHoo
hinckleyana	See A. ***chrysantha h.***
japonica	See A. ***flabellata pumila***
jonesii	NHar NKay WDav
– x ***saximontana***	EPad NHol SOkd
¶ ***laramiensis***	EPad ESis GArf SOkd WDav
longissima	CGle EDra GLoc GWic ITim MTho NHol NNrd SBla WCar WCla WDav WEas WHer
Lowdham strain	EDra
'Maxi Star'	ELan SApp
McKana hybrids	CBow CKel CSco CShe EBre EDra ELan ENot GCHN IDai MFir MWat MWgw NBar NNor NOak NVic SPer
micrantha	GCHN LGre WDav
microphylla	EDra NGre
'Modra Pisen'	EDra
'Mrs Scott Elliot's Variety'	EDra MBri MWgw
¶ 'Mrs Shaw's Double'	WEas
Music Series Hybrids	ECtt LAbb NOak NRoo SMrm SPla
nevadensis	See A. ***vulgaris n.***
nigricans	See A. ***atrata***
nivalis	See A. ***glauca***
§ ***olympica***	CSun EDra
¶ – JCA 173.600	NHol
ottonis	EDra LRHS
§ – ***amaliae***	EDra
oxysepala	CChu EDra
pyrenaica	CSam EDra LGan MBro NHol NTow WCla WWin
* ***saxatilis***	EDra
saximontana	CSun EDra GAbr GCHN MPla NHol NTow NWCA SIng SOkd WAbe WDav WOMN
'Schneekönigin' ('Snow Queen')	ELan GCHN MWgw NOak WEas WHen
schockleyi	EDra MUlv WAbe WOMN
scopulorum	CLew GAbr GLoc NRed SBar WDav
sibirica	EDra
skinneri	EDra NHol NRed WCru WDav WHil
'Snow Queen'	See A. 'Schneekönigin'
¶ sp. ACL 7781	NHol
¶ sp. from Zigana Pass	EDra
stellata	See A. ***vulgaris clematiflora***
thalictrifolia	EDra GEdr NHol NRed
– JCA 174.400	WDav
transsilvanica	EDra
triternata	EDra LGre NHol
* ***ussuriensis***	IBrk
* ***valentinianum***	GArf

viridiflora	CBot CFor CHad CHar CRow CSun EDra EFol GCHN GDra GEdr MPar NGre NHol SBla SIng SSpi WEas WOMN WThu
§ *vulgaris*	CArn CFis CHad CWGN EDra GPoy LHol NLan NNor NRoo SIde WBon WOak
– 'Adelaide Addison'	CBro EDra MTho NHol SAxl SWas WEas
– *alba*	CRow MPar
– 'Anne Calder'	EDra
– Baicalensis group	EDra GCHN
– 'Belhaven Blue Spurless'	EDra
– 'Blue Star'	CSco ECtt EFou GCHN SPer
– from Brno Czechoslovakia	EDra
§ – *clematiflora*	CBot CBre CGle CLew CRow EDra GAbr NGre NHol NNrd WDav WHal WHer WHil WPer
§ – *clematiflora alba*	CGle EDra EFou GCHN LHop
§ – *clematiflora rosea*	EDra EFou
– 'Crystal Star '	EFou
– double red	EDra
– *flore pleno*	CBre CRow EFol NOak NSti SSvw WHil WPer
– *flore pleno* 'Warwick'	MShr
– 'Gisela Powell'	EDra
*– 'Mathew Strominger'	ECro
*– 'Mrs Nicholls'	MBri
§ – *nevadensis*	EDra EPad
– 'Nivea' ('Munstead White')	CBot CHad ELan EMon GAbr IBrk NRoo SBla SSus WCla WHer WHil WRus
– 'Nora Barlow'	Widely available
♦– Olympica group	See A. ***olympica***
– 'Patricia Zavros'	EDra
– 'Pink Spurless'	See A. ***vulgaris clematiflora rosea***
– 'Red Star'	CSco ECtt EFou GCHN NOak
– 'Rev E Baty'	EDra
– from Rize, Turkey	EDra
– scented form	EDra
– 'Stellata'	See A. ***v. clematiflora***
*– 'The Bride'	WBon
– 'Tom Fairhurst'	EDra
– variegated foliage	See A. ***v.*** Vervaeneana group
– Vervaeneana group	CBot CHad CHan CHar CRow EDra EFol EFou EMon GAbr NBir NSti WCla WHil WPer WRus
– Vervaeneana group 'Woodside'	CElw GAbr LHop WHoo
– 'White Spurless'	See A. ***v. clematiflora alba***
– 'White Star'	ECtt EFou GCHN NRoo SPer

ARABIS † (Cruciferae)

albida	See A. ***caucasica***
alpina	CB&S CLew MWat
– 'Flore Pleno'	See A. ***caucasica*** 'F.P.'
– *rosea*	See A. ***caucasica rosea***
– 'Snow Cap'	See A. ***caucasica*** 'Schneehaube'
*– 'Snow White'	NGre
– 'Spring Charm'	See A. ***blepharophylla*** 'Frühlingszauber'
androsacea	EPar MCas MHig MPla NGre NTow WDav
¶ *aubrietoides*	NWCA
blepharophylla	LHop NTow WDav
– *alba*	WHoo WOMN
§ – 'Frühlingszauber' ('Spring Charm')	CB&S CHar EMNN GDra MPit NGre NKay NRoo WCla WPer
bryoides	MTho WDav
– *olympica*	SIng
§ *caucasica*	EBar MBar MWgw WOak
– 'Compinkie '	ECtt MFir NRoo WPer
– 'Corfe Castle'	CMHG EBre
§ – 'Flore Pleno'	CB&S CElw CGle CShe EBre ECha ELan EOrc EPar GAbr GLoc IDai LGro MCas MWat NKay NRoo NSti WBon WEas WHil WPer WRus WWin
¶ – 'Gillian Sharman'	EMon
– 'Pink Pearl'	CGle GAbr MRav WPer
– 'Rosabella'	CMHG EBre ECha GLoc LHop MRav
– 'Rose Frost'	EMNN
§ – *rosea*	EJud LAbb NBir WEas WPer
– 'Schneehaube' ('Snowcap')	EBar ECtt EMNN MBar NHar NKay NRoo
– 'Snowdrop'	MCas MRav
– 'Variegata'	CB&S CGle CHar CHoe CRow CShe EBre ECha EFol EFou ELan EOrc EPar EPot GLoc IDai LHop MBri MCas MTho NRoo WEas WHil WRus
§ *collina*	WHil
cypria	LRHS WOMN
ferdinandi-coburgii	CGle CRow EJud EOrc EPot ITim LGro MFir MPla NHol NVic WCla WEas WWin
– 'Aureovariegata'	CRiv GLoc
– 'Old Gold'	Widely available
– 'Variegata'	Widely available
x *kellereri*	MBro NHol SIng WDav
* *lucida* 'Variegata'	EFol LHop
muralis	See A. ***collina***
'Pink Snow'	NGre
procurrens	WHil
rosea	See A. ***collina***
¶ *scopoliana*	SIng
¶ *serrata japonica*	WHil
soyeri	NRed NTow
– *jacquinii*	NRed WHal WHil
stricta	CNat
*x *sturii*	MHig NHol NNrd WDav WHil
x *suendermannii*	MPla
¶ *turrita*	WPer

ARACHNOIDES (Aspleniaceae)

ARAIOSTEGIA (Davalliaceae)

pseudocystopteris	SApp

ARALIA (Araliaceae)

cachemirica	CHad CHan
¶ *californica*	MSal
chinensis	CB&S NHol SPer
¶ *continentalis*	CHan
elata	CBra CHEx CHad CHan CLan CLnd ELan ENot IOrc LNet MBal NNor SArc SExT SHil SPer SSpi WNor WSHC
– 'Aureovariegata'	CB&S CBow CSco EHar ELan IJoh IOrc LNet MBri SHil SSus WPat

– 'Variegata' CB&S CBot EHar ELan IBar IOrc LNet MBlu MBri NPal SGar SHil SSpi SSus WPat
racemosa GPoy GWic MSal
sieboldii See FATSIA ***japonica***
spinosa CHil SHil SMad

ARAUCARIA (Araucariaceae)
§ ***araucana*** Widely available
¶ ***augustifolia*** CHEx
excelsa See A. ***heterophylla***
heterophylla MBri
imbricata See A. ***araucana***

ARAUJIA (Asclepiadaceae)
* ***grandiflora*** SLMG
sericofera CB&S CGre CMHG ERea LHop

ARBUTUS † (Ericaceae)
andrachne ENot MBal SHil WCoo
x ***andrachnoides*** CBot CChu CCla CFor EHar IJoh LNet MBal MUlv SArc SBor SHil SPer SSpi WMou WWat
glandulosa See ARCTOSTAPHYLOS ***g.***
menziesii CBot MBal SHil SMad SSpi WBod WCoo WWat
unedo Widely available
¶ – 'Compacta' LSav SSpi
– 'Merriott' LSav
– 'Quercifolia' CFor SSta
– 'Rubra' CBra CChu CFor CSco EHar ELan IOrc LNet LSav MBal MBri SHil SPer SSpi SSta WBod

ARCHONTOPHOENIX (Palmae)
alexandrae LPal
cunninghamiana NPal

ARCTANTHEMUM (Compositae)
¶ ***arcticum*** EMon

ARCTERICA See **PIERIS**

ARCTIUM (Compositae)
lappa CArn CKin Effi GPoy LHol MChe MSal NHex SIde WHer
minus CKin MSal
pubens CKin

ARCTOSTAPHYLOS (Ericaceae)
* ***californica*** MBal SIng
'Clyde Robins' SSta
§ ***glandulosa*** SArc
x ***media*** 'Snow Camp' ELan MBal SSta
– 'Wood's Red' MBal NHar SSta WAbe
patula CCla LRHS LSav SMad
pumila SSta
pungens manzanita MBal SHil
– ***nevadensis*** MBal MBar SPer SReu SSta
uva-ursi CCla ELan ENot GEdr GPoy IDai IOrc MBal MBar MGos MPla MR&S NLan NNor NNrd SGar SHil SPer SSta WBod
¶ – 'Massachusetts' ELan
– ***myrtifolia*** EBre ECro SReu SSta WSHC
– ***nummularia*** MBal
– 'Point Reeves' SSta
– 'Vancouver Jade' MR&S MUlv SSta

ARCTOTIS (Compositae)
x ***hybrida*** 'Apricot' CHil LHop SMrm
– 'Flame' CHad CHil LHop SChu SMrm WPer
– 'Pink' CHad SChu SMrm
– 'White' CHil
– 'Wine' CHad CHil LHop SMrm

ARDISIA (Myrsinaceae)
crenata MBri

ARECA (Palmae)
aliceae LPal
catechu MBri
¶ ***triandra*** LPal

ARECASTRUM (Palmae)
§ ***romanzoffianum*** LPal NPal

ARENARIA (Caryophyllaceae)
aggregata GLoc
balearica CLew CSpe ELan EPar EPot GAbr GCHN GLoc MBro MCas MPlt MTho NGre NHar NHol NNrd SIng WEas WHil WHoo WWin
caespitosa See MINUARTIA ***verna***
fendleri MTho
grandiflora ESis GLoc WAbe WHil
ledebouriana EPot MWat NHol WAbe WThu
§ ***lithops*** ITim WWin
montana Widely available
norvegica WHil
– ***anglica*** WOMN
pinifolia See MINUARTIA ***circassica***
pulvinata See A. ***lithops***
purpurascens EMNN EPot GAbr GLoc MBro MCas NHol NKay NNrd NRoo WDav WOMN
tetraquetra EPad MTho MWat NHar NNrd NTow NWCA SIng SSmi
– ***granatensis*** EPot NTow SCro SIng WDav
– ***nevadensis*** ITim WAbe
tmolea NNrd WOMN
verna See MINUARTIA ***verna***

ARENGA (Palmae)

ARGEMONE (Papaveraceae)
grandiflora EJud ELan EMon
¶ ***mexicana*** WOMN

ARGYRANTHEMUM † (Compositae)
adauctum CCan
§ – ***canariense*** CCan EDon
– ***gracile*** LSav
* 'Blizzard' CB&S CSpe IHos
'Brontes' CCan
broussonetii CCan
'Chelsea Princess' EOrc
coronopifolium CCan
double yellow CCan CHil GWic LHil LHop NSty WPer
'Edelweiss' CB&S CBre CCan CElw CHil CSpe GWic LHil LHop SMrm WEas WHal
* 'Flamingo' CSpe IHos
foeniculaceum See A. ***frutescens foeniculaceum***

§ *frutescens* — CCla CGle CHEx CHad ELan EOrc LHil LHop LSav WWin
§ – *foeniculaceum* — CB&S CBos CBre CElw CHad CMHG CMer CSev ELan LAbb LGre NRar NSty SDix SMrm WAbe WKif
– *frutescens* — CCan
¶ – *pumilum* — GWic
¶ *gracile* — CHil
– 'Chelsea Girl' — CB&S CBre CCan CElw CHil CSev GPla LHil LHop MFir NSti WEas WHal WKif
§ 'Jamaica Primrose' — Widely available
* 'Jamaica Snowstorm' — WHal
* 'Jamaican Sunshine' — CHil
* 'Lemon Meringue' — CElw
'Levada Cream' — EDon EOrc
* *linifolium* — CMHG
§ *maderense* — CB&S CCan CHil CMHG EDon EOrc GWic IBlr LHil LHop NSty NTow SAxl SDix WEas WPer
♦ 'Margaret Lynch' — See A. ***adauctum canariense***
§ 'Mary Wootton' — CCan CElw CFis CGle CHil CMer CSev CTre ELan EOrc GAbr GPla GWic LGre LHil LHop LSav MFir NSty SChu WEas WHal WPer
mawii — See CHRYSANTHEMOPSIS ***gayanum***
'Mrs F Sanders' — CCan LHop NSty
'Nevada Cream' — See A. 'Qinta White'
ochroleucum — See A. ***maderense***
* 'Overbecks Pink' — CBos
¶ 'Penny' — LHop
* 'Pink Australian' — LHil
* 'Pink Delight' — CSpe
'Powder Puff' — CCan CElw CHil CKni CSpe LHop
¶ 'Prado' — CSpe
§ 'Qinta White' — CCan EDon
'Rollason's Red' — CB&S CCan CHil EDon LHil LHop SMrm WPer
'Rosali' — CB&S LHop
'Royal Haze' — CCan CSpe
'Sark' — CRiv CSpe LHil LHop SMrm
* 'Silver Queen' — WEas
single pink — CBos CGle LHil
§ 'Snowflake' — CB&S CBre CCan CFis CHEx CHil CMer CSev EDon EOrc GPla GWic LGre LHil LSav SAxl SMad SMrm WAbe
sundingii — CCan
'Vancouver' — Widely available
* 'Vera' — IHos
'Wellwood Park' — CCan CHil GWic LHop WPer
* 'Yellow Star' — IHos LHop

ARISAEMA † (Araceae)

amurense — GDra GEdr GHig WChr WThu
candidissimum — CBro CChu CCla ECha GLoc LAma LBow LSav MBal MPar NHol NKay NRoo SIng SPou WChr WCot
consanguineum — CBro CChu CGle LAma WCot
dracontium — ECam LAma MSal NHol WChr
flavum — LBow MPar NNrd WPer WThu
griffithii — ECam IBar LAma NHol
helleborifolium — See A. ***tortuosum***
jacquemontii — CBro LAma MTho NHol
japonicum — See A. ***serratum***
nepenthoides — LAma
ochraceum — LAma
ringens — LAma MTho WChr
§ *serratum* — LAma
sikokianum — CBro ECam EPot IBar LAma LBow NHol WChr
speciosum — CKel ECam ELan IBar LAma LBow NHol
thunbergii urashima — LAma
§ *tortuosum* — ECam LAma MBal MCab MTho
triphyllum — CBro ECam ECou EPar EPot IBar LAma LBow NHol WCar WChr

ARISARUM (Araceae)

proboscideum — Widely available
vulgare — EPot LAma NHol

ARISTEA (Iridaceae)

§ *ecklonii* — CHan GWic MCab
ensifolia — ELan EMon
♦ *major* — See A. ***ecklonii***

ARISTOLOCHIA (Aristolochiaceae)

¶ *baetica* — SSpi
clematitis — GPoy MSal NHex
¶ *contorta* — SSpi
♦ *durior* — CB&S CGre CHEx ELan MBri MUlv SSus
elegans — SLMG
heterophylla — SHil
macrophylla — CBot CSco SHil
¶ *sempervirens* — SSpi
sipho — See A. ***durior***
tomentosa — MSal

ARISTOTELIA (Elaeocarpaceae)

§ *chilensis* — CB&S SPla
¶ – G 3378 — LSav
– 'Variegata' — CBra CCla CHan CSco EBar LHop LNet LSav WSHC
fruticosa (f) — ECou
¶ – (m) — ECou
macqui — See A. ***chilensis***
¶ *serrata* — ECou

ARMERIA (Plumbaginaceae)

* *alba* — CKel
§ *alliacea* — ECha MBro MWgw NWCA WPer
– Formosa hybrids — ELan IBlr MWgw NBar NCat NOak NOrc NRoo WHil WHoo
– *leucantha* — CBot CSun
'Bee's Ruby' — CLew EFol ERou MBri MFir MTho MUlv
caespitosa — See A. ***juniperifolia***
§ *girardii* — NHol NNrd
'Glory of Holland' — EPot
§ *juniperifolia* — CMHG EMNN ESis GHig GLoc LHop MBal MBar MBro MCas MHig MPla MTho NGre NHol NKay NNor NNrd NRoo NTow SBla SIng WCla WWin
– 'Alba' — EBre ELan EPar ESis GLoc ITim MCas MHig MPla NHol NNrd NRoo SWas WAbe WHil WThu WWin
¶ – 'Ardenholme' — NKay
– 'Beechwood' — NHol SBla WThu

– 'Bevan's Variety'	CMHG CRiv EBre ECha ELan EPar EPot GLoc MFir MHig MRav MWat NHar NKay NRoo NRya WAbe WDav WHil WHoo WPat WThu
– dark form	GDra NHol WAbe
– rose form	CLew EPot
leucocephala 'Corsica'	EBre ECha
maritima	CArn CKin CMHG CRiv CRow CShe EPar LGro LHol MBar MPlt MRav NCat NLan NNor NRed NRoo NSel SIde WHil WOak
– 'Alba'	CElw CRiv EBre ECha EFou ELan EPar EPot ERou GLoc MBal MBar MBri MBro MCas NHol NNor NNrd NRoo NRya WAbe WCla WWin
¶ – ***alpina***	NHol
– 'Bloodstone'	CShe ELan EPar MWat SPla
– 'Düsseldorfer Stolz' ('D. Pride')	CShe EBre ECha ELan ERou GLoc MBri MBro NHar NHol NNrd NRoo SIng WPat
– 'La Pampa'	NOak
– 'Laucheana'	CSun MBro MFir NNrd NOak NTow WHoo
¶ – 'Ornament'	ECtt GAbr WPer
– 'Ruby Glow'	EBre NNrd
– 'Snowball'	NOak
– 'Splendens'	CHar EMNN GCHN MCas NRya SBla WCla WPer WWin
– 'Vindictive'	CKel MBal NHol WAbe
'Ornament'	EHal
pseudarmeria	ELan MBro WEas
setacea	See A. ***girardii***
tweedyi	NGre
welwitschii	CMHG CSun EFol

ARMORACIA (Cruciferae)

§ ***rusticana***	CArn CSev Effi GPoy LHol MBar MBri MSal NSel SIde WOak WSto
– 'Variegata'	EMon LRHS

ARNEBIA (Boraginaceae)

echioides	See A. ***pulchra***
§ ***pulchra***	ECro

ARNICA (Compositae)

angustifolia alpina	See A. ***angustifolia***
* – 'Iljinni'	NBir
chamissonis	GGar LHol MSal
longifolia	CSun
montana	CArn CSFH ECro GAbr GPoy MChe MSal NSel SIng WPer
¶ ***unalaschcensis***	WPer

ARONIA (Rosaceae)

arbutifolia	CCor IJoh IOrc LSav MBal MGos MR&S NBar NHol SHil SPer WAbe WBod WCoo WSHC WWat
– 'Erecta'	ENot WWat
melanocarpa	CCla CHan EBre LSav MBar MRav NHol SReu SSpi WCoo WHCG WWat
– 'Brilliant'	ELan MBar MR&S MUlv NHol SPer SReu WWat
¶ – 'Viking'	LBuc
prunifolia	CCla CSco LSav NHol WHCG WWat

ARRHENATHERUM (Gramineae)

elatius	SFis
– ***bulbosum*** 'Variegatum'	CHoe EFou ELan EMon EPla ERou GPla MCas MPar NRya SIng WEas WRus

ARTEMISIA † (Compositae)

abrotanum	Widely available
absinthium	CArn CFis CHad CSFH EEls Effi GPoy LHol MBar MBri MChe MPit NNor NSti SIde SPer WHil WOak WPer WSto
– 'Lambrook Silver'	Widely available
§ ***alba***	CRow EEls NSel SIde WPer
annua	EEls
arborescens	CFis CGle CLew CMHG CMer ECha EEls EFou ELan ERav IJoh MCot NSti SDry SHil SMad SPer SPla
– 'Brass Band'	EEls
– 'Faith Raven'	CShe EBar EEls EFou EGol ELan EMon ERou MBri MMth WHal WHer WSHC
– 'Porquerolles'	EEls LHop
armeniaca	EEls WWin
♦ ***assoana***	See A. ***caucasica***
¶ ***atrata***	EEls
brachyloba	CFis CMHG EEls
caerulescens gallica	EEls
campestris	CFis
– ***borealis***	CMer EEls Effi LHol MBri MChe NSel WHer
– ***campestris***	EEls
– ***maritima***	EEls
camphorata	See A. ***alba***
canariensis	See A. ***thuscula***
canescens	CBow CCla CFis CGle CRow CSev ECha EEls EFou EGol EMon EPla GPla GWic MBri MWgw SBla SDix SPer WBon WPer
§ ***caucasica***	CArn CFis CGle CHar CRow CSam EEls EFol GCHN GLoc IDai LGro MTho NKay NNrd NRed NRoo NSel WEas WHer WPer WRus WWat
chamaemelifolia	CArn EEls LHol SIde WPer WSto
cretacea	See A. ***nutans***
discolor	See A. ***ludoviciana incompta***
douglasiana 'Valerie Finnis'	See A. ***ludoviciana latiloba***
dracunculus	Widely available
– ***dracunculoides***	EEls
¶ ***eriantha***	EEls
frigida	EEls EOrc WEas WHCG WWin
glacialis	CMHG CRiv ECha EEls GLoc NSti SFar SIng
gmelinii	EEls
gnaphalodes	See A. ***ludoviciana***
* ***gracilis***	CFis
granatensis	NSti
judaica	EEls
¶ ***laciniata***	EEls
lactiflora	CElw CFis CGle CHad CKel CSco ECha EEls EFou ELan GWic IDai LHol NHol NKay NNor NSel NSti SDix SPer WBon
lanata	See A. ***caucasica***

§ *ludoviciana*	CElw CFis CGle CPle CShe CSun ECha EEls ELan IJoh LGro MSal MWat MWgw NNor NOak NOrc SIde WBon WHil WOld WWin
§ – *incompta*	CFis ECha EEls
– *latifolia*	See A. ***l. latiloba***
§ – *latiloba*	CCla CHad CHoe CLew CMer CRow ECha EEls EFol EFou EOrc EPla GPla GWic LHop MPar NOak NRoo NSti WCot WEas WHal WHer WPer
– 'Silver Queen'	Widely available
maritima	CTom GGar GPoy WHer
– *maritima*	EEls
¶ *molinieri*	EEls
mutellina	See A. ***umbelliformis***
§ *nutans*	CFis EBre EEls MWat NSti
palmeri	See A. ***ludoviciana***
pedemontana	See A. ***caucasica***
pontica	Widely available
'Powis Castle'	Widely available
purshiana	See A. ***ludoviciana***
rupestris	EEls
schmidtiana	CFis ECha EFol EFou LHop MCot MPar MWat NSti WEas WHen
– 'Nana'	Widely available
¶ *scoparia*	EEls
splendens	CMHG EFol ELan MCot NRar NSti SAxl WEas WRus WSHC
stelleriana	CElw CFis CGle CHad CRow CShe CTom ECha IJoh LHop MCot MTho MWgw NNor NSti SCro SPer WBon WHil WPer WRus WSHC
– 'Boughton Silver'	See A. ***s.*** 'Mori'
– 'Mori'	CMHG CSun EEls ELan GWic LGre MBri MPar NHol NNrd SCro SFir WRus WWeb
– 'Nana'	EEls EPla NCat
– *prostrata*	CFis CHoe GPla NRar
– 'Silver Brocade'	LSav
thuscula	EEls
tridentata	CFis LHop
¶ – *tridentata*	EEls
¶ – *vaseyana*	EEls
¶ – *wyomingensis*	EEls
§ *umbelliformis*	CArn EEls NRoo WPer
vallesiaca	CSun EEls EMon WHer
* *verlotiorum*	EEls
versicolor	NNor
vulgaris	CArn CSFH EEls EffI GPoy LHol MChe NSel SIde WHer WOak
¶ – 'Cragg-Barber Eye'	CNat
¶ – *crispa*	SIde
– 'Variegata'	CBre CFis CHoe CLew EFol EMon MPar MTho NSti WHer

ARTHROPODIUM (Liliaceae/Anthericaceae)

candidum	CBos CHan CRow EBul ECha ECou EPla EPot LHil MPit MTho NCat NNrd NWCA SAxl SIng SWas WEas
– *maculatum*	EBul MCot MTho
– *purpureum*	ELan EPot NHol NNrd
cirrhatum	CRow EBul ECou GWic IBar LHop LSav SWas WDav
– pink form	CSun
milleflorum	CAvo EBul MFir

ARTICHOKE, Globe See **CYNARA *scolymus***

ARTICHOKE, Jerusalem See **HELIANTHUS *tuberosus***

ARUM (Araceae)

conophalloides	See A. ***detruncatum detruncatum***
cornutum	See SAUROMATUM ***venosum***
creticum	CAvo CBot CHEx CHan ECam EMon EPar EPot IBlr LAma NHol SLHN SSpi SWas WChr WOMN WOld
– FCC form	WChr
– white form	SPou
– yellow form	SDix SPou
§ *detruncatum detruncatum*	CAvo
dioscoridis	CAvo EPar WChr
dracunculus	See DRACUNCULUS ***vulgaris***
hygrophilum	CAvo WChr
idaeum	See A. ***maculatum*** Idaeum group
italicum	ECam ECro EOrc ETub IBar LAma MBri NBar NNrd SPou SW&B WAbe WOMN
– *albispathum*	EMon EPot LAma NHol WChr WDav
– *italicum*	CAvo SMad
N– *marmoratum*	Widely available
N– *pictum*	See A. ***i. marmoratum***
§ – 'Taff's White Winter'	EMon WRus
korolkowii	WChr
maculatum	CKin EPar GPoy LAma MSal NHex
§ – Idaeum group	WChr
– *variegatum*	GPoy
nickelii	ECam SSpi WChr
nigrum	See A. ***petteri***
orientale	EPot WChr
¶ *palaestinum*	CAvo
§ *petteri*	EMon EPar
N *pictum*	CAvo ECam LAma SPou WChr
¶ – ACL 321/78	EMon
♦– 'Taff's Form'	See A. ***italicum*** 'Taff's White Winter'
– 'Tiny'	GWic MPar

ARUNCUS (Rosaceae)

aethusifolius	CCla CLew COtt CRow CSco EBre ECha EFou EGol ELan EPar LSav MUlv NHar NHol NNor NOak WEas WHil WPer WWin
§ *dioicus*	Widely available
– 'Glasnevin'	CCla CSco EBre EGol EOrc ERou MBri MUlv NHol
¶ – *kamtschaticus*	NHol
– 'Kneiffii'	Widely available
plumosus	See A. ***dioicus***
sylvester	See A. ***dioicus***

ARUNDINARIA † (Gramineae(Bambuseae))

♦ *amabilis*	See PSEUDOSASA ***a.***
♦ *anceps*	See SINARUNDINARIA ***a.***
angustifolia	See PLEIOBLASTUS ***chino angustifolius***

♦ *auricoma* See PLEIOBLASTUS *auricomus*
chino See PLEIOBLASTUS *chino*
disticha See PLEIOBLASTUS *pygmaeus distichus*
♦ *falconeri* See DREPANOSTACHYUM *f.*
fastuosa See SEMIARUNDINARIA *fastuosa*
fortunei See PLEIOBLASTUS *variegatus*
§ *funghomii* SDry
gigantea SBam SDry
hindsii See PLEIOBLASTUS *hindsii*
hookeriana See DREPANOSTACHYUM *hookerianum*
humilis See PLEIOBLASTUS *humilis*
japonica See PSEUDOSASA *japonica*
♦ *jaunsarensis* See SINARUNDINARIA *anceps*
♦ *maling* See SINARUNDINARIA *m.*
marmorea See CHIMONOBAMBUSA *marmorea*
♦ *murielae* See THANOCALAMUS *spathaceus*
nitida See SINARUNDINARIA *nitida*
palmata See SASA *palmata*
pumila See PLEIOBLASTUS *humilis pumilus*
pygmaea See PLEIOBLASTUS *pygmaeus*
quadrangularis See CHIMONOBAMBUSA *quadrangularis*
simonii See PLEIOBLASTUS *simonii*
♦ *spathiflora* See THAMNOCALAMUS *spathiflorus*
tecta SDry
♦ *tessellata* See THAMNOCALAMUS *tessellatus*
vagans See SASAELLA *ramosa*
variegata See PLEIOBLASTUS *variegatus*
veitchii See SASA *veitchii*
viridistriata See PLEIOBLASTUS *auricomus*
♦ 'Wang Tsai' See BAMBUSA *multiplex* 'Fernleaf'

ARUNDO (Gramineae)
donax CHEx CRow LMay SApp SArc
– 'Macrophylla' CRow SHil
– 'Variegata' CBot CHEx CRow CSun EFol LHop MSta MUlv SArc SHil SPou WOld
pliniana EMon LRHS

ASARINA (Scrophulariaceae)
antirrhiniflora CSpe ECro SFis
barclayana CBot CHEx CHan CHil CSpe GWic MBri SAxl SLMG WCot WPer
¶ – *alba* CBot
erubescens CBot CHEx CHan CSun ESim LHop NSti SAxl SFir SLMG WPer
– white form LHop
§ *hispanicum hispanicum roseum* CFis CSam CSpe NTow SBla SMrm WPer
lophantha SAxl WOMN
¶ *lophospermum* CSun
§ *procumbens* Widely available
scandens CHil CPle CSun ELan ERav LHil SLMG WPer

ASARUM (Aristolochiaceae)
arifolium EPar
canadense GPoy MSal
caudatum CRow EMon LHop MBri MUlv
europaeum CAvo CHEx CHad CHan EBre ECha ECro EFou EPar EPot GHig GPoy MFir MPar MSal MWat MWgw NRar SLHN SPou WEas WHer WSto
hartwegii EPot NBir SPou SWas WCot
¶ – 'Silver Heart' EMon
lemmonii ECro
¶ sp. ex Japan SPou

ASCLEPIAS (Asclepiadaceae)
albicans MSal
curassavica LAbb MSal SLMG SLon
incarnata ECro ERou GAbr GPoy MRav MSal SAxl SFis SPer WPer
physocarpa SLMG
¶ *purpurascens* LHop
speciosa MSal
subulata MSal
syriaca CArn CHan ECro MPlt MSal WPer
tuberosa CArn CHar CHil EBre ECro GPoy LGan MRav MSal SFis SMrm WPer
viridiflora MSal

ASPARAGUS (Liliaceae/Asparagaceae)
asparagoides myrtifolius SLMG
densiflorus 'Meyeri' MBri
– 'Sprengeri' MBri
falcatus MBri
¶ *officinalis* CHEx
¶ – 'Boonlim' MBen
¶ – 'Connover's Collosal' MBen
¶ – 'Lucullus' MBen
scandens MTho
setaceus MBri
– 'Pyramidalis' MBri

ASPERULA (Rubiaceae)
arcadiensis JCA 210.100 CSun GEdr NTow
aristata scabra ELan EMon
– *thessala* See A. *sintenisii*
gussonii CRiv EMNN EPot ESis GAbr GLoc ITim MCas MPit MTho MWat NHol NKay SBla SIng SSmi WAbe WDav WPat WThu
hexaphylla CArn
hirta ITim MHig NNrd NRed SIng WDav
lilaciflora CBos CRiv GLoc MHig SIng
– *caespitosa* See A. *l. lilaciflora*
– *lilaciflora* CLew CMHG EBre ELan EPot MTho NHol NKay NNrd NRoo SSmi WAbe WPat WWin
nitida CRiv ELan MTho
– *puberula* See A. *sintenisii*

odorata	See GALIUM *odoratum*
§ *perpusilla*	CShe ECou
§ *sintenisii*	EPot GEdr GLoc ITim MBro NHol NKay NTow SBla SIng SOkd SWas WDav WHoo WOMN WPat WThu
suberosa	ELan EPot GLoc MHig MTho NHol NKay NNrd NTow SSmi WAbe WOMN WThu
¶ *taurina caucasica*	SAxl
tinctoria	GPoy LHol MChe MSal SIde

ASPHODELINE † (Liliaceae/Asphodelaceae)

liburnica	CChu ECha ERou GAbr LHil MBro SDix WCot WHoo WRus
§ *lutea*	Widely available
*– 'Yellow Candle'	EBar EPot

ASPHODELUS † (Liliaceae/Asphodelaceae)

acaulis	SSpi WOMN
aestivus	WCar
albus	CChu EBul ECha ECro LGre
cerasiferus	See A. *ramosus*
fistulosus	CLew CSun ECro EMon EOrc LGan LGre LHop MTho NWCA WWin
lusitanicus	See A. *ramosus*
luteus	See ASPHODELINE *lutea*
microcarpus	See A. *aestivus*
§ *ramosus*	CHan CLew ECro MCot

ASPIDISTRA (Liliaceae/Convallariaceae)

elatior	CHEx EBak ERav MBri NRog SAxl WOak
– 'Variegata'	ERav NBir SLHN
* *lurida* 'Irish Mist'	IBlr

ASPLENIUM † (Aspleniaceae)

adiantum-nigrum	NHol NMar
alternans	See CETERACH *dalhousieae*
bulbiferum	NMar WEas WFib
¶ *cuneifolium*	NKay
* *eberlei*	NKay
* *fimbriatum*	MBri
¶ *lepidum*	NKay
nidus	MBri WFib
¶ *oblongifolium*	NMar
rhizophyllum	See CAMPTOSORUS *rhizophyllus*
ruta-muraria	CNat SIng
scolopendrium	See PHYLLITIS *scolopendrium*
trichomanes	EBre ELan GGar MBal MBri NKay NMar SApp SHil SIng SPou WFib
– Cristatum group	NMar WFib
– 'Incisum'	IOrc SApp SPou

ASTELIA (Liliaceae/Asteliaceae)

chathamica 'Silver Spear'	CB&S CHEx LHop SSpi SSus
♦ *cunninghamii*	See A. *solandri*
fragrans	ECou
grandis	EBul
nervosa	CHEx EBul ECou SSpi WWat
nivicola 'Red Gem'	SSpi
solandri	CHEx

ASTER † (Compositae)

acris	See A. *sedifolius*
§ *albescens*	CGre EHal EMon ISea MBal MPla SBor WSHC
alpinus	CHar CMHG CSun CWGN EMNN EPot GCHN GLoc MCas MPit MWat MWgw NHar NHol NKay NNrd NWCA SBla SIng WCla WOld WPer WWin
– *albus*	GCHN MPar NHol SIng WPer
– 'Beechwood'	NKay
– 'Dunkle Schöne' ('Dark Beauty')	CSun EFou NOak WCla
– 'Happy End'	MFir NHol NOak
– 'Trimix'	CSam ECtt ESis MRav NBir NRoo NRya NVic WHil
¶ – violet	WPer
– 'White Beauty'	CSun
amelloides 'Santa Anita'	See FELICIA *amelloides* 'Santa Anita'
amellus	LHil NNor
– 'Blue King'	EFou SFis
¶ – 'Breslau'	EFou WOld
– 'Brilliant'	CAll CHar CKel CLew CSco EBre EFou EOrc ERou MWat NRoo SAxl SChu SCro SPer WOld
¶ – 'Doktor Otto Petschek'	EFou
¶ – 'Empress'	WOld
¶ – 'Framfieldii'	WOld
¶ – 'Jacqueline Genebrier'	SWas WOld
– 'King George'	CAll CElw CKel CShe EBre EFou ELan EOrc ERou MWat NRoo SChu SMad SPer WEas WOld
¶ – 'Kobold'	WOld
– 'Lac de Genève'	CSco CShe EFou
– 'Lady Hindlip'	WEas
*– 'Marie Anne Neill'	SFis
– 'Moerheim Gem'	CAll SChu WEas WOld
– 'Nocturne'	CAll CSco EBre ERou SSus WOld
– 'Peach Blossom'	EFou WOld
– 'Pink Pearl'	EFou WOld
– 'Pink Zenith' ('Rosa Erfüllung')	CAll CLew CShe EBre ECha EFou ELan EOrc ERou MBri MCot MRav NRoo NVic SAxl SBla SChu SPer WEas WHil WOld WRus
– 'Praecox Junifreude'	EFou
– 'Rudolph Goethe'	CCla EFou MUlv SAxl WEas WOld
¶ – 'Schone von Ronsdorf'	WOld
– 'September Glow'	EFou EOrc
– 'Sonia'	CAll ECha EFou MCot SFis WOld
¶ – 'Sonora'	WOld
– 'Sternkugel'	WOld
– 'Ultramarine'	CAll EFou
N– 'Veilchenkönigin' ('Violet Queen')	CAll CKel EBre ECha EFou ELan ERou MBri MCot SAxl SBla SDix SWas WEas WOld
¶ – 'Weltfriede'	WOld
asper	CHan IBrk NOak WOld WPer
bellidiastrum	SIng
¶ 'Blue Star'	EFou SAxl SChu WOld WOld
canus	CHan
capensis 'Variegata '	See FELICIA *amelloides* variegated
carolinianus	CHan
coelestis	See FELICIA *amelloides*

'Coombe Fishacre'	CAll CBos EFou GWic LHil MBri MUlv NSti SWas WEas WOld
¶ ***cordifolius*** 'Aldebaran'	SAxl
– 'Elegans'	CAll EFou WCot WOld
– 'Esther'	ERou
– 'Ideal'	WOld
– 'Little Carlow'	See A. 'L. C.'
– 'Little Dorrit'	See A. 'Little Dorrit'
– 'Photograph'	See A. 'Photograph'
– 'Silver Queen'	CAll
– 'Silver Spray'	CAll CBre ERou IDai MBri WEas WOld
– 'Sweet Lavender'	CAll ERou SAxl SFis WOld
corymbosus	See A. ***divaricatus***
¶ 'Deep Pink Star'	WOld
§ ***divaricatus***	Widely available
N***dumosus***	NKay
ericoides	CGle NCat SChu SIng WHil WWin
¶ – 'Blue Wonder'	WOld
– 'Brimstone'	CAll SAxl WOld
– 'Cinderella'	CB&S CTom EBre EMon EOrc NRoo NSti SChu SPer
¶ – 'Constance'	WOld
*– 'Dainty'	CLew
– 'Enchantress'	CAll ERou
– 'Erlkönig'	MBri SChu WOld
– 'Esther'	CAll ECha EFou EMon EOrc NCat NSti SChu SDix SFis WEas WOld
– 'Golden Spray'	CAll EFou LHil WOld
¶ – 'Herbstmyrte'	SAxl
– 'Hon. Edith Gibbs'	CAll ECha EOrc
– 'Ideal'	CAll
– 'Maidenhood'	SFis WOld
*– 'Novembermyrte'	EFou
– 'Perfection'	CAll ERou
– 'Pink Cloud'	CAll CBre CTom ECha EFou EMon EOrc MUlv NRoo NSti SAxl WOld
– 'Rosy Veil'	CAll ERou WOld
¶ – 'Schneetanne'	EFou
– 'Vimmer's Delight'	CAll
– 'White Heather'	CAll CBre CSco SAxl WCot WOld
farreri	NKay
'Flora's Delight'	EBre EOrc ERou MTho NRoo
¶ ***foliaceus cusickii***	EMon
× ***frikartii***	Widely available
¶ – 'Eiger'	WOld
– 'Jungfrau'	CHan MUlv WOld
N– 'Mönch'	Widely available
– 'Wunder von Stäfa'	CSco EMon EOrc MBri MUlv SFis WOld
himalaicus	GCHN WHil
'Hon. Vicary Gibbs' (***ericoides*** ×)	CAll NSti WOld
hybridus luteus	See × SOLIDASTER ***luteus***
*'Kylie'	WOld
¶ ***laevis***	CBre
¶ – 'Blauschleier'	EFou
– 'Calliope'	WOld
lateriflorus	CGle EOrc ERou WOld
– 'Horizontalis'	Widely available
¶ – 'Prince'	EFou EMon
likiangensis	GLoc
linosyris	MPar
– 'Goldilocks'	CAll ERou SFis SPer

§ 'Little Carlow' (***cordifolius*** ×)	CAll CBre EFou GWic SAxl SBla WBon WEas WOld
§ 'Little Dorrit' (***cordifolius*** ×)	CAll NSti SAxl WOld
macrophyllus	CAll SPer WOld
– 'Twilight'	WOld
¶ ***mongolicus***	WPer
natalensis	See FELICIA ***rosulata***
novae-angliae 'Andenken an Alma Pötschke'	Widely available
¶ – 'Andenken an Paul Gerber'	EMon
– 'Barr's Blue'	EFou EMon LHop MUlv SChu SMrm WOld
– 'Barr's Pink'	CAll EFou EMon WEas WOld
– 'Barr's Violet'	CAll SAxl WCot WOld
¶ – 'Crimson Beauty'	CAll WOld
– 'Ernie Moss'	SFis
– 'Festival'	SFis
– 'Guinton Menzies'	CAll EMon WOld
– 'Harrington's Pink'	CAll CBow CBre CGle CKel EBre EFou EMon EOrc ERou IDai MBri MWat SAxl SChu SPer WEas WOld WWin
§ – 'Herbstschnee' ('Autumn Snow')	CAll CBre CShe EBre EFou EMon EOrc ERou LHil LHop MWat NHol SChu WOld WWin
– 'Lye End Beauty'	CAll EFou EMon ERou MUlv NOak SAxl SChu WOld
– 'Lye End Companion'	CAll
– 'Mrs S T Wright'	CAll EFou EMon ERou LHil WOld
*– 'Mrs S W Stern'	WOld
– 'Purple Cloud'	CAll EMon ERou
– 'Red Cloud'	EFou
¶ – 'Rosa Sieger'	EMon WOld
– 'Rubinschatz'	EFou
¶ – 'Rudelsberg'	EMon
¶ – 'Sayer's Croft'	WCot
– 'September Ruby'	CAll CKel EBre EFou EMon ERou LHop SChu WEas WOld WWin
¶ – 'Treasure'	CAll EFou EMon WOld
¶ – 'Violetta'	EMon WOld
– 'W Bowman'	EMon
N***novi-belgii*** 'Ada Ballard'	CAll CHar CKel CSco NHol SPer WOld
– 'Albanian'	CAll WOld
– 'Alderman Vokes'	CAll WOld
– 'Alex Norman'	CAll WOld
– 'Algar's Pride'	CAll EFou LHil WOld
– 'Alice Haslam'	CAll EFou MBal MBri MBro MFir MWgw NBar NHol NKay NOrc SPla WEas WOld
– 'Alpenglow'	CAll
– 'Anita Ballard'	CAll WOld
– 'Anita Webb'	WEas WOld
– 'Antwerp Pearl'	CAll
– 'Apollo'	EFou MBri
– 'Apple Blossom'	CAll EFou WOld
– 'Arctic'	CAll WOld
– 'Ashwick'	CAll
– 'Audrey'	CAll CB&S CHar CKel CLew EBre EFou ERou GAbr GCHN MBri MWgw NBar NHol NKay NOrc WOld
– 'Autumn Beauty'	CAll WOld
– 'Autumn Days'	CAll WOld

– 'Autumn Glory'	WOld
– 'Autumn Rose'	CAll WOld
– 'Autumn Snow'	See A. *n-a* 'Herbstschnee'
– 'Baby Climax'	CAll
– 'Barker's Double'	EPot
– 'Beechwood Beacon'	CAll
– 'Beechwood Challenger'	CAll NKay WOld
– 'Beechwood Charm'	CAll WOld
– 'Beechwood Lady'	CAll
– 'Beechwood Supreme'	CAll WOld
– 'Belmont Blue'	CAll
– 'Blandie'	CAll CB&S CBre CKel CSco EFou MBri MWat NHol NVic WBon WOld
– 'Blue Baby'	MBri
– 'Blue Bouquet'	CAll CKel WOld
– 'Blue Boy'	WOld
– 'Blue Danube'	CAll WOld
– 'Blue Eyes'	CAll EFou WOld
– 'Blue Gem'	CAll
– 'Blue Gown'	CAll GWic MBri SHig WOld
– 'Blue Patrol'	CAll CKel WOld
– 'Blue Plume'	CAll
– 'Blue Radiance'	CAll WOld
– 'Blue Whirl'	CAll WOld
– 'Bonanza'	CAll MBal
– 'Bonningdale Blue'	CAll WOld
– 'Bonningdale White'	CAll WOld
– 'Borealis'	CAll
– 'Bridesmaid'	CAll
– 'Brightest and Best'	WOld
– 'Cameo'	CAll
– 'Camerton'	CAll
¶ – 'Cantab'	WOld
– 'Carlingcot'	CAll WOld
– 'Carnival'	CAll CHar CSco ERou MUlv NBar NOrc SPer WOld
– 'Cecily'	CAll WOld
– 'Charles Wilson'	WCot WOld
– 'Chatterbox'	CAll CSco ECtt ERou MWat SChu WEas WOld
– 'Chelwood'	CAll
– 'Chequers'	CAll CHar EFou MBri NBar NHol WOld
– 'Chilcompton'	CAll
– 'Choristers'	CAll CBre CShe WOld
– 'Christina'	CAll WHil
– 'Cliff Lewis'	CAll CShe WOld
– 'Climax'	CAll CBre CSco ECha EFou ERou GWic MBri MUlv NSti SHig WOld
– 'Climax Albus'	See A. *n-b.* 'White Climax'
– 'Cloudy Blue'	CAll CBre EFou WOld
– 'Colin Bailey'	CAll
– 'Colonel F R Durham'	CAll
– 'Coombe Delight'	WOld
– 'Coombe Gladys'	WOld
– 'Coombe Joy'	WOld
– 'Coombe Margaret'	CAll ERou WOld
– 'Coombe Queen'	CAll
– 'Coombe Radiance'	ERou WOld
– 'Coombe Ronald'	ERou MWat WOld
– 'Coombe Rosemary'	CHar ERou MUlv WCot WOld
– 'Coombe Violet'	MWat WOld
– 'Countess of Dudley'	CAll CKel WOld
– 'Court Herald'	CAll CSco NCat WOld
– 'Crimson Brocade'	CAll CKel ELan ENot IDai MWat SAxl WOld
– 'Crimson Velvet'	CAll
– 'Dandy'	CAll CHar CKel CTom ELan LHil NHol WOld
– 'Daphne Anne'	WOld
¶ – 'Dauerblau'	WOld
– 'Davey's True Blue'	ERou WOld
– 'Dazzler'	CAll EFou WOld
– 'Destiny'	CAll WOld
– 'Diana'	WOld
– 'Diana Watts'	ERou WOld
– 'Dietgard'	MBri WOld
– 'Dora Chiswell'	CAll
– 'Dorothy Bailey'	CAll
– 'Dusky Maid'	CAll WOld
– 'Dymbro'	CAll
– 'Elizabeth'	CAll
– 'Elizabeth Bright'	CAll
– 'Elizabeth Hutton'	CAll WOld
– 'Elsie Dale'	CAll WOld
¶ – 'Elta'	WOld
– 'Emma'	CAll
– 'Erica'	CAll MWat WOld
– 'Ernest Ballard'	CAll CKel ERou WOld
– 'Eva'	CAll
– 'Eventide'	CAll CB&S CBre ENot ERou WOld
– 'F M Simpson'	IDai MBri
– 'Fair Lady'	MWat WOld
– 'Faith'	CAll WOld
– 'Farrington'	CAll WOld
– 'Felicity'	CAll
– 'Fellowship'	CAll CB&S CBre EFou ERou MBri MUlv MWat NHol NVic SPer WEas WOld
– 'Flair'	CAll
– 'Flamingo'	CAll CSco
– 'Freda Ballard'	CAll CKel ERou LHil MWat NHol WOld
– 'Gayborder Beauty'	CAll
– 'Gayborder Blue'	CAll
– 'Gayborder Royal'	CAll WOld
– 'Gayborder Spire'	CAll
¶ – 'Gayborder Splendour'	WOld
– 'Gayborder Supreme'	IDai
– 'Goliath'	CAll CKel WOld
– 'Guardsman'	CAll ERou WOld
¶ – 'Gulliver'	EFou
– 'Gurney Slade'	CAll EFou WOld
– 'Guy Ballard'	CAll NNor
– 'Happiness'	CAll
– 'Harrison's Blue'	CAll SAxl WEas WOld
– 'Heather'	CAll
– 'Heinz Richard'	ECha EFou GAbr LHop MBri MUlv NHol SBla SChu WHil WOld
– 'Helen'	WOld
– 'Helen Ballard'	CAll CSco WOld
¶ – 'Herbstpurzel'	EFou
– 'Hey Day'	CAll
– 'Hilda Ballard'	CAll EFou WOld
– 'Irene'	CAll
– 'Janet McMullen'	CAll
– 'Janet Watts'	WOld
– 'Janice Stephenson'	CAll
– 'Jean'	CAll CSco ERou MWat SChu WEas WOld
– 'Jean Gyte'	CAll WOld
– 'Jenny'	CAll CKel CLew CSco CTom EBre EFou IDai LHil LHop MBri MWat NBar NHol SPer WEas WOld

– 'Jezebel' CAll
– 'Jollity' CAll WOld
– 'Julia' CAll
– 'Juliet' CAll
– 'Karen' CAll
¶ – 'Kassel' EFou
– 'Kilmersdon' CAll
– 'King of the Belgians' CAll
– 'King's College' CAll WOld
– 'Kristina' CBre EBre ECha ECtt EFou ERou GAbr LHil MRav WOld
– 'Lady Evelyn Drummond' WOld
– 'Lady Frances' CAll CHar WHil WOld
– 'Lady in Blue' CAll CBow CCla CHar CLew CSco EBre ELan ENot ERou IHos LHil MBro MWat MWgw NBar NHol NVic SPer SPla WEas WOld WWin
– 'Lady Paget' CAll
– 'Lassie' CAll CKel ERou MWat WOld
– 'Lavender Dream' CAll
¶ – 'Lawrence Chiswell' CAll
– 'Leona' CAll
– 'Lilac Time' CAll WOld
– 'Lisa Dawn' CAll WOld
– 'Little Blue Baby' CTom
– 'Little Boy Blue' CAll CKel WOld
– 'Little Pink Beauty' CAll CCla CHar CKel EBre EFou ELan GAbr GCHN IHos LHop MBro MWat NHol NKay NVic SPer WEas WHil WOld WWin
– 'Little Pink Lady' CAll
– 'Little Pink Pyramid' CSco SFis
– 'Little Red Boy' CAll CKel CSco WOld
– 'Little Treasure' CAll WOld
– 'Lucille' CAll
– 'Lucy' CAll
– 'Mabel Reeves' CAll CShe
– 'Madge Cato' CAll WOld
– 'Maid of Athens' CAll
– 'Malvern Castle' ERou
– 'Mammoth' CAll WOld
– 'Margaret Murray' CAll
– 'Margaret Rose' CAll CB&S ELan NKay NOrc WOld
– 'Margery Bennett' CAll WOld
– 'Marie Ballard' CAll CB&S CKel CSco CShe ENot ERou GWic MBri MFir MWat NHol NKay NOak NOrc SChu WEas WOld
– 'Marjorie' CAll WOld
– 'Mars' CAll
– 'Martonie' WOld
– 'Mary' CAll
– 'Mary Dean' CAll WEas WOld
– 'May Louise' CAll
– 'Melbourne' CAll
– 'Melbourne Belle' CAll ERou WOld
– 'Melbourne Lad' CAll
– 'Melbourne Magnet' WOld
– 'Melbourne Mauve' CAll
– 'Melbourne Sparkler' CAll
– 'Michael Watts' WOld
– 'Michelle' CAll
– 'Miranda' CAll
– 'Miss Muffet' CAll
– 'Mistress Ford' CAll
– 'Mistress Quickly' CAll ERou WOld
¶ – 'Mittelmeer' WOld
– 'Mount Everest' CAll EFou WOld
– 'Mrs J Sangster' CAll
– 'Mrs Leo Hunter' CAll WOld
– 'My Smokey' CAll
– 'Nancy' CAll
¶ – 'Nesthäkchen' EFou
– 'Nightfall' CAll
– 'Niobe' CAll ELan MBro WOld
– 'Norma Chiswell' CShe
– 'Norman Thornely' CAll
– 'Norman's Jubilee' CAll ECtt WOld
– 'Norton Fayre' CAll CShe
– 'Nursteed Charm' CAll
– 'Orchid Pink' CAll
– 'Orlando' CAll CBre ERou WOld
– 'Owen Tudor' CAll
– 'Owen Wells' CAll
– 'Pamela' CAll WOld
– 'Patricia Ballard' CAll CBre CKel CLew CSco CShe MBri MWat NHol NKay NOak NVic WOld
– 'Peace' CAll WOld
– 'Peacful' CAll
– 'Peerless' CAll
– 'Penelope' CAll
– 'Pensford' CAll EFou
– 'Percy Thrower' CAll CKel EFou ERav MBri WOld
– 'Perry's White' CAll
– 'Peter Chiswell' WOld
– 'Peter Harrison' CAll CSco MBal MBri WOld
– 'Peter Pan' CAll EPot MPlt WBon WOld
– 'Petunia' CAll
– 'Picture' CAll WOld
– 'Pink Buttons' CAll
– 'Pink Cascade' CAll
¶ – 'Pink Gown' WOld
– 'Pink Lace' CAll CKel CSco ECtt ERou NHol WEas WOld
– 'Pink Perfection' CAll
– 'Pink Profusion' CAll
¶ – 'Pink Pyramid' WOld
– 'Pitcott' CAll
– 'Plenty' ERou WOld
– 'Pride of Colwall' CSco ERou
– 'Priory Blush' CAll WOld
– 'Priory Maid' CAll
– 'Professor Anton Kippenberg' CAll CSco CShe EBre ECtt EFou GAbr MBri MPlt WAbe WOld
– 'Prosperity' CAll CKel WOld
– 'Prunella' CAll ERou WOld
¶ – 'Purple Dome' WOld
– 'Purple Emperor' CAll
– 'Queen Mary' CAll WOld
– 'Queen of Colwall' CAll WOld
– 'Rachel Ballard' CAll
– 'Raspberries and Cream' CAll
– 'Raspberry Ripple' CAll CKel EFou ERav ERou MBri NHol WOld
– 'Real Pleasure' CAll
– 'Rebecca' CAll
– 'Red Greetings' CAll
– 'Red Robin' MWat
– 'Red Sunset' CAll CB&S EFou WOld
– 'Rembrandt' CAll CSco ERou NHol
– 'Remembrance' CAll EFou SAxl WOld

– 'Reverend Vincent Dale'	CAll WOld
– 'Richness'	CAll SAxl WOld
– 'Robert'	CAll
– 'Robin Adair'	CAll
– 'Rose Bonnet'	CBre CKel CTom ENot IHos MBri MWat MWgw NBar NHol SChu SPla
– 'Rose Bouquet'	CAll CLew SAxl WOld
– 'Rosebud'	CAll ELan WOld
¶ – 'Rosemarie Sallman'	EFou
– 'Rosenwichtel'	EFou MBri NBar NHol WOld
– 'Rosie Nutt'	CAll
– 'Royal Blue'	CAll
– 'Royal Ruby'	CAll CSco ECtt WOld
– 'Royal Velvet'	CAll CSco ENot WEas WOld
– 'Royal Violet'	CAll
– 'Royalty'	CAll
– 'Rufus'	CAll WOld
– 'Sailing Light'	CAll
– 'Sailor Boy'	CAll ERou SFis WOld
– 'Saint Egwin'	CAll
¶ – 'Sandford White Swan'	EFou
– 'Sandford's Purple'	CAll
– 'Sarah Ballard'	CAll MWat WOld
– 'Saturn'	CAll
– 'Schneekissen' ('Snow Cushion')	CHar CLew CSco EFou EPot ERou LHop MBal MWgw NHol SPer WOld
¶ – 'Schöne von Dietlikon'	WOld
– 'Schoolgirl'	CAll CShe WBon WOld
– 'Sheena'	WCot WOld
¶ – 'Silberblaukissen'	EFou
– 'Silver Mist'	CAll
– 'Sir Edward Elgar'	CAll
– 'Snow Drift'	CAll WOld
– 'Snowsprite'	CAll CB&S CBos CBow CKel CTom ELan ERav ERou IDai MWat NBar NOrc SChu SPer WHil WOld
– 'Sonata'	CAll ERav LHil MBri NHol SPer WOld
– 'Sophie'	WOld
– 'Sputnik'	CAll
– 'Starlight'	CAll EFou ENot WOld
– 'Stella Lewis'	CAll
– 'Stirling Silver'	CAll WOld
– 'Strawberries and Cream'	CAll
– 'Sunset'	CAll WOld
– 'Sussex Violet'	CAll
– 'Sweet Briar'	CBre EFou WOld
– 'Symbol'	CAll
– 'Tapestry'	CAll WOld
– 'Taplow Spire'	CAll
– 'Terry's Pride'	CAll WOld
– 'The Archbishop'	CAll
– 'The Bishop'	CAll WOld
– 'The Cardinal'	CAll CKel SFis WOld
¶ – 'The Dean'	CAll
– 'The Rector'	CAll
– 'The Sexton'	CAll
– 'The Urchin'	WOld
– 'Thundercloud'	CAll SAxl WOld
– 'Timsbury'	CAll WOld
– 'Tony'	CAll
– 'Tosca'	CAll SFis
– 'Tovarich'	CAll EFou WOld
– 'Triumph'	SFis WHil
– 'True Blue'	CAll
– 'Twinkle'	GHig SFis
– 'Vice Regal'	CAll
– 'Victor'	CAll CBre MBal WOld
– 'Violet Lady'	CAll CKel WOld
* – 'Violet Queen'	GHig SFis
– 'Violetta'	CB&S EFou
¶ – 'Waterperry'	MWat
§ – 'White Climax'	CAll EFou MUlv SHig WOld
– 'White Ladies'	CAll CHar ERav MBri NOrc SPer
– 'White Swan'	CAll CHan CKel EMon NOak SFis WEas WOld
– 'White Wings'	CAll ERou WCot WOld
– 'Wickwar Crimson'	CAll
– 'Winford'	CAll
– 'Winsome Winnie'	CAll
– 'Winston S Churchill'	CAll CKel CLew CSco ELan ENot IDai MWat NHol NOrc SPer SPla WEas WHil WOld
paniculatus 'Edwin Beckett'	CAll WOld
pappei	See FELICIA ***amoena***
¶ 'Pearl Star'	WOld
* ***perfoliatus***	NCat
petiolatus	See FELICIA ***petiolata***
§ 'Photograph'	CAll CHan EFou WOld
pilosus demotus	CBre CHad ERou
'Pink Star'	EFou WCot WOld
pringlei 'Monte Cassino'	COtt ECha EFou EHal LHop NHol NRoo SChu SWas WOld
procumbens	CMer CTre
¶ ***pyrenaeus*** 'Lutetia'	EFou GWic
'Ringdove' (***ericoides*** x)	CAll EFou ERou NSti SAxl WOld
¶ 'Rosa Star'	WOld
rotundifolius 'Variegatus'	See FELICIA ***amelloides*** 'Variegata'
* ***sativus atrocaeruleus***	EBre MRav NRoo
scandens	See A. ***carolinianus***
§ ***sedifolius***	CAll CBos CHar ECha EFou ELan EMon MWat SDix WBou WEas WOld
– ***nanus***	CAll CBre ECha EFou ERou MBri NBir NSti SMrm WOld
– ***roseus***	CAll
¶ 'Snow Star'	WOld
¶ ***spathulifolius***	CHan
spectabilis	SWas WOld
sp. BM&W 18	See ERIGERON ***multiradiatus*** BM&W 18
x ***thompsonii*** 'Nanus'	CGle COtt EBre ECha EFou EMon LGre NKay NNrd NRoo SBla WOld WWin
tibeticus	MDHE WCla WHil
– ***albus***	WHil
tongolensis	CHan LHil MWgw NRya WEas WOMN WWin
– 'Berggarten'	CKel CTom EFou EOrc ERou GWic MBri SCro SFis
– 'Lavender Star'	EFou
– 'Leuchtenburg' ('Shining Mountain')	ERou
– 'Napsbury'	CKel ECha EPla ERou MBri NVic SFis
– 'Sommergruss' ('Summer Greeting')	EFou
¶ – 'Wartburgstern'	WPer

tradescantii CAll CBre CGle CHad ECha EFou ELan EMon GPla GWic LHil MUlv MWgw NSti SAxl SHig SMad WEas WOld
tripolium CKin
turbinellus CAll EFou EMon ERou SChu SHig WOld
umbellatus CBre EMon SAxl SHig WOld
vahlii ECou LHop
vimineus 'Delight' CAll EFou LSav MUlv WOld
– 'Lovely' MBri
– 'Ptarmicoides' CAll EFou
yunnanensis See A. ***tongolensis***

ASTERANTHERA (Gesneriaceae)

ovata GGar LGre MBal SArc SHil SSpi WBod WWat

ASTERISCUS (Compositae)

* 'Gold Coin' IHos MPit
maritimus LHop

ASTILBE † (Saxifragaceae)

'Amethyst' (x ***arendsii***) CMHG CTom EGol ERou LHil NBar NRoo NTow SHig SPer
¶ 'Anita Pfeiffer' (x ***arendsii***) MBri
'Aphrodite' (***simplicifolia*** x) CCla COtt LSav MBri NHol SSpi
¶ x ***arendsii*** NNor WPer
astilboides NHol
'Atrorosea' (***simplicifolia*** x) CSco EBre
¶ 'Bergkristall' (x ***arendsii***) MBri
'Bonn' (***japonica*** x) CB&S CKel EPar GHig
'Brautschleier' ('Bridal Veil') (x ***arendsii***) CB&S CMHG CSco EFou EGol ENot ERou IDai MWat
'Bressingham Beauty' (x ***arendsii***) CCla CGle CKel CMHG CSco CShe EBre EHon ELan ELun ENot EOrc EPGN EPar LHop MBri MCot NHol NJap NRoo SChu SHig SPer
'Bronze Elegans' (***simplicifolia*** x) COtt CSco EBar EBre ECha EFou EOrc EPGN EPar MBal MBri MPlt MTho NBar NCat NHol NKay NNrd NOrc NRoo SMad
'Bumalda' (x ***arendsii***) MBri NHol
'Carmine King' SFis
'Ceres' (x ***arendsii***) MWat NHol NKay
chinensis CMCN
¶ – ***davidii*** LSav
– ***pumila*** Widely available
x ***crispa*** IBlr MPar NHol SSpi
¶ ***davidii*** MSF 789 SSpi
§ 'Deutschland' (***japonica*** x) CB&S CBow CMHG CTom EBre EGol ELan EOrc EPGN MBri MTho MWgw NHol NKay SBla SCro SPer SSpi WAbe WEas WWin
'Diamant' ('Diamond') (x ***arendsii***) MBri MFir SFis
'Drayton Glory' (x ***arendsii***) CKni
'Düsseldorf' (***japonica*** x) CKni ERou GGar GHig SPer
'Dunkellachs' (***simplicifolia*** x) COtt EGol EPGN GHig LSav MBri NHar NHol NOrc SHig SPla WAbe
'Emden' (***japonica*** x) MWat
'Erica' (x ***arendsii***) ERou GGar GHig MBri
'Etna' (***japonica*** x) CB&S CCla CKni CSev EPGN SCro
'Europa' (***japonica*** x) CB&S EPGN LSav MWat NBar NOak
'Fanal' (x ***arendsii***) Widely available
'Federsee' (x ***arendsii***) CB&S CGle CHar CKel CSco EBre EHon ELan EPGN LHop LSav MBri NBar NKay NRoo SCro SHig SPer WAbe
'Feuer' ('Fire') (x ***arendsii***) CB&S CKni CShe EBre ELan GGar MBri NHol NTow NVic SChu SPla
'Finale' (***chinensis pumila***) CMHG CSco EOrc LSav NHol NKay NOrc WEas
'Germania' See A. 'Deutschland'
'Gertrud Brix' (x ***arendsii***) CB&S COtt EPar GHig
glaberrima EPar SSpi
– ***saxatilis*** CRow EBre ELan EPGN GLoc ITim LHop MBal NHol NKay NNrd NOak NRoo NTow SChu SIng WAbe
– ***saxosa minor*** NNrd
'Gloria' (x ***arendsii***) CMHG MBri
'Gloria Purpurea' (x ***arendsii***) CKni CMHG NHol
'Glut' ('Glow') (x ***arendsii***) CHar CKel CMHG EPGN EPar ERou MBri NHol
'Granat' (x ***arendsii***) CB&S CMHG EPGN NHol NKay SDix WWin
grandis ELan
'Grete Pungel' (x ***arendsii***) MBri
'Hyazinth' ('Hyacinth') (x ***arendsii***) CMHG EGol ELan EPGN GHig MWgw NHol SCro
'Inshriach Pink' (***simplicifolia*** x) CMHG GDra NHar NHol NOak
'Intermezzo' (***chinensis pumila***) MBri
'Irrlicht' (x ***arendsii***) CCla CGle CHar CKel CMHG CSco CShe EBre EGol EHon ELan ELun EPGN LHop LSav MBri MCot NBar NHol NJap NRoo SChu SDix SHig
'Jo Ophurst' (***thunbergii*** x) CHar CMHG EPGN LSav SCro SHig SMad SPer WAbe
'Koblenz' (***japonica*** x) CB&S EOrc EPGN IDai LSav MBri NHol
'Kobold' See A. 'Koblenz'
'Köln' ('Cologne') (***japonica*** x) CHar EBre WAbe
¶ ***koreana*** LSav
'Kwell' (x ***arendsii***) MBri
¶ 'Lilliput' (x ***crispa***) NHar
'Mainz' (***japonica*** x) CB&S
microphylla CMCN NHol
– pink form NHol
'Montgomery' (***japonica*** x) CCla CKel EPGN LSav MBri MCot NHol SChu SCro SMad
'Nana' (***simplicifolia*** x) CRow EGol

'Peach Blossom' (x *rosea*)	CB&S CCla CMHG EGol EPar NBar NHol
'Perkeo' (x *crispa*)	CBro COtt CRow EBre ECha EOrc EPGN GDra GGar MBri NHar NKay NRoo WAbe
¶ 'Peter Barrow' (*simplicifolia* x)	EPGN
'Peter Pan' (x *crispa*)	WAbe
'Pink Curtsy' (x *arendsii*)	EBre
¶ 'Praecox Alba' (*simplicifolia*)	NHol
'Professor van der Wielen' (*thunbergii* x)	CMHG ECha GGar GWic SPer
'Purple Glory' (*chinensis*)	MBri
'Purpurlanze' ('Purple Lance') (*chinensis taquetii*)	EBre EFou ERou MBri MRav MUlv NBir SMad WCot
'Queen Alexandra' (x *rosea*)	SFis
¶ 'Queen of Holland' (x *arendsii*)	MBri
'Red Sentinel' (*japonica* x)	CB&S CSco CTom EFou EGol ELun EOrc EPGN EPar LSav NHar NHol NJap NOrc NSti SMad SPla WAbe
'Rheinland' (x *japonica*)	CB&S CBow CMHG GHig LHop MBri SBla WAbe WEas
rivularis	CChu CCla LHop LSav
'Rosa Perle' ('Pink Pearl') (x *arendsii*)	NHol
'Rosea' (*simplicifolia* x)	MBri NHol
'Rotlicht' ('Red Light') (x *arendsii*)	MBri WBon
'Salmon Queen' (x *arendsii*)	See A. 'Europa'
'Serenade' (*chinensis pumila*)	CMHG MBri
simplicifolia	CGle CRow MHig MTho NHar NKay WEas
– alba	EFou GGar NHol
– x *glaberrima*	GDra NHol
'Snowdrift' (x *arendsii*)	EBar EBre EFou EGol ELun GGar MUlv NOak NOrc
'Spartan' (x *arendsii*)	LSav NHol
'Spinell' (x *arendsii*)	MWat
'Sprite' (*simplicifolia* x)	Widely available
¶ sp. AGSJ 238	NHol
'Straussenfeder' ('Ostrich Plume') (*thunbergii* x)	CSco EBre EFou ELun EOrc EPGN GWic LSav MBri MWgw NHol NTow SHig SMad
'Superba' (*chinensis taquetii*)	CGle CMHG CRow CSco EBre ECha ELan EPGN LSav MCot NHol NNor NTow SDix SHig SMad SPer WAbe WCar WEas
'Venus' (x *arendsii*)	CCla CKel CMHG CSco CShe CTom EGol ELun EPGN LSav MCot MWgw NHol NKay NVic SChu SCro SPer
'Veronica Klose' (*chinensis pumila*)	CMHG
'Vesuvius' (x *arendsii*)	CB&S
'W E Gladstone' (*japonica* x)	CB&S MBri WAbe
'Weisse Gloria' ('White Gloria') (x *arendsii*)	CCla EGol EPGN EPar MBri MCot
'White Queen' (x *arendsii*)	GHig NHol NNrd
'William Buchanan' (*simplicifolia* x)	CGle EGol EPGN EPar GGar MBri MCas MHig NHar NHol NKay NNrd NRed WAbe
'William Reeves' (x *arendsii*)	CKni COtt NHol

ASTILBOIDES (Saxifragaceae)

§ *tabularis*	Widely available

ASTRAGALUS (Leguminosae)

¶ *alopecuroides*	EBar SPou
¶ *falcatus*	CSun
glycyphyllos	MSal
¶ *kentrophyta implexus*	WDav
¶ *purpureus*	WCar
¶ *vexilliflexus nobilis*	WDav

ASTRANTIA † (Umbelliferae)

carniolica	CHan IDai NKay
– major	CKel CShe MWat NBar WOld
– rubra	CB&S CBot CBro CCla CKel CRow ECro EPar ERou LHop MCot MFir SPer WOMN
– 'Variegata'	See A. *major* 'Sunningdale Variegated'
helleborifolia	See A. *maxima*
§ *major*	Widely available
– alba	ECha EFol EGol ERav NBir
– 'Barrister'	MUlv SSpi
¶ – *biebersteinii*	NBir
– 'Hadspen Blood'	CHad
– involucrata	ELan NHol NVic
– 'Margery Fish'	See A. *major* 'Shaggy'
¶ – 'Moira Reid'	NBir
¶ – 'Primadonna'	WPer
– rosea	CBos CBre CCla CHar EBre ECro EFou EGol LHop LSav MBri MWgw NOrc SPer
– rubra	CGle CHad CHan COtt CSco EBre ECha EGol ELan ELun EOrc ERav GWic LHop LSav MBri MCot MPar NBar NHol NOrc NRar NRoo WEas
§ – 'Shaggy'	CBro CCla CCor CShe ECro EFou EGol ELan MCot MPar NHol NKay NOak NOrc SPer SWas WHoo
§ – 'Sunningdale Variegated'	Widely available
– 'Variegata'	See A. *m.* 'Sunningdale Variegated'
§ *maxima*	Widely available
minor	CRow NBir
rubra	See A. *major*

ASYNEUMA (Campanulaceae)

canescens	EBar WPer WWin
pulvinatum	SOkd
– Mac&W 5880	EPot

ASYSTASIA (Acanthaceae)

bella	See MACKAYA *bella*
violacea	MNew SLMG

ATHAMANTA (Umbelliferae)

ATHEROSPERMA (Atherospermataceae)
moschatum CLan CPle CTre LSav WBod

ATHROTAXIS (Cupressaceae)
cupressoides MBar SHil
laxifolia MBar MBri SHil WThu

ATHYRIUM † (Aspleniaceae)
filix-femina CRow CTom EBre ECha EFou ELan MBal MBri MSta MWgw NLan NMar SHil SPer SSpi WFib
– 'Corymbiferum' NKay NMar
– Cristatum group CWGN ELan LSav MBri SPer WFib
– Cruciatum group EGol SApp
– 'Fieldii' CRow WFib
– 'Frizelliae' IOrc LSav MBri NHol NMar WFib
– 'Frizelliae Capitatum' NKay SApp WFib
– 'Grandiceps' NMar
– 'Minutissimum' CBos ECha EGol EHon ELan NMar SApp SPou SSpi SWas
– Percristatum group NHol NKay
– 'Plumosum Cristatum' NMar
– Plumosum group NMar SAxl
– 'Plumosum Percristatum' NMar
– Ramo-cristatum group NMar
– 'Setigerum Cristatum' NKay NMar
– 'Vernoniae Cristatum' MBal NHol NMar WFib
– Vernoniae group ELan MBri
– Victoriae group & clone CRow EBre EGol ELan MBri NHol NMar SApp SMad WFib
goeringianum 'Pictum' See A. *niponicum pictum*
niponicum NMar
– *metallicum* See A. *n. pictum*
§ – *pictum* CBos CFor CGle CRow EBre ECha EFou EGol EPar IOrc LHop MBal MBri NHol SBla SMad SPer SPou SSpi SWas WFib
otophorum NHol SAxl SWas
– *okonum* MBri SBla SSpi
palustre NKay

ATRAGENE See **CLEMATIS**

ATRAPHAXIS (Polygonaceae)

ATRIPLEX (Chenopodiaceae)
halimus CBot CCla CFis CGle CHad CHan CHoe CRow CSco CShe ENot LAbb LHil SHil SLHN SLon SPer SSpi WHCG WHer WRus WSHC
hortensis 'Rubra' CArn CBos CFis CGle CRow ELan EMon GPoy LHol MChe SIde WHer WSto

ATROPA (Solanaceae)
bella-donna CArn GPoy LHol MSal
– *lutea* MSal
mandragora See MANDRAGORA *officinarum*

AUBRIETA † (Cruciferae)
albomarginata See A. 'Argenteovariegata'
'Alida Vahli' ELan NHol
* 'Alix Brett' EBre ELan MMth NHol
'April Joy' CMHG MPla
§ 'Argenteo-variegata' CRow ELan LHop MWgw SBla SPla SSmi
'Astolat' CLew CRiv EBar EFol ELan MMth NHol SBla WAbe WEas WPer
§ 'Aureo-variegata' CLew CRiv CRow EBar EBre EFol ELan MCas MCot MHig MPla NHol NKay NNrd NRoo NVic SBla SChu SIng SMad WAbe WHil WPer
¶ 'Barker's Double' EPot
'Belisha Beacon' MBri NHol SIng
'Blue Cascade' ECtt
'Bob Sanders' CKel CMHG CRiv EBre MCas NVic
'Bonfire' NKay
* 'Bonsul' CShe
'Bressingham Pink' ELan EPar GLoc LHop MHig MMth NHol NNrd
'Bressingham Red' EBre
'Bright Eyes' WEas
'Britannia' NKay
'Carnival' See A. 'Hartswood Purple'
'Claret Cascade' CHar
x *cultorum* 'Aurea' GLoc
deltoidea 'Aurea' See A. x *cultorum* 'A.'
– 'Nana Variegata' EPot GLoc ITim MTho WEas WHil
– *rosea* MHig
– 'Tauricola Variegata' CShe
N– 'Variegata' CRiv CRow CShe EFol EPot ESis LHop MHig MPar MTho NHol NNrd NTow SChu SIng WDav WPat WThu
¶ – *variegata* 'Shaw's Red' WDav
'Dr Mules' CHar CKel EBre IHos MHig MPit NKay SIng
'Dr Mules Variegata' CRow GLoc MHig WHil WPer
'Dream' NHol SIng
'Elsa Lancaster' CLew EPot MHig MTho NHol
'Gloriosa' CMHG CRiv EBar SIng
¶ 'Golden Carpet' SIng
'Golden King' See A. 'Aureo-variegata'
'Greencourt Purple' CMHG CRiv EBre ELan EPar EPot MHig MWat NKay SIng WEas WPat
'Gurgedyke' ELan MHig SIng WEas
'Hartswood' SIng
'Hartswood Purple' CShe
'Henslow Purple' EBre
'Joan Allen' CMHG EBre MHig NHol SIng
'Joy' SIng
'Lavender Gem' CMHG
'Leichtlinii' GHig NNrd NOak
'Lilac Cascade' GHig NNrd
'Little Gem' MHig
'Lodge Grave' SIng
'Lucy' NKay
'Magician' NHol NKay
'Mars' ELan
'Mary Poppins' MHig NHol NKay
'Maurice Prichard' CHar CKel EBre
'Mrs Rodewald' CMHG NHol NKay WHal
'Novalis Blue' CHar CRiv GHig MCas NOak

'Oakington Lavender' ELan EPar IHos MPit
'Pennine Glory' CShe
'Pennine Heather' CShe
¶ *pinardii* WHil
'Pink Gem' NHol NKay
'Purple Cascade' ECtt EMNN GHig MMth NRoo
'Red Carpet' CKel CMHG CRiv EBre EFol ELan EMNN EPar EPot GHig IHos MCas MCot MHig MPla NHol NKay SChu SIng WEas WHil
'Red Cascade' ECtt EMNN GAbr GHig
'Red Dyke' SIng
'Riverslea' NHol SIng
'Rosea Splendens' MPla
¶ 'Royal Blue' NRoo
¶ 'Royal Red' ESis MCas MPit NRoo WPer
'Schofield's Double' ELan WEas
'Triumphante' EBre
'Vindictive' CShe
'Violet Queen' MCas
'Wanda' ELan IHos NHol SIng
'Whitewell Gem' ESis GHig NNrd
Wisley hybrid WEas

AUCUBA (Cornaceae)
japonica CHEx CHig ELan ENot SPer SReu
– 'Crassifolia' (m) CHig MBal SArc SHil
– 'Crotonifolia' (f) CB&S CBow CHEx CSco EGol ENot IJoh LAbb MBal MBar MBri MGos NWea SCro SDix SHil SPla
– 'Gold Dust' (f) CLan CShe SHil
– 'Golden King' CSco CTrw LNet
– 'Golden Spangles' CB&S
– 'Hillieri' (f) CLan CShe SHil
– 'Lance Leaf' (m) CGre SHil
¶ – 'Latiomaculata' LSav
– *longifolia* CHig SArc SDix SHil
♦– 'Maculata' See A. *j.* 'Variegata'
– 'Nana Rotundifolia' (f) SHil SMad
– 'Picturata' (m) CB&S CChu CSco CTre EGol ELan ENot IJoh LSav MBri SHil SMad SPer
– 'Rozannie' (m/f) CB&S COtt EBre MBlu MBri MGos MUlv NHol SHil SPer SReu WPat
– 'Salicifolia' (f) ENot LSav MUlv SHil SMad SPer
– 'Sulphurea Marginata' (f) CB&S CChu CSco EGol ERav MBri MUlv SPer
§ – 'Variegata' (f) CBow CFis CPle ELan ENot GRei IDai IJoh ISea LBuc LSav MBal MBar MBri MGos MR&S MWat NNor SHil SLon SPer SReu WBod
– 'Wykehurst' SCro
* 'Mr Goldstrike' CSco LNet

AUSTROCEDRUS See **LIBOCEDRUS**

AVENA (Gramineae)
candida See HELICTOTRICHON *sempervirens*
¶ *sterilis* WPer

AVENULA (Gramineae)
¶ *pratensis* EFou

AVOCADO See **PERSEA** ***americana***

AZALEA See **RHODODENDRON** Azalea

AZALEODENDRON See **RHODODENDRON** Azaleodendron

AZARA † (Flacourtiaceae)
dentata CB&S CHil CLan CMCN CMac CTrw ERea MBal SSta WSHC WWat
– 'Variegata' CMac
integrifolia CTre SArc
– G&K 4236 LSav
– 'Variegata' CGre SHil
lanceolata CB&S CHil CLan CPle IBar IOrc ISea SLon SPer SSpi WBod
microphylla Widely available
– 'Variegata' CHan CMac EHar ERav IDai IJoh IOrc ISea MBal SArc SHil SPla SSpi
paraguayensis See A. *uruguayensis*
* *patagonica* CGre
petiolaris CGre IBar WBod
serrata CBot CBow CChu CCla CHEx CHan CMCN CMHG CPle ISea MCot NTow SArc SAxl SBra SDix SLHN SLon SPer SPla WWat
§ *uruguayensis* CBot CGre CTre

AZOLLA (Azollaceae)
caroliniana CHEx CRow CWGN EHon EWav LMay MSta

AZORELLA (Umbelliferae)
filamentosa ECou
glebaria See A. *trifurcata*
gummifera ECou GEdr ITim MHig
lycopodioides ECou GCHN
§ *trifurcata* CHar CLew CRiv ELan EPot GDra MBro MTho NHol NKay NNrd NRoo SIng SSmi WAbe WDav WHoo WPat
– *nana* GGar MTho MWat NHol NNrd SIng WThu

AZORINA See **CAMPANULA**

BABIANA (Iridaceae)
¶ *cedarbergensis* CKni
hybrids CKel LBow

BACCHARIS (Compositae)
¶ *crispa* GWic
magellanica ECou
patagonica CGre CPle CTre IBar SArc SLon WBod
– prostrate form CGre

BAECKEA (Myrtaceae)
virgata CSun ISea

BAILLONIA (Verbenaceae)
juncea WSHC

BALLOTA (Labiatae)
acetabulosa CHan ECha EFou NSti SChu SDix SDry SPer

'All Hallows Green' CChu CCla ECro EFou EGol GWic LHop MCot MWgw NBar SAxl SChu SFar
nigra CArn CKin GPoy LHol MSal SIde WPer
– 'Archer's Variety' CElw CHan CSun EFol EMon MPar NHex SSpi WRus
♦– *variegata* See B. *n.* 'Archer's Variety'
– 'Zanzibar' EMon
pseudodictamnus Widely available

BALSAMITA (Compositae)
§ *major* CArn CRow CSFH CSev ECro EEls ELan EMon Effi GPoy MBri MSal NHol NSel WHal WOak WPer WSto
– *tanacetoides* LHol MSal SIde WSto
– *tomentosum* LHol SIde
vulgaris See B. *major*

BAMBUSA † (Gramineae(Bambuseae))
glaucescens See B. *multiplex*
**gracillima* CB&S CBra COtt SBam
multiplex EFul SBam WJun
– 'Alphonse Karr' CB&S CBra EFul EPla SBam SDry WJun
¶– 'Chinese Goddess' WJun
§ – 'Fernleaf' CB&S CBra EFul NPal SBam SDry WJun
♦– 'Wang Tsai' See B. *m.* 'Fernleaf'
♦*oldhamii* See B. *multiplex*
tuldoides CB&S
ventricosa SBam SDry WJun
vulgaris SBam
– 'Vittata' SBam SDry WJun
– 'Wamin' SBam SDry WJun

BANANA See **MUSA**

BANKSIA (Proteaceae)
baueri CSun
blechnifolia CSun
caleyi CSun SIgm
¶*canei* CSun
dryandroides CSun
ericifolia CSun LHop
¶*grandis* CSun
¶*integrifolia* NBar
marginata ECou
¶*ornata* CSun
petiolaris CSun
praemorsa CSun
¶*quercifolia* CGre
repens CSun
robur CSun
¶*saxicola* CSun
serratifolia SIgm
speciosa CSun SIgm
spinulosa collina CSun
¶*violacea* CSun

BAPTISIA (Leguminosae)
australis Widely available
– 'Exaltata' ECro ELan ERou LHop
leucantha MSal NBir
leucophaea MSal
tinctoria MSal

BARBAREA (Cruciferae)
praecox See B. *verna*
verna CArn GPoy
vulgaris CKin
– *variegata* Widely available

BARLERIA (Acanthaceae)
obtusa CPle MNew

BAUERA (Cunoniaceae)

BEAUCARNEA (Agavaceae)
recurvata LPal MBri

BEAUFORTIA (Myrtaceae)

BEAUMONTIA (Apocynaceae)
grandiflora MNew WCar

BEAUVERDIA See **TRISTAGMA**

BEGONIA † (Begoniaceae)
'Allan Langdon' (T) GWhi
¶*amoena* SSpi
♦*angularis* See B. *stipulacea*
'Argentea' (R) MBri
'Bali Hi' (T) GWhi
'Beatrice Haddrell' CHal
'Bertinii Compacta' SW&B
¶ 'Black Knight' CHal
¶ 'Bonaire' CHal
'Bouton de Rose' (T) SW&B
bowerae CHal
¶ 'Bush Baby' CHal
'Buttermilk' (T) GWhi
'Can-Can' (T) GWhi
'Chantilly Lace' CHal
x *cheimantha* 'Gloire de Lorraine' MBri
'City of Ballarat' (T) GWhi
'Clara' (R) MBri
'Cleopatra' CHal SLMG WEas
compta (C) CHal
x *corallina* EBak
– 'Lucerna' (C) CHal EBak SLMG
– 'Lucerna Amazon' (C) CHal IBlr
¶ 'Corbeille de Feu' CHal
'Corona' (T) GWhi
¶ 'Curly Locks' (S) CHal
'Dannebo' MBri
'Dorothy White' (T) GWhi
'Druryi' SLMG
'Elaine Tarttelin' (T) GWhi
¶ 'Emma Watson' CHal
x *erythrophylla* 'Bunchii' SLMG
– 'Helix' CHal
'Fairylight' (T) GWhi
'Falstaff' (T) GWhi
feastii helix See B. x *erythrophylla* 'Helix'
'First Love' (T) GWhi
foliosa miniata 'Rosea' CHal SLMG
fuchsioides CHal CHan CHar CSev EBak LHil WPer
– *rosea* See B. *foliosa miniata* 'Rosea'
glaucophylla See B. *limmingheiana*
grandis dark form SApp

grandis evansiana CAvo CGle CHEx ECro LHop MTho MUlv NRar SApp SAxl SDix SIng SLHN SSpi
♦– – ***alba*** CAvo LHil MTho NBir SApp SLHN SMad SSpi
'Guardsman' (T) GWhi
'Gustav Lind' (S) CHal WEas
haageana See B. ***scharffii***
x ***hiemalis*** 'Aida' MBri
– 'Aphrodite Pink' MBri
– 'Arosa' MBri
– 'Barbara' MBri
– 'Christel' MBri
– 'Elatior' MBri
– 'Elfe' MBri
– 'Heidi' MBri
– 'Ilona' MBri
– 'Korona' MBri
– 'Lara' MBri
– 'Lorina' MBri
– 'Mandela' MBri
– 'Mark Rosa' MBri
– 'Nelly' MBri
– 'Nelson' MBri
– 'Nixe' MBri
– 'Nymphe' MBri
– 'Pia Elise' MBri
– 'Radiant' MBri
– 'Rosalea' MBri
– 'Schwabenland' MBri
– 'Schwabenland Mini' MBri
– 'Schwabenland Red' MBri
– 'Schwabenland Rosa' MBri
– 'Schwabenland White' MBri
– 'Schwabenland Yellow' MBri
– 'Silvia' MBri
– 'Sirène' MBri
– 'Toran MBri
hybrids CKel
'Joc Hayden' SLMG
'Joy Towers' (T) GWhi
'Lady France' MBri
'Leopard' MBri
limmingheiana CHal MBri
listida CHal MBri
'Lucerna' See B. x ***corallina*** 'Lucerna'
'Madame Richard Gallé' (T) SW&B
'Maphil' MBri
'Margaritae' SW&B
'Marmorata' (T) SW&B
masoniana ERea MBri SLMG WEas
metallica CHal SLMG
'Mrs T White' (T) GWhi
nigramarga Sec B. ***bowerae*** 'Nigramarga'
'Peach Melba' (T) GWhi
'Président Carnot' (C) SLMG
rex MBri
'Ricky Minter' SLMG
'Rose Princess' (T) GWhi
'Roy Hartley' (T) GWhi
'Sandersonii' WEas
scharffii CHal EBak SLMG
'Scherzo' CHal
semperflorens MBri
– ***flore pleno*** LHop WPer
serratipetala EBak MBri
'Snow Bird' (T) GWhi
solananthera CHal
sonderiana ERea
§ ***stipulacea*** 'Bat Wings' SLMG
'Sugar Candy' (T) GWhi
'Sunburst' (T) GWhi
sutherlandii CFor CHal CMal EBak MBri SAxl SLHN SLMG SSpi
'Sweet Dreams' (T) GWhi
'Sweet Magic' CHal
'Switzerland' (T) LAma SW&B
'Tahiti' (T) GWhi
'Thrush' (R) SLMG
¶ 'Thunderclap' CHal
'Thurstonii' CHal
'Tiger Paws' CHal MBri
'Trout' (C) CHal SLMG
¶ 'Venus' CHal
'Zoe Colledge' (T) GWhi

BELAMCANDA (Iridaceae)

chinensis CBro CHan ECha ECro LHop MPar MSal NTow SAxl SLMG WHer WHil WHoo WOMN WOld WPer

BELLEVALIA (Liliaceae/Hyacinthaceae)

forniculata ECam SPou
paradoxa SIng
§ ***pycnantha*** EPar EPot NHol
romana MPar

BELLIS † (Compositae)

perennis CKin NNrd
– 'Alba Plena' CBos ELan EPla GPla NHol NNrd NSti SIng WHer
– 'Alice' CCot CGle GPla MTho NSti WEas WHer
– 'Aucubifolia' GAbr MShr
– 'Bunter Teppich' MShr
– 'Chevreuse' MShr
– 'Dawn Raider' EMon
– 'Double Bells' MShr
– 'Dresden China' CBos CElw CTom EBre ECha ELan GAbr GPla MCas MShr MTho NHol NNrd SIng WEas WHer WHil WOMN
– 'Lilliput Rose' MShr
– 'Miss Mason' CGle GAbr WRus
– 'Monstrosa' MWat
– 'Parkinson's Great White' GAbr MShr
– 'Pink Buttons' MShr
– 'Pomponette' MShr NRoo
– 'Prolifera' ('Hen and Chicken') CCot CGle GAbr GPla GWic LHop MShr MTho NSti WHer
– 'Rob Roy' CTom EPla GAbr GPla MCas MShr MTho NHol SIng
– 'Robert' CCot CElw GAbr GPla MCas MShr MTho WHer
– 'Roggli' MShr
– 'Shrewley Gold' MShr
– 'Single Blue' See B. ***rotundifolia*** 'Caerulescens'
– 'Stafford Pink' CBos GAbr GPla MShr WHer
– 'String of Pearls' MShr
– 'Tuberosa Monstrosa' MShr
rotundifolia CLew CRiv

§ – 'Caerulescens' CCot ECha GPla MCas MHig MTho NHol NNrd NSti SIng WEas WEas WHer WHil WOMN WRus WWin

BELLIUM (Compositae)
bellidioides CBre NHol
minutum CLew ECha GAbr MHig NGre SIng

BELOPERONE (Acanthaceae)
guttata See JUSTICIA *brandegeeana*

BENSONIELLA (Saxifragaceae)
oregona EMon LRHS

BERBERIDOPSIS (Flacourtiaceae)
corallina CB&S CChu CFor CMac CPle CSam CSco ELan EPla GWic IOrc ISea LHop MBal MBri SArc SBra SHil SLon SPer SSta WAbe WBod WSHC

BERBERIS † (Berberidaceae)
aggregata MBal SHil SPer
¶ *amurensis latifolia* LSav
x *antoniana* MBri SHil WAbe WWeb
¶ *approximata* WWeb
aquifolium See MAHONIA *aquifolium*
– *fascicularis* See MAHONIA *pinnata*
N *aristata* CCor CMCN EHal
bealei See MAHONIA *japonica* Bealei group
'Blenheim' LSav NHol WWat
* 'Boughton Red' LSav
¶ *brachypoda* NHol
* *brevipaniculata* MWat
x *bristolensis* CChu CSco MBri NHol SLon SPla WAbe WWeb
buxifolia MBal SLon
– 'Nana' See B. *b.* 'Pygmaea'
§ – 'Pygmaea' CB&S CPle CSco ELan ENot IJoh MBar MBri MPla MR&S NHol NRed NRoo SHil SPer STre
calliantha CChu CSam CSco MBri MWat SHil SMad SPla SSpi SSta WWat
candidula CBow CPle CSam ELan ENot IJoh IOrc LSav MBal MBar MBri MR&S MWat NHol NNor SHil SLon SPer WBod WWat
x *carminea* 'Barbarossa' CLan IDai SHil
– 'Bountiful' SHil
– 'Buccaneer' COtt ENot GRei ISea NKay SHil SPer
– 'Pirate King' CSco CShe ENot GRei SHil
chrysosphaera CChu CSco SHil WWat
concinna CSun
congestiflora CB&S
¶ – G&K 4237 LSav
coryi See B. *wilsoniae subcaulialata*
coxii CSam SHil
darwinii Widely available
dictyophylla CBot CCla CFor CHoe EGol EHar ELan IJoh LGre MBri MUlv SHil SLon SMad SPer SSpi SSta WSHC WWat
dulcis 'Nana' See B. *buxifolia* 'Pygmaea'
empetrifolia CLew NHar NNor SIng WHCr
* 'Fire Star' MR&S
x *frikartii* 'Amstelveen' CSam EBar ENot IJoh MR&S NTow SHil SLon
– 'Haalboom' MR&S
– 'Mrs Kennedy' MR&S
– 'Telstar' CPle CSco ELan ENot LBuc MBri MR&S MRav SHil
gagnepainii See B. *g. lanceifolia*
§ – *lanceifolia* CB&S CPle ENot IJoh IOrc MBar MGos MR&S NNor NWea SHil SLon SPer SSta
– 'Purpurea See B. x *interposita* 'Wallich's Purple'
¶ *glaucocarpa* CKni
* 'Goldilocks' CFor EHar LSav SHil SMad SSpi
hakeoides SHil
hookeri SHil
– 'Latifolia' See B. *manipurana*
x *hybrido-gagnepainii* 'Chenault' ELan SHil SPer WAbe
hypokerina CLan
x *interposita* SHil
§ – 'Wallich's Purple' EGol ENot MBar MBri MR&S NHol SPer
¶ *jamesiana* NHol
julianae CBot CBra CPle CSco EGol ELan ENot IOrc MBar MBri MGos MR&S MRav NHol NNor NWea SHil SPer SPla WSHC
– 'Mary Poppins' MBri
kawakamii SHil
knightii See B. *manipurana*
koreana CFor CMCN CSam ECtt LSav SPer SSpi
– 'Harvest Fire' EBre
lempergiana CB&S CMCN
linearifolia CBra GRei SLon
– 'Jewel' SHil
– 'Orange King' CB&S CBow CChu CGre CSco ELan ENot IJoh LHop MBri MGos MR&S MWat NBar NKay SHil SPer SReu SSpi
'Little Favourite' See B. *thunbergii* 'Atropurpurea Nana'
x *lologensis* CGre IOrc MGos SHil SPla
– 'Apricot Queen' CB&S COtt CSco IJoh LHop LSav MBri MR&S MRav SLon SMad SPer SReu SSpi WWeb
– 'Mystery Fire' CKni COtt CSco IOrc MBar MBlu MBri MGos MRav MUlv SMrm SReu
– 'Stapehill' EBre ENot LSav MBri NHol SSpi SSta WPat WWeb
¶ *lycium* EHal
§ *manipurana* ENot
x *media* 'Parkjuweel' ('Park Jewel') CB&S CBra EHal NHol SHil SPer WWeb
– 'Red Jewel' CBra CFor CSco EGol IJoh MBri MGos SHil SPla SSus WAbe WWeb
x *mentorensis* NHol
montana CGre SHil SSpi
morrisonensis SHil
x *ottawensis* CBow CHad CSco GRei
– 'Auricoma' LSav WWeb
– 'Decora' SPer
– 'Lombart's Purple' CCla SLon
N– 'Purpurea' IJoh MBri MR&S NHol

– 'Silver Mile'	CBow CFor COtt EFol ELan LHop LNet MBri SChu SDry SPla SSpi SSta WAbe
N– 'Superba'	CB&S CPle CShe CTre ELan ENot IDai LHop MBal MBar MGos NHol NNor NRoo SHil SLon SPer WPat
panlanensis	ENot MBar SHil SLon
patagonica	NNor
polyantha	See B. ***prattii***
§ ***prattii***	MBri NHol NTow
pruinosa	CPle EGol SHil
'Red Tears'	COtt MBlu MBri MGos
replicata	CB&S SLon SSpi
'Rubrostilla'	CSco ENot ISea MBri SHil
sargentiana	ELan ENot NNor SHil SLon SSpi WWat
*– 'Nana'	WPat
sherriffii	CLew
sieboldii	CBot EHar
sp. KR 1186	LSav
x ***stenophylla***	Widely available
– 'Claret Cascade'	CCla EBre LSav MBri MGos SHil SMad SSus WWeb
– 'Coccinea'	CFor IBar SHil SPer
– 'Corallina'	IDai LSav SHil WWeb
– 'Corallina Compacta'	CBow CCla CFor CLew ENot EPot GLoc IDai MBal MPla NHol NKay SBla SChu SHil SIng SSpi WAbe WPat WSHC WThu
*– 'Crawley Beauty'	CMHG
– 'Crawley Gem'	COtt CPle LNet LSav MBar MBri MPla MR&S NHol NKay NRoo SPer
– 'Cream Showers'	CCla EBre LSav SPer SSus
– 'Etna'	EBre
– 'Irwinii'	CMHG CSco CShe ENot IOrc LSav MBri MGos MWat NKay SHil SLon SPer WWeb
*– 'Lemon Queen'	NHol
*– 'Nana'	NHol
– 'Pink Pearl'	CBra CFor CShe LHop SHil
– 'Prostrata'	SHil
temolaica	CCla CFor EHar ELan LGre LSav MBri SHil SLon SMad SPer SSpi SSta WSHC WWat
thunbergii	CBra EBre ENot GRei IDai LBuc MBal MR&S NHol NKay NWea SHil SPer
– ***atropurpurea***	Widely available
– 'Atropurpurea Green Ring'	EGol
§ – 'Atropurpurea Nana'	Widely available
– 'Atropurpurea Superba'	See B. x ***ottawensis*** 'Superba'
– 'Aurea'	Widely available
– 'Bagatelle'	COtt EBre ELan ENot EPot IOrc MBar MBri MGos MR&S NRoo SPer SSpi
– 'Carpetbagger'	IOrc LHop
– 'Coronita'	LHop
♦– 'Crimson Pygmy'	See B. *t.* 'Atropurpurea Nana'
– 'Dart's Red Lady'	EBre ERav IOrc MBri NHol SHil SPer SPla WWeb
– 'Erecta'	CChu ENot IJoh MBar MBri MGos NHol SPer
– 'Golden Ring'	CB&S CCla CHoe CMHG CPle CSco EFol ELan LAbb LHop MBar MBri MWat NHol NRoo SChu SPer SPla SReu WEas WPat WSHC
– 'Green Carpet'	ENot IOrc MBar MBri NRoo SHil SPer SSta WAbe
– 'Green Ornament'	ELan MWat SPer
– 'Harlequin'	CHoe CSco EHar ELan ENot IJoh IOrc MBri MGos NHol SHil SPer SPla SSpi WPat
– 'Helmond Pillar'	CHoe CSco EBre EGol ELan ENot IJoh IOrc MBri NRoo SHil SMad SPer SReu WEas WPat WSHC
– 'Kelleriis'	COtt EBre MBar MBri SSpi
– 'Kobold'	ENot IJoh LHop MBar MBri MGos MPla NRoo SHil SPer WPat
– 'Pink Queen'	MBri MGos NHol WWeb
– 'Red Chief'	CMHG CSco CShe EBre EHar ELan ENot ERav LHop LSav MGos MR&S MRav MWat NRoo SChu SHil SLon SPer SPla SReu SSpi WPat
*– 'Red King'	ELan
– 'Red Pillar'	CB&S CLan CSco ERav MBar MBri MGos MR&S MWat NHol SPla SSpi WPat WWeb
*– 'Red Rocket'	MBri
– 'Rose Glow'	Widely available
– 'Silver Beauty'	CB&S CMHG EGol ELan MGos SChu SPer SSus WWeb
♦– 'Silver Mile'	See B. x ***ottawensis*** 'S.M.'
– 'Somerset'	CSco WWat
*– 'Tricolor'	CHoe LHop MUlv WEas WPat WSHC WWeb
– 'Vermilion'	CSco
tsangpoensis	SHil SLon
valdiviana	CBot CFor CGre LSav SMad SSpi
veitchii	SHil SSpi
verruculosa	Widely available
vulgaris	CArn
¶ ***wardii***	CB&S
wilsoniae	CB&S CBow CBra CLan CSam CSco EGol ENot IOrc MBar MPla MR&S NHol NKay NNor NTow NWea SHil SPer
– L 1738	SSpi
– L 685	LSav
– 'Graciella'	LSav
§ – ***subcaulialata***	ISea SSpi
yunnanensis	SHil

BERCHEMIA (Rhamnaceae)

racemosa	SPer SSpi WSHC

BERGENIA † (Saxifragaceae)

'Abendglocken'	SSpi
§ 'Abendglut'	CFor CLew CSco CShe EBre ECha EGol ELun GHig GPla IBar MBal MBri MCot MPlt MWgw NBar NHol NKay NOrc NSti SHig SPer SSpi
¶ ***acanthifolia***	CRow
'Admiral'	EBre ECha MUlv
¶ ***afgahanica***	CRow
'Baby Doll'	CBot CCla COtt CSco EBre EFou EGol EOrc GWic MBri MUlv NHol NOrc NTow SHig WBon
'Ballawley'	CRow IBlr MUlv SHig
N Ballawley hybrids	CB&S CBot CCla CMHG CShe EBre EGol EPar ERav ERou LGro MUlv MWat NHol SDix SPer

'Bartok'	MUlv
beesiana	See B. ***purpurascens***
'Beethoven'	ECha EGol SHig SSpi
'Borodin'	MUlv
'Brahms'	CRow MUlv SHig
'Bressingham Bountiful'	MUlv NHol SPer SSpi
¶ 'Bressingham Ruby'	COtt MUlv NRoo WCot
'Bressingham Salmon'	EBre EFol ELan ERou SSpi
'Bressingham White'	CBot CCla CHar CMHG COtt CSco EBre EGol ELan ELun EOrc ERou LHop MRav MUlv NCat NRoo SPer SPla SSpi WWin
'Britten'	MUlv
ciliata	CHEx CHad CHan CRow LGre MBal NSti SAxl SDix WEas WPer WThu
– ***ligulata***	MWgw SSpi
cordifolia	Widely available
– 'Purpurea'	CB&S CHad CHar CSco CShe EBre ECha EGol ELan ENot LGro MBri MCot MRav MWgw NKay SDix SHig SPer
– 'Redstart'	NOak
crassifolia	CB&S CGle CKel CWGN LGro MFir
– 'Autumn Red'	ECha
– ***orbicularis***	See B. x ***schmidtii***
'Croesus'	IDai
delavayi	See B. ***purpurascens***
'Delbees'	See B. 'Ballawley'
'Eric Smith'	ECha
'Evening Glow'	See B. 'Abendglut'
'Glockenturm' ('Bell Tower')	EBre MUlv
'Lambrook'	See B. 'Margery Fish'
§ 'Margery Fish'	CSco CShe SPer SPla
'Morgenröte' ('Morning Red')	CSco CShe ECha MBri NHol NKay SHig SPer
'Profusion'	SPer
'Pugsley's Pink'	MUlv
§ ***purpurascens***	CMHG CRow CSco ECha ERav GDra MBal MRav MWgw SDix SHig SPer WWin
– hybrid	SSpi
§ x ***schmidtii***	CFis LGro LHop NBir SDix
'Schneekönigin' ('Snow Queen')	ECha
'Silberlicht' ('Silverlight')	Widely available
'Snowblush'	SSpi
stracheyi	CBot CCla CHad CHan CLew CRow CSun ECha EGol EPla LSav NHol SDix WDav WHCr WHil WHoo
¶ – KBE 209	NHol
¶ – KBE 151	NHol
– ***alba***	CChu ECha SDix
'Sunningdale'	CB&S EBre ECha EGol EPar MWgw NHol NSti SChu SHig SPer
'Wintermärchen'	ECha ECtt EFou EGol ERav LSav MUlv NHol

BERLANDIERA (Compositae)

¶ ***lyrata***	ECro LGre

BESCHORNERIA (Agavaceae)

yuccoides	CHEx IBlr IFer NBir SArc

BESSEYA (Scrophulariaceae)

BETA (Chenopodiaceae)

* ***trigyna***	LRHS

BETONICA (Labiatae)

nivea	See STACHYS ***discolor***
officinalis	See STACHYS ***officinalis***

BETULA † (Betulaceae)

N ***alba***	CLnd IOrc LNet NBar SExT
albo-sinensis	CB&S ELan SExT SReu SSpi WCoo WFro WMou WNor
– W 4106	CSto
– ***septentrionalis***	CSto EHar LNet MBri SExT SGar SHil SPer SReu SSpi SSus WWat
§ ***alleghaniensis***	CMCN CSto EBre IOrc LSav MBal NWea SHil SSpi WCoo WNor
caerulea-grandis	CSto SExT SHil
calcicola B&L 12268	WHCr
celtiberica wild origin	CSto
¶ ***chichibuensis***	EPla
chinensis	WCoo
N ***costata***	CCla CLnd CMCN COtt CSam CSco CSto EBre EHar ELan ENot IBar IOrc SExT SHil SMad SPer SSpi WCoo WNor
¶ ***davurica***	SSpi WCoo
ermanii	Widely available
– 'Grayswood Form'	CSto SHil WWat
¶ – ***saitoana***	SSpi
– wild origin	CSto
'Fetisowii'	SHil
§ ***fontinalis***	CSto WCoo
grossa	CSto
jacquemontii	See B. ***utilis jacquemontii***
'Jermyns'	EHar SHil SSpi
lenta	CSto LSav MBal WCoo
lutea	See B. ***alleghaniensis***
maximowicziana	CB&S CCla CLnd CMCN CSto MBal SHil SMad SSpi SSta WCoo WFro WNor
¶ – B&L 12360	LSav
¶ – Howick 676	LSav
medwedewii	CMCN SGar SSpi SSta WCoo
nana	CLew CSto EHar ELan ESis GLoc IOrc ITim LHop MBal MBar MBri MGos MPla MTho NLan NRed NWea SHil SIng SSpi SSta STre WPat
– 'Glengarry'	EPot WAbe
nigra	CLnd CMCN CSto EHar ENot IHos IOrc LMer MBal SExT SHil SPer SSpi WCoo WFro WNor
occidentalis	See B. ***fontinalis***
papyrifera	Widely available
– ***kenaica***	MBri SHil
– wild origin	CSto
§ ***pendula***	Widely available
– ***crispa***	See B. ***p.*** 'Laciniata'
N – 'Dalecarlica'	See B. ***p.*** 'Laciniata'
– 'Fastigiata'	CSco EHar ENot GRei SExT SHil SPer SReu
– 'Golden Cloud'	CB&S COtt EBre IOrc MBar MBri MGos NBar SGar SMad SPer SReu SSus WMou

§ – 'Laciniata' CLnd COtt CSco EHar ENot GRei MBar MBri MGos MR&S NWea SExT SHil SSpi SSta WAbe WMou
– 'Purpurea' CBow CBra CLnd CMHG CSco EFol EHar ELan ENot GRei IOrc MBar MBlu MBri MGos MR&S NBar SExT SGar SHil SPer SPla SReu SSpi
– 'Tristis' CBow CLnd CSco EHar ENot GRei IOrc LSav MBal MBar MBri NWea SExT SHil SPer SPla SSpi WAbe WMou
– 'Trost's Dwarf' Widely available
– wild origin CSto
– 'Youngii' Widely available
platyphylla CMCN LHop
– *japonica* SSpi WFro WNor
– wild origin CSto
populifolia SGar WCoo
– wild origin CSto
pubescens CKin CSto IOrc MBal NWea SHil WMou
– wild origin CSto
pumila CMCN
resinifera wild origin CSto
schmidtii CSto WCoo
szechuanica CSto SHil WAbe
– W 983 CSto
tatewakiana CSto
¶ *tianschanica* LMer
utilis CBow CBra CCla CLnd CMCN EBre EHar ELan ENot LNet LSav MBal MBar MGos NBar NHol SHil SPer SSpi WAbe WCoo WNor
– B&L 5380 WHCr
– F 19505 CSto
– GWP 760 CSto
– SS&W 4382 CSto
N – *jacquemontii* Widely available
verrucosa See B. ***pendula***

BIARUM (Araceae)
carduchorum EPot LAma NHol WChr
davisii EPot LAma NHol SPou WChr
– *marmarisense* SPou
¶ *dispar* WChr
¶ *ditschianum* WChr
ochridense WChr
tenuifolium CBro ECam EPot LAma NHol SLHN WChr
– *zeleborii* CBro

BIDENS (Compositae)
atrosanguinea See COSMOS ***atrosanguineus***
aurea CGle CHil EPad LHop
cernua MSal
ferulifolia CHil CSpe ERav ERea GWic LHil LHop MFir SAxl SBor SChu WEas WHal WHea WOMN WPer
* *obstruthioides* CHil
tripartita MSal

BIGNONIA (Bignoniaceae)
capreolata CPle ERea LHop SBra SHil WSHC WWeb
unguis-cati See MACFADYENA *u-c.*

BILDERDYKIA See **FALLOPIA**

BILLARDIERA (Pittosporaceae)
longiflora CB&S CMac CSam CSun ECou ELan EOvi ERea IDai ITim LGre LHop NHar SAxl SBra SPer SSta WSHC WWat
– blue berried EBul
– 'Cherry Berry' ECou WMar
¶ – *fructu-albo* SWas
– red berried CSam EBul

BILLBERGIA (Bromeliaceae)
nutans CHEx CSun EBak ELan IBlr MBri SArc SLMG
pyramidalis 'Striata' SLMG
saundersiae See B. ***chlorosticta***
x *windii* EBak SLMG

BISCUTELLA (Cruciferae)
frutescens GAbr MHig WHil WWin

BLACKBERRY See **RUBUS** ***fruticosus***

BLACKCURRANT See **RIBES** ***nigrum***

BLACKSTONIA (Gentianaceae)
perfoliata WCla WCru

BLECHNUM (Blechnaceae)
chilense See B. ***tabulare***
gibbum MBri
magellanicum See B. ***tabulare***
occidentale minor NMar
penna-marina CBos CBro CFor EBre EBul ECou EPar MBal NHol NMar SDix SHil SPer SSpi WOMN
§ – *alpinum* NKay NMar SApp SSpi
– *cristatum* GDra NKay
spicant CKin EHon IOrc MBal MBri MWgw NMar SHil SIng SMad SPer SSpi
§ *tabulare* CB&S CHEx IBlr LSav NKay SApp SArc SDix SHig SSpi

BLETILLA (Orchidaceae)
hyacinthina See B. ***striata***
§ *striata* CAvo CKel COtt CRiv CRow CSut GAbr IBlr LAma MBri MTho NBar NHol NPer SLHN SSpi SW&B SWes WAbe WChr WOMN
– *alba* CAvo CBot CKel GAbr LAma NHol SLHN SW&B SWes WChr
– *albostriata* LAma NHol SLHN SWes WChr

BLOOMERIA (Liliaceae/Alliaceae)
¶ *crocea* WChr

BLUEBERRY See **VACCINIUM** ***corymbosum***

BOCCONIA See **MACLEAYA**

BOENNINGHAUSENIA (Rutaceae)

BOLAX See **AZORELLA**

BOLTONIA (Compositae)
asteroides CHan CLew EHal GWic MUlv NHol NSti

– *latisquama*	CHan EFou EMon GWic LRHS
– *latisquama* 'Nana'	CLew ECha WPer
– 'Snowbank'	LHop
♦ *incisa*	See KALIMERIS *incisa*

BOMAREA (Liliaceae/Alstroemeriaceae)

caldasii	CHEx MCab
multiflora	CSun
¶ *volubilis*	IBar

BONGARDIA (Berberidaceae)

chrysogonum	CAvo ECam EPot LAma LBow

BORAGO † (Boraginaceae)

alba	LHol MChe WHer
laxiflora	CElw CFor CSev ELan EMon LHol LHop MFir MPit MTho MUlv NSti SAxl SLHN WHer WHil WOMN
officinalis	CArn CSFH CSev GPoy LHol MBri MChe NSel SIde WEas WHal WHer WOak WPer WSto
– *alba*	WHal WHer

BORNMUELLERA (Cruciferae)

BORONIA (Rubiaceae)

heterophylla	CB&S CMHG ERea LHop
megastigma	CB&S CSun

BOTRYOSTEGE (Ericaceae)

bracteata	See ELLIOTTIA *bracteata*

BOUGAINVILLEA (Nyctaginaceae)

♦ 'Afterglow'	See B. 'Mrs Helen McLean'
'Alabama Sunset'	CRoc
'Albo d'Ora'	MNew SLMG
'Alexandra'	CSun ERea MBri MNew SLMG
'Amethyst'	MBri SLMG
'Barbara Karst'	CB&S CRoc MBri
¶ 'Betty Lovers'	ERea
♦ 'California Gold'	See B. 'Golden Glow'
¶ 'Canezzla Fiesta'	ERea
'Coral'	CRoc
'Dania'	MBri
'Danica Rouge'	MNew SLMG
'Doctor David Barry'	CRoc
double orange	CRoc ERea
double pink	CRoc ERea
double red	CRoc ERea
double white	CRoc ERea
'Elizabeth Angus'	ERea
¶ *floribunda*	ERea
glabra	LAbb MBri
– *variegata*	ERea
§ 'Golden Glow'	CB&S CRoc MNew
'Helen Johnson'	CRoc
'Isabel Greensmith'	CRoc
'Jamaica Orange'	CRoc
'Jamaica Red'	CRoc
¶ 'Jamaica White'	CB&S CRoc
'James Walker'	CRoc
¶ 'Jawhuri'	ERea
'Jennifer Fernie'	ERea MNew SLMG
'Juanita Hatten'	CRoc
'Killie Campbell'	CRoc MBri SLMG
'La Jolla'	CRoc
¶ 'Lady Mary Ralney'	ERea
'Mardi Gras'	CRoc
§ 'Mary Palmer'	CRoc
'Maureen Hatten'	CRoc
'Mini-Thai'	ERea
¶ 'Mrs Butt'	ERea SLMG
§ 'Mrs Helen McLean'	CB&S CRoc CSun ERea SLMG
'Murii Fitzpatrick'	SLMG
¶ 'Nina Milton'	ERea
'Orange Glow'	ERea SLMG
♦ 'Orange King'	See B. 'Mrs Helen McLean'
'Pink Pixie'	CRoc
'Poultonii Special'	ERea MNew SLMG
'Rainbow Gold'	CRoc
'Raspberry Ice'	CPle CRoc ERea
'Red Diamond'	SLMG
'Rose Parme'	ERea
'Rosenka'	CRoc
'Roy Walker'	SLMG
'Royal Purple'	CRoc
♦ 'San Diego Red'	See B. 'Scarlett O'Hara'
'Sanderiana'	CRoc NRog SLMG
'Sanderiana Variegata'	MBri
'Scarlett O'Hara'	CB&S CRoc CSun ERea MNew SLMG
'Sea Foam'	SLMG
¶ *spectabilis* 'Alison Davey'	ERea
– 'Brasiliensis'	See B. *s.* 'Lateritia'
§ – 'Lateritia'	CRoc
– 'Speciosa Floribunds'	ERea
– 'Variegata'	MNew
'Summer Snow'	CRoc
♦ Surprise ® (x *buttiana*)	See B. 'Mary Palmer'
'Tahitian Maid'	SLMG
'Temple Fire'	CRoc ERea
¶ 'Texan Dawn'	ERea
'Tropical Bouquet'	CRoc
'Vicky'	CRoc
'Weeping Beauty'	CRoc
'White Empress'	MNew
yellow	ERea

BOUSSINGAULTIA (Basellaceae)

baselloides	See ANREDERA *cordifolia*

BOUTELOUA (Gramineae)

¶ *curtipendula*	EMon
gracilis	EFou EMon ERou MPar

BOUVARDIA (Rubiaceae)

bouvardioides	CSun
¶ x *domestica*	ERea
'Jourhite'	CSun
'Lichtrose'	CSun
'Roxane'	CSun
scabrida	CPle CSun
ternifolia	CGre CSun
'Torosa'	CSun
triphylla	See B. *ternifolia*
'Zywerden'	CSun

BOWENIA (Cycadaceae)

serrulata	LPal WNor

BOWKERIA (Scrophulariaceae)

citriodora	CGre
gerrardiana	CGre

BOYKINIA (Saxifragaceae)
aconitifolia CGle ECro ELan EMon NHol NWCA SApp SSpi WPer
heucheriformis See B. *jamesii*
§*jamesii* CChu CLew EPot GEdr MBro MHig NHar NHol NTow SIng SOkd WDav WThu
- JCA 9623 CSun
rotundifolia EBar ECro ELan EMon NSti WPer
tellimoides See PELTOBOYKINIA *t.*

BOYSENBERRY See **RUBUS**

BRACHYGLOTTIS (Compositae)
§ *bidwillii* CGle
§ *buchananii* CHan CMHG WSHC
§ *compacta* CB&S ECou MCot MPla MWgw NRoo SHil SPer WEas WWat
§ *elaeagnifolia* LSav NNor SHil
N*greyi* CBow CLan CPle CSco CShe EBre ERav GRei IDai IJoh ISea MBar MCot MPla MR&S MWat MWgw NKay NNor NRoo SLon WEas WWin
§ *hectorii* LHop
§ *huntii* CBot WCru
§ *kirkii* CGre CSam
N*laxifolia* CFis CLan LHop NNor
¶ 'Leonard Cockayne' CHEx SDry
§ 'Moira Read' ELan ERav LHop SDry WEas
§ *monroi* CFis CHoe CLan CMHG CPle CSam CSco ECou ELan IBlr IDai IOrc ISea LHop MBal MCot NNor NTow SHil SLon SPer SPla WEas WSHC
¶ 'New Zealand' CBot
¶ *repanda* CHEx
¶ - *purpurea* CHEx
¶ - x *greyi* SArc
§ *rotundifolia* CGre IBlr IDai ISea SSpi WEas
* *splendens* NHol
§ 'Sunshine' CB&S CFis CHoe CMHG ELan ENot IBlr LGro LHop MBal MBri MFir MGos SDix SHil SPer SSta WAbe WWat
'Sunshine Variegated' See B. 'Moira Read'

BRACHYPODIUM (Gramineae)
pinnatum CKin
sylvaticum CKin

BRACHYSCOME (Compositae)
¶ 'Harmony' IHos
iberidifolia CGre ELan
multifida CSpe IHos LHop MBri
- *dilatata* GEdr MCas
nivalis alpina See B. *tadgellii*
rigidula CRiv ECou GAbr MCas MTho NNrd SBar SIng WOMN
stolonifera MTho
§ *tadgellii* GAbr
¶ 'Tinkerbell' IHos

BRACHYSTACHYUM (Gramineae(Bambuseae))
densiflorum SDry

BRAHEA (Palmae)
armata LPal NPal
brandegeei LPal
edulis LPal

BRASSAIA See **SCHEFFLERA**

BRASSICA (Cruciferae)
japonica See B. *juncea crispifolia*
juncea crispifolia CArn

BRAVOA See **POLIANTHES**

BRAYA (Cruciferae)
alpina GAbr WPer

BREYNIA (Euphorbiaceae)
¶ *nivosa* CPle

X BRIGANDRA (Gesneriaceae)
¶ *calliantha* SOkd

BRIGGSIA (Gesneriaceae)
muscicola ITim MHig SBla

BRIMEURA (Liliaceae/Hyacinthaceae)
amethystina EPot LRHS MPar WThu
§ - *alba* EPot ETub LRHS MBro MPar

BRIZA (Gramineae)
maxima NSti
media CHoe CKin EFou ELan EOrc EPla ERou GAbr GWic MCot NLan SApp SPer
minor CLew WHil
¶ *triloba* SPou

BRODIAEA (Liliaceae/Alliaceae)
¶ *capitata* WChr
¶ *elegans* WChr
¶ *ida-maia* WChr
¶ *ixioides ixioides* WChr
¶ - *scabra* WChr
laxa See TRITELEIA *laxa*
¶ *multiflora* WChr
peduncularis See TRITELEIA *p.*
¶ *terrestris* WChr
¶ *volubilis* WChr

BROUSSONETIA (Moraceae)
papyrifera CB&S CBot CBow CCla CCor EHar SHil SMad SPer SSpi WCoo WMou WWat

BROWALLIA (Solanaceae)
speciosa 'Major' MBri
- 'Silver Bells' MBri

BRUCKENTHALIA (Ericaceae)
spiculifolia CLew GArf MBal MBar MHig NHol WDav WThu
- 'Balkan Rose' EDen

BRUGMANSIA (Solanaceae)
§ *arborea* CGre CHEx CSun NPal SLMG
aurea MNew SLMG
x *candida* EBak
§ *chlorantha* CHEx CHan MBri MNew SLMG
- apricot ERea
§ *cornigera* 'Knightii' CBot CGre CHEx EBak ERea ESim MNew
§ hybrids SW&B
x *insignis* pink CGre CHEx MNew SHil

meteloides	See DATURA *inoxia*
§ *sanguinea*	CHEx CSun ERea ESim ISea MBri MNew SHil SLMG
– atropurpurea	ERea SLMG
§ *suaveolens*	CGre CHEx EBar ELan ERea ESim ISea SHil
§ – 'Flore Pleno'	CHan SHil
– rosea	See B. x *insignis* pink
§ *versicolor*	ERea MNew SLMG
§ – 'Grand Marnier'	CBot MBri SHil SLMG

BRUNFELSIA (Solanaceae)

americana	CPle MNew SLMG
calycina	See B. *pauciflora*
pauciflora	MBri SLMG
– 'Floribunda'	MNew
– 'Macrantha'	SLMG
undulata	MNew

BRUNNERA (Boraginaceae)

§ *macrophylla*	Widely available
– alba	See B. *m.* 'Betty Bowring'
§ – 'Betty Bowring'	CBos CRow
§ – 'Dawson's White'	Widely available
– 'Hadspen Cream'	CBot CBro CHad CRow CShe ECha EFol ELan EPar ERav MBri MRav MTho NRoo WRus
– 'Langtrees'	CChu CElw CFis CRow ECha EFol EFou ELun EPar MTho SSpi WHea WRus
– 'Variegata'	See B. *m.* 'Dawson's White'

BRYANTHUS (Ericaceae)

¶ *gmelinii*	GArf

BRYONIA (Cucurbitaceae)

dioica	GPoy MSal

BUDDLEJA † (Loganiaceae)

alternifolia	Widely available
– 'Argentea'	CBot CHan CSam CSco ELan ERav SHil SLHN SPer SSpi WSHC WWat WWeb
asiatica	CBot CGre ERea ISea MNew WTay
auriculata	CB&S CCla CHan CMCN CMal CPle ERea GWic SBor SDix SSpi SSta WSHC WWeb
bhutanica	CGre
* 'Butterfly Ball'	LHop WPer
caryopteridifolia	CGre CMal EHar EMon ENot WSHC
colvilei	CBow CCla CHEx CHan CPle CRow CTre GWic ISea MBal SBor SBra SPer SSpi WBod WEas
– 'Kewensis'	CBot CSam IBlr SDry SHil SMad WBod WSHC
crispa	CBot CBow CHad CSco ECha ELan ERav GWic LHop SBor SDry SHil SPer SSpi SSta WEas WKif WPer WSHC WWat
¶ – L 1544	NHex
– 'Variegata'	CBot
davidii	CArn CGre CKin LHol MCot NWea SPla
– 'African Queen'	MR&S SLHN SPer
– alba	CFis SLon
– 'Black Knight'	Widely available
– 'Bluegown'	CB&S
– 'Border Beauty'	CSco GWic SCro SHil SPer SPla WWeb
§ – 'Charming'	ELan NJap SPer
– 'Dartmoor'	CMHG CRow ELan ENot GWic LHop MBri MR&S SDix SHil SLHN SMad SPer SPla SSta WEas WHCG WSHC
– 'Dart's Blue Butterfly'	MBri
– 'Dart's Ornamental White'	MBri
– 'Dart's Purple Rain'	MBri
– 'Empire Blue'	CB&S CBow CSco CShe ELan ENot GRei IDai IJoh MBal MBar MR&S MUlv MWat NWea SHil SPer SPla
– 'Fascination'	CShe GWic MWat WHCG WWeb
– 'Fortune'	NNor
– 'Glasnevin Blue'	SChu SDix SPer
– 'Gonglepod'	ELan
– 'Harlequin'	Widely available
– 'Ile de France'	CB&S ELan GRei MGos MPla MWat NWea SHil WHCG
♦ – 'Nanho Blue'	See B. *d.* Petite Indigo ®
♦ – 'Nanho Petite Indigo'	See B. *d.* Petite Indigo ®
♦ – 'Nanho Petite Purple'	See B. *d.* Petite Purple ®
– 'Nanho Purple'	See B. *d.* Petite Plum ®
¶ – 'Orchid Beauty'	WWeb
– 'Peace'	CBow CLan CTre ENot ISea SPer SReu
N – Petite Indigo ®	CSco EBre EHar ELan EMon ENot EPar IOrc ISea LHil LHop MBar MPla SChu WSHC
N – Petite Plum ®	CSco EBre EHar ELan ENot EPar ISea LHop MBar MBri NRoo SHil SPer WAbe WSHC
♦ – 'Pink Charming'	See B. *d.* 'Charming'
– 'Pink Delight'	CB&S CBot CBow CSam EBre EGol EHar ELan IOrc LHop MBar MBri MPla MR&S MRav NRoo SHil WWeb
* – 'Pixie Blue'	EGol
* – 'Pixie White'	EGol
¶ – 'Purple Prince'	CB&S
– 'Royal Purple'	MGos SPla
– 'Royal Red'	Widely available
– 'Salicifolia'	SSta
– 'Variegata'	CRow NKay WPat WWeb
– 'White Bouquet'	CPle GRei MBal MCot MPla MRav MWat NRoo NWea SPer SPla WAbe WWeb
– 'White Cloud'	CBow EPar IOrc ISea MR&S SHil
– 'White Harlequin'	CRow EMon LHop SDry WEas
– 'White Perfection'	NKay
– 'White Profusion'	CB&S CHan CRow CSam CSco CShe ELan IDai IJoh LHol MBal MBar MGos NNor SLHN WEas
davidii nanhoensis	CGre CHan CMHG ERav MPla MR&S MWat SLon SPer WAbe
– – alba	EFol ELan EMon SMad
– – blue	CShe IJoh MBri SPer SPla STre WEas WHea WWat
– – 'Nanho Blue'	See B. *d.* Nanho Petite Indigo ®
N *fallowiana*	CB&S CGre CHan ISea LAbb NNor SHil SPer SReu WWeb
– alba	CBot CBow CFor CLan CRow CSco ELan ENot ERav GWic ISea LHop MRav SDix SHil SPer SSpi WBod WSHC WWat
farreri	CBot CGre CHan WBod
forrestii	CGre CHEx CHan SArc SLHN

globosa	CB&S CBow CBra CFis CHan CLan CPle CSco CShe CTre ELan ENot IJoh ISea LHol MBri MCot MGos MR&S NNor SHil SMad SPer
heliophylla	CGre CHan ERea
japonica	CGre CHan CPle
¶ x ***lewisiana***	CGre
– 'Margaret Pike'	CBot CHan
– x ***asiatica***	MNew
lindleyana	CB&S CBot CBrd CHan CMCN CMHG CMal ELan ERea GWic SBor SChu SMad SSpi WSHC
'Lochinch'	Widely available
* ***loricata***	CHan WTay
¶ ***macrostachys*** SBEC 360	NHex
§ ***madagascariensis***	CB&S CGre CHEx CHan CPle ERea LAbb LHop WWat
nicodemia	See B. ***madagascariensis***
nivea	CBot CGre CMHG CPle ELan SSpi
– ***yunnanensis***	GWic WTay
officinalis	CBot CGre ERea
§ x ***pikei*** 'Hever'	CGre CHan SMrm SPer WWat
pterocaulis	CGre
saligna	CGre CPle WTay
salviifolia	CBot CHan CMHG CPle CTre ELan GWic LHop SDry SIgm SLHN SLon SPla SSta
sp. B&L 12491	LSav
stenostachya	CGre
sterniana	CBot
tubiflora	CBot CGre ERea
'West Hill'	CGre
x ***weyeriana***	CCor CFis CLan CPle CSam ELan EPar ISea MFir MRav MWat SLHN WEas WHea WPer WSHC
– 'Golden Glow'	CB&S CHan CMCN CSco CTre ERav GWic MBri MPla NKay NNor SHil SMad SReu WAbe WWeb WWin
– 'Lady de Ramsey'	WPer
– 'Moonlight'	CRow MFir SLon
– 'Sungold'	CB&S CRow ELan IJoh IOrc MBal MBlu MGos SPer SPla
– 'Trewithen'	CB&S CTrw
* 'White Butterfly'	WWat

BUGLOSSOIDES (Boraginaceae)

§ ***purpurocaerulea***	CCla CFis CHad CKin ELan EMon SIng WEas WHal WHea WOld WWin

BULBINE (Liliaceae/Asphodelaceae)

caulescens	EBul

BULBINELLA (Liliaceae/Asphodelaceae)

¶ ***angustifolia***	NHol
hookeri	CMal CRiv ECou ELan EPot GDra GGar ITim MFir MTho NHar NHol SIng WOMN WThu

BULBOCODIUM (Liliaceae/Colchicaceae)

vernum	CAvo EPar EPot ETub GEdr LAma LBlo MBri NHol SIng WChr

BULLACE See **PRUNUS** ***institia***

BUPHTHALMUM (Compositae)

§ ***salicifolium***	CHar CKel CLew CSam CSev ELan EMon ERou LHil MBri MWgw NSti WOld
§ – 'Golden Beauty'	MRav MWat NBar
speciosum	See TELEKIA ***speciosa***

BUPLEURUM (Umbelliferae)

angulosum	LGre SIgm SSpi
falcatum	CGle CHan CNat ECha LGan MRav MUlv NKay NSti SBar
fruticosum	CBot CChu CCla CCor CHan CPle ECha ELan ERav LAbb LGre LHop NRar SBla SChu SHil SSpi WEas WPat WSHC WWat
longifolium	GGar
¶ ***rotundifolium***	MSal
salicifolium MSF 725	SSpi

BURSARIA (Pittosporaceae)

spinosa	CBot CGre CPle

BUTIA (Palmae)

capitata	CHEx LPal NPal SArc

BUTOMUS (Butomaceae)

umbellatus	CRow CWGN ECha EHon ELan EWav LMay MSta SHig

BUXUS † (Buxaceae)

aurea 'Marginata'	See B. ***sempervirens*** 'Marginata'
balearica	CChu SArc SDry SLan WSHC WWat
bodinieri	SLan
* 'David's Gold'	WEas WSHC
'Green Gem'	SLan
'Green Mountain'	SLan
'Green Velvet'	SLan
harlandii	SIng SLan
– 'Richard'	SLan
japonica 'Nana'	See B. ***microphylla***
macowanii	SLan
§ ***microphylla***	LHol SHil SIng WThu
– 'Compacta'	CChu MPlt SLan
– 'Curly Locks'	SLan
– 'Faulkner'	LHop MBri SLan
– 'Grace Hendrick Phillips'	SLan
– 'Green Pillow'	SLan
– 'Helen Whiting'	SLan
– ***insularis***	See B. ***sinica insularis***
– 'John Baldwin'	SLan
– ***koreana***	NHol WMar
– ***riparia***	See B. ***riparia***
– ***sinica***	See B. ***sinica***
¶ ***microphylla japonica***	LSav
– – 'Green Jade'	SLan
– – 'Morris Dwarf'	SLan
– – 'Morris Midget'	SLan
– – 'National'	SLan
– – 'Variegata'	CMHG
natalensis	SLan
* 'New Silver'	IDai
riparia	SLan
sempervirens	Widely available
§ – 'Angustifolia'	SLan

– 'Argentea'	See B. *s.* 'Argenteo-variegata'
– 'Argenteo-variegata'	EPla MBal MRav SLan WSHC
– 'Aurea'	See B. *s.* 'Aureo-variegata'
– 'Aurea Maculata'	See B. *s.* 'Aureo-variegata'
– 'Aurea Marginata'	See B. *s.* 'Marginata'
– 'Aurea Pendula'	CChu EHar SLan
§ – 'Aureo-variegata'	CB&S CBow CRow MBar MGos MR&S MWat SChu SIng SLan SMad SPer
– 'Blauer Heinz'	SLan
§ – 'Bullata'	SLan
– clipped ball	CSco SPer
– clipped pyramid	CSco NBar SPer
§ – 'Elegantissima'	Widely available
– 'Gold Tip'	See B. *s.* 'Notata'
– 'Handsworthiensis'	NWea SHil SLan SLon SPer
– ***hyrcana***	SLan
I – 'Langley Pendula'	SLan
– 'Latifolia'	See B. *s.* 'Bullata'
– 'Latifolia Macrophylla'	CHan ELan SLan
§ – 'Latifolia Maculata'	CSco EPla GDra ISea MBal MPla NHol NRoo SHil SLan STre WMou WOak
– 'Longifolia'	See B. *s.* 'Angustifolia'
§ – 'Marginata'	GCHN LHop MRav NHol SLan SPla WHil
– 'Memorial'	SLan
– 'Myosotidifolia'	NHol SLan WWat
– 'Myrtifolia'	CBot SLan SLon
§ – 'Notata'	CLan CRow SHil
– 'Pendula'	EHar SLan
*– 'Pendula Esveld'	SLan
– 'Prostrata'	SLan
– 'Pyramidalis'	ENot SLan WMou
– 'Rosmarinifolia'	SLan
– 'Rotundifolia'	LHol SLan WMou
– 'Salicifolia Elata'	SLan
*– 'Silver Beauty'	CB&S MGos
– 'Silver Variegated'	See B. *s.* 'Elegantissima'
– 'Suffruticosa'	CLan CSev CShe EHar ELan LBuc LHol MBri MWat NRoo SCro SHil SIde SLan SPer SPla STre WMou WOak
¶ – 'Suffruticosa Variegata'	CB&S
– 'Vardar Valley'	NHol SLan
sinica	SLan
– 'Filigree'	SLan
sinica insularis 'Justin Brouwers'	SLan
– – 'Pincushion'	SLan
– – 'Tide Hill'	SLan
– – 'Winter Beauty'	LRHS
wallichiana	SArc SBor SLan

CAESALPINIA (Leguminosae)

gilliesii	CBot CGre CHEx SHil SMad WCar
japonica	SHil

CALADIUM (Araceae)

bicolor	MBri
x ***hortulanum***	See C. ***bicolor***
§ ***lindenii***	MBri

CALAMAGROSTIS (Gramineae)

x ***acutiflora*** 'Karl Foerster'	EFol ERou GWic SApp SDix
*– 'Overdam'	CHoe ECha SApp
*– 'Stricta'	ECha SApp

CALAMINTHA † (Labiatae)

alpina	See ACINOS ***alpinus***
♦ ***clinopodium***	See CLINOPODIUM ***vulgare***
cretica	LHop MBro MTho SIng WDav WHil WPer
¶ – ***variegata***	MTho
♦ ***nepeta***	See CLINOPODIUM ***calamintha***
♦ – ***glandulosa***	See CLINOPODIUM ***calamintha***
♦ – ***nepeta***	See CLINOPODIUM ***calamintha calamintha***
♦ ***sylvatica***	See CLINOPODIUM ***ascendens***

CALAMONDIN See X CITROFORTUNELLA

CALANDRINIA (Portulacaceae)

caespitosa	GEdr MHig NGre NNrd SIng WDav WHil
¶ ***compressa***	WPer
grandiflora	EBar MHig SIng
♦ ***megarhiza nivalis***	See CLAYTONIA ***m. n.***
* ***portulacoides***	NGre
* ***rupestris***	NGre
sericea	NGre
♦ ***sibirica***	See CLAYTONIA ***sibirica***
umbellata	EBar ELan GLoc NTow SIng WDav WHil WOMN WPer WWin

CALANTHE (Orchidaceae)

aristulifera	LAma SWes WChr
bicolor	See C. ***discolor flava***
discolor	LAma NHol SSpi SWes WChr
§ – ***flava***	LAma NHol SWes
reflexa	LAma NHol SWes WChr
sieboldii	See C. ***striata***
§ ***striata***	LAma NHol SWes WChr

CALATHEA † (Marantaceae)

albertii	MBri
albicans	See C. ***micans***
bella	MBri
♦ 'Burle Marx'	See CTENANTHE ***burle-marxii***
crocata	MBri
'Exotica'	MBri
'Greystar'	MBri
kegeljanii	See C. ***bella***
lietzei	MBri
– 'Greenstar'	MBri
makoyana	MBri
* 'Mavi Queen'	MBri
'Metallica'	MBri
* 'Misto'	MBri
oppenheimiana	See CTENANTHE ***o.***
orbiculata	See C. ***truncata***
ornata	MBri
* ***pendula***	MBri
picturata 'Argentea'	MBri
– 'Vandenheckei'	MBri
roseo-picta	MBri
truncata	MBri
veitchiana	MBri
warscewiczii	MBri

'Wavestar'	MBri
zebrina	MBri

CALCEOLARIA † (Scrophulariaceae)

acutifolia	See C. ***polyrrhiza***
arachnoidea	CBot CSun GCHN GWic LGre MPar MTho WOMN WTay
× *banksii*	GWic MFir
bicolor	GWic
§ *biflora*	CLew CRiv CSam CSun GCHN GDra LHop MBal MBro MTho NKay NRed NRya NTow SBla SIng WCla WDav WHal WHil WOMN WPer WWin
* *bigibbiflora* Wr 8733	CSun
'Camden Hero'	CKni ELan SMad WOld
chelidonioides	MTho
crenatiflora	CSun WPer
darwinii	MHig MTho NNrd NTow SIng WHal WPer
falklandica	CHar CSam CSun ELan EOrc EPot GEdr GHig GLoc LHop MBal MPit NNrd NRed NTow WPer WWin
fiedleri	GEdr
fothergillii	GAbr MHig MTho NKay NTow WHil WPer
– × *darwinii*	GLoc
* 'Goldcrest'	ECtt GCHN NGre NRoo
¶ 'Hort's Variety'	MTho
integrifolia	CB&S CFis CPle CSun CTre ELan ERav MBal MFir NRar NRog SChu SHil SLon SMad SPer WEas WOMN WOld WWat WWin
– *angustifolia*	CGre SDry
– bronze form	WAbe
¶ – 'Gaines' Yellow'	GWic
'John Innes'	ELan EPad EPot ESis GEdr GWic LHop NNrd NRoo SCro WPer
'Kentish Hero'	CBot CGre CMHG ELan EMon GWic LHop MFir SChu WOMN WPat WPer
¶ *luxurians* Wr 8957	NGre
¶ *mexicana*	WPer
picta P&W 6276	CSun
♦ *plantaginea*	See C. ***biflora***
§ *polyrrhiza*	CHar CSun ELan EMNN ESis GLoc MBal MTho NHol NNrd NRoo NRya WAbe WHil WPer
scabiosifolia	See C. ***tripartita***
¶ 'Sir Daniel Hall'	SAsh
¶ sp. Wr 8745	CSun
sp. Wr 8827	NGre
sp. Wr 8875	CSun
¶ sp. Wr 8936	CSun
tenella	EPot GEdr ITim MBal MHig MTho NHol NNrd WAbe WOMN WPer WWin
§ *tripartita*	WPer
'Walter Shrimpton'	ELan EPot GEdr MTho NNrd SBla

CALENDULA (Compositae)

officinalis	CArn CSFH GPoy LHol MChe MSal NSel SIde WOak WSto
– 'Prolifera'	WHer
– 'Variegata'	MSal

CALLA (Araceae)

aethiopica	See ZANTEDESCHIA ***aethiopica***

palustris	CHEx CRiv CRow CWGN ECha EHon EWav GGar LMay MSta SHig

CALLIANDRA (Leguminosae)

eriophylla	CSun

CALLIANTHEMUM (Ranunculaceae)

kernerianum	NHol

CALLICARPA (Verbenaceae)

bodinieri	CBra EFou
– *giraldii*	CShe LSav SHil SLon SSta WBod WWat WWeb
– *giraldii* 'Profusion'	Widely available
cathayana	CMCN
dichotoma	CCla ELan LSav SHil WBod WSHC WWat WWin
japonica	WCoo
– 'Leucocarpa'	CBow CCla SHil SLon WWat
¶ × *shirasawana*	NBar
sp. B 135	LSav

CALLIRHOË (Malvaceae)

¶ *involucrata*	WDav

CALLISIA (Commelinaceae)

repens	MBri

CALLISTEMON † (Myrtaceae)

'Burning Bush'	CB&S CSun
citrinus	CPle CShe ECou ERav ISea LAbb SBar SLMG SPer WCar
– *albus*	CGre
– 'Mauve Mist'	CB&S CSun NPal
– 'Red Clusters'	CB&S
– 'Splendens'	CB&S CBow CHEx CSam ELan IOrc MR&S NPal NTow SCro SHil SLon SSta WBod WWat
§ *glaucus*	CChu NPal
'King's Park Special'	CSun
linearis	CMac CTre IOrc ISea MBal SHil SLMG SLon
pachyphyllus	ISea
pallidus	CMHG CMac CPle ISea WBod
paludosus	See C. ***sieberi***
phoeniceus	IDai
pinifolius	IBar ISea
♦ *pithyoides*	See C. ***sieberi***
rigidus	CB&S CBra CHEx CLan CMHG CSun ELan IBar ISea MBlu MGos MUlv SLMG SPer SSpi WBod
salignus	CGre CHEx CMHG CSam IOrc ISea MBal MUlv SAxl SDry SHil WSHC
¶ *shiressii*	CMHG
§ *sieberi*	CGre ECou IBar ISea MR&S NBir NHol WSHC WWat
speciosus	See C. ***glaucus***
subulatus	MBal SArc
viminalis	ERav
– 'Captain Cook'	CB&S ECou
– 'Hannah Ray'	CB&S NPal
– 'Little John '	CB&S NPal
'Violaceus'	CPle SLMG
viridiflorus	CB&S CChu CPle ECou

CALLITRIS (Cupressaceae)

¶ *rhomboidea*	ECou

CALLUNA † (Ericaceae)

vulgaris	CKin
– 'Alba Argentea'	ENHC
– 'Alba Aurea'	ENHC MBar NWin WGre
¶ – 'Alba Carlton'	EDen
– 'Alba Dumosa'	ENHC
– 'Alba Elata'	CNCN EDen ENHC MBar NHea
– 'Alba Elegans'	EDen
– 'Alba Elongata'	See C. *v.* 'Mair's Variety'
– 'Alba Jae'	EDen MBar
– 'Alba Plena'	CB&S CMac CNCN CRiv EDen ENHC GPen GSpe IDai IJoh MBal MBar NKay SHil WGre WRid
– 'Alba Praecox'	WGre
– 'Alba Pumila'	EDen MBar
§ – 'Alba Rigida'	CMac CNCN EDen ENHC MBar MBri MCra NHea WGre WRid
¶ – 'Alex Warwick'	EDen
– 'Alison Yates'	MBar
– 'Allegro'	CMac EBre EDen ENHC MBar MBri MOke
– 'Alportii'	CRiv ENHC GAng GBla GDra GSpe IDai MBar MBri MCra MOke NWin SHil WGre
– 'Alportii Praecox'	CNCN ENHC MBar NHea WGre
– 'Andrew Proudley'	ENHC
*– 'Angela Wain'	EDen
– 'Annemarie'	EBre EDen MBri MGos WGre
– 'Anthony Davis'	EBre EDen ENHC GAng MBar MCra MGos MOke NHea NWin WRid
– 'Anthony Wain'	MGos
– 'Apollo'	EDen
– 'Applecross'	EDen
– 'Argentea'	EDen MBar MCra
– 'Arina'	EDen MBri MOke
– 'Arran Gold'	EDen ENHC GBla GSpe MBar MCra
– 'August Beauty'	CNCN CRiv ENHC GBla GDra MOke NWin WRid
– 'Aurea'	EDen ENHC GSpe IJoh
– 'Baby Ben'	CMac CNCN
¶ – 'Baby Wicklow'	EDen
– 'Barbara Fleur'	EDen
– 'Barnett Anley'	CNCN EDen ENHC GDra GSpe MBal MCra
– 'Battle of Arnhem'	CNCN EDen MBar WGre
– 'Beechwood Crimson'	CNCN EDen ENHC
– 'Beoley Crimson'	CNCN ENHC GAng GDra MBar MCra MGos NWin WRid
– 'Beoley Gold'	Widely available
– 'Bernadette'	EDen
– 'Betty Baum'	MCra
– 'Blazeaway'	CMac CNCN EDen ENHC GAng GBla GDra GRei GSpe IJoh MBal MBar MBri MCra NRoo SHil WBod WGre WRid
– 'Bognie'	CNCN EDen ENHC GRei
– 'Bonfire Brilliance'	CMHG CRiv EDen MBar
– 'Boreray'	CNCN EDen
– 'Boskoop'	EDen ENHC MBar MBri SPla
– 'Braemar'	GBla
¶ – 'Braeriach'	EDen
– 'Bray Head'	CNCN MBar WGre
– 'Bud Lyle'	WGre
– 'Bunsall'	CMac EDen MCra
– 'Buxton Snowdrift'	EDen
– 'C W Nix'	CNCN EDen ENHC GPen GSpe IJoh MBar SHil WRid
– 'Caerketton White'	EDen ENHC GAng GBla GPen GSpe MBal MCra WGre
– 'Caleb Threlkeld'	EDen
– 'Calf of Man'	ENHC
– 'Californian Midge'	CNCN ENHC EPot GPen GSpe MBar MCra MGos NHol WGre
– 'Carmen'	EDen
– 'Carole Chapman'	CMHG ENHC EPot GPen MBar MCra MGos WRid
– 'Carolyn'	EDen
– 'Citronella'	EDen GPen
– 'Clare Carpet'	EDen
– 'Coccinea'	CMac ENHC MBal MBar WGre
– 'Coral Island'	MBar MCra MGos
– 'Corrie's White'	EDen
– 'Cottswood Gold'	EDen
– 'County Wicklow'	CMac CNCN EBre EDen ENHC EPot GAng GBla GPen GSpe IJoh MBal MBar MBri MCra MGos MOke NHea NHol NKay NWin SHil WBod WGre
– 'Cramond'	EDen ENHC GBla MBar MCra NKay WGre
– 'Crimson Glory'	EDen GSpe MBal MBar MPlt NWin WGre
– 'Crowborough Beacon'	EDen
– 'Cuprea'	CMac CNCN EDen ENHC GAng GBla GDra GRei GSpe MBal MBar MBri MCra MOke NHol NKay NWin WGre
– 'Dainty Bess'	CNCN MBar MPlt WGre
– 'Darkness'	CMHG CNCN EBre EDen ENHC EPot GAng GBla GPen GSpe IJoh MBal MBar MBri MCra MGos MOke MPlt NHea NRoo NWin SHil SPla WGre
– 'Darleyensis'	See ERICA x *darleyensis*
– 'Dart's Brilliant'	EDen
– 'Dart's Flamboyant'	EDen
– 'Dart's Gold'	GBla MBar NRoo
– 'Dart's Hedgehog'	EDen WGre
– 'Dart's Parakeet'	EDen
– 'Dart's Silver Rocket'	EDen GBla
– 'David Eason'	CNCN EDen ENHC MBal MCra
– 'David Hutton'	MBar
*– 'Dickson's Blazes'	EDen GSpe
– 'Dirry'	EDen GSpe
– 'Doctor Murray's White'	See C. *v.* 'Mullardoch'
¶ – 'Doris Rushworth'	EDen
– 'Drum-Ra'	CRiv EDen ENHC GAng GBla GDra GSpe MBal MBar MCra NHea WGre
– 'Dunnet Lime'	EDen SPla
– 'Dunnydeer'	ENHC
– 'Dunwood'	MBar
¶ – 'Durfordii'	EDen
– 'E F Brown'	CNCN EDen ENHC
– 'E Hoare'	MBar
– 'Edith Godbolt'	CNCN EDen ENHC
– 'Elegant Pearl'	EDen MBar MCra
– 'Elegantissima'	EDen ENHC GSpe MBri MOke
– 'Elegantissima Walter Ingwersen'	See C. *v.* 'Walter Ingwersen'
– 'Elkstone'	CNCN EDen ENHC MBal MBar MCra WGre
– 'Elsie Frye'	EDen MCra

Cultivar	Suppliers
– 'Elsie Purnell'	CMac CNCN EDen ENHC GAng GBla GPen GSpe MBal MBar MBri MCra MGos MOke NHea NHol NKay WBod WGre WRid
– 'Emerald Jack'	EDen
– 'Fairy'	CMHG CMac CNCN EDen MBri MCra MOke
§ – 'Finale'	ENHC GPen MBar MOke WGre
– 'Fire King'	MBar
– 'Firebreak'	EDen MBar MBri
– 'Firefly'	CMac CNCN CRiv EDen ENHC GAng GBla GSpe MBal MBar MBri MCra MOke NKay NRoo NWin SPla WGre WRid
– 'Flamingo'	CMac CNCN EDen MBar MBri MOke
¶ – 'Flatling'	EDen
– 'Flore Pleno'	ENHC MBar
– 'Foxhollow Wanderer'	CNCN CRiv ENHC GSpe MBal MBar MOke
– 'Foxii Floribunda'	ENHC GSpe MBar
– 'Foxii Lett's Form'	MBar
– 'Foxii Nana'	CMac CNCN CRiv ENHC GAng GBla GSpe MBal MBar MCra MPlt NHol SPla WGre WRid
– 'Fred J Chapple'	CNCN EDen ENHC GAng GBla GPen IDai MBal MBar MBri MCra MOke WBod WGre
¶ – 'Fréjus'	EDen
– 'Gerda'	SPla
– 'Ginkel's Glorie'	EDen
– 'Glencoe'	EDen ENHC GBla GSpe MBal MBar MBri MCra MOke WGre
– 'Glenfiddich'	EDen MBar MBri
– 'Glenlivet'	MBar NWin
– 'Glenmorangie'	MBar
– 'Gold Flame'	GAng MBar MBri MCra NRoo
– 'Gold Haze'	CB&S CMac CNCN EDen ENHC GAng GBla GSpe IJoh MBal MBar MBri MCra MOke NRoo SHil WBod WGre WRid
– 'Gold Knight'	MBri
– 'Gold Kup'	MBar
– 'Golden Carpet'	CB&S CMac CNCN EBre EDen ENHC EPot GAng GBla GDra GPen MBal MBar MBri MCra MGos MOke NHol NRoo NWin SPla WBod WGre WRid
– 'Golden Feather'	CB&S CMHG CMac CNCN EBre EDen ENHC GAng GBla GRei IDai MBal MBar MCra MGos NWin WGre WRid
– 'Golden Rivulet'	CMac ENHC MBar
– 'Golden Turret'	ENHC GBla GRei
– 'Goldsworth Crimson'	CRiv ENHC WGre
– 'Goldsworth Crimson Variegated'	CNCN EDen ENHC MBar
– 'Grasmeriensis'	MBar
– 'Great Comp'	MBar
– 'Grey Carpet'	GBla MBar MPlt
¶ – 'Grijsje'	EDen
– 'Guinea Gold'	EDen MBar MBri MPlt WGre
§ – 'H E Beale'	Widely available
– 'Hamlet Green'	EDen MBar
– 'Hammondii'	CNCN CRiv GPen MCra WGre
– 'Hammondii Aureifolia'	CNCN CRiv EDen GAng GBla MBal MBar MBri MCra MOke
– 'Hammondii Rubrifolia'	CNCN CRiv EDen GAng MBal MBar MBri MOke
– 'Harlequin'	MCra
– 'Heideteppich'	EDen
– 'Hester'	EDen
– 'Hibernica'	EDen GPen MBar MCra WGre
– 'Hiemalis'	EDen ENHC MBar MCra
– 'Hiemalis Southcote'	See C. *v.* 'Durfordii'
– 'Highland Rose'	GBla MCra
– 'Hillbrook Orange'	MBar
– 'Hirsuta'	GPen NWin WGre WRid
– 'Hirsuta Albiflora'	MBar
– 'Hirsuta Typica'	CNCN EDen WGre
– 'Hirta'	CNCN MBar MCra WGre
– 'Hookstone'	GPen MBar WGre
– 'Hugh Nicholson'	CNCN EDen ENHC
– 'Humpty Dumpty'	CNCN EDen ENHC NHol WRid
– 'Inchcolm'	GPen
– 'Ineke'	EDen ENHC MBar
– 'Inshriach Bronze'	CMac ENHC EPot GDra GRei GSpe MBar MCra NHea NRoo WRid
– 'Isobel Frye'	MBar
– 'Isobel Hughes'	MBar
– 'J H Hamilton'	CNCN EBre EDen ENHC GAng GBla GDra GPen GSpe MBal MBar MBri MCra MGos NHea NHol NKay NRoo SHil WGre WRid
¶ – 'Jan'	EDen
– 'Jan Dekker'	EDen MPlt SPla WGre
– 'Janice Chapman'	EDen MBar MCra WGre
– 'Jenny'	EDen
– 'Joan Sparkes'	CMac CNCN EDen ENHC GBla GPen GRei IDai MBal MBar MCra WGre
– 'John F Letts'	CMHG CMac CNCN CRiv EDen ENHC GAng GBla GRei GSpe MBal MBar MCra MGos NWin
– 'Johnson's Variety'	CNCN EDen MBar MCra WGre
– 'Joy Vanstone'	CMac CNCN EDen ENHC GAng GBla MBal MBar MBri MCra MGos MOke NHea NHol NKay SHil SPla WRid
¶ – 'Kerstin'	EDen
– 'Kinlochruel'	Widely available
– 'Kirby White'	CNCN EDen GAng GBla MBar MBri MCra NWin
– 'Kirsten'	SPla
– 'Kirsty Anderson'	MBri MOke
– 'Kit Hill'	EDen MBar
– 'Kuphaldtii'	MBar
– 'Kynance'	ENHC MBar
– 'Lambstails'	EDen MBal MBar MCra MGos
– 'Leslie Slinger'	CRiv ENHC GBla MBar MCra
– 'Lewis Lilac'	EDen WGre
– 'Llanbedrog Pride'	CNCN EDen MBar
– 'Loch Turret'	CNCN EDen ENHC GBla GSpe MBar MBri MOke NWin
– 'Loch-na-Seil'	EDen MBar MCra
– 'Long White'	EDen GSpe MBar
– 'Lyle's Late White'	CNCN EDen GPen
– 'Lyle's Surprise'	MBar
– 'Lyndon Proudley'	ENHC GPen
§ – 'Mair's Variety'	CNCN EDen ENHC GAng GBla GDra GSpe IDai MBal MBar MCra NRoo SHil WGre WRid
– 'Marion Blum'	MBar
– 'Marleen'	EDen
– 'Masquerade'	MBar
– 'Mauvelyn'	EDen
– 'Mazurka'	EDen
– 'Minima'	GPen MBar

– 'Minima Smith's Variety'	EDen ENHC MBar WRid
– 'Mirelle'	EDen
– 'Miss Muffet'	NHol
– 'Molecule'	EDen MBar
§ – 'Mousehole'	CMac CNCN ENHC GBla GSpe MBar MCra MGos MOke MPlt NHol NKay WGre
– 'Mousehole Compact'	See C. *v.* 'Mousehole'
– 'Mrs Alf'	EDen
– 'Mrs Pat'	CNCN CRiv ENHC MBar MBri MOke NWin WGre WRid
– 'Mrs Ronald Gray'	CMac CNCN EDen GDra IJoh MBar WGre WRid
– 'Mullach Mor'	EDen
§ – 'Mullardoch'	EDen GPen MBar
– 'Mullion'	EDen ENHC MBar MCra MOke SHil
– 'Multicolor'	CB&S CMac CNCN EBre EDen ENHC GAng GBla GDra GPen GSpe MBal MBar MBri MCra MOke NHea NHol NRoo NWin SPla WBod WGre WRid
– 'Murielle Dobson'	EDen MBar MCra
§ – 'My Dream'	EBre EDen ENHC GSpe MBar NHol WGre
– 'Nana'	ENHC
– 'Nana Compacta'	CMac CNCN CRiv EDen EPot GAng GPen GSpe MBal MBar MBri MOke NWin WRid
– 'Naturpark'	EDen ENHC MBar
– 'October White'	CNCN EDen ENHC
– 'Öxabäck'	MBar
¶ – 'Oiseval'	EDen
– 'Olive Turner'	EDen MCra
– 'Orange Max'	GBla
– 'Orange Queen'	CMac CNCN EBre EDen ENHC GAng GBla GRei GSpe MBal MBar MCra SHil WGre WRid
– 'Oxshott Common'	CRiv EDen ENHC EPot MBar MCra NHea WGre
– 'Pearl Drop'	MBar
– 'Penny Bun'	EDen
– 'Pepper and Salt'	EDen
– 'Peter Sparkes'	Widely available
– 'Petra'	EDen
– 'Pewter Plate'	MBar MBri NWin
– 'Pink Beale'	See C. *v.* 'H E Beale'
¶ – 'Pink Dream'	EDen
¶ – 'Pink Gown'	EDen
– 'Prizewinner'	CNCN
– 'Prostrate Orange'	CNCN EDen GSpe MBal MBar MCra NKay WRid
– 'Pygmaea'	ENHC MBar
– 'Pyramidalis'	ENHC
– 'Pyrenaica'	GPen MBar
– 'Radnor'	CMac CNCN EDen ENHC GAng GBla GSpe MBal MBar MBri MCra MGos MOke NHea NRoo WGre WRid
– 'Radnor Gold'	MBar
– 'Ralph Purnell'	CNCN CRiv EDen ENHC MBal MBar
– 'Red Carpet'	EDen MBri MOke WBod WGre
– 'Red Favorit'	EDen WGre
– 'Red Fred'	MGos
– 'Red Haze'	CMHG CMac CNCN EDen ENHC GAng MBal MBar MBri MCra MOke NHol WBod WGre
– 'Red Pimpernel'	EDen
– 'Red Star'	NHea
– 'Richard Cooper'	MBar
– 'Rigida Prostrata'	See C. *v.* 'Alba Rigida'
– 'Robert Chapman'	Widely available
– 'Roland Haagen'	EDen MBar MBri MCra MOke
– 'Roma'	EDen ENHC GPen MBar
– 'Ronas Hill'	GDra
– 'Rosalind'	CNCN EPot GBla GPen GSpe MBal MBar MCra MOke NRoo WGre
– 'Rosalind Underwood's Variety'	EDen
– 'Ross Hutton'	EDen GBla GPen
– 'Rotfuchs'	SPla
– 'Ruby Slinger'	GAng GBla MBar WGre
– 'Ruth Sparkes'	CMac CNCN CRiv EDen ENHC EPot GAng GPen MBal MBar MBri MCra MOke NWin SPla WRid
– 'Saint Kilda'	GPen GRei GSpe
– 'Saint Nick'	EDen ENHC MBar
– 'Sally Anne Proudley'	CNCN CRiv EDen ENHC MBar MCra NKay WGre
– 'Salmon Leap'	GSpe MBar MCra NHol NWin
– 'Sampford Sunset'	CSam
– 'Sandwood Bay'	EDen
– 'Schurig's Sensation'	EDen GBla GSpe MBar MBri MOke
– 'Scotch Mist'	EDen
– 'September Pink'	NWin
– 'Serlei'	CNCN EDen ENHC GPen MBal MBar MBri MCra MOke SHil
– 'Serlei Aurea'	CNCN CRiv EDen ENHC GAng GPen GSpe MBal MBar MCra NHea SPla WGre WRid
– 'Serlei Grandiflora'	GPen MBar
– 'Serlei Lavender'	EDen WGre WRid
– 'Serlei Rubra'	EDen MCra
¶ – 'Sesam'	EDen
– 'Shirley'	CMac MBar
– 'Silver Cloud'	CNCN MBar MBri NWin
– 'Silver King'	CMac CNCN CRiv MBar
– 'Silver Knight'	Widely available
– 'Silver Queen'	CMHG CMac CNCN EBre EDen ENHC GAng GBla GRei GSpe IJoh MBal MBar MBri MCra MOke NHea NHol NRoo SHil WGre WRid
– 'Silver Rose'	CNCN EBre EDen ENHC GBla GSpe MBar MCra NHea NWin WGre WRid
– 'Silver Sandra'	EDen
– 'Silver Spire'	CNCN EDen ENHC MBal MBar MCra
– 'Silver Stream'	ENHC MBar MCra NWin
– 'Sir John Charrington'	CHoe CMac CNCN EBre EDen ENHC GAng GBla GDra GPen GSpe MBal MBar MBri MCra MGos MOke NHea NHol NKay SHil WGre WRid
– 'Sirsson'	EDen MBri NWin
– 'Sister Anne'	CMac CNCN EDen ENHC EPot GAng GBla MBal MBri MGos MOke NHol NKay SHil WRid
– 'Skipper'	MBar WGre
– 'Snowball'	See C. *v.* 'My Dream'
– 'Soay'	EDen MBar
¶ – 'Spicata'	EDen
– 'Spicata Aurea'	CNCN MBar MCra
– 'Spitfire'	CMac CNCN EDen ENHC GAng GPen GSpe MBal MBar MCra NHol NKay WGre WRid
– 'Spring Cream'	CMHG EDen ENHC GAng GBla GSpe MBar MBri MCra MGos MOke WGre WRid

- – 'Spring Glow' CMac EDen GAng MBar MBri MOke NWin
- – 'Spring Torch' CMHG CNCN EDen ENHC GAng GDra GSpe IJoh MBal MBar MBri MCra MGos MOke MPlt NHea WGre WRid
- – 'Springbank' MBar
- – 'Summer Orange' CNCN EDen GAng GPen MBal MBar NHol
- – 'Sunningdale' See C. *v.* 'Finale'
- – 'Sunrise' EDen ENHC GAng MBar MCra MGos MOke NHol NKay SPla WGre
- – 'Sunset' CB&S CMHG CMac CNCN ENHC GAng GBla GDra GPen GRei GSpe MBal MBar MCra NHol NRoo NWin SHil WGre WRid
- – 'Tenuis' CNCN ENHC MBar NWin
- N– 'Terrick's Orange' EDen
- – 'Tib' CMHG CMac CNCN EDen ENHC GAng GBla GPen GSpe IJoh MBal MBar MBri MCra MOke NHea NHol NKay NWin SHil WGre WRid
- – 'Tom Thumb' MBar MCra
- – 'Torulosa' EDen ENHC GPen
- – 'Tremans' MCra
- – 'Tricolorifolia' CNCN EDen ENHC GAng GBla IDai MBal MCra
- – 'Underwoodii' ENHC GBla GPen MBar
- – 'Velvet Dome' MBal MBar MCra MPlt NHea
- ¶– 'Visser's Fancy' EDen
- §– 'Walter Ingwersen' EDen MBar
- – 'White Carpet' GPen MBar
- – 'White Gown' ENHC GDra MCra WRid
- – 'White Lawn' CMac CNCN CRiv EBre EDen MBar MGos MPlt NHol NWin
- – 'White Mite' ENHC MBar
- – 'White Princess' See C. *v.* 'White Queen'
- §– 'White Queen' EDen MBal MBar
- – 'Wickwar Flame' CMac CNCN EBre EDen ENHC EPot GAng GBla GDra GPen IJoh MBal MBar MBri MCra MOke MPlt NHol NKay NRoo SPla WBod WRid
- ¶– 'Wingate's Gem' NWin
- – 'Wingate's Gold' NWin
- – 'Winter Chocolate' CMHG CMac CNCN EDen ENHC EPot GAng GBla GPen MBal MBar MBri MCra MGos MOke NHol NKay NRoo WGre WRid

CALOCEDRUS (Cupressaceae)

- § ***decurrens*** CB&S CDoC CMac CSco EHar EHul ENot IBar IDai IJoh IOrc MBal MBar MBri MUlv NWea SExT SHil SPer SSta WCon WFro WMou WWat
- – 'Aureovariegata' CDoC CKen EHar IOrc LNet MBar MBlu SGar SHil WCon
- – 'Berrima Gold' CKen SHil
- – 'Intricata' CKen
- – 'Nana' See C. *d.* 'Depressa'
- – 'Pillar' WCon
- ***formosana*** WBod

CALOCEPHALUS (Compositae)

- ***brownii*** CMHG ECou ITim LHil MRav SChu SLon

CALOCHORTUS (Liliaceae/Liliaceae)

- ***albus*** WChr
- ***amabilis*** WChr
- ¶ ***catalinae*** WChr
- ¶ ***clavatus*** WChr
- ¶ ***kennedyi*** WChr
- ¶ ***luteus*** WChr
- ¶ ***splendens*** WChr
- ¶ ***superbus*** WChr
- ¶ ***uniflorus*** WChr WOMN
- ¶ ***venustus*** WChr
- ***vestae*** WChr
- ¶ ***weedii*** WChr

CALOMERIA (Compositae)

- ¶ ***amaranthoides*** EMon LHol

CALOSCORDUM (Liliaceae/Alliaceae)

- ***neriniflorum*** SLHN SWas

CALOTHAMNUS (Myrtaceae)

- ***quadrifidus*** CSun WTay
- ***sanguineus*** CSun
- ***validus*** CPle

CALTHA † (Ranunculaceae)

- ***introloba*** CFor CRow EPot
- ***leptosepala*** CGle
- ***palustris*** CChu CGle CHEx CHad CKin CRiv CRow CWGN EHon EPot GPoy LMay LSav MSta MWgw NHol NLan NSel SHig SLon
- – ***alba*** Widely available
- – 'Plena' Widely available
- ¶– 'Wheatfen' CNat
- ***polypetala*** CRow CWGN ECha EHon ELan EPar EWav LMay MSta SHig SPer SSpi

CALYCANTHUS (Acanthaceae)

- ***floridus*** CArn CB&S CBow CChu CCla EGol ELan ENot IOrc LSav SHil WBod
- §– ***fertilis*** CBot MUlv SGar WSHC
- – ***glauca*** See C. ***floridus fertilis***
- – 'Purpureus' MBri SHil
- ***occidentalis*** CBra CCla ELan LSav MPar SSpi

CALYPTRIDIUM (Portulacaceae)

- ***umbellatum*** See SPRAGUEA ***umbellata***

CALYSTEGIA (Convolvulaceae)

- ***hederacea*** ELan
- – 'Flore Pleno ' CBos ECha EMon EPar GWic LHop MTho SAxl SMad SPou
- ***japonica*** 'Flore Pleno' See C. ***hederacea*** 'F.P.'
- ***tuguriorum*** ECou

CALYTRIX (Myrtaceae)

- ***alpestris*** See LHOTZKYA ***alpestris***
- ***tetragona*** CPle CSun

CAMASSIA † (Liliaceae/Hyacinthaceae)

- ***cusickii*** CAvo CBro ECha ELan EPar ETub LAma LBow MBri MTho NHol WChr
- – 'Zwanenburg' ETub
- ***esculenta*** See C. ***quamash***

fraseri	See C. *scilloides*
leichtlinii	CAvo CRow ECha EOrc ERav ETub LBow NHol NRar
– *alba*	CAvo CBro LAma NHol SWas WChr
– *atroviolacea*	CHan
– 'Blue Danube'	LAma LBow
– *caerulea*	ELan EPar LAma SIng SSpi
– 'Electra'	ECha SWas
– 'Plena'	ECha WCot
– 'Semiplena'	CAvo CBro EPar ERou
¶ – *suksdorfii*	EMon
§ *quamash*	CAvo CBro ECha EFou ELan EPar ETub LAma LBlo LBow LRoo MBri MTho NHol SIng WBod WChr
¶ – *linearis*	NHol
– 'Orion'	CBro EMon
§ *scilloides*	MBri

CAMELLIA † (Theaceae)

'Aaron's Ruby' (*japonica*)	CMHG CTre SCog
'Adelina Patti' (*japonica*)	CB&S CTre SCog
'Adolphe Audusson' (*japonica*)	CB&S CMac CSco CTre CTrw ELan ENot IJoh IOrc LHyd LNet LSav MBri MMth NKay SCog SExb SHil SLon SPer SPic SPla SReu SSta
'Adolphe Audusson Special' (*japonica*)	SCog
§ 'Akashi-gata' ('Lady Clare') (*japonica*)	CMac CSco CTre CTrw ELan ENot IHos SCog SExb SHil SPer SReu SSta WBod WWat
§ 'Akebono' (*japonica*)	CTrw
'Alba Plena' (*japonica*)	CGre CMac CTre ENot IHos IOrc ISea LNet SCog SPer
'Alba Simplex' (*japonica*)	CB&S CGre CMac CTre ELan IOrc LNet MMth SCog SExb SHil SPer SReu SSta
'Alexander Blackadder' (*japonica*)	CMHG SCog
'Alexander Hunter' (*japonica*)	CTre SCog SExb
'Alice Wood' (*japonica*)	SCog
'Althaeiflora' (*japonica*)	CGre CMac CTre SCog WBod
'Ama-no-kawa' (*japonica*)	SCog
'Anemoniflora' (*japonica*)	CB&S CTre ELan IHos SPer WBod
'Angel' (*japonica*)	CMHG CTre SCog
'Angela Cocchi' (*japonica*)	SCog SExb
'Ann Sothern' (*japonica*)	CB&S
'Annie Wylam' (*japonica*)	SCog
'Anticipation' (x *williamsii*)	CB&S CMHG CSam CSco CTre CTrw EBre GArd IJoh IOrc ISea LHyd MBri SCog SHil SPic SPla SReu SSpi
'Apollo' (*japonica*)	CB&S CTrw ELan IHos MBri SExb SLon SPer SReu WBod
§ 'Apple Blossom' (*japonica*)	CGre CMac MBal SExb
'Arabella' (*japonica*)	SCog
'Arajishi' (*japonica*)	CB&S CMac CTre SCog SPla WAbe
♦ 'Auburn White'	See C. 'Mrs Bertha A Harms'
¶ 'August del Fosse' (*japonica*)	LSav
* 'Augustini Supreme' (*japonica*)	CMac
'Azuma-kagami' (*japonica*)	CSco
'Azurea (*japonica*)	CGre
'Ballet Dancer' (*japonica*)	MBri SCog SHil
'Ballet Queen' (x *williamsii*)	CB&S MBri
'Ballet Queen Variegated' (*saluenensis* x *japonica*)	SCog
'Barbara Clark' (*saluenensis* x *reticulata*)	MBri
'Barbara Hillier' (*reticulata* x *japonica*)	SHil
'Barbara Woodroof' (*japonica*)	SCog
'Baron Gomer' (*japonica*)	See C. 'Comte de Gomer'
'Baronesa de Soutelinho' (*saluenensis*)	SCog
¶ 'Baronne Leguay' (*japonica*)	LSav
* 'Bartley No 5' (x *williamsii*)	CMac
'Beatrice Michael' (x *williamsii*)	CB&S CMac CTre SCog
'Belle of the Ball' (*japonic*)	CMHG
'Ben' (*sasanqua*)	SCog
'Benten' (*japonica*)	CTrw
'Berenice Boddy' (*japonica*)	LSav SCog SLon
'Berenice Perfection' (*japonica*)	SCog
♦ 'Bertha Harms Blush'	See C. 'Mrs Bertha A Harms'
'Betty Sheffield' (*japonica*)	CGre CTre SCog SExb
'Betty Sheffield Blush' (*japonica*)	SExb
'Betty Sheffield Pink' (*japonica*)	CMHG
'Betty Sheffield Supreme' (*japonica*)	CB&S CGre CMac SCog SExb SHil
'Betty Sheffield White' (*japonica*)	SCog
'Bienville' (*japonica*)	SCog
'Black Lace' (x *williamsii* x *reticulata*)	CTre SCog
'Blackburniana' (*japonica*)	CB&S CGre
'Blaze of Glory' (*japonica*)	CGre SCog
§ 'Blood of China' (*japonica*)	CMac MBri SCog SExb SPer WBod
'Bob Hope' (*japonica*)	CGre CTre SCog

'Bob's Tinsie' (***japonica***) CGre CTre CTrw SCog SHil
'Bokuhan' (***japonica***) CGre CTre
'Bonnie Marie' (hybrid) CGre CTre
'Bow Bells' (***saluenensis***) CGre CMac CTre GArd IJoh LHyd SCog
'Bowen Bryant' (x ***williamsii***) CGre CTre CTrw SCog
'Brigadoon' (x ***williamsii***) CMHG CTre CTrw GArd IOrc ISea LHyd MRav SCog SHil
'Brushfield's Yellow' (***japonica***) CB&S MBlu
'Bryan Wright' (***japonica***) CMHG
'Burncoose' (x ***williamsii***) CB&S
'Burncoose Apple Blossom' (x ***williamsii***) CB&S
♦ 'Bush Hill Beauty' (***japonica***) See C. 'Lady de Saumarez'
'C F Coates' (x ***williamsii***) CTre SCog
§ 'C M Hovey' (***japonica***) CMHG CMac MBal SCog SExb WBod
'C M Wilson' (***japonica***) CMac CTre SCog
'Caerhays' (x ***williamsii***) CB&S CTre SCog SReu
N 'Campbellii' (***japonica***) CMac
¶ 'Campsii Alba' (***japonica***) ELan WAbe
'Can-Can' (***japonica***) CMHG LSav SCog
'Captain Rawes' (***reticulata***) CMac CTre SHil
'Cara Mia' (***japonica***) CB&S
'Cardinal's Cap' (***japonica***) CGre
'Carolyn Williams' (x ***williamsii***) CB&S GArd
'Carter's Sunburst' (***japonica***) CB&S SCog
'Cecile Brunazzi' (***japonica***) CB&S CMac SCog
'Chandleri Elegans' (***japonica***) See C. 'Elegans'
'Charlean' (***japonica*** x ***williamsii***) SCog
'Charles Colbert' (x ***williamsii***) CTrw GArd SCog
'Charles Michael' (x ***williamsii***) CB&S CGre CMac
'Charlotte de Rothschild' (***japonica***) SExb
'Charming Betty' (***japonica***) See C. 'Funny Face Betty'
* 'Cheerio' (***japonica***) SCog
'China Clay' (x ***williamsii***) CB&S CTre SCog SHil
'China Lady' (***reticulata*** x ***granthamiana***) SCog
'Christmas Beauty' (***japonica***) SCog
chrysantha CTre
'Cinderella' (***japonica***) CTre SCog
'Citation' (x ***williamsii***) CB&S CGre CMac SCog SReu WBod
'Clarise Carleton' (***japonica***) SCog SHil
'Clarrie Fawcett' (x ***williamsii***) CTre
N 'Cleopatra' (***japonica***) SBor
'Colonel Fiery' (***japonica***) See C. 'C M Hovey'
'Colonial Dame' (***japonica***) SCog
'Compton's Brow' (***japonica***) See C. 'Gauntlettii'
'Comte de Gomer' (***japonica***) CGre MBri
'Conrad Hilton' (***japonica***) SCog
'Conspicua' (***japonica***) CSco
'Contessa Lavinia Maggi' See C. 'Lavinia Maggi'
'Coquetti' (***japonica***) See C. 'Glen 40'
'Cornish Snow' (***saluenensis*** x ***cuspidata***) CB&S CGre CMac CSam CTre GArd IJoh IOrc LNet SHil SPer SPla SReu SSpi WWat
'Cornish Spring' (***japonica*** x ***cuspidata***) CMHG GArd WWat
'Coronation' (***japonica***) SCog
'Countess of Orkney' CTre
'Crimson King' (***sasanqua***) CGre MBal SHil SPer SReu WBod
'Crinkles' (x ***williamsii***) CGre
cuspidata CGre LSav SHil SSpi
'Czar' See C. 'The Czar'
'Daikagura' (***japonica***) SCog
'Daintiness' (x ***williamsii***) MBri SCog SHil
♦ 'Daitairin' (***japonica***) See C. 'Dewatairin'
'Daphne du Maurier' (***japonica***) SCog
¶ 'Dark Nite' (***japonica***) CMHG
'Daviesii' (***japonica***) SCog
'Dazzler' (***hiemalis***) CTre
'De Notaris' (***japonica***) SExb
'Dear Jenny' (***japonica***) CB&S CTre SCog
'Debbie' (x ***williamsii***) Widely available
'Debbie's Carnation' (x ***williamsii***) CMHG SCog
'Debutante' (***japonica***) CB&S CGre CMac CTre MBri SCog SExb SPer SReu SSta WBod
'Delia Williams' (x ***williamsii***) CTrw
'Devonia' (***japonica***) CGre LHyd MBal MBri SPer
§ 'Dewatairin' (***japonica***) CMac SCog SExb WBod
'Diamond Head' (***japonica*** x ***reticulata***) MBri
'Diddy Mealing' (***japonica***) SCog
¶ 'Dobrei' (***japonica***) CMac
'Doctor Burnside' (***japonica***) CMHG SCog
'Doctor Clifford Parks' (***reticulata*** x ***japonica***) CTre SCog
'Doctor Tinsley' (***japonica***) CGre SCog SExb
'Dona Herzilia de Freitas Magalhaes' (***japonica***) CTre SCog

'Dona Jane Andresson' (***japonica***)	CMHG
'Donation' (x ***williamsii***)	Widely available
♦ 'Donckelaerii'	See C. 'Masayoshi'
¶ 'Doris Ellis' (***japonica***)	CMHG
* 'Double Rose'	SCog
'Doutor Balthazar de Mello' (***japonica***)	CMHG
'Drama Girl' (***japonica***)	CB&S CGre CTre CTrw IOrc MBal SCog SExb WBod
'Dream Boat' (x ***williamsii***)	MBri SCog
'Dream Girl' (***sasanqua*** x ***reticulata***)	SCog
'Duc de Bretagne' (***japonica***)	SCog SExb
'Duchess of Cornwall'	CTre
'Duchesse Decazes' (***japonica***)	CTre SCog
'E G Waterhouse' (x ***williamsii***)	CB&S CGre CTrw SCog SExb WBod WWeb
'E T R Carlyon' (x ***williamsii***)	CB&S CTre MBri SCog SHil
♦ 'Eclipsis'	See C. 'Press's Eclipse'
'Edith Linton' (***japonica***)	SExb
* 'Effendi' (***japonica***)	CMac
¶ 'Eleanor Hagood' (***japonica***)	CB&S
§ 'Elegans' (***japonica***)	CB&S CBow CGre CHig CMHG CMac CSco CTre ENot IHos IOrc LHyd MBal MBri MMth SCog SExb SHil SReu SSta WBod
'Elegans Champagne' (***japonica***)	SCog
'Elegans Splendor' (***japonica***)	CTre
'Elegans Supreme' (***japonica***)	CGre CTre SCog
'Elegant Beauty' (x ***williamsii***)	CB&S CTre CTrw IHos MBri MRav SCog SExb
'Elisabeth' (***japonica***)	SCog
'Elizabeth Arden' (***japonica***)	CTre WBod
'Elizabeth de Rothschild' (x ***williamsii***)	SExb
'Elizabeth Dowd' (***japonica***)	CB&S SCog
'Elizabeth Hawkins'	CTre
'Elizabeth Le Bey' (***japonica***)	SCog
'Ella Drayton' (***japonica***)	SCog
'Ellen Sampson' (***japonica***)	SCog
'Elsie Jury' (x ***williamsii***)	CB&S CGre CMac CSam CSco CTrw IHos IOrc ISea LHyd SCog SExb SSta
'Emmett Pfingstl' (***japonica***)	SCog
'Emperor of Russia' (***japonica***)	MBri SCog WBod
'Erin Farmer' (***japonica***)	CB&S SCog
§ 'Etherington White' (***japonica***)	SExb
§ 'Etoile Polare' (***japonica***)	WBod
'Evelina' (***japonica***)	SCog
'Exaltation' (hybrid)	CB&S SCog
'Exo-nishiki' (***japonica***)	CTre
'Extravaganza' (***japonica***)	SCog SHil
'Faith' (***japonica***)	SCog
'Fanny Bolis' (***japonica***)	See C. 'Latifolia Variegata'
'Fatima'	CTre
'Faustine Lechii' (***japonica***)	SCog
'Felice Harris' (***sasanqua*** x ***reticulata***)	SCog
¶ 'Fimbriata' (***japonica***)	SCog
'Fimbriata Alba' (***japonica***)	See C. 'Fimbriata'
'Finlandia Variegated' (***japonica***)	SCog
'Fire Falls' (***japonica***)	CMHG
'Firebird' (***japonica***)	CTrw
'First Flush' (***saluenensis***)	SCog
¶ 'Flame' (***japonica***)	CB&S
'Flamingo' (***sasanqua***)	See C. 'Fukuzutsumi'
'Flora' (***japonica***)	SExb WBod
'Flore Pleno' (***reticulata***)	See C. 'Robert Fortune'
'Flowerwood' (***japonica***)	SCog
'Fortyniner' (***reticulata***)	SCog
'Francie L' (***saluenensis*** x ***reticulata***)	CGre CTre CTrw SCog
'Francis Hanger' (x ***williamsii***)	CB&S CMac CSam CTre CTrw IJoh IOrc ISea MBri SCog SPer SReu SSpi
♦ 'Frau Minna Seidel'	See C. 'Usu-otome'
'Freedom Bell' (hybrid)	CTre GArd ISea SCog
'Frosty Morn' (***japonica***)	SCog
§ 'Fukuzutsumi' (***sasanqua***)	CBot
§ 'Funny Face Betty' (***japonica***)	CMHG
'Furo-an' (***japonica***)	SCog
'Galaxie' (x ***williamsii***)	CB&S ISea
§ 'Gauntlettii' ('Lotus') (***japonica***)	SCog WBod
'Gay Chieftain' (***japonica***)	SCog
'Gay Time' (x ***williamsii***)	CTre
'General Leclerc' (***japonica***)	SCog
'George Blandford' (x ***williamsii***)	CB&S CMac CTre GArd
* 'Giardino Franchetti' (***japonica***)	CGre
§ 'Gigantea' (***japonica***)	IOrc SCog
'Gladys Wannamaker' (***japonica***)	SCog
§ 'Glen 40' (***japonica***)	CTre SCog
'Glenn's Orbit' (x ***williamsii*** seedling)	CB&S CGre CTre CTrw GArd LSav SCog
'Gloire de Nantes' (***japonica***)	SCog SHil WBod
'Golden Spangles' (x ***williamsii***)	CB&S CTre ELan IJoh IOrc LHyd LSav MBri SExb SPer SPla SReu SSta
'Grace Bunton' (***japonica***)	SCog
¶ 'Grace Caple' (***pitardii*** x ***japonica***)	CMHG

Cultivar	Suppliers
'Granada' (*japonica*)	SCog
'Grand Jury' (*saluenensis* x)	CTre CTrw SCog
'Grand Prix' (*japonica*)	CMHG CTrw MBri SCog
'Grand Slam' (*japonica*)	CMHG CMac CTre CTrw ISea SCog SHil
'Guest of Honor' (*japonica*)	CB&S SCog SHil
'Guilio Nuccio' (*japonica*)	CB&S CTre ISea SCog SHil SPer SPla
'Gwavas' (x *williamsii*)	CB&S CTre
¶ 'Gwenneth Morey' (*japonica*)	CMHG
§ 'Hagoromo' (*japonica*)	CGre CMac CTre ELan ENot IHos LSav MBal MBri SExb SReu WBod WWat
'Haku-rakuten' (*japonica*)	CTre ISea SCog SExb SHil SLon
'Hana-fuki' (*japonica*)	CTre SCog
'Hana-tachibana' (*japonica*)	SExb
'Hassaku' (*japonica*)	See C. 'Beni-hassaku'
'Hatsu-zakura' (*japonica*)	See C. 'Dawatairin'
'Hawaii' (*japonica*)	CB&S CGre CMac CTre SCog
'High Hat' (*japonica*)	CGre CTrw SCog
'Hikaru-genji' ('Herme') (*japonica*)	SCog
'Hilo' (x *williamsii*)	CTrw
'Hiraethlyn' (x *williamsii*)	GArd WBod
¶ 'Hi-no-maru' (*japonica*)	CMac
'Howard Asper' (*reticulata* x *japonica*)	SCog
'Hugh Evans' (*sasanqua*)	CB&S CBot CTre
'Ice Queen' (*japonica*)	SCog
§ 'Imbricata' (*japonica*)	CTre ENot IHos SCog SExb
'Imbricata Alba' (*japonica*)	SExb SLon SReu SSta
♦ 'Imbricata Rubra'	See C. 'Imbricata'
¶ 'In the Pink' (*japonica*)	CMHG
'Innovation' (x *williamsii* x *reticulata*)	CB&S CTre IJoh ISea SCog
'Inspiration' (*reticulata* x *saluenensis*)	CB&S CGre CMHG CMac CSam CSco CTre GArd IJoh ISea LHyd LSav MBri SCog SExb SHil SPic SSpi WAbe
'Iwane-shibori' (*japonica*)	SCog
'J C Williams' (x *williamsii*)	CB&S CGre CMac CSam CTre CTrw GArd IHos IJoh IOrc ISea LHyd MRav SCog SExb SHil SPer SSpi WBod
'J J Whitfield' (*japonica*)	CMac SCog
'Jack Jones Scented' (*japonica*)	SCog
'James Allan' (*japonica*)	SPer
'Janet Waterhouse' (*japonica*)	SCog
¶ 'Jean Clere' (*japonica*)	NBar
'Jean Lyne' (*japonica*)	SCog
'Jean May' (*sasanqua*)	CB&S SCog SPic
'Jennifer Carlyon' (x *williamsii*)	CTre SCog
'Jingle Bells' (*japonica*)	SCog

Cultivar	Suppliers
'Joan Trehane' (x *williamsii*)	CTrw
'Joseph Pfingstl' (*japonica*)	CGre CMHG CTre SCog SExb
'Joshua E Youtz' (*japonica*)	SCog
'Jovey Carlyton' (hybrid)	SCog
'Joy Sander' (*japonica*)	See C. 'Apple Blossom'
'Jubilation' (hybrid)	MBri SCog
'Julia France' (*japonica*)	CB&S SCog
'Julia Hamiter' (x *williamsii* seedling)	CB&S CGre CTre CTrw ELan SCog
'Juno' (*japonica*)	SCog
'Jupiter' (*japonica*)	CB&S CMac CTre CTrw ISea LHyd LNet LSav MBal SCog SExb SHil SPla WAbe WBod
'Jury's Yellow' (x *williamsii* x *japonica*)	CB&S CMHG CTrw IJoh IOrc MBri MRav SCog SHil SSta
'K Sawada' (*japonica*)	SCog
'Kate Thrash' (*japonica*)	SCog
'Katie' (*japonica*)	SCog
'Kelvingtoniana' (*japonica*)	See C. 'Gigantea'
¶ 'Kenkyo' (*sasanqua*)	SCog
'Kenny' (*japonica*)	CB&S
'Kick Off' (*japonica*)	ELan SCog
'Kimberley' (*japonica*)	WBod
§ 'Kingyo-tsubaki' (*japonica*)	SExb WBod
'King's Ransom' (*japonica*)	CMac SCog
§ 'Konronkuro' (*japonica*)	CTre LSav SBor SCog
'Kouron-jura' (*japonica*)	See C. 'Konronkuro'
¶ 'Koyoden' (*japonica*)	LSav
'Kramer's Supreme' (*japonica*)	CGre CMHG CMac CTre LNet SCog SExb
§ 'Kumasaka' (*japonica*)	CMac CSco SExb WBod
'Kyo-nishiki' (*vernalis*)	SCog
'La Pace' (*japonica*)	SExb
'Lady Campbell' (*japonica*)	CBow SExb
'Lady Clare' (*japonica*)	See C. 'Akashi-gata'
§ 'Lady de Saumarez' (*japonica*)	CMac ELan ISea LNet SCog SExb WBod
'Lady Gowrie' (x *williamsii*)	GArd
'Lady Loch' (*japonica*)	CMHG CTre SCog
'Lady Mackinnon' (*japonica*)	SCog
'Lady Marion' (*japonica*)	See C. 'Kumasaka'
'Lady McCulloch' (*japonica*)	SCog SExb
'Lady McCulloch Pink' (*japonica*)	SCog
'Lady Vansittart' (*japonica*)	CB&S CBow CMac CSam CTre ELan ENot IHos LNet MBal MBri MMth SCog SExb SPer
§ 'Lady Vansittart Pink' (*japonica*)	CMac
'Lady Vansittart Red' (*japonica*)	See C 'Lady Vansittart Pink'

'Lalla Rookh' (*japonica*) CMac SExb
'Lanarth' (*japonica*) CTre SHil
'Lasca Beauty' (***reticulata*** x ***japonica***) SCog
'Latifolia' (*japonica*) CTre ENot SCog
'Laurie Bray' (*japonica*) CGre CMHG SCog
§ 'Lavinia Maggi' (*japonica*) CMac CTre ELan IHos IOrc LHyd MBri MRav SCog SLon SPic SReu WBod
'Lavinia Maggi Rosea' (*japonica*) SCog
§ 'Le Lys' (*japonica*) SCog SExb
'Leonard Messel' (***reticulata*** x ***williamsii***) CB&S CGre CMHG CSco CTre ENot GArd IHos IJoh LHyd LSav MBri SCog SHil SPer SReu
'Leonora Novick' (*japonica*) CMHG
'Lila Naff' (***reticulata***) CTre SCog
'Lily Pons' (*japonica*) SCog
'Little Bit' (*japonica*) SCog
'Little Lavender' (hybrid) SCog
'Lucy Hester' (*japonica*) CTre MBal SCog SPer
'Lulu Belle' (*japonica*) SCog
♦ 'L'Avvenire' (*japonica*) SCog
'Ma Belle' (*japonica*) CMHG SCog
'Madame Charles Blard' (*japonica*) SCog
¶ 'Madame de Strekaloff' (*japonica*) CMac
¶ 'Madame le Bois' (*japonica*) CB&S
'Madame Martin Cachet' (*japonica*) CMHG SCog
♦ 'Madame Victor de Bisschop' See C. 'Le Lys'
'Madge Miller' (*japonica*) CTre ELan
'Magic City' (*japonica*) SCog
'Magic Moments' (*japonica*) SExb
'Magnolia Queen' (*japonica*) SCog
'Magnoliiflora' (*japonica*) See C. 'Hagoromo'
'Maiden's Blush' (*japonica*) CMac SCog
¶ 'Man Size' (*japonica*) SCog
'Marchioness of Exeter' (*japonica*) SExb
'Margaret Davis Picotee' (*japonica*) CGre CMHG CTrw MRav SCog SHil
'Margaret Waterhouse' (x ***williamsii***) CTre SCog
'Margarete Hertrich' (*japonica*) SCog
'Margherita Coleoni' (*japonica*) CB&S SExb SPla WBod
'Marguerite Gouillon' (*japonica*) ISea SCog
'Marinka' (*japonica*) CB&S
* 'Mariottii' (*japonica*) CMac
¶ 'Mark Alan' (*japonica*) NBar
'Maroon and Gold' (*japonica*) SCog
'Mars' (*japonica*) CB&S CTre SExb SPic SPla
¶ 'Martha Brice' (*japonica*) CMHG
'Mary Charlotte' (*japonica*) SCog
'Mary Christian' (x ***williamsii***) CB&S CSco CTre LHyd MBri SPer
'Mary Costa' (*japonica*) CGre
'Mary J Wheeler' (*japonica*) CTrw MBri
'Mary Jobson' (x ***williamsii***) CB&S CTre
'Mary Phoebe Taylor' (***saluenensis*** seedling) CB&S CTre CTrw MBri SCog
§ 'Masayoshi' (*japonica*) CGre CMac CTre ENot IOrc LHyd LNet MBri SCog SExb SHil SPer SReu WBod
§ 'Mathotiana' (*japonica*) CTrw MBal SCog
'Mathotiana Alba' (*japonica*) CB&S EBre MBal SCog SExb SHil SPer SReu
'Mathotiana Purple King' (*japonica*) See C. 'Julia Drayton'
'Mathotiana Rosea' (*japonica*) CB&S CGre CMac CTre ELan ENot LNet LSav SCog SHil SPer WAbe
'Mathotiana Supreme' (*japonica*) SCog SExb
'Mattie Cole' (*japonica*) CGre CTre SCog
'Mattie O'Reilly' CTre
'Maud Messel' (***reticulata***) MBri
'Melinda Hackett' (*japonica*) SCog
'Melody Lane' (*japonica*) SCog
'Mercury' (*japonica*) CMac ENot NKay SExb SLon WBod
¶ 'Mercury Variegated' (*japonica*) CMHG
'Midnight' (*japonica*) CGre SCog
'Midnight Serenade' (*japonica*) SCog
'Midsummer's Day' (*japonica*) CB&S
§ 'Mikenjaku' (*japonica*) CMac CTre ENot LNet SExb WWeb
'Mildred Veitch' (x ***williamsii***) CGre CTre
'Ming Temple' (***reticulata***) CTre
'Minnie Maddern Fiske' (*japonica*) SExb
'Miss Charleston' (*japonica*) CB&S SCog
'Miss Frankie' (*japonica*) SCog
'Miss Universe' (*japonica*) CGre SCog
'Miya' (*japonica*) SCog
'Mona Jury' (x ***williamsii*** x ***japonica***) MBri SCog
'Monica Dance' (x ***williamsii***) CB&S
¶ 'Monsieur Faucillon' (*japonica*) LSav

'Monstruosa Rubra' (*japonica*) See C. 'Gigantea'
'Monte Carlo' (*japonica*) SCog
'Moonlight' (*japonica*) IJoh
¶ 'Moonlight Bay (*japonica*)' SCog
'Morning Glow' (*japonica*) WBod
* 'Moshe Dayan' ECtt
'Moshio' (*japonica*) MBri
§ 'Mrs Bertha A Harms' (*japonica*) CGre CMHG CTrw SCog
'Mrs D W Davis' (*japonica*) CB&S CGre CTrw SCog SPer
'Mrs William Thompson' (*japonica*) SExb
'Muskoka' (x *williamsii*) CB&S CMHG ISea
'Mutabilis' (*japonica*) SCog
* 'Mywoods' (*sasanqua*) CMac
'Nagasaki' (*japonica*) See C. 'Mikenjaku'
'Narumi-gata' (*sasanqua*) CBot CMac CTrw MBlu SCog SHil SLeo SReu WBod
'New Venture' (x *williamsii*) CB&S
'Nigra' (*japonica*) See C. 'Konronkuro'
'Nobilissima' (*japonica*) CB&S CMac CTre ELan IHos ISea LSav SCog SExb SPer SPla WBod WWeb
'November Pink' (x *williamsii*) CB&S CTre
'Nuccio's Gem' (*japonica*) CMHG MBri SCog
'Nuccio's Jewel' (*japonica*) CMHG CTre SCog
'Nuccio's Pearl' (*japonica*) SCog
oleifera CTre
'Onetia Holland' (*japonica*) CB&S CTre CTrw SCog
§ 'Oniji' (*japonica*) CTre
'Optima Rosea' (*japonica*) CTre
'Otome' (*japonica*) See C. 'Usu-otome'
¶ 'Painted Lady' (*japonica*) CMac
'Paolina' (*japonica*) SCog
'Paolina Maggi' (*japonica*) SCog
'Paul Jones Supreme' (*japonica*) CMHG SCog
'Pauline Winchester' (*japonica*) SCog SPla
'Peach Blossom' (*japonica*) See C. 'Hagoromo'
¶ 'Pearl Harbour' (*japonica*) LSav
¶ 'Pearl Maxwell' (*japonica*) CMHG
'Pensacola' (*japonica*) SCog
'Philippa Forwood' (x *williamsii*) CMac WBod
'Pink Ball' (*japonica*) SExb
'Pink Champagne' (*japonica*) CMHG CTre SCog SExb
¶ 'Pink Cherub' (x *williamsii*) LSav
'Pink Clouds' (*japonica*) SCog
'Pink Diddy' (*japonica*) MBri
'Pink Pagoda' (*japonica*) SCog
'Pink Perfection' (*japonica*) See C. 'Usu-otome'
* 'Pink Spangles' LNet
¶ 'Pirate's Gold' (*japonica*) SCog
pitardii* x *cuspidata SExb
'Plantation Pink' (*sasanqua*) SExb SPer SSpi SSta
'Pompone' (*japonica*) SCog
'Pope Pius IX' (*japonica*) See C. 'Prince Eugène Napoléon'
'Powder Puff' (*japonica*) MBri SPer
§ 'Press's Eclipse' (*japonica*) SCog
'Preston Rose' (*japonica*) CB&S CGre CMac CTre ELan MBal SExb SPer
'Pride of Descanso' (*japonica*) See C. 'Yuki-botan'
'Primavera' (*japonica*) SCog SPic
'Prince of Orange' (*japonica*) SCog
* 'Princess du Mahe' (*japonica*) CMac
'Professor Sargent' (*japonica*) SCog SExb
'Purity' (*japonica*) See C. 'Shiragiku'
♦ 'Purple Emperor' (*japonica*) See C. 'Julia Drayton'
♦ 'Quercifolia' See C. 'Kingyo-tsubaki'
'R L Wheeler' (*japonica*) CB&S CGre CTre CTrw MBal SCog SHil
'Rainbow' (*japonica*) See C. 'Oniji'
'Rebel Yell' (*japonica*) SCog
'Red Dandy' (*japonica*) SCog
'Red Elephant' (*japonica*) See C. 'King Size'
'Red Ensign' (*japonica*) SCog
'Red Rogue' (*japonica*) SCog
'Reg Ragland' (*japonica*) SCog SExb
'Rendezvous' (x *williamsii* x *japonica*) SCog SPer
reticulata CGre CTre
§ 'Robert Fortune' (*reticulata*) CTre SHil
'Rogetsu' (*japonica*) CGre
'Roman Soldier' (*japonica*) CB&S
'Rose Court' (x *williamsii*) WBod
¶ 'Rose Hollard' (*saluenensis* seedling) CMHG
'Rose Parade' (x *williamsii* x *japonica*) CGre SCog SHil
* 'Rose Quartz' ELan
'Rosea Plena' (*sasanqua*) CB&S CMac CTre CTrw
'Rosemary Williams' (x *williamsii*) CB&S CTre CTrw
¶ 'Rosie Anderson' (x *williamsii*) MBri
rosiflora CTre
'Royalty' (*japonica* x *reticulata*) CTre SCog
'Rubescens Major' (*japonica*) CB&S CGre CMac LSav SCog SHil SReu WBod
¶ 'Rubra' (*sasanqua*) CMac
¶ 'Ruby Bells' (x *williamsii*) CMHG
'Sabrina' (*japonica*) SCog

'Sacco Vera' (*japonica*) SExb
'Saint André' (*japonica*) CMac SExb
'Saint Ewe' (x *williamsii*) CB&S CGre CMac CTre CTrw ELan ENot GArd IJoh ISea MBri MRav SCog SExb SHil SPla WBod
'Saint Michael' (x *williamsii*) CB&S
* 'Salonica' ISea
saluenensis CTre LSav SExb SReu
– x *japonica* See C. x *williamsii*
'Salutation' (*saluenensis* x *reticulata*) CB&S CGre CSco SCog WBod
'San Dimas' (*japonica*) SCog
'Sarah Frost' (*japonica*) SExb
sasanqua SGar
'Satan's Robe' (*reticulata*) (hybrid) CMHG CTre SCog
'Saturnia' (*japonica*) SCog
'Sayonara' (x *williamsii*) CTre
'Scentsation' (*japonica*) CMHG CTre CTrw SCog
¶ 'Sea Foam' (*japonica*) CMHG
¶ 'Seija' (*japonica*) CMac
'Senator Duncan U Fletcher' (*japonica*) CTrw
'Serenade' (*japonica*) CMHG SCog
'Shinazuma-nishiki' (*sasanqua*) SExb
'Shin-akebono' (*japonica*) See C. 'Akebono'
§ 'Shiragiku' (*japonica*) LSav SExb
'Shiro-botan' (*japonica*) MBri SCog SPla
'Shiro-daikagura' (*japonica*) SCog
'Show Girl' (*reticulata*) CTre SCog SPic
'Sierra Spring' (*japonica*) SCog
'Silver Anniversary' (*japonica*) CB&S CMHG ELan SCog SReu SSta
'Silver Waves' (*japonica*) SCog
§ *sinensis* CGre CTre
'Snow Goose' (*japonica*) SCog
'Snowflake' (*sasanqua*) SExb WBod
'Souvenir de Bahuaud Litou' (*japonica*) CGre CTre SCog SExb SLon WBod
'Sparkling Burgundy' (*sasanqua*) CB&S CTre
'Speciosissima' (*japonica*) SCog
'Spencer's Pink' (*japonica*) CB&S CTre CTrw
'Spring Festival' (*cuspidata seedling*) SCog SHil
'Spring Mist' (*japonica* x *lutchuensis*) CMHG
'Spring Sonnet' (*japonica*) CMHG SCog
♦ 'Stella Polare' See C. 'Etoile Polaire'
§ 'Suibijin' (*japonica*) SExb
'Sunset Glory' (*japonica*) SCog
'Sunset Oaks' (*japonica*) CMHG
* 'Supreme' (*japonica*) LSav
'Sweet Delight' (*japonica*) CMHG
'Sylvia' (*japonica*) CMac WBod
taliensis CB&S CGre CTre
'Taro-an' (*japonica*) SCog
'Taylor's Perfection' (*saluenensis* seedling) CTrw
'Teresa Ragland' (*japonica*) SCog
'The Czar' (*japonica*) CB&S CTrw MBri SCog
'The Pilgrim' (*japonica*) SCog
thea See C. *sinensis*
'Thomas Cornelius Cole' CTre
'Tick Tock' (*japonica*) SCog
'Tickled Pink' (*japonica*) SCog
'Tiffany' (*japonica*) CB&S CTre LNet SCog SPic SPla
'Tinker Bell' (*japonica*) CGre SCog SHil
'Tiny Princess' (*japonica* x *fraterna*) CB&S CGre
'Tiptoe' (x *williamsii* x *japonica*) SCog
'Tom Knudsen' (*japonica*) CTre
¶ 'Tom Thumb' (*japonica*) CMHG
'Tomorrow' (*japonica*) CB&S CMHG CMac CSam CTre CTrw SCog SExb
'Tomorrow Park Hill' (*japonica*) SCog
'Tomorrow's Dawn' (*japonica*) CB&S SCog
* 'Tregye' (*japonica*) CB&S
'Trewithen Red' (*saluenensis*) CTrw
'Trewithen White' (*japonica*) CTrw MRav
'Tricolor' (*japonica*) CB&S CGre CMHG CMac CTrw ENot IHos IJoh IOrc LSav SCog SExb SHil SPer SSta
'Tricolor Red' (*japonica*) SCog
♦ 'Tricolor Sieboldii' See 'Tricolor'
'Tristrem Carlyon' (hybrid) CB&S CTre MBri SCog
tsaii CB&S
'Twilight' (*japonica*) SCog SReu
§ 'Usu-otome' (*japonica*) CMac SExb SLon WBod
'Valley Knudsen' (*saluenensis* x) SCog
'Variegata' (*sasanqua*) SSta
♦ 'Victor de Bisschop' (*japonica*) See C. 'Le Lys'
'Victor Emmanuel' (*japonica*) See C. 'Blood of China'
'Virginia Carlyon' (*japonica*) CB&S CTre
'Warrior' (*japonica*) CTre SCog
'Water Lily' (x *williamsii*) CB&S CTrw GArd ISea MRav SPla SSta
♦ 'Waterloo' See C. 'Etherington White'
'White Nun' (*japonica*) SCog
'White Swan' (*japonica*) CB&S CMac CTre SExb
'Wilber Foss' (x *williamsii*) CB&S CGre CTre CTrw
'Wildfire' (*japonica*) SCog
'William Bull' (*japonica*) SExb
'William Carylon' (*japonica* x *williamsii*) CTre WAbe
'William Hertrich' (*reticulata* seedling) CGre CTre SCog
'William Honey' (*japonica*) CMHG SCog

§ x ***williamsii***	CGre
'Winter Cheer' (*japonica*)	SCog
'Winton' (*cuspidata* x *saluenensis*)	CB&S
'Wood Nymph' (*japonica*)	CBow CTre ISea
'Woodville Red' (*japonica*)	CTre
'Yesterday' (*saluenensis* x *japonica*)	SCog
'Yoibijin' (*japonica*)	See C. 'Suibijin'
'Yours Truly' (*japonica*)	CMac CTre CTrw SCog SReu
'Yukihaki' (*japonica*)	CTrw
'Yukimi-guruma' (*japonica*)	SPla WBod
§ 'Yuki-botan' (*japonica*)	SCog SExb

CAMPANULA † (Campanulaceae)

alaskana	See C. ***rotundifolia alaskana***
alliariifolia	Widely available
– 'Ivory Bells'	See C. ***alliariifolia***
allionii	See C. ***alpestris***
§ *alpestris*	EPad GArf GEdr MBro NHol SIng
– 'Grandiflora'	EPot
alpina	GDra NNrd WPer
anchusiflora	EPad MBro WDav
¶ *argaea*	WDav
arvatica	EPad GCHN GLoc MBro MHig NGre NHol NKay NNrd SIng SSmi WAbe WDav
– *alba*	EPad MBro MHig NNrd
atlantis	EPad
aucheri	EBur EPad GEdr NNrd
autraniana	EPad
'Avalon'	EPad
barbata	ECro ELan EPad GCHN GDra GLoc MBro MCas NWCA WCla WDav WHal WHoo WPer
– *alba*	MCas WDav WHil
baumgartenii	EPad
bellidifolia	EPad GDra NBir
§ *betulifolia*	CHar EPad ESis GCHN GDra GEdr MBro MPar NGre NHol NNrd NTow WDav WHil WPer WThu
'Birch Hybrid'	CHar EBre ELan EMNN EPad ESis GDra MBal MCas NHol NNrd NRoo SIng WDav WHil WRus
bononiensis	EPad WOld
'Burghaltii'	CBot CBrd CCla CGle CHad CHan EBre ECha ELan EPad LGre MPar MShr MTho MWgw NRoo SAxl SBla SChu SMad SPer SSpi SWas WEas
§ *buseri*	CSun EPad
caespitosa	NWCA WPer
§ *calaminthifolia*	CLew EPad MHig NNrd NRed NTow WAbe WHil WOMN
§ *carnica*	EPad MBro NHol
carpatha	EPad WPer
– JCA 252.700	MBro WDav
carpatica	CGle CRiv CShe GDra LAbb MBar MBri MCot MHig MWgw NNor SIng WHoo WKif WWin
– *alba*	CGle CRiv CRow CShe NNor NOak SIng WEas WHoo
– 'Bees' Variety'	NKay
– 'Blaue Clips' ('Blue Clips')	CLew ELan EMNN EPad EPar ESis MCas MPla NGre NHar NHol NKay NNrd NRoo SCro SPla WEas
– 'Blue Moonlight'	CKel EBre EOrc EPad EPot ERou
– 'Bressingham White'	CKel CLew EBre EPad ERou GDra MRav SBla WHoo
– 'Caerulea'	CB&S
– 'Chewton Joy'	EBre EOrc EPad ESis MRav NHol NRoo SSus
– 'Ditton Blue'	EPad GDra
– dwarf form	EPot
– 'Harvest Moon'	EPad NKay
– 'Lavender'	NKay
– 'Maureen Haddon'	EBre
– 'Molly Pinsent'	CKel EPad EPot NNrd WDav WMar
– 'Queen of Sheba'	EPad
– 'Queen of Somerville'	EPad NHol NKay WHil
– 'Riverslea'	EPad NKay
– 'Snowdrift'	EPad
– 'Suzie'	SBla
– 'Weisse Clips' ('White Clips')	ELan EMNN EOrc EPad EPar EPot ESis MCas MPla NGre NHar NHol NKay NNrd NRoo SCro SPla WPer
carpatica turbinata	ECha GDra MBro MPar MTho
– – *alba*	ECha NHol NNrd
– – 'Craven Bells'	EPad WDav
– – 'Georg Arends'	GLoc
– – 'Hannah'	CHar EBre EPad GDra WMar
– – 'Isabel'	CHar EBre EPad NKay NNrd
– – 'Jewel'	CLew EPad SIng SSmi
– – 'Karl Foerster'	EBre EPad MBri NRoo
– – 'Pallida'	GDra GLoc NHol SSmi
– – 'Snowsprite'	EBre LRHS
– – 'Wheatley Violet'	CHar EBre EPad ESis MRav NHol NNrd NRoo SBla WPer
cashmeriana	EPad GCHN ITim MTho NBir SIng WAbe WPer WThu
celsii	EPad
cenisia	EPad
cephalenica	See C. ***garganica c.***
cervicaria	EPad
§ *chamissonis*	EPad EPot SOkd
§ – 'Major'	EMNN EPot NHol SIng
– 'Oyobeni'	EPad
§ – 'Superba'	GArf GLoc MBal MTho NNrd NTow SPou
§ *cochleariifolia*	Widely available
§ – *alba*	CHar CLew CShe CSun EMNN EOrc EPad GCHN MBal MCas MHig MPar MShr NGre NKay NNrd NRed NVic SBla SSmi WCla WEas WHil WPer
¶ – 'Annie Hall'	WHal
– 'Blue Tit'	EBre EPad SSus
– 'Cambridge Blue'	EBre EPad NNrd NRed SSmi SSus
§ – 'Elizabeth Oliver'	Widely available
– 'Flore Pleno'	ECtt EFol EMNN EPad MBro NNrd WDav WHil
– 'Miranda'	CHar CSpe EPad GEdr GLoc MHig NNrd NTow SSmi
– 'Miss Willmott'	EBur EPad NBir SSmi SSus
– 'Oakington Blue'	CElw EPad NHol NNrd NTow SSmi WDav
¶ – *pallida*	WDav
– 'R B Loder'	EPad

Plant	Suppliers
– 'Silver Chimes'	EMNN EPad NBir NNrd WPat
– 'Tubby'	EPad NKay NNrd
– very pale blue	NHol
– ***warleyensis***	See C. x ***haylodgensis*** 'Warley White'
collina	CRiv EPad EPot MBro MCas MPlt NNrd SCro WHil WHoo WPer
'Constellation'	EPad NNrd
coriacea	WThu
¶ – JCA 253.800	EPad WDav
'Covadonga'	CTom EPad
crispa	MBro
– JCA 253.901	EPad MBro
dasyantha	See C. ***chamissonis***
divaricata	EPad
'E K Toogood'	EPad MWat NKay NNrd SBla SCro WHil
elatines	EPad
elatinoides	EPad NNrd WPer
– JCA 254.300	WDav
'Elizabeth Orange'	See C. ***cochleariifolia*** 'Elizabeth Oliver'
ephesia	EPad SPou
eriocarpa	See C. ***latifolia***
excisa	EPad EPot ITim MHig NNrd NWCA WHil WMar
fenestrellata	EMon EPad GEdr MTho NHol NSti SSmi WHil
– ***fenestrellata***	EPad
– ***istriaca***	EPad
finitima	See C. ***betulifolia***
formanekiana	CLew EBur EPad EPot GEdr MBro MFir NHol NTow SIng WDav WPer
fragilis	ELan EPad SIng
– ***hirsuta***	ELan EPad
'G F Wilson'	EMNN EPad MBal NHol NKay NNrd
garganica	CLew EFol ELan EOrc EPad ESis GLoc MBro MCas MPit MTho NHar NKay NNrd NRed NRoo SIde SIng SPla WCla WHil WHoo WPer
– 'Aurea'	See C. ***g.*** 'Dickson's Gold'
– 'Blue Diamond'	CRiv ELan EPad ESis LHop MPit SIng
– ***cephalenica***	EPad NKay
§ – 'Dickson's Gold'	EBre EFol ELan EPad EPar EPla EPot GLoc GWic LHop MCas MHig NHol NNrd NRoo SIng WPer
– 'Major'	CSun MBro
– 'W H Payne'	EBre EBur EPad NNrd
* ***glandure***	NCat
glomerata	CB&S CBot CFis CGle CKin CRow CShe EOrc EPad GDra GPla MBal MCot MFir MTho MWat NRed NRya NSel WCla WEas WHil WWin
– ***acaulis***	CLew CRiv CSun ECro EPad EPot GCHN GHig LSav MCas MPit NNrd NOak NRoo SPla WCla WHoo WPer WWin
– ***alba***	ELan EMon EPad MBal MBro WHal WHoo
– 'Alba Nana'	EPad WWin
– ***dahurica***	CSco CSun EPad NOak WPer
– 'Joan Elliott'	ECha
– 'Purple Pixie'	EPad
– 'Schneekrone' ('Crown of Snow')	CGle ECha ECro EFou EPad GHig NNor NOak NRoo WRus
– 'Superba'	CCla CHar CKel CRiv EBre EFol ELan ENot EPad EPar ERou GHig MBri MBro MWgw NBar NNor NOrc NRoo SAxl SPer WHoo WPer
– 'White Barn'	ECha
grossekii	EPad MShr
'Hallii'	EBre EPad EPot ESis GLoc MBro MPla NGre NHol NRed NRoo WDav WOld WPat WRus
x ***haylodgensis***	CElw CRiv CRow CSpe ELan EPad EPar EPot ESis GLoc IHos MBal MCas MHig NNrd SBla SIng SPou WAbe WHal WHil WOMN WPat WThu
– 'Plena'	CHan CShe LHop NHol WEas WKif WPer
§ – 'Warley White'	CGle CSam EBre EBur ECro EFol EPad GLoc LHop NNrd NRed SBla WDav WOMN WPer
hercegovina	EPad
– ***nana***	GLoc WAbe
heterophylla	EPad MBro NHol WDav
incurva	CHan EPad GEdr LHop NNrd WHil WMar
– JCA 256.800	MBro NHol
innesii	See C. 'John Innes'
isophylla	EPad ERav MBal MBri SIng SLMG WEas
– ***alba***	EPad MBal NHol SIng SLMG
– 'Balchiniana'	EPad MTho
¶ – 'Mayi'	CSpe
– 'Variegata'	See C. ***i.*** 'Balchiniana'
'Joe Elliott'	EPad GLoc SIng WAbe WHil
§ 'John Innes'	CShe EPad
kemulariae	EPad GCHN MBro MCas MShr NHol NKay NNrd SIng SSmi WEas WHil
* ***kolenatiana***	GCHN WPer
lactiflora	Widely available
– ***alba***	CBot CKel ECha EFou EOrc EPad MRav NRoo NSti SPer SSpi WBon WEas WOld
– 'Loddon Anna'	CBow CGle CHad CKel CSco CShe ECha EFou ELan EOrc EPad ERou LHop MBri MWat MWgw NBar NRoo NSti SPer SSpi WEas WOld WRus
– 'Pouffe'	CHad CKel CSco EBre ECha EFou ELan EOrc EPad ERou GGar LHop MRav MWgw NHol NNrd NRoo NSti SCro SPer WRus
– 'Prichard's Variety'	CB&S CCla CKel CSco CShe EFou ELan EPad GGar MBri MWat NBar NRoo NSti SDix SPer
¶ – 'Violet'	WPer
– 'White Pouffe'	EBre EFou EOrc EPad LHop SCro SPer
lanata	EBar ELan EPad
lasiocarpa	EBur EPad EPot MHig MTho WPer
§ ***latifolia***	CElw CHan CKin CSev EBre ECha EFou EPad LAbb MPar NNor NOrc NRed SPer SSpi WCla WEas WHoo WPer
– ***alba***	CChu CElw CGle CHan ECha EOrc EPad MCot NNor NSti SPer WBon WEas WPer

– 'Brantwood'	EFou EPad ERou GAbr MFir NOak SCro SPer
– 'Gloaming'	EPad SIde WCot
– 'Lavender'	WHil
– 'White Ladies'	EPad SAxl
latifolia macrantha	CSco EFou EHal EPad LHil MBri MBro MRav SFis WCot WOld WPer
– – ***alba***	CSco ECtt EFou MBro WPer
§ ***latiloba***	CHad EPad LGro MWgw WEas WHil WHoo WWin
– ***alba***	CBos CBre CChu CCla CElw CFis CHan CLew CTom EFou EMon EPad GAbr GWic LGre LHil MBri MRav MShr SAxl WBon WMar WOld
– 'Hidcote Amethyst'	CBos CBre CElw CHad CTom EFou ELan EMon EPad GAbr GWic MBri MShr MUlv SApp SAxl SMad WEas WHal WHoo WKif WMar WOMN
– 'Highcliffe Variety'	EPad MShr WEas WKif WOld
– 'Percy Piper'	CElw CSco ECha EFou ELan EPad GAbr GWic MBri MRav MShr NSti NVic SPer
linifolia	See C. ***carnica***
longestyla	EPad
¶ ***lusitanica***	WPer
* 'Lynchmere'	EPad NKay NNrd
makaschvilii	EPad
mirabilis	EPad GEdr
'Mist Maiden'	CShe EPad MCas NKay NNrd SBla WDav WMar
moesiaca	EPad WMar
mollis	EPad
– ***gilbraltarica***	EPad MBro WDav WMar
morettiana	EPad
¶ – 'Alba'	EPad
muralis	See C. ***portenschlagiana***
nitida	See C. ***persicifolia planiflora***
– ***alba***	See C. ***persicifolia planiflora alba***
– ***planiflora***	See C. ***persicifolia planiflora***
'Norman Grove'	EBre EPad MCas MHig NNrd
ochroleuca	EPad
olympica	See C. ***rotundifolia*** 'Olympica'
* ***orbelica***	EPad
oreadum	EPad
orphanidea	EPad NHol
♦ ***pallida tibetica***	See C. ***cashmeriana***
parryi	EPad
patula	EPad NRed NRya WCla
– ***abietina***	EPad
persicifolia	CBre CElw CGle CHar CSev CShe EFou EHon EPad EPar GCHN MWgw NBar NNor NRoo NSti SDix SPer WAbe WBon WHil WRus WWin
§ – ***alba***	Widely available
§ – 'Alba Coronata'	EPad MBal NBir NSti WAbe
– 'Alba Plena'	See C. ***p.*** 'Alba Coronata'
– blue	EOrc WEas
– 'Boule de Neige'	CBre CHad ECha EPad NOak SAxl WEas
– 'Caerulea Coronata'	See C. ***p.*** 'Coronata'
*– 'Caerulea Plena'	CBos CBre EBar EFol
– 'Carillon'	CB&S CKel EPad
*– 'China Blue'	SFis
§ – 'Coronata'	EFou GAbr GWic
N– cup & saucer white	CChu CElw ELan LGre MBri WMar WPer
– double blue	CElw CHad EOrc MBal MPar NSti SAxl WAbe WEas WRus
– double white	CChu ELan WRus
– 'Fleur de Neige'	CElw CGle CLew EFou MBri MPar WHoo WRus
– 'Flore Pleno'	EPad SApp
– 'Frances'	EFou EMon
¶ – 'George Chiswell'	LGre
– 'Grandiflora'	CSun NHol
– 'Hampstead White'	EFou EPad EPar GWic SApp WEas WHal
– 'Hetty'	See C. ***p.*** 'Hampstead White'
– 'Moerheimii'	EPad EPar
– ***nitida***	See C. ***p. planiflora***
– ***nitida alba***	See C. ***p. planiflora alba***
*– 'Peach Bells'	EBar NOak
¶ – 'Perry's Boyblue'	NPer
– 'Pike's Supremo'	LHop
§ – ***planiflora***	CHan CHar EPad MCas WHil
§ – ***planiflora alba***	EPad GEdr MCas MWat WWin
– 'Pride of Exmouth'	CGle CLew CSco CTom EFou EMon EPad ERou GWic NNor NVic WHil WHoo WPer WRus
– ***sessiliflora***	See C. ***latiloba***
– 'Telham Beauty'	CBow CKel COtt CTom EFou ELan EOrc EPad ERou LHop MCot MFir MWgw SAxl SPer WRus
– 'Wedgwood'	MBal
N– 'White Cup and Saucer'	EMon EPla SAxl WRus
– 'White Queen'	CBre EFou NVic WBon WEas
petraea	EPad
pilosa	See C. ***chamissonis***
– ***superba***	See C. ***chamissonis*** 'Superba'
piperi	EPad NGre NNrd SOkd WHal
planiflora	See C. ***persicifolia***
§ ***portenschlagiana***	CB&S CBre CCla CElw CFis CKel ELan EPad EPar LGro MBro MCas MHig MWat NNor NNrd NRoo SBla SDix SIng SSmi WEas WHil WWin
– ***bavarica***	IDai
– ***major***	CShe NKay
– 'Resholdt's Variety'	CLew CRiv CShe EBre EFou EPad EPla GCHN MPit MUlv NNrd
poscharskyana	CFis CKel CSun ELan EPad ESis IDai LBuc LGro MBal MBri MCas NGre NKay NRoo SIng SSmi WAbe WPer
– 'Blauranke' ('Blue Gown')	GCHN
– dark form	SIng
– 'E H Frost'	CLew CShe EMNN EPad MCas MHig MPla MWat NCat NHol NKay NNrd NRed SCro SIng SSmi WHil WWin
– 'Lilacina'	SIng
– 'Lisduggan'	CElw EPad MBal MCas MShr MWat NNrd SBla WAbe WHil
– 'Stella'	CShe EMNN EPad ESis GCHN MCas MRav NCat NNrd NRed NRoo NVic SChu SDix SSpi WEas
primulifolia	EPad
x ***pseudoraineri***	EPad GLoc MTho NGre NNrd

pulla	CHar CLew ELan EPad EPar EPot ESis GEdr GLoc MCas MHig MPar MPla MTho NHol NNrd SSmi WHal WPat WPer WWin
x *pulloides*	CLew EPad NNrd SSmi
punctata	CBot CBrd ECro EFol EFou EPad GCHN MCot MFir MTho NHol NSti SBla SWas WCla WPer WWin
– *alba*	EFol EPad MBri MShr
– *hondoensis*	EPad WDav
– *nana alba*	GPla WPer
– 'Pallida'	EPad
– *rosea*	CLew MPar NKay WHil
– 'Rubriflora'	CChu EGol ELan EPad LHop MShr NOak NRoo WPer
pusilla	See C. ***cochleariifolia***
pyramidalis	CBot CHad EFou EPad LAbb MShr NOrc WHil WPer
– *alba*	EFou EPad GHig MShr
¶ – *rhomboidea*	WEas
radchensis	EPad
raddeana	CRiv EPad GEdr MBal MBro MShr NGre NKay NNrd NRed SSmi WCla WDav WMar WPer
raineri	EBur EPad EPot GArf GLoc ITim NWCA SIng WAbe WThu
§ *rapunculoides*	CArn EBar EPad GGar LHop NSti SBla WHer WPer
– 'Alba'	EPad LHop
* *recurva*	CGle
reddiana	GCHN
rhomboidalis	See C. ***rapunculoides***
rotundifolia	CGle CKin CNat CRow CSun EPad NLan NNrd NRoo SCro WCla WPer
§ – *alaskana*	EPad NBir NWCA
– *alba*	CRow WHoo
♦– *caerulea plena*	See C. ***r.*** 'Flore Pleno'
*– 'Flore Pleno'	CBos CGle
– 'Olympica'	CShe EBar EPad GCHN MBro MShr NHol WHoo
rupestris	EPad EPot MBro WDav WThu
rupicola	EPad
sarmatica	CElw CGle CSun EPad NSti SIng WCar WCla WPer
sartorii	See C. ***calaminthifolia***
saxatilis	EPad NRed WHal
– *saxatilis*	EPad
saxifraga	EPad GLoc
scabrella	EPad
shetleri	EPad GEdr NNrd
sibirica	EPad WPer
spathulata	EPad
– *spruneriana*	EPad
speciosa	EPad
spicata	EPad
sp. ex Furze	MPar
sp. JCA 6872	EPad
x *stansfieldii*	EPad EPot NNrd
¶ *stevenii*	WDav
sulphurea	EPad
takesimana	Widely available
thessala	EPad EPot NWCA
thyrsoides	EPad GAbr GDra GEdr NWCA WCar WCla WDav WPer
– *carniolica*	EPad
tommasiniana	EPad WCar WHil WOMN WPer
topaliana	EPad MPar
trachelium	CGle CKin CSun EBar EOrc EPad NHol NSti WCla WHer WHil WPer
– *alba*	CElw CGle EPad WHil WPer
– 'Alba Flore Pleno'	CBos CHar CRow ECha ELan EMon EPad MCot SBla SWas
– 'Bernice'	CBos CHad CRow EFou ELan EMon EOrc EPad EPar MBri SCro SPer WBon WRus
tridentata	EPad
troegerae	EPad LRHS SBla
– JCA 265.500	WDav
* 'Tubby'	GCHN
tubulosa	See C. ***buseri***
x *tymonsii*	EBur EPad MCas MHig NBir NKay NNrd NTow WHil
'Van Houttei'	CBos EMon GWic
versicolor	EPad NHol NSti WEas WOMN WPer
– Coll 3347	EMon
§ *vidalii*	CBot CPle CSpe CSun EPad GCHN NPer WPer
*– 'Rosea'	EPad
waldsteiniana	CHar EPad EPot GEdr NNrd NTow
– JCA 266.000	MBro NHol WDav
'Warley White'	See C. x ***haylodgensis*** 'W.W.'
'Warleyensis'	See C. x ***haylodgensis*** 'Warley White'
* *witasekiana*	WDav
x *wockei*	See C. x ***w.*** 'Puck'
§ – 'Puck'	CRiv EPad GDra GLoc MCas MPla NNrd SPou WPat
* 'Yvonne'	WEas WHoo WOMN
zoysii	EPad MCas MHig

CAMPHOROSMA (Chenopodiaceae)

monspeliaca	NHol

CAMPSIS (Bignoniaceae)

* 'Flamingo'	IOrc LHop
grandiflora	CB&S CBra CPle CSco ELan ENot MR&S NPal SCro SHil SPer SSpi SSta
radicans	CArn CBot CChu CHEx CLew CMac ELan ENot MWat SHil SPer WSHC
§ – *flava*	CB&S CMac EBre ELan IHos IJoh IOrc MBri MWat NPal SBra SHil SPer SSpi SSta
– 'Yellow Trumpet'	See C. ***r. flava***
¶ x *tagliabuana* 'Guilfoylei'	CB&S NBar
– 'Madame Galen'	CB&S CCla CMac CSco CShe IJoh IOrc LHop MBri MGos NBar SBra SHil SMad SPer SSpi SSta SSus WBod WSHC

CAMPTOSORUS (Aspleniaceae)

CAMPYLOTROPIS (Leguminosae)

CANARINA (Campanulaceae)

canariensis	ERea WOMN

CANDOLLEA See HIBBERTIA

CANNA † (Cannaceae)

'Black Knight'	LAma
'Endeavour'	MSta

'Erebus'	MSta
'Firebird'	MBri
¶ x *generalis*	CHEx
'Golden Lucifer'	LAma MBri
hybrids	LBow
indica	CHEx ERav LBow LHop SLMG WCot
– 'Purpurea'	SDix WCot
– variegata	LBow
iridiflora	SDix
*– *ehrmanii*	CHEx
¶ 'Lucifer'	WCar
¶ *lutea*	WCot
malawiensis 'Variegata'	LHop
¶ *musifolia*	SDix
'Orchid'	LAma MBri WCar
'Picasso'	LAma
'President'	LAma MBri
'Ra'	MSta
¶ 'Tirol'	LHil
warscewiczii	SLMG
'Wyoming'	LAma SHig
'Yellow Humbert'	LAma LHil SHig

CANTUA (Polemoniaceae)

buxifolia	CGre CHil CPle CTre SHil SSpi

CAPSICUM (Solanaceae)

annum	MBri
*– 'Janne'	MBri

CARAGANA (Leguminosae)

arborescens	CChu ENot IJoh MBar SHil SLHN SPer
– 'Lorbergii'	CBow CSco IOrc MBlu MPla NHol SHil SPer
– 'Pendula'	CLnd CSco ELan MBar MUlv SExT SGar SHil SPer
– 'Walker'	CB&S IJoh IOrc MBlu MBri MGos MR&S MUlv NBar SHil SMrm SPer
aurantiaca	MBri
brevispina	CHan 2ok
¶	CHan franchetiana
frutex 'Globosa'	MBri SPer
pygmaea	CSco SSta

CARDAMINE (Cruciferae)

¶ *asarifolia*	CRow
bulbifera	CHan LHop
enneaphyllos	CFor GWic
§ *heptaphylla*	ECro ELan IBlr NKay
§ *kitaibelii*	ECro EPar SIng
latifolia	See C. *raphanifolia*
§ *pentaphyllos*	ECro ELan EPar GGar NKay NSti
pratensis	CArn CKin CRow CWGN EHon MSal NLan SFir WCla WHer WOak
*– 'Edith'	EMon
– 'Flore Pleno'	Widely available
¶ – 'Improperly Dressed'	EMon
¶ – 'William'	EMon
quinquefolia	SWas
§ *raphanifolia*	CBre CGle CLew CRow ECha EMon GAbr GGar GWic NCat NVic SIng
trifolia	CChu CCla CElw CFor CRiv ECha EPar GPla GWic NHol NKay NNor NNrd NTow SBla SIng SWas WEas WHer WHil WOMN
*– *digitata*	MTho

CARDIOCRINUM (Liliaceae/Liliaceae)

cordatum glehnii	EBul
giganteum	CB&S CBot CBrd CHEx EPar GEdr IBar IBlr LAma MBlu SMad SSpi WChr
– yunnanense	EBul

CARDIOSPERMUM (Sapindaceae)

¶ *grandiflorum*	CPle
¶ *halicacabum*	CHil

CARDUNCELLUS (Compositae)

¶ *mitissimus*	SIng
rhaponticoides	EBre ITim MUlv

CARDUUS (Compositae)

benedictus	See CNICUS *b.*
nutans	CKin

CAREX (Cyperaceae)

**albida*	CElw CHoe EPar MBal
atrata	CHoe SIng
berggrenii	CElw CHoe CRow ECou EPar LGre NHol NNrd NSti SBar SBla SSpi WHil
– narrow-leaved form	CHoe SApp
boottiana	GGar SApp
brunnea 'Variegata'	EPar GGar
buchananii	CElw CHad CHan CHoe CRow ELan ELun EMon EOrc EPar ERou GWic IBar IBlr MBal MPar MTho SApp SAxl SIng SMad SSpi WWat
– 'Viridis'	WHer
comans	CElw CHoe CLew EMon EPar GCHN GGar GWic IBlr MBal SApp SAxl SIng SSpi WDav WWat
– 'Bronze Form'	CHoe CRow ECou EFol EMon EPar EPla EPot MBri NNrd NSti SApp SSpi WOMN WWat
§ *conica*	CHoe EFol LHop MBri MWgw NHol SIng SSpi
♦– 'Hino-kan-sugi'	See C. *c.* 'Snowline'
§ – 'Snowline'	CElw CRow CTom ELan EMon EPla GCHN MBri MDHE NHol NWCA SApp WRus
¶ *dallii*	ECou
¶ *depauperata*	CNat EMon SApp
dipsacea	CElw CHoe CRow ECou SFar SSpi
§ *elata* 'Aurea'	CChu CCla CHad CHan CHoe CRow CSco CWGN ECha EFol EGol EHon EPar MBri MSta SApp SBla SHig SIng SSpi WEas WRus
* 'Everbright'	CB&S
firma	EPla MHig NNrd
– 'Variegata'	CRiv EPar MCas MDHE MTho NHol NTow NWCA SIng WHil WRus
flagellifera	CB&S CHoe CRow ECou EGol EMon GGar NHol WEas
fortunei 'Variegata'	See C. *morrowii* 'V.'
fraseri	GWic

* 'Frosted Curls'	CHan CHoe ELan GWic IBar MBri MUlv NHol NSti SApp SMad SSpi WWat
grayi	EMon GWic MTho SApp
N 'Hime-kan-suge'	See C. ***conica***
* *hirta*	CKin
kaloides	CHoe ECou
morrowii	ELan EOrc ERou IBlr MDHE NSti SPer
– 'Evergold'	See C. ***oshimensis*** 'E.'
– 'Fisher's Form'	CBrd CHan CHoe EGol SApp SSpi WCot
*– 'Nana Variegata'	NBir
§ – 'Variegata'	CElw CFor CGle CHan CHoe CMHG CRiv CRow EFol ELan ELun EMon ERou LSav MBal MCot SApp SIng SLon SSpi WWat
muricata	CKin
muskinguemensis	CElw CHoe EMon SApp SMad SSpi
– 'Wachtposten'	GWic
nigra	CKin
– *tornata*	SIng
ornithopoda	NNrd WHil
– *aurea*	See C. ***o.*** 'Variegata'
§ – 'Variegata'	CHoe CRiv EGol EPar GPla GWic MBal MCas NHar NHol SApp SSmi WRus WWat
§ *oshimensis* 'Evergold'	Widely available
– 'Variegata'	CElw CHoe
pendula	CElw CHoe CKin CRow CWGN ECha ELan EMon ERou GAbr GCHN MBal MFir MSta MWgw NCat NHol NLan NNor NOrc NRar SAxl SMad SSpi
petriei	CElw CHoe CRow EBar ECha ECro EGol EPla GAbr NNrd NRar NSti NVic SApp WHil
pilulifera 'Tinney's Princess'	CHoe CTom SApp SOkd SSpi
plantaginea	EMon SApp
pseudocyperus	CKin MCot MSta
riparia 'Variegata'	CHan CHoe CRiv CRow ECha EFol EPar GWic MBri SApp SCro SSpi
* *saxatilis* 'Variegata'	SApp
secta	CHoe NHol
– *tenuiculmis*	CHoe NHol
siderosticta	WSHC
– 'Variegata'	CElw CFor CGle CHoe CMHG CRow EMon IBar LHop MBri NHol NVic SApp SAxl SIng WWat
¶ *solandri*	SApp
spicata	CKin
stricta 'Bowles' Golden'	See C. ***elata*** 'Aurea'
sylvatica	CKin
testacea	CHoe ECou EFol EGol ELan EMon MBar MBri SFar SSpi
trifida	CHoe CTom GAbr GCHN GWic LSav
umbrosa 'The Beatles'	CHoe GWic SApp
¶ *uncifolia*	CHoe ECou
vulpina	CKin

CARICA (Caricaceae)

¶ *pubescens*	SArc

CARISSA (Apocynaceae)

bispinosa	SLMG

CARLINA (Compositae)

¶ *acanthifolia*	ECro GWic WPer
acaulis	ECro ECtt NSti SDix SFis SIng SPou WEas WPer
– *caulescens*	See C. ***a. simplex***
§ – *simplex*	CBrd ECha ECro MBri NHol NRar NRoo WHoo
vulgaris	CKin

CARMICHAELIA (Leguminosae)

aligera	ECou
angustata	ECou
arenaria	ECou
astonii	ECou
australis	CB&S WBod
curta	ECou
enysii	ITim SHil
– *ambigua*	ECou
– 'Pringle'	ECou
exsul	ECou
glabrata	ECou
kirkii	ECou
¶ – x *astonii*	ECou
monroi	ECou
nigrans	ECou
¶ *odorata*	ECou
orbiculata	ECou
ovata	ECou
petriei	ECou SHil SPer
uniflora	ECou
violacea	ECou
williamsii	ECou

X CARMISPARTIUM (Leguminosae)

♦ *astens*	See X C. ***hutchinsii***
§ *hutchinsii*	ECou
– 'County Park'	ECou

CARPENTERIA (Hydrangeaceae/Philadelphaceae)

californica	Widely available
– 'Bodnant'	SHil
– 'Ladhams' Variety'	CB&S LGre LHop

CARPINUS † (Carpinaceae)

betulus	CB&S CBra CKin CLnd CTre ELan ENot GRei IHos IJoh ISea LBuc MBar MBri NWea SHil SPer SReu WMou WNor
– 'Columnaris'	ENot
§ – 'Fastigiata'	CB&S CLnd CSco ENot GRei IJoh IOrc MBar MGos NWea SExT SHil SPer WMou
– 'Pendula'	WMou
– 'Purpurea'	CB&S ENot SExT
– 'Pyramidalis'	See C. ***b.*** 'Fastigiata'
¶ – 'Quercifolia'	WMou
– 'Variegata'	WMou
caroliniana	CLnd CMCN MBlu SHil WCoo WMou WNor
cordata	WCoo
coreana	WCoo
§ *fargesii*	SHil
henryana	CMCN
japonica	SHil SSpi WCoo
laxiflora	CMCN ELan SSpi WCoo WMou WNor
– *macrostachya*	See C. ***fargesii***
orientalis	CMCN WNor
schisiensis	ELan MBri

tschonoskii WCoo WNor
turczaninowii SHil WNor

CARPOBROTUS (Aizoaceae)
§ *edulis* CHEx IBlr NGre SLMG WHer

CARTHAMUS (Compositae)
tinctorius MSal SIde WHer

CARUM (Umbelliferae)
carvi CArn CSFH Effi GPoy LHol MChe NSel SIde WOak WPer WSto
petroselinum See PETROSELINUM **crispum**

CARYA † (Juglandaceae)
aquatica WCoo
cordiformis CMCN EHar LSav SHil SSpi WCoo
glabra CMCN
illinoinensis CMCN LSav SHil
laciniosa CMCN LSav
ovata CMCN EHar SHil SSpi WCoo
tomentosa CMCN LSav

CARYOPTERIS † (Verbenaceae)
x *clandonensis* CB&S CBot CBra CPle CSco CTre CTrw ELan ENot ERav GRei IDai ISea LHop MFir MR&S MWat NKay NNor WBod WEas WRus WSHC WWat
– 'Arthur Simmonds' CBow ECha EGol EHal MBal MBri SHil SLon SMad SPer
– 'Ferndown' CArn CBow CSco CShe EGol LHop NKay SPer SReu SSpi WSHC WWeb
– 'Heavenly Blue' Widely available
– 'Kew Blue' CB&S CBot CHan CSco CShe EFou EGol ELan ENot MGos SAxl SMad SPer SPla SSta WRus WSHC
– 'Worcester Gold' CBot ECha EHal ERav LHop MWat WPat WPer WRus WWeb WWin
incana CSco CShe ERav GWic LHop SDry WSHC
¶ – weeping form GWic

CARYOTA (Palmae)
mitis LPal

CASSANDRA See CHAMAEDAPHNE

CASSIA (Leguminosae)
¶ *artemisioides* CPle
N *corymbosa* CB&S CBot CHEx CPle CTre ERea LAbb SLMG
¶ *hebecarpa* MSal
marilandica LGre MSal
N *obtusa* CB&S CGre CHil MNew SHil
* *retusa* CTrw

CASSINIA (Compositae)
leptophylla CPle EBar SPer WThu
– *fulvida* CB&S CBow CHoe CMHG ECou GRei IBar IJoh IOrc ISea ITim MBar MBlu NNor NTow SBor SHil SIng SPer STre WBod WEas WThu
– *vauvilliersii* CKni CMHG NNor WSHC
– *vauvilliersii albida* CB&S ECou SHil SPer WBod
retorta ECou IBar NNor SPer
¶ *sturtii* CPle
¶ 'Ward Silver' NNor

CASSINIA X HELICHRYSUM WKif

CASSIOPE † (Ericaceae)
¶ 'Askival' ITim
'Badenoch' GDra GHig MBal NHar NHol SIng WAbe
'Bearsden' GDra GEdr GLoc MBal NHar NHol NKay NNrd WPat WThu
'Edinburgh' CRiv EPot GAbr GDra GEdr GHig GLoc MBal MBar MBri NHar NHol NNrd SGar WAbe WPat WThu
fastigiata GEdr
– B 542 MBal
– LS&H 17451 MBal
'George Taylor' WAbe
hypnoides GEdr
'Kathleen Dryden' GDra GEdr MBal NHar
lycopodioides EPot GAbr GDra GEdr GHig MBal MBar MBri MGos NHar NHol NKay NNrd SHil SIng SReu WAbe WBod WPat WThu
– 'Beatrice Lilley' CRiv EPot GEdr MBal MBar MHig NHol WPat
– 'Major' WBod
¶ – *minimus* GArf
'Medusa' EPot GDra GLoc MBal MHig SIng WAbe WPat
mertensiana CRiv MBal MBar NHol WAbe WBod
– *californica* GArf
¶ – *ciliolata* NHol
– dwarf form MBal
– *gracilis* ELan GAbr GHig GLoc MGos MHig NHar NHol SIng SPer
'Muirhead' EPot GDra GEdr GHig GLoc MBal MBar MHig NHar NHol NKay NNrd SHil SPer WAbe WBod WPat
'Randle Cooke' EPot GDra GEdr GLoc MBal MBar MBri MHig NHar NKay SIng WPat WThu
selaginoides GEdr
– LS&E 13284 GEdr
stelleriana SSta
tetragona GEdr MBal MBar MBri NHol SPer WAbe
– *saximontana* EPot MBal NHol
wardii x *fastigiata* Askival Strain GEdr

CASTANEA † (Fagaceae)
¶ *mollissima* LSav
sativa CB&S CBra CHEx CKin CLnd CPer ENot GRei IJoh IOrc ISea LBuc MBar MBri MR&S NRog NWea SHil SPer SPla WAbe WCoo WMou WOMN
– 'Albomarginata' CSco EHar MBlu SExT SHil SSpi
– 'Argenteovariegata' MBri SSta
§ – 'Aureomarginata' See C. *s.* 'Variegata'
F – 'Marron de Lyon' ESim SHil
§ – 'Variegata' ELan MBri

CASTANOPSIS (Fagaceae)
cuspidata SArc WCoo

CASUARINA (Casuarinaceae)
cunninghamiana ISea
stricta See ALLOCASUARINA *verticillata*

CATALPA † (Bignoniaceae)
bignonioides CB&S CBot CBra CHEx CLnd CSco ELan ENot IBar IOrc ISea MBri NPal SHil SPer WCoo
– 'Aurea' Widely available
– 'Purpurea' See C. x *erubescens* 'P.'
*– 'Variegata' LNet SPer SSta
bungei SExT SGar
– 'Purpurea' ELan
x *erubescens* 'Purpurea' CB&S CBot CHEx COtt EHar IOrc MBlu MBri SHil SMad SPer SSpi
fargesii GWic
– *duclouxii* SHil
ovata CBot CGre CHEx GWic LSav WCoo
speciosa CB&S CHEx CMCN SExT SHil SSpi WMou

CATANANCHE (Compositae)
caerulea CBow CBre CFis CHan CHar CSco CSev ECha EFou ELan EOrc ERou LHop MBri MBro MWgw NRoo NSti SPer WOMN WOld WWin
– *alba* CSev ECha EFou GWic LHop NBir NOak WHal WRus
– *major* CKel CShe ENot GWic MWat WEas

CATHARANTHUS (Apocynaceae)
roseus MBri
– *ocellatus* MBri

CAULOPHYLLUM (Berberidaceae)
thalictroides MSal WChr

CAUTLEYA † (Zingiberaceae)
spicata CHEx IBlr IBrk SMad
– 'Robusta' CCla CKni CSam EBre

CEANOTHUS † (Rhamnaceae)
'A T Johnson' CMHG CMac CPle ENot EPla LNet NKay SHil SPer SReu WAbe WBod WWeb
americanus CArn MSal
¶ – 'Fincham' EPla
arboreus SArc
– 'Trewithen Blue' Widely available
'Autumnal Blue' Widely available
azureus See C. *coeruleus*
'Blue Boy' LSav
* 'Blue Cushion' CB&S LHop MGos
¶ 'Blue Jeans' EMon
'Blue Mound' CBow CSco CTrw EBre EGol EPla ERav IJoh LAbb LHop MGos SHil SPer SReu SSpi WSHC
'Burkwoodii' CB&S CBow CBra CMHG CMac CPle CSco GRei IDai IOrc MBal MBri MPit NWea SBla SChu SHil SLon SPer SReu
'Burtonensis' ENot WAbe
'Cascade' CB&S CBra CChu CLan CMHG CMac CSam CSco CShe ELan ENot IOrc ISea LNet MBri MWat SHil SLon SPer SPla SSta WAbe WBod WSHC
§ *coeruleus* WWeb
'Concha' CB&S CGre CPle CTre EGol ERav LHop LSav MBri MUlv SSpi SSta WWat WWeb
cyaneus CGre
¶ 'Dark Star' LRHS
'Delight' CGre IDai IOrc LAbb MR&S NNor SChu SHil SPer WAbe WBod WWat
x *delileanus* 'Gloire de Versailles' Widely available
– 'Henri Desfossé' CSco ERav LHop MBri MR&S SHil SPer WKif WWeb
– 'Topaz' CPle CSco CShe ENot MR&S NSti SHil SLon WBod
dentatus CB&S CBra CMac CPle CSam CSco EGol ELan ENot ERav GRei IJoh IOrc MBal MGos MR&S NKay NNor SChu SHil SLon SPer WBod
– *floribundus* CBow CSco ELan SDix
*– 'Prostratus' MBal
'Dignity' CGre CLan CSco WWeb
divergens CMac LHop SPer
'Edinburgh' CBow CMac ELan ENot MBri WBod
fendleri CGre
foliosus CGre
– *austromontanus* CLan CTrw IDai
gloriosus CCla IOrc SDry WWat
– 'Emily Brown' CB&S IJoh
griseus CGre
¶ – *horizontalis* SDry
– *horizontalis* 'Yankee Point' CB&S CBra CChu CMac CPle CSam CSco LBuc LHop LNet LSav MPit SLon SPer WWeb
– 'Hurricane Point' CB&S
impressus CB&S CBow CBra CHad CLan CMHG CSco CShe EBre ELan ENot IJoh MBal MBri MR&S MWat SDix SHil SLon SPer SPla SReu SSpi WBod
'Italian Skies' CBra CLan CMHG CMac CSam CSco CShe ELan LHop LSav MR&S MRav SHil SPer WBod WWeb
'Joyce Coulter' CB&S
¶ 'Ken Taylor' LRHS
x *lobbianus* CGre SHil
– 'Russellianus' LSav SLon WBod
– 'Southmead' CB&S CBow CBra CMac IJoh IOrc ISea LSav MBri MWat SCro SHil SReu WBod WWat
x *pallidus* 'Marie Simon' CB&S CPle ECtt ELan ERav IJoh LHop MBri MR&S MRav SAxl SLon SPer WAbe WKif WSHC
– 'Perle Rose' CB&S CBow CMac IOrc SChu SPer SReu WAbe WMar
papillosus CBra CGre CLan CMHG CMac CPle CSco ELan LSav WAbe
– *roweanus* CGre CMac CPle LRHS LSav SDry SHil WWat
prostratus CBow CGre EPla IDai LGro MCot SDry SHil WAbe WWin

'Puget Blue' CB&S CBra CCla CLan CMHG CMac CSam CSco ELan IBar LHop LSav MBri MGos MWat NTow SHil SPer SSpi SSta WBod WKif WSHC
purpureus CPle MWat SDry WWeb
'Ray Hartman' CGre SMad
*x ***regius*** LHop
repens See C. ***thyrsiflorus r.***
rigidus CGre MGos SDry SHil WBod
'Sierra Blue' WBod
'Snow Flurries' CB&S ERav LHop SLon SReu
thyrsiflorus CB&S CHad CMac ELan IJoh LNet MBal MBri SArc SHil SPer WAbe WBod
§ – ***repens*** Widely available
¶ – 'Skylark' LRHS
x ***veitchianus*** CB&S CBra CChu CCla CMac CSam CSco CShe CTre ELan ENot IJoh LNet MBar MR&S MWat NHol SHil SLon SPer SPla WBod

CEDRELA See TOONA

CEDRONELLA (Labiatae)

§ ***canariensis*** CArn CFis CHan CMer CSev CTre GPoy GWic IBlr LHol LHop MSal NSel SIde WHer WOak WPer
♦ ***mexicana*** See AGASTACHE ***m.***
♦ ***triphylla*** See C. ***canariensis***

CEDRUS (Pinaceae)

atlantica See C. ***libani a.***
brevifolia EHar ELan MBar MBlu MBri NHol SHil SLHN SSta WAbe
– 'Horizon' CKen
– 'Kenwith' CKen
deodara Widely available
– 'Albospica' MBri WCon
– 'Argentea' MBar MGos
– 'Aurea' CB&S CBow CBra CDoC CSco EHar EHul IJoh MBar MBri SExT SGar SHil SPla SReu SSta WAbe WCon WMou
– 'Aurea Pendula' ENHC
¶ – 'Blue Dwarf' MBri WCon
– 'Cream Puff' EBre LLin MBri WCon
– 'Feelin' Blue' CKen LRHS MBri MGos NBar
– 'Gold Cone' EBre MGos
– 'Gold Mound' EBre MBar MBri MPla NHol WCon
– 'Golden Horizon' CBow CBra CDoC CKen CMac CSco EBre EHar EHul ENHC IJoh IOrc LLin MBar MBri MGos NHol SHil SPer SSta SSus WAbe WCon
– 'Golden Jubilee' MBri
I – 'Inversa Pendula' SExT
– 'Karl Fuchs' EBre LRHS MBri WCon
– 'Kashmir' MBri WCon
– 'Klondyke' NHol WCon
– 'Lime Glow' CKen
*– 'MacPenny's Seedling' CMac
– 'Nana Aurea' EBre
– 'Nivea' CKen
– 'Pendula' CMac EHul MBar MBri MGos SGar
N– 'Prostrata' SExT
– 'Pygmy' CKen SHil
¶ – 'Robusta' WCon
– 'Verticillata Glauca' MBri SGar
libani CB&S CBow CBra CDoC CMac CSco EHar EHul ENot IJoh IOrc ISea LSav MBar MBri NWea SHil SMad SPer WCon WMou WNor WWat
– 'Comte de Dijon' EHul SHil
– 'Nana' CKen EHul SGar WCon
– 'Sargentii' CDoC CKen CMac CSco EBre EHar EHul MBal MBar MBri MGos SExT SHil SSta WAbe WCon
– 'Taurus' NHol
§ ***libani atlantica*** CBra CDoC EHar EHul ISea MBar NWea SExT SHil WCon WMou
– – 'Aurea' CB&S CDoC CMac CSco EHar EHul IJoh MBar MBri MGos SExT SHil SPer SSta WCon
– – 'Fastigiata' CDoC CMac EHar EHul MBar MBri WCon WMou
– – 'Glauca Fastigiata' CB&S CKen EHar MBri SMad WCon
– – Glauca group Widely available
– – 'Glauca Pendula' CDoC CKen CSco EHar EHul IOrc LNet LPan MBal MBar MBri MGos MR&S SExT SGar SHil SMad SPer SSta WAbe WCon
– – 'Pendula' CMac IJoh MGos SHil

CELASTRUS (Celastraceae)

hypoleucus SSta
orbiculatus CBra CHad CHan CMCN CSco ELan EMon MFir MPla MPlt MWat SCro SHil SPer SReu SSta WBod WSHC WWat
– 'Diana' SLHN SSta
– hermaphrodite form CCla ELan EOvi SBra SDix SSpi WWat
scandens CMac ELan EOvi MSal MWat

CELMISIA (Compositae)

alpina NNrd
argentea GArf MHig
bellidioides CRiv EMNN GArf GDra GEdr GLoc ITim NHol NNrd NRed SIng SOkd WDav
brevifolia GHig
coriacea IBlr NNor SBar WEas
gracilenta GArf MHig
hectorii IBlr ITim MHig
Inshriach hybrids GAbr MBal
ramulosa GArf GEdr IBlr ITim MHig
¶ ***semicordata*** SIng WPer
¶ ***sessiliflora*** ITim WPer
§ ***walkeri*** IBlr IDai ITim WAbe
♦ ***webbiana*** See C. ***walkeri***

CELOSIA (Amaranthaceae)

cristata MBri
– Plumosa group MBri

CELSIA See VERBASCUM

X CELSIOVERBASCUM See VERBASCUM

CELTIS (Ulmaceae)

australis SExT SSpi
bungeana CMCN
occidentalis CPle EHar SHil SSpi SSta WCoo
reticulata WCoo

sinensis	CMCN WCoo

CENTAUREA (Compositae)

¶ *babylonica*	MFir
bella	CBot CCla CGle CHar EFou EGol ELan EMon EOrc GWic LGre LHop MBri MTho NHol NRoo NSti SMrm
¶ *benoistii*	EMon
cana 'Rosea'	See C. ***triumfettii cana rosea***
candidissima	See C. ***rutifolia***
§ *cheiranthifolia purpurascens*	EMon
chilensis	CHan
§ *cineraria cineraria*	CFis CSpe IDai NRar WPer
cyanus	CNat MSal
cynaroides	See LEUZEA ***centauroides***
dealbata	CHan CHar CTom EBar ECro MFir NCat NKay NOak NOrc NRoo SChu WHil WHoo WWin
– 'Steenbergii'	CSco EBre ELan MBri SCro SPer
debeauxii nemoralis	CKin
fischeri	See C. ***cheiranthifolia purpurascens***
¶ *glastifolia*	EMon
gymnocarpa	See C. ***cineraria cineraria***
hypoleuca 'John Coutts'	CHad CKel CSam CSco EBre EFol ELan EPar ERou LGre LHop MRav NOrc NSti NTow SChu SPer SSus WEas WHil WSto
* *imbricans*	NCat
¶ *jacea*	LGan
macrocephala	Widely available
montana	CBre CHad CRow ECro EFol ELan GCHN IDai MCot MFir NBar NNor NOak NOrc NVic WBon WEas WHal WHil WOak WOld WPer WWin
– *alba*	CBre CElw CSev CTom ECha EFol EGol ELan EMon EOrc GCHN LGre MBri MFir MPar NCat SChu SMad SPer WEas WHil
§ – *carnea*	CBre CElw CTom EMon WBon WWin
– 'Grandiflora'	MBri
– 'Ochroleuca'	EMon
– 'Parham'	CBre EMon ERou GCHN SChu SMrm WHil
– *purpurea*	CBre CTom SPer
– *rosea*	See C. ***m. carnea***
¶ – 'Violetta'	NBir
nigra	CArn CKin MSal NLan SFir WCla WPer
pulcherrima	ECha EFol
'Pulchra Major'	CGle CSco EBre ECha EGol ELan GWic LGre
§ *rutifolia*	EBar WHil
scabiosa	CKin CNat MSal NLan SFir WCla WPer
simplicicaulis	CBos EBre MRav NRoo SWas WAbe WCla WEas WHil WPer
§ *triumfettii cana rosea*	EFol NHol NNrd WHil
triumfettii stricta	CTom EMon GEdr GLoc LHil SFis WOMN
– – 'Macedonia'	SFis
¶ *uniflora nervosa*	CHar
¶ – *nervosa*JCA 287.000	EMon

CENTAURIUM (Gentianaceae)

erythraea	CElw GPoy MSal NSel SIde WCla WSto
scilloides	CElw CRiv CShe EBre ELan GLoc MPit MPla MTho NHol NNrd NTow NWCA WAbe WCla WPer WWin

CENTRADENIA (Melastomataceae)

inaequilateralis 'Cascade'	IHos MBri

CENTRANTHERA (Scrophulariaceae)

intermedium	CSun

CENTRANTHUS (Valerianaceae)

§ *ruber*	CArn CCla CKin EFou EMon GPoy MBro MChe MPlt MWgw NRoo NSel WHen WHil WPer
§ – *albus*	CCla CKin CSco EBre ECha EFol EFou ELan EMon EOrc MCot NRoo SPer WEas WHen WHer WPer
– *atrococcineus*	CSco ECha SPer WPer
– *coccineus*	EBre ELan EMon MCot MWat SMrm

CEPHALANTHUS (Rubiaceae)

occidentalis	CBow ELan ERav MBlu MPla SPer

CEPHALARIA (Dipsacaceae)

§ *alpina*	CElw CGle CHar EBre EPot ESis GCHN MBro MPit NNrd NRoo SIng WAbe WCla WDav WOld WWin
§ – *nana*	CShe
§ *gigantea*	CBre CChu CCor CElw CGle CHad CHan CSun ECha EFou ELan EOrc GWic LHop MCot MFir NBar NNor SBor SPer SSpi WEas WOld
tatarica	See C. ***gigantea***

CEPHALOTAXUS (Cephalotaxaceae)

fortunei	CGre SHil
– 'Prostrate Spreader'	LSav SHil
harringtonia	CMCN MRav
– *drupacea*	CMCN SHil WWat
– 'Fastigiata'	CChu CDoC CKen EHul MBar MBri NHol SExT SHil SMad
– 'Gnome'	WCon
– 'Nana'	CMCN

CEPHALOTUS (Cephalotaceae)

follicularis	WMEx

CERASTIUM (Caryophyllaceae)

alpinum	CRow ELan
– *lanatum*	CLew CSun NGre NNrd NTow WDav WHil WPer
tomentosum	CFis CRiv CRow ELan EPar LGro MWgw NRoo SIng WPer WWin
– *columnae*	CHoe CRiv EBre ECha GGar WRus WWin

CERATONIA (Leguminosae)

CERATOPHYLLUM (Ceratophyllaceae)

demersum	CRow

CERATOSTIGMA † (Plumbaginaceae)

***abyssinicum**	ERav LHop
griffithii	CB&S CBot CCla CHan CLew CPle CSco ELan ERav IOrc LAbb LHop MBro MPla NHol SHil SLon SPer SSta WAbe WOld WPer WSHC
larpentae	See C. ***plumbaginoides***
§ *plumbaginoides*	Widely available
¶ *ulicinum*	SMrm
willmottianum	Widely available

CERCIDIPHYLLUM † (Cercidiphyllaceae)

japonicum	Widely available
– *magnificum*	CBot CCla EHar LSav MBri SGar SHil WWat
– 'Pendulum'	EHar LSav MBlu MBri SSpi

CERCIS (Leguminosae)

canadensis	CBot LSav MGos SSpi
– 'Forest Pansy'	CB&S COtt CSco LRHS MBlu MBri MGos SHil SPer SSpi SSus
chinensis	CSam GWic LSav SPer SSpi WCoo
– *alba*	SPer
– 'Avondale'	CB&S LNet MBri SSpi
griffithii	CMCN
occidentalis	SSpi
siliquastrum	Widely available
– *alba*	CBot CChu CCla CMCN EHar IOrc MBlu SHil SMad SSpi WWat
– 'Bodnant'	SHil

CERCOCARPUS (Rosaceae)

brevifolius	CCor

CERINTHE (Boraginaceae)

¶ *glabra*	WPer

CEROPEGIA (Asclepiadaceae)

* *lanceolata*	SLMG
radicans	SLMG
stapeliiformis	SLMG
woodii	IBlr MBri SLMG

CEROXYLON (Palmae)

¶ *quindiuense*	LPal

CESTRUM (Solanaceae)

aurantiacum	CGre CPle CSun IBlr ISea SHil SLMG
§ *elegans*	CBot CHan CHil CPle CTre IBlr SLMG WTay
fasciculatum	CB&S IBlr
'Newellii'	CB&S CHEx CHan CHil CLan CMHG CPle ELan ERea IBlr ISea LHop SCog SHil SLMG WAbe WOMN WSHC
nocturnum	CB&S CPle CSun ERea SLMG
parqui	CBot CChu CHil CLan CMHG CPle ECha EFou EMon ERea GWic IBlr LHop MCot SDix SSpi WBod WOld WSHC
psittacinum	CGre CPle CSun SSpi
'Purpureum'	See C. ***elegans***
roseum 'Ilnacullin'	CB&S CGre ERea IBlr WTay
* *violaceum*	CB&S

CETERACH (Aspleniaceae)

officinarum	NHol

CHAENACTIS (Compositae)

CHAENOMELES (Rosaceae)

x *californica*	
'Enchantress	CShe
cathayensis	LRHS
§ *japonica*	ENot GRei IJoh LBuc MBal MBar MPla MR&S NNor NRoo WCoo WHil WWeb
¶ – *alba*	CShe
– *alpina*	CSco MPla
– 'Sargentii'	CShe MPla
maulei	See C. ***japonica***
sinensis	See PSEUDOCYDONIA *s.*
speciosa	CSam ISea MBar NNor NWea WNor
– 'Apple Blossom'	SPer
– 'Atrococcinea Plena'	WBod
– 'Aurora'	MBar WAbe
¶ – 'Brilliant'	CBra
– 'Cardinalis'	SHil
– 'Choshan'	See C. x ***superba*** 'Yaegaki'
– 'Falconnet Charlet'	CShe MR&S
– 'Geisha Girl'	CSco EPla NHol SPer WWeb
– 'Knap Hill Radiance'	CShe
– 'Moerloosei'	CChu CCla CSco CShe EHar ELan LSav MBri MRav SHil SMrm WWat WWeb
§ – 'Nivalis'	Widely available
– 'Phylis Moore'	CLan
* – 'Port Eliot'	SPla WWeb
– 'Rosea Plena'	CShe SHil
– 'Rubra Grandiflora'	CShe MPla SHil
– 'Simonii'	CBow CFor CSco CShe ENot MBri MGos MPla SHil SPer WWat
– 'Snow'	CBow CPle CSco MWat SSpi WWeb
– 'Umbilicata'	CSco ENot SPer
x *superba*	MWat
– 'Boule de Feu'	CBra CShe
¶ – 'Cameo'	EHar
– 'Coral Sea'	CSco CShe NNor
– 'Crimson and Gold'	CBra CCla CSco EHar ELan ENot IJoh IOrc LHop MBal MBar MBri MGos MR&S MRav NKay NRoo NTow SHil SLon SPer SPla SReu
– 'Elly Mossel'	CB&S CSco CShe MR&S SCro
¶ – 'Ernst Finken'	MR&S
– 'Etna'	CB&S
– 'Fire Dance'	CShe ECtt ELan ENot MBri NHol SPer SPla
– 'Hever Castle'	CShe SHil WWat
– 'Hollandia'	CSco CShe ELan MGos
– 'Issai White'	MBri
– 'Jet Trail'	CB&S CSco MBri SSta
– 'Knap Hill Scarlet'	CB&S CLan CShe CTre IOrc LAbb MPla MR&S NTow SHil SPer SPla STre WBod WWat
§ – 'Nicoline'	CB&S CSco EHar GRei IDai MBri MR&S MWat NHol SHil SSpi
§ – 'Pink Lady'	Widely available
– 'Rowallane'	CSam CSco ELan ENot IDai MRav MWat SHil SPer SPla WBod
– 'Texas Scarlet'	MBri WAbe WWin
¶ – 'Vesuvius'	NBar
§ – 'Yaegaki'	CBow CShe SPer

CHAENORRHINUM (Scrophulariaceae)
glareosum GLoc MCas MHig
§ *origanifolium* MPar SFir SIng WPer WWin
§ – 'Blue Sceptre' GLoc MCas NHar WWin

CHAEROPHYLLUM (Umbelliferae)
hirsutum CRow ELan
– *roseum* CChu CCla CHan CHar CLew EBre ECha EFol EFou LGre MPar MRav MUlv NSti SAxl SLHN SPer SSpi WEas

CHAMAEBATIARIA (Rosaceae)
millefolium CCor EHal GWic LGre WDav WThu

CHAMAECYPARIS † (Cupressaceae)
§ *funebris* CMCN
lawsoniana CBra CTre EHar EHul GRei IDai ISea MBar NWea SHil WMou
– 'Albospica' CBra CMac EBre EHul GRei MBal MBar MPla MRav MWat SPla
– 'Albospica Nana' See C. *l.* 'Nana Albospica'
– 'Albovariegata' EHul IDai MBar MPlt NHea WGre
– 'Albrechtii' ENot
– 'Allumii' CDoC CMac CSco EHar EHul ENot GRei IDai LBuc MBal MBar MCra MGos MPla MR&S MWat NGre NRya NWea SHil SPer SReu
– 'Allumii Aurea' See C. *l.* 'Alumigold'
– 'Allumii Magnificent' CB&S EHul WCon WWeb
§ – 'Alumigold' CB&S CDoC CKen EHar ENHC MBar MBri MGos MPla MR&S MWat SHil SPer WCon WWeb
– 'Argentea' See C. *l.* 'Argenteovariegata'
§ – 'Argenteovariegata' CMac WCon WThu
I – 'Aurea Compacta' MPlt
– 'Aurea Densa' CDoC CKen CMac EBre EHar EHul LSav MBar MBri MGos NHar SHil SIng SLon WCon
– 'Aureovariegata' IJoh MBal MBar NRoo
*– 'Azurea' CDoC
§ – 'Barabit's Globe' MBar MWat
– 'Barry's Gold' LSav
– 'Blom' CKen EHul MBri
§ – 'Blue Gown' CDoC EHul MBar MGos MPla SReu WWeb
§ – 'Blue Jacket' CSco
– 'Blue Nantais' CBra CDoC CKen CMHG CMac CSco EBre EHul ENHC IJoh LLin LNet MBal MBar MBri MCot MGos MPla MWat SHil SPla SReu SSmi SSta
– 'Blue Surprise' CBra CDoC CHoe CKen CMHG EHul LSav MBal MBar MBri MPla MR&S
– 'Bowleri' WCon
– 'Broomhill Gold' CBra CDoC CMac CSco EHul ENot LNet MBal MBar MBri MCra MGos MPla MRav MWat NHol SPer WAbe WCon
*– 'Burkwood's Blue' MBar
– 'Caudata' CKen LSav
– 'Chantry Gold' EHul WCon
– 'Chilworth Silver' Widely available
– 'Chingii' CDoC
– 'Columnaris' CB&S CBra CDoC CKen CMac EBre EHar ENHC ENot GRei IDai IHos MBal MBar MBri MCra MGos MOke MR&S NHea NWea SMad SReu
– 'Columnaris Aurea' See C. *l.* 'Golden Spire'
– 'Columnaris Glauca' EHul IJoh MPla MWat NRoo SPer SPla WBod WCon WWeb
– 'Croftway' EHul SCro
– 'Dik's Weeping' MBri WMou
– 'Drummondii' EHul
– 'Duncanii' MBal WCon
– 'Dutch Gold' EBre EHul WCon
*– 'Dwarf Blue' CMHG
– 'Elegantissima' CMac
*– 'Elfin' EPla
– 'Ellwoodii' Widely available
– 'Ellwood's Empire' MBri
– 'Ellwood's Gold' Widely available
– 'Ellwood's Nymph' CKen MBar
– 'Ellwood's Pillar' CBra CDoC CMac CSco EBre EHul ENHC ISea LLin MBar MBri MGos MPla MWat NHol SHil SPer SPla SSmi WAbe WCon
– 'Ellwood's Pygmy' CMac MBar SIng
– 'Ellwood's Silver' CGre ISea MR&S
– 'Ellwood's Variegata' See C. *l.* 'Ellwood's White'
§ – 'Ellwood's White' CKen CMac EBre EHul MBar MBri MPla MWat NHea SIng SSmi WAbe
I – 'Emerald' CKen MBar MBri NHol WCon
– 'Emerald Spire' CDoC CMac
– 'Erecta' CMac EHar EHul MBal MBar SHil SPer SReu
– 'Erecta Argenteovariegata' MPla
– 'Erecta Aurea' CKen EHul
– 'Erecta Filiformis' MBar
– 'Erecta Viridis' CB&S CDoC GRei MCra MPla MRav MWat NWea WCon WWeb
– 'Erika' LSav MBar MWat WCon
– 'Fantail' MWat
– 'Fleckellwood' EHul LLin MBar MGos MPla SPla WCon
– 'Fletcher Aurea' See C. *l.* 'Yellow Transparent'
– 'Fletcheri' CB&S CBra CMac CSco EHar EHul ENHC ENot IDai ISea MBar MGos MPla MRav NGre NWea SHil SLon SPer SPla SReu WBod WCon WThu
– 'Fletcher's White' EHul MBar MPla WCon
– 'Forsteckensis' CDoC CMac EHul ENHC GRei ISea LLin MBar MGos MR&S MWat NWea SCro SLon SPer WCon
I – 'Forsteckensis Aurea' WCon
– 'Fraseri' CDoC CMac EHar ENHC ISea MBar NWea SHil SPla WCon
– 'Gilt Edge' CKen
– 'Gimbornii' CDoC CMHG CMac CSco EBre EHul ENHC ISea LLin MBar MBri MPla SHil SLon SPer WAbe WCon
– 'Glauca Spek' See C. *l.* 'Spek'
– 'Globus' See C. *l.* 'Barabit's Globe'
– 'Gnome' CDoC CLew CMac EBre EHul ENHC EPot MBal MBar MGos MPla NHol SPer WAbe WCon
– 'Gold Pyramid' See C. *l.* 'Pyramidalis Lutea'

– 'Gold Splash'	CKen
– 'Golden King'	MBar
§ – 'Golden Pot'	CDoC CKen CMac EBre EHul LLin MBar MBri MGos MOke MPla MPlt MWat NRoo SPla WAbe WCon
– 'Golden Showers'	CKen
§ – 'Golden Spire'	CB&S MBar MBri MR&S
– 'Golden Triumph'	CB&S EHul WCon
– 'Golden Wonder'	CDoC CMac CSco IDai LBuc LNet MBar MBri MGos MR&S MRav SHil WCon
¶ – 'Grayswood Bronze'	LSav
– 'Grayswood Feather'	CDoC CKen CMac CSco EHul MBar MGos MPla SHil SLon WCon WWeb
– 'Grayswood Gold'	CKen EHul MBar MPla MR&S SHil
– 'Grayswood Pillar'	CKen CMac EHul MBal MBar MGos WCon
– 'Green Globe'	CDoC CKen CMHG EHul EPot MBar MBri MCas MPla NHar NHol SHil WAbe WCon
– 'Green Hedger'	CMac CSco EHar EHul ENot GRei LBuc MR&S SHil SPla SReu
– 'Green Pillar'	CKen CSco EBre EHul IJoh MBar MCra MGos MWat NRoo SReu WWeb
– 'Green Spire'	MBri
– 'Green Wall'	See C. *l.* 'Blue Gown'
– 'Greycone'	CKen
– 'Hillieri'	EHul MBar
– 'Hogger's Blue Gown'	GRei
*– 'Hogger's Gold'	CMHG EHul
– 'Howarth's Gold'	MBri
¶ – 'Imbricata Pendula'	WMou
– 'Intertexta"	EHar EHul ISea SMad
– 'Jackman's Green Hedger'	WAbe
*– 'Jackman's Variety'	See C. *l.* 'Green Pillar'
– 'Kelleriis Gold'	EHar EHul
– 'Killarney Gold'	CMac
– 'Kilmacurragh'	CMac EHar EHul ENHC ENot GRei IDai MBal MBar SHil SPer WBod WCon
– 'Knowefieldensis'	CMHG CMac IDai LLin WWeb
§ – 'Lane'	CBra CDoC CKen CMac EBre EHar EHul ENot GRei ISea MBal MBar MCra MGos MRav NHea NWea SHil SLon WCon
– 'Lanei'	See C. *l.* 'Lane'
– 'Lanei Aurea'	See C. *l.* 'Lane'
– 'Lemon Queen'	EHul LLin WCon
*– 'Limelight'	EHul
– 'Little Spire'	CDoC CMHG EBre EHul EPla LLin MBar MBri MGos MPla NHol WCon
– 'Lombartsii'	CDoC WCon
– 'Lutea'	CMac EHar EHul MBal MCra MGos SPer SPla SReu
§ – 'Lutea Nana'	CKen CMac EHul IBar IDai MBar SHil WCon
– 'Luteocompacta'	CKen
– 'Lycopodioides'	EHul MBar SSmi WThu
*– 'MacPenny's Gold'	CMac
– 'Magnifica Aurea'	ENHC
– 'Milford Blue Jacket'	See C. *l.* 'Blue Jacket'
– 'Minima'	MBar
– 'Minima Aurea'	Widely available
I – 'Minima Densa'	WAbe
– 'Minima Glauca'	Widely available
– 'Moonlight'	CBra MBar MGos MPla
– 'Naberi'	EHar SHil
– 'Nana'	CMac MBar SPla WCon
§ – 'Nana Albospica'	CDoC CKen EBre ENHC LLin MBal MBar MGos MPla WCon
– 'Nana Argentea'	CKen CMHG EHul
– 'Nana Lutea'	See C. *l.* 'Lutea Nana'
– 'Nana Rogersii'	See C. *l.* 'Rogersii'
– 'Nidiformis'	MBal MBar SLon SPla
¶ – 'Nyewoods'	WWeb
– 'Nymph'	LLin MBri WCon
– 'Parsons'	IHos SLon
¶ – 'Pelt's Blue'	CKen
– 'Pembury Blue'	Widely available
– 'Pendula'	MBar
– 'Pendula Vera'	CBra EHul
– 'Pick's Dwarf Blue'	MBar MBri WCon
– Pot of Gold ®	See C. *l.* 'Gold Pot'
– 'Pottenii'	CDoC CMac CSco EHar EHul ENHC IJoh ISea MBal MBar MCra MGos MPla MWat NHea NRya NWea SHil SPer SReu WAbe WCon
*– 'Pygmaea'	CDoC EBre EHul MBar MPla NHol WCon
– 'Pygmaea Argentea'	CKen CMac EBre EHar EHul ENHC GPen IDai LLin LSav MBal MBar MBri MPla MWat NHol SHil SPer SPla WAbe WCon WThu
§ – 'Pyramidalis Lutea'	CKen
– 'Reid's Own'	GRei
– 'Rijnhof'	EBre
– 'Rogersii'	MBar SPla
– 'Romana'	MBri
– 'Royal Gold'	EHul WCon
*– 'Silver Moon'	EHul
– 'Silver Queen'	CKen EHar EHul GRei IDai MBal MBar MCra NWea
– 'Silver Threads'	CBra CKen CMac EBre EHar EHul ENot EPla IJoh LLin MBar MBri MCas MGos MPla MWat NHol SLon SPla SReu WCon
*– 'Slocockiana'	EHul
N– 'Smithii'	CMHG ISea MBar WCon
– 'Snow Flurry'	CKen
– 'Snow White'	CDoC EHul IJoh LLin MBri MGos NHol SPla WCon
– 'Somerset'	CMac CSco IDai MBar SLon WCon WWeb
§ – 'Spek'	CB&S EHul IDai
– 'Stardust'	CDoC CMac ENHC ENot GRei IHos IJoh ISea MBal MBar MBri MGos MPla MR&S MWat NRoo SHil SPer SPla SReu WCon WGre
– 'Stewartii'	CMac CSco ENot MBal MBar MCra MGos MPla MR&S NHea NWea SHil
– 'Stilton Cheese'	MBar
– 'Summer Snow'	CDoC CMHG CMac ENot IJoh LLin MBar MBri MGos MPla MRav NHea SHil SPer SPla SReu WAbe WCon
*– 'Sunkist'	CKen
– 'Tamariscifolia'	CDoC ENHC IDai MBal MBar SHil SPer SPla WCon
*– 'Temple's White'	CKen
– 'Tharandtensis Caesia'	MBar SLon WCon
– 'Tilford'	EHul
– 'Treasure'	CKen EBre EHul EPla LLin MBar MBri MGos WCon

– 'Triomf van Boskoop'	EHul MBar
– 'Van Pelt's Blue'	CB&S CBra EHar EHul MBar MGos NHol SHil SLon SReu WCon
– 'Versicolor'	EHul MBar
– 'Westermannii'	CMac EHar EHul MBal NHea SHil SLon SPer SReu WCon
– 'White Spot'	CDoC CKen EBre EHar EHul ENHC ISea MBal MBar MBri MR&S SHil WCon
– 'Winston Churchill'	EHar MBar MCra MGos MPla NWea SHil SPer SReu WCon
– 'Wisselii'	CDoC CKen CMac EHar EHul ENHC ENot IDai ISea MBar MR&S NWea SHil SIng SLon SPer SReu WCon WMou
– 'Wisselii Nana'	LSav
– 'Witzeliana'	MBar MGos MPla SHil WCon
– 'Wyevale Silver'	MBar
*– 'Yellow Success'	EHul
§ – 'Yellow Transparent'	CMac EHul MBar MGos MWat SHil SMad SPer WCon
*– 'Yvonne'	MBri
leylandii	See X CUPRESSOCYPARIS *leylandii*
nootkatensis	EHar MBar SHil
*– 'Aurea'	CDoC CMac EHul IDai MBal MBar MR&S NHol NWea SReu WCon WWeb
– 'Aureovariegata'	EHar EHul EPla SHil
– 'Compacta'	MBar
– 'Glauca'	ENHC IDai MBar SHil
– 'Gracilis'	EHul
¶ – 'Jubilee'	WMou
– 'Lutea'	See C. ***n.*** 'Aurea'
– 'Nidifera'	MBar
– 'Pendula'	CDoC CSco EBre EHar EHul ENHC ENot IJoh LNet MBal MBar MBri NWea SHil SMad WCon WMou
– 'Variegata'	EHar EHul MBar WCon
¶ ***obtusa*** 'Albovariegata'	CKen
I – 'Aureovariegata'	MBri
¶ – 'Aurora'	CKen
*– 'Autumn Gold'	MBar
– 'Bartley'	CKen
– 'Bronze Elegance'	SIng
– 'Caespitosa'	CKen EPot SHil
– 'Chabo-yadori'	CDoC CMHG EHul EPot LLin MBal MBar MGos NHol WCon
– 'Chilworth'	CKen MBar MBri
¶ – 'Chimaamihiba'	MBri
– 'Contorta'	EPot MBri
– 'Coralliformis'	CDoC LLin MBal MBar NHol
§ – 'Crippsii'	CB&S CKen CMHG CMac EHar EHul ENot EPot IDai IJoh MBal MBar MBri MGos MPla MR&S NRoo SHil SPer WCon WMou
– 'Crippsii Aurea'	See C. ***o.*** Crippsii
– 'Dainty Doll'	CKen
– 'Densa'	CKen CMac SHil
– 'Erika'	CDoC EHul LSav MPla MPlt SIng
– 'Fernspray Gold'	CDoC CMHG CMac EHul ENot LLin MBar MBri MPla MR&S SHil SPer WCon
– 'Filicoides'	EHul
– 'Flabelliformis'	CKen
– 'Gimborn's Beauty'	MBri WCon
– 'Golden Fairy'	CKen
¶ – 'Golden Filament'	CKen
*– 'Golden Nymph'	MBri WCon
*– 'Golden Sprite'	MBri WCon
– 'Goldilocks'	EHul MBri
– 'Graciosa'	CDoC EBre EHul ENHC MBar NHol
– 'Hage'	MBri MPla WAbe
¶ – 'Hypnoides Nana'	CKen
– 'Intermedia'	EPot
– 'Juniperoides Compacta'	CKen EPot MBar MBri SHil
– 'Kosteri'	CDoC CKen CMac EBre EHul ENHC EPot LLin LSav MBar MBri MGos MPla NHol SIng WAbe WCon
– 'Little Markey'	CKen
– 'Lycopodioides'	CDoC EPot NHol
§ – 'Mariesii'	MBri NHol WCon
– 'Minima'	EPot SHil
*– 'Minima Aurea'	EPot MCas
– 'Nana'	CKen CMHG CMac EHul EPot MBar MBri MCas MPla MRav NHol SHil SIng SReu SSmi WCon
– 'Nana Aurea'	CDoC CMac CSco EBre EHul ENHC EPot LLin LSav MBar MBri MCas MRav MWat NHol SHil SLon SPer WAbe
– 'Nana Compacta'	MBri NHol
– 'Nana Gracilis'	Widely available
I – 'Nana Gracilis Aurea'	EHul
– 'Nana Lutea'	CKen EBre EHul ENHC EPot MBar MBri MPla MRav NHol NRoo SPer WAbe WCon
– 'Nana Pyramidalis'	EHul
– 'Nana Rigida'	See C. ***o.*** 'Rigid Dwarf'
– 'Nana Variegata'	See C. ***o.*** 'Mariesii'
– 'Opaal'	MBar WCon
– 'Pygmaea'	CDoC EBre EHul ENHC ENot EPot IDai MBal MBar MPla MR&S NHol SHil SPer SPla WCon
– 'Pygmaea Aurescens'	ENHC MBar MWat
¶ – 'Pygmaea Densa'	CKen
– 'Reis Dwarf'	LSav WCon
– 'Repens'	NHol
– 'Rigid Dwarf'	CKen MBar MBri
– 'Snowkist'	CKen
– 'Spiralis'	CKen LSav MBar SHil
– 'Stoneham'	CKen
– 'Tempelhof'	CBra CDoC CKen EBre EHar EHul EPot LSav MBar MBri MPla SLon WCon WWeb
– 'Tetragona Aurea'	CDoC EHar EHul ENHC IDai LSav MBar MGos MWat NHol SHil SPer WCon
– 'Tonia'	CDoC EBre EHul MBar MBri NHar NHol WWeb
¶ – 'Verdonii'	MBri NHol
¶ – 'Wissel'	CKen
– 'Yellowtip'	MBar WCon
¶ ***pisifera***	LMer
N– 'Aurea Nana'	See C. ***p.*** 'Strathmore'
*– 'Avenue'	EHul MPla SPla WWeb
– 'Boulevard'	Widely available
– 'Compacta Variegata'	EHul MBar
– 'Devon Cream'	CHoe EHul LLin MBar MPla
– 'Filifera'	CMac MBal MBar MR&S MRav NHea SLon WBod
– 'Filifera Aurea'	Widely available
*– 'Filifera Aureomarginata'	CMac EBre MBal MBar MBri NGre SPla

– 'Filifera Nana'	CDoC EBre EHul ENHC MBal MBar MBri MWat SHil SMad SPer SSmi WCon
– 'Filifera Sungold'	CKen CMHG CSco EHul MPlt WWeb
I – 'Filifera Variegata'	EHul
¶ – 'Gold Cushion'	CKen
– 'Gold Dust'	See C. *p.* 'Plumosa Aurea'
– 'Gold Spangle'	CMHG EBre ISea MBar MGos WBod
– 'Golden Mop'	MPla
¶ – 'Hime-himuro'	CKen
¶ – 'Hime-sawara'	CKen
– 'Nana'	CDoC EBre EHul GPen LLin LSav MBal MBar MBri MCot MWat NHol SHil SPer SSmi
I – 'Nana Albovariegata'	CDoC MBar MBri WCon
*– 'Nana Aurea'	See C. *p.* 'Nana Aureovariegata'
§ – 'Nana Aureovariegata'	CDoC CKen CMac EBre EHul EPot LSav MBal MBar MBri MPla MPlt MWat NHar NHol SHil SPer WCon WWeb
I – 'Nana Compacta'	CMac IDai
– 'Nana Variegata'	See C. *p.* 'Nana Aureovariegata'
¶ – 'Parslori'	CKen
– 'Pici'	CKen
– 'Plumosa'	MBal MRav SLon SPla
*– 'Plumosa Albopicta'	ENHC MBal MBar MPla MPlt
§ – 'Plumosa Aurea'	CDoC CKen EHul ENHC GPen IDai IJoh MBal MBar MCra MR&S NHea NWea SHil WGre
*– 'Plumosa Aurea Compacta Variegata'	CMac
§ – 'Plumosa Aurea Compacta'	CMac EBre ENot MBal MBar MGos MPla MPlt NRoo SHil SLon SPer SReu WCon WGre
– 'Plumosa Aurea Nana'	See C. *p.* 'Plumosa Aurea Compacta'
*– 'Plumosa Aurea Nana Compacta'	CMac
– 'Plumosa Aurescens'	CMac
§ – 'Plumosa Compressa'	CDoC CKen CMHG EBre EHul EPot MBar MBri MCas MGos MR&S NHar SHil WCon WThu
*– 'Plumosa Densa'	See C. *p.* 'Plumosa Compressa'
– 'Plumosa Flavescens'	CDoC CMac EHul LLin MBar MPla MWat SLon WCon
– 'Plumosa Juniperoides'	CKen ITim MBri MPla MPlt WCon
– 'Plumosa Purple Dome'	See C. *p.* 'Purple Dome'
– 'Plumosa Pygmaea'	MBar MPlt
– 'Plumosa Rogersii'	CDoC CSco EHul ENHC EPot MBar MCas MGos SIng WWeb
I – 'Plumosa Teddy Bear'	SCro
I – 'Purple Dome'	EBre EHul MBar MGos WCon
– 'Pygmaea'	EPot MGos SLon
*– 'Rogersii'	MPla WThu
– 'Silver and Gold'	MBar MCas
– 'Silver Lode'	CKen
– 'Snow'	CKen CMHG CMac EPot LLin MBal MBar MBri MCas MCot MPla NHar SCro SHil SIng SSmi WCon
§ – 'Squarrosa'	CDoC GPen MBal MBar NWea SLon WBod
– 'Squarrosa Argentea'	MBal
I – 'Squarrosa Blue Globe'	CKen
– 'Squarrosa Dumosa'	CKen EHul MBar MPla MWat SPer
– 'Squarrosa Intermedia'	EHul MBar MGos SLon WCon
– 'Squarrosa Lombarts'	CMac EBre EHul ENHC EPla LLin MPla MWat SIng SSmi WCon
– 'Squarrosa Lutea'	EPla MBar
– 'Squarrosa Sulphurea'	CMHG CMac CTre EBre EHul EPot GPen IDai MBal MBar MPla MR&S MWat SHil SPer WCon WGre
– 'Squarrosa Veitchii'	See C. *p.* 'Squarrosa'
§ – 'Strathmore'	CDoC CKen EHul IDai LLin MBar MBri MRav NHol
– 'Sungold'	CBra CDoC EBre EHul ENot MBar MBri MPla MR&S SHil
¶ – 'Tamu-himuro'	CKen
¶ – 'Tsukumo'	LSav
¶ – 'White Beauty'	CKen
*– 'White Brocade'	CMac
– 'White Pygmy'	EPot
thyoides	WThu
– 'Andelyensis'	CDoC CMac EHul ENHC LLin MBal MBar MPla NHol SPer SReu WCon
– 'Andelyensis Nana'	CKen SHil
– 'Aurea'	MBar MPlt
– 'Conica'	CKen WCon
– 'Ericoides'	CDoC CKen CMHG CMac EHul ENHC ENot GPen LLin LSav MBal MBar MWat SHil SPer SReu WBod WCon
§ – 'Glauca'	CMHG MBar WCon
– 'Kewensis'	See C. *t.* 'Glauca'
– 'Purple Heather'	SHil
– 'Red Star'	See C. *t.* 'Rubicon'
§ – 'Rubicon'	CKen CMac EBre EHul IJoh LLin MBar MBri MGos MPla MPlt MRav SPla WCon
– 'Variegata'	EHul MBar

CHAMAECYTISUS See CYTISUS

CHAMAEDAPHNE (Ericaceae)

§ ***calyculata***	ITim MUlv SPer WBod WSHC
– 'Nana'	MBal MBar MGos SPer SSta

CHAMAEDOREA (Palmae)

¶ ***costaricana***	LPal
elegans	LPal MBri
erumpens	NPal
metallica	LPal
seifrizii	LPal MBri

CHAMAELIRIUM (Liliaceae/Liliaceae)

luteum	MSal

CHAMAEMELUM (Compositae)

§ ***nobile***	CArn CHad CSFH CSev Effi GPoy LHol MBar MBri NNrd NRoo WEas WOak WPer WSto
– 'Flore Pleno'	CBre CElw CGle CHan CSev CShe ECha ELan GPla LHop MBri MCas NCat NHol NSti SChu SIng WEas WHal WHil WOMN WPer
– 'Treneague'	CArn CHar CLew CSFH CSev CShe CWar ELan LGro LMor MBri MRav NHol NNor NRoo NSti SIng WHal WOak WPer

CHAMAENERION (Onagraceae)
angustifolium See EPILOBIUM *angustifolium*

CHAMAEPERICLYMENUM (Cornaceae)
canadense See CORNUS *canadensis*

CHAMAEROPS (Palmae)
excelsa See TRACHYCARPUS *fortunei*
humilis CHEx IOrc LPal NPal NRog SArc SExT SHil SPer

CHAMAESPARTIUM See **GENISTA**

CHAMOMILLA See **MATRICARIA**

CHASMANTHE (Iridaceae)
aethiopica CHan GWic LHop

CHASMANTHIUM (Gramineae)
§ *latifolium* EFou ELan GWic SApp SDix

CHEILANTHES (Adiantaceae)
farinosa NMar
¶ *guanchica* SSpi
myriophylla NMar

CHEIRANTHUS (Cruciferae)
cheiri CKin CNat CRow GPoy IBlr LHol SIde WEas
N– 'Baden Powell' ELan LHop SAxl WPer
– 'Bloody Warrior' Widely available
¶ – double yellow CBot
– 'Harpur Crewe' Widely available
¶ – 'Jane's Derision' CNat
¶ – 'Malmesbury' CNat
rupestris See ERYSIMUM *pulchellum*
scoparius See ERYSIMUM *scoparium*
sempervirens See ERYSIMUM *s.*

CHELIDONIUM (Papaveraceae)
majus CKin CRow GPoy LHol MPit MSal NHex SIde WHer
– 'Laciniatum Flore Pleno' CNat CRow EMon GWic IBlr WAbe WHer
– 'Plenum' CLew CRow CWGN ELan GCHN GWic SAxl WHer WHil

CHELONE (Scrophulariaceae)
barbata See PENSTEMON *barbatus*
glabra GPoy MSal MUlv
lyonii EBre ECro ERou
obliqua Widely available
– *alba* CChu CCla CHan CLew CMal EBre ECha EFou EGol ELan EOrc GWic LHop MBri MUlv NHol SChu SPer WOld WPer WRus

CHENOPODIUM (Chenopodiaceae)
bonus-henricus CArn CSev Effi GPoy LHol MChe NSel SIde WOak WPer WSto
botrys MSal SIde

CHERRY, Duke See **PRUNUS** x *gondouinii*

CHERRY, Sour or Morello See **PRUNUS** *cerasus*

CHERRY, Sweet See **PRUNUS** *avium*

CHESTNUT, Sweet See **CASTANEA** *sativa*

CHEVREULIA (Compositae)

CHIASTOPHYLLUM (Crassulaceae)
§ *oppositifolium* Widely available
¶ – 'Jim's Pride' CElw EMon
simplicifolium See C. *oppositifolium*

CHILIOTRICHUM (Compositae)
diffusum CPle ECou GAbr GDra IBar MBlu MMth SBor SLon SPer WSHC

CHIMAPHILA (Pyrolaceae)
maculata MSal
¶ *umbellata* EBar

CHIMONANTHUS (Calycanthaceae)
fragrans See C. *praecox*
§ *praecox* Widely available
– 'Grandiflorus' ENot SHil
– 'Luteus' MBlu SHil SSpi
– 'Trenython' CFor
zhejiangensis GWic

CHIMONOBAMBUSA (Gramineae(Bambuseae))
♦ *falcata* See DREPANOSTACHYUM *falcatum*
hookeriana See DREPANOSTACHYUM *hookerianum*
§ *marmorea* NJap SBam SDry WJun
– 'Variegata' EFul SBam SDry WJun
§ *quadrangularis* EFul SBam SDry WJun
§ *tumidinoda* SBam SDry

CHIOGENES (Ericaceae)
hispidula See GAULTHERIA *hispida*

CHIONANTHUS (Oleaceae)
retusus SHil SSta
virginicus CCla CPle ELan IOrc LGre LHop MBri MUlv SGar SHil SSpi SSta WWat

CHIONOCHLOA (Gramineae)
¶ *conspicua* MFir
*– 'Rubra' CElw CHoe EMon
flavicans MUlv

CHIONODOXA † (Liliaceae/Hyacinthaceae)
albescens ECam
§ *forbesii* CBro LRHS WPer
– 'Pink Giant' CAvo CBro EPar LAma LBlo NHol SIng
– Siehei group CBro
gigantea See C. *luciliae* Gigantea group'

luciliae	CAvo CBro ECam ELan EPar EPot ETub LAma LBlo LBow LRoo MBal MBri NHol NNrd NRya SIng WAbe WHil
– *alba*	EPar ETub LAma WChr
§ – Gigantea group	ELan LAma MBri
– *rosea*	ECam EPar EPot ETub LAma LBow NHol
* *mariesii*	LAma
nana	CBro ECam WChr
sardensis	CAvo CBro CCla ECam EPar EPot ETub LAma LBlo LBow MBal NHol SIng WChr WPer
siehei	See C. ***forbesii*** Siehei group
tmolusi	See C. ***forbesii***

CHIONOHEBE (Scrophulariaceae)

* *armstrongii*	ITim
¶ *ciliolata*	NHar
densifolia	ECou ITim
x *petrimea* 'Margaret Pringle'	EPot
pulvinaris	ECou GArf ITim MHig NHol NNrd SOkd WThu

X CHIONOSCILLA (Liliaceae/Hyacinthaceae)

allenii	LRHS WChr

CHIRONIA (Gentianaceae)

baccifera	CSun

CHLIDANTHUS (Liliaceae/Amaryllidaceae)

fragrans	CAvo LBow SW&B

CHLOROPHYTUM (Liliaceae/Anthericaceae)

comosum 'Variegatum'	MBri NRog
– 'Vittatum'	MBri
§ *majus*	WChr

CHOISYA (Rutaceae)

¶ *arizonica*	SDry
'Aztec Pearl'	CBow EBar LSav MBri MGos MUlv SHil SMad SMrm SPer SSus
ternata	Widely available
– 'Sundance'	Widely available

CHORDOSPARTIUM (Leguminosae)

muratai	ECou
stevensonii	CGre CHEx ECou SArc SHil SIgm SMad SSpi

CHORISIA (Bombacaceae)

¶ *speciosa*	CPle

CHORIZEMA (Leguminosae)

ilicifolium	CB&S ERea LHop

CHRYSALIDOCARPUS (Palmae)

lutescens	LPal MBri

CHRYSANTHEMOPSIS (Compositae)

atlanticum	MBro NHol SIng WDav WEas
catananche	EPad GEdr GLoc LGre LHop SIng SMrm WOMN
§ *gayanum*	CCan CHan CHil CMHG EBar EFol ELan LHil LHop NSty NTow SAxl SChu SCro SIng WHil WKif WOMN WPer WRus WSHC
§ *hosmariense*	Widely available
* 'Tizi-n-Tichka'	LHop NBir SBla

CHRYSANTHEMUM (Compositae)

alpinum	See LEUCANTHEMOPSIS ***alpina***
♦ *arcticum*	See ARCTANTHEMUM ***arcticum***
argenteum	See TANACETUM ***argenteum***
balsamita	See BALSAMITA ***major***
cinerariifolium	See TANACETUM ***cinerariifolium***
clusii	See TANACETUM ***corymbosum clusii***
coccineum	See TANACETUM ***coccineum***
coronarium	CArn
corymbosum	See TANACETUM ***corymbosum***
foeniculaceum	See ARGYRANTHEMUM ***frutescens f.***
frutescens	See ARGYRANTHEMUM ***frutescens***
haradjanii	See TANACETUM ***haradjanii***
hosmariense	See CHRYSANTHEMOPSIS ***hosmariense***
leucanthemum	See LEUCANTHEMUM ***vulgare***
macrophyllum	See TANACETUM ***macrophyllum***
mawii	See CHRYSANTHEMOPSIS ***gayanum***
maximum	See LEUCANTHEMUM ***m.*** & L. superbum
♦ *nankingense*	See DENDRANTHEMA ***n.***
nipponicum	See NIPPONANTHEMUM ***n.***
pacificum	See DENDRANTHEMA ***pacificum***
parthenium	See TANACETUM ***parthenium***
ptarmiciflorum	See TANACETUM ***ptarmaciflorum***
roseum	See TANACETUM ***coccineum***
rubellum	See DENDRANTHEMA ***rubellum***
segetum	CNat WHer WOak
uliginosum	See LEUCANTHEMELLA ***serotina***
* *welwitzkyi*	WThu
weyrichii	See DENDRANTHEMA ***w.***
yezoense	See DENDRANTHEMA ***y.***

CHRYSOCOMA (Compositae)

¶ *coma-aurea*	WPer

CHRYSOGONUM (Compositae)

virginianum	CKel EBre ECha MRav

CHRYSOLEPIS (Fagaceae)
chrysophylla WCoo

CHRYSOPOGON (Gramineae)
¶ *gryllus* EMon

CHRYSOPSIS (Compositae)
villosa EMon LRHS

CHRYSOSPLENIUM (Saxifragaceae)
davidianum CBre CChu CFor CTom ECha EMon EPot GCHN NNrd SBla SIng SWas
¶ – SBEC 231 NHol
oppositifolium CKel EMNN GDra MWgw NKay WCla

CHRYSOTHAMNUS (Compositae)

CHRYSOTHEMIS (Gesneriaceae)
pulchella MBri

CHUSQUEA † (Gramineae(Bambuseae))
culeou CBot CBow CChu CCla CCor CGre CHEx CMCN EFul EHar ELan GWic MBlu MBri MUlv SArc SBam SDry SMad SReu SSpi SSta SSus WJun
♦– *breviglumis* See C. *c*. 'Tenuis'
– 'Tenuis' SBam SDry WJun
montana SArc SBam SSpi WJun WWat
quila SArc SBam SDry WJun
ramosissima SBam SDry

CICERBITA (Compositae)
§ *alpina* MTho

CICHORIUM (Compositae)
intybus CKin CSFH CSev ECro Effi LHol LHop MChe SIde WHer WOak WPer
– *album* EMon LRHS
– *roseum* EBre ECha ECro ELan EMon MRav MTho NRoo SMrm SPer WPer
'Rosso di Verona' ELan
spinosum ELan EMon

CICUTA (Umbelliferae)

CIMICIFUGA † (Ranunculaceae)
acerina CHan GWic WRus
americana MSal
dahurica CRow
foetida GPoy
japonica LSav
¶– Sch 171 LSav
§ *racemosa* CCla CFor CHar CKel CRow EBre ECro EGol ELan ELun ERou GPoy GWic MBro MCot MRav MSal MWgw NHol SPer SSpi
– *cordifolia* EBre ECro SBla SHig
*– 'Purple Torch' WEas
*– 'Purpurea' EFol ELun NBar SWas
§ *ramosa* CRow GWic MBri NHol SAxl WCot
– Atropurpurea group CCla CHad CHan CRow EBre ECha ECro EFou ELan EPar MBri MUlv NOak SAxl SBla SMad SMrm WRus
– 'Brunette' MUlv
simplex MBri
– 'Elstead' CFor ECha ELun EPar SBla SSpi
– 'Ramosa' See C. ***ramosa***
– 'White Pearl' CCla CHan CRow CSco EBre ECha EFou EGol ELan ELun EPar GHig IDai LHop MBri NRoo NSti NTow SMad SPer SSpi

CINERARIA (Compositae)
maritima See SENECIO ***bicolor cineraria***

CINNAMOMUM (Lauraceae)
camphora CChu CHEx ERea

CIONURA (Asclepiadaceae)
§ *erecta* SHil
¶ *oreophila* GWic

CIRCAEA (Onagraceae)
lutetiana CKin MSal NLan WHer

CIRSIUM (Compositae)
acaule CKin
diacantha See PTILOSTEMON *d.*
dissectum CKin
eriophorum CKin
falconeri WEas
♦ *helenioides* See C. ***heterophyllum***
§ *heterophyllum* CKin NLan
japonicum MFir
*– 'Pink Beauty' EFou EGol ELan SMrm WHil
– 'Rose Beauty' CHar ECro EFou ELan GWic MBri WHil WPer
palustre CKin
rivulare atropurpureum CCla COtt CSco EBre ECha ECro EGol ELan ERou MUlv NSti SPer SSus WEas
vulgare CKin

CISSUS (Vitaceae)
antarctica MBri
discolor MBri
rhombifolia MBri
– 'Ellen Danica' MBri
§ *striata* CGre CHEx IBar IJoh MUlv WSHC

CISTUS † (Cistaceae)
× *aguilari* LGre LSav WSHC
– 'Maculatus' CB&S CBot CFor CGre CSco ELan ENot LGre MBri SHil SPer SSpi WKif WWin
¶ *albanicus* GCHN
albidus CCor CFis CMHG CRiv EBar LGre SDry WEas WWat
algarvensis See HALIMIUM ***ocymoides***
'Anne Palmer' CB&S CSco CSev LGre LHop SBla SHil
atriplicifolius See HALIMIUM ***atriplicifolium***
♦ 'Barnsley Pink' See C. 'Grayswood Pink'
'Blanche' LGre LSav WKif
× *canescens* CB&S
– 'Albus' CFis CShe LGre LSav NSti SAxl
¶ 'Chelsea Pink' EBar
§ *clusii* CKni CSam LGre SAxl SCro SPla

x ***corbariensis***	Widely available
N***crispus***	CB&S CHan ECha GAbr LGre LSav MWgw NNor SSpi WEas WWeb
C– 'Prostratus'	WRus
– 'Sunset'	See CISTUS x ***pulverulentus*** 'S.'
x ***cyprius***	CBra CCla CHan CMHG CSco CShe ELan ENot ERav IBar LSav MBri MWat SDix SHil SMad SPer SPla SSpi WBod
– ***albiflorus***	CHan
'Elma'	CGre ERav LGre LHop LSav MBri NTow SDry SHil SMrm SPer WAbe WHCG WWat
x ***florentinus***	IJoh IOrc LAbb LGre LSav MRav NNor SChu WSHC
formosus	See HALIMIUM ***lasianthum***
'Grayswood Pink'	ELan MBri MPla SSpi
halimiifolius	See HALIMIUM ***halimiifolium***
hirsutus	CCla SPer WWeb
N– ***psilosepalus***	CFis EBar
§ ***incanus***	SChu WKif WSHC
– ***creticus***	CFis CHan EBar ELan ERav LGre SCro SPer WAbe WSHC WWin
¶ – ***creticus***G&K 3364	LSav
– ***incanus***	LGre
ingwerseniana	See X HALIMIOCISTUS ***ingwersenii***
N***ladanifer***	CB&S CBow CHan CPle ECha ELan IJoh IOrc LSav MBal MR&S MRav MWgw NNor NSti NTow SChu SHil SLon SPer SPla WEas
lasianthus	See HALIMIUM ***lasianthum***
laurifolius	CHan CPle CSco ENot LGre MBal MBri MGos SHil SPer SSpi WEas WSHC
x ***laxus***	LSav SPla
– 'Snow White'	CFis LGre MBri SAxl WKif
libanotis	ELan LSav NNor
Nx ***loretii***	CBra CHan CMHG ENot IBar LGre LSav MR&S SHil SPer SPla WKif WWat
x ***lusitanicus***	CSam CShe GAbr IOrc SHil WAbe
– 'Decumbens'	CBra CCla CMHG CSco ELan GWic LGre LSav MBal MBri NKay SHil SPer WAbe WHCG WSHC
'Merrist Wood Cream'	See X HALIMIOCISTUS ***wintonensis*** 'Merrist Wood Cream'
monspeliensis	CBow CHan CMHG CSev LSav SChu SPer
x ***obtusifolius***	ELan EPla LSav MBri SBla
ochreatus	LGre
ocymoides	See HALIMIUM ***ocymoides***
¶ ***osbeckiifolius***	GWic
– MSF 70	SSpi
'Paladin'	WEas
palhinhae	CPle LGre LSav SDry SHil WAbe
N***parviflorus***	CBot CCla CFis CMHG ERav LAbb LGre LHil LHop LSav MR&S NSti SAxl SChu SPer WSHC
'Pat'	CGre SHil
'Peggy Sammons'	CBot CBow CHan CSco CShe ECha EGol ELan IOrc LHop LSav MBri NSti SAxl SChu SHil SLon SPer WSHC WWat
x ***platysepalus***	LSav
populifolius	CCor CMHG SLon SPer SSpi SSta
¶ – G&K 2075	LSav
– ***lasiocalyx***	CCla ERav IOrc LGre SHil SLon
– ***major***	CFis LGre
psilosepalus G 2065	LSav
x ***pulverulentus***	CCla CGre CHan CPle ERav LSav SChu SCro SHil SPer WSHC
§ – 'Sunset'	Widely available
– 'Warley Rose'	CFis CSam CSco CShe CSun SAxl
Nx ***purpureus***	Widely available
– 'Alan Fradd'	CBra CKni CSco LSav SAxl SCro SMrm
– 'Betty Taudevin'	CB&S CFis ELan LGre LHop LSav SBar SMad WAbe
rosmarinifolius	See C. ***clusii***
sahucii	See X HALIMIOCISTUS ***sahucii***
salviifolius	CB&S CHan CPle CSam CSco LGre LSav WEas
¶ – 'Avalanche'	WAbe
– x ***monspeliensis***	SAxl
– ***prostratus***	ELan LGre LHop LSav
– 'Sienna'	CSun
'Silver Pink'	CB&S CBra EFol ELan LSav MBri MFir MWat MWgw NNor NSti SAxl SCro SMrm SPer SReu SSta WHCG WOMN
x ***skanbergii***	CB&S CBra CCla CFor CMHG CSam CSco ELan ENot LSav MWat MWgw SAxl SDix SHil SLon SMad SPer SPla SSpi WAbe WEas WWat WWin
symphytifolius	GWic LGre
– MSF 716	SSpi
tomentosus	See HELIANTHEMUM ***nummularium tomentosum***
x ***verguinii***	LGre LSav MBri SDix
villosus	See C. ***incanus***
wintonensis	See X HALIMIOCISTUS ***wintonensis***

CITHAREXYLUM (Verbenaceae)

quadrangulare	CGre

X CITROFORTUNELLA (Rutaceae)

F ***floridana*** 'Eustis'	ERea
F– 'Lakeland'	ERea
♦Limequat	See X C. ***floridana***
F ***microcarpa***	CB&S MBri SLMG WHig
F– 'Tiger'	CB&S LHop
mitis	See X C. ***microcarpa***
F ***swinglei*** 'Tavares'	ERea

CITRON See **CITRUS *medica***

X CITRONCIRUS (Rutaceae)

CITRUS † (Rutaceae)

F ***aurantiifolia*** 'Bearss'	ERea
F– 'Tahiti'	CB&S ERea MNew
F ***aurantiifolia*** x ***limon*** 'Indian Lime'	ERca

F – 'La Valette'	ERea
F *aurantium*	ERea
F – 'Bouquet'	ERea
F – *myrtifolia* 'Chinotto'	ERea
♦ – 'Seville'	See C. *a.*
Calamondin	See X CITROFORTUNELLA *microcarpa*
F *ichangensis*	SArc
japonica	See FORTUNELLA *j.*
Kumquat	See FORTUNELLA
F *limon*	LPan MBri
F – 'Garey's Eureka'	ERea MBri
F – 'Imperial'	ERea
F – 'Lemonade'	ERea
F – 'Lisbon'	ERea
– 'Quatre Saisons'	See C. *l.* 'Garey's Eureka'
F – 'Variegata'	ERea MBri
F – 'Villafranca'	ERea MNew
F – x *sinensis* 'Meyer'	CB&S CHil IJoh LHop MBri MNew NPal SGar SHil SLMG SPer SSta SSus WHig
F x *limonia* 'Rangpur'	ERea
F *maxima*	ERea
F *medica* 'Ethrog'	ERea
F – *sarcodactylis*	ERea
mitis	See X CITROFORTUNELLA *microcarpa*
F x *nobilis*	LPan
F – 'Blida'	ERea
F – 'Murcott'	ERea
F – 'Silver Hill Owari'	ERea
F – Tangor group	ERea
F x *paradisi*	LPan
F – 'Foster '	ERea
F – 'Golden Special'	CB&S ERea IOrc MNew SGar
F – 'Wheeny'	MNew
F 'Ponderosa'	ERea MNew
reticulata x *paradisi*	See C. x *tangelo*
F *reticulata* Mandarin group	IJoh
F – – 'Clementine'	CB&S ERea IOrc SGar
F – – 'Encore'	ERea
F *reticulata* Satsuma group	ERea
F *sinensis*	LPan MBri
F – 'Arnci Alberetto'	SGar
F – 'Egg'	ERea
F – 'Embiguo'	ERea
F – 'Jaffa'	ERea
F – 'Malta Blood'	ERea
F – 'Moro Blood'	ERea
F – 'Prata'	ERea
F – 'Ruby'	ERea
F – 'Saint Michael'	ERea
F – 'Shamouti'	ERea
F – 'Valencia'	ERea MBri
F – 'Valencia Late'	ERea
F – 'Washington'	CB&S ERea MBri MNew
F x *tangelo* 'Seminole'	ERea

CLADOTHAMNUS See ELLOTTIA

CLADRASTIS (Leguminosae)

lutea	CB&S CCla CMCN EHal SHil SLHN SSpi WWat
sinensis	SHil

CLARKIA (Onagraceae)

concinna	WOMN

CLAVINODUM (Gramineae(Bambuseae))

* *oedogonatum*	SDry

CLAYTONIA (Portulacaceae)

australasica	See NEOPAXIA *australasica*
caroliniana	LAma
§ *megarhiza nivalis*	GDra MAsh NGre NTow WThu
§ *parvifolia*	CLew
§ *perfoliata*	CArn GPoy WCru WHer
§ *sibirica*	CElw CFis CRow ELan NGre NNrd NOrc WBon WPer
virginica	LAma

CLEMATIS † (Ranunculaceae)

'Abundance' (V)	CBow CCla CHad CPev EOvi EPen ESco EVal IOrc LPri MBea MBri MCad NB&B SBra SDix SHil SPer SSus WAbe WSHC
¶ *addisonii*	EOvi EVal WOMN
aethusifolia	CB&S CHan EOrc EOvi EVal LGre LPri MBri MCad SBra SSpi
afoliata	CPev ECou EOvi EVal MCad SPou
akebioides	CCla CHan ELan LRHS MCad SBra SSus
'Alba Luxurians' (V)	CBow CCla CGle CHad CMac CPev EGol ELan EOrc EOvi ERav ESco EVal IOrc LPri MBri MCad NHol SBla SBra SDix SHil SPer SSus
'Alice Fisk'	EOvi ESco EVal LPri MCad NB&B SBra
'Allanah'	EOvi ESco EVal LPri MCad NB&B SBra
§ *alpina*	CMac CPev CSco EBre ESco GDra GLoc MBal MBar MBea MCad NBar SIng WAbe WDav WWat
– 'Burford White'	EOvi LPri MCad NB&B WSHC
– 'Columbine'	CPev EOrc EOvi LPri MBea MCad NB&B SBra
– 'Columbine White'	EOvi MBri MCad
– 'Frances Rivis'	Widely available
¶ – 'Frankie'	EOrc EVal LRHS MBri
– 'Inshriach Form'	CGle NHol
– 'Jacqueline du Pré'	CPev
¶ – 'Jan Lindmark'	NBir
– 'Pamela Jackman'	CCla ELan EOrc EOvi EPen EVal IOrc LPri MBea MBri MCad MGos NB&B NBar NHol SBra SDix SPer SSus
– 'Ria'	MBea MCad
– 'Rosy Pagoda'	EOvi EVal LPri MCad NBir WWat
– 'Ruby'	Widely available
– *sibirica*	CPev EOvi MCad NB&B
§ – *sibirica* 'White Moth'	CCla CFor CMac CSam CSco ELan EOvi LAbb LPri MBri MCad MGos MPar MPla NB&B NHol SBla SBra SHil SMad SPer SSta WSHC WWat
– 'Willy'	CPev EGol EOrc EOvi EPen ESco EVal LPri MBea MBri MCad MGos SBra SDix SPer WSHC
'André Devillers'	MCad
'Annabel'	EPen
* 'Anniversary'	LPri
apiifolia	CCla CPev EOvi EVal MCad SBra

aristata	ECou ESco
armandii	Widely available
– 'Apple Blossom'	CCla CHad CPev CSco EHar ELan EOvi EPen ERav ESco EVal IOrc LPri MBea MBri MCad NB&B NHol SBra SHil SPer SSpi SSta SSus
– ***biondiana***	CBow CMac EOvi SBla SSta
– 'Snowdrift'	CPev CSam CSco EOvi ESco LPri MCad NB&B SBla SHil SReu
– 'Trengwainton Form'	CBot
¶ x ***aromatica***	EOvi
'Asao'	EBre ELan EOvi EVal LPri MBea MCad NB&B SBra SHil SMad SPer WWat
'Ascotiensis'	CCla CPev EOvi ESco EVal LPri MCad SBra SDix SHil SPer
'Aureolin'	MBar MBri MCad MGos NHol SBra SSus WWeb
australis	ECou
'Barbara Dibley'	CCla CMac CPev EOvi EPen ESco EVal LPri MBea MBri MCad NB&B SBra SDix SHil
'Barbara Jackman'	CCla CPev CSco ENot EOvi EPen ESco EVal LPri MBar MBea MBri MCad MR&S NB&B NBar SBra SDix SHil SPer SSus WBod
barbellata 'Betina'	MBri
– 'Prunina'	EVal
'Beauty of Richmond'	EOvi EVal MCad SBra SDix
'Beauty of Worcester'	CCla CHad CPev EGol ELan EOvi EVal LPri MBea MCad NB&B SBra SHil SSus
'Bees' Jubilee'	Widely available
'Belle Nantaise'	CPev EBre EOvi EVal MCad
'Belle of Woking'	CCla CPev ELan EOvi ESco EVal LPri MBea MBri MCad NB&B SBra SDix SPer
'Betty Corning' (V)	EVal LRHS MBri
'Bill Mackenzie'	See C. ***tangutica*** 'B.M.'
'Blue Belle' (V)	EOvi EVal MBri MCad NB&B SBra
'Blue Bird'	CCla CHad CMac EOrc EOvi EPen ESco IOrc LPri MBea MCad NB&B NBar NHol SBra SHil SMad SPer SPla
'Blue Gem'	EOvi EPen MCad SBra SHil
x ***bonstedtii***	EPen MCad
– 'Crépuscule'	CCla EBre
'Bracebridge Star'	EOvi ESco EVal MCad SBra
brachiata	CHan LPri SBra SDix
brevicaudata	CB&S MCad
* 'Broughton's Star'	EOvi NB&B
buchananiana	CHan EVal MCad WDav
'Burford Variety'	EGol EOrc EVal LPri MBri MCad NB&B WAbe
'C W Dowman'	MCad SBra
calycina	See C. ***cirrhosa balearica***
campaniflora	CBot CCla CHad CHan CPev EOrc EOvi EVal MBri MCad NB&B SBra SHil SIng SSpi WSHC
– hybrid	MPar
'Candy Stripe'	EPen ESco
'Capitan Thuilleaux'	See C. 'Souvenir du Capitaine Thuilleaux'
'Cardinal Wyszynski'	See C. 'Kardynal Wyszynski'
'Carnaby'	ELan EOvi EPen EVal LPri MBri MCad SBra SHil SSus WBod WWeb
¶ x ***cartmanii***	ECou
¶ – 'Joe'	WAbe
'Centre Attraction'	MCad
'Chalcedony'	CPev ESco
'Charissima'	CMac CPev EOvi EPen ESco MCad SBra
chiisanensis	MCad NB&B
chinensis	EOvi ESco EVal MCad
N ***chrysocoma***	CCla CHad CHan CPev ELan EOvi ESco EVal LPri MBea MCad MGos NHol SBla SBra SDix SHil SPer SSpi SSta SSus WSHC
– B&L 12237	NB&B
– ***sericea***	See C. ***montana sericea***
– ***spooneri***	See C. ***montana sericea***
cirrhosa	CBot CBow CHan CPev ELan EOvi ERea LPri MCad SPer WSHC
§ – ***balearica***	Widely available
– ***balearica*** forms	CPev MCad
– 'Freckles'	CCla ELan EOrc EOvi ERav EVal MBri MCad NB&B SPer
– 'Wisley Form'	EGol ELan EVal LPri LRHS MCad SBra SHil SPer SSus WSHC
'Colette Deville'	ESco MCad
columbiana	MCad
'Comtesse de Bouchaud'	Widely available
connata	CBot ESco EVal MBea MCad SBra
'Continuity'	EOvi MBri WSHC
'Corona'	CPev ELan EOvi EPen EVal LPri MCad NB&B SHil
'Corry'	EVal
'Countess of Lovelace'	CB&S CCla CMac ELan EOvi EPen ESco EVal LPri MBea MBri MCad NB&B SBra SDix SHil SPer SSus
County Park hybrids	ECou
'Crimson King'	EOvi EVal MBea MCad SBra
crispa	EOvi ESco EVal MCad SBra
– ***rosea***	ESco MCad
x ***cylindrica***	EOvi ESco EVal LRHS
'Daniel Deronda'	CB&S CPev EOvi EPen ESco EVal LPri MBea MBri MCad NB&B SBra SDix SHil SPer SPla SSta SSus WBod
'Darlene'	LPri
'Dawn'	CPev EOrc EOvi EPen EVal LPri MCad NB&B SBra SPer
denticulata P&W 6287	MCad
♦ ***diascoreifolia***	See C. ***terniflora***
* 'Dilly Dilly'	MCad
'Doctor Ruppel'	CMac CPev ELan EOvi EPen ESco EVal LPri MBar MBea MBri MCad MGos NB&B SBra SDix SHil SPer SSus WAbe WSHC
'Dorothy Walton'	EOvi EPen EVal MBea MCad
douglasii	WDav
– ***scottii***	MCad MPar MUlv NB&B WOMN
'Duchess of Albany' (T)	Widely available
'Duchess of Edinburgh'	Widely available
'Duchess of Sutherland'	CPev EOvi ESco EVal LPri MBea MBri MCad SBra SDix
x ***durandii***	Widely available
'Edith'	EOvi EVal LPri MBri MCad NB&B WWat
'Edouard Desfossé'	EOvi MCad NB&B
'Edward Prichard'	EOvi MCad NB&B SDix

§ 'Elsa Späth'	CCla CPev CSco ELan ENot EOvi EPen ESco EVal IJoh LPri MBar MBea MBri MCad MGos NB&B SBra SDix SHil SPer SSus WAbe WBod
'Elvan' (V)	CPev EOvi MCad NB&B
'Empress of India'	EOvi EVal MCad NB&B
x ***eriostemon***	CCla EOvi EPen ESco EVal MCad SBla SBra SPer
– 'Blue Boy'	MBri MCad
§ – 'Hendersonii'	CCla CFor CPev CSco ECro EGol EHar ELan EOvi ERou MCad MUlv NB&B NHol SBra SHil SPer WSHC
'Ernest Markham'	Widely available
'Etoile de Malicorne'	EOvi EVal MBri MCad NB&B SBra
'Etoile de Paris'	EOvi EVal MCad SBra
'Etoile Rose' (T)	CCla CPev EOvi ESco IOrc LPri MCad NB&B SBla SBra SHil WSHC
'Etoile Violette' (V)	Widely available
'Fair Rosamond'	CHad CPev EOvi ESco EVal LPri MBri MCad NB&B SBra SDix
¶ 'Fairy' x ***indivisa***	ECou
'Fairy Queen'	EOvi EVal MCad SBra
fargesii	See C. ***potaninii***
¶ x ***fargesioides***	EVal SPer
fasciculiflora	CBot CFor CHan MCad NB&B SBla SBra SSpi
finetiana	MCad
'Fireworks'	EOvi EVal MCad NB&B
flammula	CBow CCla CPev CSco EHar ELan EPen ESco EVal LHol LHop LPri MCad NB&B SBra SDix SHil SPer SSpi SSta SSus WOak WSHC
– 'Rubra Marginata'	See C. x ***triternata*** 'Rubromarginata'
florida bicolor	See C. ***f.*** 'Sieboldii'
– 'Flore Pleno'	CCla CPev EOvi ESco EVal LGre MCad MCot NB&B SBla SBra SHil SMad SPer SSus
§ – 'Sieboldii'	Widely available
foetida	ECou EPad EVal
forrestii	See C. ***napaulensis***
forsteri	CHan CSam ESco EVal LGre LPri MCad NB&B SBra WOMN WSHC WWat
'Four Star'	LPri
fremontii	LGre
'Fuji-musume'	MCad
fusca	MCad
¶ – ***kamtschatica***	ESco
¶ – ***mandshurica***	ESco
¶ – ***violacea***	EVal
'General Sikorski'	CMac EOrc EOvi EPen ESco EVal LPri MBea MBri MCad MGos NB&B NHol SBra SDix SHil SPer SSus WBod WWat
gentianoides	EVal MBri SBra
'Gillian Blades'	EBre EOvi ESco EVal MBea MBri MCad NB&B
'Gipsy Queen'	Widely available
'Gladys Picard'	MCad
glauca	See C. ***intricata***
'Glynderek'	MCad
gouriana	CCla SBra
¶ 'Grandiflora Sanguinea' (V)	EVal SBra
grata	CMCN CPev MBea MCad WEas
'Gravetye Beauty' (T)	Widely available
'Gravetye Seedling'	EOvi
'Green Velvet'	ECou ESco
'Guiding Star'	See C. 'Lilacina Floribunda'
'H F Young'	CCla CPev CSco ELan EOvi EPen ESco EVal LPri MBea MBri MCad MGos NB&B NRoo SBra SDix SHil SPer SSta WWin
'Hagley Hybrid'	Widely available
'Haku-ookan'	CPev EOvi EPen ESco EVal LPri MBea MCad SBra
Havering hybrids	ECou
'Helsingborg'	EOrc EOvi EVal MBri MCad SBra SHil SMad
'Henryi'	CCla CHad CPev ELan EOvi EPen ESco EVal IOrc LGre LPri MBea MBri MCad NB&B NHol SBra SDix SHil SPer SSus WBod WSHC
heracleifolia	CBot CHar EPar EPot ESco MCad WSHC WWat
N– 'Campanile'	CCla CPev MCad NB&B SBra SDix
N– 'Côte d'Azur'	CBot EFol MCad NB&B SHil
– ***davidiana***	CHad CPev ELan ERav NHol
– 'Jaggards'	CBot
– 'Wyevale'	Widely available
'Herbert Johnson'	CMac CPev EOvi SBra
hexapetala	CB&S ESco WWat
'Hint of Pink'	MCad
hirsutissima	See C. ***douglasii***
hookeriana	ECou
'Horn of Plenty'	CCla EBre EOvi ESco EVal MBea MBri MCad SBra SDix
'Huldine' (V)	CCla CGle CHad CPev CSco EOvi EPen ERav ESco EVal LPri MBea MBri MCad NB&B SBra SDix SHil SPer SPla SSus WBod WSHC
§ 'Hybrida Sieboldiana'	CMac EOvi EPen ESco EVal LPri MBea MCad NB&B SBra SPer SSus
¶ ***ianthina***	ESco
*– 'Violacea'	ESco
§ ***indivisa***	CFor CGre CPev ECou MCad WSHC
integrifolia	CBow CHad CHan EOrc ESco EVal LGre LHop LPri MBri MCad MCot NHol NRoo SFis SPer WPer
– ***alba***	LPri
*– 'Finnis Form'	WSHC
– 'Hendersonii'	See C. x ***eriostemon*** 'H.'
– 'Olgae'	CCla CHan CPev EOvi ESco EVal MCad NB&B SBra SDix
– 'Pastel Blue'	CPev
– 'Pastel Pink'	CPev SBra
– 'Rosea'	CCla CPev EOvi ESco EVal LPri MBri MCad NB&B WPer
– 'Tapestry'	CPev
¶ – white form	NB&B NBir
§ ***intricata***	CB&S ESco EVal MCad WWat
'Ishobel'	LPri MCad
* ***isphahanica***	MCad SBra SIng
x ***jackmanii***	CBra CMac ENot EOvi ESco GRei IHos MCad MR&S NB&B NRoo NWea SBra SPer
'Jackmanii Alba'	CCla CPev ELan EOvi EPen EVal IJoh LPri MBar MBea MBri MCad NB&B SDix SHil SPer SSus
'Jackmanii Rubra'	CPev EOvi ESco LPri MCad NB&B SPer

'Jackmanii Superba'	Widely available
'James Mason'	CPev EVal
'Jan Pawel II'	CCla EOvi EPen ESco EVal LPri MCad NB&B SBra SPer
japonica	CPev EOrc EOvi MCad NB&B
'Jim Hollis'	EOvi EPen MCad
'Joan Picton'	EOvi EPen ESco EVal LPri MBea MCad
'John Huxtable'	CPev EBre EOvi EVal LPri MBri MCad NB&B SBra
'John Paul II'	See C. 'Jan Pawel II'
'John Warren'	CCla EOrc EOvi EPen EVal LPri MCad NB&B SBra SDix SPer
§ x *jouiniana*	CHad EOvi EVal MBal MBea MCad MCot MUlv SHil SPer SSus WSHC
§ – 'Mrs Robert Brydon'	CSco CShe EGol EVal MBri MCad NB&B NHol SBra SPer
– 'Praecox'	CCla CPev EFol EFou EGol EHar ELan EPen ESco EVal LPri MBri MCad NB&B NHol SBla SBra SDix SHil SPer SSpi SSus
¶ 'Kacper'	ESco
'Kardynal Wyszynski'	EOvi ESco EVal LPri MBea MCad NB&B SBra
'Kathleen Dunford'	EOvi EPen ESco EVal LPri MBea MCad NB&B SBra
'Kathleen Wheeler'	CMac CPev CSco EOvi EPen EVal LPri MBri MCad NB&B SBra SDix
'Keith Richardson'	CPev EOvi MCad SBra
'Ken Donson'	CMac EOvi EPen EVal MCad SBra
§ 'Kermesina' (V)	CBow CCla CMac CPev CSam CSco ELan EOvi EPen ERav EVal LPri MBea MBri MCad NB&B SBla SBra SDix SPer SSta SSus WSHC WWat
'King Edward VII'	EOvi EVal NB&B SBra
'King George V'	EOvi EVal MBea MCad NB&B SBra
koreana	MCad
¶ – *fragrans*	ESco
– *lutea*	ESco MCad SPer
ladakhiana	CHan CPev MCad NB&B NBir SBra WEas WSHC
'Lady Betty Balfour'	CCla CMac CPev CSco ELan EOvi EPen ESco EVal GRei LPri MBea MBri MCad NB&B SBra SDix SHil SSus WSHC
'Lady Caroline Nevill'	CPev EOvi EVal MCad NB&B SBra
'Lady Londesborough'	CPev EBre EGol ELan EOvi EPen EVal LPri MCad NB&B SBra SDix
'Lady Northcliffe'	CMac CPev ELan EOvi EPen EVal LPri MCad NB&B SBra SDix SPer
'Ladybird Johnson' (T)	CPev
'Lagoon'	EVal LRHS SBra
lasiandra	CHan MBea
'Lasurstern'	Widely available
'Lawsoniana'	CMac EPen ESco LPri MBea MCad NB&B SBra
ligusticifolia	CBrd
* 'Lilac Time'	LPri
§ 'Lilacina Floribunda'	CHad ELan EOvi EPen EVal LPri MBea MCad SBra SSus WSHC
'Lincoln Star'	CPev CSco ELan EOvi EPen EVal LPri MBea MBri MCad NB&B SBra SDix SHil SPer SSus WBod
'Little Nell'	CCla CHad CPev EOrc EOvi EPen ESco EVal LPri MBea MBri MCad NB&B SBra SDix SPer SPla SSta WSHC
'Lord Nevill'	CCla CPev ELan EOvi EPen ESco EVal LPri MBea MBri MCad NB&B SBra SDix SPer
'Louise Rowe'	EOvi ESco LPri MCad SBra
¶ 'Lunar Lass' x *foetida*	ECou
macropetala	Widely available
¶ – 'Anders'	EVal
♦– 'Blue Lagoon'	See C. *m.* 'Maidwell Hall'
– 'Floralia'	EVal LRHS MBri MCad SHil
– forms	CPev
– 'Jan Lindmark'	EVal LRHS MBri SHil
§ – 'Maidwell Hall'	CBow CCla CFor CMac CSco EOvi EPen ESco EVal LPri MBea MBri MCad MCot MGos NHol SBla SBra SHil SPer SSpi SSta SSus WWat
– 'Markham's Pink'	Widely available
– 'Pauline'	SBra
– 'Snowbird'	CPev EOvi MCad NB&B
– 'White Moth'	See C. ***alpina*** 'White Moth'
– 'White Swan'	CCla EPen ESco EVal MBri MCad MGos NHol SBra SHil SPer SPla SSus
'Madame Baron Veillard'	CCla CPev EOvi EPen ESco EVal LPri MBar MBea MCad NB&B SBra SDix SHil SSus
'Madame Edouard André'	CCla CMac CPev EOvi EPen ESco EVal LPri MBea MCad NB&B NHol SBra SDix WSHC
'Madame Grangé'	CPev CSco EBre EOvi EPen EVal LPri MBea MCad NB&B SBra SDix
'Madame Julia Correvon' (V)	CCla CHad CMac EGol ELan EOrc EOvi EPen ERav EVal LPri MBea MBri MCad NB&B NHol SBla SBra SDix SHil SPer SPla SSta WWat
'Madame le Coultre'	See C. 'Marie Boisselot'
marata	SBra
– 'Temple Prince' (m)	ECou
– 'Temple Queen' (f)	ECou
'Marcel Moser'	CPev EOvi EVal MBea MCad NB&B SBra SDix
'Margaret Hunt'	EOvi EPen EVal LPri MCad SBra
'Margot Koster' (V)	CCla EOvi ESco EVal LPri MBea MCad MCot NB&B SBla SBra SPla SSta WSHC
§ 'Marie Boisselot'	Widely available
marmoraria	ECou EPad EPot ESco GArf NBir NHol NRed SPou
'Maureen'	CPev EOvi ESco EVal LPri MBri MCad NB&B SDix SPer WAbe
maximowicziana	See C. ***terniflora***
¶ *microphylla*	ESco
'Minuet' (V)	CCla CHad EGol EOvi ESco EVal IOrc LPri MBea MBri MCad NB&B NHol SBra SDix SHil SPer
'Miriam Markham'	CPev SBra
'Miss Bateman'	Widely available

'Miss Crawshay'	CPev EOvi ESco EVal MBea MCad NB&B SBra SDix
N *montana*	Widely available
– *alba*	See C. ***montana***
– 'Alexander'	CSco EOrc EOvi ESco EVal LPri MBea MBri MCad MGos SBra SHil SSus
– 'Elizabeth'	Widely available
– 'Freda'	EOvi ESco EVal LPri MBri MCad MGos NB&B NHol SBra SMad SPer
– *grandiflora*	CBow CCla CHad CMac CSco EBre ELan EOvi EPen ISea LHop LPri MBea MBri MCad MGos MR&S NB&B SBra SDix SPer SSus WSHC WWat
– 'Margaret Jones'	MCad
– 'Marjorie'	CB&S EBre EOvi EPen ESco EVal LPri MBri MCad MGos NB&B NHol SBra SHil SPer
– 'Mayleen'	EOvi ESco EVal LPri MBea MBri MCad MGos NB&B SBra SPer
– 'Odorata'	EOvi EVal LRHS MBea MCad MGos SBra
– 'Peveril'	CPev
– 'Picton's Variety'	CPev CSco EOrc EOvi ESco LPri MBri MCad NB&B SBra SDix
– 'Pink Perfection'	CSco EOvi EPen EVal LPri MBea MBri MCad NB&B NHol SBra SHil SSus
– *rubens*	Widely available
– 'Rubens Superba'	CSco EPen MR&S SReu
§ – *sericea*	CB&S CBot CHad CHan CPev EOvi EPen EVal IJoh LPri MBar MCad NB&B NHol SBra SSus WWat
– 'Snow'	EOvi
– 'Spooneri'	See C. ***chrysocoma sericea***
– 'Tetrarose'	Widely available
– 'Veitch's Form'	CBot
– 'Vera'	EOvi MCad NB&B NBir
– *wilsonii*	CBot CCla CHad CLan CPev CSco CTre ELan EOvi EPen ESco EVal LHol LPri MBea MBri MCad MCot NB&B SDix SHil SPer SSus WSHC
§ 'Moonlight'	CPev EOvi MCad NB&B SBra SDix SPer
'Mrs Bush'	EOvi LRHS MCad NB&B
'Mrs Cholmondeley'	Widely available
'Mrs George Jackman'	CCla CPev EOvi EVal MBea MCad NB&B SBra SSus
'Mrs Hope'	CCla CPev EOvi EVal MCad NB&B SBra SDix
'Mrs James Mason'	CPev EOvi EVal
'Mrs N Thompson'	CMac CPev ELan EOvi EPen ESco EVal LPri MBar MBea MBri MCad MR&S NB&B NHol NRoo SBra SDix SHil SPla SSta SSus WBod
'Mrs P B Truax'	EOrc EOvi ESco EVal LPri MCad NB&B SBra SDix
'Mrs Robert Brydon'	See C. x ***jouiniana*** 'Mrs R.B.'
'Mrs Spencer Castle'	CPev EOvi EVal LPri MBea MCad NB&B SBra SDix
* 'Multi-Blue'	ELan
'Myojo'	EOvi ESco MBea MCad NB&B
§ *napaulensis*	CPev EOvi ESco EVal IBlr LPri MBea MCad SBra
'Nelly Moser'	Widely available
¶ New Zealand hybrids	ECou
'Niobe'	Widely available
'North Star'	MCad
¶ *occidentalis grosseserata*	ESco
¶ *ochotensis*	ELan
orientalis	See C. ***tibetana vernayi***
– 'Bill Mackenzie'	See C. ***tangutica*** 'Bill Mackenzie'
*– 'Helios'	EVal MBri MCad
– 'Orange Peel'	See C. ***tibetana vernayi*** 'O.P.'
*– 'Rubromarginata'	CPev
– 'Sherriffii'	See C. ***tibetana vernayi*** LS&E 13342
'Pagoda' (V)	CPev EOvi ESco MBea MCad SBra WSHC
'Pamela Jackman'	See C. ***alpina*** 'P.J.'
♦ *paniculata* Gmelin	See C. ***indivisa***
♦ – Thunberg	See C. ***terniflora***
parviflora	ECou
¶ *patens*	SBra
¶ 'Pennell's Purity'	ESco
'Percy Picton'	MCad NB&B
'Perle d'Azur'	Widely available
petriei	ECou EOvi SOkd
– 'Limelight' (m)	ECou
– 'Princess' (f)	ECou
¶ – x *foetida*	ECou
– x *forsteri*	ECou
¶ – x *parviflora*	ECou
'Peveril Pearl'	CPev EVal LPri MCad
'Pink Champagne'	EOrc EPen EVal LPri MBri MCad SBra SSus
'Pink Fantasy'	CMac CPev EOvi EPen ESco IJoh LPri MCad NHol
'Pink Flamingo'	MBea
pitcheri	CHan CPev EOrc EOvi EVal LRHS MBri MCad NB&B
'Polish Spirit' (V)	EOrc EOvi EVal MBri MCad
§ *potaninii*	ESco LPri MBri MCad NB&B SBra
§ – *souliei*	CCla CGle CHan CMHG CPev ELan EVal ISea LPri MBri MCad NB&B SBra SDix SPer WSHC
'Prince Charles'	EOvi MCad NB&B NBir SBra SDix
'Princess of Wales' (T)	CPev EOvi MCad
'Prins Hendrik'	CMac EOvi ESco EVal MBea MCad NB&B SBra
'Proteus'	CB&S CPev EOrc EOvi EPen ESco EVal LPri MCad NB&B SBra SDix SPer SSus WWat
quadribracteolata	ECou EOvi EVal NB&B
'Ramona'	See C. 'Hybrida Sieboldiana'
recta	CHad CHan CPev CSun ELan EOvi EVal LPri MBri MCad MWgw NB&B NBar NRoo SPer
– 'Grandiflora'	NHol
– 'Peveril'	CPev
– 'Purpurea'	CBot CBrd CCla CHad CHoe CSun EFol ELan ERav EVal MCad NB&B SBla SBra SDix SPer SSpi WDav
rehderiana	Widely available
'Richard Pennell'	CCla CMac CPev EOvi EPen ESco EVal LPri MBri MCad NB&B SBra SDix SSus WAbe
'Rosie O'Grady'	ELan EOrc EOvi EPen EVal LPri MBar MBea MBri MCad MFir NHol SBra SPer

'Rouge Cardinal'	Widely available
'Royal Velours' (V)	CCla CPev EOvi ESco EVal IOrc LPri MBea MCad NB&B NHol SBla SBra SDix SHil SPer SPla WWat
'Royalty'	EBre EOrc EOvi EVal LPri MBri MCad NB&B SBra SDix SSus WBod
'Ruby Glow'	EOvi EVal MCad SBra
'Sally Cadge'	MCad
'Saturn'	EPen EVal MCad SBra
'Scartho Gem'	CMac CPev EOvi EPen ESco EVal MCad SBra
'Sealand Gem'	CPev ELan EOvi ESco EVal MBea MCad MR&S NB&B NBar SBra SSta
'Serenata'	EOvi EVal LPri MBea MCad NB&B SBra
serratifolia	CCla CHan CHil CPev EGol EOvi EVal LPri MBea MBri MCad NB&B SBra SDix SPer
* 'Signe'	MCad
'Silver Moon'	EOvi EPen ESco EVal LPri MCad NB&B SBra
'Sir Garnet Wolseley'	ELan EOvi EVal MCad NB&B SBra SDix
'Sir Trevor Lawrence' (T)	CCla CPev EOvi EVal MCad NB&B SBra SDix
'Snow Queen'	EOvi ESco EVal LPri MCad NB&B
songarica	EBar EOrc EOvi EVal MBri MCad SBra
'Souvenir de J L Delbard'	EVal MCad SBra
'Souvenir du Capitaine Thuilleaux'	CPev EOvi EPen EVal LPri MBea MBri MCad NHol SBra SHil SPer SSus
spooneri	See C. ***montana sericea***
– 'Rosea'	See C. x ***vedrariensis*** 'Rosea'
stans	EVal SIng
'Star of India'	CPev ELan EOvi ESco EVal LPri MBri MCad NB&B SBra SDix
'Strawberry Roan'	EOvi
'Susan Allsop'	CPev EOvi MCad
'Sylvia Denny'	CCla ELan EOvi EVal LPri MBea MBri MCad NB&B SBra SPer
'Sympatia'	MCad
tangutica	Widely available
– 'Aureolin'	See C. 'Aureolin'
§ – 'Bill Mackenzie'	Widely available
– 'Gravetye Variety'	EPen ESco NB&B NHol
– 'Lambton Park'	EOvi LPri MCad NB&B NBir SBra
– obtusiuscula	CHan MCad NB&B
– 'Warsaw'	EOrc MBri MCad
§ ***terniflora***	CCla CHad CPev EOrc EOvi EPen ESco EVal LPri MCad NB&B SBra
¶ – 'Caddick's form'	CHan
¶ – 'Mandshurica'	ESco
texensis	CGre CHan MCad
'The President'	Widely available
¶ ***thunbergii***	EVal LRHS
§ ***tibetana***	CMac CPev ELan EOrc EPen EVal MBal MBar MBea MCad NHol NNor SHil SPer SSta WSHC WWat
§ ***– vernayi***	CHan CMHG EGol ELan EOvi EPen ESco LMer MPla NKay SBra SSus WWin
§ ***– vernayi*** LS&E 13342	CPev EOrc EOvi EVal MBri MCad NB&B NHol SBla SBra SDix SPer SSta
– vernayi 'Orange Peel'	ENot EVal IOrc MGos SPla
'Trianon'	MCad
§ x ***triternata*** 'Rubromarginata'	CBow CCla CPev CSco EPen EVal MCad NB&B NHol SBra SPer WSHC
'Twilight'	EOvi EVal MCad NB&B NHol SBra SPer
uncinata	CPev
x ***vedrariensis***	EVal MCad SPer WAbe
– 'Highdown'	CCla EPen ESco EVal LPri MBea MCad NB&B SBra
§ – 'Rosea'	CTrw EVal MCad MGos WSHC
'Venosa Violacea' (V)	CCla CHad ELan EOrc EOvi ESco EVal LPri MBri MCad MCot NB&B NBar SBla SBra SDix SHil
'Veronica's Choice'	CPev EOvi EVal MBri MCad SBra
¶ ***versicolor***	ESco
'Victoria'	CPev ELan EOvi EPen ESco EVal LPri MBea MCad NB&B SBra SDix
'Ville de Lyon'	Widely available
'Vino'	MCad
'Violet Charm'	EVal LRHS
¶ 'Violet Elizabeth'	ESco
viorna	ESco LPri NB&B SDix
virginiana	EOvi MCad NB&B SBra
vitalba	CKin CPev ESco EVal MBar MBea MCad SFir WHer
viticella	CHan CPev EOvi ESco EVal LAbb LPri MCad SBra SDix SHil SSus
– 'Mary Rose'	CPev
– 'Purpurea Plena Elegans'	Widely available
'Viticella Rubra' (V)	See C. 'Kermesina'
'Voluceau'	EBre EOvi EPen EVal MBea MCad NB&B SBra SHil SPer
'Vyvyan Pennell'	Widely available
'W E Gladstone'	CPev EOvi EPen EVal LPri MBea MCad NB&B SBra SDix SHil SPer
* 'W S Kalik'	MCad
'Wada's Primrose'	CCla CHad EBre ELan EOvi ESco EVal LPri MBea MBri MCad NB&B NHol SBra SHil SPer SSus WSHC
'Walter Pennell'	CMac CPev EOvi EPen MCad SBra
'Warszawska Nike'	MCad
'Wilhemina Tull'	EOvi ESco MCad
'Will Goodwin'	CB&S ELan EOvi EPen ESco EVal LPri MBea MBri MCad NB&B SBra SSus
'William Kennett'	CMac CPev CSco EBre ELan EOvi EPen ESco EVal LPri MBar MBea MBri MCad MGos MR&S NB&B NKay NRoo SBra SDix SHil SPer SSus
'Xerxes'	See C. 'Elsa Späth'
♦ 'Yellow Queen'	See C. 'Moonlight'
* 'Yvette Houry'	MCad

CLERODENDRUM (Verbenaceae)
bungei CB&S CBot CCla CHEx CHad CHil CPle CSco ELan ERea LGre SBor SDix SHil SLMG SPer WBod WOMN WWat
cyrtophyllum SSpi
splendens SLMG
sp. LH 391 SSpi
thomsoniae CHil CSun LAbb MBri SLMG
trichotomum CB&S CChu CCla CFis CHEx CTrw ENot IOrc ISea LSav MCot SCro SExT SHil SMad SPer SSpi SSta WBod WCoo
– fargesii CBra CHad CPle CSco ELan IOrc ISea LHop MBri MCot MGos SBor SHil SLon SPer WEas WPat WWat
ugandense CSun LHop SLMG

CLETHRA (Clethraceae)
¶ *acuminata* CB&S
alnifolia CB&S CBot CBow CChu CCla CGre CLan CMHG CSam CTre ELan IOrc MBar MR&S SBor SPer SReu WBod WWat WWin
– 'Paniculata' CSco ENot MBri SHil SSpi
– 'Pink Spire' CKni ELan MPla
– 'Rosea' CBot CBow CChu CCla CSco EGol ELan IJoh IOrc LSav MBar MBlu MBri SGar SHil SPer SSpi WAbe WBod WSHC WWat
arborea CB&S CChu CGre CHEx CPle CTre SSpi
barbinervis CB&S CBra CChu CGre CLan CSam GWic SHil SPer SSpi SSta WCoo WSHC WWat
delavayi CB&S CCla CHEx GWic MBal MBri NHol SSpi
– B&L 12547 WHCr
fargesii CB&S CCla CGre EHal MGos MUlv SHil SSpi WWat
monostachya CBow CChu CCla CGre SBor SSpi
tomentosa CCla LSav

CLEYERA (Theaceae)
§ *fortunei* CBot CMHG IBar SBor SHil SReu SSpi SSta WPat WWat
– 'Variegata' See C. ***fortunei***
japonica japonica MBal WCoo

CLIANTHUS (Leguminosae)
puniceus CBot CHEx CMac CSun CTre CTrw ECou ERea IDai IJoh LHop MBal MNew NPal SArc SAxl SHil SLMG SPer WBod WSHC
– albus CBot CHan CHil CPle CTre CTrw ELan ERea LHop MNew SLMG SPer SSus
– 'Flamingo' CB&S CBra ELan ERea IHos SHil
*– 'Red Admiral' CB&S
– 'Red Cardinal' CBra ELan ERea IHos IOrc
– roseus SSus

– 'White Heron' CB&S IHos IJoh IOrc SHil WBod

CLINOPODIUM (Labiatae)
§ ***acinos*** CArn LHol MBri MChe MSal SIde WHer WPer
§ ***ascendens*** CNat MSal WCla
§ ***calamintha*** CArn CCla CCor CHad ECha LGre MSal SBla WPer
¶ – ACL 1050/90 EMon
§ – ***calamintha*** CCla CGle CHar CSev CShe EBre ECha EFou EGol ELan EMon ERou LHol LHop MBri MPla MRav MTho SAxl SCro SIde SPer WRus WSHC
¶ – 'White Cloud' EMon
§ ***grandiflorum*** CCla CGle CHan CLew CSev CShe CTom ECha ELan EMon EOrc Effi GPoy LHol MPar MWat NSel SAxl SBla WHal WHil WHoo WPer WRus
– 'Variegata' CHan CHoe EFol EFou ELan EMon LHop MUlv NRar NSti WHal WHoo WOld WPer WRus
vulgare CArn CKin LHol MSal SIde WCla

CLINTONIA (Liliaceae/Convallariaceae)
andrewsiana GDra NHol NKay
borealis EBul EPar EPot LAma MSal
umbellulata EPot MSal SWas

CLIVIA (Liliaceae/Amaryllidaceae)
miniata hybrids ERea LAma MBri NPal SLMG

CLUSIA (Guttiferae)

CLYTOSTOMA (Bignoniaceae)
§ ***callistegioides*** CB&S

CNEORUM (Cneoraceae)
tricoccon WOMN

CNICUS (Compositae)
§ ***benedictus*** CArn GPoy LHol MSal NSel SIde

COBAEA (Polemoniaceae)
scandens CGre IBlr SMrm WCar WHal
¶ – ***alba*** CSun ELan ERea IBlr

COBNUT See **CORYLUS *avellana***

COCCULUS (Menispermaceae)

COCHLEARIA (Cruciferae)
armoracia See ARMORACIA ***rusticana***
officinalis MSal

COCONUT See **COCOS *nucifera***

COCOS (Palmae)
nucifera 'Golden Malay' LPal MBri

plumosa	See ARECASTRUM ***romanzoffianum***
weddelliana	See MICROCOELUM ***weddellianum***

CODIAEUM (Euphorbiaceae)

variegatum pictum 'Gold Moon'	MBri
– – 'Gold Sun'	MBri
– – 'Goldfinger'	MBri
– – 'Iceton'	MBri
– – 'Juliette'	MBri
– – 'Louise'	MBri
– – 'Nervia'	MBri
– – 'Petra'	MBri
– – 'Sunny Star'	MBri

CODONANTHE (Gesneriaceae)

gracilis	WEfe
¶ *paula*	WEfe

X CODONATANTHUS (Gesneriaceae)

'Aurora'	WEfe
'Fiesta'	WEfe
'Tambourine'	MBri WEfe
'Vista'	WEfe

CODONOPSIS (Campanulaceae)

bulleyana	NHol WThu
cardiophylla	MBro NHol NWCA
clematidea	Widely available
convolvulacea	CChu GDra LHop MTho NHol NKay NRar SBla SDix WHal WHoo WPer
– *alba*	CFor GDra NHol SBla SOkd SWas
forrestii	GEdr ITim LGre SOkd
handeliana	CLew NHol WPer
§ *lanceolata*	ECro SAxl WDav WPer
meleagris	ITim MTho NHol WPer
mollis	EPad NHol WPer
ovata	CBot CGle CLew ECro ELan EPad EPot GDra GLoc MTho NHol SWas WCar WEas
– KBE 225	NHol
pilosula	ECro NSti NWCA WCar WPer
rotundifolia angustifolia	NHol
subsimplex	NHol NRed NWCA
tangshen	CChu EPad EPot GPoy LGre MSal MTho NHol NSti SBla WPer
¶ *thalictrifolia*	GArf
♦ *ussuriensis*	See C. ***lanceolata***
vinciflora	ECro GDra SBla WMar
viridiflora	ECro WCla WPer WThu

COFFEA (Rubiaceae)

arabica	MBri

COFFEE See COFFEA *arabica*

COLCHICUM † (Liliaceae/Colchicaceae)

agrippinum	CAvo CBro ECam EPot ETub GHig ITim LAma LBow MBal MPar NHar SIng WAbe WChr WThu
'Antares'	LAma
atropurpureum	EPot LAma WChr
'Attlee'	LAma LBlo
'Autumn Herald'	LAma
N 'Autumn Queen'	LAma MPar NHar
autumnale	CArn CAvo CBro ELan EPot GPoy LAma LBow MBal MSal NLan SIde
– JMH 8001	WChr
§ – 'Alboplenum'	CBro ETub LAma LBlo SPou WChr
– *album*	CAvo CBro ETub LAma LBlo LBow MBal MPlt NHar NHol SIng SPou
– *atropurpureum*	CBro LAma SPou
– *major*	LAma LBlo MBri
– *minor*	ETub LAma
– *minor album plenum*	See C. ***a.*** 'Alboplenum'
– 'pannonicum'	CBro LRHS
– pink form	MPar
§ – 'Pleniflorum'	CBro EPot ETub LAma LBlo LBow
– *roseum plenum*	See C. ***a.*** 'Pleniflorum'
baytopiorum	EPot LAma WChr
'Beaconsfield'	MPar
§ *bivonae*	CBro EPot LAma WChr
boissieri	ECam SPou
– CEH 628	WChr
bornmuelleri	CAvo CBro EPot ETub LAma SIng
bowlesianum	See C. ***bivonae***
burttii	EPot WChr
byzantinum	CAvo CBro ETub LBow MPar SIng WChr
– *album*	EPot SPou
chalcedonicum	See C. ***lingulatum***
cilicicum	CBro EPot ETub LAma LBow MPar SPou WChr
– 'Purpureum'	LAma SPou
'Conquest'	LAma MPar WChr
corsicum	LAma MPar WChr WDav WThu
cupanii	CBro ECam LAma WChr
'Dandaels'	LAma MPar
'Darwin'	MPar
'Dick Trotter'	LAma MPar
doerfleri	See C. ***hungaricum***
'E A Bowles'	LAma MPar
fasciculare	LAma
giganteum	EPot LAma LBlo SIng SPou
hierosolymitanum	EPot LAma WChr
§ *hungaricum*	ECam LAma LBow SPou WChr
'Huxley'	MPar
kesselringii	CBro ECam EPot SOkd
kotschyi	EPot LAma SPou
laetum	See C. ***parnassicum***

'Lilac Wonder' CBro EPot ETub LAma MBri MPar MPlt NHol SIng
§ ***lingulatum*** EPot LAma WChr
'Little Woods' MPar
longiflorum EPot
lusitanicum LAma WChr
luteum CBro ECam EPot ETub LAma LBlo LBow WChr
macrophyllum EPot LAma WChr
micranthum EPot LAma
'Nancy Lindsay' MPar
neapolitanum LAma
parnassicum CEH 630 WChr
'Pink Goblet' EPot LAma MPar WChr
****polyphyllum*** LAma
'Prinses Astrid' LAma MPar
procurrens WChr
pusillum CBro
'Rosy Dawn' ECha LAma MPar WChr
sibthorpii See C. ***bivonae***
speciosum CAvo CBro EPot ETub LAma LBow MBal MPar NHar NOrc NRar SIng WAbe
– 'Album' CAvo CBro EBre ECha ELan EPot ETub LAma LBlo LBow MBri MPar NHar NHol SIng SPou SSpi WChr
– 'Atrorubens' ECha LAma MPar WChr
♦– 'illyricum' See C. ***giganteum***
– 'Maximum' LAma WChr
*– 'Ordii' LRHS
szovitsii SPou
tenorii LAma MPar
'The Giant' CAvo CBro EPot LAma LBlo MPar SIng
troodii EPot LAma WChr
turcicum EPot LAma WChr
umbrosum CBro EPot
variegatum CBro LAma SPou WChr
'Violet Queen' CBro LAma MPar SIng
'Waterlily' CAvo CBro ELan EPot ETub LAma LBlo LBow MBal MBri MPar NHar SIng WAbe
'William Dykes' LAma MPar
'Zephyr' LAma

COLEONEMA (Rutaceae)
pulchrum CSun LHop MNew
¶ ***virgatum*** CB&S

COLEUS See SOLENOSTEMON

COLLETIA (Rhamnaceae)
armata CB&S IBar LAbb MPar SArc SBor SLon SMad WAbe WBod
– 'Rosea' CGre MBlu SArc SHil SLHN SSus
cruciata See C. ***paradoxa***
§ ***paradoxa*** CB&S CChu CGre CHEx CTre SArc SHil SLHN SMad SSpi WBod

COLLINSONIA (Labiatae)
canadensis ELan MSal

COLLOMIA (Polemoniaceae)
¶ ***grandiflora*** MShr WOMN

COLOBANTHUS (Caryophyllaceae)
acicularis ITim NHol
buchananii ECou
canaliculatus ECou EPot ITim NHol
muscoides NHol

COLOCASIA (Araceae)
¶ ***esculenta*** CHEx

COLQUHOUNIA (Labiatae)
coccinea CCla CHEx CHan MBal MRav SSpi WBod WSHC
– ***mollis*** CGre CPle SLon
– ***vestita*** CB&S IReg NHol WPat

COLUMNEA (Gesneriaceae)
'Aladdin's Lamp' NMos WEfe
x ***banksii*** CPle CSut MBri WEfe
'Booget Stavanger' CSut WEfe
'Chanticleer' MBri WEfe
¶ 'Early Bird' WEfe
'Flamingo' WEfe
gloriosa EBak LAbb
'Heidi' MBri
hirta CSut MBri WEfe
– 'Variegata' MBri
****hosta*** MBri
'Inferno' WEfe
'Katsura' MBri WEfe
'Kewensis Variegata' MBri
¶ 'Mary Ann' WEfe
microphylla variegata MBri
¶ 'Midnight Lantern' WEfe
schiedeana MBri WEfe
'Starburst' NMos
'Stavanger' CSut EBak MBri WEfe

COLUTEA † (Leguminosae)
arborescens CArn CPle ELan ENot GPoy IBlr IHos MBar MGos MSal NNor SHil SLHN SPer SPla SReu WHer WWin
– 'Copper Beauty' CB&S CSco ELan MBri MGos SPer
¶– 'Pendula' MBar
x ***media*** CGre EHal SHil WCru
¶ ***multiflora*** CB&S
orientalis SDry SHil
persica CB&S SLon

COLUTEOCARPUS (Cruciferae)
vesicaria WDav

COMARUM See POTENTILLA

COMMELINA (Commelinaceae)
coelestis See C. ***tuberosa*** Coelestis group
dianthifolia CGle GWic ITim LGan MCas MPar MPit MTho SFir WDav WEas
¶ ***tuberosa*** ELan WEas

– 'Alba' ELan EMon GWic LGan LHop WHer
§ – Coelestis group CChu CElw CFor CGle CHan CHar ECha ECro EFol EMon GWic LHop MPlt NSti SLMG WHal WHer WHil WOMN WPer WWin
virginica ECro GWic IBlr LGan WCru

COMPTONIA (Myricaceae)
peregrina SHil

CONIUM (Umbelliferae)
¶ *maculatum* NHex

CONOPODIUM (Umbelliferae)
majus CArn CKin

CONRADINA (Labiatae)
¶ *canescens* CSun
verticillata LGre SOkd WPer

CONSOLIDA (Ranunculaceae)
§ *ajacis* CArn MSal
ambigua See C. ***ajacis***
regalis MSal

CONVALLARIA † (Liliaceae/Convallariaceae)
japonica See OPHIOPOGON ***jaburan***
majalis Widely available
§ – 'Albistriata' CBot CChu CHoe CRow CSin ELan EPar GLoc LGre MCas MPar NHol SPou SSpi WEas WHer
– 'Fortin's Giant' CAvo CBro CHad CKel CSco CSin ECro ELan EMon ERav SIng WBon
– 'Hardwick Hall' CBos CHoe CSin
– 'Prolificans' CRow ELan EMon EPar EPot LHop MCas MPar SSpi WChr
– *rosea* CAvo CFor CRow CSco CShe CSin ELan EPar EPot ERav GLoc NHol SPou WChr WEas WHil
♦ – 'Variegata' See C. ***m.*** 'Albostriata'
montana WChr
transcaucasica WChr

CONVOLVULUS (Convolvulaceae)
althaeoides CBot CHad CHan CHil CSam LGre LHil MTho SBla SChu SCro SSpi WEas
– *tenuissimus* See C. ***elegantissimus***
§ *boissieri* SIng WDav
cantabricus CSun GLoc LHop WPer
cneorum Widely available
§ *elegantissimus* EOrc GWic LHop MPar SAxl SLHN
lineatus ELan EPot GLoc LHop MTho NWCA SBla SIng
mauritanicus See C. ***sabatius***
nitidus See C. ***boissieri***
§ *sabatius* Widely available
– dark form CSpe CSun GWic LHop SIng SMrm

COOPERIA See **ZEPHYRANTHES**

COPROSMA † (Rubiaceae)
acerosa (f) See C. ***brunnea***
areolata ECou
atropurpurea (m) ECou ITim NHol
♦ *baueri* 'Picturata' See C. ***repens*** 'P.'
'Beatson's Gold' (f) CB&S CBow CBra CMHG CMer CTrw ERea IBar IJoh IOrc ISea LHop NHol NTow SChu STre WBod WSHC
'Blue Pearls' (f) ECou
'Brunette' (f) ECou
brunnea (f) ECou IJoh MHig
– x *kirkii* (m) ECou
cheesemanii ECou
'Chocolate Soldier' (m) ECou
'Coppershine' CMer
crassifolia x *repens* (m) ECou
x *cunninghamii* (f) ECou
depressa ECou
foetidissima ECou
'Green Girl' (f) ECou
'Green Globe' CTre
'Hinerua' (f) ECou
'Indigo Lustre' (f) ECou
'Jewel' (f) ECou
x *kirkii* 'Kirkii' (f) ECou IJoh
– 'Kirkii Variegata' (f) CB&S CBot CBow CHan CMer CPle CTre ECou LHop NTow SAxl SChu SCro STre WSHC
* 'Kiwi-Gold' CB&S CMer ECou
linariifolia ECou
lucida ECou
macrocarpa ECou
nitida (m) ECou
parviflora (m) ECou
'Pearly Queen' (f) EBar ECou
'Pearl's Sister' (f) ECou
petriei ECou MHig
– 'Don' (m) ECou
– 'Lyn' (f) ECou
propinqua CChu SDry WSHC
– (f) ECou
– (m) ECou
'Prostrata' (m) ECou
* *pumila* ECou
repens (f) CHEx ECou
– (m) CB&S ECou
– 'Apricot' (f) ECou
– 'Brownie' (f) ECou
– 'County Park Purple' (f) ECou
– 'Exotica' (f) ECou LHop
– 'Marble King' (m) ECou
– 'Marble Queen' (m) ECou IBar LHop SLMG
– 'Orangeade' (f) ECou
– 'Picturata' (m) ECou ERea
– 'Pink Splendour' CB&S LHop
– 'Silver Queen' (m) ECou
– 'Variegata' (m) ECou LHil
rhamnoides ECou
rigida (f) ECou

robusta (m&f)	CHEx ECou
rotundifolia (m&f)	ECou
¶ 'Roy's Red'	ECou
rugosa	ECou IBar
tenuifolia (m)	ECou
'Violet Drops' (f)	ECou
virescens (f)	ECou
'Walter Brockie'	CChu
williamsii	LHop

COPTIS (Ranunculaceae)

¶ ***laciniata***	SIng
quinquefolia	WDav

CORALLOSPARTIUM (Leguminosae)

¶ ***crassicaule***	ECou
¶ – x ***carmichaelia kirkii***	ECou

CORDYLINE † (Agavaceae)

australis	Widely available
– 'Albertii'	CB&S CHEx IOrc LNet MBri NPal SArc
*– 'Purple Tower'	CB&S IBar
– ***purpurea***	CB&S CBot CBra CHEx CTre ENot ERea IBar IOrc ISea MR&S SHil SPer WWeb
– 'Sundance'	CTor
– 'Torbay Dazzler'	CB&S CHEx CTor ELan WWeb
– 'Torbay Red'	CB&S CTor ELan MR&S WWeb
¶ – 'Torbay Sunset'	ELan IOrc
– 'Variegata'	CBot CHEx
banksii	CB&S CHEx
baueri	CHEx
fruticosa 'Atom'	MBri
– 'Baby Ti'	MBri
– 'Calypso Queen'	MBri
– 'Kiwi'	MBri
– 'Orange Prince'	MBri
– 'Red Edge'	MBri
– 'Yellow King'	MBri
§ ***indivisa***	CHEx CLan EBak MBri NPal SArc SSpi
kaspar	CHEx ECou
stricta	CHEx
terminalis	See C. ***fruticosa***

COREOPSIS † (Compositae)

¶ ***atkinsoniana***	WPer
auriculata 'Cutting Gold'	CSam IBrk SFis WPer
– 'Superba'	CTom EBre SFis
grandiflora	WOld
– 'Badengold'	CB&S ERou
– 'Domino'	NOak
*– 'Early Sunrise'	ECtt EFou NBar NRoo WHen WHil
– 'Goldfink'	CKel EBre ECha MRav NKay
– 'Mayfield Giant'	ERou NVic
– 'Sonnenkind' ('Baby Sun')	CSco MHig MPit NNor SFis
– 'Sunburst'	ELan IBrk NNor NOak WHoo
– 'Sunray'	CKel CLew CRiv EFou ERou LSav MBri MFir MPit MRav MWat NBar NOak NRoo SCro SFis WHil WPer WWin
lanceolata 'Early Sunshine'	WPer
– 'Lichtstad'	ERou MBri
– 'Sterntaler'	EFou MBri WDav
rosea	CLew
tinctoria	MSal
verticillata	CLew CSam CShe ECha EFol ENot EOrc GCHN MBal MWat NKay SDix WAbe WEas WHal WOld WRus
– 'Golden Shower'	See C. ***v.*** 'Grandiflora'
§ – 'Grandiflora'	CB&S CBow CHar CKel CSco CTom EBre EFou ELan EMon ERou MWgw NBar NHol NNor NOak NVic SChu SHig SMad SPer SPla WWin
– 'Moonbeam'	Widely available
– 'Zagreb'	CCla COtt CSco EBre GWic LHop MBri MUlv NBar NHol NRoo

CORETHROGYNE (Compositae)

californica	LHil SCro SLon WOMN WPer

CORIANDRUM (Umbelliferae)

sativum	CArn CSev GPoy LHol MChe NSel SIde WOak WPer WSto

CORIARIA (Coriariaceae)

japonica	CCla SDry SHil
kingiana	ECou
§ ***microphylla***	CHan SDry SHil
myrtifolia	CB&S SDry
terminalis xanthocarpa	CB&S CHan IBlr MBal SDry SHil WWat
thymifolia	See C. ***microphylla***

CORIS (Primulaceae)

¶ ***monspeliensis***	WPer

CORNUS † (Cornaceae)

alba	CKin CLnd CPer ENot IHos IJoh MBar MBri MR&S NWea SHil SPer WMou
*– 'Albovariegata'	CCla
– 'Aurea'	CCla CHoe CMCN CMal CSco EBre EFol EGol EHar ELan IJoh IOrc MBri MR&S NHol NRoo SHil SPer SSpi WAbe WPat
– 'Elegantissima'	Widely available
– 'Gouchaultii'	CB&S MBar NKay
– 'Kesselringii'	CCor CHoe EBre EGol EHar ELan ENot IOrc MBar MBri MR&S MWat NHol SHil SMad SPer SPla SSta WBod
§ – 'Sibirica'	Widely available
*– 'Sibirica Variegata'	CBow EBre IJoh IOrc LHop MBri MGos WPat
– 'Spaethii'	Widely available
*– 'Variegata'	CCla ISea SPer WWin
– 'Westonbirt'	See C. ***a.*** 'Sibirica'

alternifolia	CCla CMHG EHar IJoh MWat SHil SPer SSpi WWat
§ – 'Argentea'	CBra CCla CFor CSco CShe EBre EGol EHar ELan LGre SHil SLeo SMad SPer SSpi SSta WHCG WKif WWat
– variegata	See C. *a.* 'Argentea'
amomum	CB&S CChu CCla CCor NHol SHil WCoo
baileyi	CCla CCor EHar
bretschneideri	WWat
§ *canadensis*	Widely available
candidissima	See C. *racemosa*
capitata	CB&S CGre SHil SSpi
chinensis	CBra LPan
controversa	CB&S CHEx CMCN CSco CShe EHar IJoh IOrc LPan MBlu SExT SGar SHil SPer SSpi SSta WCoo WMou WWat
– 'Pagoda'	SSpi
– 'Variegata'	CBot CBra CCla CFor CSco EHar ELan IJoh LNet LPan MBlu MBri SExT SGar SHil SPer SReu SSpi SSta WHCG WSHC WWat
'Eddie's White Wonder'	CB&S CCla CFor CSco EHar MBlu MBri SHil SSpi SSta
florida	CCla CTre EGol ELan IOrc SExT SHil SPer SPla SReu SSta WCoo WNor
– 'Apple Blossom'	SHil SSpi
– 'Cherokee Chief'	CSco LPan MBri SHil SSpi
¶ – 'Cherokee Princess'	LPan
¶ – 'Clear Moon'	LPan
– 'Cloud Nine'	CB&S CSco IBar LPan MBri SHil SSpi
– 'First Lady'	LPan SSpi
¶ – 'Fragrant Cloud'	LPan
– 'Princess'	MBar SSta
– 'Rainbow'	CSco ELan IJoh LPan MBri SGar SHil SPer SSta
– rubra	CBot CBow CBra CChu CSco ELan IDai IJoh LPan MGos SExT SHil SPer SReu SSpi SSta WBod WNor
*– 'Spring Song'	MBri
¶ – 'Stoke's Pink'	SSpi
¶ – 'Sweetwater'	SSpi
– 'Tricolor'	See C. *f.* 'Welchii'
§ – 'Welchii'	SHil SSpi
– 'White Cloud'	SHil SMrm SPer SSpi
glabrata	CCor
hemsleyi	EPla
hongkongensis	ELan MBri SSta
'Kelsey's Dwarf'	See C. *stolonifera* 'Kelseyi'
kousa	CB&S CBow CBra CMCN CMHG EGol ELan ISea LNet LSav MBal MBar MWat NJap NKay NNor SExT SHil SPer SPla SReu SSpi SSta WBod
– angustata	CMHG LSav SSpi
– 'Gold Star'	ELan IOrc MBri SHil SSpi
– 'Madame Butterfly'	SSpi
*– 'Robert'	MBri
– 'Satomi'	ELan LSav MBri SHil SMad SMrm SPer SSpi
kousa chinensis	CBot CBow CChu CCla CMHG CSam CSco EHar ELan IBar IJoh LHyd LSav MBri MGos SChu SExT SHil SMad SPer SReu SSpi SSta WNor
– – 'Bodnant Form'	CFor
– – 'China Girl'	CSco IJoh LPan LSav MBri MGos SGar SPer SSpi
– – 'Milky Way'	SSpi
– – 'Snow Boy'	ELan LSav SHil SMrm SSpi SSta
– – Spinners form	SSpi
macrophylla	CMCN WCoo
mas	Widely available
– 'Aurea'	CBra CCla CFor EGol EHar ERav LSav MBri SHil SPer SSpi SSta WWat
– 'Elegantissima'	CSco EHar ELan ERav LSav MBri SHil SSpi SSta
– 'Variegata'	CBot CBra CCla CFor CShe EGol EHar ELan ERav IOrc LHyd LSav MBri MGos SHil SPer SSpi SSta WWat
N 'Norman Hadden'	CBot CBra CCla EHar LSav MBlu MBri NKay SHil SPer SReu SSpi SSta WAbe WBod WWat
nuttallii	CB&S CBot CBow CCla CMCN CSco ELan LPan MBri SGar SHil SPer SReu SSpi SSta WCoo WNor WWat
– 'Ascona'	EGol ELan MBlu MBri SPer SReu SSpi SSta
– 'Corego Giant'	SHil
– 'Gold Spot'	IOrc SExT SReu SSpi
– 'Monarch'	SSpi
– 'North Star'	MBri
– 'Portlemouth'	SHil SSpi
officinalis	CMCN MBri SHil WWat
'Ormonde'	SPer SReu SSpi
paucinervis	CMCN
pumila	LSav NHol SPla SSta
§ *racemosa*	CCor SReu WWat
sanguinea	CKin CLnd ENot LBuc NNor NWea SHil
¶ – 'Winter Beauty'	MBri SHil SSus
♦ – 'Winter Flame'	See C. *s.* 'Winter Beauty'
stolonifera	CLan EGol ERav MGos SExT
– 'Flaviramea'	Widely available
– 'Kelseyi'	EBre EGol LHop MBar MR&S NHol SGar SPer WWat
¶ – 'White Spot'	MBri SHil
walteri	CMCN
– KE 3653	SSpi
wilsoniana L/H 3653	SSpi

COROKIA (Cornaceae)

buddleioides	CChu CMHG WBod
'Coppershine'	CB&S LAbb
cotoneaster	CLan CSam CTrw ECou ELan ENot EPot ISea MBlu MUlv NHol SDry SHil SPer SReu SSpi SSta WBod WSHC WWat

– 'Little Prince'	CB&S ELan
macrocarpa	SDix SPer WSHC
x *virgata*	CB&S CBow CBra CChu CMHG CPle CTrw ECou IBar IOrc ISea MBlu MCas MGos MR&S MUlv SArc SPer SReu WBod WSHC
– 'Bronze King'	CTre IHos SPer
– 'Bronze Knight'	WPat
– 'Bronze Lady'	MBal
– 'Pink Delight'	CB&S
– 'Red Wonder'	CBra IHos SHil WBod
– 'Yellow Wonder'	CB&S LSav SHil

CORONILLA (Leguminosae)

¶ *cappadocica*	WWin
♦ *emerus*	See HIPPOCREPIS *e.*
glauca	CB&S CBot CBow CBra CGle CHil CLan CMac CPle CSam CSco ELan ENot ERav IJoh IOrc MPla NTow SHil SPer WAbe WBod WWin
– 'Citrina'	CB&S CBot CChu CHil CMHG CSam ELan ERav LAbb LHop MTho SAxl SBla SPer SSpi WAbe WRus WSHC
§ – 'Variegata'	Widely available
minima	LRHS NTow SBla SWas WAbe
valentina	CMac ITim LHop MCot MNew SBra SDix WCot WSHC
– 'Variegata'	See C. *glauca* 'Variegata'
varia	See SECURIGERA *v.*

CORREA (Rutaceae)

alba	CB&S CGre CMHG CSev ECou ERea SDry WTay
– 'Pinkie'	ECou LHop
backhouseana	CB&S CCla CHan CHil CPle CSun ECou GWic IBar IBlr IReg ISea LGre LSav SIgm SLMG WAbe WBod WSHC
calycina	CMHG ERea
decumbens	CB&S CGre ECou ISea WSHC
'Dusky Bells'	CHil CPle ECou SAxl
'Harrisii'	See C. 'Mannii'
lawrenceana	CB&S CCla ECou IBlr
– *rosea*	LAbb
§ 'Mannii'	CB&S CBot CCla CGre CHil CMHG CSam CSev CTre ECou ERea IBar IReg ISea LHop MNew SHil SLMG WAbe WBod WEas WSHC WWat
pulchella	CCla CMHG ERea LSav
§ *reflexa*	CB&S CPle CSun ECou WTay
¶ – *virens*	WEas
speciosa	See C. *reflexa*

CORTADERIA † (Gramineae)

argentea	See C. *selloana*
fulvida	IBar SSpi
§ *richardii*	CElw CHEx EFou GGar IBlr MBal
§ *selloana*	CB&S CBow CHEx CTre CWGN ELan ERou IBar ISea LNet MBar MR&S MWat NHol NKay SArc SHil SPer
¶ – 'Albo-lineata'	SMad
§ – 'Aureo-lineata'	CB&S CBra CCla CHoe CSco EGol EHar ELan ENot IBar IHos MBal MBri MR&S MUlv SHil SMad SPer SSpi SSta WAbe WPat
– 'Gold Band'	See C. *s* 'Aureo-lineata'
¶ – 'Pink Feather'	NOrc
– 'Pumila'	CB&S CCla CHoe CSco EBre ELan EMon ENot IDai ISea LSav MBal MBri MUlv NHol NTow SCro SDix SHil SPer WPat
§ – 'Rendatleri'	CB&S CHoe CSco ELan GRei LSav MBal MUlv SHil SMad SPer
– 'Rosea'	CGre CHEx CHoe ISea MBri
¶ – 'Silver Fountain'	CHoe ELan SApp SSpi
♦ – 'Silver Stripe'	See C. *s.* 'Albo-lineata'
– 'Sunningdale Silver'	CB&S CBra CHoe CSco EGol ELan ENot EOrc GHig IBar IHos ISea LSav MBal MBri MGos MR&S MUlv NHol SHil SMad SPer SSpi WAbe
– 'White Feather'	CHEx CLan ECtt
Toe Toe	See C. *richardii*

CORTUSA (Primulaceae)

matthioli	CGle CLew CSun GLoc ITim MBal MFir NGre NHar NHol NNrd NRya NTow WHal
– *alba*	CSun GLoc MBal NHol NNrd WDav
– *pekinensis*	GDra NHol WDav WPer
turkestanica	WDav

CORYDALIS (Papaveraceae)

* *afghanica*	EPot
aitchisonii	ECam
alexeenkoana	EPot LAma WChr
ambigua	EPot GDra GEdr LAma MHig NHol WChr
– Russian form	SPou
angustifolia	ECam EPot LAma NHol SPou WChr
bracteata	EPot
§ *bulbosa*	CAvo ECam EPar EPot LAma NHol SPou WHil
– *albiflora*	EPot MPar SPou
– *marschalliana*	EPot
cashmeriana	EBre GArf LAma MHig NHol SBla SPou SWas WChr
¶ – 'Kailash'	SPou
caucasica	ECam EPot LAma SPou WChr
– *alba*	EPot NBir SPou SWas
cava	See C. *bulbosa*
cheilanthifolia	Widely available
chionophila	EPot WChr
¶ *darwasica*	WChr
decipiens	SPou WChr
decumbens	EPot SPou WChr
diphylla	EPot

firouzii	EPot
¶ *flexuosa* CDR 528	LGre SWas
glauca	See C. ***sempervirens***
glaucescens	ECam EPot LAma WChr
¶ *integra*	WChr
intermedia	ECam EPot LAma WChr
* *kascgarica*	EPot WChr
ledebouriana	CBro ECam EPot SPou WChr
leariloba	EPot
♦ *lutea*	See PSEUDOFUMARIA *l.*
nobilis	LRHS
nudicaulis	WChr
♦ *ochroleuca*	See PSEUDOFUMARIA ***alba***
ophiocarpa	CLew ELan GGar GWic IBlr MRav WCot WHea WHil
paczoskii	EPot LRHS SPou WChr
parnassica	See C. ***bulbosa***
popovii	ECam EPot
pumila	EPot WChr
rutifolia	GCHN
§ *saxicola*	EPot SMrm
schanginii	EPot WChr
¶ *scouleri*	IBrk
§ *sempervirens*	CHad CSun SFis WEas WHil WWin
solida	CAvo CBro CRow EPar EPot ETub GLoc IBlr LAma LBlo LBow NHol NNrd SIng SPou WAbe WCot
– forms	EPot SPou
– 'George P Baker'	GEdr NHol SPou SWas
– *solida*	WChr
– *solida densiflora*	MHig
– *transsylvanica*	EPot NHar NHol SPou WChr
¶ sp. Gökce Beli	SPou
sp. Kartal Tepe	EPot SPou WChr
¶ sp. Yayladag	SPou
thalictrifolia	See C. ***saxicola***
tomentella	LHop SPou WAbe WDav WHil
wilsonii	CBot EFol GCHN IBlr ITim MBro MPar MRav NTow SBla SIng SLHN WAbe WDav WEas WHal WHil

CORYLOPSIS † (Hamamelidaceae)

§ *glabrescens*	CB&S CBow CFor ELan LSav MBal SHil SPer SSpi SSta WNor
– *gotoana*	CKni ELan SPer SSta
pauciflora	Widely available
platypetala	See C. ***sinensis calvescens***
– *laevis*	See C. ***sinensis calvescens***
sinensis	CTre MBri SPer SSta WWat
§ – *calvescens*	CB&S CTre MBal MBri SSpi SSta
§ – *calvescens veitchiana*	CB&S CFor CSam CTre MBal MBri SHil SSpi SSta WBod WCoo WWat
* – 'Purple Tips'	SSta
§ – *sinensis*	CB&S CCla CFor MBal MBri MGos SPer SSta WBod WWat
– 'Spring Purple'	CBow CFor EBre EHar ELan LHop LSav MBlu MBri SHil SMad SPer SSpi SSta WWat
spicata	CFor CTre ELan ENot IDai IHos IJoh MBal MBlu MBri MPla SHil SMad SPer SPla SSta
veitchiana	See C. ***sinensis calvescens v.***
willmottiae	See C. ***sinensis sinensis***

CORYLUS † (Corylaceae)

F *avellana* (cobnut)	CKin CLnd CPer ENot ERea GRei LBuc MBal MBar MBri MR&S NRog NWea SHil SKee WMou
¶ – 'Aurea'	MBlu MWat SPer
– 'Bollwyller'	See C. ***maxima*** 'Halle'sche Riesennuss'
– 'Contorta'	Widely available
F – 'Cosford Cob'	ERea ESim IJoh LBuc MBri NRog NTwe SDea SKee SPer WHig WMou
F – 'Fuscorubra'	CMac CSco EGol ELan ENot IOrc SHil SPer WMou
– 'Halle Giant'	See C. ***maxima*** 'Halle'sche Riesennuss'
– 'Heterophylla'	EGol SSta WMou
– *laciniata*	See C. ***a.*** 'Heterophylla'
– 'Merveille de Bollwyller'	See C. ***maxima*** 'Halle'sche Riesennuss'
– 'Nottingham Prolific'	See C. ***a.*** 'Pearson's Prolific'
F – 'Pearson's Prolific'	EHar ERea ESim LBuc MBri NTwe SDea
– 'Pendula'	WMou
– 'Purpurea'	See C. ***a.*** 'Fuscorubra'
F – 'Webb's Prize Cob'	CMac ERea IJoh LHol MBri NRog SDea WMou
colurna	CBow CLnd CMCN EHar ENot ESim IOrc MGos NWea SExT SHil SMad SPer SSpi WMou
¶ – x *avellana*	ESim
F *maxima* (filbert)	CLnd MBar NTwe SDea
F – 'Butler'	SKee
F – 'Ennis'	SKee
F – 'Frizzled Filbert'	ERea
– 'Frühe van Frauendorf'	See C. ***m.*** 'Red Filbert'
F – 'Garibaldi'	WMou
– 'Grote Lambertsnoot'	See C. ***m.*** 'Kentish Cob'
F – 'Gunslehert'	SKee
F – 'Halle'sche Riesennuss'	LHol NTwe SDea SKee
F – 'Kentish Cob'	CSam EHar ERea ESim LBuc MBri NBee NRog NTwe SDea SFam SKee SPer WHig WMou
F – 'Neue Riesennuss' ('New Giant')	WMou
– 'Purple Filbert'	See C. ***m.*** 'Purpurea'
F – 'Purpurea'	Widely available
F – 'Red Filbert'	EHar ERea EWar MBlu MBri NRog WMou WPat WWeb
– 'Red Zellernut'	See C. ***m.*** 'Red Filbert'
F – 'Waterloo'	WMou
F – 'White Filbert'	ERea MBri NRog WMou
– 'White Spanish Filbert'	See C. ***m.*** 'White Filbert'
– 'Witpit Lambertsnoot'	See C. ***m.*** 'White Filbert'

sieboldiana	WMou

CORYNEPHORUS (Gramineae)

¶ *canescens*	NSti

CORYNOCARPUS (Corynocarpaceae)

¶ *laevigata* 'Picturata'	CHEx
¶ – 'Variegata'	CHEx
laevigatum	CHEx ECou MBri

COSMOS (Compositae)

§ *atrosanguineus*	Widely available

COTINUS † (Anacardiaceae)

americanus	See C. ***obovatus***
§ *coggygria*	CBra CSco EGol ELan ENot IJoh IOrc LHop MBar MBri MR&S MWat NNor NRoo SHil SPer SPla WAbe WMou
– 'Foliis Purpureis'	See C. ***c. rubrifolius***
N– 'Notcutt's Variety'	EGol ENot LSav SPla WWat
– *purpureus*	CGre CLan CSco EBar ERav SHil
– 'Red Beauty'	COtt MBri
– 'Royal Purple'	Widely available
N– *rubrifolius*	CCla MBal NNor SChu SPer SPla WWeb
– 'Velvet Cloak'	EBar SHil SSpi
'Flame'	CBow CSco CShe SHil SSpi WBod WWat
'Grace'	CBow CFor COtt EBar MBri MGos MUlv SHil SSpi SSus
§ *obovatus*	CKni ENot SHil SPer SSpi SSus WWat

COTONEASTER † (Rosaceae)

adpressus	CLew EPla GDra MGos MWat NNor NWea SHil WWat
– 'Little Gem'	ESis GLoc MBro MPla
– *praecox*	See C. ***nanshan***
¶ *affinis*	SSpi
apiculatus	SHil
'Arnold Foster'	CSco
§ *ascendens*	CMCN
§ *bullatus*	CCor CPle CSam ELan ENot GRei IDai ISea MGos NNor SHil SPer WAbe WSHC WWat
♦– *floribundus*	See C. ***b.***
– *macrophyllus*	See C. ***rehderi***
buxifolius	ESis LSav MBri
– blue form	EGol
– *vellaceus*	SPer WBod
cavei	SLon
cochleatus	CHar EGol EPot ESis GDra MBal MBar MBro NHol NNrd SHil SReu SSmi WAbe WWat
N *congestus*	Widely available
– *nanus*	IBar
conspicuus	IDai
– 'Decorus'	CBra CLew CMHG CSco ELan ENot GDra IOrc MBar MGos MR&S MRav NHol NNor NRoo NWea SHil SPer SPla SReu
– 'Flameburst'	ECtt MBal MBri
– 'Highlight'	CBra SHil
– 'Red Glory'	MBri
§ *dammeri*	Widely available
– 'Oakwood'	See C. 'Eichholz'
N– *radicans*	CShe NKay SSmi
– 'Streibs Findling'	See C. ***procumbens***
dielsianus	LSav NWea
♦ *distichus*	See C. ***nitidus***
– *tongolensis*	See C. ***splendens***
divaricatus	ENot GRei SHil SPer WWat
§ 'Eichholz'	EGol ENot MBri MGos SMrm WWeb
floccosus	EHal ENot GRei IDai IJoh MBri NRoo NWea SHil SPer WWat
franchetii	CBow CLan CMHG CSco ELan IDai IOrc MBal MGos MR&S MRav MWat NWea SHil SPer WMou
– TTYü 14144	MBal
frigidus	ENot GRei NKay NWea SHil WBod WCoo
– 'Anne Cornwallis'	SPer
– *fructu-luteo*	IBlr
– 'Notcutt's Variety'	ENot
¶ – 'Sherpa'	LMer
glabratus	MBri
glaucophyllus	SMad
§ *glomerulatus*	MBar
henryanus	CSco GRei WWat
hjelmqvistii 'Major'	See C. ***h.*** 'Robustus'
§ – 'Robustus'	CSco ENot WWeb
– 'Rotundifolius'	See C. ***h.*** 'Robustus'
horizontalis	Widely available
– 'Variegatus'	Widely available
♦– *wilsonii*	See C. ***ascendens***
humifusus	See C. ***dammeri***
'Hybridus Pendulus'	See C. x ***watereri*** 'Pendulus'
§ *integrifolius*	CBow CCla CHan CMHG CSam EGol ELan ESis IDai LNet MBal MBar MBri MR&S NKay NNor NRoo SSmi SSta WWat WWin
lacteus	CCla CMHG CSam CSco CShe ELan ENot LBuc MBri MGos MRav SHil SPer SPla SReu WWat
lucidus	EHar
marquandii	EPla NNor
melanotrichus	See C. ***cochleatus***
microphyllus	CBow CLan CMCN CPle CSco ELan ENot GRei IJoh ISea MBar MBri MBro MGos MR&S NNor NRoo SDix SHil SLon STre WAbe WBod
– 'Donard Gem'	CSco
*– *inermis*	GLoc
¶ – Lowndes	WWat
– Lowndes 1496-2	LSav
– 'Menai'	CCla LSav
– 'Teulon Porter'	MBlu NKay
♦– *thymifolius*	See C. ***integrifolius***
multiflorus	NWea

§ ***nanshan***	GRei LHop MBri MPla NWea SHil SPer WWeb
– 'Boer'	LSav
¶ ***nitens***	LSav
♦ ***nitidifolius***	See C. ***glomerulatus***
§ ***nitidus***	SLon SPer
♦ ***nummularius***	See C. ***racemiflorus***
perpusillus	MBri NHol
§ ***procumbens***	CBow EBre EGol ESis NRoo
– 'Queen of Carpets'	MBri
prostratus	SPla
♦ ***pyrenaicus***	See C. ***congestus***
racemiflorus	SHil
§ ***rehderi***	CMHG
'Royal Beauty'	See C. x ***suecicus*** 'Coral Beauty'
salicifolius	CBra CLnd CPle MWat NBar NNor SPer
– 'Elstead'	SPer
– ***fructu-luteo***	EHal MBri
– 'Gnom'	CBow EGol EHar EPla LHop LNet LSav MBal MBri MGos NNor NRoo SHil SLon SPer WWat
– 'Herbstfeuer' ('Autumn Fire')	EGol MBal MWat NKay NNor SPer SPla
– 'Klampen'	MBri
– 'Merriott Weeper'	CSco WWat
– 'Parkteppich' ('Park Carpet')	EBar IDai NWea SLon SPer
– 'Red Flare'	SPer
– 'Repens'	CBow CShe ENot IDai MBal MWat NHol NNor NRoo NWea SPer SPla WAbe
¶ – 'Scarlet Leader'	MBri
serotinus	EPla LSav SHil SSta
sikangensis	CCor
simonsii	CKin CSco ELan IDai IOrc LBuc MBar MBri MGos MR&S NHol NWea SHil SPer WMou
§ ***splendens***	CGre ECtt ELan SHil
– 'Sabrina'	See C. ***splendens***
sternianus	CShe ENot MBar MBri SHil SPer WBod
x ***suecicus*** 'Coral Beauty'	CSco EBre EGol ENot GRei IJoh IOrc LBuc MBri MGos MR&S NBar NHol NNor SHil SPer SPla WWeb
– 'Skogholm'	CBow CLew CPle CSco MBal MBar MGos MR&S MWat NRoo NWea SHil SLon SPer SPla WWin
'Valkenburg'	SHil
vestitus	SHil
wardii	CSco IDai IJoh IOrc SPer
x ***watereri***	CBow CSco CShe ELan LNet MGos MR&S NBar WWat WWeb
¶ – 'Avonbank'	SPla
– 'Cornubia'	CBra CLan CSco EGol ELan ENot IDai ISea LHop LNet MBar MGos MRav MWat NKay NWea SHil SLon SPer SReu WWat
– 'Exburiensis'	CBow CBra CSam CSco CTrw LNet MBri MGos MR&S MWat SHil SPer SReu WAbe WWat
– 'Goscote'	MGos
– 'John Waterer'	CBra SHil WBod
§ – 'Pendulus'	CBow CCla CSco CShe ENot IDai IJoh ISea LNet MBar MBri MGos MWat NBar NKay NWea SHil SPer WAbe
– 'Pink Champagne'	CBow CMer LSav MBri SHil SPer
– 'Rothschildianus'	CBow CLan CMHG CShe ELan ENot IJoh LHop MBal MBar MRav NKay SCro SHil SPer

COTULA (Compositae)

atrata	See LEPTINELLA ***a.***
– ***dendyi***	See LEPTINELLA ***dendyi***
coronopifolia	CWGN LMay MSta MTho SLHN WHil WPer
'Cream Buttons'	LHil
goyenii	See LEPTINELLA ***g.***
hispida	CMHG CRiv ECtt EPot ITim MCas NNor NWCA SIgm WEas WHil WPer WRus
leariloba	See LEPTINELLA ***pyrethrifolia linearifolia***
minor	ECou NHol
pectinata	See LEPTINELLA ***p.***
§ ***perpusilla***	SSmi
potentilloides	See LEPTINELLA ***potentillina***
pyrethrifolia	See LEPTINELLA ***p.***
reptans	See LEPTINELLA ***scariosa***
rotundata	See LEPTINELLA ***r.***
scariosa	See LEPTINELLA ***s.***
sericea	See LEPTINELLA ***albida***
squalida	See LEPTINELLA ***s.***

COTYLEDON (Crassulaceae)

chrysantha	See ROSULARIA ***pallida***
oppositifolia	See CHIASTOPHYLLUM ***oppositifolium***
* ***pomedosa***	MBri
* – 'Variegata'	MBri
simplicifolia	See CHIASTOPHYLLUM ***oppositifolium***
¶ ***undulata***	WEas

COWANIA (Rosaceae)

mexicana	See C. ***stansburyana***
§ ***stansburyana***	LGre

CRAB APPLE See **MALUS**

CRAIBIODENDRON (Ericaceae)
yunnanense CTre

CRAMBE (Cruciferae)
cordifolia Widely available
koktebelica CHan ECha GWic
maritima CGle CHoe CSco ECha EPas GPoy MSal MWgw NNor NSti SLHN WHoo

CRANBERRY See **VACCINIUM** ***macrocarpon***

CRASPEDIA (Compositae)
§ *glauca* CSun GWic NHol
globoides NOrc
♦ *richea* See C. ***glauca***
sp. Max 881 CSun
uniflora See C. ***glauca***

CRASSULA (Crassulaceae)
♦ *argentea* See C. ***portulacea***
'Basutoland' MPla
coccinea CHEx SLMG
¶ *dejecta* x *coccinea* CHEx
falcata IBlr MBri
* *galanthea* SLMG
justi-corderoyi CPle
§ *milfordiae* CHar CLew ELan EPot GLoc MCas NGre NHol NNrd SSmi WHil WOMN WPer
moschata ECou
multicaulis ECou NGre
ovata See C. ***portulacea***
perforata SLMG
portulacea EBak MBri SLMG
– 'Hummel's Sunset' SLMG
– 'Variegata' EBak SLMG
rupestris MBri
§ *sarcocaulis* Widely available
– *alba* CRiv CSun ELan EPot GLoc NGre NNrd SIng STre WAbe WHal WHil WSHC
– dark form NHol
¶ – 'Ken Aslet' GAbr NGre NHol SIng
schmidtii MBri
sedifolia ELan MTho NBir SIng WWin
♦ *sediformis* See C. ***milfordiae***
¶ *socialis* ITim
tetragona SLMG

CRATAEGUS † (Rosaceae)
¶ 'Autumn Glory' MBri
F *azarolus* 'White Italian' ESim
chlorosarca SHil
coccinea NWea WMou
N *crus-galli* CLnd EHal SExT SHil SPer WJas
durobrivensis CLnd WWat
x *grignonensis* ENot SExT SHil SPer
§ *laciniata* SHil SSpi
§ *laevigata* WMou
* – 'Autumn Glory' CLnd WJas
– 'Coccinea Plena' See C. *l.* 'Paul's Scarlet'
– 'Crimson Cloud' CLnd ENot SExT SPer
¶ – 'Gireoudii' ELan EPla MGos
§ – 'Paul's Scarlet' CB&S CBow CBra CLnd ELan ENot IDai IJoh IOrc LBuc MBar MBri MGos MR&S MRav NWea SHil SPer SReu WAbe WJas WMou
– 'Plena' CB&S IHos NWea SHil SPer WMou
– 'Rosea Flore Pleno' CB&S CBow CLnd ELan ENot MBar MBri MGos NWea SExT SHil SPer WAbe WJas WMou
x *lavallei* CLnd ENot MR&S SHil SPer WAbe
– 'Carrierei' CSam NWea
mollis SHil WMou
monogyna CB&S CKin CLnd CPer ELan ENot GRei LBuc MBar MBri MGos NWea SHil SPer WMou
– 'Biflora' SHil WMou
– 'Compacta' MBlu
– 'Flexuosa' WMou
– 'Pendula Rosea' SHil WMou
– 'Stricta' CLnd ENot MBri MR&S SExT SHil
– 'Variegata' SHil
x *mordenensis* 'Toba' ENot SExT
¶ *opaca* ESim
orientalis See C. ***laciniata***
oxyacantha See C. ***laevigata***
pedicellata CLnd ENot
§ *persimilis* 'Prunifolia' CBra CSam ELan ENot IHos MBar MGos MR&S MRav NWea SHil SMad SPer SSpi WAbe WCoo WMou
phaenopyrum SHil SMad
pinnatifida WWat
– *major* SHil
prunifolia See C. ***persimilis*** 'Prunifolia'
F 'Red Italian' ESim
stipulacea WMou
tanacetifolia CLnd SHil
wattiana CLnd

CRAWFURDIA (Gentianaceae)
¶ *speciosa* ITim WCru

CREMANTHODIUM See **LIGULARIA**

CREPIS (Compositae)
aurea CCla CHar ECro EPar IBlr MTho NNrd SIng SPer WHer
incana CCla CGle CLew CRow CShe EBre ECha EPar GDra GLoc LGre LHop MPit MTho NHol NKay NNrd SDix SIng SPer WAbe WOMN

CRINITARIA See **ASTER**

CRINODENDRON (Elaeocarpaceae)
§ *hookerianum* Widely available

patagua — CB&S CBot CChu CHan CHil CMHG CPle CSam EPla GWic IBar ISea LHop MBal SArc SHil SLon SPer WSHC

CRINUM (Liliaceae/Amaryllidaceae)

aquaticum — See C. ***campanulatum***
§ *bulbispermum* — EBre ELan LHop
capense — See C. ***bulbispermum***
§ x *powellii* — CAvo CB&S CCla CKel EBak EBre ECha ELan ERav LAma LBow LHop MBri MSta MUlv SDix SHig SLHN SPer SW&B WEas
– 'Album' — CCla CHEx CKel ECha ELan ERav LBow MUlv SHig SW&B
– 'Longifolium' — See C. ***bulbispermum***
– 'Roseum' — See C. x ***powellii***

CRITHMUM (Umbelliferae)

maritimum — GPoy MSal

CROCOSMIA † (Iridaceae)

'Bressingham Beacon' — MUlv
'Bressingham Blaze' — EBre GWic NOak
¶ 'Brilliant and Best' — GWic
'Canary Bird' — CBro CChu EGol GWic NBar SChu SPer SSpi
'Carmin Brillant' — LAma MBri
¶ 'Castleward Late' — GWic
N 'Citronella' — Widely available
x *crocosmiiflora* — NOrc
¶ 'Eldorado' — GWic
'Emberglow' — CBro CChu CFor CRow CSam EBre ECro EFou ERou GHig LAma NBar NHol SAxl SPer
'Emily McKenzie' — Widely available
¶ 'Fire King' — NTow
'Firebird' — CRow EBre MUlv NRoo SAxl SMrm
'Flamenco' — CShe SBla
'George Davidson' — CB&S ECha IBlr MBro
'His Majesty' — GWic MBri WCot
'Jackanapes' — CBos CBro CRow ECha IBlr LAma MBri SAxl
'James Coey' — CChu CRow EFou IBlr LAma LBow LHop MTho NHol WCot
* 'Jenny' — COtt
'Jenny Bloom' — ERou MUlv NBir NRoo
'Lady Hamilton' — CRow GWic MBri SAxl
'Lady Wilson' — EFou LAma NHol SW&B WCot
'Lucifer' — Widely available
¶ 'Mars' — GWic
masoniorum — CAvo CB&S CBro CHEx CKel CRow CSco CShe ECha EFou ELan EOrc EPar IDai LAma MBri MCot MWat MWgw NHol NNor SPer WAbe WEas
– 'Dixter Flame' — SDix
'Mount Stewart' — IBlr WCot
'Mrs Geoffrey Howard' — IDai
'Norwich Canary' — EFou LAma LBow LHop NHol WWin
* 'Orangeade' — CB&S
§ *paniculata* — CAvo CCla CFis CSco GAbr IDai LBow MBal MUlv NHol NKay NOrc SChu SIng WCot WHoo
– 'Major' — SPer
pottsii — CB&S CChu CCor CRow IBlr
'Queen Alexandra' — LAma LHop NHol
'Queen of Spain' — MBri SAxl
* 'Red Star' — CB&S
¶ 'Rheingold' — WCot
rosea — See TRITONIA ***rubrolucens***
¶ 'Saracen' — MBri
'Sir Matthew Wilson' — GHig
N 'Solfaterre' — Widely available
'Spitfire' — CBot CChu EBre ECha ECro ERou MRav MSta NRoo SAxl WEas
'Star of the East' — CBos CChu CFor CRow GWic SAxl SBla SSpi
¶ 'Vesuvius' — MBri
'Vulcan' — CB&S EOrc SBla SPer SSpi
¶ *williamsii* — NBir

CROCUS † (Iridaceae)

abantensis — ECam EPot LAma WChr
§ *aerius* — LAma WChr
¶ – 'Cambridge' — WChr
alatavicus — CBro ECam EPot WChr
§ *ancyrensis* — CAvo CBro ECam EPar EPot ETub LAma LBlo LBow NHol SIng WChr
– 'Golden Bunch' — See C. ***a.***
§ *angustifolius* — CAvo CBro EPot LAma LBow NHol SIng WChr
– *minor* — EPot LAma WChr
antalyensis — LAma WChr
asturicus — See C. ***serotinus salzmannii***
asumaniae — ECam EPot LAma WChr
aureus — See C. ***flavus***
banaticus — CBro EPot LAma NHar NHol SPou WChr
– *albiflorus* — SPou
baytopiorum — ECam EPot LAma SPou WChr
biflorus — CBro EPar LAma
– *adamii* — ECam EPot LAma WChr
– *alexandri* — CAvo CBro ECam EPot LAma LBow WChr
– 'Argenteus' — See C. ***b. biflorus***
§ – *biflorus* — CBro LAma LBow SIng
¶ – 'Bowles' Blue' — SPou
– *crewei* — ECam LAma WChr
– *isauricus* — CAvo CBro ECam WChr
– *melantherus* — NHar SPou WChr
– *parkinsonii* — See C. ***b. biflorus***
– *pulchricolor* — CAvo ECam LAma LBow SPou WChr
– *tauri* — ECam LRHS WChr
¶ – sulphur — SPou
biflorus weldenii 'Albus' — EPar LAma LBow
– – 'Fairy' — CAvo CBro LAma LBow
biliottii — See C. ***aerius***
boryi — CAvo ECam EPot LAma LBow SPou

– PJC 168	WChr
cambessedesii	SPou
§ ***cancellatus cancellatus***	CBro ECam LAma LBow NHol SPou
– ***cilicicus***	See C. ***c. cancellatus***
– ***mazziaricus***	CAvo ECam
– ***pamphylicus***	CAvo ECam WChr
candidus	ECam
– ***subflavus***	See C. ***cancellatus cancellatus***
cartwrightianus	CBro ECam LAma SPou
– CEH 613	WChr
N– ***albus***	SPou
chrysanthus	ECam WChr
– 'Advance'	CAvo CBro ECam EPar EPot ETub EWal LAma LRoo NHol SIng
– 'Ard Schenk'	EPot LAma
– 'Blue Bird'	ECam EPar EWal LAma LBlo LBow LRoo MBri SIng
– 'Blue Giant'	LAma
– 'Blue Pearl'	CAvo CBro EPar ETub LAma LBlo LBow MBri SIng
– 'Blue Peter'	CAvo CBro EPot LAma NHol
– 'Brass Band'	LAma
– 'Canary Bird'	EPot
– 'Cream Beauty'	CAvo CBro EPar EPot ETub EWal LAma LBlo LBow MBri NHol SIng
– 'Dorothy'	LAma
– 'E A Bowles'	CBro EPot LAma LBlo NHol SIng
– 'E P Bowles'	CAvo CRiv LAma LBow MBri NHol SIng
– 'Elegance'	CBro LAma
– 'Eyecatcher'	EPot ETub LAma NHol
– ***fuscotinctus***	CBro ETub LAma MBri SIng
– 'Gipsy Girl'	CBro LAma LRoo MBri NHol SIng
– 'Gladstone'	LAma
– 'Goldilocks'	CBro LAma
– 'Herald'	LAma
– 'Jeannine'	CBro LRHS
– 'Ladykiller'	CAvo CBro ECam EPar LAma LBlo LBow MBri NHol SIng
– 'Miss Vain'	LAma NHol
– 'Moonlight'	ECam LAma NHol SIng
– 'Prins Claus'	EPot LAma SIng
– 'Prinses Beatrix'	EPot ETub LAma NHol SIng
– 'Romance'	LAma NHol
– 'Saturnus'	LAma
– 'Sky Blue'	LAma
– 'Skyline'	CBro EPot ETub NHol
– 'Snow Bunting'	CAvo CBro ECam EPar ETub EWal LAma LBlo LBow SIng
– 'Snow Storm'	LAma
– 'Snow White'	LBlo
– 'Spring Pearl'	CBro LAma
– 'Sunkist'	LAma
– 'White Beauty'	LAma
– 'White Triumphator'	EPot ETub LAma
– 'Zenith'	LAma LBlo
– 'Zwanenburg Bronze'	CAvo ECam EPar ETub EWal LAma SIng

'Cloth of Gold'	See C. ***angustifolius***
clusii	See C. ***serotinus c.***
corsicus	CAvo CBro EPar EPot ETub LAma LBow MBri NHol SIng WChr
– PJC 657	SPou
¶– ***albus***	SPou
cvijicii	LAma WChr
– CEH 560	LRHS SPou
dalmaticus	ECam LAma MPar WChr
– CEH	SPou
danfordiae	ECam LAma WChr
etruscus 'Zwanenburg'	EPot ETub LAma NHol
§ ***flavus***	EPot LAma SPou WChr
– ***flavus***	ECam
– 'Golden Yellow'	ETub LAma LBlo
fleischeri	ECam EPot LAma SPou WChr
gargaricus	EPot LAma SPou WChr WThu
– RM 3299/75	WThu
– ***gargaricus***	SPou
– ***herbertii***	CBro ECam SPou
'Golden Mammoth'	See C. ***flavus*** 'Golden Yellow'
goulimyi	CAvo CBro ECam EPot ETub LAma LBow NHol SIng SPou WChr
– ***albus***	SPou WChr
hadriaticus	ECam EPot ETub LAma LBow MBri NHol SPou WChr
– BM 8039	WChr
– AM form	SPou
– ***chrysobelonicus***	See C. ***hadriaticus***
– ***hadriaticus***	CBro
– ***lilacinus***	LRHS
– 'Tom Blanchard'	CBro LRHS
heuffelianus	See C. ***vernus vernus*** Heuffelianus group
imperati	ECam SIng SPou
– 'De Jager'	CAvo EPot LAma LBow
– ***imperati***	LRHS SPou
¶– ***suaveolens***	SPou
karduchorum	CAvo CBro ECam ETub LAma SIng SPou WChr
korolkowii	CAvo CBro EPar EPot LAma NHol SIng WChr
– forms	ECam
kosaninii	LRHS SPou WChr
kotschyanus	SPou WChr
– ***albus***	SPou
– ***cappadocicus***	ECam
– ***hakkariensis***	ECam
§ – ***kotschyanus***	CBro EPot LAma LBlo LBow MBri SIng
– ***leucopharynx***	NHol WChr
– ***suworowianus***	ECam SPou
laevigatus	ECam LBlo SPou WChr
– ***fontenayi***	CBro ECam EPot ETub LAma MBri NHol WChr
– form	CBro LAma
– white	SPou
'Large Yellow'	See C. ***flavus*** 'Golden Yellow'
lazicus	See C. ***scharojenii***
longiflorus	CAvo CBro EPot SPou WThu

malyi	ECam LAma SPou
– CEH 519	WChr
'Mammoth Yellow'	See C. ***flavus*** 'Golden Yellow'
medius	CBro EPot ETub LAma
minimus	CBro EPar EPot ETub LAma LBow MBro NHol SIng
niveus	CAvo CBro ECam LAma LBow MBro SPou
– PJC 164	WChr
¶ – blue strain	WChr
nudiflorus	EPot ETub LAma LRHS NHol WChr
ochroleucus	CAvo CBro ECam EPot LAma LBlo LBow NHol SIng WChr
olivieri	EPar EPot LAma
– ***balansae***	WChr
– ***istanbulensis***	EPot LAma WChr
§ – ***olivieri***	LAma SIng SPou WChr
¶ ***oreocreticus***	SPou
pallasii	LAma WChr
– ***pallasii***	CAvo CBro ECam
pestalozzae	EPot LAma WChr
pulchellus	CAvo CBro ECam ETub LAma SPou
– CEH 558	WChr
– ***albus***	SPou WChr
– 'Zephyr'	CBro EPot ITim LAma NHol SPou
'Purpureus'	See C. ***vernus*** 'Purpureus Grandiflorus'
reticulatus hittiticus	ECam
– ***reticulatus***	ECam EPot
robertianus	ECam LAma SPou WChr
sativus	CArn CBro ECam EPot ETub GPoy LAma LBow MBri MSal NHol SIde SIng WChr
– ***cartwrightianus albus***	See C. ***cartwrightianus albus***
scardicus	LRHS WChr
§ ***scharojanii***	ECam EPot LAma WChr
– ***flavus***	EPot WChr
serotinus clusii	CAvo CBro ECam EPot LAma NHol WChr
– forms	MPar SPou
§ – ***salzmannii***	CAvo CBro ECam EPot LAma LBow MPar SPou WChr
sibirica	See C. ***sieberi***
sieberi	CAvo EPot ETub LAma MBri
§ – 'Albus'	CAvo CBro EPot ETub LAma LBow WChr
– ***atticus***	CBro EPot LAma LBow NHol
– ***atticus***CEH 611	WChr
– 'Bowles' White'	See C. ***s.*** 'Albus'
– 'Firefly'	CBro ECam EPot LAma LBow SIng
– 'Hubert Edelsten'	CAvo CBro ECam EPar EPot LAma LBow MBri SIng
– ***sublimis***	WChr
– 'Tricolor'	CBro EPot LAma LBow SPou WChr
– 'Violet Queen'	CAvo CBro ECam ETub LAma LBlo LBow MBri
speciosus	CAvo CBro ECam ELan ETub LAma LBlo LBow MPar NHol SIng WChr
– ***aitchisonii***	CBro LAma MBri NHol SIng
– ***albus***	EPot SPou
– 'Artabir'	CBro EPot ETub NHol SIng
– 'Cassiope'	EPot LAma NHol
– 'Conqueror'	CBro LAma LBlo NHol SIng
– ***ilgazensis***	EPot
¶ – 'Keith Rattray'	SPou
– 'Oxonian'	EPot ETub LAma SPou
– x ***pulchellus*** 'Big Boy'	SPou
– ***xantholaimos***	SPou
x ***stellaris***	EPar EPot
susianus	See C. ***angustifolius***
suterianus	See C. ***olivieri olivieri***
thomasii CEH 523	SPou
tommasinianus	CAvo CBro CRiv EPar ETub LAma LBow MBri MPar MPlt SIng
– ***albus***	CAvo EPot LAma LBow SPou WChr
– 'Barr's Purple'	ECam LAma MBri SIng
– 'Bobbo'	MPar SPou WChr
¶ – 'Eric Smith'	WChr
– 'Lilac Beauty'	LAma
– ***pictus***	ECam WChr
– ***roseus***	CBro SPou WChr
– 'Ruby Giant'	CAvo CBro EPar EPot ETub LAma NHol SIng
– 'Whitewell Purple'	CAvo CBro ECam LAma LBlo LBow MBri NHol
tournefortii	CAvo CBro ECam LAma LBow SPou SWas
vallicola	LAma WChr
veluchensis	WChr
§ ***vernus albiflorus***	EPot LAma MPar WChr
– 'Enchantress'	ETub LAma
– 'Glory of Limmen'	LRHS
– ***graecus***	EPot
– 'Grand Maître'	LAma
– 'Haarlem Gem'	LAma
– 'Jeanne d'Arc'	CBro ETub LAma LBow LRoo
– 'Kathleen Parlow'	LBlo
– 'King of the Blues'	LAma
– 'Little Dorrit'	LAma
– 'Negro Boy'	LAma
– 'Paulus Potter'	LAma
– 'Pickwick'	ETub LAma LBlo LRoo
§ – 'Purpureus Grandiflorus'	CBro ETub LAma LBlo LRoo
– 'Queen of the Blues'	CBro LBlo LBow
– 'Remembrance'	ETub LAma LBlo
– ***scepusiensis***	EPot
– 'Striped Beauty'	LAma LBlo
– 'Vanguard'	CBro ETub LAma
– ***vernus*** 'Grandiflorus'	See C. ***v.*** 'Purpureus Grandiflorus'
– 'Victor Hugo'	LAma
vernus vernus Heuffelianus group	ECam
versicolor	CBro SPou
– 'Picturatus'	LAma WChr

zonatus	See C. ***kotschyanus kotschyanus***

CROSSANDRA (Acanthaceae)

infundibuliformis	MBri

CROTALARIA (Leguminosae)

capensis	CPle CSun
grevyi	CPle LAbb

CROWEA (Rutaceae)

angustifolia	CSun

CRUCIANELLA (Rubiaceae)

stylosa	See PHUOPSIS ***stylosa***

CRUCIATA (Rubiaceae)

§ *laevipes*	CKin

CRYPTANTHUS (Bromeliaceae)

bivittatus 'Pink Starlight'	MBri
bromelioides	MBri
'Lefry'	MBri
'Marion Oppenheimer'	MBri
'Red Starlight'	MBri

X CRYPTBERGIA (Bromeliaceae)

CRYPTOGRAMMA (Adiantaceae)

crispa	MBal

CRYPTOMERIA (Taxodiaceae)

fortunei	See C. ***japonica sinensis***
§ *japonica*	CBra CDoC EHar IOrc ISea LSav MBar SHil SPer WCoo WMou WNor
– 'Araucarioides'	EHul
§ – 'Aurea'	EPla
– 'Bandai-sugi'	CDoC CKen CMac EHul IJoh MBar MGos MPla SHil SIng SLon SSmi WCon
– 'Compressa'	CDoC CKen CSam EBre EHul MBar MBri MPla MR&S NHar NHol WCon
§ – 'Cristata'	CDoC CMac EHar EHul ELan IJoh ISea LLin MBal MBar NJap SGar SMad WBod WCon
– 'Dacrydioides'	LSav
– 'Elegans'	Widely available
– 'Elegans Aurea'	CDoC EHul IJoh MBal MBar MPla SPer WCon
– 'Elegans Compacta'	CDoC CHoe CSco EHul LSav MBar MPla MUlv SHil WCon WThu WWeb
§ – 'Elegans Nana'	SHil WCon
¶ – 'Fasciata'	NHol
– 'Globosa Nana'	CDoC IJoh LLin LSav MBar SExT SSmi WCon
– 'Jindai-sugi'	CMac MBal MBar MPla SIng WCon
– 'Kilmacurragh'	CKen MBar NHol WCon
– 'Lobbii'	CDoC SHil
– 'Lobbii Nana'	See C. *j.* 'Nana'
– 'Midare-sugi'	See C. *j.* 'Viridis'
– 'Monstrosa'	CMHG MBar MGos SGar
– 'Monstrosa Nana'	See C. *j.* 'Mankichi-sugi'
§ – 'Nana'	CDoC CMac EBre EHul ENHC IJoh LLin MBal MBar MPla MWat NJap SHil SLon SPer SPla WThu
¶ – 'Pygmaea'	WCon
– 'Rasen-sugi'	LSav
– 'Sekkan-sugi'	EBre LLin MBri SHil SMad WCon
– 'Sekkwa-sugi'	See C. *j.* 'Cristata'
§ – ***sinensis***	CMCN
– 'Spiralis'	CBow CBra CDoC CMHG CMac CSco EHar IOrc LLin LSav MBal MBar MBri MGos MR&S SHil SPer SSmi WBod WCon
– 'Spiraliter Falcata'	See C. *j.* 'Yore-sugi'
– 'Tansu'	WWat
– 'Tenzan-sugi'	CKen
¶ – 'Vilmorin Variegated'	EPla
– 'Vilmoriniana'	Widely available
– 'Yatsubasa'	See C. *j.* 'Tansu'
§ – 'Yenko-sugi'	LSav
¶ – 'Yokohama'	NHol WCon
– 'Yoshino'	CKen
– 'Wogon'	See C. *j.* 'Aurea'

CRYPTOTAENIA (Umbelliferae)

japonica	CArn GPoy
¶ – 'Atropurpurea'	SMrm

CTENANTHE (Marantaceae)

§ *burle-marxii*	MBri
* 'Greystar'	MBri
lubbersiana	MBri
oppenheimiana	MBri
setosa	MBri
* 'Stripe Star'	MBri

CUMINUM (Umbelliferae)

cyminum	CArn GPoy SIde

CUNILA (Labiatae)

origanoides	MSal WCot

CUNNINGHAMIA (Taxodiaceae)

lanceolata	CB&S CMCN EHar ISea LLin MBar MPla SBor SGar SHil WCoo WMou WNor
I – 'Compacta'	CChu EHar MPla SMad

CUPHEA (Lythraceae)

aequipetala	WOMN
caeciliae	CKni CMHG LHil LHop
cyanea	CMHG CMer CPle CSev CTre LHil LHop SBor SDix SLMG SLon WHea WPer
hyssopifolia	CHan CMHG CMal CMer CPle CSev CTre EBar ERea IBlr LHil LHop MBri SLMG SLon
¶ – 'Alba'	LHop
ignea	ELan GWic IBlr MBri SLMG WEas WPer
¶ – *variegata*	WEas

llavea 'Firefly' LHil WEas
macrophylla LHil
N*platycentra* WCar
* *signata variegata* CMer IBlr LAbb LHil
¶ *viscosissima* WHea

X CUPRESSOCYPARIS (Cupressaceae)
§ *leylandii* CB&S CBra CDoC CMac CSco CTre CTrw EBre EHar EHul ENHC ENot IDai ISea LBuc MBal MBar MBri MGos NRoo SHil SPer SSus WMou
– 'Castlewellan' Widely available
– 'Galway Gold' See X C. *l.* 'Castlewellan'
– 'Golconda' SMad
– 'Golden Rider' EHul IOrc MBar MBri MGos
¶ – 'Haggerston Grey' SCro
– 'Harlequin' CMHG CTrw
– 'Hyde Hall' EHar EHul MBar MGos SPla
– 'Naylor's Blue' CMac
– 'Robinson's Gold' CBra CDoC CMac CSco EHar EHul ISea MBal MBar MBri MCra NRoo NWea WMou
– 'Silver Dust' EHar IJoh ISea MBri SMad
*– 'Variegata' MBar SExT SGar
notabilis SHil WBod
*– 'Brookhill' ISea
ovensii CMHG LSav

CUPRESSUS (Cupressaceae)
arizonica 'Aurea' EHul MBar WCon
– 'Blue Ice' CBow CDoC CSco EHar EHul LSav MBar MBri MR&S WCon
§ – *bonita* CMCN CSco EHar ISea MBal SLon
– 'Compacta' CKen EHul
– 'Conica' CDoC CKen EHar SExT WWat
I – 'Conica Glauca' CMCN ENot MBar
I – 'Fastigiata' EHul MBar
– 'Pyramidalis' CMac CSco EHar EHul IOrc SHil SPer
– 'Silver Smoke' CDoC
– 'Variegata' EHul
cashmeriana See C. *torulosa* 'Cashmeriana'
chengiana LSav
duclouxiana CMHG
funebris See CHAMAECYPARIS *funebris*
glabra See C. *arizonica*
goveniana CMCN MBar WCoo
guadalupensis forbesii CMCN
lusitanica CMCN WCoo
– 'Glauca Pendula' SHil WCon
macnabiana CMCN
macrocarpa CDoC EHar EHul SArc SHil
– 'Aurea Saligna' MBri
I – 'Compacta' CMac
– 'Crippsii' LLin
– 'Donard Gold' CMac ISea MBal MBar SHil
– 'Gold Spire' CMHG
– 'Gold Spread' CDoC EHul
– 'Goldcrest' CB&S CBow CBra CDoC CMac CSco EHar EHul ENot EPot IOrc MBal MBri MPla SHil SLon SPer SPla WAbe
– 'Golden Cone' CMac IJoh MBal SHil
– 'Golden Flame' EHul
– 'Golden Pillar' CDoC CMac CSco EHul MBar MPla MWat SHil
– 'Greenstead Magnificent' EBre MBri WCon
– 'Horizontalis Aurea' CSco EHul MBar
– 'John Keown' ISea
– 'Lutea' CB&S CDoC CMac EHar MWat SPer WCon
– 'Pygmaea' CKen
sargentii CMCN WCoo
sempervirens CB&S CMCN EHar EHul IOrc SArc SGar SHil WBod WCoo
*– 'Gracilis' EHul
– 'Green Spire' SHil
♦– 'Pyramidalis' See C. *s.* 'Stricta'
– *sempervirens* See C. *s.* 'Stricta'
§ – 'Stricta' CDoC CGre CSam CSco IJoh MPla SArc SExT WCon
– 'Stricta Aurea' EHul
– 'Swane's Golden' CB&S CDoC EHar EHul MPla SHil WCon
– 'Totem Pole' EHar EHul MBar
§ *torulosa* 'Cashmeriana' CB&S CBot CDoC CGre CHEx CSam CSun SHil SSpi

CURRANT, Black See **RIBES** Black Currant group

CURRANT, Pink See **RIBES** Pink Currant group

CURRANT, Red See **RIBES** Red Currant group

CURRANT, White See **RIBES** White Currant group

CURTONUS (Iridaceae)
paniculatus See CROCOSMIA *paniculata*

CYANANTHUS (Campanulaceae)
integer NTow WAbe
– x *lobatus* 'Sherriff's Variety' GDra NBir NHol
lobatus EPad GLoc MTho NGre NKay SBla SIng
– *albus* EPot
– dark seedling GDra
– giant form EPot GDra SBla
¶ – *insignis* GLoc
– x *microphyllus* GEdr WMar
microphyllus CBow CLew EPad GDra GEdr ITim SBla SOkd
sherriffii NHol

CYANELLA (Liliaceae/Tecophilaeaceae)
¶ *orchidiformis* LBow

CYATHEA (Cyatheaceae)
cooperi CB&S
dealbata CB&S CHEx LPal NMar SArc
medullaris CB&S CHEx NPal
¶ *smithii* CHEx

CYATHODES (Epacridaceae)
colensoi See STYPHELIA ***colensoi***
empetrifolia WThu
¶ *fasciculata* ECou
fraseri See LEUCOPOGON ***fraseri***
¶ *juniperina* ECou

CYCAS (Cycadaceae)
cairnsiana LPal
circinalis LPal
kennedyana LPal
media LPal
revoluta CHEx LPal MBri NPal SArc WNor
rumphii LPal

CYCLAMEN † (Primulaceae)
africanum CAvo CBro CLCN EPot LAma LBow MAsh MTho SIng SPou STil WMar
balearicum CAvo CBro CLCN EPot LAma MBal SBla SPou STil WAbe WThu
cilicium Widely available
– *album* CBro LAma STil WChr
§ *coum* Widely available
– *abchasicum* See C. ***c. caucasicum***
– *album* (patterned leaf) STil
– 'Atkinsii' CBro EPot GLoc MBro MPlt
§ – *caucasicum* CAvo CLCN EPot LAma NHol SPou STil
– *coum* CBro MBal
– *coum album* CAvo EPot GLoc LAma MBro NGre SPou STil WChr WHoo WNor
– *coum* 'Nymans' ex EKB 371 EPot SBla SPou
– *coum* 'Pewter leaf' CBro CLCN LAma WChr WThu
– *coum* silver leaf CAvo CFor ECam EPot MBro MTho SPou SSpi STil WMar
¶ – dark pink CAvo
– 'Dazzle' SPou
– forms LAma MBro MS&S SPou
– *ibericum album* See C. ***c. caucasicum album***
¶ – from Iran (elegans) SPou
– red WChr
– *roseum* CAvo LAma LBow STil WChr
– *roseum* (plain leaf) STil
¶ – from Russia SPou
¶ – 'Tile Barn Elizabeth' SPou
¶ – from Turkey SPou
– 'Urfa' EPot
creticum CAvo CLCN EPot LAma MAsh SIng SPou SSpi STil WMar
cyprium CAvo CBro CLCN CRiv ECam EPot ETub LAma MAsh SBla SIng SPou STil WChr
– 'E.S.' CLCN SPou STil
europaeum See C. ***purpurascens***
fatrense See C. ***purpurascens purpurascens***
graecum CAvo CBro CFor CLCN CRiv ECam EPot ETub LAma MBro NHol SIng SPou STil WMar WThu
– *album* LAma LRHS STil WChr
§ *hederifolium* Widely available
§ – *album* Widely available
– 'Bowles' Apollo' CRow SBla SSpi
– forms LAma MS&S NRed SPou
– red strain SPou
– scented strain CLCN SBla SPou STil
– 'Silver Cloud' CLCN
– silver leaf EPot SPou STil
ibericum See C. ***coum caucasicum***
intaminatum CAvo CBro CLCN CRiv EPot GLoc LAma MAsh MS&S NHol NRya SBla SIng SPou SSpi STil
– EKB 628 EPot MHig
– 'E K Balls' CAvo CBro
– patterned leaved form NGre SPou STil WMar WThu
– plain leaved form NGre STil WMar WThu
latifolium See C. ***persicum***
libanoticum CAvo CBro CLCN EPot LAma LBow MAsh MBro NGre SBla SIng SSpi STil WChr WMar WThu
mirabile CAvo CLCN EPot LAma NGre SIng STil WChr WMar WThu
neapolitanum See C. ***hederifolium***
– *album* See C. ***hederifolium album***
orbiculatum See C. ***coum***
parviflorum CAvo EPot LAma NHol SPou
§ *persicum* CAvo CBro CLCN CRiv CSam EPot LAma LBow MBri STil WMar
pseudibericum CAvo CBro CLCN CRiv EPot LAma LBow MAsh SBla SIng SPou STil WChr WMar WThu
– *roseum* CLCN STil
§ *purpurascens* CBro CFor CKel CLCN EPot GLoc LAma LBow MAsh MBri NHol SBla SIng SPou SSpi STil WChr WMar WWat
– *fatrense* See C. ***purpurascens purpurascens***
– form LAma
¶ – 'Lake Garda' SSpi
§ – *purpurascens* CAvo CBro EPot LAma STil
repandum CAvo CBro CLCN CMal LAma MBal SBla SIng SPou SSpi STil SWas WChr WHoo
¶ – JCA 5157 SSpi
– *album* EPot SPou STil
§ – *peloponnesiacum* CAvo CLCN EPot LAma SPou STil
– 'Pelops' See C. ***r. peloponnesiacum***

– rhodense	CLCN LAma STil
rohlfsianum	CAvo CBro CLCN EPot MAsh SIng STil WChr WMar WThu
trochopteranthum	CAvo CLCN EPot LAma NHol SIng SPou STil WChr

CYDONIA (Rosaceae)

japonica	See CHAENOMELES ***japonica***
F *oblonga*	EMui ESim LHol
F – 'Meech's Prolific'	CSam ERea ESim MWat NTwe SDea SFam SKee SPer WHig WMou
F – 'Portugal'	NRog NTwe WMou
F – 'Vranja'	CMac EHar ERea ESim EWar GChr LBuc MBri NElm NRog NTwe SDea SFam SKee SPer WHig WMou
¶ – pear shaped	NRog

CYMBALARIA (Scrophulariaceae)

aequitriloba	NHol WAbe
– alba	MPar NTow
§ *hepaticifolia*	EFol EFou EPot GLoc NNrd SIng WHil WPer
muralis	CKin EBar EPla MPit SFis
– albiflora	ESis WOMN WWin
– 'Globosa Alba'	EPot
– 'Globosa Rosea'	MPar NNrd WHil
– 'Nana Alba'	CLew CTom ELan MDHE MPlt NNrd NWCA SIng WHil WPer
§ *pallida*	MCas NKay SAxl SBla WHea WHil WPer
pilosa	ECtt EMNN NNrd NSti SIng

CYMBIDIUM (Orchidaceae)

CYMBOPOGON (Gramineae)

citratus	CArn

CYMOPHYLLUS (Cyperaceae)

fraseri	SApp

CYNARA (Compositae)

§ *cardunculus*	CHad COtt CSco CSev ECha ECro EFou ELan EMon GPla GWic MBri MCot MUlv NNor SDix SMad WCot WEas WHer WWin
¶ – ACL 380/78	EMon
hystrix	EFou SWas
scolymus	CB&S CHad CSco GWic LHol MBri SFis SMrm SSus WEas WHer
¶ – 'Brittany Belle'	WCot
– 'Green Globe'	CSev
– 'Purple Globe'	CArn CHad
¶ – 'Vert de Laon'	MBen

CYNOGLOSSUM (Boraginaceae)

amabile	CSun ELan EMon
¶ – 'Album'	GWic
¶ *– roseum*	EMon GWic
germanicum	CKin CNat
grande	SCro
nervosum	CCla CGle CLew CSco EFou EGol ELan EPar ERou GWic MUlv NHol NSel SChu SPer WHal WHoo WWin
– roseum	CCla WCru
officinale	CKin GPoy LHol MSal NSti
wallichii	CCla LGan
¶ *zeylanicum*	CSun LHil

CYPELLA (Iridaceae)

herbertii	CAvo LAma LBow LHil MHig NWCA SAxl SWas
¶ *plumosa platensis*	LHil

CYPERUS (Cyperaceae)

§ *albostriatus*	MBri
alternifolius	See C. ***involucratus***
diffusus	See C. ***albostriatus***
§ *eragrostis*	ECha MSta WAbb
esculentus	CHoe GWic IBlr
haspan	MSta
§ *involucratus*	CHEx CKni EBak ERea MBri MSta
– gracilis	EBak MBri
longus	CHoe CRow CWGN EHon EWav LMay MSta
* *nanus*	CHEx
papyrus	CHEx ERea MBri MSta
sumula	MBri
* *variegatus*	ERea
vegetus	See C. ***eragrostis***

CYPRIPEDIUM (Orchidaceae)

acaule	CKel IBar LAma SWes WChr
calceolus pubescens	SKen
debile	LAma SW&B SWes WChr
formosanum	See C. ***japonicum***
§ *guttatum*	SW&B
– yatabeanum	See C. ***guttatum***
§ *japonicum*	LAma SW&B SWes WChr

CYRILLA (Cyrillaceae)

racemiflora	WBod

CYRTANTHUS (Liliaceae/Amaryllidaceae)

¶ *brachyscyphus*	SWas
elatus	See C. ***purpureus***
falcatus	LBow
¶ *flavidus*	LHop
♦ *parviflorus*	See C. ***brachyscyphus***
§ *purpureus*	CAvo CBro ERea LAma LBow LHop MBri SBar SLMG SW&B
speciosus	See C. ***purpureus***

CYRTOMIUM See **PHANEROPHLEBIA**

CYRTOSPERMA (Araceae)

CYSTOPTERIS † (Aspleniaceae)

bulbifera	EPot NMar NNrd NVic SBla SMad WEas
dickieana	NKay NMar NNrd

fragilis	EBul EHon MBal NKay NMar SHig
montana	NKay
regia	NKay

CYTISUS † (Leguminosae)

§ *albus*	CB&S CLan ECtt ENot NNor SBar SDix SIng SPer
'Andreanus'	ENot GRei IJoh MGos MRav NKay NNor SHil SPer
'Andreanus Splendens'	CB&S CSco
ardoinii	GDra LHop MBal MBro MCas MHig MPla NHol NKay SHil SIng WDav
– 'Cottage'	EHal EPot GDra MBri MBro MPla NHol WAbe WDav
battandieri	Widely available
– 'Yellow Tail'	SHil
x *beanii*	ENot ESis GDra IJoh MBal MBar MPar MPla MR&S MWat NBar NNor NRya NTow SHil SPer SReu WAbe WBod WWat
'Boskoop Glory'	CSco ECtt SPer
'Burkwoodii'	CB&S CSco ENot IDai IJoh ISea MBlu MBri MR&S MWat SHil
'Butterfly'	CB&S
¶ 'C E Pearson'	SHil
§ *canariensis*	ERea MBri
¶ 'Compact Crimson'	EPla
'Cornish Cream'	CB&S CSco LHop MBri SHil SPer
¶ 'Criterion'	MBri MRav
'Daisy Hill'	IDai LRHS MBri
decumbens	GLoc IOrc MBro NKay WDav WHil WWin
demissus	EPot GDra MHig WAbe
'Dorothy Walpole'	CSam CTrw
'Dragonfly'	IOrc MR&S SHil
'Dukaat'	EBre MBri NRoo
'Firefly'	IJoh MBal MBri NKay
'Fulgens'	CSco ELan IDai MBar MBri SHil SPer WWeb
'Garden Magic'	LRHS NRoo
'Golden Cascade'	CB&S MR&S MWat SPla WWeb
'Golden Showers'	MBal
'Golden Sunlight'	ECtt ELan ENot IJoh MR&S SHil
'Goldfinch'	CB&S ENot MBri MWat WWeb
'Johnson's Crimson'	MBri SHil
x *kewensis*	Widely available
– 'Niki'	MBri
'Killiney Red'	ENot GRei IJoh IOrc ISea LSav MBri MWat SHil
'Killiney Salmon'	CSco ENot LSav MGos
'La Coquette'	MBar SHil
'Lena'	CMHG EBre ECtt EPot IJoh MBri MGos MR&S NRoo SMad SPla SSta
leucanthus	See C. ***albus***
'Lord Lambourne'	LRHS SHil
'Luna'	ENot IJoh
'Maria Burkwood'	CSco IDai MBri
'Minstead'	CSco MBal SHil SPer WAbe WWeb
'Moonlight'	SPer
'Moyclare Pink'	CGle CLan CMHG
¶ 'Muldean'	WWeb
multiflorus	MBal SHil SPer SSpi WBod
– 'Toome's Variety'	SPla
– 'White Bouquet'	MBri
'Newry Seedling'	LRHS MBri
nigrescens	See C. ***nigricans***
§ *nigricans*	ENot SDry SHil SPer SSpi
'Palette'	CSco ECtt ELan ISea SPer
'Porlock'	CTre ERav SHil SPla WBod WHal
x *praecox*	See C. x ***p.*** 'Warminster'
– 'Albus'	CCla CMHG CSco ELan ENot GRei IJoh IOrc ISea LSav MBar MBri MGos MR&S MWat NRoo SHil SPer SPla WAbe WBod WWat
– 'Allgold'	CB&S CBra CMHG CSam CSco CShe EBre ENot GRei IDai IJoh MBar MBri MPla MR&S NKay NRoo SHil SPla WAbe WBod
– 'Canary Bird'	See C. x ***p.*** 'Gold Speer'
– 'Frisia'	CB&S MBar
§ – 'Gold Speer'	ENot IJoh SPer SPla WWeb
– 'Hollandia'	CB&S CSco CShe EBre EGol GRei MBar MBri MGos MR&S MRav SPer WBod WWeb WWin
N– 'Warminster'	Widely available
– 'Zeelandia'	CB&S ENot IJoh LSav MBar MR&S MRav SHil WAbe WBod WWeb
'Princess'	MBri MPla
procumbens	LHop MBal SHil SOkd SSmi WWat
purgans	IJoh MBal NNor SPer SSta WBod
purpureus	CSam ELan IDai IOrc MBal MBar MBri MGos MPla NBar NRoo NTow SHil SPer WAbe WHal WWin
– *albus*	CB&S LHop MBar MPla SHil
§ – 'Atropurpureus'	ENot MPla MR&S NHol SHil SPer SSta
– *incarnatus*	See C. ***p.*** 'Atropurpureus'
racemosus	See C. x ***spachianus***
'Red Wings'	GDra IJoh MGos MR&S SPer WBod
'Roter Favorit' ('Red Favourite')	MBar
'Royal Standard'	LRHS
scoparius	CKin ENot GRei LHol MSal NRoo NWea SIde SReu WWin
– 'Maritimus'	See C. ***s. prostratus***
§ – *prostratus*	CB&S MBri NNor NTow SHil WBod
x *spachianus*	MBri
'Sunset'	ENot
supinus	EHal EHar LHop
'Windlesham Ruby'	ELan GRei ISea MBar MPla MR&S NKay SHil SPer WAbe WBod WWeb

DABOECIA † (Ericaceae)

§ *cantabrica* CSun EBre EDen GRei MBal NHea NLan NRya
§ – *alba* CBow CMac CNCN EBre ENHC ENot GAng GBla GDra GPen GRei GSpe IDai IJoh MBal MBar MBri MOke NHol NRoo SHil SPla WBod WRid
– 'Alba Globosa' EDen ENHC MBar MCra WGre
– 'Atropurpurea' CNCN EBre EDen ENHC ENot GAng GBla GPen GSpe IDai IJoh MBal MBri MGos MOke NHea NHol NWin SHil WBod WRid
– 'Barbara Phillips' MBar
– 'Bicolor' CNCN EDen ENHC GPen GRei GSpe MBal MBri MGos MOke SHil WGre WRid
– 'Blueless' MCra NWin
– 'Charles Nelson' EDen MBar MOke
– 'Cinderella' CNCN EDen GPen GSpe MBar MCra
– 'Covadonga' CNCN EDen ENHC MBar
– 'David Moss' CMac EDen GAng GBla MBal MBar MCra WGre
– 'Donard Pink' EDen GBla MBar
– 'Early Bride' ENHC
– 'Eskdale Baron' ENHC
– 'Heather Yates' CNCN EDen ENHC GBla MBri MOke NWin
– 'Hookstone Pink' WBod
– 'Hookstone Purple' ENHC GBla GPen MBar MBri MCra MGos MOke NHol WGre
– 'Lilacina' EDen ENHC GPen MBar MFir WRid
♦– pink EDen GPen NHea
– 'Pink Lady' MBar
*– 'Polifolia' CBow EDen GBla MBri MOke
– 'Porter's Variety' GBla MBar MBri MOke SHil
– 'Praegerae' CBow CMac CNCN EDen ENHC GBla GPen GRei GSpe IDai MBal MBar MCra MGos NHea NWin SHil WGre WRid
– 'Purpurea' GBla MBar MCra
– 'Rainbow' CNCN MBar MCra
– 'Rosea' MBar
– 'Snowdrift' GPen MBar NHea NWin
– 'Waley's Red' EDen ENHC MBar NHea SPla
– 'White Blum' SPla
– 'White Carpet' EDen
– 'William Buchanan' See D. x ***scotica*** 'William Buchanan'
x *scotica* 'Bearsden' MBar
– 'Cora' ENHC GAng GPen GSpe MBar NWin
– 'Goscote' MGos
– 'Jack Drake' CSun EDen ENHC GDra GPen GSpe MBal MBar MBri MOke NKay WBod WGre
– 'Silverwells' CNCN GAng MBar MBri MGos MPlt NKay NWin
– 'Tabramhill' MBar NWin
*– 'Wayley's Red' NWin
§ – 'William Buchanan' CMac CNCN CSun EBre EDen ENHC GAng GBla GDra GPen GSpe MBal MBar MBri MCra MGos MOke MPlt NHea NHol NKay NRoo NWin WGre
– 'William Buchanan Gold' MBar MBri NWin SPla

DACRYCARPUS (Podocarpaceae)

§ *dacrydioides* ECou
– 'Dark Delight' ECou

DACRYDIUM (Podocarpaceae)

bidwillii See HALOCARPUS ***bidwillii***
cupressinum CTre ECou
franklinii See LAGAROSTROBOS *f.*
♦ *laxifolium* See LEPIDOTHAMNUS *l.*

DACTYLIS (Gramineae)

glomerata 'Variegata' CHoe EMon ERou IBlr NSti WHea

DACTYLORHIZA (Orchidaceae)

§ *elata* SPou
§ *foliosa* CFor CRow ELan MBri NHol SLHN SWes WAbe
§ *fuchsii* ELan NHol WCru
§ – 'Bressingham Bonus' EBre SBar SWes
§ *maculata* CBro ELan EPar LAma MSta SKen
§ *majalis* EBre LAma SWes WCru
* *mascula* WCru
¶ *purpurella* ELan
¶ 'Tinney's Spotted' SOkd

DAHLIA † (Compositae)

¶ 'Abridge Ben' (MinD) MBeb
'Abridge Bertie' (MinD) MBeb
'Abridge Fox' (MinD) MBeb NHal
'Abridge Natalie' (SWL) MBeb NHal
'Abridge Taffy' (MinD) MBeb
'Ace of Hearts' LAma
'Alloway Cottage' (MD) MTiv NHal
'Alltami Alpine' (MD) NHal
'Alltami Apollo' (GSC) MTiv NHal
'Alltami Cherry' (SBa) NHal
'Alltami Classic' (MD) MTiv NHal
'Alltami Corsair' (MSC) NHal
'Alltami Cosmic' (LD) NHal
'Almand's Climax' (GD) MBeb MTiv
'Alstergruss' (Col) LAma
'Alva's Doris' (SC) MBeb
'Alva's Supreme' (GD) MBeb MTiv NHal
'Amaran Pico' (MD) MBeb
'Amaran Relish' (GD) MBeb
'Amber Banker' (MC) MTiv NHal
¶ 'Anatol' CSut
'Andrew Lockwood' (Pom) MTiv
¶ 'Appenzell' (MSC) MTiv
'Appetizer' (SSC) MBeb

'Apricot Honeymoon Dress' (SD) NHal
'Arabian Night' (SD) CHad LAma SW&B
'Athalie' (SC) MBeb MTiv NHal
'B J Beauty' (MD) NHal
'Bacchus' (MSC) CKel
'Banker' (MC) MTiv NHal
¶ 'Barbarry Banker' (MinD) NHal
¶ 'Barbarry Climax' (SB) NHal
¶ 'Barbarry Flush' (MinD) NHal
¶ 'Barbarry Lavender' (MinD) NHal
'Bassingbourne Beauty' (SD) NHal
'Bednall Beauty' NBir
'Belle Epoque' (MC) CKel
'Betty Bowen' (SD) MTiv
¶ 'Bill Holmberg' (GD) MBeb
'Bishop of Llandaff (Misc) CAvo CBos CBot CChu CHad CHil LGre LHil LHop MTho MTiv NHal SLHN SMrm WEas
¶ 'Black Jack' (SD) MTiv
'Black Monarch' (GD) NHal
'Bonaventure' (GD) NHal
'Border Princess' (SC) CKel SW&B
'Border Triumph' (DwB) MTiv NHal
¶ 'Bright' CSut
'Brunton' (MinD) NHal
¶ 'Café au Lait' (LD) CSut
¶ 'Calgary' (SD) CSut
¶ 'Cameo' (WL) MBeb
'Candy Keene' (LSC) MBeb MTiv NHal
'Carstone Cobblers' (SBa) NHal
¶ 'Carstone Sunbeam' (SD) NHal
'Catherine Ireland' (MinD) NHal
'Charlie Two' (MD) MBeb NHal
¶ 'Charmant' CSut
'Cheerio' (SSC) MTiv
¶ 'Christine' CSut
'Christopher Taylor (SWL) NHal
'Clair de Lune' (Col) MBeb
'Clarion' (MC)(MSC) SW&B
'Cloverdale' (SD) MBeb NHal
coccinea (Misc) CBot GWic SSpi
¶ – hybrids SSpi
'Connie Bartlam' (MD) NHal
'Conway' (SSC) NHal
¶ 'Coral Puff' CSut
'Corona' (SSC)(DwB) MTiv NHal
¶ 'Cream Alvas' (GD) MTiv
¶ 'Cream Beauty' (SWL) NHal
'Cream Kerkrade' (SC) MBeb
'Cream Linda' (SD) NHal
'Crichton Cherry' (MinD) NHal
'Crichton Honey' (SBa) NHal
'Croydon Supreme' (LD) MTiv
'Cryfield Bryn' (SSC) NHal
'Daleko Gold' (MD) MTiv NHal
'Daleko Jupiter' (GSC) MTiv NHal
'Daleko National' (MD) NHal
'Daleko Olympic' (LD) MTiv
'Dana Iris' (SC) MBeb NHal
'Dana Louise' (MD) MBeb MTiv
'Danum Cream' (MSC) MBeb MTiv
'Danum Pinky' (MSC) MBeb MTiv
'Dauntless' (GSC) MBeb
'Davenport Anita' (MinD) NHal
'Davenport Honey ' (MinD) NHal
'Davenport Pride' (MSC) NHal
'Davenport Sunlight' (MSC) NHal
'David Howard' (MinD) CKel LAma NHal
'Debra Anne Craven' (GSC) NHal
'Deepest Yellow' (MinBa) CKel CSut
'Defile' (MD) MBeb
'Denise Willow' (Pom) MTiv
'Diamant' LAma
'Diana Gregory' (Pom) MBeb NHal
'Doc van Horn' (LSC) MTiv NHal
'Doctor Caroline Rabbitt' (SD) MTiv
'Doris Day' (SC) LAma MTiv NHal
'Duet' (MD) CSut LAma
¶ 'Dutch Baby' (Pom) MTiv
'Earl Marc' (SC) NHal
'Eastwood Moonlight' (MSC) MBeb MTiv NHal
'Edinburgh' (SD) LAma MTiv
'Edith Arthur' (SSC) MTiv
¶ 'Edna C' (MD) NHal
'Eileen Denny' (MSC) MBeb
'Emmenthal' (SD) NHal
'Emmerdale' (SC) NHal
* 'Eveline' CSut LAma SW&B
'Evelyn Foster' (MD) NHal
'Evelyn Rumbold' (GD) MTiv
¶ 'Evening Mail' (GSC) NHal
'Fernhill Champion' (MD) MBeb
'Feu Céleste' (Col) LAma
¶ 'Figurine' (WL) MBeb
¶ 'Fille du Diable' (LSC) MTiv
'Fiona Stewart' (SB) MTiv NHal
'Firebird' LAma
'Frank Holmes' (Pom) MBeb
'Frank Hornsey' (SD) MBeb MTiv
'Freestyle' (SC) NHal
* 'Friquolet' LAma
'Frits' (MinBa) MTiv
'G F Hemerik' (Sin) LAma
'Garden News' (SD) MBeb
¶ 'Gateshead Festival' (SD) NHal

¶ 'Gateshead Galaxy' (DwB) NHal
'Gay Mini' (MinD) MTiv
'Gerrie Hoek' (SWL) CKel CSut LAma MTiv SW&B
'Gilt Edge' (MD) MTiv
'Gina Lombaert' (MSC) LAma
'Giraffe' (Misc) MTiv
'Gloria Romaine' (SD) MTiv
'Glorie van Heemstede' (SWL) CKel LAma MTiv NHal
'Go American' (GD) MBeb MTiv NHal
'Gold Crown' (LSC) LAma
'Golden Emblem' (MD) SW&B
* 'Golden Festival' CKel
¶ 'Golden Impact' (MSC) MTiv
'Golden Willo' (Pom) MTiv
'Good Earth' (MC) LAma
'Good Hope' (MinD) MTiv
'Gordon Lockwood' (Pom) NHal
¶ 'Grenadier' WCot
* 'Grenidor Pastelle' (MSC) MBeb MTiv NHal
¶ 'Gypsy Boy' (LD) MTiv
'Hallmark' (Pom) MBeb
'Hamari Accord' (LSC) NHal
'Hamari Bride' (MSC) MTiv
'Hamari Fiesta' (SD) NHal
'Hamari Girl' (GD) MBeb MTiv NHal
'Hamari Gold' (GD) MBeb NHal
'Hamari Katrina' (LSC) MBeb NHal
'Hamilton Lilian' MBeb
'Hartenaas' LAma
'Hayley Jane' (SSC) MTiv NHal
'Hazard' (MSC) LAma
'Helga' (MSC) LAma
¶ 'Heljo's Flame' (SC) CSut
'Herbert Smith' (D) LAma
'Hit Parade' (MSC) CSut LAma
'Holland Festival' (GD) MTiv
'Honey' (Anem/DwB) LAma
'Honeymoon Dress' (SD) MBeb MTiv NHal
'House of Orange' (MD) SW&B
imperialis (Misc) GWic
'Inca Dambuster' (GSC) MBeb MTiv NHal
'Inca Matchless' (MD) MTiv
'Indian Summer' (SC) MTiv NHal
'Irene van der Zwet' (Sin) LAma
'Iris' (Pom) NHal
'Jacqueline Tivey' (SD) MTiv
'Jaldec Jerry' (GSC) MBeb
'Janet Goddard' (SD) MBeb MTiv
¶ 'Jean Bailiss' (MSC) MBeb
'Jean Fairs' (MinWL) NHal
'Jescot Julie' (O) MTiv
'Jim Branigan' (LSC) MTiv NHal
¶ 'Joan Beecham' (SD) MTiv NHal
'Jocondo' (GD) NHal
'Johann' (Pom) MBeb MTiv NHal
'John Prior' (SD) NHal
'John Street' (SWL) NHal
'Just Julia' (MSC) MTiv
'Just Mary' (SD) MTiv
¶ 'Karenglen' (MinD) MTiv NHal
'Kathleen's Alliance' (SC) NHal
'Kathryn's Cupid' (MinBa) MBeb MTiv NHal
'Katisha' (MinD) MTiv
¶ 'Kelvin Floodlight' (GD) CSut
'Kennemerland' (SC) LAma
'Kenora Fireball' (SB) MBeb NHal
'Kenora Valentine' (GD) MBeb
¶ 'Kenora Wildfire' (GD) MBeb
'Kidd's Climax' (GD) MBeb MTiv NHal
'Kiwi Gloria' (SC) MBeb MTiv NHal
'Klankstad Kerkrade' (SC) MBeb MTiv NHal
'Kochelsee' (MinD) LAma
'Kung Fu' (SD) MBeb MTiv NHal
'La Gioconda' (Col) LAma
'Lady Kerkrade (SC) MBeb MTiv NHal
'Lady Linda' (SD) MBeb MTiv NHal
'Laura Marie' (MinBa) MBeb
'Lavender Athalie' (SC) MBeb NHal
'Lavender Nunton Harvest' (SD) MBeb
'Lavender Perfection' (GD) CKel LAma
'Lavender Symbol' (MSC) MBeb MTiv NHal
'Lavengro' (GD) MBeb NHal
'Le Vonne Splinter' (GSC) MBeb
'Lemon Elegance' (SC) MBeb MTiv NHal
¶ 'Lemon Puff' CSut
'Leycett' (GD) MBeb
'Liberator' (GD) MBeb MTiv NHal
* 'Life Force' MTiv
'Life Size' (LD) NHal
'Lilac Athalie' (SC) MBeb
¶ 'Lilian Ingham' (SSC) MBeb
'Lilianne Ballego' (MinD) MTiv NHal
¶ 'Linda Lusardi' (SSC) MTiv
'Lipoma' (MinBa) CKel
¶ 'Lismore Peggy' (Pom) MBeb
'Little Tiger' LAma
'L'Ancresse' (MinBa) MBeb NHal
'Magic Moment' (MSC) MBeb
'Magnificat' (MinD) CKel
'Majestic Athalie' (SC) MBeb
'Majestic Kerkrade' (SC) MBeb NHal
'Majjas Symbol' (MSC) NHal
'Majuba' (MD) CKel LAma SW&B
'Margaret Ann' (MinD) MBeb MTiv
'Mark Damp' (LSC) NHal
'Mark Hardwick' NHal
'Mark Lockwood' (Pom) MTiv
'Mark Willo' (Pom) MBeb
'Match' (SSC) MBeb MTiv
'Matterhorn' (SWL) MTiv NHal
'Meiro' (SD) MTiv

merckii (Misc)	CAvo CBot CChu CFor CGle CHad CHar CHil CSun EFol GWic LGre LHil MTho MUlv NSti SLHN SSpi WEas WPer WRus WWin
– *alba*	CHad WRus
– *alba* 'Hadspen Star'	CHad
'Mi Wong' (Pom)	NHal
'Minder' (GD)	MTiv
¶ 'Minley Carol' (Pom)	NHal
'Minley Linda' (Pom)	MBeb MTiv NHal
'Miramar' (SD)	CKel
¶ 'Miss Blanc' (SD)	MTiv
'Miss Swiss ' (SD)	NHal
'Mistill Beauty' (SC)	NHal
'Mistill Delight' (MinD)	MTiv NHal
'Monk Marc' (SC)	MTiv NHal
'Moor Place' (Pom)	MBeb MTiv NHal
'Morning Dew' (SC)	SW&B
'Morning Kiss ' (LSD)	CKel SW&B
'Mrs McDonald Quill' (LD)	NHal
'Mummies Favourite' (SD)	MTiv
'Murillo'	LAma
'My Love' (SSC)	CSut LAma
'Nationwide' (SD)	MTiv
'Neil Gillson' (MD)	MBeb NHal
'Nellie Birch' (MinBa)	MTiv
'New Baby' (MinBa)	LAma
'Night Editor' (GD)	MBeb
'Nijinsky' (SBa)	MTiv
'Nina Chester' (SD)	MBeb MTiv NHal
'Noreen' (Pom)	MBeb NHal
'Nunton Harvest' (SD)	NHal
'Orange Nugget' (MinBa)	LAma
'Orfeo' (MC)	LAma
'Park Princess' (DwB)(SC)	LAma MTiv SW&B
'Paul Chester' (SC)	NHal
'Paul Damp' (MSC)	NHal
¶ 'Paul's Delight' (SD)	MBeb
'Pearl of Heemstede' (SWL)	MTiv NHal
'Pensford Marion' (Pom)	MBeb
'Pensford Willo' (Pom)	MBeb
¶ 'Periton' (MinB)	NHal
'Peter'	LAma
'Pied Piper' (MinBa)	MTiv
'Pink Frank Hornsey' (SD)	MTiv
'Pink Giraffe' (O)	MTiv
'Pink Honeymoon Dress' (SD)	NHal
'Pink Jupiter' (GSC)	MBeb MTiv NHal
'Pink Katisha' (MinD)	MTiv
'Pink Kerkrade' (SC)	MBeb NHal
'Pink Paul Chester' (SC)	NHal
'Pink Risca Miner' (SBa)	MBeb MTiv
'Pink Shirley Alliance' (SC)	MTiv
'Pink Surprise' (LSC)	SW&B
'Pink Symbol' (MSC)	MBeb
'Pink Vaguely Noble' (SBa)	MBeb
'Pioneer' (MSC)	CKel SW&B
'Piper's Pink' (SSC)(DwB)	MBeb MTiv
'Playboy' (GD)	MTiv
'Polar Sight' (GC)	CKel
'Polyand' (LD)	MBeb
'Pontiac' (SC)	MTiv
'Pop Willo' (Pom)	NHal
'Potgieter' (MinBa)	LAma
'Prefect' (MSC)	MBeb MTiv
'Preference' (SSC)	LAma
'Preston Park' (Sin)(DwB)	NHal
'Pride of Berlin'	See D. 'Stolze von Berlin'
'Primrose Rustig' (MD)	NHal
'Procyon' (SD)	LAma
'Promotion' (MC)	SW&B
'Purbeck Lydia' (LSC)	NHal
'Purple Gem'	LAma
¶ 'Queeny' (SSC)	NHal
¶ 'Quel Diable' (LSC)	MTiv
'Radfo' (SSC)	NHal
'Raiser's Pride' (MC)	NHal
'Red Alert' (LBa)	MTiv
'Red and White' (SD)	SW&B
'Red Diamond' (MD)	NHal
'Red Sensation' (MD)	MTiv NHal
'Reginald Keene' (LSC)	MBeb MTiv NHal
'Rhonda' (Pom)	MBeb MTiv NHal
'Rhonda Suzanne' (Pom)	MBeb MTiv
'Richard Marc' (SC)	MTiv
'Risca Miner' (SBa)	MBeb MTiv NHal
'Robin Hood' (SBa)	MBeb MTiv
¶ 'Rosalinde'	CSut
'Rose Cupid' (MinBa)	NHal
'Rose Jupiter' (GSC)	NHal
'Rosella' (MD)	LAma
'Rothesay Castle' (MinD)	MTiv NHal
'Rothesay Reveller' (MD)	MBeb
'Rothesay Robin' (SD)	NHal
'Rotterdam' (MSC)	MTiv NHal SW&B
'Ruby Wedding' (MinD)	NHal
'Ruskin Belle' (MSC)	NHal
'Ruskin Diane' (SD)	MBeb MTiv NHal
¶ 'Ruskin Petite' (MinBa)	MTiv
'Rustig' (MD)	MBeb MTiv NHal
'Rusty Hope' (MinD)	MTiv
'Safe Shot' (MD)	LAma
'Salmon Beauty' (D)	SW&B
'Salmon Keene' (LSC)	MBeb NHal
'Salmon Symbol' (MSC)	MBeb NHal
'Satellite' (MD)	SW&B
'Scarlet Beauty' (SD)	NHal
'Scarlet Kokarde' (MinD)	NHal
'Schweitzer's Kokarde' (MinD)	NHal

'Scottish Rhapsody' (MSC) NHal
'Senzoe Ursula' (SD) MBeb NHal
¶ 'Sherwood Monarch' (GSC) MTiv
'Sherwood Standard' (MD) NHal
'Sherwood Titan' (GSC) MTiv
'Shirley Alliance' (SC) MTiv
¶ 'Shoreline' (D) CSut
¶ 'Shy Lass' (SC) MBeb
'Siemen Doorenbos' (Anem) LAma
'Silver City' (LD) NHal
'Silver Slipper' (SSC) MTiv
'Sky High' (SD) MTiv
'Small World' (Pom) MTiv NHal
'Sneezy' (Sin) LAma
'Snowflake' (SWL) LAma
'Snowstorm' (MD) CKel LAma SW&B
'So Dainty' (MinSC) MBeb
'Spencer' (SD) NHal
'Stylemaster' (MC) MTiv
'Suffolk Bride' (MSC) NHal
¶ 'Sultan' CSut
¶ 'Sunney Boy' CSut
¶ 'Sunray Glint' (MSC) NHal
'Sunray Symbol' (MSC) MBeb
¶ 'Swan Vale' (SD) MBeb MTiv NHal
'Sweet Content' (SD) MBeb MTiv
'Sweet Symbol' (MSC) MBeb
'Symbol' (MSC) MBeb MTiv NHal
'Syston Sophia' (LBa) MTiv
'Syston Zone' (LSC) MTiv
'Tahiti Sunrise' (MSC) MTiv
'Tango' (SD) NHal
¶ 'Thais' (Col) MTiv
'Thelma Clements' (LD) MTiv
'Thomas A Edison' (MD) CSut LAma
'Tiger Tiv' (MD) MTiv
'Tommy Doc' (SSC) NHal
'Top Choice' (GSC) LAma SW&B
'Trendy' (SD) MTiv SW&B
¶ 'Trengrove Jill' (MD) MBeb MTiv NHal
¶ 'Trengrove Summer' (MD) MBeb NHal
¶ 'Twilight Time' (MD) CSut
'Union Jack' (Sin) LRHS
'Vaguely Noble' (SBa) MBeb NHal
'Vantage' (GSC) NHal
'Vazon Bay' (MinB) MBeb
'Veritable' (MSC) SW&B
'Violet' SW&B
'Violet Davies' (MSC) MTiv
'W J N' (Pom) MBeb NHal
'Wanda's Capella' (GD) MBeb MTiv NHal
¶ 'Wanda's Sunshine' (GD) MTiv
'Welcome Guest' (MSC) MBeb MTiv
¶ 'Wendy's Place' (Pom) NHal
'Whale's Rhonda' (Pom) MBeb
'White Alva's' (GD) MBeb MTiv NHal
'White Aster' (Pom) CKel
'White Hornsey' (SD) MTiv
'White Kerkrade' (SC) NHal
'White Klankstad' (SC) MBeb
'White Linda' (SD) MBeb NHal
'White Moonlight' (MSC) MBeb MTiv NHal
'White Perfection' (GD) SW&B
'White Rustig' (MD) MBeb NHal
'White Swallow' (SSC) NHal
'William John' (Pom) MBeb
'William 'B'' (GD) MBeb
'Willo's Surprise' (Pom) MBeb MTiv NHal
'Willo's Violet' (Pom) MBeb
'Wootton Carol' (SD) MTiv
'Wootton Cupid' (MinBa) MBeb MTiv NHal
'Wootton Impact' (MSC) MBeb MTiv NHal
'Worton Ann' (MinD) MBeb
'Yellow Cheer' (SD)(DwB) CKel
'Yellow Hammer' (Sin)(DwB) NHal
'Yes Sir' (MD) MTiv
¶ 'Yvonne' CSut
'Zorro' (GD) MBeb MTiv NHal

DAISWA (Liliaceae/Trilliaceae)
§ ***polyphylla*** ECro

DAMSON See **PRUNUS** ***institia***

DANAË (Liliaceae/Ruscaceae)
§ ***racemosa*** CHad ECro EGol EMon ERav IHos MBri MUlv SDry SGar SHil SPer SSpi SSta

DAPHNE † (Thymelaeaceae)
acutiloba CBow CCla CFor NRya SBla SSpi SSta
albowiana CKni SBla WMar WSHC
alpina EPad MHig NRya SBla SPou WOMN
arbuscula SBla SHil
aurantiaca SHil
bholua CBot CBow CSco ELan LHop NHar SSpi SSta WWat
– ***alba*** CB&S LHop SBla
– Daman Ridge form SSta
– Darjeeling form SBla SSpi
– 'Gurkha' CFor SHil
– 'Jacqueline Postill' LRHS SHil SSpi SSus
blagayana Widely available
x ***burkwoodii*** CB&S CBot CBow CSam ELan IBar IJoh IOrc LHol MR&S MWat SPla SSpi WWat
– 'Albert Burkwood' NWea SBla SHil
¶ – 'Astrid' MGos
– 'G K Argles' SBla
– 'Laveneri' CFor SBla
– 'Somerset' CB&S CBow CSco CShe EHar ELan ENot GAbr GLoc IHos LAbb LHop MBar MBlu MBri MGos MPar MPla NHol SBla SPer SSpi SSta WBod

– 'Somerset Gold Edge'	CSco
– 'Variegata'	CB&S CBot CFor EGol ELan ERav GAbr LGre LHop MPla MR&S SBla SHil SIgm SSpi SSta WMar WWat
caucasica	SBla SSpi WWat
cneorum	CB&S CBow CCla CSam IJoh LHol MBal MBar MBri MWat SBla SHil SPer SReu SSta WAbe WBod WWat WWin
– *alba*	SBla
– 'Eximia'	CBow CChu CFor CSco ELan EPot GAbr IOrc LNet MGos MPla NHol SBla SHil SPer SPla SSta WWat
*– 'Poszta'	LRHS SSpi
– *pygmaea*	SBla SHil SIng WPat WThu
– 'Ruby Glow'	SHil
– 'Variegata'	CBot CFor EPot GLoc MBar MGos MPla NRar SBla SHil SIng SPer SSta WRus WSHC WThu WWat
– *verlotii*	LHop
collina	CB&S CCla CFor CLan CSco CTrw ELan IBar IOrc LGre NRar SBla SHil SIng SPer SReu SSta WAbe WPat WThu
euboica	SBla
genkwa	CCla ELan SBla SHil SSpi WWeb
giraldii	CBot NHol SBla SHil SPou SSpi
¶ *gnidioides*	SIgm
gnidium	SBla SHil SSpi
x *houtteana*	CBot CCla IBar NHar SBla SSpi SSta WMar
x *hybrida*	SBla SHil SSpi
japonica 'Striata'	See D. ***odora*** 'Aureomarginata'
jasminea	EPot GLoc SBla SHil WPat
julia	SBla SHil
kamtschatica	ELan SBla SReu
– *jezoensis*	SBla SHil SSta
laureola	GPoy MGos MPla SHil SPou SReu
– *cantabrica*	SChu
¶ – 'Margaret Mathew'	SWas
– *philippi*	CShe ELan LHop MPla NHol SChu SHil SPer SReu SSpi SSta WAbe WMar
longilobata	SSta WMar
– 'Peter Moore'	SHil
x *mantensiana*	CFor MBal NHol SBla SMrm SSpi SSta WPat WThu
– 'Manten'	SHil
mezereum	Widely available
– *alba*	Widely available
– 'Bowles' White'	CBot EPot ERav MPar WOMN
– 'Grandiflora'	ELan
– *rosea*	MGos
– *rubra*	CSco EGol IOrc LNet MR&S SGar SSpi WAbe WWeb
x *napolitana*	CBot CBow CChu CCla CMHG CSam ELan EMNN IJoh IOrc LNet MGos NHol SBla SChu SHil SPer SSta
§ *odora*	CBra ERea LHol MGos SBla SChu SHil SPla SSpi SSta WMar
§ – *alba*	CB&S CBot CBra ERea IBar SBla SHil SPer
§ – 'Aureomarginata'	Widely available
– *leucantha*	See D. ***o. alba***
– 'Marginata'	See D. ***o.*** 'Aureomarginata'
– *rubra*	ERea LSav SMrm
– 'Walburton'	LRHS
oleoides	MPar SPou SSta WMar
papyracea	CCla SSta
petraea 'Flore Pleno'	SBla
– 'Grandiflora'	EPot SBla WPat
pontica	CBow CFor CPle CTre EHar ELan MBar MPar SBla SDix SHil SPer SSpi SSta WThu
retusa	Widely available
sericea	MPar NTow WThu
¶ 'Silver Y'	SBla
tangutica	Widely available
– 'Aureomarginata'	MGos
x *thauma*	SBla

DAPHNIPHYLLUM (Daphniphyllaceae)

macropodum	CChu CCla CGre CHEx EHar LSav MUlv SArc SHil SSpi WWat

DARLINGTONIA (Sarraceniaceae)

californica	CHEx EPot SSpi WMEx

DARMERA (Saxifragaceae)

§ *peltata*	CChu CCla CHad CHar CRow CWGN EBre ECha EGol EHon ELan ELun EPar LMay MBri MFir MSta MUlv NBar NKay NSti SHig SMad SSpi
– *nana*	ECha ECro NHol WOld

DASYLIRION (Agavaceae)

acrotrichum	CHEx SArc
gracile	See D. ***acrotichum***
¶ *longissimum*	SIgm
¶ *texanum*	SSpi

DASYPHYLLUM (Compositae)

¶ *dicanthoides*	LSav

DATE See PHOENIX *dactylifera*

DATURA (Solanaceae)

arborea	See BRUGMANSIA ***a.***
chlorantha	See BRUGMANSIA ***c.***
cornigera	See BRUGMANSIA ***c.***
hybrids	See BRUGMANSIA
§ *inoxia*	CSun ERea SLHN SLMG WCar
meteloides	See DATURA ***inoxia***
rosea	See BRUGMANSIA x ***insignis***
sanguinea	See BRUGMANSIA ***s.***
¶ *signata*	LHil
stramonium	CArn GPoy LHol MSal SIde WHer

– 'Tatula'	EMon
suaveolens	See BRUGMANSIA *s.*
versicolor	See BRUGMANSIA *v.*

DAUCUS (Umbelliferae)

carota	CArn CKin MSal

DAVALLIA (Davalliaceae)

bullata	See D. ***mariesii***
fejeenis	MBri WFib
§ ***mariesii***	MBri SDix
pyxidata	NMar
solida	NMar
trichomanoides	NMar
– 'Lorrainei'	NMar

DAVIDIA (Davidiaceae)

involucrata	CBot CBow CBra CHan CSco EHar ENot IDai IJoh IOrc LSav MBlu MBri MMth NBar SExT SHil SPer SReu SSpi WNor WWat
– ***vilmoriniana***	CChu CGre EHar ELan LNet MGos SHil SPer SSta WCoo WSHC

DECAISNEA (Lardizabalaceae)

fargesii	Widely available

DECUMARIA (Hydrangeaceae)

barbara	CBot CChu CCla CMac CMal EOvi IBar NBar SBra SHil SPer SSta WSHC WWeb
sinensis	CGre CHEx SArc

DEGENIA (Cruciferae)

velebitica	GEdr NTow

DEINANTHE (Hydrangeaceae)

bifida	ECro NKay WCru
¶ ***caerulea***	WCru

DELONIX (Leguminosae)

regia	CPle

DELOSPERMA (Aizoaceae)

§ ***aberdeenense***	CB&S CHEx WEas WOMN
* ***album***	CHEx
¶ ***ashtonii***	WPer
'Basutoland'	See D. ***nubigenum***
cooperi	EPot LHop NGre NNrd SIng WHil
§ ***lehmanii***	CB&S
lineare	NBir
lydenburgense	IBlr
macellum	NGre
* ***nivale***	CHar CSun
§ ***nubigenum***	CHEx CHar CLew CMHG CSun NGre NHol NNrd NRed SIng WHil WOMN WPer WThu WWin
§ ***pallidum***	CB&S
sutherlandii	NGre NRed NTow
'Wilson'	WWin

DELPHINIUM (Ranunculaceae)

'Agnes Brookes'	ERou
'Alice Artindale'	CBos ECha ERou LGre LHop WEas
'Anne Page'	ERou
'Apollo'	ERou
'Astolat'	CB&S CHar CSco EFou ELan GAbr MBri MRav MWat MWgw NNor NRoo SPer WEas WPer
¶ Avon strain	MWoo
'Baby Doll'	CBla
Belladonna 'Andenken an August Koeneman'	See D. B. 'Wendy'
– 'Bellamosum'	EFou
– 'Blue Bees'	EBre MWgw
– 'Casa Blanca'	EFou SFis
– 'Cliveden Beauty'	EFou
– hybrids	ELan
– 'Lamartine'	EBre ERou MWgw
– 'Moerheimii'	ERou
– 'Orion'	ERou
– 'Peace'	EBre
– 'Piccolo'	ERou
– 'Pink Sensation'	See D. x ***ruysii*** 'P.S.'
– 'Volkerfrieden'	ERou
§ – 'Wendy'	MWgw
bellamania	WPer
x ***bellamosum***	MWgw SMrm
'Betty Baseley'	ERou
'Black Knight'	CB&S CHad CHar CSco EBre ECtt EFou ELan GAbr MBri MFir MRav MWat MWgw NNor NRoo NVic SPer WEas WPer
'Blauwal'	EFou
'Blue Bird'	CB&S CHar GAbr MBri MRav NNor NVic SPer WPer
'Blue Butterfly'	See D. ***grandiflorum*** 'B. B.'
'Blue Dawn'	CBla ERou SOgg
'Blue Fountains'	CHad CHar CSco EBre EFou ELan LAbb MBri MFir MPit MRav MWat NOak NRoo SPer SPla WEas WPer
'Blue Heaven'	EBre NOak
'Blue Jade'	CBla NNor SOgg
'Blue Jay'	EBre EFou ELan ENot MWgw
'Blue Mirror'	CHad CSun NOrc SMrm
'Blue Nile'	CBla ERou MWoo SOgg
'Blue Tit'	CBla ERou SOgg
'Blue Triumph'	ERou
¶ 'Browne's Lavender'	SOgg
'Bruce'	ERou MWoo SOgg
brunonianum	GEdr MFir NHol SBla WOMN
'Butterball'	CBla MWoo SOgg
californicum	WWin
'Cameliard'	EBre ECtt ELan SPer
'Can-Can'	ERou
cardinale	ECro ELan LAbb LGre SIgm WPer
'Carl Topping'	ERou MWoo SOgg
cashmerianum	EFol ELan LGan NTow SIng WOMN WPer

'Cassius'	CBla ERou SOgg
caucasicum	WOMN
'Chelsea Star'	CBla ERou MWoo SOgg
'Cherub'	CBla MWoo SOgg
chinense	See D. ***grandiflorum***
'Circe'	ERou
'Clack's Choice'	ERou
¶ 'Clifford Lass'	MWoo
'Clifford Pink'	CBla MWoo SOgg
¶ 'Clifford Sky'	MWoo SOgg
Connecticut Yankees	NNor NOak
'Conspicuous'	CBla MWoo SOgg
* 'Cowan's White'	SOgg
'Creamcracker'	ERou
'Cressida'	ERou SOgg
'Cristella'	ERou MWoo
'Crown Jewel'	CBla ERou SOgg
'Cupid'	CBla SOgg
'Daily Express'	ERou
'Dairymaid'	ERou
'Demavand'	ERou SOgg
'Dolly Bird'	CBla SOgg
'Dora Larkan'	SOgg
'Duchess of Portland'	ERou
* 'Eastgrove White'	WEas
¶ ***elatum***	WHer WOMN
'Emily Hawkins'	ERou MWoo SOgg
'Eva Gower'	ERou
'F W Smith'	EFou
'Fanfare'	CBla ERou SOgg
'Father Thames'	ERou SOgg
'Faust'	CBla ERou MWoo SOgg
'Fenella'	CBla ERou MWoo SOgg
'Fred Yule'	ERou
'Galahad'	CB&S CHad CHar CSco EBre EFou ELan ENot MBri MFir MRav MWat MWgw NNor NRoo NVic SPer WEas WPer
'Garden Party'	CBla
¶ 'Gemma'	MWoo
'Gillian Dallas'	CBla ERou MWoo SOgg
'Gordon Forsyth'	CBla ERou MWoo SOgg
§ ***grandiflorum***	CHad EPad LHil LRHS WHil
– 'Azure Fairy'	MBri
§ – 'Blue Butterfly'	CRiv GWic LGan MWgw SBla WWin
'Guinevere'	CB&S ECtt MBri NBir NNor NRoo WEas WPer
'Guy Langdon'	ERou
'Harmony'	ERou SOgg
'Hilda Lucas'	ERou
'Icecap'	ERou
¶ 'Ivory Towers'	ECtt
'James Nuttall'	ECha
'Joyce Roffey'	ERou
'Judy Knight'	ERou
'Kathleen Cooke'	ERou
'Kestrel'	ERou SOgg
'King Arthur'	CB&S CHar CSco ECtt ENot GAbr MBri MRav NNor WEas WPer
'Lady Hambleden'	See D. 'Patricia Lady Hambleden'
§ 'Langdon's Royal Flush'	CBla ERou MWoo SOgg
¶ 'Layla'	MWoo
'Leonora'	ERou SOgg
¶ 'Lilian Bassett'	MWoo SOgg
'Loch Leven'	CBla ERou MWoo SOgg
'Loch Nevis'	ERou
'Loch Torridon'	ERou
'Lord Butler'	CBla ERou SOgg
'Lorna'	ERou SOgg
'M Farrand'	ERou
Magic Fountains	EFou GAbr NRoo WHil
* 'Margaret Farrand'	SOgg
'Marie Broan'	ERou
'Michael Ayres'	CBla ERou MWoo
'Mighty Atom'	CBla ERou MWoo SOgg
'Molly Buchanan'	CBla SOgg
'Moonbeam'	CBla SOgg
'Morning Cloud'	ERou
'Mrs Newton Lees'	EFou ERou
'Mrs T Carlile'	ERou
muscosum	GEdr NHol
New Century hybrids	CB&S EBre NRoo
¶ 'Nicholas Woodfield'	MWoo SOgg
'Nimrod'	CBla ERou MWoo
'Nobility'	CBla
nudicaule	CBot ELan ESis GLoc LGan MFir NRoo NWCA SIgm WPer
'Olive Poppleton'	CBla ERou MWoo SOgg
'Oliver'	ERou MWoo SOgg
¶ 'Our Deb'	MWoo SOgg
oxypetalum	MBal
Pacific hybrids	CBow CKel EBre ENot MFir MRav NOak SPer
'Patricia Lady Hambleden'	ERou
'Pericles'	CBla SOgg
'Pink Ruffles'	CBla SOgg
'Polar Sun'	ERou
'Purity'	ERou
'Purple Ruffles'	ERou
¶ 'Purple Triumph'	SOgg
'Pyramus'	ERou SOgg
'Radiance'	ERou SOgg
requienii	CBos CBot CBre ERav LHil SAxl SMrm
¶ – variegated form	CBos
'Rosemary Brock'	ERou MWoo SOgg
'Rosina'	ERou
'Royal Flush'	See D. 'Langdon's Royal Flush'
'Royal Wedding'	ERou
'Ruby'	CBla
x ***ruysii*** 'Piccolo'	NBar
– 'Pink Sensation'	ERou MUlv NBar
'Sabrina'	CBla ERou
'Samantha'	ERou
'Sandpiper'	ERou SOgg
'Sarabande'	ERou
'Shimmer'	CBla ERou SOgg
'Silver Moon'	ERou SOgg
'Skyline'	CBla ERou SOgg
'Snow White'	EFou NOak
'Solomon'	ERou
'South Seas'	ERou
'Spindrift'	ERou

staphisagria MSal WEas
'Stardust' ERou
'Strawberry Fair' CBla ERou SOgg
'Summer Haze' ERou
'Summer Skies' CB&S CHad CSco ECtt MBri MRav MWat MWgw NNor NRoo SPer WEas WPer
'Summer Wine' ERou
'Sungleam' CBla ERou SOgg
'Swan Lake' ERou
'Taj Mahal' ERou
tatsienense CHar CRiv CSun ELan EMon GDra GLoc LHop MBal MFir MPar MTho NWCA SIng WAbe WHoo WOMN
– *album* NGre SBla
'Tessa' ERou
'Thelma Rowe' ERou
'Thundercloud' ERou SOgg
'Tiddles' CBla ERou SOgg
'Tiny Tim' ERou
'Turkish Delight' CBla ERou SOgg
'Turridu' ERou
'Vespers' CBla ERou SOgg
* 'Walton Beauty' MWoo
* 'Walton Gemstone' MWoo
'Watkin Samuel' ERou
'William Richards' ERou
'Xenia Field' ERou
zalil CBot SIgm WPer

DENDRANTHEMA † (Compositae)

'Adorn' MRil
'Agnes Ann' (29K) MCol
'Albert Broadhurst' (24b) MWol NHal
'Albert's Yellow' (Rub) EUse MCol
'Alexis' (5a) MRil
'Alfreton Cream' (5b) MRil
'Aline' (29K) EHMN
'Alison' (29c) EHMN
'Alison Kirk' (23b) MCol MWol NHal
'Allison '88' (Rub) EUse
'Allouise' (25b) MCol NHal
'Allswell' (24b) NHal
'Allure' MRil
'Amy Shoesmith' (15a) MCol
'Anastasia (28) EBre ECha EFou EOrc ERou GAbr GPla LHil LHop MCol NSti SAxl SChu SCro WEas WOld WPer WSHC WWin
'Anastasia Variegated' (28) CRow EFol EHal ELan EMon LGre SMrm WEas
¶ 'Angelic' (28) MCol
'Angora' (25b) MCol
'Ann Brook' (23b) MCol
'Anna Marie' (18c) EHMN MCol MWol
'Anne' (29K) EHMN
¶ 'Anne, Lady Brockett' EMon
'Apricot' (Rub) ECtt EFou EUse SMad
¶ 'Apricot Alexis' (5a) MRil
'Apricot Cassandra' (5b) NHal
'Apricot Chessington' (25a) MRil NHal
'Apricot Courtier' (24a) MRil NHal
¶ 'Apricot New Stylist' (24b) MRil
'Apricot Vedova' MCol
'Arthur Hawkins' (24a) MRil NHal
'Audrey Shoesmith' (3a) NHal
'Aunt Millicent' (29K) MCol
'Aurora' (4a) MCol
'Autumn Days' (25b) MCol
'Balcombe Perfection' (5a) MCol MRil MWol NHal
'Bambi' (24b) MWol
'Barbara Ward' (7b) MWol
'Beacon' (5a) MRil NHal
'Belair' (9c) MCol
'Belle' (29K) EHMN
'Bessie Rowe' (25a) MCol
'Betty Wiggins' (25b) MCol
'Bill Bye' (1) MWol NHal
'Bill Florentine' (3b) MRil
'Bill Wade' (25a) MRil NHal
¶ 'Birchwood' (24b) MRil
'Black Magic' (24b) MCol
'Bonnie Jean' (9d) MCol
'Bo-Peep' (28) EMon MCol
'Brenda Rowe' (5a) MCol
'Brideshead' (13b) MRil
'Bridget' (6b) MWol
'Brietner' (24b) ECha MCol
'Bright Eye' (28) LHop MCol SCro WPer
'Bright Golden Princess Anne' (4b) NHal
'Brightness' (29K) EHMN SChu WEas WOld WWin
'Broadacre' (7a) MCol
'Bronze Belair' (9c) MCol
'Bronze Bornholm' (14b) MCol
'Bronze Bridget' (6b) MWol
'Bronze Cassandra' (5b) NHal
'Bronze Elegance' (28) CSco EBre EFou ELan EMon SIng SPer WAbe WEas WRus
'Bronze Elite' (29d) EHMN
'Bronze Fairie' (28a) MCol MWol
'Bronze Fairweather' (3b) MRil MWol
'Bronze Margaret' (29c) EHMN MCol MRil NHal
'Bronze Maria' (28a) MCol
¶ 'Bronze Wessex Charms' (29d) NHal
'Bronze World of Sport' (25a) MRil
'Bronze Yvonne Arnaud (24b) MCol
'Brown Eyes' (29K) EHMN WOld
'Bruera' (24a) MWol NHal
¶ 'Buckland' (25c) NHal
¶ 'Buff Courtier' (24a) MRil
§ 'Buff Margaret' (24b) EHMN
'Buff Peter Rowe' (23b) MRil NHal
'Bunty' (28) ECha SMrm

'Cameo' (28a) MCol MWol
'Candid' (15b) MCol
'Candylite' (14b) MCol
'Canopy' (24a) MRil NHal
'Carlene Welby' (25b) MRil NHal
'Chamoirose' EFou
'Charles Fraser' (25a) NHal
'Charles Tandy' (15a) MRil
'Cheddar' (13a) MCol
'Chempak Crimson' (24b) MRil
'Cherry Margaret' (29c) MRil NHal
'Cherry Venice' (24b) MRil NHal
¶ 'Chery Dynasty' (14a) MRil
'Chessington' (25a) MRil NHal
'Christine Hall' (25a) MCol
'Christmas Carol' (5a) MWol
'Christmas Wine' (5a) MWol
I 'Citrus' (29K) EFou
'Claire Louise' (24b) MRil
'Clara Curtis' (Rub) CCla CGle CKel CSco ECha EFou EGol ELan EMon ERou EUse GAbr LHop MBri MCol MFir NBir SChu SMad SPer WEas WOld WPer WRus
'Claudia' (24c) EHMN MCol
'Cloth of Gold' (24b) MWol
'Cloudbank' (9a) MWol
'Columbine' (29K) EHMN
'Connie Mayhew' (5a) NHal
'Contour' (24a) MWol
'Cooper Nob' (29K) EHMN
'Copeland' (14b) NHal
'Copper Hedgerow' (7b) MWol
'Copper Margaret' (29c) EHMN MWol NHal
'Coral Ryndoon' (9d) MWol
'Corngold' (5b) MWol NHal
'Cornish' (25b) MRil
'Cossack' (2) MWol
'Cottage Apricot' ERou LHop SMrm
♦ 'Cottage Pink' See D. 'Emperor of China'
'Cottingham' (25a) NHal
'Courtier' (24a) MRil NHal
¶ 'Cream Allouise' (25b) NHal
¶ 'Cream Elegance' (9c) NHal
¶ 'Cream John Hughes' (3b) MRil NHal
¶ 'Cream Margaret' (29c) NHal
'Cream Pennine Pink' (29c) NHal
¶ 'Cream West Bromwich' (14a) MRil
'Creamist' (25b) MCol
'Cricket' (25b) MCol
'Crimson Yvonne Arnaud' (24b) MCol
'Daphne' EHMN
'Darlington Jubilee' (25a) MRil
'David Higgins' (3b) MWol
'David Shoesmith' (25a) MCol MWol
'Debbie' (29K) EHMN
'Debonair ' (15a) MRil
'Dee Lemon' (24c) MCol
'Dee Pink' (29c) MCol
'Dee Prince' (29c) NHal
'Denise' (28/7b) MCol MWol
'Denise Oatridge' (5a) MRil
'Dennis Fletcher' (25a) MRil
'Derek Bircumshaw' (28a) MCol
'Deva Glow' (25a) NHal
'Diamond Wedding' (25a) MWol
'Doctor Tom Parr' (28) CElw ELan EMon LGre SAxl SMrm
'Dolly' (9c) NHal
¶ 'Donna' (3b) MRil
'Doreen Hall' (15a) MRil
'Doris' (29K) EHMN
'Dorridge Beauty' (24a) MRil MWol NHal
'Dorridge Candy' (4b) MWol
'Dorridge Choice' (5b) MWol
'Dorridge Crystal' (24a) MRil MWol NHal
'Dorridge Dream' (23b) MWol
'Dorridge King' (4b) MWol
'Dorridge Lady' (24b) MWol
'Dorridge Snowball' (3b) MWol
'Dorridge Sun' (3b) MWol
'Dorridge Velvet' (4b) MWol
'Duchess of Edinburgh' (Rub) CGle CSco EBre ELan EMon ERou EUse LHop MBri MCol MFir SChu SCro SHig SMad WEas WOld
'Duke of Kent' (1) MWol
¶ 'East Riding' (25a) NHal
'Eastleigh' (24b) MRil NHal
¶ 'Eddie Wilson' (25b) MRil
'Edelweiss' (29K) LHop
'Elegance' (9c) MCol NHal
'Elizabeth Burton' (5a) MWol
'Elizabeth Shoesmith' (1) NHal
'Ellen' (24c) NHal
'Emma Lou' (23a) MCol NHal
§ 'Emperor of China' (Rub) CElw CGle ECha EFou EMon ERou GAbr GWic LGre MCol SChu SWas WEas WRus
¶ 'Enbee Frill' (29d) MCol
'Enbee Sunray' (29d) NHal
'Enbee Wedding' (29b) MRil NHal
'Epic' (6b) MWol
'Ermine' (23a) MCol MWol NHal
'Eugene' (25b) EHMN
'Evelyn' (25a) EHMN
'Evelyn Bush' (25a) MCol MWol
'Eye Level' (5a) MRil NHal
'Fair Lady' (5a) MRil
'Fairie' (28) MCol MWol
'Fairweather' (3b) MCol MRil MWol
'Fairy Rose' (4b) MCol
§ 'Fleet Margaret' (29c) MRil MWol
'Flying Saucer' (6a) MCol
'Formcast' (24a) NHal
'Fortune' (24b) MRil

'Frank Taylor' (15a)	MWol
'Fred Brocklehurst' (25a)	MRil
'Fred Shoesmith' (5a)	MRil MWol NHal
'Frolic' (25b)	MRil
'Galaxy' (9d)	MCol
'Gambit' (24a)	MRil MWol NHal
'Gay Anne' (4b)	NHal
'Gazelle' (23a)	MCol NHal
'George Griffiths' (24b)	MRil NHal
'Gerry Milner' (23b)	MWol
'Gertrude' (19c)	MCol
'Gigantic' (1)	MWol NHal
'Gillette' (23b)	MRil
'Ginger Nut' (25b)	MCol MRil MWol NHal
'Gladys' (24b)	ELan
'Gladys Homer' (24a)	MWol
'Gladys Sharpe' (25a)	MCol MRil
'Gloria' (25a)	EHMN
'Gold Coin' (7b)	MWol
'Gold Foil' (5a)	MRil NHal
'Gold Margaret'	See D. 'Golden Margaret'
'Golden Anemone'	EHMN
'Golden Angora' (25b)	MCol
¶ 'Golden Cassandry' (5b)	NHal
'Golden Creamist' (25b)	MCol
'Golden Fred Shoesmith' (5a)	NHal
'Golden Honeyball' (15b)	MCol
'Golden Ivy Garland' (5b)	MCol NHal
'Golden Lady' (3b)	MWol
§ 'Golden Margaret' (29c)	EHMN MCol MRil NHal
'Golden Mayford Perfection' (5a)	MRil
'Golden Orfe' (29c)	MCol
'Golden Pamela' (29c)	EHMN NHal
'Golden Pennine Pink' (29c)	NHal
'Golden Pixton' (25b)	MCol
'Golden Queen' (3b)	MWol
'Golden Saskia'	MCol
'Golden Seal' (7b)	MCol
¶ 'Golden Taffeta' (9c)	NHal
'Golden Treasure' (28a)	MCol
'Grace Riley' (24a)	MCol MRil MWol
'Grandchild' (29c)	EHMN MCol
'Green Chartreuse' (5b)	MWol
'Green Nightingale' (10)	MWol
'Green Satin' (5b)	MWol
'Grenadine'	MRil
'Halloween' (4b)	NHal
'Harry Gee' (1)	MWol
'Harvest Dawn' (25)	MCol
'Harvey' (29K)	MCol
'Havelsonne'	EFou
'Hazel' (30,K)	EHMN
'Hazel Macintosh' (5a)	MRil MWol
'Hazy Days' (25b)	MCol NHal
'Heather James' (3b)	MCol NHal
'Hedgerow' (7b)	MCol
'Heide' (29c)	EHMN MCol NHal
'Helen' (29K)	EHMN
'Helmsman' (24a)	MRil
'Honey' (25b)	EHMN
'Illusion'	MRil
'Imp' (28)	MCol
'Innocence' (Rub)	CFis CGle EFou EHal ELan EMon EUse SMad WEas WOld
'International' (3a)	MRil
'Irene' (29K)	CElw EHMN SMad
'Iris Coupland' (5a)	MWol NHal
'Isabel' (15b)	EHMN
'Isabellrosa' (29K)	ECha
'Ivy Garland' (5b)	MCol
'Jack Wood' (25a)	MRil
¶ 'James Kelway'	NBir
'Jan Okum' (24b)	MRil
'Jante Wells' (28)	EMon ERou MCol WEas WOld
¶ 'Jessica' (29c)	MRil
'Jessie Cooper' (Rub)	EOrc EUse SChu SMad
'Jessie Raynor'	WOld
'Jill Collins' (24b)	MWol
'Joan' (25b)	EHMN
'John Hughes' (3b)	MCol MRil MWol NHal
¶ 'John Murray'	NBir
'John Riley' (14a)	MRil
'John Statham' (23b)	MWol
'John Wingfield' (14b)	MRil NHal
'Joy Hughes' (4b)	NHal
'Joyce Stevenson' (24b)	NHal
'Jubilee' (9c)	NHal
'Jules la Grayeur'	EMon LRHS SMrm
¶ 'Julia'	EFou
'Juliet' (24b)	EHMN
¶ 'June Wakley' (25b)	MCol
'Kampfhahn'	EFou
'Karen Riley' (25a)	MRil
'Keystone' (25b)	MCol MRil NHal
'Kimberley Marie' (15a)	MRil NHal
'Kleiner Bernstein'	EFou
'Lady Clara' (Rub)	EUse WOld
'Lady in Pink' (Rub)	EMon EUse
'Lakelanders' (3b)	MRil MWol NHal
'Leading Lady' (25b)	MWol
'Legend'	CElw
'Lemon Blanket'	EHMN
'Lemon Margaret' (29c)	EHMN MRil MWol NHal
'Lemon Tench' (29K)	EHMN
'Len Futerill' (25b)	MCol MWol
'Liberty' (15a)	MRil
'Lilian Hoek' (29c)	EHMN MWol NHal
'Lilian Jackson' (7b)	MCol
'Lilian Shoesmith' (5b)	MRil
'Little Dorrit' (29K)	EHMN MCol
'Liverpool Festival' (23b)	MCol NHal
'Long Island Beauty' (6a)	MCol
'Long Life' (25b)	MCol
'Lorraine' (24b)	MRil NHal
'Louise' (25b)	EHMN
'Lucida' (29c)	EHMN MWol
'Lucy Simpson' (29K)	MCol
'Lundy' (2)	NHal

'Lyndale' (25b)	MCol NHal
'Lynmal's Choice' (13b)	NHal
'L'Innocence' (29K)	ECha SMrm
'Mac's Delight' (25b)	MCol MRil
'Madeleine' (29c)	MWol
'Malcolm Perkins' (25a)	MRil NHal
'Mandarin'	EBre
'Margaret' (29c)	EHMN ELan MCol MRil MWol NHal
'Margaret Riley' (25a)	MRil NHal
'Maria' (28a)	MCol
'Marion' (25a)	EHMN MCol
'Mark Slater' (2)	MWol
'Marlene Jones' (25b)	MWol
'Martin Riley' (23b)	MCol MRil
'Martin Walker' (25b)	MCol
'Mary' (29K)	EHMN MCol
'Mary Stevenson' (25b)	MCol
'Mary Stoker' (Rub)	CGle CHad CSco ECha EFou EGol ELan EMon ERou EUse MBri MCol MFir SChu SCro SHig SMad SPer SWas WEas WHil WOld WRus
'Mason's Bronze' (7b)	MCol
'Matlock' (24b)	MRil NHal
'Mauve Gem' (29K)	EHMN
'Mavis' (28a)	MCol
'Max Riley' (23b)	MRil NHal
'May Shoesmith' (4b)	MCol NHal
'Megan Woolman' (3b)	MWol
'Mei-kyo' (28)	CGle CHar CSco EBre ELan EMon EOrc ERou LHop MWgw NHol NJap SAxl SIng SPer WAbe WEas WRus
'Membury' (24b)	MCol NHal
'Michelle Walker' (24b)	MCol
'Midnight' (24b)	MRil
¶ 'Milltown' (24b)	MRil
'Minaret' (3b)	MWol
'Minstrel Boy' (3b)	MRil NHal
'Mirage' (5a)	MRil
'Moira' (29K)	EHMN
'Molly Lambert' (36)	MWol
'Moonlight' (29K)	EHMN
'Mottram Barleycorn' (29d)	MCol
¶ 'Mottram Lady'	MCol
'Mottram Melody'	MCol
'Mottram Minstrel'	MCol
'Mottram Sentinel'	MCol
'Mrs Jessie Cooper' (Rub)	EFou ELan EMon LRHS
'Muriel Vipas' (25b)	MRil
'Nancy Perry' (Rub)	ELan EMon EOrc EUse LRHS MCol SChu WOld
§ ***nankingense***	EFou EMon
¶ 'Naomi'	MRil
'Nathalie' (19c)	MWol
'Nell Gwyn' (Rub)	EUse MCol
'New Stylist' (24b)	MRil
¶ 'Nicole'	MRil
'Nu Dazzler' (9d)	MCol
¶ 'Nu-Rosemary' (9d)	NHal
'Orange Allouise' (25b)	NHal
'Orange Fair Lady' (5a)	MRil NHal
'Orange Margaret' (29c)	See D. 'Fleet Margaret'
'Orange Pennine Pink' (29)	NHal
'Orangeade' (24b)	MCol
¶ 'Orno' (29b)	MCol
'Oyster Fairweather' (3b)	MWol
'Pacific' (15a)	MRil
§ ***pacificum***	CChu COtt EFou ELan EPla NBir SSus WCot
*– 'Hakai'	CHil SChu
'Packwell' (24b)	MCol
'Pamela' (29c)	EHMN NHal
'Panache' (5a)	MRil NHal
¶ 'Patricia Miller' (4b)	MRil NHal
'Paul Boissier' (Rub)	ELan EMon EOrc ERou EUse MCol SChu SMad SWas WEas WOld
'Pavilion' (25a)	MCol
'Payton Dale' (29c)	MRil NHal
¶ 'Payton Lady' (29c)	NHal
¶ 'Payton Prince' (29c)	NHal
'Payton Rose' (29c)	NHal
'Peach Allouise' (25b)	NHal
'Peach Margaret'	See D. 'Salmon Margaret'
'Pearl Celebration' (24a)	MRil NHal
'Peggy' (28a)	EHMN
'Pennine Ace' (29f)	MRil
'Pennine Amber' (29c)	MRil NHal
'Pennine Angel' (29a)	MRil
'Pennine Brenda' (29d)	MRil NHal
'Pennine Bride' (29c)	MRil
'Pennine Calypso' (29b)	MRil
'Pennine Cameo' (29a)	MRil
'Pennine Canary' (29c)	MRil
'Pennine Clarion' (29c)	MRil
'Pennine Copper' (29c)	MRil
'Pennine Crimson' (29c)	NHal
'Pennine Crystal' (29c)	MCol MRil
'Pennine Cupid' (29c)	MRil MWol
'Pennine Dell' (29d)	MCol
'Pennine Dove' (29d)	NHal
'Pennine Eagle' (29c)	MCol MRil
'Pennine Ember' (29d)	MRil
'Pennine Flute' (29f)	MRil
'Pennine Gambol' (29a)	MRil MWol
'Pennine Hannah' (29d)	MRil NHal
'Pennine Harmony' (29f)	MRil
'Pennine Ivory' (29d)	MRil
'Pennine Jade' (29d)	MRil MWol NHal
'Pennine Jude' (29a)	MRil
'Pennine Lemon' (29c)	MWol
'Pennine Light' (29d)	MRil
'Pennine Lotus' (29c)	MRil
'Pennine Magic' (29c)	MRil NHal
'Pennine Mary' (29d)	MRil
'Pennine Mavis' (29f)	MRil
'Pennine Mist' (29c)	NHal
'Pennine Orchid' (29d)	MRil
'Pennine Oriel' (29a)	MCol MRil MWol NHal
'Pennine Pet' (29f)	MRil
'Pennine Phyllis' (29b)	MRil

'Pennine Pink' (29c)	MCol NHal
'Pennine Poppet' (29a)	MRil
'Pennine Punch' (29a)	MCol
'Pennine Purple' (29c)	MCol NHal
'Pennine Rascal' (29c)	MRil
'Pennine Serene' (29d)	MRil
'Pennine Sergeant' (29c)	MWol
'Pennine Signal' (29d)	MCol MRil
'Pennine Silk' (29c)	MRil
'Pennine Silver' (29c)	MRil
'Pennine Ski' (29c)	MCol MRil
'Pennine Smoke' (29d)	MRil
'Pennine Soldier' (29d)	MRil MWol NHal
'Pennine Spice' (29c)	MRil
'Pennine Tango' (29d)	MCol MRil NHal
'Pennine Trill' (29c)	MWol
'Pennine Trinket' (29c)	MRil
'Pennine Twinkle' (29a)	MCol MRil
'Pennine Vista' (29c)	MRil
'Pennine Whistle' (29f)	MRil
'Pennine White' (29c)	MWol
'Pennine Wine' (29c)	MRil
'Percy Salter' (24b)	MCol
'Peter Rowe' (23b)	MCol NHal
'Peter White' (23a)	MCol
'Peterkin'	EBre EMon ERou SMrm WOld WRus
'Phil Houghton' (1)	MWol
¶ 'Pink Champagne' (4b)	NHal
'Pink Chessington' (25a)	NHal
'Pink Duke' (1)	MWol NHal
'Pink Gin' (9c)	MWol NHal
'Pink Margaret' (29c)	EHMN NHal
'Pink Overture'	MCol
'Pink Progression'	EBre ECtt EFou NBir
'Pink World of Sport' (25a)	MRil
'Pixton' (25b)	MCol
¶ 'Playmate' (29,k)	MCol
'Polar Gem' (3a)	MWol NHal
'Polar Queen' (3b)	MWol
'Polaris' (9c)	MCol
'Primrose Alison Kirk' (23b)	NHal
'Primrose Anemone' (29K)	EHMN
'Primrose Angora' (25b)	MCol
'Primrose Bill Wade' (25a)	MRil
'Primrose Chessington (25a)	MRil NHal
'Primrose Cricket' (25b)	MCol
'Primrose Doreen Bircumshaw' (24a)	MRil
'Primrose Ermine' (23a)	NHal
'Primrose Fairweather' (3b)	MWol
'Primrose Heide' (29c)	NHal
'Primrose John Hughes' (3b)	MRil NHal
'Primrose Margaret' (29c)	See D. 'Buff Margaret'
'Primrose Mayford Perfection' (3a)	MCol MRil
'Primrose Muriel Vipas' (5a)	MRil
'Primrose Pennine Oriel' (29a)	MRil
'Primrose Polaris' (9c)	MCol
'Primrose Sam Vinter' (5a)	MRil
'Primrose Tennis' (25b)	MRil NHal
'Primrose West Bromwich (4a)	MRil NHal
'Primrose World of Sport' (25a)	MRil
'Princess' (29K)	EHMN
'Princess Anne' (4b)	MCol NHal
'Promise' (25a)	MCol
'Pure Silk' (14b)	MRil
¶ 'Purleigh White'	SIng
'Purple Fairie' (28b)	MCol
'Purple Glow' (5a)	NHal
'Purple Margaret' (29c)	EHMN NHal
'Purple Pennine Wine' (29c)	MRil
'Queenswood' (5b)	MCol
'Quill Elegance' (9f)	MWol
'Rachel Fairweather' (3a)	NHal
'Ralph Lambert' (1)	MWol
'Raquel' (29K)	MCol
'Rayonnante' (11)	MCol
'Red Admiral' (6b)	MWol
'Red Balcombe Perfection' (5a)	MCol MWol NHal
'Red Cassandra' (5b)	NHal
'Red Claudia' (29c)	EHMN
'Red Eye Level' (5a)	MRil
'Red Formcast' (24a)	NHal
'Red Gambit' (24a)	MRil MWol NHal
'Red Keystone' (25a)	MRil
'Red Lilian Hoek' (29c)	EHMN
'Red Mayford Perfection'	MCol
'Red Pamela' (29c)	NHal
'Red Payton Dale' (29c)	MRil NHal
'Red Pennine Jade' (29d)	MRil NHal
'Red Resilient' (4b)	NHal
'Red Rosita' (29c)	MCol
'Red Shirley Model' (3a)	MWol NHal
'Red Wendy' (29c)	MCol NHal
'Redall' (4c)	MCol
'Reg Pearce' (15a)	MRil
'Regal Mist' (25b)	MCol
'Remarkable' (30)	MRil
¶ 'Resilient' (4b)	NHal
'Rheingold' (29c)	EHMN
'Riley's Dynasty' (14a)	MRil MWol NHal
'Robeam' (9c)	MWol NHal
'Robert Earnshaw' (3b)	MWol
'Roblaze' (9c)	NHal
'Roblush' (9c)	MWol
'Rockwell' (14b)	NHal
¶ 'Rolass' (9c)	NHal

'Ron James' (4a) NHal
'Rose Mayford Perfection' (5a) MCol
'Rosette' (29c) EHMN
'Rosita' (28b) MCol
'Roy Coopland' (5b) MRil MWol NHal
'Royal Command' (Rub) EUse WOld
§ ***rubellum*** EUse WRus
'Ruby Mound' (29K) EFou EHMN ERou LHop MCol
'Ruby Raynor' (Rub) EUse MCol
'Rybronze' (9d) NHal
'Ryfinch' (9d) MCol
'Ryflash' (9d) MCol MWol
'Rylands Gem' (24b) MCol NHal
'Rylands Victor' (23c) MCol
'Rynoon' (9d) MWol
'Rystar' (9d) NHal
'Rytorch' (9d) MCol
'Salmon Cassandra' (5b) NHal
'Salmon Fairie' (28) MCol MWol
'Salmon Fairweather' (3b) MWol
§ 'Salmon Margaret' (29c) MCol MRil
'Salmon Margaret Riley' (25a) MRil
'Salmon Pennine Gambol' (29a) MRil
'Salmon Pennine Pink' (29c) NHal
'Salmon Pennine Wine' (29c) MRil
'Salmon Rylands Gem' (24b) MCol NHal
¶ 'Salmon Shirley McMinn' (15a) MRil
'Salmon Susan Rowe' (24b) MCol
'Salmon Tracy Waller' (24a) MRil NHal
'Salmon Venice' (24b) MRil
'Sam Oldham' (24a) MRil MWol
'Sam Vinter' (5a) MRil NHal
¶ 'Sandy' MRil
¶ 'Sarah' MRil
¶ 'Sarah's Yellow' CSam
'Saskia' MCol
'Satin Pink Gin' (9c) NHal
¶ 'Sea Urchin' (29c) MCol
¶ 'Seashell' (28b) MCol
'Sefton' (4a) MRil NHal
'Sentry' (24b) MRil
'Sheffield Centenary' (3b) MWol
'Sheila' (29K) EHMN
'Sheila Morgan' (5b) MWol
'Shining Light' (29K) EHMN MCol
'Shirley Glorious' (24a) MWol
'Shirley McMinn' (15a) MRil
'Shirley Model' (3a) MWol
'Shirley Primrose' (1) MWol
'Shirley Sunburst' (3a) MWol
'Shirley Victoria' (25a) MWol
'Shoesmith's Salmon' (4a) MWol
¶ 'Sid Griffiths' (29c) MCol
'Silver Jubilee' (24a) MWol
¶ 'Simon Mills' (2) NHal
'Skater's Waltz' (5a) MWol
'Snooker' (23b) MRil
'Snowflake' (24a) CTre
'Snowshine' (5a) MWol
'Solarama' (9e) NHal
'Solitaire' (24a) MRil MWol
¶ 'Sonnenschein' LHop
'Spartan Flame' (29c) MWol
'Spartan Legend' (29c) MWol
'Spencer's Cottage' (13b) MCol
'Springtime' (24a) MCol
'Stan Addison' (5b) MWol
'Star Centenary' (3b) MRil NHal
'Starlet' (29K) EHMN MCol
¶ 'Stoke Festival' (25b) MCol
'Stuart Shoesmith' (4b) NHal
'Sun Spider' (29K) EHMN
'Sun Valley' (5a) MCol
'Sunbeam' (25a) EFou
'Suncharm Bronze' (22a) MWol
'Suncharm Pink' (22a) MWol
'Suncharm Red' (22a) MWol
'Suncharm White' (22a) MWol
'Suncharm Yellow' (22a) MWol
'Sundoro' MRil
'Sunflight' (25b) MCol
¶ 'Sunny Margaret' (29c) NHal
'Susan Riley' (23a) NHal
'Susan Rowe' (24b) MCol
¶ 'Sussex County' (15a) MRil
'Swansdown' (25b) MWol
'Taffeta' (9c) MCol NHal
'Talbot Bolero' (29c) MRil NHal
¶ 'Talbot Jo' (29d) MRil
'Talbot Parade' (29c) NHal
'Tanaga' MRil
'Target' (24b) MRil
'Tennis' (25b) MRil NHal
'The Favourite' MCol
'Tickled Pink' (29K) EHMN
'Toledo' (25a) MWol
'Tolima' MRil
'Tom Parr' See D. 'Doctor Tom Parr'
'Tommy Trout' (28) MCol
'Tone Dragon' (29a) NHal
'Tone Girl' (29a) NHal
'Tone Tints' (29a) NHal
'Tracy Waller' (24b) MRil NHal
'Trudie Bye' (3b) MWol
¶ 'Truro' (24a) MRil
'Twinkle' (28) EFou
¶ 'Universiade' (15a) MRil
'Vanessa Lynn' (24b) MRil
'Vanity Pink' MCol
'Vanity Primrose' MCol
'Vedova' (6a) MCol
'Venice' (24b) MRil NHal

'Violet Lawson' (15a) MWol
'Virginia' (29K) EHMN
'Vision On' (24b) MRil
'Vitax Victor' (25a) MRil
¶ 'Wedding Day' EFou WRus
'Wedding Sunshine' EHMN
'Wendy' (29c) EHMN MCol NHal
'Wendy Tench' (29d) MCol
¶ 'Wessex Charms' (29d) NHal
¶ 'Wessex Cream' (29d) NHal
'Wessex Gold' (29d) NHal
'Wessex Ivory' (29d) NHal
'Wessex Melody' (29d) NHal
'Wessex Pearl' (29d) NHal
¶ 'Wessex Prince' (29d) NHal
'Wessex Royal' (29d) NHal
¶ 'Wessex Tang' (29d) NHal
'Wessex Tune' (29d) NHal
'West Bromwich' (14a) MRil MWol NHal
§ ***weyrichii*** CHad CLew EFol ELan GCHN GEdr GLoc ITim LHop MCas MHig MTho NHol NKay NNrd NRya SBla SIng WAbe WHil WOMN WPer WRus WThu
'White Allouise' (25b) NHal
'White Bouquet' (28) MCol
'White Cassandra' (5b) NHal
'White Fairweather' (3b) MRil MWol
'White Gem' (25b) EHMN
¶ 'White Gerrie Hoek' (29c) NHal
'White Gloss' (29K) EHMN
'White Margaret' (29c) EHMN MCol MRil MWol NHal
'White Margaret Riley' (25a) MRil NHal
'White Nu Rosemary' (9d) NHal
'White Pamela' (29c) EHMN
¶ 'White Pearl Celebration' (24a) MRil
'White Spider' (10) MCol
'White Taffeta' (9c) NHal
'Win' (9c) NHal
'Winnie Bramley' (23a) MCol MRil MWol NHal
'Winning's Red' (Rub) EUse WOld
'Woolman's Celebration' (23b) MWol
'Woolman's Giant'' (14a) MWol
'Woolman's Perfecta' (3a) NHal
'Woolman's Queen' (24a) MWol
'Woolman's Star' (3a) MWol
'World of Sport' (25a) MRil
'Xenia Noelle' (4b) MWol
'Yellow Alfreton Cream' (5b) MRil
'Yellow Allouise' (25b) NHal
'Yellow Balcombe Perfection' (5a) MWol
'Yellow Cassandra' (15b) NHal
'Yellow Cornish' (25b) MRil
'Yellow Dorridge Crown' (25b) MWol
'Yellow Flying Saucer' (6a) MCol
'Yellow Fred Shoesmith' (5a) MWol
'Yellow Galaxy' (9d) MCol
'Yellow Ginger Nut' (25b) MCol MRil NHal
'Yellow Hazy Days' (25b) NHal
'Yellow Heather James' (3b) MCol
'Yellow Heide' (29c) EHMN MCol NHal
'Yellow Jack Wood' (25a) MRil
'Yellow John Hughes' (3b) MCol MRil MWol NHal
'Yellow John Wingfield' (14b) MRil NHal
'Yellow Lilian Hoek' (29c) EHMN MCol NHal
'Yellow Margaret' (29c) MCol MRil MWol NHal
¶ 'Yellow May Shoesmith' (5a) NHal
'Yellow Mayford Perfection' (5a) MCol MRil
'Yellow Pennine Oriel' (29a) MRil NHal
'Yellow Pennine Pink' (29c) NHal
'Yellow Polaris' (9c) MCol
¶ 'Yellow Resilient' (5b) NHal
'Yellow Shirley Imp' (3b) MWol
'Yellow Spider' (10) MCol
'Yellow Starlet' (29K) EHMN MCol
'Yellow Taffeta' (9c) MCol
'Yellow Tennis' (25b) MRil NHal
¶ 'Yellow Vitax Victor' (25a) MRil
'Yellowmoor' (25b) MCol
§ ***yezoense*** EFou ELan LGan LHop NKay SCro WEas
'Yvonne Arnaud' (24b) MCol MWol
¶ ***zawadaskii latilobum*** EMon

DENDRIOPOTERIUM (Rosaceae)
¶ ***benthamiana*** CHEx

DENDROBENTHAMIA See **CORNUS**

DENDROCALAMUS (Gramineae(Bambuseae))
giganteus SBam
strictus SBam

DENDROMECON (Papaveraceae)
rigida CBot ERea NRar SHil SSpi

DENDROSERIS (Compositae)
¶ ***littoralis*** CHEx

DENTARIA (Cruciferae)
californica EPar

digitata	See CARDAMINE ***pentaphyllos***
diphylla	LAma MSal
pinnata	See CARDAMINE ***heptaphylla***
polyphylla	See CARDAMINE ***kitaibelii***

DERMATOBOTRYS (Scrophulariaceae)

saunderi	CSun

DESCHAMPSIA (Gramineae)

cespitosa	CKin CTom CWGN EFou ERou SApp SMrm
– *alpina*	NHol
– 'Bronzeschleier' ('Bronze Veil')	CChu CHan COtt EBre EPla GAbr GWic IBlr SApp SMad SMrm WCot WRus
♦– 'Fairy's Joke'	See D. ***c. vivipara***
– 'Goldgehänge'	CChu CHoe GWic IBlr
– 'Goldschleier'	CWGN ECha EFou EMon EPla IBlr SMad
– 'Goldstaub'	EFou GWic NCat SSpi
¶– 'Goldtau'	EMon
– 'Tatra Gold'	ECha EFol LHop NNor SApp SFir
§ – *vivipara*	CHoe CNat GWic
flexuosa	CHoe EFou SApp

DESFONTAINIA (Loganiaceae)

§ *spinosa*	Widely available
– 'Harold Comber'	SDry SHil WBod
– *hookeri*	See D. ***spinosa***

DESMODIUM (Leguminosae)

§ *elegans*	CB&S CBow CChu CGre CHan IBrk WSHC
praestans	WSHC
♦ *tiliifolium*	See D. ***elegans***

DEUTZIA † (Hydrangeaceae)

chunii	CGre CLan SHil SPer SSpi WWat
– 'Pink Charm'	SHil
compacta	CHan SHil WBod WWat
– 'Lavender Time'	CBow CCla CMHG MPla SHil WSHC
corymbosa	CCla
– LS&T 4265	LSav
– LS&T 6668	LSav
crenata 'Nikko'	CB&S CBow CCla EBre EFol ESis GLoc LHop MBar MGos MPla SGar SPla SSta SWas WSHC
discolor 'Major'	CLan
x *elegantissima*	CLan CMHG CSco CShe IDai MRav NKay NNor SHil SPla SReu
– 'Fasciculata'	SPer WWin
– 'Rosealind'	CB&S CFor ELan ENot IOrc MPla MR&S SGar SHil SLon SPer SSta WBod WKif WSHC WWeb
forrestii	LSav
gracilis	CBow CCla CSco GRei MBar MPla MWat NNor SPer SPla WAbe WBod WHCG
– 'Carminea'	See D. x ***rosea*** 'Carminea'
¶– 'Marmorata'	WHCG
*– 'Variegata'	ECro
hookeriana	CCla SPla WWat
x *hybrida* 'Contraste'	CB&S CLan MBri MR&S SPer
– 'Joconde'	CLan LSav WKif
– 'Magicien'	CChu CFor CLan CMHG CSam CShe ECtt ENot MBri SHil SLon SPer SSpi SSta WHCG
– 'Mont Rose'	CB&S CLan CShe ENot GRei IJoh MBal MBar MBri MGos MPla MRav SHil SPer SPla SSta WAbe WSHC
– 'Perle Rose'	CLan CSco
– 'Pink Pompon'	CB&S MBri SHil SSta WWeb
– 'Reuthe's Pink'	SReu
x *kalmiiflora*	CB&S CLan CMHG CSco EHar LAbb MBar MBri MGos MR&S MRav NJap NKay NNor NTow SCro SHil SPer SWas WAbe WWeb
longifolia	CLan WSHC
– 'Veitchii'	CHan MRav SHil
x *magnifica*	CCla CSco ELan IJoh IOrc MR&S MRav SCro SHil WWeb WWin
*– 'Rubra'	CFor SBar
x *maliflora*	LSav
monbeigii	CChu ENot SBor SHil SPer WKif WWat
ningpoensis	CBow CCla LSav
pulchra	CBow CChu CFor CHan CLan CPle CShe LSav SHil SPer SSpi WHCG WWat
'Rosea Plena'	CMHG
x *rosea*	CBow CBra CTrw ENot GRei IJoh MBar MPla MR&S MWat NNor NTow SPla WKif WWin
– 'Campanulata'	ENot
§ – 'Carminea'	CB&S CBow CShe ELan LAbb LSav NHol SDix SHil SLon SPer SSpi SSta
– 'Floribunda'	CBra ELan
– 'Rosea'	CCla
scabra	CLan MGos
§ – 'Candidissima'	CBow CCla ELan IDai LSav MBri SPer SPla SReu WBod
– 'Codsall Pink'	ECtt MBri
– 'Flore Pleno'	CB&S CPle ECtt ELan NNor SGar SHil SPer
– 'Pride of Rochester'	CSco ENot GRei MBar MRav SPla WWeb
– 'Punctata'	CBow CHoe EFol NHol WThu
*– 'Variegata'	ELan
– 'Watereri'	ERav
setchuenensis	SLon SSpi WSHC
– *corymbiflora*	CBot CBow CChu CCla CFor CLan LSav SDry SHil WKif WWat
staminea	CLan
'Strawberry Fields'	SHil

x *wellsii*	See D. *scabra* 'Candidissima'
x *wilsonii*	LSav

DIANELLA † (Liliaceae/Phormiaceae)

caerulea	CFor EBul ECou GWic MCab SBar SWas
*– 'Variegata'	ECou
nigra	EBul ECou GWic SSpi WCot
revoluta	ECou SBar
tasmanica	CGle CHan CHar CRow ECou GWic IBlr MBri MUlv NOrc SArc SAxl SBor SLHN SSpi
¶– 'Variegata'	SSpi

DIANTHUS † (Caryophyllaceae)

ACW 2116	EMFP EMNN ITim MPlt
¶ 'Ada Wood' (pf)	NPin
'Admiral Crompton' (pf)	MWoo NPin SBai
'Admiration' (b)	SHay
'Afton Water' (b)	MBri SBai SHay
'Alan Titchmarsh' (p)	MBri SBai
'Albatross' (p)	SChu
'Alder House' (p)	MBro MRav NHol NRoo
'Aldersey Rose' (p)	WMar WWin
'Aldridge Yellow' (b)	MBri SBai
'Alice' (p)	CThr SAll SHay
'Alice Forbes' (b)	SAll SHay
'Allen's Ballerina' (p)	CThr LCra NPin
§ 'Allen's Huntsman' (p)	CHil CThr EBre LCra
§ 'Allen's Maria' (p)	CHil CSut CThr LCra NPin
'Alloway Star' (p)	EMFP WPer
'Allspice' (p)	CThr GAbr GWic LCra MPar NHol SChu SSvw WHoo WKin WMar WPer
'Allspice Sport' (p)	WKin
alpinus	CB&S CGle EFol GDra GEdr GLoc LAbb MBal MCot MHig MWgw NGre NHol NKay NNrd NRoo SIng SPou WAbe WWin
– 'Albus'	NNrd SBla
– 'Cherry Beauty'	LCra
– 'Drake's Red'	NGre
– 'Joan's Blood'	ECha EPot GGar GLoc LHop MHig NRed SBla WHoo WMar WWin
– 'Millstream Salmon'	NNrd
– salmon form	NGre
'Alyson'	SAll
amurensis	ITim WCla
anatolicus	ELan GLoc MCas NHol
'Andrew' (p)	SHay
'Anna' (pf)	WEas
'Anna Wyatt' (p)	CHil LCra NHol NPin NRoo
'Annabelle' (p)	MCas NKay SAll SChu WHil
¶ 'Anniversay' (p)	SBai
'Ann's Lass' (pf)	NPin
'Apricot Sue' (pf)	NPin
'Archfield'	CShe
arenarius	CLew CMHG CRiv ESis GCHN LCra MCas MWgw WPer WWin
'Argus'	MPar WPer
'Ariel' (p)	GLoc NKay
armeria	CKin CRow WOak WPer
arpadianus	EMNN MPla NGre NNrd WAbe
¶ 'Arthur' (p)	EMFP
'Arthur Leslie' (b)	SAll SHay
x *arvernensis* (p)	CMHG CRiv CSun ECha EMNN EPot GDra GHig MBro MHig MPla NGre NHol NRoo SIng WAbe WPat
atrorubens	See D. *carthusianorum* Atrorubens group
'Audrey Robinson' (pf)	MWoo NPin
'Aurora' (b)	SHay
'Autumn Glory' (b)	SHay
'Autumn Tints' (b)	SHay
'Baby Treasure' (p)	NNrd WHil
'Badenia' (p)	SPou
'Bailey's Splendour' (pf)	SBai
'Ballerina' (pf)	CHil CSco MBri NHol SBai
¶ *barbatus* Nigrescens group (p,a)	LHil SSvw
'Barleyfield Rose' (p)	MCas MTho
§ 'Bat's Double Red' (p)	CKel EMFP LCra MPar SHig SSvw WKin WPer
'Beauty of Cambridge' (b)	SAll
'Beauty of Healey' (p)	EMFP LCra MPar WKin
'Becka Falls' (p)	CGle CHil CSco CThr LCra MBri NHol NPin SBai
'Becky Robinson' (p)	MBri NPin
* 'Bella'	MBro WDav
'Betty Buckle' (p)	SChu
'Betty Day' (b)	SHay
'Betty Norton' (p)	CShe LCra MHig SBla WHoo WPer WThu
'Betty Webber' (p)	MBri SBai
§ *biflorus*	CSun
'Binsey Red' (p)	MPar SChu SSvw
* 'Blue Carpet'	WPer
'Blue Hills' (p)	ELan GLoc MCas
¶ 'Blue Ice' (b)	SHay
'Bobby' (p)	SAll
'Bobby Ames' (b)	SHay
'Bombadier' (p)	CCla CFis EBre MRav NRoo
'Bookham Beau' (b)	SHay
'Bookham Fancy' (b)	SAll SHay
'Bookham Grand' (b)	SHay
'Bookham Heroine' (b)	SHay
'Bookham Lad' (b)	SAll SHay
'Bookham Lass' (b)	SAll SHay
'Bookham Perfume' (b)	SBai SHay
'Bookham Prince' (b)	SHay
'Bookham Sprite' (b)	SAll SHay
'Bovey Belle' (p)	CB&S CGle CHad CHil CSam CThr LCra NPin NRoo SBai
'Boydii' (p)	CHil NKay NTow
'Bransgore' (p)	WHoo
* *brevicaulis*	NRed
¶ – Mac&W 5849	WOMN
'Bridal Veil' (p)	CHil CThr EMFP LCra MPar SChu WDav WKin
'Bridesmaid' (p)	SHay
'Brigadier' (p)	EBar SCro WPer WThu
'Brilliant'	See D. *deltoides* 'Brilliant'

'Brimstone' (b) SAll SHay
¶ 'Brymos' (p) CFor
'Brympton Red' (p) CFis CHil CThr ECha EFou EOrc LCra MPar SBla SChu SSvw WEas WKin
'Buckfast Abbey' (p) CHil
§ 'Caesar's Mantle' (p) MPar NGre SChu
caesius See D. ***gratianopolitanus***
– 'Compactus' See D. ***gratianopolitanus*** 'Compactus Eydangeri'
callizonus GDra NGre NKay WAbe WOMN
'Camelford' (p) LCra WKin WPer
¶ 'Camilla' SSvw
¶ 'Candy' (p) SBai
'Candy Clove' (b) SAll SHay
'Carina' (p) SHay
'Carlotta' (p) SHay
'Carmen' (b) SHay
'Caroline Clove' (b) SHay
carthusianorum CHan CSev WPer
– ***humilis*** WAbe
– 'Nanus' GDra
caryophyllus CArn CSev NSel SIde WOak
'Casser's Pink' (p) ELan EMFP MPar MPit MTho WEas WOMN
'Castleroyal Princess' (p) CHil
'Catherine Glover' (b) SAll SHay
* 'Catherine Tucker' WEas
§ 'Cedric's Oldest' (p) MPar
'Celestial' (b) SHay
'Charles' (p) SAll
'Charles Musgrave' (p) See D. 'Musgrave's Pink'
'Charm' (b) SHay
'Chastity' (p) SChu WHoo
§ 'Chelsea Pink' (p) EMFP
'Cherryripe' (p) SAxl SHay
'Cheryl' (p) See D. 'Houndspool Cheryl'
'Chetwyn Doris' (p) NPin
chinensis (p,a) MBri
'Christine Hough' (b) MBri SBai
'Christopher' (p) CB&S CHil CThr GCHN LCra SBai SHay WEas
'Cindy' (p) LHop
cinnabarinus See D. ***biflorus***
'Circular Saw' (p) SIng
'Clara' (pf) MWoo NPin
'Clara Lucinda' (pf) NPin
'Clarabelle' (b) SHay
'Clara's Choice' (pf) NPin
'Clara's Flame' (pf) NPin
'Clara's Glow' (pf) NPin
'Clara's Lass' (pf) MWoo NPin
'Clare' (p) MBri SAll SBai SHay
'Claret Joy' (p) CB&S CThr EMFP NPin NRoo
'Clarinda' (b) SAll
'Clunie' (b) SAll SHay
§ 'Cockenzie Pink' (p) EMFP SChu WEas WKin WThu
'Cocomo Sim' (pf) SAll
'Coleton Fishacre' CHil
'Constance' (p) EMFP LCra SAll SHay
'Constance Finnis' (p) CHad CHil CThr MCot MWgw SChu WEas WPer
'Consul' (b) SAll SHay
'Copperhead' (b) SHay
'Cornish Snow' (p) CMHG CSam LCra SIng
'Coste Budde' (p) MCot WMar
'Countess of Lonsdale' (b) SHay
'Cranmere Pool' (p) CB&S CGle CHil CThr LCra NHol NPin NRoo
'Cream Sue' (pf) MWoo NPin
'Crimson Ace' (p) SHay
'Crimson Velvet' (b) SAll SHay
* 'Crock of Gold' CHil
¶ 'Crompton Classic' (pf) NPin
'Crompton Princess' (pf) MWoo NPin SBai
'Crossways' (p) ESis MHig
'Crowley's Pink Sim' (pf) SAll
cruentus LHop
¶ 'Dad's Choice' (p) SBai
'Dad's Favourite' (p) CFis CGle CHil CThr ELan EOrc LCra MBri MPar SAll SAxl SBai SHay SSvw WEas WKin WPer
¶ 'Daily Mail' (p) SBai
'Dainty' (b) SHay
'Dainty Clove' (b) SHay
'Dainty Dame' SIng
'Dainty Lady' (b) MBri SBai
'Daisy Hill Scarlet' (b) IDai
'Damask Superb' (p) EMFP LCra MHig SSvw WHil WPer
'Daphne' (p) SAll
'Dartington Double' (p) ELan ESis
'Dartmoor Forest' (p) CHil CThr SBai SBla
'David' (p) SAll SHay
'Dawlish Charm' (p) CThr
'Dawn' (b) SHay
* 'Dazzler' MPla
deltoides Widely available
– 'Albus' CGle CRiv CRow CTom ECha GLoc LCra MPla NNor NOak NRed NSel SIng SSvw WCla
– 'Bright Eyes' EBre
§ – 'Brilliant' CB&S CGle CRow CSev GLoc LAbb MWgw NNor NOak
– 'Broughty Blaze' GDra
– 'Erectus' ELan SSvw WEas
– 'Hilltop Star' GLoc
– 'Leuchtfunk' ('Flashing Light') CLew CRiv EBre EMNN GDra LHil LHop MPit NKay NNrd WEas
– 'Microchip' MPit NKay NOak WHil
– 'Samos' CRiv EBre SSvw
– ***splendens*** WOMN
– 'Wisley Variety' WCla WHil
'Denis' (p) CHil CThr ELan EMFP LCra NHol WEas WHil
'Desert Song' (b) SHay
'Devon Blush' (p) CThr NPin
'Devon Cream' (p) CThr NPin NRoo
* 'Devon Dove' (p) NRoo
* 'Devon General' (p) NRoo
'Devon Glow' (p) CThr NPin NRoo

* 'Devon Maid' (p)	NRoo
* 'Devon Pride' (p)	NRoo
'Dewdrop' (p)	ESis GCHN MPar
'Diane' (p)	CB&S CGle CHil CRiv CSam CSco CShe CSut CThr ELan EMFP LCra MBri NHol NPin NRoo SAll SBai SChu SHay WEas
¶ 'Dianne Hewins' (pf)	MWoo
'Diplomat' (b)	SHay
'Doctor Archie Cameron' (b)	SHay
'Doris' (p)	Widely available
'Doris Allwood' (pf)	NPin
'Doris Elite' (p)	SAll
'Doris Majestic' (p)	SAll
'Doris Ruby'	See D. 'Houndspool Ruby'
'Doris Supreme' (p)	SAll
'Dot Clark' (b)	SHay
double dark red	CFis
'Double Irish' (p)	See D. 'Irish Pink'
double mauve	WHil
'Douglas Fancy' (b)	SHay
'Downs Cerise' (b)	SHay
'Downs Glory' (b)	SHay
'Dubarry' (p)	CShe ITim MHig NHol SBla WAbe WDav WPer
¶ 'Dunkirk' (b)	MWoo
'Dusky' (p)	LCra SChu WKin
'Dusty Sim' (pf)	SAll
'E J Baldry' (b)	SHay
'Earl of Essex' (p)	CThr EMFP LCra SAll SHay WPer
'Ebor II' (b)	SAll SHay
* ***echiniformis***	CLew
¶ 'Edan Lady' (pf)	NPin
'Edenside Scarlet' (b)	SHay
'Edenside White' (b)	SBai
¶ 'Edith Johnson' (pf)	NPin
'Edna' (p)	SAll
'Edward' (p)	SAll
¶ 'Eileen' (p)	EMFP
'Elizabeth' (p)	CGle WKin
'Emile Paré' (p)	ESis LHop MPar MTho WMar
'Emperor'	See D. 'Bat's Double Red'
'Enid Anderson' (p)	MPar SChu SHig WDav
erinaceus	CHar CLew CSun EMNN ITim MBro MPla SPou SSmi WAbe WDav WMar WThu WWin
– ***alpinus***	EPot NGre NHol
'Erycina' (b)	SAll SHay
* 'Ethel Hurford'	WHoo
'Eudoxia' (b)	SAll SHay
'Eva Humphries' (b)	SBai SHay
'Eve' (p)	SAll
'Excelsior' (p)	CHar CHil CKel CRiv CSco CThr NNor WKin WThu
'Exquisite' (pf)	MBri SBai SHay
'Fair Folly' (p)	EMFP WHil WKin WPer
'Faith Raven' (p)	EMon
'Fanal' (p)	CHar CShe NBir NNrd WAbe
'Fancy Monarch' (b)	SHay
'Farnham Rose' (p)	SChu SSvw
'Fascination' (b)	SHay
'Fenbow Nutmeg Clove' (b)	MPar SChu WKin
'Fettes Mount' (p)	EMon GAbr MPar
'Fiery Cross' (b)	MBri SAll SBai SHay
'Fimbriatus' (p)	WHoo
'Fingo Clove' (b)	SAll
'Fiona' (p)	SAll
'First Lady' (b)	SAll
'Flame' (p)	SHay
'Forest Glow' (b)	SBai
'Forest Sprite' (b)	MBri SBai
'Forest Treasure' (b)	MBri SBai
'Forest Violet' (b)	SBai
'Fortuna' (p)	SAll
'Fountain's Abbey' (p)	MPar WMar
'Fragrans' (pf)	CHil
'Fragrant Ann' (pf)	MWoo NPin
'Fragrant Lace' (p)	CThr
'Frances Isabel' (p)	LCra SAll
'Frances King' (pf)	NPin
'Frances Sellars' (b)	SHay
'Frank's Frilly' (p)	MPar SSvw
'Freckles' (p)	CHar CThr SBai SHay
¶ 'Fred Sutton' (pf)	NPin
'Freda' (p)	SAll SHay
'Freeland Crimson Clove' (b)	SAll SHay
'French'	CShe
freynii	EPot GLoc ITim MBro NGre SPou
* 'Fringed Pink'	See D. ***superbus***
¶ ***furcatus***	NWCA
'Fusilier' (p)	CHil CSam GLoc MCas
'Garland' (p)	EBre EHal NHol NNrd NRoo SIng WDav
'Garnet' (p)	SChu
'Gaydena' (b)	SHay
¶ ***giganteus***	IBlr
'Gingham Gown' (p)	MPar NBir NKay SBar SIng
'Gipsy Clove' (b)	SHay
glacialis	GEdr MCas NRed WPer
– ***gelidus***	GLoc
'Gloriosa' (p)	WKin WPer
'Glorious' (p)	SHay
gracilis	WWin
¶ ***graniticus***	NWCA
'Gran's Favourite' (p)	CHil CSam CSco EMFP MPar NRoo SChu SSvw WEas WKin WPer
§ ***gratianopolitanus***	CArn CHar CNat CRow CSev GCHN GLoc LHol MFir MHig MWgw NLan NOak NRoo NSel SIde SIng SSmi WAbe WOak
– 'Flore Pleno'	WHil
*– 'Karlik'	NWCA
– red form	GAbr
§ – 'Tiny Rubies'	WAbe
'Gravetye Gem' (b)	CHar CRiv LCra NRoo WHoo
'Green Lane' (p)	CHil
'Grenadier' (p)	WKin
¶ 'Greystone' (b)	EPla
¶ 'Gwendolen Read' (p)	SHay

* 'Gypsy Lass'	SFis
§ ***haematocalyx***	CHar EMFP GEdr ITim LCra LHil NRed SIng WDav
– 'Alpinus'	SIng
– ***pindicola***	EPot WOMN
'Hambledon' (p)	MPar
'Happiness' (b)	MBri SBai
'Harlequin' (p)	ECtt EMFP EMNN LCra NRoo
'Harmony' (b)	SAll SBai SHay
'Harvest Moon' (pf)	SAll
'Haytor' (p)	See D. 'Haytor White'
'Haytor Rock' (p)	CHil CThr LCra WPer
§ 'Haytor White' (p)	CB&S CGle CHil CSam CSut CThr GCHN LCra NHol NPin NRoo NSti SAll SBai SChu SSvw WEas
'Helen' (p)	CThr SAll SHay WEas
¶ 'Henry of Essex' (p)	EMFP SSvw
'Herbert's Pink' (p)	LCra WKin
'Hidcote' (p)	CHoe CShe ELan ESis MHig NKay SBla SChu SIng WWin
'Highland Chieftain' (p)	NKay
'Highland Fraser' (p)	CShe MHig NHol NKay NRoo WEas WHil WKif WPat WWin
'Highland Queen' (p)	SAsh WKin
'Hollycroft Fragrance' (p)	SAll
'Hollycroft Rose' (p)	EHal GWic
'Hope' (p)	EMFP EOrc LCra MPar SChu SSvw WKin WMar WPer
'Horsa' (b)	SAll SHay
* 'Horton'	MPar
'Hound Tor'	CHil
§ 'Houndspool Cheryl' (p)	CGle CHil CSco CThr GAbr LCra NHol NPin NRoo SBai SSvw
§ 'Houndspool Ruby' (p)	CGle CHil CSam CSut CThr MBri MWat NHol NOak NPin SBai SChu SSvw WEas
'Huntsman'	See D. 'Allen's Huntsman'
'Ian' (p)	CSut SAll SHay
'Ibis' (p)	SHay
'Iceberg' (p)	EMFP MPar SHay
'Icomb' (p)	MBro WHoo WPat WPer WWin
'Imperial Clove' (b)	SAll SHay
'Ina' (p)	GDra GHig
'Inchmery' (p)	CHad CShe LCra MBro MPar NKay NNor NRar NSti SAll SChu SHig SSvw WEas WHoo WKin WPer
'Inglestone' (p)	CSam MBro MCas NHol WDav
'Inshriach Dazzler' (p)	EBre GDra GEdr GLoc ITim LCra MCas NRoo WAbe WDav WEas WHil WMar WThu
'Inshriach Startler' (p)	GDra NRoo
'Isobel Templeton' (b)	SHay
'Jacqueline Ann' (pf)	MWoo NPin
'Jane Austen' (p)	LCra SChu WKin WMar WPer
¶ 'Jane Coffey' (b)	SHay
'Janet' (p)	NHol
'Janet Walker' (p)	WDav
'Jenny Wyatt' (p)	CHil CThr LCra NPin SSvw
'Jess Hewins' (pf)	MWoo NPin
'Jester' (p)	SAll
'Joanne' (pf)	NPin
'Joanne Taylor' (pf)	MWoo NPin
'Joanne's Highlight' (pf)	NPin
'Joan's Blood'	See D. ***alpinus*** 'J. B.'
'Joe Vernon' (pf)	MWoo NPin
'John Ball' (p)	EMFP MPar
'John Gray' (p)	MPar SSvw
'Joker' (pf)	SAll
'Joy' (p)	CHil CKel CSco CThr LCra MBri NPin NRoo SAll SBai SHay
'Judy' (p)	NHol
¶ 'Julian' (p)	EMFP
'Kesteven Chambery' (p)	EMNN
'Kesteven Chamonix' (p)	CHar EMNN WThu
'Kesteven Kirkstead'	CHil
'Kestor' (p)	CHil CThr GCHN LCra NOak SBai
¶ 'King of the Blacks'	WCar
kitaibelii	See D. ***petraeus petraeus***
'Kitty Jay'	CHil
knappii	CHar CSun EMFP GCHN GLoc LHil MPar WCar WCla WHil WPer WWin
§ 'La Bourboule' (p)	Widely available
'La Bourboule Alba' (p)	CCla CHar CRiv CSam EMNN EPot GLoc MHig NNrd NRed WAbe WDav WMar WWin
'La Bourbrille'	See D. 'La Bourboule'
'Laced Hero' (p)	SChu WKin WPer
laced hybrids	WCla
'Laced Joy' (p)	CGle CHad CHil CMHG CThr LCra NOak SAll SChu SHay WHoo WKin WPer
'Laced Monarch' (p)	CGle CHil CSam CThr GCHN MBri MBro NHol NPin NRoo SAll SBai SSvw WDav WPer
'Laced Prudence'	See D. 'Prudence'
'Laced Romeo' (p)	CHil EMFP LCra SAll SChu SHay WEas
'Laced Treasure' (p)	SAll
'Laddie Sim' (pf)	SAll
'Lady Diana' (p)	NKay
'Lady Granville' (p)	CHar LCra MPar SSvw WKin
'Lady Salisbury' (p)	WKin
'Lady Wharncliffe' (p)	MPar SSvw WPer
'Lancing Lady' (b)	SAll
'Lancing Lass' (p)	SHay
'Lancing Monarch' (b)	SAll SHay
'Laura' (p)	SAll SHay
'Lavender Clove' (b)	MBri SAll SBai SHay
¶ 'Lavender Lady' (pf)	MWoo
'Le Rêve' (pf)	SAll
'Leiden' (b)	SBai
'Lemsii' (p)	CMHG CRiv CSam ESis MBal MBro NHol NVic SIng WDav WHoo WPer
'Lena' (pf)	SAll
'Leslie Rennison' (b)	SAll SHay
'Letitia Wyatt' (p)	CHil CThr
'Leuchtkugel'	GLoc
'Lilac Clove' (b)	SHay
'Lilian' (p)	CFis

Name	Suppliers
* 'Linda'	SAll
¶ 'Little Diane' (p)	MWoo
'Little Gem' (pf)	LHil WCla
'Little Jock' (p)	Widely available
'Little Miss Muffet' (p)	CHil
'Little Old Lady'	See D. 'Chelsea Pink'
'London Brocade' (p)	CHil EMFP LCra SChu SIng WKin WMar WPer
'London Delight' (p)	CHil CThr EMFP EOrc LCra MPar WKin WPer
'London Glow' (p)	SAll
* 'London Joy'	WEas
'London Lovely' (p)	LCra SAll SSvw WKin WPer
'London Poppet' (p)	CRiv EMFP EOrc SAll WHoo
§ 'Lord Chatham' (b)	WKin
'Lord Grey' (b)	SAll SHay
'Loveliness' (p)	CBre GAbr WEas
'Lustre' (b)	MBri SAll SBai SHay
¶ 'Madame Dubarry' (p)	GAbr
'Madonna' (p)	CBre CThr LCra MPar SBai WKin WPer
'Mandy' (p)	EMFP SAll SBai SHay
'Manningtree Pink' (p)	ELan
'Maria'	See D. 'Allen's Maria'
'Mark' (p)	SHay
'Mars' (p)	CGle CMHG EFol ELan EPad GAbr GLoc ITim LCra MHig MPlt NRoo SAll SChu WAbe WHil
'Marshwood Mystery' (p)	CThr
* 'Martin Nest'	ITim
'Mary Jane Birrel' (pf)	MWoo NPin
* 'Mary Keene'	MPar
'Mary Livingstone' (b)	SHay
'Mary Murray' (b)	SHay
'Mary Simister' (b)	SAll SHay
* 'Mary's Gilliflower'	SSvw
'Master Stuart' (b)	SBai
'Matador' (b)	SHay
¶ 'May Jones' (p)	EMFP
'Maybole' (b)	SAll SHay
'Mendip Hills' (b)	SHay
'Merlin Clove' (b)	SBai SHay
'Microchip' (p)	NRed
microlepis	GLoc ITim MBal NRed NWCA WDav
– ***albus***	GLoc SOkd WHil
– ***musalae***	MBro WDav
'Milley' (p)	CRiv WKin
§ ***minutiflorus***	GCHN SIng
'Miss Sinkins' (p)	LCra
* 'Molly Blake'	WDav
'Monica Wyatt' (p)	CGle CHad CHil CThr LCra MBri NPin NRoo SBai
monspessulanus sternbergii	NGre
'Montrose Pink' (p)	See D. 'Cockenzie Pink'
* 'Mrs Brownhill'	CBot
'Mrs Clark'	See D. 'Nellie Clark'
'Mrs Elmhurst' (p)	LCra
'Mrs Holt' (p)	SIng
'Mrs Jackson' (p)	SBla
'Mrs N Clark'	See D. 'Nellie Clark'

Name	Suppliers
'Mrs Perkins' (b)	SAll SHay
'Mrs Shaw' (p)	LCra
'Mrs Sinkins' (p)	Widely available
'Murray's Laced Pink' (p)	CHil MPar
'Murton' (p)	WKin
N 'Musgrave's Pink' (p)	CBre CFis CGle CHil CShe CTom ECha EOrc LCra LHop SAll SChu SSvw WDav WEas WHoo WKin WMar
'Musgrave's White'	See D. 'Musgrave's Pink'
myrtinervius	ECha ESis ITim MHig MPlt NRed NRoo NWCA WHil WOMN WPer
'N M Goodall' (p)	LHop
'Nan Bailey' (p)	SBai
'Nancy Lindsay'	See D. ***pavonius*** 'N. L.'
'Napoleon III' (p)	IBar
nardiformis	LGan WPer
'Nautilus' (b)	SHay
neglectus	See D. ***pavonius***
§ 'Nellie Clark' (p)	CMHG CShe EBre MBal SChu
'Nicola Jane'	GLoc
nitidus	GDra NBir
noeanus	See D. ***petraeus n.***
'Nora Urling Clark' (pf)	WPat
* 'Norfolk Old Red Clove'	MPar
'Norman Hayward' (b)	SHay
'Nyewood's Cream' (p)	CMHG EBre EMNN ESis LCra MHig MPla MRav NGre NNrd NRed NRoo SIng SOkd WAbe WDav WPer
'Oakfield Clove' (b)	SAll
§ 'Oakington' (p)	CKel CRiv CSam EBre EMNN LCra MBal MBro MWat NKay NNrd NRoo SChu SIng WAbe WDav WHil
'Oakington Rose'	See D. 'Oakington'
'Oakwood Bill Ballinger' (p)	NPin
'Oakwood Sparkler' (p)	NPin
'Old Clove Red' (b)	EMFP SFis SSvw WDav WThu
'Old Dutch Pink' (p)	LCra SChu WKin
'Old Fringed' (p)	MPar WKin
'Old Fringed White' (p)	SAxl
'Old Mother Hubbard' (p)	CHil
§ 'Old Square Eyes' (p)	MPar SAxl SBla WEas
'Old Velvet' (p)	CBre CHar MPar MTho SChu SSvw
'Oliver' (p)	SAll
'Orange Maid' (b)	SAll SHay
'Oscar' (b)	SAll
'Osprey' (b)	SHay
'Paddington' (p)	EMFP LCra SChu WKin
'Painted Beauty' (p)	EMFP
'Painted Lady'	See D. 'Pink Damask'
'Paisley Gem' (p)	CThr EMFP LCra SChu SSvw WKin
'Pallas' (b)	SAll
'Patricia' (b)	SHay
'Paul' (p)	MBri SAll
¶ 'Paul Hayward' (p)	SHay

§ *pavonius*	CLew CSam GLoc MCas MRav NKay NWCA SBla SIng SPou WAbe WHil WWin
– *albus*	NHol WPat
§ – 'Nancy Lindsay'	MPar
– *roysii*	See D. 'Roysii'
'Peach' (p)	SHay
'Perfect Clove' (b)	SHay
§ *petraeus*	LRHS NHol NRed
– *noeanus*	SIng SPou WHal
§ – *petraeus*	CSun
'Petticoat Lace' (p)	SHay
¶ 'Phaeton' (b)	SHay
'Pheasant's Eye' (p)	CHar CHil EMFP LCra MPar WDav WKin WPer
'Philip Archer' (b)	SHay
'Picture' (b)	SHay
'Pike's Pink' (p)	Widely available
pindicola	See D. ***haematocalyx p.***
'Pink Baby' (p)	SIng
'Pink Bizarre' (b)	SHay
'Pink Calypso'	See D. 'Truly Yours'
§ 'Pink Damask' (p)	GAbr WKin WPat WPer
'Pink Jewel' (p)	CSam ECha EPad ESis ITim NHol SChu WEas
'Pink Mrs Sinkins' (p)	EMFP LCra SAll SBai SChu SSvw
'Pink Pearl' (b)	SHay
'Pink Sim' (pf)	SAll
'Pixie' (b)	EMNN EPot ITim
plumarius	NLan NRed WOak
'Portsdown Fancy' (b)	SHay
'Portsdown Lass' (b)	SHay
'Portsdown Perfume' (b)	SHay
'Portsdown Sunset' (b)	SHay
'Preston Pink'	SChu
'Pretty Lady' (p)	NRoo SIng
'Prichard's Variety' (p)	GLoc
'Prince Charming' (p)	CRiv ELan EMNN ESis GAbr ITim MCas NNrd NRoo SIng WAbe
* 'Princess Charming'	LHil
'Prudence' (p)	CHil CThr EMFP LCra NSti SBai WHoo WKin WMar
'Purley King' (p)	CThr
§ 'Queen of Hearts' (p)	ESis NNrd SAxl WAbe WPer
'Queen of Sheba' (p)	LCra NSti SChu WKin WMar
'Queen's Reward' (pf)	MWoo SBai
'Rachel' (p)	NRoo
'Rainbow Loveliness' (p,a)	WHil
'Ralph Gould' (p)	NRoo
'Red and White' (p)	WKin WPer
* 'Red Emperor' (p)	SAll WPer
* 'Red Flake'	WKin
'Red Penny' (p)	MBro NRoo WPat
'Renoir' (b)	SAll SHay
¶ *repens*	NWCA
'Richard Gibbs' (p)	EBre EHal MRav NRoo WWin
'Robert' (p)	CThr SAll SHay
'Robert Baden Powell' (b)	SHay
'Robin Thain' (b)	EBar MBri SAll SBai SHay
'Ron's Joanne' (pf)	NPin
'Rosalind Linda' (pf)	MWoo NPin
'Rose Bradwardine' (b)	SHay
'Rose de Mai' (p)	CBre CHil LCra SChu SSvw WKin
'Rose Joy' (p)	CHil CSut CThr LCra NPin NRoo SBai
¶ 'Rose Monica Wyatt' (p)	NRoo
'Rosealie' (p)	SHay
¶ 'Royal Scott' (pf)	MWoo
'Royalty' (p)	SHay
§ 'Roysii' (p)	LHil MPla MPlt NWCA WOMN WPer
'Ruby' (p)	See D. 'Houndspool Ruby'
♦ 'Ruby Castle'	See D. 'Lord Chatham'
'Ruby Doris'	See D. 'Houndspool Ruby'
'Russling Robin'	See D. 'Fair Maid of Kent'
'Saint Nicholas' (p)	LCra MPar WKin WThu
* 'Sally Anne' (b)	SHay
'Salmon Clove' (b)	SAll SHay
* 'Salmon Flake'	WKin
'Sam Barlow' (p)	CHil LCra MPar SAll SBai SChu SSvw WEas WKin WWin
¶ 'Samantha Holtom'	MWoo
'Sandra' (p)	SAll
'Santa Claus' (b)	SAll SHay
'Sappho' (b)	SHay
'Scania' (pf)	SAll
'Scarlet Fragrance' (b)	SAll SHay
'Scarlet Joanne' (pf)	MWoo NPin
* *scopulorum perplexans*	EPot
¶ *seguieri*	MBro
serotinus	GLoc
'Sevilla' (pf)	SBai
'Shaston' (b)	SHay
'Shaston Delight' (b)	SHay
'Shaston Scarletta' (b)	SHay
'Shaston Superstar' (b)	SHay
'Shocking Pink Sim' (pf)	SAll
'Show Portrait' (p)	NNor
simulans	GLoc WOMN
'Sir Arthur Sim' (pf)	SAll SHay
'Sir Cedric Morris'	See D. 'Cedric's Oldest'
'Sir David Scott' (p)	MPar
* 'Six Hills'	WPat
'Snow Clove' (b)	SHay
'Solomon' (p)	CHil SSvw WMar
'Sonata' (p)	WPer
'Sops-in-Wine' (p)	CHil CThr ECha LCra SChu SSvw WDav WKin WPer
'Southmead' (p)	CHar MHig
'Spangle' (b)	SAll SHay
'Spark' (p)	EHal ITim NRoo
'Spencer Bickham' (p)	ESis NHol WAbe
'Spindrift' (b)	SAll SHay
¶ 'Spotty' (p)	ITim
'Spring Beauty' (p)	EHal MFir NBir WPer
'Sprite' (b)	SHay
'Square Eyes'	See D. 'Old Square Eyes'
squarrosus	CHar CSun GLoc MHig NGre NNrd NWCA
¶ 'Squeeks' (p)	SChu

'Startler' (p)	SHay
'Strathspey' (b)	SAll SHay
'Strawberries and Cream' (p)	CGle CHil CThr NHol NPin
strictus brachyanthus	See D. ***minutiflorus***
§ ***subacaulis***	EPot GLoc LCra MBro SPou WAbe WPer
– ***brachyanthus***	See D. ***subacaulis***
suendermannii	See D. ***petraeus***
* 'Sullom Voe'	NRoo
'Sunray' (b)	SHay
'Sunstar' (b)	SAll SHay
§ ***superbus***	CLew CSun MTho NWCA WKin WOMN WPer WWin
'Surrey Clove' (b)	SHay
'Susan' (p)	IBar NSti SAll
'Susannah' (p)	SAll
'Swanlake' (p)	EMFP SHay
'Swansdown' (p)	NNor
* 'Sway Belle' (p)	SBai
* 'Sway Breeze' (p)	SBai
* 'Sway Gem' (p)	CSut SBai
* 'Sway Mist' (p)	SBai
'Sweet Sue' (b)	SAll SHay
'Sweetheart Abbey' (p)	CHil CThr EMFP LCra MPar SChu SSvw WDav WKin WThu
sylvestris	GDra NNrd NWCA
* 'Taffeta' (p)	CSut
'Tangerine Sim' (pf)	SAll
* ***tenerifa***	MBri
'Terry Sutcliffe' (p)	MPar SSvw WKin WMar WPer
'The Bloodie Pink'	See D. 'Caesar's Mantle'
'Thomas' (p)	CFis CGle EFou LCra NVic SAll SChu SHay
'Thomas Lee' (p)	SAll
'Timothy' (p)	SHay
'Tiny Rubies'	See D. ***gratianopolitanus*** 'T. R.'
* 'Toki Woki'	WEas
'Toledo' (p)	NPin
'Tom Bradshaw' (pf)	SBai
'Tony Langford' (pf)	NPin
'Treasure' (p)	SHay
'Trevor' (p)	SAll
¶ 'Truly Yours' (pf)	MWoo
* ***turkistanicus***	NBir
'Ursula Le Grove' (p)	CHil MPar SSvw WKin WMar
'Valda Wyatt' (p)	CCla CGle CHad CHil CSam CThr ELan GCHN LCra LHop NHol NPin NRoo SBai SChu SSvw
'Valerie' (p)	SChu
'Vanda' (p)	SAll
'Vera Woodfield' (pf)	MWoo NPin
¶ 'Victoria' (p)	EMFP GAbr ITim
'Violet Carson' (b)	SAll
'Violet Clove' (b)	SHay
'W A Musgrave' (p)	See D. 'Musgrave's Pink'
'Waithman Beauty' (p)	CFor CGle ECha EMNN ESis GAbr GLoc ITim LCra MBro MHig MPar MPla NRoo SAll WAbe WEas WHoo WKin WMar WPat WPer
'Waithman's Jubilee' (p)	CFor GCHN NKay NNrd WPer
'Warden Hybrid' (p)	EMNN MBro MHig WAbe WDav WHil
'Warrior' (b)	SAll SHay
'Water Nymph' (b)	SHay
'Weetwood Double' (p)	SIng WPer
* 'Weetwood White'	SIng
'Welcome' (b)	SHay
'Welland' (p)	NSti
'Wells next the Sea' (p)	EOrc
weyrichii	GLoc ITim SIng WAbe WOMN
'Whatfield Anona' (p)	ELan ESis
'Whatfield Brilliant'	LRHS
'Whatfield Gem' (p)	EHal ELan ESis MCas MPit NRoo SAll WPer WThu
'Whatfield Joy' (p)	MCas NTow SAll WPer
'Whatfield Magenta' (p)	EPad ESis LRHS
'Whatfield Mini' (p)	SAll WPer
'Whatfield Pom Pom' (p)	SAll
'Whatfield Ruby' (p)	LRHS
'Whatfield White' (p)	ELan EPad ESis LRHS
'Whatfield Wisp' (p)	CLew ELan LHil MPit WMar
'White Barn' (p)	ECha
'White Bouquet' (p)	SIng
'White Ladies' (p)	CSco CThr ELan ENot MPar SAll SSvw WKin
'White Sim' (pf)	SAll
'Whitecliff' (b)	SAll SHay
'Whitehill' (p)	CGle CShe EPot NKay WDav WThu WWin
'Widecombe Fair' (p)	CGle CHil CSut CThr LCra LHop NHol NPin NRoo SBai
'William Brownhill' (p)	EMFP SChu
'William Neville' (b)	SHay
'William Sim' (pf)	SAll
'Winsome' (p)	SHay
* 'Woodfield's Jewel'	MWoo
'Yellow Dusty Sim' (pf)	SAll
'Yorkshireman' (b)	SAll SHay
'Zebra' (b)	SAll SBai SHay

DIAPENSIA (Diapensiaceae)

DIASCIA (Scrophulariaceae)

anastrepta	CHan CMHG GWic MCas MFir MPit MTho SAxl SChu SWas WEas WPer WRus
barberiae	ELan GWic LHop WRus
¶ ***capensis***	WPer
cordata	Widely available
elegans	See D. ***vigilis***
felthamii	See D. ***fetcaniensis***
fetcaniensis	Widely available
flanaganii	See D. ***stachyoides***
§ ***integerrima***	CBot CChu CGle CHan CMHG CSam CSpe CSun EBar ELan EMon EOrc GGar GWic LGre LHil MFir MUlv SBla SChu WHCG WMar WPer
integrifolia	See D. ***integerrima***
'Jack Elliott'	LHop SMrm
¶ 'Katherine Sharman'	EMon
¶ 'Lilac Belle'	ELan

lilacina	CHan CHil CLew CMHG EMon ESis NOak NSti SMrm WEas WHal WPer
megathura	EMon GWic WPer
* *mollis*	CHan CMHG
* *nastopsin*	CLew
* *nigerima*	ECha
patens	EOrc ESis LHil LHop NSti WPer
¶ *pentandra*	CBot
rigescens	Widely available
* – 'Forge Cottage'	WPer
I – 'Variegata'	EFol
'Ruby Field'	Widely available
¶ – – x *stachyoides*	SIgm
'Rupert Lambert'	EMon SChu SCro SMrm WPer
¶ 'Salmon Supreme'	ELan
sp. CDR 265	LHop
§ *stachyoides*	CFis CHan CSun EBar ELan LGre LHop WPer WRus
* *stricta*	CHan
§ *vigilis*	Widely available

X DIASCIA X LINARIA See **NEMESIA** ***umbonata***

DICENTRA † (Fumariaceae)

'Adrian Bloom'	CCla CSco EPot ERou MTho NOak NSti WHoo WRus
'Bacchanal'	CMHG CRow CTom ECtt EPla MBri NOak NRoo NSti SApp SAxl SBla SSpi WHCG WRus
'Boothman's Variety'	See D. ***formosa*** 'Stuart Boothman'
'Bountiful'	CCla CGle CMHG CRow CSco EGol LSav MWgw NNor NRoo NSti SChu SPer WHoo
'Brownie'	SAxl
canadensis	EPot MSal MTho NHol
cucullaria	CBos CRow ELun EPar EPot GEdr LGre MBal MSal MTho NHol NSti SIng SOkd WChr WDav
eximia	CCla CGle CRow CShe CSun EBre ECro EGol EPar EPot MBal MBro MTho NNor NRoo NSti SChu WEas WHea WHoo WRus WWin
– *alba*	CChu CCla CGle CHan COtt CRow CShe EFou ELan EOrc EPot ERou MCot MFir NJap NOak NSti NVic SAxl SChu SPou WAbe WRus
formosa	CElw CHad CRiv CRow CWGN ECha ECro ELan EOrc LAma MFir MPar MSal MTho NOak NOrc SCro SIng WAbe WHCG
– *alba*	CBot CBre CFor CHad CSun ECha EPar LGre MBro NNor NRoo WHCG
– 'Furse's Form'	NSti SAxl
– *oregana*	CHan CRow CSun EPar GWic MBal MTho NOak NSti SChu WHCG WWin
¶ – 'Paramount'	NSti
– 'Stuart Boothman'	Widely available
'Langtrees'	CBos CCla CElw CHad CHoe CLew CRow CSco CWGN ECha ELun EOrc LSav NRar NSti SAxl SBla SChu SMad SWas WEas WMar WWat
'Luxuriant'	CCla CGle CRow CSco CShe EBre EFou EGol ELan ELun EOrc EPar MBri NBar NJap NKay NOak NRoo NSti SPer SSpi WBon WEas WRus
macrantha	CFor CGle CHar CRow EPot LGre SSpi
macrocapnos	COtt MTho NCat NSti SMrm WCru
pauciflora	GEdr
'Pearl Drops'	CBre CRow EGol ELan EOrc EPla LSav MBri MCot MRav NHol NOak NRoo SCro SPer SPou WEas WHCG WHoo WRus WWin
scandens	CBos CBot CChu CHar CRow ELan LGan LGre MFir MTho NOak SMad SSpi WSHC
¶ 'Snowflakes'	NHar NRoo
spectabilis	Widely available
– *alba*	Widely available
'Spring Morning'	CBos CElw CGle CMHG NVic SChu SPer WRus
thalictrifolia	NBir WCru

DICHELOSTEMMA (Liliaceae/Alliaceae)

¶ *congestum*	ECro
¶ *ida-maia*	ECro
¶ *multiflorum*	ECro WChr
§ *pulchellum*	ECro WChr
¶ *volubile*	ECro

DICHROA (Hydrangeaceae)

febrifuga	LGre SSpi WCru

DICKSONIA (Dicksoniaceae)

antarctica	CB&S CHEx CTre NPal SArc
fibrosa	CB&S CHEx IJoh LPal SArc
squarrosa	CB&S CHEx LPal SArc

DICLIPTERA (Acanthaceae)

DICOMA (Compositae)

¶ *zeyheri*	ECro

DICRANOSTIGMA (Papaveraceae)

lactucoides	CSun WCru

DICTAMNUS (Rutaceae)

albus	CArn CChu CCla CHad CSco EBre ECha ECro EFou ELan EOrc GWic MBri MUlv NHol SApp SChu SPer SSpi WEas WHoo
§ – *purpureus*	CBot CChu CCla CHad CSco EBre EFou ELan ENot EOrc GPla GPoy GWic LGre MBri MRav MUlv NHol NTow SChu SPer SSpi WHoo WOld
fraxinella	See D. ***albus purpureus***

DICTYOLIMON (Plumbaginaceae)
macrorrhabdos NTow WDav

DICTYOSPERMA (Palmae)
album MBri

DIDYMOCHLAENA (Aspleniaceae)
lunulata See D. ***truncatula***
truncatula MBri

DIDYMOSPERMA (Palmae)
caudata See ARENGA ***caudata***

DIEFFENBACHIA (Araceae)
'Camille' MBri
candida MBri
compacta MBri
'Jeanette' MBri
'Jupiter' MBri
'Mars' MBri
'Neptune' MBri
'Saturnus' MBri
'Schott Gitte' MBri
seguine 'Amoena' MBri
– 'Carina' MBri
– 'Katherine' MBri
– 'Tropic Snow' MBri
'Triumph' MBri
'Tropic Sun' MBri
'Tropic White' MBri
'Veerie' MBri

DIERAMA (Iridaceae)
¶ *cooperi* SSpi
§ *dracomontanum* CBro CChu CCor CGle CHad CHan CMal CSun ECha EGol ELan GAbr GWic LGre LRHS NBir SBar SBla SChu SPer WAbe WOMN
pendulum CHan CKel EFou ELan MBri MFir MPar NHol SChu SMrm SPer WAbe WRus
♦– *pumilum* See D. ***dracomontanum***
¶ 'Puck' GWic LRHS NCat SSpi
pulcherrimum Widely available
– 'Blackbird' IBar LGre LRHS SApp
– clear pink GWic LGre
¶ – dwarf forms GWic
¶ – 'Peregrine' GAbr
– Slieve Donard hybrids GWic LHop
robustum CHan
'Titania' LRHS

DIERVILLA † (Caprifoliaceae)
lonicera SHil WWat
middendorffiana See WEIGELA ***middendorffiana***
rivularis CCor GWic SCro SLon
sessilifolia CB&S CBot CBow CHan EGol EPar GWic IOrc MBal MR&S MUlv SChu WBod WKif WRus WSHC WWin

x *splendens* CBra CCla CHoe CMHG CPle EBre EGol ELan ERav IJoh MBar MPla MR&S MRav MUlv NHol SGar SPer SSta WAbe

DIETES (Iridaceae)
§ *iridioides* CGle

DIGITALIS † (Scrophulariaceae)
ambigua See D. ***grandiflora***
apricot hybrids See D. ***purpurea*** 'Sutton's Apricot'
ciliata CHan ELan NHol SSvw
cream hybrids EFou
davisiana CChu EPad SSpi WDav WHoo
dubia CBot ERav LHop NBir SSpi WRus
¶ – *minor* NWCA
eriostachya See D. ***lutea***
ferruginea Widely available
'Glory of Roundway' CBot CHan
§ *grandiflora* Widely available
– 'Temple Bells' MWgw WCla WHen WHer WPer
heywoodii See D. ***purpurea heywoodii***
kishinskyi See D. ***parviflora***
laevigata CBot CHan ERav LHop NHol SBla WHer WPer
¶ – *graeca* GAbr
lamarckii See D. ***lanata***
§ *lanata* Widely available
– JCA 408.300 CChu WDav
– *leucocephala* See D. ***leucophaea***
§ *lutea* Widely available
– 'Brickell's Form' MPar
x *mertonensis* Widely available
obscura CBot CChu CSam EBar ECro EPad ERav ESis LGre LHop NHol NSti SBla SFir SIng SMrm SSpi SSvw WCar WDav WMar WPer
¶ – dwarf form CChu
§ *parviflora* CBot CChu CCla CHan ECha ECro EFou EPad ERav LSav MFir MPar NHol NOak NSti WCar WEas
§ *purpurea* CArn CKin CNat EFou ENot ERav GPoy LHol MPit NLan NNor NSel SIde WCla WHal WHil WOak
– *alba* CBot CBow CBre CGle CHad ECha ECro EFol EFou ELan EMon GAbr NSel SAxl SSvw WCla WEas WHal WPer WRus
– Excelsior hybrids CB&S CBow CHar CKel CKni CSam CSco EFol ERou MWat MWgw NBar SPer WHen WHer WHil
¶ – Foxy hybrids EBar WHen
§ – *heywoodii* CBot CFor CHad CHan CSam ECro ERav LGan LGre MPar SBla SFis SSpi WHil WPer WRus WWin
¶ – *mariana* ELan WPer

– 'Sutton's Apricot'	CBot CBre CHad CHan CSam ECro EFou ELan EMon GAbr NBir NRoo WHen WHer WPer
purpurea gloxiniiflora	MBri
– – 'The Shirley'	ECtt EFou
thapsi	ELan EMon EPad LGan MPar
trojana	WPer
viridiflora	CElw EBar EGol EPad NHol NRoo SSvw WPer

DIMORPHOTHECA See **OSTEOSPERMUM**

DIONAEA (Droseraceae)

muscipula	CMal EPot WMEx

DIONYSIA (Primulaceae)

aretioides	EPad EPot GLoc NTow SIng WThu
– 'Phyllis Carter'	EPad EPot GLoc
¶ *involucrata*	NTow WDav
tapetodes farinose form	WAbe
– 'Peter Edwards' (Hewer 1164)	WThu

DIOON (Cycadaceae)

edule	LPal
spinulosum	LPal

DIOSCOREA (Dioscoreaceae)

¶ *japonica*	SSpi
villosa	MSal

DIOSMA (Rutaceae)

ericoides	IHos

DIOSPHAERA (Campanulaceae)

asperuloides	See TRACHELIUM *asperuloides*

DIOSPYROS (Ebenaceae)

kaki	CBot CGre SHil SSpi
lotus	SSpi
virginiana	SSpi WCoo

DIPELTA (Caprifoliaceae)

floribunda	SHil WBod
yunnanensis	SHil

DIPHYLLEIA (Berberidaceae)

cymosa	ECha MSal WChr

DIPLACUS See **MIMULUS**

DIPLADENIA See **MANDEVILLA**

DIPLARRENA (Iridaceae)

moraea	CChu ECha ECou ECro GGar GWic IBar ITim MHig MTho NHol NOrc SApp SBla SSpi WAbe WHal WOld WPer WWin
¶ – West Coast form	SWas

DIPSACUS (Dipsacaceae)

fullonum	CArn CKin CSFH CWGN ECro ENot LHol MChe NLan SIde WOak WSto
inermis	WEas
laciniatus	WPer
pilosus	CKin

DIPTERACANTHUS See **RUELLIA**

DIPTERONIA (Aceraceae)

sinensis	CCla CMCN CSam EHar ELan MBri SHil SSpi WCoo WNor

DISANTHUS (Hamamelidaceae)

cercidifolius	CCla CFor CSco ELan ERav LSav MBlu MBri MUlv SBor SHil SPer SReu SSpi SSta WBod WWat

DISCARIA (Rhamnaceae)

DISELMA (Cupressaceae)

archeri	CKen SHil

DISPOROPSIS (Liliaceae)

¶ *pernyi*	SWas

DISPORUM (Liliaceae/Convallariaceae)

* *flavens*	SWas
hookeri	SIng
– *oreganum*	CBro CRow IBlr LGre NHar NHol SBar
lanuginosum	CBro LAma WChr
maculatum	LGre WChr
sessile	WChr
– 'Variegatum'	CBro CChu CCla CRow ECha ELan EPar GWic LGre SBla SWas
smithii	EBul ECro EPot MPar SWas
¶ sp. B&L 12512	SWas

DISTICTIS (Bignoniaceae)

¶ *buccinatoria*	CPle

DISTYLIUM (Hamamelidaceae)

racemosum	CB&S CShe CTre ELan LSav SHil SSpi SSta WBod WSHC WWat
¶ – *variegatum*	SSpi

DIURANTHERA (Liliaceae/Asphodelaceae)

major	See CHLOROPHYTUM *majus*

DIZYGOTHECA See **SCHEFFLERA**

DODECATHEON † (Primulaceae)

alpinum	GEdr
– *purpureum*	GEdr
clevelandii	CBro MTho NRed NTow SWas
– *insulare*	GLoc NWCA
– *patulum*	CAvo LRHS
cusickii	See D. *pulchellum*

dentatum	CBro CFor EPar GEdr GLoc LGre MBal MCas MPar MTho SBla WAbe WHoo
¶ *– dentatum*	NHol
– ellisiae	MBri NRya WOMN
hendersonii	CBro EPar LHop MBal NBar NHol NNrd
§ *jeffreyi*	EPot NRya NWCA WCla
*x *lemoinei*	EPot
macrocarpum album	WHil
meadia	Widely available
– album	CAvo CBre CBro CHar EFou ELan EOrc EPar IBar LAma LHop MTho NHol NRed NSti SSpi WWat
¶ – 'Alpenglow'	NHol
¶ – 'Millard's Clone'	NHol
pauciflorum	See D. ***pulchellum***
poeticum	GEdr
§ *pulchellum*	CFor EBar ECro EPar EPot GDra GLoc LRHS MBro MHig NGre NHol NKay NNrd NRed NRya SBla SIng WEas
– 'Red Wings'	CRiv EBre EPot GDra GEdr GLoc MCas NNrd NTow WHoo
radicatum	See D. ***pulchellum***
redolens	GEdr
'Sooke's Variety'	GEdr GLoc
tetrandrum	See D. ***jeffreyi***

DODONAEA (Sapindaceae)

humilis (f)	ECou
– – (m)	ECou
viscosa	ECou IBlr
– angustifolia	ISea
– purpurea	CChu CGre CMCN CPle CSun CTre ECou ERea ISea SMad

DOLICHOS (Leguminosae)

lablab	See LABLAB ***purpureus***

DOLICOTHRIX (Compositae)

ericoides	CSun

DOODIA (Blechnaceae)

¶ *caudata*	NMar
¶ *media*	NMar

DORONICUM † (Compositae)

¶ *austriacum*	NCat
caucasicum	See D. ***orientale***
§ *columnae*	CB&S GDra GLoc NHar NHol NOak
cordatum	See D. ***columnae***
'Finesse'	NOak
'Frühlingspracht' ('Spring Beauty')	CBre CKel ECtt ELan ERav ERou GDra NHol NOrc WBon WEas
'Harpur Crewe'	See D. ***plantagineum*** 'Excelsum'
'Miss Mason'	CSco CShe ELan ENot EPad MWgw SPer
§ *orientale*	CBre EHal MBro MRav MWgw NBar WHil
– 'Goldzwerg'	CSco SCro
– magnificum	CHar CLew ERou MFir MPit NOak NRoo WPer WWin
¶ *pardalianches*	CBre WCot
plantagineum	ELan
§ – 'Excelsum'	CGle CKel EFou EMon GCHN IDai MWat NKay WCot WEas
'Riedels Goldkranz'	MBri

DORYANTHES (Liliaceae/Amaryllidaceae)

¶ *excelsa*	CHEx
¶ *palmeri*	CHEx

DORYCNIUM See **LOTUS**

DORYOPTERIS (Adiantaceae)

pedata	MBri

DOUGLASIA (Primulaceae)

laevigata	EPot NHar
– ciliolata	GLoc NWCA
montana	EPot MCas WHoo
vitaliana	See VITALIANA ***primuliflora***

DOXANTHA See **MACFADYENA**

DRABA (Cruciferae)

acaulis	CSun
aizoides	CHar CNat CSam CShe ECha ELan EPar GCHN GDra GLoc MBar MHig MPla MPlt NGre NHol NNrd NRya SIng WCla WHil WHoo WPat WWin
– 'Compacta'	ELan
aizoon	See D. ***lasiocarpa***
'Alaskan species'	NTow
¶ *arabisans canadensis*	NRed
§ *aspera*	GDra GHig MBro NHol WDav
athoa	MBro WDav WMar
*– *leicocarpa*	NHol
bertolonii	See D. ***aspera***
borealis	NNrd
¶ *breweri*	ITim
bruniifolia	EBre MHig MTho NHol NNrd NTow SSmi
bryoides	See D. ***rigida b.***
cappadocica	MBro SIng SOkd WDav WOMN
¶ – JCA 419.500	NHol
¶ *carinthiaca*	WHil
compacta	GLoc NNrd NWCA
crassifolia	NNrd
¶ *cretica*	NRed
dedeana	MCas NHol NTow WOMN WPer WWin
densifolia	NGre NTow SIng WDav
haynaldii	NHol
hispanica brevistyla	CSun NRed NTow
– segurensis	WDav
imbricata compacta	See D. ***rigida imbricata compacta***
¶ *incana*	NWCA
kitadakensis	GCHN

§ *lasiocarpa* EHal MBro MPit NRoo NVic NWCA SIng WHal WHil
longisiliqua CSun ITim MCas NHol NTow SOkd WHoo WOMN
– EMR 2551 EPot
magellanica GGar
mollissima CSun EPot GLoc ITim MHig NHol NNrd NTow NWCA
– x *longisiliqua* WThu
§ *norvegica* NWCA
oligosperma EPot MBro NTow SIng
parnassica GCHN NHol NRed
paysonii GArf NGre SIng
¶ – *paysonii* WDav
– *treleasii* NGre WDav
polytricha GDra MBro NHol NNrd SIng WDav WEas
repens See D. ***sibirica***
rigida EPot GDra MTho NNrd NRya NVic SIng SSmi
– *bryoides* CSun GDra NHol NNrd NTow WThu
– *bryoides imbricata* CSun EPot GArf GLoc ITim MBro NHol SSmi
§ – *imbricata compacta* EPot
rosularis ITim MBro NHol SIng WDav
rupestris See D. ***norvegica***
x *salomonii* EPot WDav
sauteri GCHN LGan
scardica See D. ***lasiocarpa***
§ *sibirica* WPer
sp. CC 238 CSun
¶ sp. Wr 8911 NGre
¶ sp. Wr 8918 NGre
¶ *stellata* WPer
stylaris MHig WPat
x *suendermannii* NKay
ventosa NGre

DRACAENA (Agavaceae)

* *compacta* 'Purpurea' MBri
*– 'Variegata' MBri
congesta See D. ***stricta***
deremensis MBri
– 'Janet Craig' MBri
– 'Lemon and Lime' MBri
– 'Warneckei' MBri
– 'Yellow Stripe' MBri
fragrans MBri
*– *glauca* MBri
– 'Massangeana' MBri
indivisa See CORDYLINE ***i.***
marginata MBri
– 'Colorama' MBri
– 'Tricolor' MBri
sanderiana MBri
* *schrijveriana* MBri
stricta MBri
* *strutneri* MBri
surculosa surculosa 'Florida Beauty' MBri
– 'Wit' MBri

DRACOCEPHALUM (Labiatae)

argunense CSun EPot LRHS SCro SWas WDav WPer WWin
botryoides NTow WDav
bullatum LHil NSti
forrestii CLew EFou ESis GLoc NHol NSti
mairei See D. ***renatii***
moldavicum MSal SFir
prattii CSco EHal GWic
§ *renatii* EPot MSal NHol
ruyschianum CLew ELan LGan NOak NRed NWCA WDav WHoo
virginicum See PHYSOSTEGIA ***virginiana***

DRACOPHYLLUM (Epacridaceae)

¶ *fiordense* CHEx
pronum ECou

DRACUNCULUS (Araceae)

§ *vulgaris* CAvo CFor CGle CHEx EMon SMad SSpi

DRAPETES (Thymelaeaceae)

dieffenbachii GDra GGar
lyallii GDra

DREGEA (Asclepiadaceae)

§ *sinensis* CBot CChu CGre CHan CMac CSam ERav ERea LGre MNew SHil SSpi WWat

DREPANOSTACHYUM (Gramineae(Bambuseae))

falcatum WJun
§ *falconeri* EFul SBam
§ *hookerianum* SArc SBam

DRIMYS (Winteraceae)

aromatica See TASMANNIA ***aromatica***
colorata See PSEUDOWINTERA ***colorata***
lanceolata See TASMANNIA ***aromatica***
winteri CB&S CBra CChu CCla CGre CHEx CMHG CTre CTrw IDai IOrc ISea LHop MUlv NHol SArc SHil SPer SSpi WSHC
– *andina* CGre CSam SPer
§ – *chilensis* CB&S CGre CLan ISea WBod
– 'Fastigiata' CChu CFor
– 'Glauca' ISea
– Latifolia group See D. ***w. chilensis***
– *punctata* See D. ***w. winteri***
§ – *winteri* CGre

DROSANTHEMUM (Aizoaceae)

¶ *floribundum* CHEx WEas
hispidum CHEx CRiv ELan EPot GLoc LHop MCot MHig MTho NGre NHol NNrd NTow SIng WPer

DROSERA (Droseraceae)

aliciae	WMEx
anglica	WMEx
binata	EPot WMEx
burmanii	WMEx
'Californian Sunset'	WMEx
capensis	EPot NWCA WHal WMEx
– alba	WMEx
– narrow leaf form	WMEx
capillaris	WMEx
cuneifolia	WMEx
dichotoma	EPot WMEx
dielsiana	WMEx
filiformis filiformis	WMEx
– tracyi	WMEx
hamiltonii	WMEx
indica	WMEx
intermedia	WMEx
– x *rotundifolia*	WMEx
'Lake Badgerup'	WMEx
'Marston Dragon'	WMEx
multifida	EPot WMEx
– extremis	WMEx
'Nagamoto'	WMEx
natalensis	WMEx
nitidula	WMEx
x *obovata*	WMEx
pulchella	WMEx
– giant form	WMEx
pygmaea	WMEx
rotundifolia	WMEx
scorpioides	WMEx
slackii	WMEx
spathulata	WMEx
– Kansai form	WMEx
– Kanto form	WMEx
x *wateri*	WMEx

DRYANDRA (Proteaceae)

¶ *formosa*	CSun
¶ *obtusa*	CSun
praemorsa	CSun
pteridifolia	CSun

DRYAS (Rosaceae)

drummondii	NBir NHol WAbe
– 'Grandiflora'	GDra WThu
octopetala	Widely available
– 'Minor'	MHig NHol NNrd SWas WAbe WDav WHoo WPat
§ – *octopetala integrifolia*	GDra GHig GLoc MBro NHol SIng WAbe WWin
x *suendermannii*	CHar EBre GLoc GWic MBal MBro MRav NHol NNrd NRoo WAbe WEas WHoo WPat
tenella	See D. ***octopetala octopetala integrifolia***

DRYOPTERIS † (Aspleniaceae)

§ *affinis*	CRow ECha EPar MBal NKay NMar WFib
– 'Congesta Cristata'	NMar
– 'Crispa Congesta'	EBre NKay
– Crispa group	IOrc NKay
– 'Cristata Angustata'	IOrc NHol NKay NMar WFib
– 'Cristata Grandiceps Askew'	NKay NMar WFib
– Cristata group	CRow LSav NMar SMad WFib WHer
– 'Cristata Ramosissima Wright'	NKay
– 'Cristata The King'	EBre EGol ELan IOrc MBri NHol NMar SApp SMad
N– *polydactyla*	NMar
– 'Stableri'	NHol NMar
atrata	See D. ***cycadina***
austriaca	See D. ***dilatata***
borreri	See D. ***affinis***
carthusiana	NMar
§ *cycadina*	CWGN EBre EFou ELan IOrc MBri SApp SSpi WFib
– hirtipes	NMar
§ *dilatata*	CKin CTom ECha EHon MBal NHol NKay NLan NMar SHil WFib
– 'Crispa'	NHol NKay
– 'Grandiceps'	CRow SPer WFib
– 'Lepidota Cristata'	CWGN IOrc NHol NMar SPer WFib
– 'Lepidota Grandiceps'	NHol NMar
erythrosora	EBre EGol ELan LSav MBri MWgw NHol NMar SBla SMad SPer SSpi WFib
filix-mas	CKin CRow CTom CWGN ECha EFou EHon ELan IOrc LHol MBal MBri MSta MWgw NHol NKay NLan NMar SHil SPer SSpi WFib WHil
– 'Barnesii'	NMar
– 'Crispa'	EHon NHol WFib
– 'Crispa Cristata'	EBre EGol ELan LSav MBri NBar NMar SCro SPer WFib
– 'Crispatissima'	NBar
– Cristata group	NMar WFib
– Cristata group 'Fred Jackson'	NHol WFib
– 'Cristata Martindale'	CRow NHol NKay NMar SApp WFib
– 'Depauperata'	SPer WFib
*– *fluctuosa*	NKay
– 'Grandiceps Wills'	NMar WFib
– 'Linearis'	EHon ELan IOrc LSav MBri SApp SMad
– 'Linearis Congesta'	NKay
– 'Linearis Cristata'	NKay NMar SApp
– 'Linearis Polydactyla'	NMar
– 'Mapplebeck'	CRow WFib
– 'Multicristata'	NMar
– 'Polydactyla Dadds'	IOrc WFib
– Polydactyla group	NKay NMar SPer WFib
goldieana	NMar
hirtipes	See D. ***cycadina***
marginalis	NKay NMar WFib
pseudomas	See D. ***affinis***
¶ *shiroumensis*	NMar
x *tavellii*	IOrc WFib
wallichiana	CKni ECha EFou EHal MBri NMar SBla SSpi WFib

DRYPIS (Caryophyllaceae)
¶ *spinosa* 'Jacquiniana' EBar

DUCHESNEA (Rosaceae)
chrysantha variegata See D. ***indica*** 'Harlequin'
§ *indica* CCor CFis CLew CTom IBar IBlr MPar NSti SAxl SIng WHoo
§ – 'Harlequin' CHoe EFol EMon MPar MTho NSti SLHN
– 'Variegata' See D. ***i.*** 'Harlequin.

DUDLEYA (Crassulaceae)
¶ *brittonii* CHEx
¶ *cymosa* JCA 11777 MBro SIgm WDav
farinosa CHEx IBlr

DURANTA (Verbenaceae)
§ *erecta* CPle
repens See DURANTA ***erecta***

EBENUS (Leguminosae)
cretica SIgm WOMN

ECBALLIUM (Curcurbitaceae)
elaterium MSal

ECCREMOCARPUS (Bignoniaceae)
scaber CGle CHar CPle CSev ELan ENot EOrc GAbr GCHN LSav MBal MBri MWat NBar SHil SLMG SLon SPer WEas WHil WHoo WMar
– *aurantiacus* CB&S CSam LHop WMar
– *coccineus* CB&S CHan CSam EBar GCHN SFir SLMG SSus WEas WMar WOMN WSHC
– *roseus* CB&S CBot CGle CSam ELan WWin

ECHEVERIA † (Crassulaceae)
affinis MBri
* 'Black Knight' SLMG
derenbergii CHEx SLMG
elegans CHEx MBri
gibbiflora metallica MBri
glauca SLMG
harmsii WEas
¶ 'Imbricata' CHEx
setosa CHEx SLMG WEas

ECHINACEA (Compositae)
angustifolia CArn GPoy MSal
pallida MSal
paradoxa MSal
§ *purpurea* Widely available
– Bressingham hybrids EBre ELan SPer
– dark stemmed form EFou
¶ – 'Magnus' WPer
– 'Robert Bloom' CShe EBre EGol LHop MUlv
– 'The King' ERou
– 'White Lustre' CSco EBre EGol MUlv SSus WCot
– 'White Swan' CCla CHad CHan COtt EFou EGol ELan LGre LHop MWgw NBar SPer WHen WHer WRus
* *simulata* MSal

ECHINOPS † (Compositae)
* *albus* ELan
§ *bannaticus* 'Blue Globe' CHan CSco ERou GWic
– 'Taplow Blue' CHan CKel CSco EBre ECro ELan ERou GWic IDai LHop MUlv MWgw NKay NOrc SCro SMad SPer
¶ *exaltus* NBir
¶ *giganteus* ECro
¶ *microcephalus* EMon
'Nivalis' CCla EFou EMon ERou GWic LGan SPer
* *perringii* GWic
ritro CB&S CBre CElw CHad CHan CHar CRow ECha EGol ELan ENot ERou GCHN MCot MWat MWgw NBar NKay NNor NRoo SPer WEas WHil WPer
¶ – ACL 149/75 EMon
– 'Blue Ball' See E. ***bannaticus*** 'Blue Globe'
– 'Veitch's Blue' CCla CSco EMon GWic MBri
sphaerocephalus ECro ELan IBlr MUlv

ECHINOSPARTIUM (Leguminosae)
¶ *horridum* SIng

ECHIUM (Boraginaceae)
¶ *fastuosum* CHEx SArc WHal
§ *pininana* CB&S CHEx CHan CMHG CTre EMon NRar SArc
– x *wildpretii* SLHN
pinnifolium See E. ***pininana***
vulgare CArn CKin GPoy LHol MChe MSal NLan SFir SIde WHer
wildpretii CBot CHEx CHan SArc

EDGEWORTHIA (Thymelaeaceae)
§ *chrysantha* SHil
papyrifera See E. ***chrysantha***

EDRAIANTHUS (Campanulaceae)
dalmaticus SBla WDav
dinaricus SPou
graminifolius ECtt EPad GDra NKay NWCA SBar SIng WDav WWin
¶ – *albus* NKay
§ *pumilio* CLew EMNN EPad EPot GLoc MBro MCas MPit NGre NHol NKay NTow SBla SIng SPou SWas WDav WHoo WOMN
¶ *serbicus* SIng
serpyllifolius EPot
– *major* EPot
tenuifolius GLoc MPlt

EHRETIA (Boraginaceae)
acuminata See E. ***ovalifolia***
§ *ovalifolia* CGre
thyrsiflora See E. ***ovalifolia***

EICHHORNIA (Pontederiaceae)
crassipes CHEx CWGN EWav LMay MSta

ELAEAGNUS † (Elaeagnaceae)
angustifolia CBot CBow CCla EHar MRav SHil SPer SSpi SSta WCoo WMou WWat
– Caspica group CBow CFor CHad CHan EGol ELan LGre SBla SPla SSpi SSta WHCG WSHC WWat
argentea See E. ***commutata***
§ *commutata* CBot CCor CHoe EGol ELan ENot EPar ERav IOrc LHop NRoo SChu SHil SMad SPer SSpi WHCG WRus WWat
x *ebbingei* Widely available
I – 'Aurea' LPan
¶ – 'Coastal Gold' CB&S MGos
¶ – 'Codsall Pink' MGos
– 'Gilt Edge' CB&S CBra CChu CHoe CMHG CPle CSco EGol ELan ENot IOrc ISea MBal MBri MPla MR&S MWat NHol SHil SMad SPer SPla SSta WPat
– 'Limelight' Widely available
– 'Salcombe Seedling' EGol LHop MBri
glabra 'Reflexa' See E. x ***reflexa***
macrophylla CCla CLan ENot NNor SDry SHil
multiflora CCla SPer SSpi
*– *gigantea* ELan SPer
pungens SHil
– 'Argenteo Variegata' See E. ***p.*** 'Variegata'
– 'Aureo Variegata' See E. ***p.*** 'Maculata'
– 'Dicksonii' CB&S CHoe CLan CSco EHar IDai LNet SCro SHil SLon SMad SSpi
– 'Frederici' CB&S CHoe CLan CMHG EHar ELan ERav LSav MBal MBri MPla SHil SPer SSpi WPat WWat
– 'Goldrim' CKni EPla IJoh MGos SHil
§ – 'Maculata' Widely available
– 'Variegata' CB&S CCla CHoe CLan CSco EGol IOrc MBal SHil SPer
§ x *reflexa* CB&S
umbellata CB&S CPle SHil SPer WCoo WHCG WWat
– *parvifolia* CChu CCla EGol ENot MPar

ELAEOCARPUS (Elaeocarpaceae)
hookerianus ECou

ELDERBERRY See **SAMBUCUS** ***nigra***

ELEOCHARIS (Cyperaceae)
acicularis ELan
palustris MSta

ELETTARIA (Zingiberaceae)
cardamomum CSun MBri

ELEUTHEROCOCCUS (Araliaceae)
senticosus GPoy MSal

§ *sieboldianus* CB&S MRav
§ – 'Variegatus' CBot CCla CHan CRow EBre EFou EGol ELan ERav IOrc LGre LHop MBri MRav SChu WSHC

ELLIOTTIA (Ericaceae)
§ *bracteata* MBal
pyroliflora MBal

ELMERA (Saxifragaceae)
racemosa WHil

ELODEA (Hydrocharitaceae)
crispa See LAGAROSIPHON ***major***

ELSHOLTZIA (Labiatae)
fruticosa CArn
stauntonii CArn CB&S CBot CBow CCla ENot SFis SHil WSHC
– *alba* SHil

ELYMUS (Gramineae)
arenarius See LEYMUS ***a.***
¶ *canadensis* NHol
glaucus See E. ***hispidus***
§ *hispidus* CHan LHil LHop MBri SApp SBla SLHN SPer SSpi
interruptus SApp
N *magellanicus* CChu CCla CCor CElw CHad CHoe CRow EBre EFol ELan EOrc ERav GCHN GWic IBar LGre MFir NCat NSti SAxl SLHN SSpi WEas

EMBOTHRIUM † (Proteaceae)
coccineum CB&S CBot CBra CCla CGre CHEx CLan CSco EBre ELan IDai IOrc MBal SBor SDry SHil SPer SReu WAbe WNor WPat
– *lanceolatum* CBow CBra CCla CFor CGre CMHG CSam ELan IJoh ISea MBal MUlv SArc SHil SPer SSta
– Longifolium group CB&S CBra CMHG CTrw IBlr IJoh IOrc ISea SPer
– 'Norquinco' CB&S CFor IOrc MBri SMad SSpi WBod

EMILIA (Compositae)
coccinea See E. ***javanica***
javanica EMon

EMINIUM (Araceae)
albertii ECam LAma WChr
lehmanii ECam WChr
rauwolffii ECam LAma WChr
stipitatum ECam

EMMENOPTERYS (Rubiaceae)
henryi CBrd

EMPETRUM (Empetraceae)
luteum MBar

nigrum GHig MBal MBar MGos NLan
– 'Lucia' NHol

ENCEPHALARTOS (Zamiaceae)
lebomboensis LPal
natalensis LPal

ENDYMION See **HYACINTHOIDES**

ENGELMANNIA (Compositae)

ENKIANTHUS † (Ericaceae)
campanulatus Widely available
– albiflorus CBot CFis ELan LSav MBal SPer SSpi SSta WWeb
– palibinii CGre MBal SSpi WPat
– 'Red Bells' SHil SMrm SSpi
cernuus rubens CB&S CCla CGre MBal MBri MUlv SHil SPer SSpi WWat
chinensis CB&S CChu CCla ELan SHil SPer SReu SSpi WWat
deflexus CKni CMHG NHol SMrm SSpi
perulatus CB&S CBra CCla CMHG MBar SHil SPer SReu SSpi SSta WBod
tectus WBod

ENSETE (Musaceae)
§ *ventricosum* CHEx LPal SArc

ENTELEA (Tiliaceae)
¶ *arborescens* CHEx CSun ECou

EOMECON (Papaveraceae)
chionanthum CBot CHan CHar CLew ECha ELan EMon EPar EPot GWic IBlr MTho MUlv NGre NSti SAxl SFar SLHN SSpi WAbe WChr WCot WHal WHer

EPACRIS (Epacridaceae)

EPHEDRA (Ephedraceae)
affinis intermedia SIgm
distachya GPoy NNor
¶ *fragilis* SDry
gerardiana NHex SBor
– sikkimensis EPla SDry SSta WBod
¶ *major* SDry
nebrodensis See E. ***major***
nevadensis MSal

EPIGAEA (Ericaceae)
asiatica MSal
repens MSal SOkd

EPILOBIUM (Onagraceae)
§ *angustifolium* CGle NNrd
– album See E. ***a. leucanthum***
§ *– leucanthum* CBot CBre CCor CElw CHan ECha GWic MBri MFir NCat SApp SAxl WPer WRus WSHC WWat
arizonicum LHop SLHN
§ *canum* CElw CHan CHar ECha ELan ERav IDai IOrc MPla NHol NKay SChu SIng SLHN WEas WPer WThu
– album CBot CHar CSpe EFou EPot LGre LHop SBla WPer
§ – 'Dublin' Widely available
*– 'Etteri' ITim
§ *– latifolium* CCla CCor CPle NHol
§ *– mexicanum* CHar GCHN GLoc NHol
– 'Sir Cedric Morris' ELan LHop
– 'Solidarity Pink' CSpe ELan LGre LHop LRHS SBla SChu SMrm SSad
chlorifolium ELan
♦ *– kaikourense* See E. ***wilsonii***
crassum CSun ESis GLoc ITim MPlt NGre NNrd WPat WWin
§ *dodonaei* CGle CLew CSun ECro ECtt EOrc LGan LHop MTho SFir WSHC WWin
fleischeri LGre MTho
glabellum Widely available
*– *aureum* MTho
– 'Sulphureum' CHan WWin
hirsutum CKin WCla
luteum WCla
montanum CKin
obcordatum CLew ELan MFir NNrd SIng WPer
rosmarinifolium See E. ***dodonaei***
§ *wilsonii* CLew GHig WOMN

EPIMEDIUM † (Berberidaceae)
¶ *acuminatum* L 575 SBla SWas
alpinum CCla CHar COtt EPar LHil MBal NGre NHol NJap SHig SIng SPer WRus
x *cantabrigiense* CBro CCla CTom EBre ELun EOrc MBal MBri MWgw NHol SPer
davidii SWas
diphyllum LGre MCas SBla
¶ *elongatum* SWas
§ *grandiflorum* CFor CHan CTom EBre ECha ECro ELan EPar MBal MBri SBla SPer SWas
– 'Crimson Beauty' SBla SWas
– koreanum CFor SBla SWas
– lilac seedling SBla SWas
– 'Nanum' CBos SBla SWas
– 'Rose Queen' CBow CBro EBre ECha MUlv NOak NRoo SBla SChu SWas WAbe
§ – 'Roseum' CFor CHad NKay
– violaceum LGre
– 'White Beauty' CFor
– 'White Queen' ECha NOak SBla SWas
macranthum See E. ***grandiflorum***
x *perralchicum* CSco MBal SChu SIng
– 'Fröhnleiten' CBro CSco ECha EOrc EPot ERav MUlv NRoo SBla SMad SPer
– 'Wisley' CChu MUlv SBla SMad

perralderianum	CChu CCla CSam EFou ELan ELun EPar EPot LGro LHil MBal MBro MCot MWgw SAxl SBla SHig SSpi WAbe WHoo WWin
pinnatum	CChu ECro MSta WHal
– colchicum	CCla CHan CKel CSco ECro ELun EPar MBal MCot MWgw SDix SHig SSpi WHoo WRus
– elegans	EPot NKay
pubigerum	ECha SHig
x ***rubrum***	Widely available
setosum	SBla SWas
x ***versicolor***	CFor MBal SIng
– 'Cupreum'	SBla SWas
– 'Neo-Sulphureum'	CBro CTrw SSpi
– 'Sulphureum'	Widely available
– 'Versicolor'	EMon
x ***warleyense***	CBos CBro CChu CSco EBre ECha ECro ELan EPot ERou LGre MBal MCot NKay NRoo SBla SHig SWas WWin
x ***youngianum***	EPot SBla SMrm
– lilacinum	See E. x ***y.*** 'Roseum'
¶ – 'Merlin'	SWas
– 'Niveum'	CChu CCla CFor CHan COtt CSco EBre ECha ECro EFou ELun ENot EPar MBal MBri MCot MUlv NKay SBla SHig SPer SSpi WEas
§ – 'Roseum'	CBos CFor CSco CTom EFou ELun GLoc LHil MBal MBri MUlv NTow SBla

EPIPACTIS (Orchidaceae)

gigantea	CChu ELan EPot MBal NHol SBla SWes WChr

EPIPREMNUM (Araceae)

§ ***aureum***	EBak MBri
pinnatum	MBri

EPISCIA (Gesneriaceae)

♦ ***dianthiflora***	See ALSOBIA ***d.***
* ***primeria***	MBri

EQUISETUM (Equisetaceae)

arvense	MSal
¶ ***hyemale***	CHEx CNat
– robustum	CNat ELan
¶ ***ramosissimum***	CNat
scirpoides	MCas
¶ ***sylvaticum***	CNat

ERANTHIS (Ranunculaceae)

§ ***hyemalis***	CAvo CBro CRiv ELan EMon EPar ETub GEdr LAma LBlo LBow MBri MSal NLan SIng WBon WChr WCot
§ – Cilicica group	CBro ELan EPar EPot LAma LBlo LBow LRoo MBri SIng
§ – Tubergenii group	LBlo
– Tubergenii group 'Guinea Gold'	MPar WChr
longistipitata	EPot WChr

ERCILLA (Phytolaccaceae)

volubilis	CChu CGre ERav LHop WSHC

EREMAEA (Myrtaceae)

purpurea	CSun

EREMURUS (Liliaceae/Asphodelaceae)

§ ***aitchisonii***	ETub LAma SBla
bungei	See E. ***stenophyllus stenophyllus***
elwesii	See E. ***aitchisonii***
himalaicus	EPar ERou ETub LAma LBow LRoo SMrm
x ***isabellinus*** 'Cleopatra'	LAma LBow SMad
– Ruiter hybrids	EFou ELan EPar ETub LAma LRoo MBri MCot MUlv MWgw SMad SPer
– Shelford hybrids	CB&S CKel ELan ERou LAma LBow MUlv NOak SBla SW&B
* 'Money Maker'	LAma
* 'Pinokkio'	ETub LAma
robustus	CB&S CBot CHEx EPar ERou ETub GGar LAma LBow MBri SMrm SPer
§ ***stenophyllus stenophyllus***	CB&S CKel ELan EPar ERou ETub LAma LBow LRoo MBri NNor NOak SPer WHil

ERICA † (Ericaceae)

arborea	CNCN EBre MBal SArc SBar SHil WWat
§ – 'Albert's Gold'	CB&S CNCN EBre EDen ELan ENHC EPla GBla IOrc MBar MBri MCra MOke NHea NHol NWin SMad SPla SSpi WGre WRid
– alpina	Widely available
*– 'Arbora Gold'	See E. ***a.*** 'Albert's Gold'
– 'Arnold's Gold'	See E. ***a.*** 'Albert's Gold'
– 'Estrella Gold'	CHoe CNCN EBre EDen ELan ENHC ERav GPen MBar NBar NHea NHol NWin SBar SPla SSta WGre WRid
– 'Spring Smile'	EDen
australis	ELan GAng GBla MBar MCra SBar SHil SPer WRid
– 'Holehird'	EDen
– 'Mr Robert'	EDen MBar SHil WGre
– 'Riverslea'	CNCN EDen ENHC GAng GBla GPen IOrc MBal MBar MBri MOke NHea NHol SHil WGre
baccans	EDen
bauera	EDen
canaliculata	CB&S CGre CSun MBal MUlv SHil
carnea 'Accent'	EDen
– 'Adrienne Duncan'	COCH EDen ENHC GAng GBla GPen MBar MBri MOke NHea NHol NKay NWin SPla WGre
– 'Alan Coates'	CMac CNCN COCH EDen ENHC MBal MBar
– alba	COCH EDen

– 'Altadena'	CNCN COCH EDen MBar
– 'Amy Doncaster'	COCH EDen
– 'Ann Sparkes'	Widely available
– 'Atrorubra'	CB&S CMac COCH ENHC MBal MBar
– 'Aurea'	Widely available
¶ – 'Barry Sellers'	EDen
– 'Beoley Pink'	CNCN COCH
– 'C J Backhouse'	ENHC GPen
– 'Carnea'	CNCN COCH EDen ENHC MBar MBri MOke NBar NGre NWin WGre
– 'Cecilia M Beale'	COCH ENHC GBla MBar MCra NWin
– 'Challenger'	COCH EDen MBri MGos NBar
– 'Christine Fletcher'	WGre
– 'Clare Wilkinson'	CNCN EDen
– 'David's Seedling'	EDen
– 'December Red'	CB&S CMac COCH EDen ENHC ENot GAng GBla GPen IJoh MBar MBri MCra MOke MWat NBar NHol NKay NRoo SPla WBod WGre WRid
– 'Early Red'	COCH
– 'Eileen Porter'	CMac COCH EDen ENHC EPot GBla IDai MBar MBri NKay NWin SHil WRid
– 'Foxhollow'	Widely available
– 'Foxhollow Fairy'	CB&S CNCN COCH CRiv EDen ENHC EPot GAng GDra GPen MBar MCra NKay NWin WGre
– 'Golden Starlet'	EDen SPla WGre
– 'Gracilis'	ENHC GPen MBar MCra NWin WGre
– 'Heathwood'	COCH ENHC ENot GAng MBar MBri NHea NHol NKay
– 'Hilletje'	COCH EDen
– 'Jack Stitt'	COCH MBar MCra WGre
– 'James Backhouse'	CMac CRiv MBri MCra
– 'Jennifer Anne'	CNCN COCH EDen ENHC MBar
– 'John Kampa'	CB&S COCH EBre EDen ENHC MBar MBri NHol WGre
– 'John Pook'	MGos
– 'King George'	Widely available
– 'Lake Garda'	EDen SPla
– 'Late Pink'	COCH
– 'Leslie Sparkes'	COCH CRiv EDen ENHC GPen MBal MBar MCra NKay NWin WGre WRid
– 'Lohse's Rubin'	WGre
– 'Loughrigg'	CMac CNCN COCH EDen ENHC EPot GAng GBla GDra GRei GSpe IJoh MBal MBar MBri MCra MGos MOke NHea NHol NRoo NWin SHil SPla
– 'March Seedling'	CB&S CNCN COCH EDen ENHC ENot GAng GBla GDra GSpe MBar MBri MCra MGos MOke MPla NHea NHol NWin WGre
– 'Mrs Sam Doncaster'	CNCN COCH CRiv MBar MCra WGre
– 'Myretoun Ruby'	Widely available
– 'Orient'	COCH
– 'Pallida'	COCH GPen
– 'Pink Beauty '	See E. *c.* 'Pink Pearl'
§ – 'Pink Pearl'	CNCN COCH EDen GPen MBar WGre
– 'Pink Spangles'	Widely available
– 'Pirbright Rose'	COCH EDen ENHC MBri MCra MPla
– 'Porter's Red'	EDen
– 'Praecox Rubra'	CB&S COCH EDen ENHC GAng GBla GDra GPen IJoh LGro MBar MBri MCra MGos MOke MPla NBar NHol NKay NWin SHil WRid
– 'Prince of Wales'	CNCN COCH EDen ENHC MCra
– 'Queen Mary'	CNCN EDen ENHC MCra
– 'Queen of Spain'	CRiv EDen ENHC GPen MBri MCra MOke
– 'R B Cooke'	CNCN COCH EDen ENHC MBar MBri NHea NWin SPla WGre
¶ – 'Red Rover'	EDen
– 'Rosalind Schorn'	COCH
– 'Rosy Gem'	EDen MBar MCra SPla WRid
– 'Rubinteppich'	COCH EDen MBri
– 'Ruby Glow'	CNCN COCH EBre EDen ENHC ENot GAng GBla GPen GSpe IJoh LGro MBal MBar MBri MCra MOke NGre NHol NKay NRoo SHil SPla
§ – 'Sherwood Creeping'	EDen ENHC MBar MCra NHol
♦ – 'Sherwoodii'	See E. *c.* 'Sherwood Creeping'
– 'Smart's Heath'	ENHC GPen
– 'Snow Queen'	CMac CNCN COCH EDen ENHC GPen MBar MCra NBar NWin WGre
– 'Spring Cottage Crimson'	COCH EDen MBar
– 'Springwood Pink'	Widely available
– 'Springwood White'	Widely available
– 'Startler'	COCH ENHC MBar MCra NKay NWin SPla
– 'Sunshine Rambler'	CNCN COCH CRiv EDen EPot GPen MBar MCra MGos NHea NWin WGre
– 'Thomas Kingscote'	CNCN COCH ENHC MBar
– 'Tybesta Gold'	CNCN COCH
– 'Viking'	COCH IJoh
– 'Vivellii'	Widely available
¶ – 'Vivellii Aurea'	EDen
– 'Walter Reisert'	COCH EDen
– 'Wanda'	COCH EDen MBar
¶ – 'Wentwood Red'	EDen
– 'Westwood Yellow'	CNCN COCH EBre EDen ENHC GAng GBla MBar MBri NHol SPla
– 'Winter Beauty'	CNCN COCH GRei IDai IJoh MBri MCra MOke MPla NBar NHol NKay NWin SHil WGre
– 'Winter Gold'	COCH
cerinthoides	CSun
ciliaris	NLan
– 'Aurea'	CMac CNCN EDen ENHC GPen MBar NWin WGre

– 'Camla'	ENHC GPen MBar MCra WGre
– 'Corfe Castle'	CMac CNCN CRiv EDen ENHC GPen IJoh MBar MCra NWin WGre
– 'David McClintock'	CMac CNCN ENHC GPen MBar MGos NWin WGre
– 'Egdon Heath'	EDen WGre
– 'Globosa'	CNCN ENHC WGre
– 'Mrs C H Gill'	CMac CNCN ENHC GPen MBal SHil WGre
– 'Stapehill'	WGre
– 'Stoborough'	CMHG CNCN CRiv EDen ENHC MBal MBar MCra SHil
– 'White Wings'	CNCN EDen ENHC GPen
– 'Wych'	GPen WGre
cinerea	NLan
– 'A E Mitchell'	MGos
– ***alba***	CMac GRei
– 'Alba Major'	MBal MBar WGre
– 'Alba Minor'	CNCN EBre EDen GAng GPen GSpe MBal MBar MBri MCra MOke MPlt NHea NHol NKay NRoo SHil WGre WRid
– 'Ann Berry'	CNCN EDen ENHC MBar MCra WGre
– 'Apple Blossom'	WGre
– 'Apricot Charm'	EDen GAng GPen MBar WGre
– 'Ashgarth Garnet'	MBar WGre
– 'Atrococcinea'	CB&S
– 'Atropurpurea'	CNCN MBar MCra NWin
– 'Atrorubens'	CMac CRiv EDen ENHC GPen GRei GSpe MBar MCra NKay SHil
– 'Atrosanguinea'	CNCN ENHC GAng GBla GSpe MBar MCra MGos NWin WGre WRid
– 'Atrosanguinea Smith's Variety'	EBre EDen SHil
– 'Baylay's Variety'	EDen MBar
– 'Blossom Time'	MBar
– 'C D Eason'	Widely available
– 'C G Best'	CMac CNCN EDen ENHC GBla GPen IDai MBal MBar NKay WGre
– 'Cairn Valley'	EDen GSpe
– 'Caldy Island'	MBar NHea NWin
– 'Carnea'	GPen
– 'Carnea Underwood's Variety'	EDen
– 'Cevennes'	CMac CNCN CRiv EDen ENHC GAng GSpe IDai MBar MBri MCra MGos MOke MPlt NKay SHil WGre
– 'Cindy'	CNCN EBre EDen ENHC GSpe MBal MBar MBri MCra MOke NHea
– 'Coccinea'	ENHC GRei IDai WGre
– 'Colligan Bridge'	GPen MBar
– 'Constance'	EDen ENHC MBar MCra
– 'Contrast'	GSpe MBar WGre
¶ – 'Daphne Maginess'	CNCN
– 'Domino'	CB&S CNCN ENHC GBla GPen MBar MBri MGos MOke SHil WBod
– 'Duncan Fraser'	CNCN EDen ENHC GSpe MBar
– 'Dunwood Sport'	MBar
– 'Eden Valley'	CMac CNCN EBre EDen ENHC GAng GBla GPen GSpe MBar MCra MGos NHea NKay NRoo SHil WGre WRid
– 'England'	ENHC
– 'Fiddler's Gold'	CNCN CRiv EBre ENHC GAng GBla GPen MBar MBri MCra MOke MPlt NHol NWin
– 'Flamingo'	EDen WGre
– 'Foxhollow Mahogany'	EBre EDen ENHC GPen GSpe MBal MBar NWin WGre WRid
– 'Frances'	EDen ENHC GBla NHea
– 'G Osmond'	ENHC GPen MBar MCra MOke
– 'Glasnevin Red'	MBar WGre
– 'Glencairn'	GAng GPen MBar MBri NHol NWin
– 'Godrevy'	EDen
*– 'Golden Charm'	MPlt NHol NKay
– 'Golden Drop'	Widely available
– 'Golden Hue'	EDen ENHC GAng GPen GSpe IJoh MBar MBri MCra MOke NHea NWin SHil WGre WRid
– 'Golden Sport'	MBri MGos
– 'Grandiflora'	MBar
– 'Guernsey Lime'	EDen ENHC MBar
– 'Guernsey Plum'	EDen
– 'Guernsey Purple'	EDen
– 'Hardwick's Rose'	CNCN MBar
– 'Harry Fulcher'	CNCN EDen ENHC MBri MOke
– 'Heidebrand'	GPen MBar
– 'Herman Dijkhuizen'	EDen
– 'Honeymoon'	ENHC GSpe MBar
– 'Hookstone Lavender'	ENHC GPen GSpe MCra
– 'Hookstone White'	CNCN EBre EDen ENHC GBla GDra GPen IJoh MBal MBar NHea NKay WGre WRid
– 'Jack London'	CNCN EDen
– 'Janet'	CNCN EDen ENHC MBar MGos NWin WGre
*– 'John Ardron'	WGre
– 'John Eason'	EDen ENHC MCra NHol
– 'Joseph Murphy'	EBre EDen GAng GBla GSpe MBar WGre
– 'Josephine Ross'	GPen GSpe MBar NHea NWin WGre
– 'Joyce Burfitt'	CNCN ENHC WGre
– 'Katinka'	CNCN EBre EDen ENHC GRei MBar NHol WGre
¶ – 'Kerry Cherry'	EDen
– 'Knap Hill Pink'	CNCN EDen ENHC GAng GBla MBar MCra NHea WGre
– 'Lady Skelton'	MBar
– 'Lavender Lady'	MCra NWin
– 'Lilac Time'	ENHC GAng GSpe MBar MCra
– 'Lilacina'	EDen ENHC GSpe MBar MBri MOke
– 'Lime Soda'	CNCN EDen ENHC MBri
¶ – 'Lorna Anne Hutton'	EDen
– 'Miss Waters'	EDen MBar NWin

– 'Mrs Dill'	ENHC MBar
– 'Mrs E A Mitchell'	EDen MBri MOke
– 'Mrs Ford'	ENHC GAng GPen MBar
– 'My Love'	EBre EDen ENHC IJoh MBar MBri MOke NHea WBod
– 'Nell'	GPen MBar
– 'Newick Lilac'	EDen MBar MBri MOke
– 'Novar'	NWin
– 'Old Rose'	MCra
– 'P S Patrick'	CNCN EDen ENHC GAng GBla GPen GSpe IJoh MBal MBar MGos NHea NKay NWin SHil SPla WRid
– 'Pallas'	GSpe IJoh
– 'Pentreath'	EDen ENHC GPen MBar MBri MOke NHea NWin WBod
– 'Pink Foam'	GBla GPen MBar
– 'Pink Ice'	CB&S CMac CNCN EBre EDen ENHC GAng GBla GDra GPen GRei GSpe IJoh MBar MBri MCra MGos MOke MPlt NHea NHol NRoo NWin WGre
– 'Pink Lace'	CRiv
– 'Plummer's Seedling'	EDen GAng GBla GSpe MBar WRid
– 'Prostrate Lavender'	EDen ENHC GPen MBal
– 'Providence'	MCra
– 'Purple Beauty'	EBre EDen ENHC GBla GSpe IJoh MBar MBri MCra MGos MOke NHea NHol NWin WGre
– 'Purple Robe'	CMac ENHC
– 'Purpurea'	GPen
– 'Pygmaea'	GBla MBar
– 'Red Pentreath'	EDen
– 'Rijneveld'	EDen
– 'Robert Michael'	EDen
– 'Rock Pool'	EBre GSpe MBal MBar MCra NWin WGre
– 'Romiley'	EDen ENHC MBar MBri MOke
– 'Rosabella'	CNCN EDen ENHC MBar NHea
– 'Rose Queen'	CMac EDen GSpe NKay NWin WGre WRid
– 'Rosea'	EDen ENHC GAng GPen GSpe MCra SHil WGre
– 'Rozanne Waterer'	CMac NWin
– 'Ruby'	CMac CNCN EDen ENHC GAng GBla GSpe MBar MCra
– 'Sandpit Hill'	MBar WGre
– 'Schizopetala'	CNCN EDen GPen MBar
– 'Sea Foam'	ENHC MBar
– 'Sherry'	CMac CNCN EDen ENHC GAng GBla GPen GRei GSpe MBar WGre
¶ – 'Smith's Lawn'	EDen
– 'Snow Cream'	EDen GPen MBar
– 'Splendens'	EDen ENHC
– 'Startler'	CB&S ENHC GSpe MBri MCra MOke NKay
– 'Stephen Davis'	CNCN EBre EDen ENHC GAng GBla GPen GSpe MBal MBar MBri MCra MOke MPlt NHol NRoo SPla WBod WGre
¶ – 'Sue Lloyd'	EDen
¶ – 'Summer Gold'	CNCN MPlt

– 'Tilford'	ENHC
– 'Tom Waterer'	MBar NWin
– 'Velvet Knight'	CMac CNCN EBre ENHC GAng GBla GPen GSpe IDai IJoh MBal MBar MBri MCra MOke NHol NKay NWin SHil WBod WGre WRid
– 'Victoria'	CMac MBar WGre
– 'Vivienne Patricia'	ENHC GAng GBla GPen GSpe MBar MCra NWin
– 'W G Notley'	EDen ENHC
– 'White Dale'	EBre EDen MBar MCra NHea WGre
– 'Windlebrooke'	EBre EDen ENHC GPen MBar MCra NHea WGre
– 'Wine'	MCra
¶ ***colorans***	CSun
¶ ***conspicua***	CSun
cruenta	CSun EDen
curviflora	CSun EDen
x ***darleyensis*** 'Ada S Collings'	CNCN COCH EBre EDen ENHC GAng GBla MBal MBar MCra MPla NHea NWin
– 'Alba'	See E. x ***d.*** 'Silberschmelze'
– 'Archie Graham'	EDen
– 'Arthur Johnson'	Widely available
– 'Cherry Stevens'	See E. x ***d.*** 'Furzey'
– 'Darley Dale'	CMac CNCN COCH EBre EDen ENHC ENot GBla GPen GSpe MBal MBar MBri MCra MOke MPla NGre NHol NRoo SHil SPla WGre WRid
¶ – 'Dunreggan'	EDen
– 'Dunwood Splendour'	MBar
– 'Erecta'	EDen
§ – 'Furzey'	Widely available
– 'George Rendall'	CB&S CMac COCH EDen ENHC GAng GDra GPen GSpe MBri MCra MPla NGre NHea NHol SHil SPla WGre WRid
– 'Ghost Hills'	CNCN COCH EBre EDen ENHC GAng GDra MBal MBar MBri MOke MPla NGre NHea NHol NRoo NWin SPla WBod WGre WRid
– 'J W Porter'	CNCN COCH EBre EDen ENHC EPot GAng GBla GPen IJoh MBal MBar MBri MCra MOke NGre NHea NHol NWin WRid
§ – 'Jack H Brummage'	Widely available
– 'James Smith'	COCH ENHC MBar MCra
– 'Jenny Porter'	CMac CNCN COCH EDen ENHC GPen MBar MBri MCra MOke NHea NHol NWin WGre WRid
– 'Kramer's Rote'	COCH EDen NHea SPla
– 'Margaret Porter'	CMHG CNCN COCH EDen ENHC GAng IJoh MBri MCra MPla NGre NHea NHol WGre WRid
– 'Mary Helen'	EDen NHol
– 'Norman R Webster'	NWin

§ – 'Silberschmelze' ('Molten Silver')	Widely available
– 'W G Pine'	COCH
– 'White Glow'	CNCN COCH EDen ENHC MBal MBri MCra NGre NHea NHol WGre WRid
– 'White Perfection'	COCH EDen MBar MBri SPla WGre WRid
densifolia	CSun
discolor	CSun EDen
doliiformis	CSun EDen
§ ***erigena***	EBre ELan ENot SBar SHil SReu
– 'Alba'	CMac COCH ENHC MBar NWin
– 'Alba Compacta'	COCH GPen
– 'Brian Proudley'	CNCN COCH EDen ENHC MBar NHea WRid
– 'Brightness'	CB&S CMac CNCN EBre EDen ENHC EPot GAng GBla GPen MBal MBar MBri MCra MOke MWat NHea NKay NWin SHil WRid
– 'Coccinea'	COCH ENHC NWin
– 'Ewan Jones'	COCH EDen ENHC IOrc MBar
– 'Glauca'	ENHC GPen
– 'Golden Lady'	CMac CNCN COCH EBre EDen ENHC EPot GAng GPen MBar MBri MGos MOke NHol SPla WGre WRid
– 'Hibernica'	GPen
¶ – 'Hibernica Alba'	MBar
– 'Irish Dusk'	CMHG CNCN COCH EBre EDen ENHC GAng GBla GPen IJoh MBar MBri MCra MGos MOke NHea NHol NWin SHil SPla WGre WRid
– 'Irish Salmon'	CB&S CMac CNCN COCH GPen IJoh MBal MBar NKay NWin
– 'Irish Silver'	COCH GPen MBar MBri NWin
– 'Mrs Paris's Lavender'	WRid
– 'Mrs Paris's Red'	WRid
– 'Mrs Paris's White'	WRid
– 'Nana Alba'	COCH GPen MBar MCra
– 'Rosea'	ENHC MBar NWin
– 'Rubra'	MCra NKay
– 'Rubra Compacta'	ENHC
– 'Superba'	CMac CNCN COCH EDen ENHC ENot GPen MBal MBar MCra MGos MOke NHea NHol NKay NWin SHil SPla WGre WRid
– 'W T Rackliff'	CB&S CNCN COCH EBre EDen ENHC ENot EPot GAng GBla GPen MBal MBar MBri MCra MGos MOke NHea NHol NKay NWin SHil SPla WGre
– 'W T Rackliff Variegated'	ENHC
glandulosa	EDen WBod
gracilis	EDen MBri
– red	CSun
hibernica	See E. ***erigena***
x ***hyemalis*** 'Limelight'	EDen
lusitanica	CB&S CMac CNCN COCH CPle EDen ELan MBar NHea NHol SHil SPer SPla SSpi WBod WRid
– 'George Hunt'	CNCN EDen ELan ENHC NHol SPer
mackayana	NLan
– 'Ann D Frearson'	EDen
– 'Dr Ronald Gray'	CNCN EDen ENHC GAng GPen MBar MBri MCra MOke WGre WRid
¶ – 'Galicia'	EDen
– 'Lawsoniana'	ENHC SHil
– 'Maura'	EDen ENHC
– 'Plena'	CMHG CRiv EDen ENHC GPen MBal MBar MBri MOke WGre
– 'Shining Light'	EDen SPla
– 'William M'Calla'	ENHC
mammosa	EDen
manipuliflora	COCH EDen GPen MBar SPla
– 'Aldburgh'	COCH
¶ – 'Korcula'	EDen
manipuliflora anthura 'Corfu'	COCH
– – 'Don Richards'	COCH EDen
– – 'Ian Cooper'	COCH EDen
¶ ***manipuliflora*** x ***vagans*** 'Elegant Spike'	EDen
– 'Heaven Scent'	COCH EDen
– 'Valerie Griffiths'	COCH EDen
¶ ***mauritanica***	EDen
mediterranea	See E. ***erigena***
¶ ***mollis***	EDen
multiflora	EDen
pageana	CSun EDen
persoluta	CSun
¶ ***perspicua***	CSun
♦ x ***praegeri***	See E. x ***stuartii*** 'Connemara'
scoparia 'Lionel Woolner'	EDen
§ – 'Minima'	EDen ENHC MBar
– 'Pumila'	See E. ***s.*** 'Minima'
sessiflora	CSun LHop
speciosa	CSun EDen
§ x ***stuartii***	CMHG ENHC GPen MBar
§ – 'Connemara'	EDen MCra
– 'Irish Lemon'	CMHG CNCN EDen ENHC GAng GDra GPen GSpe MBar MBri MCra NHol NKay NWin SPla WBod WGre WRid
– 'Irish Orange'	EDen ENHC GAng GSpe MBar MBri MCra NHol NKay SPla WGre
– 'Stuartii'	CNCN EDen MCra
subdivaricata	CSun EDen
§ ***terminalis***	CNCN COCH EDen ENHC ENot EPot GAng IOrc MBal MBar MCra NHea NHol NWin SHil SPer SPla WSHC
– ***stricta***	See E. ***terminalis.***
– 'Thelma Woolner'	CMac CNCN COCH ENHC MBar NHol WGre
tetralix	CKin NLan WCla

¶ – 'Afternoon' EDen
– 'Alba' EDen
– 'Alba Mollis' Widely available
– 'Ardy' ENHC
– 'Bala' CNCN EDen
– 'Bartinney' MBar
– 'Con Underwood' CMac CNCN CRiv EDen ENHC ENot GAng GBla GPen GSpe MBal MBar MBri MCra MOke NKay NRoo SHil WBod WGre WRid
– 'Daphne Underwood' NKay NWin WGre
¶ – 'Darleyensis' CNCN
– 'Delta' EDen ENHC MBar
– 'Foxhome' EDen ENHC GPen MBar NWin
– 'Hailstones' ENHC MBar NWin
– 'Helma' EDen ENHC
– 'Hookstone Pink' CNCN CRiv EBre EDen ENHC GPen MBal MCra MOke NKay NRoo NWin WGre
– 'Ken Underwood' CNCN ENHC GDra GPen MBar NKay NWin WGre
– 'L E Underwood' CMac ENHC EPot GAng GPen MBal MBar MCra NHol NKay NRoo NWin SHil WGre WRid
– 'Melbury White' CNCN EDen ENHC GPen MBar NWin
– 'Morning Glow' See E. x ***watsonii*** 'F White'
– 'Pink Glow' MCra SHil
– 'Pink Star' CMac CNCN CRiv EBre ENHC GAng GBla GSpe MBal MBar NHol NKay NWin SPla WGre WRid
– 'Rubra' GPen
§ – 'Ruby's Variety' GPen MBar NWin
– 'Ruby's Velvet' See E. ***t.*** 'Ruby's Variety'
– 'Ruth's Gold' MBar MBri NHol WGre
– 'Salmon Seedling' GPen
– 'Silver Bells' CMac ENHC GPen MBar WGre
– 'Swedish Yellow' SPla
¶ – 'Tina' EDen
– 'White House' EDen
¶ ***transparens*** CSun
umbellata CNCN EDen ENHC GAng GPen MBal MBar NWin SHil WGre
vagans alba MBal
– 'Birch Glow' CRiv EDen ENHC NWin WGre
– 'Cornish Cream' EBre EDen ENHC GPen MBar NHea NHol NRoo NWin WBod WGre
– 'Cream' CNCN EDen ENHC IDai MCra MOke SHil
– 'Diana Hornibrook' CNCN EDen ENHC GSpe MBal MBar MBri MOke NKay NRoo WGre
– 'Fiddlestone' CNCN EDen ENHC GPen GSpe MBar MCra NHea NKay NWin SHil WGre
– 'French White' CNCN EDen MBar
– 'George Underwood' CRiv EDen ENHC GPen MBar WBod WGre
– 'Grandiflora' CRiv EDen GPen IJoh MBal MBar MCra NHol NWin SPla WGre
– 'Holden Pink' CNCN CRiv EDen MBri MCra MOke SPla
– 'Hookstone Rosea' MBar
– 'Ida M Britten' EDen MBar MCra
– 'J C Fletcher' EDen
– 'Kevernensis Alba' CRiv EDen ENHC GPen IDai MBar MCra NHea NHol
– 'Lilacina' CMac EDen GSpe MBar
– 'Lyonesse' Widely available
– 'Miss Waterer' EDen MBar
– 'Mrs D F Maxwell' Widely available
– 'Mrs S D Donaldson' GPen
– 'Nana' EDen MBal MBar NHol
– 'Pallida' CRiv EDen ENHC MCra NHol
– 'Peach Blossom' MBar MCra
– 'Pyrenees Pink' CMac CNCN EDen GBla MBal MBar MBri MOke NHol WGre
– 'Rosea' MCra
– 'Rubra' CNCN EDen GBla MBal MBar MCra
– 'Rubra Grandiflora' ENHC
– 'Saint Keverne' CMac CNCN EBre EDen ENHC GAng GBla GPen MBal MBar MBri MCra MGos MOke NHea NHol NKay NRoo SHil SPla WGre WRid
– 'Summer Time' CNCN EDen GPen MBar
– 'Valerie Proudley' Widely available
– 'Viridiflora' EDen MBar
– 'White Lady' ENHC MBar NWin
– 'White Rocket' EDen MBar
– 'White Spire' EDen
¶ – 'Yellow John' GBla
x ***veitchii*** GPen MBal
– 'Exeter' CNCN COCH EDen MBar MCra SHil WGre
– 'Gold Tips' CNCN EDen ENHC GAng MBal MBar MBri MCra MGos MOke SPla WGre WRid
– 'Pink Joy' EDen ENHC MBal MBri MOke NBar NHol WGre
versicolor CSun
x ***watsonii*** CMHG
– 'Dawn' CNCN EDen GAng GDra GPen GSpe MBal MBar MBri MCra NHol NKay NWin SHil WGre WRid
§ – 'F White' ENHC GPen MBar NHol
– 'Gwen' CNCN CRiv EDen MBar
– 'H Maxwell' CNCN CRiv GPen GSpe MBal MCra NKay NWin WGre
– 'Rachel' MBal MCra
– 'Truro' EDen
x ***williamsii*** NKay
– 'Gwavas' CRiv EDen EPot GAng GPen MBar MCra WGre
– 'P D Williams' CNCN CRiv EDen MBal MBar MCra NWin SHil WGre WRid

ERIGERON † (Compositae)

acer CKin MSal WCla

'Adria'	CKel EBre SPer
¶ *allocatus*	NRed
alpinus	GCHN LGan MCas NGre SFis
'Amity'	EOrc SPer
¶ *annuus*	CBre
atticus	MHig
aurantiacus	CHan CSam ECtt LGan MPit MRav MWgw NCat NOak NTow WCar WHil WPer
aureus	See HAPLOPAPPUS ***brandegeei***
'Azurfee' ('Azure Fairy')	EBar ELan MBro MFir NOak NRoo WHen WHoo WPer WWin
* 'Blaauw'	WCot
borealis	NRya WEas WHil
¶ *caespitosus*	NHol
'Canary Bird'	See HAPLOPAPPUS ***brandegeei*** 'C.B.'
'Charity'	CGle CKel CSco SPer
chrysopsidis brevifolius	MBro WDav
¶ – 'Grand Ridge'	EPot
compactus JCA 10933	WDav
compositus	CHar ELan GLoc MHig NGre NHol SIng WCar WDav WHil WOMN WPer
§ – *discoideus*	CLew EPad GLoc SIng
– 'Lavender Dwarf'	NHol
delicatus	SIng
'Dignity'	CKel CShe EBre EFou EGol ELan ERou GCHN IDai MWat SChu SCro SFis WEas
'Dimity'	CGle ECha EFou ERou SFis WRus WWin
'Dunkelste Aller' ('Darkest of All')	CHar CSco CSev EBre ELan ENot ERou MBri MWgw SCro SPer WCot WEas WHil WOld WRus
elegantulus	SIng WDav
'Felicity'	MWgw WOld
¶ 'Festivity '	SFis
¶ *flettii*	NCat
'Foersters Liebling'	CKel CSev EFou ENot MUlv MWat MWgw
'Four Winds'	CLew CShe ELan EPad MCas SMad WPer
'Gaiety'	CSco LHop NSti SChu SPer
* *glaucifolius*	NWCA
glaucus	CFis CMer EPad IDai MCot MWgw NRed NVic
– *albus*	WHil WPer
– 'Elstead Pink'	CShe WEas
– *roseus*	CB&S CMer MBal
– 'Sennen'	CElw
* 'H E Beale'	LHil
¶ *humilis*	SIng
§ *karvinskianus*	CFis CHan CLew CTre ECha IDai LHop MCot MPar MWat NKay NRed NSti SAxl SCro SDix SFis SIng SPer SPla WCla WEas WHil
leiomerus	MCas MHig NKay NRed NTow SIng WCla WOMN
linearis	NRed WDav
'Mrs F H Beale'	SCro
mucronatus	See E. ***karvinskianus***
multiradiatus	CLew WPer
§ – BMW 18	MBal
nanus	MBro MHig SIng WDav
peregrinus	WEas
philadelphicus	CBre CGle GPla SAxl WRus
'Pink Jewel'	See E. 'Rosa Juwel'
pinnatisectus	MBro NRed NWCA WDav WPer
* *plenus*	WHil
'Prosperity'	CGle CKel CShe EFou WOld
'Quakeress'	CGle CKel CSam EFou EMon EOrc SWas WCot
radicatus	NNrd NRed
¶ *rhydbergii*	WDav
'Rosa Juwel' ('Pink Jewel')	CHar CSam EBar EPad GAbr GCHN LHil MFir NBar NNrd NOak NRoo WHen WPer
'Rosa Triumph' ('Pink Triumph')	ERou
'Rotes Meer'	ELan
rotundifolius 'Caerulescens'	See BELLIS ***rotundifiolia*** 'C.'
N *salsuginosus*	NOak
'Schwarzes Meer' ('Black Sea')	EBre EFou EGol EOrc ERou LHop MUlv NSti SPer
'Serenity'	CSco SFis
simplex	CLew EPad GLoc ITim LHil MBro MCas MWat NGre NHol NRed NTow SIng WDav WWin
'Sincerity'	CSco CShe
¶ 'Snow White'	LHop
¶ 'Sommerneuschnee'	MBri
speciosus	MPit NNrd WHil
¶ sp. Idaho	NRed
'Strahlenmeer'	EOrc
¶ *thunbergii*	WPer
trifidus	See E. ***compositus discoideus***
uniflorus	CLew NRed NRya NWCA
'Unity'	MWat
vagus	WPer
– JCA 8911	NRed WDav WHil
'Viridis'	MBal
'Wuppertal'	SFis

ERINACEA (Leguminosae)

§ *anthyllis*	EPot GLoc MBro NHol SHil SIng SSpi WDav
pungens	See E. ***anthyllis***

ERINUS (Scrophulariaceae)

alpinus	Widely available
– *albus*	CBot CRiv CSun GGar GHig MBro MCas MFir MPar NHol NKay NNrd NTow SIng WCla WDav WHoo WPer
– dark purple	NKay

– 'Dr Hähnle'	CSun EBre GEdr MBro MFir MHig MPit MRav NHol NKay NNrd SIng WDav WHoo WPer
– 'Mrs Charles Boyle'	CKel GDra GHig MBro MCas NKay WHoo WOld
¶ – pink form	SIng

ERIOBOTRYA (Rosaceae)

F *japonica*	CBot CGre CHEx CLan CPle CSun ERea ESim IJoh LGre MBri SArc SBor SDea SGar SHil SLon SMad SSpi SSta WWat
F – 'Benlehr'	ESim
F – 'Mrs Cookson'	ESim

ERIOCEPHALUS (Compositae)

ERIOGONUM (Polygonaceae)

¶ *caespitosum*	NTow
flavum	WPat WPer
¶ – *xanthum*	WDav
jamesii	WDav WPat
¶ *kennedyi* JCA 11697	WDav
ovalifolium nivale	WDav
umbellatum	ECha EFol NHol WPer
– *subalpinum*	MHig
– *torreyanum*	EPot GLoc MBro MHig NHol WDav WPat

ERIOPHORUM (Cyperaceae)

angustifolium	CBWG EHon EWav LMay MSta
latifolium	LMay MSta
scheuchzeri	NNrd

ERIOPHYLLUM (Compositae)

lanatum	CFis CLew EBar LHil MFir MWat MWgw NCat NSti NVic SBla SChu SIng WPer WWin

ERITRICHIUM (Boraginaceae)

¶ *howardii*	GLoc
nanum	GCHN
§ *rupestre*	SWas
strictum	See E. ***rupestre***

ERODIUM † (Geraniaceae)

absinthoides	CLew LRHS
acaule	GCHN NRog NRoo
alnifolium	GCHN
balearicum	See E. x ***variabile*** 'Album'
battandierianum	GCHN SCou
boissieri	GCHN
brachycarpum	GCHN
carvifolium	CCor CElw CLew GCHN SCou
§ *castellanum*	CCla EPad GCHN LGre LRHS NGre NHol NRog NRoo SAxl SCou
chamaedrioides	See E. ***reichardii***
N *cheilanthifolium*	GCHN GGar SIng
chium Guitt 88042202	GCHN
chrysanthum	Widely available
¶ – *sulphureum*	CHan
ciconium Guitt 85051602	GCHN
cicutarium cicutarium	GCHN
corsicum	CGle CSev EPot GLoc MHig MTho NCat NRog WAbe WOMN
– 'Album'	GCHN NHol WAbe
'County Park'	ECou
crinitum	GCHN
daucoides	See E. ***castellanum***
foetidum	GCHN NRog
N *glandulosum*	CHad CLew GCHN GLoc GWic LHop MPar NRar NRog NRya SAxl SBla SCou SWas WCar WEas WHal WHil WHoo WPer WSHC
§ *gruinum*	GCHN NSti SCou WEas WHCG WOMN
N *guttatum*	CGle CHad CHar CSun ECha EPot LHop MPla MWat NHol NKay NNrd SIng WAbe WHal WHea WHil
x *hybridum*	EFol GLoc WAbe WHal
hymenodes	See E. ***trifolium***
¶ 'Katherine Joy'	NRog
¶ x *kolbianum* 'Natasha'	GCHN NHol NRog
x *lindavicum* 'Charter House'	GCHN
macradenum	See E. ***glandulosum***
malacoides	GCHN
¶ *malviflorum*	SFis
manescavi	Widely available
'Merstham Pink'	GCHN GLoc NHol NRog NSti SAxl
moschatum Guitt 88041904	GCHN
munbyanum	GCHN
neuradifolium Guitt 86040601	GCHN
pelargoniiflorum	Widely available
N *petraeum*	CLew NGre NRoo WAbe WOld WThu
– 'Burgundy'	CElw WHCG
– *crispum*	See E. ***cheilanthifolium***
– *glandulosum*	See E. ***glandulosum***
– 'Pallidum'	CElw CSam
– *roseum*	GWic SBla WAbe WMar WPer WRus
'Pickering Pink'	GCHN NRog
pimpinellifolium	GCHN
'Rachel'	GCHN
recorderi	GCHN
§ *reichardii*	CElw CLew CRiv ESis GGar MBro MPla MTho NGre NHol NRar NRog NRoo SBla SCou SIng WCla WHal WOMN WThu
– cvs	See E. x ***variabile***
§ *rupestre*	CElw ECtt GWic MPar NKay NNor SFir SIng
salzmannii	See E. ***cicutarium cicutarium***
saxatile	GCHN
¶ x *sebaceum* 'Polly'	NSti
sibthorpianum	GLoc
'Stephanie'	GCHN

supracanum	See E. ***rupestre***
tordilioides	See E. ***gruinum***
trichomanifolium	MHig WHil
§ ***trifolium***	GWic NSti SCou WHCG
– Guitt 85051701	GCHN
*– ***montanum***	GCHN SCou
valentium	GCHN NRog
§ x ***variabile*** 'Album'	Widely available
– 'Bishop's Form'	CRiv CShe EMNN EPot ESis GHig MBro MHig MPla MPlt NGre NHol NNrd NRar NRog NRoo NSti NTow SAxl SIng WEas WHil WHoo WPat
– 'Flore Pleno'	CLew ELan ESis GCHN GLoc LHop MHig NCat NGre NHol NNrd NRog NRoo SAxl SIng WHil WHoo WOld WPer
– 'Roseum'	Widely available
¶ x ***wilkommianum***	NRog
* ***yahandierizanum***	GCHN

ERPETION (Violaceae)

reniforme	See VIOLA ***hederacea***

ERUCA (Cruciferae)

vesicaria sativa	CArn CSFH GPoy LHol MChe SIde WHer WOak

ERYNGIUM † (Umbelliferae)

§ ***agavifolium***	Widely available
alpinum	CB&S CCla CElw CGle CHad CHan CShe ECha EFou ERav GDra LSav MBal MBro MCot MTho MWgw NSti SAxl SChu SIng SPer WEas WHil
– 'Amethyst'	GWic LGre MBri MPar SFir WHil WSHC
– 'Holden Blue'	GWic
– 'Opal'	CShe MBri
– 'Superbum'	CBot ECro LGre MBro NRoo SBla SMad WDav
amethystinum	ECha EPad MBri
billardieri	CSun ECro EFou LGan
bourgatii	Widely available
– 'Oxford Blue'	MPar NTow SFir WEas WOMN
bromeliifolium	See E. ***agavifolium***
¶ ***caeruleum***	CHan CSun
I 'Calypso'	EBre MUlv
campestre	NHol
§ ***decaisneanum***	CCla CElw GWic IBlr MUlv NHol NSti SDix SIgm
§ ***eburneum***	ECha ECro LGre SSpi
giganteum	Widely available
– 'Silver Ghost'	EMon SAxl
glaciale	SPou
maritimum	ECha LGre SFir
Miss Willmott's Ghost	See E. ***giganteum***
¶ ***nivale***	EPad
x ***oliverianum***	CHan CKel ECro ELan IDai LHop MBri MBro NHol SDix WDav WSHC WWin
pandanifolium	See E. ***decaisneanum***
paniculatum	See E. ***eburneum***
planum	CElw CGle CHad CHan CHar CLew CSco CSun ECha EGol ELan ERou GCHN GPla IDai LSav MFir NGre NHol NNor NRoo NSti SPer WEas
– 'Blauer Zwerg' ('Blue Dwarf')	CBow CSco EFou MUlv
¶ – 'Flüela'	EFou
¶ – 'Seven Seas'	WPer
proteiflorum	ECro LGre SMad
spinalbum	CFor ECro MBro MTho SSpi WDav WEas
x ***tripartitum***	Widely available
variifolium	Widely available
¶ ***yuccifolium***	ECro MSal WHil
x ***zabelii***	ECro ELan GWic LHop NBir
– 'Jewel'	EMon
– 'Violetta'	GWic MBri

ERYSIMUM † (Cruciferae)

alpinum	CRiv CSam MBal WHil WHoo
arenicola torulosum	See E. ***torulosum***
¶ 'Aunt May'	SAxl
¶ 'Bicolor'	EFou NPer
'Bowles' Mauve'	Widely available
'Bredon'	EDon EFou ELan EMon LHop MRav NPer WRus WTay
'Butterscotch'	CBre CElw CGle CHar CMHG CSam LGre LHop MFir MWgw NPer NSti SAxl WHil
capitatum	MDHE NKay WOMN
'Changeling'	LRHS NPer
'Cheerfulness'	CHan
* 'Chelsea Jacket'	EDon EFou GAbr
'Chequers'	CSun ELan NHol WOMN WPer WRus
'Chevithorne'	See CHEIRANTHUS ***cheiri*** 'C.'
concinnum	LHop MDHE
'Constant Cheer'	CBre CHar CLew CMHG CRow CShe GAbr MRav NSti SAxl WHil WKif WMar WPer WRus
* 'Dorothy Elmhirst'	NSti
'Emm's Variety'	NHol
'Gold Flame'	MCas MWat
'Golden Gem'	GGar MDHE SBla
'Golden Jubilee'	NTow
§ ***helveticum***	CSun GAbr NCat NOrc NTow WOMN
'Jacob's Jacket'	CCot CGle CSam EFou EPot GAbr GCHN LHop MCot NPer SAxl SChu WPer WWin
* 'John Codrington'	EMon LGre NPer NSti SBla SChu WTay
'Jubilee Gold'	ELan MCas
kotschyanum	MCas SBla
'Lady Roborough'	CRow
linifolium	CHad MDHE NCat WHil
– 'Variegatum'	Widely available
'Miss Hopton'	CFis

'Moonlight'	CB&S CFis CGle CGre CHar CMHG CRow EDon EFou EMon ERou LGre MTho MWgw NNor NSti NVic SAxl SDix WEas WHil WOMN WOld WPer
'Mrs L K Elmhurst'	CFis CHil CRow GAbr LHop NSti
mutabile	CB&S CFis CHad CMHG CShe EMon EOrc GAbr NCat NPer SCro SSvw WEas WOMN
– 'Variegatum'	CHar EFol ELan EMon LHop NPer WEas
nivale	CCor
'Orange Flame'	CLew CMHG CRiv CRow ELan EPad GAbr GHig GLoc MHig MPla MRav NKay NRoo NSti NTow SIng SSus WDav WPer
perovskianum	WEas
'Primrose'	EFol LGre LHop NSti WPer
§ *pulchellum*	CRiv MWat WEas WHil
pumilum	See E. ***helveticum***
'Rufus'	CCot CHil CMHG CPle CRow EDon ELan EMon EOrc GAbr LGre LHop MRav MTho NSti WEas WHil WMar WOMN
rupestre	See E. ***pulchellum***
§ *scoparium*	CSun ESis GWic LHop
§ *sempervirens*	CHan
'Sissinghurst Variegated'	See E. ***linifolium*** 'Variegatum'
'Sprite'	CLew CMHG CRow CShe EOrc EPot GAbr GWic LHop MHig MPla NKay NNrd WHil
¶ *suffrutescens*	MPlt
'Sunbright'	CHar GLoc MCas NNrd
'Sunshine'	ELan
§ *torulosum*	EPad NPer NSti
N 'Variegatum'	CB&S ERou LGre WWin
'Wenlock Beauty'	CHad CMHG EDon ELan GAbr LGre LHop MCot MTho MWgw NCat NSti SAxl SChu SPer SSvw WHil WMar WOMN WPer WRus
* *wheeleri*	CSun

ERYTHRAEA See **CENTAURIUM**

ERYTHRINA (Leguminosae)

crista-galli	CB&S CBot CCla CGre CHEx CPle CSun ERea SArc SHil SIgm SMad SSpi
lysistemon	See E. ***princeps***
¶ *princeps*	CPle

ERYTHRONIUM † (Liliaceae/Liliaceae)

§ *albidum*	CAvo GLoc LAma LBow NHol WChr
americanum	CAvo CBro CHEx EPot GEdr GLoc LAma LBow MSal NHol SOkd SSpi WChr WDav
californicum	CAvo CHEx WChr
caucasicum	CBro EPot LBow WChr
citrinum	EPot
'Citronella'	CBro EPar GLoc LAma LBow MBro NHol SIng WChr
cliftonii	See E. ***multiscapoideum*** Cliftonii group
dens-canis	CAvo CBro CHEx CRiv ECha ELan EPot ETub GEdr GLoc LAma LBow MBal MBri MHig MS&S MTho NHol SIng SLHN SPou SSpi WAbe WChr
– 'Frans Hals'	EPar EPot LAma MS&S NHol WChr
– *japonicum*	CBro EPot GEdr LAma LBow MS&S NHol WChr
– 'Lilac Wonder'	CBro EPar LAma WChr
– *niveum*	LAma WChr
*– 'Pajares Giant'	LRHS
– 'Pink Perfection'	EPar EPot LAma WChr
– 'Purple King'	EPar EPot LAma LBlo MS&S NHol WChr
– 'Rose Queen'	EPar EPot GLoc LAma MTho NHol WChr
– 'Snowflake'	EPar EPot LAma MS&S NHol WChr
– 'White Splendour'	CBro
hendersonii	LAma WChr WDav
'Jeannine'	LAma LRHS WChr
'Kondo'	CCla EPot GEdr GLoc LAma MHig MS&S NHol NSti SIng SSpi SSus WAbe WHil
mesochoreum	See E. ***albidum***
* 'Miss Jessup'	MPar
§ *multiscapoideum*	MHig WChr
– Cliftonii group	WChr
oregonum	EPar EPot MS&S
'Pagoda'	Widely available
purdyi	See E. ***multiscapoideum***
revolutum	CBro EPot IBlr LAma MS&S SSpi
– Johnsonii group	CFor MS&S WChr
'Rose Beauty'	CBro LAma
tuolumnense	CAvo CBro CFor CRiv EPar EPot GLoc LAma LBow MHig MS&S NHol SIng WAbe WChr
umbilicatum	WChr
'White Beauty'	CAvo CBro CCla CFor CRiv ECha EPar EPot GEdr GLoc ITim LAma LBlo LBow MBal MBri MHig MTho NHol SIng WAbe WChr WKif

ESCALLONIA † (Escalloniaceae)

'Alice'	CGre MBri SPer
'Apple Blossom'	Widely available
'Bantry Bay'	CB&S
§ *bifida*	CGre CPle SDix WSHC WTay WWat
'C F Ball'	CSco CTre ELan ENot GRei IOrc LBuc MBri MGos MR&S NRoo NWea SHil SMad WAbe
'Compacta Coccinea'	CB&S CLan
'Crimson Spire'	CB&S CLan CSco CShe ENot GRei LHop MGos MRav MWat NHol NNor SHil SLon SPer
'Dart's Rosy Red'	MBri
'Donard Beauty'	CSco ISea SHil

'Donard Brilliance'	ISea MGos MR&S SHil
'Donard Gem'	MBri SHil
'Donard Glory'	MR&S
'Donard Radiance'	CB&S CSco CShe ELan ENot IDai IJoh ISea MGos MR&S MRav MWat NHol NKay SHil SPer WSHC
'Donard Scarlet'	CGre
'Donard Seedling'	CB&S CBow CLan CMer CPle CSco ELan ENot IDai LBuc MBal MBri MR&S NNor NRoo NWea SHil SPla WAbe
'Donard Star'	CShe ENot IOrc MGos NHol SHil
'Donard Suprise'	NNor
'Donard White'	ISea
'Edinensis'	CB&S CMHG CSco ECtt ENot ISea MBar MBri MR&S NNor SHil SPla WWat
'Erecta'	CBow
'Glory of Donard'	CSco ENot
¶ 'Greenway'	CGre
'Gwendolyn Anley'	CMer CSco NTow SPer SPla WAbe WPer WWat WWeb
illinita	CGre
'Ingramii'	CGre CHan CMHG CSco SHil
'Iveyi'	Widely available
laevis	CGre
'Lanarth Hybrid'	CGre
'Langleyensis'	CB&S CGre CMer IJoh MBri MWat NNor NRoo NWea SHil WSHC
leucantha	CGre
macrantha	See E. *rubra m.*
montevidensis	See E. *bifida*
'Newryensis'	SPer
'Peach Blossom'	CGre CSco EBar ELan ENot MGos MRav SHil SPer
'Pink Elf'	MBri
'Pink Pearl'	CGre
'Pride of Donard'	CB&S CLan CSco IDai IOrc ISea LHop SHil WWeb
pulverulenta	CGre
¶ – G&K 4716	LSav
punctata	See E. *rubra*
'Rebecca'	CGre CMer
'Red Dwarf'	WAbe
'Red Elf'	CMHG CMer EBre ELan ERav IJoh ISea MBar MBri MGos MPla MWat NHol SHil SLon SPer SSta WPat
resinosa	CGre
revoluta	CGre
'Rose Queen'	IDai
rosea	CGre
§ *rubra*	CGre SPer
¶ – G&K 4672	LSav
– *macrantha*	CB&S CBow CBra CGre CHEx CMer CSco CTre GRei IDai IJoh ISea SArc SHil SLon SPer SPla WAbe WBod
– 'Pubescens'	SLon
– 'Pygmaea'	See E. *r.* 'Woodside'
¶ – *uniflora*	SDry
§ – 'Woodside'	CPle ELan ESis GAbr GLoc LHop MGos MR&S SHil SIng SSus WBod WHCG
'Saint Keverne'	CGre
'Slieve Donard'	ENot GRei MGos MR&S MRav NHol SHil
x *stricta* 'Harold Comber'	MUlv SDry
tucamenensis	SArc
virgata	CGre CMHG CPle SDix WWat
viscosa	CGre SSpi

EUCALYPTUS † (Myrtaceae)

acaciiformis	CArn
aggregata	CArn SArc WCel
¶ *approximans condocarpa*	WCel
archeri	MBal WCel
¶ *bicostata*	IOrc
camphora	CMHG WCel
cinerea	IOrc WCel
citriodora	LHol SIde WCel WPer
coccifera	CB&S CGre CHEx CMHG CSco GAbr IOrc MBal MFir SHil SLHN SSpi WCel WNor WWeb
consideniana	CArn
cordata	MBal WCel
crenulata	WCel
dalrympleana	CMHG CSam CSco ELan ENot IOrc MBal MGos MUlv SArc SHil SPer SPla SSta WCel WWeb
¶ *deanei*	WCel
delegatensis	CMHG IOrc MFir WCel
divaricata	See E. *gunnii*
ficifolia	LRHS SLon
fraxinoides	WCel
glaucescens	EBar SArc SPer WCel
globulus	CB&S CHEx ISea LHol MBal
¶ *goniocalyx*	WCel
§ *gregsoniana*	CMHG ISea WCel WWeb
§ *gunnii*	Widely available
– *divaricata*	SArc WCel
kitsoniana	MBal WCel
kybeanensis	WCel
leucoxylon	WCel
macarthurii	WCel
¶ *mannifera elliptica*	WCel
moorei	CBow
– *nana*	IBar WNor
muelleriana	CArn
neglecta	WCel
nicholii	CGre ERav WCel
nitens	MBal WCel WPat
§ *nitida*	CArn CMHG WCel WNor
parvifolia	CB&S LHop SArc SHil WCel WHer
pauciflora	IBar MBal MUlv SArc SHil WBod WCel WNor
– *debeuzevillei*	SArc WCel
– *nana*	See E. *gregsoniana*
– *niphophila*	Widely available
– *niphophila* 'Pendula'	WCel WWeb

perriniana	CB&S CHEx ELan ENot ERav IBlr MBal MUlv SArc SLHN SPer SPla WCel WNor WWeb
pulverulenta	WCel
¶ ***radiata***	WPer
regnans	CGre ISea MBal SLHN
risdonii	NTow WNor
rubida	IOrc WCel
simmondsii	See E. ***nitida***
stellulata	CMHG IOrc WCel
stuartiana	See E. ***ovata***
subcrenulata	WCel
urnigera	ISea SSta WCel WWeb
vernicosa	WCel
– ***johnstonii***	ERav IOrc SHil WCel WWeb
viminalis	CArn IOrc SLHN WCel

EUCHARIS (Liliaceae/Amaryllidaceae)

amazonica	LAma
grandiflora	LBow SW&B

EUCODONIA (Gesneriaceae)

'Adele'	NMos
andrieuxii	NMos
– 'Frances'	NMos
'Cornell'	NMos
§ ***ehrenbergii***	LTow
'Naomi'	LTow NMos WEfe
'Tintacoma'	NMos
§ ***verticillata***	LTow

EUCOMIS (Liliaceae/Hyacinthaceae)

§ ***autumnalis***	CAvo ECro LAma
bicolor	CAvo CChu CHEx CHar CKel EBak LAma LBow LHil MBri NSti SChu WEas
– ***alba***	LBow
– hybrids	EFou
§ ***comosa***	CAvo CB&S CHEx EBul LAma LBow LHop MBri
– purple form	EMon LGre
¶ ***pole-evansii***	CAvo CHEx
punctata	See E. ***comosa***
undulata	See E. ***autumnalis autumnalis***
zambesiaca	EBul LBow

EUCOMMIA (Eucommiaceae)

ulmoides	CMCN SHil WCoo

EUCRYPHIA † (Eucryphiaceae)

'Castlewellan'	ISea
cordifolia	CB&S CGre CLan CMHG CTrw ISea MBal SCog SHil SSpi WBod
– x ***lucida***	CB&S CCla CFor CMHG CSam CTre IOrc ISea MBal SCog SPer WBod
glutinosa	CB&S CCla CFor CLan CMHG ELan IBar ISea LHyd MBal MBri SCog SHil SPer SPla SReu SSpi SSta WBod WCoo WNor WWat
– ***pleniflora***	ELan ISea
x ***hillieri***	CFor
– 'Winton'	CGre ISea SSpi
x ***intermedia***	CGre CSam CTre ELan IDai IJoh SCog SDix SPer WWat
– 'Rostrevor'	CB&S CBow CCla CFor CLan CSco ELan ISea MBal SHil SLon SPer SSta WBod
lucida	CCla CFor ISea LHyd MBal MGos SHil SSta WBod WCoo WWat
– 'Pink Cloud'	ISea
milliganii	CB&S CBow CChu CCla CFor CMHG ELan ISea MBal SBor SCog SHil SPer SSpi SSta WBod WWat
moorei	CCla ISea MBal SArc SSpi SSta WBod
x ***nymansensis***	CB&S CBow CPle MBal MMth SArc SBar SBor SCog SPla SReu WBod
– 'George Graham'	ISea
– 'Mount Usher'	CGre IJoh IOrc ISea SPer
– 'Nymansay'	CB&S CBra CCla CFor CLan CMHG CSco EHar ELan IDai IJoh ISea LHyd MBar MBri MGos SDix SHil SLon SMad SPer SSta WAbe WMou
N 'Penwith'	CFor ISea MBal SSpi

EUGENIA (Myrtaceae)

uniflora	ESim

EUMORPHIA (Compositae)

canescens	WHer WOld
sericea	CHan MCot NNor

EUNOMIA See **AETHIONEMA**

EUODIA See **TETRADIUM**

EUONYMUS † (Celastraceae)

alatus	Widely available
¶ – ***apterus***	MPla
♦ – 'Ciliodentatus'	See E. ***a.*** 'Compactus'
§ – 'Compactus'	CChu EBre EHar EPla EPla MBlu MBri MPla SHil SPla WWat
americanus	SSpi
bungeanus	CCla CMCN EPla LSav SSpi WWat
– ***semipersistens***	EPla
cornutus quinquecornutus	MPar
europaeus	CArn CBra CKin CLnd CSco CShe ELan GRei LBuc NWea SHil SPer WCoo WMou
– 'Albus'	SHil
– 'Aucubifolius'	EPla
– 'Brilliant'	IDai
– ***intermedius***	ENot
– 'Red Cascade'	Widely available
fimbriatus	CB&S
§ ***fortunei***	EBre
– 'Canadale Gold'	MBri
– 'Carrierei'	SApp

– 'Coloratus'	CLan ENot MBar MR&S NRya SHil SPer SPla
– 'Croftway	SCro
– 'Dart's Blanket'	CCla ELan ENot MBri MRav SPer
– 'Emerald Charm'	SHil
– 'Emerald Cushion'	ENot NHol NTow SPer
– 'Emerald Gaiety'	Widely available
¶ – 'Emerald Surprise'	MBri
– 'Emerald 'n' Gold'	Widely available
*– 'Gold Spot'	SCro WPat
§ – 'Gold Tip'	CCla CPle EBre EFol ENot EPla IJoh MBar MGos MRav NHol SPer SReu SSta
– 'Golden Prince'	See E. *f.* 'Gold Tip'
*– 'Highdown'	LSav
– 'Kewensis'	CLew CMHG CMer CPle ENot MBar MCas MPla MRav MWat NTow SApp SArc SPer WWat
– 'Minimus'	EBre EGol EHal EPla ESis NHol SIng SPla WPer
– 'Sarcoxie'	CCla LSav
– 'Sheridan Gold'	CCla CHoe EBre EGol EPla ERav MPla MRav NHol SPer
– 'Silver Gem'	See E. *f.* 'Variegatus'
– 'Silver Pillar'	EBar ENot ERav ESis SHil
– 'Silver Queen'	Widely available
– 'Sunshine'	CKni CSco IJoh MBri MGos
– 'Sunspot'	CHoe CMHG CSco EBre EGol ELan EPla ERav IJoh LAbb MBar MBri MGos MR&S MRav NCat NTow SLon SMad SPer SPla SSta
§ – 'Variegatus'	CMHG EFol ELan ENot MBar MCas MCot NKay NNor SPer STre WBod
– 'Variegatus' EM 85	MBri
– 'Vegetus'	NNor SPer
hamiltonianus	CCla CMCN SLon
– hians	See E. ***h. sieboldianus'***
– semiexsertus	CCla EHar NHol
§ ***– sieboldianus***	CBra CCla CMCN EBre EGol EHar ENot LHop LSav MR&S MRav SCro SSpi WCoo WWat
– sieboldianus 'Coral Charm'	EGol SHil
– yedoensis	See E. ***h. sieboldianus***
japonicus	ENot SArc SHil
– 'Albomarginatus'	CB&S MBar MPla SCro
– 'Aureopictus'	See E. *j.* 'Aureus'
– 'Aureovariegatus'	See E. *j.* 'Ovatus Aureus'
§ – 'Aureus'	CB&S CBow CHoe CSco ELan ENot IDai IJoh MBal MBri NJap SHil SLon WAbe
– 'Duc d'Anjou'	CB&S CHoe CRow ELan EPla SDry SMad SMrm
§ – 'Latifolius Albomarginatus'	CHoe ERav SHil SPer
♦– 'Luna'	See E. *j.* 'Aureus'
– 'Macrophyllus Albus'	See E. *j.* 'Latifolius Albomarginatus'
– 'Maricke'	SHil
– 'Mediopictus'	MBri
– 'Microphyllus'	MBal NCat SArc
§ – 'Microphyllus Albovariegatus'	CBow CHoe CMHG ECtt EFol ELan EPla ERav MBal MBar MGos MR&S MRav NHol NTow SAxl SHil SLon SPla SPla WAbe WHCG WPat WThu
– 'Microphyllus Aureovariegatus'	MR&S WPat WThu WWin
♦– 'Microphyllus Aureus'	See E. *j.* 'Microphyllus Pulchellus'
§ – 'Microphyllus Pulchellus'	CB&S CHoe EFol EPla EPot IJoh MBar MRav NTow SHil SLon SMad SPer SPla WHCG
♦– 'Microphyllus Variegatus'	See E. *j.* 'Microphyllus Albovariegatus'
– 'Ovatus Albus'	CHoe CPle
§ – 'Ovatus Aureus'	CBra CFis CHoe CLan CSco ELan ENot ERav IJoh MBal MGos MPla MR&S MRav SHil SPer SReu WPat
– 'Président Gauthier'	CRow LHop
– robustus	EPla
*– 'Silver Princess'	NHol
kiautschovicus	EGol
latifolius	CMCN
– x ***hamiltonianus***	CMCN
§ ***lucidus***	CChu CHil CTre SSpi
myrianthus	SSpi WWat
§ ***nanus***	CPle MBal SSpi WPat WSHC
– turkestanicus	CBrd EPla SPer
oxyphyllus	CMCN LSav SHil SSpi WWat
pendulus	See E. ***lucidus***
phellomanus	CSco GDra LNet MBar MBlu SHil WWat
§ ***planipes***	CBow CCla CSco EHar ELan ENot LSav MBri NHol SHil SPer SSpi WWat
radicans	See E. ***fortunei radicans***
rosmarinifolius	See E. ***nanus***
sachalinensis	See E. ***planipes***
wilsonii	SHil WWat
yedoensis	See E. ***hamiltonianus sieboldianus***

EUPATORIUM (Compositae)

ageratoides	See E. ***rugosum***
¶ ***altissimum*** JLS 88029	EMon
aromaticum	CArn ELan EMon GPoy WPer
cannabinum	CArn CKin CWGN EHon ELan GPoy LHol MFir MSal MSta NSti WOak WPer WSto
– 'Flore Pleno'	ECha EFou EMon SFis
¶ ***coelestinum***	CSun
fraseri	CChu NSti
§ ***ligustrinum***	CB&S CChu CCla CGle CHan CHil CLan CPle CSun CTre ELan IBar IOrc ISea LHol LHop LSav SDix SPer WBod WSHC
maculatum	EFou EMon GWic IBrk MUlv SSvw
§ ***– atropurpureum***	CCla CHad CSco CSev ECha EFol EFou ELan ERou GWic MBri MFir

micranthum	See E. ***ligustrinum***
perfoliatum	GPoy LHol MSal
purpureum	CArn CTom CWGN ECha GPoy IDai LHol MCot MSal MWat SIde SMrm SPer SSvw WEas WHer WOld WPer WSHC
– *atropurpureum*	See E. ***maculatum a.***
§ *rugosum*	CCla CGle CHan EFou ELan EMon EPar GWic MCot MSal SPer WEas WOld WWat
– *album*	CBot CHad SChu
¶ – 'Braunlaub'	EFou
sordidum	MNew SLMG
¶ *triplinervis*	CTom
weinmannianum	See E. ***ligustrinum***

EUPHORBIA † (Euphorbiaceae)

¶ *acanthothamnos*	LGre
amygdaloides	CKin CRow
– *purpurea*	See E. ***a. rubra***
– *robbiae*	Widely available
§ – *rubra*	Widely available
– 'Variegata'	CRow ELan EMon EOrc LGre MCot MTho SSpi
biglandulosa	See E. ***rigida***
capitulata	CHoe CLew EFol ELan GLoc LHop MCas MHig NHol NNrd WOld WPer WThu WWin
ceratocarpa	EMon GWic LRHS
characias	CB&S CBot CBow CGle CRow ELun EMon ERav GPla MCot MPar MWgw NBar NNor NOak NPer WBon WHoo WWat
– 'Blue Hills'	GWic IBlr
– 'Perry's Winter Blusher'	NPer
¶ – 'Variegata'	CRow
characias wulfenii	Widely available
¶ – – 'Boscawen'	CMHG SAxl
– – 'H E Bates'	NBir SDix
– – 'Humpty Dumpty'	NPer
¶ – – 'John Tomlinson'	EPla
– – Kew form	WEas
– – 'Lambrook Gold'	CCla CFis CHad CMHG CRow CSam EBre EGol ELan EMon EOrc LSav MCot NPer SChu SMad SPer
– – 'Lambrook Yellow'	EMon
¶ – – 'Margery Fish'	EFou EPla
– – 'Minuet'	CHad CHan CShe
– – 'Purpurea'	CFor CHad NRar WRus
– – *sibthorpii*	ERav GWic WCot WEas WOld
corallioides	CElw CFis CHar CSco CTom EBre ECha EGol IBlr WHer
¶ *cornigera*	GWic IBlr
cyparissias	Widely available
* – 'Betten'	GWic
– 'Bush Boy'	IBlr
¶ – 'Orange Man'	EMon
– 'Tall Boy'	IBlr
dulcis	CFis CGle CLew CRow CSun CTom ECha EFol ELun EOrc NOak NSti WBon WCot WEas WOld WRus WWat
– 'Chameleon'	CChu CFor CHad CHan CHil CHoe CRow CSun ERav IBlr LGre NSti SMad WBon WRus WTay
epithymoides	See E. ***polychroma***
glauca	ECou IBlr
griffithii	CRow CSun SBor WCru
– 'Dixter'	CCla CFor CSam EBre ECha EGol ELan ENot EOrc LGre MBri MTho MWgw NOak NRoo NTow SAxl SDix SMad SSpi SSta WCot WWat
– 'Fireglow'	Widely available
– 'Fireglow' Wickstead's form	GWic LHop
horrida	SLMG
hyberna	CFis CFor CTom IBlr MFir
jacquemontii	LGan WWat
x *keysii*	MBri
lathyrus	CArn CFis CRow ERav LHol MCot NPer SIng WEas WSto
N *longifolia*	CCla CFor ELan EMon LHop LSav SBor SSpi WAbb
mammillaris	SLMG
¶ *marginata*	CHan
x *martinii*	Widely available
mellifera	CB&S CBot CChu CGle CHad CHan CMHG CTre ELan EMon GPla GWic ISea LGre LHop NPer NSti SArc SAxl SBor SChu SLHN SSpi
milii	EBak
* – *koeniger*	MBri
myrsinites	Widely available
nicaeensis	CChu CFis CMHG COtt EBre EOrc LGre LHop MRav SBla SChu SSpi WWat
oblongata	EFou EMon IBlr LRHS
palustris	Widely available
pilosa	CNat ERav NSti
– *major*	See E. ***polychroma*** 'Major'
§ *polychroma*	Widely available
¶ – 'Emerald Jade'	IBlr
§ – 'Major'	CFis CMHG CTom ECha GWic MBri MUlv SPer
– 'Midas'	SSpi
– 'Purpurea'	CBot CFor CHar CMHG CMer CRow EBre ECha EFol ELun EOrc ERav ERou GGar LHop MUlv NHol NOak NRoo NSti SBla SChu SCro SMad
– 'Sonnengold'	GWic
* – 'Variegata'	EPla WSHC
portlandica	CFis WHer
§ *pseudovirgata*	SAxl
pugniformis	MBri
pulcherrima	MBri
* *reflexa*	NCat NNor
resinifera	SLMG

§ *rigida*	CBot CFis CHad CHar CMHG ERav LGre NRar NSti SAxl SBla SIgm SSpi SWas
robbiae	See E. ***amygdaloides r.***
schillingii	CChu CFor CHad CHil CMHG ECha ELan GWic LHop MRav SAxl SBla SDix SLHN SMad SSpi SWas WWat
seguieriana	ECha NCat
– *niciciana*	CChu CFor CHan CMHG CSam CSco ERav IBlr LGre MRav NSti SAxl SBla SDix SSpi WEas
♦ *serrulata*	See E. ***stricta***
sikkimensis	Widely available
stricta	CNat CRow CTom IBlr MCot NRar NSti WEas
* *submammillaris* 'Variegata'	MBri
¶ *tenuissimus*	CHil
uralensis	See E. ***pseudovirgata***
§ *virgata*	EMon
x *waldsteinii*	See E. ***virgata***
N *wallichii*	Widely available

EUPTELEA (Eupteleaceae)

franchetii	See E. ***pleiosperma***
pleiosperma	ERav WCoo
polyandra	CChu CCla CGre EHar MBri NHol SSpi WCoo

EURYA (Theaceae)

japonica	CTre
– KE3653	SSpi
– 'Variegata'	See CLEYERA ***fortunei***

EURYOPS (Compositae)

abrotanifolius	CMHG WPer
§ *acraeus*	Widely available
chrysanthemoides	CB&S CHil CMHG CPle CSam CSpe CTre ERea IBlr LHil LHop NRar NTow SDix SLHN WPer
*– 'Carl'	LSav
evansii	See E. ***acraeus***
¶ *linearis*	WPer
pectinatus	Widely available
♦ *sericea*	See URSINIA ***s.***
¶ *tysonii*	SIng
virgineus	CB&S CHil CMHG CMer CTre IBlr WPer

EUSTEPHIA (Liliaceae/Amaryllidaceae)

* *jujuyensis*	LBow

EUSTOMA (Gentianaceae)

grandiflorum	MBri
russellianum	See E. ***grandiflorum***

EVOLVULUS (Convolvulaceae)

¶ *convolvuloides*	ERea
glomeratus 'Blue Daze'	CHil LHil SSad
* *passenimoides*	CGre

EWARTIA (Compositae)

¶ *nubigena*	CSun NWCA

EXACUM (Gentianceae)

affine	MBri
– 'Rococo'	MBri

EXOCHORDA (Rosaceae)

giraldii wilsonii	CBot CSco EHar SHil WWat
korolkowii	SHil
x *macrantha* 'The Bride'	Widely available
racemosa	CGre ISea MGos NNor SGar SHil SLon SPer WBod
– 'The Pearl'	ERav

FABIANA (Solanaceae)

imbricata	CBot CBra CCla CLan CPle ERav GAbr LAbb MBar SHil SLon SPer SSpi SSta WAbe WBod WKif WPat
¶ – *alba*	WThu
– 'Prostrata'	CPle SDry SHil SSpi WThu WWat
– *violacea*	CB&S CPle LAbb MBar MUlv SBla SHil SLon SSpi SSta WBod

FAGOPYRUM (Polygonaceae)

cymosum	See F. ***dibotrys***
§ *dibotrys*	ELan LGan

FAGUS † (Fagaceae)

crenata	SHil WNor
engleriana	CMCN CSco SExT SHil
orientalis	SHil
sylvatica	CB&S CBow CKin CLnd CPer ELan ENot GRei IDai IOrc ISea LBuc MBar MBri MFir MGos MR&S NWea SHil SPer SReu WMou WNor
§ – 'Albomarginata'	IOrc SHil
– 'Albovariegata'	See F. ***s.*** 'Albomarginata'
– 'Ansorgei'	CMCN MBri
§ – 'Aspleniifolia'	CB&S CBow CMCN CSco EGol EHar ELan ENot IOrc LSav MBal MBri MR&S SExT SHil SPer WAbe WMou
– 'Atropunicea'	See F. ***s. purpurea***
– 'Aurea Pendula'	CFor CMCN EHar SHil WMou
*– 'Black Swan'	CMCN
– 'Bornyensis'	EHar WMou
– 'Cochleata'	CMCN
– 'Cristata'	CMCN SExT
§ – 'Dawyck'	CB&S CBow CLnd CMCN COtt CSco EHar ELan ENot IHos IOrc LSav MBal MBar MBri MR&S NWea SExT SHil SPer
– 'Dawyck Gold'	CMCN CSco EHar IOrc LSav MBlu MBri MR&S SHil SMad SSpi WMou
– 'Dawyck Purple'	CMCN COtt CSco EHar IOrc MBlu MBri MGos SHil SMad SPer SSpi WMou
– 'Fastigiata'	See F. ***s.*** 'Dawyck'
– ***heterophylla***	See F. ***s.*** 'Aspleniifolia'

– 'Horizontalis'	WMou
§ – *laciniata*	CMCN WMou
– *latifolia*	MR&S SHil
– 'Luteovariegata'	WMou
– 'Miltonensis'	WMou
N– 'Pendula'	CB&S CBra CLnd CMCN EHar ELan ENot GRei IJoh IOrc LSav MBal MBri MR&S MRav NWea SExT SHil SMad SPer WAbe WMou
– 'Prince George of Crete'	SHil
– 'Purple Fountain'	CMCN COtt CSco EHar IJoh IOrc LHop MBri WMou
§ – *purpurea*	CB&S CBra ELan ENot GRei IDai IOrc LBuc MBal MBar MBri MGos MR&S NWea SHil SPer WAbe WCoo WMou
– 'Purpurea Pendula'	CBow CCla CSco EHar ELan ENot GRei IJoh IOrc LSav MBal MBar MBri MGos MR&S NWea SExT SHil SPer SPla WAbe
– 'Quercifolia'	See F. ***s. laciniata***
– 'Riversii'	CB&S CBow CLnd CMCN CSco EHar ELan ENot IDai IJoh IOrc MBal MBri NWea SExT SHil SPer SReu SSta WAbe
– 'Rohan Gold'	CMCN WMou
*– 'Rohan Obelisk'	MR&S
*– 'Rohan Trompenburg'	CMCN
– 'Rohanii'	CB&S CBow CLnd CMCN COtt CSco EHar ELan IHos IJoh IOrc LHop MBal MBlu MBri MR&S SExT SGar SHil SPer SSpi WMou
– 'Roseomarginata'	CBow CMCN CSco EGol EHar IOrc LSav SExT SHil SPer
– 'Rotundifolia'	LSav NWea
*– 'Silver Wood'	CMCN
– 'Spaethiana'	MBri
– *tortuosa*	WMou
– 'Tricolor'	CB&S COtt ELan ENot LHop MBal MBri MR&S MUlv NBar NHol
*– 'Trompenburg'	SSpi
*– 'Variegata'	MBri
– 'Zlatia'	CB&S CBow CLnd CMCN CSco EHar ELan ENot IJoh IOrc LSav MBal MBar MBri MGos SExT SGar SHil SPer WMou

FALLOPIA † (Polygonaceae)

aubertii	See F. ***baldschuanica***
§ *baldschuanica*	CBow CCla CMac CSco CShe ELan ENot ERav GRei IDai IHos MBar MGos MPla MWat NHol NKay NRoo SBra SHil SLon SPer SPla WBod
§ *japonica*	CFis CRow ELan ERou SAxl WMar
– *compacta*	CRow MFir MUlv
– 'Spectabilis'	CRow EFol EGol ELan MUlv
– 'Variegata'	IBlr SMad
sachalinensis	CRow ELan EMon

FALLUGIA (Rosaceae)

FARFUGIUM (Compositae)

§ *tussilagineum*	CB&S MTho
¶ – 'Argenteum'	CBos CHEx
¶ – 'Aureo-maculatum'	CBos CHEx MTho

FARGESIA (Gramineae(Bambuseae))

dracocephala	SArc SBam WJun
robusta	SBam SDry
utilis	SBam SDry WJun

FARSETIA (Cruciferae)

clypeata	See FIBIGIA ***clypeata***

FASCICULARIA (Bromeliaceae)

♦ *andina*	See F. ***bicolor***
§ *bicolor*	CB&S CGre CHEx CHil IBlr LGre LHil MTho MUlv SLMG SSpi WEas
kirchhoffiana	SLMG
pitcairniifolia	CGre CHEx EBak IBlr LRHS MBri SArc SLMG

X FATSHEDERA (Araliaceae)

lizei	CB&S CBot CHEx CLan CRow CSam CSco IBlr ISea MBal MBri NNor NRog SArc SAxl SBra SHil SPla WWat
– 'Anne Mieke'	MBri SHil
§ – 'Aurea'	CHoe LHop
– 'Aureopicta'	See X F. ***l.*** 'Aurea'
§ – 'Lemon and Lime'	CB&S CBot IBlr WWat
– *maculata*	See X F. ***l.*** 'Lemon and Lime'
– 'Pia'	MBri
– 'Variegata'	CB&S CGre CHEx CHoe CRow CSco IBlr MBal MBri SHil SSta

FATSIA (Araliaceae)

§ *japonica*	Widely available
– 'Variegata'	CBot EGol MBri MUlv SArc SHil SPer
papyrifera	See TETRAPANAX ***papyriferus***

FAUCARIA (Aizoaceae)

tigrina	MBri

FEIJOA See ACCA

FELICIA (Compositae)

§ *amelloides*	CHil CMer CRiv CSev EMon ERea ESis GWic LAbb MPit SAxl SChu SLMG WPer
*– 'Read's Blue'	LHop
*– 'Read's White'	CB&S CSpe ERea LHil LHop SCro
§ – 'Santa Anita'	CHil CSev CSpe EDon EMon EOrc ERea IBar LHil LHop LSav SAxl SCro WEas WHal WPer

– 'Santa Anita Variegated'	CHil LHop SMrm
§ – variegated	CCla CHan CLew CRiv CSev EBar EDon ELan EMon ERav ERea ESis IBlr LHil MBri SAxl SCro WEas WHal WPer WRus
* ***amethystina***	WWin
§ ***amoena***	CCla CFis CHad CHan CMer CTre EDon ELan LHil LHop LSav MCot MTho SChu SCro SDix SIng SLon WEas WHal WPer WWin
– 'Variegata'	CFis CMer EOrc GLoc LAbb LSav MCas MCot MPit SChu
bergeriana	CHil WOMN
capensis 'Variegata'	See F. ***amelloides*** variegated
¶ ***echinata***	WPer
¶ ***filifolia***	CHil
natalensis	CHan
pappei	See F. ***amoena***
§ ***petiolata***	CHan CRiv EMon GPla IBlr LHil LHop NSti SCro WWin
* ***plena ensbergensis***	MPit
§ ***rosulata***	CMHG CSun EBre ELan GDra GEdr GHig GLoc LHil LHop MCas MHig MPit MTho NKay NNrd NRoo NTow SIng WBon WHil WWin
* 'Snowmass'	MTho
uliginosa	CHar GEdr GGar MTho SBar WEas

FERRARIA (Iridaceae)

§ ***crispa***	LBow WMar
undulata	See F. ***crispa***

FERULA (Umbelliferae)

assa-foetida	MSal
communis	CSco EMon LHol SDix
*– 'Gigantea'	CHad ECha
'Giant Bronze'	See FOENICULUM ***vulgare*** 'G.B.'
* ***purpurea***	EOrc

FESTUCA (Gramineae)

amethystina	CHoe CLew EFou MBro NHol NSti WHoo
arundinacea	CKin
erecta	CHoe
eskia	CHoe NHol
¶ ***filiformis***	EMon
§ ***gautieri***	ECro ELan LHil MFir MUlv NOrc
glacialis	EPad MBal MDHE NHol NNrd NRed
§ ***glauca***	Widely available
¶ – 'Azurit'	EFou EMon
– 'Blaufuchs' ('Blue Fox')	CElw CHoe MBri SApp
– 'Blausilber'	GWic
– 'Harz'	CElw CHoe IBlr
– 'Meerblau' ('Sea Blue')	CElw
– ***minima***	EFol NHol NNrd
¶ – 'Pallens'	EFou
– 'Seven Seas'	IBlr SApp SMad
¶ ***mairei***	IBlr SApp
ovina	See F. ***glauca***
paniculata	EMon SApp
punctoria	CElw CHoe CLew CTom ECha MDHE SBla SIng SSmi SSpi
rubra viridis	SIng
scoparia	See F. ***gautieri***
¶ ***valesiaca glaucantha***	SMad WWat
§ – 'Silbersee' ('Silver Sea')	CHoe CLew ECha EPla MWat NCat NHol NNrd SApp SIng
vivipara	CHoe NHol NLan
– ***glauca***	NLan

FIBIGIA (Cruciferae)

§ ***clypeata***	ELan ESis LGan NSti WEas

FICUS † (Moraceae)

australis	See F. ***rubiginosa***
benghalensis	MBri
benjamina	MBri
– 'Exotica'	MBri
– 'Flandriana'	MBri
– 'Golden King'	MBri
– 'Golden Princess'	MBri
– 'Green Gem'	MBri
– ***nuda***	MBri
F ***carica***	MBri
F – 'Angélique'	ERea
F – 'Black Ischia'	ERea
F – 'Black Mission'	ERea
F – 'Bourjassotte Grise'	ERea
F – 'Brown Turkey'	Widely available
F – 'Brunswick'	ERea ESim GBon NTwe SFam WHig
F – 'Castle Kennedy'	ERea
F – 'Figue d'Or'	ERea
F – 'Lisa'	ERea
F – 'Malcolm's Giant'	ERea
F – 'Malta'	ERea
F – 'Negro Largo'	ERea
F – 'Osborn's Prolific'	ERea
F – 'Panachée'	ERea
F – 'Rouge de Bordeaux'	ERea
F – 'Saint Johns'	ERea
F – 'San Pedro Miro'	ERea
F – 'Sugar 12'	ERea
F – 'Violette Sepor'	ERea
F – 'White Ischia'	ERea
F – 'White Marseilles'	ERea ESim NTwe SDea SFam
cyathistipula	MBri
§ ***deltoidea***	MBri
diversifolia	See F. ***deltoidea***
elastica 'Belgica'	MBri
– 'Schrijveriana'	MBri
– 'Zulu'	MBri
* ***foliole***	MBri
leprieurii 'Westland'	MBri
lyrata	MBri
microcarpa 'Hawaii'	MBri
* ***minor*** 'Variegata'	LHop
pumila	CHEx EBak MBal MBri NHol

– 'Minima'	MBal
– 'Sonny'	MBri
– 'Variegata'	CHEx MBri
radicans	See F. ***sagittata***
robusta	MBri
rubiginosa	MBri
§ *sagittata* 'Variegata'	MBri
* 'Starlight'	MBri
triangularis	See F. ***leprieurii***

FIG See **FICUS** ***carica***

FILBERT See **CORYLUS** ***maxima***

FILIPENDULA (Rosaceae)

alnifolia 'Variegata'	See F. ***ulmaria*** 'Variegata'
camtschatica	CRow CWGN EBre ELan
– *rosea*	IBlr LHop
digitata 'Nana'	See F. ***palmata*** 'Nana'
hexapetala	See F. ***vulgaris***
– 'Flore Pleno'	See F. ***vulgaris*** 'Plena'
palmata	CBre CWGN ECha SFis SSpi
– 'Digitata Nana'	See F. ***p.*** 'Nana'
§ – 'Elegantissima'	CChu CRow ECha GGar
§ – 'Nana'	CChu CCla CRow ECha ECro MBal MBri WHoo
– *purpurea*	EFou ELun
– 'Rosea'	CGle NBir NCat
– 'Rubra'	CSco
purpurea	CCla CRow CWGN GGar MBri MUlv SBla WAbe WEas
– *alba*	EGol MUlv
* – *splendens*	NKay
rubra	CHan CRow CWGN NOrc
– 'Venusta'	CBre CChu CCla CRow EBre ECha EFol EGol ELan EPar GWic MUlv NKay SChu SPer SSpi WHal WRus
§ – 'Venusta Magnifica'	EFou MWat SFis SHig
§ *ulmaria*	CArn CFis CKin CSFH CWGN EHon Effi GPoy LHol MChe MTho NHol NLan NSel SIde WCla WOak WPer WSto
– *aurea*	Widely available
– 'Flore Pleno'	CBre CHar CWGN LHil NHol
– 'Rosea'	CCla MUlv NSel
§ – 'Variegata'	CCor CHoe CRow EFol EGol ELan ELun EOrc EPar EPla LHop MTho MUlv NRoo NSti SPer WAbe WEas WHal WRus
§ *vulgaris*	CFis CHan CKin CWGN GPoy LHol LMay MSal MWgw NLan NNor NOrc SIde SPer WCla WHoo WPer
– 'Grandiflora'	CHar EOrc ERou NCat
§ – 'Plena'	CBre CCla CGle CLew CSco ECha EGol ELan EOrc EPar ERou MBal MFir MTho MUlv NHol NSti SPer WEas WRus WWat

FIRMIANA (Sterculiaceae)

simplex	CHEx GWic

FITTONIA (Acanthaceae)

verschaffeltii argyroneura	MBri
– *argyroneura nana*	MBri

FITZROYA (Cupressaceae)

cupressoides	CMac IOrc MBal MBar NHol SBor SHil SLon WBod WThu

FOENICULUM (Umbelliferae)

vulgare	CArn CCor CFis CHad CHan ECha EEls ELan Effi GPoy LHol MChe MCot MSal NRoo NSel SIde WOak WPer WSto
– black form	CFis CHad
– 'Bronze'	See F. ***v. purpureum***
– *dulce*	CArn CSev GPoy MChe
– 'Giant Bronze'	CSco ELan LAbb SPer
§ – *purpureum*	CArn CBre CGle CHoe CSev ECha EEls GPla GPoy LHol MCot MFir MPit MSal NHol NOak NRoo NSti WEas WHal WOak WPer WSto
¶ – 'Smokey'	ECro EFou

FOKIENIA (Cupressaceae)

hodginsii	CKen CMCN SBor SSpi

FORSYTHIA † (Oleaceae)

'Arnold Dwarf'	CSun EHal IDai SCro WWeb
'Arnold Giant'	CShe WBod WWeb
N 'Beatrix Farrand'	ECtt ELan MGos MPla MR&S MWat NHol NNor SHil SPer SPla WWeb
europaea	WWeb
giraldiana	LSav WBod WWeb
'Golden Nugget'	EBre ELan ESis IOrc NRoo SHil SLon SPer SReu
x *intermedia*	IJoh WWeb
– 'Densiflora'	WWeb
– 'Goldzauber'	ERav WWeb
– 'Lynwood'	Widely available
– 'Mertensiana'	WWeb
– 'Mini-gold'	CBra EPla IJoh MGos MUlv WWeb
– 'Spectabilis'	CSco ELan IOrc LBuc MBar MR&S NWea SHil SPer WWeb
– 'Spectabilis Variegated'	EFol EPla LHop SDry WWeb
– 'Spring Glory'	ENot MBri MRav WWeb
– 'Variegata'	CBow CHoe MUlv SPer SSta WAbe
– 'Vitellina'	WWeb
japonica saxatilis	WWeb
'Karl Sax'	CBow CBra CSco NHol WWeb
I 'Melissa'	MBri MGos
'Northern Gold'	WWeb
ovata	CBow CChu EPla GRei MBar SHil
– forms	LSav MUlv WWeb
– 'Tetragold'	CB&S CBow CSco MBal MBar MR&S NHol WWeb
* 'Paulina'	CBow
* 'Spring Beauty'	EHal WWeb

suspensa	CB&S CBow CBra CSco CShe ENot IJoh IOrc MBar MWat SHil SPer WAbe WWeb
– L 275	WWeb
– *atrocaulis*	CBow EBre LSav SSpi SSta WWeb
– 'Decipiens'	WBod WWeb
– *fortunei*	WWeb
– 'Nymans'	CBra CCla CSco MBri NRoo SMad WTay WWeb
– *sieboldii*	WWeb
§ – 'Taff's Arnold'	ELan
♦– 'Variegata'	See F. *s.* 'Taff's Arnold'
'Tremonia'	CMer EHar MBal MGos MPla NHol NNor NRoo WWeb
viridissima	NNor WWeb
– 'Bronxensis'	CLew ELan EPar EPot GLoc MPla SHil SMad WPat WWeb
– *koreana*	WWeb

FORTUNEARIA (Hamamelidaceae)

¶ *sinensis*	LSav

FORTUNELLA (Rutaceae)

F *japonica*	LPan
F – 'Meiwa'	ERea
F *margarita*	MBri
F – 'Nagami'	ERea

FOTHERGILLA (Hamamelidaceae)

gardenii	ELan EPar IOrc MBri MUlv NBar SHil SPer SPla SSpi SSta WWat
* 'Hunstman'	CCla MUlv SSta
major	CB&S CBow CBra CSco EBre ELan IJoh LSav MBri MGos MR&S MRav MUlv NBar NTow SChu SHil SPer SReu WNor WWat
– Monticola group	CBra CCla CFor ELan ENot IBar IHos MBar MBri MPla MRav SChu SPer SSpi SSta WBod

FRAGARIA † (Rosaceae)

alpina	See F. *vesca* 'Semperflorens'
– *alba*	See F. *vesca* 'Semperflorens Alba'
F x *ananassa* 'Aromel'	EMui MBri NTwe SDea WHig WWeb
F – 'Bogota'	EMui GRei NBar NTwe
F – 'Bounty'	EMui SDea
F – 'Cambridge Favourite'	CMac CSut EMui ESha GRei IJoh MBri NBar NElm NRog NTwe SDea WHig WWeb
F – 'Cambridge Vigour'	CSam EMui IJoh NBar NBee NRog NTwe SDea WWeb
F – 'Cantata'	EMui
F – 'Domanil'	EMui
F – 'Elsanta'	EMui GRei MBri NTwe WHig WWeb
F – 'Elvira'	EMui WHig
– 'Fraise des Bois'	See F. *vesca*
F – 'Gento'	EMui
F – 'Gorella'	NBar SDea WWeb
F – 'Hapil'	CSam EMui NBee NTwe
F – 'Hedley'	CSut
F – 'Honeoye'	EMui NTwe WHig
F – 'Idil'	EMui NBee NTwe
F – 'Korona'	EMui NTwe
F – 'Kouril'	EMui
F – 'Maxim'	EMui
F – 'Ostara'	CSut EMui GRei NTwe
F – 'Pandora'	EMui NTwe WHig
F – 'Pantagruella'	EMui GRei NTwe SDea WHig
F – 'Pegasus'	CSut NTwe
F – 'Rabunda'	EMui
F – 'Rapella'	EMui MBri
F – 'Redgauntlet'	MBri NBar NRog SDea WWeb
F – 'Rhapsody'	NTwe
F – 'Royal Sovereign'	CMac CSam EMui NBee NRog NTwe SDea
F – 'Serenata'	EMui
F – 'Sweetheart'	NBee
F – 'Tamella'	EMui NTwe SDea
F – 'Tenira'	EMui
F – 'Totem'	NTwe
F – 'Variegata'	CCor CElw CGle CRiv CSev CShe ECro EFol ELan EOrc EPar EPla LHop MCot MFir MRav NRoo NSti SAxl SIng WRus WThu WWin
F – 'Vigour'	WHig
F 'Baron Solemacher'	NHol SCro WCla WHer
'Bowles' Double'	See F. *vesca* 'Multiplex'
F *chiloensis*	EMon
¶ – 'Chaval'	EMon
N– 'Variegata'	GWic WEas
¶ – x *virginiana*	CArn
daltoniana	SAxl SIng SWas
indica	See DUCHESNEA *indica*
* *japonica*	EPla
F 'Pink Panda'	MBri NRoo SMrm
'Variegata'	See F. x *ananassa* 'V.'
F *vesca*	CArn CKin EMui GPoy LHol MSal NLan NSel SIde WCla WOak
F – 'Alexandria'	MChe NHol NRog
F – 'Delicious'	WHig
– 'Flore Pleno'	See F. *v.* 'Multiplex'
F – *monophylla*	CElw CFis CMal CRow ELan EMon NHol
§ – 'Multiplex'	CCor CElw CFis CGle CRow CSev CSun CTom ELan EMon EOrc GWic MCot MPar NHol NSti SSvw WHer
§ – 'Muricata'	CBos CElw CRow GPla NSti WHer
♦– 'Plymouth Strawberry'	See F. *v.* 'Muricata'
F – 'Rügen'	WHoo
F – 'Semperflorens'	MCot
¶ – 'Variegata'	MWgw NHol

FRANCOA (Saxifragaceae)

appendiculata	See F. *sonchifolia*
ramosa	CElw CGre CHan CSun ECro GAbr IBar IBlr ITim NRog NRoo NSti NWCA WCar WEas WHal
– *alba*	CGle

§ *sonchifolia* Widely available
– Rogerson's form CGle

FRANKENIA (Frankeniaceae)
laevis CShe GGar MBro NVic SLHN WWin
thymifolia Widely available

FRANKLINIA (Theaceae)
alatamaha CGre CMCN ELan SHil SMrm SSpi SSta WNor

FRAXINUS † (Oleaceae)
americana CMCN EHar
– 'Autumn Purple' SHil
§ *angustifolia* 'Raywood' CB&S CLnd EHar ENot IOrc LSav NWea SExT SHil SPer WMou
chinensis rhyncophylla SHil
dipetala WCoo
excelsior CB&S CKin CLnd CPer ENot GRei IJoh ISea LBuc MBar MBri MGos MR&S NWea SHil SPer WMou
¶ – 'Crispa' EMon
– *diversifolia* SHil WMou
– 'Geesink' ENot IHos SExT
– 'Jaspidea' CB&S CLnd COtt CSco EHar ENot IDai IJoh IOrc LSav MBar MBlu MBri MGos MR&S SExT SHil SPer SSta WJas WMou WWat
– 'Pendula' CLnd CSco EHar ELan ENot GRei IJoh IOrc MBri SExT SHil SPer WJas WMou
¶ – 'Pendula Wentworthii' WMou
– 'Westhof's Glorie' CSco ENot MBri MR&S SExT SHil WJas
lanuginosa WCoo
latifolia SHil WCoo
mandshurica WCoo
mariesii See F. ***sieboldiana***
ornus CBot CLnd CSco EHar ENot GRei IOrc ISea MBri MR&S SExT SHil WCoo WMou
oxycarpa 'Raywood' See F. ***angustifolia* 'Raywood'**
pennsylvanica EHar SExT WCoo
– *lanceolata* See F. ***p. subintegerrima***
– 'Summit' SHil
– 'Variegata' SHil
§ *sieboldiana* IOrc SHil WCoo WMou
velutina CBot ISea LHop SHil WCoo WMou

FREESIA (Iridaceae)
'Diana' LAma
'Fantasy' LAma
¶ hybrids CSut
N *refracta alba* LAma
'Romany' LAma
'White Swan' LAma
¶ *xanthospila* LBow

FREMONTODENDRON (Sterculiaceae)
'Californian Glory' Widely available
californicum CBow CBra CChu CCla CHEx CPle CSun EBre ELan IOrc ISea LSav MBlu MBri MGos MRav MUlv NHol SHil SPer WNor WWin
– 'Pacific Sunset' CCla CKni LHop
'Ken Taylor' ERea
mexicanum CB&S CBot CChu SHil SPla
'San Gabriel' LRHS

FREYLINIA (Scrophulariaceae)
cestroides See F. ***lanceolata***
§ *lanceolata* CHan CPle CSun CTre

FRITILLARIA † (Liliaceae/Liliaceae)
acmopetala CAvo CBro CRiv EPar EPot ETub ITim LAma LBow MHig MPar MS&S NHol SIng WCar WChr WDav
– *wendelboi* LAma WChr
§ *affinis* ECam EPot ETub ITim LAma NHol WDav
§ – *gracilis* ECam LAma WChr WDav
¶ – *tristulis* WChr
– 'Wayne Roderick' ECam EPot
¶ *agrestis* WChr
alburyana WChr
alfredae glaucoviridis ITim LAma WChr
armena EPot LAma WChr
assyriaca CAvo ELan EPar EPot ETub ITim NHol SIng WChr
aurea CAvo EPot LAma WChr
¶ *biflora* WChr
¶ – 'Martha Roderick' MS&S
§ *bithynica* CBro EBul EPar EPot LAma NHol WChr WDav
* *brandegeei* LAma
bucharica CAvo EPot WChr
camschatcensis CAvo CBro ECha ELan EPar EPot ETub GEdr LAma LBow MPar MS&S NHar SIng SMad SSpi WAbe WChr
– *multiflora* WDav
– yellow LRHS
carduchorum See F. ***minuta***
carica EPot WChr
– *serpenticola* LRHS
caucasica CAvo LAma WChr
cirrhosa CAvo LAma NHol
citrina See F. ***bithynica***
§ *collina* ECam EPot NBar WChr
conica LAma
crassifolia CRiv EPot LAma MS&S WDav
– *kurdica* CAvo MS&S WChr
davisii CAvo CBro EBul EPot ETub LAma MHig WChr
delphinensis See F. ***tubiformis***
drenovskii ECam LAma WChr
* *eastwoodii* LAma
eduardii ECam
ehrhartii LRHS
elwesii WChr
epirotica LAma LRHS WChr

forbesii	WChr
¶ *gibbosa*	NHol
glauca	LAma
graeca graeca	WChr
– ionica	See F. ***g. thessala***
§ *– thessala*	CAvo LAma LRHS MPar WChr WDav
§ *grayana*	LAma SOkd WChr WDav
gussichae	LAma
hermonis amana	EPot LAma WChr
hispanica	See F. ***lusitanica***
imperialis	CAvo CB&S CHEx ERav LRoo MBal MBri SIng
– 'Argentea Variegata'	CBot ETub
– 'Aureo-marginata'	EPar LAma LBow MBri
– 'Aurora'	CAvo EPar LAma LBlo LBow MS&S SIng WHil
– 'Blom's Orange Perfection'	LBlo
– 'Crown upon Crown'	EPar LAma LBow LRHS
§ – 'Lutea Maxima'	CBro CCla CHEx ELan EPar ETub LAma LBlo LBow LRoo MS&S SIng SMad
– 'Maxima'	LAma
– 'Rubra'	CCla ELan EPar ETub LAma LBlo LBow LRoo MS&S
– 'The Premier'	EPar LAma LBow SIng SMad
involucrata	CBro LAma MTho NHol SIng WChr WDav
ionica	See F. ***graeca thessala***
japonica	LAma
karadaghensis	See F. ***crassifolia kurdica***
kotschyana	LAma LRHS WChr
lanceolata	See F. ***affinis***
latakiensis	LAma WChr
§ *latifolia*	CAvo EPot LAma WChr
– nobilis	See F. ***latifolia***
liliacea	CBro EPot LAma MS&S NHol
§ *lusitanica*	LAma MS&S NHol
lutea	See F. ***collina***
meleagris	Widely available
– alba	CBro CHad ECtt EPot ETub GLoc LAma LBow MBri MBro MHig MPar MS&S SIng WPer
– 'Aphrodite'	CAvo EPot LBlo MBro NHol WChr
messanensis	LAma MS&S WChr WDav
– gracilis	LAma MPar NHol
– messanensis	CBro
michailovskyi	CAvo CBro ELan EPar EPot ETub GHig LAma LBlo LBow LRoo MBri MPlt MS&S MTho NHol SIng WAbe WCar WChr WCla WHil WPat
micrantha	EBul ECam LAma WChr
§ *minuta*	CAvo LRHS NHol
nigra	See F. ***pyrenaica***
¶ *olgae*	WChr
olivieri	CAvo ECam NHol WChr
§ *orientalis*	WChr
pallidiflora	CAvo CBro EPar EPot ETub ITim LAma MPar MS&S NHol SOkd SPou WChr WDav
persica	CB&S CCla EPar EPot LAma LBlo LRoo MBri MS&S NHol WDav WHil
– 'Adiyaman'	CAvo CBro ELan ETub LBow SIng
*– 'Senkoy'	LRHS
phaeanthera	See F. ***affinis gracilis***
pinardii	CBro EPot WChr
pluriflora	ECam
pontica	CAvo CBro EPar EPot ETub ITim LAma LBow MPar NHol SSpi WChr WDav
– Pras 1276	LRHS
pudica	CAvo ETub ITim LAma MS&S NHol WChr WDav
§ *pyrenaica*	CBro EPar GEdr LAma LBow MBal MPar MS&S MTho NHol SChu SOkd WChr
raddeana	EPar LAma WChr
roderickii	See F. ***grayana***
roylei	LAma NHol
rubra major	See F. ***imperialis*** 'Maxima'
ruthenica	EBul LRHS MS&S WChr
sewerzowii	CAvo ECam EPot LAma WChr
sibthorpiana	CBro EPot LAma SIng WChr
– HS 2147	ECam
stenanthera	CAvo ECam EPot LAma WChr WDav
stribrnyi	LAma LRHS WChr
tenella	See F. ***orientalis***
thunbergii	CRiv LRHS
§ *tubiformis*	WChr
tuntasia	LRHS
uva-vulpis	CBro EBul ECam LAma LBow MS&S SPou
verticillata	CAvo CBro ECam ECha EPar EPot ETub LAma LBow MS&S NHol SPou WChr
walujewii	ECam EPot WChr
whittallii	ECam EPot LAma WChr

FUCHSIA † (Onagraceae)

N 'A 1'	MPen WPau
'A M Larwick'	EBak WPau
'A W Taylor'	EBak
'Abbé Farges'	CCla CLoc EBak EBly EGou EKMF MPen MSmi MWar MWhe NMGN NPor SKen SLBF SOld SPla WPau
N 'Abundance'	WPau
'Achievement'	CLoc EBly EKMF LHig MJac MPen SKen SOld
'Achilles'	EBly EGou
'Ada Perry'	EKMF MSmi WPau
'Adagio'	CLoc WPau
'Admiration'	MPen WPau
'Ailsa Garnett'	EBak
'Aintree'	NPor WPau
'Ajax'	EBly EGou
'Al Stettler'	WPau
'Alabama Imp'	SKen
'Alan Ayckbourn'	EBly MWar NPor SLBF
'Alan's Joy'	EGou

	Cultivar	Suppliers
	'Alaska'	CCla EBak EKMF MPen MWhe SKen SOld WPau
	'Albion'	CCla
	'Alde'	EBly EGou
	'Alexandra Dyos'	SLBF
	'Alf Thornley'	EKMF MWar MWhe NPor
	'Alfred Rambaud'	NMGN WPau
	'Alice Ashton'	EBak EKMF NMGN WPau
	'Alice Hoffman'	Widely available
	'Alice Mary'	EBly
¶	'Alice Topliss'	EGou
	'Alice Travis'	EBak EGou
	'Alison Ewart'	CLoc EBak EKMF MPen MWar MWhe NPor SKen SOld WPau
¶	'Alison Patricia'	EKMF SLBF
	'Alison Reynolds'	WPau
	'Alison Ryle'	EBak
	'Alison Sweetman'	MJac MWhe SKen
	'Allegra'	WPau
	'Alpestris'	See F. ***regia alpestris***
	'Alsa Garnett'	WPau
	'Althea Green'	EKMF
	'Altmark'	EBly
	'Alwin'	MWhe WPau
	'Alyce Larson'	CCla EBak ECtt MJac MWhe NMGN NPor WPau
	'Amanda Bridgland'	CCla EKMF WPau
	'Amanda Jones'	MWhe WPau
	'Ambassador'	EBak ECtt MPen SKen
¶	'Amber Supreme'	SKen
	'Amelie Aubin'	CLoc EBak EKMF WPau
	'America'	EBak EGou
	'American Flaming Glory'	CCla WPau
	'Amethyst Fire'	CCla CTab
	'Amigo'	EBak WPau
	'Amy Lye'	CCla CLoc EBak EKMF MPen MSmi NMGN NPor SKen WPau
	'Andenken an Heinrich Henkel'	WPau
	'André Le Nostre'	EBak
	'Andrew'	EBak
	'Andrew Carnegie'	CLoc
	'Andrew George'	MJac
	'Andrew Hadfield'	EKMF MWar SLBF
	'Andrew Ryle'	WPau
N	'Andromeda'	CCla
	'Angela Leslie'	CCla CLoc EBak EKMF MBri WPau
	'Angela Rippon'	EKMF MJac MWhe SKen SOld
	'Angeline'	EGou
	'Angel's Dream'	WPau
	'Angel's Flight'	CLoc EBak EKMF MSmi SOld WPau
	'Ann Adams'	EBly MJac
	'Ann H Tripp'	CLoc MBri MJac MPen MWar MWhe NMGN NPor SLBF WPau
	'Ann Lee'	CLoc EBak
	'Ann Margaret'	SOld
¶	'Ann Roots'	EGou
	'Anna of Longleat'	CCla CLoc EBly SKen SLBF WPau
	'Annabel'	CCla CLoc EBak EBly EKMF MBri MJac MLab MPen MSmi MWar MWhe NMGN NPor SKen SLBF SOld WPau
	'Anne Porter'	NPor WPau
	'Anne Smith'	SOld
	'Ann's Beauty'	MSmi
	'Anthea Day'	CLoc
	'Antigone'	SLBF
	'Antonella Merrills'	EKMF
	'Aphrodite'	CLoc EBak WPau
	'Apollo'	SOld
	'Applause'	CLoc EBak EBly EGou EKMF MSmi NMGN NPor SOld WPau
¶	***aprica***	CCla
	'Aquarius'	MPen MWhe
	'Arabella'	WPau
	'Arabella Improved'	EGou EKMF WPau
	arborescens	CLoc CPle EBak EGou EKMF ERea MPen SLBF SOld
	'Arcadia'	CLoc MWar WPau
	'Arcadia Gold'	EKMF
	'Arcadia Lady'	EKMF MJac
¶	'Arcady'	WPau
	'Archie Owen'	EKMF MSmi WPau
	'Ariel'	NMGN
	'Ark Royal'	SLBF WPau
	'Arlendon'	MPen MWhe WPau
	'Army Nurse'	CCla CLoc MLab MPen MWhe NPor SKen SLBF SOld SPla WPau WWeb
	'Arthur Cope'	WPau
	'Ashley and Isobel'	NPor
	'Athela'	EBak
	'Atlantic Star'	EBly MJac MPen NPor SLBF SOld WPau
	'Atlantis'	MJac WPau
	'Atomic Glow'	EBak WPau
	'Aubrey Harris'	EBly
	'Audrey Hepburn'	EKMF WPau
	'Aunt Juliana'	EBak WPau
	'Auntie Maggie'	WPau
	'Aunty Jinks'	CCla EBak EBly EGou EKMF MWar MWhe NMGN NPor SKen SLBF SOld WPau
	'Aurora Superba'	CLoc EBak ECtt EKMF MPen NMGN NPor SLBF WPau
	'Australia Fair'	CLoc EBak WPau
	austromontana	EKMF
	'Autumnale'	CCla CLoc EBak EBly EFol EKMF MBri MLab MPen MSmi MWhe NMGN NPor SKen SLBF SOld WPau
	'Avalanche'	CLoc EBak WPau
	'Avocet'	CLoc EBak
	'Avon Celebration'	CLoc
	'Avon Gem'	CLoc WPau
	'Avril Lunn'	MLab
	ayavacensis	EKMF
	'Azure Sky'	EKMF
¶	'Baby Blue Eyes'	SLBF
	'Baby Chang'	MWhe
¶	'Baby Face'	MPen

'Baby Lilac'	WPau
'Baby Pink'	EBly WPau
bacillaris	CCla CGre CHil CMHG EBak MBri SBor SLBF WPer
'Bagworthy Water'	CLoc
'Baker's Tri'	EBak WPau
¶ 'Bali Hi'	MSmi
'Balkonkönigin'	CCla CLoc EBak SKen WPau
'Ballerina'	MPen WPau
'Ballet Girl'	CCla CLoc EBak EKMF MPen MSmi SLBF SOld WPau
'Bambini'	EBly NPor WPau
'Banstead Bell'	SLBF WPau
'Barbara'	CCla EBak EKMF MJac MPen MWar MWhe NPor SKen SOld WEas WPau
'Barbara Anne'	SOld
'Barbara Edwards'	CTab
'Barbara Pountain'	MJac
'Baron de Ketteler'	SLBF WPau
'Baroque Pearl'	EKMF
'Barry's Queen'	EBak SKen SOld
'Bashful'	CTab EBly MBri SIng SKen SOld WWeb
'Basketfull'	WPau
'Beacon'	CCla CLoc EBak EBly EKMF IHos MBri MLab MPen MSmi MWhe NMGN NPor SKen SOld SPla WPau
¶ 'Beacon Kon'	CSut
'Beacon Rosa'	CLoc EBly EGou MBri MJac MLab MPen MWar MWhe NPor SKen SLBF SOld WPau
'Bealings'	CCla EBly EGou EKMF MWar NPor SOld WPau
'Beau Nash'	CLoc
'Beauty of Bath'	CLoc EBak WPau
'Beauty of Clyffe Hall'	EBak WPau
'Beauty of Exeter'	CCla EBak EKMF SKen
'Beauty of Prussia'	CLoc ECtt
'Beauty of Swanley'	EBak
'Beauty of Trowbridge'	MPen NPor SKen WPau
'Beauty Queen'	WPau
'Bedford's Park'	EBly
'Bella'	CGle
'Bella Forbes'	CLoc EBak SOld
'Bella Mia'	WPau
'Bella Rosella'	MSmi
'Bellbottoms'	WPau
'Belsay Beauty'	CCla MJac MLab NPor WPau
'Belvoir Beauty'	CLoc ECtt MJac WPau
'Belvoir Elf'	ECtt MLab
¶ 'Belvoir Lakes'	ECtt
'Benjamin Pacey'	EBly
'Beranger'	EBak WPau
¶ 'Berba's Coronation'	EKMF
'Berba's Delight'	EGou
'Berg Nemf'	EGou EKMF
'Berliner Kind'	EBak
'Bermuda'	EKMF WPau
'Bernadette'	WPau
¶ 'Bernisser Stein'	SLBF
¶ 'Bertha Gadsby'	EKMF
'Beth Robley'	CCla EBly NPor WPau
¶ 'Betsy Ross'	WPau
'Bette Sibley'	SLBF
'Betty Wass'	EBak EBly
'Beverley'	EBak EBly SLBF
'Beverley Baby'	EBly
'Bewitched'	EBak WPau
'Bianca'	SOld WPau
'Bicentennial'	CCla CLoc EBak EBly EKMF MJac MLab MPen MSmi MWar MWhe NMGN NPor SKen SOld WPau
'Biddy Lester'	WPau
'Bill Kennedy'	MSmi
'Billie Roe'	NMGN
'Billy Green'	CCla CLoc EBak EBly EKMF MJac MPen MSmi MWar MWhe NMGN NPor SKen SLBF SOld
'Bishop's Bells'	MJac SKen
'Bits'	WPau
'Bittersweet'	SLBF WPau
'Black Beauty'	WPau
'Black Prince'	CCla EKMF MWar WPau
'Blanche Regina'	CCla MJac MWhe NPor WPau
'Bland's New Striped'	EBak EKMF SLBF WPau
'Blaze'	WPau
'Blowick'	MPen NMGN NPor WPau
'Blue Anchor'	WPau
'Blue Beauty'	EBak WPau
'Blue Bonnet'	CTab SOld
'Blue Boy'	WPau
'Blue Bush'	EKMF MJac MPen NMGN NPor WPau
'Blue Butterfly'	EBak WPau
'Blue Gown'	CLoc EBak EBly EKMF MLab MPen MSmi MWar SHil SKen WPau
¶ 'Blue Halo'	EGou
'Blue Ice'	EBly MLab WPau
'Blue Lace'	CCla CTab
N 'Blue Lagoon'	MLab WPau
'Blue Lake'	MLab WPau
'Blue Mink'	EBak WPau
'Blue Mirage'	EGou MLab NMGN WPau
'Blue Mist'	EBak WPau
'Blue Pearl'	CCla EBak NMGN WPau
'Blue Petticoat'	CLoc
'Blue Pinwheel'	EBak WPau
'Blue Satin'	SLBF WPau
'Blue Tit'	SKen SLBF
'Blue Veil'	CCla ECtt MBri MSmi MWar NMGN NPor SKen SLBF WPau
'Blue Waves'	CCla CLoc EBak EBly EKMF MJac MPen MWar MWhe NMGN NPor SOld WPau
'Blush o' Dawn'	CCla CLoc EBak EBly EKMF MSmi NMGN SKen SLBF SOld WPau
'Blythe'	EBly
¶ 'Bob Armbruster'	MSmi
'Bobby Boy'	EBak WPau
'Bobby Dazzler'	EKMF MJac WPau
'Bobby Shaftoe'	CLoc EBak EKMF MWhe NMGN WPau

'Bobby Wingrove'	EBak WPau
'Bobolink'	EBak WPau
'Bob's Best'	EBly MJac SLBF
'Bob's Choice'	WPau
'Boerhaave'	EBak WPau
boliviana	CCla CGre CHil CSun EBak EKMF MWhe
– 'Luxurians Alba'	CHil CLoc EGou EKMF
'Bon Accorde'	CCla CLoc EBak EBly EKMF MPen NPor SKen SLBF SOld WPau
'Bon Bon'	CCla EBak WPau
'Bonanza'	WPau
'Bonita'	MJac MLab MSmi WPau
'Bonnie Berrycloth'	SOld
'Bonnie Doan'	MSmi
'Bonnie Lass'	EBak WPau
'Bonny'	CLoc
'Bora Bora'	CCla EBak EKMF WPau
'Border Queen'	CCla CLoc EBak EBly EGou EKMF MJac MLab MPen MWhe NPor SKen SLBF WPau
'Border Reiver'	EBak
'Born Free'	WPau
'Bornemann's Beste'	EBak EGou EKMF NPor SKen
'Bouffant'	CLoc MJac WPau
'Bountiful'	CCla CLoc EKMF MWhe NMGN NPor SKen SLBF SOld WPau
'Bouquet'	EKMF MPen SKen
'Bow Bells'	CLoc MJac MPen MWhe NMGN NPor WPau
'Boy Blue'	CTab
'Brandt's 500 Club'	CLoc EBak WPau
'Breckland'	EBak MJac MPen WPau
¶ 'Breeder's Delight'	WPau
'Breeder's Dream'	EBak WPau
'Brenda'	EBak EBly WPau
'Brenda Megan Hill'	EBly
'Brenda Pritchard'	ECtt WPau
'Brenda White'	EBly EGou EKMF MWhe NMGN NPor SLBF SOld
'Brentwood'	EBak
'Brian Stannard'	EGou
'Bridal Veil'	EBak
'Bridesmaid'	CCla EBak EKMF MSmi SOld WPau
'Brigadoon'	CCla CLoc EBak SLBF WPau
'Brighton Belle'	EBly EGou
N 'Brilliant'	CCla CLoc EBak MGos MPla MWat MWhe NPor SKen WPau
¶ 'Briony Caunt'	EKMF
'British Jubilee'	EKMF MJac NMGN NPor SLBF WPau
'British Sterling'	WPau
'Brodsworth'	MLab NMGN
'Brookwood Belle'	EBly MJac NPor SLBF
'Brookwood Joy'	EBly EGou MJac SLBF SOld WPau
'Brutus'	CCla CLoc EBak EBly EKMF ISea LHig MPen MSmi MWhe NPor SKen SLBF SOld WPau
¶ 'Bubble Hanger'	MSmi
'Buddha'	EBak WPau
'Buenos Aires'	EBly EGou
'Bunny'	EBak EGou NPor WPau
'Buttercup'	CLoc EBak EGou MWhe SKen SOld WPau
'Buttons and Bows'	NMGN WPau
'C J Howlett'	EBak
'Caballero'	EBak
'Cable Car'	WPau
'Caesar'	EBak EKMF SOld WPau
'Caledonia'	EBak NMGN WPau
'Callaly Pink'	CCla EBly MJac NPor WPau
'Cambridge Louie'	EBak MBri MLab MPen MWar MWhe NMGN NPor SKen SLBF SOld WPau
'Camelot'	EBak MJac
'Cameron Ryle'	WPau
'Candlelight'	CLoc EBak MPen MSmi NPor WPau
'Candy Stripe'	CLoc
§ ***canescens***	CCla EKMF
'Capri'	EBak SLBF WPau
'Cara Mia'	CLoc NPor SKen SLBF
'Cardinal Farges'	CCla CLoc EGou EKMF NMGN SKen SLBF SOld WPau
'Carefree'	NMGN WPau
'Carioca'	EBak WPau
'Carl Wallace'	EKMF
'Carla Johnson'	CLoc EBly EGou EKMF MJac MLab NPor SLBF SOld
'Carlisle Bells'	NMGN
'Carmel Blue'	CCla CLoc MPen MWhe SKen SOld WPau
'Carmen Maria'	CCla MJac SKen WPau
'Carmine Bell'	EKMF
'Carnival'	EGou SOld WPau
'Carnoustie'	EBak EBly EGou WPau
'Carol Grace'	CLoc
'Carol Roe'	EKMF MPen SOld
'Carole Scott'	MLab
'Caroline'	CCla CLoc EBak EBly EKMF MSmi MWhe NMGN SKen SLBF SOld WPau
'Cascade'	CCla CLoc EBly EGou EKMF MBri MJac MLab MPen MSmi MWar MWhe NMGN NPor SKen SOld WEas WPau
'Caspar Hauser'	EGou EKMF NPor SLBF WPau
'Catherine Bartlett'	EKMF SLBF
'Cathie MacDougall'	EBak WPau
'Cecile'	EKMF MLab MSmi SLBF WPau
'Celadore'	EKMF MJac NMGN NPor SKen WPau
'Celebration'	EBly EGou
'Celia Smedley'	CCla CLoc EBak EBly EGou EKMF MBri MJac MPen MWar MWhe NMGN NPor SKen SLBF SOld WPau
'Centenary'	SOld
'Centerpiece'	EBak WPau
'Ceri'	CCla CLoc EBly
'Champagne Celebration'	CLoc
'Chandleri'	CCla EKMF NPor SLBF SOld WPau

'Chang'	CCla CLoc CMHG EBak EKMF MPen MWar MWhe NMGN NPor SLBF WPau
'Charisma'	SOld
'Charles Edward'	EBly
'Charleston'	SLBF WPau
'Charlie Gardiner'	EBak EBly EGou MWhe NMGN SLBF WPau
'Charlie Girl'	EBak
'Charming'	CCla CLoc EBak MJac MPen MWhe NMGN SLBF SOld WPau
'Checkerboard'	CCla CLoc EBak EGou EKMF MJac MLab MPen MSmi MWar MWhe NPor SKen SLBF SOld WPau
'Cheers'	EBly EGou EKMF MLab MSmi MWar NMGN NPor SOld WPau
'Cherry Pie'	CTab
'Chessboard'	CCla CLoc
'Cheviot Princess'	WPau
'Chillerton Beauty'	CCla CLoc CSco EKMF IDai LHig MJac MPen MWhe SHil SLBF SOld SPer WPau
'China Doll'	EBak MWhe SKen WPau
'China Lantern'	CLoc EBak
'Chiquita Maria'	MSmi
¶ 'Christ Driessen'	EGou
'Christine Pugh'	WPau
'Christine Windsor'	WPau
'Christmas Holly'	WPau
'Christmas Ribbons'	EGou MSmi
'Churchtown'	EKMF NPor
'Cicely Ann'	WPau
'Circe'	EBak EKMF MPen WPau
'Circus'	EBak SOld WPau
'Citation'	CCla CLoc EBak EBly EKMF MJac MPen MSmi NMGN NPor SLBF SOld WPau
'City of Adelaide'	EKMF MWhe SKen WPau
'City of Derby'	WPau
'City of Leicester'	EBly EKMF MPen NPor SLBF WPau
'Claire de Lune'	EBak EKMF MWhe NPor SLBF WPau
'Claire Evans'	CLoc
'Classic Jean'	MWhe WPau
'Clifford Gadsby'	EBak WPau
'Cliff's Hardy'	CCla EKMF MPen
'Cliff's Own'	CCla MLab MPen WPau
'Cliff's Supreme'	CGre
'Cliff's Unique'	CCla EBly MWar NPor WPau
'Clifton Beauty'	MJac WPau
'Clifton Belle'	MJac WPau
'Clifton Charm'	EBly MJac
'Cloth of Gold'	CCla CLoc EBak MJac MLab MWhe NMGN NPor SKen SLBF SOld
'Clouds'	CCla CTab
'Cloverdale Delight'	SKen
'Cloverdale Jewel'	CCla EBak MJac MLab MWhe SKen WPau
'Cloverdale Joy'	EBak
'Cloverdale Pearl'	EBak EKMF MJac MPen MWhe NPor SKen SLBF SOld WPau
'Cloverdale Pride'	WPau
'Cloverdale Star'	SKen
'Coachman'	CCla CLoc EBak EBly EKMF MBri MLab MPen MSmi MWar MWhe NMGN NPor SKen SLBF SOld SPla WPau
coccinea	CCla EKMF
colensoi	CSun CTre ECou
– forms	CMal
'Collingwood'	CLoc EBak EKMF WPau
'Come Dancing'	MLab MPen SKen SLBF WPau
N 'Comet'	CLoc EBak WPau
'Conchilla'	EBak
'Concorde'	CLoc WPau
'Confection'	MSmi NMGN WPau
'Connie'	CCla EBak WPau
'Conspicua'	EBak EGou EKMF ELan SKen
'Constable Country'	EBak EGou WPau
'Constance'	CCla CLoc EGou EKMF MJac MPen MSmi MWar MWhe SKen SLBF SOld SPla WPau
N 'Constellation'	CCla CLoc EBak MBri MJac MWhe NPor SKen SOld WPau
'Contamine'	EKMF
'Continental'	EBly EGou WPau
'Contramine'	WPau
'Cookie'	WPau
'Copycat'	WPau
'Coquet Bell'	EBak EBly EGou MJac NPor
'Coquet Dale'	EBak EBly EGou EKMF MJac MPen MWhe NMGN NPor SOld
'Coquet Gold'	ECtt EGou MSmi NMGN
'Coral Rose'	CTab
'Coral Seas'	EBak
'Coralle'	See F. 'Koralle'
'Corallina'	CBra CCla CLoc CMHG EBak EKMF IHos MFir MPen MWgw MWhe NMGN SHil SKen SLBF SPla WEas
cordifolia	CGre CHil CPle CTre EBak
'Core'ngrato'	CLoc EBak WPau
'Cornelian Fire'	CTab
'Corsage'	MSmi WPau
'Corsair'	EBak EKMF MSmi NMGN SLBF WPau
§ ***corymbiflora***	CCla EBak EKMF
– ***alba***	CCla EBak MPen MWhe SLBF
'Cosmopolitan'	EBak WPau
'Costa Brava'	CCla CLoc
'Cotta Bella'	EKMF MJac NPor WPau
'Cotta Fairy'	EKMF WPau
'Cotta Princess'	EKMF
'Cottinghamii'	CCla ITim WSHC
'Cotton Candy'	CCla CLoc EBly MBri MLab MWhe SLBF SOld WPau
'Countess of Aberdeen'	CLoc EBak EGou EKMF NPor SLBF SOld WPau
'Countess of Maritza'	CLoc WPau
'Court Jester'	CLoc EBak
'Cover Girl'	MSmi WPau
'Coxeen'	EBak

¶ 'Cracker'	WPau
'Crackerjack'	CLoc EBak MSmi WPau
'Creampuff'	WPau
'Crescendo'	CLoc SKen
'Crinoline'	EBak WPau
'Cropwell Butler'	WPau
'Crosby Soroptimist'	EGou MPen MWar NPor SLBF
'Crosscheck'	CCla EKMF MJac NPor WPau
'Crusader'	CSut NMGN
'Crystal Blue'	EBak
'Crystal Stars'	CCla SKen
'Cupcake'	EKMF WPau
'Cupid'	EBak
'Curly Q'	CCla EBak EKMF WPau
'Curtain Call'	CCla CLoc EBak EGou MPen WPau
'Cymon'	EBly MWhe
'Cyndy Robyn'	EKMF WPau
'Cyril Holmes'	WPau
'Dainty'	EBak
'Dainty Lady'	EBak WPau
'Daisy Bell'	CLoc EBak EGou EKMF MJac MLab MPen MWhe NPor SKen SLBF SOld
'Dalton'	EBak
'Dancing Flame'	CCla CLoc EBly EGou EKMF MLab MSmi MWar MWhe NMGN NPor SKen SLBF SOld WPau
'Danish Pastry'	WPau
'Danny Boy'	CCla CLoc EBak MPen MWhe NMGN SOld WPau
'Daphne Arlene'	SLBF WPau
'Dark Eyes'	CCla CLoc EBak EKMF MJac MLab MSmi MWhe NMGN SKen SLBF SOld WPau
'Dark Secret'	EBak WPau
'David'	EKMF SKen WPau
'David Alston'	CLoc EBak
'David Lockyer'	CLoc WPau
'David Ward'	EGou
'Dawn'	EBak SKen SOld WPau
'Dawn Redfern'	MJac
'Dawn Sky'	EBak
'Dawn Star'	EBly MJac MLab MWhe WPau
'Dawn Thunder'	MSmi WPau
'Day Star'	EBak
'Daytime Live'	EBly
'De Bono's Pride'	WPau
'Debbie'	EBak WPau
'Deben'	EGou
'Deborah'	MSmi WPau
'Deborah Louise'	EBly
'Deborah Young'	EKMF
'Debra Hampson'	MLab
'Debra Imp'	MLab
§ *decussata*	CGle EBak EKMF
'Dedham Vale'	EBak EGou WPau
'Dee Copley'	EBak WPau
¶ 'Dee Star'	WPau
'Deep Purple'	MSmi
'Delaval Lady'	WPau
'Delicia'	WPau
'Delilah'	MJac WPau
'Deltaschön'	WPau
'Denis Bolton'	SLBF
denticulata	CHil CLoc CMHG CPle CSun EKMF IBar SLBF
dependens	See F. *corymbiflora*
'Derby Imp'	MWar NMGN SKen WPau
'Devonshire Dumpling'	CCla CGre CLoc EBly EGou EKMF MJac MLab MPen MWhe NMGN SLBF SOld WPau
'Diablo'	EBak WPau
'Diamond Fire'	CTab
'Diamond Wedding'	SOld
'Diana'	EBak WPau
¶ 'Diana Goodwin'	EGou
'Diana Wills'	CCla MWhe SKen WPau
¶ 'Diane Brown'	EKMF
'Diane Christiansen'	CTab
'Dilly-Dilly'	MBri MJac MPen WPau
'Dimples'	NMGN
'Dipton Dainty'	CLoc EBak WPau
'Dirk van Delen'	WPau
'Display'	CCla CLoc CMHG EBak EBly EGou EKMF IHos LHig MBri MJac MLab MPen MWar MWhe NMGN NPor SKen SLBF SOld WPau
'Doc'	CTab EBly SOld WWeb
'Doctor'	See F. 'The Doctor'
'Doctor Brendan Freeman'	MJac
'Doctor Foster'	CCla CLoc CMHG CSco EBak MSmi SKen SOld WEas WPau
'Doctor Olson'	CLoc EBak
'Doctor Robert'	EBly MJac NPor
'Doctor Topinard'	CLoc EBak
§ 'Dollar Princess'	CCla CLoc CMHG EBak EBly EGou EKMF IHos LHig MBri MLab MPen MSmi MWar MWhe NMGN SKen SLBF SOld SPla WPau
'Dolly Daydream'	EKMF WPau
'Domacine'	MSmi MWhe NMGN WPau
'Dominyana'	CCla CPle EBak EKMF
'Don Peralta'	EBak WPau
'Dopey'	CTab EBly SOld
'Doreen Redfern'	CCla CLoc EKMF MJac MWhe NPor SOld WPau
'Doris Coleman'	SLBF SOld
'Doris Hobbs'	EKMF
'Dorothea Flower'	CLoc EBak
'Dorothy'	MR&S SLBF
'Dorothy Day'	CLoc WPau
'Dorothy M Goldsmith'	EBly EGou
'Dorothy Shields'	EBly MJac NPor
¶ 'Dove Cottage'	MPen
¶ 'Drake 400'	CLoc
'Drama Girl'	EKMF WPau
'Drame'	CCla EBak ECtt EKMF MSmi NMGN SKen SOld SPla WPau
'Dreamy Days'	EGou
'Drooping Lady'	WEas
'Drum Major'	EBak
'Du Barry'	EBak WPau
'Duchess of Albany'	CCla CLoc EBak

'Duchess of Cornwall'	CTab
'Duet'	EBly MSmi SLBF WPau
N 'Duke of Wellington'	CLoc
'Dulcie Elizabeth'	EBak EKMF MJac MPen MWar MWhe SOld WPau
'Dunrobin Bedder'	SLBF
'Dusky Beauty'	EKMF MJac MWar NPor SLBF WPau
'Dusky Rose'	CCla CLoc EBak MJac MLab MWar MWhe
'Dutch Mill'	CLoc EBak WPau
'Dutch Pearl'	WPau
'Dutch Shoes'	WPau
'Duyfken'	WPau
'Earl of Beaconsfield'	CLoc EGou
'East Anglian'	CLoc EBak
'Easter Bonnet'	CCla CLoc
'Easterling'	SLBF WPau
'Ebbtide'	CCla CLoc EBak WPau
'Ecstasy'	SOld
'Ed Largarde'	EBak EKMF NPor WPau
'Edale'	MSmi
'Eden Dawn'	EBly
'Eden Lady'	CLoc MWar MWhe SOld WPau
'Eden Princess'	MJac MWhe SKen
'Edith'	SLBF
'Edith Emery'	WPau
¶ 'Edith Hall'	EGou
'Edith Jack'	CTab WPau
'Edith of Kimbolton'	MLab
'Edna'	MSmi
'Edna May'	EKMF MPen MWar NPor WPau
'Edna W Smith'	ECtt MLab
'Edwin Miles'	SOld
'Eileen Raffill'	EBak
'Eileen Saunders'	EBak
'El Camino'	CCla ECtt MJac WPau
'El Cid'	CLoc EBak EKMF MPen
'Elaine Ann'	EBly MJac NPor
'Eleanor Clark'	EKMF MPen NPor WPau
'Eleanor Leytham'	EBak EKMF MPen NMGN SOld WPau
'Eleanor Rawlins'	EBak EKMF MLab NMGN NPor SKen SOld
'Elf'	CCla CTab EBly
'Elfin Glade'	CLoc EBak NBir
'Elfrida'	EKMF NMGN SKen
'Elfriede Ott'	CCla EBak EKMF MSmi MWhe SLBF SOld WPau
'Elise Mitchell'	EBly MPen MWar MWhe NMGN NPor SLBF SOld WPau
N 'Elizabeth'	EBak MPen WPau
'Elizabeth Broughton'	CCla EKMF WPau
'Elizabeth Travis'	EBak WPau
'Elsa'	MJac
'Elsie Johnson'	MLab
§ 'Emile de Wildeman'	EBak EGou EKMF MJac MPen MWhe NPor SKen WPau
'Emile Zola'	SPla
'Emily Austen'	EKMF
'Empress of Prussia'	CCla CLoc EBak EKMF MLab MPen SKen SLBF SPla WPau
'Enchanted'	EBak WPau
encliandra encliandra	EGou
§ 'Enfant Prodigue'	CCla CLoc EKMF EMon SLBF WPau
'English Rose'	EBly
'Erica Julie'	WPau
'Erica Memlis'	WPau
'Eric's Hardy'	SLBF
'Ernestine'	CCla EBly MPen MWhe SOld WPau
'Ernie Bromley'	EGou
'Errol'	CLoc
'Eschott Elf'	WPau
'Esme Tabraham'	CTab
'Estelle Marie'	CCla CLoc EBak EBly EGou EKMF MJac MLab MPen MWar NPor SKen SLBF SOld WPau
'Esther'	WPau
'Esther Devine'	WPau
'Eternal Flame'	EBak MBri MPen MWhe NMGN NPor SKen WPau
N 'Ethel'	WPau
'Ethel May Lester'	SOld
'Eurydice'	CLoc
'Eusebia'	EKMF MJac MSmi WPau
–	NMGN
'Eva Boerg'	CCla CLoc CSco EBak EKMF ERav IHos MBri MLab MPen MSmi MWar MWhe NMGN NPor SKen SOld WKif WPau
'Evanson's Choice'	SKen
'Evening Sky'	EBak EKMF WPau
'Evensong'	CCla CLoc EBak EBly EKMF MPen NMGN SLBF SOld WPau
'Excalibur'	EBak EGou WPau
excorticata	CB&S CGre CHil CMer CTre CTrw ECou EKMF GWic WSHC
'Exeter'	CSut EBly EGou
'Expo '86'	MSmi
'Fairplay'	EKMF
'Fairytales'	EKMF
'Falling Stars'	CCla CLoc EBak ECtt MWhe NPor WPau
'Fan Dancer'	EBak WPau
'Fan Tan'	MSmi WPau
'Fancy Flute'	WPau
'Fancy Pants'	CLoc MBri SKen
'Fancy Sockeye'	WPau
'Fanfare'	CCla EBak
'Fascination'	See F. 'Emile de Wildeman'
'Fashion'	EBak WPau
'Favourite'	EBak
'Felixstowe Display'	EBly WPau
'Feltham's Pride'	EBly
'Fenman'	EBly EGou EKMF MJac SLBF WPau
'Fenrother Fairy'	WPau
'Fergie'	SOld
'Festoon'	EBak
'Fey'	EGou EKMF SLBF
'Fiery Spider'	EBak EKMF
'Filligrain'	CCla MJac

'Finn' EBly EGou
'Fiona' EBak MJac MPen WEas WPau
¶ 'Fiona Jane' EKMF
'Fire Mountain' EGou MPen MWhe NMGN NPor SKen WPau
'Firebird' EKMF WPau
'Firecracker' MLab
'Firelite' CCla EBak
'Firenza' CCla MWar
'First Kiss' WPau
'First Lady' MBri MPen MSmi WPau
'First Sucess' EKMF
'Fizzy Lizzy' WPau
'Flair' CCla CLoc WPau
'Flame' EBak WPau
'Flash' CCla CLoc EBak ECtt EKMF MJac MPen MWhe NMGN SIng SLBF SOld WPau
'Flashlight' ELan WPau
¶ 'Flat Jack o'Lancashire' EKMF
'Flavia' EBak SOld
'Flirtation Waltz' CCla CLoc EBak EGou EKMF MBri MJac MPen MSmi MWhe NMGN NPor SKen SLBF SOld WPau
'Flocon de Neige' EBak
'Floral City' CLoc EBak EKMF WPau
'Florence Mary Abbott' EBak EBly EGou MWar NMGN SLBF SOld WPau
'Florence Taylor' WPau
'Florence Turner' EBak EBly EKMF MPen MWhe NPor SKen
'Florentina' CLoc EBak EKMF NPor WPau
'Florrie Bambridge' WPau
'Flowerdream' MJac
'Fluffy Frills' WPau
'Fluffy Ruffles' WPau
'Fly by Night' CCla
'Flyaway' EBak NPor WPau
'Flying Cloud' CCla CLoc EBak EBly EKMF MBri MPen MWhe NMGN SKen WEas WPau
'Flying Scotsman' CCla CLoc EBak EBly EGou SLBF SOld WPau
'Folies Bergères' WPau
'Foline' EGou
¶ 'Foolke' EGou
N 'Forget-me-not' CLoc EBak EKMF MWhe SLBF WPau
'Fort Bragg' EBak MSmi SKen WPau
'Forward Look' CCla MWhe SKen
'Fountains Abbey' NPor WPau
'Foxtrot' MBri MWar WPau
'Frank Saunders' EKMF SLBF WPau
'Frank Unsworth' ECtt EKMF MWar MWhe NMGN NPor SOld WPau
'Frau Hilda Rademacher' CCla EBak EBly EKMF MPen MPla SLBF WPau
'Fred Swales' EKMF WPau
'Freefall' EBak
'Freeland Ballerina' MJac
'Friendly Fire' EKMF WPau
'Frosted Amethyst' WPau
'Frosted Flame' CLoc EBly EKMF MJac MWar MWhe NPor SLBF SOld WPau
'Frühling' EBak
'Fuchsia Fan' EBly
'Fuchsiade '88' EGou SLBF
'Fuchsiarama' EKMF MSmi WPau
'Für Elise' EBak WPau
'Fuksie Foetsie' EGou EKMF
fulgens CCla CMHG EKMF MBal MPen MWhe SOld
– gesneriana CCla CLoc EBak
– rubra grandiflora EBak EKMF SLBF
'Gabriel Rose' CTab
'Gala' EBak WPau
¶ 'Galadriel' EGou
'Galahad' EBak
'Garden News' CCla CLoc EBly EGou EKMF MJac MPen MPla MSmi MWar MWhe NMGN NPor SHil SKen SLBF SOld SPla WPau
'Garden Week' MSmi MWhe SLBF SOld WPau
'Gartenmeister Bonstedt' CCla CLoc EBak EBly EKMF MLab NMGN NPor SKen SMad SOld WEas
'Gay Anne' EKMF
'Gay Fandango' CLoc EBak ECtt MPen MWar NMGN SKen SOld WPau
'Gay Future' EKMF
'Gay Parasol' CLoc EGou MLab MSmi WPau
'Gay Paree' EBak WPau
'Gay Senorita' EBak WPau
'Gay Spinner' CLoc
¶ 'Gazebo' MSmi
gehrigeri EBak EKMF
'General Monk' CCla EBak EKMF MBri MJac MPla MSmi SKen SOld WPau
'Général Voyron' MPla
'General Wavell' WPau
'Genii' Widely available
'Geoffrey Smith' EKMF
'Georgana' ECtt MSmi MWhe WPau
'George Barr' SKen
¶ 'George Bunstead' MPen
'George Humphrey' SOld
'George N Joe' WPau
'George Robinson' MPen
'George Travis' EBak MBri MPen WPau
'Giant Falls' CLoc MSmi
'Giant Pink Enchanted' CLoc EBak WPau
'Gilda' EGou MJac NPor SLBF WPau
'Gilt Edge' CLoc
'Gipping' EBly EGou
'Gladiator' EBak MPen WPau
'Gladys Miller' CLoc
'Glenby' NPor WPau
¶ 'Glendale' MPen
'Glitters' CCla EBak ECtt EKMF NMGN NPor WPau
'Globosa' CCla CMHG EBak SKen
'Glow' EBak
'Glowing Embers' EBak WPau
'Glowing Lilac' EKMF MSmi WPau
'Glyn Jones' EKMF
'Göttingen' EBak

'Gold Brocade'	CCla CTab EBly SKen WPau
'Gold Crest'	CTab EBak SKen
'Gold Runner'	CCla MJac MWar NPor WPau
'Golden Anniversary'	CLoc EBly EKMF MJac MSmi MWar NMGN SOld WPau
'Golden Arrow'	EGou
'Golden Border Queen'	CLoc WPau
'Golden Dawn'	CCla CLoc EBak ECtt NPor SKen SOld WPau
'Golden Eden Lady'	MPen MWhe WPau
'Golden La Campanella'	CLoc ECtt SKen SOld
'Golden Lena'	CCla EKMF SOld WPau
'Golden Marinka'	CCla CLoc EBak EBly EKMF MBri MJac MPen MSmi MWar MWhe NMGN NPor SKen SOld WEas
'Golden Melody'	CCla CTab SKen
'Golden Swingtime'	EBly EGou MBri MLab MWar MWhe NMGN NPor SOld WPau
'Golden Tolling Bell'	MLab
'Golden Treasure'	CCla CLoc CSco EBly EKMF MBri MPen MWhe NMGN NPor
'Golden Wedding'	EKMF WPau
'Golondrina'	EBak MPen MWhe
'Goody Goody'	EBak WPau
'Goose Girl'	CTab
'Gordon Thorley'	EBly MJac MWhe NPor SLBF
'Gordon's China Rose'	EBly SKen
'Governor Pat Brown'	EBak WPau
'Grace Darling'	CCla EBak MWhe
'Grace Durham'	EBak EGou WPau
gracilis	See F. ***magellanica gracilis***
'Grady'	WPau
'Graf Spee'	EBly EGou
'Graf Witte'	EGou MPen MWhe SHil WPau
'Granada'	WPau
'Grand Prix'	MLab SKen SOld WPau
'Grand Slam'	SKen SOld WPau
'Grandma Sinton'	EBly MBri MJac MPen MWar MWhe NPor SKen WPau
'Grandpa George'	SOld
¶ 'Grange Farm'	EGou
'Grasmere'	EKMF NPor WPau
'Gray Dawn'	WPau
'Great Scott'	CCla CLoc SKen WPau
'Green 'n' Gold'	EBak
'Greenpeace'	EKMF SLBF WPau
'Greg Walker'	WPau
'Gretna Chase'	WPau
'Grey Lady'	CTab SOld
'Groene Kans Glorie'	EKMF MWhe SLBF
'Grumpy'	CTab EBly MBri NPor SKen SOld WWeb
'Gruss aus dem Bodethal'	CCla CLoc EBak EBly EKMF SKen
'Guinevere'	EBak WPau
'Gustave Doré'	EBak WPau
'Guy Dauphine'	EBak WPau
'Gwen Dodge'	EBly SLBF
'Gypsy Girl'	SKen WPau
'Gypsy Prince'	CLoc WPau
'H G Brown'	EBak MJac MWhe NPor
'Hampshire Beauty'	MJac SOld
'Hampshire Blue'	SLBF WPau
'Hampshire Prince'	EKMF WPau
'Hampshire Treasure'	EBly MPen SLBF WPau
'Hanna'	CCla
'Happiness'	NMGN
'Happy'	CCla CTab EBly SIng SOld
'Happy Fellow'	CLoc EBak
'Happy Wedding Day'	CLoc EKMF MPen MSmi MWhe SLBF WPau
'Hapsburgh'	EBak WPau
'Harlow Car'	EKMF SLBF
'Harmony'	CTab EBak
'Harnser's Flight'	EGou
'Harriett'	MSmi WPau
'Harrow Pride'	SKen SLBF
'Harry Dunnett'	EBak
'Harry Gray'	CCla EBak EBly EGou EKMF MBri MPen MSmi MWar MWhe NMGN NPor SKen SLBF SOld WPau
'Harry Lye'	EGou WPau
hartwegii	EGou EKMF
'Harvest Glow'	EBak EGou WPau
'Hathersage'	MPen
¶ 'Hathor'	EGou
'Haute Cuisine'	EGou SLBF
'Hawaiian Night'	WPau
'Hawkshead'	CCla CMal CRow EGou EKMF ELan LGre MJac MWhe NPor SChu SOld WPau
'Hay Wain'	EBak WPau
'Hazel'	EKMF MSmi MWhe WPau
'Heart Throb'	EBak MBri WPau
'Hebe'	EBak MWhe WPau
'Heidi Ann'	CCla CLoc EBak EBly EGou EKMF IHos MBri MJac MLab MSmi MWar NMGN NPor SKen SLBF SOld WPau
'Heidi Weiss'	EKMF MLab NMGN SKen SOld
'Heinrich Heinkel'	CCla CLoc EBak MWhe NMGN SOld
'Heirloom'	EKMF MSmi NMGN WPau
'Helen Clare'	CCla CLoc EBak WPau
'Hello Dolly'	CLoc
'Hemsleyana'	CCla LHig MLab MWhe SKen SLBF SOld WPau
'Henri Poincaré'	EBak EKMF MSmi
'Herald'	EBak NMGN SLBF SOld WPau
'Herbe de Jacques'	EBly EKMF SKen
'Heritage'	CLoc EBak
¶ 'Hermiena'	EGou EKMF SLBF WPau
'Hermione'	MPen NPor
'Heron'	EBak EKMF MPen NMGN SKen WPau
'Hessett Festival'	EBak EBly WPau
'Heston Blue'	EKMF MWhe NMGN WPau
'Heydon'	WPau
'Hi Jinks'	MSmi WPau
hidalgensis	See F. ***microphylla hidalgensis***

'Hidcote Beauty'	CLoc EBak EKMF MPen MWar MWhe NPor SKen SLBF WPau
'High Peak'	WPau
'Highland Beauty'	WPau
'Highland Pipes'	EGou EKMF SLBF WPau
'Hilda Fitzsimmons'	EGou WPau
'Hill Top'	WPau
'Hindu Belle'	EBak EKMF MSmi WPau
¶ 'Hinnerike'	EGou
'His Excellency'	EBak
'Hobson's Choice'	MWar SLBF SOld WPau
'Hollywood Park'	EBak
'Horatio'	MJac NMGN
'Howlett's Hardy'	CLoc EBak EKMF LHig MBal MBri MPen MSmi NMGN NPor WPau
'Hula Girl'	CCla EBak EKMF MJac MLab MWar MWhe NMGN NPor SKen SLBF WPau
'Humboldt Holiday'	CCla EBly MLab MSmi NMGN WPau
'Humpty Dumpty'	CTab
'Ian Brazewell'	CLoc
'Ian Leedham'	EBak EKMF NPor WPau
'Ice Cream Soda'	EBak WPau
'Ice Festival'	WPau
'Iceberg'	EBak EBly WPau
'Icecap'	EKMF MPen
'Iced Champagne'	CLoc EBak MJac MWar NMGN NPor SKen WPau
'Ichiban'	CLoc WPau
'Ida'	WPau
'Ida Dixon'	EBak
'Igloo Maid'	CLoc EBak EBly EKMF MJac MLab MPen MWar MWhe NPor SKen SOld WPau
'Imperial Fantasy'	MSmi SLBF WPau
'Improved Hannah'	WPau
'Impudence'	CCla CLoc EBak NMGN
'Impulse'	ECtt EKMF SKen WPau
'Independence'	NPor WPau
'Indian Maid'	EBak EBly EKMF MBri MJac NMGN SKen SOld WPau
'Indian Princess'	WPau
'Inferno'	EKMF MSmi
'Ingram Maid'	CCla NMGN
'Interlude'	EBak WPau
'Iris Amer'	CLoc EBak MWar NPor WPau
'Isabel Ryan'	CTab
'Isis'	CCla SKen
'Isle of Mull'	EGou MPen SKen WPau
'Italiano'	MJac NPor WPau
¶ 'J M Scales'	MPen
'Jack Acland'	ECtt EGou EKMF MPen NPor SKen WPau
'Jack Coast'	SOld
'Jack Horner'	CTab
'Jack Shahan'	CCla CLoc EBak EBly EKMF IHos MBri MJac MPen MSmi MWhe NMGN SKen SLBF SOld WEas WPau
'Jack Sprat'	CTab
'Jack Stanway'	WEas WMar
'Jackie Bull'	EBak WPau
'Jackpot'	EBak WPau
'Jackqueline'	EBly EGou EKMF SOld
'Jam Roll'	WPau
'Jamboree'	EBak WPau
'James Lye'	EBak
'James Travis'	EBak MPen NPor SKen
'Jandel'	MSmi WPau
'Jane Elizabeth'	WPau
'Jane Humber'	EKMF WPau
'Jane Lye'	EBak SKen WPau
'Janet Williams'	CTab
'Janice Revell'	EBly MJac
'Janie'	MPen
'Jayne Rowell'	NPor SKen
'Jean'	EKMF WPau
'Jean Campbell'	EBak
'Jean Dawes'	EBly EGou
'Jean Ewart'	NMGN
'Jennie Rachael'	NMGN
'Jenny Sorensen'	EKMF NPor SLBF
'Jess'	SLBF
'Jessimae'	CCla MLab NMGN WPau
'Jester'	CLoc CTab
'Jet Fire'	EBak WPau
N 'Jewel'	CTab
'Jezebel'	MSmi WPau
'Jill Whitworth'	NMGN
'Jim Coleman'	MPen NPor SLBF SOld
'Jim Dowers'	EGou
'Jimmy Carr'	NPor
'Joan Barnes'	MPen WPau
'Joan Cooper'	CCla CLoc EBak EKMF NPor
'Joan Gilbert'	WPau
'Joan Goy'	EKMF MJac NPor SLBF
'Joan Leach'	CCla CTab
'Joan Pacey'	EBak MJac SKen
'Joan Smith'	EBak MPen NPor SLBF
'Joe Browning'	CTab
'Joe Kusber'	EBak EKMF NMGN SKen SOld WPau
'John Baker'	WPau
'John Lockyer'	CLoc EBak WPau
'John Maynard Scales'	EBly EGou MJac MWhe
'John Suckley'	EBak
'John Waugh'	EBly
'Johnny'	CLoc WPau
'Jolly Jorden'	MPen
'Jomam'	EBly MWhe NPor
'Jon Oram'	CLoc
'Joseph Holmes'	SOld
'Jose's Joan'	CCla MLab MWhe NMGN WPau
'Joy Bielby'	EKMF MWhe NPor WPau
'Joy Patmore'	CLoc EBak EBly EKMF MJac MPen MWhe NPor SKen SLBF SOld WPau
'Joy White'	CTab
'Joyce Sinton'	EKMF NPor SLBF
'Jubie-Lin'	WPau
'Judith Alison Castle'	WPau
'Jules Daloges'	EBak
'Julia'	EBly EKMF NMGN WPau
'Julia Deitrich'	EKMF WPau
¶ 'Julie Adams'	MPen

	Cultivar	Suppliers
	'Julie Marie'	MJac SLBF
	'June Gardner'	EKMF
	'Juno'	EBak MSmi WPau
	'Jupiter Seventy'	CCla EBak SOld
	'Justin's Pride'	EKMF MLab NMGN WPau
	'Kaleidoscope'	EBak MSmi WPau
	'Karen Bielby'	EKMF SLBF
	'Karen Louise'	CLoc
	'Kathleen Colville'	CLoc
	'Kathleen Muncaster'	EKMF MWar WPau
	'Kathleen Saunders'	SOld
	'Kathleen Smith'	EKMF WPau
	'Kathryn Maidment'	EKMF
	'Kathy's Sparkler'	EGou EKMF WPau
	'Katrina'	CLoc EBak WPau
	'Keepsake'	CCla CLoc EBak WPau
	'Kegworth Carnival'	MJac MLab NPor SKen SOld WPau
	'Kegworth Clown'	WPau
	'Kegworth Delight'	NPor WPau
	'Kegworth Supreme'	MJac MWhe
¶	'Ken Goldsmith'	EGou
	'Ken Jennings'	MJac NPor WPau
	'Ken Sharp'	MJac
	'Kenny Dalglish'	EKMF
	'Kernan Robson'	CLoc EBak WPau
	'Kerry Anne'	EBly EKMF MLab MWar
	'Keystone'	CCla EBak
	'Khada'	EKMF MPen MWhe WPau
	'Kim Hampson'	WPau
	'Kim Wright'	MWhe WPau
	'Kimberly'	EBak
	'King of Hearts'	EBak WPau
¶	'King of Siam'	SLBF
	'King's Ransom'	CLoc EBak MPen MWhe NMGN NPor SKen SLBF SOld WPau
¶	'Kit Oxtoby'	EKMF
	'Kiwi'	EBak NMGN SKen SLBF WPau
	'Knight Errant'	SLBF
	'Knockout'	EGou EKMF MSmi NPor SLBF WPau
	'Kolding Perle'	SOld WPau
	'Kon-Tiki'	EKMF NMGN WPau
§	'Koralle'	CCla EBak EBly EGou EKMF MJac MLab MSmi MWar MWhe NPor SKen SLBF SOld WEas
	'Kursal'	WPau
	'Kwintet'	EBak MJac NPor SKen WPau
	'La Bergère'	EKMF WPau
	'La Bianca'	EBak WPau
	'La Campanella'	CCla CLoc EBak EBly EKMF MBri MJac MLab MPen MSmi MWar MWhe NMGN NPor SKen SLBF SOld WPau
	'La Fiesta'	EBak MSmi NMGN WPau
	'La France'	EBak
N	'La Neige'	CCla EBak MSmi SKen SOld WPau
	'La Porte'	CLoc
	'La Rosita'	EBak MSmi SLBF WPau
N	'La Traviata'	CCla EBak WPau

	Cultivar	Suppliers
	'Lace Petticoats'	CLoc EBak MSmi WPau
	'Lady Beth'	WPau
	'Lady Boothby'	CPle EBak EKMF NMGN NPor SKen SOld SPla WPau
	'Lady in Grey'	EKMF
	'Lady Isobel Barnett'	CCla CLoc EBak EBly EKMF IHos MBri MJac MPen MSmi MWar MWhe NPor SKen SLBF SOld WPau
	'Lady Kathleen Spence'	EBak EGou EKMF MJac MPen MWhe NMGN NPor SKen SOld WPau
¶	'Lady Pamela Mountbatten'	CSut
	'Lady Patricia Mountbatten'	ECtt EGou EKMF MJac MPen MWar NPor SOld
	'Lady Ramsay'	EBak EGou EKMF MJac NMGN WPau
	'Lady Rebecca'	CLoc
	'Lady Thumb'	Widely available
	'Lady's Smock'	EGou SLBF
	'Lakeland Princess'	EBak WPau
	'Lakeside'	CLoc EBak
	'Lancashire Lass'	EBly MBri NPor WPau
	'Lancelot'	CCla EBak EBly EGou NMGN SKen SLBF WPau
	'Lark'	EBly EGou EKMF
¶	'Larkfield Skylark'	EGou
	'Lassie'	CLoc EBak MJac MSmi WPau
N	'Laura'	EKMF MSmi MWhe NMGN SLBF
	'Laurie'	SOld WPau
	'Lavender Blue'	CCla CTab
	'Lavender Kate'	CLoc EBak MJac
	'Lazy Lady'	EBak
	'Le Berger'	EKMF
	'Lechlade Apache'	EGou
	'Lechlade Debutante'	EGou
¶	'Lechlade Fire Eater'	EGou
	'Lechlade Gorgon'	EKMF
	'Lechlade Martianess'	EKMF
	'Lechlade Rocket'	EKMF
	'Lechlade Tinkerbell'	EGou
	'Lemacto'	EBak
	'Len Bielby'	EKMF MWar
	'Lena'	CCla CLoc CMHG EBak EBly EGou EKMF LHig MBal MBri MJac MLab MPen MPla MSmi MWhe NMGN NPor SHil SKen SLBF SOld SPer WEas
	'Lena Dalton'	CCla CLoc EBak EBly EGou EKMF IHos MBri MJac MSmi MWar MWhe SKen SOld WPau
	'Leonora'	CCla CLoc EBak EBly EKMF MBri MLab MPen MSmi MWar MWhe NPor SKen SLBF SOld WPau
¶	'Letty Lye'	EBak
	'Lett's Delight'	EBly EGou
	'Leverhulme'	See F. 'Leverkusen'
§	'Leverkusen'	CCla CLoc EBak EKMF MJac MPen MWhe SKen SOld WPau
	'Libra'	MSmi WPau
	'Liebestraum'	EBak

'Liebriez'	EBak EBly EKMF LHig SOld
'Lilac'	EBak WPau
'Lilac Lady'	MJac
'Lilac Lustre'	CLoc EBak EKMF MBri WPau
'Lilac Princess'	MJac SKen WPau
'Lilac Queen'	EBak
'Lilac Sceptre'	CTab
'Lillibet'	CLoc EBak SKen WPau
'Lillydale'	EGou MSmi WPau
'Lilo Vogt'	EKMF
'Linda Copley'	WPau
'Linda Goulding'	CMHG EBak EBly EGou NMGN SOld WPau
'Lindisfarne'	EBak EGou EKMF MJac MLab MPen MWar NPor SKen SLBF SOld WPau
'Lindy'	WPau
'Linet'	EBak EGou
'Lisa'	EBly MSmi WPau
'Little Beauty'	EKMF MLab MWhe NPor
'Little Gene'	EBak
'Little Jewel'	MPen SLBF WPau
§ 'Little Miss Muffet'	CTab
'Little Ouse'	EBly EGou
'Little Ronnie'	MWhe
'Liz'	EBak SOld WPau
'Lochinver'	EKMF MJac MWar MWhe SLBF
'Loeky'	EBak EKMF NPor SLBF SOld WPau
'Logan Garden'	SLBF
'Lolita'	EBak SKen
'Lonely Ballerina'	CLoc WPau
'Long Wings'	EKMF NMGN
'Loni Jane'	WPau
'Lord Byron'	CCla CLoc EBak SOld
¶ 'Lord Leverhulme'	MPen
'Lord Lonsdale'	CCla EBak EBly MWhe NMGN SKen SOld WEas WPau
'Lord Roberts'	CLoc SKen WPau
'Lorna Doone'	MWhe
¶ 'Lorna Swinbank'	SLBF
'Lorraine's Delight'	ECtt WPau
'Lottie Hobby'	CLoc EBly EKMF ISea MPen SBar SKen WBod WHea
'Louise Emershaw'	EBak MJac NMGN WPau
'Lovable'	EBak
'Love Knot'	MSmi WPau
'Loveliness'	CLoc EBak EKMF MWhe WPau
'Love's Reward'	MJac MWar NPor SLBF
loxensis	CCla EBak EKMF LHop SKen SOld WPau
'Lucerowe'	WPau
'Lucie Harris'	EBly
'Lucinda'	WPau
'Lucky Strike'	CLoc EBak MPen SKen WPau
'Lucy Harris'	MJac
'Lumière'	EGou
'Lunter's Glorie'	WPau
'Lunter's Klokje'	EGou
'Lunter's Roehm'	WPau
'Luscious'	WPau
'Lustre'	EBak MPen NPor
lycioides	CCla CGre EBak EGou EKMF
'Lye's Excelsior'	EBak WPau
'Lye's Favourite'	NMGN
'Lye's Own'	EBak MPen NMGN SLBF
'Lye's Unique'	CLoc CMHG EBak EBly EGou EKMF MJac MLab MPen MWar MWhe NMGN NPor SKen SLBF SOld WPau
'Lylac Sunsa'	EKMF
'Lynette'	CCla CLoc
'Lynn Ellen'	EBak WPau
'Lynne Marshall'	CCla CTab
'L'Arlésienne'	CLoc EBly
'Mabel Greaves'	MWhe NPor WPau
¶ 'Mabel Grey'	CCla
'Machu Picchu'	EBly EKMF MSmi WPau
macrophylla	CMCN WEas
'Madame Butterfly'	CLoc
'Madame Cornelissen'	CCla CLoc CSco EBak EBly EKMF ENot IJoh MBar MBri MJac MPen MR&S MWhe NKay NMGN NPor SHil SKen SOld SPer SPla WPau
'Madame Eva Boye'	EBak WPau
'Madame Theobald'	SPer
'Madame van der Strasse'	WPau
magellanica	CFis CGle CMHG CRow EBre NNor NSti SHil SKen WBod WRus WWat
– 'Alba'	See F. ***m. molinae***
I – 'Alba Aureovariegata'	LHop
– 'Alba Variegata'	See F. ***m.*** 'Sharpitor'
– 'Aurea'	CBot CCla CHoe EGou EHar EKMF ERav MPen MPla MWhe NPor SIng SKen SLBF SPer WRus
– conica	EKMF
§ ***– molinae***	Widely available
– pumila	NPor SChu SIng
– purpurea	CRow
– 'Riccartonii'	See F. 'Riccartonii'
§ – 'Sharpitor'	Widely available
§ – 'Versicolor'	Widely available
'Magellanica Alba'	See F. ***magellanica molinae***
magellanica gracilis	CCla CLoc EKMF SHil SLon
§ ***– – aurea***	CGle CRow CTre EFou EGol ELan ENot ISea MPen MR&S SPla WWat
– – 'Variegata'	Widely available
magellanica macrostema	EKMF
§ – – 'Tricolor'	LHig SLBF
– – 'Variegata'	EGou
'Magenta Flush'	MJac MSmi WPau
'Magic Flute'	CLoc MJac MWhe SOld
'Maharaja'	EBak WPau
'Major Heaphy'	CCla EBak EBly MPen NMGN NPor
'Malibu Mist'	EKMF MJac MSmi WPau
'Mama Bleuss'	EBak
'Mancunian'	ECtt WPau
N 'Mandarin'	EBak SKen

'Mantilla'	CLoc EBak EKMF MJac MSmi MWhe NMGN SKen SOld WPau
'Maori Pipes'	EGou
¶ 'Marbled Sky'	MJac
'Marcus Graham'	EKMF MPen MSmi SLBF WPau
'Marcus Hanton'	ECtt EKMF MWar NPor SLBF WPau
'Mardale'	MLab
'Mardi Gras'	EBak WPau
'Margaret'	CLoc CSco EBak EGou EKMF ENot ISea MBal MPen MWgw MWhe NMGN SChu SCro SHil SKen SLBF SLon SOld WPau
'Margaret Brown'	CCla CLoc EBak EKMF MPen MPla MR&S MWgw MWhe NMGN NPor SHil SKen SLBF SPla WPau
'Margaret Pilkington'	EKMF MWar NPor SLBF WPau
'Margaret Roe'	EBak EKMF MJac MPen MWar MWhe NPor SKen SOld WPau
'Margaret Rose'	MJac
'Margaret Susan'	EBak WPau
'Margaret Swales'	EKMF WPau
'Margarita'	CCla WPau
'Margery Blake'	CCla EBak
¶ 'Maria Landy'	EKMF SLBF
¶ 'Maria Merrills'	EKMF
'Marie Julie'	WPau
'Marilyn Olsen'	EBly EKMF MWar NPor SLBF WPau
'Marin Belle'	EBak WPau
'Marin Glow'	CLoc EBak EBly EKMF MBri NMGN NPor SLBF SOld WPau
'Marinka'	CCla CLoc EBak EBly EGou EKMF IHos MBri MJac MPen MSmi MWar NMGN NPor SKen SLBF SOld WEas WPau
'Mark Kirby'	EKMF WPau
¶ 'Marlene Gilbee'	ECtt
'Marlies'	WPau
'Marshside'	NPor WPau
'Marta Frädrich'	CTab
'Martin Hayward'	SKen
'Martin's Midnight'	NMGN
'Marty'	EBak
'Mary'	CCla CLoc EBly EGou EKMF MPen MSmi MWar MWhe NPor SKen SLBF SOld
'Mary Ellen'	WPau
¶ 'Mary Fairclo'	MSmi
'Mary Joan'	NMGN
'Mary Kipling'	WPau
'Mary Lockyer'	CLoc EBak WPau
'Mary Reynolds'	MWar
'Mary Rose'	EKMF
'Mary Thorne'	EBak WPau
'Mary Wright'	MWhe
'Masquerade'	EBak EKMF MWhe WPau
'Maureen Munro'	NMGN
'Mauve Beauty'	CCla EGou EKMF WPau

'Mauve Lace'	CCla CTab EBly
'Mauve Wisp'	CCla CTab SOld WPau WWeb
'Mayblossom'	EBly EKMF SLBF WPau
'Mayfayre'	CLoc
'Mayfield'	EBly EKMF MJac MWhe SKen WPau
'Mazarine'	WPau
'Mazda'	MWhe WPau
'Meadowlark'	EKMF WPau
'Medalist'	NMGN WPau
'Meditation'	CLoc
'Medocino Rose'	WPau
'Meike Meursing'	CCla NMGN SKen
'Melody'	EBak MWhe SKen WPau
'Melody Ann'	EBak
'Melting Moments'	WPau
'Mendocini Mini'	EGou EKMF
'Meols Cop'	MWhe NPor WPau
'Merry England'	EKMF WPau
'Merry Mary'	EBak EKMF NPor WPau
'Mexicali Rose'	CLoc WPau
'Michael'	EBly
'Michelle Wallace'	EBly
'Micky Goult'	CLoc EBly EKMF MBri MJac MPen MWar MWhe NMGN NPor SLBF SOld WPau
microphylla	CB&S CCla CGle CHad CLoc CMHG CTre EBak EKMF ERav ERea GRei LHig MPen SLon WPau
– aprica	CGre EGou WPau
§ ***– hidalgensis***	CCla EGou EKMF SLBF
– microphylla	EGou
'Midas'	MPen NPor
'Midnight Sun'	EBak EBly
'Mieke Meursing'	CLoc EBak EKMF MJac MPen MWar MWhe NPor SLBF SOld WPau
'Miep Alhuizen'	EGou
N 'Mikado'	EBly
'Mike Oxtoby'	EKMF
'Ming'	CLoc
minimiflora	CCla EKMF LHig NHol
'Minirose'	EKMF MWar MWhe NPor SKen SLBF WPau
'Miniskirt'	WPau
'Minnesota'	CCla EBak
'Minx'	WPau
'Mipam'	SLBF WPau
'Miranda Morris'	WPau
'Mischief'	CTab WWeb
'Miss California'	CLoc EBak EBly EKMF MBri MLab MPen MSmi MWar NMGN SKen SOld WEas WPau
'Miss Great Britain'	MSmi SOld WPau
'Miss Leucadia'	WPau
'Miss Muffet'	See F. 'Little Miss Muffet'
'Miss Vallejo'	EBak
'Mission Bells'	CCla CLoc EBak EGou EKMF MJac MSmi MWhe NMGN SKen SLBF SOld WPau
'Misty Blue'	EKMF SLBF WPau
'Misty Haze'	EBly

'Misty Morn'	EGou
'Misty Pink'	EKMF MSmi
'Molesworth'	EBak MJac MLab MWhe NPor SKen SOld WPau
'Mollie Beulah'	EBly EKMF MPen
'Money Spinner'	CLoc EBak WPau
'Monsieur Thibaut'	CCla SKen SOld
'Monte Rosa'	CCla CLoc SKen
'Monterey'	MWhe
'Montezuma'	MSmi SOld WPau
'Montrose Village'	MSmi MWhe WPau
'Monument'	WPau
'Mood Indigo'	EGou NPor SLBF WPau
'Moonbeam'	CLoc EBly MLab MWhe NPor WPau
'Moonlight Sonata'	CLoc MJac MPen MSmi SKen WPau
'Moonraker'	ECtt MPen WPau
'Moonshot'	NMGN SKen WPau
'Mordred'	EBak WPau
'Morning Glow'	WPau
'Morning Light'	CLoc EBak MSmi NPor SKen WPau
'Moth Blue'	EBak NPor WPau
'Mount Stewart'	CCla
'Mountain Mist'	EKMF MJac NPor WPau
'Moyra'	EKMF
'Mr A Huggett'	CLoc EBly EGou MPen NPor SLBF SOld WPau
'Mr W Rundle'	EBak EBly
'Mrs Churchill'	CLoc
'Mrs Lawrence Lyon'	EBak WPau
'Mrs Lovell Swisher'	CCla EBak EKMF MBri MJac MPen MWar MWhe NPor SLBF SOld WPau
'Mrs Marshall'	EBak EGou MWar SKen SLBF SOld WEas WPau
'Mrs Minnie Pugh'.	CLoc
'Mrs Popple'	Widely available
'Mrs W Castle'	NPor
'Mrs W P Wood'	CLoc SHil
'Mrs W Rundle'	CLoc EBak EBly EKMF MWhe NPor SLBF
'Muriel'	CLoc EBak EKMF MWhe SKen WPau
'My Beauty'	MSmi
'My Dear'	CLoc
'My Fair Lady'	CLoc EBak WPau
'Nancy Lou'	CCla CLoc EBly EGou EKMF MJac MSmi MWar MWhe NMGN NPor SKen SLBF SOld WPau
'Natalie Jones'	EGou
¶ 'Natasha Sinton'	SLBF
'Native Dancer'	EBak
'Nautilus'	EBak
'Navy Blue'	CCla CTab
'Neapolitan'	EKMF SKen SLBF
'Neil Clyne'	MWhe
'Nell Gwyn'	CCla CLoc EBak NPor
'Nellie Nuttall'	CLoc EBak EBly EGou EKMF MBri MJac MPen MWar MWhe NMGN NPor SLBF SOld WPau
'Neopolitan'	CCla EGou MPen NPor WPau
'Neue Welt'	EBak WPau
'New Constellation'	WPau
'New Fascination'	CCla EBak SKen
'Nice 'n' Easy'	MPen WPau
'Nicholas Hughes'	NPor
'Nicola'	EBak
'Nicola Claire'	NPor
'Nicola Jane'	CCla EBak EBly EKMF LHig MBri MJac MSmi NMGN NPor SLBF WPau
'Nicolette'	MJac
'Nightingale'	CLoc EBak WPau
nigricans	**See F. *sylvatica***
'Nikki'	SKen WPau
¶ 'Nikkis Findling'	EGou
'Nimue'	EBak EGou WPau
'Nina Wills'	EBak
'Niobe'	EBak
'No Name'	EBak
'Noblesse'	WPau
'Norah Henderson'	MLab WPau
'Normandy Bell'	CCla EBak MSmi
'Northern Pride'	NMGN SOld WPau
'Northumbrian Belle'	EBak MJac SOld WPau
'Northway'	CLoc EBly EKMF MJac MWhe NPor SKen SLBF WPau
'Norvell Gillespie'	EBak
'Novato'	MPen WPau
'Novella'	EBak MSmi NPor WPau
'Obergartner Koch'	EBly SKen SOld
'Ocean Beach'	EBly MSmi
'Oetnang'	WPau
'Old Rose'	WPau
'Old Somerset'	CCla SOld
'Oldbury'	SOld
'Oldbury Delight'	SOld
'Oldbury Galore'	SOld
'Oldbury Gem'	SOld
'Oldbury Pearl'	SOld
'Olive Moon'	SLBF
'Olive Smith'	EBly MJac MLab NMGN SLBF WPau
'Olympic Lass'	EBak WPau
'Omeomy'	NPor WPau
'Oosje'	EGou EKMF
'Opalescent'	CLoc WPau
'Orange Bell'	NMGN
'Orange Blossom'	SLBF
'Orange Cocktail'	EKMF
'Orange Crush'	CCla CLoc EBak MSmi MWar MWhe SLBF
'Orange Crystal'	CCla EKMF IHos MBri MJac MWhe NMGN SKen SOld WPau
'Orange Drops'	CLoc EBak EBly EKMF MPen MWhe NPor SKen SOld WPau
¶ 'Orange Flame'	WPau
'Orange Flare'	CCla CLoc EBak EBly EKMF MJac MSmi MWar MWhe NMGN SLBF SOld WPau
* 'Orange Flash'	SOld
'Orange King'	EGou NMGN WPau

'Orange Mirage'	CCla CLoc EBak EBly MBri MLab MPen MSmi MWhe SKen SLBF SOld WPau
'Orangy'	WPau
'Oranje Boven'	EKMF
'Oranje Van Os'	MJac MWhe NPor
'Orient Express'	EBly EGou EKMF MWhe WPau
'Oriental Flame'	EKMF MSmi WPau
'Oriental Lace'	WPau
'Oriental Sunrise'	CCla MSmi MWhe NPor SKen
'Ornamental Pearl'	CLoc EBak EBly ECtt MPen SKen SLBF SOld
'Ortenburger Festival'	EKMF WPau
'Orwell'	EBly EGou
'Other Fellow'	EBak EBly EKMF MLab MPen NMGN NPor SKen SLBF SOld WPau
'Our Darling'	EBly MPen MWhe NPor
'Our Ted'	SOld
'Ovation'	MSmi WPau
'Overbecks'	See F. ***magellanica*** 'Sharpitor'
¶ 'Overbecks Ruby'	EMon
'P J B'	EBly
'Pacific Grove'	EBak WPau
'Pacific Queen'	CLoc EBak EKMF WPau
'Pacquesa'	EBak EBly EKMF IHos MJac MLab MWar MWhe NMGN NPor SKen SLBF SOld WPau
'Padre Pio'	EBly MJac
'Pale Beauty'	EKMF
'Pale Flame'	MSmi MWhe WPau
'Palford'	EBak
'Pamela Knights'	EBak EGou
'Pan America'	EBak
paniculata	CCla CGre CHan CSun EBak EGou EKMF LHop
'Pantaloons'	EBak WPau
'Papa Bleuss'	CLoc EBak NMGN SOld WPau
'Papoose'	CCla EBak EKMF MPen MPla NMGN SLBF SOld WPau
¶ 'Paramour'	CCla
'Party Frock'	CLoc EBak MSmi NMGN SOld WPau
N ***parviflora***	EBak
'Passing Cloud'	SKen
'Pastel'	EBak
'Pat Meara'	CLoc EBak WPau
'Pathetique'	CLoc
'Patience'	EBly EGou EKMF NMGN SLBF SOld WPau
'Patio Princess'	MPen NPor SLBF
N 'Patricia'	EBak WPau
'Patricia Ann'	EKMF MWar WPau
'Patty Evans'	EBak MBri SKen
'Paul Baylis'	CTab
'Paul Gambon'	EBak EKMF
'Paul Roe'	MJac NPor
'Paula Jane'	MWar SLBF SOld WPau
'Paula Johnson'	MJac
'Pauline Flint'	CTab
'Pauline Rawlins'	CLoc EBak
'Peace'	EBak
'Peachy Keen'	EBak WPau
'Peacock'	CLoc
'Pearl Farmer'	EBly MLab WPau
'Pee Wee Rose'	EBak EKMF MSmi
'Peggy King'	EBak
'Peloria'	CLoc EBak SKen WPau
'Pennine'	MBri MPen MWar WPau
'Pepi'	CLoc EBak SOld WPau
'Peppermint Candy'	MSmi
'Peppermint Stick'	CCla CLoc EBak EBly EKMF MBri MJac MPen MSmi MWhe NMGN NPor SKen SOld WPau
'Perky Pink'	EBak EBly MBri MLab MPen MWhe NMGN SKen SLBF SOld WPau
'Perry Park'	EBak MBri MJac MLab MPen SKen WPau
perscandens	ECou EKMF ISea
'Personality'	EBak MSmi WPau
'Peter Bielby'	EGou EKMF MWar WPau
'Peter Crooke'	EGou EKMF NPor SLBF WPau
'Peter Pan'	EBly SIng SKen SPer
'Petite'	EBak
'Petronella'	MWar SLBF SOld WPau
'Pharaoh'	CLoc WPau
'Phenomenal'	EBak EBly EKMF SKen SOld WPau
'Phyllis'	CCla CLoc EBak EBly EGou EKMF MBal MJac MLab MPen MSmi NMGN SChu SKen SLBF SOld SPla WPau
'Phyllis Stevens'	CTab
'Phyrne'	EBak
'Piet Hein'	SLBF
'Pinch Me'	CCla EBak ECtt EKMF MWar NMGN NPor SKen SOld WPau
'Pink Aurora'	CLoc WPau
'Pink Ballet Girl'	CLoc EBak
'Pink Bon Accord'	CCla CLoc WPau
'Pink Bouquet'	MJac MPen WPau
¶ 'Pink Chiffon'	MSmi
'Pink Claws'	CTab
'Pink Cloud'	CLoc EBak
'Pink Darling'	CCla CLoc EBak MWhe SKen WPau
'Pink Dessert'	EBak SKen
'Pink Domino'	CTab EKMF
'Pink Fairy'	EBak NMGN NPor
'Pink Fandango'	CLoc WPau
'Pink Fantasia'	EGou EKMF MJac MWar NPor
'Pink Flamingo'	CLoc EBak NMGN SKen
'Pink Galore'	CCla CLoc EBak EBly EGou EKMF IHos MBri MJac MPen MSmi MWhe NMGN NPor SKen SLBF SOld WEas WPau
'Pink Goon'	EKMF SLBF WPau
'Pink Haze'	CTab
'Pink Jade'	CCla EBak LHig NPor WPau
'Pink La Campanella'	EKMF MJac NMGN NPor
'Pink Lace'	CCla CTab SOld
N 'Pink Lady'	MWhe NPor
'Pink Marshmallow'	CCla CLoc EBak EBly EGou EKMF MJac MSmi MWar MWhe NPor SLBF SOld WPau

'Pink Most'	EKMF
'Pink Panther'	EKMF
N 'Pink Pearl'	CTab EBak EKMF MJac
'Pink Profusion'	EBak
'Pink Quartet'	CLoc EBak EBly NMGN SOld
'Pink Rain'	EGou EKMF
'Pink Ruffles'	WPau
'Pink Spangles'	IHos MBri WPau
'Pink Temptation'	CLoc EBak MPen SOld WPau
'Pink Veil'	MLab
'Pinto'	WPau
'Pinwheel'	CLoc EBak WPau
'Piper'	EBly MWar WPau
'Pirbright'	EKMF SLBF WPau
'Pixie'	CCla CLoc EBak EGou EKMF MJac NMGN SHil SKen SLBF SOld WPau
'Playford'	EGou WPau
'Plenty'	CLoc EBak MWar MWhe NPor WPau
'Pluto'	CCla CTab
'Pole Star'	CCla CTab
'Pop Whitlock'	CCla EKMF SKen SLBF WPau
'Poppet'	SLBF SOld WPau
'Port Arthur'	EBak
'Postiljon'	EKMF SLBF WPau
'Powder Puff'	CCla CLoc CTab EBly EKMF MBri MSmi NMGN SKen SOld WPau WWeb
N 'Prelude'	CLoc EBak
'President'	EBak SKen
'President B W Rawlins'	EBak
'President Elliot'	MWhe
'President Leo Boullemier'	EBak EKMF MJac SKen WPau
'President Margaret Slater'	EBak MWar MWhe SKen SLBF WPau
'President Norman Hobbs'	EKMF
'President Roosevelt'	EBly ECtt
'President Stanley Wilson'	EBak EBly EKMF SLBF
'President Wilf Sharp'	CCla MPen SKen WPau
'Preston Guild'	CCla CLoc EBak EKMF MPen MWhe NMGN NPor SKen SOld WPau
'Pretty Belinda'	WPau
'Pretty Grandpa'	WPau
'Pride of the West'	EBak
'Prince of Orange'	CLoc EBak NPor SOld WPau
'Prince of Peace'	MSmi NMGN WPau
'Princess Dollar'	See F. 'Dollar Princess'
'Princess of Bath'	CLoc
'Princess Pat'	CCla EKMF WPau
'Princess Saranntoe'	MWar
'Princessita'	EBak EKMF MBri MJac MLab MSmi MWar MWhe SKen SLBF WPau
procumbens	Widely available
'Prodigy'	See F. 'Enfant Prodigue'
'Prosperity'	CLoc EBak EBly EGou EKMF LHig MJac MLab MPen MSmi MWar MWhe NMGN SHil SLon SOld SPla
'Pumila'	CCla EGou EKMF ELan MBal MPla SKen SLBF WHea WPau
'Purple Ann'	NMGN
'Purple Emperor'	CLoc
'Purple Heart'	CLoc EBak NMGN SKen
'Purple Lace'	CCla CTab
¶ 'Purple Rain'	EGou
'Purple Showers'	WPau
'Purple Splendour'	CSco ELan
'Pussycat'	CLoc EKMF NMGN SKen WPau
'Putt's Folly'	EBak MJac SKen WPau
putumayensis	EKMF
'Quaser'	EKMF NMGN SLBF SOld WPau
'Queen Mabs'	EBak
'Queen Mary'	CLoc EBak EKMF MPen WPau
'Queen of Derby'	WPau
'Queen of Hearts'	CTab WPau
'Queen's Park'	EBak
'Query'	EBak SKen
'R A F'	CCla CLoc EBak EBly EKMF MJac MPen MWar SKen SLBF SOld WPau
¶ 'Radcliffe Beauty'	MWhe WPau
'Radcliffe Bedder'	EKMF NMGN SKen
¶ 'Rading's Inge'	EGou
¶ 'Rading's Karin'	EGou SLBF
'Rahnee'	CCla MJac NPor WPau
'Raintree Legend'	CCla
'Rambling Rose'	CCla CLoc EBak MJac MLab SKen SLBF SOld WPau
'Rams Royal'	EBly MJac
'Raspberry'	CLoc EBak EKMF MSmi MWar NMGN SKen WPau
'Ratae Beauty'	CCla
¶ 'Ratatouille'	EGou
ravenii	EGou EKMF
'Ray Redfern'	EBly MJac
'Razzle Dazzle'	EBak EKMF WPau
'Reading Show'	EBly MPen SLBF
'Rebecca Louise'	NMGN
'Rebecca Williamson'	EGou MJac NMGN NPor SLBF WPau
'Red Imp'	CTab NPor WWeb
'Red Jacket'	CLoc EBak
'Red Ribbons'	EBak
'Red Shadows'	CCla CLoc EBak EBly MBri MJac MWhe NMGN SLBF WPau
'Red Spider'	CCla CLoc EBak EGou EKMF MLab MPen MSmi MWar MWhe NMGN NPor SKen SOld WPau
'Red Wing'	CLoc
'Reg Dickenson'	MJac MWhe
'Reg Gubler'	SLBF WPau
'Regal'	CLoc
'Regal Robe'	WPau
¶ ***regia***	CCla
§ – ***alpestris***	EBak
'Remus'	EKMF MBri MLab WPau
'Requiem'	CLoc IHos

'Reverend Doctor Brown'	EBak WPau
'Reverend Elliott'	See F. 'President E A Elliot'
N 'Rhapsody'	CLoc
¶ 'Ri Mia'	EGou
§ 'Riccartonii'	CB&S CCla CHad CLoc CSco EBak EKMF ELan ENot IDai IJoh ISea MBar MBri MLab MPen MR&S NMGN NWea SIng SMad WBod WEas WPau
'Richard Livesy'	WPau
'Ridestar'	CCla CLoc EBak EBly MJac MSmi MWhe NMGN SLBF WPau
'Rigoletto'	WPau
'Rika'	WPau
'Ringwood Gold'	SOld
'Ringwood Market'	EBly EKMF MWhe NMGN SKen SOld WPau
'River Plate'	EBly EGou
'Robbie'	EKMF NMGN SLBF WPau
'Robert Bruce'	WPau
¶ 'Robin'	MSmi
'Robin Pacey'	WPau
'Rolla'	EBak
'Roman City'	CLoc
'Romance'	EKMF NMGN WPau
'Ron Ewart'	EKMF NPor WPau
'Ronald L Lockerbie'	CLoc EKMF MSmi MWhe SKen WPau
'Ron's Pet'	SOld
'Rosamunda'	CLoc
'Rose Aylett'	EBak
'Rose Bower'	NMGN
'Rose Bradwardine'	EBak
'Rose Churchill'	CCla EKMF MBri MJac MPen
'Rose Lace'	CTab
'Rose Marie'	CLoc
'Rose of Castile'	CCla CLoc EBak EKMF LHig MJac MPen MWhe NMGN WPau
'Rose of Castile Improved'	CCla EBak EBly EKMF MJac MWar NPor SKen SOld WPau
'Rose of Denmark'	CCla EBak MJac MSmi MWar SLBF SOld WPau
'Rose Reverie'	EBak WPau
'Rosebud'	EBak EKMF WPau
'Rosecroft Beauty'	EBak EBly EKMF LHig MWhe SKen SOld
'Rosemary Day'	CLoc WPau
'Rosetta'	CTab
'Roslyn Lowe'	EKMF WPau
'Rosy Frills'	EGou EKMF MJac MSmi MWhe NMGN NPor SOld WPau
'Rosy Morn'	CLoc EBak
'Rosy Ruffles'	MSmi WPau
'Rough Silk'	CLoc EBak SOld WPau
'Roy Walker'	CCla CLoc EGou EKMF MJac MPen MWar MWhe NMGN NPor SKen SOld WPau
'Royal and Ancient'	EGou
¶ 'Royal Orchid'	WPau
'Royal Purple'	EBak EKMF MBri
'Royal Splendour'	MWar
'Royal Touch'	EBak WPau
'Royal Velvet'	CCla CLoc CMHG EBak EBly EGou EKMF MJac MLab MPen MSmi MWar MWhe NMGN NPor SKen SLBF SOld WEas WPau
'Royal Wedding'	WPau
'Rubens'	MWar WPau
'Ruby'	SOld
'Ruby Glow'	CTab
'Ruddigore'	EBly EGou SLBF SOld WPau
'Ruffles'	EBak MSmi WPau
§ 'Rufus'	CCla CLoc CMHG EBak EBly EFou EKMF MJac MWar MWhe NMGN SKen SLBF WPau
'Rufus the Red'	See F. 'Rufus'
'Ruth Brazewell'	CLoc
'Ruth King'	EBak NMGN NPor SKen SOld WPau
'Ruthie'	WPau
'Rutland Water'	EBly EKMF
'Sacramento Bells'	MSmi
'Sahara'	NMGN
'Sally Ann'	NPor WPau
¶ 'Salmon Cascade'	EKMF
'Salmon Glow'	MJac MWhe
'Sampson's Delight'	WPau
'Samson'	EBak WPau
'San Diego'	MPen MSmi WPau
'San Francisco'	EBak WPau
'San Leandro'	EBak NMGN WPau
'San Mateo'	EBak
sanctae-rosae	EKMF
'Sandboy'	SLBF SOld WPau
'Santa Barbara'	NMGN
'Santa Claus'	WPau
'Santa Cruz'	CCla EBak EKMF MPen MWhe SOld WPau
'Santa Lucia'	CLoc EBak WPau
'Santa Monica'	EBak WPau
'Sapphire'	EBak MSmi WPau
'Sara Helen'	CLoc EBak NPor WPau
'Sara Jayne'	EBak WPau
'Sarah Ann'	MWar
'Sarah Greensmith'	EKMF
'Sarah Louise'	EKMF
¶ 'Sarina'	EGou
'Sarong'	EBak MSmi WPau
¶ 'Satchmo'	EGou
'Satellite'	CLoc EBak EKMF MJac MSmi WPau
'Saturnus'	EBak LHig SLBF SOld WPau
scandens	See F. ***decussata***
¶ 'Scarborough Rosette'	EGou
'Scarcity'	EBak MBri SKen
'Schneeball'	EBak EBly EKMF
'Schneewittchen'	EBak EBly EKMF WPau
'Schönbrunner Schuljubiläum	EBak EKMF
'Scotch Heather'	MSmi WPau
'Sea Shell'	EBak WPau

	'Seaforth'	EBak MPen
	'Sealand Prince'	WPau
	'Sebastopol'	CLoc EKMF MSmi NPor WPau
	'Sensation'	EBly WPau
	'Serendipity'	WPau
N	***serratifolia***	EBak SKen SOld
	sessilifolia	EKMF
	'Seventh Heaven'	CLoc MSmi NMGN SLBF WPau
	'Shady Lady'	MSmi
	'Shangri-La'	EBak
	'Shanley'	EKMF
	'Sharon Allsop'	MJac MLab MWhe WPau
¶	'Sharon Caunt'	EKMF
	'Sharpitor'	See F. ***magellanica*** 'Sharpitor'
	'Sheila Crooks'	EBak MPen NPor WPau
	'Sheila Joy'	SLBF
	'Shell Pink'	CTab WPau
	'Shelley Lyn'	SKen WPau
	'Shellford'	EBly EKMF MWar NPor SLBF
	'Shining Knight'	EBly
	'Shooting Star'	EBak
	'Shuna'	NPor WPau
	'Shuna Lindsay'	WPau
	'Shy Lady'	EBly MWhe SKen WPau
	'Sierra Blue'	CCla CLoc EBak EKMF SKen WPau
	'Silver Anniversary'	EKMF MSmi
	'Silver Dawn'	EBly EKMF MWhe NMGN NPor SLBF WPau
	'Silver Dollar'	MWar MWhe NMGN NPor SKen SLBF SOld WPau
	'Silver Jubilee'	WPau
	'Silver Pink'	CTab
	'Silverdale'	EKMF MWar MWhe WPau
	'Simple Simon'	CTab
	simplicicaulis	EBak EKMF SOld
	'Sincerity'	CLoc MWhe WPau
	'Siobhan'	MJac
	'Sir Alfred Ramsey'	EBak EGou MJac MWhe WPau
N	'Siren'	EBak
	'Sister Ann Haley'	EKMF
	'Skylight'	MLab
	'Sleepy'	CTab EBly EKMF MBri SKen SOld
	'Sleigh Bells'	CCla CLoc EBak EKMF MWhe NMGN SKen SOld WPau
	'Small Pipes'	EGou
	'Smoky'	WPau
	'Smoky Mountain'	MSmi
	'Sneezy'	CTab EBly SKen WWeb
¶	'Snow Burner'	MSmi
	'Snow White'	CCla EBly NMGN WPau
§	'Snowcap'	CCla CLoc CMHG EBak EBly EGou EKMF IHos LHig MBri MJac MLab MPen MSmi MWar MWhe NMGN SKen SLBF SOld SPla WEas WPau
	'Snowdon'	MWar
N	'Snowdrift'	CCla CLoc EBak MWhe NMGN WPau
	'Snowfall'	WPau
	'Snowfire'	CCla CLoc EBly EKMF MSmi MWhe NMGN SLBF WPau
	'Snowstorm'	CMHG ECtt EKMF MPen NMGN
	'Snowy Summit'	MSmi WPau
	'So Big'	EKMF WPau
	'Software'	MSmi
	'Soldier of Fortune'	CCla
	'Son of Thumb'	CCla CLoc EBly EKMF ELan GHig LHig MBar MBri SKen SLBF SOld WPau
	'Sonota'	CCla CLoc EBak EKMF MSmi NMGN SLBF SOld WPau
¶	'Sophie Claire'	EGou
	'Sophisticated Lady'	CLoc EBak EBly EKMF MJac MPen MSmi MWar NMGN SKen SOld WPau
	'South Seas'	EBak WPau
	'Southgate'	CCla CLoc EBak EBly EGou EKMF NMGN NPor SLBF WPau
	'Southwell Minster'	EKMF NMGN
	'Space Shuttle'	EKMF WPau
	'Sparks'	WPau
	'Speciosa'	EKMF MPen WPau
	'Spion Kop'	CCla EBak EKMF MLab MPen MWar MWhe NMGN SKen SLBF WPau
	splendens	CCla CSun EBak EKMF MPen SLBF SOld WEas
	– 'Karl Hartweg'	CCla CHil CSun
	'Spoutsknight'	EBly EGou
	'Spring Bells'	CCla
	'Springtime'	CSco
	'Squadron Leader'	EBly SOld
	'Square Peg'	WPau
*	'Stad Elburg'	MJac
	'Stanley Cash'	CCla EBly EKMF MBri MJac MLab MWar MWhe NMGN NPor SKen SLBF SOld WEas WPau
	'Star of Pink'	MSmi MWhe
	'Star Rose'	EKMF
	'Stardust'	EBak EKMF MJac MWhe NPor SKen SLBF SOld WPau
*	'Stathern Surprise'	EBly MJac NPor
	'Steeley'	MSmi MWhe WPau
	'Stella Ann'	EBak EBly EGou EKMF MWhe
	'Stella Marina'	CLoc EBak
	'Stephanie'	WPau
	'Stevie Doidge'	WPau
	'Storm'	CTab
	'Stormy Sunset'	SLBF WPau
	'Strawberry Delight'	CCla CLoc CMHG EBak EKMF LHig MJac MLab MWhe NPor SKen SOld WPau
	'Strawberry Fizz'	MSmi WPau
	'Strawberry Sundae'	CLoc EBak NMGN WPau
	'Strawberry Supreme'	EKMF WPau
	'String of Pearls'	EKMF MBri MJac MPen NPor SKen SLBF SOld WPau
	'St. Andrews'	EGou
	'Sugar Almond'	MJac NPor
	'Sugar Blues'	EBak

'Sugar Plum'	WPau
'Suikerbossie' ('Sugarbush')	MJac MPen
'Summer Snow'	WPau
'Sunkissed'	CCla EBak WPau
'Sunlight Path'	EGou
'Sunningdale'	EGou
'Sunny'	SKen WPau
'Sunny Smiles'	CCla EKMF NMGN NPor
'Sunray'	CCla CLoc EBak EFol EKMF LHop MSmi MWhe NMGN SKen SOld
'Sunset'	CCla CLoc EBak EKMF MWhe NPor SKen SPer WPau
'Supernova'	MSmi NMGN NPor
'Superstar'	MPen NPor SLBF WPau
¶ 'Susan'	MPen
'Susan Daley'	NPor
'Susan Ford'	EKMF MLab NPor SKen WPau
'Susan Green'	EBly EGou EKMF MWhe NMGN NPor SLBF WPau
'Susan Jill'	SLBF
'Susan McMaster'	CLoc
'Susan Travis'	CCla CLoc EBak EKMF LHig MWhe NMGN SKen SOld
'Susan Young'	WPau
'Susie Olcese'	EBak NPor WPau
¶ 'Suzy'	MSmi
¶ 'Swanland Candy'	ECtt
'Swanley Gem'	CCla CLoc EBak EKMF MPen NMGN NPor SKen SLBF WPau
'Swanley Pendula'	CCla CLoc
'Swanley Yellow'	EBak MPen SKen SOld WPau
'Sweet Leilani'	CLoc EBak NMGN SKen WPau
'Sweet Sixteen'	CLoc WPau
N 'Sweetheart'	EBak
¶ 'Sweetie Dear'	EGou
'Swingtime'	CCla CLoc CMHG EBak EBly EKMF IHos MJac MLab MPen MSmi MWar MWhe NMGN NPor SKen SLBF SOld WEas WPau
'Swiss Miss'	WPau
sylvatica* x *gehrigeri	EKMF
¶ 'Sylvia Barker'	EGou
'Sylvy'	SLBF
'Symphony'	CLoc EBak WPau
'S'Wonderful'	CLoc EBak MSmi WPau
'T S Tabatha'	MLab
'Taddle'	EBly EKMF MJac NPor SLBF WPau
'Taffeta Bow'	CLoc MSmi WPau
'Taffy'	WPau
'Tahiti'	MBri WPau
'Tahoe'	WPau
'Tam O'Shanter'	WPau
'Tamar Isobel'	WPau
'Tamworth'	CLoc EBak MJac MPen NPor WPau
'Tangerine'	CCla CLoc EBak EKMF MPen MWhe NPor WPau
'Tanya'	CLoc
'Tanya Bridger'	EBak WPau
'Tartan'	MLab
'Task Force'	NMGN SKen
'Tausendschön'	CCla CLoc EKMF MPen WPau
'Ted Heath'	WPau
'Ted Perry'	EBly ECtt MJac NMGN
'Television'	CLoc NMGN SLBF WPau
'Temple Bells'	CTab
N 'Temptation'	CCla CLoc EBak EKMF MBri NPor WEas WPau
'Tennessee Waltz'	CCla CLoc CMHG EBak EBly EGou EKMF LHig MJac MLab MPen MSmi MWar MWhe NMGN NPor SChu SHil SKen SLBF SOld SPer SPla WEas
'Terrysue'	EKMF
'Texas Longhorn'	CCla CLoc EBak EBly EKMF MPen MSmi NMGN SKen SOld
'Thalia'	CCla CLoc EBak EBly EGou EKMF ERea IHos MBri MJac MLab MPen MSmi MWar MWhe NMGN NPor SKen SLBF SOld SPla WPau
'Thames Valley'	EGou WPau
'That's It'	EBak
'The Aristocrat'	CLoc EBak NPor
§ 'The Doctor'	CCla CLoc EBak EKMF MWhe SLBF SOld WPau
'The Jester'	EBak WPau
'The Madame'	EBak WPau
'The Observer'	CCla
'The Patriot'	MWhe WPau
'The Phoenix'	WPau
'The Rival'	MSmi NMGN WPau
'The Speedbird'	WPau
'The Spoiler'	MSmi WPau
'The Tarns'	EBak EKMF
¶ 'Therese Dupois'	EKMF
'Théroigne de Méricourt'	EBak
'This England'	WPau
'Thompsonii'	EMon SKen
'Thornley's Hardy'	EKMF MBri MPen NMGN NPor SLBF SOld WPau
'Three Cheers'	CLoc EBak
'Three Counties'	EBak
'Thunderbird'	CLoc EBak EGou
thymifolia	CCla ELan EMon GLoc LHop MBal MPen MPla SPla WKif WPer
'Tiara'	EBak WPau
N 'Tiffany'	EBak
'Tillmouth Lass'	EKMF
'Timlin Brened'	CCla EBak MWhe
'Ting-a-Ling'	CCla CLoc EBak EBly EKMF MBri MJac MSmi MWar MWhe NMGN NPor SKen SLBF SOld WEas WPau
N 'Tinker Bell'	CTab EBak EKMF SOld
'Tintern Abbey'	NPor
'Toby Bridger'	CLoc EBak
'Tolemac'	EGou WPau
'Tolling Bell'	CCla EBak EBly EKMF MJac MPen MSmi MWhe NMGN NPor SKen SOld WPau
'Tom H Oliver'	EBak
'Tom Hobson'	WPau

'Tom Knights'	EBak EBly EGou EKMF MWhe SLBF SOld WPau
'Tom Redfern'	EBly MJac NPor
'Tom Thorne'	EBak
'Tom Thumb'	Widely available
'Tom West'	CCla CLoc CMHG EBak EFol EGou EKMF MLab MPen MSmi MWhe NMGN NPor SKen SLBF SOld SPla WPau
'Tom Woods'	MLab MSmi MWhe NPor WPau
'Tommy Tucker'	CTab
'Top Score'	NMGN
'Topaz'	CLoc EBak WPau
'Topper'	EKMF WPau
'Torch'	CLoc EBak EGou MJac MLab MSmi NMGN WPau
'Torchlight'	EBly MJac MLab
¶ 'Torotino'	EKMF
'Torville and Dean'	CCla CLoc EBly EKMF MJac MLab MPen MSmi MWhe NMGN NPor SLBF WPau
'Tour Eiffel'	EGou WPau
'Tower of London'	SKen
'Tracid'	CLoc
'Tracie Ann'	EKMF
'Tradewinds'	MSmi
'Trailblazer'	CLoc EBak MJac MLab MPen MWhe NPor SKen WPau
'Trailing Queen'	CCla EBak EKMF MJac WPau
'Tranquillity'	MSmi WPau
'Trase'	CCla EBak EBly EKMF LHig MLab NMGN NPor
'Traudchen Bonstedt'	CCla CLoc EBak EBly MPen MWhe NMGN SLBF SOld
'Treasure'	EBak WPau
'Trewince Twilight'	SLBF
'Tricolor'	See F. ***magellanica macrostema*** 'Tricolor'
'Tricolorii'	EBly EKMF
'Trio'	CLoc
triphylla	EBak EKMF IReg SOld
'Trisha'	WPau
'Tristesse'	CLoc EBak MJac MSmi MWhe NMGN SOld WPau
'Trixie Coleman'	MSmi
'Troika'	EBak EKMF WPau
'Troon'	EGou
'Tropic Sunset'	CCla MBri MSmi MWhe SKen SLBF WPau
'Tropicana'	CLoc EBak MSmi MWhe NPor WPau
'Troubadour'	CLoc MSmi
'Troutbeck'	WPau
'Trudy'	EBak EKMF NMGN SKen
N 'Trumpeter'	CLoc EBak EBly EGou EKMF MJac MPen MSmi MWhe NMGN NPor SKen SLBF SOld WPau
'Tsjiep'	EKMF NPor SLBF WPau
'Tuonela'	CLoc EBak EGou EKMF MWhe NMGN NPor SKen WPau
'Tutone'	MJac SLBF WPau
'Tutti-Frutti'	CLoc MWhe
'Tutu'	EKMF WPau
'Twiggy'	WPau
'Twinkling Stars'	EKMF MJac
'Two Tiers'	EKMF NPor SLBF WPau
'U F O'	EKMF SOld WPau
'Ullswater'	EBak WPau
'Ultramar'	EBak WPau
'Uncle Charlie'	CLoc EBak WEas
'Uncle Jinks'	EBly
'Uncle Steve'	EBak WPau
'Unique'	WPau
'Upward Look'	EBak EKMF
'Valda May'	EKMF
'Valentine'	EBak WPau
'Valerie'	WPau
'Valerie Ann'	EBak SKen SOld WPau
'Valiant'	EBak
'Vanessa'	CLoc
'Vanessa Jackson'	CCla CLoc MJac MWar MWhe NPor SKen
'Vanity Fair'	CLoc EBak
vargarsiana	EKMF
'Variegated Snowcap'	CCla MPen MWhe
'Variegated Swingtime'	EBak MPen WPau
¶ 'Variegated White Joy'	EKMF
'Varty's Pride'	NPor
N 'Venus'	CCla CTab EKMF
'Venus Victrix'	EBak EKMF SLBF WPau
venusta	EGou EKMF
'Versicolor'	See F. ***magellanica*** 'Versicolor'
'Vespa'	SOld
'Vi Whitehouse'	EBly
'Victorian'	WPau
'Victory'	EBak WPau
'Vincent van Gogh'	EGou
'Violacea'	MSmi
'Violet Bassett-Burr'	CCla CLoc EBak WPau
'Violet Gem'	CLoc WPau
'Violet Lace'	CTab
'Violet Mist'	WPau
'Violet Rosette'	EBak SLBF WPau
'Viva Ireland'	EBak EKMF MJac
'Vivian Miller'	NPor
'Vivien Colville'	CLoc
'Vivien Harris'	MJac
'Vivienne Thompson'	MWar WPau
'Vobeglo'	EKMF SLBF WPau
'Vogue'	EBak SOld WPau
'Voltaire'	EBak
'Voodoo'	CLoc EBak EBly EKMF NMGN NPor SKen SLBF SOld WPau
'Vulcan'	WPau
vulcanica	See F. ***canescens***
'Vyvian Miller'	MJac
'Waldfee'	CCla MWhe
'Walsingham'	EBak EBly MJac MWhe NMGN NPor SKen SLBF WPau
'Waltzing Matilda'	WPau
'Walz Freule'	MJac
'Walz Harp'	EGou
¶ 'Walz Parasol'	EGouS

'Walz Waterval'	EGou WPau
'War Dance'	MWhe WPau
'Warpaint'	CLoc EBak WPau
'Warton Crag'	NPor WPau
'Waternymph'	CCla CLoc SLBF WPau
'Wave of Life'	EKMF MWhe SKen SLBF WPau
'Waveney Gem'	CSut EBak EBly EGou EKMF MJac MWar NMGN SLBF SOld
'Waveney Queen'	EGou
'Waveney Sunrise'	ECtt EGou EKMF MJac MWar SLBF
'Waveney Valley'	EBak EGou MWhe NMGN
'Waveney Waltz'	EBak EBly EKMF MJac MWar MWhe SLBF WPau
'Waxen Beauty'	EBly EKMF WPau
'Wedding Bells'	SOld
'Wee One'	EBly
'Welsh Dragon'	EBak WPau
'Wendy'	See F. 'Snowcap'
'Wendy Atkinson'	EKMF
'Wendy Harris'	EBly MJac WPau
'Wendy Leedham'	EKMF
'Wendy's Beauty'	MSmi
'Wentworth'	EGou WPau
'Westergeest'	EKMF WPau
'Westgate'	EKMF WPau
'Westminster Chimes'	CLoc EBly EKMF MJac MWar MWhe NMGN NPor SLBF SOld WPau
'Whirlaway'	CCla CLoc EBak EKMF MSmi NMGN SOld WPau
'White Ann'	CLoc MBri SLBF WPau
'White Bride'	WPau
'White Fairy'	WPau
'White Galore'	EBly MPen MSmi SKen SLBF SOld WPau
'White Gold'	EBak WPau
¶ 'White Haven'	SLBF
'White Joy'	EBak EBly EKMF MJac MWhe SKen WPau
'White King'	CLoc EBak EKMF MSmi MWhe NMGN NPor SLBF SOld WPau
'White Lace'	CCla CTab
'White Locky'	NPor
'White Marshmallow'	EBly
'White Pixie'	CCla EBly EGou EKMF ELan MJac MPen MPla SKen SOld WPau
'White Pixie' Wagtails	EBak MWhe
N 'White Queen'	EBak MJac MWhe NPor WPau
'White Spider'	CLoc EBak EKMF MWhe SKen SOld WPau
'White Surprise'	SOld
'White Swan'	CTab
'White Water'	WPau
'Whiteknights Amethyst'	WPau
'Whiteknights Blush'	CCla SKen
'Whiteknights Cheeky'	EKMF
'Whiteknights Goblin'	See F. ***denticulata*** 'W.G.'
'Whiteknights Pearl'	EKMF SLBF
'Wicked Queen'	CTab
'Wild and Beautiful'	EKMF WPau
'Wildfire'	WPau
'William Caunt'	EKMF
'Willie Lot'	EGou
'Willy Winkey'	CTab
'Wilson's Joy'	WPau
'Wilson's Pearls'	SLBF SOld
'Wilson's Sugar Pink'	EBly
'Win Oxtoby'	EKMF
'Wine and Roses'	CCla EBak MSmi WPau
'Wingrove's Mammoth'	WPau
'Wings of Song'	EBak WPau
'Winston Churchill'	CCla CLoc EBak EBly EKMF IHos MBri MJac MPen MSmi MWar MWhe NMGN NPor SKen SLBF SOld WPau
'Woodnook'	MLab SLBF SOld
wurdackii	EKMF
¶ 'Yolande Franck'	EKMF
'Yorkshire Rally'	MJac
'Yuletide'	EBly SKen WPau
'Zaza'	MWhe NPor
'Ziegfield Girl'	EBak SLBF WPau

FUMARIA (Fumariaceae)

♦***lutea***	See PSEUDOFUMARIA ***lutea***
officinalis	CKin GPoy MSal

FURCRAEA (Agavaceae)

longaeva	CGre CHEx CMal SArc
selloa	SArc

GAGEA (Liliaceae)

GAHNIA (Cyperaceae)

GAILLARDIA (Compositae)

aristata	See G. x ***grandiflora***
¶ – JCA 11449	EMon
'Burgunder'	CHar ECtt EHal ELan GCHN GWic MBri NOak WRus
'Dazzler'	ECtt ELan ENot MBri MWat
'Golden Queen'	ERou
'Goldkobold' ('Yellow Goblin')	EMon MPit
§ x ***grandiflora***	CGle CHar CSco NOak NVic SLHN
¶ – JCA 9096	CSun
– 'Nana Nieske'	GWic NTow
Kelway's hybrids	CKel
'Kobold' ('Goblin')	CB&S CHar CKel EBre ELan EPar ERou MBri MRav NRoo WEas WHen WHil WPer WWin
'Mandarin'	CSco EBre ERou
* 'Summer Fire'	EHal
'Tokajer'	GCHN
'Wirral Flame'	WEas

GALACTITES (Compositae)

tomentosa	CBos CHad CRow EBar ECha ECro EFou ELan EMon MPar SFir SLHN WEas WPer

GALANTHUS † (Liliaceae/Amaryllidaceae)

allenii	CAvo ECam LAma WChr

alpinus	ECam EPot LAma WChr
x ***atkinsii***	CAvo CBro ECam EMor EOrc EPot ERav LAma LFox MPar WChr
– 'Moccas'	WOld
– 'Mrs Backhouse's Spectacles'	LFox
'Augustus'	EMor
'Bitton'	CBro ECam
bortkewitschianus	CBro
'Brenda Troyle'	CBro EPot LFox WChr
byzantinus	See G. ***plicatus b.***
cabardensis	See G. ***lagodechianus***
caucasicus	CAvo CBro ECam EPot LAma LFox
– early form	WChr
– ***hiemalis***	CBro ECam EMor
¶ – late form	WChr
– x ***elwesii***	CBro EMor
corcyrensis	See G. ***reginae-olgae vernalis***
'Cordelia'	LFox
'Dionysus'	CBro EMor ERav LAma LFox LRHS MPar WChr
elwesii	CBro ECam EMon ETub LAma LBlo LBow MBri MBro MPar SIng
– 'Kite'	CBro
'Ermine Street'	EPot
fosteri	CAvo CBro ECam EPot LAma
– PD 26830	EMor
'Galatea'	EMor
§ ***gracilis***	CAvo CBro EBul EMon EMor EPot LAma MPar SPou WOld WThu
– Highdown form	SWas
graecus	See G. ***gracilis***
'Hill Poë'	CBro ERav LFox MBro
'Hippolyta'	CBro ECam EMor LAma LFox
ikariae ikariae	EOrc EPot LAma
§ – Latifolius group	CAvo EBul ECam EMon EMor EOrc EPot LAma LFox WChr
– Woronowii group	ECam EPot LAma LRHS WChr
'Jacquenetta'	CBro EMor LAma LFox
'John Gray'	EMor LFox
kemulariae	ECam EPot LAma NHol WChr
'Ketton'	EOrc LFox
'Lady Beatrix Stanley'	CAvo CBro ECam EMon EMor EPot LAma LFox MPar SWas WChr
§ ***lagodechianus***	CBro WChr
latifolius	See G. ***ikariae*** Latifolius group
'Lavinia'	MPar
'Lime Tree'	EMor LAma LFox
lutescens	See G. ***n.*** 'Lutescens'
'Magnet'	CAvo CBro EBul EMor EPot LAma LFox MPar SWas WChr WThu
'Maidwell L'	EMor WChr
'Melvillei'	WChr
'Merlin'	EMor EOrc LFox MPar
'Mighty Atom'	ECam
'Mrs Backhouse'	MPar
'Neill Fraser'	LFox
'Nerissa'	LAma
nivalis	Widely available
– ***angustifolius***	CBro EPot
– 'Boyd's Double'	EMor
– dwarf form	LFox
– 'Flore Pleno'	CAvo CBro CRiv CRow EMon EPar EPot ERav ETub LAma LBlo LBow LFox LRoo MBri MBro SIng SMad WHil
– 'Humberts Orchard'	LFox
– ***imperati***	CBro ECam EPot LFox LRHS
– ***imperati*** 'Ginn's Form'	EMor
– 'Lady Elphinstone'	CAvo CBro CRow EMor ERav LFox MPar WChr
§ – 'Lutescens'	CBro EMor EPot LAma
– ***poculiformis*** 'Sandhill Gate'	EMor
– 'Pusey Green Tip'	CBro EBul EMor ERav ITim LFox MPar WChr
§ – Scharlockii group	CBro ECam EMor EOrc EPot LAma LFox MPar NHar SWas WChr
– 'Tiny'	EMor
– ***vernalis***	LFox
– ***virescens***	LFox
– 'Virescens'	EMor MPar
– 'Viridapicis'	CAvo CBro EBul EMor EPot ERav ETub LAma LBlo LBow MPar SIng WChr
'Ophelia'	CAvo CBro EPar ERav LAma LFox WChr
'Peg Sharples'	ECam EPot
'Pewsey Vale'	EMor
platyphyllus	See G. ***ikariae*** Latifolius group
plicatus	CAvo EBul ECam ERav MPar WChr WDav
§ – ***byzantinus***	CAvo CBro ECam EMor EOrc EPot LAma LFox WChr
– large form	EOrc
– 'Silverwells'	SPou
– 'Warham'	CBro CRow EOrc SWas WOld
reginae-olgae	CBro ECam EMor EPot LAma LBow LFox MPar SPou WChr
N – Corcyrensis group	CAvo EBul ECam EMor LAma LBow LFox SPou
– ***vernalis***	ECam EMor
– ***vernalis*** AJM 75	EMor
§ – ***vernalis*** CEH 541	EMor
rizehensis	CBro EPot MPar WHil
'Robin Hood'	EMor LFox MPar WChr
'S Arnott'	CAvo CBro ECam EMor EPot ERav LAma LBlo LFox MPar NHar SIng SWas WChr WCot WOld WThu
'Scharlockii'	See G. ***nivalis*** Scharlockii group
'Straffan'	CBro EMor EOrc EPot LAma LFox MPar NHar WChr WOld
'Trotter's Merlin'	EMor

GALAX (Diapensiaceae)

aphylla	See G. ***urceolata***
§ ***urceolata***	GLoc MBal SSpi

GALEGA (Leguminosae)

¶ ***bicolor***	ECro
x ***hartlandii*** 'Alba'	IBlr
– 'Candida'	CFor CGle GWic NTow WTay
'Her Majesty'	EBre
* 'His Majesty'	GWic
'Lady Wilson'	CGle SFis WRus
officinalis	CArn CBot CCla CHad CHan CHar CSev CSun ECro EFou ELan EOrc Effi GPoy IBlr LHil LHol MChe NSti SIde WEas WHea WHoo WOak
– 'Alba'	CBot CElw CHan CSun EFol EMon IBlr WEas WHea WHer WHoo WRus
orientalis	CGle CHad CHan ECha ECro EFol EMon GWic LHop

GALEOBDOLON (Labiatae)

luteum	See LAMIUM ***galeobdolon***

GALIUM (Rubiaceae)

cruciatum	See CRUCIATA ***laevipes***
mollugo	CArn CKin MSal NLan SIde
§ ***odoratum***	Widely available
palustre	CKin
♦ ***perpusillum***	See ASPERULA ***perpusilla***
verum	CArn CKin CNat MChe MSal NLan NSel SFir WOak

GALTONIA (Liliaceae/Hyacinthaceae)

candicans	Widely available
princeps	CAvo ECha ECro NSti SChu SDix SLHN WEas
viridiflora	CAvo CChu ECha ECro ELan SAxl SBar SDix SIgm SLHN WBon

GAMOLEPIS See STEIRODISCUS

GARDENIA (Rubiaceae)

florida	See G. ***jasminoides***
* ***gloriosa***	SLMG
grandiflora	See G. ***jasminoides***
§ ***jasminoides***	CB&S EBak LAbb MBri MNew SLMG
– ***veitchiana***	ERea
thunbergia	MNew

GARRYA † (Garryaceae)

elliptica	Widely available
– 'James Roof' (m)	CB&S CCla CSco EBre ELan ERav IJoh IOrc LNet MBal MBri MWat NHol SBra SHil SLon SMad SPer SPla SSta WAbe WPat WWat
fremontii	CB&S CKni CMHG ISea
x ***issaquahensis*** 'Pat Ballard' (m)	IOrc
x ***thuretii***	SArc SHil SSta

X GAULNETTYA See GAULTHERIA

GAULTHERIA † (Ericaceae)

adenothrix	EPot MBal MPlt WDav
antipoda	ECou MBal NHol
* ***coriacea***	NHol
crassa	ECou
cuneata	CFor ELan EPot GDra GEdr GHig GLoc IBar IDai MBal MBar MBri MGos MHig SHil SPer SSta WAbe
depressa	GArf IBar MBal NHol
¶ – pink form	NHol
– x ***crassa***	MBal
§ ***eriophylla***	CCla LSav
forrestii	CTrw SHil
♦ ***furiens***	See G. ***insana***
'Glenroy Maureen'	MBal
griffithiana BM&W 69	MBal
§ ***hispida***	ECou GArf GDra MBal NHar NHol SIng
hookeri	MBri SHil
– B 547	MBal
humifusa	MBal
§ ***insana***	MBal
itoana	CMHG GArf GDra MBal MPlt WAbe
♦ ***leucocarpa***	See G. ***pumila***
macrostigma	IBar MBal
miqueliana	CSun IBar MBal MBar MDHE MGos SHil SIng SPla SSta WAbe
mucronata	CBow CLan CMHG CPle ELan ENot IDai ISea MBal MBar NHol NNor NWea SIng SReu WBod
– (m)	CB&S CBow CSco ELan GRei IJoh MBar MBri MGos MMth MR&S MRav MUlv NKay SHil SIng SPer SReu WPat
– 'Alba' (f)	CSco GRei MR&S MRav SIng SPer
¶ – 'Barry Lock'	WPat
– 'Bell's Seedling' (m/f)	CB&S CSco ENot GRei MBri MMth NKay SHil SPer SReu SSta WAbe WPat
– 'Cherry Ripe' (f)	CSco IOrc LSav MPlt NHol SHil SPer
– 'Crimsonia' (f)	CB&S CGre ELan LSav MPlt NHol SLon SPer WPat
– Davis's hybrids	MGos
¶ – 'Indian Lake'	MPlt
– 'Lilacina' (f)	CB&S CBow MBri NKay SHil
– 'Lilian'	CGre LSav MBri MUlv NHol SPla WWeb
– 'Mulberry Wine'	IOrc SHil
¶ – 'October Red'	MPlt
– 'Parelmoer' ('Mother of Pearl') (f)	CB&S ELan ENot LSav MBri MPlt NHol NKay SPer WPat WWeb
– 'Pink Pearl' (f)	CBow MBri SHil
– 'Rosalind' (f)	MPlt SPer WWeb
– 'Rosea' (f)	CB&S GRei MR&S SPer
– 'Rosie' (f)	MBri SHil WBod

– 'Sea Shell' (f)	IOrc MBri NHol SHil
– 'Signaal' ('Signal') (f)	CB&S ELan ENot MBri MPlt SPer WPat WWeb
– 'Sneeuwwitje' ('Snow White') (f)	CB&S ENot MBri MPlt SPla
– 'Stag River'	GDra LSav WDav
– 'Thymifolia' (m)	LSav SHil SPer SPla
– 'White Magic'	SLon
– 'White Pearl' (f)	IOrc LSav MBri NHol SHil
– 'Wintertime' (f)	ELan LSav NHol WWeb
¶ ***myrsinioides*** 'Geoffrey Herklots'	MBri
§ ***myrsinoides***	GDra GEdr IBar MBal NHol SHil SIng
* ***myrtilloides racemosa***	SSta
♦ ***nana***	See G. ***parvula***
nummularioides	GEdr MHig NHol NNrd WBod
– B 673	MBal
§ – ***elliptica***	SSta
– ***minor***	MBal
– 'Minuta'	See G. ***n. elliptica***
¶ 'October Red'	WWeb
ovalifolia	See G. ***fragrantissima***
* ***paraguayensis***	MBal
§ ***parvula***	ECou
phyllyreifolia	CFor SSpi SSta
'Pink Pixie'	CCla ECro EPla IDai MBar MBri SHil SIng SPer SSta WAbe
procumbens	Widely available
♦ ***prostrata***	See G. ***myrsinoides***
♦ – ***purpurea***	See G. ***myrsinoides***
pumila	ECou MBal MBar MBri NHol NNrd SIng WAbe
§ – CW 5226	MBal NHol
– 'E K Balls'	WDav
pyroloides	MBal WPer
– BMW 5	MBal
rupestris	MBal
semi-infera	SHil WSHC
shallon	CB&S CLan CTom ENot GRei IDai IJoh MBar MBri MPla MR&S SHil SLon SPer SPla SReu SSpi SSta WWin
– dwarf form	MBal
sinensis	MBal NHol
sp. Gillanders 110	NHol
¶ sp. PW 6142	NHol
¶ sp. Wr 8710	WDav
tasmanica	ECou GDra MBal MBar
– ***alba***	GDra
– x ***pumila***	MBal
– yellow fruited form	MBal
tetramera	CB&S
thymifolia	MBal
trichophylla	GArf GDra GHig MBal NHol WAbe WDav WWin
willisiana	See G. ***eriophylla***
x ***wisleyensis***	CCla CLan MBal MUlv SLon SPer SSta WAbe WBod WPat
– 'Wisley Pearl'	GDra GLoc IBlr IDai IJoh MBar MBri MGos MR&S MRav SDry SHil SIng WThu

GAURA (Onagraceae)

lindheimeri	CElw CGle CHad CHan CHil CSam CSun ECha ECro ELan GWic IBrk LGre LHop MBri MPar MUlv SAxl SChu SDix SMrm WEas WPer WRus
¶ – 'Whirling Butterflies'	EMon

GAYLUSSACIA (Ericaceae)

¶ ***ursinum***	SMrm

GAZANIA (Compositae)

* 'Cookei'	ELan LHop SMad WEas
cream	LHop
'Cream Beauty'	CHad GWic LHil NTow SChu
cream & purple	CHad ELan LHop SChu WPer
¶ 'Dorothy'	LHil
'Flash'	WEas
'Flore Pleno'	WHer WPer
hybrids	ELan LHop SDix WPer
krebsiana	CBos LGre WEas WPer
* ***madeira***	LHop
¶ 'Mini Star White'	WHen
¶ 'Mini Star Yellow'	WHen
¶ 'New Magic'	IHos
'Orange Beauty'	ELan SMad
rigens	CB&S CSam MBri NTow
– 'Aureo Variegata'	LHop
– 'Variegata'	CB&S CRiv ELan EOrc ERav MPit NSti WPer
'Silver Beauty'	CBot CHad CHil LAbb NTow SChu
¶ 'Slate'	SMrm
'Snuggle Bunny'	GWic
splendens	See G. ***rigens***
uniflora	EOrc GWic LHop WEas
'Vinner's Variegated'	GWic
'Yellow Buttons'	LHop

GELASINE (Iridaceae)

coerulea	EBur

GELIDOCALAMUS (Gramineae(Bambuseae))

fangianus	SBam SDry

GELSEMIUM (Loganiaceae)

rankinii	CChu CMCN CPle
sempervirens	CB&S CMCN ERea IBar MNew MSal
– 'Flore Pleno'	CB&S ERea
– 'Pride of Augusta'	CMCN

GENISTA † (Leguminosae)

aetnensis	Widely available
anglica	CKin
– 'Cloth of Gold'	GLoc MPla WDav
cinerea	CFor CShe LSav MBro SMad SPer
¶ ***decumbens***	MBro
delphinensis	See G. ***sagittalis delphinensis***
N ***depressa moesiaca***	ITim
'Emerald Spreader'	See G. ***pilosa*** 'Lemon Spreader'
¶ ***florida***	WHCG

fragrans	See CYTISUS ***canariensis***
hispanica	CB&S CBow CBra CSam CSco ELan ENot IDai IJoh IOrc MBal MBar MGos MR&S MRav MWat NHol NNor SHil SLon SPla SReu WAbe
– 'Compacta'	CLew EBre SIng SPer
N ***humifusa***	EPot ITim MBro WDav
januensis	LRHS SHil
lydia	Widely available
¶ ***monosperma***	WTay
pilosa	Widely available
– 'Goldilocks'	CBra ECtt MBar MBri MPlt SHil SSta WBod WWeb
§ – 'Lemon Spreader'	CBra CMHG COtt EBre ECtt ESis IJoh LHop LSav MBri MPlt MRav MWat SPer WBod WWat WWeb
*– ***major***	MHig
– ***minor***	NNrd WAbe
– 'Procumbens'	CLew GLoc MBal NHol WEas WPat
*– 'Superba'	NNrd
– 'Vancouver Gold'	CB&S COtt CSam CTre EHal ELan ERav ESis IHos IJoh IOrc LHop MBri MGos MRav NHol NTow SBla SCro SLon SMad SPer WSHC WWat
'Porlock'	CB&S ELan
sagittalis	CBot CHan CLew CMHG LHop MBal MR&S NHol NNor NNrd SBla SHil SIng SPer WHil WWat
§ – ***delphinensis***	CLew ELan GHig GLoc MCas MHig NKay NNrd SOkd WAbe
– ***minor***	See G. ***s. delphinensis***
sericea	CHan
tenera	CHan SPer SSta WHCG
– 'Golden Showers'	CSco SHil
tinctoria	CArn CBra CCor CGle CKin EEls ERav GPoy IJoh LHol MBar MChe MSal NNor NSel SIde SPla WHer WOak
– 'Flore Pleno'	EMon ESis GLoc IJoh ITim MBal MBar MPla MPlt NHol NKay NNrd SHil SPer WHil WPat
– 'Golden Plate'	SHil
N– ***humilis***	MHig NHol
N– ***prostrata***	WOak
– 'Royal Gold'	CBow CBra CSco EBre ENot MBri MPla MR&S MRav MWat NNor SHil WBod WWeb
– ***virgata***	CHan
tournefortii	CShe MBal WPat
villarsii	LSav MBro NHol NKay SIng WDav

GENTIANA † (Gentianaceae)

§ ***acaulis***	Widely available
¶ – JCA 515.005	GLoc
– ***alba***	WThu
– ***angustifolia***	GAng WAbe WThu
– 'Belvedere'	EMNN EPot GLoc MBro WAbe WThu
– 'Coelestina'	GAng
– 'Dinarica'	See G. ***dinarica***
– 'Gedanensis'	GAng
– 'Helzmannii'	GLoc
– 'Holzmann'	EPot GAng NNrd WDav
– 'Krumrey'	EMNN GDra GLoc NNrd WThu
– 'Rannoch'	EMNN EPot GLoc NNrd WThu
– 'Trotter's Form'	GAng
– 'Undulatifolia'	WThu
¶ – ***alba*** A G Week's form	GLoc
affinis	NHol
algida	CPla NGre
alpina	GAng
¶ ***altaica***	NHol
andrewsii	CPla CRiv NRya WHil
¶ ***angustifolia***	EPot
¶ – from Priin Mountains	GLoc
¶ – from Scoulor Pass	GLoc
'Ann's Special'	GAng NHar NHol
asclepiadea	Widely available
– ***alba***	Widely available
– 'Knightshayes'	GAng MBri MBro WHoo WRus
– 'Nymans'	ELan SPer
¶ – pale blue	SSpi WHoo WOMN
– 'Phyllis'	MBro MTho WHoo WRus
'Barbara Lyle'	GAng NRoo
x ***bernardii***	See G. x ***stevenagensis*** 'Bernardii'
bisetaea	NHol
'Blauer Diamant'	GAng
'Blauer Edelstein'	GAng
'Blue Flame'	GAng GDra GEdr
'Blue Heaven'	CLew EPot GAng GDra GEdr NRoo WAbe
§ ***burseri villarsii***	WHil
cachemirica	GLoc MTho NHol NRoo
¶ Cambrian hybrids	WAbe
'Carolii'	GAng GEdr NHar NKay NRoo WAbe WMar WPat
'Christine Jean'	GAbr NHar NHol WDav
clusii	EPot GAng NHol WAbe WDav
¶ – ***alba***	GLoc
¶ – ***corbariensis***	GLoc
– ***costei***	GLoc
'Coronation'	NRoo
crinita	See GENTIANOPSIS ***crinita***
§ ***cruciata***	CPla MTho NWCA WHil
§ ***dahurica***	CLew CPla ELan GLoc SBla
decumbens	CPla CSun NHol NRed
dendrologi	CPla SIng
depressa	MTho WAbe
'Devonhall'	GEdr WAbe
§ ***dinarica***	GAng GDra MTho
– 'Harlin'	GLoc
Drake's strain	GAbr GAng GDra GEdr GHig GLoc NGre
'Drumcairn White'	EPot
'Dusk'	GAng GDra
'Eleanor'	GAng
'Elizabeth'	GAng GEdr NNrd NRed WMar
'Exploi'	GAng

x *farorna*	GAng NRoo
farreri	GEdr MBal NKay WMar
'Fasta Highlands'	GAbr GAng GEdr NRoo
freyniana	GAng NWCA SIng
¶ *frigida*	NHol
'Glendevon'	GAng
§ *gracilipes*	ELan MBro MWat WHoo
– 'Yuatensis'	See G. ***wutaiensis***
gracilis	CPla
grossheimii	GLoc WAbe
♦x *hascombensis*	See G. ***septemfida lagodechiana*** 'Hascombensis'
hexaphylla	GAng
x *hexa-farreri*	GAng GEdr
§ – 'Alpha'	GAng GEdr
'Ida K'	GAng
Inshriach hybrids	GDra GHig NHar NHol
'Inverleith'	ELan GAng GEdr MBri NHol NKay SIng WThu
kesselringii	See G. ***walujewii***
kochiana	See G. ***acaulis***
kurroo	CPla ELan WDav
– *brevidens*	See G. ***dahurica***
lagodechiana	CCla CLew CSam EBar LAbb NGre NPer NRoo NVic WHil
'Leslie Delaney'	GAng
lutea	CArn CBot CHar CPla CSun ECha ELan GDra GEdr GPoy LHol MSal SIng SSpi
x *macaulayi*	CLew CPla CRiv EBre GAng MBri MHig MRav NHar NHol NKay NRoo NTow
– 'Blue Bonnets'	GAng GEdr NHar
– 'Edinburgh'	GAng GEdr NRoo
– 'Elata'	ELan GEdr MBri NHol
– 'Kidbrooke Seedling'	NGre NHol NKay NRya WAbe
– 'Kingfisher'	CPla CRiv EBre ECha GAng GDra GEdr MBal NHol NNrd NRoo SBla SIng
– 'Praecox'	GAng GCHN GEdr MBri NHol
§ – 'Wells's Variety'	EPot GAbr GEdr MBri MPla NKay WAbe
macrophylla	See G. ***burseri villarsii***
'Magnificent'	GAng
makinoi	GAng
'Mary Lyle'	GAng WMar
'Maryfield'	GAng
'Midnight'	GAng
'Multiflora'	GAng
ochroleuca	See G. ***villosa***
olivieri	ECam
oreodoxa	EPot GEdr ITim WAbe
ornata	GEdr
pannonica	GDra
paradoxa	CSun GEdr
phlogifolia	See G. ***cruciata***
pneumonanthe	CRiv GEdr NRoo
¶ *prolata* K 214	GArf
– forms	GArf
przewalskii	WBon WEas
¶ *punctata*	NHol
purdomii	See G. ***gracilipes***
robusta	ELan
'Royal Highlander'	GAng
saxosa	CLew CSun ECou GAng GEdr GLoc ITim LHop MCas MPar MTho NGre NHar NHol NNrd NRed NTow SPou SWas WAbe WDav WOMN
'Sensation'	GAng
septemfida	Widely available
– 'Doeringiana'	CHar MRav NRoo
§ – *lagodechiana* 'Hascombensis'	CPla ELan NGre NWCA WOld
– *latifolia*	CHar EBre MRav
sino-ornata	Widely available
– *alba*	CPla EPot GDra GEdr NHol NKay NRoo WDav WMar WWin
– 'Angel's Wings'	ELan GAng GEdr MBri NHol
– 'Blauer Dom'	GAng
– 'Brin Form'	CRiv EBre GLoc MBal MHig NKay NNrd NRoo SIng SWas WAbe
¶ – 'Downfield'	NHol
– 'Edith Sarah'	ELan EPot GAng GEdr GLoc ITim MBri NHar NHol NKay NNrd NRoo WAbe WMar
– 'Mary Lyle'	EBre EPot GEdr GGar MBri MTho NHol NRoo WAbe
– 'Praecox'	See G. x ***macaulayi*** 'P.'
– 'Trogg's Form'	EPot NHol
– 'Woolgreaves'	EPot GLoc
x *stevenagensis*	CPla CRiv EMNN GAng MBal MBri MFir MHig NNrd NRoo NTow SIng WPat WThu
§ – 'Bernardii'	GAng GEdr MBri NHar SIng WAbe
– dark form	NRoo WAbe
– 'Frank Barker'	GAng GEdr MBri
straminea	NRoo NRya WHil
'Strathmore'	GAng MBri NHar NHol
'Susan'	GAng
'Susan Jane'	GAng GDra GEdr
ternifolia	ELan EPot GAng GArf GDra GEdr GHig ITim NKay NRoo SIng WDav
– SBEC 1053	NHol
¶ – 'Cangshan'	NHar
¶ – 'Dali'	MBri NBir NHar NHol
'Thunersee'	GAng
tibetica	CBot CPla EBar GAbr WEas WHil
¶ *triflora montana*	GArf
'Tweeddale Strain'	GEdr
veitchiorum	MBri NRoo
* *velkokvesii*	GLoc
verna	CGle CLew CSam ELan GAng GEdr GLoc ITim LHop MBro MPla MTho MWat NKay NRoo SSpi SWas WAbe WOMN WOld WPat
¶ – *alba*	WPat
– *angulosa*	CHar CPla CSun EPot GAbr GAng GDra GLoc MBro MCas MHig MTho NGre NHar NHol NRed SBla SIng WDav WHoo
– *tergestina*	GEdr

– x ***pumila***	GLoc
villosa	SIng
waltonii	CLew ELan
walujewii	CCla
♦ ***wellsii***	See G. x ***macaulayi*** 'Wells's Variety'
'Wendy Jean'	GLoc
¶ 'White Wings'	ELan NHol
§ ***wutaiensis***	ELan GDra NRed WHil
'Zauberland'	GAng

GENTIANOPSIS (Gentianaceae)

GEOGENANTHUS (Commelinaceae)

GERANIUM † (Geraniaceae)

aconitifolium	See G. ***rivulare***
albanum	CCor GCHN SCou
albiflorum	GCHN SAxl
anemonifolium	See G. ***palmatum***
'Ann Folkard'	CElw CLew CSev EFol ELan EOrc ERav ERou GAbr MRav NRoo NSti SAxl SBla SCou WCot
argenteum	MDHE NHar SPou
– 'Purpureum'	See G. x ***lindavicum*** 'P.'
aristatum	GCHN SAxl SCou
armenum	See G. ***psilostemon***
asphodeloides	CChu CCor CElw CFis CHar CSun EMou EOrc GAbr GCHN NCat NSti SAxl WCar WEas WHal WHea WHoo WRus WToa
¶ – ***album***	WRus
– forms	NCat SCou
¶ – ***asphodeloides*** white form	SCou
atlanticum	See G. ***malviflorum***
biuncinatum	SCou
bohemicum	EBar GCHN MDHE NVic SAxl SCou SSus WCar WCru WEas WHal WHer
'Brookside'	CElw NSti SAxl
brutium	CFis GCHN SAxl SCou WHen
'Buxton's Blue'	See G. ***wallichianum*** 'Buxton's Variety'
caffrum	CElw GCHN SAxl SCou
canariense	GGar SAxl SCou WCru
candicans	See G. ***lambertii***
§ x ***cantabrigiense***	Widely available
– 'Biokovo'	CGle CHad CMHG CSev CShe ECha EGol EMou EPla GCHN LSav MPar NSti SAxl SChu SCou SHig SSpi SWas WEas WHen WOld WRus WToa
– 'Cambridge'	EPla NCat NRoo NVic SAxl SSpi
¶ – 'Carmina'	GWic
cataractarum	CFis GCHN NCat SAxl SCou
cinereum	CGle CSev WToa
– ***album***	MBal
– 'Apple Blossom'	See G. ***lindavicum*** 'A.B.'
– 'Ballerina'	Widely available
– ***cinereum***	GCHN
– 'Giuseppii'	CCla CLew EBre GCHN MBri MRav MTho NNrd NRoo SCou WHoo WRus WToa
– 'Lawrence Flatman'	CCla CElw CLew CSco EBre EFol ELan ERou GCHN MBri MRav NRoo SBla SMad WHen WPat WRus WToa WWin
– 'Splendens'	CCla CLew EBre ECha EFou GCHN MBri MBro WHoo WRus WToa
– ***subcaulescens***	Widely available
'Claridge Druce'	See G. x ***oxonianum*** 'Claridge Druce'
* ***clarkei*** 'Kashmir Blue'	SCro SMrm
– 'Kashmir Pink'	CBos SBla SMrm WToa
– 'Kashmir Purple'	CBos EFou GWic MBri NSti SAxl SBla SCou SMrm SSpi WToa
§ – 'Kashmir White'	Widely available
collinum	GCHN SAxl SCou WCru WHen
columbinum	SCou
dalmaticum	Widely available
– ***album***	Widely available
¶ – Coombeland form	EPla
dalmaticum x ***macrorrhizum***	See G. x ***cantabrigiense***
delavayi	CBot CHad
dissectum	MSal
donianum	SCou
– ES 179	GLoc
drakensbergense	CHan
§ ***endressii***	CBre CFis CSev CSun ECha ELan EMou EPar ERav GCHN LBuc LGro LSav MBro MCot MFir NNor NNrd SAxl SDix STre WHil WOld WToa
¶ – dark form	NCat
¶ – 'Rose'	CSun WToa
– 'Wargrave Pink'	Widely available
erianthum	GCHN MPar SAxl SSpi WDav
N ***eriostemon***	CElw CFis CFor CGle CHar CSev GCHN LGre MPar NSti SAxl SCou WHal WHea WHen
farreri	CElw CGle GCHN MTho NKay SAxl SBla SCou SWas WDav WEas WHal
* ***flanaganii***	GCHN SAxl
fremontii	CBos SAxl SCou
gracile	CMal GCHN NVic SAxl SCou
¶ – pale form	GWic
grandiflorum	See G. ***himalayense***
– ***alpinum***	See G. ***himalayense*** 'Gravetye'
§ ***himalayense***	CCla CCor CFis CSco CSun CWGN ELan EMou MBri MPar MWgw NHol NNor SAxl SWas WBon WHen WHil
– ***alpinum***	See G. ***h.*** 'Gravetye'
– 'Birch Double'	See G. ***h.*** 'Plenum'
§ – 'Gravetye'	Widely available
– 'Irish Blue'	CFis SAxl SCou
§ – 'Plenum'	Widely available
ibericum	CCla CElw CFis CHar CKel CRow CShe CSun MBal MCot MWat NRoo SCou SPer WEas WHen WToa WWin

– jubatum	GCHN SAxl
– platypetalum	See G. x ***magnificum***
incanum	CHan CMHG CShe CSpe CTre ECou GCHN LGre LHop NSti SAxl SBar SBor SCou
'Johnson's Blue'	Widely available
kishtvariense	CSev GCHN SAxl SBla SCou
§ ***lambertii***	CElw NBir NCat SAxl SCou WEas WHoo
¶ – 'Coombland White'	SCou
– 'Swansdown'	GWic SCou
¶ ***lanuginosum***	SCou
libani	CHan CRow EMou GCHN GWic NSti SAxl SCou WCot WEas
'Lily Lovell'	CBos CElw CRow ERav GCHN GWic IBlr LGre MBri MUlv NCat SAxl SCou SMrm SWas WEas WHal WHea WHer WToa
x ***lindavicum***	SPou
§ – 'Apple Blossom'	CCla CFis MCot NNrd NRoo SCou
¶ – 'Purpureum'	WDav
lucidum	GCHN MSal NSti SCou
macrorrhizum	CArn CCla CHan CSco CShe CSun EPar GCHN GWic LHol MCot MPar MWgw NHol SApp SBor SCou SPla STre WEas WHal WHen WWin
– album	Widely available
– 'Bevan's Variety'	CChu CCla CCor CFis CRow EBre ECha EFou EGol ELan EOrc GCHN GHig GPla GWic NRoo SCou SHig SMad SPer SWas WHea WHer WRus
– 'Czakor'	CHar CLew CSun EMon EOrc MUlv NCat NRoo NSti SAxl SCou WHer WToa
– 'Ingwersen's Variety'	Widely available
¶ – 'Lohfelden'	SAxl SWas
¶ – 'Ridsko'	SAxl
– roseum	CRow CSco CShe MUlv WWin
– 'Spessart'	CCla CFis GWic LSav MUlv NCat NSti SCou SHig
– 'Variegatum'	Widely available
macrostylum	CCor GCHN MPar SAxl WCot
maculatum	CFor CSev ELan EMou GCHN GPoy GWic MRav MSal SAxl SCou SSpi
– album	CBre CFor GCHN SAxl SCou SSpi
maderense	CHEx CPle CTre ERea GCHN GWic IBlr SAxl SCou SDix SMad SSpi WEas WHal WKif WTay
§ x ***magnificum***	Widely available
§ ***malviflorum***	CBre CElw CFis CHad CHan ECha EFou ELan EMou EPar EPot GCHN LGre LHop MBro MPar MTho SAxl SBor SCou SSpi WHoo WKif WOMN
'Maxwelton'	GCHN
molle	MSal
§ x ***monacense***	CBos CBre CElw CFis CHan CTom EFou ELan GGar NRoo NSti SAxl SCou SSus WHer
– anglicum	CCor GCHN NSti SAxl SCou WBon
§ – 'Muldoon'	CElw CFis CSev ECha EFou EGol GWic LHop MBri MUlv NHol NOak NRoo NSti SCou SPer SSus WBon WEas WHer WRus WToa
– 'Variegatum'	See G. x ***m.*** 'Muldoon'
'Mourning Widow'	See G. ***phaeum***
nepalense	CTom SCou
¶ 'Nimbus'	SAxl
nodosum	CBow CCla CElw CFis CGle CHad CHan CSev CShe ECha EFou EGol ELan EMou GCHN MPar NSti SAxl SCou SPer SSpi WHea WHoo WToa
ocellatum	NCat
oreganum	CCor SAxl SCou
§ ***orientalitibeticum***	Widely available
x ***oxonianum***	CLew EBar SAxl SCou
– 'A T Johnson'	Widely available
§ – 'Claridge Druce'	CB&S CFis CGle CHar CSun EBre ECha EFou ELan EMou EOrc ERav GCHN LGro MWgw NSti SAxl SChu SCou SPer WBon WHen WHer WHoo
– 'Hollywood'	ELan EMon SAxl
¶ – 'Lady Moore'	SAxl
– 'Rose Clair'	CShe CSun EFou NHol SChu SCou SCro WEas WHen
– 'Southcombe Double'	GWic MUlv SAxl SChu WHal
– 'Southcombe Star'	CElw GWic NSti SCou SMrm
§ – 'Thurstonianum'	CChu CCor CElw CFis CHan ELan EOrc GCHN GWic NCat SAxl SCou WAbb WEas WWin
¶ – 'Wageningen'	GWic
¶ – 'Walter's Gift'	CHan EMon GWic SAxl
– 'Winscombe'	CElw CSun CTom EOrc GCHN GWic NCat SAxl SCou SWas
§ ***palmatum***	CBot CElw CHad CHan CSpe EPad LHil MFir MPar NCat NSti SAxl SCou WEas WHer WKif WOMN
palustre	CCor EMou GCHN GWic SAxl SCou
Pelargonium	See PELARGONIUM
peloponnesiacum	SCou
§ ***phaeum***	Widely available
– album	Widely available
– black form	SAxl
– forms	CBos EMou SAxl WBon
¶ – ***hungaricum***	GWic NCat
– 'Langthorn's Blue'	ELan
– 'Lily Lovell'	See G. 'L. L.'
*– 'Taff's Jester'	CHad NSti SCou
– 'Variegatum'	CFis CFor CHad CHan CRow ECro ELan EMon ERav SAxl
phaeum lividum	CFor CRow GCHN GPla MUlv NSti SChu SCou SCro SPer SWas WHal WHen WHer
– – 'Majus'	NCat SAxl SCou

platypetalum	CHan ELan ENot GCHN MBro MPar MPit NKay SAxl SCou STre
pogonanthum	CElw GCHN GWic NSti SAxl SCou WHal
polyanthes	CSun EMou GDra MBro NHol WDav
pratense	CArn CBre CFis CKin CRow CShe CWGN ECro ELan EMou EOrc GCHN LHol MSal MWgw NLan SCou WCla WPer WToa
– ***albiflorum***	CBot CCla CCor CElw CGle GCHN GWic MSal NRoo SAxl SBor SCou SPer SSpi WHal WHoo WPer WToa WWin
– 'Bittersweet'	EMon
– 'Blue Chip'	EMon
– 'Flore Pleno'	See G. ***p.*** 'Plenum Violaceum'
– forms	GCHN SCou
– 'Galactic'	CHan EMon WOMN
– 'Mrs Kendall Clark'	Widely available
– 'Plenum Album'	CFis
§ – 'Plenum Caeruleum'	CB&S CCla CFis CGle CHad CHar CKel CSco EBre ERou GCHN MBri NSti SCou SPer WEas WHoo WToa
– 'Plenum Purpureum'	See G. ***p.*** 'Plenum Violaceum'
§ – 'Plenum Violaceum'	Widely available
– ***rectum album***	See G. ***clarkei*** 'Kashmir White'
– ***roseum***	ELan NBir NSti WHoo WToa
– ***ruprech***	NCat
– 'Silver Queen'	CBre CSco ELan EOrc GCHN GGar SAxl WHen WToa
– 'Striatum'	CElw CFis ECha ELan EMou NCat SAxl SCou WEas WHal WHoo WKif WWin
– 'Wisley Blue'	SCou SCro
procurrens	Widely available
§ ***psilostemon***	Widely available
– 'Bressingham Flair'	EBre MBri NRoo SAxl SCou WRus
pulchrum	CElw EMon GWic NCat SAxl SCou SWas
punctatum	See G. x ***monacense***
– ***variegatum***	See G. x ***monacense*** 'Muldoon'
pusillum	CKin MSal
pylzowianum	CCor CElw CShe CTom EBre EMou EPla GGar GLoc MBri NHol NRoo NRya NVic SAxl SBor SChu SCou SIng SSmi WHer WHil WToa
pyrenaicum	CBre CElw CFis CKin EPad GAbr GCHN MSal NSti NVic SCou WHen WToa
– ***albiflorum***	CBre CCor CElw CLew CNat GCHN NSti NVic SAxl WHen WToa
¶ – 'Bill Wallace'	CLew MTho NCat SAxl
rectum 'Album'	See G. ***clarkei*** 'Kashmir White'
reflexum	CElw CFis CSev EGol GCHN SAxl SCou SMrm WEas WToa
renardii	Widely available
– blue form	See G. ***r.*** 'Whiteknights'
§ – 'Whiteknights'	EGol EPla WEas
¶ – 'Zetterland'	ECro
richardsonii	GCHN GWic SAxl SCou
¶ x ***riversleaianum*** 'Jean Armour'	GCHN
– 'Mavis Simpson'	CCla CFis CMHG EMon GCHN MPar NSti SAxl SSpi WBon WToa
– 'Russell Prichard'	Widely available
§ ***rivulare***	CFis GCHN GPla WHer WToa
– 'Album'	MPar
'Robert Burns'	GCHN
robertianum	CFis CKin EFol LHol MChe SIde WHen
– ***album***	CFis MPar NCat NSti NVic WBon
– ***bernettii***	SCou
– 'Celtic White'	CBre CFis CTom EMon GWic NCat NHol NSti SAxl
robustum	CElw CHan GCHN GWic NSti SAxl SCou WCar WEas WHal WToa
rubescens	EMon NSti SAxl SCou WEas WHal
¶ ***rubicaule***	NCat
¶ ***rubifolium***	SAxl
'Salome'	SAxl SCou
sanguineum	Widely available
– ***album***	Widely available
¶ – 'Cedric Morris'	SWas
* – ***compactum tuberosum***	EPot
– 'Elsbeth'	SAxl SCou
– 'Glenluce'	GCHN NCat NOrc SAxl SCou
– 'Jubilee Pink'	SAxl SBla SCou WToa
– ***lancastrense***	See G. ***sanguineum striatum***
– ***lancastrense*** 'Splendens'	See G. ***s. striatum*** 'Splendens'
– 'Max Frei'	EFou EGol GWic NHol SChu SCou SSpi
– 'Minutum'	CFis LGre SCou SIng
– 'Nanum'	EPar NHar NHol NKay
– 'Nyewood'	SAxl
– ***prostratum***	MTho NRoo SBla SCro WAbe WHil
– 'Shepherd's Warning'	CCla CSco CSev EBre GCHN GLoc LHop MRav NRoo SCou SSpi WHoo WOld WPat WPer WRus
§ – ***striatum***	Widely available
§ – ***striatum*** 'Splendens'	CCla CFis CFor CKel CSco EBre ECha EGol EHar ELan ERou GDra IDai LHop MCot MWat NKay NNor NRoo SAxl SCou SPer SSmi WEas
* ***schikonianum***	SCou
¶ 'Sea Pink'	GCHN
sessiliflorum	CHad CMal ECou EPar MCot SCou WCar WHoo WToa

– ***novae-zelandiae nigricans***	Widely available
– ***novae-zelandiae*** green form	CElw GCHN
– ***novae-zelandiae*** red form	CBos GCHN LHop
*– 'Porter's Pass	EFol GLoc MPit SCou
sessiliflorum novae-zelandiae nigricans x ***traversii elegans***	GCHN WCru
sibiricum	GCHN WToa
sinense	CBre CFis CFor CHar EBar EMon GCHN GWic MPar MRav SAxl SCou SSpi SWas WHoo
¶ – B&L 12466	EMon
soboliferum	NBir SAxl SCou WEas
¶ 'Southcombe Beauty'	SSpi
'Southcombe Star'	See G. x ***oxonianum*** 'S. S.'
¶ 'Spinners'	SAxl SCou
'Standhoe'	NSti SAxl SCou
stapfianum roseum	See G. ***orientalitibeticum***
swatense	SAxl WCru
– SEP 131	GCHN
sylvaticum	CBow CBre CCla CSev EMon EMou MBal MSal SAxl SCou SSpi WHen WPer
§ – ***albiflorum***	CBot CBre CCla CElw CFor CHad CHan CHar CSco CSun EGol ELan EMou GCHN MCot NRoo NSti SCou WEas WOld WToa WWin
– 'Album'	CFis CGle ECha LHop LSav NHol SApp SAxl WBon WEas
– 'Amy Doncaster'	SAxl SCou SWas
¶ – 'Angulatum'	SCou
– 'Baker's Pink'	CCor SAxl
¶ – 'Birch Lilac'	GWic
– ***caeruleatum***	SAxl
– 'Mayflower'	CFis CHad CSco EBre ECha EFou ELan EMou ERav GCHN LGre MUlv NHol NSti SAxl SCou SHig SPer WHal WHen WHil WHoo WToa
– 'Meran'	SCou
– ***roseum***	GCHN NCat SAxl SPer WHen
– 'Silva'	GWic SAxl SCou
– ***wanneri***	CFis CGle CHar CSun CTom NCat SCou WHoo
thunbergii	CElw CHan CLew ELan EMon GAbr GCHN GWic MSal NHol NOak NSti SAxl SCou WCar WHil WPer WToa
thurstonianum	See G. x ***oxonianum*** 'T.'
¶ ***transbaicalicum***	GCHN SAxl
traversii	CBot CCor EPot MDHE
– ***elegans***	CBos CFis CFor CHad CHan CSpe ELan GCHN GWic LGre LHop MPar MRav MTho NSti NTow SAxl SCou SWas WEas WHal WHen WHer WOMN
tuberosum	Widely available
– 'Carlesii'	GWic
versicolor	CCor CFis CHad CSev CShe CTom EMou GWic MRav NVic SAxl SCou SCro STre WToa
– ***album***	CHan NCat
violareum	See PELARGONIUM 'Splendide'
viscosissimum	SAxl SCou
wallichianum	WHal WToa
§ – 'Buxton's Variety'	Widely available
¶ – pink form	CBos
¶ – 'Syabru'	SWas
wilfordii	CFis
wlassovianum	CCor CFis CSco CTom EGol GCHN MPar NHol NSti SAxl SCou SPer WHea WHoo WToa
yesoense	EGol GCHN NSti SAxl SCou SWas WHal WHea
yunnanense	GGar NCat SCou

GESNERIA (Gesneriaceae)

cardinalis	See SINNINGIA ***c.***
♦x ***cardosa***	See SINNINGIA x ***c.***

GEUM † (Rosaceae)

'Borisii'	Widely available
– x ***montanum***	LHop
bulgaricum	MBri NHol
¶ ***calthifolium***	WPer
§ ***chiloense***	GGar
– 'Dolly North'	CGle ERou GGar GWic MBri NHol
– 'Feuermeer'	LHop
– 'Mrs Bradshaw'	CB&S CBow CHar CKel CSco CShe EBre ELan ENot ERou GCHN LHop LSav MBri MBro MFir MWat MWgw NNor NRoo SMad SPer WEas WHil
♦ ***coccineum***	See G. ***chiloense***
elatum	MCab
– SEP 304	CHan
'Fire Opal'	CSco ERou GWic
'Georgenberg'	CB&S CElw CGle CKel CSco EBre ELun ERou LHil LSav MBri MWgw NBar NHol NOak NSti SAxl SChu WBon WHal WHil WOld
* ***hybrida luteum***	NSti
x ***intermedium***	CChu CElw CTom ECha SChu SCro WCot
japonicum	See G. ***macrophyllum***
'Lady Stratheden'	CB&S CBow CHar CKel CSco EBre ELan ENot ERou GCHN LAbb LSav MBri MFir MWat NNor NRoo SMad SPer WAbe WEas
leiospermum	ECou
'Lemon Drops'	ECha EGol
macrophyllum	CLew
¶ – ***sachalinense***	IBrk
'Marika'	CRow
montanum	CGle CHar CLew CSam ECha ELan GAbr GLoc MBro MCas MFir NHol NKay SIng SWas WCla WHal WHoo WPer WWin

*– ***maximum***	SWas
¶ ***pentapetalum***	GArf WDav
'Prinses Juliana'	ERou GWic NHol
pyrenaicum	WHil
♦ ***quellyon***	See G. ***chiloense***
reptans	CLew EPad GAbr NHol WDav WPer WThu
x ***rhaeticum***	NKay NTow
¶ 'Rijnstroom'	MUlv
rivale	CCor CElw CHar CKin CRiv CRow EHon ELun EMon GAbr LGro MFir MSal MSta NLan NNor WCla WHal WHoo WRus WWin
– 'Album'	CChu CCla CElw CGle CHar CRow CSam CWGN EGol ELan EMon GAbr GWic MBal MCot MFir MShr NHol NSti WEas WHer WHil
– 'Coppertone'	CGle CTom EBre ECha ELan GWic IBlr MFir SAxl SWas
– 'Leonard's Variety'	CBre CChu CElw CGle CHad CRow CSam CWGN ECha ELan EOrc GWic MBal MBri MCot MWat MWgw NOrc NRar NSti NVic SWas WAbe WBon
– 'Leonard's Variety Double'	CGle
– 'Lionel Cox'	CBre CChu CElw CGle CHad CLew CRow CTom ECha EGol EOrc NSti SWas WWin
rossii	WDav
¶ 'Rubin'	EFou
* 'Tangerine'	EBre EPla MRav NRoo
x ***tirolense***	NKay
triflorum	WRus
* 'Two Ladies'	NBar
urbanum	CArn CKin CSFH GPoy LHol MSal NLan NSel SIde WCla WHer WSto

GEVUINA (Proteaceae)

avellana	CB&S CChu CGre CTrw SArc WPat

GIBASIS (Commelinaceae)

GILIA (Polemoniaceae)

aggregata	See IPOMOPSIS ***a.***

GILLENIA (Rosaceae)

trifoliata	CArn CCla CRow ECha EFou ELan ERou GPoy MBri MCot MSal MUlv NKay SChu SDix SLHN SPer SSpi WCot WEas WOld WSHC

GINKGO (Ginkgoaceae)

biloba	Widely available
– 'Autumn Gold'	See G. ***b.*** 'Saratoga'
– 'Fastigiata'	SHil
– 'Horizontalis'	WMou
– 'Pendula'	LRHS MBri
§ – 'Saratoga'	LNet MBri SExT
– 'Tremonia'	SHil
– 'Variegata'	SSta

GLADIOLUS † (Iridaceae)

'Alice' (Min)	LAma
'Amanda Mahy' (N)	CBro LAma LBlo LBow WHil
'Andorra' (B)	CKel
'Anglia' (B)	CKel
'Anitra' (P)	LAma
'Applause' (L)	LAma
'Apricot Queen'	LAma
'Atom' (P)	CBro LAma
'Avalanche'	LAma
'Bell Boy'	LAma
'Blackpool'	LAma
'Blushing Bride' (N)	LBlo
Butterfly hybrids	LBow
byzantinus	See G. ***communis byzantinus***
§ ***callianthus***	CAvo CBro CKel CSut LAma LBow SLHN SW&B
'Camborne' (Min)	LAma
'Campanella' (B)	CKel
'Carmen' (G)	CKel
carmineus	LBow
carneus	CAvo CBro LBow
'Charm' (N)	CBro LAma LBlo
'Chatres'	LAma
'Christabel' (L)	LBow
'Cindy'	LAma
'Columbine' (P)	CKel LAma
'Comet' (N)	LBow
communis	CAvo CRiv ETub LAma NHol
§ – ***byzantinus***	CAvo CB&S CBro CGle CHEx CHad CTom ELan EMon EPar ETub LAma LBow MBri MUlv NHol NSti SIng WAbe WEas
'Confetti' (B)	CKel
'Deciso' (L)	CKel
'Desirée'	CBro LAma
'Dream Party'	LAma
¶ 'Dutch Parade'	CSut
'Dyanito'	LAma
'Edward van Beinum'	LAma
'Elvira' (N)	LAma
¶ 'Erin'	CSut
'Essex' (S)	CKel
¶ 'Esta Bonita' (G)	CSut
'Fidelio' (L)	LAma
'Firebird'	LAma
floribundus	LBow
'Flower Song' (L)	CKel LAma
'Friendship' (L)	CKel
'Georgette ' (S)	LAma
'Gillian' (L)	LBow
'Good Luck' (N)	CBro
grandis	See G. ***liliaceus***
'Green Woodpecker' (M)	CKel LAma
'Greenland' (B)	CKel
'Guernsey Glory' (N)	LAma
¶ 'Gypsy Baron' (G)	CSut
'Helene' (P)	LAma
'Her Majesty'	LAma
'Holland Pearl' (Min)	LAma
'Hunting Song' (L)	LAma

'Hypnose' (B)	LAma
'Imperialis'	IBlr
'Impressive' (N)	LAma
'Introspection' (L)	CKel
¶ *italicus*	EBar
'Jacksonville Gold'	LAma
'Jessica' (L)	LAma
'Lady Godiva' (Min)	LAma
'Leonore' (P)	LAma
§ *liliaceus*	LBow
'Little Darling' (P)	CKel
longicollis	CHan
'Lorena'	LAma
¶ 'Love Letter'	CSut
¶ 'Madonna' (L)	CSut
'Madrilene' (B)	CKel
¶ 'Mandy'	CSut
'Mary Housley'	LAma
'Mascagni'	LAma
'Misty Eye'	CKel
murielae	See G. ***callianthus***
'My Love' (G)	LAma
§ *natalensis*	GWic IBlr
'Nicole'	LAma
'Nova Lux'	LAma
'Nymph' (N)	CAvo LAma LBow SIng
'Obelisk' (P)	LAma
'Oscar' (G)	CKel LAma
¶ 'Ovation'	CSut
'Pandion' (L)	CKel
papilio	CChu CHad ECha EOrc GPla GWic MPar SAxl SBla SLHN SSpi WEas WHal WOMN
¶ – 'Grey Ghost'	WEas
§ – *purpureoauratus*	CBro CGle CMal IBlr MFir
¶ 'Passion'	CSut
'Peach Blossom' (N)	LBlo
'Pegasus' (N)	LAma
'Perky'	LAma
'Perseus' (P)	CKel LAma
'Peter Pears' (L)	CKel LAma
'Piccolo' (B)	CKel
'Picture'	LAma
'Picturesque'	LAma
'Pink Lady' (L)	CKel
¶ 'Pink Perfection' (L)	CSut
'Piquant'	LAma
'Praha' (L)	LAma
primulinus	See G. ***natalensis***
Primulinus hybrids	LBow SW&B
'Prince Claus' (N)	CBro LAma WHil
'Princess Margaret Rose' (Min)	LAma
'Priscilla'	LAma
¶ 'Promise' (M)	CSut
purpureoauratus	See G. ***papilio p.***
'Queen of Night' (G)	CKel
'Red Jewel'	LAma
'Robinetta' (*recurvus* x)	CAvo LAma
'Rose Supreme' (G)	LAma
¶ 'Royal Beauty' (L)	CSut
¶ 'Royal Dutch' (L)	CSut
'Royal Violet' (G)	CKel
'Sancerre' (G)	CKel
¶ 'Saxony' (L)	CSut
segetum	See G. ***italicus***
'Shakespeare'	LAma
'Shamrock' (B)	CKel
'Spic and Span' (G)	CKel LAma
'Spitfire' (N)	LBlo
'Storiette' (B)	CKel
'Tangerine' (G)	CKel
'The Bride' (Colv.)	CAvo CBro CGle LAma LBlo LBow MUlv
'Trader Horn' (G)	CKel LAma
'Treasure' (P)	CKel
tristis	CBro ECha LBow SDix WAbe
undulatus	ETub LBow NHol
'Velvet Joy' (P)	LAma
'Victor Borge'	LAma
'Violetta' (M)	LAma
'White City' (P)	CKel LAma
'White Friendship' (L)	CKel LAma
'White Prosperity' (L)	CSut LAma
'Wind Song' (L)	LAma
'Yellow Special' (P)	CKel

GLANDULARIA See VERBENA

GLAUCIDIUM (Paeoniaceae)

palmatum	GEdr GLoc ITim MBal SPou
– 'Album'	See G. ***p. leucanthum***

GLAUCIUM (Papaveraceae)

§ *corniculatum*	CGle ECro ERav LGan MPar SFir WEas WHer WHoo
flavum	CGle CNat EBar ECha ECro LGan MPar NHex SFir WHer WOMN
– *aurantiacum*	ECha
¶ – red form	SBar
phoenicium	See G. ***corniculatum***

GLAUX (Primulaceae)

maritima dwarf form	CSun NRya

GLECHOMA (Labiatae)

hederacea	CArn CKin GPoy IHos
– 'Rosea'	EMon LRHS
§ – 'Variegata'	CHoe CRow CTom ECro EFol EFou ELan MBri MRav SFar SIng SLMG SPla WPer
¶ *hirsuta*	EMon

GLEDITSIA (Leguminosae)

japonica	WCoo
triacanthos	CBra CPle ENot IOrc SHil WMou WNor
– 'Bujotii'	SHil
– 'Elegantissima'	EHar SHil
*– 'Emerald Kascade'	SGar
– *inermis*	ENot SHil
– 'Rubylace'	CBra CSco EHar ELan MBar MBlu MGos SGar SHil SMad SSpi SSta
– 'Shademaster'	SHil
– 'Skyline'	SGar
– 'Sunburst'	Widely available

GLOBULARIA (Globulariaceae)

aphyllanthes	GLoc
bellidifolia	See G. ***meridionalis***
cordifolia	CLew CMHG CRiv EBre GLoc MTho NGre NHol NTow SWas WDav WHoo WOld
incanescens	WPer WWin
§ ***meridionalis***	GLoc ITim MBro MHig MWat SBla WHal WOld WPer
– 'Hort's Variety'	MTho
nana	See G. ***repens***
nudicaulis	CLew CSun MBro NGre WDav
punctata	NTow NWCA SBar
pygmaea	See G. ***meridionalis***
§ ***repens***	CLew CSun GAbr
trichosantha	CLew GAbr MHig NHol SIng

GLORIOSA (Liliaceae/Colchicaceae)

caramii	LBow
carsonii	See G. ***superba***
lutea	See G. ***superba superba***
rothschildiana	See G. ***superba***
§ ***superba***	CAvo CKel IBlr LAma LBow LHop MBri SLMG SW&B
– ***superba***	LAma LBow

GLOXINIA (Gesneriaceae)

perennis	NMos
sylvatica	WEfe

GLYCERIA (Gramineae)

aquatica 'Variegata'	See G. ***maxima*** 'Variegata'
fluitans	CKin
§ ***maxima*** 'Variegata'	CElw CHoe CRiv CRow CWGN ECha EFou EHon ELan EMon EPot ERou GCHN GWic LMay MSta MUlv NHol NSti SHil SPer SSpi WEas
§ ***notata***	CKin
♦ ***plicata***	See G. ***notata***
spectabilis 'Variegata'	See G. ***maxima*** 'Variegata'

GLYCYRRHIZA (Leguminosae)

echinata	MSal
glabra	CArn ECro GPoy MSal
glandulifera	MSal
lepidota	MSal
missouriensis	MSal

GLYPTOSTROBUS (Taxodiaceae)

lineatus	See G. ***pensilis***

GNAPHALIUM (Compositae)

'Fairy Gold'	See HELICHRYSUM ***thianschanicum*** 'Goldkind'
♦ ***keriense***	See ANAPHALIS ***keriensis***
♦ ***subrigidum***	See ANAPHALIS ***subrigida***
♦ ***trinerve***	See ANAPHALIS ***trinervis***

GODETIA See **CLARKIA**

GONIOLIMON (Plumbaginaceae)

§ ***tataricum angustifolium***	CCla ECtt ELan GHig WHil WPer

GOODENIA (Goodeniaceae)

humilis	ECou
repens	NHol

GOODYERA (Orchidaceae)

GOOSEBERRY See **RIBES** ***uva-crispa***

GOOSEBERRY, Cape See **PHYSALIS** ***peruviana***

GORDONIA (Theaceae)

axillaris	CHEx CHil ERea SHil SSpi

GOSSYPIUM (Malvaceae)

sturtianum	CSun

GRANADILLA See **PASSIFLORA** ***quadrangularis***

GRAPE See **VITIS** ***vinifera***

GRAPEFRUIT See **CITRUS** ***paradisi***

GRAPTOPETALUM (Crassulaceae)

paraguayense	NSed SLMG
¶ – ***bernalense***	NSed

GRATIOLA (Scrophulariaceae)

nana	ECou
officinalis	CArn CWGN GPoy LHol MSal SIde WHil WPer

GREENOVIA (Crassulaceae)

§ ***aurea***	CWil SIng SSpi

GREVILLEA † (Proteaceae)

alpina	MBal SBla SHil
* 'Apricot Queen'	CB&S
banksii forsteri	CSun
bipinnatifida	CSun
'Canberra Gem'	CHan CSun ECou LHop SDry
fasciculata	CSun
juniperina	CHan
¶ – prostrate yellow form	CB&S
– ***sulphurea***	CB&S CBra CHEx MBal SDix SHil SIgm WAbe WBod WSHC WTay
pilulifera	CSun
* 'Red Cloud'	CB&S
robusta	MBri WCar
rosmarinifolia	CBow CBra CCla CGre CHEx CTrw MBal SArc SHil SIgm SLon SSpi WBod WSHC
– 'Jenkinsii'	CB&S
x ***semperflorens***	CGre
¶ ***thelemanniana***	ECou
thyrsoides	CB&S SDry

GREWIA (Tiliaceae)
parviflora CMCN

GREYIA (Greyiaceae)
¶ *radlkoferi* CHEx
¶ *sutherlandii* CHEx

GRINDELIA (Compositae)
chiloensis CGre CHan CHil ECha GWic SAxl SBla SBor SChu SDix SDry SHil WPer
integrifolia EPad MSal
* *lanceolata* MSal
* *oregana* MSal
robusta MSal
squarrosa SCro SLHN
stricta CArn MSal

GRISELINIA (Griseliniaceae)
* 'Crinkles' SDry SMad
littoralis Widely available
– 'Bantry Bay' CChu CLan ECtt EPla IOrc SPer WAbe
– 'Dixon's Cream' CB&S CGre CRiv SDry SHil SLon
– 'Gold Edge' MPar
*– 'Green Jewel' CB&S SDry
– 'Variegata' Widely available
lucida CGre CHEx MUlv
* *ruscifolia* CMCN ISea
* *scandens* WSHC

GUAVA See **PSIDIUM**

GUICHENOTIA (Sterculiaceae)
¶ *ledifolia* CSun
macrantha CSun

GUNNERA (Gunneraceae)
¶ *arenaria* GGar
chilensis See G. ***tinctoria***
hamiltonii CBos CHEx CHar ECou SWas
magellanica CCla CHEx CHan CHar COtt CTom CWGN ECha ECro EPot IBar LSav MBal NHol NNor NNrd SIng SPer WWat
manicata Widely available
prorepens CTre ECou SSpi SWas
scabra See G. ***tinctoria***
§ *tinctoria* CHEx CWGN ECha ERav GAbr LSav MSta SDix

GUZMANIA (Bromeliaceae)
'Amaranth' MBri
'Cherry' MBri
'Claret' MBri
dissitiflora MBri
'Festival' MBri
'Grand Prix' MBri
lindenii MBri
lingulata MBri
– 'Empire' MBri
– *minor* MBri
* *marlebecka* MBri
'Mini Exodus' MBri
monostachya MBri
'Orangeade' MBri
sanguinea MBri
'Surprise' MBri
* *vulkana* MBri
* 'Wittn Lila' MBri

GYMNOCARPIUM (Aspleniaceae)
dryopteris EBul EPar EPot MBri MWgw NHol NKay NLan NMar NNrd SDix
– 'Plumosum' CFor NKay NMar WFib
robertianum NKay NLan NMar NNrd

GYMNOCLADUS (Leguminosae)
dioica CB&S CChu CCla ELan LGre LSav MBlu MBri SHil SMad SPer SSpi WCoo

GYMNOSPERMIUM (Berberidaceae)
alberti ECam EPot LAma

GYNANDRIRIS (Iridaceae)
sisyrinchium CAvo

GYNERIUM (Gramineae)
argenteum See CORTADERIA ***selloana***

GYNURA (Compositae)
aurantiaca 'Purple Passion' MBri SLMG
sarmentosa See G. ***aurantiaca*** 'Purple Passion'

GYPSOPHILA (Caryophyllaceae)
acutifolia ELan EMon
altissima EMon LRHS
aretioides NHar NNrd
§ – *caucasica* EPot MHig NHol NTow WDav WOMN
– *compacta* See G. ***a. caucasica***
briquetiana Mac&W 5920 EPot NNrd
cerastioides CElw CFor CMHG EMNN ESis GArf GLoc MCas MHig NGre NHol NKay NNrd NTow WDav WHal WHil WHoo WPer WWin
– *farreri* CShe WEas
dubia See G. ***repens*** 'Dubia'
¶ *libanotica* NRed
nana SIng
pacifica ECtt ELan NOak
paniculata CHar CLew MWat MWgw NNor WHil WWin
– 'Baby's Breath' ERav WEas
– 'Bristol Fairy' Widely available
– 'Compacta Plena' CCla CSco EFou GWic LHop NRoo WPer
– 'Flamingo' CB&S CBow CMer CSco EBre EFou EOrc ERou IDai MBri MUlv MWgw NBar NOrc NRoo SPer
– 'Pink Star' CSco NHol

– 'Rosenschleier' ('Rosy Veil')	CCla CHad CHar ECha EFou ELan NBar NKay NNrd NRoo SFis WEas
– 'Schneeflocke' ('Snowflake')	ECtt GHig NRoo SFis WHil WHoo
– 'Snow White'	LHop NOrc
repens	CLew EPad EPot IDai MHig MPla MRav MTho MWat MWgw NWCA
– ***alba***	CLew EFou ELan EPad ESis GArf MBro MPla NNor NNrd WAbe WDav WHil
– 'Dorothy Teacher'	CKel CShe EBre EMNN MCas MHig MPar MPit MTho NHol SIng WAbe WEas
§ – 'Dubia'	CMHG CShe ECha EFol ELan EMNN EPot ESis MBro MCas MHig MPla NHol SIng WAbe WDav WEas WPer WWin
– ***fratensis***	ELan EMNN MPla NHol NKay SIng WDav
– 'Letchworth Rose'	SIng
– 'Monstrosa'	SIng
– 'Rosa Schönheit' ('Rose Beauty')	EBre ECha
– 'Rose Fountain'	SFis WPat WThu
– 'Rosea'	CHar CMHG EFou EMNN ESis MCas MWat NHol NKay NNor NOak NRed NRoo NRya NTow SBla SFis WHal
tenuifolia	CSun EMNN EPot GLoc ITim MBro MCas MHig MPla MWat NGre NHol NRed NTow NVic NWCA SIng WDav WPer WThu WWin
transsylvanica	See G. ***petraea***

HAASTIA (Compositae)

HABENARIA (Orchidaceae)

radiata	SW&B SWes

HABERLEA (Gesneriaceae)

ferdinandi-coburgii	CGle GLoc NKay SIng SPou
rhodopensis	CChu CFor CRiv GLoc IDai MBal MCas MHig MWat NTow SBla SIng SOkd SPou WOMN WThu
– 'Virginalis'	CChu EPot GLoc SIng WOMN WThu

HABRANTHUS (Liliaceae/Amaryllidaceae)

andersonii	See H. ***tubispathus***
gracifolius	CBro
§ ***robustus***	CAvo CBro LAma MBri SW&B
texanus	CBro
§ ***tubispathus***	CBro NWCA SOkd WMar WThu

HACQUETIA (Umbelliferae)

epipactis	CCla CHar CRow EBre ECha ELan EPar EPot GLoc GPla LHop MBal MCot MTho MUlv NNrd SChu SIng SWas WAbe WEas WHea WOld WRus

HAEMANTHUS (Liliaceae/Amaryllidaceae)

albiflos	CAvo SLMG
kalbreyeri	See SCADOXUS ***multiflorus multiflorus***
katherinae 'King Albert'	See SCADOXUS ***multiflorus katherinae*** 'King Albert'
natalensis	See SCADOXUS ***puniceus***

HAKEA (Proteaceae)

francisiana	CSun
lissosperma	SArc
microcarpa	SHil
sericea	CHan CPle ISea SArc SBor
stenocarpa	CSun
suaveolens	SArc
teretifolia	ISea

HAKONECHLOA (Gramineae)

§ ***macra*** 'Alboaurea'	Widely available
– 'Aureola'	CChu CHan CHoe ECtt GLoc MBal MBri MPar NHol SAxl SIng SSus SWas WCot WEas
– ***variegata***	See H. ***m.*** 'Alboaurea'

HALESIA (Styracaceae)

carolina	See H. ***tetraptera***
diptera magniflora	SHil WCoo
monticola	CB&S CSco EBre ELan GRei IJoh ISea LSav MBal MBri SHil SPer WNor WWat
– ***rosea***	SHil
– ***vestita***	CBow CBra CCla CFor CMHG CPle CSam CSco IOrc LSav MBlu SHil SPer SSpi SSta WBod
¶ ***parviflora***	WCoo
§ ***tetraptera***	CB&S CBow CFor CLnd CSam EHar ELan IBar IJoh IOrc MBri MGos MRav MUlv SHil SPer SSpi SSta WSHC WWat

X HALIMIOCISTUS (Cistaceae)

♦ ***algarvensis***	See HALIMIUM ***ocymoides***
§ 'Ingwersenii'	CFis CHan CLew CMHG CSco ELan IDai LGre LSav MBro MGos NHol NSti SHil SIng SPer WAbe WBod WDav WPer WSHC
revolii	EPla ERav LGre LSav MR&S WKif
§ ***sahucii***	CBow CCla CPle CSco CShe CSun ECha GCHN LHop LSav MBal MBro MHig MPla MWat NKay NSti SAxl SHil SMad SPer WHil WRus WSHC

♦ 'Susan'	See HALIMIUM 'S.'
§ *wintonensis*	CB&S CHan CMHG CSco CSun ELan EOrc LGre LHop LSav MBri MWat NSti SAxl SHil SMad SPer SSpi WAbe WPat WRus WSHC WWat
§ – 'Merrist Wood Cream'	Widely available

HALIMIUM (Cistaceae)

§ *atriplicifolium*	LHop MR&S SChu
§ *commutatum*	LSav SAxl SHil
formosum	See H. ***lasianthum***
§ *halimiifolium*	CSco GWic WSHC
§ *lasianthum*	CB&S CCla CHan CShe ELan ENot LGre LHop MBal MR&S SChu SHil SLon SPer WAbe WBod WEas WWin
– *concolor*	ITim LHop LSav SAxl SDry SSta WAbe WWin
– *formosum*	CKni GWic MBri SAxl SPla WSHC
– 'Sandling'	ELan
libanotis	See H. ***commutatum***
§ *ocymoides*	CB&S CCla CFis CSco CSun ELan ENot ERav LGre LSav MBro MGos MPla MWat NKay SHil SLon SPer WBod WSHC WWat
'Susan'	CBra ELan ITim LGre LHop LSav MBri NHex NNor NSti SPer WAbe WPer
§ *umbellatum*	CSam ERav LGre LSav MBro NSti SPer WAbe WDav WHCG WHil WKif
wintonensis	See X HALIMIOCISTUS ***wintonensis***

HALIMODENDRON (Leguminosae)

halodendron	CB&S CBow CCla ELan MBlu SHil SSpi

HALOCARPUS (Taxaceae)

§ *bidwillii*	ECou NHol

HAMAMELIS † (Hamamelidaceae)

'Brevipetala'	NHol SSta
x *intermedia* 'Advent'	SHil SSta
– 'Allgold'	SHil SSta
– 'Arnold Promise'	ELan LSav MBri NHol SPer SSpi SSta
– 'Aurora'	SSta
– 'Barmstedt Gold'	LRHS MBri SSpi SSta
– 'Boskoop'	SSta
– 'Carmine Red'	SHil SSta WNor
– 'Copper Beauty'	See H. x ***i.*** 'Jelena'
– 'Diane'	CB&S CBow CFor CSco EHar IJoh IOrc LSav MBar MBri MR&S NHol SHil SLon SMad SPer SPla SSpi SSta WBod
– 'Feuerzauber'/('Magic Fire')	IOrc NBar SSta
– Hillier's clone	SSta
– 'Hiltingbury'	SSta
§ – 'Jelena'	CBra CFor CSam CSco EBre EHar ELan ENot IHos IOrc LNet LSav MBri MR&S NHol SHil SLon SPer SSpi SSta WBod
– 'Luna'	SSta
– 'Moonlight'	SHil SSpi SSta
– 'Orange Beauty'	CB&S MGos NBar SSta
– 'Pallida'	Widely available
– 'Primavera'	LRHS NHol SMrm SSpi SSta
– 'Ruby Glow'	CB&S EGol ELan MR&S SHil SMad SPer SSta
– 'Sandra'	SPer SSta
– 'Sunburst'	IJoh MBri SHil SSta
– 'Vezna'	MBlu SSta
– 'Westerstede'	EPar IOrc LSav MBri MGos NHol SSpi SSta
– 'Winter Beauty'	SSta
japonica	MBal NHol WWat
– *arborea*	SHil SSta WNor
– *flavopurpurascens*	SSta
– 'Sulphurea'	SSta
– 'Zuccariniana'	CB&S LSav SSpi SSta
mollis	Widely available
– 'Brevipetala'	See H. 'Brevipetala'
– 'Coombe Wood'	SHil SSta
– 'Goldcrest'	CBra SHil SSpi SSta
– Henry form	SSta
– 'James Wells'	SSta
– Renken form	SSta
– 'Select'	See H. x ***intermedia*** 'Westerstede'
– 'Superba'	SSta
– Wilson Clone	SSta
vernalis	CCla NHol WCoo
– 'Carnea'	SSta
– 'Christmas Cheer'	SSta
– Compact form	SSta
– 'January Pride'	SSta
– 'Lombart's Weeping'	SSta
– 'New Year's Gold'	SSta
– 'Orange Glow'	SSta
– 'Pendula'	SSta
– 'Red Imp'	SSta
– 'Sandra'	CFor EHar MBri NHol SHil SSpi SSta
– 'Squib'	SSta
– *tomentella*	SSta
virginiana	CB&S GPoy LHol WCoo WMou WWat

HAPLOCARPHA (Compositae)

rueppellii	CTom SIng WHea WHil WPer

HAPLOPAPPUS (Compositae)

¶ *acaulis*	WDav
§ *brandegeei*	GLoc MHig
§ – 'Canary Bird'	GLoc WAbe
coronopifolius	CHar CLew CRiv ECha EFol EFou EPla EPot GLoc LHil MBro MHig MTho MWat SChu SLHN SSmi WEas
glutinosus	CHan
hirsutus	CHil
lyallii	WDav WHil WPer WWin

rehderi	CCor
¶ sp. P&W 6545	CSun

HAPLOPPAPUS

§ ***pygmaeus***	WDav

HARDENBERGIA (Leguminosae)

comptoniana	CSun
– ***rosea***	CSun ERea
violacea	CSun ELan ERav ERea IBlr IReg WBod
– 'Happy Wanderer'	ERea
– 'White Crystal'	ERea

HARRIMANELLA See CASSIOPE

HAWORTHIA (Liliaceae/Aloeaceae)

cuspidata	SLMG

HEBE † (Scrophulariaceae)

albicans	Widely available
– 'Cranleigh Gem'	CMHG ECou MCot SSmi
– 'Pewter Dome'	CHoe CMHG ECou EGol ERav ESis IJoh IOrc LHop MGos MPlt NHol NNor NRed SDix SHil SIng SLHN SPer SPla WAbe WWat
– prostrate form	ECou
♦– 'Red Edge'	See H. 'R.E.'
§ – 'Sussex Carpet'	CBow EPla SPer SSta
§ 'Alicia Amherst'	CLan CSam ECou ENot IBar LHop MCot NHol SHil WAbe WBod
allanii	ECou GDra MBro NNor SIng WDav
'Amanda Cook'	CHoe ECou EMon EPla LHop MPla MTho MUlv SDry SFar
N 'Amy'	CLan CMHG CPle ECou LHop MBri MGos MUlv MWgw NHol NSti WEas WRus WSHC WThu
x ***andersonii***	IJoh
– 'Anne Pimm'	WSHC
– 'Argenteovariegata'	See H. x ***a.*** 'Variegata'
– 'Aureovariegata'	CFis SDry
*– 'Heida'	MBri
§ – 'Variegata'	CMer CPle CTrw ECou ELan IOrc MBri NSti NTow SDry SHil SPla WEas
*– 'White Summer'	MBri
N ***anomala***	ENot EPla NNor
'Aoira'	See H. ***recurva*** 'A.'
* 'April Joy'	MUlv
armstrongii	CBot CBow CHoe CMHG CRiv ECou ELan ERav GAbr GLoc IJoh MBar NHol NNor SHil SPer
– x ***selaginoides***	MCot
¶ 'Autumn Blush'	MPla
'Autumn Glory'	Widely available
¶ 'Autumn Joy'	EBar MPla
* 'Autumn Queen'	NNor
¶ 'Azurea'	MBri MRav WPer
'Baby Marie'	CMHG ECou ELan ESis GLoc SChu SSta
barkeri	ECou
'Beatrice'	ECou
x ***bishopiana***	ECou
'Blue Clouds'	ECou EHal EPla SHil WEas WRus
¶ 'Blue Diamond'	WEas
* 'Blue Streak'	ELan
'Blue Wand'	MBal
'Bluebell'	ECou
'Blush Wand'	WAbe
bollonsoi	ECou
'Boscawenii'	CMHG
§ 'Bowles's Hybrid'	CElw CMHG CShe ECou LHil MCot MFir MPla MR&S MRav NSti SChu SHil WAbe WEas
brachysiphon	CFis ECou ENot ISea MGos MPla SHil SLon SPer
breviracemosa	ECou
'Brill Blue'	CMHG EMNN ESis NRed NTow WWin
brockiei	ECou SIng
buchananii	CBow CElw CMal ECou EMNN ESis GAbr GDra LSav MGos MTho NHol NNor SPla SSmi WBod WPer
– 'Minima'	MBar NHol WAbe
– 'Minor'	CLew ECou EPla EPot GAbr GLoc LHop MBar MHig NHar NHol NNrd SChu SIng WOMN
buxifolia	CFis CMHG ELan ENot GAbr GCHN IHos IJoh LHil MBal MWat MWgw NNrd NSti NWea WHil
– 'Nana'	CHoe CSam EHar EPad EPla ESis GLoc MBri NHar SPer SPla
*– ***patens***	MGos
N 'C P Raffill'	ECou MPar MUlv SFir
§ 'Caledonia'	CHoe CLew CMHG CShe ECou ERav ESis GAbr LHop MGos NHol NRya NTow SBla SChu SPer WEas WHoo WPer WSHC
'Candy'	ECou
¶ ***canterburiensis***	ECou EHal
N 'Carl Teschner'	See H. 'Youngii'
'Carnea'	CElw ERav MCot
'Carnea Variegata'	CHoe ECou LHop MCot SHil
carnosula	CHoe CMHG ECou EPla ERav IJoh MGos MR&S NNor SPer WAbe WPer
catarractae	See PARAHEBE ***catarractae***
chathamica	CLew CMHG ECou EMNN ESis GAbr GWic MBal MCas MPla MPlt NNrd NRed NTow SDry SIng WHil
cheesemanii	ECou MHig
'Christabel'	ECou
'Christensenii'	CSun ECou
ciliolata	ECou
coarctata	CSun ECou
cockayneana	ECou EPad
¶ ***colensoi***	ECou

– 'Glauca'	See H. 'Leonard Cockayne'
'Colwall'	CBow ESis LHop MHig WOMN
'Cookiana'	See H. ***stricta macroura***
corrigana	ECou
'County Park'	ECou EMNN ESis GAbr MCot MGos MUlv MWgw NNrd NTow SIng WAbe WSHC
'Cranleighensis'	EBar ECou
'Croftway Emberglow'	SCro
cupressoides	CMHG CSco ECou ELan LHil MBal MBar MGos MR&S NNor SHil
– 'Boughton Dome'	CHoe ECha ECou EFou EMNN ESis GAbr GLoc MBri MBro MCot MGos MHig MPla MPlt MTho NTow SDix SHil SIng SPla WDav WEas WHoo
– 'Glauca'	CMHG
– 'Golden Dome'	CB&S CMHG EPla NHol WAbe
– 'Nana'	ECou GLoc NNrd SPer
darwiniana	See H. ***glaucophylla***
¶ 'Debbie'	ECou
decumbens	ECou ESis GDra
dieffenbachii	ECou SDry
diosmifolia	CBow CLan ECou ESis ISea LSav WSHC
¶ – 'Marie'	ESis
divaricata	ECou
× ***divergens***	CLan
'Dorothy Peach'	GAbr SChu WAbe WHea
'E A Bowles'	ECou MWgw
'E B Anderson'	See H. 'Caledonia'
'Edinensis'	CFis CMHG CMer ECou ELan GAbr IJoh MR&S NNor SSmi WPer WSHC WWin
¶ 'Edington'	ECou
elliptica	ECou IBlr
– 'Anatoki'	ECou
¶ – 'Bleaker'	ECou
– 'Charleston'	ECou
¶ – 'Kapiti'	ECou
– 'Variegata'	See H. × ***franciscana*** 'Variegata'
¶ 'Emerald Dome'	GAbr
§ 'Emerald Gem'	CMHG CRiv CSam EBre ECou EGol ELan ESis GAbr GLoc IJoh ITim LHop LSav MBar MBri MBro MGos MPla NHar NSti SLHN SMad SSpi
epacridea	ECou GAbr GDra GHig GLoc MHig NHar NHol NNrd SSmi WAbe WThu
§ 'Eveline'	CPle ELan ENot IJoh LAbb MBal SChu WEas WSHC
evenosa	ECou
'Eversley Seedling'	See H. 'Bowles' Hybrid'
'Fairfieldensis'	IBlr MUlv SDry WSHC
'Fairlane'	ECou
'Fragrant Jewel'	CChu CPle SMrm SPla
× ***franciscana***	ECou WAbe
– 'Blue Gem'	CLan ENot IJoh NBir SHil
§ – 'Variegata'	CHoe CMer ECou ELan ENot ERav IJoh MBal MCot MGos MR&S MRav NHol NSti NTow SHil SLon SPer WAbe WBod WPer
'Franjo'	ECou MCot SSmi
'Gauntlettii'	See H. 'Eveline'
gibbsii	ECou
– × ***pimeleoides***	ECou
¶ ***glaucophylla*** 'Clarence'	ECou
N 'Glaucophylla'	ECou IJoh SHil
'Glaucophylla Variegata'	CFis CHoe ECou GAbr MCot NRoo NSti SHil SMad SPer SPla WEas WHer WHil WKif WPer WRus WSHC
'Glengarriff'	CChu NHol
'Gloriosa'	CSam IOrc LHop MR&S SHil WBod
'Gnome'	ECou
gracillima	CMHG ECou GWic LSav
'Gran's Favourite'	ECou
'Great Orme'	CBot CBow CFis CMHG CSam CSco CShe ECou ELan ENot LHop MBal MBri MCot MMth NHol NRoo NTow SHil SMad SPer SSta WAbe
'Green Globe'	See H. 'Emerald Gem'
'Greensleeves'	CBow CMHG CSam ECou GAbr LSav MGos
haastii	ECou ITim NHol NNor
'Hagley Park'	CPle CSam ECou ERav ESis LGre LHil LHop MCot SPla WKif WPat WPer WSHC
'Havering Green'	ECou MHig NHol NTow
'Headfortii'	ECou
hectori	CBow CSco EMNN IJoh MBal MHig SPer
– ***demissa***	ECou
'Highdownensis'	CPle ECou
¶ 'Hinerua'	ECou
hookeriana	See PARAHEBE ***h.***
hulkeana	CBot CFor CPle CSam ECou ELan GLoc GPla LGre MPar MPla MUlv NTow SBla SHil SMad SSpi WEas WKif WPer WSHC WWat
– 'Sally Blunt'	ECou
¶ 'Imposter'	ECou
insularis	ECou
'James Platt'	ECou MPar SFir
'James Stirling'	See H. ***ochracea*** 'James Stirling'
'Jane Holden'	CSco SBla WSHC
¶ 'Jasper'	ECou ESis
'Joan Lewis'	ECou
'Johny Day'	ECou MCot
'Joyce Parker'	ECou
'Killiney Variety'	CLan ECou MBal
'Kirkii'	ECou MUlv SPer
'Knightshayes'	See H. 'Caledonia'
§ 'La Seduisante'	CB&S EBar ECou ENot IOrc MBri MCot SChu SHil SPer WBod WSHC
'Lady Ardilaun'	See H. 'Amy'
'Laevis'	CMHG

laingii	CSun ECou
lapidosa	See H. ***rupicola***
* ***latifolia***	NNor
lavaudiana	ECou WDav WWat
§ 'Leonard Cockayne'	CGre CHoe IBar NSti SHil WSHC
'Lewisii'	ECou
ligustrifolia	ECou
'Lilac Haze'	NHol
'Lilac Wand'	CMer
'Lindsayi'	CGre CMHG CPle ECou SHil
loganioides	CLew CRiv ECou EMNN ESis GAbr GLoc MBal MCas MCot MPlt NNor SIng SSmi WPer
'Long Acre Variety'	ECou
¶ 'Lopen'	ECou
lyallii	See PARAHEBE ***lyallii***
lycopodioides	CMHG ECou MHig WPer WThu
– 'Aurea'	CHoe WPer
– patula	ECou
– 'Peter Pan'	ECou GAbr ITim SIng WAbe
¶ 'Macewanii'	GAbr
mackenii	See H. 'Emerald Gem'
macrantha	Widely available
macrocarpa	ECou
– brevifolia	ECou
– latisepala	ECou
¶ 'Margaret'	MGos SMrm
'Margery Fish'	See H. 'Primley Gem'
'Marjorie'	CChu CMHG CPle CSco ECou ELan ENot GAbr LAbb MBal MCot MGos MPla MR&S MRav NNor NRoo SHil SLon SPer
'Marlene'	MBri
matthewsii	CMHG ECou NNor
'Mauvena'	SPer
'McEwanii'	CMHG ECou EPla
♦ 'McKean'	ECou
¶ 'Mercury'	ECou
'Midsummer Beauty'	CChu CSco ECou ELan ENot IOrc ISea LGro MBri MCot MGos MR&S MRav MWat MWgw NNor NTow SDix SHil SMad SPer SSta WAbe
'Milmont Emerald'	See H. 'Green Globe'
'Mini'	ECou
'Miss E Fittall'	CFis ECou
'Monica'	ECou GCHN
* 'Moppets Hardy'	SPer SPla
'Morning Clouds'	ECou NHol
* 'Mrs Barton'	IJoh
'Mrs Winder'	CMHG CPle CSco CShe ECou GRei IJoh LHop MBri MCot MR&S MWgw NNor NRoo NSti SHil SLon SPer WHea WWin
x ***myrtifolia***	GRei NNrd
¶ 'Mystery'	ECou
'Neil's Choice'	ECou
'Nicola's Blush'	CElw EBar ECou LHop MBri MPla MWgw SMrm SSta WRus
obtusata	ECou
§ ***ochracea***	ECou MGos NSti SLon SPer STre
§ – 'James Stirling'	Widely available
odora	CHoe ECou
– 'New Zealand Gold'	CMHG CSam ECou EGol NHar SIng SLon
– prostrate form	ECou
– 'Stewart'	ECou
¶ 'Oratio Beauty'	IJoh
'Otari Delight'	CMHG
'Pageboy'	ECou
parviflora	CMHG MMth
– angustifolia	ECou WMar
¶ – 'Christine Eggins'	WMar
'Pauciflora'	EMNN MPlt NHol SPer
pauciramosa	CSun ECou NTow
'Penny Day'	ECou
perfoliata	See PARAHEBE ***p***
'Perryhill Lilac'	SPer
'Perryhill White'	SPer
'Petra's Pink'	ECou ESis WEas
'Pewter Dome'	See H. ***albicans*** 'P.D.'
'Pimeba'	NHol SIng
pimeleoides	ECou ESis MHig NCat NNor WHil
– 'Glauca'	WWin
– 'Glaucocaerulea'	CHoe ECou EGol ESis GRei MBar MPla SHil SIng SPer
– 'Minor'	ECou WPer
– 'Quicksilver'	Widely available
– rupestris	ECou
pinguifolia	ECou MCot
– 'Godfroyana'	ECou
¶ – 'Hutt'	ECou
– 'Mount Dobson'	ECou
– 'Pagei'	Widely available
– 'Sutherlandii'	ECou GLoc IJoh MBri NSti SLon
* 'Pink Payne'	LHop
'Pink Wand'	CB&S IJoh MBri
'Polly Moore'	MBal MCot NNrd NTow WAbe
¶ ***poppelwellii***	ITim
'Porlock Purple'	See PARAHEBE ***catarractae*** 'Delight'
§ 'Primley Gem'	CFis CLan EBar MCot MWat MWgw WAbe WSHC
'Princess'	ECou
propinqua	ECou SIng
§ – 'Aurea'	MBal MCot
– 'major'	MCot
'Prostrata'	ECou
* ***pulchella***	CSam
'Purple Picture'	ECou SDry
'Purple Queen'	CSam ECtt GAbr IJoh IOrc MBri MR&S NTow SFar SHil WAbe WBod
N 'Purple Tips'	CHoe CMer ECou IBlr NHol NSti SHil WEas WWin
rakaiensis	Widely available
raoulii	CShe ECou MBro MCas NHol SFir WDav WHoo
– maccaskillii	ECou ESis
– pentasepala	ECou ESis

§ ***recurva***	CBow CChu CHoe CMHG CMer CPle ECou EFol ESis GAbr LAbb LHop MCot NNor SHil WAbe WBod WPer WRus
§ – 'Aoira'	ECou NTow SPer
*– 'Boughton Silver'	SDry SHil
§ 'Red Edge'	Widely available
♦ 'Red Ruth'	See H. 'Eveline'
rigidula	ECou ESis
'Ronda'	ECou
'Royal Purple'	See H. 'Alicia Amherst'
'Ruddigore'	See H. 'La Seduisante'
§ ***rupicola***	CMHG
salicifolia	CFis CMer CPle ECou ELan ENot GAbr GCHN IJoh LGro MR&S MWat NNor SArc SHil SPer
– 'Snow Wreath'	ECou IBlr WThu
– 'Variegata'	CPle SHil
salicornioides	ECou
– 'Aurea'	See H. ***propinqua*** 'A.'
'Sapphire'	ECou MGos
¶ 'Silver Gilt'	CBot
'Simon Delaux'	CB&S CChu CElw CSam ECou EPad IJoh LHop MBal MBri NTow SHil SPer WAbe WBod WEas WSHC WTay
speciosa 'Dial Rocks'	ECou
¶ – 'Kapiti'	ECou
N– 'Tricolor'	ECou SDry
'Spender's Seedling'	CLan CMHG CMer ECou NSti SHil SPer WHea WRus
¶ ***stricta***	ECou
– cookiana	See H. ***s. macroura***
§ ***– macroura***	ECou IBar SDry
subalpina	CFis CLan CPle CShe EBre ECou MWgw NCat NWea
subsimilis astonii	MHig
'Sussex Carpet'	See H. ***albicans*** 'Sussex Carpet'
tetrasticha	WAbe
'Tiny Tot'	ECou MCot MTho NHol
♦ 'Tom Marshall'	See H. ***canterburiensis***
topiaria	CCla CElw COtt ECou EGol EPla ESis IJoh LHop MCot NNor SPer SSpi SSta
townsonii	ECou
traversii	ECou GAbr GRei MWgw WWin
'Tricolor'	See H. ***speciosa*** 'Purple Tips'
'Trixie'	ECou MUlv MWat
tumida	ECou
'Veitchii'	See H. 'Alicia Amherst'
venustula	CMHG ECou
vernicosa	CElw CLew CMHG CMer EBre ECou EGol EPla GDra GHig LHop LSav MBar MBri MCas MHig NNor NTow SIng SPer WAbe WHil
'Waikiki'	CHoe CLan CMer CSam GAbr LAbb MRav MWat NCat SMad SPla
'Walter Buccleugh'	ECou MR&S NNrd WSHC
'Wardiensis'	CMHG ECou MBar SIng
'Watson's Pink'	ECou ENot SPer WKif
'White Gem'	CMHG CMer CSam ECou ESis GRei MCot MFir MGos MR&S NHol NNor SHil
'White Wand'	CB&S MCot
'Willcoxii'	CMal
'Wingletye'	CElw CHoe CMHG EBre ECou EPla GAbr LHop LSav MBal MCas MGos MWat NTow SSta WAbe WPer
'Winter Glow'	ECou SPla SSta
* 'Wintergreen'	ELan MR&S
* 'Wootten'	WPer
§ 'Youngii'	Widely available

HEBENSTRETIA (Globulariaceae)

¶ ***dentata***	NWCA

HECTORELLA (Hectorellaceae)

HEDEOMA (Labiatae)

pulegioides	MSal

HEDERA † (Araliaceae)

algeriensis 'Gloire de Marengo'	See H. ***canariensis*** 'G. de M.'
azorica	EWhi WFib WWat
– 'Pico'	EWhi
– 'typica'	EWhi
– 'Variegata'	EWhi
§ ***canariensis***	CHEx CSco EWhi IJoh SArc SHil
– 'Algeriensis'	See H. ***algeriensis***
– 'Cantabrian'	EWhi
§ – 'Gloire de Marengo'	Widely available
– 'Margino Maculata'	EWhi SHil
– 'Montgomery'	MBri WFib
– 'Ravensholst'	CB&S CMac EWhi
– 'Variegata'	See H. ***canariensis*** 'Gloire de Marengo'
caucasigena	EWhi
– 'Telavi'	EWhi
chinensis 'typica'	EWhi
colchica	CHEx CRow CTom ENot SPer
– 'Dentata'	CHEx EWhi MBal NKay SHil SPer SPla WFib
– 'Dentata Aurea'	See H. ***c.*** 'Dentata Variegata'
§ – 'Dentata Variegata'	Widely available
– 'Paddy's Pride'	See H. ***c.*** 'Sulphur Heart'
§ – 'Sulphur Heart'	Widely available
– variegata	See H. ***c.*** 'Dentata Variegata'
cristata	See H. ***h.*** 'Parsley Crested'
helix	CKin CRow EWhi MBar MGos MR&S NLan NWea WFib WHer
– '238th Street'	EWhi
– 'Abundance'	EWhi
– 'Adam'	CBow CFis EMon ESis MBri MGos MPar MWgw SHil STre WFib WWat WWeb
– 'Ahorn'	EWhi

– 'Albany'	EWhi
– 'Alpha'	EWhi
– 'Alt Heidelberg'	EWhi WFib
– 'Alten Brucken'	EWhi
– 'Ambrosia'	EWhi WFib
– 'Anchor'	EWhi
– 'Angularis'	EWhi
– 'Angularis Aurea'	CHoe CSco EGol EWhi MPla WFib
– 'Anna Marie'	CMac EWhi MBri WEas WFib WWin
– 'Anne Borch'	MBri
– 'Annette'	MBri
– 'Apaloosa'	EWhi
– 'Aran'	EWhi WFib
– 'Arapahoe'	EWhi
– 'Arborescens'	SArc SHil
– 'Ardingly'	EMon EWhi SPer WFib
¶ – 'Argyle Street'	EWhi
– 'Asterisk'	EWhi
– 'Astin'	EWhi WFib
– 'Atropurpurea'	EPla EWhi MBar WFib
– 'Aurea Variegata'	CMac EWhi
– 'Avon'	EWhi WFib
– 'Baby Face'	EWhi
– 'Baccifer'	EWhi WFib
– 'Baden-Baden'	EWhi
– 'Baltica'	EWhi
– 'Bates'	EWhi
– 'Big Deal'	EWhi
– 'Bill Archer'	EPla EWhi WFib
N – 'Bird's Foot'	See H. ***h.*** 'Pedata'
– 'Blarney'	EWhi
– 'Bodil'	EWhi WFib
– 'Boskoop'	EPla EWhi
¶ – 'Bowles Ox Heart'	EWhi
– 'Brigette'	EWhi MBri
– 'Brightstone'	EWhi
– 'Brokamp'	EWhi MWgw WFib
– 'Bruder Ingobert'	EWhi
– 'Bulgaria'	EWhi
– 'Buttercup'	Widely available
§ – 'Caecilia'	CB&S CBow COtt EHar ELan EPla EWhi LHop MBri MGos NSti SPla WFib WHal
N – 'Caenwoodiana'	See H. ***h.*** 'Pedata'
– 'Caenwoodiana Aurea'	EWhi
– 'Calico'	EWhi
– 'California'	EWhi
– 'California Fan'	EWhi
– 'California Gold'	ESis EWhi MBri WFib
– 'Carolina Crinkle'	EWhi WFib
– 'Cascade'	EWhi
– 'Cathedral Wall'	EWhi
§ – 'Cavendishii'	EWhi SHil WFib
¶ – 'Ceridiven'	EWhi
– 'Chester'	EWhi MBri WFib WWat
– 'Chicago'	MR&S SHil WFib
– 'Chicago Variegata'	See H. ***h.*** 'Harald'
– 'Christian'	EWhi
– 'Chrysanna'	EWhi
– 'Chrysophylla'	WFib
– 'Clotted Cream'	See H. ***h.*** 'Caecilia'
– 'Clouded Gold'	SPer
– 'Cockle Shell'	EWhi
– 'Compacta'	EWhi
§ – 'Congesta'	CCla CFis CHar EPla EWhi GDra GWic MBal MPlt MTho SBar SSmi STre WEas WFib
– 'Conglomerata'	CLew CSam ELan EPla EWhi ISea MBal MBri MPar MR&S NNor SMad SPer WEas WFib WHil
– 'Conglomerata Erecta'	See H. ***h.*** 'Erecta'
– 'Corrugata'	EWhi
– 'Crenata'	EWhi
– 'Crispa'	EWhi NNor WFib
– 'Cristata'	See H. ***h.*** 'Parsley Crested'
♦ – 'Cristata Melanie'	See H. ***h.*** 'Melanie'
– 'Curleylocks'	See H. ***h.*** 'Manda's Crested'
– 'Curvaceous'	EWhi
– 'Cuspidata Major'	EWhi
– 'Cuspidata Minor'	EWhi
– 'Cyprus'	WFib
– 'Dark Knight'	EWhi
– 'Dealbata'	CMac EWhi
– 'Deltoidea'	EPla MBal NHol SHil SPla WFib WHil
– 'Denticulata'	EWhi
– 'Diana'	EWhi
– 'Dicke von Stauss'	EWhi
– 'Digitata'	WFib
– 'Digitata-Hesse'	EWhi
– 'Direktor Badke'	EWhi
– 'Discolor'	See H. ***h.*** 'Minor Marmorata'
– 'Domino'	EFol EWhi WFib
§ – 'Donerailensis'	EWhi
– 'Dorado'	EWhi
– 'Dragon Claw'	EWhi
– 'Duckfoot'	CLew EWhi IReg MWgw NSti WFib
– 'Edison'	EWhi
– 'Elegance'	EWhi
– 'Elfenbein'	EWhi
– 'Emerald Gem'	CSco EWhi
– 'Emerald Globe'	EWhi
– 'Emerald Jewel'	EWhi
§ – 'Erecta'	CCor CMac ECha EPla EPot ESis MBar MBri MTho MWgw NHol SIng SPer SReu WFib WHil WThu
– 'Erin'	EWhi
– 'Ester'	EWhi MBri
– 'Eugen Hahn'	EGol EWhi WCot WFib
– 'Eva'	CFis CMac EWhi MBal MBri MGos MWgw SHil SIng WFib WWeb
– 'Evesham'	WFib
– 'F C Coates'	EWhi
– 'Fan'	EWhi
– 'Fantasia'	CMac EWhi
– 'Feenfinger'	EWhi
– 'Ferney'	EWhi
– 'Fiesta'	EWhi
– 'Filigran'	EPla EWhi
– 'Finger Point'	MWgw WFib

– 'Flamenco'	EWhi
– 'Flava'	EWhi
– 'Fleur de Lis'	EWhi
– 'Fluffy Ruffles'	EWhi
– 'Francis'	MBri
– 'Fringette'	EWhi WFib
– 'Frosty'	EWhi
¶ – 'Galaxy'	EWhi
– 'Garland'	EWhi
– 'Gavotte'	EWhi WFib
– 'Geranium'	EWhi
– 'Gertrud'	MBri
– 'Gertrude Strauss'	EWhi
– 'Glache'	EWhi
– 'Glacier'	CBow CBra CFis CHoe CMac CRow CSam CSco ELan IHos IJoh MBal MBar MBri MGos MR&S MWgw NKay NNor NSti SHil SLon SPer WFib
– 'Glacier Improved'	EWhi
– 'Gladiator'	EWhi
§ – 'Glymii'	EWhi WFib
¶ – 'Gold Dust'	EWhi
§ – 'Gold Harald'	MBri
– 'Gold Knight'	EWhi
– 'Gold Snow'	MBri
– 'Goldchild'	CB&S EWhi IJoh MBar MBri MGos MTho MWgw NCat SHil WFib
– 'Goldcraft'	EWhi
– 'Golden Ann'	MBri
– 'Golden Emblem'	EWhi
– 'Golden Envoy'	EWhi
– 'Golden Ester'	EWhi MBri
– 'Golden Fleece'	EWhi
– 'Golden Inger'	MBri
– 'Golden Ingot'	EWhi MGos
– 'Golden Kolibri'	MBri
– 'Golden Medal'	EWhi
§ – 'Golden Pittsburgh'	EWhi
¶ – 'Golden Snow'	EWhi
– 'Goldfinger'	EWhi
♦ – 'Goldheart'	See H. ***h.*** 'Oro di Bogliasco'
– 'Goldstern'	EFou EWhi LHop MWgw WFib
– 'Goldtobler'	EWhi
– 'Goldwolke'	EWhi
– 'Good's'	EWhi
– 'Gracilis'	EWhi WFib
§ – 'Green Feather'	ESis EWhi MFir NHol
– 'Green Finger'	EWhi
– 'Green Heart'	EWhi
– 'Green Ripple'	CBow CMac CSam CSco IJoh IOrc MBar NCat NNor SHil SPer SSta WAbe WFib
– 'Green Spear'	WFib
– 'Green Survival'	EWhi
– 'Guinevere'	EWhi
– 'Hahn Variegated'	EWhi
– 'Hahn's Green Ripple'	EWhi
§ – 'Hamilton'	ESis EWhi WFib
§ – 'Harald'	CBow CHoe EBar EWhi MBal MBri MCot WEas WFib WWeb
– 'Hazel'	EWhi WFib
– 'Hebron'	EWhi
– 'Heise'	EWhi WFib
– 'Helena'	EWhi
– 'Helford River'	EWhi
– 'Helvig'	MBri
§ – 'Heron'	ELan EMon SPla WFib
– ***hibernica***	CB&S ELan LBuc MBar MBri MR&S MRav MWgw NNor SBra SHil SPer WAbe WFib WWat
– 'Hibernica Hamilton'	See H. ***h.*** 'Hamilton'
– 'Hibernica Maculata'	EWhi
¶ – 'Hibernica Rona'	EWhi
– 'Hibernica Sark'	EWhi
– 'Hibernica Sulphurea'	EWhi
– 'Hibernica Variegata'	EWhi
– 'Hispanica'	WFib
– 'Hite's Miniature'	EWhi
– 'Holly'	EWhi
– 'Humpty Dumpty'	MBar
– 'Ideal'	EWhi
– 'Imp'	EWhi
– 'Ingelise'	MBri
– 'Ingrid'	See H. ***h.*** 'Hamilton'
– 'Irish Lace'	EWhi
– 'Itsy Bitsy'	EWhi
– 'Ivalace'	CB&S CTom ECha ELan ESis MBal MGos MR&S MRav MWgw NSti SHil WAbe WEas WFib
– 'Jack Frost'	EWhi
– 'Jersey Doris'	EWhi
– 'Jerusalem'	WFib
– 'Jubilee'	CSco EWhi WFib
– 'Knobby Eight'	EWhi
– 'Knulch'	EWhi WFib
– 'Kobold'	EWhi
– 'Kolibri'	CSam EHar ESis EWhi MBri SHil SSus WFib
– 'Konigers'	EWhi MBar WFib
¶ – 'Konsforth'	EWhi
– 'Kurios'	EWhi WFib
– 'La Plata'	EWhi
– 'Lady Kay'	See H. ***h.*** 'Lucy Kay'
– 'Lalla Rookh'	EWhi MWgw WFib
– 'Laubfrosch'	EWhi
– 'Lee's Silver'	EWhi
– 'Lemon Swirl'	EWhi
– 'Leo Swicegood'	EPla EWhi MWgw WFib
– 'Light Fingers'	SPer
– 'Lise'	EWhi
– 'Little Diamond'	CFis CHoe CSam EGol EPla MBri MGos MWgw SApp SHil SMad WFib WThu WWat
– 'Little Eve'	WHea
– 'Little Gem'	EWhi
§ – 'Little Luzii'	WFib
– 'Little Picture'	ESis EWhi
– 'Liz'	EWhi
– 'Lobata Major'	EWhi
– 'Lucida Aurea'	EWhi
§ – 'Lucy Kay'	EWhi WFib

§ – 'Luzii'	CFis CHoe ECha EWhi IJoh MBar MGos MR&S NNor NSti SPer WFib WHea
– 'Mabel Quin'	MBri
– 'Maculata'	See H. ***h.*** 'Minor Marmorata'
– 'Maegheri'	See H. ***h.*** 'Green Feather'
§ – 'Manda's Crested'	CFis ELan ESis MBal MBar MWgw SHil SLon WFib WWeb
– 'Manda's Star'	EWhi
– 'Maple Leaf'	EWhi WFib
– 'Maple Queen'	EWhi
– 'Marginata'	SIng
– 'Marginata Elegantissima'	CBow SHil SPer
– 'Marginata Major'	WFib
– 'Marginata Minor'	See H. ***h.*** 'Cavendishii'
– 'Marie Luise'	EWhi
– 'Marmorata'	See H. ***h.*** 'Luzii'
– 'Masquerade'	EWhi
– 'Mein Herz'	MBri
§ – 'Melanie'	ECha EWhi
– 'Merion Beauty'	CFis EPla EWhi
– 'Microphylla Picta'	EWhi
– 'Midas Touch'	EWhi LHop
– 'Midget'	EWhi WEas WFib
– 'Milford'	EWhi
– 'Mini Ester'	EWhi MBri
– 'Mini Heron'	MBri
– 'Miniature Knight'	EWhi
* – 'Miniature Needlepoint'	NHol
– 'Minigreen'	EWhi
♦ – 'Minima'	See H. ***h.*** 'Donerailensis'
§ – 'Minor Marmorata'	EPla EWhi MBal SHil WFib
– 'Miss Maroc'	EWhi WFib
– 'Misty'	EWhi
– 'Modern Times'	EWhi
– 'Mount Vernon'	EWhi
– 'Mrs Pollock'	EWhi
– 'Mrs Ulin'	EWhi
– 'Nebulosa'	EWhi
– 'Needlepoint'	EWhi IOrc WHea
– 'Neilson'	EWhi SPer STre WFib
– 'Neptune'	EWhi
– 'New Ripples'	EWhi
– 'Nigra'	EWhi
– 'Nigra Aurea'	EWhi
– 'Northington Gold'	EWhi WFib
– 'Obscura'	EWhi
– 'Old English'	EWhi
– 'Old Lace'	EWhi
– 'Olive Rose'	EPla EWhi WCot WFib
§ – 'Oro di Bogliasco'	Widely available
– 'Pallida'	WFib
– 'Palmata'	EWhi WFib
– 'Paper Doll'	EWhi
– 'Parasol'	EWhi
§ – 'Parsley Crested'	CRow ECha EGol ELan MBal MBar MGos NKay NSti SPer WEas WFib
N – 'Pedata'	ELan ENot EWhi WFib
– 'Pedata Heron'	See H. ***h.*** 'Heron'
– 'Pencil Point'	EWhi

– 'Pennsylvanian'	EWhi
¶ – 'Peppermint'	EWhi
– 'Perfection'	EWhi
– 'Perkeo'	EPla EWhi WFib
– 'Perle'	EWhi MWgw
– 'Permanent Wave'	EWhi
– 'Persian Carpet'	EWhi LMer
– 'Peter'	EWhi WFib
– 'Pin Oak'	EWhi ISea NHol
¶ – 'Pink 'n' Curley'	WCot
– 'Pirouette'	EWhi
§ – 'Pittsburgh'	EWhi WFib
– 'Pixie'	EWhi
– 'Plattensee'	EWhi
– 'Plimpton'	EWhi
– 'Plume d'Or'	EWhi MTho WFib
– 'Poetica'	EWhi IOrc SHil WFib
– 'Poetica Arborea'	ECha
– 'Preston Tiny'	EWhi
– 'Professor F Tobler'	EWhi WFib
– 'Quatermas'	EWhi
– 'Ralf'	EWhi
– 'Rambler'	EWhi
– 'Rauschgold'	EWhi
– 'Ray's Supreme'	See H. ***h.*** 'Pittsburgh'
– 'Reef Shell'	EWhi
– 'Regency'	EWhi
– 'Ritterkreutz'	EWhi
– 'Rochester'	EWhi
– 'Romanze'	EWhi WFib
– 'Rottingdean'	EWhi
– 'Rubaiyat'	EWhi
– 'Rumania'	EWhi
– 'Rusche'	EPla EWhi
– 'Russell's Gold'	EWhi
– 'Sagittifolia'	CBow CMac CRow CSco MBal MCot MFir MR&S MWgw NNor SCro SHil SMad SPer WAbe WEas WFib
– 'Sagittifolia Variegata'	CBow CHoe CMac ECha EHal ESis EWhi SHil SPer WAbe WEas WFib
– 'Sally'	EWhi
– 'Salt and Pepper'	WEas
– 'Sark'	EWhi
– 'Schafer Four'	EWhi
– 'Schafer One'	EWhi
– 'Schafer Three'	EWhi WFib
– 'Schafer Two'	EWhi
– 'Scutifolia'	See H. ***h.*** 'Glymii'
– 'Serenade'	EWhi
– 'Shamrock'	EPla MBri MWgw SHil SPer WFib
– 'Shannon'	EWhi
– 'Silver Emblem'	EWhi
– 'Silver King'	EWhi MWgw WFib
– 'Silver Kolibri'	EWhi
– 'Silver Queen'	See H. ***h.*** 'Tricolor'
– 'Small Deal'	EWhi
– 'Spear Point'	EWhi
– 'Spectabilis Aurea'	EWhi
– 'Spectre'	EWhi WFib
– 'Spetchley'	CLew EMon EPla EWhi SPla
– 'Spinosa'	EPla EWhi

– 'Staghorn'	EWhi
– 'Star'	EWhi
– 'Star Dust'	EWhi
– 'Sterntaler'	EWhi
– 'Stift Neuberg'	EWhi WFib
– 'Stiftpark'	EWhi
– 'Student Prince'	EWhi
– 'Stuttgart'	EWhi WFib
¶ – 'Succinata'	EPla
– 'Suzanne'	EWhi
– 'Sylvanian'	EWhi WFib
– 'Tango'	EWhi WFib
– 'Telecurl'	EWhi MWgw WFib
¶ – 'Tenerif'	ELan EWhi
– 'Tess'	EWhi
– 'Thorndale'	EWhi
– 'Tiger Eye'	EWhi
– 'Tomboy'	EWhi
– 'Transit Road'	EWhi
– 'Très Coupé'	CMHG ISea MBal MGos NHol SPer SPla SReu WFib
– 'Tribairn'	EWhi
§ – 'Tricolor'	CB&S CHoe CMac CSco ELan EWhi IDai ISea SBra SReu
– 'Triloba'	EWhi
– 'Trinity'	EWhi NHol WFib
¶ – 'Tristram'	EWhi
– 'Triton'	EWhi MBal MTho WFib
– 'Trustee'	EWhi
– 'Tussie Mussie'	EWhi
– 'Ustler'	EWhi
– 'Victoria'	SHil
– 'Walthamensis'	EWhi
– 'Wanda's Fan'	WFib
– 'Welsomii'	EWhi
– 'White Knight'	EWhi
– 'Wichtel'	EWhi
– 'William Kennedy'	EWhi WEas WFib
– 'Wilson'	EWhi
– 'Wingertsberg'	EWhi
– 'Wlliamsiana'	EWhi
– 'Woener'	EWhi
– 'Woodsii'	EWhi
– 'Yalta'	EWhi
– 'Zebra'	EWhi
nepalensis	ISea MBal MBlu WFib
– sinensis	EWhi
– 'Susanne'	EWhi WFib
pastuchovii	EMon EWhi
– 'Cyprus Taxon Troodos'	EWhi
rhombea	EWhi WFib
– 'Japonica'	EWhi
– 'Variegata'	EWhi WFib

HEDYCHIUM (Zingiberaceae)

chrysoleucum	LAma
coccineum	CB&S CRow LAma LBow
– aurantiacum	LAma LBow MNew
– 'Tara'	CChu CFor SSpi
coronarium	CAvo CHil LBow LGan MNew NOak WOMN
densiflorum	CChu CCla CRow CTre GWic LSav SMad SSpi
– 'Assam Orange'	CB&S CChu CFor CHEx LSav MNew NRar SMad SSpi
ellipticum	LAma LBow
flavescens	LAma MNew
forrestii	CChu CFor CHEx CTre LSav SSpi
gardnerianum	CGre CHEx ERea GWic LAma LBow LHop MNew SArc SDix WTay
greenei	CHEx CHan CRow LBow
longicornutum	MNew
spicatum	CChu CHEx CHan SSpi
villosum	LAma LBow

HEDYOTIS (Rubiaceae)

N ***caerulea***	CFor CLew CRiv CSam EBar ELan GGar GHig GLoc MPit MPla MTho NGre NNrd WOld WPer WWin
– alba	CLew GLoc MTho NHol NNrd
'Fred Millard'	CSun EPot ITim NHol NNrd SIng WHoo

HEDYSARUM (Leguminosae)

coronarium	CArn CCla CHan EBar EHal ELan GCHN SAxl WEas WHil
– album	CBot
multijugum	CCla CPle CSco ENot SDry SHil
– apiculatum	ELan

HEDYSCEPE (Palmae)

§ ***canterburyana***	NPal

HEIMERLIODENDRON See PISONIA

HEIMIA (Lythraceae)

salicifolia	CArn CFor CGre CHan CLew

HELENIUM † (Compositae)

autumnale	CLew EBar EHal MPit
¶ – JLS 88007	EMon
'Baudirektor Linne'	CKel CSam MBri
¶ ***bigelovii***	LSav
'Bruno'	CB&S ERou
'Butterpat'	CSco EFou ERou MWgw SPer
'Chipperfield Orange'	ERou
'Coppelia'	CKel CSam CShe ERou
'Crimson Beauty'	ELan MBri NBar NRoo WRus
'Croftway Variety'	SCro
* 'Dark Beauty'	MBri
'Gartensonne'	ERou
'Gold Fox'	CKel CSam
'Goldene Jugend' ('Golden Youth')	EFou ELan NRoo
hoopesii	CHar CShe EBar EFou EMon ERou GHig GWic SCro WCar WPer
'July Sun'	CB&S CBre ERou
¶ 'Kupferzwerg'	EFou
'Mahogany'	CSco LHil
¶ 'Margot'	EFou

'Moerheim Beauty'	CBre CHad CKel CSam CSco CSev CShe EFou ELan ERav ERou IDai LHop MWat MWgw NKay NRoo SChu SDix SPer WEas WOld WRus
'Pumilum Magnificum'	CBow CKel CSam CSco MBri MWat NKay NRoo SPer
'Red and Gold'	ECtt GHig IBrk NOak WPer
'Riverton Gem'	ECtt ERou
¶ 'Rupperkuppel'	EFou
'Sonnenwunder'	ECha
'Sunshine'	CHar GCHN MFir
'The Bishop'	CSco EFou ERou LHil MBri NBar
'Waldtraut'	CKel EFou ELan ERou MBri MWgw SCro
'Wyndley'	CSam CSco ERou MBri MRav
'Zimbelstern'	ECha EFou

HELIAMPHORA (Sarraceniaceae)

nutans	WMEx

HELIANTHELLA (Compositae)

¶ ***quinquenervis***	EMon GWic

HELIANTHEMUM † (Cistaceae)

'Alice Howarth'	CShe ESis SIng WHCG WHoo
alpestre serpyllifolium	See H. ***nummularium glabrum***
amabile 'Plenum'	GDra
'Amy Baring'	EMNN GAbr GDra LHop MPlt NCat NKay NRoo SHil SIng WHil WSHC
'Annabel'	CCla CElw CHar CRiv EBre EOrc GCHN MPit MPla NRoo NSti SAxl SChu WHCG WPer
apenninum	LGan NLan WCla WPer
– ***roseum***	WCla
'Beech Park Red'	CRiv CShe MBro MWat MWgw NNrd SAsh WHoo
'Ben Afflick'	CRiv GAbr IDai MBro NKay NSty SHil
'Ben Alder'	NSty
'Ben Attow'	NKay
'Ben Dearg'	ECtt EMNN ESis GAbr MPlt MR&S NKay NSty
'Ben Fhada'	CMHG CRiv EMNN GAbr GDra GHig MBal MBro MCas NKay NNrd NSti NSty SSvw WAbe WEas WHil WPer WWin
'Ben Heckla'	CKel CRiv CSam EBre GAbr GGar GHig NHol NRed SAxl WEas WPer
'Ben Hope'	EBar EMNN GAbr GDra GLoc ITim MBal MCas MR&S NKay NRoo NSty SChu SIng WPer WWin
'Ben Lawers'	MBro WDav
'Ben Ledi'	CB&S CRiv EFol ELan EMNN ESis GAbr GCHN GDra MBal MBro MFir MPlt NKay NRed NSty WAbe WHoo WPer WWin
'Ben Lomond'	CRiv MBal
'Ben Macdui'	GAbr GHig
'Ben More'	CB&S CRiv EMNN ESis GAbr GDra GHig GLoc IDai IHos ITim MBal MCas MFir MPla MR&S MWat NHol NKay NNrd NSti SIng WWin
'Ben Nevis'	CRiv CShe EBre ELan ESis GAbr GDra LHop MBro WHoo WWin
'Ben Vane'	CRiv EMNN NKay
¶ 'Birch White'	SIng
'Boughton Double Primrose'	CElw CGle ELan GAbr LGre LHop NHol SChu SSvw WDav WEas WSHC
'Brilliant'	CHar
'Broughty Beacon'	GAbr GDra
'Broughty Sunset'	GAbr MBro NBir WHoo
'Brown Gold'	EOrc
'Butter and Eggs'	CB&S
'Butterball'	MDHE NKay
¶ ***canum***	WPer
¶ – ***balcanicum***	NTow
'Captivation'	EFol MBro WDav
'Cerise Queen'	CHar CKel CRiv EBre GAbr LHop MBro MCas MPla NKay NRed SAxl SIng WCla WHil WHoo
chamaecistus	See H. ***nummularium***
'Cheviot'	MDHE WEas WWat
'Chocolate Blotch'	EBar ECtt EMNN GAbr GHig LBuc MTho NCat NRed NSty SChu WHil WPer
'Coppernob'	SHil
¶ 'Cornish Cream'	SIng
cupreum	CMHG EFou
'Doctor Phillips'	CShe WHCG WHoo WPer
double apricot	CRiv CShe GAbr WHil WSHC
double cream	ECtt EMNN EOrc GAbr ITim MDHE NSti
double orange	LHop MWat
¶ double pink	GAbr
double red	MPla
double yellow	MPla NSti
'Etna'	STre
'Fairy'	NRed
'Fire Dragon'	See H. 'Mrs Clay'
'Fireball'	See H. 'Mrs C W Earle'
'Firefly'	NRed
¶ 'Firegold'	WAbe
'Gaiety'	CRiv MTho WDav WPer
'Georgeham'	CMHG CShe LHop NNrd WEas WHCG WHil
globulariifolium	See TUBERARIA ***globulariifolia***
§ 'Golden Queen'	ECtt MCas NHol NSty SChu SHil SIng
'Henfield Brilliant'	CCla CHad CRiv CShe EBre GAbr GDra LHop MBar MBro MCas MPit NRoo SIng SMad SSmi WDav WEas WHil WHoo WPer WSHC
'Highdown'	GAbr WAbe
¶ 'Honeymoon'	SAxl
'Jubilee'	Widely available
'Jubilee Variegatum'	EFol MPla

'Kathleen Druce' EBar MCas MWat SIng
¶ *ledifolium* WPer
'Lemon Queen' CShe EFou EMon
'Lucy Elizabeth' GAbr MCas WHil
lunulatum CLew EMon GLoc MCas MHig MPla NKay NNrd SHil WAbe WPat WSHC
'Magnificum' LHop MWat
'Moonbeam' WWin
§ 'Mrs C W Earle' CRiv EBre ELan EMNN EOrc GAbr IDai LAbb LBuc LHop MPlt MWat NKay NNrd NRoo NSti NSty SHil STre WAbe WHil WPer WWin
'Mrs C W Earle Variegated' EFol ELan LHop WWin
§ 'Mrs Clay' CCla CKel CSam EBre ECtt ELan GAbr GCHN MWgw NRoo SChu WAbe WDav
'Mrs Jenkinson' LHop MBro
'Mrs Lake' EMNN NSty
¶ *mutabile* WPer
§ *nummularium* CKin GPoy LGan MCas MHig NLan SFir WCla WHil WPat
§ – *glabrum* CLew,CMHG EMNN GAbr MBro NKay NRoo SIng WDav WHil WHoo WPat
– *grandiflorum* 'Variegatum' MWat
§ – *tomentosum* MWat
oblongatum MBro WDav
oelandicum piloselloides WWin
oelandicum alpestre ESis MBro NHol NKay NNrd SHil SSmi WPer
¶ – – 'Baby Buttercup' MPla
'Old Gold' CB&S CRiv ELan MCas MHig NHol NRoo WAbe WDav WPer
'Orange Surprise' NRed
ovatum See H. ***nummularium obscurum***
'Pink Perfection' CMHG CSam
'Praecox' CHar CKel EBre EMNN ESis MBal MBro MCas MPla NHol NRoo NSty SHil SIng STre WHil WHoo WPer
'Raspberry Ripple' CCla CMHG CShe EBre EFol ELan EOrc EPot GAbr ITim LHop MPla MTho NHol NRoo SChu SIng WHil WHoo WPat WPer WWin
'Red Orient' See H. 'Supreme'
'Rhodanthe Carneum' See H. 'Wisley Pink'
'Rosa Königin' ('Rose Queen') EMNN NKay NRed NSty WAbe
'Rose of Leeswood' CShe ELan EOrc GHig LBuc LGre LHop NKay NRed SIng SSvw WEas WHCG WHil WHoo WKif WWin
'Rushfield's White' WHCG WRus
'Saint John's College Yellow' CMHG CSam CShe EBar GHig NHol WHCG
'Salmon Bee' CShe
'Salmon Queen' CMHG CRiv EMNN ESis ITim MCas MFir NCat NKay NRoo SMad WWin
* *scardicum* EPot MBro NHol WDav
serpyllifolium See H. ***nummularium glabrum***
¶ 'Shot Silk' NRoo
¶ 'Silvery Salmon' WAbe
'Snow Queen' See H. 'The Bride'
'Southmead' EMNN WPer
'Sterntaler' GAbr GDra GGar GHig NHol SIng WDav WHil
'Sudbury Gem' CRiv EBre LHop MHig SHil WSHC
'Sulphureum' NLan
'Sunbeam' CRiv CSam EMNN GAbr ITim MCas NSty
§ 'Supreme' CRiv CShe ELan GLoc IDai LHop MWat NKay SChu SHil
§ 'The Bride' CElw EBar EFou ELan EOrc GLoc LHop MWat MWgw NSty WAbe WPer WSHC
'Tigrinum Plenum' ESis NRed WWin
¶ 'Tomato Red' SMrm
umbellatum See HALIMIUM ***umbellatum***
* 'Valerie Finnis' WAbb
'Venustum Plenum' MBro WEas
'Voltaire' EMNN GAbr LBuc NKay NRoo WHil WWin
'Watergate Rose' MWat NBir NKay
¶ 'Westfield Wonder' CBot
¶ 'White Queen' WPer
§ 'Wisley Pink' Widely available
'Wisley Primrose' Widely available
'Wisley White' CHar CRiv EBre EFou LHop MBal MBro NRoo SAxl SHil SIng WHil WHoo WPer WRus
♦ 'Yellow Queen' See H. 'Golden Queen'

HELIANTHUS † (Compositae)

atrorubens MBri
– 'Monarch' CKel ERou
decapetalus 'Capenoch Star' EFou MUlv SDix
– 'Loddon Gold' CKel CSco EBre EFou ELan ENot ERou NVic SFis WCot
¶ – 'Maximus' EMon
§ *lactiflorus* ELan EMon NOrc WOak
'Lemon Queen' CBre EFou
* 'Limelight' WEas
'Morning Sun' CBre CHar EBre EMon ERou
orgyalis See H. ***salicifolius***
quinquenervis See HELIANTHELLA ***q.***
rigidus See H. ***lactiflorus***
§ *salicifolius* CBre ELan EMon MBri SFis
scaberrimus See H. ***lactiflorus***
¶ 'Soleil d'Or' ECtt
'Triomphe de Gand' EMon MWat
¶ *tuberosus* NRog

HELICHRYSUM † (Compositae)

acuminatum CSun NHol
§ *aggregatum* ECou
alveolatum See H. ***splendidum***

ambiguum CFis EFou GLoc MPla NNor NRoo
amorginum CSun NSti WPer
– 'Pink Bud' CSun
– 'White Bud' CSun
– 'Yellow Bud' CSun
angustifolium See H. *italicum*
– Cretan Form See H. *italicum microphyllum*
arenarium SSmi
¶ *argyrophyllum* LHil SIng
arwae ESis ITim LHop MHig NTow SBla SIng SOkd
§ *asperum* CFis
bellidioides CGle CHar CLew CShe EBre ECha ECou ELan ESis GAbr GHig GLoc IDai MBal MHig MTho NGre NHol NKay NNrd NTow WPer
bellum CSun LHop
bracteatum WPer
– 'Dargan Hill Monarch' ERav LHop WEas WPer
chionophyllum NTow
* 'Coco' IHos
* *confertum* EMNN ITim MHig NTow SIng
coralloides ITim MHig SIng WEas
'County Park Silver' ECou NNrd NTow WDav
depressum ECou
diosmifolium CSun
¶ *doerfleri* MHig
'Elmstead' See H. *stoechas* 'White Barn'
* *emelinii* CHan CSun
ericifolium See H. *asperum*
ericoides See DOLICOTHRIX *ericoides*
foetidum CHan
fontanesii CFis LHil NKay SPer
frigidum EPot ITim MHig NNrd NTow SBla SIng WOMN
♦ *glomeratum* See H. *aggregratum*
gunnii CSco SSpi
hookeri ECou ITim MHig SChu SIng WMar
§ *italicum* Widely available
§ – *microphyllum* CGle CSev ECha EFou ELan GAbr GPoy SIde SPla WEas WMar
– 'Nanum' See H. *i. microphyllum*
§ – *serotinum* CBow COtt ITim LHop SHil SPer SPla WAbe WWeb
lanatum See H. *thianshanicum*
§ *ledifolium* Widely available
lobbii ELan EMon SPou
marginatum See H. *milfordiae*
microphyllum See PLECOSTACHYS *serpyllifolia*
§ *milfordiae* Widely available
orientale CHan NHol NKay NTow SIng WThu
pagophilum WDav
§ *petiolare* CB&S CCla CFis CHad CTre EBak IHos LAbb NRoo SDix SIng WEas WHal WHea
– 'Aureum' See H. *p.* 'Limelight'
§ – 'Limelight' CB&S CCla CFis CTre IHos LAbb NRoo SDix SIng SLon WEas WHal WMar
– 'Roundabout' LHop WEas
– 'Skynet' LHop WPer
– 'Variegatum' CB&S CCla CFis CTre ERav IHos LAbb NRar NRoo SDix SIng WEas WHal
petiolatum See H. *petiolare*
plicatum CFis EBar SHil WSto
¶ *plumeum* GArf ITim MHig
* *populifolium* CKni EMon
praecurrens ITim NHol
§ *rosmarinifolium* CB&S CBow CCla CHar CMHG CPle ELan IBar IDai IOrc ISea MR&S NNor NRar SChu SHil SLon SPer SPla WHCG WPer WSHC WWat
– 'Purpureum' CMHG
– 'Silver Jubilee' CB&S CCla CElw CHan CLan CMHG CSun CTre IJoh ISea NTow SAxl SBla SCro SHil SLon SPer WAbe WHCG WPer WSHC WWat
'Schweffellicht' ('Sulphur Light') CFis CGle CHad CKel CLew CSco CShe EBre ECha EFou EOrc ERav ERou LHop MWgw NHol NRoo SPer WEas WHal WSHC
scorpiodes ECou
scutellifolium ECou
§ *selago* GLoc ITim MCot MWat SBla
* – *macrophyllum* ITim
– 'Major' SHil
¶ – *minor* NWCA
serotinum See H. *italicum serotinum*
serpyllifolium See PLECOSTACHYS *serpyllifolia*
* *sessile* CSun EMNN ITim MHig NHol SBla SIng SPou WDav
§ *sibthorpii* CMHG CRiv CShe GLoc ITim LGre MHig SIng SSmi WAbe WDav
siculum See H. *stoechas barrelieri*
§ *splendidum* Widely available
¶ sp. from Drakensburg Mountains CLew GAbr NHol NKay
stoechas IDai
§ – 'White Barn' ECha
§ *stoechas barrelieri* CFis
'Sulphur Light' MBri MRav
'Sussex Silver' LHop SSpi
¶ *thianschanicum* NHol
§ – 'Goldkind' ('Golden Baby') CRiv CSun LHil NNrd NRoo SFis WHil
thyrsoideum CB&S WWat
trilineatum See H. *splendidum*
tumidum See H. *selago*
* *virginale* ITim
virginicum See H. *sibthorpii*
woodii See H. *arwae*

HELICHRYSUM X RAOULIA (Compositae)

¶ 'Rivulet' ECou
¶ 'Silver Streams' ECou

HELICTOTRICHON (Gramineae)

§ ***sempervirens*** Widely available
¶ – 'Pendula' EMon

HELIOPSIS † (Compositae)

helianthoides 'Gigantea' CSco ERou WCot
– 'Hohlspiegel ' MBri
¶ – 'Sonnenschild' MBri
– 'Spitzentänzerin' MBri
¶ – 'The Monarch' ERou
helianthoides scabra
'Ballerina' EFou
– – 'Goldgefieder' ('Golden Plume') CKel LRHS MBri
– – 'Goldgrünherz' LRHS MBri
– – 'Incomparabilis' CKel
– – 'Light of Loddon' MWat
– – 'Patula' NBar
– – 'Sommersonne' ('Summer Sun') CSco EBre EFou EHal ERou LHop MFir SCro SPer WPer WWin

HELIOTROPIUM (Boraginaceae)

§ ***arborescens*** CArn CKni CSev MPit
'Chatsworth' CCla CHad CPle ERea SIde SLHN SMrm
'Gatton Park' ERea SLHN SMrm
'Lord Roberts' ERea SLHN SMrm
'P K Lowther' ERea SLHN WEas
peruvianum See H. ***arborescens***
'Princess Marina' ERea SLHN WEas
'W H Lowther' MNew
¶ 'White Lady' ERea SLHN

HELIPTERUM (Compositae)

albicans albicans incanum GDra NNrd
– ***alpinum*** GDra
anthemoides CSun ECou LGre
roseum LHop WPer

HELLEBORUS † (Ranunculaceae)

§ ***argutifolius*** Widely available
– large flowered SPou
atrorubens CCla CSco IDai MPhe SHig
colchicus See H. ***orientalis abchasicus***
corsicus See H. ***argutifolius***
cyclophyllus SBla SPou SWas
¶ ***dumetorum*** MPhe SPou
foetidus Widely available
– Bowles' form CBro
– Italian form CCla GPla WRus
– Wester Flisk group CAvo CBot CBro CSco ERav MBri MCou MPar MPhe NHol SAxl SBla SSpi WAbe WBal WHoo WRus WWat
lividus CAvo CBos CBot CBro CGle EMon MPhe MUlv SBla SWas WAbb WOld
– ***corsicus*** See H. ***argutifolius***
– dwarf SPou
multifidus bocconei SBla SSpi
¶ – ***hercegovinus*** MPhe
– hybrids SSpi
– ***istriacus*** MPhe SBla SPou SWas
¶ – ***multifidus*** MPhe SPou
niger Widely available
– 'Higham's Variety' CGle
§ – ***macranthus*** MPhe
– ***major*** See H. ***n. macranthus***
– 'Potter's Wheel' CBro CHan EPad SBla SPou SSpi
– 'Trotter's Form' SPou
– 'White Magic' GHig SAxl SBla
x ***nigercors*** SBla
x ***nigristern*** NRoo SBla WCot
odorus MPhe SBla
orientalis Widely available
¶ – DS&T 89080T EMon
§ – ***abchasicus*** CRow MBri MCot NRoo SPou
– 'Agnes Brook' MCou
– 'Albin Otto' EBre
– Anderson's Red Hybrids CLCN
– 'Angela Tandy' MCou
– ***antiquorum*** NHol
– 'Apple Blossom' ECha
– 'Baby Black' LRHS
– Ballard's strain WRus
– black seedlings CGle GDra MPar
¶ – 'Blue Showers' WBal
– 'Button' WBal
– 'Carlton Hall' MCou
– 'Christmas Lantern' LRHS
– 'Citron' WBal
– 'Darley Mill' MCou
– 'Dawn' WBal
– Draco strain CLCN
– 'Elizabeth Coburn' MCou
– 'Eric's Best' ECha
– 'Freckleface' ECha
– 'Fred Whitsey' MCou
– 'Gertrude Raithby' MCou
– 'Gladys Burrow' MCou
– 'Greencups' WBal
– ***guttatus*** CAvo CBow CHad CLCN COtt CSco ELun MUlv SBla SPou SSpi
– ***guttatus*** cream ECha
– ***guttatus*** pink ECha
– Hadspen hybrids CHad
– 'Hazel Key' MCou
– 'Helen Ballard' WBal
– 'Hercules' MUlv
– 'Ian Raithby' MCou
– ivory CLCN
– 'John Raithby' MCou
– Kochii group COtt EBre ELun MUlv WRus
– 'Lavinia Ward' MCou
– 'Leo' MUlv
– 'Little Black' SBla
– 'Mary Petit' MCou

- 'Maureen Key' MCou
¶ – Midnight Sky strain WWat
¶ – 'Mystery' WBal
¶ – 'Nancy Ballard' WBal
– olympicus See H. ***o. orientalis***
– orientalis SFis SPou WWat
– 'Pebworth White' MCou
– 'Philip Ballard' WBal
– 'Philip Wilson' WBal
¶ – pink strain CLCN
– 'Plum Stippled' ECha
– purple CLCN ECha MPar NHol
– 'Rembrandt' WBal
– 'Richard Key' MCou
– 'Sarah Ballard' WBal
¶ – 'Saturn' WBal
¶ – 'Tom Wilson' WBal
– 'Trotter's Spotted' GDra MPar
– 'Ushba' LRHS WBal
– 'Victoria Raithby' MCou
– 'Vulcan' WBal
– white strain CGle EBre ECha MBal MPar
– Zodiac strain CLCN
purpurascens CHad ECha SPou SWas
x ***sternii*** CBot CBow CChu CCla EGol ELan GWic MBal MBri NBar NHol NRoo SBla SFis SMad SSus SWas WAbe WWat
– Blackthorn strain SAxl SBla SWas
– 'Boughton Beauty' CAvo CBos CBro LGre SAxl WSHC
– Boughton strain CBot
torquatus MPhe SPou
– BM 5279 SPou
¶ – hybrids MPhe
¶ – 'Pluto' SBla
viridis CRow GWic SBla
– occidentalis CAvo CBro MPhe SBla

HELONIOPSIS (Liliaceae/Melanthiaceae)
breviscapa CFor SWas
japonica See H. ***orientalis***
§ ***orientalis*** CFor EPot LGre
– yakusimensis CFor SWas

HELWINGIA (Cornaceae/Helwingiaceae)
¶ ***himalaica*** EMon
japonica CBot LGre WWat

HELXINE See **SOLEIROLIA**

HEMEROCALLIS †
(Liliaceae/Hemerocallidaceae)
¶ '23rd Psalm' WHal
'Admiral' MAus
'Adoration' SPer
'Alan' CKel SCro
'Amazon Amethyst' MAus
'Ambassador' CKel LSav
'Amber Star' LMay
'Angel Flight' MAus
'Anzac' CB&S CHar EBre ECha ERou LSav MBlu MBri MSta NHol SMad WCot
'Apple Court Damson' SApp
¶ 'Apple Tart' SApp
'Apricot Beauty' SFis WAbe
'Arkansas Post' EGol
aurantiaca CB&S
¶ 'Aurora' WAbe
'Autumn Red' ERou
'Ava Michelle' SApp
'Avanti' CB&S
'Azor' CB&S
'Back Boy' MAus
'Bald Eagle' SApp
'Ballet Dancer' ERou
'Baroni' EGol
'Battle Hymn' MAus
'Bejewelled' EGol LSav MSta SApp
'Beloved Returns' MAus
'Bess Ross' MAus
'Bess Vestale' ERou NHol
'Bibury' SCro
'Bitsy' SApp
'Black Falcon' CKel
'Black Knight' CRow
'Black Magic' CBow CBro CGle CHar EBre EGol ELan ERou MAus MBri MCot MRav NHol SChu SPer
'Blaze of Fire' MAus
'Blushing Belle' WWin
'Bold Courtier' CKel MAus
'Bonanza' CBro CCla CSco CTom EBre ECha EHon ELan ERou LSav MAus MBri NBar NHol SApp SChu SHig SPer WAbe
'Bourbon King' EBre ERou
'Brass Cup' MAus
'Bright Banner' MAus
'Bright Spangles' SApp
'Buffy's Doll' SApp
'Burlesque' CKel
'Burning Daylight' CB&S CKel CSco EBre ERou MAus NHol NVic SApp SPer WOld
'Buttons' CShe
'Buzz Bomb' EBre SHig SPer
'By Jove' MAus
'By Myself' SApp
'Canary Glow' EBre LSav
'Cartwheels' CKel CRiv SPer
'Catherine Woodbury' CCla CHar COtt EBre EGol ELan MRav MSta NRoo SApp SMad
'Chartreuse Magic' CRiv EBre ERou NHol SPer
'Cherry Cheeks' CB&S EBre EGol ELan ERou LSav MRav SFis
¶ 'Chestnut Lane' SApp
'Chic Bonnet' SPer
¶ 'Chicago Cameo' SApp
'Chicago Petticoats' EGol
'Chicago Robe' EBre MSta SApp WCot WWin
'Chicago Sugar Plum' SApp
'Chicago Sunrise' EBre MSta NOrc
'Chief Sarcoxie' MAus
¶ 'Children's Festival' ECtt EGol
'Chinese Coral' CKel

'Chloe's Child'	SCro
'Christmas Candles'	MAus
citrina	CBow EMon MCot
'Classic Simplicity'	MAus
'Colonial Dame'	CKel LSav
'Conspicua'	CShe CWGN SFis
'Constitutional Island'	MAus
'Contessa'	CBro ELan SCro SPer
'Corky'	ECha SChu SDix SPer
¶ 'Corsican Bandit'	SApp
'Countess Zora'	MAus
¶ 'Cream Drop'	ECtt EFou EGol NOrc
¶ 'Crimson Icon'	SApp
'Crimson Pirate'	ERou NBar
'Croesus'	MAus NHol SCro
'Curls'	SApp
'Dawn Play'	CKel
'Delicate Splendor'	CCla MAus
'Devon Cream'	SPer
'Diamond Dust'	CRiv SPer
'Dido'	CSco ERou
'Dorothy McDade'	CB&S EGol
'Double Coffee'	SApp
§ 'Doubloon'	CKel EBul ERou GAbr MAus MWgw NHol
'Down Town'	MAus
'Dresden Doll'	SPer
'Dresden Gleam'	CRiv
dumortieri	CBot CBro CChu CCla EBul ECha EFou ELan EOrc EPla MAus MUlv MWat NHol NSti NVic SAxl SHig SPer SSpi
'Dutch Beauty'	NBar
'Edelweiss'	EGol
'Eenie Weenie'	ECtt EGol NOrc
¶ 'Eeny Non Stop'	SWas
'Esther Walker'	CKel
'Evelyn Claar'	CKel SCro
'Fairy Delight'	MAus
'Fairy Wings'	SPer
'Fandango'	SPer
'Far East'	CB&S
'Fashion Model'	CB&S CRow
'Fire Dance'	SCro
'First Formal'	SPer
flava	See H. ***lilio-asphodelus***
* ***flavescens***	LHop
'Folklore'	MAus
'Frans Hals'	COtt EBre EPla ERou MBri MRav SPer
'Full Reward'	MAus
fulva	CRow CWGN ELan NCat SChu SHig
N– 'Flore Pleno'	CBre CHan CKel CRow CWGN EFou EGol EHon ELan EMon EOrc ERou LHop MAus NSti SAxl SFis SPer WEas WHoo WWin
N– 'Green Kwanso'	EMon
N– 'Kwanzo Variegata'	CBot CChu CGle ELan ERou LGre LHop MTho NHol SApp WCot
'Garnet Garland'	CKel
'Gateway'	MAus
* 'Gay Nineteen'	CKel
'Gay Rapture'	SPer
'Gay Troubadour'	CKel
'George Cunningham'	CGle CRiv EBre EGol ELan ERou MAus MBri MCot NBar SChu
'Giant Moon'	EBre EGol ELan ERou MBri SPer WRus
'Glowing Gold'	MAus
'Gold Dust'	GHig
'Gold Imperial'	CShe
'Golden Bell'	NBar NHol SChu
'Golden Chance'	CCla MAus
'Golden Chimes'	Widely available
'Golden Gate'	SHig
'Golden Orchid'	See H. 'Doubloon'
'Golden Prize'	EBre
'Green Magic'	EGol SApp
¶ 'Grumbly'	ELan
'Gusto'	MAus
'Halo Light'	CKel SPer
¶ 'Heartthrob'	MAus
'Heaven Knows'	MAus
'Heirloom Lace'	MAus
'Helios'	CSco SHig
¶ 'Hemlock'	SApp
'Her Majesty'	CKel
'Holiday Harvest'	MAus
'Holiday Mood'	ELan ERou
'Home Run'	MAus
'Hornby Castle'	CBro CKel EBre NHol NVic
'Hyperion'	CB&S CCla CShe EBre EGol MAus MRav NBar NHol NRoo SChu SPer WOld
'Imperator'	CWGN LMay MAus NHol
'Indian Serenade'	CRow
¶ 'Iron Gate Glacier'	SApp
'Iron Gate Iceberg'	SApp
'Jo Jo'	MAus
'Joan Senior'	EGol SApp
'Kathleen Ormerod'	LSav
'Kelway's Gold'	CKel
'Kinfolk'	MAus
N 'Kwanso Flore Pleno'	See H. ***fulva*** Green Kwanso
N 'Kwanso Flore Pleno Variegata'	See H. ***fulva*** 'Kwanzo Variegata'
'Lady Inara'	MAus
'Larksong'	EBre EGol
'Late Advancement'	SApp
'Lavender Bonanza'	MAus
'Lilac Wine'	ECha EFou
§ ***lilio-asphodelus***	CBre CGle CHad CHan ECha ELan GWic MAus MBri MBro MFir MWgw NTow SApp SAxl SDix SHig SMad SPer SSpi STre WHoo
'Linda'	ERou LSav MAus MBri NHol
'Little Grapette'	SApp
'Little Men'	MAus
¶ 'Little Sally'	EGol
'Little Wart'	EGol
'Little Wine Cup'	ECtt EGol NOrc SApp

'Lively Set'	MAus
'Lotus Land'	CKel
'Luxury Lace'	EBre ECtt EGol ELan EOrc LSav MSta SApp
'Lynn Hall'	EBre EGol
'Mabel Fuller'	SCro SPer
'Magic Dawn'	CKel LSav
'Mallard'	EBre ECtt MRav SApp WCot
'Marcus Perry'	SApp
'Marion Vaughn'	EBre EGol LHop MAus SApp SDix
'Mavoureen Nesmith'	SCro
¶ 'May Colven'	EGol
'Melody Lane'	EGol
'Michele Coe'	SApp
middendorfii	EBul EMon MAus
'Mikado'	MWgw
minor	CBro CChu CCla CHar EGol SIng SPla
'Misty'	MAus
'Mormon Spider'	SApp
'Morocco Red'	CBow CWGN ELan LSav MAus WAbe
'Mount Joy'	SPer
'Mrs David Hall'	CKel LSav SCro
'Mrs Hugh Johnson'	CHad MWgw NHol
'Mrs John J Tigert'	CSco ERou
'Mrs Lester'	CKel
multiflora	CCla LHop NHol
'Nashville'	CBro CHar CKel ELan ERou
'Neyron Rose'	EBre ERou WRus
'Night Hawk'	SPer
'Nigrette'	LMay MWat NHol
'Nob Hill'	EBre EGol
'Ophir'	LSav
'Orford'	WWin
¶ 'Oriontio'	ECtt
'Ozark Lass'	MAus
'Painted Lady'	CKel
'Paradise Prince'	EGol
¶ 'Pardon Me'	SApp
'Party Partner'	MAus
'Patricia Fay'	CKel
'Peach Supreme'	CB&S
'Persian Princess'	CKel
'Persian Shrine'	EGol
'Pink Charm'	CBow CCla CGle CRow CWGN GHig LHop LMay MAus MBal MSta MWat MWgw NHol NOrc
'Pink Damask'	Widely available
'Pink Dream'	MBri NBar NHol
'Pink Lady'	CSco ERou SPer
'Pink Prelude'	CKel NHol
'Pink Sundae'	ECha
'Prairie Blue Eyes'	CB&S EGol
'Prairie Sunset'	MAus
'Precious Treasure'	CKel
'Premier'	MAus
'Prima Donna'	CKel
'Primrose Mascotte'	NBir
'Raspberry Pixie'	SApp
¶ 'Red Precious'	EGol
'Red Torch'	CKel CSco SPer
'Revolute'	MAus
'Romany'	LMay
'Royal Ruby'	CSco
'Royalty'	CKel EBul
'Ruffled Pinafore'	LSav
'Russell Prichard'	ERou
'Salmon Sheen'	CKel LSav
'Sammy Russell'	CB&S CBow CGle CWGN EGol EOrc GHig LHop MAus MBal MBri NHol WHoo
'Shooting Star'	CKel EGol
'Silent World'	MAus
¶ 'Siloam Bo Peep'	SApp
¶ 'Siloam Pocket Size'	SApp
'Siloam Purple Plum'	EGol
¶ 'Siloam Tiny Mite'	SApp
'Sirius'	MWat NHol
'Soft Whisper'	MAus
'Soledad'	CB&S
'Solid Scarlet'	CSco
'Sound of Music'	MAus
'Spanish Gold'	CBow CSco
'Stafford'	CB&S CBow CKel CSco EFou EHon ELan ERou GAbr LGro LHop LSav MBri MSta NHol NOrc SChu SHig SPer
¶ 'Starling'	EGol
'Stella de Oro'	CBro CChu CTom EBar EBre EGol ELan EOrc EPla ERou MAus MBri MRav MTho MUlv NRoo SApp SSpi WRus
'Stoke Poges'	SApp
'Stolen Hours'	MAus
'Summer Interlude'	MAus
'Sweet Refrain'	CBot LSav
'Tasmania'	SPer
'Tejas'	CSco
'Telstar'	CSco
'Thelma Perry'	CHad
'Thumbelina'	ECha
§ ***thunbergii***	CHad EBul
'Tinker Bell'	SApp
'Towhead'	EGol MAus
'Triple Treat'	CCla MAus
'Varsity'	CCla EGol SPer
vespertina	See H. ***thunbergii***
'Vicountess Byng'	SFis
'Virgins Blush'	SPer
'Wally Nance'	MBri
'Water Witch'	EGol
'Waxwing'	CKel
'Whichford'	CBro CKel EBre EGol ELan LSav NHol SApp SChu SHig SSpi WWin
'Wild Welcome'	MAus
'Windsor Tan'	MAus
'Winnie the Pooh'	MAus
¶ 'Wishing Well'	WCot
¶ 'Woodbury'	WRus
'World of Peace'	MAus
¶ 'Yellow Rain'	WCot
'Young Countess'	MAus
'Zampa'	CB&S
'Zara'	CRiv SPer

HEMIPHRAGMA (Scrophulariaceae)

HEPATICA † (Ranunculaceae)
acutiloba CBro EPar LAma NHol NKay WChr
'Ada Scott' MCot
americana CBro EPar LAma LHop MSal NHol WChr WWat
angulosa See H. ***transsilvanica***
x *media* 'Ballardii' IBlr MTho WChr
§ *nobilis* CAvo CRiv ECha ECro EPar EPot GLoc IBlr LHop MBri MCot MTho MWat NBar NKay NOrc SWas
– *alba* CAvo EPar MHig MS&S NHol SPou
– blue MS&S SPou SWas
¶ – double pink MBri
– *japonica* CBro EPar GLoc LAma NHol NRed SSpi WChr WWat
– marbled leaf SOkd
– pink form MS&S SOkd SPou SWas
¶ – *rubra* GLoc
¶ – 'Tabby' GLoc
§ *transsilvanica* CAvo CBro CHad ELan EPar GLoc LAma LGre LHop MBri MBro MHig MUlv NHol NKay SPou WChr WOld
triloba See H. ***nobilis***

X HEPPIMENES (Gesneriaceae)
'Purple Queen' NMos

HEPTACODIUM (Caprifoliaceae)
¶ *jasminoides* ERav SSpi

HEPTAPLEURUM See **SCHEFFLERA**

HERACLEUM (Umbelliferae)
* *antasiaticum* EMon LRHS
mantegazzianum CRow ERav
minimum roseum ELan MTho NGre WEas WOMN WPat

HERMANNIA (Sterculiaceae)
verticillata LHop

HERMODACTYLUS (Iridaceae)
§ *tuberosus* CBro CCla CHan ECam ECha EPar ETub LAma LBlo LBow LRoo MTho NRar SAxl SCro SIng SLHN

HERNIARIA (Caryophyllaceae)
glabra CLew EPar GPoy LHol MSal NCat NHol NSel SIng WHer

HERPOLIRION (Liliaceae)

HERTIA See **OTHONNA**

HESPERALOË (Agavaceae)
parviflora rubra SArc

HESPERANTHA (Iridaceae)
buhrii CElw
¶ *huttonii* GWic MFir
¶ *moysii* WHal

HESPERIS † (Cruciferae)
matronalis CArn CBre CGle CKin CLew CNat CRow CSFH CSev EEls EFou ELan ERav ERou LHol MCot MSal MWgw NSti SIde WCla WHer WOak WPer
– *alba* CCla EFou EPad MFir SSvw WHer
– Alba Plena WRus
– double form CSun MBri NHol SSpi WHer
– Lilacina Flore Pleno CBos CBre CRow NBir SSvw

HETEROCENTRON (Melastomataceae)
§ *elegans* CTre

HETEROMELES (Rosaceae)
¶ *arbutifolia* CPle

HETEROPAPPUS (Compositae)
¶ *altaicus* WPer

HEUCHERA † (Saxifragaceae)
§ *americana* CRow CShe EFol EOrc LHil MUlv NHol SAxl WEas WThu WWat
'Apple Blossom' CSco
Bressingham hybrids CHar EBre EFou EHon ERou GDra LHil MBri NHol NOak SCro SFis SPer SPla WHil WHoo WWin
x *brizoides* 'Gracillima' CGle
¶ – 'Widar' NHol
'Coral Bells' See H. ***sanguinea***
'Coral Cloud' CB&S CKel ENot IDai
cylindrica CChu CSun GCHN SIng
– *alpina* NHol
¶ – 'Chartreuse' SWas
– 'Greenfinch' CB&S CGle CHan CKel CRow CSco CWGN ECha EFol EFou EGol ELan ERou GWic NCat NSti SApp SMad WCar WCla WEas WHal WHer WKif
– 'Hyperion' CSco MUlv
'Firebird' CKel CSco ELan NVic
'Firefly' CHar EFou ESis MFir MRav NBar SFis WHil WHoo
glauca See H. ***americana***
'Gloriana' CSco
'Green Ivory' CCla CGle ECro EFou EGol ELan ELun ERou MBri MRav MUlv NCat NRoo NSti SPer SPla WHil
grossulariifolia GLoc
¶ *hispida* CSun
¶ 'Huntsman' MUlv
* *maritima* SIng
'Mary Rose' CSco
* *micans* WDav WThu
micrantha CHoe CSun ELan EMon GGar GWic MUlv MWgw

N– 'Palace Purple' Widely available
* 'Moondrops' CRow
'Mother of Pearl' EFol
parvifolia GWic
¶ 'Pluie de Feu' EHal
'Pretty Polly' ENot
pubescens LRHS
– alba CChu WHoo
pulchella LGre SBla
– JCA 9508 NHol SWas WDav
'Red Spangles' CGle CKel
richardsonii MTho WWin
rubescens GLoc MTho WWin
§ *sanguinea* CGle EFol GCHN MBal MBro MWgw NBar NNor NRoo SPla WDav WEas WHal WPer
– dwarf form GAbr
¶ 'Schneewitchen' EFou
'Scintillation' CB&S CKel CSco
'Shere Variety' EFol
'Snow Storm' Widely available
'Sparkler' CKel
'Taff's Joy' CBos CLew CRow EFol LGre LHil LHop MTho SApp
versicolor CCor CHar GWic MBro WDav

X HEUCHERELLA (Saxifragaceae)

alba 'Bridget Bloom' CHar COtt CSco CShe ECha ECro ELan ELun ERou GCHN LGro MBri MUlv NBar NRoo NSti NTow SFis SPer WRus
tiarelloides EFol ELan LSav MWgw SPer WHoo

X HIBANOBAMBUSA (Gramineae(Bambuseae))

tranquillans EFul SDry WJun
– 'Shiroshima' SDry

HIBBERTIA (Dilleniaceae)

aspera CGre CPle CSun
§ *cuneformis* CHil
cuneiformis ERea
dentata SLMG
procumbens ITim SBla
– BH 2260 SOkd
scandens CGre CHEx CSun CTre ERea
volubilis See H. ***scandens***

HIBISCUS † (Malvaceae)

diversifolius CSun
geranioides CSun
huegelii 'Santa Cruz' See ALYOGYNE ***h.*** 'S.C.'
leopoldii SPer
¶ *militaris* CSun
* *moesiana* MBri
moscheutos CSun
rosa-sinensis EBak MBri SLMG
– 'Casablanca' MBri
– 'Helene' MBri
– 'Holiday' MBri
– 'Kardinal' MBri
– 'Koeniger' MBri
– 'Rose of China' MBri
– 'Tivoli' MBri
– 'Weekend' MBri
rubis ELan SPer
schizopetalus CSun MNew SLMG
sinosyriacus 'Autumn Surprise' SHil
– 'Lilac Queen' CFor SHil
*– 'Red Centre' CBot
¶ – 'Ruby Glow' MGos
syriacus CHEx CHad
– 'Ardens' ELan MRav
– 'Blue Bird' See H. ***s.*** 'Oiseau Bleu'
– 'Coelestis' COtt SPer
– 'Diana' CCla CSco SHil
– 'Dixie Belle' WCar
– 'Dorothy Crane' ENot
– 'Duc de Brabant' SPer
– 'Elegantissimus' See H. ***s.*** 'Lady Stanley'
– 'Hamabo' CBra CCla ELan ENot IHos MBri MGos MR&S MRav MWat SHil SPer SReu
– 'Hinomaru' SHil
– 'Jeanne d'Arc' CBot
§ – 'Lady Stanley' CCla ECtt SHil SPer
– 'Meehanii' EGol LGre
– 'Monstrosus' IOrc SHil
§ – 'Oiseau Bleu' ('Blue Bird') CB&S CBow CBra CCla CHad CSco CShe EBre EGol ELan ENot IHos IOrc MBri MGos MR&S MWat SHil SPer SReu SSpi
– 'Pink Giant' CB&S CBow CCla CHad ELan MR&S SHil SPer
– 'Red Heart' CBow CCla CSco CShe ECtt ELan MPla MR&S MRav MWat SHil SMrm SPer WWeb
– 'Russian Violet' CSco ELan MRav WWeb
– 'Speciosus' SPer
– 'Totus Albus' CBow SMrm
*– 'Variegatus' CBot MBri
– 'Weekend' MNew
– 'William R Smith' CCla EGol ELan ENot WWeb
– 'Woodbridge' CB&S CBow CBra CCla CHad CSco CShe ELan ENot IHos MBri MGos MR&S MRav SHil SPer SReu SSpi WSHC
trionum CHad ECou LHop SLMG
– 'Spirits Bay' ECou
– 'Sunny Day' ELan SMrm WEas

HIERACIUM (Compositae)

alpinum CTom
aurantiacum CCor CFis CRiv CRow CSun CTom EFol ELan MBri MFir MSal NCat NLan NRya SIng SSmi WCla WEas WHer WPer
§ *– carpathicola* SFir
¶ *bombycinum* NWCA
brunneocroceum See H. ***aurantiacum carpathicola***
¶ *candidum* LHil
¶ *glabra* WPer
§ *lanatum* CCor CGle EBar ECro EPot WEas WHal WPer WWin

maculatum	CRow ECro ELan EPar MFir MUlv MWat NCat NSti SIng WOak WPer
mixtum	CSun
¶ ***murorum***	NWCA
pilosella	CKin CRow WPer
praecox	CFis CRiv EFou NHol WEas WWin
¶ ***scotostictum***	EMon
sp. from Afghanistan	NKay
*x ***stoloniferum***	CRow
* ***variegatum***	EFol
villosum	CRow CSam EFou MBri NNor NSti SIng WEas WHer WPer WWin
waldsteinii	MPar NNor SIng WHoo
welwitschii	See H. ***lanatum***

HIEROCHLOË (Gramineae)

redolens	GAbr

HILDABERRY See **RUBUS** 'Hildaberry'

HIPPEASTRUM (Amaryllidaceae)

'Amadeus'	LRoo
'Apple Blossom'	LAma
'Beautiful Lady'	LAma
'Bestseller'	LAma
§ ***bifidum***	LBow
'Bouquet'	LAma
'Bright Red'	LAma
'Byjou'	LRoo
'Cantate'	LRoo
'Christmas Gift'	LRoo
'Dark Red'	LAma
'Dutch Belle'	LAma
'Fantastica'	LAma
'Fire Dance'	LAma
gracile 'Donau'	ETub
– 'Pamela'	ETub
'King of the Stripes'	LAma
'Lucky Strike'	LAma
'Ludwig's Goliath'	LAma
'Maria Goretti'	LAma
'Minerva'	LRoo
'Orange Souvereign'	LAma
'Orange Star'	LRoo
'Oscar'	LAma
'Oskar'	LRoo
papilio	LAma
'Papillon'	LAma
phycelloides	CHan
'Picotee'	LAma
¶ ***roseum***	SIgm
'Salmon Beauty'	LRoo
'Star of Holland'	LRoo
'Striped Vlammenspel'	LAma
'United Nations'	LAma
'Valentine'	LRoo
'Vera'	LAma
'White Dazzler'	LAma
'Wonderful'	LAma
'Wonderland'	LAma LRoo
'Yellow Pioneer'	LAma

HIPPOBROMA (Campanulaceae)

¶ ***longiflora***	WPer

HIPPOCREPIS (Leguminosae)

comosa	CKin WHil
– 'E R James'	EPot MPla
§ ***emerus***	CB&S CBra CMHG CSco EBre ECro ELan SHil WAbe WSHC

HIPPOPHAË (Elaeagnaceae)

rhamnoides	Widely available
¶ ***salicifolia***	EHal WDav

HIPPURIS (Hippuridaceae)

vulgaris	EHon

HISTIOPTERIS (Dennstaedtiaceae)

¶ ***incisa***	SSpi

HOHERIA † (Malvaceae)

§ ***angustifolia***	CB&S CBot SSpi WBod WSHC
glabrata	CB&S CBot CFor CSco ECou ISea MBal MBar SHil SPer SSpi
'Glory of Amlwch'	CChu CFor CSam GWic MRav SHil SSpi WSHC
§ ***lyallii***	CB&S CCla ECou ELan IDai IOrc ISea LSav MBri SHil SPer SReu SSpi SSta WCoo
microphylla	See H. ***angustifolia***
populnea	SHil WBod
– 'Variegata'	SHil
sexstylosa	CBot CCla CFor CPle EHar ELan IOrc ISea SHil SPer SSpi WCoo
– ***pendula***	CB&S

HOLBOELLIA (Lardizabalaceae)

coriacea	CBot CChu CRow SArc SBor SBra SHil SPer WSHC
* ***hex***	CHil
latifolia	CSam ERea SArc SSpi

HOLCUS (Gramineae)

mollis 'Albovariegatus'	Widely available

HOLODISCUS (Rosaceae)

discolor	CBow CCla ELan GWic LGre MBlu SHil SLon SPla SSta WEas WHCG
dumosus	CCor

HOMERIA (Iridaceae)

§ ***breyniana***	EBul ETub
– ***aurantiaca***	See H. ***flaccida***
collina	ETub
flaccida	LAma LBow
ochroleuca	LAma LBow

HOMOGYNE (Compositae)

¶ ***alpina***	WPer

HORDEUM (Gramineae)

jubatum	NSti SLHN WHil

murinum CKin

HORMINUM (Labiatae)

pyrenaicum CHar CLew CRiv CSun GDra GLoc MHig MTho NGre SBla SIng SSmi WAbe WCla WEas WHil WOMN WPat WThu WWin

¶ – pale blue WDav

HOSTA † (Liliaceae/Funkiaceae)

aequinoctiiantha EBul SPou
'Alba' (*sieboldiana*) EGol MCot
albomarginata See H. ***sieboldii***
'Albomarginata' (*fortunei*) CB&S CMal CWGN EPGN MBar SApp
'Amanuma' EGol
'Anne Arett' CMal
'Antioch' (*fortunei*) CBdn CMal SApp
'Aoki' (*fortunei*) CB&S CMal EPGN
'Argentea' (*lancifolia thunbergiana*) NKay
'Argentea variegata' (*undulata*) See H. ***undulata undulata***
'August Moon' Widely available
'Aurea' (*lancifolia thunbergiana*) See H. ***sieboldii subcrocea***
aureafolia CMal
'Aureo Alba' (*fortunei*) See H. 'Spinners'
'Aureomaculata' (*fortunei*) See H. ***fortunei albopicta***
§ 'Aureomarginata' (*elata*) CBdn CFor CHad EPGN SApp SMad SSpi
§ – (*ventricosa*) CBdn CCla CFor CHad CHan CMal EBre ECha EGol EPGN MCot MCuc NHol NRoo SDix SHig SMad SPer SSpi WRus
'Baby Blue' (x *tardiana*) CHad
bella EGol
'Besançon' (*ventricosa*) CMal
'Betsy King' CBdn CMal GKit MWgw
'Big Daddy' (*sieboldiana*) COtt EBre ECtt EGol ELan EOrc EPGN MBri MCuc NHol NOrc SApp SMad SPer SSpi WRus
'Big Mama' (*sieboldiana*) EGol
§ 'Birchwood Parky's Gold' CBdn CFor CHad CHan CMal CTom EGol EPGN GKit MCuc SApp SPou SSpi SWas
'Blue Angel' (*sieboldiana*) CHoe EBar EFou EGol ELan EOrc MWat NHol NOrc SApp SSpi
'Blue Belle' (x *tardiana*) CBdn EGol
'Blue Blush' (x *tardiana*) EGol
'Blue Boy' CBdn CHad CMal EGol EPGN MCot SSpi
'Blue Cadet' CHad EGol SSpi
'Blue Diamond' (x *tardiana*) CHad EGol
'Blue Dimples' (x *tardiana*) EGol
'Blue Fandancer' CSin
'Blue Mammoth' (*sieboldiana*) SApp
'Blue Moon' (x *tardiana*) CChu CMHG EFou EGol ELan EOrc EPGN LGre SApp SMad SSpi SWas WEas
'Blue Piecrust' MCuc
¶ 'Blue Seer' (*sieboldiana*) EGol
'Blue Skies' (x *tardiana*) EBre EGol ELan EPGN
'Blue Umbrellas' (*sieboldiana*) CMal EBre EGol ELan EOrc GKit MCuc NJap SPer SSpi WRus
'Blue Wedgwood' (x *tardiana*) CBdn CFor CMHG CMal CRow EGol ELan EOrc GKit NHol SApp SIng SSpi WRus
¶ 'Bold Ribbons' EGol
'Bold Ruffles' EGol LRHS
¶ 'Bouquet' EGol
'Bressingham Blue' CWGN EBre EGol
'Bright Glow' (x *tardiana*) CBdn
¶ 'Bright Lights' EGol
¶ 'Brim Cup' EGol
'Buckshaw Blue' CHan CMal ECha EGol EPGN MCuc SApp SDix
¶ 'Butter Rim' EGol
'Candy Hearts' CBdn CFor CHan CMal EGol EPGN GKit MCuc
capitata CMal
'Carol' (*fortunei*) CBdn CMal SApp
'Celebration' CMal EGol ELan EPGN
¶ 'Chartreuse Wiggles' EGol
'Chinese Sunrise' (*lancifolia*) CBdn EGol EPGN
'Christmas Tree' EGol
'Claudia' SApp
clausa normalis EBre EGol SApp
'Condensata' (*sieboldiana*) CMal
'County Park' ECou
'Cream Delight' (*undulata*) MCuc
crispula CB&S CBow CHad CMal CRow CSco CShe EHon EOrc EPGN EPar MBal MCot MCuc NHol SApp SHig SSpi
'Dark Victory' CMal
decorata CCla CHar CHoe EBre EGol LGro LSav MCuc WPat
'Devon Blue' (x *tardiana*) CBdn CHad CHan EGol
'Diamond Tiara' EGol
'Dorothy' CMal GHig
'Dorset Charm' (x *tardiana*) CMal EGol
'Dorset Flair' (x *tardiana*) CMal
§ *elata* CBos CHad CMal EPar MCuc MUlv WWat
'Eldons' CSin
♦ 'Eldorado' See H. 'Frances Williams'

Name	Suppliers
'Elegans'	See H. ***sieboldiana elegans***
¶ 'Elizabeth Campbell' (*fortunei*)	SApp
'Ellerbroek' (*fortunei*)	CMal
'Emerald Skies'	CMal EGol
'Eric Smith' (x ***tardiana***)	EGol GKit MUlv
'Eric Smith Gold'	CMal
'Excitation'	EGol GKit
¶ 'Floradora'	CBdn
fluctuans	SPou
– variegated	EGol
'Fond Hope'	CMal
fortunei	CBdn CHad CHan CHar CMHG CMal CRow CShe CWGN EBre EOrc EPGN ERou MBal MCuc NGre NHol SChu SHig SPer WEas WOld
§ – ***albopicta***	Widely available
§ – ***albopicta aurea***	CBdn CCla CHad CHoe CKel CMal CRow EBre ECha EGol ELan EPGN LHyd MBal MCot MCuc NHol SApp SChu SHig SPer SPla SSpi WRus
– ***albopicta viridis***	CMal MCuc
– ***aurea***	See H. ***fortunei albopicta aurea***
§ – ***aureomarginata***	Widely available
– ***gigantea***	CMal
§ – ***hyacinthina***	CBdn CCla CGle CHad CMal CSco EGol EOrc EPGN GGar GKit MBar MCuc NBar NSti SApp SHig SSpi WRus WWin
– ***hyacinthina*** variegated	CBdn EGol EPGN MCuc NHol SApp WAbe
– ***obscura***	CMal CShe EPGN LHyd LSav
– ***rugosa***	CHad CMal EPGN
'Fragrant Gold'	CBdn
'Francee' (*fortunei*)	Widely available
§ 'Frances Williams' (***sieboldiana***)	Widely available
'Frances Williams Improved' (***sieboldiana***)	EGol
'Freising' (*fortunei*)	CMal
'Fringe Benefit'	CMal EBre EGol MCuc
¶ 'Frosted Jade'	EGol
¶ 'Geisha'	EGol
'Ginko Craig'	CBdn CBro CFor CHad CMal COtt CRow EBre EFou EGol ELan EOrc EPGN GKit LHop MCuc NHol NJap SApp SIng SPer SPou SSpi WRus
glauca	See H. ***sieboldiana elegans***
'Glauca' (*fortunei*)	CMal
'Gloriosa' (*fortunei*)	EGol
'Gold Drop'	CBdn EGol
'Gold Edger'	CBdn CBro CHan CMHG CMal CRiv EBre EGol ELan EOrc EPGN GKit LSav MCuc NBar NHol NJap SApp SChu SPer SSpi WOld WRus
§ 'Gold Haze' (*fortunei*)	EGol EOrc GKit MCuc NHol
¶ 'Gold Leaf' (*fortunei*)	EGol
'Gold Regal'	CBdn EGol SApp
'Gold Standard' (*fortunei*)	CBdn CMal ECha EGol ELan EPGN MCuc MWat SApp WRus
¶ 'Gold Streak' (***tardiflora***)	NHol
'Goldbrook' (*fortunei*)	EGol
¶ 'Goldbrook Glimmer' (x ***tardiana***)	EGol
'Goldbrook Grace'	EGol
§ 'Golden' (***nakaiana***)	CBdn CFor CHad CHan CMal CTom EGol EPGN MCuc SApp SPou SSpi SWas
♦ 'Golden Age'	See H. 'Gold Haze'
'Golden Circles'	See H. 'Frances Williams'
'Golden Medallion' (***tokudama***)	CBro CMal CSin EBar EGol ELan EOrc EPGN MBri MCuc NHol NJap SApp SIng SMad SSpi
♦ 'Golden Nakaiana'	See H. 'Birchwood Parky's Gold'
'Golden Prayers' (***tokudama***)	Widely available
'Golden Scepter'	CBdn EGol GKit MCuc SApp
'Golden Sunburst' (***sieboldiana***)	CBdn CHad CMal CSco EGol ELan EPGN GGar GHig LSav MBri NBar NJap NRoo SApp WRus
'Golden Tiara'	CBdn CHan CMal EGol ELan EPGN GKit MCuc NJap SApp SSpi WRus
'Goldsplash'	MCuc
gracillima	CMal CRow EBul GKit LHyd NKay SPou
'Great Expectations' (***sieboldiana***)	EGol EPGN
'Green Acres'	SApp
'Green Formal'	CMal
'Green Fountain' (***kikutii***)	CBdn CSin EBre EGol MCuc SApp
'Green Gold' (*fortunei*)	CBdn MCuc
¶ 'Green Piecrust'	EGol
'Green Ripples' (x ***tardiana***)	CHad CMal
¶ 'Green Sheen'	EGol
'Grenfell's Greatest' (***sieboldiana***)	SApp
'Ground Master'	CBdn CMal COtt ECtt EGol ELan EOrc EPGN GKit MBri MCuc NHol NJap NOrc SApp WAbe WRus
¶ 'Gum Drop'	CBdn
'Hadspen Blue' (x ***tardiana***)	CBdn CHad CMHG CMal EBar EGol EOrc EPGN MCot NHol NJap NSti SSpi WRus
'Hadspen Blue Jay' (x ***tardiana***)	CHad
'Hadspen Dolphin' (x ***tardiana***)	CHad
'Hadspen Heron' (x ***tardiana***)	CBdn CHad CMal EGol EPGN GKit SApp SPou

I	'Hadspen Nymphaea'	CHad
	'Hadspen Samphire'	CBdn CHad CHan EGol
	'Hadspen Seersucker'	CHad
	'Hadspen White' (*fortunei*)	EPGN
	'Hakujima' (*sieboldii*)	EGol
§	'Halcyon' (x *tardiana*)	Widely available
	'Happiness' (x *tardiana*)	CBdn CHad CHoe MCuc SPla
	'Happy Hearts'	CMal
¶	'Harmony' (x *tardiana*)	EGol
	'Heartleaf'	CMal
	'Helen Field Fisher'	See H. ***fortunei hyacinthina***
	helonioides albopicta	CBdn CMal EGol ELan EPGN EPar MPar SPou
	'Herifu'	CMal EGol
♦	'Holstein'	See H. 'Halcyon'
§	'Honeybells'	Widely available
	'Hydon Gleam'	EPGN
	'Hydon Sunset'	CBdn CFor CHan CMHG CMal EBar EGol EOrc EPGN GKit LHyd MBri MCot MCuc NHol NOrc SApp SIng SSpi WWat
¶	***hypoleuca***	EGol
§	'Inaho' (***lancifolia***)	EBre EGol
	'Invincible'	CBdn EGol SApp
	'Janet'	CBdn CMal EGol ELan NHol SSpi
¶	'Japan Boy'	SPou
¶	'Japan Girl'	SPou
	'Julie Morss'	CBdn SApp
	'June Beauty'	CMal
	'Kabitan'	See H. ***sieboldii kabitan***
	'Kath's Gold'	CBdn
	kikutii	CHad CMal EGol
¶	– ***caput-avis***	EGol MBro NHol WDav
	– ***polyneuron***	See H. ***k. yakusimensis***
§	– ***yakusimensis***	EBul GKit GLoc SPou
	kiyosumiensis	CRow EBul EGol
	'Krossa Regal'	Widely available
	'Lady Helen'	CMal
	lancifolia	Widely available
	'Lemon Lime'	CBdn CWGN EGol SApp
*	***lilacina***	SCro
	'Little Aurora'	CBdn SIng WRus
	'Little Blue'	CBdn EGol
	'Little Fatty'	CMal
	longipes	CMal EGol SIng SPou
	– ***longipes***	EBul
	longissima	CMal EBul EGol LHyd MCuc SPou WWin
	– ***brevifolia***	EPGN LHyd
	– broad leaf	CMal
	'Louisa'	CMal ECha EGol EPGN NHol
	'Love Pat'	EGol
	'Lucky Charm'	CMal
	'Lunar Eclipse'	CBdn CMal EGol LRHS SApp SSpi
¶	'Maekawa'	EGol
¶	'Maple Leaf'	GKit
N	'Marginata Alba' (*fortunei*)	CBdn CBot CHad CKel EBul ECha LMay MCot MCuc SPer SPla WAbe WOld WWin
	'Mediovariegata' (*undulata*)	See H. ***undulata undulata***
	'Mentor Gold'	CMal
	'Midas Touch' (*tokudama*)	EFou EGol EPGN GKit LSav MCuc NBar NHol NJap NVic SSpi WRus
¶	'Mildred Seaver'	EGol
	'Minnie Klopping'	CMal SApp
§	***minor***	CBro CMal CTom EBre EGol ELan EPGN EPot MCuc NHol SPou WWin
	– ***alba***	See H. ***sieboldii alba***
	'Moerheim' (*fortunei*)	EPar MBri
N	***montana***	SApp WDav
§	– KR 875	LSav WWat
	– Mount Fuji form	CMal
	'Moon Glow'	EGol
¶	'Moonlight' (*fortunei*)	EGol SApp
	'Mount Kirishima' (*sieboldii*)	EPGN NKay SPou
	nakaiana	CMal SIng
	'Nakaimo'	CMal
	'Nana' (*ventricosa*)	See H. ***minor***
§	'Nancy Lindsay' (*fortunei*)	LHyd SApp
	'Neat Splash'	SApp
	'Neat Splash Rim'	SApp
	'Nicola' (x ***tardiana***)	EGol EPGN
	nigrescens	CMal EGol
	'North Hills' (*fortunei*)	CMal
	'Northern Halo' (*sieboldiana*)	CBdn EGol ELan SApp
¶	'Northern Lights' (*sieboldiana*)	EGol
	'Obscura Marginata' (*fortunei*)	See H. ***f. aureo-marginata***
	'Oriana' (*fortunei*)	CBdn EGol
¶	'Osprey' (x ***tardiana***)	EGol
	'Pastures New'	CBdn CFor CHad CMal EGol SApp
	'Pearl Lake'	CBdn CMal EGol SApp SSpi
	'Phyllis Campbell' (*fortunei*)	CFor EGol GKit
	'Picta' (*fortunei*)	See H. ***f. albopicta***
	'Piedmont Gold'	CBdn CSin EBre EPGN GKit LGre MCuc SApp
	'Pineapple Poll'	CMal EPGN
¶	'Pizzazz'	EGol
	plantaginea	CBrd CHad CWGN EGol ERav MCot MPar WEas
	– ***grandiflora***	CBot CGle CHan CMal CSco EPar NHol SSpi WPat WRus WWat
	rectifolia	CMal WKif
	'Resonance'	CMal EBre GKit SApp
	'Richland Gold' (*fortunei*)	EGol
	'Royal Lady'	CMal
	'Royal Standard'	Widely available

'Royal Tiara'	EGol
rupifraga	CMal GKit
'Russell's Form' (*ventricosa*)	EBre
'Ryan's Big One'	CMal LRHS
'Saishu Jima' (*sieboldii*)	CBdn EGol SApp
'Sazanami' (*crispula*)	See H. *crispula*
¶ 'Sea Dream'	EGol
'Sea Drift'	CMal EBre EGol
'Sea Gold Star'	EGol
'Sea Lotus Leaf'	EGol
¶ 'Sea Monster'	EGol
'Sea Octopus'	EGol
'Sea Sprite'	CMal EGol EPGN WRus
'See Saw' (*undulata*)	EGol SApp
'Sentinels'	CMal
'Shade Fanfare'	CBdn CBro CMal COtt CSin EBre EGol ELan EOrc EPGN MCuc MWat NJap NRoo SApp SPer WRus
'Shade Master'	WRus
'Sharmon' (*fortunei*)	CMal
sieboldiana	Widely available
§ – *elegans*	Widely available
– *mira*	CHad CMal
§ *sieboldii*	CBdn CCla CFor EBul ECha EGol EPGN GKit IDai LHyd MCuc MFir MWgw SApp SBla WRus
§ – *alba*	CBdn CCla CHad CHan CMal EBre EGol ELan MCuc SApp SPou
– *elegans*	See H. *sieboldiana e.*
– *kabitan*	CBdn CFor CMal CSin ECou EGol ELan EPGN LRHS MCuc SApp SPou SSpi
– *shiro-kabitan*	EGol
§ – *subcrocea*	EPGN SApp
'Silver Lance'	SApp
'Snowden'	CFor CHad CMHG CMal COtt EBre ECha EGol EPGN MCot MCuc NHol SSpi WRus
'Snowflakes' (*sieboldii*)	EGol MBri MWgw SPer
¶ 'So Sweet'	EGol
'Special Gift'	CMal
§ 'Spinners' (*fortunei*)	CHad CMal ECha EGol MCuc SApp SSpi
'Sprengeri'	CMal
¶ 'Spritzer'	EGol
'Sugar & Cream'	CMal EGol SApp SSpi
'Sum and Substance'	CBdn CMal COtt CSin EGol MUlv SApp
'Summer Fragrance'	EGol SApp
'Sun Power'	CBdn CMal EGol EPGN MCuc MWat NJap SApp SPer WRus
¶ 'Sundance' (*fortunei*)	EGol
'Susy'	CMal
* 'Sweet Strain' (*plantaginea*)	CMal SSpi
'Sweet Susan'	GKit MUlv
'Tall Boy'	CBdn CHad CMHG CMal EBre ECha EGol LSav MCuc MWgw NHol SHig SPer SSpi
x *tardiana*	CBro CCla CHad CRiv CShe EBre EGol ELan EPGN MCuc NHol SHig SPer SSpi WAbe WKif
tardiflora	CHad CSco EBre EGol MBal MCuc NHol NKay SApp WChr
tardiva	See H. 'Inaho'
'The Twister'	GKit SApp
'Thomas Hogg'	See H. *undulata albo-marginata*
'Tiny Tears'	EGol SApp
tokudama	CBdn CChu CHad CMal EBul EGol ELan EPGN ERav IHos MBri MCuc NBar NSti SApp SChu SPla SSpi WAbe WKif WRus WWat
§ – *aureonebulosa*	CBdn CHad CMal EGol EPGN GKit MPar SApp
– *flavocircinalis*	EGol SApp
– forms	CMal
*– *viridis circinalis*	EPGN
'True Blue'	EPGN WRus
undulata	GKit SApp SSpi
§ – *albomarginata*	Widely available
– *erromena*	CBdn CCla CHad CMal CWGN EHon EPGN LMay LSav MCot MCuc MWgw NKay SChu SHig SPer WAbe
§ – *undulata*	Widely available
– *univittata*	CRow ECha EGol EPGN LHop LHyd LSav MCuc SApp WKif WRus
'Variegata' (*gracillima*)	See H. 'Vera Verde'
¶ – (*longissima*)	MCab
– (*tokudama*)	See H. *tokudama aureonebulosa*
– (*undulata*)	See H. *undulata undulata*
– (*ventricosa*)	See H. 'Aureomarginata' (ventricosa)
ventricosa	CB&S CBdn CBro CHad CKel CMal CSco EGol EPGN ERav GDra LHyd LMay MCuc NHol SDix SHig SPla SSpi WChr WOld WWat
– *aureomaculata*	CCla CFor CHad CSco EGol EPGN MCuc WRus
– *minor*	See H. *minor*
venusta	CBdn CBro CChu CHad CHan CMal CRiv CRow EBul EGol ELan EPGN EPar MCuc NKay NNrd SHig SIng SPou WChr WEas
– forms	CMal
– *yakushimensis*	See H. *kikutii y.*
N 'Venusta Variegated'	EGol
§ 'Vera Verde'	CBdn CMal EGol EPGN MCuc SApp SIng WRus
'Verte' (*sieboldii*)	CMal
'Viette's Yellow Edge' (*fortunei hyacinthina*)	CMal
'Vilmoriniana'	CMal
'Viridis Marginata' (*lancifolia thunbergiana*)	See H. *sieboldii kabitan*
♦ 'Wayside Perfection'	See H. 'Honeybells'

'Weihenstephan' (*sieboldii alba*) GKit
'Wide Brim' CBdn CHoe CSin ECtt EGol ELan EOrc EPGN GKit MBri MWat NHol NJap WAbe WRus
'Willy Nilly' CMal
♦ 'Windsor Gold' See H. 'Nancy Lindsay'
♦ 'Wogon Giboshi' See H. 'Wogon Gold'
'Wogon Gold' (*sieboldii*) CRow EFou EGol EPGN GKit MCuc NHol SApp
'Wold Gold' SApp
¶ 'Yakushima-mizu' (*sieboldii*) CBdn
'Yellow Edge' (*fortunei*) See H. *f. aureo-marginata*
¶ 'Yellow River' EGol
'Yellow Splash' CMal ECha EPGN SApp
'Yellow Splash Rim' EGol SApp
'Zounds' CHoe CMHG CMal EBre EFou EGol ELan EOrc EPGN GKit IHos MBri MCuc NJap NSti SApp SMad SSpi WRus WWat

HOTTONIA (Primulaceae)
palustris ELan LMay

HOUSTONIA See **HEDYOTIS**

HOUTTUYNIA (Saururaceae)
cordata CFis CHan CSun CTom IBlr MUlv MWgw
– 'Chameleon' Widely available
– 'Flore Pleno' Widely available
*– 'Tricolor' CHEx MSta SLon
– *variegata* GEdr IBar IBlr MPit NVic

HOVENIA (Rhamnaceae)
dulcis CB&S CMCN CPle ELan ESim

HOWEIA (Palmae)
forsteriana LPal MBri

HOYA † (Asclepiadaceae)
australis MNew SLMG
bandaensis SLMG
bella CB&S ERea LAbb MBri NRog SLMG WEas
§ *carnosa* CB&S EBak ERea ESim LAbb MNew NRog SLMG
– 'Exotica' SLMG
*– 'Jungle Garden' SLMG
– 'Krinkle Eight' SLMG
– 'Red Princess' MBri
– 'Rubra' SLMG
– 'Variegata' CB&S MBri SLMG
compacta CB&S MBri SLMG
engleriana SLMG
fusca 'Silver Knight' SLMG
imperialis SLMG
linearis MNew
longifolia MNew
– *shepherdii* MNew
motoskei MNew
multiflora MBri MNew
* *neo-caledonica* LAbb SLMG
polyneura MNew SLMG
pubicalyx 'Red Buttons' MNew SLMG
'Shibata' MNew

HUGUENINIA (Cruciferae)
alpina See H. *tanacetifolia*

HUMATA (Davalliaceae)
tyermannii NMar

HUMEA (Compositae)
elegans See CALOMERIA *amaranthoides*

HUMULUS (Cannabidaceae)
japonicus MSal NHex
lupulus CArn CB&S GPoy LHol MSal SIde WHer
– *aureus* Widely available
– 'Fuggle' GPoy
¶ – 'Hip-Hop' EMon
– variegated CSco
– 'Wye Challenger' GPoy

HUTCHINSIA (Cruciferae)
alpina CLew CShe ELan EMNN EPot MBro MCas MPla MWat NKay NNrd NRya SIng WHil WPer
– *brevicaulis* NKay

HYACINTHELLA (Liliaceae/Hyacinthaceae)
acutiloba EPot LAma WChr
heldreichii WChr
lineata LRHS WChr

HYACINTHOIDES (Liliaceae/Hyacinthaceae)
§ *hispanica* CAvo CBro NHol SIng
– 'Azalea' LBlo
– 'Danube' ('Donau') LBow
– 'Excelsior' ETub
– 'La Grandesse' CBro
– 'Mount Everest' LBlo
– 'Myosotis' LBlo
– 'Queen of the Pinks' LBow
– 'Rosabella' CBro
– 'White City' LBow
§ *italica vicentina* WChr
– *vicentina alba* WChr
§ *non-scripta* CAvo CBro CKin EPar ERav ETub LAma LBlo LBow LFox MBri NLan NSel SIng WBon WCla
– pink bell LBlo
– white bell LBlo

HYACINTHUS † (Liliaceae/Hyacinthaceae)
amethystinus See BRIMEURA *amethystina*
azureus See MUSCARI *azureum*
comosum 'Plumosum' See MUSCARI *comosum* 'Plumosum'
orientalis 'Amethyst' ETub LAma LRoo
– 'Amsterdam' LAma
– 'Anne Marie' CBro ETub LAma LBlo LRoo MBri
– 'Apollo' LBlo

– 'Ben Nevis'	LAma MBri
– 'Bismarck'	LAma
– 'Blue Giant'	LAma
– 'Blue Ice'	LRoo
– 'Blue Jacket'	CBro LAma LBlo LRoo
– 'Blue Magic'	LAma LBlo
– 'Blue Orchid'	LAma
– 'Blue Star'	LAma
– 'Blushing Dolly'	LBlo
– 'Borah'	LAma
– 'Carnegie'	CBro ETub LAma LBlo LRoo
– 'Cherry Blossom'	LBlo
– 'Chestnut Flower'	ETub LRoo
– 'City of Haarlem'	CBro ETub LAma LBlo LRoo
– 'Colosseum'	LAma
– 'Concorde'	LAma LBlo
– 'Debutante'	LBlo
– 'Delft Blue'	CBro ETub LAma LBlo MBri
– 'Distinction'	LAma LBlo
– 'Edelweiss'	LAma
– 'Fireball'	LBlo
– 'Fondante'	LAma
– 'General Koehler'	LRoo
– 'Gipsy Queen'	LAma LBlo LRoo MBri
– 'Grace Darling'	LBlo
– 'Hollyhock'	ETub LAma LBlo LRoo MBri
– 'Indian Prince'	LBlo
– 'Jan Bos'	ETub LAma LBlo LRoo
– 'King Codro'	LAma MBri
– 'King of the Blues'	LAma LRoo
– 'La Victoire'	LAma
– 'Lady Derby'	LAma LBlo
– 'Lord Balfour'	LAma LBlo
– 'L'Innocence'	CBro LAma LBlo
– 'Madame Kruger'	LAma
– 'Madame Sophie'	ETub LRoo
– 'Marconi'	LAma LRoo
– 'Marie'	LAma
– 'Maryon'	LBlo
– 'Morning Star'	LBlo
– 'Mulberry Rose'	LAma
– 'Myosotis'	LAma
– 'Orange Queen'	LBlo
– 'Oranje Boven'	ETub LAma LBlo
– 'Ostara'	CBro ETub LAma LBlo MBri
– 'Paul Herman'	LBlo
– 'Pink Pearl'	CBro ETub LAma LBlo
– 'Pink Royal'	LAma
– 'Princess Margaret'	LAma
– 'Princess Victoria'	LBlo
– 'Prins Hendrik'	LAma
– 'Queen of the Pinks'	LAma LRoo
– 'Rosette'	LAma
– 'Salmonetta'	See H. ***o.*** 'Oranje Boven'
– 'Skyjacket'	LBlo
– 'Sneeuwwitje' ('Snow White')	LAma LBlo
– 'Tubergen's Scarlet'	ETub
– 'Violet Pearl'	CBro ETub LAma LBlo
– 'Vuurbaak'	LAma
– 'White Pearl'	LAma

HYDRANGEA † (Hydrangeaceae)

¶ ***anomala***	CChu
§ ***anomala petiolaris***	Widely available
§ – – ***cordifolia***	CChu EPla SSta WWeb
– – dwarf form	See H. ***p. cordifolia***
arborescens	MRav NNor SPla
– 'Annabelle'	CB&S CCla COtt EBre EFou EGol ELan ENot ERav IJoh IOrc ISea LHop LSav MBri MGos MPla SHil SMad SPer SSpi SSta WPat
– ***discolor*** 'Sterilis'	EPla SHil SSpi
– 'Grandiflora'	CB&S CBot CBow CCla ELan IJoh LSav SHil SPer SSpi SSta WBod WPat WSHC WWin
¶ – 'Hills of Snow'	SSpi
– ***radiata***	CHan ELan NHlc SPla SSpi
aspera	CFor CSco EGol IJoh IOrc MBar MMth SChu SHil SPer SSpi SSta
¶ – ***kawakamii***	EPla
– ***macrophylla***	MBri SSpi WBod
– 'Mauvette'	CKni LHop MBlu MUlv SSpi SSta
– ***robusta***	CCla
– 'Taiwan'	NHlc SSpi
§ – ***villosa***	Widely available
cinerea	See H. ***arborescens discolor***
heteromalla	CBot CCla LSav SSpi
– Bretschneideri group	CB&S CMCN IJoh LSav NHlc SHil SSpi SSta WBod WWat
– 'Morrey's Form'	SSpi
– 'Snowcap'	EGol ERav NHlc SSpi
– ***wilsonii***	SHil
– ***xanthoneura***	CB&S CBot SSpi WSHC
– 'Yarlbury Ridge'	NHlc SSpi
integerrima	See H. ***serratifolia***
involucrata	MBal MPla NHlc SHil SSpi SSta
– 'Hortensis'	CFor CHan CShe IOrc MMth SHil SSpi WBod WKif
japonica 'Macrosepala'	SSpi
§ ***macrophylla*** 'Adria'	MR&S
– 'Albury Purple'	MBri
– 'Alpenglühn' ('Alpen Glow') (H)	ELan ENot ESis IOrc MBri NHlc SPla WBod
– 'Altona' (H)	CB&S CSco IOrc ISea MBal MGos NHlc NKay SHil SPer SReu
– 'Ami Pasquier' (H)	CB&S CBow CSco IOrc NHlc SHil SSpi
– 'Ayesha' (H)	CB&S CBot CBow CBra CChu CCla CHan CMHG CPle CSco CTrw EBre EGol MRav SChu SDix SHil SMad SPer SPla SSpi WBod
– 'Beauté Vendômoise' (L)	SSpi
– 'Belzonii' (L)	LSav NHlc
– 'Benelux' (H)	CB&S IJoh MR&S WAbe
– 'Blauer Prinz' ('Blue Prince') (H)	CB&S IJoh IOrc MBri
– 'Blaumeise'	NHlc SHil

– 'Blue Bonnet'	MGos SPer
– 'Blue Deckle'	CCla CFor CMHG CSco EPla NHlc SHil SPla SSpi SWas
¶ – 'Blue Prince'	NHlc
– 'Blue Wave' (L)	See H. *m.* 'Mariesii Perfecta'
– 'Bodensee' (H)	ELan MBri MRav SHil SPla WWeb
– 'Bouquet Rose' (H)	CSco ECtt EHal MGos MR&S
– 'Chinensis'	SSpi
¶ – 'Cordata'	WWeb
– 'Deutschland' (H)	IOrc SHil
*– 'Dwaag Pink'	WWeb
– 'Enziandom' ('Gentian Dome') (H)	CFor SSpi WAbe
– 'Europa' (H)	CB&S CTrw IOrc MGos MR&S MRav NHlc SHil SReu WPat
– 'Fisher's Silverblue' (H)	WAbe
– 'Générale Vicomtesse de Vibraye' (H)	CB&S CBot CBow CFor CMHG ISea LSav MBar MBri NHlc SHil SLon SPer WAbe WBod WWin
– 'Geoffrey Chadbund' (L)	CB&S CCla ECtt IHos MBri NHlc SChu SDix SHil SMad SPer SSpi SSta WWeb
– 'Gertrude Glahn' (H)	CBow
– 'Goliath' (H)	MBri SHil
– 'Grant's Choice'	NHlc SSpi
– 'Hamburg' (H)	CB&S CBow CSco ECtt ENot IDai IOrc MGos MPla MR&S NHlc NKay SDix SHil SLon SReu WAbe
– 'Heinrich Seidel' (H)	CB&S NHlc SHil
– 'Holstein' (H)	COtt NRoo SPla
¶ – 'Intermezzo'	WWeb
– 'James Grant'	NHlc
– 'Joseph Banks' (H)	See H. *m.* 'Otaksa'
*– 'Khudnert'	WWeb
– 'King George' (H)	CBow CSco ENot IDai IOrc MBar MGos MRav NHlc SHil SPer WWeb
– 'Kluis Superba' (H)	CPle CSco IOrc MRav NHlc NRoo WAbe
– 'La France' (H)	EHal MBar MR&S NRoo WAbe WWeb
– 'Lanarth White' (L)	CB&S CBow CCla CSco LSav MPla MRav NHlc SDix SHil SLon SPer SReu SSpi WBod WWeb
– 'Libelle' (L)	CB&S LSav MBri MPla NHlc SHil SPer SSpi WKif
– 'Lilacina'	CCla CGre NHlc SCro SPer SSpi
§ – 'Maculata'	EFol ELan IOrc LHop SCro
– 'Madame Emile Mouillère' (H)	CB&S CBot CBow CCla CHan CSco ENot IDai IOrc MBri MPla NHlc SChu SDix SHil SLon SMad SPer SPla SSta WAbe WBod
*– 'Magic Light'	MBri
– 'Maréchal Foch'	IOrc SHil
– 'Mariesii' (L)	CB&S CBot CCla CSco ELan ENot IDai ISea MBal NHlc NKay SDix SHil SLon SPer SSpi WKif WWat
§ – 'Mariesii Perfecta' (L)	CBot CBow CFor CPle CSco CTre ELan ENot IDai IJoh ISea MGos MR&S NKay SDix SPer SPla WBod
– 'Mariesii Variegata' (L)	WAbe
– 'Masja'	COtt IHos IOrc MBri MGos
– 'Matilda Gutges' (H)	MPla SSpi WAbe WWeb
– 'Miranda'	CBrd CFor CMHG EPla ERav LSav NHlc SHil SSpi
– 'Miss Belgium' (H)	IDai IOrc MBal MBri MUlv
– 'Miss Hepburn'	COtt EHal LRHS SPer
– 'Niedersachsen' (H)	MRav SHil
– 'Nigra' (H)	CCla CPle CTre ELan IOrc ISea SChu SDix SHil SLon SPer SPla SSpi SSta WAbe
¶ – 'Nikko Blue'	CB&S
§ – 'Otaksa' (H)	MBri NHlc
– 'Parzival' (H)	CB&S CSco CTrw NHlc
– 'Pia' (H)	CB&S CLew ELan ESis GLoc IOrc MBal MBri MCot MHig MPla MTho MUlv SIng SMad SPer SPla SSta WAbe WOMN WPat WThu WWat
– 'Pink Wave' (L)	CB&S
– 'President Doumer'	CBow CSco
¶ – 'Prinses Beatrix'	MR&S
– 'Quadricolor' (L)	CChu CCla CHoe EGol EPla IJoh LGre MUlv SDix SPer SPla SSpi
– 'Red Emperor' (H)	SReu
– 'Regula'	CTrw SSta
– 'Rheinland'	WBod
– 'Sea Foam' (L)	IJoh IOrc NHlc SHil
– 'Seascape'	NHlc
♦– 'Sir Joseph Banks'	See H. *m.* 'Otaksa'
– 'Soeur Therèse' ('Sister Therese') (H)	CPle IOrc MGos MR&S WBod WWeb
– 'Sybilla'	MPla NHlc WAbe
– 'Teller's Blue'	MBri NHlc
– 'Teller's Red'	IHos MBri
– 'Teller's Variegated'	MBri
¶ – 'Teller's White'	MBri NBar
– 'Tokyo Delight'	CBrd IOrc NHlc SSpi SSta
– 'Tovelit'	EBre MBri
– 'Tricolor' (L)	CB&S CBot CBow CBra CCla CMal ERav ISea MBri MTho SChu SHil SLon SMad SPer SReu SSpi WKif
– 'Variegata'	IOrc MPla NKay SPla
– 'Veitchii' (L)	CBot CCla CHan CMHG CSco ENot IJoh MBri SCro SDix SHil SPla SSpi WBod WWat
– 'Vicomte de Vibraye'	See H. ***macrophylla*** 'Générale Vicomtesse de Vibraye'
– 'Westfalen' (H)	NHlc SDix SPla SSpi
– 'White Lace' (L)	ELan
– 'White Swan'	MBri MGos WBod
– 'White Wave' (L)	CCla CPle CSco EGol ENot MBar MR&S SHil SPer SPla SSpi

- 'Wryneck' (H) NHlc
maculata 'Variegata' See H. ***macrophylla*** 'Maculata'
paniculata CMCN CPle CTrw LSav SLon
¶ – 'Brussels Lace' CKni LSav SSpi
– 'Everest' LSav
– 'Floribunda' CCla CFor MBri SPer SSpi
– 'Grandiflora' Widely available
– 'Green Spire' LSav
– 'Kyushu' CB&S CCla CFor COtt EBre EGol ELan ERav IOrc MBlu MBri MGos NHlc NRoo SHil SPer SPla SSpi SSta WPat WWat
– 'Pink Diamond' EHar LSav
– 'Praecox' CCla CSco ENot IDai LSav NKay SDix SHil SPer SSpi WWin
– 'Tardiva' CB&S CBot CFor CSam CSco EHar LSav MBri MRav NHlc SDix SHil SPer SPla SSpi WBod WPat
– 'Touchard' CSco
– 'Unique' CB&S EBre IJoh LHop LSav NHlc SHil SSpi
– 'Vera' EGol ENot
– 'White Moth' CKni EHar MBri SSpi
petiolaris See H. ***anomala p.***
– tiliifolia MBlu SSpi WSHC
'Preziosa' Widely available
quelpartensis CB&S CChu CPle LHop
quercifolia Widely available
– 'Snowflake' ELan ERav LGre NBar SSpi WWat
'Rocklon' SSpi
sargentiana CB&S CBot CBow CCla CHEx COtt CSco EHar ELan ERav LSav MBlu MBri MCot SArc SBor SHil SMad SPer SSpi SSta WBod WKif WWat
scandens CGre SSpi
§ *– chinensis* SPer
seemannii CB&S CBot CChu CHEx CHil CMac CSam CTrw ISea SSpi SSta WSHC WWat
serrata CTrw NHlc WHCr
– 'Acuminata' See H. ***s.*** 'Bluebird'
– 'Belle Deckle' See H. ***macrophylla*** 'Blue Deckle'
§ – 'Bluebird' CBot CBow CBra CCla CFor ELan ISea MBal MBri MGos NHlc NKay SDix SHil SMad SPer SPla SSta WAbe
– chinensis NHlc SHil
– 'Diadem' CBrd CPle EPla LSav NHlc SDix SSpi
– 'Grayswood' CBot CCla CHad CHig CPle CSam CSco ENot LHop MPla NHlc NKay SDix SHil SPer SSpi WKif WWat
– 'Intermedia' CCla ENot SHil
– koreana SHil
– 'Rosalba' CCla IJoh MRav SChu SHil SPer SSpi WHCr WSHC
– thunbergii CB&S CFor CMHG
– 'Preziosa' See H. 'P.'
serratifolia CB&S CBot CChu LHop SArc SHil SSpi WSHC
sinensis See H. ***scandens chinensis***
sp. GUIZ 146 LSav
tiliifolia See H. ***anomala petiolaris***
* *umbellata* SPer
villosa See H. ***aspera villosa***

HYDRASTIS (Ranunculaceae)
canadensis GPoy MSal

HYDROCHARIS (Hydrocharitaceae)
morsus-ranae CWGN EHon LMay MSta

HYDROCLEYS (Limnocharitaceae)
nymphoides MSta

HYDROCOTYLE (Umbelliferae/Hydrocotylaceae)
* *americana* NHol
moschata CRiv NHol SIng WPer WWin

HYDROPHYLLUM (Hydrophyllaceae)
appendiculatum MSal
canadense EMon
virginianum MSal WEas

HYLOMECON (Papaveraceae)
japonicum CLew EBar ELun EPar EPot GEdr GHig GLoc MCot MTho MUlv NHol NKay WOMN

HYMENANTHERA See **MELICYTUS**
crassifolius CBot CChu CPle ECou NHol SCro WHCG WSHC
obovatus ECou

HYMENOCALLIS (Liliaceae/Amaryllidaceae)
caroliniana LAma MSta
× *festalis* CAvo CSut LAma LBow MBri SW&B WBod
– 'Sulphur Queen' LBow SW&B
harrisiana LBow
longipetala LBow
narcissiflora 'Advance' LAma LBow
occidentalis See H. ***caroliniana***

HYMENOSPORUM (Pittosporaceae)
flavum CGre CPle

HYMENOXYS (Compositae)
¶ *acaulis caespitosa* WDav
– caespitosa JCA 9467 CLew
grandiflora CSun MBro NHol WDav
¶ – JCA 11422 SBla
§ *scaposa* EBre LHil

HYOPHORBE (Palmae)
§ *lagenicaulis* LPal

HYOSCYAMUS (Solanaceae)
albus LHol WHer
niger CArn CSev GPoy LHol MChe MSal NSel WHer

HYPERICUM † (Guttiferae)	
acmosepalum	EMon LSav
– SBEC 93	CChu CCla
¶ ***addingtonianum***	EPla
adenotrichum	GCHN SIng
aegypticum	CRiv ELan EPad EPot ESis GCHN GLoc LHop MHig NHar NHol NTow WPer
androsaemum	CArn CFis CKin ECha ELan ENot ISea MFir MSal NRoo SHil SLon WHil
– 'Albury Purple'	EFol LMer
*– 'Autumn Blaze'	CB&S
– 'Dart's Golden Penny'	EBre
§ – 'Gladys Brabazon'	CHan CHoe EBre ERav IJoh MBar MBri MUlv NSti SPla
– 'Variegatum'	See H. ***a.*** 'Gladys Brabazon'
§ ***annulatum***	ELan EMon ERav
athoum	GCHN LHop MBro MHig MPla NHol NTow SIng WPer
augustinii	CChu CCla CPle CTre
balearicum	CHan EPad LGre LHop MBro MCas MFir MPla SChu SDry SPla SSta WPer WSHC WWin
beanii	CChu EBar ELan EMon LRHS
¶ ***bellum***	EBar GWic
¶ – ***latisepalum***	ELan
¶ ***buckleyi***	GCHN MHig
calycinum	Widely available
– ***aureum***	WWin
§ ***cerastioides***	CLew CMHG GCHN GHig GLoc MBro MPla NHol SChu SIng WHil WHoo WPer WWin
choisyanum B&L 12469	CChu LSav
coris	CLew CShe CSun EBre ECha EPot ESis GLoc LGre LHop MBro MCas MTho MWat NKay WCla WHoo WOMN
cuneatum	See H. ***pallens***
x ***cyathiflorum*** 'Gold Cup'	CTre MBal SHil
¶ ***delphicum***	SIng
x ***dummeri*** 'Peter Dummer'	CChu LSav
'Eastleigh Gold'	SHil
elatum	See H. ***inodorum***
empetrifolium	CLew GLoc MHig
§ – ***oliganthum***	ECha ESis GCHN SIng WOMN WPer
– 'Prostatum'	See H. ***e. oliganthum***
¶ ***ericoides***	MBro WDav
§ ***forrestii***	CBot CCla CHan CLan EHar ELan ENot EPla MBal MGos SHil SSpi STre WWat
¶ – SBEC 472	LSav
N ***fragile***	See H. ***olympicum minus***
frondosum Sunburst ®	LBuc MBri
'Gold Penny'	See H. ***androsaemum*** 'Dart's Golden Penny'
grandiflorum	See H. ***kouytchense***
¶ ***henryi*** L 753	CChu
'Hidcote'	Widely available
'Hidcote Variegated'	CMal CMer CPle ELan IJoh MUlv SSus WWeb
hircinum cambessedesii	EMon LRHS
¶ – ***majus***	EMon
hirsutum	CKin
hookerianum	CLan
humifusum	WCla
hyssopifolium	EBar WPer
inodorum 'Elstead'	CB&S CBow CLan CShe ELan IDai IJoh ISea LHop MBal MBar MGos MR&S MWat NKay NNor NRoo SHil SPer SPla WEas WWin
– 'Summergold'	ENot IBar NHol SMad WSHC
– 'Ysella'	CMer CRow EBre EFol ELan SDry SPer
kalmianum	CBot CBow CMal CTre EHar
kamtschaticum	CChu WOMN
kelleri	CLew GCHN MBro NHol WDav
§ ***kouytchense***	CGle CLan CSco EMon IBar SDry SHil SSpi WKif
lagarocladum	CChu ELan EMon
¶ – L 807	LSav
lancasteri	EMon LRHS
– L 750	CChu
leschenaultii	CLan SSpi WSHC
manolatum	See H. ***annulatum***
x ***moserianum***	CB&S CHan CLan CMHG CSco CShe ELan ENot IDai IJoh MBar MCot MR&S NNor NRoo SHil SPer WAbe
§ – 'Tricolor'	Widely available
– 'Variegatum'	See H. x ***m.*** 'Tricolor'
'Mrs Brabazon'	See H. ***androsaemum*** 'Gladys Brabazon'
¶ ***nanum***	SIng
nummularium	MHig WAbe
olympicum	CArn CShe CSun ECha ELan EPot GCHN GDra GLoc IDai MFir MHig MPla MPlt MWat NNor SBla SIng SLon SPer SPla SSmi WEas
– 'Edith'	CLew NCat NHol SAsh SWas
– 'Grandiflorum'	See H. ***o. uniflorum***
§ ***olympicum minus***	CHar EBre ECha ELan EMNN ENot EPot GCHN GLoc IDai MCas MCot MHig MPlt MRav NHol NKay NRoo SIng STre WDav WHil WPer WWin
§ – – 'Sulphureum'	CChu CRiv EBre ESis MRav NRoo SAxl SPer WSHC WWin
§ – – 'Variegatum'	CHoe EFol ELan MHig SIng WPat
§ ***olympicum uniflorum***	EBre MBal MBar MBro NHol NRoo NVic WAbe WCla WHoo
– – 'Citrinum'	CHan ECha EFol EGol GCHN GLoc LHop MBal MWat NKay NRoo SBar SBla WAbe WCla WEas WOMN WWat
orientale	CLew CMHG EMNN GCHN GLoc LHop MBro MMth MPla MPlt NNrd NRoo SChu WCla WDav WHoo WPer
¶ ***patulum***	EBar LSav
– ***forrestii***	See H. ***forrestii***
– ***henryi***	See H. ***pseudohenryi***

- – 'Variegatum' CCla CMHG EPla LHop MUlv SPer
- ***perforatum*** CArn CKin CSFH Effi GPoy LHol MChe NLan NSel SIde WCla WHer WOak
- ***polyphyllum*** See H. ***olympicum minus***
- – ***citrinum*** See H. ***olympicum minus*** 'Sulphureum'
- – 'Grandiflorum' See H. ***olympicum uniflorum***
- – 'Sulphureum' See H. ***olympicum minus*** 'Sulphureum'
- – 'Variegatum' See H. ***olympicum minus*** 'Variegatum'
- ***prolificum*** CChu CCla CMHG CSco EBre EHal NHol SChu SOkd WPat WSHC
- § ***pseudohenryi*** CBow EBar ELan EMon
- – L 1029 CChu CCla
- ***pseudopetiolatum*** WPer
- – ***yakusimense*** See H. ***y.***
- ***pulchrum*** CKin WHil
- ¶ ***quadrangulum*** EHal
- ***reptans*** See H. ***olympicum minus***
- ***rhodoppeum*** See H. ***cerastioides***
- 'Rowallane' CB&S CBot CBow CCla CFor CLan CPle CSco CTre CTrw EPla ISea MBri MR&S SDix SHil SPer SSpi WAbe WBod
- sp. B&L 12009 CChu LSav
- ***stellatum*** CGre EBre SLon
- ***subsessile*** ELan EMon
- * 'Sungold' WWeb
- ***tenuicaule*** KR 743 ISea
- ***tetrapterum*** CKin MSal NLan
- ***trichocaulon*** CLew ELan EMNN EPot ESis GCHN GHig GLoc MBro MHig MPit NHol NNrd NRoo SIng WAbe WOMN WPat WPer WThu
- ***uralum*** EPla MBal NSti
- ***wilsonii*** CCla
- ***yakushimense*** CHar CSun EPla GCHN MBar NGre NTow SIng WCla WHil

HYPOCHOERIS (Compositae)

- ***radicata*** CKin

HYPOCYRTA See NEMATANTHUS

HYPOESTES (Acanthaceae)

- ***phyllostachya*** MBri
- – 'Bettina' MBri
- – 'Carmina' MBri
- – 'Purpuriana' MBri
- – 'Wit' MBri
- ***sanguinolenta*** See H. ***phyllostachya***

HYPOLEPIS (Dennstaedtiaceae)

- ***millefolium*** ECha EMon
- ¶ ***rugulosa*** EMon

HYPOXIS (Liliaceae/Amaryllidaceae)

- ***hirsuta*** WChr
- ***hygrometrica*** ECou MFir WAbe

HYPSELA (Campanulaceae)

- ***longiflora*** See H. ***reniformis***
- § ***reniformis*** CHar CSun ELan EMNN EPar EPot ESis GLoc MCas MHig MMth MPar MPit MTho NNrd NOak NRed SCro SIng SSmi WHal WHil WWin
- – 'Greencour White' GGar MCas

HYSSOPUS (Labiatae)

- ***officinalis*** CArn CCor CSFH CSev ECha ELan EPar Effi GPoy LHol MBri MChe NRoo NSel SIde WEas WHer WHil WOak WPer WSto
- – ***albus*** NNor SChu WHer WMar WPer WSHC WWin
- – ***angustifolius*** See H. ***o. officinalis***
- – ***aristatus*** CLew CSco EBre EMon ESis GPoy LHol NRoo SIde WEas WPer WSto WWin
- ¶ – ***decussatus*** MBar
- § – ***purpurascens*** ECha WPer
- – ***roseus*** NNor NSti SChu WHer WKif WMar WPer WSHC WWin
- – ***ruber*** See H. ***o. purpurascens***
- ***seravshanicus*** MBro

HYSTRIX (Gramineae)

- ***patula*** GWic WHea

IBERIS (Cruciferae)

- ***amara*** CFis GPoy
- ***candolleana*** See I. ***pruitii***
- ***commutata*** See I. ***sempervirens***
- * ***correvoniana*** WEas
- ***gibraltarica*** CLew CRiv EFou ELan EMon GLoc NNor NTow SIng WCar WPer
- ***jordanii*** See I. ***pruitii***
- § ***pruitii*** CLew CRiv CSun GLoc MBal NKay WCla
- ***saxatilis*** ECha MBro NHol WPat
- – ***candolleana*** See I. ***pruitii***
- § ***sempervirens*** CB&S CFis CKel CRiv EBre ELan LAbb LGro LHil MBal MBro MPit MWat MWgw NGre NNor NNrd WHil WPer
- – 'Pygmaea' EMNN ITim MPlt MWat
- – 'Schneeflocke' ('Snowflake') CShe ENot EPar IDai MBri MCas MFir SIng SPer WHoo WPat
- – 'Weisser Zwerg' ('Little Gem') CLew CShe EBre ECha EFou ELan EMNN EPar EPla EPot GLoc MBro MCas MHig MPla MTho NKay NTow SBla SIng WHoo WOld WWin

IDESIA (Flacourtiaceae)

- ***polycarpa*** CHEx EHar SHil SSpi WCoo WWat

ILEX † (Aquifoliaceae)

Nx *altaclerensis* 'Belgica Aurea' (f) — CB&S CBow CMHG CRos CSam EGol EHar LNet LSav MBar MBri MWat SBla SHil SMad SSpi
– 'Camelliifolia' (f) — CMCN LSav MRav MUlv MWat SHil SMad SPer SSpi WWat
– 'Camelliifolia Variegata' (f) — CChu SHil
– 'Golden King' (f) — Widely available
– 'Hendersonii' (f) — NWea
– 'Hodginsii' (m) — CRos IOrc IReg LSav MBar MUlv NWea SHil
– 'Howick' (f) — LSav
– 'Lady Valerie' (f) — IReg
– 'Lawsoniana' (f) — CB&S CHoe CMHG CPle CRos CShe EGol ELan ERav LAbb LNet LSav MBal MBri MR&S MWat NHol NWea SBla SHil SLon SMad SPer WPat
– 'Maderensis Variegata' — See I. ***aquifolium*** 'M.V.'
– 'Moira' (f) — LSav
– 'Mundyi' (m) — EGol SHil
– 'Nigrescens' (m) — MWat
– 'Purple Shaft' (f) — SHil WMou
– 'Ripley Gold' (f) — SSpi
– 'Silver Sentinel' — See I. x ***a.*** 'Belgica Aurea'
– 'W J Bean' (f) — LSav
– 'Wilsonii' (f) — CMHG IOrc IReg LSav MWat NWea SHil SMad

§ ***aquifolium*** — CB&S CKin CSco GRei LNet MBar MBri MGos MR&S MWat SHil SLon WMou
– 'Alaska' (f) — CMCN CRos EGol IHos LBuc NHol WMou
¶ – 'Alcicornis' (m) — LSav
– 'Amber' (f) — CBow COtt LSav NWea SHil SMad SPer
– 'Angustifolia' (m or f) — CB&S EHar IOrc MBar MWat SArc WThu WWeb
¶ – 'Angustimarginata Aurea' (m) — LSav
– 'Apricot' (f) — LSav
§ – 'Argentea Marginata' (f) — CB&S CBra CSam CSco CShe ECtt ENot ISea LSav MBri MGos MRav NWea SHil SPer SPla WAbe WPat
– 'Argentea Marginata Pendula' (f) — CBow CSco CShe EGol EHar LSav MBri SHil SLon SMad SPer SSpi WPat WWat WWeb
♦ – 'Argentea Pendula' (f) — See I. ***a.*** 'Argentea Marginata Pendula'
– 'Argentea Variegata' (f) — See I. ***a.*** 'Argentea Marginata'
– 'Atlas' (m) — CB&S CRos LBuc MBri
– 'Aurea Marginata' (f) — ECtt LSav WAbe WPat
¶ – 'Aurea Marginata Stricta' — LSav
♦ – 'Aurea Ovata' — See I. ***a.*** 'Ovata Aurea'
– 'Aurea-regina' — See I. ***a.*** 'Golden Queen'
– 'Aurifodina' (f) — IReg
§ – 'Bacciflava' (f) — CPle CSam ECtt EHar IOrc IReg ISea MBlu MBri MWat NHol SHil SPer SPla WMou
¶ – 'Cookii' (f) — LSav
– 'Crispa' (m) — CRos ISea MBal NHol
– 'Donningtonensis' (m) — CRos LSav
– 'Ferox' (m) — CBra CLan EHar ELan MBal SHil SMad
– 'Ferox Argentea' (m) — CBow CCla CMHG CRos EGol EHar ELan ERav IJoh IOrc ISea LNet LSav MBal MBar MBri MWat NHol NKay SHil SMad SPer SPla SReu
– 'Ferox Aurea' (m) — CBra CCla EGol EHar MR&S MWat SHil SPer
– 'Flavescens' (f) — CBot EHar EPla SHil
– 'Fructu-luteo' — See I. ***a.*** 'Bacciflava'
– 'Gold Flash' (f) — ECtt MBri
– 'Golden Milkboy' (m) — CB&S CHoe CRos CSco ENot IHos LNet LSav MBal MWat SHil SPer SReu WPat
– 'Golden Milkmaid' (f) — ELan IOrc
§ – 'Golden Queen' (m) — CB&S CShe ELan ENot IJoh LNet MBri NHol SHil SPer SReu
– 'Golden Tears' — ELan
– 'Golden van Tol' (f) — CB&S CBow CBra CSco ECtt ENot IJoh IOrc ISea LHol LNet MBal MBar MBri SHil SPer WMou
¶ – 'Grandis' — LSav
– 'Green Sentinel' (f) — LSav
* – 'Green Spire' — LSav SHil
– 'Handsworth New Silver' (f) — Widely available
§ – 'Hascombensis' — CLew CRos GDra LGre MBal MGos MPla NHol WDav WWat
¶ – 'Hastata' (m) — CRos EPla SMad
– 'Heterophylla Aureo-marginata' (m) — LSav
– 'Ingramii' (m) — CRos EHar SMad
– 'J C van Tol' (f) — CBow CSco EGol ELan ENot IDai IJoh IOrc MBal MBar MBri MGos MWat NHol NRoo NTow NWea SHil SMad SPer SReu SSta WMou WWat
– 'Madame Briot' (f) — CBow CSco EGol EHar ELan ENot IOrc LHol LSav MBal MBar MBri NHol NRoo SCro SHil SPer SSpi WAbe
§ – 'Maderensis Variegata' (m) — LSav SDry SHil
– 'Monstrosa' (m) — MWat
– 'Myrtifolia' (m) — CBow ELan IBar LSav MBar
– 'Myrtifolia Aureo-maculata' (m) — CBow CHoe CLan EHar LNet LSav NHol NWea SChu SHil SMad WPat
§ – 'Ovata Aurea' (m) — CBra CRos LSav SHil SSta
– 'Pendula' (f) — CRos MBri SHil SReu WMou
– 'Pendula Medio Picta' — See I. ***a.*** 'Weeping Golden Milkmaid'

§ – 'Pyramidalis' (f)	CBow CSco CShe ELan ENot GRei IHos LSav MBar MBri NHol NWea SHil SPer SReu WAbe WMou
– 'Pyramidalis Fructuluteo' (f)	CSco MBar SHil
– 'Recurva ' (m)	LSav MWat WWeb
¶ – 'Rubricaulis Aurea Variegata' (f)	CRos
¶ – 'Scotica'	CRos
– 'Silver King'	See I. *a.* 'Silver Queen'
– 'Silver Milkboy' (f)	CB&S CMHG ELan MBal MBri
– 'Silver Milkmaid' (f)	CHoe CMHG IJoh LSav NTow SHil SPer SSta
§ – 'Silver Queen' (m)	Widely available
– 'Silver van Tol' (f)	MBri SHil WMou
§ – 'Watereriana' (m)	CLan ISea LSav
– 'Waterer's Gold'	See I. *a.* 'Watereriana'
§ – 'Weeping Golden Milkmaid' (f)	LSav
x *attenuata*	CRos
– 'Sunny Foster' (f)	CRos LSav
buergeri	CMCN
cassine	IReg
ciliospinosa	CMCN CRos
¶ *colchica*	CRos
cornuta	CMCN CRos LSav SHil
– 'Burfordii' (f)	CRos LSav SHil
crenata	CBra CMCN LHol MGos SArc SReu WBod WWat
– 'Aureovariegata'	See I. *c.* 'Variegata'
– 'Compacta'	CMHG
*– 'Congesta'	CRos
– 'Convexa' (f)	ENot EPla GDra LSav MBal MBar NHol NWea SHil WPat
¶ – 'Firefly' (m)	LSav
– 'Fukarin'	See I. *c.* 'Shiro-fukurin'
– 'Golden Gem' (f)	Widely available
¶ – 'Green Island' (m)	EPla
¶ – 'Green Lustre' (m)	CRos
– 'Helleri' (f)	CRos LSav MBar
– 'Ivory Hall' (f)	CRos
– 'Mariesii' (f)	CFor CRos LSav MHig MPar MPla SIng WPat
– 'Microphylla'	CMHG CSam
¶ – *paludosa*	LSav
¶ – 'Piccolo' (f)	CRos
– 'Sentinel' (f)	CLew CMHG CSam
§ – 'Shiro-fukurin' (f)	CMHG LGre WPat
– 'Stokes' (m)	CRos NHol WPat
– upright form	CMCN
§ – 'Variegata'	CChu CRos MBar SMad WWat
¶ – *watanabeana* (f)	CRos
decidua	CMCN
* *dimorphophylla*	CChu LGre LSav
– 'Somerset Pixie'	SSpi
dipyrena	SArc
'Elegance' (f)	LSav
fargesii	SHil
ficoidea	CMCN
¶ *georgei*	CRos
¶ *glabra*	CRos
¶ – 'Leucocarpa'	LSav

¶ – 'Nana'	LSav
'Good Taste' (f)	CRos LSav
hascombensis	See I. *aquifolium* 'Hascombensis'
¶ *hookeri*	CMHG
'Indian Chief' (f)	CMHG CRos CSam SMad WWat
¶ *insignis*	CB&S
integra	LSav
¶ 'John T Morris'	CRos
kingiana	CRos SHil WWat
x *koehneana*	CBot CRos
– 'Chestnut Leaf'	CMCN EGol EHar EPla LSav MBri SHil SMad WMou
latifolia	CHEx CMCN SArc SHil SMad
'Lydia Morris' (f)	CMHG CSam EPla SHil WWat
macropoda	CMCN LSav
x *makinoi*	CMCN
x *meserveae*	ELan
– 'Blue Angel' (f)	CBow COtt CSco EBre ENot IOrc LSav MBri MMea MR&S MWat NHol NNor SPer SReu SSta WPat
– 'Blue Boy' (m)	CRos
¶ – 'Blue Girl' (f)	LSav
– 'Blue Prince' (m)	CB&S CHoe CMHG COtt CSco EBre IJoh IOrc MBar MBri MMea MR&S NHol SPer
– 'Blue Princess' (f)	CB&S CMHG COtt EGol ENot IJoh MBar MBri MMea MR&S NHol SPer SReu SSta WAbe
¶ – 'Blue Stallion' (m)	LSav
¶ – 'Goliath' (f)	CRos
*– 'Red Darling'	COtt CSco
muchagara	CMCN CRos LSav
¶ *myrtifolia*	LSav
'Nellie R Stevens' (f)	CRos ENot IHos SReu
opaca	CMCN CRos
¶ – 'Natalie Webster'	LSav
¶ – 'Villanova' (f)	CRos
pedunculosa	CMCN
perado latifolia	See I. *p. platyphylla*
§ – *platyphylla*	CB&S CHEx CMCN CRos
pernyi	CB&S CRos IOrc IReg MBal MBri SCro SHil SLon SMad SPer SPla WThu WWat WWeb
– 'Jermyns Dwarf' (f)	SHil
– *veitchii*	CMCN CRos NWea
poneantha	CMCN CRos LSav
'Pyramidalis'	See I. *aquifolium* 'Pyramidalis'
rotunda	CMCN
rugosa	CMCN
'September Gem' (f)	LSav
serrata	CMCN IReg
'Shin Nien' (m)	LSav
¶ 'Sparkleberry' (f)	CRos
verticillata (f)	CBow CRos ELan
– (m)	ELan
vomitoria	CMCN
x *wandoensis*	CMCN CRos
yunnanensis	CMCN

ILIAMNA (Malvaceae)

¶ *rivularis*	WOMN

ILLICIUM (Illiciaceae)

anisatum	CB&S CBot CChu CCla CFor CPle EPla LSav NHol SBor SHil SSpi SSta WPat WSHC WWat
– laurifolium	SSta
floridanum	CBow CChu CCla CFor LSav MBal SHil SSpi SSta WBod WWat
henryi	SHil SSpi SSta

IMPATIENS (Balsaminaceae)

aurigona	EBak
¶ 'Ballerina'	CSut
¶ 'Cardinal Red'	CSut
congolensis	CPle
double flowered forms	EBak
¶ 'Evening Blush'	CSut
glandulifera 'Candida'	EMon
hawkeri	EBak
New Guinea hybrids	EBak MBri
niamniamensis	EBak
¶ 'Salmon Princess'	CSut
¶ *scabrida*	WPer
¶ 'Strawberry Ripple'	CSut
tinctoria	CChu CGre CHil CPle CTre EMon LHil
walleriana	EBak MBri

IMPERATA (Gramineae)

cylindrica	SApp
– 'Red Baron'	See I. *c.* 'Rubra'
§ – 'Rubra'	CBos CChu CFor CHoe ECha ECro EFol EFou ELan EPla MBri SApp SAxl SBar SBla SChu SFar SPou SSpi WRus

INCARVILLEA (Bignoniaceae)

arguta	CChu CHan GWic IBrk LGre SBla SMrm SSpi WEas WOMN WWin
brevipes	See I. ***mairei***
compacta	WHoo
delavayi	Widely available
emodi	SBla
§ *mairei*	GDra GWic MBro MTho NHar NHol SBar WDav WPer
– 'Bees' Pink'	CAvo NSti
– 'Frank Ludlow'	GDra GEdr GLoc MTho
– *grandiflora*	MTho SBla WHoo
– 'Nyoto Sama'	GDra GEdr MTho NHol SBla
¶ – pink form	NHol
olgae	ELan LHop SMrm WHoo
¶ *sinensis*	WPer

INDIGOFERA (Leguminosae)

amblyantha	CPle GWic LGre SDry SSpi WKif WSHC WTay
dielsiana	CB&S CPle SSpi WSHC
gerardiana	See I. ***heterantha g.***
hebepetala	ECtt SHil WBod WSHC
§ *heterantha gerardiana*	Widely available
kirilowii	CGre LGre WSHC
potaninii	CSco SHil
pseudotinctoria	SHil

INDOCALAMUS (Gramineae(Bambuseae))

latifolius	SBam SDry
longiauritus	SBam SDry
solidus	SBam SDry WJun
§ *tessellatus*	EFul SBam SDry SHil

INULA (Compositae)

acaulis	MBro MHig MTho
conyzae	CKin WCla
¶ *crithmoides*	WHer
ensifolia	CBre CHan CLew CSam ELan IBlr LHop MPit MTho SFis SIng WEas WHal WHoo
– 'Compacta'	MBri NNrd WHen
– 'Gold Star'	ECtt LHil NNor NOak NVic WPer
glandulosa	See I. ***orientalis***
'Golden Beauty'	See BUPHTHALMUM ***salicifolium*** 'G.B.'
helenium	CArn CFis CKin CSev EEfi GPla GPoy LHol MChe MFir MSal NSel SIde WHal WHer WOak WPer WSto
hookeri	CBos ECha ELan EMon LHil MBri MFir MTho NHol NSti WEas WHal WOld WWin
magnifica	CHan CLew CSam EBre ECha ELan EMon ERou LHil MBri NHol WBon WHoo WOld
* 'Mediterranean Sun'	EPad WHil
§ *orientalis*	CHan CKel CSco ECro EFou GAbr MBri MBro NCat NNor WHoo WOld
racemosa	ECha EMon GWic NHol
rhizocephala	SIng WThu
– rhizocephaloides	CSun NHol
royleana	CHan CSam CSun GWic LSav MBri MBro NSti WDav WHil WHoo WPer

IOCHROMA (Solanaceae)

coelestis	CHil
¶ *cyaneum*	CHEx CHil
¶ *purpurea*	CHEx

IPHEION See **TRISTAGMA**

IPOMEA

¶ *quamoclit*	CHEx

IPOMOEA (Convolvulaceae)

learii	CHEx CKni CMer CSun GWic LAbb MNew SLMG
palmata	ECou
tuberosa	See MERREMIA ***t.***

IPOMOPSIS (Polemoniaceae)

aggregata	WDav

IRESINE (Amaranthaceae)

herbstii	EBak IBlr SLMG
– aureoreticulata	SLMG
lindenii	SLMG

IRIS † (Iridaceae)

'Abracadabra' (SDB)	LBro MS&S
'Abridged Version' (MTB)	NZep
'Ace of Clubs' (SDB)	NZep
'Action Front' (TB)	ERou MS&S SFis
'Actress' (TB)	EFou
acutiloba	ECam EPot LAma
– ***lineolata***	ECam
'Adobe Sunset' (Spuria)	LBro MS&S
'Adrienne Taylor' (MDB)	LBro WWin
* 'Ahakugyoruro'	CRow
'Alba' (***sibirica***)	CSun ECha EPar EWav GDra MAus NKay SBla
¶ ***albicans***	MAus
albomarginata	WChr
'Alien' (IB)	LBro
'Allegiance' (TB)	MAus WEas
'Alpine Lake' (MDB)	NZep
'Alsterquelle' (SDB)	NZep
'Amaranth Gem' (SDB)	LBro
'Amazon Princess' (SDB)	NZep
'Ambassadeur' (TB)	ERou
¶ 'Amber Blaze' (SDB)	NZep
'Amber Queen' (DB)	ECtt ELan
'American Heritage' (TB)	NZep
'Amethyst Flame' (TB)	EBre ERou MAus MS&S
'Amethyst Sunset' (MTB)	LBro
'Amigo' (TB)	SCro
'Amphora' (SDB)	CBro NNrd
'Ancilla' (Aril)	EPot
'Angel Eyes' (MDB)	LBlo
¶ 'Angel Unawares' (TB)	MAus
'Angelic' (SDB)	LBro MAus
'Angel's Kiss' (SDB)	NZep
'Angel's Tears'	See I. ***histrioides*** 'A.T.'
anglica	See I. ***latifolia***
'Ann Dasch' (***sibirica***)	EFou LBro
'Annabel Jane' (TB)	LBro MAus MBri
¶ 'Anne Marie Troeger' (***sibirica***)	LBro
'Annikins' (IB)	NZep
'Anniversary' (***sibirica***)	LBro
aphylla	MAus NOrc WThu
'Appledore' (SDB)	CBro
¶ 'Apricot Silk' (IB)	NZep
'April Ballet' (MDB)	LBro NZep
¶ 'April Sweetheart' (SDB)	NZep
'Apropos'	MAus
'Arabi Pasha' (TB)	MAus MS&S
'Arabi Treasure' (IB)	LBro MAus MS&S
'Arabic Night' (IB)	CHad MAus
'Archie Owen' (Spuria)	LBro MAus
'Arctic Star' (TB)	CShe
¶ 'Arctic Tern' (TB)	LBro
'Arctic Wine' (TB)	MAus
arenaria	See I. ***humilis***
'Arnold Sunrise' (CH)	LBro
'Arnold Velvet' (SDB)	LBro MS&S
'Arsonist' (TB)	NZep
'Art Gallery' (IB)	NZep
'Ask Alma' (IB)	LBro NZep
'Astralite' (SDB)	NZep
attica	CBro LAma WDav
¶ 'Auburn Valley' (SDB)	NZep
§ ***aucheri***	CBro EPot LAma WChr
'Audacious' (BB)	NZep
'Aunt Martha' (BB)	MAus
'Austrian Sky' (SDB)	CBot CCor CHad CSam EGol ELan LBro MAus MBri MS&S SIng
'Autumn Leaves' (TB)	MAus
'Avanelle' (IB)	EFou LBro
'Az Ap' (IB)	NZep
'Aztec Star' (SDB)	LBro
babadagica	SOkd
'Babe' (SDB)	NZep
'Baby Baron' (SDB)	NZep
'Baby Blessed' (SDB)	NZep
'Baccarat' (TB)	MAus
bakeriana	LAma LRHS SPou
¶ 'Ballerina'	SOkd
¶ 'Ballerina Blue'	ERou
'Ballyhoo'	MAus
'Banbury Fair' (CH)	LBro
'Banbury Melody' (CH)	LBro
'Banbury Ruffles' (SDB)	MAus MBri
'Bang' (TB)	MS&S
'Barbara's Kiss' (Spuria)	LBro
'Barbushka' (SDB)	LBro
'Baria' (SDB)	CBot LBro
'Barletta' (TB)	MAus
'Barnet Anley'	MAus
barnumae polakii (Oncocyclus)	See I. ***polakii***
'Baxteri' (***sibirica***)	CRow
¶ 'Bay Ruffles' (SDB)	NZep
'Be Dazzled' (SDB)	EFou LBro
'Beauty Mark' (SDB)	NZep
'Bee Wings' (MDB)	NZep WEas
'Belise' (Spuria)	LBro
'Benton Arundel' (TB)	SCro
'Benton Dierdre' (TB)	SCro
'Benton Lorna' (TB)	SCro
'Benton Nigel' (TB)	MAus
'Benton Sheila' (TB)	SCro
'Berkeley Gold' (TB)	CHar CSco EBre ECtt LHil MAus SPer
'Betsey Boo' (SDB)	NZep
'Betty Chatten' (TB)	MHig NNrd
'Betty Cooper' (Spuria)	LBro MS&S
'Betty Wood' (SDB)	LBro
'Bibury' (SDB)	MAus
'Birthstone' (TB)	NZep
'Black Forest' (TB)	MCot
'Black Hills' (TB)	MAus MBri MUlv
'Black Knight' (***chrysographes***)	CBot EBre ECha ELan GWic LHop MS&S NNor NOrc NSti WDav
'Black Lady' (MTB)	LBro
'Black Onyx' (TB)	MAus

¶ 'Black Star' (SDB)	NZep
'Black Swan' (TB)	EBre ELan MAus MS&S SPer SSus
'Black Velvet' (*chrysographes*)	ECha
'Black Watch' (IB)	NZep
'Blazing Saddles' (TB)	NZep
'Blitz' (SDB)	NZep
'Blockley' (SDB)	MAus
¶ 'Blood Dance' (SDB)	NZep
'Blue Asterisk' (IB)	LBro MS&S
¶ 'Blue Brilliant' (*sibirica*)	LSav
'Blue Denim' (SDB)	CBro CHar CSco EBre EGol ENot GLoc LBro LHil MAus MBri MS&S NNrd SIng WBon
'Blue Doll' (MDB)	NZep
'Blue Elegance' (Dutch)	LAma
'Blue Eyed Brunette'	LHil MAus
¶ 'Blue Hendred' (SDB)	MAus NBir
'Blue Icing' (IB)	NZep
'Blue King' (*sibirica*)	CKel
'Blue Line' (SDB)	NZep
¶ 'Blue Luster' (TB)	LBro
'Blue Magic' (Dutch)	LAma
'Blue Mere' (*sibirica*)	LBro LSav MCot
'Blue Moon' (SDB)	NZep
'Blue Petticoat' (TB)	MAus
'Blue Pigmy' (SDB)	CSco EPar MAus MBro MCot NBar SPer
'Blue Pools' (SDB)	EFou LBro NZep SCro
'Blue Rhythm' (TB)	CSco ERou MAus MBri MS&S SCro SPer
'Blue Sapphire' (TB)	CHad MAus
'Blue Shimmer' (TB)	CHar CRow ELan ENot MAus MS&S SCro SPer
'Blue Smoke' (TB)	MS&S
'Blue Sparks' (SDB)	LBro
'Blue Wind' (MDB)	NZep
'Blue Zephyr' (Spuria)	LBro
'Blushes' (IB)	NZep
'Bold Lassie'	MAus MBri
'Bold Print' (IB)	NZep
'Boo' (SDB)	MAus MBri NZep
'Born Graceful'	SSpi
'Bracknell' (*sibirica*)	CWGN
bracteata	MHig SIng
'Braithwaite' (TB)	EBre ELan ERou MBri SSus
'Brannigan' (SDB)	CBro EGol LHil NBir NNrd
'Brass Tacks' (SDB)	LBro MAus NZep
'Brassie' (SDB)	CRiv LBro LHil SIng
'Bright Bauble' (SDB)	NZep
¶ 'Bright Chic' (SDB)	NZep
'Bright Moment' (SDB)	LBro NZep
'Bright Spring' (DB)	EBre
'Bright Vision' (SDB)	NZep
'Bright White' (MDB)	CBro EPot LBro
'Bright Yellow' (DB)	EBre
'Brighteyes' (IB)	CCor CHar CSco ELan ENot EPar GLoc LBro LHil MAus MHig MS&S MTho SChu SCro
'Brilliant Excuse' (TB)	NZep
'Broad Grin' (SDB)	LBro NZep
'Broadleigh Ann' (CH)	CBro
'Broadleigh Dorothy' (CH)	CBro
'Broadleigh Emily' (CH)	CBro
'Broadleigh Florence' (CH)	CBro
'Broadleigh Joan' (CH)	CBro
'Broadleigh Lavinia' (CH)	CBro
'Broadleigh Mitre' (CH)	CBro
'Broadleigh Nancy' (CH)	CBro
'Broadleigh Peacock' (CH)	CBro
'Broadleigh Rose' (CH)	CBos CBro EOrc GWic SApp
'Broadleigh Sybil' (CH)	CBro SBar WBon
'Broadleigh Victoria' (CH)	CBro
'Broadway' (TB)	NZep
'Bromyard' (SDB)	MAus
'Bronze Bird' (TB)	CSco
'Bronze Cloud' (TB)	MS&S
'Bronze Perfection' (Dutch)	LAma
'Bronze Queen' (Dutch)	LAma LBlo
¶ 'Broseley' (TB)	LBro
'Brown Chocolate'	MAus
'Brown Doll' (IB)	NZep
'Brown Lasso' (BB)	LBro
'Brummit's Mauve'	MAus
'Bubbly Blue' (IB)	NZep
N ***bucharica***	CAvo CBro ECam EPar EPot ETub GLoc LAma LBow MBro NHol WChr WDav WHil WThu
¶ – x ***aucheri***	EPot
'Buckeye Blue' (SDB)	NZep
'Bumblebee Deelite' (MTB)	NZep
'Bunny Hop' (SDB)	NZep
'Burgundy Brown' (TB)	NZep
'Butter Pecan' (IB)	NZep
'Buttercup Bower' (TB)	MAus
'Buttercup Charm' (MDB)	NZep
'Buttered Chocolate' (Spuria)	LBro
'Butterpat' (IB)	NZep
'Butterscotch Kiss' (TB)	ELan ERou MAus MS&S
'Button Box' (SDB)	NZep
'Byword' (SDB)	LBro
caerulea	See I. ***albomarginata***
'Caesar' (*sibirica*)	CKel CSco LBro
'Caesar's Brother' (*sibirica*)	GWic MSta MUlv SPer WWin
'Caliente' (TB)	MAus
¶ 'California Style' (IB)	NZep
§ Californian hybrids	CChu CCla CGle EMon GAbr LHil MBal MPar NHol NSti SChu SSpi
'Camberley' (*sibirica*)	LSav
'Cambridge' (*sibirica*)	EFou LBro NHol
'Cambridge Blue' (Spuria)	MAus
'Camelot Rose' (TB)	MAus

'Campbellii'	See I. **lutescens** 'C.'
'Canary Bird' (TB)	LHil NZep
'Candy Apple' (SDB)	NZep
'Cantab' (Reticulata)	CAvo CBro ECam ELan EPar EPot ETub LAma LBlo LBow NHol SIng WChr WPer
'Can't Stop' (SDB)	NZep
'Capetown'	MAus
¶ 'Captain Gallant' (TB)	MAus
'Captive Heart' (SDB)	NZep
'Caramba' (TB)	NZep
'Caress' (SDB)	NZep
'Carilla' (SDB)	LBro
'Carnaby' (TB)	MAus
'Carnival Glass' (BB)	LBro
¶ 'Carnival Time' (TB)	EFou
'Carnton' (TB)	MAus WEas
'Carolyn Rose' (MTB)	LBro MS&S NZep
¶ 'Cascading Skies'	ERou
caucasica	ECam EPot WChr
'Celestial Glory' (TB)	MAus MBri
'Centre Court' (TB)	NZep
'Centrepiece' (SDB)	LBro
chamaeiris	See I. **lutescens**
– 'Campbellii'	See I. **lutescens** 'Campbellii'
'Champagne Music'	MAus
'Chantilly'	ELan SCro
'Chapeau' (TB)	MAus
'Chapel Hill' (SDB)	LBro
'Char True' (Spuria)	MAus
'Charm Song' (IB)	LBro
'Cheers' (IB)	EFou LBro MS&S NZep
'Cherry Falls' (TB)	LBro
'Cherry Gardens' (DB)	CBro CHar EBre EGol LHil MS&S
'Cherry Orchard' (TB)	NNor
'Cherub Tears' (SDB)	NZep
'Chickee' (MTB)	NZep
'Chief Chickasaw' (TB)	LBro
'Chief Moses' (TB)	MAus
'Chieftain' (TB)	EPar MAus
'Chinese Coral' (TB)	MAus
'Chione' (Aril)	WChr
'Chippendale' (TB)	NZep
* 'Chitosenotomo'	CRow
¶ 'Chivalry' (TB)	MAus SCro
'Christmas Angel' (TB)	EBre ECtt ERou MAus SSus
'Christmas Rubies' (TB)	NZep
¶ 'Christmas Tree' (TB)	NZep
chrysographes	CCla CGle CHad CSam ELan ELun EMNN GLoc LBro MAus MBal MTho NHol NNor SIng SWas WMar WWin
¶ – ***alba***	NBir
– black form	CHar CRow CSam EFou ELun EPot GAbr GDra GWic LGre MAus MBal MFir NHar NHol NNrd SBla SIng SPer WHoo
¶ – purple form	MAus
– red form	CSam MBal
¶ – yellow form	MAus
'Chubby Cheeks' (SDB)	NZep
'Chubby Cherub' (MDB)	NZep
'Circus Stripes' (TB)	NZep
¶ 'Cirrus'	LHil
'City Girl' (SDB)	NZep
'Clairette' (Reticulata)	CAvo CBro EPar LAma NHol SIng WChr
'Clap Hands' (DB)	LBro NZep
clarkei	CHan ELan NHol NNrd NWCA SCro WOld
¶ 'Classy Babe' (SDB)	NZep
'Clay's Caper' (SDB)	LBro MS&S
'Cliffs of Dover' (TB)	MCot MS&S
¶ 'Closed Circuit' (TB)	NZep
'Cloud Fluff' (IB)	LBro
¶ 'Cloudless Sunrise'	ERou
'Colonial Gold' (TB)	MAus
'Combo' (SDB)	LBro
¶ 'Comma' (SDB)	NZep
'Concord Touch' (SDB)	NZep
'Confederate Soldier' (IB)	LBro
confusa	CGle CHEx CHad CHan GWic LGre MTho MUlv SArc SIng
'Connoisseur' (Spuria)	EFou LBro
'Consummation' (MTB)	NZep
'Copper Classic' (TB)	NZep
¶ 'Coquette Doll' (SDB)	NZep
¶ 'Coral Chalice'	ERou
'Coral Strand'	MAus
'Corn Harvest' (TB)	NZep
'Cotaty' (BB)	LBro
'Cotton Blossom' (SDB)	EGol LBro NZep
'Court Magician' (SDB)	NZep
cretensis	See I. **unguicularis** 'Cretensis'
¶ 'Cricker Lane' (SDB)	NZep
'Crimson Velvet'	MAus
'Crispette' (TB)	MAus
¶ 'Crispin' (SDB)	NZep
cristata	CBro CSun ITim LAma NNrd SBar SIng SSpi WOMN
– ***alba***	CBro CFor LGre MBal SIng SWas
¶ – x ***lacustris***	CHan
'Crocus' (MDB)	NZep
'Croftway Lemon' (TB)	SCro
'Cross Stitch' (TB)	NZep
'Crushed Velvet' (TB)	MAus
'Crystal Bright' (SDB)	NZep
'Cup Race' (TB)	MAus NZep
'Curio' (MDB)	LBro
¶ 'Curlew' (IB)	SCro
'Cutie' (IB)	NZep
'Cycles' (TB)	NZep
cycloglossa	LRHS SOkd WChr
'Dainty Belle' (MDB)	NZep
'Daisy Powell' (TB)	MAus
'Dale Dennis' (DB)	LBro
'Dancer's Veil' (TB)	EBre EFou ELan ERou LBro MAus NVic SCro SPer SSus
'Dancing Eyes' (SDB)	LBro
'Dancing Gold' (MTB)	NZep
'Dancin'' (IB)	NZep

danfordiae	CAvo CB&S CBro ECam EPar EPot ETub LAma LBlo LBow LRoo MBri MS&S NHol NRya SIng WChr
'Dappled Pony' (MTB)	NZep
'Dardanus' (Aril)	EPot
'Daring Eyes' (MDB)	NZep
'Dark Blizzard' (IB)	NZep
'Dark Fairy' (SDB)	MAus
'Dark Fury' (TB)	MAus
¶ 'Dark Rosaleen' (TB)	LBro
'Dark Spark' (SDB)	MAus
* 'Dark Vader' (SDB)	NZep
'Darkover' (SDB)	LBro
'Dash Away' (SDB)	NZep
'Dawn Candle' (Spuria)	LBro
'Dawn Favour' (SDB)	LBro
'Debra Jean' (TB)	MAus
decora	NVic WDav
'Deep Black' (TB)	CHad CSco MAus SCro
'Deep Pacific' (TB)	MAus
'Deep Space' (TB)	MAus
'Deft Touch' (TB)	CHad MAus
delavayi	CKel EMon NKay SIng
– 'Didcot'	LBro MS&S
'Delicate Air' (SDB)	EGol LBro MAus MS&S
'Demon' (SDB)	EFou LBro
'Deputé Nomblot' (TB)	CShe LHil
'Derring Do' (SDB)	LBro MS&S
'Derry Down' (SDB)	LBro
'Derwentwater' (TB)	MAus MS&S
'Desert Dream' (AB)	GDra
¶ 'Desert Echo' (TB)	EFou
'Desert Quail' (MTB)	LBro
'Desert Song' (TB)	MAus
¶ 'Designer Gown'	ERou
'Dew Point' (IB)	LBro
'Die Braut' (DB)	See I. 'Bride'
'Diligence' (SDB)	NZep
¶ 'Disco Jewel' (MTB)	NZep
'Ditto' (MDB)	NZep
'Dixie Pixie' (SDB)	NZep
¶ 'Doll Dear' (SDB)	LBro
'Doll Dress' (TB)	MAus
'Doll Ribbons' (MTB)	NZep
'Doll Type' (IB)	EFou LBro NZep
¶ 'Dotted Doll' (MTB)	NZep
'Dotted Swiss'	MAus
'Double Lament' (SDB)	CBro LBro
'Douglas 402' (TB)	SCro
douglasiana	CChu CSun EMon EPar IBlr LBro MS&S MWgw NNrd NRed SSpi WDav WHoo
'Doxa' (IB)	LBro SCro
'Dragonfly' (*sibirica*)	CSun
'Dream Builder' (TB)	NZep
'Dreaming Spires' (*sibirica*)	LBro
'Dreaming Yellow' (*sibirica*)	LBro NRoo SCro WRus
'Dresden Candleglow' (IB)	CWGN MAus
'Dresden China'	CRow
'Driftwood' (Spuria)	LBro
¶ 'Dumpling' (MDB)	NZep
'Dunlin' (MDB)	CBro LHil
'Dusky Dancer' (TB)	MAus
dykesii	CRow
'Eagle's Flight' (TB)	NZep
'Early Edition' (IB)	LBro
¶ 'Early Light' (TB)	LBro
'Early Snowbird' (TB)	NZep
'East Indies' (TB)	EBre MAus MS&S
'Easy Grace'	MAus
'Easy Strolling' (SDB)	LBro NZep
¶ 'Eccentric' (SDB)	NZep
'Echo Pond' (MTB)	NZep
'Ecstatic Night' (TB)	MAus
'Edward' (Reticulata)	ECam LAma NHol WChr WPer
'Edward of Windsor' (TB)	CHad ELan ERou MAus SCro
'Ego' (*sibirica*)	EBre ECha MBri
'Egret Snow' (MDB)	NZep
'Eleanor's Pride' (TB)	MAus
'Elegans' (TB)	LHil MCot
'Elegante' (*laevigata* x)	CRow EGol
elegantissima	See I. ***iberica e.***
'Elixir' (Spuria)	LBro MS&S
¶ 'Elizabeth Poldark' (TB)	LBro
'Ellen Manor'	MAus
'Elusive Quest' (IB)	MAus
'Emerald Fountain'	MAus
'Emperor' (*sibirica*)	CB&S CBre CKel CRow EHon ERou LMay MAus MS&S MWgw NHol NKay
'Emphasis' (TB)	NZep
'Empress of India' (TB)	SFis
'Enchanted Blue' (SDB)	LBro NZep
'Enchanted Gold' (SDB)	NZep
§ ***ensata***	CB&S CCla CCor CHad CKel CMHG CWGN ELan LHil LMay MAus MBri MSta NRoo SHig SSpi WAbe WDav WWin
– 'Alba'	CBot CGle CRow CWGN ECha
– 'Apollo'	CRow
– 'Blue Peter'	CRow
– 'Galatea'	CRow CWGN
¶ – 'Gei-sho-ui'	CWGN
* – 'Glory of Aiichi'	EBre
– 'Hana-aoi'	CRow IBlr
¶ – 'Hatsu-shimo'	CRow IBlr
– 'Hercule'	CWGN
– Higo hybrids	CGle CRow IBlr LHop MSta SCro SPer SSpi
– 'Hokkaido'	CGle CRow CWGN
¶ – 'Kuma-funjin'	CWGN NHol
– 'Laced'	SPer
– 'Landscape at Dawn'	EHon
– 'Mandarin'	CRow
– 'Moonlight Waves'	CRow CWGN EGol EHon ELan GWic MAus NRoo SApp SCro SSpi WRus
– 'Nirihira'	CRow
¶ – 'Oku-banri'	CWGN NHol
– pale mauve	SPer
– 'Pink Frost'	CHad EBre
– purple	SPer
– 'Purple East'	CKni CRow CWGN NHol

– 'Rampo'	CRow
¶ – 'Rowden'	CRow
– 'Royal Purple'	CGle NHol
¶ – ruby form	MHig
– 'Variegata'	CRow CWGN ECha EGol EHon IBlr LMay MSta MUlv SBla WRus
¶ – 'Waka-muasaki'	WRus
– 'Yakontama'	CRow
¶ 'Eric the Red' (*sibirica*)	CB&S
'Essay' (Spuria)	LBro
'Esther Fay' (TB)	MAus
'Etched Apricot' (TB)	MAus
'Evening Pond' (MTB)	NZep
¶ 'Everything Plus'	ERou
ewbankiana	EPot
'Ewen' (*sibirica*)	EFou LBro
'Excelsior' (DB)	CSco CShe
'Exotic Gem' (TB)	MAus
'Exotic Isle' (TB)	NZep
'Exotic Shadow' (SDB)	LBro
¶ 'Eye Opener' (SDB)	NZep
'Eye Shadow' (SDB)	MAus
¶ 'Eyebright' (SDB)	MAus
¶ 'Fairy Footsteps' (SDB)	NZep
'Fairy Time' (IB)	LBro
¶ 'Fall Primrose' (TB)	LBro
'Fancy Capers' (IB)	MAus
¶ 'Fancy Tales' (TB)	NZep
'Fantasy Fair'	MAus
'Fantasy World' (IB)	LBro
'Farolito' (Spuria)	LBro
'Fashion Fling'	MAus
'Fashion Lady'	GLoc
'Fashion Show' (TB)	MAus
¶ 'Favorite Angel' (SDB)	NZep
'Feminine Charm' (TB)	MAus
¶ ***fernaldii*** JCA 11790	WDav
'Festive Skirt' (TB)	MAus
filifolia	CBro
'Fire and Flame' (TB)	MAus
'Fire One' (SDB)	LBro
'Firecracker' (TB)	EBre ERou MAus MS&S SCro SPer
'First Lilac' (IB)	LBro
¶ 'First Step' (SDB)	NZep
'First Violet' (TB)	MAus
'Flamenco' (TB)	NZep
'Flare Up' (TB)	MAus
'Flashing Beacon' (MTB)	NZep
¶ ***flavescens***	MAus
'Flea Circus' (MDB)	NZep
'Flight of Butterflies' (*sibirica*)	CRow CTom EBre EGol ELan MBri MS&S NRar WRus
'Flirty Mary' (SDB)	MAus
'Flivver' (IB)	NZep
'Florentina'	CArn CBro CRow EBre EFou Effi GPoy LBro LHil LHol
'Focus' (TB)	NZep
§ ***foetidissima***	Widely available
– ***chinensis***	See I. ***f. citrina***
§ – ***citrina***	CFis CRow ECha EFou EGol GWic MBal MWgw NSti SChu SSpi WOMN
– 'Fructo-alba'	EGol SCro
– 'Variegata'	Widely available
'Foggy Dew' (TB)	MAus
'Forest Light' (SDB)	CBro LBro NNrd
¶ ***formosana***	CHEx
¶ 'Forncett Moon' (*sibirica*)	EFou
forrestii	CHan CRow CSun CWGN ECam ELan EMNN EPar GDra GLoc GWic LHop LMay LSav MAus MBri NHol NNrd SSpi WAbe WCla WDav
¶ – L 1696	SSpi
forrestii x ***chrysographes***	GDra NBir
¶ 'Fort Regent' (TB)	LBro
'Forte' (SDB)	NZep
'Foxfire' (TB)	MAus
'Fracas' (SDB)	NZep
'Frank Elder' (Reticulata)	LAma NHol WChr
'Fresno Flash' (TB)	NZep
'Fresno Frolic' (TB)	NZep
'Friendly Welcome' (*sibirica*)	LBro
'From the Heart' (IB)	NZep
'Frost and Flame' (TB)	CHar EBre ELan ERou MAus MFir MS&S SCro SPer
'Frosty Crown' (SDB)	NZep
'Full Time'	MAus
fulva	CFor GWic MUlv NSti SSpi WEas WWat
x ***fulvula***	CCor CFor GWic MAus WRus
'Fun Time' (SDB)	MAus MS&S
¶ 'Funny Face' (MDB)	NZep
'Furnaceman' (SDB)	CBro
'Gala Gown' (TB)	MAus
§ ***galatica bracteata***	EPot LAma WChr
¶ 'Galillee' (TB)	MAus
'Galleon Gold' (SDB)	NZep
¶ 'Garden Gnome' (MDB)	NZep
gatesii	EPot LAma
'Gatineau' (*sibirica*)	GDra
'Gay Prince' (TB)	MS&S
'Gay Trip' (TB)	MS&S NZep
'Gemini' (BB)	MAus
'George' (Reticulata)	CAvo CBro EPar EPot ETub LBow NHol SIng WChr
'Gerald Darby' (x ***robusta***)	CBro CCor CFis CRow ECha EFol EGol ELun EPar GWic LSav MS&S MUlv SApp SCro SHig SSpi WEas WRus
germanica	LBro NNor
– 'Kochii'	GWic
'Gigglepot' (SDB)	NZep
'Gilston Guitar' (TB)	MAus
'Gilston Gulf' (TB)	MAus
¶ 'Gingerbread Castle' (TB)	MAus
'Gingerbread Man' (SDB)	EFou LBro LGre LHil MAus MS&S

'Glad Rags' (TB)	NZep
'Gleaming Gold' (SDB)	MAus
'Gleanings' (SDB)	NZep
¶ 'Glee Club' (IB)	NZep
'Glen' (TB)	MS&S
'Going My Way' (TB)	MAus NZep
'Gold Burst' (TB)	NZep
¶ 'Gold Canary' (MDB)	NZep
'Gold Flake' (TB)	MS&S
¶ 'Gold Galore' (TB)	NZep
'Gold Intensity' (BB)	LBro
'Golden Alps' (TB)	ENot MAus
'Golden Chord'	MAus
'Golden Dewdrops' (SDB)	LBro
'Golden Emperor' (Dutch)	LBlo
'Golden Encore' (TB)	MAus NZep
¶ 'Golden Eyelet' (MDB)	NZep
¶ 'Golden Fair' (DB)	NBir SIng
'Golden Forest' (TB)	MAus
'Golden Harvest' (Dutch)	CB&S LAma LRoo
'Golden Hind' (TB)	MAus
'Golden Lady' (Spuria)	LBro
'Golden Muffin' (IB)	LBro NZep
'Golden Planet' (TB)	MS&S
'Golden Ruby' (SDB)	LBro NZep
'Golden Spice' (TB)	LBro
'Golden Starlet' (SDB)	LBro
'Good Morning America' (TB)	NZep
'Good Nature' (Spuria)	LBro
'Gordon' (Reticulata)	LAma LBow MS&S NHol
'Gosau' (TB)	MAus
'Gossamer Steel'	MAus
gracilipes	CRiv GLoc MBal WOMN
– ***alba***	SWas
¶ 'Graclac'	SIng
graeberiana	EPot
graminea	Widely available
¶ – 'Hort's Variety'	GWic
'Grandpa's Girl' (MTB)	LBro NZep
¶ 'Grape Orbit' (SDB)	NZep
¶ 'Grapelet' (MDB)	NZep
¶ 'Grapesicle' (SDB)	NZep
'Graphic Arts' (TB)	NZep
'Green Halo' (DB)	EGol LBro MS&S
'Green Ice' (TB)	MS&S
'Green Jungle' (TB)	LBro
'Green Spot' (IB)	CBot CChu CHar ECtt ELan GLoc LBro LHil MAus MBri MHig MWat NNrd SChu SCro SPer SWas WEas
'Gringo' (TB)	MAus
'Gudrun' (TB)	ERou SPer
'Gypsy Boy' (SDB)	NZep
'Gypsy Eyes' (SDB)	NZep
'Gypsy Jewels' (TB)	MAus
'H C van Vliet' (Dutch)	LAma
¶ 'Hafnium' (SDB)	NZep
'Hagari's Helmet' (IB)	LBro
'Happening' (SDB)	NZep
'Happy Choice' (Spuria)	LBro
'Happy Crowd' (SDB)	NZep
'Happy Mood' (IB)	LBro
'Happy Song' (BB)	NZep
'Harbor Blue' (TB)	MAus MBri MWat
'Harlow Gold' (IB)	NZep
'Harmony' (Reticulata)	CAvo CBro ECam EPot ETub LAma LBlo LBow LRoo MBri NHol SIng WChr
¶ ***hartwegii columbiana***	WDav
'Harvest Festival' (SDB)	LBro
'Hazy Skies' (MTB)	LBro
'Headlines'	MAus
'Heather Hawk'	MAus
'Heavenly Blue' (***sibirica***)	CKel CSco EHon LMay MAus
'Helen Astor' (***sibirica***)	CHar CRow CSco CWGN GAbr GDra
'Helen Proctor' (IB)	NZep
'Helen Traubel' (TB)	MAus
'Helge'	SFis
'Hellcat' (IB)	NZep
'Hercule' (Reticulata)	CRow LAma NHol WChr
¶ 'Hermosa Rose' (SDB)	NZep
'High Barbaree' (TB)	MAus
'High Command' (TB)	LHil MS&S SCro
¶ 'Highland Cascade' (TB)	MAus
'Hildegarde' (Dutch)	LAma
'Hills of Lafayette' (IB)	NZep
histrio aintabensis	LAma MPar NHol
histrioides	MS&S
§ – 'Angel's Tears'	EPot LAma WChr
– 'Lady Beatrix Stanley'	SOkd SPou
– 'Major'	CBro ECam EPar EPot LAma LBlo LBow MBal MBri NRya WChr
– ***sophenensis***	LRHS SPou WChr
'Hocus Pocus' (SDB)	LBro
'Holden Clough'	CBot ELan ELun GWic LBro MAus MUlv MWgw NHol NSti SApp SSpi WRus
¶ 'Holiday Flame' (IB)	NZep
'Honey Glazed' (IB)	EFou LBro NZep
'Honeydip' (SDB)	NZep
'Honington' (SDB)	MAus MBri
'Honorabile' (MTB)	MAus
'Hoodwink' (SDB)	LBro NZep
hoogiana	EPot ETub LAma LBow MTho NHol WChr WThu
– ***alba***	EPot
– 'Bronze Beauty'	EPot
– ***purpurea***	LRHS WChr
¶ ***hookeriana***	NWCA
'Hot Fudge' (IB)	NZep
'Hot Spice' (IB)	NZep
'Hugh Miller' (TB)	MAus
'Hula Doll' (MDB)	LBro
§ ***humilis***	SIng SOkd WThu
Hyrcana group (Reticulata)	CBro EPot LAma LBow WChr
'I Do' (TB)	NZep
§ ***iberica***	EPot
– ***elegantissima***	ECam EPot
'Ice Chip' (SDB)	NZep
'Ida' (Reticulata)	LAma NHol WChr

'Ideal' (Dutch)	LAma
'Immortal Hour'	MAus
'Impelling' (BB)	LBro
'Imperator' (Dutch)	CB&S LBlo
'Imperial Bronze' (Spuria)	MAus
'Impetuous' (BB)	LBro
'Indeed' (IB)	LBro NZep
'Indian Chief' (TB)	ENot MAus MBri MS&S
'Indian Jewel' (SDB)	LBro
'Indian Pow Wow' (SDB)	LBro
'Ingenuity' (SDB)	LBro
innominata	CCla CGle CRow ECha EPar EPot GLoc ITim MCot MHig MTho MWgw NNrd NRed NSti NTow SIng WCla WEas
– 'Doctor Riddle's Form'	CSun GDra LSav MBal
¶ – rose form	MHig
– 'Spinners'	SSpi SWas
'Inscription' (SDB)	LBro NZep
'Inshriach' (***chrysographes***)	GDra
¶ 'Instructor'	ERou
'Interpol'	MAus
'Invisible Ink' (MDB)	NZep
'Iris King' (TB)	ERou
'Irish Doll' (MDB)	EGol LBro MAus
'Irish Lullaby' (TB)	MAus
'Ishmael' (SDB)	LBro
'Ivory Gown' (TB)	MAus
'J S Dijt' (Reticulata)	CAvo CBro ECam EPar EPot LAma LBlo LBow MBri MS&S NHol SIng WChr
'Jack o' Hearts' (SDB)	LBro
'Jade Mist' (SDB)	LBro MS&S
'Jan Reagan' (SDB)	NZep
'Jana White'	MAus
'Jane Phillips' (TB)	CHad CSco CShe EBre ELan ENot ERou LBro MAus SChu SCro SPer SSus
'Jane Taylor' (SDB)	CBro NNrd
'Janice Chesnik' (Spuria)	LBro MS&S
'Janice Ruth'	MAus
japonica 'Ledger's Variety'	CAvo CBro CHad CHan CRow CSco CSun ECha ELan EPar GWic MBro MUlv NHol SCro SIng SSpi WEas WHoo WOMN WWat
– 'Rudolph Spring'	GWic
– 'Variegata'	CBot CHan CRow ECha EFol EPar GPla GWic LBro LHop MBal MPar MUlv NHol NOrc NRar NSti SBla WHer WWin
'Jared' (SDB)	NZep
'Jasper Gem' (MDB)	LBro MS&S
'Jean Guymer' (TB)	LBro NZep
'Jeannine (Reticulata)	LAma LRHS WChr
'Jeremy Brian' (SDB)	NZep
'Jersey Lilli' (SDB)	MAus MBri
'Jesse's Song' (TB)	NZep
'Jewel Baby' (SDB)	NZep
¶ 'Jill Welch' (MTB)	NZep
'Joan Lay' (TB)	CSco
'Joanna Taylor' (MDB)	CBro MAus NZep
'Joette' (MTB)	LBro
'Jolly Fellow' (SDB)	LBro
'Joyce' (Reticulata)	CBro ECam ELan EPar EPot LAma MBri NHol SIng WChr
'Joyce McBride' (SDB)	NZep
'Joyce Terry' (TB)	MAus
'Joyful' (SDB)	LBro NZep
'Joyous Isle' (SDB)	LBro NZep
'Jungle Fires' (TB)	MAus
'Jungle Shadows' (BB)	MAus
¶ 'Jungle Warrior' (SDB)	NZep
'Just Jennifer' (BB)	LBro MAus
'Just So' (SDB)	MAus
kaempferi	See I. ***ensata***
'Karen Maddock' (TB)	LBro
'Kashmir White'	EGol LAma
¶ 'Kate Izzard'	LHil
'Katharine Hodgkin' (Reticulata)	CAvo ECam EPot GEdr LAma LBow MBro MTho NHar NHol SIng SOkd WChr
'Katy Petts' (SDB)	MAus MBri NZep
'Kayo' (SDB)	EFou LBro MAus MS&S NZep
kemaonensis	GDra WDav
'Kent Pride' (TB)	CSco EBre EFou ERou SPer
'Kentucky Bluegrass' (SDB)	EFou EGol LBro NZep WWin
kerneriana	CBro ELan EPot LBro LSav MWgw NRed WEas
'Kharput'	EGol LBro
'Kildonan' (TB)	MAus
¶ 'Kirkstone' (TB)	MAus
'Kista' (SDB)	MAus MBri
¶ 'Kiwi Capers' (SDB)	NZep
klattii	See I. ***spuria musulmanica***
'Knick Knack' (MDB)	CCor ELan GLoc MAus MHig NNrd SChu
'Knotty Pine' (SDB)	MAus
'Kochii'	See I. ***germanica*** 'K.'
kolpakowskiana	ECam EPot LAma WChr
kopetdagensis	EPot WChr
korolkowii violacea	WChr
kuschakewiczii	ECam EPot
'La Nina Rosa' (BB)	MAus
'La Senda' (Spuria)	MAus
'Laced Lemonade' (SDB)	LBro
lactea	MAus
lacustris	CRiv EPot GLoc MCot NKay NWCA WHil WMar WOMN WPat
– x ***gracilipes***	SWas WOMN
'Lady Bell' (MTB)	LBro
¶ 'Lady Friend'	ERou
'Lady Ilse'	MAus
'Lady Mohr' (AB)	MAus
'Lady of Nepal' (IB)	LBro NZep
§ ***laevigata***	CHad CRow ECha EGol EHon ELan LMay MAus MSta NBar SHig SSpi WDav
– 'Alba'	CRow CWGN EGol LMay

– 'Atropurpurea' CRow EGol IBlr LMay MSta SBar
– 'Colchesterensis' CRow CWGN EGol EHon LMay MSta
– 'Dorothy' CWGN MSta
– 'Midnight' CRow CWGN EGol
– 'Monstrosa' EGol
– 'Mottled Beauty' CRow MSta
– 'Richard Greeny' CRow
– 'Rose Queen' See I. 'R.Q.'
– 'Snow Drift' See I. 'S.D.'
– 'Variegata' CBot CChu ECha EGol EHon EWav LMay MSta SSpi WWat
– 'Violet Garth' CRow
– 'Weymouth' CRow CWGN EGol
'Langport Chief' (IB) MS&S
'Langport Chimes' (IB) NZep
'Langport Finch' (IB) MS&S NZep
'Langport Flame' (IB) MS&S
'Langport Girl' (IB) MS&S NZep
'Langport Kestrel' (IB) EPar
'Langport Lady' (IB) LHil
'Langport Magic' (IB) MS&S
'Langport Minstrel' (IB) NZep
'Langport Prince' (IB) MS&S
'Langport Romance' (IB) NZep
'Langport Secret' (IB) EPar
'Langport Smoke' (IB) MS&S
'Langport Storm' (IB) EFou
'Langport Vale' (IB) EPar MS&S
'Langport Warrior' (IB) MS&S
'Langport Wren' (IB) CBro LGre LHop MS&S
'Langthorn's Pink' (*sibirica*) ELan
¶ ***latifolia*** SAxl
– alba ELan
'Laurenbuhl' (*sibirica*) SCro
'Lavanesque' (TB) MAus
¶ 'Lavender Ribbon' ERou
'Lavendula Plicatee' CBro
§ ***lazica*** CAvo CBro EPot MUlv NHol NSti SChu SPou SWas WEas WRus
¶ 'Lemon Blossom' (SDB) NZep
'Lemon Brocade' MAus
¶ 'Lemon Charm' (SDB) NZep
'Lemon Flame' MCot
'Lemon Flare' (SDB) EGol LBro MAus MS&S
'Lemon Flurry' (IB) LBro
'Lemon Ice' (TB) EPar
'Lemon Lark' (SDB) NZep
'Lemon Mist' (TB) MAus
'Lemon Puff' (MDB) CBro LBro NZep
'Lemon Queen' (Dutch) LBlo
'Lemon Tree' (TB) MAus
'Letitia' (*sibirica*) WThu
'Libation' (MDB) LBro
'Light Cavalry' (IB) NZep
¶ 'Lighten Up' (SDB) NZep
'Lilac and Lavender' (SDB) NZep
'Lilac Festival' (TB) MAus
'Lilac Lulu' (SDB) NZep
'Lilac Mist' (TB) MAus
'Lilli-White' (SDB) EBre EGol EPar LBro MAus NNrd
'Lima Colada' (SDB) NZep
'Lime Grove' (SDB) EPar SCro
'Lime Heart' (*sibirica*) EBre ELan LBro MBri SPer SSus WRus
'Lime Ripples' (IB) MAus
'Limelight' (*sibirica*) EFou
'Liquid Smoke' EFou
'Liquorice Stick' MAus
'Listowell' (IB) LBro
'Little Amigo' (SDB) NZep
'Little Annie' (SDB) NZep
'Little Bill' (SDB) EFou
'Little Bishop' (SDB) NZep
'Little Black Belt' (SDB) EFou LBro MS&S NZep
'Little Blackfoot' (SDB) CHad MAus MBri MS&S
'Little Chestnut' (SDB) LBro MAus
'Little Cottage' (IB) SCro
'Little Dandy' (SDB) MAus
'Little Dogie' (SDB) LBro
'Little Dream' (SDB) NZep
'Little Episode' (SDB) NZep
'Little Paul' (MTB) LBro
'Little Pearl' (MDB) NZep
'Little Rosy Wings' (SDB) LBro MS&S SCro
'Little Shadow' (IB) CSco EBre LBro MAus MS&S
'Little Sheba' (AB) MAus
¶ 'Little Sir Echo' (BB) MAus
'Little Snow Lemon' (IB) NZep
'Little Vanessa' MAus
'Little Wonder' (IB) EFou
'Live Jazz' (SDB) NZep
'Lively Rose' (MTB) LBro
'Living Desert' (TB) NZep
'Llanthony' (SDB) MAus NZep
'Lodestar' (TB) LBro MS&S
'Lodore' (TB) MAus
'Logo' (IB) NZep
'Lollipop' (SDB) NZep
¶ ***longipetala*** NBir
'Lookin' Good' (IB) NZep
'Lord Warden' (TB) EFou GPla
'Lord Wolsely' (Spuria) LBro
'Lorna Lee' (TB) MAus
¶ ***lortetii*** SIng
'Los Angeles' MAus
'Lothario' (TB) MS&S
'Loud Mouth' (AB) LBro
'Loud Music' MAus
'Louise Hopper' (MTB) NZep
'Love Lisa' (SDB) NZep
'Lovely Again' (TB) MAus
'Lovely Letty' (TB) MAus
'Lovely Light' MAus
¶ 'Lovely Me' (SDB) NZep
'Loveshine' (SDB) NZep
'Love's Allure' (TB) NZep
'Low Snow' (SDB) NZep
'Lucinda' (TB) MS&S

'Lucky Charm' (MTB) LBro
'Lucky Duck' (SDB) NZep
'Lunar Fire' (TB) MAus
'Luscious One' (SDB) LBro
lutescens LHil MAus NRed SIng WChr WDav
§ – 'Campbellii' CBro EGol EPar MHig NBar NNrd WDav
– ***cyanea*** NKay
– 'Jackanapes' NKay
§ – 'Nancy Lindsay' CAvo
'Lydia Jane' (Spuria) LBro
'Lynn Hall' (TB) MS&S
'Mabel Cody' (*sibirica*) LBro
¶ ***macrosiphon*** WDav
'Madeira Belle' MAus
¶ 'Mademoiselle Yvonne Pelletier' (TB) MAus
'Magenta and Peach' MAus
¶ 'Maggie Me Darlin'' (MTB) NZep
'Magic Flute' (MDB) LBro
¶ 'Magic Man' (TB) LBro
magnifica EPot WChr WDav WThu
– ***alba*** WDav
'Mahogany Rush' (TB) NZep
'Mahogany Snow' (SDB) NZep
'Mandarin' (TB) GDra SBla
'Mandarin Purple' (***chrysographes***) GWic SPer
¶ ***maracandica*** EPot
'Marcus Perry' (*sibirica*) CRow LSav
'Margot Holmes' (***chrysographes***) GDra GWic
'Marhaba' (MDB) CBro
'Maritima' (Spuria) CCor
'Marmalade Skies' (BB) LBro MS&S NZep
'Maroon Caper' (IB) MAus
¶ 'Marshlander' (TB) EFou SCro
'Marty' (IB) LBro
'Mary Frances' (TB) MAus
'Mary McIlroy' (DB) CBro
'Mary Randall' (TB) ERou MAus MS&S SSus
'Maui Moonlight' (IB) NZep
'May Melody' (TB) MAus
'Meadow Court' (SDB) CBro CHad EPar
'Meadow Moss' (SDB) EGol
'Media Luz' (Spuria) LBro MAus
'Melbreak' (TB) EBre ERou MAus MS&S
mellita See I. ***suaveolens***
– ***rubromarginata*** See I. ***suaveolens***
'Melon Honey' (SDB) LBro MS&S NZep WWin
'Memphis Delight' (TB) MAus
'Merry Day' (IB) MS&S
¶ 'Merseyside' (SDB) LHil
'Michael Paul' (SDB) NZep
'Midas Kiss' (IB) LBro
¶ 'Midnight Fire' ERou
'Midnight Madness' (SDB) NZep
¶ ***milesii*** NBir
¶ 'Mill Pond' (MDB) LBro
'Mini Dynamo' (SDB) NZep
'Minnie Colquitt' (TB) MAus MS&S SCro
'Mirror Image' (TB) NZep
'Mission Sunset' (TB) EBre MAus
'Missouri Gal' (Spuria) LBro
missouriensis CRow SIng WDav
'Mister Roberts' (SDB) LBro NZep
'Mockingbird' (MTB) MS&S
¶ 'Monaco' (TB) EFou
monnieri SDix
'Moon Shadows' (SDB) MAus
'Moonlight' (TB) EGol LBro MAus NNor NNrd
'Moonlight Waves' See I. ***ensata*** 'M.W.'
'Morning Sunlight' (TB) MAus
'Mrs Nate Rudolph' (SDB) EFou LBro
'Mrs Perry' (*sibirica*) MAus
'Mrs Rowe' (*sibirica*) CBre CRow EFou LBro
'Mrs Saunders' (*sibirica*) CBre CRow
'Muffin' (IB) NZep
'Mulberry Rose' (TB) MS&S
'Muriel Neville' (TB) MAus
'Murmuring Morn' (TB) MAus
'Music Box' (SDB) NZep
'Music Caper' (SDB) LBro
'Music Maker' (TB) MS&S
'My Girl Friend' (TB) NZep
'My Honeycomb' (TB) MAus
'My Mary' (TB) MS&S
'my seedling' (DB) CBro
¶ 'My Smoky' (TB) SCro
'Myra's Child' (SDB) MAus
'Nambe' (MTB) LBro
¶ 'Nampara' (TB) LBro
'Nancy Hardy ' (MDB) CBro
'Nancy Lindsay' See I. ***lutescens*** 'N.L.'
¶ 'Narnia' (SDB) NZep
'Nashborough' (TB) MAus MBri MS&S
'Natascha' (Reticulata) EPot ETub LAma LBlo NHol SIng WChr WPer
'Navy Doll' (MDB) NZep
'Nectar' (TB) MS&S
¶ 'Neon Pixie' (SDB) NZep
'Neophyte' (Spuria) LBro
nepalensis See I. ***decora***
nertschinskia See I. ***sanguinea***
'New Idea' (MTB) LBro MAus MS&S
'New Snow' (TB) ENot MAus
'New Wave' (MTB) NZep
'Nice 'n' Nifty' (IB) NZep
nicolai ECam EPot LRHS WChr
'Night Shift' (IB) NZep
'Nightfall' SFis
'Nineveh' (AB) MAus MS&S NSti
'Normandie' (TB) MAus
'Nottingham Lace' (*sibirica*) LBro MAus
'Nuggets' (MDB) NZep
nusairiensis LRHS WChr
'Nylon Ruffles' (SDB) EGol LBro
ochroleuca See I. ***orientalis***
¶ 'Offenham' (TB) LBro
¶ 'Oh Jay' (SDB) NZep

'Ohio Belle' (SDB) NZep
'Ola Kala' (TB) CSco ERou MAus SCro SFis
'Old Flame' (TB) NZep
'Oliver' (SDB) LBro MAus MS&S NSti
'Olympic Torch' (TB) LHil MAus MS&S
'On Fire' (SDB) NZep
'One Desire' (TB) MAus NZep
'Open Sky' (SDB) NZep
'Orange Caper' (SDB) NZep
¶ 'Orange Dawn' (TB) LBro
'Orange Empire' (TB) NZep
'Orange Maid' (Spuria) LBro
¶ 'Orange Tiger' (SDB) NZep
¶ 'Orangerie' ERou
'Orchid Flare' (MDB) EPar
orchioides WChr
¶ 'Oregold' (SDB) NZep
'Oriental Blush' (SDB) LBro
'Oriental Glory' (TB) MAus
§ ***orientalis*** CBot CCor CHan CRiv CRow ELan LBro LMay MAus MBal MWgw NHol SChu SCro SDix WWat WWin
– 'Alba' See I. ***sanguinea*** 'A.'
'Ornament' (SDB) LBro MS&S NZep
'Oroville' (Spuria) LBro
'Orville Fay' (***sibirica***) EFou LBro MAus SCro
'Ottawa' (***sibirica***) CCla CHad CKel CRiv CRow ELan ERou EWav LSav MS&S NRoo SChu SCro SPer WRus
'Ouija' (BB) LBro
¶ 'Out Yonder' (TB) MAus
'Outstep' (SDB) NZep
'Owlet' (SDB) MAus
'Pacer' (IB) NZep
'Pacific Coast Hyb' See I. Californian Hybrids
'Pagan Princess' (TB) MAus
'Painted Rose' (MTB) LBro
'Palamino' MAus
'Pale Primrose' (TB) CHad MAus WEas
'Pale Suede' (SDB) LBro
pallida LHol MAus
– 'Argentea Variegata' CGle CHad CKel ERav LHop MUlv NRoo SDix SSpi WHoo WRus
– 'Aurea' See I. ***p.*** 'Variegata'
– 'Aurea Variegata' See I. ***p.*** 'Variegata'
– ***dalmatica*** See I. ***pallida pallida***
§ – ***pallida*** CBot CBre CCla EBre EGol MAus MBri MUlv MWgw NSti SDix SPer
N– 'Variegata' Widely available
– x ***tectorum*** MPar
pamphylica LAma WChr
¶ 'Panda' (MTB) NZep
'Papillon' (***sibirica***) CCla CHad EBre ELan LHop MAus MUlv NHol WHea WRus
¶ 'Paradise' (TB) LBro
¶ 'Paradise Bird' (TB) LBro
'Paradise Pink' (TB) CSco
paradoxa ECam EPot
– ***choschab*** ECam
'Parakeet' (MTB) LBro
'Paricutin' (SDB) CBro NNrd
'Party Dress' (TB) CHad EBre ELan ENot ERou MAus MS&S SPer WAbe
parvula ECam
'Passport' (BB) MAus MS&S
¶ 'Patacake' (SDB) NZep
'Path of Gold' (DB) CBro LBro MAus NNrd WHil
'Patterdale' (TB) MAus MS&S NBar NVic
'Pauline' (Reticulata) CAvo CBro ECam EPot LAma MS&S SIng WChr
¶ 'Peach ala Mode' (BB) MAus
¶ 'Peach Band' ERou
'Peach Float' (TB) CHad MAus
'Peach Spot' (TB) MAus
'Peach Sundae' (TB) NZep
'Peaches 'n' Topping' (BB) LBro
'Peachy Face' (IB) LBro NZep
¶ 'Peacock' LGre
'Pearl Queen' (***sibirica***) MCot
'Pearly Dawn' (TB) CCla CHad ECtt MS&S NVic SPer SSus
'Pecan Spot' (SDB) NZep
'Pegasus' (TB) SCro
¶ 'Peggy Chambers' (IB) EFou
'Pennies' (MDB) NZep
'Penny Bunker' LBro
'Penny Candy' (MDB) NZep
'Peppermint Twist' (SDB) NZep
'Perry's Blue' (***sibirica***) CB&S CCla CHar CKel CWGN EFou EPar GAbr GDra MWgw NKay NOrc SCro SPer WHea WRus WWat
'Perry's Favourite' (***sibirica***) CBre CRow
'Perry's Pygmy' (***sibirica***) CRow LSav
'Persian Doll' (MDB) NZep
'Persian Fancy' (TB) NZep
persica LAma
'Persimmon' (***sibirica***) EBre MAus
'Pet' (SDB) NZep
'Pigmy Gold' (IB) LBro MAus
'Pink Bubbles' (BB) LBro NZep
'Pink Clover' (TB) LBro
'Pink Kitten' (IB) LBro NZep
'Pink Lavender' (TB) SCro
'Pink Pleasure' (TB) NZep
'Pink Pussycat' MAus
'Pink Randall' (TB) SCro
'Pinnacle' (TB) MAus MS&S
'Piper's Flute' (TB) NZep
'Piper's Tune' (IB) NZep
'Pipes of Pan' (TB) MAus
'Pippi Longstockings' (SDB) NZep
'Pirate Prince' (***sibirica***) LBro
'Pixie Plum' (SDB) MAus
'Pixie Princess' (SDB) MAus
'Play Girl' MAus
¶ ***plicata*** MAus
'Poet' (TB) NZep
'Pogo' (SDB) EBre EGol ELan ENot MAus MBri NZep SCro

Name	Suppliers
'Pogo Doll' (AB)	LBro
¶ 'Polly Dodge' (*sibirica*)	LBro
'Pony' (IB)	LBro MS&S
'Port of Call' (Spuria)	LBro
'Pot Luck' (IB)	LBro MS&S
'Prairie Sunset' (TB)	MS&S
'Praise the Lord' (TB)	MAus
'Pretender' (TB)	MAus
'Primrose Drift' (TB)	MAus
'Prince' (SDB)	EFou LBro
'Princely' (TB)	MAus
'Princess Beatrice'	See I. ***pallida pallida***
prismatica	CBre CElw CSun EPot SWas
¶ 'Priviledged Character' (SDB)	NZep
'Prodigy' (MDB)	LBro
'Professor Blaauw' (Dutch)	CB&S LAma LRoo
'Prophetic Message' (AB)	LBro
'Protégé' (Spuria)	LBro
'Proud Land'	MAus
pseudacorus	CHar CKin CRow CSco CSun CWGN EHon ELan EWav GPoy LMay MAus MCot MSta MUlv NLan NNor NSel WAbe WEas WHer WOak WSto WWin
– ***bastardii***	CChu CRow CWGN ECha EGol MS&S MUlv SHig SPer
– cream form	EGol MUlv NBir
– 'Golden Fleece'	SPer
– 'Golden Queen'	CRow MSta MUlv
¶ – 'Mandshurica'	LSav
– 'Variegata'	Widely available
pseudopumila	WThu
pumila	CChu ITim MBro NKay NNor NNrd WAbe WBon WCla WDav
– ***atroviolacea***	MBro MCas
– ***attica***	See I. ***attica***
– ***aurea***	MBro MCas
– 'Violacea'	CTom MBro SCro SPer
¶ 'Pumpkin Center' (SDB)	NZep
'Puppet' (SDB)	EFou EGol LBro NZep
'Puppet Baby' (MDB)	NZep
'Puppy Love' (MTB)	NZep
¶ ***purdyi*** JLS 860165	EMon
'Purple Cloak' (*sibirica*)	LBro LSav SMad
'Purple Gem' (Reticulata)	LAma NHol
'Purple Mere' (*sibirica*)	CBre CHar EFou LBro
'Purple Sensation' (Dutch)	CB&S LAma
'Purple Song' (TB)	MS&S
purpurea bracteata	See I. ***galatica bracteata***
'Pussycat' (MDB)	NZep
'Pussytoes' (MDB)	NZep
'Queechee' (TB)	EBre ERou MS&S SCro
¶ 'Queen's Ivory' (SDB)	MAus
'Queen's Pawn' (SDB)	LBro NZep
'Quiet Lagoon' (SDB)	NZep
¶ 'Quiet Thought' (TB)	LBro
'Quip' (MDB)	NZep
'Rabbit's Foot' (SDB)	NZep
'Rain Dance' (SDB)	NZep
¶ 'Rainbow Rock'	ERou
'Rainbow Sherbet' (SDB)	NZep
¶ 'Rainbow Trout' (TB)	LBro
¶ 'Raindance Kid' (IB)	NZep
'Rajah' (TB)	CRow EBre ERou LBro
'Ranger' (TB)	LHil MS&S
'Rare Edition' (IB)	EFou LBro MS&S NZep
¶ 'Rare Treat' (TB)	NZep
'Raspberry Acres' (IB)	MAus MS&S
'Raspberry Blush' (IB)	NZep
'Raspberry Jam' (SDB)	EFou LBro MS&S NZep
'Raspberry Ripples' (TB)	MAus
'Raspberry Rose' (IB)	NZep
'Raspberry Sundae' (BB)	NZep
¶ 'Rathke Primrose' (IB)	SCro
'Raven Hill' (TB)	CHad MAus
'Real Jazzy' (MTB)	NZep
'Red Atlast' (MDB)	EFou
'Red Flag' (*sibirica*)	EFou NHol
'Red Flare' (*sibirica*)	ELan LBro LHop MS&S
'Red Flash' (TB)	MS&S
'Red Heart' (SDB)	EBre ECtt
'Red Lion' (TB)	NZep
'Red Oak' (Spuria)	MAus
'Red Orchid' (IB)	MS&S
'Red Revival'	MAus
¶ 'Red Rufus' (TB)	EFou
'Red Tempest' (IB)	NZep
¶ 'Reddy Maid' (*sibirica*)	LBro
'Redwing' (TB)	MWat
'Redwood Falls' (Spuria)	LBro
'Redwood Supreme' (Spuria)	LBro MS&S
'Regal Splendour'	MAus
'Regards' (SDB)	LBro
§ ***reichenbachii***	ECam
– Balkana group	SIng
¶ 'Reluctant Dragon' (SDB)	NZep
§ ***reticulata***	CAvo CBro EPar EPot ETub LBlo LRoo MBro MPlt WChr
– cvs.	See under ***cultivar name***
'Revved Up' (IB)	NZep
'Reward'	CSco
'Riches' (SDB)	NZep
'Rickshaw' (SDB)	LBro
'Right Royal' (TB)	MAus
'Rimouski' (*sibirica*)	LBro
'Ringo' (TB)	NZep
¶ 'Rio Tulare'	LBro
'Ripple Chip' (SDB)	NZep
'Risque' (TB)	MAus
¶ 'River Patrol' (TB)	EFou
'Roanoke's Choice' (*sibirica*)	LBro
'Rob' (*chrysographes*)	GWic
'Robert Graves' (TB)	MAus
§ 'Rocket' (TB)	CRow MAus MS&S SCro SPer
'Roger Perry' (*sibirica*)	CRow

¶ 'Roman Emperor' (TB)	EFou
'Romance' (TB)	ERou
'Rose Queen' (*laevigata* x)	CCla CRow CSco CWGN ECha ELan ELun EPar ERou EWav GWic LMay MSta NKay NRoo SChu SSpi WRus
'Rose Violet' (TB)	MAus MS&S
'Rosemary's Dream' (MTB)	NZep
rosenbachiana	WChr
'Rosie Lulu' (SDB)	NZep
'Rosy Air' (SDB)	NZep
'Rosy Wings' (TB)	EGol EPar
'Roustabout' (SDB)	LBro
¶ 'Roy Elliott'	NHol
¶ 'Royal Ascot' (TB)	LBro
'Royal Blue' (Reticulata)	EPot LAma LBow MS&S
– – (*sibirica*)	ECha SBla
'Royal Contrast' (SDB)	NZep
'Royal Elf' (SDB)	NZep
'Royal Eyelash' (SDB)	NZep
'Royal Ruffles' (TB)	MAus
'Royal Sparks' (SDB)	NZep
'Royal Touch' (TB)	EFou MFir
¶ 'Royal Velours'	LHil
'Royal Yellow' (Dutch)	LAma
'Rubella' (*chrysographes*)	CRow GDra LGre
'Rubens' (*chrysographes*)	SChu
'Ruby Chimes' (IB)	MAus MS&S
'Ruby Contrast' (TB)	MAus MS&S
'Ruby Gem' (TB)	MS&S
¶ 'Ruby Locket' (SDB)	NZep
'Ruby Mine' (TB)	MAus
rudskyi	See I. ***variegata***
¶ 'Ruffled Velvet' (*sibirica*)	LBro
¶ 'Rumbling Thunder' (TB)	MAus
¶ 'Runaway' (IB)	MAus
'Rushing Stream'	MAus
¶ 'Rusty Dusty' (SDB)	NZep
'Ruth Couffer' (BB)	LBro MS&S
* 'Ruth Nies Cabeen' (Spuria)	LBro
ruthenica	MPar NKay NWCA SChu WOMN
'Sable' (TB)	CHad CHar CSco MAus MBro SPer SSus
'Sable Night' (TB)	ERou
'Saffron Charm' (AB)	MAus
'Saint Crispin' (TB)	CSco EBre ERou GHig MUlv MWat SPer SSus
'Saint Teresa' (IB)	LBro
'Saintbury' (SDB)	MAus
'Saltwood' (SDB)	CBro
'Sam' (SDB)	NZep
§ x ***sambucina***	MAus
'San Jose' (TB)	NZep
'San Leandro' (TB)	MAus
'Sand and Sea' (TB)	LBro
'Sandy Caper' (IB)	MAus MS&S
§ ***sanguinea***	CAvo SSpi WDav
§ – 'Alba'	CRow
'Sapphire Beauty' (Dutch)	LAma
'Sapphire Jewel' (SDB)	NZep
sari	EPot LAma WChr
'Sass with Class' (SDB)	NZep
'Satin Gown' (TB)	MAus
'Saturnus' (Dutch)	LAma
'Saucy Peach' (BB)	LBro MS&S
'Savoir Faire' (*sibirica*)	CWGN ECha LBro
¶ 'Saxon Princess' (TB)	LBro
'Scented Air' (SDB)	NZep
schachtii	ECam WChr
'Scintilla' (IB)	SCro
'Scribe' (MDB)	CBro GLoc MAus NZep
¶ 'Scrimmage' (SDB)	NZep
¶ 'Sea Horse' (*sibirica*)	WHea
¶ 'Sea Shadows' (*sibirica*)	NBir NSti
'Sea Urchin' (SDB)	NZep
'Seawolf' (TB)	NZep
serbica	See I. ***reichenbachii***
¶ 'Serenity Prayer' (SDB)	NZep
setosa	CBro CCla CCor CRiv CRow CSun ECam ECha EGol EMNN GAbr ITim LHil LSav MAus MHig MSta NKay NNrd SIng
– ***alba***	CRow
§ – ***arctica***	CCla CTom EGol ELan ELun EPot GDra GLoc LGre MBal NHol NNrd NTow SBla SPer WAbe WHoo WOMN
§ – ***canadensis***	NNrd
– dwarf form	See I. ***s. arctica***
– 'Hookeri'	See I. ***s. canadensis***
*– ***major***	SIng
– ***nana***	See I. ***s. arctica***
'Shampoo' (IB)	EFou NZep
'Shawsii'	EFou
'Sheer Class' (SDB)	NZep
'Sheer Energy' (SDB)	NZep
'Shepherd's Delight' (TB)	MAus
'Sherbourne' (SDB)	MAus
'Short Distance' (IB)	LBro
¶ 'Show Me Yellow' (SDB)	NZep
'Showcase' (TB)	NZep
'Showdown' (*sibirica*)	EBre MBri
¶ 'Showman'	ERou
'Shrawley' (*sibirica*)	MAus
'Shrinking Violet' (MTB)	LBro MS&S
¶ 'Shy Violet' (SDB)	NZep
sibirica	CElw CFis CHad CShe CSun CWGN EHon GPla LAma LHil MBro MFir MWat NHol NNor NSel NSti SMad WEas WHer WHoo WWin
'Sierra Nevada' (Spuria)	EFou LBro
¶ 'Sigh' (SDB)	NZep
'Silent Strings' (IB)	LBro
¶ 'Silver True'	WEas
'Silvery Moon' (TB)	SCro

sindjarensis	See I. ***aucheri***
'Sing Again' (IB)	MAus
sintenisii	CSun EPar MPar NHol SIng
¶ –	CHan
'Siva Siva' (TB)	EBre ERou MAus MBri MS&S
'Skip Stitch' (SDB)	LBro MAus
'Sky and Snow' (SDB)	NZep
'Sky Bolt' (SDB)	MAus
'Sky Wings' (***sibirica***)	CWGN ECha
'Skyfire' (TB)	NZep
¶ 'Slap Bang' (SDB)	NZep
'Sleepy Time' (MDB)	NZep
'Slim Jim' (MTB)	LBro
'Small Sky' (SDB)	CBro LBro
'Small Wonder' (SDB)	LBro MS&S
'Smart Girl' (TB)	NZep
'Smarty Pants' (MTB)	LBro MS&S
¶ 'Smell the Roses' (SDB)	NZep
'Smoky Valley' (BB)	LBro MS&S
'Smooth Orange' (TB)	MAus
'Snappie' (IB)	NZep
¶ 'Sneak Preview' (TB)	NZep
'Snow Crest' (***sibirica***)	CCla EFou LHop LSav NHol SMad
'Snow Elf' (SDB)	LBro
'Snow Festival' (IB)	NZep
'Snow Fiddler' (MTB)	NZep
¶ 'Snow Gambit' (MTB)	NZep
'Snow Queen' (***sibirica***)	CBre CCla CHad CKel CRow CSco CSun CWGN ELan EPot ERou EWav GHig LMay LSav MAus MWgw NSti SPer
'Snow Troll' (SDB)	MAus MBri
'Snowcone' (TB)	NZep
'Snowcrest' (***sibirica***)	CHad MAus
§ 'Snowdrift' (***laevigata*** x)	CRow CWGN EGol EHon EWav LMay MSta SHig
¶ 'Snowshill' (TB)	LBro
'Snowy Owl' (TB)	MAus MBri
¶ 'Snowy River' (MDB)	NZep
'Snowy Wonderland' (TB)	NZep
'Soaring Kite' (TB)	LBro MAus
'Soft Blue' (TB)	LBro MAus
¶ 'Soft Breeze' (SDB)	NZep
'Solar Song' (SDB)	NZep
'Solid Mahogany' (TB)	MAus MUlv
'Somerset Vale' (TB)	MS&S
'Something Special' (BB)	NZep
'Song of Norway' (TB)	NZep
¶ 'Soul Power'	ERou
'Sounder' (BB)	LBro
'Southcombe White' (***sibirica***)	CRow SWas
'Southern Clipper' (SDB)	MAus MS&S
'Space Odyssey' (TB)	NZep
'Spanish Coins' (MTB)	LBro NZep
'Sparkling Cloud' (SDB)	MAus
'Sparkling Rose' (***sibirica***)	CTom EBre EFou MBri MS&S NOrc
'Spartan'	See I. ***germanica*** 'S.'

'Speckled Bird' (AB)	MAus MS&S
'Splash of Red' (SDB)	LBro NZep
'Spring Bells' (SDB)	EFou
'Spring Fern' (SDB)	MAus
'Spring Festival' (TB)	MAus
'Spring Signal' (TB)	LBro MS&S
'Spring Wine' (IB)	LBro
'Springtime' (Reticulata)	CAvo LAma LBow NHol SIng WChr
¶ ***spuria***	ELan
– ***halophila***	LBro
– ***maritima***	NNrd SIng
§ – ***musulmanica***	CHar LBro MAus SPer
– ***ochroleuca***	See I. ***orientalis***
x ***squalens***	See I. x ***sambucina***
'Squeaky Clean' (SDB)	NZep
'Stability' (Spuria)	LBro
'Stapleford' (SDB)	CBro
¶ 'Stardate' (SDB)	NZep
'Starlight Waltz' (SDB)	NZep
¶ 'Starlit River' (TB)	EFou
'Starry Eyed' (SDB)	LBro MS&S
'Starshine' (TB)	MAus NZep
'Staten Island' (TB)	ELan ENot LHil MAus MBri MS&S
'Stella Polaris' (TB)	SCro
§ ***stenophylla***	EPot
'Stepping Little' (BB)	NZep
'Stepping Out' (TB)	MAus MFir
'Sterling Silver' (TB)	MAus
'Stockholm' (SDB)	LBro NZep
stolonifera	EPot
'Storrington' (TB)	SCro
¶ 'Strange Child' (SDB)	NZep
¶ 'Strawberry Love' (IB)	NZep
'Strawberry Sensation' (TB)	NZep
'Strawberry Sundae' (TB)	MAus
¶ 'Striking Gold' (MTB)	NZep
¶ 'Strum' (IB)	NZep
stylosa	See I. ***unguicularis***
§ ***suaveolens***	CBro ELan EPot MHig MPar SIng WMar
subbiflora	CCor WDav
'Sugar' (IB)	MAus
'Sugar Candy' (CH)	LBro
¶ 'Sugar Please' (SDB)	NZep
¶ 'Sullom Voe' (TB)	LBro
'Summer Luxury' (TB)	NZep
¶ 'Sun Dappled'	ERou
'Sun Doll' (SDB)	NZep
'Sun King'	MAus
'Sun Miracle' (TB)	MAus
¶ 'Sunbrella' (SDB)	NZep
'Sunlit Sea' (Spuria)	LBro
'Sunlit Trail' (SDB)	MAus
¶ 'Sunny Dawn' (IB)	NZep
'Sunny Day' (Spuria)	LBro
'Sunny Heart' (SDB)	NZep
'Sunny Honey' (IB)	NZep
'Sunnyside' (Spuria)	LBro
'Sunrise Point' (TB)	MAus

'Superlation' (TB)	MAus SCro
¶ 'Supreme Sultan' (TB)	NZep
¶ 'Surprise Blue' (MTB)	NZep
'Surprise Orange' (MDB)	NZep
'Susan Bliss' (TB)	GHig
susiana	LAma NHol SIng
'Suspense' (Spuria)	LBro
'Svelte' (IB)	LBro
'Swank' (***sibirica***)	LBro
'Sweet Lavender' (TB)	SCro
¶ 'Sweet Tears' (SDB)	NZep
'Swizzle' (IB)	LBro
'Sylvia Murray' (TB)	MAus
'Symphony' (Dutch)	LRoo
'Tall Chief' (TB)	EBre MAus MBri SCro
'Tan Tingo' (IB)	NZep
'Tantara' (SDB)	NZep
'Tarheel Elf' (SDB)	LBro NZep
'Tarn Hows' (TB)	MAus MS&S
'Taupkin' (SDB)	LBro
tauri	See I. ***stenophylla***
'Tea Rose' (TB)	SCro
¶ 'Tease' (SDB)	LBro
¶ 'Techny Chimes' (TB)	MAus
tectorum	CSun EMNN LGre MPar NRar SCro WOMN
– ***alba***	WThu
– 'Variegata'	MBri SCro
'Ten' (SDB)	NZep
tenax	EPot MBal MFir MHig
– ***alba***	EPot GLoc
tenuis	MHig NNrd WDav
'The Bride'	See I. 'Bride'
'The Citadel' (TB)	SCro
'The Desert' (TB)	MS&S
¶ 'The Gower'	LSav
'The Rocket'	See I. 'Rocket'
'Theatre' (TB)	NZep
¶ 'Thelma Perry' (***sibirica***)	MAus
'Theseus' (Aril)	EPot
'Thor' (Aril)	EPot
'Threepio' (SDB)	NZep
'Thrice Blessed' (SDB)	NZep
¶ 'Thriller' (TB)	NZep
thunbergii	See I. ***sanguinea***
'Thundercloud' (TB)	MAus
'Tic Tac' (MDB)	NZep
'Tidbit' (DB)	LBro MS&S
'Tiddle de Winks' (BB)	LBro MS&S
¶ 'Tides In'	ERou
'Tillamook'	MAus
'Time for Love' (TB)	NZep
'Timmie Too' (BB)	LBro
¶ ***timowejewii***	WOMN
tingitana fontanesii	SPou
'Ting-a-Ling' (MTB)	NZep
'Tinkerbell' (SDB)	EBre EGol LBro MS&S
'Tiny Freckles' (MDB)	NZep
¶ 'Titan's Glory' (TB)	LBro
'Toasty' (SDB)	NZep
'Tom Tit' (TB)	MAus
'Tomingo' (SDB)	MAus MFir MS&S
'Toni Lynn' (MDB)	NNrd
'Toots' (SDB)	LBro MS&S
'Top Flight' (TB)	ENot ERou SPer
'Topsy Turvy' (MTB)	LBro NZep
'Torchlight' (TB)	MS&S
¶ 'Torchy' (SDB)	NZep
¶ 'Toy Boat' (SDB)	NZep
¶ 'Transcribe' (SDB)	NZep
'Treasure' (TB)	MAus
¶ 'Tricks' (SDB)	NZep
¶ 'Triple Crown'	ERou
¶ ***trojana***	MAus SIng
'Tropic Night' (***sibirica***)	CCla CRiv CSco CWGN EFou GAbr LSav MBri MSta NHol NRoo NRya SCro SMad SPer SSus WRus WWat
¶ 'Truly' (SDB)	MAus
¶ 'Tu Tu Turquoise' (SDB)	NZep
tuberosa	See HERMODACTYLUS ***tuberosus***
¶ 'Tulare' (BB)	SCro
¶ 'Tumbleweeds' (SDB)	NZep
'Tupelo Honey' (TB)	NZep
'Tuscan' (TB)	NZep
'Twist of Lemon' (MDB)	NZep
¶ 'Two Bits' (MTB)	LBro
'Tycoon' (***sibirica***)	CWGN NHol SPer
'Tyke' (MTB)	NZep
'Ultrapoise' (TB)	MAus
§ ***unguicularis***	CAvo CBro CCla CFis CHar CKel CShe CSun EBre ELan EPar EPot ERav IHos LBro LSav MAus MCot MPar NSti SDix SIng SMad SPou
– 'Abington Purple'	CAvo CBro
– ***alba***	CBro SPou
– 'Bob Thompson'	CAvo SPou
¶ – broken form	WCot
§ – 'Cretensis'	CAvo ECha SPou
– ***lazica***	See I. ***lazica***
– 'Mary Barnard'	CAvo CBro CHan CSam CSco EBre ECha EFou GPla MUlv SPer SPou SWas
– 'Oxford Dwarf'	CBro SPou
– 'Walter Butt'	CAvo ECha SPou SSpi SWas
urmiensis	See I. ***barnumae u.***
¶ 'Ursula Vahl' (TB)	LBro
'Valimar' (TB)	MAus
'Vanity' (TB)	NZep
¶ 'Vanity's Child'	ERou
§ ***variegata***	EPar MAus MPar NRed
– ***alba***	EPar
* – ***pontica***	SCro
¶ 'Vegas Showgirl' (SDB)	NZep
'Veiled Prophet' (BB)	NZep
'Velvet Robe' (TB)	MAus
'Velvet Toy' (MDB)	LBro
'Vera' (Aril)	EBre EPot ETub WChr
verna	NHol WDav
versicolor	CBWG CCla CElw CRow CSun CWGN EGol EHon EPar EPot EWav LMay MSta NSti
¶ – ***alba***	NHol

– ***kermesina***	CRow CWGN ECha EGol EHon EPar GGar GWic MSta SHig
– violet form	EGol
'Vi Luihn' (***sibirica***)	CB&S LBro
vicaria	ECam
'Victoria Falls' (TB)	NZep
¶ 'Vim' (SDB)	LBro
'Vintage Year' (Spuria)	LBro
violacea	See I. ***spuria musulmanica***
'Violet Beauty' (Reticulata)	CAvo CBro ECam EPot LAma LBow NHol SIng WChr WPer
'Violet Bouquet' (MTB)	LBro
¶ 'Violet Classic' (TB)	EFou
'Violet Lass' (SDB)	NZep
'Violet Lulu' (SDB)	NZep
'Violet Zephyr' (Spuria)	LBro
'Violetmere' (***sibirica***)	LBro
¶ ***virginica*** 'Shrevei'	MAus
'Virtue' (IB)	MAus
viscaria	EPot
'Voila' (IB)	EFou LBro NZep
'Wabash' (TB)	CSco ERou MAus MBri MS&S NZep
¶ 'Wake Up' (SDB)	NZep
'Walter Butt'	See I. ***unguicularis*** 'W.B.'
'Warlsind' (Juno)	EPot
¶ 'Waterboy' (SDB)	NZep
'Watercolor' (SDB)	NZep
'Webelos' (SDB)	LBro LGre
'Wee Doll' (MDB)	NZep
¶ 'Well Suited' (SDB)	NZep
'Wenlock' (IB)	MAus
'Westar' (SDB)	NZep
'Westwell' (SDB)	MAus
'Whisky' (MDB)	NZep
'White Bridge' (Dutch)	LAma
'White Canary' (MTB)	LBro MAus
'White City' (TB)	CRow CSco LHil MAus MBri SCro
'White Excelsior' (Dutch)	CB&S LAma LBlo
'White Gem' (SDB)	NZep WWin
'White Heron' (Spuria)	LBro
'White Queen' (***sibirica***)	LBro
* 'White Sails' (***sibirica***)	CB&S
'White Swirl' (***sibirica***)	CBot CCla CHar EBar EBre EGol LBro MBri MUlv NRoo SPer WHoo WRus WWat WWin
'White van Vliet' (Dutch)	LRoo
'White Wedgwood' (Dutch)	LAma
'Whoop 'em Up' (BB)	LBro NZep
'Why Not' (IB)	LBro MS&S NZep
'Widdicombe Fair' (SDB)	EPar
¶ 'Widget' (MTB)	LBro
'Wigit' (IB)	MS&S
'Wild Echo' (TB)	MS&S
'Wild Ginger' (TB)	MAus
¶ ***willmottiana***	EPot
– 'Alba'	CBro EPot WChr
¶ 'Willow Mist' (SDB)	NZep
¶ x ***wilsonii*** 'Gelb Mantel'	NBir
'Winged Melody' (TB)	MAus
'Winkieland' (IB)	NZep
winogradowii	GEdr SDix WChr
'Winter Olympics' (TB)	EFou
'Wisley White' (***sibirica***)	CSco LBro LSav MWgw
'Wisteria Sachet' (IB)	MAus
'Wizard of Id' (SDB)	NZep
¶ 'Woodling' (SDB)	NZep
'Wow' (SDB)	LBro
¶ 'Wrights Pink' (SDB)	MAus
'Wyckhill' (SDB)	MAus
xiphioides	See I. ***latifolia***
xiphium 'Lusitanica'	WDav
'Yellow and White'	MAus MBri
'Yellow Girl' (SDB)	NZep
'Yo-Yo' (SDB)	NZep
'Zantha' (TB)	MAus
'Zipper' (MDB)	NZep
¶ 'Zounds' (SDB)	NZep
'Zowie' (SDB)	NZep
'Zua' (IB)	LGre MUlv

ISATIS (Cruciferae)

tinctoria	CArn CSFH CTom ELan EMon GPoy LHol MChe MSal NSel NSti SIde WHer WOak WPer

ISCHYROLEPIS (Restionaceae)

¶ ***subverticillata***	CHEx

ISMENE See **HYMENOCALLIS**

ISOCOMA See **HAPLOPAPPUS**

ISOPLEXIS (Scrophulariaceae)

¶ ***canariensis***	CSun WEas

ISOPOGON (Proteaceae)

¶ ***anethifolius***	CSun

ISOPYRUM (Ranunculaceae)

affine-stoloniferum	EPot
§ ***nipponicum sarmentosum***	EPot
ohwianum	See I. ***nipponicum sarmentosum***
thalictroides	NHol SPou

ISOTOMA See **SOLENOPSIS**

ITEA (Iteaceae)

ilicifolia	Widely available
japonica 'Beppu'	NHol
virginica	CBow CCla CFor CMHG ECro ELan LHop MGos MUlv SGar SHil SPer SReu SSpi SSta WBod WSHC WWat
¶ – Swarthmore form	LMer
yunnanensis	CGre CTre IOrc

IVESIA (Rosaceae)

IXIA (Iridaceae)

'Bird of Paradise'	LAma
'Blue Bird'	LAma LBow
'Hogarth'	LAma
'Hubert'	LBow
hybrids	SW&B
'Mabel'	ETub
paniculata	ETub LBow
'Rose Emperor'	LAma LBow
'Uranus'	LBow
'Venus'	LAma LBow

IXIOLIRION (Liliaceae/Ixioliriaceae)

pallasii	See I. *tataricum*
§ *tataricum*	ETub LAma LBlo LRoo MBri
– Ledebourii group	CAvo LAma

JABOROSA (Solanaceae)

integrifolia	EMon SLHN SMrm WCru

JACARANDA (Bignoniaceae)

acutifolia	MBri
mimosifolia	CPle SLMG WCar

JACOBINIA See **JUSTICIA**

JAMESIA (Hydrangeaceae)

americana	CBot CCla ELan

JASIONE (Campanulaceae)

§ *crispa*	NHol
– *crispa*	NRed
§ *heldreichii*	CHan CLew CRiv CSun GDra GLoc MBro MHig NKay NNrd NRoo NTow SBla SChu SIng SLHN WCla WHil WHoo WWin
humilis	See J. *crispa*
jankae	See J. *heldreichii*
§ *laevis*	EHal ELan MRav SLHN WHal WHil WWin
– 'Blue Light'	CFis EBar EFou ESis NOak NRed SFis WPer
montana	CKin WCla
perennis	See J. *laevis*

JASMINUM † (Oleaceae)

angulare	CGre ERea
azoricum	CSun ERea SHil
beesianum	CArn CB&S CBot CBra CPle CRow CSco CTre ERav GWic ISea LHol MBea MCot MPla MRav SBra SHil SLon SPer SPla STre WBod WHer
¶ *dispermum*	LHop
floridum	IOrc LHop
fruticans	CMac ECro ELan EPla NKay
grandiflorum 'De Grasse'	ERea
humile	IBlr SLon WBod WKif
– B&L 12086	CBot
– KR 709	ISea
§ – 'Revolutum'	Widely available
– *wallichianum*	CGle
§ *mesnyi*	CB&S CBot CCla CHan CMac CSco EBak ELan EOvi ERea GWic IOrc LAbb LHop MBea NTow SBra SHil SLMG SSta WSHC
¶ *nitidum*	ERea
nudiflorum	Widely available
– 'Aureum'	EGol EHar ELan EPla SPou SSpi SSta WEas WRus WSHC
– 'Nanum'	ELan
¶ *odoratissimum*	ERea
officinale	Widely available
§ – *affine*	CB&S CPle EBre ELan ENot ERea GWic IBar IDai IOrc MR&S SDix SHil SMad WWat
§ – 'Argenteovariegatum'	Widely available
– 'Aureovariegatum'	See J. *o.* 'Aureum'
§ – 'Aureum'	Widely available
– 'Grandiflorum'	See J. *o. affine*
– 'Variegatum'	See J. *o.* 'Argenteovariegatum'
parkeri	CB&S CBot GLoc IDai MBro MCas MHig MPla NHol NKay SHil SPou SReu WAbe WDav WPat WSHC WThu WWat
polyanthum	CArn CB&S CGle CHan CPle CSco CTre CTrw EBak ELan ERav ERea IReg ISea LAbb LHop MBea MBri NRog NTow SHil SLon WEas WWat
primulinum	See J. *mesnyi*
reevesii	See J. *humile* 'Revolutum'
sambac	CHil CSun MNew
¶ – 'Maid of Orleans'	ERea
simplicifolium suavissimum	MNew SHil
x *stephanense*	Widely available

JEFFERSONIA (Berberidaceae)

diphylla	CHEx EPar LAma LRHS MSal MTho NHol NRed WChr WWat
dubia	EPot MTho NHol SBla SOkd SWas

JOVELLANA (Scrophulariaceae)

punctata	CHan WTay
sinclairii	CBos ECou GWic MRav NGre SWas WBod WPer
violacea	Widely available

JOVIBARBA (Crassulaceae)

§ *allionii*	CWil EPad EPot GEdr MCas MFir NKay NNor SIng SMit SSmi WAbe WDav WHil WThu
– from Estang x *hirta* from Biele	SMit
– x *hirta*	CWil
– x *hirta glabrescens* from Smeryouka	SMit
¶ – x *hirta* 'Oki'	CWil
– x *sobolifera*	SMit
§ *arenaria*	CRow CWil NKay SIng SSmi
– from Murtal	CWil MDHE SSmi
¶ – 'Opiz'	MCas

'Emerald Spring'	CWil
§ ***heuffelii***	CWil MCas NBra NWCA SMit
– 'Aquarius'	CWil
– 'Beacon Hill'	CWil SMit
– 'Belcore'	SMit
– 'Bermuda'	CWil
– 'Brocade'	SMit
– 'Bronze King'	CWil SMit
– 'Chocoleto'	CWil
– 'Cloverdale'	SMit
– 'Fandango'	CWil
– 'Gento'	CWil
– 'Giuseppi Spiny'	CWil SMit
¶ – 'Grand Slam'	CWil
– 'Greenstone'	CWil SMit
– 'Henry Correvon'	CWil SMit
– 'Hystyle'	SMit
– 'Inferno'	CWil SMit
– 'Kapo'	SMit
– ***kopaonikensis***	CWil
– 'Miller's Violet'	CWil SMit
– 'Minuta'	CWil SMit
– 'Orion'	SMit
– ***patens***	SMit
– 'Prisma'	CWil
– 'Purple Haze'	CWil
– 'Sundancer'	CWil SMit
– 'Tan'	CWil SMit
– 'Tancredi'	SMit
– 'Torrid Zone'	CWil NBar SMit
– 'Tuxedo'	CWil NBar SMit
– 'Violet'	CWil
– 'Vulcan'	CWil
heuffelii glabra from Anabakanak	CWil SIng SMit
– – from Anthoborio	CWil
– – from Kosova × ***hirta glabra*** from Smeryouka	SMit
– – from Haila	CWil SMit
– – from Jakupica	CWil SMit
– – from Koprovnik	CWil
– – from Ljubotin	CWil SMit
– – from Pasina Glava	CWil
– – from Rhodope	CWil
– – from Treska Gorge	CWil SMit
– – from Vitse	CWil SMit
§ ***hirta***	CRiv CWil MDHE NBar NHol SIng
– ***borealis***	CWil
– from Col d'Aubisque	SMit
– 'Preissiana'	CWil NBar
hirta glabrescens from Belansky Tatra	CRow CWil NGre SSmi
– – from High Tatra	CRow
– – ***neilreichii***	CRow SIng SMit
– – from Smeryouka	CWil SIng SSmi
× ***kwediana*** 'Pickwick'	SMit
× ***nixonii*** 'Jowan'	SMit
§ ***sobolifera***	CRiv CWil EPot ESis NBar NGre NHol NKay SMit SSmi
– 'Green Globe'	CWil MDHE NBar NGre SSmi WEas

JUANIA (Palmae)

JUANULLOA (Solanaceae)

aurantiaca 'Gold Finger'	MBri
¶ ***mexicana***	CGre

JUBAEA (Palmae)

chilensis	CHEx LPal SArc

JUGLANS † (Juglandaceae)

ailantifolia	CHEx ESim SHil SSta
¶ × ***bixbyi***	ESim
F ***cinerea***	ESim LSav SHil SSta WCoo
♦ – × ***ailantifolia***	See J. × ***bixbyi***
microcarpa	LSav SHil
F ***nigra***	CB&S CBow CBra CLnd EHar ESim IOrc LNet NRog NTwe SDea SHil SKee SPer SSta WCoo WMou
F ***regia***	Widely available
F – 'Broadview'	ESim MBri NTwe WHig
F – 'Buccaneer'	ESim NTwe SDea WHig
¶ – 'Franquette'	SKee
– 'Laciniata'	SHil WMou
sieboldiana	WCoo

JUNCUS (Juncaceae)

articulatus	CKin
compressus	CKin
¶ ***concinnus***	SSpi
– SEP 187	CSun
§ ***decipiens*** 'Curly-Wurly'	EFou GWic MFir
♦ – 'Spiralis'	See J. ***d.*** 'Curly-Wurly'
effusus	CKin NLan
– 'Spiralis'	CRow EHon ELan EMon GDra IBlr LMay MBal MSta NNrd SIng SSpi
ensifolius	MSta
inflexus	CKin EHon
– 'Afro'	EMon
¶ ***xiphioides*** JLS 860161	EMon

JUNIPERUS † (Cupressaceae)

ashei	CMCN
chinensis	CFis CMac NWea
– 'Aurea'	CKen CMHG CMac EBre EHar EHul GPen IJoh LLin LNet MBar MBri MGos SHil SIng SLon WCon WMou WThu
– 'Blue Alps'	CDoC CMHG EBre EHar EHul EPla IJoh LNet LSav MBar MBri MGos MR&S NHol SHil WCon
– 'Blue Point'	EHul MBar MR&S
– 'Densa Spartan'	See J. ***c.*** 'Spartan'
– 'Echiniformis'	CKen CMac
– 'Iowa'	CMHG
– 'Japonica'	EHul MBar
– 'Japonica Variegata'	EHul
– 'Kaizuka'	CDoC CMHG EBre EHul ENHC MBal MBar SHil WCon WMou
– 'Keteleeri'	WCon

– 'Kuriwao Gold'	CDoC CMHG CMac CSco EBre EHul ENHC GRei LLin LNet MBar MBri MGos MOke MPlt MR&S MRav NHol NRoo SPer SPla WAbe WCon
– 'Kuriwao Sunbeam'	NHol
– 'Obelisk'	CDoC EHul MBar MGos NHol SHil WCon
– 'Oblonga'	EHul LLin MBar
– 'Pyramidalis'	CDoC CMac EBre EHar EHul ENHC ENot LLin MGos MWat NHea NRoo SHil WCon
– 'Rockery Gem'	EHul MBar NHea
– 'San José'	CDoC EHul EPot MBar MPla WCon WWeb
§ – 'Spartan'	EHul
– 'Stricta'	CKen CMHG CSco EHul ENHC GPen IHos LSav MBal MBar MBri MOke MPla
– 'Stricta Variegata'	See J. *c* 'Variegata'
– 'Variegata'	CFis EHul MBar MPla
– 'Variegated Kaizuka'	EBre EHul MBar NHol
communis	CArn CKin CSev GPoy ITim LHol MPla NHex NSel NWea SIde SPer WMou
– 'Arnold'	WCon
I – 'Aureopicta'	EBre WCon
* – 'Barton'	LLin MPla NHol
¶ – 'Berkshire'	EPla
– 'Clywd'	WThu
– 'Compressa'	Widely available
– 'Constance Franklin'	EHul MBar MCas
– 'Corielagan'	MBar MCas MGos MPla MWat
– ***depressa***	GPoy LLin MBal MBar SHil
– 'Depressa Aurea'	Widely available
– 'Depressed Star'	MBar
– 'Gelb'	See J. ***c.*** 'Golden Showers'
– 'Gold Cone'	CDoC CKen EBre LLin MBar MBri MCas MPla NHol SPla WCon
§ – 'Golden Showers'	EBre EPla
– 'Green Carpet'	EBre MBri NHol SHil
– 'Greenmantle'	SPla
– 'Hemispherica'	MBar
– 'Hibernica'	Widely available
– 'Hornibrookii'	CDoC CMac CSco EHul ENot GDra IDai LLin MBal MBar MGos MPla MR&S MWat NWea SHil SLon SPla SReu SSmi STre WWin
– 'Horstmann'	EPla MBri SMad
§ – 'Minima'	ENHC WCon
§ – ***montana***	EPla EPot SSta
– 'Nana Prostrata'	See J. ***c.*** 'Minima'
– 'Oblonga Pendula'	MBri
♦ – 'Prostrata'	See J. ***c.*** 'Depressed Star'
– 'Prostrata Nana'	LSav MOke
– 'Pyramidalis'	LLin MR&S
– 'Repanda'	Widely available
I – 'Repanda' Waddon clone	CChu
– 'Sentinel'	CBra CDoC EBre EHul ENHC IHos IJoh MBar MBri MPla SHil WBod WCon WWeb
– 'Silver Lining'	See J. ***c.*** 'Minima'
– ***suecica***	EHul ENot IHos LSav MBar NHol NWea WCon
¶ – 'Suecica Aurea'	EHul EPla
– 'Zeal'	CKen LSav
conferta	CBra CDoC CTre EHar EHul IDai LLin MBri MWat SHil SLon SPer SPla WMou
– 'Blue Pacific'	CMac EBre MBar SHil
davurica	EHul
– 'Expansa'	CMHG CMac EHul LSav MBar NKay STre
– 'Expansa Albopicta'	See J. ***d.*** 'Expansa Variegata'
– 'Expansa Aureospicata'	CBra CDoC CKen CMac EBre EHar EHul ENHC LLin MBar NRoo SPla SSmi WCon
– 'Expansa Variegata'	CBra CMac EBre EHar EHul LLin MBal MBar MGos MPla SLon SSmi WAbe WCon
deppeana 'Silver Spire'	MBar MPla SMad
drupacea	SHil
'Grey Owl'	CBra CDoC CMHG CMac CSco EBre EHar EHul ENot GRei ISea LLin MBal MBar MBri MGos MPla MR&S SHil SLon SPer SPla STre WAbe
horizontalis	NWea
– 'Alpina'	CKen LSav
§ – 'Andorra Compact'	CKen CMac LSav MBar
– 'Banff'	CKen EBre WCon
– 'Bar Harbor'	CB&S CKen CMac ENHC MBar MGos MPla MPlt SHil SPla
§ – 'Blue Chip'	CDoC CHoe CKen CMac EBre EHar EHul ENHC ENot LSav MBar MBri MGos MPla NHol NRoo SHil SPla SSmi
– 'Blue Moon'	See J. ***h.*** 'Blue Chip'
– 'Blue Rug'	See J. ***h.*** 'Wiltonii'
– 'Coast of Maine'	SHil
– 'Douglasii'	CMac EHul LLin MBal MBar SHil
– 'Emerald Spreader'	CDoC CKen EHul ENHC ENot LSav MBar MGos SSmi
– 'Glauca'	See J. ***h.*** 'Wiltonii'
– 'Glomerata'	CKen MBar
– 'Grey Pearl'	CDoC CKen EBre EHar EHul EPla MBri WCon WWeb
– 'Hughes'	CDoC CMac CSco EBre EHul ENot IHos LLin MBar MBri MGos MOke MPla MR&S MRav NRoo SHil WCon
– 'Jade River'	CKen MBri
– 'Jade Spreader'	EHul
– ***montana***	EHul SHil
– 'Petraea'	LSav
– 'Plumosa'	EHal GPen SSmi
– 'Plumosa Compacta'	See J. ***h.*** 'Andorra Compact'
– 'Prince of Wales'	CDoC EBre MBri MGos WCon
– 'Prostrata'	IDai
– 'Saxatalis'	See J. ***communis montana***
– ***saxatilis***	See J. ***communis montana***
– 'Turquoise Spreader'	CKen EBre MBar MPla
– 'Variegata'	EPla MBar

– 'Venusta'	CKen
– 'Webberi'	CDoC MBar MBri WWeb
– 'Wilms'	EPla MBri
– 'Wiltonii'	CDoC CKen CMac CSco EBre EHul ENHC ENot GDra IDai IHos LGro LLin MBal MBri MGos MPla MWat NHol NRoo SHil SPla WWin
– 'Winter Blue'	EHul ENHC
– 'Youngstown'	CMac EBre MBar SPer SPla SSta WCon
¶ – 'Yukon Belle'	CKen
* *maritima*	EPot
x *media* 'Armstrongii'	EHul
– 'Blaauw'	CDoC CMac CSco ENHC ENot IHos IJoh LLin MBar MGos NHea SHil STre WCon
– 'Blue and Gold'	CKen EBre EPla MBri
§ – 'Carbery Gold'	CDoC CMac EHul LLin MBar MGos NHol WCon
– 'Globosa Cinerea'	MBar
– 'Gold Coast'	CDoC CKen CMac CSco EBre EHul ENHC ENot IHos MBar MBri MGos MWat NHol SHil WCon
– 'Gold Sovereign'	MGos NBar
– 'Gold Star'	EBre
¶ – 'Golden Saucer'	MBri
¶ – 'Goldkissen'	MBri
– 'Hetzii'	CB&S CBra CMac CSco EHar EHul ENHC MBal MBar MBri MGos MR&S NWea SHil SPer SPla WCon
¶ – 'Mathot'	LSav
– 'Milky Way'	LSav MWat
* – 'Mint Julep'	CDoC CMac CSco EBre EHul ENHC ENot IDai IJoh LLin MBar MGos MPla MPlt MR&S NHea NRoo SHil SPer WCon WMou
– 'Mordigan Aurea'	SHil
– 'Old Gold'	Widely available
– 'Old Gold Carbery'	See J. 'Carbery Gold'
– 'Pfitzeriana'	CBra CMac EHar EHul ENHC ENot LLin MBal MBar MBri MGos MOke MR&S NWea SHil SLon SPer SPla SReu WWin
– 'Pfitzeriana Aurea'	Widely available
– 'Pfitzeriana Compacta'	CDoC CMac EHul MBar SHil
– 'Pfitzeriana Glauca'	CDoC CSco EHul MWat WAbe WCon
– 'Plumosa'	MBar SHil
– 'Plumosa Albovariegata'	EBre MBar WCon
– 'Plumosa Aurea'	CSco EHar EHul ENHC ENot MBar MBri WCon
– 'Plumosa Aureovariegata'	CKen EBre MBar WCon
– 'Richesson'	MBar
– 'Shimpaku'	CKen MBar
– 'Sulphur Spray'	CDoC CMHG CMac EBre EHul ENHC GPen IJoh MBar MBri MOke MPla MRav MWat NHea NRoo SHil SPer SSmi WCon
oxycedrus	CMHG
phoenicia G&G 2365	LSav
pinchotii	LSav
procumbens	MBri SHil SLon WAbe WBod
– 'Bonin Isles'	MBal MBar MGos WAbe
– 'Nana'	CDoC CKen CLew CMac EBre EHar EHul ISea LLin LSav MBal MGos MPla MRav MWat NHar NHol NKay SHil SPla SSmi SSta WCon
recurva 'Castlewellan'	SHil
– ***coxii***	CBra CChu CDoC CMac EHar EHul EPla ISea MBar MBri MGos MPar SHil SIng SLon SMad WCon WMou WThu
– 'Densa'	CDoC EBre EHul LLin STre
– 'Embley Park'	EHul LSav MBar MBri SHil
– 'Nana'	CKen LSav MBar SPla WCon
rigida	MBar SHil SIng
sabina	GPoy NWea
– 'Arcadia'	CMac
– 'Blue Danube'	CMac EHul IDai MBar MGos NGre
– 'Buffalo'	EHul
– 'Cupressifolia'	MBar
– 'Hicksii'	CMac EHul MBar MGos NWea WCon
– 'Skandia'	CKen
– 'Tamariscifolia'	Widely available
– 'Variegata'	CMac EBre EHul MBar
– 'Von Ehren'	LSav
sargentii	EHul MBal WWeb
scopulorum 'Blue Heaven'	CSco EBre EHar EHul ENHC ENot MBal MBar NHol SHil WCon WMou
– 'Blue Pyramid'	MBri
– 'Boothman'	EHul
* – 'Frosty Moon'	CDoC MBar
– 'Gray Gleam'	EHul ENHC MBri
– 'Moonlight'	LSav MBar
– ***repens***	MBar MGos
– 'Repens'	EHul
– 'Silver Star'	EHar EHul MGos
– 'Skyrocket'	Widely available
– 'Springbank'	CMac EHar EHul ENHC MBar SHil WCon
– 'Table Top'	EHul MBar SPer
– 'Tolleson's Weeping'	SHil
– 'Wichita Blue'	EBre SHil
¶ ***seravshanica***	LMer
squamata	NWea
– 'Blue Carpet'	Widely available
– 'Blue Spider'	EHul LLin MBar MBri WCon
– 'Blue Star'	Widely available
– 'Blue Swede'	CSco EBre EHul IJoh LLin MBri MPlt WCon
– 'Chinese Silver'	EBre MBar NHol SHil
– 'Filborna'	CDoC CKen LSav MBar MWat NHol
– 'Glassell'	CLew MBar
¶ – 'Golden Flame'	CKen
– 'Holger'	CDoC CKen CMac EBre EPla EPot LLin MBri MGos MPla MWat SHil WCon

– 'Hunnetorp' MBar MBri MGos WCon
– 'Loderi' CKen EBre EHar EHul IJoh MBar SSta WCon
– 'Meyeri' CB&S CBra CDoC CMac EHul ENHC ENot GDra GPen IDai ISea LLin MBal MBar MBri MCot MCra MWat NWea SHil SLon SMad SPer WCon
– 'Pygmaea' CDoC MBar MPla WCon
– 'Wilsonii' CKen MBar SMad WCon
taxifolia lutchuensis EHar MBal MPla MWat WCon
virginiana CBra CMCN NWea WCoo
– 'Blue Cloud' CDoC CSco EHul LLin MBar
– 'Burkii' EHar MBal SHil WCon
*– 'Cline's Dwarf' LSav
– 'Glauca' EHul NWea SHil SLon
– 'Helle' See J. ***chinensis*** 'Spartan'
– 'Hillii' MBar
– 'Hillspire' EHul
– 'Moon Glow' EBre EHul MBri
– 'Nana Compacta' MBar
– 'Pendula' EPla
– 'Robusta Green' ENHC MBar
– 'Silver Spreader' CDoC LLin MGos SPer WCon
– 'Tripartita' MBar

JURINEA (Compositae)
ceratocarpa WWin

JUSTICIA (Acanthaceae)
§ ***brandegeeana*** MBri SLMG
– lutea See J. ***b.*** 'Yellow Queen'
§ – 'Yellow Queen' SLMG
§ ***carnea*** CGre EBak ERea MBri SLMG
guttata See J. ***brandegeeana***
* 'Norgard's Favourite' MBri
pauciflora See J. ***rizzinii***
****plumbaginifolia*** CSun
pohliana See J. ***carnea***
§ ***rizzinii*** CB&S CKni CPle CSun CTre ERea IBar IBlr LHop MNew SLMG
suberecta ERea LHop

KADSURA (Schisandraceae)
japonica CGre CHan CPle SSpi WSHC
– 'Variegata' SSpi SSta WSHC

KALANCHOE (Crassulaceae)
beharensis MBri SLMG
blossfeldiana MBri
– 'Annetta' MBri
– 'Attraction' MBri
– 'Bali' MBri
– 'Beta' MBri
– 'Calypso' MBri
– 'Caprice' MBri
– 'Charm' MBri
– 'Cinnabar' MBri
– 'Flores' MBri
– 'Fortyniner' MBri
– 'Inspiration' MBri
– 'Lucky Island' MBri
– 'Pollux' MBri
– 'Regulus' MBri
– 'Sensation' MBri
– 'Sentosa' MBri
– 'Seraya' MBri
– 'Siam' MBri
– 'Singapore' MBri
– 'Tessa' MBri SLMG
– 'Wendy' MBri
– 'Yellow Nugget' MBri
pumila IBlr WEas
tomentosa SLMG

KALIMERIS (Compositae)
¶ 'Yemeno Variegated' EMon

KALMIA † (Ericaceae)
angustifolia CLan IJoh LNet MBar
– rubra CB&S CBow CBra CCla CFor CSco EBre ELan MBal MGos NBar NHol NKay NRoo NWea SHil SPer SReu SSpi SSta WPat WThu
cuneata SOkd
latifolia CB&S CBow CBra CFor CLan CSco CTre ELan ENot IJoh ISea LHyd LNet LSav MBal MBar MGos NWea SHil SPer SPla SReu SSta WBod
– 'Alpine Pink' MBri MLea SSpi
– 'Bullseye' EBre IOrc LNet MBri
– 'Carousel' EBre LNet MGos MLea
– 'Clementine Churchill' CFor SSpi
– 'Elf' CFor EBre MBri MLea SSpi
– 'Freckles' EBre LNet MBri MLea SSpi
– 'Fresca' CFor ISea
– 'Goodrich' CB&S LSav MGos SPer SSpi
¶ – 'Minuet' MLea
– myrtifolia CFor MBri SSpi
– 'Nipmuck' CFor IBar LHyd LMil MGos MLea SSpi
– 'Olympic Fire' CFor EBre IBar IOrc LNet MBri MGos MLea SPer SSpi
– 'Ostbo Red' CB&S CBra CChu CFor CSco CTre EHar ELan IBar IOrc ISea LHyd LNet MBri MGos MLea SHil SPer SReu SSpi SSta WBod
– 'Pink Charm' CCla CFor MBri MGos MLea SPer SPla SSpi
– 'Pink Frost' LMil LNet MGos MLea MRav SPer SSpi WWeb
– 'Pink Star' IOrc MLea
¶ – 'Pinwheel' MLea
– 'Sarah' LMil MLea SSpi
– 'Shooting Star' IBar MBri MGos SPer
– 'Silver Dollar' ELan SSpi
¶ – 'Willowcrest' LMil
§ ***microphylla*** MBal SBar SSta WThu
N ***polifolia*** CB&S CFor GCHN ISea ITim MBar SHil SReu SSpi SSta
– 'Glauca' See K. ***microphylla***

KALMIOPSIS (Ericaceae)
leachiana EPot GArf ITim MBal MBri MGos SHil SLHN

– 'Glendoick'	SReu WPat
– 'La Piniec'	MGos SSpi
– Umpqua Valley form	EPot

KALOPANAX (Araliaceae)

pictus	CBot CHEx EHar ELan LGre SArc SHil
– *maxomowiczii*	CHEx MBlu MBri SMad
septemlobus	MBri

KECKIELLA (Scrophulariaceae)

¶ *antirrhinoides* 'Microphylla'	LGre
¶ *cordifolia*	LGre WPer
¶ *corymbosa* JCA 11618	LGre WDav

KELSEYA (Rosaceae)

¶ *uniflora*	WDav

KENNEDIA (Leguminosae)

coccinea	CSun
nigricans	LHop WPer
prostrata	CSun

KENTIA (Palmae)

belmoreana	See HOWEIA *b.*
canterburyana	See HEDYSCEPE *c.*

KENTRANTHUS (Valerianaceae)

ruber	See CENTRANTHUS *ruber*

KERNERA (Cruciferae)

KERRIA (Rosaceae)

§ *japonica*	CB&S CBra CChu CLan CSco CTre CTrw ELan ENot IDai IOrc ISea MCot MGos NKay NWea SDix SHil SReu WWin
– 'Golden Guinea'	EBre ERav IOrc LRHS NBar SSpi WWeb
§ – 'Picta'	Widely available
– 'Pleniflora'	Widely available
– 'Simplex'	See K. *japonica*
– 'Variegata'	See K. *j.* 'Picta'

KIRENGESHOMA (Hydrangeaceae)

koreana	CSco ECro MBri MCot
palmata	Widely available

KITAIBELA (Malvaceae)

vitifolia	CHan ELan EMon LGan LHop SFis SMrm SSpi

KITCHINGIA See **KALANCHOE**

KIWI FRUIT See **ACTINIDIA** ***deliciosa***

KNAUTIA (Dipsacaceae)

arvensis	CArn CKin CRiv EBre LHol NLan SFir WCla WHer WOak
§ *macedonica*	Widely available

KNIPHOFIA † (Liliaceae/Asphodelaceae)

'Ada'	CChu EBre ELan ERou
'Alcazar'	EFou EPar MBri
¶ 'Apricot'	LGre SWas
'Atlanta'	EBre EMon IBlr
'Bees' Sunset'	ELan MBri MWgw SHig
'Border Ballet'	ECtt GHig LHop MFir MPit MWgw NOak WHil
Bressingham hybrids	EBre IBlr NKay
'Buttercup'	CChu EBul LGre MBri
'C M Prichard'	See K. *rooperi*
'Candlelight'	EBre WWin
caulescens	CBot CHEx CHan CSam EBre EBul EMon LGre MUlv MWgw SApp SAxl SCro SDix SHig SIgm SMrm SSpi WCot
¶ 'Comet'	EOrc
'Corallina'	ELan MBri
'Dr E M Mills'	CKni COtt ELan
'Early Buttercup'	CCla CHad CSam CWGN EFou EGol EOrc MUlv MWgw NBar SCro
¶ *elegans*	SIgm
¶ *ensifolia*	MWgw
'Fiery Fred'	COtt EBre EFou ELan ERou WCot WHil
'Fireking'	MBri
¶ *foliosa*	SSpi
N *galpinii*	CGle ENot MBal NSti SApp SMad WCot WWat
'Gold Else'	CChu EOrc IBlr SAxl SBla SWas
¶ 'Goldfinch'	SAxl SMrm SWas
'Green Jade'	CChu CLew CRow ECha EFou EGol EPar MUlv SApp SBla
'H E Beale'	GWic
¶ *hirsuta* H&B 16444	EMon
'Ice Queen'	COtt EGol EOrc ERou MUlv NRoo SApp SMad SMrm
'Jenny Bloom'	SWas
late orange	MUlv
'Limelight'	EOrc MBri MWgw
'Little Maid'	Widely available
macowanii	See K. *triangularis triangularis*
'Maid of Orleans'	IBlr
'Mermaiden'	MBri
'Modesta'	GWic IBlr
'Mount Etna'	WAbe
nelsonii	See K. *triangularis triangularis*
'Nobilis'	See K. *uvaria* 'N.'
northiae	CBot ECha SAxl
'Percy's Pride'	EFou EOrc ERou MBri SApp SAxl SMrm WCot
'Prince Igor'	CRiv ECha EFou MBal
¶ *pumila*	SSpi
§ *rooperi*	CBot EBre GWic LGre MUlv
'Rougham Beauty'	ERou
'Royal Standard'	CHEx ELan ENot IBlr IDai MBri MWgw SHig SMrm
rufa	GWic
'Samuel's Sensation'	MBri
'September Sunshine'	EFou
'Shining Sceptre'	CChu COtt EBre ECtt ELan ERou MBri MUlv NRoo SBla
'Sir C K Butler'	IBlr

'Star of Baden-Baden'	MBri
'Strawberries and Cream'	CChu LGre SBla SWas
'Sunningdale Yellow'	ECha WEas
thomsonii snowdenii	CBot CChu CHan CSun ECha IBlr NRar SApp SSpi
'Toffee Nosed'	EFou ERou GWic
¶ ***triangularis***	CBot
§ – ***triangularis***	CBot CChu ELan EPar NSti SHig SSpi
'Tuckii'	CSun
uvaria	CHEx CShe EBre MWgw SPer WCot
– 'Nobilis'	ERou SDix WCot
'Yellow Hammer'	CBot CSam ECha EGol ERou GWic IBlr SSpi

KOBRESIA (Cyperaceae)

KOELERIA (Gramineae)

¶ ***alpina***	WPer
glauca	CHoe ECha ERou MWgw NHol NSti WHil

KOELLIKERIA (Gesneriaceae)

'Red Satin'	NMos

KOELREUTERIA (Sapindaceae)

bipinnata	CHEx GWic
paniculata	Widely available
– Apiculata group	CMHG MBri NHol
– 'Fastigiata'	MBri SHil

KOHLERIA (Gesneriaceae)

digitaliflora	WEfe
eriantha	MBri SLMG WEfe
– 'Clythe'	MBri
– 'Strawberry Flieds'	MBri
* x ***hybrida***	NMos
¶ 'Linda'	WEfe
'Longwood'	SLMG
'Strawberry Fields'	NMos

KOLKWITZIA (Caprifoliaceae)

amabilis	CB&S CFis CLan CSco CTrw ELan GRei IDai IJoh MCot MGos MPla MWat NHol NNor NRoo NWea SHil SSta WWin
– 'Pink Cloud'	Widely available

KUMMEROWIA (Leguminosae)

KUNZEA (Myrtaceae)

ambigua	CSun
baxteri	CHEx CHil
ericifolia	CSun
§ ***ericoides***	CTre ECou
¶ ***muelleri***	CSun
parvifolia	CSun

LABICHEA (Leguminosae)

punctata	CSun

LABLAB (Leguminosae)

purpureus	SPou

+ **LABURNOCYTISUS** (Leguminosae)

adamii	CBra COtt CSco EHar ELan GRei IOrc MUlv SHil SPer

LABURNUM † (Leguminosae)

alpinum	NWea SHil
– 'Pendulum'	CBow ELan IJoh IOrc LNet MBri MGos NBar SHil SPer
§ ***anagyroides***	GRei ISea MR&S NWea
– 'Aureum'	SHil
– 'Pendulum'	SHil
vulgare	See L. ***anagyroides***
¶ x ***watereri*** 'Alford's Weeping'	MBar MGos
– 'Vossii'	CB&S CBow CLnd CSco ELan ENot GRei IJoh IOrc LNet MBar MBri MGos MR&S MRav NBar NWea SFam SHil SPer SPla SReu SSta SSus

LACCOSPADIX (Palmae)

australasica	NPal

LACHENALIA (Liliaceae/Hyacinthaceae)

§ ***aloides***	EDon EPot ETub LBow MBri WOMN
– ***aurea***	ETub LBow
¶ – ***luteola***	LBow
– 'Nelsonii'	LBow
– 'Pearsonii'	EDon
– ***quadricolor***	EDon LBow
– ***vanzyliae***	EDon LBow
§ ***bulbifera***	ETub LBow MBri
– 'George'	LBow
contaminata	LBow
glaucina	EDon
hybrid Lac. 213	LBow
¶ ***liliiflora***	SLHN
mediana	LBow
pendula	See L. ***bulbifera***
tricolor	See L. ***aloides***

LACTUCA (Compositae)

alpina	See CICERBITA ***alpina***
perennis	CElw CHan SChu WPer
¶ ***sibirica***	WPer

LAGAROSIPHON (Hydrocharitaceae)

§ ***major***	CRow ELan

LAGAROSTROBOS (Podocarpaceae)

§ ***franklinii***	CB&S SHil WBod

LAGENOPHORA (Compositae)

LAGERSTROEMIA (Lythraceae)

indica	CGre CPle SGar SLMG SPer
¶ – 'Little Chief'	WCar
– Petite Orchid ®	CSun
– Petite Red ®	CSun
– 'Rosea'	CB&S
– 'Watermelon'	CSun
* ***subcordata***	CB&S

LAGUNARIA (Malvaceae)
patersonii MNew

LAGURUS (Gramineae)
ovatus SMrm WHil

LALLEMANTIA (Labiatae)
canescens NWCA

LAMIASTRUM See **LAMIUM**

LAMIUM † (Labiatae)
¶ 'Alan Leslie' GWic
♦ *album aureovariegatum* See L. *a.* 'Goldflake'
– 'Friday' EMon LRHS
§ – 'Goldflake' EFol
flexuosum EMon
§ *galeobdolon* CArn CGle CKin EMon LGro MWat SPer WOak
§ – 'Florentinum' CFis CGle CHoe CKel CRow CSco CShe ECha ECro EFol ELan ENot EPar ERou LHil MCot MFir NHol SBar SDix SIng STre
– 'Hermann's Pride' CMHG COtt EBre EMon GWic MBri MUlv
– 'Silberteppich' ('Silver Carpet') CHar CHoe CRow EBre ECha EFol EFou ELan EMon EOrc GGar LHop MCot MTho NKay NNor NRar NSti SBla SMad WWat
– 'Silver Angel' ELan EMon NSti
– 'Variegatum' See L. *g.* 'Florentinum'
¶ *garganicum garganicum* EMon
– 'Golden Carpet' EMon
– *pictum* EFol ELan GLoc WBon
¶ – *reniforme* DS&T 89011 EMon
maculatum CArn CFis CMer CRow CTom EBre EJud EMon WEas WOak
– *album* CCla CFis CGle CHad CHar CLew CRow CSco EFou ELan EMon LGro MCot NHol NSti SPer WBon
§ – 'Aureum' Widely available
– 'Beacon Silver' Widely available
– 'Beedham's White' CBre CHoe SCro
*– 'Cannon's Gold' CHoe ECha ELan EMon NSti WBon
N– 'Chequers' CSco EFou ELan EMon ENot NHol SPer SSpi
– 'Dingle Candy' EFol
♦– 'Gold Leaf' See L. *m.* 'Aureum'
– 'Hatfield' ELan EMon
¶ – 'Immaculate' EMon
¶ – 'James Boyd-Parselle' EMon
¶ – 'Pink Nancy' WAbb
– 'Pink Pewter' CBre ECha EFou EMon SCro
– 'Red Nancy' EMon GWic
§ – *roseum* Widely available
– 'Shell Pink' See L. *m. roseum*
– 'Silver Dollar' EMon MBri
¶ – 'Sterling Silver' EMon
– 'White Nancy' Widely available
¶ – 'Wootton Pink' WEas
orvala CHan EBre ECro EFou NSti SIng WHea
– *album* CHan ECro ELan EMon

LAMPRANTHUS (Aizoaceae)
aberdeenensis See DELOSPERMA *aberdeenense*
aurantiacus CB&S CHEx
blandus CB&S CHEx
§ *brownii* CB&S CHEx ELan SLMG
* 'Carn Brae' CB&S
§ *deltoides* CHEx MRav SLMG WEas
edulis See CARPOBROTUS *e.*
falcatus roseus SLMG
glaucus CB&S CHEx
haworthii CRiv SLMG
lehmanii See DELOSPERMA *l.*
oscularis See L. *deltoides*
pallidus See DELOSPERMA *pallidum*
spectabilis CB&S SLMG
– 'Tresco Apricot' CB&S
– 'Tresco Brilliant' CB&S CRiv
– 'Tresco Red' CB&S WPer
zeyheri CB&S

LANTANA (Verbenaceae)
¶ 'Arlequin' IHos
camara CPle ERea ESim ISea LAbb MBri
– 'Brazier' ERea
– 'Drap d'Or' ('Cloth of Gold') ESim
– 'Feston Rose' ERea
– 'Firebrand' ESim SLMG
– forms IBlr
– 'Mine d'Or' ERea
– 'Snow White' ERea SLMG
'Gold Dust' SLMG
§ *montevidensis* ERea LHop SLMG WEas
– forms SLMG
* 'Mr Bessieres' ERea
¶ 'Naide' IHos
'Radiation' ERea
♦ *sellowiana* See L. *montevidensis*
¶ 'Sunkiss' IHos

LAPAGERIA (Liliaceae/Philesiaceae)
rosea CB&S CFor CGre CHEx CMac CTre EBak ERea LGre MBal MNew SArc SHil SPer SReu SSpi WNor WWat
¶ – G&K 4083 LSav
– *alba* CB&S CSun MNew SSpi SSus
– *albiflora* 'White Cloud' CGre
*– 'Beatrice Anderson' SSpi
– 'Flesh Pink' CGre MNew SHil SSpi SSus
– 'Nash Court' CBot CChu CMac ERav ERea IBar IJoh IOrc ISea SHil SSpi SSus WSHC WWeb
– 'Penheale' SSpi SSus

LAPEIROUSIA (Iridaceae)
cruenta See ANOMATHECA *laxa*

laxa	See ANOMATHECA *laxa*

LAPSANA (Compositae)

¶ *communis* 'Inky'	CNat

LARDIZABALA (Lardizabalaceae)

biternata	CGre

LARIX † (Pinaceae)

¶ *kaempferi* 'Blue Rabbit Weeping'	MBri
decidua	CB&S CBow CBra CSco EHar ENHC ENot GRei IDai IHos MBal MBar NWea SHil SMad SPer WCon WMou
– 'Corley'	CKen
– 'Pendula'	CB&S WMou
x *eurolepis*	EHar ENot GRei MBar MBri MR&S NRoo NWea SExT SHil WMou
gmelinii	CMCN LRHS LSav
– *principis-ruprechtii*	SHil
§ *kaempferi*	CBra CDoC CLnd CPer CSco CTre EHar ENHC ENot GRei IJoh LBuc LNet MBar MGos NWea SHil SMad SPer WMou WNor
*– 'Bambino'	CKen
*– 'Blue Ball'	CKen
– 'Blue Dwarf'	MBri
– 'Blue Haze'	SHil
¶ – 'Blue Rabbit Weeping'	MBri
– 'Cruwys Morchard'	CKen
– 'Dervaes'	EHar
– 'Diana'	EBre MBlu
– 'Nana'	CKen EBre
*– *nana prostrata*	CKen
– 'Pendula'	CBra CDoC EHar IBar IJoh IOrc MBar MBlu MBri SExT SHil
– 'Varley'	CKen
¶ – 'Wolterdingen'	CKen
leptolepis	See L. *kaempferi*
sibirica	MBar
sukaczevii	WNor

LASERPITIUM (Umbelliferae)

¶ *halier*	WPer

LASIAGROSTIS (Gramineae)

splendens	See STIPA *splendens*

LATHYRUS (Leguminosae)

aureus	See L. *luteus* 'Aureus'
chloranthus	SFir SSad
**fremontii*	CSpe NRed SSad
grandiflorus	CGle CSev EMon LGre NRar SSad SWas WCot WOak
inermis	See L. *laxifolius*
japonicus	SFir
latifolius	CBow CCla CGle CSun ELan ERav GCHN GWic MCot MFir MWat NSti SIng SLHN WCot WEas WHal WHer WOak WPer WWin
– *albus*	CBot CHad ELan EMon LGre MPar SAxl SFir SSpi SWas WCot WHal
¶ – 'Blushing Bride'	WCot
– pale pink	MPar SIng WEas WHal
*– 'Red Pearl'	ECro ECtt EFou GWic MBri SMrm SPer SSvw
– 'Rosa Perle' ('Pink Pearl')	ECro ECtt EFou GAbr GWic MBri SMrm SPer WRus
– 'Weisse Perle' ('White Pearl')	CCla CGle ECha ECro EFou EOrc GAbr GWic LAbb MBri NSti SBla SLHN SMad SPer SSvw WHer WPer WRus
§ *laxifolius*	EOrc GWic LGre SAxl
§ *luteus* 'Aureus'	GWic MPar NHol SAxl SFar SFir WEas
♦ *magellanicus*	CBos
montanus	CKin
nervosus	CBot CHan CPla CSun ECro EFou EPla IBrk LGre MTho SAxl SBla SLHN SMad SSad WEas WRus
niger	EMon
nissolia	ELan
odoratus	CGle
– 'Bicolor'	ELan
¶ – 'Painted Lady'	SFir
rotundifolius	EPad ERav GDra MPar MTho NHol SAxl SBar SFir SSad SWas WOMN
sativus	CHad MPar NSti SFir WEas
– *azureus*	ELan LHop SSad
sylvestris	CHan CKin ELan
tingitanus	ECro MPar SFir WEas
tuberosus	ELan EMon LGre MWat WCot WOld
vernus	CHad CHan CTom EFou ELan EPot MCot MPar MTho SAxl SLHN WHal WHea WPer WRus WThu
– *alboroseus*	CChu CFis EFou ELan LGre MBri SAxl SBla WCot WHCr WHoo WKif WOMN WPat WRus WThu
– *albus*	GLoc MPar
– *aurantiacus*	See L. *luteus* 'Aureus'
– 'Caeruleus'	MPar
– *cyaneus*	CHad WRus
– 'Flaccidus'	WKif WRus
– *roseus*	ECha ECro MPar MPlt NTow SFir WPer
¶ – 'Spring Melody'	WCot

LAURELIA (Atherospermataceae)

sempervirens	SArc
serrata	CB&S CGre CTrw SBor

LAURUS (Lauraceae)

§ *azorica*	CTre SSpi
canariensis	See L. *azorica*
nobilis	Widely available
– *angustifolia*	CBow CPle EHar LAbb LHol SArc SDry SHil SLon

– 'Aurea'	CB&S CBow COtt CPle CSco CSev EHar ELan ERav IJoh IOrc LHol LNet SHil SPer WPat WWat

LAVANDULA † (Labiatae)

N 'Alba'	Widely available
§ *angustifolia*	CArn CBow CFis CLan CRow CSFH CShe ENot GPoy MBar MBri MGos MPla MWgw NNor NSel SHil SLon WAbe WHil WPer
– 'Alba Nana'	See L. *a.* 'Nana Alba'
– 'Baby Blue'	EFol LHop
– 'Bowles' Early'	CJer CMHG CSam
– 'Bowles' Variety'	See L. *a.* 'Bowles' Early'
– 'Folgate'	CJer CSco LHol
§ – 'Hidcote'	Widely available
– 'Hidcote Pink'	CArn CGle CHan CJer CRow EBre EFou EGol ELan EMon EOrc EPar LHol LHop MCot MWgw NHol NNor NRoo NSti SMad WPer
– 'Jackman's Dwarf'	MCot
– 'Munstead'	Widely available
§ – 'Nana Alba'	Widely available
– 'Nana Atropurpurea'	CJer
§ – 'Rosea'	Widely available
dentata	Widely available
– *candicans*	CJer LHol WSto
– silver form	GWic LGre LHop SCro SDry SIde SMrm SSad WHal WPer
'Hidcote Blue'	See L. *angustifolia* 'Hidcote'
§ x *intermedia* Dutch group	CArn CBow CFis CJer EBre EFou ELan EMon ENot MBri MChe MCot NHol NSel SChu SHil SPer WEas WHer WHil WSto
– 'Fring A'	CJer
– 'G4'	CJer
– 'Grappenhall'	CArn CHad CJer CSco CShe EBre ENor EOrc GAbr LHol MCot SChu SHil WOak WPer
– 'Grey Hedge'	LHol
– 'Grosso'	CJer LHol NHex
¶ – 'Hidcote Giant'	EHal ENor SMad
– 'Imperial Gem'	CCla CJer ENor SIde SSus
– 'Loddon Blue'	CJer LHol
* – 'No. 9'	CJer
– Old English group	CArn ELan SPla WEas WOak WWeb
– 'Princess Blue'	CJer ENor SIde
– 'Royal Purple'	CArn CJer CSev ENor LHol SIde
– 'Seal'	CArn CJer GPla LHol NSti SPla WPer
– 'Twickel Purple'	CBow CCla CJer CMHG CSco CSev EMon ENot LHol SChu SHil WAbe WOak WPer
– 'Vera'	See L. x *i.* Dutch group
'Jean Davis'	See L. *angustifolia* 'Rosea'
lanata	CArn CBot CFis CHoe CJer CMer CSun ECha ELan EMon ERav ESis GWic LGre LHol MPla NRar NSel NSti SDry SMad WHal WPer
¶ – 'Richard Grey'	EMon LHop
latifolia	CArn LGre MSal WSto
♦ 'Loddon Pink'	See L. *angustifolia* 'Rosea'
¶ *lusitanica*	ENor
* *multifida*	CFis CJer ERea LHol SSad
officinalis	See L. *angustifolia*
pink	LGre
pinnata	CFis CSun LGre LHil LHol LHop SDry SSad WPer
'Rosea'	See L. *angustifolia* 'Rosea'
* 'Sawyer's'	ENor
spica	See L. *angustifolia*
stoechas	Widely available
– *alba*	Widely available
– 'Nana'	CArn
– *pedunculata*	CArn CBow CChu CCor CFis CJer CMHG CSun ECha EGol ELan GWic LGre LHol LHop MBri NRar NSti SAxl SMad SPer WHer WOMN WPer
¶ – *pedunculata* 'James Compton'	EMon
viridis	CArn CBow CChu CFis CHan CJer CRow CSFH CSev CTre EEls ELan ENor EPla ERav LGre LHol LHop MSal SFis SSad WPer
¶ – *alba*	CHan

LAVATERA (Malvaceae)

arborea	CGre EMon ISea SPla WHer
– 'Ile d'Hyères'	NPer
– *rosea*	See L. 'Rosea'
– 'Variegata'	CB&S CHan EFou ELan EMon ERav LHop NPer SFis WEas WHer
assurgentiflora	EMon LHop NPer
'Barnsley'	Widely available
'Barnsley Perry's Dwarf'	NPer
bicolor	CGre COtt CSco CShe ELan SMad SSpi WOMN WPer WSHC
'Bredon Springs'	ELan EMon LHop MBri MGos SAxl
* 'Bressingham Pink'	LHop SMad
'Burgundy Wine'	CB&S CBra CKni CMHG CSco EGol ELan LHil MBri MGos NHol NPer NRoo SAxl SCro SHil SMad SPer SSus WPat WWeb
'Candy Floss'	CKni CMHG CSco EBar ELan LHop MBri NHol SHil SMrm SPer SSpi SSus WWeb
'Ice Cool'	CBow CKni ELan EMon EOrc LHop MBri MMth NPer NRar SHil SMad SMrm SSpi SSus WWat

kashmiriana	CGle CHan CSun MWgw NHol NPer SFis SMad SMrm WPer
'Kew Rose'	CKni EOrc LHop NPer SMad SMrm
§ ***maritima***	CBot CGle CHad CHil CMHG LHil LHop SDry SFir WOld
¶ – ***bicolor***	SFis SMrm
*– 'Princesse de Ligne'	CSun
N***olbia***	CBot CGle EMon MPla MWat SDix WSHC
'Peppermint Ice'	See L. 'Ice Cool'
* 'Pink Frills'	CBot EPla ERav LHop
§ 'Rosea'	Widely available
* 'Shorty'	ELan EMon MMth
N***thuringiaca***	EMon
'Variegata'	See L. 'Wembdon Variegated'
§ 'Wembdon Variegated'	CMal EFol ELan EMon NPer NRar NSti SMad SMrm

LAWSONIA (Lythraceae)

inermis	MChe

LEDEBOURIA (Liliaceae/Hyacinthaceae)

§ ***cooperi***	EBre EBul ELan ESis IBlr MPar SIng WMar WOMN
§ ***ovalifolia***	EBul
§ ***socialis***	CHEx EBul IBlr

X LEDODENDRON (Ericaceae)

¶ 'Arctic Tern'	WAbe

LEDUM (Ericaceae)

columbianum	MBal SSta
glandulosum	NHol SPer SSta
groenlandicum	MBar MBri NHol NTow SHil SPer SSpi WPat WSHC
– 'Compactum'	CKni LNet LRHS MBal
palustre	EPot GPoy MBal SSta WThu
– ***dilatatum***	CLew SHil
– ***hypoleucum***	SSta

LEEA (Leeaceae)

coccinea	MBri

LEIOPHYLLUM (Ericaceae)

buxifolium	MBal MBri MHig SBar SHil SReu SSpi WThu
¶ – ***nanum***	GArf
– ***prostratum***	NHol SHil WPat

LEMBOTROPIS See **CYTISUS**

LEMNA (Lemnaceae)

gibba	LMay MSta
minor	EWav LMay MSta
polyrhiza	See SPIRODELA ***polyrhiza***
trisulca	LMay MSta

LEONOTIS (Labiatae)

leonurus	See L. ***oxymifolia***
§ ***oxymifolia***	CB&S CGre CHil CMer CPle CTre LAbb LHop SAxl SLMG WHer WTay

LEONTICE (Berberidaceae)

alberti	See GYMNOSPERMIUM ***a.***
¶ ***leontopetalum***	NHol
– ***ewersmannii***	ECam
¶ sp. BSBE 864	WDav

LEONTODON (Compositae)

¶ ***autumnalis***	CKin
hispidus	CKin

LEONTOPODIUM (Compositae)

alpinum	CB&S CHar CKel EBre ELan EMNN EPar EPot GAbr GCHN IDai MBal MCas MPit NHol NKay NNor NNrd NRoo SIng WCla WHoo WPer WWin
– 'Mignon'	CLew CRiv ELan EMNN EPad GAbr GDra GLoc MHig NHol NKay NNrd NRoo NRya NVic SIng SSmi WHil WPer
§ ***discolor***	WOMN
hayachinense miyabeanum	ITim WHoo
himalayanum	CLew WDav
§ ***leontopodioides***	GLoc
sibiricum	See L. ***leontopodioides***
tataricum	See L. ***discolor***

LEONURUS (Labiatae)

cardiaca	CArn CSev EMon Effi GPoy LHol MChe MSal NSel SIde WHer WPer WSto
sibiricus	MSal

LEOPOLDIA (Liliaceae/Liliaceae)

comosa	See MUSCARI ***comosum***

LEPECHINIA (Labiatae)

chamaedryoides	SLHN

LEPIDOTHAMNUS (Podocarpaceae)

§ ***laxifolium***	SHil SIng WThu

LEPIDOZAMIA (Zamiaceae)

¶ ***hopei***	LPal
peroffskyana	LPal

LEPTINELLA (Compositae)

§ ***albida***	GGar
§ ***atrata***	MTho SIng
§ – ***luteola***	MCas MHig NGre WHil
§ ***dendyi***	ECou GLoc NHol NNrd
§ – forms	ECou
§ ***goyenii***	MHig NHol
¶ ***maniototo***	ECou
§ ***pectinata***	ECou
– ***sericea***	See L. ***albida***
perpusilla	See COTULA ***p.***
§ ***potentillina***	CHoe ECha ELan EMon ESis MMth NHol NKay NNrd SChu SIng WHil WPer WWin

§ ***pyrethrifolia linearifolia*** CHar CLew GLoc LGre LHil LHop NSti SBla SCro SFar SIng
♦***reptans*** See L. ***scariosa***
§ ***rotundata*** CKni ECou NCat WPer
§ ***scariosa*** ECou LHop
§ ***squalida*** CLew CRiv ECha ECou IBlr LHil MCas NCat NHol NNrd NVic SIng SLHN SSmi WHil WPer

LEPTODACTYLON (Polemoniaceae)

¶***pungens*** WDav

LEPTOSPERMUM † (Myrtaceae)

arachnoides CSun
cunninghamii See L. ***lanigerum***
ericoides See KUNZEA ***ericoides***
N***flavescens*** See L. ***polygalifolium***
§ ***grandiflorum*** CFor CGre CPle ELan ERav ISea SSpi WSHC
humifusum See L. ***rupestre***
juniperinum CPle CSun
laevigatum CSun ISea
§ ***lanigerum*** CB&S CCla CFor CMHG CPle ECou IOrc ISea NHol SHil SLon SPer WBod WSHC WWin
¶– 'Citratum' ECou
¶– 'Cunninhamii' CFor ECou IBar LSav
*– 'Macrocarpum' ISea
¶– 'Wellington' ECou
liversidgei CPle ECou SSta
¶– x ***scoparium*** ECou
minutifolium CSun
N***nitidum*** CSun
obovatum CMHG
petersonii ECou
phylicoides See KUNZEA ***ericoides***
N***polygalifolium*** CSun
prostratum See L. ***rupestre***
pubescens See L. ***lanigerum***
rodwayanum See L. ***grandiflorum***
§ ***rupestre*** CChu CCla CMHG CPle CSun CTre ECou EPot IBar IDai IJoh ISea ITim MBal MBar MBro MGos NHar SHil SIng SSpi WBod WDav WSHC
scoparium CLan CPle ECou IOrc LSav MSal NWCA SBar SHil
– 'Autumn Glory' CPle CTre
*– 'Black Robin' IHos
– 'Blossom' CB&S ECou
¶– 'Bunting' ECou
– 'Burgundy Queen' CB&S ECou
– 'Chapmanii' CMHG SHil
– 'Cherry Brandy' CB&S ELan EPot
¶– 'Chiff Chaff' ECou
– 'Elizabeth Jane' CB&S MR&S
– 'Fascination' CB&S CGre
¶– 'Firecrest' ECou
– 'Gaiety Girl' CGre ISea
– 'Grandiflorum' CGre CTrw
¶– 'Jubilee' CB&S
– 'Karekare' CB&S
– 'Keatleyi' CGre ECou LAbb SHil SPla
– 'Leonard Wilson' CSun ECou
¶– 'Lyndon' ECou
– 'Martinii' CB&S CTre MR&S
¶– 'McLean' ECou
– 'Nichollsii' CB&S CGre CMHG CSco CTre ENot EPot ITim SIng SLon WAbe WEas WSHC
– 'Nichollsii Grandiflorum' IDai SHil
– 'Pink Cascade' CB&S SPer
– 'Pink Champagne' ECou LAbb
– ***prostratum*** GLoc
– 'Red Damask' CB&S CBow CChu CGre CLan CPle CSam CSco ELan ENot EPot ESis IBar IDai IOrc LAbb MRav SHil SPer SPla SReu WSHC
– 'Red Ensign' ENot
– 'Red Falls' ECou
¶– 'Redpoll' ECou
¶– 'Redstart' ECou
¶– 'Robin' ECou
– 'Roland Bryce' ECou
– 'Rosy Morn' ISea LHop
– 'Silver Sheen' CChu CFor CGre LGre SPla SSpi SSta
– 'Snow Flurry' CB&S CGre CTre ENot MR&S SPer
– 'Sunraysia' CChu CSam CSun CTrw SPer
– 'Winter Cheer' MR&S
scoparium nanum CRiv EPot SHil SIng SPla WThu
– – 'Huia' CTre ECou ENot IOrc
– – 'Kea' CLew ECou ELan EPot GLoc WPat
– – 'Kiwi' CB&S CTre ECou ELan ENot EPot IOrc ITim MR&S SAxl SHil SLon SMad
– – 'Kotoku' ELan EPot GLoc ITim
– – 'Tui' CTre
squarrosum CSun

LESPEDEZA (Leguminosae)

bicolor CB&S CCla CLew SSpi
buergeri ELan
¶***davurica*** CB&S
****floribunda*** CB&S CPle
****hedysaroides*** CB&S
thunbergii CBow CCla CSco CShe ECro EHar ELan ENot ERav LHop MBlu MBri MGos MPla SHil SPer SReu SSpi SSta WBod
¶– 'Albiflora' WSHC
tiliifolia See DESMODIUM ***elegans***
yakushima MPla

LESQUERELLA (Cruciferae)

¶***fendleri*** NTow
¶***multiceps*** WDav

LEUCADENDRON (Proteaceae)

argenteum CHEx CSun
¶***discolor*** CSun
sessile CSun

tinctum CSun

LEUCAENA (Leguminosae)
§ *latisiliqua* CPle
leucocephala See L. *latisiliqua*

LEUCANTHEMELLA (Compositae)
§ *serotina* CBre CGle CHan CLew ECha ELan SApp SPer WBon WEas WWin

LEUCANTHEMOPSIS (Compositae)
§ *alpina* CLew MHig WPer
hosmariensis See CHRYSANTHEMOPSIS *hosmariense*

LEUCANTHEMUM † (Compositae)
hosmariense See CHRYSANTHEMOPSIS *hosmariense*
mawii See CHRYSANTHEMOPSIS *gayanum*
§ *maximum* EFou GCHN MCot MWgw NNor SApp WEas WHil WOak WWin
– *uliginosum* See LEUCANTHEMELLA *serotina*
nipponicum See NIPPONANTHEMUM *nipponicum*
x *superbum* 'Aglaia' MBri SFis
– 'Alaska' SMrm SPer
– 'Antwerp Star' MFir
– 'Beauté Nivelloise' CKel ECha
– 'Bishopstone' ELan ERou LHil MWgw WEas
– 'Cobham Gold' NOrc
§ – 'Esther Read' CBow CGle CKel CShe ELan ERou NNor NRoo SApp WAbe
– 'Fiona Coghill' CSco
– 'H Siebert' CKel
– 'Horace Read' ECha ELan EMon LHil
¶ – 'John Murray' MBri WBon
¶ – 'Little Princess' MBro
¶ – 'Little Princess' WHal
– 'Manhattan' EMon
– 'Marion Collyer' GWic
– 'Mayfield Giant' ERou
¶ – 'Mount Everest' LHil WCot
– 'Phyllis Smith' CBre CGle CHan CSco ECha EJud GWic MBri NCat SApp SFis WAbb WBon WHal WHil
– 'Polaris' WHil
– 'Shaggy' WSHC
§ – 'Silberprinzesschen' CShe EJud LHil MFir NHol NOak NRoo WHen
– 'Snow Lady' GCHN MPit WHen WHil
– 'Snowcap' CCla CHar EBre ECha ENot EPla ERou MBri NBar SApp SMrm SPer
– 'Starburst' EFou MBri NRoo WHen
– 'T E Killin' CGle CSco ECha EMon WHil
¶ – 'Wirral Pride' LHil
§ – 'Wirral Supreme' CBre CCla CHar CKel EBre ELan ENot EOrc ERou IDai LHil MBro MFir MWat NNor SCro SFis SPer WEas
§ *vulgare* CArn CKin CNat EBre EJud NLan WCla WEas WHen WHer WOak
– 'Hullavington' CNat
– 'Maikönigin' ('May Queen') EMon GWic

LEUCOCORYNE (Liliaceae/Alliaceae)
ixioides LBow

LEUCOGENES (Compositae)
grandiceps EPot GEdr ITim
leontopodium GGar GLoc ITim MHig NHar NRoo

LEUCOJUM † (Liliaceae/Amaryllidaceae)
aestivum CB&S CBro ECam ELun EOrc LAma LBlo LBow MBri MBro MSta NLan SIng WBod WCla
– 'Gravetye Giant' CAvo CBro CHad ECha ELan EPar EPot ERav ETub LAma LBlo LBow LFox LRoo MPar NHol SIng WThu
autumnale CAvo CBos CBro CFor CTom ELan GLoc ITim LAma LBow MBal MHig MPit NHol SAxl SIng SPou SSpi SWas WChr WOMN
– 'Cobb's Variety' LHop
– *oporanthum* EPot MPlt NHol
– *pulchellum* CBro CRiv EPot
nicaeense CAvo CBro EBul ECam EPot GLoc LBow LHop MHig SOkd WChr WMar WOMN WThu
roseum CAvo ECam EPot LAma LBow SOkd SWas WChr WMar
¶ *trichophyllum* JCA NHol
– pink form EPot WChr
valentinum CBro WChr
vernum CBro ECam ELan EPar EPot ETub LAma LBow MBri MHig NHol NLan SIng SSpi
– *carpathicum* CAvo CBro EBul GEdr LAma WChr
– *vagneri* CBro EPot GEdr LFox LHop MPar NHol SFir WChr

LEUCOPOGON (Epacridaceae)
ericoides SIng
§ *fraseri* ECou IBar
¶ *parviflorus* ECou

X LEUCORAOULIA (Compositae)
R. hectorii x L. grandiceps EPot ITim MHig NHol SOkd
loganii EPot GArf GDra ITim MHig NHar NHol SOkd WDav

LEUCOSPERMUM (Proteaceae)
¶ *cordifolium* yellow CSun

LEUCOTHOË (Ericaceae)

axillaris	CSun
davisiae	IDai MBal SSta
fontanesiana	CCla MBal MGos SHil SPer SReu WSHC WWat
– 'Nana'	SHil SPer
– 'Rainbow'	Widely available
– 'Rollissonii'	MBal MBar NHol SPer SPla SSta WBod
greyana	NHol SHil
keiskei	ECro NHol SHil SOkd SSpi
* 'Lovita'	GWic MBri MUlv SSpi SSta
populifolia	See AGARISTA ***p.***
'Scarletta'	CBow CKni COtt IBar IJoh MBar MBri MGos MUlv NHol SHil SSpi SSta SSus WWeb

LEUZEA (Compositae)

§ *centauroides*	MFir

LEVISTICUM (Umbelliferae)

officinale	CArn CCor CSFH CSev ECha EJud ELan Effi GPoy LHol MBar MChe NSel SDix SIde WEas WHal WHer WOak WPer WSto

LEWISIA † (Portulacaceae)

¶ 'Ashwood Pearl'	MAsh
'Ben Chace'	MAsh
Birch strain	CB&S ELan EPad SIng
brachycalyx	EPad EPot GAbr GArf GLoc MAsh MBal MTho NHar SIng WDav
cantelovii	EMNN ESis GLoc ITim MAsh NGre NNrd NRoo WThu
columbiana	CPla EMNN ESis MAsh MBro NGre NHol NRed NRoo NTow SIng WCla WHal
– 'Rosea'	ESis MAsh MCas MHig NGre NHol WAbe WMar WThu
– rupicola	EPot ESis ITim MAsh NGre NHol NNrd NRya
– wallowensis	CLew EPot MAsh NHol NRed WCla WThu
congdonii	NGre
cotyledon	CPla ESis MAsh NNrd WHil
– alba	CPla ESis GAbr GDra GLoc LHop MAsh NGre NHol NRed NTow WCla WHoo WThu
– Ashwood strain	CSun ESis GEdr MAsh MBri NRoo SIng WAbe WHoo
– cotyledon	NNrd
– 'Harold Judd'	CHar CRiv EPot NNrd
– heckneri	GAbr GDra LHop NHol SIng WEas
– howellii	CPla ELan EPot GAbr NHol NNrd SIng WPer
– hybrids	CCla CHar CMHG EBre EMNN EPad EPot GDra GLoc ITim MBro MHig NGre NHol NRed SSmi WAbe WMar WOld WThu WWin
– magenta strain	MAsh NHol
– 'Rose Splendour'	ELan EPad EPar EPot MAsh SIng
– 'Sundance'	GDra
– Sunset strain	CSam ELan ESis GAbr GCHN GDra GEdr GLoc MBal MBri NGre NHar NHol NKay NTow SBla WCla WDav WEas WHoo WPer
'Edithae'	WAbe
'George Henley'	CRiv EPot MAsh NHol SIng WAbe WDav WThu
'Joyce Halley'	NHol
'Karen'	SIng
* 'L W Brown'	SIng
leeana	MAsh
longifolia	See L. ***cotyledon cotyledon***
§ *longipetala*	EBar EMNN EPot ESis GAbr GDra GLoc MAsh MHig NGre NHar NHol NNrd NRed WAbe WHal WThu
*– *arizonica*	GArf
* *longiscapa*	ESis MAsh NGre
nevadensis	Widely available
oppositifolia	MAsh
'Oxstalls Lane'	WThu
'Paula'	SIng
'Phyllellia'	MAsh
'Pinkie'	CRiv EPot MAsh SIng
pygmaea	EPot ESis GAbr GCHN GLoc ITim MAsh MBri NGre NHol NNrd NRed NRoo SIng WAbe WHil WHoo WThu
– longipetala	See L. ***longipetala***
rediviva	GLoc ITim MAsh NGre NHol SIng WAbe WDav
– JCA 9269	WDav
– Jolon strain	MAsh
– pink form	NRed
sierrae	MAsh NGre NNrd NRed WThu
stebbinsii	MAsh
¶ 'Susan'	SIng
'Trevosia'	CRiv EPot MAsh MHig NHol NNrd SIng WThu
triphylla	MAsh NGre
tweedyi	EMNN EPad EPot GDra ITim MAsh NGre NHol SIng WDav
– alba	GDra MAsh
*– 'Elliott's Variety'	MAsh
– Mount Wenatchee form	GLoc
– rosea	EMNN GDra MAsh NGre NTow WThu

LEYCESTERIA (Caprifoliaceae)

crocothyrsos	CGre CHan CPle GWic IBrk MFir WTay
formosa	Widely available

LEYMUS (Gramineae)

§ *arenarius*	CElw CHad CHoe ECha EFol ELan EOrc ERou GWic MUlv MWgw NOrc SApp SLHN SMad WEas WRus WWat

LHOTSKYA (Myrtaceae)

alpestris	CSun

LIATRIS (Compositae)

pycnostachya	EBar ECro WWin
scariosa 'Alba Magnifica'	CB&S CCla
'Snow Queen'	ERou
spicata	CArn CB&S CChu CShe CSun CTom ECha EFol EFou ELan GCHN GPoy LAma LHol MPit MSal MWgw NNor SIde SW&B WOld WPer
– 'Alba'	CChu CCla ECha ECro EFol EFou EGol ELan EOrc GGar LAma LHol LHop MWgw NBar SPer SW&B WHal WHoo WPer
– *callilepis*	CHar CKel CSco EBre ELan LHop MWat NKay SPer WEas
– 'Floristan Weiss'	CElw CHad CTom EBre ECro GAbr GCHN MBri NOak NRoo WHil
– 'Kobold' ('Goblin')	CB&S CShe EBre ENot EOrc ERou IDai LSav MBri MWgw NBar NRoo SAxl WHoo

LIBERTIA † (Iridaceae)

caerulescens	CHan EBar EBul IBlr LHop
chilensis	See L. ***formosa***
¶ *elegans*	SSpi
§ *formosa*	CCla CElw CGle CHan CSun EBre ECha EGol EPot LHop MBal MBri MUlv NHol NSti SArc SAxl SChu SPer WDav WHer WHil WOld WWin
– form	GWic IBlr
grandiflora	CB&S CHEx CHan ECha ELan EPar GWic IBlr ISea NCat SPer SPla SSpi WAbe WBod WHal WPer
ixioides	CAvo CGre CHan ECou IBar IBlr WHoo WOld
¶ 'Nelson Dwarf'	ECou
paniculata	CHan EGol IBlr
peregrinans	CChu CHan ECha EMon GWic IBlr LSav SChu SDix WAbe WHil WOld
– 'Gold Leaf'	CB&S SLHN
pulchella	CHan MHig SWas
sp. ex New Zealand	GWic

LIBOCEDRUS (Cupressaceae)

chilensis	CGre SBor SHil
decurrens	See CALOCEDRUS ***decurrens***

LIBONIA (Acanthaceae)

floribunda	See JUSTICIA ***rizzinii***

LICUALA (Palmae)

grandis	LPal MBri

LIGULARIA † (Compositae)

clivorum	See L. ***dentata***
§ *dentata*	CBow CHEx CHan CRow ELun MFir WHoo WOld
– 'Desdemona'	Widely available
– 'Orange Princess'	CSco
– 'Othello'	CCla CRow CSco MBal MBri NKay WCot
'Gregynog Gold'	CHad CHan CHar CRow CSco ECha EGol ELun ENot ERou MBri NKay SCro SMad SPer WHoo
x *hessei*	CRow GGar
hodgsonii	CSam CSco MBri MCot NHol NSti SLHN
japonica	CRow CSco
macrophylla	EBre ECro WCru
x *palmatiloba*	GWic LRHS WCot
§ *przewalskii*	CGle CHEx CHan CSun EFol EFou ELun EPar GWic LMay MBal MBri MFir MWat NKay NNor NOak NTow SLHN SMad WEas WHoo WOld
– 'The Rocket'	Widely available
smithii	See SENECIO ***smithii***
stenocephala	CCla CHEx CRow EGol
tangutica	See SENECIO ***tanguticus***
♦ *tussilaginea*	See FARFUGIUM ***tussilagineum***
veitchiana	CCla CRow CSco CSun GDra GGar GWic SApp SFis WBon WCru WDav
wilsoniana	CCla CRow SFis

LIGUSTICUM (Umbelliferae)

scoticum	CTom GPoy

LIGUSTRUM † (Oleaceae)

chenaultii	SHil SMad WMou WWat
delavayanum	EMon MUlv WWat
x *ibolium* 'Midas'	CMHG
japonicum	CHil EHar ENot ISea LSav SHil WBod WWat
– 'Coriaceum'	See L. ***j.*** 'Rotundifolium'
♦– 'Macrophyllum'	SHil
§ – 'Rotundifolium'	CBow CCla CSco EHar LNet MUlv SHil SIng SPer
– 'Texanum'	SGar
§ *lucidum*	CBra CCla CMCN CPle CShe EHar ELan ENot MBar MGos MUlv SArc SCro SHil SPer SSpi WMou WWat
– 'Excelsum Superbum'	CSco ECtt EHar ELan LPan MBar MBri SHil SPer SSpi SSta
¶ – 'Golden Wax'	MUlv
*– 'Latifolium'	MUlv SHil
– 'Tricolor'	CBow CLan CSco EHar ELan IOrc MBal MBri SChu SHil SPer SPla SSpi WWat
obtusifolium regelianum	MR&S
ovalifolium	CB&S CBra CCla CLnd CSco IDai ISea LBuc MBar MBri MGos NNor NWea SHil SPer WMou
§ – 'Argenteum'	CB&S CBra CFis CGle CHoe CLan CSco EGol EPla ERav ISea MBar MBri NHol SLon SPer SPla SReu WEas WPat WWin
– 'Aureo Marginatum'	See L. ***o.*** 'Aureum'
§ – 'Aureum'	Widely available

*– 'Lemon and Lime' SPla
– 'Variegatum' See L. *o.* 'Argenteum'
quihoui CCla CHan EGol EMon MGos MUlv SDix SHil SSpi WHCG WWat
§ *sempervirens* CBow CCla LHop MUlv SSta WBod
sinense CHan CMCN CMHG WWat
– 'Pendulum' NHol
– 'Variegatum' CMHG CRow EPla IDai SHil SMad WWat
– 'Wimbei' EPla SSpi
stongylophyllum SArc
x *vicaryi* CHoe EPla NHol SPer SSpi WPat
vulgare CKin LBuc MBri SHil WHer WMou

LILAEOPSIS (Umbelliferae)
macloviana ECou NHol

LILIUM (Liliaceae/Liliaceae)
'Achilles' (Ia) MLin
African Queen (VIa) CKel EWal LAma LBlo MLin SW&B
amabile (IX) CBro CKel LBlo SW&B
'Amber Gold' (Ic) CKel
amoenum (IX) WChr
'Apeldoorn' (Ie) ETub EWal LAma SW&B
'Apollo' (Ia) ETub SW&B
**argenteum* CHEx
'Aristo' See L. 'Orange Aristo'
Asiatic hybrids (VI/VII) LAma LBlo SW&B
'Attila' (Ib) CKel EWal SW&B
auratum (IX) CB&S CBro CKel EWal LAma LBow SW&B
– 'Cinnabar' (IX) CKel
– 'Crimson Beauty' (IX) LAma SW&B
– *platyphyllum* (IX) SW&B
– 'Red Band' EWal
'Avignon' (Ia) LAma
'Ballade' (Ia) LBlo
'Beckwith Tiger' (Ic) EBul
Bellingham hybrids (IV) EBul LBlo SSpi
Bellmaid hybrids (IV) EBul
'Black Beauty' (VIId) LAma MLin SW&B
'Black Dragon' (VIa) CKel LAma LBlo
Black Magic (VIa) SW&B
'Bonfire' (VIIb) CKel SW&B
'Brandywine' (Ib) EWal
'Bright Star' (VIb) CBro CKel EWal LAma LBlo SW&B
bulbiferum croceum (IX) LBlo SW&B
Bullwood hybrids (IV) EBul
'Bull's Eye' (Ib) SW&B
¶ Burgundy (Ic) EFou
'Cambridge' (Ic) EWal
§ *canadense* (IX) EBul LAma MBal MS&S SW&B WChr
– *editorum* LAma
– *flavum* See L. *canadense*
'Canasta' (Ia) LBlo
candidum (IX) CAvo CB&S CBro CFor CHEx CRiv ECha ELan EMon ETub EWal LAma LBlo LBow MBri SMad SW&B WCla
¶ – 'Plenum' EMon
'Carla Luppi' (Ia) LBlo
'Casablanca' (VIIb) CB&S EWal LAma LBlo MLin SW&B
cernuum (IX) LBlo SW&B
chalcedonicum (IX) CRiv MPar WChr
'Cherrywood' (IV) EBul
'Chinook' (Ia) EWal LAma MBri
Citronella (Ic) CBro EWal LAma LBlo MS&S SW&B
'Coachella' (IV) EBul
'Cocktail' (Ia) LBlo
¶ *concolor* 'Partheneion' (IX) EPot
'Concorde' (Ia) SW&B
'Connecticut King' (Ia) CAvo CB&S CBro CKel ETub EWal LAma LBlo LBow SW&B
'Connecticut Yankee' (Ic) CKel
'Corina' (Ia) MBri SW&B
'Corsage' (Ib) CAvo CKel EWal LBlo SW&B
'Côte d'Azur' (Ia) ETub EWal LAma SW&B
¶ 'Crimson Sun' (VIb) EFou
* 'Crystal Palace' SW&B
x *dalhansonii* (II) MPar
* 'Daphne' SW&B
davidii willmottiae (IX) LAma MS&S
'Destiny' (Ia) CKel EWal LAma
'Discovery' (Ic) LBlo MS&S SW&B
'Dominique' (VII) LAma
duchartrei (IX) GEdr MPar
* 'Elvin's Son' ETub LAma
'Enchantment' (Ia) CAvo CB&S CBro CKel EWal LAma LBlo LBow MBri MLin SW&B
'Esther' (Ia) EWal
'Eurovision' (Ia) EWal
'Exception' (Ib) LAma
'Festival' (Ia) CB&S EWal LAma MS&S
'Fire King' (Ib) EWal LAma LBlo SW&B
'Firebrand' (I) EWal LAma
'Firecracker' (Ia) EWal LAma
* 'Flamenco' MS&S
formosanum (IX) EBul NSti NWCA WHal WHoo
– *pricei* (IX) COtt CRiv CSam EBul ELan EPot GEdr ITim LGre LHop MBal MBri MCas MFir MTho NHol NNrd SAxl WChr WCla WPer
– 'Snow Queen' (IX) CKel
'Fuga' (Ic) SW&B
'Genève' EWal
'Gold Medal' (Ia) EWal
Golden Splendor (VIa) CAvo EWal LAma LBlo MLin SW&B
'Gran Paradiso' (Ia) CB&S LAma
'Grand Cru' EWal SW&B
grayi (IX) EBul
'Green Dragon' (VIa) CBro CKel LAma LBlo
Green Magic (VIa) EWal LAma SW&B

'Hallmark' (Ic)	CKel
'Hannah North' (Ic)	EBul
hansonii (IX)	CBro CKel LAma LBlo
Harlequin hybrids (Ic)	CKel SW&B
'Harvest' (Ia)	ETub WAbe WHil
henryi (IX)	CAvo CKel EWal LAma LBlo LBow MLin SAxl SW&B
'Hornback's Gold' (Ic)	EBul
Imperial Crimson (VIIc)	SW&B
Imperial Gold (VIIc)	LAma LBlo SW&B
Imperial Silver (VIIc)	EWal LAma SW&B
¶ 'Iona' (Ic)	EBul
§ 'Jacques S Dijt' (II)	LAma LBlo
Jamboree (VIId)	SW&B
'Jetfire' (Ia)	CB&S ETub LAma SW&B
§ 'Joanna' (Ia)	EWal
'Journey's End' (VIId)	CB&S CSut ETub EWal LAma SW&B
'Joy' (VIIb)	CB&S EWal LAma
'Karen North' (Ic)	EBul
'King Pete' (Ib)	CSut SW&B
'Lady Ann' (VIb)	LBlo SW&B
'Lady Bowes Lyon' (Ic)	CFor EBul MLin
'Ladykiller' (Ia)	LAma
¶ 'Lake Tahoe' (IV)	EBul
'Lake Tulare' (IV)	EBul
§ ***lancifolium*** (IX)	EWal GPla LAma LBow SPla SW&B
– 'Flore Pleno' (IX)	LHop WCot
§ – ***splendens*** (IX)	CAvo CBro CKel ETub EWal LAma LBow MLin MPar SMad SW&B
¶ ***lankongense*** (IX)	WPer
'Le Rêve'	See L. 'Joy'
'Levant' (Ic)	CKel LAma SW&B
'Liberation' (I)	LAma LBlo NBir WHil
'Limelight' (VIa)	CKel LAma LBlo
'Little Snow White' (V)	GLoc
longiflorum (IX)	CAvo CB&S EWal LAma WHal
¶ – 'Casa Rosa'	EWal
– 'Gelria' (IX)	SW&B
– 'White American' (IX)	LBlo
'Luxor'	CB&S CSut
Mabel Violet (VIa)	CKel LAma SW&B
mackliniae (IX)	CBos CChu GEdr MBal NBir NHar NHol
'Manuella' (Ia)	LAma
'Marhan' (II)	LAma MPar
x ***marhan*** 'J S Dijt'	See L. 'Jacques S Dijt'
¶ 'Maria Callas' (Ia)	CSut
¶ 'Marie North' (Ic)	EBul
'Marilyn Monroe' (Ia)	EWal MLin
martagon (IX)	CAvo CBro CKel ECha EFou ELan ELun EMon ETub GAbr GPla LAma LBlo LBow MBal MS&S SW&B
– ***album*** (IX)	CAvo CBro ECha GEdr LAma LBlo LBow MPar MS&S MTho SW&B WChr
– ***cattaniae*** (IX)	ECha GAbr WChr
– ***pilosiusculum*** (IX)	MPar
– x ***hansonii*** (II)	EBul
'Maxwill' (Ic)	SW&B
'Medaillon' (Ia)	CKel EWal LAma MBri MLin SW&B
¶ 'Mona Lisa'	EWal
§ ***monadelphum*** (IX)	CBro LAma LBlo LBow LHop MPar SSpi SW&B
'Mont Blanc' (Ia)	CB&S EWal LAma NBir SW&B WAbe WHil
¶ 'Monte Negro' (Ia)	CSut
'Monte Rosa' (Ic)	SW&B
'Montreux' (Ia)	CB&S EWal LAma
'Moonflower' (Ia)	CB&S
Moonlight (VIa)	LBlo SW&B
'Mrs R O Backhouse' (II)	CKel LAma
§ ***nanum*** (IX)	CAvo GEdr NHol WDav
¶ – deep purple (IX)	NKay
– ***flavidum*** (IX)	NHol
– 'Len's Lilac' (IX)	NHol NKay
¶ – McBeath's form (IX)	NHol NKay
* 'Nell Gwyn'	EWal MLin
nepalense (IX)	GEdr LAma SW&B
* 'Nivea'	SW&B
'Olivia' (Ia)	LAma SW&B
Olympic Hybrids (VIa)	CKel EWal LAma SW&B
'Omega' (VII)	LAma SW&B
'Orange Aristo' (Ia)	LBlo
'Orange Pixie' (Ia)	CBro
* 'Orange Sensation'	LBlo
'Orange Triumph' (Ia)	EWal LAma
'Orange Wattle ' (Ic)	EBul
'Orchid Beauty' (Ia)	EWal MBri
'Orestes' (Ib)	LSav
* Oriental Superb	LBlo
oxypetalum (IX)	CAvo CBro GEdr NHol WDav
– ***insigne*** (IX)	GEdr NHol WDav
'Pan' (Ic)	MLin
'Pandora' (Ia)	EWal
'Paprika' (Ib)	LBlo
pardalinum (IX)	CAvo CBro CGle ECha ELan SAxl
– ***giganteum*** (IX)	CKel
'Peachblush' (Ia)	EWal LAma SW&B
'Peggy North' (Ic)	EBul
philadelphicum (IX)	WChr
philippinense (IX)	WHil
'Phoebus' (Ia)	EWal MLin
'Pink Beauty' (VIIc)	CBro SW&B
* 'Pink Panther'	LBlo
Pink Pearl Trumpets (VIa)	SW&B
Pink Perfection (VIa)	CAvo CB&S CBow CBro CKel EWal LAma LBlo MLin SW&B
'Pink Sunburst'	SW&B
'Pink Tiger' (Ib)	CKel
'Pirate' (Ia)	EWal LAma MS&S
* 'Pixie's Gold'	CTab
polyphyllum (IX)	NHol
'Prins Constantijn' (Ib)	CKel
'Prominence'	See L. 'Firebrand'
§ ***pumilum*** (IX)	CAvo CBro ETub LAma LBlo LHop MTho SW&B WCla
¶ 'Purple Sensation' (Ia)	CSut
pyrenaicum (IX)	CAvo EBul ELan LHop MPlt MS&S NHol WChr

– ***aureum*** (IX)	LBlo
'Rangoon' (Ia)	EBul
'Red Carpet' (Ia)	CBro EFou ETub NBir WAbe WHil
'Red Fox' (Ic)	SW&B
Red Jewels (Ic)	LAma
'Red Lion' (Ia)	CKel MLin SW&B
* 'Red Marvel'	LBlo
* 'Red Sentinel'	CTab
'Redstart' (Ib)	MPar
regale (IX)	CAvo CB&S CBow CBro CKel CSam CSut EBre EFol EFou ETub EWal LAma LBlo LBow LHop MBal MLin MS&S SW&B WEas WHal
– ***album*** (IX)	CAvo CKel EFou LAma LBlo LBow SW&B
§ – Royal Gold (IX)	CB&S CBow CKel LAma LBlo MLin SW&B
'Roma' (Ia)	CSut EWal LAma
'Rosefire' (Ia)	LAma
'Rosemary North' (I)	EBul
'Rosepoint Lace' (Ic)	SW&B
'Rosita' (Ia)	EWal LAma MBri SW&B
'Roter Cardinal' ('Red Knight') (Ia)	EWal
Royal Gold strain	See L. ***regale*** 'Royal Gold'!
'Sans Pareil'	SW&B
'Sans Souci' (VIId)	LBlo
* 'Scallop'	CTab
'Scentwood' (IV)	EBul
* 'Sea Urchin'	CTab
shastense (IX)	MS&S
'Simoen' (Ia)	SW&B
'Sirocco' (Ia)	CKel
'Snow Princess'	LAma
'Snow Trumpet' (V)	CSam
¶ 'Sorrento'	CSut
speciosum album (IX)	CBro CKel EWal LAma LBlo SW&B
– 'Grand Commander' (IX)	CKel LAma LBlo SW&B
– 'Ida Uchida' (IX)	LBlo
– 'Rosemede' (IX)	LBlo
– ***roseum*** (IX)	LAma LBlo MLin SW&B
– ***rubrum*** (IX)	CAvo CB&S CBro CKel ECha EWal LAma LBlo LBow MLin SW&B
– 'Twinkle' (IX)	SW&B
– 'Uchida' (IX)	CB&S EWal LAma SW&B
'Star Gazer' (VIIc)	CB&S CBro EWal LAma LBlo MLin SW&B
'Starfish' (I)	CTab
* 'Sterling Silver'	LAma
'Sterling Star' (Ia)	CB&S ETub EWal LAma LBlo MLin SW&B
'Sun Ray' (Ia)	LAma WAbe WHil
'Sunset' (Ia)	SW&B
superbum (IX)	EBul LAma WChr
szovitsianum	See L. ***monadelphum***
'Tabasco' (Ia)	MS&S
'Tamara' (Ib)	CSut EWal LAma MBri MS&S SW&B
* 'Tandy'	MLin
tenuifolium	See L. ***pumilum***
x ***testaceum*** (IX)	CAvo ETub LAma LBlo LBow MPar SW&B
'Tiger White' (Ic)	LBlo
tigrinum	See L. ***lancifolium***
– 'Splendens'	See L. ***lancifolium splendens***
'Trance' (VIb)	LBlo
'Tropicana' (Ia)	SW&B
'Troubadour' (VIIc)	LBlo
¶ 'Unique'	CSut
wallichianum (IX)	LAma SW&B
¶ 'Wattle Bird' (Ia)	EBul
'White Happiness' (Ia)	LAma
'White Henryi' (VId)	SW&B
'White Journey's End' (VIId)	CB&S
'White Lady' (VIa)	CBro CKel
'White Mountain' (VIIc)	SW&B
'White Prince' (Ia)	EWal
willmottiae	See L. ***davidii willmottiae***
'Yellow Blaze'	LAma SW&B
'Yellow Giant'	See L. 'Joanna'
* 'Yellow Imp'	CTab
'Yellow Present'	SW&B
* 'Yellowhammer'	LBlo

LIME See CITRUS *aurantiifolia*

LIMNANTHES (Limnanthaceae)

douglasii	CKni CRiv ELan EMon IBlr LHil MPit SIng WBod WEas WHal WHer WHil

LIMONIUM (Plumbaginaceae)

bellidifolium	CShe ECha GLoc MHig NNrd NTow SBla SFir SLHN WEas
cosyrense	CSun
§ ***dregeanum***	WThu
♦ ***dumosum***	See GONIOLIMON ***tataricum angustifolium***
globulariifolium	See L. ***ramosissimum***
¶ ***gmelinii***	WPer
¶ ***gougetianum***	MCas
latifolium	CCla CGle CSco CSun EGol IDai MFir MWat MWgw SDix SFis SPer WEas WHoo WOld
– ***grandiflorum***	CKel
– 'Violetta'	CKel CSco ECha ELan ERav ERou MBri SMrm SPer
¶ ***minutum***	GLoc
paradoxum	ELan
¶ ***platyphyllum***	WPer
§ ***ramosissimum***	WThu
♦ ***tartaricum angustifolium***	See GONIOLIMON ***t. a.***
tetragonum	See L. ***dregeanum***

LINANTHASTRUM See LINANTHUS

LINANTHUS (Polemoniaceae)

nuttallii	WPer

LINARIA (Scrophulariaceae)

alpina	CRiv CTom ECro ELan EMNN GLoc MBar MPit MTho NHar NKay NOak NWCA SIng WCla WPer WWin
– *rosea*	NKay WCla WCru
* 'Blue Pygmy'	MPit
* *cyana*	SFis
cymbalaria	See CYMBALARIA ***muralis***
dalmatica	CSev ELan GPla LGan NCat SMrm SWas WOMN WPer
x *dominii* 'Carnforth'	EMon
– 'Yuppie Surprise'	EFou ELan EMon LRHS
genistifolia dalmatica	CChu CCor CGle CHan CHar CSun ERou GWic MFir NRed NSti NWCA SAxl SChu SWas WKif
hepaticifolia	See CYMBALARIA ***h.***
maroccana 'Fairy Bouquet'	WPer
nevadensis	WCla WHil
origanifolia	See CHAENORHINUM ***origanifolium***
pallida	See CYMBALARIA ***pallida***
pilosa	See CYMBALARIA ***pilosa***
purpurea	CCor CGle CHar CKin CRiv EFou EJud ELan EMon LHol MFir NCat NNor WCla WHea WPer WWin
– 'Alba'	See L. ***p.*** 'Radcliffe Innocence'
– 'Canon Went'	Widely available
– 'Radcliffe Innocence'	ECha ECro
¶ – 'Springside White'	EMon
repens	CCor CKin WCot
supina	EMNN GLoc MWat NKay NNrd WCla WHer WPer
triornithophora	CGle ECha ECro LGan MBri NSti SMrm WBon WCar WCot WWin
– cream form	CSun
– pink form	CBot CGle MPar WBon WEas WPer
– purple form	CSun ELan
¶ *tristis*	SFir
– 'Toubkal'	ITim MDHE MPar SWas WWin
vulgaris	CKin CNat CRiv EBre EJud GWic LHol MChe NLan NSel SIde WHer

LINDELOFIA (Boraginaceae)

anchusoides	CSun WHoo
longiflora	GWic WPer
¶ *spectabilis* 'Hartington White'	EMon

LINDERA (Lauraceae)

angustifolia LH 126	SSpi
benzoin	SHil SSpi
erythrocarpa	CMCN SSta WCoo
¶ – MSF 819	SSpi
– USNA 3768	SSpi
obtusiloba	CFor SHil SSpi SSta WCoo
umbellata	WCoo

LINNAEA (Caprifoliaceae)

borealis	CElw GDra GEdr ITim MBal MHig WAbe WOMN
– *americana*	CLew MHig NNrd NWCA SIng

LINUM † (Linaceae)

arboreum	ECha MBro MPla NHol SBla SHil SIng SLHN WOMN WPat WThu WWat
capitatum	WOMN
flavum	CGle CShe IDai WHoo WPer
– 'Compactum'	CCla CKel CSun EBre ECha EFou ELan GLoc LAbb MBro MPit MRav NHol NKay NRoo SBla SPer WDav WHal WOld WWin
'Gemmell's Hybrid'	CShe EPot GLoc MBro MCas MHig NHol SBla WDav WPat WThu
leonii	ELan EMon LRHS
¶ *mongolicum*	WPer
monogynum	ECou MPar NHol NWCA SChu SFir
§ – *diffusum*	ECou
– dwarf form	MTho
♦ – 'Nelson'	See L. ***m. diffusum***
narbonense	CHar CKel CSam CShe ELan ERou LGre LGro MBro MFir MUlv NHol NNrd NOak SCro SMrm SSpi SSus WHoo WKif WOld WPer
– 'Heavenly Blue'	ECtt ELan EOrc GWic LHop WEas WHen
perenne	CHad CHar ECha ELan GPla GWic IDai LAbb LHol MBri MChe MPit MPla MWgw NNor SIde SPer WEas WHer WPer WWin
– *album*	CHad EFou ELan GWic NSel SPer WHer WPer WRus
– *alpinum*	LGre WCla WPer
– *alpinum* 'Alice Blue'	SBla WDav
– *anglicum*	CNat NSel
– 'Blau Saphir' ('Blue Sapphire')	EFou EOrc ESis MPit NHol NRoo NRya WCla
– *lewisii*	CSun LGre NBir NHol NRya WDav WOMN
sibiricum	See L. ***perenne***
suffruticosum salsoloides nanum	WOld WThu
– *salsoloides* 'Prostratum'	ECha
usitatissimum	SIde
viscosum	EBar WPer

LIPPIA (Verbenaceae)

canescens	See PHYLA ***c.***
chamaedrifolia	See VERBENA ***peruviana***
citriodora	See ALOYSIA ***triphylla***
nodiflora	See PHYLA ***nodiflora***
repens	See PHYLA ***nodiflora***

LIQUIDAMBAR (Altingiaceae)

formosana	CGre CMCN MBlu MBri SSpi SSta WCoo WNor WWeb
– Monticola group	SHil SSta
orientalis	CMCN CSco LMer SSta
styraciflua	Widely available
*– *acalycina**	SSta
– 'Aurea'	IOrc SHil SMrm SPer SSta WPat
*– *festeri**	SSta
– 'Golden Treasure'	SSta
– 'Gumball'	EHar SSta
– 'Lane Roberts'	CCla CSco EHar LHop LSav MBri MUlv SHil SReu SSta WPat
– 'Moonbeam'	SHil SSta
– 'Moraine'	SSta
– 'Palo Alto'	SSta
– 'Pendula'	SSta
– 'Variegata'	SExT SGar SHil SMad SPer SSta
– 'Worplesdon'	CSco EHar ENot IHos LMer LSav MBri SMad SPer SSpi SSta WAbe WWat

LIRIODENDRON † (Magnoliaceae)

chinense	CMCN EHar ELan MBri SHil SSpi WCoo
tulipifera	Widely available
– 'Aureomarginatum'	Widely available
– 'Fastigiatum'	CSco EHar ELan ENot MBri SHil SPer SSpi SSta WMou
¶ – 'Mediopictum'	ELan

LIRIOPE † (Liliaceae/Convallariaceae)

¶ *exiliflora* 'Silvery Sunproof'	WCot
gigantea	SApp
graminifolia	See L. ***muscari***
hyacinthifolia	See REINECKEA ***carnea***
minor	SApp WCot
§ *muscari*	Widely available
– 'Monroe White'	SApp
– *variegata*	CAvo CRow ELan
platyphylla	ECro SApp SSpi
spicata	SSpi WHoo
– 'Alba'	CCla CHad CRow ECro EGol GWic MTho MUlv

LITHOCARPUS † (Fagaceae)

densiflorus	LSav SArc WCoo
edulis	CHEx SArc
§ *glaber*	CHEx
henryi	SBor

LITHODORA (Boraginaceae)

§ *diffusa*	LHil MPit NKay SBla SSpi
– *alba*	CMHG EPot GLoc MBri MPla NHol SIng WDav WHal WHil
– 'Cambridge Blue'	CSam LGre LHop MPla SAxl WSHC
¶ – 'Compacta'	LHop
– 'Grace Ward'	CCla CGle CRiv EPot IDai MCas MPla NHol SAxl SIng SMrm WDav WHal WPat WSHC WThu
– 'Heavenly Blue'	Widely available
¶ – 'Inverleith'	LHop
hispidula	ELan GLoc
♦ x *intermedia*	See MOLTKIA x ***i.***
§ *oleifolia*	CSam CShe ELan EPot GLoc LGre MHig MTho NHol NKay SHil SIng SMrm WDav WPat
– 'Barker's Form'	WOld
rosmarinifolia	ELan EPot LHop SHil WOMN
zahnii	ELan EPad EPot GLoc LHop MTho NHol NTow WHil

LITHOPHRAGMA (Saxifragaceae)

parviflora	CRiv EPot GDra GLoc MTho NHol SBar WDav WHil WOMN

LITHOSPERMUM (Boraginaceae)

arvense	MSal
diffusum	See LITHODORA ***diffusa***
doerfleri	See MOLTKIA ***doerfleri***
officinale	GPoy MSal WCla WSto
oleifolium	See LITHODORA ***oleifolia***
purpureo-caeruleum	See BUGLOSSOIDES ***purpurocaerulea***

LITTONIA (Liliaceae/Colchicaceae)

modesta	LBow

LIVISTONA (Palmae)

australis	CHEx LPal NPal
chinensis	LPal
decipiens	NPal

LOASA (Loasaceae)

LOBELIA † (Campanulaceae)

anatina	GWic IBrk
N *angulata*	GLoc MTho NGre NNrd SIng SSmi WAbe WHil
– 'Jack's Pass'	MTho
– 'Ohau'	ECou ESis NHol WOMN
§ – 'Tim Rees'	MTho NRya SBla SIng WCru WPer
– 'Woodside'	ECou
'Bees' Flame'	CB&S CChu ERou MTho
'Brightness'	ELan GWic SAxl
cardinalis	CArn CBWG CHad CHar CKel CRow CSun CWGN EHon EMon EPot ERav EWav GWic LGre LHol LMay MSal MSta MWat SChu SSpi WOld WWin
¶ – JLS 88010	EMon
'Cherry Ripe'	CChu CRiv ELan MTho SAxl SBla SChu
¶ 'Compliment Scarlet'	GCHN
'Dark Crusader'	CChu CHad CRow ECha EFou ELan GWic LGre LHil MBri MTho NHol NOrc NSti SChu
'Flamingo'	See L. 'Pink Flamingo'

fulgens	CHad CWGN IBlr MFir SCro SMrm SSpi WEas WHil
– 'Illumination'	GWic
* 'Galen'	CRow
¶ x *gerardii*	NHol
¶ – 'Eastgrove Pink'	WEas
– 'Vedrariensis'	Widely available
* *gibberosa*	CHEx
¶ 'Hadspen Royal Purple'	CHan
'Huntsman'	IDai
inflata	CArn MSal
'Jack McMaster'	CChu GWic LGre LHop MTho NSti
'Kathleen Mallard'	CCla CElw CGle CRow CSev ELan EMon EPla ERav GWic WEas
laxiflora	CBos CBot CHan MTho SBla SMrm WEas
– *angustifolia*	CChu CGre CHEx CMHG ELan EMon EPla GWic IBlr LHil LHop WMar WPer WRus
lindblomii	CElw CRiv CTom EPar NHar NNrd SIng WHal
linnaeoides	EPot MTho NNrd NTow WEas WOMN WPer
macrodon	NGre NRya
nicotinifolia	GWic
§ *oligodon*	NKay
♦–	See LOBELIA *o.*
pedunculata	Widely available
– 'Blue Stars'	ECou
– 'Clear Skies'	ECou
– 'County Park'	CLew CRiv ECou ELan ESis GLoc LRHS NWCA SBla SCro SIng SSmi WHal WPer WRus
– 'Kinsey'	ECou
– 'Tom Stone'	ECou NHol
perpusilla	ECou
– 'Fragrant Carpet'	ECou NHol WHer
– 'Summer Meadows'	CLew ECou NHol
'Pink Flamingo'	CBre CChu CGre CRow CSun ECha EFou GCHN GWic LGre LHop MTho NSti SAxl SBla SChu SMrm WHCG WHal WHil
'Queen Victoria'	Widely available
repens	ECou
'Russian Princess'	LHop MBri MTho NHol SBor SChu SMad
* *sequinii* 'Doniana'	WEas
sessilifolia	CHar GDra NGre SBla WPer
siphilitica	Widely available
– *alba*	CBrd CBre CRow EMon GWic SAxl WEas WHil
– 'Nana'	GWic
¶ x *speciosa*	WPer
'Tania'	CChu CRow EFou GWic IBlr LGre LHop MUlv NSti SAxl SChu SHig
tenuior	WPer
treadwellii	ECha ESis MPar MTho WAbe WHal WPer WWin
tupa	CBot CChu CFor CHEx CHad CHan CRow ELan ERav GGar GWic IBlr LGre LHop MTho SAxl SBla SChu SHig SMad SSpi WWat
– G&K 4253	CCla
valida	CHil ELan SMrm WPer
vedrariensis	See L. x *gerardii* 'Vedrariensis'
'Will Scarlet'	CChu GWic MTho SAxl SBla

LOGANBERRY See RUBUS

LOISELEURIA (Ericaceae)

LOMANDRA (Xanthorrhoeaceae)

longifolia	ECou

LOMARIA (Blechnaceae)

alpina	See BLECHNUM *penna-marina alpinum*
magellanica	See BLECHNUM *magellanicum*

LOMATIA (Proteaceae)

dentata	CGre ISea
ferruginea	CFor CHEx CLan CPle IBar ISea MUlv SArc SHil SSpi
longifolia	See L. *myricoides*
§ *myricoides*	CBow CCla CFor CHEx CTre CTrw ECro ELan ERav ISea SArc SDry SHil SSpi WBod WWat
– glaucous form	CFor
silaifolia	CTre SArc SDry SHil
tinctoria	CFor CHEx CPle CTre CTrw ERav LSav SArc SBor SHil SSpi

LONICERA † (Caprifoliaceae)

alseuosmoides	CChu SBra SLon WWeb
N x *americana*	CB&S CChu CCla CFor CMac CPle CSco CShe EBre EHar ELan ENot LHol MBri SBla SBra SHil SLon SPer SReu SSta WBod WSHC WWat
* 'Anne Fletcher'	MBri WEas WWeb
x *brownii*	CBra CMac IDai
– 'Dropmore Scarlet'	Widely available
– 'Fuchsioides'	CBow CCla ELan ENot EOvi ERav SBra SHil SPer SPla WSHC WWeb
caerulea edulis	ESim
caprifolium	CSco CShe EHal LGre LHol MBar MBri SBra SHil SPer WWat
– 'Pauciflora'	CBot CBow CCla CSco SBla SBra SHil SSpi SSta WSHC
chaetocarpa	CBot CMHG LGre WPat
ciliosa	CGre SBra
'Clavey's Dwarf'	IOrc NHol SPer WPat
'Early Cream'	CSco MMth
etrusca	CHan CSco EHal MBri NRar SBra SHil WWeb
– 'Donald Waterer'	LHop SBra SHil SPer SSpi
– 'Michael Rosse'	SBra SHil

– 'Superba'	CCla ECtt GWic MUlv SBla SBra SSpi WSHC
flexuosa	See L. ***japonica repens***
fragrantissima	CB&S CBot CCla CShe EFol EGol EHar ELan ENot ISea MBea MGos MWat NNor SChu SHil SPer SPla SReu SSta STre WHCG WHea
giraldii	CB&S CBot CHan SBra WSHC
glabrata	SBra WWat
grata	See L. x ***americana***
x *heckrottii* ('Gold Flame')	CB&S CHad CHan CMHG CMac CMer CSco IDai ISea MBal MBar MBea MBri MGos MR&S NBar NHol NKay NRoo SBra SHil SPer WAbe WSHC
henryi	CBow CCla CHan CMac CSco EGol ELan EPla GWic IOrc LHop MBar MBri MMth MRav NHol SBra SLon SPer SSpi WBod WSHC
– *subcoriacea*	SHil
* 'Hidcote'	CMac
hildebrandiana	CGre CHEx
implexa	CHan ELan SBra
insularis	CMCN
involucrata	CChu CCla CCor CHan CMCN CMHG CPle LHop MBar MRav NTow SCro SPer SReu WBod WHal
– *ledebourii*	CHan EPla GRei WPat
japonica	WOak WWat
– 'Aureoreticulata'	Widely available
– 'Dart's World'	SBra
– 'Halliana'	Widely available
¶ – 'Peter Adams'	LHop
§ – *repens*	CBow CBra CMac CSco CShe CTre ECtt ENot EPla IHos MBri MPla SBra SCro SHil SPer SPla WWeb
– 'Variegata'	CLan
korolkowii	CBow CMCN CSam NBir SSpi
– *zabelii*	ELan LGre
maackii	CHad CHan CMCN MRav
¶ *nigra*	EPla
nitida	CB&S CHan CKin CLan CSco ELan MR&S MRav NNor NRya SLon SPer WHen WMou
– 'Baggesen's Gold'	Widely available
– 'Elegant'	ELan IOrc LBuc
– 'Ernest Wilson'	MBar SHil
– 'Fertilis'	SPer
– 'Maigrün' ('Maygreen')	MBri
¶ *obovata*	WPer
periclymenum	CArn CKin GPoy NNor NWea WMou WOak WWin
N– 'Belgica'	Widely available
¶ – 'Cornish Cream'	EGol
♦– 'Florida'	See L. ***p.*** 'Serotina'
– 'Graham Thomas'	CBot CCla CHad CSam EFol ELan EPla ERav GWic IHos ISea LHop MBri MRav MUlv SBra SHil SMad SSpi SSus WSHC WWat WWeb
¶ – 'La Gasnérie'	EPla
*– 'Lyden'	SBra
*– 'Red Gables'	MBri
N– 'Serotina'	Widely available
§ – 'Serotina'EM 85	MBri
*– 'Serpentine'	SBra
¶ – *sulphurea*	EPla
– yellow form	SPer
pileata	Widely available
– 'Moss Green'	MR&S
x *purpusii*	CBow CBra CCla CHan CHil CPle CSam CSco LAbb MBar MCot MPla SHil SPer WBod WEas WHal WSHC WWin
– 'Winter Beauty'	ECtt ELan MBlu MBri SHil SLon SSpi SSta
pyrenaica	SHil
¶ *quinquelocularis*	EHal
reflexa	EHar LHop
rupicola syringantha	Widely available
– *syringantha* 'Grandiflora'	MPla
sempervirens	EGol LGre MRav SBra SHil SSpi WSHC WWat
– 'Sulphurea'	CMCN SBra WWeb
setifera	CBot SHil
similis delavayi	CBot SBra
splendida	CBot CCla CFor CSam SBra SSpi WEas
sp. L 1604	SSpi
standishii	CB&S LHol MBea MR&S MRav MUlv SHil SPer WOld WWat WWin
syringantha	See L. ***rupicola s.***
tatarica	CHan WHCG
– 'Arnold's Red'	CB&S CBow CPle CSco ELan MBlu MPla
– 'Hack's Red'	CB&S CBow CBra CCla COtt ECtt NKay SHil SPer STre WHCG
– 'Rosea'	SPer
– *sibirica*	SPer
– 'Zabelii'	CCor MGos
x *tellmanniana*	Widely available
tragophylla	CB&S CBow CChu CCla CFor CMac EBre EHar ELan EOvi ERav IOrc MBri MRav SBla SBra SHil SPer SSpi SSta WBod WSHC WWat
trichosantha deflexicalyx	CHan
¶ *webbiana*	ELan
x *xylosteoides* 'Clavey's Dwarf'	MGos
– 'Miniglobe'	EPla
xylosteum	SAxl WBod

LOPHOMYRTUS (Myrtaceae)

§ *bullata*	CChu CGre CPle CTre ECou EPla
'Gloriosa'	CB&S CGre

* 'Lilliput'	CB&S
§ *obcordata*	CB&S CGre ERav WCoo
'Pinkalina'	CB&S
* 'Pixie'	CB&S
x *ralphii*	CTre WWat
§ – 'Kathryn'	CB&S CGre CHan CPle ERea ISea WSHC
– 'Variegata'	ERea
§ 'Traversii'	CCla CGre CTrw
'Tricolor'	CTre
'Versicolor'	CB&S CMer CSun LAbb

LOQUAT See **ERIOBOTRYA** ***japonica***

LOROPETALUM (Hamamelidaceae)

chinense	CCla SSta

LOTUS (Leguminosae)

berthelotii	Widely available
– Kew form	LHop
– x *maculatus*	LHop
corniculatus	CArn CKin CNat GAbr NLan SFir
– 'Plenus'	CLew CMer CRiv ELan EPot GWic IBlr ITim WPer
¶ 'Gold Flash'	IHos
§ *hirsutus*	Widely available
¶ *jacobaeus*	LGre
maculatus	CHil CSpe CSun LGre LHil LHop WTay
¶ *maritimus*	MSal NWCA
mascaensis	ERea NTow SIgm
♦ *pedunculatus*	See L. ***uliginosus***
§ *pentaphyllus pentaphyllus*	NRar
suffruticosus	See L. ***pentaphyllus pentaphyllus***
§ *uliginosus*	CKin

LUCULIA (Rubiaceae)

gratissima	CB&S CBot CHEx CHan CSun LAbb LHop SHil
– *rosea*	CSun SLMG

LUDWIGIA (Onagraceae)

¶ *longifolia*	IBrk
¶ *octovalvis*	LGre

LUETKEA (Rosaceae)

pectinata	CLew EPot GCHN GDra GGar MHig NHol SIng WAbe WPat WThu

LUMA (Myrtaceae)

§ *apiculata*	CHil CLan CMHG CPle CTre CTrw IJoh MBal MMth MR&S SArc SDix SHil SPer STre WBod WCoo WMou WSHC WWat
§ – 'Glanleam Gold'	Widely available
– 'Penwith'	CBow CGre
– 'Variegata'	CMHG NHol WWat
§ *chequen*	CChu CMHG CPle CTre WWat

LUNARIA (Cruciferae)

§ *annua*	NCat WEas WHer WHil WOak
– *alba*	ECro EFou NBir NCat SIde WHer WOak
¶ – *alba-variegata*	EMon WHil
¶ – 'Croftacre Purple Pod'	ECro
¶ – 'Ken Aslet'	NHol
¶ – 'Stella'	GWic
– *variegata*	GWic IBlr MPar MTho NBir SFir WEas WHal WHer WHil WOMN WOld
– violet	GWic NBir
biennis	See L. ***annua***
rediviva	ECha ECro EMon ERav GGar IBlr SAxl SSpi WEas

LUPINUS † (Leguminosae)

albifrons	LGre SBla SMrm
¶ – *collinus*	CMHG
– *douglasii*	LGre
arboreus	Widely available
– 'Golden Spire'	SMad
– 'Snow Queen'	CCla
¶ *argenteus*	ELan
'Band of Nobles'	ECtt GAbr LAbb MRav NVic
¶ 'Barnsdale'	MWoo
¶ 'Beryl, Viscountess Cowdrey'	EMon
'Blushing Bride'	CSco EMon
'Boningale Lass'	CSco
'Catherine of York'	CSco
chamissonis	CBos LHop MTho
'Chandelier'	CHad CSco EBre ECtt EFou ELan MBri MRav NBar NRoo SPer WHil WPer
¶ 'Chelsea Pensioner'	MWoo
¶ 'Clifford Star'	MWoo
¶ 'Deborah Woddfield'	MWoo
Dwarf Gallery hybrids	NOak
'Dwarf Lulu'	See L. 'Lulu'
'Fred Yule'	CSco
'Gold Dust'	CSco
¶ 'Halina'	MWoo
¶ 'Household Brigade'	MWoo
¶ 'Judith Chalmers'	MWoo
'Lady Fayre'	CSco
¶ 'Little Eugenie'	MWoo
littoralis	CHar GDra
'Loveliness'	CSco
§ 'Lulu'	EBre ECtt ELan LAbb MPit MRav NOak NRoo SFis SPer WHil
'Minarette'	ECtt MBri
¶ 'Misty'	MWoo
¶ 'Moonraker'	MWoo
'My Castle'	CSco EBre ECtt EFou ELan MBri MRav NBar NRoo SMad SPer WHil WPer
'Nellie B Allen'	CSco
'Noble Maiden'	ECtt EFou ELan MBri MRav NBar NOak NRoo SMad SPer WPer
¶ 'Olive Tolley'	MWoo
¶ 'Orangeade'	MWoo

¶ 'Party Dress' MWoo
¶ 'Pope John Paul' MWoo
¶ *princei* ELan
'Royal Parade' CSco
¶ 'Royal Wedding' MWoo
Russell hybrids CB&S CBow CHar CKel CSco ELan MWgw NRoo WHer
¶ 'Sunset' MWoo
'Sunshine' CSco
'The Chatelaine' CHad CSco EBre ECtt EFou ELan MBri MRav NBar NRoo SPer WPer
'The Governor' CSco EBre ECtt ELan MBri MRav NBar NRoo SMad SPer WPer
'The Page' EBre EFou ELan MBri MRav NBar NRoo SPer WHil WPer
'Thundercloud' CHad CSco
¶ 'Troop the Colour' MWoo
¶ 'Walton Lad' MWoo

LUZULA (Juncaceae)
alopecurus ECou SApp
x *borreri* 'Botany Bay' CHoe EMon
campestris CKin
¶ *canariensis* SSpi
celata CHoe ECou
– *NZ* Ohau EPar
maxima See L. *sylvatica*
'Mount Dobson' EPar
¶ *nivalis* CHan
nivea CHoe ECha ERou GAbr GWic MFir NCat NHol NSti SApp SFar SIng SSpi WCar WHea WHil WOMN
pilosa GWic IBlr
* *plumosa* SApp SSpi
pumila ECou
rufa ECou
§ *sylvatica* CKin CRow ERou MFir MWgw NLan SSpi WHea
*– 'Aurea' ECha SApp
– 'Marginata' CB&S CBre CElw CHEx CHoe CKel CRow ECha ECro EFol EGol EMon GAbr MBal NSti SApp SCro SMrm SSpi WHea WRus WWat WWin
¶ – 'Select' SApp
– 'Tauernpass' EMon GPla
¶ *ulophylla* CHoe ECou

LUZURIAGA (Liliaceae/Philesiaceae)
¶ *radicans* SIng WCru WSHC

X LYCENE (Caryophyllaceae)

LYCHNIS † (Caryophyllaceae)
alpina CLew CSun EFol ELan GDra GLoc MBro MFir NGre NHar NKay NRoo NRya WCla WHil WHoo WPer WWin
¶ – *americana* NTow
– *rosea* CHan NHol SIng
x *arkwrightii* CGle CHar CHoe CKel CLew CRow CSun EBre ECha EFou ELan ERou MBri MPit NOak NSti SIng SPer WHil WHoo WOMN WOld WWin
§ – 'Vesuvius' CB&S CGle CSun GGar NRoo WHoo WPer
chalcedonica Widely available
– *alba* CCor CElw CSam ECha EFou ELan EMon ERav ERou IBlr MFir NCat NOak NSti SPer WBon WEas WHen WHil WHoo WPer
– *carnea* EMon NCat
– 'Plena' CHar EFol WOld
– *rosea* CElw CGle CLew ECro EFou EMon ERou GPla MUlv NHol NSti WHen
§ *coronaria* CArn CBre CFis CGle CHad CHoe CRow ECha ELan EPar ERav MBri MCot MFir NKay NNor NOak NSti SIng SPer WCla WEas WHil WOld
– 'Abbotswood Rose' See L. x *walkeri* 'A.R.'
– *alba* Widely available
¶ – 'Angel's Blush' ECro GCHN
– *atrosanguinea* EBre ECro EFou EPad ERou GCHN IBlr LHil NHol SCro SPla WPer
– *oculata* CBre CBro CCor CGle CHad CHan CHil CLew ELan EMon ERou GCHN IBlr LHop MFir MTho NOak NSti SLHN SSvw WEas WHen WHer WHoo
¶ *coronata sieboldii* WPer
dioica 'Rosea Plena' See SILENE *dioica* 'Rosea Plena'
flos-cuculi CArn CBre CKin CRow CWGN ECro EFou EHon EPar GCHN MSal MSta NLan SFis SLHN WBon WCla WHen WHer WSto
– *albiflora* CBre CElw CRow CSam EFou EMon EPar NSel NSti SLHN WBon WCla WHer WHil
– dwarf form EMon LHop WCla WOMN WPat WPer
flos-jovis CGle CHad CLew CSco CSun ECha ECro ELan EMon LHop MSal NOak SIng WEas WHea WPat WPer
– 'Alba' CBow
– 'Hort's Variety' CHar CKel ECro EFou ERou MUlv NSti SBla WCla WHil
– *minor* GCHN WOMN
– 'Nana' CRow GLoc GWic LHop NRed WHoo
x *haageana* CSun EOrc ERou LHil MBri MWgw NWCA SIng
kubotae See X LYCENE *k.*
lagascae rosea See PETROCOPTIS *glaucifolia rosea*
miqueliana EBar EMon MFir NGre WPer
* *nutans* MSal
¶ *sculata nana* 'Rose Angel' WPer
sp. Andes WOMN

§ *viscaria*	CGle CKin CLew ECha ECro GPla MSal NGre NLan NNor NNrd NSti WCla
– *alba*	ECha ECro EPla GWic NSti
– *alpina*	EFou
¶ – *atropurpurea*	GWic
¶ – 'Firebird'	EFou
– 'Plena'	CSco ELan NCat SFis WHil WOld
¶ – 'Snowbird'	EFou
– 'Splendens Plena'	CGle CLew CShe ECha EFol ELan EMon EPla IDai MBal MWat NKay NVic WEas
§ × *walkeri* 'Abbotswood Rose'	NBar
¶ – 'Abbotswood Rose'	EMon
¶ *wilfordii*	CBot NGre NRed
yunnanensis	CCor CLew GCHN MFir NHol SFis WCar WPer

LYCIUM (Solanaceae)

barbarum	ELan SFir SHil

LYCOPSIS See **ANCHUSA**

LYCOPUS (Labiatae)

europaeus	CArn GPoy MChe MSal

LYCORIS (Liliaceae/Amaryllidaceae)

albiflora	CKel SW&B
aurea	CKel SW&B

LYGODIUM (Schizaeaceae)

¶ *japonicum*	NMar

LYONIA (Ericaceae)

ligustrina	CCla ELan LSav SHil SSpi SSta
mariana	SReu

LYONOTHAMNUS (Rosaceae)

floribundus aspleniifolius	CChu SArc SHil SSpi WSHC WWat

LYSICHITON (Araceae)

americanus	Widely available
camtschatcensis	CChu CCla CHEx CRiv CRow CWGN ECha EHon ELan EPar LMay LSav MSta SMad SPer SSpi WWat

LYSIMACHIA † (Primulaceae)

¶ *atropurpurea*	WCot
barystachys	EMon LHop MRav WCot
ciliata	CBre CChu CCor CFor CGle CHan CHoe CMHG CRow ECha EFol EFou EGol ELan ERav MBri NSti SChu WEas WHal WHoo WOld WRus WWin
clethroides	Widely available
ephemerum	Widely available
henryi	LHil WEas WHal
japonica minutissima	MTho NKay NRya WCru WOMN WPer WWin
¶ *lichiangensis* B&L 12464	EMon
nemorum	CKin
nummularia	CShe CWGN ECtt EHon EJud GPla GPoy LHol LMay MBar MBri MFir MWgw NNor NNrd SIde
– 'Aurea'	Widely available
* – *nana*	MPit
¶ *ovata*	NHol
pseudohenryi	GLoc LHop
punctata	CFis CHar CKel CRow CSco CShe CWGN ECha EHon ELan ERou MBri MCot MFir MPit MWat MWgw NHol NKay NNor NSti WEas WOld WWin
thyrsiflora	CRow MSta
vulgaris	CArn CWGN EHon NSel WHil

LYSIONOTUS (Gesneriaceae)

pauciflorus	SOkd

LYTHRUM (Lythraceae)

'Croftway'	SCro
salicaria	CArn CGle CKin CRow CSun CWGN EHon GCHN MChe MFir MSal NLan NNor NSel SLHN WCla WHer WHil
– 'Brightness'	CSco NCat
– 'Feuerkerze' ('Firecandle')	CKel EBre EFou ELan EPad ERou MRav MUlv MWgw NHol SChu SPer
– 'Happy'	GWic
– 'Lady Sackville'	EFou GWic SFis WAbe
– 'Morden's Pink'	EFou MBri
– 'Red Gem'	EFou
– 'Robert'	CShe ECha ELan ERou MBri MWat MWgw NHol NOak NSti SChu SPer WEas
– 'Rose'	ELan MWgw
– 'The Beacon'	CGle CRow ERou SFis WCot
– Ulverscroft form	MUlv
virgatum 'Rose Queen'	ECha EFol GWic SPer WBon
– 'Rosy Gem'	CRow ECtt EPad MFir NOak SFis STre WHoo WPer WRus
– 'The Rocket''	CHar CSco EBre NHol SPer WWin

MAACKIA (Leguminosae)

amurensis	CB&S CBow CChu CCla ELan SHil WCoo

MACFADYENA (Bignoniaceae)

§ *unguis-cati*	CGre

MACHAERANTHERA (Compositae)

♦ *pattersonii*	See M. ***bigelovii***

MACHILUS See **PERSEA**

MACKAYA (Acanthaceae)

bella	CSun ERea LHop

MACLEAYA (Papaveraceae)

N*cordata*	CArn CHEx CWGN EFou ELan EPar LAbb MFir MWgw SPer WEas WHal WHer WHoo
– 'Flamingo'	CCla EBre ECha EFou GWic MUlv SAxl SSus
microcarpa	EMon
§ – 'Kelway's Coral Plume'	Widely available

MACLURA (Moraceae)

pomifera	CPle EHar MSal WCoo

MACRODIERVILLA See **WEIGELA**

MACROPIPER (Piperaceae)

crocatum	See PIPER *ornatum*
excelsum	CHEx ECou
¶ – 'Aureo-pictum'	CHEx

MACROZAMIA (Cycadaceae)

communis	LPal WNor
miquelii	LPal
moorei	LPal
reidlei	LPal WNor

MAGNOLIA † (Magnoliaceae)

acuminata	SHil SSpi
– *subcordata*	LRHS SHil
'Ann'	LSav SSpi
'Betty'	CFor LNet MGos MR&S SSpi SSta
biondii	SSpi
'Caerhays Belle'	CB&S CGre
¶ 'Caerhays Surprise'	CB&S
campbellii	CB&S ELan ISea SPer SSpi
– *alba*	CB&S LSav SHil SPer SSta
– 'Charles Raffill'	CBow EHar IBar SHil SPer SSpi SSta
– 'Darjeeling'	SHil
– 'Ethel Hillier'	SHil
– 'Kew's Surprise'	CGre SLHN SSpi
– *mollicomata*	CB&S CSam CTrw IBar ISea SHil SSta
– *mollicomata* 'Lanarth'	CB&S SHil SSpi SSta
– 'Princess Margaret'	SHil
*– 'Wakehurst'	SHil
'Charles Coates'	CLan LHyd SHil SSpi
'Coral'	SSpi
¶ *cordata* 'Miss Honeybee'	SSpi
cylindrica	CB&S CGre LSav SHil SSpi SSta
dawsoniana	CB&S CMCN SHil
¶ – 'Ruby Rose'	SSpi
delavayi	CHEx LRHS SArc SHil SSpi WBod
§ *denudata*	CB&S CCla CMCN CTrw EHar LSav MBal SGar SHil SPer SReu SSpi SSta WNor WSHC
– late form	SSpi
'Elizabeth'	SHil SSpi
¶ 'Eva Maria'	SSpi
fraseri	SHil
'Freeman'	LSav
'Galaxy'	SSpi
'George Henry Kern'	COtt MGos SGar SSpi
globosa	CBow CMCN SHil SSpi WWat
'Glow'	SSpi
grandiflora	CHEx CMCN IJoh ISea LSav MRav MWat SArc SLon SSta WNor
– 'Charles Dickens'	SHil SSpi
– 'Exmouth'	Widely available
– 'Ferruginea'	CLan SHil SSpi
– 'Gallissonière'	LSav SGar SPic
– 'Goliath'	CB&S CHEx CLan CTre EHar ELan IOrc ISea LNet MBal MR&S SArc SHil SPer SSpi SSta WBod
– 'Little Gem'	SHil
– 'Russet'	LNet SPer
– 'Saint George'	LSav SPic
– 'Saint Mary'	LRHS SPic
– 'Samuel Sommer'	CMCN LNet LRHS SPic
– 'Undulata'	SHil
¶ – 'Victoria'	ELan SSpi
'Heaven Scent'	CBow CMCN COtt EHar IOrc LHop LSav MBar MBri SHil SPer SSpi SSta
heptapeta	See M. *denudata*
N x *highdownensis*	CGre
hypoleuca	CB&S CHEx LSav SHil SPer SSpi SSta
'Iolanthe'	CMCN MBri SHil SSpi
'Jane'	COtt EBre LSav MBri SHil SPer SSpi SSta
'Judy'	LSav
x *kewensis* 'Kewensis'	CB&S SHil
– 'Wada's Memory'	CB&S CCla CMCN CMHG LHyd LRHS LSav MBri SHil SSpi WWeb
* 'Koban Dori'	SSpi
kobus	CB&S CBot CBra CFor CGre CMCN CTre EHar LHyd LSav SGar SHil SLeo WBod WNor WWat
'Lilenny'	SPic SSpi
§ *liliiflora*	CSco CTre CTrw MBar SHil SPic
§ – 'Nigra'	CB&S CBow CFor CLan CMHG ELan ENot IJoh LSav MBri MGos MR&S MRav MWat NBar SBla SDix SHil SPer SPla SReu SSpi WWat
x *loebneri*	CB&S CFor CLan CTre EHal ELan LHyd SPla WCoo
– 'Ballerina'	CMCN MBri SSpi
– 'Leonard Messel'	Widely available
– 'Merrill'	CB&S CBow CCla CFor CMCN CMHG CSam CSco CTre EGol EHar IOrc ISea LSav MBal MBri MR&S MRav SBla SHil SPer SPla SSta WBod
– 'Snowdrift'	CMCN
– 'Star Bright'	CLan CMCN SSpi
macrophylla	SArc SHil SSpi
¶ – 'Sara Gladney'	CHEx
'Manchu Fan'	LRHS SHil SSpi

'Mark Jury'	CMCN SSpi SSta
'Maryland'	CTre LSav SHil SSpi
'Michael Rosse'	SHil
N *obovata*	WBod
officinalis biloba	SHil
¶ 'Orchid'	SSpi
'Peppermint Stick'	LRHS MBri SHil SSpi SSta
'Peter Smithers'	SSpi
'Pickard's Coral'	MBlu SPic WWeb
'Pickard's Firefly'	MBlu SPic WWeb
'Pickard's Garnet'	SPic WWeb
'Pickard's Glow'	MBlu SPic WWeb
'Pickard's Maime'	SPic
'Pickard's Opal'	SPic SSpi
'Pickard's Pearl'	SPic
'Pickard's Ruby'	SPic
'Pickard's Schmetterling'	See M. 'Schmetterling'
'Pinkie'	LHop LSav MBri SHil
x *proctoriana*	
'Proctoriana'	CBra LHyd SLeo SPer SPla SSpi
– 'Slavin's Snowy'	CTrw
'Purple Eye'	SHil
quinquepeta	See M. *liliiflora*
'Raspberry Ice'	LRHS MBri
'Ricki'	CMCN COtt LRHS LSav MBri MGos SSpi
'Royal Crown'	CKni EHar LSav MBri SSpi SSta
'Ruby'	SSpi
salicifolia	CBra CFor CTre ISea LSav SHil SPer SPla SSpi SSta WPat
– 'Jermyns'	CChu CFor LHyd SHil SLeo
sargentiana	CGre SHil SSpi
– *robusta*	CB&S CTrw EHar NHlc SHil SPer SReu SSpi SSta
– *robusta alba*	CTrw
'Sayonara'	IOrc SHil SSpi
§ 'Schmetterling'	MBlu SPic SSpi WWeb
¶ 'Serene'	SSpi
* 'Seyu'	SSpi
sieboldii	CB&S CBra CGre CMCN CSco EHar ELan IOrc LSav MBal MBar MBri MGos SBla SHil SPer SReu SSpi SSta WAbe WBod WCoo WNor
– *sinensis*	CB&S CMCN CSco ELan LSav SHil SPer SSpi WSHC
x *soulangeana*	Widely available
– 'Alba'	See M. x *s.* 'Alba Superba'
§ – 'Alba Superba'	CB&S CBra CGre COtt CSco CTre ENot IOrc ISea LSav MGos MR&S SBla SHil SPer SReu SSpi WBod
– 'Alexandrina'	CFor CTre ELan IOrc LSav MBri SPer WBod WWeb
– 'Brozzonii'	CB&S CGre CMCN CMHG CSam CTre IOrc ISea LSav SHil SSpi WBod
N – 'Burgundy'	CB&S CBot SBla SPic SSpi WBod
– 'Coimbra'	CFor SSpi
– 'Garnet'	SSpi
– 'Just Jean'	SSpi
– 'Lennei'	CB&S CBra CMCN CMHG CSco CTre EHar ENot IOrc ISea LSav MGos NKay SBla SHil SPer SPic SPla SReu SSpi WBod WNor
– 'Lennei Alba'	CMCN CSco ELan IOrc ISea LSav SHil SSpi
– 'Nigra'	See M. *liliiflora* 'Nigra'
– 'Picture'	CB&S CMCN CSco IOrc SBla SHil SPic SSpi WBod
– 'Rose Superb'	LSav
– 'Rubra'	See M. x *s.* 'Rustica Rubra'
§ – 'Rustica Rubra'	CB&S CBow CBra CLan CMCN CMHG CSam CSco EHar ELan ENot IOrc ISea LNet LSav MBri SBla SHil SPer SPla SSpi SSta WBod
– 'San Jose'	CMCN LSav MBri MR&S SPer SSpi SSta
– 'Sundew'	CB&S CFor CMCN IOrc ISea MBri SGar SPer SPic SSpi SSta WWeb
– 'Verbanica'	CTre LRHS SPic SSpi SSta
sprengeri	CGre CTrw SHil SSpi
– *diva*	CB&S CMCN SSpi
– *diva* 'Burncoose'	CB&S
§ *stellata*	Widely available
– 'Centennial'	LHop MBri SSta
– *chrysanthemiflora*	SSpi
– 'King Rose'	CB&S CBow CFor CMHG MBlu MBri SBla SPer SPic SSta WBod WSHC
– 'Massey'	CChu CFor SCro WBod
– 'Norman Gould'	CMCN LHop MBri SSpi
– 'Rosea'	CBow CSco EHar ELan IOrc SHil SPla WBod
– 'Royal Star'	CB&S CBot CFor CLan CSco CTrw EBre ENot IOrc ISea LSav MBri MGos MR&S SPer SPic SReu SSpi SSta WBod
– 'Water Lily'	CB&S CBot CBow CFor CMCN CSam CSco EGol EHar ELan IOrc ISea MBri SBla SHil SPer SSpi WBod WWeb
'Susan'	CMCN COtt IJoh IOrc LSav MBri MGos MR&S MWat SGar SHil SPer SPla SSpi SSta WBod WWeb
x *thompsoniana*	CMCN SHil SReu SSpi
'Tina Durio'	SSpi
tripetala	CHEx CMCN SHil SSpi WWat
– 'Woodlawn'	SSpi
x *veitchii*	CGre SSpi
– 'Isca'	WBod
– 'Peter Veitch'	SHil
virginiana	CGre CHEx CMCN SArc SHil SSpi WOMN
x *watsonii*	See M. x *wieseneri*
§ x *wieseneri*	CFor ELan MBlu MBri SHil SPer SPic SSpi SSta WBod
wilsonii	Widely available

X MAHOBERBERIS (Berberidaceae)
aquisargentii CBra CSam EGol EHar ENot IOrc LHop MGos MPla MR&S MRav NHol SHil SLon WPat WSHC WWat
'Dart's Treasure' MBri
'Magic' MBri MGos SMad WWeb
miethkeana CMHG CSam MBar SMad SPer
¶ ***neubertii*** SSta

MAHONIA † (Berberidaceae)
♦ ***acanthifolia*** See M. ***napaulensis***
§ ***aquifolium*** CBow CBra ELan ENot GRei IDai IJoh MBal MBar MBri MGos MR&S MWat NKay NNor NRoo NWea SHil SLon SPer SPla SReu WWin
– 'Apollo' CSco CShe EGol EHar ELan ENot IJoh IOrc MBar MBri MGos MR&S SHil SPer SReu SSpi SSta WPat WWat
– 'Atropurpurea' CSco EHar ENot IDai NKay SHil SPer WPat WWat
– 'Donewell' MBri
– 'Fascicularis' See M. x ***wagneri*** 'Pinnacle'
– 'Green Ripple' MBri NBar
– 'Orange Flame' MBri
– 'Scallywag' MBri
– 'Smaragd' CCla CSco EBre GRei MBlu MR&S MUlv SGar WPat
'Cantab' LSav NHol SSpi
confusa SSpi
fortunei CBot MBal SArc SMad WSHC
fremontii CGre LGre SHil SSpi WPat
haematocarpa LGre
higginsae SMad
japonica Widely available
§ – Bealei group CB&S CBow CCla CLan ELan GRei IOrc ISea LHyd MGos MR&S SCro SHil SLon WWeb
– 'Hiemalis' See M. ***j.*** 'Hivernant'
§ – 'Hivernant' CChu EHar ELan LSav MBri MUlv NHol WAbe WPat WWat WWeb
lomariifolia CB&S CBot CBra CHEx CLan CSco ENot IHos IOrc LSav MBal MRav MUlv SArc SHil SPer SReu SSpi SSta WSHC
x ***media*** 'Arthur Menzies' LSav MBri
– 'Buckland' CB&S CBra CChu CFor CSam CSco CTrw ENot ISea LSav MBal MBri SHil SLon SPer WBod WPat WSHC
– 'Charity' Widely available
– 'Charity's Sister' LSav MBri WAbe
– 'Faith' LSav
– 'Hope' LSav
– 'Lionel Fortescue' CB&S CBow CChu CFor COtt CSam CSco CTre CTrw EHar ELan ISea LHop LHyd LSav MBri SBla SHil SMad SPer SSpi SSta WBod WWat
– 'Underway' CBow ELan LSav MBri WAbe WBod
– 'Winter Sun' CB&S CSco EHar ELan IOrc LHop LSav MBlu MBri MGos MR&S MWat NHol NRoo SHil SPer SSpi WAbe WBod WWat
§ ***napaulensis*** SHil
*– 'Grayswood Hybrid' LSav
– 'Maharajah' LSav SSpi
nervosa CBow CChu CSco LSav MBlu MBri MHig MUlv NHol SHil SSpi SSta SSus WPat WSHC WWat
pallida T&K 553 CChu LSav
N ***pinnata*** CBow ELan ENot IOrc LSav MBal MBar NWea SHil SPer SSpi
piperiana LSav
pumila CBrd SHil
repens EGol EPla SLHN
– ***rotundifolia*** CCla SHil
¶ ***siamensis*** CGre
trifoliolata LGre LSav
– ***glauca*** SHil
x ***wagneri*** 'Fireflame' MBri
– 'Hastings Elegant' SHil
– 'Moseri' CChu CFis CSco MBri MUlv SHil SSpi
§ – 'Pinnacle' CSco MBri MGos
– 'Undulata' CCla CSco EGol ENot IHos LSav MBri MUlv SDix SHil SPer

MAIANTHEMUM (Liliaceae/Convallariaceae)
bifolium CFor CRow EBul ELun EMon EPar EPot MCas NHol NKay SLHN WDav WOld WWat
– British form WThu
§ – ***kamtschaticum*** EBul ECro EMon EPar
¶ – Yakushima form SOkd
¶ ***canadense*** MSal
dilatatum See M. ***bifolium kamtschaticum***

MALEPHORA (Aizoaceae)
lutea GLoc MHig

MALPIGHIA (Malpighiaceae)

MALUS † (Rosaceae)
'Aldenhamensis' MGos SDea SExT
'Almey' SIgm
x ***atrosanguinea*** NWea SHil
baccata CMCN SSpi WMou
– ***manshurica*** EHar SHil
brevipes CCor
'Butterball' EHar
F 'Charlotte' SKee
'Cheal's Crimson' NRog
'Coralburst' MBri
coronaria 'Charlottae' CLnd COtt CSco EHar ENot SHil SPer
'Cowichan' LRHS MBri NBar WJas
'Crittenden' SHil
'Dartmouth' CLnd CSco NRog SFam SKee SPer
F ***domestica*** SNTN

Cultivar	Suppliers
F– 'Acme' (D)	SDea SKee
F– 'Adam's Pearmain' (D)	EEde NTwe SDea SFam SIgm SKee SNTN WJas
F– 'Advance' (D)	SKee
F– 'Akane' (D)	SDea
F– 'Alford' (Cider)	SKee
F– 'Alkmene' (D)	NTwe
F– 'Allen's Everlasting' (D)	NTwe SDea SKee
F– 'Allington Pippin' (D)	NRog SDea SKee WJas
– 'American Mother'	See M. *d.* 'Mother'
F– 'Anna Boelens' (D)	SDea
F– 'Anne-Marie' (C)	SKee
F– 'Annie Elizabeth' (C)	EEde NTwe SDea SFam SKee SNTN WJas
F– 'Ard Cairn Russet' (D)	NTwe SDea
F– 'Arthur Turner' (C)	EEde NRog NTwe SDea SFam SKee WJas
F– 'Ashmead's Kernel' (D)	EEde MWat NRog NTwe SDea SFam SIgm SKee SNTN WHig WJas
F– 'Autumn Peamain' (D)	SDea
F– 'Baker's Delicious' (D)	EEde SDea SIgm
– 'Balsam'	See M. *d.* 'Green Balsam'
F– 'Barnack Beauty' (D)	SKee SNTN
F– 'Baumann's Reinette' (D)	SKee
F– 'Baxter's Pearmain' (C/D)	SKee
F– 'Beauty of Bath' (D)	CSam EEde EHar IJoh IOrc MBea NRog NTwe SFam SKee WJas
F– 'Beauty of Kent' (C)	SDea SKee
F– 'Beeley Pippin' (D)	NTwe SDea
F– 'Belle de Boskoop' (C/D)	SKee
F– 'Bess Pool' (D)	SKee
F– 'Bismarck' (C)	EEde SKee
F– 'Blenheim Orange' (C/D)	CSam EEde EHar EWar GBon LBuc MBri MCls MR&S MWat NRog NTwe SDea SFam SIgm SKee SNTN SPer WHig WJas
– 'Blenheim Red'	See M. *d.* 'Red Blenheim'
F– 'Bloody Ploughman'	EEde SKee
F– 'Blue Pearmain' (D)	EEde
F– Bolero ®/ 'Tuscan' (D/Ball)	ELan MBri SDea SSus WWeb
¶– 'Bolingbroke Beauty' (D)	EEde
F– 'Bountiful'	WHig
F– 'Braeburn' (D)	SKee
F– 'Bramley's Seedling' (C)	Widely available
F– 'Broad-Eyed Pippin' (C)	SKee
F– 'Brownlees Russet' (D)	EEde NRog NTwe SDea SFam SKee SNTN
F– 'Bushey Grove' (C)	SDea SKee
F– 'Calagolden Elbee' (D)	SKee
F– 'Calville Blanc d'Hiver' (D)	SKee
F– 'Calville des Femmes' (C)	SKee
F– 'Catherine' (C)	SKee
F– 'Catshead' (C)	SDea SKee SNTN WJas
F– 'Cellini' (C)	SDea SKee
F– 'Charles Eyre' (C)	SKee
F– 'Charles Ross' (C/D)	CMac CSam EWar GBon GRei MBea MCls NRog NTwe SDea SFam SIgm SKee WJas WWeb
F– 'Cheddar Cross' (D)	SKee
F– 'Chivers Delight' (D)	NBee NTwe SDea SNTN WJas
F– 'Christmas Pearmain' (D)	NTwe SDea WJas
F– 'Cinderella'	WHig
F– 'Claygate Pearmain' (D)	EEde NTwe SDea SFam SKee SNTN
F– 'Cockle Pippin' (D)	NTwe SDea
F– 'Coeur de Boeuf' (C)	SKee
F– 'Colonel Vaughan' (C)	SNTN
F– 'Compact Mac'	EMui
F– 'Compact Sue'	EMui
F– 'Cornish Aromatic' (D)	NTwe SDea SFam SKee SNTN WJas
F– 'Cornish Gilliflower' (D)	SDea SFam SKee WJas
F– 'Cornish Pine' (D)	SDea SKee
F– 'Coronation' (D)	SDea
F– 'Cortland' (C)	SKee
F– 'Costard' (C)	SKee
F– 'Cottenham Seedling' (C)	SKee
F– 'Coul Blush' (C)	EEde
F– 'Court Pendu Plat' (D)	EEde NRog SDea SFam SKee SNTN WJas
F– 'Cox's Orange Pippin' (D)	Widely available
F– 'Cox's Pomona' (C/D)	SDea SKee SNTN
F– 'Cox's Red Sport' (D)	SKee
F– 'Cox's Rouge de Flandres' (D)	SKee
F– 'Crawley Beauty' (C)	EEde NTwe SDea SFam SKee WJas
F– 'Crimson Bramley' (C)	CSam SKee
– 'Crispin'	See M. *d.* 'Mutsu'
F– 'Crown Gold'	SKee
F– 'Dabinett' (Cider)	SDea SKee WJas
F– 'Deacon's Blushing Beauty' (C/D)	SDea
F– 'Decio' (D)	SKee
F– 'Devonshire Quarrenden' (D)	CSam SDea SFam SKee WJas
F– 'Discovery' (D)	Widely available
F– 'Doctor Harvey' (C)	EHar SNTN
F– 'Doctor Kidd's Orange Red' (D)	SDea
F– 'Domino' (C)	SKee
F– 'Duchess of Oldenburg' (C/D)	SKee
F– 'Duchess's Favourite' (D)	SKee
F– 'Duke of Devonshire' (D)	CSam SDea SFam SKee

N– 'Dumeller's Seedling' (C)	NTwe SDea SKee SNTN
F– 'Dunn's Seedling' (D)	SDea
F– 'D'Arcy Spice' (D)	SDea SFam SIgm SKee WJas
F– 'Early Julyan' (C)	SKee
– 'Early Victoria'	See M. *d.* 'Emneth Early'
– 'Early Worcester'	See M. *d.* 'Tydeman's E. W.'
F– 'Easter Orange' (D)	SKee
F– 'Ecklinville' (C)	SDea SKee
F– 'Edward VII' (C)	NTwe SDea SFam SKee SNTN WJas
F– 'Egremont Russet' (D)	CMac CSam EMui EWar GBon GChr IOrc LBuc MBea MBri MCls MR&S MWat NBee NElm NRog NTwe SDea SFam SIgm SKee SPer WHig WJas
F– 'Ellison's Orange' (D)	CSam EEde EWar GBon MCls NRog NTwe SDea SFam SKee SPer WJas
F– 'Elstar' (D)	EMui IOrc NTwe SDea SIgm SKee WHig
F– 'Elton Beauty' (D)	EEde SDea
F– 'Emneth Early' (C)	GChr MCls NRog NTwe SDea SFam SKee WHig WJas
F– 'Encore' (C)	SDea
F– 'Epicure' (D)	CSam EEde GBon IOrc NElm NRog NTwe SFam SKee
F– 'Ernie's Russet' (D)	SDea
F– 'Evening Gold' (C)	SDea
F– 'Eve's Delight' (D)	SDea
F– 'Exeter Cross' (D)	SDea SFam SKee
F– 'Falstaff'	NTwe WHig
F– 'Fearn's Pippin' (D)	SFam
F– 'Fiesta' (D)	CSam EMui LBuc MBri NBar NTwe SDea SFam SIgm SKee WHig
F– 'Firmgold' (D)	SDea
F– 'Five Crowns'	SKee
F– 'Flower of Kent' (C)	SDea SKee
F– 'Forge' (D)	SDea SKee
F– 'Fortune' (D)	CMac CSam EMui GChr GRei MCls NElm NRog NTwe SDea SFam SIgm SKee SPer WHig WJas
F– 'French Crab' (C)	SDea
F– 'Fuji' (D)	SDea
F– 'Gala' (D)	CSam EMui MBri NTwe SDea SFam SIgm SKee SNTN
F– 'Gala Royal'	SKee
F– 'Gascoyne's Scarlet' (D)	SDea SFam SKee
F– 'Gavin' (D)	NTwe SDea SKee
F– 'Genesis II' (D/C)	SDea
F– 'Geneva' (Crab)	SKee
F– 'George Cave' (D)	GChr NBee NRog NTwe SDea SFam SIgm SKee WJas
F– 'George Neal' (C)	SDea SFam SIgm
F– 'Gladstone' (D)	SKee SNTN
F– 'Gloria Mundi' (C)	SDea SKee
F– 'Gloster '69' (D)	NTwe SDea SIgm SKee
F– 'Golden Delicious' (D)	CB&S CMac CSam ELan EWar IJoh LBuc MBea MBri MCls MR&S NElm NRog SDea SKee SPer WWeb
F– 'Golden Knob' (D)	SKee
F– 'Golden Noble' (C)	EEde NTwe SDea SFam SIgm SKee SNTN WJas
F– 'Golden Pippin' (C)	SNTN
F– 'Golden Reinette' (D)	SKee SNTN
F– 'Golden Russet' (D)	SDea WJas
F– 'Golden Spire' (C)	EEde NRog SKee
F– 'Goldilocks'	GChr SKee WHig
F– 'Gooseberry' (C)	SKee
F– 'Granny Smith' (D)	MBea MBri MR&S NTwe SDea SIgm SKee SPer WWeb
F– 'Gravenstein' (D)	SDea SFam SKee
F– 'Green Balsam' (C)	NRog
– 'Green Roland'	See M. *d.* 'Greenup's Pippin'
F– 'Greensleeves' (D)	CSam EEde EMui IJoh LBuc MBea MBri NBee NRog NTwe SDea SFam SIgm SKee SPer WHig WJas
F– 'Greenup's Pippin' (D)	SKee
F– 'Grenadier' (C)	EWar GChr GRei IJoh IOrc LBuc MBri MCls NBee NElm NRog NTwe SDea SIgm SKee SPer WHig
F– 'Hambledon Deux Ans' (C)	SDea
F– 'Harry Masters Jersey' (Cider)	SDea
F– 'Harvey' (C)	SDea
F– 'Hawthornden' (C)	EEde SKee
F– 'Herefordshire Beefing' (C)	SKee
F– 'Herring's Pippin' (D)	NTwe SDea SNTN
F– 'Histon Favourite' (D)	SKee
F– 'Hoary Morning' (C)	SDea
F– 'Holland Pippin' (C)	SKee
F– 'Holstein' (D)	NTwe SDea SIgm SKee
F– 'Howgate Wonder' (C)	CSam EMui GBon GChr IJoh IOrc LBuc MWat NBar NBee NElm NRog NTwe SDea SFam SIgm SKee SPer WHig WJas
F– 'Idared' (D)	MR&S NTwe SDea SKee
F– 'Improved Cockpit' (D)	NRog
F– 'Ingrid Marie' (D)	SDea SIgm SKee WJas
F– 'Invicta' (D)	SKee
F– 'Irish Peach' (D)	EEde NTwe SDea SFam SKee SNTN WJas
– 'Isaac Newton's Tree'	See M. *d.* 'Flower of Kent'
F– 'Isle of Wight Pippin' (D)	SDea
F– 'Isle of Wight Russet' (D)	SDea
F– 'James Grieve' (D)	Widely available
F– 'Jerseymac' (D)	SDea
F– 'Jester' (D)	NTwe SDea SKee WHig
F– 'John Apple' (C)	SKee
F– 'John Standish' (D)	SDea
F– 'Jonagold' (D)	EEde IJoh MBea MBri NTwe SDea SFam SIgm SKee SNTN SPer WWeb
F– 'Jonagold Crowngold' (D)	NTwe
F– 'Jonagored' (D)	SKee
F– 'Jonared' (D)	NTwe

F– 'Jonathan' (D)	SDea SKee WJas
F– 'Jordan's Weeping'	SDea WJas
F– 'Joybells' (D)	SKee
– 'Jubilee'	See M. *d.* 'Royal Jubilee'
F– 'Jupiter' (D)	CSam EMui GBon IOrc LBuc MBea MBri MR&S MWat NBar NRog NTwe SDea SFam SIgm SKee WHig WJas WWeb
F– 'Kapai Red Jonathan' (D)	IJoh SDea
F– 'Karmijn de Sonnaville' (D)	SDea SKee
F– 'Katja' (D)	CSam EMui GBon IJoh IOrc LBuc MBea MBri NBar NBee NTwe SDea SFam SIgm SKee SPer WHig
– 'Katy'	See M. *d.* 'Katja'
F– 'Kent' (D)	NTwe SDea SKee
F– 'Kentish Fillbasket' (C)	SKee
– 'Kentish Pippin'	See M. *d.* 'Colonel Vaughan'
F– 'Kentish Quarrenden' (D)	SKee
F– 'Keswick Codling' (C)	CSam NRog SDea SKee SNTN WJas
F– 'Kidd's Orange Red' (D)	EEde NTwe SFam SIgm SKee SNTN WHig
F– 'King Charles' Pearmain' (D)	SKee
F– 'King Luscious' (D)	SDea
F– 'King of the Pippins' (D)	EEde NTwe SDea SKee SNTN WJas
F– 'King Russet' (D)	SDea
F– 'Kingston Black' (Cider)	SDea SKee
F– 'King's Acre Bountiful' (C)	SKee
F– 'King's Acre Pippin' (D)	EEde SDea SFam SKee WJas
F– 'Lady Henniker' (D)	EEde SDea SKee WJas
F– 'Lady Lambourne' (C/D)	SKee
F– 'Lady Stanley' (D)	SDea
F– 'Lady Sudeley' (D)	SDea SFam SKee WJas
F– 'Lady's Finger of Lancashire' (C/D)	SKee
F– 'Lane's Prince Albert' (C)	CSam EHar EWar GBon IJoh MCls MWat NRog NTwe SDea SIgm SKee WJas
F– 'Langley Pippin' (D)	SDea
– 'Laxton's Fortune'	See M. *d.* 'Fortune'
F– 'Laxton's Royalty' (D)	SDea SFam
F– 'Laxton's Superb' (D)	CB&S CSam EHar ELan EWar GBon IJoh IOrc LBuc MBea MBri MCls MR&S NBee NElm NRog NTwe SDea SFam SKee SPer WJas WWeb
F– 'Leathercoat Russet' (D)	SKee
F– 'Lemon Pippin' (C)	SDea SKee SNTN
F– 'Lewis's Incomparable' (C)	SKee
F– 'Liberty' (D)	SDea
F– 'Loddington' (C)	SKee
F– 'Lodi' (C)	SDea SKee
F– 'Lord Burghley' (D)	NTwe SDea
F– 'Lord Derby' (C)	CMac CSam LBuc MBri MCls NBar NRog NTwe SDea SKee
F– 'Lord Grosvenor' (C)	NTwe SKee
F– 'Lord Hindlip' (D)	NTwe SDea SKee
F– 'Lord Lambourne' (D)	CSam EHar EWar GChr IOrc LBuc MCls MWat NBee NRog NTwe SFam SIgm SPer WHig
F– 'Lord Stradbroke' (C)	SKee
F– 'Lord Suffield' (C)	SKee
F– 'Lucombe's Seedling' (D)	SKee
F– 'Madresfield Court' (D)	SDea WJas
F– 'Maidstone Favourite' (D)	SKee
F– 'Malling Kent' (D)	CSam EMui SDea SFam
F– 'Maltster' (D)	SKee
F– 'Manks Codlin' (C)	SKee
F– 'Mannington's Pearmain' (D)	SKee
F– 'Margil' (D)	EEde NTwe SDea SFam SKee SNTN WJas
F– 'May Queen' (D)	EEde SDea SFam SKee
F– 'Maypole' (D/Ball)	ELan MBri MGos SDea SSus WWeb
F– 'McIntosh Red' (D)	SKee
F– 'Melba' (D)	CSam SKee
F– 'Melon' (D)	SDea
F– 'Melrose' (D)	NTwe SKee
F– 'Merton Charm' (D)	SFam SKee
F– 'Merton Knave' (D)	NTwe SDea
F– 'Merton Russet' (D)	EEde SDea SNTN
F– 'Merton Worcester' (D)	SDea SKee
F– 'Michaelmas Red' (D)	NTwe SKee WJas
F– 'Michelin' (Cider)	SDea WJas
F– 'Miller's Seedling' (D)	SKee WJas
F– 'Millicent Barnes' (D)	SDea
F– 'Monarch' (C)	NRog NTwe SDea SFam SKee
F– 'Morgan's Sweet' (C/Cider)	SDea SKee
F– 'Moss's Seedling' (D)	NTwe SDea WJas
F– 'Mother' (D)	EEde NTwe SDea SFam SKee SNTN WJas
F– 'Mutsu' (D)	GBon MBri MWat NRog NTwe SDea SIgm SKee
F– 'Nettlestone Pippin' (D)	SDea
F– 'Newton Wonder' (D/C)	CMac CSam EEde EWar IJoh MCls NElm NRog NTwe SDea SFam SIgm SKee
F– 'Nittany Red' (D)	SDea
F– 'Nonpareil' (D)	SKee SNTN
F– 'Norfolk Beauty' (C)	SKee
F– 'Norfolk Beefing' (C)	SKee
F– 'Norfolk Royal' (D)	EHar NTwe SDea SFam SKee WHig
F– 'Northern Greening' (C)	SKee
F– 'Old Pearmain' (D)	SDea SKee SNTN
F– 'Orange Goff' (D)	SKee

F – 'Orleans Reinette' (D)	EEde MWat NTwe SDea SFam SIgm SKee SNTN WHig WJas
F – 'Oslin' (D)	EEde
F – 'Owen Thomas' (D)	SKee
F – 'Paroquet' (D)	SKee
F – 'Patricia' (D)	SKee
F – 'Paulared' (D)	SDea
F – 'Peacemaker' (D)	SKee
F – 'Peasgood's Nonsuch' (C)	EEde NTwe SDea SFam SKee WJas
F – 'Peck's Pleasant' (D)	SKee
F – 'Pitmaston Pine Apple' (D)	EEde SDea SFam SKee
F – 'Pixie' (D)	NTwe SIgm SKee WJas
F – Polka ®/ 'Trajan' (D/Ball)	ELan MBri SDea SSus WWeb
F – 'Pott's Seedling' (C)	SKee
F – 'Queen' (C)	EEde SKee SNTN
F – 'Queen Caroline' (C)	SKee
F – 'Queen Cox' (D)	EEde MBri SDea SFam SIgm SKee
F – 'Red Blenheim' (C/D)	SKee
F – 'Red Bramley' (C)	EEde
F – 'Red Charles Ross' (C/D)	SDea
F – 'Red Devil' (D)	SKee WHig
F – 'Red Ellison' (D)	NRog NTwe SDea
F – 'Red James Grieve' (D)	SDea
F – 'Red Jonagold'	EMui
F – 'Red Miller's Seedling' (D)	SDea
F – 'Red Siberian' (Crab)	SDea
F – 'Red Superb' (D)	SKee
F – 'Redsleeves' (C)	SDea WHig
F – 'Reinette du Canada' (D)	SKee
F – 'Reinette Rouge Etoilée' (D)	SDea
F – 'Reverend Greeves'	SDea
F – 'Reverend W Wilks' (C)	EEde EMui NRog SFam SIgm SKee WJas
F – 'Ribston Pippin' (D)	EEde MWat NRog NTwe SDea SFam SIgm SKee SNTN
F – 'Rival' (D)	SDea SKee SNTN
F – 'Rome Beauty' (D)	SDea
F – 'Rosemary Russet' (D)	EEde NTwe SDea SFam SKee WJas
F – 'Ross Nonpareil' (D)	NTwe SDea
F – 'Roundway Magnum Bonum' (D)	EEde SDea SKee
F – 'Roxbury Russet' (D)	SKee
– 'Royal Gala'	See M. *d.* 'Tenroy'
F – 'Royal Jubilee' (C)	SKee
F – 'Royal Russet' (C)	SDea
F – 'Rubinette'	MBri NBar NTwe WHig
F – 'Saint Albans Pippin' (D)	SKee
F – 'Saint Cecilia' (D)	SDea SKee SNTN
F – 'Saint Edmund's Pippin' (D)	SKee
F – 'Saint Edmund's Russet' (D)	EEde NTwe SDea SFam SIgm SKee SNTN WJas
F – 'Sandringham' (C)	SKee
F – 'Sanspareil' (D)	SKee
F – 'Scarlet Pimpernel' (D)	EEde WJas
F – 'Scotch Bridget' (C)	SKee WJas
F – 'Sheep's Nose' (C)	SDea SKee
F – 'Shortymac' (D)	SKee
– 'Sir Isaac Newton's'	See M. ***domestica*** 'Flower of Kent'
F – 'Sir John Thornycroft' (D)	SNTN
F – 'Smart's Prince Arthur' (C)	SDea
F – 'Spartan' (D)	CSam GBon LBuc MCls MWat NRog NTwe SDea SFam SIgm SKee SNTN SPer WHig
F – 'Spur Mac' (D)	SDea
F – 'Stark' (D)	SDea
F – 'Starking' (D)	SKee
F – 'Starkrimson' (D)	SKee
F – 'Starkspur Golden Delicious' (D)	SKee
F – 'Stark's Earliest' (D)	SKee
F – 'Stirling Castle' (C)	EEde NTwe SKee
– 'Stone's'	See M. ***d.*** 'Loddington'
F – 'Sturmer Pippin' (D)	CSam EEde MWat NTwe SDea SFam SIgm SKee SNTN
F – 'Summer Golden Pippin' (D)	SKee
F – 'Summer Granny'	SDea
F – 'Summerred' (D)	SKee
F – 'Sunburn' (D)	SKee
F – 'Sunset' (D)	CMac CSam EEde EMui LBuc MBea MBri MR&S NBee NRog NTwe SDea SFam SIgm SKee SNTN SPer WHig
F – 'Suntan' (D)	CSam MWat NTwe SDea SKee WHig
– 'Superb'	See 'M. ***d.*** 'Laxton's Superb'
F – 'Taylor's' (Cider)	SDea
F – 'Ten Commandments' (D)	WJas
F – 'Tenroy'	SDea
F – 'Tom Putt' (C)	SDea WJas
F – 'Tower of Glamis' (C)	EEde SKee
F – 'Tremlett's Bitter' (Cider)	SDea
F – 'Twenty Ounce' (C)	WJas
F – 'Tydeman's Early Worcester' (D)	GRei IJoh MR&S NBee NRog NTwe SDea SKee WJas
F – 'Tydeman's Late Orange' (D)	LBuc MWat NRog NTwe SDea SFam SKee WJas
F – 'Tyler's Kernel' (C)	SKee
F – 'Upton Pyne' (D)	CSam SDea SKee SNTN
F – 'Vickey's Delight' (D)	SDea
F – 'Vista-Bella' (D)	NBee NTwe SDea SKee
F – 'Wagener' (D)	SDea SFam
F – Waltz ®/ 'Telamon' (D/Ball)	ELan SDea SSus WWeb

F – 'Wanstall Pippin' (D)	EEde SKee
F – 'Warner's King' (C)	SDea SKee SNTN WJas
F – 'Wealthy' (D)	SDea
– 'Wellington'	See M. *d.* 'Dumeller's Seedling'
F – 'Wellspur Delicious' (D)	WJas
F – 'Wellspur Red Delicious'	NTwe
F – 'Welsh Russet' (D)	SDea
F – 'White Melrose' (C)	EEde SDea SKee
F – 'White Transparent' (C/D)	EEde NTwe SDea SKee
F – 'William Crump' (D)	SDea SKee WJas
F – 'Winston' (D)	CMac NRog NTwe SDea SFam SIgm SKee SNTN
F – 'Winter Banana' (D)	SDea SKee WJas
F – 'Winter Quarrenden' (D)	SDea
F – 'Worcester Pearmain' (D)	CSam EWar GBon GChr GRei IJoh LBuc MBea MBri MCls NBar NElm NRog NTwe SDea SFam SIgm SKee SNTN SPer WHig WJas WWeb
F – 'Wormsley Pippin' (D)	SKee
F – 'Wyken Pippin' (D)	NTwe SDea SFam SKee SNTN
F – 'Yarlington Mill' (Cider)	SDea SKee
F – 'Yellow Ingestrie' (D)	SKee
F – 'Yellowspur' (D)	SKee
F – 'Zabergäu Renette' (D)	SKee
§ 'Echtermeyer'	SHil
'Eleyi'	CBra CLnd ENot GRei MGos MR&S NWea
'Elk River'	WJas
'Evereste'	CBow CLnd CSco GChr MBlu MBri MRav SExT WAbe
'Excellenz Thiel'	SIgm
floribunda	CBow CBra CLnd CSam CSco ELan ENot IDai IHos IOrc MBar MBri MGos MR&S SChu SHil SKee SPer SReu WJas WMou
'Gardener's Gold'	MBri
'Golden Gem'	SIgm WJas
'Golden Hornet'	Widely available
'Gorgeous'	COtt CSco MBri MR&S NBar SIgm
'Hillieri'	CBow CLnd IDai SExT SFam SHil
'Hopa'	WJas
hupehensis	CB&S CFor CLnd CMCN EHar ENot IHos SExT SFam SHil SIgm SPer SSpi WCoo WJas WMou WWat
F 'John Downie'	Widely available
'Kaido'	See M. × ***micromalus***
kansuensis	CLnd SSpi WCoo
'Katherine'	COtt ENot SHil
'Lady Northcliffe'	CLnd SExT SFam
'Lemoinei'	GRei IOrc SDea SHil WJas
'Liset'	CLnd ECtt ENot GChr NBar SExT SHil SPer
'Magdeburgensis'	NWea SExT SIgm WJas
'Makamik'	COtt IJoh WJas
§ × ***micromalus***	CLnd SHil
× ***moerlandii***	CLnd
'Montreal Beauty'	LRHS MBri SFam
'Neville Copeman'	CLnd SExT
niedzwetzkyana	CLnd
'Pink Perfection'	CLnd ENot SPer
'Prince George's'	SHil
'Profusion'	CBra CLnd CSco ELan ENot GRei IDai IOrc MBar MBri MGos MR&S NWea SExT SFam SHil SIgm SKee SPer SReu WAbe WJas
'Purple Wave'	LRHS MBri WJas
× ***purpurea*** 'Pendula'	See M. 'Echtermeyer'
¶ 'Red Flash'	LBuc
'Red Glow'	CLnd COtt CSco MBri SExT SKee WJas
'Red Jade'	CLnd CSco ELan ENot IJoh IOrc LBuc MBar MBri MGos MR&S MRav NTwe SFam SHil SPer SPla SReu WAbe WJas
'Red Sentinel'	CLnd COtt CSco ELan ENot LNet MBri MR&S SFam SHil SKee SPer WJas
× ***robusta***	CLnd MBal NTwe NWea SExT SNTN SPla WJas
– 'Red Siberian'	SHil SPer
– 'Yellow Siberian'	CLnd SHil
'Royal Beauty'	COtt CSco NTwe SHil
'Royalty'	CBra CLnd CSco ELan ENot GRei IHos LBuc LNet MBar MGos MR&S MRav NTwe SFam SHil SKee SMad SPer SPla SSta WJas
sargentii	See M. ***toringo s.***
sieboldii	See M. ***toringo***
'Simcoe'	GChr MBri MR&S SExT SKee
'Snowcloud'	CLnd ENot SExT SPer
'Strathmore'	WJas
sylvestris	CKin CLnd GChr LBuc NRog NWea SKee
§ ***toringo***	COtt CSto SKee WCoo
§ – ***sargentii***	CMCN ENot MGos SFam SHil SIgm SKee SPer SSpi WJas WNor WThu WWat
toringoides	CLnd CMCN SFam SHil SIgm SPer SSpi WMou WNor WWat
transitoria	CLnd MBri SExT SHil SSpi WWat
trilobata	SHil
tschonoskii	CBra CLnd ELan ENot IOrc LSav MBal MBri MGos MR&S MRav NBar NTwe NWea SExT SHil SKee SPer SSta WAbe WJas WMou WWat
'Van Eseltine'	CBra CLnd ENot GChr MBri MR&S NTwe SExT SHil SReu
'Veitch's Scarlet'	CLnd NRog SFam SIgm WJas
'Weeping Red Jade'	SKee
'Wintergold'	CLnd CSam ECtt SExT SFam SKee SSus
'Wisley'	CLnd GChr LRHS NTwe SDea SFam SKee
yunnanensis veitchii	SHil

MALVA (Malvaceae)

alcea	CShe
– fastigiata	CArn CGle CHan ELan EMon ERav ERou MBri MRav NCat NHol NPer NRoo NVic SPer SSpi WHal WPer
bicolor	See LAVATERA ***maritima***
crispa	See M. ***verticillata***
hispida	CNat
moschata	Widely available
– alba	Widely available
¶ *– alba* 'Pirovette'	WHen
¶ – 'Romney Marsh'	MRav NRar WSHC
– rosea	ECha ELan NNor SFis
'Primley Blue'	CB&S CElw CFis CGle CHad CHan CHar ECha ECro EFol ERav LGre LHop MBri MTho NPer NRar NRoo NSti SMad SMrm WOld WPer WWin
pyramidalis	CSco
sylvestris	CHad CHar CKin CLew CTom ELan EMon GCHN MChe MPit NLan NOak NSti SMad WBon WEas WHer WPer WWin
¶ – 'Alba'	EMon
– 'Brave Heart'	EMon LRHS SAxl
– 'Cottenham Blue'	ELan EMon LRHS NRar
– mauritiana	CSun ECro ELan EPad LHop MFir MPit NRoo SFis SMrm WHer WOMN
¶ – 'Zebrina'	LHil
§ *verticillata*	EJud ELan SFis
– 'Crispa'	EMon

MALVASTRUM (Malvaceae)

hypomadarum	See ANISODONTEA ***hypomadarum***
lateritium	Widely available
– 'Eastgrove Silver'	NSti
¶ – 'Hopley's Variegated'	LHop
– 'Variegatum'	WPer
latifolium	SPer

MALVAVISCUS (Malvaceae)

¶ *arboreus mexicanus*	CSun

MANDARIN See **CITRUS** ***reticulata*** Mandarin group

MANDEVILLA (Apocynaceae)

x *amabilis* 'Alice du Pont'	CB&S CHEx ERea IHos IOrc LHop MNew
§ *laxa*	CB&S CBot CChu CHEx CHil CPle CSun ECro ERea IHos IOrc MNew NPal SBra SHil SLMG SSpi WBod WOMN WSHC WWat
sanderi	MBri
splendens	CHEx EBak LHil SLMG
suaveolens	See M. ***laxa***

MANDRAGORA (Solanaceae)

autumnalis	GPoy MSal
§ *officinarum*	CSun EEls GPoy

MANETTIA (Rubiaceae)

inflata	LHop SLMG

MARANTA (Marantaceae)

bicolor	EBak
leuconeura erythroneura	MBri
– kerchoviana	MBri

MARGYRICARPUS (Rosaceae)

§ *pinnatus*	CLew CRiv ELan GLoc GWic MCas NHol NWCA SIng WHil WPer
setosus	See M. ***pinnatus***

MARKHAMIA (Bignoniaceae)

¶ *platycalyx*	CPle

MARRUBIUM (Labiatae)

candidissimum	See M. ***incanum***
cylleneum	ECha ECro EFol EMon WHea WWin
*– 'Velvetissimum'	CHad EFou LHop NRar SChu SCro WTay
* *cynoglossum*	EOrc
'Gold Leaf'	EBar ECha EFol NSti
§ *incanum*	CGle CHan CSun EMon LHil MCot MPar NSti NTow SFis
¶ *libanoticum*	EMon
supinum	EFou NSti WHea
velutinum	EMon
vulgare	CArn CSev EEls EJud Effi GPoy LHol MChe MSal NSel SIde WHer WOak WPer WSto
– variegated	EFol NRar

MARSDENIA See **CIONURA**

MASCARENA See **HYOPHORBE**

MATRICARIA (Compositae)

chamomilla	See MATRICARIA ***recutita***
§ *maritima*	CKin
§ *recutita*	EJud GPoy LHol MChe NSel SIde
'White Snowball'	See TANACETUM ***parthenium*** 'W. S.'

MATTEUCCIA (Aspleniaceae)

orientalis	NMar
struthiopteris	Widely available

MATTHIOLA (Cruciferae)

¶ *fruticulosa*	WPer
– perennis	NSti
incana	CNat SSvw WRus
* 'Les Merriennes'	WOMN
¶ *scapifera*	WDav
sinuata	CNat CSun
thessala	SPou
white perennial	CGle CHad CHan GPla MPar NCat SFir WBon WEas WHea

MAURANDYA See **ASARINA**

MAYTENUS (Celastraceae)
boaria CBot CGre CMCN CTre EHar SArc SBor SHil WWat
– G&K 4177 LSav
¶ – 'Worplesdon Fastigiate' LMer
magellanica SArc

MAZUS (Scrophulariaceae)
pumilio ECou NKay SIng
radicans ECou NKay SIng WCru
reptans CLew CRiv CRow CShe CTom EBre ECha ELan EPar EPot ESis GLoc MBar MHig MPit NHol NNrd NRoo SBla SLHN WHer WHil WHoo
– 'Albus' CLew CMer CRiv CRow CTom ELan GLoc NHol NNrd SIng WHil WHoo WMar WPer

MECONOPSIS † (Papaveraceae)
aculeata MBal SSpi
baileyi See M. ***betonicifolia***
x *beamishii* EBre
§ *betonicifolia* Widely available
– *alba* CB&S CSam EBre ELan GArf GHig MBal MBri NHol NLin NRoo SBla
– Harlow Carr strain GAbr IBrk NRar
cambrica CCla CGle CKin CRow EJud ELan MPar MPit NCat NGre NHol NLan SIng SMrm WAbe WBon WCla WHal WHer WPer
– *aurantiaca* ELan EMon NBir WBon WPer
– *flore pleno* CGle CRow EMon EPar GAbr MBal MFir MTho NCat NVic WBon
¶ – 'Frances Perry' GAbr
chelidoniifolia CFor NHar NHol SAxl SSpi WCru
dhwojii GAbr NBir NTow SBar WOMN
grandis CCla CElw CGle CShe ELan GArf MBri NBar NLin NRar NRoo SLHN SSpi WEas WPer
¶ – GS 600 NBir
horridula ELan GEdr MBri MTho NKay NRoo SIng SLHN WDav
integrifolia GEdr
napaulensis CB&S CCla CRiv CSam CSun ELan GArf GDra MBal MBri NCat NKay NRoo NSti NVic WAbe WEas WHal WPer WThu WWin
– forms GArf NHol
– red form LHop NBir NWCA
nudicaule 'Oregon Rainbow' See PAPAVER ***nudicaule*** 'O. R.'
paniculata ITim NBir NLin
quintuplinervia CBos CSun GArf GDra MBal NBir NRoo SBla
regia CBot ELan GArf NRar WRus
x *sarsonsii* EBre GGar WRus
x *sheldonii* ELan GGar MFir NBir NRoo NVic SSpi
– 'Branklyn' CCla IBlr
– Crewdson hybrids GDra MBri WEas
– 'Ormswell' NKay
– 'Slieve Donard' CFor GDra GEdr IBar IBlr SBla
superba MBal
villosa CFor GArf SBla

MEDEOLA (Liliaceae/Convallariaceae)
virginica LAma MSal NHol WChr

MEDICAGO (Leguminosae)
arborea CPle ELan GWic IBlr
echinus See M. ***intertexta***
* *falcata* 'Cambot' CNat
sativa CKin WHer
¶ – *sativa* IBlr

MEDINILLA (Melastomataceae)
magnifica MBri

MEDLAR See **MESPILUS** ***germanica***

MEEHANIA (Labiatae)
¶ *urticifolia* EMon MPar

MELALEUCA (Myrtaceae)
acuminata CSun
armillaris CPle CSun CTre
§ *biconvexa* CSun
* *capitata* ISea
coccinea CSun
decussata ECou
* – *ovoidea* CSun
diosmifolia CSun
ericifolia CGre CSun
– *nana* CSun
erubescens CSun
gibbosa CPle CSun CTre
glaberrima CSun
hypericifolia CGre CMer CSun ECou
lateritia CSun
pauciflora See M. ***biconvexa***
pulchella CSun
scabra CSun
spathulata CSun
squamea CSun ECou
squarrosa CGre CSun
striata CSun
thymifolia CSun
viridiflora CB&S

MELANDRIUM See **SILENE**

MELANOSELINUM (Umbelliferaceae)
¶ *decipiens* CHEx

MELANTHIUM (Liliaceae/Melanthiaceae)
virginicum MSal

MELASPHAERULA (Iridaceae)
♦ *graminea* See M. ***ramosa***
¶ *ramosa* CAvo

MELIA (Meliaceae)	
§ *azedarach*	CFor CPle SLMG
– *japonica*	See M. ***azedarach***
MELIANTHUS (Melianthaceae)	
major	CBot CChu CFor CHEx CHad CHan CHoe ECha ECro EFou ERav IJoh LGre SArc SAxl SBla SChu SDix SHil SLHN SMad SPer SSpi
minor	CHEx ECro ERav LGre SChu SMad SMrm
MELICA (Gramineae)	
altissima	ECha
– 'Atropurpurea'	CElw CHoe ECha EMon EPla MPar NSti SApp
ciliata	CElw CLew EFou SApp WCar WHil
nutans	CElw CHoe NLan
¶ *sylvanica*	CLew
uniflora	CKin
¶ – *albida*	EMon
– 'Variegata'	CElw CHoe EMon SApp SSpi
MELICOPE (Rutaceae)	
ternata	ECou
MELICYTUS (Violaceae)	
alpinus	ECou
angustifolius	ECou SDry
MELILOTUS (Leguminosae)	
officinalis	CArn CKin CSFH Effi GPoy LHol MChe SIde WHer WSto
MELIOSMA (Meliosmaceae)	
§ *dilleniifolia flexuosa*	WBod
myriantha	CMCN WCoo
parviflora	CMCN
♦ *pendens*	See M. ***dilleniifolia flexuosa***
pinnata oldhamii	SSpi
veitchiorum	CHEx SHil
MELISSA (Labiatae)	
officinalis	CArn CRow CSFH EJud Effi GCHN GPoy LHol MBal MBar MBri MChe MCot MPar MPit NSel SIde WEas WOak WPer WSto
– 'All Gold'	CBre CHoe CLew CMal CRiv CSev EFou EJud ELan EMon LHol MBri MCot NHol NRoo NSti SSpi
§ – 'Aurea'	Widely available
– 'Variegata'	See M. ***o.*** 'Aurea'
MELITTIS (Labiatae)	
melissophyllum	CFor SAxl SSpi
MENISPERMUM (Menispermaceae)	
MENTHA † (Labiatae)	
* *angustifolia* 'Variegata'	MWgw
aquatica	CKin CRow CWGN EHon EJud EWav GPoy LMay MSal MSta NSel WHer WOak WSto
arvensis	CArn CKin SIde WHer
¶ *asiatica*	SIde
* *buddleia*	See M. ***longifolia***
citrata 'Variegata'	See M. x ***gentilis*** 'Variegata'
cordifolia	See M. x ***villosa***
* *corsica*	CTom
'Eau de Cologne'	See M. x ***piperita citrata***
x *gentilis*	CArn EOrc Effi GPla LHol MChe NOak NSel SIde WPer
– 'Aurea'	MBal NRoo NSti SIng WEas
§ – 'Variegata'	CFis CGle CHar CHoe CSFH CSev CTom CWGN ECha ELan EMon EPar GPoy MCot MFir MSal NNor NRya WEas WHer WHil WOak WPer
§ *longifolia*	CFis CGle CSun ECha EFol ELan EOrc LHop NSti SIng WEas WHer WOak WPer
* – 'Variegata'	NSti
x *piperita*	CArn CHoe CRiv CSFH CSev ECha EJud Effi GPoy MBri MChe MCot MPit MSal NNor NOak NRoo NSel WHal WOak WPer WSto
§ – *citrata*	Widely available
– *citrata* 'Lemon'	MBri
– *officinalis*	NHol
pulegium	CArn CRiv CRow CSFH CSev CWGN ECha EJud EPar Effi GPoy LHol MChe MCot MPit MSal NOak NSti SIde WHer WOak WPer WSto
requienii	Widely available
x *rotundifolia*	CArn CFis EJud Effi GPoy LHol MBal MBri MCot MFir MPar MPit NRoo NSel WHal WHer WHil WPer
– 'Bowles'	See M. x ***villosa alopecuroides***
– 'Variegata'	See M. ***suaveolens*** 'Variegata'
rubra raripila	See M. x ***smithiana***
§ x *smithiana*	CArn GPoy WHer WPer
§ *spicata*	CArn CSFH CSev ELan Effi GPoy LHol MBal MBri MChe MCot MOak MPit NNor NRoo NSel WEas WHal WHer WHil WOak WSto
– *crispa*	See M. ***spicata***
– 'Moroccan'	CArn CSev SIde WHer WOak WPer
sp. Nile Valley Mint	CArn
suaveolens	CSFH CWGN WOak WSto
§ – 'Variegata'	Widely available
sylvestris	See M. ***longifolia***
§ x *villosa alopecuroides* Bowles' Mint	CBre CHad GPoy LHol MChe WEas WHer WPer
viridis	See M. ***spicata***

MENYANTHES (Menyanthaceae)
trifoliata CRiv CRow CWGN EHon EWav GPoy LMay MSta SFir SLon WOak

MENZIESIA (Ericaceae)
alba See DABOECIA ***cantabrica alba***
ciliicalyx CGre MBlu SBar SHil SSta
– dwarf form NHol
– *lasiophylla* See M. ***c. purpurea***
– *multiflora* GDra MBal SSta WThu
§ – *purpurea* GDra MBal SHil SSpi WBod
ferruginea MBal SSta
polifolia See DABOECIA ***cantabrica***

MERCURIALIS (Euphorbiaceae)
perennis CKin CNat GPoy

MERENDERA (Liliaceae/Colchicaceae)
attica LBow WChr
eichleri See M. ***trigyna***
¶ *hissarica* WChr
kurdica EPot LAma WChr
montana WMar
* *nivalis* WChr
* *oliveri* ECam
raddeana EPot WChr
robusta ECam
sobolifera EPot WChr WThu
trigyna EPot LAma WChr

MERREMIA (Convolvulaceae)
tuberosa MNew

MERTENSIA (Boraginaceae)
ciliata EFol ELan MRav
echioides NTow
maritima CSun EPad GPoy NWCA WCru WOMN WWin
– *asiatica* CBos CBot CHad CHan CHil CLew COtt CSun EBre ELan GLoc GWic LGre MPit MRav MTho NGre SAxl SBla SIng SPer WAbe WCru
primuloides CHad WCru
pterocarpa EPot GWic LGre MCot NKay WHoo
§ *pulmonarioides* CBot CBre CBro CHad CHan CHar CRiv EFol ELan EPot GDra LAma LHop MTho NHol SAxl SIng WWat
¶ *simplicissima* WPer
virginica See M. ***pulmonarioides***

MERYTA (Araliaceae)
sinclairii CHEx SArc
¶ – 'Variegata' CHEx

MESEMBRYANTHEMUM (Aizoaceae)
'Basutoland' See DELOSPERMA ***nubigenum***
brownii See LAMPRANTHUS ***brownii***
ornatulum See DELOSPERMA ***ornatulum***

MESPILUS (Rosaceae)
F *germanica* CB&S CBow CLnd ELan IJoh IOrc LHol MWat WMou
F – 'Dutch' SDea SKee
F – 'Large Russian' ERea ESim
F – 'Monstrous' NTwe SDea
F – 'Nottingham' EHar ERea ESim EWar GChr LBuc MBea NBee NTwe SDea SKee SPer WHig WMou
* – 'Westerveld' CMac

METASEQUIA
♦ *glytostroboides* 'Fastigiata' See M. ***g.*** 'National'

METASEQUOIA (Taxodiaceae)
glyptostroboides Widely available
– 'Emerald Feathers' SHil
* – 'Green Mantle' EHul
§ – 'National' CSam
– 'Sheridan Spire' CB&S LNet LSav

METROSIDEROS (Myrtaceae)
¶ *carminea* CHEx
– 'Carousel' ERea
– 'Ferris Wheel' ERea
excelsa CGre CHEx ECou SHil
– *aurea* ECou
– 'Scarlet Pimpernel' SLon
fulgens ECou
¶ 'Goldfinger' ERea
kermadecensis ECou LHop
¶ – 'Radiant' WTay
– 'Variegata' CB&S CMer ECou ERea LGre LHop
lucida See M. ***umbellata***
'Minstrel' CB&S
robusta CHEx ISea SHil
§ *umbellata* CGre CHEx CHan ECou SHil

MEUM (Umbelliferae)
athamanticum COtt EBre EFou EGol LHop MTho MUlv NRoo SAxl

MIBORA (Gramineae)
mimima SIng

MICHAUXIA (Campanulaceae)
campanuloides EMon EPad LRHS SMrm
laevigata EPad
tchihatchewii CBot CSun ECro EPad SMrm WMar
– JCA 677.300 CSun

MICHELIA (Magnoliaceae)
doltsopa CB&S CGre CHEx SHil WBod
– 'Silver Cloud' CB&S
figo CB&S CGre ERea

MICROBIOTA (Cupressaceae)
decussata Widely available

MICROCACHRYS (Podocarpaceae)
tetragona ECou SHil SIng SSta WCon

MICROCOELUM (Palmae)
§ *weddellianum* MBri NPal

MICROGLOSSA (Compositae)
albescens See ASTER *albescens*

MICROLEPIS (Dennstaedtiaceae)
speluncae MBri

MICROMERIA (Labiatae)
corsica See ACINOS *corsicus*
croatica WDav
rupestris See M. *thymifolia*
§ *thymifolia* LHil MPla
varia ELan MWat

MICROSERIS (Compositae)
lanceolata alpina CSun

MICROSORIUM (Polypodiaceae)
diversifolium CHEx SApp SArc

MICROSTROBOS (Podocarpaceae)
fitzgeraldii CKen
¶ *niphophilus* WThu

MIKANIA (Compositae)
scandens MSal
ternata MBri

MILIUM (Gramineae)
effusum CKin NNrd
– *aureum* Widely available

MILLIGANIA (Liliaceae/Asparagaceae)

MIMULUS (Scrophulariaceae)
'A T Johnson' CKel CSam EBre GPla NCat NHol NVic SIng
§ 'Andean Nymph' (ex Mac&W 5257) CHar CWGN EBre ELan EPot ESis GCHN MBal MCas NHol NKay NNrd NRed SIng WAbe WCla WOMN WOld
§ 'Andean Nymph' forms CGle GLoc GWic NTow WCla
§ *aurantiacus* CBot CCla CGre CHan CHil CPle EBak EBar ELan ERea GWic IBlr ITim LHop MPla SHil SLHN SLMG SMad SMrm WEas WHal WHea WPer
x *bartonianus* CCla CRow ELun NVic SPer
'Bees' Scarlet' MBri WPer
bifidus CSun LGre LHop
boydii NKay WPer
x *burnetii* CGle CKel CRow GLoc LMay MFir MRav NNrd NVic
cardinalis CHar CHil CRow CWGN EBre EHon ELan LHop MFir MTho NCat NHol NNor SIng SPer SSpi WPer
¶ 'Caribbean Cream' WCla
cupreus CRow MBal SHig
– Wr 8732 CSun
– 'Whitecroft Scarlet' CSun CWGN ECha ELan ERou GDra LMay MBar NGre NHol NNrd SIng WCla WDav WHil WHoo WPer WWin
¶ 'Doreen's Delight' SIng
glutinosus See M. ***aurantiacus***
– *atrosanguineus* See M. ***puniceus***
– *luteus* See M. ***aurantiacus***
– orange See M. ***aurantiacus***
§ *guttatus* CBWG CKin CRow CSun GAbr MFir NKay SFir SIng WCla WPer
'Highland Pink' CSun ECtt ESis NHol NNrd NRoo WCla WPer
'Highland Red' CGle CRow ECtt GDra MPit NHol NNrd NRed NRoo SIng WHoo WPer WWin
'Highland Yellow' CGle CRiv ECtt MPit NRoo WCla WOMN WPer
hose in hose CMer CRow ECha EFou GPla GWic MTho NCat WEas WHer WPer
* 'Inca Sunset' NHar NHol
'Inshriach Crimson' CSun GDra NHol WDav WOMN
langsdorfii See M. ***guttatus***
lewisii CHar CRiv CSun ELan GDra LGan MTho NHol NOak NWCA WCar WCla WHal WHoo WPer
longiflorus CBot LGre
luteus CMer CRiv CRow CWGN ECha EHon LMay MBal MSta NHar NHol NNor NNrd WHal WHil
¶ 'Magnifique' SIng
* 'Major Bees' GWic
'Malibu' CRow NNor NNrd NRoo
¶ 'Malibu Ivory' NRoo
'Mandarin' EBre MRav NNrd
moschatus CRiv CRow CSam NCat NKay WCla WEas
'Old Rose' ECha
'Orange Glow' MBri NHar
'Plymtree' CGle NCat NKay NNrd WCla
primuloides CRow CSun ELan EPot GLoc ITim MBar MPit MTho NGre NHar NNrd NTow SIng SPla WAbe WCla WHal WOMN WOld WPer WWin
§ *puniceus* CBot CCla CPle LHop NNrd SHil SIng SLMG WPer WSHC
– Verity hybrid CHil ERea
ringens CRiv CRow CSun CWGN EBar EHon LMay MSta WBon WPer WRus
'Royal Velvet' NNrd
'Shep' NNrd WPer
sp. CW5233 NTow
sp. JCA 64 NHol NNrd
sp. Mac&W 5257 See M. 'Andean Nymph'
¶ sp. WW 233 WPer
¶ 'Tigrinus Queen's Prize' WPer
tilingii NNrd WHil
– *caespitosus* NGre NNrd NTow

'Wisley Red' CHar CKel EBre ECha ELan SIng WRus

MINUARTIA (Caryophyllaceae)
§ ***circassica*** GHig MHig NTow WPat
¶ ***imbricata*** ITim
¶ ***juniperina*** ITim
kashmirica WCla WEas
laricifolia NHol
parnassica See M. ***stellata***
§ ***stellata*** EPot NHol NNrd NTow SIng
§ ***verna*** CLew EMNN NNrd NRya SIng WOMN WPer
– ***aurea*** See SAGINA ***subulata*** 'Aurea'
– ***gerardii*** See M. ***verna verna***

MIRABILIS (Nyctaginaceae)
jalapa CArn ECro LAma MBri SLMG

MISCANTHUS (Gramineae)
floridulus EFou GWic MBri SApp SAxl SDix SMad WCot
¶ ***litoralis*** 'Zuneigung' SApp
sacchariflorus CB&S CHEx CHoe CRow CWGN EBre ECha ECro ELan LMay MBri MUlv MWgw NHol NJap NVic SApp SHig SHil SMad SPer SSpi WWat
sinensis CHEx
¶ – 'Cabaret' SApp
¶ – ***condensatus*** EFou
– dwarf form MUlv
¶ – 'Goldfeder' SApp
¶ – 'Goliath' EFou
– 'Gracillimus' CB&S CHEx CHoe CRow CWGN ECha EFou ELan ENot ERou MBal MBri MWgw NHol SApp SAxl SDix SHil SMad SPer SSpi
– 'Graziella' EFou SApp
¶ – 'Grosse Fontane' EFou
¶ – 'Hercules' EFou
– 'Kascade' CHoe SApp
– 'Klein Fontane' SApp
¶ – 'Kleine Silberspinne' EFou
– 'Malepartus' CRow SApp SAxl
¶ – 'Morning Light' SApp
– 'Nippon' CHoe EFou SApp
¶ – 'Punktchen' SApp
– ***purpurascens*** CHoe EBre ECha EGol MUlv SApp SSpi
– 'Rotsilber' EFou SApp
– 'Silberfeder' ('Silver Feather') CCla CHoe CRow EBre ECha EFou ELan MBri MUlv MWgw NHol NVic SAxl SDix SHil SMad SPer SSpi WCot WWat
¶ – 'Silberpfeil' SApp
– 'Silberspinne' CHoe EFou SApp
– 'Sirene' SApp
– 'Strictus' ERou MBri SDix
¶ – 'Undine' EFou
– 'Variegatus' CHEx CHad CHoe CRow ECha ECro EFou EGol ENot ERou GWic LSav MBal MBri MSta MUlv NHol NJap SApp SAxl SBla SDix SHil SMad
– 'Zebrinus' Widely available
yakushimensis CHoe LSav SApp

MISOPATES (Scrophulariaceae)
orontium WCla

MITCHELLA (Rubiaceae)
repens LSav MHig MSal WWat

MITELLA (Saxifragaceae)
breweri CElw CGle CLew ECha ECro EFol ELan ELun ESis GWic NHol NKay NSti SIng SLHN SSpi WEas WOMN WWat WWin
caulescens ECha NCat NSti
diphylla LGro
stauropetala NCat WHea

MITRARIA (Gesneriaceae)
coccinea Widely available
– Lake Puye form CHan GWic LHop LSav SSpi

MODIOLASTRUM See **MALVASTRUM**

MOLINIA (Gramineae)
altissima See M. ***caerulea arundinacea***
* ***caerulea aurea*** SCro
¶ – 'Carmarthen' CNat
§ ***caerulea arundinacea*** ECha EFou SPer
¶ – – 'Bergfreund' GWic
– – 'Karl Foerster' EFou GWic SApp
– – 'Windspiel ' GWic NHol
caerulea caerulea
'Heidebraut' CHoe ECha NHol
– – 'Moorhexe' CHoe ECha
– – 'Variegata' Widely available

MOLTKIA (Boraginaceae)
§ ***doerfleri*** COtt CSco
§ × ***intermedia*** MWat NKay SIgm WOld WPer WWin
petraea ECha MWat

MONADENIUM (Euphorbiaceae)
lugardae MBri
'Variegata' MBri

MONARDA † (Labiatae)
'Adam' CSco GWic
'Aquarius' ECha EFou EMon
'Beauty of Cobham' CHad ECha EFou EOrc MBri MUlv MWat NOrc NRoo NSti SChu SDix SMrm
'Blaustrumpf' ('Blue Stocking') CRow CSco EFou MBri NHol SMrm SPer
'Cambridge Scarlet' Widely available
'Capricorn' EMon

citriodora	CArn EEls LHol MChe MSal SIde WHil WPer
'Croftway Pink'	CBow CFis CGle CRow CSco CSev CShe ECha EFou ELan EPar ERou Effi IDai MCot MWat NHol NKay NRoo NSti SCro SPer WBon WOld
¶ 'Dark Ponticum'	EMon
didyma	CArn CHan CSFH Effi LHol MChe MFir MSal NSel SIde WHoo WOak WOld WSto
¶ – 'Alba'	WBon
¶ 'Elsie's Lavender'	EMon
¶ 'Feuernschopf' ('Firecrown')	MUlv
fistulosa	CArn CCor CRow EJud GPoy LHol MSal SIde WHer
¶ 'Hartswood Wine'	CSun
'Libra'	EMon
'Loddon Crown'	CBre EFou EMon GWic
'Mahogany'	CRow EFou EMon GHig LHop SPer
¶ 'Maiden's Pride'	EMon
* 'Meerswogan'	GWic SAxl
I 'Melissa'	EFou
¶ 'Mrs Perry'	EFou
¶ 'Pale Ponticum'	EMon
'Panorama'	CBre CFis ECtt EJud GAbr GHig MSal NRoo WHil WPer
¶ 'Pink Tourmalin'	MBri
'Pisces' ('Fishes')	ECha EFou EMon
'Poyntzfield Pink'	GPoy
'Prärienacht' ('Prairie Night')	CGle CHad CHar CRow CSev ECha EFol ELan ERou Effi GAbr MBri MFir MTho MWat NHol NKay NOrc NRoo NVic SChu SPer WEas WOld
punctata	CArn CChu ELan EMon LGre MSal SIde
russeliana	CElw
'Saggitarius' ('Bowman')	EMon
§ 'Schneewittchen' ('Snow White')	CCla CRow CSev ECha EFou EGol ELan EMon EOrc EPar GAbr GWic LHop NHol NRoo NSti SChu SPer WHil WRus WWin
'Scorpio' ('Scorpion')	EMon
'Snow Maiden'	See M. 'Schneewittchen'
'Squaw'	ECha
¶ 'Talud'	EMon
¶ 'Thundercloud'	EMon
'Vintage Wine'	ELan EMon

MONARDELLA (Labiatae)

macrantha	LGre LRHS MTho
¶ *odoratissima*	MHig
¶ – JCA 11724	CSun
villosa 'Sheltonii'	EOrc LHop WPer

MONSONIA (Geraniaceae)

emarginata	GCHN

MONSTERA (Araceae)

deliciosa	MBri
– 'Variegata'	MBri

MONTBRETIA See CROCOSMIA

MONTIA (Portulacaceae)

australasica	See NEOPAXIA ***a.***
californica	ELan
¶ *chamissoi*	LHil
parvifolia	See CLAYTONIA ***parvifolia***
sibirica	See CLAYTONIA ***s.***

MORAEA (Iridaceae)

§ *aristata*	LBow
§ *bellendenii*	LBow
glaucopsis	See M. ***aristata***
iridioides	See DIETES ***i.***
pavonia lutea	See M. ***bellendenii***
ramosissima	LBow
spathulata	CBro CCla GWic LHop SBla
¶ *villosa*	LBow

MORINA (Morinaceae)

¶ *alba*	GCHN
longifolia	CBot CChu CCla CElw CFis CGle CHar EBre ECha EFou ELan EOrc GEdr LGre MFir NHol NRoo NSti NTow SAxl SSpi WEas WOld WPer
¶ *persica*	EBar ECro
¶ *ramallyi*	WPer

MORISIA (Cruciferae)

hypogaea	See M. ***monanthos***
§ *monanthos*	CLew CShe EPad EPot GCHN GLoc ITim MBro MCas MHig NNrd NTow WHil WHoo
– 'Fred Hemmingway'	EBre EPot NHol WAbe

MORUS (Moraceae)

alba	CHEx CLnd EHal EHar ELan ERea IOrc SHil SPer WCoo WMou WWat
– 'Globosa'	See M. ***a.*** 'Nana'
¶ – 'Laciniata'	MBri
– *multicaulis*	ERea
§ – 'Nana'	MBri
– 'Pendula'	CBow CSco ELan ERea LHol LNet MBri MWat NTwe SExT SGar SHil SPer SSpi
australis	WCoo
F *nigra*	Widely available
F – 'Chelsea'	ERea
F – 'Wellington'	WMou
platanifolia	SGar SSus
¶ *rubra* x *alba* 'Illinois Everbearing'	ESim

MUEHLENBECKIA (Polygonaceae)

astonii	ECou ISea LGre
§ *axillaris*	ECou IBar ITim MUlv NCat NHol SDry SHil

complexa CB&S CHEx CHan CPle CSun ECou EFol IBlr ISea MUlv SArc SBra SCro SHil SIng WSHC
– 'Nana' See M. ***axillaris***
– *trilobata* GWic IBlr
ephedroides ECou
¶ – 'Clarence Pass' ECou
¶ – prostrate form ECou

MUKDENIA (Saxifragaceae)
§ *rossii* CChu ECro GWic LSav SSpi WCot WOld

MULBERRY See **MORUS** ***nigra***

MURBECKIELLA (Cruciferae)
¶ *pinnatifida* MPlt

MUSA (Musaceae)
F *acuminata* LPal MBri
basjoo CB&S CHEx SArc
cavendishii See M. ***acuminata*** (AAA group) 'Dwarf Cavendish'
ensete See ENSETE ***ventricosum***
nana See M. ***acuminata***

MUSCARI † (Liliaceae/Hyacinthaceae)
ambrosiacum See M. ***muscarimi***
'Argaei Album' LAma
§ *armeniacum* CAvo CBro EPar ETub LBow LRHS LRoo MBri NHol WPer
– 'Blue Spike' CBro EPar LAma LBlo LBow LRoo MBri NHol SIng WPer
– 'Cantab' CAvo
– 'Dark Eyes' WChr
– 'Saphir' ETub LAma
♦ – 'Sky Blue' See M. ***pallens*** 'S.B.'
– 'White Beauty' WChr
§ *aucheri* CBro EPar ETub LAma LBlo NHol SIng WThu
§ *azureum* CAvo CBro ECam ELan LAma LBlo
– *album* CAvo CBro EPar ETub LAma LRoo
'Blue Pearl' LBlo
botryoides LAma
– *album* CAvo CBro ELan ETub GLoc LAma LBlo LBow MBri NHol SIng WHil WPer
bourgaei ECam
caucasicum WChr
chalusicum BSBE See M. ***pseudomuscari*** BSBE
§ *comosum* CAvo CBro EPar ETub LBow WPer
– 'Monstrosum' See M. ***c.*** 'Plumosum'
§ – 'Plumosum' CAvo CBro ELan EMon EPar ETub LAma LBow LRoo MBri NHol SIng
'Early Giant' LAma SIng
'Heavenly Blue' LAma LBlo LRoo
latifolium CAvo CBro ETub LAma
§ *macrocarpum* CAvo CBro ECam LBow SPou WChr WThu
moschatum See M. ***muscarimi***
– *flavum* EPot LAma
– 'Major' LBow
§ *muscarimi* CAvo CBro EPar GLoc LAma LBow NHol SIng WChr
§ *neglectum* CAvo ETub LAma SIng
§ *pallens* 'Sky Blue' CBro WChr
paradoxum See BELLEVALIA ***pycnantha***
§ *pseudomuscari* BSBE WChr
racemosum See M. ***neglectum***
tubergenianum See M. ***aucheri***

MUSCARIMIA (Liliaceae/Hyacinthaceae)
ambrosiacum See MUSCARI ***muscarimi***
macrocarpum See MUSCARI ***macrocarpum***

MUSSCHIA (Campanulaceae)
¶ *aurea* CHEx
¶ *wollastonii* CHEx

MUTISIA (Compositae)
* *coccinea* EOvi
¶ *decurrens* CHEx EOvi MTho
ilicifolia CMac EOvi IBlr WMar WSHC
oligodon CGre EOvi ERav IBlr SHil
retusa CGre EOvi

MYOPORUM (Myoporaceae)
¶ *acuminatum* CPle
debile ECou
laetum CGre CHEx CPle CTre ECou

MYOSOTIDIUM (Boraginaceae)
hortensia CBos CHEx CSun LHop

MYOSOTIS (Boraginaceae)
alpestris 'Ruth Fischer' NNrd
australis CRiv GGar GLoc NHol NNrd SLHN WBon WEas WHil WPer
colensoi ECou EPot GLoc MTho NHol NKay NNrd SCro WAbe WDav WPer
¶ *elderi* CBot
explanata NNrd NTow WEas
macrantha WHil
♦ *palustris* See M. ***scorpioides***
'Popsy' ECou
¶ *pygmaea* WPer
rakiura NRar NSti SIng WCla WPer
rupicola See M. ***alpestris***
saxosa ECou
§ *scorpioides* CBre CRow CWGN ECha EHon ELan EPar EWav LMay MSta NCat SHig SSpi
– 'Mermaid' EBre ECha ESis GPla LHop MFir MSta MTho NHol NNrd NSti SDix WBon WPer WWin
¶ – 'Pinkie' CBre
* *secunda* CKin
¶ *sylvatica* EMon
– *alba* CRow WBon

MYOSURUS (Ranunculaceae)

MYRCEUGENIA (Myrtaceae)
§ *exserta* CHil CLan CMHG CPle CTrw SDry WBod

MYRICA (Myricaceae)
californica ERav SLon SSta
cerifera SHil WCoo
gale GPoy LHol MGos SHil
pensylvanica CCla LHol MBal NHol SSpi WCoo

MYRICARIA (Tamaricaceae)
§ *germanica* SHil

MYRIOPHYLLUM (Haloragidaceae)
§ *aquaticum* CHEx CRiv CRow CWGN EHon ELan LMay MSta SHig
♦ *brasiliense* See M. ***aquaticum***
elatinoides ECou
♦ *proserpinacoides* See M. ***aquaticum***
¶ *verticillatum* CHEx

MYRRHIS (Umbelliferae)
odorata CArn CHad CKin CLew CSFH CSev EJud ELan GPla GPoy LHol MChe MCot MSal NSel SIde WEas WHal WHer WOak WSto

MYRSINE (Myrsinaceae)
africana CTre LHop SArc
nummularia ECou

MYRTEOLA (Myrtaceae)
§ *nummularia* GDra ITim MBal MHig SHil WWat

MYRTUS (Myrtaceae)
apiculata See LUMA ***apiculata***
bullata See LOPHOMYRTUS ***bullata***
chequen See LUMA ***chequen***
communis Widely available
*– *citrifolia* SArc
– 'Flore Pleno' LHol MPla SHil
– 'Jenny Reitenbach' See M. ***c. tarentina***
– 'Microphylla' See M. ***c. tarentina***
– 'Nana' See M. ***c. tarentina***
– 'Tricolor' See M. ***c.*** 'Variegata'
§ – 'Variegata' CArn CBot CBow CFis CMCN CRow CTre ECtt ERav ISea LHop LSav SDry SHil SLMG SLon SPer SSta WWat
§ *communis tarentina* Widely available
– – *compacta* CSun
§ – – 'Variegata' CHan CMHG CPle EJud ELan EPla ERav LGre LHop MBal MPla MTho SArc SHil WHal WOak WSHC WWat
'Glanleam Gold' See LUMA ***apiculata*** 'Glanleam Gold'
lechleriana See MYRCEUGENIA ***exserta***
luma See LUMA ***apiculata***
nummularia See MYRTEOLA ***n.***
obcordata See LOPHOMYRTUS ***obcordata***
x *ralphii* See LOPHOMYRTUS x ***ralphii***
'Traversii' See LOPHOMYRTUS 'Traversii'
ugni See UGNI ***molinae***

NANDINA (Nandinaceae)
domestica CB&S CBot CBow CBra CFor ECro ELan IOrc ISea LHop LPan MBri MUlv NKay NRog SHil SSpi SSta WBod WPat WSHC WWat
– 'Firepower' CB&S CBra EBre ELan ENot IBar IHos IOrc LHop LNet MR&S MUlv NHol SPer SPla SSta WWat
– 'Harbor Dwarf' LRHS SSta
– 'Nana Purpurea' SHil
§ – 'Pygmaea' CBra CSam ECro SSus
– 'Richmond' CB&S ECro ELan MBlu MMea MR&S MUlv NHol SPer SSpi
– 'Wood's Dwarf' CB&S
♦ – 'Nana' See N. ***d.*** 'Pygmaea'

NANNORRHOPS (Palmae)
ritchieana LPal

NARCISSUS † (Liliaceae/Amaryllidaceae)
'Abalone' (2) EWal
¶ 'Accent' (2) ICar
'Acclamation' (4) EWal
'Accolade' (3) ECop
'Achduart' (3) ECop ICar IDun
'Achentoul' (4) ICar
'Achnasheen' (3) ICar
'Acropolis' (4) ECop EWal ICar LAma LBlo
'Actaea' (9) ETub LBlo LRoo MBri SIng
'Advocat' (3) IDun
¶ 'Affable' (4) ICar
'Aflame' (3) LAma MBri
'Aircastle' (3) IBal ICar
¶ 'Alba Pax' (2) ECop
'Albus Plenus Odoratus' See N. ***poeticus*** 'Plenus'
¶ 'Algarve' (2) IDun
'Alice's Pink' (2) ICar
'Alliance' (1) EWal
alpestris See N. ***pseudonarcissus moschatus***
¶ 'Alpha' (9) EWal
'Altruist' (3) ECop EWal
'Amber Light' (2) EWal
'Ambercastle' (2) ECop ICar IDun
'Ambergate' (2) EWal LAma
'Amberglow' (2) EWal LBlo
'Amor' (3) EWal LRoo
'Andalusia' (6) ECop SIng
Angel's Tears See N. ***triandrus triandrus***
¶ 'Angkor' (4) ICar
'Ann Abbott' (2) EWal

'Annalong' (3)	IBal
'Anniversary' (2)	EWal
'Anthea' (2)	EWal
'Apotheose' (4)	EWal
'Apricot' (1)	CBro
'Apricot Sundae' (4)	ICar
'April Charm' (2)	ICar
'April Love' (1)	ECop IBal ICar
'April Snow' (2)	CBro
'April Tears' (5)	CBro CCla ECop EWal LAma LBlo SIng
'Aranjuez' (2)	LAma
'Arbar' (2)	EWal LAma
'Arcady' (2)	EWal
¶ 'Arctic Char' (2)	ICar
'Arctic Gold' (1)	ECop ICar LBlo
'Ardbane' (2)	ICar
'Ardglass' (3)	IBal ICar
'Ardour' (3)	ICar
'Ardress' (2)	IDun
'Arie Hoek' (2)	LBlo
'Arish Mell' (5)	EWal ICar IDun
'Arkle' (1)	ECop ICar LBlo
'Armagh' (1)	ECop ICar
¶ 'Armynel' (2)	EWal
'Arndilly' (2)	ECop
'Arpege' (2)	ECop
'Arragon' (2)	ECop
'Artillery' (3)	EWal
'Ashmore' (2)	ICar IDun
¶ 'Aslan' (4)	ICar
'Aspasia' (8)	CBro
§ ***assoanus***	CBro EPar EPot LAma MPar NHol WChr
§ ***asturiensis***	CBro ECam ELan EPar EPot GLoc IBlr LAma LBow MBal NHol SIng WChr
– 'Fuente De'	WChr
*– 'Giant'	ETub
'Atholl Palace' (4)	IDun
atlanticus	SPou
'Attrus' (2)	EWal
'Audubon' (3)	EWal
¶ 'Aurum' (1)	ICar
'Avalanche' (8)	EWal IDun
¶ 'Avalon' (2)	IDun
'Avenger' (2)	ECop ICar
'Ayston' (2)	ECop
'Baby Doll' (6)	EWal
'Baby Moon' (7)	CB&S CCla ECam ELan EPar EPot ETub LAma MBri NHol SIng
'Baccarat' (11)	EWal LAma MBri
'Badbury Rings' (3)	IDun
¶ 'Baily' (2)	ICar
'Ballintoy' (2)	ICar
'Ballyarnett' (1)	ICar
'Ballycastle' (3)	ICar
'Ballyfrema' (1)	ICar
'Ballygarvey' (1)	EWal
'Ballyrobert' (1)	ECop
'Ballytrim' (2)	ICar
'Balvenie' (2)	ECop IDun
'Bambi' (1)	CBro ETub
'Banbridge' (1)	ECop IBal ICar
'Bandleader' (2)	EWal
'Bantam' (2)	CBro EWal
'Barley Cove' (2)	ICar
'Barley Sugar' (3)	ICar
¶ 'Barleythorpe' (1)	EWal
'Barnby Moor' (3)	IBal
'Barnsdale Wood' (2)	ECop
'Barnwell Alice' (2)	ICar
'Baronscourt' (1)	ICar
'Barrett Browning' (3)	ETub LBlo MBri
'Bartley' (6)	EWal
'Bastion' (1)	EWal
¶ 'Beauticol' (11)	IDun
'Beauvallon' (4)	IDun
'Bebop' (7)	CBro
'Beefeater' (2)	EWal
'Beersheba' (1)	MBri
'Beige Beauty' (3)	EWal ICar
'Belisana' (2)	LAma
'Bell Song' (7)	ETub EWal
'Beltrim' (2)	ICar
'Ben Vorlich' (2)	ICar
¶ 'Bencarden' (3)	ICar
¶ 'Bergerac' (11)	IDun
'Bermuda' (2)	EWal
¶ 'Berry Gorse' (3)	ECop
'Beryl' (6)	CAvo CBro ECop EWal ICar LAma LBow NHol
'Best of Luck' (3)	IBal
'Bethany' (2)	EWal ICar
* 'Big Cycla' (6)	ETub
¶ 'Big John' (1)	IDun
'Bilbo' (6)	IDun
'Binkie' (2)	CBro EWal LAma MBri
'Birdsong' (3)	ICar
'Birkdale' (2)	IDun
'Birma' (3)	EWal LAma MBri
'Birthday Girl' (2)	IDun
'Birthright' (1)	EWal
'Biscayne' (1)	EWal
¶ 'Bishopstone' (1)	ICar
'Bit O'Gold' (2)	ICar
'Bithynia' (3)	EWal
¶ 'Bittern' (2)	ICar
'Bizerta' (2)	EWal
'Blarney' (3)	EWal
'Blessing' (2)	EWal
'Blue Bird' (2)	EWal
¶ 'Bob Minor' (1)	EWal
'Bobbysoxer' (7)	CAvo CBro EWal ICar LAma MBri NHol
'Bodilly' (2)	EWal
'Bonamargy' (2)	ICar
'Border Chief' (2)	ICar
'Borrobol' (2)	ECop
'Bossa Nova' (3)	IDun
'Boudoir' (1)	ICar
'Bovagh' (2)	ICar
'Bowles' Sulphur'	CRow
'Bracken Hill' (2)	ICar
'Braddock' (3)	IBal
'Brave Journey' (2)	ICar

'Bravoure' (1)	EWal LBlo
'Breakthrough' (2)	EWal
'Bridal Crown' (4)	EWal LAma
'Bridesmaid' (2)	IBal
'Brighton' (1)	LAma
'Broadland' (2)	ECop
¶ 'Broadway Rose' (2)	IDun
'Broadway Star' (11)	EWal LAma
'Brookfield' (2)	ICar
'Broomhill' (2)	ECop
'Broughshane' (1)	ICar
'Brunswick' (2)	EWal LAma
'Bryanston' (2)	ECop IDun
'Bryher' (3)	ICar
'Buffawn' (7)	EWal
'Bulbarrow' (2)	IDun
bulbocodium	CBro CRiv ECam ETub LBow MBri SOkd WCla
– bulbocodium	CBro SIng WChr
– citrinus	SPou
– conspicuus	CAvo CBro EPar EPot GLoc LAma LBlo MBal MBri MS&S NHol SIng WChr
*– ***filifolius***	CBro
– mesatlanticus	See N. ***romieuxii m.***
– nivalis AB&S 4519	SPou
¶ ***– praecox paucinervis***	WChr
– tananicus	See N. ***tananicus***
– 'Tenuifolius'	GLoc LAma MS&S NHol SPou
'Bullseye' (3)	EWal
'Bunclody' (2)	ECop ICar
'Buncrana' (2)	ECop ICar
'Bunting' (7)	ICar IDun
'Burgemeester Gouverneur' (1)	LAma
'Burma Star' (2)	ICar
'Burning Heart' (11)	EWal
'Burning Torch' (2)	ICar
¶ 'Burntollet' (1)	IDun
'Bushmills' (3)	ICar
'Buster' (2)	EWal
'Buttercup' (7)	CBro
'By Jove' (1)	EWal
'Cabra' (1)	ICar
¶ 'Cadence' (3)	ICar
'Cairn Toul' (3)	ECop
'Cairndhu' (2)	ICar
'Calabar' (2)	EWal
¶ 'Callaway' (3)	ICar
'Camelot' (2)	ECop EWal ICar
'Campion' (9)	IDun
'Canaliculatus' (8)	CBro EPar LAma LBlo LBow LRoo MBri SIng WHil WPer
'Canarybird' (8)	CBro
'Canasta' (11)	ETub
'Canby' (2)	ICar
'Candida' (4)	EWal
'Canford' (3)	IDun
'Canisp' (2)	ECop ICar
'Cantabile' (9)	ECop IBal SIng
¶ ***cantabricus cantabricus***	CRiv
– cantabricus petunioides	LAma
– foliosus	EPot LBow SPou WChr
– monophyllus	SPou
'Cantatrice' (1)	LBlo
'Canticle' (9)	IBal
'Cape Cool' (2)	ICar
'Capisco' (3)	IBal
'Carbineer' (2)	LAma LBlo
'Carlton' (2)	ETub LAma LBlo LRoo MBri
'Caro Nome' (2)	EWal
'Carrickbeg' (1)	LBlo
'Carrigeen' (2)	ICar
'Caruso' (2)	LAma
'Cassata' (11)	EWal LAma LBlo LRoo
'Casterbridge' (2)	IDun
'Castle Dobbs' (4)	ICar
'Castlehill' (3)	IBal
'Cavoda' (1) or (2)	ICar
'Celtic Song' (2)	ECop
¶ 'Cernuus Plenus' (4)	ICar
'Ceylon' (2)	EWal LAma
'Chagall' (2)	ICar
'Chania' (1)	ICar
'Chanterelle' (11)	EWal LAma
'Chapeau' (2)	ICar
'Charade' (2)	ICar
'Charity Fair' (6)	IBal
'Charity May' (6)	CAvo CBro ECop EWal IBal ICar LAma MBri SAxl SIng
'Charleston' (2)	IDun
'Charter' (2)	ECop EWal
¶ 'Chat' (7)	ICar
¶ 'Cha-Cha' (6)	IDun
'Checkmate' (2)	ICar
'Cheer Leader' (3)	IDun
'Cheerfulness' (4)	ETub EWal LAma LBlo MBri SIng
'Chelsea Derby' (2)	ICar
'Chérie' (7)	CBro
'Cherrygardens' (2)	ECop
'Chesterton' (9)	IDun
'Chickerell' (3)	IDun
¶ 'Chief Inspector' (1)	IDun
'Chig' (2)	EWal
'Chiloquin' (1)	ECop
'Chinchilla' (2)	IDun
'Chinese Sacred Lily' (8)	ETub
'Chinese White' (3)	ICar
'Chinita' (8)	CBro EWal IDun
'Chivalry' (1)	EWal
'Chungking' (3)	ICar
'Church Bay' (2)	ICar
'Churchfield' (2)	ICar
'Churchman' (2)	IBal ICar
'Clady Cottage' (2)	ICar
'Clare' (7)	CBro
'Clare Park' (2)	ICar
'Clockface' (3)	EWal
'Cloud Nine' (2)	EWal ICar
'Cloudcap' (2)	ICar
¶ 'Cloud's Hill' (4)	IDun
'Cloyfin' (2)	ICar
'Collector's Choice' (3)	ICar
¶ 'Colloggett' (2)	ECop
¶ 'Colorama' (11)	IDun

'Coloratura' (3)	ICar
'Columbus' (2)	ICar
§ ***concolor***	CBro ECam EPar EPot MBal NHol SIng
– SB 202	SPou
'Congress' (11)	EWal
'Connor' (2)	ICar
'Cool Autumn' (2)	ICar
'Cool Crystal' (3)	ECop ICar IDun
'Coolattin' (2)	ICar
'Cophetua' (1)	ICar
'Cora Ann' (7)	CBro
'Coral Fair' (2)	IBal
¶ 'Coral Light' (2)	ICar
'Coraline' (6)	IDun
'Corbridge' (2)	EWal
'Corinthian' (1)	LAma
'Cornerstone' (2)	EWal
'Country Morning' (3)	ICar
'Coverack Perfection' (2)	EWal
'Crackington' (4)	IDun
'Cragford' (8)	ETub EWal LAma
'Craigdun' (2)	ICar
'Craigtara' (2)	ICar
'Craigywarren' (2)	EWal
'Cranbourne' (2)	IDun
'Creagh Dubh' (2)	IDun
'Crenelet' (2)	IDun
'Crimson Chalice' (3)	IDun
'Crinoline' (2)	EWal
'Cristobal' (1)	ECop LBlo
'Crock of Gold' (2)	EWal
'Croila' (2)	ECop
'Crown Royalist' (2)	IBal
'Crystal River' (3)	EWal
cuatrecasasii	WChr
'Curly' (1)	ETub
'Cushendall' (3)	EWal ICar
'Cushendun' (3)	IBal
cyclamineus	CBro EPot LAma SIng SWas WChr
'Cyclope' (1)	LRoo
¶ 'Cyros' (1)	IDun
'Dailmanach' (2)	ECop IDun LBlo
'Dalliance' (2)	ICar
'Dancer' (2)	EWal
'Dancing Partner' (2)	EWal
'Danes Balk' (2)	ICar
* 'Darlow Dale' (2)	ECop
'Dateline' (3)	IDun
'Davlyn' (2)	EWal
'Dawn' (5)	CBro ICar
'Dawn Mist' (2)	EWal
'Daydream' (2)	ECop EWal ICar IDun LAma LBlo
¶ 'Debrett' (2)	IDun
'Debutante' (2)	LBlo
¶ 'Decoy' (2)	ICar
'Delamont' (2)	ICar
'Delia' (6)	IDun
'Delibes' (2)	LAma LBlo
¶ 'Delnashaugh' (4)	ICar IDun
¶ 'Delos' (3)	IDun
'Delta Wings' (6)	IDun
'Derg Valley' (1)	IDun
'Descanso' (1)	ECop EWal
¶ 'Desdemona' (2)	EWal
'Desert Rose' (2)	ICar
'Diane' (6)	IDun
'Dick Wilden' (4)	ETub EWal LAma
¶ 'Dickcissel' (7)	ICar
'Dilemma' (3)	IDun
'Dinkie' (3)	CBro
'Diversion' (3)	ICar
'Divertimento' (7)	ICar
'Doctor Alexander Fleming' (2)	EWal
'Doctor Hugh' (3)	EWal IDun
'Dolly Mollinger' (11)	EWal LAma LBlo
'Don Carlos' (2)	ICar LBlo
'Double Blush' (4)	ICar
'Double Event' (4)	ICar LBlo
'Doubtful' (3)	ECop ICar
'Dove of Peace' (6)	IBal
'Dove Wings' (6)	CBro ECam ECop ETub EWal IBal LAma NHol SIng
¶ 'Dovekie' (12)	ICar
'Dover Cliffs' (2)	ECop
'Downhill' (3)	ICar
'Downpatrick' (1)	ECop ICar
'Dream Castle' (3)	EWal ICar
'Drenagh' (2)	ICar
'Drumadarragh' (1)	ICar
'Drumadoon' (2)	ICar
'Drumawillan' (2)	ICar
'Drumnabreeze' (2)	ICar
'Drumnasole' (3)	ICar
'Drumragh' (1)	IDun
'Drumrunie' (2)	ICar
'Drumtullagh' (2)	ICar
'Duet' (4)	EWal
'Duke of Windsor' (2)	LBlo
'Dulcie Joan' (2)	ECop
'Dundarave' (2)	ICar
'Dunlambert' (2)	IBal
'Dunskey' (3)	IDun
'Dutch Master' (1)	ETub EWal LAma LBow MBri
'Dynamite' (2)	EWal
'Early Blossom' (1)	IBal
'Early Splendour' (8)	LAma
'Easter Bonnet' (2)	LAma
¶ 'Easter Moon' (2)	ICar
¶ 'Eaton Park' (3)	IDun
¶ 'Edge Grove' (2)	ICar
'Edwalton' (2)	ECop
'Edward Buxton' (3)	ETub LAma LBlo MBri
'Egard' (11)	EWal
'Egg Nog' (4)	ICar
¶ 'Eland' (7)	IDun
¶ 'Elfin Gold' (6)	IDun
'Elizabeth Ann' (6)	IDun
¶ 'Elphin' (4)	ICar
'Elrond' (6)	IDun
'Elvira' (8)	CBro
'Elwing' (6)	IDun

'Elysian Fields' (2)	EWal
'Emily' (2)	IBal ICar
'Eminent' (3)	EWal
'Empress of Ireland' (1)	ECop EWal IBal LBlo
'Entrancement' (1)	EWal
'Ernevale' (3)	IDun
'Eskylane' (2)	ICar
'Estio Pinza' (2)	EWal
'Estrella' (3)	ECop
¶ 'Estremadura' (2)	IDun
'Euphony' (2)	ICar
'Evendine' (2)	EWal
'Exception' (1)	LBlo
¶ 'Exemplar' (1)	EWal
'Eyecatcher' (3)	ICar
'Eystettensis' (4)	CBro
'Fair Head' (9)	IBal
'Fair Prospect' (2)	ICar IDun LBlo
'Fairgreen' (3)	IBal ICar
'Fairmaid' (3)	IBal
'Fairmile' (3)	ICar LAma
'Fairy Footsteps' (3)	IBal ICar
¶ 'Fairy Island' (3)	ICar
'Falstaff' (2)	EWal ICar
'Far Country' (2)	ICar
'Faraway' (3)	IBal ICar
'Faro' (1)	IBal
'Farranfad' (2)	IBal
'Favor Royal' (3)	IBal
'Favourite' (2)	EWal
'February Gold' (6)	CAvo CBro ECam EPar ETub EWal IBal LAma LBlo LBow LRoo MBri NHol SIng WPer
'February Silver' (6)	CAvo CBro EPar ETub EWal LAma LBow NHol SIng
'Feeling Lucky' (2)	EWal
'Felindre' (9)	EWal IBal
'Fellowship' (2)	IDun
'Fergie' (2)	EWal
fernandesii (10)	CBro SPou WChr
'Ferndown' (3)	ECop IDun
'Festivity' (2)	ECop EWal ICar
'Fiji' (4)	ECop ICar
'Filly' (2)	EWal
¶ 'Finchcocks' (2)	ECop
'Fionn' (2)	ICar
'Fire Flash' (2)	ICar
¶ 'Fire Raiser' (2)	ICar
'Firestorm' (2)	IBal
'Firgrove' (3)	ICar
'First Date' (3)	ICar
'Flaming Meteor' (2)	ICar
'Flirt ' (6)	ICar
'Flomay' (7)	CBro
'Florida Manor' (3)	IBal
'Flower Carpet' (1)	LAma
'Flower Drift' (4)	ETub LAma MBri
'Flower Record' (2)	ETub LAma LRoo
* 'Flowerdream'	LAma
¶ 'Flycatcher' (7)	IDun
'Flying Saucer' (2)	EWal
¶ 'Fool's Gold' (4)	ICar
'Foray' (2)	EWal
'Foresight' (1)	ICar LAma LBlo LRoo
'Forge Mill' (2)	ICar
'Fort Knox' (1)	EWal
'Fortissimo' (2)	LRoo
'Fortune' (2)	EWal LAma LBlo LRoo
'Foundling' (6)	ECop EWal IBal ICar IDun SIng
'Fount' (2)	ICar
'Fourways' (3)	IBal
'Foxfire' (2)	ICar
'Fragrant Rose' (2)	EWal ICar IDun
'Frank's Fancy' (9)	IBal
'Frigid' (3)	IBal ICar
'Frolic' (1)	EWal
'Front Royal' (2)	ECop.ICar
'Frou-Frou' (4)	ICar
'Fuego' (2)	ICar
¶ 'Fulwell' (4)	IDun
¶ 'Gabriël Kleiberg' (11)	IDun
gaditanus (10)	CBro
'Gainsborough' (2)	ICar
'Galway' (2)	ECop EWal
'Ganaway' (3)	IBal
'Garden Princess' (6)	CBro LAma
'Gay Challenger' (4)	LBlo
'Gay Kybo' (4)	ECop IDun
'Gay Mood' (2)	ECop EWal
'Gay Song' (4)	ICar
¶ 'Gay Time' (4)	EWal
¶ 'George's Pink' (2)	ICar
¶ 'Georgie Girl' (6)	IDun
'Geranium' (8)	CBro ECop ETub EWal LAma LBlo LRoo MBri SIng
¶ 'Gettysburg' (2)	IDun
'Gigantic Star' (2)	EWal LAma MBri
'Gilda' (2)	IBal
'Gilford' (3)	ICar
'Gimli' (6)	IDun
'Gin and Lime' (1)	ICar IDun
'Gipsy Moth' (2)	ICar
¶ 'Gipsy Queen' (1)	ICar
'Glacier' (1)	LBlo
'Glad Day' (2)	ICar
¶ 'Glaston' (2)	ICar
'Glen Clova' (2)	LBlo
'Glenamoy' (1)	ICar
'Glencraig' (2)	ICar
'Glendermott' (2)	ICar
'Glenfarclas' (1)	ICar LBlo
'Glorious' (8)	IBal
'Glowing Embers' (2)	ICar
'Gold Bullion' (1)	ICar
'Gold Medal' (1)	EWal LAma
'Gold Mine' (2)	IBal
'Gold Phantom' (1)	ICar
'Gold Strike' (1)	ICar
'Golden Amber' (2)	IBal ICar
'Golden Aura' (2)	ECop EWal IBal ICar
'Golden Ducat' (4)	EWal LAma LBlo MBri
'Golden Halo' (2)	IBal
'Golden Harvest' (1)	ETub LAma LBlo MBri
'Golden Jewel' (2)	ECop IDun
'Golden Joy' (2)	ICar IDun

'Golden Orchid' (11)	LAma
'Golden Perfection' (7)	LAma LRoo
'Golden Radiance' (1)	IBal
¶ 'Golden Ranger' (2)	IDun
'Golden Rapture' (1)	ECop LBlo
¶ 'Golden Riot' (1)	EWal
'Golden Rupee' (1)	ECop
'Golden Sands' (1)	ECop
'Golden Sheen' (2)	IDun
'Golden Showers' (1)	IBal
'Golden Sovereign' (1)	IBal
'Golden Vale' (1)	ECop IDun
'Golden Wings' (6)	IBal
¶ 'Goldfinger' (1)	IDun
'Golly' (4)	EWal
'Good Measure' (2)	EWal
'Goose Green' (3)	IBal
'Gossamer' (3)	EWal
'Gourmet' (1)	LAma
gracilis	See N. x ***tenuior***
¶ 'Gracious Lady' (2)	IDun
'Grand Prospect' (2)	IBal
'Grand Soleil d'Or' (8)	LAma
'Gransha' (3)	IBal
'Great Expectations' (2)	IBal
'Green Glens' (2)	ICar
'Green Gold' (2)	EWal
'Green Howard' (3)	ECop
'Green Ice' (2)	IDun
* 'Green Orchid'	LAma
'Green Peace' (3)	IBal
'Green Rival' (2)	EWal
'Greenfinch' (3)	ICar
¶ 'Greenholm' (2)	IDun
'Greenstar' (4)	EWal
'Greenvale' (2)	IDun
'Greeting' (2)	ECop
¶ 'Grey Lady' (3)	ICar
¶ 'Grosvenor' (4)	IDun
'Halolight' (2)	EWal
'Halstock' (2)	IDun
'Hambledon' (2)	ECop IDun
'Hammoon' (3)	EWal
'Happy Face' (2)	ICar
'Hartington' (2)	ECop
'Hawaii' (4)	IBal
'Hawera (5)	CAvo CBro CCla CSam ECam ECop EPar ETub EWal LAma LBow LRoo MBri MBro NHol SAxl SIng WHil WOMN
'Hazel Winslow' (2)	IDun
'Heart's Desire' (4)	EWal
'Heat Haze' (2)	ICar
henriquesii	See N. ***jonquilla h.***
'Hero' (1)	EWal IDun
'Hesla' (7)	ICar
'High Church' (2)	IBal
'High Note' (7)	EWal
'High Society' (2)	EWal IDun
'Highfield Beauty' (8)	ECop EWal IDun
'Highland Wedding' (2)	ECop ICar
'Highway Song' (2)	ICar
'Hilford' (2)	IBal
¶ 'Holbeck' (4)	IDun
'Holiday Fashion' (2)	EWal
'Holland Sensation' (1)	LAma
'Holly Berry' (2)	ICar
'Homage' (2)	EWal
'Home Fires' (2)	LBlo
'Honeybird' (1)	ECop EWal ICar
'Hoodsport' (11)	LBlo
¶ 'Hoopoe' (8)	ICar
'Hope' (4)	EWal
'Horace' (9)	ICar
'Hors d'Oeuvre' (8)	CBro
'Hot Sun' (3)	ECop
'Hot Toddy' (4)	IBal ICar
'Hotspur' (2)	ICar
'Howard's Way' (3)	IBal
'Ibberton' (3)	ECop
'Ice Follies' (2)	ETub EWal LAma LBlo LBow LRoo MBri
'Ice King' (11)	EWal
'Ice Wings' (5)	CBro IDun SIng
¶ 'Ida May' (2)	IDun
¶ 'Indian Maid' (7)	ICar
'Inglescombe' (4)	LAma
¶ 'Initiation' (1)	ICar
¶ 'Innis Beg' (2)	ICar
¶ 'Innisfree' (3)	ICar
'Inniswood' (1)	ICar
'Interim' (2)	EWal ICar
'Interval' (2)	IBal
¶ 'Intrigue' (7)	ICar IDun
'Inverpolly' (2)	ICar
'Ireland's Eye' (9)	IBal
'Irene Copeland' (4)	EWal LBlo
'Irish Charm' (2)	ECop
'Irish Light' (2)	ICar
'Irish Linen' (3)	ICar
'Irish Luck' (1)	EWal LAma
'Irish Mist' (2)	ECop ICar
'Irish Nymph' (3)	ICar
'Irish Ranger' (3)	ICar
¶ 'Irish Splendour' (3)	ICar
'Islandhill' (3)	IBal
'It's True' (1)	EWal
'Ivy League' (1)	ICar
'Jack Snipe' (6)	CAvo CBro CCla ECam ECop ETub EWal LAma LBlo LBow LRoo MBri MBro NHol SAxl SIng
'Jamestown' (3)	IBal
¶ 'Janis Babson' (2)	ICar
'Jeannine Hoog' (1)	LRHS
'Jenny' (6)	CAvo CBro ECop EPar ETub EWal IBal ICar LAma LBlo LRoo SIng
'Jessamy' (12)	SPou
'Jetfire' (6)	CBro ECop ETub EWal IDun LAma
'Jewel Song' (2)	ECop ICar
'John of Salisbury' (2)	EWal
§ 'Jolity' (2)	EWal
'Jolly Roger' (2)	ICar
Jonquil Single	LBlo

jonquilla	CAvo CBro EPar EPot LAma LBow MBri SIng
§ – *henriquesii*	CBro
'Joseph Macleod' (1)	EWal
'Joy'	See N. 'Jolity'
'Joy Bishop' (10)	SOkd SPou WChr
'Jubilation' (2)	EWal
'Jules Verne'	LAma
§ 'Julia Jane' (10)	EPot
'Jumblie' (6)	CAvo CBro CCla ECop EPot EWal LAma LRoo MBri SAxl
'Jumbo Gold' (1)	IDun
juncifolius	See N. ***assoanus***
¶ 'Kanchenjunga' (1)	ICar
'Karachi' (2)	ICar
¶ 'Karamudli' (1)	ICar
'Karelia' (1 or 2)	LRoo
'Kaydee'	IDun
'Kehelland' (4)	CBro
¶ 'Kelanne' (2)	IDun
¶ 'Ken's Favourite' (2)	IDun
'Kildavin' (2)	ICar
'Kildrum' (3)	EWal ICar
'Kilkenny' (1)	EWal
'Killeen' (2)	IBal
'Kilmorack' (2)	ICar
'Kilworth' (2)	EWal LAma LBlo
'Kimmeridge' (3)	ECop IDun
'Kindled' (2)	ICar
'King Alfred' (1)	LAma LBlo MBri
'Kinglet' (7)	ICar
'Kingscourt' (1)	ECop
'King's Bridge' (1)	IDun
¶ 'King's Grove' (1)	IDun
¶ 'King's Stag' (1)	IDun
'Kirkinriola' (3)	ICar
'Kirklington' (2)	IBal
'Kissproof' (2)	LAma LBlo
'Kitten' (6)	EWal
'Klamath' (2)	EWal
'Knockstacken' (1)	ICar
'Krakatoa' (2)	EWal
'La Riante' (3)	LAma
'Ladybank' (1)	IDun
'Lanarth' (7)	CBro
'Lancaster' (3)	IBal ICar
'Landmark' (2)	EWal
'Langford Grove' (3)	ECop IBal
'Larkelly' (6)	CBro ICar
'Larkfield' (2)	ICar
'Last Word' (3)	EWal
'Late Call' (3)	IBal
'Lavender Lass' (6)	ECop ICar IDun
'Lemnos' (2)	EWal
'Lemon Beauty' (11)	EWal
'Lemon Cloud' (1)	EWal
'Lemon Express' (1)	IDun
'Lemon Heart' (5)	CBro ICar
'Lemon Meringue' (1)	ICar
'Lemon Sherbet' (2)	ICar
'Lemonade' (3)	ICar
¶ 'Lennymore' (2)	IDun
'Leonaine' (2)	EWal

'Leslie Hill' (1)	ICar
'Liberty Bells' (5)	CAvo CBro ECop EWal LAma MBri NHol SIng
'Lichfield' (3)	EWal
'Lighthouse' (3)	IDun
'Lilac Charm' (6)	IDun
¶ 'Lilac Hue' (6)	IDun
'Limbo' (2)	EWal IDun
'Limeade' (2)	ICar
'Limelight' (1)	EWal
'Limerick' (3)	EWal ICar
'Lintie' (7)	CBro EWal LAma MBri SAxl SIng
'Lionheart' (4)	EWal
¶ 'Lisanore' (2)	ICar
'Lisbane' (3)	IBal
'Lisbarnett' (3)	IBal
¶ 'Lisrenny' (1)	ICar
'Little Beauty' (1)	CAvo CBro EPot ETub LAma
'Little Dancer' (1)	CBro
'Little Gem' (1)	CAvo CBro LAma LRoo
'Little Princess' (6)	ICar
'Little Sentry' (7)	CBro
'Little Witch' (6)	CAvo CBro ECop EWal LAma LBow MBri NHol SAxl SIng WHil
'Lizard Light' (2)	EWal
lobularis	See N. ***pseudonarcissus*** 'Lobularis'
'Loch Assynt' (3)	ECop ICar
'Loch Fada' (2)	ICar
'Loch Garvie' (2)	ICar
'Loch Hope' (2)	ECop ICar IDun
¶ 'Loch Lundie' (2)	ICar IDun
¶ 'Loch Naver' (2)	IDun
'Loch Owskeich' (2)	ECop
'Loch Stac' (2)	ECop ICar
'Loth Lorien' (3)	IDun
'Lothario' (2)	LAma MBri
'Lough Bawn' (2)	ICar
'Lough Cuan' (1)	IBal
'Loughanisland' (1)	IBal
'Loughanmore' (1)	ICar
'Louise de Coligny' (2)	ETub
'Lovable' (3)	EWal
'Lunar Sea' (1)	ECop EWal
'Lurgain' (1)	EWal
'Lusky Mills' (3)	IBal
'Lydwells' (2)	ECop
'Lyles' (2)	ECop
'Lynwood' (1)	ICar
'Lyric' (9)	IDun
¶ 'Lysander' (2)	IDun
'L'Amour'	See N. 'Madelaine'
§ 'Madelaine' (2)	EWal
¶ 'Madrigal' (2)	EWal
'Magic Flute' (2)	ICar
¶ 'Magic Maiden' (2)	IDun
¶ 'Magna Carta' (2)	IDun
'Magnet' (1)	ETub LAma MBri
'Magnificence' (1)	LAma
'Mahmoud' (3)	ICar
'Maiden Over' (2)	ECop
¶ 'Majestic Star' (1)	IDun

'Manchu' (2)	EWal
'Manly' (4)	EWal LBlo LRoo
'Mantle' (2)	IDun
'Maraval' (1)	EWal ICar
'March Madness' (2)	ICar
'March Sunshine' (6)	CBro EWal ICar LAma NHol
'Marcola' (2)	ICar
'Marie-José' (11)	ETub LAma
'Marshfire' (2)	ICar
'Martha Washington' (8)	CBro ECop
marvieri	See N. ***rupicola m.***
'Mary Bohannon' (2)	ETub EWal
'Mary Copeland' (4)	EWal LAma MBri
'Mary Kate' (6)	IDun
'Mary Sumner' (1)	ICar
'Mary's Pink' (2)	ICar
'Medalist' (2)	ICar
¶ 'Megalith' (2)	IDun
'Melbury' (2)	ECop IDun
'Mellon Park' (3)	IDun
'Melody Lane' (2)	EWal
'Mentor' (2)	IDun
'Menucha' (2)	ICar
'Mercato' (2)	LAma
'Merlin' (3)	ECop IBal LBlo
¶ 'Merlin's Castle'	ICar
'Mermaid's Spell' (2)	ICar
'Merry Bells' (5)	ICar
'Merrymaker' (4)	EWal
'Mexico City' (2)	IBal
'Midas Touch' (1)	IDun
'Millennium' (1)	CBro
¶ 'Millgreen' (1)	EWal
'Minikin' (3)	ICar
minimus	See N. ***asturiensis***
'Minnow' (8)	CAvo CBro CCla ECam ECop EPot ETub EWal LAma LBlo LRoo MBri NHol SIng WHil
§ ***minor***	CBro LAma LBlo MPar
– 'Cedric Morris'	ECha
¶ – ***pumilus***	WPer
– ***pumilus plenus***	See N. 'Rip van Winkle'
'Mint Cup' (3)	ICar
'Missouri' (2)	EWal
'Mistral' (11)	ETub LRoo
'Misty Glen' (2)	ECop ICar
¶ 'Misty Moon' (3)	ICar
¶ 'Mockingbird' (7)	IDun
'Moina' (3)	ICar
'Mol's Hobby' (11)	EWal LAma
'Mondaine' (2)	EWal
'Moneymore' (2)	ICar
'Montalto' (2)	ICar
'Montego' (3)	ECop
¶ 'Monterrico' (4)	IDun
'Monument' (2)	ICar
'Monza' (4)	IDun
'Moon Goddess' (1)	IBal
'Moon Jade' (3)	IBal
'Moon Orbit' (2)	LBlo
'Moon Rhythm' (4)	IBal
'Moon Tide' (3)	IBal
'Moon Valley' (2)	IDun
'Moonshine' (5)	CBro
'Moonshot' (1)	EWal
'Moonspell' (2)	IBal ICar
'Moralee' (4)	IDun
'Mother Catherine Grullemans'	LAma
'Mount Angel' (3)	IDun
'Mount Fuji' (2)	IDun
'Mount Hood' (1)	ETub EWal LAma LBlo LRoo MBri
'Mount Ida' (2)	IBal
'Mount Vernon' (2)	ICar
'Mountjoy' (7)	EWal
'Mountpleasant' (2)	IBal
'Moyle' (9)	IBal
'Moyola' (2)	ICar
'Mrs R O Backhouse' (2)	LAma MBri
'Mrs William Copeland' (4)	EWal
'Muirfield' (1)	IDun
'Mulatto' (1)	EWal
'Murlough' (9)	IBal
'Murrayfield' (3)	IDun
'My Lady' (2)	EWal
'My My' (2)	EWal
¶ 'My Word' (2)	ICar
'Nampa' (1)	ECop EWal
¶ 'Namraj' (2)	IDun
'Nancegollan' (7)	CBro ECop
nanus	See N. ***minor***
¶ 'Nether Barr' (2)	IDun
'Nevta' (2)	IDun
'New Song' (2)	EWal
'New Star' (2)	EWal
'New World' (2)	EWal
'Newcastle' (1)	ECop IDun
'Nirvana' (7)	CBro
'Niveth' (5)	ICar
¶ 'Northern Light' (2)	ICar
'Northern Sceptre' (2)	IBal ICar
'Notable' (3)	IBal
'Noweta' (3)	ICar
'Nuage' (2)	EWal
'Nylon' (12)	CBro ECop SPou WChr
'Nymphette' (6)	IDun
'Oadby' (1)	ECop
'Oakwood' (3)	EWal
¶ 'Obelisk' (11)	IDun
obesus	MS&S WChr
x ***odorus*** 'Campernelli Plenus'	LAma SIng
– ***rugulosus***	CAvo CBro EPar LAma NHol
¶ 'Odyssey' (4)	ICar
Old Pheasant's Eye	See N. ***poeticus recurvus***
'Old Satin' (2)	ICar
'Olympic Gold' (1)	ECop
'Omaha' (3)	IBal
'Oneonta' (2)	ICar
'Orange Beacon' (2)	ICar
'Orange Lodge' (2)	IDun
'Orange Sherbet' (2)	ICar
'Orangery' (11)	LAma LBlo MBri
'Oratorio' (2)	EWal

¶ 'Oryx' (7)	IDun
'Osmington' (3)	ECop IDun
'Ottoman Gold' (2)	IBal
'Owen Roe' (1)	IBal
¶ 'Oykel' (3)	ICar
'Painted Desert' (3)	ECop ICar
¶ 'Pale Sunlight' (2)	ICar
¶ ***pallidiflorus***	WChr
¶ 'Palmares' (11)	EWal
'Palmyra' (3)	ICar
'Panache' (1)	ECop EWal ICar
'Pankot' (2)	ICar
¶ 'Paolo Veronese' (2)	EWal
'Paper White' (8)	ETub EWal LAma LBow LRoo MBri
'Papillon Blanc' (11)	EWal LAma LRoo
'Parcpat' (7)	CBro
¶ 'Parfait' (4)	ICar
'Paricutin' (2)	EWal
'Parisienne' (11)	LAma LRoo
'Park Springs' (3)	ECop IBal ICar
¶ 'Parterre' (2)	IDun
'Parthenon' (4)	ICar
'Passionale' (2)	ECop EWal IBal ICar LAma LBlo LBow
'Pastorale' (2)	EWal
'Patabundy' (2)	IDun
'Paula Cottell' (3)	CBro
¶ 'Pay Day' (1)	ICar
¶ 'Peacock' (2)	ICar
'Pearlax' (11)	EWal
'Pearly King' (1)	ECop
'Peeping Tom' (6)	CAvo CB&S CBro ECam EPar ETub LAma LBlo LBow LRoo MBri MBro NHol SAxl SIng
'Pencrebar' (7)	CAvo CBro EPot LAma LBlo MBri NHol
'Pennine Way' (1)	ECop
'Penpol' (7)	CBro
'Penvose' (2)	EWal
'Pepper' (2)	CBro
'Perimeter' (3)	ECop IBal ICar
'Perseus' (1)	ICar
'Pet Finch' (7)	EWal
'Petit Four' (4)	ETub EWal LAma LBlo LRoo
'Petrel' (5)	ETub ICar
'Petsamo' (1)	ICar
'Picasso' (3)	ICar
¶ 'Pick-Up' (11)	ICar
¶ 'Pinafore' (2)	EWal
¶ 'Pink Angel' (7)	ICar
'Pink Champagne' (4)	ECop
¶ 'Pink Charm'	EWal
'Pink Gin' (4)	EWal
'Pink Mink' (2)	IDun
'Pink Monarch' (2)	EWal
'Pink Pageant' (4)	EWal IDun
'Pink Panther' (2)	ICar
'Pink Paradise' (4)	IDun
'Pink Whispers' (2)	IBal
'Pinza' (2)	ICar LBlo
'Pipe Major' (2)	EWal IBal
'Piper's Barn' (7)	CBro
'Pipit' (7)	CBro EWal ICar IDun LAma MBri SIng
'Pismo Beach' (2)	ECop ICar IDun
'Pitchroy' (2)	ECop
'Playboy' (2)	ICar
'Playschool' (3)	ICar
poeticus	CAvo ECam LAma
– ***hellenicus***	EWal
– Old Pheasant's Eye	See N. ***poeticus recurvus***
§ – 'Plenus'	CBro
§ – ***recurvus***	CBro CGle ETub EWal ICar LAma LBlo LBow MBri SIng
¶ 'Poet's Way' (9)	ECop
'Polar Circle' (2)	ICar
'Polar Imp' (3)	ICar
'Polglass' (3)	CBro
'Polindra' (2)	EWal
'Polnesk' (7)	CBro
'Pomona' (3)	LAma
'Pontresina' (2)	ICar LBlo
'Portavo' (2)	ICar
'Porthchapel' (7)	ECop
¶ 'Portnagolan' (2)	ICar
'Portrush' (3)	EWal
'Portstewart' (3)	IBal
¶ 'Post House' (4)	IDun
'Prairie Fire'	IDun
'Preamble' (1)	ECop IBal ICar LBlo
'Premiere' (2)	IDun
'President Carter' (1)	LAma
'Pretty Polly' (2)	ICar
'Pride of Cornwall' (8)	CBro
'Prince of Brunswick' (2)	IBal
'Professor Einstein' (2)	ETub LAma LBlo LBow LRoo
'Prologue' (1)	EWal
'Prophet' (1)	EWal
pseudonarcissus	CBro CGle CRow LAma LBow NLan SIng WChr
– ***gayi***	CBro
§ – 'Lobularis'	CAvo CBro LBlo NHol SIng
– ***moschatus***	CBro
– ***nevadensis***	WOMN
§ – ***obvallaris***	CAvo CBro ECam ETub LBow NHol NLan SIng WCla
'Pueblo' (7)	ICar
x ***pulchellus***	SIng
pumilus	See N. ***minor pumilus***
'Puppet' (5)	ICar
'Puppy' (6)	EWal
'Purbeck' (3)	ECop EWal IDun
'Quail' (7)	CBro ICar LAma
¶ 'Quasar' (2)	ICar
♦ 'Queen Anne's Double'	See N. 'Eystettensis'
'Queen of Bicolors' (1)	LAma
'Queenscourt' (1)	ECop ICar
¶ 'Quetzal' (9)	ICar
'Quick Step' (7)	EWal
'Quiet Day' (2)	ICar
'Quince' (6)	CBro
'Quirinus' (2)	ETub LAma
'Radiation' (2)	EWal
'Radical' (6)	EWal
'Rainbow' (2)	ECop EWal ICar LBlo

'Rame Head' (1)	ECop
'Rameses' (2)	ECop
'Rarkmoyle' (2)	ICar
'Rathgar' (2)	ICar
'Rathowen Flame' (2)	ECop
¶ 'Ravenhill' (3)	IDun
'Reckless' (3)	ICar
'Red Arrow' (1)	IBal
'Red Bay' (2)	ICar
'Red Cottage' (2)	ICar
'Red Devil' (2)	ICar
'Red Devon' (2)	LBlo MBri
¶ 'Red Ember' (3)	IDun
'Red Goblet' (2)	LAma
'Red Hall' (3)	ICar
¶ 'Red Haze' (2)	IDun
'Red Rascal' (2)	LBlo MBri
'Red Spartan' (2)	IDun
¶ 'Redlands' (2)	ICar
'Redman' (2)	IBal
'Redstart' (3)	EWal
'Regal Bliss' (2)	IDun
'Reggae' (6)	ICar IDun
'Reliance' (2)	EWal
'Rembrandt' (1)	LAma LBlo MBri
¶ 'Replete' (4)	ICar IDun
requienii	See N. ***assoanus***
¶ 'Resplendent' (2)	ICar
'Revelry' (2)	ECop
'Revival' (4)	EWal
'Richhill' (2)	IBal
'Riding Mill' (3)	EWal
'Rijnveld's Early Sensation' (1)	ECop EWal
'Rima' (1)	ECop
'Rimmon' (3)	IDun
'Ringleader' (2)	EWal ICar IDun
¶ 'Ringmaster' (2)	ICar
'Ringmer' (3)	ECop
'Ringway' (3)	IDun
'Rio Bravo' (2)	IBal
'Rio Gusto' (2)	IBal
'Rio Rouge' (2)	IBal ICar
§ 'Rip van Winkle' (4)	CAvo CBro EPar EPot ETub LAma LBlo LBow LRoo MBri NHol WHil
'Rippling Waters' (5)	CBro ECam ECop LAma LBlo NHol
'Riptide' (1)	ICar
'Rivendell' (3)	ICar IDun
'Rob Roy' (3)	EWal
'Rockall' (3)	ECop ICar LBlo
¶ 'Rockport' (2)	ICar
'Rococo' (2)	EWal
'Roger' (6)	CBro ICar
'Roman Tile' (2)	EWal
'Romance' (2)	EWal LAma LBlo LRoo
'Romany Red' (3)	IDun
romieuxii	CAvo ECam EPot ITim LBow SIng SPou
¶ – AGS 4384	NHol
– JCA 805	EPot NHol WChr
¶ – ***albidus***	WChr
§ – ***mesatlanticus***	EPot SPou SWas
'Rosapenna' (2)	ICar
¶ 'Roscarrick' (2)	ECop
¶ 'Rose Gold' (1)	IDun
'Rose Noble' (2)	MBri
'Rose Royale' (2)	IBal ICar
¶ 'Roseate Tern' (2)	IDun
'Rosedew' (2)	LBlo
'Rosedown' (5)	CBro
'Roseworthy' (2)	LAma LBlo
'Rossferry' (2)	IBal
'Rosy Sunrise'	LAma
'Rosy Trumpet' (1)	CBro
¶ 'Rosy Wonder' (2)	EWal
¶ 'Rotarian' (3)	IDun
'Roulette' (2)	LBlo
'Round Robin' (2)	ICar
¶ 'Rousillon' (11)	IDun
'Royal Ballet' (2)	IDun
'Royal Coachman'	ICar
'Royal Command' (2)	See N. 'Royal Decree'
§ 'Royal Decree' (2)	EWal
'Royal Oak' (1)	ECop
'Royal Orange' (2)	EWal
'Royal Regiment' (2)	ICar
'Royal Wedding' (2)	ICar
'Rubh Mor' (2)	ECop
'Ruby Tail' (2)	EWal
rupicola	ECam EPot LAma LBow MS&S NHol SIng
¶ – ***marvieri***	WChr
'Rushlight' (2)	EWal
¶ 'Ruth Haller' (5)	ICar
'Ryan Son' (3)	IBal
¶ 'Saberning' (5)	ICar
* 'Sabik' (2)	ETub
'Sabine Hay' (3)	ICar IDun
'Sacajawea' (2)	EWal
'Safari' (2)	ICar
'Saint Keverne' (2)	ECop EWal IBal LAma
'Saint Patrick's Day' (2)	EWal LAma
'Salmon Leap' (2)	ICar
'Salmon Spray' (2)	LBlo
'Salmon Trout' (2)	ECop ETub EWal LAma
'Salomé' (2)	EWal LAma LBlo MBri
'Samantha' (4)	ECop ICar
'Samaria' (3)	CBro
'Samba' (5)	ETub
¶ 'Samite' (1)	EWal
'Sammy Boy' (2)	ECop
'Sarah' (3)	EWal
'Sateen' (2)	EWal
'Satellite' (6)	EWal ICar
'Satin Pink' (2)	ETub EWal MBri
'Saturn' (3)	ICar
scaberulus	CBro EPot LAma LBow NHol SIng WChr
'Scarlet Elegance' (2)	LAma
'Scarlet Gem' (8)	ETub EWal LAma LRoo SIng
'Scarlett O'Hara' (2)	LAma
'Scoreline' (1)	IDun
'Scotney Castle' (1)	ECop
¶ 'Sea Dream' (3)	IDun
'Sea Gift' (7)	CBro

'Sea Green' (9)	ECop
'Sea Princess' (3)	IBal
'Sealing Wax' (2)	ECop EWal
'Segovia' (3)	CBro
'Sempre Avanti' (2)	ETub LAma LBlo MBri
'Sextant' (6)	EWal IDun
'Shandon' (2)	IDun
'Shanes Castle' (1)	ICar
'She' (2)	EWal
'Sheerline' (2)	IDun
'Sheik' (2)	ICar
¶ 'Sherborne' (4)	IDun
'Sherpa' (1)	IDun
'Shining Light' (2)	ECop ICar
'Shot Silk' (5)	LAma
'Showboat' (2)	ICar
'Shuttlecock' (6)	IDun
'Shy Face' (2)	ICar
'Sidley' (3)	IDun
'Sigrid Undset' (3)	LAma
'Silent Valley' (1)	ICar IDun
'Silk Cut' (2)	IDun
'Silken Sails' (3)	ICar
'Silver Blaze' (2)	IDun
'Silver Chimes' (8)	CAvo CBro ETub EWal LAma LBlo SIng
'Silver Princess' (3)	EWal
¶ 'Silver Shell' (11)	IDun
¶ 'Silver Standard' (2)	EWal
'Silver Surf' (2)	IDun
'Silvermere' (2)	IDun
'Silverwood' (3)	IDun
'Sir Winston Churchill' (4)	EWal LAma LBlo LRoo
'Slaney' (3)	ICar
'Slowcoach' (3)	IDun
¶ 'Small Fry' (1)	EWal
'Smokey Bear' (4)	IDun
'Snoopie' (6)	IDun
'Snow Dream' (2)	EWal ICar
¶ 'Snow Gleam' (1)	IDun
¶ 'Snowcrest' (3)	IDun
'Snowfire' (4)	ICar
'Snowshill' (2)	ICar LBlo
'Solar Tan' (3)	IDun
'Soldier Brave' (2)	EWal
'Soledad' (2)	ICar
'Soleil d'Or' (8)	ETub EWal MBri
¶ 'Solferique' (2)	IDun
'Sorcerer' (3)	ICar
¶ 'Southease' (2)	ECop
'Southgrove' (2)	ECop
¶ 'Sovereign' (11)	IDun
¶ 'Space Age' (2)	ICar
'Spanish Moon' (1)	EWal
'Sparkling Eye' (8)	IBal
'Spellbinder' (1)	ECop EWal LAma LBlo MBri
'Spey Bay' (3)	IDun
'Sportsman' (2)	IDun
'Spring Valley' (3)	ICar
'Springston Charm' (2)	ICar
'Springwood' (2)	IDun
'Sputnik' (6)	IDun
¶ sp. ABS 4450	SPou
¶ sp. ABS 4656	SPou
sp. C M Stocken (10)	CBro
¶ sp. PJC 445	SPou
'Stadium' (2)	EWal
'Stainless' (2)	IBal
'Standard Value' (1)	LAma
¶ 'Starfire' (7)	ICar
'Starship' (2)	IDun
'State Express' (2)	IDun
'Statue' (2)	EWal
¶ 'Stoke Charity' (2)	ICar
¶ 'Stormy Weather' (1)	ECop
'Strangford' (3)	IBal
'Strathkanaird' (1)	ICar
'Stratosphere' (7)	ECop ICar
'Strephon' (1)	ICar
'Strines' (2)	ECop EWal
'Stromboli' (2)	EWal
'Suda Bay' (2)	ICar
'Sugarbush' (7)	CAvo CBro LAma LBlo MBri NHol SIng
'Suilven' (3)	ICar
'Sun Chariot' (2)	LBlo
'Sun Disc' (7)	CBro ECam EWal MBri SIng WPat
'Sun Salver' (2)	IBal
'Sunbather' (2)	ICar
'Sundial' (7)	CAvo CBro ECop EPot EWal ICar LAma LBlo LRoo NHol
'Sundisc' (7)	LAma
'Sunlover' (2)	ETub
¶ 'Suntory' (3)	IDun
¶ 'Surrey' (2)	IDun
¶ 'Susan Pearson' (7)	ICar
'Suzy' (7)	CAvo CBro ETub EWal ICar LAma LBlo LRoo MBri SIng
'Swallowcliffe' (6)	IDun
'Swallownest' (1)	ECop
'Swansdown' (4)	EWal ICar
'Sweet Harmony' (2)	ETub
'Sweet Pepper' (7)	CBro ECop ICar
'Sweetness' (7)	CAvo CBro ECop EWal IBal IDun LAma
'Swing Wing' (6)	IDun
'Sydling' (5)	IDun
'Sylvan Hill' (1)	IBal
'Symphonette' (2)	ICar
'Syracuse' (3)	ECop ICar
'Taffeta' (12)	CAvo ECam SPou WChr
'Tahiti' (4)	ECop EWal LAma LBlo LRoo MBri
'Tamar Fire' (4)	ECop
§ ***tananicus***	SPou WChr
'Tanera' (2)	ICar
'Tangent' (2)	EWal ICar
'Tardree' (1)	ICar
'Tarlatan' (12)	CBro SPou
'Tedstone' (1)	EWal
¶ 'Tekapo' (2)	ICar
§ 'Telamonius Plenus' (4)	CBro LAma LRHS
§ x ***tenuior***	CAvo
'Testament' (2)	EWal

'Tête-à-Tête' (12)	CAvo CB&S CBro CCla CSam ECop EPar EPot ETub EWal IBal LAma LBlo LBow MBri MPlt NHol SAxl SIng WHil
'Texas' (4)	ETub LAma MBri
'Thalia' (5)	CAvo CBro ETub EWal ICar LAma LBow LRoo MBri SIng WHil
'Theano' (2)	ICar
'Thoughtful' (5)	CBro EWal
'Thunderbolt' (1)	EWal
'Tibet' (2)	EWal IBal
'Tiger Moth' (6)	IDun
'Timolin' (3)	ICar
'Tingford' (3)	IBal
'Tiri Tomba' (11)	EWal IDun LBlo
'Tittle Tattle' (7)	CBro EWal IBal ICar LAma
'Toby' (2)	EWal
'Tollymore' (2)	IBal
'Tonga' (4)	ECop ICar
'Top Gallant' (3)	IBal
'Top Notch' (2)	ICar
'Top of the Hill' (3)	IBal ICar
'Topkapi' (2)	IBal
'Topolino' (1)	CBro ETub LAma LRoo WHil
'Torcross' (3)	IDun
¶ 'Torridon' (2)	ICar IDun
¶ 'Torrish' (3)	ICar
'Tranquil Morn' (3)	EWal
¶ 'Trena' (6)	IDun
'Tresamble' (5)	CBro ECop EWal ICar LAma
'Trevithian' (7)	CAvo CBro ECop EWal IBal LAma LBlo LRoo NHol
'Trewirgie' (6)	CBro
triandrus	WChr
– albus	See N. ***triandrus triandrus***
– concolor	See N. ***concolor***
– pulchellus	LAma NHol
§ ***– triandrus***	CBro ECam ELan EPar EPot GLoc LBow MBal NHol SIng
'Trillick' (3)	IDun
¶ 'Trilune' (11)	IDun
'Tripartite' (11)	ECop EWal ICar NZep
'Tristram' (2)	ICar
¶ 'Tropic Isle' (4)	ICar
'Trousseau' (1)	EWal LAma LBlo
'Troutbeck' (3)	IBal
¶ 'Tudor Grove' (2)	IDun
'Tudor Minstrel' (2)	EWal
'Tudor Rose' (2)	ECop
'Tuesday's Child' (5)	ECop ETub EWal ICar IDun
'Tullybeg' (3)	IBal
'Tullycore' (2)	ICar
'Tullygirvan' (2)	ICar
'Tullyglass' (2)	ICar
¶ 'Tullynog' (4)	ICar
'Tullyroyal' (2)	IBal
'Turncoat' (6)	IDun
'Tutankhamun' (2)	ECop IBal
'Tweedsmouth' (9)	ECop
¶ 'Twicer' (2)	IDun
'Tynan' (2)	ICar
'Tyneham' (3)	IDun
'Ulster Bank' (3)	IDun
'Ulster Bullion' (2)	IBal
'Ulster Prince' (1)	ICar
'Ultimus' (2)	EWal
'Uncle Ben' (1)	IBal
'Uncle Remus' (1)	EWal
'Unique' (4)	ECop EWal ICar IDun LAma LBlo
'Unsurpassable' (1)	LAma LBlo
¶ 'Urchin' (6)	IDun
'Val d'Incles' (3)	IDun
'Valdrome' (11)	MBri
¶ 'Valediction' (3)	IDun
'Valinore' (2)	IDun
'Van Sion'	See N. 'Telamonius Plenus'
¶ 'Vantage' (2)	ICar
'Verdant' (1)	IDun
'Verdin' (7)	ICar
'Verger' (3)	LAma LBlo MBri
'Vernal Prince' (3)	IDun
'Verona' (3)	ECop ICar LBlo
'Vers Libre' (9)	IDun
'Verwood' (3)	IDun
'Victory' (2)	EWal
'Vigilante' (1)	IDun
'Viking' (1)	ECop LBlo
'Vilna' (2)	EWal
'Vincent van Gogh' (1)	ETub
'Violetta' (2)	EWal ICar IDun
¶ 'Vireo' (7)	ICar
'Virgil' (9)	EWal
'Vivarino' (11)	EWal
'Vocation' (2)	IDun
'Vulcan' (2)	EWal LBlo
'W P Milner' (1)	CAvo CBro ECam LAma MBri NHol SIng WChr WOMN
'Wahkeena' (2)	ICar
¶ 'Waldorf Astoria' (4)	IDun
'Waterperry' (7)	CBro LAma SIng
watieri	EPot GEdr LAma SPou WChr
¶ 'Waxwing' (5)	IDun
'Webster' (9)	IDun
'Wee Bee' (1)	EWal
¶ 'Welvan' (3)	ICar
¶ 'Wendy Walsh' (2)	ICar
'Westholme' (2)	IDun
¶ 'Westward' (4)	EWal
'Wetherby' (3)	IDun
'Whang-hi' (6)	ECop
'Whisper' (5)	EWal
'Whitbourne' (3)	EWal
'White Butterfly' (2)	EWal
'White Empress' (1)	IBal ICar
'White Ermine' (2)	IDun
'White Hill' (2)	IBal
'White Lion' (4)	ETub EWal LAma LBlo
'White Majesty' (1)	IBal
'White Marvel' (4)	CBro EWal LAma
'White Phantom' (1)	ICar
¶ 'White Plume' (2)	EWal
'White Spray' (2)	ICar
'White Star' (1)	IBal ICar IDun

'Whiteabbey' (2) IBal
'Widgeon' (2) EWal
willkommii SPou
'Winchester' (2) EWal
'Windjammer' (1) EWal
'Winfrith' (2) EWal
'Witch Doctor' (3) IBal
'Woodcock' (6) CBro
'Woodgreen' (2) EWal
'Woodland Prince' (3) ECop ICar
'Woodland Star' (3) ECop
'Woodvale' (2) IBal
'Worcester' (2) EWal
'Xanthin Gold' (1) IDun
'Xit' (3) GLoc WChr
'Yellow Cheerfulness' (4) ETub EWal LAma LBlo MBri SIng
'Yellow Standard' (2) LAma
'Yellow Sun' (3) LAma
'Yes Please' (2) EWal
¶ 'Young Blood' (2) IDun
'Young Idea' (7) EWal
'Zeus' (2) ICar

NARDOPHYLLUM (Compositae)
bryoides ITim SOkd

NASSELLA (Gramineae)
trichotoma EMon LRHS

NASTURTIUM (Cruciferae)
officinale WHer

NECTARBERRY See **RUBUS**

NECTARINE See **PRUNUS *persica nectarina***

NECTAROSCORDUM (Liliaceae/Alliaceae)
§ ***siculum*** CAvo CBro CTom ECam ELan EOrc EPar ERav SLHN
§ – ***bulgaricum*** CBro CHad ECha EFou EPot ETub IBlr LBow SIng

NEILLIA (Rosaceae)
affinis CCla CMCN EBre MUlv SCro WHCG
longiracemosa See N. ***thibetica***
sinensis CMCN EGol MRav
§ ***thibetica*** CB&S CBow CCla CLan CPle ELan ENot IOrc ISea LAbb MBri NHol SAxl SChu SHil SPer SPla SSta WAbe WBod WWin
thyrsiflora ERav

NELUMBO (Nelumbonaceae)
nucifera MSta

NEMASTYLIS (Iridaceae)
¶ ***pringlei*** WPer

NEMATANTHUS (Gesneriaceae)
'Bijou' WEfe
'Black Magic' MBri WEfe
'Christmas Holly' WEfe
'Freckles' WEfe
* ***glabra*** MBri
gregarius MBri WEfe
– 'Variegatus' MBri WEfe
'Jungle Lights' WEfe
radicans See N. ***gregarius***
strigillosa MBri
'Tropicana' MBri WEfe

NEMESIA (Scrophulariaceae)
foetens See N. ***fruticans***
fruticans CSam EMon MTho WWin
¶ 'Hermione' EMon
§ ***umbonata*** CHil CMHG CSam ELan EMon GWic LHil LHop MFir MHig SAxl SChu WEas WOMN WPer

NEMOPANTHUS (Aquifoliaceae)

NEODYPSIS (Palmae)
decaryi LPal

NEOLITSEA (Lauraceae)
glauca See N. ***sericea***
§ ***sericea*** SArc

NEOMARICA (Iridaceae)

NEOPANAX See **PSEUDOPANAX**

NEOPAXIA (Portulacaceae)
§ ***australasica*** ECou EPot GAbr SIng
¶ – 'Arthur' ECou
♦ – blue leaved form See N. ***a.*** 'Koscuisko'
♦ – bronze form See N. ***a.*** 'Ohau'
¶ – 'Great Lake' ECou
♦ – green form See N. ***a.*** 'Great Lake'
♦ – grey form See N. ***a.*** 'Kosciusko'
§ – 'Kosciusko ' ECou GDra GLoc NBir NNrd
¶ – 'Lakeside' ECou
¶ – 'Lomond' ECou
¶ – 'Lyndon' ECou
§ – 'Ohau' ECou GGar

NEOREGELIA (Bromeliaceae)
carolinae MBri
– 'Flandria' MBri
– 'Meyendorffii' MBri
– ***tricolor*** MBri

NEPENTHES (Nepenthaceae)
alata WMEx
– x ***merrilliana*** WMEx
– x ***ventricosa*** WMEx
albomarginata WMEx
ampullaria WMEx
bicalcarata WMEx
x ***coccinea*** MBri WMEx
hirsuta WMEx
khasiana WMEx
leptochilia WMEx
maxima WMEx

merrilliana	WMEx
mirabilis	WMEx
rafflesiana	WMEx
– ampullaria	WMEx
– gigantea	WMEx
reinwardtiana	WMEx
stenophylla × *reintwardiana*	WMEx
ventricosa	WMEx

NEPETA † (Labiatae)

'Blue Beauty'	See N. *sibirica* 'Souvenir d'André Chaudron'
camphorata	CHar SIde WWin
cataria	CArn CFis CSev EJud Effi GPoy LHol MChe MSal NSel SIde WHer WOak
– 'Citriodora'	CArn EJud GPoy GWic LHol MSal SChu WHil
**clarkei*	CCor CHan SWas
× *faassenii*	CCla EMon LBuc MSal NKay NVic SChu SCro SIng
– 'Superba'	ELan
floccosa	WPer
♦*gigantea*	See N. 'Six Hills Giant'
glechoma 'Variegata'	See GLECHOMA *hederacea* 'Variegata'
govaniana	Widely available
♦*grandiflora*	See N. *sibirica*
hederacea 'Variegata'	See GLECHOMA *hederacea* 'Variegata'
lanceolata	See N. *nepetalla*
¶ *longiflora*	WPer
**longipes*	SChu SCro
macrantha	See N. *sibirica*
¶ *melissifolia*	EMon
mussinii	Widely available
– 'Little Titch'	EFou GWic SChu WSHC
– 'Snowflake'	CBre CCla CSco EFou ELan EMon GWic SChu SMrm
– 'Superba'	EFou EMon WCot
– 'Walker's Low'	EFou
§ *nepetella*	EMon WPer
nervosa	CCla CHan CSam EBre ECha ELan EMon ERou MFir NOak NSti SBla SDix WEas WHal WHer WHoo WPer WRus
§ *nuda*	ELan EMon GWic
– albiflora	EMon LRHS
pannonica	See N. *nuda*
§ *phyllochlamys*	CBot CFis EMon EPot LGre MPar SApp SBla SCro
– Mac&W 5882	WOMN
'Pool Bank'	EMon
'Porzellan'	EMon
§ *sibirica*	ECha EFou LHil MBri SChu SIde WCot WEas WHal WPer
§ – 'Souvenir d'André Chaudron'	CHad CMHG CSam CSco EFou EGol ERou GWic MBri SCro WEas WHer WHil WPer
§ 'Six Hills Giant'	Widely available
subsessilis	CHan
teydea	NHol WPer
'Thornbury'	CShe
¶ *ukranica*	NHex

NEPHROLEPIS (Davalliaceae)

cordifolia	MBri NMar WFib
– plumosa	WFib
exaltata	WFib
– 'Bostoniensis'	MBri
– 'Rooseveltii'	MBri
– 'Smithii'	MBri
– 'Smithii Linda'	MBri
– 'Teddy Junior'	MBri
– todeoides	NMar
– 'Whitmanii'	WFib

NERINE † (Liliaceae/Amaryllidaceae)

bowdenii	Widely available
– 'Alba'	CBot ECha
– 'Mark Fenwick'	CB&S EPot ERav WCot
– 'Pink Triumph'	CAvo CB&S CKel LAma LBlo LBow NHol SW&B WAbe
¶ 'Clare'	ERea
corusca major	See N. *sarniensis corusca*
crispa	See N. *undulata*
filifolia	CBro EPot LGre
flexuosa	MTho SLMG
– alba	CAvo CBro LAma LGre SW&B
¶ 'Hera'	EPot
¶ 'Joan'	CAvo
masonorum	MTho WOMN
pudica	LHop
¶ 'Rosée du Ventoux'	ERea
sarniensis	CKel ECha SLMG
§ *– corusca*	LAma LBow
¶ 'Snowflake'	ERea
¶ 'Soleil Levant'	ERea
§ *undulata*	CAvo CBro ECha LAma LBow MBri NHol

NERIUM † (Apocynaceae)

'Emile Sahut'	CSun
'Emilie'	CSun ERea
'Géant des Batailles'	CSun ERea
'Luteum Plenum'	CSun ERea
'Madame Léon Blum'	CSun
'Mont Blanc'	CSun
oleander	CHEx CPle EBak ESim LAbb SGar WOMN
*– 'Avalanche'	CB&S
¶ – 'Belle Helene'	CSun
¶ – double apricot	CSun
– double white	CBot
– forms	MNew SLMG
– 'Hardy Red'	ERea
– 'Isle of Capri'	ERea
– 'Italia'	ERea
¶ – 'Madame Allen'	CSun
¶ – 'Magaly'	CSun ERea
– 'Margaritha'	ERea
¶ – 'Marie Gambetta'	CSun
¶ – 'Papa Gambetta'	CSun
– 'Peach Blossom'	ESim SLMG
– 'Professor Granel'	CSun ERea
¶ – 'Rosario'	CSun
– roseum	SLMG

– 'Roseum Plenum' CB&S CSun ESim SLMG
– 'Rouge Cardinal' CB&S
¶ – 'Souvenir des Iles Canaries' CSun
¶ – 'Souvenir d'Emma Schneider' CSun
– 'Splendens' ERea
– 'Variegatum' CB&S CBot ERea LHop NHex SLMG
– 'Ville de Carpentras' ERea
– 'Yellow Queen' CB&S
'Provence' CSun ERea
'Soeur Agnes' CSun ERea
'Tito Poggi' CSun

NERTERA (Rubiaceae)
depressa ECou MBri
granadensis MBri

NEVIUSIA (Rosaceae)

NICANDRA (Solanaceae)
physalodes CArn EJud NBir SIde
¶ ***– alba*** NBir

NICOTIANA (Solanaceae)
glauca CB&S CHan CHil CPle SFir SLMG WEas WSHC
¶ 'Hopley's' SFir
langsdorfii CB&S CHad CHan CHil CRow ECro EMon NSti SMrm WEas WHal WOMN WRus
¶ ***noctiflora*** EBar
rustica MSal
¶ ***suaveolens*** SFir
sylvestris CHEx CHad CHan CHil EBar ECro LHil SFir SMrm WEas WHal WRus
¶ ***tabacum*** CHEx CPle EJud
* ***viridis*** CTrw

NIDULARIUM (Bromeliaceae)
flandria See NEOREGELIA ***carolinae*** 'Flandria'

NIEREMBERGIA (Solanaceae)
¶ ***caerulea*** SLHN
frutescens CGle CHad EMon EOrc ITim LHop MTho WRus
♦ ***hippomanica*** See N. ***caerulea***
§ ***repens*** Widely available
rivularis See N. ***repens***
'Violet Queen' ELan LHop MTho

NIPHAEA (Gesneriaceae)
oblonga NMos

X NIPHIMENES (Gesneriaceae)
'Lemonade' NMos

NIPPONANTHEMUM (Compositae)
§ ***nipponicum*** CFis CHan CLew CSam CSco CSev EBre ECha EGol EMon GWic MTho NRoo SApp WAbe WBon WEas

NOLANA (Nolanaceae)
¶ ***paradoxa*** MHig

NOLINA (Agavaceae)
¶ ***humilis*** SArc
¶ ***longifolia*** SArc

NOMOCHARIS (Liliaceae/Liliaceae)
aperta CAvo CBro GCHN GEdr NHol
farreri CAvo NHol
x ***finlayorum*** GEdr
mairei See N. ***pardanthina***
nana See LILIUM ***nanum***
§ ***pardanthina*** CAvo GEdr NHol
– punctulata CAvo
saluenensis CAvo NHol

NOTHOFAGUS † (Fagaceae)
alessandrii CGre SSpi
§ ***alpina*** CB&S CGre CLnd CSco GRei IOrc ISea LSav MBal NWea SExT SHil SPer SSpi WCoo WMou WNor
antarctica CB&S CGre CLnd CMHG ELan IOrc LSav MBal MBar MBri MGos NBar NWea SExT SGar SHil SMad SPer SSpi WBod WCoo
*– 'Prostrata' CCla
betuloides SHil
cunninghamii CB&S LSav SSpi WNor
dombeyi CGre CMHG IOrc SArc SHil
fusca LSav SHil WNor
menziesii CB&S CGre CMHG LSav SArc SSpi WCoo
obliqua CGre CLnd CSam CSco IOrc ISea LSav MBal NWea SExT SHil SPer SSpi WMou WNor
procera See N. ***alpina***
pumilio CB&S CGre ISea WNor WWat
solandri SArc SHil WNor
¶ ***truncata*** WNor

NOTHOLIRION (Liliaceae/Liliaceae)
bulbuliferum CAvo ECro GEdr ITim NHol
macrophyllum CAvo EBul GEdr NHol
thomsonianum EBul

NOTHOPANAX See **PSEUDOPANAX**

NOTHOSCORDUM (Liliaceae/Alliaceae)
bivalve MSal
inodorum CBro
neriniflorum See CALOSCORDUM ***n.***

NOTOSPARTIUM (Leguminosae)
carmichaeliae CHan ECou SHil
glabrescens ECou
torulosum ECou

NOTOTRICHE (Malvaceae)
compacta MTho

NUPHAR (Nymphaeaceae)
lutea CRow LMay

¶ *pumila variegata*	MSta

NUT, Cob See **CORYLUS** ***avellana***

NUT, Filbert See **CORYLUS** ***maxima***

NYMPHAEA † (Nymphaeaceae)

'Afterglow'	MSta
alba	CRow EHon EWav LMay MSta SFir
– occidentalis	MSta
'Albatros'	EHon LMay MSta SLon
'Amabilis'	CRiv CRow LMay MSta SHig
'American Star'	MSta
'Andreana'	LMay MSta
¶ 'Arc-en-ciel'	MSta
'Atropurpurea'	EWav LMay
'Attraction'	CBWG CRiv CRow CWGN EHon EWav LMay MSta SHig
'August Koch'	MSta
'Aurora'	EWav LMay MSta
'Brackleyi Rosea'	LMay MSta
candida	LMay MSta
'Candidissima'	MSta
capensis	MSta
'Caroliniana Nivea'	MSta
'Caroliniana Perfecta'	LMay MSta
'Charlene Strawn'	MSta
'Charles de Meurville'	CRow EWav LMay MSta SLon
'Colonel A J Welch'	CRow EHon EWav LMay MSta
colorata	MSta
'Colossea'	EHon EWav LMay MSta
'Comanche'	MSta
'Conqueror'	LMay MSta SHig SLon
x ***daubenyana***	MSta
'Director George T Moore'	MSta
'Ellisiana'	LMay MSta
'Escarboucle'	CBWG CRow CWGN EWav LMay MSta SHig SLon
'Evelyn Randig'	MSta
'Fabiola'	LMay
'Firecrest'	EWav LMay MSta SHig SLon
'Froebelii'	CRiv CRow EHon EWav LMay MSta SHig SLon
'General Pershing'	MSta
'Gladstoneana'	CRow CWGN EHon EWav LMay MSta SHig
'Gloire de Temple-sur-Lot'	MSta
'Gloriosa'	LMay MSta
'Gonnère'	CRow CWGN EWav LMay MSta SHig
'Graziella'	CWGN LMay
x ***helvola***	CRow CWGN EHon EWav LMay MSta SHig
'Hermine'	MSta
'Hollandia'	MSta
'Indiana'	CWGN LMay MSta SLon
'James Brydon'	CRiv CRow CWGN EHon EWav LMay MSta SHig SLon
'Laydekeri Fulgens'	LMay MSta
'Laydekeri Lilacea'	CRow EWav LMay MSta SHig
'Laydekeri Purpurata'	LMay MSta
'Laydekeri Rosea'	LMay
'Lucida'	LMay MSta
'Madame Wilfon Gonnère'	EHon EWav LMay MSta
'Marliacea Albida'	CBWG CRiv CWGN EHon EWav LMay MSta
'Marliacea Carnea'	CBWG CRiv CRow CWGN EHon EWav LMay MSta
'Marliacea Chromatella'	CBWG CRiv CRow CWGN EHon EWav LMay MSta SHig SLon
'Marliacea Ignea'	MSta
'Marliacea Rosea'	EWav MSta SHig
'Martin E Randig'	MSta
'Masaniello'	CBWG CRow CWGN EHon EWav LMay MSta SLon
mexicana	MSta
'Moorei'	CWGN EHon LMay MSta SHig
'Mrs Richmond'	CRow EHon EWav LMay MSta SHig
§ ***odorata***	CRow CWGN LMay MSta SHig
– rosea	MSta
– rubra	MSta
'Odorata Alba'	See N. ***odorata***
'Odorata Eugène de Land'	MSta
'Odorata Gigantea'	MSta
'Odorata Juliana'	MSta
'Odorata Minor'	CRow LMay MSta
'Odorata Sulphurea Grandiflora'	CRow CWGN EHon EWav LMay MSta
'Odorata Turicensis'	CRiv LMay MSta
'Odorata W B Shaw'	CWGN EHon LMay MSta SLon
'Pamela'	MSta
'Paul Hariot'	CWGN EWav LMay MSta SLon
'Pearl of the Pool'	MSta
'Perry's Pink'	MSta
'Peter Slocum'	MSta
'Pink Opal'	LMay MSta
'Pink Sensation'	MSta
'Princess Elizabeth'	LMay
'Pygmaea Alba'	See N. ***tetragona***
'Pygmaea Rubis'	CRow EHon EWav LMay MSta
'Queen of the Whites'	MSta
'Radiant Red'	MSta
'Ray Davies'	MSta
'Red Cup'	MSta
'Red Flare'	MSta
'Rembrandt'	MSta
'René Gérard'	CBWG CRiv EHon EWav LMay MSta SHig
'Rose Arey'	CBWG CRow CWGN EHon EWav LMay MSta SHig SLon
'Rosennymphe'	LMay
'Sioux'	CWGN EHon LMay MSta SHig
'Sir Galahad'	MSta
'Solfatare'	EWav
'Sunrise'	EWav LMay MSta
¶ 'Syrius'	MSta
§ ***tetragona***	CRow LMay MSta

tuberosa LMay
¶– 'Alba' MSta
– 'Richardsonii' CWGN EHon
– 'Rosea' CWGN LMay MSta
'William Falconer' CWGN EWav LMay MSta SLon
'Yellow Dazzler' MSta

NYMPHOIDES (Menyanthaceae)
peltata CRiv SFir
§– 'Bennettii' CWGN EHon EWav IBlr LMay MSta

NYSSA (Nyssaceae)
aquatica CMCN
sinensis CCla CFor EHar MBri SHil SPer SSpi SSta WWat
sylvatica Widely available
– 'Jermyns Flame' MBri SHil SSpi

OAKESIELLA (Liliaceae/Convallariaceae)
sessilifolia See UVULARIA ***sessilifolia***

OCHAGAVIA (Bromeliaceae)
¶*rosea* CHEx

OCHNA (Ochnaceae)
serrulata CPle CSun

OCIMUM (Labiatae)
americanum WHer
basilicum CArn CSFH CSev EEls EJud GPoy LHol MBri MChe MPit MSal NSel SIde WHal WHer WPer WSto
– 'Cinnamon' CSev MSal WHal WHer WPer
– *citriodorum* CArn MChe MSal SIde WHal WOak WPer
¶– 'Dark Opal' WHal
– 'Genovese' NSel
– *glycyrrhiza* MSal
¶– 'Green Ruffles' MChe WHal
– *minimum* CArn CSFH CSev EEls EJud LHol MBri MChe MSal SIde WHer WPer
*– *neapolitanum* MChe SIde WPer
¶– 'Purple Ruffles' MChe SIde WHal
– *purpurascens* CArn CSev EEls GPoy LHol MBri MChe MSal NSel SIde WHer WOak WPer WSto
sanctum CArn GPoy MChe MSal SIde WPer

OEMLERIA (Rosaceae)
§ *cerasiformis* CB&S CBow CCla ELan LSav SHil SSta WEas WWat

OENANTHE (Umbelliferae)
¶*japonica* 'Flamingo' EMon

OENOTHERA † (Onagraceae)
§ *acaulis* CBot CChu CTom EPad GLoc IBrk LHop MCas MPar SAxl SChu SIng SMrm WOMN WPer WThu
§– *aurea* MFir SFir SMrm WCla WHil WPer
– *lutea* See O. ***a. aurea***
§ *berlandieri* CGle CLew EMon NRed SFir SIng SMrm WAbe WOMN WPer
§ *biennis* CHar CHoe CKin CRow EBre ECha GPoy LHol MChe NSel NSti SIde SIng SPer WEas WHer WOak WPer WRus
caespitosa EPad MTho WOld
childsii See O. ***berlandieri***
cinaeus See O. ***tetragona fraseri***
§ *elata* EPad IBrk SMrm WCla WHer WHil
erythrosepala See O. ***glazoviana***
flava EPad GLoc MTho NHol NNrd
fruticosa GWic
glaber See O. ***biennis***
§ *glazoviana* CSev EMon GAbr IBlr SFir
**grandiflora* GWic
*'Greencourt Lemon' WPat
*'Hollow Meadows' EPot
hookeri See O. ***elata***
kunthiana NHol NTow NWCA WAbe WPer
lamarckiana See O. ***glazoviana***
linearis EBre GWic
macrocarpa See O. ***missouriensis***
§ *missouriensis* Widely available
¶– *alba* WHil
nuttallii NHol
odorata CArn CHad CSev EFol GWic IBlr LHil MPar NOrc SFir WEas
– *sulphurea* CHad CHan CHil CTom ELan EMon GWic IBlr LRHS NPer SChu SMrm
pallida CRiv ELan IBlr NRed SMrm WHil
§ *perennis* CHar CLew CRiv CTom EBre MCas MTho NHol NKay NNrd NTow SIng WCla WEas WHil WHoo WPer WThu WWin
pumila See O. ***perennis***
rosea LHop WOMN WRus
speciosa EMon EPad SAxl SMrm WCot WHal WMar
– *childsii* See O. ***berlandieri***
stricta CKin EPad
sulphurea CBre
taraxacifolia See O. ***acaulis***
§ *tetragona* CHad EBar EMon IDai MTho SIng WEas WHoo
¶– cream form WHoo
– 'Feuerverkeri' ('Fireworks') CGle CKel CSco CShe ECro EFou ELan ENot ERav LHop NHol NKay SPer WOld WPer WRus WWin
§– *fraseri* CElw LHol NCat NHol NTow
– 'Hoheslicht' ('Highlight') EBre MRav
– 'Lady Brookborough' LHop MRav
*– *longistipata* MFir

– *riparia*	ELan EPad GLoc GWic IDai LHop NHol NKay SAxl SFir SMrm SSpi WPer WRus
– 'Yellow River'	CB&S CSco EOrc MBri MWgw
– 'Youngii'	See O. ***tetragona***
texensis 'Early Rise'	ELan EMon LHop NSti SMrm WEas
trichocalyx	LHol

OLEA (Oleaceae)

europaea	EPad ERea LHol SArc SHil STre WNor
– 'Cipressino'	CSun
– 'El Greco'	CB&S ERea
– 'Picholine'	ERea
– 'Pyramidalis'	ERea

OLEARIA † (Compositae)

albida	ERav WWat
¶ – x *paniculata*	CPle
¶ *arborescens*	IBar
¶ *argophylla*	ECou
avicenniifolia	CChu CMHG ECou EPla SHil WBod WSHC
– 'White Confusion'	WWat
¶ *bidwellii*	MHig
capillaris	CMHG ECou GAbr ISea SDry SLon WWat
chathamica	GWic
cheesemanii	CCla CHan
erubescens	CTre
¶ *floribunda*	CPle
frostii	CSun WSHC
¶ *furfuracea*	CB&S CHEx
glandulosa	ECou
gunniana	See O. ***phlogopappa***
x *haastii*	Widely available
¶ – 'McKenzie'	ECou
§ 'Henry Travers'	CFor CGre IBar IBlr IDai ISea MBal SHil WBod
ilicifolia	CCla IDai SHil SSpi
lepidophylla	ECou GLoc NHol
¶ – green form	ECou
¶ – silver form	ECou
¶ *lirata*	ECou
macrodonta	Widely available
– 'Major'	SHil SSus
– 'Minor'	ECou
x *mollis*	CTre NNor SHil SLon SPer SSpi WSHC WWat
moschata	ECou GRei SLon SSpi WSHC
myrsinoides	CCla CMHG
§ *nummulariifolia*	CHil CLew CMHG CPle CSco ECou EPla ISea MBal NNor SBor SIng WBod WPer WSHC
– *cymbifolia*	ECou
– hybrids	ECou
odorata	ECou GWic
paniculata	CB&S CChu CGre CMHG ISea SDix SDry
§ *phlogopappa*	CHan CMHG ECou IBar IJoh ISea NTow SBar SHil
– 'Comber's Blue'	CB&S CCla CGre GWic IBar IBlr ISea SCro SPer SSta
– 'Comber's Pink'	IBar IBlr ISea SSta WBod
– 'Rosea'	CB&S SPer
– 'Splendens'	CLew NRar SHil WPer
– *subrepanda*	CB&S CGre CTre
§ *ramulosa*	CB&S CGre CLew CPle LHil
– 'Blue Form'	See O. ***ramulosa***
– *ramulosa*	ECou
rani	CChu CFor CGre CPle WSHC
x *scilloniensis*	See O. ***stellulata***
– 'Master Michael'	CCla CPle CTrw GWic SPer WBod
semidentata	See O. 'Henry Travers'
solandri	CBow CBra CHan CMHG CMer CPle CSam ECou EMon GAbr LAbb MCot MR&S MRav SDix SLon SPer
– 'Aurea'	CB&S
§ *stellulata*	Widely available
– blue	CTre
– pink	CTre
traversii	CChu CMHG CPle CTre IOrc SHil WSHC
– 'Variegata'	ECou
virgata	CMHG CPle ECou ELan ISea MCot
– 'Laxifolia'	CTre
– *lineata*	CMer SHil WSHC
* *virginens*	CHil
viscosa	CTre
'Waikariensis'	CBot CChu CFor CMHG CPle CTre ECou ERav MR&S SChu SHil SLon SSpi WPat WSHC WWat
'Zennorensis'	CB&S CGre CLan CMHG CPle CTre IBar ISea NNor NTow SHil SSpi

OMPHALODES (Boraginaceae)

cappadocica	Widely available
¶ – *alba*	MTho
¶ – 'Anthea Bloom'	IBlr
¶ – 'Bridget Bloom'	SAxl
– 'Cherry Ingram'	CElw NBir NCat SAxl SWas WCot
¶ – 'Starry Eyes'	IBlr
§ *linifolia*	CBos CTom ECro EJud LHil LHop MPar NSti SAxl SFir SLHN WEas WHil WWin
– *alba*	See O. ***linifolia***
luciliae	WHoo
¶ – *alba*	MTho
nitida	CTom
verna	Widely available
– *alba*	CBot CCla CGle CLew CRow CSco CShe ECha EFol EFou ELan EPar GLoc GPla GWic LHop LSav MTho NNrd NSti SIng SPer WHal WRus

OMPHALOGRAMMA (Primulaceae)

ONOBRYCHIS (Leguminosae)

viciifolia	CHar CKin CNat ECro ELan MSal SFir SMrm

ONOCLEA (Aspleniaceae)
sensibilis CRow CWGN ECha EGol EHon EPar IOrc LSav MBri NHol NKay NMar NNrd SAxl SHig SHil SPer SSpi WEas WFib
¶ – copper form NKay

ONONIS (Leguminosae)
cenisia See O. ***cristata***
§ *cristata* WPer
fruticosa MPla
repens CArn CKin MSal
rotundifolia NTow WOMN WWin
spinosa CKin MSal WHil WPer

ONOPORDUM (Compositae)
acanthium CCla CKin COtt ECha ECro ELan EMon LHol MPar SFis SIde SLHN SMad WHer WHil
acaule LHop SLHN
arabicum See O. ***nervosum***
§ *nervosum* CFis CSpe ECro ERav LHil NSti NVic SFir SMad SMrm WEas

ONOSMA (Boraginaceae)
albopilosum CHan
alboroseum ECha EFol EFou ELan EOrc GWic LHop NHol NSti NTow SChu WEas WOMN WPat WPer
¶ *echioides* EPad
helvetica WPat
nanum LHop WCru
– Mac&W 5785 CLew NKay WOMN WPer
pyramidalis CArn
stellulata CLew GLoc GWic
tauricum EBar WDav WWin

ONYCHIUM (Adiantaceae)
japonicum CBos SApp SSpi SWas

OPHIOPOGON † (Liliaceae/Convallariaceae)
'Black Dragon' See O. ***planiscapus nigrescens***
* *bodinieri* EMon
graminifolius See LIRIOPE ***muscari***
intermedius EMon SApp
– *parviflora* EBul
§ *jaburan* CHan GLoc LAma MUlv NHol SApp WWat
– 'Variegatus' See O. ***j.*** 'Vittatus'
– 'Vittatus' CHEx
japonicus CBro CElw CRiv CRow EBul NSti SApp
– 'Albus' SIng
planiscapus CHan CSun EBul EPad EPar GLoc GWic MTho MWat SApp SSpi
– green SCro
– *leucanthus* CRow
§ – *nigrescens* Widely available
sp. DF 617 EBul
sp. DF 86127 EBul

OPITHANDRA (Gesneriaceae)
¶ *primuloides* SOkd

ORANGE, Sour or Seville See **CITRUS** ***aurantium***

ORANGE, Sweet See **CITRUS** ***sinensis***

ORCHIS (Orchidaceae)
foliosa See DACTYLORHIZA ***foliosa***
fuchsii 'Bressingham Bonus' See DACTYLORHIZA ***f.*** 'B.B.'
maculata See DACTYLORHIZA ***maculata***
maderensis See DACTYLORHIZA ***foliosa***
majalis See DACTYLORHIZA ***majalis***

OREOBOLUS (Cyperaceae)

OREOPANAX (Araliaceae)
¶ *epremesnilianus* CHEx

ORIGANUM † (Labiatae)
acutidens WPer
– JCA 735.000 EMon WDav
amanum ELan EPot GLoc NHol SBla SChu SOkd SPou WDav WOMN WPat WPer WThu
– *album* SBla SPou WOMN
'Barbara Tingey' CSev CSun ECou ELan GLoc LHop MHig MTho SBla SChu SIng SPou WDav WHer
* 'Bristol Cross' SIng
'Buckland' NRar SBla SPou
* *caespitosum* NCat
§ *calcaratum* CLew CShe GLoc NRar SBla SIng SOkd SPou SWas WHea WOld
dictamnus CHad EEls MPar SPou WOMN
'Emma Stanley' SPou
¶ 'Erntedank' EFou
heracleoticum See O. ***vulgare hirtum***
'Herrenhausen' ECha EFou EMon LHop SChu
x *hybridum* EGol GLoc LHop MPar NHol SBla SChu SPou WPat WWat WWin
'Kent Beauty' CSun ECha ELan EPot GLoc MTho SBla SChu SPou SWas WOMN
kopatdaghense See O. ***vulgare gracile***
laevigatum Widely available
– 'Hopleys' CHad CSev CSun ECha EFou EMon EOrc GWic LGre LHop NHol SBla SChu SIng WHer WOld WPer WSHC
majorana CArn CSFH CSev ELan Effi GPoy LHol MChe MSal NSel SIde WOak WPer WSto

microphyllum	CArn CBot EMon ESis ITim MHig MTho SBla SChu SIng SPou WDav WHer WOMN WThu
¶ ***minutiflorum***	GLoc
¶ 'Nymphenburg'	LHop SWas
onites	CArn CSFH EEls Effi GPoy LHol MChe MSal NRoo SIde WHer WOak WPer WSto
pulchellum	EFol SPou
rotundifolium	CArn CElw CGle CHan CLew CSev ECha EFol ELan GLoc LGre LHop NRar NSti SBla SChu SIng SPou WEas WKif WOMN WRus WThu
– JCA 736.300	CSun
scabrum	CArn
– ***pulchrum***	LHop
sp. Mac&W 5882	See NEPETA ***phyllochlamys***
tournefortii	See O. ***calcaratum***
* ***villosum***	CBot
vulgare	CArn CFis CKin CSev EJud Effi GPoy LHol MChe MCot NLan NRoo NSel SIde WEas WHal WHer WOak WSto
– ***album***	WHer
– ***aureum***	Widely available
– 'Aureum Album'	WHer
– 'Aureum Crispum'	EOrc NSti SIde
– 'Compactum'	CArn CSFH CSev GPoy LHol NHol SBla SIde SPou WPer
– 'Gold Tip'	CArn CElw CHad CHoe CMer CSev EFol EJud EOrc GPla NRoo NSel NSti WHal WHer WPer
§ – ***gracile***	NHol SIng
§ – ***hirtum***	EEls GPoy MSal WPer WSto
– 'Nanum'	LHop WCla
– 'Tracy's Yellow'	CCor
– 'Variegatum'	MCot WRus

ORIXA (Rutaceae)

japonica	CBot CCla SSpi

ORNITHOGALUM (Liliaceae/Hyacinthaceae)

arabicum	CAvo LAma LBow MBri SW&B
balansae	CAvo EPot ETub
caudatum	CHEx ELan WHer
lanceolatum	CAvo ECam
magnum	LRHS
nanum	See O. ***sigmoideum***
narbonense	CAvo CBro
nutans	CAvo CBro EMon EPar EPot ETub LAma LBlo LBow LRoo MBri MSal MTho NHol NLan NNrd SIng
oligophyllum	CBro
¶ ***pyramidale***	EPot
pyrenaicum	CAvo NLan
¶ ***reverchonii***	MPar
¶ ***saundersiae***	LBow
sibthorpii	See O. ***sigmoideum***
¶ ***sigmoideum***	CAvo
thyrsoides	CKel LAma LBow MBri SW&B
umbellatum	CAvo CBro CCla CRiv ELan EPar ETub GPoy LAma LBlo LBow LRoo MBri MFir MSal NHol NLan NNrd SIng WOMN

ORONTIUM (Araceae)

aquaticum	CHEx CWGN EHon EWav LMay MSta SHig

OROSTACHYS (Crassulaceae)

§ ***aggregatus***	NGre NSed
chanetii	GLoc NBra
furusei	NSed SIng
iwarenge	ESis NTow WHil
malacophyllus	See O. ***aggregatus***
§ ***spinosus***	CHar CRow NGre NSed SSmi WOMN WThu

ORPHIUM (Gentianaceae)

frutescens	CSun

ORTHROSANTHUS (Iridaceae)

chimboracensis	CHan LHop
multiflorus	CHan CSun
polystachyus	CHan

OSCULARIA See **LAMPRANTHUS**

OSMANTHUS (Oleaceae)

armatus	CHan NNor SArc SHil SPla WWat
§ x ***burkwoodii***	Widely available
§ ***decorus***	CB&S CBow EGol ELan ENot LSav MGos MRav MUlv SCro SHil SLon SPer SSta WBod WWat
– 'Angustifolius'	SLon
delavayi	Widely available
– 'Latifolius'	LSav
x ***fortunei***	SHil SSta
– 'Variegatus'	SBla
fragrans	CBot CGre
§ ***heterophyllus***	CB&S CBow CChu CLan CPle CSco EHar ELan ENot IJoh MBar MR&S MUlv NNor SHil SPer SSpi SSta WWat
– 'Argenteomarginatus'	See O. ***h.*** 'Variegatus'
– 'Aureomarginatus'	CPle CSco ELan IOrc MBal SHil SPer
– 'Aureus'	CB&S
– 'Goshiki' ('Tricolor')	EHar ELan IOrc LHop MBri SHil SPer
– 'Gulftide'	CCla ELan LSav MGos MUlv SHil SSpi
– 'Latifolius Variegatus'	SHil
¶ – 'Purple Shaft'	CKni
– 'Purpureus'	CB&S CMHG EGol EHar ELan IBar LHop LSav MBal MRav SHil SSpi SSta
§ – 'Variegatus'	Widely available
ilicifolius	See O. ***heterophyllus***
serrulatus	CBot SHil
suavis	LSav

yunnanensis CHan MBlu SArc SHil SSpi

X OSMAREA (Oleaceae)
burkwoodii See OSMANTHUS x ***burkwoodii***

OSMARONIA (Rosaceae)
cerasiformis See OEMLERIA ***cerasiformis***

OSMORHIZA (Umbelliferae)
¶ *claytonii* MSal

OSMUNDA † (Osmundaceae)
cinnamomea LSav NKay NMar
claytoniana NKay NMar
regalis CHEx CHad CRow CWGN EBre ECha EGol EHar EHon ELan IOrc LHol LMay LSav MBri MSta MWgw NHol SHil SMad SPer SSpi WFib WHer
– 'Crispa' NMar
– Cristata group ELan LSav MBri NHol SMad WFib
¶ – 'Gracilis' LSav
– *purpurascens* CRow ELan IOrc LSav MBri MWgw NHol NMar SSpi WFib
* – *spectabilis* SSpi
¶ – *undulata* ELan NHol

OSTEOMELES (Rosaceae)
subrotunda LGre

OSTEOSPERMUM † (Compositae)
'African Queen' See O. 'Tresco Purple'
'Ballyrogan Pink' IBlr
barberae See O. ***jucundum***
'Bloemhoff Belle' CCan CMHG MBri SBor WEas
* 'Blue Eyes' WTay
'Blue Streak' CB&S CCan CFis CHad CHil CMHG CMer CSam CSpe CTre ELan GAbr LAbb SAxl SBor SChu SMrm WHea WPer WRus
'Bodegas Pink' CCan CHil CRow EFol ELan EMon EOrc ERav GWic LHop MBri NRar SChu SMad SMrm
'Brickell's Hybrid' CCan CHil CMHG CSam CSev CTre EOrc GWic NSti WHal
* 'Buttercup' GAbr
'Buttermilk' Widely available
'Cannington John' CCan CMHG EMon EOrc LHop SChu
'Cannington Joyce' CSpe LHop
'Cannington Katrina' CCan
'Cannington Roy' CB&S CCan CElw CGle CHil CMHG CSam CTre CTrw ELan EMon GWic LHop MBri SMrm WPer
'Cannington Sally' CCan
'Cannington Vernon' CCan
caulescens See O. ***ecklonis prostratum***
'Croftway Blush' SCro
'Croftway Coconut Ice' SCro WRus
'Croftway Eveningstar' SCro
'Croftway Goldback' SCro
'Croftway Hall' SCro
'Croftway Halo' SCro
'Croftway Humbug' SCro
'Croftway Silverspoons' SCro WRus
'Croftway Snow' SCro
'Croftway Tufty' SCro
'Croftway Velvetspoons' SCro
'Croftway Wonderwhirls' SCro
ecklonis CB&S CCla CFis CGle CHEx CHil CMHG CRiv CSam CShe CTre IDai ISea LAbb MTho NHol SBla SBor SCro SHil SIng WHea WWin
* – deep pink form GWic MBri
– 'Giant' CCan CHan
– *prostratum* Widely available
– 'Starshine' CElw EOrc
¶ 'Edna Bond' WEas
'Falmouth' CFis
* 'Golden Beauty' CCan
'Goulds' CHil
* 'Gweek Variegated' LHil
¶ 'Hampton Court Purple' LHop
'Hopley's' CCan CTre EBar EOrc WCru
'James' CHil
§ *jucundum* Widely available
– 'Blackthorn Seedling' SBla
– *compactum* CCan ECha ELan GWic MHig SAxl SBla SMrm WAbe WDav WPer WRus
'Killerton Pink' CCan CMHG EOrc SCro WPer
'La Mortola' CCan CHad CTre LAbb
§ 'Lady Leitrim' CB&S CBow CCan CHEx CMHG CSam CTre CTrw EBar ECha EOrc GWic LHop MBri NSti SAxl SBla SChu WAbe WRus
'Langtrees' CCan EFol GAbr GPla LHop SMrm WPer
* 'Lilac Whirleygig' LHil
♦ 'Nairobi' See O. 'Tresco Purple'
♦ 'Pale Face' See O. 'Lady Leitrim'
'Peggyi' See O. 'Tresco Purple'
'Penny Pink' LHop
'Pink Whirls' Widely available
prostratum See O. ***ecklonis prostratum***
'Silver Sparkler' CHan CHil CMHG CSpe CSun EBar EFol EOrc ERav IBar IHos LHop LSav MRav MTho SAxl SBla SChu SCro SMad WHal WPer WRus
'Sparkler' CB&S CHEx CHil EOrc LHil NRar
'Tauranga' See O. 'Whirligig'
tresco See O. 'Tresco Purple'
'Tresco Pink' CB&S IBlr
§ 'Tresco Purple' Widely available
'Tresco Sally' CFis
'Valerie Finnis' CHil
'Weetwood' CHil CMHG GAbr GWic LHop MBri SChu SIng SWas WAbe WEas WPer WRus

'Whirligig'	Widely available
* 'White Pim'	LHil
'Wine Purple'	See O. 'Tresco Purple'
Wisley hybrids	LAbb WEas WRus

OSTROWSKIA (Campanulaceae)

magnifica	EPad

OSTRYA (Carpinaceae)

carpinifolia	CLnd CMCN CMHG EHar ELan IOrc LSav MBri SExT SHil SSpi WCoo WMou WNor
virginiana	CMCN EHar LSav MBri SHil SSpi WNor

OTANTHUS (Compositae)

maritimus	CSun NHol

OTHONNA (Compositae)

§ ***cheirifolia***	CBot CFis CHan CHil CLew CPle CSam EFol EFou ELan EMon EOrc ERav GWic NNor NRar NSti SIgm SLon WEas WHal WPer WRus

OTHONNOPSIS See **OTHONNA**

OURISIA † (Scrophulariaceae)

caespitosa	ECou GGar GHig
– ***gracilis***	GArf ITim WMar
coccinea	CBot CChu CGle GDra GEdr IBar MTho NRya SAxl WOMN WPer
'Loch Ewe'	CChu GAbr GDra GEdr GGar GWic MTho MUlv NCat NKay SAxl SWas
macrophylla	GDra GGar GWic
microphylla	GEdr ITim WAbe WPer
¶ – WR 8819	NGre
'Snowflake'	CBos GDra GEdr GGar MRav MTho SBla SWas WAbe

OXALIS (Oxalidaceae)

acetosella	CKin CRow MSal NGre NLan SIng WHer
– ***subpurpurascens***	EMon
adenophylla	Widely available
¶ – x ***laciniata***	WAbe
§ ***articulata***	CTom EBre GLoc LGro MFir MTho NPer WHil WWin
* 'Beatrice Anderson'	MTho NHar
'Bowles' White'	WHil WThu
brasiliensis	EPot MTho WDav
chrysantha	CRow ELan MCas NNrd SIng WAbe
¶ ***corniculata purpurea***	MTho
deppei	See O. ***tetraphylla***
depressa	See O. ***inops***
enneaphylla	CAvo ECou EPar EPot GEdr IDai MCas MTho NRya SPou WThu
– ***alba***	GEdr MHig NNrd
– ***minutifolia***	EPot GLoc MHig NGre NHol NKay NNrd SPou SSmi SWas WAbe
– ***rosea***	CBro EPot GDra MBal NGre NHol NRya SIng SPou
– ***rubra***	GDra NKay WAbe
– 'Ruth Tweedie'	GEdr NRya
– x ***adenophylla***	GDra NGre
floribunda	See O. ***articulata***
hirta	CRiv LBow MTho NHol NNrd
– 'Gothenburg'	EPot
§ ***inops***	CRow ELan EPot GLoc MCas MPlt NHol NNrd NRya SIng SPou WHil
'Ione Hecker'	CBro CRiv EPot GAbr GEdr GLoc MHig MTho NGre NHar NHol NNrd SPou SWas WAbe
* ***japonica*** 'Picta'	WThu
laciniata	EPot GAbr GArf GEdr GLoc MHig MTho NHar NHol SBla SIng SPou WAbe WChr WOMN
lactea double form	See O. ***magellanica*** 'Flore Pleno'
lobata	CAvo CRow EPot GLoc LBow NHol SIng SPou
magellanica	CRiv CTom EBre ELan ESis GAbr GCHN MCas MMth MTho NHol NNrd SAxl SIng WDav WHil WPer
§ – 'Flore Pleno'	CElw CGle CLew CRiv CRow CSpe ECou GLoc MCas MTho WPer
– 'Nelson'	NHol
– 'Old Man Range'	ECou
¶ ***melanosticta***	CAvo LBow
obtusa	CRiv ELan EPot MCas MTho SIng SWas WOMN
oregana	CAvo CGle SBar
ortgiesii	SLMG
patagonica	GEdr NHol NKay SPou WHil
pes-caprae	CAvo
purpurata 'Bowiei'	EPot NNrd
purpurea	LHop NPer
– 'Ken Aslet'	CBro EPot MCas MTho NNrd NTow SBla SOkd SWas WOMN WThu
¶ ***regnellii***	WHal
speciosa	See O. ***purpurea***
§ ***tetraphylla***	CRiv CRow CSam EPar LAma MBri MTho NOrc NPer SIng SLMG SW&B WOMN
– 'Iron Cross'	CAvo ECro ELan LAma MPlt NBir SMrm WCot WEas WHal WPer
* ***triangularis***	LAma
tuberosa	GPoy WCru
versicolor	CRiv EPot MCas MTho SBla SPou
vespertilionis	GWic

OXYCOCCUS (Ericaceae)

macrocarpus	See VACCINIUM ***macrocarpon***
palustris	See VACCINIUM ***oxycoccos***

OXYDENDRUM (Ericaceae)
arboreum CB&S CBow CChu CCla CFor EHar ELan IBar LSav MBri MGos SHil SLHN SPer SReu SSpi SSta WFro WWat

OXYLOBIUM (Leguminosae)

OXYPETALUM (Ascleiadaceae)
caeruleum See TWEEDIA ***caerulea***

OXYRIA (Polygonaceae)
digyna GCHN GGar NWCA

OXYTROPIS (Leguminosae)
campestris SPou
¶ *halleri* ITim NTow
¶ *lambertii* MHig WDav
* *magellanica* LRHS
* *todomoshirensis* SPou
uralensis WEas

OZOTHAMNUS See **HELICHRYSUM**

PACHYPHRAGMA (Cruciferae)
macrophyllum ECha EFol ELan EMon WEas

PACHYPODIUM (Apocynaceae)
lamerei MBri

PACHYSANDRA (Buxaceae)
terminalis Widely available
– 'Green Carpet' EFou EGol EPla MBar MBri SPla WWat
– 'Variegata' Widely available

PACHYSTACHYS (Acanthaceae)
lutea MBri

PACHYSTEGIA (Compositae)
¶ *insignis* ECou

PAEDERIA (Rubiaceae)
scandens CHad

PAEDEROTA (Scrophulariaceae)
§ *bonarota* CLew

PAEONIA † (Paeoniaceae)
albiflora See P. ***lactiflora***
anomala EPot SSpi
arietina See P. ***mascula a.***
'Avant Garde' WKif
¶ *bakeri* MAus
¶ *banatica* MAus
¶ *beresovskii* MPhe
broteroi CCor MPar SSpi
cambessedesii LGre MPar SBla SHig SPou SSpi WKif
¶ 'Carol' MAus
¶ 'Chocolate Soldier' MAus
¶ 'Coral Fay' MAus
daurica See P. ***mascula triternata***
¶ 'Defender' MAus
delavayi (S) CB&S CBow COtt IBlr MBal MBri MPar NHol SCro SHil SMad SMrm SPer SSpi WEas WHal WSHC
¶ – Trollioides group (S) EPla
§ – *ludlowii* (S) CB&S CCla CGle CLan COtt CSco EHar ELan GWic ISea MBal SBla SHil SMad SPer SSpi SSta WBod WEas WHoo WOMN WPat
§ – *lutea* (S) CBow CCla CHad CRiv ELan EPad GPla MMth MPar SHil STre WEas WSHC
§ – Potaninii group (S) CBrd MPar SPou
¶ – 'Yellow Queen' NBar
¶ 'Ellen Cowley' MAus
emodi ECha
'Empress of India' ELan
¶ 'Horizon' MAus
¶ *humilis* MAus SPou
¶ – *villosa* SPou
¶ 'Illini Warrior' MAus
♦ *japonica* See P. ***lactiflora***
¶ 'Jenny' MPhe
kevachensis See P. ***mascula mascula***
'Kinkaku' See P. × ***lemoinei*** 'Souvenir de Maxime Cornu'
'Kinko' See P. × ***lemoinei*** 'Alice Harding'
'Kinshi' (S) See P. × ***lemoinei*** 'Chromatella'
'Kintei' See P. × ***lemoinei*** 'L'Esperance'
§ *lactiflora* MAus SPou WCot
– 'Adolphe Rousseau' MAus
– 'Agida' EBre ELan MAus MRav
– 'Albert Crousse' IDai NKay
– 'Alexander Fleming' CBow CSco MAus MUlv NBar
– 'Alice Harding' MAus
¶ – 'Auten's Pride' MAus
– 'Baroness Schroeder' ELan
¶ – 'Belle Center' MAus
– 'Blush Queen' EBre ELan ERou MAus
– 'Border Gem' EBre ELan MRav
– 'Bowl of Beauty' CCla CSco EBre ELan MAus MBri MUlv NBar NKay NRoo NVic SPer WEas WKif
¶ – 'Bright Knight' MAus
– 'Bunker Hill' CCla CShe MAus NHol
– 'Butter Ball' MAus
– 'Carnival' ELan
– 'Cherry Hill' CBow MAus
– 'Claire Dubois' EBre ERou
– 'Colonel Heneage' SPer
– 'Cornelia Shaylor' EBre ELan
– 'Couronne d'Or' EBre NKay
– 'Dandy Dan' MAus
– 'Dinner Plate' MAus
¶ – 'Duchess of Kent' CBow
¶ – 'Duchess of Marlborough' CBow MRav
– 'Duchesse de Nemours' CBow CCla CSco EBre ECtt MAus MMth MUlv NBar NHol NRoo SPer WAbe

– 'Edulis Superba'	EBre EGol ELan MAus SPer
– 'Eugénie Verdier'	MUlv
– 'Eva'	SHig
– 'Evening World'	ELan
– 'Felix Crousse'	CShe EBre ELan ERou MAus NHol NVic SPer WAbe
– 'Festiva Maxima'	EBre ELan MAus MBri NKay
– 'François Ortegat'	MAus
– 'Gay Paree'	MAus
– 'Gayborder June'	MAus
– 'Gilbert Barthelot'	MAus
– 'Globe of Light'	CCla
– 'Great Sport'	ELan
– 'Helen Hayes'	MAus
– 'Hiawatha'	MAus
– 'Inspecteur Lavergne'	CSco EBre EFou ERou MAus MRav SPer
– 'Instituteur Doriat'	CSco
– 'Karl Rosenfield'	CBow CSam CSco IDai MAus NBar
– 'Lady Alexandra Duff'	MAus NBar
– 'Le Cygne'	EBre
– 'Lois Kelsey'	MAus
– 'Lord Kitchener'	SPer
– 'Louis Barthelot'	MAus
– 'Madame Calot'	EFou MAus MRav
– 'Madame Claude Tain'	MBri
– 'Madame Emile Debatène'	MAus
– 'Madame Jules Dessert'	MAus
– 'Madame Lemoine'	NHol NRoo
¶ – 'Marie Lemoine'	MAus
– 'Matilda Lewis'	MAus
– 'Minnie Shaylor'	MAus
– 'Miss Eckhart'	CSco MAus
¶ – 'Mistral'	MBri
– 'Monsieur Jules Elie'	CSco EFou MAus MBri SPer
– 'Monsieur Martin Cahuzac'	EBre
– 'Mr G F Hemerik	CSco SHig
– 'Mrs F J Hemerik'	MAus
¶ – 'Mrs Sarson'	CCla SBla SMad
– 'Nancy Nicholls'	MAus
– 'Nymph'	MUlv
– 'Peter Brand'	MBri
– 'Philomèle'	MAus
– 'Pink Lemonade'	MAus
– 'President Franklin D Roosevelt'	EBre ECtt ELan MAus MRav NKay NRoo SPer
– 'Président Poincaré'	EBre MAus SPer
– 'President Taft'	See P. *l.* 'Reine Hortense'
– 'Queen of Sheba'	MAus
– 'Raspberry Sundae'	EBre ECtt MAus MRav
§ – 'Reine Hortense'	MAus
– 'Richard Carvel'	MAus
– 'Sante Fe'	MAus
– 'Sarah Bernhardt'	CBow CHad CSam CShe EBre ELan ERou IDai IHos MAus MBri MRav MUlv NBar NHol NRoo NVic SPer WAbe WEas
– 'Shirley Temple'	EFou ELan MAus MBri
– 'Sir Edward Elgar'	ELan
– 'Snow Cloud'	EBre IDai
¶ – 'Snow Mountain'	MAus
¶ – 'Solange'	EGol
– 'Surugu'	MBri
– 'Top Brass'	MAus
– 'Victoire de la Marne'	MAus NBar
– 'Vogue'	MAus
– 'Westerner'	MAus
– 'White Wings'	EBre EGol ELan MAus MBri MUlv
¶ – 'Wiesbaden'	MAus
– 'Zuzu'	MAus
¶ 'Laddie'	MAus
x ***lemoinei*** 'Alice Harding' (S)	MBri SHil
§ – 'Chromatella' (S)	EBre LAma SHil
– 'L'Esperance'	LAma
§ – 'Souvenir de Maxime Cornu' (S)	CBow EBre LAma SHil
lutea	See P. ***delavayi lutea***
– ***ludlowii***	See P. ***delavayi ludlowii***
'Mai Fleuri'	SHig
§ ***mascula mascula***	EPot
– ***russii***	MPar
§ – ***triternata***	MPar NTow SSpi WHoo
§ ***mascula areitina***	MAus NHol
– – 'Northern Glory'	EBre MAus SHig WCot
¶ – – 'Purple Emperor'	MAus
mlokosewitschii	CCla CHad COtt CRiv ECha EPot GLoc LGre MBal MPar MRav NBar NTow SSpi WEas WHoo
¶ ***obovata***	SPou
– ***alba***	MPar NHol WEas
– 'Grandiflora'	ELan
officinalis	EBre WEas
– 'Alba Plena'	CSco MAus
– 'Anemoniflora Rosea'	SHig
– 'James Crawford Weguelin'	CSco
– 'Lize van Veen'	EBre ELan SPer
– 'Mutabilis Plena'	IBlr
¶ – 'Rosea Plena'	MBri
– 'Rosea Superba Plena'	CSco EBre MMth NKay NRoo
– 'Rubra Plena'	CSco EBre MAus MBri MMth NKay WHoo
¶ 'Paula Fay'	MAus
peregrina	MAus
– 'Fire King'	MAus
– 'Sunshine'	EBre ELan MAus MBri NKay SHig SPer
♦***potaninii***	See P. ***delavayi*** Potaninii group
¶ 'Roselette'	MAus
russii 'Corallina'	See P. ***mascula***
¶ 'Scarlett O'Hara'	MAus
* 'Shimasaijin'	MBri
sp. ex Stern	MPar
suffruticosa (S)	CSco ELan MGos SHil
¶ – 'Gessekai' ('Moon World')	MAus
– 'Godaishu' (S)	EBre LAma

¶ – 'Gosho-zakura' ('Cherries of Imperial Palace') (S) MAus
¶ – 'Hakuo-jisi' ('King of White Lions') (S) MAus
– 'Hana-daigin' ('Magnificent Flower') (S) EBre LAma MAus
– 'Hana-kisoi' ('Floral Rivalry') (S) EBre LAma MAus
– 'Higurashi' ('Twilight') (S) LAma
¶ – 'Howki' ('Charming Age') (S) MAus
– 'Kamada-fuji' ('Wisteria at Kamada') (S) LAma
¶ – 'Kamada-nishiki' ('Kamada Brocade') (S) EBre MAus
– 'Kaoh' (S) EBre
¶ – 'Kaow' ('King of Flowers') (S) MAus
– 'Koku-ryu-nishiki' ('Black Dragon Brocade') (S) LAma
¶ – 'Mrs William Kelway' (S) CBow
¶ – 'Naniwa-nishiki' ('Brocade of the Rapid Waves') (S) MAus
¶ – 'No-kagura' ('Knight's Dance') (S) MAus
¶ – 'Renkaku' ('Flight of Cranes') (S) EBre MAus
– 'Rimpo' ('Bird of Rimpo') (S) LAma
¶ – 'Shugyo-kuden' ('Palace of Gems') (S) MAus
– 'Sitifukujin' ('Seven Gods of Fortune') (S) EBre MAus
¶ – 'Taisyo-no-hokori' ('Pride of Taisho') (S) MAus
¶ – 'Taiyo' ('The Sun') (S) LAma MAus
– 'Tama-fuyo' ('Jewel in the Lotus') (S) LAma
¶ – 'Tama-sudare' ('Jewelled Screen') (S) MAus
¶ – 'Yachiyo-tsubaki' ('Eternal Camellias') (S) LAma MAus
– 'Yae-zakura' ('Very Double Cherry') (S) LAma MAus
¶ – 'Yatsu-kazishi' (S) MAus
¶ 'Tango' MAus
tenuifolia EPot SPou
* 'Trojiman' MBri
veitchii LGre MBal NSti
– woodwardii GDra GLoc NHol WHoo
¶ ***wittmanniana*** MPhe
– wittmanniana MPar

PAESIA (Dennstaedtiaceae)
scaberula NMar SSpi SWas

PALIURUS (Rhamnaceae)
spina-christi SHil SLHN

PANAX (Araliaceae)
quinquefolius GPoy MSal

PANCRATIUM (Liliaceae/Amaryllidaceae)
maritimum CAvo ECam WHil

PANDANUS (Pandanaceae)

PANDOREA (Bignoniaceae)
jasminoides CSun IBlr MNew SLMG
– alba ERea
– 'Lady Di' CB&S
– 'Rosea Superba' CB&S ERea MNew
♦ ***lindleyana*** See CLYTOSTOMA ***callistegioides***
pandorana CB&S ERea LRHS SLMG

PANICUM (Gramineae)
* ***bulbosum*** CHan
¶ ***clandestinum*** EPla SApp
miliaceum EFou
¶ ***virgatum*** EMon EPla SMrm WHil
¶ – 'Hänse Hermes' EFou
¶ – 'Rehbraun' EFou
¶ – 'Rotstrahlbusch' EFou
– rubrum CHoe ECha EFou ELan NSti SApp SPer
– 'Strictum' CHoe ERou

PAPAVER † (Papaveraceae)
alboroseum GEdr WPer
alpinum CCla CHar EBre EMNN ESis GCHN GDra GLoc MBal MWat NGre NHol NKay NOak SIng WCla WEas WHil WOMN WPer WWin
¶ ***– album*** ECro
¶ – 'Flore Pleno' NBir
* ***arboreum*** WPer
§ ***atlanticum*** EBar GCHN GPla NOak NSti SWas WPer
– flore pleno MRav NSti WCot WOld
bracteatum See P. ***orientale b.***
§ ***commutatum*** ELan EMon LHol MRav SFir SMrm WEas WOMN
– 'Ladybird' See P. ***commutatum***
corona-sancti-stephani WCla
¶ ***dubium*** WPer
faurei See P. ***miyabeanum***
§ 'Fireball' CBos CHad ECha EFol ELan EPad GWic LHop MWat SSus
* 'French Grey' MPar
heldreichii See P. ***spicatum***
¶ × ***hybridum*** 'Flore Pleno' EMon
kerneri GEdr
♦ ***lateritium*** See P. ***atlanticum***

§ ***miyabeanum***	CGle ELan EPot GCHN GDra GLoc LHop MPlt NKay NTow NWCA SIng WCar WCla WEas WHal WHil WOMN WPer WWin
– ***tokewokii***	See P. ***miyabeanum***
nanum 'Flore Pleno'	See P. 'Fireball'
nudicaule	CCla ELan WPer
¶ – 'Constance Finnis'	EMon
¶ – 'Gartenzwerg' ('Garden Gnome')	MPit
§ – 'Oregon Rainbow'	ECro
¶ – 'Pacino'	MPit
– Wonderland hybrids	MBri NRoo
orientale	CB&S CHad EBre EHal LHil MFir WBod WEas WPer
– 'Allegro'	CBow CCla CSam CSco CShe ECro EFou EHal GHig MBri MPit NBar NRoo SPer
– 'Avebury Crimson'	MWat
§ – 'Beauty of Livermere'	CFis CHad CKel EFou ELan ERou MUlv NOak NVic SDix SPer WEas WRus
– 'Beauty Queen'	CTom ERou MBri NBar SMrm
– 'Black and White'	CCla CHad CKel CSco CSev CShe EBre ECha EFou ELan ERou MUlv NBar NRoo SChu SCro SPer
– 'Blue Moon'	CHad EBre SChu SMrm
§ – ***bracteatum***	ECha EHal EMon GCHN GDra NBir
– ***bracteatum***JCA 752.250	CSun
– ***carneum***	WHer
– 'Cedar Hill'	EFou
– 'Cedric's Pink'	ECha MUlv
– 'Constance Finnis'	GPla LHop WOMN
– 'Curlilocks'	EBre EFou ELan ERou GGar MBri MUlv NKay NRoo SMrm SPer
– 'Doubloon'	EBre
– 'Dwarf Allegro'	CHar MFir NNor NOak
– 'Flore Pleno'	EFou EMon
– 'Glowing Embers'	EBre SPer
* – 'Goldie'	ELan
– 'Goliath'	See P. *o.* 'Beauty of Livermere'
– 'Harvest Moon'	CShe EBre ECro ERou MBri MRav
– 'Helen Elisabeth'	EBre EFou MRav
– 'Indian Chief'	ERou
– 'King George'	MWat
¶ – 'Ladybird'	ERou NRoo WCot
– 'Marcus Perry'	CBow CKel CSco EBre ERou GGar GHig MWgw SCro
– 'Midnight'	EBre ERou
– 'Mrs George Stobart'	LHop
– 'Mrs Marrow's Plum'	CHad
– 'Mrs Perry'	CBow CHad CKel CSam CSco CSev CShe EBre EFou ELan ERou GHig LHop MBri MFir MUlv MWat MWgw NKay NRoo NSti SChu SHig SPer
– 'Nanum Flore Pleno'	See P. 'Fireball'
– 'Orange Glow'	GHig

– 'Oriana'	EBre ERou MBri SMrm
– 'Perry's White'	CKel CSam CSco CShe ECha ECro ELan ERou MBri MWat MWgw NBar NKay NOak NSti NVic SChu SPer WEas
– 'Picotée'	CHar CKel CSco CShe EBre ECha ECro EFou ELan EMon ERou GHig LHop MUlv MWat NBar NOak WCot WPer
– 'Pink Chiffon'	CGle WEas
– 'Prinzessin Victoria Louise'	WEas
– 'Redizelle'	EBre
– 'Salmon Glow'	CSco ERou GHig
¶ – 'Scarlet King'	MBri
– 'Sultana'	ECha NOak SPer
N – 'Türkenlouis' ('Turkish Delight')	CCla CHad CSco EBre ELan EMon ERou MBri SPer WRus
pilosum	CLew NCat WPer
¶ ***radicatum***	WPer
rhaeticum	ELan WCla WPer
rhoeas	CArn EFol GPoy LHol
¶ – 'Mother of Pearl'	ECro
– 'Valerie Finnis'	ELan
rupifragum	CGle CTom ECha GCHN MFir MWgw WCar WEas WHer WPer WWin
– 'Flore Pleno'	SSvw WCru WHer WHil
sendtneri	CSun
somniferum	CArn GPoy LHol NSel SIde
§ ***spicatum***	CSun ECha ECro LHop NBir NSti SLHN WEas
suaveolens	WCla
triniifolium	LGan

PARABENZOIN See **LINDERA**

PARADISEA † (Liliaceae/Asphodelaceae)

liliastrum	CGle CSun EBar ECro NHol SBar WCla WCot
– 'Major'	MPar NHol
lusitanica	CMHG

PARAHEBE † (Scrophulariaceae)

bartleyi	WRus
x ***bidwillii***	CHar CLew CMHG CRiv ECou EMNN GGar MPlt WOMN
– 'Kea'	ECou ECtt EMNN ESis GCHN GLoc GWic LHop MHig MPlt SAxl SBla WPer
¶ – 'Rosea'	MRav
canescens	ECou WHoo
§ ***catarractae***	CCla CFis CHan CMHG CMer CShe ECou ELan EMNN LAbb MCas MFir MPla MPlt MR&S NNor NRar NTow SAxl SHil SPer SPla WHoo WPer
– ***alba***	CBot CCla CHan ECha ELan EMNN ESis GCHN GWic IBlr MPlt NCat SAxl WEas WPer
– blue form	SPer
§ – 'Delight'	CGre ECou ESis GGar LHop MCot SDix SLon WEas WHoo

– ***diffusa***	CMHG ECou EMNN IOrc LHop MCas MPlt NVic SHil
– dwarf form	SSmi
– garden form	ECha SBla WAbe
– ***martinii***	ECou
– 'Porlock Purple '	See P. *c.* 'Delight'
– ***rosea***	CSun NHol NRed SBla SIng
– 'Tiny Tot'	MCot
– 'Tinycat'	GWic MCot NHol
decora	ECou EMNN GAbr LGre MPlt NCat NTow WHil
formosa	CGre ECou
¶ – erect form	ECou
¶ – lax form	ECou
¶ – white	ECou
'Gillian'	GGar
'Greencourt'	GCHN GWic
§ ***hookeriana***	CFis CShe CSun GAbr LGre NHol NTow WHoo
linifolia	EMNN GLoc MHig NHol WDav
– 'Blue Skies'	ECou GAbr
§ ***lyallii***	CBot CHar CMer ECou ELan EMNN EMon ERav ESis GAbr LHop MCas MPit MPla MPlt MR&S MRav NGre NHol NNor NNrd NRar SSmi WAbe
– 'Julie-Anne'	ECou GWic
– 'Rosea'	GGar MBal SSmi WPer
'Mervyn'	ECou ESis GCHN GGar GLoc LHop MCas MPlt NHol NRed NRya SFis WAbe WPer
'Miss Willmott'	CLew CShe EBre MCas NNrd NRar NVic WBod WPer
olsenii	ECou GGar
§ ***perfoliata***	Widely available
– dark blue form	GWic NCat

PARAJUBAEA (Palmae)

¶ ***cocoides***	LPal

PARAQUILEGIA (Ranunculaceae)

adoxoides	See SEMIAQUILEGIA ***adoxoides***
§ ***anemonoides***	GDra
grandiflora	See P. ***anemonoides***

PARASYRINGA See **LIGUSTRUM**

X PARDANCANDA (Iridaceae)

norrisii	IBrk

PARIETARIA (Urticaceae)

§ ***judaica***	GPoy MSal
officinalis	See P. ***judaica***

PARIS (Liliaceae/Trilliaceae)

incompleta	MPlt SPou WChr
polyphylla	See DAISWA ***p.***
quadrifolia	GPoy MSal WHer

PARNASSIA (Saxifragaceae)

nubicola	MBal
¶ ***palustris***	ECro WHoo

PAROCHETUS (Leguminosae)

communis	CB&S CBre CElw CGle CHar CLew CMer CRiv CSun CTre ELan GDra GLoc LAbb NKay NNrd SIng SLHN WEas WHal WPer WWat
¶ – dark form	GWic
– Himalayan form	IBlr

PARONYCHIA (Caryophyllaceae)

argentea	GLoc LHil WPer
§ ***capitata***	CLew CRiv CSun ELan EMNN MHig NHol NKay NNrd WHil WPer WWin
§ ***kapela***	MCas NHol
nivea	See P. ***capitata***
serpyllifolia	See P. ***kapela***

PARROTIA (Hamamelidaceae)

persica	Widely available
– 'Pendula'	CBow EHar IJoh IOrc SPer SSpi
¶ – 'Prostrata'	LSav

PARROTIOPSIS (Hamamelidaceae)

jacquemontiana	CB&S CCla CHan MBri MUlv SSpi SSta

PARRYA (Cruciferae)

menziesii	See PHOENICAULIS ***cheiranthoides***

PARSONSIA (Apocynaceae)

capsularis	ECou

PARTHENIUM (Compositae)

integrifolium	MSal

PARTHENOCISSUS † (Vitaceae)

§ ***henryana***	Widely available
himalayana	ECtt SHil
– ***rubrifolia***	CMac SHil
§ ***quinquefolia***	Widely available
– ***engelmannii***	MGos MR&S SPer SPla WAbe
¶ ***semicordata***	CHEx
thomsonii	SHil
tricuspidata	CGre CHEx CShe ECtt MBal MCot MGos NNor SHil SMrm SPer SReu WBod
– 'Beverley Brook'	CBow CMac CSco CShe MBri SBra SPer WAbe WBod
– 'Green Spring'	CSco EHal IHos MBri MGos SBra
– 'Lowii'	CMac EHal SPer
§ – 'Veitchii'	CBra CMac EHar ELan ENot IDai IHos IJoh MBar MGos MMth MR&S MRav MWat NHol NKay NWea SBra SHil SLon SPer SSta WPat WWat

PASSIFLORA † (Passifloraceae)

alata	CGrh SLMG
♦ x ***alatocaerulea***	See P. x ***belotii***
'Allardii'	CGre CGrh SHil
amethystina	CB&S CGrh CSun ERea SLMG SSus WWcb

antioquiensis	CB&S CBot CGre CGrh CHEx CHil CSun ERea IBlr ISea MNew NRar SHil SLMG
§ ***aurantia***	CGrh ERea
♦ ***banksii***	See P. ***aurantia***
§ x ***belotii***	CGrh CGrh ERea MNew NRar WWeb
♦– 'Impératrice Eugénie'	See P. x ***b.***
¶ ***biflora***	CGrh
¶ ***bryonioides***	CGrh
§ ***caerulea***	Widely available
– 'Constance Elliott'	CB&S CBot CCla CGrh CHil CMac CSco ELan LHop MGos SBra SHil SLMG SMad SPer SPla SReu SSta WWeb
– forms	SLMG
– ***rosea***	SHil
¶ – ***rubra***	ECtt
x ***caeruleo-racemosa***	CB&S CCla CGrh CKni ISea LHop NTow
– 'Eynsford Gem'	IOrc
x ***caponii***	ERea
capsularis	CGrh CHil SLMG
♦ ***chinensis***	See P. ***caerulea***
¶ ***cinnabarina***	CGrh
¶ ***cirrhifolia***	CGrh
coccinea	CGre CGrh
¶ x ***colvillei***	CGrh CHil
¶ ***coriacea***	CGrh
¶ ***costaricensis***	CGrh
edulis	CGrh CHil EBak ERea LAbb SHil SLMG WHer
– 'Alice'	ESim
– 'Crackerjack'	CB&S CHEx ERea
F – ***edulis***	CB&S
F – ***flavicarpa***	CGrh
– 'Supreme'	CB&S
¶ ***eichleriana***	CGrh
♦ 'Empress Eugenie'	See P. x ***belotii***
x ***exoniensis***	CBot CGre CGrh ESim LAbb
¶ ***foetida***	CGrh
¶ ***glandulosa***	CGrh
¶ ***gracilis***	CGrh
¶ ***hartwiesiana***	CGrh
¶ ***helleri***	CGrh
herbertiana	CGrh SLMG
¶ ***holoserica***	CGrh
incana	CArn
incarnata	CArn CGrh CSun MSal
¶ x ***innesii***	CGrh CSun
¶ x ***kewensis***	CGrh
¶ ***laurifolia***	CGrh
'Lavender Lady'	IOrc
ligularis	CGrh ESim
¶ ***lutea***	CGrh
¶ ***maliformis***	CGrh
¶ ***manicata***	CGrh
♦ ***mayana***	See P. ***caerulea***
♦ ***menispermifolia***	See P. ***pilosa***
¶ ***misera***	CGrh
¶ ***mixta***	CGrh ERea
¶ – x ***antioquiensis***	CGrh
mollissima	CB&S CBot CGre CGrh CHil CSun ERea LHop SHil SLMG
¶ ***morifolia***	CGrh
¶ ***nitida***	CGrh
¶ ***oerstedii***	CGrh
onychina	See P. ***amethystina***
§ ***pilosa***	CGrh
¶ ***platyloba***	CGrh
'Purple Passion'	See P. ***edulis edulis***
quadrangularis	CBot CGre CGrh CHil CSun ERea ESim SHil SLMG
– 'John Innes'	SLMG
racemosa	CGre CGrh CHil CSun ERea IBlr SHil
rubra	CGrh CMac ELan MUlv SPer WWeb
¶ – forms	CGrh
¶ ***sanguinolenta***	CGrh
¶ ***seemannii***	CGrh
¶ 'Star of Bristol'	CGrh
¶ 'Star of Clevedon'	CGrh
¶ 'Star of Kingston'	CGrh
¶ ***suberosa***	CGrh
¶ ***subpeltata***	CGrh
§ ***tetrandra***	CGrh ECou WCoo
¶ ***trifasciata***	CGrh
¶ ***trifoliata***	CGrh
truxilensis	ERea
¶ ***tuberosa***	CGrh
umbilicata	CBot CGre CGrh CHil SHil
violacea	CGrh ERea MBri
vitifolia	CGrh CSun MNew
¶ 'Wilcrowl'	WWeb

PASSION FRUIT, Purple See **PASSIFLORA** ***edulis edulis***

PASSION FRUIT, Yellow See **PASSIFLORA** ***edulis flavicarpa***

PASTINACA (Umbelliferae)

sativa	CKin

PATRINIA (Valerianaceae)

gibbosa	LGan MHig NHol SIng SSus
¶ ***scabiosifolia***	WHil
triloba palmata	CShe NKay WHil
– ***triloba***	CChu CGle CLew CTom GLoc GWic MCas MHig MPar MTho NNrd SSpi WWin

PAULOWNIA (Scrophulariaceae)

coreana	CGre
N ***fargesii***	CChu CGre CHEx GWic SHil SSpi SSta
lilacina	CGre
* ***simmular***	CHil
tomentosa	Widely available

PAVONIA (Malvaceae)

¶ ***praemosa***	NBar

PAW PAW See **CARICA** ***papaya***

PAXISTIMA (Celastraceae)

canbyi	MBal MUlv WWin

PEACH See **PRUNUS** ***persica***

PEAR See **PYRUS** ***communis***

PEAR, Asian See **PYRUS** ***pyrifolia***

PECAN See **CARYA** ***illinoinensis***

PEDICULARIS (Scrophulariaceae)

canadensis	MSal

PEGANUM (Zygophyllaceae)

harmala	CArn EBar MSal WPer

PELARGONIUM † (Geraniaceae)

§ 'A Happy Thought' (Z/V)	IHos LTho LVer MBri MWhe SDen SKen WEas
'A M Mayne' (Z/D)	LVer SDen WFib
'Abel Carrière' (I/D)	LVer SDen SKen WFib
abrotanifolium (Sc)	CCla SKen
acerifolium	See P. ***vitifolium***
acetosum	CSpe GCHN SMrm
¶ 'Ada Sutcliffe' (Min)	SKen
'Ada Sutterby' (Dw/D)	SBro WFib
'Adagio' (Dw)	ESul
'Adam's Quilt' (Z/C)	SKen SOld WEas
'Adele' (Min/D)	ESul SBro WFib
'Aerosol Improved' (Min)	CSpe LTho
'Aida' (R)	CCla
'Ailsa' (Min/D)	ESul MBri SBro
¶ 'Ainsdale Angel' (A)	LTho
'Ainsdale Beauty' (Z)	LTho
'Ainsdale Claret' (Z)	LTho WFib
¶ 'Ainsdale Eyeful' (Z)	LTho
'Ainsdale Happiness' (Z/D)	LTho
'Ainsdale Sixty' (Z)	LTho
'Akela' (Min)	ESul SBro
'Alan West' (Z/St)	SDen
'Alba'	See P. PELFI Alba ®
'Albert Sheppard' (Z/D/C)	LVer WFib
'Alberta' (Z)	SKen WFib
'Albert's Choice' (R)	WFib
'Alcyone' (Dw/D)	CCla ESul IHos LVer SBro SKen
'Alde' (Min)	ESul LVer MWhe SBro SDen SKen
¶ 'Aldham' (Min)	SBro
'Aldwyck' (R)	LTho
'Alex' (Z)	SKen
'Alex Kitson' (Z)	LTho
'Algenon' (Min/D)	ESul SBro WFib
'Alice Crousse' (I/D)	SKen WFib
¶ 'Alison' (Dw)	SBro
'Alison Jill' (Z/D)	LVer
'All My Love' (R)	LVer WFib
'Alma' (Min/C)	ESul SBro
'Alpine Glow' (Z/D)	IHos LVer MSmi MWhe SKen SOld
'Alpine Orange' (Z/D)	SDen
'Alta Bell' (R)	WFib
'Altair' (Min/D)	CCla LVer MWhe SBro
¶ 'Always' (Z/D)	LVer
'Ambrose' (Dw/D)	ESul SBro WFib
¶ 'Amelia' (Min)	SBro
'Amethyst' (I/D)	CSut ECtt IHos LTho MWhe WFib
– (R)	LTho LVer MBri MPen MSmi MWhe SDen SKen SOld WEas WFib
'Ami' (R)	WFib
'Amour' (R)	SDen
'Anabell Stephenson' (Dw/D)	WFib
'Andenken an Emil Eschbach' (I/D)	LVer
'Andersonii' (Sc)	WFib
'Andrew Salvidge' (R)	LTho SDen WFib
I 'Andromeda' (Min)	SBro WFib
'Ange Davey' (Z/D)	WFib
¶ 'Angela' (Min)	SBro
¶ 'Angela Mitchell' (Z/D/C)	SBro
'Angela Read' (Dw)	ESul LTho SBro
'Angelique' (Dw/D)	LTho SBro
'Anglia' (Dw)	ESul SBro SDen
'Ann Hoysted' (R)	WFib
'Ann Redington' (R)	WFib
'Anna' (Dw)	ESul SBro
'Antigua' (R)	WFib
'Antoinette' (Min)	ESul SBro
'Apache' (Z/D)	WFib
¶ 'Aphrodite' (Z)	CCla
appendiculatum	GCHN
'Apple Blossom Rosebud' (Z/D)	LVer MBri MWhe SDen SKen SOld WFib
'Appledram' (R)	LTho
'Apricot' (Z/St/D)	ESul LVer SDen SKen
'Apricot Queen' (I/D)	LTho LVer
'Aquarell' (R)	CCla
'Arctic Star' (Z/St)	CSpe ESul LTho LVer SDen SOld
'Arcturus' (Min)	SBro
'Aries' (Min/C)	MWhe SBro
'Arizona' (Min/D)	ESul SBro SDen SKen WFib
'Arthings Slam' (R)	SKen
'Arthur Biggin' (Z)	LVer MWhe SKen
'Ashdown Forest' (Dw)	LVer SBro
'Ashfield Blaze' (Z/D)	LVer WFib
'Ashfield Jubilee' (Z/C)	LVer SKen
'Ashfield Monarch' (Z/D)	LVer MWhe WFib
'Ashfield Serenade' (Z)	LTho LVer SKen WFib
'Ashley Stephenson' (R)	WFib
'Askham Fringed Aztec' (R)	LTho
asperum	See P. ***graveolens***
'Athabasca' (Min)	ESul SBro
'Atomic Snowflake' (Sc/V)	CCla ESul LVer SDen WFib
'Attar of Roses' (Sc)	CCla ESul GPla IHos LTho LVer MWhe NSty SDen SKen WEas WFib

'Attraction' (Z/St/D) WFib
'Aubusson' (R) WFib
'Audrey' (Z/D) WFib
'Audrey Clifton' (I/D) SDen WEas WFib
¶ 'Augusta' LHop
'Aurora' (Z/D) MWhe
'Aurore' See P. 'Unique Aurore'
australe EPad GCHN IHos WHer
¶ – Tasmanian form SSpi
'Autumn' (Z/D) IHos MWhe
¶ 'Autumn Colours' (Min) SBro
'Autumn Festival' (R) WFib
'Autumn Mist' (R) WFib
'Avalon' (Dw/D) WFib
'Aztec' (R) LTho LVer SKen WFib WPer
'Baby Birds Egg' (Min) CSpe ESul SBro
'Baby Brocade' (Min/D) ESul LVer SBro
'Baby Clare' (Min) LTho SBro
¶ 'Baby Doll' (Min/D) SBro
'Baby Helen' (Min) ESul LTho SBro SDen
'Baby James' (Min) CCla SBro SKen
'Babylon' (R) WFib
'Badley' (Dw) ESul SBro
Balcon Imperial ® See P. 'Roi des Balcons Impérial'
'Balcon Royale' (I) See P. 'Roi des Balcons Impérial'
'Ballerina' (Dw/D) CCla MWhe WFib
'Ballet Dancer' (Min/D) ESul SBro
♦ 'Bandit' See P. ***'Bandit'***
§ 'Bantam' (Min/D) ESul LVer SBro WFib
'Barbara Rice' (Z/D) LVer
§ 'Barbe Bleu' (I/D) ECtt LTho MSmi MWhe SDen SKen WFib
'Barcelona' (R) SKen
'Barham' (Min/D) ESul LTho SBro
'Barking' (Min) ESul SBro
'Baron de Layres' (Z/D) WFib
'Baronne A. de Rothschild' (Z/D) WFib
'Bashful' (Min) ESul SBro
'Bath Beauty' (Dw) LVer SBro SDen SKen WEas
'Baylham' (Min) ESul LTho SBro
'Beacon Hill' (Min) LTho SBro
'Beatrice Cottington' (I/D) LVer SKen
'Beatrix' (Z/D) ESul SBro SKen
'Beau Geste' (R) LVer MPen
'Beauty of Bath' (R) WFib
'Beauty of Calderdale' (Z/C) WFib
'Beauty of Coldwell' (Z/C) MWhe
N 'Beauty of Eastbourne' See P. 'Lachskönigin'
'Beauty of El Segundo' (Z/D) SKen WFib
'Beauty of Jersey' (I/D) LTho WFib
'Beckwith's Pink' (Z) SDen SKen
'Belinda Adams' (Min/D) ESul LVer MWhe SBro
'Belstead' (Min) ESul SBro SDen
'Belvedere' (R) CCla
'Ben Franklin' (Z/V) IHos LVer MWhe
'Ben Nevis' (Dw/D) SBro SDen

'Benedict' (Min) SBro
'Bengal Fire' (Z/C) LVer
'Bentley' (Dw) ESul SBro
'Berliner Balkon' (I) SDen SKen
'Beronmunster' (A) LTho LVer SOld WFib
'Bert Pearce' (R) LTho
'Beryl Gibbons' (Z/D) LTho LVer MWhe
'Beryl Read' (Dw) ERea LTho SBro
'Beryl Reid' (R) LTho
'Berylette' (Min/D) SBro
'Bess' (Z/D) LVer SBro SDen SKen
'Beta' (Min/C) ESul SBro
¶ 'Betsy Trotwood' (Dw) SBro
¶ 'Bette Shellard' (Z/D) LTho
¶ 'Betty Dollery' (Z/D) SDen
'Betty Hulsman' (A) ESul SBro
'Betty Read' (Dw) ESul SBro
'Betty West' (Min/D) SBro SDen
betulinum GCHN
'Bewerley Park' (Z/D/C) LVer SKen WFib
'Bianca' (Min/D) ESul LVer SBro
'Biedermeier' (R) CCla
'Bildeston' (Z/C) ESul LVer SBro
'Bill West' (I) SDen
'Billie Read' (Dw/D) ERea ESul LTho SBro
'Bingo' (Min) ESul LTho SBro
'Bird Dancer' (Dw/St) CCla CSpe ESul LTho LVer MWhe SBro SDen SKen SOld WFib
'Birthday Girl' (R) WFib
'Bi-Coloured Startel' (Z/St/D) CBot LVer MWhe
'Black Butterfly' (R) See F. 'Brown's Butterfly'
¶ 'Black Knight' (R) CSpe
'Black Magic' (R) WFib
'Black Velvet' (R) LVer
'Black Vesuvius' See P. 'Red Black Vesuvius'
¶ 'Blackcurrant Sundae' LVer
'Blakesdorf' (Dw) CSpe ESul MWhe SBro
'Blanchland Cerise' (Dw) CCla SBro
¶ 'Blanchland Dazzler' (Min) SBro
§ 'Blandfordianum' (Sc) CCla SIgm WHer
§ 'Blauer Frühling' (I/D) IHos LTho LVer MWhe SDen SKen WFib
'Blazonry' (Z/V) CCla LTho SDen
'Blisworth Mrs Mappin' (Z/V) MWhe
'Blooming Gem' (Min/I/D) LTho LVer SBro
'Blossomtime' (Z/D) LVer
'Blue Beard' (I) See P. 'Barbe Bleu'
¶ 'Blue Peter' (I/D) SKen
'Blue Spring' See P. 'Blauer Frühling'
'Blues' (Z/D) See P. PELFI Blues ®
'Blush Mariquita' (R) WFib
'Blush Petit Pierre' (Min) ESul SBro
'Blushing Bride' (I/D) IHos LVer SKen
¶ 'Blushing Emma' (Z) LTho
'Bob Legge' (Z/D) WFib
'Bodey's Picotee' (R) LTho

¶ 'Bold Romance' (Z)	LTho
'Bold Sunset' (Z/D)	LTho
'Bolero' (U)	IHos LTho
¶ 'Bonanza' (Z/D)	SBro
'Bosham' (R)	LTho
'Botley Beauty' (R)	LTho
'Boudoir' (Z/C/D)	SBro
'Brackenwood' (Min/D)	LTho SBro
'Bramford' (Dw)	ESul SBro
'Braque' (R)	WFib
'Bravo' (Z/D)	MWhe
'Break o' Day' (R)	CCla SDen SKen WEas
'Bredon' (R)	WFib
'Brenda' (Min/D)	ESul LVer SBro
'Brenda Hyatt' (Dw/D)	ESul LVer SBro
'Brenda Kitson' (Z/D)	LTho LVer MWhe WFib
¶ 'Brett' (Min)	SBro
'Brettenham' (Min)	ESul SBro
¶ 'Bridal Veil' (Min/C)	SBro
'Bridesmaid' (Dw/D/C)	CCla ESul LTho LVer SBro SOld WEas WFib
'Brightwell' (Min/D)	ESul SBro WFib
'Brixworth Boquet' (Min/D/C)	MWhe
¶ 'Brixworth Charmer'	MWhe
'Brixworth Gold' (Min/D/C)	MWhe
¶ 'Brixworth Melody'	MWhe
¶ 'Brixworth Rhapsody'	MWhe
'Brixworth Serenade' (Min/D/C)	MWhe
'Brixworth Starlight' (I/V)	MWhe
'Brocade' (Z/D)	IHos LVer WFib
'Bronze Corinne' (Z/D/C)	LVer SDen SKen
¶ 'Bronze Queen' (Z/C)	MWhe
'Bronze Velvet' (R)	WFib
'Brookside Betty' (Dw/D/C)	LTho
¶ 'Brookside Bolero' (Z)	LTho
'Brookside Flamenco' (Min/D)	LTho SBro
¶ 'Brookside Jupiter' (Z)	LTho
'Brookside Primrose' (Min/D/C)	LTho SBro
¶ 'Brookside Serenade' (Z)	LTho
'Brook's Purple'	See P. 'Royal Purple'
¶ 'Brownie' (Min)	SBro
§ 'Brown's Butterfly' (R)	LHop LVer SMrm WFib
'Brunii' (Z/D)	IHos LVer MWhe WFib
'Brunswick' (Sc)	LTho LVer SDen
'Bucklesham' (Dw)	ESul SBro
'Bumblebee' (Dw)	ESul SBro
'Burgenlandmädel' (Z/D)	SDen SKen WFib
'Burgundy' (R)	CCla WFib
'Burstall' (Min/D)	ESul LTho SBro SDen
'Butley' (Min)	ESul SBro
'Cal' (Z/D)	See P. 'Salmon Irene'
'Caledonia' (Z)	LVer SDen SKen
'Caligula' (Min/D)	LVer SBro WFib
¶ 'Cally' (Min/D)	SBro
'Cameo' (Dw/D)	LVer MWhe SBro WFib
'Camilla' (Dw)	SBro SDen
'Camphor Rose' (Sc)	ESul
candicans	GCHN
'Candy' (Min/D)	CCla ESul LVer SBro
¶ 'Candy Kisses' (D)	LVer SBro
canescens	See P. 'Blandfordianum'
'Can-Can' (I/D)	WFib
'Capel' (Dw/D)	ESul SBro
¶ 'Capella' (Min)	SBro
– (Min/D)	SBro
capitatum (Sc)	GCHN SDen WFib
'Caprice' (R)	SKen WFib
'Capricorn' (Min/D)	ESul LVer SBro
'Captain Starlight' (A)	ESul LTho SBro
'Cardinal' (Z/D)	See P. 'Kardinal'
'Carefree' (U)	LTho
'Cariboo Gold' (Min/C)	LTho SKen
'Carisbrooke' (R)	CCla LVer SDen SKen WEas WFib
'Carnival' (R)	See P. 'Marie Vogel'
– (Z)	WFib
'Carol'	SOld
'Carol Ann' (Z)	LTho
'Carol Cooper' (Fr/D)	LTho
'Carol Gibbons' (Z/D)	LTho MWhe
'Carol Plumridge' (Dw/C)	WFib
'Carole Munroe' (Z/D)	LTho LVer
'Caroline Schmidt' (Z/D/V)	CCla LTho LVer MBri MWhe SDen SKen WFib WPer
'Carolyn' (Min)	SBro
'Carol's Treasure' (Z/C)	LVer
'Carousel' (Z/D)	LVer
¶ 'Cassio' (Min/D)	SBro
'Catford Belle' (A)	CSpe ESul LTho LVer MWhe SBro SDen SKen SOld WFib
'Cayucas' (I/D)	SKen
'Celebration' (Z/D)	ESul LTho SBro
'Celia' (Min)	ESul SBro SDen
'Cerise' (I/D)	MWhe
'Cézanne' (R)	CCla IHos LVer SDen SKen WFib
'Champagne' (Z/D)	See P. PELFI Champagne ®
'Chang' (Z)	WEas
'Chantilly Lace' (R)	LTho
§ 'Charles Gounod' (Z/D)	LVer SDen
'Charlie Boy' (R)	CCla SDen WFib
'Charlotte Read' (Dw)	ERea LTho SBro
'Charmer' (R)	SDen
'Chattisham' (Min)	ESul SBro
'Chelmondiston' (Min/D)	ESul MWhe SBro
§ 'Chelsea Gem' (Z/D/V)	LTho LVer SDen SKen SOld WFib
'Chelsworth' (Min/D)	ESul SBro
'Chelvey' (R)	WFib
'Cherie' (Min)	ESul LVer SBro WFib
– (R)	WFib
¶ 'Cherie Maid' (Z/V)	CSpe
¶ 'Cherie Mitchell' (Min)	SBro
'Cherie Salmon'	WEas

¶ 'Cherry' (Min) SBro WFib
– (Z/D) LVer WFib
'Cherry Blossom' (Z/D) LVer SKen
'Cherry Galilee' (I/D) LTho SKen
'Cherry Hazel Glory' (R) LTho
'Cherry Orchard' (R) CCla LTho LVer SDen SKen WFib
'Chew Magna' (R) WFib
'Chieko' (Min/D) ESul LTho SBro SDen WFib
'Chiltern Beacon' (Min/D) LTho SBro
¶ 'Chime' (Min/D) SBro
'China Doll' (Dw/D) WFib
'Chiquita' (R) WFib
'Chi-Chi' (Min) ESul LVer SBro
'Chocolate Blotch' (Z/C) SBro
§ 'Chocolate Peppermint' (Sc) CCla CSev ESul IHos LTho LVer SDen SKen WFib WHer WPer
'Chocolate Tomentosum' See P. 'Chocolate Peppermint'
'Chorus Girl' (R) WEas
'Christine Read' (Dw) ESul
'Christopher Ley' (Z) LTho LVer SKen
¶ 'Christopher Mitchell' (Min) SBro
'Cindy' (Dw/D) ESul SBro
'Circus Day' (R) MPen WFib
'Citriodorum' (Sc) CCla WFib
'Citronella' (Sc) WFib
citronellum (Sc) NSty SKen WFib WHer WPer
'Clair' (Min) WFib
'Clara Read' (Dw) ESul LTho LVer SBro
¶ 'Clare' (Min) SBro
'Claret Rock Unique' (U) LVer SDen SKen WFib
'Clarissa' (Min) ESul
'Claude Read' (Dw) ERea ESul SBro
¶ 'Claudette' (Min) SBro
'Claudius' (Min) ESul SBro SDen WFib
'Claydon' (Dw/D) CSpe ESul LVer SBro
'Clorinda' (U/Sc) CCla CSev ESul LTho LVer SDen SKen WFib WHer
♦ 'Clorinda Variegated' See P. 'Variegated Clorinda'
'Coddenham' (Dw/D) ESul LTho SBro WFib
'Colonel Baden Powell' (I/D) WFib
'Colour Sergeant' (Min) LTho SBro
'Concolor Lace' (Sc) LTho LVer SKen
'Contrast' (Z//D/C/V) LVer MWhe SKen WFib
'Copdock' (Min/D) ESul SBro
'Copthorne' (Sc) LTho LVer WFib WHer
'Coral Frills' (Dw) SBro
'Coral Island' (Z/D) SDen
'Coralglow' (Z/D) IHos LVer
coriandrifolium WHer
'Cornell' (I/D) IHos MBri MWhe
'Coronia' (Z/Ca) LVer
'Corsair' (Z/D) MWhe WFib
'Cotswold Queen' (Z/D) WFib
'Cotton Candy' (Dw/D) ESul LVer SBro
'Cottontail' (Min/D) ESul LTho LVer SBro
cotyledonis GCHN
'Countess Mariza' See P. 'Gräfin Mariza'
♦ 'Countess of Scarborough' See P. 'Lady Scarborough'
'Country Girl' (R) IHos
¶ 'County Girl' (Z) CCla
'Cover Girl' (Z/D) WFib
'Cramdon Red' (Dw) LVer SKen SOld
'Crampel's Master' (Z) LVer SKen
¶ 'Cransley Blends' (R) LTho
¶ 'Cransley Star' (A) LTho
crassipes GCHN
'Creamery' (Z/D) LTho SKen WFib
'Creamy Nutmeg' See P. x *fragrans* 'C.N.'
'Creed's Seedling' (Z/C) LVer
'Creeting St Mary' (Min) ESul SBro
'Creeting St Peter' (Min) ESul SBro
¶ 'Crestfield Pink' (Min) SBro
'Crimson Fire' (Z/D) LVer MBri MWhe SKen
¶ 'Crimson Glow' (Dw/D) SBro
'Crimson Unique' (U) LVer SKen WFib
§ *crispum* (Sc) SDen WEas WFib
– *major* (Sc) CCla ESul GPoy LTho NSty SDen SKen WFib WHer WPer
♦ – *minor* See P. *crispum*
– 'Peach Cream' (Sc/V) CCla MWhe SDen
– 'Variegatum' (Sc/V) CCla CSev GCHN IHos LHil LVer MWhe NRoo NSty SBro SDen SKen SOld WEas WFib WHer WPer
crithmifolium GCHN
'Crocketta' (I/D) LTho LVer
♦ 'Crocodile' See P. 'The Crocodile'
'Crowfield' (Min/D) ESul SBro
'Crystal Palace Gem' (Z/V) CCla LVer MWhe SDen SKen
cucullatum strigifolium GCHN WHer
'Culpho' (Min/D/C) ESul SBro
'Cupid' (Min/Dw/D) ESul LVer SBro WFib
'Cynthia' (Min) ESul SBro
'Cyril Read' (Dw) ERea ESul SBro
'Dainty Lassie' (Dw/V) ESul LTho
'Dale Queen' (Z) LTho WFib
'Dame Anna Neagle' (Dw/D) LTho LVer
'Dancer' (Dw) ESul LVer SBro
'Dark Red Irene' (Z/D) LTho LVer MWhe WFib
'Dark Secret' (R) CCla CSpe LTho SDen SKen WFib
'Darmsden' (A) ESul LVer SBro
'David John' (Dw/D) SBro SDen
¶ 'David Mitchell' (Min/Ca/D/V) SBro
'Davina' (Min/D) ESul LVer SBro WFib
'Deacon Arlon' (Z/D) ESul LTho MWhe SDen SKen
'Deacon Barbecue' (Z/D) ESul LTho LVer SBro SDen
'Deacon Birthday' (Z/D) ESul LTho LVer MWhe SBro
'Deacon Bonanza' (Z/D) ESul LTho LVer MWhe SDen SKen WFib
'Deacon Clarion' (Z/D) ESul LTho LVer SBro SKen

'Deacon Constancy' (Z/D)	ESul LTho LVer MWhe SBro SDen
'Deacon Coral Reef' (Z/D)	ESul LTho LVer MWhe SBro SDen SKen SOld
'Deacon Finale' (Z/D)	ESul LTho LVer SBro SDen
'Deacon Fireball' (Z/D)	ESul LTho LVer MWhe SDen SKen SOld
'Deacon Flamingo' (Z/D)	ESul LTho LVer MWhe SDen
'Deacon Gala' (Z/D)	ESul LTho LVer MWhe SBro SDen
'Deacon Golden Bonanza' (Z/D/C)	ESul LTho SBro
'Deacon Golden Gala' (Z/D/C)	ESul LTho SBro
'Deacon Golden Lilac Mist' (Z/D/C)	ESul LTho SDen
'Deacon Jubilant' (Z/D)	ESul LTho LVer MWhe SBro SDen SKen
'Deacon Lilac Mist' (Z/D)	ESul LTho LVer MWhe SBro SDen SKen SOld
'Deacon Mandarin' (Z/D)	CCla ESul LTho LVer MWhe SBro SDen SKen SOld
'Deacon Minuet' (Z/D/C)	ESul LTho LVer MWhe SBro SDen SKen
'Deacon Moonlight' (Z/D)	ESul LTho MWhe SBro
'Deacon Peacock' (Z/D/V)	ESul LTho LVer MWhe SBro SDen SKen
'Deacon Picotee' (Z/D)	ESul IHos LTho LVer MBri SBro SDen SKen
'Deacon Regalia' (Z/D)	ESul LTho LVer MWhe SDen SKen
'Deacon Romance' (Z/D)	ESul LTho LVer MWhe SBro SDen SKen
'Deacon Summertime' (Z/D)	ESul LTho LVer MWhe SBro
'Deacon Sunburst' (Z/D)	ESul LTho LVer MWhe SBro SKen SOld
'Deacon Suntan' (Z/D)	ESul LTho LVer MWhe SBro SKen SOld
'Deacon Trousseau' (Z/D)	ESul LTho LVer SBro SDen
'Decora Impérial' (I)	LTho SKen
§ 'Decora Lilas' (I)	ECtt LTho SKen WFib
'Decora Mauve' (I)	See P. 'Decora Lilas'
'Decora Rose' (I)	ECtt IHos LTho SKen
§ 'Decora Rouge' (I)	CSpe ECtt LTho SKen WFib
'Degas' (R)	WFib
¶ 'Delilah' (Z)	CCla
¶ 'Della' (Min/D)	SBro
¶ 'Delta' (Min/D)	SBro
'Denebola' (Min/D)	ESul LVer SBro SDen WFib
N *denticulatum* (Sc)	LTho SDen SKen WFib
§ – 'Filicifolium group' (Sc)	CCla CSev CSpe GCHN IHos LTho LVer SDen SKen WFib WHer WPer
'Destiny' (R)	WFib
¶ 'Dewit's' (Dw)	SBro
¶ 'Di' (Min/D)	SBro
'Diadem' (R)	SKen WFib
'Diana Palmer' (Z/D)	LTho
'Diane' (Min/D)	SBro SDen WFib
¶ 'Dibbinsdale' (Z)	LTho
dichondrifolium	WFib
¶ 'Dick's White' (Dw/D)	SBro
'Didden's Improved Picardy' (Z/D)	MWhe
'Diddi-Di' (Min/D)	LTho SBro
¶ 'Didi' (Min)	SBro
'Dinky' (Min/D)	LVer SBro
'Disco' (Z)	See P. PELFI Disco ®
'Distinction' (Z)	IHos LVer MWhe SDen SKen WFib
'Doctor A Chipault' (I/D)	LVer WFib
'Dodd's Super Double' (Z/D)	IHos
'Dollar Bute' (R)	LVer
'Dollar Princess' (Z/C)	LVer SKen
'Dolly Read' (Dw)	ERea ESul LTho SBro WFib
'Dolly Varden' (Z/V)	IHos LHop LTho LVer MBri MWhe SDen SKen WFib
dolomiticum	GCHN
'Dolphin' (Min)	SBro WFib
¶ 'Dondo' (Dw/D)	SBro
'Dopey' (Min)	ESul SBro
'Doreen Featherby' (R)	CCla
'Doris Brook' (Z/D)	WFib
'Doris Frith' (R)	SKen WFib
'Doris Hancock' (R)	WFib
'Doris Shaw' (R)	WFib
'Double Grace Wells' (Min/D)	ESul LTho SBro
'Double Jacoby' (Z/D)	LVer WFib
'Double Lilac White' (I/D)	IHos MWhe
'Double Orange' (Z/D)	SKen
'Double Pink Bird's Egg' (Z/D)	SDen SKen
'Dove' (Z)	WFib
'Dovedale' (Dw/C)	LTho SBro
'Downlands' (Z/D)	LVer SDen
'Dream' (Z)	WFib
'Dresden Pink' (Dw)	LVer SBro WFib
'Dresden White' (Dw)	CSpe LVer SBro
'Drummer Boy' (Z)	SDen SKen
drummondii	GCHN
'Dryden' (Z)	LVer SDen SKen
'Dubonnet' (R)	WFib
¶ 'Duchess' (I)	CSpe
'Duchess of Devonshire' (Z)	SKen
'Duke of Buckingham' (Z/D)	SDen
'Duke of Devonshire' (Z/D)	CCla LTho
♦ 'Duke of Edinburgh'	See P. 'Hederinum Variegatum'
'Dulcie' (Min)	ESul LVer SBro
'Dunkery Beacon' (R)	WFib
¶ 'Dusty Rose' (Min)	SBro

¶ 'Dutch Vermillion' (Min) SBro
§ 'Dwarf Miriam Baisey' (Min) LTho SBro SDen WFib
♦ 'Dwarf Miriam Read' See P. 'Dwarf Miriam Baisey'
'E Dabner' (Z/D) SKen WFib
'Earl of Chester' (Min/D) LTho
'Earleana' (Dec) CSpe ESul SBro SKen
'Earth Magic' (Z/V) SDen
'Eastbourne Beauty' (I/D) WFib
'Easter Greeting' See P. 'Ostergruss'
echinatum GCHN
– stapletonii MFir
'Eclipse' (Min/D) MWhe SBro SDen SKen
'Eden Gem' (Min/D) ESul LTho LVer SBro
'Edgar Chisnall' (Z) LTho
'Edith Steane' (Dw/D) LVer SBro
'Edmond Lachenal' (Z/D) WFib
'Edward Humphris' (Z) SDen SKen
¶ 'Edwin Clarke' (Dw/Min) SBro
'Eileen Postle' (R) WFib
'Eleanor' (Z/D) LVer SDen
'Electra' (Z/D) LVer SDen SKen WFib
'Elfin Rapture' (R) SMrm WFib
'Elgar' (R) WFib
'Elizabeth Angus' (Z) SDen SKen WFib
'Elizabeth Cartwright' (Z) WFib
¶ 'Elizabeth Iris' (Dw) LVer
'Elizabeth Read' (Dw) ERea ESul LTho SBro
'Elmsett' (Z/D/C) ESul LTho LVer SBro
'Elna' (Min) ESul LVer SBro
elongatum GCHN
'Els' (Min/St) ESul LVer SBro SKen
'Elsi' (I/D/V) LVer WFib
¶ 'Elsie' (Z/D/C) SBro
'Elsie Hickman' (R) SDen SKen WFib
'Elsie Portas' (Z/D/C) LVer SKen
'Embassy' (Dw) ESul SBro WFib
'Emerald' (I) MSmi SKen
¶ 'Emma' (Min/D/C) SBro
♦ 'Emma Hössle' See P. 'Frau Emma Hössle'
'Emma Jane Read' (Dw/D) ERea ESul LTho MWhe SBro WFib
'Emma Louise' (Z) LVer SKen
'Empress' (Z) SKen
'Ena' (Min) ESul LVer SBro
'Enchantress' (I) LTho MBri MWhe WEas
endlicherianum EPot GCHN SApp SPou SSpi
'Endora' (Min) SBro SDen
'Endsleigh' (Sc) SDen
'Enid Blackaby' (R) WFib
'Enid Read' (Dw) ERea ESul LTho SBro
'Eric Ellis' (Dw/D) WFib
'Erwarton' (Min/D) ESul LTho LVer SBro
'Escapade' (Dw/D) ESul LVer SBro
¶ 'Etna' (Min) SBro
'Evesham Wonder' (Z/D) WFib
§ 'Fair Ellen' (Sc) CCla ESul SKen WFib WPer
¶ 'Faircop' (Sc) LTho
'Fairey Princess' (R) LTho
¶ 'Fairy Orchid' (A) SBro
¶ 'Fairy Princess' (Min) SBro
'Fairy Tales' (Dw) ESul SBro
'Falkenham' (Min) ESul SBro
'Falklands Hero' (Z/V) LTho MWhe SBro SKen SOld WFib
'Fandango' (Z/St/D) LTho
'Fanny Eden' (R) WFib
'Fantasie' (Dw/D) ESul LTho LVer MWhe SBro WFib
'Fareham' (R) LTho
'Fascination' (Z/Ca) WFib WPer
¶ 'Feneela' (Dw/D) SBro
'Fenton Farm' (Z/C) LTho
'Festal' (Min/D) ESul SBro
'Feu d'Amour' (I/D) WEas
¶ 'Feuerriese' (Z) LVer
'Fiat' (Z/D) SKen
'Fiat Queen' (Z/D) SKen WFib
'Fiat Supreme' (Z/D) SKen WFib
'Fidelio' (Z) See P. PELFI Fidelio ®
'Fiery Sunrise' (R) CCla LTho
¶ 'Fiesta' (Z) LVer
¶ 'Fifth Avenue' (R) CSpe
♦ 'Filicifolium' See P. ***denticulatum*** Filicifolium group
'Filigree' (Dw/V) IHos SBro
¶ 'Finger' SBro
'Finito' (Dw/D) ERea LTho SBro
'Fire Cascade' (I) LVer
'Fire Dragon' (Z/St/D) MWhe SDen SKen WFib
¶ 'Fireball' SBro
'Firebrand' (Z/D) LVer
'Firefly' (Min/D) ESul SBro WFib
'Fireglow' (Z/D) ESul
'First Blush' (R) WFib
'First Love' (Z) LTho
'Flakey' (I/D/V) CSpe ESul LTho LVer MWhe SBro SDen SKen
'Flamboyant' (I/D) LVer
'Flame' (Z) WFib
¶ 'Flamingo Dancer' (Z/Ca) SBro
'Flash' (Min) SBro
'Fleur d'Amour' (R) WFib
'Fleurette' (Dw/D) ESul LVer MWhe SBro SDen SKen SOld WFib
'Flirt' See P. PELFI Flirt ®
'Floral Cascade' (Fr/D) LTho WFib
'Florence Storey' (Z/C/D) WFib
'Flower of Spring' (Z/V) LVer MWhe SDen SKen WEas WFib
'Flowerfield' (Z) SDen
'Flowton' (Dw/D) ESul SBro
'Flynn' (Min) ESul
'Fox' (Z) CCla
'Foxhall' (Dw) ESul SBro

x *fragrans* (Sc) CCla CSev ESul GCHN GPla GPoy LTho LVer MWhe NSty SDen SKen WFib WHer WPer
– 'Creamy Nutmeg' (Sc/V) CCla
♦– 'Snowy Nutmeg' See P. x *f.* 'Variegatum'
§ – 'Variegatum' (Sc/V) CCla CSev CSpe ESul GPla LHop LTho LVer MWhe NSty SDen SKen WFib WPer
'Francis Parrett' (Min/D) ESul LTho LVer MWhe SBro WFib
'Francis Read' (Dw/D) ERea ESul LTho SBro
'Frank Headley' (Z/V) CCla CSpe ESul IHos LTho LVer MWhe SBro SDen SKen SOld WEas WFib
'Frank Parrett' (Min/D) ESul SBro
§ 'Frau Emma Hössle' (Dw/D) CCla ESul LVer MWhe SDen WFib
'Frau Käthe Neubronner' (Z/D) SDen
'Freak of Nature' (Z/V) ESul IHos LTho MWhe SDen SKen WEas WFib
'Freckles' (Z/D) LVer
'Frensham' (Sc) ESul IHos
'Freston' (Dw) ESul
¶ 'Freya' (Min) SBro
'Friary Wood' (Z/D/C) LTho LVer SKen WFib
'Friesdorf' (Dw) CCla ESul LVer MWhe SBro SDen SKen WEas WFib
¶ 'Friesian Beauty' (Z) CSpe
'Frills' (Min/D) ESul LVer MWhe SBro SKen WFib
'Fringed Aztec' (R) LTho LVer SDen SOld
'Frosty' (Min/V) LVer SBro
fruticosum WHer
fulgidum GCHN
¶ 'Fynn' (Dw) SBro
'Galilee' (I/D) IHos LTho LVer SDen SKen WFib
'Gallant' (Z/D) LVer
'Galway Star' (Sc/V) MWhe SDen WFib
¶ 'Gama' (Min) SBro
'Garibaldi' (Z/D) WFib
¶ 'Garland' (Dw/D) SBro
– (R) SDen SKen
'Garnet' (Z/D) LVer WFib
'Garnet Rosebud' (Min/D) ESul LVer SBro
'Garnet Wings' (R) WFib
'Gauguin' (I/D) IHos
'Gay Baby' (DwI) ESul LTho MWhe SBro SDen SKen
'Gay Baby Supreme' (DwI) CSpe ESul SDen SKen
'Gazelle' (Z) SDen SKen
¶ 'Gemini' (Z/St/D) SKen
¶ 'Gemma' (Min/C) SKen
– (R) LTho LVer
'Genetrix' (Z/D) WFib
'Genie' (Z/D) LTho LVer MWhe SDen SKen WFib
'Geoff May' (Dw) ESul SBro SDen WFib
'Geoffrey Horsman' (R) WFib WPer
'Georgia Peach' (R) WFib
¶ 'Geo's Pink' MWhe
'Gerald Portas' (Dw/C) SBro
¶ 'Gerald Wells' (Min) SBro
'Geraldine' (Min) ESul LVer SBro
¶ 'Geratus' (Min/Ca/D) SBro
'Gess Portas' (Z/V) SKen
gibbosum GCHN
'Gilbert West' (Z) SDen SKen
¶ 'Gilda' (Z) CCla
'Gill' (Min/Ca) ESul SBro
'Gillian Clifford' (Z/D) SDen
¶ 'Gina' (Min) SBro
¶ 'Glacier Claret' IHos
'Gladys Evelyn' (Z/D) LVer WFib
'Gladys Stevens' (Min/D) SBro SDen
'Gladys Washbrooke' (Z/D) LVer
'Gleam' (Z/D) LVer
¶ 'Glen' (Z/D) LVer
'Glenn Barker' (Z/D) WFib
'Glenshree' (R) SKen
'Glenys Carey' (Z/D) LVer
'Gloria Pearce' (R) CCla WFib
'Glory' (Z/D) WFib
'Glowing Embers' (R) WFib
§ *glutinosum* CCla CSev
'Goblin' (Min/D) ESul IHos LVer SBro SDen SKen WFib
¶ 'Golden Bonanza' SBro
'Golden Brilliantissimum' (Z/C) LTho SKen WFib
'Golden Butterfly' (Z/C) CCla LVer SBro
¶ 'Golden Chalice' (Min/V) MWhe SBro SKen
'Golden Clorinda' (U/Sc/C) LTho LVer SDen
'Golden Crest' (Z/C) SDen SKen
'Golden Ears' (Dw/St/C) CCla ESul LTho LVer MWhe SBro SKen SOld WFib
'Golden Everaarts' (Dw/C) ESul SBro
'Golden Fleece' (Min/D/C) ESul LVer SDen SKen
¶ 'Golden Gala' SBro
'Golden Gates' (Z/C) LTho SBro SDen SKen
'Golden Gleam' (Z/C) SDen
'Golden Harry Hieover' (Z/C) ESul LVer SDen SKen WEas
¶ 'Golden Lilac Mist' SBro
'Golden Magaluf' (I/D/C/V) LTho
'Golden Mirage' (Z/V) SDen
'Golden Mist' (Dw/D/C) LVer
¶ 'Golden Orange' (Dw/C) SBro
'Golden Orfe' (Dw/C) SBro WFib
'Golden Oriole' (Dw/C) SKen
'Golden Petit Pierre' (Min/C) ESul LTho LVer SBro SDen
'Golden Princess' (Min/C) ESul SBro WFib
'Golden Roc' (Min/C) ESul SBro

'Golden Staphs' (St/C) CCla ESul LTho LVer SBro SDen
'Golden Tears' (MinI/D/C) ESul SDen
'Goldie' (R) WFib
¶ 'Goldilocks' (A) LTho
'Gordano Midnight' (R) WFib
'Gosbeck' (A) ESul MWhe SBro
¶ 'Gottweig' (Z) CCla
¶ 'Grace Read' (Min) SBro
'Grace Wells' (Min) ESul LTho WFib
'Gräfin Mariza' (Z/D) IHos LVer SDen SKen WFib
'Granada' (R) IHos
'Grand Slam' (R) IHos LTho LVer MPen SDen SKen SOld WFib WPer
¶ -- (Z) CCla
grandiflorum GCHN
'Grandma Fischer' See P. 'Grossmama Fischer'
'Grandma Ross' (R) LTho
'Granny Hewitt' (Min/D) ESul LVer MWhe SBro
¶ 'Grasmere Beauty' (Z) LTho
§ ***graveolens*** (Sc) CCla CSev GCHN GPoy LTho LVer MWhe NSty SDen SKen WFib
'Great Bricett' (Min/D) ESul LVer SBro
'Green Eyes' (I/D) SDen
'Green Goddess' (I/D) LTho SKen
§ 'Greengold Kleine Liebling' (Min/C/V) LVer SBro SKen
'Greengold Petit Pierre' See P. 'Greengold Kleine Liebling'
'Greetings' (Min/V) LTho
'Grenada' (R) MPen SKen
'Grenche Belle' (I/D) LTho LVer
'Grey Lady Plymouth' (Sc/V) CCla SDen WFib
'Grey Sprite' (Min/V) ESul SBro WFib
§ 'Grossmama Fischer' (R) WEas WFib
grossularioides NSty
'Grozser Garten' (Dw) ESul
'Grozser Garten Weiss' (Dw) ESul
'Guernsey' WEas
'Gustav Emich' (Z/D) LVer SDen SKen WFib
¶ 'Gwen' (Min/V) SBro
'H Guinier' See P. 'Charles Gounod'
'Hadleigh' (Dw) ESul SBro
¶ 'Haidee' (Min) SBro
'Hamble Lass' (R) LTho
'Hans Rigler' (Z/D) LVer
'Happy Thought' See P. 'A Happy Thought'
'Happy Valley' (R) WFib
'Harbour Lights' (R) LTho
'Harewood Slam' (R) CCla LTho WFib
'Harkstead' (Min) ESul SBro
'Harlequin Alpine Glow' (I) LVer MWhe SDen WFib
'Harlequin Hilda Day' (I) LVer
'Harlequin Mahogany' (I/D) IHos LTho LVer MBri MWhe SDen SKen SOld WFib
'Harlequin Miss Liver Bird' (I) LVer MSmi MWhe SDen SKen SOld
'Harlequin My Love' (I) SDen SKen
'Harlequin Picotee' (I/D) LTho LVer MWhe SDen
'Harlequin Pretty Girl' (I) IHos LTho LVer MWhe SDen SKen WFib
'Harlequin Rosie O'Day' (I) LTho LVer MWhe SDen SKen WFib
'Harlequin Ted Day' (I) LVer
'Harold Headley' (Z/V) WFib
'Harriet Le Hair' (Z) SKen
'Harvey' (Z) MWhe
¶ 'Hayley Clover' MWhe
'Hazel' (R) CCla LVer SDen SKen WFib
'Hazel Birkby' (R) LTho
¶ 'Hazel Blake' (R) LTho
'Hazel Candy' (R) LTho
'Hazel Cherry' (R) LTho SDen WFib
'Hazel Choice' (R) LTho
'Hazel Dream' (R) LTho
'Hazel Gipsy' (R) LTho
'Hazel Herald' (R) LTho
'Hazel Orchid' (R) LTho
'Hazel Peach' (R) LTho
'Hazel Perfection' (R) LTho
'Hazel Saga' (R) LTho
'Hazel Satin' (R) LTho LVer
§ 'Hederinum' (I) IHos LTho MWhe SDen SKen WEas WFib
§ 'Hederinum Variegatum' (I/V) CSpe LTho LVer MWhe SKen WFib
'Heidi' (Min/D) ESul SBro SDen SKen WFib
'Helena' (I/D) LTho MWhe SDen SKen
'Hemingstone' (A) ESul SBro
'Henhurst Gleam' (Dw/D/C) WFib
'Henley' (Min/D) ESul
'Henri Joignot' (Z/D/V) LTho
'Henry Jacoby' (Z) WEas WPer
'Henry's Rose' (Z/C) LVer
'Hermione' (Z/D) LVer MWhe WFib
'High Tor' (Dw/D/C) LTho LVer SKen WEas
'Highfields Always' (Z/D) IHos LVer WFib
'Highfields Appleblossom' (Z/D) IHos LVer SKen
'Highfields Attracta' (Z/D) CCla LTho LVer SDen SKen
'Highfields Ballerina ' (Z/D) LTho LVer
'Highfields Cameo (Z/D) LVer
'Highfields Candy Floss' (Z/D) LTho LVer
'Highfields Charisma' (Z/D) LVer
'Highfields Choice' (Z) LTho LVer SDen SKen
'Highfields Comet' (Z) LVer SKen
'Highfields Concerto' (Z) LVer

'Highfields Contessa' (Z/D) LTho LVer SDen SKen
'Highfields Delight' (Z) LVer
'Highfields Fancy' (Z/D) IHos LVer SKen
'Highfields Fantasy' (Z) LTho SKen
¶ 'Highfields Fashion' (Z) LVer
'Highfields Festival' (Z/D) LVer MWhe SDen
'Highfields Flair' (Z/D) LTho LVer
'Highfields Flash' (Z/D) LVer
'Highfields Harmony' (Z) LVer
'Highfields Jazz' (Z/D) LVer
'Highfields Joy' (Z/D) LTho SDen WFib
'Highfields Melody' (Z/D) LVer SDen
'Highfields Orange' (Z) LVer
'Highfields Paramount' (Z) MWhe SDen SKen
'Highfields Pearl' (Z) LVer SDen
'Highfields Peerless' (Z) LVer
'Highfields Perfecta' (Z) LVer
'Highfields Pink' (Z) LVer
'Highfields Prestige' (Z) SKen
'Highfields Pride' (Z) LTho LVer SDen SKen
'Highfields Prima Donna' (Z/D) LTho LVer MWhe SKen
¶ 'Highfields Progress' (Z) LVer
'Highfields Promise' (Z) LVer SDen SKen
'Highfields Romance' (Z) LVer
'Highfields Salmon' (Z/D) LVer
¶ 'Highfields Sensation' (Z) LVer
¶ 'Highfields Serenade' (Z) LVer
'Highfields Snowdrift' (Z) LTho SKen
'Highfields Sonata' (Z/D) LVer
'Highfields Sugar Candy' (Z/D) ECtt IHos LTho LVer SDen SKen
'Highfields Symphony' (Z) LTho LVer
'Highfields Vogue' (Z) LVer
'Hildegard' (Z/D) LVer SKen WFib
'Hills of Snow' (Z/V) LTho LVer SDen SKen
'Hillscheider Amethyst' (I/D) See P. 'Amethyst'
'Hindoo' (R) WFib
'Hintlesham' (Min) ESul SBro
hirtum GCHN
'Hitcham' (Min/D) ESul SBro
'Holbrook' (Min/D/C) ESul LTho LVer SBro
'Hollywood Star' (Z) MWhe
'Honeywood Hannah' (R) LTho
'Honeywood Jonathan' (R) LTho
'Honeywood Lindy' (R) LTho LVer SDen
'Honeywood Margaret' (R) LTho
'Honeywood Matthew' (Dw) LTho LVer SBro
'Honeywood Suzanne' (Min/Fr) LTho LVer SBro
'Honne Früling' (Z) LVer SKen WFib
'Honneas' (Min) ESul
'Honnestolz' (Min) ESul SBro SKen
'Hope' (Z) WFib
'Hope Valley' (Dw/D/C) CCla ESul LTho LVer MWhe SBro SDen SKen
'Horace Parsons' (R) WFib
'Horace Read' (Dw) ERea ESul LTho SBro
'House and Garden' (R) LVer WFib
'Howard Stanton' (R) WFib
'Howard's Orange' (R) SKen
'Hugo de Vries' (Z/D) WFib
'Hula' (U) LTho
'Hunter's Moon' (Z/C) LTho SBro SKen
'Hurdy-Gurdy' (Z/D/V) LTho WFib
¶ HWD Corelli ® IHos
¶ HWD Gabrieli ® IHos
¶ HWD Monteverdi ® CCla IHos
¶ HWD Onyx ® IHos
¶ HWD Romanze ® IHos
¶ HWD Vivaldi ® IHos
'Ian Read' (Min/D) ERea ESul SBro WFib
¶ 'Ice Cap' (Min) SBro
'Icing Sugar' (I/D) LVer MWhe
'Immaculatum' (Z) WFib
'Imperial Butterfly' (A) LTho SBro
'Improved Goertz' WEas
'Improved Petit Pierre' (Min) ESul LVer
'Improved Ricard' (Z/D) WFib
'Improved Rubin' (Z/D) LVer
'Inca' (R) SDen
incrassatum GCHN
'Ingres' (I/D) ECtt IHos
inquinans GCHN
'Ione' (Z/D) LVer
'Ipswich Town' (Dw/D) ESul
'Irene' (Z/D) LTho LVer WFib
'Irene Cal' (Z/D) SKen
'Irene Corsair' (Z/D) SKen
'Irene Hardy' (Z/D) LVer
'Irene La Jolle' (Z/D) SKen
'Irene Lollipop' (Z/D) SKen
'Isaac Middleton' (Z) LVer
¶ 'Isaac Read' (Dw) SBro
'Isidel' (I/D) MSmi SKen WFib
'Isobel Gamble' (Z/D) LTho LVer SKen
'Italian Gem' (I) SKen
'Ivalo' (Z/D) IHos LVer MWhe SKen WFib
'Ivory Snow' (Z/D/V) LTho SKen
'Jacey' (Z/D) LVer SDen SKen
'Jack Cox' (Dw/D) LVer
'Jack of Hearts' (I) LVer
'Jack Read' (Dw) ERea ESul SBro
'Jack Wood' (Z/D) LTho
'Jackie's Gem' (I/D) MWhe
'Jacky Gauld' (I/D) IHos LVer MBri MWhe SKen
'Jacqueline' (Z/D) LVer SDen SKen
'Jan Portas' (Min/C) MWhe

'Jane Biggin' (Dw/D/C) CCla ESul LTho LVer MWhe SBro SKen SOld
'Jane Shoulder' (Min) SBro SDen
'Janet Kerrigan' (Min/D) ESul SBro WEas WFib
¶ 'Jasmine' (R) CCla
'Jaunty' (Min/D) LVer SBro SDen
¶ 'Jay' (Dw) SBro
'Jayne' (Min/D) SBro
'Jayne Eyre' (Min/D) ESul LTho LVer MWhe SBro SDen WFib
'Jean Beatty' (Dw/D) LVer
'Jean Oberle' (Z/D) SDen SKen
¶ 'Jean Viaud' (Z/D) LVer
'Jeanne d'Arc' (I/D) SKen WFib
'Jenifer' (Min) ESul SBro SDen
'Jenifer Read' (Dw) ERea ESul LTho SBro
'Jessel's Unique' (U) LVer SDen
'Jewel' (Z/D) SDen
'Jeweltone' (Z/D) WFib
'Jill Portas' (Z/C) LTho SKen
'Jim Field' (R) WFib
'Jim Small' (Z/C) LTho
'Jimmy Read' (Min) ERea ESul LTho LVer SBro
'Jim's Delight' (Z/C) LVer
'Joan Cashmore' (Z/D) LVer
'Joan Fairman' (R) WFib
'Joan Hayward' (Min) ESul SBro
'Joan Morf' (R) CCla LHop SKen WFib
'Joan of Arc' (I/D) See P. 'Jeanne d'Arc'
¶ 'Joan Shearman' (Min) SBro
'Joanna Pearce' (R) LTho SKen
¶ 'John's Dilys' LVer
¶ 'John's Pride' LVer
¶ 'Joseph Haydn' (R) CCla
'Joseph Paul' (R) SDen
'Joseph Warren' (I/D) LTho
'Joy' (R) LTho LVer WFib
'Joy Lucille' (Sc) CCla CSev ESul LTho SDen WFib
'Joy Thorp' (I) LTho
'Joyce Delamere' (Z/D/C) WFib
¶ 'Joyce Headley' (Dw/C) LVer SBro
'Joyden' LVer
¶ 'Joyful' (Min) SBro
'Jubel Parr' (Z/D) SDen
'Judith Thorp' (R) LTho LVer
¶ 'Judy Read' (Dw) SBro
'Julia' (R) LTho
'Julie' (A) ESul SBro SKen
'Julie Smith' (R) WFib
'Jupiter' (Min/D) LVer SBro WFib
'Just William' (Min/D/C) LTho SBro
'Kamahl' (R) WFib
¶ 'Kardinal' (Z/D) IHos LVer
¶ 'Karen' (Dw/C) SBro
'Karen Gamble Improved' (Z) LVer
'Karl Hagele' (Z/D) LTho LVer SKen WFib
karrooense 'Graham Rice' See P. ***quercifolium*** 'Grollie's Cream'
'Kathleen Gamble' (Z) LVer SKen
¶ 'Kathleen Gamble Improved' (Z) LVer
'Kathleen Mott' (Z/C) WFib
'Kathryn' (Min) ESul
'Kathryn Portas' (Z/V) SKen
'Kayleigh West' (Min) SDen
'Keepsake' (Dw/D) ESul LTho LVer SBro WFib
'Keith Vernon' (Fr/D) LTho LVer
¶ 'Kelvedon Beauty' (Min) SBro
¶ 'Ken Salmon' (DW/D) SBro
'Kerensa' (Min/D) ESul SBro SKen
'Kershy' (Min) ESul SBro
'Kesgrave' (Min/D) ESul LVer SBro
'Kettle Baston' (A) ESul LTho LVer MWhe SBro
'King Edmund' (R) SDen
'King of Balcon' See P. 'Roi des Balcons Rose'
'King of Denmark' (Z/D) LTho LVer SDen SKen WFib
'Kingswood' (Z) SDen
'Kirton' (Min/D) ESul SBro
§ 'Kleine Liebling' (Min) CSev LHop LTho MWhe SBro SKen
¶ 'Koora' (Min/D) SBro
¶ 'Kosset' (Min/D) SBro
'Krista' (Min/D) ESul LVer SBro SDen WFib
'Kyra' (Min/D) ESul LVer SBro WFib
'L E Wharton' (Z) SDen SKen
'La France' (I/D) LTho LVer MBri MSmi MWhe SDen SKen SOld WEas WFib
'La Jolla' (Z/D) SDen
'La Paloma' (R) SKen WEas
'Lachskönigin' (I/D) IHos LVer MPen MSmi MWhe SKen SOld WFib
♦ 'Lady Churchill' SDen WFib
¶ 'Lady Cullum' (Z/C/V) MWhe
'Lady Ilchester' (Z/D) LVer SDen SKen WFib
¶ 'Lady Lexington' (I) SKen
'Lady Mary' (Sc) CCla LVer SDen WFib
'Lady Mavis Pilkington' (Z/D) LTho
'Lady Plymouth' (Sc/V) CCla CSpe ESul IHos LHop LTho LVer MWhe NRoo NSty SDen SKen SOld WEas WFib WHer WPer
§ 'Lady Scarborough' (Sc) CCla SKen WFib
¶ 'Lakeland' (I) SBro
'Lamorna' (R) SKen
'Langley' (R) CCla MPen SDen
'Lanham Royal' (Min/D) LTho
'Lark' (Min/D) ESul SBro
N 'Lass o' Gowrie' (Z/V) CCla LTho LVer MWhe SDen SKen WFib
¶ 'Lass O'Gowrie' (American) (Z/V) WFib
'Laura' (Z) CCla
'Lauripen' (Z/D) WFib
'Lavender Grand Slam' (R) IHos LTho LVer SDen SKen SOld WFib
'Lavender Mini Cascade' See P. 'Lila Mini Cascade
'Lavender Sensation' (R) WFib
'Layham' (Dw/D) ESul SBro
'Layton's White' (Z/D) LVer SKen

'Le Lutin' (Z/D)	WFib
¶ 'Legende' (R)	CCla
'Lemon Fancy' (Sc)	CCla IHos LVer MWhe SDen WFib
¶ 'Lemore' (Min/D)	SBro
'Len Chandler' (Min)	ESul SBro SDen
'Leo' (Min)	ESul SBro
'Leonie Holbrow' (Min)	ESul SBro
'Leopard' (I/D)	SKen
'Lerchenmuller' (Z/D)	LTho LVer
¶ 'Lesando' (Z)	LTho
'Leslie Judd' (R)	WFib
'Leslie Salmon' (Min/C)	MWhe SBro
'Letita' (A)	ESul
'Leucht-Cascade'	See P. 'Decora Rouge'
¶ 'Levington' (Min/D)	SBro
'Lila Mini Cascade' (I)	CCla ESul LTho MWhe
'Lilac Cascade'	See P. 'Roi des Balcons Lilas'
'Lilac Domino'	See P. 'Telston's Prima'
'Lilac Gem' (Min/I/D)	IHos LTho LVer MWhe SDen SKen SOld WFib
'Lilac Gemma' (R)	LTho
¶ 'Lilac Mini Cascade' (I)	SBro
'Lilac Ricard' (Z/D)	WFib
'Lili Marlene' (I)	SKen
¶ 'Lilian' (Dw)	LVer SBro
'Lilian Pottinger' (Sc)	CCla LTho LVer SDen SKen WFib WHer
'Lilian Woodberry' (Z)	WFib
'Limoneum' (Sc)	CCla LTho LVer SDen SKen WFib WPer
'Lin Davis' (Z/C)	WFib
'Linda' (R)	LTho
'Lindy Portas' (I/D)	LTho SKen
'Lisa' (Min/C)	ESul SBro
'Little Alice' (Dw/D)	LTho SBro WFib
'Little Blakenham' (A)	ESul SBro
¶ 'Little Dandy'	LHop
'Little Fe Fine' (Min)	ESul SBro
'Little Gem' (Sc)	CCla LVer SDen
¶ 'Little John' (Min/D)	SBro
'Little Love' (A)	SBro SKen
'Little Margaret' (Min/V)	ESul LTho SBro SDen
¶ 'Little Primular' (Min)	SBro
'Little Trot' (Z/V)	SBro WFib
'Lively Lady' (Dw/C)	ESul LTho SBro SDen
'Liverbird' (I)	See P. 'Harlequin Miss Liver Bird'
lobatum	GCHN
'Lollipop' (Z/D)	SDen WFib
'Lord Baden Powell' (I/D)	See P. 'Colonel Baden Powell'
'Lord Bute' (R)	CBos LVer SMrm WEas
'Lord de Ramsey'	WPer
'Lorelei' (Z/D)	LVer WFib
'Loretta' (Dw)	ESul
'Lorna' (Dw/D)	ESul
'Lorraine' (Dw)	ESul SBro
'Louise' (Min)	ESul SBro
'Love Song' (Dw/V)	LTho
¶ 'Love Story'	SBro
'Loveliness' (Z)	SDen
* 'Loverly' (Min/D)	ESul SBro
'Lowood' (R)	MPen WFib
'Lucilla' (Min)	ESul SDen
'Lucinda' (Min)	ESul SBro
¶ 'Lucy' (Min)	ESul SBro
'Lucy Gunnet' (Z/D/V)	MWhe
'Luscious' (Min)	ESul
'Lustre' (R)	WFib
'Luz del Dio' (R)	WFib
'Lyric' (Min/D)	ESul LTho LVer SBro WFib
'L'Elegante' (I/V)	CSpe IHos LTho LVer MBri MSmi MWhe SDen SKen SOld WEas WFib
'L'Enfer' (Min/C)	See P. 'Mephistopheles'
I 'M A F F' (Min)	SBro
'M J Cole' (I/D)	WFib
'Mabel Grey' (Sc)	CCla CSev CSpe ESul IHos LTho LVer MWhe SDen SKen WEas WFib WHer WPer
'Madame Butterfly' (Z/D/V)	LTho MWhe SDen SKen SOld
'Madame Crousse' (I/D)	LVer SDen WEas WFib
'Madame Dubarry' (Z)	WFib
'Madame Fournier' (Min/C)	ESul SBro
♦ 'Madame Guinier'	See P. 'Charle Gounod'
'Madame Hibbault' (Z)	SKen
'Madame Irene' (Z/D)	MPen
'Madame Layal' (A)	CSpe ESul LVer SBro SDen SKen WFib
♦ 'Madame Margot'	See P. 'Hederinum Variegatum'
'Madame Nonin' (Sc)	LVer SDen SMrm WFib
'Madame Recamier' (Z/D)	WFib
'Madame Salleron' (Min/V)	LHil LVer MPar SKen
'Madame Thibaut' (Z/D)	WFib
'Madeline Crozy'	WEas
'Madge Hill' (Min)	ESul SBro WFib
'Magaluf' (I/D/V)	LTho LVer WFib
'Magda' (Z/D)	LVer
'Magic Lantern' (Z/C)	IHos LVer MWhe SKen
'Magic Moments' (R)	WFib
'Magnum' (R)	WFib
¶ 'Mahogany' (I/D)	MSmi
'Maid of Honour' (Min)	ESul SBro SDen
'Mairi' (A)	SBro SKen
'Maloja' (Z)	SDen SKen
'Mamie' (Z/D)	LVer SDen SKen
'Mangles' Variegated' (Z/V)	SDen
'Manta' (Min)	SBro
'Mantilla' (Min)	SBro SKen
'Manx Maid' (A)	ESul LVer SBro SDen SKen WFib
♦ 'Marble Sunset'	See P. 'Wood's Surprise'
§ 'Maréchal MacMahon' (Z/C)	LVer SDen SKen
'Margaret Bryan' (Z/C)	LTho SKen
'Margaret Pearce' (R)	SDen WFib
'Margaret Salvidge' (R)	LTho SDen WFib

'Margery Stimpson' (Min/D)	ESul LVer SBro SDen WFib
'Maria Wilkes' (Z/D)	WFib
'Marie Rober' (R)	SKen WFib
§ 'Marie Vogel' (R)	WFib
'Marion' (Min)	ESul SBro
'Mariquita' (R)	WFib
'Marktbeherrscher' (Z/D)	WFib
'Marmalade' (Dw/D)	ESul LTho LVer MWhe SBro SDen WFib
'Martin Parrett' (Min/D)	ESul LVer SBro
'Mary Ellen Tanner' (Min/D)	ESul SBro
'Mary Godwin' (Z)	WFib
'Mary Read' (Min)	ERea ESul SBro
'Mary Webster' (Min)	SBro
¶ 'Masquerade' (R)	SBro
'Masterpiece' (Z/D/C)	ESul LTho SDen SKen
'Mataranka' (Min/D/C/V)	MWhe
¶ 'Maureen' (Min)	SBro
'Mauve Beauty' (I/D)	IHos LTho LVer SKen WFib
'Mauve Duet' (A)	ESul SBro
'Maxime Kovalevski' (Z)	WFib
'May Magic' (R)	WFib
'Medallion' (Z/C)	LTho SDen SKen WFib
¶ 'Meditation' (Dw)	SBro
'Medley' (Min/D)	ESul LVer MWhe SBro WFib
¶ 'Meill Jamison' (Min)	SKen
'Melanie' (Min/D)	ESul LVer SBro
I 'Melissa' (Min)	CSpe ESul MPen SBro WEas
¶ 'Memento' (Min/D)	SBro SKen
'Memories' (Z/D)	LVer
'Mendip' (R)	SKen WFib
§ 'Mephistopheles' (Min/C)	ESul IHos SBro
'Mere Casino' (Z)	LTho
'Mere Greeting' (Z/D)	MWhe
'Mere Seville' (Z)	LTho
'Merry-Go-Round' (Z/C/V)	ESul LTho WFib
'Mexican Beauty' (I)	LVer MWhe SDen SKen WFib
'Mexicanerin'	See P. 'Rouletta'
¶ 'Mia' (Min/D)	SBro
'Michelle' (Min/C)	SBro WFib
'Michelle West' (Min)	SDen
'Mickey' (R)	CCla
'Mikado' (R)	CCla
'Milden' (Z/C)	ESul LVer SBro
'Milkmaid' (Min)	SBro WFib
'Mill Purple' (I)	MWhe
'Mill Wine' (I/D)	MWhe
¶ 'Millbern Clover'	MWhe
'Millbern Engagement' (Min/D)	MWhe
¶ 'Millbern Sharna'	MWhe
'Millfield Gem' (I/D)	LTho LVer SDen SKen WFib
'Millfield Rose' (I/D)	IHos LTho LVer MWhe SDen SKen
'Millie' (Z/D)	LVer WFib
'Mimi' (Min/D)	ESul SBro
Minipel	See P. PAC Minipel
'Mini-Czech' (Min/St)	LVer SBro
'Minstrel Boy' (R)	LTho WFib
'Minx' (Min/D)	LTho LVer SBro WFib
'Miranda' (Dw)	ESul SBro
♦ 'Miriam Basey'	See P. 'Dwarf Miriam Baisey'
'Miss Australia' (R/V)	CCla SKen WFib
'Miss Burdett Coutts' (Z/V)	ESul IHos LTho LVer
¶ 'Miss Muffett' (Min/D)	SBro
¶ 'Miss Prim' (Min)	SBro
'Miss Wackles' (Min/D)	ESul LVer SBro SDen WFib
'Misty' (Z)	CCla SBro
¶ 'Mitzi' (Min)	SBro
¶ 'Mixed Blessings' (Min/C)	SBro
'Modesty' (Z/D)	LVer SDen SKen WEas WFib
'Modigliani' (R)	SKen
'Mollie' (R)	SKen WFib
¶ 'Monarch' (Dw/V)	SBro
'Monica Bennett' (Dw)	ESul SBro SDen SKen WEas
'Monkwood Delight' (R)	SDen
'Monkwood Rhapsody' (R)	SOld
'Monsal Dale' (Dw/D/C)	ESul LTho LVer SKen
'Mont Blanc' (Z/V)	LTho MWhe SBro WFib
'Monty' (I/D)	WFib
'Moon Maiden' (A)	LTho SBro WFib
'Moor' (Min/D)	ESul LVer SBro
¶ 'Moppet' (Min/D)	SBro
'More Mischief' (Dw/Ca/D)	ESul
'Morello' (R)	WFib
'Morning Cloud' (Min/D)	SBro
'Morning Sunrise' (Min/V)	ESul SBro
'Morval' (Dw/C)	CCla ESul LTho LVer MWhe SBro SKen SOld WFib
'Morwenna' (R)	SDen WFib
¶ 'Mountie' (Dw)	SBro
'Mozart' (R)	CCla
'Mr Everaarts' (Dw/D)	ESul LVer MWhe WEas WFib
'Mr Henry Cox' (Z/V)	IHos LTho LVer MWhe SKen SOld WFib
¶ 'Mr Pickwick' (Dw)	SBro
'Mr Ritson' (Min)	ESul SBro
'Mr Wren' (Z)	IHos LHop LVer MWhe SDen SKen SMrm WFib
'Mrs Cannell' (Z)	SKen
'Mrs Dumbrill' (A)	ESul SDen
'Mrs Farren' (Z/V)	SKen WFib
'Mrs G H Smith (A)	CSpe ESul LTho SBro SDen SKen SOld
'Mrs G More' (R)	SOld WFib
'Mrs J C Mappin' (Z/V)	SDen SKen
'Mrs Kingsbury' (U)	SKen WEas WPer
'Mrs Kingsley'	See P. 'Mrs Kingsbury'
'Mrs Lawrence' (Z/D)	SDen SKen WFib
'Mrs Margaret Thorp' (R)	LTho
'Mrs Martin' (I)	WFib
'Mrs Mayne'	WEas

Name	Suppliers
'Mrs Parker' (Z/V)	CCla IHos LVer MWhe SDen SKen WFib WPer
'Mrs Pat' (Min/St/C)	ESul LTho LVer MWhe SBro
'Mrs Pollock' (Z/V)	CCla LTho LVer MWhe NRoo SDen SKen WFib
'Mrs Quilter' (Z/C)	CCla LTho LVer MWhe SDen SKen WFib WPer
'Mrs Salter Bevis' (Z/Ca/D)	ESul LVer SDen WFib
'Mrs Strang ' (Z/D/V)	LTho LVer SKen SOld WEas
'Mrs Tarrant' (Z/D)	WFib
'Mrs W A R Clifton' (I/D)	SDen SKen WFib
multicaule multicaule	GCHN
'Music Man' (R)	WFib
'Mustang'	IHos
'Mutzel' (I/V)	LTho
¶ 'My Choice' (R)	CCla
myrrhifolium coriandrifolium	GCHN
'Nacton' (Min)	ESul LVer SBro
'Nadine' (Dw/D/C)	SBro WFib
'Nan Greeves' (Z/V)	SDen
'Nancy Grey' (Min)	ESul SBro WFib
'Nancy Hiden' (R)	MPen WFib
'Naomi' (R)	CCla
'Naughton' (Min)	ESul SBro
'Naunton Velvet' (R)	WFib
'Naunton Windmill' (R)	WFib
'Nedging Tye' (A)	ESul LTho LVer SBro
'Needham Market' (A)	CSpe ESul LTho SBro
'Neene' (Dw)	ESul MWhe SBro
¶ 'Nella' (Min)	SBro
'Nellie' (R)	SKen
'Neon Fiat' (Z/D)	WFib
'Nervosum' (Sc)	ESul
'New Life' (Z)	ESul MWhe SKen
'Nicholas Purple' (R)	LTho
¶ 'Nicor Star' (Min)	SBro
¶ 'Night and Day' (Dw)	SBro
'Nimrod' (R)	LTho
'Nina West' (Z)	SDen
'Noche' (R)	MPen WFib
'Noel' (Z/Ca/D)	LVer SDen WFib
'Noele Gordon' (Z/D)	WFib
'Nono' (I)	WFib
'Northern Lights' (R)	LTho
'Notting Hill Beauty' (Z)	SKen
'Nuhulunbuy' (R)	LTho WFib
'Obergarten' (Z/D)	WFib
'Occold Embers' (Dw/D/C)	CCla ESul LTho LVer SBro SOld
'Occold Lagoon' (Dw/D)	CCla ESul LTho LVer SBro SDen SKen
'Occold Orange Tip' (Min/D)	SBro
'Occold Profusion' (Min/D)	ESul LVer SBro
'Occold Ruby' (Dw/C)	LVer SBro
'Occold Shield' (Dw/D/C)	ESul LTho LVer SBro
'Occold Surprise' (Min/D)	ESul SBro
'Occold Tangerine' (Dw)	ESul SBro
'Occold Volcano' (Dw/D)	ESul LTho SBro
odoratissimum (Sc)	CCla GPoy IHos LTho LVer MWhe NSty SDen SKen WEas WFib
– ***variegatum*** (Sc)	WEas
'Offton' (Dw)	ESul SBro
'Old Spice' (Sc/V)	WFib
'Olga' (R)	CCla IHos MPen SKen
'Olympia' (Z/D)	WFib
'Onnalee' (Dw)	ESul SBro
'Orange' (Z/St)	SDen
'Orange Glow' (Dw/D)	LVer SBro
'Orange Imp' (Dw/D)	SBro
'Orange Ricard' (Z/D)	LVer MWhe SDen SKen SOld WFib
'Orange River' (Dw/D)	ESul MWhe SBro SKen
'Orangeade' (Dw/D)	LTho SKen
'Orangesonne' (Z/D)	SDen WFib
'Orchid Paloma' (Dw/D)	ESul LTho LVer SBro
'Orion' (Min/D)	ESul LTho LVer MWhe SBro SDen SKen WFib
¶ 'Orwell' (Min)	SBro
¶ 'Ostergruss' (R)	SDen
¶ 'Otley' (Min)	SBro
¶ 'Oyster Maid' (Min)	SBro
PAC Isobel ® (Z)	LTho
¶ PAC Minipel Karminrot ® (Dw)	SBro
PAC Minipel Orange ® (Dw)	SBro
* PAC Minipel Red ® (Dw)	SBro
¶ PAC Minipel Rosa ® (Dw)	SBro
PAC Minipel Scharlach ® (Dw)	ESul SBro
PAC Pearl Necklace ® (Z)	LTho
PAC Purpurball ® (Z/D)	LTho SKen SOld
PAC Rosepen ® (Z)	LTho
PAC Velvet ® (I)	LTho
'Paddie' (Min)	ESul SBro
'Pagoda' (Z/St/D)	ESul LVer SBro SDen SKen
'Paisley Red' (Z/D)	LTho
'Palais' (Z/D)	SKen WFib
'Pamela Underwood' (R)	WFib
panduriforme	GCHN WFib
¶ ***papilionaceum***	CHEx
¶ 'Paradise Moon' (Min/D)	SBro
'Parasol' (R)	WFib
'Parisienne' (R)	SDen
'Party Dress' (Z/D)	MWhe SDen SKen WEas WFib
'Pascal' (Z)	SKen
'Patience' (Z/D)	IHos LVer SKen WFib
'Paton's Unique' (U/Sc)	CCla IHos LHop LVer SDen SKen SOld WEas WFib
'Patricia Andrea' (T)	LTho LVer SDen SOld
'Patricia Read' (Min)	ERea ESul LTho SBro
'Patsy 'Q'' (Z/C)	IHos LTho SKen
patulum	GCHN
'Paul Crampel' (Z)	LTho LVer WFib

'Paul Gotz' (Z)	SKen
'Paul Humphries' (Z/D)	MPen WFib
'Paul West' (Min/D)	SBro SDen
'Pauline' (Min/D)	ESul LVer MWhe SBro SDen
'Pavilion' (Min)	LTho SBro
'Peace' (Min/C)	ESul LVer SBro WFib
'Peace Palace' (Dw)	ESul SBro
'Pearl Brocade' (R)	WFib
'Pearl Eclipse' (I)	SDen SKen
'Pearly Queen' (Min/D)	LVer SBro
'Pegasus' (Min)	LVer SBro
¶ 'Peggy Franklin' (Min)	SBro
'Peggy Sue' (R)	LTho SDen
'Peggy West' (Min/D/C)	SBro SDen
PELFI Alba ® (Z/D)	LTho WFib
PELFI Barock ® (I)	LTho
¶ PELFI Belladonna ®	IHos
PELFI Blues ® ® (Z/D)	CCla IHos LTho WFib
¶ PELFI Brun ® (Z)	CSpe
¶ PELFI Butterfly ®	IHos
PELFI Cabaret ® (Z/D)	IHos LTho MBri WFib
PELFI Casino ® (Z/D)	IHos WFib
PELFI Champagne ® (Z)	CCla LTho
¶ PELFI Charleston ® (Z)	CCla IHos
PELFI Coco-Rico ® (I)	SDen WFib
PELFI Columbia ® (Z/Sc)	IHos LTho
PELFI Disco ® (Z/D)	CCla IHos LTho WFib
PELFI Fidelio ® (Z/D)	CCla IHos LTho WFib
PELFI Flirt ® (Min)	ESul MBri WFib
PELFI Flirtpel ® (Z/D)	WFib
PELFI Fortuna ® (Z)	LTho
PELFI Gemini ® (Z/St)	IHos LTho
PELFI Gloria ® (Z/D)	LTho WFib
¶ PELFI Jazz ®	CCla IHos
PELFI Leucht-Cascade ®	See P. 'Decora Rouge'
PELFI Lila Compakt-Cascade ®	See P. 'Decora Lilas'
PELFI Mars ® (Z/D)	LTho WFib
PELFI Polka ® (Z/D)	LTho WFib
PELFI Rio ® (Z)	LTho WFib
¶ PELFI Rokoko ®	IHos
PELFI Romy ® (I)	WFib
PELFI Rosais ® (I/D)	LTho WFib
PELFI Rote Mini-Cascade ®	See P. 'Rote Mini-Cascade'
PELFI Satellite ® (Z/St)	IHos LTho
PELFI Schöne Helena ® (Z/D)	CCla LTho WFib
PELFI Solidor ® (I)	CSut LTho WFib
PELFI Tango ® (Z/D)	IHos LTho WFib
PELFI Tutti Frutti ® (Z)	IHos LTho WFib
PELFI Twist ® (Z/I)	LTho WFib
PELFI Vulcan ® (Z/D)	IHos LTho WFib
PELFI Waltz ® (Z)	LTho
peltatum	SDen
'Penny' (Z/D)	LTho LVer MWhe SDen SKen WFib
'Penny Serenade' (Dw/C)	LTho SKen
'Percival' (Dw/D)	LVer SBro SDen SOld
'Perfect' (Z)	SDen SKen
'Persian Queen' (R)	WFib
'Petals' (Z/V)	LVer SKen
¶ 'Peter Godwin' (R)	LTho
'Peter Read' (Dw/D)	ERea ESul SBro
'Petit Pierre' (Dw)	See P. 'Kleine Liebling'
'Petite Blanche' (Dw/D)	SBro WFib
'Petronella' (Z/D)	LTho
'Philomel' (I/D)	SKen WFib
'Phlox New Life' (Z)	ESul SBro
'Phyllis Mary' (R)	WFib
'Phyllis Read' (Min)	ERea ESul LTho LVer MWhe SBro WFib
'Phyllis Richardson' (R/D)	SDen WFib
'Picardy' (Z/D)	LVer
Picasso ®	IHos
'Pickaninny' (Min)	ESul SBro
'Pier Head' (Z)	LTho
'Pin Mill' (Min/D)	ESul LVer SBro
'Pink Aurore' (V)	LVer
'Pink Bonanza' (R)	CCla LTho SDen SKen SOld WFib
'Pink Bouquet' (R)	WFib
-- (Z/D)	IHos LVer
'Pink Carnation' (I/D)	IHos SKen
'Pink Cascade' (I)	See P. 'Roi des Balcons Rose'
'Pink Champagne' (Sc)	ESul SDen WFib WHer
'Pink Cloud' (Z/D)	LVer
'Pink Countess Mariza' (Z)	SDen SKen
'Pink Floral Cascade' (Fr/D)	LTho
'Pink Fondant' (Min/D)	ESul LTho SBro
'Pink Gay Baby' (I)	See P. 'Sugar Baby'
¶ 'Pink Golden Ears' (Dw/St/C)	SBro
¶ 'Pink Golden Harry Hieover' (Z/C)	SBro
-- (Z/C)	ESul LVer SBro SDen
'Pink Grace Wells' (Min)	ESul SBro
'Pink Happy Thought' (Z/V)	LTho SKen SOld WFib
'Pink Ice' (Min/D)	ESul LTho LVer SBro
¶ 'Pink Kewense' (Min)	LVer SBro
'Pink Lady' (Z)	LVer
'Pink Lady Harold' (Z)	SDen
¶ 'Pink Lively Lady' (Dw/C)	SBro
'Pink Margaret Pearce' (R)	LTho SDen
'Pink Mini Cascade'	See P. 'Rose Mini Cascade'
'Pink Moon'	MSmi
'Pink Pandora' (T)	LTho
'Pink Rambler' (Z/D)	MPen MWhe SKen SOld WFib
'Pink Raspail' (Z/D)	WFib
'Pink Rosebud' (Z/D)	IHos SDen SKen WFib
¶ 'Pink Satisfaction' (Z)	CCla IHos
'Pink Slam' (R)	WFib
¶ 'Pink Snow' (Min/D)	SBro
'Pink Splash' (Min/D)	SBro SDen

¶ 'Pink Splendour' (Min/D)	SBro
'Pixie' (Dw)	ESul SBro
'Platinum' (Z/V)	SBro
¶ 'Playboy Blush' (Dw)	SBro
¶ 'Playboy Candy' (Dw)	SBro
¶ 'Playboy Cerise' (Dw)	SBro
¶ 'Playboy Coral' (Dw)	SBro
¶ 'Playboy Coral Orange' (Dw)	SBro
¶ 'Playboy Mauve' (Dw)	SBro
¶ 'Playboy Powder Pink' (Dw)	SBro
¶ 'Playboy Salmon' (Dw)	SBro
¶ 'Playboy Salmon Eyed' (Dw)	SBro
¶ 'Playboy Scarlet' (Dw)	SBro
¶ 'Playboy White' (Dw)	SBro
'Playford' (Dw)	ESul SBro
'Playmate' (Min/St)	LTho LVer SBro SKen
'Plenty' (Z/D)	WFib
'Plum Rambler' (Z/D)	LVer SKen WFib
'Poetesse' (A)	LTho
¶ 'Polaris' (Min)	SBro
'Polka' (U)	CCla LTho
'Pompeii' (R)	CCla SMrm WFib
'Portsmouth' (R)	LVer
'Potpourri' (Min)	SBro SKen
Prelude ® (Z)	CCla
'Presto' (Min)	CSpe ESul SBro
'Preston Park' (Z/C)	SKen WFib
'Pride of the West' (Z)	SKen
'Prim' (Min/D)	ESul LVer
'Prince Harry' (I)	SKen
'Prince of Orange' (Sc)	CCla CSev GPoy IHos LTho LVer NSty SDen SKen WEas WFib WHer WPer
'Prince of Wales' (Z)	WFib
¶ 'Princess Alexandra' (R)	WFib
– – (Z/D/V)	LTho LVer MWhe SDen SKen WFib
¶ 'Princess Anne' (Z)	CSpe
'Princess Josephine' (R)	LTho WFib
'Princess Margaretha' (Z)	LVer MWhe
'Princess of Balcon' (I)	See P. 'Roi des Balcons Lilas'
'Princess Pink' (Z)	LVer SKen
'Princess Virginia' (R/V)	LTho
'Professor Eckman' (R)	WFib
'Promenade' (Z/D)	WFib
'Prudence' (Min)	SBro SKen
pulverulentum	GCHN
punctatum	GCHN
'Purple Emperor' (R)	WFib
'Purple Gem' (Min)	ESul
'Purple Light'	See P. 'Purple Gem'
'Purple Orchid' (R)	LTho
¶ 'Purple Pat' (Min/D)	SBro
'Purple Rambler' (Z/D)	MWhe
'Purple Unique' (U/Sc)	CCla IHos LVer SDen SKen WFib
'Pygmalion' (Z/D/V)	WFib
'Quakermaid' (Min)	ESul SBro
'Quantock' (R)	WFib
'Queen Ingrid' (Z)	IHos LVer
'Queen of Denmark' (Z/D)	LVer SDen SKen WFib
'Queen of Hearts' (I/D)	LVer WFib
N ***quercifolium*** (Sc)	CSev ESul GPoy LTho NSty SDen SKen SSpi WEas
– 'Fair Ellen'	See P. 'Fair Ellen'
§ – 'Grollic's Cream'	LHop
quinquelobatum	GCHN
'Rachel' (Min)	ESul SBro
'Rachel Fisher' (Z)	WFib
radens (Sc)	WFib
'Radiance' (Z/D)	WFib
'Radiant' (Z/D)	WFib
'Radio' (Z/D)	SDen
'Rads Star' (Z/St)	LTho
§ 'Radula' (Sc)	CCla ESul GCHN LTho SKen WFib WPer
¶ 'Radula group' (Sc)	CCla LVer MWhe SDen
'Ragamuffin' (Min/D)	LTho
'Rager's Pink' (Dw/D)	ESul LVer SBro
'Rager's Star' (Min)	LVer SBro
rapaceum	GCHN
'Rapture' (R)	WEas WFib
'Raspberry Parfait' (R)	SDen
¶ 'Raspberry Ripple' (A)	SBro
'Raspberry Sundae' (R)	LVer
'Raviro' (I)	MSmi WFib
'Ray Coughlin' (Z/D/C)	WFib
'Raydon' (Min)	ESul SBro
¶ 'Rebecca' (Min/D)	LVer SBro
– (R)	LVer
'Red Admiral' (Min/D/V)	ESul SBro SKen
§ 'Red Black Vesuvius' (Min/C)	CCla CSpe ESul LTho LVer MWhe NRoo SDen SKen WEas WFib
¶ 'Red Brooks Barnes' (Dw/C)	SBro
'Red Cascade' (I)	MWhe SKen
¶ 'Red Comet' (Min)	SBro
'Red Dollar' (Z/C)	LVer
¶ 'Red Dwarf' (Min/D)	SBro
¶ 'Red Fox' (Min)	SBro
'Red Galilee' (I/D)	MWhe SKen
'Red Gem' (Min)	ESul
¶ 'Red Ice' (Min/D)	SBro
¶ – – (Z)	LTho
'Red Light' (Z/D)	WFib
'Red Magic Lantern' (Z/C)	LVer SKen
'Red Mini Cascade' (I)	See P. 'Rote Mini-Cascade'
'Red Pandora' (T)	LTho LVer
¶ 'Red Pearl' (Min)	SBro
'Red Rambler' (Z/D)	LVer MWhe SDen SKen WFib
¶ 'Red Satisfaction' (Z)	CCla IHos
'Red Spider' (Min/Ca/D)	CSpe ESul SBro
'Red Star' (Z)	LVer
'Red Startel' (Z/D)	LVer MWhe SKen
¶ 'Red Streak' (Min/Ca)	SBro
¶ 'Red Tiny Tim' (Min)	SBro

'Red Velvet' (R)	WFib
'Red Witch' (Dw/St)	CSpe ESul LVer SBro
'Redondo' (Min/D)	CCla CSpe ESul LVer MWhe SBro SDen WEas WFib
¶ 'Reg 'Q'' (Z/C)	SBro
¶ 'Regal Perchance'	SDen
'Regi' (I/D)	IHos LVer
'Regina' (Z/D)	LTho LVer SDen SKen SOld WFib
'Rembrandt' (R)	CCla LVer SDen SKen WEas WFib
'Renee Ross' (I/D)	LTho WFib
'Rhineland' (I)	SKen
'Rhodamant' (I/D)	WFib
'Rhodamine' (R)	SKen
'Rhodo' (R)	WFib
'Richard Key' (Z/D/V)	WFib
¶ 'Richard West' (I/D)	SDen
'Ric-Rac'	WEas
'Rietje van der Lee' (A)	ESul SBro
'Rigel' (Min/D)	ESul LVer MWhe SBro SKen WFib
'Rigi' (I)	LTho MBri MSmi SDen SKen WEas
¶ 'Rigoletta'	MWhe
'Rimfire' (R)	WFib
¶ 'Ringo Rose' (Z)	SKen
'Rio' (Z)	CCla
'Rio Grande' (I/D)	CSpe LTho LVer MWhe SDen SKen SOld WEas WFib
'Rita Brook' (Z/D)	WFib
'Rita Coughlin' (R)	WFib
'Rita Scheen' (A)	ESul LVer MWhe SBro SDen WFib
'Robbie Hare' (R)	WFib
'Robert Fish' (Z/C)	ESul SBro SDen
'Rober's Lavender' (Dw)	ESul LVer SBro
'Rober's Lemon Rose' (Sc)	CCla ESul LTho LVer SDen WFib WHer
¶ 'Rober's Salmon Coral' (Dw/D)	SBro
'Robinson Crusoe' (Dw/C)	WFib
rogersianum	See P. ***worcesterae***
'Rogue' (R)	LTho WFib
♦ 'Roi des Balcons' (I)	See P. 'Hederinum'
'Roi des Balcons Impérial' (I)	IHos LTho MWhe
§ 'Roi des Balcons Lilas' (I)	IHos LTho LVer MPen MWhe SKen WFib
'Roi des Balcons Rouge' (I)	LTho
'Roller's David' (I)	LVer
'Roller's Echo' (A)	LTho SBro
'Roller's Pathfinder' (I/V)	LTho
'Roller's Pioneer' (I/V)	LTho LVer SDen SKen
'Rollisson's Unique' (U)	LVer SDen SKen WFib
¶ 'Romance'	SBro
¶ 'Rosaleen' (Min)	SBro
'Rosalie' (Min)	ESul SBro
'Rosamunda' (Z/D)	WFib
'Roscobie' (Z/D)	SDen SKen
'Rose Bengal' (A)	ESul LVer NSty SDen SKen SMrm SOld WEas WFib WPer
'Rose Crousse' (I/D)	MWhe
'Rose Irene' (Z/D)	MWhe SDen WFib
'Rose Lady Lexington' (I/V)	LTho
'Rose Mini Cascade' (I)	CCla ESul LTho LVer MWhe SBro SDen
'Rose of Amsterdam' (Min/D)	LTho SBro
¶ 'Rose Silver Cascade'	LVer
'Rose Slam' (R)	SDen
¶ 'Rose Startel' (Z/St)	LVer
'Rosee Normande' (Z/D)	WFib
¶ 'Rosemarie'	MWhe
'Rosenpen' (Z/D)	WFib
'Rosette' (Dw)	SBro SKen WFib
'Rosina Read' (Dw)	ERea ESul LTho LVer SBro
'Rosita' (Dw/D)	LTho LVer SBro SDen
* 'Rosmaroy' (R)	LTho
* 'Rosseau' (Min)	SBro
¶ 'Rosy Dawn' (Min/D)	SBro
§ 'Rote Mini-Cascade' (I)	CCla IHos LTho LVer MWhe SBro SDen SKen SOld WFib
'Rotlieb' (Z/D)	WFib
'Rouge' (R)	SDen
'Rouletta' (I)	CSut IHos LTho LVer MPen MSmi MWhe SDen SKen SOld WEas WFib
'Rousillon' (R)	WFib
'Royal Ascot' (A)	LTho LVer
'Royal Blaze' (Z/V)	SDen SKen
'Royal Carpet' (Min/D)	ESul SBro
'Royal Fiat' (Z/D)	WFib
'Royal Norfolk' (Min/D)	ESul LTho LVer MWhe SBro SKen SOld WFib
'Royal Oak' (Sc)	CCla CSev ESul LVer MWhe WFib WHer WPer
§ 'Royal Purple' (Z/D)	SKen WFib
¶ 'Royal Sovereign' (Z/D/V)	LVer
'Royal Wedding' (R)	LTho
'Rubella' (Z/D)	WFib
'Ruben' (I/D)	LTho
'Rubin' (Z/D)	SKen
'Ruby' (Min/D)	SBro WFib
'Rushmere' (Dw/D)	ESul
¶ 'Rusty' (Dw/D/C)	SBro
'Ruth Bessley'	LVer
¶ 'Ryan Dollery' (Z)	SDen
'Ryecroft Pride' (Z/D)	WFib
'Sabrina' (Z/D)	CCla
'Sally Anne'	WEas
'Sally Read' (Dw/D)	ERea ESul LVer SBro
'Salmon Beauty' (Min/D)	NRoo SBro WFib
'Salmon Black Vesuvius' (Min/C)	SBro WEas
'Salmon Comet' (Min)	ESul SBro
'Salmon Grozser Garten' (Dw)	ESul
§ 'Salmon Irene' (Z/D)	MWhe SDen WFib

'Salmon Queen'	See P. 'Lachskönigin'
¶ 'Salmon Satifaction' (Z)	CCla
'Salmon Slam' (R)	LVer SDen WFib
'Salmon Startel' (Z/St/D)	LVer MWhe
'Saltford' (R)	WFib
'Sancho Panza' (Dec)	CSpe ESul LVer SBro SDen SKen SOld WFib
'Santa Maria' (Z/D)	LVer SDen SKen WFib
'Santa Paula' (I/D)	LVer MWhe SDen SKen
'Sante Fe' (Z/C)	SDen
¶ 'Sarah Mitchell' (Min)	SBro
'Sarkie' (Z/D)	LTho
'Sasha' (Min)	SBro WFib
'Saxifragoides'	GCHN SBro
'Scarlet Breakway' (Z)	MWhe
'Scarlet Crousse' (I/C)	WFib
'Scarlet Galilee' (I/D)	LVer
'Scarlet Pet' (U)	ESul MWhe
'Scarlet Pimpernel' (Z/D/V)	ESul SBro WFib
'Scarlet Rambler' (Z/D)	LVer MPen SKen SOld WFib
'Scarlet Unique' (U)	CCla LVer SDen SKen WFib
¶ 'Scarlett O'Hara' (Min)	SBro
'Schneekönigin' ('Snow Queen') (/I/D)	CSpe CSut ECtt IHos LTho
'Schöne Helena' (Z)	See P. PELFI Schöne Helena ®
x *schottii*	See P. x ***sanguineum***
'Schwarzwalderin' (I)	LVer
'Seeley's Pansy' (A)	CSpe ESul LTho SBro
'Sefton' (R)	LTho SKen
'Selby' (Z/D/C)	WFib
'Selina'	LVer SBro
'Semer' (Min)	ESul LVer SBro SKen
senecioides	GCHN
'Senorita' (R)	LVer
'Sensation' (Z)	SDen SKen
'Serena' (Min)	ESul SBro
¶ 'Serenade' (Z/D)	CCla
¶ 'Shalimar' (St)	CSpe
'Sharon' (Min/D)	ESul SBro
'Sharon Louise' (Min)	SDen
'Shaun Jacobs' (Min/D)	SBro SDen
'Shaunough' (Min)	ESul SBro
'Sheila' (Dw)	ESul LTho SBro
'Sheila Thorp' (Dw/D)	LTho SBro
'Shelley' (Dw)	ESul LVer SBro
'Shenandoah' (Min)	WFib
'Sheraton' (Min/D)	ESul MWhe SBro
'Shimmer' (Z/D)	IHos MWhe SKen SOld WFib
'Shiraz' (R)	SKen
'Shirley Anne' (Dw/D)	SBro SDen
'Shirley Ash' (A)	ESul SBro
'Shirley Maureen' (R)	LTho
'Shocking' (Z/D)	LVer
'Shotley' (Min)	ESul SBro
'Shrubland Pet' (U/Sc)	CCla LVer SDen SKen
¶ 'Silas Marner' (Dw)	SBro
'Silberlachs' (Z/D)	SDen WFib
'Silipen' (Z/D)	WFib
'Silver Kewense' (Dw/V)	ESul IHos LVer SBro SDen SKen SOld WFib
'Silver Wings' (Z/V)	LTho MWhe SDen
'Silvia' (R)	CCla
'Simon Portas' (I/D)	LTho LVer
'Simon Read' (Dw)	ERea ESul LTho LVer SBro
'Simplicity' (Z)	LVer
'Sir Arthur Hort' (I)	WFib
'Sister Teresa' (Z/D)	IHos LTho LVer SKen
'Skelly's Pride' (Z)	LVer SDen SKen WEas
'Skies of Italy' (Z/D/C)	LTho SDen
'Sleuring's Robin' (Min/D)	LVer SBro
¶ 'Small Fortune' (Dw)	SBro SKen
'Sneezy' (Min)	ESul SBro
'Snow Queen' (I)	See P. 'Schneekönigin'
'Snow White' (Min)	SBro
'Snowball' (Z/D)	SDen
¶ 'Snowdon' (Min)	SBro
'Snowdrift' (I/D)	LTho LVer WFib
'Snowflake' (Min)	ESul LVer SBro SDen WPer
'Snowmass' (Z/D)	LVer MWhe SKen
'Snowstorm' (Z)	SKen WFib
¶ 'Snowy Baby' (Min/D)	ESul LTho LVer SBro SDen SOld WFib
'Sofie'	See P. 'Deacon Rose'
'Solano' (R)	WFib
'Solent Sunrise' (Z/C)	LVer SDen
¶ 'Solent Waves' (R)	LTho
'Solferino' (A)	ESul LTho SBro SKen
'Somersham' (Min)	ESul SBro
'Something Special' (Z/D)	LTho LVer MWhe SDen SOld
'Sonata' (Dw/D)	LVer SBro
'Sophie Dumaresque' (Z/V)	LTho LVer SDen SKen SOld
'Sophie Koniger' (Z/D)	LVer WFib
'Sorcery' (Dw/C)	ESul IHos LVer MWhe SBro SKen
'South American Bronze' (R)	CCla LVer SDen SKen WFib WPer
'Southampton' (Z)	LTho
'Southern Belle' (Z/D)	SDen WFib
'Souvenir' (R)	LVer SDen
¶ 'Spanish Angel' (A)	LTho
¶ 'Sparkle' (Dw)	SBro
¶ 'Speckled Egg' (Dw)	SBro
¶ 'Speckled Hen' (Dw)	SBro
¶ 'Speckled Orange' (Dw)	SBro
'Speckles' (Z)	MWhe SBro
'Spellbound' (R)	WFib
'Spitfire' (Z/Ca/V)	ESul LVer SDen WFib
§ 'Splendide'	CSun SKen SMrm SSad WEas
¶ 'Sporwen' (Min)	SBro
'Spot-on-Bonanza' (R)	LTho SOld
'Spring Park' (A)	ESul LVer SBro SDen
'Springfield Black' (R)	LVer
'Springtime' (Z/D)	LVer MPen MWhe SDen SKen WFib
¶ 'Sprite' (Min/V)	SBro
'St Helen's Favourite' (Min)	ESul SBro
'Stadt Bern' (Z/C)	CCla IHos LVer MBri MWhe SKen WEas WFib
'Stanton Drew' (Z/D)	WFib
'Staplegrove Fancy' (Z)	SKen

'Star of Persia' (Z/Ca) LVer
¶ 'Starry Eyed' (Dw) SBro
'Stella Read' (Dw/D) ERea ESul LTho SBro
'Stellar Arctic Star' (Z/St/D) See P. 'Arctic Star'
'Stellar Cathay' (Z/St/D) LVer WFib
'Stellar Dawn Star' (Z/St) LVer SOld WFib
'Stellar Grenadier' (Z/St/D) See P. 'Grenadier'
§ -- (Z/St/D) SDen
'Stellar Hannaford Star' (Z/St/D) See P. 'Hannaford Star'
§ -- (Z/St) ESul SDen
'Stellar Ragtime' (Z/St/D) LTho LVer SDen
stenopetalum GCHN
'Stephen Read' (Min) ERea ESul LTho SBro
'Stewart Read' (Dw) ERea ESul LTho SBro
'Strawberry Sundae' (R) LVer MPen SDen WFib WPer
'Stuart Gamble' (Z/D) LVer
'Stutton' (Min) ESul SBro
sublignosum GCHN
'Suffolk Gold' (Min/C) SDen
§ 'Sugar Baby' (DwI) ESul IHos LTho LVer MBri MSmi MWhe SBro SDen SKen SOld WEas WFib
'Summer Cloud' (Z/D) LVer SDen SKen WFib
'Summer Idyll' WEas
'Sun Rocket' (Dw) ESul MWhe SBro WFib
'Sunbeam' (Dw/D) SBro
'Sunday's Child' WEas
'Sundridge Moonlight' (Z/C) LTho
'Sundridge Surprise' (Z) LTho
'Sunrise' (R) SDen SKen SOld WEas WFib
¶ 'Sunset' (Z) CCla
'Sunset Snow' (R) WFib
'Sunspot Petit Pierre' (Min/V) LTho LVer SBro SKen SOld
'Sunstar' (Min/D) CCla ESul LTho LVer SBro WFib
'Super Rose' (I) LVer MBri MSmi SDen SKen
'Supernova' (Min/D) ESul LVer
¶ - (Z/St/D) SBro
'Surcouf' (I) WFib
'Susan' (Dw) SBro WFib
'Susan Baldwin' See P. 'Salmon Kovalevski'
'Susan Jane' (Z/D) LVer
'Susan Payne' (Dw/D) ESul LVer SBro SDen
'Susan Pearce' (R) LVer SDen SKen
'Susan Read' (Dw) ERea ESul LTho SBro
¶ 'Susie' (Z/C) CCla
'Susie 'Q'' (Z/C) CCla ESul LTho LVer MWhe SBro SDen SKen
¶ 'Sussex Beauty' (Dw/D/V) LVer SBro
'Sussex Delight' (Min) LVer SBro SKen
¶ 'Sussex Gem' (Min) SBro SKen
¶ 'Sussex Jewel' (Min) SBro SKen
♦ 'Sussex Lace' See P. 'White Mesh'
¶ 'Sussex Surprise' (Dw/V) SBro
'Swan Song' (Z) LTho
'Swedish Angel' (A) LVer SBro SKen
'Sweet Mimosa' (Sc) CCla LVer SKen WFib
'Sweet Miriam' (Sc) LTho
'Sweet Sue' (Min) ESul LVer SBro
'Swilland' (A) ESul LTho LVer MWhe SBro
'Swing' (Z) CCla
'Sybil Bradshaw' (R) WFib
'Sybil Holmes' (I/D) IHos LTho LVer MBri MSmi MWhe SKen SOld WFib
'Sylvia Gale' (R) CCla WFib
'Sylvia Marie' (Dw/D) LTho LVer MWhe SKen
'Sylvia Mariza' IHos
¶ 'Tami' (Min) SBro
¶ 'Tamie' (Dw/D) SBro
'Tamie D' (Min) LTho SKen
'Tammy' (Dw/D) ESul LVer MWhe SBro WFib
'Tangerine' (Min/Ca/D) ESul WFib
¶ 'Tanya' (Min) SBro
'Tanzy' (Min) ESul SBro
'Tapestry' (Min/V) LTho WEas
'Tattingstone' (Min) ESul SBro
'Tattoo' (Min) LTho SBro
'Tavira' (I/D) CSut IHos LTho MSmi SDen SKen SOld WFib
'Ted Brooke' (Z/D) WFib
'Ted Dutton' (R) WFib
'Telstar' (Min/D) ESul LTho LVer SBro WFib
'Telston's Prima' (R) WFib
¶ 'Tenderly' (Dw/D) SBro
¶ 'Tenerife Magic' (MinI/D) SBro
'Terence Read' (Min) ERea ESul LTho LVer SBro
tetragonum EPad GCHN
'The Boar' (Fr) LVer WEas WHea WPer
§ 'The Crocodile' (I/D/V) IHos LTho LVer MWhe SDen SKen WEas WFib
♦ 'The Czar' WFib
'The Mary Rose' (R) LTho SDen
'The Prince' (Min) ESul SBro
'The Speaker' (Z/D) SDen SKen WFib
'Thomas Gerald' (Min/C) LTho SKen
'Tiberias' (I/D) WFib
'Tilly' (Min) ESul SBro
'Tim' (Min) ESul SBro
¶ 'Timmy Griffin' (Min) SBro
'Timothy Clifford' (Min/D) ESul LVer MWhe SBro SDen WFib
¶ 'Tiny Tim' SBro
'Tip Top Duet' (A) ESul LTho LVer MWhe SBro SDen SKen WFib
'Token' (Z) IHos LVer
'Tom Portas' (Dw/D) LTho LVer
¶ 'Tom Tit' (Dw) SBro
tomentosum (Sc) CHEx CSev CSpe GCHN GPla LHop LTho LVer MWhe NSty SDen SKen WEas WFib
– 'Chocolate' See P. 'Chocolate Peppermint'
¶ 'Tommays Delight' (R) LTho
tongaense GCHN
¶ 'Toni' (Min) SBro

'Tony' (Min)	ESul SBro
'Topscore' (Z/D)	SKen WFib
'Torento' (Sc)	CCla ESul LTho LVer SDen
¶ 'Tornado' (R)	LTho
'Tortoise Shell' (R)	WFib
'Toyon' (Z/D)	LVer SKen WFib
'Tracy' (Min/D)	LTho SBro
'Trautlieb' (Z/D)	WFib
'Treasure Chest' (Z/D)	LTho LVer SDen SKen
♦ ***tricolor***	See P. 'Splendide'
trifidum	GCHN
'Trimley' (Dw/D)	ESul SBro
'Trinket' (Min/D)	IHos SBro SKen
'Triomphe de Nancy' (Z/D)	WFib
triste	GCHN
'Trudie' (Dw)	CSpe ESul SBro SKen WFib
'Trulls Hatch' (Z/D)	LVer MWhe SDen SKen
¶ 'Trumps' (Min)	SBro
'Tu Tone' (Dw/D)	ESul
'Tuddenham' (Min/D)	ESul LTho LVer SBro
'Tuesday's Child' (Dw/C)	LTho SKen
'Tunias Perfecta' (R)	WFib
'Turkish Delight' (Dw/V)	ESul LTho LVer SOld
'Turtle's Surprise' (Z/D/V)	LVer SKen
'Turtle's White' (R)	SKen
'Tweedle-Dum' (Dw)	ESul MWhe
'Twinkle' (Min/D)	ESul LTho SBro WFib
'Tyabb Princess' (R)	WFib
§ 'Unique Aurore' (U)	LVer SKen WFib
'Urchin' (Min)	CSpe ESul LTho LVer SBro
'Ursula Key' (Z/V)	SKen WFib
'Vagabond' (R)	WFib
'Valanza' (A)	ESul SBro
'Valcandia' (Dw)	ESul SBro
'Valencia' (R)	WEas
'Valenciana' (R)	CCla WFib
'Valentin' (R)	CCla
'Valentina' (Dw/D)	ESul SBro
'Valerie' (Z/D)	CCla
'Vancouver Centennial' (Dw/St/C)	CCla LTho LVer SBro SOld
§ 'Variegated Clorinda' (Sc/V)	CCla WHer
'Variegated Fragrans'	See P. x ***fragrans*** 'Variegatum'
§ 'Variegated Kleine Liebling' (Min/V)	CSpe ESul LTho LVer SKen
'Variegated Madame Layal' (A/V)	LVer SBro
'Variegated Oak' (Sc/V)	LTho
'Variegated Petit Pierre'	See P. 'Variegated Kleine Liebling'
'Vasco da Gama' (Dw/D)	ESul SBro
'Velvet' (Z)	IHos
'Velvet Duet' (A)	ESul LTho LVer SBro SDen SKen
'Venus' (Dw/D)	LVer SBro
'Vera Dillon' (Z)	SKen WFib
'Vera Vernon' (Z/V)	LTho
'Verona' (Z/C)	LVer SDen SKen
'Veronica' (Z)	MPen MWhe SKen
* 'Vesuvius' (Min)	SBro WPer
'Vicky Claire' (R)	CCla LTho SDen SKen
'Vicky Town' (R)	SKen SOld WFib
'Victoria' (Z/D)	CCla
'Victoria Regina' (R)	WFib
'Vida' (Min)	ESul SBro
¶ 'Video Blush' (Min)	CSpe SBro
¶ 'Video Red' (Min)	SBro
¶ 'Video Rose' (Min)	SBro
¶ 'Video Salmon' (Min)	SBro
¶ 'Viking' (Min/D)	LVer SBro SKen
'Viking Red' (Z)	MWhe
'Village Hill Oak' (Sc)	ESul LVer
♦ 'Ville de Paris' (I)	See P. 'Hererinum'
'Vina' (Dw/D/C)	LTho LVer SKen WFib
♦ ***violareum***	See P. 'Splendide'
'Violet Lambton' (Z/V)	WFib
'Violetta' (Z/D)	CCla WFib
'Virginia' (R)	CCla IHos LTho MPen
'Virginia Ley' (Z)	SKen
viscosissimum	See P. ***glutinosum***
vitifolium	GCHN
'Vivat Regina' (Z/D)	MPen WFib
'Voodoo' (U)	LTho
'W H Heytman' (R)	WFib
'Wallace Fairman'	LVer
'Wallace's Pink' (Fr)	LTho
'Wallis Friesdorf' (Dw/D/C)	LVer MWhe SBro SOld
'Waltz' (Z)	CCla IHos
'Wantirna' (Z/V)	LVer
'Warrior' (Z/D)	WFib
'Washbrook' (Min/D)	ESul SBro
'Waveney' (Min)	ESul SBro
'Wayward Angel' (A)	ESul LTho SBro SKen
'Wedding Royale' (Dw/D)	LTho LVer
'Wellington' (R)	SDen WFib
'Wembley Gem' (Z)	MWhe
'Wendy' (Min)	LTho SBro
'Wendy Read' (Dw/D)	ERea ESul LTho MWhe SBro
'Wensum' (Min/D)	ESul SBro WFib
¶ 'Westerfield' (Min)	SBro
'Wherstead' (Min)	ESul SBro
'White Bird's Egg' (Z)	WFib
¶ 'White Boar' (Fr)	LVer
'White Bonanza' (R)	LTho SDen SOld
'White Chiffon' (R)	CSpe LVer
¶ 'White Eggshell' (Min)	LVer SBro
¶ 'White Gem' (Min)	SBro
'White Glory' (R)	WFib
¶ 'White Lively Lady' (Dw/C)	SBro
§ 'White Mesh' (I/V)	CSpe GPla LTho LVer MBri MWhe SDen SKen WEas WFib
'White Pearl Necklace' (Z/D)	LVer WFib
¶ 'White Roc' (Min/D)	SBro
'White Unique' (U)	CCla LVer NSty SDen SKen WFib
¶ 'Wilf Vernon' (Min/D)	SBro

'William Sutton' (R)	WFib
'Winford Festival'	LVer
'Winnie Read' (Dw/D)	ERea ESul LTho LVer SBro
'Wirral Cascade' (Fr/D	LTho
¶ 'Wirral Target' (Z/D)	LTho
'Witnesham' (Min/D)	ESul SBro
§ 'Wood's Surprise' (MinI/D)	LTho LVer MWhe SBro SDen SKen WFib
'Wookey' (R)	WFib
worcesterae	GCHN
'Wrington' (R)	WFib
'Wyck Beacon' (I/D)	SKen
'Wycombe Maid' (Min/D)	LTho LVer SBro WFib
'Xenia Field' (Z)	SDen SKen
'Yale' (I/D)	CSpe IHos LVer MBri MWhe SDen SKen SOld WFib
'Yhu' (R)	LVer
'Yolanda' (Min/C)	ESul SBro
¶ 'York Minster' (Dw/V)	SBro SKen
'Yours Truly' (Z)	MWhe SKen
'Yvonne' (Z)	SKen
'Zinc' (Z/D)	WFib

PELLAEA (Adiantaceae)

falcata	MBri
rotundifolia	MBri NMar WFib
sagittata	NMar

PELLIONIA (Urticaceae)

pulchra	MBri

PELTANDRA (Araceae)

§ ***undulata***	CRow CWGN EHon LMay MSta
virginica	See P. ***undulata***

PELTIPHYLLUM (Saxifragaceae)

peltatum	See DARMERA ***peltata***

PELTOBOYKINIA (Saxifragaceae)

§ ***tellimoides***	LGre NHol SSpi WBon

PENNANTIA (Icacinaceae)

corymbosa	ECou

PENNISETUM (Gramineae)

§ ***alopecuroides***	CCor CKel COtt EGol GWic SApp SSpi WWat
– 'Hameln'	EFou EMon ERou LHop MBri SApp
¶ – ***viridescens***	ELan SApp WWat
– 'Woodside'	EBre SApp
compressum	See P. ***alopecuroides***
longistylum	See P. ***villosum***
¶ ***macrourum***	CHan
orientale	CHEx ECha NBir WCot WOMN
¶ ***setaceum***	SApp
§ ***villosum***	EBar ECha EMon GWic SApp SPou

PENSTEMON † (Scrophulariaceae)

acaulis	EPad
albertinus	EPad
albidus JCA 9164	WDav
'Alice Hindley'	Widely available
alpinus	EPad LGre NOak
¶ ***ambiguus***	WPer
¶ – JCA 9501	SBla
§ 'Andenken an Friedrich Hahn'	Widely available
§ ***angustifolius***	MSal WPer
antirrhinoides	NNrd
– ***microphyllus***	NNrd
'Apple Blossom'	CChu CCla CElw CFis CGle CHan CSev CSun ELan EPad ERou GPla LGre LHil LHop LSav MWgw NSti NVic SAxl SCou WHCG WOld WPer
arizonicus	See P. ***whippleanus***
¶ ***attenuatus***	SCou
azureus	EPad SCou WDav WPer
baccharifolius	LGre
'Barbara Barker'	CChu CElw ELan EOrc LHop LSav SCou
§ ***barbatus***	CBot CGle CHar CHil CKel CSco CSun EBre ECha EFol EGol ELan ERou IBar LGre MCot MWgw SAxl SCou SPer WEas WHCG WHil
– 'Coccineus'	MBri NOak SCou WPer
¶ – 'Praecox'	WPer
– 'Praecox Nanus'	CLew EPad WPer
barrettae	EPad NRoo
'Bisham Seedling'	CSco
'Blackbird'	CElw CHan CHil CSun EBar ELan EOrc LGre LHil NCat NSti SAxl SMrm WEas WHoo WRus
'Blue Eye'	EPad WEas WPer
'Blue King'	SCro
'Blue Spring'	CBot CHan MBri SFis
'Breitenbrush Blue'	LHop SMrm
¶ ***bridgesii***	SCou
¶ 'Bridget's White'	CSam
'Burford Seedling'	CElw CMHG LHil LSav SBor SCou SPer WAbe WRus
'Burgundy'	CHan CSam EOrc GCHN GPla GWic IHos MBri NHol NSti SAxl SChu SCou WBod WRus
caeruleus	See P. ***angustifolius***
¶ ***caespitosus***	SCou
§ ***campanulatus***	CHan CHar CRiv CSam EMNN EPad EPla EPot ESis GLoc LGre LHil LHop MHig MPit MTho NHol NNrd NRed NTow SCou WAbe WDav WPer
– ***chihuahuensis***	EPad GWic
– ***pulchellus***	See P. ***campanulatus***
¶ – ***roseus***	WEas
cardwellii	EPad GCHN LGan LGre NHol WPer
'Castle Forbes'	CElw WEas
'Catherine de la Mare'	CElw CHan COtt EBar EDon EFou ELan EOrc GAbr LHil NVic SAxl SChu SCro WPer WRus
'Charles Rudd'	CElw EPad GWic NRar NVic SBor SChu SCou SMrm

'Cherry Ripe'	EBar SCou WHoo WKif WRus
'Chester Scarlet'	CChu CElw CFis CGle CHan CSun GCHN GGar GWic NHol SAxl WHCG WRus
clutei	LGre
comarrhenus	LGre SBla
compactus	EPad
confertus	CMHG CSun EBar ELan EMNN EPad GLoc MCas MHig MPla MPlt NGre NNrd NRed NRoo NSti WAbe WHal WPer
cordifolius	LGre
crandallii glabrescens	LGre WDav
§ *– – taosensis*	SMrm WAbb WAbe WTay
cristatus	See P. ***eriantherus***
davidsonii	CMHG EMNN EPad MHig WAbe WOMN
– menziesii	CSam EPad WEas WPer
– menziesii 'Microphyllus'	CHar EPad GDra SChu SMrm WDav WHea
'Dazzler'	CGre CHil
deustus	EPad WDav
diffusus	See P. ***serrulatus***
digitalis	CGle CHan ECha EPad LGre LHop WHea WPer
– purpureus	ECro SBla
* *discolor*	LGre SIgm
dissectus	EPad
'Drinkstone'	CChu CGle CMHG CRiv CSam EFou LHop LSav SDix SMrm WPer
eatonii	CHan EPad LGre SBla
'Edithae'	CGre CLew CMHG EOrc MBal MPlt SBor SChu WEas WMar WPer
§ *eriantherus*	EBar EPad MHig WDav WPer
– redactum	WDav
§ 'Evelyn'	Widely available
¶ *federici augusti*	WDav
fendleri	See P. ***nitidus***
'Firebird'	See P. 'Schoenholzeri'
* 'Flame'	CGle CSco NHol
fruticosus	EPad
fruticosus scouleri	CShe EPad GLoc ITim NHol NRed NSti SCou WPat WPer
– – albus	CBot EMon GDra GLoc LGre LHop NSti SBla SChu SHil SWas WAbe WEas WMar WOMN WPer WRus WThu
– – 'Hopleys'	EPad LHop WPer
¶ *– – roseus*	GLoc
– – ruber	WOMN
* 'Gaff's Pink'	SChu
'Garnet'	See P. 'Andenken an Friedrich Hahn'
¶ *gentianoides*	WCot WRus
'George Home'	SCou
glaber	CBow CElw CRiv CSev EDon EPad LGre LHil LHop MRav NRed SCou SMrm WDav WEas WKif WPer WRus
– JCA 9290	CSun
¶ *glacialis*	WPer
¶ *gracilis*	WDav
hallii	CSun EPad LGre LHop WPer
hartwegii	CGre EOrc LHop NCat SChu SMrm WAbe WRus
¶ *– albus*	EOrc SChu
harvardii	LGre
§ *heterophyllus*	Widely available
– 'Blue Gem'	CHar EBre EFol IDai NRoo SHil SIgm SIng SMrm WAbe WHoo WRus
– 'Blue Springs'	CElw CGle CMHG CSam EBar SBla SChu WAbe WEas WRus
– 'Heavenly Blue'	CElw EHal LHop SLon
– purdyi	ECha EFol LHop SMrm
– 'True Blue'	See P. ***heterophyllus***
'Hewell's Pink'	CGle ECro EFou EGol ERou LHil NRoo SChu SCou WHal WRus
¶ 'Heythrop Park'	WHoo
'Hidcote Pink'	Widely available
* 'Hidcote Purple'	CElw LHil SChu
* 'Hidcote White'	CBot CSun EBar WAbe WRus WWin
§ *hirsutus*	CGle CSun EBar LHil NRed SCou WOMN
– minimus	NTow SFir
– pygmaeus	CHar CHoe CSun GLoc MBro MPar MPit MPla NHol NRed SBla WCar WDav WHoo WOMN WThu WWin
'Hopleys Variegated'	EFol EHal EOrc NSti SMrm
humilis	WPer
– albus	WPer
– 'Pulchellus'	LGre
'Hyacinth'	ELan
¶ *impressus*	WPer
* *isophyllus*	CHan SChu SCou SFir WEas WOld WPer WRus
jamesii	EPad LGre LHil SBla
'John Nash'	CElw CFis CHan EBar LGre SMrm
¶ 'Joy'	WHoo WRus
'King George'	CFis CGre CHan CSam EBar EBre EPad ERou GPla IHos LHil LSav MBri NRoo SBla SBor SCou WEas WOld
kunthii	See P. ***campanulatus***
¶ *labrosus*	WDav
laetus roezlii	CLew GDra MBro MHig MPla NNrd SIng WAbe WDav WPer WSHC WWin
laricifolius	CLew
leonardii	EPad
linarioides JCA 9694	EPad WDav
– taosensis	EOrc LGre LHop SChu
lyallii	CElw CSun ELan EMon EPad LHil
* 'Lynette'	WOld
'Margery Fish'	CChu CHan
¶ 'McPenny's Pink'	SAxl
'Midnight'	LGre LHil WBon WEas WMar WPer WTay WWin
'Modesty'	CHan NHol
montanus	EPad

'Mother of Pearl' CChu CElw EFou EOrc GPla GWic IBar LGre LHil LHop NRoo NSti SAxl SChu SMrm WRus
* 'Mountain Wine' LRHS
'Mrs Morse' See P. 'Souvenir d'André Torres'
mucronatus LGre
'Myddelton Gem' CGle EPad MWat SAxl SCou WHCG
newberryi CGle ELan EPad GGar GLoc LGre LHop NRar NRoo NTow SHil WKif WMar WPat WPer WSHC WWin
– ***berryi*** EPad
– ***humilior*** EPad
§ ***nitidus*** EPad LGre
'Oaklea Red' EDon
* old candy pink EOrc EPad WPer
oliganthus LGre WDav
¶ 'Osprey' LHil WEas
ovatus CElw ELan EPad GWic MFir MPar NRar NSti SFir SMrm
palmeri EPad LGre WDav
¶ – JCA 9550 SLHN
– ***eglandulosus*** JCA 9527 EPad
'Papal Purple' CChu CMHG EBar NCat SChu WOld WRus
parryi LGre
paysoniorum EPad
'Peace' SCou
'Pennington Gem' CChu CElw CGle CHil CSam CSun ELan LGre LHil LHop NRar SCou SPer WEas WMar WRus
'Phyllis' See P. 'Evelyn'
pinifolius Widely available
– 'Mersea Yellow' Widely available
¶ pink and cream CHan
'Pink Dragon' EPad GCHN GDra LGre MBal MHig MPla WPat WPer WRus
'Pink Endurance' CElw ELan EOrc EPad LGan NRar NSti SChu SCou WEas WHCG
'Plum Beauty' EDon
'Port Wine' CGle CSam CSco GCHN NHol SCou
'Prairie Fire' GWic
¶ 'Priory Purple' WHCG
procerus EPad GLoc SCou WDav WPer
– ***tolmiei*** CElw EPad EPot GWic LGre NTow WCla WDav
pseudospectabilis LGre
pubescens See P. ***hirsutus***
pulchellus See P. ***campanulatus***
* 'Purple and White' LGre SAxl SCou
'Purple Bedder' CGle CGre EPad MWat
'Purple Dragon' MPla SBla
'Purple Gem' GDra WMar
¶ ***purpusii*** LGre
* ***radicosus*** EPad
¶ 'Raven' LHil WHoo WRus
'Red Emperor' CMHG SFis SPla WPer
I 'Red Knight Number 2' WHCG
'Rich Ruby' CChu CElw CHan CSun EDon ELan LHop LSav SAxl SChu SMrm WCot WRus
richardsonii EPad LHop
* ***roseocampanulatus*** GWic SFir WAbe WMar
rostriflorus CLew EPad
¶ – JCA 9548 SWas
* 'Roy Davidson' EPad GLoc
¶ 'Royal White' LHil
'Rubicundus' CChu CHan EBar LHil LHop SCou WAbe WRus WTay
'Ruby' See P. 'Schoenholzeri'
rupicola GDra MPla NRoo WPer
– ***albus*** LGre
– mauve hybrid GDra
* 'Russina River' SChu SMrm
* 'Scarlet 'n' White' WAbe
§ 'Schoenholzeri' Widely available
scouleri See P. ***fruticosus s.***
secundiflorus JCA 9484 CSun
§ ***serrulatus*** ECha SCou
– ***albus*** LHil NRed
'Sissinghurst Pink' See P. 'Evelyn'
'Six Hills' CLew EPad LHop MBro MHig MPla NHol NRoo WDav WMar WPat WPer WSHC
* 'Skyline' EBar SMrm WHil
smallii CElw EHal EPad WPer
'Snow Storm' Widely available
'Snowflake' See P. 'White Bedder'
'Sour Grapes' Widely available
'Southgate Gem' CMHG MWat SCro
'Souvenir d'Adrian Regnier' WOld
§ 'Souvenir d'André Torres' MBri SChu WEas
speciosus kennedyi EPad
spectabilis WPer
sp. KR 637A CGre
'Stapleford Gem' CGle ELan WAbe WRus
* ***stenophyllus*** LGre
strictus CSun EBar EHal LGre WPer
subulatus LGre
superbus LGre
taosensis See P. ***crandallii glabrescens t.***
ternatus EMon
teucrioides EPad LGre
– JCA 9619 NHol WDav
'Thorn' CGle SCou WRus
'Threave Pink' CChu CHan WPer
* 'Threave White' CSun
thurberi LGre
'Torquay Gem' CElw LSav
utahensis LGre WPer
venustus CCor CSam EBar EPad GWic NSti WPer
virens CElw EFol EPad NRoo WAbe WDav
– ***albus*** EPad MPla NHol WDav WHil WWin
virgatus arizonicus EPad WDav
– ***asa-grayi*** EPad SBla

watsonii	EPad LHop SBla SCou SMrm WPer WSHC
§ *whippleanus*	CBre CChu CElw CHan ECro EPad GWic LGre NSti WCla WPer
– JCA 9504	CSun
– dark form	CSun
§ 'White Bedder'	CChu CElw CGle CHan CMHG CSco EBar MWat NVic SMrm WEas WHoo WRus
'Whitethroat'	CGre GPla WPer WTay
'Windsor Red'	CChu CMer GWic NTow SAxl
wislizenii	LGre

PENTAGLOTTIS (Boraginaceae)

§ *sempervirens*	CKin Effi MSal NSel WHen WSto

PENTAPTERYGIUM See AGAPETES

PENTAS (Rubiaceae)

lanceolata	MBri

PEPEROMIA (Piperaceae/Peperomiaceae)

§ *argyreia*	MBri
caperata	MBri
– 'Little Fantasy'	MBri
– 'Luna'	MBri
* *columbiana*	MBri
– 'Carnival'	MBri
* *deppeana*	MBri
glabella	MBri
'Green Valley'	MBri
* *jeli*	MBri
maculosa	MBri
* *miqueliana*	MBri
obtusifolia 'Golden Gate '	MBri
– 'Greengold'	MBri
– 'Jamaica'	MBri
– 'Tricolor'	MBri
– 'USA'	MBri
I *orba* 'Pixie Variegata'	MBri
– 'Pixie '	MBri
'Pauline'	MBri
pereskiifolia	MBri
pulchella	See P. *verticillata*
puteolata	MBri
* *rauvema*	MBri
resediflora	See P. *fraseri*
rubella	MBri
sandersii	See P. *argyreia*
scandens	MBri
– 'Variegata'	MBri
'Teresa'	MBri
'Tine'	MBri
tristachya	MBri
verticillata	MBri

PERESKIA (Cactaceae)

¶ *aculeata variegata*	CSun

PEREZIA (Compositae)

¶ *linearis*	GCHN
recurvata	ECou EPot GLoc MCas MHig WAbe
* *sessiliflora* P+W 6190	WDav

PERICALLIS (Compositae)

§ *lanata*	CBos CFis CGre CHan CHil CMer ELan EOrc ERav LAbb LGre LHil LHop

PERILLA (Labiatae)

¶ *frutescens crispa*	CArn
¶ – *rubra*	CArn

PERIPLOCA (Asclepiadaceae)

graeca	CB&S CCla CMac SBra SPer WSHC

PERISTROPHE (Acanthaceae)

speciosa	ERea SLMG

N PERNETTYA See GAULTHERIA

PEROVSKIA (Labiatae)

atriplicifolia	CArn CBot CHan CShe ERav GPoy LGre LHol MBri MR&S NNor SIde SPer WHal WHil WKif WOld WPer
'Blue Spire'	Widely available
¶ 'Superba'	WWeb

PERSEA (Lauraceae)

ichangensis	CHEx SArc

PERSICARIA See POLYGONUM

affinis	CB&S CFis CHad CHar CShe CTom CWGN ECha EFol LSav MBar MTho NKay NSel NSti SAxl SCro WEas WOld WWat WWin
– 'Darjeeling Red'	CB&S CCla CGle CRow CSco ECro ELan ENot GWic IDai LGro MBal MBri MWgw NBar NNrd SChu SCro WAbe
♦– 'Dimity'	See P. *a.* 'Superba'
– 'Donald Lowndes'	Widely available
§ – 'Superba'	CCla CLew CRow EBre ECro EFou EGol EHon EMon EPar ERou GLoc MBri MFir MWgw NBar NHol SFis SIng SMrm SSpi WHoo WPer WRus
alata	CRow EPla NHol
alpina	CRow
amphibia	CRow
amplexicaulis	CArn CBre CElw CFis CHar CRow CShe ELan ELun LGro MBal MCot MWgw NHol NNor NOrc SChu WHea WHoo
– 'Alba'	CRow ECha
♦– 'Arun Gem'	See P. *a. pendula*
– *atrosanguinea*	CKel CRow CSco ECha MBri MFir NKay NTow NVic SFis SHig SMrm SPer WOld WWin
– 'Firetail'	CCla CHan CLew CRow EBre EFou ERou MBri NHol NRoo NSti SMrm WHil WOld WRus

– 'Inverleith'	CBre CHad CHan CRow CSun EBre ECha EGol NRoo
§ – ***pendula***	CHan COtt CRow CShe EBre ECro EGol MBri NRoo SAxl
– ***rosea***	CFis CRow ECha ELan
bistorta	CRow CSFH CShe Effi GPoy LHol MChe MSal NLan SIde WBon
– ***carnea***	CRow EBre ECha EFol ELan NBir
– 'Superba'	Widely available
§ ***campanulata***	Widely available
– ***alba***	CFis CGle CRow ELan EMon EOrc GWic NSti SAxl SChu WWat
– pale pink form	GWic
– 'Rosenrot'	CBre CRow EGol ELan EOrc GWic IBlr NHol SCro WOld
– 'Southcombe White'	CRow
capitata	CGle CRiv CRow CTre EFol ELan LSav MFir NRar NRoo SAxl SIng SMrm WEas WHea WPer
¶ ***elata***	GGar
emodi	CRow LSav WWat
– 'George Taylor'	LSav
§ ***macrophylla***	CRow EBre ECha ERou GDra MCot NRoo SPer
¶ ***microcephala***	CRow LGre
milletii	CGle CRiv CRow ECha ERou GDra LSav MBri MCot MTho NOak NSti SAxl SPer
* ***nepalensis***	SAxl
runcinata	CRow LHop NSti SAxl SChu WEas WHer WOld
♦ ***scoparia***	See POLYGONUM ***scoparium***
sphaerostachya	See P. ***macrophylla***
tenuicaulis	CGle CLew CRiv CRow CSun CTom ECro EMon EPar EPla MBal MCot MHig NKay SIng WOMN
vacciniifolia	Widely available
§ ***virginiana*** 'Painter's Palette'	CArn CB&S CBot CChu CGle CHad CHan CHoe CKel CRow CSco EBre ECha ECro EFou ELan ERav LHop NSti NVic SLon SMad WEas WOld
§ – ***variegata***	CBot CHan CHoe CRow ECha EFou GWic LHop WOld
vivipara	CRow MCot NHol NLan WEas
wallichii	CRow IBlr SAxl
weyrichii	GWic NBir

PETASITES (Compositae)

albus	EMon GPoy LRHS MSal
fragrans	CHEx CNat EJud ELan EMon EPar SCro WHal
hybridus	CKin MSal MSta WHer
japonicus	SLHN
– ***giganteus***	CHad CWGN ECha EGol ELan EMon EPar MBri MUlv NVic
– 'Variegatus'	EMon IBlr MUlv
palmatus	EMon
paradoxus	SApp

PETROCALLIS (Cruciferae)

§ ***lagascae***	EPot GLoc MHig NHol NTow WDav WPer
pyrenaica	See P. ***lagascae***

PETROCOPTIS (Caryophyllaceae)

glaucifolia	EBar GAbr GLoc MBro MCas MPla NGre NRed NWCA WDav WWin
pyrenaica	NGre WOMN

PETROCOSMEA (Gesneriaceae)

kerrii	GLoc SOkd

PETROMARULA (Campanulaceae)

PETROPHYTON (Rosaceae)

caespitosum	GArf NHol WDav
cinerascens	SIng
§ ***hendersonii***	EPot GArf GEdr NHol NKay WDav WOMN

PETRORHAGIA (Caryophyllaceae)

¶ ***nanteuilii***	CNat
§ ***saxifraga***	CHar MPit MSal NGre NKay NRya NVic WHil WPer WThu
§ – 'Rosette'	ECha MTho WAbe WWin

PETROSELINUM (Umbelliferae)

§ ***crispum***	CArn CSFH CSev EJud Effi GPoy LHol MChe SIde WHal WPer WSto

PETTERIA (Leguminosae)

ramentacea	EHal MPla SSpi

PHACELIA (Hydrophyllaceae)

PHAEDRANTHUS See **DISTICTIS**

PHAIOPHLEPS (Iridaceae)

biflora	NHol

PHALARIS (Gramineae)

arundinacea	CKin CWGN EHal
– 'Elegantissima'	See P. ***a. picta*** 'Picta'
¶ – 'Streamlined'	EMon
arundinacea picta 'Aureovariegata'	CB&S CKel CRow EMon
– – 'Feesey'	CHoe EMon IBlr
§ – – 'Picta'	CHoe CRow CSco EHon ELan EPot ERou IBlr LGro MBal MBar MCot MFir MPar MWgw NHol NNor NSti SHil SIng SPer WEas WWin
– – 'Tricolor'	CHoe

PHANEROPHLEBIA (Aspleniaceae)

caryotidea	NMar WFib
§ ***falcata***	CHEx MBri MWgw NKay SMrm SSpi
– 'Rochfordiana'	CRow WFib

fortunei	IOrc NHol NMar SBla SSpi WCot WFib

PHARBITIS See **IPOMOEA**

PHEGOPTERIS (Thelypteridaceae)

§ *connectilis*	MBal NKay NLan NMar NNrd WFib
decursive-pinnata	NMar

PHELLODENDRON (Rutaceae)

amurense	CB&S CCla EHar LSav SGar SHil SSpi
– *sachalinense*	WCoo
chinense	LSav WCoo

PHILADELPHUS † (Philadelphaceae)

'Albâtre'	CB&S
¶ *argyrocalyx*	LSav
'Atlas'	EGol LHop
'Avalanche'	CMHG ELan ISea LAbb SPer WHCG
'Beauclerk'	CB&S CBow CLan CMHG CSco CShe EBre ENot LSav MBri MGos NHol NKay SHil SLon SMad SPer SPla SReu SSpi WWat WWin
'Belle Etoile'	Widely available
'Boule d'Argent'	CFor CMHG
'Bouquet Blanc'	IDai MBri SHil WKif
brachybotrys	IOrc LSav
'Buckley's Quilt'	EBre MUlv SHil
'Burfordensis'	CCla SLon SPer WBod WWeb
coronarius	CSco EHar MWat NNor SHil SPer SPla
– 'Aureus'	Widely available
– 'Bowles' Variety'	CCla CHoe ELan MBri MGos SCro SMad SPer SSta WPat WSHC WThu
– 'Gold Mound'	MGos
– 'Variegatus'	CCla CRow CSco CShe EFol EGol ELan ENot ERav IJoh IOrc LGre LHop MBri MPla MRav MWat SHil SPla SSta WAbe WSHC WWat WWin
'Coupe d'Argent'	MRav
¶ *delavayi*	SSpi
– B&L 12331	LSav
– SBEC 0182	LSav
– *calvescens*	See P. ***purpurascens***
'Enchantment'	SDix SHil
'Erectus'	CSco ENot ISea MBal MRav NWea SHil SPla WHCG
x *falconeri*	CMCN
'Frosty Morn'	CB&S CCla IJoh MBri SPer
'Galahad'	LRHS MBri
incanus	CMCN
§ 'Innocence'	CBot CCla CHoe CPle EFol ELan EPla LHop MBri MUlv SPla SSpi SSta WHCG WWeb
♦ 'Innocence Variegatus'	See P. 'Innocence'
§ *insignis*	WBod
x *lemoinei*	IDai IJoh MGos MR&S NNor SLon SMad
lewisii	LSav WHCr WWat
'Manteau d'Hermine'	Widely available
microphyllus	CBot CCla CHan CMHG CSco CShe EHar ELan ERav LAbb LGre MPla NHol SDry SHil SLon SPer SSpi WHCG WKif WPat WSHC WWat
'Minnesota Snowflake'	SHil
'Mrs E L Robinson'	CFor LSav
'Natchez'	EBre
'Pentagon'	LSav SSta
'Perryhill'	SPer
x *purpureomaculatus*	WAbe
'Rosace'	SPer
satsumi	LSav
'Silberregen' ('Silver Showers')	CCla CPle CSco EGol IJoh IOrc ISea LSav MBar MBri MGos MUlv NHol WAbe WPat WWat
'Silver Slipper'	ISea
'Snowbelle'	SHil
'Souvenir de Billiard'	See P. ***insignis***
'Sybille'	CCla CFor CSco ENot IDai ISea LSav MBri MRav SHil SSpi SSta WAbe WHCG WSHC WWat
tomentosus	WHCG
– LS&T 4265	LSav
'Virginal'	Widely available
– LA82	MUlv

PHILESIA (Liliaceae/Philesiaceae)

buxifolia	See P. ***magellanica***
§ *magellanica*	CB&S CCla CFor CTrw IBar IDai MBal SArc SHil SLHN SPer SSpi SSta WBod

PHILLYREA (Oleaceae)

angustifolia	LSav
– *rosmarinifolia*	SHil
decora	See OSMANTHUS ***decorus***
§ *latifolia*	SArc SHil SSpi WCoo WWat
media	See P. ***latifolia***

PHILODENDRON (Araceae)

angustisectum	MBri
§ *bipennifolium*	MBri
'Burgundy'	MBri
elegans	See P. ***angustisectum***
'Emerald Queen'	MBri
epipremnum	See EPIPREMNUM ***pinnatum***
erubescens	MBri
– 'Imperial Red'	MBri
– 'Red Emerald'	EBak MBri
– 'Valeria'	MBri
melanochrysum	MBri
'New Red'	MBri
panduriforme	See P. ***bipennifolium***
pedatum	MBri
'Purple Queen'	MBri
radiatum	MBri
sodiroi	See P. ***ornatum***

tuxtlanum 'Royal Queen'	MBri
– 'Tuxtla'	MBri

PHLEBODIUM (Polypodiaceae)

PHLEUM (Gramineae)

pratense	CKin

PHLOMIS † (Labiatae)

anatolica	CBow CHan CKni ELan
– 'Lloyd's Variety'	CChu CKni ELan EMon EPla GWic LHop WKif WSHC WWat
¶ *borei morrocana*	CBot EMon
cashmeriana	CChu CPle CSco SSpi WCru
chrysophylla	CB&S CBot CBow CChu CFis CHan CPle ELan EMon GWic LSav SDix SDry SHil SLon SPer WWat
¶ *crinita*	SWas
fruticosa	Widely available
– 'Edward Bowles'	CSco GWic LHop SHil WTay
grandiflora	CB&S CChu ELan
italica	Widely available
lanata	CFis CHan CMer CSco LGre LHop SBla SDry SPer WHer WSHC WWat
¶ *leucopacta*	CBow CKni
¶ *longifolia*	CBot
– *bailanica*	CKni EBre EMon LSav WWat
lycia	CCla CKni CSun ERav LGre
* 'Nova'	CBot
¶ *orientalis*	NBir
purpurea	CHan NBir WSHC WTay
– *alba*	CBot CHan LHop
rigida	SWas
§ *russeliana*	Widely available
samia	See P. ***russeliana***
tuberosa	CCor CHan CSun ECha WCru
¶ – 'Amazone'	ECha
viscosa	See P. ***russeliana***

PHLOX † (Polemoniaceae)

adsurgens	CFor GLoc ITim MHig NNrd SBla WPer
– *alba*	SBla
– 'Black Buttes'	EPot NHol
– 'Red Buttes'	GLoc LGre SBla
– 'Wagon Wheel'	CRiv ECha EPad EPla EPot ITim LHop MHig SIng WPat WPer WThu WWin
amoena	See P. × ***procumbens***
– *variegata*	See P. × ***procumbens*** 'Variegata'
¶ × *arendsii* 'Anja'	WCot
¶ – 'Lisbeth'	SWas
bifida	ITim MHig WDav WThu WWin
¶ – blue form	ELan
– 'Colvin's White'	LHop MCas NHol
– 'Mina Colvin'	NHol
– 'Starbrite'	EPot ITim MHig WHil WHoo WPat WPer
borealis	CShe ELan GDra GLoc ITim NRed
caespitosa	EMNN EPot GLoc ITim MHig NHol NTow SOkd
¶ – *pulvinata*	ITim
canadensis laphamii	See P. ***divaricata laphamii***
¶ *carolina* 'Bill Baker'	EMon SAxl SWas
– 'Miss Lingard'	SDix WCot
'Charles Ricardo'	CFor EFou ERav MCas NTow WEas WOMN
'Chattahoochee'	Widely available
'Daniel's Cushion'	See P. ***subulata*** 'McDaniel's Cushion'
divaricata	GLoc MRav NKay WPer WWin
– *alba*	ELan
¶ – 'Blue Dreams'	SWas
– 'Dirigo Ice'	CFor CHad ERav SBla WPer
§ – *laphamii*	EPot MCot MHig MPar NVic SBar SBla WDav
¶ – 'May Breeze'	SWas
douglasii	EBar NHol
– 'Apollo'	EMNN EPot GAbr GDra GEdr MHig NHol NNrd WAbe WDav WWin
– 'Boothman's Variety'	CGle CHar CShe ECha ELan EMNN EPar EPot GLoc MHig MPar MPit MPla MWat NHar NHol NKay SIng WEas WHil WWin
– 'Concorde'	GDra
– 'Crackerjack'	CHar CSam CShe ELan EMNN EPot ESis GAbr GDra GEdr GLoc ITim MCas MHig MPla MWat NHar NKay NRed SIng STre WAbe WDav
– 'Eva'	CB&S CHar ELan EMNN EPot GEdr LAbb MHig MRav NGre NHar NHol NKay NRoo WAbe WHil WPer WWin
– 'Galaxy'	GDra NHol
– 'Holden Clough'	NHol
– 'Iceberg'	EPot GAbr GDra GEdr ITim NHol NRed NTow WDav WOMN WWin
– 'J A Hibberson'	EPot LRHS MHig
– 'Lilac Cloud'	NHol
– 'Lilakönigin' ('Lilac Queen')	WHil
– 'Red Admiral'	CMHG CShe EBre EMNN GCHN GDra GEdr IHos MCas MHig NHol NRoo SChu
– 'Rose Cushion'	GDra LRHS MPla NHol SIng
– 'Rose Queen'	CHar CMHG GDra NHol
– 'Rosea'	ELan EMNN EPar GLoc MBal MBro MCas MPla MRav NGre NKay NRed NRoo SIng SSmi WAbe
– 'Star Dust'	GDra
– 'Tycoon'	GDra GEdr LGre WAbe
– 'Violet Queen'	EMNN EPot GDra NHol
– 'Waterloo'	CTom EBre EPot GLoc ITim LHop MCas MRav NHol SChu WAbe WPer WWin
– 'White Drift'	WThu
– × *nana depressa*	EPot NHol SBla WDav
'Geddington Cross'	MWgw
hoodii	CRiv EPot ITim
'Ice Mountain'	GLoc IHos WPer

'Kelly's Eye'	CMHG CSam EBre EMNN EPot GAbr GEdr GLoc ITim LHop MBro MHig NRoo SWas WPer
kelseyi	WOMN
– 'Rosette'	CHar EPot MCas MHig NHol WAbe WHil WPer
maculata	NOrc
– 'Alpha'	CHan CKel CSco EBre EFou ERou GCHN GWic MBri MUlv NHol NRoo NVic SChu SCro SHig SPer WBon WOld
– 'Omega'	CBre CHad CHan CSco EFou EOrc ERou GCHN GWic MBri MTho MUlv NHol NRoo SChu SMrm SPer SSpi WOld
¶ – 'Rosalinde'	NRoo
mesoleuca	See P. ***nana ensifolia***
Mexican hybrids	See P. ***nana***
'Millstream'	See P. x ***procumbens*** 'M.'
§ *nana*	EPad
– 'Arroya'	GLoc NHol SBla
– 'Chameleon'	GLoc NHol
§ – *ensifolia*	EPad GLoc WThu
– 'Lilacina'	IDai
– *lutea*	GLoc
– 'Manjana'	GLoc NHol SBla WThu
– 'Mary Maslin'	CSun GLoc NHol SBla WPer WThu
– 'Paul Maslin'	GLoc NHol SBla
– 'Tangelo'	GLoc NHol
– 'Vanilla Cream'	GLoc NHol SBla WOMN WThu
nivalis 'Camla'	EPot GEdr ITim LHop NNrd WAbe
– 'Jill Alexander'	NHol
– 'Nivea'	ITim NGre NHol NTow WPer
ovata	EPot
paniculata	CShe NCat NNor SChu SDix SMrm SSpi WEas WOld WPer
– 'Aida'	CB&S CKel ERou MWat
– *alba*	GWic NCat SDix WCot
¶ – 'Alba Grandiflora'	WEas
– 'Albert Leo Schlageter'	CShe ERou IDai
– 'Amethyst'	ERou MBri WPer
– 'Annie Laurie'	CKel
¶ – 'Anthony Six'	WPer
– 'Balmoral'	CGle EBre ECtt ERou
– 'Barnwell'	ERou NBar
– 'Betty Symons-Jeune'	ERou SFis
– 'Bill Green'	EBre ERou MRav
– 'Blue Boy'	EFou ERou SApp WPer
– 'Blue Ice'	EBre EFou ELan ERou
– 'Blue Mist'	CKel
– 'Border Gem'	CB&S EFou ENot ERou SApp WCot
– 'Branklyn'	EBre ERou
– 'Brigadier'	CKel CSco ELan ENot ERou MWat NBar NKay NVic SPer
– 'Bright Eyes'	CBla CBow ERou
– 'Buccaneer'	CBla
– 'Charmaine'	CBla
– 'Cherry Pink'	EBre ERou
– 'Chintz'	CKel ERou
– 'Cinderella'	ERou

– 'Cool of the Evening'	CBla ERou
– 'Dodo Hanbury Forbes'	CBla CKel ERou
¶ – 'Dresden China'	MUlv
– 'Dusterlohe'	NBar
– 'Elizabeth Arden'	ERou NBar
– 'Europa'	CB&S CGle ELan ERou GHig
– 'Eva Cullum'	EBre EFou EPad ERou GAbr NRoo WCot
– 'Eventide'	CSco ECtt EFou ENot SMrm SPer
– 'Excelsior'	CHar EBre ERou MRav
– 'Fairy's Petticoat'	CKel MWat WEas
– 'Firefly'	CKel ENot SFis
– 'Flamingo'	NBar
– 'Franz Schubert'	EBre EFou ERou SApp SMrm WCot
§ – 'Frau A von Mauthner'	ERou NKay
– 'Frau Antoine Buchner'	SFis
§ – 'Fujiyama'	CCla CHar CSam EBre ECha EFou EMon EOrc EPad ERou NSti SChu SMrm WCot WEas
– 'Gaiety'	CBla CSco
– 'Glamis'	CBla MWat
– 'Graf Zeppelin'	ELan ERou MWat
– 'Hampton Court'	CKel ERou
– 'Harewood'	ERou GHig
– 'Harlequin'	ECha MPit NVic SSpi
– 'Inspiration'	EBre ERou
– 'Juliglut' ('July Glow')	ERou MWat WCot
– 'Kelway's Cherub'	CKel
– 'Kirmesländler'	CB&S ERou
* – 'Latest Red'	EFou
– 'Le Mahdi'	EFou ELan ERou MWat
– 'Lilac Time'	CBla CBow CSco MWat
– 'Marlborough'	CKel ERou NRoo
– 'Mary Fox'	CSam ERou NRoo SPer
– 'Mia Ruys'	EFou NVic WEas
– 'Mies Copijn'	CSco ERou NBar
– 'Mother of Pearl'	CBla CGle CHad CKel CSco EFou ELan ERou MWat NVic SApp SPer
– 'Mount Fujiyama'	See P. ***p.*** 'Fujiyama'
¶ – 'Mrs Campbell'	ECtt
– 'Mrs Fincham'	SFis
– 'Newbird'	ERou
– 'Norah Leigh'	Widely available
¶ – 'Orange Perfection'	CB&S
– 'Othello'	CBla
– 'Otley Choice'	EFou ERou MWat NVic
– 'Pastorale'	CHar CKel MWat WCot
¶ – 'Pike'	WCot
– 'Pink Gown'	ERou
– 'Prince of Orange'	CBla CCla CGle CHar CKel CSam EBre EFou ELan ERou MRav MUlv MWat NKay NRoo SPer WCot
– 'Prospero'	CBla CHar CRiv EBre EOrc ERou GAbr MRav NRoo SChu SFis SPer WOld
– 'Rapture'	MWat
– 'Red Indian'	EBre ELan ERou MWat
– 'Rembrandt'	CSco CShe ERou MUlv WCot
¶ – 'Rheinländer'	WPer
– 'Rijnstroom'	CB&S EBre EFou

– 'Russian Violet'	CKel CSco MWat
– 'San Antonio'	CSco ERou
– 'Sandringham'	CKel CSam EBre ELan ENot ERou LHop MUlv NBar NKay NRoo NVic SApp SChu SPer
– 'Shenstone'	MWat
– 'Sir John Falstaff'	CSco SFis
– 'Sir Malcolm Campbell'	ERou
– 'Skylight'	CHar CShe ERou NKay SFis
– 'Snowball'	ERou
– 'Spitfire'	See P. *p.* 'Frau A von Mauthner'
– 'Starfire'	CB&S CGle CKel CSam CSco EBre EFou ELan ENot ERou MFir NBar NKay NRoo SApp SChu SCro SFis SPer WCot
– 'Tenor'	CBow EFou
– 'The King'	ERou
– 'Toits de Paris'	MWat
– 'Vintage Wine'	CKel SPer
– 'White Admiral'	CB&S CBla CBow CGle CHad CKel EBre ENot EOrc ERou LHop MRav MUlv MWat NKay NRoo SCro SPer WEas
– 'Windsor'	CBla CHar EBre EFou MBri NBar SFis WPer
pilosa	ECha LHop NSti
* 'Pleu de Pervanche'	CSco
x ***procumbens***	CHar
§ – 'Millstream'	EBre ECha ELan EPad GEdr GLoc ITim LHop MCas NHar NHol SBla WPer WWin
§ – 'Variegata'	Widely available
x ***rugellii***	ECha NHol WHil WPer WWin
stolonifera	CHan GGar MTho WPer
– 'Ariane'	CRiv CSun ECha EPar LHop MHig MPar NVic SAxl SBla SWas WMar WPer WThu WWin
– 'Blue Ridge'	CSun ECha EPar LHop NVic SAxl SBla SMrm WHil WWin
– 'Mary Belle Frey'	ECha LHop SAxl SBla SWas WMar WPer WWin
¶ – 'Violet Vere'	SBla
subulata 'Alexander's Surprise'	CGle CHar CRiv CSam CShe EPot ESis GCHN GHig LHop MBal MCas MPit NGre NHol NKay SCro
– 'Amazing Grace'	CGle ECtt EPad ESis GLoc ITim NHol SIng WAbe WHil WHoo WPer WWin
– 'Apple Blossom'	GAbr GDra GHig NHol SChu
– 'Atropurpurea'	CHar GCHN NKay NNor WWin
– 'Beauty of Ronsdorf'	See P. *s.* 'Ronsdorfer Schöne'
– 'Betty'	ECtt EMNN NNrd NRoo WHil
– 'Blue Eyes'	See P. *s.* 'Oakington Blue Eyes'
¶ – 'Blue Saucer'	WDav
– 'Bonita'	EBre EMNN EMon ESis GAbr MRav NHol NRoo SChu
– 'Bressingham Blue Eyes'	See P. *s.* 'Oakington Blue Eyes'
– 'Brightness'	CRiv LRHS MRav NKay SChu
– ***brittonii*** 'Rosea'	EPot ITim NHol WDav WOMN WPer
– 'Drumm'	LRHS
– 'Emerald Cushion Blue'	CRiv EBar EPad MBal MRav NHol NRoo WAbe WHoo WPer
– 'Fairy'	NHol
– 'G F Wilson'	CHar CShe CTom ECha ELan EPad IDai LGro MBal MHig MWat NGre NHol NKay NNor NRoo SChu WAbe WDav WHil WPer WWin
– 'Greencourt Purple'	ESis NCat NHol WHil
¶ – 'Lavinia'	NHol
§ – 'Maischnee' ('May Snow')	Widely available
– 'Marjorie'	EBar ECtt ELan EMNN MBal MCas NHar NKay SChu SIng
§ – 'McDaniel's Cushion'	CGle CHar CMHG CShe EBre ECha ELan EMNN ESis GEdr GLoc ITim LGre MCas MHig MPla NHol NNrd NRoo SBla SIng WHoo WPer
– 'Model'	LGro MWat NHol
– 'Nelsonii'	CShe IDai
§ – 'Oakington Blue Eyes'	CHar CMHG EBre EPar GAbr GDra MBro NHol NRoo WHoo WPer
– 'Red Wings'	EBre GLoc MBal MCas MPit MRav NHol NKay NRoo STre WHil
§ – 'Ronsdorfer Schöne'	EPad EPot MBro MCas NHol WDav WPer
– 'Rose Mabel'	GHig NVic
– 'Samson'	ELan GAbr GHig IDai MRav NHol NKay STre WWin
– 'Scarlet Flame'	CB&S CHar EBre ECha ELan EMNN EPot GDra GHig LGro MBal MPit MRav MWat NHol NKay WHil WHoo WPer WWin
– 'Schneewitchen'	MCas NHol
– 'Snow Queen'	See P. *s.* 'Maischnee'
– 'Star Glow'	NHol
¶ – 'Tamanongalei'	SChu
– 'Temiskaming'	CB&S CGle CHar CKel EBre ECha EMNN ESis GDra GLoc IDai LAbb LGro MWat NHol NKay NRoo SChu SIng WAbe WEas WHil WHoo
– violet seedling	NHol NKay
– 'White Delight'	CHar EBre ELan EMNN GCHN GLoc MCas MHig NHol NKay NNrd NRoo SChu WDav
– 'Winifred'	LMer
'Vivid'	EPad NHol WAbe

PHOEBE (Lauraceae)

shearii	CMCN

PHOENICAULIS (Cruciferae)

¶ ***cheiranthoides***	EHal WOMN

PHOENIX (Palmae)
canariensis — CHEx LPal MBri NPal SMad WNor
F *dactylifera* — LPal
reclinata — NPal
roebelenii — LAma LPal MBri
sylvestris — LPal
theophrasti — LPal

PHORMIUM † (Agavaceae/Phormiaceae)
'Apricot Cream' — IJoh LNet
'Apricot Queen' — SHil
'Bronze Baby' — CB&S CSam CSco MBal SBla SHil
'Burgundy' — CB&S
colensoi — See P. ***cookianum***
§ *cookianum* — CHEx CHan CTrw EFou IBlr MBal MGos SArc
– 'Alpinum Purpureum' — SWas
– 'Tricolor' — CB&S CBot CBra CHEx ELan ENot IBar IJoh MBal MR&S SArc SHil SPla SSpi WCot WWat
'Cream Delight' — CB&S CHoe CSco ENot IJoh IOrc MBal MGos MR&S SHil SLon SPer SSpi SSta WCot
'Dark Delight' — CB&S LNet SHil SMad
'Dazzler' — ENot IJoh IOrc LNet MBal SHil
'Duet' — LNet
'Guardsman' — MBri
'Jack Sprat' — ECou IBar IBlr
§ 'Maori Chief' — CB&S EGol IJoh SHil SPer SSpi SSus
'Maori Maiden' — CB&S CHoe MBal SHil SSpi
'Maori Queen' — CB&S SHil SSpi SSus
'Maori Sunrise' — CB&S ENot IJoh LNet SHil SLon SPer WCot
'Pink Panther' — CB&S MBri MR&S SHil
♦ 'Rainbow Chief' — See P. 'Maori Chief'
Rainbow Hybrids — IJoh MBal
'Smiling Morn' — LNet
'Sundowner' — CB&S CSco EGol ENot IBar IBlr IJoh IOrc LHop LNet MBal MBri MR&S SHil SPer
'Sunset' — CB&S
tenax — Widely available
– *purpureum* — CB&S CBot CBra CFis CHEx CHad CSco CTre EGol ELan ENot IBar IJoh IOrc LHop MBal MR&S SHil SLon SMad SPer SSpi WCot
– 'Radiance' — MBal SBla SSta
– 'Variegatum' — CHEx LPal MBal SArc SGar SHig SHil
– 'Veitchii' — SHig
'Thumbelina' — CB&S MFir
'Yellow Wave' — CB&S CHEx CHoe CSco ELan IBlr IJoh IOrc LHop MBal SHil SMad SSpi WCot

PHOTINIA † (Rosaceae)
arbutifolia — See HETEROMELES ***a.***
beauverdiana — CMHG EHar SHil SSpi WWat
§ *davidiana* — CCla CMCN CPle CSco CShe CTrw ELan ENot IDai LHop LSav MBal MBar MBri MGos MWat SHil SPer SPla WBod WHCG WPat WSHC WWat
¶ – L 541 — LSav
– 'Fructu Luteo' — CBow CCla CMHG CTrw EHar LHop LSav MBri MRav SHil SPer WWat
– 'Palette' — CCla CFor CHoe CMHG CPle CSco CTrw EBre EFol EGol EHar ELan ERav IJoh LHop MBar MBri MGos MPla NHol SHil SPer SSta WPat
– *undulata* — CMCN MRav
– *undulata* 'Prostrata' — CCla EHar ELan ENot LSav MBar MBri SHil WSHC WWat
x *fraseri* — IDai ISea
– 'Birmingham' — CChu CLan EHar MBal WSHC WWeb
– 'Red Robin' — Widely available
– 'Robusta' — CChu CMHG MBal MCot SHil WWat
glabra 'Pink Lady' — MUlv SSta
– 'Rubens' — CChu CFor EHar ELan LSav MBri MUlv NTow SHil SPer SPla SSpi SSta WPat WWat
– 'Variegata' — CFor CSco EBre EGol ELan ERav LHop SDry SPer SSpi
¶ *glomerata* — CHEx CMHG
lasiogyna — CMCN
§ 'Redstart' — CFor EHar MGos MUlv SHil SLon SSpi SSta WHCG WWat
serrulata — CBot CHEx EHar MBal SHil SReu SSta WBod WWat
villosa — CBow CCla CSco EHar IDai IOrc MBal MBar NHol SHil SPer SSpi WBod WCoo WWat
– *longipes* USNA 3680 — SSpi
– *maximowicziana* — CCla

PHRAGMITES (Gramineae)
§ *australis* — LMay
¶ – *pseudodonax* — GWic
– 'Variegatus' — CHoe GWic SApp
communis — See P. ***australis***

PHUOPSIS (Rubiaceae)
§ *stylosa* — CBre CElw CFis CGle CMer CRiv CSun ECha EFou ELan ESis GLoc LAbb MPar MRav NBar NHol NRoo NSti SChu STre WHal WPer WWin
– 'Purpurea' — CBos CBre ECha ELan EMon ESis NCat

PHYGELIUS (Scrophulariaceae)
aequalis — Widely available
– *alba* — See P. ***a.*** 'Yellow Trumpet'
– 'Aureus' — See P. ***a.*** 'Yellow Trumpet'
– 'Cream Trumpet' — See P. ***a.*** 'Yellow Trumpet'
– 'Indian Chief' — See P. x ***rectus*** 'African Queen'

*– 'Pink Trumpet'	CMal EFou
§ – 'Yellow Trumpet'	Widely available
capensis	Widely available
– albus	CGle
*– 'Angel's Tears'	ERou
– coccineus	CB&S CHEx CSco CSun CTrw EOrc IDai IJoh LAbb MBal MPla SCro SHil SMad WBod
¶ – orange form	EPla
– roseus	CTrw
– x ***aequalis***	See P. x ***rectus***
x ***rectus***	CGre EPla SPla
– 'African Queen'	Widely available
– 'Devil's Tears'	CB&S CChu CCla CSam CSun CTre EBar EOrc EPla GHig GWic MBri SHil SLon SPla SSpi SSus WRus
– 'Moonraker'	CChu CCla CMHG EBar ELan EOrc EPla ERav MBri SHil SMad SSpi SSus
– 'Pink Elf'	ELan EOrc SHil SSus
– 'Salmon Leap'	CChu CMHG EBar ECha EOrc GHig GWic LHil SHil SSus
§ – 'Winchester Fanfare'	CB&S CChu CHan CMHG CSam EOrc EPla GHig GWic LAbb SChu SCro SHil SLon SPer SSpi SSus WOld WPer WSHC WWat
– 'Winton Fanfare'	See P. x *r.* 'Winchester Fanfare'
'Trewidden Pink'	LHop

PHYLA (Verbenaceae)

§ ***canescens***	CLew EFol NHol SLHN WHal
§ ***nodiflora***	CMer CRow ECha LGan SIng WPer

PHYLICA (Rhamnaceae)

X PHYLLIOPSIS (Ericaceae)

hillieri	GArf
– 'Coppelia'	CFor WAbe
– 'Pinocchio'	CFor EPot GDra MBri SSpi SSta

PHYLLITIS (Aspleniaceae)

****furcata***	MWgw NBar
§ ***scolopendrium***	Widely available
– Crispa group	EBul ECha ELan MBri NHol NKay SSpi WFib
– 'Crispa Nobilis'	NMar WEas WFib
– Cristata group	EBre ELan IOrc MBri MWgw NKay NMar SPer WFib
– 'Digitata'	WFib
– 'Kaye's Lacerated'	EGol ELan MBri NMar
– Marginata group	CWGN NMar
– Marginata group 'Irregularis'	NHol WFib
– 'Muricata'	NMar
– 'Ramo-Cristata'	NMar
– 'Ramo-Marginata'	CWGN ELan MBri
– 'Sagittato-Cristata'	NKay
– 'Undulata'	EBre EGol NMar SMrm SSpi

PHYLLOCLADUS (Podocarpaceae)

aspleniifolius alpinus	CKen SHil

PHYLLODOCE † (Ericaceae)

§ ***aleutica***	CFor CRiv EPot GAbr GArf GHig MBal MBar MHig NHar SHil SIng WBod WPat WThu
– 'Flora Slack'	GHig MHig SSta
§ ***– glanduliflora***	GArf GDra MBal NHol SSta WThu
– white form	MBal WThu
breweri	GDra GHig
caerulea	GAbr GDra GHig MBal SHil WAbe
– japonica	See P. ***nipponica***
empetriformis	CRiv GDra GLoc MBal MBar MBri MGos MHig SIng WAbe WBod WPat WThu
glanduliflora	See P. ***aleutica***
x ***intermedia***	GDra MBal
– 'Drummondii'	GHig
– 'Fred Stoker'	GHig MHig SSta
§ ***nipponica***	GDra MBal NHol SHil

PHYLLOSTACHYS † (Gramineae(Bambuseae))

angusta	SBam SDry WJun
arcana	SBam SDry WJun
aurea	CHEx EFul LPan MBri SArc SBam SDry SHil SSus WJun
¶ – 'Albovariegata'	WJun
– 'Flavescens Inversa'	SBam SDry
¶ ***– formosana***	WJun
– 'Holochrysa'	EFul SBam SDry WJun
– 'Koi'	SBam SDry
– 'Variegata'	EFul SBam SDry
aureosulcata	EFul NJap SBam SDry WJun
– 'Aureocaulis'	SBam SDry
– 'Spectabilis'	EFul SBam SDry
bambusoides	NJap SBam SDry SHil WJun
§ – 'Allgold' ('Holochrysa')	SBam SDry SHil
– 'Castillonis'	EFul SArc SBam SDry WJun
– 'Castillonis Inversa'	SBam SDry
¶ – 'Katashibo'	WJun
¶ – 'Slender Crook Stem'	WJun
– subvariegata	SBam SDry
– 'Sulphurea'	See P. ***b.*** 'Allgold'
* ***bissettii***	SBam SDry WJun
Congesta	SBam SDry
decora	SBam SDry WJun
dulcis	SBam WJun
§ ***edulis***	NJap SArc SBam SDry SSpi
– 'Bicolor'	SBam SDry
♦ ***– pubescens***	See P. ***e.***
flexuosa	EFul SArc SBam SDry SHil WJun
¶ ***fulva***	WJun
¶ ***glauca*** 'Yunzhu'	WJun
§ ***heteroclada***	SBam SDry WJun
– 'Solid Stem'	SBam SDry WJun
– 'Straight Stem'	SBam SDry WJun
heterocycla	See P. ***edulis***
humilis	SBam SDry WJun

mannii SBam SDry

meyeri SBam SDry

nidularia SBam SDry WJun

¶ – Smooth Sheath WJun

nigra CHEx EFul LPan MBri SArc SBam SDry SReu SSus WJun

– 'Boryana' SBam SDry SHil WJun

¶ – 'Hanchiku' WJun

– *henonis* SArc SBam SDry WJun

– 'Megurochiku' SBam SDry WJun

– *punctata* SBam WJun

nuda SBam SDry

– *localis* SBam SDry

propinqua SBam

♦*purpurata* See P. ***heteroclada***

rubromarginata SBam SDry

sulphurea 'Houzeau' SBam SDry

– 'Robert Young' SBam SDry WJun

♦– 'Sulphurea' See P. ***bambusoides*** **'Allgold'**

– *viridis* EFul SBam SDry

– *viridis* 'Mitis' MBri SBam

violascens SBam SDry WJun

viridiglaucescens CHEx EFul SArc SBam SDry WJun

vivax SBam SDry WJun

X PHYLLOTHAMNUS (Ericaceae)

erectus EPot GDra MHig NHar SHil SIng WAbe

PHYMOSIA

§ *umbellata* CBot CSun

PHYODINA (Commelinaceae)

¶ *rosea graminifolia* WCot

PHYSALIS (Solanaceae)

alkekengi franchetii CBow CHar CKel CRiv CSco ELan ENot ERav LAbb MBri MCot MFir MWgw NBar NJap NRoo SPer WHal WHil WWin

– – *gigantea* CSco ERou NNor

– – *variegata* ERav IBlr

F *peruviana* LHop

PHYSARIA (Cruciferae)

¶ *acutifolia* JCA 8648 WDav

¶ *alpestris* NHar

¶ *bellii* WDav

didymocarpa CSun WDav

¶ *floribunda* GLoc

¶ *vitulifera* WDav

PHYSOCARPUS (Rosaceae)

¶ *capitatus* EMon

opulifolius EGol MSal

– 'Dart's Gold' Widely available

§ – 'Luteus' CB&S CBot CPle CSam ECha ELan ENot ISea MBar MR&S NHol NNor NRoo SLon SPer SPla SReu SSpi WBod WRus WSHC

ribesifolius 'Aureus' See P. ***opulifolius*** **'Luteus'**

PHYSOPLEXIS (Campanulaceae)

§ ***comosa*** EPad GLoc MBro MCas SIng SPou WHoo

PHYSOSTEGIA (Labiatae)

virginiana ECro GCHN MSal

§ – 'Alba' CChu CElw CRiv EBre ECro MWgw NRoo WEas

*– 'Crown of Snow' CHar EBar ECro IBrk SIng SPla WCot

¶ – pale pink form EFou

*– 'Snow Queen' MWat NVic

– 'Summer Snow' CCla CKel CSco ECha EFou EGol ELan ENot EOrc ERou IDai LHop LSav MBri MFir NHol SPer WHal WHil WOld WRus WWin

– 'Summer Spire' CKel ECro ELan ERou NHol NKay SPer

– 'Variegata' CB&S CHoe CMHG ECha ECro EFol EFou EGol ELan EMon GPla LHop MUlv NHol NOak NRoo NSti SBla SPer WCot WEas WRus WWin

– 'Vivid' CElw CSco EBre ECro EFou ELan ERou MCot MRav MWat NHol NOak NRoo SChu SDix SPer WEas WHoo WWin

¶ *virginiana speciosa* EMon

– – 'Bouquet Rose' ('Rose Bouquet') CHar EBre ECha IDai LSav MBri MFir MRav NCat NKay SChu SFis WRus

– – 'Variegata' EMon

PHYTEUMA (Campanulaceae)

balbisii NBir WHil

charmelii WPer

comosum See PHYSOPLEXIS ***comosa***

halleri See P. ***ovatum***

hemisphaericum MTho WPer

humile NGre SIng

orbiculare MSal WHoo

scheuchzeri CRiv EFol ELan GLoc LGan NCat NHol NKay SBla SFis SLHN WCla WPer

sieberi GDra NBir

spicatum EBar WPer

– *nigrum* CLew NSti

tenerum CKin GAbr

PHYTOLACCA (Phytolaccaceae)

acinosa EBar IBlr

§ *americana* CArn CHEx CSev ECha ECro ELan ERav GPoy IBlr LHol MFir MSal NSti SIde SMrm SSpi WEas WOld

clavigera See P. ***polyandra***

decandra See P. ***americana***

§ *polyandra* ECha ECro LHol MCot NHex SMrm

PICEA † (Pinaceae)	
§ ***abies***	CPer EHar EHul ENot GRei IDai ISea LBuc MBar MBri MGos MR&S NRoo NWea SHil WMou WThu
– 'Acrocona'	CDoC EBre EHar EHul IJoh MBar MBri MGos MPla NHol SHil SSta WCon
– 'Argenteospica'	EBre MBri NHol WCon
– 'Aurea'	EHul IJoh
– 'Capitata'	CKen MBar SPla WCon
*– 'Cinderella'	MBri
– 'Clanbrassiliana'	CKen MBar WAbe WCon
– 'Columnaris'	EBre
¶– 'Crippsii'	CKen
– 'Cruenta'	CKen
¶– 'Cupressina'	CKen
– 'Diffusa'	MBar WAbe WCon
¶– 'Dumosa'	WAbe
– 'Elegans'	MBar WCon
– 'Excelsa'	See P. ***abies***
– 'Finedonensis'	NHol WCon
¶– 'Formanek'	CKen
– 'Frohburg'	CDoC EBre EHul ENHC IBar MBar MBri NHol
– 'Globosa'	MBar WCon
– 'Globosa Nana'	MGos
– 'Gregoryana'	CDoC CKen CSco MBar MBri MPla MWat NHol SHil SPla WAbe WCon
§– 'Gregoryana Veitchii'	SIng
– 'Humilis'	SHil
– 'Inversa'	CDoC EHul ENHC IJoh IOrc LPan MBar SHil SMrm
¶– 'Kamon'	WCon
– 'Little Gem'	CDoC CKen CMac EBre EHul ENHC LLin MBar MBri MGos MPla MWat NHol SHil SIng WAbe WCon WThu
– 'Maxwellii'	CMHG EHul MBar MGos WCon
– 'Merkii'	WAbe
– 'Nana'	MBar WCon
– 'Nana Compacta'	CKen MBar NHol WAbe
– 'Nidiformis'	CDoC CKen CMac EBre EHul ENHC ENot EPot IJoh IOrc LLin MBal MBar MBri MGos MPla MR&S MWat NRoo NWea SHil SLon SPer SPla
– 'Norrkoping'	CKen
– 'Ohlendorffii'	CKen EHul ENHC MBar MBri MPla MWat NHol NRoo WCon
– 'Pachyphylla'	CKen
¶– 'Pendula Major'	NHol
– 'Procumbens'	MBar
– 'Pumila'	IDai
– 'Pumila Nigra'	CMac EHul LLin MBar MGos MPla WAbe WCon
– 'Pygmaea'	CKen GDra MBar MGos MPla WAbe WCon
– 'Pyramidata'	MBar
– 'Reflexa'	EHul WThu
– 'Remontii'	NWea
– 'Repens'	MBar MBlu MGos WCon
– 'Rubrospicata'	SHil
– 'Saint James'	NHol
– 'Saint Mary's Broom'	CKen
– 'Tabuliformis'	MBar SHil
♦– 'Veitchii'	See P. *a.* 'Gregoryana Veitchii'
– 'Waugh'	MBar WCon
– 'Wills Zwerg' ('Will's Dwarf')	EBre MBri
asperata	CMCN
bicolor	MBri
– 'Prostrata'	MBal
brachytyla	CMCN LSav SHil WCoo
breweriana	Widely available
engelmannii	MBar MPla NWea WCoo
– ***glauca***	EHar EHul SHil SSta WCon
glauca	NWea
– 'Alberta Globe'	CBow CDoC CFor CSco EBre EHul ENHC EPot IJoh LLin MBar MBri MGos MPla NHar NHol WAbe WCon
– ***albertiana*** 'Conica'	Widely available
– 'Caerulea'	MBar SHil
– 'Echiniformis'	CKen EPot IJoh LLin MBal MBar MBri SHil WAbe WCon
– 'Laurin'	CKen EBre MBri SSta WAbe WCon
– 'Lilliput'	EPot MBar MBri NHol WAbe WCon
¶– 'Nana'	CKen
¶– 'Piccolo'	CKen
– 'Tiny'	CKen EHul MBar WAbe
¶– 'Zuckerhut'	MBri
glehnii 'Sasanosei'	CKen
– 'Shimezusei'	CKen
jezoensis	CMCN LSav MBri MGos
– ***hondoensis***	EHar SHil WCoo WNor
– ***hondoensis*** 'Mrs Cesarini'	CKen
koraiensis	See P. ***koyamae***
kosteri 'Glauca'	See P. ***pungens*** 'Koster'
§ ***koyamae***	CMCN SHil STre WHCr
likiangensis	CGre SHil WWat
– ***balfouriana***	MBri
– ***purpurea***	CMCN MBri SHil WCon
mariana	CMCN NWea SHil WCoo
– 'Ericoides'	MPla NHol WCon
– 'Fastigiata'	CKen
– 'Nana'	Widely available
x ***mariorika***	MBar
– 'Machala'	CDoC MBri
meyeri	CMCN
morrisonicola	WCoo
omorika	Widely available
– 'Glauca'	CFor
– 'Gnom'	EBre
– 'Nana'	CMac EBre EHar ENHC LNet MBar MBri NHol SGar SHil WCon
– ***pendula***	EBre EHar IOrc MBar MBri NHol SHil SSta WCon
¶– 'Pimoko'	CKen MBri
¶– 'Treblitzsche'	CKen
orientalis	CBow CMCN LSav NWea SHil WCoo

§ – 'Aurea'	CBra CDoC CMac EBre EHar EHul ELan ENHC IJoh IOrc LLin LPan MBar MBri NHol SHil WThu
– 'Aureospicata'	See P. *o.* 'Aurea'
– 'Early Gold'	SSta
– 'Gowdy'	MBar
– 'Gracilis'	EHul WCon
– 'Kenwith'	CKen
– 'Pendula'	NHol SHil
*– 'Skylands'	EBre NHol
pungens	EBre EHal MBar NWea WNor
– 'Endtz'	CKen
– 'Erich Frahm'	CDoC EBre ENHC MBri SMad WCon
– 'Glauca'	CBra CMCN CSam EHul GRei IBar MBal MBar NWea WMou
– 'Glauca Globosa'	See P. *p.* 'Globosa'
N– 'Glauca Pendula'	MBri
– 'Glauca Procumbens'	EHar LNet NHol SHil
§ – 'Glauca Prostrata'	CMac EHul MBal SSta WCon
§ – 'Globosa'	CBow CDoC CKen CSam CSco EBre EHar EHul ELan ENHC IJoh IOrc LLin MBar MBri MGos MWat NHol SHil SPer SPla SSta WAbe WCon
I – 'Globosa Viridis'	EHul
– 'Gloria'	CKen
– 'Hoopsii'	Widely available
– 'Hotto'	CMac EBre EHul ENHC IOrc MBar SSta
– 'Hunneywelliana'	CSam
§ – 'Koster'	CBra CDoC CFor CMac EHar EHul ENHC ENot GRei IJoh IOrc LLin LNet MBar MGos NWea SExT SHil SPer SReu SSta WAbe WCon WMou
*– 'Koster's Prostrate'	MBal NHol
– 'Lucky Strike'	CKen MBri WCon
– 'Moerheimii'	CBra CMac EHul LNet MBar MGos SExT WCon
– 'Montgomery'	CKen MBar WCon
– 'Pendula'	SHil
*– 'Procumbens'	WCon
– 'Prostrata'	See P. *p.* 'Glauca Prostrata'
– 'Schovenhorst'	MBri
– 'Spek'	SHil WAbe
– 'Thomsen'	CKen MBal MBri
– 'Thuem'	WCon
rubens	LSav
schrenkiana	CMCN
sitchensis	CPer GRei IDai LBuc MGos NWea SHil WMou
*– 'Papoose'	EBre WCon
¶ – 'Strypemonde'	CKen
– 'Tenas'	NHol
smithiana	EHar IBar ISea MBal MBri SHil WCoo
spinulosa	SHil
tianschanica	CMCN
wilsonii	CMCN

PICRASMA (Simaroubaceae)

quassioides	SHil

PICRIS (Compositae)

echioides	CKin

PIERIS † (Ericaceae)

'Bert Chandler'	CCla CHig ELan LSav SHil SPer SSpi
'Brouwer's Beauty'	MBri SSpi SSta
'Debutante'	CFor CHig ELan IJoh MPla SPla SSpi
'Firecrest'	CB&S CBra CCla CFor CHig CMHG ECtt EGol IJoh IOrc LSav MBal MBri MPlt NRoo SExb SHil SPic SPla SSpi WAbe
'Flaming Silver'	CB&S CBra CHig CHoe CKni COtt CSam ELan IHos IOrc MBar MBri MGos NHol NRed SGar SHil SMad SPic SSpi WAbe WPat WWeb
floribunda	IDai IOrc MBal MBar SPer SPla
– 'Elongata'	SHil
'Forest Flame'	Widely available
formosa	CBow CFor CHig SExb
formosa forrestii	CSco CTre CTrw ENot GRei IBar IJoh ISea LSav MPlt MR&S NRoo NWea SExb SPic WAbe
– – 'Ball of Fire'	SSpi
– – 'Charles Michael'	CB&S CLan SHil
– – 'Fota Pink'	WSHC
– – 'Jermyns'	CB&S CFor IOrc LSav MBal SExb SHil SPic SSpi
– – 'Wakehurst'	CBra CCla CFor CHig CLan ERav IBar IOrc LHyd LSav MBal MR&S NHol NKay SArc SExb SHil SLon SPer SPic SPla SReu SSpi WBod
¶ 'Havila'	IOrc
japonica	CB&S CBow CCla CHig CLan CTrw LSav MBal MBar MGos NHol NWea SArc SExb SPer WBod
– 'Bisbee Dwarf'	NHol WPat WThu
– 'Blush'	CCla CHig LSav MRav NHol SHil SPer SPla SSta WSHC
§ – 'Christmas Cheer'	CHig CSco IOrc LSav MBal MGos NHol NKay SHil SSpi
– 'Coleman'	LSav
– 'Compact Crimson'	LRHS MBal
– 'Compacta'	LSav NHol
– 'Crystal'	SSpi SSta
¶ – 'Cupido'	MGos
– 'Daisen'	CLan CTrw NHol SHil
*– 'Debutante'	EBre LSav SExb WWat
– 'Don'	SSta
– 'Dorothy Wyckoff'	CB&S CFor CMHG CTrw LSav SPla SSpi SSta WBod
– 'Flaming Star'	SPer
– 'Flamingo'	CB&S CBra CHig CTrw LSav MBal MBri MGos NHol SHil SReu SSpi SSta WAbe WPat
– 'Grayswood'	CFor CMHG IBar IOrc LSav MBri MPlt NHol SPer SSpi
– 'Hino Crimson'	CB&S CHig
¶ – 'Kakashima'	WSHC

– 'Little Heath'	CBra CCla CFor CHig CHoe CMHG ERav IOrc LSav MBar MBri MGos MHig SHil SPer SPic SSpi SSta WAbe WBod WWeb
– 'Little Heath Green'	CFor CHig CMHG COtt EPla LHyd LSav MBar MBri NHar NHol SGar SPer SSta WPat
¶ – 'Minor'	NHol WPat
– 'Mountain Fire'	CB&S CBow CBra CHig CMHG CSco EBre GRei IBar IOrc MBar MBri MGos MMth NJap SHil SPer SPic SSta WPat WWeb
* – 'Nana'	CFor NHol
– 'Pink Delight'	CB&S CBra IBar LSav MBal MBar MGos MMth MPla MRav NHol NKay SPer SReu SSpi WPat
– 'Prelude'	LSav MBri MRav WPat
– 'Purity'	CB&S CBow CFor CHig CMHG EBre IOrc LSav MBal MBar MGos MPlt MR&S NHol NJap NTow SExb SHil SPer SPla SReu SSta WBod WPat
– 'Pygmaea'	CFor MBal NHol WPat WThu
– 'Red Mill'	CHig CSco LSav MMth NHol SPer SSpi SSta
– 'Robinswood'	SSpi SSta
– 'Rosalinda'	LSav MR&S
– 'Rosea'	LHyd LSav
– 'Sarabande'	EPla LSav MBri SSpi SSta WPat
– 'Scarlett O'Hara'	CB&S IBar LSav MBri MGos SHil SSta
– 'Select'	MGos
– 'Snowdrift'	CKni SPer
– 'Spring Candy'	MGos
– Taiwanensis group	CCla CHig CMHG CSco CTre ENot GRei IOrc LHyd LSav MBal MBar MPlt MR&S MRav NWea SExb SHil SLon SPer SPla SSta WAbe WBod
– 'Tickled Pink'	CB&S
– 'Tilford'	CCla CHig MBri SPla SSpi SSta
– 'Valley Rose'	CBra CSam ENot MGos MR&S SHil SSpi
– 'Valley Valentine'	COtt LRHS LSav MBri SHil SSpi SSta
– 'Variegata'	Widely available
– 'Wada's Pink'	See P. ***j.*** 'Christmas Cheer'
¶ – 'Weeping Bride'	LRHS
¶ – 'Weeping Groom'	LRHS
– 'White Caps'	CHig LSav
– 'White Cascade'	LSav MBar WWat
– 'White Pearl'	CKni EBre IJoh MBri MGos SSta
– 'White Rim'	See P. ***j.*** 'Variegata'
– 'William Buchanan'	MHig NHol WPat WThu
nana	GLoc MBal MBar NHol
– 'Redshank'	MBal
ryukuensis 'Temple Bells'	CB&S IBar LSav
yakushimensis	CMHG LSav SPic WBod

PILEA (Urticaceae)

* 'Anette'	MBri
cardierei	MBri SLMG WEas
– ***nana***	SLMG
* 'Ellen'	MBri
involucrata	MBri
– 'Moon Valley'	MBri
– 'Norfolk'	MBri
nummulariifolia	MBri
peperomioides	CSev EPad
repens	MBri
'Silver Tree'	MBri
* ***spruceana*** 'Bronze'	MBri

PILEOSTEGIA (Hydrangeaceae)

viburnoides	Widely available

PILGERODENDRON (Cupressaceae)

PILULARIA (Marsileaceae)

globulifera	CNat

PIMELEA (Thymelaeaceae)

¶ ***arenaria***	ECou
coarctata	See P. ***prostrata***
¶ ***ferruginea*** 'Magenta Mist'	LHop
filiformis	ECou
§ ***prostrata***	ECou EPot GAbr GLoc MHig NHar NHol SHil SIng WOMN WPat WPer WThu
¶ – ***parvifolia***	ECou
¶ ***suteri***	ECou

PIMPINELLA (Umbelliferae)

anisum	CArn GPoy LHol MChe MSal SIde WPer
major rosea	EFol ELan MPar SFir WEas
¶ ***minima rosea***	SBar
sanguisorba	EEls
saxifraga	LHol SIde

PINELLIA (Araceae)

cordata	SPou
pedatisecta	SAxl
pinnatisecta	SAxl
ternata	EPar EPot SIng WOld WThu
tripartita	See P. ***pinnatisecta***

PINGUICULA † (Lentibulariaceae)

caerulea	WMEx
caudata	WMEx
cyclosecta	WMEx
ehlersiae	WMEx
grandiflora	CHar CRiv EPot MHig NKay NRya NWCA WMEx WThu
lutea	WMEx
¶ ***vulgaris***	ECro

PINUS † (Pinaceae)

albicaulis 'Nana'	See P. ***a.*** 'Noble's Dwarf'
§ – 'Noble's Dwarf'	CKen SHil

N ***aristata***	CBow CDoC CMCN EBre EHar EPot IBar IJoh LSav MBal MBar MBri MGos NHol SGar SHil SMad SReu SSta STre WCon WCoo WMou WThu
armandii	CMCN SHil WCoo
attenuata	LSav
austriaca	See P. ***nigra nigra***
ayacahuite	CBow LSav SHil
banksiana	MBal STre WCon
– 'Chippewa'	CKen
I – 'Compacta'	CKen
– 'Manomet'	CKen
– 'Neponset'	CKen
– 'Wisconsin'	CKen
bungeana	CMCN EHar MBlu SHil WFro
canariensis	EHul
cembra	CDoC EHar ENHC LSav MBar NWea SHil WCon
– 'Aurea'	See P. ***c.*** 'Aureovariegata'
§ – 'Aureovariegata'	CKen EHar WAbe
– 'Barnhourie'	CKen
– 'Blue Mound'	CKen
– 'Chalet'	CKen
¶ – 'Compacta Glauca'	WCon
*– 'Glauca'	EBre NHol
I – 'Inverleith'	CBra CKen MBri
– 'Jermyns'	CKen
– 'King's Dwarf'	CBow CKen
– nana	See P. ***pumila*** 'Nana'
¶ – 'Roughills'	CKen
– sibirica	See P. ***sibirica***
– 'Stricta'	CKen SHil
cembroides	EHar LSav
– edulis	LSav SHil
– monophylla	EHar SGar
contorta	CB&S CDoC CPer GRei MBal MBar MGos NWea SGar STre WMou
– 'Frisian Gold'	EBre
– latifolia	SHil
– 'Spaan's Dwarf'	CKen LLin MBar MBri MGos
corsicana	See P. ***nigra maritima***
coulteri	EHar LSav SHil WCoo WNor
densiflora	CDoC EHul ENHC LSav MBal SHil WNor
– 'Alice Verkade'	LLin MBri WCon
– 'Aurea'	WCon
*– 'Jeffreyi'	WCon
– 'Oculis-draconis'	MBar MBri SHil WCon
– 'Pendula'	CKen MBal NHol
– 'Umbraculifera'	EHul IOrc LLin MBar MBri SHil SSta WCon
flexilis	LSav SHil
– 'Firmament'	MBri
– 'Glenmore Dwarf'	CKen
– 'Nana'	CKen
¶ – 'Pendula'	SMad
gerardiana	EHal EHar
griffithii	See P. ***wallichiana***
halepensis	SHil
– brutia	WCoo
heldreichii 'Aureospicata'	MBar
– 'Compact Gem'	CKen EBre IOrc LLin MBar MBri MGos SHil SSta
§ ***– leucodermis***	CDoC CMac EHar IJoh LNet LSav MBal MBar SHil SSta WCon
– 'Pygmy'	CKen SHil
– 'Satellit'	CDoC CSco ENHC IOrc MBri SGar WAbe
– 'Schmidtii'	CKen EBre LLin MBri
x ***holfordiana***	SHil
x ***hunnewellii***	SHil
jeffreyi	EHar LSav MBal MBar SHil WCoo
koraiensis	CMCN LSav NWea WNor
– 'Bergman'	CKen
– 'Compacta Glauca'	SHil
¶ – 'Dragon Eye'	CKen
– 'Jack Corbit'	CKen
– 'Shibamichi'	CKen
¶ – 'Silveray'	CKen
– 'Winton'	CKen SHil
kwangtungensis	CMCN
lambertiana	SHil
leucodermis	See P. ***heldreichii leucodermis***
luchuensis	WCoo
magnifica	See P. ***montezumae***
monophylla	CKen EHar
§ ***montezumae***	CB&S IOrc ISea MUlv SArc SHil SMad SSpi WBod WCoo
monticola	CMCN LSav NWea SHil
*– 'Pendula'	MBar
– 'Skyline'	MBar MBri
mugo	CB&S CBra EHul ENot GRei MBal MBar MBri MGos MR&S SHil WMou
– 'Carsten's Wintergold'	See P. ***m.*** 'Winter Gold'
– 'Corley's Mat'	CKen NHol SSta
– 'Gnom'	CMac CSco EHul IJoh LLin MBar MBri NBar SHil WCon WWat
– 'Humpy'	CKen EBre EHul ENHC LLin MBri WCon
– 'Jacobsen'	CKen
– 'March'	CKen NHol
– 'Mops'	CBow CDoC CMac CSco EBre EHar EHul ENHC IHos LLin MBar MBri MGos NHol SHil SPer SSta WCon
– mugo	GRei MBar WCon
– 'Ophir'	CBow CKen CSco EBre EHar EHul ENHC IOrc LLin LNet MBar MBri SGar SHil SSta WCon
– prostrata	See P. ***m. rostrata***
– pumilio	CDoC CMac EHul ENot GRei IOrc LLin MBar MBro MGos MR&S NWea SHil SPer STre WCon WNor
§ ***– rostrata***	GRei NWea WMou
– 'Spaan'	CKen
– 'Trompenburg'	SHil

§ – 'Winter Gold'	CKen EBre EHul IOrc MBri SSta WCon
– 'Yellow Point'	MBri
– 'Zundert'	MBar MBri MGos
muricata	CDoC MBal MGos SHil WCoo
§ ***nigra***	CB&S CDoC CKin CSco ENHC ENot GRei IJoh LBuc LNet MBar MGos MR&S NWea SHil SPer WCon WMou
– 'Aurea'	CBow EBre WMou
– ***austriaca***	See P. ***nigra nigra***
– 'Black Prince'	CKen LLin
– 'Bright Eyes'	CKen EHul LLin
N– 'Cebennensis Nana'	CKen
– ***corsicana***	See P. ***n. maritima***
¶ – 'Géant de Suisse'	WMou
– 'Hornibrookiana'	CKen MBri SHil SSta
– ***laricio***	See P. ***n. maritima***
¶ – 'Moseri'	CKen
– 'Nana'	MBri
– 'Pygmaea'	CKen
– 'Wurstle'	CKen
§ ***nigra maritima***	CDoC CKen CKin CPer CSco ENot GRei IHos LBuc MBri NWea SHil SMad WMou
– – 'Spingarn'	CKen
– – 'Talland Bay'	CKen
– – 'Yaffle Hill'	CKen
§ ***nigra nigra***	LBuc MBri NWea
¶ – – 'Bright Eyes'	CKen
¶ – – 'Helga'	CKen
– – 'Schovenhorst'	CKen
– – 'Strypemonde'	CKen
palustris	SHil WCoo
parviflora	CDoC EPot LSav NWea SHil STre WCoo WNor
– 'Adcock's Dwarf'	CKen MBri SHil WAbe
¶ – 'Azuma-goyo'	CKen
I – 'Baasch's Form'	CKen
– 'Blue Giant'	NHol WCon
*– 'Bonny Bergman'	CKen
– ***brevifolia***	CBow SHil
¶ – 'Dai-ho'	CKen
¶ – 'Diaset-susan'	CKen
*– 'Fukai Seedling'	CKen
¶ – 'Fukushima-goyo'	CKen
– ***glauca***	CMac CSco EHul ENHC IHos IOrc MBar MBri SHil
*– 'Goykusen Seedling'	CKen
¶ – 'Goyoku-sui'	CKen
¶ – 'Gyok-ka-sen'	CKen
– 'Gyok-uei'	CKen
– 'Gyok-ukan'	CKen
– 'Hagaromo Seedling'	CKen
– 'Hakko'	CKen
¶ – 'Ibo-can'	CKen
¶ – 'Ichi-no-se'	CKen
– 'Irifune'	CKen
¶ – 'Janome'	CKen
– 'Kiyomatsu'	CKen
– 'Kobe'	CKen
– 'Kokonde'	CKen
¶ – 'Ko-raku'	CKen
¶ – 'Mei-ko'	CKen

– 'Negishi'	EHul MBal MBlu MBri
– 'Ryo-kuho'	CKen
¶ – 'Ryuju'	CKen
– 'Saphir'	NHol
¶ – 'Setsu-gekka'	CKen
– 'Shika-shima'	CKen
– 'Shizakagoten'	CKen
– 'Tempelhof'	ENHC LNet MBri NHol SHil WCon
patula	CGre CTre ISea MBal MBlu SArc SHil SMad WCoo WWat
peuce	IJoh LSav MBar NWea STre WCon WCoo
¶ – 'Arnold Dwarf'	CKen
pinaster	CB&S CDoC MBal SHil
pinea	CHEx CMac EHar IOrc MBal MGos SArc SHil WCon WCoo WNor
ponderosa	CBow EHar NWea SHil WCon WCoo
– ***scopulorum***	LSav
* ***pumila*** 'Compacta'	SHil
– 'Draijer's Dwarf'	NHol
– 'Dwarf Blue'	See P. ***p.*** 'Glauca'
§ – 'Glauca'	CKen EBre IDai LNet MBri NHol
– 'Globe'	EBre MBar MBri
– 'Säntis'	CKen
– 'Saphir'	CKen MBri
radiata	CB&S CDoC CHEx CSco CTre CTrw ENot IHos IJoh IOrc ISea MBal SArc SHil SPer WCoo
– 'Aurea'	CKen
– 'Marshwood'	CKen
resinosa 'Joel's Broom'	CKen
– 'Nobska'	CKen
– 'Quinobequin'	CKen
– 'Watnong'	CKen
x ***schwerinii***	CDoC WCon
sibirica	LSav
strobus	CBow CCor CDoC CSco EPot GRei IJoh IOrc LSav MBar MR&S NWea SHil SMad STre WCon
§ – 'Alba'	SHil SMrm
¶ – 'Bergman's Mini'	CKen
I – 'Bergman's Sport of Prostrata'	CKen
¶ – 'Densa'	CKen
¶ – 'Fastigiata'	CKen
¶ – 'Hillside Gem'	CKen
– 'Horsford'	CKen
¶ – 'Jericho'	CKen
¶ – 'Krügers Liliput'	MBri
– 'Macopin'	NHol
– 'Merrimack'	CKen
– 'Minima'	CDoC MBar MBlu MBri WCon
*– ***minuta***	CKen
– 'Nana'	See P. ***s.*** 'Radiata'
– 'Nivea'	See P. ***s.*** 'Alba'
– 'Northway Broom'	CKen
¶ – 'Pendula'	MBri
– 'Prostrata'	SHil

§ – 'Radiata'	EBre EHul ENHC IHos IJoh IOrc LLin LNet MBri SHil WAbe WCon
– 'Reinshaus'	EBre WAbe
¶ – 'Sea Urchin'	CKen
– 'Uncatena'	CKen
– 'Verkade's Broom'	CKen
sylvestris	Widely available
– 'Argentea'	EHar LNet SHil
– 'Aurea'	CMac CSco EHar EHul IOrc LLin LNet MBal MBar NHol SHil SPer SSta WAbe WMou
– 'Beuvronensis'	CMac CSco EHar EHul LNet MBlu MBri MGos NHol SHil SSta STre WAbe WMou
¶ – 'Burghfield'	CKen
– 'Chantry Blue'	LLin MBar NHol
¶ – 'Compressa'	NHol WCon
¶ – 'Dereham'	CKen
– 'Doone Valley'	CKen SHil
– 'Fastigiata'	CDoC CKen CSco EBre EHar EHul LLin MBar MBri SHil SSta WCon WMou
– 'Frensham'	CKen
– 'Globosa Viridis'	NHol
– 'Gold Coin'	CBra CKen LLin MBar MBri NHol WCon
* – 'Hensley's Dwarf'	MBar
– 'Hibernia'	EBre ENHC
– 'Hillside Creeper'	CKen
– 'Jade'	See P. *s.* 'Iceni'
– 'Jeremy'	CKen LLin
– 'Kenwith'	CKen
¶ – 'Lodge Hill'	WCon
¶ – 'Martham'	CKen
– 'Mongolia'	CMCN
§ – 'Moseri'	MBri SSta WCon
– 'Nana'	See P. *s.* 'Watereri'
– 'Pixie'	CKen
I – ***prostrata***	WCon
¶ – 'Pyramidalis Compacta'	WCon
– 'Repens'	CKen
– 'Saxatilis'	WCon
* – 'Sei'	LRHS
– 'Sentinel'	CKen
I – 'Skjak II'	CKen
¶ – 'Spaan's Slow Column'	CKen
– 'Tabuliformis'	CMCN WCon
– 'Tage'	CKen
– 'Viridis Compacta'	SHil
§ – 'Watereri'	CDoC CMac EHul ENHC ENot IDai IHos IOrc LNet MBar MBri MGos NBar NHol SHil SPer SSta WCon
taeda	WCoo
§ ***thunbergii***	CDoC EHar LSav MBal MBar MGos SHil STre WCon WCoo WNor
– 'Kotobuki'	CKen
– 'Kujaku'	CKen
– 'Oculus-draconis'	SHil
– 'Sayonara'	CKen NHol
¶ – 'Shio-guro'	CKen
– 'Sunsho'	CKen
– 'Yatsubusa'	See P. *t.* 'Sayonara'
uncinata	See P. ***mugo rostrata***
virginiana	MBal
§ ***wallichiana***	CChu CDoC CKen CMCN CSco EHar EHul ENHC IBar IOrc LSav MBal MBar MGos MR&S NHol SGar SHil SMad SReu WCon WCoo WMou
– 'Nana'	SHil
– 'Umbraculifera'	MBal
¶ – 'Zebrina'	WCon
yunnanensis	CMCN

PIPER (Piperaceae)

ornatum	MBri

PIPTANTHUS (Leguminosae)

laburnifolius	See P. ***nepalensis***
§ ***nepalensis***	Widely available

PISONIA (Nyctaginaceae)

♦ ***brunoniana***	See P. ***umbellifera***
¶ ***umbellifera***	CHEx
¶ – 'Variegata'	CHEx

PISTACIA (Anacardiaceae)

chinensis	CB&S ELan LGre SHil SSpi

PISTIA (Araceae)

stratiotes	MSta

PITTOSPORUM † (Pittosporaceae)

anomalum	ECou
colensoi	WCoo WHCr
crassifolium	CB&S ECou SHil
– 'Variegatum'	CGre LHop SHil
¶ – x ***tenuifolium***	ECou
¶ ***cuneatum***	LHop
dallii	CHEx SArc SHil
divaricatum	ECou
eugenioides	CB&S CGre MFir
– 'Variegatum'	CB&S CGre IOrc MUlv SHil WSHC
'Garnettii'	Widely available
¶ 'Green Flame'	WSHC
michiei	ECou
* ***molvocata***	CHan
obcordatum kaitaiaensis	ECou
* ***oniensis***	SArc
patulum	SArc
phillyreoides	CPle
pimeleoides	ECou
ralphii	ECou IBlr SHil
– 'Green Globe'	ECou
– 'Variegatum'	SHil SLon SSpi
tenuifolium	CB&S CBow CBra CHoe CPle CSco CShe ECou ELan ENot IDai LHop MBal MBri MR&S NTow SChu SDix SHil SLon SReu WAbe WOMN WSHC
– 'Abbotsbury Gold'	CBot CBow CCla CHoe CSam ELan SPer WSHC WWeb
– 'All Gold'	SPla
– 'Arundel Green'	LRHS
– 'Atropurpureum'	CB&S CSco

– 'County Park Dwarf'	ECou
– 'Deborah'	CB&S CBra LHop WSHC
– 'Dixie'	CMHG CMer CTre ECou
§ – 'Eila Keightley'	CMHG IOrc MBal SHil
– 'Golden King'	CB&S CGre CMHG IJoh MBal MRav SPer
– 'Irene Paterson'	CB&S CCla CMHG CSam CSco CTrw EGol ELan ERav IJoh IOrc LHop MBal MR&S MRav SHil SLon SPer SSta WSHC
– 'James Stirling'	CMHG IOrc SLon SPla
– 'John Flanagan'	See P. *t.* 'Margaret Turnbull'
– 'Limelight'	CB&S CGre
– 'Margaret Turnbull'	CB&S COtt ECou IReg LHop MR&S
– 'Marjory Channon'	CB&S
– 'Nigricans'	CB&S CLan CMHG
– 'Purpureum'	CBot CBra CGre CHoe CMHG CMer CPle CSam CTrw ELan ERav IJoh IOrc ISea MBal SHil SPer SPla WSHC
– 'Saundersii'	CGre CKni ENot ISea MBal SHil
*– 'Silver Dollar'	MBri
– 'Silver Magic'	CB&S
– 'Silver Queen'	CBow CBra CGre CLan CMHG CSam CSco IBar IDai IJoh IOrc MBal MRav NKay NTow SHil SPer SPla WBod WKif WSHC
¶ – 'Stirling Gold'	CB&S
– 'Sunburst'	See P. *t.* 'Eila Keightley'
– 'Tom Thumb'	CB&S CBow CHoe CMHG CTrw ECou EGol IBar IJoh IOrc IReg LHop MPla MR&S NRoo SHil SPer SPla SSta WWat
– 'Tresederi'	CMHG CSco CTrw MBal
– 'Variegatum'	CB&S SHil
– 'Warnham Gold'	CB&S CMHG COtt CSco CTrw IOrc ISea SHil SSpi
– 'Wendle Channon'	CB&S CBra CCla CMHG CSam CSco IJoh SPer WWeb
– 'Winter Sunshine'	SSta
tobira	CB&S CBra CCla CHEx CHan CMCN CPle CTre LSav MNew SArc SBor SGar SHil SPer SSpi SSta WSHC
– 'Nanum'	MUlv
– 'Variegatum'	CB&S CBot CGre CHEx CPle LHop MBri SGar SHil SPer
undulatum	CB&S CHEx CPle
– 'Variegatum'	CGre

PITYROGRAMMA (Adiantaceae)

chrysophylla	NMar
triangularis	SBla

PLAGIANTHUS (Malvaceae)

♦***betulinus***	See P. ***regius***
lyallii	See HOHERIA ***lyallii***
§ ***regius***	ECou ISea SHil
¶ – ***chatamica***	IReg

PLANTAGO (Plantaginaceae)

¶ ***arborescens maderensis***	SAxl
argentea	SIng
asiatica 'Variegata'	See P. ***major*** 'V.'
¶ ***barbata***	WDav
coronopus	CKin
cynops	EMon
lanceolata 'Streaker'	CRow
¶ ***major*** B&L 12649	EMon
– ***atropurpurea***	See P. ***m. rubrifolia***
§ – 'Rosularis'	CArn CBre CCor CFis CGle CHan CRiv CRow ECha ECro ELan EMon GPla GWic MTho NHol NSti SLHN SSvw WBon WHal WHer WHil WRus
§ – ***rubrifolia***	Widely available
§ – 'Variegata'	CHoe CRiv CRow ECro EFol ELan NHar NHol NRar WDav WHer WHil
maritima	CKin
media	CKin LHil
nivalis	EPot NTow WEas WHer WThu
rosea	See P. ***major*** 'Rosularis'
sempervirens	NHol

PLATANUS † (Platanaceae)

♦× ***acerifolia***	See P. × ***hispanica***
§ × ***hispanica***	CB&S CKin CLnd CSco EHar ENot IDai IJoh LBuc MBri MGos MR&S NWea SHil SMad SPer WMou
– 'Suttneri'	SHil WMou
occidentalis	WCoo
orientalis	CLnd EHar IOrc ISea MBri SExT SHil SMad SSpi WCoo WMou
§ – ***digitata***	MBri SHil
– ***insularis***	EHar
– 'Laciniata'	See P. ***o. digitata***
'Pyramidalis'	SMad WMou

PLATYCARYA (Juglandaceae)

strobilacea	CMCN SHil WMou
¶ – MSF 804	SSpi

PLATYCERIUM (Polypodiaceae)

alcicorne	See P. ***bifurcatum***
§ ***bifurcatum***	MBri
grande	See P. ***superbum***
§ ***superbum***	MBri

PLATYCLADUS See **THUJA**

PLATYCODON † (Campanulaceae)

grandiflorus	CGle CSco ECha EPad LHop LSav MFir MSal NKay NNor SAxl SDix SFis SIng WCla WHoo WOld
– ***albus***	CSco CSun ECro EFou ELan EPad LAbb MBri MBro NOak SPer WHoo WWin
– ***apoyama***	EPad GLoc MBro MCas NKay SWas WHil WHoo WPer
– ***apoyama albus***	LGre SWas
¶ – 'Baby Blue'	ECro

¶ – blue	ECro LAbb
– 'Blue Pearl'	WHoo
¶ – double blue	ECro
– 'Florist Rose'	EPad NOak WCar
– 'Florist Snow'	NOak WCar
¶ – 'Fuji Pink'	NHol WHil
¶ – 'Hakone'	ECro LHop WHil
– 'Mammoth Blue'	ECro
¶ – 'Mammoth White'	ECro
– ***mariesii***	CGle CHar CKel CSun EFou ELan ENot EPad ERou LSav MBal MBro MWgw NBar NHol NSti SDix SHig SPer WEas WHoo WOMN WRus WWin
– ***mariesii albus***	CCla ERou GWic NBar WEas WRus
– 'Park's Double Blue'	LGan NOak SMrm WCar WHer WHoo
– 'Perlmutterschale' ('Mother of Pearl')	CGle ECro ELan EPad MBri
¶ – ***pumilus***	GArf NWÇA
– ***roseus***	CSco CSun ECro EFou WHoo WRus
¶ – 'Zwerg'	LGre

PLECOSTACHYS (Compositae)

§ ***serpyllifolia***	CCla CFis CSun IHos LAbb SDix SIng WPer

PLECTRANTHUS (Labiatae)

australis	SLMG
behrii	SLMG
§ ***coleoides*** 'Marginatus'	ERea GAbr LHil MRav SLMG WHal WPer
– 'Variegatus'	See P. *c.* 'Marginatus'
oertendahlii	EBak SLMG

PLEIOBLASTUS † (Gramineae(Bambuseae))

akebono	SBam SDry
§ ***auricomus***	Widely available
– 'Bracken Hill'	SBam SDry
– 'Chrysophyllus'	SBam SDry
§ ***chino***	SBam SDry WJun
§ – ***angustifolius***	SBam SDry
– 'Aureostriatus'	SBam SDry
♦ – ***chrysanthus***	See SASA ***chyrsantha***
– ***elegantissimus***	SBam SDry WJun
– 'Murakamianus'	SBam SDry
'Gauntlettii'	See P. ***humilis pumilus***
♦ ***glaber*** 'Albostriata'	See SASAELLA ***masamuneana*** 'Albostriata'
gramineus	SBam SDry
§ ***hindsii***	SArc SBam SDry SHil
§ ***humilis***	ELan SBam
§ – ***pumilus***	CRow CSco ELan EPar MBlu MBri SArc SBam SDry SHil WJun WNor WPat
kongosanensis 'Aureostriatus'	SBam SDry
linearis	SBam SDry
§ ***pygmaeus***	CB&S CLew CRow ECro EFul ELan IOrc MBri MGos SBam SCro SDry SHil SIng SPer WJun WRus
§ – ***distichus***	EFul SArc SBam SDry WJun
§ – 'Mirrezuzume'	EPla SBam WWat
shibuyanus 'Tsuboi'	SDry
§ ***simonii***	CHEx EFul SBam SDry SHil
♦ – ***heterophyllus***	See P. *s.* 'Variegatus'
§ – 'Variegatus'	MBlu SBam SDry WJun
§ ***variegatus***	CB&S CBra CElw CHoe CKel EFul EGol ELan ENot GWic LHop MBal MBri MGos NJap NNrd SArc SBam SDry SHil WHil WJun WRus
* – ***viridis***	SDry
viridistriatus	See P. ***auricomus***

PLEIONE † (Orchidaceae)

¶ ***aurita***	WChr
bulbocodioides	IBlr
– Pricei group	CBro CRiv NTow
– 'Yunnan'	LAma NTow
bulbocodioides Formosana group	CAvo CBro CRiv ELan IBlr LAma MBri NTow SIng SW&B WAbe WChr
– – 'Alba'	CAvo CBro IBlr NHol NWCA SWes
– – 'Clare'	CAvo CBro
– – 'Iris'	SWes
– – 'Lilac Beauty'	SWes
– – 'Lilac Jubilee'	CBro
– – 'Oriental Jewel'	CBro SWes
– – 'Oriental Splendour'	SIng SWes WAbe
– – 'Polar Star'	WAbe
– – 'Serenity'	WAbe
bulbocodioides Limprichtii	CBro CRiv NTow WAbe
– – 'Primrose Peach'	CBro SWes
x ***confusa***	WChr
Etna	SWes
forrestii	LAma WChr
Fuego	SWes
Hekla	SWes
hookeriana	LAma
humilis	LAma SW&B
Jorullo	SWes
maculata	LAma SW&B
¶ ***pinkepankii***	WChr
pogonoides	See P. ***speciosa***
¶ ***scopulorum***	WChr
speciosa	SWes
Tolima	SWes
Tongariro	SWes
Versailles	CBro SWes
– 'Muriel Turner'	CBro SWes

PLEUROSPERMUM (Umbelliferae)

brunonis	CFor NTow

PLUM See **PRUNUS** ***domestica***

PLUMBAGO (Plumbaginaceae)

§ ***auriculata***	CB&S CCla CHan CHil CPle CSun CTre EBak EEls ELan ERav ERea LAbb LHol LHop MBri MNew MRav NPal NRog SIde SLMG SLon WBod
– ***alba***	CB&S CBot CCla CSun EBak ERav ERea IBlr LAbb MNew SLMG
capensis	See P. ***auriculata***
indica	CPle SLMG
– ***rosea***	ERea MNew
larpentae	See CERATOSTIGMA ***plumbaginoides***

PLUMERIA (Apocynaceae)

forms	MNew
rubra	MNew
'Singapore'	MNew

PNEUMATOPTERIS (Thelipteridaceae)

¶ ***pennigera***	NMar

POA (Gramineae)

acicularifolia	NHol
alpina	NLan
chaixii	CElw CHoe EMon SApp
colensoi	CHoe SApp
x ***jemtlandica***	CHoe NHol

PODANTHUS (Compositae)

¶ ***ovatifolius*** G&K 4386	LSav

PODOCARPUS (Podocarpaceae)

acutifolius	ECou WCon
N ***alpinus***	CDoC ECou EHul EHul GLoc IOrc MBar MBar SBor SHil SReu
– 'Blue Gem' (f)	ECou LLin MBri WWat
– 'Bluey'	LLin LSav
andinus	See PRUMNOPITYS ***andina***
chilinus	See P. ***salignus***
§ ***cunninhamii*** (f)	ECou IBar
dacrydioides	See DACRYCARPUS ***dacrydioides***
ferrugineus	See PRUMNOPITYS ***ferruginea***
'Golden Dwarf'	See PRUMNOPITYS ***ferruginea*** 'G.D.'
♦ ***hallii***	See P. ***cunninghamii***
§ ***lawrencei*** (f)	ECou LSav MBar MGos MPla SSmi WWat
♦– ***alpinus***	See P. ***alpinus***
macrophyllus	CGre CMCN CTre SArc SHil SMad WWat
¶– 'Angustifolius'	CHEx
nivalis (f)	CDoC CMac CSco ECou EHar MBar MHig MPla SBor SHil SLon SPer SSmi SSta WThu WWat
– 'Bronze'	MBri
¶– 'Clarence' (m)	ECou
¶– 'Green Queen' (f)	ECou
– 'Jack's Pass' (m)	ECou
¶– 'Little Lady' (f)	ECou
– 'Otari' (m)	ECou
¶– 'Park Cover'	ECou
¶– 'Princess' (f)	ECou
nubigenus	SHil
§ ***salignus***	CB&S CChu CDoC CGre CHEx CLan CMer CPle CTre IOrc SArc SHil WCoo
spicatus	See PRUMNOPITYS ***taxifolia***
totara	CHEx CHan CTre ECou STre WCoo
– 'Aureus'	CB&S ECou EHul MBal MBar SMad WSHC
– ***hallii*** (f)	ECou WBod WThu
– 'Pendulus'	ECou

PODOPHYLLUM (Podophyllaceae)

emodi	See P. ***hexandrum***
– ***chinense***	See P. ***hexandrum c***
§ ***hexandrum***	CChu CCla CElw CHEx CHar CRow CSun ECha EFou EPar GAbr GDra GEdr GPoy GWic MBal MBri MCot MHig MPar MSal MTho NKay SAxl
§ – ***chinense***	LGre SMad WWat
– ***majus***	NHol SHig
peltatum	ECro GPoy LAma MSal SSpi WChr WWat
¶ ***versipelle***	ECro

PODRANEA (Bignoniaceae)

§ ***ricasoliana***	LHop LRHS MNew SLMG

POGONATHERUM (Gramineae)

paniceum	See P. ***saccharoideum***
saccharoideum	MBri

POGOSTEMON (Labiatae)

¶ ***heyneanus***	CSun

POINSETTIA See **EUPHORBIA** ***pulcherrima***

POLEMONIUM (Polemoniaceae)

brandegeei	MHig NRed
¶– JCA 9510	WDav
caeruleum	Widely available
– ***album***	Widely available
– 'Blue Bell'	CGle NNrd
– Himalayan	WPer
– 'Hopleys'	LHop
carneum	CChu CElw CGle ECha EOrc LHop MPar MTho NTow SSpi WOMN WWin
cashmerianum	CChu CHan CSun GCHN MFir NOak NSti WEas WHoo
¶ ***confertum***	LHil NHol
delicatum	MTho NHar
flavum	CHan GAbr MFir MHig NSti SCro SSpi

foliosissimum	CBot CGle CHan CKel CSco CSun ECha EJud MCot MPar MWgw NTow WHen WKif WRus
– 'Album'	See P. ***f. alpinum***
§ – *alpinum*	IBrk NBir
¶ – *alpinum* JCA 41518	SBla
mellitum	WCar WPer
pauciflorum	Widely available
'Pink Beauty'	LHil SPer
pulcherrimum	CBre CSun CTom EBre ECro ELan EPla GAbr GWic LHil NHol NRed WPer
– *tricolor*	CElw SSpi WDav WPer
reptans	CArn CFis GLoc GPoy LHol MSal MTho NHar SIde WEas WPer
– 'Blue Pearl'	CBre CFis CGle CHar CSco ECro EFol ERou NRoo SIng SPer WHen
¶ – 'Dawn Flight'	ECro
♦– 'Lambrook Manor'	See P. ***r.*** 'Lambrook Mauve'
§ – 'Lambrook Mauve'	CBre CChu CGle CHan ECha EOrc ERav GAbr GWic MTho MUlv SWas WHoo WRus
¶ – 'Pink Beauty'	EFou
x *richardsonii*	NKay WEas
'Sapphire'	CSco ECro EFol ELan EMon GWic NNor
¶ *viscosum*	GCHN NHar WDav
yezoense	CCor CFis

POLIANTHES (Agavaceae)

geminiflora	LAma LBow
tuberosa	CB&S CKel
– 'The Pearl'	LAma SLMG

POLYGALA (Polygalaceae)

calcarea	MHig NKay WOMN
– 'Lillet'	ELan EPot GLoc LHop LMer SBar SOkd SWas
chamaebuxus	GDra GEdr GLoc MBal MBar MHig MPla NCat NKay SHil SMrm WDav
– *alba*	WAbe
§ – *grandiflora*	Widely available
¶ – 'Kamniski'	CMHG
– 'Loibl'	EPot
– 'Purpurea'	See P. ***c. grandiflora***
– 'Rhodoptera'	See P. ***c. grandiflora***
x *dalmaisiana*	ERea
§ *myrtifolia*	CB&S CFis CGre CHil CPle CSun CTre IBlr SChu SLHN
– 'Grandiflora'	See P. ***m.***
vayredae	SHil
virgata	WBod
vulgaris	CKin IOrc

POLYGONATUM †
(Liliaceae/Convallariaceae)

§ *biflorum*	CBro CChu CCla EBre ELan MBri MCot MSal NRoo SMad
– dwarf form	WChr
canaliculatum	See P. ***biflorum***
cirrhifolium	SOkd
commutatum	See P. ***biflorum***
¶ *curvistylum*	SWas
cyrtonema	See DISPOROPSIS ***pernyi***
§ *falcatum*	CRiv CRow EBul ELan GLoc MBal NHar NOak SIng WAbe WChr WThu
– 'Variegatum'	CChu EFou EPar LGre SBla SSpi WBon WRus
¶ 'Falcon'	WRus
giganteum	See P. ***biflorum***
* *graminifolium*	EPot
§ *hirtum*	EBul
hookeri	Widely available
humile	EPot SWas
§ x *hybridum*	Widely available
§ – 'Striatum'	CAvo CBos CBot CCor CHoe CRow EBre ECha IDai LHop MBal MPar NBar NOak NOrc NRoo SBla SSpi
♦– 'Variegatum'	See P. x ***h.*** 'Striatum'
latifolium	See P. ***hirtum***
multiflorum	See P. x ***hybridum***
– *giganteum*	See P. ***biflorum***
§ *odoratum*	CBro CRow EBul EPar EPot MPar MSal NHar NLan SPou SSpi WHil
*– *albopictum*	WChr
– 'Flore Pleno'	MCas
♦– 'Grace Barker'	See P. x ***hybridum*** 'Striatum'
*– *pluriflorum*	SSpi
*– 'Silver Wings'	MPar SPou
N– 'Variegatum'	CBro CChu CCla CHar EBul EFol EGol ELun EOrc ERou LGre LHop MBri MCas MCot MPar MWgw NHar NHol NRoo SAxl SPla WChr WRus
officinale	See P. ***odoratum***
pumilum	See P. ***falcatum***
racemosum	SIng
roseum	MPar WThu
¶ sp. Ewlat	SPou
stewartianum	LGre WChr
verticillatum	ECha EPot MBal NHol WWat
– *rubrum*	CArn LGre SPou WChr

POLYGONUM † (Polygonaceae)

aubertii	See FALLOPIA ***baldschuanica***
baldschuanicum	See FALLOPIA ***baldschuanica***
cuspidatum	See FALLOPIA ***japonica***
equisetiforme	See P. ***scoparium***
polystachyum	See PERSICARIA ***wallichii***
reynoutria	See FALLOPIA ***japonica compacta***
§ *scoparium*	CHar CRow EPla LHop MUlv NSti SDry

POLYMNIA (Compositae)

POLYPODIUM † (Polypodiaceae)

aureum	See PHLEBODIUM ***aureum***
§ *australe*	NKay NMar WCot WFib
§ – 'Barrowii'	NKay NMar
§ – 'Cristatum'	SApp
– 'Wilharris'	NKay
¶ – 'Oakley'	SWas
cambricum	See P. ***australe***
cristatum 'Cambricum'	See P. ***australe*** 'Cristatum'
glycyrrhiza 'Longicaudatum'	NMar
interjectum	NMar WFib
x *mantoniae*	NKay
¶ *scouleri*	SApp
x *shivasiae*	NKay
vulgare	CKin CWGN EHon GPoy MBal MWgw NKay NMar NNrd SHil SPer WFib
– 'Acutum'	NMar
– 'Bifido-Cristatum'	NHol NKay NNrd WFib
– 'Bifido-Grandiceps'	NMar
– *cambricum barrowii*	See P. ***australe*** 'Barrowii'
– 'Congestum Cristatum'	NKay
– 'Cornubiense'	CBos CFor CWGN ECha EMon NHol NKay NMar NVic SPer SSpi WFib
– 'Cornubiense Multifidum'	NKay
– Cristatum group 'Forster'	NKay
– 'Longicaudatum'	WFib
– 'Pulcherrimum'	EBre EGol NKay
– Ramosum group	NMar
– 'Semilacerum Falcatum O'Kelly'	NMar
– 'Semilacerum Jubilee'	NMar

POLYSCIAS (Araliaceae)

balfouriana 'Pennockii'	MBri
fruticosa	MBri
– 'Elegans'	MBri

POLYSTICHUM † (Aspleniaceae)

acrostichoides	IOrc
aculeatum	EBre EBul ECha EHon ELan IOrc MBri MWgw NHol NKay NMar SBla SHil SSpi WFib
– Grandiceps group	WFib
andersonii	LSav
braunii	CB&S EGol LSav
falcinellum	NKay
lonchitis	NKay SHil
munitum	IOrc NHol WFib
polyblepharum	EBre ELan IOrc LSav MBri SBla SSpi WCot WFib
♦ *proliferum*	See P. ***setiferum*** Acutilobum group
rigens	NMar
setiferum	CKin CSam CWGN EBre EGol ELan IOrc MBri MCot MWgw NHol NOrc SArc SBla SIng SPer SSpi WEas WFib
§ – Acutilobum group	CB&S CFor EBul ECha EPot LSav MCot MPar NHar NKay SApp SDix SMad SSpi WCot
– Congestum group	IOrc MBri NHol NKay NMar SAxl WFib
– *cristato-gracile*	See P. *s.* Percristatum group
– Dahlem group	LSav
– 'Divisilobum Densum'	MBal MPar NMar
– Divisilobum group	CFor CWGN EBre ELan EPar LHop LSav MBri NHol NKay NMar SMad SPer SPla WEas WFib WHoo
– Divisilobum group 'Herrenhausen'	MBri NMar
– Divisilobum group 'Mrs Goffy'	NMar
– 'Divisilobum Iveryanum'	NMar WFib
– 'Foliosum'	NKay SWas
– 'Imbricatum'	NKay
– Lineare group	NKay
§ – Percristatum group	NMar
– Perserratum group	NKay
– Plumoso-Divisilobum group	EGol MCot NHar SDix SHil SPla SWas
– Plumoso-divisilobum group 'Baldwinii'	NMar
– Plumosum group	CSam CWGN WFib
– *proliferum*	See P. *s.* Acutilobum group
– 'Pulcherrimum Bevis'	CFor NKay NMar SApp
– *ramo-pinnatum*	NMar
– *ramulosum*	NMar
N– 'Wollaston'	NBar
tsus-simense	MBri MWgw NMar SMad WFib

POLYXENA (Liliaceae/Hyacinthaceae)

ensifolia	LBow
odorata	LBow

POMEGRANATE See **PUNICA** ***granatum***

PONCIRUS (Rutaceae)

§ *trifoliata*	CB&S CBra CChu CCla CLan EHar ELan ENot ERea IBar LGre SArc SHil SMad SPer SSpi SSta STre WPat WWat

PONTEDERIA (Pontederiaceae)

cordata	CRiv CRow CWGN ECha EHon ELan EWav LMay MSta SHig
– *lancifolia*	CRiv MSta
lanceolata	See P. ***cordata lancifolia***

POPULUS † (Salicaceae)

alba	CKin CLnd ENot IDai LBuc MBar MBri NWea SExT SHil SPer WMou WWin

– ***bolleana***	See P. ***a.*** 'Pyramidalis'
§ – 'Pyramidalis'	CB&S CCor SHil WMou
– 'Raket' ('Rocket')	CLnd CSco EHar ELan ENot IJoh MGos SExT SPer
– 'Richardii'	CBot CCla CSco EBre EHar MBar SHil SMad SPer SSpi WMou
§ 'Balsam Spire'	CLnd ENot LBuc MBri NWea SExT SHil WMou
§ ***balsamifera***	ELan ENot MGos NWea SExT SHil SPer SPla
x ***canadensis***	See P. x ***euroamericana***
candicans	SHil
– 'Aurora'	Widely available
x ***canescens***	WMou
– 'De Moffart'	ENot
deltoides 'Cordata'	CCor
x ***euroamericana*** 'Aurea'	CLnd CSco ENot MRav SHil SPer WMou
– 'Eugenei'	ENot SHil
– 'Robusta'	CKin CLnd ENot LBuc MBri NWea SHil WMou
– 'Serotina'	EHar NWea SHil
x ***generosa***	SHil
lasiocarpa	CBot EHar ELan ENot IJoh MBri SExT SHil SPer
§ – ***tibetica***	SHil WMou
nigra	CNat EHar ELan ENot
– ***betulifolia***	CKin MBri MGos SHil
N– ***italica***	CB&S CLnd CMHG ELan ENot ISea LBuc MBri MGos NWea SExT SHil SMad SPer
♦– 'Italica Aurea'	See P. 'Lombardy Gold'
§ – 'Lombardy Gold'	LMer SMad WBod WMou
– 'Pyramidalis'	See P. ***n. italica***
¶ ***simonii*** 'Fastigiata'	CB&S
tacamahaca	See P. ***balsamifera***
'Tacatricho 32'	See P. 'Balsam Spire'
tremula	CKin CLnd EHar ELan ENot IJoh LBuc MBar MBri NWea SExT SHil SPer WMou
– 'Erecta'	EHar SExT WMou
– 'Fastigiata'	See P. ***t.*** 'Erecta'
– 'Pendula'	CLnd SHil SPer WMou
trichocarpa	EHar SHil
– 'Fritzi Pauley'	WMou
violascens	See P. ***lasiocarpa tibetica***
wilsonii	SHil

PORTULACA (Portulacaceae)

grandiflora	MBri

PORTULACA (Portulacaceae)

grandiflora	MBri
oleracea	CArn GPoy MChe SIde WHer WSto

POTATO See **SEED** Supplier's Index

POTENTILLA † (Rosaceae)

alba	CGle CHad CSev CShe EBre ECha EFou ELan GLoc ISea LGro LSav MCas MRav MTho MWgw NHol NRoo NSti SPer
alchemilloides	CLew CTom MHig WHil
alpicola	MCot
ambigua	See P. ***cuneata***
anserina	CKin WHer
♦***arbuscula***	See P. ***fruticosa*** 'Elizabeth'
argentea	CFor EBar IJoh NHol WCla WPer
– 'Calabre'	EFol GAbr
– ***glabra***	WWin
argyrophylla	See P. ***atrosanguinea a.***
– ***leucochroa***	See P. ***atrosanguinea leucochroa***
atrosanguinea	CBre CGle CHad CHan CHar CSco CShe CSun ECha ELun EOrc GLoc GWic MBal MPar MWgw NHol NKay NNor NSti SAxl SIng WEas WHoo
– CC 184	CSun
§ – ***argyrophylla***	CGle CHan ECro ELan GAbr MBri NOak NRed SCro SIng
§ – ***leucochroa***	CMHG GWic NHar
§ – ***leucochroa*** SSW 7768	CSun GAbr GDra GLoc MPla NGre NHol
§ ***aurea***	CElw CLew ELan EMNN GLoc LHop MTho NNrd SIng SSmi WWin
– 'Aurantiaca'	EBre LHop MRav NNrd NRoo
– ***chrysocraspeda***	NHol NKay NNrd NRoo SIng
§ – 'Goldklumpen'	EFou GAbr LHop NBar
– 'Plena'	EBre EMNN GDra GLoc MHig MRav NNrd WWin
bifurca	WPer
– CC 102	CSun
'Blazeaway'	EBre ERou MBri
¶ ***brauniana***	SIng
calabra	ECha GLoc WPer
§ ***cinerea***	CHar CLew CRiv CShe CSpe CTom ELan MCas SSmi
§ ***crantzii***	CSun CTom ESis MCas MHig NLan NNrd NTow SIng WCla WHil WThu
¶ – ***nana***	WPer
¶ – 'Pygmaea'	MPlt
§ ***cuneata***	CLew CRiv CTom ELan EMNN ESis GDra GLoc MHig MPla MTho NKay SIng SSmi WHil WPer WWin
¶ – ***aurea***	ECro
delavayi	NHol WDav
dickinsii	NTow
§ ***erecta***	CArn CKin GPoy MChe MSal
eriocarpa	EBre EMNN ESis GDra MBro MHig MPla MWat NGre NKay NNrd NRoo SSmi WAbe WCla WHil
'Etna'	CElw CSco ELan LGre SFir
'Everest'	See P. 'Mount Everest'
'Fireflame'	ECha
fissa	CSun MBri
'Flamenco'	CB&S CSco EBre ELan ERou MBri MCot MRav NRoo WHoo WOld
fragiformis	See P. ***megalantha***
fruticosa 'Abbotswood'	Widely available

– 'Abbotswood Silver'	CB&S CBow CCla CHoe CPle EBre EFol ELan MBri MGos MRav NHol SPer SPla WHCG WPat WSHC WWat
– 'Annette'	CSco WHCG
♦– ***arbuscula***	See P. *f.* 'Elizabeth'
– 'Argentea Nana'	See P. 'Beesii'
– 'Barnbarroch'	EBre
– 'Beanii'	NHol WWeb
§ – 'Beesii'	CBot CHad CHoe CSco CShe CTom EHar ELan EMNN ESis IDai MBar MBro MPla NHol NKay NRoo SHil SPer WAbe WHCG WPer WWat WWeb
– 'Beverley Surprise'	SPer WWeb
– 'Buttercup'	NHol WHCG WWeb
– 'Cascade'	LHop
*– 'Chelsea Star'	LHop
– 'Clotted Cream'	MBar
– 'Dart's Cream'	MBri
– 'Dart's Golddigger'	CB&S ECtt NHol NRoo WHCG WWeb
¶ – 'Dart's Nugget'	NHol WHCG
– 'Daydawn'	Widely available
*– 'Donard Orange'	NNor
– 'Eastleigh Cream'	CCla LSav SHil SPer
§ – 'Elizabeth'	Widely available
– 'Farreri'	See P. 'Gold Kugel'
§ – 'Farreri Prostrata'	SIng
– 'Floppy Disc'	CKni ELan
– 'Frances Lady Daresbury'	ISea MPla WWeb
– 'Friedrichsenii'	WWeb
– 'Glenroy Pinkie'	WAbe
§ – 'Gold Kugel' ('Gold Drop')	ENot NHol NNor SPla WHCG WWeb
– 'Goldcharm'	NKay
– 'Goldfinger '	CMer EBre ELan ENot IJoh IOrc LHop MBri MGos MR&S MRav MWat SHil SPla STre WAbe WHCG WWeb
– 'Goldstar'	CBot EBre IOrc MBri MGos SHil SSta WHCG WPat WWeb
– 'Goldteppich'	MBar NBar
– 'Goscote'	MGos
– 'Hachmann's Gigant'	WWeb
¶ – 'Honey'	WHCG
– 'Hopleys Little Joker'	EMNN WPat WWin
– 'Hopleys Orange'	LHop MBri WHCG WPat WWin
– 'Hurstbourne'	WWeb
– 'Jackman's Variety'	CSam CSco ECtt ENot SPer WBod WWeb
– 'Judith'	WWeb
– 'Katherine Dykes'	CBow CPle CSco ELan ENot GRei IDai MBal MBar MR&S NHol SHil SLon SPer WBod WWeb
– 'Klondike'	CB&S CLan CSco ELan GRei IDai ISea MBar MR&S NNor NRoo NWea SHil SPla WAbe WBod WWeb
– 'Knaphill'	ENot SReu WWeb
*– 'Knaphill Buttercup'	ELan EPar GDra GRei MPit WWeb
– 'Kobold'	EBre MBar WWeb
– 'KW 5774'	WWeb
– 'Logan'	WWeb
– 'London Town'	CMHG SLon
– 'Longacre Variety'	CBow CSco GDra GRei ISea MBar MR&S NHol NWea SHil SLon WBod WWat WWeb
– 'Maanelys' ('Moonlight')	CPle CSco CTrw ECtt ELan IJoh MBal MWat NWea SPer SPla WHCG WWeb
– 'Macpenny's Cream'	ENot
§ – 'Manchu'	Widely available
*– 'Medicine Wheel Mountain'	CKni EHal ELan NTow WHCG WPat WWeb
– 'Milkmaid'	WWeb
§ – 'Mount Everest'	ELan MPla MWat MWgw NHol NWea WBod WHCG WWeb
– 'Nana Argentea'	See P. ***fruticosa*** 'Beesii'
– 'Northman'	WWeb
– 'Nugget'	WWeb
– 'Ochroleuca'	WWeb
– 'Orange Star'	MPla NHol WWeb
– 'Orange Stripe'	WWeb
– 'Orangeade'	CKni
– ***parvifolia***	LSav
– 'Pastel Pink'	LHop
– 'Peaches & Cream'	WWeb
– 'Perryhill'	SPer
– 'Pink Glow'	GDra
– 'Pink Pearl'	EBre WWin
*– 'Pink Queen'	CB&S
– 'Pretty Polly'	CBow CCla CMHG COtt CSco EBre ELan IOrc LHop MBlu MBri MGos MPla NRoo SLon SPer SPla SSta SSus WHCG WPat WSHC WWeb
– 'Primrose Beauty'	Widely available
§ – 'Princess' ('Blink')	Widely available
¶ – 'Prostrate Copper'	NHol
– ***pumila*** CC 312	CSun
– 'Red Ace'	Widely available
¶ – 'Red Robin'	MBri SSus
– 'Rhodocalyx'	CCla EMNN MGos WHCG WWat
– 'Royal Flush'	CBra CCla CPle EBre ELan IJoh LHop MBar MBri MR&S SPer WHCG
– 'Ruth'	SHil WWeb
– 'Sandved'	IDai WWeb
– 'Silver Schilling'	LHop
– 'Snowflake'	CB&S WHCG WWeb
– 'Sophie's Blush'	ISea NHol NRoo WSHC WWeb
– 'Sunset'	CB&S CCla CSam CSco ECha ELan EMNN ENot ERav GDra MBal MBar MBri MGos MPla MR&S NHol NKay NNor NWea SHil SPer SReu SSta
– 'Tangerine'	Widely available
– 'Tilford Cream'	Widely available
– 'Tom Conway'	WPat

– 'Veitchii' CCla CPle CSco ISea NHol SHil SPer WHCG WWeb
– 'Vilmoriniana' CBow CHad CSco ELan IDai NNor SChu SHil SLon SMad SPer SSpi WAbe WHCG WSHC WWat WWeb
– 'Walton Park' MBal WWeb
¶ – 'Wessex Silver' WHCG
– 'Whirligig' CPle WHCG
– 'White Rain' CMer GDra MR&S NNor WWeb
– 'William Purdom' WHCG WWeb
¶ – 'Yellow Carpet' WHCG
– 'Yellow Giant' WWeb
– 'Yellow Star' LHop
¶ ***fruticosa davurica*** WHCG
– – 'Farrer's White' CSam SHil
♦ – – 'Hersii' See P. *f.* 'Snowflake'
♦ – – ***mandshurica*** See P. *f.* 'Manchu'
– – ***veitchii*** See P. *f.* 'Veitchii'
gelida See P. ***crantzii ternata***
'Gibson's Scarlet' CBow CCla CHad CKel CSam CSco EBre ECha EFou ELan ELun ERou GWic IDai LSav MBri MWgw NBar NHol SMad SPer WEas WHea WSHC
'Gloire de Nancy' EBre ELan ERou MRav SAxl
'Gold Clogs' See P. ***aurea*** 'Goldklumpen'
'Helen Jane' EBre MRav NHol WPer
x ***hopwoodiana*** LGre SWas
* 'Limelight' CKni ELan
* ***magnifica alba*** NNrd
'Mandschurica' See P. ***fruticosa*** 'Manchu'
* 'Maroon Variety' GWic
§ ***megalantha*** Widely available
'Melton' CSco EHal NOak WHen
'Monsieur Rouillard' MWat WHoo
montana CTom GCHN NHol
nepalensis CHan CShe CSun ECha ECro EFou GAbr MFir NNor NSti SAxl WHoo
§ – 'Miss Willmott' CB&S CCla CFor CGle CSco CShe CSun ELan LGre MBri MPit MRav MWgw NBar NHol NKay NRoo SBla SPer WEas WHen WPer WRus WWin
– 'Roxane' CFor CGle CHar CKel CSco CShe EBre ELan EOrc MBri MFir MPar MRav WHil WHoo
¶ – 'Salmon Seedling' GWic
§ ***neumanniana*** NTow WAbe
– ***aurea*** STre
– 'Goldrausch' ECha MBri SIng
– ***nana*** Widely available
nevadensis GLoc NHol WHil WPer WThu
nitida NHol NKay SIng WDav WPer
– 'Alannah' SIng
– 'Lissadell' WOMN
– ***rubra*** CShe EFol EPot GEdr GLoc MWat NHol NTow SBla SSmi WAbe WPer WWin
* 'Olympic Mountains' WPer
palustris MSta WCla
¶ ***peduncularis*** SWas
♦ 'Pink Panther' See P. ***fruticosa*** 'Princess'
♦ 'Pyrenaica' See P. ***fruticosa*** 'Farreri Prostrata'
recta CHad CHan ELan MCot MRav WBon WHil
– 'Citrina' See P. ***recta pallida***
♦ – ***macrantha*** See P. ***r.*** 'Warrenii'
§ – ***pallida*** CElw CFis CGle EBar EMon ERav LHop NSti SIng WBon WCar WHea WHoo
– ***sulphurea*** See P. ***r. pallida***
– 'Warrenii' CElw CHar CSam EBre ERou GAbr LHil MBro MFir MPar MWat NSti SIng SPer WCar WHal WHoo
reptans CKin
– 'Pleniflora' EMon
rupestris CCor CGle CNat CSco ECha IBrk MFir NHol NLan NRed NSti WAbe WCla WHil WPer WSHC
speciosa EPad LGre WOMN
sterilis CKin ELan
¶ 'Sungold' ESis
♦ ***tabernaemontani*** See P. ***neumanniana***
ternata See P. ***aurea chrysocraspeda***
thurberi EPad LGre
tommasiniana See P. ***cinerea***
x ***tonguei*** CHar CKel CShe EBre ECha ELan EMNN ESis GDra GLoc LHop MBal MBri MCas NHol NKay NNrd NRoo NSti SBla SIng SSmi WDav WHil
tormentilla See P. ***erecta***
tridentata See SIBBALDIOPSIS ***tridentata***
verna pygmaea See P. ***neumanniana nana***
verna See P. ***neumanniana***
'Versicolor Plena' NHol
villosa See P. ***crantzii***
* 'White Beauty' CKni
'Wickwar Trailer' CShe MGos MPla WHCG WSHC
'William Rollison' CB&S CBow CKel CSam EBre ECro EFou ELan ERou GAbr GWic MBri MFir MRav NHol NSti SChu SCro WSHC
willmottiae See P. ***nepalensis*** 'Miss Willmott'
'Yellow Queen' CB&S CBow CHar CKel CSco EBre EFou ERou MBri MRav NHol NRoo SChu SCro SPer

POTERIUM See **SANGUISORBA**

PRATIA See **LOBELIA**

PRIMULA † (Primulaceae)
acaulis See P. ***vulgaris***
'Alan Robb' (D.Prim) CFis CRow CSam EMNN GAbr GGar GHig NHol NJap NRoo SIng SPla SSus WCla WHal WHil

'Alba Plena' (D.Prim)	CGle GAbr GGar GSta IBlr WEas WRus
algida (11)	CPla MHig NGre
allionii (2)	CSun EMNN EPot GEdr GLoc ITim LCra LFox MBro MCas MHig NHar NHol NNrd NRya WAbe WWin
¶ – JCA 416.22 (2)	EPot
¶ – JCA 416.21 (2)	EPot
– ***alba*** (2)	GLoc MCas SIng WHil
– 'Anna Griffith' (2)	EPot ITim MCas NHol WDav
– 'Anne' (2)	GLoc
– 'Austen' (2)	EPot LFox NHol SIng
– 'Avalanche' (2)	EPot ITim LFox WAbe WDav WHil
– 'Beatrice Wooster' (2)	EPot LFox MCas NHar NHol NNrd SIng SSmi SWas WAbe WDav WHil WPat WThu
– 'Clarkes' (2)	NHar
– 'Crowsley Variety' (2)	EPot MCas MHig NHol NNrd NRya SIng WAbe WDav WHil WThu
¶ – 'Edrom' (2)	ITim
– 'Elliott's Variety' (2)	EPot ITim NHar
– 'Ethel Barker' (2)	EPot GEdr MCas MHig NHar NNrd SIng WHil WThu
¶ – ***forma*** (2)	ITim WHil
– 'Frank Barker' (2)	NHol
– 'Jane' (2)	GLoc
– 'K R W' (2)	EPot NHol WDav WHil
¶ – 'Ken's Seedling'	WAbe WHil
– 'Marion' (2)	EPot ITim LFox NNrd WDav
– 'Martin' (2)	EPot MBro NHol NNrd WDav
– 'Mary Berry' (2)	EPot WDav WHil
¶ – 'Peggy Wilson'	EPot
– 'Pennine Pink' (2)	EPot MBro NHol NNrd SIng WDav
– 'Picton's Variety' (2)	EPot
– 'Praecox' (2)	MCas WDav
– 'Snow Flake' (2)	EPot MCas WDav WThu
– 'William Earle' (2)	EPot MBro NHol SIng WDav WThu
¶ – x ***auricula*** (2)	NHol
§ – x ***hirsuta*** (2)	EPot MBro NHol WDav
– x ***marginata*** (2)	NHar WDav WHil
– x ***rubra*** (2)	See P. ***a.*** x ***hirsuta***
alpicola (26)	Widely available
– ***alba*** (26)	CPla CRow MBal NGre NRoo NRya
– hybrids (26)	NHol
– ***violacea*** (26)	CPla CRow ELun GAbr GDra GLoc MBal MBri NHol WDav
altaica grandiflora	See P. ***elatior meyeri***
'Altaica'	See P. ***elatior meyeri***
¶ American Pink Hose-in-Hose (Prim)	GSta
'Amethyst' (Poly)	EDon
amoena	See P. ***elatior meyeri***
angustifolia (20)	WDav
anisodora (4)	CBre CPla CRiv ELan ELun GAbr GEdr MBal NHol NKay NRya
'April Rose' (D.Prim)	CFis CGle CRow EMNN GAbr NHar NHol NJap NRoo NSti SIng SSus WCla WHil
'April Snowflake' (Prim)	CShe
aurantiaca (4)	CHar CPla EHon GAbr GEdr MSta NGre WDav
– hybrids (4)	CCla CSun
aureata (21)	EPar GEdr GLoc LCra NHar WAbe
– ***fimbriata*** (21)	GEdr WAbe
Auricula (2)	CArn CBow CCla CHar CSun ELan EPar ERou ESis GDra GLoc LAbb LCra MBal MTho MWgw NRoo SPer SSmi WCla WDav WThu WWin
auricula 'A Delbridge' (A)	SHya
– A74 (A)	MFie
– 'Adrian' (A)	EDon GAbr LCra LFox MCas NHar NJap SHya
– ***albocincta*** (2)	WDav
– 'Albury' (D)	EDon MFie
– 'Alfred Niblett' (S)	SHya
– 'Alice Haysom' (S)	NNrd SHya WHil
– 'Alison Jane' (A)	EDon LCra NNrd SHya
– 'Almondbury' (S)	SHya
– Alpine mixed (A)	CSun EHon GDra LCra
– 'Amethyst' (S)	SHya
– 'Andrea Julie' (A)	CRow EDon LCra LFox MCas MFie NHol NJap NRar NRed SHya WHil
¶ – 'Ann Hill' (S)	SHya
– 'Ann Taylor' (A)	LCra MFie
– 'Antoc' (S)	LCra MFie
– 'Applecross' (A)	ESis GAbr LCra LFox MCas MFie NJap NNrd NRed SHya
¶ – 'Archer'	NHol
– 'Argus' (A)	CShe EDon ELan EMNN GAbr LCra LFox MCas MFie NHar NJap NNrd NRed SHya WRus
¶ – 'Arundel Stripe' (S)	SHya
– 'Astolat' (S)	LCra MFie SHya
– 'Aurora' (A)	MCas SHya
– 'Aviemore' (A)	MFie
– 'Balihai' (S)	NHar
– 'Ballet' (S)	SHya
– 'Banana Split'	CGle
– 'Basuto' (A)	SHya
– ***bauhinii***	MBro NHol WDav
– 'Baupaume' (S)	LCra
– 'Beatrice' (A)	LCra LFox NNrd NRed
– 'Beauty of Bath' (S)	SHya
– 'Beechen Green' (S)	SHya
– 'Ben Wyves' (S)	SHya
– 'Betty Sheriff' (B)	SHya
– 'Big Ben' (S)	SHya
– 'Bilton' (S)	EDon LCra MFie WHer
– 'Black Ice' (S)	SHya
– 'Blairside Yellow'	CShe GLoc LFox MHig NHar NHol NRya SIng SPou WAbe WHil WThu WWin
– 'Blakeney' (D)	SHya
– 'Blossom' (A)	EDon LCra LFox MFie NJap NNrd SHya
– 'Blue Bonnet' (A)	LCra
– 'Blue Jean' (S)	CGle EDon LCra LFox MFie NHol NJap NRed

– 'Blue Nile' (S)	EDon LCra MFie SHya
¶ – 'Blue Steel' (S)	SHya
– 'Blue Velvet' (B)	ECha MCas SHya WHil
– 'Blue Wave' (D)	NNrd
– 'Bluebird' (S)	SHya
– 'Bookham Firefly ' (A)	LCra LFox MCas MFie NHar NJap NNrd
¶ – 'Bookham Star' (S)	SHya
– 'Bramshill' (S)	SHya
– 'Brass Dog' (S)	SHya
– 'Brazil' (S)	EDon ESis LCra LFox MCas MFie NHol NRed WHil
– 'Broadwell Gold' (B)	LFox SHya WDav WHil
¶ – 'Brookfield'	NHol
– 'Broughton' (S)	SHya
– 'Brown Bess ' (A)	LCra MCas NHar
– 'Bunty' (A)	MFie
¶ – 'Buttermilk'	NHol
– 'C G Haysom' (S)	CRow EDon ELan LCra LFox MFie NHar NJap NRed SHya
– 'C W Needham' (A)	EDon GAbr LCra LFox MFie NJap NNrd NRed SHya WHil
– 'Café au Lait' (A)	MFie
– 'Camelot' (D)	CRow EDon ELan LCra MCas MFie NHol NJap NRed SHya WHer
– 'Camilla' (A)	MFie
– 'Carcerot' (A)	MFie
– 'Carole' (A)	LFox NNrd SHya
– 'Catherine' (D)	CFor CMal CRow EDon ELan LCra MFie NHol NJap NRed WHer
– 'Chaffinch' (S)	LFox SHya
– 'Chamois' (B)	MFie
– 'Cherie' (S)	SHya
– 'Cherry' (S)	LCra LFox MFie SHya WHil
– 'Chirichua' (S)	LCra SHya
– 'Chloe' (S)	NHol NJap SHya
– 'Chloris' (S)	SHya
– 'Chorister' (S)	EDon ELan EPot ESis LCra LFox MBro MCas MFie NHar NNrd NRed SHya WDav WRus
– 'Citron' (S)	SHya
– 'Clare' (S)	MPar
– 'Colbury' (S)	LCra LFox
– 'Coll' (A)	SHya
– 'Colonel Champney' (S)	GAbr MFie SHya
– 'Comet' (S)	NNrd
– 'Commander' (A)	SHya
– 'Conservative' (S)	SHya
– 'Consett' (S)	LCra SHya
– 'Coppernob' (S)	SHya
– 'Coral' (S)	LCra MCas SHya
– 'Cortina' (S)	LCra LFox MFie NHol NJap NNrd
– 'County Park' (B)	SHya
– 'County Park Cream' (B)	SHya
– 'County Park Red' (B)	ECou SHya
– 'Crackley Tagetes' (D)	SHya
– 'Craig Vaughan ' (A)	LCra LFox MFie NHar NNrd
– 'Cream Blush' (D)	CRow EDon MFie
– 'Creenagh Stripe' (A)	MFie
– 'Crimson Cavalier'	CGle
– 'Crimson Velvet'	NNrd
– 'Daftie Green' (S)	SHya
– 'Dakota' (S)	LCra
– 'Daphnis' (S)	LFox SHya
– 'Delilah' (D)	EDon
– 'Devon Cream' (D)	CFor CGle CPla CRow EDon ELan ESis GLoc LCra MCas MFie NHol NJap NRed WHil WKif WRus
– 'Diane'	LCra NRed WDav
– 'Donhead' (A)	MCas NHol SHya WHil
– 'Doublet' (D)	EDon EMNN LCra MCas MFie NNrd SHya WDav WHil
– 'Douglas Black' (S)	SHya
– 'Douglas Blue' (S)	SHya
– 'Douglas Green' (S)	SHya
– 'Douglas Rose' (S)	SHya
– 'Douglas Salmon' (S)	SHya
– 'Douglas White' (S)	MFie
– 'Downlands' (S)	SHya
– 'Dunlin' (S)	SHya
– 'Durness' (S)	SHya
– 'Dusky Yellow'	MCas MPar SIng
– E82 (S)	MFie
– 'Ed Spivey' (A)	NHar
– 'Elegance' (S)	MFie NNrd SHya
– 'Elizabeth Ann' (A)	GAbr LCra SHya
– 'Ellen Thompson' (A)	MFie NHar NNrd SHya
– 'Elsie' (A)	SHya
– 'Elsie May' (A)	LCra LFox MFie NRed SHya WHer WRus
– 'Elsinore' (S)	SHya
– 'Embley' (S)	LCra SHya
– 'Emerald' (S)	SHya
– 'Emery Down' (S)	SHya
– 'Esso Blue' (S)	SHya
– 'Ettrick' (S)	SHya
– 'Everest Blue' (S)	EDon SHya
– 'Fairy' (A)	SHya
¶ – 'Falcon' (S)	SHya
– 'Fanciful' (S)	EDon MFie SHya WHil
– 'Fanny Meerbeck' (S)	CGle EDon LCra LFox MFie NHol NJap NRed
– 'Finchfield' (A)	SHya
– 'Flamingo' (S)	SHya
– 'Fleminghouse' (S)	CGle EDon ELan MFie NJap NRed SHya WHil
– 'Frank Crosland' (A)	LCra MFie NHar NNrd NRya SHya WHil
– 'Frank Faulkner ' (A)	LCra
– 'Freda' (S)	SHya
¶ – 'Frittenden Yellow' (B)	LFox
– 'G Douglas' (A)	LCra
– 'G Swinford' (B)	SHya
– 'Galen' (A)	EDon LCra NNrd SHya
– 'Geldersome Green' (S)	MFie
– 'Gem' (A)	SHya
– 'George Edge' (B)	SHya
– 'George Harrison' (B)	MFie SHya
– 'George Swinnerton's Leathercoat'	CGle
– 'Geronimo' (S)	SHya
– 'Girlguide' (S)	SHya

– 'Gizabroon' ELan LCra LFox MCas MFie NRed
– 'Gleam' (S) MFie SHya
¶ – 'Glenluce' (S) SHya
¶ – 'Gnome' NHol
– 'Gold Blaze' (S) SHya
– 'Goldcrest' (S) SHya
¶ – 'Golden Chartreuse' (S) NHol WHil
¶ – 'Golden Gleam' (A) WHil
– 'Golden Lilliput' (S) SHya
– 'Gooseberries and Cream' CGle
– 'Gordon Douglas' (A) EDon SHya
– 'Graisley' (S) MFie
– 'Green Edge Pin Eye' CRow
– 'Green Isle' (S) NHar SHya
– 'Green Jacket' (S) NHar SHya WHil
– 'Green Mouse' (S) MFie SHya
– 'Green Parrot' (S) LFox WHil
– 'Green Shank' (S) SHya
– 'Green Woodpecker' (S) SHya
– 'Greenheart' (S) EDon SHya
– 'Greensleeves' (S) SHya
– 'Greta' (S) EDon ELan SHya
– 'Gretna Green' MFie
¶ – 'Grey Bonner' (S) LFox
– 'Grey Edge' NHar
– 'Grey Monarch' (S) MFie SHya
– 'Gueldersome Green' (S) LFox MCas NNrd SHya
– 'Guinea' (S) EDon LCra LFox MCas MFie NHar NNrd SHya
– 'Hardley' (S) LCra
¶ – 'Harrison Weir' (S) SHya
¶ – 'Harry 'O'' (S) SHya
– 'Hawkswood' (S) LCra LFox NHar NNrd NRya
– 'Hawkwood Fancy' (S) MCas SHya
– 'Hazel' (A) ESis LCra MFie
– 'Headdress' (S) LFox MFie
¶ – 'Helen' (S) SHya
¶ – 'Helen Barter' (S) SHya
– 'Helena' (S) LFox MCas MFie NNrd SHya
– 'Holrood' (S) MFie
– 'Hurstwood Majesty' (S) NNrd
– 'Hyacinth' (S) NJap SIng SSmi WDav WRus
– 'Ibis' (S) MFie
– 'Ida' (A) LCra
– 'Idmiston' (S) SHya
– 'James Arnot' (S) LCra LFox MCas NHar NNrd SHya
– 'Jeannie Telford' (A) LCra SHya
– 'Jenny' (A) NRya SHya WHil
– 'Jezebel' (B) SHya
– 'Joan Elliott' (A) GAbr SHya WHil
– 'Joanne' (A) SHya
– 'John Gledhill' (A) NHar
– 'Joy' (A) EDon ELan LCra LFox MCas MFie NRed SHya
– 'Jungfrau' (D) EDon
– 'K H B' (S) NNrd
– 'Kathy' (A) SHya
– 'Kelso' (A) SHya
– 'Kercup' (A) LCra NHar NRar SHya
– 'Kim' (A) LCra NNrd SHya
– 'Kingcup' (A) LCra SHya
– 'Kinloch' (A) SHya
– 'Kirklands' (D) EDon MFie
– 'Lady Croft' (S) SHya
– 'Lady Daresbury' (A) LCra
– 'Lady Joyful ' (S) EDon
– 'Lady Zoë' (S) LCra
– 'Lamplugh' NNrd
– 'Lechistan' (S) LCra MCas MFie NHol NJap NNrd NRed
– 'Lee' (A) LCra SHya
¶ – 'Lee Paul' (A) EDon LCra
¶ – 'Lemon Drop' (S) SHya
– 'Light Sussex' (S) SHya
– 'Lilac Domino' (S) SHya
– 'Lime 'n' Lemon' CGle
– 'Lindley' (S) LCra
– 'Ling' (A) LCra LFox SHya
– 'Lisa' (A) EDon EMNN GAbr LCra MCas MFie NRed SHya WHer
– 'Lisa's Red' (S) NHar SHya
– 'Lisa's Smile' (S) LCra LFox NNrd SHya
¶ – 'Little Rosetta' (D) EDon
– 'Lovebird' (S) EDon LCra LFox MCas MFie NHar NJap NNrd NRed SHya WEas
– 'Maid Marion' (D) SHya
– 'Mandan' (S) SHya
– 'Manka' (S) LCra SHya
– 'Margaret Faulkner' (A) LCra LFox NRar SHya
– 'Margot' (S) SHya
– 'Marigold' (D) CRow EDon LCra MFie NJap NRed
– 'Mark' (A) EDon LCra MCas NJap SHya
¶ – 'Marmion' (S) SHya
– 'Marsco' (S) LFox
– 'Martin's Red' MPar
– 'Mary' (D) EDon NHar SHya
– 'Matley' (S) NHar SHya
¶ – 'Matthew Yates' (D) EDon LCra
– 'Maureen Millward' MCas MFie NNrd
– 'McWatt's Blue' GEdr
– 'Mermaid' CPla EDon LCra MFie NRed
– 'Merridale' (A) EDon GAbr LCra MCas SHya
– 'Midnight' (S) CBot CGle CRow ELan LCra MFie NHol
– 'Mikado' (S) EDon MFie SHya
– 'Mink' (A) LFox SHya
– 'Minley' (S) LFox SHya
– 'Minsmere' (S) SHya
– 'Mipsie Miranda' (D) MFie
¶ – 'Mmonglow' (S) SHya
– 'Mojave' (S) LCra LFox MBro MFie NHar NNrd WDav
¶ – 'Moneymoon' (S) SHya
– 'Monk' (A) MFie
– 'Moonglow' (S) CGle CRow CShe EDon ELan LCra MFie NJap SHya
– 'Moonstone' (D) EDon MFie
– 'Mr 'A'' (S) SHya WHil
¶ – 'Mrs C Warne' NRar

– 'Mrs L Hearne' (A) EDon LCra MFie NHar NHol NNrd NRed SHya
– 'Natham Silver' (A) MFie
– 'Neat and Tidy' (S) CRow EDon LCra LFox MCas MFie NJap NNrd NRar NRed NRya SHya
¶ – 'Nigel' (D) EDon
– 'Night and Day' (S) LCra
– 'Night Heron' (S) SHya
– 'Nocturne' (S) CGle ELan LCra LFox MCas MFie NHar NHol NRed SHya
– 'Norah' (A) SHya
– 'Norma' (A) NNrd
– 'Oake's Blue' (S) LCra
– 'Old Gold' (S) LFox SHya
– 'Old Gold Dusty Miller' (B) ECha
– 'Old Irish Blue' (B) CShe MCas NHol SHya SIng
– 'Old Mustard' MCas
– 'Old Pink Lace' CGle
– 'Old Red Dusty Miller' (B) GEdr LFox MCas NBir NHar SHya
– 'Old Suffolk Bronze' (B) LFox SHya
– 'Old Wine' (A) MFie
– 'Old Yellow Dusty Miller' (B) LFox MBro MCas MHig MPar NHar NHol SHya SIng WDav WHil
– 'Orb' (S) EDon LFox MCas MFie NHar NJap NNrd NRed SHya
– 'Ower' (A) MFie
– 'Paradise Yellow' (B) EPar GEdr LFox NHol SHya
¶ – 'Parchment' (S) SHya
¶ – 'Party Time' (S) SHya
– 'Pat' (S) EDon LCra LFox MFie NHol SHya
– 'Pat Berwick' (A) MFie
– 'Patience' (S) SHya
– 'Peggy' (A) EDon EPot LCra MCas MFie NNrd
– 'Philip Green' (S) SHya
– 'Phyllis Douglas' (A) LCra LFox MFie SHya
– 'Pink Lady' (A) SHya
– 'Pippin' (A) SHya
– 'Pixie' (A) LCra
– 'Plush Royal' (S) SHya
– 'Pot of Gold' (S) EDon LCra LFox MFie SHya
¶ – 'Prague' (S) EDon
– 'Prince Charming' (S) EDon
– 'Prince John' (A) EDon LCra LFox MCas MFie NHar NJap NRya SHya
– 'Proctor's Yellow' (B) SHya
– 'Purple Emperor' (A) SHya
– 'Purple Frills' CGle
¶ – 'Purple Mermaid' (D) EDon
– 'Purple Velvet' (S) MFie NHol SHya
¶ – 'Queen Bee' (S) LFox
– 'Queen of Sheba' (S) LCra
– 'Rabley Heath' (A) EDon LFox MFie SHya
– 'Radiance' (A) MFie
– 'Rajah' (S) CGle EDon ELan LCra MCas MFie NHol NJap NRed SHya WHer WHil
– 'Red Beret' (S) LCra LFox NJap WHil
– 'Red Gauntlet' (S) EDon ELan LCra LFox MCas MFie NHol NJap NNrd NRed SHya
– 'Red Rum' (S) LCra MFie NHar SHya
– 'Redstart' (B) MFie
– 'Remus' (S) EDon LCra LFox MCas MFie NHar NHol NNrd NRed NRya SHya WHil
– 'Riatty' (D) MFie
– 'Richard Shaw' (A) NNrd
¶ – 'Roberto' (S) SHya
– 'Rock Sand' (S) NNrd
– 'Rodeo' (A) EDon LCra MFie SHya
– 'Rolts' (S) EDon LCra LFox MCas MFie NHar NNrd SHya
– 'Rosalie Edwards' (S) LCra LFox NNrd SHya
– 'Rosanna' (S) SHya
– 'Rosebud' (S) MFie
¶ – 'Rossiter's Grey' (S) SHya
– 'Rowena' (A) EDon GAbr LCra MCas MFie NHar NJap NNrd NRar SHya WHil
– 'Roxburgh' (A) SHya
– 'Royal Purple' (S) SHya
– 'Royalty' (S) MFie SHya
¶ – 'Ruffles' (S) SHya
– 'Sailor Boy' (S) LCra LFox MFie NHar SHya
– 'Saint Boswells' (S) SHya
– 'Saint Elmo' (D) MFie NHol
– 'Saint Gerrans' White' (B) MFie
– 'Salome' (A) SHya
– 'Sandmartin' (S) SHya
– 'Sandra' (A) GAbr LFox MFie SHya
– 'Sandwood Bay' (A) EDon LCra LFox MCas MFie NRar NRed SHya WRus
– 'Sarah Lodge' (D) SHya
– 'Senorita' (A) SHya
– 'Serenity' (S) LFox MFie NHar SHya
¶ – 'Shako' (A) LFox
– 'Shalford' (D) EDon MFie SHya
– 'Sheila' (S) EDon LFox MFie NHar NNrd NRed NRya SHya WAbe
– 'Shere' (S) EDon LCra LFox MCas MFie SHya
– 'Sherwood' MCas NHar
– 'Shogun' (A) SHya
– 'Sir Robert Ewbank' (D) LCra MCas
– 'Sirius' (A) LCra LFox MCas MFie SHya
– 'Slioch' (S) MFie SHya
– 'Snooty Fox' CGle MCas MFie
– 'Sonya' (A) EMNN MFie NHol
– 'South Barrow' (D) MFie WHil
– 'Sphinx' (A) SHya
– 'Spinney Lane' (A) SHya
¶ – 'Spitfire' (S) SHya
– 'Spring Meadows' (S) CShe EDon ELan LCra NHol SHya
– SS TY 72 (S) MFie
– 'Standish' (D) LCra MFie NHol NJap WHer
– 'Stant's Blue' (S) LCra LFox MCas MFie NHar NHol NJap SHya

– 'Stella' (S)	EDon LCra LFox SHya
– 'Stonnal' (A)	SHya
– 'Sue' (A)	NNrd
– 'Summer Sky' (A)	SHya
¶ – 'Sunflower' (S)	LFox
– 'Sunny Boy' (S)	LCra SHya
– 'Super Para' (S)	MCas MFie SHya
– 'Superb' (S)	SHya
¶ – 'Susan' (A)	LFox SHya
– 'Susannah' (D)	EDon MFie
– 'Swale' (A)	SHya
– 'Sweet Pastures' (S)	LCra MCas MFie NHar NJap SHya WEas
– 'Tally-ho' (A)	SHya
– 'Tarantella' (A)	GAbr LCra LFox MCas MFie NJap NRar
– 'Tavistock' (S)	SHya
– 'Ted Roberts' (A)	LCra MCas MFie SHya
– 'Teem' (S)	LCra MFie NJap SHya
– 'Tenby Grey' (S)	SHya
– 'The Baron' (S)	CGle LFox MCas MFie NHar NHol NJap NRed
– 'The Bishop' (S)	LCra
– 'The Bride' (S)	EDon LCra MCas MFie NJap SHya
– 'The Cardinal' (D)	SHya
– 'The Czar' (A)	SHya
– 'The Snods' (S)	LCra MFie
– 'Thetis' (A)	LCra LFox MFie NHar NNrd NRar SHya
– 'Tinkerbell' (S)	MFie NHar NJap
– 'Tony Murloch'	WHer
– 'Trojan' (S)	NHar SHya
¶ – 'Trouble' (D)	EDon LCra
– 'Trudy' (S)	LCra SHya
– 'True Briton' (S)	SHya
¶ – 'Turnbull' (A)	LFox
– 'Tye Lea' (S)	NNrd
– 'Valerie' (A)	EDon LCra MCas MFie NNrd SHya WHil
– 'Vee Too' (A)	MFie SHya
– 'Verdi' (A)	LCra MFie NJap
¶ – 'Victoria de Wemyss'	NRar
– 'Vivien' (S)	SHya
– 'Vulcan' (A)	EDon LCra LFox MCas NHar SHya
– 'Waincliffe Red' (S)	MFie
– 'Walhampton' (S)	SHya
– 'Walton' (A)	SHya
– 'Walton Heath ' (D)	EDon MFie NHol SHya
– 'Watt's Purple' (D)	EDon MFie
– 'Westcott Pride' (D)	EDon
– 'Wexland ' (S)	LCra
– 'White Ensign' (S)	MFie NHar SHya
– 'White Wings' (S)	LCra MFie NNrd SHya
– 'Winifrid' (A)	CShe EDon LCra LFox MCas MFie NHol NRar SHya WHil WRus
– 'Yellow Hammer' (S)	SHya
– 'Yorkshire Grey' (S)	EDon MFie
– 'Zambia' (D)	EDon MFie SHya WHil
auriculata (11)	GEdr
'Barbara Barker' (2)	ITim WDav
* 'Barnard's Crimson' (Prim)	CCot
Barnhaven Blues (Prim)	GAbr WEas
Barnhaven doubles (D.Poly)	CSun
'Barnhaven Reds' (Prim)	See P. Tartan Reds
Barnhaven Traditional (Poly)	CSun
¶ 'Barrowby Gem' (Poly)	GSta
'Beamish Foam' (Poly)	GSta
beesiana (4)	CArn CCla CHar CRow EHon ELan LMay MBri MSta NHol NKay NRoo SHig SPer WDav WEas WRus
'Belle Watling' (D.Prim)	NHol
bellidifolia (17)	CPla CRow MBal
beluensis	See P. x ***pubescens*** 'Freedom'
x ***berninae*** (2)	NHol
– 'Windrush' (2)	MPar NNrd WAbe WDav
'Betty Green' (Prim)	MBri NHol
'Bewerley White'	See P. ***pubescens*** 'Bewerley White'
bhutanica (21)	GArf IBlr LCra
¶ 'Big Red Giant'	NHol
bileckii	See P. x ***forsteri b.***
'Blue Riband' (Prim)	CCot CGle COtt EBre EPot GSta LCra LFox MHig NCat NHol SBla SPer WRus
Blue Striped Victorians (Poly)	GAbr
'Blue Triumph'	LHop
'Blutenkissen' (Prim)	CBow EPot LFox NNrd
¶ 'Bon Accord Cerise' (D.Poly)	GSta
'Bon Accord Elegance' (D.Poly)	CGle CRow
'Bon Accord Gem' (D.Poly)	CCot CGle CRow GAbr GSta
¶ 'Bon Accord Lavender' (D.Poly)	GSta
¶ 'Bon Accord Lilac' (D.Poly)	GSta
'Bon Accord Purple' (D.Poly)	CBos CCor CCot CGle EJud
'Bonfire' (4)	GDra GEdr
¶ – (Poly)	ELun
boothii (21)	EPar GArf
– ***alba*** (21)	EPar
bracteosa	EPar GEdr ITim NHar
Bressingham (4)	EBre
'Brimstone' (Poly)	CGle CRow
'Buckland Enchantress'	CRow
'Buckland Wine' (Prim)	CCot CRow GSta
¶ x ***bulleesiana*** (4)	NKay
– Asthore hybrids (4)	EHon
bulleyana (4)	Widely available
burmanica (4)	CHar CPla CSam CSun EBre ELun GEdr GHig LCra MBal MSta NKay SIng
¶ 'Butterscotch'	NHol WEas
'Caerhays Ruby' (Prim)	CB&S
'Caerulea Plena' (D.Prim)	GWic

calderiana (21)	GDra
Candelabra hybrids (4)	CBro EMNN LCra LFox LHop MTho NNrd WDav
Candy Pinks (Prim)	GAbr WHil
capitata (5)	CArn CBot CBow CGle CHar CPla ELun GAbr GDra GEdr GHig GLoc LCra MBal MBri MBro MFir MPlt NGre NLin WCla WEas
¶ – *crispata* AGW/ES 407 (5)	NHol
– *mooreana* (5)	CBre CElw CWGN ELan LMay NVic WCla WHoo
¶ – *sphaerocephala*	NWCA
'Captain Blood' (D.Prim)	CBot CCot CFis CGle EOrc GAbr NHar NHol SIng SSpi SSus WHer WHil WRus
'Carmen' (Prim)	LFox
'Carnation' (Poly)	NJap
x *carueli* (2)	NHol
¶ 'Casquet'	WEas
cawdoriana (8)	GAbr GDra
¶ *cernua* (17)	CPla
¶ 'Charlene (D.Prim)	GAbr
'Charlotte' (Prim)	NHol SIng
Chartreuse (Poly)	CGle CRow EDon GAbr NJap NSti
'Cherry' (Prim)	CCot ECha GSta
'Chevithorne Pink' (Poly)	CGle EMNN GSta NRoo
chionantha (18)	Widely available
§ – purple form (18)	CCla CGle CPla CRow CSam CSun ELun EMNN GDra LCra MBal NHol NKay NLin WDav
'Chocolate Soldier' (D.Prim)	CCot CFis CGle ELan MCas NHar NHol NJap NSti WHil
chungensis (4)	CCla CGle COtt ELun GEdr GHig MBri MRav MSta NHar NKay NLin NRya SIng WDav WHal
§ – x *pulverulenta* (4)	GEdr
x *chunglenta*	See P. ***chungensis*** x ***pulverulenta***
clarkei (4)	EPot GEdr GLoc LCra MHig NHar NHol SIng WAbe
¶ 'Cluny'	GArf
clusiana (2)	GDra GEdr MBal NHol SIng
cockburniana (4)	CHar CRow CSun ELun EPar GAbr GDra GEdr LCra LSav MBal MBri NGre NHol NLin NRya
concholoba (17)	CPla CRow GEdr GGar LCra MBro NGre NLin
'Corporal Baxter' (Prim)	CFis CGle CSam ELan ELun EMNN EOrc GHig MCas NHar NHol WHer WHil
cortusoides (7)	CPla LCra WDav
Cowichan Amethyst (Poly)	EDon
Cowichan Blue (Poly)	EDon GAbr WHil
Cowichan Garnet (Poly)	EDon GAbr NHol
¶ Cowichan Red	WHil
Cowichan Strain (Poly)	CCot EFou GAbr LCra LFox MBri NJap NRed WHoo

¶ Cowichan Venetian (Poly)	EDon
Cowichan Yellow (Poly)	EDon GAbr WHil
'Craven Gem' (Poly)	CFis NKay
'Crescendo' (Poly)	MPit NRoo WHil
'Crimson Beauty' (D.Prim)	LHop
crispa	See P. ***glomerata***
¶ 'Crispii' (Prim)	GSta
daonensis (2)	GEdr
darialica (11)	CBre CGle CPla ELan GAbr GDra GLoc LCra NHol NRya
¶ dark scarlet (Prim)	GSta
¶ 'David Green' (Prim)	GSta
¶ 'David Valentine'	CCor
'Dawn Ansell' (Prim)	CB&S CBot CBre CChu CCla CFis CGle CRow EDon EFou ELan ELun EMNN EOrc GAbr GGar LHop MBri MRav NHol NRoo SSus WHer WHil
Daybreak (Poly)	CSun
denticulata (9)	Widely available
– *alba* (9)	CB&S CCla CGle CSco EBre ECha EGol ELan EMNN EPar EPot GAbr GEdr GLoc LCra MBal MBri MWat MWgw NHol NJap NNrd NRoo WHea
– 'Bressingham Beauty' (9)	EBre NNrd
– *cashmeriana* (9)	ELan MBro WCla
– 'Glenroy Crimson' (9)	MBal
– 'Inshriach Carmine' (9)	GDra NNrd
– lilac (9)	EHon NHol NJap
– purple (9)	EMNN GAbr IBlr NRoo
– red (9)	CB&S CRow EMNN EPar NHar
¶ – 'Robinson's Red' (9)	EPot
– rose (9)	GLoc
– 'Rubinball' (9)	CBre NHol NRoo
– ruby (9)	CSco EHon GAbr MBri NJap NOak WHen WHoo
– 'Snowball' (9)	CBre NOak WHen
x *deschmannii*	See P. x ***vochinensis***
'Desert Sunset' (Poly)	EDon NSti WEas
'Dianne'	See P. x ***forsteri*** 'D.'
¶ 'Doctor Molly' (Prim)	GSta
'Dorothy' (Prim)	CBro SIng
'Double Lilac' (D.Prim)	See P. 'Lilacina Plena'
¶ 'Double Red' (D.Poly)	GSta
¶ 'Double Sulphur' (D.Prim)	GSta
¶ 'Dr Mary' (Prim)	GSta
¶ 'Duckyls Red' (Prim)	GSta SSpi
¶ 'Dusky Lady'	MBri
¶ 'Early Irish Yellow' (Prim)	GSta
'Eastgrove's Gipsy' (Poly)	WEas
¶ *edelbergii*	EPot
edgeworthii (21)	ELun EPar GArf
– *alba* (21)	GLoc NKay
elatior (30)	Widely available
– *leucophylla* (30)	ELun EPad MHig WHil
§ – *meyeri*	CFis CShe LRHS NHol

Name	Suppliers
– ***ruprechtii*** (30)	NNrd
¶ 'Elizabeth Dickey' (D.Poly)	GSta
ellisiae (21)	CSun NHol
¶ 'Elyahelham'	NCat
¶ 'Enchantress' (Poly)	GSta
'Erin's Gem' (Poly)	CGle CRow
'Ethel Barker' (2)	GLoc ITim LFox WAbe
'Ethel M Dell' (D.Prim)	CFis EOrc NHol SIng WHil
'Eugénie' (D.Prim)	CFis CGle NHar NHol NSti SSus WHil
¶ 'Evonne' (D.Poly)	GSta
¶ 'Exhilaration'	NHol
farinosa (11)	CArn CElw CPla CSun ELun GAbr LCra MBal MBri MSal NGre NHol NKay NRed NRya SIng WAbe WCla WHil
¶ 'Fife Yellow' (D.Poly)	GSta
'Finesse' (Prim)	WHil
¶ 'Fire Dance' (Poly)	EDon
Firefly (Poly)	CSun GAbr LFox NHol
firmipes (26)	EPot NHol
§ ***flaccida*** (28)	ELan GDra GEdr GLoc ITim LCra MBal MBro NHar WAbe
Flamingo (Poly)	EDon GAbr NJap
x ***floerkeana biflora*** (2)	GEdr
– ***biflora alba*** (2)	GEdr
florindae (26)	Widely available
– hybrids (26)	LFox NHol WHal
– orange form (26)	IBlr
– red form (26)	CCor MSta NKay NOak
Footlight Parade (Prim)	CSun GAbr NCat
forrestii (3)	EPot WCla
– RL 1688 (3)	GLoc
§ x ***forsteri*** (2)	CShe ELan GEdr GLoc ITim MHig NHar NHol NKay WAbe
§ – ***bileckii*** (2)	GLoc MBal MBro MHig NHar NHol NKay NNrd SIng SWas WAbe WDav WHil
– 'Dianne' (2)	EPot GEdr MBro MHig NHar NHol NNrd SIng WAbe WThu
'Freckles' (Prim)	CFis ELun NHol SIng WCla WHil
'Freedom'	See P. x ***pubescens*** 'F.'
frondosa (11)	Widely available
'Frühlingszauber' (Prim)	NHol
Fuchsia Victorians (Poly)	GAbr NJap
Galligaskins (Poly)	CCot
Garryard	See P. 'Guinevere'
¶ ***gaubaeana*** (12)	CBre
geraniifolia (7)	GDra NGre
glabrescens JCA 786.900	NHol
glaucescens (2)	GEdr MBro NHar NHol SIng WDav
¶ – JCA 786.900 (2)	NHol
– ***calycina*** (2)	NHol
§ ***glomerata*** (5)	CLew GAbr GEdr NKay NRed WHil
– BM&W 35 (5)	NHol
¶ 'Gloria' (Prim)	GSta
'Gloriosa' (Prim)	CCot LFox
'Glowing Embers' (4)	ELun NSti
¶ ***glutinosa*** (2)	ITim
gold laced (Poly)	Widely available
gracilipes (21)	CFor CGle EPar GArf GEdr NHar NKay
– ***minor***	See P. ***petiolaris***
– 'Winter Jewel' (21)	GEdr NHol
Grand Canyon (Poly)	GAbr NJap WEas
¶ 'Granny Graham' (Prim)	NHol SIng WCla WHil
griffithii (21)	GEdr NHar
'Groeneken's Glory' (Prim)	CGle CRiv GEdr GSta LCra MBri NHol NNrd SIng SPer
§ 'Guinevere' (Poly)	Widely available
halleri (11)	CPla GAbr GEdr GLoc LCra MBal NHol NKay NNor NRed WCla WHoo WPat
– 'Longiflora'	See P. ***h.***
Harbinger (Prim)	GAbr NNrd WEas WHil
¶ 'Harbour Lights'	GAbr WEas
Harlow Carr hybrids (4)	CBre NHol NRoo NSti WBon WHil
Harvest Yellows (Poly)	EDon GAbr NCat
x ***heerii*** (2)	EPot
helodoxa	See P. ***prolifera***
heucherifolia (7)	CBot CCla CHar CPla CSam GAbr LFox NHol NLin
'Hipperholme'	NHar
hirsuta (2)	MPar WAbe
¶ – 'Dyke's Variety'	LRHS
'Hose in Hose' (Poly)	CBos CCla CCot CGle LCra LFox NNrd NRoo WEas WRus
* 'Husky'	MPit NRoo
¶ ***hyacinthina*** (17)	GArf
Indian Reds (Poly)	EDon NJap
'Ingram's Blue' (Prim)	CRow
Inshriach hybrids (4)	CChu CMHG CSun GAbr GDra GGar MBri NHol NSti SPer
integrifolia (2)	GEdr SIng WAbe
x ***intermedia*** (2)	MHig WHil
'Inverewe' (4)	CBro CKel CRiv CSun GDra GGar MCot NHar NKay SSpi
involucrata (11)	CBot CCla CFor CGle CRiv GEdr NKay NNrd NTow WCla
– Yargongensis group (11)	CFor CGle CPla CRow GEdr MBal MBri NHol NNrd NWCA SIng WHil
ioessa (26)	CPla GEdr GLoc MBal MBri NHar NHol NJap NTow SBar
'Iris Mainwaring' (Prim)	EPot GSta LCra NKay NNrd WHil
Jack in the Green (Poly)	CCot CGle GAbr LCra LFox NNrd WEas WHil WRus
¶ 'Janie Hill' (A)	LFox
japonica (4)	CCla CCor CGle CMHG CRow CSun CWGN ELun GEdr LAbb LCra LMay MCot MFir MPlt NNor NRoo SBla SHig SPla SSpi WCla WDav WEas
– 'Apple Blossom' (4)	CSun NNrd
– 'Fuji' (4)	CSun ELun ENot GDra GEdr MBal MBri MSta NJap SIng WHal
– 'Glowing Embers' (4)	CGle MBri NJap

– 'Miller's Crimson' (4)	Widely available
– 'Oriental Sunrise' (4)	NJap SPer
– 'Postford White' (4)	Widely available
– red shades (4)	NJap NSti WAbe
– 'Valley Red' (4)	GGar
jesoana (7)	NTow
'Johanna' (11)	EBre EPot GArf GEdr GLoc
juliae (30)	CGle CPla CRiv NGre NHol NKay NNrd WEas
– white form (30)	CGle
– x ***elatior*** (30)	CCor
'Julian'	NNrd
x ***juribella*** (2)	NHar
'Ken Dearman' (D.Prim)	CChu CFis CGle CRow EFol EJud ELan ERav GGar MRav NHar NHol NJap NSti WHer WHil WRus
¶ ***kewensis***	NWCA
'Kinlough Beauty' (Poly)	CCot CFis CRow CShe ECha ELun EMNN EPar GAbr GSta LCra LFox NHol NNrd NRoo NSti SIng WEas WHil
¶ ***kisoana*** (7)	CPla WCru
– ***alba*** (7)	CBre CPla SWas WCru
'Lady Greer' (Poly)	Widely available
'Lambrook Lilac' (Poly)	CRow
¶ 'Lambrook Pink' (Poly)	GSta
'Lambrook Yellow' (Poly)	CGle
§ ***latifolia*** (2)	CShe LCra NHol SIng
– 'Crimson Velvet' (2)	EPot GLoc MHig WThu
laurentiana	See P. ***mistassinica macropoda***
'Lemon Soufflé' (Prim)	CRow WHer
leucophylla	GLoc
¶ lilac purple (D.Poly)	GSta
§ 'Lilacina Plena' (D.Prim)	CBot CCor CFis CGle CRow CSam EDon GAbr IBlr NHol NNrd NSti SIng WEas WHer WHil WRus
'Lilian Harvey' (D.Prim)	CChu CFis CGle ELan MCas MRav NHar NHol NJap NRoo SSus WHil
Limelight (Poly)	CGle GAbr NJap
'Lingwood Beauty' (Prim)	GSta LFox NHol NKay
'Linnet' (21)	GEdr ITim NHol
'Lismore Yellow' (2)	ITim WAbe WDav
Lissadel hybrids (4)	GAbr
'Little Egypt' (Poly)	CGle EDon NCat WHil
littoniana	See P. ***vialii***
'Lizzie Green' (Prim)	GLoc LCra NHol
'Lopen Red' (Poly)	CFis GSta
luteola (11)	GEdr NKay
macrophylla (18)	MBal SIng
– H 78 (18)	CSun GDra NGre NHar
'Madame Pompadour' (D.Poly)	CGle
malacoides (3)	MBri
marginata (2)	CGle EPar EPot GDra GEdr GLoc LCra LFox LHop MCot NGre NHar NHol NNrd NRed SIng SSmi WAbe WOMN
– ***alba*** (2)	EPot GLoc LCra MBro MCas MHig NKay NRed SIng SPou SSmi WAbe WDav
¶ – 'Arthur Branch' (2)	WAbe
– 'Beamish' (2)	EPot MCas SPou WDav WHil
– 'Beatrice Lascaris' (2)	EPot GLoc ITim MBro MCas MHig NHol SPou WAbe WDav WHil
– 'Caerulea' (2)	EPot GEdr ITim MCas MHig NHol SPou WAbe WThu
– 'Clear's Variety' (2)	EPot MCas MHig NHol SPou WDav WHil
– 'Correvon's Variety' (2)	LCra
– 'Doctor Jenkins' (2)	WDav
– 'Drake's Form' (2)	EMNN EPot GEdr ITim MCas MPar NHol SPou
– 'Earl L Bolton' (2)	EPot NHol NNrd SPou WAbe WDav
– 'Elizabeth Fry' (2)	LFox MCas MPar SPou
¶ – 'Gold Plate' (2)	SIng
– 'Grandiflora' (2)	NHol WDav
– 'Highland Twilight' (2)	NHar SPou
– 'Holden Variety' (2)	MBal MHig NHol NNrd SIng WDav
– 'Hyacinthia' (2)	CShe EPot NHol SPou WAbe
– 'Ivy Agea' (2)	WDav
– 'Janet' (2)	GEdr MHig NHol NRed WDav WHil
– 'Jenkins Variety' (2)	SIng SPou
– 'Kesselring's Variety' (2)	ELan EPot GLoc MBro MCas MHig NHol NRed SPou SSmi WAbe WDav WHil WWin
– 'Lilac' (2)	GDra LFox NNrd
– 'Linda Pope' (2)	CGle CShe EPot GEdr ITim LCra MCas MPar NHar NHol NRed SIng SPou WDav
– 'Longifolia' (2)	GEdr
– maritime form (2)	SPou
– 'Marven' (2)	EPot GEdr LCra MCas SPou
– 'Millard's Variety' (2)	SPou WDav
– 'Prichard's Variety' (2)	CGle CShe ELan EMNN EPot GDra ITim LCra LFox MBro MCas NHol NKay NNrd NRed SIng SPou SSmi WAbe WCla WDav WEas WHil WOMN
– 'Rheniana' (2)	SPou WDav
¶ – 'Rosea' (2)	NHol
– 'Sharp's Variety' (2)	NHar
– 'Violet Form' (2)	GDra MBro WDav WHil
– 'Waithman's Variety' (2)	NHar WDav
'Marianne Davey' (D.Prim)	CB&S CFis CGle CRow EJud ELan EMNN EOrc GHig MBri MRav NHol NRed NRoo NSti SIng WHer WHil WRus
'Marie Crousse' (D.Prim)	CChu CCot CFis CGle ELun MBal MPlt NHol NRed SApp SIng SSpi WHer WHil WRus
Marine Blues (Poly)	GAbr NCat NJap
mauve (Poly)	NJap
'McWatt's Claret' (Poly)	CCot EPot GSta LCra LFox NNrd

'McWatt's Cream' (Poly)	CRiv EMon GEdr LCra LFox SIng
melanops (18)	CGle CPla ELan GAbr NGre NRed NRya WDav
Midnight (Poly)	GAbr
minima (2)	GEdr MHig NHar NHol NRed NWCA WDav
– *alba* (2)	GArf GEdr NHar NHol
¶ – x *hirsuta* (2)	NHar
– x *villosa* (2)	NHar
– x *wulfeniana* (2)	See P. x ***vochinensis***
'Miss Indigo' (D.Prim)	CB&S CFis CGle CHad CRow CSam EDon ELan ELun EMNN EOrc GHig MCas MRav NHol NJap NRed NSti SIng SSus WEas WHal WHer WHil
§ *mistassinica macropoda* (11)	MHig
modesta (11)	EMNN NHol NTow
– *alba* (11)	GLoc
– *fauriae* (11)	CBre GEdr NNrd WHil WHoo
* – *saximontana* (11)	NGre
– *yuparensis alba* (11)	NHol
¶ 'Morton'	NGre
'Mrs McGillivray' (Prim)	NNrd
'Mrs Peggy Wilson' (*allionii*) (2)	GLoc
muscarioides (17)	CGle CPla NLin
nepalensis	See P. ***tanneri n.***
New Pinks (Poly)	EDon GAbr NCat NJap NSti WHil
nivalis (18)	CPla LCra
nutans	See P. ***flaccida***
obconica (19)	MBri
'Old Port' (Poly)	CFis NHar NNrd
'Old Rose' (Poly)	NJap
'Olive Wyatt' (D.Prim)	CB&S CChu CFis CGle CRow EMNN EOrc MPit MPlt NHar NHol NJap SSus WHal
'Oriental Sunrise' (4)	LAbb MBri
Osiered Amber (Prim)	CRow GAbr LFox NHol NJap
'Our Pat' (D.Poly)	GAbr GSta GWic IBlr WHer
Pagoda hybrids (4)	MBri NHol NJap
'Pale Blue'	NHar
*pale pink Juliae (D.Poly)	GSta
palinurii (2)	WDav
¶ 'Paris '90' (Poly)	EDon
parryi (20)	EMNN GEdr LCra NHol
pedemontana (2)	GEdr NGre WDav
¶ 'Penlan Cream' (D.Poly)	GSta
'Perle von Bottrop' (Prim)	GSta LFox NKay
'Peter Klein' (11)	CRiv ELun GEdr GLoc ITim MBal MBro MCas NHar NHol WAbe WDav WOMN
§ *petiolaris* (21)	EMNN EPar GArf GEdr ITim LCra MPit NHol
– LS&H 19856 (21)	EPot GArf GGar
¶ 'Petticoat'	NHol
¶ 'Pink Lady'	NHol
¶ 'Pink Profusion' (Prim)	GSta
poissonii (4)	CBot CGle CPla CSun CTom CWGN ELun EMon EPar GEdr GHig IBlr LMay MBal NGre NHol NJap NKay NLin
Polyanthus (30)	CSun ECha ENot GDra LCra NKay
polyneura (7)	CBot CCla CPla CSun GEdr LSav MBal MBro MHig NHol NSti NTow WEas WWat
praenitens	See P. ***sinensis***
'Prince Silverwings' (D.Poly)	WEas
§ *prolifera* (4)	CCla CFor CLew CMHG CTrw ELan LMay MFir MSta NHol NLin NSti SBla SMad SSpi WHal
x *pruhonicensis*	See under ***cultivar name***
x *pubescens* (2)	EMNN GDra LFox MBro SSmi WHil WOMN
– 'Apple Blossom' (2)	MCas MFie NHar NHol SIng
– 'Balfouriana' (2)	LFox MBro MPar WDav
§ – 'Bewerley White' (2)	CBre CShe CSun EPot ITim LCra MBal MBro NHar NNrd NRed SSmi WHil WRus WThu WWin
– 'Boothman's Variety' (2)	EMNN EPot ITim LCra MBro MCas MHig NGre NHar NHol NKay NNrd SBla SIng SSmi WAbe WCla WDav WEas WHil WOMN WPat WRus WThu
– 'Carmen' (2)	MBro WDav WHil WPat WWin
– 'Chamois' (2)	NHar
– 'Christine' (2)	EPot LCra LHop MBro MHig NHar NHol NNrd NRed WDav WHil WThu
– 'Cream Viscosa' (2)	EMNN MCas MPlt NNrd WHil
– 'Elphenor' (2)	NNrd
– 'Faldonside' (2)	CRiv CShe EPot GLoc LCra MBro MCas MHig NHar NHol NKay NNrd NRed WAbe WDav WHil WThu
§ – 'Freedom' (2)	CBre CShe ELan EMNN EPot GEdr GLoc ITim LCra MBro MHig MPlt NHar NHol NNrd NRya SIng SSmi WDav WHil WPat WThu WWin
– 'Gnome' (2)	SPou WThu
– 'Harlow Car' (2)	CShe EPot GEdr ITim LFox NHol NNrd WAbe WDav WDav WHil
– 'Henry Hall' (2)	NHol
– 'Joan Gibbs' (2)	LCra NHol WDav
– 'Mrs J H Wilson' (2)	CRiv CShe GEdr GLoc ITim LCra MBal MHig NHar NHol NKay SSmi WDav WRus
– 'Nivea' (2)	MPar
– 'Pat Barwick' (2)	EPot LFox WDav
– 'Peggy Fell' (2)	GEdr
– 'Pink Freedom' (2)	WDav
– 'Rufus' (2)	CRiv CShe GEdr GLoc ITim LCra MBal MCas MHig SBla SIng SPou WDav WOld WThu
– 'The General' (2)	GEdr LCra MCas MHig NHol WHil

– 'Wharfedale Gem' (2)	NNrd
– x ***allionii*** (2)	NHar
– yellow form (2)	CCor
pulverulenta (4)	Widely available
– Bartley hybrids (4)	CBot CGle CSun ELun NKay WEas WHal
– 'Bartley Pink' (4)	CPla LRHS NSti
'Purpurkissen' (Prim)	NHol
'Quaker's Bonnet' (Poly)	See P. 'Lilacina Plena'
¶ 'Queen of the Whites' (Prim)	GSta
'Ravenglass Vermilion' (4)	CRow
'Red Paddy' (D.Prim/Poly)	CBos CCot GAbr GSta MPit
'Red Sunset' (4)	GDra
'Red Velvet' (D.Prim)	CRow LHop MRav
¶ 'Red Warbler' (Prim)	GSta
reidii (28)	LCra MBri NHar NHol
– hybrids (28)	NHol
– ***williamsii*** (28)	CPla CSun ELun GDra GEdr GLoc ITim MBal MBri NGre NHol NRed WAbe WDav
– ***williamsii alba*** (28)	CSun ELun GDra GLoc MBal MBri NGre NHol
reptans (16)	GEdr
'Reverie' (Poly)	EDon NJap
'Rhapsody' (D.Prim)	CFis CRow LHop WHer
'Rhubarb and Custard' (Poly)	CGle
'Romeo' (Prim)	GSta LCra
'Rose O'Day' (D.Prim)	CB&S CFis CGle EDon ELan EOrc MPlt NHar NHol NJap NRoo NSti SIng WHil
rosea (11)	CBot CHar CPla CRow ELun GDra GEdr LCra LHop MBal MHig NGre NHar NJap NKay NSti NVic SBla SIng SSpi WEas WRus
– 'Delight'	See P. *r.* 'Micia Visser de Geer'
– ***elegans*** (11)	GDra
– 'Gigas' (11)	MSta NHol
– ***grandiflora*** (11)	CBow CGle CSam CSun CWGN EFou EHon ELan EMNN EPar GAbr GLoc LMay MBri MCas MPit MPlt NHol NLin NRed NRoo NTow WHil
§ – 'Micia Visser-de Geer' (11)	CKel EBre NKay SPer
– ***splendens*** (11)	IDai
rotundifolia	See P. ***sibirica***
'Rowallane Rose' (4)	CBro CSun GWic
'Roy Cope' (D.Prim)	CFis CSam ERav GGar GHig MPit MRav NHar NHol SIng WHil
rubra	See P. ***erythra***
rusbyi (20)	SIng
Rustic Reds (Poly)	NJap WEas
¶ 'Sandy's Form' (21)	NHol
saxatilis (7)	CLew MCas NRya SIng WDav
¶ ***scapeosa*** (21)	GArf
x ***scapeosa*** (21)	MBal
scapigera (21)	NHol
– DF 614 (21)	EBul
'Schneekissen' (Prim)	CBre CCla CCot CTom EBre EOrc GAbr LHop SApp SIng WHer WRus
scotica (11)	CRiv EMNN GArf GDra GEdr GLoc LCra LFox MBal NHar NTow WCla WThu
'Sea Way' (Prim)	MRav
secundiflora (26)	Widely available
x ***serrata*** (2)	GLoc MBro NHol SIng WDav
serratifolia	NHol
¶ 'Shocking Pink'	NHol
§ ***sibirica*** (25)	GDra GEdr LCra
sibthorpii	See P. ***vulgaris sibthorpii***
sieboldii (7)	CBre CGle CHad CRiv CRow CShe EGol ELun EMNN GLoc LAbb LCra LFox MBal MBri MSta NHar NRya NVic SIng SSpi WEas WHil
– 'Carefree' (7)	CGle NNrd
– 'Cherokee' (7)	NNrd
– 'Cherubim' (7)	EBre NNrd SBla
– 'Dancing Ladies' (7)	CGle ELan GAbr NHol NJap NRed
– 'Galaxy' (7)	GAbr NHol NRed
– 'Geisha Girl' (7)	CTom EBre MRav NNrd SBla
– 'Lilac Sunbonnet' (7)	CGle
– 'Manankoora' (7)	CGle ELan NHol NJap NRed
– 'Mikado' (7)	EBre MRav NNrd
– 'Pago-Pago' (7)	CGle NHol NJap NRed
*– 'Seraphim' (7)	EBre SBla
– 'Snowflake' (7)	CGle EBre NNrd NRed
*– 'Spring in Kyoto' (7)	SBla
– 'Tah-ni' (7)	CTom ELan NHol NJap NNrd NRed
– 'Winter Dreams' (7)	CGle NHol NJap
sikkimensis (26)	CBot CCla CGle CHad CHar CSun ELun EMNN ENot EPar ERou GEdr LCra LMay MBal MBri MBro MSta NGre NHol NKay NLin NTow SHig
¶ – BM&W 40 (26)	NHol
¶ – crimson and gold (26)	GAbr NHol
– ***hopeana*** (26)	GEdr
– ***pudibunda*** (26)	GEdr MPlt
– 'Tilman Number 2' (26)	CBre CSun ELun GDra NHol SIgm WDav
Silver Dollar hybrids (Poly)	CSun WEas
silver laced (Poly)	CGle EFou ELan EOrc EPar GLoc WEas WHer
'Silverwells' (4)	GEdr
sinensis (27)	MBri
¶ single green (Prim)	GSta
sinoplantaginea (18)	CPla GAbr GEdr GGar GLoc
sinopurpurea	See P. ***chionantha*** 'purple form'
¶ 'Sir Bedivere' (Prim)	GAbr
'Sir Galahad' (Prim)	NHol
smithiana	See P. ***prolifera***
* 'Snow Carpet' (Prim)	CB&S
'Snow Cushion' (Prim)	See P. 'Schneekissen'
soldanelloides (28)	LCra
sonchifolia (21)	GArf GDra GEdr GGar GLoc NHar NHol

– Tibetan form	NHol
'Soup Plate' (21)	CFor NHol
spectabilis (2)	GEdr GLoc MBro NHol WAbe WHoo
Spice Shades (Poly)	EDon GAbr NJap
Springtime (Prim)	CSun WHil
x ***steinii***	See P. x ***forsteri***
'Sue Jervis' (D.Prim)	CBos CHad CTom ELun GSta GWic WEas WRus
'Sunshine Susie' (D.Prim)	CFis CGle CRow ELan ELun GAbr MBri MPlt NCat NHol NJap NRoo NSti SIng SSus WHer WHil WRus
'Sylvia' (Prim)	NHol NNrd
takedana (24)	NHol
tanneri nepalensis (21)	ITim NHar
'Tantallon' (21)	EPot GEdr
§ Tartan Reds (Prim)	GAbr NHol NJap WHil
'Tawny Port' (Poly)	CBrd CCot CGle CRiv CRow EPot GAbr GLoc GSta LCra LFox SApp WRus
'Techley Red' (Prim)	EPot
¶ 'The Grail' (Prim)	NKay
'Tipperary Purple' (Prim)	CCot GAbr GSta
'Tomato Red' (Prim)	CBrd COtt CRow GAbr GSta LCra LFox NKay
'Torchlight' (Prim)	LHop
tsariensis alba	NHol
'Tyrian Purple' (D.Poly)	CGle
uralensis	See P. ***veris macrocalyx***
'Val Horncastle' (D.Prim)	CB&S CChu CFis CHad EOrc GAbr NHol NJap NRoo NSti SIng SSpi WHal WHil WRus
Valentine Victorians (Poly)	GAbr NJap
veris (30)	Widely available
§ – ***macrocalyx*** (30)	NHol
vernalis	See P. ***vulgaris***
verticillata (12)	LGre
§ ***vialii*** (17)	Widely available
Victorian shades (Poly)	CSun NCat WHil
§ ***villosa*** (2)	GEdr NHol
– ***commutata*** (2)	NHol
– ***cottica*** (2)	See P. ***villosa***
Violet Victorians (Poly)	GAbr NJap
viscosa	See P. ***latifolia***
§ x ***vochinensis*** (2)	CRiv GEdr MBro MHig NHar NHol NKay NWCA SIng WAbe
§ ***vulgaris*** (30)	CArn CBre CBro CGle CPla CSFH ECha ELun ENot EPar LCra LFox LHol MBri MWgw NHol NJap NLan SIng SPer WCla WEas WOak WRus
– ***alba*** (30)	CGle ECha
¶ – Balltrogan cream edge	IBlr
¶ – 'Brendon Hills'	CRow
– Cornish pink (Prim)	GAbr
– double yellow (30)	ELan
¶ – green flowered	IBlr
– ***sibthorpii*** (30)	CBro CCla CElw CGle COtt EJud ELun GEdr LCra LFox NHol NNrd SBla WAbe
waltonii (26)	CBot CBre COtt CPla GEdr MBal MHig NRya WHal
'Wanda' (D.Prim)	Widely available
'Wanda Cherry Red' (Prim)	GAbr
'Wanda Hose in Hose' (Prim)	CElw CGle CTom ELan GSta LFox NHol WHer WHil WRus
¶ 'Wanda Improved' (Prim)	GSta
warshenewskiana (11)	CPla EMNN GAbr GDra GEdr GLoc LCra MBal MCas MHig NGre NHar NHol NKay NNrd NRed NRya NTow SIng WAbe WDav WEas
¶ 'Wedgwood'	NHol
¶ 'Westmorland Blue' (Prim)	GSta
¶ 'Whipped Cream'	NHol
'White Wanda' (Prim)	CRow ECha
whitei (21)	CBot CBrd EPar GGar GHig MBal SBar
– 'Arduaine' (21)	CFor GEdr
'William Gender' (Poly)	CBro GSta WRus
wilsonii (4)	CCla CPla GAbr GArf GEdr NHol
'Windrush'	See P. x ***berninae*** 'W.'
'Wisley Red' (Prim)	CBos CTom EBre GSta
wulfeniana (2)	CRiv GEdr MBro NHol NWCA SIng
yargongensis	See P. ***involucrata*** Yargongensis group

PRINSEPIA (Rosaceae)

PRITCHARDIA (Palmae)

pacifica	LPal

PROSOPIS (Leguminosae)

chilensis	CGre

PROSTANTHERA (Labiatae)

cuneata	Widely available
¶ ***eurybiodes***	CSun
lasianthos	CHan CPle ECou SSpi
– ***coriacea***	CSun
melissifolia	CSun ERav
§ – ***parvifolia***	CB&S CBow CTre CTrw GWic LHil WBod WHer WSHC
nivea	CGre CPle CSun CTre WTay
ovalifolia	ECou
¶ 'Poorinda Ballerina'	LHop
'Poorinda Pixie'	CBot WBod
rotundifolia	CArn CB&S CBrd CChu CGre CHan CPle CSun CTre EPad ERea LAbb LHop SHil SIgm SLMG WBod
– ***alba***	CBot
– ***rosea***	CB&S CGre CPle CSun CTre ERea LHop SLMG
sieberi	See P. ***melissifolia parvifolia***
walteri	ECou LGre SIgm SSpi

PROTEA (Proteaceae)

¶ *burchellii* CSun
¶ *compacta* CSun
cynaroides CHEx SIgm SSpi
¶ *eximia* CSun

PRUMNOPITYS (Podocarpaceae)

§ *andina* SHil SLon WBod WWat
♦ *elegans* See P. ***andina***
§ *ferruginea* ECou SBor
§ – 'Golden Dwarf' CMer CSun
§ *taxifolia* ECou

PRUNELLA (Labiatae)

grandiflora CLew CRiv MBri NKay WHoo
– alba NKay WHil
– 'Pagoda' CBow CHar EHal NOak
– rosea NSel WHil
incisa See P. ***vulgaris***
* 'Inshriach Ruby' NBir
laciniata WHer
§ *vulgaris* CArn CKin EJud Effi GPoy LHol MChe MSal NLan NSti SIde WCla WHer WHil
– alba WHer
– lilacina CSun
x *webbiana* CFis CRow CSco MWat SIng WPer
– 'Blue Loveliness' GDra
– 'Little Red Riding Hood' See P. x *w.* 'Rotkäppchen'
– 'Loveliness' CBow CGle CSco CTom ECha ELan EOrc EPar MWgw NNrd SPer WHal WHil WWin
– 'Pink Loveliness' CFis CGle CHar CKel CRow CSco EBre ECha EGol EOrc EPar GDra MBal SIng SPer WEas WWin
§ – 'Rotkäppchen' CGle CTom ERou GCHN MRav SPer
– 'White Loveliness' CGle CRow ECha EGol EOrc EPar GDra SPer WEas WRus WWin

PRUNUS † (Rosaceae)

'Accolade' CB&S CLnd COtt CSam CSco ECtt ENot GRei IOrc LSav MBri MR&S MRav NWea SExT SFam SHil SIgm SPer SSta WMou
§ 'Amanogawa' Widely available
*– 'Baggesen's Variety' CLnd
x *amygdalo-persica* MBri
– 'Pollardii' ELan ENot NWea SHil SReu WJas
amygdalus See P. ***dulcis***
F *armeniaca* 'Alfred' EHar EMui MBri NTwe SDea SPer
F – 'Bredase' SDea
– 'De Nancy' See P. ***a.*** 'Gros Pêche'
F – 'Early Moor Park' EWar GRei IJoh MBea NElm NTwe SDea SFam SIgm WWeb
F – 'Farmingdale' SDea SKee
F – 'Goldcot' SDea
F – 'Gros Pêche' CMac
F – 'Hongaarse' SDea
– mandshurica WCoo
F – 'Moor Park' EHar ERea IJoh LBuc NRog NTwe SDea SKee WHig
F – 'New Large Early' NTwe SDea SKee
F – 'Royal' CMac
F – 'Tross Orange' SDea
'Asano' ENot SHil
avium CB&S CBra CKin CLnd CPer EHar ENot GRei ISea LBuc MBar MBri MGos MR&S NWea SExT SHil SPer WAbe WMou
F – 'Amber Heart' MCls SDea SKee
F – 'Bigarreau Gaucher' SDea SKee
F – 'Bigarreau Napoléon' IJoh MCls NElm NTwe SDea SKee
F – 'Black Heart' SKee
F – 'Bradbourne Black' SKee
♦– 'Cherokee' See P. ***a.*** 'Lapins'
F – 'Early Rivers' EWar IJoh MCls NTwe SDea SKee
F – 'Emperor Francis' SKee
F – 'Florence' SKee
F – 'Frogmore Early' MCls
F – 'Governor Wood' NElm NTwe SKee
F – 'Inge' MBea
F – 'Ironsides' SKee
F – 'Lapins' EMui NTwe SKee SNTN WHig
– 'May Duke' See P. x ***gondouinii*** 'M.D.'
F – 'Merchant' NTwe SKee
F – 'Mermat' NTwe
F – 'Merpet' NTwe
F – 'Merton Bigarreau' CMac MCls SDea
F – 'Merton Bounty' CMac
F – 'Merton Favourite' SKee
F – 'Merton Glory' EHar EWar GChr NTwe SDea SKee
F – 'Merton Heart' CMac SDea SKee
F – 'Merton Marvel' SKee
F – 'Merton Reward' SKee
– 'Napoléon' See P. ***a.*** 'Bigarreau Napoléon'
F – 'Noble' SKee
F – 'Noir de Guben' GChr NTwe SKee
F – 'Nutberry Black' SKee
– 'Plena' CBow CLnd ELan ENot GRei IOrc MBal MGos MR&S NWea SExT SHil SPer WAbe
F – 'Roundel' SDea SKee
F – 'Stella' CMac CSam EEdc EHar EMui EWar GBon GChr GRei IJoh LBuc MBea MBri MCls MR&S NBar NBee NElm NRog NTwe SIgm SKee SPer WHig
F – 'Stella Compact' MBri SKee WHig
F – 'Sunburst' LBuc MBri NTwe SKee SNTN WHig
F – 'Van' EHar NTwe SKee
F – 'Waterloo' SKee
F – 'White Heart' NElm SKee
besseyi CCor MGos
* 'Birch Bark' GRei

x ***blireana***	CBra CLnd CSco ECtt IDai MBri MRav SExT SHil SPer SReu
'Blushing Bride'	See P. 'Shogetsu'
capuli	See P. ***salicifolia***
cerasifera	CSco LBuc NWea SHil WMou
F – 'Cherry Plum'	SKee
– 'Hessei'	WPat
F – 'Kentish Red'	SKee
F – Myrobalan	CKin SDea SKee
N – 'Nigra'	CBow CBra CLnd CSam CSco EHar ELan IDai IOrc LNet MBri MGos NBar SDea SHil SKee SPer SPla WAbe WJas
¶ – 'Pendula'	WMou
§ – 'Pissardii'	CBra CSco GRei LBuc MBar MR&S MRav NNor NWea SExT SHil SIgm SPer
– 'Rosea'	SHil
F ***cerasus*** 'Montmorency'	SDea SKee
F – 'Morello'	Widely available
F – 'Nabella'	EWar
– 'Rhexii'	EHar MGos SHil SPer WAbe
F – 'Wye Morello'	SKee
'Cheal's Weeping'	CBow CLnd IJoh MBal SExT SIgm WAbe
§ 'Choshia-hizakura'	SDea SHil
x ***cistena***	CB&S CBot CBow CPle CSam CSco CShe ELan ENot ERav IJoh IOrc LHop MBar MGos MR&S MWat NKay SHil SPla WAbe WPat
– 'Crimson Dwarf'	MBri NRoo SPer
F ***domestica*** 'Angelina Burdett' (D)	NRog SKee
F – 'Anna Späth' (C/D)	SKee
F – 'Ariel' (C/D)	SDea SKee
¶ – 'Avalon'	NTwe WHig
F – 'Belgian Purple' (C)	SKee
F – 'Belle de Louvain' (C)	NRog NTwe SDea SKee
F – 'Blue Imperatrice' (C/D)	SKee
F – 'Blue Tit' (C/D)	SKee
F – 'Bonne de Bry' (D)	SKee
F – 'Brandy Gage' (C/D)	SKee
F – 'Burbank' (C/D)	SDea
F – 'Bush' (C)	SKee
F – 'Cambridge Gage' (D)	CSam EHar EMui ERea GBon LBuc MBri MR&S MWat NRog NTwe SDea SFam SIgm SKee SPer WHig WWeb
F – 'Coe's Golden Drop' (D)	EEde EMui MBri MCls NTwe SDea SFam SIgm SKee
F – 'Count Althann's Gage' (D)	EHar NRog SDea SIgm SKee
F – 'Crimson Drop' (D)	SKee
– 'Cropper'	See P. ***d.*** 'Laxton's Cropper'
F – 'Curlew' (C)	SDea
F – 'Czar' (C)	CSam EEde EHar EMui EWar GChr IJoh IOrc LBuc MBea MCls MR&S NElm NRog NTwe SDea SIgm SKee SPer WWeb
– 'Delicious '	See P. ***d.*** 'Laxton's Delicious'
– 'Denniston's Superb'	See P. ***d.*** 'Imperial Gage'
F – 'Diamond' (C)	SKee
F – 'Dittisham Ploughman' (C)	SKee
F – 'Early Laxton' (C/D)	NTwe SDea SFam SKee
F – 'Early Orleans' (C)	SKee
– 'Early Prolific'	See P. ***d.*** 'Rivers's Early Prolific'
– 'Early Rivers'	See P. ***d.*** 'Rivers's Early Prolific'
F – 'Early Transparent Gage' (C/D)	EEde NTwe SDea SFam SIgm
F – 'Edwards' (C/D)	EWar MBri NBee NTwe SDea SFam SIgm WHig
F – 'Excalibur'	NTwe WHig
F – 'German Prune' (C)	SKee
F – 'Giant Prune' (C)	NRog NTwe SKee
F – 'Godshill Blue' (C)	SDea
F – 'Golden Transparent' (D)	NRog NTwe SFam
F – 'Goldfinch' (D)	NRog SFam SKee
F – Green Gage (C/D)	EEde EHar MBea MCls NElm NRog NTwe SDea SFam SKee SPer
F – 'Grove's Late Victoria' (C/D)	SKee
F – 'Herman' (C/D)	CSam NTwe
F – 'Imperial Gage' (C/D)	CMac GRei LBuc NTwe SDea SFam SIgm SKee WHig
– ***institia***	See P. ***institia***
F – 'Jefferson' (D)	MCls NRog NTwe SDea SFam SIgm SKee
F – 'Kirke's' (D)	MBri NTwe SDea SFam SIgm SKee
F – 'Laxton's Cropper' (C)	NBee NRog NTwe SKee
F – 'Laxton's Delight' (D)	NTwe
F – 'Laxton's Gage' (D)	SKee
F – 'Marjorie's Seedling' (C)	EEde EHar EMui LBuc MWat NBee NElm NTwe SDea SFam SIgm SKee SPer WHig
F – 'Merton Gem' (C/D)	NTwe SFam SKee
F – 'Monarch' (C)	NTwe SKee
F – 'Ontario' (C/D)	NTwe SKee
F – 'Opal' (D)	EEde EWar IJoh IOrc MCls MWat NElm NTwe SDea SKee WHig
F – 'Ouillins Gage' (C/D)	CMac CSam EEde EHar EMui ERea EWar GChr IJoh LBuc MBri MCls MWat NBee NElm NRog NTwe SDea SFam SIgm SKee SPer
F – 'Peach Plum' (D)	SKee
F – 'Pond's Seedling' (C)	SDea SKee
F – 'President' (C/D)	SDea SKee
F – 'Prince Englebert' (C)	SKee
F – 'Priory Plum' (D)	SDea
F – 'Purple Pershore' (C)	NRog NTwe SDea SKee
– 'Quetsche d'Alsace'	See P. ***d.*** 'German Prune'
F – 'Reeves' (C)	NBee NTwe SIgm SKee
F – 'Reine Claude de Bavay' (D)	NRog SFam
– 'Reine Claude d'Orée'	See P. ***d.*** Green Gage

F– 'Reine Claude Violette' (D)	SKee
F– 'Rivers's Early Prolific' (C)	GBon LBuc MBri MWat NRog NTwe SDea SIgm SKee
F– 'Royale de Vilvoorde' (D)	SKee
F– 'Ruth Gerstetter' (C)	SKee
F– 'Sanctus Hubertus' (D)	EWar NTwe SDea SIgm SKee
F– 'Severn Cross' (D)	NTwe SKee
F– 'Stint' (C/D)	SKee
F– 'Transparent Gage' (D)	SKee
F– 'Utility' (D)	SKee
F– 'Victoria' (C(D)	Widely available
F– 'Warwickshire Drooper' (C)	CSam EWar GBon LBuc NTwe SDea SKee SPer
F– 'Washington' (D)	SKee
F– 'White Magnum Bonum' (C)	SDea
F– 'Wyedale' (C)	NTwe
F– 'Yellow Egg' (C)	NTwe SDea SFam
F– 'Yellow Pershore' (C)	MBea NRog SKee
§ ***dulcis***	CBra CLnd EMui ENot MBar MR&S NWea SDea SExT SKee
F– 'Macrocarpa'	EHar ESim SFam SHil
– 'Roseoplena'	SHil
'Fudan-zakura'	SHil
'Fugenzo'	SHil
glandulosa 'Alba Plena'	Widely available
§ – 'Rosea Plena'	Widely available
– 'Sinensis'	See P. ***g.*** 'Rosea Plena'
F x ***gondouinii*** 'May Duke'	SKee
'Hally Jolivette'	CChu COtt CShe ELan MBri SHil WAbe
'Hillieri'	MBar MGos MR&S SExT SHil
'Hillieri Spire'	See P. 'Spire'
'Hisakura'	See P. 'Choshia-hizakura'
'Hokusai'	SHil
'Ichiyo'	CLnd ECtt IOrc LNet LSav SHil SPer WAbe
incisa	IOrc SHil SPer
– 'February Pink'	SSta
– 'Fujima'	WPat WWat
– 'Konjo-no-mai'	EPla MBri
¶ – 'Oshidori'	MBri
– 'Praecox'	LRHS LSav SHil SSpi
F ***institia***	EHar
F– 'Black Bullace'	SKee
F– 'Blue Violet Damson'	SKee
F– 'Bradley's King Damson'	MCls
F– 'Farleigh Damson' (C)	EEde NBee NTwe SDea SIgm SKee SPer
F– 'Godshill Damson' (C)	SDea
– 'Golden Bullace'	See P. ***i.*** 'White Bullace'
– 'King of Damsons'	See P. ***i.*** 'Bradley's King Damson'
F– 'Merryweather Damson' (C)	CMac EEde EHar ERea GChr GRei LBuc MBea MBri MCls NBar NBee NRog NTwe SDea SFam SKee
F– Mirabelle de Nancy (C)	SDea SKee
F– 'Mirabelle de Nancy (Red)' (C)	SDea
F– 'Prune Damson'	CSam EHar EMui EWar GBon LBuc MBri MCls MWat NBee NRog NTwe SDea SFam SIgm SKee
– 'Shropshire Damson'	See P. ***i.*** 'Prune Damson'
F– 'Small Bullace'	SKee
F– 'White Bullace'	SKee
'Jo-nioi'	SHil
x ***juddii***	SHil
N 'Kanzan'	Widely available
§ 'Kiku-shidare-zakura'	CB&S CBra CSam CSco ECtt ELan GRei IDai LBuc LNet MBar MBri MGos MR&S NBar NJap NWea SExT SFam SHil SPer SReu
'Korean Hill'	See P. ***serrulata pubescens***
'Kursar'	COtt EHar IOrc LNet LRHS MBri SGar SHil
laurocerasus	CB&S CBra CKin CSco ELan GRei IDai LNet MR&S MWat NNor NWea SArc SExT SHil SPer SReu WAbe WMou WWin
♦– 'Aureovariegata'	See P. ***l.*** 'Taff's Golden Gleam'
– 'Barnstedt'	MWal
– 'Camelliifolia'	CChu CFis EPla ISea WHCG
N– 'Castlewellan'	Widely available
– 'Caucasica'	IDai WWeb
– 'Cherry Brandy'	MWal SPer
– 'Goldglanz'	MWal
– 'Green Marble'	MUlv SSpi WSHC
– 'Greenmantle'	SHil
– 'Herbergii'	CBow MWal
– 'Holstein'	MWal
– 'Latifolia'	SHil
– 'Magnoliifolia'	MWal SArc SHil
– 'Marbled White'	See P. ***l.*** 'Castlewellan'
– 'Mischeana'	MBri MWal
– 'Mount Vernon'	ELan MBar MBri MWal
– 'Otto Luyken'	Widely available
– 'Reynvaanii'	LHop MBri MGos MWal
– 'Rotundifolia'	EBar ELan ENot LBuc MBar MBri MWal SHil
– 'Rudolf Billeter'	MWal
– 'Schipkaensis'	CSco MWal NNor SPer
§ – 'Taff's Golden Gleam'	CHoe EMon
– 'Van Nes'	IOrc MUlv MWal WWeb
N– 'Variegata'	EMon
– 'Zabeliana'	CLan CMHG CSco ENot MBar MR&S MWal NRoo SHil SLon SPer SPla SReu WPat WWin
lusitanica	Widely available
– ***azorica***	SHil SLon SPer WMou WWat
– 'Myrtifolia'	EHar MUlv SHil WMou
– 'Variegata'	Widely available
maackii	EHar LSav SSpi WMou WWat
– 'Amber Beauty'	SHil
mandshurica	See P. ***armeniaca m.***

'Mount Fuji'	CLnd CSam ELan ENot IDai IJoh IOrc MBal MGos MR&S NWea SHil SPer SReu
mume	WNor
– 'Alba Plena'	LRHS SHil
– 'Alphandii'	SHil
– 'Beni-chidori'	ELan ERav LRHS MBri SHil SSpi
§ – 'Omoi-no-mama'	LRHS SSpi
– 'Omoi-no-wac'	See P. ***mume*** 'Omoi-no-mama'
– 'Pendula'	CLnd EHal MBri
myrobalan	See P. ***cerasifera*** Myrobalan
nipponica kurilensis 'Ruby'	SHil
'Ojochin'	SHil
'Okame'	CLnd CSam EHar MBri NBar NWea SHil SPer
'Okumiyako'	See P. 'Shogetsu'
padus	CKin CLnd EHar IDai IOrc LBuc LNet LSav MBri MGos NWea SExT SHil SMad WMou
– 'Albertii'	SExT SGar SHil
– 'Colorata'	CMHG ELan IOrc LNet MBri MR&S SExT SHil SPer SPla SSpi WJas
– ***grandiflora***	See P. ***p.*** 'Watereri'
– 'Purple Queen'	ENot MGos
§ – 'Watereri'	CLnd EHar ELan ENot IDai IOrc MBri SExT SHil SPer SReu SSta WJas
'Pandora'	CB&S CLnd ECtt ELan ENot GRei LSav MBal NWea SFam SHil SPer WAbe
§ ***pendula*** 'Pendula Rosea'	CB&S CBow ECtt ENot MBar SHil SPer WAbe WJas
§ – 'Pendula Rubra'	COtt ENot LNet MBri MGos SFam SHil SPer
persica 'Alboplena'	SExT
F – 'Amsden June'	ELan ERea NTwe SDea SFam
F – 'Bellegarde'	ERea NTwe SDea SFam
F – 'Bonanza'	ELan ERea
– 'Cardinal'	SExT
F – 'Doctor Hogg'	SDea
F – 'Duke of York'	ERea EWar GBon NTwe SDea SFam SKee
F – 'Early Alexander'	NTwe
F – 'Early Rivers'	CMac EHar NRog NTwe SDea
F – 'Francis Miriam'	SKee
F – 'Garden Anny'	ELan MBri
F – 'Garden Lady'	ERea WHig
F – 'Hale's Early'	ERea MBri NTwe SDea SFam SKee
– 'Klara Mayer'	MBri SExT SHil
F – 'Peregrine'	CMac EEde EHar EMui ERea EWar GBon GRei IJoh LBuc MBea MBri MR&S NBee NElm NRog NTwe SDea SFam SIgm SKee SMad WHig WWeb
– 'Red Peachy'	NBar
F – 'Reliance'	SDea
F – 'Robin Redbreast'	SDea
F – 'Rochester'	EHar EMui ERea EWar GBon MBea MBri NElm NTwe SDea SFam SIgm SKee WHig WWeb

F – 'Royal George'	NRog NTwe SFam SKee
* – 'Rubra'	MBri
F – 'Saturne'	WHig
– 'Spring Glow'	MBri
F – 'Springtime'	SDea
– 'White Peachy'	NBar
– 'Windle Weeping'	CB&S
F ***persica nectarina*** 'Crimson Gold'	SDea
F – – 'Early Gem'	SDea
F – – 'Elruge'	ERea NTwe SFam
F – – 'Fantasia'	SDea
F – – 'Fire Gold'	SDea
F – – 'Fuzalode'	SDea
F – – 'Humboldt'	NTwe SFam
F – – 'John Rivers'	ERea NTwe SFam
F – – 'Lord Napier'	EHar EMui ERea IJoh LBuc MBea SDea SFam SIgm SKee SPer WHig WWeb
F – – 'Nectared'	SKee
F – – 'Nectarella'	ERea
F – – 'Pineapple'	EHar ERea NElm NTwe SDea SFam SKee WHig
F – – 'Red Haven'	NTwe SFam SKee
F – – 'Rivers Prolific'	SDea
F – – 'Ruby Gold'	SDea
'Pink Perfection'	CBow CBra CLnd CSco GRei LSav MBri MR&S SExT SFam SHil SPer WAbe WMou
'Pink Shell'	MBri SExT SFam SHil
pissardii	See P. ***cerasifera*** 'Pissardii'
'Pissardii Nigra'	See P. ***cerasifera*** 'Nigra'
prostrata	EHal NHol SHil WPat WThu
pumila depressa	EGol ERav LHop MBar MPla SHil SPla SSpi SSta
'Red Cascade'	SDea
rufa	SHil
¶ ***salicifolia***	SDry
sargentii	CBra CLnd EHar ELan ENot IDai IHos IJoh IOrc LSav MBri MGos MR&S NWea SExT SFam SHil SPer SPla SReu SSta STre WAbe WMou
– 'Rancho'	ENot MBri SHil SPer
x ***schmittii***	CLnd SExT SHil SPer
'Sekiyama'	See P. 'Kanzan'
serotina	NWea
§ ***serrula***	CBra CLnd EHar ELan ENot IDai IOrc MBal MBar MBri MGos NBar NWea SExT SGar SHil SKee SMad SPer SSta WAbe WMou WWat
– ***tibetica***	See P. ***serrula***
serrulata 'Autumn Glory'	SHil
– 'Erecta'	See P. 'Amanogawa'
– 'Grandiflora'	See P. 'Ukon'
– ***hupehensis***	SHil
– 'Longipes'	See P. 'Shogetsu'
N – ***pubescens***	CLnd LSav MBri MR&S SExT SPer
♦ – 'Rosea'	See P. 'Kiku-shidare-zakura'
– ***spontanea***	SHil

'Shidare-zakura'	See P. 'Kiku-shidare-zakura'
'Shimidsu-zakura'	See P. 'Shogetsu'
'Shirofugen'	CB&S CBra CLnd ECtt EHar GRei IDai IOrc LSav MBri SDea SExT SFam SPer SReu
'Shirotae'	See P. 'Mount Fuji'
§ 'Shogetsu'	CB&S CLnd CSco ELan ENot IOrc MBal MBri SFam SHil SPer WAbe
'Shosar'	CLnd CSco MBri MR&S SGar SHil SPer WAbe
'Snow Goose'	LSav MBri SExT SHil
spinosa	CKin CPer LBuc MBri NNor NWea SHil SPer WMou
– 'Purpurea'	SHil WMou WPat WWat
'Spire'	CBow CBra CLnd CSco EHar ELan ENot IOrc SFam SHil SPer SPla WAbe
x ***subhirtella ascendens*** 'Rosea'	SHil WAbe
– 'Autumnalis'	CB&S CBow CBra CLnd CSco EGol EHar ELan ENot IDai IHos IJoh ISea MBal MRav NWea SDea SExT SFam SHil SPer SReu SSta WWat
– 'Autumnalis Rosea'	CB&S CSam EHar ELan ENot GRei IJoh LBuc LNet MBar MBri MGos MR&S NBar NJap NWea SHil SPer SPla WAbe WJas WMou WWat
– 'Fukubana'	CB&S CLnd COtt ELan MBri SHil
– 'Pendula'	See P. ***pendula*** 'Pendula Rosea'
– 'Pendula Rubra'	See P. ***pendula*** 'Pendula Rubra'
– 'Rosea'	CLnd SReu
– 'Stellata'	SHil
'Tai-haku'	CB&S CLnd CSam CSco EHar ELan ENot IOrc LNet LSav MBri MGos NBar NWea SExT SFam SHil SPer SPla SReu WAbe
¶ 'Tao-yoma'	WAbe
tenella	CB&S CBra CCla CSco ELan GLoc MBri MGos SDix SGar SPla SSpi WWat
– 'Fire Hill'	CCla CFor CShe EHar ELan GLoc IJoh LNet MGos NHol SHil SPer SSpi WPat
tibetica	See P. ***serrula***
tomentosa	EBre EPla WAbe
F 'Trailblazer' (C/D)	CLnd CSco IOrc MGos MR&S NHol NWea SKee
triloba	CB&S CBow CBra CLnd CSco ELan IJoh LBuc MBar MBri MGos MPla SExT SHil SIgm SKee SPer SSpi WAbe
– 'Multiplex'	EGol ENot IHos WJas
§ 'Ukon'	CB&S CLnd CSco EHar ENot IOrc LNet MBal MBar MBri MR&S MRav NWea SExT SFam SHil SPer SReu WAbe
'Umineko'	CLnd ENot IOrc MGos MR&S SExT SPer
virginiana 'Shubert'	CLnd EHar ELan ENot EPla IOrc LHop MBri SExT SGar SHil SSpi SSta WJas
♦ 'Wood's Variety'	See P. ***cerasifera*** 'Woodii'
x ***yedoensis***	CBra CLnd ENot SExT SFam SHil SPer WWat
– 'Erecta'	ENot
– 'Ivensii'	CSco ECtt SHil
– ***pendula***	See P. x ***y.*** 'Shidare-yoshino'
– 'Perpendens'	See P. x ***y.*** 'Shidare-yoshino'
§ – 'Shidare-yoshino'	CLnd CSco ECtt LNet MBri SHil SPer WWat
'Yedo-zakura'	SHil

PSEUDOCYDONIA (Rosaceae)

¶ ***sinensis***	CB&S LNet

PSEUDOFUMARIA (Papaveraceae)

§ ***alba***	EPot MPar SApp SFir SPou WBon
lutea	CHad ECro EHal IBlr LGro MPit MUlv MWat NNrd WCot WOak WPer

PSEUDOLARIX (Pinaceae)

§ ***amabilis***	CGre CMCN EHar LNet MBri SHil SMad SSpi WCon WCoo WNor WWat
♦ ***kaempferi***	See P. ***amabilis***

PSEUDOMERTENSIA (Boraginaceae)

sp. SEP 234	WDav

PSEUDOMUSCARI (Liliaceae/Hyacinthaceae)

azurea	See MUSCARI ***azureum***

PSEUDOPANAX † (Araliaceae)

'Adiantifolius'	CHEx IBar
¶ ***arboreus***	CHEx
¶ ***chathamicus***	CHEx
crassifolius	CBot CHEx ECou IBar MBal SArc
davidii	SHil
ferox	CHEx SHil
laetivirens	CCla
¶ ***laetus***	CHEx
¶ ***lessonii***	CB&S CHEx ECou
– 'Gold Splash'	NPal
– hybrids	CHEx
¶ 'Sabre'	SMad

PSEUDOPHEGOPTERIS (Thelypteridaceae)

* ***levingei***	EMon LRHS

PSEUDOPHOENIX (Palmae)

* ***nativo***	MBri

PSEUDOSASA (Gramineae(Bambuseae))

§ ***amabilis***	SBam SDry
§ ***japonica***	CBow CHEx EFul ELan ERav IDai MBal NJap SBam SDry SHil SMad SPer SReu WJun
– 'Tsutsumiana'	SBam SDry WJun
– 'Variegata'	EFul SBam SDry

pleioblastoides	SBam SDry

PSEUDOTSUGA (Pinaceae)

**flahaultii*	WHCr
macrocarpa	SHil
§ *menziesii*	CPer EHar IDai IOrc LBuc MBar NWea SExT SHil WCon WMou
– 'Blue Wonder'	MBri
¶ – 'Densa'	CKen
– 'Fletcheri'	CKen MBar MBri SHil
– *glauca*	EHar IBar MBar WCon
– 'Glauca Pendula'	EHar MBar MGos SHil
I – 'Gotelli's Pendula'	CKen
¶ – 'Graceful Grace'	CKen
– 'Little Jon'	MBar MBri WCon
– 'Nana'	CKen
– 'Pendula group'	MBri WCon
– 'Viridis'	GRei
taxifolia	See P. ***menziesii***

PSEUDOWINTERA (Winteraceae)

§ *colorata*	CB&S CBra CCla CFor CLan CMHG CTrw IBar IDai IJoh IOrc ISea MBal MUlv SHil SSus WBod

PSIDIUM (Myrtaceae)

F *littorale*	ERea ESim
¶ – *lucidum*	ESim

PSILOSTROPHE (Compositae)

¶ *tagentinae*	WPer

PSORALEA (Leguminosae)

¶ *affinis*	CHEx

PSYCHOTRIA (Rubiaceae)

capensis	SLMG

PTELEA (Rutaceae)

**isophylla*	LSav
¶ *nitens*	LSav
trifoliata	CB&S CChu CCla CLnd CSco EHar LHol LSav SHil SPer SSpi WBod WCoo WNor WOMN
– 'Aurea'	CCla CFor CSco EHar ELan ERav LGre MBri SHil SPer SSpi WPat

PTERACANTHUS (Acanthaceae)

§ *attenuatus*	CCla
urticifolius	CHan

PTERIDIUM (Dennstaedtiaceae)

aquilinum Percristatum group	IOrc NKay

PTERIDOPHYLLUM (Fumariaceae)

racemosum	EPot

PTERIS (Adiantiaceae)

argyraea	NMar
cretica	MBri SArc
– *albolineata*	MBri NMar WFib
– *cristata*	MBri
– 'Gautheri'	MBri
– 'Major'	WFib
– 'Parkeri'	MBri
– 'Rivertonia'	MBri WFib
– 'Rowei'	MBri
– 'Wimsettii'	MBri
ensiformis	MBri NMar
– 'Arguta'	MBri
– 'Victoriae'	MBri
quadriaurita argyraea	MBri WFib
tremula	MBri NMar
umbrosa	MBri
vittata	WFib

PTEROCARYA (Juglandaceae)

fraxinifolia	CB&S CLnd CSam EHar ENot IBar IOrc LHop LSav MBlu SHil SSpi WMou
x *rehderiana*	WMou
rhoifolia	CCor EHar SSpi WCoo WMou
stenoptera	CB&S EHar LSav MBri SMad SSpi WCoo WMou

PTEROCELTIS (Ulmaceae)

PTEROCEPHALUS (Dipsacaceae)

parnassi	See P. ***perennis perennis***
§ *perennis*	CShe EFol MPar MPit NKay NRar WAbe WDav WPat WPer
§ – *perennis*	CLew EPot GCHN GLoc MBro MCas SBla SCro SIng WCar WEas WHoo WOMN WWin
¶ *pinardii*	WPer

PTEROSTYLIS (Orchidaceae)

¶ *curta*	CRiv

PTEROSTYRAX (Styracaceae)

corymbosa	CMCN
hispida	CChu CCla CMCN CPle ELan LSav MBri MRav SHil SSpi SSta WBod WCoo WWat

PTILOSTEMON (Compositae)

¶ *afer*	ECro
diacantha	ECro LHil

PTILOTRICHUM (Cruciferae)

cappadocicum	SCro
pyrenaicum	MHig NWCA WHil
§ *spinosum*	MBro MHig MTho NKay STre WAbe
– *roseum*	CHar CMHG CShe EFol ELan EPad EPot GLoc LHop MPla MWat NGre NTow SBla SIng SPou WAbe WHal WPat WPer WSHC WWin

PTYCHOSPERMA (Palmae)

macarthurii	LPal

PULICARIA (Compositae)	
dysenterica	CArn CKin LGan MSal WOak
PULMONARIA † (Boraginaceae)	
angustifolia	CFis CHEx CHad CRow CSam EFol GDra GEdr MFir MPlt MSal MWat NHol NOrc SChu SSpi WBon WEas WRus WWin
– azurea	CBro CElw CKel CLew CRow EBre EFou EGol ELan ELun ERou IDai MBri NKay NRoo NSti NTow SIng SPer SSpi
– 'Beth's Blue'	ECha EOrc MBri
– 'Beth's Pink'	ECha NCat
– 'Blaues Meer'	SSpi
– 'Mawson's Blue'	CTom ECha EMon MBri WHea WWat
– 'Munstead Blue'	CGle CSco CShe ECha EGol ENot EPar GPla MCot MTho MWgw WOld
*– 'Rubra'	CLew ELun ERou MCot SIng
* 'Beth Chatto'	EOrc
'Blauhimmel'	See P. ***saccharata*** 'Frühlingshimmel'
¶ 'Blue Ensign'	EMon
'Blue Mist'	NCat
¶ 'Fiona'	LHil
'Glacier'	EMon NSti
'Highdown'	See P. 'Lewis Palmer'
¶ 'Leopard'	SSpi
§ 'Lewis Palmer'	CBre CHan EBre EFol EGol ELan EOrc MTho NHol NRoo NSti SAxl SBla SPer SSpi WHoo WRus
****linifolia***	WHil
longifolia	CBot CBro CGle CHan CMHG CRow EFol EGol ELan EPar EPla GLoc GWic MBri MCot MSal MUlv NCat NVic SChu SIng SMad WBon WEas
– 'Bertram Anderson'	CBos CHad EMon MUlv SAxl SBla SWas WCot
¶ – 'Roy Davidson'	SWas
¶ 'Mary Mottram'	NSti
mollis	CBot CHan EOrc GWic NCat NSti
'Mournful Purple'	CRow ECha MUlv NSti
officinalis	Widely available
– alba	MWgw NCat
– 'Bowles' Blue	CRow WRus
– 'Cambridge'	CBos CBre CBro CElw CHan ECha EFol EFou EGol EMon EOrc ERav GPla NHol NSti SAxl WBon WEas
– rubra	EOrc NBir
– 'Sissinghurst White'	Widely available
'Patrick Bates'	NSti
'Roy Davidson'	CHad
rubra	CElw CFis CGle CHan CHil CSam CShe ECha ELan EPar MFir NHol NOak NOrc NSti SChu SFis SSpi WHea WHil WHoo
¶ ***– alba***	EPla
– albocorollata	EMon LRHS NSti
– 'Barfield Pink'	CHan CRow ELan EMon ERav GWic NSti SChu SSpi WRus
– 'Bowles' Red'	CBot CBre CBro CCla CHar CKel CSco EBre EJud ENot ERav ERou LHop MBri MWgw NRoo SCro SPer WHal
– 'David Ward'	ECha EOrc
– 'Redstart'	CBro CHad CSun EBre ECtt EFou EGol GLoc MUlv NHol NRoo NSti SAxl SHig SPer SSpi WEas WRus
§ ***saccharata***	CBre CElw CHEx CRow CShe CSun ECha ELan GPla LGro NHol SChu WEas WHea WHoo WWat WWin
– 'Alba'	CBro CRow ECha EFol EPar NNrd NOak
– argentea	CBro CGle CHan CHar CRow CWGN ECha EFol EGol ELan EOrc ERav MCot MPit MTho NHol SSpi WOld
¶ – 'Brentor'	CRow
– 'Frühlingshimmel'	EOrc GLoc NCat NSti SBla SWas
– 'Mrs Moon'	CCor ECro ECtt EFou ENot ERou GPla LSav NHol NOrc NSti SChu SFis SPer
– 'Picta'	See P. ***s.***
– 'Pink Dawn'	CHad CKel CSco EOrc MBri MUlv NCat NSti WRus
– 'Reginald Kaye'	ECha NSti
¶ – 'Snow Queen'	NHol
– 'Tim's Silver'	ECha
* 'Salmon Glow'	MTho
¶ 'Skylight'	LHil
vallarsae 'Margery Fish'	CBro COtt EBre EGol EOrc LHil MBri MUlv NRoo SAxl SPer WEas WRus
'Weetwood Blue'	CChu
'White Wings'	CHan CSco NHol SChu SSpi WEas
PULSATILLA (Ranunculaceae)	
albana	SOkd SPou
¶ – 'Lutea'	SPou
– white form	SOkd
alpina	CBot NRoo
§ ***– apiifolia***	CBot CHar ELan GArf GDra MBro NHol NRoo WAbe WHoo WOMN
– sulphurea	See P. ***a. apiifolia***
halleri	GPla NTow SCro
– slavica	CSun SWas
montana	LGre
¶ ***occidentalis***	WOMN
patens	CLew MBro MSal WDav WHoo
pratensis	MTho NRoo
– nigricans	LRHS
§ ***vernalis***	MBro NHol WAbe WDav WEas WHoo WMar
§ ***vulgaris***	Widely available

– alba	CAvo CBow CCla CGle EFou ELan EPar GLoc LHop MBri MBro MHig NHol NOak NRoo SBla SSpi WAbe WDav WHal WHil WPat WPer WRus
– Balkan form	GEdr
– 'Ena Constance'	LHop LRHS
– 'Gotlandica'	NHol
– 'Röde Klokke' ('Rote Glocke')	NHol SPou
– rubra	Widely available
wallichiana CHA 128	WEas

PUMMELO See **CITRUS** ***grandis***

PUNICA (Punicaceae)

granatum	ERea LAbb LHop SHil STre WSHC
– nana	CArn ERea LGre MPla SHil WPat
– 'Plena'	CB&S SPla

PUSCHKINIA (Liliaceae)

libanotica	See P. ***scilloides***
§ *scilloides*	CAvo CBro CCla EPar EPot ETub LAma LBlo LRoo MBal SIng WPer
– alba	CAvo EPar EPot LAma LRoo NHol SIng

PUTORIA (Rubiaceae)

¶ *calabrica*	WOMN

PUYA (Bromeliaceae)

alpestris	CHEx SArc SSpi
¶ *berteroniana*	CHEx
caerulea	CHEx SIgm
chilensis	CHEx SArc WTay
conquimbensis	CSun GWic MUlv SSpi
lanata	MTho
¶ *laxa*	CHEx
mirabilis	CHEx WTay
¶ *raimondii*	CHEx
¶ *venusta*	CHEx WTay
¶ *weberbauri*	CHEx

PYCNANTHEMUM (Labiatae)

pilosum	CArn GPoy MSal WPer

PYCNOSTACHYS (Labiatae)

PYGMAEA See **CHIONOHEBE**

PYRACANTHA † (Rosaceae)

'Alexander Pendula'	CSco ENot LHop LSav MGos MRav NJap SLon
angustifolia	CB&S CMac CSco ELan EMon LHop SHil WWat
§ *atalantioides*	CB&S CBow CBra CMac CPle CSam CSco CShe IDai MRav MWat SLon SPer SPla WPat WWat
§ – 'Aurea'	CBow CSco SLon WWin
– 'Nana'	LHop MRav
'Brilliant'	CB&S CBra
coccinea	CTrw WWin
– 'Lalandei'	CBra CMac CSam MGos NNor SPer WBod
– 'Sparkler'	ERav LHop SHil SMad
crenulata	MFir
* 'Fiery Cascade'	SHil
gibbsii	See P. ***atalantioides***
– 'Flava'	See P. ***atalantioides*** 'Aurea'
'Golden Charmer'	CSco ECtt ELan IJoh MBal MGos NKay NTow SHil SPer WAbe WBod
'Golden Dome'	CBra SHil
'Golden Sun'	See P. 'Soleil d'Or'
'Harlequin'	CB&S CHoe CMHG CMac ELan EPla ERav IJoh MBal MBar MGos MRav NHol WPat WSHC
§ 'Kasan'	MWat SPla
'Knap Hill Form'	SPer
koidzumii 'Victory'	SHil
'Lavinia Rutgers'	SHil
'Mohave'	CB&S CBow CMac CSco ELan ENot GRei IJoh MBal MBar MBri MGos MR&S MWat NKay NNor NRoo SHil SLon SPer SReu WAbe WBod WPat
* 'Mozart'	WWeb
'Navaho'	CBow CSco MPla MR&S MRav SHil WBod
N 'Orange Charmer'	CPle CSco CShe ELan ENot IJoh MBal MBar MGos MR&S SHil SPer WAbe
'Orange Giant'	See P. 'Kasan'
'Orange Glow'	CBow CMac CSco CShe EBre ENot GRei IDai IHos IJoh LBuc MBar MBri MGos MR&S NKay NNor NTow NWea SHil SLon SPer WBod WPat
* 'Orange Sun'	CMer
'Red Column'	CMac CMer ECtt GRei IJoh LBuc MBar MGos MR&S MRav SHil WPat
'Red Cushion'	ENot IHos
'Red Delight'	MPla WAbe
* 'Red Pillar'	CSco MBri
'Renault d'Or'	SHil
rogersiana	CBra ELan ENot IJoh MPla SHil
– flava	CBra ELan ENot IDai LHop MBal MBar MGos NKay SHil SPla WBod
'Shawnee'	CB&S CBow CMac MRav MWat WWeb
§ 'Soleil d'Or'	CMac CPle CSam CSco CShe EBre ECtt ENot IHos MBar MBri MPla MR&S MRav NRoo SHil SPer SPla SReu WAbe WPat WSHC
'Sparkler'	CBra CMac SGar SPer
'Telstar'	CB&S SPer WPat

'Teton'	CBra CMHG CMac CSco ELan ENot MBar MBri MGos MR&S MRav NHol SHil SLon SPer WAbe WBod WPat
'Watereri'	ELan NWea SHil SPer SPla
'Yellow Sun'	See P. 'Soleil d'Or'

X PYRACOMELES (Rosaceae)

PYRENARIA (Theaceae)

PYRETHRUM See **TANACETUM**

PYROSTEGIA (Bignoniaceae)

venusta	MNew

PYRUS † (Rosaceae)

betulifolia	CMCN SHil
calleryana 'Chanticleer'	CLnd ECtt EHar ENot IJoh IOrc SExT SHil SPer WJas WMou WWat
caucasica	WCoo
F ***communis***	CKin MBlu WMou
F – 'Admiral Gervais'	SKee
F – 'Autumn Bergamot' (D)	SKee
F – 'Baronne de Mello' (D)	SFam SKee
F – 'Beech Hill'	CLnd EHar ENot SExT SHil
F – 'Belle Guérendais'	SKee
F – 'Belle Julie' (D)	SKee
F – 'Bellissime d'Hiver' (C)	SNTN
F – 'Bergamotte d'Automne' (D)	SKee
F – 'Bergamotte Esperen' (D)	SKee SNTN
F – 'Beth' (D)	EMui EWar GChr MBea MBri NBee NElm NRog NTwe SDea SFam SIgm SKee SPer WHig WWeb
F – 'Beurré Alexandre Lucas' (D)	SKee
F – 'Beurré Bedford' (D)	NRog SKee
F – 'Beurré Bosc' (D)	SKee
F – 'Beurré Clairgeau' (C/D)	SKee
F – 'Beurré de Jonghe' (D)	SKee
F – 'Beurré de Naghin' (C/D)	SKee
F – 'Beurré Dumont' (D)	SFam
F – 'Beurré d'Amanlis' (D)	SKee
F – 'Beurré Hardy' (D)	ERea IJoh LBuc MBri MWat NRog NTwe SDea SFam SIgm SKee
F – 'Beurré Mortillet' (D)	SKee
F – 'Beurré Superfin' (D)	NTwe SFam SKee SNTN
F – 'Black Worcester' (C)	SKee SNTN
F – 'Blakeney Red' (Perry)	SDea
F – 'Blickling'	SKee
F – 'Bonne de Beugny'	SKee
F – 'Brandy' (Perry)	SDea
F – 'Bristol Cross' (D)	SKee
F – 'Catillac' (C)	NRog NTwe SFam SKee
– 'Chalk'	See P. *c.* 'Crawford'
F – 'Chaumontel' (D)	SKee
F – 'Clapp's Favourite' (D)	IOrc NRog NTwe SIgm SKee
F – 'Comte de Lamy' (D)	SFam SKee
F – 'Concorde' (D)	CSam EHar EMui EWar LBuc MBri NBee NElm NTwe SDea SIgm WHig
F – 'Conference' (D)	Widely available
F – 'Crawford' (D)	SKee SNTN
F – 'Deacon's Pear' (D)	SDea
F – 'Doctor Jules Guyot' (D)	SKee
F – 'Doyenné du Comice' (D)	CMac CSam EHar EMui ERea EWar GBon IOrc LBuc MBea MBri MCls MR&S MWat NBar NRog SDea SFam SIgm SKee SNTN SPer WHig WWeb
F – 'Doyenne d'Eté' (D)	SFam SKee
F – 'Duchesse de Bordeaux' (D)	SKee
F – 'Duchesse d'Angoulême' (D)	SFam SKee
F – 'Durondeau' (D)	NRog NTwe SKee
F – 'Emile d'Heyst' (D)	NTwe SIgm SKee
– 'Fertility Improved'	See P. *c.* 'Improved Fertility'
F – 'Fondant d'Automne' (D)	SKee
F – 'Forelle' (D)	SKee SNTN
F – 'Glou Morceau' (D)	NRog NTwe SDea SFam SIgm SKee SNTN
F – 'Glow Red Williams' (D)	SFam
F – 'Gorham' (D)	NBee NTwe SFam SKee
F – 'Green Pear of Yair' (D)	SNTN
F – 'Gros Blanquet' (D)	SNTN
F – 'Hacon's Imcomparable' (D)	SKee
F – 'Hessle' (D)	NRog SFam SKee
F – 'Highland'	SKee SNTN
F – 'Improved Fertility' (D)	NTwe SDea SKee
F – 'Jargonelle' (D)	NRog SFam SKee SNTN
F – 'Jeanne d'Arc'	SNTN
F – 'Joséphine de Malines' (D)	NTwe SDea SFam SIgm SKee SNTN
F – 'Laxton's Foremost' (D)	SKee
F – 'Laxton's Satisfaction'	SFam
F – 'Louise Bonne of Jersey' (D)	EWar MBri MCls NRog NTwe SDea SFam SIgm SKee
F – 'Marguérite Marillat'	NTwe SKee
F – 'Marie Louise d'Uccle' (D)	SKee
F – 'Marie-Louise' (D)	SFam SKee
F – 'Marquise' (D)	SNTN
F – 'Martin Sec' (C/D)	SNTN
F – 'Merton Pride' (D)	NTwe SDea SFam SIgm SKee
F – 'Merton Star' (D)	SKee
F – 'Messire Jean' (D)	SNTN
F – 'Nouveau Poiteau' (C)	NTwe SKee
F – 'Nouvelle Fulvie' (D)	SKee

F – 'Olivier de Serres' (D)	SFam SKee SNTN
F – 'Onward' (D)	EMui GChr MCls NBee NRog NTwe SDea SFam SIgm SKee
F – 'Packham's Triumph' (D)	GBon NRog NTwe SKee SPer
F – 'Passe Crassane' (D)	SKee
F – 'Pear Apple' (D)	SDea
F – 'Pierre Corneille'	SNTN
F – 'Pitmaston Duchess' (C/D)	NTwe SDea SIgm SKee
F – 'Red Comice' (C)	NBee NTwe SKee
F – 'Robin' (C/D)	ERea SKee
F – 'Santa Claus'	SFam SKee
F – 'Seckle' (D)	SFam SKee
F – 'Souvenir du Congrès' (D)	NRog
F – 'Swan's Egg' (D)	SNTN
F – 'Thompson's' (D)	NTwe SFam SKee SNTN
F – 'Triomphe de Vienne' (D)	SFam
– 'Triumph'	See 'P. *c.* 'Packham's Triumph'
F – 'Uvedale's St Germain' (C)	SKee
F – 'Vicar of Winkfield' (D)	SDea SKee
F – 'Williams Red' (D)	CSam IJoh NTwe SKee WHig
F – 'Williams' Bon Chrétien' (D)	CMac EHar EMui ERea EWar GBon GChr GRei IOrc LBuc MBea MBri MCls MR&S NBar NElm NRog SDea SFam SIgm SKee SNTN WWeb
F – 'Windsor' (D)	SNTN
F – 'Winter Nelis' (D)	EHar NTwe SDea SFam SKee SNTN
cordata	CNat
nivalis	EHar ENot SHil SPer SSpi
¶ ***pashia***	EHal
pyraster	EHar
¶ ***pyrifolia***	WHig
F – '20th Century'	IOrc SKee
F – 'Chojura'	IOrc SKee
F – 'Hosui'	SNTN WHig
F – 'Kumoi'	ESim WHig
F – 'Nijusseiki'	SNTN
F – 'Shinko'	IOrc SNTN
F – 'Shinseiki'	SKee
F – 'Yakumo'	SNTN
salicifolia 'Pendula'	Widely available

QIONGZHUEA (Gramineae(Bambuseae))

♦ ***tumidinoda***	See CHIMONOBABUSA ***t.***

QUERCUS † (Fagaceae)

acuta	CHEx CMCN SArc
acutissima	CMCN SHil SSpi WCoo WNor
aegilops	See Q. ***macrolepis***
agrifolia	CMCN LSav WCoo
alba	CMCN SHil WCoo
aliena	SHil WCoo
alnifolia	CMCN SBor
bicolor	CMCN IOrc SHil WCoo
borealis	See Q. ***rubra***
canariensis	CMCN SHil WMou
castaneifolia	SHil SPer WMou
– 'Greenspire'	CMCN EHar MBri SHil WMou
cerris	CB&S CKin CLnd CMCN CSco EHar ENot IOrc NWea SExT SHil SMad SPer SSta STre WCoo WMou
– 'Variegata'	CMCN EHar SHil SSpi WMou
chrysolepis	WCoo
coccifera	CMCN SHil WCoo
coccinea	CMCN EHar ELan IBar IOrc SGar SMad SPer WCoo WNor
– 'Splendens'	CSco EHar ELan IOrc LSav MBlu MBri SHil SPer SSpi
dentata	CMCN SHil WCoo
douglasii	CMCN WCoo
dumosa	WCoo
durifolia	CMCN
ellipsoidalis	CMCN LSav SHil WCoo
falcata	CMCN LSav
– ***pagodifolia***	LSav
frainetto	CLnd CMCN EHar IOrc MBri SExT SHil SPer SSpi WCoo WMou WWat
¶ – 'Trump	SMad
§ ***fruticosa***	CMCN
garryana	CMCN
georgiana	CMCN
glabra	See LITHOCARPUS ***glaber***
glandulifera	CMCN WCoo
x ***hispanica*** 'Ambrozyana'	SHil
– 'Diversifolia'	WMou
– 'Lucombeana'	CMCN EHar SHil SPer WMou
hypoleucoides	SHil
ilex	Widely available
imbricaria	CMCN LSav
incana	CMCN
x ***kewensis***	SHil
x ***libanerris*** 'Rotterdam'	CMCN WMou
libani	CMCN SHil WCoo WMou
lobata	CMCN WCoo
x ***ludoviciana***	SArc SHil WMou
lusitanica	See Q. ***fruticosa***
macranthera	CMCN SHil WMou
macrocarpa	CMCN LSav SHil SSpi WCoo WNor
§ ***macrolepis***	CMCN SHil WCoo
marilandica	CMCN SHil
michauxii	CMCN LSav
mongolica	SHil WCoo
– ***grosseserrata***	CMCN
muehlenbergii	WCoo
myrsinifolia	CMCN SArc SBor SHil SSpi WCoo
nigra	CMCN LSav SHil WCoo
palustris	CLnd CMCN EHar IOrc LPan LSav MBal SExT SHil SPer SSpi STre WNor WWat
pedunculata	See Q. ***robur***
§ ***petraea***	CKin CLnd EHar GRei IOrc LBuc MBal NWea SExT SHil SPer WMou

– 'Columna'	SHil
§ – 'Insecata'	CMCN
– 'Laciniata'	See Q. *p.* 'Insecata '
– 'Purpurea'	CMCN SHil WMou
phellos	CMCN ISea LSav SHil SSpi WNor
¶ – ***latifolia***	IOrc
phillyreoides	CMCN LSav SBor SHil SSpi WCoo WWat
pontica	SHil
prinus	WCoo
pubescens	SHil WCoo
*****pumila***	CMCN
pyrenaica	CMCN SHil
*– 'Argenteomarginata'	CMCN
§ ***robur***	CB&S CBra CKin CLnd CPer CSco ENot GRei IJoh IOrc LBuc MBar MBri MGos NWea SExT SHil SMad SPer SPla WAbe WCoo WMou
– 'Atropurpurea'	SHil SPer WMou
– 'Concordia'	CMCN COtt CSco EHar ELan MBri SHil SSpi WMou
– 'Cristata'	CMCN
– 'Cucullata'	CMCN
– ***fastigiata***	CBow CLnd CSco EHar ENot IOrc MBri NWea SExT SHil SMad SPer WMou
– 'Fastigiata Kassel'	CSco
– 'Fastigiata Koster'	CMCN
– 'Fastigiata Purpurea'	CMCN IOrc SHil
¶ – 'Hungaria'	MBri
– ***pendula***	CMCN CSco SHil WMou
¶ – 'Salicifolia Fastigiata'	WMou
– 'Strypemonde'	CMCN
– ***variegata***	SHil
x ***rosacea*** 'Filicifolia'	SHil
§ ***rubra***	Widely available
– 'Aurea'	CMCN CSco SHil WMou
sadleriana	CMCN
x ***schochiana***	SHil
sessiliflora	See Q. ***petraea***
shumardii	CMCN LSav SHil SSpi
suber	CGre EHar SArc SExT SHil SSpi WMou
trojana	CMCN SHil
x ***turneri***	CMCN EHar LSav MBri SExT SHil WMou
vacciniifolia	MBal
variabilis	CMCN SHil WCoo
velutina	CGre CMCN LSav WWat
– 'Rubrifolia'	SHil
virginiana	CMCN
¶ ***wislizenii***	IOrc WCoo

QUESNELIA (Bromeliaceae)

QUILLAJA (Rosaceae)

saponaria	CGre CHil CPle

QUINCE See **CYDONIA** ***oblonga***

RACOSPERMA See **ACACIA**

RAMONDA (Gesneriaceae)

§ ***myconi***	CFor CLew CRiv ECro EPot GDra GLoc NHol NKay SBla SIng SPou SSpi WKif
– ***rosea***	NKay SPou
nathaliae	ECro
– 'Alba'	GLoc SOkd
pyrenaica	See R. ***myconi***
serbica	GDra

RANUNCULUS † (Ranunculaceae)

abnormis	SWas
aconitifolius	CAvo CGle EBre ECha
– 'Flore Pleno'	CBos CRow IBlr LGre WHea
– ***platanifolius***	CBre CElw CTom EBre
acris 'Farrer's Yellow'	CRow
– 'Flore Pleno'	CAvo CGle CHar CRow CSco ECha EMon EPar EPla ERou GWic NRya
– 'Sulphureus'	EMon NRed
¶ ***adoneus***	WDav
alpestris	NKay
amplexicaulis	GDra NHar SIng SWas
¶ ***anemoneus***	SOkd
asiaticus red form	ECam WChr
*– Tecolote hybrids	LAma LBlo
– white form	WChr
bilobus	NHar
bulbosus	CKin
– 'F M Burton'	CBos CElw EMon MPar SAxl
– 'Speciosus Plenus'	See R. ***constantinopolitanus*** 'Plenus'
cadmicus	ECam
calandrinioides	CMHG CSun SPou
§ ***constantinopolitanus*** 'Plenus'	CGle CHan CRow ECha GPla GWic MBri NTow SPer
crenatus	CElw GEdr ITim MBal MHig NHar NHol NNrd NRya NTow WAbe WHal
creticus	MPar
ficaria	CArn CKin CRow CSFH GWic MChe NNrd SIde WHer WOak
– ***albus***	CBre CCor CFor CGle CLew CRow NHol SIng WCot
– anemone centred	See R. *f.* 'Collarette'
– ***aurantiacus***	See R. *f.* ***cupreus***
– 'Brazen Hussy'	CAvo CBos CBre CCor CFor CGle CLew CRow ECha EFou EPot GWic MTho NTow SBla SDix SIng SSpi SWas WCot WHal
§ – 'Collarette'	CBre CRow EMon EPar EPot MTho NNrd SIng WCot WHil
§ – ***cupreus***	CBre CFor CLew CRow ECha EMon EPot GDra GLoc GWic MPar SBla SIng
– double bronze	EMon
– double cream	CBre SBla SIng WCot

– double green eye	CRow
– 'E A Bowles'	CFor SBla SIng WCla
– *flore pleno*	CBro CFor CGle ECha ELan EMon EPar GAbr GDra GLoc GWic MPar NHol NNrd NSti SIng WCot WEas WHil
– 'Green Petal'	EMon MTho NHol SIng
– 'Hoskins Miniature'	CRow
– 'Hoskins Spider'	CRow
– 'Lemon Queen'	NHol SIng
– 'Major'	CRow EPot SIng
– 'Picton's Double'	CFor CRow
– 'Primrose'	CBre CFor MTho NHol
– 'Randall's White'	MTho NTow WCot
– 'Rowden Magna'	CRow
– 'Salmon's White'	CBos EPot NNrd SBla
– 'Wisley Double Yellow'	CFor CLew
¶ – 'Wyatt's White'	CCor
¶ – 'Yaffle'	CBre
flammula	CArn CKin CRow EHon LMay MSal MSta
¶ *glacialis*	EBar
gouanii	CSun EPot NGre NHol NKay SIng WHoo
gramineus	CHar CLew CSun EFou ELan EPad EPot GAbr GEdr GLoc MBro MPar NGre NHol NNrd SChu SIgm SIng WCot WDav WHea WHoo WThu
illyricus	EMon
¶ *kochii*	EPot
lingua	CKin
– 'Grandiflorus'	CRiv CRow CWGN EHon LMay MSta WOak
lyallii	CRow
millefoliatus	NNrd SIng WHil
montanus	MBal
– 'Molten Gold'	EBre ELan EPad GLoc MHig MRav MTho NHar NHol NKay NNrd NRya NTow
parnassifolius	NGre NHar
¶ *pygmaeus*	NHar
pyrenaeus	MBal
repens	CKin
– 'Joe's Golden'	CHoe EMon
– *pleniflorus*	CBre CElw CGle CMal CRow ELan EMon EPar GWic NSti SSvw WBon WEas
rupestris	SOkd WOMN
sceleratus	CKin
speciosus 'Flore Pleno'	See R. ***constantinopolitanus*** 'Plenus'

RANZANIA (Berberidaceae)

japonica	NHol

RAOULIA (Compositae)

N *australis*	Widely available
– 'Calf'	ITim NHol
– Lutescens group	ECha EPot GLoc ITim MHig NHol NTow WAbe
– Saxon Pass form	NHol
glabra	ECou EPot GAbr ITim MCas NHol NKay NTow SIng
haastii	ECou GDra GGar
hectorii x Leucogenes grandiceps	See X LEUCORAOULIA R. hectorii x *L.* ***grandiceps***
hookeri	CHar CLew EBre ECha ECou ELan EMNN EPot GCHN GLoc ITim MBro MHig MRav NHol NNrd NTow SBla SIng WAbe WDav WHil WOMN WPat
¶ – *apice-nigra*	NHol
¶ – *hookeri*	NHol
x *loganii*	See X LEUCORAOULIA ***loganii***
lutescens	See R. ***australis*** Lutescens group
monroi	ECou ELan ITim NHol WEas WMar WOMN
nova	EPot GDra NKay
parkii	GDra
subsericea	ECou MHig NGre NHol NNrd
tenuicaulis	ECha ECou EPot GAbr NHol NKay WHil WHoo

RASPBERRY See **RUBUS** ***idaeus***

RASPBERRY, Black See **RUBUS**

RATIBIDA (Compositae)

columnifera	CSun ECro

RAVENALA (Strelitziaceae)

madagascariensis	LPal

RAVENEA (Palmae)

rivularis	LPal

REEVESIA (Sterculiaceae)

REGELIA (Myrtaceae)

cymbifolia	CSun
inops	CSun
megacephala	CSun
velutina	CSun

REHDERODENDRON (Stryracaceae)

macrocarpum	SHil

REHMANNIA (Gesneriaceae)

angulata	See R. ***elata***
§ *elata*	CBot CCla CSev ECro EGol GWic LAbb LGan LHil LSav NBar SBar SMrm WCot WHal WHil WPer WRus
glutinosa	WOMN

REINECKEA (Liliaceae/Convallariaceae)

§ *carnea*	CElw CFis CFor EBul ECha ELan EPar EPla GWic MPar MTho NRar SIng WBon WHal

REINWARDTIA (Linaceae)

¶ *indica*	CHil

RESEDA (Resedaceae)
lutea CArn CKin MSal
luteola CArn CKin CSFH GPoy LHol MChe MSal SIde WHer WOak
odorata WSto

RESTIO (Restionaceae)
♦*subverticillatus* See ISCHYROLEPIS ***subverticillata***
**tetraphyllus* ECou

RETAMA (Leguminosae)
sphaerocarpa CCor

REYNOUTRIA See **FALLOPIA**

RHABDOTHAMNUS (Gesneriaceae)
solandri ECou

RHAGODIA (Chenopodiaceae)
triandra ECou

RHAMNUS (Rhamnaceae)
alaternus EMon SHil
§ – 'Argenteovariegata' Widely available
– *variegata* See R. ***a.*** 'Argenteovariegata'
cathartica CKin LBuc SHil WMou
citrifolia WCoo
frangula CArn CKin EHal ENot GPoy LBuc SHil WMou
imeretina SHil
procumbens SHil

RHAPHIOLEPIS (Rosaceae)
x *delacourii* IJoh LGre SReu SSta
– 'Coates Crimson' CBow CCla SHil SSpi SSta
– 'Spring Song' MUlv SHil
¶ *indica* CHEx
– 'Enchantress' CGre IBlr
umbellata CBot CChu CCla CHEx CMCN CPle CSam LHop MNew MUlv SHil WAbe WBod WHCG WSHC

RHAPHITHAMNUS (Verbenaceae)
cyanocarpus See R. ***spinosus***
§ *spinosus* CGre CHan CPle CTre ERea IBar IJoh SArc WBod WCoo WTay

RHAPIDOPHYLLUM (Palmae)
hystrix LPal

RHAPIS (Palmae)
excelsa LPal

RHAZYA (Apocynaceae)
orientalis CGle ECha EMon EPar ERea ERou LHop MCot SChu SWas WHal WOld WPer WWin

RHEKTOPHYLLUM (Araceae)

RHEUM † (Polygonaceae)
'Ace of Hearts' CBot CHad CRow ECha ECtt EGol ELan MBri
'Ace of Spades' See R. 'Ace of Hearts'
acuminatum CRow
alexandrae CRow CWGN EBre ECha ECro GEdr MBri MUlv NNor WCot
§ *australe* CArn CChu CCla CRow MBri MBro SSpi WCot WHer WHoo WWat
♦x *cultorum* See R. x ***hybridum***
delavayi EMon LRHS
emodi See R. ***australe***
'Green Knight' SPer
Nx *hybridum* 'Cawood Delight' NTwe
– 'Early Albert' GChr
– 'Early Champagne' CMac
– 'Harbinger' NTwe
– 'Stockbridge Arrow' NTwe
– 'Strawberry' EMui
– 'The Sutton' LBuc
– 'Timperley Early' CSam ECtt EMui GChr LBuc MBea NElm NTwe SDea WHig
– 'Victoria' GChr
kialense ECha ECro
¶ *nobile* CHEx
¶ *officinale* CHEx
palmatum CB&S CHEx ECha ECro EHal MCot MSal MTho MWgw NNor NSti SHig SLHN WHal
– 'Atropurpureum' See R. ***p.*** 'Atrosanguineum'
§ – 'Atrosanguineum' CBot CHEx CRow CSco CShe ECha EGol ELan ELun EPar ERou NNor SSpi WWin
– 'Bowles' Crimson' CHad
– 'Hadspen Crimson' CHad
– *rubrum* CBow CWGN EFou SPer WCot
– *tanguticum* CBow CRow ECha ECro MBri MSta MUlv WCot WHoo WWat
webbianum EHal WWat

RHODIOLA (Crassulaceae)
crassipes NGre NSed NTow SSmi
– *stephanii* NSed
¶ *fastigiata* NGre
§ *heterodonta* CSun CTom ECha ITim LHop NSed SPer SWas
himalensis SSmi
¶ *kirilowii* WPer
– *rubra* NGre
♦*pachyclados* See SEDUM ***p.***
♦*primuloides* See SEDUM ***p.***
rhodantha NGre WPer
§ *rosea* CElw CKel CSco ECha ECro EFou EGol ELan GWic MBal MFir MWgw NGre NNor NRoo NSed NSti SCro SIng SSmi
§ – *integrifolia* NGre
sp. CC 284 CSun

¶ *trollii* NSed

RHODOCHITON (Scrophulariaceae)

§ ***atrosanguineus*** CB&S CChu CGle CGre CHad CHil CMac CSun ELan ESim LAbb LGre LHop NTow SAxl SHil SMad WAbe WEas WHal WMar WPer
volubilis See R. ***atrosanguineus***

RHODODENDRON † (Ericaceae)

aberconwayi CWal IOrc ISea SLeo SReu
– 'His Lordship' LHyd
adenogynum CWal LMil SLeo
§ – Adenophorum group CWal SLeo
– Adenophorum group F 20444 SLeo
adenophorum See R. ***adenogynum*** Adenophorum group
adenopodum CWal SLeo
adenosum LMil
– Kuluense group SLeo
adroserum R/USDA 59201 See R. ***lukiangense*** R 11275
aeruginosum See R. ***campanulatum a.***
aganniphum SLeo
– ***flavorufum*** SLeo
aganniphum aganniphum Doshongense group CWal SLeo
agastum SLeo
albrechtii LHyd LSav MBri SHil SReu
alutaceum russotinctum SLeo
alutaceum aleutaceum Globigerum group R 11100 SLeo
¶ ***amagianum*** LSav
– x ***reticulatum*** SSta
ambiguum CHig CWal LMil LSav SLeo SReu
– best form LSav
¶ – 'Jane Banks' LSav
amesiae CWal SLeo
annae LMil SLeo
– Hardingii group CWal
anthopogon GEdr GK&P LMil SLeo
– AGS/ES 561 NHol
– 'Annapurna' LMil
– 'Betty Graham' LMil
§ – ***hypenanthum*** CWal GArd LMil
anthosphaerum F 26432 SLeo
– Eritimum group CWal
anwheiense See R. ***maculiferum a.***
aperantum F 26933 SLeo
araiophyllum SLeo
arborescens LKna LMil SHil SLeo
arboreum CB&S CWal IOrc ISea LMil SLeo SReu
– B 708 MBal
– BMW 172 MBal
¶ – KR 938 LSav
¶ – KR 966 LSav
– Sch 1111 CWal
– 'Blood Red' CWal SHil
– ***delavayi*** LRHS SLeo
– 'Goat Fell' CWal
*– ***nigrescens*** SLeo
§ – ***peramoenum*** LSav
§ – 'Sir Charles Lemon' CWal MBri MLea SHil SLeo SReu SSta
– 'Tony Schilling' CWal LHyd SLeo
– ***zeylanicum*** SLeo
arboreum cinnamomeum CWal LSav SLeo SReu
– – Campbelliae group SLeo
– – ***roseum*** CWal
x ***arbutifolium*** See R. Hybrid Arbutifolium
argipeplum CWal SLeo
argyrophyllum CWal SLeo
– 'Chinese Silver' CWal LHyd LMil SLeo
§ – ***hypoglaucum*** SLeo SReu
– ***nankingense*** IOrc LMil
arizelum See R. ***rex arizelum***
atlanticum CCla CFor CWal MBar SSpi
– 'Seaboard' LMil
augustinii CB&S CBow CTre CTrw GArd IOrc ISea LHyd LMil LSav MBal MBri MLea SCog SExb SHil SLeo SReu SSpi SSta WAbe WBod
– ***chasmanthum*** CWal WBod
– 'Dartington Form' CWal
– 'Electra' SHil
¶ – Exbury best form SReu
– ***hardyi*** CWal LHyd SLeo
– Reuthe's dark form SReu
– ***rubrum*** LMil
§ – ***rubrum*** 'Papillon' CWal
augustinii augustinii Vilmorinianum group CWal
aureum LMil SLeo
auriculatum CSam CWal LHyd LMil MBal MLea SHil SLeo SReu SSpi SSta
auritum CWal
– KW 7431 * SLeo
Azalea 'Addy Wery' (E) CB&S CHig CMac CSco CWal IDai IJoh IOrc ISea LHyd LKna LSav MBal MBar MGos SCog SExb SHil SLeo SPer SPla SReu WBod
– 'Adonis' (E) CMac IOrc MBar NJap SCog SPer SReu SSta
– 'Adorable' (E) IOrc
– 'Advance' (O) LSav MPlt SExb SHil SLeo SReu SSta WAbe WPat
– 'Ageeth' (E) MBri
– 'Aida' (R) MBri SHil SReu
– 'Aladdin' (E) IJoh IOrc SHil
– 'Alexander' (E) CB&S IOrc LMil MBri MGos MPlt SSta WWeb
– 'Alice' (E) CMac IHos LHyd LKna SReu WBod
– 'Amethystinum' (E) LKna

Plant	Suppliers
Azalea 'Amoenum' (E)	CB&S CBow CMHG CMac CSam CTrw LHyd LKna MBar MBri MGos NHol SCog SExb SHil SLeo WBod
– 'Amoenum Coccineum' (E)	LHyd MBri SCog SReu
– 'Angelus' (E)	SExb
– 'Annabella' (K)	CWal LHyd MBri MMor NBar SReu
– 'Anne Frank' (E)	MBri
– 'Anne Rothwell'	LHyd
– 'Anneke' (K)	MBar MBri MMor SSta
¶ – 'Anny' (E)	CMac LKna
¶ – 'Anthony Koster' (M)	SReu
§ – 'Antilope' (V)	CFor LKna MMor SPer SSpi SSta
N – 'Appleblossom' (E)	See R. Azalea 'Ho-o'
– 'Arabesque'	MBri MMor
– 'Arborescens'	See R. ***arborescens***
– 'Arcadia' (E)	CSco LKna
– 'Ardeur'	MBri
– 'Arpege'	LKna MBri SPer SReu SSpi
– 'Asa-gasumi' (E)	LHyd
– 'Audrey Wynniatt' (E)	SExb
¶ – 'Aurora' (K)	MLea
– 'Azuma-kagami' (E)	CB&S LHyd LKna LSav SCog SHil WBod
– 'Babeuff' (M)	CB&S
– 'Baby Scarlet'	SSta
– 'Ballerina' (K)	CWal MBal SExb SHil SReu
– 'Balzac' (K)	CWal IJoh IOrc MBri MGos
– 'Banzai' (E)	CWal LSav SLeo
– 'Barbara Coates'	LHyd
– 'Barbecue'	SExb
– 'Basilisk' (K)	CWal
– 'Beaulieu' (K)	SExb SHil
– 'Beethoven' (E)	LHyd LKna MBal MBar MBri NBar SExb SLeo SReu
– 'Ben Morrison' (E)	SSta
– 'Bengal Beauty' (E)	LMil LSav
– 'Bengal Fire' (E)	CMac SExb
– 'Benigasa' (E)	SReu WPat
– 'Beni-giri' (E)	CMac SHil
– 'Berryrose' (K)	CSco CWal GRei IDai IJoh IOrc LHyd LKna LMil MBal MBar MBri MLea MMor MRav NBar SExb SHil SPer SReu WAbe
– 'Betty' (E)	LHyd SReu
– 'Betty Anne Voss' (E)	LHyd SExb
¶ – 'Betty Kelly' (K)	LKna
– 'Bijou de Ledeberg'	SSta
– 'Blaauw's Pink' (E)	CBow CCla CHig CMac CSco CWal GRei IDai IJoh IOrc ISea LHyd LKna LMil MBar MBri MGos NKay SCog SExb SHil SLeo SPer SPic
– 'Black Hawk' (E)	CB&S SExb
– 'Blaue Donau' ('Blue Danube') (E)	CMac CSco CWal EBre IJoh IOrc LHyd LKna MBal MBar MBri MMor MRav NKay SCog SExb SHil SLeo SPer SPic SPla SReu SSta WAbe
– 'Blazecheck'	NHol
– 'Blue Monday'	EBre MBri NHol
– 'Bob White' (E)	SExb
– 'Bouquet de Flore' (G)	CSco LMil MBar MBri SReu
– 'Brazier' (E)	LHyd SLeo
– 'Brazil' (K)	CWal LKna SExb SHil SPic SReu
– 'Breslau' (E)	SSta
– 'Bridesmaid White'	NKay
– 'Bright Forecast' (K)	LMil MBri SExb
– 'Brilliant' (E)	MBri NBar SPla
*– 'Brilliant Crimson'	SSta
*– 'Brilliant Pink'	SSta
– 'Buccaneer' (E)	CSco CSut CWal LHyd LKna MBal SExb SPer SReu SSta
– 'Bungo-nishiki' (E)	CMac CWal SReu
¶ – 'Buzzard' (K)	LKna
– 'Caerhays Lavender'	CB&S IOrc
– 'Campfire' (E)	MBar NKay
– 'Carat'	MBri SReu
¶ – 'Carnival' (E)	LSav
– 'Cavalier' (E)	SExb
– 'Cayenne' (E)	SExb
– 'Cecile' (K)	CB&S CBow CSam CSco CWal IJoh ISea LHyd LKna LMil MBal MBri MGos MMor NBar SExb SHil SPer SPic SPla SReu
– 'Celestial' (E)	CMac
¶ – 'Chaffinch' (K)	LKna
¶ – 'Chameleon' (E)	LKna LSav
– 'Chanel' (V)	MMor SSta
– 'Chanticleer' (E)	LSav SExb SHil SPer
¶ – 'Charlemagne' (G)	LKna
– 'Charlotte de Rothschild'	SExb
¶ – 'Chelsea Reach' (K)	LKna
¶ – 'Chenille' (K)	LKna
¶ – 'Chicago' (M)	LKna
– 'Chippewa' (E)	LMil MBri NKay SReu WAbe
¶ – 'Chocolate Ice' (K)	LKna
– 'Chopin' (E)	WBod
¶ – 'Chorister' (K)	LKna
– 'Christina' (E)	CMac MBri MMor NHol NKay SPer SPla
– 'Christmas Cheer' (E)	See R. Azalea 'Ima-shojo'
– 'Christopher Wren' (K)	CSco ELan MBal MBri SReu
– 'Citroen'	SExb
– 'Coccineum Speciosum' (G)	CSco CWal IDai IOrc LHyd LMil MBar MBri MGos SExb SHil SPer SReu SSta WBod
¶ – 'Cockade' (E)	LKna
¶ – 'Cockatoo' (K)	LKna
¶ – 'Colin Kenrick' (K)	LKna
¶ – 'Colleen' (E)	LSav
– 'Colyer' (E)	LHyd LMil
– 'Commodore' (E)	LSav SExb SHil WAbe
– 'Con Amore' (E)	LSav
– 'Congo'	See R. A. 'Robin Hill Congo'
– 'Conversation Piece' (E)	LHyd
– 'Cora Grant' (E)	SExb
– 'Corneille' (G)	LKna SHil SReu

Azalea 'Coronation Lady' (K)	LKna MBri MMor
– 'Corringe' (K)	LMil SExb
– 'Crimson Glory'	See R. A. 'Natalie Coe Vitetti'
– 'Crinoline' (K)	SExb SPer SSta WWeb
– 'Crown Supreme'	SExb
– 'Cytherea' (E)	ISea SExb
– 'Daimio' (E)	CMHG LHyd SPer
– 'Dandy' (E)	SExb
– 'Daphne' (E)	SExb
– 'Darkness' (E)	SExb
– 'Daviesii' (G)	CB&S CSam LKna LMil MBri MLea MMor MRav SHil SPer SPla WBod WWeb
– 'Dawn's Glory'	SExb
N– 'Daybreak' (K)	See R. Azalea 'Kirin'
N– 'Debutante'	IHos MMor
– 'Delectable'	SExb
– 'Delicatissimum' (O)	LMil SExb
¶– 'Desert Pink' (K)	LKna
¶– 'Diabolo' (K)	LKna
– Diamant group (lilac) (E)	MBri
– Diamant group (rosy-red) (E)	COtt MBri
– 'Diorama' (V)	CSco MBar MBri MMor NBar SReu SSta
§– 'Directeur Moerlands' (M)	IDai
– 'Doctor M Oosthoek' (M)	CSco LHyd MMor SHil SReu
– 'Doctor Reichenbach' (M)	MBri
¶– 'Dorothy Corston' (K)	LKna
– 'Dorothy Hayden' (E)	LHyd
– 'Dorothy Rees' (E)	LHyd
– 'Double Beauty' (E)	LKna MMor SCog SPer SReu SSta
– 'Double Damask' (K)	LHyd LKna
– 'Driven Snow' (E)	SExb
– 'Early Beni' (E)	LHyd
– 'Easter Parade' (E)	SExb
– 'Eddisbury' (K)	MMor
– 'Eddy' (E)	LKna SExb SLeo
¶– 'Edna B' (E)	LMil
N– 'Elizabeth' (E)	ISea MGos MPlt SCog SExb WAbe
– 'Elizabeth Gable' (E)	NKay
– 'Elsie Lee' (E)	SReu SSta
– 'Elsie Pratt' (K)	MBar MBri MMor NBar SSta
N– 'Esmeralda'	CMac IJoh
¶– 'Eucharis' (E)	SReu
– 'Eunice Updike' (E)	LHyd
¶– 'Eva Goude' (K)	LKna
– 'Evensong' (E)	LKna
– 'Everest' (E)	CWal GRei LHyd MBar MBri WAbe
– 'Everest White'	NKay
– 'Exbury White' (K)	LMil SExb
– 'Explorer' (E)	MBri
– 'Exquisitum' (O)	LKna MBri SHil
– 'Fanny'	See R. A. 'Pucella'
– 'Favor Major' (K)	SReu
– 'Favorite' (E)	CMac CTrw LKna MBar MBri MMor SExb SHil SLeo SPer SSta
– 'Fawley' (K)	SExb
– 'Fedora' (E)	CB&S CTre LHyd LKna MBar MRav SExb SHil SPer SReu
– 'Ferndown Beauty' (E)	LHyd
¶– 'Feuerwerk' (K)	SReu
– 'Fireball' (K)	CB&S CSco EBre GRei IJoh ISea LHyd LMil MBri MLea NKay SExb WWeb
– 'Firefly' (K)	IOrc LMil SExb
– 'Fireglow'	MBri
¶– 'Flaming June' (K)	LKna
– 'Floradora' (M)	SExb SReu
– 'Florida' (E)	CMac CSco LKna LSav MRav SCog SPer SReu SSta WAbe
– 'Frans van der Bom' (M)	IDai MBri
– 'Freya' (R)	SReu
¶– 'Frieda' (E)	LKna
– 'Frills' (K)	CWal SExb
¶– 'Frome' (K)	LKna
– 'Fudetsukasi'	SLeo
– 'Fuko-hiko' (E)	CWal LSav SLeo
– 'Gabriele' (E)	SSpi
– 'Gaiety' (E)	LMil SCog
– 'Galathea' (E)	GRei LSav MBri
– 'Gallipoli' (K)	SExb SReu
– 'Gardenia' (E)	SHil
– 'Gauche'	SExb
– 'Gaugin'	SExb
*– 'Geisha Lilac' (E)	CSut MBri
*– 'Geisha Orange' (E)	MBri
*– 'Geisha Red' (E)	MBri
– 'Gekkeikan' (E)	CB&S
– 'General Wavell' (E)	CMac CWal LKna SExb SHil
– 'Georg Arends'	IJoh
– 'George Reynolds' (K)	CWal SExb SHil
– 'Gibraltar' (K)	Widely available
– 'Gilbert Mullier'	MBri
– 'Ginger' (K)	CWal LMil SExb
– 'Girard's Hot Shot' (E)	SSta
– 'Girard's Pink' (E)	SReu
– 'Glamora' (E)	LHyd
– 'Glencora' (E)	LHyd
¶– 'Glockenspiel' (K)	LKna
¶– 'Gloria Mundi' (G)	WAbe
– 'Glowing Embers' (K)	CMHG CSam GRei MBri MLea MMor NBar NKay SExb SPer SReu WWeb
¶– 'Gnome' (E)	NHol
– 'Gog' (K)	CSam CWal LHyd LKna SHil
¶– 'Gold Crest' (K)	LKna
– 'Goldball'	See R. A. 'Christopher Wren'
– 'Golden Eagle' (K)	CB&S COtt LKna MBri MGos MLea SPer
*– 'Golden Emma'	IJoh
¶– 'Golden Eye' (K)	LKna
– 'Golden Flare' (K)	CB&S CMHG ISea MBri WWeb
– 'Golden Horn' (K)	CWal
– 'Golden Lights'	LMil

Azalea 'Golden Oriole' (K) LKna SExb SReu
– 'Golden Sunlight' (M) See R. Azalea 'Directeur Moerlands'
– 'Golden Sunset' (K) CSco IJoh LKna LMil MBri MMor NBar SExb SReu
¶– 'Goldfinch' (K) LKna
– 'Gosho-zakura' (E) LHyd
– 'Graciosum' (O) LKna
– 'Greenway' (E) CB&S CGre CTre LHyd SPer
– 'Greenwood Yukon' (E) COtt
– 'Greta' (E) LHyd
– 'Gumpo' (E) CMac EPot NHol SCog SPer SReu WAbe
– 'Gumpo Pink' (E) GEdr SPla SReu SSta WBod
– 'Gumpo White' (E) SSta WAbe WBod
– 'Gumpo' x ***nakaharae*** SSta
– 'Gwenda' (E) LHyd
– 'H H Hume' (E) SPic
– 'H O Carre' (E) CMac SExb
– 'Hachika-tsugi' (E) LSav
– 'Hana-asobi' (E) CB&S CBow EPot LHyd SExb WBod
– 'Harbinger' (E) SExb SLeo
– 'Hardy Gardenia' (E) SCog SPla SSta
– 'Harkwood Orange' SExb
– 'Harkwood Red' SExb
– 'Haro-no-yuki' CGre
– 'Harumiji' (E) CWal LSav SLeo
– 'Harvest Moon' (K) IHos NBar SReu
– 'Hatsugiri' (E) CHig CMac GRei IJoh IOrc LHyd LKna LSav MBar MBri MMor SCog SHil SReu SSta WBod WPat
– 'Heather Macleod' (E) LHyd
– 'Helen Close' (E) LSav SExb SHil
¶– 'Helen Curtis' (E) SReu
– 'Helena' (E) SExb
¶– 'Herbert' (E) CMac
– 'Hexe' (E) WBod
¶– 'Hiawatha' (K) LKna
– 'Hinode-giri' (E) CB&S CHig CMac CSut CTrw CWal LHyd LKna LSav SExb SHil SLeo SReu WBod
– 'Hinode-no-kumo' (E) CWal LSav SLeo
– 'Hinode-no-taka' (E) LSav
– 'Hino-Crimson' (E) CMac CSco CWal GRei IDai IJoh IOrc LKna LMil MBar MBri MGos MMor NJap NKay SHil SPer SReu SSta WPat
– 'Hino-mayo' (E) CB&S CMac CSco CSut CTre CWal GRei IOrc LHyd LKna LMil LSav MBri MRav NJap NKay NRoo SCog SExb SHil SLeo SPic SReu SSta
– 'Hino-Scarlet' See R. A. 'Campfire'
– 'Hino-tsukasa' (E) CWal SLeo
*– 'Hojo-ngodor-akako' (E) LSav
– 'Hojo-no-odorikarako' (E) SLeo
– 'Homebush' (R) CB&S CCla CMHG CSam CWal GRei IJoh IOrc ISea LHyd LKna LMil MBal MBri NRoo SHil SPer SPic SReu SSta WBod WWeb
– 'Honeysuckle' (K) IOrc MBar MMor NBar SExb
– 'Hopeful' (E) LSav SExb
– 'Hortulanus H Witte' (M) MMor NBar SReu
– 'Hot Shot' See R. A. 'Girard's Hot Shot'
– Hotspur group (K) ELan GRei SHil WWeb
– 'Hotspur Red' (K) CWal LKna LMil MBri SReu
– 'Hotspur Yellow' (K) CWal LHyd
§– 'Ho-o' (E) CB&S CGre CMac LSav SCog SExb SHil
– 'Hugh Wormald' (K) SExb
– 'Hyde and Seek' SExb
– 'Hyde Park' SExb
– 'Ightham Pink' SReu
¶– 'Il Tasso' (R) LKna
§– 'Ilam Melford Lemon' LMil
§– 'Ilam Ming' LMil
¶– 'Imago' (K) LKna
§– 'Ima-shojo' (E) CB&S CGre CMac IHos LHyd LSav SExb WBod
¶– 'Impala' (K) LKna
– 'Indicum' See R. ***indicum***
– 'Irene Koster' (O) CMHG CWal ELan ISea LHyd LKna LMil MBri SExb SHil SPer SReu WWeb
– 'Iro-hayama' (E) CBow CMac CTrw LHyd LKna LMil LSav NRoo SCog SExb SPer SReu SSta
¶– 'Ishiyama' (E) SCog
– 'Ivette' (E) CMac LHyd LKna LMil LSav SExb
– 'Iwato-kagami' (E) CWal SLeo
– 'Izayoi' (E) WBod
– 'J Jennings' (K) SExb WAbe
– 'Janet Baker' SExb
– 'Jean Read' LHyd
– 'Jeanette' (E) LKna LMil NRoo
– 'Jeff Hill' (E) IJoh
¶– 'Jock Coutts' LKna
– 'Johann Sebastian Bach' (E) WBod WWeb
– 'Johann Strauss' (E) WBod
– 'Johanna' (E) CMac EBre MBri MMor MRav SExb SPer
– 'John Cairns' (E) CMac CWal LHyd LKna LMil LSav MBal MBar SCog SExb SHil SPer SReu WBod
– 'Jolie Madame' (V) MBri SReu
– 'Joseph Haydn' (E) WBod
– 'Joseph Hill' (E) LMil SExb SSpi SSta
– 'Kakiemon' (E) LHyd SPer
– 'Kasane-kagaribi' (E) LHyd
N– 'Kathleen' CWal IOrc LHyd LKna LMil LSav MBar MMor SCog SExb
– 'Katinka' (E) MBal MGos
– 'Katisha' (E) LHyd
– 'Katsura-no-hana' (E) LSav
*– 'Keija' SCog
– 'Keinohana' (E) CWal SLeo

¶ Azalea 'Kentucky Minstrel' (K) LKna
– 'Kermesinum' (E) COtt MBar MBri NBar SReu WPat
– 'Kermesinum Album' (E) MBri NBar
– 'Keston Rose' SSta
– 'Kijei' CB&S
¶ – 'Kilauea' (K) LKna
– 'Killarney' (E) SHil
– 'Kimigayo' (E) LHyd LSav
– 'King's Red' (K) LMil
§ – 'Kirin' (E) CMac CTrw CWal IJoh IOrc LHyd LKna LSav MBri SCog SExb SHil WBod WPat
– 'Kirishima' (E) CHig LKna SReu
– 'Kiritsubo' (E) LHyd LSav
– 'Kiusianum' See R. ***kiusianum***
– 'Klondyke' (K) CB&S CSco EBre ELan IOrc LKna LMil MBri MGos SHil SReu
– 'Knap Hill Apricot' (K) LKna LMil
– 'Knap Hill Red' (K) LKna LMil
– 'Kobold' (E) SLeo SSta
– 'Komurasaki' (E) CWal SLeo
– 'Koningin Emma' ('Queen Emma') (M) LMil MBri
– 'Koningin Wilhelmina' (E) SExb WBod
– 'Kormesing' IJoh
– 'Koster's Brilliant Red' (M) CSco MBal MBri SHil SReu
– 'Krishna' ISea
– 'Kumo-no-ito' (E) LHyd
– 'Kurai-no-himo' (E) LHyd
– 'Kure-no-yuki' (E) CGre CHig CMac CWal LHyd LKna LSav SCog SExb SHil SReu SSta WBod
– 'Lady Elphinstone' (E) LHyd
– 'Lady Louise' (E) LHyd
– 'Lady Robin' (E) LHyd
¶ – 'Lady Rosebery' (K) LKna
¶ – 'Langmans' LKna
– 'Lapwing' (K) LHyd LKna
– 'Late Love' (E) IJoh SExb SSpi SSta
– 'Laura Morland' (E) LHyd
* – 'Lavender Brilliant' LSav
– 'Ledifolium' See R. Azalea 'Mucronatum'
– 'Ledifolium Album' See R. Azalea 'Mucronatum'
– 'Lemonora' (M) ELan MBri SHil SPer
– 'Lemur' (E) MBri WThu
– 'Leo' (E) CBow CWal LHyd LKna LMil LSav SCog SExb SLeo SPer SPla SReu WAbe WWeb
– 'Lilac Time' (E) MBar
¶ – 'Lilacinum' CSut SCog
– 'Lilliput' (E) SPer SSta
– 'Lily Marleen' (E) CWal MBar MMor SReu
– 'Linearifolium' See R. ***macrosepalum*** 'L.'
¶ – 'Linnet' LKna
– 'Litany' (E) SExb
– 'Little Beauty' (E) SExb
– 'Lobster Pot' SExb
– 'Lorna' (E) CSco LMil LSav MGos
– 'Lotte' (E) SReu
– 'Louis B Williams' SPer
– 'Louisa' (E) IJoh SExb SSpi SSta
– 'Louise Dowdle' (E) MMor SPer
– 'Louise Gable' (E) LMil LSav
¶ – 'Lullaby' (E) LKna MPlt
I – 'Mac Ovata' CMac
– 'Macranthum' See R. ***indicum***
– 'Macranthum Roseum' (E) SExb
– 'Macrosepalum' See R. ***macrosepalum***
– 'Macrostemon' See R. ***obtusum macrostemon***
– 'Madame Ad van Hecke' (E) COtt MBri NBar SHil SReu
N – 'Magnificum' LMil MBri SCog SExb
– 'Mahler' (E) LHyd
– 'Malvaticum' (E) SExb WBod
– 'Margaret George' (E) LHyd LSav
– 'Marie' (E) CMac LSav SCog SExb
– 'Marina' (K) SPic
¶ – 'Marion Merriman' (K) LKna
– 'Martha Hitchcock' (E) LKna LMil MPlt SExb SHil WAbe
– 'Martine' MBri MGos
– 'Mary Helen' (E) LHyd LSav SExb SReu WBod
– 'Mary Meredith' (E) LHyd
¶ – 'Master of Elphinstone' (E) SCog
¶ – 'Mauna Loa' (K) LKna
– 'Maxwellii' (E) CMac SCog SExb WBod
¶ – 'Mazurka' (K) LKna
– 'Melford Lemon' See R.A. 'Ilam Melford Lemon'
¶ – 'Mephistopheles' (K) LKna
N – 'Merlin' (E) LMil LSav MBal SExb SHil WWeb
– 'Michael Hill' (E) CB&S SExb SPer SSpi SSta WWeb
– 'Midori' (E) SExb
– 'Mikado' (E) CMHG CWal SPer SPla SReu SSta
– 'Mimi' (E) CMac MBri
– 'Ming' See R. A. 'Ilam Ming'
– 'Misomogiri' CHig
– 'Miss Muffet' (E) SExb
– 'Mizu-no-yamabuki' (E) CWal SLeo
– 'Moira' (E) LSav
– 'Moira Salmon' (E) LHyd
– Mollis orange MBri
– Mollis pink MBri
– Mollis red MBri
– Mollis yellow MBri
– 'Moon Maiden' (E) MMor
¶ – 'Motet' LKna
– 'Mother's Day' (E) Widely available
¶ – 'Mount Rainier' (K) SReu
– 'Mount Saint Helens' ISea LHyd LMi
– 'Mozart' (E) WBod
¶ – 'Mrs Anthony Waterer' (O) LKna

¶ Azalea 'Mrs Doorenbos' CMac
– 'Mrs Emil Hager' (E) LHyd
– 'Mrs Peter Koster' (M) IJoh
§ – 'Mucronatum' (E) CHig CMCN CSto CTre EPot LHyd LMil MBar SExb SLeo SMad SPer SPic WBod
♦ – 'Mucronatum Amethystinum' See R. A. 'Amethystinum'
– 'Multatuli ' (M) MBri
– 'Multiflorum' NBar
– ***nakaharae*** x Kin-no-zai' SSta
– 'Nakahari Orange' See R. ***nakaharae*** Orange form
– 'Nakahari-mariko' See R. ***nakaharae*** 'Mariko'
– 'Nancy Buchanan' (K) SExb SReu
– 'Nancy of Robinhill' (E) LHyd
– 'Nancy Waterer' (G) CSco MBri MMor SHil SReu
¶ – 'Nani-wagata' (E) LSav
– 'Nanki Poo' (E) LHyd SPer
– 'Naomi' (E) IOrc LKna LMil MRav NJap SCog SExb SHil SPer
– 'Narcissiflorum' (G) CSco CWal IOrc LHyd LKna LMil MBri SExb SHil SReu
¶ – 'Natalie Coe Vitetti' (E) CMac
¶ – 'Nettie' (E) SCog
– 'Niagara' (E) LHyd LSav MBal SCog SExb WBod
– 'Nico' CMac EBre MBar MBri MRav SPer
¶ – 'Niphetos' (E) LSav
¶ – 'Nishiki' (E) CMac
– 'Noordtianum' (E) MBar
N – 'Norma' (G) LMil MBri
– 'Northlight' MBri SReu
– 'Oino-mezame' (E) LHyd
¶ – 'Old Gold' (K) SReu
– 'Opal' (E) SExb
¶ – 'Optima' (E) SCog
– 'Orange Beauty' (E) Widely available
– 'Orange King' (E) MBar
* – 'Orange Scout' IJoh
– 'Orangeade' (K) ISea SExb SReu
– 'Oregon Trail' SExb
¶ – 'Oryx' (O) LKna
– 'Otome' (E) LHyd
¶ – 'Ouchiyama' LKna
– 'Oxydol' (K) CWal ISea LHyd LKna MLea SExb
– 'Palestrina' (E) CB&S CHig CMac CSco CWal EPot IDai IOrc LHyd LKna LSav MBal MBar MBri MMor SCog SExb SHil SLeo SPer SReu SSta WBod WPat
– 'Pallas' (G) CSco MBri SReu
– 'Pamela Miles' LHyd LSav
– 'Panaché' SExb
¶ – 'Pancake' CMac
– 'Panda' (E) CMac EBre MBri SReu
– 'Papineau' (E) LHyd
¶ – 'Paramount' (K) LKna
¶ – 'Pavane' (K) LKna
– 'Peach Blossom' (E) See R. Azalea 'Saotome'
– 'Peach Blow' (E) ISea
– 'Pearl Bradford' SExb
– 'Peep-Bo' (E) LHyd SPer
– 'Perfect' MBal SPer
– 'Persil' (K) CB&S CSco CWal EBre ELan GRei IDai IJoh ISea LHyd LKna MBar MBri MGos MMor NBar SHil SPer SReu
– 'Petrouchka' (K) LKna MBri
– 'Pettychaps' (E) SReu
¶ – 'Piccolo' (K) LKna
– 'Pickard's Gold' SPic
– 'Pink Beauty' SExb
N – 'Pink Delight' LHyd LKna
– 'Pink Mimosa' (V) SSta
– 'Pink Pancake' (E) CB&S IJoh LMil SExb SSpi SSta WWeb
N – 'Pink Ruffles' SReu WBod
¶ – 'Pippa' (E) CMac
– 'Polar Bear' (E) IJoh MBal
¶ – 'Polar Haven' (E) LKna LSav
– 'Polar Sea' (E) SExb SHil
¶ – 'Polonaise' (E) LKna
– ***ponticum*** See R. ***luteum***
– 'Pooh-Bah' (E) LHyd
¶ – 'Port Knap' (E) LKna
¶ – 'Port Wine' (E) LKna
– 'Princess Ida' (E) LHyd
I – 'Princess Margaret of Windsor' (K) SExb
– 'Prins Bernhard' (E) LKna SExb
– 'Prinses Juliana' (E) MMor SExb SReu WAbe WBod
§ – 'Pucella' (G) MLea
– purple Glenn Dale (E) SExb
– 'Purple Splendor' (E) CMac CWal IOrc LKna MGos NHol
– 'Purple Triumph' (E) CB&S CHig CWal IJoh LKna LMil SHil SLeo SReu SSta WBod
¶ – 'Purple Velvet' LSav
¶ – 'Quaker Maid' (K) MBri
¶ – 'Raphael de Smet' (G) LKna SReu
– 'Rasho-mon' (E) LHyd LKna LSav SLeo WBod
– 'Red Bird' (E) CMac
– 'Red Fountain' (E) COtt
– 'Redmond' (E) LHyd SExb
– 'Redwing' (E) SExb SPer
– 'Renne' (E) SExb
– 'Rêve d'Amour' (V) MMor SSta
– 'Rex' (E) CWal MBar SPer
§ – 'Robin Hill Congo' (E) LHyd
– 'Robin Hill Frosty' (E) LHyd SExb
– 'Robin Hill Gillie' (E) LHyd
– 'Rosalie' (E) NBar
– 'Rosata' (V) MBri MMor NBar SReu SSta
– 'Rose Glow' MMor
– 'Rose Greeley' (E) CHig CSco SExb SPla SReu SSta
– 'Rose Haze' MMor
– 'Rose Torch' MMor

Azalea 'Rosebud' (E)	CB&S CBow CHig CMac CSco CTrw CWal ISea LHyd LKna LMil LSav MBar MGos MMor NKay SCog SExb SHil SLeo SPer SPla SReu WBod
– 'Rosiflorum'	See R. ***indicum*** 'Balsaminiflorum'
– 'Rosy Lights'	LMil
– 'Royal Command' (K)	CSco GRei MBar MBri MMor NBar SExb
– 'Royal Lodge' (K)	CWal SPer
– 'Royal Ruby' (K)	LMil MMor NBar
¶ – 'Rozanne Waterer'	LKna
– 'Rubinetta' (E)	NHol
– 'Rubinstern' (E)	MBri NBar
¶ – 'Rumba' (K)	LKna
– 'Sabina'	NBar NHol
– 'Sahara' (K)	LKna SPic
– 'Sakata Red' (E)	CGre CMac IOrc SExb
– 'Sakon' (E)	CWal SLeo
– 'Salmon King' (E)	MBar
– 'Salmon Sander' (E)	LKna SExb
– 'Samuel Taylor Coleridge' (M)	IDai MBri MMor
– 'Sang de Gentbrugge' (G)	MBri
– 'Santa Maria'	COtt SReu SSta
§ – 'Saotome' (E)	CMac LHyd SExb
– 'Saroi' (E)	CWal SLeo
¶ – 'Saskia' (K)	LKna
– 'Satan' (K)	CB&S CWal ELan LKna MBri MMor NBar SHil SReu
– 'Satsuki' (E)	CGre IJoh LNet SExb SSta WWeb
– 'Saturnus' (M)	ELan MBri
¶ – 'Scarlatti' (K)	LKna
– 'Scarlet Pimpernel' (K)	CWal NKay SExb
– 'Schubert' (E)	MGos WAbe WBod
– 'Seikai' (E)	SExb
¶ – 'Shanty' (K)	LKna
– 'Sherbrook' (E)	LHyd
– 'Shiko' (E)	SReu
– 'Shinimiagagnoo' (E)	CWal SLeo
– 'Shintoki-no-hagasane' (E)	LHyd LSav WBod
– 'Shintsune' (E)	CWal LSav SLeo
– 'Shin-seikai' (E)	CB&S CTre LSav SHil
– 'Shin-utena' (E)	LHyd LSav
– 'Shi-no-noe' (E)	LSav SLeo
– 'Shukishima' (E)	CWal SLeo
¶ – 'Silver Glow' (E)	CMac
– 'Silver Moon' (E)	IOrc LSav SCog SExb SHil SLeo SPer SReu SSta
– 'Silver Slipper' (K)	CWal LHyd LKna LMil MBal MBar MBri MLea MMor NBar SHil SReu SSta
¶ – 'Silverwood' (K)	LMil
– 'Silvester' (E)	COtt MBri MMor NRoo WAbe WPat
– 'Sir William Lawrence' (E)	LKna SExb SReu
* – 'Sissley'	SExb
– 'Snow' (E)	CBow CMac COtt IJoh
– 'Snow Hill' (E)	LHyd LMil LSav
– 'Snowflake'	See R. A. 'Kure-no-yuki'
– 'Soho' (E)	LNet SExb
– 'Soir de Paris' (V)	MBar MBri MMor SSta
¶ – 'Sophie Hedges'	LKna
¶ – 'Souvenir du Président Carnot' (G)	LKna
– 'Spek's Brilliant' (M)	MBri
– 'Spek's Orange' (M)	CWal LHyd MGos SHil
– 'Spicy Lights'	LMil
¶ – 'Spoonbill'	LKna
– 'Spring Beauty' (E)	CBow CMac MMor SExb
– 'Squirrel' (E)	CMac LHyd MBri MGos SCog SReu SSta WPat
– 'Stewartstonian' (E)	CMac CWal IJoh IOrc LHyd LMil MBal MBar MBri MMor NBar SSta
– 'Stranraer'	MBri MLea
– 'Strawberry Ice' (K)	CMHG CSco CWal IJoh IOrc LKna LMil MBri MGos SExb SHil SPer SPla
– 'Sugared Almond' (K)	CWal LMil MBal SPer SPic SReu
– 'Sugi-no-ito'	See R. A. 'Kumo-no-ito'
– 'Summer Fragrance' (O)	SReu SSta
– 'Sun Chariot' (K)	CB&S CSam CWal GRei ISea LHyd LKna LMil MBri SPer SReu
– 'Sunbeam'	See R. Azalea 'Benifude'
– 'Sunset Pink' (K)	ISea LHyd MLea SExb SPer WWeb
– 'Sunte Nectarine' (K)	LMil SExb
– 'Surprise' (E)	ISea NHol SCog SExb SLeo SPer SReu SSta WWeb
– 'Susannah Hill' (E)	CB&S LMil MBri SPer SSta
¶ – 'Swansong' (E)	CMac SCog
– 'Sword of State'	SExb
– 'Sylphides' (K)	EBre LKna MBri
– 'Sylvester'	MGos NBar
– 'Takasago' (E)	LMil SCog
– 'Tama-no-utena' (E)	LHyd
– 'Tanager' (E)	LKna SExb
– 'Tangiers' (K)	SExb
– 'Tay' (K)	SReu
– 'Tebotan' (E)	CB&S
– 'Tender Heart'	SExb
– 'Tinsmith'	SExb
– 'Tit Willow' (E)	CWal LHyd SPer
– 'Titipu' (E)	CWal LHyd
– 'Tonkonatsu' (E)	CWal LSav SLeo
– 'Toreador' (E)	CMac LKna SExb
¶ – 'Toucan' (K)	LKna
– 'Tower Beauty' (C)	LHyd
– 'Tower Dainty' (C)	LHyd
– 'Tower Daring' (C)	LHyd
– 'Tower Dexter' (C)	LHyd
– 'Tower Dragon' (C)	LHyd
– 'Trent' (K)	SReu
* – 'Troll'	SReu
¶ – 'Troupial' (K)	LKna
– 'Tsuta-momiji' (E)	LHyd
– 'Tunis' (K)	CWal MBri MLea SHil
– 'Twilight'	MBri SExb
– 'Ukamuse' (E)	LHyd

Azalea 'Umpqua Queen' (K)	ISea
– 'Unique' (G)	LKna SReu
– 'Velvet Gown' (E)	MBri
– 'Venetia' (K)	MBri MMor
– 'Vida Brown' (E)	CMac LKna LSav MBri SCog SHil SPer SPic SReu SSta WThu
– 'Viking' (E)	LHyd
– 'Violet Longhurst'	LHyd LSav
– 'Violetta' (E)	ISea SExb WAbe
– 'Vuyk's Rosyred' (E)	CB&S CBow CHig CMac CSco CWal IJoh IOrc ISea LKna LMil LSav MBar MBri MGos MMor MRav NKay SExb SHil SPer SPic SReu WAbe
– 'Vuyk's Scarlet' (E)	Widely available
– 'W E Gumbleton' (M)	MBri SReu
– 'Ward's Ruby' (E)	CTrw SReu
¶ – 'Waxwing'	LKna
– 'Wee Willie' (E)	LHyd
– 'Werrington'	CFor
¶ – 'Westminster' (O)	LKna LMil
– 'White Jade' (E)	SExb
– 'White Lady' (E)	IJoh LKna SExb SReu
¶ – 'White Lights'	LMil
– 'White Moon' (E)	LHyd
– 'White Swan'	CSco ISea
– 'Whitethroat' (K)	IOrc LKna MBri SHil SPer SReu
– 'Willy' (E)	LHyd LKna MBri SExb SPer SReu SSta
– 'Winston Churchill' (M)	MBar MMor
– 'Wintergreen' (E)	CB&S SSta WWeb
– 'Wombat' (E)	GEdr LHyd MBri MGos SCog SReu SSta WPat
– 'Wryneck' (K)	LHyd LMil MBri SReu
– 'Yaye-giri' (E)	IJoh
¶ – 'Yaye-hiryu' (E)	LSav
¶ – 'Yoga' (K)	LKna
– 'Yorozuyo' (E)	LSav
– 'Yo-zakura' (E)	CWal LSav SLeo
Azaleodendron 'Broughtonii Aureum'	SReu
¶ – 'Cameronian'	LKna
– 'Galloper Light'	LKna
– 'Glory of Littleworth'	LKna SHil SReu
– 'Govenianum'	CLan LKna SReu
¶ – 'Hammondii'	LKna
§ – 'Hardijzer Beauty'	CB&S CBow LKna MBal SSta
¶ – 'Joy's Delight'	LKna
– 'Martha Isaacson'	MBal SReu
– 'Martine'	LHyd LKna MBri SLeo
– 'Ria Hardijzer'	LKna MBri SSta
¶ – 'Wilsonii'	LKna
baileyi	CWal LHyd LMil LSav SLeo
bainbridgeanum R/USDA 59184/R 11190	CWal SLeo
bakeri	LHyd LMil SLeo
balfourianum Aganniphoides group	CWal SLeo
barbatum	CWal LHyd LMil SExb SHil SLeo
– BMW 152	MBal
– DF 525	MBal
¶ – KR 931	LSav
§ *basilicum*	CWal LMil SLeo WBod
beanianum	CWal SLeo
– compact form	See R. ***piercei***
beesianum	SLeo
bergii 'Papillon'	See R. ***augustinii rubrum*** 'Papillon'
¶ *bhutanense* EGM 077	LMil
bodinieri	LSav SLeo
brachyanthum	CWal SExb SLeo
– *hypolepidotum*	CWal LMil LSav MBal SLeo
§ *brachyanthum* L&S 2764	LMil
brachycarpum	CWal MBal SLeo
– *fauriei*	CWal SLeo
– pink form	SLeo
brachysiphon	See R. ***maddenii maddenii***
bullatum	See R. ***edgeworthii***
bureaui	CWal IOrc LHyd LMil MBlu SHil SLeo SReu SSpi SSta
burmanicum	CTre CWal LMil WBod
calendulaceum	LSav MBal SHil
callimorphum	CWal LHyd
– *myiagrum*	CWal
– *myiagrum*F 21821A	SLeo
calophytum	CHEx CWal LHyd LMil SHil SLeo
calostrotum	CHig CWal GK&P LMil MBlu MBri MPlt SIng WAbe WBod
– 'Gigha'	CWal EPot GArd LHyd MBri SHil
§ – *keleticum*	CHig CSun GAbr GArd GDra GEdr LHyd MBal MBar NKay SIng SReu WAbe WBod
– *keleticum*F 19915	LSav
– *keleticum*F 21757	LSav
– *keleticum*F 21756	CWal SLeo
– *keleticum*R 58	NHar NHol
– *riparioides*	LMil
– *riparium*	CWal GAbr MBal
– *riparium* Rock's form R 178	GArd LSav
§ *calostrotum keleticum* Radicans group	CWal EPot GK&P LHyd LMil MLea MPlt NHar NHol SHil SPla SSta WAbe WBod WPat
– – Radicans group R 59182	MLea SOkd
– – *Radicans group* mound form	SOkd
calostrotum riparium Calciphilum group	GArd MBar MLea
§ – – Nitens group	CMHG LMil
caloxanthum	See R. ***campylocarpum caloxanthum***
camelliiflorum	CWal GK&P
campanulatum	IOrc LHyd LKna LMil SLeo SReu
– B 643	MBal
– DF 563	MBal

– SS&W 9107 CWal SLeo
– TSS 11 SLeo
– TSS 45 * CWal
– TSS 7 SLeo
– ***aeruginosum*** CWal LMil SReu
– ***album*** CWal SLeo
– 'Knap Hill' CWal LHyd SHil SReu
– 'Waxen Bell' LHyd SLeo
campylocarpum CHig CWal LHyd LMil SCog SLeo SReu
– BMW 150 MBal
– DF 558 MBal
– ***caloxanthum*** CWal IOrc LHyd
– ***caloxanthum*** forms SLeo
– Elatum group CWal
§ ***campylocarpum caloxanthum*** Telopeum group KW 5718B SLeo
campylogynum CB&S CBow CFor CMHG CTrw CWal GK&P IOrc LMil MBri NKay SExb SLeo SReu WBod
– KW 21481 NHol
– 'Album' See R. ***c.*** 'Leucanthum'
– 'Beryl Taylor' LMil
– 'Bodnant Red' EPot GArd GEdr LHyd SLeo WBod
– Celsum group LMil
– Charopoeum group CWal GArd MBal MGos MLea MPlt SSta WBod
– claret form MLea
§ – Cremastum group CWal LHyd LMil SLeo SReu
– 'Hillier's Pink' CFor
§ – 'Leucanthum' GArd LMil
– Myrtilloides group CWal EGol EPot LHyd LMil MBal MBri SExb SLeo
¶ – Myrtilloides group Farrer 1046 LSav
– pink form MBar
– salmon pink CWal GEdr MLea NHar NHol WBod
– yellow form MBar
camtschaticum GArd GArf GDra GEdr GK&P MBal MLea SOkd
– ***album*** NHol
– Murray-Lyon form NHol
canadense NHol SLeo
x ***candelabrum*** SLeo
canescens CWal LSav
¶ ***carneum*** LMil
carolinianum See R. ***minus minus*** Carolinianum group
catacosmum SLeo
– R 11185 SLeo
catawbiense CHig CMCN LHyd SLeo
– 'Powell Glass' CWal
caucasicum CWal MBal
cephalanthum EPot
– ***cephalanthum*** MBal
cerasinum SLeo
– KW 5830 SLeo
– KW 6923 CWal
– 'Cherry Brandy' CWal LHyd
– 'Coals of Fire' CWal SLeo
– deep pink SLeo
– x ***forrestii forrestii*** MBal
chaetomallum KW 6955 SLeo
chamaethomsonii CSam CWal GArd GK&P LMil MBal SExb SLeo
chameunum See R. ***sanguineum c.***
charitopes CWal GArd GK&P LMil MBal MBri SExb
– ***tsangpoense*** CWal LMil NHol SHil
chlorops SLeo
chrysodoron CWal LMil
chrysomanicum See R. H. 'Chrysomanicum'
ciliatum CB&S CHig CWal GArd GK&P IOrc LHyd MBal SHil
¶ – T 149 LSav
– 'Multiflorum' See R. Hybrid 'Multiflorum'
ciliicalyx CTre CWal GK&P
§ – ***lyi*** CTre CWal GK&P SLeo
cinnabarinum CWal LMil LSav SExb SHil SLeo SReu
– B 652 MBal
– BL&M 234 LMil LSav
¶ – LS&H 21283 LSav
– 'Aestivale' LMil
– ***cinnabarinum*** Blandfordiiflorum gr. LMil SExb SLeo
– 'Magnificum' LMil LSav
§ – 'Mount Everest' CWal GArd LHyd LSav SLeo SReu SSta
– 'Nepal' CWal LMil SLeo
– ***tamaense*** LMil SLeo
– 'Vin Rosé' CWal LMil LSav
cinnabarinum cinnabarinum Roylei group CHig CWal GArd LHyd LMil MBlu MLea SLeo SReu
§ ***cinnabarinum xanthocodon*** CHig CWal LMil MBal SCog SLeo SReu WBod
¶ – – EGM 088 LMil
– – KW 6026 LSav WThu
– – LS&H 17521 LSav
– – Concatenans group CWal EGol LHyd LMil SHil SLeo SSta
– – 'Daffodilly' CWal LHyd SLeo
– – Exbury AM form SReu
– – forms CWal SLeo
– – Purpurellum group CWal LHyd SLeo
citriniflorum CWal GK&P LRHS SReu
clementinae SLeo
– F 25705 SLeo
coelicum CWal
– F 21830 SLeo
concatenans CHig CSam LMil SExb WBod
– KW 5874 LRHS LSav
– copper LS&T 6560 LSav SLeo
– mustard yellow form SLeo
– ***xanthocodon*** See R. ***cinnabarinum xanthocodon***
concinnum CHig CTre CTrw CWal LHyd LMil MBal SLeo

- Pseudoyanthinum group — CWal GK&P SLeo
cookeanum — SLeo
coriaceum — CWal LMil SLeo
coryanum — CWal
crassum — See R. ***maddenii crassum***
cremastum — See R. ***campylogynum*** Cremastum group
crinigerum — CWal LMil SLeo
cubittii — See R. ***veitchianum*** Cubittii group
cuneatum — CWal
– F 27119 * — SLeo
cyanocarpum — CWal SLeo
dalhousieae — CTre CWal SLeo
§ – *rhabdotum* — SLeo
dasypetalum — MBal MLea
dauricum — EPot LMil MBal MBlu MPlt SExb SLeo WBod
– *album* — LHyd
– 'Hokkaido' — LHyd
– 'Midwinter' — CWal LHyd SHil SLeo
– 'Nanum' — MBal
– 'Suzuki' — SLeo
– x *formosum* — SSta
davidsonianum — CB&S CBow CTre CTrw CWal GArd IOrc ISea LHyd LMil MBal MBlu MMor SExb SHil SLeo SSpi SSta WBod
*– 'Bodnant' — LMil
¶ – 'Ruth Lyons' — LMil
¶ – 'Serenade' — LMil
decorum — CBow CWal IOrc LHyd LMil SHil SLeo SReu
– 'Cox's Uranium Green' — SReu
degronianum degronianum — CWal SLeo
– *degronianum* 'Gerald Loder' — CWal
§ – *heptamerum* — CWal SExb SLeo
– 'Metternianum' — See R. ***d.*** Kyomaruense group
♦ *delavayi peramoenum* — See R. ***arboreum peramoenum***
dendricola Taronense group — CWal SLeo
desquamatum — See R. ***rubiginosum*** Desquamatum group
x *detonsum* — CWal SLeo
– Edinburgh select form — SReu
diaprepes — IOrc LHyd
– Farrer 979 — SLeo
– 'Gargantua' — CWal SExb SLeo SReu
dichroanthum — CHig CWal IOrc LHyd MBal SLeo SReu
– *apodectum* — CWal GK&P LMil SLeo
– *scyphocalyx* — CWal LMil SLeo
– *scyphocalyx* F 27657 — LSav
didymum — See R. ***sanguineum didymum***
diphrocalyx — CWal SLeo
drumonium — See R. ***telmateium***
dryophyllum — See R. ***phaeochrysum levistratum***
eclecteum — CWal SLeo
– *bellatulum* — CWal
edgarianum — CWal LMil SLeo
§ *edgeworthii* — CTrw CWal SLeo
elegantulum — CWal SLeo
elliottii — SLeo
erubescens — See R. ***oreodoxa fargesii*** Erubescens group
x *erythrocalyx* Panteumorphum group — SLeo
euchaites — See R. ***neriiflorum neriiflorum*** Euch. group
eudoxum — LRHS SLeo
eurysiphon — CWal
exasperatum — CWal SLeo
eximium — See R. ***falconeri e.***
faberi — CWal LMil SLeo SSta
– *prattii* — CWal SLeo
facetum — SLeo
falconeri — CHEx CWal IOrc LMil SHil SLeo SReu
– BMW 66 — MBal
– DF 526 — MBal
¶ – EGM 055 — LMil
– *eximium* — LMil SSpi
fargesii — See R. ***oreodoxa f.***
fastigiatum — CHig CWal EPot GAbr GArd GDra GEdr LMil LSav MBal MBar MLea SHil SLeo
– SBEC 0840* — NHar WThu
*– 'Harry White' — LMil
ferrugineum — COtt CSco CWal GArd GK&P LHyd LKna LMil MBal MBar MGos MPlt SLeo SReu SSta WAbe
– *album* — CWal LSav
¶ – 'Glenarn' — NHol
fictolacteum — See R. ***rex fictolacteum***
fimbriatum — See R. ***hippophaeoides hipp.*** Fimbriatum group
flavidum — CWal GArd MBal SExb SSta WBod
– 'Album' — CWal LMil SExb SOkd WBod
fletcherianum R 22302 — CWal GEdr SLeo
flinkii — See R. ***lanatum*** Flinkii group
floccigerum — CWal SLeo
– F 20305 — SLeo
– R 18465/6 — LSav
floribundum — SLeo
formosum — CB&S CGre CWal ERea LMil SSta
§ – formosum Iteaphyllum group — CWal GK&P SLeo WBod
forrestii — GAbr GK&P LHyd SReu
forrestii forrestii Repens group — CWal LHyd LMil MBal SLeo WAbe WBod
– – Tumescens group — CWal LHyd SLeo
fortunei — CBow IOrc LHyd LMil SHil SLeo SReu
– McLaren S 146 — CWal
– *discolor* — CWal LHyd SLeo SReu

§ – discolor Houlstonii group	CWal LMil SLeo
– 'Foxy'	SLeo
– 'Mrs Butler'	CWal LMil
fulgens	CWal LHyd SLeo
– DF 543	MBal
fulvum	CWal IOrc LHyd LMil SExb SLeo SReu SSta
– F 24110	SLeo
galactinum	CWal SLeo
genestierianum	CWal SLeo
x ***geraldii***	SLeo
glaucophyllum	CFor CWal GK&P LHyd LMil SLeo SPer SReu SSta
– (Branklyn)	LMil
– L&S 2764	See R. ***brachyanthum*** L&S 2764
– BH form	LMil
– ***tubiforme***	See R. ***tubiforme***
glischrum	SLeo
– ***glischroides***	SLeo
– ***rude***	SLeo
glomerulatum	See R. ***yungningense*** Glomerulatum group
grande	CGre CWal IOrc
– DF 524	MBal
¶ – EGM 058	LMil
griersonianum	CWal IOrc ISea LHyd MBal SExb SHil SLeo
griffithianum	CWal SLeo
grothausii	GK&P
gymnocarpum	See R. ***microgynum*** Gymnocarpum group
habrotrichum	CWal SLeo
haematodes	CWal LMil LSav MBal MBri SLeo
– F 6773	SLeo
– McClaren S124A	SLeo
haematodes chaetomallum KW 21077	SLeo
– – KW 5431	CWal
– – R 18359	SLeo
hanceanum	CB&S CHig LHyd NKay SLeo
– 'Canton Consul'	LHyd LSav SSta
– Nanum group	CWal EPot GAbr LHyd MBal SIng WBod WThu
– x ***lutescens***	WBod
hardyi	See R. ***augustinii h.***
heliolepis	CWal IOrc LMil MBal SLeo
– ***brevistylum***	CWal
§ – ***brevistylum*** Pholidotum group F 6762	SLeo
x ***hemigynum***	SLeo
hemitrichotum Yu 14843	SLeo
hemsleyanum	CWal IOrc SLeo
hippophaeoides	CHig CSco CWal LKna LMil MBri NHol SLeo SSta
– 'Inshriach'	SHil
hippophaeoides hippophaeoides F 22197A	SLeo
§ – – Fimbriatum group	CWal GK&P MGos
hirsutum	CHig CWal LHyd MBal MBar NHol SReu SSpi WBod
– ***album***	LHyd
– 'Flore Pleno'	CHig GK&P MBal NKay WAbe
hirtipes KW 5659	SLeo
– KW 6223	SLeo
hodgsonii	IOrc LHyd LMil SLeo
– B 653	MBal
– DF 532	MBal
¶ – EGM 081	LMil
hongkongense	SLeo
hookeri	SLeo
¶ ***horlickianum***	LMil
houlstonii	See R. ***fortunei discolor*** Houlstonii group
hunnewellianum	CWal SExb
– Wilson A 4248	SLeo
N Hybrid 'A Bedford'	LHyd LKna
♦ – 'A J Ivens'	See R. H. 'Arthur J Ivens'
¶ – 'Abe Arnott'	MLea
– 'Abegail'	SLeo
– 'Abendrot'	SSta
– 'Achilles'	CWal SLeo
– 'Actress'	CWal SLeo
– 'Adamant'	CWal
– Adelaide (g.&cl.)	CWal SExb
– 'Admiral Piet Hein'	SReu
– 'Adriaan Koster'	CWal SExb
* – 'Ahren's Favourite'	SSta
– 'Airy Fairy'	LHyd
– 'Aksel Olsen'	MBal MBar MPlt MR&S NHol WBod
– Albatross (g.&cl.)	LKna LMil MBlu SLeo SReu SSta
– 'Albatross Townhill Pink'	LMil SHil
– 'Albatross Townhill White'	SHil
– 'Albert Schweitzer'	CWal IJoh LMil MBal MBar MR&S SLeo SReu SSta
– 'Album'	WBod
– 'Alice'	CWal LHyd LKna MMor SCog SExb SHil SLeo SPer SReu
* – 'Alice Gilbert'	CWal
– 'Alice Street'	SLeo SReu
– Alison Johnstone (g.&cl.)	CB&S CBow COtt CTrw CWal GArd LHyd LMil MLea NHol SCog SExb SHil SLeo SPer SSpi SSta WThu
– Alix (g.&cl.)	SLeo
¶ – 'Aloha'	LMil MLea WWeb
– 'Alpine Glow'	CWal NHol SLeo
– Amalfi (g.&cl.)	CWal
– Amaura	WBod
– 'America'	CB&S IJoh MBar MGos MRav SLeo WWeb
– 'Amethyst'	CWal LHyd LSav
– Amor (g.&cl.)	LHyd SLeo SReu
– 'Analin'	See R. H. 'Anuschka '
– 'Andre'	MBri SLeo SSta
– Angelo	LMil SCog SReu
– Anita	CWal SLeo
¶ – 'Anita Dustan'	LMil

Hybrid 'Ann Aberconway' WBod
– 'Anna Baldsiefen' CSam EBre GEdr LMil LSav MBri NHol SSta
¶– 'Anna H Hall' LMil SReu WWeb
– 'Anna Rose Whitney' CB&S CSam GRei LHyd LKna LMil MBar MBri MGos MLea MR&S SExb SLeo SReu SSta WBod
– 'Annapurna' SReu
– 'Anne Dring' MLea
– 'Anne George' LHyd
– 'Annette' SReu
– 'Antje' LRHS
– Antonio (g.&cl.) CWal SCog
– 'Antoon van Welie' SSta
– 'Anuschka' LRHS MGos
– 'Apotrophia' CWal
– 'Apple Blossom' CWal LKna
§– 'April Glow' LHyd MR&S NKay SLeo
– 'April Showers' See R. Hybrid 'April Glow'
– Arbcalo SLeo
– Arblact CWal
– 'Arborfield' LMil SLeo
– Arbsutch SLeo
– Arbutifolium NHol
– 'Arctic Snow' MLea
– 'Arctic Tern' CSam EBre GArd ITim LHyd LMil NHol SLeo SReu WThu
– Argosy CWal LMil SReu
– Ariel SLeo
– 'Arkle' LHyd
¶– 'Armantine' LKna
– Armia CWal
– 'Arthur Bedford' MBri SExb SLeo SReu
– 'Arthur J Ivens' CWal LSav
– 'Arthur Osborn' CHig CWal SLeo SSpi
– 'Arthur Stevens' CWal SLeo
¶– 'Arthur Warren' LKna
– 'Ascot Brilliant' SExb SLeo
– Augfast CB&S CTrw CWal EPot IJoh IOrc ISea LMil SHil SReu WBod
– Aurora (g.&cl.) SLeo
– 'Autumn Gold' GRei LMil MBri MLea NHol SExb
– Avalanche (g.&cl.) CWal SLeo SReu
– Avocet CWal
– Ayesha SExb
– Azor (g.&cl.) CWal LHyd LMil SReu SSpi SSta
*– 'Azorazie' SLeo
– 'Babylon' SLeo
– 'Bad Eilsen' NWea SSta
– 'Baden-Baden' CBow CSco CWal ELan EPot GArd GRei IJoh ISea LHyd LKna MBal MBar MBri MGos MMor MR&S NBar NKay SCog SExb SPer SSta WAbe
– 'Bagshot Ruby' LKna SExb SHil SReu
– 'Bali' LMil
– 'Balsaminiflorum' See R. ***indicum*** 'Balsaminiflorum'
– 'Bambi' CWal MBri SCog SHil SLeo SSta
– 'Bambino' LMil LNet MLea SLeo
*– 'Bandoola' SReu
¶– 'Barbara Reuthe' SReu
– 'Barclayi Helen Fox' CWal
– 'Barclayi Robert Fox' CWal SLeo
– 'Bashful' CB&S CWal ELan GRei LHyd MBal MBlu MBri MGos MMor SCog SLeo SPer SPic SReu
– 'Bastion' SExb
– Bauble SExb
– 'Beatrice Keir' CWal LHyd SHil SLeo SReu
– Beau Brummel (g.&cl.) LMil
– 'Beauty of Littleworth' CBow CWal LHyd LKna SExb SLeo SPer SReu
– 'Belle Heller' CSam LMil MBri MLea SSta
– 'Belle of Tremeer' CWal LHyd
– 'Ben Moseley' SSta
– 'Bengal' ISea MBar MLea MPlt SCog SReu
– 'Bernard Shaw' SReu
– Berryrose (g.&cl.) CWal SExb
– 'Bert's Own' CWal
*– 'Betty Robertson' NKay
– 'Betty Stewart' SLeo
– 'Betty Wormald' CBow CHig CSco CWal IHos LHyd LKna LMil MGos SCog SExb SHil SLeo SPer SReu SSta
– Bibiani (g.&cl.) LHyd SExb
– 'Billy Budd' LHyd SCog
– 'Binfield' SLeo
– 'Birthday Greeting' SExb
– 'Biscuit Box' SExb SLeo
– 'Bishopsgate' LHyd
– Biskra (g.&cl.) CWal LMil SReu
– 'Black Magic' LMil SExb
– 'Blewbury' CWal LHyd LMil LSav SCog SExb SSpi SSta
– 'Blitz' MBri SLeo
¶– 'Blue Bell' LKna
– 'Blue Boy' LMil MBlu
– 'Blue Chip' LHyd LMil SLeo
– 'Blue Danube' CWal LKna
– Blue Diamond (g.&cl.) Widely available
– 'Blue Ensign' CWal
*– 'Blue Gown' LKna LSav
¶– 'Blue Haze' LHyd LSav
– 'Blue Jay' MBlu NKay SReu
– 'Blue Mountain' GArd GDra MBal NHar WThu
– 'Blue Peter' CB&S CHig CSco CWal IHos IOrc ISea LKna MBar MBri MGos MMor SExb SHil SLeo SPer SReu SSta
– 'Blue Pool' LMil MBal MBar MLea WBod
– Blue Ribbon CB&S CTrw ISea
– 'Blue Star' CMHG CWal LHyd LSav SPer
– 'Blue Steel' See R. ***impeditum*** 'Blue Steel'
– Blue Tit Widely available

Hybrid Bluebird (g.&cl.)	CWal IOrc LSav MBal MBar MGos MLea MMor NHol SExb SReu WBod
¶ – Bluebird (g.&cl.)	LKna
– Bluestone	MBar MMor SExb
– 'Bluette'	IJoh ISea SLeo
– Boadicea	CWal
– 'Bob's Blue'	ISea SReu
– 'Boddaertianum'	CWal LHyd
– 'Bodnant Yellow'	CSam CWal LMil
– 'Bonfire'	CWal SReu
– Bonito (g.&cl.)	SCog
– 'Borderer'	SCog SLeo
– 'Boule de Neige'	SLeo
– Bow Bells (g.&cl.)	Widely available
– 'Bow Street'	LHyd
– Bo-peep (g.&cl.)	CB&S CHig CSam CWal LHyd LMil MBal MLea NKay SExb SLeo SPla SReu
– Break of Day (g.&cl.)	CWal SLeo
– 'Bremen'	SExb
– 'Brentor'	SLeo
– 'Brets Own'	SLeo
– Bric-a-brac (g.&cl.)	CB&S CTrw CWal LHyd MBal SExb SLeo SPer SPla SReu
– 'Brightwell'	SPer
– 'Britannia'	CB&S CSam CSco IJoh LHyd LKna LNet MBar MBlu MBri MGos MMor MR&S NBar NWea SExb SHil SLeo SPer SReu SSta
– Brocade	CWal LHyd LKna LMil LSav NHol SCog SHil SLeo
– 'Brookside'	CWal SHil
– 'Broughtonii'	SExb SLeo
– 'Bruce Brechtbill'	CSco MLea NHol SSta
– 'Bud Flanagan'	MBlu SExb
– Burning Bush	CWal
– Bustard	SLeo
– 'Butter Yellow'	NHar SLeo
– 'Butterfly'	CBow LKna SLeo
– 'Buttermint'	CSam LHyd LMil MBri MLea SExb SLeo SReu SSpi SSta
– 'Buttersteep'	SLeo
– 'C B van Nes'	CWal
– 'C I S'	MBlu MBri MLea SLeo SSpi
– Caerhays John	CWal
– 'Caerhays Lawrence'	CBow CWal MBal SLeo
– 'Caerhays Philip'	CWal MBal
– Calfort (g.&cl.)	CWal SLeo
– Calrose	WBod
– Calstocker	SLeo
– Calsutch	SLeo
– Campirr	LHyd
– 'Canadian Beauty'	LMil
– 'Canary'	LKna SLeo SReu
¶ – 'Caperci Special'	LSav
– 'Captain Jack'	SLeo
– 'Caractacus'	MBar SLeo SSta
– Cardinal (g.&cl.)	CWal
– Carex (g.&cl.)	SCog
– Carita	CWal LKna SReu
– 'Carita Charm'	SExb SHil
– 'Carita Golden Dream'	CWal LKna LMil SExb SLeo
– 'Carita Inchmery'	CWal LHyd LKna SCog SExb SLeo SSpi
– Carmen	Widely available
¶ – 'Caroline'	LMil
– 'Caroline Allbrook'	CMHG CSam CWal LHyd LMil SCog SLeo SReu SSta WWeb
– 'Caroline de Zoete'	LHyd
– 'Cary Ann'	CSco GRei ISea MLea NHar SLeo SSta
– 'Castle of Mey'	SExb
¶ – 'Catalode'	LMil
– 'Catawbiense Grandiflorum'	IJoh
– Cauapo	CWal
– 'Caucasicum Pictum'	LMil MBri
– 'Cavalcade'	CWal
– 'Cetewayo'	SLeo SReu
– 'Champagne'	CWal LHyd MLea SCog SExb SLeo SReu SSpi SSta
– Chanticleer	CBow
– 'Charlotte Currie'	SLeo
– 'Charlotte de Rothschild'	CWal LMil SExb
– Charmaine (g.&cl.)	EPot GArd MBri NHol WBod
– 'Cheer'	IJoh IOrc MBar MBri SSta
– 'Chelsea Seventy'	CWal ELan IHos NHol SCog SLeo SReu SSta
¶ – 'Cherry Pink'	ISea
– 'Chevalier Felix de Sauvage'	CWal LMil SExb SLeo SReu SSta
– 'Cheyenne'	CWal SLeo
– 'Chiffchaff'	EPot GArd NHar SLeo WAbe
– 'Chikor'	Widely available
– China (g.&cl.)	CWal LKna SLeo SReu
¶ – 'China A'	LKna
– 'Chink'	CB&S CSam CWal GArd GRei LHyd LSav MBal MBar MPlt SCog SExb SHil SLeo SReu WBod WThu
– 'Chionoides'	CBow CWal ISea LKna
– 'Chippewa'	GEdr
– 'Choremia'	CTrw GArd SCog SExb SLeo WBod
– 'Christmas Cheer'	CB&S CHig CWal ELan IOrc ISea LHyd LKna LMil MBlu MBri NKay SExb SHil SLeo SPer SReu
– 'Christobel Maude'	LHyd
– Chrysomanicum (g.&cl.)	CTrw CWal LMil SLeo
– Cilpinense	Widely available
– Cinnkeys (g.&cl.)	CTrw CWal GArd LHyd LMil
– Cinzan	LHyd LMil SReu
– 'Cliff Garland'	LMil
– Clio	CWal SLeo
¶ – 'Colonel Coen'	LMil
– Colonel Rogers	CWal LHyd SLeo SReu
– Comely	CWal LHyd SLeo
– 'Comte de Gomer'	CB&S
– 'Concerto'	SExb
– 'Concessum'	LKna MBri
– 'Concorde'	LHyd MBar MMor SCog

Hybrid 'Conroy'	CBow GArd ISea LHyd LMil LSav MBal SPer WBod
– 'Constable'	CWal LHyd SLeo
¶ – 'Constant Nymph'	LKna
– Conyan	LHyd
– 'Cool Haven'	SHil
– 'Coral Reef'	LHyd SLeo SReu
– 'Cornish Cracker'	SLeo
– Cornish Cross	CWal LHyd SCog SExb SHil SLeo SReu
– Cornish Early Red	See R. Hybrid Smithii group
– 'Cornish Red'	See R. Hybrid Smithii group
– Cornsutch	CWal
– Cornubia	CWal SLeo
– 'Corona'	CWal LKna SCog SReu
¶ – 'Coronation Day'	SReu
– Coronet	SExb
– 'Corry Koster'	LKna SExb
– 'Cosmopolitan'	IJoh MGos MR&S MRav SExb SSta
– 'Costa del Sol'	SLeo
– 'Cotton Candy'	LMil MLea SSpi
– 'Countess of Athlone'	CWal LKna
– 'Countess of Derby'	SPer SReu
– 'Countess of Haddington'	CB&S CTre ERea ISea LMil SLeo
– 'County of York'	See R. H. 'Catalode'
– Cowslip	CBow CSam EBre ELan IJoh LHyd LKna LMil LSav MBal MBar MBri MGos NHar NHol SCog SHil SLeo SPer SReu WBod
– 'Cranbourne'	SReu
¶ – 'Crater Lake'	LSav
– 'Cream Crest'	ISea SLeo SPer
– 'Cream Glory'	LHyd LMil MLea SReu WWeb
– 'Creamy Chiffon'	CSam ISea LHyd LMil MLea SLeo SPer SReu SSpi SSta
§ – 'Creeping Jenny'	CBow CWal EPot GEdr LHyd LMil LSav MBal MBar MLea MPlt NHol SCog SHil SPer SPla WBod
– 'Crest'	CSco CWal IOrc ISea LHyd LKna LMil MBlu MGos MLea SHil SLeo SPer SReu SSpi SSta WThu WWeb
¶ – 'Crete'	SReu
– Crossbill	CB&S MBal NKay SExb SLeo
– 'Crowthorne'	SCog
– 'Crushed Strawberry'	WBod
– 'Cunningham's Sulphur'	See R. ***caucasicum*** 'C.S.'
– 'Cunningham's White'	CBow CHig CSam CWal ELan GRei IJoh LKna LMil MBar MBri MGos MMor MRav SExb SLeo SReu
– 'Curlew'	Widely available
– 'Cutie'	SLeo SSta
– 'Cynthia'	CB&S CSam CSco CWal GRei IJoh IOrc ISea LHyd LKna MBal MBar MBri MGos MMor MR&S NBar NWea SExb SHil SLeo SPer SReu SSta
– 'Dairymaid'	CWal LHyd LKna SLeo SReu
– Damaris	CBow CWal SLeo
– 'Damaris Logan'	See R. Hybrid 'Logan Damaris'
– Damozel (g.&cl.)	CWal SCog SExb SPer
¶ – 'Dandy'	LKna
– Dante	CWal SLeo
– 'Daphne'	SLeo
– 'Daphne Jewiss'	SReu
– 'Daphne Magor'	SLeo
¶ – 'Daphnoides'	MLea
– 'David'	CWal LHyd LKna SLeo SPer SReu
– 'David Rockefeller'	SExb
– Day Dream (g.&cl.)	CWal LHyd LKna LSav SExb SPer SReu SSpi
– 'Dayan'	SExb
– 'Diana Colville'	CBow CWal
– 'Diana Pearson'	SLeo
– 'Diane'	LKna SLeo SReu
– Dicharb	CWal SLeo
¶ – 'Dido'	LHyd
– 'Diny Dee'	LMil MGos SExb SSpi SSta
– Diva (g.&cl.)	SExb
– 'Doc'	CB&S CWal ELan GRei IOrc ISea LMil MBal MBar MGos MMor NBar NKay SCog SHil SLeo SPer SReu
– 'Doctor Arnold W Endtz'	MBar MMor SExb SLeo
– 'Doctor H C Dresselhuys'	IJoh MBri
– 'Doctor Stocker'	CTrw CWal SLeo
– 'Doctor Tjebbes'	ISea
– 'Doctor V H Rutgers'	MGos
– 'Dollar Princess'	SExb
– 'Doncaster'	CBow CWal LKna MBar MGos NHol NWea SCog SExb SHil SLeo SPer
– 'Dopey'	CSco CWal GRei IHos IJoh IOrc ISea LHyd LMil MBar MBri MLea MMor NBar SCog SHil SLeo SPer SPic SReu
– 'Dora Amateis'	Widely available
– Dormouse	LMil SExb
– 'Dorothea'	CWal SLeo
– 'Dorothy Amateis'	SSta
– 'Douglas McEwan'	ISea MBri
– Dragonfly	CWal SReu
– 'Drake's Mountain'	MBar MPlt MRav
– 'Dreamland'	LHyd SReu SSpi
– 'Duchess of Portland'	CWal
– 'Dusky Dawn'	CWal SLeo
– 'Dusty Miller'	COtt CWal IHos LMil MBal MBri SCog SLeo SReu
– 'Earl of Athlone'	LHyd LKna SReu
– 'Earl of Donoughmore'	CWal IDai LHyd LKna LMil MBri MMor SExb SPer SReu SSta

¶ Hybrid Early Brilliant LKna
– 'Early Gem' ISea MBri
– *edgeworthii* x *leucaspis* CB&S
– *edgeworthii* x *moupinense* CB&S
*– 'Edith Bosley' LMil
– 'Edith Mackworth Praed' CWal
¶ – 'Edmond Amateis' LMil
– Edmondii LHyd
– 'Egret' CSam EPot GEdr ISea ITim LMil MBri NHar NHol SLeo SSta
– 'Eider' GArd LHyd MLea NHar SLeo SPer SReu
– 'Eileen' LMil SReu
– 'El Alamein' CWal SLeo
– 'El Camino' MBlu MLea SLeo SReu SSpi SSta
– Eldorado SExb
– Eleanore (g.&cl.) ISea SExb
– Electra (g.&cl.) CWal LHyd SCog SLeo
– 'Elisabeth Hobbie' GDra GRei LKna LMil MBal MBar MGos MLea NBar SCog SExb SHil WAbe WBod
– Elizabeth Widely available
– 'Elizabeth de Rothschild' CB&S SExb
– 'Elizabeth Jenny' See R. Hybrid 'Creeping Jenny'
– 'Elizabeth Lockhart' CWal LHyd MGos MLea SHil SLeo SSpi
¶ – 'Elsa Crisp' LKna
– Elsae (g.&cl.) CWal SLeo
– 'Elsie Straver' IJoh MBri NHol SExb SLeo SPer SReu SSta
– 'Elspeth' CWal LHyd LKna
– 'Emasculum' CGre CSam CWal LKna LSav SPer SReu WThu
¶ – 'Empire Day' LKna
– 'Ems' GArd
– 'Enborne' SLeo
– 'Endre Ostbo' CWal SLeo
– 'Endsleigh Pink' WBod
– 'Ernest Inman' CWal LHyd SLeo
– Ethel (g.&cl.) CHig CWal WBod
– 'Etta Burrows' MLea SLeo SSpi
– 'Euan Cox' LMil NHar
¶ – 'Europa' SReu
– 'Evening Glow' MLea NHol
– 'Everestianum' LKna MBar SLeo SSta
– Exburiense LSav
¶ – 'Exbury Albatross' LKna
§ – 'Exbury Lady Chamberlain' LHyd SHil SReu
– 'Exbury May Day' SReu
– F C Puddle (g.&cl.) SLeo
– Fabia (g.&cl.) CBow CWal GArd IJoh IOrc LHyd LKna LMil SExb SHil SLeo SPer SReu SSpi SSta
– 'Fabia Roman Pottery' SPer
– 'Fabia Tangerine' MBal MLea WBod
– 'Fabia Waterer' SSta
– 'Faggetter's Favourite' CWal LKna LMil MMor SLeo SReu SSta
– Fairy Light CGre CWal SExb
– 'Faltho' SLeo
– Fandango CWal
– 'Fastuosum Flore Pleno' CHig CSco CWal LHyd LKna LMil MBal MBar MBlu MBri MGos MMor MR&S NBar NWea SExb SHil SLeo SPer SReu SSta
– Fire Bird LHyd SReu
– 'Fireball' CWal SLeo
¶ – Firedrake SReu
– 'Fireman Jeff' ISea MLea SPer
– 'Fittra' SHil
– Flamingo CWal
– 'Flare' CWal
– Flashlight CWal SLeo
§ – Flava (g.&cl.) CWal MBri MGos SSta
¶ – *flavidum* x Lady Rosebery 'Biscuit' NHol
– 'flavidum 'Album' x Lady Rosebery LMil
¶ – 'Flavour' LKna
– 'Florence Archer' SSta
– 'Floriade' LHyd LKna SExb
– Fortorb SLeo
– Fortune (g.&cl.) CWal LKna SLeo
¶ – 'Fox Hunter' LKna
– 'Fragrantissimum' CB&S CTre CTrw CWal ELan ERea GArd IOrc ISea LMil MBal MRav SExb SHil SReu SSpi SSta WBod WMar
– Francis Hanger (Reuthe's) CWal SExb SLeo SReu
– 'Frank Baum' MBri MLea SLeo SSta
– 'Frank Galsworthy' LKna SExb SLeo SReu SSta
¶ – 'Fred Peste' LMil MLea SSpi
– 'Fred Rose' SLeo
– Fred Wynniatt (FCC) LMil SExb
– 'Frill' CTrw
– 'Frilled Petticoats' MLea
– 'Frontier' LMil
– 'Frühlingszauber' CWal SExb
– 'Fuju-kaku-no-matsu' LRHS
– 'Fulbrook' CWal LHyd
– 'Fulgarb' CWal SLeo
¶ – Full House LHyd
– 'Furnivall's Daughter' CSam CSco LHyd LKna LMil MBar MBlu MBri MGos MMor SHil SLeo SPer SReu SSta WWeb
– Fusilier (g.&cl.) CWal LHyd SExb SReu
– 'Galactic' SLeo
– Garnet CWal
– 'Gartendirektor Glocker' CSam MR&S SHil SSta
¶ – 'Gartendirektor Rieger' LMil NHol
– 'General Eisenhower' SReu
– 'General Eric Harrison' CWal LHyd SCog SLeo
– 'General Sir John du Cane' SExb
¶ – 'Gene's Favourite' SReu
– 'Genghis Khan' MLea
– 'George Hardy' CWal SExb

Cultivar	Suppliers
Hybrid 'George Johnstone'	CTrw LMil
– 'Georgette'	CWal LHyd SLeo
– Gertrud Schale	CWal MBal MBar MLea MPlt SReu
– Gibraltar	SExb
– 'Gill's Crimson'	SExb
– 'Ginny Gee'	CSam EPot LMil MBri MLea NHol NRoo SReu SSpi SSta
– 'Gipsy King Memory'	SExb
– 'Glad Tidings'	SLeo
– Gladys (g.&cl.)	SCog
– Glamour (g.&cl.)	SExb
– 'Gleam'	CWal LHyd
– 'Glen's Orange'	SExb
– 'Gloriana'	LHyd SReu
– 'Glory of Leonardslee'	SLeo
– 'Glory of Penjerrick'	CWal SLeo
– Goblin (g.&cl.)	SExb
– 'Gold Mohur'	SLeo SReu
– 'Golden Belle'	LMil MBri MLea SLeo SPer
– 'Golden Fleece'	CWal LKna SLeo SReu
– 'Golden Gate'	NHol SLeo
– Golden Horn (g.&cl.)	IOrc MBal SExb SLeo
– 'Golden Horn Persimmon'	See R. Hybrid 'Persimmon'
– 'Golden Orfe'	CWal LHyd LMil NKay
– Golden Oriole	CB&S CTre LSav NHol SLeo SPer
– 'Golden Oriole Talavera'	CB&S CWal MBal SCog
§ – 'Golden Queen'	CWal
– 'Golden Spur'	LHyd
– 'Golden Star'	LMil SReu
– 'Golden Torch'	CMHG COtt CSam CSco CWal IOrc ISea LMil LNet MBlu MBri MLea SCog SHil SLeo SPer SPic SReu SSpi SSta WWeb
¶ – 'Golden Wedding'	LMil MBri MLea SReu
– 'Golden Wit'	MBri MLea
¶ – Goldfinch	MRav
– Goldfinger	MBal
– 'Goldfort'	LKna SLeo SReu
¶ – 'Goldika'	LMil
– 'Goldkrone'	LMil
– 'Goldstrike'	LMil
– 'Goldsworth Orange'	CBow CWal LHyd LKna LMil MBar MBlu MGos MMor SPer SReu SSta
– 'Goldsworth Pink'	LKna SReu
– 'Goldsworth Yellow'	LKna SExb SHil SLeo SPer SReu SSta
– 'Gomer Waterer'	CB&S CBow CHig CSam CSco CWal IJoh ISea LHyd LKna LMil MBal MBar MBri MGos MMor MR&S NWea SExb SHil SLeo SPer SReu SSta
– 'Goosander'	LHyd
– 'Grace Seabrook'	LHyd LMil MBlu MBri MLea SExb SLeo SPer SReu
*– 'Grafton'	SExb
– 'Grayswood Pink'	CSam LHyd SPer
*– 'Great Dane'	LHyd
– 'Green Eye'	CWal
¶ – 'Greensleeves'	LKna
– Grenadier (g.&cl.)	CWal SExb
– Grenadine (g.&cl.)	LHyd
– Gretia (g.&cl.)	WBod
– 'Gretzel'	SLeo
– Grierocaster	SCog
– 'Grilse'	LHyd
– 'Grisette'	SLeo
– 'Gristede'	LMil MBri NHol SReu SSta WBod
– Grosclaude (g.&cl.)	CWal LHyd SCog SLeo SSpi
– 'Grouse'	GArd LHyd
– 'Grumpy'	CB&S CBow CMHG CWal EBre ELan GRei IHos LHyd LMil LNet MBal MBar MBri MLea MMor NHol SCog SLeo SPer SPic SReu SSta
– Guardsman	SLeo
¶ – 'Gwen Bell'	LMil
– 'Gwillt-King'	CWal SLeo
– 'H Whitner'	SLeo
– 'Haida Gold'	LMil MBri MGos MLea NKay SSta WWeb
– Halcyone	CWal SLeo
– 'Halfdan Lem'	ISea LHyd LMil MGos MLea SHil SLeo SPer SReu SSta WWeb
– 'Hallelujah'	CBow ISea LMil
– 'Handsworth Scarlet'	SLeo
– Happy	CWal ELan IJoh IOrc ISea MMor SPer WWeb
– 'Hardijzer's Beauty'	See R. Azaleodendron 'Hardijzer's Beauty'
– 'Harvest Moon'	CSam CWal LHyd MBal MBar MBlu MBri MGos NKay SExb SLeo SPer SReu SSta
– 'Hawk Jervis Bay'	See R. Hybrid 'Jervis Bay'
¶ – Hawk 'Crest'	See R. H. 'Crest'
*– ***Hawk*** 'Falcon'	SReu
– 'Haze'	SLeo
– 'Hazel'	LRHS
– Hebe	CWal SExb
*– 'Helen Koster'	LKna
– 'Helene Schiffner'	SExb SLeo SReu
*– 'Henry Street'	SLeo
– Hesperides	CWal SExb
¶ – 'High Gold'	LMil SReu
– 'High Summer'	LMil
¶ – 'Hilda Margaret'	SReu
– 'Hill Ayah'	CWal
– 'Hollandia'	MMor
– 'Honey'	CWal LKna SLeo
– 'Honey Bee'	LMil LRHS SSta
– 'Hope Findlay'	LHyd
– 'Hoppy'	CMHG CSco CWal MBlu MBri MLea SCog SHil SLeo SReu SSta WWeb
¶ – 'Horizon Snowbird'	LMil
– 'Hotei'	CB&S CBow CSco CWal IJoh LHyd LMil MBal MBar MBri MLea MMor NKay SExb SHil SLeo SPer SReu SSpi SSta

Hybrid 'Hugh Koster'	CB&S CSam CWal ISea LHyd LKna MGos MRav SExb SHil SLeo SPer WWeb
– Humming Bird	CB&S CBow CMHG CSam CSco CWal EPot GArd ISea LHyd LKna LSav MBal MBar MBri MGos MLea MMor MPlt NHol SExb SLeo WBod
– 'Hurricane'	LMil MBlu MBri
– 'Hydon Ball'	CWal LHyd SReu
– 'Hydon Ben'	LHyd
– 'Hydon Dawn'	CWal LHyd LMil MGos SCog SLeo SPer SPla SReu SSta
– 'Hydon Glow'	CWal LHyd SLeo
¶ – 'Hydon Gold'	LHyd
– 'Hydon Harrier'	LHyd LSav
– 'Hydon Hunter'	CWal LHyd LMil LNet SCog SLeo SPla SReu SSta
– 'Hydon Mist'	LHyd
– 'Hydon Pink'	LHyd
– 'Hydon Rodney'	LHyd
– 'Hydon Salmon'	LHyd LSav SLeo
– 'Hydon Snowflake'	CWal LHyd
– 'Hydon Velvet'	LHyd
– Hyperion	LKna SReu SSta
– Ibex (g.&cl.)	CWal MLea SExb
– Icarus	CWal
– 'Ice Cream'	LHyd SCog
– 'Iceberg'	See R. H. 'Lodauric Iceberg'
– 'Icecream Flavour'	See R. H. 'Flavour'
– 'Icecream Vanilla'	See R. H. 'Vanilla'
– Idealist (g.&cl.)	CBow CWal LHyd MBri MLea SExb SLeo SPer SReu
¶ – 'Ightham Gold'	SReu
*– 'Ightham Peach'	SReu
*– 'Ightham Purple'	SReu
– 'Ightham Yellow'	CFor CWal MMor SLeo SPer SReu SSpi SSta
– 'Ilam Violet'	LKna LMil
– Impi (g.&cl.)	CWal LKna MBri SExb SLeo
– Inamorata	SExb
– Indiana	SExb
– Intermedium	MBal
– Intrepid	SExb SLeo
– Intrifast	CWal GEdr LHyd LSav MBri NKay SHil SReu
– 'Irene'	SSta
– 'Isabel Pierce'	CSam LMil SLeo SSta WWeb
– Isabella (g.&cl.)	SExb SHil
– 'Isabella Mangles'	LHyd
– Italia	SLeo
– Ivanhoe (g.&cl.)	CWal ISea SExb
– 'Ivery's Scarlet'	CWal SExb
¶ – Iviza	SReu
*– 'J C Williams'	CB&S
– 'J G Millais'	LHyd
– 'J H Agnew'	SExb
– 'J H van Nes'	SPer
– 'J M de Montague'	See R. Hybid 'The Hon. Jean Marie de Montague'
*– 'Jack'	CTrw
*– 'Jack Skelton'	CWal LHyd
– 'Jacksonii'	CWal ISea LKna MBar MBri SLeo SReu
– Jacques	SReu
– Jacquetta	WBod
– 'Jade'	SLeo
– Jaipur	CWal
– Jalisco (g.&cl.)	CFor CWal SExb SLeo
– 'Jalisco Eclipse'	CWal LKna SExb
– 'Jalisco Elect'	LKna LMil SHil
– 'Jalisco Goshawk'	SLeo
– 'Jalisco Janet'	CWal SHil
– 'Jalisco Jubilant'	LHyd LMil SExb
– 'James Barto'	CWal LHyd LMil LSav SLeo SPer SSta
– 'James Burchett'	LKna LMil SLeo
¶ – 'Jan Dekens'	SReu
– Jan Steen (g.&cl.)	SExb
– Janet	SHil SLeo
¶ – 'Janet Blair'	SReu
¶ – 'Janet Ward'	LHyd LKna
– 'Janine Alexandre Debray'	SCog SLeo
– 'Jasper Pimento'	SExb
– Jean	SCog
– 'Jean Mary Montague'	See R. Hybrid 'The Hon. Jean Marie de Montague'
– 'Jenny'	See R. Hybrid 'Creeping Jenny'
– 'Jerez'	SExb
§ – 'Jervis Bay'	SLeo
– 'Joan Scobie'	CWal SLeo
– Jock	CB&S CMHG LHyd
– 'John Barr Stevenson'	LHyd SLeo
– 'John Keats'	CWal
– 'John Tremayne'	SLeo
– 'John Walter'	GRei MBar MGos SSta
– 'John Waterer'	LKna SPer
– Johnnie Johnston (g.&cl.)	CWal SLeo
– 'Johnny Bender'	MLea
– 'Johnson's Impeditum'	SExb
– 'Joseph Whitworth'	CWal
¶ – Josephine	LMil
– 'Joyful'	SExb
¶ – 'Jubilee'	LKna
– Jubilee Queen (g.&cl.)	SLeo
– 'Jungfrau'	SExb
– 'Juwel'	CSco MGos
– 'Karin'	CSco IJoh MBal MR&S
– Karkov (g.&cl.)	SExb
– 'Kate Waterer'	CWal LKna MBar MGos SLeo SPer SSta
– Keiskrac	CWal
– 'Ken Janeck'	See R. ***yakushimanum*** 'Ken Janeck'
N– Kewense	See R. H. Loderi
– Kilimanjaro (g.&cl.)	SCog SLeo SReu SSpi SSta
– 'Kingston'	LMil LRHS SSpi
– 'Kluis Sensation'	CB&S CBow CSam LHyd LKna MGos MMor SExb SHil SLeo SReu
– 'Kluis Triumph'	CSco LKna SReu
– 'Koichiro Wada'	See R. ***yakushimanum*** 'Koichiro Wada'
– 'Lacs'	SLeo
– 'Lady Adam Gordon'	CWal SLeo

Hybrid 'Lady Alice Fitzwilliam' CB&S CGre CMHG CWal ERea ISea LHop LMil MBal SLeo
¶– 'Lady Annette de Trafford' LKna
– Lady Berry (g.&cl.) SExb
¶– Lady Bessborough (g.&cl.) LHyd
– 'Lady Bessborough Roberte' See R. H. 'Roberte'
– 'Lady Bowes Lyon' CWal LHyd SCog SLeo SPer SReu
– 'Lady Cathcart' SLeo
– Lady Chamberlain (g.&cl.) CBow CWal GArd LHyd LMil MBal MBlu MGos SLeo SReu
– 'Lady Chamberlain Exbury' See R. Hybrid 'Exbury Lady Chamberlain'
– 'Lady Chamberlain Golden Queen' See R. Hybrid 'Golden Queen'
– 'Lady Chamberlain Salmon Trout' See R. Hybrid 'Salmon Trout'
– 'Lady Clementine Mitford' CBow CSam CWal IHos LHyd LKna LMil MBri MLea SExb SHil SLeo SReu SSta
– 'Lady Eleanor Cathcart' CHig CWal LKna SExb SLeo
– 'Lady Grey Egerton' CWal LKna MMor
– Lady Jean CWal
– Lady Linlithgow LMil SCog
– 'Lady Longman' CWal SSta
– Lady Montagu (g.&cl.) SExb
¶– 'Lady Primrose' SReu
– 'Lady Rosebery' (g.&cl.) CBow CHig CSam CWal LMil MLea SHil SLeo SReu
– 'Lady Rosebery Pink Delight' See R. H. 'Pink Lady Rosebery'
¶– Ladybird (g.&cl.) SReu
– Lamellen CWal LHyd SLeo
– 'Lamplighter' LMil SLeo SPer SReu
¶– 'Langworth' LKna
– 'Lascaux' SReu
– Laura Aberconway (g.&cl.) SLeo
– 'Lava Flow' CWal LHyd NHol SCog SPer
– 'Lavender Girl' GRei IJoh LHyd LKna LMil MGos SHil SLeo SPer SReu SSta
¶– 'Lavender Princess' LMil
¶– 'Lavender Queen' MBlu
*– 'Laverette Pichards' MLea
– 'Lea Rainbow' MLea
– 'Lee's Dark Purple' IJoh ISea MBlu SExb SPer
– 'Lee's Scarlet' LKna LMil
– 'Lemon Ice' IJoh SCog
– 'Lem's 121' MLea SReu
– 'Lem's Cameo' SSta
– 'Lem's Monarch' LMil MGos SReu SSta
– 'Lem's Stormcloud' LMil MLea SSta
– 'Leny' NHol SSta
– Leo (g.&cl.) CWal SLeo
– 'Leonardslee Brilliant' SLeo
– 'Leonardslee Giles' SLeo
– 'Leonardslee Pink Bride' SLeo
– 'Leonardslee Primrose' SLeo
– Leonore (g.&cl.) SReu
– Letty Edwards (g.&cl.) CWal LKna SLeo SReu
– 'Lila Pedigo' LMil MLea SReu
– 'Lillian Peste' LMil
– 'Lincill' CWal
– 'Linda' CBow CSam CSco EBre MBal MBar MBri MGos MLea MRav NHol SCog SReu
– Lionel's Triumph (g.&cl.) CWal LMil SLeo
*– 'Lissabon Rosa' SExb
– 'Little Ben' GK&P MBal MBar MPlt WBod
– 'Little Bert' SLeo
¶– 'Little Bert' SReu
*– 'Little Jock' MBal
¶– 'Llenroc' ISea
– Lodauric SHil
§– 'Lodauric Iceberg' CWal LKna LMil SReu
*– 'Lodbrit' SReu
N– Loderi LMil
– 'Loderi Fairy Queen' SLeo
– 'Loderi Fairyland' CWal LHyd SLeo
§– 'Loderi Game Chick' CBow LHyd SExb SLeo SPer SReu SSta
– 'Loderi Georgette' SLeo
– 'Loderi Helen' SLeo
§– 'Loderi Julie' SHil SLeo SReu
– 'Loderi King George' CB&S CBow CFor CSam CSco ISea LHyd LKna LMil MBlu MBri MLea SExb SHil SLeo SMad SPer SReu SSta
– 'Loderi Patience' LHyd SLeo
– 'Loderi Pink Topaz' CKni LHyd LMil SExb SLeo
– 'Loderi Pretty Polly' SLeo
– 'Loderi Princess Marina' SLeo
– 'Loderi Sir Edmund' LHyd SLeo
– 'Loderi Sir Joseph Hooker' LHyd SLeo
– 'Loderi Titan' SReu
§– 'Loderi Venus' CWal IOrc LHyd LKna LMil MLea SExb SHil SLeo SPer SReu SSta
– 'Loderi White Diamond' CBow CWal LHyd SLeo
– 'Loder's White' CBow CWal IHos LHyd LKna LMil MBlu MLea SCog SExb SHil SLeo SPer SReu SSta
§– 'Logan Damaris' CWal LHyd SHil SLeo SReu
– 'Loki' SLeo
– 'Lord Roberts' CB&S CBow CHig CSam CWal ELan GRei IOrc LKna LMil MBal MBar MBri MGos MMor MR&S NBar NHol SExb SHil SLeo SPer SSta
– 'Lord Swaythling' LHyd
– 'Lori Eichelser' CSam NHol

Hybrid 'Louis Pasteur'	SReu SSta
– 'Lovely William'	CSam LHyd LMil MBal
– ***lowndesii*** x Yaku Fairy	SSta
– 'Lucy Lockhart'	CTre
¶ – ***ludlowii*** x ***mekongense*** Viridescens group	NHol
– 'Lunar Queen'	CWal LHyd
– Luscombei	LHyd SLeo
¶ – 'Madame Albert Moser'	LKna
– 'Madame de Bruin'	CWal LKna MBal SExb SLeo SReu
– 'Madame Fr V Chauvin'	ISea
– 'Madame Masson'	CHig MBar MLea NHol SLeo SPer SReu SSta
– 'Madison Snow'	LRHS SSta
– 'Maestro'	CWal
– Mai	CWal
¶ – 'Manda Sue'	LMil MLea
– Mandalay	CWal LHyd LMil LSav MBri SExb SLeo
– 'March Sun'	SLeo
– 'Marchioness of Lansdowne'	CBow MGos
– 'Marcia'	LMil SHil SLeo
– Margaret Dunn (g.&cl.)	CWal SLeo
– 'Margaret Falmouth'	LHyd
– Marie Antoinette	CWal LMil
– Mariloo	CWal SExb SLeo
– 'Mariner'	LHyd
– 'Marinus Koster'	CWal LKna MBri MMor NBar SHil
– 'Marion Street'	CWal LHyd LMil SCog SLeo SReu
– 'Markeeta's Prize'	ISea LMil MBri
– 'Mars'	SReu
– Marshall	CWal
– 'Mary Fleming'	LHyd MBlu MBri MLea SReu SSta
– 'Mary Forte'	SExb SLeo
*– 'Master Mariner'	LHyd
– Matador (g.&cl.)	CBow CWal LHyd LMil NKay SCog SExb SSpi WBod
– May Day (g.&cl.)	Widely available
*– 'May Glow'	MGos
– Medea	CWal
– Medusa	CWal NHol SReu
– 'Merganser'	GEdr NHol SReu
– Merops	CWal
– 'Michael Waterer'	CWal ELan SExb SLeo
– 'Michael's Pride'	CB&S CWal
– 'Midsummer'	SLeo
– 'Minterne Cinnkeys'	MBal
– 'Moerheim'	CBow CSco CWal EBre GAbr IJoh LSav MBal MBar MMor MRav NBar NHol NKay NRoo SHil SIng SReu SSta
§ – 'Moerheim's Pink'	ELan LHyd LKna LMil MBri WThu
¶ – 'Moerheim's Scarlet'	LKna
– Mohamet (g.&cl.)	CWal LMil MLea SExb
¶ – 'Molly Ann'	LMil MLea SReu
– 'Molly Buckley'	SExb
– 'Molly Miller'	SReu
– 'Monica'	SCog SReu
– 'Monica Wellington'	LHyd
– 'Montreal'	SExb
¶ – Moonbeam	LKna
– Moonshine (g.&cl.)	LHyd
– 'Moonshine Bright'	LHyd SLeo SReu
– 'Moonshine Crescent'	LHyd SLeo SReu
¶ – 'Moonshine Supreme'	LKna
– Moonstone	CHig CWal GArd MBal MBar MLea MPlt SCog SExb SHil SLeo WBod
– 'Moonstone Pink'	CWal SExb
– 'Moonstone Yellow'	SExb
– 'Moonwax'	LMil
– 'Morgenrot' ('Morning Red')	MBri MGos MLea SHil SReu
– 'Morning Cloud'	CWal LHyd LMil MBri SLeo SReu WWeb
– 'Morning Magic'	CWal LHyd SCog SLeo
– 'Mortimer'	LHyd
– 'Morvah'	SLeo
– 'Mosaique'	SExb
– 'Moser's Maroon'	CBow LKna MGos SExb SLeo
¶ – 'Moser's Strawberry'	LKna
– 'Mother of Pearl'	CBow CWal LKna SCog SPer SReu
*– 'Mother Theresa'	LKna
– 'Mount Everest'	LHyd LKna SExb SHil SReu SSta
– 'Mountain Dew'	SReu
– 'Mountain Star'	SLeo
– 'Mrs A M Williams'	SHil
– 'Mrs A T de la Mare'	IDai IOrc LHyd LKna MBri MMor SLeo SPer SReu SSta
– 'Mrs Anthony Waterer'	LKna SSta
– 'Mrs Ashley Slocock'	SReu
– 'Mrs Betty Robertson'	MBri MLea SReu
– 'Mrs C B van Nes'	SPer SReu
– Mrs C Whitner	SLeo
– 'Mrs Charles E Pearson'	CB&S CBow CWal LHyd LKna LMil MLea MR&S SCog SHil SLeo SReu
– 'Mrs Davies Evans'	LHyd LKna MBar MMor SReu SSta
– 'Mrs Donald Graham'	SReu
– 'Mrs E C Stirling'	CBow GArd LKna SExb
– 'Mrs Furnival'	LKna LMil MBri MGos SExb SLeo SReu
– 'Mrs G W Leak'	CSam CWal LHyd LKna LMil MBri MLea MMor SCog SExb SHil SLeo SPer SReu SSta
– 'Mrs Henry Agnew'	SLeo
– 'Mrs J C Williams'	LKna LMil SLeo
– 'Mrs J G Millais'	LKna LMil SLeo
– 'Mrs James Horlick'	CWal SLeo
– 'Mrs John Kelk'	CWal
– 'Mrs Kingsmill'	CWal SLeo
¶ – 'Mrs Lindsay Smith'	LKna
– Mrs Lionel de Rothschild (g.&cl.)	CBow CWal ELan LKna LMil SExb SReu

Plant	Suppliers
Hybrid 'Mrs P D Williams'	LKna SExb SReu
¶ – 'Mrs Philip Martineau'	LKna
– 'Mrs R S Holford'	CBow CWal LKna SExb SLeo
– 'Mrs T H Lowinsky'	CBow MBri SPer
– 'Mrs Tom H Lowinsky'	LKna LMil MGos SLeo SReu SSta WWeb
– 'Mrs W C Slocock'	CBow CWal LHyd LKna SLeo SPer SReu SSta
– 'Mrs William Agnew'	LKna SLeo
§ – 'Multiflorum'	SReu
– 'Muncaster Mist'	ISea LHyd LRHS SSpi SSta
– 'Muriel'	SLeo
– 'Myrtifolium'	CSco MBar SReu
– 'Mystic'	CWal
*– 'Nancor'	CB&S
– 'Nancy Evans'	LMil MLea SSpi
– Naomi (g.&cl.)	LHyd LKna LMil MLea SReu
– 'Naomi Astarte'	LKna SExb SLeo
– 'Naomi Exbury'	CWal LKna LMil SExb SHil SLeo
– 'Naomi Glow'	CWal LMil
– 'Naomi Pink Beauty'	MBlu SExb
– 'Naomi Stella Maris'	CWal LMil SHil
– Neda	WBod
– Neriihaem	SLeo
– 'Nero'	MBar
– 'New Comet'	LHyd SHil SLeo SReu
– 'New Moon'	CWal SLeo SReu
– 'Newcomb's Sweetheart'	LMil
– 'Night Sky'	SLeo
– 'Nightingale'	LMil SReu
– 'Nimbus'	LKna LMil SLeo
– Nimrod	SExb SLeo
§ – Nobleanum	ISea LHyd LKna LMil MMor SHil SLeo SSta WThu
– 'Nobleanum Album'	LHyd LKna LMil MBal SLeo SReu
– 'Nobleanum Coccineum'	ISea SExb SLeo SReu
– 'Nobleanum Lamellen'	CWal SLeo
– 'Nobleanum Venustum'	ISea LHyd LKna LMil SReu WBod
– Norman Shaw (g.&cl.)	LHyd
¶ – 'Normandy'	LMil
– 'Northern Star'	CWal SLeo
– 'Nova Zembla'	CSam IJoh ISea MBar MBlu MGos MR&S SExb SLeo SReu SSta
– 'Odee Wright'	CGre LMil MBlu MLea SExb SLeo SSpi SSta
– Oklahoma	SExb
– 'Old Copper'	LNet MBri MLea NHol
– 'Old Port'	CWal MBar SReu SSta
– Oldenburgh	CWal SLeo
– 'Olga'	LHyd LKna LMil SReu SSta
¶ – 'Olga Mezitt'	LHyd LMil
– 'Olive'	LHyd LKna LMil SLeo SReu
– 'Olive Judson'	SLeo SReu
¶ – 'Oliver Cromwell'	SReu
– Olympic Lady	CWal LHyd LMil MLea SLeo SSpi
– Omar	MBar MR&S NKay
¶ – 'One Thousand Butterflies'	LMil
¶ – 'Ooh Gina'	SReu
– ***orbiculare*** × ***decorum***	CWal
– Oregonia	SExb
– Oreocinn	MBal
– 'Organdie'	SExb
– 'Osmar'	MBri MGos
– 'Oudijk's Favorite'	MBar MBri MGos SExb
– 'Oudijk's Sensation'	CBow CSco CWal IDai LKna MGos MLea MMor MR&S
– Oxlip	SExb SLeo
– P J M	CSam ISea MBri MLea SExb SSta
– 'P J Mezitt'	See R. H. 'Peter John Mezitt'
– 'Palma'	See R. ***parmulatum*** 'Palma'
– 'Pamela-Louise'	LHyd
¶ – 'Paprika Spiced'	LMil MBlu MLea MRav
– 'Parisienne'	SCog SExb
– 'Patricia's Day'	SReu
– 'Patty Bee'	LHyd LMil MBlu MBri MLea MRav NHar NHol SReu SSpi SSta
¶ – 'Paul Vossberg'	LMil
– 'Peace'	CWal GArd LHyd MBal SLeo WBod
– 'Pearl Diver'	LHyd
– 'Peeping Tom'	LMil SLeo
– 'Pematit Oxford'	SReu SSta
– Penelope	SReu
– 'Penheale Blue'	CB&S CBow CTre CWal ISea LMil MBri SLeo WBod WWeb
– Penjerrick (g.&cl.)	SCog
– 'Penjerrick Cream'	CWal SHil SLeo
– 'Penjerrick Pink'	CWal SLeo
– 'Penrose'	CB&S
– 'Percy Wiseman'	Widely available
§ – 'Persimmon'	CWal LKna SExb SLeo
– 'Peter John Mezitt'	LHyd LMil LSav SExb SLeo WThu
– 'Peter Koster'	CB&S IJoh SExb SLeo
– 'Phalarope'	CSam CWal GAbr GArd GEdr GRei LHyd LMil MBal MBar MBlu MBri MGos NHol NKay SReu SSpi WBod
– 'Pheasant Tail'	SCog SLeo
– 'Phyllis Korn'	LMil MLea
¶ – Pilgrim (g.&cl.)	LKna
– 'Pink Bee'	LRHS
– 'Pink Bountiful'	LKna WAbe
– 'Pink Cherub'	CMHG CWal ELan IHos MBar MBri NBar SCog SHil SLeo SReu WWeb
– 'Pink Drift'	Widely available
– 'Pink Frills'	CB&S
– 'Pink Ghost'	CWal SLeo
– 'Pink Gin'	LMil
– 'Pink Glory'	SLeo
§ – Pink Lady Rosebery	SReu
– 'Pink Pearl'	Widely available
– 'Pink Pebble'	CTrw CWal LHyd LSav SLeo SReu SSpi
– 'Pink Perfection'	MGos SExb SLeo

Hybrid 'Pink Petticoats' CBow MBlu
¶ – 'Pink Rosette' LKna
– 'Pink Sensation' MBri
– 'Pinkerton' LKna
– 'Pipaluk' CWal LHyd LSav
– 'Pipit' EPot GArd MBal WAbe
– 'Piquante' CWal
¶ – 'Point Defiance' MLea
– Polar Bear (g.&cl.) COtt CWal LHyd LMil SHil SLeo SReu SSpi
– 'Polaris' MGos SHil
*– 'Polgrain' CB&S
*– 'Polycinn' SCog
– 'Ponticum' See R. ***ponticum***
– 'Pook' CWal LHyd LSav
– 'Popacatapetl' SReu
– Portia (g.&cl.) WBod
– 'Powder Puff' LMil
– 'Praecox' Widely available
– 'Prawn' LKna SReu
– Prelude (g.&cl.) CWal SExb
– 'President Roosevelt' CWal EGol GArd IHos IJoh IOrc LKna LNet MBal MGos MMor SExb SLeo SPer SReu SSta
¶ – 'Pretty Girl' LKna
¶ – 'Prima Donna' SReu
– 'Prince Camille de Rohan' LMil SExb
– 'Princess Alice' CB&S COtt ERea ISea LMil MBal WBod
– 'Princess Anne' Widely available
– 'Princess Elizabeth' SExb
– 'Princess Juliana' SExb
– 'Professor Hugo de Vries' LKna MGos SReu
– 'Professor J H Zaayer' CWal IDai MGos SExb SLeo
– 'Prostigiatum' CWal GDra LMil MGos
– Psyche See R. H. Wega
– 'Ptarmigan' CB&S CMHG CTrw CWal EPot GArd GEdr LHyd LMil MBal MBar MBri MGos MLea MMor MPlt NHol SExb SHil SLeo SPer SReu SSta WBod
– 'Puget Sound' SLeo
*– 'Purple Carpeter' SReu SSta
– 'Purple Emperor' LKna SExb
– 'Purple Gem' ISea SReu SSta
– 'Purple Splendour' Widely available
*– 'Purple Split' ISea
– Quaver SExb
– 'Queen Alice' LMil SPer
– 'Queen Anne's' LRHS SSpi SSta
– 'Queen Elizabeth II' CWal LHyd LMil SHil SPer SReu SSta
– 'Queen Mary' MBar MMor
– 'Queen Mother' See R. H. 'The Queen Mother'
– Queen of Hearts (g.&cl.) CWal LHyd SExb SLeo
– 'Queen Souriya' SReu
– 'R W Rye' CTre
– 'Racil' LHyd LKna LSav MBal MBar MGos MLea MMor MPlt SExb SHil
– 'Radmosum' LSav SSta
¶ – 'Rainbow' LKna
– 'Ramapo' CBow EBre GArd ISea LMil LSav MBri MGos MLea NHar NHol SOkd SReu SSta WBod
¶ – 'Raspberry Ripple' LKna
– 'Razorbill' EPot GArd LHyd LMil MBri MGos NHol
– Red Admiral CWal SExb SLeo
– Red Argenteum SLeo
– Red Cap CWal
– 'Red Carpet' SSta
– 'Red Dragon' LHyd SLeo
– 'Red Glow' LHyd SLeo
– 'Red Poll' LHyd
– 'Red Riding Hood' CWal LKna SExb
– 'Red Velour' SSta
¶ – 'Red Walloper' MBlu
– Remo CWal LHyd MBal MR&S SLeo SReu
– Remus CWal
– 'Renoir' LHyd LMil SLeo SReu SSta
¶ – Repose (g.&cl.) LKna
– 'Reuthe's Purple' See R. ***lepidotum*** 'Reuthe's Purple'
– Rêve Rose (g.&cl.) SCog
– Review Order CWal LMil SSta
– 'Revlon' LHyd SReu
– ***rex*** x Sincerity SLeo
– Rickshaw SLeo
– 'Rijneveld' LRHS
– 'Ripe Corn' LHyd LKna SLeo SReu
– Riplet EPot NHar
– 'Robert Keir' CWal LHyd SLeo
§ – 'Roberte' CWal LHyd NKay SCog SExb
– 'Robin Redbreast' LHyd SLeo
– 'Rocket' MLea WWeb
– Romany Chai CWal LHyd LMil NKay SExb
– Romany Chal CWal LHyd SCog SHil SPer
– 'Romy' LMil SLeo
– 'Rosa Regen' LRHS
¶ – Rosalind (g.&cl.) ISea
– 'Rose Elf' NHar NHol
*– 'Rosebud' GEdr
– 'Roseum Elegans' IJoh MBar MR&S SLeo
– 'Rosevallon' CWal SLeo
– 'Rosy Bell' LKna
*– 'Rosy Lea' MLea
– 'Rothenburg' LHyd LMil SExb SLeo SReu WThu
– 'Royal Blood' LHyd
– Royal Flush CWal ISea MBlu
– Royal Flush pink form CWal
– Royal Flush yellow form CWal
¶ – 'Royal Pink' SHil
– 'Royal Purple' CTrw
– Royalty WBod
– 'Roza Stevenson' CWal LHyd LMil SHil SLeo SReu
– Rubicon LMil SReu WWeb
– Rubina CWal SLeo SSpi
– 'Ruby F Bowman' CSam CSco MGos MLea SExb SLeo SReu

	Hybrid 'Ruby Hart'	NHol SExb SReu SSta
	– Russautinii	LMil SHil
	– 'Sacko'	NHol
	– 'Saffron Queen'	CB&S CGre CTrw ISea MBal
	– 'Saint Breward'	CB&S CWal LHyd MLea SCog SExb SPer SReu WBod
	– 'Saint Keverne'	CWal
	– 'Saint Kew'	CWal
	– 'Saint Merryn'	CTrw CWal LHyd MBri NHol SLeo SPer SSpi WSHC
¶	– 'Saint Michael'	SReu
	– 'Saint Minver'	CWal LHyd MBri
	– 'Saint Tudy'	CB&S CWal LHyd LKna LSav MBar MMor MPlt SExb SHil SLeo SPer WAbe WBod
	– 'Saint Wenn'	CWal
§	– 'Salmon Trout'	CWal LHyd SHil SReu
	– 'Salute'	CSco
	– 'Sandling'	LHyd
	– 'Santa Claus'	CWal
	– Sapphire (g.&cl.)	CBow CMHG CWal EPot GAbr GArd GRei LKna LMil LSav MBal MBar MLea MPlt NHar NKay SHil SLeo SPer SReu WAbe WBod WThu
	– 'Sappho'	CB&S CSco CWal ELan IDai IHos IOrc ISea LHyd LKna LMil MBal MBar MGos MMor SCog SExb SHil SLeo SReu SSta
	– Sarita Loder (g.&cl.)	SLeo
	– Sarled	CMHG CSam CWal EPot GArd GDra GEdr LHyd LMil MBal MBri NHol SLeo SReu SSpi WWat
	– 'Scandinavia'	SExb
	– 'Scarlet Wonder'	Widely available
	– 'Scintillation'	CSam CSco LMil MLea SExb SSpi
	– Seagull (g.&cl.)	SLeo
	– 'Sea-Tac'	MLea
	– 'Second Honyemoon'	ISea MLea SSta
	– 'Sennocke'	CBow LMil LSav SReu SSta
*	– 'September Song'	LMil
	– 'Sesterianum'	CWal
	– Seta (g.&cl.)	CB&S CHig CTrw CWal LHyd MBal MLea MPlt NHol SExb SHil SLeo SReu WBod
	– 'Seven Stars'	CWal LHyd LMil MBri SCog SLeo SReu
*	– 'Sevenac'	LHyd
	– 'Seville'	CWal LHyd
	– 'Shamrock'	CSam ISea LMil LSav MBri NHar NHol SPer SSpi SSta
	– 'Sham's Candy'	CWal
	– Sheperd's Delight	CWal
	– Shilsonii	CWal LHyd WBod
	– 'Shrimp Girl'	CWal ELan IHos LHyd MBri MLea NHol SLeo SReu
	– 'Silberwolke' ('Silver Cloud')	SHil
*	– 'Silky'	MBal
	– 'Silver Jubilee'	LHyd
	– 'Silver Sixpence'	CB&S CBow CMHG CSam CSco CWal IHos ISea LMil MBal MBlu MBri MLea SCog SLeo SPic SReu SSta WWeb
*	– 'Simmon's Classic'	LMil
¶	– 'Simona'	LHyd
	– 'Sinbad'	SLeo
	– 'Sir Charles Lemon'	See R. ***arboreum*** 'Sir Charles Lemon'
	– Sir Frederick Moore (g.&cl.)	SCog SReu
*	– 'Sir G E Simpson'	SLeo
	– 'Sir George Sansom'	CWal
*	– 'Sir John Tremayne'	CWal
	– Siren (g.&cl.)	CWal MBal WBod
	– 'Sirius'	LHyd SReu
	– 'Skookum'	SPer
	– 'Sleepy'	CSam CWal ELan IHos MBri SCog SLeo SPer SReu
§	– Smithii group	CWal
	– 'Sneezy'	CB&S CWal EBre ELan GRei IHos ISea LHyd MBal MBlu MBri MGos NHol SCog SLeo SPer SReu SSta
	– 'Snipe'	CSam EPot GArd LHyd LMil MBri MGos NHol SSta
	– 'Snow Lady'	CBow GEdr MBal MBar MLea MPlt NKay WBod WThu
	– Snow Queen (g.&cl.)	GArd LKna MLea SHil SReu SSpi
	– 'Soldier Sam'	SReu SSta
	– Solent Queen	SHil
¶	– 'Solidarity'	WWeb
	– 'Sonata'	CWal MBal MBri NKay SReu SSta
	– 'Songbird'	CSam CWal GAbr GArd GDra GEdr LHyd LKna LMil MBal MBar MBri MLea MPlt NHol NKay SExb SPer SReu WBod
	– 'Songster'	SLeo
	– Souldis	CWal LMil
	– Soulking	WBod
	– 'Southern Cross'	LHyd
	– 'Souvenir de Doctor S Endtz'	CBow CWal LKna MBal MBar MMor NBar SReu SSta
	– 'Souvenir of Anthony Waterer'	LHyd LKna MBar MMor SReu SSta
	– 'Souvenir of W C Slocock'	LKna MR&S SLeo SReu SSta
	– 'Sparkler'	CMHG COtt CSam EBre ISea LMil MBlu MLea SReu WWeb
	– 'Spinulosum'	LHyd
	– 'Spitfire'	MMor SLeo SReu
*	– 'Spring Dream'	LHyd
	– 'Spring Magic'	LMil WThu
	– 'Spring Parade'	SExb
	– 'Spring Pearl'	See R. H. 'Moerheim's Pink'
*	– 'Spring Rose'	LSav
	– 'Springbok'	LHyd
*	– 'Springday'	CWal
	– 'Squirrel'	GEdr
	– Stadt Essen (g.&cl.)	LMil

Hybrid 'Stanley Rivlin'	CWal LHyd SCog SLeo
– 'Stanway'	LMil
– 'Starcross'	LHyd
– 'Starfish'	SReu
– 'Stella'	SLeo
¶ – 'Stephanie'	MBlu
– 'Strategist'	CWal
– 'Streatley'	CWal LSav SLeo SReu
*– 'Striped Beauty'	MBal SSta
¶ – 'Suede'	SReu
– 'Sugar Pink'	LMil
– 'Sunbeam'	LKna SReu
– 'Surrey Heath'	CB&S CMHG CSam CWal LHyd LMil LNet MBri MGos MLea SCog SHil SLeo SPer SPla SReu SSta
– 'Susan'	CTrw CWal LHyd LKna LMil MBri MMor SCog SLeo SReu
– 'Sussex Bonfire'	SLeo
– 'Swansdown'	LMil SReu
– 'Sweet Simplicity'	IJoh LKna
– 'Sweet Sixteen'	SLeo SSta
– 'Sweet Sue'	CWal SCog SLeo SReu
– Tally Ho (g.&cl.)	CB&S CWal SHil SLeo SReu
– 'Tan Crossing'	SReu
– Tasco	SExb
– 'Taurus'	LMil MLea WWeb
– 'Teal'	GArd ISea LMil NHol SPer
– Temple Belle	CSam CWal GArd ISea LHyd LKna LMil LSav MBal MBri MLea SCog SHil SLeo SReu WBod
– 'Tensing'	SReu
¶ – 'Tequila Sunrise'	LMil
*– 'Terra-Cotta'	LKna
– Tessa (g.&cl.)	LKna LMil MGos SExb
¶ – 'Tessa Bianca'	LMil
– Tessa pink form	LSav
– 'Tessa Roza'	EPot LHyd LMil MBri SOkd
§ – 'The Hon Jean Marie de Montague'	CSam CWal IDai LKna MBri MLea MMor NBar SLeo WWeb
¶ – 'The Lizzard'	LKna
– 'The Master'	CWal LHyd LKna SLeo SReu
§ – 'The Queen Mother'	CWal LHyd
– 'The Warrior'	SExb
– Thomdeton	CWal
– Thomwilliams	CWal LKna LMil MBal NHar
– Thor (g.&cl.)	MMor SLeo
– 'Thunderstorm'	LKna LRHS SReu SSta
– 'Tibet'	GArd MBar MR&S
– 'Tidbit'	LHyd LKna LMil MBal MGos MLea SLeo SSpi
– 'Tiger'	SReu
*– 'Tilford Seedling'	LKna
– 'Timothy James'	NHol SReu
– 'Titian Beauty'	CB&S CMHG COtt CSam CSco CWal ELan IHos LHyd LMil LNet MBri MGos MLea MMor NHol NKay SCog SLeo SPer SPic SReu SSta
– 'Tolkien'	SSta
¶ – 'Top Banana'	MLea
*– 'Top Bonanza'	LMil
– 'Top Hat'	LMil MLea
– 'Topsvoort Pearl'	SReu
– 'Torch'	LKna SPer SReu
– 'Tortoiseshell Biscuit'	CWal
– 'Tortoiseshell Champagne'	See R. H. 'Champagne'
– 'Tortoiseshell Orange'	CWal LHyd LKna LMil MBri SCog SReu SSta
¶ – 'Tortoiseshell Pale Orange'	LKna
– 'Tortoiseshell Salome'	LHyd LKna LMil SLeo SSta
– 'Tortoiseshell Scarlet'	LKna SReu
– 'Tortoiseshell Wonder'	CWal LHyd LKna LMil MGos SLeo SReu SSta
– 'Tottenham'	MGos
– 'Tow Head'	LMil
– Treasure	CWal GArd GDra MBal NHar SLeo
– 'Trebah Gem'	CWal SLeo
– 'Tregedna'	SLeo
– 'Tretawn'	CWal SLeo
– 'Trewithen Orange'	CB&S CBow CSam CTrw CWal LHyd LMil MBal MBlu NHol SCog SLeo SPer WAbe
*– 'Trewithen Purple'	CTrw CWal
– 'Trianon'	SExb
– 'Trilby'	LMil SLeo SReu
– 'Trude Webster'	CSam LMil MLea SLeo SSta
¶ – 'Tulyar'	LKna
– 'Turkish Delight'	MLea
– 'Twilight Pink'	MBlu MLea
– 'Tyermannii'	CWal SLeo
– Ungerio	SLeo
– 'Unique'	CB&S CSam CSco CWal GArd ISea LHyd LKna LMil LNet MBri MLea MMor NKay SExb SHil SLeo SPer SReu SSta WThu
– 'Unknown Warrior'	CWal MMor SExb SReu
*– 'V M H'	CWal
¶ – 'Van'	MLea
¶ – 'Van Nes Sensation'	LMil
– 'Van Weerden Poelman'	MR&S SSta
– Vanessa (g.&cl.)	CWal GArd LHyd LMil SCog SHil SReu WBod
– 'Vanessa Pastel'	CBow CGre CHig CWal LHyd LMil LSav MBal SCog SHil SLeo SReu WBod
– Vanguard	ISea
¶ – 'Vanilla'	LKna
– Varna	WBod
¶ – 'Veesprite'	LSav
– Vega	WBod
– 'Veldtstar'	LHyd
– 'Vellum'	SExb
¶ – 'Venapens'	LSav
– 'Venetian Chimes'	CMHG CWal ELan IHos ISea LMil MBri MLea SCog SLeo SPer SReu SSta WWeb
– 'Veryan Bay'	CB&S LMil LSav
– 'Victoria de Rothschild'	SExb
– 'Vincent van Gogh'	MBlu MLea
– 'Vinestar'	LHyd

Hybrid 'Vintage Rose'	CBow CWal ELan LMil MBri MLea SCog SLeo SReu
– Virginia Richards (g.&cl.)	LHyd LMil MBal MBri MLea SExb SHil SLeo SReu SSta
– 'Viscy'	LHyd LRHS
– Volker	See R. H. Flava
¶ – 'Voodoo'	MBlu
– 'Vulcan'	CB&S CSco LMil MLea SHil SSta
¶ – 'Vulcan's Flame'	MBlu
– W F H	LMil SCog SHil SLeo SSpi
– Walloper	SLeo SReu
– 'Wally Miller'	SSta
¶ – 'Wantage'	LSav
– 'Waterfall'	MBal
¶ – 'Wee Bee'	LMil
– Wega	CWal GArd LHyd LKna
– 'Wellesleyanum'	SLeo
– 'Werei'	SLeo
– 'Weybridge'	SLeo
– 'Whisperingrose'	CSam LMil NHol
– White Glory (g.&cl.)	SLeo
¶ – 'White Olympic Lady'	LKna
– 'White Swan'	CBow LKna LMil MBlu SReu
– 'White Wings'	SLeo
– 'Whitney's Dwarf Red'	SLeo
– 'Wigeon'	LMil LRHS NHol SPer
– 'Wild Affair'	LRHS
– 'Wilgen's Ruby'	CSam CWal IJoh LKna LMil MBri MGos MMor MR&S NBar SExb SPer SSta WWeb
– 'Willbrit'	LHyd MBri SCog
– Wilsonii	CWal
– 'Windlesham Scarlet'	LHyd LMil SPer
– 'Windsor Hawk'	CFor
¶ – 'Windsor Lad'	LKna SReu
– Winsome (g.&cl.)	CB&S CHig CSam CTrw CWal GArd IOrc LHyd LKna LMil LSav MBal MBar MMor NHol SCog SHil SLeo SPer SSta WBod
– 'Wishmoor'	CWal LHyd LMil SCog SLeo
– 'Witch Doctor'	LRHS MBlu MBri
¶ – 'Wonderland'	LKna
– 'Woodcock'	LHyd SPer WBod
– 'Woodside'	CWal SLeo
¶ – 'Wren'	CSam MBri WWeb
– 'Xenophile'	CWal
§ – 'Yaku Fairy'	CWal EPot LMil MBal NHar NHol SSta
– 'Yaku Prince'	MBri
– 'Yaku Princess'	MBri MLea SLeo SPer SReu WWeb
– 'Yaku Queen'	MBri SLeo SReu
– ***yakushimanum* x *decorum***	GArd MMor SReu
* – 'Yellow By Trailer'	MLea
– Yellow Hammer	Widely available
– 'Yellow Petticoats'	IJoh LMil MBri SLeo SSpi
– 'Youthful Sin'	CWal GArd ISea WBod
– Yuncinn	CWal
– Yvonne	CWal
– 'Yvonne Dawn'	SLeo

– Zelia Plumecocq (g.&cl.)	SExb
– Zuiderzee	CBow SLeo SReu
hylaeum	SExb
– KW 6833	SLeo
hypenanthum	See R. ***anthopogon hypenanthum***
hyperythrum	CWal LHyd LMil SExb SLeo
hypoglaucum	See R. ***argyrophyllum hypoglaucum***
– 'Heane Wood'	See R. ***argyrophyllum*** 'H.W.'
imberbe	SLeo
impeditum	Widely available
– F 20454	LSav
§ – 'Blue Steel'	COtt ELan LMil LSav SLeo SReu WAbe
– compact form	LKna LSav
– 'Drake's Hybrid'	EPot NHar
¶ – 'Harry White's Purple'	WThu
– 'Indigo'	CMHG LMil WThu
¶ – 'Johnston's Impeditum'	LKna
– Litangense group	GK&P
– 'Moerheim'	CSam MBri NKay WAbe
– 'Pygmaeum'	GArd GLoc SOkd WAbe
¶ – Reuthe's form	SReu
– 'Russell's Blue'	SOkd SReu
imperator	See R. ***uniflorum imperator***
§ ***indicum***	CWal LHyd MBal SPic
§ – 'Balsaminiflorum'	CMac SReu WAbe WBod
– ***eriocarpum*** 'Gumpo'	See R. Azalea 'Gumpo'
inopinum	SLeo
insigne	CWal IOrc LMil MGos SExb SLeo SSpi SSta
¶ – Reuthe's form	SReu
intricatum	GK&P
– KW 4184	SLeo
irroratum	CWal LHyd LMil SExb SLeo
– 'Polka Dot'	SExb SLeo
iteaphyllum	See R. ***formosum formosum*** Iteaphyllum group
japonicum	LHyd
– ***japonicum***	See R. ***degronianum heptamerum***
– ***pentamerum***	See R. ***degronianum degronianum***
johnstoneanum	CB&S CGre CWal GK&P LMil SExb SLeo
– doubled flowered form	CGre CWal MBal
– 'Rubrotinctum' KW 7723	SLeo
kaempferi	LHyd LMil WBod
– 'Damio'	LMil
¶ – 'Eastern Fire'	LSav
– 'Firefly'	See R. Azalea 'Hexe'
– 'Mikado'	SHil
keiskei	CHig CWal GK&P LMil LSav MBal NHol SExb SHil SSta
¶ – Windsor Great Park form	SReu
keleticum	See R. ***calostrotum keleticum***

§ *kendrickii*	CWal
¶ *kesangiae*	LMil
keysii	CB&S CWal LHyd LMil SExb SLeo
– KR 954	LSav
– 'Unicolor'	SLeo
§ *kiusianum*	CWal GK&P LHyd SLeo SReu
– 'Album'	LHyd LMil LSav SOkd SReu SSta
– 'Benichidori'	LMil
– 'Hillier's Pink'	LMil
– 'Mountain Gem'	LSav SSta
– 'Mountain Pride'	LSav SReu
– 'Tenshi'	LSav
– 'Troll'	LSav
kotschyi	See R. ***myrtifolium***
kyawii	SLeo
lacteum	CWal LMil SLeo
– forms	SLeo
lanatum	CWal LHyd LMil SLeo
– Cooper 2148	SLeo
– DF 538	MBal
¶ – Flinkii group EGM 083/090	LMil
lanigerum	CWal SLeo
– 'Chapel Wood'	CWal
– pink form	SLeo
– 'Round Wood'	LHyd
§ *latoucheae*	MBal SLeo
laudandum temoense	CWal
ledifolium 'Bulstrode'	See R. Azalea 'Bulstrode'
– 'Magnificum'	See R. Azalea 'Magnificum'
– 'Ripense'	See R. ***ripense***
lepidostylum	CB&S CHig CWal EPot GAbr GArd GK&P LHyd LMil MBar MBri NBar SExb SLeo SMad SPla SReu SSta WAbe WBod WThu
lepidotum	CGre CMHG CWal EPot GArf GEdr GK&P LHyd LMil SLeo
– AGS/ES 637	NHol
– BLM 279	MBal
– Sch 2251	LSav
§ – 'Reuthe's Purple'	LSav MBal SLeo SPer SReu SSta
leptothrium	CWal LMil SLeo
leucaspis	CBow CHig CWal EPot ERea IOrc LHyd MBal SExb SIng SReu SSta
– KW 7171	SLeo
liliiflorum Guiz 163	LSav
lindleyi	CB&S CWal LMil SLeo
litiense	See R. ***wardii wardii*** Litiense group
loderi	See R. Hybrid 'Loderi'
longesquamatum	CWal LMil SLeo
lopsangianum	See R. ***thomsonii l.***
lowndesii x *keiskei* 'Yaku Fairy'	See R. Hybrid 'Yaku Fairy'
lukiangense	SLeo
§ – R 11275*	SLeo
luteiflorum	CWal LMil SLeo WBod
– KW 21040	LSav SExb
lutescens	CB&S CHig CTre CWal GArd IBlr IOrc ISea LMil LSav MBal MBri NBar SCog SExb SHil SPer SReu SSpi SSta WAbe WBod WWat
– 'Bagshot Sands'	CBow CWal LHyd
– 'Exbury'	CWal SReu
– pink form	CWal
§ *luteum*	CB&S CCla CSam CTre CWal GDra ISea LKna LMil LSav MBar MBri MGos SExb SHil SLeo SMad SReu SSta WBod WWat
lyi	See R. ***ciliicalyx l.***
lysolepis	GK&P
¶ – 'Woodland Purple'	NHol
macabeanum	CB&S CWal LHyd LMil MBal SHil SLeo SReu SSpi SSta
– KW 7724	SLeo
¶ – Reuthe's form	SReu
macranthum	See R. ***indicum***
macrophyllum	GK&P
macrosepalum 'Linearifolium'	CMac CWal SLeo SMad WBod
§ *macrosmithii*	CWal SLeo
§ *maculiferum anwheiense*	CWal LHyd SLeo
maddenii	CWal GArd SLeo
§ – *crassum*	CTrw CWal GK&P LMil MBal
§ – *maddenii*	CWal SLeo
– pink form	CWal
§ *maddenii crassum* Obtusifolium group	CWal
§ *maddenii maddenii* Polyandrum group	CWal ISea
magnificum	LMil SLeo
makinoi	CHig CWal LHyd LMil MBri NHol SLeo SReu SSta
– x *bureaui*	LRHS
mallotum	CWal LMil SLeo SReu
manipurense	See R. ***maddenii crassum*** Obtusifolium group
martinianum	SLeo
maximum	SLeo
meddianum	CWal SLeo
– *atrokermesinum*	CWal SLeo
– *atrokermesinum* F 26476	SLeo
megacalyx	CWal LMil SLeo
megaphyllum	See R. ***basilicum***
megeratum	CB&S CWal SReu WAbe WBod
§ *mekongense melinanthum*	CWal SLeo
– *rubrolineatum*	LMil SLeo
– *Viridescens group* 'Doshang La'	LMil
– 'Yellow Fellow'	LMil
mekongense mekongense Rubroluteum group	GK&P LMil
§ – – Viridescens group	GArd LMil MBal

– – Viridescens group KW 5829	CWal SLeo
melinanthum	See R. ***mekongense melinanthum***
metternichii	See R. ***degronianum heptamerum***
micranthum	CWal
– Wilson V 1218	SLeo
microgynum	SLeo
– F 14242	SLeo
– Gymnocarpum group	CWal LMil
micromeres C&H 420	SLeo
mimetes	SLeo
minus	CWal LHyd
– chapmanii	LHyd
§ ***minus minus*** Carolinianum group	CWal LHyd
§ – – Punctatum group	GRei MBar
mollicomum F 30940	SLeo
monosematum W V1522	CWal SLeo
montroseanum	LMil SLeo
morii	CWal LHyd SExb SLeo
– Wilson A 10955	SLeo
§ ***moulmainense***	CWal SLeo
moupinense	CB&S CHig CWal ERea GK&P LHyd LSav SCog SLeo SPer SReu
– pink	SHil SReu
¶ – white form	LSav
mucronatum	See R. Azalea 'Mucronatum'
mucronulatum	CB&S CSto CTre LHyd LMil LSav SHil SLeo SSpi WBod
– Cheju Island form	CWal
– 'Dwarf Cheju'	CFor SSta
– Reuthe's form	SReu
– 'Winter Brightness'	CWal
§ x ***myrtifolium***	COtt LHyd SLeo SPla SSta
nakaharae	CWal MBal SCog SLeo SReu WAbe
§ – 'Mariko'	CWal EPot GEdr LHyd LMil MGos WAbe WPat WThu
– 'Mount Seven Stars'	LHyd LMil SSta WPat
§ – orange form	LMil SCog SPer SReu SSta
– pink	LHyd SCog SSta
– Starborough form	SSta
neriiflorum	CWal ISea SCog SExb SLeo
§ ***neriiflorum neriiflorum*** Euchaites group	SLeo
– – Euchaites group KW 6854	CWal
– – 'Lamellen'	CWal
neriiflorum phaedropum C&H 422	SLeo
– – KW 6845*	SLeo
– – KW 8521	SLeo
– – LS&T 6563	LSav
nigropunctatum	See R. ***nivale*** Nigropunctatum group
nitens	See R. ***calostrotum riparium*** Nitens group
nitidulum omeiense KR 185	LMil LSav

nivale	SLeo
§ ***nivale boreale*** Nigropunctatum group	LMil SIng
§ – – Stictophyllum group	LMil
niveum	CWal LMil SLeo SSta
– 'Clyne Castle'	SHil
– 'Nepal'	LHyd
nobleanum	See R. Hybrid Nobleanum
nudiflorum	See R. ***periclymenoides***
¶ ***nuttallii***	LMil
¶ ***oblongifolium***	LSav
obtusum	CHig CWal LHyd
– 'Macrostemon'	GEdr WBod
occidentale	LMil NHol
oldhamii	CTre CWal SLeo
oleifolium 'Penheale Pink'	See R. ***virgatum o.*** 'P.P.'
orbiculare	CWal LHyd LMil LSav SCog SHil SLeo SReu SSta
– W V 1519	SLeo
¶ – Sandling Park form	SReu
oreodoxa	CBow CWal LMil SLeo
– fargesii	CWal IOrc LHyd SExb SHil SLeo
§ ***oreodoxa fargesii*** Erubescens group	CWal SLeo
oreotrephes	CWal IOrc LMil MBal SExb SHil SIng SLeo SReu WBod
– McL P 69	LSav
¶ – Exquisetum group	SReu
¶ – Timeteum group	SReu
orthocladum	CHig CWal LHyd LMil
– F 20488	SLeo
– microleucum	CWal MBal SLeo
ovatum	CB&S CWal SExb SLeo WBod
– W A 1391	SLeo
§ ***pachypodum***	CTre LMil
pachysanthum RV 72/001	CWal LMil SLeo
pachytrichum	SLeo
panteumorphum	See R. x ***erythrocalyx*** Panteumorphum group
paradoxum	SLeo
parmulatum	CWal LMil NHol SLeo
– KW 5875	LSav NHol
– mauve form	CWal
– 'Ocelot'	CWal
parryae	CTre
patulum	See R. ***pemakoense*** Patulum group
pemakoense	CSam CWal EPot GArd GEdr GK&P LHyd LMil MBal MBar MGos NHar NKay SExb SHil SIng SLeo SReu WAbe WBod WThu
§ – Patulum group	GEdr GK&P MBar MLea MPlt
pennivenium	See R. ***tanastylum p***
pentaphyllum	CWal SSta
peregrinum	SLeo
– 'Wilson'	CWal
§ ***periclymenoides***	LMil LSav SHil
phaeochrysum	CWal SLeo
§ ***– levistratum***	CWal

– McLaren cup winner	SLeo
pholidotum	See R. ***heliolepis brevistylum*** Pholidotum group
§ ***piercei***	GK&P LMil SLeo
– KW 11040	SLeo
planetum	SLeo
pocophorum	CWal SLeo
– forms	SLeo
– ***hemidartum***	SLeo
polyandrum	See R. ***maddenii maddenii*** Polyandrum group
§ ***polycladum***	CSam EPot GArd LHyd LKna LMil MBal MLea MMor
– Compactum group	GK&P
– Scintillans group	CMHG GDra MBar MBri MLea NHar NHol SHil SLeo WAbe WThu
polylepis	SLeo
ponticum	CKin CWal IDai ISea LHyd MBar MBri MMor SExb SHil SPer SPla
– (Azalea)	See R. ***luteum***
– 'Cheiranthifolium'	CWal SLeo
¶ – 'Gilt Edge'	SReu
– 'Variegatum'	CB&S CHig CWal IOrc ISea MBal MBar MBri MMor SExb SHil SPer SPla SReu SSta WThu
poukhanense	See R. ***yedoense p.***
praestans	CWal LMil SLeo
praevernum	CWal SReu
preptum	CWal SLeo
– F 25064	SLeo
primuliflorum	CWal LMil
principis	LMil
– Vellereum group	CWal SLeo
§ ***prinophyllum***	LMil LSav
prostratum	See R. ***saluenense chameunum*** Prostratum group
proteoides	SReu
protistum	SLeo
– ***giganteum***	CWal LMil SLeo
pruniflorum	CWal LMil SLeo
¶ ***prunifolium***	LSav
przewalskii	LMil MBri SLeo
– Cox 2545	NHol
pseudochrysanthum	CFor CWal LHyd LMil MBal SCog SExb SLeo SSta
– AM 1956 Form	CWal SSpi
pubescens	CWal SLeo
¶ – 'Fine Bristles'	SReu
pumilum	EPot GArd GDra MBal
punctatum	See R. ***minus minus*** Punctatum group
quinquefolium	CGre CWal SHil SLeo SSpi SSta
racemosum	CB&S CWal EPot LMil MBar SExb SIng SLeo SPer SPla SSpi SSta
¶ – F 21321	LSav
– Forrest's dwarf form	MBar NBar SHil SReu
– 'Glendoick'	NHol
– 'Rock Rose'	LHyd SExb
– x ***tephropeplum***	GArd MBal MBar MLea MPlt
¶ – x ***trichocladum*** SBEC	NHol
radicans	See R. ***calostrotum keleticum*** Radicans group
ramsdenianum	CWal SLeo
ravum	See R. ***cuneatum*** Ravum group
recurvoides	GK&P LHyd LMil SReu SSta
– KW 7184	CWal SLeo
reticulatum	CB&S CWal LSav SLeo SReu SSpi SSta
– 'Sea King'	LHyd
rex	CWal IOrc LHyd LMil MBal SLeo
§ ***rex arizelum***	LMil SLeo SSpi
– F 21861	CWal
– KW 20922	CWal
– 'Brodick'	CWal
– Rubicosum group	SLeo
§ ***rex fictolacteum***	CWal LHyd LMil MBal SHil SLeo SReu SSpi
– R/USDA 59104/R11043	SLeo
– 'Cherry Tip' R 11395	SLeo
rhabdotum	See R. ***dalhousieae rhabdotum***
rigidum	CWal GK&P LHyd LMil LSav SCog SLeo
– ***album***	CHig
ripense	GK&P
ririei	CWal
– W 5254A	CWal SLeo
roseum	See R. ***prinophyllum***
rothschildii	SLeo
roxieanum	CWal SExb SLeo SReu
– R 25422	SLeo
– R/USDA 59159/R11141	SLeo
– ***cucullatum*** SBEC 0345	SLeo
¶ ***roxieanum roxieanum*** Oreanastes group Nyman's form	SReu
– – Oreonastes group	CWal LHyd LMil SHil SLeo SSta
rubiginosum	CKin CWal IOrc ISea LHyd LMil MBal SLeo SReu SSta
§ – Desquamatum group	CFor CWal SExb SLeo
rubroluteum	See R. ***mekongense m.*** Rubroluteum group
rude	See R. ***glischrum rude***
rufum	CWal SLeo
– W V 1808 *	SLeo
rupicola	CWal GArd GDra LMil MBal SLeo
– ***chryseum***	LMil SLeo
– ***muliense***	LMil
russatum	CSam CWal EPot GArd GEdr GK&P LHyd LMil MBri MPlt SExb SHil SLeo
– R 11284	NHol
¶ – ***album***	SReu
– black violet form	GK&P
– 'Collingwood Ingram'	NHol SCog

– good form	LSav
saluenense	CWal LHyd LMil LSav MBal SExb SHil SLeo
– R 11238	LSav
saluenense chameunum	CHig CWal LMil MBal SLeo
§ – – Prostratum group	GEdr MBal NHol WBod
sanctum	SLeo
sanguineum	CWal GArd LMil SLeo
– R/USDA 59096/R 11029	SLeo
– ***chameunum***F 25560	NHol
– ***didymoides***R 10903	LMil SLeo
§ – ***didymum***	SLeo
¶ – ***didymum***R 18464	LSav
– ***melleum***R 10906	LMil
sanguineum aff. R/USDA 59553/R 11212	SLeo
sanguineum cloiophorum F 25521	LMil
– – R 10899	LSav SLeo
– – R 11052	LSav
sanguineum Consanguineum group	SLeo
– – KW 6831	LMil LSav
– – R 10900*	LSav
¶ ***sanguineum didymoides*** Roseotinctum group	LMil
sanguineum haemaleum	LMil SLeo
– – F 21735	SLeo
– – F 21732	SLeo
– – R 10893	SLeo
– – R/USDA 59453/R 10938	SLeo
– – ***haemaleum***R/USDA 59303/R 10895	SLeo
sargentianum	CWal GArd GEdr MLea SLeo SOkd
¶ – Leonardslee form	SReu
– 'Whitebait'	GArd
scabrifolium	SLeo
– ***spiciferum***	CWal LMil MBal SLeo
schlippenbachii	CB&S CFor CWal LHyd LMil MBri SHil SLeo SReu SSpi SSta WWat
scintillans	See R. ***polycladum***
scopulorum	SLeo
– Magor's hardy form	CWal
scottianum	See R. ***pachypodum***
searsiae	CWal SLeo
seinghkuense	MBal
selense	CWal
– ***dasycladum***	SLeo
selense selense Probum group	CWal
selense setiferum	CWal
– – F 14458	SLeo
semnoides	CWal SLeo
serotinum	CWal SLeo SReu
serpyllifolium	CB&S CWal SLeo SSta
¶ ***serrulatum***	LSav
setosum	GArd LMil MBal SLeo

shepherdii	See R. ***kendrickii***
sherriffii	CWal LHyd SLeo
– AM 1966 Form	CWal
shweliense	SReu
sidereum	CWal LMil SLeo
– KW 13649	SLeo
siderophyllum	SLeo
simiarum	CWal SLeo
simsii	CMac CWal
¶ – double form	LSav
sinogrande	CB&S CWal IOrc MBal SHil SLeo
– KW 21111	SLeo
smirnowii	CWal LHyd LMil MBal NHol SExb SLeo SReu SSta
smithii	See R. ***macrosmithii***
– Argipeplum group	See R. ***argipeplum***
souliei	CWal GArd IOrc LMil SHil SLeo
sperabile	CWal
– F 26446	SLeo
– F 26453	SLeo
– ***weihsiense***	SLeo
sphaeranthum	See R. ***trichostomum***
sphaeroblastum	CWal SLeo
– F 20416	SLeo
spilotum	SLeo
spinuliferum	CWal LHyd SExb SLeo
– 'Jack Hext'	CWal
stamineum W V 887	SLeo
stenaulum	See R. ***moulmainense***
stewartianum	CWal SLeo
stictophyllum	See R. ***nivale boreale*** Stictophyllum group
strigillosum	CWal SLeo
¶ – Reuthe's form	SReu
subansiriense C&H 418	CWal SLeo
succothii	CWal LHyd SLeo
– LS&H 21295	SLeo
sulfureum	CWal
– F 15782	SLeo
sutchuenense	CWal LMil SLeo
taggianum	CWal GK&P
taliense	CWal LHyd SLeo
– F 6772	SLeo
§ ***tanastylum pennivenium***	SLeo
tashiroi	CWal
tatsienense	LMil SLeo
telmateium F 15370	SLeo
telopeum	See R. ***campylocarpum caloxanthum*** Telopeum group
temenium R 10909	LSav SLeo
– ***gilvum*** 'Cruachan' R 22272	LMil SLeo
– ***temenium***F 21734	SLeo
temenium dealbatum Glaphyrum group F 21902	SLeo
tephropeplum	CWal LHyd SLeo
– KW 6303	SLeo
thayerianum	CWal
– W A 4273	SLeo
thomsonii	CWal LHyd LMil SHil SLeo

– BMW 153	MBal
– DF 540	MBal
– T 142	LSav
thomsonii	
lopsangianum	GK&P
– – LS&T 6561	CWal SLeo
tosaense 'Ralph Clarke'	SLeo
traillianum	CWal LMil SLeo
– F 5881 *	SLeo
trichanthum	CHig CWal IOrc LMil SLeo
– 'Honey Wood'	LHyd
trichocladum	CWal SLeo
§ ***trichostomum***	MLea SExb WBod
– deep form	SSta
– Ledoides group	CWal LMil SLeo SReu
– Radinum group	CWal SSta
triflorum	CTre CWal IOrc ISea LMil MBal SLeo WThu
– ***bauhiniiflorum***	CWal LMil SLeo
– Mahogani group	SLeo
tsangpoense	SExb
tsariense forms	SLeo
– 'Yum Yum'	CWal LHyd SLeo
N ***tubiforme***	CWal LHyd SCog SLeo SReu
ungernii	SLeo
uniflorum	CWal SReu WThu
– KW 5876	SLeo
§ – ***imperator***	GEdr
uvariifolium	CWal LMil SLeo
– 'Reginald Childs'	CWal
– 'Yangtze Bend'	CWal
valentinianum	CB&S CSam CWal GK&P MBal SLeo WBod
– F 24347	SLeo
vaseyi	LHyd LMil LSav MBal SHil
veitchianum Cubitii group	CWal SLeo
– Cubitii group 'Ashcombe'	CWal
venator	CWal GK&P SLeo
vernicosum	CWal LMil SLeo
– F 5881	SLeo
verruculosum	SLeo
vesiculiferum	SLeo
virgatum	CWal
– ***album***	MBal
– ***oleifolium*** KW 6279	SLeo
viridescens	See R. ***mekongense mekongense*** Viridescens group
viscosum	CB&S CWal LHyd LKna LMil SHil SPer SSpi
– ***aemulans***	LMil LSav SReu
– 'Antilope'	See R. Azalea 'Antilope'
– 'Arpege'	See R. Azalea 'A.'
– hybrids	LMil
– ***rhodanthus***	LMil LSav SReu
wallichii LS&H 17527	CWal SLeo
– McB	GArd
wardii	CWal IOrc LHyd LMil MBal MLea SHil SLeo
– L&S form *	CWal SLeo SReu
– ***puralbum***	CWal
§ ***wardii wardii*** Litiense group	CWal SLeo
wasonii	CWal
– ***rhododactylum***	LSav SLeo
– white form	SLeo
watsonii	SLeo
weyrichii	CWal
wightii	CWal LHyd SLeo
– BMW 153	MBal
– DF 542	MBal
¶ – KR 877	LMil
williamsianum	Widely available
– Caerhays form	CWal MPla
– 'Exbury White'	CFor
– white form	CTre CWal SLeo SSpi
– x ***martinianum***	CTre
wilsoniae	See R. ***latoucheae***
wiltonii	CWal LMil SLeo
wongii	CWal SExb SLeo SOkd
xanthostephanum	CWal
yakushimanum	CB&S CBow CSam GArd IOrc LKna LMil MBar MBri MMth SExb SHil SMad SPer SReu SSpi SSta
– Exbury form	SReu
– FCC form	CFor MUlv SReu
§ – 'Koichiro Wada'	CWal NHol SLeo
– ***makinoi***	See R. ***makinoi***
– Tremeer tall form	CWal
– x ***bureaui***	MLea SSpi
yungningense	CWal
yunnanense	CWal EHar GArd GK&P IOrc LHyd LMil SCog SHil SLeo SReu
¶ – R 25381	LSav
– 'Diana Colville'	CWal
– Hormophorum group	CWal GK&P
– 'Openwood'	LMil
– selected form	SReu
– 'Tower Court'	CWal
– white	SCog
¶ ***zaleucum*** F 24562	LSav
– F 27603	SLeo
– Flaviflorum group KW 20837	SLeo

RHODOHYPOXIS (Hypoxidaceae)

'Albrighton'	CBro CRiv ELan EPot GEdr LAma NHol NKay WAbe WChr
'Appleblossom'	SIng
baurii	CAvo CCla CRiv ELan EPad EPar EPot GLoc IDai MBro MHig NHar NHol NKay NRoo NTow WEas WHal WHil WWin
– 'Alba'	CBro CCla
– 'Dulcie'	SWas WAbe
¶ – 'Pinkeen'	WChr
– ***platypetala***	CRiv EPot NHol WAbe
¶ – 'Susan Garnett-Botfield'	CRiv WChr
'Dawn'	EPot GEdr LAma NHol SBla WAbe WChr
'Douglas'	CRiv EPot GEdr LAma NHol WChr WHil

'E A Bowles' WAbe
'Eva-Kate' LAma NHol SBla WChr
'Fred Broome' CBro CCla CMal CRiv ELan EPot GEdr LAma NHol SBla WAbe WChr WEas
'Garnett' NHol NKay WAbe
'Great Scott' WChr
'Harlequin' CBro ELan EPot GEdr LAma NHol WChr WHil
hybrids CKel ELan LBow SW&B
* 'Knockdolian Red' NHol
¶ *milloides* WChr
'Perle' EPot GEdr
'Picta' CRiv CSam EPot GEdr LAma NHol SBla WAbe WChr WHil
¶ 'Pink Pearl' EPot
'Ruth' GEdr LAma NHol SBla WAbe WChr
'Shell Pink' NKay SBla
'Stella' CRiv EPot GEdr WAbe WHil
'Tetra Pink' WAbe WChr
'Tetra Red' EPot NHol WAbe WChr
'Tetra White' EPot NHol WAbe

RHODOPHIALA See HIPPEASTRUM

RHODORA (Ericaceae)
canadensis See RHODODENDRON ***canadense***

RHODOTYPOS (Rosaceae)
kerrioides See R. ***scandens***
§ *scandens* CBot CMHG CPle EPla LSav MGos MPla NTow SHil SPla SSpi WBod WHea WWin

RHOEO See TRADESCANTIA

RHOICISSUS (Vitaceae)

RHOPALOBLASTE (Palmae)
ceramica LPal

RHOPALOSTYLIS (Palmae)
baueri LPal NPal
sapida CHEx LPal NPal

RHUBARB See RHEUM x *hybridum*

RHUS † (Anacardiaceae)
aromatica MSal WCoo
copallina CB&S CBow CKni CMHG LSav SHil SSpi WPat
cotinus See COTINUS ***coggygria***
glabra CCla IJoh MBlu SHil SSta
– 'Laciniata' CSco MBri MGos SHil WPat
N *hirta* CB&S CBra CLnd ELan ENot EPar GPoy IDai IJoh IOrc ISea MBar MBri MGos MR&S MWat NNor SHil SPer SSta WAbe WWin
– *laciniata* CB&S CBra CCla CLnd CSco ELan ENot GRei IJoh IOrc MBar MBri MR&S MWat NKay SHil SMad SPer SReu WAbe WPat
integrifolia CArn
potaninii WWat
punjabensis CB&S CMHG SSpi
¶ *radicans* GPoy
¶ *succedanea* CKni
toxicodendron See R. ***radicans***
trichocarpa CBow CKni CMHG ELan LSav SHil SSpi
¶ *trilobata* MSal
♦ *typhina* See R. ***hirta***
verniciflua CB&S CChu CCla LSav SSpi

RIBES † (Grossulariaceae)
alpinum CBow ELan ENot ESis GRei IOrc NWea SHil
– 'Aureum' CCla CMHG EFol ELan ISea LSav MHig MPar MPla MWat NNor SHil WSHC
americanum 'Variegatum' CHoe EFol ELan EPla LHop SDry WPat
atrosanguineum See R. ***sanguineum*** 'Atrorubens'
aureum See R. ***odoratum***
F x *culverwellii* Jostaberry EMui NTwe
F *divaricatum* Worcesterberry CMac EMui GChr IJoh MBri NBar NRog SDea WHig
¶ *fasciculatum chinense* EMon SSpi
gayanum LHop SHil SPla WThu
glandulosum CCor
x *gordonianum* CChu CCor CMHG CSco EHar ERav LHop MBal MCot MRav NTow SLon WWat WWeb
grossularia See R. ***uva-crispa***
henryi SHil
laurifolium CBot CBow CChu CCla CMHG CPle CSam ELan EPla ERav GWic IOrc LHop MBal MBri SAxl SChu SHil SMad SPer SSpi SSta WSHC WWat
menziesii LHop WWat
F *nigrum* 'Amos Black' SKee
F – 'Baldwin' CMac EWar GBon IJoh MBea SDea SKee SPer WWeb
F – 'Ben Lomond' CSam EHar EMui EWar GRei IJoh LBuc MBea MBri NBee NElm NRog NTwe SDea SKee SPer WHig WWeb
F – 'Ben More' GChr GRei LBuc MBri NBee NTwe SDea SKee SPer
F – 'Ben Nevis' GRei MBea NBar NElm NRog NTwe SDea SKee
F – 'Ben Sarek' CSam EMui GChr LBuc MBri NTwe SDea SKee WHig WWeb
*– 'Ben Tirran' CSut
F – 'Black Reward' SKee
F – 'Blackdown' SDea
F – 'Boskoop Giant' CMac EWar NBar NElm NRog
F – 'Green's Black' SKee
F – 'Jet' NTwe SDea SKee WHig

F – 'Laxton's Giant'	NTwe SDea
F – 'Malling Jet'	EHar NElm NRog SPer
F – 'Mendip Cross'	NRog
F – 'Seabrook's'	EWar WHig
F – 'Wellington XXX'	CSam EHar ESha EWar IJoh LBuc MBea MBri NBar NBee NRog NTwe SDea SKee SPer WWeb
F – 'Westwick Choice'	SKee
§ ***odoratum***	CB&S CBow CCor CPle CSam CSco ELan ENot ERav GRei LSav MBar MFir MGos MPla NWea SHil SLon SMad SPer SPla SSpi WWat
* ***praecox***	CB&S
F Red Currant group 'Jonkheer van Tets'	EMui GRei IJoh LBuc SDea SKee
F – – 'Laxton No 1'	CMac CSam EHar ESha GBon GChr MBea NBar NElm NRog SDea SKee SPer WHig
F – – 'Red Lake'	CMac EMui GRei LBuc MBea NBee NElm NRog SDea SKee SPer WHig
¶ – – 'Redstart'	EMui SDea SKee
F – – 'Rondom'	SDea
F – – 'Rovada'	EMui
F – – 'Stanza'	CSut SDea SKee
roezlii cruentum	SAxl
sanguineum	CPle CSam ISea LBuc MBal MBar MFir NNor WWin
– 'Albescens'	CBow CCla EHar LSav SPer
– 'Brocklebankii'	CCla CSco EGol EHar ENot EPar EPla LHop LSav MBar MBri MFir MGos NHol SHil SLon SMad SPer SPla WAbe WSHC WWat
¶ – ***glutinosum***	LSav
– ***glutinosum*** 'Albidum'	CGre CSco ERav LHop SChu WWat
– 'King Edward VII'	CHan CSco ECtt IJoh MBar MBri MGos MWat NNor NRoo NWea SHil SMad SPer SPla SReu WWeb
– 'Lombartsii'	CShe SLon
– 'Pulborough Scarlet'	CB&S CBow CSco CShe EFol ELan ENot MBri MGos MPla MRav MWat NKay SHil SPer SPla WAbe WWeb
– 'Pulborough Scarlet Variegated'	LHop MUlv SDry
– 'Red Pimpernel'	EBre
– ***roseum***	See R. *s.* 'Carneum'
– 'Splendens'	GRei IDai MGos SHil
– 'Tydeman's White'	CCla EBre ECtt MBar MBri SHil SSpi
speciosum	CB&S CBot CBrd CCla CPle ELan ENot EOrc EPar GWic ISea LHop MBal MFir MPla MWat SHil SPer WEas WKif WSHC WWin
F ***uva-crispa*** 'Achilles' (C/D)	ERou NTwe
F – 'Admiral Beattie'	NRog
F – 'Ajax'	ERou
F – 'Alma' (D)	ERou NRog
F – 'Angler'	ERou
F – 'Annelii'	SDea
F – 'Antagonist'	ERou
– 'Aston Red'	See R. ***u-c.*** 'Warrington'
F – 'Australia'	ERou NRog
F – 'Beauty'	ERou
F – 'Beauty Red' (D)	ERou
F – 'Bedford Red' (D)	NRog NTwe
F – 'Bedford Yellow' (D)	ERou NTwe
F – 'Beech Tree Nestling'	ERou NTwe
F – 'Belle de Meaux'	ERou
F – 'Bellona' (C)	ERou NRog
F – 'Berry's Early Giant' (C)	ERou
F – 'Black Seedling'	ERou
F – 'Black Velvet'	CMac MBea MBri SPer WWeb
F – 'Blucher'	ERou NRog
F – 'Bobby'	ERou
F – 'Bright Venus' (D)	ERou
F – 'British Oak' (D)	ERou
F – 'Broom Girl' (D)	ERou NRog NTwe
F – 'Brown's Red' (D)	ERou
F – 'Captivator'	ERou
F – 'Careless' (C)	CMac CSam EHar EMui ERou ESha EWar GRei IOrc MBea MBri NBar NBee NElm NRog NTwe SDea SKee SPer WWeb
F – 'Catherina'	ERou SDea
F – 'Champagne Red'	NTwe
F – 'Champion'	ERou
F – 'Clayton'	ERou NRog
F – 'Coiner'	ERou
F – 'Colossal'	ERou
F – 'Conquering Hero'	ERou
F – 'Cook's Eagle' (C)	ERou
F – 'Criterion' (C)	ERou NRog
F – 'Crown Bob' (C/D)	ERou NRog NTwe
F – 'Dan's Mistake' (D)	ERou NRog
F – 'Drill'	ERou NTwe
F – 'Early Green Hairy' (D)	ERou
F – 'Early Sulphur' (D)	ERou GRei IJoh NRog NTwe SDea SKee
F – 'Echo' (D)	ERou
F – 'Edith Cavell'	ERou
F – 'Emerald' (D)	ERou
F – 'Faithful' (C)	ERou
F – 'Fascination'	ERou
F – 'Firbob' (D)	ERou NRog
F – 'Forester' (D)	ERou
F – 'Forever Amber' (D)	ERou
F – 'Freedom' (C)	ERou NRog NTwe
F – 'Gautrey's Earliest'	ERou
F – 'Gem' (D)	ERou
F – 'Gipsey Queen'	ERou NTwe
F – 'Glencarse Muscat' (D)	ERou
F – 'Glenton Green'	ERou NTwe
F – 'Globe Yellow'	ERou
F – 'Golden Ball' (D)	ERou SDea
F – 'Golden Drop' (D)	ECtt ERou NTwe
F – 'Golden Lion'	ERou
– 'Green Gascoigne' (D)	See R. ***u-c.*** 'Early Green Hairy'
F – 'Green Gem' (C/D)	ERou NRog NTwe
F – 'Green Ocean'	ERou NRog NTwe

F– 'Green Overall' (C) ERou
F– 'Green Walnut' ERou
F– 'Greengage' (D) ERou NRog
F– 'Gretna Green' ERou
F– 'Grüne Flashen Beere' ERou
F– 'Grüne Kugel' (C) ERou
F– 'Grüne Reisen' (C) ERou
F– 'Guido' ERou NRog
F– 'Gunner' (D) ERou NRog
F– 'Guy's Seedling' (D) ERou
F– 'Hamamekii' SDea
F– 'Heart of Oak' ERou NRog NTwe
F– 'Hebburn Prolific' (D) ERou
F– 'Hedgehog' (D) ERou
F– 'Helgrüne Samtbeere' (C) ERou
F– 'Hero of the Nile' (C) ERou NRog NTwe
F– 'High Sheriff' (D) ERou
F– 'Highlander' (D) ERou
F– 'Höning Früheste' (D) ERou
F– 'Hot Gossip' ERou
F– 'Hough's Supreme' ERou
F– 'Howard's Lancer' (C/D) ERou NRog NTwe SDea SKee
F– 'Hue and Cry' (C) ERou
F– 'Improved Mistake' ERou
F– 'Independence' ERou
F– 'Ingal's Prolific Red' (C) ERou
F– 'Invicta' (C) CMac EMui EWar GBon GChr IJoh LBuc MBea MBri NBar SDea SKee WHig WWeb
F– 'Jenny Lind' ERou
F– 'Jolly Angler' ERou
F– 'Jolly Potter' ERou
F– 'Jubilee' LBuc MBri NRog SKee
F– 'Katherina Ohlenburg' (C) ERou
F– 'Kathryn Hartley' (C) ERou
F– 'Keen's Seedling' (D) ERou NTwe
F– 'Keepsake' (C/D) ERou NRog NTwe
F– 'King of Trumps' ERou NRog
F– 'Lady Delamere' (C) ERou
F– 'Lady Haughton' (D) ERou
F– 'Lady Leicester' (D) ERou
F– 'Lancashire Lad' (C/D) ERou NRog NTwe
F– 'Langley Gage' (D) ERou NRog
F– 'Langley Green' (C) ERou
F– 'Lauffener Gelbe' ERou
F– 'Laxton's Amber' (D) ERou
F– 'Leader' (C) ERou
F– 'Leveller' (C/D) CMac CSut EHar EMui ERou EWar LBuc MBea MBri NElm NRog NTwe SDea SKee SPer WHig WWeb
F– 'Lily of the Valley' ERou
F– 'Lloyd George' ERou
F– 'London' (C/D) ERou NRog
F– 'Lord Audley' (D) ERou
F– 'Lord Derby' (C/D) ERou NRog NTwe
F– 'Lord Elcho' ERou
F– 'Lord George' ERou
F– 'Lord Kitchener' NRog
F– 'Macherauch's Seedling' NRog
F– 'Marigold' ERou NRog
F– 'Marmorierte Goldkugel' (D) ERou
F– 'Matchless' (D) ERou NRog
F– 'Maurer's Seedling' (D) ERou
F– 'May Duke' (C/D) ERou IJoh NRog SDea
F– 'Mertensis' ERou
F– 'Mischief' ERou
F– 'Mitre' (C) ERou NTwe
F– 'Monarch' (D) ERou
F– 'Montgomery' ERou
F– 'Mrs Westlon' ERou
F– 'Muttons' (D) ERou
F– 'Nailer' ERou
F– 'Napoléon le Grand' (D) ERou
F– 'Norden Hero' (D) ERou
F– 'Ostrich' (C) ERou
F– 'Pitmaston Green Gage' (D) ERou NTwe
F– 'Pixwell' ERou
F– 'Plain Long Green' ERou
F– 'Plunder' ERou NRog
F– 'Postman' ERou
F– 'Pottage' ERou
F– 'Preston's Seedling' (D) ERou
F– 'Prince Charles' ERou
F– 'Profit' ERou
F– 'Queen of Hearts' ERou NRog
F– 'Queen of Trumps' (C) ERou NRog NTwe
F– 'Railway' ERou
F– 'Ries von Kothen' (C) ERou
F– 'Rifleman' (D) ERou
F– 'Roaring Lion' ERou
F– 'Robustenda' ERou
F– 'Roseberry' (D) ERou NTwe
F– 'Rushwick Seedling' (C) ERou
F– 'Scotch Red Rough' (D) ERou
F– 'Scottish Chieftan' (D) ERou
F– 'Sensation' (C) ERou
F– 'Shiner' ERou
F– 'Sir George Brown' (D) ERou NRog
F– 'Slap Bang' (C) ERou
F– 'Smaragdbeere' (C) ERou
F– 'Smiling Beauty' (C) ERou
F– 'Snow' ERou
F– 'Snowdrop' (C) ERou
F– 'Souter Johnny' ERou
F– 'Speedwell' ERou NRog
F– 'Spinefree' ERou
F– 'Stockwell' ERou
F– 'Sulphur' (D) ERou
F– 'Sultan Juror' NRog
F– 'Surprise' (C) ERou NRog
F– 'Suter Johnny' NRog
F– 'Talfourd' (D) ERou
F– 'Telegraph' ERou NTwe
F– 'Thatcher' ERou
F– 'The Leader' NRog

F– 'Tom Joiner' ERou NTwe
F– 'Trumpeter' (C) ERou NRog
F– 'Victoria' ERou NRog
F– 'Viper' (C) ERou
F– 'Warrington' (D) ERou NRog NTwe
F– 'Weisse Riesen' ERou
F– 'Weisse Volltriesen' (C) ERou
F– 'Werdersche Frühemarkt' (D) ERou
F– 'Whinham's Industry' (C/D) CMac CSam EHar EMui ERou EWar GChr GRei IJoh IOrc LBuc MBri NBee NElm NRog NTwe SDea SKee SPer WHig
F– 'White Eagle' (C) ERou NRog
F– 'White Fig' (C) ERou
F– 'White Lion' (C/D) ERou NRog NTwe
F– 'White Swan' (C) ERou
F– 'White Transparent' (C) ERou NTwe
F– 'Whitesmith' (C/D) EMui ERou GRei IJoh LBuc NRog NTwe SDea SKee WHig
F– 'Woodpecker' NRog
F– 'Yellow Champagne' ERou NRog
viburnifolium CGre CHan CMHG CPle LSav
F White Currant group
'White Grape' NElm NRog
F– – 'White Pearl' GRei IJoh
F– – 'White Versailles' CMac EMui LBuc MBea MBri SDea SKee SPer WHig WWeb

RICHEA (Epacridaceae)
dracophylla CSun SArc
scoparia SArc SBor SHil SSpi

RIGIDELLA (Iridaceae)

ROBINIA † (Leguminosae)
× *ambigua* 'Bella-rosea' MUlv SHil
– 'Decaisneana' SHil
hispida CBot CSco ELan ENot LNet MUlv SHil SMad SPer SSpi WMou WSHC
– 'Macrophylla' SHil
N– 'Rosea' CB&S CBot
kelseyi CSco IOrc MUlv SHil SPer WAbe
¶ *luxurians* CB&S
§ × *margaretta* 'Casque Rouge' ('Pink Cascade') CCla CSco EHar LNet SChu SExT SPer
pseudoacacia CB&S CHEx CLnd ELan ENot SHil WCoo WNor
– 'Bessoniana' CLnd ENot SExT SHil SMad SPer
– 'Fastigiata' See R. *p.* 'Pyramidalis'
– 'Frisia' Widely available
– 'Inermis' See R. *p.* 'Umbraculifera'
§ – 'Pyramidalis' EHar ENot SExT SHil
– 'Rozynskiana' SHil
– 'Semperflorens' CSco
– 'Tortuosa' EHar ELan IJoh MBri SMad SPer WMou
§ – 'Umbraculifera' SExT SHil
– 'Unifolia' CLnd SHil
× *slavinii* 'Hillieri' CCla CLnd CSco IOrc SHil SPer WWat

ROCHEA See **CRASSULA**

RODGERSIA † (Saxifragaceae)
aesculifolia CFor CGle CHEx CHad CRow CSco CWGN EGol ELan ELun EPar MBri NSti SBla SHig SPer SSpi WAbe WWat
– 'Irish Bronze' CHad EBre
henrici hybrid MBri
'Parasol' ELan SSpi
pinnata CBow CFor CGle CHEx CHad CKel CRow CSco CWGN EBre EFol EGol ERav MBal MBri MSta NVic SAxl SBla SChu SHig SLon SPer WHoo
– L 1670 SSpi
– 'Alba' MBro NHol WDav
– *elegans* CBro CCla CHad CHar EBre ELan ELun EPar ERou GWic NHol NJap NOrc SMad SPer WDav WWin
– 'Superba' CCla CHEx CHad CSco CShe ECha GWic IDai LGro MBri MBro MCot MUlv NSti SBla SHig SPer SSpi WAbe WHoo WKif WWat
podophylla CChu CCla CFor CHEx CHad CKel EBre ECha EFol EGol EHon ELun LSav NHol NJap SAxl SBla SDix SHig SPer SSpi WHer WMar
– 'Pagode' CHad
– 'Rotlaub' MBri
– 'Smaragd' CHad CRow
purdomii CHad CRow SSpi
sambucifolia CCla CHEx CHad CRow CShe MBri MFir SMad SPer SSpi WWat
tabularis See ASTILBOIDES *tabularis*

ROHDEA † (Liliaceae)
japonica SApp

ROMANZOFFIA (Hydrophyllaceae)
californica GLoc WHal
sitchensis CSun EBar NRed WHoo
tracyi WEas
unalaschkensis CRiv CSun ECro ELan EPot ESis GAbr NGre NNrd NTow NWCA SIng WAbe WHil WOMN WPer

ROMNEYA (Papaveraceae)
coulteri Widely available
– *tricocalyx* CGre LGre
§ – 'White Cloud' CCla ECro SSpi
× *hybrida* See R. *coulteri* 'White Cloud'

ROMULEA (Iridaceae)
bulbocodium CBro CRiv GLoc LBow MHig
– *clusiana* LAma NHol

– leichtliniana ECam
linaresii EPot LAma NHol
♦*longituba* See R. ***macowanii***
♦*macowanii* MHig WAbe
– alticola GLoc WOMN
nivalis ECam GLoc LAma NHol WChr
ramiflora LAma
sabulosa CBro
tempskyana LAma
'Zahnii' LAma

ROSA † (Rosaceae)
'Abbandonata' MRTP
Abbeyfield Rose ® (HT) CDoC ESha MRos SHil SPer
'Abbotswood' (***canina*** x) EBls
Abraham Darby ® (S) CDoC CSam EOrc EWar LGod MAus MBri MHay MRea MRui SHil SPer SSus
'Abundance' (F) MGan
Ace of Hearts ® (HT) CSan
acicularis WAct
– engelmannii CCor
– nipponensis EBls
'Adam' (T/Cl) EBls
'Adam Messerich' (Bb) CCor EBls ETWh IHos MAus
'Adélaïde d'Orléans' (Ra) CCMG EBls MAus MRTP SPer SRum WAct WHCG
'Admiral Rodney' (HT) EWar LPlm MGan MHay MRea NBat NRog
Adolf Horstmann ® (HT) ESha MGan NBar WWar
'Agatha' (G) EBls
¶ 'Agatha Christie' (F/Cl) CGre MMat
'Agnes' (Ru) CBow CCMG CHad CSan EBls ETWh IHos LGre MAus MGan MMat MRTP NSty SHil SPer SSus WAct WHCG
'Aimée Vibert' (Ra) CCMG EBls ETWh MAus MRTP SPer WAct WHCG WSHC
Air France ® (Min) EWar MR&S
'Akebono' (HT) MHay
'Alain Blanchard' (G) CCor EBls MAus
'Alba Maxima' (A) CBow CCMG CCla EBls ELeG ETWh MAus MMat MRTP NSty SFam SHil SPer SSus WAct WHCG
N Alba Meidiland ® (GC) EWar
'Alba Semiplena' (A) CCMG EBls ELeG ETWh MAus NSty SPer SSus WAct WHCG
x ***alba*** EBls MR&S NRog WWeb
'Albéric Barbier' (Ra) Widely available
'Albertine' (Ra) Widely available
'Alchymist' (S/Cl) CCMG CCor CHad EBls ETWh MAus MBri MMat SPer SSus WAct WHCG
Alec's Red ® (HT) Widely available
Alec's Red, Climbing ® (HT/Cl) SPer
'Alexander Von Humbolt' (Cl) MGan
Alexander ® (HT) Widely available
'Alexandre Girault' (Ra) CCMG EBls EBro ETWh MAus SPer WHCG
'Alfred Colomb' (HP) EBls
'Alfred de Dalmas' See R. 'Mousseline'
'Alida Lovatt' (Ra) EBls MAus
'Alison Wheatcroft' (F) SHen
'Alister Stella Gray' (N) CCMG EBls ETWh LHol MAus MGan SFam SHil SPer WAct WHCG
All in One ® See R. 'Exploit'
'Allen Chandler' (HT/Cl) EBls MAus NSty SPer WHCG
Allgold ® (F) CB&S CGro CMac EBls ELeG ESha GTra MGan MHls MMor MR&S NBar SHen SRum WWeb
'Allgold, Climbing' (F/Cl) CCMG CDoC CSan EBls ELeG ETWh EWar GGre IHos IJoh MAus MGan MHay MHls MR&S MRea SRum WWeb
Allotria ® (F) MGan
'Aloha' (F/Cl) Widely available
alpina See R. ***pendulina***
Alpine Sunset ® (HT) EBls ELeG ESha EWar MAus MGan MR&S MRos NBar NElm SHil SPer SRum
altaica See R. ***pimpinellifolia altaica***
Altissimo ® (Cl) CHad EBls ELeG ETWh LPlm MAus MBri MGan MHay MHls MMat MRea SPer
'Amadis' (Bs) EBls WHCG
Amanda ® (F) MBri
'Amatsu-otome' (HT) MHay
'Amazing Grace' (HT) GGre
Amber Queen ® (F) Widely available
'Amberlight' (F) ELeG MAus
¶ 'Ambridge Rose' MAus
'Amélia' (D) See R. 'Celsiana'
'American Pillar' (Ra) Widely available
'Améthyste' (Ra) See R. 'Rose-Marie Viaud'
'Amy Robsart' (HSwb) EBls ELeG ETWh MAus
¶ Anabell ® (F) WWar
'Andersonii' (***canina*** x) EBls ISea MAus SHil WAct
¶ 'Andrea' (Min) MHay
'Andrea, Climbing' (MinCl) MRos
'Andrewsii' (HScB) MAus WAct
§ 'Anemone' (Cl) EBls MAus SHil
♦***anemoniflora*** See R. x ***beanii***
anemonoides See R. 'Anemone'
– ramona See R. 'Ramona'
Angela Rippon ® (Min) ELeG EWar IHos MBri MGan MHay MHls MMat MRea MRui NRed SHil SIng SPer
'Angela's Choice' (F) MGan
'Angèle Pernet' (HT) EBls
'Angelina' (S) EBls EWar MMat
Anisley Dickson ® (F) CDoC ELeG IDic LGod MGan MHay MRea NBat SHil SPer
'Ann Aberconway' (F) CDoC MMat
'Anna de Diesbach' (HP) EBls

Anna Ford ® (Min/F)	CDoC ELeG EWar GGre IHos LGod LPlm MAus MGan MHay MHls MRea NBat NRed SPer SRum WWar
Anna Livia ® (F)	IHos MMat
'Anna Olivier' (T)	EBls
'Anna Pavlova' (HT)	EBls SSus
Anna Zinkeisen ® (S)	ELeG
Anne Cocker ® (F)	CDoC EBls MGan MHay MHls NBar NBat
Anne Harkness ® (F)	CDoC EWar LPlm MAus MGan MHay MHls MRos NBar NBat NRog SHil SPer WWar
Anne Moore ® (Min)	MHay
'Anne of Geierstein' (HSwB)	EBls MAus MGan
'Anne Watkins' (HT)	EBls
¶ Antique '89 ® (F/Cl)	MMat
'Antoine Rivoire' (HT)	EBls
'Antonia d'Ormois' (G)	EBls
Anvil Sparks ® (HT)	MGan
Apothecary's Rose	See R. ***gallica officinalis***
'Apple Blossom' (Ra)	EBls
'Apricot Nectar' (F)	MAus MGan MR&S SPer
'Apricot Silk' (HT)	CB&S CGro EBls EWar IHos IJoh MAus MGan MHay MHls MR&S MRos NBar NRog SPer SRum WWeb
Apricot Spice ® (HT)	CSan
Apricot Sunblaze ® (Min)	EBls EWar IHos IJoh MHay MR&S MRea MRui NElm WWar
'Arabesque' (F)	CSan
Arcadian ® (F)	MMat WWar
♦ 'Archiduc Joseph' (T)	See R. 'Général Schablikine'
'Archiduchesse Elisabeth d'Autriche' (HP)	EBls WHCG
Arctic Sunrise ® (Min)	MHls MRui
'Ardoisée de Lyon' (HP)	EBls
Ards Beauty ® (F)	CDoC ELeG IDic SPer WWar
'Ards Rover' (HP/Cl)	EBls
'Arethusa' (Ch)	EBls
'Arizona Sunset' (Min)	MHay
arkansana suffulta	EBls WHCG
Armada ® (S)	MAus SHil SPer
Arnold Greensitt ® (HT)	MHay
'Arthur Bell' (F)	Widely available
'Arthur Bell, Climbing' (F/Cl)	NRog SPer
'Arthur de Sansal' (D/Po)	EBls MAus MRTP WAct
'Arthur Hillier' (S)	CCor SHil
¶ 'Arthur Scargill' (Min)	MHay
arvensis	CKin EBls ETWh SBra
'Ash Wednesday' (Cl)	EBls
'Assemblage des Beautés' (G)	EBls MAus SFam
'Astrid Späth Striped' (F)	EBls
¶ Audrey Gardner ® (Min/Patio)	MRea

'August Seebauer' (F)	EBls MAus
'Auguste Gervais' (Ra)	EBls MAus SRum WHCG
'Augustine Guinoisseau' (HT)	EBls MAus
'Augustine Halem' (HT)	EBls
'Aunty Dora' (F)	EWar
Austrian Copper	See R. ***foetida*** 'Bicolor'
Austrian Yellow	See R. ***foetida***
'Autumn' (HT)	NRog
'Autumn Bouquet' (S)	EBls
'Autumn Delight' (HM)	EBls MAus
'Autumn Fire'	See R. 'Herbstfeuer'
'Autumn Sunlight' (HT/Cl)	ELeG MGan MHay SPer
¶ 'Autumn Sunset' (S)	EBls
♦ 'Autumnalis' (Ra)	See R. 'Princesse de Nassau'
'Aviateur Blériot' (Ra)	EBls MAus
Avocet ® (F)	CDoC ELeG MBri MHls NBat
¶ 'Awakening' (Cl)	EBls
'Ayrshire Splendens'	See R. 'Splendens'
'Baby Bio' (F)	CB&S MGan MR&S MRos NElm NRog SRum
'Baby Darling' (Min)	MAus MGan MHls MRea MRos MRui
'Baby Faurax' (Poly)	ELeG MAus
¶ 'Baby Gold' (Min)	CGro
'Baby Gold Star' (Min)	ELeG MAus MGan MHls SPer
Baby Masquerade ® (Min)	CGro CSan ELan ELeG EWar GGre IHos LGod LPlm MAus MBur MGan MHay MHls MMat MMor MR&S MRea MRos MRui NBar NElm NRog WWeb
¶ 'Baby Princess' (Min)	MRui
Baby Sunrise ® (Min)	MMat
Baccará ® (HT)	MGan
'Bad Neuenahr' (Cl)	MGan
'Bakewell Scot's Briar' (HScB)	NSty
'Ballerina' (HM)	Widely available
'Baltimore Belle' (Ra)	EBls MAus
'Bambino' (Min)	MHay MHls
banksiae (Ra)	ELeG SHil
♦ – ***alba***	See ROSA ***b. banksiae***
§ – ***banksiae*** (Ra)	CBot ERea
– 'Lutea' (Ra)	Widely available
– 'Lutescens' (Ra)	SBra SHil WKif
– ***normalis*** (Ra)	SHil
Bantry Bay ® (HT/Cl)	CCMG CSan EBls EBro ETWh MGan MMat SRum WWeb
'Barbara Richards' (HT)	EBls MAus
¶ Barkarole ® (HT)	WWeb
'Baron de Bonstetten' (HP)	EBls
'Baron de Wassenaer' (Ce/Mo)	EBls MGan
'Baron Girod de l'Ain' (HP)	CCMG CCor EBls EBro ETWh IHos MAus MRTP NSty SHil SPer SSus WHCG

'Baroness Rothschild' (HT) — See R. Baronne Edmond de Rothschild ®
§ 'Baronne Adolph de Rothschild' (HP) — CBow CCMG CCor CGro CSam EBls ETWh EWar IHos IOrc MAus MGan MRTP SSus WHCG
'Baronne de Rothschild' (HP) — See R. 'Baronne Adolph de Rothschild'
'Baronne Henriette de Snoy' (T) — EBls
'Baronne Prévost' (HP) — CCor EBls MAus SFam SSus WAct WHCG
'Bashful' (Co) — MGan
Basildon Bond ® (HT) — CDoC
'Bayreuth' (S) — MGan
§ x *beanii* (Ra) — EBls LGre SHil
'Beauté' (HT) — EBls ESha MAus MGan NElm SRum
Beautiful Britain ® (F) — CDoC EBls ELeG GGre IDic IHos LGod MAus MBri MGan MHay MHls MR&S MRea MRos NBar NRog SHen SHil SPer SRum WWar
'Beauty of Rosemawr' (T/Cl) — EBls
Beauty Queen ® (F) — EWar
'Beauty Secret' (Min) — MR&S
'Bel Ange' (HT) — MGan
'Belle Amour' (D x A) — CCor EBls MAus MRTP NSty WHCG
'Belle Blonde' (HT) — MBur MGan NElm SPer
'Belle de Crécy' (G) — CCMG CCla CDoC EBls ELeG ETWh IOrc MAus MMat MRTP NSty SFam SHil SPer SSus WAct WHCG
'Belle des Jardins' — See R. 'Centifolia Variegata'
'Belle Isis' (G) — CCMG CCor EBls MAus MRTP SPer
'Belle Lyonnaise' (T/Cl) — EBls
'Belle Poitevine' (Ru) — EBls MAus NSty WAct
'Belle Portugaise' (Cl) — EBls MAus
Belle Story ® (S) — MAus SPer
Belle Sunblaze ® (Min) — NBar NElm
'Belvedere' (Ra) — MAus
Benevolence ® (HT) — CSan
'Bengal Beauty' — ELan WWat WWeb
¶ 'Bennett's Seedling' (Ra) — MAus
Benson and Hedges Gold ® (HT) — EWar GGre MGan MHls MMat MR&S
Benson and Hedges Special ® (Min) — ELan MHay MHls MMat NBar
Bettina ® (HT) — MAus MBur MGan MRea NRog SRum
Bettina, Climbing ® (HT/Cl) — EBls MAus
Betty Driver ® (F) — MBri MGan SPer
* 'Betty Hussey' — LGre
'Betty Prior' (T) — MGan SPer
'Betty Uprichard' (HT) — EBls EBro MAus NSty
'Bharami' (Min) — MGan
Bianco ® (Patio) — MAus MRea NRed
Bibi Mezoon ® (S) — ELeG MRui SPer
¶ Biddulph Grange ® (S) — WWar
biebersteinii — EBls
'Big Chief' (HT) — ESha IDic LGod MRea NRog
Big Purple ® (HT) — ELeG MBri MGan MRea SRum WWar
Bischofsstadt Paderborn ® (S) — MGan
'Bishop Darlington' (HM) — EBls
'Bit o'Sunshine' (Min) — ELeG MGan MMor
'Black Beauty' (HT) — IJoh MAus MRos NBar
'Black Ice' (F) — MGan
'Black Jack' — See R. 'Tour de Malakoff'
'Black Prince' (HP) — EBls
'Blairii Number 1' (Bb) — EBls NSty
'Blairii Number 2' (Bb/Cl) — CCor CHad EBls ETWh MAus MRTP NSty SPer SSus WAct WHCG WSHC
'Blanche de Vibert' (DPo) — EBls
'Blanche Double de Coubert' (Ru) — Widely available
'Blanche Moreau' (CeMo) — CCMG CSan EBls EBro ELeG IHos MAus MBur MGan MHls MRTP NElm NSty SHil SPer WAct
'Blanchefleur' (Ce) — CCor EBls IHos MAus MRTP NSty WHCG
blanda — EBls
'Blaze Away' (F) — CSan
Blessings ® (HT) — Widely available
Blessings, Climbing ® (HT/Cl) — EBls
'Bleu Magenta' (Ra) — CCMG CHad EBls MAus MRTP WHCG
'Bloomfield Abundance' (Poly) — CCMG CMac CSan EBls ELeG MAus MMat MRTP NSty SPer SRum SSus WHCG WWat
'Blossomtime' (Cl) — NRog SPer
'Blue Diamond' (HT) — MGan
Blue Moon ® (HT) — Widely available
'Blue Moon, Climbing' (HT/Cl) — MBur MGan MRea SHen
Blue Parfum ® (HT) — ELeG MAus MRea
Blue Peter ® (Min) — IHos MRea MRui
'Blush Boursault' (Bs) — EBls MAus
'Blush Damask' (D) — CCMG CCor EBls
♦ 'Blush Noisette' — See R. 'Noisette Carnée'
'Blush Rambler' (Ra) — CCMG EBls ETWh MAus SPer
¶ 'Blushing Lucy' (Cl) — WSHC
'Bob Collard' (F) — SRum
'Bobbie James' (Ra) — CCMG CHad EBls ETWh IHos MAus MHay MHls MMat MRTP NBat NSty SPer SPla SRum SSus WAct WHCG
'Bobby Charlton' (HT) — ELeG ESha MBri MGan MHay MRea NRog
'Bobolink' (Min) — GGre MGan
'Bon Silène' (T) — EBls

Bonfire Night ® (F)	CGro MGan MHls MMat
Bonica ® (GC)	CCor CDoC EBls ELan IHos LGod MAus MBur MMat MR&S MRos NBar SHen SHil SPer SRum SSus
'Bonn' (HM)	CB&S CDoC MAus MGan MHls NRog
'Bonnie Scotland' (HT)	MBri MBur MGan
Bonsoir ® (HT)	GTra MAus MGan MHay
'Border Coral' (F)	NRog
'Born Free' (Min)	CSan MBur MRea MRos
'Botzaris' (D)	CCMG EBls SFam
'Boule de Nanteuil' (G)	CCor EBls
'Boule de Neige' (Bb)	CCMG CCla CSan EBls ELeG ETWh LHol MAus MBur MHls MMat MRTP MRos NSty SFam SHil SPer SSus WAct WHCG WSHC WWeb
'Bouquet d'Or' (N)	EBls MAus
'Bourbon Queen' (Bb)	CBow CCMG CCor EBls ETWh MAus NSty SPer SSus WHCG
Boys' Brigade ® (Patio)	EWar LGod MAus MGan NBat WWeb
bracteata	CHil EBls GWic ISea LGre MAus MPar SHil WWat
Breath of Life ® (HT/Cl)	CGro ELan ELeG ESha EWar GGre LGod MAus MBri MBur MGan MHay MHls MRea NBar NBat SPer SRum
Bredon ® (S)	MAus MBri
'Breeze Hill' (Ra)	EBls MAus
'Brenda Colvin' (Ra)	CBot MAus MRTP
'Brennus' (Ch x)	EBls
'Briarcliff' (HT)	EBls
'Bridgwater Pride' (F)	CSan
Bright Eyes ® (F)	CSan
Bright Smile ® (F)	CDoC ELeG GTra IDic MAus MGan MHay MMat MRos NBar SPer WWeb
¶ Bright Spark ® (Min)	MRui
'Brindis' (F/Cl)	MGan
'Bristol Post' (HT)	CSan
¶ 'Brother Cadfael'	MAus MRui
Brown Velvet ® (F)	ELeG MMat WAct
'Brownie' (F)	ELeG MAus
'Browsholme Rose' (Ra)	NSty
brunonii (Ra)	EBls MAus MRTP
– 'La Mortola' (Ra)	CHad MAus SHil SPer WHCG
'Buccaneer' (HT)	MAus MGan
¶ Buck's Fizz ® (F)	MBur
'Buff Beauty' (HM)	Widely available
'Bullata'	See R. ***centifolia*** 'Bullata'
§ 'Burgundiaca' (Ce/G)	CCMG CCor EBls ETWh MAus MPar WAct WHCG
Burgundian Rose	See R. 'Burgundiaca'
'Burma Star' (F)	ESha EWar WWat
Burnet, Double Pink	See R. ***pimpinellifolia*** 'Double Pink'
Burnet, Double White	See R. ***pimpinellifolia*** 'Double White'
'Burning Love' (F)	MGan
Bush Baby ® (Min)	LGod MHay MRea MRos MRui NBat

Buttons ® (Patio)	IDic IHos MBur MHay MR&S SPer
'C F Meyer'	See R. 'Conrad Ferdinand Meyer'
'Café' (F)	ELeG MAus WAct
'Cairngorm' (F)	ESha MGan
californica	MAus SPer WHCG
– 'Plena'	See R. ***nutkana*** 'Plena'
'Callisto' (HM)	CCor EBro ETWh
'Camaïeux' (G)	CBow CCMG CCor EBls EBro ETWh MAus MMat MRTP SHil SPer WAct WHCG
'Camelia Rose'	EBls
'Cameo' (Poly)	EBls MAus MGan
'Canary Bird'	See R. ***xanthina spontanea*** 'C.B.'
Candy Rose ® (S)	EWar MR&S MRea NBar NElm SHen SPer
canina	CKin LBuc MAus MBri MRTP NWea SHil WMou
– 'Abbotswood'	See R. 'Abbotswood'
– 'Andersonii'	See R. 'Andersonii'
'Cantabrigiensis' (S)	CMac CSam EBls ELeG MAus NRog SHil SPer WAct WWat WWeb
'Canterbury' (S)	MAus
Can-Can ® (HT)	ELeG ESha EWar MGan NBar SRum WWar
'Capitaine Basroger' (Mo)	EBls MAus
'Capitaine John Ingram' (Mo)	CCor EBls ETWh MAus NSty SFam SPer WAct
'Captain Christy, Climbing' (HT/Cl)	EBls MAus
Captain Cook ® (F)	NBat
'Captain Hayward' (HP)	EBls
'Cardinal de Richelieu' (G)	CBow CCMG CDoC EBls EBro ELeG ETWh IOrc MAus MBur MMat MRTP NSty SFam SHil SPer SRum SSus WAct WHCG
Cardinal Hume ® (S)	EBls ELeG MAus MGan MHay SPer
Carefree Beauty ® (S)	EWar
'Carmen' (S)	EBls MAus
'Carmenetta' (S)	EBls EWar MAus
♦ 'Carol'	See R. 'Carol Amling'
§ 'Carol Amling' (Gn)	EBls ELeG MHls
Carol Ann ® (F)	MRea WWeb
carolina	LHop
¶ Caroline Davison ® (F)	MAus
♦ 'Caroline Testout'	See R. 'Madame Caroline Testout'
Casino ® (HT/Cl)	CCMG CCla CMac CSan EBls ELeG ESha EWar IJoh LPlm MAus MBur MGan MHay MHls MMor MR&S MRea MRui NBar NElm SPer SRum WWeb
¶ Catherine Cookson ® (HT)	NBat
'Catherine Mermet' (T)	EBls MAus

Name	Suppliers
'Catherine Seyton' (HSwB)	EBls
caudata	CCor
'Cécile Brunner' (Poly)	Widely available
'Cécile Brunner, Climbing' (Poly/Cl)	CCMG CHad CSan EBls ELeG ETWh MAus MHay MHls MMat NSty SHil SPer SPla SSus WAct WHCG WSHC WWat
'Cécile Brunner, White' (Poly)	EBls LGre MAus WHCG WWat
§ 'Céleste' (A)	CB&S CBow CCMG CCla CSan EBls ELan ELeG ETWh IHos MAus MHay MMat MPar MRTP NSty SFam SHil SPer SSus WAct WHCG WWeb
'Celestial'	See R. 'Céleste'
'Célina' (Mo)	CCor EBls MGan
'Céline Forestier' (N)	CCMG EBls ETWh MAus MRTP SFam SPer WAct
'Celsiana' (D)	CBow CCMG CCor CDoC EBls MAus SFam SPer WAct WHCG
Centenaire de Lourdes ® (F)	EBls SSus
§ 'Centifolia Variegata' (Ce)	EBls MAus MGan MHay WHCG
x ***centifolia***	CBow CCMG EBls ETWh IOrc LHol MAus MRTP NRog SHil SSus WAct WHCG
– 'Bullata'	EBls ELeG MAus SFam
§ – 'Cristata'	CCla CSan EBls ELeG ETWh IHos MAus MBur MHls MMat MRTP NRog SFam SHil SPer SSus WHCG
§ – 'Muscosa'	CCMG CDoC EBls ETWh IHos IOrc MAus MGan MHls MMat NRog NSty SFam SHil SRum SSus WAct WHCG WWeb
– 'Parvifolia' (G)	See R. 'Burgundiaca'
'Centurion' (F)	MMat
¶ *cerasocarpa* (Ra)	ETWh
'Cerise Bouquet' (S)	CCMG CCla EBls MAus MMat MRTP NSty SHil SPer SSus WWeb
¶ Cha Cha ® (Patio/Min)	CGro
¶ 'Chami' (HM)	EBro
Champagne Cocktail ® (F)	EHar ELeG EWar NBat WWar WWeb
'Champion' (HT)	ELeG MAus MGan MHay NElm
'Champneys' Pink Cluster' (Ch x)	EBls LGre WKif
Champs Elysées ® (HT)	MGan SRum
'Chanelle' (F)	EBls ELeG MAus MBur MGan MRea NRog SPer
Chapeau de Napoléon	See R. x ***centifolia*** 'Cristata'
'Chaplin's Pink Climber' (Cl)	EBls EBro ETWh MGan MHay
Chardonnay ® (HT)	MBri MRea

Name	Suppliers
Charles Austin ® (S)	CCMG MAus MBri NSty SPer SSus
Charles Aznavour ® (F)	EWar
Charles de Gaulle ® (HT)	SRum
'Charles de Mills' (G)	CBow CCMG CCla CCor CMac CSan EBls EBro ELeG ETWh MAus MHay MMat NSty SFam SHil SPer SPla SRum SSus WAct WHCG WWeb
'Charles Gater' (HP)	EBls
'Charles Lefèbvre' (HP)	EBls
'Charles Mallerin' (HT)	EBls MHls
Charles Rennie ® (S)	CCla MAus
Charleston ® (F)	MGan MR&S
Charleston '88 ® (HT)	EWar SHen
'Charley's Aunt' (HT)	MHay
'Charm of Paris' (HT)	SRum WWeb
Charmian ® (S)	CCMG MAus SSus
¶ 'Château de Clos-Vougeot' (HT)	MGan
– – Climbing (HT/Cl)	EBls EBro MAus SPer
'Chatterbox' (F)	CSan
'Chaucer' (S)	CCMG MAus MBri
Chelsea Pensioner ® (Min)	LPlm MHls MMat
Cherry Brandy ® (HT)	MBur MRea MRos SRum WWar
'Cherry Pie' (HT)	GTra MGan
'Cherryade' (S)	MGan
'Cherryade, Climbing' (HT/Cl)	MGan
'Cheshire Life' (HT)	ELeG ESha GGre GTra LGod MAus MBri MBur MGan MHls MMor MR&S MRea NBar SHen SRum WWeb
'Chianti' (S)	CCla EBls MAus NSty
Chicago Peace ® (HT)	CB&S CDoC CMac EBls ELeG ESha EWar GGre GTra IHos IJoh LGod LPlm MAus MBur MGan MMor MR&S NBar NElm NRog SHen SRum WWeb
Chinatown ® (F/S)	Widely available
♦ ***chinensis***	See R. x ***odorata*** 'Pallida'
– 'Mutabilis'	See R. x ***odorata*** 'Mutabilis'
'Chloris' (A)	EBls
'Chorus Girl' (F)	MGan
Chorus ® (F)	MR&S MRea
Christian Dior ® (HT)	EBls MGan SRum
'Christine Gandy' (HT)	MGan
'Chrysler Imperial' (HT)	EBls MAus MGan NElm
'Chuckles' (F)	EBls
Cider Cup ® (Patio)	CDoC CGro ELeG ESha EWar GGre IDic MBur MR&S MRea MRos NBat SPer WWar
'Cinderella' (Min)	ELeG MAus MGan MHls MR&S MRea
cinnamomea	See R. ***majalis***
'Circus' (F)	MAus MGan SRum
'City of Bath' (HT)	CSan MHay
City of Belfast ® (F)	CGro EBls ELeG IHos MAus MGan NBar NElm

¶ City of Birmingham ® (S/HT)	MMat
'City of Glasgow' (HT)	MHay
'City of Gloucester' (HT)	MGan MHay
'City of Leeds' (F)	EBls ESha EWar GGre MAus MGan MHay MHls MMat MR&S MRea NBar NBat NRog SHen SPer WWeb
City of London ® (F)	ESha EWar MBur MHay SHil
'City of Portsmouth' (F)	CB&S ELeG MBur MGan MHls
'City of Worcester' (HT)	MHay
'City of York' (Ra)	EBls
Clair Matin ® (S/Cl)	CCor EBls ETWh MAus SPer
'Claire Jacquier' (N)	CCMG EBls MAus SFam SPer WHCG
Claire Rose ® (S)	EOrc EWar IHos MAus MRea SHil SPer SSus
Clarissa ® (F)	ELeG IHos MAus MRea SHil SPer SRum
'Clementina Carbonieri' (T)	EBls
'Clio' (HP)	EBls
'Cloth of Gold' (N)	EBls MAus
¶ 'Clytemnestra' (HM)	EBro
'Coalite Flame' (HT)	MHay
Cocktail ® (S)	EBls MGan MRea SSus
Colibri ® (Min)	GGre LGod MGan SHil SPer
Colibri '79 ® (Min)	ELan ELeG EWar GGre LPlm MGan MHay MRui WWar
Colibri '80 ®	See R. Colibri '79 ®
'Colonel Fabvier'	EBls
'Colonial White'	See R. 'Sombreuil, Climbing'
Colorama ® (HT)	MBri MR&S
'Columbian' (Cl)	ERav SPer
'Commandant Beaurepaire' (Bb)	CCor EBls ELeG MAus NSty SFam SPer SSus
Common Moss	See R. x *centifolia* 'Muscosa'
'Compassion' (HT/Cl)	Widely available
'Complicata' (G)	CBow CCMG CHad CSam CSan EBls EBro ELeG ETWh LHol MAus MBri MGan MHls MMat MRTP NRog NSty SFam SHil SMad SPer SSus WAct
'Comte de Chambord'	See R. 'Madame Knorr'
'Comtesse Cécile de Chabrillant' (HP)	EBls
'Comtesse de Lacépède'	See R. 'Du Maître d'Ecole'
'Comtesse de Murinais' (D/M)	CCMG CCor EBls MAus SFam SSus WAct
'Comtesse du Cayla' (Ch)	MAus
'Comtesse d'Oxford' (HP)	EBls
'Comtesse O'Gorman' (HP)	EBls
'Comtesse Vandal' (HT)	MAus SRum

'Comtesse Vandal, Climbing' (HT/Cl)	EBls MAus
'Conditorum' (G)	EBls SFam
Congratulations ® (F)	CSan ELeG EWar GGre IHos IJoh LGod LPlm MGan MHls MMat NElm SPer WWar
'Conrad Ferdinand Meyer' (Ru)	CCMG EBls IHos MAus MGan NSty SHen SPer SSus WAct
Conservation ® (Patio)	ESha MRea NBat
'Constance Spry' (S/Cl)	Widely available
'Cooper's Burmese'	See R. ***laevigata*** 'Cooperi'
'Copenhagen' (S)	EBls MAus MBri MBur
'Copper Delight' (F)	NRog
Copper Pot ® (F)	ELeG MBur MGan SPer SRum
'Coral Cluster' (Poly)	EBls MAus MGan
Coral Dawn ® (HT/Cl)	EBls MAus MHls MRui
Coral Reef ® (Patio)	GGre MRea MRos
'Coral Satin' (Cl)	MGan
'Coral Star' (HT)	MGan MR&S
'Coralie' (D)	EBls
'Coralin' (Min)	CGro ELeG IJoh LGod MGan MR&S MRea
'Cornelia' (HM)	Widely available
'Coronation Gold' (F)	ESha
'Coronet' (F)	WAct
Corsair ® (F)	CSan
x ***coryana***	EBls
♦ 'Corylus' (Ru)	See R. 'Hazel Le Rougetel'
corymbifera	EBls
corymbulosa	EBls
'Cosimo Ridolfi' (G)	EBls
'Cottage Maid'	See R. 'Centifolia Variegata'
¶ Country Heritage ® (HT)	SHen
¶ Country Lady ® (HT)	MBur
'Country Maid' (F)	EWar
'Countryman' (S)	SHil
'Coupe d'Hébé' (Bb)	EBls ETWh MAus SHil SSus
covillei	CCor
'Cramoisi Picotée' (G)	CCor EBls MAus
'Cramoisi Supérieur' (Ch)	EBls ETWh MAus MMat WHCG
'Cramoisi Supérieur Grimpant' (Ch/Cl)	EBls WHCG
'Crarae' (HT)	CSan
'Crépuscule' (N)	EBls
'Cressida' (S)	CCMG MAus
Crested Moss	See R. ***centifolia*** 'Cristata'
Cricri ® (Min)	CGro MAus MGan MR&S
'Crimson Conquest' (HT/Cl)	EBls
'Crimson Damask'	See R. ***gallica officinalis***
Crimson Gem ® (Min)	MGan NBat
'Crimson Globe' (Mo)	EBls ELeG MGan MHls
'Crimson Glory' (HT)	EBls MAus MBur MGan
'Crimson Glory, Climbing' (HT/Cl)	EBls ELeG ETWh MAus MGan MHay NRog SRum SSus

Name	Suppliers
'Crimson Rambler' (Ra)	MAus
'Crimson Shower' (Ra)	ETWh EWar GGre IHos LGod MAus MGan MMat NRog SHil SPer
Crimson Wave ® (F)	MGan
'Cristata'	See R. ***centifolia*** 'Cristata'
♦ 'Cuisse de Nymphe'	See R. 'Maiden's Blush'
'Cupid' (HT/Cl)	EBls ETWh MAus
Curiosity ® (HT)	CCor
Cymbeline ® (S)	MAus SPer
'Cynthia Brooke' (HT)	EBls
Daily Express ® (HT)	MRea
'Daily Mail'	See R. 'Madame Edouard Herriot'
Daily Sketch ® (F)	MGan SRum
'Dainty Bess' (HT)	CHad EBls EBro ELeG MAus NSty
Dainty Dinah ® (Patio)	CGro MAus MRea
'Dainty Maid' (F)	ELeG MAus
'Dairy Maid' (F)	ELeG ERav MAus
'Daisy Hill' (***macrantha*** x)	CCMG EBls
¶ 'Dale Farm' (F/Patio)	MBur
x ***damascena bifera***	EBls MRTP
§ – ***semperflorens***	CCMG CCor EBls EBro ETWh IHos MAus WAct WHCG
§ – 'Trigintipetala'	CCor EBls ELeG ETWh IHos MAus NSty SHil WAct WHCG
– ***versicolor***	CCMG CGro EBls ELeG ETWh IHos LHol MAus MGan NSty SHil SPer SSus WAct WWeb
'Dame de Coeur' (HT)	IJoh SRum
'Dame Edith Helen' (HT)	EBls
Dame of Sark ® (F)	ESha
Dame Vera Lynn ® (F)	MRea
¶ 'Dame Wendy' (F)	LGod
'Danaë' (HM)	CCMG EBls EBro ETWh MAus WHCG
'Danny Boy' (HT/Cl)	SRum
'Danse des Sylphes' (Cl)	EBls EBro MHay NBat
'Danse du Feu' (Cl)	Widely available
'Daphne Gandy' (F)	MGan
'Dapple Dawn' (S)	MAus MBri SPer
Darling Flame ® (Min)	ELan EWar GGre LGod MAus MGan MHay MHls MMat MR&S MRui NElm SPer WWar
davidii	EBls MAus
davurica	CCor
'Daybreak' (HM)	EBls EBro MAus NRog WAct WHCG
'De Meaux' (Ce)	CBow CCMG CSan EBls ETWh MAus MMat MRTP NSty SHil SPer SSus WHCG
'De Meaux, White' (Ce)	CCMG EBls MAus
§ 'De Rescht' (DPo)	CCla CCor EBls EBro ETWh LHol MAus MBri MGan MHay MRea SPer WAct WHCG
'Dearest' (F)	CB&S CCMG CDoC ESha EWar GGre GTra IJoh LPlm MAus MGan MHay MHls MMor MR&S MRea NBar NElm NRog SHen SRum WWeb
'Debutante' (Ra)	EBls MAus
Deb's Delight ® (F)	ELeG EWar MRea WWeb
'Deep Secret' (HT)	CCMG CDoC CGro CSan ELeG ESha EWar GGre LPlm MBur MGan MMor MR&S MRea MRos NBar NRog SHen SPer SRum WWeb
'Delambre' (DPo)	EBls MAus
'Dembrowski' (HP)	EBls
Denman ® (HT)	MRea NBat
'Dentelle de Malines' (S)	MAus
'Deschamps' (N)	EBls
'Desprez à Fleur Jaune' (N)	CCMG EBls EBro ETWh MAus MRTP SPer WHCG WSHC
'Deuil de Paul Fontaine' (Mo)	EBls
'Devon Maid' (Cl)	WWar
'Devoniensis, Climbing' (T/Cl)	CCMG EBls MAus
Diamant ® (F)	MGan
'Diamond Jubilee' (HT)	EBls MAus MHay
♦ 'Dicbar'	See R. Memento ®
'Dickson's Flame' (F)	MGan
Die Welt ® (HT)	MHay NBat
'Dimples' (F)	NSty
'Diorama' (HT)	CDoC ELeG IJoh MAus MBri MGan MR&S NElm NRog SRum
'Directeur Alphand' (HP)	EBls
Disco Dancer ® (F)	IDic IHos MRea WWar
'Doc' (Co)	MGan
'Docteur Andry' (HP)	EBls
'Docteur Grill' (T)	EBls MAus
'Doctor A J Verhage' (HT)	ELeG MGan SRum
Doctor Dick ® (HT)	MHay NBat
'Doctor Eckener' (Ru)	EBls MAus MGan
'Doctor Edward Deacon' (HT)	EBls
Doctor Goldberg ® (HT)	MGan
'Doctor Jackson' (S)	MAus
'Doctor John Snow' (HT)	MGan
Doctor McAlpine ® (HT)	MBri MR&S MRea MRos SRum
'Doctor W Van Fleet' (Ra/Cl)	EBls MAus
¶ 'Don Charlton' (HT)	NBat
'Don Juan' (Cl)	MGan
doncasteri	EBls ISea MAus
'Dopey' (Co)	MGan
'Doreen' (HT)	NRog
Doris Tysterman ® (HT)	Widely available
'Dornröschen' (Cl)	MGan
'Dorothy Perkins' (Ra)	Widely available

'Dorothy Wheatcroft' (F)	ELeG ESha IHos LPlm MBri MGan MHay MMor SHen SRum WWeb
Dortmund ® (HScB/Cl)	CMac EBls ETWh GTra LPlm MAus MGan MHay MMat MMor SPer
Double Delight ® (HT)	CGro ELan ELeG ESha GGre IJoh MBri MGan MHay MR&S MRos NElm NRog SRum WWar
'Double Joy' (Min)	CSan MBur MHay MRea MRos
Dove ® (S)	MAus MBri
'Dream Time' (HT)	MHay MRea NBat
'Dream Waltz' (F)	MHay
'Dreamgirl' (Cl)	MAus NSty SPer
'Dreamglo' (Min)	MHay
'Dreaming Spires' (Cl)	IHos MHls MMat SPer WAct
Dreamland ® (F)	MGan NElm
'Dresden Doll' (Min/Mo)	CSan EBls MAus MHls MRos MRui SHil SPer
Drummer Boy ® (F/Patio)	ESha GGre NElm WWar
'Du Maître d'Ecole' (G)	CCMG CCor EBls ELeG ETWh MAus
Dublin Bay ® (Cl)	CDoC CSan EBls ELeG ESha EWar IHos IJoh LGod LPlm MBri MGan MHay MHls MMat MR&S MRea NBar NRog SHil SPer WWar
'Duc de Fitzjames' (G)	EBls
'Duc de Guiche' (G)	CCMG CCor CSan EBls ETWh MAus SFam SPer WHCG
'Duchess of Portland'	See R. 'Portlandica'
'Duchesse de Buccleugh' (G)	CCor EBls MAus MRTP
'Duchesse de Montebello' (G)	CCMG CCor EBls ETWh MAus NSty SPer SSus WHCG
'Duchesse de Rohan' (Ce/HP)	EBls
'Duchesse de Verneuil' (Mo)	EBls MAus SFam
'Duchesse d'Albe' (T)	EBls
'Duchesse d'Angoulême' (G)	CCMG EBls ETWh MAus NSty
'Duchesse d'Auerstädt' (N)	EBls
'Düsterlohe' (R)	CCor EBls
'Duke of Edinburgh' (HP)	EBls MAus
'Duke of Wellington' (HP)	EBls WHCG
'Duke of Windsor' (HT)	CDoC GGre IHos IJoh MGan MHls MR&S NBar NElm NRog SPer SRum
'Duke of York' (Ch)	EBls
Duke Sunblaze	See R. Duke Meillandina ®
'Dundee Rambler' (Ra)	EBls MAus
'Dunwich Rose' (HScB)	CCMG CCor EBls MAus MBri
'Dupontii' (S)	EBls ELeG MAus MRTP SFam SPer
'Dupuy Jamain' (HP)	EBls SSus WAct WHCG
¶ 'Durham Prince Bishop' (HT)	NBat
'Dusky Maiden' (F)	CBos EBls ELeG MAus
'Dutch Gold' (HT)	CDoC CGro EWar MAus MGan MHay MHls MRea MRos NBar NElm NRog SHen SPer
'Dwarf King'	See R. 'Zwergkönig'
Dwarf Queen '82 ® /Zwergkönigin '82 ® (Min)	MGan
'D'Aguesseau' (G)	EBls EBro MAus SPer WHCG
'E H Morse'	See R. 'Ernest H Morse'
'Easlea's Golden Rambler' (Ra)	CMac EBls ETWh MAus NSty SHil SPer SSus WHCG
'Easter Morning' (Min)	CGro CSan ELan GGre LGod MAus MBur MGan MHay MRos MRui NBar NBat NElm SPer WWeb
'Eblouissant' (Poly)	MGan
ecae	EBls MAus SHil
– 'Helen Knight'	See R. 'Helen Knight'
'Eclair' (HP)	EBls
'Eddie's Jewel' (moyseii x)	EBls MAus MGan NSty
Eden Rose ® (HT)	EBls IHos MGan SPla SRum
Eden Rose '88 ® (HT/Cl)	SHen SPer
'Edith Bellenden' (HSwB)	EBls
Edith Holden ® (F)	ELeG MAus NBat WAct WWar WWeb
eglanteria	CBow CBre CCMG CCor CSan EBls ETWh GPoy LHol MAus MBri MMat MR&S SHil SPer SRum WAct WMou
'Egyptian Treasure' (F)	MGan
'Eiffel Tower' (HT)	MGan
'Elegance' (HT/Cl)	EBls MAus MGan SPer SSus
Elegant Pearl ® (Patio)	SHil
§ ***elegantula***	CCor MMat
– 'Persetosa'	CCMG EBls ELeG MAus MPar SHil SPer SSus WAct WHCG
Elina ® (HT)	See R. Peaudouce ®
Elizabeth Harkness ® (HT)	EBls GTra LPlm MAus MGan MMat NBar SPer WWar
Elizabeth Heather Grierson ® (HT/Cl)	MMat
Elizabeth of Glamis ® (F)	Widely available
'Elizabeth Philp' (F)	LPlm
'Ellen Mary' (HT)	ELeG
'Ellen Poulsen' (Poly)	MGan
'Ellen Willmott' (HT)	EBls ETWh MAus
Ellen ® (S)	MAus MBri SPer
'Ellinor LeGrice' (HT)	ELeG
'Ellinor LeGrice, Climbing' (HT/Cl)	ELeG
'Elmshorn' (S)	CB&S CCMG CDoC CSan GTra MGan MHls MMat NBar WHCG
¶ Elsie Warren ® (F)	NBat

Emanuel ® (S)	CCMG MAus SPer
'Embassy' (HT)	CSan MHay
'Embassy Regal' (HT)	CSan
'Emily Carter'	CMac
'Emily Gray' (Ra)	Widely available
Eminence ® (HT)	MGan
'Emma Wright' (HT)	MAus
'Emmerdale' (F)	ESha
'Empereur du Maroc' (HP)	CCMG EBls MAus MMat MRTP NSty WHCG
'Empress Josephine'	See R. x ***francofurtana***
'Ena Harkness' (HT)	CGro CMac EBls EBro ELan ESha EWar GGre IJoh MBur MGan MHay MR&S MRos NBar NElm NRog SHen SRum WWeb
'Ena Harkness, Climbing' (HT/Cl)	CGro CMac EBls ELeG GGre GTra IHos MAus MBri MBur MGan MHay MRos NRog SPer SRum WWeb
§ 'Enfant de France' (HP)	EBls
English Elegance ® (S)	MAus
English Garden ® (S)	CCla CSam ETWh EWar MAus MBri MMat MRea MRui SPer SSus WAct WWeb
'English Miss' (F)	CCMG CDoC EBls ELeG EWar IHos MAus MGan MRea MRos SPer SRum WWeb
'Eos' (*moyesii* x)	EBls MAus
'Erfurt' (HM)	CCMG EBls ETWh MAus NSty SPer
'Ernest H Morse' (HT)	Widely available
'Ernest H Morse, Climbing' (HT/Cl)	MGan MRea NElm
'Eroica' (HT)	EBro MGan NRog WWeb
Escapade ® (F)	EBls ELeG MAus
Esperanto Jubileo ®	CSan
Essex ® (GC)	CCla CCor CSut ELeG EOrc IHos MGan MMat MR&S SPer WWar
Esther Ofarim ® (F)	EWar
Esther's Baby ® (Patio)	MAus
'Etoile de Hollande, Climbing' (HT/Cl)	CBow CCMG CCor EBls ETWh LHol MAus MHls MRTP NRog NSty SHen SPer SRum SSus WAct
'Etoile de Lyon' (T)	EBls
'Etude' (Cl)	CSan
'Eugène Fürst' (HP)	EBls WAct WHCG
'Eugénie Guinoisseau' (Mo)	EBls WHCG
Euphrates ® (S)	MGan
Europeana ® (F)	CDoC CGro MAus MGan MHay SRum
'Eva' (HM)	EBls
'Evangeline' (Ra)	EBls MAus NSty SPer WAct
Evelyn Fison ® (Irish Wonder ®) (F)	Widely available
'Evening Star' (HT)	ELeG IDic MAus MMat
'Evening Telegraph' (HT)	MHay

'Everest Double Fragrance' (F)	EBls
'Excelsa' (Ra)	Widely available
Exploit ® (Cl)	EWar
Eye Paint ® (F)	ELeG EWar MAus MGan MMat NRog
'Eyecatcher' (F)	GTra
Eyeopener ® (S/GC)	CGro EWar IDic WWar
'F E Lester'	See R. 'Francis E Lester'
'F J Grootendorst' (Ru)	CCMG EBls ELeG EWar IHos IOrc LGod MAus MGan MHls MMor NRog NSty SRum SSus WAct
'Fabvier'	See R. 'Colonel Fabvier'
Fair Bianca ® (S)	CCMG IJoh IOrc MAus MBri SSus
'Fairlight' (F)	MGan
Fairy Changeling ® (Poly)	MAus
Fairy Damsel ® (Poly/GC)	CDoC EBls MAus
Fairyland ® (Poly)	EBls ESha EWar MAus MRea
'Falkland' (HScB)	EBls MAus
Fantan ® (HT)	ELeG MAus
'Fantin-Latour' (Ce x)	Widely available
fargesii	See R. ***moyesii*** 'Fargesii'
farreri	See R. ***elegantula***
– ***persetosa***	See R. ***elegantula*** 'Persetosa'
'Fashion' (F)	MGan
'Fashion Flame' (Min)	MGan MHls MRea NBar
'Fashion, Climbing' (F/Cl)	EBls
Father's Day ® (Min)	NElm
¶ Favorite Rosamini ® (Min)	MRui
fedtschenkoana	CCor EBls ELeG MAus MGan NSty SPer WHCG
'Felicia' (HM)	Widely available
'Félicité Parmentier' (A/D)	CCMG EBls MAus MRTP NSty SPer SSus WAct
§ 'Félicité Perpétue' (Ra)	CBow CCMG CCla CCor CMac EBls ERav ETWh IHos LHol MAus MBri MGan MMat MRTP NSty SFam SHil SPer SSus WAct WHCG
Felicity Kendal ® (HT)	CDoC MBri MGan MHay NBat
'Fellenberg' (Ch)	EBls ELeG MAus MMat
'Femina' (HT)	MGan
'Ferdinand de Lesseps' (HP)	EBls
'Ferdinand Pichard' (HP)	CBow CCMG CCor EBls EBro ERav ETWh MAus MMat MRTP NSty SHil SPer SSus WAct WHCG
Ferdy ®	CCMG CDoC EBls ELan ETWh EWar MMat MR&S NBar SHen SPer SSus
Fergie ® (F/Patio)	ESha MBri MGan MRos
filipes 'Brenda Colvin'	See R. 'Brenda Colvin'
– 'Kiftsgate' (Ra)	Widely available
– 'Toby Tristram' (Ra)	SBra
'Fillette' (F)	MGan

'Fimbriata' (Ru)	CBow CCor EBls ETWh MAus MBri WAct WHCG
Financial Times Centenary ® (S)	IHos MAus
Fiona ® (S/GC)	EBls EWar IHos MBur MMat MR&S MRea NBar SHen SHil SPer SRum SSus WHCG
'Fire Princess' (Min)	CSan MHay MRea MRos MRui NBar NElm WWeb
'Firecracker' (F)	EBls
Firefly ® (Min)	MRea MRui WWar
'First Love' (HT)	EBls MGan
'Fisher and Holmes' (HP)	EBls MAus WHCG
Fisherman's Friend ® (S)	CDoC ETWh EWar IHos MAus MHay SHil SPer
'Fleet Street' (HT)	MHay
'Fleur Cowles' (F)	MBur MRos
'Flora' (Ra)	EBls MAus
'Flora McIvor' (HSwB)	EBls MAus MGan
Florence Nightingale ® (F)	MBur MGan WWeb
'Florida von Scharbeutz' (F)	MGan
¶ Flower Carpet ® (GC)	MRui NBat
foetida	EBls MAus NSty SHil
– 'Bicolor'	CCMG CDoC EBls ERav ETWh MAus MMat NRog NSty SHil SPer SSus WAct
– 'Persiana'	EBls LHol MAus MGan SHil SPer SSus
foliolosa	EBls SHil WHCG
Fontainebleau ® (HT)	MHay
'Forgotten Dreams' (HT)	MHay
forrestiana	CCor EBls MAus MMat
x *fortuneana*	EBls
'Fosse Way' (HT)	MHay
'Fountain' (S)	EBls ELeG ESha EWar MAus MGan NElm SPer SRum
'Fräulein Octavia Hesse' (Ra)	CCMG EBls
Fragrant Cloud ® (HT)	Widely available
'Fragrant Cloud, Climbing' (HT/Cl)	CB&S ELan LPlm MGan NElm SRum
Fragrant Delight ® (F)	CCMG CCla ELeG ESha EWar IHos LPlm MGan MRea MRos NBar NBat NElm SHil SPer WWar WWeb
Fragrant Dream ® (HT)	IDic MRea WWar
Fragrant Gold ® (HT)	MR&S SRum
'Fragrant Hour' (HT)	MGan MMat
'Francesca' (HM)	EBls EBro ETWh MAus MGan NSty SPer WHCG
Francine Austin ® (S)	CCla IHos MAus MRui SPer SSus WAct
'Francis Dubreuil' (T)	EBls
'Francis E Lester' (HM/R)	CBow CSam EBls EBro ETWh MAus MBri MHay NSty SPer SSus WAct WHCG
§ x *francofurtana*	CCMG CCla EBls ETWh IHos SFam SSus WAct WHCG
'François Juranville' (Ra)	CCMG CHad CSan EBls EBro ERav ETWh LHol MAus MBri MGan MHls MMat NElm NRog SHil SPer SSus
'Frank Naylor' (S)	EWar MAus MMat
'Frau Astrid Späth' (F)	NElm NRog
'Frau Karl Druschki' (HP)	CSan EBls ETWh MAus MGan MHay NSty SHil SPer
'Frau Karl Druschki, Climbing' (HP/Cl)	EBls NRog
'Fred Gibson' (HT)	CSan MHay
'Fred Loads' (S)	EBls ELeG ESha EWar MAus MGan MHay MHls MMat NBat SHil SPer SSus
Freddy ® (F)	MRea
Freedom ® (HT)	CDoC ELeG EWar IDic LGod MBur MGan MRea MRos NBat NRog WWar WWeb
'Freiherr von Marschall' (T)	EBls
'Frensham' (F)	CB&S CGro EBls ELeG MGan MHls MMat SHen SRum
'Fresh Pink' (Poly)	MGan
Friction Lights ® (F)	NBat
'Fringette' (Min)	MGan MMor
'Fritz Nobis' (S)	CBow CCMG CCla CCor CHad CSan EBls ETWh IHos MAus MGan MHay MHls MMat MRTP NSty SHil SPer SSus WHCG
¶ 'Frosty' (Min)	MRui
'Fru Dagmar Hastrup' (Ru)	Widely available
'Frühlingsanfang' (HScB)	EBls MAus MBri SSus
'Frühlingsduft' (HScB)	CBow CCor EBls ELan ETWh NRog NSty SPer
'Frühlingsgold' (HScB)	Widely available
'Frühlingsmorgen' (HScB)	CBow CCMG CHad EBls ELeG ETWh EWar IHos LPlm MAus MBri MBur MGan MHls MMat MMor NBar NElm NRog NSty SHil SPer SSus WHCG
'Frühlingsschnee' (HScB)	EBls
'Frühlingszauber' (HScB)	EBls
'Fulgens'	See R. 'Malton'
Fulton Mackay ® (HT)	ESha WWar
Fyvie Castle ® (HT)	ESha MGan WWar
'Gail Borden' (HT)	ESha MAus MGan MR&S SPla SRum
§ *gallica*	CBre EBls ELan MHay
– 'Beckett's Single'	CCor
– 'Complicata'	See R. 'Complicata'
– 'Conditorum'	See R. 'Conditorum'
§ – *officinalis*	CBow CCMG CCor CDoC EBls EBro ELeG ETWh GPoy LHol MAus MBri MHls MMat NRog NSty SHil SPer SSus WAct WHCG
– *velutiniflora*	EBls

§ – 'Versicolor'	Widely available
Galway Bay ® (HT/Cl)	CMac CSan IJoh MAus MGan MMat SPer
'Garden Princess'	IJoh
§ 'Garnette' (Gn)	ELeG MHls
'Garnette Apricot' (Gn)	ELeG MHls SPer
♦ 'Garnette Carol'	See R. 'Carol Amling'
'Garnette Golden' (Gn)	MHls
♦ 'Garnette Pink'	See R. 'Carol Amling'
♦ 'Garnette Red' (Gn)	See R. 'Garnette'
'Garnette Rose' (Gn)	ELeG
'Garnette Salmon' (Gn)	MHls
'Garnette Yellow' (Gn)	ELeG
¶ 'Gary Lineker' (F)	MRea
'Gary Player' (HT)	MHay MRea NBat
'Gateshead Festival' (HT)	NBat
'Gaujard'	See R. 'Rose Gaujard'
'Gavotte' (HT)	CSan MHay
'Gay Gordons' (HT)	MHls NBar
'Gay Vista' (S)	MGan
'Général Galliéni' (T)	EBls
'Général Jacqueminot' (HP)	EBls SSus WAct WHCG
'Général Kléber' (Mo)	EBls IHos MAus MRTP NSty SFam SPer WAct WHCG
'General MacArthur, Climbing' (HT/Cl)	EBls MAus
§ 'Général Schablikine' (T)	EBls ETWh MAus WWat
gentiliana (Ra)	CCor EBls MAus SHil WHCG
Gentle Touch ® (Min/Patio)	CCla CDoC EBls ESha EWar GGre IDic LGod MBri MBur MGan MHay MMat MR&S MRea MRos MRui NBar NBat SHen SHil SPer SRum WWeb
'Geoff Boycott' (F)	ESha
¶ Geordie Lad ® (HT)	NBat
'Georg Arends' (HP)	CCMG EBls MAus SFam SHil SPer SSus WAct WHCG
'George Dickson' (HT)	MAus
¶ 'George R Hill' (HT)	NBat
'Georges Vibert' (G)	EBls MAus WHCG
Geraldine ® (F)	CDoC ELeG ESha MBri MGan MR&S MRea MRos SPer SRum
'Geranium' (*moyesii* x)	Widely available
'Geranium Red' (F)	MAus
Gerbe d'Or ®	See R. 'Casino'
'Gerbe Rose' (Ra)	EBls MAus NSty
Gertrude Jekyll ® (S)	CDoC CHad CSam EWar IJoh IOrc MAus MMat MRea MRui SHil SPer WAct
'Ghislaine de Féligonde' (S/Ra)	EBls
gigantea	EBls
– cooperi	See R. ***laevigata*** 'Cooperi'
Gilda ® (F)	MRea
Gingernut ® (Patio)	CGro ESha
♦ 'Gipsy Boy'	See R. 'Zigeunerknabe'
Glad Tidings ® (F)	CGro ELeG ESha EWar GGre LPlm MBri MBur MGan MHay MMat MRea NBat SHil SRum WWar WWeb
§ ***glauca***	Widely available
'Glenfiddich' (F)	CBow CGro EBls ESha EWar GGre GTra IHos LGod LPlm MAus MBri MGan MHay MHls MR&S NBar NBat NElm NRog SHen SPer SRum WWeb
'Gloire de Bruxelles' (HP)	EBls
'Gloire de Dijon' (T/Cl)	Widely available
'Gloire de Ducher' (HP)	ETWh MAus MGan MRTP SFam SPer WHCG
'Gloire de France' (G)	CCMG CCor EBls ETWh MAus MRTP WHCG
'Gloire de Guilan' (D)	EBls MAus MRTP NSty SHil WAct
'Gloire des Mousseuses' (Mo)	CBow CCMG CCor EBls EBro ELeG ETWh IHos MAus SFam SHil SSus WAct WHCG
'Gloire du Midi' (Poly)	MAus
'Gloire Lyonnaise' (HP)	CBow CCor EBls ETWh
'Gloria Mundi' (Poly)	EBls MGan
'Glory of Edzell' (HScB)	EBls MAus SHil WSHC
Glowing Embers ® (F)	GTra
glutinosa	See R. ***eglanteria***
'Godfrey Winn' (HT)	WWeb
'Goethe' (Mo)	EBls
Gold Bunny ® (F)	EWar MGan
'Gold Coin' (Min)	MR&S
'Gold Pin' (Min)	ELeG MMat NRed
Gold Topaz ® (F)	MGan
'Goldbusch' (S)	EBls MGan MMat
'Golden Angel' (Min)	MHay MRos
Golden Chersonese ® (S)	EBls MAus NRog NSty SHil
'Golden Dawn' (HT/Cl)	ELeG MAus
Golden Days ® (HT)	EWar LGod MBri
'Golden Glow' (Cl)	EBls GTra MGan
Golden Jubilee ® (HT)	ELan EWar GGre GTra LPlm MBur MHay MRea NBat
'Golden Melody' (HT)	EBls SSus
'Golden Moss' (Mo)	EBls
'Golden Ophelia' (HT)	EBls MAus
'Golden Rambler'	See R. 'Alister Stella Gray'
¶ Golden Rosamini ® (Min)	MRui
'Golden Salmon' (Poly)	MGan
'Golden Salmon Supérieur' (Poly)	EBls
'Golden Shot' (F)	ESha MGan
Golden Showers ® (Cl)	Widely available
'Golden Slippers' (F)	CB&S LPlm MAus MGan MHay
'Golden Sunblaze'	See R. 'Rise 'n' Shine'
'Golden Times' (HT)	MRos WWeb
'Golden Wings' (S)	Widely available
¶ Golden Years ® (F)	MBur NBat
'Goldfinch' (Ra)	CBow CCMG CHad CSan EBls ETWh LGre MAus MRTP NSty SPer WAct WHCG
Goldilocks ®	NElm NRog SPer
'Goldkrone' ('Gold Crown')	MGan SRum
Goldstar ® (HT)	ELeG EWar LPlm MGan WWar

'Goliath' (HT) MHay
'Grace Abounding' (F) EWar MHay NBat
'Grace Darling' (T) EBls
Grace de Monaco ® (HT) EBls MAus MGan
Graham Thomas ® (S) Widely available
'Granadina' MHls
Grand Hotel ® (HT/Cl) EWar IHos MBri MMat SPer
'Grandpa Dickson' (HT) Widely available
'Grandpa's Delight' (F) MRea
'Grand-mère Jenny' (HT) EBls LPlm MGan
'Grand-mère Jenny, Climbing' (HT/Cl) EBls MHls
'Great Maiden's Blush' (A) CSan EBls MBur MMat MRTP NElm NSty WAct WWeb
'Great News' (HT) ELeG MAus SRum
'Great Western' (Bb) EBls
'Green Diamond' (Min) ELeG MAus MBur MMat MRea MRos
¶ Green Snake ® (S/GC) ELan
¶ Greenall's Glory ® (F/Patio) WWeb
'Greenmantle' (HSwB) EBls MAus MGan
Greensleeves ® (F) EBls ELeG MAus SPer
'Grey Dawn' (F) ELeG
'Grootendorst Supreme' (Ru) LPlm MAus SPer
N 'Gros Choux de Hollande' (Bb) EBls
Grouse ® (S/GC) CCMG CCor EBls ETWh IHos LHop MAus MBri MGan MMat MR&S MRos SPer SSus
'Grumpy' (Co) MGan
'Gruss an Aachen' (Poly) CCMG EBls ETWh MAus MGan NSty SPer WAct WHCG
'Gruss an Teplitz' (Ch x) CSan EBls EBro MAus SFam SPer
¶ Guiding Spirit ® (Min/Patio) MBur WWeb
'Guinée' (HT/Cl) CCMG CCor CHad CMac CSan EBls EBro ELan ELeG ETWh IHos MAus MBur MGan MHay MHls MMat MRTP NSty SPer SSus WAct
Guletta ® See R. 'Rugul'
'Gustav Grünerwald' (HT) EBls MAus
♦ 'Gypsy Boy' See R. 'Zigeunerknabe'
'Gypsy Jewel' (Min) CGro NBar NElm
'Gypsy Moth' (F) MBur SRum
'Hakuun' (Min) MAus
'Halley's Comet' (HT) MRea
¶ 'Hamburg Love' (F) MBur
'Hamburger Phönix' (Ra) CGro EBls ELeG MGan NElm SPer
Hampshire ® (GC) CSut IHos MGan MMat
Handel ® (Cl) Widely available
Hannah Gordon ® (F) CDoC ESha EWar MGan MHay MHls MMat MR&S MRea NBar NBat SRum
¶ 'Hannah Hauwxell' (Patio) NBat
'Hannes' (HT) NRog
'Hansa' (Ru) EBls IHos LBuc MAus MGan MMat
§ 'Hansestadt Lübeck' (S) MGan
'Happy' (Co) MGan
'Happy Thought' (Min) MHls MR&S
Happy Wanderer ® (F) EWar
x *harisonii* 'Harison's Yellow' (HScB) CHad EBls MAus SHil SSus
– 'Lutea Maxima' (HScB) EBls MAus SHil
§ – 'Williams' Double Yellow' (HScB) CCMG EBls ELeG ETWh MAus
Harkness Marigold ® (F) CDoC
Harold Macmillan ® (F) NBat
'Harriny' (HT) MGan MMor
'Harry Maasz' (GC) EBls
Harry Wheatcroft ® (HT) CB&S CGro EBls ESha GGre IHos LGod MAus MBri MGan NBat NElm NRog
Harvest Fayre ® (F) CGro ELeG GGre IDic LGod MBri MBur MGan MHay MMat MR&S NBat SPer SRum WWeb
Harvest Home ® (Ru) EWar
'Harvester' (HT) MHay
§ 'Hazel Le Rougetel' (Ru) EBls
x *headleyensis* EBls ETWh MAus
¶ 'Heart of England' (F) MBur
'Heather' (Min) LGod
¶ Heather Honey ® (HT) ELeG
'Heather Muir' EBls MAus NSty WKif
'Heaven Scent' (F) IJoh NBat
'Hebe's Lip' (D x SwB) EBls ELeG MAus
'Hector Deane' (HT) EBls MGan NSty
Heidelberg ® (S) NBar SHil SMad
'Heidi Jayne' (HT) MGan NBar SRum
Heidi ® (Min) MR&S
'Heinrich Schultheis' (HP) EBls
'Helen Knight' (*ecae* x) CSan EBls EHar MAus MBri MMat NSty SHil SPer SSus WHCG
'Helen Traubel' (HT) EBls EBro MGan
helenae CCor EBls ELeG MAus SHil SPer WHCG
Helga ® (HT/F) MGan
'Help the Aged' (HT) MRos
hemisphaerica CBow EBls EMon ETWh MAus MRTP WAct
'Henri Fouquier' (G) EBls
'Henri Martin' (Mo) CCMG CCor EBls IOrc MAus NRog SHil SPer WAct WHCG
'Henry Nevard' (HP) EBls
'Her Majesty' (HP) EBls
'Herbstfeuer' (HSwB) CCor EBls MAus NSty
Heritage ® (S) CDoC CSam EBls ELeG ETWh IHos LGod LHol MAus MBri MHay MMat MRea MRos MRui NBat SHil SPer SSus WHCG

'Hermosa' (Ch)	EBls ETWh MAus MRTP SSus WHCG
Hero ® (S)	MAus
'Hiawatha' (Ra)	EBls ERav ETWh MAus WHCG
'Hibernica' (*canina* x)	MAus
'Hidcote Gold'	EBls MAus
'Highdownensis' (*moyesii* x)	CCla EBls ELan MAus MMat SHil SPer
Highfield ® (Cl)	CDoC ELeG ESha EWar LGod MAus MBri MRea NBat SPer
'Highlight' (F)	MGan
Hilda Murrell ® (S)	MAus
'Hillieri' (*moyesii* x)	EBls MAus SHil WSHC
'Hippolyte' (G)	EBls MAus WSHC
holodonta	See R. ***moyesii rosea***
Holy Rose	See R. ***richardii***
'Home Sweet Home' (HT)	EBls MAus
¶ 'Home Sweet Home, Climbing' (HT/Cl)	MAus
'Homère' (T)	EBls MAus
¶ 'Honey Bunch' (F/Patio)	MBri NBat
'Honey Favorite' (HT)	MAus
'Honeymoon' (F)	CB&S GTra IJoh MAus MGan MMor NElm SRum WWeb
'Honorine de Brabant' (Bb)	CBow CCMG CCor CHad CSan EBls ETWh MAus MMat SFam SHil SPer SSus WHCG
'Horace Vernet' (HP	EBls
horrida	See R. ***biebersteinii***
'Horstmanns Rosenresli' (F)	EBls ERav
'Hot Pewter' (HT)	MHay
¶ Hotline ® (Min)	MRui
'Hugh Dickson' (HP)	CBow CCMG EBls EBro ETWh MAus NSty
hugonis	CBow CCMG CCla CCor EBls ELan ETWh LHol MAus MGan MHls MMat NRog SHil SPer WAct WHCG
'Hula Girl' (Min)	CSan ELeG LGod MBur MHay MHls MRea MRos MRui NRed
Hume's Blush	See R. x ***odorata*** 'Odorata'
'Hunslet Moss' (Mo)	EBls
'Hunter' (Ru)	MHls WAct
'Hutton Village' (HT)	EWar
hypoleuca	CCor
Ice Fairy ® (GC)	CSan
'Ice White' (F)	MGan
Iceberg ® (Schneewittchen ®) (F)	Widely available
Iceberg, Climbing ® (F/Cl)	Widely available
'Iced Ginger' (F)	CCMG ELeG EWar MAus MGan NBar SPer WAct WWar
'Ideal Home' (HT)	MMor
IGA '83 München ® (GC)	MR&S
iliensis	CCor
'Illusion' (Cl)	MGan
Ilse Krohn Superior ® (Cl)	EBls
'Indian Sunblaze' (Min/Patio)	IHos IJoh WWeb
Ingrid Bergman ® (HT)	CDoC EWar LGod MBri MGan MMat MRea MRos SPer WWar WWeb
'Intermezzo' (HT)	CDoC MBur MGan
International Herald Tribune ® (Patio)	ELeG ESha MAus
Intrigue ® (F)	MHay MMat WWar
Invincible ® (F)	EWar MGan MRea WWar
'Invitation' (HT)	MBur MGan
'Ipsilanté' (G)	CCor EBls MAus WAct WHCG
'Irene of Denmark' (F)	EBls
'Irène Watts' (Ch)	EBls ETWh
Irene's Delight ® (HT)	MHay NBat
Iris Webb ® (F)	ELeG
¶ 'Irish Brightness' (HT)	MAus
'Irish Elegance' (HT)	EBls MAus
'Irish Fireflame' (HT)	EBls MAus
¶ 'Irish Fireflame, Climbing' (HT/Cl)	MAus
Irish Mist ® (F)	GTra MGan
'Isabel de Ortiz' (HT)	MGan MRea
'Isis' (F)	MBri
¶ 'Isobel' (HT)	MAus
'Ispahan' (D)	CCMG CCla CCor CSam EBls EBro ELeG ETWh MAus NSty SFam SPer SSus WAct WHCG WSHC
¶ 'Ivory Fashion' (F)	EBls MAus
'Ivory Tip Top' (F)	MHay
¶ 'J C Bell' (HT)	MHay
x ***jacksonii*** 'Max Graf'	Widely available
– 'White Max Graf'	EOrc IHos MMat
Jacobite Rose	See R. 'Alba Maxima'
Jacqueline du Pré ® (S)	ELeG EWar MAus WWar
'Jacquenetta' (S)	LHol
'Jacques Cartier'	See R. 'Marquise Boccella'
'James Bourgault' (HP)	EBls
'James Mason' (G)	EBls MAus
'James Mitchell' (Mo)	EBls MAus MBur SFam WHCG
'James Veitch' (DP/Mo)	EBls
'Jan Guest' (HT)	MHay MRea NBat
Jane Asher ® (Patio)	CGro MRea
'Janet's Pride' (HSwB)	EBls MAus
'Janice Tellian' (Min)	MHay MRos
'Japonica' (Mo)	MAus
¶ 'Jayne Austin'	MAus MRui
'Jean Mermoz' (Poly)	MAus NElm NRog NSty SPer SRum
'Jean Rosenkrantz' (HP)	EBls
'Jean Sisley' (HT)	EBls
'Jeanne de Montfort' (Mo)	EBls MAus WHCG
¶ 'Jeannie Deans' (HSwB)	MAus
¶ 'Jenny Charlton' (HT)	NBat
'Jenny Duval' (G)	See R. 'Président de Sèze'
'Jenny Wren' (F)	EBls MAus
'Jenny's Dream' (HT)	MRea
'Jersey Beauty' (Ra)	EBls

'Jiminy Cricket' (F)	EBls
'Jimmy Greaves' (HT)	MGan MHay
Jimmy Savile ® (F)	MRea
¶ Joan Ball ® (Min)	MRui
'Joanna Hill' (HT)	EBls
'Joanne' (HT)	EWar MHay MRea
'Jocelyn' (F)	EBls ELeG MAus MBri
'John Abrams' (F)	CSan
'John Hopper' (HP)	EBls ETWh MAus NSty
John Hughes ® (F)	CSan
'John Waterer' (HT)	ELeG MAus MGan
Johnnie Walker ® (HT)	ELeG MBri MGan MHls
'Josephine Bruce' (HT)	CB&S CGro CMac EBls ELeG ESha EWar GTra LGod LPlm MAus MBur MGan MHay MHls MR&S NRog SHen SRum
'Josephine Bruce, Climbing' (HT/Cl)	MAus MGan MHay SHen
'Josephine Wheatcroft'	See R. 'Rosina'
Joseph's Coat ® (S/Cl)	CSan EBls IHos LGod LPlm MGan MHay MHls MMat MMor MRui SRum SSus WWar WWeb
'Journey's End' (HT)	MGan
'Joybells' (F)	MAus MGan
Joyfulness ® (F)	GTra MGan NElm WWeb
'Judy Fischer' (Min)	EWar LGod MHay MRui NElm WWeb
Judy Garland ® (F)	MRea
'Julia Mannering' (HSwB)	MAus
Julia's Rose ® (HT)	CGro CHad ELeG EWar MAus MBur MGan MRea MRos NBar NElm SPer
Julie Cussons ® (F)	MRea NBat
'Juliet' (HP)	EBls
'June Bride' (F)	MGan
'June Park' (HT)	MGan
'June Time' (Min)	CGro MMor NBat NElm
'Juno' (Ce)	EBls MAus SFam WHCG
Just Joey ® (HT)	Widely available
'Karl Förster' (HScB)	EBls MAus
'Kassel' (S/Cl)	EBls MAus MBri MGan MMat SPer
'Katharina Zeimet' (Poly)	EBls MAus MGan NRog NSty WAct WHCG
'Kathleen' (HM)	EBls EBro
'Kathleen Ferrier' (F)	EBls MGan MHay MMat MMor
'Kathleen Harrop' (Bb)	CCMG CHad EBls IHos MAus MMat NSty SFam SHil SPer SSus WHCG WSHC WWat WWeb
'Kathleen O'Rourke' (HT)	EWar
¶ 'Kathryn Morley'	MAus MRui
'Katie' (F/Cl)	MGan
'Kazanlik'	See R. ***damascena*** 'Trigintipetala'
Keepsake ® (HT)	LPlm MGan MHay MMat NBat NElm NRog SHil WWar
Kent ® (S/GC)	CCor CSut IHos LGod MMat MR&S SPer
'Kerrygold' (F)	IJoh MGan
Kerryman ® (F)	EWar MGan
'Kew Rambler' (Ra)	CBow CCMG EBls ETWh MAus SPer SSus WHCG
'Kiese' (canina x)	CCor ELeG
'Kiftsgate'	See R. ***filipes*** 'Kiftsgate'
'Kilworth Gold' (HT)	MGan SRum
'Kim' (Patio)	MAus NRog
King's Ransom ® (HT)	Widely available
'Kitchener of Khartoum'	See R. 'K of K'
x ***kochiana***	EBls
'Köln am Rhein' (Cl)	MGan
§ 'Königin von Dänemark' (A)	CCMG CCla CHad EBls ELeG ETWh MAus MBri MBur MMat NSty SHil SSus WAct WHCG
'Korbell' (F)	MGan NBat
'Kordes Robusta'	See R. Robusta ®
Korona ® (F)	EBls GTra MGan NRog
'Korona, Climbing' (F/Cl)	EBls.
'Korp' (F)	ELeG MGan MHls MMat
'Korresia' (F)	CCMG CSan EHar ELeG ESha EWar GGre IHos IJoh LGod MAus MBri MGan MHay MHls MMat MMor MRea MRos NBat NRog SHil SPer SRum
Kronenbourg ® (HT)	EBls MAus MBur SRum
'Kronprinzessin Viktoria' (Bb)	CBow CCor EBls ETWh MAus
L D Braithwaite ® (S)	ELeG LGod MAus MGan MRui SPer WWeb
'La Belle Distinguée' (HSwB)	EBls WHCG
'La Belle Sultane'	See R. 'Violacea'
'La Follette' (Cl)	EBls
'La France' (HT)	EBls EBro MAus MRTP SHil
¶ 'La France, Climbing' (HT/Cl)	MAus
¶ 'La Jolla' (HT)	MBur
'La Mortola'	See R. ***brunonii*** 'La M.'
'La Noblesse' (Ce)	EBls WHCG
¶ 'La Perle' (Ra)	MAus
'La Plus Belle des Ponctuées' (G)	CCor
'La Reine' (HP)	EBls NSty
'La Reine Victoria'	See R. 'Reine Victoria'
'La Rêve' (Cl)	EBls MAus
'La Rubanée'	See R. 'Centifolia Variegata'
La Sevillana ® (GC)	EBls EWar MR&S SHen SPer
'La Ville de Bruxelles' (D)	CCMG CCor EBls EBro ETWh IHos MAus NSty SFam SPer WAct WHCG
'Lady Alice Stanley' (HT)	EBls MAus MBur
'Lady Barnby' (HT)	EBls
'Lady Belper' (HT)	EBls MAus
'Lady Curzon' (Ru)	EBls IHos MAus NSty WAct
'Lady Elgin'	See R. 'Thaïs'
'Lady Forteviot' (HT)	EBls
'Lady Godiva' (Ra)	CDoC MAus

'Lady Helen' (HT) CGro
'Lady Hillingdon' (T) ETWh MAus MRTP NSty
'Lady Hillingdon, Climbing' (T/Cl) CBow CCMG EBls EBro MAus NSty SHen SHil SPer SSus WAct WHCG
'Lady Iliffe' (HT) MGan
'Lady Mary Fitzwilliam' (HT) EBls
Lady Meillandina ® MR&S
'Lady of Stifford' (F) EWar
'Lady Penzance' (HSwB) CB&S CCMG CDoC CSam EBls ELeG EWar MAus MBur MGan NSty SHen SHil SPer SSus WAct
'Lady Romsey' (F) EBls
'Lady Seton' (HT) MGan SPer
'Lady Sylvia' (HT) EBls ELeG MAus MGan NRog NSty SHen SPer SSus
'Lady Sylvia, Climbing' (HT/Cl) EBls ELeG ETWh MAus MGan MHls NElm NRog SPer SSus
Lady Taylor ® (F/Patio) MRea MRos
'Lady Waterlow' (HT/Cl) CBow CCMG EBls EBro ETWh MAus SPer WAct WHCG
laevigata CBot EBls MAus
– 'Anemonoides' See R. 'Anemone'
– 'Cooperi' CCMG CHad EBls ETWh LGre MAus WSHC WTay
'Lafter' (S) EBls
'Lagoon' (F) EBls
'Lakeland' (HT) MAus MBri NRog
'Lamarque' (N) MAus
Lancashire Life ® (F) MBri
'Lanei' (Mo) EBls
Langford Light ® (Min/GC) MBri
Laughter Lines ® (F) IDic MBri WWar
¶ Laura Ashley ® (Min/Cl) MBur NBat
Laura Ford ® (Min/Cl) ELeG MBri MBur MHls MRui NBat WWar WWeb
¶ 'Laura Jane' (HT) MGan
Laura ® (HT) EWar
'Lavender Jewel' (Min) CSan ELeG MAus MBur MHay MMat MRos MRui
'Lavender Lace' (Min) MHay
'Lavender Lassie' (S) CHad EBro ELeG ERav IOrc MAus MBur MGan MHay MHls MMat MRui SSus WAct WHCG
'Lavender Pinocchio' (F) MAus WAct
Lavinia ® (Cl) EWar LGod MBri NElm SPer
'Lawrence Johnston' (Cl) CCla MAus NSty SPer WAct WHCG
'Le Havre' (HP) EBls
¶ 'Le Rêve' (Cl) ETWh
'Le Vésuve' (Ch) EBls MAus
Leander ® (S) CCMG MAus MBri
Leaping Salmon ® (HT/Cl) CDoC CGro ELeG EWar IHos IJoh IOrc LGod MBri MHay MRea NBat SRum
'Leda' (D) CBow CCMG CCor EBls ETWh MAus SFam WAct
'Lemon Pillar' See R. 'Paul's Lemon Pillar'
'Lemon Yellow' (F) MGan
Len Turner ® (F) CDoC ELeG IDic IHos LGod MBri
'Léonie Lamesch' (Poly) EBls
'Léontine Gervais' (Ra) MAus MRTP WAct WHCG
¶ Letchworth Garden City ® (F) WWar
'Leuchtstern' (Ra) EBls
'Leverkusen' (Cl) CBow CDoC CHad CSan EBls ELeG ETWh MAus MGan MHls MRea NElm NSty SPer SRum SSus WAct WSHC
'Leweson Gower' (Bb) EBls
'Ley's Perpetual' (Cl) CCMG EBls ETWh MAus WHCG
'Liberty Bell' (HT) MGan
Lichtkönigin Lucia ® (S) MMat WWar
Lilac Airs ® (HT) CSan
'Lilac Charm' (F) CHad EBls ELeG MAus SRum
¶ 'Lilac Rose' MAus
Lilian Austin ® (S) IHos MAus MBri SPer
Lilli Marlene ® (F) CB&S CCMG CDoC EBls ELeG ESha GGre GTra IHos IJoh LGod LPlm MAus MBur MGan MHls MMat MMor MR&S NElm NRog SHen SRum WWeb
Lincoln Cathedral ® (HT) ELeG ESha MGan MHay MRea NBat SPer WWar
Little Artist ® (Min) MHay MRui WWeb
'Little Buckaroo' (Min) CGro ELan EWar GGre LGod MGan MHay MMor MR&S NBar NElm NRed SPer
'Little Dorrit' (Poly) CDoC NElm NRog
'Little Flirt' (Min) ELeG EWar GGre IJoh LPlm MAus MGan MR&S MRui NBat
'Little Gem' (DPMo) EBls EBro MAus MGan
Little Jewel ® (Patio) MAus MRea
Little Marvel ® (Patio) MBri MRea
Little One ® CSan
Little Prince ® (Patio) MAus WWar
Little Russel ® (Min) NBat
'Little Stephen' (HT) CSan
'Little White Pet' (Poly) CBow CCMG CCla CCor CHad ETWh IHos MAus MBri MBur MGan MRTP MRea SPer SPla SSus WAct WHCG
♦ 'Little White Pet, Climbing' See R. 'Félicité Perpétue'
Little Women ® (Patio) CDoC ELeG IDic IHos MRos
'Liverpool Echo' (F) ESha MHay NBat SHen
'Living Fire' (F) EBls MGan NBar
'Lollipop' (Min) MGan
'Long John Silver' (Cl) EBls

longicuspis (Ra)	CCMG CCla CHil EBls ELan ETWh ISea MRea SHil SPer SPla SSus WWat
Longleat ® (Min)	MHay MMat
'Lord Penzance' (HSwB)	CCMG EBls ELeG ETWh MAus MGan MRTP NSty SPer SSus WAct
Lordly Oberon ® (S)	SPer
'Lorraine Lee' (T)	EBls
'Los Angeles' (HT)	EBls
'Louis Gimard' (Mo)	EBls IHos MAus SPer WAct WHCG
'Louis Philippe' (Ch)	EBls
'Louis XIV' (Ch)	EBls WHCG
'Louise Odier' (Bb)	CCMG CCla EBls ELeG ETWh MAus MBri MHls MMat MRTP NSty SFam SHil SPer SRum SSus WAct WHCG
¶ 'Love Affair' (Min)	MBur
¶ 'Love Token' (F)	MBur
Lovely Lady ® (HT)	CDoC ELeG ESha IDic MGan MHay MRos SHil
'Lover's Meeting' (HT)	CSan ELeG ESha GGre IJoh LPlm MBri MBur MGan MHay MHls MMat MRea MRos NBar NBat SHil SPer WWar WWeb
Loving Memory ® (HT)	ELeG EWar MGan MHay MHls MMat SHil SRum WWar
Loving Touch ® (Min)	MHay
'Lucetta' (S)	LHol MAus SPer
luciae	EBls
♦ 'Lübeck'	See R. 'Hansestadt Lübeck'
'Luis Brinas' (HT)	NSty
'Lutea Maxima'	See R. x ***harisonii*** 'L.M.'
'Lykkefund' (Ra)	CCor CHad EBls MAus
'Lyon Rose' (HT)	EBls
L'Oréal Trophy ® (HT)	ELeG MAus MGan NBar WWar
'L'Ouche'	See R. 'Louise Odier'
'Ma Perkins' (F)	EBls MAus
'Ma Ponctuée' (DPMo)	EBls
'Mabel Morrison' (HP)	EBls MAus WHCG
Macartney Rose	See R. ***bracteata***
'Macrantha' (G x)	CCor EBls MAus SHil SPer SSus WAct
'Macrantha Raubritter'	See R. 'Raubritter'
'Macrexy'	See R. Sexy Rexy ®
macrophylla	CCor MAus MMat
– 'Doncasteri'	See R. 'Doncasteri'
¶ 'Macshana' (Min)	WWar
'Madame Abel Châtenay' (HT)	EBls MAus SHil
'Madame Abel Châtenay, Climbing' (HT/Cl)	CCMG EBls MAus NElm SPer WWeb
'Madame Alfred Carrière' (N)	Widely available
'Madame Alice Garnier' (Ra)	EBls ETWh
'Madame Antoine Mari' (T)	EBls
'Madame Berkeley' (T)	EBls
'Madame Bravy' (T)	EBls MAus
'Madame Butterfly' (HT)	EBls EBro MAus MBur MGan MHls NSty SHil SPer SRum
'Madame Butterfly, Climbing' (HT/Cl)	CBow CMac EBls LPlm MAus MGan SPer
§ 'Madame Caroline Testout, Climbing' (HT/Cl)	EBls ELeG LHol MAus NRog NSty SHil SPer SSus WAct WSHC
'Madame de Watteville' (T)	EBls
'Madame Delaroche-Lambert' (DPMo)	EBls MAus WAct WHCG
'Madame Driout' (T/N/Cl)	EBls WHCG
'Madame d'Arblay' (Ra)	EBls
'Madame Edouard Herriot, Climbing' (HT/Cl)	CCMG EBls ETWh GTra MAus MGan
'Madame Eliza de Vilmorin ' (HT)	EBls
'Madame Ernst Calvat' (Bb)	CCMG CSan EBls MAus NSty SFam SPer WHCG
'Madame Eugène Résal' (Ch)	MAus
'Madame Gabriel Luizet' (HP)	EBls
'Madame Georges Bruant' (Ru)	EBls MAus
§ 'Madame Grégoire Staechelin' (HT/Cl)	CBow CCMG CGro CSan EBls EBro ELeG ETWh MAus MBri MGan MHay MMat MRTP MRea NRog NSty SHen SHil SPer SRum SSus WAct WHCG
'Madame Hardy' (D/Cl)	Widely available
'Madame Henri Guillot' (HT/Cl)	EBls
'Madame Isaac Pereire' (Bb/Cl)	Widely available
'Madame Jules Bouché, Climbing' (HT/Cl)	MGan
'Madame Jules Gravereaux' (T/Cl)	EBls MAus
N 'Madame Knorr' ('Comte de Chambord') (D/P)	CBow CCMG EBls ETWh IHos MAus NSty SHil SSus WAct
'Madame Laurette Messimy ' (Ch)	CCMG EBls MAus SFam WHCG
'Madame Lauriol de Barny' (Bb)	CCMG EBls ETWh MAus MGan SPer SSus WHCG

	Cultivar	Suppliers
	'Madame Legras de Saint Germain' (A/N)	CCMG CCla EBls ETWh IHos MAus NSty SFam SPer SSus WAct WHCG
	'Madame Lombard' (T)	EBls
	'Madame Louis Laperrière' (HT)	EBls LPlm MAus MGan MHls MMor NSty SPer WWeb
	'Madame Louis Lévêque' (DPMo)	EBls
	'Madame Pierre Oger' (Bb)	CBow CCMG CMac CSan EBls EBro ELeG ETWh EWar IHos LHol MAus MHls MMat MRTP MRea NSty SFam SHil SPer SRum SSus WAct WHCG
	'Madame Plantier' (A/N)	CCla CCor CHad EBls ETWh LHol MAus MMat MRTP SPer SSus WAct WHCG
	'Madame Sancy de Parabère' (Bs)	CCor EBls ETWh MAus
	'Madame Scipion Cochet' (HP)	EBls WHCG
	'Madame Victor Verdier' (HP)	EBls
	'Madame Wagram, Comtese de Turenne' (T)	EBls
	'Madame William Paul' (PMo)	EBls
	'Madame Zoëtmans' (D)	CCMG EBls MAus WHCG
	'Madeleine Selzer' (Ra)	EBls MAus MGan MHay
	'Märchenland' (S)	EBls MAus
	Maestro ® (HT)	EHar MAus NBar
	'Magenta' (S)	EBls ELeG MAus MHay SPer
	Magic Carrousel ® (Min)	CSan ELeG LPlm MAus MBri MBur MHay MHls MMor MRos MRui NBat NRed WWar WWeb
¶	'Magna Charta' (HP)	EBls
	'Magnifica' (HSwB)	EBls MAus MGan
N	'Maiden's Blush' (A)	CBow CCMG CDoC CHad EBls ELan ELeG ETWh LHol MAus MGan SFam SHil SPer SRum SSus WHCG
	'Maiden's Blush, Great'	See R. 'Great Maiden's Blush'
	'Maigold' (HScB/Cl)	Widely available
	'Mainzer Wappen' (HT)	MGan
	majalis	CCor
	'Mala Rubinstein' (HT)	ELeG IDic
	'Malaga' (HT/Cl)	MMat SRum
	Malcolm Sargent ® (HT)	NBar SPer
	'Malmesbury' (HT)	CSan
	'Maltese Rose'	See R, 'Cécile Brunner'
§	'Malton'	EBls
	'Maman Cochet, Climbing' (T/Cl)	EBls MAus
¶	Mandy ® (HT)	MRea
	'Manettii' (N)	EBls
	Mannheim ® (S)	MGan

	Cultivar	Suppliers
	'Manning's Blush' (HSwB)	CCor EBls ELeG MAus MRTP NSty SSus WAct
	Manou Meilland ® (HT)	EWar MGan
	Manuela ® (HT)	MGan
	'Manx Queen' (F)	CSan GTra MGan
	'Marbrée' (D/P)	EBls
	'Marcel Bourgouin' (G)	CCor EBls ELeG
¶	'Marchioness of Salisbury' (HT)	CCMG
	'Marcie Gandy' (HT)	MGan
	'Maréchal Davoust' (Mo)	EBls ELeG MAus MRTP NSty SFam
	'Maréchal Niel' (N)	CCMG EBls ERea ETWh MAus MGan MRTP NSty SPer
	'Margaret' (HT)	ELeG MBur MGan
	Margaret Merril ® (HT/F)	Widely available
	Margaret Thatcher ® (HT)	CDoC MMat SRum
	'Margo Koster' (Poly)	MAus NRog SPer SRum
	'Marguerite Guillard' (HP)	EBls
	'Marguerite Hilling' (S)	Widely available
	'Marianne Powell' (HT)	NBat
	'Marie de Blois' (Mo)	EBls
	'Marie Louise' (D)	CBow CCMG CCor EBls EBro ETWh IHos MAus SFam WAct WHCG
	'Marie Pavié' (Poly)	CCla EBls MAus
	'Marie van Houtte' (T)	EBls MAus
	'Marie-Jeanne' (Poly)	EBls MAus
	Marion Harkness ® (HT)	MBri
	Maritime Bristol ® (HT)	CSan
	Marjorie Fair ® (S/GC)	CSan EBls ELeG ERav ESha EWar MAus MGan MHay MMat MRea SHil SPer SRum
	'Marlena' (Patio)	ELeG MAus MBri MGan MHay
N	'Marquise Boccella' ('Jacques Cartier') (DPo)	CBow CCMG CCla CCor EBls EBro ETWh LHol MAus MGan SPer SSus WAct WHCG
	'Marshall P Wilder' (HT)	NSty
	'Martha' (Bb)	EBls
	'Martian Glow' (F/S)	MGan
	'Martin Frobisher' (S)	CCor EBls MAus
¶	'Marty' (F)	MRea
	'Mary Barnard' (F)	CSan
	Mary Donaldson ® (HT)	EWar MGan
	Mary Hayley Bell ® (S)	ELeG WWeb
	'Mary Manners' (Ru)	EBls SPer
	'Mary Queen of Scots' (HScB)	EBls NSty
	Mary Rose ® (S)	Widely available
¶	Mary Sumner ® (F)	WWar
	'Mary Wallace' (Cl)	EBls MAus SPer
	Mary Webb ® (S)	MAus MBri

'Masquerade' (F)	CB&S CGro EBls EBro ELeG ESha GGre IJoh LPlm MAus MGan MHay MHls MMat MMor MR&S NBar NElm NRog SHen SRum WWeb
'Masquerade, Climbing' (F/Cl)	CMac CSan EBls EBro ELeG GGre LPlm MAus MGan MHay MHls NRog SHen SRum WWeb
'Master Hugh' (***macrophylla*** x)	EBls MAus NSty SHil
Matangi ® (F)	EWar LGod LPlm MGan MHay MHls MMat MR&S WWar
Matthias Meilland ® (F)	EWar
'Max Graf'	See R. x ***jacksonii*** 'Max Graf'
'Maxima'	See R. 'Alba Maxima'
May Lyon ® (HT)	LGod MGan
'May Queen' (Ra)	CBow EBls ETWh MAus MRTP SFam SPer WAct WHCG
'McGredy's Sunset' (HT)	NRog
'McGredy's Yellow' (HT)	EBls MBur MGan
'McGredy's Yellow, Climbing' (HT/Cl)	MGan
'Meg' (Cl)	CCMG CCla CHad EBls ETWh MAus MBur MGan MRea NBar NSty SPer SRum WHCG
'Meg Merilees' (HSwB)	EBls LHol MAus MGan SSus
'Megiddo' (F)	MGan WWeb
Meirov ® (Min)	MGan
melina	EBls
Melinda ® (HT)	MBri
¶ Melody Maker ® (F)	ELeG MBur NBat
§ Memento ® (F)	CDoC ELeG EWar IDic MBri MHay MHls MMat SPer WWar
'Memoriam' (HT)	MGan MHay SHen
'Mermaid' (Cl)	Widely available
'Merveille de Lyon' (HP)	EBls
Message ® (HT)	ELeG MAus MGan NBar NElm SHen
Meteor ® (F)	ESha MGan MMor WWeb
¶ 'Mevrouw G A van Rossem, Climbing' (HT/Cl)	EBls MAus
§ 'Mevrouw Nathalie Nypels' (Poly)	CCla CHad CMac EBls ELeG ERav ETWh MAus MRTP SHil SPer WAct WHCG WSHC
'Michèle Meilland' (HT)	EBls ELeG MAus MGan NSty SRum
x ***micrugosa***	EBls MAus
– ***alba***	EBls
Midas ® (HT)	ELeG
Mimi ® (Min)	MGan
Mini Metro ® (Min)	ELeG MRea MRui
Minijet ® (Min)	EWar IHos MGan NBat
Minilights ® (Patio)	CDoC ELeG EWar GGre IDic MRui SPer
'Minnehaha' (Ra)	CSan EBls EBro ELeG LGod MAus
Minnie Pearl ® (Min)	MHay
mirifica stellata	See R. ***stellata mirifica***
Mischief ® (HT)	CDoC CGro CMac CSan EBls EWar GGre GTra IJoh LPlm MAus MBur MGan MHls MR&S NBar NElm NRog SHen SPer SRum WWeb
'Miss Edith Cavell' (HT)	EBls
Miss Harp ® (HT)	MGan NBar NElm NRog
Miss Ireland ® (HT)	MGan NRog SRum
'Miss Lowe' (Ch)	CCor EBls
Miss Pam Ayres ® (S)	MMat
'Mission Supreme' (HT)	CSan
§ Mister Lincoln ® (HT)	CGro EBls EBro IHos LGod MAus MBri MBur MGan MHls MR&S NElm SHen SPer WWar
Modern Art ® (HT)	WWar WWeb
'Modern Times' (HT)	MBur MGan
'Mojave' (HT)	MAus MGan MR&S SRum
Moje Hammarberg ® (Ru)	IHos MMat
Molly McGredy ® (F)	GTra LPlm MGan
'Mona Ruth' (Min)	MGan
'Monique' (HT)	EBls MBur MGan NSty
'Monsieur Tillier' (T)	EBls
'Montezuma' (HT)	MGan
'Moon Maiden' (F)	MMat
¶ 'Moonbeam' (S)	MAus
'Moonlight' (HM)	CCMG CCor CHad EBls EBro ERav ETWh EWar IHos MAus MGan MHay MMat MRTP NElm NRog NSty SHil SPer SRum WAct WHCG
'Morgengruss' (Cl)	MGan SPer WWar
Moriah ® (HT)	MGan
'Morletii' (Bs)	EBls
'Morning Jewel' (F/Cl)	CB&S ELeG EWar MRea NElm NRog SHil SPer SRum
moschata (Ra)	CCMG CSan EBls ETWh MAus MRTP SHil WAct
– ***autumnalis***	See R. 'Princesse de Nassau'
♦ – ***nastarana***	See R. 'Nastarana'
– ***nepalensis*** (Ra)	EBls
Mother and Baby ® (HT)	CSan
'Mothers Day' (F)	ELan NElm
Mountain Snow ® (Ra)	MAus MBri
Mountbatten ® (F)	Widely available
§ 'Mousseline' (D/PMo)	CCMG EBls EBro ELeG ETWh MAus NSty WAct WHCG
moyesii	Widely available
– 'Evesbatch'	WAct
– ***fargesii***	EBls ELeG SPer
– 'Geranium'	See R. 'Geranium'
– 'Highdownensis'	See R. 'Highdownensis'
– 'Hillieri'	See R. 'Hillieri'
– ***holodonta***	See R. ***m. rosea***
§ – ***rosea***	EBls
– 'Sealing Wax'	See R. 'Sealing Wax'

'Mr Bluebird' (Min)	ELeG EWar IJoh LGod MAus MGan MMor MR&S MRea
'Mr Chips' (HT)	MBur MGan
'Mr Lincoln'	See R. Mister Lincoln ®
'Mrs Aaron Ward, Climbing' (HT/Cl)	EBls
'Mrs Anthony Waterer' (Ru)	EBls IHos MAus MMat NSty SPer SSus WAct
¶ 'Mrs Arthur Curtiss James' (HT/Cl)	ETWh
'Mrs Colville' (HScB)	EBls MAus
'Mrs Eveline Gandy' (HT)	MGan
♦ 'Mrs G A van Rossem, Climbing'	See R. 'Mevrouw G A van Rossem, Climbing'
'Mrs Herbert Stevens, Climbing' (HT/Cl)	CCMG EBls ETWh MAus MRTP NRog NSty WHCG
'Mrs John Laing' (HP)	CBow CCMG EBls EBro ELeG ETWh MAus NSty SFam SHil SPer SSus WHCG
'Mrs Oakley Fisher' (HT)	CHad EBls ERav MAus NSty SHil WAct
'Mrs Paul' (Bb)	EBls MAus
'Mrs Pierre S du Pont' (HT)	EBls
'Mrs Sam McGredy' (HT)	MAus MBur MGan
'Mrs Sam McGredy, Climbing' (HT/Cl)	CBow CGro CMac EBls ETWh MAus MBri MGan MHay MMor NBar NElm NRog SRum SSus
'Mrs Walter Burns' (Patio)	MGan
'München' (S)	MAus
'Mullard Jubilee' (HT)	ELeG EWar MAus MGan NBar
mulliganii	EBls MAus
multibracteata	CCor EBls MAus MPar WHCG WWeb
multiflora	CCMG CCor EBls MAus WHCG
– 'Carnea'	EBls
– ***cathayensis***	EBls
– 'Grevillei'	EBls ETWh MAus SPla
– 'Platyphylla'	See R. ***m.*** 'Grevillei'
– ***watsoniana***	See R. ***watsoniana***
– 'Wilsonii'	CSan
mundi	See R. ***gallica*** 'Versicolor'
– ***versicolor***	See R. ***gallica*** 'Versicolor'
'Munster' (S)	MGan
* ***muriculata***	CCor
'Mutabilis'	See R. x ***odorata*** 'Mutabilis'
'My Choice' (HT)	ELeG MGan MR&S SHen
'My Guy' (HT)	NBat
'My Joy' (HT)	MHay
¶ 'My Little Boy' (Min)	MBur
'My Love' (HT)	GGre GTra MBur MGan MHay MRos WWeb
'My Love, Climbing' (HT/Cl)	MGan SRum
My Valentine ® (Min)	MHay
'Myra' (F)	NBat
nanothamnus	See R. ***webbiana microphylla***
'Naomi' (HT)	MRea
'Narrow Water' (Ra)	EBls WAct WHCG
§ 'Nastarana' (N)	EBls
'Nathalie Nypels'	See R. 'Mevrouw Nathalie Nypels'
'National Trust' (HT)	EBls ELeG ESha EWar GGre IHos LGod MAus MBri MGan MHay MHls MMat MMor NBar NElm NRog SHen SPer WWeb
'Nestor' (G)	EBls MAus
'Nevada' (S)	Widely available
Neville Gibson ® (HT)	MHay
§ 'New Dawn' (Cl)	Widely available
'New Look' (F)	MGan
'New Penny' (Min)	ELeG EWar GGre IJoh MAus MBur MGan MMor MR&S MRui SPer WWeb
News ® (F)	ELeG ESha IHos LGod MAus MGan
'Nicola' (F)	EWar MGan MHay
Night Light ® (Cl)	CDoC EWar MBri MGan
'Nikki' (F)	MRos
Nimbus ® (F)	ELeG
Nina Weibull ® (F)	MGan
'Niphetos' (T/Cl)	EBls WTay
nitida	CCor EBls EBro ELan ELeG IHos MAus MMat NSty NWea SHil SPer SSus WHCG
– 'Kebu'	MR&S
§ 'Noisette Carnée' (N)	CCMG CCor EBls ETWh MAus MRTP SFam SPer SSus WAct WHCG
¶ Nona ® (F)	MRea
'Norfolk' (GC)	CCor ELeG IHos LGod MMat SPer
¶ Northamptonshire ® (GC)	LGod MMat
¶ 'Northumberland WI' (HT)	NBat
'Norwich Castle' (F)	EBls
'Norwich Pink' (Cl)	MAus
'Norwich Salmon' (Cl)	MAus
'Norwich Union' (F)	EBls
'Nova Zembla' (Ru)	CCMG EBls MAus NSty
'Nozomi' (GC)	Widely available
'Nuits de Young' (Mo)	CBow CCMG CCor EBls ELeG ETWh MAus MMat NSty SFam SHil WHCG
'Nur Mahal' (HM)	EBls EBro MAus WHCG
nutkana	EBls MAus
§ – ***hispida***	EBls
§ – 'Plena'	CCMG CCla CCor EBls ELeG MAus NSty SHil WAct
'Nymphenburg' (S)	CBow CCMG EBls ETWh IHos MAus SHil SPer SSus
'Nypels' Perfection' (Poly)	MAus
'Nyveldt's White' (Ru)	EBls IHos MAus

'Oakington Ruby'	CCor
'Octet'	CCor
¶ x *odorata* 'Bengal Crimson'	EMon
– 'Fortune's Double Yellow' (Cl)	EBls MAus SHil WSHC
¶ – 'Miss Willmott's Crimson China'	EMon
– 'Mutabilis' (Ch)	CCMG CHad EBls ELeG ETWh LGre MAus MMat MRTP NSty SHil SPer SSus WHCG WKif WWat
– 'Ochroleuca' (Ch)	EBls
– 'Odorata' (Ch)	EBls WHCG
§ – 'Pallida' (Ch)	CCMG CCla CHad EBls ELeG ETWh IHos MAus MMat MRTP SHen SHil SSus WHCG
– Sanguinea group (Ch)	EBls WHCG
§ – 'Viridiflora'	CSan EBls ELeG IHos LGre MAus MBur SHil SMad SPla SRum WHCG
'Oeillet Flamand'	See R. 'Oeillet Parfait'
'Oeillet Parfait' (G)	EBls MAus
officinalis	See R. ***gallica o.***
'Oh La La' (F)	WWeb
'Ohl' (G)	EBls
'Oklahoma' (HT)	MGan
♦ 'Old Blush China'	See R. x ***odorata*** 'Pallida'
Old Cabbage	See R. x ***centifolia***
Old Master ® (F)	MAus MBur MGan
Old Pink Moss	See R. x ***centifolia*** 'Muscosa'
Old Velvet Moss	See R. 'William Lobb'
Old Yellow Scotch	See R. x ***harisonii*** 'Williams' Double Yellow'
Olympiad ® (HT)	MBri MGan MHay
Olympic Spirit ® (F)	MRea
'Omar Khayyám' (D)	EBls IHos MAus MMat MRTP SPer SSus
'Ombrée Parfaite ' (G)	EBls
omeiensis pteracantha	See R. ***sericea pteracantha***
'Only You' (HT)	MGan
'Opera' (HT)	MGan SPla SRum
'Ophelia' (HT)	EBls MAus MGan MHls NSty SHil
'Ophelia, Climbing' (HT/Cl)	EBls ETWh MAus MHls
'Orange Goliath' (HT)	MGan
'Orange Honey' (Min)	CSan MBur MHay MHls MRos MRui WWeb
Orange Sensation ® (F)	EBls ELeG ESha EWar GGre GTra IJoh LPlm MAus MBri MGan MHay MMor MR&S MRos NElm NRog SRum WWeb
Orange Sunblaze ® (Min)	EBls ELeG EWar GGre IHos IJoh LGod MGan MHay MR&S MRea MRui NBar NElm SHen WWeb
Orange Sunblaze, Climbing ® (Min/Cl)	ELeG EWar MBri MRui
Orange Triumph ® (Poly)	EBls ELeG
'Orangeade' (F)	EBro MGan SHen
'Orangeade, Climbing' (F/Cl)	CDoC MGan SRum
'Oriana' (HT)	CGro MGan MRea
'Orient Express' (HT)	NBat
'Ormiston Roy' (HScB)	MAus NSty
'Orpheline de Juillet'	See R. 'Ombrée Parfaite'
Othello ® (S)	CDoC CSan MAus MBri MHay SPer
Our Love ® (HT)	GGre
'Over the Rainbow' (Min)	CSan MBur MHay
'Oxfam' (HT)	MHay
Pacemaker ® (HT)	MHay
Paddy McGredy ® (F)	CGro EBro ESha EWar GGre GTra IJoh MAus MGan MHay MHls MMor MR&S NElm NRog SRum
Paint Box ® (Min)	SRum
¶ Painted Moon ® (HT)	IDic
¶ Paint-Pot ® (Min)	MRui
'Pam Ayers' (S)	WWar
¶ Pandora ® (Min)	MRui
¶ 'Panorama Holiday' (F)	MBur
'Papa Gontier' (T)	EBls MAus
'Papa Hémeray' (Ch)	EBls
Papa Meilland ® (HT)	CB&S CGro EBls EBro GGre MAus MGan MHay NElm NRog SPer SRum WWeb
'Papillon' (T)	EBls
Paprika ® (F)	ELeG MAus MMor
'Pâquerette' (Poly)	EBls
§ 'Para Ti' (Min)	ELeG EWar GGre LGod LPlm MAus MBur MGan MHay MHls MMat SHil SPer
'Parade' (Cl)	ELeG MAus MGan MHay MMat MRui
Paradise ® (HT)	MGan MMat
Parkdirektor Riggers ® (Cl)	Widely available
Parks' Yellow China	See R. x ***odorata*** 'Ochroleuca'
'Parkzierde' (Bb)	EBls
'Parsons' Pink China'	See R. x ***odorata*** 'Pallida'
Partridge ® (GC)	CCMG EBls IHos MAus MGan MMat SPer SSus
'Party Girl' (Min)	MHay
parvifolia	See R. 'Burgundiaca'
Pascali ® (HT)	Widely available
'Pascali, Climbing' (HT/Cl)	CB&S MGan
Patricia ® (F)	SRum
'Paul Crampel' (Poly)	EBls MAus MGan NElm NRog NSty SPer
'Paul Lédé, Climbing' (T/Cl)	CCMG EBls ETWh MAus
'Paul Neyron' (HP)	CCor EBls EBro ETWh MAus MMat NSty SPer SSus WHCG
'Paul Ricault' (Ce/HP)	CCor EBls MAus
Paul Shirville ® (HT)	CDoC ELeG EWar GGre IHos MAus MGan MHay MMat MRea MRos NBar NBat NRog SHil SPer SRum WWar WWeb

'Paul Transon' (Ra)	CBow EBls EMon ETWh MAus MBri SPer WAct
'Paul Verdier' (Bb)	EBls
'Paulii' (Ru)	CSan EBls EHar ELan ELeG ETWh IHos MAus MBur MHls MMat MMor MRea SHil SPer SSus WAct WHCG WWeb
'Paulii Alba'	See R. 'Paulii'
'Paulii Rosea' (Ru/Cl)	EBls ELeG MAus MBri MHls SPer SSus WAct WHCG
'Paul's Early Blush' (HP)	EBls
'Paul's Himalayan Musk' (Ra)	CBow CCMG CSam CSan EBls EBro EHar ELeG ETWh LGre MAus MBri MRTP MRui NSty SPer SSus WAct WHCG WKif
'Paul's Lemon Pillar' (HT/Cl)	CCMG CHad EBls EBro ETWh MAus NRog NSty SPer SPla SRum
'Paul's Perpetual White' (Ra)	EBls ETWh
'Paul's Scarlet Climber' (Ra/Cl)	Widely available
'Pax' (HM)	CCMG EBls EBro ELeG MAus NSty SPer WHCG
Peace Sunblaze ® (Min)	EWar
Peace ® (HT)	Widely available
¶ 'Peach Blossom'	MAus
'Peaches 'n' Cream' (Min)	MHay WWar
'Peachy White' (Min)	MAus MRos
Pearl Drift ® (GC)	EBls ELeG EWar MAus MRea SPer SRum WHCG
§ Peaudouce ® (HT)	ELeG ESha EWar IDic IHos LGod MAus MGan MHay MHls MMat MRea NElm NRog SHil SPer WWar
Peek A Boo ® (Min/Patio)	CDoC ELan ELeG EWar GGre IDic IHos LGod LPlm MAus MGan MMat MRea MRos MRui SPer WWar
Peer Gynt ® (HT)	ELeG ESha GTra IHos MAus MGan MHls MMat MR&S
'Pélisson' (Mo)	CCor EBls WHCG
pendulina	EBls MAus MMat MPar WHCG
'Penelope' (HM)	Widely available
Penelope Keith ® (Min/Patio)	MHls MMat MRea
Penelope Plummer ® (F)	EBls
'Penny' (F)	CSan
¶ Pensioner's Voice ® (F)	WWeb
x ***penzanceana***	See R. 'Lady Penzance'
'Percy Thrower' (HT)	MHls SRum
Perdita ® (S)	CCMG IHos IOrc MAus MBri SPer SSus
¶ 'Perestroika' (F)	MMat
Perfecta ® (HT)	EBls MGan MHay SRum
'Perla de Montserrat' (Min)	ELeG EWar MR&S SPer
'Perla d'Alcañada' (Min)	EWar IHos MAus MMat MR&S
'Perle des Jardins' (T)	EBls MAus
'Perle des Panachées' (G)	EBls
'Perle d'Or' (Poly)	CBow CCMG CHad ELeG ETWh MAus MHls MMat MPar NRog NSty SPer SPla SSus WAct WHCG WWat
'Perle von Hohenstein' (Poly)	EBls
Pernille Poulsen ® (F)	EBls ELeG MGan
'Persian Yellow'	See R. ***foetida*** 'Persiana'
Peter Frankenfeld ® (HT)	MHay
Petit Four ® (Min/Patio)	IDic MAus SHil
'Petite de Hollande' (Ce)	CBow CCMG EBls ELeG ETWh MAus NSty SHil SPer WAct WHCG
Petite Folie ® (Min)	GGre MGan
'Petite Lisette' (Ce)	EBls MAus SPer WHCG
'Petite Orléannaise' (Ce)	EBls
'Pharisäer' (HT)	EBls
Pheasant ® (GC)	ELeG IHos MAus MBri MGan MMat MR&S SPer
'Phoebe' (S)	WAct
'Phyllis Bide' (Ra)	CBow CCMG EBls ETWh MAus MGan MHls NSty SPer WHCG WSHC
Picasso ® (F)	EBls ELeG MAus MGan MR&S
Piccadilly ® (HT)	Widely available
Piccolo ® (F/Patio)	EWar GGre MBri MGan MHay MMor MRea MRos WWar WWeb
'Picture' (HT)	EBls MAus MGan NRog NSty SPer
'Picture, Climbing' (HT/Cl)	EBls MAus MGan
'Pierre Notting' (HP)	EBls
Pigalle '84 ® (F)	SRum
Pillar Box ® (F)	LGod MGan MRos WWar
pimpinellifolia	CCMG EBls ETWh MAus MBri MGan MMat NLan NWea SHil SPer SRum SSus WAct WHCG
– ***altaica***	CCor EBls ETWh
– 'Andrewsii'	See R. 'Andrewsii'
– double pink	CCor EBls WHCG
– double white	CCMG EBls MAus SHil WAct
– double yellow	See R. x ***harisonii*** 'Williams' Double Yellow'
– 'Dunwich Rose'	See R. 'Dunwich Rose'
– 'Glory of Edzell'	See R. 'Glory of Edzell'
– 'Grandiflora'	MAus SSus
– 'Harisonii'	See R. x ***harisonii*** 'Harison's Yellow'
– ***lutea***	See R. x ***harisonii*** 'Lutea Maxima'
– 'Marbled Pink'	CCor MAus
– 'Mary Queen of Scots'	MAus
– 'Robbie Burns'	See R. 'Robbie Burns'
– 'Stanwell Perpetual'	See R. 'Stanwell Perpetual'
– 'William III'	LHop MAus SHil
– x ***pendula***	See R. x ***reversa***

'Pineapple Poll' (F)	CDoC MGan
Pink Bells ® (GC)	CCMG CCla CDoC CGro EBls ELeG EOrc EWar IHos LBuc MAus MBri MGan MHls MMat MR&S MRea MRos SPer SSus WHCG WWeb
Pink Drift ® (Min/GC)	IHos MMat
'Pink Elizabeth Arden' (F)	SHen
'Pink Favorite' (HT)	CSan ELeG IHos IJoh MAus MGan MHay MHls MMor MR&S NBat NElm NRog SPer SRum WWeb
'Pink Grootendorst' (Ru)	CB&S CBow CCMG CCla CSan EBls ELeG EWar IHos IOrc LPlm MAus MGan MHls MMat MMor MRea NRog NSty SPer SRum SSus WAct WHCG
Pink La Sevillana ® (F/GC)	EWar MR&S SHen SPer SRum
'Pink Meteor' (F)	ESha
Pink Moss	See R. ***centifolia*** 'Muscosa'
Pink Nevada ® (S)	CSan
Pink Panther ® (HT)	EWar MR&S
'Pink Parfait' (F)	CSan EBls ELeG GGre GTra IHos IJoh LPlm MAus MBri MBur MGan MHls MMor MRea NBar NBat NElm NRog SHen SPer SRum WWeb
Pink Peace ® (HT)	CB&S ESha GGre MAus MGan MMor MRea NBar NElm SRum WWeb
¶ 'Pink Pearl' (HT)	MMat WWar
'Pink Perpétué' (Cl)	Widely available
'Pink Petticoat' (Min)	MHay WWar
Pink Posy ® (Patio)	MAus
'Pink Prosperity' (HM)	CCMG EBls LGre MAus
'Pink Showers' (HT/Cl)	WAct
Pink Sunblaze ® (Min/Patio)	EWar MRea NBar NElm WWeb
Pink Wave ® (GC)	IHos MMat MRea
'Pinocchio' (F)	EBls
'Pinta' (HT)	EBls
pisocarpa	CCor
'Pixie Rose' (Min)	IHos IJoh MR&S
Playgroup Rose ® (F)	MRos NBat
Pleine de Grâce ® (S)	MAus
'Plentiful' (F)	EBls ELeG MAus
Polar Star ® (HT)	Widely available
'Polly' (HT)	EBls MAus MGan NElm NRog
polyantha grandiflora	See R. ***gentiliana***
pomifera	See R. ***villosa***
– 'Duplex'	See R. 'Wolley-Dod'
'Pompon Blanc Parfait' (A)	CCMG EBls MAus SFam
'Pompon de Bourgogne' (Ce)	See R. 'Burgundiaca'
'Pompon de Paris, Climbing' (Ch/Cl)	CBot CCor EBls EPad ERav LHop MAus MPar MRTP NSty SPer SSus WHCG WSHC WThu
'Pompon Panaché' (G)	CCMG EBls MAus
Portland Rose	See R. 'Portlandica'
'Portlandica'	CCMG EBls ETWh MAus SPer SSus WAct WHCG
Pot o'Gold ® (HT)	CDoC ESha EWar IDic IHos MAus MGan MHls MRea MRos SPer WWar
Potter and Moore ® (S)	IHos MAus SSus
Potton Heritage ® (HT)	MHay
♦ 'Pour Toi'	See R. 'Para Ti'
Prairie Rose	See R. ***setigera***
prattii	CCor
'Precious Platinum' (HT)	CDoC ELeG IDic IHos LGod MAus MBri MGan MHay MHls MMat MR&S NBar SPer WWar
§ 'Président de Sèze' (G)	CBow CCMG CCor EBls ETWh MAus MBri MRTP NSty SFam SHen WHCG
'President Herbert Hoover' (HT)	WWat
'Prestige' (S)	NRog
'Pretty Jessica' (S)	IHos MAus SHil SSus
Pretty Polly ® (Patio)	GGre MRui
'Prima Ballerina' (HT)	Widely available
primula	CCMG CHad CSan EBls EBro EHar ELeG ETWh IHos LHol MAus MMat NSty SHil SPer WAct WHCG WKif
'Prince Camille de Rohan' (HP)	EBls MAus WAct WHCG
'Prince Charles' (Bb)	CCMG CCor EBls ELeG ETWh MAus NSty WHCG
Princess Alice ® (F)	EWar LGod MGan MHay
'Princess Margaret of England' (HT)	EWar
Princess Michael of Kent ® (F)	MBur SHen WWar
'Princess Michiko' (F)	EWar MGan MMor
§ 'Princesse de Nassau' (Ra)	EBls MAus
'Princesse Louise' (Ra)	MAus
'Princesse Marie' (Ra)	EBro MBri
Prins Claus ® (HT)	MGan
Priscilla Burton ® (F)	ELeG EWar MAus MGan
Pristine ® (HT)	CDoC EWar IDic IHos LPlm MAus MGan NBar SPer WWar
'Prolifera de Redouté'	See R. 'Duchesse de Montebello'
'Prosperity' (HM)	CCor CHad CSan EBls EBro ETWh IOrc MAus MBur MGan MHay MMat MRos MRui NElm NRog SHil SPer SSus WAct WHCG WWeb
Prospero ® (S)	CCMG MAus MBri SPer
Proud Titania ® (S)	MBri SPer
x ***pruhoniciana*** 'Hillieri'	See R. 'Hillieri'
Pucker Up ® (Min)	MHay
pulverulenta	EBls
'Purity' (Ra)	CCor CSan
'Purple Beauty' (HT)	MGan
'Purple Elf'	IJoh
'Purple Splendour' (F)	ELeG MAus
Quatre Saisons	See R. x ***damascena semperflorens***

'Quatre Saisons Blanche Mousseuse' (D/Mo) EBls ETWh
¶ Queen Charlotte ® (HT) ELeG MBur
Queen Elizabeth ® (F) Widely available
'Queen Elizabeth, Climbing' (F/Cl) EBls MGan MRea SHen SRum
'Queen Esther' (HT) MRea
Queen Nefertiti ® (S) IHos MAus
'Queen of Bedders' (Bb) EBls
'Queen of Denmark' See R. 'Königin von Dänemark'
'Queen of Hearts' See R. 'Dame de Coeur'
'Radway Sunrise' (S) EBls
'Rainbow' (S) MMat
'Ralph Tizard' (F) CSan
'Rambling Rector' (Ra) CBow CCMG CCla CHad EBls ELan ETWh LGod MAus MBri MRTP NSty SFam SPer SPla SRum SSus WAct WHCG
'Ramona' (Cl) EBls ETWh MAus WHCG WSHC
'Raubritter' (*macrantha x*) CBos CBow CCMG CCor EBls ETWh IHos MAus MBri MMat NSty SPer SSus WAct WHCG
Ray of Sunshine ® (Patio) ESha GGre MBri
'Raymond Chenault' (Cl) MGan
'Rebecca Claire' (HT) CDoC MGan MRos SPer
Red Ace ® (Min) LGod MHay MRea MRui SHil
'Red Beauty' (Min) MHay
Red Bells ® (Min/GC) CCla CDoC CGro EBls ELeG EOrc EWar IHos MAus MGan MHls MMat MR&S MRea MRos SPer SSus WHCG WWeb
Red Blanket ® (S/GC) CGro CSam CSan EBls ELeG EWar IDic IHos LGod MAus MGan MMat SPer SRum WAct
'Red Coat' (S) IHos LHol MAus WAct
'Red Dandy' (F) MGan
Red Devil ® (HT) CSan ELeG ESha EWar GGre LPlm MAus MGan MHay MRea NBar NBat NElm NRog SHen SRum
'Red Gold' (F) MBur MR&S WAct
'Red Grootendorst' See R. 'F J Grootendorst'
'Red Lion' (HT) MGan MHay
'Red Maid' (F) CSan
Red Minimo ® (Min) IHos
Red Moss See R. 'Henri Martin'
'Red Queen' (HT) MHay
Red Rascal ® (Patio) EWar IDic MBri SPer
Red Rose of Lancaster See R. ***gallica officinalis***
'Red Splendour' (F) MHay
'Red Sprite' (F) ELeG
Red Sunblaze ® (Min) EWar IHos IJoh MR&S WWar WWeb
'Red Wing' (***hugonis x***) EBls MAus WAct
'Redcliffe' (F) CSan
Redgold ® (F) GGre LGod MGan NBar
Rediffusion Gold ® (F) CDoC
'Redland Court' (F) CSan
Regensberg ® (F/Patio) ESha EWar IHos LPlm MAus MBri MGan MHay MHls MMat MRea MRos NBar NRog SPer
'Reine des Cent-feuilles' (Ce) EBls SFam
'Reine des Violettes' (HP) CBow CCMG CCor CSan EBls EBro ELeG ETWh MAus MRTP NSty SFam SHil SPer SSus WHCG
'Reine Marie Henriette' (HT/Cl) EBls
§ 'Reine Victoria' (Bb) CBow CCMG CCor CSam CSan EBls EBro ETWh IHos MAus MBur MGan MHay NSty SHil SPer SSus WHCG
Remember Me ® (HT) CDoC ELeG ESha GGre LGod LPlm MGan MHay MMat MRea MRos NBar NBat NRog SHil SPer WWar
'René André' (Ra) EBls ETWh MAus
'René d'Anjou' (Mo) EBls MAus
Repens Meidiland ® EWar
'Rescht' See R. 'De Rescht'
'Rêve d'Or' (N) CBow CCMG EBls ETWh MAus SPer WSHC
'Reveil Dijonnais' (HT/Cl) EBls MAus
'Reverend F Page-Roberts' (HT) EBls
§ x ***reversa*** white form MPar
'Rhodes Rose' NSty
x ***richardii*** EBls MAus MBri MRTP WHCG
'Richmond, Climbing' (HT/Cl) EBls MAus
'Ripples' (F) ELeG
'Rise 'n' Shine' (Min) CSan ELeG EWar LGod MGan MHay MR&S MRos MRui NBat NElm WWar
'Ritter von Barmstede' (Cl) ELeG MGan MHls MMor
'Rival de Paestum' (T) EBls MAus
Rob Roy ® (F) CCMG EBls MGan SHen SPer
'Robbie Burns' (HScB) CHad MAus WAct
'Robert le Diable' (Ce) CCor EBls ELeG MAus NSty SPer SSus WAct WHCG
'Robert Léopold' (DPMo) EBls
'Robin' (Min) ELeG IJoh
'Robin Hood' (HM) EBls EBro
Robin Redbreast ® (Patio) EBls ELeG IDic IHos MAus MBri MRea SHil SPer WWeb
Robusta ® (Ru) EBls ELeG MAus MHls MMat
'Roger Lambelin' (HP) EBls ELeG MAus MMat NSty SPer SSus WAct
Romance ® (F/S) WWeb
¶ 'Rosamini Gold' (Patio) CSut
¶ 'Rosamini Orange' (Patio) CSut
¶ 'Rosamini Pink' (Patio) CSut
¶ 'Rosamini Red' (Patio) CSut
¶ 'Rosamini White' (Patio) CSut

'Rose à Parfum de l'Hay' (Ru)	EBls
'Rose de Meaux'	See R. 'De Meaux'
'Rose de Meaux White'	See R. 'De Meaux White'
'Rose de Rescht'	See R. 'De Rescht'
'Rose des Maures'	See R. 'Sissinghurst Castle'
'Rose du Maître d'Ecole'	See R. 'Du Maître d'Ecole'
'Rose du Roi' (HP/D)	EBls MAus NSty WHCG
'Rose du Roi à Fleur Pourpre' (HP)	EBls MAus
'Rose d'Amour'	CCor EBls ETWh EWar ISea MAus SHil WHCG
'Rose d'Hivers' (D)	EBls
'Rose d'Orsay'	EBls
¶ 'Rose Edouard' (Bb)	EBls
Rose Gaujard ® (HT)	CMac CSan EBls ELeG ESha EWar GGre GTra IJoh LGod LPlm MAus MBur MGan MHay MHls MMor NElm SHen SRum WWeb
'Rose of Clifton' (F)	CSan
'Rose of Tralee' (F)	CDoC
'Rosemary Gandy' (F)	MGan
Rosemary Harkness ® (HT)	CDoC EWar IHos MBur MHay MMat MRea SHil SPer WWar
'Rosemary Rose' (F)	EBls ELeG ERav MAus MBri MRos NRog SPer SSus WAct
'Rosenelfe' (F)	EBls
'Roseraie de l'Haÿ' (Ru)	Widely available
'Rosette Delizy' (T)	EBls MAus
§ 'Rose-Marie Viaud' (Ra)	MAus NSty SPer WHCG
'Rosina' (Min)	ELeG EWar LPlm MGan MMat MRea NRed SHil
'Rosmarin' (Min)	LPlm
'Rosy Cheeks' (HT)	GGre GTra LPlm MBur MGan MRea WWeb
Rosy Cushion ® (S/GC)	CGro EWar IDic IHos IJoh LGod MAus MMat MRea NBar SHil SPer WAct
Rosy Gem ® (Min)	GGre
'Rosy Mantle' (Cl)	CB&S ELeG EWar LPlm MGan SPer SRum
Rote Max Graf ® (GC)	EBls ELeG EOrc EWar IHos MHls MMat SHil WAct
'Roundelay' (S)	EBls MAus
roxburghii	CB&S CCor CGre CMCN EBls GWic MAus MMat NSty WAct WHCG
'Royal Albert Hall' (HT)	EBls MGan NBar
¶ 'Royal Baby' (Min)	MBur
'Royal Bath and West' (F)	CSan
'Royal Gold' (Cl)	CCMG CGro CMac EBls ERav EWar IHos IJoh LPlm MAus MBri MGan MHay MHls MMor MRea MRos MRui NElm NRog SRum WWeb
'Royal Highness' (HT)	CGro EBls ESha MGan MHay MRea NBat SRum WWeb
'Royal Lavender' (HT/Cl)	ELeG
Royal Meillandina ® (Min/Patio)	EWar
'Royal Occasion' (F)	MGan SPer
Royal Romance ® (HT)	MRea
Royal Salute ® (Min)	ELeG EWar MHay MMat NElm NRog SPer
'Royal Smile' (HT)	EBls
Royal William ® (HT)	Widely available
'Rubens' (HP)	EBls
rubiginosa	See R. ***eglanteria***
rubra	See R. ***gallica***
rubrifolia	See R. ***glauca***
– 'Carminetta'	See R. 'Carminetta'
'Rubrotincta'	See R. 'Hebe's Lip'
rubus (Ra)	MAus
'Ruby Wedding' (HT)	CSan ELan EWar GGre GTra LPlm MAus MGan MHay MMor MRea MRos NBat NElm NRog SHen SPer SRum SSus WWeb
'Ruga' (Ra)	EBls MAus
rugosa	CCor CSam CSan IHos ISea LHol MAus MBri MR&S SHil WAct
– 'Alba'	Widely available
– ***kamtschatica***	See R. ***r. ventenatiana***
– ***rubra***	CCor CDoC ETWh IJoh LBuc MHls MMat MRea NRoo NSty SHil SPer SRum WAct WMou
– 'Scabrosa'	See R. 'Scabrosa'
– ***ventenatiana***	CCor
'Rugosa Atropurpurea' (Ru)	NRog
'Rugul' (Min)	IHos MGan MRui
'Ruhm von Steinfurth' (HP)	EBls MGan
Rumba ® (F)	MGan SHen
Running Maid ® (S/GC)	MAus WAct
'Ruskin' (Ru x HP)	EBls MAus SPer
'Russelliana' (Ra)	CCMG EBls ETWh MAus WHCG
Rutland ® (Min/GC)	IHos MMat MR&S
'Sadler's Wells' (S)	EBls
'Safrano' (T)	EBls
'Saga' (F)	SPer
Saint Boniface ® (F/Patio)	ESha MHay MHls MMat
Saint Cecilia ® (S)	ETWh EWar IHos MAus MRea MRui SHil SSus
'Saint Hugh's' (HT)	MHls MMat
Saint John's Rose	See R. x ***richardii***
Saint Mark's Rose	See R. 'Rose d'Amour'
'Saint Nicholas' (D)	CCor EBls MAus WHCG
'Saint Prist de Breuze' (Ch)	EBls
'Salet' (DPMo)	CBow CCMG EBls EBro ETWh MAus WAct WHCG
¶ Salita ® (Cl)	WWar
Sally Holmes ® (S)	CCor CHad EBls ELeG MAus MGan MHay NBat
'Salmon Sprite' (F)	ELeG
sancta	See R. x ***richardii***

'Sanders' White Rambler' (Ra)	CBow CCMG CDoC CMac CSan EBls EBro ERav ETWh GGre IHos MAus MGan MHay MHls MMor NRog NSty SHil SPer SRum SSus WAct WHCG
'Sandringham Centenary' (HT)	EBls
'Sanguinea'	See R. x ***odorata*** Sanguinea group
Sarabande ® (F)	MGan
'Sarah van Fleet' (Ru)	CBow CCMG CCla CGro CMac EBls ELeG ETWh MAus MGan MMat MMor MRTP MRui NElm NRog NSty SHil SPer SPla SRum SSus WAct WHCG
Sarah ® (HT)	EWar
Satchmo ® (F)	ELeG ESha EWar IHos
'Saul' (HT)	MGan
Savoy Hotel ® (HT)	ELeG GGre LGod MAus MBur MHay MRea NBar NBat SPer WWar
'Scabrosa' (Ru)	CCMG CCla CSan EBls EBro ELeG ETWh IHos MAus MGan MMat SHil SSus WAct WHCG
'Scarlet Fire'	See R. 'Scharlachglut'
Scarlet Gem ® (Min)	CGro ELan ELeG EWar GGre LPlm MGan MMor SPer
'Scarlet Glow'	See R. 'Scharlachglut'
Scarlet Meidiland ® (S/GC)	EWar IHos MMat MR&S
'Scarlet Pimpernel'	See R. 'Scarlet Gem'
Scarlet Queen Elizabeth ® (F)	CB&S CGro CMac EBls GGre GTra IJoh LPlm MBur MGan MHls MMor NBar NElm SHen SRum WWeb
'Scarlet Showers' (Cl)	MGan
Scarletta ® (Min)	GGre IHos MHay MMor
'Scented Air' (F)	MGan MHls MMat SPer
§ 'Scharlachglut' (S/Cl)	CBow CCMG EBls ELan ELeG ETWh MAus MBur MGan MMat NSty SHil SPer WAct WHCG WSHC
Scherzo ® (F)	MGan
'Schneelicht' (Ru)	EBls MAus
'Schneewittchen'	See R. 'Iceberg'
'Schneezwerg' (Ru)	EBls ELeG ETWh IHos IOrc LHol MAus MGan MHls MMat MMor NSty SHil SPer SSus WAct WHCG WWeb
'Schoolgirl' (Cl)	Widely available
'Scintillation' (S/GC)	CCMG CCor MAus MBri WAct
Scottish Special ® (Min/Patio)	CGro MRea
'Sea Pearl' (F)	MGan MHls MMat SPer
¶ Seafarer ® (F)	MR&S
'Seagull' (Ra)	CCMG EBls EBro ELan ELeG ESha ETWh EWar LGod MAus MGan NElm NRog NSty SPer WAct WHCG
§ 'Sealing Wax' (*moyesii* x)	EBls ELeG MAus WAct
Seaspray ® (F)	MMat
Selfridges ® (HT)	MMat
'Semi-Plena'	See R. 'Alba Semi-plena'
sempervirens (Ra)	CCor
'Sénateur Amic' (Cl)	EBls
serafinii	CCor
'Serenade' (HT)	MGan
sericea	CCor MAus
– 'Heather Muir'	See R. 'Heather Muir'
– ***pteracantha***	CCMG CHad CSan EBls EHar ELan ELeG ETWh EWar LHol MAus MGan MHls MMat NRog NSty SHil SPer SSus WAct WHCG WWeb
¶ – ***pteracantha atrosanguinea***	ELeG
– 'Red Wing'	See R. 'Red Wing'
'Serratipetala' (Ch)	CCor
setigera	EBls MAus
setipoda	EBls ISea MAus WAct
¶ 'Seven Seas' (F)	MBur
Seven Sisters Rose	See R. ***multiflora*** 'Grevillei'
Sexy Rexy ® (F)	CGro ELeG EWar IHos IJoh MBri MHay MRos NBar NBat SPer WWeb
'Shailer's White Moss' (Ce/Mo)	CBow CCMG CDoC EBls EBro ELeG ETWh MAus MGan MHls NRog NSty SFam SHil WAct
Shareefa Asma ® (S)	MRui WAct WWeb
¶ 'Sharifa Asma'	MAus
Sheila's Perfume ® (HT/F)	CDoC EWar GGre LPlm MGan MHay MRea NRog SHen SHil SPer WWar
'Shepherdess' (F)	MMat
'Shepherd's Delight' (F)	MGan SRum
Sheri Anne ® (Min)	ELeG MAus MHay MRos MRui
Shocking Blue ® (F)	ELeG LPlm MGan MMat SPer WWar
Shona ® (F)	IDic MRea MRos
'Shot Silk' (HT)	CMac EBls ELeG MAus MBur MGan SSus
'Shot Silk, Climbing' (HT/Cl)	CCMG CSan EBls EBro ETWh MAus MGan MHay MHls SHen SPer SRum
Showman ® (HT)	MHay
'Shropshire Lass' (S)	MAus MBri MRTP SPer
'Sidonie' (HP)	EBls
'Silver Cloud'	ELeG
Silver Jubilee ® (HT)	Widely available
'Silver Lining' (HT)	CMac EBls LPlm MAus MBur MHay SRum
'Silver Moon' (Cl)	CCMG EBls ETWh MAus
'Silver Tips' (Min)	MAus MGan
'Silver Wedding' (HT)	EBls ELan GGre MBur MGan MHay MMor MRea MRos NBat NElm NRog SPer SSus WWeb
Simba ® (HT)	CSan ELeG ESha EWar MBri MGan MHay MMat MRea MRos SPer

Simon Robinson ® (Min/GC) EBls
'Single Cherry' (HScB) EBls MAus
sinowilsonii (Ra) EBls GWic MAus WHCG
'Sir Cedric Morris' (Ra) EBls
'Sir Clough' (S) MAus
'Sir Frederick Ashton' (HT) EBls
Sir Harry Pilkington ® (HT) NElm
'Sir Lancelot' (F) MGan
Sir Walter Raleigh ® (S) MAus MBri MHay SHil SSus
¶ 'Sir Wiliam Leech' (HT) NBat
'Sissinghurst Castle' (G) CSan EBls WHCG
'Sleepy' (Co) MGan
Smarty ® (S/GC) EBls ELeG IDic IHos MAus MHls MMat MRea SPer WAct
'Sneezy' (Co) MGan
'Snow Bride' (Min) MHay
Snow Carpet ® (Min/GC) CBow CCor CSan EBls ELeG EOrc IHos LGre MAus MBri MGan MMat MRui SHil SPer SPla WAct
'Snow Dwarf' See R. 'Schneezwerg'
'Snow Queen' See R. 'Frau Karl Druschki'
Snow White ® (HT) CDoC MBri MRea
Snowball ® (Min/GC) MMat
¶ 'Snowdon' (Ru) MAus
Snowdrop ® (Min/Patio) MHay MHls MRui
'Snowflake' (Ra) ELeG
'Snowgoose' (Min) MHls
'Snowline' (F) EWar MGan SPer
'Soldier Boy' (Cl) EBro ELeG MGan
'Soleil d'Or' (HT) MAus
Solitaire ® (HT) MBri MHay MRea WWar
'Sombreuil, Climbing' (T/Cl) CCMG EBls ETWh MAus MRTP SRum WAct WHCG
'Sonatina' (F) CSan
'Sophie's Perpetual' (Ch/Cl) EBls MAus MGan MMat SPer WHCG WWeb
Soraya, Climbing ® (HT/Cl) CMac MAus
soulieana (Ra) EBls ETWh MAus MMat WKif
'Soupert et Notting' (PMo) EBls MAus MRTP SPer WHCG
'Southampton' (F) CMac CSan EBls ELeG EWar MAus MBri MGan MHay MHls MMat NElm NRog SHil SPer WWar
'Souvenir de Claudius Denoyel' (HT/Cl) CCMG EBls MAus MMat NRog SPer SSus
'Souvenir de François Gaulain' (T) EBls
'Souvenir de Jeanne Balandreau' (HP) EBls WHCG
'Souvenir de la Malmaison' (Bb) CBow CCMG CCla CCor EBls EBro ETWh IHos IOrc LHol MAus MGan MMat NSty SHil SPer SSus WAct WHCG WWeb
'Souvenir de la Malmaison, Climbing' (Bb/Cl) CBow CCMG EBls EBro ETWh MAus WAct WHCG
'Souvenir de Madame Léonie Viennot' (T/Cl) EBls MAus MRTP
'Souvenir de Philémon Cochet ' (Ru) EBls ETWh LGre MAus WAct
'Souvenir de Pierre Vibert' (DPMo) EBls
'Souvenir de Saint Anne's' (Bb) CCMG CHad EBls EBro ETWh MAus SHil WAct WHCG
'Souvenir di Castagneto' MRTP
'Souvenir du Docteur Jamain' (HP/Cl) CCMG EBls EBro ETWh LGre MAus MMat MRTP NSty SFam SHil SPer WHCG
'Souvenir du Président Carnot' (HT) EBls MAus
'Souvenir d'Alphonse Lavallée' (HP/Cl) CSan EBls WAct WHCG
'Souvenir d'Elise Vardon' (T) EBls
'Souvenir d'un Ami' (T) EBls
spaldingii See R. ***nutkana hispida***
'Spanish Beauty' (HT/Cl) See R. 'Madame Grégoire Staechelin'
Sparkling Scarlet ® (Ra) ELan EWar MGan
'Sparrieshoop' (S/Cl) EWar
'Spartan' (F) MGan
'Spartan, Climbing' (F/Cl) MGan
'Spectabilis' (Ra) CCor EBls MAus WHCG
'Spek's Yellow' (HT) CB&S EBls MGan SRum
'Spek's Yellow, Climbing' (HT/Cl) MAus MGan
♦ 'Spencer' See R. 'Enfant de France'
spinosissima See R. ***pimpinellifolia***
'Splendens' (N) CCMG EBls ELan ETWh SSus
'Spong' (G) CCMG CCor EBls ETWh MAus WAct
'Stacey Sue' (Min) CSan MAus MHay MRea MRos
'Stanley Duncan' (Min) MHls
'Stanwell Perpetual' (HScB) CCor CSam EBls ELeG ETWh IHos MAus MMat MRTP NSty SHil SPer SSus WAct WHCG WWeb
Star Child ® (F) EWar IDic WWar
Starina ® (Min) CSan ELeG EWar MGan MHay MR&S MRos MRui SHil WWeb
'Stars 'n' Stripes' (Min) CGro CSan ELeG LGod LPlm MAus MBur MRea MRos MRui NElm
Stella ® (HT) EBls MGan NBar SRum
stellata mirifica EBls MAus MGan MMat
'Stephanie Diane' (HT) MHay MRea
'Stephen Langdon' (F) CSan GTra
'Sterling Silver' (HT) EBls MAus MGan
'Strawberry Ice' (F) IHos IJoh MHay

'String of Pearls' (Co)	MRea SPer
'Stromboli' (F)	IJoh
Sue Lawley ® (F)	MGan MMat MR&S NRog
Sue Ryder ® (F)	MHay
Suffolk ® (S/GC)	CCor CSut ELeG EOrc IHos LGod MMat MR&S
suffulta	See R. ***arkansana suffulta***
'Sugar Sweet' (F)	CSan
Suma ® (GC)	ELeG GGre MRui NBat WWeb
Summer Fragrance ® (HT)	EWar MRea WWar
Summer Holiday ® (HT)	MBur MGan MRos SPer
Summer Love ® (F)	MRos
¶ Summer Sérénade ® (F)	WWar
'Summer Song' (F)	MGan
'Summer Sunshine, Climbing' (HT/Cl)	LPlm MBri NElm SHen
Summer Wine ® (Cl)	ELeG EWar MBri MGan MMat MRea WWar
'Sun Blush' (HT)	GGre
'Sunblaze'	See R. 'Orange Sunblaze'
Sunblest ® (HT)	ELan ESha GGre IHos IJoh LGod MAus MBri MGan MMor MRos NBar NRog SHen WWar WWeb
'Sunday Times' (F)	EBls
Sunderland Supreme ® (HT)	MHay
Sunmaid ® (Min)	MMor
'Sunny South' (HT)	EBls
¶ Sunny Sunblaze ® (Min)	MRui
Sunset Song ® (HT)	CDoC ESha
'Sunshine' (Poly)	MGan
'Sunsilk' (F)	MBri MGan
Super Star ® (HT)	CB&S CGro CMac EBls EBro ESha EWar GTra IJoh LPlm MAus MBur MGan MHls MMat MMor MR&S MRea NBar NRog SPla SRum WWeb
Super Star, Climbing ® (HT/Cl)	CMac ELeG MAus MGan MHay MHls MMor MRea NElm SHen SRum
'Super Sun' (HT)	ESha MBur MGan NBar NElm SRum
'Surf Rider' (S)	MMor
'Surpasse Tout' (G)	EBls MAus
'Surpassing Beauty of Woolverstone' (HP/Cl)	EBls WHCG
Surrey ® (GC)	CSut ELeG IHos MGan MMat
Susan Hampshire ® (HT)	EBls EWar MGan SRum
Suspense ® (HT)	MGan
'Sutter's Gold' (HT)	EBls ELeG MAus MBur MGan MHls MR&S NElm NRog
'Sutter's Gold, Climbing' (HT/Cl)	MAus MGan
'Swan Lake' (Cl)	Widely available
Swan ® (S)	IHos MAus
Swany ® (Min/GC)	CCMG CGro CHad EBls EHar ELan ELeG ERav EWar IHos MAus MBri MGan MMat MR&S MRea NBar SHen SHil SPer SRum SSus WAct WHCG
¶ 'Swedish Doll' (Min)	MBur
Sweet Dream ® (Patio)	CCla CDoC CGro ELeG ESha EWar GGre LGod LPlm MAus MBri MGan MHls MMor MRea MRos MRui NBar NBat SHil SRum WWar WWeb
'Sweet Fairy' (Min)	ELeG LPlm MMat
'Sweet Honesty'	MBur NRed
Sweet Juliet ® (S)	LGod MAus MRui NBat WAct WWeb
Sweet Magic ® (Patio)	CDoC CGro ELeG ESha GGre IDic IHos LGod MBri MBur MGan MMat MRea MRos MRui NBat NElm SHen SHil SPer SRum WWar WWeb
Sweet Nell ® (F)	LGod
'Sweet Promise' (F)	ELeG MGan NElm SPer
'Sweet Repose' (F)	ELeG MGan
'Sweet Velvet' (F)	MGan
N Sweetheart ® (HT)	MGan MR&S NBat WWar
sweginzowii	CCor MAus MMat
– macrocarpa	EBls
'Swinger' (Min)	MHay
Sympathie ® (HT/Cl)	ELeG IHos IJoh LPlm MAus MGan MMat MMor SPer SRum
Symphony ® (S)	MAus
'Talisman' (HT)	EBls
'Talisman, Climbing' (HT/Cl)	EBls
Tall Story ® (S/GC)	EWar IDic MRea MRos SPer SRum
'Tallyho' (HT)	EBls
'Tamora' (S)	CCMG MAus MBri
'Tango' (F)	NBat WWar WWeb
'Tausendschön' (Ra)	CSan EBls
'Tea Rambler' (Ra)	CCor EBls NSty
Tear Drop ® (Min/Patio)	IDic MBur MGan NBat
'Telstar' (F)	MGan
'Temple Bells' (Min/GC)	EBls MAus NRog
Tender Night ® (F)	MGan
'Tenerife' (HT)	ESha GTra MBur MGan MRea NElm SRum WWeb
Tequila Sunrise ® (HT)	ESha IDic MBri MGan MHay NBat SPer WWar
'Texas Centennial' (HT)	EBls
'Thaïs' (HT)	EBls SRum
¶ 'Thalia'	MAus
'The Bishop' (Ce/G)	EBls
'The Bride' (T)	EBls NSty
The Countryman ® (S)	CCla ELeG EWar MAus MRea MRui SSus
'The Doctor' (HT)	EBls MAus MGan
'The Doctor, Climbing' (HT/Cl)	MGan
'The Fairy' (Poly)	Widely available
'The Garland' (Ra)	CCMG EBls ETWh MAus MMat SFam SPer WHCG
'The Havering Rambler'	EBro
'The Honorable Lady Lindsay' (S)	NSty
'The Knight' (S)	NSty
The Lady ® (S)	MAus MHay NBat
'The Maid Marion'	EBro
'The Miller' (S)	MAus
'The New Dawn'	See R. 'New Dawn'

'The Nun' (S)	IHos MAus
¶ 'The Prince'	MAus MRui
¶ 'The Prioress' (S)	MAus
'The Queen Alexandra'	EBro
'The Queen Elizabeth Rose'	See R. 'Queen Elizabeth'
'The Reeve' (S)	MAus SSus
The Seckford Rose ® (S)	MMat
'The Squire' (S)	MAus
The Times Rose ® (F)	CDoC ELeG EWar IHos LGod MGan MHay MMat SPer WWar
¶ 'The Valois Rose' (F)	MMat
'The Wife of Bath' (S)	MAus MBri SPer WHCG
'The Yeoman' (S)	MBri
'Thelma' (Ra)	CDoC EBls MAus
'Thérèse Bugnet' (Ru)	EBls
'Thisbe' (HM)	CCMG EBls EBro MAus SPer
Thora Hird ® (F)	MRos WWeb
'Thousand Beauties'	See R. 'Tausendschön'
Threepenny Bit Rose	See R. ***elegantula*** 'Persetosa'
'Tiara' (HSwB)	MHls SPer
'Till Uhlenspiegel' (S)	EBls
¶ 'Tina Turner' (HT)	NBat
'Tinker Bell' (Min)	MR&S
Tip Top ® (F/Patio)	Widely available
'Tipo Ideale'	See R. x ***odorata*** 'Mutabilis'
¶ 'Tipsy Imperial Concubine' (HT)	EBls
'Toby Tristam' (Ra)	WWat
'Tom Brown' (F)	ELeG MRea
'Tom Tom'	IJoh
'Topeka' (F)	MRea SRum
Topsi ® (F/Patio)	CDoC ESha EWar GGre IHos IJoh LGod LPlm MAus MBri MHay MMor NBar NElm SHen SPer SRum WWeb
Torville and Dean ® (HT)	CDoC IHos MGan NRog
§ 'Tour de Malakoff' (Ce)	CCMG CCla CCor EBls ELeG ETWh LHol MAus MHay MRTP SFam SHil SPer SSus WHCG
'Toy Clown' (Min)	MAus
Toynbee Hall ® (F)	MMat
'Trade Winds' (HT)	MGan
Tranquillity ® (HT)	MHls WWar
'Treasure Trove' (Ra)	CCor EBls MAus
'Tricia's Joy' (Cl)	CSan
'Tricolore de Flandre' (G)	EBls MAus
'Trier' (Ra)	CCor EBls MHls MMat WHCG
'Trigintipetala'	See R. x ***damascena*** 'Trigintipetala'
'Triomphe du Luxembourg' (T)	EBls MAus
triphylla	See R. ***anemoniflora***
Troika ® (HT)	ELeG ESha IJoh MAus MBur MGan MHay MHls MMat MR&S MRos SPer WWar
'Troilus' (S)	CCMG MAus
'Truly Yours' (HT)	MGan SRum

Trumpeter ® (F)	ELeG ESha EWar GTra IHos IJoh LGod LPlm MBri MGan MHay MHls MMat MRea MRos NBar NBat SPer WWar
* 'Turkestan'	WSHC
'Tuscany' (G)	CHad CSan MAus SPer WAct
'Tuscany Superb' (G)	CBow CCMG CCor EBls EBro ELeG ETWh IHos LHol MAus MMat MRTP NSty SHil SPer SPla SSus WAct WHCG WKif WSHC WWeb
'Twinkles' (Min)	ELeG
Tynwald ® (HT)	CDoC EWar MMat
'Typhoo Tea' (HT)	ELeG
'Typhoon' (HT)	ESha WWar
'Tyrius' (HT)	MGan
'Ulrich Brunner Fils' (HP)	EBls MAus
ultramontana	CCor
'Uncle Bill' (HT)	EBls
'Uncle Joe' (HT)	MHay
Uncle Walter ® (HT)	CMac EBls ELeG ESha GTra MGan MMor NElm NRog SHen SRum
'Unique Blanche' (Ce)	CCMG EBls ETWh WHCG
'Vagabonde' (F)	MGan
¶ Valentine Heart ® (F)	IDic
'Vanda Beauty'	MHls
'Vanguard' (Ru)	EBls MAus MMat SPer
'Vanity' (HM)	CHad EBls EBro IHos MAus SPer WHCG
'Variegata di Bologna' (Bb)	CCMG CCla EBls EBro ELeG ETWh LHol MAus MBur MHls MMat MRTP NSty SFam SHil SSus WAct WHCG
'Veilchenblau' (Ra)	CBow CCMG CCla CCor CHad CSan EBls EBro ELan ELeG ETWh MAus MBri MGan MHay MRTP NSty SHil SPer SRum WAct WHCG WKif WSHC
Velvet Fragrance ® (HT)	MAus MRea
'Velvet Hour' (HT)	ELeG
'Venusta Pendula' (Ra)	EBls
versicolor	See R. ***gallica*** 'Versicolor'
'Vesper' (F)	ELeG
'Vesuvius' (HT)	MAus
'Vick's Caprice' (Bb)	EBls MAus NSty
'Vicomtesse Pierre de Fou' (HT/Cl)	EBls MAus NSty
'Victoriana' (F)	ELeG MAus
'Village Maid'	See R. 'Centifolia Variegata'
villosa	CMac EBls MAus MMat NSty
– 'Duplex'	See R. 'Wolley-Dod'
'Violacea' (G)	CCor EBls WHCG
'Violet Carson' (F)	ESha MAus MGan
'Violette' (Ra)	CCMG CHad EBls EBro MAus NSty SPer WAct WHCG
'Violinista Costa' (HT)	EBls ELeG MAus
virginiana	CCor EBls ELan ELeG ETWh MAus MGan SHil SPer SSus WHCG

– 'Plena'	See R. 'Rose d'Amour'
'Virgo' (HT)	EBls IJoh MAus MHls SRum
'Viridiflora' (Ch)	See R. × *odorata* 'V.'
Vital Spark ® (F)	MGan
'Vivid' (Bb x)	EBls
'W E Lippiat' (HT)	EBls
Wagbi ® (F)	MHls
Wandering Minstrel ® (F)	MGan
¶ *wardii culta*	MAus
'Warley Jubilee' (F)	EWar
¶ 'Warm Welcome'	ELeG MBur MRui NBat
'Warrior' (F)	ELeG EWar MGan NBat SPer WWeb
Warwick Castle ® (S)	MAus MBri MHay SHil SPer SSus
watsoniana	EBls
webbiana	CCor EBls MAus SHil WHCG
§ – *microphylla*	CSun
'Wedding Day' (Ra)	CBow CCMG CDoC CSan EBls EBro ELan ELeG ETWh MAus MBri MBur MGan MMat NBar NSty SHil SPer SPla SRum SSus WAct WHCG WWeb
Wee Barbie ® (Min)	MRea MRui NElm
Wee Jock ® (F/Patio)	CDoC MAus MRea
'Wee Man' (Min)	WWeb
'Weetwood' (Ra)	MAus SPer
'Weisse aus Sparrieshoop' (S)	MGan
'Welcome Guest' (HT)	MHay
'Wembley Stadium' (HT)	MGan
'Wendy Cussons' (HT)	Widely available
'Wendy Cussons, Climbing' (HT/Cl)	CMac EBro MHls
Wenlock ® (S)	CSam EOrc EWar MAus MRea
Westerland ® (F/S)	LPlm MGan MHay MHls MMat WWar
'Westfield Star' (HT)	MAus
'Whippet' (HT)	MHay
'Whisky Gill' (HT)	ESha MGan MRea
Whisky Mac ® (HT)	Widely available
♦ 'White Bath' (CeMo)	See R. 'Shailer's White Moss'
White Bells ® (Min/GC)	CCMG CCla CCor CDoC EBls ELeG EWar IHos LBuc MAus MGan MHls MMat MRea MRos SPer WWeb
'White Cécile Brunner'	See R. Cécile Brunner, White'
'White Christmas' (HT)	ELan ESha MBur MGan SRum
'White Cockade' (Cl)	CB&S CCMG CDoC EBls ELeG LPlm MAus MGan MHls MRea NElm SHil SPer SSus
'White Flight' (Ra)	EBls
'White Grootendorst' (Ru)	EBls LGre MAus WAct
White Meidiland ® (S/GC)	CCMG MR&S
White Moss	EWar MMat
'White Pet'	See R. 'Little White Pet'
White Provence	See R. 'Unique Blanche'
'White Queen Elizabeth' (F)	EBls
White Rose of York	See R. 'Alba Semiplena'
White Spray ® (F)	EBls ELeG
'White Sunblaze' (Min)	MR&S
'White Wings' (HT)	CCMG CHad EBls MAus MBri MGan MHls NSty SPer WAct
¶ Whitley Bay ® (F)	NBat
wichuraiana (Ra)	CCor EBls ELeG LHol MAus SHil SRum SSus WHCG
– 'Variegata' (Ra)	CB&S EBar EBro EFol EPot ERav MPla
– 'Variegata Nana' (Ra)	GLoc LHop SMad SSus
'Wickwar' (Ra)	CHad EBls ELan GWic WAct WHCG
Wild Flower ® (S)	MAus MBri
'Wilhelm' (HM)	CCor EBls EBro IHos MAus NSty SHen
'Will Scarlet' (HM)	ELeG IHos MAus SHil
'Willhire Country' (F)	EBls
'William Allen Richardson' (N)	EBls ETWh MAus MMat WHCG
'William and Mary' (S)	EBls
'William III' (HScB)	EBls
'William Lobb' (Mo)	Widely available
'William R Smith' (T)	EBls
William Shakespeare ® (S)	CCMG CCla ETWh EWar IHos LGod MAus MBri MMat MRea MRui SPer SSus WWeb
♦ 'Williams' Double Yellow' (HScB)	See R. × *harisonii* 'W. D. Y'
willmottiae	EBls ELeG MAus MGan MMat NSty SHil SPer WHCG
Wimi ® (HT)	EWar LPlm MGan MHay NBat
Winchester Cathedral ® (S)	ETWh EWar LGod MAus MRui NBat SHil SSus WWeb
Windrush ® (S)	LHol MAus MBri SPer WAct WHCG
'Winefred Clarke' (HT)	MGan
Wise Portia ® (S)	CCMG MAus
Wishing ® (F/Patio)	IDic LGod MHay MRea MRos SHil SPer WWeb
'Woburn Abbey' (F)	CGro CMac EBls ESha GGre MGan MHls MMor MR&S NBar NElm NRog SRum
'Woburn Gold' (F)	MGan
§ 'Wolley-Dod'	EBls ELeG MAus MRTP SFam WAct
'Woodrow's Seedling' (Cl)	MMor
Woods of Windsor ® (HT)	CDoC MMat
woodsii	CCor CMCN EBls ELeG MAus MBur MMat SHil SPer WHCG
– *fendleri*	See R. *woodsii*
'Woolverstone Church Rose'	See R. 'Surpassing Beauty of Woolverstone'
xanthina	EBls ETWh MGan MMat SHil

¶ – ***spontanea*** 'Canary Bird'	Widely available
'Xavier Olibo' (HP)	EBls
yainacensis	CCor
'Yellow Button' (S)	CCMG CMac MAus MBri SHil SPer SSus
'Yellow Charles Austin' (S)	CCMG MAus MBri SPer
'Yellow Cushion' (F)	EWar MAus
'Yellow Doll' (Min)	ELan ELeG GGre IJoh MAus MBur MGan MHls MR&S MRea MRos
¶ 'Yellow Fru Dagmar Hastrup' (Ru)	CCor
'Yellow Pages' (HT)	MAus
'Yellow Petals' (HT)	MBur MGan
'Yellow Pixie' (Patio)	LPlm
¶ 'Yellow Queen Elizabeth' (F)	CCor
'Yellow Ribbon' (F)	ESha
'Yellow Scotch'	See R. x ***harisonii*** 'Williams' Double Yellow'
Yellow Sunblaze ® (Min)	EWar IHos MR&S NElm WWeb
Yesterday ® (F/S)	CCMG CHad EBls ELeG ERav ESha ETWh EWar LGod MAus MGan MMat SHil SPer SPla SRum SSus
'Yolande d'Aragon' (HP)	EBls
York and Lancaster	See R. x ***damascena versicolor***
Yorkshire Sunblaze ® (Min)	ELeG EWar
Young Quinn ® (HT)	IHos MBur
Young Venturer ® (F)	MMat
Yves Piaget ® (HT)	EWar
'Yvonne Rabier' (Poly)	CCla EBls MAus MMat MRTP SHil SPer SSus WAct WHCG
Zambra ® (F)	CB&S
'Zéphirine Drouhin' (Bb)	Widely available
§ 'Zigeunerknabe' (S)	CCMG CCla CCor CHad EBls ELeG ETWh MAus MMat MRTP NSty SHil SPer SSus WAct WHCG
Zitronenfalter ® (S)	MGan
'Zola' (S)	CSan
'Zorina' (F)	MHls
'Zweibrücken' (Cl)	MGan
'Zwergkönig' (Min)	ELeG EWar IHos MAus MGan MRea

ROSCOEA † (Zingiberaceae)

alpina	CFor GEdr LHop NHol NKay NWCA SBla SWas WChr WHer WPer
auriculata	EBre GEdr
'Beesiana'	SHig WCot
capitata	See R. ***scillifolia***
cautleoides	CAvo CGle EPad ERou GEdr IBrk LAma LGre MPar NHol NKay SAxl SBla SHig SMad SOkd SPou SSpi WChr
– 'Grandiflora'	EPot ERou
– 'Kew Form'	EBre MUlv WCot
humeana	EBre EPad SMrm SPou
§ ***purpurea***	CAvo CGle CHEx CHar EBre ECro EGol ELan ELun EPar EPot GWic ITim LHop MFir MUlv NHol SBla SPou WChr WCot WPer WWin
– ***procera***	See R. ***purpurea***
§ ***scillifolia***	EPad LAma NHol WChr WThu
* ***tibetica***	WHer

ROSMARINUS † (Labiatae)

angustifolius	See R. ***officinalis angustissimus***
* ***calabriensis***	WHer
* ***capicanalli***	CHan
corsicus 'Prostratus'	See R. x ***lavandulaceus***
§ x ***lavandulaceus***	Widely available
¶ – 'Vicomte de Noailles'	ERea
officinalis	Widely available
§ – ***albus***	CArn CB&S CBow CRow CSFH CSev GPla GPoy IBar MPar NSti SBla SChu SLon SMad SSta WHer WHil WOMN WSHC WSto
§ – ***angustissimus*** 'Corsican Blue'	CArn SCro SPer
– 'Aureovariegatus'	See R. ***o. aureus***
§ – ***aureus***	CB&S CFis CHil CMer CSun EFol ELan ERav IBlr WHer WOMN WPer
§ – 'Benenden Blue'	CBow CGle CPle CSFH CSco CSev CTre EFou GPoy LHop MGos NSel SBla SChu SDix SLon SMad SPer SPla STre WHer WSHC WWat
– 'Collingwood Ingram'	See R. ***o.*** 'Benenden Blue'
¶ – 'Corsicus Prostratus'	CB&S
– 'Fastigiatus'	See R. ***o.*** 'Miss Jessopp's Upright'
– 'Fota Blue'	SCro SIde SSus
– 'Frimley Blue'	See R. ***o.*** 'Primley Blue'
– 'Guilded'	See R. ***o. aureus***
– 'Jackman's Prostrate'	CB&S SPla
– 'Majorca'	SIde WOMN
– 'Majorcan Pink'	CB&S SPer WMar
– 'McConnell's Blue'	EBre ELan MGos
§ – 'Miss Jessopp's Upright'	Widely available
§ – 'Primley Blue'	CArn CBow CRow CSam CSev LSav SChu SHig WHer WOak WWeb
– ***prostratus***	See R. x ***lavandulaceus***
– ***pyramidalis***	See R. ***o.*** 'Miss Jessopp's Upright'
– ***roseus***	CBow CHan CMer CSun LHop NSti SBla SChu SLon SMad WHer WSHC
– 'Russell's Blue'	WHer
– 'Severn Sea'	CArn CB&S CBot CGle CHan CMer CSco CSev CShe ELan GPoy LHop LSav NNor SHil SLon SMad SPer WEas WSto WWat

– 'Sissinghurst'	CArn CBow CKni CSev CShe SSus WWat
– 'Sudbury Blue'	WEas
¶ – 'Trusty'	CKni
– 'Tuscan Blue'	CShe LSav NHex SHil SLon WWat
– 'Variegatus'	See R. ***o. aureus***
¶ ***repens***	NSti

ROSTRINUCULA (Labiatae)

dependens GUIZ 18	EMon LSav

ROSULARIA (Crassulaceae)

♦ ***acuminata***	See SEMPERVIVELLA ***a.***
¶ ***adenotricha adenotricha***	NGre
aizoon	MBro WDav
alpestris	CWil
§ ***chrysantha***	CRiv MHig NGre NNrd SIng SSmi WHil WPer
– Number 1	CWil SMit WThu
– Number 2	CWil SMit WThu
crassipes	See RHODIOLA ***c.***
¶ ***globulariifolia***	NGre SIgm WDav
¶ ***haussknechtii***	NGre
muratdaghensis	CWil
pallida	See R. ***chrysantha***
platyphylla	ITim SIng SSmi
* ***rechingeri***	CWil
sedoides	SMit SSmi WPer
§ – ***alba***	CHar CLew CMHG CRow CSun CWil EMNN EPar EPot GCHN MBar MCas MHig NGre NHol NKay NNrd SChu SIng SMit WHil WHoo WOMN WThu
sempervivum	CWil NGre NHol SMit WThu
¶ – ***amanensis***	NGre
* – ***glaucophylla***	CWil
¶ ***serpentinica***	CWil
– from Sandras Dag	SMit
serrata	NGre
– from Crete	SMit
spathulata	NTow WThu

RUBIA (Rubiaceae)

peregrina	CKin MSal
tinctorum	CArn GPoy LGan LHol MChe MSal NHex SIde WHer WSto

RUBUS † (Rosaceae)

arcticus	CGle ESim MBal MHig SReu SSta WAbe WPat WThu
¶ x ***barkeri***	ECou
'Betty Ashburner'	CHan EGol GWic IBar MBri MGos MR&S WWat
biflorus	EMon ERav
F 'Boysenberry, Thornless'	EMui SDea
§ ***calycinoides***	Widely available
cockburnianus	CB&S CCla CCor CGle EHar ELan ENot EPar IOrc MBri MFir MR&S MRav SHil SPer SSpi WEas WWat
¶ – 'Golden Vale'	CB&S EPla
coreanus 'Dart's Mahogany'	MBri
crataegifolius	CBrd EPla WWat
deliciosus	CSco GRei SHil
flagelliflorus	MBar
fockeanus	See R. ***calycinoides***
¶ x ***fraseri***	EPla
fruticosus	CKin
F – 'Ashton Cross'	EMui LBuc NBee NTwe SDea
F – 'Bedford Giant'	EHar EMui MBea NBar NTwe SDea SKee SPer WHig WWeb
F – 'Black Satin'	CSam EMui GChr GRei MBea MBri NTwe WWeb
F – 'Denver Thornless'	EWar
F – 'Fantasia Blackberry'	EMui
F – 'Godshill Goliath'	SDea
F – 'Himalayan Giant'	CSam EWar GRei MBea NBar NRog NTwe SDea SPer WHig
F – 'John Innes'	NElm NRog
F – 'Loch Ness'	CSam EMui GChr MBri NBar NTwe
F – 'Merton Thornless'	CMac EHar MBea NBee NElm NRog SDea SKee WHig WWeb
F – 'No Thorn'	SDea
F – 'Oregon Thornless'	EMui EWar IJoh LBuc MBea MBri NTwe SDea SPer WHig WWeb
F – 'Parsley Leaved'	SDea
F – 'Sylvan'	CSut WHig
F – 'Thornfree'	SDea
– 'Variegatus'	CBot EFol ELan EPla LHop MBal
¶ ***henryi***	CBot EPla
– ***bambusarum***	CHan CMal ELan EPar EPla GWic SHil SSpi SSus WWat
F 'Hildaberry'	WHig
ichangensis	CBot CHan CMCN GWic ISea
idaeus	CKin
F – 'Aureus'	CBos CCor CHoe ECha EFol EHal ELan GPla GWic LHop NRoo WRus
F – 'Autumn Bliss'	CSam CSut ECtt EMui IJoh LBuc NBee NTwe SDea SKee WHig WWeb
F – 'Fallgold'	EMui IJoh NTwe SDea SPer
F – 'Glen Clova'	CMac EHar EMui EWar GChr GRei IJoh LBuc MBri NBar NBee NRog NTwe SDea SKee SPer WHig WWeb
F – 'Glen Coe'	WHig
F – 'Glen Moy'	CSam CSut EMui GChr GRei IJoh LBuc MBri NRog NTwe SKee SPer
F – 'Glen Prosen'	EMui IJoh LBuc MBri NRog NTwe SKee SPer WHig
F – 'Golden Everest'	EWar NTwe SDea SPer
F – 'Heritage'	EHar IJoh SDea SPer
F – 'Leo'	CSut EMui NBee NTwe SDea SKee SPer WHig
F – 'Malling Admiral'	CMac CSam EHar EMui ESha MBri NBar NRog NTwe SKee SPer
F – 'Malling Delight'	EMui GChr GRei NBar NRog NTwe SDea SKee SPer WHig WWeb
F – 'Malling Jewel'	EMui EWar IJoh NBee NTwe SDea SKee SPer WHig WWeb
F – 'Malling Joy'	EMui NTwe

F – 'Malling Orion' CMac ESha
F – 'Malling Promise' EWar NBar NTwe SDea SPer
F – 'September' EWar SPer
F – 'Zeva' CMac EMui EWar NBar NBee NTwe SDea SPer
F ***illecebrosus*** CCor CSun ESim WPat
irenaeus CHan
'Kenneth Ashburner' CBow ERav MBri WWat
F 'King's Acre Berry' EMui
lambertianus CHan CMCN
lineatus CBot CBrd CFor CHan LHop SDix SDry
F Loganberry 'LY 59' EHar NElm NRog NTwe SDea SPer
F – 'LY 654' CSam GRei LBuc MBea MBri NElm NTwe SDea SPer WHig WWeb
F – 'New Zealand Black' SDea
F 'Loganberry Thornless CMac EMui IJoh NRog NTwe SDea
'Margeret Gordon' IBar IJoh
microphyllus
'Variegatus' ELan ERav IJoh MBri SHil WWeb
§ ***nepalensis*** CGle WHea WWat
– Sch 2074 CBow
nutans See R. ***nepalensis***
odoratus CCla CHEx CSco ELan NRar SHil SPer
parviflorus CCor
parvus ECou
F ***phoenicolasius*** Japanese Wineberry CCla CHan CMac CTre ELan EMui ESim MBri NBar NHol NRog NTwe SDea SHil SPer WHig WPat WWat
setchuenensis SBra
F 'Silvanberry' EMui NTwe
spectabilis CChu CGre CMHG CMal ELan LHop MBal MR&S MRav NHol WHal
– 'Flore Pleno' CChu CCla LHop LSav NHol WPat WWeb
squarrosus ECou LHop SDry
* ***stellarcticus*** ESim
¶ – 'Anna' ESim
¶ – 'Beata' ESim
¶ – 'Linda' ESim
¶ – 'Sofia' ESim
F 'Sunberry' EMui SKee WHig
F Tayberry CMac CSam EMui EWar GChr GRei IJoh MBea MBri NBar NElm NRog NTwe SKee SPer WHig WWeb
F – 'Medana Tayberry' CSut LBuc SDea
thibetanus CB&S CBot CHad CHan CSco ECha EOrc GWic LSav MBri NHol SDix SHil SPer SSus WPat WSHC
– 'Silver Fern' CCla EBre EGol EHar ELan ERav MRav SLon SMad WWat
treutleri CCor CHan
tricolor Widely available
– 'Dart's Evergreen' MBri
Tridel 'Benenden' Widely available
trilobus CCla SLon
F 'Tummelberry' EMui
ulmifolius 'Bellidiflorus' CBot CCla ELan ENot EPla GWic MBal MPar NNor SChu SDix SHil
F 'Veitchberry' EMui NRog
F 'Youngberry' SDea

RUDBECKIA (Compositae)
echinacea purpurea See ECHINACEA ***purpurea***
fulgida deamii CGle CHar CKel EBre ECha EFou ELan ELun ERou MWat NBar NKay NOak NRoo NSti SChu SPer WEas WHoo
§ – ***speciosa*** CGle CKel CSco CShe EBre ECha EJud ELan IDai MPit NBar NRoo WOld WRus
– ***sullivantii*** 'Goldsturm' CBos CHar CKel CSam CSco CSun EBre EFou GAbr LAbb MBri MFir MRav MWat NKay NOrc NRoo SBla SDix SMad SPer WEas WHoo WOld
gloriosa See R. ***hirta***
§ ***hirta*** IBrk LHil NCat
¶ – 'Irish Eyes' EPad
laciniata ELan LHil NOrc SFis
– 'Golden Glow' CSco EMon
maxima MBri
newmannii See R. ***fulgida speciosa***
nitida 'Goldquelle' CBow CGle CSco EBre EFou ELan ERou MWgw NOrc SCro SPer WWin
– 'Herbstsonne' ('Autumn Sun') CSco ECha ERou IDai MWat NVic SFis SMad SPer WEas
¶ – 'Juligold' ('July Gold') EFou
purpurea See ECHINACEA ***purpurea***
subtomentosa EFou EMon ERou GWic

RUELLIA (Acanthaceae)
devosiana MBri
makoyana IBlr MBri SLMG

RUMEX (Polygonaceae)
acetosa See R. ***rugosus***
¶ ***alpinus*** WCot
flexuosus EFol EMon GWic WCot
hydrolapathum MSta
montanus 'Ruber' See R. ***arifolius*** 'R.'
§ ***rugosus*** CArn CKin CSev ECha EJud Effi GPoy LHol NBir NSel SIde WOak WSto
¶ – 'Hortensis' MBar
sanguineus sanguineus CHoe CRow ELan EMon GPla LHol MTho NHol NSti SIng WHer WRus
scutatus CArn CSFH CSev Effi GPoy LHol MChe MPar MTho NHol SIde WOak WSto
– silver form EFol ELan GWic
– 'Silver Shield' EMon IBlr LRHS

RUMOHRA (Davalliaceae)
adiantiformis WFib

RUPICAPNOS (Fumariaceae)
africanus EPot SBla WOMN

RUSCHIA (Aizoaceae)
¶ *schollii* pale pink LHop

RUSCUS † (Liliaceae/Ruscaceae)
aculeatus CHad ECro ENot GPoy IJoh MBri MRav MUlv SArc SHil SSta WOMN WOak WWat
– andromonoecious SLHN
hypoglossum MUlv SHil
racemosus See DANAE ***racemosa***

RUSSELIA (Scrophulariaceae)
equisetiformis CPle ERea SIgm
juncea See R. ***equisetiformis***

RUTA (Rutaceae)
chalepensis CArn ELan LHol WHil
– 'Dimension Two' EFol EMon EPla LHol SCro
– prostrate form See R. *c.* 'Dimension Two'
¶ *corsica* WPer
graveolens CArn CCor CGle CMer CSFH ECha EJud LHol MBro MChe NOak NSel SIde WEas WHal WHer WOak WPer
– 'Jackman's Blue' Widely available
– 'Variegata' CBot CBow CBra CBre CSFH ECha EFol EFou EGol ELan ERav GPoy LHop MCot NNor NOak NSel SPla WAbe WHer WHoo WPer WSHC
prostrata See R. ***chalepensis*** 'Dimension Two'

RUTTYA (Acanthaceae)
¶ *fruticosa* CSun

SABAL (Palmae)
minor LPal NPal
palmetto CArn LPal NPal WNor
texensis NPal

SACCHARUM (Gramineae)
¶ *ravennae* EMon

SAGERETIA (Rhamnaceae)
§ *thea* STre
♦ *theezans* See S. ***thea***

SAGINA (Caryophyllaceae)
boydii EMNN GArf GEdr GLoc ITim MHig NHol NTow WThu
glabra 'Aurea' See S. ***subulata*** 'Aurea'
subulata CLew ECro
§ – 'Aurea' CHoe CKel CRiv EBar ECha EFol ELan EPar GLoc IDai LGro LHop MCas NHol NVic SIng WEas WHal WPer WWin

SAGITTARIA (Alismataceae)
japonica See S. ***sagittifolia***
¶ *latifolia* CHEx
§ *sagittifolia* CRow CWGN EHon LMay MSta SHig
– 'Flore Pleno' CRow EHon LMay MBal MSta SHig

SAINTPAULIA (Gesneriaceae)
¶ 'Alma' CSut
¶ 'Bella' EAVC
¶ 'Bertini' CSut
¶ 'Blue Nymph' EAVC
¶ 'Bright Eyes' EAVC
¶ 'Celebration' EAVC
¶ 'Delft' EAVC
¶ 'Fred' EAVC
¶ 'Fusspot' EAVC
¶ 'Garden News' EAVC
¶ 'Gisela' CSut
¶ 'Ice Maiden' EAVC
¶ 'Lotte' CSut
¶ 'Ma Cherie' EAVC
¶ 'Maria' EAVC
¶ 'Meteor Trail' EAVC
¶ 'Midnight Trail' EAVC
¶ 'Miki' CSut
¶ 'Rococo Pink' EAVC
¶ 'Sarah' EAVC
¶ 'Silver Milestone Star' EAVC
¶ 'Starry Trail' EAVC
¶ 'Susi' CSut
¶ 'Wonderland' EAVC

SALIX † (Salicaceae)
acutifolia ELan ENot IOrc SExT SPla
– 'Blue Streak' CCor CMHG CSco IOrc NBir SHil
– 'Pendulifolia' IOrc
adenophylla See S. ***syrticola***
'Aegma Brno' WMou
aegyptiaca CCor CLnd ENot NWea WMou
alba CLnd LBuc MR&S SExT SHil SPer WMou
– *argentea* See S. ***a. sericea***
– 'Aurea' CSam WMou
§ – 'Britzensis' CCor CKin CLnd CMHG EHar ELan ENot GRei IOrc LSav MBal MBri MGos MRav NNor NWea SHil SPer SSta WMou WWat
– *caerulea* ENot NWea SHil WMou
– 'Cardinal' ISea
– 'Chermesina' See S. *a.* 'Britzensis'
– 'Hutchinson's Yellow' EHar
– 'Liempde' ENot MBri SExT
¶ – 'Orange Spire' LMer
– 'Richmond' SPer
§ – *sericea* CCor CLnd CSam EBre EFol EGol EHar ENot IOrc MBal MBri MRav NNor SHil SMad SPer WMou WWat
– 'Splendens' See S. ***a. sericea***
N– 'Tristis' CKin CLnd ELan IJoh MBri NWea SPer WMou
– *vitellina* CCor CKin CSam EBar EGol EHar ELan MBri MR&S NWea SExT SHil WMou

– 'Vitellina Pendula'	See S. ***a.*** 'Tristis'
– 'Vitellina Tristis'	See S. ***a.*** 'Tristis'
§ ***alpina***	CShe EPot ITim MBal MCas MHig MPla MPlt NHar NHol NNrd NRoo WPat
apoda	ELan MBal NHol WAbe WHal WPat WPer
arbuscula	CLew CShe EBre ELan EPad GLoc IJoh MBal MBri MPla NLan SSta
aurita	WMou
babylonica	ELan NWea SExT WMou
– 'Annularis'	See S. ***b.*** 'Crispa'
§ – 'Crispa'	CGre EHar ELan EPla LHop NBar SGar
§ – ***pekinensis***	SHil
– ***pekinensis*** 'Pendula'	SHil
– ***pekinensis*** 'Tortuosa'	CCla CLnd CSco EGol EHar ELan ENot ERav IDai IJoh IOrc ISea MBal MBar MGos MWat NNor NWea SHil SPer SSpi WThu WWat
x ***balfourii***	SPla WMou
bicolor	CChu
bockii	CBra COtt ELan LHop MBar MBri MGos MR&S SHil WAbe WMar WPer
§ 'Bowles' Hybrid'	CCor EHar LBuc MBri WMou
'Boydii'	CSam EHar ELan EPot GDra GLoc ITim MBal MBar MBri MBro NHol NNor NRoo SHil SIng WAbe WDav WPat WThu
'Boyd's Pendulous'	EHar EPla MBal MBar
breviserrata	GDra
burjatica 'Korso'	WMou
candida	WPat
caprea	CBrd CKin CLnd ENot GRei LBuc MBri MR&S NWea SHil WMou
– 'Kilmarnock'	See S. ***c. pendula***
N – ***pendula***	Widely available
* – ***variegata***	CRow IBar
¶ ***capusii***	LMer
cascadensis	MBal
* ***cashmiriana***	WPat WThu
'Chrysocoma'	See S. x ***sepulcralis chrysocoma***
cinerea	CKin GRei MBri NWea SHil
– 'Tricolor'	See S. ***c.*** 'Variegata'
– 'Variegata'	EBre EFol EGol ERav LHop MBri WPat
x ***cottetii***	CBra IJoh MBri SHil WMar WMou
daphnoides	CLnd CSam EHar ELan ENot GRei IHos IOrc MBar MCot MR&S NHol NWea SExT SHil SPer STre WMou WWat
– 'Aglaia'	CB&S MBal
– 'Oxford Velvet'	MBri
♦ 'E A Bowles'	See S. 'Bowles' Hybrid'
♦ ***elaeagnos***	WMou
§ – ***angustifolia***	CCla CLnd EGol EHar ELan ENot EPar IOrc LHop MBal NNor NWea SHil SMad SSpi STre WAbe WPat WWat WWin
'Elegantissima'	See S. ***pendulina blanda***
§ 'Erythroflexuosa'	CB&S CBow CCor CShe EGol EHar ELan MBri MFir SExT SHil SLon SPer WOak
exigua	CCla EBre EGol EHar ELan ENot IJoh IOrc LSav MBar MBri NBar SHil SMad SPer SSpi SSus WMou WPat WWat
fargesii	CBot CChu CFor EBre EGol EHar ISea LHop MBal MGos NHol SDix SHil SIng SMad WAbe WPat WWat
§ x ***finmarchica***	MPlt
formosa	See S. ***arbuscula***
fragilis	CKin SHil WMou
fruticulosa	See S. ***lindleyana***
'Fuiri-koriyanagi'	See S. ***integra*** 'Hakuro-nishiki'
furcata	CChu CGle CLew EFol EPar GDra MBal MBar MBro MCot MHig NKay NNrd WHil WPer WThu
glauca	WMou
glaucosericea	CCor NHol
'Golden Curls'	See S. 'Erythroflexuosa'
gracilistyla	CFor CSco EHar SHil WMou WWat
§ – ***melanostachys***	Widely available
x ***grahamii***	CLew MBal WMar
– ***moorei***	EPot MBal NNrd NRed
* ***greyi***	CSam EPla
'Hagensis'	See S. 'The Hague'
hastata 'Wehrhahnii'	Widely available
helvetica	Widely available
herbacea	MBal MCas NLan
hookeriana	CCor EHar SSpi WHCr WMar WMou WPat WWat
§ ***humilis***	ELan LSav SHil
hylematica	See S. ***lindleyana***
incana	See S. ***elaeagnos***
integra 'Albomaculata'	See S. ***i.*** 'Hakuro-nishiki'
§ – 'Hakuro-nishiki'	Widely available
irrorata	CBot CCor CMHG EHar IOrc ISea LSav MPar SHil SMad WMar WMou
'Jacquinii'	See S. ***alpina***
N ***japonica***	CFor EGol WWin
kinuyanagi	ELan LHop
kurome	See S. ***gracilistyla melanostachys***
lanata	Widely available
– Kew form	LHop
– 'Stuartii'	See S. 'Stuartii'
lapponum	MBri NHol NLan SIng SLon WPat
x ***laurina***	CMHG SPer
§ ***lindleyana***	CHan CRiv EPla EPot GLoc MPla NHar NKay NOak NRed NRoo NRya WMar WWat
lucida	WMou
magnifica	CBot CChu EHar ELan EPar MBal SHil SMad SSpi WMou
matsudana	See S. ***babylonica pekinensis***
– 'Tortuosa Aureopendula'	See S. 'Erythroflexuosa'

– 'Tortuosa Aureopendula'	See S. 'Erythroflexuosa'
melanostachys	See S. ***gracilistyla m.***
moupinensis	IOrc LSav MBri SHil WMou
**myricoides* 'Hastata'	WMou
§ *myrsinifolia*	EHar
¶ *myrsinites*	NRya
– 'Jacquiniana'	See S. ***alpina***
myrtilloides	NNrd
– 'Pink Tassels'	ELan LHop MBal SSpi WAbe
– x *repens*	See S. x ***finmarchica***
nakamurana yezoalpina	CBrd CChu CCla CFor EPla LHop SSta SWas WPat
nepalensis	See S. ***lindleyana***
nigricans	See S. ***myrsinifolia***
occidentalis	See S. ***humilis***
x *ovata*	EHal EMNN MPlt NRed NRoo
pentandra	CKin IOrc SHil WMou WWat
phylicifolia	CCor EGol SPer WMou
polaris	EPot MBal
procumbens	NHol
prunifolia	See S. ***waldsteiniana***
§ *purpurea*	CB&S EHal EPad IOrc WMou
– *gracilis*	See S. ***p.*** 'Nana'
– 'Helix'	See S. ***p.***
– 'Howki'	WMou
– *lambertiana*	CCor
– 'Nana'	CBow CCor CHad CPle ELan MBal MGos MPar NHol SChu SHil SPer SPla SSpi STre WPat
– 'Nancy Saunders'	EFol EPla ERav GWic MPar SAxl SWas
– 'Pendula'	CBra CMer EHar ENot IJoh ISea LSav MBal MBar MBri MPla NBar NNor NWea SHil SPer SSpi WWat
*– 'Richartii'	MPar
pyrenaica	MCot
pyrifolia	WMou
repens	ERav ITim LHil NCat NRed SGar STre
– *argentea*	Widely available
– 'Iona'	SIng
– 'Voorthuizen'	IJoh NHar
reticulata	GDra GEdr LHop MBal MBro NHar WPat
retusa	CSam GDra MHig MPla NHol NNrd WPat
– *pygmaea*	GLoc
N*rosmarinifolia*	See S. ***elaeagnos angustifolia***
x *rubens* 'Basfordiana'	CLnd EBar EGol EHar LSav SHil WMou
x *rubra* 'Eugenei'	CCor CSam EHar SHil WWat WWin
sachalinensis	See S. ***udensis***
¶ x *sadleri*	LHil
schraderiana	CSam SSta
x *sepulcralis*	EHar NWea
§ – *chrysocoma*	CBow CSco EHar ELan ENot IDai LBuc MBal MBar MGos MWat SExT SHil SMad
– 'Salamonii'	NWea
serpyllifolia	CLew ITim LHop MBal MBro MCas MPlt NHar NRed SIng WAbe WPat WPer
– *chamonii*	EPot
setsuka	See S. ***udensis*** 'Sekka'
x *simulatrix*	CSam
Nx *smithiana*	CLnd SPer
x *stipularis*	CMHG
'Stuartii'	EPot MBar WBod
subopposita	ELan MBar MBri NBar NHar SHil SIng
§ 'The Hague'	WMou
triandra	SHil WMou
– 'Black Maul'	WMou
– 'Champion'	WMou
tristis	See S. ***humilis***
x *tsugaluensis* 'Ginme'	CMHG WMou WWat
¶ *udensis*	WWat
§ – 'Sekka'	CLnd CMer EGol EHar ELan EPar IOrc MBal MBri NRoo NWea SPer SPla SSta STre WMou
uva-ursi	MBal SHil WMou
viminalis	CKin ENot GRei MR&S NWea SHil WMou
– 'Bowles' Hybrid'	See S. 'Bowles' Hybrid'
vitellina 'Pendula'	See S. ***alba*** 'Tristis'
§ *waldsteiniana*	CB&S IJoh
x *wimmeriana*	EGol IJoh MBri
'Yelverton'	SPer

SALVIA † (Labiatae)

acetabulosa	See S. ***multicaulis***
aethiopis	CPle ELan EMon EPad NSti WHea WHil WPer
**africana lutea*	CHan
ambigens	See S. ***guaranitica*** 'Blue Enigma'
¶ *amplexicaulis*	WPer
angustifolia	CFis CPle MR&S
argentea	Widely available
arizonica	CFis CPle CSun LGre
¶ *aucheri*	GWic
aurea	CPle CSco CTre LGre LHop WHal WPer
azurea	CHan LHol LHop
♦ *bacheriana*	See S. ***buchananii***
♦ *bicolor*	See SALVIA ***barrelieri***
blancoana	CBot ECha EFol EMon ERav GPla GWic LGre LHop NSti WHer
blepharophylla	CB&S CCan CGre CHan CPle LHil LHop WHea
¶ *broussonettii*	LHil
§ *buchananii*	CB&S CBrd CCan CGre CHil CPle CSun ERav ERea LGre LHil LHop SAxl SCro SMrm WHea
bulleyana	CCla CHan CPle CSev EBre ELan EMon GWic LHol SIde WAbb WHea
cacaliifolia	CCan CFis CHan CHil CMer CPle CSpe CTre GWic LHol LHop SCro WEas WHea WPer

caerulea	See S. ***guaranitica*** 'Black and Blue'
caespitosa	GLoc ITim NTow
campanulata	EMon
canariensis	GWic
candelabra	CHan LGre MPar WHer WKif WPer WSHC
¶ ***cardinalis***	NHex
clevelandii	WPer
coccinea	CBot CHil CSev EBar EFol ELan EMon MFir WEas WHea WPer
– 'Alba'	CCan EMon
concolor	See S. ***guaranitica***
confertiflora	CCan CFis CGre CHil CPle CSun ELan EMon GWic LHop SAxl SMrm WEas
discolor	CBot CGre CHil CPle CSev ELan ERav ERea LGre LHil LHol LHop MPar MRav MTho SMrm SSpi WHal
dombeyi	CCan CFis CPle GWic LHop
dorisiana	CFis CHan CPle CSev ELan SMrm WTay
elegans	CCan CCla CFis CGre CPle CSev EBar GWic LGre LHol SCro SIde WOak
¶ ***farinacea*** 'Victoria'	CBow
¶ ***ferruginea*** 'Porcelain'	CB&S
forsskaolii	CGle CPle CSev ELan EMon EPad GWic IBrk LHil MPar NSti SAxl SChu SCro WCar WEas WHea WHil WPer
fulgens	CCan CCla CHan CPle CSam CSev LGre LHil SIde SMrm WHea
gesneriiflora	CCan CHan CHil CPle CSev GWic LHil LHol SCro SHil SIde
glutinosa	CChu CHad CHan CPle CSun ELan EMon GWic LGan LHol NSti SSvw WEas WPer
grahamii	Widely available
greggii	CFis CHil CPle ERav LGre LHil SPer
– 'Alba'	LHop WHer
¶ – 'Keter's Red'	EMon
– peach	CB&S LAbb LHop
¶ – 'Raspberry Royal'	LHop
¶ – x ***lycioides***	LHop
§ ***guaranitica***	CB&S CBot CCan CChu CFis CHad CHan CHil CMer CPle CSun ECha ELan GWic LAbb LHol MRav SAxl SHil SLMG WEas WHea WHer WPer
§ – 'Black and Blue'	CCan WPer
§ – 'Blue Enigma'	CCan CHad EHal EMon LHop SCro
haematodes	See S. ***pratensis*** Haematodes group
hians	EBar EPad GWic NSti SBla WAbb WEas WPer
hispanica	See S. ***lavandulifolia***
horminoides	EMon WCla
horminum	See S. ***viridis***
interrupta	EHal EMon LGre LHil SChu SDix SPer WEas WHea
involucrata	CB&S CHan CPle CSev GWic LHil LHol WEas WSHC
– 'Bethellii'	Widely available
– 'Boutin'	CCan
– dark form	GWic
– 'Hadspen'	CCan CSam
– 'Mrs Pope'	CBot CCan CSam ECro
¶ 'James Compton'	SIgm
§ ***lavandulifolia***	CArn CHad CMHG ECha EFou EMon LSav MCot MRav NSti SAxl SCro SLon SPer SPla WBon WDav WHer WHil WOak WPer
lemmonii	SCro
leptophylla	CFis CHan CHil CPle CSpe LHop WHea WPer
– ***reptans***	CCan
leucantha	CCan CCla CFis CHil CMCN CMer CPle CSam CSun CTre ELan ERea GWic LHol LHop LSav MFir SIde SLMG WHer WOMN WPer
¶ ***lycioides***	LGre
¶ ***lyrata***	MSal
macrosiphon	CHan
mellifera	CArn CPle
mexicana minor	CCan CFis CGre CHil CPle
microphylla	CCan CCla CFis CGle CHan CMHG CMal CMer CPle CSun MFir SChu SLMG SLon
– ***microphylla***	CPle LGre SMrm
– ***neurepia***	CB&S CFis CGle CHan CPle CSam ECro EMon ERav GCHN LHol LHop LSav NSti SHil SPer WHal WPer WSHC
– 'Newby Hall'	LHil
¶ – 'Pink Blush'	ELan LHil
– ***wislizeni***	LGre LHop
moorcroftiana	CPle GWic NCat WDav WPer
§ ***multicaulis***	CBrd CHan CSev CSun ECha EFou EMon EPla ERav NSti SAxl WAbb WOMN WOld WPer WSHC
nelsonii	SMrm
¶ ***nemorosa***	WHil
¶ – 'Amethyst'	SWas
– 'Lubecca'	CCla CHad CSco CSev CShe EFou ERou SPer WOld WRus WSHC
– 'Ostfriesland' ('East Friesland')	CCla CKel CSco EBre ECha EFou ELan GCHN MWat NBar NKay SChu SDix SPer SPla WHoo WPer WRus WWin
– ***tesquicola***	ECha
¶ ***nilotica***	EPad WHer
* ***ningpo***	CPle
nubicola	CHan WPer
officinalis	CArn CHad CHoe CSFH CShe ENot ERav ESis Effi GPoy LSav MBal MBar MBri MChe NNor NSel SHil SLon WEas WOak WPer WSto WWat
– 'Alba'	See S. ***o.*** 'Albiflora'

– 'Albiflora' CBot CFis EFou LHil NSti SBla
N– 'Aurea' CHad CRiv GPoy LHop MCot MFir NSel SMad WWin
– 'Berggarten' ECro EFou EMon GWic WHer
– broadleaved variety EJud NSti
– 'Cedric' MWgw
¶– 'Grete Stoltze' GWic
§– 'Icterina' Widely available
– 'Kew Gold' EMon LHop NSti
– 'Minor' EFou GWic WHer
– narrow-leaved See S. ***lavandulifolia***
– 'Purpurascens' Widely available
– 'Purpurascens Variegata' CFis CGle CHoe EFol GPla NSti WEas
– Tomentosa group CArn
– 'Tricolor' Widely available
– 'Variegata' See S. ***o.*** 'Icterina'
****oppositifolia*** CCan CFis CPle LHop
patens Widely available
– 'Cambridge Blue' Widely available
¶– 'Chilcombe' LHop
– 'Royal Blue' CCla ECha EFol
pratensis CArn CKin EFou EJud ELan EMon MPit MSal NCat SIde WPer
– Haematodes group CHad CKel CKin CSco CSun ECha ELan EMon LHil MFir MPar MRav MShr MWgw NKay NSti SCro SDix SPer WHoo WOld WPer WRus
****prostrata*** MCot
przewalskii CPle EMon GGar
recognita CBot LGre
¶ ***regeliana*** NBir
roemeriana CBos CHan WDav WHer WPer
rutilans Widely available
****scabra*** GWic
sclarea CArn CGle EFou EJud EMon Effi GPoy LHol MChe NSel SFis SIde WHer WHoo WOak WPer
– JCA 847.400 CSun
– ***turkestanica*** CArn CCla CHad CHan CPle CSam CSco CSev EFou ELan EMon EOrc GPla MFir MWgw NSti SPer WEas WHal WHil WPer WRus WSHC
****semiatrata*** GWic
¶ ***sinaloensis*** GWic LGre LHop
sp. Iran WOMN
¶ sp. T&K 550 CBot
x ***superba*** CGle CKel CRow CShe EFol ELan MBri MWat NRoo SAxl SCro SDix SFis WEas WHea WHoo
¶– 'Rubin' EFou
– 'Superba' CSco CSev ECha EFou SPer
– 'Tänzerin' MPar
x ***sylvestris*** 'Blauhügel' CCla CSev EFou MBri NHol NRoo NVic SChu
– 'Blaukönigin' ('Blue Queen') CBow CGle CHar ECro EFou MWat NOak NRoo SFis SPla WPer
– 'Indigo' EFou
– 'Lye End' CHar EBre GWic WRus
– 'Mainacht' ('May Night') CSco ECro EFou ERou MBri NBar NHol SMrm SPer WEas
– 'Rose Queen' CHar EBar ECha EFou ELan EMon ERou GCHN GHig NCat NOak NOrc NRoo SFis WHoo WPer
¶– 'Rügen' MBri
¶ ***taraxacifolia*** SLHN
¶ ***tesquicola*** CBrd
¶ ***transcaucasica*** SIde
¶ ***transsylvanica*** WPer
****trijuga*** EMon
triloba CArn EEls LHol SIde
uliginosa Widely available
– 'African Skies' GWic
verbanaca MSal
verticillata CPle EBar ECha ELan EMon LHol NHol NNor NSti WPer
– ***alba*** CHan LHol MPar NHol WHer
*– 'Purple Rain' EFou LHil SWas
virgata CPle
§ ***viridis*** CArn LHol MChe SIde
****wardii*** WKif

SALVINIA (Salviniaceae)

braziliensis MSta

SAMBUCUS † (Caprifoliaceae)

alba 'Variegata' ERav IJoh
canadensis ESim
F– 'Adams' ESim
– 'Aurea' ELan IOrc NWea WAbe
– 'Maxima' CCor CHEx ERav GWic SDix SHil
¶– 'Rubra' EPla
F– 'York' ESim
ebulus CKin CRow ERav
****koreana*** CMCN
¶ ***mexicana*** EMon
nigra CKin EHar ENot GPoy GRei LHol MBri NNor NSel NWea SHil SIde WMou
– 'Albomarginata' See S. ***n.*** 'Marginata'
– 'Albovariegata' See S. ***n.*** 'Marginata'
*– 'Aspleniifolia' CMHG
N– 'Aurea' CB&S CCla CCor CFis CLnd CMHG CRow CSco EHar ELan ENot ERav GRei LHol MBar MR&S SHil SPer
– 'Aureo-marginata' CHan CMal EBre ELan EPla ERav MBal NNor SHil SLon
¶– 'Bimble' EMon
*– 'Cae Rhos Lligwy' WHer
¶– 'Din Dryfol' CNat
– 'Fructu-Luteo' EPla
§– 'Guincho Purple' Widely available
– 'Heterophylla' See S. ***n.*** 'Linearis'

– *laciniata*	CCla CCor CMHG CRow CSco EHar ELan EPar EPla ERav LHol NNor NWea SDix SHil SMad SPer SPla SSpi SSta WSHC WWat
§ – 'Linearis'	EGol EHal ELan EPla ERav GWic LGre SMad
¶ – 'Madonna'	CNat
§ – 'Marginata'	Widely available
– 'Nana'	SLon
– 'Pulverulenta'	CChu CRow EBre EFol EGol EHar ELan EPar EPla ERav GWic LGre LHop MBri SHil SSpi WSHC
– 'Purpurea'	See S. *n.* 'Guincho Purple'
– 'Pygmy'	EHal EPla LHop NHol WPat
– 'Pyramidalis'	CCor EHar EMon
*– 'Tenuifolia'	CKni
– 'Variegata'	See S. *n.* 'Marginata'
– 'Witches Broom'	EMon
racemosa	NHol SHil WMou
– *aurea*	CBow CSco ECtt EPad GRei NKay NSel
– 'Goldenlocks'	EHal WPat
– 'Plumosa Aurea'	Widely available
– 'Sutherland Gold'	Widely available
– 'Tenuifolia'	EHal ELan LGre MUlv SHil SMad SSpi WHCG WPat WWat
* *wightiana*	CSun EPad

SANDERSONIA (Liliaceae/Colchicaceae)

aurantiaca	ECro LAma LBow

SANGUINARIA (Papaveraceae)

canadensis	CAvo CBro CChu CCla CGle ECro EPar EPot GPoy LAma LBow MSal NKay NNor SIde SPer SPou WAbe WMar WWat
– 'Plena'	CAvo CBrd CBro CCla CFor EPar EPot GLoc LGre MBri MCot MHig MTho NHar NHol NKay NRya SPer SPou SSpi SWas WAbe WEas

SANGUISORBA (Rosaceae)

canadensis	CHan CRow ECha GAbr GWic MFir
hakusanensis	See S. *obtusa*
* *magnifica alba*	CCla EBre ECro EFou ERou NRoo
minor	CArn CKin GPoy LHol MBar MChe MSal NSel SIde WCla WEas WHer WPer
§ *obtusa*	CCla CKel CRow CSco CShe EBre ECha ECro EFol EFou ELan GAbr GWic MBri MUlv NHol NSti SFis SMad SPer SSus WEas
– *albiflora*	ELan
officinalis	CArn CHad CLew CSev EGol Effi NLan NSel WCla WSto WWin
sitchensis	See S. *stipulata*
stipulata	MUlv
tenuifolia	MUlv

SANICULA (Umbelliferae)

europaea	CArn CKin GPoy LHol WHer

SANIELLA (Liliaceae/Amaryllidaceae)

¶ *verna*	MHig SIng

SANSEVIERIA (Agavaceae)

trifasciata gigantea	MBri
– 'Golden Hahnii'	MBri
– 'Laurentii'	MBri
– 'Moonshine'	MBri

SANTOLINA † (Compositae)

§ *chamaecyparissus*	Widely available
– *corsica*	See S. *c. nana*
– 'Lambrook Silver'	CGle ECtt NH&H NHol WHer
*– 'Lemon Queen'	CArn EOrc MR&S NH&H SIde SMad WOak
§ – *nana*	CB&S ECha ENot EPla GLoc LHop MBar NH&H NNor NNrd NRya SAxl SHil SLon SPer WAbe
– *nana* 'Weston'	CLew CShe MCas NHol NTow
– 'Pretty Carol'	CBow CKni CSco ELan NH&H SMad SPla WWat
¶ *impressa*	NH&H
incana	See S. *chamaecyparissus*
¶ 'Little Ness'	EMon
¶ 'Oldbury hybrid'	NH&H
pectinata	See S. *rosmarinifolia canescens*
§ *pinnata*	CFis CSev LHol NH&H SBor WTay
– 'Sulphurea'	CFis NCat NH&H NHol SPer WPer WRus
pinnata neapolitana	Widely available
– – cream form	See S. *p. n.* 'Edward Bowles'
– – 'Edward Bowles'	CCla CFor CGle EFou EJud ELan EOrc EPad GWic IJoh LHop NHol NRar NSel SAxl SChu SHil SLon SPla WAbe WHer WSHC
¶ *rosmarinifolia canescens*	NH&H
– 'Primrose Gem'	CLew CSam ECha EFol EFou EPad GHig IJoh LHop MPla NCat NH&H NHol SAxl SPer WPer
§ – *rosmarinifolia*	Widely available
*– 'Nana'	WWat
* *serratifolia*	CSco LHol NH&H
tomentosa	See S. *pinnata*
virens	See S. *rosmarinifolia rosmarinifolia*
viridis	See S. *rosmarinifolia rosmarinifolia*

SAPINDUS (Sapindaceae)

drummondii	WCoo

SAPIUM (Euphorbiaceae)

japonicum	SSpi

SAPONARIA (Caryophyllaceae)

¶ x *boissieri*	SIng

'Bressingham'	EBre ECha EMNN EPot GEdr GLoc NHol NTow SBla SIng WPat WThu WWin
caespitosa	MHig NHol WOMN
¶ ***lutea***	WCar
ocymoides	Widely available
– 'Rubra Compacta'	WPer
officinalis	CArn CBre CKin CRow CSFH EJud Effi GPoy LHol MChe MSal NSti SIde WHal WHer WOak WSto
– 'Alba Plena'	CGle EMon GPla NBar NSti SChu WHer WPer WWin
§ – 'Dazzler'	CHoe EBar EFol ELan EMon MTho NRar NSti SIde WCot WPer WRus
– 'Rosea Plena'	CBre CGle CHad CLew CRow EJud ELan EMon MBri MCot NCat NHol SCro SPer WCot WHal WHer WHil WRus
– 'Rubra Plena'	CGle ELan EMon SChu WCot
– 'Variegata'	See S. *o.* 'Dazzler'
x ***olivana***	CHar ECha EMNN GEdr GLoc MHig MPla NHol NKay SOkd WOMN WPat WPer WThu WWin
pulvinaris	See S. ***pumilio***
pumilio	GCHN MHig NHol NNrd WPer WWin
sicula	WPer
zawadskii	See SILENE *z.*

SARCOCAPNOS (Fumariaceae)

¶ ***enneaphylla***	WHil

SARCOCOCCA † (Buxaceae)

confusa	Widely available
hookeriana	CCla CFor IOrc SHil SReu WOMN
– ***digyna***	Widely available
– ***digyna*** 'Purple Stem'	SHil
¶ – ***hookeriana***	SSpi
humilis	CFis CHan CSco ELan ENot EPar IJoh MBal MBar MBri MCas MCot MGos MPla MR&S MWat NNor SHil SPer SPla WBod WSHC WWat
orientalis	CMCN
ruscifolia	CB&S CMCN CSam CSco EGol ELan ENot IHos IOrc LSav MBri MGos SHil SLon SPer SPla SSpi WWat
– ***chinensis***	CBot SApp SHil
saligna	CMCN LSav WBod

SARCOPOTERIUM (Rosaceae)

SARRACENIA † (Sarraceniaceae)

'Ahlsii'	WMEx
alata	WMEx
x ***areolata***	WMEx
x ***catesbyi***	SSpi WMEx
– x ***popei***	WMEx
– x ***rubra***	WMEx
x ***chelsonii***	EPot WMEx
x ***comptonensis***	WMEx
'Evendine'	WMEx
excellens x ***wrigleyana***	WMEx
x ***exornata***	EPot WMEx
flava	EPot SSpi WHal WMEx
– 'Maxima'	WMEx
x ***formosa*** x ***excellens***	WMEx
'Gulf Rubra' x ***leucophylla*** x ***excellens***	WMEx
x ***harperi***	WMEx
leucophylla	WMEx
– x ***catesbyi***	WMEx
– x ***popei***	WMEx
x ***melanorhoda***	WMEx
x ***miniata***	WMEx
minor	WHal WMEx
– 'Okefenokee Giant'	WMEx
– x ***wrigleyana***	WMEx
x ***mitchelliana***	WHal WMEx
x ***mooreana***	WMEx
– 'Marston Select'	WMEx
– x ***readii***	WMEx
¶ ***oreophila***	EPot
– x ***minor***	EPot WMEx
popei x ***flava***	EPot WMEx
– x ***purpurea venosa***	WMEx
psittacina	WMEx
purpurea	EPot WMEx
– ***purpurea***	WMEx
– ***venosa***	WHal WMEx
x ***readii***	WMEx
– x ***excellens***	WMEx
'Red Burgundy'	WMEx
x ***rehderi***	WMEx
rubra	WMEx
– ***jonesii***	EPot WMEx
– x ***excellens***	WMEx
x ***swaniana***	WMEx

SASA † (Gramineae(Bambuseae))

borealis	See SASAMORPHA ***borealis***
disticha 'Mirriezuzume'	See PLEIOBLASTUS ***pygmaeus*** 'M.'.
glabra 'Albostriata'	See SASAELLA ***masamuneana*** 'Albostriata'
kurilensis	SBam SDry
– 'Shimofuri'	SBam SDry
megalophylla 'Nobilis'	SBam SDry
nana	See S. ***veitchii minor***
nipponica	SBam SDry
– 'Aureostriata'	SBam SDry
§ ***palmata***	CB&S CHad CHan ENot SBam SReu
– ***nebulosa***	CHEx SArc SBam SDry WJun
– variegated form	SBam SDry
quelpaertensis	SBam SDry
senanensis	SBam SDry
tessellata	See INDOCALAMUS ***tessellatus***
tsuboiana	SBam SDry

nipponica SBam SDry
– 'Aureostriata' SBam SDry
§ *palmata* CB&S CHad CHan ENot SBam SReu
– *nebulosa* CHEx SArc SBam SDry WJun
– variegated form SBam SDry
quelpaertensis SBam SDry
senanensis SBam SDry
tessellata See INDOCALAMUS *tessellatus*
tsuboiana SBam SDry
§ *veitchii* CGre CHEx ECha EPar ERav IOrc LNet MBri MUlv NJap SBam SDry SHil WJun
§ – *minor* SBam

SASAELLA (Gramineae(Bambuseae))
glabra See S. ***masamuneana***
§ *masamuneana* 'Albostriata' SBam SDry WJun
– 'Aureostriata' SBam SDry
§ *ramosa* CHoe MBal SBam SDry SHil WJun
'bitchuensis' SBam SDry

SASAMORPHA (Gramineae(Bambuseae))
§ *borealis* SBam

SASSAFRAS (Lauraceae)
albidum CArn CBot CCla CHEx ERav LSav MBri SHil SSpi
tzumu CHEx CMCN SMad SSpi

SATSUMA See **CITRUS** ***reticulata*** Satsuma group

SATUREJA (Labiatae)
coerulea CKel GLoc SIde WPer
cuneifolia MCas
hortensis GPoy LHol LHop MChe MSal NSel WHer
montana CArn CRiv EEls ELan Effi GPoy LHol MBri MChe MHig MPla MSal NHol NRoo NSel NSti SDix SIde WHer WOak WPer WSto
§ – *illyrica* NHol
– *subspicata* See S. ***m. illyrica***
parnassica WPer
repanda See S. ***spicigera***
selleriana CHan LHop MHig WPer
§ *spicigera* CArn CLew CRiv EMNN EPot LHol MHig NKay NNrd NTow SIde WPer WWin
spinosa SOkd
thymbra EEls

SATYRIUM (Orchidaceae)
¶ *nepalense* EPot

SAURAUIA (Actinidiaceae)
¶ *subspinosa* CHEx

SAUROMATUM (Araceae)
guttatum See S. ***venosum***
§ *venosum* CAvo ELan LAma MBri

SAURURUS (Saururaceae)
cernuus CWGN EHon ELan LMay MSta

SAUSSUREA (Compositae)
¶ *chinophylla* WDav WPer

SAXEGOTHAEA (Podocarpaceae)
conspicua CGre EHar IBar SBor SHil SLon WThu

SAXIFRAGA † (Saxifragaceae)
'Aemula' (x *borisii*) (8) MWat NHol WAbe
aizoides atrorubens (6) MBal MBro MWat NGre NHol NNrd WAbe WHil WPer WWin
¶ – *aurantiana* NGre
aizoon See S. ***paniculata***
¶ 'Aladdin' (x *borisii*) (8) MWat
* 'Alan Hayhurst' NHol
'Alba' (x *apiculata*) (8) Widely available
– (x *arco-valleyi*) See S. 'Ophelia'
– (*oppositifolia*) (9) ELan EPot NGre NHol SIng SSmi WAbe WThu WWin
♦– (*sempervivum*) See S. 'Zita'
¶ 'Albert Einstein' (x *apiculata*) (8) MWat
'Albertii' (*callosa*) (7) CShe EBre GLoc MHig NBar NHol NNrd SIng SPou SSmi WHil WWin
¶ 'Aldebaran' EPot
'Alfons Mucha' MWat NHol NRed WAbe
'Amitie' (x *gloriana*) (8) NHol
'Anagales Sunset' WThu
andersonii (8) EPot ITim MBal NHol NNrd NRya NTow WAbe
x *andrewsii* (7) MHig NBar NHol WHil
§ *androsacea* (12) NTow
¶ 'Anne Beddall' (*cinerea*) MWat
'Aphrodite' (*sempervivum*) (8) MWat
x *apiculata* See S. 'Gregor Mendel'
'Apple Blossom' (12) GHig NBar
aquatica (11) CSun GAbr
¶ 'Arabella' (x *edithae*) (8) MWat
§ 'Arco' (x *arco-valleyi*) (8) EPot NHol NNrd WAbe WHil
x *arco-valleyi* See S. 'Arco'
x *arendsii* (12) MPit WEas
§ 'Aretiastrum' (x *boydii*) (8) EPot NGre NHol NNrd SIng SPou WAbe WDav WThu
aretioides (8) WThu
'Ariel' (x *hornibrookii*) (8) LRHS SPou WHil
'Assimilis' (x *petraschii*) (8) MBro NHol WAbe WHil
§ 'Aureopunctata' (x *urbium*) (3) CArn CBre CGle CKel CShe ECha ELan GWic MBal MCot MFir MWat MWgw NGre NHol NRoo WBon
'Avoca Gem' IDai

'Balcana'	See S. ***paniculata orientalis***
'Baldensis'	See S. ***paniculata baldensis***
¶ 'Balkan' (***marginata rocheliana***) (8)	MWat NHol
'Ballawley Guardsman' (12)	EPar IDai MBal NKay NRoo SIng
§ 'Beatrix Stanley' (x ***anglica***) (8)	EMNN EPot MBal MBro NGre NHar NHol NRya SPou WAbe
'Beauty of Letchworth'	ELan
¶ 'Ben Lawers' (***oppositifolia***) (9)	NHol
* 'Bettina'	MWat
¶ 'Biegleri'	EPot
'Birch Baby' (12)	SIng
'Birch Yellow'	See S. 'Pseudo-borisii'
'Black Beauty' (12)	CMHG EPot GLoc SIng WBon
* 'Blackhouse White'	NBar NGre
'Bob Hawkins' (12)	CElw CMHG CMer EFol ELan EPar EPot ERav GDra GLoc MCas MCot NBar NNrd NRed NVic SPla WWin
'Bodensee' (x ***hofmannii***) (8)	WAbe
x ***borisii***	See S. 'Sofia'
'Boston Spa' (x ***elizabethae***) (8)	CKel EMNN GCHN GLoc ITim MBro MCas MHig MPit MPlt NGre NHar NHol NKay NNrd NRed NRoo NTow SIng WAbe WDav WEas WHil WHoo
'Bridget' (x ***edithae***) (8)	CShe EBre ELan EPar GLoc ITim MBal MBro MCas NGre NHar NNrd NTow SIng SPou WAbe WThu
bronchialis (5)	NHol SIng
*– ***pseudoburseriana*** (5)	NHol
'Brookside' (***burseriana***) (8)	EPot NHol SPou WAbe
brunonis (2)	EPot NNrd SIng
– AGS/ES 590 (2)	NHol
bryoides (5)	MHig NBar
'Buchholzii' (x ***fleischeri***) (8)	WHil
x ***burnatii*** (7)	EBre EPot MBro MHig NHar NHol NKay NNrd SIng
burseriana (8)	GCHN NBar NRed NRya WAbe
'Buttercup' (x ***kayei***) (8)	EPot MBro MWat NHol NWCA WAbe WDav WHoo WPat
caesia (7)	NHol SPou
§ ***callosa*** (7)	EMNN EPot MBro NBar NGre NHar NKay SBla WAbe WPat WPer
§ – ***australis*** (7)	CRiv EPot MCas MHig NHar NHol NNrd SIng WHoo
– ***bellardii***	See S. ***callosa***
§ – ***catalaunica*** (7)	MBro SPou WDav
– ***lantoscana***	See S. ***c. australis***
– ***lingulata***	See S. ***callosa.***
'Cambria Jewel' (12)	NNrd
'Cambridge Seedling' (8)	MWat NHol
§ ***camposii*** (12)	GAbr SIng
'Camyra' (8)	MWat NHol WAbe
canaliculata (12)	NBar SIng
x ***canis-dalmatica*** (7)	CMHG ECtt EMNN ESis GGar MBro MHig NBar NHol NNrd SIng WAbe
§ 'Carmen' (x ***elizabethae***) (8)	CShe EBre ELan EMNN EPot GLoc IDai ITim MBro MCas MHig MWat NHol NKay NNrd NRya WAbe WThu
¶ 'Carnival'	ESis
'Castor' (x ***bilekii***) (8)	SIng WAbe WThu
catalaunica (7)	See S. ***callosa catalaunica***
'Caterhamensis' (***cotyledon***)	WEas
§ ***caucasica*** (8)	NKay
– ***desoulavyi*** (8)	MHig NNrd WHil
cebennensis (12)	EPad EPot NHol NRed NRya SIng SPou
– dwarf form	WAbe
* 'Cervinia' (***oppositifolia***) (9)	NHol
'Chamber's Pink Pride'	See S. 'Miss Chambers'
§ ***cherlerioides*** (5)	EBar ELan GHig GLoc NRed NRya WCla WEas WWin
'Cherrytrees' (x ***boydii***) (8)	MCas NHar WAbe
'Chetwynd' (***marginata***) (8)	WAbe
¶ 'Chez Nous' (x ***gloriana***)	MWat
'Christine' (x ***anglica***) (8)	MWat SIng
¶ ***chrysospleniifolium***	WPer
x ***churchillii*** (7)	NKay
cinerea (8)	SIng
¶ 'Clare' (x ***anglica***) (8)	WAbe
'Clare Island' (12)	SIng
'Clarence Elliot' (***umbrosa primuloides***) (3)	NHol
§ 'Cloth of Gold' (***moschata***) (12)	Widely available
cochlearis (7)	CShe ESis MBal NNor SIng SPou SSmi WEas WWin
*– ***probinii*** (7)	SPou
'Compacta' (***moschata***) (12)	SIng
'Coningsby Queen' (x ***hornibrookii***) (8)	ITim
* x ***correvensis***	ECtt GCHN NNrd
'Correvoniana' (***paniculata***) (7)	CHar CSun EMNN ESis GHig GLoc MBar MBro NHar NHol NKay SIng WAbe WCla WHoo WPer WWin
corsica cossoniana	WOMN
§ ***cortusifolia*** (4)	CChu CFor CHEx CKel EBre MBal MWgw NHar NKay NNrd SIng WHer
– dwarf form	CFor EPot LGre
– ***fortunei***	NHol SBar SIng WHal WRus
§ ***corymbosa*** (8)	EPad MWat NKay

cotyledon (7)	GDra NKay NNor SIng SPou WAbe WCla WEas
§ 'Cranbourne' (x ***anglica***) (8)	CRiv CShe CSun EBre EMNN EPar EPot GLoc MBro MCas NBar NGre NHar NHol NNrd NRed SBla SIng SPou WAbe WHil WHoo WPat WThu
'Cream Seedling' (8)	MBro MWat NRed
'Crenata' (***burseriana***) (8)	EPot GLoc MBro MWat NGre NHar NHol NKay NNrd SPou WAbe WHoo
* 'Crinkle'	NHol
crispa (4)	MCot SIng
crustata (7)	NKay SIng WThu
– ***vochinensis*** (7)	NKay
'Crystalie' (x ***biasolettoi***) (8)	EPot MBro NGre NHol SPou WAbe WPat
cuneata (12)	EPot
cuneifolia (3)	CHEx CHar CRiv GDra MBal MCas MWat NGre NHol NRoo NSti NWCA SIng SSmi WPer
– ***capillipes*** (3)	NKay SIng
cuscutiformis (4)	ERav MCot WCru WThu
'Cwm Idwal' (***rosacea***) (12)	CNat
cymbalaria (13)	SFir SIng WCla WHil
'Dainty Dame' (x ***arco-valleyi***) (8)	MWat NGre NHol SIng WAbe
¶ 'Dana' (x ***megaseiflora***)	MWat NRed
'Dartington Double' (12)	CElw CLew CRow EBre GDra MBal MCas NHar NKay NNrd NRed WAbe
§ 'Denisa' (x ***pseudokotschyi***) (8)	MBal MWat WAbe
densa	See S. ***cherlerioides***
'Dentata' (x ***geum***) (3)	CBos ECha ECro GAbr GGar NVic SWas
desoulavyi	See S. ***caucasica d.***
¶ 'Diana' (x ***lincoln-fosteri***) (8)	MWat
¶ ***diapensioides*** (8)	WAbe
Dixter form (x ***geum***) (3)	ECha
'Doctor Clay'	WAbe
'Doctor Ramsey' (7)	CElw ESis ITim MCas NKay NRed SIng SPou
'Dorothy Milne'	WThu
'Drakula' (***ferdinandi-coburgii***) (8)	MWat WAbe WHil
'Dubarry' (12)	CHar NGre NKay SIng
¶ 'Edgar Irmscher' (8)	MWat WAbe
'Edie Campbell' (12)	NGre SIng
¶ 'Edward Elgar' (x ***megasaeaflora***)	MWat NRed
'Elf' (12)	CRiv ELan MBro NHar NHol NKay NNrd NRoo SIng WCla
'Eliot Hodgkin' (x ***millstreamiana***) (8)	MWat WAbe
x ***elizabethae***	See S. 'Carmen'
¶ 'Ellie Brinkerhoff'	NGre
'Elliott's Variety' (x ***urbium primuloides***) (3)	CHar CShe EBre ELan EPot GDra MCas MHig NBar NCat NGre NHar NKay NNrd NVic NWCA STre WCla WOMN WThu
'Esther' (7)	CHar CRiv EBre ELan ESis GLoc MBro MHig MPit MPla NBar NHol NKay NNrd NRed NTow SBla SIng SSmi WDav WEas WThu
'Eulenspiegel' (x ***geuderi***) (8)	NKay NRya
exarata (12)	ITim
– ***pyrenaica***	See S. ***androsacea***
♦ Fair Maids of France	See S. ***granulata*** 'Flore Pleno'
'Fairy' (12)	CRiv ELan MBro MCas
'Faldonside' (x ***boydii***) (8)	CRiv EPot MBro NHol NNrd NRed SBla SPou WAbe WHoo WPat
'Falstaff' (***burseriana***) (8)	LRHS MWat NHol SIng
§ 'Faust' (x ***borisii***) (8)	MBro NGre NKay NNrd SIng WDav
Federici-Augusti (8)	SBla
'Ferdinand' (x ***hofmannii***) (8)	WAbe
ferdinandi-coburgii (8)	NGre NRya NTow WAbe
– ***pravislavia***	See S. ***f-c. rhodopea***
– ***radoslavoffii***	See S. ***f-c rhodopea***
§ – ***rhodopea*** (8)	EPot LRHS MCas SIng WThu
ferruginea (1)	NHol
'Findling' (12)	CHar CMHG ESis GCHN GLoc MBro MPlt NKay NNrd NRoo SIng WAbe WEas WPat WWin
flagellaris (2)	WCla
– ***crassiflagellata***CHA 298 (2)	NTow WDav
– ***flagellaris*** (2)	NNrd
x ***fleischeri*** (8)	SPou
¶ 'Florissa' (***oppositifolia***)	LRHS
'Flowers of Sulphur'	See S. 'Schwefelblüte'
fortunei	See S. ***cortusifolia fortunei***
'Four Winds' (12)	GAbr GHig NHol NNrd SBla SIng WDav
'Francis Cade'	ITim NGre NHar
'Franzii' (x ***paulinae***) (8)	NHar NHol
¶ 'Frederici-augustii	WHil
'Friesei' (x ***salmonica***) (8)	CShe EPot NHol
§ x ***fritschiana*** (7)	CMHG NHol NKay NNrd SCro SPou WAbe
¶ 'Funkii' (x ***petraschii***) (8)	NHol WAbe
'Gaiety' (12)	CElw CHar CRiv EBre ELan ESis GDra GHig NHol NRoo SIng SPla
¶ 'Galaxie' (x ***megaseiflora***)	EPot NGre WAbe WHil
'Ganymede' (***burseriana***) (8)	SIng

x ***gaudinii*** (7)	NKay
'Gem' (x ***irvingii***) (8)	EPot
♦ 'Geoides'	See S. ***hirsuta paucicrenata***
x ***geuderi***	See S. 'Eulenspiegel'
x ***geum*** (3)	EPar GLoc MCas SIng
'Gladys'	ELan
'Gloria' (***burseriana***) (8)	CRiv CShe GLoc MBal MBro MCas NGre NHol NNrd SBla SIng WAbe WPat WThu
x ***gloriana*** (8)	EPot
¶ 'Godiva' (x ***gloriana***)	EPot MWat NHol WAbe
'Goeblii' (8)	SIng WAbe
'Gold Dust' (x ***eudoxiana***) (8)	CRiv GLoc MBro MHig MWat NHar NHol NKay NNrd SIng WAbe WDav WWin
'Golden Falls' (12)	CLew EFol EPot GLoc LHop NHar NNrd SIng
'Golden Prague' (x ***pragensis***) (8)	MWat SIng WAbe
* 'Grace'	GLoc
'Grace Farwell' (x ***anglica***) (8)	CRiv EPot GLoc ITim MBar MBro MCas MWat NBar NHar NRya SIng SPou WAbe WHil
¶ 'Grandiflora' (***burseriana***) (8)	MWat
granulata (11)	CCla CRow EPot GLoc MCas NNrd SFir WCla WHil WOak
§ – 'Flore Pleno' (11)	GAbr GLoc LGre NBir NRya SBar WAbe WCla
'Gratoides' (x ***grata***) (8)	MWat NHol WAbe
§ 'Gregor Mendel' (x ***apiculata***) (8)	Widely available
grisebachii (8)	EPot MPlt NBar NHol SBar SPou WCla WDav
'Gustav Hegi' (x ***anormalis***) (8)	NHol WAbe
'Haagii' (x ***eudoxiana***) (8)	CRiv ELan EMNN EPar EPot MBal MBro MCas NBar NGre NHar NHol NKay NNrd NRed NTow SBla SIng SSmi WAbe WDav WEas WHoo WWin
* ***hallii***	WWin
'Harlow Car'	NHol
'Harry Marshall' (x ***irvingii***) (8)	MWat NHol
'Hartswood White' (12)	NGre SIng
x ***hausmannii*** (1x6)	NKay
'Herbert Cuerdon' (x ***elizabethae***) (8)	MWat NGre
'Highdownensis' (7)	NHol
'Hindhead Seedling' (x ***boydii***) (8)	ITim LRHS MWat WAbe
hirsuta (3)	WBon WHil
'Hirsuta' (x ***geum***)	See S. x ***geum***
'Hirtella' (***paniculata***) (7)	SIng
'His Majesty' (x ***irvingii***) (8)	NHol SIng WAbe WThu
'Hi-Ace' (12)	ELan EPot GEdr GHig GLoc MBar MBro MCas MHig MPit NGre NRoo NTow SBla SIng SSmi WAbe WDav WHoo WPat WPer WThu WWin
'Hocker Edge' (x ***arco-valleyi***) (12)	ITim MHig MWat NRya WAbe WThu
'Holden Seedling' (12)	EMNN EPot
x ***hornibrookii*** (8)	NKay
hostii (7)	ESis ITim MBro MCas MHig NHol NKay SIng WAbe WHoo
– ***altissima*** (7)	EPad NHol NTow STre
¶ – ***hostii***	EPad
– ***rhaetica*** (7)	NHol NNrd
hypnoides (12)	GAbr NHol NLan NRya SSmi WCla
§ – ***egemmulosa*** (12)	MBal
'Ingeborg' (12)	ECha SIng
'Ingwersen's Variety' (x ***urbium primuloides***) (7)	SIng
iranica (8)	MWat SIng WAbe
'Iris Prichard' (x ***hardingii***) (8)	CShe CSun EPot ITim MBro MCas MWat NBar NGre NHol SIng SPou WAbe WThu
x ***irvingii***	See S. 'Walter Irving'
'James Bremner' (12)	MCas NHol NNrd SIng WDav
'Jason' (x ***elizabethae***) (8)	NHol
'Jenkinsiae' (x ***irvingii***) (8)	Widely available
§ 'Johann Kellerer' (x ***kellereri***) (8)	EPot MHig MWat NGre NHol NRoo SIng WAbe WHil WWin
'John Tomlinson' (***burseriana***) (8)	MWat NBar SPou
¶ 'Josef Capek' (x ***megaseiflora***)	MWat
¶ 'Josef Manes' (x ***borisii***) (8)	MWat
'Joy'	See S. 'Kaspar Maria Sternberg'
¶ 'Judith Shackleton' (8)	MBro MWat WAbe
'Juliet'	See S. 'Riverslea'
§ ***juniperifolia*** (8)	CHar EBre EMNN ITim MBro MCas MPlt NGre NHol NKay NNrd NRoo NRya NWCA SChu SIng SSmi WDav
– ***macedonica***	See S. ***juniperifolia***
¶ 'Jupiter'	NGre WAbe
¶ 'Karasin'	MWat
'Karel Capel' (x ***megaseiflora***) (8)	EPot MWat NGre NRed
¶ 'Karel Stivin' (***edithae***)	MWat NRed
¶ 'Karlstejn' (x ***borisii***) (8)	MWat WAbe
§ 'Kaspar Maria Sternberg' (x ***petraschii***) (8)	ITim MBro NHol NKay NRya SPou WPat
'Kath Dryden' (x ***anglica***) (8)	SIng WAbe

'Kathleen Pinsent' (7)	CShe EPad EPot GLoc MBro NHol NNrd NVic SIng SPou SSmi WAbe WHil
x ***kellereri***	See S. 'Johann Kellerer'
¶ 'Kew Green'	MWat
'Kewensis' (x ***kellereri***) (8)	SIng WAbe
¶ 'King Lear' (x ***bursiculata***) (8)	WAbe
'Kingii'	See S. ***hypnoides egemmulosa***
'Kingscote White'	NGre SIng
'Klondike' (x ***boydii***) (8)	LRHS MWat NHol WAbe
'Knapton Pink' (12)	CMHG MCas MWat NGre NHol NRya SIng SSmi
'Knapton Red' (12)	MWat
'Knapton White' (12)	SIng WCla
¶ 'Knebworth' (***longifolia***) (7)	SIng
§ 'Kolbiana' (x ***paulinae***) (8)	NHol
'Koprvnik' (***paniculata***) (7)	CSun SIng
kotschyi (8)	WAbe
¶ 'Krasava' (x ***megaseiflora***)	EPot MWat NGre
'Kyrillii' (x ***borisii***) (8)	MWat
¶ 'Labe'	NHol
'Lady Beatrix Stanley'	See S. 'Beatrix Stanley'
'Lagraveana' (***paniculata***) (7)	ELan NGre NHol SIng WWin
x ***landaueri***	See S. 'Leonore'
¶ ***latepetiolata*** (11)	WHil
¶ 'Lenka'	ITim NGre
'Leo Gordon Godseff' (x ***elizabethae***) (8)	MBro MHig NHol NKay WDav
'Leonore' (x ***landaueri***) (8)	MWat NHol
'Letchworth Gem' (x ***urbium***) (3)	CBos CRiv GWic NHol
¶ 'Lidice'	MWat NGre
lilacina (8)	NGre NHol WAbe WHil WPat
lingulata	See S. ***callosa***
'Lissmore Carmine' (8)	MWat
¶ 'Lissmore Pink' (8)	MWat
¶ 'Loeflingii' (x ***grata***) (8)	NHol
longifolia	EBar EPad GEdr NHol SIng SPou WDav
* 'Louise' (***marginata***) (8)	LRHS
'Luna' (x ***millstreamiana***) (8)	WAbe
¶ 'Lusanna' (x ***irvingii***)	MWat
'Lutea' (***paniculata***) (7)	CSun EBre EMNN GDra GLoc MBal MCas NGre NHar NHol NNrd NRoo SBla SIng SSmi WHil
§ 'Luteola' (x ***boydii***) (8)	EPot MWat SPou WAbe
luteoviridis	See S. ***corymbosa***
lyallii (1)	NHol
x ***macnabiana*** (7)	GLoc NKay SOkd SPou
major lutea	See S. 'Luteola'
'Major' (***paniculata cartilaginea***) (7)	SPou
– (***cochlearis***) (7)	GLoc ITim NHol NKay NNrd SIng SPou WAbe
'Major Lutea' (***burseriana***)	See S. 'Luteola'
mandschuriensis (1)	CFor EPot GDra NKay
¶ 'Mangart' (***burseriana***) (8)	MWat
'Margarete' (x ***borisii***) (8)	NNrd WAbe WDav
§ ***marginata*** (8)	NHol WAbe WHil WThu
– ***balcanica***	See S. ***m. rocheliana***
– ***boryi***	See S. ***marginata***
– ***coriophylla***	NBar NHol WAbe
– ***karadzicensis*** (8)	LRHS WAbe
– ***lutea***	See S. 'Faust'
§ – ***rocheliana*** (8)	CMHG ELan EPot MCas NGre NHar NHol NKay SIng WAbe WEas
'Maria Luisa' (x ***salmonica***) (8)	CRiv EPot GLoc MBro MWat NHol NKay NNrd SPou WAbe
x ***mariae-theresiae*** (8)	GLoc
'Marianna' (x ***borisii***) (8)	EMNN MWat NHol WHil
'Mars' (x ***elizabethae***) (8)	MWat NHol
'Martha' (x ***semmleri***) (8)	NHol
media (8)	NGre NHol
x ***megaseiflora***	See S. 'Robin Hood'
mertensiana	WDav
* 'Meteor'	NHol WAbe
¶ 'Midas' (x ***elizabethae***) (8)	MWat
'Millstream Cream' (x ***elizabethae***) (8)	EPot WAbe
¶ 'Minihaha' (x ***elizabethae***) (8)	MWat
¶ 'Minor' (***marginata coriophylla***) (8)	NHol
– (***cochlearis***) (7)	Widely available
– (***paniculata***)	See S. ***p. brevifolia***
'Minor Glauca' (***paniculata***) (7)	NGre SIng
'Minutifolia' (***paniculata***) (7)	CLew EPot ESis MBal NHol SIng
'Miss Chamberlain'	MCot
'Mona Lisa' (x ***borisii***) (8)	NHol SIng WAbe
¶ 'Mondscheinsonate' (x ***boydii***) (8)	MWat WAbe
¶ 'Monika' (***webrii***)	MWat
¶ 'Moonlight'	NBra
♦ 'Moonlight Sonata' (x ***boydii***)	See S. 'Mondscheinsonate'
¶ 'Morava'	MWat
moschata (12)	MWgw NGre
'Mother of Pearl' (x ***irvingii***) (8)	EPot MBro NBar NHol WAbe
'Mother Queen' (x ***irvingii***) (8)	MBro WAbe WHoo WPat
'Mount Nachi' (***cortusifolia fortunei***) (4)	CBos CFor SOkd SSpi SWas
'Mrs E Piper' (12)	NKay WCla

'Mrs Gertie Prichard' (× *megaseiflora*) (8) MWat WAbe
'Mrs Helen Terry' (× *salmonica*) (8) EPot LRHS MWat NHol
'Mrs Leng' (× *elizabethae*) (8) MWat NHol
¶ 'Muffet' (*burseriana*) (8) MWat
'Multipunctata' (*paniculata*) (7) WHil
'Myra' (× *anglica*) (8) CRiv EMNN EPot MBro NHol NNrd SPou WAbe WEas WHil WHoo WPat WThu
'Myra Cambria' (× *anglica*) (8) NHol WAbe
'Nancye' (*cinerea* × *'Winifrid'*) MWat
§ *nelsoniana* (1) NHol
'Norvegica' (*cotyledon*) (7) NGre NNrd SPou WHil WWin
* 'Nottingham Gold' (× *boydii*) (8) MWat WAbe
* 'Nugget' SIng
'Obristii' (× *salmonica*) (8) MWat NHol WAbe
¶ *obritsii* ITim
§ *obtusa* (8) NHol NKay WAbe
'Ochroleuca' (× *elizabethae*) (8) CRiv ITim MPlt MWat NHol WAbe WThu
'Opalescent' MWat WAbe
§ 'Ophelia' (× *arco-valleyi*) (8) MWat NHar NHol SIng WEas WHil
oppositifolia (9) CRiv ITim MHig NKay WEas WWin
– *latina* (9) ELan EMNN EPot GDra GHig GLoc NHar NHol WAbe WHoo WWin
– *major* (9) NNrd
– *pyrenaica* (9) EMNN EPad NHar
– *rudolphiana* (9) NHol
– Skye form (9) NHol WAbe
'Orientalis' (*paniculata*) (7) SIng
¶ 'Oriole' (× *boydii*) (8) NHol
'Orjen' (*paniculata orientalis*) (7) EPot NNrd
§ *paniculata* (7) CShe ELan ESis GLoc MBal MBro MCas NKay NRoo SIng WCla WHoo
§ – *baldensis* (7) CHar CSun EBre ELan EMNN GDra ITim MBar MBro MCas NGre NHar NKay NNrd SBla SSmi WCla WDav WHoo WWin
§ – *brevifolia* (7) CTom NKay NNrd NRya SIng SSmi
– *carniolica* (7) MCas MHig NHol NRed SBla SPou WHil
§ – *cartilaginea* (7) EPot SPou WHil
– *cultrata* (7) NKay
– *eriophylla* (7) NKay
– *kolenatiana* See S. *p. cartilaginea*
– *labradorica* (7) NKay NNrd
*– *minima* (7) IDai
– *notata* (7) NKay
§ – *orientalis* (7) SSmi WAbe WCla
– *punctata* (7) NHol
paradoxa (14) MCas SBla SIng
¶ – (14) NBra
'Parcevalis' (× *finnisiae*) (8x6) NHol WAbe
* 'Parsee' (× *margoxiana*) (8) MWat
¶ × *patens* (6x7) WAbe
'Paula' (× *paulinae*) (8) NKay
'Peach Blossom' (8) MWat NBar NHol WAbe WThu
* 'Pearly Gates' (× *irvingii*) (8) MWat WHil
'Pearly Gold' EBar MCas MPlt NHol NRoo WThu
'Pearly King' (12) CKel EBre ELan ESis MBal MPlt NHol NKay NVic SChu SCro WAbe WCla WHoo
× *pectinata* See S. × *fritschiana*
'Penelope' (× *boydilacina*) (8) ITim NGre NHol SPou WAbe WEas WPat WThu
'Peter Pan' (12) CHar CMer ELan EMNN EPot GDra ITim MCas NHar NHol NKay NNrd NRoo NRya SSmi WAbe WPat
'Petra' (8) MWat NHol NKay
¶ *petraea* ESis
× *petraschii* (8) ITim MCas NRed
¶ 'Phoenix' (× *biasolettoi*) MWat
'Pilatus' (× *boydii*) (8) SIng
'Pixie' (12) CMer EBre EMNN EPar ITim MBal MBar MPla MWat NGre NKay NNrd NRoo NRya SIng SSmi WHoo
'Pixie Alba ' See S. 'White Pixie'
'Plena' (*granulata*) (12) CElw ELan EPot MCas MTho NHar NKay NNrd SIng
'Pollux' (× *boydii*) MWat
poluniniana (8) CSun GLoc ITim NGre NRed WAbe WThu
¶ 'Popelka' NRed
porophylla (8) GDra NGre NWCA SPou WAbe WThu
– × *sempervivum* (8) WThu
'Portae' (*paniculata*) (7) NKay NNrd
'Priestwood White' (10) MBro
'Primrose Bee' (× *apiculata*) (8) EPot MWat NKay WAbe
'Primrose Dame' (× *elizabethae*) (8) CSam CShe GLoc ITim MBal MBro MCas MWat NHar NHol SIng WAbe
× *primulaize* (6x3) ITim MBro NGre NHol NKay SIng WOMN
– salmon form CLew
'Primulina' (× *malbyana*) (8) MWat NHol WAbe
'Prince Hal' (*burseriana*) (8) EPot ITim MWat NNrd
'Princess' (*burseriana*) (8) MHig NBar NNrd
'Prospero' (× *petraschii*) (8) MWat

x ***prossenii***	See S. 'Regina'
§ 'Pseudoborisii' (x ***borisii***) (8)	EPot ITim WDav
x ***pseudoforsteri*** (7x3)	NHol
¶ 'Pseudofranzii' (x ***paulinae***) (8)	MWat
¶ 'Pseudokellereri' (8)	NHol
x ***pseudokotschyi***	See S. 'Denisa'
¶ 'Pseudopungens' (x ***apiculata***) (8)	NHol
¶ ***pseudosalomonii***	EPot
¶ 'Pseudo-paulinae' (x ***paulinae***) (8)	MWat
¶ 'Pseudo-scardica' (x ***wehrhahnii***) (8)	MWat
pubescens iratiana (12)	EPot WDav WThu
punctata	See S. ***nelsoniana***
'Pungens' (x ***apiculata***) (8)	MWat NHol NKay
¶ – (x ***apiculata***) (8)	WAbe
'Purpurea' (***cortusifolia***)	See S. 'Rubrifolia'
§ 'Pygmalion' (x ***webrii***) (8)	MPlt MWat NBar NHol NNrd NRed WDav WHil WPat WThu
'Pyramidalis' (***cotyledon***) (7)	NHol SPou
* 'Pyrenaica' (***oppositifolia***) (9)	NHol
'Rainsley Seedling' (7)	NHol
¶ 'Red Poll' (8)	MWat
§ 'Regina' (x ***prossenii***) (8)	ITim MHig MWat SIng WAbe
retusa (9)	EPot GEdr NGre NHar NHol NWCA WAbe WHil
'Rex' (***paniculata***) (7)	CSun EBre EMNN NBar NHar NHol NNrd SIng
§ 'Riverslea' (x ***hornibrookii***) (8)	CGle CSun EPot MWat NGre NHol SPou WAbe WHil WPat
§ 'Robin Hood' (x ***megaseiflora***) (8)	CRiv ITim LRHS MWat NGre NHar NHol NKay SIng SPou
'Rokujo' (***cortusifolia fortunei***) (4)	LGre WEas
¶ 'Romeo' (x ***hornibrookii***) (8)	MWat
rosacea (12)	NLan
– ***hartii*** (12)	SIng
¶ 'Rosamunda'	WAbe
'Rosea' (***cortusifolia fortunei***) (8)	CFor GLoc SOkd SSpi
– (x ***stuartii***) (8)	MWat WAbe
– (***callosa***) (7)	WEas
– (***paniculata***) (7)	CElw CSun EBre GDra MBal MBro MCas NGre NHar NHol NKay NRed NRoo SBla SIng SSmi STre WAbe WCla WHoo WWin
'Rosemarie' (x ***anglica***) (8)	ITim MHig MWat
'Rosina Sündermann' (x ***rosinae***) (8)	EPot LRHS MWat WAbe
rotundifolia (10)	NHol NNrd WCot WCru
¶ 'Roy Clutterbuck'	MWat
'Rubella' (x ***irvingii***) (8)	EPot MCas SPou
'Rubrifolia' (***cortusifolia fortunei***) (8)	CFor EBre ECha EPar MCot NHar NRoo SSpi SWas
* ***ruchiana***	WEas
'Russell Vincent Prichard' (x ***irvingii***) (8)	MWat
'Ruth Draper' (***oppositifolia***) (9)	CLew CRiv CShe EPot GLoc NGre NHol NKay NNrd NTow SBla WAbe WThu
'Ruth McConnell' (12)	MCas NNrd
'Saint John' (***caesia***)	CRiv NHol NNrd SPou WHil WWin
'Salmon' (x ***primulaize***) (6x3)	EPot ESis GLoc MCas MHig NHar SIng WHil
'Salomonii' (x ***salmonica***) (8)	EPot ITim MHig NBar NHar NHol NNrd NRya SIng SPou WAbe WHil WThu
sancta (8)	CRiv EPot MBal MBro MHig NHol NNrd SSmi WAbe WHil WThu
– ***macedonica***	See S. ***juniperifolia***
¶ 'Sandpiper' (8)	MWat
'Sanguinea Superba' (x ***arendsii***) (12)	GDra IDai MBro NHar NKay NNrd SIng WDav
'Sara Sinclair' (x ***arco-valleyi***) (8)	NNrd
sarmentosa	See S. ***stolonifera***
'Sartorii'	See S. 'Pygmalion'
¶ 'Saturn' (x ***megaseaeflora***)	MWat NGre
* 'Savernake'	GLoc
scardica (8)	NRed SIng
– ***dalmatica***	See S. ***scardica obtusa***
– ***erythrantha*** (8)	NBar WDav
– ***obtusa***	See S. ***obtusa***
'Schelleri' (x ***petraschii***) (8)	MWat NHol WAbe
'Schleicheri' (x ***kellereri***) (8)	MWat NHol NKay SPou
§ 'Schwefelblüte' (12)	CKel EBre ESis MBal NNrd NRoo SSmi WAbe WCla WDav WPat
¶ 'Seissera' (***burseriana***) (8)	MWat
x ***semmleri***	See S. 'Martha'
sempervivum (8)	EPot MBro SIng SPou WThu
– JCA 864.003 (8)	MBro WDav
¶ – ***sempervivum*** (8)	WAbe
¶ – ***stenophylla*** (8)	NHol WAbe
sibirica (11)	EPot WDav
* 'Silver Cushion'	ESis SIng
'Silver Dome'	CMHG
'Sir Douglas Haig' (12)	NKay NNrd SIng WCla
* 'Snowcap' (***pubescens***)	EPot
'Snowflake' (7)	MCas MHig WHil
§ 'Sofia' (x ***borisii***) (8)	MWat NKay NNrd
§ 'Southside Seedling' (7)	Widely available
'Spartacus' (x ***apiculata***) (8)	MWat WAbe

spathularis (3) NCat NRar SFir SIng WCot WEas WWin
'Splendens' (***oppositifolia***) (9) ELan EMNN EPar EPot GLoc ITim MBal NHol NNrd NRed SIng WAbe
'Sprite' (12) GCHN
spruneri (8) CRiv NRya WThu
sp. BM&W 118 GDra
¶ ***squarrosa*** (7) SPou
'Stansfieldii' (12) CHar CKel CRiv EMNN GHig MRav NBar NGre NHol SSmi WDav WWin
'Stella' (x ***stormonthii***) (8) NHol NKay SBla WThu
stellaris WCla
stolitzkae (8) EPot GLoc NGre NHar NHol NRed WThu
§ ***stolonifera*** (4) CArn ELan SBar SSpi WEas
'Stormont's Variety' See S. 'Stella'
stribrnyi (8) EPot NKay
'Sturmiana' (***paniculata***) (7) NBar NHol NKay SIng
'Suendermannii' (x ***kellereri***) (8) CRiv MWat SIng SPou
¶ 'Suendermannii Major' (x ***kellereri***) (8) NHol NRya
§ 'Sulphurea' (x ***boydii***) (8) CRiv CShe EPot MBro MCas NBar NHar NHol NNrd NWCA SIng SPou WAbe WEas WHoo WPat WThu
'Superba' (***callosa australis***) (8) GDra SPou SSmi WHil
'Sylvia' (x ***elizabethae***) (8) MWat NGre
taygetea (10) EPot
x ***tazetta*** (10x3) MCas NRed
¶ 'Thorpei' (8) ITim
'Timballii' (7) SIng
'Tom Thumb' (12) NNrd
tombeanensis (8) NHol WDav
'Tricolor' (***stolonifera***) (4) EBak WEas
trifurcata (12) GAbr
'Triumph' (x ***arendsii***) (12) EBre EMNN GCHN GDra GHig NHar NKay NNrd NRoo NVic WCla
'Tulley' (x ***elizabethae***) (8) NHol WPat
'Tumbling Waters' (7) CGle GAbr MCas MHig NBar NHar NHol NKay NTow SIng SMrm SPou WAbe WDav WEas WThu WWin
umbrosa (3) CKel EMon EPar ERav IDai MCas NGre NNor SApp SPer STre WHil WOak WWin
– ***variegata*** See S. 'Aureopunctata'
* 'Unique' WPat
x ***urbium*** (3) CHar EJud ELan ERav ESis GDra MBal MWgw NRar NSti NVic SIng WAbe WBon
– ***primuloides*** (3) CGle CShe SCro WEas WHil

'Vaccarina' (***opositifolia***) (9) CHar GAbr NHol NNrd NVic WAbe
'Vaclav Hollar' (x ***gusmusii***) (8) NGre
'Vahlii' (x ***smithii***) (8) WAbe
'Valborg' See S. 'Cranbourne'
'Valentine' See S. 'Cranbourne'
'Valerie Finnis' See S. 'Aretiastrum'
¶ 'Valgeri' EPot
'Variegata' (***exarata moschata***) (12) NNrd
– (x ***urbium***) (3) CCor CHoe CMer ELan EPar ESis GDra LGro MBal MCas NBar NCat NHol NNor NNrd NSti SIng SPer SSmi WAbe WCla WEas WHil WWin
– (***cuneifolia***) (3) CElw ECtt EFol ELan ESis GCHN MBar MCas MPlt NHol NKay NNrd NRoo NTow NVic SIng WHil WHoo WPer WThu
vayredana (12) MBro SIng
veitchiana (4) EMon MHig NKay NNrd WHil
'Venetia' (***paniculata***) (7) NKay NNrd SSmi
'Vesna' (x ***borisii***) (8) EMNN MBro MCas MHig MWat NBar NHar NKay NNrd NRya NTow WAbe WThu WWin
'Vincent van Gogh' (x ***borisii***) (8) ITim NKay
'Vladana' (x ***megaseiflora***) (8) EMNN NGre NRed WHil
¶ 'Vlasta' MWat
¶ 'Vltava' MWat
'W A Clark' (***oppositifolia***) (9) MBal WAbe
'Wada' (***cortusifolia fortunei***) (8) CChu CFor EBre EPar EPot GCHN MBal NHol NRoo SCro SPer SSpi WWin
'Waithman's Variety' (7) NHol NNrd
wallacei See S. ***camposii***
'Walpole's Variety' (***longifolia***) (7) EPot NHar NHol NNrd SPou
§ 'Walter Irving' (x ***irvingii***) (8) NHol WAbe
'Welsh Dragon' (12) WAbe
'Welsh Red' (12) WAbe
'Welsh Rose' (12) WAbe
wendelboi (8) EPot GLoc NGre NHol SIng WAbe WDav WHil WThu
'Wendrush' (x ***wendelacina***) (8) MWat WAbe
'Wendy' (x ***wendelacina***) (8) MWat WAbe
'Wetterhorn' (***oppositifolia***) (9) EBre ITim MBal MRav NHol NNrd WAbe
'Wheatley Rose' (8) LRHS
'White Imp' (8) NHol
'White Pixie' (12) CMer EPar ESis ITim MBro MCas MWat NGre NHol NNrd SBla SIng SSmi WCla WDav
'White Star' (x ***salmonica***) See S. 'Schelleri'

'Whitehill' (7) Widely available
'Whitlavei Compacta' (*hypnoides*) (12) CRiv EMNN MCas NKay
* 'William Bevington' EBre WDav
'William Boyd' (x *boydii*) (8) MWat WAbe
¶ 'William Tell' (x *malbyana*) (8) MWat
'Winifred' (x *anglica*) (8) EPot MWat NHol NNrd SPou WAbe
'Winifred Bevington' (7x3) EMNN ESis GLoc LHop MBro NHol NNrd NRed SChu SIng SOkd SPla WCla WHil WHoo
'Winston Churchill' (12) SIng
'Winter Fire' (7) See S. 'Winterfeuer'
'Winterfeuer' (*callosa*) (7) CShe
¶ 'Winton' SPou
'Wisley' (*grisebachii*) (8) CLew GCHN MBal MCas NHar NKay SPou WEas WHoo WPat
'Wisley Primrose' See S. 'Kolbiana'
* 'Witham's Compact' CHar
* 'Yellow Rock' (8) MWat NHol WAbe
x *zimmeteri* (7x3) NHol NRed NTow
¶ *zohlenschaferi* NBra

SCABIOSA † (Dipsaceae)

alpina See CEPHALARIA *alpina*
anthemifolia CHan
* Blue Beauty ® EFou
'Butterfly Blue' EFol MBri MPit NCat SChu WRus
caucasica CBow CSam LAbb LGan MBro MFir NCat SBla WHoo WOld WPer WWin
– *alba* LGre MBri MBro MFir NNor NRoo WHoo
– 'Bressingham White' ECha
– 'Clive Greaves' CB&S CCla CHad CKel CSco CSev CShe EBre ECha EFol EFou EGol ELan EOrc ERou GWic IDai LHop MBri MBro MWat MWgw NBar SPer
– 'Fama' EBar ECro MPit MRav NRoo SBla
– 'Floral Queen' ECha
¶ – 'Goldingensis' EBar NRoo
– 'Kompliment' MUlv
– 'Miss Willmott' CBow CCla CHad CSco CSev EBre EFou EGol ELan ERou GWic LHop MUlv MWgw NBar SPer WEas WRus
– 'Moerheim Blue' ERou MBri
– 'Penelope Harrison' CSco CShe
– 'Stäfa' GWic LGre LHop MBri MUlv SChu SMrm WRus
cinerea WWin
columbaria CKin GPla MBro MCot MSal NLan NTow SFir WCla WRus
– 'Nana' LHop NBir SSmi WHoo
– *ochroleuca* CChu CGle CHan EBar MPar NSti SMrm SWas WDav WWin
– *webbiana*JCA 862.850 CLew
gigantea See CEPHALARIA *gigantea*
graminifolia ELan LGan MBro NRoo SBar SChu SMrm WHil WHoo WOld
¶ *japonica* WPer
¶ – *alba* CSun
lucida CGle CSev CSun EBre ECro ELan GDra GLoc LHop MBro MCas MFir MHig MPit NKay NRoo SBla SMrm WAbe WEas WHoo WPer
¶ *minoana* EMon
ochroleuca See S. *columbaria o.*
parnassi See PTEROCEPHALUS *perennis*
* 'Pink Mist' MBri MPit
pterocephala See PTEROCEPHALUS *perennis*
rumelica See KNAUTIA *macedonica*
succisa See SUCCISA *pratensis*
tatarica See CEPHALARIA *gigantea*

SCADOXUS (Liliaceae/Amaryllidaceae)

multiflorus LAma LBow MBri
§ – *multiflorus* SW&B
puniceus SLMG

SCAEVOLA (Goodeniaceae)

¶ *aemula* 'Blue Fan' CSpe
¶ 'Blue Jade' SSad
§ *calendulacea* LHil
suaveolens See S. *calendulacea*

SCHEFFLERA (Araliaceae)

actinophylla EBak MBri
arboricola MBri
– 'Beauty' MBri
– 'Compacta' MBri
– 'Diane' MBri
– 'Golden Capelle' MBri
– 'Henriette' MBri
– 'Jacqueline' MBri
– 'Milena' MBri
– 'Trinetta' MBri
– 'Worthy' MBri
digitata CHEx SArc
elegantissima MBri
– 'Castor' MBri
– 'Castor Variegata' MBri

SCHIMA (Theaceae)

argentea SHil WBod
khasiana ISea

SCHINUS (Anacardiaceae)

SCHISANDRA (Schisandraceae)

chinensis CChu CMCN WSHC
grandiflora EOvi SPer
– *cathayensis* See S. *sphaerandra*
propinqua chinensis CBot SHil

rubriflora (f)	CChu CCla EHar ELan EOvi LGre MGos NHol SBla SBra SDix SHil SLon SPer SSpi SSta WBod WSHC WWat
¶ – (m)	SBla
§ ***sphaerandra***	SHil
sphenanthera	CChu ELan EOvi SBla SSta

SCHIVERECKIA (Cruciferae)

podolica	MCas NHol WDav

SCHIZOCENTRON (Melastomataceae)

elegans	See HETEROCENTRON ***elegans***

SCHIZOCODON See **SHORTIA**

SCHIZOPHRAGMA (Hydrangeaceae)

hydrangeoides	CBow CCla CHEx CSco EHar ELan MBri MGos SBra SHil SMad SPer SSpi SSta
– 'Roseum'	SBla SHil SSpi
integrifolium	CBot CBow CCla CFor CHEx CMac CSco EHar ELan MBri MRav SBla SBra SDix SHil SSpi WPat WSHC WWat

SCHIZOSTYLIS † (Iridaceae)

coccinea	CAvo CB&S CBow CBro CHan CKel CRow CSco EFol ELan EMon ERou LAma MBal MCot MFir NHol NKay NNor NRoo SChu SIng WEas WHil
– ***alba***	CAvo CBos CChu CElw CHan CRow CSco ECha ELan GWic LAma LGre MBri MPit SApp SAxl SChu SDix SLHN SMad SSpi SWas WOMN WWat
– 'Cardinal'	CHan CHar CRow
– 'Gigantea'	See S. ***c***. 'Major'
– 'Grandiflora'	See S. ***c***. 'Major'
– 'Jennifer'	CAvo CBro CElw COtt EMon GAbr SApp
– 'Major'	Widely available
– 'Mrs Hegarty'	Widely available
– 'November Cheer'	CCla IBlr NRoo
– 'Pallida'	CChu CRow ECha GWic SIng
– 'Professor Barnard'	CChu CRow GAbr GWic IBlr SHig
§ – 'Sunrise'	CAvo CB&S CChu CFis CHan CRow ECha EGol ELan ELun EMon GWic MWgw NHol NNor NRoo NSti SApp SAxl SBla SChu SIng SWas WAbe
– 'Sunset'	See S. ***c***. 'Sunrise'
– 'Tambara'	CHan MFir NCat SSpi
– 'Viscountess Byng'	CAvo CB&S CBro CChu CCla CFis CGle CHar CKel CRow CShe EPot GWic MBri NOrc SApp SAxl SChu SDix SHig SLHN SPer WAbe WBon
– 'Zeal Salmon'	CBow CBro CRow SApp SSpi

SCHOENUS (Cyperaceae)

pauciflorus	CHoe ECou EPar SSpi

SCHOTIA (Leguminosae)

¶ ***brachypetala***	CPle

SCIADOPITYS (Taxodiaceae)

verticillata	CB&S CDoC CKen IJoh IOrc LLin LNet LPan MBri NHol SGar SHil WNor

SCILLA (Liliaceae/Hyacinthaceae)

adlamii	See LEDEBOURIA ***cooperi***
* ***allionii***	LAma
amethystina	See S. ***litardierei***
amoena	LAma NHol WChr
autumnalis	EPot LAma LBow NHol WChr WOMN WThu
bifolia	CBro EPar EPot ETub LAma LBlo LBow NHol
– ***rosea***	CAvo ECam EPar EPot LAma LBow MBri NHol SIng
bithynica	LBow
campanulata	See HYACINTHOIDES ***hispanica***
cilicica	CAvo ECam LAma
greilhuberi	CAvo ECam NHol
hohenackeri	LAma
japonica	See S. ***scilloides***
lilio-hyacinthus	CBro CCor SSpi WChr
– ***alba***	MPar WChr
lingulata aliata	CBro
¶ – ***ciliolata***	WChr
§ ***litardierei***	ECam EPot ETub LAma MPar NHol WChr
§ ***mischtschenkoana***	CAvo CBro ECam EPar EPot ETub LAma LBlo LBow LRoo MBri MBro MPar NHol SIng
monanthos	WChr
monophyllos	LAma
non-scripta	See HYACINTHOIDES ***n-s.***
nutans	See HYACINTHOIDES ***non-scripta***
ovalifolia	See LEDEBOURIA ***ovalifolia***
paucifolia	SLMG
¶ ***persica*** BSBE	CAvo WChr
peruviana	CAvo CBrd CBro CHEx EBul EPar EPot ETub LAma
– ***alba***	CAvo LAma SWas
pratensis	See S. ***litardierei***
puschkinioides	ECam EPot LAma NHol WChr
ramburei	EPot LAma NHol WChr
reverchonii	WChr
rosenii	ECam EPot WChr
§ ***scilloides***	CBro WOMN
siberica	CAvo CCla ECam ETub LAma LBlo LBow NHol NRya SIng
– ***alba***	CAvo CBro CCla ECam EPar LAma LBow LRoo NHol SIng
– 'Spring Beauty'	CAvo CBro ECam EPar ETub LAma LBlo LRoo MBri NHol SIng
tubergeniana	See S. ***mischtschenkoana***
vicentina	See HYACINTHOIDES ***italica vicentina***

violacea	See LEDEBOURIA ***socialis***
* *vvedenskyi*	ECam

SCINDAPSUS (Araceae)

aureus	See EPIPREMNUM ***aureum***
pictus	MBri

SCIRPUS (Cyperaceae)

cernuus	MBri
cespitosus	MBal
lacustris 'Albescens'	CWGN EHon LMay MSta SHig
– *tabernaemontani* 'Zebrinus'	CRiv CWGN EHon ELan EWav LMay MSta SHig SSpi
mucronatus	MSta
¶ *variegata*	CBot

SCLERANTHUS (Caryophyllaceae)

biflorus	ECou ELan ESis GLoc MHig SIng
brockiei	NHol
singuliflorus	ECou WPat
uniflorus	CLew GAbr NHol NWCA

SCOLIOPUS (Liliaceae/Trilliaceae)

¶ *bigelovii*	SWas

SCOLYMUS (Compositae)

cardunculus	See CYNARA ***c.***

SCOPOLIA (Solanaceae)

carniolica	EMon GDra GPoy GWic MSal
– forms	IBlr
– *hladnikiana*	CHan ECro
lurida	MSal

SCORZONERA (Compositae)

humilis	GPoy
* *minima*	MFir

SCROPHULARIA (Scrophulariaceae)

aquatica	See S. ***auriculata***
– 'Variegata'	See S. ***auriculata*** 'Variegata'
auriculata	LHol MSal NLan NOrc
¶ – 'Burdung'	EMon
§ – 'Variegata'	Widely available
coccinea	EMon
grandiflora	CHan
nodosa	CArn CKin LHol MChe MSal NLan SIde WCla WHer WSto
– *variegata*	See S. ***auriculata*** 'V.'
scorodonia	CKin
umbrosa	MSal
vernalis	NSti

SCUTELLARIA (Labiatae)

alpina	CLew CRiv CSun ESis MHig MSal NHol SIng WDav WPer WWin
– *alba*	GLoc
altissima	CGle EMon MSal NWCA WPer
baicalensis	CHan EBre ERou IBlr LHil
canescens	See S. ***incana***
¶ *diffusa*	ESis MBro WDav WPer
galericulata	CKin CTom Effi GPoy MSal
hastata	See S. ***hastifolia***
§ *hastifolia*	ECtt EMNN LHil LHop NHol SIng
incana	EFou ELan SBor SFis SPer
indica japonica	See S. ***indica parvifolia***
§ – *parvifolia*	CLew CRiv ELan GLoc MBro MHig MTho NHol WDav WPer
lateriflora	CArn GPoy LHol MSal NSel SIde WPer
minor	MSal WPer
novae-zelandiae	ECou
orientalis	MBro NGre SBla WDav WOMN WPer WWin
¶ – *carica*	WOMN
ovata	WSto
pontica	SBla WDav
* *prostrata*	MBro NHol NRed WDav WOMN
* *rentenatii*	SLMG
scordiifolia	CKel CLew CRiv CSam ECha EFou ELan EMNN EPot ESis GLoc MCas NHol NKay NNrd SBla WCla WHil WPer WWin
* *serrata*	CArn
¶ *supina*	MBro WDav

SEAKALE See **CRAMBE** ***maritima***

SECURIGERA (Leguminosae)

§ *varia*	CSun SIng WCot WPer

SEDASTRUM (Crassulaceae)

§ *hemsleyanum*	NSed

SEDUM † (Crassulaceae)

acre	ELan GPoy LHol MBar NGre SIde WWin
– (diploid)	NSed
– (tetraploid)	MPit NSed
– *aureum*	CRiv ECha EFol ELan EPar EPot MCas MWat NHol NKay NRed NSed NVic SIng WHil WHoo WPat
– *elegans*	ECtt GDra MBal NGre NSed SSmi
§ – *majus*	NGre NHol NNrd NSed SIde SSmi
– 'Minus'	NGre NHol NSed SIde SSmi
– *neglectum sopianae*	NSed
adenotrichum	NSed
adolphi	NSed
aggregatum	See OROSTACHYS ***malacophyllus***
§ *aizoon*	MCot NGre NKay NSed NVic SChu SIng WEas
♦ – 'Aurantiacum'	See S. ***a. euphorbioides***
§ – *euphorbioides*	ECtt ELan EMon GGar NSed SChu SPer WCot
– *maximowiczii*	See S. ***aizoon***
alamosanum	NSed
♦ *albescens*	See S. ***forsterianum purpureum***

alboroseum NGre NHol NRoo NSed
§ – 'Mediovariegatum' CBot CHoe EFol EGol ELan EMon EPla ERou LHop NGre NHol NSed NSti SCro WEas WHil WPer
§ *album* GGar NLan NSed NSel SCro WHil
– *album balticum* NSed
– *album* Faro form NSed
– 'Chloroticum' CRiv GGar NGre NSed SSmi WHil
– *clusianum* See S. ***gypsicola glanduliferum***
– 'Coral Carpet' ELan EPot GDra MCas MWat NGre NHol NKay NNrd NSed SChu SIng SSmi STre WHil
– *gypsicola* imbricate form NSed
– *gypsicola* Portugese form NSed
– *gypsicola* Spanish form NSed
– *ibizicum* NSed
– *micranthum* See S. ***a.*** 'Chloroticum'
§ – *teretifolium murale* CRiv CSun ECha NGre NKay NSed SIng SSmi
– *teretifolium turgidum* NSed
alfredii nagasakianum NSed
allantoides NSed
alpestre NSed
alsinefolium fragrans NSed
altissimum See S. ***sediforme***
amecamecanum NSed
amplexicaule ibericum See S. ***tenuifolium i.***
anacampseros CHEx CHar CLew CRiv CTom ECha EPad GLoc MCas NGre NHol NKay NSed SIde SIng SSmi WCla WEas WPer
anglicum GGar NGre NSed SIng WCla
– *anglicum hibernicum* NSed
– *microphyllum* NSed
– *pyranaicum* Portugese form NSed
– *pyrenaicum* NSed
anopetalum See S. ***ochroleucum***
– alpine form See S. ***ochroleucum montanum***
– decumbent form See S. ***ochroleucum*** 'd.f.'!
– *glabrum* See S. ***ochroleucum ochroleucum glabrum***
– *glaucum* See S. ***ochroleucum ochroleucum glaucum***
apoleipon NSed
athoum See S. ***album***
♦ *atlanticum* See S. ***dasyphyllum mesatlanticum***
'Autumn Joy' See S. 'Herbstfreude'
batallae ISI 1496 NSed
batesii See VILLADIA ***hemsleyana***
*x *battandieri* NSed
'Bertram Anderson' EPot LHop MCas NCat NGre NRoo NSti SApp
¶ *beyrichianum* NGre
borissovae NSed
borschii NSed
brevifolium CSun GGar NSed SChu WHil WOMN
¶ – *induratum* NSed
– *novum* NSed
– *quinquefarum* NSed SSmi
brissemoretii NSed
burrito NSed
caducum NSed
caucasicum EMon NGre
cauticola CHar CLew CMHG CShe GEdr GWic ITim MBro MCas MCot MHig MRav NGre NKay NNor NRoo NSed SIng SSmi WHil WWin
– 'Lidakense' CHar CLew CRiv CRow CSam EBre EFol ELan EMon GLoc MBar MBri MFir NGre NHar NSed NVic SBla SSmi WDav
cepaea gracilescens NSed
chontalense NSed
clavatum NSed
clusianum See S. ***gypsicola glanduliferum***
cockerellii NSed
commixtum NSed
compactum NSed
compressum NSed
confusum NHol NSed
craigii NSed
crassipes See RHODIOLA ***crassipes***
♦ *crassularia* See CRASSULA ***milfordiae***
cyaneum GCHN NGre NSed
dasyphyllum CLew CMer CRiv CRow CSun CTom ELan EPot MBal MBar MCas MRav MWat NGre NNrd NSed SSmi WCla WHil
– *dasyphyllum glanduliferum* CHEx NSed SIng
– *dasyphyllum macrophyllum* NGre NSed
– hairy form NSed
§ – *mesatlanticum* CRiv NGre NSed WThu
¶ – *mucronatis* NBir
– *oblongifolium* NSed
– 'Riffense' NHol
¶ – *suendermannii* NSed
debile NSed
decumbens NSed
dendroideum NSed
diffusum NSed
– U 2986 NSed
divergens NGre SIng SSmi
– forms NSed
douglasii NNrd SCro
'Dudley Field' GCHN NGre
¶ 'Eleanor Fisher' WCot
ellacombeanum CRiv ELan EMNN EMon IDai MPlt NGre NKay NNrd NSed SCro SIng SSmi WHil

ewersii	CLew CMHG CRiv CSam CTom EBre ELan EMNN ESis MCas MRav NGre NRar NSed SSmi WEas WHil
– ***cyclophyllum***	NSed
– ***hayesii***	NKay
§ – ***homophyllum***	MHig NGre NKay NSed SSmi
fabaria	NSed WEas
farinosum	NSed SIng
floriferum	See S. ***kamtschaticum***
§ ***forsterianum***	MBar NGre NHol NLan NSed SSmi WCla WEas WHil
– ***elegans***	LGro NSed
fosterianum purpureum	NSed
frutescens	NSed
furfuraceum	NSed
fusiforme	NSed
gracile	CSun NGre NSed SSmi
greggii	NSed
gypsicola	CHEx MDHE NSed
– ***glanduliferum***	GAbr NSed
¶ 'Harvest Moon'	NSed
§ 'Herbstfreude'	Widely available
heterodontum	See RHODIOLA ***heterodonta***
hidakanum	CHoe ECha EMNN EPot GCHN GDra NGre NHol NNrd WPat
♦ ***hillebrandtii***	See S. ***urvillei*** Hillebrandtii group
hirsutum	NSed
– ***baeticum***	NSed
§ ***hispanicum***	CRow CSun ELan EMNN EPar ITim NKay NSed SIng STre WHil
– 'Albescens	NGre
¶ – ***bithynicum***	SIng
♦ – ***glaucum***	See S. ***h. minus***
– 'Pewter'	NSed
§ ***hispanicum minus***	ECtt EJud NGre NHol NNrd NRar NSed SIng SSmi STre WPer
§ – – 'Aureum'	CB&S CRiv CRow ECha EPot MCas MHig NGre NHol NKay NNrd NSed SIng SSmi STre WDav WHil WPer
humifusum	NSed NTow SIng SSmi WAbe WHil WOMN WThu
♦ ***hybridum***	CShe NGre NSed SIng
hyperaizoon	NGre NSed
indicum densirosulatum	NSed
– ***yunnanense***	NSed
♦ ***integrifolium***	See RHODIOLA ***rosea integrifolia***
¶ ***japonicum***	NSed
– ***senanense***	NSed
kamtschaticum	CRow MBar MCas NGre SSmi
– ***floriferum*** 'Weihenstephaner Gold'	CElw CFis CLew EBre EMNN ESis MBal MCas MHig MPit NGre NHol NKay NNor NNrd NRoo NSed SChu SIng SSmi WAbe WCla WEas WHil
– forms	NSed
– 'Variegatum'	Widely available
kostovii	NSed
laconicum	NSed
lanceolatum	NSed
lancerottense	NSed
¶ ***laxum***	NSed
– ***heckneri***	NGre NSed
¶ – ***laxum***	NHol
lidakense	See S. ***cauticolum*** 'Lidakense'
– 'Bertram Anderson'	See S. 'B.A.'
liebmannianum	NSed
lineare	SLMG
– 'Variegatum'	MBri NSed SIde
litorale	NGre
'Little Gem'	NSed
longipes	NSed
lucidum	NSed
¶ – 'Obesum'	NSed
x ***luteolum***	NSed
x ***luteoviride***	NSed
lydium	CHar CLew CRiv CSun ECha EMNN MBal MBar MCas MHig MWat NGre NKay NNrd NRoo NSed SIng SSmi STre WCla
♦ – ***aureum***	See S. ***hispanicum minus*** 'Aureum'
magellense	NSed
¶ ***makinoi makinoi***	NSed SSmi
– 'Variegatum'	NSed
maweanum	See S. ***acre majus***
maximum	See S. ***telephium maximum***
mexicanum	MBri NSed
middendorfianum	CTom ECha ELan EMon GLoc ITim LHop MCas MDHE MHig NGre NHol NKay NSed SSmi WHil WHoo WWin
– ***diffusum***	NGre NSed SSmi
monregalense	NSed
♦ ***montanum rubrum***	See S. ***m.*** 'Red Mountain'
* 'Moonglow'	NSed SSmi
moranense	CRiv NGre NHol NSed SIde SSmi WHil
moranii	NSed
morganianum	EBak MBri NSed
multiceps	NGre NSed SSmi
multiflorum	NSed
murale	See S. ***album murale***
nanifolium	NSed
N ***nevii***	CLew CShe NKay NTow
nicaeense	See S. ***sediforme***
– 'Gran Canaria'	See S. ***sediforme*** 'G.C.'
nussbaumerianum	NSed
nutans	NSed
oaxacanum	NSed
obcordatum	NSed
obtusatum	NSed
– ***boreale***	See S. ***oreganum b.***
– ***retusum***	See S. ***retusum***
ochroleucum	NSed SIng SSmi
¶ – 'Green Spreader'	SSmi
– ***montanum***	NSed WHil

– *ochroleucum glaucum*	NGre
§ *oppositifolium*	CLew CRow ELan NCat NGre NSed SIde SIng WHil
§ *oreganum*	Widely available
– *procumbens*	NHol NSed
– 'Variegatum'	EFol
¶ *oregonense*	NGre
oryzifolium	NSed
– forms	NSed
oxycoccoides	NSed
oxypetalum	NSed
§ *pachyclados*	CHoe GAbr MDHE MPlt NBir NGre NSed SSmi WCla WPer
pachyphyllum	NSed
– x *treleasei*	NSed
palmeri	NBir NSed SIng SSmi
parvum	See VILLADIA *parva*
pilosum	CLew CRiv NGre SIng WOMN WThu
pluricaule	CHar EBre EMNN GCHN MBar MCas NGre NHol NKay NNrd NSed WCla WHil
– from Rebun	NSed
polytrichoides	See RHODIOLA *komarovii*
populifolium	CHar CLew CMHG ECha ITim MCas MPla NGre NHol NSed SDry SIng SSmi STre WEas WHil
potosinum	NSed
praealtum	NSed
§ *primuloides*	NHol NSed SSmi WHil
pruinatum	NGre NHol NKay NSed
pruinosum	See S. *spathulifolium p.*
pulchellum	CShe CTom NGre NSed SIde SSmi
purdyi	NGre NHol NSed
quinquefarium	See S. *brevifolium q.*
♦ *ramossisima*	See VILLADIA *r.*
reflexum	CRiv EBar ELan EMon GGar GLoc NCat NGre NHol NKay NSed SIde SIng SSmi WHil
– 'Monstrosum Cristatum'	CLew MBal NBir NSed SMad
– 'Viride'	NSed
reptans	NSed
– ISI 1222	NSed
– *carinatifolium*	NSed
retusum	NSed
rhodiola	See RHODIOLA *rosea*
rosea	See RHODIOLA *rosea*
rosulatobulbosum	NSed
rosulatum ISI 1223	NSed
rubens	NSed
– *praegeri*	NSed
rubroglaucum	CRiv NNrd SSmi WHil
rubromucronatum	See S. sp. RBGE 736791
x *rubrotinctum*	NSed SLMG
– *aurora*	NSed
'Ruby Glow'	Widely available
rupestre	See S. *forsterianum*
rupifragum	NSed
ruprechtii	CMHG MBri NSti WEas
ruwenzoriense	NSed
♦ *sarcocaule*	See CRASSULA *sarcocaulis*
sarmentosum	NGre NSed SIng SSmi
§ *sediforme*	CTom ECha LHop MBro NCat NGre NKay SSmi
– *nicaeense*	See S. *sediforme*
selskianum	CLew GDra GHig NSed
sempervivoides	NGre SIng
serpentinii	NSed
sexangulare	CHar CLew CRiv CSun EMNN ESis GDra GHig MBar MCas MPlt NGre NHol NKay NNrd NSed SIng SSmi WHil
– *elatum*	NSed
sichotense	NGre NSed SIng
sieboldii	CHar CRow CSam LGro MBri NGre NSed SIng SSmi
– *ettyuense*	NSed
– 'Mediovariegatum'	CRow ELan GLoc NGre NNrd NSed SLMG SSmi WHil WPer
'Silvermoon'	NGre NHol SIng SSmi WHil WPer
spathulifolium	CLew ECha ELan ESis MPlt NKay NSed SChu WEas WOld
– *aureum*	CRiv ECtt EMNN MBar MHig MWat NGre NHol NNor NNrd NSed SSmi WHil
N– 'Cape Blanco'	Widely available
– 'Major'	SIng SPla
§ – *pruinosum*	NGre NHol NSed SSmi
– 'Purpureum'	Widely available
– 'Roseum'	CRow CTom NHol SSmi
spectabile	CArn CCla CHar CKel CRiv CRow EJud ELan MCot NBar NSti SCro SIng WHil WHoo WWin
– 'Brilliant'	CKel CSco CShe EBre ECha EFou ELan EMon MBri MCot NGre NOrc SDix SMad SPla WEas
¶ – 'Carmen'	EMon
– 'Humile'	EMon
– 'Iceberg'	CHad EFou EMon
♦– 'Indian Chief'	See S. 'Herbstfreude'
– 'Meteor'	EBar MWat SCro WAbe
*– 'Mini'	ELan
¶ – 'Septemberglut' ('September Glow')	EMon
– 'Stardust'	ECha SIde
– 'Variegatum'	See S. *alboroseum* 'Mediovariegatum'
spinosum	See OROSTACHYS *spinosum*
spurium	CRiv CTom EJud ELan GLoc LGro NGre NNor SIng STre WEas WHil
– *album*	See S. *oppositifolium*
*– 'Atropurpureum'	ECha NNor NRoo SHig SPla WOld WPat
– 'Bronze Carpet'	NSed
– *carneum*	NSed
– 'Coccineum'	CRiv MBar NSed WOMN
– 'Erdblut'	EBre GGar MHig NGre NNrd NRoo NSed WDav
¶ – 'Fool's Gold'	EMon

- 'Fuldaglut' CHoe CRow NGre NHar NRed NSed SChu WDav WPer WWin
- 'Glow' STre
- 'Green Mantle' ECha MPit NHol NSed
- 'Purpureum' CHan CRow ELan GDra NCat
- 'Purpurteppich' ('Purple Carpet') CHar CShe CTom EBre EPot ESis GLoc LGro MHig NGre NHol NKay NSed SAxl WCla WThu
- 'Ruby Mantle' CRiv GGar NSed SIng WCot
- ***salmoneum*** NSed
- 'Schorbuser Blut' ('Dragon's Blood') CElw CRiv EMon GLoc LHop MBal MCas MWat NGre NHol NKay NSed NVic SCro WAbe WEas WHil WHoo

♦– 'Tricolor' See S. ***s.*** 'Variegatum'
§– 'Variegatum' Widely available
§ sp. RBGE 736791 from Taiwan NSed
stahlii NSed SLMG
stefco NSed
stelliforme NSed
stenopetalum NSed
– 'Douglasii' NSed
stephanii See RHODIOLA ***crassipes s.***
♦***stoloniferum*** NGre NSed SSmi
stribrnyi See S. ***urvillei*** Stribrnyi group
subtile NSed
'Sunset Cloud' CMHG LHop WOld
tatarinowii GLoc NSed WPer
¶***telephioides*** WCot
telephium CRow EBar WCla WHil WPer
– 'Arthur Branch' EMon SSpi WCot
– ***fabaria*** See S. ***fabaria***
§– ***maximum*** CRow ECha EMon NSed
– ***maximum*** 'Atropurpureum' CBot CGle CHad CLew CRow CSev EBre ECha EGol ELan MBri MCot MWgw NSti SAxl WEas WWin
– 'Munstead Dark Red' CRiv CSco EMon MUlv NGre SFis SHig
*– 'Roseum' EFol LHop
– 'Variegatum' CCor CMHG COtt CRow CSco ECha EFol MCot MPlt NRoo SPer SPla WWin
tenuifolium GGar NHol NSed SSmi
§– ***ibericum*** NGre NHol NSed
ternatum NGre NKay NSed
¶***treleasei*** NSed
****trollii*** NGre
tuberiferum NSed
urvillei NSed
§– Hillebrandtii group NSed
– Sartorianum group NSed
– Stribrnyi group NSed
'Vera Jameson' CElw CHoe CKel CMHG CSco CShe ECha EGol ERav ITim MCas MCot MFir MWgw NHar NHol NKay NSti SApp SBla SIng WDav WEas WPer
versadense NSed
– ***villadioides*** NSed
'Weihenstephaner Gold' See S. ***kamtschaticum floriferum*** 'W.G.'
weinbergii See GRAPTOPETALUM ***paraguayense***
winkleri See S. ***hirsutum baeticum***
yesoense NSed
zentaro-tashiroi NSed

SEEMANNIA See **GLOXINIA**

SELAGINELLA (Selaginellaceae)

apoda MBri
braunii NMar
douglasii NMar
emmeliana See S. ***pallescens***
helvetica NHol
kraussiana MBal MBri NMar SIng
– 'Aurea' MBri NMar
– 'Brownii' MBri NMar
– 'Variegata' MBri
martensii 'Variegata' MBri
– 'Watsoniana' MBri NMar
§***pallescens*** NMar
– 'Aurea' NMar
****sanguinolenta*** SIng
vogellii NMar

SELAGO (Globulariaceae)

¶***thunbergii*** LHop

SELINUM (Umbelliferae)

¶***carvifolia*** NRar
tenuifolium CFor CGle CHad CHan EFou GWic MPar NCat NRar SBar SMrm SPer WEas WHer

SELLIERA (Goodeniaceae)

¶***radicans*** forms ECou WPer

SEMELE (Liliaceae/Ruscaceae)

¶***androgyna*** CHEx

SEMIAQUILEGIA † (Ranunculaceae)

§***adoxoides*** EDra NHol NNrd NRya WAbe WHil
§***ecalcarata*** CBot CGle CHan CHar CRiv CRow CSun EDra EFol EFou GAbr GWic MPar MPlt NOak SAxl SBla WDav WHil WMar WPer WThu WWin
– 'Flore Pleno' CBos CMHG CSun GWic LGan MBro WCar WEas
simulatrix See S. ***ecalcarata***

SEMIARUNDINARIA † (Gramineae(Bambuseae))

§***fastuosa*** CHEx EFul NJap SArc SBam SDry WJun
– ***viridis*** SBam SDry
nitida See SINARUNDINARIA ***nitida***
♦***villosa*** See S. ***okuboi***
yamadorii SBam SDry

yashadake SBam SDry WJun

SEMPERVIVELLA (Crassulaceae)

§ ***acuminata*** WOMN WThu
alba See ROSULARIA ***sedoides alba***

SEMPERVIVUM † (Crassulaceae)

'Abba' CRow CWil NBar
'Alaric' NBar
¶ 'Alcithoë' CWil NBar SSmi
'Aldo Moro' CWil NBar SMit SSmi
allionii See JOVIBARBA ***allionii***
'Alluring' CWil SMit
'Alpha' CRiv CRow CWil MCas NBar NGre NHol NKay SIng SSmi
altum CWil MCas NBar SSmi
'Amanda' CWil NBar SIng
'Ambergreen' CWil SSmi
¶ 'Amtmann Fischer' NBra
andreanum CWil MCas NBar NGre SIng SMit SSmi
'Apache' CWil SSmi
'Apple Blossom' CWil NBar SIng SMit SSmi
arachnoideum CHar CRow CSam CShe CWil ELan ESis GAbr GEdr MBar MCas MWat NBar NRoo SBla SIng SLMG SPla SSmi WEas WHil WHoo WWin
– ***bryoides*** CWil NBar
¶ – 'Clairchen' NBra
– ***doellianum*** See S. ***a. glabrescens***
– 'Form No 1' SSmi
§ – ***glabrescens*** MCas SSmi
– ***glabrescens*** 'Album' CRiv WThu
– 'Laggeri' See S. ***a. tomentosum***
– 'Minor' MCas NBar NHol SIng
¶ – ***minuatum*** NHol
¶ – 'Rubrum' NBra
– 'Stansfieldii' CRiv CRow GAbr MCas NBar NGre NHol NKay SLMG
– 'Sultan' SSmi
N– ***tomentosum*** CRiv CRow CWil EBre ECro EMNN EPar ESis GCHN MCas NBar NGre NHar NHol NKay SIng SSmi WPer WWin
– x ***calcareum*** CWil SMit SSmi
– x ***grandiflorum*** SIng
– x ***nevadense*** CRiv CWil SIng SMit SSmi
– x ***pittonii*** CWil NBar NGre NHol SMit SSmi
arenarium See JOVIBARBA ***arenaria***
'Arlet' SMit
armenum CLew CWil
– ***insigne*** from Akyarma Gecidi SMit
¶ 'Aross' NBra
'Arrowheads Red' NBar SSmi
arvernense See S. ***tectorum***
'Ashes of Roses' CRow CWil NBar NTow SSmi WAbe WHal
¶ 'Asteroid' NBar SSmi
atlanticum CWil NBar SIng SSmi
– 'Edward Balls' SIng
– from Oukaimaden CWil NHol SMit
¶ 'Atlantis' NHol
¶ 'Atropurpureum' NBra
¶ 'Atroviolaceum' CWil NBar
'Aureum' See GREENOVIA ***aurea***
§ 'Aymon Correvon' NBra SSmi
ballsii CWil NBar WHil
– from Kampechio SIng
– from Smolika SSmi
– from Tschumba Petzi SIng SSmi
¶ 'Banderi' CWil NBar
¶ 'Banyan' SSmi
x ***barbulatum*** SSmi
§ – ***barbulatum*** GCHN MCas NKay SIng WAbe WHoo WThu
§ – ***hookeri*** CWil MCas SIng SMit SSmi
¶ 'Bascour Zilver' CWil
'Bedivere' CElw CRow CWil NBar NGre SSmi
'Bella Meade' CWil NGre SMit SSmi
'Belladonna' CWil MCas NHol NTow SSmi
'Bellotts Pourpre' SMit
¶ 'Bennerbroek' SSmi
'Bernstein' CWil NBar SIng
'Beta' CKel CRow CWil MCas NBar NKay NRoo SIng SSmi
¶ 'Birchmaier' CWil NBar
¶ 'Black Mini' CWil NBar
'Black Prince' CRow CWil SSmi
¶ 'Black Velvet' NBar SSmi
'Blari' SSmi
'Blood Tip' CRiv CRow EBre GAbr NBar NHar WHal
¶ 'Blue Boy' CWil NBar
'Blue Moon' MFir
'Boissieri' See S. ***tectorum tectorum*** 'B.'
'Booth's Red' NBar SSmi
borissovae CWil SSmi
'Boromir' CWil SMit SSmi
'Brock' CWil NBar NHol
'Bronco' CWil ELan EPad NBar SMit SSmi
'Bronze Pastel' CWil MCas NBar NGre SMit SSmi
'Bronze Tower' SMit
¶ 'Brown Owl' CWil NBar
'Brownii' CRow GAbr NRya
¶ 'Burgundy' NBra
¶ 'Burnatii' CWil NBar
'Café' CWil NHar SIng SSmi
x ***calcaratum*** NBar SIng
calcareum CWil EPar NGre NKay SIng SSmi WHoo WThu
– from Ceuze CWil
– from Col de la Michael CWil
– from Gleiza CWil
– from Gorges du Cains CWil SSmi
– 'Greenii' CWil NBra NGre SMit SSmi
– 'Grigg's Surprise' CRow CWil NBar NBra SMit
– from Guillames Mont Ventoux CWil
– from La Mata de la Riba SMit

– 'Limelight'	CWil NBar SIng SMit SSmi
– 'Monstrosum'	See S. *c*. 'Grigg's Surprise'
– 'Mrs Giuseppi'	CRiv CRow EPar ESis GAbr GCHN MCas NOak SChu SSmi WThu
– 'Nigricans'	NKay
¶ – 'Pink Pearl'	SSmi
– from Queyras	CWil
– from Roote Annote	CWil SSmi
– 'Sir William Lawrence'	CRow CWil NBar SIng SSmi WHal WThu
– 'Spinulifolium'	SMit
– from Trioria	CWil
– from Ventous	SSmi
'Canada Kate'	CWil NBar SMit SSmi
'Cancer'	SSmi
'Candy Floss'	CWil SSmi
cantabricum	CWil NBar SSmi
– ***cantabricum*** from Leitariegos	CWil SMit
– ***cantabricum*** from Someido No 1	SMit
– ***guadarramense*** from Lobo No 2	SMit SSmi
– ***guadarramense*** from Lobo No 1	CWil SMit SSmi
– ***guadarramense*** from Morcuera No 1	SMit
– ***guadarramense*** from Morcuera No 3	SMit
– ***guadarramense*** from Navafria No 1	SMit
– ***guadarramense*** from Valvanera No 1	SMit SSmi
– from Lago de Enol	CWil SSmi
¶ – from Pena Prieta	SSmi
– from Piedrafita	CWil SMit SSmi
¶ – from Riano	CWil
– from San Glorio	CWil SSmi
– from Santander	SSmi
– ***urbionense*** from Picos de Urbion	CWil SMit
– from Valvernera	CWil
– x ***montanum stiriacum***	CWil NGre SMit SSmi WEas
¶ 'Canth'	CWil NBra
'Carluke'	CWil
'Carmen'	CHar CWil EPar NBar SSmi
¶ 'Carneus'	NBra
'Carnival'	MCas NBar SSmi
caucasicum	CWil NKay SSmi
'Cavo Doro'	CWil NGre SSmi
'Celon'	CWil NBar
charadzeae	SMit
'Cherry Frost'	MFir NBar NGre SSmi WHil
'Cherry Tart'	CWil NBar
'Chocolate'	CWil SSmi WAbe
x ***christii***	CWil NHol SSmi WThu
* 'Chrysanthum'	NBra
ciliosum	CHar CWil NGre NKay SSmi
– from Ali Botusch	MCas WThu
¶ – ***borisii***	ESis NBar NRoo NTow
– ***galicicum*** from Mali Hat	CWil NBar NHol SSmi
– x ***ciliosum borisii***	CHar CWil WOld
– x ***marmoreum***	CWil SSmi
– x ***marmoreum*** from Sveta Peta	SMit
'Circlet'	SSmi
* ***cistaceum***	WEas
'Clare'	NBar NGre SSmi
'Cleveland Morgan'	CWil EBre ECro NHar SSmi
¶ 'Climax'	NBra
¶ 'Cobweb Capers'	NBra
'Collage'	CWil NBar SSmi
'Collecteur Anchisi'	SMit SSmi
'Commander Hay'	CCor CRiv EPar GWic MCas NHol NTow SChu SSmi WEas WHil WThu
¶ 'Compte de Congae'	NBra SPla
'Congo'	CWil NBar SMit SSmi
'Cornstone'	CWil NBar SMit
¶ 'Corona'	NBra
'Coronet'	NBar SSmi
♦ 'Correvons'	See S. 'Aymon Correvoa'
'Corsair'	CWil SIng SSmi
'Crimson Velvet'	CWil NBar NGre SSmi
§ 'Crispyn'	CWil MCas MFir NBar NHol SIng SSmi WEas
'Cupream'	CWil NBra NGre
¶ 'Dakota'	CWil
'Dallas'	CWil NBar
'Damask'	NBar NGre SSmi
'Dame Arsac'	SMit
'Dark Beauty'	CWil NBar SMit SSmi WHal
'Dark Cloud'	CWil SCro SMit SSmi
'Dark Point'	CWil MCas NBar SMit SSmi
'Darkie'	CWil
¶ x ***degenianum***	NBra
* ***densum***	ELan
'Director Jacobs'	CRiv CWil GAbr NBar NGre SIng SMit SSmi WEas
'Disco Dancer'	CWil
dolomiticum	NBar
– x ***montanum***	CWil SMit SSmi
'Downland Queen'	CWil NBar SMit
'Dragoness'	SMit
'Duke of Windsor'	CWil NBar NGre SSmi
'Dusky'	CWil SMit SSmi
¶ 'Dyke'	CWil
dzhavachischilii	SMit
¶ 'Edge of Night'	CWil
¶ 'El Greco'	CWil NBar
'El Toro'	CWil NBar
'Elgar'	CWil MCas NBar NHar SIng
¶ ***elianum***	NHol
'Elvis'	CRow CWil NBar SSmi
'Emerald Giant'	CWil
¶ 'Emerson's Giant'	CWil NBar
¶ 'Engle's 13-2'	CWil NBar
'Engle's Rubrum'	CLew CRow NBar
erythraeum	CLew NGre NHol SIng
– from Pirin	NGre
– 'Red Velvet'	NBar
¶ – from Rila	MCas
'Excalibur'	CWil NBar SSmi
* ***excelsum***	NKay
'Exhibita'	CWil NBar SSmi

'Exorna' CWil NBar SIng SSmi WEas
¶ 'Fair Lady' NBra
'Fame' CWil MDHE NBar SSmi
x ***fauconnettii*** CRow CWil NBra SIng SSmi WThu
– ***thompsonii*** NGre NHol SSmi
'Festival' CWil NBar
¶ 'Fiesta' CWil
fimbriatum See S. x ***barbulatum barbulatum***
'Finerpointe' CWil SMit SSmi
¶ 'Fire Giant' CWil
'Firebird' CWil NBar
'Flaming Heart' CWil SSmi
¶ 'Flander's Passion' NBar SSmi
'Flasher' CWil NBar WEas
¶ 'Forden' NBra
'Ford's Amability' CWil SSmi
'Ford's Giant' CWil NBar
¶ 'Ford's Shadows' SSmi
'Ford's Spring' CWil SSmi
'Frosty' CWil
¶ 'Fuego' CWil NBar
x ***funckii*** CRiv CRow CWil NGre NHol SIng
¶ 'Fusilier' NBra
'Fuzzy Wuzzy' SSmi
'Gamma' NHol SSmi
'Garnet' CWil
'Gay Jester' CWil NBar NGre SSmi
'Gazelle' CRiv CWil
'Georgette' NBar SSmi
'Ginnie's Delight' CWil NBar SSmi
'Gipsy' CWil NBar
giuseppii CRiv CShe CWil NBar NGre NHol SIng SSmi WThu
– from Pena Espiguita CWil
– from Pena Prieta CWil SMit
glabrifolium SMit
¶ 'Gleam' NBra
'Gloriosum' NGre SSmi
'Glowing Embers' CWil NBar SSmi
¶ 'Godaert' CWil
'Gollum' SMit SSmi
'Granada' CWil NBar NGre
'Granat' CKel CWil MCas NBar SIng
grandiflorum CWil EBar NGre NRed SIng SSmi WThu
– ***fasciatum*** CWil SIng SMit SSmi
– 'Keston' CWil NGre SSmi
– x ***montanum*** SIng
– x ***tectorum*** NKay
'Grapetone' CWil NBar NGre SSmi
'Green Apple' CWil NGre SSmi
'Green Gables' CWil SMit SSmi
* 'Green Globe' WEas
'Greenwich Time' MCas SSmi
'Grey Dawn' CHar SSmi
'Grey Ghost' CWil
¶ 'Grey Green' CWil NBar
'Grey Lady' CWil SSmi
'Greyfriars' CWil NBar NHol SMit SSmi
¶ 'Greyolla' NBar SSmi
'Gruaud Larose' SMit
'Hall's Hybrid' MCas NBar NHar SIng
¶ 'Happy' CWil
* 'Hart' CWil NBar
'Haullauer's Seedling' CWil NBar
'Hayling' CWil NHol SSmi
¶ 'Hayter's Red' NBra
'Heigham Red' CWil NBar NGre SIng SMit SSmi
¶ 'Hekla' NBra
helveticum MCas NBar
'Hester' CWil MDHE NBar SIng SSmi
'Hey-Hey' CRiv NBar NKay
'Hidde' CWil NBar SSmi
¶ 'Hiddes Roosje' SSmi
'Highland Mist' SMit
hirtum See JOVIBARBA ***hirta***
♦ 'Hookeri' See S. x ***barbulatum hookeri***
¶ 'Hortulanus Smit' NBar SSmi
'Hullabaloo' NBar SSmi
¶ 'Hyacintha' NBra
'Icicle' CWil MCas NBar NHol SSmi
* ***imbricatum*** SIng
'Imperial' CWil NBar SSmi
ingwersenii CWil NGre SSmi
– x ***marmoreum*** from Sveta Peta SMit
¶ 'Interlace' SSmi
'Iophon' SSmi
¶ 'Irazu' CWil NBar
italicum CWil
'Itchen' NBar SSmi
¶ 'IWO' CWil
'Jack Frost' CWil NGre NHar SIng SSmi
¶ 'Jane' NBra
¶ 'Jelly Bean' CWil NBar
¶ 'Jet Stream' CWil
'Jewel Case' CWil NBar SIng SMit SSmi
'Jolly Green Giant' CWil SSmi
¶ 'Jo's Spark' CWil
'Jubilee' ELan GAbr MCas MPlt NBar NHol NRed NRoo SSmi WEas WPer WWin
'Jubilee Tricolor' NBar
'Jungle Fires' MCas
'Kalinda' NBar SSmi
'Kappa' CWil SSmi
'Kelly Jo' CWil NBar NGre SIng
'Kermit' CWil NBar SSmi
kindingeri CWil MCas SMit SSmi
'King George' CRiv CRow CWil ESis LHil NBar NGre SSmi
'Kip' CWil NBar SIng SMit SSmi
'Kismet' SSmi
'Kolibri' GAbr MDHE
kosaninii CRow CWil NGre NKay SSmi
– from Koprivnik CWil SMit SSmi WAbe
'Kramers Spinrad' CWil NBar SMit SSmi WEas
'Kubi' CWil
'Lady Kelly' CWil SSmi SWas
'Lavender and Old Lace' CWil NBar SMit SSmi
'Le Clair's Hybrid No 4' NBar
'Leneca' NGre SSmi
'Lennik's Glory' See S. 'Crispyn'

'Lennik's Time'	SSmi
¶ 'Lentezon'	CWil NBar
¶ 'Leocardia's Nephew'	CWil
'Lilac Time'	CWil NBar SSmi
'Liliane'	SMit
¶ 'Lipari'	CWil
'Lipstick'	CWil GAbr NGre SMit
'Lively Bug'	CWil MCas NBar SMit SSmi
¶ 'Lou Bastidou'	NBar SSmi
¶ 'Lowe's Rubicundum'	ESis
'Lynn's Choice'	CWil NBar
macedonicum	CWil NGre SSmi
– from Ljubotin	SSmi
¶ 'Magic Spell'	SSmi
'Magnificum'	CWil
'Mahogany'	CRiv CWil MBro MCas MPlt NBar NHol WHal WHoo
¶ 'Maigret'	CWil
'Majestic'	NGre SSmi
'Malabron'	CWil SSmi
* 'Malby's Hybrid'	CShe MDHE
¶ 'Marella'	CWil
'Marijntje'	SSmi
¶ 'Marjorie Newton'	CWil
'Marmalade'	NBar SSmi
§ ***marmoreum***	CWil NBar SIng SPla WEas
– ***angustissimum***	SMit
– ***blandum***	NKay
– 'Brunneifolium'	CWil ESis MCas NGre NHol SChu SIng SMit SSmi
– from Kanzas Gorge	NBra NGre NHol SIng SSmi
– ***marmoreum dinaricum***	CWil
§ – ***marmoreum*** 'Rubrifolium'	CRow CShe CWil NHar SMit
– from Monte Tirone	CWil SSmi
– from Okol	CWil SMit SSmi
§ – 'Ornatum'	ITim NBar NGre SSmi WAbe WEas WHil
– from Sveta Peta	NGre SMit SSmi
¶ 'Mary Ente'	NBra
'Mate'	SSmi
'Mauna Kea'	NBar SSmi
¶ 'Mauvine'	NBra
'Medallion'	CWil
'Meisse'	NBar SSmi
¶ 'Melanie'	CWil
'Mercury'	CWil NBar NHol SIng SMit SSmi
¶ 'Merkur'	NBra
'Merlin'	CWil NBar SSmi
¶ 'Midas'	CWil NBar
'Mila'	CWil
'Mini Frost'	CWil NBar
'Moerkerk's Merit'	CWil NBar SSmi
¶ 'Mondstein'	CWil NBar
montanum	CRiv CRow CWil NBar SCro SIng
– from Anchisis	CWil
– from Arbizion	CWil
– ***burnatii***	NGre SSmi WThu
– ***montanum braunii***	CHar
§ – 'Red Mountain'	MCas MWat NKay
– ***stiriacum***	CRow CWil EPar SIng
– ***stiriacum*** from Mauterndorf	SSmi
– ***stiriacum*** 'Lloyd Praeger'	CWil NGre SSmi
– from Windachtal	CWil
¶ 'More Honey'	CWil
¶ 'Mount Hood'	CWil
* 'Moyin'	SMit
¶ 'Mulberry Wine'	CWil NBar
'Mystic'	CWil NBar SIng
nevadense	CWil NBar NGre NHol NKay SSmi
– ***hirtellum***	CWil SIng SMit SSmi
– from Puerto de San Francisco	SMit
'Night Raven'	CWil MCas NBar SMit
♦ 'Nigrum'	See S. ***tectorum*** 'N.'
¶ 'Niobe'	CWil NBar
¶ 'Nixes 27'	NBra
'Noir'	CRiv GAbr NGre NKay SCro SIng SSmi
¶ 'Norbert'	CWil NBar
'Nouveau Pastel'	CWil NBar SMit
¶ 'Octet'	NBra
octopodes	ESis MDHE
– ***apetalum***	CWil MCas SIng SSmi
'Oddity'	CWil NBar SMit
'Ohio Burgundy'	CWil MDHE NBar SSmi WAbe
'Olivette'	CWil NBar SSmi
'Omega'	SIng SSmi
¶ 'Opitz'	CWil
¶ ***oreostachys chanettyi***	NBra
'Ornatum'	ITim ITim NBar NGre SSmi WAbe WEas WHil
ossetiense	CWil
'Othello'	CRow MCas NBar NVic SSmi WAbe
'Packardian'	CWil NBar SMit SSmi
'Palissander'	CWil NGre SMit SSmi
'Pastel'	CWil MCas NBar
♦ ***patens***	See JOVIBARBA ***heuffelii***
'Patrician'	CWil NBar SSmi
'Pekinese'	CWil EPar NBar SIng SSmi WEas WWin
'Peterson's Ornatum'	NGre SSmi
¶ 'Pilatus'	CWil
¶ 'Pilosella'	NBra
¶ 'Pink Cloud'	CWil NBar SSmi
¶ 'Pink Puff'	CWil NBar SSmi
'Pippin'	CWil SIng SMit
pittonii	CWil ESis GAbr NBar SSmi
'Pixie'	CWil
'Plumb Rose'	CWil NBar SIng SSmi
'Pluto'	SSmi
'Poke Eat'	SSmi
'Polaris'	CWil NBar SSmi
'Pottsii'	CRow CWil GAbr
x ***praegeri***	CWil
'President Arsac'	CWil NBar SIng SSmi
'Proud Zelda'	CWil SSmi
'Pumaros'	CWil SSmi
pumilum	CWil MCas NBra
– from Adyl Su No 1	MCas SSmi

– from Adyl Su No 2	SSmi
– from Armchi	SSmi
– from Armchi × *ingwersenii*	SMit
– from Elbruz No 1	SSmi
– from Elbruz No 2	SSmi
¶ 'Purdy'	WAbe
'Purdy's 50-6'	CWil NBar
¶ 'Purple Beauty'	NBra
'Purple King'	CWil NBar
'Purple Passion'	SSmi
¶ 'Purpurriese'	CWil
'Queen Amalia'	See S. ***reginae-amaliae***
¶ 'Query'	NBra
¶ 'R H I'	NBra
¶ 'Racey'	CWil
* 'Ramis'	MCas
'Raspberry Ice'	CWil MCas NBar NHol WAbe WHal
'Red Ace'	CWil EBar NBar SSmi
'Red Beam'	MDHE NGre SSmi
¶ 'Red Cap'	NBra
'Red Delta'	CWil NBar SSmi
'Red Devil'	CWil NBar SSmi
'Red Giant'	NBar NBra
'Red Mountain'	NBar SSmi
¶ 'Red Shadows'	CWil NBar
¶ 'Red Skin'	CWil NBar
'Red Wings'	GAbr NBar NGre SSmi
¶ 'Regal'	NBra
'Regina'	SSmi
reginae	See S. ***reginae-amaliae***
§ ***reginae-amaliae***	CRow ELan NBar NHol SSmi
– from Kambeecho No 1	CWil SSmi
– from Kambeecho No 2	CWil MCas
– from Marvi Petri	CWil SIng SMit SSmi
– from Peristeria	SMit SSmi
– from Sarpun	CWil SMit SSmi
– from Vardusa	SMit
'Reginald Malby'	CWil MCas NGre SSmi
¶ 'Reinhard'	CWil SIng
¶ 'Remus'	CWil NBar SIng
¶ 'Rex'	NBra
* ***richardii***	MBar
¶ 'Risque'	CWil
'Rita Jane'	CWil EBar MCas NBar SSmi
* ***roavis***	CRow
'Robin'	CRow CWil MCas NBar NHol SSmi
¶ 'Ronny'	CWil
¶ × ***roseum***	NBar
– ***fimbriatum***	CWil NHol SSmi WEas
'Rosie'	CWil GAbr NBar NGre NRoo SMit SSmi
'Rotkopf'	CWil SMit
'Rotmantel'	CWil SSmi
¶ 'Rotsand'	NBra
'Rotund'	CWil
'Rouge'	CWil
'Royal Flush'	CWil SSmi
¶ 'Royal Mail'	NBra
'Royal Opera'	CWil SMit SSmi
'Royal Ruby'	CWil EBre ECtt NHar NRoo SIng SSmi
¶ 'Rubellum'	NBra
'Rubikon Improved'	CWil SChu SSmi
'Rubin'	CHar CRiv EPad EPar NBar NGre NHar SCro WAbe WEas WThu
'Rubra Ash'	NBar SMit
* ***rubra-compacta***	CRow
'Rubrifolium'	See S. ***marmoreum marmoreum*** 'R.'
'Ruby Heart'	NGre SSmi
'Rule Britannia'	SMit
¶ 'Rusty'	CWil
¶ 'Ruth'	NBra
ruthenicum	NBar NGre
'Saga'	CWil NBar
¶ 'Saturn'	CWil SSmi
schlehanii	See S. ***marmoreum***
*– 'Hall's Seedling'	NKay
¶ 'Seminole'	CWil NBar
¶ 'Shawnee'	CWil NBar
'Shirley's Joy'	CWil GAbr NBar SSmi WEas
¶ 'Sigma'	NBra
'Silberspitz'	CWil NHar SIng
'Silver Jubilee'	CWil MDHE SSmi
¶ 'Silver Spring'	NBra
'Silver Thaw'	CWil NBar NTow SSmi WHil
* 'Simonkaianum'	MCas
'Sioux'	CWil GAbr NBar NGre SIng SSmi
'Skrocki's Bronze'	SMit SSmi
¶ 'Slabber's Seedling'	CWil
¶ 'Smokey Jet'	SSmi
'Snowberger'	CWil EBre GAbr NBar NHar SIng
soboliferum	See JOVIBARBA ***sobolifera***
¶ 'Sopa'	CWil NBar
sosnowskyi	CWil
¶ 'Soul'	CWil NBar
'Spanish Dancer'	CWil NBar SSmi
'Spherette'	CWil SIng SSmi
'Spice'	SSmi
'Spinnelli'	WThu
'Spode'	SSmi
'Spring Mist'	CWil NBar SIng
'Sprite'	CWil SMit SSmi
¶ sp. Sierra del Cordi'	NHol
stansfieldii	See S. ***arachnoideum*** 'Stansfieldii'
'Starshine'	CWil NBar SIng SSmi
'State Fair'	CWil NBar NGre SIng SSmi
¶ 'Strawberry Sundae'	NBra
'Strider'	MCas SMit
'Stuffed Olive'	SSmi
'Sun Waves'	SSmi
'Sunkist'	SSmi
'Superama'	CWil NBar SSmi
¶ 'Tarn Hows'	CWil
¶ 'Teck'	NBra
§ ***tectorum***	CRiv CSFH CShe CWil EJud EPar GAbr GPoy MBar MDHE SIde SIng SMad WAbe WHoo WOak
– ***alpinum***	CWil MCas NKay SIng SSmi

– from Andorra	CWil
¶ – 'Atrorubens'	NBra
– 'Atroviolaceum'	ESis NHol SIng SMit
– ***glaucum***	CWil NBar NKay SSmi
– from Mount Ventoux	CWil
– from Neuveglise	SMit
– 'Nigrum'	CRow CWil EBar ESis NBra NGre NHol SIng SMit SSmi
– 'Red Flush'	CWil NBar SIng SMit SSmi
– 'Robustum'	NKay
– 'Royanum'	NBar SAxl WEas
– from Sierra del Cadi	CWil SSmi
– 'Sunset'	CWil MCas NBar SIng SMit SSmi WAbe WEas
– 'Violaceum'	CCor NBar WAbe
§ ***tectorum tectorum*** 'Atropurpureum'	CRow CWil MCas NBra SIng SSmi
– – 'Boissieri'	CWil NKay SMit SSmi
– – 'Triste'	CRow CWil MCas NBar NHol SSmi
'Theo'	SMit
thompsonianum	CWil NBar NGre SIng SSmi WThu
¶ 'Tiffany'	NHol
'Tina'	SSmi
'Titania'	CWil SIng SSmi
¶ 'Topaz'	CWil
'Tordeur's Memory'	CWil SMit SSmi
'Traci Sue'	CWil SMit SSmi
transcaucasicum	CRow CWil SSmi
'Tristesse'	SMit SSmi
¶ 'Tristram'	NBar SSmi
'Truva'	CWil NBar
'Twilight Blues'	CWil
x ***vaccarii***	NGre SSmi
'Vanbaelen'	CWil NBar SSmi
¶ 'Vaughelen'	NBra
¶ 'Victorian'	NBra
'Video'	CWil NBar SSmi
vincentei	CWil
'Virgil'	CWil NBar SIng SSmi
'Virginus'	CWil
¶ 'Vulcano'	CWil NBar
¶ 'Webby Ola'	NBra
'Webbyola'	SSmi
'Weirdo'	CWil
'Wendy'	CWil SSmi
'Westerlin'	CWil GAbr NBar NGre SIng SSmi
'Whitening'	CWil SSmi
x ***widderi***	SIng SSmi
'Wollcott's Variety'	CRow EBre GAbr NBar NHar SIng
wulfenii	CWil SIng SMit
zeleborii	CWil MDHE NBar
¶ 'Zenocrate'	CWil
'Zeppelin'	CWil
'Zone'	CWil NBar SSmi
'Zulu'	NBar SSmi

SENECIO † (Compositae)

§ ***abrotanifolius***	LHil NTow
– ***tiroliensis***	See S. ***abrotanifolius***
aquaticus	CKin
§ ***bicolor cinerarian***	CFis CHEx LHil MBri SCro WHen
– – 'Alice'	EFou
– – 'Ramparts'	LHop
– – 'Silver Filigree'	ENot
¶ – – 'Sleights Hardy'	NPer
– – 'White Diamond'	CFis CKel ECha LGro MCot NRar WEas WWin
bidwillii	See BRACHYGLOTTIS ***bidwillii***
¶ ***canus***	WDav
chilensis	CGre CSam MBro WDav
chrysanthemoides	See EURYOPS ***c.***
compactus	See BRACHYGLOTTIS ***compacta***
confusus	SLMG
¶ ***crassulifolius***	CBot
doria	SAxl
♦ ***elaeagnifolius***	See BRACHYGLOTTIS ***elaeagnifolia***
¶ ***formosus***	CBot WDav
¶ – WR 8906	CSun
glastifolius	See BRACHYGLOTTIS ***kirkii***
'Gregynog Gold'	See LIGULARIA 'G.G.'
greyi	See BRACHYGLOTTIS ***greyi***
heritieri	See PERICALLIS ***lanata***
herreianus	MBri SLMG
* ***huteri***	WEas
incanus carniolicus	SOkd
¶ ***jacquemontianus***	WCar
kirkii	See BRACHYGLOTTIS ***k.***
laxifolius	See BRACHYGLOTTIS ***laxifolia***
♦ 'Leonard Cockayne'	See BRACHYGLOTTIS 'L.C.'
leucostachys	See S. ***vira-vira***
macroglossus 'Variegatus'	SLMG
maritimus	See S. ***bicolor cineraria***
¶ ***mikanioides***	CHEx
monroi	See BRACHYGLOTTIS ***monroi***
¶ ***petasitis***	CHEx
¶ ***populnea***	CBot
przewalskii	See LIGULARIA ***przewalskii***
pulcher	CChu CGle CHan CSam LGre SHig SOkd SSpi
reinoldii	See BRACHYGLOTTIS ***rotundifolia***
rowleyanus	EBak
scandens	CMac ELan ERea ISea MTho NTow SHil WHil WSHC
serpens	MBri
§ ***smithii***	CMHG CRow ECha MSta WCru
'Sunshine'	See BRACHYGLOTTIS 'Sunshine'
¶ ***takedanus***	ITim WDav
¶ ***tamoides***	CHil
– 'Variegatus'	ERea

§ *tanguticus* CElw CFis CGle CHEx CHan CRow ELan GGar MBal NHol SDix WHer
§ *vira-vira* CFis CGle CHan CPle ELan ERea LHop MCot MRav NSti SChu SDix SPer WAbe WHal WOld WRus WSHC WWat

SEQUOIA (Taxodiaceae)
sempervirens CDoC EHar EHul IJoh IOrc ISea LSav SExT SHil SMad WCon WCoo WMou WNor
– 'Adpressa' CBow CBra CDoC CMac CSco EHar EHul LLin MBal MBar MBri MGos MPla MR&S NHar SHil SPer WCon
– 'Prostrata' CGre CMac CSco EHar EHul EPla LLin MBar MBri SHil WAbe

SEQUOIADENDRON (Taxodiaceae)
giganteum CB&S CDoC CMac CSco EHar EHul ELan GRei IBar IJoh IOrc ISea LNet MBar MBri NWea SExT SGar SHil SMad SPer WCoo WMou WNor
– 'Glaucum' EHar MBri SMad WCon WMou
– 'Pendulum' CDoC EHar MBar SGar SHil WCon WMou

SERENOA (Palmae)

SERIPHIDIUM See **ARTEMISIA**

SERISSA (Rubiaceae)
foetida STre

SERRATULA (Compositae)
§ *seoanei* CLew EMon LHop MCas MHig MUlv MWat SDix SFir SIng SLHN WHil
shawii See S. *seoanei*
tinctoria CKin SIde
– macrocephala CLew

SESAMUM (Pedaliaceae)
indicum CArn

SESLERIA (Gramineae)
caerulea CHoe ELan ERou GPla GWic MPar MWgw SFar SFir
glauca CHoe
heufleriana EMon LRHS
insularis EMon LRHS
nitida EMon

SETCREASEA See **TRADESCANTIA**

SHADDOCK See **CITRUS** *grandis*

SHEPHERDIA (Elaeagnaceae)
argentea CBot CHoe LSav

SHERARDIA (Rubiaceae)
arvensis MSal

SHIBATAEA † (Gramineae(Bambuseae))
kumasasa CB&S CBra IOrc LNet MBal MBri MGos MUlv NHol NJap SArc SBam SDry SHil WJun

SHORTIA (Diapensiaceae)
soldanelloides GDra NKay
– dwarf form GDra NKay
soldanelloides ilicifolia IBlr
– – 'Askival' GDra
uniflora CFor
– 'Grandiflora' IBlr NKay

SIBBALDIA (Rosaceae)

SIBBALDIOPSIS (Rosaceae)
§ *tridentata* SCro SIng

SIDA (Malvaceae)
¶ *hermaphrodita* EMon
napaea EMon

SIDALCEA † (Malvaceae)
'Brilliant' CGle CHar
candida CBos CElw CGle CHad CHan CHar CSco EFou ELan EPar ERou GGar GWic LGre MBri NRoo NSti SAxl SPer WBon
'Crimson King' CSco
'Croftway Red' CGle ELan GGar MWgw NRoo NVic SChu SCro SPer
'Elsie Heugh' CHan ERou GWic IDai MBri NBar WRus
¶ 'Interlaken' NOrc
'Loveliness' CGle CHad CSco EFou ELan MWat MWgw NHol SPer WHal
malviflora CBos CLew MFir NNor SChu WEas WHoo WPer
'Monarch' CSco
'Mrs Borrodaile' CTom NKay NRoo
'Mrs Cadman' SFis
'Mrs Galloway' CSco
'Mrs T Alderson' CGle ERou
¶ *neomexicana* GWic
'Oberon' CHan GWic NHol SPer WEas
'Party Girl' ECtt NRoo WPer
'Reverend Page Roberts' CFor CShe NVic SFis
¶ 'Rosanna' WHil
'Rose Queen' CGle CKel CSco CTom EBre MCot MWat NHol NKay NRoo SPer WHoo
Stark's hybrids MPit
¶ 'Sussex Beauty' CBos
'The Duchess' CSco CShe
'Twixt' SFis
'William Smith' CGle CSco EBre MWat NHol NKay NOrc SPer WEas

SIDERITIS (Labiatae)
¶ *hyssoppifolia* WPer
syriaca ECha

SILAUM (Umbelliferae)
silaus CKin

SILENE (Caryophyllaceae)

acaulis	CHar CLew CSun EMNN EPot ESis GCHN GLoc ITim MBro MCas MPla MTho NGre NRya SIng WAbe WPat WThu WWin
– 'Alba'	CHar ESis GDra MBro MHig NHol NNrd NRed WDav
¶ – ***elongata***	NHol
¶ – ***exscapa***	WPer
– 'Frances'	GAbr GArf GCHN GDra GLoc ITim NHol NNrd WAbe
¶ – from Pfiezujoch	NHol
– ***longiscapa***	CMHG GAbr GDra MCas NHol NNrd NRed SSmi WPer
* – ***minima***	CLew
– 'Mount Snowdon Form'	ELan EMNN GLoc NHol NNrd NRed NWCA
– 'Pedunculata'	WPer
alba	CKin WCla WHen WHer
alpestris	CGle CLew CSun EMNN ESis MBro MCas MFir MHig MPla MTho NGre NKay NNrd NRya WAbe WCla WHil
– 'Flore Pleno'	CGle CShe CSun EOrc ESis GLoc MDHE MHig NKay WWin
altaica	SIng
x ***arkwrightii*** 'Vesuvius'	See LYCHNIS x ***a.*** 'V.'
armeria	WHer
asterias	CHil CSun EBar NSti SAxl WPer
'Bill Mackenzie'	MCot
¶ ***caryophylloides***	WPer
– ***echinus***	EPot SOkd WPer
compacta	EPad WEas WKif
dioica	CArn CGle CKin CNat CSFH ELan MChe NLan WCla WEas WHen WHer WPer
– ***compacta***	ELan WBon
¶ – 'Flore Pleno'	CBot
– 'Graham's Delight'	EMon
¶ – 'Perkin'	CNat
– 'Richmond'	CFor ECha
§ – 'Rosea Plena'	CBre CChu CGle CLew CSam ELan EMon EOrc GPla LHop MTho NKay NSti SChu WBon WHer
– 'Rubra Plena'	CHan MTho
– ***variegata***	EFol ELan
elisabethae	LRHS NGre NRed WOMN WPer
¶ – 'Alba'	WCla
§ ***fimbriata***	CCor CHan ELan EMon MPar SAxl
¶ ***flavescens***	NRed
* ***foliosa***	CLew NRed
frivaldskyana	CHan GCHN LGan
¶ ***hifacensis***	EPad
hookeri	CLew EPad EPot WPer
ingramii	GArf MDHE NHol
italica	CKin
keiskii	ECha LGan NKay NTow SBla WPer
– ***akaisialpina***	ITim SOkd
– ***minor***	MCas MTho NHol NWCA SOkd WAbe WOMN
¶ ***lerchenfeldiana***	WHil
♦ ***maritima***	See S. ***uniflora***
moorcroftiana	WPer
multifida	See S. ***fimbriata***
* ***nigrescens***	WPer
noctiflora	CKin WCla
nutans	CKin CNat NLan WPer
¶ ***pendula*** 'Compacta'	WPer
¶ – ***rosea***	LHil
petersonii petersonii	WDav
pusilla	NHol WPer
rubra 'Flore Pleno'	See S. ***dioica*** 'F.P.'
¶ ***rupestris***	SIng
saxatilis	NHol NKay
schafta	CHar CSun ECha EFol ELan EMNN GAbr GCHN ITim MBro MCas MCot MFir MPla MWat NGre NHol NKay NRoo SIng WCla WHil WHoo WWin
– 'Abbotswood'	See LYCHNIS x ***walkeri*** 'Abbotswood Rose'
– 'Shell Pink'	LHop MHig WHoo WOMN
¶ ***scouleri***	LGre
♦ ***sieboldii***	See LYCHNIS ***coronata sieboldii***
¶ sp. L 887	NHol
suksdorfii	CLew MCas
¶ ***undulata***	CHan
§ ***uniflora***	CGle CHan CKin CNat CSun ELan EMNN ESis GAbr MFir MPar NGre NKay NLan NNor NOak NSti WCla WHen WHer WHil WWin
– 'Alba Plena'	See S. ***u.*** 'Flore Pleno'
§ – 'Flore Pleno'	CGle CHar CLew CRiv ECha EFol ELan GAbr GWic LHop MWat NHol NSti NVic SIng WDav WEas WHil WPer WWin
– 'Robin Whitebreast''	CFis CMHG CRiv EBar ECro ECtt EOrc MWat NOak SIng WEas WPer
– ***rosea***	CGle CTom ECtt EMNN EPot NHol NNrd NRed SAxl SMrm SWas WHil
– 'Silver Lining'	ELan EMon LRHS
§ – 'Variegata'	SIng
– 'White Bells'	NNrd WHoo
vallesia	WCar WPer
vulgaris	CKin NLan
– ***alpina***	See S. ***v. prostrata***
♦ – ***maritima***	See S. ***uniflora***
§ – ***prostrata***	CCor
zawadskii	EBar GLoc ITim NGre NHol NTow WPer

SILPHIUM (Compositae)

¶ ***laciniatum***	WCar
¶ ***perfoliatum***	ECro GPoy
* ***trifoliatum***	MSal

SILYBUM (Compositae)
marianum CArn CFis CGle ECro EJud ELan GPoy LHil LHol NRar NSel SAxl SFir SIde SMrm WEas

SIMMONDSIA (Simmondsiaceae)
chinensis MSal

SINARUNDINARIA † (Gramineae(Bambuseae))
§ *anceps* CHEx CHad CSco IOrc MBri MGos MUlv SArc SBam SDry SHil SPer SReu
♦ *jaunsarensis* See S. ***anceps***
§ *maling* SBam SDry
♦ *murieliae* See THAMNOCALAMUS ***spathaceus***
§ *nitida* Widely available

SINNINGIA (Gesneriaceae)
'Arion' NMos
'Blanche de Meru' NMos SW&B
'Blue Wonder' MBri
'Boonwood Yellow Bird' NMos
¶ 'Brilliant Scarlet' CSut
cardinalis EBak WEfe
§ x *cardosa* MBri
'Cherry Belle' NMos
'Chic' NMos
'Diego Rose' MBri
¶ 'Duchess of York' CSut
¶ 'Duke of York' CSut
'Etoile du Feu' LAma MBri NMos
'Hollywood' LAma NMos SW&B
'Island Sunset' NMos
'Kaiser Friedrich' LAma MBri NMos
'Kaiser Wilhelm' LAma MBri NMos
'Medusa' NMos
'Mont Blanc' CSut LAma MBri NMos SW&B
'Pegasus' NMos
'Princess Elizabeth' SW&B
¶ 'Red Tiger' CSut
'Reine Wilhelmine' SW&B
¶ 'Royal Crimson' CSut
¶ 'Royal Pink' CSut
¶ 'Royal Purple' CSut
¶ 'Royal Tiger' CSut
'Tigrina' NMos SW&B
'Violacea' MBri NMos
'Waterloo' NMos

SINOBAMBUSA (Gramineae(Bambuseae))
tootsik SBam SDry

SINOFRANCHETIA (Lardizabalaceae)
¶ *chinensis* WWat

SINOWILSONIA (Hamamelidaceae)
henryi SSta

SISYMBRIUM (Cruciferae)
luteum CLew

SISYRINCHIUM † (Iridaceae)
* *album* CGle
* x *anceps* See S. ***angustifolium***
§ *angustifolium* CCla CGle CMCN CRiv CRow CWGN EBur ECha EFol ELan EMNN GCHN LAma MBar MCot MPit NBar NHol NNor NNrd NRya SIng SSmi STre
arenarium CRow
atlanticum EBur ESis WCar
* *bellum* CBro CKel EBre EBur ELan GCHN MBal MCas SCro SIng WCla WHil WHoo
* *bermudianum* CFis CGle CHan CRiv CShe EBur EMNN MBal MSal MWat NGre NHol NKay NLan WAbe WCla WEas WHil WSto
*– 'Album' CCor WCla
'Biscutella' CGle CLew CRiv CTom EBur ELan ESis GAbr LHop NHol SAxl SBla SChu SCro SIng SLHN SSmi SSvw WBon WCla WHal WHil WOMN
* 'Blue Ice' CLew WHoo
boreale See S. ***californicum***
brachypus See S. ***californicum*** Brachypus group
'Californian Skies' SAsh SAxl SWas
§ *californicum* Widely available
§ – Brachypus group CBro CCla CMal EBar ECtt GAbr GCHN GPla LHil MPit MWgw NGre NRed NSti SCro SFir
. – British Columbia form CSun WHil
§ *chilense* SIng
coeleste EBur ESis
coeruleum See GELASINE ***coerulea***
cuspidatum See S. ***arenarium***
¶ *depauperatum* ESis NRed WAbe WHoo
§ *douglasii* CBro EPot GDra GEdr LAma NTow SIng SPou WAbe WCar
– *album* EBur EPot GDra GEdr ITim NHol SPou
'E K Balls' CLew EBre EBur ELan EPla EPot MBro MTho NHol NKay NRya SSmi WAbe WCla WPat WWin
filifolium CSun GAbr LHop MBal MDHE SIng WCar
– *junceum* MTho
¶ *graminoides* WPer
¶ – 'Album' WPer
grandiflorum See S. ***douglasii***
§ *idahoense* CSun EBur ECha EMNN EPar ESis GPla ITim MBal MCas MHig NRya NWCA WAbe WPer
§ – *album* Widely available
– 'blue' ELan ITim
iridifolium CBro LHil SCro
littorale CSun EBur WCla
macounii See S. ***idahoense***
macrocarpon CBro EBur EMNN EPot ESis MPlt NGre NHol NNrd SIng SWas WAbe WCla WHal WOMN WPat WPer

'May Snow' See S. ***idahoense album***
montanum CCla SIng
– JCA 9434 CSun
'Mrs Spivey' CAvo CBro CRiv CRow EBur EMNN ESis MBal MBar NGre NHol NOak SIng WAbe WCla WOMN
§ 'North Star' CTom EBur ESis IBlr NHol NNrd SFir SIng WHal WPer
nudicaule* x *montanum CSam EBur EMNN EPot ESis GWic ITim MCas MDHE NHol NNrd
patagonicum EBur NRed NWCA WCla
'Pole Star' See S. 'North Star'
'Quaint and Queer' CCor CRow EBur ECha EFol EOrc EPla GCHN MTho SSmi WAbe WCar WPer WRus WWin
scabrum See S. ***chilense***
striatum Widely available
§ – 'Aunt May' Widely available
– ***variegatum*** See S. ***striatum*** 'Aunt May'
* 'Tierra del Fuego' CRow

SIUM (Umbelliferae)

sisarum GPoy LHol SIde WOak WSto

SKIMMIA † (Rutaceae)

anquetilia ISea LSav
x ***confusa*** EGol MBri
– 'Kew Green' (m) LRHS LSav MBri NHol SBla SPer SSus WWat
§ ***japonica*** Widely available
– 'Alba ' See S. ***j.*** 'Fructu-albo'
– 'Bowles' Dwarf' (f) CBot CChu CHig ECou LSav MBar MBri MGos MPar MPla SPer SSta WWat
– 'Bowles' Dwarf' (m) CBot CCla LSav MBri MPla SPer SSpi SSta WWat
*– 'Bronze Beauty' SReu
– 'Bronze Knight' (m) IHos LSav NHol SPer
– 'Cecilia Brown' (f) LRHS LSav WWat
N– 'Foremanii' See S. ***j.*** 'Veitchii'
– 'Fragrans' (m) CBra CHig CSam CSco CTrw IOrc LSav MBar MBri MGos MPar NHol SBla SHil SPla SReu WBod WThu WWat
§ – 'Fructu Albo' (f) CB&S CHig CTrw EGol IBar LSav MBar MBri SLon SPla SSpi SSta WWat
– 'Highgrove Redbud' (f) CHig MBar MGos
¶ – 'Kew White' (f) MBri
– 'Nymans' (f) CBot CBow CFor EGol IOrc ISea LSav MBal MBar MBri MRav NHol SArc SBla SHil SPer SPla SReu SSpi SSta WWat
– 'Obovata' (f) MBri
– 'Pigmy' (f) CB&S
– 'Red Princess' (f) MBri
*– 'Red Riding Hood' SLon
– 'Redruth' (f) CB&S CLan IOrc LSav MBar MBri MGos NHol SMad
– ***reevesiana*** CBow CBra CCla CHig CSco EBre EHar IJoh IOrc ISea MBar MBri NHol NKay NTow SBla SHil SMad SPer SSpi SSta WBod WThu
¶ – ***reevesiana*** 'Robert Fortune' WWat
– 'Rubella' (m) Widely available
– 'Ruby Dome' (m) LSav MBar MBri WWat
– 'Scarlet Dwarf' (f) MBri
– 'Tansley Gem' (f) LRHS LSav MBar
– 'Thelma King' MBri
§ – 'Veitchii' (f) LSav MBar
¶ – ***viridis*** NBar
– 'Winifred Crook' (f) LRHS LSav MBar WWat
– 'Winnie's Dwarf' CHig MGos
– 'Wisley Female' (f) EGol EPla LSav
§ ***japonica*** Rogersii group EBre ENot GRei IDai IHos IOrc MBal MBar MGos MPla MWat SBla SChu SHil SLon SPer SPla SReu WBod WWat
– – 'Dunwood' MBar
– – 'George Gardner' MBar
– – 'Helen Goodall' (f) MBar
– – 'Nana Femina' (f) MBri
– – 'Nana Mascula' (m) MBri MGos NKay SSpi
– – 'Rockyfield Green' MBar
– – 'Rogersii Femina' (f) CSam IHos SBla
– – 'Rogersii Mascula' (m) SBla
– – 'Snow Dwarf' MBar
laureola CChu CFor EBre ENot MGos SArc SHil SLon WSHC
– Taylor 132 LSav SSta WWat
– 'Fragrant Cloud' MBar
* ***mica*** ISea
reevesiana See S. ***japonica r.***

SMILACINA (Liliaceae/Convallariaceae)

racemosa Widely available
stellata CBos CBre CBro CRow EBul EPar EPot NHol NKay WChr

SMILAX (Smilacaceae)

asparagoides nanus See ASPARAGUS ***a. myrtifolius***
¶ ***china*** SSpi
discotis CB&S
¶ ***sieboldii*** SSpi

SMITHIANTHA (Gesneriaceae)

'Calder Girl' NMos
'Carmel' NMos
'Carmello' NMos
'Castle Croft' NMos
'Cinna Barino' NMos
'Corney Fell' NMos
'Dent View' NMos
'Ehenside Lady' NMos
'Harecroft' NMos
'Little One' NMos
'Matins' NMos
'Meadowcroft' NMos
'Multiflora' NMos

'New Yellow Hybrid'	NMos
'Orange King'	NMos
'Orangeade'	NMos
'Pink Lady'	NMos
'Sandybank'	NMos
'Santa Clara'	NMos
'Starling Castle'	NMos
'Summer Sunshine'	NMos
'Vespers'	NMos
'Zebrina Hybrid'	NMos

X SMITHICODONIA (Gesneriaceae)

§ 'Cerulean Mink'	NMos

SMYRNIUM (Umbelliferae)

olusatrum	CArn CKin CSev LHol MChe MSal SIde WHer WOak
perfoliatum	EFou ELan MPar

SOLANDRA (Solanaceae)

hartwegii	See S. *maxima*
maxima	ERea MNew

SOLANUM (Solanaceae)

¶ *aculeatissimum*	LHop
crispum	CHan CSco ELan ISea WEas
– *autumnale*	See S. *c.* 'Glasnevin'
– 'Glasnevin'	Widely available
– 'Variegatum'	IJoh NTow
dulcamara	CArn CMer GPoy
– 'Variegatum'	CB&S CHan CMac CRow CTre EBre EFol ELan EMon EPla ERav IBlr IOrc MBri SLon SMad SPer WEas WSHC
jasminoides	CB&S IBar IJoh SHil SLon WSHC
– 'Album'	Widely available
laciniatum	CGle CGre CPle ERea GWic IBlr LHil LHop LRHS NHex SArc SMad WEas
muricatum 'Ryburn'	ESim
pseudocapsicum	MBri
– 'Ballon'	MBri
– 'Mandarin'	MBri
– 'Thurino'	MBri
rantonnetii	CB&S CHad CSun ERea LHop WMar
sisymbrifolium	CFis GWic
valdiviense 'Variegatum'	CB&S
¶ *wendlandii*	CB&S ERea

SOLDANELLA (Primulaceae)

alpina	CHar CRiv CShe CSun ELan EPot GDra GEdr LHop MBal MBro NHol NNrd NRya NVic SBla SIng WDav
austriaca	GLoc NHol NTow
carpatica	CRiv EPot MBal NNrd NRed NRya WAbe
– *alba*	CRiv EPot
cyanaster	NBir
¶ x *ganderi*	GLoc
hungarica	MBal MHig NHol NNrd SIng WDav
minima	GEdr MHig NNrd NRed WAbe WDav
¶ – *alba*	ITim
montana	CRiv GDra GEdr NKay NNrd NRed SIng WAbe WDav
pindicola	EPot GEdr MBal MBro NHar NHol NNrd NRed SIng WAbe WDav
¶ – *dimoniei*	EPot ITim
pusilla	CHar ITim NHol WDav
villosa	CHar CSun EBre MHig NNrd NRed NTow SOkd WOMN

SOLEIROLIA (Urticaceae)

soleirolii	CHEx CMer EPot LMay MBri WEas WOak
– 'Argentea'	See S. *s.* 'Variegata'
§ – 'Aurea'	CB&S CHEx CHoe CMer
– 'Golden Queen'	See S. *s.* 'Aurea'
– 'Silver Queen'	See S. *s.* 'Variegata'
§ – 'Variegata'	CB&S

SOLENOMELUS (Iridaceae)

sisyrinchium	NHol WDav

SOLENOPSIS (Campanulaceae)

¶ *auxillaris*	CSpe LHil LHop
¶ *erianthum*	CPle
* *hirsuta*	CPle

SOLENOSTEMON (Labiatae)

¶ *aromaticus*	CHal
¶ 'Beckwith's Gem'	CHal
¶ 'Crimson Ruffles'	CHal
¶ 'Glory of Luxembourg'	CHal
¶ 'Kiwi Fern'	CHal
¶ 'Lemondrop'	CHal
¶ *pentheri*	CHal
¶ 'Picturatum'	CHal
¶ 'Pineapple Beauty'	CHal
scutellarioides	MBri
¶ *thyrsoideus*	CHal
¶ 'Walter Turner'	CHal
¶ 'Winter Sun'	CHal

SOLIDAGO (Compositae)

altissima	See S. *canadensis scabra*
brachystachys	See S. *cutleri*
caesia	EBre EGol ERou NKay
canadensis	ELan
§ – *scabra*	WOak
'Cloth of Gold'	CKel CLew EBre ECro IDai MBri NBar WOld
'Crown of Rays' ('Strahlenkrone')	CHar CTom EBre ECtt ERou MRav NBar NHol SCro WWin
§ *cutleri*	CHar CLew EBre ELan EMon IDai MPit MTho MWat NGre NHol NKay NNrd NRoo NVic SCro SIng WHil WWin
flexicaulis 'Variegata'	See S. *latifolia* 'V.'
¶ *glomerata*	EMon

'Golden Baby' ('Goldkind') ECtt GAbr MBri MFir NCat NOak NOrc NRoo SFis SPla WEas WHil
'Golden Dwarf' ('Goldzwerg') CBow CSco EBre EFou EPar
'Golden Falls' IDai WOld
'Golden Shower' CKel MWat
'Golden Thumb' See S. 'Queenie'
'Golden Wings' LHil MWat
'Goldenmosa' CSco CShe ERou MWat MWgw NKay SChu SPer
hybrida See X SOLIDASTER ***luteus***
latifolia 'Variegata' CBos ELan EMon LHop NSti SFar
'Laurin' NHol
'Leda' SFis
'Lemore' See X SOLIDASTER ***luteus*** 'Lemore'
'Lesden' CSco IDai
'Loddon Gold' CSco
¶ ***microcephalus*** EMon
'Mimosa' NHol NKay NVic
minutissima CLew ITim MTho
¶ ***multiradiata scopulorum*** WDav
'Peter Pan' ERou
§ 'Queenie' CHoe CKel CLew CMal EBre ECha ECro ELan GCHN MBri MTho MWat NHol NKay NVic SPer WHal
spathulata nana JCA 9627 CLew CSun MBro NHol WDav
'Tom Thumb' CShe MRav WEas
virgaurea CArn CKin CRiv GPoy LHol NLan SIde WCla
– ***cambrica*** WCla
¶ – 'Variegata' WCot
* ***vulgaris*** 'Variegata' CHoe EFol

X SOLIDASTER (Compositae)

hybridus See X S. ***luteus***
§ ***luteus*** CAll CB&S COtt EFou WEas WHal
§ – 'Lemore' CChu CRow CSco CShe CTom EBre ECha EFou ELan ERou MUlv MWat NBar SPer

¶ X SOLIDAGO 'Super ' EFou EMon

SOLLYA (Pittosporaceae)

fusiformis See S. ***heterophylla***
§ ***heterophylla*** Widely available
– form WMar
parviflora ECou

SONCHUS (Compositae)

¶ ***platylepsis*** CHEx

SOPHORA (Leguminosae)

§ ***davidii*** SHil
japonica CB&S CLnd EHar ELan ENot ISea SExT SHil SLHN WNor
– 'Pendula' ELan LNet MBri SGar SHil
'Little Baby' IJoh NBar
¶ – – EHal
macrocarpa CHan ISea WBod
* ***macropoda*** G&K 4175 LSav
microphylla CGre ECou IBar LSav SArc SHil SLHN SSpi WBod
¶ – G&K 4178 LSav
– 'Dragon's Gold' ECou
– 'Earlygold' CB&S
– ***fulvida*** ECou
– 'Goldilocks' CB&S IBar
– ***longicarinata*** ECou
mollis SIgm
N ***prostrata*** CBot CChu ECou ITim
¶ – Pukaki form ECou
tetraptera CB&S CBot CCla CHEx CHan CMac CPle CTre ECou ELan IOrc ISea LHop SPer SSpi WBod WWat
– 'Gnome' CB&S ECou LHop
– 'Goughensis' WBod
– 'Grandiflora' SHil
viciifolia See S. ***davidii***

SORBARIA † (Rosaceae)

♦ ***aitchisonii*** See S. ***tomentosa***
♦ ***arborea*** See S. ***kirilowii***
¶ ***kirilowii*** CCor CHad CSco CShe IOrc MRav NNor SHil
lindleyana See S. ***tomentosa***
sorbifolia CCla CSco MR&S SLHN SPer SSta
§ ***tomentosa*** CB&S CCla CSco EFol EHal ELan ENot MBar MBri MRav NBar NHol SHil SLon SMad SPer SSpi SSta WBod WEas WWat

SORBUS † (Rosaceae)

alnifolia CMCN LSav SHil WCoo WNor WWat
americana CLnd GAbr LSav NWea SExT SHil
– 'Belmonte' MBri SExT
– ***erecta*** See S. ***decora***
anglica SSpi
'Apricot Lady' SHil SSpi
aria CBra CKin CLnd EHar GRei LBuc MBar NWea SHil SPer WMou
– 'Chrysophylla' MBri SExT SHil SMad SPer WAbe
– 'Decaisneana' See S. ***a.*** 'Majestica'
– 'Lutescens' CB&S CBow CBra CLnd CSam EGol EHar ELan ENot GRei IDai IJoh MBar MBri MGos MR&S NBar NWea SHil SMad SPer SReu WAbe WJas
– 'Magnifica' ENot SExT WJas
§ – 'Majestica' CLnd ELan ENot MGos SExT SHil SPer WJas
– 'Mitchellii' See S. ***thibetica*** 'John Mitchell'
aucuparia CB&S CBow CBra CKin CLnd CPer EHar ELan ENot GRei IDai IJoh ISea LBuc MBal MBar MBri MGos MR&S NBar NWea SHil SReu WAbe

– 'Aspleniifolia'	CB&S CBra CLnd EGol ENot GRei MBar MR&S MRav NWea SExT SHil SPer WAbe WJas
§ – 'Beissneri'	CLnd EHar MBri MGos SExT SHil WMou WWat
– 'Cardinal Royal'	SExT SHil
– 'Dirkenii'	CLnd COtt SMad WJas WMou
– 'Edulis'	ESim IOrc SExT SHil
– 'Fastigiata'	IOrc MBar MBri MGos SHil WMou
§ – 'Fructu Luteo'	CB&S ENot MBar MGos SExT
– gold form	MPar
– ***pluripinnata***	See S. ***scalaris***
– 'Sheerwater Seedling'	CB&S CBra CLnd ELan ENot IOrc MBri MGos MR&S SExT SHil SPer WAbe
¶ – 'Winterdown'	CNat
– 'Xanthocarpa'	See S. ***a.*** 'Fructu Luteo'
bristoliensis	CNat
'Carpet of Gold'	CBra CLnd IOrc SSpi
cashmiriana	Widely available
* – 'Molly Sanderson'	EBre
chamaemespilus	GAbr GDra
'Chinese Lace'	EHar MBri SExT SSpi WJas
§ ***commixta***	CB&S CBra CLnd CMCN CSam ENot GAbr GRei IJoh IOrc MBar MR&S MUlv NBar SExT SHil SPer WAbe WCoo WJas
– ***rufo-ferruginea***	WAbe
'Coral Beauty'	CLnd
cuspidata	CLnd CMCN SHil SSpi WCoo WWat
* ***decora*** 'Grootendorst'	MBri
discolor	CBra CLnd CMCN CSam ECtt ELan GRei IDai MBar MGos MR&S MUlv NWea SExT SPer SReu
domestica	EHar NWea SExT SHil SSpi WMou WThu
– 'Maliformis'	EHar
– 'Pyriformis'	EHar
'Eastern Promise'	SHil
'Embley'	CB&S CLnd ENot IHos MBri SExT SHil SSpi
esserteauiana	CSam ENot MPar SHil WAbe
– 'Flava'	SHil
'Ethel's Gold'	SHil
folgneri	SHil
forrestii	CChu CCor MBri SSpi WWat
¶ ***fruticosa***	CChu SSpi
'Ghose'	IOrc MBri SHil SPer
♦ ***glabrescens***	See S. ***hupehensis***
'Golden Wonder'	CBow MGos SExT SHil WAbe WJas
graeca	SSpi
* 'Harry Smith'	MBri
hedlundii	IBlr
x ***hostii***	ENot SPer
§ ***hupehensis***	Widely available
§ – ***obtusa***	ENot LSav MBri SHil SSpi SSta WWat
– 'Rosea'	See S. ***h. obtusa***
– 'Rufus'	LSav
hybrida	NWea
– 'Gibbsii'	MBri SExT SHil
insignis	SHil
intermedia	CB&S CKin CLnd ENot GRei ISea LSav MBal MGos MR&S NWea SExT SHil SPer
– 'Brouwers'	ELan SGar SHil
'Joseph Rock'	Widely available
x ***kewensis***	CSam SHil SPer SSpi
'Kirsten Pink'	CLnd MGos SSpi
koehneana	EBre EGol EHar MBri NHol NTow NWea SSpi
lanata	SSpi
lancastriensis	CNat
latifolia	EHal ENot LSav NWea SExT SSpi WAbe WThu
'Leonard Springer'	ENot
matsumarana	ENot IHos
megalocarpa	CBot CGre CMCN SHil SSpi WWat
* ***megalophylla***	LGre
meliosmifolia	SHil
moravica 'Laciniata'	See S. ***aucuparia*** 'Beissneri'
'November Pink'	IOrc NHol
'Pearly King'	SHil
pohuashanensis	CCla EHar GAbr IBar MBlu SSpi WNor
poteriifolia	SHil
§ ***prattii***	EHar NHol SSpi SSta WWat
– ***tatsienensis***	See S. ***p.***
randaiensis	SSpi WMou
'Red Marbles'	SHil
'Red Tip'	MGos NBar SSpi
reducta	Widely available
reflexipetala	See S. ***commixta***
rehderiana	MBal MBri WNor
– 'Pink Pearl'	LSav MBri WAbe
* – 'Rock's Yellow'	MBri
'Salmon Queen'	CLnd ECtt SSpi
sargentiana	CBot CLnd CSam EHar ENot IHos MBri NHol NWea SHil SMad SPer SSpi WJas WWat
§ ***scalaris***	CCor CSam ECtt IJoh IOrc MBri NHol SHil SPer SSpi WWat
'Schouten'	ENot MBlu MBri
'Signalman'	SPer
sp. HS 12799	CChu
'Sunshine'	LSav SExT SHil SSpi WJas
thibetica	CGre CMCN SHil SSpi
§ – 'John Mitchell'	CLnd EHar ENot MBri MGos NBar SExT SHil SMad SPer SSpi
x ***thuringiaca*** 'Fastigiata'	CB&S CBra CLnd ENot MBri MR&S SExT SHil SPer
torminalis	CKin CLnd EHar LSav MBri NWea SHil SPer SSpi SSta WCoo WMou WThu
'Tundra'	SHil
umbellata cretica	See S. ***graeca***
ursina	IOrc SSpi
vestita	CLnd
vexans	CNat
vilmorinii	Widely available

'White Wax' CBow ECtt MGos SHil
'Wilfrid Fox' SHil
willmottiana CNat
'Winter Cheer' SHil WWat
zahlbruckneri SSpi

SORGHASTRUM (Gramineae)
avenaceum CHoe ECha
nutans See S. ***avenaceum***

SORGHUM (Gramineae)
¶ *halepense* SApp

SPARAXIS (Iridaceae)
elegans 'Coccinea' LBow
hybrids LAma LBlo
tricolor EPar MBri

SPARGANIUM (Sparganiaceae)
§ *erectum* CRow CWGN LMay MSta WHer
ramosum See S. ***erectum***

SPARMANNIA (Tiliaceae)
africana CHEx CPle CSun CTre ERea MBri SArc WOak

SPARTINA (Gramineae)
pectinata
'Aureomarginata' CHoe EBre ECha EFou EGol ELan EMon ERou GWic MSta NHol SHig SPer SSpi
¶ – 'Variegata' SApp

SPARTIUM (Leguminosae)
junceum Widely available

SPARTOCYTISUS (Leguminosae)
nubigenus See S. ***supranubius***
§ *supranubius* SHil

SPATHICARPA (Araceae)

SPATHIPHYLLUM (Araceae)
'Adagio' MBri
'Viscount' MBri
wallisii MBri

SPEIRANTHA (Liliaceae/Convallariaceae)
§ *convallarioides* EBul EMon GWic SLHN SSpi WCot
gardenii See S. ***convallarioides***

SPERGULARIA (Caryophyllaceae)
rupicola CKin CRiv

SPHACELE (Labiatae)
chamaedryoides See LEPECHINIA ***c.***

SPHAERALCEA (Malvaceae)
(Malvaceae)
ambigua ELan LGre SMrm

fendleri CBot CHad CHan CMHG CMer CSun EOrc LGre LHop SAxl SMrm WAbe WMar WOMN
– *venusta* CBot CSun LHop WSHC
¶ *malviflora* WPer
miniata CMHG ELan LGre SMrm
munroana CBot CHan CMHG CSev CSun EOrc GAbr LGre LHop MPar MUlv NTow SAxl SMrm WEas WHea WMar WOMN WSHC WWin
¶ – pale pink form SMrm
¶ *parvifolia* LHop
* *prostrata* WOld

SPHENOTOMA (Epacridaceae)
gracilis CSun

SPIGELIA (Loganiaceae)
marilandica MSal

SPILANTHES (Compositae)
acmella MSal

SPIRAEA † (Rosaceae)
albiflora See S. ***japonica*** 'Albiflora'
arborea See SORBARIA ***kirilowii***
arcuata MBri MR&S
§ 'Arguta' Widely available
x *arguta* 'Bridal Wreath' See S. 'Arguta'
– 'Compacta' See S. x ***cinerea***
– *nana* See S. x ***cinerea***
bella ISea MBar WHCG
* *betonicifolia* WPer
betulifolia MBri MRav WHCG WPer WWeb
– *aemiliana* CCla CMHG EBre ECtt EGol IJoh MPla SSta
x *billiardii* 'Macrothyrsa' CB&S
– 'Triumphans' ENot NNor SHil WWin
x *bumalda* See S. ***japonica***
– 'Crispa' See S. ***japonica*** 'Crispa'
– *wulfenii* See S. ***japonica*** 'Walluf'
callosa 'Alba' See S. ***japonica*** 'Albiflora'
canescens EGol WPer
cantoniensis 'Lanceata' CFor EMon
§ x *cinerea* MR&S SSta WAbe WEas
– 'Grefsheim' CB&S CShe ECtt MBri MR&S SHil SPer SPla SSta
crispifolia See S. ***japonica*** 'Bullata'
decumbens EBre MBri
douglasii NRoo
fritschiana LHop WHCG
hendersonii See PETROPHYTUM ***hendersonii***
japonica 'Alba' See S. ***j.*** 'Albiflora'
§ – 'Albiflora' CB&S CBow CPle ESis MBal MPla MR&S NRoo SChu SHil SPer WEas
*– 'Allgold' COtt
– 'Alpina' See S. ***j.*** 'Nana'
– 'Anthony Waterer' Widely available

§ – 'Bullata'	CMHG ELan GHig MBal MBar MBri MBro MPla MR&S NKay NRoo SHil SIng SLon SPer SPla SReu SSta WBod WSHC WThu
– 'Coccinea'	IDai
§ – 'Crispa'	CMHG EPla MBar MBri
– 'Dart's Red'	IOrc MBri NBar SSta
– 'Froebelii'	GRei ISea LBuc
– 'Glenroy Gold'	MBal WAbe
– 'Gold Mound'	CBow CMHG CRow CShe EGol EHar ELan EPla IJoh MBar MBri MGos MRav NRoo SChu SIng SPer SPla WHCG WSHC
– 'Gold Rush '	EBar WRus
– 'Golden Dome'	SHil
– 'Golden Princess'	CCla CHoe CRow CSco EBre ELan GRei IJoh IOrc MPla MUlv NHol NRoo SPer SPla SReu SSta
– 'Goldflame'	Widely available
¶ – 'Little Maid'	CBot
– 'Little Princess'	Widely available
§ – 'Nana'	CBow CSco ENot MBri MPla SHil SPla WEas WHCG WPat WWeb
– 'Nyewoods'	ELan LHop MBal MBri MTho NHol NKay NNor NRya WDav WPer
¶ – 'Pamela Harper'	SPla
– 'Pink Ice'	CHoe EFol EGol ELan LHop MBri SLon SMrm
– 'Ruberrima'	NKay
– 'Shirobana'	Widely available
¶ – 'Shirobana sport'	EPla
§ – 'Walluf'	CPle NNor SLon WHCG
– 'Wyndbrook Gold'	NHol WPat
'Margaritae'	GHig NKay SPer
nipponica	CB&S ERav MBar MGos WHCG WPer
– 'Halward's Silver'	LHop
– 'June Bride'	WHCG
– 'Rotundifolia'	ISea
– 'Snowmound'	Widely available
– tosaensis	CSam LHop LSav MR&S MWat NHol SCro SHil SPer SReu WBod WHCG WWat
palmata elegans	See FILIPENDULA ***palmata*** 'Elegantissima'
§ ***prunifolia***	CCla CSco CShe EHar ELan ENot LHop MPla MRav SPer WBod WHCG
– 'Plena'	See S. ***prunifolia***
salicifolia	MRav
sp. B&L 12210	LSav
¶ sp. B&L 12325	LSav
stevenii	SPer SPla
thunbergii	CBow CCla CPle CSco EHar ELan ENot IOrc ISea LHop MBri MPla MRav NNor NWea SHil SIng SLon SMad SPer
trilobata	NHol
ulmaria	See FILIPENDULA ***ulmaria***
x ***vanhouttei***	CB&S ELan ENot GRei IDai IJoh IOrc MBal MBar MR&S MRav MWat NHol NKay NNor NRoo SHil SLon SMad SPer SPla WWin
veitchii	MBal MRav SHil
venusta 'Magnifica'	See FILIPENDULA ***rubra*** 'Venusta Magnifica'
wilsonii	CHan

SPIRODELA (Lemnaceae)

SPODIOPOGON (Gramineae)

¶ ***sibiricus***	SApp

SPRAGUEA (Portulacaceae)

§ ***umbellata glandulifera***	NGre

SPREKELIA (Liliaceae/Amaryllidaceae)

formosissima	CAvo LAma LBow LHop

STACHYS (Labiatae)

§ ***affinis***	GPoy
alpina	CKin MSal NLan
betonica	See S. ***officinalis***
§ ***byzantina***	Widely available
§ – 'Big Ears'	EMon SApp
§ – 'Cotton Boll'	CBre CHar CRow EBre ECha EFou EMon EPla GAbr GWic LSav NVic SPer
– large-leaved form	See S. ***b.*** 'Big Ears'
– 'Margery Fish'	CHar
– 'Primrose Heron'	CRow EBre EHal GGar GHig NHol NSti SPer
– 'Sheila McQueen'	See S. ***b.*** 'Cotton Boll'
– 'Silver Carpet'	CB&S CFis CGle CHad CHoe CKel CSco CShe EBre ECha EFou EGol ELan EOrc ERou LGro MBri MCot MWgw NOrc SApp SPer WHea
– 'Striped Phantom'	EMon
– 'Variegata'	CHan CRow EFol ELan GPla NPer NRar SApp WRus
candida	MPar WOMN WPer
chrysantha	CHar LGre
citrina	GWic MPar WHea WHil
coccinea	CCor CGle CHan CSun EMon SAxl WEas WHea
densiflora	See S. ***monieri***
§ ***discolor***	EGol MBri MCas WPer
germanica	CNat
grandiflora	See S. ***macrantha***
¶ ***iva***	ESis NTow
lanata	See S. ***byzantina***
§ ***macrantha***	CCla CKel CLew CShe ECha GGar MBro MPar MWgw NOak NOrc WEas WHal WHoo WOld WWin
– 'Nivea'	EGol GWic NTow WPer
– 'Robusta'	ELan EMon SApp SPer
– rosea	CHad CKel CRiv CSco EFol EFou ELan MBri SCro SPer WEas WOld WPer
– 'Rosea Compacta'	WOld

– *superba*	CGle CHan CHar EPla MBri WHil
§ *officinalis*	CArn CKin CSev Effi GPoy LHil MChe MSal MWgw NLan SIde SIng WCla WHal WHer WSto
– *alba*	CBre CFis NHol SIng
– 'Rosea Superba'	ECha EFou EGol ELan ERou
olympica	See S. ***byzantina***
palustris	CKin MSta NLan
spicata	See S. ***grandiflora***
sylvatica	CArn CKin GPoy NLan WCla WHer
tuberifera	See S. ***affinis***

STACHYTARPHETA (Verbenaceae)

jamaicensis	SLMG

STACHYURUS (Stachyuraceae)

chinensis	CGre CMCN GWic MBri MUlv SHil WBod WCoo WWat
– 'Magpie'	CBot CBow CRow EGol ELan LGre MBri SHil SSpi SSus
leucotrichus	SSpi
praecox	CB&S CBot CBow CCla CFis CSco EGol EHar ELan ENot IOrc MBar MBri SHil SPer SPla SReu SSpi SSta WCoo WSHC WWat
rubriflorus	CKni SSpi

STAEHELINA (Compositae)

uniflosculosa	LGre

STANLEYA (Cruciferae)

STAPHYLEA (Staphyleaceae)

bumalda	WCoo
colchica	CB&S CCla IOrc MCot SHil WKif WSHC WWat
holocarpa	CHil WWat
– *rosea*	EHar ENot IHos SHil WSHC
pinnata	ELan WNor
trifolia	CMCN

STATICE See **LIMONIUM**

STAUNTONIA (Lardizabalaceae)

hexaphylla	CChu CCla CHEx CHil SBra SHil SLon SPer SSpi SSta WSHC

STEIRODISCUS (Compositae)

* *euryopoides*	CKni

STELLARIA (Caryophyllaceae)

graminea	CKin
holostea	CKin MChe NLan
¶ *ruscifolia*	ITim

STENANTHIUM (Liliaceae/Melanthiaceae)

STENOCHLAENA (Blechnaceae)

palustris	MBri

STENOTAPHRUM (Gramineae)

secundatum	
'Variegatum'	CMer CSun IBlr

STEPHANANDRA (Rosaceae)

incisa	CB&S CGle CLan CShe IOrc MPar SChu SHil SPla WHCG
§ – 'Crispa'	Widely available
– 'Prostrata'	See S. ***i.*** 'Crispa'
tanakae	CCla CGle CSco EGol ELan IOrc LAbb MBar MPar MUlv NHol NNor SChu SHil SLon SPer SPla STre WBod WHCG

STEPHANOTIS (Asclepiadaceae)

floribunda	CB&S EBak MBri SLMG

STERNBERGIA (Amaryllidaceae)

candida	CBro ECam LAma
clusiana	ECam ELan EPot LAma SIng WChr
colchiciflora	WChr
fischeriana	EPot LAma
lutea	CBro CHan ECam ELan EPot LAma LBlo LBow MBri MPar SDix SIng SLHN SPou WChr WThu
– Angustifolia group	EMon SPou
macrantha	See S. ***clusiana***
sicula	CBro ECam EPot SPou WThu
– JRM 3186	WThu
– 'Dodona Form'	WChr

STEWARTIA † (Theaceae)

koreana	See S. ***pseudocamellia k.***
malacodendron	CCla MBri SHil SPer SSpi SSta WWat
monadelpha	CB&S ELan SPer SSpi SSta WCoo WNor
ovata	CB&S CGre MUlv SHil SSpi WNor WWat
N– *grandiflora*	SPer SSta
pseudocamellia	CB&S CBow CCla CGre EHar IOrc LHyd LSav MBri MUlv SGar SHil SMad SPer SReu SSpi SSta WBod WNor WWat
– *koreana*	CGre CMCN MBri SHil SPer SSpi SSta WNor WWat
serrata	CB&S CCla LSav MBri SHil SPer SSpi SSta WCoo WNor WWat
sinensis	CCla EHar LSav MBri SHil SSpi SSta WBod WNor WWat

STICTOCARDIA (Convolvulaceae)

beraviensis	MNew

STIPA (Gramineae)

arundinacea	CElw CHoe CRow CSam CTom EBar ECha EFol EFou EMon EPla GWic IBar IBlr LHop MFir NSti SAxl SSpi WCar
– 'Autumn Tints'	ECou
– 'Gold Hue'	CHoe ECou
¶ *atropurpurea*	WPer

∗ ***brachytricha***	CHoe
§ ***calamagrostis***	CHoe ECha EMon GWic NSti SApp SHil WHea
capillata	EFou
gigantea	Widely available
lasiagrostis	See S. ***calamagrostis***
pennata	CB&S GArf MWgw SHil SPou WHoo
§ ***splendens***	CKel EFou MCot MPar NHol NKay SDix SFir
tenacissima	CHoe
¶ ***tenuifolia***	CElw
¶ ***tenuissima***	EMon
¶ ***turkestanica***	GWic

STOKESIA (Compositae)

laevis	CChu ECha EHal ELan NNor NRoo SAxl SCro WRus
– ***alba***	CChu EMon LGre MBri NRoo SMrm
– 'Blue Star'	CGle CHan CKel CSam CSco CShe EFou EGol ELan LGre MBri MFir MTho MUlv NBar NHol NOak NRoo SChu SMrm SPer WWin
– 'Wyoming'	EBre ERou NOak

STRANVAESIA (Rosaceae)

davidiana	See PHOTINIA ***davidiana***

X STRANVINIA (Rosaceae)

'Redstart'	See PHOTINIA 'Redstart'

STRATIOTES (Hydrocharitaceae)

aloides	CHEx CRow CWGN EHon EWav LMay MSta WOak

STRAWBERRY See **FRAGARIA** x ***ananassa***

STRAWBERRY, Alpine See **FRAGARIA** ***vesca***

STRELITZIA (Strelitziaceae)

nicolai	LPal
reginae	CCla CHEx ERea IBlr LPal MNew WCar

STREPTOCARPUS (Gesneriaceae)

'Albatross'	WEfe
'Amanda'	WEfe
¶ 'Anna'	EPla
¶ 'Athena'	WEfe
'Blue Gem'	WEfe
¶ 'Blue Nymph'	EPla
candidus	WEfe
'Carol'	MBri WEfe
caulescens	WEfe
– ***pallescens***	WEfe
'Cobalt Nymph'	MBri
'Concord Blue'	MBri WEfe
'Constant Nymph Seedling'	MPit WEfe
cyanandrus	WEfe
'Cynthia'	MBri WEfe
'Diana'	WEfe
'Eira'	WEfe
'Elsi'	EPla WEfe
'Falling Stars'	MBri WEfe
fanniniae	WEfe
'Fiona'	WEfe
gardenii	WEfe
glandulosissimus	WEfe
¶ 'Gloria'	WEfe
grandis	MNew
'Heidi'	MBri WEfe
'Helen'	WEfe
hybrids	LAbb
'Joanna'	MBri WEfe
¶ ***johannis***	EPla
'Julie'	WEfe
¶ 'Kim'	WEfe
'Lisa'	MBri WEfe
'Lynne'	WEfe
'Marie'	WEfe
'Mini Nymph'	WEfe
'Myba'	MBri
'Neptune'	MBri
¶ 'New Buckenham'	EPla
'Nicola'	MBri WEfe
¶ 'Olga'	EPla
'Paula'	MBri WEfe
primulifolius formosus	WEfe
rexii	WEfe
'Rosebud'	MPit WEfe
'Ruby'	MBri WEfe
'Sandra'	MBri WEfe
'Sarah'	WEfe
saxorum	MBri MNew WEfe
'Snow White'	WEfe
¶ ***solenanthus***	EPla
'Stella'	WEfe
'Susan'	WEfe
'Tina'	MBri WEfe
'Weismoor Red'	MBri WEfe
'Winifred'	WEfe

STREPTOPUS (Liliaceae/Convallariaceae)

roseus	LAma

STREPTOSOLEN (Solanaceae)

jamesonii	CGre CPle CSev CSun ERea IBlr LAbb MNew NRog SLMG WBod WHea
– yellow form	ERea

STROBILANTHES (Acanthaceae)

atropurpureus	CBot CHan CPle EBre ECha ECro EFou EHal ELan GWic LAbb SAxl SBor SMrm SSus SSvw WOld WPer
♦ ***attenuatus***	See PTERACANTHUS ***a.***
dyerianus	MBri
sp. from Nepal TSS	SWas
violaceus	ERea LHop

STROMANTHE (Marantaceae)

amabilis	MBri
'Freddy'	MBri
sanguinea	MBri
'Stripestar'	MBri

STUARTIA See **STEWARTIA**

STYLIDIUM (Stylidiaceae)
graminifolium alpine form — WDav

STYLOPHORUM (Papaveraceae)
diphyllum — CHar LAma SBar SSpi WCar WCru WRus
lasiocarpum — CSun SAxl SWas WCru

STYPHELIA (Epacridaceae)
§ *colensoi* — CGre ECou EPot GWic ITim MBal MBar MBri MPla MPlt NHol SIng SSpi WAbe WBod WDav WPat WSHC WWat

STYRAX (Styracaceae)
dasyantha — CMCN SBor
hemsleyana — CChu CCla LHyd LSav MBri SHil SSpi
japonica — Widely available
– 'Benibana' — ELan SPer SSpi SSta
– 'Pendula' — SSpi SSta
obassia — CChu CCla CFor CMCN LSav MBri SHil SSpi SSta WNor WWat
wilsonii — SHil

SUCCISA (Dipsacaceae)
Orkney dwarf form — CSun
§ *pratensis* — CArn CKin ITim MFir MHig MSal NLan SFir WHil WOak
– dwarf form — GDra MTho NGre NTow WDav

SUNBERRY See **RUBUS** Sunberry

SUTERA (Scrophulariaceae)
* *pristisepala* — SIgm

SUTHERLANDIA (Leguminosae)
frutescens — CGre SMrm WHer WPer
* *montana* — CCor SAxl SIgm

SWAINSONA (Leguminosae)
¶ *procumbens* — WPer

SWERTIA (Gentianaceae)
¶ *perennis* — WPer
¶ *petiolata* — EBar

X SYCOPARROTIA (Hamamelidaceae)
semidecidua — CKni SSta

SYCOPSIS (Hamamelidaceae)
sinensis — CTre EHar SBor SHil SSpi SSta WBod WSHC
tutcheri — SSta

SYMPHORICARPOS (Caprifoliaceae)
albus — CGre CKin CMer ENot MBri NWea WWin
– 'Constance Spry' — MUlv
§ – *laevigatus* — CB&S ENot GRei LBuc MBar NKay SHil
– 'Turesson' — MBar
*– 'Variegatus' — CMer
x *chenaultii* 'Hancock' — CB&S CMer CSco EGol ELan ENot GRei IJoh MBar MBri MR&S MRav MWat SCro SHil SPer
x *doorenbosii* 'Erect' — SHil
– 'Magic Berry' — CSco ENot ERav MBar MR&S NKay SHil
– 'Mother of Pearl' — CBow CSco ECha ELan ENot IJoh MBar MGos MR&S NWea SHil SPer
– 'White Hedge' — CSco ELan ENot ERav LBuc MR&S NWea SHil SPer
orbiculatus — SHil
♦– 'Albovariegatus' — See S. *o.* 'Taff's White'
♦– 'Argenteovariegatus' — See S. *o.* 'Taff's White'
– 'Bowles' Golden Variegated' — EPla
– 'Foliis Variegatis' — CB&S CHoe CPle EHal EHar ELan LHop MBal SCro SHil SSpi WWin
§ – 'Taff's White' — Widely available
– 'Variegatus' — See S. *o.* 'Foliis Variegatis'
rivularis — See S. *albus laevigatus*

SYMPHYANDRA (Campanulaceae)
armena — ELan EPad LGan MBro MPar NHol WPer
cretica alba — NTow
hofmannii — CCla CFis CGle CHan CRiv ECro ELan EPad ERou ITim MPar MTho NHol NSti SAxl SIng WPer WWin
ossettica — CGle CLew EPad MTho SWas
pendula — ELan EPad SBar WPer
wanneri — EPad LGan MPar NHol WOMN WPer WWin

SYMPHYTUM † (Boraginaceae)
asperum — ELan EMon
caucasicum — CCla CCor CFis CHad CHan CSco ECha EPad EPar GPoy MBri NKay SAxl SSpi WEas WHer WOak WSto
– 'Eminence' — EMon
§ 'Goldsmith' — CFor CHad CHan CLew CSev ECha EFol ELan EMon EOrc EPar EPla ERav GPla LHop MBri NOrc NRoo SAxl SChu SSpi SWas WHer WRus
grandiflorum — See S. *ibericum*
'Hidcote Blue' — EMon EPla MBri NHol NSti SChu WHea
§ 'Hidcote Pink' — CGle EBre EPla ERav LHol LHop NSti SAxl SChu WSto
'Hidcote Variegated' — CGle ECha
§ *ibericum* — Widely available
– 'Jubilee' — ELan ERav LHop WCru
– 'Lilacinum' — CCla CFis WHer
♦– 'Variegatum' — See S. 'Goldsmith'
'Langthorns Pink' — ELan EMon GWic
officinale — CArn CKin CSev CShe EJud Effi GPoy LHol MChe MSal NPer SIde WHer WOak WSto

– 'Bohemicum'	SIng
orientale	EMon WSto
peregrinum	See S. x *uplandicum*
¶ 'Pink Robins'	EMon
'Roseum'	See S. 'Hidcote Pink'
'Rubrum'	CCla CSco ECha ELan EOrc EPar NRoo NSti SChu SPer WSto
tuberosum	CBre GPoy MFir NHol NSti WHer WSto
§ x *uplandicum*	CGle CLew CRow CSco CSev Effi MSal NSel SCro WSto WWin
– 'Variegatum'	CArn CBot CChu CGle CHad CHan CMHG CSam CSco CSev ECha EFol EGol ELan EOrc LHop MWgw SChu SPer SSpi WEas WRus WSto WWat

SYMPLOCARPUS (Araceae)

foetidus	MSal

SYMPLOCOS (Symplocaceae)

paniculata	ELan LSav SHil SSpi WBod

SYNEILESIS (Compositae)

palmata	SSpi

SYNGONIUM (Araceae)

'Jenny'	MBri
'Maya Red'	MBri
podophyllum 'Silver Knight'	MBri
– 'Variegatum'	MBri
'White Butterfly'	MBri

SYNTHYRIS (Scrophulariaceae)

missurica stellata	GGar
reniformis	IBlr

SYRINGA † (Oleaceae)

afghanica	See S. *protolaciniata*
♦ *amurensis*	See S. *reticulata a.*
x *chinensis* 'Saugeana'	SHil SPer
¶ + *correlata*	IOrc
emodi	CBot WHCG
¶ – 'Aurea'	EPla
'Fountain'	CBrd SHil
x *henryi*	SCro
x *hyacinthiflora* 'Blue Hyacinth'	MR&S
– 'Clarke's Giant'	ELan
– 'Esther Staley'	CSco ENot SFam SHil
x *josiflexa* 'Bellicent'	CSco EGol ELan ENot EPad ISea MBal MBar MGos MR&S MRav MUlv SChu SHil SMad SPer SPla SSta WHCG
¶ – 'Lynette'	EPla
josikaea	SPer SSpi WHCG
julianae	SHil
laciniata	CBot CBow CCla CHan LSav MBri NHol SChu SHil SReu WHCG WKif
§ *meyeri* 'Palibin'	Widely available
microphylla	CPle CSco
– 'Superba'	Widely available
palibiniana	See S. *meyeri* 'Palibin'
§ *patula*	CCla ELan IHos IJoh IOrc LNet LSav MBal MPar MR&S MWat NRoo SHil SPer SPla SSta WHCr
pekinensis	CBot
x *persica*	CMHG CSco EHal ERav ISea LSav MGos MPar MWat SHil SPer SPla WWat WWin
– 'Alba'	CBot LSav MR&S SHil SPla WSHC
– *laciniata*	See S. *laciniata*
pinnatifolia	CBot CBrd CHan
x *prestoniae* 'Audrey'	MGos SPer
¶ – 'Coral'	MBri
– 'Elinor'	CMHG CSco EGol ENot SCro SHil SPer
– 'Isabella'	MGos SHil
¶ – 'James Macfarlane'	MBri
– 'Kim'	MBri
¶ – 'Nocturne'	MBri
– 'Redwine'	MBri
§ *protolaciniata*	CChu CGre CSco EPla ERav ESis IBar MPar MPla WSHC WWeb
reflexa	EGol LSav MBar MGos MRav NKay SHil SSpi
reticulata	CMCN
§ – *amurensis*	CCla LSav WCoo
¶ – 'Ivory Silk'	MBri
♦ – *mandshurica*	See S. *r. amurensis*
sweginzowii	CSam MBal SBla SCro SPer WWat
– 'Superba'	SHil
tomentella	CCla IJoh SSta
velutina	See S. *patula*
villosa	LSav
vulgaris	CShe GRei LBuc NNor NWea
– 'Andenken an Ludwig Späth'	CB&S CSco ECtt ENot IJoh IOrc MBar MBri MGos NWea SDix SHil SPer
* – 'Aurea'	EMon EPla MRav
– 'Belle de Nancy' (d)	ECtt ELan MBri MR&S
– 'Charles Joly' (d)	CB&S CBow CBra CSam CSco ELan ENot GRei IDai IHos IJoh IOrc LHol LNet MBal MBar MBri MR&S MRav NWea SHil SPer WAbe
– 'Condorcet' (d)	LNet
– 'Congo'	ENot
¶ – 'Edward J Gardner' (d)	SHil
– 'Firmament'	CSco ELan ENot SHil SPer
– 'Glory of Horstenstein'	See S. *v.* 'Ruhm von Horstenstein'
– 'Katherine Havemeyer' (d)	CB&S CCor CSco ELan ENot GRei IDai MBri MGos MRav SFam SHil SPer SReu
– 'Madame Antoine Buchner' (d)	CSco ENot MR&S SFam SHil SReu

- 'Madame Lemoine' (d) CB&S CBow CBra CSco ELan ENot GRei IDai IJoh LHol LNet MBal MBar MBri MGos NWea SDix SFam SHil SPer SPla SReu WAbe
- 'Masséna' ENot SFam SPer
- 'Maud Notcutt' CSco ENot SFam SHil SPer
- 'Michel Buchner' (d) CB&S CBow ECtt ENot GRei IHos IJoh IOrc LHol MBar MBri MR&S NBar SHil
- 'Mrs Edward Harding' (d) ECtt ENot LNet MBri MGos MRav SFam SHil SPer SReu
- 'Paul Thirion' (d) SHil
- 'Président Grévy' (d) NTow
- 'Primrose' CBow CBra CCla CSco EGol ELan ENot SFam SHil SPer WAbe
- 'Sensation' CSco ENot SHil SPer
- 'Souvenir de Louis Spaeth' See S. *v.* 'Andenken an Ludwig Späth'
- variegated double EFol
- 'Vestale' ENot SDix SHil

yunnanensis ELan WBod
- 'Rosea' ISea SHil

TACITUS (Crassulaceae)

bellus MBri

TAIWANIA (Taxodiaceae)

cryptomerioides SHil

TALINUM (Portulacaceae)

calycinum NGre
okanoganense ITim NGre SIng SOkd WOMN
¶ – pink stem form SOkd
parviflorum NGre
¶ ***rugospermum*** EPot
spinescens NGre SIng WOMN
¶ ***teretifolium*** NWCA
* 'Zoe' GLoc SIng

TAMARIX (Tamaricaceae)

africana WWin
gallica ENot SArc SHil
germanica See MYRICARIA ***germanica***
§ ***parviflora*** CB&S IOrc SHil WPat
pentandra CBra CSco CShe ELan ISea LAbb MBri MUlv SHil SMrm WWeb
ramosissima 'Pink Cascade' ENot MBri MR&S
- 'Rubra' CSco ENot IOrc MGos MR&S SHil SLon SPer WPat

tetrandra CBow CBra CMHG CSco ELan ENot LNet MWat NNor SHil SLon SPer SReu SSta WAbe WBod WWeb
- 'Purpurea' See T. ***parviflora***

TAMUS (Dioscoreaceae)

communis CArn

TANACETUM † (Compositae)

§ ***argenteum*** IDai MTho NTow SAsh SSmi
¶ – ***canum*** CKni MBri
balsamita See BALSAMITA ***major***
§ ***cinerariifolium*** CArn GPoy WOak
§ ***coccineum*** GPoy MSal WWin
- 'Brenda' MWat
- 'Eileen May Robinson' MWat NBar WRus
- 'James Kelway' MBri NBar
¶ – 'King Size' MPit
¶ – 'Robinson's Pink' NRoo
- 'Sam Robinson' MWat
- 'Scarlet Glow' MWat
- 'Snow Cloud' EFou MWat

§ ***corymbosum*** CGle EBre ECha EMon GWic WHil
densum ELan WWeb
– ***amani*** CHoe ECha EFol EFou ELan EOrc EPot ERav ESis GPla LSav MCas MPar MPla MPlt MWat NNrd NRoo NSti SIng SSmi WHoo WRus WThu
§ ***haradjanii*** CFis CGle CSam CSun ELan EMNN GCHN LGro MCot NKay NNor SAxl SBla SChu WEas WHil WPat WPer WSHC
§ ***herderi*** CFis EFol LHop MPar NRoo SChu
§ ***macrophyllum*** EMon GWic MCot
pallidum spathulifolium See LEUCANTHEMOPSIS ***pallida spathulifolia***
§ ***parthenium*** CArn CKin EEls EJud Effi GPoy LHol MChe NRoo NSel SIde WHer WOak
– ***aureum*** CRow ECha EEls EFou ELan ERav MBri MChe MCot NHol NSel NSti SIng SMad SPer SPla WBon WEas WHal WHer WHil WOak WWin
- 'Ball's Double White' CBre
¶ – double white EPad
- 'Golden Moss' GWic LHil
- 'Plenum' EPad MBri MFir NSel NSti SIng WBon WHil WOMN WOak
§ – 'Rowallane' CHan ELan EMon GWic SIng
♦ – 'Sissinghurst White' See T. ***p.*** 'Rowallane'
- 'Snowball' ELan
- 'White Bonnet' CGle CHan ECha ELan EMon ERav GWic MCot WEas

praeteritum ECha
§ ***ptarmiciflorum*** EMon MCot
vulgare CArn CCor CSFH CSev EEls EJud Effi LHol MBar MChe MSal NLan NSel SIde SPer WCla WHal WOak
– ***crispum*** ELan GPla GWic MBri WHil WSto
- 'Silver Lace' EMon

TANAKAEA (Saxifragaceae)

radicans ELan NHol

TANGELO See **CITRUS** x *tangelo*

TANGERINE See **CITRUS** *reticulata* Tangerine group

TANGOR See **CITRUS** x *nobilis*

TARAXACUM (Compositae)
¶ *albidum* NRar
officinale LHol SIde

TASMANNIA (Winteraceae)
§ *aromatica* CChu CCla CMHG CPle CTrw ECou ELan IDai ISea MBal SBor SCro SPer SSta WBod
– (f) CTre
– (m) CTre
lanceolata See T. *aromatica*

TAXODIUM (Taxodiaceae)
ascendens See T. *distichum*
§ *distichum* Widely available
– *nutans* EHar IOrc MBlu SHil
– 'Pendens' SHil

TAXUS † (Taxaceae)
baccata Widely available
– 'Adpressa' SHil
– 'Adpressa Aurea' MPla WMou
– 'Adpressa Variegata' EHul SHil
– 'Amersfoort' MBri SSpi
– 'Argentea Minor' NHol SHil
– 'Aurea' CGre SExT SHil
*– 'Aurea Pendula' ENHC
*– 'Aureomarginata' CBra ENHC WCon
– 'Cheshuntensis' LSav
¶ – 'Compacta' EPla
– 'Corley's Copper Tip' CDoC CKen CSam EBre EHul NHol
¶ – 'David' WMou
– 'Dovastoniana' CDoC CMac IJoh ISea MBar NWea SHil SMad WAbe WBod WMou
– 'Dovastonii Aurea' CBow CDoC CMac EBre EHul IJoh LHol LSav MBar MBri SHil SLon SMad SPer SReu WCon WMou
*– 'Drinkstone Gold' EHul
– 'Elegantissima' MPla NKay NWea SHil
§ – 'Fastigiata' CB&S CBow CDoC CMac CSco EHar EHul ENHC ENot GRei IJoh ISea LNet MBar MBri MGos MWat SExT SHil SPer WAbe WCon WMou WWin
– 'Fastigiata Aurea' EHar EHul IHos IJoh LLin NRoo SPla WAbe
– 'Fastigiata Aureomarginata' CBow CDoC CMac CSco EHul GRei IDai ISea LHol MBal MBar MBri MGos MR&S MWat NHol NKay NWea SHil SSta WMou
– 'Fastigiata Robusta' EBre EPla NHol WMou
– 'Glauca' LSav
– 'Glenroy New Penny' MBal
– 'Gracilis Pendula' LSav WCon
– 'Hibernica' See T. *b.* 'Fastigiata'
– 'Lutea' MR&S SHil
– 'Nutans' CKen LLin MBar
– 'Overeynderi' EHul
*– 'Pendula' MBal
– 'Pumila Aurea' MBri
– 'Pygmaea' IOrc SHil
– 'Repandens' CDoC EHul ENHC MBar SHil SPer
– 'Repens Aurea' CDoC CHig CKen CMHG CSco EBre EHul ENHC LLin MBar MBri MGos MPla NHol SHil SPer SPla
– 'Rushmore' LSav
– 'Semperaurea' CB&S CBra CMac EBre EHul ENHC ENot IJoh LHol MBal MBar MBri MGos NHol NWea SHil SPla WCon WWin
– 'Silver Spire' CB&S CKen
– 'Standishii' CDoC CHoe CKen CSco EBre EHar EHul ENHC IJoh IOrc LLin LNet MBal MBar MBri MGos MPla MWat NHol SHil SPer WAbe WCon WMou
– 'Strait Hedge' EHul WCon WMou
– 'Summergold' CBra CDoC CSco EBre EHul ENHC ENot IDai IJoh IOrc MBar MBri MGos MR&S NHol NRoo SPer WCon
– 'Variegata' See T. *b.* 'Aurea'
*– 'Windsor Gold' EHul
cuspidata 'Aurescens' EPla
– 'Golden Jubilee' LRHS MBri
– 'Luteobaccata' EPla
– 'Minima' LSav
– *nana* CDoC EHul EPot LLin MBar NHol
x *media* 'Brownii' EHul
– 'Hicksii' CBow CSco ENHC LNet LPan MBar NHol SExT SHil WCon WMou
– 'Hillii' EHul MBar WCon
– 'Kelseyi' LSav
– 'Skalborg' LSav

TAYBERRY See **RUBUS**

TECOMA (Bignoniaceae)
garrocha CPle
ricasoliana See PODRANEA *r.*
stans CPle CSun

TECOMANTHE (Bignoniaceae)
¶ *speciosa* ECou

TECOMARIA (Bignoniaceae)
capensis CHEx CPle CSun EBak ERea SHil SLMG
– 'Aurea' ERea

TECOPHILAEA (Liliaceae/Tecophilaeaceae)
cyanocrocus CAvo EPot LAma WChr
– 'Leichtlinii' CAvo

violiflora EPot

TECTARIA (Aspleniaceae)
gemmifera NMar

TELEKIA (Compositae)
§ *speciosa* CBre CHan CHar CSco EBre ELan EMon MFir SAxl SDix SFis WOld WPer

TELESONIX (Saxifragaceae)
jamesii See BOYKINIA *jamesii*

TELLIMA (Saxifragaceae)
grandiflora CElw CFis CGle CMHG CSam CSun CTom EHon EJud ELan ELun EMon GCHN GPla MCot MFir MWgw NNor NRar SCro WHen WOak
– *alba* EGol
– *odorata* CElw ECha GWic NCat NSti
– 'Perky' EMon
– 'Purpurea' See T. ***grandiflora rubra***
– 'Purpurteppich' ECha
§ – *rubra* Widely available

TELOPEA (Proteaceae)
oreades CSun SSpi
¶ *speciosissima* CHEx
truncata CB&S CGre CHEx CSun ISea SHil SSpi

TERNSTROEMIA (Theaceae)
gymnanthera LRHS

TETRACENTRON (Tetracentraceae)
sinense CB&S CCla CGre CMCN EHar LSav SHil SSpi WWat

TETRADIUM (Rutaceae)
§ *daniellii* CCla CMCN EHar LSav SHil SSpi WCoo
hupehense CMCN GWic SHil SSpi WCoo WHCr
sp. L 1597 SSpi

TETRAGONOLOBUS See **LOTUS**

TETRAPANAX (Araliaceae)
papyriferus CHEx SArc SMad

TETRAPATHAEA (Passifloraceae)
♦ *tetrandra* See PASSIFLORA *t.*

TETRASTIGMA (Vitaceae)
voinierianum CHEx MBri

TEUCRIUM (Labiatae)
ackermannii CLew CShe ESis LHop MBro MCas MTho NHol NVic SBla SChu SIgm WPat
aroanum GAbr MBro MHig MPla MWat NTow SBla WDav WOMN WPer
¶ *bicolor* CGre
botrys MSal WPer
canadense LHop
N *chamaedrys* Widely available
– 'Nanum' CLew SIng
– 'Variegatum' CHan CLew CRow CSev EFol NRar SIng WHil WPer WRus
§ *creticum* WDav
flavum WOMN WPer WSHC
fruticans Widely available
– 'Album' CGle SBla WSHC
– 'Azureum' CB&S CFor LGre SBra SChu SHil SPer SSpi WAbe WBod WPat
¶ – 'Compactum' LHop SDry
hircanicum ELan EMon LHop
lucidum WCla WOak
majoricum See T. ***polium pii-fontii***
marum NHol
montanum CLew ESis MHig WDav WHoo WPer
musimosum MBro MHig NTow WDav
polium CFis CShe EBar ESis MBro MPar MWat SFar SIng WEas WPat WPer
¶ *pulveolentum* NRar
pyrenaicum CHar GLoc MBro MCas MHig NHol NKay NNrd NRed SIng WPat
rosmarinifolium See T. ***creticum***
scolymus crispum variegatum See T. ***scorodonia*** 'Crispum Marginatum'
¶ *scordium* CNat
¶ *scoridifolia* WPer
scorodonia CArn CKin EJud GPoy LHol MChe MSal NLan SIde WCla WHer WPer
– 'Crispum' CB&S CFis CHan CHar CMer CRiv ELan EOrc MBri MPar MWat SAxl SMrm WPer
§ – 'Crispum Marginatum' CBot CHoe CLew ECha ECro EFol EFou EGol ELan ESis GAbr IBlr LHop LSav NOak NRar NRoo NSti WBon WEas WHer WRus
– 'Winterdown' CNat
subspinosum ITim LGre MHig MPla SLon WPat WThu
webbianum WDav WPer

THALIA (Marantaceae)
dealbata CHEx MSta

THALICTRUM † (Ranunculaceae)
adiantifolium See T. ***minus a.***
angustifolium EFol ELan
aquilegiifolium Widely available
– *album* CCor EBre ECha EFou ELan NTow SCro SSpi WEas
*– 'Hybridum' ECro
– 'Purpureum' CSco SSpi
– 'Thundercloud' ('Purple Cloud') CCla ECro EFou MBri
§ *chelidonii* CFor EPot NTow SBla SSpi
– dwarf form GDra
coreanum See T. ***ichangense***

§ ***delavayi***	Widely available
– 'Album'	CSco ECha ELan ERou LGre NOak
– 'Hewitt's Double'	Widely available
diffusiflorum	GDra NHar SBla
dipterocarpum	See T. ***delavayi***
flavum	CGle CHan EFou ELan NHol NKay WCar
– 'Chollerton'	See T. sp. Afghanistan
§ – ***glaucum***	CBot CChu CCla CElw CHad CSco CShe ECha ECro ELan GWic NOak SSpi WCar WEas WOak WOld WWin
§ ***ichangense***	CFor
¶ ***isopyroides***	ECro SBla SWas
¶ ***javanicum***	NOak
kiusianum	CBos LGre MTho NTow SBar SBla
– Kew form	SWas
¶ ***koreanum***	GArf
minus	CHan EBre ECro ELan EMon GAbr MBri NLan NOak NRoo SIng WBon
§ – ***adiantifolium***	EHal EJud MFir MWgw NHol
¶ – ***saxatile***	WPer
polygamum	MSal NHol
reniforme	See T. ***chelidonii***
rochebrunnianum	CChu CHad CHan CSun EOrc MBri MUlv WCar
speciosissimum	See T. ***flavum glaucum***
sp. Afghanistan	ELan EMon NHol WDav
tuberosum	LGre NHol SIng WCot

THAMNOCALAMUS (Gramineae(Bambuseae))

falcatus	See DREPANOSTACHYUM ***falcatum***
falconeri	See DREPANOSTACHYUM ***falconeri***
funghomii	See ARUNDINARIA ***f.***
khasianus	See DREPANOSTACHYUM ***khasianum***
maling	See SINARUNDINARIA ***maling***
§ ***spathaceus***	CBow CBra CFor CHEx CHan CLew EHar ELan ENot ERav LNet MBri NJap SBam SDry SHil SPer SPla SReu SSpi SSta WJun
– 'Simba'	EPla
– 'Variegata'	SDry
§ ***spathiflorus***	EFul SBam SDry SHil
§ ***tessellatus***	SBam SDry WJun

THELYPTERIS (Thelypteridaceae)

¶ ***palustris***	SMrm
phegopteris	See PHEGOPTERIS ***connectilis***

THERMOPSIS (Leguminosae)

caroliniana	See T. ***villosa***
lanceolata	See T. ***lupinoides***
§ ***lupinoides***	CSun ECha ECro EFou NOrc
¶ ***mollis***	MPlt
montana	CCla CElw CFis ECro EFol EFou ELan EMon ERav LHop NOrc NSti SChu SIng SPer WRus WSto
§ ***villosa***	CChu CGle CHan CSun GWic

THEVETIA (Apocynaceae)

peruviana	CPle

THLASPI (Cruciferae)

bellidifolium	GDra NBir WDav
* ***biebersteinii***	GAbr
densiflorum	NWCA
¶ ***nevadense***	NWCA
rotundifolium	GLoc NGre NHol NWCA SBar WOMN
– ***cenisium***	WOMN
– ***limosellifolium***	NKay
¶ ***stylosum***	GLoc NWCA

THRINAX (Palmae)

THUJA (Cupressaceae)

koraiensis	CMHG EHar IBar ISea LSav SHil
occidentalis	SExT
– 'Aurea'	IJoh MBar
*– 'Baurmanii'	NBar
– 'Beaufort'	CKen EHul LSav MBar MPla WCon
*– 'Brabant'	EHul
– 'Caespitosa'	CMHG LLin WCon
*– 'Copper Kettle'	EHul MPla
– 'Cristata Argenteovariegata'	EHul
– 'Cristata Aurea'	CKen
– 'Cuprea'	WCon
– 'Danica'	CMac CSco EBre EHar EHul ENHC ENot IJoh LLin MBar MGos MPla MR&S MWat NRoo SHil SPer WCon
¶ – 'Douglasii Aurea'	CKen
– 'Ellwangeriana Aurea'	ENHC MGos SPla
– 'Emerald'	See T. ***o.*** 'Smaragd'
– 'Ericoides'	CSco EHul ENHC EPot IJoh MBal MBar SSmi
– 'Europe Gold'	CDoC EBre EHul MBar MBri MGos SHil
– 'Fastigiata'	EHul ISea MBar
– 'Filiformis'	WCon
– 'Globosa'	CMac LLin MBar MGos NHea SPer
I – 'Globosa Compacta Nana'	CDoC
*– 'Globosa Variegata'	LLin MBar WCon
– 'Golden Globe'	CSco EHul ENHC ENot LNet MBar MR&S SPer WCon
*– 'Golden Minaret'	EHul
– 'Hetz Midget'	CDoC EBre EHul LLin MBar MGos NHol SPer SPla WCon

– 'Holmstrup'	CDoC CMac CTre EBre EHul ENHC ENot MBal MBar MBri MOke MR&S MWat NHea SHil SPer SPla SSta WAbe WCon
– 'Holmstrup Yellow'	EBre EHul MBri MPla SPla WCon WWeb
– 'Hoveyi'	CDoC EHul ENHC MBar
– 'Indomitable'	SHil
– 'Little Champion'	EHul NHol
– 'Little Gem'	EHul ENHC IDai MGos NHol SHil
– 'Lutea Nana'	CMac EHul ENHC MBal MBar MCra WCon WGre
– 'Lutescens'	CMac EHul ENHC MGos MPla SPer WCon
– 'Madurodam'	MBri
– 'Malonyana'	SHil
– 'Marrison Sulphur'	EBre WCon
– 'Meinekes Zwerg'	CKen
– 'Milleri'	EPot
– 'Ohlendorffii'	CKen EHul EPot LLin MBar MWat SPer SPla SSmi WCon
– 'Orientalis Semperaurescens'	See T. ***orientalis*** 'Semperaurea'
– 'Pygmaea'	MBar
*– 'Pyramidalis Compacta'	EHul LNet
– 'Recurva Nana'	CMHG LLin MBal MBar NRya SLon
– 'Rheingold'	Widely available
*– 'Silver Beauty'	CMHG
– 'Smaragd'	CSco EBre EHul ENHC ENot LBuc LNet MBar MGos MPla MR&S NRoo SHil SPer WCon WMou
*– 'Smaragd Variegated'	EPla
– 'Southport'	MBri WCon
– 'Sphaerica'	MPla
– 'Spiralis'	CMHG EHar MBar
– 'Stolwijk'	MGos
– 'Sunkist'	Widely available
– 'Tiny Tim'	CDoC CMac EHul EPot LLin LSav MBar MGos NHea SIng SSta WCon
¶– 'Trompenburg'	MBri
– 'Vervaeneana'	CSco
– 'Wansdyke Silver'	CMac EHar EHul MBar MPla WCon
– 'Wareana'	CDoC CMac SPer
– 'Wareana Aurea'	See T. ***o.*** 'Wareana Lutescens'
§– 'Wareana Lutescens'	MBal MBar SHil SLon
– 'Woodwardii'	MBar SHil WCon
– 'Yellow Ribbon'	CDoC EBre IJoh NHol SSta
orientalis	NWea
§– 'Aurea Nana'	Widely available
¶– 'Berckman'	WWeb
– 'Beverleyensis'	CDoC MBri
¶– 'Carribean Holiday'	MBri
– 'Collen's Gold'	EBre EHul MBar SPla
– 'Conspicua'	CDoC EHar EHul ENHC LSav MBar MBri MWat SHil SPer SPla WCon
– 'Elegantissima'	CMHG CMac EHul MBar MBri MGos MR&S NHea SHil WCon
*– 'Filiformis Erecta'	EBre WCon
*– 'Golden Ball'	EBre LSav MBri
¶– 'Golden Minaret'	MBri
*– 'Golden Pillar'	EHul
¶– 'Golden Pygmy'	CKen
*– 'Golden Wonder'	ENHC
*– 'Grasmere'	LSav
¶– 'Green Cone'	LSav
– 'Juniperoides'	EHul IDai LLin MBar SHil
– 'Magnifica'	EHul WMou
*– 'Marrison Sulphur'	EHul
– 'Meldensis'	CDoC CLew CMHG CSco EBre EHul ENHC GPen LLin MBal MBar SHil WCon
– 'Miller's Gold'	See T. ***o.*** 'Aurea Nana'
– 'Minima'	CDoC EHul MBri MWat WCon
– 'Minima Glauca'	CKen CSco MBar SHil
¶– 'Purple King'	EPla
– 'Pyramidalis Aurea'	EBre IJoh MBri
– 'Rosedalis'	CDoC CHoe CKen CMac EBre EHul ENHC IDai IJoh LLin LSav MBal MBar MBri MPla MWat NHea SHil SPer WCon
*– 'Rowneri'	LSav
– 'Sanderi'	MBar MBri WCon
§– 'Semperaurea'	CMac LSav SHil
– 'Sieboldii'	EHul MBri WCon
– 'Summer Cream'	EHul MBar MGos
– 'Westmont'	EPla MBri
plicata	CPer CTre EHar EHul GRei IDai MBal MBar MGos MR&S NWea SExT SHil SPer WMou WWin
– 'Atrovirens'	CSam EHar ENot LBuc MBri MR&S SExT WCon WMou WWeb
– 'Aurea'	EHul SHil WMou
I – 'Cole's Variety'	CSco MBar
– 'Collyer's Gold'	EHul LSav MBri SPla WCon WMou
– 'Copper Kettle'	MBri MPlt NHol WCon
– 'Cuprea'	EHul LLin MBar SHil
*– 'December Gold'	LSav
– 'Doone Valley'	CDoC CMHG EBre EHul LSav MBar NHol WMou WThu
*– 'Dura'	CDoC EHul IJoh
*– 'Excelsa'	EHul
– 'Fastigiata'	CMac EHar MBar SHil
*– 'Globosa'	WCon
– 'Gracilis Aurea'	EHul WCon
– 'Hillieri'	EHul EPla MBar NHol WCon
– 'Irish Gold'	CMac EPla SHil
– 'Rogersii'	CDoC CKen CMHG CMac EBre EHul EPot IJoh LLin MBar MGos MPla NGre NHar NHea NHol SHil SLon SPer SPla SReu SSmi WAbe WCon
– 'Semperaurescens'	CSco EHar SHil WMou
I – 'Stolwyck's Variety'	MBar

– 'Stoneham Gold'	CDoC CMHG CMac CSco EBre EHar EHul ENHC EPla LLin MBar MBri MPla MPlt NHol SHil SLon SPer SSmi WCon WMou
*– 'Windsor Gold'	EHar
– 'Winter Pink'	CKen
– 'Zebrina'	CB&S CBra CDoC CMHG CMac CSco EHar EHul ENot IDai IJoh MBal MBar MGos MPla MR&S MWat NWea SHil SLon SPer SReu WCon WWin
* 'Stalworts'	EHul
standishii	SHil

THUJOPSIS (Cupressaceae)

dolabrata	CMer EHar EHul ELan ENot IBar IDai IOrc MBar NWea SHil SPer WWat
– 'Aurea'	CKen EHar EHul SHil WCon
§ – 'Laetevirens'	CDoC CKen CMac CSco EHar LLin MBar MBri MPla NHol SLon STre WAbe
– 'Nana'	See T. *d.* 'Laetevirens'
– 'Variegata'	CDoC CMHG CMac EHar EHul IBar LLin MBal MBar WCon
koraiensis	MBar SReu WThu

THUNBERGIA (Acanthaceae)

alata	MBri
grandiflora	SLMG
– alba	SLMG

THYMUS † (Labiatae)

* 'Albus'	CArn GPoy MPla WWin
'Anderson's Gold'	See T. x ***citriodorus*** 'Bertram Anderson'
* 'Aureus'	CFis CKni CSev GPoy WOak
azoricus	See T. ***cilicicus***
'Belle Orchard'	WEas
caespititius	CArn GAbr GDra IDai MBar MBro MCas MHig NHol NNrd WEas WHil WHoo WOMN WPer
– 'Aureus'	ECha EKal GAbr SIde
camphoratus	LHop SIde
carnosus	NHol SFis SIng SSmi STre WDav WEas WHil
¶ – 'Argenteus'	NHol
§ ***cilicicus***	ESis GCHN GGar GPoy LHop NRoo NRya NSel SBla SWas WOMN WPer
– azoricus	See T. ***c.***
x ***citriodorus***	CArn CGle CRow CSFH GAbr GCHN GPoy MChe MCot NHol NOak SCro WAbe WHoo WOak WSto
– 'Archer's Gold'	CHoe EKal ELan GAbr LGro LHop MBri MCas MPit MRav NKay SSmi WHil WPer
– 'Argenteus'	CKni MBro NHol
– 'Aureus'	CHar CKel CSFH CSco CShe EBre EKal EMNN GDra GPla MBal MBar MBri MBro MCas MRav NHol NKay NNrd NRoo NRya SBla WHoo
§ – 'Bertram Anderson'	CMer CShe EBre EFol EKal EMNN EPot GCHN MBro MHig NGre NHol NKay NRed NRoo SBla WAbe WDav WEas WHil WHoo WOld WThu WWin
– 'Golden King'	CHoe ECha EKal ELan EPar GLoc GPoy MBar MBri MBro NGre NHol NRya SIng WHil WHoo WPer
– 'Golden Lemon'	CArn GPoy
– 'Golden Queen'	CMer ECha EKal EMNN NHol NKay NRoo WWin
– 'Nyewoods'	CRow CSFH GAbr
¶ ***– repandia***	SIde
– 'Silver Posie'	See T. x ***c.*** 'Variegatus'
– 'Silver Queen'	Widely available
§ – 'Variegatus'	Widely available
comosus	ESis GLoc NHol SCro SIde WEas WHil WHoo WPer
* ***compactus albus***	CTom MBro MPla MPlt WHil
'Desboro'	GAbr NNrd
doerfleri	CLew CShe ECha EKal GAbr NKay NNrd SSmi WHil WPer
– 'Bressingham Pink'	CHad EBre ECtt EMNN GAbr LBuc LGro MBar MBro MHig MPla MRav NGre NHol NKay NNrd NRoo SBla SIng WHil WHoo WPat
'Doone Valley'	Widely available
drucei	See T. ***praecox arcticus***
– albus	See T. ***praecox arcticus albus***
– minus	See T. ***praecox arcticus minus***
'E B Anderson'	See T. x ***citriodorus*** 'Bertram Anderson'
* ***epiroticus***	CHar CLew
erectus	See T. ***vulgaris*** 'Erectus'
* ***ericoides*** 'Aureus'	EPot MBro WDav WHil
herba-barona	CArn CHad CSFH EBre ECha EJud EKal ESis GAbr GDra GPoy MBal MCas MRav NHol NRoo NVic SIde SIng SSmi WAbe WOak WPer
¶ ***hirsutus***	EKal
hyemalis	GPoy MSal SIde
¶ – 'Albus'	SIng
lanuginosus	See T. ***pseudolanuginosus***
leucotrichus	GAbr MHig SFir WOMN WPat
longicaulis	CArn EBar ECha EKal
mastichina	CArn CSun EKal LHop MPar SBla SChu SFar WPer
membranaceus	WOMN
micans	CShe EBre EJud EKal EMon GAbr WEas
montanus	See T. ***pulegioides***
neicefferi	CHar ECha EKal GAbr MHig MPar WOMN WPer
odoratissimus	See T. ***pallasianus pallasianus***

'Onyx'	EMNN NNrd WPer
§ ***pallasianus pallasianus***	GWic SIde WOak
'Pincushion'	EKal NHol SIng WDav WPer
praecox	GAbr NHol
§ – ***albus***	ELan MPar
§ – ***arcticus***	EEls EKal EPot GAbr GPoy MPar NLan WPer
– 'Porlock'	CTom EBre EKal ESis GPoy MCas MRav NHol NKay SCro SPla WDav WHil WHoo WPer
§ ***pseudolanuginosus***	Widely available
– 'Hall's Variety'	MBro
§ ***pulegioides***	CArn CHar CSFH CSev EKal GPoy MBri WOak WPer
richardii nitidus	CShe EKal IDai NHol NKay STre WAbe
– ***nitidus albus***	SSmi WPer
– ***nitidus*** 'Peter Davis'	CArn EBar EBre EKal LHop MCas MPla MRav NHol NKay SBla WPer
serpyllum	CRiv CSFH ELan ESis Effi GAbr GCHN MBri MChe MCot MWgw NOak NSel WHil WOld WSto
– ***albus***	Widely available
– 'Annie Hall'	CRiv CTom EBre EJud EKal EMNN EPot ESis GAbr LGro MBro MRav NHol NNrd NRoo NRya NSel SIng SSmi WDav WPat
– 'Carol Ann'	NHol
– ***coccineus***	Widely available
– ***coccineus*** 'Major'	Effi GDra SCro
– ***coccineus*** 'Minor'	EBre EKal MRav NRoo
– 'Dartmoor'	GWic
– 'East Lodge'	MBro
– 'Elfin'	CHar EKal EPar EPot GAbr GLoc MBri MBro MCas NGre NNrd SIng WAbe WCla WDav WEas WHil WHoo WPer WThu
– 'Goldstream'	CLew EKal EMNN GAbr LBuc MBar MBri NHol NNrd NRoo NRya SIng WHal WPer
– ***lanuginosus***	See T. ***pseudolanuginosus***
– 'Lemon Curd'	GAbr SIde
– 'Minimus'	CArn CLew CRiv CRow CSFH ECha GAbr MBri SIde WOMN WPer
§ – 'Minor'	CArn CLew ELan EMNN ESis GDra MBro MCas MHig NHol NKay NSel SIng SSmi WCla WDav WHil WHoo WWin
– 'Minus'	See T. *s.* 'Minor'
– 'Pink Chintz'	Widely available
– 'Pink Ripple'	NHol
– 'Rainbow Falls'	EMNN GAbr NHol NRed NRoo WHil
– 'Ruby Glow'	NHol
– 'Russetings'	CLew CTom EKal EMNN EOrc MBar MBro MCas MPit MRav NHol NKay NNrd NRoo NRya SIng WAbe WHil WOak WPat WWin
– 'September'	NHol
¶ – 'Silver Dew'	NHol
– 'Snowdrift'	GGar MBar NHol SCro SSmi WAbe WPat
– 'Vey'	EFol EKal EOrc ESis GLoc NHol SIng SPla WHil
N 'Silver Posie'	See T. x ***citriodorus*** 'Variegatus'
¶ sp. from Turkey	NHol
vulgaris	CSFH CSev ECha EKal GPoy MBri MChe NHol NRoo NSel SCro SDix WEas WHil WPer WSto
¶ – ***albus***	SIde
– ***aureus***	EKal LGro MChe NRoo
§ – 'Erectus'	CArn ELan EMon MCas SIde WPer
zygis	CArn WPer

TIARELLA (Saxifragaceae)

collina	See T. ***wherryi***
cordifolia	Widely available
polyphylla	ECro EGol ELan GAbr MRav NHol SWas WCla
trifoliata	CChu CFis ECro ELan EMon SBla WRus
– 'Incarnadine'	EMon
¶ ***unifoliata***	NCat
§ ***wherryi***	Widely available

TIBOUCHINA (Melastomataceae)

* 'Edwardsii'	MNew
* ***organensis***	CB&S CHil ERea MNew
* ***paratropica***	CPle
semidecandra	CB&S CCla CHEx CPle CSpe CSun CTre ERea IOrc IReg ISea LHil SLMG WBod
– 'Grandiflora'	CTre ERea IBlr WBod
urvilleana	EBak LAbb MNew SArc SHil SLon SSus

TIGRIDIA (Iridaceae)

hybrids	CSut SW&B
lutea	SW&B
pavonia	LAma LBow MBri SBar

TILIA † (Tiliaceae)

americana	CLnd CMCN ENot SExT WCoo
'Chelsea Sentinel'	SHil
cordata	CKin CLnd CPer EHar ELan ENot GRei IOrc LBuc MBal MBri MR&S NWea SExT SHil SPer WMou
– 'Erecta'	SExT
– 'Greenspire'	ENot IOrc MBri SExT SMad SPer WMou
x ***euchlora***	CLnd EHar ENot IDai MBri MGos MR&S SExT SHil SPer WMou
x ***europaea***	EHar ELan WMou
– 'Pallida'	EHar SExT SHil WMou
– 'Wratislaviensis'	SHil WMou
x ***flavescens***	SExT
henryana	CMCN SHil WMou
insularis	CMCN WMou
japonica	WMou

kuisiana	CMCN WMou
maximowicziana	SSta
'Moltkei'	SHil WMou
mongolica	EHar ENot SHil WMou
¶ ***neglecta***	WMou
oliveri	SHil WMou
'Petiolaris'	CLnd EHar ELan ENot IOrc SExT SHil SMad SPer SSta WMou
platyphyllos	CKin ENot GRei IJoh LBuc MBri MR&S SExT SHil SPer WMou
– 'Aurea'	SHil
– 'Corallina'	See T. ***p.*** 'Rubra'
– ***erecta***	See T. ***p.*** 'Fastigiata'
§ – 'Fastigiata'	ENot SHil WMou
– 'Laciniata'	WMou
– 'Prince's Street'	SHil
§ – 'Rubra'	CLnd ENot IDai IOrc MBar MBri MGos SExT SHil SPer
¶ – 'Tortuosa'	WMou
'Redmond'	SHil
tomentosa	CLnd EHar ENot SExT WMou
– 'Brabant'	EHar ENot IOrc SHil SPer
tuan	SSta WMou

TILLAEA See CRASSULA

TILLANDSIA † (Bromeliaceae)

acestae	MBri
argentea	MBri
baileyi	MBri
balbisiana	MBri
brachycaulos	MBri
*– ***abdita***	MBri
*– ***multiflora***	MBri
bulbosa	MBri
butzii	MBri
caput-medusae	MBri
circinnata	MBri
cyanea	MBri
x ***erographica***	MBri
* ***fasciculata*** 'Tricolor'	MBri
filifolia	MBri
flabellata	MBri
ionantha	MBri
– ***scaposa***	MBri
juncea	MBri
magnusiana	MBri
matudae	MBri
oaxacana	MBri
polystachya	MBri
punctulata	MBri
seleriana	MBri
sphaerocephala	MBri
tricolor melanocrater	MBri
vicentina	MBri
wagneriana	MBri
xerographica	MBri

TIPUANA (Leguminosae)

¶ ***tipu***	CPle

TITHONIA (Compositae)

¶ ***rotundifolia***	SMrm
¶ – 'Torch'	SMrm

TOFIELDIA (Liliaceae/Melanthiaceae)

¶ ***calyculata***	NHol

TOLMIEA (Saxifragaceae)

'Goldsplash'	See T. ***menziesii*** 'Taff's Gold'
menziesii	CArn CB&S CBow CGle CHEx CWGN EBar ECha EMon LGro MBri MCot NHol NOrc
– 'Maculata'	GWic NHol
§ – 'Taff's Gold'	Widely available
– 'Variegata'	See T. ***m.*** Taff's Gold'

TOLPIS (Compositae)

barbata	MSal

TONESTUS See HAPLOPAPPUS

TOONA (Meliaceae)

sinensis	CBot CGre CMCN LSav MBri SHil SSpi WCoo
– 'Flamingo'	CB&S EHar LHop MR&S MRav SHil SSpi

TORREYA (Taxaceae)

californica	SHil WCoo
nucifera	SHil

TOVARA See PERSICARIA

TOWNSENDIA (Compositae)

'Boulder'	WEas
¶ ***eximia***	MBro WDav
exscapa	MHig WDav
florifera	GLoc NWCA
formosa	CRiv ELan GAbr GLoc NHol NNrd NTow WDav WOMN WPer
¶ ***grandiflora***	WOMN
¶ – JCA 9166	WDav
¶ ***hookeri***	NWCA
incana	NTow
¶ ***leptotes***	WDav
¶ ***montana***	NTow
parryi	EPad GEdr NTow
¶ ***rothrockii***	GLoc NGre NHol
§ – JCA 9464	NTow WDav
* ***uniflora***	MBro WDav
wilcoxiana	See T. ***rothrockii***

TRACHELIUM (Campanulaceae)

§ ***asperuloides***	SIng
jacquinii rumelianum	NTow WPer

TRACHELOSPERMUM (Apocynaceae)

asiaticum	Widely available
jasminoides	Widely available
– Wilson 776	CBot CHan CMac ERav IOrc NRar SPer SSpi SSta WSHC
♦ – 'Tricolor'	ERav

♦– 'Variegatum' Widely available
majus GWic SSpi
sp. from Nanking EPla

TRACHYCARPUS (Palmae)
§*fortunei* Widely available
wagnerianus LPal SArc

TRACHYMENE (Umbelliferae)

TRACHYSTEMON (Boraginaceae)
orientalis CGle CHar EBre ECha ECro EFol EFou EGol ELan EPar MFir MRav MUlv SAxl SIng WWat WWin

TRADESCANTIA (Commelinaceae)
albiflora See T. ***fluminensis***
§ x *andersoniana* CHad CRiv EFol MFir MSal MWgw WEas WHil WWin
¶ – 'Bilberry Ice' NTow
– 'Blue Stone' CSco ECha ERou WHoo
– 'Croftway Blue' SCro
– 'Innocence' CAvo CBow CCla CFor CSco EBre ECha EFou EOrc EPla LHop LSav MBri MUlv SAxl SFis SPer WHoo WRus
– 'Iris Prichard' CHan CSco EBre ELan EPar ERou GGar MWat NHol SChu SCro
– 'Isis' CAvo CB&S CBow CCor CHar CSco EBre EFou ELan EPar MCot MUlv NHol NOrc NRoo SAxl SChu SPer WHil WOld WRus WWin
– 'J C Weguelin' CCla CSco LSav MBri WHoo
– 'Karminglut' ('Carmine Glow') CHar EBre ELan EOrc EPar ERou MWat NRoo NVic WHil WRus
– 'Leonora' CSco ENot ERou
– 'Osprey' Widely available
– 'Pauline' CSco CTom EBre EFou ERou NHol NRoo WWin
– 'Purewell Giant' CKel ERou NBar NHol SChu SPer WHoo
– 'Purple Dome' CHan CHar CKel CSco CTom EBre GCHN LSav MCot MRav NHol SChu WHal WHoo WRus
– 'Rubra' CCla NOrc SChu SCro
– 'Zwanenburg Blue' EBre ECha EFou EOrc LSav MBri MUlv NHol SFis
¶ *bracteata* NTow
– alba CHar
brevicaulis CSco ECha GDra SFis
canaliculata See T. ***ohiensis***
fluminensis 'Albovittata' SLMG
– 'Aurea' MBri
– 'Laekenensis' MBri
– 'Quicksilver' MBri
§ *ohiensis* LMay
§ *pallida* IBlr
sillamontana CMal MBri
§ *tabulaemontana* CSun
virginiana See also T. x ***andersoniana***
– 'Alba' CRiv CSam GWic WPer
– 'Caerulea Plena' CCla CHad CTom EFou ELan LHop LSav NKay
– 'Rubra' CHan CSco

TRAGOPOGON (Compositae)
porrifolius GPoy
pratensis CArn CKin
roseus See T. ***ruber***

TRAPA (Trapaceae)
natans CHEx CWGN MSta

TREVESIA (Araliaceae)

TRICUSPIDARIA (Elaeocarpaceae)
dependens See CRINODENDRON ***hookerianum***
lanceolata See CRINODENDRON ***hookerianum***

TRICYRTIS † (Liliaceae/Convallariaceae)
bakeri See T. ***latifolia***
flava CBro
– ohsumiensis EPar EPot
formosana CAvo CFor CGle CHan CTom EBre ECha ECro EGol ELan ELun MBri MCot MUlv NRoo SIng WEas WPer
§ – Stolonifera group Widely available
hirta CB&S CBro CCla CHad CHan CRiv CSam ECro EPot MBri MBro MRav MTho MUlv NHol SCro WHoo WRus
§ *– alba* CBro CChu CFor CHan CRiv EBre ECha ECro ELan EPot ERou MBal MPlt WWin
¶ – 'Miyazaki' EFou
– 'Variegata' CAvo ECha EFou EGol LGre WHal
N Hototogisu SWas
japonica alba See T. ***hirta alba***
– 'Kinkazan' CBro
§ *latifolia* CAvo CChu EBul ECro ELun EPar LGre LHop LSav MPar SBla WCot
macrantha SHig WPer
– macranthopsis CBro EPot SWas
* *macrocarpa* CAvo NKay
N *macropoda* CChu CCla CGle ECha ECro MBri MPar MWgw NHol NSti WCar WHoo
ohsumiensis CFor LGre NHol WCot
perfoliata SWas
pubila MPar
stolonifera See T. ***formosana*** Stolonifera group
'White Towers' CChu CSpe EPar LGre MRav SAxl SBla SWas

TRIENTALIS (Primulaceae)
europaea rosea WDav

TRIFOLIUM (Leguminosae)
campestre CKin

incarnatum	LHop SIde WHer
pannonicum	GWic NSti
***pratense* 'Dolly North'**	See T. ***p.*** 'Susan Smith'
§ – 'Susan Smith'	CArn CHan CRow EJud EPla GAbr GWic IBlr LHop MTho NSti SAxl SIng SMrm WHer WPer
repens	CHEx NGre
– 'Aureum'	MBal
– 'Gold Net'	See T. ***pratense*** 'Susan Smith'
¶ – 'Good Luck'	CRow
– ***pentaphyllum***	See T. ***r.*** 'Quinquefolium'
– 'Purpurascens'	Widely available
§ – 'Purpurascens Quadrifolium'	CLew ECha ELan SIng SPer WHea WRus WWin
– 'Quadrifolium'	CHoe EPar GLoc IBar
§ – 'Quinquefolium'	WEas WPer
– 'Tetraphyllum Purpureum'	See T. ***r.*** 'Purpurascens Quadrifolium'
*– 'Variegatum'	EFol
– 'Wheatfen'	CNat
uniflorum	WThu

TRIGONELLA (Leguminosae)

foenum-graecum	CArn GPoy MSal SIde

TRILLIUM † (Liliaceae/Trilliaceae)

apetalon	WChr
§ ***catesbyi***	ELan EPot LAma MSal NHol WChr
cernuum	CAvo CBro EPot LAma NKay WChr
chloropetalum	CBro GDra WChr WDav
cuneatum	CB&S ELan EPar EPot LAma NHol NOak SAxl SPer SSpi WChr
decumbens	WChr
discolor	WChr
erectum	CArn CAvo CBro CCla COtt EPar EPot GDra GEdr GLoc GPoy IBar LAma LBow MBal MSal NHol NKay SAxl SIng SPer SSpi SW&B WChr
♦– ***albiflorum***	See T. ***e. album***
§ – ***album***	CBro EPot LAma MSal NHol NKay WChr
– ***luteum***	CBro EPot LAma NHol WChr
– ***roseum***	WChr
grandiflorum	Widely available
– ***flore-pleno***	EBre SPou SSpi SWas WThu
kamtschaticum	CAvo LAma NHol WChr
lancifolium	WChr
§ ***luteum***	CAvo CB&S CBro ELan EPar EPot IBar LAma LBow NHol NKay NSti SAxl SIng SPer SW&B WChr
nervosum	See T. ***catesbyi***
nivale	CBro EPot NHol WChr
ovatum	EPot GDra LAma WChr
– ***hibbersonii***	CAvo GDra NHol SWas
pusillum	CBro GLoc NHol WChr
– ***virginianum***	LAma NHol WChr
recurvatum	EPar EPot GLoc LAma NHol NSti SAxl SIng SPer WChr
rivale	EPot LAma NHol SWas WChr WOMN
rugelii	LAma NHol WChr
– pink form	WChr
sessile	CAvo CBro CCla CHEx CKel COtt ELan EPot GEdr LAma LBow MCot NKay SPer SW&B
– ***luteum***	See T. ***luteum***
– ***rubrum***	SWas
smallii	LAma NHol
stylosum	See T. ***catesbyi***
tschonoskii	LAma NHol WChr
undulatum	CBro CHEx EPar EPot GLoc LAma LBow NHol NKay WChr
vaseyi	CBro LAma NHol WChr
viride	ELan LAma NHol WChr

TRINIA (Umbelliferae)

* ***grandiflora***	EMon

TRIOSTEUM (Caprifoliaceae)

erythrocarpum	CChu

TRIPETALEIA See ELLIOTTIA

TRIPLEUROSPERUM (Compositae)

maritimum	See MATRICARIA ***maritima***

TRIPTERYGERUM (Celastraceae)

¶ ***regelii*** MSF 833	LSav SSpi

TRISTAGMA (Liliaceae/Alliaceae)

§ 'Rolf Fielder'	CAvo CBro EPot MTho NHol SPou WChr
§ ***sellowianum***	SOkd
§ ***uniflorum***	CAvo CBro CCla CRiv ECha EFol ETub LAma LRoo MBri MBro NHol NNrd SApp SIng SLHN WCla WHea WPer
– ***album***	CAvo CBro ECha ELan EPar EPot GLoc MTho SBla SIng SPou WChr
– 'Froyle Mill'	CAvo CBro CRiv EPot GLoc LBow MTho SBla SPou WChr WOMN
§ – 'Wisley Blue'	CAvo CBro CRiv ECam ECha ELan EPar EPot ETub LAma LBlo LBow MPlt MTho NHol SApp SBla SIng WBon WChr WHea WWat

TRITELEIA (Liliaceae/Alliaceae)

bridgesii	LBow
* ***californica***	ETub WChr
hyacinthina	LAma LBow WChr
§ ***laxa***	CAvo CCla LAma NWCA
¶ – C&R 951	WChr
– 'Konigin Fabiola' ('Queen Fabiola')	CCla ETub LAma LBow MBri
§ ***peduncularis***	LAma LBow WChr
× ***tubergenii***	EPot LAma LBow
uniflora	See TRISTAGMA ***uniflorum***

TRITONIA (Iridaceae)
crocata GWic LBow
rosea See T. ***rubrolucens***
§ ***rubrolucens*** CB&S CBro CChu CCor CHan EBre ECha ERou GWic IDai MFir NRoo SApp

TROCHETIOPSIS (Sterculiaceae)
¶ ***melanoxylon*** EPad

TROCHODENDRON (Trochodendraceae)
aralioides CCla EGol EHar ENot MUlv SArc SBor SHil SLon SMad SReu SSpi SSta WBod WHCr WWat

TROLLIUS † (Ranunculaceae)
acaulis CRiv GDra GLoc MBro MTho NGre WDav
'Baudirektor Linne' CHar NKay
Bressingham hybrids EBre NRoo
§ ***chinensis*** ECha MBro
– 'Golden Queen' CSco ELan IBrk IDai LSav MUlv MWat NRoo SPer SSpi WEas WHoo
– 'Imperial Orange' CGle LSav
x ***cultorum*** 'Alabaster' CRow EBre ECha
– 'Canary Bird' CSco EGol ELan GHig MWgw SPer
– 'Earliest of All' CCla CGle CSco IDai LSav MWgw NKay SHig
– 'Etna' GHig MBri
– 'Feuertroll' ('Fireglobe') CCla CHar CKel CWGN EBre ECha ERou NRoo SHig WEas
– 'Golden Cup' WHal
– 'Golden Monarch' CWGN EPar GHig
¶ – 'Golden Queen' LSav WHen
– 'Goldquelle' EHon MWat NVic SHig
– 'Goliath' CGle GHig LSav
– 'Helios' CGle CSam ECha GWic
– 'Lemon Queen' CCla CSco CWGN EPar ERou GHig SLon WRus
– 'Maigold' MBri
– 'Orange Princess' CBow CWGN ERou GHig MBal MWgw NHol SBla SHig SLon SPer SPla
– 'Prichard's Giant' CSco GHig
– 'Salamander' NKay
– 'Superbus' CKel ELan EPar MBri MRav MWat NKay NRoo SHig SSpi WRus
europaeus CBot CRow CSam CSun ECha EPad GEdr GPla MBal MBro NRya WBon WCla WHoo
ledebourii See T. ***chinensis***
pumilus CGle CSun ECha ELan EPad EPar MBro MHig NHol NNrd WAbe WDav
– 'Wargrave' NNrd WEas
yunnanensis CGle EBre ELan GDra MBal NGre NHol NSti SLon

TROPAEOLUM † (Tropaeolaceae)
* ***ciliatum*** SSpi WChr WCru WNor
majus CHEx LHol SIde
– 'Alaska' EMon
*– 'Clive Innes' ERea
– 'Hermine Grashoff' ELan EOrc ERea GWic SAxl SDix WEas
– 'Variegatum' EMon ERea
pentaphyllum CFor GWic IBlr
peregrinum ELan LHil
polyphyllum CFor SOkd
speciosum Widely available
¶ ***sylvestre*** LBow
tricolorum CRiv EPot GWic WAbe WChr
tuberosum CB&S CGle CHad CRiv CSam EPot LHil MBal MFir SLon WAbe WCla WEas
– 'Ken Aslet' Widely available
– 'Pilifera Sidney' CGle IBlr NCat WCru

TSUGA (Pinaceae)
canadensis CGre EHar EHul ENHC IDai MBal MBar SExT SPer WCoo
¶ – 'Abbot's Dwarf' CKen
– 'Bennett' EBre EPot MBar SHil
¶ – 'Brandley' CKen
¶ – 'Cinnamonea' CKen
– 'Coffin' CKen
– 'Cole' CKen EHar MBar MBri NHol
¶ – ***compacta*** WCon
¶ – 'Curtis Ideal' CKen
– 'Dwarf Pyramid' MBar
– 'Dwarf Whitetip' SHil
¶ – 'Everitt Golden' CKen
– 'Fantana' EHul LLin MBar WCon
– 'Gentsch Snowflake' CKen
– 'Golden Splendour' EPla
– 'Horsford' CKen MPla SHil
– 'Hussii' CKen
¶ – 'Jacqueline Verkade' CKen
– 'Jeddeloh' CDoC CMac EHar EHul ENHC ENot EPot IJoh LLin MBal MBar MBri MGos MPla MR&S NHol SMad SPer SReu WAbe WCon WThu
¶ – 'Jervis' CKen
– 'Lutea' CKen SHil
– 'Minima' MBar NHol
– 'Minuta' CKen EHul SHil
– 'Nana' CMHG CMac EHul IOrc
– 'Nana Gracilis' SHil
¶ – 'Palomino' CKen
– 'Pendula' CDoC CSco EHar ENot MBar MBri SHil SPla WThu
– 'Prostrata' CKen SHil
– 'Rugg's Washington' CKen MPla
– 'Verkade Recurved' CKen
– 'Von Helms Dwarf' CKen
*– 'Warnham' CKen
caroliniana LSav SHil WCoo
– 'La Bar Weeping' CKen
chinensis CMCN SHil WCoo
diversifolia EPot
– 'Nana' CKen

heterophylla	CBra CDoC CMCN CPer CTre EHar GRei IOrc LBuc MBar NWea SExT SHil SMad SPer STre WCon WCoo
– 'Greenmantle'	SHil
– 'Laursen's Column'	SHil
menziesii	See PSEUDOTSUGA ***menziesii***
mertensiana	LRHS LSav WCoo
– 'Glauca'	CKen SHil

TSUSIOPHYLLUM (Ericaceae)

¶ *tanakae*	WAbe

TUBERARIA (Cistaceae)

guttata	CNat WCru
lignosa	MBro NHol WCla WCru WHil

TULBAGHIA † (Liliaceae/Alliaceae)

capensis	LGre
– 'Variegatus'	LHop
¶ *coddii*	LGre
cominsii	LGre
fragrans	CSam EBul ITim
* 'Tricolor'	EBul
violacea	CAvo CChu CHan CRow EBul GWic IBlr IBrk LAma SAxl SMrm SSpi SSus SWas WMar
– Capacea group	GWic
– *pallida*	CAvo CChu LGre SAxl SMrm
§ – 'Silver Lace'	CHan ERea LGre LHop
– *variegata*	See T. *v.* 'Silver Lace'

TULIPA † (Liliaceae/Liliaceae)

'Abu Hassan' (3)	LAma LRoo
acuminata	CAvo CBro EPar LAma LBow LRoo SIng
'Ad Rem' (4)	IDun LAma
'Addis' (14)	LAma
'African Queen' (3)	IDun LBlo
aitchisonii	See T. ***clusiana***
'Akela' (3)	LRoo
'Aladdin' (6)	LAma LBlo LRoo
'Alaska' (6)	LAma
albertii	ECam LAma
'Albino' (3)	LAma
aleppensis	LAma
'Aleppo' (7)	LAma
'Alfred Cortot' (12)	LAma LRoo
'Ali Baba' (14)	LRoo MBri
'Alice Leclercq' (2)	LAma
'All Bright' (5)	LAma
'Allegretto' (11)	LAma
altaica	ECam EPar EPot LAma
'Amulet' (3)	LAma
'Ancilla' (12)	CBro LAma LBlo LRoo
'Angélique' (11)	ETub IDun LAma LBlo LRoo MBri
'Anne Claire' (3)	LAma
'Anneke' (3)	LAma
'Antwerp' (3)	LAma
'Apeldoorn' (4)	ETub LAma LBlo MBri
'Apeldoorn's Elite' (4)	LAma LBlo
'Apricot Beauty' (1)	ETub LAma LBlo LBow LRoo MBri
'Apricot Jewel'	See T. ***linifolia*** 'A.J.'
'Apricot Parrot' (10)	LAma LBlo
'Arabian Mystery' (3)	LRoo
'Arie Alkemade's Memory (2)	LBlo
'Aristocrat' (5)	LAma
'Arlington' (5)	LAma
'Arma' (7)	LAma
'Artist' (8)	CAvo IDun LAma LBlo LBow
'Asta Nielsen' (5)	LAma
¶ 'Astarte' (3)	IDun
'Athleet' (3)	LAma
'Attila' (3)	ETub IDun LAma LBlo LRoo
aucheriana	CBro ECam EPar EPot ETub LAma LBow MBro SIng SOkd WChr
'Aurea'	See T. ***greigii*** 'A.'
'Aureola' (3)	LAma
'Baby Doll' (2)	LRoo
bakeri	ECam EPot LAma
'Balalaika' (5)	LAma
'Ballade' (6)	IDun LBlo LRoo
¶ 'Ballerina' (6)	IDun
'Bandoeng' (3)	LAma
¶ 'Baronesse' (3)	IDun
batalinii	See T. ***linifolia*** Batalinii group
* 'Beauty' (7)	LAma
'Beauty of Apeldoorn' (4)	LAma LBlo LRoo
¶ Beauty Queen ® (1)	IDun
'Belcanto' (3)	LAma
'Bellflower' (7)	IDun LAma
'Bellona' (1)	ETub LAma LRoo
'Berlioz' (12)	LAma LBlo LRoo
biebersteiniana	ECam LAma WChr
§ *biflora*	CAvo CBro ECam EPar EPot ETub LAma LBow SIng WChr
– forms	ECam WChr
'Big Chief' (4)	ETub LAma MBri
'Bing Crosby' (3)	ETub LAma
'Bird of Paradise' (10)	LRoo
'Black Diamond' (5)	LRoo
'Black Parrot' (10)	LAma LBlo LBow LRoo
'Black Swan' (5)	LBlo
'Bleu Aimable' (5)	ETub LAma LBlo
'Blizzard' (1)	LBlo
'Blue Heron' (7)	IDun LAma LRoo
'Blue Parrot' (10)	LAma LBlo LRoo
'Bonanza' (11)	LAma LRoo
'Boule de Neige' (2)	LAma
'Bravissimo' (2)	MBri
'Brilliant Star' (1)	LAma LBlo LRoo MBri
'Bruno Walter' (3)	LAma
buhseana	ECam
'Burgundy' (7)	ETub LAma
'Burgundy Lace' (7)	LAma LBlo
'Burns' (7)	LAma
butkovii	LAma
'Cabaret' (6)	LAma
'Caland' (10)	LAma
'Candela' (13)	CBro LAma
'Cantata' (13)	CBro LAma LBlo LRoo MBri
'Cantor' (5)	LAma

'Cape Cod' (14)	LAma
'Caprice' (10)	LAma
'Captain Fryatt' (6)	LAma
carinata	LAma
'Carlton' (2)	ETub LAma
'Carnaval de Nice' (11)	IDun LAma LBlo MBri
'Cashmir' (5)	LAma
'Cassini' (3)	LAma LBlo
§ ***celsiana***	CAvo EPar EPot ETub LAma
'César Franck' (12)	LAma
'Charles' (1)	LAma
'Charles Needham' (5)	LAma
'China Lady' (14)	LRoo
'China Pink' (6)	ETub LAma LBlo LBow
'Chopin' (12)	LAma
¶ 'Christmas Dream' (1)	IDun
'Christmas Marvel' (1)	ETub LAma LRoo
chrysantha	See T. ***clusiana c.***
'Clara Butt' (5)	LAma LBlo
§ ***clusiana***	CAvo CBro ECam EPar ETub LAma LBlo LBow LRoo SIng WChr
§ – ***chrysantha***(15)	CAvo ECam EPar ETub IDun LAma LBlo LBow LRoo SIng
– ***chrysantha*** 'Diplomate' (4)	LRoo
– ***chrysantha*** 'Tubergen's Gem'	EPar LAma MBri
– ***clusianoides***	LRHS WChr
– 'Cynthia'	EPar EPot LAma SIng
– ***stellata***	LAma LRHS MBro
'Compliment' (6)	LAma
'Concerto' (13)	ETub LAma
'Coriolan' (3)	LAma
'Corona' (12)	LAma
'Corrie Kok' (3)	LAma
'Corsage' (14)	LAma LBlo LRoo
'Couleur Cardinal' (1)	ETub LAma LBow
* 'Crispa Pink' (7)	LAma
'Dancing Show' (8)	LAma
dasystemon	EPot LAma NHol WHil
'Daydream' (4)	ETub LBlo
* 'Delano' (3)	LAma
'Diana' (1)	ETub LAma
'Diantha' (14)	LAma
didieri	CAvo LAma NHol
'Dillenburg' (5)	LAma
'Dix' Favourite' (5)	LAma
'Doctor James Parkinson' (3)	LAma
'Doctor Plesman' (1)	LAma LBlo
'Doll's Minuet' (8)	LAma
'Don Quichotte' (3)	LAma
'Donna Bella' (14)	LAma
'Douglas Bader' (3)	LAma
'Dreaming Maid' (3)	LAma LBlo
¶ 'Dreamland' (5)	IDun
'Duke of Wellington' (5)	LAma
* 'Dutch Gold' (3)	LAma
¶ 'Dyanito' (6)	IDun LAma
¶ Early Glory ® (3)	IDun
'Early Harvest' (12)	LAma LRoo
'Early Light' (1)	IDun LAma
'Easter Fire' (3)	LAma

'Easter Parade' (13)	EWal LAma
'Easter Surprise' (14)	LAma
§ ***edulis***	LAma WChr
eichleri	See T. ***undulatifolia***
'El Toreador' (2)	LAma
'Electra' (2)	IDun LAma LRoo MBri
'Elegant Lady' (6)	ETub
'Elizabeth Arden' (4)	ETub IDun LAma LBlo LRoo
'Elmus' (3)	LAma
'Esperanto' (8)	ETub LBlo LRoo
'Estella Rijnveld' (10)	IDun LAma LBlo LBow
'Esther' (5)	LAma
'Etude' (3)	LAma
'Fair Lady' (12)	LAma
'Fancy Frills' (7)	IDun LBlo LRoo
'Fantasy' (10)	LAma LBlo LBow
'Fashion' (12)	LAma
ferganica	ECam EPot LAma LBow WChr
'Feu Superbe' (13)	LAma
'Fidelio' (3)	LBlo
¶ Fire Queen ® (1)	IDun
'Fireside'	See T. 'Vlammenspel'
'First Lady' (3)	LAma
'Flair' (1)	IDun LAma
'Flaming Parrot' (10)	IDun LAma LBlo LBow LRoo
'Floradale' (4)	LAma
'Florosa' (8)	ETub LAma
'Flying Dutchman' (5)	LAma
fosteriana	MBri
¶ 'Françoise' (5)	IDun
'Franfurt' (3)	LAma
'Franz Léhar' (12)	LAma LRoo
'Frasquita' (5)	LAma
'Fresco' (14)	LAma
'Fringed Beauty' (2)	LRoo MBri
'Fringed Elegance' (7)	LAma
'Fritz Kreisler' (12)	LAma LRoo
fulgens	ECam LAma
'G W Leak' (5)	LAma
'Gaiety' (12)	LAma
'Galata' (13)	LAma
galatica	LAma WChr
'Garanza' (2)	LAma LBlo
'Garden Party' (3)	ETub LAma LBlo
'Generaal de Wet' (1)	ETub LAma LBlo LRoo MBri
'General Eisenhower' (4)	LAma
'Georgette' (5)	ETub LAma LBlo LRoo MBri
'Gerbrand Kieft' (11)	LRoo
'Giuseppe Verdi' (12)	EWal LAma LBow MBri NHol
'Glück' (12)	IDun LAma LBlo LRoo
'Gold Medal' (11)	LAma MBri
'Golden Age' (5)	LAma LBlo
'Golden Apeldoorn' (4)	ETub LAma LBlo LRoo MBri
'Golden Artist' (8)	ETub LAma LBlo LRoo MBri
'Golden Eagle' (13)	LAma
'Golden Eddy' (3)	LAma
'Golden Emperor' (13)	LAma
'Golden Harvest' (5)	LAma
'Golden Melody' (3)	LAma LBlo
'Golden Oxford' (4)	LAma
'Golden Parade' (4)	LAma
* 'Golden Show' (3)	LAma

'Golden Springtime' (4)	LAma
'Goldenes Deutschland' (4)	LAma
'Gordon Cooper' (4)	IDun LAma
'Goudstuk' (12)	LAma
'Goya' (2)	LAma LRoo
'Graceful' (14)	LAma
'Grand Prix' (13)	LAma
'Green Eyes' (8)	LAma
'Green Spot' (8)	LAma
greigii	CBro
– 'Aurea'	LRHS
grengiolensis	CAvo EPar LAma NHol
'Greuze' (5)	LAma
'Grevel' (3)	LAma
'Groenland' (8)	LAma LBlo LRoo
'Gudoshnik' (4)	LAma LBow
'Hadley' (1)	LAma
hageri	ECam EPar ETub LAma MBri SIng
– 'Splendens'	EPar ETub LAma
'Halcro' (5)	ETub LAma
¶ 'Hamilton' (7)	IDun
'Happy Family' (3)	ETub LRoo
'Heart's Delight' (12)	CAvo CBro ETub EWal LAma LBlo LBow LRoo
'Henry Ford' (5)	LAma
'Hermione' (11)	LBlo
'Hibernia' (3)	LAma
'High Society' (3)	LBlo
hissarica	ECam EPot WChr
'Hit Parade' (13)	LAma
'Hoangho' (2)	LAma
'Holland's Glorie' (5)	LAma
'Hollywood' (8)	LAma LBlo LBow
hoogiana	LAma
humilis	CAvo CBro ECam EPar EPot ETub GLoc LAma LBow SIng WChr
– Albacoerulea-oculata group	ECam EPar EPot LAma WChr
– 'Eastern Star'	LAma MBro
– 'Odalisque'	EPot LAma
– 'Pallida'	LRHS
– 'Persian Pearl'	EPar EPot LAma
– 'Violet Queen'	LBlo
– yellow centre	LAma LBow
humilis Violacea group	CAvo ECam EPar ETub GLoc LAma LRoo SIng
– – black centre	CBro LRHS
– – dark yellow centre	CBro LRHS SIng
'Humming Bird' (8)	LBlo LBow
'Humoresque' (13)	LAma
'Hytuna' (2)	LAma
'Ibis' (1)	LAma
'Ile de France' (5)	LAma
ingens	LAma LRHS
'Inglescombe Yellow' (5)	LAma
'Inzell' (3)	LAma
¶ 'Ivory Floradale' (4)	IDun
'Jacqueline' (6)	LAma
'James V Forrestal' (10)	LAma
'Jan Vermeer' (2)	LAma
'Jeantine' (12)	LAma LRoo
'Jenny' (1)	LRoo
'Jewel of Spring' (4)	LAma LBlo
'Jockey Cap' (14)	LAma
'Joffre' (1)	LAma MBri
'Johann Gutenberg' (7)	LBlo
'Johann Strauss' (12)	CBro ETub LAma LBlo MBri
'Johanna' (3)	LAma
'Juan' (13)	LAma LRoo MBri
julia	ECam
'Juri Gagarin' (14)	LRoo
kalpakowskiana	ECam
'Kansas' (3)	ETub LAma
'Karel Doorman' (10)	LAma LBlo
'Kareol' (2)	LAma
kaufmanniana	CAvo CBro ETub LBow SIng
§ 'Kees Nelis' (3)	LAma LBlo LRoo MBri
'Keizerskroon' (1)	LAma LBlo LRoo
'Kingsblood' (5)	LAma LRoo
kolpakowskiana	CAvo EPar LAma MBri WChr
'Koningin Wilhemina' (4)	LBlo LRoo
'Kryptos' (5)	LBlo
kurdica	LAma
'La Tulipe Noire' (5)	LAma
'Lady Diana' (14)	LAma MBri
'Lady Montgomery' (11)	LRoo
lanata	LAma LRHS
'Landseadel's Supreme' (5)	LAma LBlo
'Large Copper' (14)	LAma
'Laverock' (7)	LRoo
'Leen van der Mark' (3)	IDun LRoo
'Lefeber's Favourite' (4)	LAma
'Libretto' (3)	LAma
'Lighting Sun' (5)	LBlo
'Lilac Perfection' (11)	LBlo
'Lilac Time' (6)	LAma
'Lilac Wonder'	See T. ***bakeri*** 'L.W.'
linifolia	CAvo ECam EPar EPot ETub LAma LBlo LBow LRoo MBro SIng WAbe WChr WHil
§ – 'Apricot Jewel'	CAvo CBro EPar
§ – Batalinii group	CAvo CBro ECam EPar EPot LAma LBow SIng WChr
– 'Bright Gem'	CAvo CBro EPot ETub LAma LBow LRoo NHol SIng
– 'Bronze Charm'	CAvo CBro EPar LAma
– Maximowiczii group	CBro EPar
– 'Red Jewel'	CBro LAma
– 'Yellow Jewel'	EPar LAma
'London' (4)	LAma
'Longfellow' (14)	LAma
'Love Song' (12)	LAma LBlo
'Lucifer' (7)	IDun LAma
'Lucky Strike' (3)	LAma
§ 'Lustige Witwe' (3)	LAma
§ 'Madame Lefeber' (13)	CBro ETub EWal LAma LBlo LBow LRoo MBri
'Madame Spoor' (3)	LAma
'Magier' (5)	LAma
'Maja' (7)	LAma LBlo
'Majestic' (14)	LRoo
'Mamasa' (5)	LAma

'March of Time' (14)	MBri
'Marechal Niel' (2)	LAma
'Mariette' (6)	LAma LBlo LRoo
'Marilyn' (6)	ETub LBlo
'Marjolein' (6)	LBlo
marjoletii	CAvo CBro ETub LAma LBow SIng
'Marquette' (2)	LAma
'Mary Ann' (14)	LAma
'Maskerade' (5)	LAma
'Maureen' (5)	ETub IDun LAma
mauritiana	LAma
maximowiczii	LAma LBow
'Maytime' (6)	LAma LBlo LRoo
'Maywonder' (11)	LAma LRoo
'Meissner Porzellan' (3)	LBlo
'Menton' (5)	ETub
'Merry Widow'	See T. 'Lustige Witwe'
'Mirella' (5)	LBlo
'Mirjoran' (3)	LAma
'Miss Holland' (3)	MBri
¶ 'Modern Style' (5)	IDun
§ ***montana***	CBro ECam EPar EPot LAma LBow WChr
'Monte Carlo' (2)	ETub LAma LBlo
'Most Miles' (5)	LAma
'Mount Tacoma' (11)	IDun LAma LBlo LRoo MBri
'Mr van der Hoef' (2)	LAma LRoo MBri
'Mrs John T Scheepers' (5)	LAma LBlo
'Murillo' (2)	LAma
'Murillo Maxima' (2)	LAma
'My Lady' (4)	LAma
* 'Nefertete' (11)	LRoo
'Negrita' (3)	LAma LRoo
neustreuvae	WChr
'New Design' (3)	ETub LAma LBlo LRoo MBri
'Noranda' (7)	IDun LRoo
'Olympic Flame' (4)	LBlo LRoo
'Olympic Gold' (4)	LBlo
'Orange Bouquet' (5)	LAma LBlo LRoo
'Orange Cassini' (3)	LAma
'Orange Elite' (14)	LAma MBri
'Orange Emperor' (13)	ETub LAma LBlo LRoo MBri
'Orange Favourite' (10)	LAma LBlo LBow
'Orange Goblet' (4)	LAma
'Orange King' (5)	LAma
'Orange Monarch' (3)	ETub LAma
'Orange Sun'	See T. 'Oranjezon'
'Orange Toronto' (14)	ETub
'Orange Triumph' (11)	MBri
'Orange Wonder' (3)	LAma
'Oranje Nassau' (2)	LAma LBlo LRoo MBri
'Oranjezon' (4)	LAma LRoo
'Oratorio' (14)	ETub LAma LBlo LRoo MBri
'Oriental Beauty' (14)	LAma
'Oriental Splendour' (14)	EWal LAma LRoo
'Ornament' (3)	LAma
orphanidea	ECam EPar LAma LBow SIng
– ***flava***	CAvo CBro EPar ETub LAma
– Whittallii group	CAvo CBro EPar ETub LAma LBow SIng
'Oscar' (3)	LRoo
ostrowskiana	LAma
'Oxford' (4)	LAma
'Oxford's Elite' (4)	LAma
'Page Polka' (3)	LAma
'Palestrina' (5)	LAma LBlo
* 'Pandit Nehru' (3)	LAma
'Pandour' (14)	LAma MBri
'Parade' (4)	IDun LAma MBri
'Paris' (3)	LAma
'Paul Crampel' (2)	LAma LRoo
'Paul Richter' (3)	LAma
'Pax' (3)	LAma
'Peach Blossom' (2)	ETub IDun LAma LBlo LBow LRoo MBri
'Peerless Pink' (3)	LAma
'Perfecta' (10)	LBow
'Perlina' (14)	LAma LRoo
persica	See T. ***celsiana***
'Philippe de Comines' (5)	LAma
'Picture' (5)	ETub IDun LAma LBlo LRoo
'Pimpernel' (8)	LAma
'Pink Beauty' (1)	LAma LBlo LRoo
'Pink Impression' (4)	IDun LAma
'Pink Trophy' (1)	LAma
'Pinkeen' (13)	LAma
'Pinocchio' (14)	EWal
'Plaisir' (14)	ETub IDun LAma LBlo LRoo MBri
platystigma	CAvo ECam LAma LBow
'Polo' (13)	LAma
polychroma	See T. ***biflora***
praestans	LAma SIng
– 'Fusilier'	CAvo CBro EPot ETub EWal LAma LBlo LBow LRoo MBri
– 'Unicum'	ETub IDun LAma LBlo LRoo MBri SIng
– 'Van Tubergen's Variety'	ETub LAma
'Preludium' (3)	LAma
'President Kennedy' (4)	LAma
'Prince of Austria' (1)	LAma
'Princeps' (13)	CBro EWal LAma LRoo MBri
'Princess Elizabeth' (5)	LAma
'Princess Margaret Rose' (5)	LAma
'Princesse Charmante' (14)	ETub
'Prins Carnaval' (1)	LAma LRoo
'Prinses Irene' (1)	ETub LAma LBlo LBow LRoo MBri
'Prinses Margriet' (1)	LBlo
'Prominence' (3)	LAma
pulchella	See T. ***humilis pulchella***
– ***humilis***	See T. ***humilis***
§ 'Purissima' (13)	CBro ETub LAma LBlo LBow LRoo
'Purple Cupland' (5)	LAma
'Queen' (4)	LAma
'Queen Ingrid' (14)	LAma
'Queen of Bartigons' (5)	LAma LBlo
'Queen of Night' (5)	ETub LAma LBlo LBow LRoo MBri
'Queen of Sheba' (6)	LAma LBlo LRoo

'Queen Wilhelmina'	See T. 'Koningin Wilhelmina'
'Recreado' (3)	ETub LAma
'Red Champion' (10)	LAma
'Red Emperor'	See T. 'Madame Lefeber'
'Red Georgette' (5)	MBri
'Red Matador' (4)	LAma
'Red Parrot' (10)	LAma
'Red Present' (3)	LAma
¶ 'Red Reflection' (14)	IDun
'Red Riding Hood' (14)	CAvo CBro ETub EWal LAma LBlo LBow LRoo MBri WHil
'Red Sensation' (10)	LAma LRoo
'Red Shine' (6)	ETub LAma LBlo LRoo
'Red Wing' (7)	IDun LBlo LRoo
'Reforma' (3)	ETub LAma
Rembrandt	MBri
'Renown' (5)	LAma
'Rheingold' (2)	LAma LBlo
rhodopea	See T. ***urumoffii***
'Rhodos' (5)	ETub
'Rijnland' (3)	LAma
'Ringo'	See T. 'Kees Nelis'
'Robinea' (3)	LBlo
'Rockery Beauty' (13)	LAma
'Rockery Master' (14)	LAma
'Rockery Wonder' (14)	LAma
'Rococo' (10)	LRoo
'Rosanna' (14)	LRoo
* 'Rose Emperor' (13)	LAma
'Rosella' (5)	LRoo
'Rosy Queen' (2)	LRoo
'Rosy Wings' (5)	LAma LBlo
'Salmon Parrot' (10)	LRoo
'San Marino' (5)	LBlo
saxatilis	CAvo CBro ECam EPar EPot LAma MBri SIng
– Bakeri group	EPar WChr
– 'Lilac Wonder'	CBro EPar ETub LAma LBlo LRoo MBri SIng
'Scarlet Cardinal' (2)	LAma LBlo
'Scarlett O'Hara' (5)	LAma
'Schoonoord' (2)	ETub LAma LRoo MBri
schrenkii	ECam EPar ETub LAma SIng
'Scotch Lassie' (5)	LAma
'Shakespeare' (12)	CBro LAma LBlo LBow
'Shirley' (5)	ETub LAma LBlo LRoo MBri
'Showwinner' (12)	CBro ETub LAma LBlo LRoo MBri
'Sigrid Undset' (5)	LAma
'Silentia' (3)	LAma
'Sint Maarten' (1)	IDun LAma
'Smiling Queen' (5)	LAma LBlo LRoo
¶ 'Smyrna' (14)	IDun
'Snow Queen' (2)	LBlo
'Snowflake' (3)	LAma
'Snowpeak' (5)	LAma LBlo LRoo
sogdiana	LAma
'Sorbet' (5)	LAma LBlo
sosnowskyi	LRHS
'Sothis' (7)	LAma
'Spalding' (3)	LAma
'Sparkling Fire' (14)	ETub LAma
'Spectacular Gold'	See T. 'Goldenes Deutschland'
sprengeri	CAvo CBro EPar LAma SSpi WChr
¶ – 'Trotter's form'	WCot
'Spring Green' (8)	ETub IDun LAma LBlo LBow LRoo MBri
'Spring Pearl' (13)	LAma LBlo
'Spring Song' (4)	LAma
stellata	See T. ***clusiana s.***
'Stockholm' (2)	LAma LBlo
'Stresa' (12)	CBro LAma LBlo LRoo
'Striped Apeldoorn' (4)	LAma
subpraestans	EPot LAma
'Success' (3)	LAma
'Summit' (13)	LAma
'Sun Dance' (14)	LRoo
'Sundew' (7)	LAma
'Sunkist' (5)	LAma
'Sunray' (3)	LAma
'Susan Oliver' (8)	LAma
'Sussex' (5)	LBlo
'Swan Wings' (7)	LAma
'Sweet Harmony' (5)	ETub LAma LBlo MBri
'Sweet Lady' (14)	LAma
'Sweetheart' (13)	LAma LBlo
sylvestris	CAvo CBro ECam EPar ETub LAma LBow NLan SIng
'Sylvia Warder' (14)	ETub
'Tamara' (3)	LAma
'Tango' (14)	LAma
tarda	CAvo CBro CCla ECam EPar EPot ETub EWal LAma LBlo LBow LRoo MBri MBro SIng WPat
'Teenager' (14)	LAma
'Teheran' (3)	LAma
¶ 'Temple of Beauty' (5)	IDun
'Tender Beauty' (13)	ETub LAma
tetraphylla	LAma WChr
'Texas Flame' (10)	LAma
'Texas Gold' (10)	LAma LBlo LBow
'The First' (12)	CBro LAma
'Thule' (3)	LAma
'Topscore' (3)	LAma
'Toronto' (14)	ETub LAma LBlo LRoo MBri
'Toulon' (13)	LRoo MBri
'Towa' (14)	LAma
'Trance' (3)	LAma
'Treasure' (14)	LRoo
¶ Trendsetter ® (3)	IDun
'Trinket' (14)	LAma
'Triumphator' (2)	LAma
tschimganica	ECam LAma
tubergeniana	LAma
– 'Keukenhof'	LAma
turkestanica	CAvo CBro CCla EPar EPot ETub LAma LBow LRoo MBri MPlt SIng WPat
'Uncle Tom' (11)	IDun LAma LRoo MBri
§ ***undulatifolia***	CBro LAma LBow MBri SIng
'Union Jack' (5)	LAma LBlo

urumiensis CAvo CBro CCla ECam EPar EPot ETub LAma LRoo MBri MBro NHol SIng WAbe WHil WPat
urumoffii LAma
'Valentine' (3) LAma LBlo
'Van der Neer' (1) ETub LAma
'Varinas' (3) LAma
* 'Vianen' (6) LRoo
violacea See T. ***humilis*** Violacea group
viridiflora NHol
'Vivaldi' (12) LAma
'Vivex' (4) LAma LRoo
'Vlammenspel' (1) LAma
'Vuurbaak' (2) LAma
vvedenskyi CBro EPar LAma SIng
¶ – 'Blanka' EPot
¶ – 'Hanka' EPot
¶ – 'Lenka' EPot
¶ – 'Tangerine Beauty' SIng
'West Point' (6) ETub IDun LAma LBlo LBow LRoo
* 'White Alba' (7) LAma
'White Dream' (3) LAma LBlo
'White Emperor' See T. 'Purissima'
'White Parrot' (10) LAma LBlo LRoo
'White Swallow' (3) LRoo
'White Triumphator' (6) ETub IDun LAma LBlo LBow LRoo
'White Virgin' (3) LAma
whittallii See T. ***orphanidea*** Whittallii group
'Wienerwald' (3) LRoo
'Wilhelm Kordes' (2) LAma
'Willem van Oranje' (2) LAma
'Willemsoord' (2) LAma LRoo MBri
wilsoniana See T. ***montana***
'Wim van Est' (5) LAma
¶ 'Wirosa' (11) IDun
'Yellow Dawn' (14) LAma
'Yellow Dover' (4) LAma
'Yellow Emperor' (13) CBro MBri
'Yellow Empress' (13) LAma LRoo
'Yellow Parrot' (10) LRoo
'Yellow Present' (3) LAma
'Yellow Purissima' (13) ETub
'Yokohama' (1) LAma
'Zampa' (14) LAma
zenaidae EPot WChr
'Zombie' (13) LAma
'Zwanenburg' (5) LAma

TUNICA (Caryophyllaceae)
'Rosette' See PETRORHAGIA ***saxifraga*** 'Rosette'
saxifraga See PETRORHAGIA ***saxifraga***

TUSSILAGO (Compositae)
farfara CArn CKin LHol MSal SIde WHer

TUTCHERIA See **PYRENARIA**

TWEEDIA (Asclepiadaceae)
§ ***caerulea*** CB&S CBow CHan CPle CSam CSun ECro ELan IBlr LAbb LGre LHop MNew NSti SAxl SLMG SMad SPer SSus WEas WPer

TYPHA (Typhaceae)
angustifolia CKin CRow CWGN EHon EWav LMay MSta SHig
latifolia CHEx CRow CWGN EHon EWav LMay MSta WHer
– 'Variegata' ELan MSta
§ ***laxmannii*** CRiv EHon LMay MSta
minima CBWG CRiv CRow CWGN EHon EWav LMay MSta SHig WHer
shuttleworthii IDai
stenophylla See T. ***laxmannii***

UGLI See **CITRUS** x ***tangelo*** 'Ugli'

UGNI (Myrtaceae)
§ ***molinae*** CB&S CHil CMer CPle ERea ESim ISea MBal SHil SSpi WSHC WWat
– G&K 4131 LSav
– G&K 4255 LSav

ULEX (Leguminosae)
europaeus ENot GRei SHil SPla SSta WMou
*– 'Aureus' CB&S CHoe GWic SPer
¶ – 'Dubloon' MR&S
§ – 'Flore Pleno' CB&S CShe ENot IJoh MBal MR&S NTow SHil SPer WWeb
– 'Plenus' See U. ***e.*** 'Flore Pleno'
– 'Prostratus' MBar
gallii MPla SHil
¶ – 'Mizzen' MBri
§ ***minor*** ISea SHil
nanus See U. ***minor***

ULMUS (Ulmaceae)
¶ 'Dodoens' LBuc
§ ***glabra*** CKin GRei NWea WMou
– 'Camperdownii' ELan SPer WMou
– 'Nana' NHol WPat
x ***hollandica*** 'Jacqueline Hillier' Widely available
– 'Lobel' MGos
– 'Wredei' See U. ***minor*** 'Dampieri Aurea'
'Louis van Houtte' WMou
§ ***minor*** 'Dampieri Aurea' CBot CLnd ELan IJoh LNet MBar MBlu SExT SHil SMad SPer WMou WPat
montana See U. ***glabra***
nana 'Variegata' EPot
parvifolia SChu SMad STre WCoo WFro WNor
– 'Frosty' CKni ELan EPad GLoc WAbe

– 'Geisha' EHar GLoc LHop MBar MGos MPla NBar NHar NHol SBla SChu SMad SSpi WPat WWeb
– 'Hokkaido' LGre SBla SIng STre WAbe
– *pygmaea* See U. *p.* 'Hokkaido'
procera CKin WCoo
¶ – 'Argenteo-variegata' SMad
pumila WNor
– 'Sapporo Autumn Gold' EHar MR&S

UMBELLULARIA (Lauraceae)
californica CArn CMCN IBar SArc SBor SHil SPla SSus

UMBILICUS (Crassulaceae)
erectus CChu
rupestris CNat CSun ELan GAbr GCHN NGre NWCA SIde WBon WCla WHer

UNCINIA (Cyperaceae)
egmontiana GLoc SSpi
N *rubra* CHan CHoe CMHG CSam CTom CTre EFol EMon EPla GWic IBlr LGre MRav NHol NSti SApp SMad WHal WHer
uncinata CHoe EPar LGre LHil SApp SLHN SSpi

UNGNADIA (Sapindaceae)

UNIOLA (Gramineae)
latifolia See CHASMANTHIUM *latifolium*

URCEOLINA (Liliaceae/Amaryllidaceae)
miniata See U. *peruviana*
peruviana EPot

URGINEA (Liliaceae/Hyacinthaceae)
maritima CAvo GPoy LAma

UROSPERMUM (Compositae)
delachampii CChu CTom MUlv SAxl

URSINIA (Compositae)
chrysanthemoides See EURYOPS *c.*
¶ *sericea* CMHG

UTRICULARIA (Lentibulariaceae)

UVULARIA (Liliaceae/Convallariaceae)
caroliniana WChr
disporum LAma
grandiflora CBro CCla CFor EBul ECha ELan EPar EPot GDra LAma LGre MBri MSal MUlv NHol SPer SWas WChr
– *pallida* EFou EPar IBlr
perfoliata CBro ECha EPot LAma SBla SOkd SPou WChr WThu WWat
pudica See U. *carolininana*
§ *sessilifolia* EBul LAma SPou WChr

VACCINIUM (Ericaceae)
angustifolium SHil
arctostaphylos SHil SSpi
bracteatum LSav MBri
caespitosum GDra
constablei NHol
corymbosum CB&S ELan LSav MBal MBar MGos NHol SHil SPer SReu SSta
F – 'Berkeley' LBuc MBri NTwe
F – 'Blue Crop' CMac EMui GRei LBuc MBri NBar NTwe WHig WWeb
F – 'Blue Ray' MBri
F – 'Bluetta' NTwe
F – 'Coville' EMui
F – 'Earliblue' EMui
F – 'Goldtraube' WHig
F – 'Herbert ' EMui
F – 'Parrot' NTwe
F – 'Pioneer' MBar
F – 'Trovor' ELan
cylindraceum CChu CFor LSav MBri SHil SOkd SSta WBod WPat
delavayi GArf MBal MBar MHig SHil SReu SSta
– 'Drummondii' NHol
deliciosum SHil
donianum See V. *sprengelii*
duclouxii CB&S
* *eriophyllum* SSta
erythrinum SSta
erythrocarpum NHol
floribundum CGre CMHG GAbr GDra MBal SHil SPer SSpi SSta WAbe
glaucoalbum CFor CKni GAbr IBar LSav SHil SMad SPer SReu WBod
– BMW 173 MBal
§ *macrocarpon* CMac CSun ELan ESim MBal MBar NTwe SHil SSpi SSta WThu
F – 'Early Black' ESim SSta
F – 'Hamilton' NHol WThu
F – 'Pilgrim' ESim SSta
* 'McMinn' MBal
membranaceum NHol
moupinense CCla GHig IBar ITim MBal MGos SPer SPla SSpi SSta WThu
– small leaved form MBal
myrsinites SHil SSta
myrtillus MBal SHil
'Nimo Pink' MBar
nubigenus SSta
nummularia CCla CFor EPot MBal MHig NHar SHil SIng SSpi SSta WAbe WBod WThu
– L&S 17294 NHol
ovatum CCla CFor CMHG IBar MBal MBar NHol SHil SPer SSpi SSta WThu
§ *oxycoccos* CArn MGos NLan SHil
padifolium CFor MBal NHol
praestans GEdr ITim NHol SHil SOkd

retusum	CTrw MBal SSpi SSta WAbe WBod
sikkimense	CFor
§ ***sprengelii***	CB&S
uliginosum	NLan
virgatum	MBal
vitis-idaea	CSto GPoy IJoh MBal MBar MGos MHig SHil SLon SPer SReu WHig WPer WThu
– 'Compactum'	MBal NHar WDav
– 'Koralle'	CCla IBar MBal MBar MBri MGos MRav NBar NHol SHil SPer SSta WAbe WPat
– ***minus***	ECou GArf MBal MPlt NHar NHol SReu SSta WAbe WDav WThu
* 'Well's Delight'	MBri

VALERIANA (Valerianaceae)

'Alba'	See CENTRANTHUS ***ruber albus***
¶ ***alliariifolia***	GWic
arizonica	MTho NCat NKay
'Coccinea'	See CENTRANTHUS ***ruber***
montana	EPar MCas NHol NNrd NRya WHal WHil WPer
officinalis	CArn CKin Effi GPoy LHol MChe NSel SIde WHal WHer WOak WSto
– ***sambucifolia***	CHan
phu 'Aurea'	CBot CBre CGle CHan CHoe ECha EFol EFou ELan ELun EOrc GWic IBlr LHop MBal MFir MPar MWgw NHol NNor NSti WBon WEas WRus
pyrenaica	EFol
saxatilis	EFol NRoo
supina	GLoc NWCA

VALERIANELLA (Valerianaceae)

eriocarpa	CArn EJud
§ ***locusta***	GPoy
olitoria	See V. ***locusta***

VALLEA (Elaeocarpaceae)

stipularis	IBar IJoh
– ***pyrifolia***	CGre CPle

VALLOTA See **CYRTANTHUS**

VANCOUVERIA (Berberidaceae)

chrysantha	CBos ECha EMon SBla SWas WCot
hexandra	CCla CHEx ECha EMon GWic MBal MUlv MWgw NCat NHol NKay NRya NSti SSpi WBon WOld WWin
planipetala	CBos

VEITCHIA (Palmae)

merrillii	LPal

VELTHEIMIA (Liliaceae/Hyacinthaceae)

bracteata	CAvo EBak ETub LBow
capensis	SLMG

X VENIDIO-ARCTOTIS See **ARCTOTIS**

VENIDIUM See **ARCTOTIS**

VERATRUM † (Liliaceae/Melanthiaceae)

album	CBot ECha
nigrum	CBro CCla CHEx COtt EBre ECro ELan ELun ERou GDra MBri MPar MUlv SChu SPer WCot

VERBASCUM † (Scrophulariaceae)

* ***adzharicum***	WHoo
'Arctic Summer'	See V. 'Polarsommer'
arcturus	LAbb WCla WPer
* ***bakerianum***	EBar MPit WEas
¶ 'Bill Bishop'	SIng
blattaria	CFis CHan CTom LGan MWgw NWCA WEas WHer WHil
– ***album***	CHad LGan NSti SFir SSvw WHer WHoo WRus
§ ***bombyciferum***	CBre ERav MWgw NSel NSti SSvw WEas WHil
– 'Silver Lining'	NNor SFir
'Broussa'	See V. ***bombyciferum***
chaixii	CBre CHad ECha ECro
– 'Album'	CChu CCla CFor CGle CHad CLew ECro EFou EOrc ERou LGan LGre LHop MUlv MWgw NCat SMrm WHal WHen WHil WPer WRus
Cotswold hybrid	
'Boadicea'	CSco CShe
– – 'Bridal Bouquet'	CKel
– – 'C L Adams'	CSco
– – 'Cotswold Beauty'	CB&S CSco
– – 'Cotswold Gem'	CSco ERou
– – 'Cotswold Queen'	CB&S CGle CHan CKel CSev EBre ELan ERou MBri NKay SFis SMrm SPer WHil
– – 'Gainsborough'	CGle CHar CKel CSco CSev EBre ECha ELan ERou MBri MWat MWgw SFis SMrm SPer WEas WRus
– – 'Hartleyi'	CKel
– – 'Mont Blanc'	CBot CGle CKel CSco EBre EFou MWgw SPer
– – 'Pink Domino'	CGle CHad CHar CKel CSco CSev EBre EFou ELan ERou GHig MBri MWgw SMrm SPer
– – 'Royal Highland'	CGle CHad CSco EFou ELan GHig SMrm WRus
§ ***densiflorum***	CArn CSco EBre ERou Effi LHol SIde SPer WCla WHer
dumulosum	ECha NHol WAbe
elegantissimum	CSco
§ 'Golden Wings'	ITim NHol
'Jackie'	SBla
'Letitia'	CGle CHan CRiv EPad EPot GLoc GWic MPar MTho NNrd NSti NTow SBla SIng WAbe WEas WPer WThu WWin
longifolium pannosum	See V. ***olympicum***
¶ ***lychnitis***	CArn

nigrum	CArn CCor CKin CRow ECro EOrc LHil MChe MSal SFir
§ ***olympicum***	CBow CGle EBar ECha ERav ERou GPla MFir NOak NSel NSti WHer WPer
phlomoides	EPad MSal
phoeniceum	CBre CGle ELan MPit MWgw NOak NSel NSti NWCA WCla WEas WHen WPer WWin
§ 'Polarsommer'	CHad CSam EHal ERou NBir
pulverulentum	CKin
spinosum	CGle
thapsiforme	See V. ***densiflorum***
thapsus	CKin EJud GPoy WOak
'Turkey'	NKay
¶ ***undulatum***	EPad
'Vernale'	CBot CSco
virgatum	CKin

VERBENA † (Verbenaceae)

* 'Aveyron'	SChu
bipinnatifida	SCro
* 'Blue Knight'	CB&S
♦ ***bonariensis***	See V. ***patagonica***
¶ 'Boughton House'	CSpe
canadensis	MSal
¶ – 'Perfecta'	EBar WPer
* 'Cardinal'	CB&S
* 'Carousel'	CB&S CCla
chamaedrifolia	See V. ***peruviana***
corymbosa	CGre CHil ECha LHop SChu SMrm WEas WHea WPer WSHC
¶ 'Cupido'	CSpe MPit
* 'Foxhunter'	LHop
'Gravetye'	EHal EMon GWic
hastata	CHad CHan EMon ERou MSal SCro SMrm WPer
¶ – JLS 88010	EMon
– 'Alba'	EMon
– 'Rosea'	EMon
¶ 'Hecktor'	SMad
'Hidcote Purple'	CGle GWic SAxl SMrm WEas WPer
'Huntsman'	CGle GWic WPer
N 'Kemerton'	LHop
¶ 'Kurpfalz'	IHos
* 'La France'	SChu SMrm
* 'Lavender Blue'	CB&S
'Lawrence Johnston'	CGle EOrc GWic MRav SChu WEas
'Loveliness'	GWic IBlr LHop MUlv SAxl SChu SMrm WEas
x ***maonettii***	CRiv CSpe ELan EOrc LHop WPer
officinalis	CArn CSFH EJud Effi GPoy LHol MChe NSel SIde WHer WOak WPer WSto
¶ 'Othello'	CSpe
§ ***patagonica***	CArn CChu CCla CHad CHan CHil CSam CSun ECha EFou EMon GPla GWic LHop MBri MUlv NCat SDix SMad SSvw WBon WHal WHea WSHC
§ ***peruviana***	CFor CHad CSam EBre ELan GCHN GLoc GWic LHop MCot MPit NRar NTow SAxl SChu SCro SIng WAbe WEas WHoo WOMN WPer WWin
– ***alba***	CRiv CSpe ELan EPla GLoc GWic LHop MPit SAxl SChu SIde WPer
¶ – Japanese form	WMar
phlogiflora	SLHN
'Pink Bouquet'	See V. 'Silver Anne'
pulchella	See V. ***tenera***
¶ 'Purple Kleopat'	IHos
§ ***rigida***	CGre CHad CHil ECha EMon NCat SIde SMrm WPer
¶ – 'Lilacina'	EMon
* 'Rose du Barry'	SAxl
* 'Royal Purple'	CB&S
¶ ***scabrida glandulosa***	WPer
'Silver Anne'	CB&S CBos CCla CElw CGle CHad CHil CSam ECtt EOrc GWic LAbb LHop MUlv NRar NTow SAxl SChu SDix SMrm WEas WPer
'Sissinghurst'	Widely available
¶ sp. WR 8833	WDav
stricta	MSal
¶ – JLS 88008	EMon
§ ***tenera***	CSpe LHop
'Tenerife'	See V. x ***hybrida*** 'Sissinghurst'
tenuisecta	SChu SLHN WPer
– 'Alba'	CHad SChu
venosa	See V. ***rigida***
¶ 'White Cascade'	EOrc
* 'White Knight'	CB&S CCla

VERNONIA (Compositae)

crinita	ECha ECro ERou SFis
¶ ***mespilifolia***	ECro

VERONICA † (Scrophulariaceae)

'Amethystina'	See V. ***spuria***
armena	CShe EBre GLoc MBro MRav MWat WHil
austriaca Corfu form	SBar WPer
– ***dubia***	See V. ***prostrata***
¶ – 'Ionian Skies'	SWas
austriaca teucrium	MWgw NNor NWCA SChu
– – 'Blue Fountain'	MPit WHil
– – 'Crater Lake Blue'	CB&S CHad CKel EBre ECha EFou ELan ESis MFir NNor SPer WCot WEas WWin
– – 'Kapitän'	CKel ECha LHop MFir WPer
– – 'Royal Blue'	CKel CLew CSco EFou ELan IDai LAbb MBro NKay NSti SIng WHoo
– – 'Shirley Blue'	See V. 'Shirley Blue'
beccabunga	CKin COtt CRiv CWGN EHon GPoy LMay MSal MSta NSel SHig WHer
'Blue Spire'	EBre ERou IBrk LHil WPer
bombycina	NTow SIng WDav WOMN
bonarota	See PAEDEROTA ***bonarota***

caespitosa Mac&W 5849	EPot
candida	See V. ***spicata incana***
x *cantiana* 'Kentish Pink'	EMon
caucasica	ELan EMon NCat
chamaedrys	CKin
– 'Variegata'	CMal ELan
cinerea	CShe CSun CTom EBre ECha MCas NHol NKay NNrd SIgm SSmi WAbe WEas WHil WOld WPat
dabneyi	NHol SIng
**dichroa*	ELan
exaltata	EMon
filifolia	WHoo
filiformis	SIng
formosa	See PARAHEBE ***f.***
§*fruticans*	EMNN NKay WCla
fruticulosa	SSmi WPer
gentianoides	Widely available
– 'Alba'	EGol EOrc GWic NSti
– 'Nana'	EOrc
– 'Variegata'	Widely available
x *guthrieana*	WPer
¶ *hastata rosea*	EFou
hendersonii	See V. ***subsessilis h.***
incana	See V. ***spicata incana***
kellereri	See V. ***spicata***
liwanensis	CSun ELan GCHN MBro NTow
– Mac&W 5936	EPot GDra MHig NHol WHil WOMN
longifolia	CBre CKel ELan GWic LHil MFir SFis WEas WOak WOld
– 'Alba'	CSco ELan EMon
– 'Blauriesen'	EOrc MBri NHol SFis
– 'Foerster's Blue'	CSco GWic
¶ – 'Incarnata'	EMon
– 'Schneeriesen'	ECtt EFou EOrc MBri NHol NOrc SFis
¶ – *subsessilis*	GWic
lyallii	See PARAHEBE ***l.***
montana	CKin
nummularia	ESis
officinalis	CKin GPoy NHol
oltensis	WEas WPat
– JCA 984.150	MBro NHol NTow WDav WPer
pectinata	CHar ESis GDra NCat
– *rosea*	CRiv CSun CTom EBre ESis GAbr GDra MCas MRav NHar NKay NNrd SBar SSmi WWin
peduncularis	LRHS SBla SChu SWas WEas
¶ – 'Oxford Blue'	LHop
perfoliata	See PARAHEBE ***perfoliata***
§*prostrata*	Widely available
¶ – *alba*	WHoo
¶ – 'Blue Ice'	SSmi
– 'Blue Sheen'	EBre ECtt MPlt SChu WWin
– 'Loddon Blue'	CHar CKel CSun IDai MRav NVic SBla
– 'Miss Willmott'	CKel
– 'Mrs Holt'	CSam CShe CTom EMNN MCas MPlt NCat NNrd NVic SAxl SBla SSmi WHal WWin
– 'Nana'	EMNN EPot ESis MCas MHig MPla NKay NNrd
– *rosea*	CHar GLoc MBro MPla NHol NKay NRed SIng WDav WHil WPer
¶ – 'Silver Sheen'	CTom
– 'Spode Blue'	CShe GGar LHil LHop MBro MRav NHol SBla WDav
– 'Trehane'	CRiv CShe CTom EBre ECha ELan EPar EPla ESis GHig GLoc LGro LHop MPar MRav MWat NKay NNrd NSti SPer WDav WHoo WPer WWin
♦*repens*	See V. ***reptans***
§ *reptans*	EHal EMNN ESis LHil MCas NCat NHar NNrd
* 'Romany'	CB&S
'Rosalinde'	CBot ECtt ELan EOrc LHop NHol NOrc SFis
rupestris	See V. ***prostrata***
saturejoides	MBro NRya WDav WOMN WPer
saxatilis	See V. ***fruticans***
schmidtiana	GEdr
– *nana*	CHar CLew CSun GLoc MBro NHol WOMN WPat
– *nana rosea*	WEas WOMN WPer
selleri	See V. ***wormskjoldii***
'Shirley Blue'	CHar CShe CSun CTom EBar EBre ECro EFou GCHN GGar MBro MFir MWat NBar SFis WHil WPer
spicata	CFis CHar ELan GDra MBro NNor WCla WHal
– 'Barcarolle'	EFol ELan SFis
– 'Blaufuchs' ('Blue Fox')	EFou NRoo
*– 'Corali'	SFis
– 'Erika'	ECha EOrc
– 'Heidekind'	Widely available
– 'Icicle'	LHop NTow SApp SAsh
– 'Minuet'	SFis
– 'Mori's Form'	WWin
– 'Pavane'	SFis
– 'Romiley Purple'	EFou EMon ERou GWic
– *rosea*	EFou NOak WCla
– 'Rotfuchs' ('Red Fox')	CCla CGle EBre ECha EFol EFou ELan EPar ERou GHig NHol NRoo NSti SCro SPer WEas WHal WWin
– 'Sarabande'	CSco
– *spicata*	CNat
*– *variegata*	EMon
§ *spicata incana*	CCla CGle CHoe CKel CShe CSun EFol EGol ELan ENot EPar GAbr MBro MCas NKay NNor NRya NSti SBla SPer WAbe WEas WPer WRus
– – 'Nana'	ECha LGre SSmi WCot WHal
– – 'Silver Carpet'	EFou EGol EOrc SMrm
– – 'Wendy'	GWic
§ *spuria*	EMon MFir
stelleri	See V. ***wormskjoldii***
subsessilis hendersonii	EHal GWic
¶ *sumiliensis*	EPla

tauricola Mac&W 5835 EPot
telephiifolia CHoe CLew EMNN ESis GLoc MPla MPlt NNrd NTow NWCA WHil
teucrium See V. *austriaca t.*
¶ *virense* CHan
virginica See VERONICASTRUM *virginicum*
* *waldsteinii* EMon
'Waterperry Blue' EBre MRav
¶ *wherryi* WPer
¶ 'White Spire' CBot
whitleyi GAbr MCas MPar NHol NKay NNrd NOrc WHil WPer WWin
§ *wormskjoldii* CHan CRiv CSun EFol ELan ESis LHop MBro MHig MPar NHol NKay NNrd WAbe WCla WDav WHil WOMN WPat WWin

VERONICASTRUM (Scrophulariaceae)
§ *virginicum* CRow ECha EFol EFou MPar MSal NSti WPer WWin
– *album* CCla CKel CLew CShe ECha EFol ELan GWic MBri MCot MPar MUlv MWat SAxl SPer WEas WHoo
– *roseum* EFou MBri
– *sibiricum* EMon

VESTIA (Solanaceae)
§ *foetida* CB&S CBra CGre CHan CPle CTrw ELan GWic IBlr IReg ISea NRar SMrm SSpi WOMN
lycioides See V. *foetida*

VIBURNUM † (Caprifoliaceae)
acerifolium WWat
'Allegheny' SHil
alnifolium See V. *lantanoides*
'Anne Russell' CFor CSco CShe EHar IOrc NHol SHil SPer SSta WAbe WSHC
atrocyaneum CCla LSav MBri
betulifolium CB&S CCla CTrw MBal NHol SHil SPla SReu SSpi SSta WBod WCoo WHCG WWat
bitchiuense ELan LSav
x *bodnantense* CBot CChu CPle CTrw ELan ENot GRei IDai IJoh MCot MRav MWat NNor SLon WEas WWat WWin
– 'Charles Lamont' CBot CBow EBre EHar IBlr LSav MBri SBla SHil SSpi WBod WWeb
– 'Dawn' Widely available
– 'Deben' EGol EHar ENot LSav MBri MCot SHil SPer
¶ *bracteatum* LSav
buddlejifolium CCla EHal LSav WWat
¶ *burejaeticum* LSav
x *burkwoodii* Widely available
– 'Chenaultii' EHal ELan LSav SPer
– 'Park Farm' CCla CFor CTre EGol ENot IJoh LSav MCot NHol NKay SHil SPer WBod WWat
¶ *calvum* LSav
x *carlcephalum* CB&S CBow CSco EGol ELan ENot GRei IDai IJoh LHop MBri MGos MR&S MRav MUlv MWat NKay NNor SHil SLon SPer SPla WBod WSHC
carlesii CB&S CBow CBra CPle ENot GRei LHol MBri MCot MR&S SHil SPer SReu WWat
– 'Aurora' CBow CCla CFor CSco ELan ENot IDai IJoh IOrc LSav MBar MBri MGos MR&S MUlv MWat NJap NKay SHil SPer SReu SSpi SSta WPat
– 'Charis' CFor LSav NBar SMad SSpi WBod
– 'Diana' CFor SHil SSpi SSta WWat
cassinoides WPat
'Chesapeake' CChu CCla EHar LSav MBri SHil
chingii ELan WWat
cinnamomifolium CBow CLan CSco LNet LSav SArc SBor SHil SLon SPer SReu SSpi WWat
¶ *congestum* ELan
cotinifolium LSav
cylindricum CBot CBrd CFor ELan SBor SSpi SSta WWat
¶ *dasyanthum* EPla
davidii Widely available
– (m) CB&S CSco ELan MUlv NHol SHil SPer SPla SReu SSta WBod WWat WWeb
– (f) CB&S CSco ELan MUlv NKay SHil SPer SPla SReu SSta WBod WWat WWeb
dentatum LSav
dentatum pubescens 'Longifolium' LSav
dilatatum EHar ELan SSpi
¶ *erubescens* CCla LSav WWat
– *gracilipes* SHil WWat
'Eskimo' SHil
§ *farreri* Widely available
– 'Album' See V. *f.* 'Candidissimum'
§ – 'Candidissimum' CBot CCla EFol EHar ELan ENot LHop LSav MBri MPar NHol SSpi WPat WThu
– 'Farrer's Pink' MBri WWat
– 'Nanum' CBow EGol LHop LSav MPar MPla NHol SChu SSta WHCG WPat WThu WWat
foetidum WHCr
fragrans See V. *farreri*
'Fulbrook' EBre EHar LSav MBri MUlv NHol SMrm SSpi WBod
furcatum SHil WBod WWat
x *globosum* 'Jermyns Globe' CBow CSco EGol IBar MBar MBri NHol SHil SLon SMad WWat
grandiflorum SHil SLon WBod WWat
¶ – Cooper 3023 LSav
– Foetens group SHil SSta
harryanum CBow CCla ECou IOrc LGre LSav MBal MUlv SSta

henryi	CBow CCla EHar LSav MBri NHol SHil SPla SSta WWat
× ***hillieri***	MPar SLon SSpi WBod
– 'Winton'	ISea MBri SHil SPla SReu
hupehense	LSav SCro
¶ ***ichangense***	LSav
japonicum	CChu CHEx LSav SHil SSpi WWat
× ***juddii***	Widely available
¶ ***kansuense***	LSav
* ***koreanum***	WBod
lantana	CKin CPer ENot IJoh IOrc LBuc MBar NWea SHil SPer WMou
– 'Aureum'	CHoe LSav
– 'Mohican'	LSav
– 'Xanthocarpum'	CSco ISea WMou
§ ***lantanoides***	LSav SHil
lobophyllum	MFir
macrocephalum	SHil WBod
¶ ***macrophyllum keteleeri***	SSpi
mariesii	GRei IJoh LGro
'Mohawk'	LSav
mullaha	LSav
nudum	CCla
– 'Pink Beauty'	CChu CCla WWat
odoratissimum	CB&S CGre CHEx SMad SSpi WSHC
opulus	CB&S CBra CKin CPer CSam ELan ENot GPoy GRei LBuc LHol MBar MBri MCot MFir MR&S MWat NNor NWea SHil SPer WMou
¶ – 'Andrews'	LSav
¶ – 'Apricot'	LRHS
– 'Aureum'	CBra CCla CCor CMHG CSam CSco EBre EGol EHar ELan IJoh IOrc LSav MBal MBri MGos MPla MUlv NHol NRoo SHil SPla SSta WPat
– 'Compactum'	Widely available
*– 'Flore Pleno'	GRei
N– 'Fructu-luteo'	See V. ***o.*** 'Xanthocarpum'
¶ – 'Hans'	LSav
*– 'Harvest Gold'	SSta
– 'Nanum'	CCla EGol ELan EPot MBal MBar MBri MPla SPla WHCG
– 'Notcutt's Variety'	CBow CSco ENot LSav SHil
*– 'Park Harvest'	EPla MUlv
§ – 'Roseum'	CB&S CBot CBow CCla CSco EBre EGol ELan ENot IDai IJoh ISea LSav MBar MBri MGos MPla MR&S MWat NNor NWea SHil SPer SSta
– 'Sterile'	See V. ***o.*** 'Roseum'
N– 'Xanthocarpum'	CChu CCla CMHG CSam CSco EBre EGol ELan IOrc LHop LSav MBar MR&S MRav MUlv MWat NHol SHil SLon SPer SPla WBod WSHC WWin
¶ ***parvifolium***	LSav
N ***plicatum***	CB&S CShe EHar ENot IJoh MBar
– 'Cascade'	EBre EGol EPla SSpi
– 'Grandiflorum'	CPle CSco EGol EHar IDai MBar NHol SBla SHil SPla SReu SSpi WBod
– 'Lanarth'	CB&S CBra CCla CFor CHil CPle CSco CShe CTre EGol EHar ENot LHop LSav MBri MPla NTow SHil SLon SPer SPla SReu SSta WEas
– 'Mariesii'	Widely available
– 'Nanum'	See V. ***p.*** 'Nanum Semperflorens'
§ – 'Nanum Semperflorens'	CB&S CSco EBre EHar ELan IJoh IOrc LHop MBri MGos MPla MUlv NTow SHil SLon SPer SSpi WHCG WKif WPat WSHC WWat
– 'Pink Beauty'	Widely available
*– 'Pink Prelude'	SReu
*– 'Prostratum'	EPla
¶ – 'Rosace'	MBri
*– 'Roseum'	LSav
– 'Rotundifolium'	MBri SPer WPat
– 'Rowallane'	CSco NHol SHil WBod WWat
¶ – 'Shasta'	LSav
N– 'Sterile'	SHil
– 'Summer Snowflake'	CB&S CFor IOrc LRHS SHil SMrm SSpi WWeb
– ***tomentosum***	CBra CHil CLan ISea MCot MR&S NNor SHil
– 'Watanabe'	See V. ***p.*** 'Nanum Semperflorens'
'Pragense'	CChu CMCN EGol EHar LSav MBar MBri SHil SLon SSpi
propinquum	SHil
¶ ***prunifolium***	ESim LSav
♦ ***pubescens***	See V. ***dentatum p.***
recognitum	LSav
× ***rhytidophylloides***	CSco MCot NNor WWat
– 'Dart's Duke'	MBri
rhytidophyllum	Widely available
*– 'Aldenhamense'	CB&S
– ***roseum***	CShe MRav WWat
– 'Variegatum'	CBot ELan
rigidum	LSav SSpi
sargentii	ELan IOrc LSav
– 'Onondaga'	Widely available
*– ***puberellum***	LSav
– 'Susquehanna'	LSav SPer
semperflorens	See V. ***plicatum*** 'Nanum Semperflorens'
setigerum	CBow CChu CCla LSav MBri SHil SMad
¶ – ***sulcatum***	SSpi
'Shasta'	CCla EHar LSav MBri SSpi SSta
sieboldii	LRHS LSav
– 'Seneca'	LSav SSpi
theiferum	See V. ***setigerum***
tinus	Widely available
*– 'Bewley's Variegated'	CB&S IBar MGos
– 'Eve Price'	Widely available
– 'French White'	CGre IJoh SHil WWat

– 'Gwenllian'	CCla CSco EGol EHar ELan ENot IJoh LSav MBal MGos MUlv NTow SHil SLon SPer WAbe WBod WPat
– *hirtellum*	CTre
– 'Israel'	CB&S EGol MPlt SMad SPer
¶ – 'Little Bognor'	SCro
– 'Lucidum'	CB&S CGre CSco CShe LSav MGos MUlv NNor SHil SLon SMad SPla
– 'Lucidum Variegatum'	CLan EMon SDry
– 'Pink Prelude'	LSav SPer SSta
– 'Purpureum'	EGol ELan EPla ERav MBri MUlv SHil SLon SMad SPer SPla
– 'Pyramidale'	SLon
– 'Variegatum'	Widely available
tomentosum	See V. ***plicatum***
♦ *trilobum*	See V. ***opulus***
utile	EHal LSav SSpi WThu WWat
veitchii	LSav SSta
wrightii	LSav WPat
– 'Hessei'	MBri SHil

VICIA (Leguminosae)

angustifolia	See V. ***sativa nigra***
cracca	CKin NLan SFir
§ *sativa nigra*	CKin
sepium	CKin

VICTORIA (Nymphaeaceae)

regia	See V. ***amazonica***

VIGNA (Leguminosae)

VILLADIA (Crassulaceae)

♦ *hemsleyana*	See SEADSTRUM ***hemsleyanum***
parva	NSed
– *diminutum*	NSed
§ *ramossisima*	NSed

VILLARSIA (Menyanthaceae)

♦ *bennettii*	See NYMPHOIDES ***peltata*** 'Bennettii'

VINCA † (Apocynaceae)

difformis	CCor CFis CHad CRow ELan IDai LHop LSav SDix WHal WHer
– *argentea*	NKay
¶ – *difformis*	EMon
¶ – 'Jenny's Pym'	EMon
'Hidcote Purple'	See V. ***major oxyloba***
major	CB&S CHar CRow CSco CShe ELan ENot EOrc ERav GPoy GRei IJoh ISea MBri MCot MFir MGos MR&S MWat NHol SPer SReu WOak WWin
– *alba*	IBlr LHop NSti WPer
¶ – 'Caucasian Blue'	LMer
– 'Elegantissima'	See V. ***m.*** 'Variegata'
§ – *hirsuta*	CFis CRow CShe CTom EMon EOrc WCot
– 'Jason Hill'	ELan EMon LRHS
§ – 'Maculata'	CElw CHoe CRow EFol ELan EMon ENot EPla IBar MBri NRoo NSti SAxl WAbe
– 'Oxyloba'	CBre CHil CRow ECtt ELan EMon LHop MRav
– *pubescens*	See V. ***m. hirsuta***
– 'Reticulata'	ELan EMon NSti
– 'Surrey Marble'	See V. ***m.*** 'Maculata'
§ – 'Variegata'	Widely available
minor	Widely available
– *alba*	CB&S CBot CCla CRow ECha ECro ELan EOrc EPar IJoh MBar MBri MBro MGos MWgw NNor NOak SIng SPer STre WCot WEas WOak WWat
– 'Alba Aureavariegata'	See V. ***m.*** 'Alba Variegata'
§ – 'Alba Variegata'	CBre CCla CRow CTom EGol EJud EOrc EPar EPla ESis MBar MFir NHol NKay STre WAbe WEas WHer WWat
– 'Argenteovariegata'	Widely available
§ – *atropurpurea*	Widely available
– 'Aurea'	EPla
– 'Aureovariegata'	Widely available
§ – 'Azurea Flore Pleno'	Widely available
– 'Bowles' Variety'	See V. ***m.*** 'La Grave'
– 'Burgundy'	CBre CShe EPar MBal MWgw SIng WWat
– 'Caerulea Plena'	See V. ***m.*** 'Azurea Flore Pleno'
– 'Dartington Star'	See V. ***major*** 'Oxyloba'
– 'Double Burgundy'	See V. ***m.*** 'Multiplex'
– 'Gertrude Jekyll'	CCla CFis CRiv CRow CSco EGol ELan EPla ERav GHig GPla IBar MBri MPar NHol NRoo NSti SChu SHil SIng SPer WAbe WHer
– 'Grüner Teppich' ('Green Carpet')	MBri
§ – 'La Grave'	CCla CLew CRiv CRow CSco CShe ECha ENot EPla LSav MBri MBro MCot MPlt MWgw NHol SHil SIng SPer STre WWat
– 'Maculata'	ELan
§ – 'Multiplex'	CCla CRow CTom ECtt EGol ELan EPar EPla MBri NRoo WWeb
– 'Purpurea'	See V. ***m. atropurpurea***
– 'Rubra'	See V. ***m. atropurpurea***
– 'Silver Service'	EMon
– 'Variegata'	See V. ***m.*** 'Argenteovariegata'
– 'Variegata Aurea'	See V. ***m.*** 'Aureovariegata'

VINCETOXICUM (Asclepiadaceae)

hirundinaria	GPoy MSal
nigrum	EMon LRHS
officinale	GPoy

VIOLA † (Violaceae)

¶ 'Abigail' (Vtta)	SCaw
'Achilles' (V)	SCaw
'Adelina' (V)	SCaw
'Admiral Avallon'	See V. 'Amiral Avallon'

'Admiration' (V)	CFul GMac SCaw WBou
adunca	WPer
aetolica	CPla EBar EFol ITim NCat NKay NRed
¶ 'Agnes Susannah'	CFul
'Agneta' (V)	SCaw
'Alanta' (V)	SCaw
albanica	See V. ***magellensis***
I 'Alcea'	SCaw
'Alethia' (V)	SCaw
'Alexia' (V)	SCaw
'Alice Woodall' (V)	SCaw
'Alma' (V)	SHaz
altaica	CSun SCaw
'Alwyn' (V)	SCaw
'Alys' (V)	SHaz
'Amelia' (V)	CFul GMac SCaw
'Amethyst' (C)	LHop SMrm
'Amiral Avellan' (Vt)	CCot CCra CGro CPla GMac WRus
'Anita' (V)	CFul CGle GMac
'Ann' (ExV)	SHaz
'Ann Kean' (Vtta)	SCaw
'Ann Robb' (ExV)	SHaz
'Anna' (V)	SHaz
'Annabelle' (V)	SCaw
'Anne Mott' (V)	SCaw
'Annette Ross' (V)	SCaw
I 'Annona' (V)	SCaw
'Anthea' (V)	SCaw
'Antique Lace' (V)	GMac
'Aphrodite' (V)	SCaw
'Apollo' (V)	SCaw
'Arabella' (V)	SCaw SMrm
arborescens	NHol
'Ardross Gem' (V)	Widely available
arenaria rosea	See V. ***rupestris rosea***
'Arkwright's Ruby' (V)	EBar MFir NNrd WRus
'Artemis' (V)	SCaw
'Aspasia' (V)	CFul CHar CShe GMac NHol SCaw SHaz WBou
'Atalanta' (Vtta)	SCaw
'Athena' (V)	SCaw
'Aurelia' (V)	SCaw
'Aurora' (V)	SCaw
'Baby Blue'	CGro
'Barbara' (V)	CFul CShe SCaw WBou
'Baronne Alice de Rothschild' (Vt)	CBre CCot CGro GMac
¶ 'Beatrice' (Vtta)	SHaz
§ 'Belmont Blue' (C)	Widely available
'Benjie' (V)	SHaz
bertolonii	CCor EBar MHig NHol SCaw WBou WMar
'Beshlie' (V)	GMac SCaw WBou
'Bessie Cawthorne' (C)	SCaw
'Bessie Knight' (V)	SCaw
betonicifolia	CSun NRed WPer WThu
'Bettina' (V)	SCaw
'Betty'	CFul SHaz
'Betty Grace' (V)	SCaw
'Bianca' (Vtta)	SCaw
biflora	CMHG CPla EPar GDra MCot MTho NGre NNrd WEas
'Bishop's Belle' (FP)	SHaz
'Black Ace' (V)	SCaw
'Black Diamond' (V)	SHaz
* 'Black Velvet'	NRed
'Blue Carpet' (V)	CFul GMac
'Blue Cloud' (V)	SCaw
'Blue Lace' (V)	SHaz
'Blue Ripple'	SChu
¶ 'Blue Skies' (C)	CBre
'Blue Tit' (V)	CFul WBou
'Bonna Cawthorne' (V)	SCaw
'Bonnie Heather' (V)	CFul
bosniaca	See V. ***elegantula***
♦ 'Boughton Blue'	See V. 'Belmont Blue'
¶ 'Bournemouth Gem' (Vt)	CCra
'Bowles' Black' (T)	Widely available
'Boy Blue' (Vtta)	SCaw
'Brenda Hall' (V)	SCaw
'Bronwen' (V)	SCaw
bubanii	CMHG SCaw
'Bullion' (V)	SCaw SHaz SMrm
'Buttercup' (Vtta)	CBos CCot CFul GMac SCaw SHaz WBou WMar WWin
'Buxton Blue' (V)	CFul NTow SCaw SChu SHaz
'Byrony' (Vtta)	GMac SCaw
'Calantha' (Vtta)	SCaw
calcarata	ELan SCaw WThu
§ – ***zoysii***	GDra GLoc ITim NGre NNrd NTow
'California' (Vt)	CCot
'Callia' (V)	SCaw
I 'Calypso' (V)	SCaw
'Candida' (Vtta)	SCaw
canina	CKin
'Carberry Seedling' (V)	SCaw
'Carina' (Vtta)	SCaw
'Carnival' (V)	GMac
'Caroline' (V)	SHaz SMrm
I 'Cassandra' (Vtta)	SCaw
¶ 'Chantal' (Vtta)	SCaw
'Chantreyland' (V)	LAbb MTho NCat NNrd SIng WRus
'Charity' (V)	SCaw
'Charlotte Mott' (V)	SCaw
'Chelsea Girl' (V)	SHaz SMrm
'Chloe' (Vtta)	CFul GMac SCaw
'Christobel' (V)	SCaw
'Cinderella (V)	CFul CShe
'Cindy' (V)	SHaz
'Citrina' (V)	SCaw
'Clementina' (V)	CCot CHar EBre MRav NNrd NRoo SCro
'Cleo' (V)	CBos GMac MRav SHaz
'Clive Groves' (Vt)	CGro
'Clodagh' (V)	SCaw
'Clover' (V)	SCaw
'Coeur d'Alsace' (Vt)	CCot CGro CHad CPla ELan EPar SHaz WEas WHer WRus
'Colleen' (Vtta)	SCaw
'Columbine' (V)	SCaw
'Colwall' (C)	WOld
§ 'Comte Brazza' (DVt)	CCot CCra CGro CPla GMac SHaz

'Connie' (V)	CFul SCaw SHaz
'Constellation'	CSam
'Coralie' (Vtta)	SCaw
'Cordelia' (V)	SCaw
cornuta	CBre CFul CGle CHad CPla EOrc MBro MCot MFir MWgw NKay NNrd NRoo SCaw SDix SIng SPer WBou WHoo
– ***alba***	Widely available
§ – 'Alba Minor'	CFul CGle GLoc GMac NRoo SCaw SChu
– blue	GPla SCaw WMar WWat
– 'Foliis Aureis'	EFol MFir
– ***lilacina***	CFul CGle CHar CTom ECha GMac NCat SCaw SChu SHaz WPer
– 'Minor'	CFul CPla GLoc GMac MBro SBla SCaw SHaz SSpi WBou WDav WHil WHoo WRus
– 'Minor Alba'	See V. *c.* 'Alba Minor'
– ***purpurea***	ECha WRus
– 'Rosea'	CFul SCaw SWas WMar
– ***rotundiflora***	CBre
– 'Variegata'	SCaw
– 'Violacea'	SCaw
*– 'White Perfection'	ECro
'Coronation'	CMHG CSam
corsica	MBro SCaw WDav
'Cox's Moseley' (ExV)	SHaz
crassa	EPot
'Cream Sensation' (V)	SHaz
'Cressida' (V)	SCaw
cucullata	See V. ***obliqua***
– ***alba***	See V. ***obliqua alba***
– ***rosea***	See V. ***obliqua rosea***
cunninghamii	CHar NNrd
curtisii	See V. ***tricolor c.***
¶ CW 5021	WDav
'Cyril Bell' (V)	SCaw
'Czar' (Vt)	CCot CGro CPla ECro GAbr NRed SHaz
'Daena' (Vtta)	SCaw
'Daisy Smith' (V)	CFul GMac
'Dartington Hybrid' (V)	SCaw
¶ 'Daveron' (C)	SCaw
'David Wheldon' (V)	CFul SCaw SHaz SMrm
'Davina' (V)	SCaw SChu
'Dawn' (Vtta)	CCot SCaw SHaz
'Decima' (V)	SCaw
'Delia' (V)	CFul GMac SCaw WBou
'Delicia' (Vtta)	SCaw
'Delmonden' (V)	CCla EPot GLoc
delphinantha	NKay
'Delphine' (V)	SCaw
'Demeter' (V)	SCaw
'Desdemona' (V)	GMac SHaz
'Desmonda' (V)	SCaw SChu
'Devon Cream' (V)	GMac
'Dimity' (V)	SCaw
'Dione' (Vtta)	SCaw
I 'Diosma' (V)	SCaw
'Dirty Molly'	CGle
dissecta	WPer

'Dobbie's Bronze' (V)	CFul GMac SCaw SHaz WBou
'Dobbie's Red' (V)	SCaw WBou
'Doctor Smart' (C)	SCaw
doerfleri	SCaw
'Dominy' (Vtta)	SCaw
'Double Russian' (DVt)	CGro
'Double White' (DVt)	MPar
¶ 'Dubyana'	SBar
'Duchesse de Parme' (DVt)	CGro GMac SHaz
'Dulcie Rhoda' (V)	SHaz
'Dusk'	CFul WBou
'E A Bowles'	See V. 'Bowles' Black'
'Eastgrove Blue Scented (V)	GMac WEas
'Ednaston Gem'	CSam
eizenensis	CCla GLoc SIng WDav WHal WOMN
§ ***elatior***	CCor CHar CPla MPar MPla NHol NSti SChu SHaz SIng WMar WOld WPer
elegantula	SCaw
– ***bosniaca***	SCaw WEas
'Elizabeth' (V)	CFul GMac SCaw WBou
¶ 'Elizabeth Cawthorne' (C)	SCaw
'Elizabeth Robb' (FP)	SHaz
'Emily Mott' (V)	SCaw
'Emma' (V)	SCaw
'Enterea' (V)	SCaw
erecta	See V. ***elatior***
'Eris' (V)	SCaw
'Eros' (V)	SCaw
'Etain' (V)	SCaw
'Ethena' (V)	SCaw
'Etienne' (V)	SCaw
'Evelyn Cawthorne' (C)	SCaw
'Evelyn Jackson' (V)	WBou
eximia	SCaw
'Fabiola' (Vtta)	GMac SCaw
'Felicity' (V)	SCaw
'Finola Galway' (V)	SCaw
'Fiona' (V)	CBos CFul CMHG GMac NCat SCaw WBou WMar
flettii	NKay WHal WOMN
'Florence' (V)	SCaw
'Foxbrook Cream' (C)	CFul CHar GMac SHaz WBou WRus
'Francesca' (V)	SCaw
'Freckles'	Widely available
'Gatina' (V)	SCaw
I 'Gazania' (V)	SCaw
'Gazelle' (Vtta)	ECha LHop SCaw
'Gemma' (V)	SHaz
'Genesta Gambier' (V)	CFul CMHG CSam SCaw
'George Rowley' (FP)	SHaz
'Georgina' (V)	SCaw
'Geraldine' (Vtta)	SCaw
¶ 'Geraldine Cawthorne' (C)	SCaw
'Gina' (Vtta)	SCaw
'Giselle' (V)	SCaw
glabella	GLoc WOMN

'Gladys Findlay' (V)	CFul GMac SCaw SHaz WBou WHer
'Glenroyd Fancy' (ExV)	SHaz
'Governor Herrick' (Vt)	CB&S CShe ECro EFou MShr
'Grace' (V)	SHaz
§ ***gracilis***	ELan SBla SCaw WOMN
– ***lutea***	CMHG CSam SBla
*– 'Magic'	CElw NTow SMrm
– 'Major'	GMac SCaw SHaz
'Grey Owl' (V)	SCaw
grisebachiana	CPla GAbr NGre
'Griselda' (Vtta)	SCaw
'Grovemount Blue' (C)	NCat NHol NKay WDav
'Gustav Wermig' (C)	CFul GAbr NCat SCaw SHaz WBou
¶ 'Gwen Cawthorne' (C)	SCaw
'Hansa' (C)	CGle SMrm
♦ 'Haslemere'	See V. 'Nellie Britton'
I 'Hebe' (Vtta)	SCaw
§ ***hederacea***	CArn CCot CElw CHan CMHG CPla CShe CSun ECou EFol ELan ELun EPar EPot ESis GCHN GLoc GMac GWic MPar SHaz SIng WEas WHer
– blue form	CElw CPla ECou SAxl SIng WHal WOMN WPer
¶ – 'Putty'	ECou
♦ – ***sieberi***	See V. ***sieberiana***
'Helen' (V)	SHaz
'Helen W Cochrane' (ExV)	SHaz
'Helena' (V)	SCaw
'Hera' (V)	SCaw
'Hespera' (V)	SCaw
I 'Hesperis' (V)	SCaw
heterophylla epirota	See V. ***bertolonii***
'Hextable' (C)	SCaw
hirta	CKin WCla
hispida	SCaw
'Honey' (V)	SHaz
'Horrie' (V)	CFul
'Hudsons Blue'	CElw
'Hugh Campbell' (ExV)	SHaz
'Huntercombe Purple' (V)	CBos CCla CCot CFul CSam CSun GMac MCot NNrd SBla SCaw WBou
'Hyacintha' (C)	CFul
'Hyperion' (V)	SCaw
'Iantha' (Vtta)	SCaw
'Iden Gem' (V)	CFul GMac SCaw SHaz
'Inverurie Beauty' (V)	SCaw WBou
'Inverurie Mauve' (V)	SCaw
'Iona' (V)	SCaw
'Irene Missen'	CGle
¶ 'Irina' (V)	CFul
¶ 'Irish Elegance' (Vt)	WHal
'Irish Molly' (V)	Widely available
'Isata' (V)	SCaw
¶ 'Isla' (Vtta)	SCaw
'Ita' (V)	SCaw
'Iver Grove' (V)	SCaw
'Ivory Queen' (V)	CCla CFul SCaw
'Ivory White' (V)	SCaw WOMN
'Jack Frost' (FP)	SHaz
'Jackanapes' (V)	CBot CCla CCot CFul CGle CMHG CSam CShe CSun ECha ELan ERav GMac LHop MCot MHig NNrd SCaw SHaz SMrm WBou WMar WWin
'James Christie' (FP)	SHaz
'James Pilling' (V)	CFul GMac SCaw SHaz
'Jamie' (V)	SHaz
'Jane Askew' (V)	SCaw
'Jane Mott' (V)	SCaw
'Janet' (V)	SCaw WBou
'Janine' (Vtta)	SCaw
'Janna' (V)	SCaw
'Jeannie' (V)	SHaz
'Jeannie Bellew' (V)	CSun GMac NNrd NTow SCaw SChu WBou WKif WMar WRus
'Jemma' (V)	SCaw
'Jenelle' (Vtta)	SCaw
'Jenny' (Vtta)	SCaw
'Jersey Gem' (V)	GMac SCaw SHaz
'Jessie East'	WEas
'Jimmie's Dark' (ExV)	SHaz
'Joan Christie' (FP)	SHaz
'Joe Millet' (FP)	SHaz
'Joella' (V)	SCaw
'John Raddenbury' (Vt)	CCra CGro GMac
'John Rodger' (SP)	SHaz
'John Yelmark' (V)	SCaw SMrm
'John Zanini' (Vtta)	SCaw
'Johnny Jump Up' (T)	LAbb MPit SSus WBou
¶ Joker strain (P)	NOak
jooi	EPot GLoc MCot MPar NNrd NWCA SIng WOMN WPer WThu
'Josie'	CFul
'Joyce Gray' (V)	SHaz SMrm
'Julia' (V)	SCaw
'Julian' (V)	CFul GMac GPla NHol NKay NNrd NSti SBla SIng WAbe WBou WHer WMar WPer
'Juno' (V)	GMac SCaw
'Jupiter' (V)	SCaw
'Kadischa' (V)	SCaw
'Karen' (V)	SHaz
'Kate' (V)	CFul GMac LHil
'Kathleen Hoyle' (ExV)	SHaz
'Kathy' (Vtta)	SCaw
'Katinka' (V)	SCaw
'Kerrie' (V)	SCaw
'Kilruna' (V)	SCaw
'King of the Blues' (V)	SHaz
'Kitty White' (V)	SCaw
'Kizzy' (V)	SHaz
koraiensis	MTho SPou
¶ ***koreana***	CPla NWCA
labradorica	CBro CCla CCor CCot CCra CFis CGle CGro CPla ECha EFol EFou ELan ERav GAbr LGro MCot MTho MWgw NRoo SPer WAbe WEas WRus
– ***purpurea***	Widely available
'Lady Finnyoon' (V)	SHaz

'Lady Tennyson' (V)	CFul GMac LGre SBla SCaw SHaz WBou
'Lamorna' (Vtta)	SCaw
¶ ***lanceolata***	CPla
'Larissa' (V)	SCaw
'Latona' (V)	SCaw
'Laura' (C)	CFul EFol GMac
¶ 'Lavender Lady'	CGro
'Laverna' (V)	SCaw
'Lavinia' (V)	CHar ERav GMac SCaw SHaz WBou
'Leander' (V)	SCaw
'Leda' (V)	SCaw
'Lee' (V)	SHaz
'Leora' (Vtta)	CFul GMac SCaw
'Leora Hamilton' (C)	SCaw
'Lerosa' (Vtta)	SCaw
'Leta' (Vtta)	SCaw
'Letitia' (V)	CFul GMac SCaw SHaz WAbe WBou
'Leto' (V)	SCaw
'Lewisa' (V)	SCaw
'Lianne' (Vt)	CCra CGro GMac SHaz
'Lilac Rose' (V)	CFul GMac
'Liliana' (V)	SCaw
'Liriopa' (V)	SCaw
'Lisa Cawthorne' (C)	SCaw
'Little David' (Vtta)	CBos CCot CFul CMHG CShe GMac LGre SCaw SHaz SMrm WBou WEas WRus
'Little Johnny' (V)	GMac
'Little Liz' (V)	GMac SHaz
'Livia' (Vtta)	SCaw WBou
'Lizzie's Favourite' (V)	CFul
'Lola' (V)	SCaw
'Lord Nelson' (C)	CCot
'Lord Plunket' (V)	CFul NCat SCaw WBou
♦ 'Lorna' (V)	See V. 'Mauve Radiance'
¶ 'Lorna Cawthorne' (C)	SCaw
'Lorna Moakes' (V)	SCaw SMrm
'Louisa' (V)	SCaw
'Louise Gemmell' (V)	SCaw SChu
¶ 'Love Duet'	NBir
'Luca' (V)	SCaw
'Lucinda' (V)	SCaw
'Lucy' (V)	SCaw
'Ludy May' (V)	SCaw
'Lulu' (V)	SHaz
'Luna' (Vtta)	SCaw
lutea	CShe ECha SCaw SIng WBou WRus
– elegans	See V. ***lutea lutea***
§ ***– lutea***	SCaw
'Luxonne' (Vt)	CCot SHaz
lyallii	ECou
'Lydia' (V)	CFul CShe SCaw SChu SHaz WBou
'Lydia Groves'	CGro
'Lysander' (V)	SCaw
macedonica	See V. ***tricolor macedonica***
¶ 'Madame Armandine Pages' (Vt)	CBre CCra CGro
'Madelaine' (V)	SCaw
'Madge' (V)	SCaw
'Maera' (Vtta)	SCaw
§ ***magellensis***	CPla MPit
'Magenta Maid' (V)	CFul GMac
'Maggie' (V)	SCaw
'Maggie Mott' (V)	Widely available
¶ 'Majella' (Vtta)	SCaw
'Malise' (V)	SCaw
'Malvena' (Vtta)	SCaw
mandschurica	MPar WHal WThu
'Margaret' (V)	SHaz
'Margaret Cawthorne' (C)	SCaw
'Marian' (V)	SCaw
'Marie Louise' (DVt)	CCot CCra CGro CHad CPla EPar
'Marika' (V)	SCaw
'Mark Talbot' (V)	CFul
'Maroon Picotee'	ELan
'Mars' (V)	SCaw
'Marsland's Yellow' (Vtta)	SCaw
'Martin' (V)	CBre CCla CFis CFul CMHG CShe ECha GMac LHop MCas NKay SCaw SChu SHaz WBou WMar WRus WWin
'Mary Cawthorne' (C)	SCaw
'Mary Dawson' (V)	SCaw
¶ 'Mary Ellen'	CFul
'Mattie' (V)	SHaz
'Mauve Beauty' (V)	SCaw
'Mauve Haze' (V)	CCla CFul CSun ERav GMac MTho NHol WBou WMar
§ 'Mauve Radiance' (V)	CBos CCot CFul CShe GMac NVic SCaw SHaz WBou
'Mavis Tuck'	CSam
'May Mott' (V)	GMac WAbe
'May Roberts' (ExV)	SHaz
'Mayfly' (V)	GMac
'Meena' (Vtta)	SCaw
'Megumi' (V)	SCaw
'Melinda' (Vtta)	SCaw WBou
I 'Melissa' (V)	CFul CMHG GMac SMrm
'Mercury' (V)	SCaw
'Midnight' (V)	GMac
'Midnight Turk' (V)	SHaz
'Milkmaid' (V)	CBos CFul ECha GAbr NBir SPer WKif
'Mina Walker' (ExV)	SHaz
'Minerva' (V)	SCaw
'Miranda' (Vtta)	SCaw
'Miss Brookes' (V)	CFul GMac SCaw SMrm WBou
'Mistral' (V)	SCaw
¶ 'Mitzel' (Vtta)	SCaw
'Molly Sanderson' (V)	Widely available
'Monica' (V)	SCaw
'Moonlight' (V)	Widely available
'Moonraker'	CCot NCat NKay NTow
* 'Moonshine'	GMac
'Morvana' (V)	SCaw
'Morwenna' (V)	SCaw
'Moscaria' (V)	SCaw
¶ 'Moseley Bedder'	CFul
'Moseley Ideal' (ExV)	SHaz

'Moseley Perfection' (V)	CFul SCaw
'Mrs Chichester' (V)	CFul EFou GMac LHop SCaw WBou
¶ 'Mrs David Lloyd George'	CGro
'Mrs Lancaster' (V)	CFor CFul CMHG CSam GMac SCaw WBou
'Mrs R Barton' (Vt)	CCot CCra CGro CPla GMac SHaz
'Myfawnny' (V)	CSam SCaw WBou
'Mylene' (V)	SCaw
'Myntha' (Vtta)	SCaw
'Mysie' (V)	CFul
'Nadia' (V)	SCaw
'Natasha' (V)	SCaw
'Nell' (V)	CFul
§ 'Nellie Britton' (V)	CCla CElw CFul CGle CShe EOrc GLoc GMac LGre LHop MCot MHig NKay NNrd SBla SCaw SChu SHaz SPer WAbe WBou WEas WMar WRus
'Nemesis' (V)	SCaw
'Neptune' (V)	SCaw
'Nerena' (Vtta)	SCaw
'Nesta' (Vtta)	SCaw
'Netta Stracham' (C)	WBou
'Nicole' (V)	SCaw
'Nigra' (V)	SCaw
'Nimrod' (V)	SCaw
'Nina' (V)	SCaw
'Nona' (V)	SCaw
¶ 'Nora May'	CFul
'Norah Church' (Vt)	CGro GMac SHaz
'Norah Leigh' (V)	CCra EBre NRoo WBou
§ ***obliqua***	CHar EPar ERav MPlt NHol NVic SHaz SPer WOMN
§ – ***alba***	CGro CPla CRiv EFou ELan EPar NHol NSti NVic SCro WBon WPer WWin
§ – ***rosea***	CBre CRiv NHol
'Octavia' (V)	SCaw
'Odile' (V)	SCaw
odorata	CB&S CGro CHad CKin CRow EPar ERav GPoy LHol MBri MSal NKay NRoo NSel NSti SIde SIng WCla WOak
– 'Alba'	CCla CRow ELan EPad EPar MPar MWgw NCat NRoo SIng WCla
– 'Alba Plena'	MShr WHer
– 'Aurea'	MPar
– ***dumetorum***	CKin
– ***flore pleno***	CRow EFol EPar MPar SBla
– pink	MPar WCla
¶ – ***rosea***	WOMN
– 'Sulphurea'	ELan GMac WOMN
¶ – ***wellsii***	GArf
'Olive Edmonds' (V)	SCaw
'Opera' (Vt)	CBre CCra CGro GMac
oreades	SCaw WDav
'Oriana' (V)	SCaw
orphanidis	GMac SCaw
ossea	SCaw
'Palmer's White' (V)	CFul GMac SCaw SHaz
palustris	CKin CRow CShe
'Pamela' (V)	SHaz
¶ 'Pamela Zambra' (Vt)	SHaz
'Pam's Fancy' (ExV)	WBou
'Pandora' (V)	SCaw
papilionacea	CRow WHal WOMN
– ***priceana***	CCla CHad NRed SAxl SHaz SPer WWat
'Pat Creasy' (V)	GMac SHaz
'Patricia Brookes' (V)	SCaw
pedata	EPot WWat
pedatifida	CCla CHad CHan CRiv EFol ELan GLoc NSti SChu SHaz WPer WRus WThu
'Penny Black' (V)	SCaw WBou
pensylvanica	CBro CKni
'Perle Rose' (Vt)	CCot CCra CGro MShr
¶ 'Pete'	SChu
'Petra' (Vtta)	SCaw
'Philippa Cawthorne' (C)	SCaw
'Phoebe' (V)	SCaw WBou
'Phyllida' (V)	SCaw
'Pickering Blue' (V)	CCot CFul GMac SCaw SHaz WBou
'Piper' (V)	SHaz
'Pippa' (Vtta)	SCaw SChu
'Pixie' (V)	SHaz
'Poppy' (V)	SCaw
'Priam' (V)	SCaw
'Primrose Cream' (V)	SCaw
'Primrose Dame' (V)	CFul GMac SCaw SHaz WBou
'Primrose Pixie' (V)	GMac
'Prince Henry' (T)	EFou LAbb MPit NKay SPer WBou WCla WHil
'Prince John' (T)	MPit NCat NKay SPer WBou
'Princess Mab' (Vtta)	CBos CFul GMac SCaw SHaz WBou
♦ 'Princess of Wales'	See V. 'Princesse de Galles'
§ 'Princesse de Galles' (Vt)	CB&S CCra CGro ECro EPar GMac SHaz WRus
'Purity' (Vtta)	SCaw
'Purple Dove' (V)	SHaz
'Purple Radiance'	CCla
'Purple Wings' (V)	GMac
'Queen Charlotte' (Vt)	ECro GCHN MBri
'Queen Disa' (Vtta)	SCaw
'Quink' (V)	CFul
'Ramona' (V)	SCaw
'Raven (Vtta)	GMac
'Ravenna' (V)	SCaw
'Rawson's White' (Vt)	CGro GMac NCat
'Rebecca' (Vtta)	CBos CCot CFul CGle CMHG CPla CSam GMac NCat SCaw SChu WBou WHer
'Rebecca Cawthorne' (C)	SCaw
'Red Charm ' (Vt)	MBri
¶ 'Red Lion'	CGro
'Red Queen' (Vt)	CCot CGro
reichenbachiana	ELan EPar
'Remora' (Vtta)	SCaw WBou
'Rhoda' (V)	SCaw

'Richard Vivian' (V)	SCaw
'Richard's Yellow' (V)	SCaw
riviniana	CArn CKin CTom MFir NLan WBon WHer WHil WOak
– 'Autumn White'	MPar
'Romilly' (V)	SCaw
'Rosine' (Vt)	CCra CGro GMac
'Rowan Hood' (ExV)	SHaz
'Rowena' (V)	SCaw
¶ 'Royal Delft'	GCHN
'Royal Robe' (VT)	CCra CGro
rupestris	NHol NRed
¶ – blue	NCat
§ – ***rosea***	CBre CHar CPla CTom NCat NGre NRed NSti WBon WCla WEas WHal
'Russian Superb' (Vt)	CCot
'Ruth Blackall' (V)	SCaw
'Ruth Elkans' (V)	CFul GMac SCaw SHaz
¶ 'Saint Helena' (Vt)	CGro
'Sally' (Vtta)	SCaw
'Samantha' (Vtta)	SCaw
'Sammy Jo' (V)	SHaz WBou
'Sarah' (V)	CFul SHaz
saxatilis	See V. ***tricolor subalpina***
selkirkii	CPla CRiv WThu
sempervirens	WPer
¶ ***sempervivoides***	WOMN
septentrionalis	CCla CCot CCra ECha EGol ELan EPot ERav MCas MCot MPar NGre SAxl SHaz SSmi WCla WHal WHil WOld WRus
– ***alba***	CBre CFis CMHG NNrd WPer
'Septima' (V)	SCaw
'Serena' (V)	SCaw
'Sheila' (V)	SHaz WBou
§ ***sieberiana***	ECou
'Sigrid' (V)	SCaw
'Sissinghurst' (V)	SCaw
'Sky Blue' (V)	SCaw
'Sophie' (V)	SHaz
sororia 'Albiflora'	WDav
'Soula' (Vtta)	SCaw
'Spey' (C)	SPer
'Stewart William' (FP)	SHaz
'Steyning' (V)	SCaw
stojanowii	ELan EMon GLoc GMac SBla SIng WEas WOMN WPer
striata	WWat
'Sulphurea' (Vt)	CGro CPla ECro ELan
¶ 'Sunshine' (V)	CFul
'Susan' (SP)	SHaz
'Susannah' (V)	GMac SHaz
'Susie' (V)	CShe SHaz
'Swanley White'	See V. 'Comte de Brazza'
'Sybil' (ExV)	SHaz
'Sybil Cornfield'	WWin
'Sylvia Hart'	MTho
'Talitha' (V)	GMac SCaw
'Tamsin' (V)	SCaw
'Tara' (V)	SCaw
'Thalia' (Vtta)	CFul SCaw WBou
'The Clevedon Violet' (Vt)	WWat
'Thea' (V)	SCaw
'Thelma' (V)	SCaw
'Thetis' (V)	SCaw
'Tiffany' (V)	SCaw
'Tina' (V)	GMac SHaz WBou
'Titania' (Vtta)	SCaw
'Tom Tit' (V)	SCaw WBou
'Tony Venison' (C)	CBos CElw CHoe EFol MTho NNrd SHaz WHer WRus
¶ 'Translucent Blue'	MShr
tricolor	CKin CRow GPoy LHol MCot MSal NGre NSel NWCA SFir SIde WHer
§ – ***curtisii***	SCaw
§ – ***macedonica***	CSun NGre SIng
– 'Sawyer's Blue'	WPer
'Tropical Waves'	EFou
'Tullia' (Vtta)	SCaw
'Una' (V)	SCaw
'Unity' (V)	SCaw
'Velleda' (Vtta)	SCaw
velutina	See V. ***gracilis***
'Venetia' (V)	CFul SCaw
'Venus' (V)	SCaw
§ ***verecunda yakusimana***	CRiv CTom EPot ESis NGre NNrd SIng WAbe WDav
'Victoria' (Vt)	LGre
'Victoria Cawthorne' (C)	SCaw SChu
'Vignette' (V)	SHaz
'Virginia' (V)	CFul GMac SCaw SHaz WBou
'Virgo' (V)	SCaw
x ***visseriana lutea***	GMac WKif
'Vita' (V)	CFul CHad CShe CSun EFou ERav GMac GWic LGre SCaw SChu SHaz WBou WMar WPer
'Wanda' (V)	SCaw
'Wheatley White'	SPer
'White Gem' (V)	SHaz
'White Ladies' (Vt)	See V. ***obliqua alba***
'White Pearl' (V)	GMac
'White Swan' (V)	GMac SCaw
'White Waves'	EFou
'William Fife' (ExV)	SHaz
'William Wallace' (V)	SCaw
'Windward' (Vt)	CCot CGro NCat
'Winifred Jones' (V)	SHaz
'Winifred Wargent' (V)	SCaw
'Winona' (Vtta)	SCaw
'Winona Cawthorne' (C)	SCaw SChu
'Woodlands Cream' (V)	GMac SHaz
'Woodlands Gold' (V)	SHaz
'Woodlands Lilac' (V)	SCaw WBou
'Woodlands White' (V)	SCaw
'Xantha' (V)	SCaw
yakusimana	See V. ***verecunda yakusimana***
yedoensis	CPla CSun
'Yoyo' (V)	SHaz
'Zalea' (V)	SCaw
'Zara' (V)	GMac SHaz WBou
'Zepherine' (V)	SCaw
'Zeta' (V)	SCaw
'Ziglana' (V)	SCaw
'Zoe' (Vtta)	CFul GMac SCaw WBou

'Zona' (V) SCaw
zoysii See V. ***calcarata zoysii***

VISCARIA (Caryophyllaceae)
vulgaris See LYCHNIS ***viscaria***

VITALIANA (Primulaceae)
§ ***primuliflora*** CLew CRiv CSun GEdr GLoc MBro NKay NNrd WHil WHoo WOMN WPat
– ***cinerea*** EPot
– ***praetutiana*** EPot GDra GHig ITim MBro MCas MHig NHar NHol SIng WAbe WDav
– silver leaf form EPot
– ***tridentata*** EPot

VITEX (Verbenaceae)
agnus-castus CB&S CBow CCla CGre CHan ELan GPoy LHol MSal SHil SPer SSpi WHer
¶ ***lucens*** CHEx
negundo GWic
– ***cannabinifolia*** See V. ***n. heterophylla***
– ***heterophylla*** GWic

VITIS † (Vitaceae)
F 'Abouriou' (***vinifera***) (O/B) WStA
F 'Alden' (O/W) CYea
F 'Alicante' (***vinifera***) (G/B) CB&S ERea NTwe WStA
F 'Alzey Red' (***vinifera***) (O/R) CYea
amurensis CHEx SHil WMou WWat
F 'Angers Frontignan' (***vinifera***) (G/O/B) ERea
'Apiifolia' (***vinifera***) See V. 'Ciotat'
F 'Appley Towers' (***vinifera***) (G/B) ERea
F 'Aris' (O/W) CYea
F 'Ascot Citronelle' (***vinifera***) (G/W) ERea
F 'Aurora' (Seibel 5279) CYea
F 'Auvergne Frontignan' (***vinifera***) (G/O/W) ERea
F 'Auxerrois' (***vinifera***) (O/W) CYea WStA
F 'Bacchus' (***vinifera***) (O/W) WStA
F 'Baco Noir' (O/B) CYea NTwe WStA
betulifolia SHil
'Black Alicante' (***vinifera***) See V. 'Alicante'
F 'Black Corinth' (***vinifera***) (G/B) ERea
F 'Black Frontignan' (***vinifera***) (G/O/B) ERea WStA
♦ 'Black Hamburgh' ('Trollinger') See V. 'Schiava Grossa'
F 'Black Monukka' (***vinifera***) (G/B) ERea ESim
F 'Black Prince' (***vinifera***) (G/B) ERea
F 'Blauburger' (***vinifera***) (O/B) CYea WStA
'Blue Portuguese' (***vinifera***) See V. 'Portugieser'
F 'Boskoop Glory' (***vinifera***) CMac IJoh NTwe SDea
F 'Brant' Widely available
F 'Buckland Sweetwater' (***vinifera***) (G/W) ERea MBri NTwe SCra
F 'Cabernet Sauvignon' (***vinifera***) (O/B) WStA
F ***californica*** ERea
¶ 'Canadice' ESim
F 'Canon Hall Muscat' (***vinifera***) (G/W) ERea
F 'Cardinal' (***vinifera***) ERea
'Cascade' (Seibel 13053) (O/B) CYea ERea LBuc
F 'Chaouch' (***vinifera***) (G/W) ERea
F 'Chardonnay' (***vinifera***) (O/W) CYea SCra WStA
F 'Chasselas' (***vinifera***) (G/O/W) CB&S CMac ERea EWar SCra WStA
'Chasselas d'Or' (***vinifera***) See V. 'Chasselas'
F 'Chasselas Rosé' (***vinifera***) (G/R) ERea WStA
F 'Chasselas Vibert' (***vinifera***) (G/W) ERea
F 'Chenin Blanc' (***vinifera***) (O/W) WStA
F 'Ciotat' (***vinifera***) EPla ERea WSta
coignetiae Widely available
F 'Concord' (***labrusca***) (O/B) ERea
F 'Cot' (***vinifera***) (O/B) WStA
F 'Cote House Seedling' (***vinifera***) (O/W) ERea
* 'Csabyongye' (***vinifera***) (W) WStA
davidii SHil
– ***cyanocarpa*** MGos
F 'Dunkelfelder' (***vinifera***) (O/R) CYea WStA
F 'Early Van der Laan' (***vinifera***) LHol
F 'Ehrenfelser' (***vinifera***) (O/W) CYea WStA
F 'Elbling' (***vinifera***) (O/W) WStA
F 'Emerald Riesling' (***vinifera***) (O/W) CYea
F 'Espiran' (***vinifera***) ERea
F 'Excelsior' (***vinifera***) (W) WStA
F 'Faber' (***vinifera***) (O/W) CYea WStA
F 'Forta' (***vinifera***) (O/W) WStA
F 'Foster's Seedling' (***vinifera***) (G/W) ERea NTwe SPer WStA
F 'Fragola' (***vinifera***) (O/R) CCor CMac ERav ERea NTwe SDea WStA
F 'Gagarin Blue' (***vinifera***) (O/B) CYea ERea SCra WStA

F 'Gamay Hatif' (***vinifera***) (O/B)	ERea
F 'Gamay Noir' (***vinifera***) (O/B)	CYea WStA
F Gamay Tienturier group (***vinifera***) (O/B)	WStA
F 'Gewürztraminer' (***vinifera***) (O/R)	CYea WStA
¶ 'Glenora'	ESim
'Glory of Boskoop' (***vinifera***)	See V. 'Boskoop Glory'
'Golden Chasselas' (***vinifera***)	See V. 'Chasselas'
F 'Golden Queen' (***vinifera***) (G/W)	ERea
F 'Goldriesling' (***vinifera***) (O/W)	WStA
F 'Grizzley Frontignan' (***vinifera***) (G/R)	ERea
F 'Gros Colmar' (***vinifera***) (G/B)	ERea
F 'Gros Maroc' (***vinifera***) (G/B)	ERea
F 'Gutenborner' (***vinifera***) (O/W)	CYea WStA
henryana	See PARTHENOCISSUS ***henryana***
F 'Himrod' (O/W)	CYea ERea ESim NTwe SCra SDea
F 'Incana' (***vinifera***) (O/B)	CSco LGre SHil
inconstans 'Veitchii'	See PARTHENOCISSUS ***tricuspidata*** 'Veitchii'
F 'Interlaken' (***vinifera***)	ERea
F 'King's Ruby' (***vinifera***)	ERea
F 'Kuibishevski' (O/R)	CYea WStA
F 'Lady Downe's Seedling' (***vinifera***) (G/B)	ERea
F 'Lady Hastings' (***vinifera***) (G/B)	ERea
F 'Lady Hutt' (***vinifera***) (G/W)	ERea
F Landot 244 (O/B)	WStA
F 'Léon Millot' (***vinifera***) (O/G/B)	CYea EMui ERea SKee WStA
F 'Lucombe' (***vinifera***)	SDea
F 'Madame Mathias Muscat' (***vinifera***)	SCra
F 'Madeira Frontignan' (***vinifera***) (G/R)	ERea
* 'Madeleine' (***vinifera***)	EMui
F 'Madeleine Angevine' (***vinifera***) (O/W)	CYea ERea NTwe WStA
F 'Madeleine Royale' (***vinifera***) (G/W)	ERea WStA
F 'Madeleine Silvaner' (***vinifera***) (O/W)	CYea ERea LBuc NTwe SCra SDea SKee WStA
F 'Madresfield Court' (***vinifera***) (G/B)	ERea NTwe WStA
♦ 'Malbec' (***vinifera***)	See V. 'Cot'
F 'Maréchal Foch' (O/B)	CYea
F 'Maréchal Joffre' (O/B)	CYea NTwe WStA
F 'Melon de Bourgogne' (***vinifera***) (O/W)	WStA
F 'Mireille' (***vinifera***)	NTwe WStA
F 'Morio Muscat' (***vinifera***) (O/W)	CYea WStA
F 'Mrs Pearson' (***vinifera***) (G/W)	ERea
F 'Mrs Pince's Black Muscat' (***vinifera***) (G/B)	ERea
F 'Müller-Thurgau' (Riesling-Silvaner) (***vinifera***) (O/W)	CB&S CYea ERea LBuc MBri NElm NTwe SCra SDea SKee SPer WStA
♦ 'Muscadet' (***vinifera***)	See V. 'Melon de Bourgogne'
F 'Muscat Blanc à Petits Grains' (***vinifera***) (O/W)	WStA
F 'Muscat Bleu' (***vinifera***) (O/B)	ERea
F 'Muscat Champion' (***vinifera***) (G/R)	ERea
F 'Muscat Hamburg' (***vinifera***) (G/B)	ERea WStA
F 'Muscat of Alexandria' (***vinifera***) (G/W)	CB&S CMac CSam ERea EWar IJoh
F 'Muscat of Hungary' (***vinifera***) (G/W)	ERea
F 'Muscat Ottonel' (***vinifera***) (O/W)	WStA
F 'Muscate de Saumur' (***vinifera***) (W)	WStA
F 'New York Muscat' (***vinifera***) (O/B)	ERea
F 'Nobling' (***vinifera***) (O/W)	CYea
F 'Noir Hatif de Marseilles' (***vinifera***) (O/B)	CYea ERea
F 'No. 69' (***vinifera***) (W)	WStA
F Oberlin 595 (O/B)	CYea WStA
F 'Oliver Irsay' (***vinifera***) (O/W)	ERea WStA
F 'Optima' (***vinifera***) (O/W)	CYea WStA
F 'Ortega' (***vinifera***) (O/W)	CYea WStA
♦ parsley leaved	See V. 'Ciotat'
F 'Perle' (***vinifera***) (O/W)	CYea WStA
F 'Perle de Czaba' (***vinifera***) (G/O/W)	ERea
F 'Perlette' (***vinifera***) (O/W)	WStA
F 'Phoenix' (***vinifera***) (O/W)	CYea
F 'Pinot Blanc' (***vinifera***) (O/W)	CYea SCra WStA
F 'Pinot Gris' (***vinifera***) (O/B)	CYea WStA
F 'Pinot Meunier' (***vinifera***) (O/B)	CYea
F 'Pinot Noir' (***vinifera***)	CYea WStA

F 'Pirovano 14' (O/B) CYea ELan ERea NTwe WStA
F 'Plantet' (O/B) WStA
F 'Portugeiser' (*vinifera*) WStA
F 'Portugieser' (*vinifera*) (O/B) CYea
F 'Précoce de Bousquet' (*vinifera*) (O/W) WStA
F 'Précoce de Malingre' (*vinifera*) (O/W) CYea ERea
F 'Primavis Frontignan' (*vinifera*) (G/W) ERea WStA
F 'Prince of Wales' (*vinifera*) (G/B) ERea
'Pulchra' LGre SHil WAbe
F 'Purpurea' (*vinifera*) (O/B) Widely available
quinquefolia See PARTHENOCISSUS ***quinquefolia***
F 'Ramdas' (O/W) CYea
F Ravat 51 (O/W) WStA
F 'Regner' (*vinifera*) (O/W) WStA
F 'Reichensteiner' (*vinifera*) (O/G/W) CYea WStA
F 'Reine Olga' (*vinifera*) (O/R) ERea
F 'Rembrant' (*vinifera*) (R) WStA
F 'Riesling' (*vinifera*) (O/W) CYea WStA
F 'Rotberger' (*vinifera*) (O/G/B) CYea
F 'Royal Muscadine' (*vinifera*) See V. 'Chasselas'
F 'Saint Laurent' (*vinifera*) (G/O/W) ERea
F 'Sauvignon Blanc' (*vinifera*) (O/W) CYea WStA
F 'Scheurebe' (*vinifera*) (O/W) CYea WStA
F 'Schiava Grossa' (*vinifera*) (G/B) CB&S CMac CSam ELan ERea EWar GChr GRei IJoh ISea LBuc LHol MBri NElm NRog NTwe SCra SDea SKee WStA
F 'Schönburger' (*vinifera*) (O/W) CYea WStA
F 'Schuyler' (O/B) CYea
F 'Seibel' EMui NTwe SCra
Seibel 13053 See V. 'Cascade'
F Seibel 138315 (*vinifera*) (R) WStA
F Seibel 5409 (*vinifera*) (W) WStA
♦ Seibel 5455 See V. 'Plantet'
F 'Septimer' (*vinifera*) (O/W) CYea WStA
F 'Seyval Blanc' (Seyve Villard 5276) (O/W) CYea ELan ERea NTwe SCra SDea WStA
♦ Seyve Villard 12.375 See V. 'Villard Blanc'
F Seyve Villard 20.473 (*vinifera*) (W) WStA
F 'Siegerrebe' (*vinifera*) (O/W) CYea EMui ERea NTwe SCra SDea WStA
F 'Silvaner' (*vinifera*) (O/W) CYea WStA
'Strawberry Grape' (*vinifera*) See V. 'Fragola'
'Sultana' (*vinifera*) ERea WStA
F 'Syrian' (*vinifera*) (G/W) ERea
F Teinturier (*vinifera*) (O/B) ERea
F 'Tereshkova' (O/B) ERea SCra WStA
'Thompson Seedless' (*vinifera*) See V. 'Sultana'
F 'Traminer' (*vinifera*) (O/W) CYea
F 'Trebbiano' (*vinifera*) (G/W) ERea
F 'Triomphe d'Alsace' (O/B) CYea SCra WStA
¶ 'Vanessa' ESim
¶ 'Venus' ESim
F 'Villard Blanc' (O/W) WStA
F 'West's St Peter's' (*vinifera*) (G/B) ERea
F 'Wrotham Pinot' (*vinifera*) (O/B) CYea WStA
F 'Würzer' (*vinifera*) (O/W) CYea WStA
F 'Zweigeltrebe' (*vinifera*) (O/B) CYea WStA

VRIESEA (Bromeliaceae)
carinata MBri
hieroglyphica MBri
x ***poelmanii*** MBri
'Polonia' MBri
saundersii MBri
splendens MBri
– 'Fire' MBri
'Vulkana' MBri

WACHENDORFIA (Haemodoraceae)
thyrsiflora CHEx IBlr IBrk SAxl
– 'Trengwainton Form' GWic

WAHLENBERGIA (Campanulaceae)
albomarginata CRiv ECou EPad EPla GCHN GGar GLoc NHol NTow NWCA WDav WHal WPer
– 'Blue Mist' ECou EPad
congesta GCHN LRHS SIng
gloriosa CLew EPad WAbe
¶ – white form CLew
¶ ***lobelioides*** WPer
pumilio See EDRAIANTHUS ***pumilio***
§ ***saxicola*** CHar CLew CRiv CRow CShe CSpe MCas NTow NVic SBla WHil WPer
species ECou
tasmanica See W. ***saxicola***
trichogyna LRHS
¶ ***unduriata*** WPer

WALDHEIMIA (Compositae)
¶ *glabra* ITim NGre WPer

WALDSTEINIA (Rosaceae)
¶ *fragarioides* MFir
¶ *rosaceae* WPer
ternata Widely available

WALNUT, Common See **JUGLANS** *regia*

WASABIA (Cruciferae)
japonica CArn GPoy

WASHINGTONIA (Palmae)
filifera CHEx LPal MBri SArc

WATSONIA † (Iridaceae)
angusta CHan GWic
♦ *ardernei* See W. *borbonica a.*
♦ *beatricis* See W. *pillansii*
§ *borbonica* CChu CFor IBlr
– *ardernei* LGre
marginata CHan IBrk
– *alba* CFor
meriana IBlr IBrk CHan CFor
§ *pillansii* CChu CHan CHan GWic IBlr SSpi SSvw
♦ *pyramidata* See W. *borbonica*
'Stanford Scarlet' GWic LGre
Tresco hybrids WEas
versfeldii CHan

WATTAKAKA See **DREGEA**

WEIGELA † (Caprifoliaceae)
'Abel Carrière' CBow CRow CSco CShe ELan ENot GRei SHil SSta WWeb
'Abel Carrière Golden' EPla
'Avalanche' CRow ECtt MR&S MRav SHil
'Boskoop Glory' CSco MBri NCat SPer WWeb
Briant Rubidor ® See W. Olympiade ®
'Bristol Ruby' Widely available
'Candida' ELan EPla MBri NHol SPer
'Carnival' COtt MR&S SSta
'Centennial' MBri MGos
coraeensis 'Alba' CChu CCla
'Dart's Colourdream' CCla COtt EBre ECtt IOrc MGos
¶ 'Espérance' EPla
'Eva Rathke' CB&S CBra CFis ELan EPla ISea MBri NHol NWea SHil SSta
* 'Evita' CSco EBre GRei IJoh IOrc MGos MPla SHil SPer SSta WPat WWat
¶ 'Féerie' WWeb
florida CTrw MR&S MWat
– *alba* CB&S CMHG MBar
*– 'Albovariegata' CFis SMad
§ – 'Aureovariegata' CMHG CSco ECha EPar IJoh ISea MBal NHol NJap SLon SPer SPla WHil WPat
– 'Bicolor' CB&S
– 'Bristol Snowflake' CCla CSco EBre LHop LSav SLon
– 'Foliis Purpureis' Widely available
– 'Gustave Malet' ISea
*– 'Langtrees' EFol
– 'Magee' CMCN
*– 'Minuet' EBre SGar WPat
– 'Nana Variegata' CBow CSco EHal ERav MBar MBri SMad
– 'Rubigold' See W. Olympiade ®
*– 'Rumba' EBre
¶ – 'Tango' ECtt
*– 'Variegata Aurea' See W. *f.* 'Aureovariegata'
*– 'Variegata Compacta' WWat
– *venusta* SHil
*– 'Versicolor' CChu CCor CMHG LHop SHil
'Florida Variegata' Widely available
'Guiz 122' CCla
hortensis 'Nivea' CPle EPla SHil
lonicera CRow
'Looymansii Aurea' CBow CCla CFor CPle CRow CSco ECha EHar ELan ERav MPla NHol SHil SLon SPer SPla WSHC WWat
'Lucifer' EBre MR&S SSta WWeb
'Majestueux' SHil SSta
maximowiczii CBot CBow CCla CPle EBre NHol SSta WHCG
§ *middendorffiana* CBot CBow CChu CCla CHad CMHG CPle CRow CSco EBre ELan ENot ISea MBar MPla MWat SHil SPer SPla WHCG WSHC WWin
'Mont Blanc' CBot SHil
'Newport Red' CBow CCla CSco ENot IDai MBri MR&S MRav MWat NHol SHil SPla
§ Olympiade ® EBar EBre ECtt EFol ELan ERav IJoh IOrc LSav MBar MBri MGos SHil SPer SSta
praecox SHil
'Praecox Variegata' CChu CMHG ECha EHar LHop MBri NHol SHil SLon SPer SSpi SSta WHCG WPat WWat WWeb
'Red Prince' MBri
'Rubidor' See W. Olympiade ®
'Snowflake' CBow CPle ECtt MPla WWeb
'Victoria' COtt ECtt MBri

WEINMANNIA (Cunoniaceae)
trichosperma CGre CHEx IBlr SArc

WELDENIA (Commelinaceae)
candida LRHS

WESTRINGIA (Labiatae)
angustifolia ECou
brevifolia ECou
– Raleighii group ECou
§ *fruticosa* CMer CPle CTre ELan LHop
– 'Variegata' CPle CTre LHop
rosmariniformis See W. *fruticosa*

WHITE CURRANT See **RIBES** White Currant group

WIDDRINGTONIA (Cupressaceae)
§ ***cupressoides*** LRHS
nodiflora See W. ***cupressoides***
whytei MBri

WIGANDIA (Hydrophyllaceae)
¶ ***caracasana*** CHEx
urens CHEx SArc

WINEBERRY See **RUBUS** ***phoenicolasius***

WISTERIA † (Leguminosae)
floribunda CB&S ELan NKay SLon WNor
§ – 'Alba' CB&S CBow CCla CFor CSco EHar ELan MR&S NHol SBra SHil SPer SReu SSpi SSta
*– 'Burford' MMea
– 'Domino' CCla LNet MMea SSus
– 'Hichirimen' MMea
*– 'Lipstick' ELan LNet
– 'Macrobotrys' See W. *f.* 'Multijuga'
§ – 'Multijuga' CFor EHar IOrc LNet MBri MMea MUlv MWat NHol SHil SMad SPer SSpi WAbe WWat
¶ – 'Murasaki Noda' MGos
– 'Peaches and Cream' CB&S CCla LNet MMea SPer SSus
– 'Pink Ice' CCla IJoh MBri MMea SSpi SSus
– 'Purple Patches' CCla LNet MMea SPer SSus
– 'Rosea' ('Honko') CBow CFor CMac EHar ELan ENot MBar MMea MR&S SBra SHil SPer
– 'Snow Showers' CBow IHos IJoh LNet MBri MMea SPer SSus
– 'Violacea Plena' MBri MMea SHil
x ***formosa*** 'Issai' CB&S CSam ELan LNet MBar MGos MMea MUlv SPer
– 'Kokkuryu' ('Black Dragon') CB&S CBow ELan LNet MGos SHil SMad SPer SSpi SSta
frutescens WNor
multijuga 'Alba' See W. ***floribunda*** 'Alba'
sinensis Widely available
– 'Alba' ('Shiro-capital') CSco CShe ELan IOrc ISea LNet MBar MBri MMea MWat SHil SPer SSpi WBod
– 'Caroline' LNet MMea MR&S MUlv SMad SPer SSpi SSta SSus
– 'Plena' SHil
– 'Prematura' CBow CSco NHol SSpi
– 'Prematura Alba' CSco WWat
– 'Prolific' CHad MBri MMea
*– 'Rosea' LNet
venusta EHar LNet MMea MUlv SHil SPer
* ***vestita*** MMea

WITHANIA (Solanaceae)
¶ ***somnifera*** MSal

WITTSTEINIA (Alseuosmiaceae)
vacciniacea MBal

WOODSIA (Aspleniaceae)
obtusa NMar

WOODWARDIA † (Blechnaceae)
martinezii SApp
* ***orientalis formosana*** NMar
radicans CHEx NMar SApp SArc
¶ ***virginica*** CB&S

WORCESTERBERRY See **RIBES** ***divaricatum***

WULFENIA (Scrophulariaceae)
¶ ***amherstiana*** NHol
baldaccii SIng
carinthiaca CGre EBar MHig NHol SIng WHil WHoo

XANTHOCERAS (Sapindaceae)
sorbifolium CBot CChu CMCN CPle EHar ELan GWic LGre MBri SHil SLHN SSpi WWat

XANTHORHIZA (Ranunculaceae)
simplicissima CBot CChu CCla CFor CGle CRow LSav MBri MUlv SHil SMad WWat

XANTHOSOMA (Araceae)
lindenii See CALADIUM ***lindenii***
¶ ***sagittifolium*** CHEx

XERONEMA (Liliaceae/Phormiaceae)
callistemon ECou

XEROPHYLLUM (Liliaceae/Phormiaceae)
tenax CSun MBro WDav

YOUNGBERRY See **RUBUS**

YUCCA † (Agavaceae)
aloifolia CCan CHEx MBri MUlv SArc SIgm
– 'Variegata' CCan CHEx LPal
angustifolia See Y. ***glauca***
§ ***elephantipes*** CCan CHEx MBri SArc
filamentosa Widely available
– 'Bright Edge' CCan CSam EGol ELan EOrc IHos IOrc LHop LSav MBri MR&S MUlv SArc SHil SPla
¶ – 'Garlands Gold' CHEx
– 'Schneefichte' MUlv
– 'Variegata' CB&S CBot CBow CCan CTre EGol ELan ENot IBar IJoh IOrc LHop MBal MBri MGos MR&S MRav SDix SHil SPer SSta
flaccida CCan CHar CShe MR&S SDix SPer WThu
– 'Golden Sword' CCan CSco EGol IHos IJoh IOrc MBri MUlv SArc SBla SHil WAbe

– 'Ivory' CB&S CCan CSco CShe EGol ELan ENot ERav GWic IOrc LSav MBri MUlv NHol NKay SBla SHil SPer SPla SSpi SSta WThu
– striated cultivar CCan
x ***floribunda*** SArc
'Garland's Gold' LRHS SMad SSpi
§ ***glauca*** CB&S CCan CHEx GWic NHol SArc SHil SIgm
gloriosa CB&S CBow CCan CHEx CSco CShe CTre ENot LNet MUlv SArc SHil SLon
– 'Aureovariegata' See Y. ***g.*** 'Variegata'
– 'Nobilis' SDix
§ – 'Variegata' CBot CBow CCan CHEx CSco ENot IBar IJoh ISea LSav MBri MUlv SArc SHil SMad SPer SSpi
guatemalensis See Y. ***elephantipes***
harrimaniae MUlv SIgm
neomexicana WThu
recurvifolia CB&S CCan CHEx CLan NRar SArc SHil
– 'Marginata' CCan
– 'Variegata' CCan CHEx
treculeana SArc
* 'Tricolor' CB&S
'Vittorio Emmanuele II' CCan MUlv SArc
'Vomerensis' CCan
whipplei CBot CCan CHEx EMon SArc SHil SIgm SLHN SLMG SSpi WHCr
– ***parishii*** CCan

YUSHANIA (Gramineae(Bambuseae))
maculata SBam SDry
§ 'Pitt White' SBam SDry WJun

ZALUZIANSKYA (Scrophulariaceae)
ovata CHan EPot LHop SBla WMar WPer

ZAMIA (Araceae)
furfuracea LPal

ZAMIOCULCAS (Araceae)

ZANTEDESCHIA † (Araceae)
§ ***aethiopica*** CHEx CWGN EHon ELun EWav GWic LAma LMay MSta SDix WEas
– 'Apple Court Babe' SApp
– 'Crowborough' Widely available
– ***gigantea*** SLMG
– 'Little Gem' EMon GWic
– 'White Sails' CRow EMon GWic MUlv
albomaculata CAvo LAma MBri MCab
§ ***angustiloba*** CAvo
'Aztec Gold' CB&S
'Best Gold' LAma MBri
'Black Magic' CB&S LAma
'Black-eyed Beauty' LAma MBri
'Bridal Blush' LAma
'Cameo' LAma
¶ 'Carmine Red' MBri
'Dusky Pink' CB&S
elliottiana CAvo CB&S CSut LAma MBri SW&B
¶ 'Galaxy' MBri
'Golden Affair' CB&S
¶ 'Golden Sun' MBri
'Green Goddess' CB&S CChu CHan CRow CWGN ECha EFou ELan SApp SLHN SMad
'Harvest Moon' LAma MBri
'Helen O'Connor' SLMG
¶ 'Lady Luck' MBri
'Lavender Petit' LAma MBri
'Majestic Red' CB&S
'Maroon Dainty' LAma
¶ 'Oriental Sun' MBri
'Pacific Pink' LAma
pentlandii See Z. ***angustiloba***
rehmannii CB&S LAma MBri SW&B
– ***superba*** SLMG
¶ 'Ruby' MBri
'Shell Pink ' LAma
'Solfatare' LAma
¶ 'Treasure' MBri

ZANTHORRHIZA See **XANTHORHIZA**

ZANTHOXYLUM (Rutaceae)
acanthifolium B&L 12460 LSav
coreanum CCla SSpi
piperitum SHil SSpi
schinifolium CCla SHil
simulans WCoo

ZAUSCHNERIA (Onagraceae)
californica 'Albiflora' See EPILOBIUM ***canum*** 'Albiflorum'
– 'Glasnevin' See EPILOBIUM ***canum*** 'Dublin'
– ***latifolia*** See EPILOBIUM ***canum latifolium***
– 'Mexicana' See EPILOBIUM ***canum mexicanum***
microphylla See EPILOBIUM ***canum***
villosa See EPILOBIUM ***canum mexicanum***

ZEBRINA (Commelinaceae)
pendula See TRADESCANTIA ***zebrina***
tabulaemontana See TRADESCANTIA ***t.***

ZELKOVA † (Ulmaceae)
carpinifolia SHil WMou WNor
schneideriana CMCN LSav
serrata CB&S CLnd CMCN EHar IOrc MBal NBar NHol NWea SGar SHil SPer SSpi STre WBod WCoo WMou WNor WPat
– 'Goblin' NHol SSpi WPat

ZENOBIA (Ericaceae)

pulverulenta	CB&S CChu CCla CFor ELan ERav IOrc MBal MBar MBri MUlv NHol SHil SPer SReu SSpi SSta WPat WSHC WWat

ZEPHYRANTHES (Liliaceae/Amaryllidaceae)

candida	CAvo CBro ERea LAma LBow NHol SDix SW&B WMar WThu
citrina	LAma LBow
¶ *drummondii*	CAvo WOMN
flavissima	CAvo CBro
grandiflora	CAvo LBow WCot
robusta	See HABRANTHUS ***robustus***
rosea	LAma

ZIERIA (Rutaceae)

ZIGADENUS (Liliaceae/Melanthiaceae)

elegans	CCla CGle COtt EBul ECro MBro NHol NWCA SAsh WDav WHoo WThu
fremontii	LGre
muscitoxicus	WCot
nuttallii	LGre MBro NHol WDav

ZINGIBER (Zingiberaceae)

¶ *officinale*	NHex

ZINNIA (Compositae)

¶ *grandiflora*	EPad

NURSERY CODE INDEX

Nurseries that are included in **THE PLANT FINDER** for the first time this year (or have been reintroduced) are marked in **Bold Type**.

Full details of the nurseries with a four letter Code will be found in the CODE-NURSERY Index on page 559.

Nurseries with a number are detailed in the ADDITIONAL NURSERY Index on page 610.

Those marked SEED are listed in the SEED Index on page 618.

Abbey Dore Court Gardens	WAbb
Abbot's House Garden	LAbb
Aberconwy Nursery	WAbe
Abriachan Nurseries	GAbr
Acton Beauchamp Roses	WAct
Addisford Hardy Plant Nursery	82
African Violet Centre	EAVC
Misses I Allen & J Huish	CAll
Allwood Bros	SAll
Allwoods Bros	SEED
Jacques Amand Ltd.	LAma
Angus Heathers	GAng
Apple Court	SApp
Architectural Plants	SArc
Ard Daraich Shrub Nursery	GArd
Ardfearn Nursery	GArf
Arne Herbs	CArn
Ashenden Nursery	SAsh
Ashwood Nurseries	MAsh
Ashwood Nurseries	SEED
David Austin Roses	MAus
Avon Bulbs	CAvo
Axletree Nursery	SAxl
Aylings of Trotton	2
Steven Bailey	SBai
B & H M Baker	EBak
Ballagan Nursery	3
Ballalheannagh Gardens	MBal
Helen Ballard	WBal
Ballydorn Bulb Farm	IBal
Ballyrogan Nurseries	IBlr
Bamboo Nursery	SBam
Barkers Primrose Nurseries & GC	NBar
Barkleigh Nurseries	IBrk
Barncroft Nurseries	MBar
Barnhawk Nursery	SBar
Barnsdale Plants	EBar
Barons Court Nurseries	IBar
Battersby Roses	NBat
John Beach (Nursery) Ltd.	MBea
Peter Beale's Roses	EBls
Tom Bebbington Dahlias	MBeb
Beechcroft Nurseries	NBee
R F Beeston	86
Beetham Nurseries	5
Bennett & Brown (Clematis)	NB&B
Michael Bennett	MBen
Birkheads Cottage Garden Nursery	NBir
Blackmore & Langdon Ltd	CBla
Blackthorn Nursery	SBla
Blagdon Water Garden Centre Ltd	CBWG
Blairhoyle Nursery	GBla
Walter Blom and Son Ltd.	LBlo
Blooms of Bressingham	EBre
The Bluebell Nursery	MBlu
R J Blythe	EBly
Bodnant Garden Nursery Ltd.	WBod
S & E Bond	WBon
Bonhard Nursery	GBon
Borde Hill Garden Ltd.	SBor
Bosvigo Plants	CBos
The Botanic Nursery	CBot
Bouts Cottage Nurseries	WBou
Ann & Roger Bowden	CBdn
Rupert Bowlby	LBow
Bowood Garden Centre	CBow
Brackenwood Nurseries	CBra
J Bradshaw & Son	SBra
Brambling House Alpines	NBra
Bregover Plants	CBre
Bretby Nurseries	9
Bridgemere Nurseries	MBri
Broadleas Gardens Ltd.	CBrd
Broadleigh Gardens	CBro
Broadstone Alpines	MBro
Brokenbacks Roses	EBro
Jarvis Brook Geranium Nurseries	SBro
D T Brown & Co Ltd.	SEED
Mrs P J Brown	LBro
Buckingham Nurseries	LBuc
Bullwood Nursery	EBul
J M Burgess	EBur
Burncoose & South Down Nurseries	CB&S
Burrows Roses	MBur
C E & D M Nurseries	81
The Cabbage Patch	MCab
Caddick's Clematis Nurseries	MCad
Cambridge Bulbs	ECam
Cannington College Plant Centre	CCan
Carmel Court Nurseries	WCar

Nursery	Code
Little Creek Nursery	CLCN
Little Horsted Nursery	SLHN
Lochside Alpine Nursery	SEED
Lochside Alpine Nursery	GLoc
C S Lockyer	CLoc
Long Man Gardens	SLMG
Longacre Nursery	41
Longstock Park Nursery	SLon
Lower Severalls Herb Nursery	CSev
Lower Kenneggy Nurseries	93
Mrs Ann Lunn	ELun
Elizabeth MacGregor	GMac
Macpennys	CMac
Madrona Nursery	SMad
Mallet Court Nursery	CMCN
Mallorn Gardens	CMal
Manningford Nurseries	42
Markham Grange Nurseries	NMGN
Marle Place Plants	43
Marley Bank Nursery	WMar
S E Marshall & Co Ltd.	SEED
J & D Marston	NMar
Marston Exotics	WMEx
Martin Nest Nurseries	EMNN
J E Martin	SEED
Marwood Hill Gardens	CMHG
S E Matthews	MMth
Mattock's Roses	MMat
Maydencroft Aquatic Nurseries	LMay
Mears Ashby Nurseries Ltd.	MMea
Merlin Rooted Cuttings	CMer
Merriments Nursery	SMrm
Merrist Wood Plant Shop	LMer
Mill Hill Plants	83
Millais Nurseries	LMil
Mills' Farm Plants & Gardens	EMFP
Mary & Peter Mitchell	SMit
Monksilver Nursery	EMon
Morehavens	LMor
John Morley	EMor
John Morley	SEED
F Morrey & Sons	MMor
Stanley Mossop	NMos
Frances Mount Perennial Plants	EMou
Mount Pleasant Trees	WMou
Mugswell Nursery	21
Ken Muir	EMui
Kathleen Muncaster Fuchsias	EKMF
Naked Cross Nurseries	CNCN
Natural Selection	CNat
Nettletons Nursery	LNet
New Trees Nurseries	SNTN
Newington Nursery	MNew
K P Nichols	46
Norden Alpines	NNrd
Nordybank Nurseries	48
Andrew Norfield Trees & Seeds	WNor
Andrew Norfield Trees & Seeds	SEED
Norfolk Lavender	ENor
Northumbria Nurseries	NNor
Norwich Heather & Conifer Centre	ENHC
Notcutts Nurseries	ENot
Oak Cottage Herb Garden	WOak
Oak Tree Nursery	NOak
Oakdene Nursery	SOkd
Stuart Ogg	SEED
Stuart Ogg	SOgg
Okell's Nurseries	MOke
Old Court Nurseries Ltd	WOld
The Old Manor Nursery	WOMN
The Old Mill Herbary	77
Oldbury Nurseries	SOld
Orchard House Nursery	NOrc
Orchard Nurseries	EOrc
Orchardstown Nurseries	IOrc
Otter Nurseries Ltd.	COtt
Otters' Court Heathers	COCH
M Oviatt-Ham	EOvi
P W Plants	EPla
Padlock Croft	EPad
The Palm Centre	LPal
The Palm Farm	NPal
A J Palmer & Son	LPlm
Pantiles Nurseries Ltd.	LPan
Paradise Centre	EPar
J & E Parker-Jervis	MPar
Park Green Nurseries	EPGN
Parkinson Herbs	50
A R Paske	EPas
Chris Pattison	WPat
Paul's Fuchsias	WPau
Pendennis Fuchsia Nursery	MPen
Pennells Nurseries	EPen
Pennyacre Nurseries	GPen
Perhill Nurseries	WPer
Perrie Hale Forest Nursery	CPer
Perryhill Nurseries	SPer
Perry's Plants	NPer
Peveril Clematis Nursery	CPev
Phedar Nursery	MPhe
Pickard's Magnolia Gardens	SPic
Pinks & Carnations	NPin
Pitts Farm Nursery	MPit
Plant World Botanic Gardens	SEED
Plant World	CPla
Plantables	MPlt
E L F Plants Cramden Nursery Ltd.	MPla
Plants from the Past	GPla

Plaxtol Nurseries	SPla
Pleasant View Nursery	CPle
J V Porter	NPor
Porthpean House Gardens	52
Potterton & Martin	EPot
Roger Poulett	SPou
Poyntzfield Herb Nursery	GPoy
Priorswood Clematis	LPri
The Priory	53
Rarer Plants	NRar
Raveningham Gardens	ERav
Ravensthorpe Nursery	MRav
Reads Nursery	ERea
Rearsby Roses	MRea
Redhouse Nurseries	NRed
Regional Nurseries	IReg
Ben Reid and Co	GRei
G Reuthe Ltd	SReu
Ridgeway Heather Nursery	WRid
Rileys' Chrysanthemums	MRil
Rivendell Alpines	CRiv
W Robinson & Sons Ltd.	SEED
Rock Park Nurseries	CRoc
Rock Park Nurseries	SEED
R V Roger Ltd	NRog
Rookhope Nurseries	NRoo
Frans Roozen (Holland)	LRoo
Rose du Temps Passé	MRTP
Rosemary Roses	MRos
Roses & Shrubs Ltd. Garden Centre	MR&S
Rougham Hall Nurseries	ERou
Rowden Gardens	CRow
Royal Horticultural Society's Garden	CRos
Andrew de Ruiter (Rose Specialist)	MRui
Rumwood Nurseries	SRum
Rushfields of Ledbury	WRus
Ryal Nursery	NRya
Ryans Nurseries	56
S & S Perennials	MS&S
Mrs Jane Sadler	SSad
Salley Gardens	SEED
Salley Gardens	MSal
Sampford Shrubs	CSam
John Sanday (Roses) Ltd.	CSan
Savill Garden	LSav
Scotland Farmhouse Herbs	CSFH
Scotts Nurseries (Merriott) Ltd	CSco
Scott's Clematis Nursery	ESco
Seaforde Gardens	ISea
Sedum Specialist	NSed
Seeds by Size	SEED
Sellet Hall Herbs	NSel
Shaw Rose Trees	ESha
Shepton Nursery Garden	CShe
Shrewley Gardens	MShr
Clive Simms	ESim
John Sinden	CSin
Siskin Plants	ESis
Smallscape Nursery	96
Alan C Smith	SSmi
Elizabeth Smith	60
John Smith & Son	MSmi
Southcombe Garden Plant Nursery	61
Southfarthing Alpines	76
Southview Nurseries	SSvw
Southwick Country Herbs	62
Special Plants	CSpe
Speyside Heather Garden Centre	GSpe
Spinners	SSpi
St Annes Vinyard	WStA
Stapeley Water Gardens Ltd	MSta
Starborough Nursery	SSta
Fiona Stark	GSta
Stewart's (Nottingham) Ltd.	SEED
Stillingfleet Lodge Nurseries	NSti
Stoke Lacy Herb Garden	SEED
Stoke Lacy Herb Garden	WSto
Stone House Cottage Nurseries	WSHC
Stone Lane Gardens	CSto
Stydd Nursery	NSty
Suffolk Herbs	SEED
Pearl Sulman	ESul
Sunbeam Nurseries	CSun
Sussex Country Gardens	SSus
Suttons Seeds Ltd.	CSut
Suttons Seeds Ltd.	SEED
A P & E V Tabraham	CTab
A P & E V Tabraham	SEED
J Mann Taylor	WTay
Thompson & Morgan	SEED
A & A Thorp	MTho
Thorp's Nurseries	LTho
Three Counties Nurseries	CThr
Thuya Alpine Nursery	WThu
Thuya Alpine Nursery	SEED
Tile Barn Nursery	STil
Timpany Nurseries	ITim
Philip Tivey & Son	MTiv
Toad Hall Produce	WToa
Tomperrow Farm Nurseries	CTom
The Torbay Palm Farm	CTor
Totties Nursery	64
Town Farm Nursery	NTow
Mr K J Townsend	LTow
John Train & Sons	GTra
Treasures of Tenbury Ltd	95
Peter Trenear	STre
Trewidden Estate Nursery	CTre

CODE-NURSERY INDEX

Please note that all these nurseries are listed in alphabetical order of their Codes. All nurseries are listed in alphabetical order of their name in the NURSERY-CODE INDEX on page 553.

CAll **Misses I Allen & J Huish,** Quarry Farm, Wraxall, Bristol, Avon BS19 1LE
TEL: (0275) 810435 *CONTACT:*
W/SALE or RETAIL: Retail *OPENING TIMES:* By appt. only.
MAIL ORDER: Yes *MIN VALUE:* None *CAT. COST:* 20p + Sae *EXPORT:* No
SPECIALITIES: National Reference Collection of Aster. *MAP PAGE:* **2/4**

CArn **Arne Herbs,** Limeburn Nurseries, Limeburn Hill, Chew Magna, Avon BS18 8QW
TEL: (0272) 333399 *CONTACT:* A Lyman-Dixon & H Lee
W/SALE or RETAIL: Both *OPENING TIMES:* Most times. Check first.
MAIL ORDER: Yes *MIN VALUE:* None *CAT. COST:* 40p *EXPORT:* Yes
SPECIALITIES: Herbs, Wild Flowers & Cottage Flowers. *MAP PAGE:* **2/4**

CAvo **Avon Bulbs,** Burnt House Farm, mid-Lambrook, South Petherton, Somerset TA13 5HE
TEL: (0460) 42177 *CONTACT:* C Ireland-Jones
W/SALE or RETAIL: Retail *OPENING TIMES:* Thu, Fri, Sat mid Sep-end Oct 1991 & mid Feb-end Mar 1992 or by appt.
MAIL ORDER: Yes *MIN VALUE:* None *CAT. COST:* 4 x 2nd class *EXPORT:* Yes
SPECIALITIES: Smaller & unusual Bulbs. NOTE: Address applicable from June 1990.
MAP PAGE: **2**

CBdn **Ann & Roger Bowden,** Cleave House, Sticklepath, Okehampton, Devon EX20 2NN
TEL: (083784) 0481 *CONTACT:* Ann & Roger Bowden
◆ *W/SALE or RETAIL:* Both *OPENING TIMES:* Appt only.
MAIL ORDER: Yes *MIN VALUE:* None *CAT. COST:* Sae *EXPORT:* Yes
SPECIALITIES: Hosta only. *MAP PAGE:* **1**

CBla **Blackmore & Langdon Ltd,** Pensford, Bristol Avon BS18 4JL
TEL: (0272) 332300 *CONTACT:* J S Langdon
◆ *W/SALE or RETAIL:* Both *OPENING TIMES:* 0900-1700 Mon-Fri. 1300-1700 Sun only Easter to end-Jun.
MAIL ORDER: Yes *MIN VALUE:* None *CAT. COST:* Sae *EXPORT:* Yes
SPECIALITIES: Phlox & Delphinium. *MAP PAGE:* **2/4**

CBos **Bosvigo Plants,** Bosvigo House, Bosvigo Lane, Truro, Cornwall TR1 3NH
TEL: (0872) 75774 *CONTACT:* Wendy Perry
W/SALE or RETAIL: Retail *OPENING TIMES:* 1100-dusk daily.
MAIL ORDER: No *MIN VALUE:* *CAT. COST:* 4 x 2nd class *EXPORT:* No
SPECIALITIES: Rare & unusual Herbaceous. *MAP PAGE:* **1**

CBot **The Botanic Nursery,** Rookery Nurseries, Atworth, Nr Melksham, Wiltshire SN12 8NU
TEL: (0225) 706597 *CONTACT:* T & M Baker
W/SALE or RETAIL: Both *OPENING TIMES:* 1000-1700 Summer, 1000-1500 Winter daily ex Thu & Sun. Thu & Sun by appt. only
MAIL ORDER: Yes *MIN VALUE:* *CAT. COST:* £1.50* *EXPORT:* No
SPECIALITIES: Rare hardy Shrubs & Perennials for lime soils. Also Conservatory plants. NOTE: Mail Order only Oct-Mar. * Cat cost refundable. *MAP PAGE:* **2**

CBow **Bowood Garden Centre,** Bowood Estate, Calne, Wiltshire SN11 0LZ
TEL: (0249) 816828 *CONTACT:* Peter Edmonds
◆ *W/SALE or RETAIL:* Retail *OPENING TIMES:* 0900-1800 daily Apr-Oct. 0900-1700 daily Nov-Mar.
MAIL ORDER: No *MIN VALUE:* *CAT. COST:* None issued *EXPORT:* No
SPECIALITIES: Wide range of Old Fashioned Roses, Rhododendrons, Shrubs, Climbers & herbaceous Perennials. Many interesting & unusual plants. *MAP PAGE:* **2**

CBra **Brackenwood Nurseries,** 131 Nore Road, Portishead, Nr Bristol, Avon BS20 8DU
TEL: (0272) 843484 *CONTACT:* Mr J Maycock
W/SALE or RETAIL: Both *OPENING TIMES:* 0900-1730 daily ex Xmas period.
MAIL ORDER: No *MIN VALUE:* *CAT. COST:* *EXPORT:* No
SPECIALITIES: Trees, Shrubs, Conifers & Alpines. Many unusual varieties. *MAP PAGE:* **2/4**

◆ **See also Display Advertisements**

CBrd **Broadleas Gardens Ltd.,** Broadleas, Devizes, Wiltshire SN10 5JQ
TEL: (0380) 722035 *CONTACT:* Lady Anne Cowdray
W/SALE or RETAIL: Both *OPENING TIMES:* 1400-1800 Wed, Thu & Sun Apr-Oct.
MAIL ORDER: No *MIN VALUE:* *CAT. COST:* *EXPORT:* No
SPECIALITIES: General range. *MAP PAGE:* **2**

CBre **Bregover Plants,** Hillbrooke, Middlewood, North Hill, Launceston, Cornwall PL15 7NN
TEL: (0566) 82661 *CONTACT:* Jennifer Bousfield
W/SALE or RETAIL: Retail *OPENING TIMES:* Wed-Fri Mar-midOct and by appt.
MAIL ORDER: Yes *MIN VALUE:* None *CAT. COST:* 2 x 1st class *EXPORT:* No
SPECIALITIES: Hardy Perennials inc. Asters, Geraniums, Primulas. Small supply of Show Auriculas, named Primroses & Violets. *MAP PAGE:* **1**

CBro **Broadleigh Gardens,** Bishops Hull, Taunton, Somerset TA4 1AE
TEL: (0823) 286231 *CONTACT:* Lady Skelmersdale
W/SALE or RETAIL: Retail *OPENING TIMES:* 0900-1600 Mon-Fri for viewing ONLY. Orders collected if prior notice given.
MAIL ORDER: Only *MIN VALUE:* *CAT. COST:* 2 x 1st class *EXPORT:* BO
SPECIALITIES: Two Catalogues. (Jan) - Bulbs in growth, (Galanthus, Cyclamen etc.) & Herbaceous. (June) - Dwarf Bulbs.

CBWG **Blagdon Water Garden Centre Ltd,** Bath Road, Upper Langford, Avon BS18 7DN
TEL: (0934) 852973 *CONTACT:* Peter Wheeler
W/SALE or RETAIL: Retail *OPENING TIMES:* 0900-1730 Mon-Fri 1000-1700 Sat & Sun
MAIL ORDER: Yes *MIN VALUE:* None *CAT. COST:* £1.00 *EXPORT:* No
SPECIALITIES: Aquatics. *MAP PAGE:* **2/4**

CB&S **Burncoose & South Down Nurseries,** Gwennap, Redruth, Cornwall TR16 6BJ
TEL: (0209) 861112 *FAX:* (0209) 860011 *CONTACT:* C H Williams & D Knuckey
W/SALE or RETAIL: Both *OPENING TIMES:* 0900-1700 Mon-Sat & 1400-1700 Sun.
MAIL ORDER: Yes *MIN VALUE:* £10.00 + p&p *CAT. COST:* £1.00 inc p&p *EXPORT:* Yes
SPECIALITIES: Extensive range of 2000 Ornamental Trees & Shrubs and Herbaceous. 30 acre garden. *MAP PAGE:* **1**

CCan **Cannington College Plant Centre,** Cannington, Bridgwater, Somerset TA5 2LS
TEL: (0278) 652226 *CONTACT:* Horticultural Enterprise Manager
W/SALE or RETAIL: Retail *OPENING TIMES:* 1400-1700 Tue-Sun Easter-Sept.
MAIL ORDER: No *MIN VALUE:* *CAT. COST:* *EXPORT:* No
SPECIALITIES: Abutilon, Argyranthemum, Buddleja, Ceanothus, Osteospermum, Salvia, Yucca. *MAP PAGE:* **1/4**

CChu **Churchills Garden Nursery,** Exeter Road, Chudleigh, South Devon TQ13 0DD
TEL: (0626) 852585 *CONTACT:* Mr M J S Henry
◆ *W/SALE or RETAIL:* Retail *OPENING TIMES:* 1400-1700 Mon-Fri, 1000-1700 Sat & Sun. Mid Mar-Mid Oct. Also by appt.
MAIL ORDER: No *MIN VALUE:* None *CAT. COST:* 50p *EXPORT:* No
SPECIALITIES: Extensive & interesting range of Trees, Shrubs, Climbers & Herbaceous - many unusual. *MAP PAGE:* **1**

CCla **Clapton Court Gardens,** Crewkerne, Somerset TA18 8PT
TEL: (0460) 73220/72200 *CONTACT:* Capt. S Loder
◆ *W/SALE or RETAIL:* Retail *OPENING TIMES:* 1030-1700 Mon-Fri, 1400-1700 Sun Mar-Oct. 1400-1700 Easter Sat only.
MAIL ORDER: No *MIN VALUE:* *CAT. COST:* £1.35 *EXPORT:* No
SPECIALITIES: Rare & unusual Plants, Shrubs, Trees, Clematis, Pelargoniums & Fuchsias. *MAP PAGE:* **2**

CCMG **Cranborne Manor Garden Centre,** Cranborne, Nr Wimborne, Dorset BH21 5PP
TEL: (07254) 248 *FAX:* (07254) 764 *CONTACT:* Mrs Janet Burnell (Manager)
W/SALE or RETAIL: Retail *OPENING TIMES:* 0900-1700 Tue-Sat 1000-1700 Sun. Closed Sun Jan & Feb.
MAIL ORDER: Yes* *MIN VALUE:* *CAT. COST:* 50p (Roses) *EXPORT:* Yes
SPECIALITIES: Roses, Clematis, Herbaceous incl unusual varieties, Topiary, Fan & Espalier Fruit, Shrubs & Trees. *NOTE: Mail Order for Roses only. *MAP PAGE:* **2**

CCor **Corsley Mill,** Corsley, Warminster, Wiltshire BA12 7QA
TEL: (0373) 832787 *CONTACT:* B E P Quest-Ritson
W/SALE or RETAIL: Both *OPENING TIMES:* By appt.
MAIL ORDER: Yes *MIN VALUE:* None *CAT. COST:* 50p *EXPORT:* No
SPECIALITIES: Plants grown from wild collected seed. Roses on own root-stock. NOTE: Mail Order in winter only. *MAP PAGE:* 2

CCot **Cottage Garden Plants Old & New,** Cox Cottage, Lower Street, East Norden, Wareham, Dorset BH20 7DL
TEL: (092945) 496 *CONTACT:* Mrs Alex Brenton
W/SALE or RETAIL: Retail *OPENING TIMES:* 0900-1200 Mon & Tue all year. Please phone to check first at other times.
MAIL ORDER: Yes *MIN VALUE:* None *CAT. COST:* 2 x 1st class *EXPORT:* No
SPECIALITIES: Primroses, Cheiranthus, Viola & Violets. *MAP PAGE:* 2

CCra **Crankan Nurseries,** New Mill, Penzance, Cornwall TR20 8UT
TEL: (0736) 62897 *CONTACT:* Mr J J Jelbert
W/SALE or RETAIL: Both *OPENING TIMES:* Daily by appt.
MAIL ORDER: Yes *MIN VALUE:* None *CAT. COST:* Sae *EXPORT:* Yes
SPECIALITIES: Violets. *MAP PAGE:* 1

CDoC **Duchy of Cornwall,** Penlyne Nursery, Cott Road, Lostwithiel, Cornwall PL22 08W
TEL: (0208) 872668 *CONTACT:* Eric Baker
W/SALE or RETAIL: Retail *OPENING TIMES:* 0900-1700 Mon-Sat ex Bank Hols.
MAIL ORDER: No *MIN VALUE:* *CAT. COST:* 50p *EXPORT:* No
SPECIALITIES: General, particularly Conifers. *MAP PAGE:* 1

CElw **Elworthy Cottage Garden Plants,** Elworthy Cottage, Elworthy, Lydeard St Lawrence, Taunton, Somerset TA4 3PX
TEL: (0984) 56427 *CONTACT:* Mrs J M Spiller
W/SALE or RETAIL: Retail *OPENING TIMES:* Tues & Fri afternoon & by appt mid Mar-mid Oct.
MAIL ORDER: No *MIN VALUE:* *CAT. COST:* 3 x 2nd class *EXPORT:* No
SPECIALITIES: Unusual Herbaceous plants esp. Penstemon & hardy Geranium & Grasses. *MAP PAGE:* 1

CFis **The Margery Fish Plant Nursery,** East Lambrook Manor, East Lambrook, S. Petherton, Somerset TA13 5HL
TEL: (0460) 40328 *CONTACT:* Mr M Stainer
W/SALE or RETAIL: Retail *OPENING TIMES:* 1000-1700 Mon-Sat & Bank Hols Sun.
MAIL ORDER: Yes *MIN VALUE:* £10.00 *CAT. COST:* 4 x 1st class *EXPORT:* Yes
SPECIALITIES: Hardy Geranium, Euphorbia, Helleborus, Primula vulgaris, Penstemon, Salvia & Herbaceous. *MAP PAGE:* 2

CFor **The Fortescue Garden Trust,** The Garden House, Buckland Monachorum, Yelverton, Devon PL20 7LQ
TEL: (0822) 854769 *CONTACT:* The Fortescue Garden Trust
W/SALE or RETAIL: Retail *OPENING TIMES:* 1030-1700 daily Apr 1-Sep 30. 1400-1700 Oct, Nov, Feb, Mar.
MAIL ORDER: Yes *MIN VALUE:* None *CAT. COST:* 4 x 1st class *EXPORT:* No
SPECIALITIES: General Herbaceous, Trees & Shrubs. *MAP PAGE:* 1

CFul **Rodney Fuller,** Coachman's Cottage, Higher Bratton Seymour, Wincanton, Somerset BA9 8DA
TEL: *CONTACT:* R Fuller
W/SALE or RETAIL: Retail *OPENING TIMES:* Not open.
MAIL ORDER: Only *MIN VALUE:* None *CAT. COST:* Sae *EXPORT:* No
SPECIALITIES: Violas & Violettas. Please note that stocks are strictly limited.

CGle **Glebe Cottage Plants,** Pixie Lane, Warkleigh, Umberleigh, North Devon EX37 9DH
TEL: (07694) 554 *CONTACT:* Carol Klein
W/SALE or RETAIL: Both *OPENING TIMES:* 1000-1700 Wed-Sun, please check first.
MAIL ORDER: Yes *MIN VALUE:* £10 *CAT. COST:* 65p *EXPORT:* Yes
SPECIALITIES: Species Primula, Primula vulgaris, doubles, Geranium, Violas & Penstemon. *MAP PAGE:* 1

CGre **Greenway Gardens,** Churston Ferrers, Brixham, Devon TQ5 0ES
TEL: (0803) 842382 *CONTACT:* Roger Clark (Manager)
W/SALE or RETAIL: Retail *OPENING TIMES:* 1400-1700 Tue, Wed, Fri, 1000-1200 Sat.
MAIL ORDER: Yes *MIN VALUE:* None *CAT. COST:* 50p *EXPORT:* No
SPECIALITIES: Unusual Trees & Shrubs particulary from temperate South America. *MAP PAGE:* 1

CGrh **Greenholm Nurseries,** (Off.) Lampley Road, Kingston Seymour, Clevedon, Avon BS21 6XS
TEL: (0934) 833350 *FAX:* (0934) 838237 *CONTACT:* John Vander Plank
W/SALE or RETAIL: *OPENING TIMES:* 0900-1730 daily
MAIL ORDER: Yes *MIN VALUE:* None *CAT. COST:* Free *EXPORT:*
SPECIALITIES: Passiflora. National Collection of over 100 species & varieties. NOTE: Nursery at Smallway Congresbury, Yatton, Avon. *MAP PAGE:* 2

CGro **C W Groves & Son,** West Bay Road, Bridport, Dorset DT6 4BA
TEL: (0308) 22654 *CONTACT:* C W Groves
W/SALE or RETAIL: Retail *OPENING TIMES:* 0830-1300 & 1400-1700 daily.
MAIL ORDER: Yes *MIN VALUE:* None *CAT. COST:* Free *EXPORT:* Yes
SPECIALITIES: Garden Centre specialising in Parma & Hardy Viola. *MAP PAGE:* 2

CHad **Hadspen Garden & Nursery,** Hadspen House, Castle Cary, Somerset BA7 7NG
TEL: (0963) 50939 *CONTACT:* N & S Pope
◆ *W/SALE or RETAIL:* Retail *OPENING TIMES:* 0900-1800 Thu-Sun & Bank Hols, Mon Mar 1st-Oct 1st. Garden open at the same time.
MAIL ORDER: No *MIN VALUE:* *CAT. COST:* 2 x 1st class *EXPORT:* No
SPECIALITIES: Large leaved Herbaceous. Old fashioned and shrub Roses. *MAP PAGE:* 2

CHal **Halsway Nursery,** Halsway, Nr Crowcombe Taunton, Somerset TA4 4BB
TEL: (0984) 243 *CONTACT:* T A & D J Bushen
W/SALE or RETAIL: Retail *OPENING TIMES:* Most days - please telephone first.
MAIL ORDER: Yes* *MIN VALUE:* None *CAT. COST:* Sae *EXPORT:* No
SPECIALITIES: Coleus & Begonias (excl. tuberous & winter flowering). Also small range of Rock plants. *NOTE: Mail Order for Coleus & Begonias only. *MAP PAGE:* 1

CHan **The Hannays of Bath,** Sydney Wharf Nursery, Bathwick, Bath, Avon BA2 4ES
TEL: (0225) 462230 *CONTACT:* Mr V H S & Mrs S H Hannay
◆ *W/SALE or RETAIL:* Retail *OPENING TIMES:* 1000-1700 Wed & Fri-Sun, and by appt.
MAIL ORDER: No *MIN VALUE:* *CAT. COST:* £1.00+40p p&p *EXPORT:* Yes*
SPECIALITIES: Unusual Perennials in specimen sizes and uncommon shrubs. *NOTE: For Export items, Certificates arranged but collection only. *MAP PAGE:* 2

CHar **W & L Harley,** Parham Nursery, The Sands, Market Lavington, Wiltshire SN10 4QA
TEL: (038 081) 3712/2443 *CONTACT:* W & L Harley
◆ *W/SALE or RETAIL:* Both *OPENING TIMES:* 0930-1700 Fri & Sat, Mar-Nov incl. (Dec-Feb & Aug by appt. only).
MAIL ORDER: Yes *MIN VALUE:* None *CAT. COST:* Free *EXPORT:* Yes
SPECIALITIES: Wide range of Alpine & Perennial in traditional and unusual varieties.
MAP PAGE: 2

CHEx **Hardy Exotics,** Trebah Gardens, Trebah, Mawnan Smith, Falmouth, Cornwall TR11 5JZ
TEL: (0326) 250915 *CONTACT:* Clive Shilton & Julie Smith
W/SALE or RETAIL: Retail *OPENING TIMES:* 0900-1700 daily
MAIL ORDER: Yes *MIN VALUE:* £20 + carriage *CAT. COST:* Free *EXPORT:* Yes
SPECIALITIES: Trees, Shrubs & Herbaceous plants to create tropical & desert effects. Hardy & half-Hardy for gardens patios & conservatories. *MAP PAGE:* 1

CHig **The High Garden,** Courtwood, Newton Ferrers, South Devon PL8 1BW
TEL: (0752) 872528 *CONTACT:* F Bennett
W/SALE or RETAIL: Both *OPENING TIMES:* By appt.
MAIL ORDER: Yes *MIN VALUE:* None *CAT. COST:* 60p *EXPORT:* Yes
SPECIALITIES: Pieris & Rhododendron. *MAP PAGE:* 1/2

CHil **Hill House Nursery & Gardens,** Landscove, Nr Ashburton, Devon TQ13 7LY
TEL: (080 426) 273 *CONTACT:* Mr & Mrs R Hubbard
W/SALE or RETAIL: Retail *OPENING TIMES:* 1100-1800 daily, all year.
MAIL ORDER: No *MIN VALUE:* *CAT. COST:* Free *EXPORT:* No
SPECIALITIES: Large range of unusual & Conservatory plants. *MAP PAGE:* **1**

CHoe **Hoecroft Plants,** Fosse Lane, Welton, Midsomer Norton, Avon BA3 2UZ
TEL: Not on phone *CONTACT:* N J Taylor
◆ *W/SALE or RETAIL:* Retail *OPENING TIMES:* 0930-1300 & 1400-1730 Fri, 1400-1730 Sat Mar-Nov. (Closed 4/17/18/12 May, 19/20 July 1991).
MAIL ORDER: Yes *MIN VALUE:* None *CAT. COST:* £1.10 *EXPORT:* No
SPECIALITIES: 240 varieties of Variegated and 300 varieties of Coloured-leaved plants in all species. 125 Grasses. *MAP PAGE:* **2**

CJer **Jersey Lavender Ltd.,** Rue du Pont Marquet, St Brelade, Jersey, Channel Isles
TEL: (0534) 42933 *FAX:* (0534) 45613 *CONTACT:* David Christie
W/SALE or RETAIL: Retail *OPENING TIMES:* 1000-1700 Mon-Sat Jun-Sep. Also by appt.
MAIL ORDER: No *MIN VALUE:* *CAT. COST:* Free *EXPORT:* No
SPECIALITIES: National Collection of Lavandula *MAP PAGE:* **1**

CKel **Kelways Nurseries,** Langport, Somerset TA10 9SL
TEL: (0458) 250521 *FAX:* (0458) 253351 *CONTACT:* Barry Moignard
W/SALE or RETAIL: Both *OPENING TIMES:* 0900-1300 & 1400-1700 Mon-Fri.
MAIL ORDER: Yes *MIN VALUE:* None *CAT. COST:* 2 x 1st class *EXPORT:* Yes
SPECIALITIES: (Spring) Lilium, Gladioli, Dahlias, Spring Bulbs, Border & Alpine plants. (Autumn) Paeonies, Iris, 300 Autumn bulbs, Herbaceous perennials *MAP PAGE:* **2**

CKen **Kenwith Nursery (Gordon Haddow),** The Old Rectory, Littleham, Bideford, North Devon EX39 5HW
TEL: (02372) 473752 *CONTACT:* G Haddow
◆ *W/SALE or RETAIL:* Retail *OPENING TIMES:* 1000-1200 & 1400-1630 Wed-Sat & by appt.
MAIL ORDER: Yes *MIN VALUE:* £10.00 *CAT. COST:* 2 x 2nd class *EXPORT:* Yes
SPECIALITIES: All Conifer genera. Grafting a speciality. Many new introductions to UK. *MAP PAGE:* **1**

CKin **Kingsfield Conservation Nursery,** Broadenham Lane, Winsham, Chard, Somerset TA20 4JF
TEL: (0460) 30697/30620 *CONTACT:* G & J E Peacock & Y Saunders
W/SALE or RETAIL: Both *OPENING TIMES:* Please phone for details.
MAIL ORDER: Yes *MIN VALUE:* None *CAT. COST:* Free *EXPORT:* No
SPECIALITIES: Native Trees, Shrubs and Wildflowers. *MAP PAGE:* **1/2**

CKni **Knightshayes Garden Trust,** The Garden Office, Knightshayes, Tiverton, Devon EX16 7RG
TEL: (0884) 259010 (Shop) *FAX:* (0884) 253264 *CONTACT:* M Hickson
W/SALE or RETAIL: Retail *OPENING TIMES:* 1100-1630 Wed-Sun Mar-Apr 1st, 1100-1800 daily Apr 1-Oct 31 & 1100-1600 Oct 31st-Dec 23rd.
MAIL ORDER: No *MIN VALUE:* *CAT. COST:* *EXPORT:* No
SPECIALITIES: Bulbs, Shrubs & Herbaceous. *MAP PAGE:* **1**

CLan **The Lanhydrock Gardens (NT),** Lanhydrock, Bodmin, Cornwall PL30 5AD
TEL: (0208) 72220 *CONTACT:* The National Trust
W/SALE or RETAIL: Both *OPENING TIMES:* Daily Easter (or Apr 1st) - Oct 31.
MAIL ORDER: No *MIN VALUE:* *CAT. COST:* Free *EXPORT:* No
SPECIALITIES: Shrubs, especially Camellia, Azalea, Rhododendron, Magnolia, Deutzia. Philadelphus & Ceanothus. *MAP PAGE:* **1**

CLCN **Little Creek Nursery,** 39 Moor Road, Banwell, Weston-super-Mare, Avon BS24 6EF
TEL: (0934) 823739 *CONTACT:* Rhys & Julie Adams
W/SALE or RETAIL: Retail *OPENING TIMES:* By appt. only
MAIL ORDER: Yes *MIN VALUE:* None *CAT. COST:* Sae *EXPORT:* No
SPECIALITIES: Species Cyclamen (from seed) & Helleborus. *MAP PAGE:* **2/4**

CLew **Lewdon Farm Alpine Nursery,** Medland Lane, Cheriton Bishop, Nr Exeter, Devon EX6 6HF
TEL: (0647) 24283 *CONTACT:* Betty Frampton
W/SALE or RETAIL: Retail *OPENING TIMES:* Daily, end Mar-end Oct. By appt. in winter.
MAIL ORDER: Yes *MIN VALUE:* £3.00 + p&p *CAT. COST:* 2 x 2nd class *EXPORT:* No
SPECIALITIES: Alpines, miniature Shrubs, dwarf Conifers & unusual perennials. *MAP PAGE:* **1**

CLnd **Landford Trees,** Landford Lodge, Landford, Salisbury, Wiltshire SP5 2EH
TEL: (0794) 390808 *CONTACT:* C D Pilkington
W/SALE or RETAIL: Both *OPENING TIMES:* 0800-1700.
MAIL ORDER: No *MIN VALUE:* *CAT. COST:* Free *EXPORT:* Yes
SPECIALITIES: Deciduous ornamental Trees. *MAP PAGE:* **2**

CLoc **C S Lockyer,** Lansbury, 70 Henfield Road, Coalpit Heath, Bristol, Avon BS17 2UZ
TEL: (0454) 772219 *CONTACT:* C S Lockyer
W/SALE or RETAIL: Both *OPENING TIMES:* Appt only. (Many open days & coach parties).
MAIL ORDER: Yes *MIN VALUE:* 6 plants + p&p *CAT. COST:* 2 x 1st class *EXPORT:* Yes
SPECIALITIES: Fuchsia. *MAP PAGE:* **2**

CMac **Macpennys,** 154 Bransgore, Christchurch, Dorset BH23 8DB
TEL: (0425) 72348 *CONTACT:* T & V Lowndes
W/SALE or RETAIL: Both *OPENING TIMES:* 0800-1700 Mon-Fri, 0900-1700 Sat 1400-1700 Sun.
MAIL ORDER: No *MIN VALUE:* *CAT. COST:* Free *EXPORT:* No
SPECIALITIES: General. *MAP PAGE:* **2**

CMal **Mallorn Gardens,** Lanner Hill, Redruth, Cornwall TR16 6DA
TEL: (0209) 215931 *CONTACT:* John
W/SALE or RETAIL: Both *OPENING TIMES:* By appt. only.
MAIL ORDER: Yes *MIN VALUE:* None *CAT. COST:* 3 x 1st class *EXPORT:* No
SPECIALITIES: Very wide & often changing general range. *MAP PAGE:* **1**

CMCN **Mallet Court Nursery,** Curry Mallet, Taunton, Somerset TA3 6SY
TEL: (0823) 480748 *CONTACT:* J G S & P M E Harris F.L.S.
W/SALE or RETAIL: Both *OPENING TIMES:* 0900-1300 & 1400-1700 Mon-Fri. Sat & Sun by appt.
MAIL ORDER: Yes *MIN VALUE:* None *CAT. COST:* £1.00 *EXPORT:* Yes
SPECIALITIES: Maples, Oaks, Magnolias, Hollies & other rare and unusual plants including those from China & South Korea. *MAP PAGE:* **1**

CMer **Merlin Rooted Cuttings,** Little Drym, Praze, Camborne, Cornwall TR14 0NU
TEL: (0209) 831 704 *CONTACT:* Liz & Roger Jackson
◆ *W/SALE or RETAIL:* Both *OPENING TIMES:* 1000-1700 Wed-Fri, 0900-1300 Sat Mar-mid Oct & by appt.
MAIL ORDER: Only *MIN VALUE:* *CAT. COST:* 3 x 1st class *EXPORT:* No
SPECIALITIES: Rooted cuttings.

CMHG **Marwood Hill Gardens,** Barnstaple, North Devon EX31 4EB
TEL: (0271) 42528 *CONTACT:* Dr. Smart
W/SALE or RETAIL: Retail *OPENING TIMES:* 1100-1300 & 1400-1700 daily.
MAIL ORDER: No *MIN VALUE:* *CAT. COST:* 70p *EXPORT:* No
SPECIALITIES: Large range of unusual Trees & Shrubs. Eucalyptus, Alpines, Camellia, & Bog plants. *MAP PAGE:* **1**

CNat **Natural Selection,** (Off.) 1 Station Cottages, Hullavington, Chippenham, Wiltshire SN14 6ET
TEL: (0666) 837369 *CONTACT:* Martin Cragg-Barber
W/SALE or RETAIL: Retail *OPENING TIMES:* Wed Apr-Sep & by appt. Please telephone first.
MAIL ORDER: Yes *MIN VALUE:* £6.00 *CAT. COST:* 2 x 1st class *EXPORT:* No
SPECIALITIES: British native plants, familiar & unusual. *MAP PAGE:* **2**

CNCN **Naked Cross Nurseries,** Waterloo Road, Corfe Mullen, Wimborne, Dorset BH21 3SR
TEL: (0202) 693256 *CONTACT:* Mr P J French & Mrs J E Paddon
W/SALE or RETAIL: Both *OPENING TIMES:* 0900-1730 daily.
MAIL ORDER: No *MIN VALUE:* *CAT. COST:* Free *EXPORT:* No
SPECIALITIES: Heathers and Herbaceous. *MAP PAGE:* **2**

COCH **Otters' Court Heathers,** Otters' Court, West Camel, Yeovil, Somerset BA22 7QF
TEL: (0935) 850285 *CONTACT:* Mrs D H Jones
W/SALE or RETAIL: Both *OPENING TIMES:* 0900-1700 Wed-Sun and by appt.
MAIL ORDER: Yes *MIN VALUE:* None *CAT. COST:* 3 x 1st class *EXPORT:* Yes
SPECIALITIES: Lime-tolerant Heathers. *MAP PAGE:* **2**

COtt **Otter Nurseries Ltd.,** Gosford Road, Ottery St. Mary, Devon EX11 1LZ
TEL: (0404) 815815 *CONTACT:* M J White
W/SALE or RETAIL: Retail *OPENING TIMES:* 0800-1700 daily ex Xmas.
MAIL ORDER: No *MIN VALUE:* *CAT. COST:* Free *EXPORT:* No
SPECIALITIES: Large Garden Centre & Nursery with extensive range of Trees, Shrubs, Conifers, Climbers, Roses, Fruit & hardy Perennials. *MAP PAGE:* **1**

CPer **Perrie Hale Forest Nursery,** Northcote Hill, Honiton, Devon EX14 8TH
TEL: (0404) 43344 *CONTACT:* N C Davey & Mrs J F Davey
W/SALE or RETAIL: Both *OPENING TIMES:* 0800-1630 Mon-Fri, 0800-1300 Sat. Retail sales by appt. please.
MAIL ORDER: Yes *MIN VALUE:* £6.00 *CAT. COST:* Sae *EXPORT:* No
SPECIALITIES: Forest Trees, Hedging plants & Shrubs. *MAP PAGE:* **1**

CPev **Peveril Clematis Nursery,** Christow, Exeter, Devon EX6 7NG
TEL: (0647) 52937 *CONTACT:* Barry Fretwell
W/SALE or RETAIL: Retail *OPENING TIMES:* 1000-1300 & 1400-1730 Fri-Wed, 1000-1300 Sun. Dec-Mar by appt..
MAIL ORDER: No *MIN VALUE:* *CAT. COST:* 2 x 1st class *EXPORT:* No
SPECIALITIES: Clematis. *MAP PAGE:* **1**

CPla **Plant World,** St Marychurch Road, Newton Abbot, South Devon
TEL: (0803) 872939 *CONTACT:* Ray Brown
◆ *W/SALE or RETAIL:* Both *OPENING TIMES:* 0900-1700.
MAIL ORDER: SO *MIN VALUE:* *CAT. COST:* 70p *EXPORT:* SO
SPECIALITIES: Alpines & unusual Herbaceous plants. Choice seed list also available (Meconopsis, Gentians, Primulas, Lewisias). 4 acre world botanic map. *MAP PAGE:* **1**

CPle **Pleasant View Nursery,** Two Mile Oak, Nr Denbury, Newton Abbot, Devon TQ12 6DG
TEL: (0803) 813388 *CONTACT:* Mrs B D Yeo
W/SALE or RETAIL: Both *OPENING TIMES:* 1000-1700 Wed-Sat Mar-end Nov.
MAIL ORDER: Yes *MIN VALUE:* £10.00 + p&p *CAT. COST:* £1.00 (coin) *EXPORT:* No
SPECIALITIES: Unusual Shrubs, Salvias & Conservatory plants. *MAP PAGE:* **1**

CRiv **Rivendell Alpines,** Horton Heath, Wimborne, Dorset BH21 7JN
TEL: (0202) 824013 *CONTACT:* John & Claire Horsey.
W/SALE or RETAIL: Both *OPENING TIMES:* 1000-1700 Sat-Thu Mar-Oct, 1000-1700 Sat & Sun Nov-Feb or by appt.
MAIL ORDER: Yes *MIN VALUE:* None *CAT. COST:* Sae *EXPORT:* Yes
SPECIALITIES: Alpines, Heathers, & Aquatics. *MAP PAGE:* **2**

CRoc **Rock Park Nurseries,** Church Lane, Calstock, Cornwall PL18 9QH
TEL: (0822) 833238 *CONTACT:* Vince & Marilyn O'Neill
W/SALE or RETAIL: Retail *OPENING TIMES:* 0900-2100 ex Xmas day.
MAIL ORDER: Yes *MIN VALUE:* None *CAT. COST:* 2 x 1st class *EXPORT:* SO
SPECIALITIES: Bougainvillea. Exotic seed & plants. Unusual Trees & Shrubs. For Flowers by post tel. FREEPHONE 0800 378644. Regular newsletter. *MAP PAGE:* **1**

CRos **Royal Horticultural Society's Garden,** Rosemoor, Great Torrington, Devon EX38 8PH
TEL: (0805) 24067 *CONTACT:* Plant Sales Manager
W/SALE or RETAIL: Retail *OPENING TIMES:* Mar 1st-Dec 16th.
MAIL ORDER: No *MIN VALUE:* *CAT. COST:* *EXPORT:* No
SPECIALITIES: National Cornus and part Ilex collections. Many rare & unusual plants.
MAP PAGE: **1**

◆ **See also Display Advertisements**

CRow **Rowden Gardens,** Brentor, Nr Tavistock, Devon PL19 0NG
TEL: (0822 810) 275 *CONTACT:* John R L Carter
W/SALE or RETAIL: Both *OPENING TIMES:* 1000-1700 Sat-Sun & Bank Hols Mar 25th-end Sep. Other times by appt.
MAIL ORDER: Yes *MIN VALUE:* None *CAT. COST:* £1.50 *EXPORT:* Yes
SPECIALITIES: Aquatics, Bog, unusual & rare specialist plants. NCCPG Polygonum Collection. *MAP PAGE:* **1**

CSam **Sampford Shrubs,** Sampford Peverell, Tiverton, Devon EX16 7EN
TEL: (0884) 821164 *CONTACT:* M Hughes-Jones & S Proud
W/SALE or RETAIL: Retail *OPENING TIMES:* 0900-1700 (dusk if earlier) Thur-Sun ex Dec 25-end Jan.
MAIL ORDER: Yes *MIN VALUE:* £10.00 *CAT. COST:* Sae *EXPORT:* No
SPECIALITIES: Common & uncommon plants. *MAP PAGE:* **1**

CSan **John Sanday (Roses) Ltd.,** Over Lane, Almondsbury, Bristol, Avon BS12 4DA
TEL: (0454) 612195 *CONTACT:* Thomas Sanday
W/SALE or RETAIL: Both *OPENING TIMES:* 0900-1900 Mon-Sat May-Aug. 0900-1700 Mon-Sat Sep-Apr. 1000-1700 Sun Mar-Dec.
MAIL ORDER: Yes *MIN VALUE:* None *CAT. COST:* Free *EXPORT:* No
SPECIALITIES: All types of Roses. *MAP PAGE:* **2/4**

CSco **Scotts Nurseries (Merriott) Ltd,** Merriott, Somerset TA16 5PL
TEL: (0460) 72306 *FAX:* (0460) 77433 *CONTACT:* Mark Wallis
◆ *W/SALE or RETAIL:* Both *OPENING TIMES:* 0900-1700 Mon-Sat, 1000-1700 Sun.
MAIL ORDER: Yes *MIN VALUE:* None *CAT. COST:* £1.50 *EXPORT:* No
SPECIALITIES: Wide general range. *MAP PAGE:* **2**

CSev **Lower Severalls Herb Nursery,** Crewkerne, Somerset TA18 7NX
TEL: (0460) 73234 *CONTACT:* Mary R Pring
W/SALE or RETAIL: Retail *OPENING TIMES:* 1000-1700 Fri-Wed (1400-1700 Sun).
MAIL ORDER: Yes *MIN VALUE:* £7.00 *CAT. COST:* 3 x 2nd class *EXPORT:* No
SPECIALITIES: Herbs, Herbaceous & Conservatory plants. *MAP PAGE:* **2**

CSFH **Scotland Farmhouse Herbs,** Virginstow, Beaworthy, North Devon EX21 5EA
TEL: (040921) 585 *CONTACT:* Peter Charnley
W/SALE or RETAIL: Both *OPENING TIMES:* Telephone for appt.
MAIL ORDER: Yes *MIN VALUE:* *CAT. COST:* 50p *EXPORT:* No
SPECIALITIES: Herbs, culinary, medicinal & dye plants. Scented foliage plants for the wild garden. (Nursery formally HERBS & SPICES). *MAP PAGE:* **1**

CShe **Shepton Nursery Garden,** Old Wells Road, Shepton Mallet, Somerset BA4 5XN
TEL: (0749) 3630 *CONTACT:* Mr & Mrs P W Boughton
W/SALE or RETAIL: Retail *OPENING TIMES:* 0930-1730 Tue-Sat and by appt.
MAIL ORDER: No *MIN VALUE:* *CAT. COST:* Free *EXPORT:* No
SPECIALITIES: Herbaceous, Alpines & Chaenomeles. *MAP PAGE:* **2**

CSin **John Sinden,** 10 Derwentwater Road, Merley Ways, Wimbourne, Dorset BH21 1QS
TEL: (0202) 885841 *CONTACT:* John Sinden
W/SALE or RETAIL: Both *OPENING TIMES:* 0900-1700 daily.
MAIL ORDER: Yes *MIN VALUE:* None *CAT. COST:* Sae *EXPORT:* No
SPECIALITIES: Convallaria & Hosta. *MAP PAGE:* **2**

CSpe **Special Plants,** Laurels Farm, Upper Wraxall, Chippenham, Wiltshire SN14 7AG
TEL: (0225) 891686 *CONTACT:* Derry Watkins
W/SALE or RETAIL: Retail *OPENING TIMES:* Most days. Please ring first to check.
MAIL ORDER: Yes *MIN VALUE:* £10.00 *CAT. COST:* 50p *EXPORT:* No
SPECIALITIES: Tender Perennials, Argyranthemum, Felicia, Diascia, Dimorphotheca, Lewisia, Salvia. *MAP PAGE:* **2**

CSto **Stone Lane Gardens,** Stone Farm, Chagford, Devon TQ13 8JU
TEL: (064723) 311 *CONTACT:* K B Ashburner
W/SALE or RETAIL: Retail *OPENING TIMES:* Appt only.
MAIL ORDER: Yes *MIN VALUE:* *CAT. COST:* List £1.00* *EXPORT:* Yes
SPECIALITIES: Wide range of wild provenance Betula and Alnus. Also interesting varieties of Rubus, Vaccinium, Sorbus etc. *£2.00 for full descriptive Cat. *MAP PAGE:* **1**

CSun **Sunbeam Nurseries,** Bristol Road, Frampton Cotterell, Avon BS17 2AU
TEL: (0454) 776926 *CONTACT:* Nöel Kingsbury
◆ *W/SALE or RETAIL:* Retail *OPENING TIMES:* 1000-1800 Mon-Sat but please telephone first.
MAIL ORDER: Yes *MIN VALUE:* None *CAT. COST:* £1.00 each* *EXPORT:* Yes
SPECIALITIES: Unusual hardy & Conservatory plants, many rarities & unusual plants. *NOTE: Hardy & Conservatory lists £1.00 each £1.80 for both. *MAP PAGE:* 2

CSut **Suttons Seeds Ltd.,** Hele Road, Torquay, Devon TQ2 7QJ
TEL: (0803) 612011 *FAX:* (0803) 615747 *CONTACT:* Mr P J McDermott
W/SALE or RETAIL: Both *OPENING TIMES:* (Office) 0830-1700.
MAIL ORDER: Only *MIN VALUE:* None *CAT. COST:* Free *EXPORT:* Yes
SPECIALITIES: Over 1,200 varieties of flower & vegetable seed, bulbs, plants & sundries.

CTab **A P & E V Tabraham,** Porth Mellon, St. Mary's, Isles of Scilly TR21 0JY
TEL: (0720) 22759 *CONTACT:* A P & E V Tabraham
W/SALE or RETAIL: Both *OPENING TIMES:* 0900-1700.
MAIL ORDER: Yes *MIN VALUE:* *CAT. COST:* Sae *EXPORT:* Yes
SPECIALITIES: Fuchsias, Miniature & Rock Garden. *MAP PAGE:* 1

CThr **Three Counties Nurseries,** Marshwood, Bridport, Dorset DT6 5QJ
TEL: (02977) 257 *CONTACT:* A & D Hitchcock
W/SALE or RETAIL: Both *OPENING TIMES:* Not open.
MAIL ORDER: Only *MIN VALUE:* None *CAT. COST:* 2 x 2nd class *EXPORT:* No
SPECIALITIES: Pinks & Dianthus.

CTom **Tomperrow Farm Nurseries,** Tomperrow Farm, Threemilestone, Truro, Cornwall TR3 6BE
TEL: (0872) 560344 *CONTACT:* Mrs S C Goodswen
W/SALE or RETAIL: Retail *OPENING TIMES:* 1000-Dusk most days. Dec, Jan & Aug by appt.
MAIL ORDER: Yes *MIN VALUE:* None *CAT. COST:* 60p inc p&p *EXPORT:* No
SPECIALITIES: Wide range of hardy Herbaceous plants, some unusual. *MAP PAGE:* 1

CTor **The Torbay Palm Farm,** St Marychurch Road, Coffinswell, nr Newton Abbot, South Devon TQ12 4SE
TEL: (0803) 872800 *CONTACT:* T A Eley
W/SALE or RETAIL: Both *OPENING TIMES:* 0900-1700.
MAIL ORDER: Yes *MIN VALUE:* £3.80 *CAT. COST:* Free *EXPORT:* Yes
SPECIALITIES: Cordyline australis, Trachycarpus fortuneii & new varieties of Cordyline. *MAP PAGE:* 1

CTre **Trewidden Estate Nursery,** Trewidden Gardens, Penzance, Cornwall TR20 8TT
TEL: (0736) 62087 *FAX:* (0736) 68142 *CONTACT:* Mr M G Snellgrove.
W/SALE or RETAIL: Both *OPENING TIMES:* 0800-1300 & 1400-1700 Mon-Sat.
MAIL ORDER: Yes *MIN VALUE:* None *CAT. COST:* 50p *EXPORT:* Yes
SPECIALITIES: Camellia & unusual Shrubs. *MAP PAGE:* 1

CTrw **Trewithen Nurseries,** Grampound Road, Truro, Cornwall
TEL: (0726) 882764 *CONTACT:* M Taylor
W/SALE or RETAIL: Both *OPENING TIMES:* 0800-1630 Mon-Fri.
MAIL ORDER: No *MIN VALUE:* *CAT. COST:* 60p *EXPORT:* No
SPECIALITIES: Shrubs, especially Camellia & Rhododendron. *MAP PAGE:* 1

CWal **Wall Cottage Nursery,** Lockengate, Bugle, St. Austell, Cornwall PL26 8RU
TEL: (0208) 831259 *CONTACT:* Mrs J R Clark
W/SALE or RETAIL: Both *OPENING TIMES:* 0830-1700 Mon-Sat.
MAIL ORDER: Yes *MIN VALUE:* £15.00 *CAT. COST:* 60p *EXPORT:* Yes
SPECIALITIES: Specialist Rhododendron & Azalea plus general range. *MAP PAGE:* 1

CWar **Mrs M Warrick,** Lower Trenode, Widegates, Looe, Cornwall PL13 1QA
TEL: (050 34) 270 *CONTACT:* Mrs M Warrick
W/SALE or RETAIL: Retail *OPENING TIMES:* Anytime.
MAIL ORDER: Yes *MIN VALUE:* None *CAT. COST:* Free *EXPORT:* No
SPECIALITIES: Chamomile. *MAP PAGE:* 1

CWGN **The Water Garden Nursery,** Highcroft, Moorend, Wembworthy, Chulmleigh, Devon EX18 7SG
TEL: (0837) 83566 *CONTACT:* J M Smith
W/SALE or RETAIL: Both *OPENING TIMES:* 0800-1700 Fri-Wed Apr-Sep & by appt.
MAIL ORDER: Yes *MIN VALUE:* None *CAT. COST:* 3 x 1st class *EXPORT:* No
SPECIALITIES: Plants for shade, wetlands, bog & water. *MAP PAGE:* **1**

CWil **H & J Wills,** 2 St Brannocks Park Road, Ilfracombe, Devon EX34 8HU
TEL: (0271) 863949 *CONTACT:* H Wills
W/SALE or RETAIL: Retail *OPENING TIMES:* Appt only.
MAIL ORDER: Only *MIN VALUE:* £3.00 *CAT. COST:* 3 x 1st class *EXPORT:* Yes
SPECIALITIES: Sempervivum, Jovibarba & Rosularia.

CYea **Yearlstone Vineyard,** Chilverton, Coldridge, Crediton, Devon EX17 6BH
TEL: (0363) 83302 *CONTACT:* Miss G Pearkes
W/SALE or RETAIL: Retail *OPENING TIMES:* Appt only.
MAIL ORDER: Yes *MIN VALUE:* None *CAT. COST:* Sae *EXPORT:* No
SPECIALITIES: Vines. *MAP PAGE:* **1**

EAVC **African Violet Centre,** Terrington St Clement, King's Lynn, Norfolk PE34 4PL
TEL: (0553) 828374 *FAX:* (0553) 827273 *CONTACT:* Tony Clements or M Garford
W/SALE or RETAIL: Retail *OPENING TIMES:* 1030-1630 daily. Closed Dec 23rd-Jan 2nd.
MAIL ORDER: Yes *MIN VALUE:* *CAT. COST:* Free *EXPORT:* No
SPECIALITIES: African violets (Saintpaulia ionantha). *MAP PAGE:* **6**

EBak **B & H M Baker,** Bourne Brook Nurseries, Greenstead Green, Halstead, Essex CO9 1RJ
TEL: (0787) 472900/476369 *CONTACT:* B & H M Baker
W/SALE or RETAIL: Both *OPENING TIMES:* 0800-1630 Mon-Fri, 0900-1200 & 1400-1630 Sat & Sun.
MAIL ORDER: No *MIN VALUE:* *CAT. COST:* 15p+stamp *EXPORT:* No
SPECIALITIES: Fuchsia & Conservatory Plants. *MAP PAGE:* **6**

EBar **Barnsdale Plants,** Exton Avenue, Exton, Oakham, Rutland LE15 8AH
TEL: (0572) 813200 *FAX:* (0872) 813346 *CONTACT:* Mr Hamilton
W/SALE or RETAIL: Retail *OPENING TIMES:* 1000-1700 Thu-Sun & Bank Hols.
MAIL ORDER: Yes *MIN VALUE:* None *CAT. COST:* 1 x 27p stamp *EXPORT:* No
SPECIALITIES: Choice & unusual Garden Plants *MAP PAGE:* **6**

EBls **Peter Beale's Roses,** London Road, Attleborough, Norfolk NR17 1AY
TEL: (0953) 454707/455881 *FAX:* (0953) 456845 *CONTACT:* Mr Peter Beales
W/SALE or RETAIL: Both *OPENING TIMES:* 0900-1700 Mon-Fri, 0900-1630 Sat, 1000-1600 Sun. Jan & Aug closed Sun.
MAIL ORDER: Yes *MIN VALUE:* None *CAT. COST:* Free *EXPORT:* Yes
SPECIALITIES: Old fashioned Roses. *MAP PAGE:* **6**

EBly **R J Blythe,** Potash Nursery, Cow Green, Bacton, Stowmarket, Suffolk IP14 4HJ
TEL: (0449) 781671 *CONTACT:* R J Blythe
W/SALE or RETAIL: Retail *OPENING TIMES:* 1000-1700 Sat, Sun & Mon mid Feb-end June.
MAIL ORDER: Yes* *MIN VALUE:* £3.10 *CAT. COST:* 25p *EXPORT:* No
SPECIALITIES: Fuchsias. *NOTE: Mail Order Feb-Apr only. *MAP PAGE:* **6**

EBre **Blooms of Bressingham,** Diss, Norfolk IP22 2AB
TEL: (037988) 464 *CONTACT:* Ken Marsh
W/SALE or RETAIL: Both *OPENING TIMES:* 1000-1730 daily. (Direct retail Plant Centre)
MAIL ORDER: Yes *MIN VALUE:* £10.00 *CAT. COST:* £1.75 *EXPORT:* Yes
SPECIALITIES: Very wide general range. A proportion also available through Garden Centres. Many own varieties. *MAP PAGE:* **6**

EBro **Brokenbacks Roses,** Broxhill Road, Havering-atte-Bower, Romford, Essex RM4 1QH
TEL: (04023) 77744 *CONTACT:* A Carter
W/SALE or RETAIL: Retail *OPENING TIMES:* 0900-1700 Thu-Mon.
MAIL ORDER: Yes *MIN VALUE:* None *CAT. COST:* Sae *EXPORT:* No
SPECIALITIES: Old fashioned and Hybrid musk Roses. *MAP PAGE:* **3**

EBul **Bullwood Nursery,** 54 Woodlands Road, Hockley, Essex SS5 4PY
TEL: (0702) 203761 *CONTACT:* D & E Fox
W/SALE or RETAIL: Retail *OPENING TIMES:* 0930-1730 Wed-Sun.
MAIL ORDER: Yes *MIN VALUE:* *CAT. COST:* Sae *EXPORT:* No
SPECIALITIES: Mainly Liliaceae, also a wide range of other Perennials, some uncommon and rare.
MAP PAGE: **3**

EBur **J M Burgess,** Rectory Cottage, Sisland, Norwich, Norfolk NR14 6EF
TEL: (0508) 20724 *CONTACT:* Jenny Burgess
W/SALE or RETAIL: Both *OPENING TIMES:* Any time by appt.
MAIL ORDER: No *MIN VALUE:* *CAT. COST:* Sae *EXPORT:* No
SPECIALITIES: Alpines, Sisyrinchium & Campanula. *MAP PAGE:* **6**

ECam **Cambridge Bulbs,** 40 Whittlesford Road, Newton, Cambridgeshire CB2 5PH
TEL: (0223) 871760 *CONTACT:* N Stevens.
W/SALE or RETAIL: Retail *OPENING TIMES:*
MAIL ORDER: Only *MIN VALUE:* None *CAT. COST:* 2 x 1st class *EXPORT:* Yes
SPECIALITIES: Arum, Crocus, Corydalis, Fritillaria, Gallanthus, Iris & Tulipa.

ECha **Unusual Plants,** Beth Chatto Gardens, Elmstead Market, Colchester, Essex CO7 7DB
TEL: (0206) 822007 *FAX:* (0206) 825933 *CONTACT:* Rosemary Shelley
W/SALE or RETAIL: Retail *OPENING TIMES:* 0900-1700 Mon-Sat Mar 1-Oct 31. 0900-1600 Mon-Fri Nov 1- Mar 1. Always closed Sun & Bank Hols.
MAIL ORDER: Yes *MIN VALUE:* £20.00 + p&p *CAT. COST:* £2.00 incl p&p *EXPORT:* No
SPECIALITIES: Predominantly Herbaceous. Many unusual for special situations. *MAP PAGE:* **6**

ECop **Copford Bulbs,** Dorsetts, Birch Road, Copford, Colchester, Essex CO6 1DR
TEL: (0206) 330008 *CONTACT:* D J Pearce
W/SALE or RETAIL: Retail *OPENING TIMES:* By appt.
MAIL ORDER: Yes *MIN VALUE:* *CAT. COST:* 50p credited *EXPORT:* Yes
SPECIALITIES: Daffodil bulbs & Cyclamen tubers. *MAP PAGE:* **6**

ECou **County Park Nursery,** Essex Gardens, Hornchurch, Essex RM11 3BU
TEL: (04024) 45205 *CONTACT:* G Hutchins
W/SALE or RETAIL: Retail *OPENING TIMES:* 0900-dusk Mon-Sat ex Wed. 1000-1700 Sun.
MAIL ORDER: No *MIN VALUE:* *CAT. COST:* 3 x 1st class *EXPORT:* No
SPECIALITIES: Alpines & rare and unusual plants from New Zealand, Tasmania & Falklands.
MAP PAGE: **3**

ECro **Croftacre Hardy Plants,** Croftacre, Ellingham Road, Scoulton, Norfolk NR9 4NT
TEL: (0953) 850599 *FAX:* (0953) 851399 *CONTACT:* Mrs V J Allen
◆ *W/SALE or RETAIL:* Retail *OPENING TIMES:* Most days. Please telephone first.
MAIL ORDER: Yes *MIN VALUE:* No *CAT. COST:* 3 x 1st class *EXPORT:* Yes
SPECIALITIES: Good range of Perennials, Shrubs & Grasses. Many unusual. *MAP PAGE:* **6**

ECtt **Cottage Nurseries,** Thoresthorpe, Alford, Lincolnshire LN13 0HX
TEL: (0507) 466968 *CONTACT:* W H Denbigh
W/SALE or RETAIL: Both *OPENING TIMES:* 0900-dusk daily.
MAIL ORDER: Yes *MIN VALUE:* £5.00 *CAT. COST:* 2 x 1st class *EXPORT:* No
SPECIALITIES: Wide general range. *MAP PAGE:* **7**

EDen **Denbeigh Heather Nurseries,** All Saints Road, Creeting St. Mary, Ipswich, Suffolk IP6 8PJ
TEL: (0449) 711220 *CONTACT:* D J & A Small
W/SALE or RETAIL: Both *OPENING TIMES:* By appt. only.
MAIL ORDER: Yes *MIN VALUE:* None *CAT. COST:* £1.00 *EXPORT:* Yes
SPECIALITIES: Rooted Heather cuttings & Cape Heaths. *MAP PAGE:* **6**

EDon **Donington Plants,** Donington House, Main Road, Wrangle, Boston, Lincolnshire PE22 9AT
TEL: (0205) 870015 *CONTACT:* D W Salt
W/SALE or RETAIL: Retail *OPENING TIMES:* 1000-1800 Wed-Sun Mar-Oct.
MAIL ORDER: Yes *MIN VALUE:* None *CAT. COST:* Sae *EXPORT:* No
SPECIALITIES: Auricula, Hardy Geranium, Cheiranthus, Argyranthemum, Lachenalia, Penstemon & Barnhaven Polyanthus. *MAP PAGE:* **7**

EDra **John Drake,** Hardwicke House, Fen Ditton, Cambridgeshire CB5 8TF
TEL: *CONTACT:* John Drake
W/SALE or RETAIL: Retail *OPENING TIMES:*
MAIL ORDER: Only *MIN VALUE:* £10.00 *CAT. COST:* 60p *EXPORT:* No
SPECIALITIES: Aquilegia.

EEde **Eden Nurseries,** Rectory Lane, Old Bolingbroke, Spilsby, Lincolnshire PE23 4EY
TEL: (07903) 582 *CONTACT:* Marjorie Stein
W/SALE or RETAIL: Both *OPENING TIMES:* By appt.
MAIL ORDER: Yes *MIN VALUE:* *CAT. COST:* Sae *EXPORT:* No
SPECIALITIES: Hardy varieties of English Apple trees. *MAP PAGE:* **7**

EEls **Elsworth Herbs,** Avenue Farm Cottage, 31, Smith Street, Elsworth, Cambridgeshire CB3 8HY
TEL: (09547) 414 *CONTACT:* Drs J D & J M Twibell
W/SALE or RETAIL: Retail *OPENING TIMES:* Advertised weekends & by appt. only.
MAIL ORDER: Yes *MIN VALUE:* £10.00 *CAT. COST:* 2 x 1st class *EXPORT:* No
SPECIALITIES: Herbs, Artemisia (NCCPG Collection), & Cottage garden plants. *MAP PAGE:* **6**

Effi **Daphne ffiske Herbs,** Rosemary Cottage, Bramerton, Norwich, Norfolk NR14 7DW
TEL: (05088) 8187 *CONTACT:* D ffiske
W/SALE or RETAIL: Retail *OPENING TIMES:* 1000-1600 Thu-Sun.
MAIL ORDER: Yes *MIN VALUE:* None *CAT. COST:* Sae *EXPORT:* No
SPECIALITIES: Herbs including own cultivars and rarities. *MAP PAGE:* **6**

EFol **Foliage & Unusual Plants,** The Dingle, Pilsgate, Stamford, Lincolnshire PE9 3HW
TEL: (0780) 740775 *CONTACT:* Margaret Handley
◆ *W/SALE or RETAIL:* Retail *OPENING TIMES:* 1000-1800 (dusk if earlier) daily Mar-Nov & Bank Hols.
MAIL ORDER: Yes* *MIN VALUE:* £10.00 *CAT. COST:* 3 x 1st class *EXPORT:* No
SPECIALITIES: Variegated, coloured foliage & unusual plants. *NOTE: Mail Order only available for some months. *MAP PAGE:* **6**

EFou **Four Seasons,** Forncett St Mary, Norwich, Norfolk NR16 1JT
TEL: *CONTACT:* J P Metcalf & R W Ball
W/SALE or RETAIL: Retail *OPENING TIMES:* No callers.
MAIL ORDER: Only *MIN VALUE:* £15.00 *CAT. COST:* 75p *EXPORT:* No
SPECIALITIES: Herbaceous.

EFul **Fulbrooke Nursery,** 43 Fulbrooke Road, Cambridgeshire CB3 9EE
TEL: (0223) 311102 *CONTACT:* Paul Lazard
W/SALE or RETAIL: Both *OPENING TIMES:* By appt. most times.
MAIL ORDER: Yes *MIN VALUE:* Varies on plant *CAT. COST:* Free *EXPORT:* No
SPECIALITIES: Bamboos *MAP PAGE:* **6**

EGol **Goldbrook Plants,** Hoxne, Eye, Suffolk IP21 5AN
TEL: (037975) 770 *CONTACT:* Sandra Bond
W/SALE or RETAIL: Retail *OPENING TIMES:* 1030-1800 or dusk Thu-Sun ex. Jan, or by appt.
MAIL ORDER: Yes* *MIN VALUE:* £10.00 *CAT. COST:* 4 x 1st class *EXPORT:* Yes
SPECIALITIES: Very large range of Hosta (over 300), Hemerocallis & Bog Iris. Interesting Shrubs & Hardy plants. *NOTE: M.O. Perennials and Grasses only. *MAP PAGE:* **6**

EGou **Goulding's Fuchsias,** West View, Link Lane, Bentley, Nr Ipswich, Suffolk IP9 2DP
TEL: (0473) 310058 *CONTACT:* Mr E J Goulding
W/SALE or RETAIL: Retail *OPENING TIMES:* 1000-1700 Sat, Sun & Bank Hols. Wed Feb 17th-July 22nd
MAIL ORDER: Yes *MIN VALUE:* £5.00 *CAT. COST:* 3 x 1st class *EXPORT:* No
SPECIALITIES: Fuchsia - new introductions, Hardy, Encliandra, Terminal flowering (Triphylla), Basket & Bedding. *MAP PAGE:* **6**

EHal **Hall Farm Nursery,** Harpswell, Nr Gainsborough, Lincolnshire DN21 5UU
TEL: (042773) 412 *CONTACT:* Pam & Mark Tatam
W/SALE or RETAIL: *OPENING TIMES:* 0900-1800 daily. Please telephone in winter to check.
MAIL ORDER: Yes *MIN VALUE:* None *CAT. COST:* Sae *EXPORT:*
SPECIALITIES: Wide range of Shrubs, Trees & Perennials. *MAP PAGE:* **7**

EHar **Hartshall Nursery Stock,** Hartshall Farm, Walsham-le-Willows, Nr Bury St Edmunds, Suffolk IP31 3BY
TEL: (0359) 259238 *FAX:* (0359) 259238 *CONTACT:* J D L & M A Wight
W/SALE or RETAIL: Retail *OPENING TIMES:* 1000-1630 Tue-Sat. Ex all Bank Hols & all July.
MAIL ORDER: No *MIN VALUE:* *CAT. COST:* 3 x 1st class *EXPORT:* No
SPECIALITIES: Hardy Shrubs, Trees & Conifers. Wide general range & rare, esp. Acer, Betula, Fagus, Prunus, Quercus, Salix & Sorbus, Viburnum. *MAP PAGE:* **6**

EHMN **Home Meadows Nursery Ltd,** Martlesham, Suffolk IP12 4RD
TEL: (0394) 382419 *CONTACT:* S D & M I O'Brien Baker & I D Baker
W/SALE or RETAIL: Both *OPENING TIMES:* 0800-1700 Mon-Sat.
MAIL ORDER: Yes *MIN VALUE:* None *CAT. COST:* Free *EXPORT:* No
SPECIALITIES: Small general range plus Chrysanthemum esp. Korean. *MAP PAGE:* **6**

EHon **Honeysome Aquatic Nursery,** The Row, Sutton, Nr Ely, Cambridgeshire CB6 2PF
TEL: (0353) 778889 *CONTACT:* D B Barker & D B Littlefield
W/SALE or RETAIL: Both *OPENING TIMES:* 0930-1700 Mon-Fri. 0930-1200 Sat. Mid Apr-end Oct.
MAIL ORDER: Yes *MIN VALUE:* None *CAT. COST:* 45p *EXPORT:* No
SPECIALITIES: Hardy Aquatic, Bog & Marginal. *MAP PAGE:* **6**

EHul **Hull Farm,** Spring Valley Lane, Ardleigh, Colchester, Essex CO7 7SA
TEL: (0206) 230045 *CONTACT:* J Fryer & Sons
W/SALE or RETAIL: Both *OPENING TIMES:* 1000-1630 daily ex Xmas.
MAIL ORDER: No *MIN VALUE:* *CAT. COST:* 50p + Sae *EXPORT:* No
SPECIALITIES: Conifers, Heathers, Rhododendron, Azalea, Camellia, and choice Shrubs. *MAP PAGE:* **6**

EJud **Judy's Country Garden,** The Villa, Louth Road, South Somercotes, Louth, Lincolnshire LN11 7BW
TEL: (0507) 358487 *CONTACT:* M J S & J M Harry
W/SALE or RETAIL: Retail *OPENING TIMES:* 0900-dusk most days Mar-Nov.
MAIL ORDER: No *MIN VALUE:* *CAT. COST:* 2 x 1st class *EXPORT:* No
SPECIALITIES: Herbs, old-fashioned & unusual plants. *MAP PAGE:* **7**

EKal **Kalm Oak Nursery,** Hunters Chase, Ardleigh, Colchester, Essex CO7 7LW
TEL: (0206) 322877 *CONTACT:* Andrew Stalham
W/SALE or RETAIL: Both *OPENING TIMES:* 0900-1700 daily Feb-Nov, 0900-1600 or dusk Mon-Fri Dec-Jan.
MAIL ORDER: Yes *MIN VALUE:* £5.00 *CAT. COST:* Sae-Thyme list*EXPORT:* No
SPECIALITIES: Extensive range of Thymes. Large selection of Shrubs, Trees, Herbaceous & Alpines. *MAP PAGE:* **6**

EKMF **Kathleen Muncaster Fuchsias,** 18 Field Lane, Morton, Gainsborough, Lincolnshire DN21 3BY
TEL: (0427) 612329 *CONTACT:* Kathleen Muncaster
W/SALE or RETAIL: Retail *OPENING TIMES:* 1000-Dusk.
MAIL ORDER: Yes* *MIN VALUE:* None *CAT. COST:* 2 x 1st class *EXPORT:* No
SPECIALITIES: Fuchsia. *NOTE: Mail Orders to be received before April 1st. *MAP PAGE:* **7**

ELan **Langthorns Plantery,** High Cross Lane West, Little Canfield, Dunmow, Essex CM6 1TD
TEL: (0371) 872611 *CONTACT:* P & D Cannon
W/SALE or RETAIL: Retail *OPENING TIMES:* 1000-1300 & 1400-1700 or dusk (if earlier) daily ex Xmas fortnight.
MAIL ORDER: No *MIN VALUE:* *CAT. COST:* 3 x 1st class *EXPORT:* No
SPECIALITIES: Wide general range with many unusual plants. *MAP PAGE:* **6**

ELeG **LeGrice Roses,** Norwich Road, North Walsham, Norfolk NR28 0DR
TEL: (0692) 402591 *CONTACT:* Bill LeGrice
◆ *W/SALE or RETAIL:* Both *OPENING TIMES:* 0900-1700 Mon-Sat, 1000-1700 Sun & Bank Hols.
MAIL ORDER: Yes *MIN VALUE:* None *CAT. COST:* Free *EXPORT:* No
SPECIALITIES: Roses. NOTE: Mail Order for Roses only. *MAP PAGE:* **6**

◆ **See also Display Advertisements**

ELun **Mrs Ann Lunn,** The Fens, Old Mill Road, Langham, Colchester, Essex CO4 5NU
TEL: (0206) 272259 *CONTACT:* Mrs Ann Lunn
W/SALE or RETAIL: Retail *OPENING TIMES:* Thu, Fri & Sat and by appt.
MAIL ORDER: Yes *MIN VALUE:* *CAT. COST:* 3 x 1st class *EXPORT:* No
SPECIALITIES: Primula, Woodland and moisture loving plants. *MAP PAGE:* **6**

EMFP **Mills' Farm Plants & Gardens,** Norwich Road, Mendlesham, Suffolk IP14 5NQ
TEL: (0449) 766425 *CONTACT:* Peter & Susan Russell
W/SALE or RETAIL: Retail *OPENING TIMES:* 0900-1730 Wed-Mon.
MAIL ORDER: *Yes *MIN VALUE:* None *CAT. COST:* 1 x 2nd class *EXPORT:* No
SPECIALITIES: Pinks, Old Roses, Wide general range. *NOTE: Mail Order for Pinks only.
MAP PAGE: **6**

EMNN **Martin Nest Nurseries,** Grange Cottage, Harpswell Lane, Hemswell, Gainsbor'o, Lincolnshire DN21 5UP
TEL: (042 773) 369 *CONTACT:* M & M A Robinson
W/SALE or RETAIL: Both *OPENING TIMES:* 1000-1800 Wed-Sun.
MAIL ORDER: Yes *MIN VALUE:* None *CAT. COST:* 3 x 2nd class *EXPORT:* No
SPECIALITIES: Alpines especially Auricula, Primula, Lewisia, & Saxifraga. *MAP PAGE:* **7**

EMon **Monksilver Nursery,** Oakington Road, Cottenham, Cambridgeshire CB4 4TW
TEL: *CONTACT:* Joe Sharman & Alan Leslie
W/SALE or RETAIL: Both *OPENING TIMES:* Open 1000-1600 May 3rd, 4th, 17th, 18th, 31st, June 1st, 14th, & 15th 1991
MAIL ORDER: Yes *MIN VALUE:* £10.00 *CAT. COST:* 5 x 1st class *EXPORT:* Yes
SPECIALITIES: Herbaceous plants, Grasses, Lamium, Nepeta, Malva, Monarda, Salvia, Vinca, Sedges & Variegated plants. Many NCCPG 'Pink Sheet' plants. *MAP PAGE:* **6**

EMor **John Morley,** North Green Only, Stoven, Beccles, Suffolk NR34 8DG
TEL: *CONTACT:* John Morley
W/SALE or RETAIL: Retail *OPENING TIMES:* By appt. ONLY.
MAIL ORDER: Only *MIN VALUE:* None *CAT. COST:* 50p + stamp *EXPORT:* No
SPECIALITIES: Galanthus, species & hybrids.

EMou **Frances Mount Perennial Plants,** 1 Steps Farm, Polstead, Colchester, Essex CO6 5AE
TEL: (0206) 262811 *CONTACT:* Frances Mount
W/SALE or RETAIL: Retail *OPENING TIMES:* 1000-1700 Tue Wed Sat Sun & Bank Hols. 1400-1800 Fri. Check weekends & Hols.
MAIL ORDER: Yes *MIN VALUE:* £4.00 *CAT. COST:* Sae *EXPORT:* No
SPECIALITIES: Geraniums. *MAP PAGE:* **6**

EMui **Ken Muir,** Honeypot Farm, Rectory Road, Weeley Heath, Essex CO16 9BJ
TEL: (0255) 830181 *FAX:* (0255) 831534 *CONTACT:* Ken Muir
W/SALE or RETAIL: Both *OPENING TIMES:* 1000-1600.
MAIL ORDER: Yes *MIN VALUE:* Min for each spec*CAT. COST:* 2 x 1st class *EXPORT:* No
SPECIALITIES: Fruit. *MAP PAGE:* **3/6**

ENHC **Norwich Heather & Conifer Centre,** 54a Yarmouth Road, Thorpe, Norwich, Norfolk NR14 6PU
TEL: (0603) 39434 *CONTACT:* B Hipperson
W/SALE or RETAIL: Retail *OPENING TIMES:* 0900-1700 Mon Tue Wed Fri Sat, 1400-1700 Sun Mar-Dec.
MAIL ORDER: Yes *MIN VALUE:* None *CAT. COST:* 40p *EXPORT:* No
SPECIALITIES: Conifers and Heathers. *MAP PAGE:* **6**

ENor **Norfolk Lavender,** Caley Hill, Heacham, King's Lynn, Norfolk PE31 7JE
TEL: (0485) 70384 *FAX:* (0485) 71176 *CONTACT:* Joy Warner
W/SALE or RETAIL: Retail *OPENING TIMES:* 0930-1700 daily. Closed two weeks at Xmas.
MAIL ORDER: Yes *MIN VALUE:* None *CAT. COST:* Free *EXPORT:* No
SPECIALITIES: National collection of Lavandula. *MAP PAGE:* **6**

ENot **Notcutts Nurseries,** Woodbridge, Suffolk IP12 4AF
TEL: (0394) 383344 *FAX:* (0394) 385460 *CONTACT:* J A Dyter
W/SALE or RETAIL: Both *OPENING TIMES:* 0845-1730 Mon-Sat, 1000-1700 Sun.
MAIL ORDER: Yes *MIN VALUE:* £30 *CAT. COST:* £2.70 *EXPORT:* Yes
SPECIALITIES: Wide general range. *MAP PAGE:* **6**

EOrc **Orchard Nurseries,** Tow Lane, Foston, Grantham, Lincolnshire NG32 2LE
TEL: (0400) 81354 *CONTACT:* R & J Blenkinship
◆ *W/SALE or RETAIL:* Retail *OPENING TIMES:* 1000-1800 Mar-Oct daily.
MAIL ORDER: Yes *MIN VALUE:* *CAT. COST:* £1.00 *EXPORT:* Yes
SPECIALITIES: Unusual herbaceous. *MAP PAGE:* **6**

EOvi **M Oviatt-Ham,** (Office) Ely House, 15 Green Street, Willingham, Cambridgeshire CB4 5JA
TEL: (0954) 60481 *CONTACT:* M Oviatt-Ham
W/SALE or RETAIL: Both *OPENING TIMES:* Sat & Sun from Easter-end Sept, other times by appt. only.
MAIL ORDER: Yes *MIN VALUE:* £8.00 *CAT. COST:* 50p *EXPORT:* Yes
SPECIALITIES: Clematis & climbing plants. Nursery address: Rampton Rd., Willingham. *MAP PAGE:* **6**

EPad **Padlock Croft,** 19 Padlock Road, West Wratting, Cambridgeshire CB1 5LS
TEL: (0223) 290383 *CONTACT:* Susan & Peter Lewis
W/SALE or RETAIL: Retail *OPENING TIMES:* 1000-1800 Mon, Tue, Thu-Sat. Mar 1st-Nov 1st. Aug, Weds & winter by appt.
MAIL ORDER: Yes *MIN VALUE:* £10+p&p *CAT. COST:* 4 x 2nd class *EXPORT:* No
SPECIALITIES: National Collection of Campanula. Campanulaceae. Penstemon. Many other less common Alpines & Perennials. *MAP PAGE:* **6**

EPar **Paradise Centre,** Twinstead Road, Lamarsh, Bures, Suffolk CO8 5EX
TEL: (0787 269) 449 *CONTACT:* Cees & Hedy Stapel-Valk
W/SALE or RETAIL: Retail *OPENING TIMES:* 1000-1700 Sat-Sun & Bank Hols or by appt. Easter-Nov 1st.
MAIL ORDER: Yes *MIN VALUE:* £5.00 *CAT. COST:* 3 x 1st class *EXPORT:* No
SPECIALITIES: Unusual bulbous & tuberous plants including shade & bog varieties. *MAP PAGE:* **6**

EPas **A R Paske,** The South Lodge, Grazeley Road, Kentford, Suffolk CB8 7QB
TEL: (0638) 750613 *CONTACT:* A R Paske
W/SALE or RETAIL: Both *OPENING TIMES:* (Office) 0900-1700 Mon-Fri.
MAIL ORDER: Yes *MIN VALUE:* £6.00 *CAT. COST:* None *EXPORT:* Yes
SPECIALITIES: Seakale thongs only. (Crambe maritima) *MAP PAGE:* **6**

EPen **Pennells Nurseries,** Newark Road, South Hykeham, Lincoln, Lincolnshire LN6 9NT
TEL: (0522) 500091 *CONTACT:* Pennell & Sons Ltd
W/SALE or RETAIL: Both *OPENING TIMES:* 0830-1730 Mon-Sat, 1000-1700 Sun.
MAIL ORDER: No *MIN VALUE:* *CAT. COST:* *EXPORT:* No
SPECIALITIES: Clematis & Climbers. Garden centres at Newark Rd, Lincoln & Humberstone Rd, Cleethorpes. *MAP PAGE:* **7**

EPGN **Park Green Nurseries,** Wetheringsett, Stowmarket, Suffolk IP14 5QH
TEL: (0728) 860139 *CONTACT:* Richard & Mary Ford
W/SALE or RETAIL: Both *OPENING TIMES:* 1000-1730 Thu-Sun and Bank Hol Mons.
MAIL ORDER: Yes *MIN VALUE:* None *CAT. COST:* Sae *EXPORT:* No
SPECIALITIES: Hosta, Astilbe & Herbaceous. *MAP PAGE:* **6**

EPla **P W Plants,** Sunnyside Nurseries, Heath Road, Kenninghall, Norfolk NR16 2DS
TEL: (095 387) 8212 *CONTACT:* Paul Whittaker
◆ *W/SALE or RETAIL:* Both *OPENING TIMES:* By appt. only please.
MAIL ORDER: Yes *MIN VALUE:* None *CAT. COST:* £1 refundable *EXPORT:* Yes
SPECIALITIES: Choice Shrubs, Perennials, Grasses, Climbers, Bamboos, Hedera & Streptocarpus. Also wide range of unusual hardy ornamental Shrubs.. *MAP PAGE:* **6**

EPot **Potterton & Martin,** The Cottage Nursery, Moortown Road, Nettleton, Caistor, Lincolnshire LN7 6HX
TEL: (0472) 851792 *CONTACT:*
W/SALE or RETAIL: Both *OPENING TIMES:* 0900-1700 daily.
MAIL ORDER: Yes *MIN VALUE:* £1 handling under£10 *CAT. COST:* 50p *EXPORT:* Yes
SPECIALITIES: Alpines, Dwarf Bulbs, Conifers, & Shrubs and Carnivorous. *MAP PAGE:* **7**

◆ **See also Display Advertisements**

ERav **Raveningham Gardens,** Norwich, Norfolk NR14 6NS
TEL: (0508 46) 206 *FAX:* (0508 46) 8958 *CONTACT:* Tessa Hobbs
◆ *W/SALE or RETAIL:* Both *OPENING TIMES:* 0900-1600 Mon-Fri, Sats in Mar-Jun & Sep-Nov. Gardens open 1400-1700 Sun & Bank Hols Mar24th-Sep15th
MAIL ORDER: Yes *MIN VALUE:* None *CAT. COST:* 3 x 1st class *EXPORT:* Yes
SPECIALITIES: Plants noted for Foliage, Berries, Bark & Texture. Variegated & coloured leaf plants & shrubs. *MAP PAGE:* **6**

ERea **Reads Nursery,** Hales Hall, Loddon, Norfolk NR14 6QW
TEL: (050846) 395 *CONTACT:* Terence & Judy Read
◆ *W/SALE or RETAIL:* Both *OPENING TIMES:* 1000-1700 (or dusk if earlier) Tue-Sat & by appt.
MAIL ORDER: Yes *MIN VALUE:* £10.00 *CAT. COST:* 4 x 1st class *EXPORT:* Yes
SPECIALITIES: Conservatory plants, Vines, Citrus, Figs & unusual Fruits & Nuts. Wall Shrubs & Climbers. Scented & aromatic Hardy plants. *MAP PAGE:* **6**

ERou **Rougham Hall Nurseries,** (RHN Ltd), Ipswich Road, Rougham, Bury St. Edmunds, Suffolk IP30 9LZ
TEL: (0359) 70577/70153 *FAX:* (0359) 71149 *CONTACT:* A A & K G Harbutt
W/SALE or RETAIL: Retail *OPENING TIMES:* Special advertised weekends & by appt only.
MAIL ORDER: Yes *MIN VALUE:* None *CAT. COST:* 65p inc p&p *EXPORT:* No
SPECIALITIES: Hardy Perennials & Gooseberries. NOTE: Gooseberry cat. 40p. *MAP PAGE:* **6**

ESco **Scott's Clematis Nursery,** 40 Roman Road, Moulton Chapel, Spalding, Lincolnshire PE12 0XQ
TEL: (0406) 380457 *CONTACT:* John Scott
W/SALE or RETAIL: Both *OPENING TIMES:* 1000-1700 Mon-Fri, 0900-1700 Sat, 1000-1600 Sun Mar-Nov
MAIL ORDER: Yes *MIN VALUE:* *CAT. COST:* Free *EXPORT:* Yes
SPECIALITIES: Clematis only. *MAP PAGE:* **6**

ESha **Shaw Rose Trees,** 2 Hollowgate Hill, Willoughton, Gainsborough, Lincolnshire DN21 5SF
TEL: (042 773) 230 *CONTACT:* Mr K Shaw
W/SALE or RETAIL: Both *OPENING TIMES:* Vary, please check.
MAIL ORDER: Yes *MIN VALUE:* None *CAT. COST:* Sae *EXPORT:* No
SPECIALITIES: Roses & soft Fruit. *MAP PAGE:* **7**

ESim **Clive Simms,** Woodhurst, Essendine, Stamford, Lincolnshire PE9 4LQ
TEL: (0780) 55615 *CONTACT:* Clive & Kathryn Simms
W/SALE or RETAIL: Retail *OPENING TIMES:* Telephone appt. only
MAIL ORDER: Only *MIN VALUE:* None *CAT. COST:* 3 x 2nd class *EXPORT:* No
SPECIALITIES: Unusual Trees, Shrubs & Conservatory plants, esp. fruiting varieties.

ESis **Siskin Plants,** April House, Davey Lane, Charsfield, Woodbridge, Suffolk IP13 7QG
TEL: (0473 37) 567 *CONTACT:* Chris & Valerie Wheeler
W/SALE or RETAIL: Retail *OPENING TIMES:* 1000-1800 Tue-Sat. Sun by appt. Please telephone first during Nov-Jan.
MAIL ORDER: Yes* *MIN VALUE:* None *CAT. COST:* 3 x 1st class *EXPORT:* No
SPECIALITIES: Wide range of Alpines & dwarf Shrubs, esp. Hebe, Parahebe & Lewisia. *NOTE: Young plants also available by Mail Order. *MAP PAGE:* **6**

ESul **Pearl Sulman,** 54 Kingsway, Mildenhall, Bury St Edmunds, Suffolk IP28 7HR
TEL: (0638) 712297 *CONTACT:* Pearl Sulman
W/SALE or RETAIL: Retail *OPENING TIMES:*
MAIL ORDER: Only *MIN VALUE:* £8.00 incl p&p*CAT. COST:* 2 x 1st class *EXPORT:* No
SPECIALITIES: Miniature, Dwarf & Scented-leaf Geraniums.

ETub **Van Tubergen UK Ltd.,** Bressingham, Diss, Norfolk, Norfolk IP22 3AA
TEL: (0379) 888282 *CONTACT:* General Manger
W/SALE or RETAIL: Retail *OPENING TIMES:*
MAIL ORDER: Only* *MIN VALUE:* *CAT. COST:* Free *EXPORT:* Yes
SPECIALITIES: Bulbs. *NOTE: Retail sales by Mail Order only. *MAP PAGE:*

ETWh **Trevor White Old Fashioned Roses,** Chelt Hurst. 10 Sewell Road, Norwich, Norfolk NR3 4BP
TEL: (0603) 418240 *CONTACT:* Mr T A & Mrs V J White.
W/SALE or RETAIL: Both *OPENING TIMES:* 0900-1700 by appt only.
MAIL ORDER: Only *MIN VALUE:* None *CAT. COST:* Free *EXPORT:* Yes
SPECIALITIES: Old-fashioned, Shrub, Climbing & Rambling Roses

EUse **The Useful Plant Co.,** 3 Church Street, Buckden, Huntingdon, Cambridgeshire PE18 9TE
TEL: (0480) 810548/861342 *CONTACT:* Sue Roe & Bill Wallis
W/SALE or RETAIL: Both *OPENING TIMES:* Please phone first.
MAIL ORDER: No *MIN VALUE:* *CAT. COST:* 2 x 1st class *EXPORT:*
SPECIALITIES: Chrysanthemum rubellum. NCCPG collection holders. Propagation to order.
MAP PAGE: **6**

EVal **The Valley Clematis Nursery,** Willingham Road, Hainton, Lincolnshire LN3 6LN
TEL: (0507) 313398 *CONTACT:* Mr Keith Fair
◆ *W/SALE or RETAIL:* Retail *OPENING TIMES:* 1000-1800 (Dusk in winter) daily. Closed Xmas to New Year.
MAIL ORDER: Yes *MIN VALUE:* £12.00 *CAT. COST:* 75p *EXPORT:* Yes
SPECIALITIES: Clematis. *MAP PAGE:* **7**

EWal **J Walkers Bulbs,** Broadgate, Weston Hills, Spalding, Lincolnshire PE12 6DQ
TEL: (0406) 380420 *CONTACT:* M B Clare & J W Walkers
W/SALE or RETAIL: Both *OPENING TIMES:* See Daffodil Catalogue for details of field viewing.
MAIL ORDER: Only *MIN VALUE:* None *CAT. COST:* 35p *EXPORT:* Yes
SPECIALITIES: Daffodils & Lilies.

EWar **Warley Rose Garden Ltd.,** Warley Street, Great Warley, Brentwood, Essex CM13 3JH
TEL: (0277) 221966/219344 *CONTACT:* J H G Deamer
W/SALE or RETAIL: Both *OPENING TIMES:* 0900-1730 Mon-Sat.
MAIL ORDER: Yes *MIN VALUE:* None *CAT. COST:* Free-20p atshop *EXPORT:* No
SPECIALITIES: Roses & container grown Nursery Stock.. *MAP PAGE:* **3**

EWav **Waveney Fish Farm,** Park Road, Diss, Norfolk IP22 3AS
TEL: (0379) 642697 *FAX:* (0379) 651315 *CONTACT:* D G Laughlin
W/SALE or RETAIL: Both *OPENING TIMES:* 1000-1700 daily.
MAIL ORDER: Yes *MIN VALUE:* £5.00 *CAT. COST:* Free *EXPORT:* Yes
SPECIALITIES: Aquatic & Marginals. *MAP PAGE:* **6**

EWhi **Whitehouse Ivies,** Hylands Farm, Rectory Road, Tolleshunt Knights, Maldon, Essex CM9 8EZ
TEL: (0621) 815782 *CONTACT:* R Whitehouse
W/SALE or RETAIL: Both *OPENING TIMES:* Appt. only, please telephone
MAIL ORDER: Yes *MIN VALUE:* None *CAT. COST:* £1 refundable *EXPORT:* Yes
SPECIALITIES: Hedera only. Over 300 varieties. *MAP PAGE:* **3/6**

GAbr **Abriachan Nurseries,** Loch Ness Side, Invernesshire IV3 6LA
TEL: (046 386) 232 *CONTACT:* Mr & Mrs D Davidson
W/SALE or RETAIL: Both *OPENING TIMES:* 0900-1900 daily.
MAIL ORDER: Yes *MIN VALUE:* No *CAT. COST:* 3 x 1st class *EXPORT:* No
SPECIALITIES: Rockery & Herbaceous. Primulas, Helianthemum & Hebe. *MAP PAGE:* **9**

GAng **Angus Heathers,** 10 Guthrie Street, Letham, Forfar, Tayside DD8 2PS
TEL: (030781) 504 *CONTACT:* George, Joyce & David Sturrock
W/SALE or RETAIL: Both *OPENING TIMES:* 1000-1700 daily.
MAIL ORDER: No *MIN VALUE:* *CAT. COST:* Free *EXPORT:* Yes
SPECIALITIES: Heathers & Gentians. *MAP PAGE:* **9**

GArd **Ard Daraich Shrub Nursery,** Ardgour, by Fort William, Invernesshire PH33 7AB
TEL: (085 55) 248 *CONTACT:* David Maclaren
W/SALE or RETAIL: Retail *OPENING TIMES:* 1000-1730 Tue-Sun.
MAIL ORDER: No *MIN VALUE:* *CAT. COST:* 2 x 1st class *EXPORT:* No
SPECIALITIES: Dwarf Rhododendron, Camellia, Acer & Shrubs. *MAP PAGE:* **9**

◆ **See also Display Advertisements**

GArf **Ardfearn Nursery,** Bunchrew, Inverness Highland IV3 6RH
TEL: (0463) 243 250 *CONTACT:* James Sutherland
W/SALE or RETAIL: Both *OPENING TIMES:* 0900-1700 Mon-Sat, 1300-1700 Sun Mar-Nov & by appt.
MAIL ORDER: Yes* *MIN VALUE:* None *CAT. COST:* 2 x 1st class *EXPORT:* No
SPECIALITIES: Alpines & Ericaceae, rare & unusual. *NOTE: Mail Order Oct-Mar only.
MAP PAGE: **9**

GBla **Blairhoyle Nursery,** Port of Menteith, Stirling, Central FK8 3LF
TEL: (08775) 669 *CONTACT:* B A & G W Cartwright
W/SALE or RETAIL: Both *OPENING TIMES:* 1000-dusk ex Tue & Sat Mar-Nov.
MAIL ORDER: No *MIN VALUE:* *CAT. COST:* Sae *EXPORT:* No
SPECIALITIES: Heathers, Alpines & Dwarf Conifers. *MAP PAGE:* **9**

GBon **Bonhard Nursery,** Murrayshall Road, Scone, Perth, Tayside PH2 7PQ
TEL: (0738) 52791 *CONTACT:* Mr & Mrs Hickman
W/SALE or RETAIL: Retail *OPENING TIMES:* 1000-1800, or dusk if earlier, daily.
MAIL ORDER: No *MIN VALUE:* *CAT. COST:* Free *EXPORT:* No
SPECIALITIES: Herbaceous, Conifers & Alpines. Fruit & ornamental Trees. *MAP PAGE:* **9**

GCHN **Charter House Nursery,** 2 Nunwood, Stepford Road, Dumfries & Galloway DG2 7RE
TEL: (0387) 720363 *CONTACT:* John Ross
W/SALE or RETAIL: Retail *OPENING TIMES:* Appt. only
MAIL ORDER: Yes *MIN VALUE:* None *CAT. COST:* 9inx4in Sae *EXPORT:* No
SPECIALITIES: Aquileagia, Hypericum, Geranium, Erodium, Pelargonium species and Campanula. Erodium National Collection. *MAP PAGE:* **9**

GChr **T & W Christie (Forres) Ltd,** The Nurseries, Forres, Moray, Grampian IV36 0EA
TEL: (0309) 72633 *FAX:* (0309) 76846 *CONTACT:* Donald W Williamson
W/SALE or RETAIL: Both *OPENING TIMES:* 0800-1200 & 1300-1700 Mon-Fri, 0800-1200 Sat.
MAIL ORDER: Yes *MIN VALUE:* £15.00 *CAT. COST:* Free *EXPORT:* No
SPECIALITIES: Hedging & screening plants. Woodland & less common Trees, Shrubs & Fruit.
MAP PAGE: **9**

GDra **Jack Drake,** Inshriach Alpine Nusery, Aviemore, Invernesshire PH22 1QS
TEL: (05404) 287 *CONTACT:* J C Lawson
◆ *W/SALE or RETAIL:* Both *OPENING TIMES:* 0900-1700 Mon-Fri, 0900-1230 Sat.
MAIL ORDER: Yes *MIN VALUE:* None *CAT. COST:* 60p *EXPORT:* No
SPECIALITIES: Rare and unusual Alpines & Rock plants. Especially Primula, Meconopsis, Gentian, Heathers etc. *MAP PAGE:* **9**

GEdr **Edrom Nurseries,** Coldingham, Eyemouth, Berwick, Borders TD14 5TZ
TEL: (08907) 71386 *CONTACT:* J Jermyn
W/SALE or RETAIL: Retail *OPENING TIMES:* 1000-1700 Mon-Sat, 1400-1700 Sun Mar 1-Sept 30.
MAIL ORDER: Yes *MIN VALUE:* None *CAT. COST:* 60p *EXPORT:* No
SPECIALITIES: Primula, Gentiana, Meconopsis, Anemone & other Alpines. *MAP PAGE:* **9**

GGar **Garden Cottage,** Tournaig, Poolewe, Achnasheen, Highland IV22 2LH
TEL: (044 586) 339 *CONTACT:* R Rushbrooke
W/SALE or RETAIL: Retail *OPENING TIMES:* 1200-1900 Mon-Sat (Mar-Oct) or by appt.
MAIL ORDER: Yes *MIN VALUE:* None *CAT. COST:* 3 x 1st class *EXPORT:* No
SPECIALITIES: Large range of Herbacous & Alpines esp. Primula, Geranium & moisture lovers. Range of West Coast Shrubs. *MAP PAGE:* **9**

GGre **Greenhead Roses,** Greenhead Nursery, Old Greenock Road, Inchinnan, Renfrew, Strathclyde PA4 9PH
TEL: (041 812) 0121 *CONTACT:* C N Urquhart
W/SALE or RETAIL: Both *OPENING TIMES:* 1000-1700 daily.
MAIL ORDER: Yes *MIN VALUE:* £3.00 *CAT. COST:* Sae *EXPORT:* No
SPECIALITIES: Roses. Wide general range, dwarf Conifers, Azaleas, Rhododendrons, Shrubs, Alpines, Fruit, hardy Herbaceous & Spring & Summer bedding. *MAP PAGE:* **9**

GHig **Highland Liliums,** Kiltarlity-by-Beauly, Inverness Highland IV4 7JQ
TEL: (046374) 365 *CONTACT:* Neil MacRitchie
W/SALE or RETAIL: Both *OPENING TIMES:* 0900-1700 Mon-Sat.
MAIL ORDER: Yes *MIN VALUE:* £10.00 *CAT. COST:* 25p *EXPORT:* No
SPECIALITIES: Shrubs, Herbaceous, Alpines, Ferns, Grasses, Bamboo, Primula & Herbs.
MAP PAGE: **9**

GKit **Kittoch Plants,** Kittoch Mill, Busby Road, Carmunnock, Glasgow, Strathclyde G76 9BJ
TEL: 041-644 4712 *CONTACT:* Mrs P A Jordan
W/SALE or RETAIL: Retail *OPENING TIMES:* Appt. only.
MAIL ORDER: Yes *MIN VALUE:* None *CAT. COST:* Sae *EXPORT:* No
SPECIALITIES: Hostas from the Scottish National Collection. *MAP PAGE:* **9**

GK&P **King & Paton,** Barnhourie Mill, By Dalbeattie, Dumfries & Galloway DG5 4PU
TEL: (038778) 269 *CONTACT:* Miss E King & Dr M Paton
W/SALE or RETAIL: Retail *OPENING TIMES:* Appt only.
MAIL ORDER: Yes *MIN VALUE:* None *CAT. COST:* Sae *EXPORT:* No
SPECIALITIES: Rhododendron species. *MAP PAGE:* **9**

GLoc **Lochside Alpine Nursery,** Lochside, Ulbster, Caithness, Highland KW2 6AA
TEL: (095 585) 320 *CONTACT:* Terry & Jane Clarke
W/SALE or RETAIL: Retail *OPENING TIMES:* 1000-1800 daily.
MAIL ORDER: Yes *MIN VALUE:* *CAT. COST:* Sae *EXPORT:* SO
SPECIALITIES: Cyclamen species, Primulaceae, Phlox species & dwarf alpine Shrubs & Cyclamen.
MAP PAGE: **9**

GMac **Elizabeth MacGregor,** Ellenbank, Tongland Road, Kirkcudbright, Dumfries & Galloway DG6 4UU
TEL: (0557) 30620 *CONTACT:* Elizabeth MacGregor
W/SALE or RETAIL: Retail *OPENING TIMES:* Please phone.
MAIL ORDER: Yes *MIN VALUE:* £8.40 + p&p *CAT. COST:* 75p *EXPORT:* No
SPECIALITIES: Violets, Violas & Violettas, old and new varieties. Cottage garden plants.
MAP PAGE: **9**

GPen **Pennyacre Nurseries,** Station Road, Springfield, Fife KY15 5RU
TEL: (0334) 55852 *CONTACT:* C P Piper
W/SALE or RETAIL: Retail *OPENING TIMES:* Telephone before visiting.
MAIL ORDER: Yes *MIN VALUE:* None *CAT. COST:* Sae *EXPORT:*
SPECIALITIES: Heathers, Dwarf Conifers. *MAP PAGE:* **9**

GPla **Plants from the Past,** The Old House, 1 North Street, Belhaven, Dunbar, Lothian EH42 1NU
TEL: (0368) 63223 *CONTACT:* J Sutherland
W/SALE or RETAIL: Retail *OPENING TIMES:* Mar-Sept 1300-1700 ex Tues.
MAIL ORDER: Yes *MIN VALUE:* 5 plants *CAT. COST:* 3 x 1st class *EXPORT:* No
SPECIALITIES: Old fashioned plants. *MAP PAGE:* **9**

GPoy **Poyntzfield Herb Nursery,** Nr Balblair, Black Isle, Dingwall, Ross & Cromarty, Highland IV7 8LX
TEL: (03818) 352 evs *CONTACT:* Duncan Ross
W/SALE or RETAIL: Retail *OPENING TIMES:* 1300-1700 Mon-Sat.
MAIL ORDER: Yes *MIN VALUE:* None *CAT. COST:* Sae+3x1st cls. *EXPORT:* Yes
SPECIALITIES: Over 350 popular, unusual & rare Herbs, esp. Medicinal. *MAP PAGE:* **9**

GRei **Ben Reid and Co,** Pinewood Park, Countesswells Road, Aberdeen, Grampian AB9 2QL
TEL: (0224) 318744 *FAX:* (0224) 310104 *CONTACT:* John Fraser
W/SALE or RETAIL: Both *OPENING TIMES:* 0900-1700 Mon-Sat. 1000-1700 Sun.
MAIL ORDER: Yes *MIN VALUE:* £10.00 *CAT. COST:* Free *EXPORT:* No
SPECIALITIES: Trees & Shrubs. *MAP PAGE:* **9**

GSpe **Speyside Heather Garden Centre,** Dulnain Bridge, Highland PH26 3PA
TEL: (047 985) 359 *FAX:* (047 985) 396 *CONTACT:* D & B Lambie
W/SALE or RETAIL: Retail *OPENING TIMES:* 0900-1730 daily in Summer. 0900-1700 Mon-Sat Nov-Mar.
MAIL ORDER: Yes *MIN VALUE:* *CAT. COST:* £1.75 *EXPORT:* Yes
SPECIALITIES: Heathers. *MAP PAGE:* **9**

GSta **Fiona Stark,** The Neuk, Torphins, Grampian AB31 4JR
TEL: (03398) 82405 *CONTACT:* Fiona Stark
W/SALE or RETAIL: Retail *OPENING TIMES:* Appt. only
MAIL ORDER: Yes *MIN VALUE:* None *CAT. COST:* 2 x 1st class *EXPORT:* Yes
SPECIALITIES: Single & Double Primroses. *MAP PAGE:* **9**

GTra **John Train & Sons,** Benston, Tarbolton, Strathclyde KA5 5NT
TEL: (0292) 541336 *FAX:* (0292) 541808 *CONTACT:* Mr Adam & Matt Train.
W/SALE or RETAIL: Both *OPENING TIMES:* 0900-1700 daily Mar-Dec. 0900-1600 Mon-Fri Jan & Feb.
MAIL ORDER: Yes *MIN VALUE:* None *CAT. COST:* Free *EXPORT:* No
SPECIALITIES: Rose bushes & bedding plants. *MAP PAGE:* **9**

GWhi **T White & Son,** Park Main Nursery, Erskine, Strathclyde
TEL: (041 812) 1246 *CONTACT:* R T White
W/SALE or RETAIL: Both *OPENING TIMES:* Always.
MAIL ORDER: Yes *MIN VALUE:* *CAT. COST:* Free *EXPORT:* No
SPECIALITIES: Begonias. *MAP PAGE:* **9**

GWic **M C Wickenden,** Cally Gardens, Gatehouse of Fleet, Castle Douglas, Dumfries & Galloway DG7 2DJ
TEL: Not on phone. *CONTACT:* M C Wickenden
W/SALE or RETAIL: Both *OPENING TIMES:* 1000-1750 Sat & Sun only, Mar 30th - Oct 20th 1991.
MAIL ORDER: Yes *MIN VALUE:* £10 *CAT. COST:* 3 x 1st class *EXPORT:* Yes
SPECIALITIES: Unusual perennials. Agapanthus, Crocosmia, Erodium, Eryngium, Euphorbia, Geranium. Some rare Shrubs, Climbers & Conservatory plants. *MAP PAGE:* **9**

IBal **Ballydorn Bulb Farm,** Killinchy, Newtownards, Co. Down, N Ireland BT23 6QB
TEL: (0238) 541250 *CONTACT:* Sir Frank & Lady Harrison
W/SALE or RETAIL: Retail *OPENING TIMES:* Not open.
MAIL ORDER: Only *MIN VALUE:* £10.00 *CAT. COST:* £1.00 *EXPORT:* Yes
SPECIALITIES: New Daffodil varieties for Exhibitors and Hybridisers.

IBar **Barons Court Nurseries,** Abercorn Estates, Newtownstewart, Co. Tyrone, N Ireland
TEL: (06626) 61683 *FAX:* (06626) 62059 *CONTACT:* David Wilson
W/SALE or RETAIL: Both *OPENING TIMES:* 1000-1630 Mon-Sat & 1400-1630 Sun.
MAIL ORDER: Yes *MIN VALUE:* £5.00 *CAT. COST:* Free *EXPORT:* Yes
SPECIALITIES: Meconopsis 'Slieve Donard'. Specimen Trees & container grown Shrubs & Conifers. *MAP PAGE:* **10**

IBlr **Ballyrogan Nurseries,** The Grange, Ballyrogan, Newtownards, Co. Down, N Ireland BT23 4SD
TEL: (0247) 810451 eves *CONTACT:* Gary Dunlop
◆ *W/SALE or RETAIL:* Both *OPENING TIMES:* Not open except for collection.
MAIL ORDER: Yes *MIN VALUE:* £5.00 *CAT. COST:* 2 x 1st class *EXPORT:* No
SPECIALITIES: Conservatory & choice Herbaceous & Shrubs. Abutilon, Agapanthus, Crocosmia, Euphorbia, Geranium & Grasses. *MAP PAGE:* **10**

IBrk **Barkleigh Nurseries,** Richmond Wood, Glanmire, Co. Cork, Eire
TEL: (010 353) 21 821547 *CONTACT:* Niall O'Neill
W/SALE or RETAIL: Both *OPENING TIMES:*
MAIL ORDER: Only *MIN VALUE:* £10.00 *CAT. COST:* 50p *EXPORT:* Yes
SPECIALITIES: Unusual Herbaceous perennials.

ICar **Carncairn Daffodils,** Broughshane, Ballymena, Co. Antrim, N Ireland BT43 7HF
TEL: (0266) 861216 *CONTACT:* Mr & Mrs R H Reade
W/SALE or RETAIL: Both *OPENING TIMES:*
MAIL ORDER: Yes *MIN VALUE:* None *CAT. COST:* Free *EXPORT:* Yes
SPECIALITIES: Old and new Narcissus cultivars, mainly for show. *MAP PAGE:* **10**

IDai **Daisy Hill Nurseries Ltd,** Hospital Road, Newry, Co. Down, N Ireland BT35 8PN
TEL: (0693) 62474 *CONTACT:* W A Grills
W/SALE or RETAIL: Retail *OPENING TIMES:* 0800-1700 Mon-Fri.
MAIL ORDER: Yes *MIN VALUE:* £5.00 *CAT. COST:* Free *EXPORT:* No
SPECIALITIES: Wide variety Trees, Shrubs, Herbaceous, Alpines & Heathers especially Camellia, Ceanothus. *MAP PAGE:* **10**

IDic **Dickson Nurseries Ltd.,** Milecross Road, Newtownards, Co. Down, N Ireland BT23 4SS
TEL: (0247) 812206 *CONTACT:* A P C Dickson OBE.
W/SALE or RETAIL: Both *OPENING TIMES:* 0800-1230 & 1300-1700 Mon-Thur. 0800-1330 Fri.
MAIL ORDER: Yes *MIN VALUE:* None *CAT. COST:* Free *EXPORT:* Yes
SPECIALITIES: Roses, especially modern Dickson varieties. *MAP PAGE:* **10**

IDun **Brian Duncan,** Novelty & Exhibition Daffodils 15 Ballynahatty Road, Omagh, Co. Tyrone, N Ireland BT78 1PN
TEL: (0662) 242931 *CONTACT:* Brian Duncan
W/SALE or RETAIL: Both *OPENING TIMES:* By appointment.
MAIL ORDER: Yes *MIN VALUE:* £10.00 *CAT. COST:* £1.00 inc p&p *EXPORT:* Yes
SPECIALITIES: New hybrid Narcissus & Exhibition Tulips. *MAP PAGE:* **10**

IFer **Fernhill Nursery,** Sandyford, Co. Dublin, Eire
TEL: (0001) 956158 *CONTACT:* Robert Walker
W/SALE or RETAIL: Both *OPENING TIMES:* 1100-1700 Tue-Sat all year & 1400-1700 Sun Mar-Nov.
MAIL ORDER: No *MIN VALUE:* *CAT. COST:* *EXPORT:* No
SPECIALITIES: Wide general range. *MAP PAGE:* **10**

IHos **Hosford's Geraniums & Garden Centre** Cappa, Enniskeane, Co. Cork, Eire
TEL: (010 353) 23 39159 *FAX:* (010 353) 23 39300 *CONTACT:* John Hosford
W/SALE or RETAIL: Retail *OPENING TIMES:* 0900-1800 Mon-Sat (all year inc. Bank Hols). 1430-1830 Sun Mar-Jun, 1430-1730 mid-Sep-Xmas.
MAIL ORDER: Yes *MIN VALUE:* IR£1.80 *CAT. COST:* IR£1.50 *EXPORT:* Yes
SPECIALITIES: Geraniums, Pelargoniums, Basket & Window box plants, Bedding & Roses. NOTE: Express Courier service available within Ireland. *MAP PAGE:* **10**

IJoh **Johnstown Garden Centre,** Johnstown, Naas, Co. Kildare, Eire
TEL: (010 353) 45 79138 *FAX:* (010 353) 45 79073 *CONTACT:* Jim Clarke
W/SALE or RETAIL: Retail *OPENING TIMES:* 1000-1800 Mon-Sat & 1400-1800 Sun.
MAIL ORDER: No *MIN VALUE:* *CAT. COST:* Free *EXPORT:* No
SPECIALITIES: Very wide range of Shrubs, Conifers, Alpines, Herbs & Aquatics. Newest introductions. *MAP PAGE:* **10**

IOrc **Orchardstown Nurseries,** 4 miles out, Cork Road, Waterford, Eire
TEL: (010 353) 51 84273 *FAX:* (010 353) 51 84422 *CONTACT:* Ron Dool
W/SALE or RETAIL: Retail *OPENING TIMES:* 0900-1800 Mon-Sat, 1400-1800 Sun.
MAIL ORDER: Yes* *MIN VALUE:* None *CAT. COST:* IR£1.50 *EXPORT:* Yes
SPECIALITIES: Unusual hardy plants incl. Shrubs, Shrub Roses, Trees, Climbers, Rhododendron species & Water plants. *NOTE: Only SOME plants Mail Order. *MAP PAGE:* **10**

IReg **Regional Nurseries,** Rockfield House, Sandyford Road, Dundrum, Dublin 16, Eire
TEL: (0001) 982667 *FAX:* (0001) 982667 *CONTACT:* Neil Murray & S Coone
W/SALE or RETAIL: Both *OPENING TIMES:* 0900-1200 Sat.
MAIL ORDER: No *MIN VALUE:* *CAT. COST:* Sae *EXPORT:* Yes
SPECIALITIES: Trees & Shrubs esp. Ilex. NOTE: This is a Wholesale nursery that is only open for Retail sales on Saturday morning. *MAP PAGE:* **10**

ISea **Seaforde Gardens,** Seaforde, Co. Down, N Ireland
TEL: (039 687) 225 *CONTACT:* P Forde
W/SALE or RETAIL: Both *OPENING TIMES:* 1000-1700 Mon-Fri all year. 1000-1700 Sat & 1400-1800 Sun mid Mar-end Sep.
MAIL ORDER: Yes *MIN VALUE:* None *CAT. COST:* Free *EXPORT:* Yes
SPECIALITIES: Over 600 varieties of self-propagated Trees & Shrubs, especially Eucryphia.
MAP PAGE: **10**

ITim **Timpany Nurseries,** 77 Magheratimpany Road, Ballynahinch, Co. Down, N Ireland BT24 8PA
TEL: (0238) 562812 *CONTACT:* Susan Tindall
W/SALE or RETAIL: *OPENING TIMES:* 1400-1600 Tue-Fri, 1000-1700 Sat & Bank Hols.
MAIL ORDER: Yes *MIN VALUE:* £10.00 + p&p *CAT. COST:* 50p *EXPORT:*
SPECIALITIES: Celmisia, Androsace, Primula, Saxifraga, Helichrysum & Dianthus. *MAP PAGE:* **10**

LAbb **Abbot's House Garden,** 10 High Street, Abbots Langley, Hertfordshire WD5 0AR
TEL: (0923) 264946/262167 *CONTACT:* Dr Peter Tomson & Mrs Joan Gentry
W/SALE or RETAIL: Retail *OPENING TIMES:* 0900-1300 & 1400-1600 Sat Mar-Nov and by appt. Please check before visiting.
MAIL ORDER: Yes* *MIN VALUE:* None *CAT. COST:* 2 x 2nd class *EXPORT:* No
SPECIALITIES: Conservatory, Tender and Patio plants. Flower arranger's plants. Small nursery. *NOTE: Only SOME plants by Mail Order. *MAP PAGE:* **3**

LAma **Jacques Amand Ltd.,** The Nurseries, 145 Clamp Hill, Stanmore, Middlesex HA7 3JS
TEL: (081) 954 8138 *FAX:* (081) 954 6784 *CONTACT:*
W/SALE or RETAIL: Both *OPENING TIMES:* 0900-1700 Mon-Fri, 0900-1300 Sat-Sun.
MAIL ORDER: Yes *MIN VALUE:* Under£30+£2p&p *CAT. COST:* Free *EXPORT:* Yes
SPECIALITIES: Rare and unusual species Bulbs. *MAP PAGE:* **3**

LBlo **Walter Blom and Son Ltd.,** Coombelands Nurseries, Leavesden, Watford, Hertfordshire WD2 7BH
TEL: (0923) 672071/673767 *FAX:* (0923) 894247 *CONTACT:*
W/SALE or RETAIL: Retail *OPENING TIMES:* 0900-1300 & 1400-1700 Mon-Fri.
MAIL ORDER: Yes *MIN VALUE:* None *CAT. COST:* Free *EXPORT:* Yes
SPECIALITIES: Tulips, Lilies, Narcissus & Hyacinthus. *MAP PAGE:* **3**

LBow **Rupert Bowlby,** Gatton, Reigate, Surrey RH2 0TA
TEL: (0737) 642221 *CONTACT:* Rupert Bowlby
W/SALE or RETAIL: Retail *OPENING TIMES:* Sat & Sun pm in Mar-Apr & Sep-Oct.
MAIL ORDER: Yes *MIN VALUE:* None *CAT. COST:* 2 x 2nd class *EXPORT:* No
SPECIALITIES: Unusual Bulbs & Corms. *MAP PAGE:* **3**

LBro **Mrs P J Brown,** V H Humphrey-Iris Specialist, Westlees Farm, Logmore Lane, Westcott, Dorking, Surrey RH4 3JN
TEL: (0306) 889827 *FAX:* (0306) 889371 *CONTACT:* Mrs P J Brown
◆ *W/SALE or RETAIL:* Both *OPENING TIMES:* Appt only. Open day 1000-1700 May 12th 1991.
MAIL ORDER: Yes *MIN VALUE:* None *CAT. COST:* Large Sae 9x6 *EXPORT:* Yes
SPECIALITIES: Dwarf Bearded, Median, Border, Intermediate, Tall Bearded, Spuria, Siberian, Pacific Coast, Water & Species Iris. *MAP PAGE:* **3**

LBuc **Buckingham Nurseries,** 14 Tingewick Road, Buckingham, Buckinghamshire MK18 4AE
TEL: (0280) 813556 *FAX:* (0280) 815491 *CONTACT:* R J & P L Brown
W/SALE or RETAIL: Retail *OPENING TIMES:* 0830-1730 (1800 in summer) Mon-Fri, 0930-1730 (1800 in summer) Sun.
MAIL ORDER: Yes *MIN VALUE:* None *CAT. COST:* Free *EXPORT:* No
SPECIALITIES: Bare rooted and container grown hedging. Trees & Shrubs. *MAP PAGE:* **2**

LCha **Chanctonbury Nurseries,** Rectory Lane, Ashington, Pulborough, Sussex RH20 3AS
TEL: (0903) 892870 *FAX:* (0903) 893036 *CONTACT:* Peter J Smith
W/SALE or RETAIL: Both *OPENING TIMES:* Not open.
MAIL ORDER: Only *MIN VALUE:* £2.50 *CAT. COST:* 20p *EXPORT:* No
SPECIALITIES: Hybrid Alstroemeria for conservatory & garden.

LCra **Craven's Nursery,** Hall Barn Nurseries, Windsor End, Beaconsfield, Buckinghamshire HP9 2SG
TEL: (0494) 674139 *CONTACT:* S R Craven & M Craven
W/SALE or RETAIL: Both *OPENING TIMES:* 1000-dusk Wed-Sun but please ring first.
MAIL ORDER: Yes *MIN VALUE:* £5.00 *CAT. COST:* 54p *EXPORT:* Yes
SPECIALITIES: Show Auricula, Primula, Pinks, Alpines and specialist Seeds. *MAP PAGE:* **3**

LFox **Foxgrove Plants,** Foxgrove, Enborne, Nr Newbury, Berkshire RG14 6RE
TEL: (0635) 40554 *CONTACT:* Miss Louise Vockins
W/SALE or RETAIL: Retail *OPENING TIMES:* 1000-1700 Wed-Sun & Bank Hols.
MAIL ORDER: Yes *MIN VALUE:* £1.90 *CAT. COST:* 65p *EXPORT:* No
SPECIALITIES: Alpines, Foliage plants, Galanthus & Auriculas. *MAP PAGE:* **2**

LGan **Gannock Growers,** Gannock Thatch, Sandon, Buntingford, Hertfordshire SG9 0RH
TEL: (076 387) 386 *CONTACT:* Penny Pyle
W/SALE or RETAIL: Both *OPENING TIMES:* 1000-1600 Tue-Sun & Bank Hol Mons.
MAIL ORDER: Yes *MIN VALUE:* None *CAT. COST:* 3 x 1st class *EXPORT:* No
SPECIALITIES: Unusual & some rare herbaceous plants. *MAP PAGE:* **3/6**

LGod **Godly's Roses,** Redbourn, St Albans, Hertfordshire AL3 7PS
TEL: (0582) 792255 *CONTACT:* Colin Godly
W/SALE or RETAIL: Retail *OPENING TIMES:* 0900-1900 Summer, 0900-dusk Winter Mon-Fri. 0900-1800 Sat & Sun.
MAIL ORDER: Yes *MIN VALUE:* £2.50 *CAT. COST:* Free *EXPORT:* No
SPECIALITIES: Roses. *MAP PAGE:* **3**

LGre **Green Farm Plants,** Bentley, Farnham, Surrey GU10 5JX
TEL: (0420) 23202 *CONTACT:* J Coke
W/SALE or RETAIL: Retail *OPENING TIMES:* 1000-1800 Wed-Sat, end Mar-early Oct.
MAIL ORDER: No *MIN VALUE:* *CAT. COST:* 3 x 1st class *EXPORT:* No
SPECIALITIES: Small Shrubs, Alpines, Sub-shrubs and Perennials. Many uncommon.
MAP PAGE: **2/**

LGro **Growing Carpets,** The Old Farmhouse, Steeple, Morden, Hertfordshire SG8 0PP
TEL: (0763) 852417 *CONTACT:* Mrs P D Milne
W/SALE or RETAIL: Retail *OPENING TIMES:* 1100-1300 & 1400-1800 daily.
MAIL ORDER: Yes *MIN VALUE:* £5.00 *CAT. COST:* 70p stamps/PO*EXPORT:* No
SPECIALITIES: Wide range of Ground-covering plants. *MAP PAGE:* **6**

LHig **High Trees Nurseries,** Buckland, Reigate, Surrey RH2 9RE
TEL: (0737) 247217 *FAX:* (0737) 222521 *CONTACT:* S Head
W/SALE or RETAIL: Retail *OPENING TIMES:* 0900-1730 Mon-Sat ex Bank Hols. 1000-1700 Sun & Bank Hols.
MAIL ORDER: No *MIN VALUE:* *CAT. COST:* None issued *EXPORT:* No
SPECIALITIES: Fuchsia, Geranium, Summer Bedding. Alpines, Heathers, Trees, Shrubs & Roses, Top & Soft Fruit. *MAP PAGE:* **3**

LHil **Brian Hiley,** 25 Little Woodcote Estate, Wallington, Surrey SM5 4AU
TEL: (081) 647 9679 *CONTACT:* Brian & Heather Hiley
W/SALE or RETAIL: Both *OPENING TIMES:* 0900-1700 Wed-Sat (ex Bank Hols). Please check beforehand.
MAIL ORDER: Yes *MIN VALUE:* None *CAT. COST:* 3 x 1st class *EXPORT:* No
SPECIALITIES: Penstemon, Alpines, Herbaceous, tender & unusual plants. *MAP PAGE:* **3**

LHol **Hollington Nurseries,** Woolton Hill, Newbury, Berkshire RG15 9XT
TEL: (0635) 253908 *FAX:* (0635) 254990 *CONTACT:* S & J Hopkinson
W/SALE or RETAIL: Both *OPENING TIMES:* 1000-1700 Mon-Sat, 1100-1700 Sun & Bank Hols Apr-Sep. 1000-dusk Mon-Fri Oct-Mar.
MAIL ORDER: No *MIN VALUE:* *CAT. COST:* £1.50 *EXPORT:* No
SPECIALITIES: Herbs, Thymes, Old fashioned Roses & Salvia. Cool conservatory plants.
MAP PAGE: **2**

LHop **Hopleys Plants Ltd,** High Street, Much Hadham, Hertfordshire SG10 6BU
TEL: (0279 84) 2509 *FAX:* (0279 84) 2509 *CONTACT:* A Barker
W/SALE or RETAIL: Both *OPENING TIMES:* 0900-1700 Mon & Wed-Sat. 1400-1700 Sun. Closed Jan & Aug.
MAIL ORDER: Yes *MIN VALUE:* None *CAT. COST:* £1.00 *EXPORT:* No
SPECIALITIES: Wide range of Hardy & Half-hardy Shrubs & Perennials. *MAP PAGE:* **3/6**

LHyd **Hydon Nurseries Ltd.,** Clock Barn Lane, Hydon Heath, Godalming, Surrey GU8 4AZ
TEL: (0483 860) 252 *CONTACT:* A F George
◆ *W/SALE or RETAIL:* Both *OPENING TIMES:* 0800-1700 Mon-Sat. Sun by appt. only.
MAIL ORDER: Yes *MIN VALUE:* None *CAT. COST:* £1.50 *EXPORT:* Yes
SPECIALITIES: Large and dwarf Rhododendron & Yakushimanum hybrids. *MAP PAGE:* **3**

LKna **Knaphill & Slocock Nurseries,** Barrs Lane, Knaphill, Woking, Surrey GU21 2JW
TEL: (04867) 81212/5 *CONTACT:* Mrs Joy West
W/SALE or RETAIL: Both *OPENING TIMES:* 0900-1700 Mon-Sat & 1000-1700 Sun.
MAIL ORDER: Yes *MIN VALUE:* £20.00 *CAT. COST:* 50p* *EXPORT:* Yes
SPECIALITIES: Wide variety Trees & Shrubs especially Rhododendron, Azalea & Ericaceous.
*NOTE: Catalogue refunadable Rhodos & Azaleas only. *MAP PAGE:* 3

LLin **Lincluden Nursery,** Bisley Green, Bisley, Woking, Surrey GU24 9EN
TEL: (0483) 797005 *FAX:* (0276) 74311 *CONTACT:* Mr & Mrs J A Tilbury
W/SALE or RETAIL: Both *OPENING TIMES:* Any time by appt.
MAIL ORDER: No *MIN VALUE:* *CAT. COST:* 40p *EXPORT:*
SPECIALITIES: Dwarf, slow-growing & unusual Conifers. *MAP PAGE:* 3

LMay **Maydencroft Aquatic Nurseries,** Maydencroft Lane, Gosmore, Hitchin, Hertfordshire SG4 7QD
TEL: (0462) 456020 *CONTACT:* P Bromfield
W/SALE or RETAIL: Both *OPENING TIMES:* 0900-1300 & 1400-1730 daily summer. Same Mon-Fri but 1000-1300 Sat-Sun winter.
MAIL ORDER: Yes *MIN VALUE:* None *CAT. COST:* 50p *EXPORT:* Yes
SPECIALITIES: Water Lilies, Marginals, Bog, Alpines, dwarf Conifer. *MAP PAGE:* 6

LMer **Merrist Wood Plant Shop,** Merrist Wood College, Worplesdon, Guildford Surrey GU3 3PE
TEL: (0483) 232424 *FAX:* (0483) 236518 *CONTACT:* Danny O'Shaughnessy
W/SALE or RETAIL: Both *OPENING TIMES:* 0900-1700 Mon-Fri
MAIL ORDER: No *MIN VALUE:* *CAT. COST:* *EXPORT:* Yes
SPECIALITIES: *MAP PAGE:* 3

LMil **Millais Nurseries,** Crosswater Lane, Churt, Farnham, Surrey GU10 2JN
TEL: (025125) 2698 *CONTACT:* David Millais
◆ *W/SALE or RETAIL:* Both *OPENING TIMES:* 1000-1300 & 1400-1700 Tue-Sat also Sun & Bank Hols in May & June.
MAIL ORDER: Yes *MIN VALUE:* £20.00 *CAT. COST:* £1.00 *EXPORT:* Yes
SPECIALITIES: Rhododendron & Azalea. *MAP PAGE:* 3

LMor **Morehavens,** 28 Denham Lane, Gerrards Cross, Buckinghamshire SL9 0EX
TEL: (024 07) 3601 *CONTACT:* B Farmer
W/SALE or RETAIL: Both *OPENING TIMES:* Only for collection.
MAIL ORDER: Yes *MIN VALUE:* £13.90 inc p&p *CAT. COST:* Free *EXPORT:* No
SPECIALITIES: Chamomile 'Treneague'. *MAP PAGE:* 3

LNet **Nettletons Nursery,** Ivy Mill Lane, Godstone, Surrey RH9 8NF
TEL: (0883) 742426 *CONTACT:* Johathan Nettleton
W/SALE or RETAIL: Both *OPENING TIMES:* 0830-1300 & 1400-1730 Mon Tue Thu-Sat, 1000-1300 Sun Mar-Jun. Bank Hols by appt.
MAIL ORDER: No *MIN VALUE:* *CAT. COST:* *EXPORT:* Yes
SPECIALITIES: Trees & Shrubs. Especially Conifers, Azalea, Camellia, Rhododendron, Vines, Climbers. 100 Japanese Acers. 16 Wisteria. *MAP PAGE:* 3

LPal **The Palm Centre,** 563 Upper Richmond Rd West, London SW14 7ED
TEL: (081) 876 3223 *FAX:* (081) 876 6888 *CONTACT:* Martin Gibbons
W/SALE or RETAIL: Both *OPENING TIMES:* 1000-1800 daily.
MAIL ORDER: Yes *MIN VALUE:* £5.00 *CAT. COST:* £1.95/£1.85 *EXPORT:* Yes
SPECIALITIES: Palms & Cycads, exotic & sub-tropical, hardy, half-hardy & tropical. Seedlings to mature trees. Two cats., one for Palms & one for Cycads. *MAP PAGE:* 3

LPan **Pantiles Nurseries Ltd.,** Almners Road, Lyne, Chertsey, Surrey KT16 0BJ
TEL: (0932) 872195 *FAX:* (0932) 874030 *CONTACT:* Brendan Gallagher
W/SALE or RETAIL: Both *OPENING TIMES:* 0900-1730 daily.
MAIL ORDER: No *MIN VALUE:* *CAT. COST:* Sae *EXPORT:* No
SPECIALITIES: Large Trees, Shrubs & climbers in containers. *MAP PAGE:* 3

LPlm **A J Palmer & Son,** Denham Court Nursery, Village Road, Denham, Uxbridge, Middlesex UB9 5BQ
TEL: (0895) 832035 *CONTACT:* Sheila Palmer
W/SALE or RETAIL: Both *OPENING TIMES:* 0900-dusk Jul-Oct daily. 0900-1700 Mon-Sat, 0900-1300 Sun Nov-Jun.
MAIL ORDER: Yes *MIN VALUE:* None *CAT. COST:* Free *EXPORT:* No
SPECIALITIES: Roses. *MAP PAGE:* **3**

LPri **Priorswood Clematis,** Priorswood, Widbury Hill, Ware, Hertfordshire SG12 7QH
TEL: (0920) 461543 *CONTACT:* G S Greenway
◆ *W/SALE or RETAIL:* Both *OPENING TIMES:* 0800-1700 Tue-Sun & Bank Hol Mondays..
MAIL ORDER: Yes *MIN VALUE:* None *CAT. COST:* 65p + Sae *EXPORT:* Yes
SPECIALITIES: Clematis & other climbing plants. *MAP PAGE:* **3/6**

LRHS **Wisley Plant Centre,** RHS Garden, Nr Ripley, Woking, Surrey GU23 6QB
TEL: (0483) 211113 *FAX:* (0483) 211003 *CONTACT:*
◆ *W/SALE or RETAIL:* Retail *OPENING TIMES:* 1000-1830 daily Summer, 1000-1730 Winter.
MAIL ORDER: No *MIN VALUE:* *CAT. COST:* None issued *EXPORT:* No
SPECIALITIES: Very wide range, many rare & unusual. *MAP PAGE:* **3**

LRoo **Frans Roozen (Holland),** c/o 34 Friars Road, Braughing, Ware, Hertfordshire SG11 2NN
TEL: (0920) 822875 *FAX:* (0920) 822876 *CONTACT:* Mrs Evans
W/SALE or RETAIL: Retail *OPENING TIMES:*
MAIL ORDER: Only *MIN VALUE:* *CAT. COST:* *EXPORT:* Yes
SPECIALITIES: Flower Bulbs.

LSav **Savill Garden,** Crown Estate Office, The Great Park, Windsor, Berkshire SL4 2HT
TEL: (0753) 860222 *FAX:* (0753) 859617 *CONTACT:* J D Bond
◆ *W/SALE or RETAIL:* Both *OPENING TIMES:* 1000-1800 (sunset if earlier).
MAIL ORDER: No *MIN VALUE:* *CAT. COST:* *EXPORT:* No
SPECIALITIES: An exceptionally wide range of choice and rare Trees, Shrubs & hardy Perennials. Wholesale list also produced. *MAP PAGE:* **3**

LTho **Thorp's Nurseries,** 257 Finchampstead Road, Wokingham, Berkshire RH11 3JT
TEL: (0734) 781181 *CONTACT:* J E & S J Thorp
W/SALE or RETAIL: Retail *OPENING TIMES:* 0900-1300 & 1400-1700 Mon-Wed & Fri-Sat. Feb-Oct except Aug.
MAIL ORDER: Yes *MIN VALUE:* 6 plants *CAT. COST:* 2 x 1st class *EXPORT:* Yes
SPECIALITIES: Pelargoniums & tender Geraniums. *MAP PAGE:* **3**

LTow **Mr K J Townsend,** 17 Valerie Close, St Albans, Hertfordshire AL1 5JD
TEL: *CONTACT:* Mr K J Townsend
W/SALE or RETAIL: Retail *OPENING TIMES:* Not open.
MAIL ORDER: Only *MIN VALUE:* None *CAT. COST:* Sae *EXPORT:* No
SPECIALITIES: Over 100 varieties of Achimenes - 'Hot Water Plants'.

LVer **The Vernon Geranium Nursery,** Cuddington Way, Cheam, Sutton, Surrey SM2 7JB
TEL: *CONTACT:* Janet & Derek James
W/SALE or RETAIL: Both *OPENING TIMES:* 0930-1730 Mon-Sat, 1000-1600 Sun, Easter to end-Aug.
MAIL ORDER: Yes *MIN VALUE:* None *CAT. COST:* 2 x 1st class *EXPORT:* No
SPECIALITIES: Pelargoniums. *MAP PAGE:* **2**

MAsh **Ashwood Nurseries,** Greenforge, Kingswinford, West Midlands DY6 0AE
TEL: (0384) 401996 *CONTACT:* John Massey & Philip Baulk
◆ *W/SALE or RETAIL:* Both *OPENING TIMES:* 0900-1800 Mon-Sat & 0930-1800 Sun. ex Xmas & Boxing day.
MAIL ORDER: SO *MIN VALUE:* *CAT. COST:* 9"x6" Sae *EXPORT:* SO
SPECIALITIES: Lewisias (Holder of NCCPG Collection). Also large range of hardy plants.
MAP PAGE: **5**

MAus **David Austin Roses,** Bowling Green Lane, Albrighton, Wolverhampton, Staffordshire WV7 3HB
TEL: (0902) 373931 *FAX:* (0902) 372142 *CONTACT:* D Austin
◆ *W/SALE or RETAIL:* Both *OPENING TIMES:* 0900-1700 Mon-Fri, 1000-1800 Sat, Sun & Bank Hols. Til dusk Nov-Jan.
MAIL ORDER: Yes *MIN VALUE:* None *CAT. COST:* Free *EXPORT:* Yes
SPECIALITIES: Paeonia, Roses, Iris & Hemerocallis. Also Herbaceous perennials at Nursery. NOTE: Only Roses are available for export. *MAP PAGE:* **5**

MBal **Ballalheannagh Gardens,** Glen Roy, Lonan, Isle of Man
TEL: (0624) 861875 *CONTACT:* Cliff & Maureen Dadd
W/SALE or RETAIL: Retail *OPENING TIMES:* 1000-1300 & 1400-1700 or dusk if earlier in Winter. Closed w/ends Nov-Mar. Please telephone first.
MAIL ORDER: Yes *MIN VALUE:* £5.00 *CAT. COST:* £1.00 *EXPORT:* No
SPECIALITIES: Rhododendrons & Ericaceous Shrubs. Small number of rare trees and shrubs for callers not in catalogue. *MAP PAGE:* **4**

MBar **Barncroft Nurseries,** Dunwood Lane, Longsdon, Nr Leek, Stoke-on-Trent, Staffordshire ST9 9QW
TEL: (0538) 384310/372111 *CONTACT:* R & S Warner
W/SALE or RETAIL: Both *OPENING TIMES:* 0900-1900 or dusk if earlier Fri-Sun.
MAIL ORDER: No *MIN VALUE:* *CAT. COST:* None issued *EXPORT:* No
SPECIALITIES: Very large range of Heathers, Conifers & Shrubs. *MAP PAGE:* **5**

MBea **John Beach (Nursery) Ltd.,** (Office) 9 Grange Road, Wellesbourne, Warwickshire CV35 9RL
TEL: (0926) 624173 *CONTACT:* John Beach
◆ *W/SALE or RETAIL:* Both *OPENING TIMES:* 1000-1300 & 1430-1700 Mon-Sat Mar-Oct. 1000-1300 & 1430-dusk Mon-Sat Nov-Feb.
MAIL ORDER: Yes *MIN VALUE:* 2 plants *CAT. COST:* 10 x 2nd class *EXPORT:* Yes
SPECIALITIES: Clematis, Trees & Shrubs inc Fuchsia. (Nursery address:- Thelsford Farm, Charlcote, Warwick.) *MAP PAGE:* **2**

MBeb **Tom Bebbington Dahlias,** Lady Gate Nursery, 47 The Green, Diseworth, Derbyshire DE7 2QN
TEL: (0332) 811565 *CONTACT:* T & M Bebbington
W/SALE or RETAIL: Both *OPENING TIMES:* Appt only.
MAIL ORDER: Yes *MIN VALUE:* £10.00 *CAT. COST:* 28p *EXPORT:* No
SPECIALITIES: Dahlias. *MAP PAGE:* **5**

MBen **Michael Bennett,** Long Compton, Shipston-on-Stour, Warwickshire CV36 5JN
TEL: (060 884) 676 *CONTACT:*
W/SALE or RETAIL: Both *OPENING TIMES:*
MAIL ORDER: Only *MIN VALUE:* *CAT. COST:* Sae *EXPORT:* No
SPECIALITIES: Asparagus & Globe Artichoke.

MBlu **The Bluebell Nursery,** Blackfordby, Burton-on-Trent, Leicestershire DE11 8AJ
TEL: (0283) 222091 *CONTACT:* Robert & Suzette Vernon
W/SALE or RETAIL: Retail *OPENING TIMES:* 0900-1230 & 1330-1700 daily. Closed Dec 25th-Jan 2nd.
MAIL ORDER: No *MIN VALUE:* *CAT. COST:* 2 x 1st class *EXPORT:* No
SPECIALITIES: Shrubs & Climbers. *MAP PAGE:* **5**

MBri **Bridgemere Nurseries,** Bridgemere, Nr Nantwich, Cheshire CW5 7QB
TEL: (09365) 381/239 *FAX:* (09365) 215 *CONTACT:* John Ravenscroft
W/SALE or RETAIL: Both *OPENING TIMES:* 0900-2000 Mon-Sat, 1000-2000 Sun summer, until 1700 latest in winter, dusk if earlier.
MAIL ORDER: No *MIN VALUE:* *CAT. COST:* *EXPORT:* No
SPECIALITIES: Largest variety of Plants, Bulbs & Seeds on one site in UK. Especially dwarf Rhododendrons, Conifers, Heathers, Alpines Trees & Shrubs. *MAP PAGE:* **5**

MBro **Broadstone Alpines,** 13 The Nursery, High Street, Sutton Courtenay, Abingdon, Oxfordshire OX14 4UA
TEL: (0235) 847557 *CONTACT:* J Shackleton
W/SALE or RETAIL: Retail *OPENING TIMES:* 1500-1900 Fri & Sat (except Show days) & by appt.
MAIL ORDER: Yes *MIN VALUE:* None *CAT. COST:* 3 x 1st class *EXPORT:* No
SPECIALITIES: Plants for rock garden, scree, troughs & borders. Lime tolerant Alpines & unusual plants. *MAP PAGE:* **2**

MBur **Burrows Roses,** Meadow Croft, Spondon Road, Dale Abbey, Derbyshire DE7 4PQ
TEL: (0332) 668289 *CONTACT:* Mr Stuart Burrows
W/SALE or RETAIL: *OPENING TIMES:* 0900-1700
MAIL ORDER: Only *MIN VALUE:* £2.00 *CAT. COST:* 20p+1st class *EXPORT:*
SPECIALITIES: Roses

MCab **The Cabbage Patch,** 14 Greenoak Drive, Sale, Cheshire M33 3QA
TEL: (061) 962 4230 *CONTACT:* Mrs Thelma Kay
W/SALE or RETAIL: Retail *OPENING TIMES:* By appt. only.
MAIL ORDER: Yes* *MIN VALUE:* None-p&p at cost *CAT. COST:* *EXPORT:* No
SPECIALITIES: Bomarea caldasii, and a few other rare plants in small quantities. *NOTE: Mail Order for small plants only. *MAP PAGE:* **5**

MCad **Caddick's Clematis Nurseries,** Dyer's Lane, Rushgreen Road, Lymm, Cheshire WA13 9QL
TEL: (0925 75) 7196 *CONTACT:* H Caddick
◆ *W/SALE or RETAIL:* Both *OPENING TIMES:* 1000-1700 daily.
MAIL ORDER: Yes *MIN VALUE:* £3.95 + p&p *CAT. COST:* 3 x 1st class *EXPORT:* Yes
SPECIALITIES: Clematis. *MAP PAGE:* **5**

MCas **Castle Alpines,** Castle Road, Wootton, Woodstock, Oxfordshire OX7 1EG
TEL: (0993) 812162 *CONTACT:* M S & F E Castle
W/SALE or RETAIL: Retail *OPENING TIMES:* 1000-1700 Tue-Sat Mar 1-Sep 30. Appt only Oct 1-Feb 28.
MAIL ORDER: Yes *MIN VALUE:* None *CAT. COST:* 2 x 2nd class *EXPORT:* No
SPECIALITIES: Alpines. *MAP PAGE:* **2**

MChe **Cheshire Herbs,** Fourfields, Forest Road, Little Budworth, Cheshire CW6 9ES
TEL: (0829) 760578 *CONTACT:* Mr & Mrs Ted Riddell
W/SALE or RETAIL: Both *OPENING TIMES:* 1000-1700 daily Jan 3-Dec 24th.
MAIL ORDER: SO *MIN VALUE:* *CAT. COST:* 20p *EXPORT:* Yes
SPECIALITIES: Display Herb garden & Elizabethan knot garden. *MAP PAGE:* **5**

MCls **James Coles & Sons Ltd.,** The Nurseries, Thurnby, Leicestershire LE7 9QB
TEL: (0533) 412115 *FAX:* (0533) 432311 *CONTACT:* Janet Thompson
W/SALE or RETAIL: Both *OPENING TIMES:* 0900-1645 Mon-Fri.
MAIL ORDER: No *MIN VALUE:* *CAT. COST:* *EXPORT:* Yes
SPECIALITIES: Fruit, Ornamental Trees & Shrubs. *MAP PAGE:* **5**

MCol **Collinwood Nurseries,** Mottram St. Andrew, Macclesfield, Cheshire SK10 4QR
TEL: *CONTACT:* A Wright
W/SALE or RETAIL: Retail *OPENING TIMES:* 0830-1800 Mon-Sat 1400-1800 Sun.
MAIL ORDER: Yes *MIN VALUE:* None *CAT. COST:* Free *EXPORT:* No
SPECIALITIES: Chrysanthemums. *MAP PAGE:* **5**

MCot **Coton Manor Garden,** Nr Guilsborough, Northampton, Northamptonshire NN6 8RQ
TEL: (0604) 740219 *CONTACT:* Mr & Mrs Ian Pasley-Tyler
W/SALE or RETAIL: Retail *OPENING TIMES:* 1400-1800 Sun & Bank Hols, Apr-Oct. 1400-1800 Wed Jun-Aug other times in working hours by appt.
MAIL ORDER: No *MIN VALUE:* *CAT. COST:* Large Sae *EXPORT:* No
SPECIALITIES: Herbaceous, Foliage & Shrubs especially for clay soils. *MAP PAGE:* **2**

MCou **Court Farm Nurseries (Pebworth)Ltd.** Honeybourne Road, Pebworth, Nr Stratford-on-Avon, Warwickshire CV37 8XT
TEL: (0789) 720788 *FAX:* (0789) 721162 *CONTACT:* Mr & Mrs R J Key
W/SALE or RETAIL: Retail *OPENING TIMES:* Not open.
MAIL ORDER: Only *MIN VALUE:* None *CAT. COST:* 2 x 2nd class *EXPORT:* No
SPECIALITIES: Hellebore.

◆ **See also Display Advertisements**

MCra **Crail Nurseries Ltd,** Newstead Abbey Park, Nottingham, Nottingham NG15 8GD
TEL: (0623) 792866 *CONTACT:* Mr & Mrs Lunn
W/SALE or RETAIL: Both *OPENING TIMES:* 0900-1300 & 1400-1700 Mon-Fri.
MAIL ORDER: No *MIN VALUE:* *CAT. COST:* Free *EXPORT:*
SPECIALITIES: Heathers & Conifers. *MAP PAGE:* **5/7**

MCuc **The Cuckoo Pen Nursery,** Preston Crowmarsh, Nr Wallingford, Oxfordshire OX10 6SL
TEL: (0491) 35971/25557 *CONTACT:* I R Burles
W/SALE or RETAIL: Both *OPENING TIMES:* For order collection only.
MAIL ORDER: Only *MIN VALUE:* None *CAT. COST:* Sae *EXPORT:* Yes
SPECIALITIES: Hostas & native Wildflowers for retail Mail Order.

MDHE **DHE Plants,** Rose Lea, Darley House Estate, Darley Dale, Matlock, Derbyshire DE4 2QH
TEL: (0629) 732512 *CONTACT:* Peter M Smith
W/SALE or RETAIL: Retail *OPENING TIMES:* By appt. only, essential to phone first.
MAIL ORDER: Yes *MIN VALUE:* None *CAT. COST:* 40p *EXPORT:* No
SPECIALITIES: Small range of Rock Garden plants. NOTE: Nursery may be moving, please check first by phone. *MAP PAGE:* **5/7**

MFie **Field House Nurseries,** Leake Road, Gotham, Nottingham NG11 0JN
TEL: (0602) 830278 *CONTACT:* Doug Lochhead
W/SALE or RETAIL: Retail *OPENING TIMES:* 0900-1700 Wed-Mon or by appt.
MAIL ORDER: Yes* *MIN VALUE:* *CAT. COST:* 3 x 1st class *EXPORT:* SO
SPECIALITIES: Auriculas, Primulas, Alpines & Rock plants. *NOTE: Mail Order for Auriculas, Primulas & Seeds ONLY. *MAP PAGE:* **5**

MFir **The Firs Nursery,** Chelford Road, Henbury, Macclesfield, Cheshire SK10 3LH
TEL: (0625) 426422 *CONTACT:* Fay J Bowling
W/SALE or RETAIL: Retail *OPENING TIMES:* 1000-1800 Thu-Tue, Mar-Sep.
MAIL ORDER: No *MIN VALUE:* *CAT. COST:* 2 x 1st class *EXPORT:* No
SPECIALITIES: Herbaceous Perennials, Alpines, Hebe, some unusual. *MAP PAGE:* **5**

MGan **Gandy's (Roses) Ltd.,** North Kilworth, Nr Lutterworth, Leicestershire LE17 6HZ
TEL: (0858) 880398 *CONTACT:* Miss R D Gandy
W/SALE or RETAIL: Both *OPENING TIMES:* 0900-1700 Mon-Sat & 1400-1700 Sun.
MAIL ORDER: Yes *MIN VALUE:* None *CAT. COST:* Free *EXPORT:* Yes
SPECIALITIES: 600 Rose varieties. *MAP PAGE:* **2**

MGos **Goscote Nurseries Ltd,** Syston Road, Cossington, Leicestershire LE7 8NZ
TEL: (050981) 2121 *CONTACT:* D C & R C Cox
◆ *W/SALE or RETAIL:* Retail *OPENING TIMES:* 0800-1630 Mon-Fri, 0900-1200 & 1400-1630 Sat, 1000-1300 & 1400-1630 Sun.
MAIL ORDER: Yes *MIN VALUE:* £5.00 *CAT. COST:* 50p in stamps *EXPORT:* No
SPECIALITIES: Trees, Shrubs, Heathers, Conifers, Alpines, Herbaceous. Especially Ericaceae. *MAP PAGE:* **5**

MHay **F Haynes & Partners Ltd.,** (Off.) 56 Gordon Street, Kettering, Northamptonshire NN16 0RX
TEL: (0536) 519836 *CONTACT:* Mr Maple
W/SALE or RETAIL: Both *OPENING TIMES:* 0800-1530 daily.
MAIL ORDER: Yes *MIN VALUE:* £2.50 *CAT. COST:* Free *EXPORT:* No
SPECIALITIES: Roses, especially exhibition & miniature. NOTE: Nursery at Drayton Road, Lowick, Nr Thrapston. *MAP PAGE:* **6**

MHig **Highgates Nursery,** 166a Crich Lane, Belper, Derbyshire DE5 1EP
TEL: (0773) 822153 *CONTACT:* R E & D I Straughan
W/SALE or RETAIL: Retail *OPENING TIMES:* 1030-1630 Mon-Sat mid Mar-mid Oct. Closed Sun.
MAIL ORDER: No *MIN VALUE:* *CAT. COST:* 40p *EXPORT:* No
SPECIALITIES: Alpines. *MAP PAGE:* **5/7**

MHls **Hills Nurseries,** Netherton Road, Appleton, Nr Abingdon, Oxfordshire OX13 5QN
TEL: (0865) 862081 *CONTACT:* Mrs Hill
W/SALE or RETAIL: Both *OPENING TIMES:* 0730-1700 winter, 0730-dusk summer.
MAIL ORDER: Yes *MIN VALUE:* £2.50 *CAT. COST:* Free *EXPORT:* No
SPECIALITIES: Roses and standard Fuchsias & Gooseberries. *MAP PAGE:* **2**

MJac **Jackson's Nurseries,** Clifton Campville, Nr Tamworth, Staffordshire B79 0AP
TEL: (082786) 307 *CONTACT:* N Jackson
W/SALE or RETAIL: Both *OPENING TIMES:* 0900-1800 Mon Wed-Sat, 1000-1700 Sun.
MAIL ORDER: Yes *MIN VALUE:* £7.45 *CAT. COST:* 2 x 1st class *EXPORT:* No
SPECIALITIES: Fuchsia. *MAP PAGE:* **5**

MLab **Laburnum Nurseries,** c/o 6 Manor House Gardens, Main Street, Humberstone Village, Leicestershire LE5 1AE
TEL: (0533) 766522 *CONTACT:* Mr W Johnson
W/SALE or RETAIL: Both *OPENING TIMES:* 0900-1600 Mon-Sat 0900-1200 Sat & Sun.
MAIL ORDER: Yes *MIN VALUE:* £6.00 *CAT. COST:* Free *EXPORT:* Yes
SPECIALITIES: Fuchsia. *MAP PAGE:* **5**

MLea **Lea Rhododendron Gardens Ltd.,** Lea, Matlock, Derbyshire DE4 5GH
TEL: (0629 534) 380/260 *CONTACT:* Jon Tye
W/SALE or RETAIL: Retail *OPENING TIMES:* 1000-1900.
MAIL ORDER: Yes *MIN VALUE:* £10.00 *CAT. COST:* 25p *EXPORT:* Yes
SPECIALITIES: Rhododendron, Azalea & Kalmia. *MAP PAGE:* **5/7**

MLin **Linfield Nurseries of Barton,** Holly Road, Barton-under-Needwood, Staffordshire DE13 8LP
TEL: (028371) 6292 *CONTACT:* Peter C Mullis.
W/SALE or RETAIL: Both *OPENING TIMES:*
MAIL ORDER: Only *MIN VALUE:* £15.00 *CAT. COST:* Free *EXPORT:* Yes
SPECIALITIES: Lilium, including virus tested. Hybrid Alstroemeria, garden & commercial cut-flower varieties.

MMat **Mattock's Roses,** The Rose Nurseries, Nuneham Courtenay, Oxford, Oxfordshire OX9 9PY
TEL: (086 738) 265 *FAX:* (086 738) 267 *CONTACT:* Mr Mattock
W/SALE or RETAIL: Both *OPENING TIMES:* 0900-1730 Mon-Sat, 1030-1730 Sun. Closes 1700 Nov-Feb.
MAIL ORDER: Yes *MIN VALUE:* None *CAT. COST:* Free *EXPORT:* Yes
SPECIALITIES: Roses. *MAP PAGE:* **2**

MMea **Mears Ashby Nurseries Ltd.,** Glebe House, Glebe Road, Mears Ashby, Northamptonshire NN6 0DL
TEL: (0604) 811811/812371 *FAX:* (0604) 812353 *CONTACT:* John B & J E Gaggini
W/SALE or RETAIL: Both *OPENING TIMES:* 0800-1700 Mon-Fri (Wholesale & Retail). 0930-1730 Sat & Sun (Retail only).
MAIL ORDER: No *MIN VALUE:* *CAT. COST:* £1.00 + 20p *EXPORT:* No
SPECIALITIES: Specialist growers of container Trees, Shrubs, Conifers & Fruit, esp. Wisteria. Tree Ferns. *MAP PAGE:* **6**

MMor **F Morrey & Sons,** Forest Nursery, Kelsall, Tarporley, Cheshire CW6 0SW
TEL: (0829) 51342 *FAX:* (0829) 52449 *CONTACT:* D F Morrey
W/SALE or RETAIL: Both *OPENING TIMES:* 0830-1730 Mon-Sat.
MAIL ORDER: No *MIN VALUE:* *CAT. COST:* 20p *EXPORT:*
SPECIALITIES: Azaleas, Rhododendrons & ornamental Trees. *MAP PAGE:* **4/5**

MMth **S E Matthews,** Alderley Park Nurseries, Nether Alderley, Nr Macclesfield, Cheshire SK10 4TH
TEL: (0625) 582087 *FAX:* (0625) 586411 *CONTACT:* I D Urquhart
W/SALE or RETAIL: Both *OPENING TIMES:* 0900-1800 Summer, 0900-1730 Winter daily.
MAIL ORDER: No *MIN VALUE:* *CAT. COST:* 50p *EXPORT:* No
SPECIALITIES: Specimen Confiers up to 2.5m Ht. Extensive range of Shrubs & modern varieties of herbaceous Perennials. *MAP PAGE:* **5**

MNew **Newington Nursery,** Newington, Wallingford, Oxfordshire OX10 7AW
TEL: (0865) 891401 *CONTACT:* C J & C A Colbourne
W/SALE or RETAIL: Retail *OPENING TIMES:* 1000-1600 Sat & Sun by appt.
MAIL ORDER: Yes *MIN VALUE:* None *CAT. COST:* £1.50 *EXPORT:* No
SPECIALITIES: Conservatory plants. *MAP PAGE:* **2**

MOke **Okell's Nurseries,** Duddon Heath, Nr Tarporley, Cheshire CW6 0EP
TEL: (0829) 41512 *FAX:* (0829) 41587 *CONTACT:* Gary & Donna Okell
W/SALE or RETAIL: Both *OPENING TIMES:* 0900-1730.
MAIL ORDER: Yes *MIN VALUE:* None *CAT. COST:* Free *EXPORT:* No
SPECIALITIES: Heathers. NOTE: Rooted cuttings only by Mail Order. *MAP PAGE:* **4/5**

MPar **J & E Parker-Jervis,** Marten's Hall Farm, Longworth, Abingdon, Oxfordshire OX13 5EP
TEL: (0865) 820376 *CONTACT:* J & E Parker-Jervis
W/SALE or RETAIL: Retail *OPENING TIMES:* By appt. only.
MAIL ORDER: No *MIN VALUE:* *CAT. COST:* 3 x 1st class *EXPORT:* No
SPECIALITIES: Cottage garden plants, Galanthus & Colchicum. *MAP PAGE:* **2**

MPen **Pendennis Fuchsia Nursery,** 14 Pendennis Road, Heaton Norris, Stockport, Cheshire SK4 2QA
TEL: (061 431) 7934 *CONTACT:* Mrs K M Whittaker.
W/SALE or RETAIL: Retail *OPENING TIMES:* 0900-1300 & 1600-2000 Mon, 1300-1900 Tue, 1700-2000 Wed, 0900-2000 Sat, 1400-1600 Thur, Fri & Sun.
MAIL ORDER: Yes *MIN VALUE:* £8.00 *CAT. COST:* 3 x 1st class *EXPORT:* Yes
SPECIALITIES: Fuchsia & Pelargoniums. *MAP PAGE:* **5**

MPhe **Phedar Nursery,** Bunkers Hill, Romily, Stockport, Cheshire SK6 3DS
TEL: (061 430) 3772 *CONTACT:* Will McLewin
W/SALE or RETAIL: Both *OPENING TIMES:* Frequent in Spring but irregular. Please telephone.
MAIL ORDER: Yes *MIN VALUE:* None *CAT. COST:* Sae *EXPORT:* No
SPECIALITIES: Helleborus, Paeonia, Erythronium. *MAP PAGE:* **5**

MPit **Pitts Farm Nursery,** Shrewley, Warwick, Warwickshire CV35 7BB
TEL: (0926 84) 2737 *CONTACT:* Mrs J Farmer
W/SALE or RETAIL: Retail *OPENING TIMES:* 1000-1800 daily.
MAIL ORDER: No *MIN VALUE:* *CAT. COST:* Sae *EXPORT:* No
SPECIALITIES: Perennials & Bedding. *MAP PAGE:* **2**

MPla **E L F Plants Cramden Nursery Ltd.,** Harborough Road North, Northampton, Northamptonshire
TEL: (0604) 846246 Eve. *CONTACT:* E L Fincham-Nichols
W/SALE or RETAIL: Both *OPENING TIMES:* 1000-1700 Wed-Sat ex Dec & Jan.
MAIL ORDER: Yes *MIN VALUE:* £4.00 *CAT. COST:* 70p *EXPORT:* No
SPECIALITIES: Dwarf and slow growing Shrubs & Conifers, many unusual. Some Alpines & Heathers. *MAP PAGE:* **2**

MPlt **Plantables,** The Old Orchard, Hall Lane, Hurst Hill, Coseley, West Midlands WV14 9RJ
TEL: (0902) 662647 *CONTACT:* Alan Rumble
◆ *W/SALE or RETAIL:* Both *OPENING TIMES:* By appt. please.
MAIL ORDER: Only *MIN VALUE:* None *CAT. COST:* 2 x 2nd class *EXPORT:* No
SPECIALITIES: Alpines, Dwarf Shrubs, Dwarf Rhododendron & Hardy plants

MRav **Ravensthorpe Nursery,** 6 East Haddon Road, Ravensthorpe, Northamptonshire NN6 8ES
TEL: (0604) 770548 *CONTACT:* Jean & Richard Wiseman
W/SALE or RETAIL: Retail *OPENING TIMES:* 1000-1800 Tue-Sun Mar 1st-Oct 31st. 1000-1700 Tue-Sat Nov 1st-Feb 28th. Also Bank Hol Mons.
MAIL ORDER: Yes *MIN VALUE:* None *CAT. COST:* 4 x 1st class *EXPORT:* No
SPECIALITIES: Wide range of Trees, Shrubs, & Perennials with many unusual varieties.
MAP PAGE: **2**

MRea **Rearsby Roses,** Melton Road, Rearsby, Leicestershire LE7 8YP
TEL: (0533) 601211 *FAX:* (0533) 640013 *CONTACT:* R W Boswijk
◆ *W/SALE or RETAIL:* Both *OPENING TIMES:* 0900-1700 Mon-Fri, 1000-1630 Sat & 1330-1700 Sun.
MAIL ORDER: Yes *MIN VALUE:* None *CAT. COST:* Free *EXPORT:* No
SPECIALITIES: Roses, Rose understocks and Rugosa stems. Comprehensive list of Roses for amateur exhibitors. *MAP PAGE:* **5**

MRil **Rileys' Chrysanthemums,** Alfreton Nurseries, Woolley Moor, Derbyshire DE5 6FF
TEL: (0246) 590320 *CONTACT:* C A & G K Riley
W/SALE or RETAIL: Both *OPENING TIMES:* 0900-1700 Mon-Fri, Mail Order only. 0900-1700 Sun Feb-May, collection only. 0900-1600 Sun in Sept.
MAIL ORDER: Yes *MIN VALUE:* None *CAT. COST:* 35p *EXPORT:* Yes
SPECIALITIES: Chrysanthemum. *MAP PAGE:* **5/7**

MRos **Rosemary Roses,** The Rose Nurseries, Stapleford Lane, Toton, Beeston, Nottingham NG9 5FD
TEL: (0602) 491 100 *CONTACT:* Mrs Rosemary McCarthy
W/SALE or RETAIL: Retail *OPENING TIMES:* 1000-1600 Winter, 1000-1700 Summer.
MAIL ORDER: Yes *MIN VALUE:* None *CAT. COST:* 1 x 2nd class *EXPORT:* Yes
SPECIALITIES: Roses, half-standard, miniature & ground-cover. *MAP PAGE:* **5**

MRTP **Rose du Temps Passé,** Woodland House, Stretton, Nr Stafford Staffordshire ST19 9LG
TEL: (0785) 840217 *FAX:* (0902) 850193 *CONTACT:* John Scarman
W/SALE or RETAIL: Both *OPENING TIMES:* 0900-1800.
MAIL ORDER: Yes *MIN VALUE:* One rose + p&p*CAT. COST:* £1.00 *EXPORT:* Yes
SPECIALITIES: Roses. *MAP PAGE:* **5**

MRui **Andrew de Ruiter (Rose Specialist),** 9 Ingersley Road, Bollington Cheshire SK10 5RE
TEL: (0625) 574389 *CONTACT:* Andrew de Ruiter
W/SALE or RETAIL: Both *OPENING TIMES:*
MAIL ORDER: Only *MIN VALUE:* None *CAT. COST:* 1 x 1st class *EXPORT:* No
SPECIALITIES: Roses, esp. Miniature, also good range of English Roses.

MR&S **Roses & Shrubs Ltd. Garden Centre,** Newport Road (A41), Albrighton, Nr Wolverhampton, West Midlands WV7 3ER
TEL: (0902 37) 3233) *FAX:* (0902 37) 3151 *CONTACT:* Mrs Jill Troth
W/SALE or RETAIL: Both *OPENING TIMES:* 1000-1700 daily.
MAIL ORDER: No *MIN VALUE:* *CAT. COST:* *EXPORT:*
SPECIALITIES: Container grown hardy Trees, Shrubs & Roses. (M54 Exit 3 then A41 one mile towards Wolverhampton on rt.) *MAP PAGE:* **5**

MSal **Salley Gardens,** 8 Radcliffe Mount, West Bridgford, Nottingham NG2 5FY
TEL: (0602) 813690 *CONTACT:* Richard Lewin
W/SALE or RETAIL: Retail *OPENING TIMES:* By appt.
MAIL ORDER: Yes *MIN VALUE:* None *CAT. COST:* Sae *EXPORT:* SO
SPECIALITIES: Wildflowers & Medicinal Herbs. *MAP PAGE:* **5**

MShr **Shrewley Gardens,** Crossways, Shrewley, nr Warwick, Warwickshire CV35 7AU
TEL: (092684) 2402 *CONTACT:* Mrs Jean Andrews.
W/SALE or RETAIL: Retail *OPENING TIMES:*
MAIL ORDER: Only *MIN VALUE:* 6 plants *CAT. COST:* 90p *EXPORT:* Yes
SPECIALITIES: Campanula. National Collection of Bellis perennis cvs. Unusual hardy plants.

MSmi **John Smith & Son,** Hilltop Nurseries, Thornton, Leicestershire LE6 1AN
TEL: (0530) 230331 *CONTACT:* J Smith
W/SALE or RETAIL: Both *OPENING TIMES:* 0800-1730 Mon-Sat.
MAIL ORDER: Yes *MIN VALUE:* None *CAT. COST:* Sae *EXPORT:* No
SPECIALITIES: Hardy & Half-hardy Fuchsia, dwarf Conifers, Heathers, Hardy Plants, Shrubs & Trees. *MAP PAGE:* **5**

MSta **Stapeley Water Gardens Ltd,** London Road, Stapeley, Natwich, Cheshire CW5 7LH
TEL: (0270) 623868 *FAX:* (0270) 624919 *CONTACT:* Mr Mayor (Manager)
W/SALE or RETAIL: Both *OPENING TIMES:* 0900-1800 Mon-Fri, 1000-1900 Sat-Sun Easter-Sep 1. Till 1700 Winter.
MAIL ORDER: Yes *MIN VALUE:* None *CAT. COST:* £1 refundable *EXPORT:* Yes
SPECIALITIES: World's largest Water Garden Centre. Full range of Hardy & Tropical Water Lilies, Aquatic, Bog & Poolside plants. Also large general stock. *MAP PAGE:* **5**

MS&S **S & S Perennials,** 24 Main Street, Normanton Le Heath, Leicestershire LE6 1TB
TEL: (0530) 62250 *CONTACT:* Shirley Pierce
W/SALE or RETAIL: Retail *OPENING TIMES:* 0900-1730 daily.
MAIL ORDER: Yes *MIN VALUE:* None *CAT. COST:* Sae *EXPORT:* No
SPECIALITIES: Erythronium, Fritillaria, hardy Cyclamen, Lilies & Iris. *MAP PAGE:* **5**

MTho **A & A Thorp,** Bungalow No 5, Main Street, Theddingworth, Leicestershire LE17 6QZ
TEL: (0858) 880496 *CONTACT:* Anita & Andrew Thorp
W/SALE or RETAIL: Retail *OPENING TIMES:* Dawn to Dusk all year.
MAIL ORDER: No *MIN VALUE:* *CAT. COST:* 50p + Sae *EXPORT:* No
SPECIALITIES: Unusual plants or those in short supply. *MAP PAGE:* **2**

MTiv **Philip Tivey & Son,** 28 Wanlip Road, Syston, Leicestershire LE7 8PA
TEL: (0533) 692968 *CONTACT:*
W/SALE or RETAIL: Both *OPENING TIMES:* 1000-1500 daily.
MAIL ORDER: Yes *MIN VALUE:* £8.00 *CAT. COST:* Sae *EXPORT:* No
SPECIALITIES: Dahlia. *MAP PAGE:* **5**

MUlv **Ulverscroft Grange Nursery,** Priory Lane, Ulverscroft, Leicestershire LE6 0PH
TEL: (0530) 243635 *CONTACT:* Ted Brown
W/SALE or RETAIL: Both *OPENING TIMES:* From 1000 Wed-Sun Mar-Nov.
MAIL ORDER: No *MIN VALUE:* *CAT. COST:* None isued *EXPORT:* No
SPECIALITIES: Herbaceous & Shrubs. *MAP PAGE:* **5**

MWal **T Walker,** 118 Peel Drive, Loughborough, Leicestershire LE11 1DF
TEL: (0509) 235375 *CONTACT:* T Walker
W/SALE or RETAIL: *OPENING TIMES:* By appt. ONLY
MAIL ORDER: No *MIN VALUE:* *CAT. COST:* Sae *EXPORT:*
SPECIALITIES: Prunus laurocerasus & other shade tolerant evergreens. *MAP PAGE:* **5**

MWar **Ward Fuchsias,** 5 Pollen Close, Sale, Cheshire M33 3LP
TEL: (061973) 6467 *CONTACT:* K Ward
W/SALE or RETAIL: Retail *OPENING TIMES:* 0930-1800 Tue-Sun Feb-Jun incl Bank Hols.
MAIL ORDER: Yes *MIN VALUE:* None *CAT. COST:* Free *EXPORT:* No
SPECIALITIES: Fuchsia. *MAP PAGE:* **5**

MWat **Waterperry Gardens Ltd.,** Nr. Wheatley, Oxfordshire OX9 1JZ
TEL: (08447) 339226/254 *CONTACT:* Miss S Elliott
W/SALE or RETAIL: Retail *OPENING TIMES:* 1000-1730 Mon-Fri, 1000-1800 Sat & Sun Summer. 1000-1630 Winter.
MAIL ORDER: No *MIN VALUE:* *CAT. COST:* 35p *EXPORT:* No
SPECIALITIES: General plus National Reference Collection of Saxifraga Porophyllum.
MAP PAGE: **2**

MWgw **Wingwell Nursery,** Top Street, Wing, Oakham, Leicestershire LE15 8SE
TEL: (057 285) 400 *CONTACT:* Rose Dejardin
W/SALE or RETAIL: Retail *OPENING TIMES:* 1000-1300 & 1400-1730 Wed-Fri & Sun & Bank Hols Mar-Dec. Also by appt.
MAIL ORDER: Yes *MIN VALUE:* £5.00 *CAT. COST:* Large Sae *EXPORT:* No
SPECIALITIES: Specialists in Herbaceous Perennials, Ground Cover & small Shrubs.
MAP PAGE: **6**

MWhe **A D & N Wheeler,** Pye Court, Willoughby, Rugby, Warwickshire CV23 8BZ
TEL: (0788) 890341 *CONTACT:* Mrs N Wheeler
W/SALE or RETAIL: Retail *OPENING TIMES:* 1000-1900 or dusk Oct 1st-Jun 1st. From Jun 1st-Oct 1st please phone first for appt.
MAIL ORDER: Yes *MIN VALUE:* *CAT. COST:* 2 x 2nd class *EXPORT:* No
SPECIALITIES: Fuchsia & Pelargonium. New varieties of coloured leaf & double flowers introduced each year. *MAP PAGE:* **2**

MWol **H Woolman Ltd,** Grange Road, Dorridge, Solihull, West Midlands B93 8QB
TEL: (0564) 776283 *FAX:* (0564) 770830 *CONTACT:* John Woolman
W/SALE or RETAIL: Both *OPENING TIMES:* 0730-1615 Mon-Fri.
MAIL ORDER: Yes *MIN VALUE:* None *CAT. COST:* Free *EXPORT:* Yes
SPECIALITIES: Chrysanthemum. *MAP PAGE:* **2**

MWoo **Woodfield Bros,** Wood End, Clifford Chambers, Stratford-on-Avon, Warwickshire CV37 8HR
TEL: (0789) 205618 *CONTACT:* B Woodfield
W/SALE or RETAIL: Both *OPENING TIMES:* Weekends for plant collection only.
MAIL ORDER: Yes *MIN VALUE:* Carnations only*CAT. COST:* Sae *EXPORT:* No
SPECIALITIES: Carnations, Lupins & Delphiniums. *MAP PAGE:* **2**

NBar **Barkers Primrose Nurseries & Garden Centre,** Whalley Road, Clitheroe, Lancashire BB7 1HT
TEL: (0200) 23521 *CONTACT:* W & G M Barker
◆ *W/SALE or RETAIL:* Retail *OPENING TIMES:* 0830-1730 Mon-Sat, 1000-1700 Sun.
MAIL ORDER: No *MIN VALUE:* *CAT. COST:* 3 x 2nd class *EXPORT:* No
SPECIALITIES: Trees, Shrubs, many Roses and uncommon, Perennials etc. *MAP PAGE:* **5**

NBat **Battersby Roses,** Peartree Cottage, Old Battersby, Great Ayton, Cleveland TS9 6LU
TEL: (0642) 723402 *CONTACT:* Eric & Avril Stainthorpe
W/SALE or RETAIL: Retail *OPENING TIMES:* 1000-dusk most days.
MAIL ORDER: Yes *MIN VALUE:* None *CAT. COST:* Sae *EXPORT:* No
SPECIALITIES: Exhibition Roses. *MAP PAGE:* **7/8**

NBee **Beechcroft Nurseries,** Bongate, Appleby-in-Westmorland, Cumbria CA16 6UE
TEL: (07683) 51201 *CONTACT:* Roger Brown
W/SALE or RETAIL: Retail *OPENING TIMES:* Daily until sunset. 1100-dusk Sun.
MAIL ORDER: Yes *MIN VALUE:* None *CAT. COST:* £1.00 *EXPORT:* No
SPECIALITIES: Hardy field-grown Trees & Shrubs. *MAP PAGE:* **8**

NBir **Birkheads Cottage Garden Nursery,** Birkheads Lane, Nr Sunniside, Newcastle upon Tyne, Tyne & Wear NE16 5EL
TEL: (0207) 232262 *CONTACT:* Mrs Christine Liddle
W/SALE or RETAIL: Retail *OPENING TIMES:* 1000-1800 Fri-Sun & Bank Hols Mar-mid Oct & by appt.
MAIL ORDER: No *MIN VALUE:* *CAT. COST:* None *EXPORT:* No
SPECIALITIES: Allium, Campanula, Digitalis, Euphorbia, Hardy Geraniums, Meconopsis, Primula & Herbs. *MAP PAGE:* **7/8**

NBra **Brambling House Alpines,** 119 Sheffield Road, Warmsworth, Doncaster, South Yorkshire DN4 9QX
TEL: (0302) 850730 *CONTACT:* Tony & Jane McDonagh
W/SALE or RETAIL: Both *OPENING TIMES:* 0900-dusk Tue-Sun.
MAIL ORDER: Yes *MIN VALUE:* £2.70 *CAT. COST:* Large Sae *EXPORT:* No
SPECIALITIES: Saxifraga, Lewisia, Sempervivum (over 150 varieties). Unusual Alpine House plants. *MAP PAGE:* **5/7**

NB&B **Bennett & Brown (Clematis),** Stoney Lane, Beamish, Co Durham DH9 0SJ
TEL: (091) 3700202 *CONTACT:* T H Bennett & C F Brown
W/SALE or RETAIL: Both *OPENING TIMES:* 0900-1700 Mon-Sat & 1000-1700 Sun & Bank Hols.
MAIL ORDER: Yes *MIN VALUE:* None *CAT. COST:* 2 x 1st class *EXPORT:* No
SPECIALITIES: 180 varieties of Clematis. *MAP PAGE:* **7/8**

NCat **Catforth Gardens,** Roots Lane, Catforth, Preston, Lancashire PR4 0JB
TEL: (0772) 690561 *CONTACT:* Judith Bradshaw & Chris Moore
W/SALE or RETAIL: Retail *OPENING TIMES:* 1030-1700 Mar 15th-end Sep.
MAIL ORDER: No *MIN VALUE:* *CAT. COST:* 2 x 1st class *EXPORT:* No
SPECIALITIES: Unusual Herbaceous, esp. Campanula, Erysimum, Euphorbia, Geranium, Pulmonaria & Viola. *MAP PAGE:* **5**

NElm **Elm Ridge Gardens Ltd.,** Coniscliffe Road, Darlington, Co Durham DL3 8DJ
TEL: (0325) 462710 *CONTACT:* Mr C Blake & M Blake
W/SALE or RETAIL: Both *OPENING TIMES:* 0800-1830 Mon-Sat Apr-Jul, 0800-1730 Aug-Mar.
MAIL ORDER: No *MIN VALUE:* *CAT. COST:* Free *EXPORT:* No
SPECIALITIES: Very large selection of Pot Plants for home & industry, bedding plants, cut flowers & floristry. *MAP PAGE:* **7/8**

NGre **Greenslacks Nurseries,** Ocot Lane, Scammonden, Huddersfield, Yorkshire HD3 3FR
TEL: (0484) 842584 *CONTACT:* Mrs V K Tuton
W/SALE or RETAIL: Both *OPENING TIMES:* By appt. only
MAIL ORDER: Yes *MIN VALUE:* None *CAT. COST:* £1.00 *EXPORT:* Yes
SPECIALITIES: Unusual & Hardy plants esp. Succulents *MAP PAGE:* **5**

NHal **Halls of Heddon,** (Off.) West Heddon Nurseries, Heddon-on-the-Wall, Newcastle-upon-Tyne, Northumberland NE15 0JS
TEL: (0661) 852445 *CONTACT:* Judith Lockey
W/SALE or RETAIL: Retail *OPENING TIMES:* 0900-1700 Mon-Sat 1000-1700 Sun Oct-Mar, 0900-1800 Mon-Sat 1000-1800 Sun Apr-Sep.
MAIL ORDER: Yes* *MIN VALUE:* £10.00 *CAT. COST:* 2 x 2nd class *EXPORT:* Yes
SPECIALITIES: Chrysanthemum & Dahlia. Wide range of small and mature Herbaceous & Alpine plants. *NOTE: Mail Order Dahlia & Chrysanthemum only. *MAP PAGE:* **8**

NHar **Hartside Nursery Garden,** Nr Alston, Cumbria CA9 3BL
TEL: (0434) 381372 *CONTACT:* S L & N Huntley
W/SALE or RETAIL: Retail *OPENING TIMES:* 0900-1730 Mon-Fri, 1000-1600 Sat, 1230-1600 Sun & B/Hols Mar 1-Oct 31. 1000-1530 Mon-Fri Nov 1-Xmas
MAIL ORDER: Yes *MIN VALUE:* None *CAT. COST:* 3 x 2nd class *EXPORT:* Yes
SPECIALITIES: Alpines grown at altitude of 1100 feet in Pennines. *MAP PAGE:* **8**

NHea **The Heather Garden,** 139 Swinston Hill Road, Dinnington, Sheffield, South Yorkshire S31 7RY
TEL: (0909) 565510 *CONTACT:* Peter Vickers
W/SALE or RETAIL: Both *OPENING TIMES:* 1000-1800 or dusk (if earlier) daily ex Mon & Thurs.
MAIL ORDER: No *MIN VALUE:* *CAT. COST:* Free *EXPORT:* No
SPECIALITIES: Heathers, Dwarf Conifers, Alpines, Potentilla, Hebe, Hardy Fuchsia.
MAP PAGE: **5/7**

NHex **Hexham Herbs,** Chesters Walled Garden, Chollerford, Hexham Northumberland
TEL: (0434) 681 483 *CONTACT:* Susie & Kevin White
W/SALE or RETAIL: *OPENING TIMES:* 1000-1700 Easter-Oct daily. Please phone for Winter opening times.
MAIL ORDER: No *MIN VALUE:* *CAT. COST:* £1.00 *EXPORT:*
SPECIALITIES: Herbs & National Collection of Thymus. Unusual Perennials & Wild Flowers.
MAP PAGE: **8**

NHlc **Halecat Garden Nurseries,** Witherslack, Grange over Sands, Cumbria LA11 6RU
TEL: (044 852) 229 *CONTACT:* Mrs M Stanley
◆ *W/SALE or RETAIL:* Retail *OPENING TIMES:* 0900-1630 Mon-Fri, 1400-1600 Sun & parties by appointment.
MAIL ORDER: No *MIN VALUE:* *CAT. COST:* 30p *EXPORT:* No
SPECIALITIES: Hosta, Euphorbia, grey foliage and perenial border plants. *MAP PAGE:* **5/8**

NHol **Holden Clough Nursery,** Holden, Bolton-by-Bowland, Clitheroe, Lancashire BB7 4PF
TEL: (02007) 615 *CONTACT:* P J Foley
◆ *W/SALE or RETAIL:* Both *OPENING TIMES:* 1300-1630 Mon-Thu, 0900-1630 Sat & Sun. 1400-1630 Apr & May & Easter Sun.
MAIL ORDER: Yes *MIN VALUE:* £20 + £3.20 p&p *CAT. COST:* £1.00 inc p&p *EXPORT:* Yes
SPECIALITIES: Large general list including Primula, Saxifrage, Pulmonaria, Androsace, Astilbe, Gentiana & Hosta. *MAP PAGE:* **5**

NH&H **Herb & Heather Centre,** West Haddlesey, Nr Selby, North Yorks YO8 8QA
TEL: (0757) 228279 *CONTACT:* Carole Atkinson
W/SALE or RETAIL: Both *OPENING TIMES:* 1000-1800 Thu-Tue Mar-Oct. 1000-dusk Thu-Tue Nov-Feb.
MAIL ORDER: Yes *MIN VALUE:* £10 *CAT. COST:* * *EXPORT:* Yes
SPECIALITIES: 450 Herbs, 150 Heathers. *NOTE: Herb Catalogue 25p, Heathers 40p, each + 15p for p&p. National Collection of Santolina *MAP PAGE:* **5/7**

NJap **The Japanese Garden Co.,** Sellet Hall Gardens, Kirkby Lonsdale, via Carnforth, Lancashire LA6 2QF
TEL: (05242) 71865 *CONTACT:* Keith & Susan Gott
W/SALE or RETAIL: Retail *OPENING TIMES:* 0900-1700 daily.
MAIL ORDER: Yes *MIN VALUE:* None *CAT. COST:* £1.00 *EXPORT:* Yes
SPECIALITIES: Primula, Acer, Bamboo, Conifers & Herbaceous, mainly of oriental origin. Japanese garden design service. Booklet on design £3.75. *MAP PAGE:* **5**

NKay **Reginald Kaye Ltd,** Waithman Nurseries, Silverdale, Carnforth, Lancashire LA5 0TY
TEL: (0524) 701252 *CONTACT:* Reginald, J J & L M Kaye
W/SALE or RETAIL: Both *OPENING TIMES:* 0800-1230 & 1400-1700 Mon-Fri all year. 1000-1230 & 1400-1700 Sat & 1430-1700 Sun Mar-Nov only.
MAIL ORDER: No *MIN VALUE:* *CAT. COST:* 50p *EXPORT:* No
SPECIALITIES: Hardy ferns, Alpines, Herbaceous, some Shrubs. *MAP PAGE:* **5/8**

NLan **Landlife Wildflowers Ltd.,** The Old Police Station, Lark Lane, Liverpool, Lancashire L17 8UU
TEL: (051 728) 7011 *FAX:* (061) 794 8072 *CONTACT:* Dr K Chambers & G Watson
W/SALE or RETAIL: Both *OPENING TIMES:* By appt for collection only.
MAIL ORDER: Yes *MIN VALUE:* *CAT. COST:* Free *EXPORT:* No
SPECIALITIES: Wild herbaceous plants. *MAP PAGE:* **4/5**

NLin **Lingholm Gardens,** Lingholm, Keswick, Cumbria CA12 5UA
TEL: (07687) 72003 *CONTACT:* Mr M J Swift
W/SALE or RETAIL: Both *OPENING TIMES:* 1000-1700 daily Apr-Oct. Mar-Nov by appt. only.
MAIL ORDER: No *MIN VALUE:* *CAT. COST:* No retail cat. *EXPORT:* No
SPECIALITIES: Meconopsis & Primula. Other unusual plants from the garden. *MAP PAGE:* **8**

NMar **J & D Marston,** Culag, Green Lane, Nafferton, Driffield, East Yorkshire YO25 0LF
TEL: (0377) 44487 *CONTACT:* J K & D Marston
◆ *W/SALE or RETAIL:* Retail *OPENING TIMES:* 1350-1700 Easter-mid Sep, Sat, Sun & other times by appt.
MAIL ORDER: Yes *MIN VALUE:* £15.00 *CAT. COST:* 60p *EXPORT:* Yes
SPECIALITIES: Hardy & Greenhouse Ferns only. *MAP PAGE:* **7**

NMGN **Markham Grange Nurseries,** Long Lands Lane, Brodsworth, Nr Doncaster, South Yorkshire DN5 7XB
TEL: (0302) 722390 *CONTACT:* V T Nuttall
W/SALE or RETAIL: Both *OPENING TIMES:* 0900-1630 daily, later in summer.
MAIL ORDER: Yes *MIN VALUE:* £1.50 + p&p *CAT. COST:* 20p *EXPORT:* No
SPECIALITIES: Fuchsia. *MAP PAGE:* **5/7**

NMos **Stanley Mossop,** Boonwood Garden Centre, Gosforth, Seascale, Cumbria
TEL: (0946) 821817 *CONTACT:* Stanley & Gary Mossop.
W/SALE or RETAIL: Both *OPENING TIMES:* 1000-1700 daily.
MAIL ORDER: Yes *MIN VALUE:* None *CAT. COST:* Free *EXPORT:* Yes
SPECIALITIES: Achimenes, Achimenantha, Eucodonia, Gloxinia (incl. species) & Smithiantha. *MAP PAGE:* **8/9**

NNor **Northumbria Nurseries,** Castle Gardens, Ford, Berwick-upon-Tweed, Northumberland TD15 2PZ
TEL: (089 082) 379 *CONTACT:* Hazel M Huddleston
◆ *W/SALE or RETAIL:* Both *OPENING TIMES:* 0900-1700 Mon-Fri all year, & 1300-1700 Sat-Sun & Bank Hols Mar-Oct & by appt..
MAIL ORDER: No *MIN VALUE:* *CAT. COST:* £1.25 PO/Chq.*EXPORT:* No
SPECIALITIES: Container grown hardy ornamental Shrubs & Perennials. *MAP PAGE:* **8/9**

NNrd **Norden Alpines,** Hirst Road, Carlton, Nr Goole, Humberside DN14 9PX
TEL: (0405) 861348 *CONTACT:* Norma & Denis Walton
W/SALE or RETAIL: Both *OPENING TIMES:* 1000-1700 Sat-Sun & Bank Hols Mar-Sep, or by appt.
MAIL ORDER: No *MIN VALUE:* *CAT. COST:* None *EXPORT:* No
SPECIALITIES: Many unusual Alpines esp. Campanula, Primula & Saxifraga. *MAP PAGE:* **5/7**

NOak **Oak Tree Nursery,** Mill Lane, Barlow, Selby, North Yorks YO8 8EY
TEL: (0757) 618409 *CONTACT:* Gill Plowes
W/SALE or RETAIL: Retail *OPENING TIMES:* 1000-1700 Thu-Tue, Easter-end Oct.
MAIL ORDER: No *MIN VALUE:* *CAT. COST:* 2 x 1st class *EXPORT:* No
SPECIALITIES: Herbaceous & unusual Perennials. *MAP PAGE:* **5/7**

◆ **See also Display Advertisements**

NOrc **Orchard House Nursery,** Orchard House, Wormald Green, Nr Harrogate, North Yorks HG3 3PX
TEL: (0765) 87541 *CONTACT:* Mr B M Corner
W/SALE or RETAIL: Both *OPENING TIMES:* 0830-1800 all year.
MAIL ORDER: Yes* *MIN VALUE:* £15.00 + p&p *CAT. COST:* £1.00 *EXPORT:* No
SPECIALITIES: Herbaceous, Heathers, Herbs, Alpines, unusual cottage garden plants. *NOTE: Mail Order Autumn & Winter only. *MAP PAGE:* **5/7**

NPal **The Palm Farm,** Thornton Hall Gardens, Station Road, Thornton Curtis, Nr Ulceby, Humberside DN39 6XF
TEL: (0469) 31232 *CONTACT:* W W Spink
◆ *W/SALE or RETAIL:* Both *OPENING TIMES:* 1400-1700 daily ex Winter when by appt.
MAIL ORDER: Yes *MIN VALUE:* £14.25(incl p&p) *CAT. COST:* 1 x 2nd class *EXPORT:* Yes
SPECIALITIES: Hardy & half-Hardy Palms, Meconopsis & unusual Trees & Shrubs, Citrus.
MAP PAGE: **7**

NPer **Perry's Plants,** The River Garden, Sleights, Whitby, North Yorks YO21 1RR
TEL: (0947) 810329 *CONTACT:* Pat Perry
◆ *W/SALE or RETAIL:* Retail *OPENING TIMES:* 1000-1700 Easter to October.
MAIL ORDER: No *MIN VALUE:* *CAT. COST:* Sae for list *EXPORT:* No
SPECIALITIES: Lavatera, Malva, Cheiranthus, Euphorbia, Anthemis. *MAP PAGE:* **7/8**

NPin **Pinks & Carnations,** 22 Chetwyn Avenue, Bromley Cross, Bolton, Lancashire BL7 9BN
TEL: (0204) 56273 *CONTACT:* R & T Gillies
◆ *W/SALE or RETAIL:* Both *OPENING TIMES:* Appt only.
MAIL ORDER: Yes *MIN VALUE:* None *CAT. COST:* Free *EXPORT:* No
SPECIALITIES: Pinks and Perpetual Flowering Carnations. *MAP PAGE:* **5**

NPor **J V Porter,** 12 Hazel Grove, Southport, Merseyside PR8 6AX
TEL: (0704) 533902 *FAX:* (07048) 32196 *CONTACT:* John Porter
W/SALE or RETAIL: Both *OPENING TIMES:* 1030-1600 Thu-Sun Jan-May & by appt. (Wholesale open all year 0800-1615)
MAIL ORDER: Yes *MIN VALUE:* £4.00 (6 plants) *CAT. COST:* 2 x 1st class *EXPORT:* Yes
SPECIALITIES: Fuchsia. *MAP PAGE:* **5**

NRar **Rarer Plants,** Ashfield House, Austfield Lane, Monk Fryston, Leeds, North Yorkshire LS25 5EH
TEL: (0977) 682263 *CONTACT:* Anne Watson
W/SALE or RETAIL: Retail *OPENING TIMES:* 1330-1730 Thu-Mon Easter -Oct 18th.
MAIL ORDER: No *MIN VALUE:* *CAT. COST:* Sae *EXPORT:* No
SPECIALITIES: Unusual plants, variegated plants and Penstemons. *MAP PAGE:* **5/7**

NRed **Redhouse Nurseries,** Woodside, High Whinholme, Streetlam, Northallerton, North Yorks DL7 0AS
TEL: (0325) 378721 *CONTACT:* C Elliott
W/SALE or RETAIL: Both *OPENING TIMES:* Daily - but please check first.
MAIL ORDER: Yes *MIN VALUE:* None *CAT. COST:* 30p *EXPORT:* No
SPECIALITIES: Show Auriculas, minature Roses, Alpines (beginners & collectors) & Shrubs.
MAP PAGE: **5/7**

NRog **R V Roger Ltd,** The Nurseries, Pickering, North Yorks YO18 7HG
TEL: (0751) 72226 *CONTACT:* C Cook S Peirson & A G & I M Roger
W/SALE or RETAIL: Both *OPENING TIMES:* 0900-1700 Mon-Sat, 1300-1700 Sun.
MAIL ORDER: Yes *MIN VALUE:* None *CAT. COST:* 75p *EXPORT:* No
SPECIALITIES: General list, hardy in North of England. Co-holders of National Erodium Collection.
MAP PAGE: **7/8**

NRoo **Rookhope Nurseries,** Rookhope, Upper Weardale, Co Durham DL13 2DD
TEL: (0388) 517272 *CONTACT:* Karen Blackburn
W/SALE or RETAIL: Retail *OPENING TIMES:* 0830-1800 daily Apr-Oct, 1000-1700 daily Nov-Mar.
MAIL ORDER: No *MIN VALUE:* *CAT. COST:* 60p *EXPORT:* No
SPECIALITIES: Wide range of Hardy plants grown at 1,100 feet in the northern Pennines.
MAP PAGE: **8**

NRya **Ryal Nursery,** East Farm Cottage, Ryal, Northumberland NE20 0SA
TEL: (0661) 886562 *CONTACT:* R F Hadden
W/SALE or RETAIL: Both *OPENING TIMES:* 1300-1700 Tue, 1000-1700 Sun Mar-Aug & by appt.
MAIL ORDER: Yes *MIN VALUE:* None *CAT. COST:* Sae *EXPORT:* No
SPECIALITIES: Alpines, Primula & Saxifraga. *MAP PAGE:* **8/9**

NSed **Sedum Specialist,** 55 Beverley Drive, Choppington, Northumberland NE62 5YA
TEL: (0670) 817901 *CONTACT:* Ray Stephenson
W/SALE or RETAIL: Retail *OPENING TIMES:* Not open.
MAIL ORDER: Only *MIN VALUE:* None *CAT. COST:* Sae *EXPORT:* Yes
SPECIALITIES: National reference collection of Tender & Hardy Sedum. Collected clone propagations. The Ron Evans Memorial Collection.

NSel **Sellet Hall Herbs,** Whittington, via Carnforth, Lancashire LA6 2QF
TEL: (05242) 71865 *FAX:* (05242) 72208 *CONTACT:* Judy Gray
W/SALE or RETAIL: Retail *OPENING TIMES:* 1000-1800 daily all year. Please telephone to check winter weekend openings.
MAIL ORDER: Yes *MIN VALUE:* £6.00 + p&p *CAT. COST:* £1.00 *EXPORT:* No
SPECIALITIES: Herbs. *MAP PAGE:* **5/8**

NSti **Stillingfleet Lodge Nurseries,** Stillingfleet, Yorkshire YO4 6HW
TEL: (0904) 87506 *CONTACT:* Vanessa Cook
W/SALE or RETAIL: Retail *OPENING TIMES:* 1000-1600 Tue Wed Fri & Sat Apr 1- Oct 18th, or by appt.
MAIL ORDER: Yes *MIN VALUE:* £3.50 + p&p *CAT. COST:* 5 x 1st class *EXPORT:* No
SPECIALITIES: Foliage & unusual perennials. Hardy Geranium, Pulmonaria, variegated plants & Grasses. Holder of National Pulmonaria Collection. *MAP PAGE:* **5/7**

NSty **Stydd Nursery,** Stoneygate Lane, Ribchester, Nr Preston, Lancashire PR3 3YN
TEL: (0254) 878797 *CONTACT:* Mr & Mrs J A Walker
W/SALE or RETAIL: Both *OPENING TIMES:* 1330-1700 Tue-Fri, 0900-1700 Sat all year, 1400-1700 Sun Apr 1st-Dec 23rd.
MAIL ORDER: Yes *MIN VALUE:* *CAT. COST:* 50p *EXPORT:* No
SPECIALITIES: Old Roses & ornamental foliage. *MAP PAGE:* **5**

NTow **Town Farm Nursery,** Whitton, Stillington, Stockton on Tees, Cleveland TS21 1LQ
TEL: (0740) 31079 *CONTACT:* F D Baker
◆ *W/SALE or RETAIL:* Retail *OPENING TIMES:* 1000-1800 Fri-Mon Mar-Oct.
MAIL ORDER: Yes *MIN VALUE:* £3.00 *CAT. COST:* Sae *EXPORT:* No
SPECIALITIES: Unusual Alpines, Border Perennials, Shrubs & Conservatory plants.
MAP PAGE: **7/8**

NTwe **J Tweedie Fruit Trees,** 504 Denby Dale Road West, Calder Grove, Wakefield, Yorkshire WF4 3DB
TEL: (0924) 274630 *CONTACT:* John Tweedie
W/SALE or RETAIL: Both *OPENING TIMES:* 0930-1600 Sat Oct-Mar & by appt.
MAIL ORDER: Yes *MIN VALUE:* None *CAT. COST:* Sae *EXPORT:* No
SPECIALITIES: Fruit trees & bushes. A wide range of old & new varieties. *MAP PAGE:* **7**

NVic **The Vicarage Garden,** Carrington, Urmston, Manchester, Lancashire M31 4AG
TEL: (061 775) 2750 *CONTACT:* Miss M Zugor
W/SALE or RETAIL: Both *OPENING TIMES:* 1000-1800 Fri-Wed Apr-Sept. 1030-1700 Fri-Wed Oct-Mar.
MAIL ORDER: Yes *MIN VALUE:* £3.00 *CAT. COST:* 75p *EXPORT:* No
SPECIALITIES: Herbaceous & Alpines. *MAP PAGE:* **5**

NWCA **White Cottage Alpines,** Eastgate, Rudston, Driffield, East Yorkshire YO25 0UX
TEL: (026282) 668 *CONTACT:* Sally E Cummins
W/SALE or RETAIL: Both *OPENING TIMES:* 1000-1700 (or dusk) Thu-Sun, 1000-1700 (or dusk) Bank Hol Mons. Closed Dec 15th -Jan 16th.
MAIL ORDER: Yes *MIN VALUE:* None *CAT. COST:* Large Sae *EXPORT:* No
SPECIALITIES: Alpines *MAP PAGE:* **7**

NWea **Weasdale Nurseries,** Newbiggin-on-Lune, Kirkby Stephen, Cumbria CA17 4LX
TEL: (05873) 246 *FAX:* (05873) 277 *CONTACT:* Andrew Forsyth
W/SALE or RETAIL: Retail *OPENING TIMES:* 0900-1700 Mon-Fri.
MAIL ORDER: Yes *MIN VALUE:* £11(min carriage) *CAT. COST:* £2.25 *EXPORT:* No
SPECIALITIES: Hardy forest trees, hedging & ornamental Shrubs grown at 850 feet. *MAP PAGE:* **8**

NWin **Wingates,** 62A Chorley Road, Westhoughton, Bolton, Lancashire BL5 3PL
TEL: (0942) 813357 *CONTACT:* G Lambert
W/SALE or RETAIL: Retail *OPENING TIMES:* 1400-dusk daily. Check during winter months.
MAIL ORDER: No *MIN VALUE:* *CAT. COST:* 30p *EXPORT:* No
SPECIALITIES: Mainly Heathers, also Dwarf Conifers & Shrubs, Ericaceous plants, Alpines & dwarf Rhododendrons. *MAP PAGE:* **5**

NZep **Zephyrwude Irises,** 48 Blacker Lane, Crigglestone, Wakefield, West Yorkshire WF4 3EW
TEL: (0924) 252101 *CONTACT:* Richard L Brook
◆ *W/SALE or RETAIL:* Retail *OPENING TIMES:* Display garden 0900-dusk daily May-June. Check first. Orders taken Feb-Sep. Delivery Jul-Oct.
MAIL ORDER: Yes *MIN VALUE:* £10 + £3.50 p&p *CAT. COST:* 3 x 1st class *EXPORT:* Yes
SPECIALITIES: Bearded Iris (dwarf intermediate & tall). Mainly modern varieties from USA. 450 varieties. *MAP PAGE:* **5/7**

SAll **Allwood Bros,** Mill Nursery, Hassocks, West Sussex BN6 9NB
TEL: (07918) 4229 *CONTACT:*
W/SALE or RETAIL: Both *OPENING TIMES:* 0900-1700 Mon-Fri.
MAIL ORDER: Yes *MIN VALUE:* None *CAT. COST:* 2 x 1st class *EXPORT:* Yes
SPECIALITIES: Dianthus, incl Hardy Border Carnations, Pinks, Perpetual & Allwoodii. Heathers, Gypsophila, most available as Seed. *MAP PAGE:* **3**

SApp **Apple Court,** Hordle Lane, Hordle, Lymington, Hampshire S041 0HU
TEL: (0590) 642130 *CONTACT:* Diana Grenfell
◆ *W/SALE or RETAIL:* Retail *OPENING TIMES:* Normally Thu-Mon Feb-Nov. Closed Dec & Jan & two weeks end-Aug. Suggest telephone first.
MAIL ORDER: Yes* *MIN VALUE:* £10.00 *CAT. COST:* 3 x 1st class *EXPORT:* No
SPECIALITIES: Hosta, Grasses, Ferns, Hemerocallis. National Collection Woodwardia, Anthericum/Paradisea, Camassia & Hosta. *NOTE: MO Spring/Autumn only. *MAP PAGE:* **2**

SArc **Architectural Plants,** Cooks Farm, Nuthurst, Horsham, West Sussex RH13 6LH
TEL: (0403) 891772 *FAX:* (0403) 991056 *CONTACT:* Angus White
◆ *W/SALE or RETAIL:* Both *OPENING TIMES:* 0900-1700 Mon-Sat, but please phone first.
MAIL ORDER: Yes *MIN VALUE:* £11.50 carriage *CAT. COST:* Free *EXPORT:* Yes
SPECIALITIES: Architectural plants & hardy Exotics. *MAP PAGE:* **3**

SAsh **Ashenden Nursery,** Cranbrook Road, Benenden, Cranbrook, Kent TN17 4ET
TEL: (0580) 241792 *CONTACT:* Kevin McGarry
W/SALE or RETAIL: Retail *OPENING TIMES:* 1000-1300 & 1400-1700 Mon-Sat.
MAIL ORDER: Yes *MIN VALUE:* *CAT. COST:* Sae *EXPORT:* No
SPECIALITIES: Rock garden & perennials *MAP PAGE:* **3**

SAxl **Axletree Nursery,** Starvecrow Lane, Peasmarsh, Rye, East Sussex TN31 6XL
TEL: (079721) 470 *CONTACT:* D J Hibberd
W/SALE or RETAIL: Retail *OPENING TIMES:* 1000-1700 Wed-Sat Apr-Sep.
MAIL ORDER: Yes* *MIN VALUE:* *CAT. COST:* 3 x 1st class *EXPORT:* No
SPECIALITIES: Herbaceous plants, esp. Geranium & Euphorbia. Mail Order catalogue available Sep-Feb, visitors list from April. *NOTE: Not ALL items by M.O. *MAP PAGE:* **3**

SBai **Steven Bailey,** Silver Street, Sway, Lymington, Hampshire SO41 6ZA
TEL: (0590) 682227 *FAX:* (0590) 683765 *CONTACT:*
W/SALE or RETAIL: Both *OPENING TIMES:* 1000-1300 & 1400-1630 Mon-Fri all year. 1000-1300 & 1400-1600 Sat Mar-Jun ex Bank Hols.
MAIL ORDER: Yes *MIN VALUE:* None *CAT. COST:* 2 x 2nd class *EXPORT:* No
SPECIALITIES: Carnations, Pinks & Alstroemeria. *MAP PAGE:* **2**

SBam **Bamboo Nursery,** Kinsgate Cottage, Wittersham, Tenterden, Kent TN30 7NS
TEL: (0797) 270607 *FAX:* (0797) 270825 *CONTACT:* A Sutcliffe
W/SALE or RETAIL: Both *OPENING TIMES:* Appt only.
MAIL ORDER: Yes *MIN VALUE:* None *CAT. COST:* Sae *EXPORT:* Yes
SPECIALITIES: Bamboo. *MAP PAGE:* **3**

SBar **Barnhawk Nursery,** Little Barn, Woodgreen, Fordingbridge, Hampshire SP6 2QX
TEL: (0725) 22213 *FAX:* (0725) 22213 *CONTACT:* R & V Crawford
◆ *W/SALE or RETAIL:* Both *OPENING TIMES:* 0900-1800 Fri & Sat Mar-end Oct only.
MAIL ORDER: No *MIN VALUE:* *CAT. COST:* 3 x 1st class *EXPORT:* No
SPECIALITIES: Choice plants for peat and scree, dwarf shrubs. Two acre garden to visit during opening times. *MAP PAGE:* **2**

SBla **Blackthorn Nursery,** Kilmeston, Alresford, Hampshire SO24 0NL
TEL: (0962) 771796 *CONTACT:* A R & S B White
W/SALE or RETAIL: Retail *OPENING TIMES:* 0900-1700 Fri & Sat Mar-end Oct.
MAIL ORDER: No *MIN VALUE:* *CAT. COST:* 75p *EXPORT:* No
SPECIALITIES: Choice perennials, Shrubs & Alpines esp. Daphne & Helleborus. *MAP PAGE:* **2**

SBor **Borde Hill Garden Ltd.,** Haywards Heath, West Sussex RH16 1XP
TEL: (0444) 450326 *CONTACT:* Claire Reaney
W/SALE or RETAIL: Retail *OPENING TIMES:* 1000-1700 Mar 31-Oct 31, as Garden.
MAIL ORDER: No *MIN VALUE:* *CAT. COST:* None issued *EXPORT:* No
SPECIALITIES: Rhododendron, hardy Ferns & unusual Trees & Shrubs, evergreen Oaks.
MAP PAGE: **3**

SBra **J Bradshaw & Son,** Busheyfield Nursery, Herne, Herne Bay, Kent CT6 7LJ
TEL: (022737) 5415 *CONTACT:* D J Bradshaw
W/SALE or RETAIL: Both *OPENING TIMES:* Not open to public except to collect phone or letter orders.
MAIL ORDER: No *MIN VALUE:* *CAT. COST:* 4 x 2nd class *EXPORT:* No
SPECIALITIES: Clematis & Climbers. Mainly wholesale. NCCPG collection of climbing Lonicera.
MAP PAGE: **3**

SBro **Jarvis Brook Geranium Nurseries,** Tubwell Lane, Jarvis Brook, Crowborough, Sussex TN6 3RH
TEL: (0892) 662329 *CONTACT:*
W/SALE or RETAIL: Both *OPENING TIMES:* 0930-1730 Tue-Sun Apr-Aug.
MAIL ORDER: Yes *MIN VALUE:* None *CAT. COST:* 2 x 1st class *EXPORT:* Yes
SPECIALITIES: Miniature & Dwarf Pelargonium. *MAP PAGE:* **3**

SCaw **R G M Cawthorne,** Lower Daltons Nursery, Swanley Village, Swanley, Kent BR8 7NU
TEL: *CONTACT:* R G M Cawthorne
W/SALE or RETAIL: Retail *OPENING TIMES:* Written appt. only.
MAIL ORDER: Only *MIN VALUE:* 12 plants + p&p *CAT. COST:* 50p *EXPORT:* Yes
SPECIALITIES: 450 named Violas & Violettas. (Largest collection in the world). Holder of NCCPG Viola collection

SChu **Church Hill Cottage Gardens,** Charing Heath, Ashford, Kent TN27 0BU
TEL: (023 371) 2522 *CONTACT:* Mr & Mrs Michael Metianu.
W/SALE or RETAIL: Retail *OPENING TIMES:* 1000-1700 daily Mar-May, 1000-1700 Wed-Sun Jun-Apr. Closed Dec & Jan & Bank Hols.
MAIL ORDER: No *MIN VALUE:* *CAT. COST:* 3 x 1st class *EXPORT:* No
SPECIALITIES: Unusual hardy plants, Dianthus, Alpines & Shrubs. *MAP PAGE:* **3**

SCog **Coghurst Nursery,** Ivy House Lane, Near Three Oaks, Hastings, East Sussex TN35 4NP
TEL: (0424) 425371/437657 *CONTACT:* J Farnfield, L A & D Edgar
W/SALE or RETAIL: Both *OPENING TIMES:* 1400-1630 Mon-Fri, 1000-1630 Sun.
MAIL ORDER: Yes *MIN VALUE:* None *CAT. COST:* 30p *EXPORT:* No
SPECIALITIES: Camellias, Rhododendrons & Azaleas. *MAP PAGE:* **3**

SCou **Coombland Gardens,** Coombland, Coneyhurst, Billingshurst, West Sussex
TEL: (0403 741) 549 *CONTACT:* Mrs Rosemary Lee
◆ *W/SALE or RETAIL:* Both *OPENING TIMES:* By appt. only.
MAIL ORDER: Yes *MIN VALUE:* £10.00 + p&p *CAT. COST:* 4 x 1st class *EXPORT:* No
SPECIALITIES: Hardy Geranium, Erodium and choice Herbaceous. *MAP PAGE:* **3**

◆ See also Display Advertisements

SCra **Cranmore Vine Nursery,** Yarmouth, Isle of Wight PO41 0XS
TEL: (0983) 760080 *CONTACT:* N Poulter
W/SALE or RETAIL: Both *OPENING TIMES:* Appt only.
MAIL ORDER: Yes *MIN VALUE:* None *CAT. COST:* Sae *EXPORT:* No
SPECIALITIES: Grape vines (Dessert & Wine) only. *MAP PAGE:* **2**

SCro **Croftway Nurseries,** Yapton Road, Barnham, Bognor Regis, West Sussex PO22 0BH
TEL: (0243) 552121 *CONTACT:* Graham Spencer
◆ *W/SALE or RETAIL:* Both *OPENING TIMES:* 0900-1730 daily.
MAIL ORDER: Yes* *MIN VALUE:* 5 plants + p&p *CAT. COST:* £1.00 *EXPORT:* No
SPECIALITIES: Wide general range incl. Shrubs, Climbers & Herbaceous esp. Iris. *NOTE: Mail Order for Bearded Iris ONLY - Send stamp for colour brochure. *MAP PAGE:* **3**

SDea **Deacon's Nursery,** Moor View, Godshill, Isle of Wight PO38 3HW
TEL: (0983) 840750/522243 *CONTACT:* G D & B H W Deacon
W/SALE or RETAIL: Both *OPENING TIMES:* 0800-1600 Mon-Sat.
MAIL ORDER: Yes *MIN VALUE:* None *CAT. COST:* 1 x 2nd class *EXPORT:* Yes
SPECIALITIES: Over 200 varieties of Apple, old & new varieties. Pears, Plums, Gages, Damsons etc. Fruit & Nut trees, triple Peaches, Ballerinas. *MAP PAGE:* **2**

SDen **Denmead Geranium Nurseries,** Hambledon Road, Denmead, Waterlooville, Hampshire PO7 6PS
TEL: (0705) 240081 *CONTACT:* I H Chance
W/SALE or RETAIL: Both *OPENING TIMES:* 0800-1300 & 1400-1700 Mon-Fri, 0800-1230 Sat (ex Aug), 1400-1700 Sat May-Jun & 0930-1230 Sun Apr-May
MAIL ORDER: Yes *MIN VALUE:* 6 plants *CAT. COST:* 2 x 2nd class *EXPORT:* No
SPECIALITIES: Pelargoniums - Ivy-leaved, Scented, Unique, Rosebud, Stellars, Miniature, Dwarf, Swiss Balcony, Mini Cascade, Ornamental & Regals. *MAP PAGE:* **2**

SDix **Great Dixter Nurseries,** Northiam, Rye, East Sussex TN31 6PH
TEL: (0797) 253107 *CONTACT:* C Lloyd
W/SALE or RETAIL: Retail *OPENING TIMES:* 0900-1230 & 1330-1700 Mon-Fri ex Bank Hols. 0900-1200 Sat.
MAIL ORDER: Yes *MIN VALUE:* £10.00 *CAT. COST:* 60p *EXPORT:* No
SPECIALITIES: Clematis, Shrubs and Plants. (Gardens open). *MAP PAGE:* **3**

SDry **Drysdale Nursery,** Bowerwood Road, Fordingbridge, Hampshire SP6 1BN
TEL: (0425) 653010 *CONTACT:* David Crampton
W/SALE or RETAIL: Both *OPENING TIMES:* 0930-1730 Wed-Fri, 1000-1730 Sun & Bank Hols. Closed Dec 24 - Jan 2 incl.
MAIL ORDER: Yes *MIN VALUE:* £10.00 *CAT. COST:* 2 x 1st class *EXPORT:* No
SPECIALITIES: Shrubs, Conifers and National Reference Collection of Bamboo. *MAP PAGE:* **2**

SExb **Exbury Enterprises Ltd.,** Exbury, Nr. Southampton, Hampshire SO4 1AZ
TEL: (0703) 898625/891203 *FAX:* (0703) 243380 *CONTACT:*
W/SALE or RETAIL: Both *OPENING TIMES:* 1000-1730 Plant Centre. 0900-1700 Office.
MAIL ORDER: Yes *MIN VALUE:* None *CAT. COST:* Sae *EXPORT:* Yes
SPECIALITIES: Rhododendron, Azalea, Camellia. *MAP PAGE:* **2**

SExT **Exbury Trees,** Otterwood, Exbury Road, Beaulieu, Hampshire SO42 7YS
TEL: (0590) 612278 *CONTACT:* Kevin Ruane
W/SALE or RETAIL: Both *OPENING TIMES:* 0900-1700 Mon-Fri.
MAIL ORDER: Yes *MIN VALUE:* £75.00 *CAT. COST:* 50p *EXPORT:* Yes
SPECIALITIES: Heavy & semi-mature Trees, Deciduous & Coniferous. *MAP PAGE:* **2**

SFam **Family Trees,** PO Box 3, Botley, Hampshire SO3 2EA
TEL: (0489) 895674 *CONTACT:* P F W House
◆ *W/SALE or RETAIL:* Retail *OPENING TIMES:* 0900-1200 Wed & Sat. Closed Oct.
MAIL ORDER: Yes *MIN VALUE:* £30.00 *CAT. COST:* Free *EXPORT:* Yes
SPECIALITIES: Fruit & Ornamental trees. Old Roses & trained Fruit trees. *MAP PAGE:* **2**

SFar **Farmhouse Plants,** Royal Farm House, Elstead, Godalming, Surrey GU8 6LA
TEL: (0252) 702460 *CONTACT:* Mrs S Cole
W/SALE or RETAIL: *OPENING TIMES:* By appointment.
MAIL ORDER: No *MIN VALUE:* *CAT. COST:* 2 x 1st class *EXPORT:*
SPECIALITIES: General range, esp. Grasses & Euphorbia. *MAP PAGE:* **3**

SFir **Firecrest Nursery,** 104 Newtown Road, Woolston, Southampton, Hampshire SO2 9HQ
TEL: (0703) 685192 *CONTACT:* Marina H Christopher
W/SALE or RETAIL: Retail *OPENING TIMES:* Appt. only.
MAIL ORDER: Yes *MIN VALUE:* None *CAT. COST:* 2 x 1st class *EXPORT:* No
SPECIALITIES: Unusual Cottage Garden plants. Alpines and plants to attract butterflies.
MAP PAGE: 2

SFis **Kaytie Fisher,** The Nursery, South End Cottage, Long Reach, Ockham, Surrey GU23 6PF
TEL: (04865) 2304 *CONTACT:* Kaytie Fisher
W/SALE or RETAIL: Retail *OPENING TIMES:* 1000-1700 Thu-Sun.
MAIL ORDER: Yes *MIN VALUE:* £10.00 *CAT. COST:* 35p in stamps *EXPORT:* Yes
SPECIALITIES: Mainly hardy Herbaceous & some Shrubs. Old Shrub Roses & Climbers.
MAP PAGE: 3

SGar **Gardeners World & English Water Garden,** Rock Lane, Washington, West Sussex RH20 3BL
TEL: (0903) 892006/892408 *FAX:* (0903) 892006 *CONTACT:* K S Quick
◆ *W/SALE or RETAIL:* Both *OPENING TIMES:* 0900-1730 daily.
MAIL ORDER: Yes *MIN VALUE:* None *CAT. COST:* *EXPORT:* Yes
SPECIALITIES: Specimen Trees, Shrubs, Waterplants & unusual species. Some Trees & Shrubs available in very large sizes. *MAP PAGE:* 3

SHay **Hayward's Carnations,** The Chace Gardens, Stakes Road, Purbrook, Portsmouth, Hampshire PO7 5PL
TEL: (0705) 263047 *CONTACT:* A N Hayward
W/SALE or RETAIL: Both *OPENING TIMES:* 0930-1700 Mon-Fri.
MAIL ORDER: Yes *MIN VALUE:* £12.00 *CAT. COST:* 1 x 1st class *EXPORT:* No
SPECIALITIES: Hardy Pinks & Border Carnations. Greenhouse perpetual Carnations.
MAP PAGE: 2

SHaz **Hazeldene Nursery,** Dean Street, East Farleigh, Maidstone, Kent ME15 0PS
TEL: (0622) 726248 *CONTACT:* Mr W W Adams
W/SALE or RETAIL: Retail *OPENING TIMES:* 1000-1600 Mar-Sep. Oct-Feb by appt. only
MAIL ORDER: Yes *MIN VALUE:* None *CAT. COST:* Sae *EXPORT:* No
SPECIALITIES: Pansies, Viola & Violets. *MAP PAGE:* 3

SHen **C E Henderson & Son,** Leydens Nursery, Stick Hill, Edenbridge, Kent TN8 5NH
TEL: (0732) 863318 *CONTACT:* K A Henderson
W/SALE or RETAIL: Both *OPENING TIMES:* 0900-1700 daily.
MAIL ORDER: Yes *MIN VALUE:* Carriage at cost*CAT. COST:* Free list *EXPORT:* No
SPECIALITIES: Hardy Trees & Shrubs. Roses, Heathers, Conifers, Fruit & Hedging. Wild British flowers, Cowslips, Primula & Polyanthus. *MAP PAGE:* 3

SHig **Higher End Nursery,** Hale, Fordingbridge, Hampshire SP6 2RA
TEL: (0725) 22243 *CONTACT:* D J Case
W/SALE or RETAIL: Both *OPENING TIMES:* 1000-1700 Wed-Sat 1400-1700 Sun Apr-Aug.
MAIL ORDER: Yes *MIN VALUE:* £10.00 *CAT. COST:* 2 x 1st class *EXPORT:* No
SPECIALITIES: Water Lilies, Bog & Marginal, Hellebore, Rodgersia, Trollius, Bergenia.
MAP PAGE: 2

SHil **Hillier Nurseries (Winchester) Ltd,** Ampfield House, Ampfield, Nr. Romsey, Hampshire SO51 9PA
TEL: (0794) 68733 *FAX:* (0794) 68813 *CONTACT:*
W/SALE or RETAIL: Both *OPENING TIMES:* Office 0830-1700 Mon-Fri. Garden Centres 0900-1730 Mon-Sat, 1000-1730 Sun.
MAIL ORDER: Yes *MIN VALUE:* £50. £30 collctd*CAT. COST:* 2 x 1st class *EXPORT:*
SPECIALITIES: Very large range of Trees, Shrubs, Conifers, Climbers, Roses, Fruit. *MAP PAGE:* 2

SHya **Brenda Hyatt,** 1 Toddington Crescent, Bluebell Hill, Chatham, Kent ME5 9QT
TEL: (0634) 863251 *CONTACT:* Mrs Brenda Hyatt
W/SALE or RETAIL: Retail *OPENING TIMES:* Appt only.
MAIL ORDER: Yes *MIN VALUE:* None *CAT. COST:* 49p *EXPORT:* No
SPECIALITIES: Show Auricula. *MAP PAGE:* 3

SIde **Iden Croft Herbs,** Frittenden Road, Staplehurst, Kent TN12 0DH
TEL: (0580) 891432 *FAX:* (0580) 892416 *CONTACT:* Rosemary & D Titterington
W/SALE or RETAIL: Retail *OPENING TIMES:* 0900-1700 or dusk Mon-Sat all year & 1100-1700 Sun Mar 1st-Sep 30th.
MAIL ORDER: Yes *MIN VALUE:* None *CAT. COST:* £2.50 inc p&p *EXPORT:* Yes
SPECIALITIES: Herbs & Aromatic plants. National Origanum collection. Export orders undertaken for dispatch during Spring months. *MAP PAGE:* **3**

SIgm **Tim Ingram,** Copton Ash, 105 Ashford Road, Faversham, Kent ME13 8XW
TEL: (0795) 535919 *CONTACT:* Dr T J Ingram
◆ *W/SALE or RETAIL:* Retail *OPENING TIMES:* 1400-1800 Tue-Thur & Sat-Sun Mar-Oct. Nov-Feb by appt.
MAIL ORDER: Yes *MIN VALUE:* £5.00 *CAT. COST:* 2 x 1st class *EXPORT:* No
SPECIALITIES: Unusual hardy Perennials, Alpines & Australasian plants. *MAP PAGE:* **3**

SIng **W E Th. Ingwersen Ltd,** Birch Farm Nursery, Gravetye, E. Grinstead, West Sussex RH19 4LE
TEL: (0342) 810236 *CONTACT:* M P & M R Ingwersen
W/SALE or RETAIL: Retail *OPENING TIMES:* 0900-1300 & 1330-1600 daily Mar 1-Oct 31. 0900-1300 & 1330-1600 Mon-Fri Nov-Feb.
MAIL ORDER: Yes* *MIN VALUE:* £3.50 *CAT. COST:* £1.00 *EXPORT:* No
SPECIALITIES: Very wide range of hardy plants mostly alpines. *NOTE: Mail Order only during Mar-May & Sep-Nov. *MAP PAGE:* **3**

SKee **Keepers Nursery,** 446 Wateringbury Road, East Malling, Kent ME19 6JJ
TEL: (0622) 813008 *CONTACT:* Anne & Mike Cook
W/SALE or RETAIL: Retail *OPENING TIMES:* All hours by appt.
MAIL ORDER: Yes *MIN VALUE:* None *CAT. COST:* Sae *EXPORT:* No
SPECIALITIES: Old & unusual Top Fruit varieties. Budding & grafting as required. Wide range of Soft Fruit. *MAP PAGE:* **3**

SKen **Kent Street Nurseries,** Sedlescombe, Battle, East Sussex TN33 0SF
TEL: (0424) 751134 *CONTACT:* Mrs D Downey
W/SALE or RETAIL: Both *OPENING TIMES:* 0900-1800 daily all year.
MAIL ORDER: Yes *MIN VALUE:* £5.00 *CAT. COST:* Sae* *EXPORT:* No
SPECIALITIES: Fuchsia, Pelargonium, Bedding & Perennials. *NOTE: Please specify Fuchsia or Pelargonium list. *MAP PAGE:* **3**

SLan **Langley Boxwood Nursery,** Langley Court, Rake, Liss, Hampshire GU33 7JL
TEL: (0730) 894467 *CONTACT:* E Braimbridge
◆ *W/SALE or RETAIL:* Both *OPENING TIMES:* By appt. only.
MAIL ORDER: Yes *MIN VALUE:* £30.00 *CAT. COST:* 5 x 1st class *EXPORT:* Yes
SPECIALITIES: Buxus species & cultivars, topiary and hedging. *MAP PAGE:* **2/3**

SLBF **Little Brook Fuchsias,** Ash Green Lane West, Ash Green, Nr Aldershot, Hampshire GU12 6HL
TEL: (0252) 29731 *CONTACT:* Carol Gubler
W/SALE or RETAIL: Both *OPENING TIMES:* 0900-1700 Wed-Sun Jan 1st-Aug 27th.
MAIL ORDER: No *MIN VALUE:* *CAT. COST:* 15p + Sae *EXPORT:* No
SPECIALITIES: Fuchsia old & new. *MAP PAGE:* **3**

SLeo **Leonardslee Gardens,** 1 Mill Lane, Lower Beeding, West Sussex RH13 6PX
TEL: (0403) 891 412 *CONTACT:* A J Clark
W/SALE or RETAIL: Retail *OPENING TIMES:* 1000-1800 Tue Thu & Sun BY APPOINTMENT ONLY.
MAIL ORDER: Yes *MIN VALUE:* £20.00 *CAT. COST:* £2.00 *EXPORT:* Yes
SPECIALITIES: Rhododendron & Azalea in all sizes. *MAP PAGE:* **3**

SLHN **Little Horsted Nursery,** Home Farm, Little Horsted, Uckfield, East Sussex
TEL: (0825) 75577 *CONTACT:* Peter A Boys
W/SALE or RETAIL: Retail *OPENING TIMES:*
MAIL ORDER: Only *MIN VALUE:* £10.00 *CAT. COST:* Sae *EXPORT:* No
SPECIALITIES: Rare & unusual Hardy & Conservatory plants.

SLMG **Long Man Gardens,** Lewes Road, Wilmington, Polegate, East Sussex BN26 5RS
TEL: (0323) 870816 *CONTACT:* O Menzel
W/SALE or RETAIL: Both *OPENING TIMES:* 0900-1200 & 1430-1700 daily. Please check day before visit.
MAIL ORDER: Yes *MIN VALUE:* 1 plant+£3.50 p&p *CAT. COST:* Free *EXPORT:* Yes
SPECIALITIES: Mainly conservatory plants. Some hardy climbers. *MAP PAGE:* **3**

SLon **Longstock Park Nursery,** Stockbridge, Hampshire SO20 6EH
TEL: (0264) 810894 *FAX:* (0264) 810439 *CONTACT:* General Manager
W/SALE or RETAIL: Both *OPENING TIMES:* 0830-1630 Mon-Sat.
MAIL ORDER: No *MIN VALUE:* *CAT. COST:* £1.50 inc p&p *EXPORT:* No
SPECIALITIES: Shrubs & Conifers. Herbaceous and moisture loving and Aquatics. *MAP PAGE:* **2**

SMad **Madrona Nursery,** Tara Lodge, Harden Road, East Rype, Lydd, Kent TN29 9LT
TEL: (0679) 20868 *CONTACT:* Liam MacKenzie
W/SALE or RETAIL: Retail *OPENING TIMES:* 1400-2000 Tue-Thu Apr 1st-Oct 31st.
MAIL ORDER: Yes *MIN VALUE:* None *CAT. COST:* 80p *EXPORT:* No
SPECIALITIES: Unusual Shrubs, Conifers & Perennials. *MAP PAGE:* **3**

SMit **Mary & Peter Mitchell,** 11 Wingle Tye Road, Burgess Hill, West Sussex RH15 9HR
TEL: (0444) 236848 *CONTACT:* Mary & Peter Mitchell
W/SALE or RETAIL: Retail *OPENING TIMES:* Appt only.
MAIL ORDER: Yes *MIN VALUE:* None *CAT. COST:* Stamp *EXPORT:* No
SPECIALITIES: Sempervivum, Jovibaba, Rosularia. *MAP PAGE:* **3**

SMrm **Merriments Nursery,** Hawkhurst Road, Hurst Green, East Sussex TN19 7RA
TEL: (058 086) 666 *FAX:* (058 086) 324 *CONTACT:* Mark Buchner
◆ *W/SALE or RETAIL:* Retail *OPENING TIMES:* 0830-1730.
MAIL ORDER: No *MIN VALUE:* *CAT. COST:* 50p *EXPORT:* No
SPECIALITIES: Tendy & Hardy Perennials. *MAP PAGE:* **3**

SNTN **New Trees Nurseries,** 2 Nunnery Road, Canterbury, Kent CT1 3LS
TEL: (0227) 761209 *CONTACT:* P H Harding
W/SALE or RETAIL: Retail *OPENING TIMES:* By appt. only.
MAIL ORDER: Yes *MIN VALUE:* £12.50 *CAT. COST:* Large Sae *EXPORT:* No
SPECIALITIES: Apples, Pears, Plums, Cherries. Unusual varieties grafted to order. *MAP PAGE:* **3**

SOgg **Stuart Ogg,** Hopton, Fletching Street, Mayfield, East Sussex TN20 6TL
TEL: (0435) 873322 *CONTACT:* Stuart Ogg
W/SALE or RETAIL: Retail *OPENING TIMES:* Appt. only, unless advertised in local press.
MAIL ORDER: SO *MIN VALUE:* *CAT. COST:* Sae *EXPORT:* SO
SPECIALITIES: Delphiniums. *MAP PAGE:*

SOkd **Oakdene Nursery,** Scotsford Road, Broad Oak, Heathfield, East Sussex TN21 8TU
TEL: (0435) 864382 *CONTACT:* David Sampson
W/SALE or RETAIL: Retail *OPENING TIMES:* 0900-1700 Wed-Sat ex Bank Hols. Sun by appt.
MAIL ORDER: Yes *MIN VALUE:* £10.00 *CAT. COST:* 2 x 1st class *EXPORT:* Yes
SPECIALITIES: Alpines, Bulbs, Shrubs & dwarf Rhododendron. *MAP PAGE:* **3**

SOld **Oldbury Nurseries,** Brissenden Green, Bethersden, Kent TN26 3BJ
TEL: (023382) 416 *CONTACT:* Peter & Wendy Dresman
W/SALE or RETAIL: Both *OPENING TIMES:* 0930-1700 daily Feb 1-Aug 23.
MAIL ORDER: No *MIN VALUE:* *CAT. COST:* 36p *EXPORT:* No
SPECIALITIES: Fuchsia. *MAP PAGE:* **3**

SPer **Perryhill Nurseries,** Hartfield, East Sussex TN7 4JP
TEL: (0892) 770377 *FAX:* (0892) 770929 *CONTACT:* Mrs S M Gemmell
W/SALE or RETAIL: Retail *OPENING TIMES:* 0900-1700 daily March 1-Oct 31. 0900-1630 Nov 1-Feb 28.
MAIL ORDER: No *MIN VALUE:* *CAT. COST:* £1.34 *EXPORT:* No
SPECIALITIES: Over 900 Herbaceous varieties & 300 shrub & climbing roses. Wide range of Trees, Shrubs, Conifers, Rhododendron etc. *MAP PAGE:* **3**

SPic **Pickard's Magnolia Gardens,** Stodmarsh Road, Canterbury, Kent CT3 4AG
TEL: (0227) 463951 *CONTACT:* Mr & Mrs A A Pickard
W/SALE or RETAIL: Retail *OPENING TIMES:* 1000-dusk Winter, 1000-1700 Summer ex Mon, Wed & Fri. 1200-dusk winter Wed & Fri. Please check.
MAIL ORDER: No *MIN VALUE:* *CAT. COST:* Sae *EXPORT:* No
SPECIALITIES: Own registered Magnolia hybrids and others. All from cutting or micro-propagation.
MAP PAGE: **3**

SPla **Plaxtol Nurseries,** The Spoute, Plaxtol, Sevenoaks, Kent TN15 0QR
TEL: (0732) 810550 *CONTACT:* Tessa N & Donald M Forbes.
W/SALE or RETAIL: Retail *OPENING TIMES:* 1000-1700 daily. Closed two weeks from Xmas eve.
MAIL ORDER: Yes* *MIN VALUE:* £5 + £5 p&p *CAT. COST:* 50p *EXPORT:* Yes
SPECIALITIES: Plants for Flower arrangers. *NOTE: Mail Order Nov-Mar only. *MAP PAGE:* **3**

SPou **Roger Poulett,** Nurse's Cottage, North Mundham, Chichester, Sussex PO20 6JY
TEL: *CONTACT:* Roger Poulett
W/SALE or RETAIL: Retail *OPENING TIMES:* By arrangement only.
MAIL ORDER: Yes *MIN VALUE:* £10 *CAT. COST:* 3 x 1st class *EXPORT:* No
SPECIALITIES: Helleborus, Corydalis, Crocus, Cyclamen, Origanum and many unusual plants. List in June. *MAP PAGE:* **3**

SReu **G Reuthe Ltd,** Crown Point Nursery, Sevenoaks Road, Ightham, Nr Sevenoaks, Kent TN15 0HB
TEL: (0732) 810694 *CONTACT:* E W Reuthe
◆ *W/SALE or RETAIL:* Retail *OPENING TIMES:* 0900-1630 Mon-Sat. 1000-1630 Sun & Bank Hols during Apr & May ONLY. Occasionally in June; check.
MAIL ORDER: Yes *MIN VALUE:* £15.00 + p&p *CAT. COST:* £1.00 *EXPORT:* Yes
SPECIALITIES: Rhododendrons, Azaleas, Trees, Shrubs & Conifers. *MAP PAGE:* **3**

SRum **Rumwood Nurseries,** Langley, Maidstone, Kent ME17 3ND
TEL: (0622) 861477 *FAX:* (0622) 863123 *CONTACT:* Mr R Fermor
W/SALE or RETAIL: Both *OPENING TIMES:* 0800-1700 Mon-Sat 1000-1700 Sun.
MAIL ORDER: Yes *MIN VALUE:* £3 p&p *CAT. COST:* Sae *EXPORT:* Yes
SPECIALITIES: Roses & Trees. *MAP PAGE:* **3**

SSad **Mrs Jane Sadler,** Ingrams Cottage, Wisborough Green, Billingshurst, West Sussex RH14 0ER
TEL: (0403) 700234 *CONTACT:* Mrs Jane Sadler
W/SALE or RETAIL: Retail *OPENING TIMES:* Daily.
MAIL ORDER: No *MIN VALUE:* *CAT. COST:* Sae *EXPORT:* No
SPECIALITIES: Many unusual or hard to find plants incl. Evolvulus glomeratus 'Blue Daze'
MAP PAGE: **3**

SSmi **Alan C Smith,** 127 Leaves Green Road, Keston, Kent BR2 6DG
TEL: (0959) 72531 *CONTACT:* A C Smith
W/SALE or RETAIL: Retail *OPENING TIMES:* Appt only.
MAIL ORDER: Yes *MIN VALUE:* None *CAT. COST:* 50p *EXPORT:* No
SPECIALITIES: Over 1000 kinds of Sempervivum & Jovibarba. *MAP PAGE:* **3**

SSpi **Spinners,** Boldre, Lymington, Hampshire SO41 5QE
TEL: (0590) 673347 *CONTACT:* P G G Chappell
W/SALE or RETAIL: Retail *OPENING TIMES:* 0900-1800 Apr-Sept. 0900-1700 (or dusk) Sept-Apr daily.
MAIL ORDER: No *MIN VALUE:* *CAT. COST:* 3 x 1st class *EXPORT:* No
SPECIALITIES: Rare Tree and Shrubs especially for shade. Acer, Magnolia, Hosta, Geranium, Hydrangea, Ferns etc. *MAP PAGE:* **2**

SSta **Starborough Nursery,** Starborough Road, Marsh Green, Edenbridge, Kent TN8 5RB
TEL: (0732) 865614 *CONTACT:* C Tomlin & P Kindley
◆ *W/SALE or RETAIL:* Retail *OPENING TIMES:* 1000-1600 Thu-Mon. Closed Jan & Jul.
MAIL ORDER: Yes *MIN VALUE:* £20.00 *CAT. COST:* 85p *EXPORT:* Yes
SPECIALITIES: Rare and unusual Shrubs especially Daphne, Acer, Rhododendron, Azalea, Magnolia & Hamamelis. *MAP PAGE:* **3**

SSus **Sussex Country Gardens,** Newhaven Road, Kingston, Nr Lewes, East Sussex BN7 3NE
TEL: (0273) 473510 *FAX:* (0273) 477135 *CONTACT:* Mr P Thurman
◆ *W/SALE or RETAIL:* Retail *OPENING TIMES:* 0900-1730 Mon-Thu, 0930-1730 Fri, 0900-1800 Sat & Sun.
MAIL ORDER: No *MIN VALUE:* *CAT. COST:* 95p (Roses) *EXPORT:* No
SPECIALITIES: Over 200 varieties of Old English Roses, 90 Clematis, extensive range of Alpines, Herbaceous & Shrubs. *MAP PAGE:* **3**

SSvw **Southview Nurseries,** Chequers Lane, Eversley Cross, Basingstoke, Hampshire RG27 0NT
TEL: (0734) 732206 *CONTACT:* Mark Trenear
◆ *W/SALE or RETAIL:* Retail *OPENING TIMES:* 0900-1300 & 1400-1630 Mon-Sat.
MAIL ORDER: Yes *MIN VALUE:* None *CAT. COST:* Free *EXPORT:* No
SPECIALITIES: Unusual Hardy plants, good selection of old named Pinks. *MAP PAGE:* **2/3**

STil **Tile Barn Nursery,** Standen Street, Iden Green, Benenden, Kent TN17 4LB
TEL: (0580) 240221 *CONTACT:* Peter Moore
W/SALE or RETAIL: Both *OPENING TIMES:* 0900-1700 Wed-Sat.
MAIL ORDER: Yes *MIN VALUE:* None *CAT. COST:* Sae *EXPORT:* Yes
SPECIALITIES: Cyclamen species. *MAP PAGE:* **3**

STre **Peter Trenear,** Chantreyland, Chequers Lane, Eversley Cross, Hampshire RG27 0NX
TEL: (0734) 732300 *CONTACT:* Peter Trenear
W/SALE or RETAIL: Both *OPENING TIMES:* 0900-1630 Mon-Sat.
MAIL ORDER: Yes *MIN VALUE:* None *CAT. COST:* 1 x 1st class *EXPORT:* No
SPECIALITIES: Geranium, Vinca, Trees, Shrubs & Conifers. *MAP PAGE:* **2**

SWas **Washfield Nursery,** Horn's Road (A265), Hawkhurst, Kent TN18 4QU
TEL: (0580) 752522 *CONTACT:* Elizabeth Strangman
W/SALE or RETAIL: Retail *OPENING TIMES:* 1000-1700 Wed-Sat.
MAIL ORDER: Yes *MIN VALUE:* None *CAT. COST:* 3 x 1st class *EXPORT:* No
SPECIALITIES: Alpine, Herbaceous & Woodland, many unusual & rare. Helleborus, Epimedium, Geranium. *MAP PAGE:* **3**

SWes **Westwood Nursery,** 65 Yorkland Avenue, Welling, Kent DA16 2LE
TEL: 081 301-0886 *CONTACT:* Mr S Edwards
W/SALE or RETAIL: Retail *OPENING TIMES:* Not open.
MAIL ORDER: Only *MIN VALUE:* None *CAT. COST:* Sae *EXPORT:* No
SPECIALITIES: Pleiones & Hardy Orchids.

SW&B **Wallace & Barr Ltd.,** The Nurseries, Marden, Kent TN12 9BP
TEL: (0622) 831235 *FAX:* (0622) 832416 *CONTACT:* Wallace & Barr Ltd.
W/SALE or RETAIL: Both *OPENING TIMES:* 0900-1700 Mon-Fri.
MAIL ORDER: Yes *MIN VALUE:* None *CAT. COST:* Free *EXPORT:* Yes
SPECIALITIES: Wide general range, esp. Bulbs. Lillium, Tulipa, Narcissus species & miscellaneous. Large range of Perennials. *MAP PAGE:* **3**

WAbb **Abbey Dore Court Gardens,** Abbeydore, nr Hereford, Herefordshire HR2 0AD
TEL: (0981) 240419 *CONTACT:* Mrs C Ward
W/SALE or RETAIL: Retail *OPENING TIMES:* 1100-1800 Thu-Tue 3rd Sat Mar-3rd Sun Oct.
MAIL ORDER: No *MIN VALUE:* *CAT. COST:* None issued *EXPORT:* No
SPECIALITIES: Shrubs & hardy Perennials, many unusual, which may be seen growing in the garden. National Collection of Sedum & Euphorbia. *MAP PAGE:* **2/4**

WAbe **Aberconwy Nursery,** Graig, Glan Conwy, Colwyn Bay, Clwyd LL28 7TL
TEL: (0492) 580875 *CONTACT:* Dr & Mrs K G Lever
W/SALE or RETAIL: Retail *OPENING TIMES:* 0900-1700 Tue-Sun.
MAIL ORDER: No *MIN VALUE:* *CAT. COST:* 1 x 2nd class *EXPORT:* No
SPECIALITIES: Alpines, including specialist varieties, esp. Autumn Gentians. Trees, Shrubs, Conifers & Herbaceous plants. *MAP PAGE:* **4**

◆ **See also Display Advertisements**

WAct **Acton Beauchamp Roses,** Acton Beauchamp, Worcestershire WR6 5AE
TEL: (053 186) 433 *CONTACT:* Lindsay Bousfield
W/SALE or RETAIL: Both *OPENING TIMES:* 1000-1800 Wed, 1400-1800 Sun Apr-Sep, 1000-1800 Sat, Sun, Mon Bank Hol W/ends.
MAIL ORDER: Yes *MIN VALUE:* None *CAT. COST:* 2 x 1st class *EXPORT:* Yes
SPECIALITIES: Old Rose species & hybrids. Also modern shrub, new English Roses, climbers, ramblers & ground-cover Roses. *MAP PAGE:* **2**

WBal **Helen Ballard,** Old Country, Mathon, Malvern, Worcestershire WR13 5PS
TEL: (0886 880) 215 *CONTACT:* Helen Ballard
W/SALE or RETAIL: Retail *OPENING TIMES:* Fri & Sat Jan-Apr only by appt.
MAIL ORDER: Yes *MIN VALUE:* £10.00 *CAT. COST:* Free *EXPORT:* No
SPECIALITIES: Hellebores, mainly hybrid Orientalis. *MAP PAGE:* **2**

WBod **Bodnant Garden Nursery Ltd.,** Tal-y-Cafn, Colwyn Bay, Clwyd LL28 5RE
TEL: (0492) 650460 *FAX:* (0492) 650448 *CONTACT:* Martin Puddle (Gen. Man.)
W/SALE or RETAIL: Retail *OPENING TIMES:* All year.
MAIL ORDER: Yes *MIN VALUE:* £10.00 + p&p *CAT. COST:* Sae *EXPORT:* Yes
SPECIALITIES: Rhododendron, Camellia & Magnolia. Wide range of unusual Trees and Shrubs. *MAP PAGE:* **4**

WBon **S & E Bond,** Upper Travelly, Beguildy, Knighton, Powys LD7 1UW
TEL: (05477) 658 *CONTACT:* Mrs E Bond
W/SALE or RETAIL: Retail *OPENING TIMES:* 1000-1700 Sun Easter - last weekend of Sep.
MAIL ORDER: Yes *MIN VALUE:* At cost *CAT. COST:* 2 x 1st class *EXPORT:* No
SPECIALITIES: Shade plants. *MAP PAGE:* **4**

WBou **Bouts Cottage Nurseries,** Bouts Lane, Inkberrow, Worcestershire WR7 4HP
TEL: (0386) 792923 *CONTACT:* M & S Roberts
W/SALE or RETAIL: Retail *OPENING TIMES:* Not open to the public.
MAIL ORDER: Only *MIN VALUE:* None *CAT. COST:* Sae *EXPORT:* No
SPECIALITIES: Viola.

WCar **Carmel Court Nurseries,** Kings Turning Road, Presteigne, Powys
TEL: (0544) 267205 *FAX:* (0544) 260306 *CONTACT:* Nicola Humphries
W/SALE or RETAIL: Retail *OPENING TIMES:* 1000-1800 Wed-Sun.
MAIL ORDER: Yes *MIN VALUE:* £8.00 *CAT. COST:* Sae *EXPORT:* No
SPECIALITIES: Unusual Herbaceous Perennials & Wild flowers. *MAP PAGE:* **4**

WCel **Celyn Vale Nurseries,** Carrog, Corwen, Clwyd LL21 9LD
TEL: (0490) 83671 *CONTACT:* Andrew McConnell
W/SALE or RETAIL: Both *OPENING TIMES:* Please telephone first. March to end-Oct.
MAIL ORDER: Yes *MIN VALUE:* 3 Plants *CAT. COST:* 1 x 1st class *EXPORT:* Yes
SPECIALITIES: Hardy Eucalyptus & Acacia. *MAP PAGE:* **4**

WChr **Paul Christian - Rare Plants,** PO Box 468, Wrexham, Clwyd LL13 9XR
TEL: (0978) 366399 *FAX:* (0978) 366399 *CONTACT:* P Christian
W/SALE or RETAIL: Both *OPENING TIMES:* Not open.
MAIL ORDER: Only *MIN VALUE:* None *CAT. COST:* 3 x 1st class *EXPORT:* Yes
SPECIALITIES: Bulbs, Corms, Tubers, especially Colchicum, Crocus, Erythronium, Fritillaria, Iris, Rhodohypoxis & Trillium.

WCla **John Clayfield,** Llanbrook Alpine Nursery, Hopton Castle, Clunton, Shropshire SY7 0QG
TEL: (05474) 298 *CONTACT:* John Clayfield
W/SALE or RETAIL: Both *OPENING TIMES:* Daily, but please check first.
MAIL ORDER: Yes *MIN VALUE:* None *CAT. COST:* 2 x 1st class *EXPORT:* No
SPECIALITIES: Alpines, Wildflowers & native Fern species. *MAP PAGE:* **2/4**

WCon **The Conifer Garden,** Saltway Farm, Northleach, Gloucestershire GL54 3QB
TEL: (0285) 720387 *CONTACT:* Mr & Mrs M P S Powell
W/SALE or RETAIL: Retail *OPENING TIMES:* 1100-1600 Oct-Mar, 1100-1800 Apr-Sep.
MAIL ORDER: No *MIN VALUE:* *CAT. COST:* Free *EXPORT:* No
SPECIALITIES: Conifers only. *MAP PAGE:* **2**

WCoo **Mrs Susan Cooper,** Churchfields House, Cradley, Malvern, Worcestershire WR13 5LJ
TEL: (0886) 880223 *CONTACT:* Mrs S Cooper
W/SALE or RETAIL: Retail *OPENING TIMES:* Appt only.
MAIL ORDER: Yes *MIN VALUE:* £20.00 *CAT. COST:* Sae *EXPORT:* No
SPECIALITIES: Rare & unusual Trees & Shrubs. Provenances on request. *MAP PAGE:* 2

WCot **Cotswold Garden Flowers,** 1 Waterside, Evesham, Worcestershire WR11 6BS
TEL: (0386) 47337 *CONTACT:* Bob Brown
W/SALE or RETAIL: Retail *OPENING TIMES:* Not open to public.
MAIL ORDER: Only *MIN VALUE:* None *CAT. COST:* Free *EXPORT:* Yes
SPECIALITIES: Easy & unusual Perennials for the Flower Garden.

WCru **Crûg Farm Plants,** Griffith's Crossing, Nr Caernarfon, Gwynedd LL55 1TU
TEL: (0248) 670232 *CONTACT:* Mr B Wynn-Jones
◆ *W/SALE or RETAIL:* Both *OPENING TIMES:* 1000-1800 Thu-Sun Apr-Oct or by appt.
MAIL ORDER: No *MIN VALUE:* *CAT. COST:* Sae *EXPORT:* NO
SPECIALITIES: Plants for shade, climbers, Geraniums, Hebaceous, native & bulbous *MAP PAGE:* 4

WDav **Kim W Davis,** Lingen Alpine Nursery, Lingen, Bucknell, Shropshire SY7 0DY
TEL: (0544) 267720 *CONTACT:* Kim W Davis
◆ *W/SALE or RETAIL:* Both *OPENING TIMES:* 1000-1800 daily Feb-Oct. Fri-Sun Nov-Jan by appt.
MAIL ORDER: Yes *MIN VALUE:* 5 plants *CAT. COST:* Sae *EXPORT:* Yes
SPECIALITIES: Alpines & Rock Plants, esp. Androsace, Aquilegia, Campanula, Primula & Penstemon. Export enquiries welcome. *MAP PAGE:* 2/4

WEas **Eastgrove Cottage Garden Nursery,** Sankyns Green, Nr Shrawley, Little Witley, Worcestershire WR6 6LQ
TEL: (0299) 896389 *CONTACT:* Malcolm & Carol Skinner
W/SALE or RETAIL: Retail *OPENING TIMES:* 1400-1700 Thu-Mon Apr 1-Nov 1st ex Aug.
MAIL ORDER: No *MIN VALUE:* *CAT. COST:* 80p stamps *EXPORT:* No
SPECIALITIES: Hardy plants displayed in 'old world country flower garden'. *MAP PAGE:* 2

WEfe **Efenechtyd Nurseries,** Llanelidan, Ruthin, Clwyd LL15 2LG
TEL: (097 888) 677 *CONTACT:* R Dibley
W/SALE or RETAIL: Both *OPENING TIMES:* 0900-1700 daily May-Sept.
MAIL ORDER: Yes *MIN VALUE:* None *CAT. COST:* Sae *EXPORT:* No
SPECIALITIES: Streptocarpus, Columneas & other Gesneriads. *MAP PAGE:* 4

WFib **Fibrex Nurseries Ltd,** Honeybourne Road, Pebworth, Stratford-on-Avon, Warwickshire CV37 8XT
TEL: (0789) 720788 *FAX:* (0789) 721162 *CONTACT:* R J & H Key & U K-Davis
W/SALE or RETAIL: Both *OPENING TIMES:* 1200-1700.
MAIL ORDER: Yes *MIN VALUE:* None *CAT. COST:* 2 x 2nd class *EXPORT:* Yes
SPECIALITIES: Ivys, Ferns & Pelargoniums. *MAP PAGE:* 2

WFro **Fron Nursery,** Fron Isa, Rhiwlas, Oswestry, Shropshire SY10 7JH
TEL: (069176) 605 *CONTACT:* Thoby Miller
W/SALE or RETAIL: Both *OPENING TIMES:* By appt. only.
MAIL ORDER: Yes *MIN VALUE:* £10.00 *CAT. COST:* Sae *EXPORT:* Yes
SPECIALITIES: Ornamental Trees & Shrubs, Perennials & Hedging. *MAP PAGE:* 4

WGre **Greenacres Nursery,** Bringsty, Worcestershire WR6 5TA
TEL: (0885) 482206 *CONTACT:* D & M Everett
W/SALE or RETAIL: Both *OPENING TIMES:* Appt only.
MAIL ORDER: No *MIN VALUE:* *CAT. COST:* Free *EXPORT:* Yes
SPECIALITIES: Heathers. *MAP PAGE:* 2

WHal **Hall Farm Nursery,** Kinnerley, Nr Oswestry, Shropshire SY10 8DH
TEL: (069185) 219 *CONTACT:* Mrs C Ffoulkes-Jones
W/SALE or RETAIL: Both *OPENING TIMES:* 1000-1700 Tue-Sat Mar 1st-Oct 31st. Open Bank Hols & by appt.
MAIL ORDER: No *MIN VALUE:* *CAT. COST:* 4 x 1st class *EXPORT:* No
SPECIALITIES: Unusual plants. Perennials, Alpines, Herbs & Patio plants. Small selection of Insectivorous plants. *MAP PAGE:* 5

WHCG Hunts Court Garden & Nursery, North Nibley, Dursley, Gloucestershire GL11 6DZ
TEL: (0453) 547440 *CONTACT:* T K & M M Marshall
◆ *W/SALE or RETAIL:* Retail *OPENING TIMES:* Nursery 0900-1700 Tue-Sat ex Aug. Garden 1400-1800 ex Aug. Also by appt.
MAIL ORDER: No *MIN VALUE:* *CAT. COST:* 50p *EXPORT:* No
SPECIALITIES: Old Rose species & climbers. Hardy Geranium. Shrubby Potentilla & unusual shrubs. *MAP PAGE:* **2**

WHCr Hergest Croft Gardens, Kington, Herefordshire HR5 3EG
TEL: (0544) 230160 *CONTACT:* John Potts
W/SALE or RETAIL: Retail *OPENING TIMES:* 1330-1830 daily Apr-Oct.
MAIL ORDER: No *MIN VALUE:* *CAT. COST:* None issued *EXPORT:* No
SPECIALITIES: Acer, Betula & unusual woody plants. *MAP PAGE:* **2**

WHea Heath Garden, Heath Hill, Sheriffhales, Shifnal, Shropshire TF11 8RR
TEL: (095270) 341 *CONTACT:* Gordon Malt
W/SALE or RETAIL: Retail *OPENING TIMES:* 0900-1800 Sat & 1300-1800 Sun Mar 1st-Oct 1st.
MAIL ORDER: No *MIN VALUE:* *CAT. COST:* 50p *EXPORT:* No
SPECIALITIES: Unusual herbaceous esp. Geranium & Salvia. *MAP PAGE:* **5**

WHen Henllys Lodge Plants Henllys Lodge, Beaumaris, Anglesey, Gwynedd LL58 8HU
TEL: (0248) 810106 *CONTACT:* Mrs E Lane
W/SALE or RETAIL: Retail *OPENING TIMES:* 1100-1700 Tue, Wed, Fri, Sat, Sun & by appt. Apr-Oct.
MAIL ORDER: Yes *MIN VALUE:* None *CAT. COST:* 2 x 1st class *EXPORT:* No
SPECIALITIES: Hardy Geranium, Ground cover & cottage style Perennials. *MAP PAGE:* **4**

WHer The Herb Garden, Plant Hunter's Nursery, Capel Ulo, Pentre Berw, Gaerwen, Anglesey, Gwynedd LL60 6LF
TEL: (0248) 421064 *CONTACT:* Corinne & David Tremaine-Stevenson
W/SALE or RETAIL: Retail *OPENING TIMES:* 0900-dusk daily Mar-Sep 30th. 1000-1700 Oct-Apr & Bank Hols & by appt. (Please ring out of season).
MAIL ORDER: Yes *MIN VALUE:* £5.00 *CAT. COST:* £1.00. List 50p*EXPORT:* No
SPECIALITIES: Wide range of Herbs, Wild flowers, unusual Perennials. Scented Pelargoniums, Aquilegia, Salvia, old Roses & hardy Geraniums *MAP PAGE:* **4**

WHig Highfield Nurseries, Whitminster, Gloucestershire GL2 7PL
TEL: (0452) 740266 *CONTACT:* Mrs S Gray
W/SALE or RETAIL: Retail *OPENING TIMES:* 0800-1700 Mon-Sat, 1100-1600 Sun Nov-end Mar. 0900-1800 Mon-Sat, 1100-1600 Sun Apr-end Oct.
MAIL ORDER: Yes *MIN VALUE:* None *CAT. COST:* Free *EXPORT:* No
SPECIALITIES: Wide general range including Fruit. *MAP PAGE:* **2**

WHil Hillview Hardy Plants, Worfield, Nr Bridgenorth, Shropshire WV15 5NT
TEL: (074 64) 454 *CONTACT:* Ingrid Millington
W/SALE or RETAIL: Retail *OPENING TIMES:* 1000-1700 Tue-Sun also Bank Hol Mondays Mar-mid Oct. By appt. mid Oct-Feb.
MAIL ORDER: Yes *MIN VALUE:* None *CAT. COST:* 2 x 1st class *EXPORT:* No
SPECIALITIES: Hardy Perennials & Alpines. Contract growing for Wholesale. *MAP PAGE:* **5**

WHoo Hoo House Nursery, Hoo House, Gloucester Road, Tewkesbury, Gloucestershire GL20 7DA
TEL: (0684) 293389 *CONTACT:* Robin & Julie Ritchie
◆ *W/SALE or RETAIL:* Both *OPENING TIMES:* 1400-1700 Mon-Sat.
MAIL ORDER: No *MIN VALUE:* *CAT. COST:* 3 x 1st class *EXPORT:* No
SPECIALITIES: Wide range of Herbaceous & Alpines - some unusual. *MAP PAGE:* **2**

WJas Paul Jasper (Trees & Roses), The Lighthouse, Bridge Street, Leominster, Herefordshire HR6 8DU
TEL: *CONTACT:* Paul Jasper
W/SALE or RETAIL: Both *OPENING TIMES:*
MAIL ORDER: Only *MIN VALUE:* £25.00 *CAT. COST:* 2 x 1st class *EXPORT:* Yes
SPECIALITIES: Worthy old Apple & flowering Crab Apple varieties, modern Fruit varieties & ornamental Trees.

WJun **Jungle Giants,** Plough Farm, Wigmore, Herefordshire HR6 9UW
TEL: (0568) 86708 *FAX:* (0568) 86383 *CONTACT:* Michael Brisbane
◆ *W/SALE or RETAIL:* Both *OPENING TIMES:* Daily - by appt. only please.
MAIL ORDER: Yes *MIN VALUE:* Postage cost *CAT. COST:* £4.32 info.pack *EXPORT:* Yes
SPECIALITIES: Bamboo and hardy plants for tropical effect gardens. *MAP PAGE:* **3**

WKif **Kiftsgate Court Gardens,** Kiftsgate Court, Chipping Camden, Gloucestershire GL55 6LW
TEL: *CONTACT:* Mrs J Chambers
W/SALE or RETAIL: Retail *OPENING TIMES:* 1400-1800 Wed, Thu & Sun Apr 1st-Sep 30th & Bank Hol Mons.
MAIL ORDER: No *MIN VALUE:* *CAT. COST:* *EXPORT:* No
SPECIALITIES: Small range of unusual plants. *MAP PAGE:* **2**

WKin **Kingstone Cottage Plants,** Weston-under-Penyard, Ross-on-Wye, Herefordshire HR9 7NXL
TEL: (0989) 65267 *CONTACT:* Mrs S Hughes
W/SALE or RETAIL: Retail *OPENING TIMES:* By appt. and as under National Garden Scheme.
MAIL ORDER: Yes *MIN VALUE:* None *CAT. COST:* Sae *EXPORT:* No
SPECIALITIES: Dianthus. *MAP PAGE:* **2/4**

WMar **Marley Bank Nursery,** Bottom Lane, Whitbourne, Worcestershire WR6 5RU
TEL: (0886) 21576 *CONTACT:* Roger & Sue Norman
W/SALE or RETAIL: Retail *OPENING TIMES:* By appt. and as for National Garden Scheme.
MAIL ORDER: No *MIN VALUE:* *CAT. COST:* Sae *EXPORT:* No
SPECIALITIES: Alpines, Cyclamen, tender Perennials, Penstemon & Violas. *MAP PAGE:* **2**

WMEx **Marston Exotics,** Brampton Lane, Madley, Herefordshire HR2 9LX
TEL: (0981) 251140 *FAX:* (0432) 274023 *CONTACT:* Paul Gardner & M Luscombe
W/SALE or RETAIL: Both *OPENING TIMES:* 0800-1700 Mon-Sat Apr-Sept, Mon-Fri Oct-Mar.
MAIL ORDER: Yes *MIN VALUE:* £15.00 *CAT. COST:* 60p *EXPORT:* Yes
SPECIALITIES: Carnivorous plants. *MAP PAGE:* **2/4**

WMou **Mount Pleasant Trees,** Rockhampton, Berkeley, Gloucestershire GL13 9DU
TEL: (0454) 260348 *CONTACT:* G Locke
◆ *W/SALE or RETAIL:* Both *OPENING TIMES:* Appt only.
MAIL ORDER: Yes *MIN VALUE:* £4.50 *CAT. COST:* 3 x 1st class *EXPORT:* No
SPECIALITIES: Common & rare Trees & Shrubs for hedging, arboreta, forestry and gardens. Specimens of Yew & Box. *MAP PAGE:* **2**

WNor **Andrew Norfield Trees & Seeds,** Lower Meend, St Briavels, Gloucestershire GL15 6RW
TEL: (0594) 530134 *CONTACT:* Andrew Norfield
W/SALE or RETAIL: Both *OPENING TIMES:*
MAIL ORDER: Only *MIN VALUE:* None *CAT. COST:* 1 x 1st class *EXPORT:* SO
SPECIALITIES: Wide range of Trees from seed. Acer, Betula, Stewartia & pregerminated seed.

WOak **Oak Cottage Herb Garden,** Nesscliffe, nr Shrewsbury, Shropshire SY4 1DB
TEL: (074381) 262 *CONTACT:* Jane & Edward Bygott.
◆ *W/SALE or RETAIL:* Retail *OPENING TIMES:* Usually 1500-1800 weekdays, 1030-1800 weekends.
MAIL ORDER: Yes *MIN VALUE:* £3.50 *CAT. COST:* 25p + Sae *EXPORT:* No
SPECIALITIES: Herbs, Wild flowers, Old Roses and Cottage plants. *MAP PAGE:* **4/5**

WOld **Old Court Nurseries Ltd,** Colwall, Nr Malvern, Worcestershire WR13 6QE
TEL: (0684) 40416 *CONTACT:* Paul & Meriel Picton
W/SALE or RETAIL: Retail *OPENING TIMES:* 1000-1300 & 1415-1730 Wed-Sun Apr-Oct. 1415-1700 Wed-Fri (by appt.) Nov-Mar.
MAIL ORDER: Yes *MIN VALUE:* None (p&p £4) *CAT. COST:* 2 x 1st class *EXPORT:* No
SPECIALITIES: National collection of Michaelmas Daisies. Herbaceous Perennials & Alpines. (Mail order for Asters only). *MAP PAGE:* **2**

WOMN **The Old Manor Nursery,** Twyning, Gloucestershire GL20 6DB
TEL: (0684) 293516 *CONTACT:* Mrs Joan Wilder
W/SALE or RETAIL: Retail *OPENING TIMES:* 1400-1800, or dusk if earlier, Mon all year.
MAIL ORDER: No *MIN VALUE:* *CAT. COST:* 25p+Large Sae *EXPORT:* No
SPECIALITIES: Predominately Alpines, small supply of unusual and rare varieties of other Perennial plants. *MAP PAGE:* **2**

WPat **Chris Pattison,** Brookend, Pendock, Gloucestershire GL19 3PL
TEL: (0531) 650480 *CONTACT:* Chris Pattison
◆ *W/SALE or RETAIL:* Both *OPENING TIMES:* 0900-1700 Mon-Fri. Weekends by appt. only.
MAIL ORDER: No *MIN VALUE:* *CAT. COST:* 3 x 1st class *EXPORT:* No
SPECIALITIES: Choice & rare Shrubs and Alpines. *MAP PAGE:* **2**

WPau **Paul's Fuchsias,** Gors Farm, Rhydargaeau, Carmarthen, Gwynedd SA32 7AP
TEL: (0267) 253361 *CONTACT:* Paul Newman
W/SALE or RETAIL: Both *OPENING TIMES:* 0900-1800.
MAIL ORDER: Yes *MIN VALUE:* None *CAT. COST:* Free *EXPORT:* No
SPECIALITIES: Fuchsia. *MAP PAGE:* **4**

WPer **Perhill Nurseries,** Worcester Road, Great Witley, Worcestershire WR6 6JT
TEL: (0299) 896329 *CONTACT:* Jon Baker
W/SALE or RETAIL: Both *OPENING TIMES:* 0900-1800 Mon-Sat 0900-1700 Sun.
MAIL ORDER: No *MIN VALUE:* *CAT. COST:* Sae for list *EXPORT:* No
SPECIALITIES: Rare & unusual Alpines & Herbaceous Perennials. Over 1500 grown. Old fashioned Dianthus, Penstemon, Salvia, Thymes, Herbs & Pelargoniums. *MAP.PAGE:* **2**

WRid **Ridgeway Heather Nursery,** Park House, Plaish, Church Streeton, Shropshire SY6 7HY
TEL: (06943) 574 *CONTACT:* Mrs N Cordingley
W/SALE or RETAIL: Retail *OPENING TIMES:* 1000-1800 Tue-Sun.
MAIL ORDER: No *MIN VALUE:* *CAT. COST:* Free *EXPORT:* Yes
SPECIALITIES: Heathers *MAP PAGE:* **2/4**

WRus **Rushfields of Ledbury,** Ross Road, Ledbury, Herefordshire HR8 2LP
TEL: (0531) 2004 *CONTACT:* B & J Homewood
W/SALE or RETAIL: Both *OPENING TIMES:* 1100-1700 Wed-Sat.
MAIL ORDER: Yes *MIN VALUE:* £10.00 + p&p *CAT. COST:* £1.00 inc p&p *EXPORT:* No
SPECIALITIES: Unusual Herbaceous & foliage plants. *MAP PAGE:* **2**

WSHC **Stone House Cottage Nurseries,** Stone, Nr Kidderminster, Worcestershire DY10 4BG
TEL: (0562) 69902 *CONTACT:* J F & L N Arbuthnott
◆ *W/SALE or RETAIL:* Retail *OPENING TIMES:* 1000-1800 Wed-Sat, & Sun in May & June. Appt. only in Nov. Closed Dec-Feb.
MAIL ORDER: No *MIN VALUE:* *CAT. COST:* Sae *EXPORT:* No
SPECIALITIES: Small general range, especially wall Shrubs, Climbers and unusual plants. *MAP PAGE:* **2**

WStA **St Annes Vineyard,** Wain House, Oxenhall, Newent Gloucestershire GL18 1RW
TEL: (098 982) 313 *CONTACT:* B R Edwards
W/SALE or RETAIL: Both *OPENING TIMES:* 1400-1900 Wed-Fri, 1000-1900 Weekends & Bank Hols.
MAIL ORDER: Yes *MIN VALUE:* *CAT. COST:* Sae *EXPORT:* Yes
SPECIALITIES: Vines *MAP PAGE:* **2**

WSto **Stoke Lacy Herb Garden,** Bromyard, Herefordshire HR7 4JH
TEL: (0432) 820232 *CONTACT:* Madge Hooper
W/SALE or RETAIL: Retail *OPENING TIMES:* 1000-1630 Sat only.
MAIL ORDER: Yes *MIN VALUE:* None *CAT. COST:* 3 x 1st class *EXPORT:* No
SPECIALITIES: Herbs. *MAP PAGE:* **2**

WTay **J Mann Taylor,** Sunningdale, Grange Court, Westbury-on-Severn, Gloucestershire GL14 1PL
TEL: (045 276) 268 *CONTACT:* J Mann Taylor
W/SALE or RETAIL: Retail *OPENING TIMES:* Appt. only.
MAIL ORDER: No *MIN VALUE:* *CAT. COST:* 2 x 2nd class *EXPORT:* No
SPECIALITIES: Buddleja saligna, Calomanthus quadrifolius, Geranium maderense, Hedychium gardnerianum, Puyas and other seldom offered plants. *MAP PAGE:* **2**

WThu **Thuya Alpine Nursery,** Glebelands, Hartpury, Gloucestershire GL19 3BW
TEL: (045270) 548 *CONTACT:* S W Bond
W/SALE or RETAIL: Retail *OPENING TIMES:* 1000-dusk Sat & Bank hol. 1100-dusk Sun, Weekdays appt. advised.
MAIL ORDER: Yes *MIN VALUE:* £3.00 *CAT. COST:* 4 x 2nd class *EXPORT:* SO
SPECIALITIES: Wide and changing range including rarities. *MAP PAGE:* **2**

WToa **Toad Hall Produce,** Frogmore, Weston-under-Penyard, Herefordshire HR9 5TQ
TEL: (098981) 214 *CONTACT:* S V North
◆ *W/SALE or RETAIL:* Retail *OPENING TIMES:* 1000-1800 Mon Apr-Oct.
MAIL ORDER: Yes *MIN VALUE:* None *CAT. COST:* Sae *EXPORT:* No
SPECIALITIES: Hardy Geranium & Ground cover plants. *MAP PAGE:* **2**

WWar **Warners Roses,** Greenfields, Brockton, Newport, Shropshire
TEL: (0952) 604217 *CONTACT:* Mr C H Warner
W/SALE or RETAIL: Both *OPENING TIMES:* 1000-1930 Mon-Sat & 1430-1830 July 10th-Apr 10th.
MAIL ORDER: Yes *MIN VALUE:* £4.00 *CAT. COST:* *EXPORT:* Yes
SPECIALITIES: New and climbing Rose varieties. *MAP PAGE:* **5**

WWat **Waterwheel Nursery,** Bully Hole Bottom, Usk Road, Shirenewton, Chepstow, Gwent NP6 6SA
TEL: (02917) 577 *CONTACT:* Desmond & Charlotte Evans
◆ *W/SALE or RETAIL:* Retail *OPENING TIMES:* Almost always, but please phone to check & for directions.
MAIL ORDER: Yes* *MIN VALUE:* None *CAT. COST:* 2 x 1st class *EXPORT:* No
SPECIALITIES: Wide range of Trees, Shrubs & Perennials - many unusual. *NOTE: Mail Order Oct-Mar only. *MAP PAGE:* **2/4**

WWeb **Webbs Garden Centres Ltd,** Wychbold, Droitwich, Worcestershire WR9 0DG
TEL: (0527 86) 777 *FAX:* (0527 86) 284 *CONTACT:* Mr W R B Webb
◆ *W/SALE or RETAIL:* Both *OPENING TIMES:* 0900-1700 Mon-Sat 1000-1700 Sun Winter. 0900-1745 Mon-Sat 1000-1700 Sun Summer
MAIL ORDER: No *MIN VALUE:* *CAT. COST:* £1.95 *EXPORT:* No
SPECIALITIES: Hardy Trees & Shrubs, Alpines, Heathers, Herbaceous, Herbs, Roses & Fruit. *MAP PAGE:* **2**

WWin **Wintergreen Nurseries,** Bringsty Common, Worcestershire WR6 5UW
TEL: (0885) 482358 eves. *CONTACT:* S Dodd
W/SALE or RETAIL: Both *OPENING TIMES:* 1000-1730 Wed-Sun 1st Mar-29th Oct & by appt.
MAIL ORDER: Yes *MIN VALUE:* None *CAT. COST:* 2 x 2nd class *EXPORT:* No
SPECIALITIES: General, especially Alpines & Herbaceous. *MAP PAGE:* **2**

ADDITIONAL NURSERY INDEX

Please note that all these nurseries are listed in ascending order of their numeric Codes. All nurseries are listed in alphabetical order of their name in the NURSERY-CODE INDEX on page 553.

2 **Aylings of Trotton,** Trotton Garden Centre, Rogate, Petersfield, Hampshire GU31 5ES
TEL: (0730) 813621 *CONTACT:* Anthony Ayling.
W/SALE or RETAIL: Retail *OPENING TIMES:* 0800-1700 Mon-Sat. 0900-1700 Sun.
MAIL ORDER: No *MIN VALUE:* *CAT. COST:* None issued *EXPORT:* No
SPECIALITIES: Wide range of unusual Shrubs. Also old-fashioned Roses & Rhododendron. American import Hostas. Specimen size house-plants. *MAP PAGE:* **2/3**

3 **Ballagan Nursery,** Gartocharn Road, Nr Balloch, Alexandria, Strathclyde G83 8NB
TEL: (0389) 52947 *CONTACT:* Mr G Stephenson
W/SALE or RETAIL: Retail *OPENING TIMES:* 0830-1830 daily.
MAIL ORDER: No *MIN VALUE:* *CAT. COST:* None issued *EXPORT:* No
SPECIALITIES: Home grown bedding and general nursery stock. *MAP PAGE:* **9**

5 **Beetham Nurseries,** Pool Darkin Lane, Beetham, Nr Milnthorpe, Cumbria
TEL: (05395) 63630 *CONTACT:* S J & A J Abbit
W/SALE or RETAIL: Retail *OPENING TIMES:* 0900-1800 Summer, 0900-dusk Winter.
MAIL ORDER: No *MIN VALUE:* *CAT. COST:* *EXPORT:*
SPECIALITIES: Comprehensive range of Trees, Shrubs & Herbaceous Plants. Many unusual varieties. *MAP PAGE:* **5/8**

9 **Bretby Nurseries,** Bretby Lane, Burton-on-Trent, Staffordshire
TEL: (0283) 703355 *FAX:* (0283) 704035 *CONTACT:* Mr David Cartwright
W/SALE or RETAIL: Both *OPENING TIMES:* 0900-1700 daily.
MAIL ORDER: No *MIN VALUE:* *CAT. COST:* 3 x 1st class *EXPORT:* No
SPECIALITIES: Wide range of shrubs. *MAP PAGE:* **5**

11 **Colemans Nurseries,** 6 Old Ballyclare Road, Templepatrick, Ballyclare, Co Antrim, N Ireland BT39 0BJ
TEL: (08494) 32513 *FAX:* (08494) 32151 *CONTACT:* Mr Rodney Coleman
W/SALE or RETAIL: Both *OPENING TIMES:* 0900-1730 Mon-Fri, 0900-1700 Sat, 1400-1700 Sun.
MAIL ORDER: No *MIN VALUE:* *CAT. COST:* Free *EXPORT:* Yes
SPECIALITIES: Over 2000 varieties of plants. *MAP PAGE:* **10**

12 **Cottage Gardens,** Langham Road, Boxted, Colchester, Essex CO4 5HU
TEL: (0206) 272269 *CONTACT:* Alison Smith
W/SALE or RETAIL: Retail *OPENING TIMES:* 0800-1900 daily Spring & Summer. 0800-1800 Thu-Sun Jul-Feb.
MAIL ORDER: No *MIN VALUE:* *CAT. COST:* Free *EXPORT:* Yes
SPECIALITIES: 400 varieties of Shrubs, 390 varieties of Herbaceous. Huge range of Trees, Alpines, Herbs, Hedging - all home grown. Garden antiques. *MAP PAGE:* **6**

13 **Cowcombe Farm Herbs,** Gipsy Lane, Chalford, Stroud, Gloucestershire GL6 8HP
TEL: (0285 76) 544 *CONTACT:* Mrs C M Barnett
W/SALE or RETAIL: Both *OPENING TIMES:* 1000-1700 Wed-Sat, 1400-1700 Sun, Easter Sat-end Sep or by appt.
MAIL ORDER: Yes *MIN VALUE:* *CAT. COST:* 2 x 2nd class *EXPORT:* No
SPECIALITIES: Herbs, Wild flowers & Cottage garden plants. Herb and wild Seed. *MAP PAGE:* **2**

16 **Daleside Nurseries,** Ripon Road, Killinghall, Harrogate, North Yorks HG3 2AY
TEL: (0423) 506405 *FAX:* (0423) 527872 *CONTACT:* Messrs Darley & Townsend.
W/SALE or RETAIL: Retail *OPENING TIMES:* 0900-1700 Mon-Sat, 1000-1200 & 1330-1630 Sun.
MAIL ORDER: No *MIN VALUE:* *CAT. COST:* *EXPORT:* No
SPECIALITIES: Many plants & trees not generally available. Container grown Fruit, Apples, Pears & Soft Fruit. *MAP PAGE:* **5/7**

19 **Denmans Ltd. (Denmans Garden),** Clock House, Denmans, Fontwell, Nr Arundel, West Sussex BN18 0SU
TEL: (0243 68) 2808 *CONTACT:* John Brookes
W/SALE or RETAIL: Retail *OPENING TIMES:* 1000-1700 daily Mar 4th - Dec 15th.
MAIL ORDER: No *MIN VALUE:* *CAT. COST:* £2.50 *EXPORT:* No
SPECIALITIES: Rare and unusual plants. *MAP PAGE:* **3**

20 **Devon Herbs,** Burn Lane, Brentor, Tavistock, Devon PL19 0ND
TEL: (0822) 810285 *CONTACT:* Mrs S A Wetherbee
W/SALE or RETAIL: Retail *OPENING TIMES:* 1100-1700 Fri-Sun Apr 1st-Sep 30th.
MAIL ORDER: No *MIN VALUE:* None *CAT. COST:* 75p *EXPORT:* No
SPECIALITIES: Herb plants. *MAP PAGE:* **1**

21 **Mugswell Nursery,** Bisley, Stroud, Gloucestershire GL6 7AN
TEL: (0452) 770105 *CONTACT:* Peter Dinning
W/SALE or RETAIL: Both *OPENING TIMES:* 1000-1800 (dusk if earlier) Wed-Sun. Please check.
MAIL ORDER: No *MIN VALUE:* *CAT. COST:* £1.00 + Sae *EXPORT:* No
SPECIALITIES: Mainly Alpines and Herbaceous Perennials. *MAP PAGE:* **2**

22 **Elly Hill Herbs,** Elly Hill House, Barmpton, Darlington, Durham DL1 3JF
TEL: (0325) 464682 *CONTACT:* Mrs Nina Pagan
W/SALE or RETAIL: Retail *OPENING TIMES:* By appt. only
MAIL ORDER: No *MIN VALUE:* None *CAT. COST:* 50p+large Sae *EXPORT:* No
SPECIALITIES: Herbs. *MAP PAGE:* **7/8**

23 **Christopher Fairweather Ltd.,** High Street, Beaulieu, Hampshire SO42 7YB
TEL: (0590) 612113 *FAX:* (0590) 612615 *CONTACT:* C Fairweather
W/SALE or RETAIL: Both *OPENING TIMES:* 0900-1700 daily.
MAIL ORDER: No *MIN VALUE:* *CAT. COST:* No retail Cat. *EXPORT:* Yes
SPECIALITIES: Shrubs & Trees. *MAP PAGE:* **2**

26 **The Flower Centre,** 754 Howth Road, Raheny, Dublin 5, Eire
TEL: (0001) 313740 *CONTACT:* Eugene Higgins
W/SALE or RETAIL: Both *OPENING TIMES:* 1000-1300 & 1430-1800 Summer, 1000-1300 & 1430-1700 Winter daily. Mon-Sat only Jan & Feb.
MAIL ORDER: No *MIN VALUE:* *CAT. COST:* Free *EXPORT:* No
SPECIALITIES: Impatiens, Universal pansies, Fuchsia & hanging baskets. *MAP PAGE:* **10**

27 **Garden & Landscape Advice,** 33 School Lane, Kirkella, Hull, Yorkshire HU10 7NP
TEL: (0482) 655710 *CONTACT:* Dr I G & Dr R Tinklin
W/SALE or RETAIL: Both *OPENING TIMES:* By appt for collection only.
MAIL ORDER: Yes *MIN VALUE:* £3.00 + p&p *CAT. COST:* 30p *EXPORT:* No
SPECIALITIES: British native plants, mostly field grown. *MAP PAGE:* **7**

28 **Diana Gilbert,** 25 Virginia Road, South Tankerton, Whitstable, Kent CT5 3HY
TEL: (0227) 273128 *CONTACT:* Diana Gilbert.
◆ *W/SALE or RETAIL:* Retail *OPENING TIMES:* 1000-1800 Wed-Sun. Also by appt.
MAIL ORDER: No *MIN VALUE:* *CAT. COST:* 2 x 1st class *EXPORT:* No
SPECIALITIES: Ilex cultivars, Pittosporum, Hebe, Hosta, Herbs, Foliage & Flower arrangers plants. *MAP PAGE:* **3**

29 **Glebe Cottage Gardens,** Church Lane, Stockerston, Oakham, Leicestershire LE15 9JD
TEL: (0572) 821253 *CONTACT:* A V Burwood
W/SALE or RETAIL: Retail *OPENING TIMES:* 1000-1700 Sat, Sun & Bank Hols, Mar-Sep or by appt. Closed Aug 1st-14th.
MAIL ORDER: No *MIN VALUE:* *CAT. COST:* 2 x 1st class *EXPORT:* No
SPECIALITIES: Alpines & Cottage garden plants. Only small quantities of each, please check availability. *MAP PAGE:* **6**

30 **Glen Haven Gardens,** 21 Dark Lane, Backwell, Bristol, Avon BS19 3NT
TEL: (027546) 2700 *CONTACT:* D G Everitt
W/SALE or RETAIL: Both *OPENING TIMES:* Appt only.
MAIL ORDER: Yes *MIN VALUE:* None *CAT. COST:* None issued *EXPORT:* No
SPECIALITIES: General herbaceous, many unusual items. *MAP PAGE:* **2/4**

32 **Grange Farm Nursery,** Guarlford, Malvern, Worcestershire
TEL: (0684) 562544 *CONTACT:* Mrs C Nicholls
W/SALE or RETAIL: Retail *OPENING TIMES:* 0900-1730 daily Summer. 0900-1700 daily Winter. ex Xmas & 2 weeks in Jan.
MAIL ORDER: No *MIN VALUE:* *CAT. COST:* Free pamphlet *EXPORT:* No
SPECIALITIES: Wide general range of container grown hardy Shrubs, Trees, Conifers, Heathers, Alpines & Herbaceous. *MAP PAGE:* **2**

33 **The Herb Farm,** Peppard Road, Sonning Common, Reading, Berkshire RG4 9NJ
TEL: (0734) 724220 *CONTACT:* R Scott
W/SALE or RETAIL: Retail *OPENING TIMES:* 1000-1700 Tue-Sun Summertime. 1000-1600 Tue-Sat Wintertime
MAIL ORDER: No *MIN VALUE:* *CAT. COST:* Sae *EXPORT:* No
SPECIALITIES: Herbs & fragrant Plants. *MAP PAGE:* **2/3**

35 **The Herbary Prickwillow,** Ely, Cambridgeshire CB7 4SJ
TEL: (0353 88) 456 *FAX:* (0353 88) 451 *CONTACT:* Peter Petts
W/SALE or RETAIL: Both *OPENING TIMES:* 0900-dusk all year.
MAIL ORDER: Yes *MIN VALUE:* £5.95 *CAT. COST:* Free *EXPORT:* Yes
SPECIALITIES: Culinary Herbs. Will propagate any not on list; minimum of six plants.
MAP PAGE: **6**

36 **Herterton House Garden Nursery,** Hartington, Cambo, Morpeth, Northumberland NE61 4BN
TEL: (067074) 278 *CONTACT:* Mrs M Lawley
W/SALE or RETAIL: Retail *OPENING TIMES:* 1330-1730 Mon Wed Fri-Sun May 1st-end Oct. (Earlier or later in the year weather permitting).
MAIL ORDER: No *MIN VALUE:* *CAT. COST:* None issued *EXPORT:* No
SPECIALITIES: Achillea, Aquilegia, Daisies, Geum, Geranium, Polemonium & aromatics.
MAP PAGE: **8/9**

37 **Caroline Holmes,** Denham End Farm, Denham, Bury St Edmunds, Suffolk IP29 5EE
TEL: (0284) 810653 *CONTACT:* Caroline Holmes
♦ *W/SALE or RETAIL:* Both *OPENING TIMES:* Any time.
MAIL ORDER: Yes *MIN VALUE:* £2.00 *CAT. COST:* 3 x 1st class *EXPORT:* No
SPECIALITIES: Herbs. *MAP PAGE:* **6**

38 **The Laurels Nursery,** Benenden, Cranbrook, Kent TN17 4JU
TEL: (0580) 240463 *CONTACT:* Mr P H Kellett
W/SALE or RETAIL: Both *OPENING TIMES:* 0800-1200 & 1300-1700 Mon-Fri, 0900-1200 Sat, Sun by appt. only.
MAIL ORDER: No *MIN VALUE:* *CAT. COST:* Free *EXPORT:* No
SPECIALITIES: Flowering Cherries, open ground ornamental Trees & Shrubs *MAP PAGE:* **3**

40 **Layham Garden Centre,** Lower Road, Staple, Canterbury, Kent CT3 1LH
TEL: (0304) 813267 *FAX:* (0304) 615349 *CONTACT:* L W Wessel
W/SALE or RETAIL: Both *OPENING TIMES:* 0900-1700 Mon-Sat 1000-1700 Sun.
MAIL ORDER: Yes *MIN VALUE:* £5.00 *CAT. COST:* Free *EXPORT:* No
SPECIALITIES: Roses, Herbaceous, Shrubs, Trees, Conifers, Liners & Whips. Aquatic plants.
MAP PAGE: **3**

41 **Longacre Nursery,** Perry Wood, Selling, Nr Faversham, Kent ME13 9SE
TEL: (0227) 752254 *CONTACT:* Dr & Mrs G G Thomas
◆ *W/SALE or RETAIL:* Retail *OPENING TIMES:* 1400-1700 daily, Apr 1st - Oct 31st.
MAIL ORDER: No *MIN VALUE:* *CAT. COST:* 50p + stamp *EXPORT:* No
SPECIALITIES: Hardy Herbaceous only. *MAP PAGE:* **3**

42 **Manningford Nurseries,** Manningford Abbots, Nr Pewsey, Wiltshire SN9 5PB
TEL: (0672) 62232 *CONTACT:* Peter Jones
W/SALE or RETAIL: Both *OPENING TIMES:* 0830-1700 Mon-Sat, 1030-1300 & 1400-1700 Sun.
MAIL ORDER: Yes *MIN VALUE:* £5.00 *CAT. COST:* None issued *EXPORT:* Yes
SPECIALITIES: Plants of the 18th & 19th century. Digitalis, Penstemon, Hemerocallis, Nepeta, Aconitum volubile, Maurandya. *MAP PAGE:* **2**

43 **Marle Place Plants,** Marle Place, Brenchley, Nr Tonbridge, Kent TN12 7HS
TEL: (0892 72) 2304 *CONTACT:* Mrs L M Williams
W/SALE or RETAIL: Both *OPENING TIMES:* 1000-1700 Easter-Oct. Gardens open 1000-1700 Mon-Sat (not Bank Hols) or by appt.
MAIL ORDER: Yes *MIN VALUE:* None *CAT. COST:* *EXPORT:* No
SPECIALITIES: Herbs & Wild Flowers. *MAP PAGE:* **3**

46 **K P Nichols,** Coniston Lodge, 20 Rider Haggard Lane, Kessingland, Suffolk NR33 7PD
TEL: (0502) 741190 *CONTACT:* K P Nichols
W/SALE or RETAIL: Retail *OPENING TIMES:* Written appt. only.
MAIL ORDER: Yes *MIN VALUE:* None *CAT. COST:* 60p *EXPORT:* No
SPECIALITIES: Rare, common & unusual Perennials & Alpines. *MAP PAGE:* **6**

48 **Nordybank Nurseries,** Clee St Margaret, Craven Arms, Shropshire SY7 9EF
TEL: (0584 75) 322 *CONTACT:* P J Bolton
W/SALE or RETAIL: Both *OPENING TIMES:* 1000-1800 Wed & Sun Easter - October.
MAIL ORDER: No *MIN VALUE:* *CAT. COST:* 30p *EXPORT:* No
SPECIALITIES: Native & Hardy Herbaceous plants. *MAP PAGE:* 2/4

50 **Parkinson Herbs,** Barras Moor Farm, Perran-ar-Worthal, Truro, Cornwall TR3 7PE
TEL: (0872) 864380 *CONTACT:* Elizabeth Parkinson
W/SALE or RETAIL: Retail *OPENING TIMES:* 0900-1700 daily.
MAIL ORDER: Yes *MIN VALUE:* None *CAT. COST:* Free *EXPORT:* No
SPECIALITIES: Herbs. *MAP PAGE:* **1**

52 **Porthpean House Gardens,** Porthpean, St. Austell, Cornwall PL26 6AX
TEL: (0726) 72888 *CONTACT:* Mrs Petherick
W/SALE or RETAIL: Both *OPENING TIMES:* 0900-1700 Mon-Fri. Sat & Sun by appt.
MAIL ORDER: Yes *MIN VALUE:* None *CAT. COST:* None issued *EXPORT:* Yes
SPECIALITIES: Camellia & Shrubs for acid soils. *MAP PAGE:* **1**

53 **The Priory,** Kemerton, Tewkesbury, Gloucestershire GL20 7SN
TEL: (038689) 258 *CONTACT:* P Healing
W/SALE or RETAIL: Retail *OPENING TIMES:* Thurs afternoons.
MAIL ORDER: No *MIN VALUE:* *CAT. COST:* None issued *EXPORT:* No
SPECIALITIES: Rare and unusual plants. *MAP PAGE:* **2**

◆ See also Display Advertisements

56 **Ryans Nurseries,** Lissivigeen, Killarney, Co. Kerry, Eire
TEL: (0001) 6433507 *CONTACT:* Mr T Ryan
W/SALE or RETAIL: Retail *OPENING TIMES:* 0900-1800 Mon-Sat 1400-1800 Sun.
MAIL ORDER: No *MIN VALUE:* *CAT. COST:* *EXPORT:*
SPECIALITIES: Camellias, Pieris, Azaleas, Acacia, Eucalyptus, Dicksonia & many tender & rare plants. *MAP PAGE:* **10**

60 **Elizabeth Smith,** Downside, Bowling Green, Constantine, Falmouth, Cornwall TR11 5AP
TEL: (0326) 40797 *CONTACT:* Elizabeth Smith
W/SALE or RETAIL: Retail *OPENING TIMES:*
MAIL ORDER: Only *MIN VALUE:* None *CAT. COST:* *EXPORT:* Yes
SPECIALITIES: Scented Violets. NOTE: Telephone or Postal enquiries please.

61 **Southcombe Garden Plant Nursery,** Widecombe-in-the-Moor, Newton Abbot, Devon TQ13 7TU
TEL: *CONTACT:* C & T Wood
W/SALE or RETAIL: Retail *OPENING TIMES:* 1000-dusk daily.
MAIL ORDER: No *MIN VALUE:* *CAT. COST:* None issued *EXPORT:* No
SPECIALITIES: General, especially Alpines. *MAP PAGE:* **1**

62 **Southwick Country Herbs,** Southwick Farm, Nomansland, Nr Tiverton, Devon EX16 8NW
TEL: (0884) 861099 *CONTACT:* Martin & Tricha Menist
W/SALE or RETAIL: Both *OPENING TIMES:* 1000-1730 Mon-Sat, 1100-1730 most Sun. Please phone first for directions.
MAIL ORDER: Yes *MIN VALUE:* 6 plants + £3 p&p *CAT. COST:* Sae *EXPORT:* No
SPECIALITIES: Over 200 Herbs. *MAP PAGE:* **1**

64 **Totties Nursery,** Greenhill Bank Road, New Mill, Holmfirth, West Yorkshire HD7 1UN
TEL: (0484) 683363 *CONTACT:* David A Shires
W/SALE or RETAIL: Both *OPENING TIMES:* 0900-1915 Mon-Fri & 0900-1800 Sat & Sun Summer. 0900-1700 daily Winter.
MAIL ORDER: No *MIN VALUE:* *CAT. COST:* *EXPORT:* No
SPECIALITIES: Large selection of ornamental Trees, field and container grown Conifers. Rhododendron & Azalea. Huge range of herbaceous Perennials. *MAP PAGE:* **5**

65 **Triscombe Nurseries,** West Bagborough, Nr Taunton, Somerset TA4 3HG
TEL: (098 48) 267 *CONTACT:* S Parkman
◆ *W/SALE or RETAIL:* Retail *OPENING TIMES:* 0900-1300 & 1400-1730 Mon-Sat. 1400-1730 Sun & Bank Hols.
MAIL ORDER: No *MIN VALUE:* *CAT. COST:* None issued *EXPORT:* No
SPECIALITIES: Rock plants & Alpines, Herbaceous, Conifers and unusual Shrubs. *MAP PAGE:* **1**

66 **Westdale Nurseries,** Holt Road, Bradford-on-Avon, Wiltshire BA15 1TS
TEL: (02216) 3258 *CONTACT:* C W & P A Clarke
W/SALE or RETAIL: Both *OPENING TIMES:* 0830-1800 daily Summer. 0900-1630 daily Winter
MAIL ORDER: No *MIN VALUE:* *CAT. COST:* *EXPORT:* No
SPECIALITIES: Geranium & Conservatory plants. *MAP PAGE:* **2**

67 **Westhall Herbs,** Church Lane, Westhall, Nr Halesworth, Suffolk IP19 8NU
TEL: (050 279) 646 *CONTACT:* Miss Mildred Durne
W/SALE or RETAIL: Both *OPENING TIMES:* 1000-1700 Sat & Sun, 1400-1700 Mon, Wed, Thu, Fri Apr-Oct & by appt.
MAIL ORDER: Yes *MIN VALUE:* No *CAT. COST:* 60p *EXPORT:* No
SPECIALITIES: Herbs. *MAP PAGE:* **6**

72 **Eden Plants,** Eden, Rossinver, Co. Leitrim, Eire
TEL: (010 353) 72 54122 *CONTACT:* Rod Alston & Dolores Keegan
W/SALE or RETAIL: Both *OPENING TIMES:* 1400-1800 daily & by appt.
MAIL ORDER: Yes *MIN VALUE:* None *CAT. COST:* Sae for list *EXPORT:* Yes
SPECIALITIES: Large range of hardy Herbs. NOTE: £1.00 for Catalogue & growing guide.
MAP PAGE: **10**

75 **Fold Garden,** 26 Fold Lane, Biddulph, Staffordshire ST8 7SG
TEL: (0782) 513028 *CONTACT:* M P Machin
W/SALE or RETAIL: *OPENING TIMES:* By appt. only
MAIL ORDER: Yes *MIN VALUE:* £2.75 *CAT. COST:* 30p *EXPORT:*
SPECIALITIES: Herbs & Wild Flowers. *MAP PAGE:* **5**

76 **Southfarthing Alpines,** Southfarthing, Hawkenbury, Staplehurst, Kent TN12 0ED
TEL: (0580) 892140 *CONTACT:* Ivan Smith
W/SALE or RETAIL: Retail *OPENING TIMES:* Most days - please check first.
MAIL ORDER: No *MIN VALUE:* *CAT. COST:* None issued *EXPORT:* No
SPECIALITIES: Alpines. *MAP PAGE:* **3**

77 **The Old Mill Herbary,** Helland Bridge, Bodmin, Cornwall PL30 4QR
TEL: (020 884) 206 *CONTACT:* Mrs B Whurr
W/SALE or RETAIL: *OPENING TIMES:* 1000-1700 Apr-Oct
MAIL ORDER: No *MIN VALUE:* *CAT. COST:* £1.00 *EXPORT:*
SPECIALITIES: Culinary, Medicinal & Aromatic Herbs, Shrubs, Climbing & Herbaceous plants.
MAP PAGE: **1**

78 **Ty'r Orsaf Nursery,** Maentwrog Road, Gellilydan, Gwynedd LL41 4RB
TEL: (076 685) 233 *CONTACT:* A G & M Faulkner
W/SALE or RETAIL: Retail *OPENING TIMES:* 1000-dusk Mon-Sat, 1430-dusk Sun.
MAIL ORDER: Yes *MIN VALUE:* None *CAT. COST:* Sae *EXPORT:* No
SPECIALITIES: Hardy herbaceous & Shrubs. *MAP PAGE:* **4**

79 **Worth Trees,** Fleet Estate Office, Fleet, Spalding, Lincolnshire PE12 8LR
TEL: (0406) 22778 *FAX:* (0406) 25402 *CONTACT:* Stuart Gray
W/SALE or RETAIL: Both *OPENING TIMES:* 0800-1730
MAIL ORDER: No *MIN VALUE:* *CAT. COST:* Free *EXPORT:* Yes
SPECIALITIES: Native Trees in all sizes from Seed. *MAP PAGE:* **6**

80 **Kinlochlaich House,** Garden Plant Centre, Appin, Argyll PA38 43D
TEL: (063 173) 342 *CONTACT:* D E Hutchison
W/SALE or RETAIL: Retail *OPENING TIMES:* 0930-1800 Mon-Sat 1030-1800 Sun Apr-Oct, 0930-1700 Mon-Sat Nov-Mar.
MAIL ORDER: No *MIN VALUE:* *CAT. COST:* *EXPORT:* No
SPECIALITIES: Wide general range of Shrubs & Perennials (over 2000 plants varieties). Particularly suitable for West coast locations i.e. damp and acid. *MAP PAGE:* **9**

81 **C E & D M Nurseries,** The Walnuts, 36 Main Street, Baston, Peterborough, Northamptonshire PE6 9PB
TEL: (0778 36) 483 *CONTACT:* Mrs D M Fletcher
W/SALE or RETAIL: Retail *OPENING TIMES:*
MAIL ORDER: Only *MIN VALUE:* None *CAT. COST:* 2 x 1st class *EXPORT:* No
SPECIALITIES: Hardy Herbaceous Perennials.

82 **Addisford Hardy Plant Nursery,** West Lane, Dolton, Devon EX19 8QU
TEL: (08054) 365 *CONTACT:* Mrs K A Taylor
W/SALE or RETAIL: *OPENING TIMES:* 1000-1700 Sun, Mon, Wed, Thu, Fri. mid-March - mid-Oct.
MAIL ORDER: Yes *MIN VALUE:* None *CAT. COST:* 50p *EXPORT:*
SPECIALITIES: Hardy Perennials, Ground cover & moisture lovers *MAP PAGE:* **1**

83 **Mill Hill Plants,** Mill Hill House, Elston Lane, East Stoke, Newark, Nottinghamshire NG23 5QJ
TEL: (0636) 525460 *CONTACT:* G M Gregory
◆ *W/SALE or RETAIL:* Retail *OPENING TIMES:* 1000-1800 Wed-Sun & Bank Hols Mar-Oct & by appt.
MAIL ORDER: No *MIN VALUE:* *CAT. COST:* 3 x 1st class *EXPORT:* No
SPECIALITIES: General range. *MAP PAGE:* **7**

85 **Hunters Oak Nursery,** Bere Alston, Yelverton, Devon PL20 7HT
TEL: (0822) 840289 *CONTACT:* Denise Dion
◆ *W/SALE or RETAIL:* Both *OPENING TIMES:* 1100-1800 Mon, Tue, Thu, Fri, 1000-1800 Sat & Sun Mar 1st-Sep 30th. Winter by appt.
MAIL ORDER: Yes *MIN VALUE:* £5.00 *CAT. COST:* 50p *EXPORT:* No
SPECIALITIES: Alpines (250 varieties), Herbs (130 varieties) & hardy Perennials. *MAP PAGE:* **1**

86 **R F Beeston,** (Office) 294 Ombersley Rd., Worcestershire WR3 7HD
TEL: (0905) 53245 *CONTACT:* R F Beeston
W/SALE or RETAIL: Retail *OPENING TIMES:* 1000-1300 & 1400-1700 Wed-Fri Mar 1-Oct 31 & by appt.
MAIL ORDER: Yes *MIN VALUE:* None *CAT. COST:* Sae *EXPORT:* No
SPECIALITIES: Rare Alpines, esp. Androsace, Dionysia, Primula, Saxifraga,Gentiana & Daphne. NOTE: Nursery at Bevere Nursery, Bevere, Worcester. *MAP PAGE:* **2**

89 **Cranesbill Nursery,** White Cottage, Stock Green, Nr. Redditch, Worcestershire
TEL: (0386) 792414 *CONTACT:* Mrs S M Bates
W/SALE or RETAIL: Retail *OPENING TIMES:* 1000-1730 Fri-Wed Easter-mid Oct. Except August.
MAIL ORDER: Yes *MIN VALUE:* None *CAT. COST:* 4 x 1st class *EXPORT:* No
SPECIALITIES: Hardy Geraniums *MAP PAGE:* **2**

91 **The Wildlife Gardening Centre,** The Apple Centre, Kingston Bagpuize, Abingdon, Oxfordshire OX13 5AN
TEL: (0865) 249414 evngs. *CONTACT:* Jenny Steel & Alan Pottinger
W/SALE or RETAIL: Both *OPENING TIMES:* 1000-1700 or dusk Wed-Mon.
MAIL ORDER: Yes *MIN VALUE:* None *CAT. COST:* 2 x 1st class *EXPORT:* No
SPECIALITIES: Native Wild Flowers & Shrubs, Cottage garden plants, Herbs, barerooted Hedging & Trees. *MAP PAGE:* **2**

92 **The Herbary Plant Centre,** 89 Station Road, Herne Bay, Kent CT6 5QQ
TEL: (0227) 362409 *CONTACT:*
◆ *W/SALE or RETAIL:* Retail *OPENING TIMES:* 1000-1700 Wed, Fri & Sat Mar-Oct.
MAIL ORDER: No *MIN VALUE:* *CAT. COST:* *EXPORT:* No
SPECIALITIES: Plants suitable for Tufa growing. Aromatic Herbs, interesting Shrubs & Herbaceous. *MAP PAGE:* **3**

93 **Lower Kenneggy Nurseries,** Halzephron, Germoe Crossroads, Penzance, Cornwall TR20 9AA
TEL: (0736) 762382 *CONTACT:* Stephen Mules
W/SALE or RETAIL: Both *OPENING TIMES:* 0900-1700 Tue-Sun Apr-Oct, 1400-1700 Tue-Sun Nov-Mar.
MAIL ORDER: No *MIN VALUE:* None *CAT. COST:* Sae *EXPORT:* No
SPECIALITIES: Broad range, esp. for milder coastal areas, many unusual. *MAP PAGE:* **1**

94 **Hill Farm Herbs,** Park Walk, Brigstock, Kettering, Northants NN14 3HH
TEL: (0536) 373694 *FAX:* (0536) 373246 *CONTACT:* Mrs Eileen Simpson
W/SALE or RETAIL: *OPENING TIMES:* 1030-1730 daily Easter - New Year
MAIL ORDER: No *MIN VALUE:* *CAT. COST:* 5 x 1st class *EXPORT:*
SPECIALITIES: Herbs & Cottage garden plants *MAP PAGE:* **6**

95 **Treasures of Tenbury Ltd,** Burford House Gardens, Tenbury Wells, Worcestershire WR15 8HQ
TEL: (0584) 810777 *CONTACT:* General Manager
W/SALE or RETAIL: Retail *OPENING TIMES:* 1000-1800 Mon-Sat, 1400-1800 Sun. Until dusk in Winter.
MAIL ORDER: Yes* *MIN VALUE:* *CAT. COST:* None available *EXPORT:* Yes
SPECIALITIES: Clematis and Herbaceous, many unusual. *NOTE: Clematis plants ONLY by Mail Order. *MAP PAGE:* **2/4**

96 **Smallscape Nursery,** 3 Hundon Close, Stradishall, Nr Newmarket, Suffolk CB8 9YF
TEL: (0440) 820336 *CONTACT:* Stephen & Leigh Sage
W/SALE or RETAIL: *OPENING TIMES:* Most times, but please telephone first.
MAIL ORDER: Yes *MIN VALUE:* None *CAT. COST:* 4 x 1st class *EXPORT:*
SPECIALITIES: Interesting, unusual & rare Alpines, Herbaceous, Shrubs, Trees & tender Perennials sold Mail Order as rooted plants. *MAP PAGE:* **6**

SEED SUPPLIERS

A **Vegetable Variety Finder** is due to be published by the Henry Doublday Research Association in November 1991. For details please write to:

HDRA (Sales) Ltd.
National Centre for Organic Gardening
Ryton-on-Dunsmore
Coventry CV8 3LG

Allwoods Bros, Hassocks, West Sussex BN6 9NB
TEL: (079 18) 4229 *CONTACT:* W Rickaby *CAT. COST:* 2 x 1st class
SPECIALITIES: Carnations, Pinks & Dianthus

Ashwood Nurseries, Greenforge, Kingswinford, West Midlands DY6 0AE
TEL: (0384) 401996 *CONTACT:* John Massey & Philip Baulk *CAT. COST:* 9 x 6 Sae
SPECIALITIES: Lewisias

D T Brown & Co Ltd., Station Road, Poulton-le-Fylde, Blackpool, FY6 7HX
TEL: (0253) 882371 *FAX:* (0253) 890923 *CONTACT:* *CAT. COST:* Free
SPECIALITIES: Flowers, Grass, & Vegetable seed..

Carters Seeds Ltd., Hele Road, Torquay, Devon TQ2 7QJ
TEL: (0803) 616156 *FAX:* (0803) 615747 *CONTACT:* D G Arnold *CAT. COST:* Free
SPECIALITIES: General range especially Pansies.

Cheshire Herbs, Fourfields, Forest Road, Little Budworth, Cheshire CW6 9ES
TEL: (0829) 760578 *CONTACT:* Mr & Mrs Ted Riddell *CAT. COST:* 20p
SPECIALITIES: Herbs

Chiltern Seeds, Bortree Stile, Ulverston, Cumbria LA12 7PB
TEL: (0229) 581137 *FAX:* (0229) 54549 *CONTACT:* *CAT. COST:* 3 x 2nd class
◆ *SPECIALITIES:* Nearly 4,000 items of all kind - Wild Flowers, Trees, Shrubs, Cacti, Annuals, Houseplants, Vegetables & Herbs.

Cowcombe Farm Herbs, Gipsy Lane, Chalford, Stroud, Gloucestershire GL6 8HP
TEL: (0285 76) 544 *CONTACT:* Mrs C M Barnett *CAT. COST:* 2 x 2nd class
SPECIALITIES: Herbs & Wild flowers.

B & D Davies, 2 Wirral View, Connah's Quay, Deeside, Clwyd CH5 4TE
TEL: (0244) 818833 *CONTACT:* Mr B Davies *CAT. COST:* Sae
SPECIALITIES: Trees & Shrubs especially Conifers.

Samuel Dobie & Sons Ltd., Broomhill Way, Torquay, Devon TQ2 7QW
TEL: (0803) 616281 *CONTACT:* Mr T J Sharples *CAT. COST:* Free
SPECIALITIES: Flower & Vegetable seeds, Plants, Bulbs & Garden sundries.

Emorsgate Seed, Terrington Court, Terrington St Clement, Kings Lynn Norfolk PE34 4NT
TEL: (0553) 829028 *CONTACT:* Donald Macintyre *CAT. COST:* Free
SPECIALITIES: Wild British Flowers & Grasses.

Field House Nurseries, Leake Road, Gotham, Nottingham NG11 0JN
TEL: (0602) 830278 *CONTACT:* Doug Lochhead *CAT. COST:* 3 x 1st class
SPECIALITIES: Primulas & Alpines.

Mr Fothergill's Seeds Ltd., Gazeley Road, Kentford, Newmarket, Suffolk CB8 7QB
TEL: (0638) 751161 *CONTACT:* Gillie Gray or Ann Loads *CAT. COST:* Free
SPECIALITIES: Annual, Biennials, Perennials, Herbs, Vegetables & Bulbs.

HDRA (Sales) Ltd., National Centre for Organic Gardening, Ryton-on-Dunsmore, Coventry, Warwickshire CV8 3LG
TEL: (0203) 303517 *FAX:* (0203) 639229 *CONTACT:* Mr J Vyse *CAT. COST:* Free
SPECIALITIES: Untreated Seeds. Old & unusual varieties of Vegetables & Oriental Salad Vegetables.

James Henderson & Sons, Kingholm Quay, Dumfries DG1 4SU
TEL: (0387) 52234 *FAX:* (0387) 62302 *CONTACT:* *CAT. COST:* Free
SPECIALITIES: Over 30 varieties of Scottish Seed Potatoes

W W Johnson & Son Ltd., London Road, Boston, Lincolnshire PE21 8AD
TEL: (0205) 365051 *FAX:* (0205) 310148 *CONTACT:* R W Johnson *CAT. COST:* Free
SPECIALITIES: Flower & Vegetable & Lawn Grass seed.

Lancashire Propagators, 147 Liverpool Old Road, Much Hoole, Nr Preston, Lancashire PR4 4GB
TEL: (0772) 613016 *CONTACT:* Miss Shirley Ogden *CAT. COST:* Sae.
SPECIALITIES: Flower & Vegetable seeds, some rare and not available in UK.

Landlife Wildflowers Ltd., The Old Police Station, Lark Lane, Liverpool, West Midlands L17 8UU
TEL: (051 728) 7011 *CONTACT:* Gillian Watson *CAT. COST:* Free
SPECIALITIES: Native Herbaceous plants.

Lochside Alpine Nursery, Lochside, Ulbster, Caithness, Highland KW2 6AA
TEL: (095 585) 320 *CONTACT:* Terry & Jane Clarke *CAT. COST:* Sae
SPECIALITIES: Alpine plants

S E Marshall & Co Ltd., Regal Road, Wisbech, Cambridgeshire PE13 2RF
TEL: (0945) 583407 *FAX:* (0945) 588235 *CONTACT:* *CAT. COST:* Free
SPECIALITIES: Vegetable seed, Onion Sets & Shallots, seed Potatoes.

J E Martin, 4 Church Street, Market Harborough, Leicestershire LE16 7AA
TEL: (0858) 462751 *FAX:* (0858) 434544 *CONTACT:* *CAT. COST:* Free (List)
SPECIALITIES: Over 30 varieties of Scotch & Dutch Seed Potatoes.

John Morley, North Green Only, Stoven, Beccles, Suffolk NR34 8DG
TEL: *CONTACT:* John Morley *CAT. COST:* 50p + stamp
SPECIALITIES: Small specialist range of Galanthus, Allium, Fritillaria and choice shrubs.

Andrew Norfield Trees & Seeds, Lower Meend, St Briavels, Gloucestershire GL15 6RW
TEL: (0594) 530134 *CONTACT:* Andrew Norfield *CAT. COST:* 1 x 1st class
SPECIALITIES: Germinated & pretreated Seed of hardy Trees, Shrubs, Herbaceous & House plants.

Stuart Ogg Hopton, Fletching Street, Mayfield, East Sussex TN20 6TL
TEL: (0435) 873322 *CONTACT:* Stuart Ogg *CAT. COST:* Sae
SPECIALITIES: Delphiniums.

Plant World Botanic Gardens, Seed Dept. (PF) St Marychurch Road, Newton Abbot, Devon
TEL: (0803) 872939 *CONTACT:* Ray Brown *CAT. COST:* 80p in stamps
◆ *SPECIALITIES:* Meconopsis, Gentiana, Primula, Aquilegia, Campanula, Viola, Lewisia, Salvia, Eryngium.

W Robinson & Sons Ltd., Sunny Bank, Forton, Nr Preston, Lancashire PR3 0BN
TEL: (0524) 791210 *FAX:* (0524) 791933 *CONTACT:* Miss Robinson *CAT. COST:* Free
SPECIALITIES: Mammoth Vegetable seed.

Rock Park Nurseries, Church Lane, Calstock, Cornwall PL18 9QH
TEL: (0822) 833238 *FAX:* (0822) 833238 *CONTACT:* V & M O'Neill *CAT. COST:* 2 x 1st class
SPECIALITIES: Exotic seeds collected from around the world, promulgated in a periodical newsletter. To register, send details to above address.

◆ See also Display Advertisements

Salley Gardens, 8 Radcliffe Mount, West Bridgford, Nottingham NG2 5FY
TEL: (0602) 813690 *CONTACT:* Richard Lewin *CAT. COST:* Sae
SPECIALITIES: Wildflower & Medicinal Herbs.

Seeds by Size, 70 Varney Road, Hemel Hempstead, Hertfordshire HP1 1TB
TEL: (0422) 251458 *CONTACT:* Mr John Robert Size *CAT. COST:* Free
SPECIALITIES: Flowers & Vegetables. 900 varieties of Vegetable, (147 Cabbage, 93 Cauliflower, 56 Onion) & 230 varieties of Sweet Pea.

Stewart's (Nottingham) Ltd., 3 George Street, Nottingham NG1 3BH
TEL: (0602) 476338 *CONTACT:* Brenda Lochhead *CAT. COST:* Sae
SPECIALITIES: Large general range esp. Vegetables.

Stoke Lacy Herb Garden, Bromyard, Herefordshire HR7 4JH
TEL: (0432) 820232 *CONTACT:* Madge Hooper *CAT. COST:* 30p
SPECIALITIES: Herbs.

Suffolk Herbs, Sawyers Farm, Little Cornard, Sudbury, Suffolk CO10 0NY
TEL: (0787) 227247 *FAX:* (0787) 227258 *CONTACT:* John Stevens *CAT. COST:* Free
SPECIALITIES: Herbs, Wildflowers & Conservation seeds & unusual vegetables. Cottage Flowers,

Suttons Seeds Ltd., Hele Road, Torquay, Devon TQ2 7QJ
TEL: (0803) 612011 *FAX:* (0803) 615747 *CONTACT:* Customer Services *CAT. COST:* Free
SPECIALITIES: Wide general range.

A P & E V Tabraham, Porth Mellon, St. Mary's, Isles of Scilly TR21 0JY
TEL: (0720) 22759 *CONTACT:* A P & E V Tabraham *CAT. COST:* Sae for list
SPECIALITIES: Unusual Seed of plants growing in the Isles of Scilly.

Thompson & Morgan, London Road, Ipswich, Suffolk IP2 0BA
TEL: (0473) 688588 *FAX:* (0473) 680199 *CONTACT:* Martin Thrower *CAT. COST:* Free
SPECIALITIES: Largest Seed catalogue in the world.

Thuya Alpine Nursery, Glebelands, Hartpury, Gloucestershire GL19 3BW
TEL: (045270) 548 *CONTACT:* S W Bond *CAT. COST:* Sae
SPECIALITIES: General range.

Edwin Tucker & Sons, Brewery Meadow, Stonepark, Asburton, Devon TQ13 7DG
TEL: (0364) 52403 *FAX:* (0364) 52403 Ext22 *CONTACT:* Geoff Penton *CAT. COST:* Free
SPECIALITIES: Over 40 varieties of Seed Potatoes. Wide range of Vegetables, Green Manures & sprouting seeds in packets.

Unwins Seeds Ltd., Mail Order Dept. Histon, Cambridgeshire CB4 4ZZ
TEL: (0945) 588522 *CONTACT:* *CAT. COST:* Free
SPECIALITIES: Wide general range particularly Sweet Peas.

Wildseeds, Branas Llandderfel, Gwynedd LL23 7RF
TEL: (06783) 427 *CONTACT:* Mr M Thorne *CAT. COST:* Free
SPECIALITIES: Wild Flower seeds.

REVERSE SYNONYMS

In order to assist users to establish from which Genera an unfamiliar plant name may have been transferred, the following list of reverse synonyms may help.
For further details see D J Mabberley ***The Plant-Book***, Cambridge University Press, 1987

ACACIA from	RACOSPERMA	BLECHNUM	LOMARIA
ACCA	FEIJOA	BOYKINIA	TELESONIX
ACHILLEA	ANTHEMIS	BRACHYGLOTTIS	SENECIO
ACINOS	CALAMINTHA	BRIMEURA	HYACINTHUS
ACINOS	MICROMERIA	BRODIAEA	TRITELEIA
ACINOS	THYMUS	BRUGMANSIA	DATURA
ACTINIDIA	KIWI FRUIT	BRUNNERA	ANCHUSA
AEONIUM	SEMPERVIVUM	BUGLOSSOIDES	LITHOSPERMUM
AETHIONEMA	EUNOMIA	BUPHTHALMUM	INULA
AGAPETES	PENTAPTERYGIUM	CALADIUM	XANTHOSOMA
AGARISTA	LEUCOTHOE	CALAMINTHA	CLINOPODIUM
AGASTACHE	CEDRONELLA	CALOCEDRUS	LIBOCEDRUS
AICHRYSON	AEONIUM	CALOMERIA	HUMEA
ALBIZIA	ACACIA	CALOSCORDUM	NOTHOSCORDUM
ALLOCASUARINA	CASUARINA	CAMPANULA	AZORINA
ALOYSIA	LIPPIA	CAMPTOSORUS	ASPLENIUM
ALSOBIA	EPISCIA	CARDAMINE	DENTARIA
ALYOGYNE	HIBISCUS	CARICA	PAWPAW
X AMARYGIA	AMARYLLIS	CARYA	PECAN
AMPELOPSIS	VITIS	CASSIOPE	HARRIMANELLA
ANAPHALIS	GNAPHALIUM	CASTANEA	CHESTNUT, Sweet
ANCHUSA	LYCOPSIS	CENTAURIUM	ERYTHRAEA
ANISODONTEA	MALVASTRUM	CENTRANTHUS	KENTRANTHUS
ANOMATHECA	LAPEIROUSIA	CENTRANTHUS	VALERIANA
ANREDERA	BOUSSINGAULTIA	CEPHALARIA	SCABIOSA
APHANES	ALCHEMILLA	CERATOSTIGMA	PLUMBAGO
ARCTOTIS	VENIDIUM	CETERACH	ASPLENIUM
ARCTOTIS	X VENIDIO-ARCTOTIS	CHAENOMELES	CYDONIA
ARECASTRUM	COCOS	CHAENORHINUM	LINARIA
ARENGA	DIDYMOSPERMA	CHAMAECYPARIS	CUPRESSUS
ARGYRANTHEMUM	ANTHEMIS	CHAMAEDAPHNE	CASSANDRA
ARGYRANTHEMUM	CHRYSANTHEMUM	CHAMAEMELUM	ANTHEMIS
ARMORACIA	COCHLEARIA	CHASMANTHIUM	UNIOLA
ARUNDINARIA	THAMNOCALAMUS	CHEIRANTHUS	ERYSIMUM
ASARINA	ANTIRRHINUM	CHIASTOPHYLLUM	COTYLEDON
ASARINA	MAURANDYA	CHIMNOBAMBUSA	ARUNDINARIA
ASPARAGUS	SMILAX	CHIMONOBAMBUSA	ARUNDINARIA
ASPERULA	GALIUM	CHIMONOBAMBUSA	THAMNOCALAMUS
ASPHODELINE	ASPHODELUS	CHIONOHEBE	PYGMAEA
ASTER	MICROGLOSSA	CHLOROPHYTUM	DIURANTHERA
ASTER	CRINITARIA	CHRYSANTHEMOPSIS	ARGYRANTHEMUM
ASTILBOIDES	RODGERSIA	CHRYSANTHEMOPSIS	LEUCANTHEMUM
AZORELLA	BOLAX	CHRYSANTHEMOPSIS	LEUCANTHEMOPSIS
BALSAMITA	CHRYSANTHEMUM	CHRYSANTHEMOPSIS	CHRYSANTHEMUM
BALSAMITA	TANACETUM	CICERBITA	LACTUCA
BAMBUSA	ARUNDINARIA	CIONURA	MARSDENIA
BELLEVALIA	MUSCARI	X CITROFORTUNELLA	CALAMONDIN

X CITROFORTUNELLA	CITRUS
CITRUS	MANDARIN
CITRUS	GRAPEFRUIT
CITRUS	SATSUMA
CITRUS	UGLI
CITRUS	ORANGE, Bittersweet
CITRUS	ORANGE, Sour or Seville
CITRUS	CITRON
CITRUS	MANDARIN, Sour
CITRUS	SHADDOCK
CITRUS	LIME, Rangpur
CITRUS	TANGERINE
CITRUS	TANGOR
CITRUS	LIME
CITRUS	PUMMELO
CITRUS	TANGELO
CLARKIA	GODETIA
CLAYTONIA	MONTIA
CLAYTONIA	CALANDRINIA
CLEMATIS	ATRAGENE
CLEYERA	EURYA
CLINOPODIUM	ACINOS
CLINOPODIUM	CALAMINTHA
CNICUS	CARDUUS
COCOS	COCONUT
COFFEA	COFFEE
CONSOLIDA	DELPHINIUM
CORDYLINE	DRACAENA
CORNUS	CHAMAEPERICLYMENUM
CORTADERIA	GYNERIUM
CORYLUS	NUT, Cob & Filbert
COSMOS	BIDENS
COTINUS	RHUS
COTULA	LEPTINELLA
CRASSULA	SEDUM
CRASSULA	TILLAEA
CRINODENDRON	TRICUSPIDARIA
CROCOSMIA	CURTONUS
CROCOSMIA	MONTBRETIA
CROCOSMIA	ANTHOLYZA
CRUCIATA	GALIUM
CTENANTHE	CALATHEA
X CUPRESSOCYPARIS	CHAMAECYPARIS
CYDONIA	QUINCE
CYMBALARIA	LINARIA
CYNARA	SCOLYMUS
CYRTANTHUS	VALLOTA
CYTISUS	LEMBOTROPIS
CYTISUS	CHAMAECYTISUS
CYTISUS	GENISTA
DABOECIA	MENZIESIA
DACRYCARPUS	PODOCARPUS
DACTYLORHIZA	ORCHIS
DAISWA	PARIS

DANAE	RUSCUS
DARMERA	PELTIPHYLLUM
DELOSPERMA	MESEMBRYANTHEMUM
DELOSPERMA	LAMPRANTHUS
DENDRANTHEMA	CHRYSANTHEMUM
DESMODIUM	LESPEDEZA
DICHELOSTEMMA	TRITELEIA
DICLIPTERA	JUSTICIA
DIETES	MORAEA
DISPOROPSIS	POLYGONATUM
DOLICOTHRIX	HELICHRYSUM
DRACUNCULUS	ARUM
DREGEA	WATTAKAKA
DREPANOSTACHYUM	ARUNDINARIA
DREPANOSTACHYUM	THAMNOCALAMUS
DREPANOSTACHYUM	THAMNOCALAMUS
DUCHESNEA	FRAGARIA
ECHINACEA	RUDBECKIA
EDRAIANTHUS	WAHLENBERGIA
ELEUTHEROCOCCUS	ACANTHOPANAX
ELLIOTTIA	CLADOTHAMNUS
ELLIOTTIA	BOTRYOSTEGE
ELLIOTTIA	TRIPETALEIA
ELYMUS	AGROPYRON
ELYMUS	LEYMUS
ENSETE	MUSA
EPILOBIUM	ZAUSCHNERIA
EPILOBIUM	CHAMAENERION
EPIPREMNUM	PHILODENDRON
EPIPREMNUM	SCINDAPSUS
EPISCIA	ALSOBIA
ERANTHIS	ACONITUM
ERICA	CALLUNA
ERIGERON	ASTER
ERYBOTRYA	LOCQUAT
ERYSIMUM	CHEIRANTHUS
EURYOPS	URSINIA
EURYOPS	SENECIO
FALLOPIA	BILDERDYKIA
FALLOPIA	POLYGONUM
FARFUGIUM	LIGULARIA
FATSIA	ARALIA
FELICIA	AGATHAEA
FELICIA	ASTER
FIBIGIA	FARSETIA
FICUS	FIG
FILIPENDULA	SPIRAEA
FOENICULUM	FERULA
FORTUNELLA	CITRUS
FRAGARIA	STRAWBERRY
GALIUM	ASPERULA
GAULTHERIA	PERNETTYA
GAULTHERIA	X GAULNETTYA
GAULTHERIA	CHIOGENES

GELASINE	SISYRINCHIUM
GENISTA	CHAMAESPARTIUM
GENTIANOPSIS	GENTIANA
GLADIOLUS	ACIDANTHERA
GLECHOMA	NEPETA
GONIOLIMON	LIMONIUM
GRAPTOPETALUM	SEDUM
GREENOVIA	SEMPERVIVUM
GYMNOSPERMUM	LEONTICE
HABRANTHUS	ZEPHYRANTHES
X HALIMIOCISTUS	HALIMIUM
X HALIMIOCISTUS	CISTUS
HALIMIUM	HELIANTHEMUM
HALIMIUM	X HALIMIOCISTUS
HALIMIUM	CISTUS
HALOCARPUS	DACRYDIUM
HAPLOPAPPUS	ERIGERON
HAPLOPAPPUS	ISOCOMA
HAPLOPAPPUS	TONESTUS
HEDYOTIS	HOUSTONIA
HEDYSCEPE	KENTIA
HELICHRYSUM	GNAPHALIUM
HELICHRYSUM	OZOTHAMNUS
HELICTOTRICHON	AVENA
HEPATICA	ANEMONE
HERMODACTYLUS	IRIS
HETEROCENTRON	SCHIZOCENTRON
HETEROMELES	PHOTINIA
HIERACIUM	ANDRYALA
HIPPEASTRUM	RHODOPHIALA
HIPPEASTRUM	AMARYLLIS
HIPPOCREPIS	CORONILLA
HOHERIA	PLAGIANTHUS
HOWEIA	KENTIA
HYACINTHOIDES	SCILLA
HYACINTHOIDES	ENDYMION
HYMENOCALLIS	ISMENE
HYMENOXYS	ACTINELLA
HYOPHORBE	MASCARENA
INDOCALAMUS	SASA
INDOCALAMUS	THAMNOCALAMUS
IPHEION	BEAUVERDIA
IPHEION	TRITELEIA
IPOMOEA	PHARBITIS
IPOMOPSIS	GILIA
JOVIBARBA	SEMPERVIVUM
JUGLANS	WALNUT, Common
JUSTICIA	BELOPERONE
JUSTICIA	JACOBINIA
JUSTICIA	LIBONIA
KALANCHOE	KITCHINGIA
KALIMERIS	BOLTONIA
KNAUTIA	SCABIOSA
KUNZEA	LEPTOSPERMUM
LABLAB	DOLICHOS
LAGAROSIPHON	ELODEA
LAGAROSTROBOS	DACRYDIUM
LAMIUM	GALEOBDOLON
LAMIUM	LAMIASTRUM
LAMPRANTHUS	OSCULARIA
LAMPRANTHUS	MESEMBRYANTHEMUM
LAVATERA	MALVA
LEDEBOURIA	SCILLA
LEMBOTROPIS	CYTISUS
LEPTINELLA	COTULA
LEUCANTHEMELLA	LEUCANTHEMUM
LEUCANTHEMELLA	CHRYSANTHEMUM
LEUCANTHEMOPSIS	CHRYSANTHEMUM
LEUCANTHEMOPSIS	TANACETUM
LEUCANTHEMUM	CHRYSANTHEMUM
LEUCOPOGON	CYATHODES
LEUCORAOULIA	RAOULIA
LEUZEA	CENTAUREA
LHOTZKYA	CALYTRIX
LIBOCEDRUS	AUSTROCEDRUS
LIGULARIA	CREMANTHODIUM
LIGULARIA	SENECIO
LIGUSTRUM	PARASYRINGA
LILIUM	NOMOCHARIS
LIMONIUM	STATICE
LINANTHUS	LINANTHASTRUM
LINDERA	PARABENZOIN
LIRIOPE	OPHIOPOGON
LITHOCARPUS	QUERCUS
LITHODORA	LITHOSPERMUM
LOBELIA	PRATIA
LOPHOMYRTUS	MYRTUS
LOTUS	DORYCNIUM
LUMA	MYRTUS
LYCENE	LYCHNIS
LYCHNIS	VISCARIA
LYCHNIS	AGROSTEMMA
LYCHNIS	SILENE
MACFADYENA	BIGNONIA
MACFADYENA	DOXANTHA
MACLEAYA	BOCCONIA
MACROPIPER	PIPER
MAHONIA	BERBERIS
MALUS	APPLE
MALVASTRUM	MODIOLASTRUM
MANDRAGORA	ATROPA
MATRICARIA	TRIPLEUROSPERMUM
MATRICARIA	CHAMOMILLA
MELICYTUS	HYMENANTHERA
MERREMIA	IPOMOEA
MESPILUS	MEDLAR
MICROCOELUM	COCOS
MIMULUS	DIPLACUS

MINUARTIA	ARENARIA
MOLTKIA	LITHODORA
MOLTKIA	LITHOSPERMUM
MONTIA	CLAYTONIA
MORUS	MULBERRY
MUKDENIA	ACERIPHYLLUM
MUSA	BANANA
MUSCARI	HYACINTHUS
MUSCARI	LEOPOLDIA
MUSCARI	PSEUDOMUSCARI
MUSCARI	MUSCARIMIA
MYRCEUGENIA	MYRTUS
MYRICARIA	TAMARIX
MYRTEOLA	MYRTUS
NECTAROSCORDUM	ALLIUM
NEMESIA	DIASCIA X LINARIA
NEMESIA	DIASCIA
NEOPAXIA	MONTIA
NEOPAXIA	CLAYTONIA
NEOREGALIA	NIDULARIUM
NEPETA	ORIGANUM
NIPPONANTHEMUM	LEUCANTHEMUM
NIPPONANTHEMUM	CHRYSANTHEMUM
OEMLERIA	OSMARONIA
OPHIOPOGON	CONVALLARIA
ORNITHOGALUM	CHINCHERINCHEE
OROSTACHYS	SEDUM
OSMANTHUS	PHILLYREA
OSMANTHUS	X OSMAREA
OSTEOSPERMUM	DIMORPHOTHECA
OTHONNA	HERTIA
OTHONNA	OTHONNOPSIS
PAEDEROTA	VERONICA
PAPAVER	MECONOPSIS
PARAHEBE	HEBE
PARAHEBE	VERONICA
PARTHENOCISSUS	AMPELOPSIS
PARTHENOCISSUS	VITIS
PARTHENOCISSUS	AMPELOPSIS
PASSIFLORA	TATRAPATHAEA
PASSIFLORA	PASSION FRUIT
PASSIFLORA	GRANADILLA
PELARGONIUM	GERANIUM
PELTOBOYKINIA	BOYKINIA
PENSTEMON	CHELONE
PENTAGLOTTIS	ANCHUSA
PERICALLIS	SENECIO
PERSEA	AVOCADO
PERSEA	MACHILUS
PERSICARIA	POLYGONUM
PERSICARIA	TOVARA
PETROCOPTIS	LYCHNIS
PETROPHYTUM	SPIRAEA
PETRORHAGIA	TUNICA

PETROSELINUM	CARUM
PHANEROPHLEBIA	CYRTOMIUM
PHEGOPTERIS	THELYPTERIS
PHLEBODIUM	POLYPODIUM
PHOENICAULIS	PARRYA
PHOENIX	DATE
PHOTINIA	X STRANVINIA
PHOTINIA	STRANVAESIA
PHUOPSIS	CRUCIANELLA
PHYLA	LIPPIA
PHYLLITIS	ASPLENIUM
PHYMOSIA	SPHAERALCEA
PHYSALIS	GOOSEBERRY, Cape
PHYSOPLEXIS	PHYTEUMA
PHYSOSTEGIA	DRACOCEPHALUM
PIERIS	ARCTERICA
PISONIA	HEIMERLIODENDRON
PLECOSTACHYS	HELICHRYSUM
PLEIOBLASTUS	SASA
PLEIOBLASTUS	ARUNDINARIA
POLIANTHES	BRAVOA
POLYGONUM	PERSICARIA
POLYGONUM	ACONOGONUM
POLYGONUM	TOVARA
PONCIRUS	AEGLE
PORANEA	TECOMA
POTENTILLA	COMARUM
PRUMNOPITYS	PODOCARPUS
PRUNUS	AMYGDALUS
PRUNUS	PEACH
PRUNUS	BULLACE
PRUNUS	ALMOND
PRUNUS	NECTARINE
PRUNUS	CHERRY, Sweet
PRUNUS	PLUM
PRUNUS	DAMSON
PRUNUS	APRICOT
PSEUDOCYDONIA	CHAENOMELES
PSEUDOFUMARIA	CORYDALIS
PSEUDOFUMARIA	FUMARIA
PSEUDOPANAX	NEOPANAX
PSEUDOPANAX	NOTHOPANAX
PSEUDOSASA	ARUNDINARIA
PSEUDOTSUGA	TSUGA
PSEUDOWINTERA	DRIMYS
PSIDIUM	GUAVA
PTERACANTHUS	STROBILANTHES
PTEROCEPHALUS	SCABIOSA
PTILOSTEMON	CIRSIUM
PTILOTRICHUM	ALYSSUM
PULSATILLA	ANEMONE
PUNICA	POMEGRANATE
PYRENARIA	TUTCHERIA
PYRUS	PEAR

REINECKEA	LIRIOPE
REYNOUTRIA	POLYGONUM
RHEUM	RHUBARB
RHODIOLA	SEDUM
RHODODENDRON	RHODORA
RHODODENDRON	AZALEA
RHODODENDRON	AZALEODENDRON
RIBES	BLACKCURRENT
RIBES	GOOSEBERRY
RIBES	WORCESTERBERRY
RIBES	CURRANT, Black, Red, White
ROSULARIA	COTYLEDON
ROSULARIA	SEMPERVIVELLA
ROSULARIA	SEDUM
RUBUS	LOGANBERRY
RUBUS	YOUNGBERRY
RUBUS	SUNBERRY
RUBUS	MARIONBERRY
RUBUS	BOYSENBERRY
RUBUS	WINEBERRY, Japanese
RUBUS	BLACKBERRY
RUBUS	NECTARBERRY
RUBUS	TAYBERRY
RUBUS	RASPBERRY
RUELLIA	DIPTERACANTHUS
SAGINA	MINUARTIA
SAMBUCUS	ELDERBERRY
SANGUISORBA	POTERIUM
SASA	ARUNDINARIA
SASAELLA	ARUNDINARIA
SASAELLA	SASA
SASAMORPHA	SASA
SAUROMATUM	ARUM
SCADOXUS	HAEMANTHUS
SCHEFFLERA	DIZYGOTHECA
SEDASTRUM	VILLARDIA
SEDUM	CRASSULA
SEMIAQUILEGIA	PARAQUILEGIA
SEMIAQUILEGIA	AQUILEGIA
SEMIARUNDINARIA	ARUNDINARIA
SEMPERVIVELLA	ROSULARIA
SENECIO	LIGULARIA
SENECIO	CINERARIA
SHORTIA	SCHIZOCODON
SIBBALDIOPSIS	POTENTILLA
SILENE	LYCHNIS
SILENE	SAPONARIA
SINARUNDINARIA	SEMIARUNDINARIA
SINARUNDINARIA	ARUNDINARIA
SISYMBRIUM	HESPERIS
SOLEIROLIA	HELXINE
SOLENOPSIS	ISOTOMA
SOLENOSTEMON	COLEUS
X SOLIDASTER	SOLIDAGO
X SOLIDASTER	ASTER
SORBARIA	SPIRAEA
SPRAGUEA	CALYPTRIDIUM
STACHYS	BETONICA
STACHYS	BETONICA
STEIRODISCUS	GAMOLEPSIS
STEWARTIA	STUARTIA
STIPA	LASIAGROSTIS
STIPA	ACHNATHERUM
STYPHELIA	CYATHODES
SUCCISA	SCABIOSA
TANACETUM	ACHILLEA
TANACETUM	PYRETHRUM
TANACETUM	CHRYSANTHEMUM
TANACETUM	MATRICARIA
TASMANNIA	DRIMYS
TELEKIA	BUPHTHALMUM
TETRADIUM	EUODIA
TETRAPANAX	FATSIA
THAMNOCALAMUS	SINARUNDINARIA
THAMNOCALAMUS	ARUNDINARIA
THAMNOCALAMUS	FARGESIA
TOONA	CEDRELA
TRACHELIUM	DIOSPHAERA
TRACHYCARPUS	CHAMAEROPS
TRADESCANTIA	SETCEASEA
TRADESCANTIA	ZEBRINA
TRADESCANTIA	RHOEO
TRISTAGMA	IPHEION
TRITELEIA	BRODIAEA
TRITONIA	CROCOSMIA
TUBERARIA	HELIANTHEMUM
TULIPA	AMANA
TWEEDIA	OXYPETALUM
UGNI	MYRTUS
URSINIA	EURYOPS
UVULARIA	OAKESIELLA
VACCINIUM	CRANBERRY
VACCINIUM	BLUEBERRY
VACCINIUM	OXYCOCCUS
VERBASCUM	CELSIA
VERBASCUM	X CELSIOVERBASCUM
VERBENA	LIPPIA
VERONICASTRUM	VERONICA
VILLADIA	SEDUM
VIOLA	ERPETION
VITALIANA	ANDROSACE
VITALIANA	DOUGLASIA
VITIS	GRAPE
WEIGELA	DIERVILLA
WEIGELA	MACRODIERVILLA
XANTHORHIZA	ZANTHORRHIZA
ZANTEDESCHIA	CALLA

PLANT DELETIONS

Plants marked with a '7', '8', '9' or '0' were listed in the 1987, 1988, 1989 or 1990/91 editions respectively. Back editions of THE PLANT FINDER may be obtained from Lakeside, Whitbourne, Worcester, WR6 5RD. Price £6.00 each inclusive of p&p.

ABELMOSCHUS
0 ***esculentus***

ABIES
0 ***balsamea*** 'Prostrata'
7 ***chensiensis chensiensis***
0 ***cilicica***
9 ***concolor*** 'Aurea'
7 ***durangensis coahuilensis***
9 ***firma***
9 ***fraseri***
7 × ***insignis*** 'Beissneriana'
koreana 'Inverleith'
9 – 'Prostrate Beauty'
0 ***nebrodensis***
8 ***procera*** 'Noble'
7 ***recurvata***
7 × ***shastensis***

ABROMEITIELLA
9 ***brevifolia***

ABROTANELLA
0 ***emarginata***
0 ***forsterioides***

ABUTILON
9 'Lopen Red'
7 'White Swan'

ACACIA
0 ***adunca***
7 ***implexa***
9 ***jonesii***
7 ***longifolia sophorae***
9 ***myrtifolia***
0 ***neriifolia***

ACAENA
9 'Greencourt Hybrid'

ACALYPHA
0 ***godseffiana***

ACANTHOLIMON
8 ***confertiflorum***
0 ***hohenackeri***

ACER
9 ***capillipes morifolium***
0 ***japonicum*** 'O-taki'
7 ***palmatum*** 'Bonfire'
7 – 'Dissectum Rubrifolium'
0 – 'Hamaotome'
8 – 'Junihitoye'
0 – 'Kagero'
9 – 'Koshimino'
9 – 'Matukagami'
7 – 'Mizu-kagiri'
7 – 'Monzukushi'
7 – 'Ogon-sarasa'
9 – 'Sango-nishiki'
8 – 'Schichihenge'
7 – 'Tatsuta-gawa'
7 – 'Tsuchigumo'
7 – 'Yezo-nishiki'
0 ***platanoides*** 'Palmatifidum'
7 – 'Reitenbachii'
9 ***rubrum*** 'Morgan'
0 ***sieboldianum*** 'Kinugasayama'
9 ***tataricum ginnala*** 'Durand Dwarf'

ACHILLEA
8 ***hausmannii***
0 'Heidi'
9 ***millefolium*** 'Purpurea'
0 × ***obristii***
0 ***oxyloba***
7 × ***prichardii***

ACHIMENES
9 'Tetra Altrote Charm'
9 'Tetra Dark Violet Charm'
9 'Tetra Rokoko Elfe'

ACIPHYLLA
0 ***congesta***
8 ***dobsonii***
0 ***ferox***
8 ***lecomtei***
0 ***montana***
8 – ***montana***
0 ***similis***
9 ***spedenii***
0 ***subflabellata***

ACONITUM
9 ***chasmanthum***
8 ***heterophyllum***
9 ***hookeri***
0 ***lycoctonum neapolitanum***
9 ***spicatum***

ACORUS
0 ***graminifolius tanguticus***

ACTINIDIA
9 ***callosa***
8 ***deliciosa*** 'Abbot' (f)
8 – 'Bruno' (f)
8 – 'Matura' (m)
8 ***purpurea***

ADENOPHORA
0 ***takedae howozara***

ADIANTUM
0 ***raddianum*** 'Goldelse'

ADONIS
0 ***aestivalis***

AECHMEA
0 ***blumenavii***
0 ***cylindrata***
0 ***fulgens discolor***
0 ***gamosepala***
0 ***lueddemanniana***
9 ***recurvata recurvata***

AEONIUM
0 ***lindleyi***

AESCHYNANTHUS
0 'Black Pagoda'
0 ***marmoratus***

AESCULUS
7 ***flava vestita***
7 × ***hybrida***
9 ***wilsonii***

AETHIONEMA
9 ***armenum*** 'Mavis Holmes'
8 ***stylosum***
0 ***thomasianum***

AGAPANTHUS
8 ***africanus minor***
8 'Ben Hope'
9 ***campanulatus*** 'Slieve Donard Variety'
8 ***inapertus intermedius***
7 – ***pendulus***
0 ***praecox***
9 – 'Albiflorus'
8 – ***minimus***
0 'Underway'

AGASTACHE
8 ***mexicana*** 'Rosea'

AGAVE
9 ***parviflora***
0 ***shawii***

AGLAONEMA
0 ***commutatum maculatum***
0 – 'Pseudo-bracteatum'
0 ***nitidum*** 'Curtisii'

ALANGIUM
9 ***chinense***

ALBUCA
0 ***spiralis***

ALCEA
0 ***rosea*** single white
0 – 'Sutton's Single Brilliant'

ALCHEMILLA
8 ***glaucescens***
9 ***hoppeana***
7 ***mollis*** 'Variegata'

ALKANNA
9 ***aucheriana***

ALLIUM
0 ***auctum***
9 ***campanulatum***
9 ***carinatum pulchellum*** dwarf
0 ***cyaneum*** 'Cobalt Blue'
8 ***douglasii***
9 ***griffithianum***
0 ***nutans***
0 ***sp.*** AC&W dwarf

ALNUS
9 ***acuminata arguta***
7 ***hirsuta sibirica***
0 ***lanata***
9 ***nepalensis***
0 ***sinuata***
9 ***tenuifolia***

ALOCASIA
0 × ***argyraea***
0 × ***chantrieri***
0 ***cuprea***
0 'Green Velvet'
0 ***korthalsii***
0 ***longiloba***
0 ***macrorrhiza***
0 ***watsoniana***
0 ***wentii***

ALSTROEMERIA
9 Annabel ®
9 Appelbloesem ®
0 Atlas ® / 'Stalrama'
0 Canaria ® / 'Stagelb'
0 Isabella ® / 'Stalis'
0 Jubilee ® / 'Stalilas'
0 Libelle ® / 'Stalbel'
0 Mandarin ® / 'Stalrin'
0 Manon ® / 'Zelanon'
0 Mona Lisa ® / 'Stablaco'
0 Monika ® / 'Stalmon'
0 Pink Triumph ® / 'Stapink'
0 Ramona ® / 'Stadaram'
0 Red Sunset ® / 'Stamarko'
0 'Regina'
0 Rita ® / 'Zelido'
0 Rosita ® / 'Starosello'
0 Samora ® / 'Stalsam'
0 Tango ® / 'Staltang'
0 Zebra ® / 'Stazeb'

ALYSSUM
0 ***markgrafii***
8 ***montanum*** 'Prostratum'
9 ***murale***
7 ***petraeum***
9 ***troodii***

AMELANCHIER
9 ***asiatica sinica***

AMPELOPSIS
8 ***bodinieri***
8 ***chaffanjonii***

AMPELOPSIS
8 ***bodinieri***
8 ***chaffanjonii***

ANANAS
0 ***comosus***

ANDROMEDA
0 ***glaucophylla*** 'Latifolia'
8 ***polifolia angustifolia***
9 – 'Compacta Alba'

ANDROSACE
9 ***alpina***
0 ***armeniaca macrantha***
8 ***chamaejasme lehmanniana***
0 ***hausmannii***
0 x ***heeri*** pink form
0 ***helvetica***
9 ***lactiflora***
0 ***lehmannii***
8 ***rotundifolia*** 'Elegans'
9 ***saximontana***
8 ***spinulifera***
0 ***tapete***
8 ***wulfeniana***

ANEMONE
8 ***baicalensis***
0 ***biflora***
0 ***blanda*** 'Blue Pearl'
8 – ***scythinica***
9 coronaria 'De Caen' 'Die Braut' ('The Bride')
9 – – 'Sylphide'
8 ***elongata***
9 'French Hill'
0 ***hortensis***
0 ***lithophila***
9 ***mexicana***
9 ***nemorosa*** 'Celestial'
0 – 'Wyatt's Pink'
0 ***nikoensis***
7 ***obtusiloba patula***
0 ***pavonina ocellata***
9 ***raddeana***

ANETHUM
9 ***sowa***

ANTENNARIA
9 ***plantaginifolia***

ANTHERICUM
9 ***baeticum***

ANTHRISCUS
0 ***sylvestris*** 'Moonlight Night'

ANTHURIUM
0 ***andreanum album***
0 – 'Aztec'
0 – 'Brazilian Sunrise'
0 – 'Flamingo'
0 – 'Nova'
0 ***crystallinum***
0 x ***ferrierense***
0 ***leuconeurum***
0 ***magnificum***
0 ***scherzerianum album***
0 – ***minimum***
0 – 'Rothschildianum'
0 – 'Wardii'
0 ***veitchii***
9 ***warocqueanum***

ANTHYLLIS
9 ***barba-jovis***

APHELANDRA
0 'Snow Queen'

APIUM
9 ***nodiflorum***

APONOGETON
0 ***desertorum***

AQUILEGIA
9 ***bernardii***
8 ***caerulea daileyae***
7 'Edelweiss'
9 ***hirsutissima***
8 Langdon's Rainbow hybrids
0 ***longissima*** 'Flore Pleno'
0 ***vulgaris*** double pink
9 – 'Millicent Bowden'

ARABIS
9 ***breweri***
7 ***caucasica*** 'Snowflake'
ferdinandi-coburgii 'Reversed'
9 ***pumila***

ARACHNOIDES
0 ***standishii*** 'Variegata'

ARBUTUS
7 ***xalapensis***

ARCTOSTAPHYLOS
8 ***auriculata***
0 'Emerald Carpet'

ARENARIA
8 ***longifolia***
0 ***procera***
0 ***purpurascens*** 'Elliott's Variety'

ARENGA
9 ***caudata***

ARGEMONE
9 ***ensifolia***
0 ***platyceras***

ARISAEMA
8 ***kiushianum***
8 ***thunbergii***

ARISTOLOCHIA
8 ***colchica***

ARISTOTELIA
0 ***peduncularis***

ARMERIA
9 ***alliacea*** 'Grandiflora'
0 – ***plantaginea***
7 ***arctica***
9 'Bloodgood'
0 ***leucocephala***
0 ***maritima*** 'Birch Pink'
7 – ***sibirica***
8 – 'Splendens Alba'

ARNICA
0 ***angustifolia***
0 ***cordifolia***

ARTEMISIA
7 ***absinthium*** 'Poland's Variety'
9 ***genipi***
7 ***lactiflora*** 'Variegata'

ARTHROPODIUM
9 ***cirrhatum*** bronze form

ARUM
0 ***byzantinum***
0 ***maculatum*** 'Pleddel'

ARUNCUS
0 ***dioicus*** 'Aphrodite'

ASARINA
0 ***hispanicum hispanicum*** white form

ASPLENIUM
8 ***dareoides***
7 ***fontanum***
9 ***marinum***
0 ***squamulatum***

ASTELIA
7 ***nivicola***

ASTER
9 ***ageratoides***
0 ***alpinus dolomiticus***
7 ***amellus*** 'Mrs Ralph Woods'
8 – 'Rotfeuer'
0 – 'September Glory'
0 ***cordifolius***
8 ***ericoides*** 'Yvette Richardson'
0 ***falconeri***
0 'Lovely'
0 ***nana*** 'Variegatus'
0 ***novae-angliae*** 'Roter Stern'
0 ***novi-belgii*** 'Amethyst'
9 – 'Autumn Princess
0 – 'Blue Jacket'
0 – 'Blue Orb'
0 – 'Bridget'
0 – 'Candelabra'
0 – 'Catherine Chiswell'
0 – 'Charnwood'
0 – 'Desert Song'
0 – 'Dunkerton'
0 – 'Fair Trial'
8 – 'Gayborder Rapture'
8 – 'Gayborder Rose'
9 – 'Glorious'
0 – 'Goblin Coombe'
0 – 'Grey Lady'
0 – 'Minster'
0 – 'Moderator
0 – 'Monkton Coombe'
0 – 'Newton's Pink'
0 – 'Pink Bonnet'
0 – 'Powder Puff'
0 – 'Princess Marie Louise'
9 – 'Queen of Sheba'
0 – 'Red King'
0 – 'Rosy Dreams'
0 – 'Ruby Glow'
0 – single blue
0 – 'Walkden's Pink'
0 ***sp.*** CC 170

ASTILBE
0 x ***crispa rosea***
9 'Purple Splendour' (***x urendsii***)
0 'Robinson's Pink'

ASTRAGALUS
0 ***arnotii***
9 ***crassicarpus paysonii***

ASTRANTIA
0 ***major*** 'Rosensinfonie'
0 ***maxima alba***

ASYNEUMA
0 ***linifolium***
9 – ***eximium***

ATHAMANTA
0 ***cretensis***
0 ***turbith***

ATHYRIUM
0 ***distentifolium***
0 ***vidalii***

ATRAPHAXIS
0 ***billardierei tournefortii***

ATRIPLEX
0 ***canescens***

AUBRIETA
8 Bengal hybrids
9 'Blue Beauty'
7 'Bridesmaid'
9 ***canescens macrostylla***
9 'Church Knowle'
8 'Crimson Bedder'
7 'Crimson Queen'
7 'Eileen Longster'
9 Eversley hybrids
0 'Godstone'
8 'Graeca Superba'
0 'Prichard's A1'
7 'Purple Splendour'
8 'Rosanna Miles'
9 'Rose Cascade'

AUCUBA
9 ***japonica*** 'Dentata'

AZORELLA
0 ***sp.*** WR 88101

BALLOTA
9 ***frutescens***

BAUERA
0 ***rubioides***

BEAUFORTIA
0 ***sparsa***

BEGONIA
0 ***acutifolia***
0 ***albopicta*** (C)
0 'Aruba'
0 'Barclay Griffiths'
8 'Bertinii'
0 'Black Velvet'
0 ***bowerae nigramarga***
0 'Bow-Mag'
0 ***burle-marxii***
0 'Camouflage'
0 'Chimbig'
0 'Chumash'
0 'Clifton'
0 ***coccinea*** (C)
0 ***cucullata***
0 ***dichroa*** (C)

0 ***echinosepala***
0 'Enchantment'
0 ***epipsila***
0 ***formosana***
0 'Fuscomaculata'
0 ***grandis*** 'Claret Jug'
0 ***hispida cucullifera***
0 'Holmes Chapel'
0 'Ingramii'
0 'Lexington'
0 'Linda Harley'
0 'Linda Myatt'
0 ***lindeniana***
0 'Mac MacIntyre'
0 ***maculata*** 'Wightii' (C)
0 'Mac's Gold'
0 ***manicata***
0 'Medora' (C)
0 'Mirage'
0 'Norah Bedson'
0 'Panther'
0 ***partita***
0 'Paul Harley'
0 ***plagioneura***
0 ***polyantha***
0 ***pustulata*** 'Argentea'
0 'Queen of Olympus'
0 'Raquel Wood'
0 'Richard Robinson'
0 'Richmondensis'
0 'Royal Lustre'
0 ***shepherdii***
0 'Silbreen'
0 Skeezar
0 Skeezar 'Brown Lake
0 ***stipulacea***
0 x ***superba*** (C)
0 'Universe'
0 x ***verschaffeltii***
0 'Weltoniensis'

BELAMCANDA
0 ***chinensis*** 'Hello Yellow'

BELLIS
9 ***perennis*** 'Red Alice'
9 ***sylvestris***

BERBERIS
0 ***amurensis*** 'Flamboyant'
7 ***atrocarpa***
9 ***dumicola***
8 ***erythroclada***
9 ***francisci-ferdinandi***
0 'Georgei'
9 ***hookeri viridis***
0 ***ilicifolia***
9 ***orthobotrys canescens***
7 ***poiretii***
0 ***sanguinea***
0 x ***stenophylla*** 'Autumnalis'
8 – 'Cornish Cream'
9 – 'Pendula'
7 – 'Semperflorens'
8 ***thunbergii*** 'Dart's Purple'
7 – 'Dart's Red Devil'
0 – 'Pearly Queen'
9 ***valdiviana*** x darwinii

BERGENIA
9 ***crassifolia pacifica***
9 'Milesii'
7 'Perfect'
0 'Summer Mountain'
7 'White Dwarf'

BESSEYA
0 ***wyomingensis***

BETULA
7 ***apoiensis***
7 ***austrosinensis***
0 ***fontinalis*** 'Inopina'
9 ***fruticosa***
9 ***glandulosa***
9 ***luminifera***
9 ***nana*** 'Walter Ingwersen'

BILLARDIERA
9 ***scandens***

BILLBERGIA
0 ***bucholtzii***
0 ***chlorosticta***
0 ***distachia***
0 ***leptopoda***
0 'Santa Barbara'

BLECHNUM
0 ***moorei***

BOENNINGHAUSENIA
0 ***albiflora***

BORNMUELLERA
9 ***tymphaea***

BORONIA
0 'Heaven Scent'

BOYKINIA
8 ***orientalis***

BRACHYGLOTTIS
0 ***kirkii*** 'Variegatus'
0 ***spedenii***

BRACHYSCOME
0 ***diversifolia***

BRIMEURA
0 ***fastigiata***

BRIZA
7 ***subaristata***

BROUSSONETIA
8 ***papyrifera*** 'Laciniata'

BUDDLEJA
8 ***caryopteridifolia*** 'Variegata'
7 ***davidii*** 'Opéra'
9 – 'Pink Pearl'
7 – 'Southcombe Splendour'
7 – 'Widecombe'
7 – 'Windtor'
9 ***fallowiana*** 'Town Foot'
0 ***globosa*** 'Lemon Ball'
8 ***latifolia***
0 ***nevinii***
7 x ***weyeriana*** 'Golden Tassels'

BULBINE
9 ***bulbosa***

BUPLEURUM
9 ***triradiatum***

BUXUS
0 ***microphylla rugulosa***
9 ***sempervirens*** 'Elegans'

CALADIUM
0 ***bicolor*** 'John Peel'
0 – 'June Bride'
0 – 'Mrs Arno Nehrling'
0 – 'Pink Beauty'
0 – 'Postman Joyner'
0 – 'Rosebud'
0 ***candidum***

CALATHEA
0 ***carlina***
0 ***eximia***
0 ***insignis***
0 ***leopardina***
0 ***louisae***
0 ***micans***
0 ***musaica***
0 ***ornata*** 'Sanderiana'
0 ***rotundifolia*** 'Fasciata'
0 ***rufibarba***
0 ***vittata***

CALCEOLARIA
9 ***corymbosa***
0 ***darwinii*** WR 8849

CALLIANTHEMUM
9 ***angustifolium***

CALLICARPA
0 ***mollis***

CALLISTEMON
0 ***citrinus*** purple form
9 ***macropunctatus***
9 ***montanus***
0 ***pallidus*** lilac form

CALLUNA
0 See also ERICA
8 ***vulgaris*** 'Adrie'
8 – 'Alba'
8 – 'Alba Erecta'
8 – 'Alba Minor'
9 – 'Allegretto'
8 – 'Alys Sutcliffe'
8 – 'Amilto'
8 – 'Anton'
8 – 'Ariadne'
8 – 'Ashgarth Amber'
8 – 'Asterix'
8 – 'Autumn Glow'
9 – 'Ben Nevis'
8 – 'Beoley Crimson Variegated'
8 – 'Blueness'
8 – 'Catherine Anne'
8 – 'Christina'
8 – 'Coby'
9 – 'Con Brio'
8 – 'Copper Glow'
8 – 'Crimson Sunset'
8 – 'Dark Star'
8 – 'Dart's Amethyst'
0 – 'Dart's Parrot'
8 – 'Dart's Squirrel'
8 – 'David Platt'
8 – 'Desiree'
8 – 'Diana'
8 – 'Discovery'
0 – 'Easter Bonfire'
8 – 'Elegantissima Lilac'
8 – 'Elkstone White'
8 – 'Findling'
9 – 'French Gray'
8 – 'Glentock Silver'
8 – 'Gnome'
0 – 'Gold Carmen'
0 – 'Gold Charm'
8 – 'Gold Spronk'
8 – 'Golden Max'
9 – 'Goldsworth Purple'
8 – 'Grizzly'
8 – 'Gynodioica'
8 – 'Harten's Findling'
8 – 'Hayesensis'
8 – 'Heidberg'
8 – 'Heidezwerg'
8 – 'Hetty'
8 – 'Hollandia'
8 – 'Holstein'
8 – 'Ingrid Bouter'
8 – 'Japanese White'
0 – 'Jimmy Dyce'
8 – 'Joseph's Coat'
8 – 'Karin Blum'
0 – 'Lemon Gem'
8 – 'Lemon Queen'
8 – 'Lime Gold'
0 – 'L'Ancresse'
8 – 'Mallard'
8 – 'Manitoba'
8 – 'Mies'
9 – 'Minty'
8 – 'Monstrosa'
9 – 'Orange Beauty'
9 – 'Orange Carpet'
8 – 'Pallida'
8 – 'Parson's Gold'
0 – 'Platt's Surprise'
8 – 'Procumbens'
9 – 'Rannoch'
8 – 'Red Max'
8 – 'Rica'
0 – 'Rivington'
8 – 'Robber Knight'
8 – 'Roodkapje'
9 – 'Sedlonov'
0 – 'Sonja'
8 – 'Spicata Nana'
8 – 'Spook'
8 – 'Stranger'
8 – 'Talisker'
8 – 'Tomentosa'
8 – 'Velvet Fascination'
8 – 'Whiteness'
8 – 'Winter Fire'
8 – 'Yellow One'

CALOCEDRUS
0 ***decurrens*** 'Depressa'

CALTHA
0 ***sagittata***

CALYTRIX
9 ***glutinosa***
8 ***rhomboidea***

CAMELLIA
9 'Ada Pieper' (***japonica***)
9 'Alba Superba' (***japonica***)
9 'Alta Gavin' (***japonica***)
9 'Anna Bruneau' (***japonica***)
9 'Anna M Page' (***japonica***)
9 'Anne Smith' (***japonica***)

9 'Arbutus Gum' (*reticulata* x japonica)
0 'Arch of Triumph' (*reticulata seedling*)
0 'Australis' (*japonica*)
9 'Ave Maria' (*japonica*)
9 'Beni-hassaku' (*japonica*)
9 'Benten-kagura' (*japonica*)
9 'Bernadette Karsten' (*reticulata* x japonica)
9 'Bert Jones' (*sasanqua*)
9 'Billie McCaskill' (*japonica*)
9 'Blue Danube' (*x williamsii* x reticulata)
9 'Bridal Gown' (*x williamsii*)
0 'Bride's Bouquet' (*japonica*)
9 'Bright Buoy' (*japonica*)
7 'Candy Stripe' (*japonica*)
9 'Captain Folk' (*japonica*)
7 'Cardinal Variegated' (*japonica*)
0 *caudata*
9 'Centenary' (*japonica*)
0 'Charity' (*x williamsii*)
7 'Charlean Variegated' (*japonica* x williamsii)
7 'Charles Bland' (*japonica*)
9 'Charlotte Bradford' (*japonica*)
9 'Cheryl Lynn' (*japonica*)
7 'Clarissa' (*japonica*)
9 'Clark Hubbs' (*japonica*)
9 'Commander Mulroy' (*japonica*)
7 'Coral Pink Lotus' (*japonica*)
7 'Coral Queen' (*japonica*)
8 'Cornish Cream' (*japonica*)
9 *crapnelliana*
0 'Dainty Dale' (*japonica*)
9 'Debut' (*reticulata*)
9 'Desire' (*japonica*)
9 'Dixie Knight' (*japonica*)
0 'Doctor Louis Pollizzi' (*saluenensis* x reticulata)
7 'Dorothy James' (hybrid)
9 'Drama Girl Variegated' (*japonica*)
9 'Dream Castle' (*reticulata* x japonica)
9 'Eden Roc' (*reticulata*)
9 'El Dorado' (*pitardii* x japonica)
7 'Elena Nobile' (*japonica*)
9 'Ellamine' (*williamsii*)
9 'Elsie Dryden' (*reticulata* x japonica)
9 'Emmett Barnes' (*japonica*)
9 'Eugène Lize' (*japonica*)
7 'Evelyn' (*japonica*)
0 'Fimbriata Blush' (*japonica*)
9 'Flower Girl' (*sasanqua* x reticulata)
0 'Fortune Teller' (*japonica*)
9 'Fragrant Pink' (*lutchuensis* x japonica)
8 *fraterna*
9 'Free Style' (*x williamsii*)
9 'Gay Marmee' (*japonica*)
9 'Geisha Girl' (*japonica*)
9 'Gosho-guruma' (*japonica*)
7 'Grand Prix Variegated' (*japonica*)
9 'Grand Sultan' (*japonica*)
0 *granthamiana*
7 'Gus Menard' (*japonica*)
9 'Harold L Paige' (*japonica* x reticulata)
7 'Helen Bower' (*japonica*)
9 'Henry Turnbull' (*japonica*)
9 'High Wide 'n' Handsome' (*japonica*)
9 'Hishi-karaito' (*japonica*)
9 'Hody Wilson' (*reticulata*)
9 'Hope' (*x williamsii*)
9 'Interval' (*japonica* x reticulata)
9 *japonica*
9 'Jennifer Turnbull' (*japonica*)
9 'Jill Totty' (*x williamsii*)
9 'Judge Solomon' (*japonica*)
7 'Julia Drayton' (*japonica*)
9 'K O Hester' (*reticulata*)
7 'Katherine Nuccio' (*japonica*)
9 'King Size' (*japonica*)
9 *kissi*
9 'Kitty' (*japonica*)
9 'La Belle France' (*japonica*)
9 'Lady Kay' (*japonica*)
9 'Lady's Maid' (*x williamsii*)
9 'Latifolia Variegated' (*japonica*)
9 'Laura Boscawen' (*x williamsii*)
9 'Lillian Ricketts' (*japonica*)
9 'Lisa Gael' (*reticulata seedling*)
9 'Little Pearl' (*sasanqua*)
9 'Lois Shinault' (*reticulata* x granthamiana)
9 'Lookaway' (*japonica*)
9 'Louise Wilson' (*japonica*)
9 'Lovelight' (*japonica*)
9 'Lucinda' (*sasanqua*)
9 *lutchuensis*
7 'Mabel Blackwell' (*japonica*)
9 *maliflora*
9 'Mandalay Queen' (*reticulata seedling*)
7 'Margaret Rose' (*japonica*)
9 'Margaret Short' (*japonica*)
7 'Marion Mitchell' (*japonica*)
9 'Marjorie Magnificent' (*japonica*)
8 'Mary Agnes Patin' (*japonica*)
0 'Mary Larcom' (*x williamsii*)
0 'Mary Williams' (*reticulata seedling*)
7 'Masterpiece' (*japonica*)
9 'Matterhorn' (*japonica*)
9 'Mildred Pitkin' (*reticulata* x japonica)
0 'Mine-no-yuki' (*sasanqua*)
9 'Miss Anaheim' (*japonica*)
9 'Miss Betty' (*japonica*)
9 'Miss Tulare' (*reticulata seedling*)
9 'Momiji-gari' (*japonica*)
9 'Mrs Baldwin Wood' (*japonica*)
9 'Mrs George Bell' (*japonica*)
9 'Mrs Swan' (*japonica*)
7 'Mrs Tingley' (*japonica*)
9 'Nancy Bird' (*japonica*)
9 'Navajo' (*sasanqua*)
9 'Nodami-ushiro' (*sasanqua*)
9 'Nuccio's Ruby' (*reticulata seedling*)
9 'Otto Hopfer' (*reticulata* x japonica)
9 'Paulette Goddard' (*japonica*)
9 'Perfecta' (*x williamsii*)
9 'Phyl Doak' (*saluenensis* x reticulata)
9 'Pink Sparkle' (*reticulata* x japonica)
0 'Premier' (*japonica*)
0 'Prince Eugene Napoléon' (*japonica*)
8 'Prince Murat' (*japonica*)
9 'Princess Lear' (*japonica*)
9 'Purple Swirl' (*japonica*)
0 'Queen's Escort' (*japonica*)
9 'Red Cardinal' (*japonica*)
9 'Richard Nixon' (*japonica*)
0 'Richfield' (*japonica*)
9 'Rosemary Elsom' (*japonica*)
0 'Rosina Sobeck' (*japonica*)
9 'Ruddigore' (*japonica*)
7 'Sawada's Dream' (*japonica*)
9 'Senorita' (*x williamsii*)
9 'Sheridan' (*japonica*)
9 'Shinomome' (*sasanqua*)
9 'Shiro Chan' (*japonica*)
9 'Shiro-wabisuke' (*wabiske*)
7 'Showa-no-sakae' (*hiemalis*)
9 'Simeon' (*japonica*)
8 'Snow Chan' (*japonica*)
9 'Snowflake' (*japonica*)
9 'Splendens' (*japonica*)
7 'Spring Fever' (*japonica*)
9 'Tanya' (*sasanqua*)
9 'Teringa' (*japonica*)
9 'Terrell Weaver' (*reticulata*)
0 'The Mikado' (*japonica*)
9 'Tomorrow Park Hill Var.' (*japonica*)
9 'Touchdown' (*japonica*)
0 'Tregrehan' (hybrid)
9 'Valentine Day' (*reticulata* x japonica)
0 x *vernalis*
9 'Ville de Nantes Variegata' (*japonica*)
8 'Virginia Robinson' (*japonica*)
9 'Vittorio Emanuele II' (*japonica*)
7 'Waltz Time' (*x williamsii* x japonica)
9 'Waverley' (*japonica*)
0 'White Giant' (*japonica*)
9 'Wilamina' (*japonica*)
9 'Wild Silk' (*reticulata*)
9 'Wildwood' (*japonica*)
9 'William Bartlett' (*japonica*)
9 'Yae-arare' (*sasanqua*)
9 'Yuletide' (*vernalis*)

CAMPANULA

7 'Abundance'
0 *alliariifolia* x makaschvilii
7 *alpestris* 'Rosea'
0 *arvatica* x cochleariifolia
0 *barbata* deep blue
0 *bornmuelleri*
9 *carpatica* 'Albescens'
9 – 'Jingle Bells'
7 – 'Loddon Bell'
7 *carpatica turbinata* 'Grandiflora'
7 *cochleariifolia* 'Patience Bell'
7 – 'Temple Bells'
9 *davisii*
9 *glomerata* 'Wisley Supreme'
8 *hawkinsiana*
7 'Iceberg'
9 *kladniana*
8 *lactiflora* 'Superba'
8 *lyrata*
0 *persicifolia* 'Curiosa'
0 *petrophila*
0 *pulla alba*

0 *pyramidalis* 'Aureovariegata'
0 *rigidipila*
0 *sp.* Bolgar Dag
0 *sp.* Kilma 203
7 'Warley Gem'

CAMPTOSORUS
9 *rhizophyllus*

CAMPYLOTROPIS
8 *macrocarpa*

CAREX
0 *buxbaumii*

CARPINUS
9 *betulus* 'Incisa'
8 *caroliniana virginiana*

CARYA
9 *reticulata*

CASSIA
8 *acutifolia*
9 *didymobotrya*

CASSINIA
9 *quinquefaria*

CASSIOPE
9 *wardii*

CATALPA
9 *speciosa* 'Pulverulenta'

CATANANCHE
0 *caerulea* 'Bicolor'

CEANOTHUS
0 *burfordiensis*
0 'Mary Lake'
0 x *mendocinensis*
9 x *pallidus* 'Plenus'
8 'Percy Picton'

CEDRUS
0 *brevifolia* 'Epsteiniana'
8 *deodara* 'Glauca Pendula'
0 – Paktia group
0 – 'Polar Winter'

CELMISIA
0 *armstrongii*
0 *asteliifolia*
8 *dallii*
0 *densiflora*
0 *haastii*
0 *holosericea*
0 *longifolia*
9 *ramulosa tuberculata*
0 *spectabilis argentea*

CELTIS
7 *caucasica*
9 *tournefortii*

CENTAUREA
9 *cineraria* 'Colchester White'
0 *ruthenica*
0 *triumfettii cana*
7 *triumfettii stricta alba*

CENTAURIUM
8 *chloodes*

CERASTIUM
8 *biebersteinii*
0 *candidissimum*
9 *tomentosum* 'Silberteppich'

CERATONIA
8 *siliqua*

CERATOSTIGMA
0 *minus*

CERCIS
7 *chingii*
0 *racemosa*
9 *siliquastrum* 'Rubra'

CERCOCARPUS
9 *montanus*

CETERACH
0 *dalhousieae*

CHAENACTIS
9 *alpina*
9 *jamesii*

CHAENOMELES
8 *japonica* 'Orange Beauty'
0 *speciosa* 'Rosemoor Seedling'
0 x *superba* 'Alba'

CHAMAECYPARIS
0 *formosensis*
9 *lawsoniana* 'Annesley'
9 – 'Booth'
7 – 'Boy Blue'
9 – 'Darleyensis'
0 – 'Ellwood's Glauca'
8 – 'Ellwood's Prize'
9 – 'Ericoides'
8 – 'Filiformis Compacta'
0 – 'Gold Lace'
8 – 'Green Monarch'
8 – 'Holden Gold'
0 – 'Juvenilis Stricta'
9 – 'Kilbogget Gold'
8 – 'Killiney Gold'
0 – 'Lemon Pillar'
8 – 'Lissellii'
0 – 'Moerheimii'
0 – 'Shawii'
8 – 'Suffolk Belle'
7 – 'Tilgate'
7 – 'Trentham Gold'
9 – 'Van Eck'
8 – 'Watereri'
9 *nootkatensis* 'Tatra'
0 *obtusa* 'Albospica'
7 – 'Ericoides'
9 – 'Goldspire'
0 – 'Heinrich'
9 – 'Tetragona'
0 *pisifera* 'Compacta'
8 – 'Plumosa Floral Arts'
8 *thyoides* 'Marwood'
0 – 'Schumacher's Blue Dwarf'

CHAMAEDOREA
0 *elegans* 'Bella'

CHASMANTHIUM
0 *latifolium* 'Variegatum'

CHEILANTHES
9 *argentea*
0 *distans*
9 *lanosa*

CHEIRANTHUS
0 *cheiri* 'Chevithorne'

CHELONE
8 *obliqua* 'Praecox Nana'

CHENOPODIUM
8 *ambrosioides*
9 *bonus-henricus* 'Variegatum'

CHEVREULIA
0 *lycopodioides*

CHIMONANTHUS
7 *nitens*
praecox 'Mangetsu'

CHIONOHEBE
0 *takatima*

CHRYSANTHEMUM
7 *cordifolium*
9 *praeteritium*

CHRYSOTHAMNUS
0 *nauseosus*

CICUTA
9 *virosa*

CIRSIUM
9 *spinosissimum*

CISTUS
0 'Elma Colicte'
0 x *glaucus*
0 *heterophyllus*
0 *ladanifer* 'Albiflorus'
0 x *nigricans*
0 *varius*

X CITROFORTUNELLA
0 *floridana*

X CITRONCIRUS
9 *webberi*

CITRUS
F x *nobilis* Ortanique group
F x *tangelo* 'Ugli'

CLEMATIS
8 *alpina* 'Prairie River'
9 'Blue Diamond'
0 *denticulata*
0 'Elizabeth Foster'
8 *florida*
0 *grata argentilucida*
9 *lanuginosa*
0 'Lucey'
9 *macropetala* 'Ballet Skirt'
9 – 'White Lady'
7 *occidentalis occidentalis*
9 *parviflora depauperata*
0 'Perryhill Pearl'
8 'Ruby'

CLETHRA
0 *alnifolia* 'Nana'

CLINTONIA
0 *uniflora*

CLUSIA
9 *rosea*

COCCULUS
7 *trilobus*

CODIAEUM
0 *variegatum pictum*
0 – – 'Excellent'
0 – – 'Gold Star
0 – – 'Norma'

CODONOPSIS
9 *bhutanica*
9 *dicentrifolia*

COLCHICUM
0 *bornmuelleri* F&S
9 'Lilac Bedder'
9 *parlatoris*
0 *parnassicum*

COLOBANTHUS
0 *strictus*
0 *subulatus*

COLOCASIA
0 *esculenta antiquorum*

COLUMNEA
0 'Apollo'
fendleri
0 'Mercury'
0 *microphylla*

COLUTEA
0 *arborescens* 'Variegata'

CONVALLARIA
9 *majalis* 'Flore Pleno'

COPROSMA
9 *ciliata*
0 *serrulata*
0 *spathulata* (m)
0 'Tuffet' (f)
0 *viridiflora* (f)

CORDYLINE
0 *banksii* 'Purpurea'
0 *fruticosa*
0 – 'Negri'
0 *parryi purpurea*
9 *pumilio*

COREOPSIS
8 *grandiflora* 'Schnittgold' ('Golden Gain')

CORIARIA
0 *angustissima*
9 *napalensis*

CORNUS
0 *drummondii*
0 *florida* 'Barton's White'
0 *kousa* 'Variegata'
0 *kousa chinensis* 'Rosea'
9 x *unalaschkensis*

CORREA
8 'Kane's Hybrid'

CORYDALIS
9 *bulbosa blanda*
9 – *blanda alba*
9 *conorhiza*
9 *vittae*

CORYLOPSIS
9 *himalayana griffithii*

7 *koreana*

COTINUS

9 *coggygria* 'Drinkstone Form'

COTONEASTER

0 *amoenus*
9 *conspicuus* 'Red Pearl'
0 'Eastleigh'
9 *harrovianus*
7 *pannosus*
9 *rugosus*
0 'Saldam'
0 *salicifolius* 'Afterglow'
9 – 'Perkeo'
9 x *suecicus* 'Greensleeves'
8 – 'Jürgel'
7 *tomentosus*
7 x *watereri* 'Inchmery'
0 – 'Saint Monica'

CRASSULA

0 *lactea*
7 *rigginsiana*

CRATAEGUS

9 *arnoldiana*
9 *laevigata* 'Cheal's Crimson'
9 – 'Masekii'
9 – 'Punicea'
9 – 'Rosea'
9 *punctata*

CRINUM

0 *campanulatum*

CROCOSMIA

N 'Honey Angels'
9 'Orange Flame'

CROCUS

8 *biflorus weldenii*
0 *caspius*
9 *etruscus*
9 *imperati* 'form'
9 *korolkowii* 'Unicoloratus'
0 *niveus* 'Cape Mataplan'
0 *pestalozzae caeruleus*
9 *reticulatus*
9 *speciosus* 'Globosus'
0 *tommasinianus* forms
9 *vernus* 'Early Perfection'
0 – 'Flower Record'
9 – 'King of the Striped'

CROWEA

8 *exalata* x saligna

CRYPTANTHUS

0 *acaulis*
0 – *ruber*
0 *bivittatus lueddemannii*
0 – *minor*
0 *bromelioides* 'Tricolor'
0 *zonatus* 'Zebrinus'

X CRYPTBERGIA

0 *rubra*

CRYPTOMERIA

9 *japonica* 'Elegantissima'
9 – 'Enko-sugi'
0 – 'Globosa'
0 – 'Knaptonensis'
0 – 'Mankichi-sugi'
7 – 'Viminalis'
9 – 'Viridis'

CTENANTHE

0 *kummeriana*
0 *oppenheimiana* 'Tricolor'

CUNNINGHAMIA

8 *lanceolata* 'Glauca'

CUPHEA

0 'Mickey Mouse'

X CUPRESSOCYPARIS

0 *leylandii* 'Leighton Green'

CUPRESSUS

8 *arizonica* 'Sulphurea'
9 *bakeri* 'Matthewsii'
9 *goveniana abramsiana*
9 *macrocarpa* 'Barnham Gold'
7 – 'Lutea Horizontalis'
7 – 'Nana Aurea'
9 – 'Pendula'
8 *torulosa*
8 'Vladivostok'

CYANANTHUS

8 *lobatus* 'Inshriach Blue'

CYATHEA

0 *cuninghamii*
0 *kermadecensis*

CYCLAMEN

0 *cilicium* patterned leaf
9 *coum caucasicum album*
0 *hederifolium* Corfu form
9 – x africanum
0 *repandum peloponnesiacum vividum*

CYDONIA

F *oblonga* 'Broadview'
F – 'Champion'

CYMBIDIUM

9 *goeringii*

CYMBOPOGON

0 *flexuosus*

CYNARA

0 *scolymus* 'Glauca'

CYPERUS

9 *ustulatus*

CYRTANTHUS

0 *luteus*

CYRTOSPERMA

0 *johnstonii*

CYSTOPTERIS

8 *fragilis* 'Cristata'

CYTISUS

9 'Baronscourt Amber'
9 'Boskoop Ruby'
7 'Charmaine'
7 'Donard Seedling'
7 'Eastern Queen'
9 *hirsutus*
8 *jeffsii*
9 'Lady Moore'
9 *maderensis magnifoliosus*
0 *monspessulanus*
9 'Mrs J Rodgers'
7 'Orange Arch'
7 x *praecox* 'Buttercup'
7 'Southcombe Apricot'
9 *subspicatus*

DABOECIA

8 *azorica*
8 *cantabrica blummii*
8 – 'Creeping White'
8 – 'Globosa Pink'
8 – 'Harlequin'
8 – 'Heraut'
8 – 'Pink Blum'
8 – 'Rodeo'
8 – 'Wijnie'
8 x *scotica* 'Red Imp'
8 – 'Robin'

DACTYLORHIZA

0 *sambucina*

DAHLIA

0 'Aladdin' (SD)
8 'Alfred C' (GSC)
9 'Alltami Coral' (MSC)
9 'Alltami Ruby' (MSC)
0 'Amanda' (SC)
9 'Amaran Guard' (LD)
8 'Amelisweerd' (MSC)
7 'Anchorite' (SD)
8 'Andries' Orange' (MinSC)
8 'Ann Hilary' (SD)
8 'Anniversary Doc'
9 'Apple Blossom' (MC)
8 'Armgard Coronet'
9 'Arthur Lashlie' (MC)
9 'Bach' (MC)
7 'Barbara Schell' (GD)
0 'Baseball' (MinBa)
9 'Belle of Barmera' (GD)
0 'Bettina' (SSC)
8 'Betty Ann' (Pom)
7 'Birchwood'
7 'Bitsa' (MinBa)
0 'Blaisdon Red' (SD)
7 'Bob Fitzjohn'
9 'Bonne Esperance' (Sin)(Lil)
9 'Brookfield Dierdre (MinBa)
9 'Brownie' (Sin)(Lil)
9 'Bulls Pride' (GD)
9 'Bushfire' (Pom)
9 'Camano Choice' (SD)
8 'Cantab Symbol' (MSC)
8 'Carol Channing'
9 'Caroussel' (MC)
8 'Cefn Glow' (SSC)
8 'Centenary Symbol' (MSC)
8 'Cherida' (MinBa)
0 'Cherry Wine' (SD)
8 'Chiltern Amber' (SD)
7 'Chinese Lantern' (SD)
0 'Chorus Girl' (MinD)
8 'Claire' (Misc)
0 'Cocktail' (SC)
9 'Color Spectacle' (LSD)
7 'Corfu'
8 'Corrine'
7 'Cortez Silver'
0 'Cream Pontiac' (SC)
0 'Crossfield Sceptre' (MSC)
9 'Cryfield Jane'
9 'Cryfield Max' (SC)
7 'Cryfield Rosie' (SBa)
9 'Curiosity' (Col)
8 'Dad's Delight' (MinD)
7 'Daleko Adonis' (GSC)
0 'Daleko Tangerine' (MD)
9 'Daleko Venus' (MSC)
8 'Dana Audrey' (MinC)
8 'Dana Judy' (SSC)
9 'Dana Peerless'
8 'Dancing Queen'
8 'Dandy' (Sin)(Lil)
7 'Danum Cupid'
9 'Davenport Lesley' (MinD)
8 'Dedham' (SD)
9 'Delectus' (SD)
9 'De-la-Haye' (MSC)
8 'Diane Nelson'
0 'Doctor John Grainger' (MinD)
0 'Donald van de Mark' (GD)
8 'Doris Knight' (SC)
0 'Dorothy Whitney Wood' (SSC)
7 'Downham Royal' (MinBa)
8 'Duncan'
0 'Early Bird' (SD)
0 'Eastwood Pinky' (MSC)
7 'Eastwood Star' (MSC)
8 'Eden Marc'
8 'Elizabeth Hammett' (MinD)
0 'Elizabethan' (SD)
0 'Elmbrook Rebel' (GSC)
9 'Exotic Dwarf' (Sin)(Lil)
9 'Flying Picket'
9 'Formby Perfection' (MD)
0 'Fred Sheard' (MinD)
0 'Free Lance' (MSC)
9 'Gale Lane' (Pom)
0 'Gerald Grace' (LSC)
0 'Ginger Nut' (Pom)
8 'Ginger Willo'
8 'Glenafton' (Pom)
8 'Glenbank Honeycomb'
0 'Golden Fizz' (MinBa)
0 'Golden Hope' (MinD)
0 'Hamari Saffron' (MSC)
0 'Hamari Sunset' (MSC)
0 'Haseley Cameo' (SD)
0 'Haseley Pearl' (DBa)
0 'Haseley Triumph' (SD)
8 'Hazel' (Pom)
0 'Hazel's Surprise' (SD)
8 'Higherfield Crown' (SC)

0 'Highgate Lustre' (MSC)
8 'Highgate Torch' (MSC)
8 'Hilda Clare' (Col)
0 'Holland Herald' (LSC)
7 'Horn of Plenty' (MinD)
0 'Hot Spot' (MinD)
8 'Ice Queen' (SWL)
9 'Imp' (Sin)(Lil)
7 'Inca Metropolitan' (LD)
9 'Inflammation' (Sin)(Lil)
9 'Invader' (SC)
9 'Jancis' (MinSC)
8 'Jane Horton' (Col)
8 'Janet Clarke' (Pom)
8 'Jescot Jess' (MinD)
0 'Jescot Jim' (SD)
8 'Jescot Nubia' (SSC)
8 'Jill Day' (SC)
9 'Jill Doc' (MD)
9 'Joy Bennett' (MD)
9 'Joyce Green' (GSC)
8 'Jo's Choice' (MinD)
9 'Kenn Emerland'
8 'Kenora Carousel'
8 'Kenora Sunburst'
8 'Kimi' (O)
0 'Kim's Marc' (SC)
9 'Kiwi Nephew' (SSC)
8 'Kym Willo' (Pom)
9 'La Cierva' (Col)
9 'La Corbiere' (DwBa)
0 'Lady Orpah' (SD)
8 'Lady Sunshine' (SSC)
0 'Laurence Fisher' (MSC)
0 'Lavendale' (MinD)
7 'Lavender Leycett'
0 'Lavender Pontiac' (SC)
8 'Lemon Hornsey' (SD)
0 'Leverton Chippy' (SD)
7 'Limited Edition'
8 'Little Conn' (Pom)
9 'Little Dorrit' (Sin)(Lil)
0 'Little Sally' (Pom)
9 'Lloyd Huston' (GSC)
7 'Louise Bailey'
9 'Love's Dream' (SWL)
9 'Lula Pattie' (GD)
8 'Madame Vera' (SD)
7 'Madelaine Ann' (GD)
7 'Margaret Duross' (GD)
7 'Margaret Jean' (GD)
8 'Mariposa' (Col)
8 'Masons' (SWL)
8 'Mauvine'
8 'Meiktila' (SWL)
0 'Melanie Jane (MSC)
9 'Melton' (MinD)
9 'Merriwell Topic' (MD)
0 'Millbank Inferno' (SD)
8 'Minley Iris' (Pom)
0 'Miranda' (MSC)
8 'Moonlight' (SD)
9 'Morley Lady' (SD)
0 'Morley Lass' (SSC)
7 'Mrs Silverston' (SD)
9 'Nescio' (Pom)
0 'Nettie' (MinBa)
8 'Neveric' (LSC)
0 'Newby' (MinD)
8 'Norm Williams'
9 'Omo' (Sin)(Lil)
7 'Onslow Linda Ann'
8 'Ornamental Rays' (SC)
8 'Pamela' (SD)
0 'Pastel Pontiac' (SC)
0 'Pat Seed' (MD)
0 'Patti-Pink' (SSC)
9 'Peace Pact' (SWL)
0 'Peach Pontiac' (SC)
9 'Peachette' (Misc)(Lil)
0 'Pearl Hornsey' (SD)
9 'Pearl Sharowean' (MSC)
9 'Peters Glorie' (MD)
9 'Pink Leycett' (GD)
0 'Pink Worton Ann' (MinD)
8 'Pippa' (SC)
7 'Pop Stretton' (GSC)
7 'Poppa Jim'
8 'Porcelain' (SWL)
9 'Pot Black' (MinBa)
8 'Primrose Bryn' (SSC)
0 'Promise' (MSC)(Fim)
0 'Purple Doris Day' (SC)
7 'Purple Joy' (MD)
7 'R Nash'
8 'Rachel's Place'
7 'Raffles' (SD)
8 'Rani'
0 'Readley' (SWL)
8 'Red Admiral' (MinBa)
8 'Red Delight' (Col)
9 'Red Dwarf' (Sin)(Lil)
9 'Red Lotus'
8 'Red Schweitzer'
8 'Regal Kerkrade' (SC)
0 'Robbie Huston' (LSC)
8 'Roberta' (LD)
8 'Rokesley Mini ' (MinC)
9 'Rosalie' (Pom)
9 'Rose Newby' (MinD)
7 'Rose Symbol'
8 'Rose Willo' (Pom)
8 'Rosewood' (SSC)
8 'Rotonde' (SC)
0 'Ruskin Dynasty' (SD)
9 'Ruskin Emil' (SC)
8 'Ruskin Melody'
9 'Saint Croix' (GSC)
7 'Salmon Athalie'
7 'Salmon Kerkrade'
9 'Samantha' (DwB)
0 'Sandra Chapman' (MSC)
0 'Sango' (MinBa)
8 'Scarborough'
9 'Scaur Princess' (SD)
9 'Scott's United' (MinD)
7 'Senzoe Jenny'
9 'Sharowean Pride' (MSC)
9 'Sherwood Sunrise' (SD)
9 'Shy Princess' (MC)
0 'Sonia' (MinBa)
9 'Stoke Festival '86' (SSC)
9 'Stolze von Berlin (MinBa)
9 'Stoneleigh Cherry' (Pom)
8 'Stoneleigh Joyce' (Pom)
8 'Strawberry Gem'
7 'Stump Cross'
8 'Sue Willo' (Pom)
8 'Suffolk Punch' (MD)
0 'Sugar Candy' (MSC)
8 'Sunburst' (Col)
0 'Supermarket' (MSC)
9 'Sure Thing' (MC)
7 'Swallow Falls'
9 'Sweetheart' (SD)
7 'Symbol Jim'
8 'Teatime' (MSC)
0 'The Bride' (SC)
0 'Tinker's White' (SD)
9 'Tiny Tot' (Misc)(Lil)
9 'Topaz Puff'
0 'Tourbillon' (LC)
0 'Trelawny' (GD)
7 'Twiggy' (SWL)
0 'Val Saint Lambert' (MC)
8 'Vicky Crutchfield' (SWL)
7 'Vicky Jackson' (SWL)
9 'Vidal Rhapsody' (MSC)
8 'Vidal Tracy' (SSC)
0 'Vigor' (SWL)
8 'Walter Hardesty'
8 'Weston Aramac'
9 'Weston Forge' (SC)
8 'White Lady Linda' (SD)
7 'White Marc'
8 'William Gregory'
8 'Willo Fairy'
9 'Willo Flecks' (Pom)
8 'Willo's Flame'
8 'Willo's Night' (Pom)
8 'Winston Churchill' (MinD)
8 'Winter Dawn' (SWL)
9 'Wood Plumpton'
8 'Wootton Amber'
8 'Worton Bluestreak' (SSC)
7 'Worton Ruth' (SD)
7 'Wyndal Horizon'
0 'Yellow Frank Hornsey' (SD)
8 'Yellow Jubilee'
8 'Yellow Symbol' (MSC)
8 'Yelno Harmony' (SWL)

DAPHNE
9 ***cneorum*** 'Major'
0 ***jasminea*** forms
0 ***kiusiana***
0 'Louis Mountbatten'
0 ***mezereum*** 'Variegata'
0 ***petraea***
9 'Rosetii'

DELOSPERMA
9 ***deschampsii***
9 ***ornatulum***

DELPHINIUM
8 'Antares'
8 'Aphrodite'
9 Belladonna 'Capri'
8 'Blue Springs'
8 'Ceylon'
8 ***cheilanthum***
0 'Cinderella'
8 'Claire'
9 ***denudatum***
7 ***glareosum***
8 'Gossamer'
8 'Great Expectations'
0 'Horizon'
0 'Jennifer Langdon'
0 'Jo Jo'
0 'Jumbo'
0 'Lady Eleanor'
0 'Loch Katrine'
8 'Loch Lomond'
0 'Loch Maree'
0 'Loch Morar'
0 'Magic Moment'
0 ***menziesii***
8 'Moody Blues'
0 'Patricia'
0 'Peacock'
0 'Peter Pan'
0 ***pylzowii***
0 'Rev E Lascelles'
8 'Rosy Future'
0 'Round Table'
8 'Sarah Edwards'
0 'Savrola'
0 'Sentinel'
0 'Silver Jubilee'
8 'Wheatear'
8 'Zeus'

DENDRANTHEMA
9 'Alf Price' (25b)
7 'Alice Fitton' (7b)
9 'Alison McNamara' (3b)
7 'Amanda' (11)
8 'Amber Chessington' (25a)
7 'Amber Leading Lady' (25b)
7 'Amy Fitton' (4a)
8 'Ann Dickson' (25a)
7 'Apricot Harry Gee' (1)
0 'Apricot Madeleine' (29c)
0 'Apricot Margaret' (29c)
0 'Arcadia'
9 'Ark Royal' (24b)
9 'Arkle' (25a)
7 'Arnold Fitton' (1)
0 'Arthur' (25a)
9 'Bambino' (29c)
7 'Barbara Hall' (23a)
7 'Barker's Wine' (24c)
7 'Barnsley' (5a)
8 'Batley Centenary' (25b)
7 'Beaujolais' (24b)
7 'Bergerac' (24b)
9 'Betty Saxton' (24a)
7 'Birmingham' (2)
7 'Blanche Poitevine' (5b)
8 'Bonus' (24a)
7 'Bowers Jim'
0 'Bravo' (25a)
7 'Breakaway'
8 'Brighton' (25b)
7 'Broadway Flare' (29c)
7 'Broadway Magic' (19e)

7 'Broadway Peach' (29c)
7 'Broadway Royal' (29c)
8 'Broadway Sovereign ' (29c)
7 'Bronze Eda Fitton' (23a)
8 'Bronze Emilia' (29c)
9 'Bronze Juweeltje'
0 'Bronze Mayford Perfection' (4a)
7 'Bronze Miss World' (24a)
9 'Bronze Nathalie' (29c)
7 'Bronze Shoesmith Salmon (4a)
0 'Bronze Venice' (24b)
7 'Bullfinch' (12a)
7 'Candy' (7a)
9 'Capulet' (3b)
8 'Carmine Margaret' (24b)
9 'Carol Moonlight' (29b)
7 'Carrie' (25a)
9 'Chaffinch' (22a)
7 'Chanelle' (25a)
0 'Chatsworth' (29c)
7 'Cheltenham Show' (25a)
9 'Cherry Chintz' (24a)
7 'Chesswood Beauty' (7b)
8 'Chintz' (24b)
8 'Chippendale' (24a)
9 'Christina' (25b)
8 'Clarette'
7 'Conderton' (15a)
0 'Copper Rylands Gem' (24b)
8 'Copper Spoon'
7 'Coral Rynoon' (9d)
9 'Countdown' (5a)
7 'Countryman' (24b)
7 'Cranforth' (24b)
9 'Crimson Daily Mirror' (5a)
0 'Crimson Purple Glow' (5a)
9 'Crimson Venice' (24b)
7 'Crimson Woolman's Glory ' (7a)
8 'Cropthorne'
0 'Crown Derby' (15a)
9 'Daily Mirror' (5a)
7 'Dark Eve Gray' (24b)
8 'Dark Pennine Pink' (29c)
0 'Doreen Bircumshaw' (24a)
8 'Dorridge Jewel' (15a)
0 'Dragoon' (9c)
0 'Early Bird' (24b)
9 'Early Red Cloak' (24b)
7 'Eda Fitton' (23a)
7 'Edith Goodall' (24a)
9 'Elsie Prosser' (1)
8 'Emilia' (29c)
0 'Encore'
7 'Enid Whiston' (4b)
9 'Eve Gray' (24b)
9 'Fairisle' (24b)
0 'Fairway' (15a)
7 'Far North' (5a)
0 'Fiona Lynn (24a)
9 'Flambard' (24b)
9 'Flo Cooper' (25a)
7 'Forest Flare' (24b)
7 'Fred Raynor'
9 'Gemma Jones' (5b)
7 'Gerrie Hoek' (29c)
7 'Gillian Gore' (23b)
0 'Ginger' (30)
9 'Glorie'
9 'Goldcrest' (25b)
9 'Golden Echo' (4a)
7 'Golden Elegance' (5a)
9 'Golden Oyster' (25b)
9 'Golden Salter'
7 'Golden Shoesmith Salmon (4a)
0 'Golden Stardust' (24b)
7 'Golden Woolman's Glory' (7a)
0 'Goldmine' (24b)
7 'Goldway' (25b)
9 'Granny Gow' (29d)
9 'Graphic' (23b)
9 'Green Goddess' (1)
9 'Greensleeves' (11)
0 'Hamburg' (25a)
9 'Hardwick Lemon' (29c)
0 'Hardwick Primrose' (29c)
8 'Harford'
7 'Harry Whiston' (1)
9 'Hayley Boon' (25b)
0 'Hekla'
9 'Highland Skirmish' (29d)
9 'Honey Margaret' (29e)
0 'Horace Martin'
0 'James Hall' (5a)
7 'Jessie Gilmour' (23a)
9 'Jessie Habgood' (1)
7 'Jinx' (7b)
7 'John Wood' (5a)
7 'Julie Ann' (25b)
7 'Just Tom' (24b)
7 'Kingfisher' (12a)
7 'Kissy'
8 'Lady Anna' (25a)
7 'Lapley Blush' (29b)
7 'Lapley Bracken' (29d)
7 'Lapley Hallmark' (29c)
7 'Lapley Princess' (29c)
7 'Lapley Rose' (29b)
7 'Lapley Snow' (29d)
7 'Lapley Sunset'
0 'Lemon Drop' (23a)
7 'Linda Young' (5b)
7 'Lipstick' (28)
7 'Littleton'
9 'Lovely Charmer' (7b)
7 'Lydia' (25a)
9 'Madge Welby' (25b)
0 'Manito'
7 'Margaret Fitton' (23b)
0 'Marian Gosling' (24b)
9 'Marie Taylor' (29c)
0 'Martina' (24b)
0 'Mary Dyer' (24a)
7 'Mason's Golden'
0 'Mayford Perfection' (5a)
8 'Michael Fish' (25b)
7 'Michael Pullom' (25a)
7 'Morning Star' (12a)
7 'Mosquito' (28b)
8 'Mrs Farley'
8 'Munsel'
9 'Muriel Foster' (29d)
7 'My Jeanie' (25a)
7 'My Love' (7b)
7 'Naden Pound'
9 'Ned Holdaway' (25b)
7 'Nora Brook'
8 'Olga Williams' (25b)
7 'Olwyn' (4b)
0 'Orchid Helen'
8 'Orlando' (25a)
9 'Oyster' (25b)
8 'Paint Box' (24b)
7 'Pandora' (5a/ 12a)
8 'Pat' (6b)
7 'Pat Amos' (23a)
9 'Peach Chessington' (25a)
9 'Peach Juweeltje'
0 'Pelsall Imperial' (3a)
7 'Pelsall Lady' (25a)
0 'Pennine Air' (29d)
9 'Pennine Alfie' (29f)
9 'Pennine Ann' (29a)
9 'Pennine Belle' (29d)
9 'Pennine Brandy' (29c)
8 'Pennine Brighteye' (29c)
8 'Pennine Bronze' (29c)
9 'Pennine Cadet' (29a)
8 'Pennine Champ' (29c)
9 'Pennine Chorus' (29c)
9 'Pennine Chum' (29d)
8 'Pennine Dancer'
0 'Pennine Dandy' (29c)
9 'Pennine Darkeye' (29c)
9 'Pennine Dew' (29c)
9 'Pennine Dixie' (29d)
9 'Pennine Dream' (29d)
8 'Pennine Echo' (29d)
9 'Pennine Elf' (29c)
8 'Pennine Fairy' (29c)
9 'Pennine Flirt' (29b)
9 'Pennine Gem' (29c)
9 'Pennine Globe' (29a)
8 'Pennine Gloss' (29d)
7 'Pennine Gold' (29c)
0 'Pennine Jewel' (29f)
9 'Pennine Marvel' (29c)
8 'Pennine Model' (29c)
8 'Pennine Penny ' (29d)
9 'Pennine Plume' (29d)
8 'Pennine Polka' (29c)
9 'Pennine Prince' (29c)
9 'Pennine Prize' (29a)
9 'Pennine Quiver' (29d)
9 'Pennine Rave' (29a)
7 'Pennine Red' (19c)
9 'Pennine Rose' (29c)
0 'Pennine Salute' (29d)
8 'Pennine Sand' (29c)
7 'Pennine Shell' (29c)
9 'Pennine Shield' (29c)
8 'Pennine Smile' (29c)
8 'Pennine Solo' (29d)
0 'Pennine Sweetheart' (29c)
9 'Pennine Tan' (29c)
9 'Pennine Torch' (29d)
8 'Pennine Tune' (29a)
0 'Pennine Waltz' (29c)
7 'Penny Lane' (25b)
9 'Peter Pan' (24b)
0 'Phil Oultram' (5b)
7 'Pilsley Queen' (29c)
9 'Pink Gambit' (24a)
7 'Pink Mason' (7b)
7 'Plushred' (4b)
7 'Poppet' (28a)
0 'Port Stanley' (5b)
7 'Primrose Olwyn' (4b)
7 'Purple Gerrie Hoek'
0 'Rebecca Walker' (25a)
9 'Red Claire Louise' (24b)
8 'Red Cropthorne'
0 'Red Early Bird' (24b)
7 'Red Fair Lady' (5a)
7 'Red Glory' (7a)
9 'Redwing' (4b)
7 'Ringdove' (12a)
0 'Romantika'
7 'Romany' (2)
7 'Ronald Rowe' (24b)
8 'Rose Madeleine' (29c)
7 'Rosedew' (25a)
0 'Rutland' (24a)
7 'Rychart' (9d)
7 'Rychoice' (9d)
0 'Ryfire' (9d)
9 'Sally Ball' (29a)
0 'Sally Duchess' (25a)
0 'Salmon Allouise' (25b)
7 'Salmon Chessington' (25a)
0 'Salmon Orpheus' (1)
7 'Salmon Primrose'
8 'Salmon Rutland' (24a)
0 'Sassen'
0 'Scarlet Pennine Crimson' (29c)
0 'Schaffhausen'
7 'Seychelle' (2)
0 'Sheffield Anniversary' (24a)
9 'Sherwood Forester' (24a)
9 'Shirley Imp' (3b)
7 'Sierra' (25b)
9 'Skylark'
7 'Snow Elf' (28)
9 'Snowcap' (14a)
7 'Snowdon' (5b/ 9c)
0 'Soccer' (25a)
0 'Southway Seville' (29c)
8 'Spartan Bronze' (29c)
8 'Spartan Orange' (29d)
8 'Spartan Pink' (29c)
8 'Spartan Rose'
8 'Spartan White'
8 'Spartan Yellow' (29c)
9 'Standby' (24b)
0 'Stardust' (24b)
9 'Sun Blaze' (29a)
0 'Suncharm Orange' (22a)
7 'Sunflash' (5b/ 12a)
8 'Sunset Rylands Gem' (24b)
0 'Susan Freestone' (24b)
9 'Susan Pullom' (25a)
9 'Sydenham Girl' (24b)
7 'Tang' (12)

7 'Terry Morris' (7b)
7 'Tiara' (28a)
7 'Tinkerbelle' (24b/ 12a)
9 'Tom Stillwell'
9 'Tone Glow' (29a)
9 'Tone Sail' (29a)
0 'Triumph'
0 'Vanity Apricot'
0 'Vanity Yellow'
9 'Wagtail' (22a)
0 'Wessex Sentry' (29d)
0 'Wessex Shell' (29d)
8 'White Len Futerill' (25a)
0 'White Sally Duchess' (25a)
0 'Winchcombe' (29c)
7 'Winter Queen' (5b)
9 'Woody's Choice' (5b)
7 'Woolman's Glory' (7a)
9 'Worcester' (14b)
0 'Yellow Broadway Sovereign' (29c)
9 'Yellow Chessington' (25a)
7 'Yellow Cricket' (25b)
8 'Yellow Emilia' (29c)
7 'Yellow Fair Lady' (5a)
9 'Yellow Jemma Wilson' (23b)
8 'Yellow Juweeltje'
0 'Yellow Pamela' (29c)
9 'Yellow Salter'
7 'Yellow Sam Vinter' (5a)
9 'Yorkshire Television' (5a)

DESCHAMPSIA

9 ***cespitosa*** 'Tardiflora'
9 – 'Tauträger'

DEUTZIA

0 'Avalanche'
8 ***crenata nakaiana***
9 × ***kalmiiflora*** 'Pom Pom'
8 ***purpurascens***
0 ***sp.*** B&L 12275
8 ***vilmoriniae***

DIANTHUS

9 'Achievement' (p)
9 'Alfred Galbally' (b)
9 'Alfriston' (b)
0 ***alpinus*** 'Adonis'
9 – 'Ascreavie Form'
9 – 'Ruby Venus'
0 – x callizonus
8 'Amarinth' (p)
0 ***angulatus***
9 'Anne Jones' (b)
9 'Anthony' (p)
9 'Apollo' (b)
8 'Avoca Purple' (p)
9 'Barbara Norton' (p)
0 ***barbatus*** 'Wee Willie'
9 'Barton's Pink' (p)
9 'Belle of Bookham' (b)
7 'Beryl Giles' (pf)
9 'Bressingham Pink' (p)
9 'Brilliance' (p)
9 'Bryony Lisa' (b)
9 'Can-Can' (pf)
0 ***carthusianorum*** Atrorubens group
9 'Charles Edward' (p)
7 'Cherry Heldenbrau' (pf)
9 'Cherry Pie' (p)
9 'Chris Crew' (b)
9 'Cranborne Seedling' (p)
9 'Crimson Clove' (p)
9 'Crimson Treasure' (p)
0 'Crusader' (b)
9 'David Saunders' (b)
9 ***deltoides*** 'Steriker' (p)
0 – 'Vampir'
7 'Diane Marie' (pf)
9 'Dianne' (pf)
9 'Dicker Clove' (b)
0 'Doctor Danger'
8 'Donizetti' (p)
9 'Doris Galbally' (b)
0 'Double Devon' (p)
9 'Downs Souvenir' (b)
9 'Downs Unique' (b)
0 'Duchess of Fife' (p)
0 'Duke of Argyll'
9 'Edenside Glory' (b)
9 'Eileen Neal' (b)
9 'Eileen O'Connor' (b)
9 'Elizabeth Jane' (p)
0 'Favourite Lady' (p)
9 'Fay' (p)
0 'Firefly' (b)
9 'Flanders' (b)
7 'G J Sim' (pf)
9 'Gaiety' (p)
8 'George Vernon' (pf)
9 'Glenda' (p)
9 'Glory'
9 'Goblin' (p)
9 'Golden Cross' (b)
9 'Grace How' (b)
0 'Grace Mather' (p)
7 'Grandad' (p)
0 ***gratianopolitanus*** 'Compactus Eydangeri' (p)
0 – x subacaulis
9 'Grey Dove' (b)
9 'Grome' (p)
9 'Hannah Louise' (b)
7 'Hardwicke's Pink' (p)
9 'Hazel Ruth' (b)
9 'Heidi' (p)
9 'Heldenbrau' (pf)
9 'Helen Keates' (b)
9 'Helga' (p)
9 'Highland Gem' (p)
8 'Houstan House' (p)
9 'Howard Hitchcock' (b)
0 'Indios' (pf)
8 'Ipswich Crimson' (p)
9 'Irene Della-Torré' (b)
0 'Irish Pink' (p)
0 'J M Bibby' (pf)
8 'Jack Wood' (pf)
9 'Jack's Lass' (pf)
0 'Jacqueline's Delight' (p)
9 'Jane Bowen' (p)
9 'John Malcolm' (p)
9 'Kathleen Hitchcock' (b)
9 'Katy' (b)
9 'Lily Lesurf' (b)
9 'Little Beauty' (pf)
9 'Lord Nuffield' (b)
9 ***lumnitzeri***
9 'Maggie' (p)
9 'Maisie Neal' (b)
9 'Margaret Curtis' (p)
9 'Maudie Hinds' (b)
8 'Maurice Prichard' (p)
7 'Maythorne' (p)
9 'Mercury' (p)
9 'Messines White' (p)
9 'Michael Saunders' (b)
8 'Monarch' (pf)
0 ***monspessulanus***
9 'Mrs Blarney's Old Pink' (p)
8 'Mrs Dunlop's Old Pink '
8 'Mrs Macbride' (p)
7 'Oakwood Dainty' (p)
9 'Oakwood Dorothy' (p)
0 'Old Crimson Clove' (b)
8 'Old Fringed Pink' (p)
0 'Old Irish'
9 'Orchid Lace' (p,a)
9 ***pavonius*** 'Roaschia'
9 'Peter Adamson' (b)
9 'Peter Wood' (b)
9 'Petula' (p)
9 'Pink Bouquet' (p)
0 'Pink Delight' (p)
0 'Plum Diadem' (p)
9 'Pluto' (p)
9 'Portrait Sim' (pf)
8 'Pride of Ayrshire' (p)
8 'Raeden Pink' (p)
9 'Raspberry Ripple' (p)
9 'Riccardo' (b)
9 'Richard Pollak' (b)
9 'Robert Douglas' (b)
9 'Robert Smith' (b)
0 'Rubin' (pf)
8 ***rupicola***
0 'Ruth' (p)
9 'Sacha' (pf)
9 'Salmon Fragrant Ann' (p)
9 'Salmon Queen' (b)
9 'Sandra Neal' (b)
9 'Shaston Supreme' (b)
9 'Sheila Short' (pf)
0 'Sheila Weir' (b)
9 'Show Ideal' (p)
9 'Shrimp' (b)
9 'Snowflake' (p)
0 'Snowshill Fringed' (p)
7 ***spiculifolius***
9 'Stanley Stroud' (b)
0 ***superbus longicalycinus***
9 'Syston Beauty' (p)
9 'Tamsin Fifield' (b)
8 'Taunton' (p)
0 'Tayside Red' (m)
9 'Tom Welborn' (p)
9 'Tony Cutler' (b)
9 'Uncle Teddy' (b)
8 'Welwyn' (p)
9 'Whatfield Pretty Lady' (p)
9 'Whitesmith' (b)
9 'William of Essex' (p)
9 'Winnie Lesurf' (b)
9 'Wisp' (p)
0 ***xylorrizus***
9 'Zephyr' (b)

DIAPENSIA

9 ***lapponica obovata***

DICENTRA

0 ***peregrina***
8 – ***alba***

DICKSONIA

0 ***lanata***

DIEFFENBACHIA

0 × ***bausei***
0 'Janet Weidner'
0 ***seguine*** 'Exotica'
0 – 'Jenmanii'
0 'Wilson's Delight'

DIETES

7 ***grandiflora***

DIGITALIS

9 ***leucophaea***
9 ***lutea*** 'Sarah'
0 ***purpurea nevadensis***

DIONYSIA

9 ***archibaldii***
9 ***aretioides*** 'Paul Furse'
0 ***bryoides***
0 ***curviflora***
0 ***denticulata***
0 ***janthina***
0 ***michauxii***
0 ***revoluta canescens***
0 – ***revoluta***
0 ***tapetodes***

DIOSPYROS

7 ***glaucifolia***

DIPELTA

9 ***ventricosa***

DISCARIA

0 ***toumatou***

DISPORUM

8 ***sessile yakushimense***

DISTYLIUM

9 ***myricoides***

DODECATHEON

0 ***conjugens***

DOUGLASIA

0 ***nivalis***

DRABA

8 ***alpina***
0 ***daurica***
0 ***dedeana mawii***
8 ***fladnizensis***
0 ***hispanica***
0 ***oreibata***
0 ***setosa***
0 ***sp.*** AGST 214
9 ***streptocarpa***

DRACAENA

0 ***deremensis*** 'Compacta'
0 ***fragrans*** 'Lindenii'
0 ***reflexa***

DRACOCEPHALUM

0 ***heterophyllum***

9 *integrifolium*
8 *nutans*

DREPANOSTACHYUM
9 *khasianum*

DRYAS
9 *octopetala lanata*

DRYOPTERIS
9 *dilatata* 'Crispa Whiteside'
7 *filix-mas* Grandiceps group

DURANTA
9 *plumieri* 'Variegata'

ECHINOPS
0 *chantavicus*
9 *ritro ruthenicus*

EHRETIA
0 *dicksonii*

EICHHORNIA
7 *crassipes* 'Major'

ELAEAGNUS
0 *angustifolia orientalis*
8 × *ebbingei* 'Tricolor'

ELAEOCARPUS
9 *decipiens*
0 *pusillus*

ELEUTHEROCOCCUS
9 *henryi*

ELLIOTTIA
9 *racemosa*

EMPETRUM
8 *hermaphroditum*
8 *nigrum* 'Bernstein'
8 – 'Compactum'
8 – *japonicum*
8 – 'Smaragd'
0 *rubrum*

ENGELMANNIA
0 *pinnatifida*

ENKIANTHUS
9 *campanulatus matsudae*
9 – *sikokianus*
0 *cernuus*
9 *serrulatus*

EPACRIS
0 *pauciflora*

EPHEDRA
0 *intermedia*

EPIGAEA
9 *gaultherioides*

EPILOBIUM
9 *canum* 'Splendens Plenum'
0 *glabellum* 'Roseum'
9 *gunnianum*

EPIMEDIUM
0 *grandiflorum* 'Rose Glow'

EQUISETUM
9 *telmateia*

ERICA
0 See also CALLUNA
8 *andevalensis*
8 *carnea* 'Amy Backhouse'
8 – 'Margery Frearson'
8 – 'Mayfair White'
8 – 'Mr Reeves'
8 – 'Rosy Morn'
8 – 'Urville'
8 – 'Winter Red'
8 *ciliaris alba*
8 – 'Jennifer Anne'
8 – 'Maweana'
8 – 'Ram'
8 – 'Rock Pool'
8 *cinerea* 'Alette'
0 – 'Angarrack'
8 – 'Anja Blum'
8 – 'Aquarel'
8 – 'Atrorubens Daisy Hill'
8 – 'Atrosanguinea Reuthe's Variety'
9 – 'Creel'
8 – 'Discovery'
0 – 'Electra'
8 – 'Guernsey Pink'
8 – 'Heatherbank'
8 – 'Heathfield'
9 – 'Hutton Pentreath'
8 – 'Hutton Seedling'
8 – 'Iberian Beauty'
7 – 'Lankidden'
0 – 'Lilian Martin'
8 – 'Marina'
0 – 'Michael Hugo'
8 – 'Pallida'
8 – 'Penaz'
0 – 'Rock Ruth'
8 – 'Rose Gem'
8 – 'Uschie Ziehmann'
8 – 'Violetta'
0 – 'Yvonne'
0 × *darleyensis*
9 *erigena* 'Ivory'
8 *mackayana* 'Donegal'
8 *maderensis*
8 *oatesii*
8 *perlata*
0 *scoparia*
9 – *azorica*
9 × *stuartii* 'Nacung'
8 *taxifolia*
8 *tetralix* 'Alba Praecox'
8 – 'Humoresque'
8 – 'Mary Grace'
8 – 'Rosea'
8 – 'Terschelling'
9 *vagans* 'Alba Nana'
8 – 'Bianca'
8 – 'Carnea'
8 – 'Elegant Spike'
9 *verticillata*
8 *vestita*
0 × *watsonii* 'Cherry Turpin'

ERIGERON
9 'Blue Beauty'
0 *glabellus*
9 *myosotis*
0 *polymorphus*

8 *roylei*
9 *speciosus* 'Roseus'
9 'White Quakeress'

ERIOCEPHALUS
8 *africanus*

ERIOGONUM
9 *giganteum*
0 *gracilipes*
8 *ovalifolium*
0 *umbellatum* JCA 9247

ERIOPHORUM
0 *brachyantherum*

ERODIUM
0 'Bedderi'
9 *petraeum petraeum*
9 *romanum*

ERYNGIUM
0 *creticum*
0 *dichotomum* Caeruleum group
8 *ebracteatum*
7 *serra*
0 *sp. ex* Todhunter
7 × *zabelii* 'Spring Hills'

ERYSIMUM
0 *(See also* CHEIRANTHUS)
0 *amoenum*
8 *concinnum* cream
0 *linifolium glaucum*
9 *odoratum*
0 'Wenlock Beauty Variegated'

ESCALLONIA
0 'Glasnevin Hybrid'
0 *laevis* 'Gold Ellen'
0 'Lord Headfort's Seedling'
0 'Red Guard'
0 'Red Hedger'
0 *rubra macrantha* 'Sanguinea'
0 'William Watson'
0 'Wintonensis'

EUCALYPTUS
8 *amygdalina*
0 *caesia*
8 *lehmannii*
8 *maculata*
8 *mitchelliana*
8 *nova-anglica*
9 *ovata*
9 *populnea*
8 *preissiana*
0 *pulchella*
8 *rodwayi*
9 *rossii*
8 *tenuiramis*

EUONYMUS
8 × *buxifolius* 'Nanus'
0 *europaeus* 'Chrysophyllus'
0 *fortunei* 'Dart's Covergirl'
9 – *radicans*
0 *grandiflorus*
9 *hamiltonianus maackii*

7 *japonicus* 'Macrophyllus'

EUPHORBIA
8 *dendroides*
0 'Goldburst'
0 *macrostegia*
9 *millotii*

EXOCHORDA
7 *giraldii*

FAGUS
0 *moesiaca*
0 *sylvatica* 'Cockleshell'

FALLOPIA
0 *elliptica*

FALLUGIA
9 *paradoxa*

FESTUCA
7 *curvula crassifolia*

FICUS
0 *elastica*
0 *leprieurii*
0 *religiosa*

FILIPENDULA
0 *palmata* 'Alba'

FITTONIA
0 *verschaffeltii*

FORSYTHIA
9 × *intermedia* 'Phyllis'

FRAGARIA
F × *ananassa* 'Grandee'
F – 'Tantallon'
8 *vesca* 'Reine des Vallées'
9 – 'Semperflorens Alba'

FRAXINUS
9 *bungeana*
9 *chinensis*
7 *cuspidata*
9 *excelsior* 'Argenteovariegata'
9 – 'Aurea Pendula'
0 *paxiana*
9 *pennsylvanica subintegerrima*
7 *quadrangulata*
7 *rotundifolia* 'Flame'
7 *sogdiana* Potamophila group
0 *spaethiana*
0 'Veltheimii'

FRITILLARIA
8 *alfredae platyptera*
9 *ariana*
0 *caucasica caucasica*
8 *graeca*
8 *imperialis* 'Sulphurino'
9 *meleagris* 'Jupiter'
9 – 'Poseidon'
9 – 'Purple King'
9 – 'Saturnus'
9 *montana*

FUCHSIA
0 'Aad Franck'
9 'Aber Falls'
9 'Abt. Koloman Holzinger'

9 'Airball'
0 'Aladna's Marina'
0 'Aladna's Sander'
0 'Albert H'
0 'Albertina'
0 'Alma Hulscher'
0 'American Prelude'
9 ***americana elegans***
9 'Angela'
0 'Anjo'
0 'Ann Pacey'
0 'Anne Howard Tripp'
0 'Anniek Geerlings'
0 'Anthea Bond'
0 'Anthonetta'
0 'Arc en Ciel'
9 'Architect Ludwig Mercher'
0 'Arels Fleur'
0 'Art Deco'
0 'Art Nouveau'
0 'Aubergine'
0 'Avon Gold'
0 'Axel of Denmark'
0 'Baby Love'
0 'Baby Veerman'
0 'Barry Sheppard'
0 'Belinda Allen'
0 'Belle de Lisse'
0 'Berbanella'
0 'Berba's Fleur'
0 'Berba's Francis Fenke'
0 'Berba's Happiness'
0 'Berba's Impossible'
0 'Berba's Inge Mariel'
0 'Berba's Ingrid'
0 'Berba's Love'
0 'Berba's Trio'
0 'Bernard Rawdin'
9 'Beryl's Jewel'
0 'Betma Whitison'
0 'Bill Gilbert'
0 'Blue Ranger'
0 'Bob Paisley'
9 'Bohémienne'
9 'Bosun's Superb'
9 'Bridal Pink'
0 'Brightling'
0 'Brunette'
0 'Carl Drude'
9 'Carmen'
0 'Caroline Imp'
0 'Catherine Claire'
0 'Cecil Glass'
0 'Cees van Braunschott'
9 'Chance Encounter'
0 'Chaos'
0 'Chartwell'
0 'Chatsworth'
0 'Checkmate'
0 'Chris'
0 'Chris van der Linden'
0 'Christine Clements'
0 'Cindy Robijn'
0 'Cinnabarrina'
0 'Cinnamon'
0 'Cissbury Gem'
9 'Clipper'
9 'Coconut Ice'
9 'Country Girl'
0 'Crown Derby'
0 'Dark Spider'
0 'Dark Treasure'
9 'Day by Day'
9 'Deben Petite'
0 'Deltaschön'
0 'Delta's Fellow'
0 'Delta's Rien'
0 'Delta's Robijn'
0 'Delta's Wonder'
0 'Derby Belle'
0 'Derby Countess'
0 'Derby Star'
9 'Diana Wright'
9 'Diana's Calypso'
0 'Didi'
0 'Diny Hetterscheid'
9 'Donauweibchen'
9 'Dorothy Woakes'
9 'Duchess of Petitport'
0 'Dutch Firebird'
0 'Dutch Flamingo'
0 'Earre Barre'
0 'Eelco Brinkman'
0 'El Matador'
9 'Elisabeth Nutzinger'
9 'Ellen Morgan'
0 'Elsine'
0 'Elsstar'
0 ***encliandra tetradactyla***
9 'Enstone'
9 'Erika Köth'
0 'Eroica'
0 'Ethel Weeks'
9 'Ethel Wilson'
0 'Eva Watkins'
0 'Fatima'
0 'Firenzi'
9 'Flamingo'
9 'Flarepath'
9 'Flim Flam'
0 'Flirt'
0 'Francois Villon'
0 'Frank Veerman'
0 'Frauke'
0 'Fred Standen'
9 'Fred's First'
0 'Freestyle'
0 'Frosty Bell'
0 'Garden Beauty'
0 'Gazette'
0 'Geertien'
0 'Geertje'
0 'Général Negrier'
0 'Geoff Barnett'
9 'Georg Bornemann'
0 'George Johnson'
0 'George Roe'
0 'Gidding'
0 'Gillian Shepherd'
9 'Gleneagles'
0 'Göttingen'
0 'Gold Leaf'
0 'Golden Lye's Favourite'
0 'Golden Spade'
9 'Goldsworth Beauty'
0 'Gondolier'
0 'Grace'
9 'Grace Groom'
9 'Grand Duke'
9 'Grayrigg'
0 'Guurtje'
9 'H M S Victorious'
0 'Harbour Bridge'
9 'Harlequin'
0 'Harriet Lye'
0 'Heather'
0 'Helene Houwen Claessen'
8 'Henriette Ernst'
0 'Hiawatha'
0 'Hilda May Salmon'
0 'HMS Victorious'
9 'Hobson'
0 'Ina Buxton'
0 'Iolanthe'
0 'Irene van Zoeren'
0 'Ivan Gadsby'
0 'Jack King'
9 'James Shurvell'
0 'Jan Bremer'
0 'Jan Houtsma'
0 'Janneke'
0 'Jaspers Donderslag'
9 'Jaunty'
0 'Je Maintiendrai'
9 'Jean Burton'
9 'Jean Pidcock'
0 'Joanne'
0 'Joan's Delight'
0 'Johannes Novinski'
0 'Joker'
0 'Jolanda Weeda'
0 'Julie Horton'
0 'Karen'
0 'Karin de Groot'
0 'Kathleen'
0 'Kathy Louise'
9 'Kentish Belle'
0 'Kentish Maid'
0 'Kiekeboe'
0 'King George V'
0 'Klein Beekestein'
9 'Kocarde'
0 'Kolibrie'
9 'Komeet'
0 'Lady Bower'
9 'Lady Dorothy'
0 'Larissa'
0 'Lavender Thumb'
0 'Lechlade Chinaman'
9 'Lechlade Fairy'
0 'Lechlade Magician'
0 'Lechlade Maiden'
0 'Lechlade Potentate'
0 'Lechlade Violet'
0 'Leo Goetelen'
9 'Liemers Lantaern'
0 'Lila Sunsa'
9 'Lilac Dainty'
0 'Lilian Windsor'
9 'Linda Pratt'
9 'Little One'
0 'Little Witch'
0 'Liver Bird'
0 'Lonneke'
0 'Look East'
0 'Loulabel'
0 'Love in Bloom'
9 'Love It'
0 'Loverdale'
0 'Lunter's Trots'
9 'Lustre Improved'
0 'Lye's Elegance'
0 'Lye's Perfection'
0 'Lynhurst'
0 'L'Ingenue'
0 'Madame Danjoux'
0 'Madame Lanteime'
0 'Madurodam'
0 ***magdalenae***
9 ***magellanica*** 'Ghostly Pink'
9 – 'Longipedunculata'
8 – ***myrtifolia***
0 'Margaret Thatcher'
9 'Margie'
0 'Marja'
0 'Martha Franck'
0 'Martyn Smedley'
0 'Mary Poppins'
0 'Max Jaffa'
9 'Medusa'
0 'Melissa Heavens'
0 'Mendocino Rose'
7 'Mephisto'
9 'Mercurius'
0 'Mia van der Zee'
0 ***microphylla hemsleyana***
0 'Millie Butler'
0 'Mistique'
0 'Mon Ami'
9 'Monsieur Joule'
0 'Montevideo'
9 'Morrells'
0 'Mosedale Hall'
9 'Mrs John D Fredericks'
0 'Muirfield'
9 'My Love'
0 'Nanne'
9 'Naomi Adams'
0 'Nemerlaer'
0 'Nettala'
0 'Nicolina'
0 'Night and Day'
0 'Oddfellow'
0 'Olympia'
0 'Omar Giant'
0 'Pamela Hutchinson'
0 'Panylla Prince'
0 'Patricia Bardgett'
0 'Patricia Ewart'
0 'Peper Harow'
9 'Pèredrup'
0 ***petiolaris***
9 'Petit Point'
0 'Piet G Vergeer'
9 'Pink Cornet'
9 'Pink Trumpet'
0 'Piquant'
0 'Pixie Bells'
0 'Playboy'
9 'Präsident Walter Morio'
9 'Prince Syray'
0 'Pukkie'
0 'Purper Klokje'
9 'Puttenden Manor'
9 'Queen of Bath'
0 'R L Lockerbie'
0 'Rachel Catherine'
9 'Rading's Michelle'
0 'Rambo'
9 'Ravensbarrow'
0 'Recy Holmes'
0 'Red Rain'
0 'Red Rover'
9 'Red Rum'
0 'Reflexa'
0 'Regina van Zoeren'
0 'Revival'
0 'Rhanee'

9 'Riccartonii Variegated'
0 'Rina Felix'
0 'Robert Hall'
0 'Robert Lutters'
9 'Ron Holmes'
0 'Rosabell'
0 'Rosedale'
9 'Rothbury Beauty'
9 'Royal Ruby'
9 'Royal Sovereign'
0 'Sangria'
0 'Saxondale'
8 'Schnabel'
0 'Schneewitcher'
9 'Severn Queen'
0 'Shady Blue'
9 'Sheila Hobson'
0 'Sherwood'
0 'Shower of Stars'
0 'Showtime'
0 'Shy Look'
0 'Skyway'
0 'Slender Lady'
9 'Snowcap Variegated'
0 'Snowflake'
8 'Spangles'
9 'Spotlight'
9 'Steve Wright'
0 'Storm Petrel'
0 'Summer Mist'
0 'Summer Night'
0 'Sundance'
0 'Susan Allen'
0 'Sweet Revenge'
0 ***sylvatica***
9 'Ted's'
8 'Telegraph'
0 'Tempo Doelo'
0 ***tetradactylla***
0 'Thomos'
9 ***thymifolia minimiflora***
9 – ***thymifolia***
I 'Tillettiana'
0 'Tina Head'
0 'Topsin'
9 'Tourtonne'
0 'Toven'
0 'Towi'
0 'Traviata'
9 'Tresco'
0 'Trubell'
0 'Ultralight'
0 'Vale of Belvoir'
0 'Valerie Cotterell'
0 'Vera Wilding'
0 'W F C Kampionen'
0 'Waltraud Strumper'
0 'Walz Blaukous'
0 'Walz Bugel'
0 'Walz Doedelzak'
0 'Walz Gitaar'
0 'Walz Gong'
0 'Walz Hobo'
0 'Walz Kalebas'
0 'Walz Kattesnoor'
0 'Walz Knipperbol'
0 'Walz Luit'
0 'Walz Mandoline'
0 'Walz Meermin'
0 'Walz Piano'
0 'Walz Ratel'
0 'Walz Tam Tam'
0 'Walz Toeter'
0 'Walz Triangl'
0 'Walz Viool'
0 'Wassernymph'
9 'Waveney Unique'
0 'Wee Lass'
0 'Wentelwieck'
0 'Whistling Rufus'
8 'White Clove'
0 'White Falls'
8 'White Gem'
0 'Whiteknights Glister'
0 'Whiteknights Ruby'
8 'Wicked Lady'
9 'Wild Glove'
0 'Wilf Tolley'
0 'Wilma Versloot'
9 'Winifred'
0 'Wise Choice'
0 'Yankee Clipper'
0 'Zaanlander'
0 'Zulu Queen'

GAGEA

9 ***lutea***

GAHNIA

0 ***grandis***

GAILLARDIA

9 'Aurea'
7 'Bremen'
9 'Chloe'
9 'Croftway Yellow'
9 'Fackelschein' ('Torchlight')
8 'Ipswich Beauty'

GALANTHUS

0 'Desdemona'
0 ***elwesii*** 'Whitallii'
9 'Maidwell C'
8 'Titania'

GALTONIA

9 ***princeps praecox***

GARDENIA

0 ***jasminoides*** 'Belmont'

GARRYA

0 ***laurifolia macrophylla***

GAULTHERIA

9 ***cordifolia***
9 ***erecta***
9 ***fragrantissima***
9 ***mucronata*** 'Goldsworth Pink'
9 – 'Goldsworth Red'
0 ***procumbens*** 'Darthuizer'
0 ***wardii***

GAYLUSSACIA

9 ***brachycera***

GAZANIA

8 ***rigens*** 'Torquay Silver'

GENISTA

8 ***berberidea***
0 ***falcata***
8 ***radiata***

GENTIANA

9 ***acaulis*** 'Harlin'
9 – 'Leith Vale'
8 – 'Nora Bradshaw'
0 ***algida igarishii***
9 ***alpina*** Trotter's form
0 ***brachyphylla***
8 'Bucksburn Azure'
9 ***burseri***
0 ***calycosa***
8 ***clusii*** 'Mount Rax'
8 ***cruciata phlogifolia***
8 'Elizabeth Brand'
9 ***gelida***
0 'Inverdevon'
9 'Mount Everest'
9 ***occidentalis***
0 ***pumila***
9 ***pyrenaica***
7 'Queen of the Blues'
0 ***sceptrum***
0 'Sinorna'
7 'The Souter'
0 ***tianschanica***
9 'Utterby Seedling'
9 ***wilsonii***

GENTIANOPSIS

0 ***crinita***

GEOGENANTHUS

0 ***undatus***

GERANIUM

8 x ***cantabrigiense*** 'Ingwersen'
9 – 'Ridsko'
0 ***collinum*** x clarkei
9 ***divaricatum***
9 ***himalayense*** 'Frances Perry'
0 x ***lindavicum*** 'Lissadel'
9 ***mascatense***
0 ***napuligerum***
0 x ***oxonianum*** Form B
0 ***pratense*** pale mauve form
9 ***sanguineum*** 'Hadspen'
9 ***schlechteri***

GEUM

9 ***chiloense*** 'Red Wings'
9 ***rivale*** cream form
7 ***triflorum campanulatum***

GIBASIS

9 ***linearis***

GLADIOLUS

7 'Ali Baba' (B)
9 'Blue Conqueror' (L)
0 ***cardinalis***
9 'Chanson'
9 'City Lights'
9 ***imbricatus***
9 'Invitation'
9 'Lovely Day' (G)
9 'Merry'
9 'Pink Pearl' (S)
9 'Plum Tart' (L)
9 'Prince Carnival' (L)
9 'Prosperity'
9 'Scout'
9 'Shell Pink'
9 'Shocking Pink'
9 'Spring Gem'
9 'Wine and Roses' (L)

GLAUCIDIUM

0 ***palmatum leucanthum***

GLAUCIUM

0 ***flavum*** orange form

GLEDITSIA

9 ***sinensis***

GLOBULARIA

7 ***vulgaris***

GLYPTOSTROBUS

0 ***pensilis***

GNAPHALIUM

0 ***andicolum***

GOODENIA

9 ***lunata***

GOODYERA

0 ***pubescens***

GREVILLEA

9 ***aspleniifolia*** 'Robin Hood'
9 – 'Robyn Gordon'
7 'Claret'
8 'Desert Flame'
7 ***jephcottii***
8 ***lanigera***
0 'Olympic Flame'

GRISELINIA

9 ***lucida*** 'Variegata'

GUNNERA

0 ***flavida***
9 ***monoica***

GUZMANIA

0 ***musaica***

GYPSOPHILA

0 ***briquetiana***
9 ***petraea***

HAASTIA

7 ***sinclairii***

HAEMANTHUS

0 ***carneus***

HAKEA

0 ***epiglottis***
8 ***macraeana***
8 ***nitida***
8 ***platysperma***
8 ***victoriae***

HALIMIUM

0 ***alyssoides***

HAPLOPAPPUS

9 ***clementis***
8 ***lanuginosus andersonii***

HEBE

0 ***(See also*** PARAHEBE)
8 ***amplexicaulis***
8 'Balfouriana'
8 'Barnettii'
7 'Brian Kessell'
0 ***buchananii*** 'Major'
7 'Cilsouth'
8 'Cupins'
8 'Diamond'
9 ***diosmifolia*** 'Variegated'
8 'Ettrick Shepherd'

8 'Gillanders'
9 ***giselli***
8 'Greenway Purple'
7 'Harlequin'
9 'Hartii'
8 'Hidcote'
9 'Hielan Lassie'
8 'Kewensis'
9 ***leiophylla***
8 'Lycing'
7 'Mist Maiden'
9 'Mrs E Tennant'
7 'Obora Gold'
7 ***plano-petiolaris***
9 'Purple Princess'
7 'Southcombe Pink'
0 ***subsimilis***
8 ***tetragona*** 'Southcombe Dwarf'
8 ***treadwellii***
7 'Wakehurst'
0 'Wendy'
7 'Widecombe'

HECTORELLA
8 ***caespitosa***

HEDERA
9 ***algeriensis***
0 ***colchica*** 'Dendroides'
0 ***helix*** 'Arborescens Variegata'
0 – 'Arrowhead'
0 – 'Cavendishii Latina'
0 – 'Schimmer'
0 – 'Sinclair Silverleaf'
0 – 'Teena'

HEDYOTIS
7 ***serpyllifolia***

HEDYSARUM
0 ***hedysaroides exaltatum***

HELENIUM
8 'Kupfersprudel' ('Copper Spray')
8 'Tawny Dwarf'

HELIANTHEMUM
8 'Apricot'
8 'Bishopsthorpe'
7 'Cherry Pink'
0 'Cupreum'
0 'Harlequin'
8 'Low Yellow'
0 'Loxbeare Gold'
8 ***nummularium grandiflorum***
0 – ***obscurum***
8 'Peach'
0 'Pink Beauty'
8 'Prima Donna'
7 'Rose Perfection'
8 Trenear's hybrids
8 'Wisley Yellow'

HELIANTHUS
0 ***angustifolius***

HELICHRYSUM
9 ***bellidioides gracile***
7 – 'Major'
9 ***cooperi***
7 'Darwin Gold'
9 ***dealbatum***
8 ***frigidum*** 'Miffy Beauty'
8 ***purpurascens***
9 ***retortum***
0 ***selaginoides***
0 ***thyrsoideum*** 'Variegatum'

HELIOPSIS
8 ***helianthoides*** 'Mid West Dream'
9 ***helianthoides scabra*** 'Sunburst'

HELIOTROPIUM
0 x ***hybridum***

HELIPTERUM
9 ***albicans***

HELLEBORUS
9 ***bocconei*** Apennine form
9 ***foetidus*** compact form
0 ***multifidus***
0 ***niger*** 'Madame Fourcade'
9 ***orientalis*** 'Amethyst'
0 – 'Blowsy'
0 – 'Blue Spray'
7 – 'Blue Wisp'
9 – 'Cheerful'
9 – 'Cosmos'
9 – 'Dick Crandon'
7 – 'Dotty'
0 – 'Dusk'
9 – 'Ernest Raithby'
9 – 'Garnet'
9 – 'Hades'
9 – 'John Cross'
9 – 'Lady Bonham Carter'
0 – 'Laura'
9 – 'Lynne'
8 – 'Mercury'
9 – 'Nocturne'
9 – 'Parrot'
0 – 'Patchwork'
9 – 'Peggy Ballard'
9 – 'Rosa'
9 – 'Rossini'
0 – 'Rubens'
9 – 'Sirius'
0 – 'Sunny'
0 – 'Sylvia'
0 – 'Tommie'
0 – 'Upstart'
9 – 'Yellow Button'
9 x ***sternii*** dwarf form
0 ***torquatus*** ex Nero

HEMEROCALLIS
8 'A la Mode'
8 'After Glow'
8 'Angel Face'
7 'Apollo'
8 'Applause'
9 'Ariadne'
9 'Atlas'
9 'Atomic Age'
8 'August Pink'
0 'Bees Rose'
8 'Belinda'
8 'Bellringer'
9 'Black Prince'
8 'Bold Ruler'
8 'Bonnie Rose'
8 'Bourbon Prince'
8 'Bright Charm'
8 'Brilliant Red'
9 'Broad Ripples'
9 'Brunette'
8 'Buried Treasure'
9 'Candle Glow'
8 'Candy Fluff'
8 'Capri'
8 'Carriage Trade'
7 'Chantilly Lace'
8 'Charlotte Holman'
8 'Chetco'
8 'Childscraft'
9 'Christmas Isle'
9 'Claret Cup'
8 'Coquinna'
7 'Cuddlesome'
8 'Dauntless'
8 'Dawn Supreme'
9 'Delft Rose'
8 'Demure'
0 'Deva'
0 'Double Firecracker'
9 'Double Pleasure'
8 'Dynamo'
8 'Eden'
9 'Elaine Strutt'
9 'Esther Murray'
8 'Far Afield'
8 'Felicity'
8 'Finlandia'
8 'First Romance'
7 'Flair'
8 'Fond Caress'
8 'Fortyniner'
9 'Fox Grape'
8 'Gay Music'
8 'Georgia Peach'
9 'Golden Dewdrop'
9 'Golden Glory'
8 'Goldensong'
8 'Grecian Gift'
8 'High Glory'
8 'High Time'
8 'Hippity Hop'
0 'How About That'
8 'Illinois'
8 'Inlaid Gold'
8 'Irene Felix'
8 'Jack Frost'
9 'Jake Russell'
8 'Janet'
8 'Joan Durelle'
8 'July Gold'
8 'June Royalty'
0 'Kathleen Woodbury'
9 'King Haiglar'
8 'Late Date'
8 'Laurel Anne'
8 'Lester Pastel'
7 'Lilac Chiffon'
7 'Lilly Dache'
9 'Lusty Leland'
9 'Mantra'
0 'Margaret Perry'
8 'Mary Anne'
9 'Mascot'
8 'Melotone'
8 'Momento'
9 'Mrs B F Bonner'
9 'Multinomah'
8 'Nehoiden'
8 'Northfield'
7 'Old Vintage'
8 'Pecheron'
7 'Pink Perfection'
8 'Polar Bear'
9 'Pony'
8 'Powder Puff'
9 'Precious'
0 'President'
0 'Purple Water'
7 'Radiant'
8 'Rare China'
9 'Rose Motif'
8 'Rosetta'
8 'Roseway'
0 'Royal Robe'
8 'Sanders Walker'
8 'Satin Glass'
7 'Sawanne Belle'
7 'Sea Gypsy'
8 'Shell Cameo'
8 'Sherwood'
8 'Sleeping Beauty'
8 'Snappy Rhythm'
9 'Star Ruby'
8 'Sweetheart Supreme'
9 'Taj Mahal'
8 'Temple Bells'
8 'Theresa Hall'
7 'Tiny Tex'
8 'Torpoint'
8 'War Clouds'
8 'Whir of Lace'
0 'Winnetka'
8 'Yellow Beacon'

HEMIPHRAGMA
9 ***heterophyllum***

HERPOLIRION
9 ***novae-zelandiae***

HESPERIS
0 ***matronalis*** pink double form

HEUCHERA
7 'Damask'
8 'Edge Hill'
7 'Freedom'
9 ***glabra***
7 'Ibis'
7 'Lady Romney'
8 'Pruhoniciana'
0 ***sanguinea*** 'Superba'
8 – 'Variegata'
9 ***villosa***

HIBISCUS
8 ***moscheutos palustris***
0 ***rosa-sinensis*** 'Colombo'
0 – 'Cooperi'
0 – 'Nairobi'
0 – 'Paramaibo'
0 – rose
9 ***sabdariffa***
7 ***syriacus*** 'Admiral Dewey'
9 – 'Caeruleus Plenus'
0 – 'Violet Clair'

HIERACIUM
8 x ***rubrum***

HIPPEASTRUM
0 ***bifidum spathaceum***

HOHERIA
7 ***populnea sinclairii***

HOSTA
9 'Blue Danube' (***x tardiana***)
8 'Crown Jewel'
0 ***longipes mira***
7 'Midwest Gold'
0 ***minuta*** forms
8 'Pixie Power'
0 'Sherbourne Swift' (***x tardiana***)
9 ***tsushimensis***

HOWEIA
9 ***belmoreana***

HUGUENINIA
9 ***tanacetifolia***

HUTCHINSIA
9 ***alpina auerswaldii***

HYACINTHELLA
0 ***leucophaea***

HYACINTHOIDES
0 ***hispanica*** 'Rose'

HYACINTHUS
9 ***orientalis*** 'Cote d'Azur'
9 – 'Eros'
9 – 'Rosalie'
9 – 'Yellow Hammer'

HYDRANGEA
9 ***arborescens discolor***
0 – ***radiata*** 'Robusta'
9 ***aspera*** 'Rosthornii'
0 – ***strigosa***
9 ***longipes***
9 ***macrophylla*** 'Covent Garden'
9 – 'Draps Pink'
9 – 'Fargesii'
7 – 'Harry's Pink Topper'
7 – 'Madame A Riverain'
8 – 'Max Löbner'
8 – 'Mousseline'
8 – 'Oamacha'
0 – 'Queen Elizabeth'
7 – 'Ursula'
7 – 'Val de Loire'
9 – 'Yodogawa'
0 ***quercifolia*** 'Flore Pleno'
0 – sterile
0 ***serrata*** 'Amagyana'

HYMENOXYS
0 ***acaulis glabra***

HYPERICUM
8 ***canariense***
0 ***elodeoides***
9 ***elongatum***
0 ***frondosum***
8 ***hircinum albimontanum***
9 ***inodorum***
9 – 'Hysan'
9 – 'Summer's End'
0 ***montanum***
0 ***oblongifolium***
9 ***pallens***
8 ***pulchrum procumbens***
0 ***sp.*** B&L 12508
9 'Summer Sunshine'
9 ***xylosteifolium***

HYPSELA
9 ***rivalis***

HYSSOPUS
0 ***officinalis officinalis***

IBERIS
0 ***sempervirens*** 'Correifolia'
7 – 'Garrexiana'
8 – 'Gracilis'
7 – 'Zwergschneefloke' ('Snowdrift')

ILEX
0 x ***altaclerensis*** 'Atkinsonii' (m)
7 – 'Balearica'
9 – 'Maderensis'
0 ***aquifolium*** 'Crassifolia' (m)
7 – 'Ovata' (m)
0 ***chinensis***
0 'Clusterberry' (f)
0 ***corallina***
8 ***cornuta*** 'O'Spring'
8 – 'Rotunda'
8 ***crenata*** 'Dwarf Pagoda'
0 – 'Fastigiata'
0 – 'Twiggy' (f)
8 'Dazzler'
8 'Doctor Kassab' (f)
0 ***integra leucoclada***
0 ***verticillata*** 'Christmas Cheer' (f)
0 – 'Nana' (f)

IMPATIENS
9 ***glandulifera*** white form
9 ***pseudoviola***

INDIGOFERA
0 ***australis***
9 ***decora alba***

INULA
9 ***obtusifolia***

IPOMOEA
0 ***coccinea***

IRIS
9 'Ablaze' (DB)
9 'Airy Fancy' (Spuria)
8 'Alenette' (TB)
9 'Already' (MDB)
7 'Amber' (TB)
8 'Arab Chief' (TB)
0 'Arctic Fancy' (IB)
0 'Autumn Primrose' (TB)
9 ***barnumae urmiensis***
9 'Belief' (Spuria)
9 'Bellboy' (MTB)
0 'Belvi Queen' (TB)
8 'Benton Yellow' (TB)
8 'Bibelot' (BB)
0 'Black Ink' (TB)
0 'Blue Admiral' (TB)
0 'Blue Beret' (MDB)
8 'Blue Valley' (TB)
9 'Bride' (DB)
8 'Britomas' (TB)
9 'Bronze Charm' (TB)
0 ***bulleyana***
8 'Buster Brown' (DB)
0 'Butter Cookie' (IB)
9 'Calypso Clown' (AB)
8 'Candy Cane' (BB)
0 'Catani' (SDB)
0 'Chain White' (SDB)
8 'Church Stoke' (SDB)
9 'Cinnamon Roll' (Spuria)
9 'Cinnamon Stick' (Spuria)
9 'Circlette' (SDB)
9 'City of Lincoln' (TB)
8 'Clotho' (Aril)
0 'Clouded Moon' (***sibirica***)
9 'Confetti' (TB)
8 'Constance Meyer' (TB)
0 'Copper Pot' (TB)
8 'Craithie' (TB)
9 'Doll House' (MDB)
9 ***douglasiana*** 'Apple Court White'
0 'Elizabeth Arden' (TB)
8 'Ellesmere' (***sibirica***)
9 'Encanto' (SDB)
9 'Ennerdale' (TB)
0 ***ensata*** aff. SEP 6
9 – 'Balathea'
9 – 'Buri-cho'
9 – 'Chidori'
9 – 'Chigesyo'
0 'Ethel Hope' (Spuria)
0 ***foetidissima*** 'Moonshy seedling'
0 'Fourfold White' (***sibirica***)
9 'Frenchii' (BB)
9 'Gentle Grace' (SDB)
0 ***germanica*** 'Spartan'
9 'Golden Chocolate' (Spuria)
9 'Golden Glow' (TB)
8 'Grace Sturtevant' (TB)
8 'Gypsy Smoke' (IB)
8 ***haynei***
8 ***hermona***
8 'Hipermestra' (Aril)
9 ***hoogiana*** 'Noblesse'
0 'In the Buff' (IB)
0 ***innominata*** 'Alba'
0 'I'm Yellow' (SDB)
0 ***japonica***
7 'Jirovette' (***sibirica***)
8 'Joanna' (TB)
8 ***jordana***
9 ***korolkowii*** 'Concolor'
9 ***laevigata*** 'Murakumo'
9 'Langport Carnival' (IB)
0 'Langport Chapter' (IB)
9 'Langport Duchess' (IB)
0 'Langport Flash' (IB)
0 'Langport Pagan' (IB)
0 'Langport Sultan' (IB)
9 'Lavender Light' (***sibirica***)
9 'Little Swinger' (BB)
8 'Louvois' (TB)
0 ***lutescens*** white
8 'L'lita' (TB)
0 'Magic Hills' (TB)
9 'Mariposa Tarde' (Spuria)
8 'Marmot' (MTB)
0 'Mary B' (MDB)
9 'Masked Ball' (TB)
0 'Mini Plic' (MDB)
8 'Miss Underwood' (***sibirica***)
7 'Mountain Lake' (***sibirica***)
0 'Nancy's Khaki' (TB)
8 ***nigricans***
9 'Of Course' (IB)
8 'Oracle' (BB)
9 'Pepper Mill' (SDB)
8 'Pink Charm' (TB)
8 'Pink Ruffles' (IB)
0 ***planifolia***
9 ***polakii***
0 'Powder Pink' (TB)
0 'Princess of Love' (SDB)
9 ***purdyi***
8 'Real Gold' (AB)
9 'Reuthe's Bronze' (CH)
9 'Ripe Wheat' (Spuria)
8 'Rippling Waters' (TB)
9 'Sahara Sands' (Spuria)
8 ***samariae***
9 'Sand Princess' (MTB)
8 'Silver Edge' (***sibirica***)
8 'Silver Shower' (TB)
0 'Sindpers' (Juno)
8 'Snow Princess' (***sibirica***)
0 'Southcombe Velvet'
0 'Sparkling Water' (TB)
9 'Spring Reverie (Spuria)
9 'Steve' (***sibirica***)
8 'Sugar Pie' (BB)
0 'Tequila Sunrise' (TB)
0 'Tetra-white Rose' (***sibirica***)
0 'The Monarch' (TB)
9 'Three Cherries' (MDB)
8 'Three Oaks' (TB)
0 Tol-Long
9 'Turquoise Cup' (***sibirica***)
9 ***unguicularis angustifolia***
0 ***virginica***
9 'Wedgwood' (Dutch)
9 'White Knight' (TB)
8 'Whiteladies' (IB)
9 'Wine Wings' (***sibirica***)
0 'Witch Doctor' (TB)
0 ***xiphium***
9 'Yellow Queen' (Dutch)

IVESIA
9 ***gordonii***

JASIONE
8 ***laevis orbiculata***
9 ***tuberosa***

JEFFERSONIA
0 ***dubia alba***

JOVIBARBA
0 ***heuffelii*** 'Cameo'
9 – 'Nannette'
8 – 'Pink Skies'
9 – 'Wotan'
0 – 'Xanthoheuff'
0 ***heuffelii glabra***
9 – – from Kosovo

8 – – from Osljak
9 – – from Sapka
9 – – from Stogovo

JUANIA
0 ***australis***

JUNCUS
0 ***pusillus***

JUNIPERUS
0 ***chinensis*** 'Belvedere'
0 – 'Kuriwao Mist'
0 ***communis*** 'Edgbaston'
8 – 'Effusa'
7 – 'Gimborn'
7 – 'Hibernica Variegata'
7 – 'Inverleith'
9 – 'Nana Aurea'
0 – ***oblonga***
0 – 'Windsor Gem'
8 ***flaccida***
0 ***horizontalis*** 'Schoodic Point'
9 x ***media*** 'Arctic'
7 – 'Globosa'
0 ***recurva***
8 ***sabina*** 'Broadmoor'
9 – 'Knap Hill'
0 ***salturaria***
8 ***sargentii*** 'Viridis'
0 ***scopulorum*** 'Hillborn's Silver Globe'
8 – 'Lakewood Globe'
8 – 'Mrs Marriage's Form'
0 ***silicicola***
8 ***squamata*** 'Blue Spreader'
7 – 'Forrestii'
0 ***virginiana*** 'Canaertii'
7 – 'Straver'

KALANCHOE
8 ***uniflora***

KALIMERIS
0 ***incisa***

KALMIA
9 ***latifolia*** 'Richard Jaynes'
0 ***microphylla occidentalis***

KENNEDIA
0 ***beckxiana***
0 ***eximia***
0 ***prostrata*** West Australian form
0 – West Coast form
0 ***rubicunda***

KERNERA
9 ***saxatilis***

KNIPHOFIA
0 'Apple Court'
7 'Bees' Lemon'
8 'Brimstone'
7 'David'
8 'Dorset Strain'
7 'Earliest of All'
9 'Firefly'
9 'Lye End'
0 'Nancy's Red'
9 'Ross Sunshine'
8 'Saturn'
8 'Sunset'
8 'Timothy'
0 'Torchbearer'
0 'Tubergeniana'
0 'Underway'

KOBRESIA
9 ***simpliciuscula***

KUMMEROWIA
8 ***stipulacea***

KUNZEA
8 ***capitata***

LACHENALIA
0 ***arbuthnotiae***
0 ***bachmanii***
9 ***unifolia***
9 'Violet Queen'
9 ***zeyheri***

LACTUCA
0 ***macrantha***
8 ***tenerrima***
0 ***virosa***

LAGENOPHORA
9 ***pumila***

LAGERSTROEMIA
7 ***fauriei***
0 ***indica*** 'Berlingot Menthe'

LAMIUM
0 ***garganicum*** 'Laevigatum'

LANTANA
0 ***camara*** 'Miss Tibbs'

LARIX
0 ***griffithiana***
9 ***laricina***
9 ***occidentalis***

LATHYRUS
9 ***aphaca***
0 ***azureus***
9 ***cyaneus alboroseus***
0 ***davidii***
9 ***pratensis***
0 ***sativus caeruleus***

LAVANDULA
0 ***angustifolia*** 'Alba'
7 – 'Nana Rosea'
8 – 'Norfolk'
0 x ***intermedia*** 'Alba'
8 – 'Fring Favourite'
9 – 'Heacham No 4'

LAVATERA
9 ***cretica***

LEEA
0 ***rubra***

LEIOPHYLLUM
0 ***buxifolium hugeri***

LEONTOPODIUM
9 ***alpinum nivale***
8 ***palibinianum***
0 ***souliei***

LEPTOSPERMUM
8 ***micromyrtus***
7 ***scoparium*** 'Big Red'
8 – 'Flore Pleno'
9 – 'Gaiety'
0 – Jervis Bay form
9 – 'Pink Pearl'
7 ***scoparium nanum*** 'Elizabeth Jane'
9 – – 'Ruru'

LESQUERELLA
9 ***kingii sherwoodii***

LEUCANTHEMOPSIS
7 ***pallida spathulifolia***

LEUCANTHEMUM
0 x ***superbum*** 'Everest'
0 – 'Flore Pleno'
0 – 'Juno'
9 – 'Moonlight'

LEUCOPOGON
9 ***collinus***

LEUCOTHO_
0 ***keiskei*** 'Minor'

LEWISIA
8 'Chastity'

LIBERTIA
0 ***stolonifera***

LICUALA
0 ***spinosa***

LIGULARIA
9 ***oblongata***
9 ***reniformis***

LIGUSTRUM
0 ***lucidum*** 'Macrophyllum'

LILIUM
9 'Anne Boleyn' (Ia)
9 'Apricot' (Ia)
9 'Apricot Beauty' (Ib)
9 Aurelian hybrids (VIIa)
0 ***bulbiferum*** (IX)
8 ***concolor*** (IX)
9 'Damson' (VIa)
9 'Escapade' (Ia)
0 Golden Clarion (VIa)
0 x ***imperiale*** (VIa)
9 'John Dix' (Ib)
0 'Langtry' (Ic)
9 'Magic Fire' (VId)
9 ***michiganense*** (IX)
0 Mid-Century Hybrids (Ia)
0 ***regale*** yellow (IX)
8 ***rubellum*** (IX)
9 'Staccato' (Ia)
9 'Vermilion Brilliant' (Ia)

LIMONIUM
7 ***chilwellii***

LINARIA
0 ***anticaria***
9 ***genistifolia***
7 ***lilacina***
8 ***nobilis***
0 ***tristis lurida***
8 ***vulgaris*** 'Flore Pleno'

LINDERA
8 ***praecox***
0 ***triloba***

LINUM
9 ***narbonense album***
0 ***perenne*** dwarf form
9 ***suffruticosum*** 'Nanum'
0 ***tenuifolium***

LIRIOPE
0 ***koreana***

LIVISTONA
0 ***rotundifolia***

LOASA
9 ***nana***
0 ***vulcanica***

LOBELIA
0 ***angulata*** 'Messenger'
9 – 'Tennyson'
9 ***begonifolia***
9 ***linnaeoides*** 'Dobson'
9 ***pedunculata*** 'Tunnack'
0 ***physaloides***
8 ***puberula***
0 ***villosa***

LOISELEURIA
0 ***procumbens***

LONICERA
8 ***albertii***
7 ***alpigena***
0 ***arizonica***
0 ***caerulea***
0 ***discolor***
9 ***morrowii***
9 ***myrtillus***
8 ***nitida*** 'Hohenheimer Findling'
7 ***trichosantha***
9 ***utahensis***

LUMA
7 ***apiculata*** purple form

LUNARIA
0 ***annua*** purple stem

LUPINUS
9 'Cherry Pie'
9 'Comet'
9 'Daydream'
0 'Freedom'
0 Gallery series
9 'Guardsman'
9 'Harlequin'
9 'Harvester'
0 ***hirsutissimus***
9 'Joy'
9 'Lilac Time'
9 'Limelight'
0 ***longifolius***
9 'Mystic Charm'
9 'Pat Baird'
8 'Rougham Beuaty'
9 'Serenade'
0 ***succulentus***
7 ***texensis***

LUZULA
0 ***banksiana***

X LYCENE
0 ***kubotae***

LYCHNIS
9 ***alpina*** 'Alba'

0 *viscaria* 'Splendens Rosea'

LYCIUM
8 *pallidum*

LYCORIS
8 *radiata*
8 *squamigera*

LYONIA
9 *lucida*

LYTHRUM
8 *virgatum* 'Dropmore Purple'

MACHAERANTHERA
9 *bigelovii*

MAGNOLIA
7 *campbellii* 'Visa'
9 *dawsoniana* 'Caerhays'
0 *grandiflora* 'Edith Bogue'
0 – 'Rosemoor'
7 x *loebneri* 'Spring Snow'
7 *nitida*
0 'Rouged Alabaster'
7 x *soulangeana* 'Purple Dream'
9 – 'Triumphans'
9 *sprengeri elongata*

MAHONIA
0 *aquifolium* dwarf form
0 *eutriphylla*
0 x *wagneri*
0 – 'Vicaryi'

MALPIGHIA
9 *glabra* 'Fairchild'

MALUS
9 'Elise Rathke'
9 *halliana* 'Parkmanii'
0 *hupehensis rosea*
7 'Professor Sprenger'
9 *sikkimensis*
9 *spectabilis*
9 *tschonoskii* 'Bonfire'

MALVA
0 *sylvestris* 'Mest'

MALVASTRUM
7 *peruvianum*

MARANTA
0 *leuconeura massangeana*

MATTHIOLA
8 East Lothian

MAZUS
9 *miquelii*

MECONOPSIS
9 *latifolia*
0 'White Swan'

MEDICAGO
9 *intertexta*

MELALEUCA
9 *citrina*
9 *halmaturorum*

MELIANTHUS
8 *comosus*

MELICYTUS
0 *ramiflorus*

MELILOTUS
9 *officinalis albus*

MELIOSMA
7 *cuneifolia*

MENISPERMUM
7 *davuricum*

MENZIESIA
9 *pentandra*

MERTENSIA
8 *alpina*

MESPILUS
F *germanica* 'Breda Giant'

MICHELIA
0 *champaca*
7 *maudiae*

MICROMERIA
0 *cristata*

MILLIGANIA
8 *densiflora*

MIMULUS
7 'Burgess'
0 Calypso hybrids
9 'Fire King'
8 'Firedragon'
9 *minimus*
7 'Wildwood's'
8 'Yellow Velvet'

MITELLA
9 *pentandra*

MOLINIA
9 *caerulea*

MONARDA
8 'Cerise Pink'
0 'Kardinal'

MONARDELLA
0 *villosa neglecta*

MONSTERA
0 *obliqua*
0 – *expilata*

MORINA
9 *coulteriana*

MUSA
F *acuminata (AAA group)* 'Dwarf Cavendish'

MUSCARI
8 *parviflorum*

MYOSOTIS
9 *alpestris*
8 – 'Nana'
9 *arvensis*
8 *azorica*
0 *forsteri*
9 *petiolata*
7 *pulvinaris*
9 *symphytifolia*
0 *uniflora*

MYOSURUS
9 *minimus*

NANDINA
0 *domestica* 'Little Princess'
9 – 'Umpqua Chief'

NARCISSUS
9 'Akala' (1)
9 'Albacrest' (3)
9 'Aldringham' (2)
9 'Alray' (1)
9 'Andrew Marvell' (9)
9 'Ann Cameron' (2)
9 'April Message' (1)
9 'Arctic Flame' (2)
9 'Backchat' (6)
9 'Balalaika' (2)
9 'Ballyroan' (2)
9 'Bandolier' (2)
9 'Bar None' (1)
9 'Ben Hee' (2)
9 'Ben Rinnes' (3)
9 'Birdalone' (2)
9 'Brave Adventure' (2)
9 'Bright Spark' (3)
0 'Brindisi' (2)
0 *bulbocodium AB&S* forms
9 'Cairngorm' (2)
9 'Capstan' (2)
9 'Caracas' (2)
9 'Carrara' (3)
9 'Carrickmannon' (2)
9 'Celtic Gold' (2)
9 'Citronita' (3)
9 'City Lights' (2)
9 'Colblanc' (11)
9 'Cold Overton' (2)
9 'Comal' (1)
9 'Como' (9)
9 'Coral Ribbon' (2)
9 'Coylum' (3)
9 'Crater' (2)
9 'Dalinda' (1)
9 'Dawncrest' (2)
9 'Debbie Rose' (2)
9 'Delightful' (3)
9 'Deseado' (1)
9 'Dorada Dawn' (2)
9 'Dress Circle' (3)
9 'Dumbleton' (1)
9 'Earlicheer' (4)
9 'Earthlight' (3)
9 'El Camino' (6)
9 'Elmley Castle' (1)
9 'Fiery Flame' (2)
9 'Fly Half' (2)
0 'Fontmell' (1)
9 'Galahad' (1)
9 'Gambler's Gift' (2)
9 'Gay Record' (4)
9 'Gay Symphony' (4)
9 'Glandore' (2)
9 'Glenside' (2)
9 'Gunsynd' (2)
9 'High Tower' (3)
9 'Irish Minstrel' (2)
9 'Irish Rover' (2)
9 'Itzim' (6)
9 'Ivory Crown' (2)
9 'Kelpie' (6)
9 'Kentucky Cardinal' (2)
9 'King's Ransom' (1)
9 'Kipling' (3)
9 'Knowehead' (2)
9 'Lancelot' (1)
9 'Leader' (2)
9 'Leonora' (3)
9 'Limegrove' (3)
0 'Limehurst' (2)
9 'Loch Brora' (2)
9 'Lucky Star' (3)
9 'L'Innocence' (8)
9 'Maid of Ulster' (2)
9 'Mandolin' (2)
9 'Matapan' (3)
9 'May Queen' (2)
9 'Milestone' (2)
9 'Mill Grove' (2)
0 'Mint Julep' (3)
9 'Modest Maiden' (2)
9 'Moonlight Sonata' (1)
9 'Mrs Ernst H Krelage' (1)
9 'Music Hall' (1)
9 'My Love' (2)
9 'Navarone' (1)
9 'Norval' (2)
9 'Ocean Spray' (7)
9 'Ohio' (2)
9 'Owston Wood' (1)
9 'Papua' (4)
9 'Park Royal' (2)
9 'Parkdene' (2)
9 'Parkridge' (2)
9 'Perky' (6)
9 'Pimm' (2)
9 'Polonaise' (2)
9 'Privateer' (3)
9 'Queen of Spain' (10)
9 'Queensland' (2)
0 'Ramada' (2)
9 'Raspberry Ring' (2)
9 'Rathowen Gold' (1)
9 'Red Curtain' (1)
9 'Red Hot' (2)
9 'Red Mars' (2)
9 'Red Rum' (2)
9 'Revenge' (1)
9 'Rich Reward' (1)
9 'Right Royal' (2)
9 'Rimski' (2)
9 'Rimster' (2)
9 'Rubythroat' (2)
9 'Rutland Water' (2)
9 'Santa Rosa' (2)
9 'Scarlet Thread' (3)
9 'Sealed Orders' (3)
9 'Sedate' (2)
8 *serotinus*
9 'Shell Bay' (2)
9 'Silent Cheer' (3)
9 'Silent Morn' (3)
9 'Silver Bells' (5)
9 'Silversmith' (2)
9 'Sir Ivor' (1)
9 'Snow Magic' (3)
9 'Spring Fashion' (2)
9 'Standfast' (1)
9 'Star War' (2)
9 'Suave' (3)
9 'Sunapee' (3)
9 'Tara Rose' (2)
9 'The Prince' (2)
9 'Timandaw' (3)

9 'Tomphubil' (2)
9 'Torch Bearer' (2)
9 'Touch of Silver' (2)
9 'Trelay' (3)
0 'Troon' (2)
0 'Undertone' (2)
9 'Verve' (2)
9 'Viennese Rose' (4)
9 'White Prince' (1)
9 'Woodland Splendour' (3)

NEMOPANTHUS
8 ***mucronatus***

NEOLITSEA
0 ***caerulea***

NEOREGELIA
0 ***concentrica*** 'Plutonis'
9 ***cyanea***
0 ***spectabilis***
0 ***tristis***

NEPENTHES
0 ***stenophylla***

NEPETA
8 ***tuberosa***
0 'Valerie Finnis'

NERINE
0 'Lady de Walden'
0 'Miss France Clarke'
0 'Mrs Cooper'
0 'Mrs Dent Brocklehurst'
8 ***sarniensis fothergillii***
0 'Zeal Giant'

NEVIUSIA
8 ***alabamensis***

NICANDRA
9 ***physalodes violacea***

NICOTIANA
0 'Sissinghurst Green'

NIDULARIUM
0 ***billbergioides*** 'Flavum'
0 ***burchellii***
0 ***fulgens***
0 ***regelioides***

NOTHOFAGUS
7 ***solandri cliffortioides***

NYMPHAEA
7 'Newton'
9 'Robinsoniana'

NYSSA
9 ***sylvatica*** 'Sheffield Park'

OENANTHE
9 ***pimpinelloides***

OENOTHERA
9 ***laciniata***
9 ***tetragona*** 'Sundrops'
0 ***texensis***

OLEARIA
9 ***megalophylla***
9 ***phlogopappa*** 'Comber's Mauve'

OMPHALOGRAMMA
9 ***elegans***
7 ***minus***

ONONIS
7 ***crispa balearica***

ONOSMA
0 ***aucherianum***

OPHIOPOGON
0 ***japonicus*** 'Silver Dragon'

OREOBOLUS
8 ***pauciflorus***

ORIGANUM
0 'French'
0 'Gold Splash'
9 'Roding'
0 ***vulgare*** 'Curly Gold'

OSMANTHUS
7 ***heterophyllus*** 'Rotundifolius'

OSTEOSPERMUM
0 'Croftway Whirlydots'
0 ***ecklonis*** x jucundum
8 'Lilac Beauty'
0 'Pink Whirls' low form

OTHONNA
7 ***coronopifolia***

OURISIA
9 ***breviflora***
8 ***macrocarpa***
9 ***racemosa***

OXALIS
0 ***laciniata*** blue form
7 ***racemosa*** 'Aureoreticulata'
0 ***rubra***
0 ***tetraphylla alba***

OXYLOBIUM
0 ***parviflorum***

PACHYSTEGIA
9 ***minor***

PAEONIA
9 ***anomala intermedia***
9 ***chamaeleon***
0 ***clusii***
0 ***lactiflora*** 'Amo-no-sode'
0 – 'Argentine'
0 – 'Auguste Dessert'
9 – 'Balliol'
0 – 'Bowl of Cream'
0 – 'Break o' Day'
0 – 'Bridal Gown'
0 – 'Butch'
0 – 'Carolina Moon'
0 – 'Charles' White'
0 – 'Charm'
0 – 'Cheddar Cheese'
8 – 'Crimson Glory'
0 – 'Do Tell'
0 – 'Doreen'
0 – 'Dresden'
0 – 'Edith Cavell'
0 – 'Elsa Sass'
0 – 'Emma Klehm'
0 – 'Fairy's Petticoat'
0 – 'Fuji-no-mine'
0 – 'Gay Ladye'
8 – 'General Wolfe'
0 – 'Germaine Bigot'
0 – 'Gleam of Light'
0 – 'Gloriana'
0 – 'Glory Hallelujah'
0 – 'Grace Loomis'
0 – 'Honey Gold'
7 – 'James Kelway'
9 – 'Jan van Leeuwen'
0 – 'John Howard Wigell'
0 – 'June Rose'
0 – 'Kansas'
0 – 'Kelway's Glorious'
8 – 'Kelway's Supreme'
8 – 'Kestrel'
0 – 'King Midas'
0 – 'King of England'
0 – 'Krinkled White'
0 – 'La France'
0 – 'La Lorraine'
0 – 'Lady Orchid'
0 – 'Lake of Silver'
0 – 'Largo'
0 – 'Laura Dessert'
0 – 'Lora Dexheimer'
0 – 'Lotus Queen'
0 – 'Lowell Thomas'
0 – 'Madame Ducel'
0 – 'Marguérite Gerard'
0 – 'Marietta Sisson'
0 – 'Mary Brand'
0 – 'Mischief'
0 – 'Miss America'
0 – 'Mister Ed'
9 – 'Moon River'
0 – 'Moonglow'
0 – 'Mr Thim'
0 – 'Mrs Franklin D Roosevelt'
0 – 'Mrs J V Edlund'
0 – 'My Pal Rudy'
0 – 'Nice Gal'
0 – 'Paul M Wild'
0 – 'Philippe Rivoire'
0 – 'Pink Dawn'
0 – 'Pink Parfait'
9 – 'President Wilson'
0 – 'Primevere'
0 – 'Rose of Delight'
0 – 'Souvenir d'A Millet'
0 – 'Sweet Sixteen'
0 – 'The Moor'
0 – 'Thérèse'
0 – 'Thura Hires'
0 – 'Toro-no-maki'
0 – 'Victoria'
0 – 'Wilbur Wright'
0 ***mascula***
9 ***officinalis*** 'China Rose'
0 – ***humilis***
9 'Smouthii'
0 ***tenuifolia*** 'Plena'
9 ***veitchii alba***

PALIURUS
0 ***ramosissimus***

PANDANUS
0 ***veitchii***

PAPAVER
7 ***aprokinomenton***
7 ***kwanense***
7 ***nudicaule*** 'Meadhome Strain'
0 ***orientale*** 'Lavender Girl'
9 – 'Lighthouse'
7 – 'Salome'
7 – 'Snowflame'
7 – 'Stormtorch' ('Sturmfackel')
0 ***pyrenaicum degenii***
0 ***rhoeas*** 'Whispering Fairies'
9 ***thianschanicum***

PARAHEBE
0 ***hookeriana compacta***

PARONYCHIA
8 ***cephalotes***

PARTHENOCISSUS
8 ***inserta***

PASSIFLORA
8 x ***tresederi*** 'Lilac Lady'

PAULOWNIA
0 ***fortunei***

PAXISTIMA
0 ***myrtifolia***

PELARGONIUM
9 'Annette Kellerman' (Z)
0 'Autumn Haze' (R)
0 'Black Pearl' (Z/ D)
9 'Bold Sunrise' (Z)
0 'Bovey Beauty'
^ 'Burge' (R)
0 'Cardinal Pink' (Z/ D)
0 'Cézanne' (I/ D)
9 'Clown' (R)
0 'Copper Flair' (Z/ C)
9 ***cordifolium***
0 'Corot' (I/ D)
0 'Dark Venus' (R)
0 'David Gamble' (Z)
0 'Daydream' (Z/ D/ C)
0 'Desert Dawn' (Z/ C)
0 'Double Skies of Italy' (Z/ D/ C)
0 'Emily De Sylva' (I/ D)
9 ***exhibens***
0 'Fabel' (Z)
0 'Fortuna' (Z)
0 'Francis James' (Z)
9 'Fraulein Gruss' (R)
0 'Fringed Rouletta' (I)
0 'Frosty Petit Pierre'
9 'Gaudy' (Z)
0 'Gemma' (Z/ C)
0 'Giant Butterfly' (R)
0 'Gloria' (Z/ D)
0 'Great Blakenham' (Min)
0 'Green Woodpecker' (R)
0 'Harvest Moon' (Z)
^ 'Hazel Fire' (R)
0 'Hazel Glory' (R)
0 'Hazel Harmony' (R)
0 'Hazel White' (R)
^ 'High Glow' (R)
9 'Highfields Dazzler' (Z)
0 'Highfields Fiesta' (Z)
9 'Highfields Glory' (Z)
9 'Highfields Glow' (Z/ D)
0 'Highfields Supreme' (Z)
9 'Janet Hofman' (Z/ D)

^ 'Jennifer Strange' (R)
9 'Joyrider' (Z/ D)
0 'Katina' (Z)
9 'Kelly's Eye' (Z/ C)
9 'Kelvendon Wonder' (Min)
0 'Kewensis' (Z)
^ 'Lavender Harewood Slam' (R)
0 'Lee Gamble' (Z)
0 'Lesley Kefford' (Z)
9 'Lethas'
^ 'Lucy Jane' (R)
0 'Lyrik' (Z/ D)
0 'Market Day' (R)
9 'Mary Screen' (Min)
0 'May Rushbrook' (Z)
9 'Mere Ripon' (R)
0 'Milka' (R)
0 'Muttertag' (R)
0 'Nanette' (Z)
0 'Noir' (R)
0 'North Star' (Dw)
0 'Orange Fizz' (Z/ D)
0 'Otley Slam' (R)
0 'Our Jim' (Z)
9 'Pam Screen'
^ 'Partisan' (R)
0 'Pearl Necklace' (Z/ D)
^ 'Phyllis Brooks' (R)
0 'Phyllis Variegated'
^ 'Pink Delight' (Z/ D)
0 'Poetic' (Z)
0 'Prima Vera' (R)
0 'Quakeress (R)
9 'Red Doll'
0 'Red Grande' (I)
0 'Red Patricia Andrea' (T)
9 *ribifolium*
0 'Robin Hood' (Dw/ D)
0 'Ron' (R)
0 'Ron's Delight' (R)
0 'Rose Star' (Z/ D)
9 'Royal Pageant'
0 'Royal Surprise' (R)
0 'Salmon Kovalevski' (Z)
9 x *sanguineum*
0 'Sea Mist' (Min)
^ 'Sienna' (R)
0 'Silver Monarch'
9 'Single New Life' (Z)
9 'Spray Paint' (Min)
0 'Stellar Pixie Rose' (St)
0 'Stellar Red Devil' (Z/ St/ D)
9 'Stellar Snowflake' (Z/ St)
9 *stipulaceum*
9 'Sugar Plum Fairy' (I)
0 'Suntrap' (Z/ C)
0 'Treasure' (Z/ D)
0 'Treasure Trove' (Z/ V)
0 'Twist (Z)
0 'Velley Court' (I/ V)
0 'Whistling Dancer' (Z/ C)
0 'White Startel' (Z)
0 'Zoe Washbrooke' (Z/ D)

PENSTEMON
8 'Claret'
0 *crandallii*
0 *digitalis nanus*
8 'Eva'
8 *fruticosus scouleri* 'Boulder'
0 *gormanii*
8 'Greencourt Purple'
9 *grinnellii*
9 *hirsutus* 'Darnley Violet'
0 'Lilactime'
8 *mexicanus*
8 'Newbury Gem'
8 *rydbergii*
0 *strictus* 'Bandera'
8 'Waterloo'

PENTAS
0 *lanceolata* 'Kermesina'
0 – 'Quartiniana'

PEPEROMIA
0 *caperata* 'Variegata'
0 *fraseri*
0 *griseo-argentea*
0 *obtusifolia* 'Variegata'

PERIPLOCA
8 *sepium*

PERSEA
0 *thunbergii*

PERSICARIA
9 *affinis* 'George Taylor'
0 *amplexicaulis oxyphylla*
7 *mollis*

PETROMARULA
0 *pinnata*

PHACELIA
8 *sericea*

PHANEROPHLEBIA
9 *lonchitoides*

PHILADELPHUS
7 'Burkwoodii'
0 *coronarius* Threave form
9 'Etoile Rose'
0 *microphyllus* 'Superbus'
0 'Mrs Reid'
7 'Norma'
9 *pubescens*
0 *purpurascens*
9 *schrenkii*
0 *sericanthus*

PHILODENDRON
0 *bipennifolium* 'Variegatum'
0 *ilsemannii*
0 *imbe* 'Variegatum'
0 *ornatum*
0 'Painted Lady'
0 *scandens oxycardium*

PHLEBODIUM
0 *aureum* 'Glaucum'
0 – 'Undulatum'

PHLEUM
9 *alpinum*

PHLOMIS
0 *samia maroccana*

PHLOX
8 'Boris'
0 'Chequers'
9 *condensata*
0 *diffusa*
0 – 'Octopus'
0 *douglasii* 'Petra'
9 'Lee Raden'
0 *missoulensis*
8 'Moonlight'
7 *paniculata* 'Ann'
0 – 'Blue Moon'
0 – 'Caroline van den Berg'
9 – 'Cecil Hanbury'
9 – 'Denny'
0 – 'Eclaireur'
7 – 'Glow'
0 – 'Jules Sandeau'
0 – 'Little Lovely'
7 – 'Scheerausch'
9 – 'Silver Salmon'
8 'Snowflake'
9 *stolonifera* 'Pink Ridge'
0 *subulata* 'Brilliant'
7 – 'Jill Alexander'
7 – 'Pink Delight'
0 – pink seedling
9 – 'Sensation'
0 – 'White Drift'
0 – 'Woodside'

PHOENIX
9 *rupicola*

PHORMIUM
7 'Gold Spike'
0 'Tom Thumb'

PHOTINIA
0 *lasiogyna* Hangzhou 11818
0 *villosa longipes*

PHYLICA
0 *ericoides*

PHYLLITIS
0 *scolopendrium* 'Apple Court'

PHYLLOSTACHYS
8 *bambusoides* 'Kronberg'
8 *edulis subconvexa*
7 *elegans*

PHYSALIS
9 *alkekengi*

PHYSARIA
0 *alpina*

PHYTEUMA
0 *cordatum*
9 *ovatum*

PICEA
7 *abies* 'Gregoryana Parsonsii'
0 – 'Mariae Orffiae'
0 – 'Pseudoprostrata'
0 *glauca* 'Densata'
0 *glehnii*
0 *mariana* 'Beissneri'
9 *pungens* 'Compacta'

PIERIS
0 *formosa* 'Charles Williams'
0 *japonica* 'Cavatine'
0 – 'Crispa'
0 – 'Stockman'
9 – 'Valley Fire'
9 – 'Whitecaps'

PILEA
0 *microphylla*

PILGERODENDRON
0 *uviferum*

PINUS
7 *balfouriana*
7 *banksiana* 'Schoodic'
8 *bhutanica*
7 *flexilis* 'Van der Woolf's Pyramid'
7 *gordoniana*
9 *greggii*
9 *hartwegii*
7 *heldreichii* 'Groen'
0 *koraiensis* 'Silver Mop'
7 *mugo* 'Hesse'
7 – 'Spingarn's Form'
0 *nigra caramanica* 'Pyramidata'
7 – 'Globosa'
7 – 'Strypemonde'
7 *parviflora* 'Fukusumi'
7 – 'KA-HO'
7 – 'Kukuhow'
0 – 'Shikoku'
7 *peuce* 'Nana'
0 *pseudostrobus*
0 *pungens*
0 *resinosa*
0 *rigida*
9 *rudis*
7 *sabiniana*
7 *strobus* 'Compacta'
7 – 'Pumila'
7 – 'Umbraculifera'
7 *sylvestris* 'Corley'
0 – 'Gold Medal'
0 – 'Iceni'
7 – 'Longmoor'
7 – 'Nana Compacta'
7 – 'Scott's Dwarf'
I – 'Skjak I'
7 – 'Umbraculifera'
7 *tabuliformis densata*
7 – *mukdensis*
7 *wincesteriana*

PITTOSPORUM
0 *bicolor*
9 *chathamicum*
9 *heterophyllum*
0 – *aculeatum*
0 *tenuifolium* 'Silver Sheen'
9 – 'Snowflake'

PLAGIANTHUS
7 *divaricatus*

PLECTRANTHUS
0 *coleoides*

PLEIOBLASTUS
8 'Chigogasa'

PLEIOBLASTUS
8 'Chigogasa'

PLEIONE
0 ***bulbocodioides*** Formosana group 'Blush of Dawn'
0 – – 'Snow White'
0 Shantung 'Ducat'
0 – 'Muriel Harberd'
0 Versailles 'Bucklebury'

POA
9 ***flabellata***

PODOCARPUS
0 ***latifolius***
7 ***macrophyllus*** 'Aureus'
9 ***nivalis*** dwarf form

PODOPHYLLUM
9 ***pleianthum***

POLEMONIUM
7 ***boreale***
0 ***californicum***
8 ***lanatum***
9 ***pulcherrimum calycinum***
0 x ***richardsonii*** 'Album'

POLYGONATUM
0 ***geminiflorum***
9 x ***hybridum*** 'Flore Pleno'
9 – 'Nanum'
9 ***involucratum***
9 ***oppositifolium***
9 ***orientale***

POLYMNIA
0 ***sonchifolia***

POLYSCIAS
0 ***filicifolia***

POLYSTICHUM
8 ***setiferum cristato-gracile*** 'Moly'
0 – Cristatum group
8 – 'Divisilobum Grandiceps'
8 – Divisilobum group 'Oakfield'
8 – 'Gracile'
9 – ***Perserratum group*** 'Schroeder'
9 – 'Thompsoniae'

POPULUS
0 x ***canescens*** 'Macrophylla'
9 ***ciliata***
9 ***grandidentata***
9 ***koreana***
9 ***szechuanica***
8 ***tomentosa***
9 ***yunnanensis***

POTENTILLA
9 ***crantzii ternata***
9 'Cyril'
9 'Daphne'
9 ***fruticosa*** 'Daisy Hill Variety'
0 – 'Glenroy Seashell'
0 – 'Yellow Dome'
9 ***gracilis***
0 – ***nuttallii***
0 ***hyparctica nana***
8 ***lignosa***
9 ***multifida***
9 ***nitida*** 'Alba'
8 'Orange Glow'
0 ***pamirica***
8 ***pensylvanica***
9 'Roulette'
8 ***salesoviana***
8 'Southcombe White'

PRIMULA
0 ***allionii*** 'Elizabeth Earle' (2)
9 – 'Joan Hughes' (2)
0 – 'Miniera' (2)
0 – Stanton's form (2)
0 – 'Viscountess Byng' (2)
0 – x pubescens (2)
8 ***alpicola luna*** (26)
9 ***apennina*** (2)
9 ***atrodentata*** (9)
9 ***auricula*** 'Alpine Violet' (A)
9 – 'Aubergine' (B)
9 – 'Barnhill' (D)
9 – 'Blackcock' (S)
0 – 'Blue Lagoon' (S)
9 – 'Carolina Duck' (S)
9 – 'Crackley Seashell' (D)
9 – 'Desert Dawn' (A)
9 – 'Desert Magic' (A)
9 – 'Desert Peach' (A)
9 – 'Desert Queen' (A)
9 – 'Desert Rose' (A)
9 – 'Desert Sands' (A)
9 – 'Desert Star' (A)
9 – 'Elizabeth Saunders' (D)
9 – 'Firecrest' (S)
9 – 'Greenfinger' (S)
9 – 'Grey Lady' (S)
9 – 'Holne' (A)
9 – 'King Cole' (S)
0 – 'Milk Chocolate' (S)
0 – 'Moonlight' (S)
0 – 'Pathan' (A)
0 – 'Peach Blossom'
9 – 'Pennant's Parakeet' (S)
9 – 'Purple Heron' (S)
9 – 'Purple Lake' (S)
7 – 'Queen Alexandar' (B)
0 – 'Sam Gordon'
9 – 'Scarlet Ibis' (S)
9 – 'Scarlet Lancer' (S)
9 – 'Shaheen' (S)
8 – 'Show Red' (S)
9 – 'Sunburst' (S)
9 – 'Sungold' (S)
0 – 'Tiphareth' (A)
9 – 'Velvet Knight' (B)
7 – 'Victoria' (S)
9 – 'Violetta' (S)
9 – 'Woodpigeon' (S)
0 'Blue Diamond'
9 'Butter-pat' (Prim)
9 ***calderiana strumosa*** (21)
0 ***capitellata*** (11)
9 ***carniolica*** (2)
9 'Charmian' (D.Prim)
9 'Cheerleader'
9 'Cherry Pie' (Prim)
0 ***chionantha*** x sinoplantaginea (18)
9 'Coerulea' (Prim)
0 Cottage Mixed (Prim)
9 'Crimson Queen' (Prim)
7 ***cuneifolia*** (8)
9 ***denticulata*** 'Cashmeriana Rubin' (9)
8 – 'Prichard's Ruby' (9)
7 ***deorum*** (2)
7 ***deuteronana*** (21)
8 ***duthieana*** (18)
0 ***ellisiae alba*** (21)
0 ***erythra*** (26)
0 ***erythrocarpa***
9 x ***facchinii*** (2)
0 ***fedtschenkoi*** (11)
0 Gallygaskins (Prim)
9 'Garnet' (D.Prim)
9 ***hidakana*** (24)
0 'Highland Jewel' (D.Prim)
0 ***ianthina*** (4)
9 'Jubilee' (D.Prim)
0 'Ladybird' (Prim)
9 'Lambrook Peach' (Poly)
0 ***latifolia*** cream form (2)
0 – ***cynoglossifolia*** (2)
7 ***latisecta*** (7)
9 ***magellanica*** (11)
0 ***megaseifolia***
0 ***minima*** x glutinosa (2)
9 ***minutissima*** (16)
9 ***modesta*** 'Flore Pleno' (11)
9 x ***muretiana dinyana*** (2)
7 ***nipponica***
9 'Pink Ruffles' (Prim)
9 x ***pubescens*** 'Old Rose' (2)
7 – 'The Fawn' (2)
0 ***pulverulenta*** Pyramid Pinks (4)
9 'Quarry Wood' (4)
9 'Royal Purple' (Prim)
9 'Ruby Button' (Prim)
9 ***scandinavica*** (11)
0 'Schneekissen Improved' (Prim)
0 ***sieboldii alba*** (7)
0 – 'Chinese Mountain' (7)
7 – 'Deechin' (7)
7 – 'Hakutsuri' (7)
7 – 'Harunuyuki' (7)
9 – 'Joan Jervis' (7)
9 – 'Shironyi' (7)
7 – 'Sunrokumare' (7)
9 – 'Tsu-no-motana' (7)
9 – 'Ykiguruma' (7)
0 ***specuicola*** (11)
9 'Stardust' (Prim)
9 ***stricta*** (11)
0 ***suffrutescens*** (8)
0 Sunset strain
0 ***tanneri*** (21)
9 'The Bride' (Poly)
0 'Tina' (Prim)
9 'Tinney's Apple Blossom' (21)
7 'Tinney's Dairymaid'
0 ***tyrolensis*** (2)
8 ***veris*** 'bronze' (30)
0 – red form (30)
9 ***yuparensis alba*** (11)

PRINSEPIA
7 ***utilis***

PROSTANTHERA
7 ***caerulea***
9 ***chlorantha***
8 ***stricta***

PRUNUS
8 ***americana***
0 ***armeniaca ansu*** 'Flore Pleno'
F ***avium*** 'Grandiflora'
0 ***cerasifera*** 'Mirage'
8 – 'Woodii'
9 ***conradinae*** 'Semiplena'
7 ***davidiana*** 'Alba'
7 – 'Rubra'
F ***domestica*** 'Pixy'
9 'Gyoiko'
7 'Hilling's Weeping'
0 ***incisa*** 'Rubra'
7 ***mahaleb***
7 ***persica*** 'Crimson Cascade'
9 – 'Foliis Rubris'
0 – 'New Award'
0 – 'Pink Peachy'
0 – 'Weeping Flame'
7 ***virginiana***
7 x ***yedoensis*** 'Moerheimii'

PSEUDOMERTENSIA
9 ***moltkioides***

PSEUDOTSUGA
7 ***guinieri***
9 ***menziesii*** 'Knap Hill Seedling'
8 – 'Oudemansii'
7 ***rehderi***

PTERIS
0 ***cretica*** 'Wilsonii'
0 ***longifolia*** 'Mariesii'

PTEROCELTIS
9 ***tatarinowii***

PULMONARIA
0 ***saccharata*** 'White Barn'
9 – 'Wisley White'

PULSATILLA
0 ***alba***
0 ***albana armena***
0 ***campanella***
9 ***halleri*** 'Budapest'
9 ***montana australis***
0 ***turczaninovii***
8 ***vulgaris*** 'Barton's Pink'

PYCNOSTACHYS
0 ***urticifolia***

PYRACANTHA
0 ***augustifolia variegata***
0 'Buttercup'
0 ***fortunei***

X PYRACOMELES
8 ***vilmorinii***

PYRENARIA
9 *spectabilis*

QUERCUS
7 *glauca*
7 *ilicifolia*
7 *laurifolia*
0 Macon
0 *stellata*

QUESNELIA
0 *liboniana*

RAMONDA
0 *myconi alba*

RANUNCULUS
9 *amplexicaulis* 'Grandiflorus'
7 *eschscholtzii*
0 *hirtellus*
9 *insignis*
9 *lappaceus*
9 *macrophyllus*
9 *muelleri brevicaulis*
0 *seguieri*
0 *traunfellneri*

REEVESIA
9 *pubescens*

RHAMNUS
9 x *hybrida* 'Billardii'

RHAPIS
0 *humilis*

RHEKTOPHYLLUM
0 *mirabile*

RHODIOLA
0 *komarovii*

RHODODENDRON
0 *alabamense*
9 *alutaceum*
9 *ambiguum* 'Keillour Castle'
9 *aperantum*
9 *arboreum* 'Patterson'
9 *argyrophyllum hypoglaucum* 'Heane Wood'
9 Azalea 'Agamujin' (E)
9 – 'Alice de Stuers' (M)
9 – 'Ambrosia' (E)
9 – 'Ambush'
8 – 'Anne van Hoeke'
9 – 'Apollo' (E)
9 – 'Apricot Surprise'
0 – 'Atalanta' (E)
9 – 'B Y Morrison' (E)
0 – 'Benifude' (E)
0 – 'Bridesmaid' (O)
0 – 'Bulstrode' (E)
9 – 'Buttercup' (K)
0 – 'Challenger' (E)
0 – 'Chichibu' (E)
9 – 'Comte de Gomer' (M)
9 – 'Comte de Papadopoli' (M)
0 – 'Coquille'
9 – 'Crepello'
0 – 'Crystal Violet'
7 – 'Dart' (K)
0 – 'Dawn's Chorus' (K)
0 – 'Dayspring' (E)
9 – 'Devon' (K)
9 – Diamant group (pink) (E)
9 – Diamant group (salmon pink) (E)
9 – 'Drury Lane'
9 – 'Embley Crimson' (K)
0 – 'Everbloom' (E)
0 – 'Flaire' (K)
8 – 'Fraseri' (M)
7 – 'Garden Beauty' (E)
0 – 'Geisha' (E)
0 – 'Glacier' (E)
9 – 'Gold Dust' (K)
8 – 'Golden Hind'
0 – 'Gorbella'
0 – 'Gretchen' (E)
9 – 'Gwynidd Lloyd' (E)
0 – 'Hamlet' (M)
9 – 'Hanio-no-shion' (E)
9 – 'Harwell' (K)
9 – 'Hershey's Bright Red'
9 – 'Hikkasen' (E)
9 – 'Hollandia' (G)
8 – 'Hotspur Orange' (K)
9 – 'Igneum Novum' (G)
0 – 'Imazuma' (E)
9 – 'Imperator' (M)
9 – 'Jan Steen' (M)
0 – 'Joho-ngodor-akako'
9 – 'Kumoidori' (E)
9 – 'La France' (E)
7 – 'Louisa Hill'
0 – 'Matsukasa Pink'
9 – 'Medway' (K)
8 – 'Megan' (E)
9 – 'Midsummer Beauty' (E)
9 – 'Miyagino' (E)
0 – Mollis salmon (M)
0 – 'Nichola' (E)
9 – 'Orchid Lights'
8 – 'Perfection' (E)
8 – 'Peter Koster' (M)
7 – 'Phoebe'
0 – 'Picotee' (E)
9 – 'Pink Treasure' (E)
8 – 'Pure Gold' (K)
9 – 'Queen Louise' (K)
N– 'Rhapsody' (E)
0 – 'River Belle'
7 – 'Rogue River Belle' (O)
9 – 'Rosella' (K)
9 – 'Salmon Queen' (M)
9 – 'Satrap' (E)
7 – 'Shinto' (E)
8 – 'Soft Lips' (K)
9 – 'Spinoza' (M)
0 – 'Splendens' (E)
0 – 'Star of Zaffelare'
0 – 'Sui-yohi' (E)
0 – 'Sun Charm'
8 – 'Sunset Boulevard' (K)
0 – 'Superbum' (O)
9 – 'Tamarind'
9 – 'Tyrian Rose' (E)
0 – 'Van Heka'
0 – 'Viscosepalum' (G)
9 – 'Wadai-akasuba' (E)
9 – 'Wada's Pink Delight'
0 – 'Wye' (K)
0 – 'Yellow'
9 – 'Yokohama' (E)
0 – 'Yokora'
0 Azaleodendron 'Tottenham'
9 *balfourianum*
9 *brachycarpum brachycarpum* Tigerstedii group
0 *caesium*
0 *campylogynum* Brodick form
9 – Charopoeum group 'Patricia'
0 – 'Crushed Strawberry'
9 *canadense albiflorum*
9 *caucasicum*. 'Cunningham's Sulphur'
8 *cuneatum* Ravum group
9 *dauricum* dwarf
9 *davidsonianum* 'Caerhays Pink'
9 *degronianum* Kyomaruense group
9 *degronianum heptamerum* 'Oki Island'
0 – – 'Wada'
9 *faucium*
9 *ferrugineum* 'Ascreavie'
8 – 'Plenum'
0 *fittianum*
9 *forrestii* 'Branklyn'
0 *fortunei* 'Lu-Shan'
0 *fulgens* Leonardslee form
0 *glaucophyllum* 'Prostratum'
0 *haematodes* FCC form
9 *hippophaeoides* 'Bei-ma-shan'
0 – 'Haba-shan'
9 *hirtipes*
0 Hybrid Aladdin (g.&cl.)
9 – 'Alice Martineau'
8 – 'Anah Kruschke'
0 – 'Apricot Lady Chamberlain'
9 – 'April Chimes'
9 – 'Arlie'
9 – 'Azurika'
9 – 'Azurwolke'
9 – 'Balta'
9 – 'Barmstedt'
8 – 'Beautiful Day'
0 – 'Beefeater'
0 – 'Bernstein'
9 – 'Black Beauty'
0 – 'Blue Pacific'
9 – 'Blue Silver'
0 – 'Bray'
0 – 'Brown Eyes'
0 – 'Buketta'
9 – 'Cadis'
7 – 'Caerhays Yellow'
0 – 'Candi'
0 – 'Carex White'
8 – Cavalier
0 – 'Chelsea'
9 – 'Contina'
0 – 'Cunningham's Album Compactum'
9 – 'Cunningham's Blush'
7 – 'Dawn's Delight'
0 – 'Director Dorsman'
0 – 'Double Date'
9 – 'Duchess of Teck'
9 – Duke of Cornwall (g.&cl.)
9 – Dusky Maid
0 – Elena
0 – Emerald Isle
0 – 'Esveld Select'
0 – 'Exbury Matador'
9 – 'Feespite'
9 – 'Flip'
0 – 'Gladys Rose'
0 – 'Goldbukett'
9 – 'Golden Bee'
9 – 'Good News'
0 – 'Hachmann's Porzellan'
7 – 'Halopeanum'
0 – 'Hansel'
9 – 'Harry Tagg'
0 – Hawk (g.&cl.)
8 – Hawk 'Buzzard'
9 – 'Helen Johnson'
0 – hemsleyanum x 'Polar Bear
8 – 'Hillcrest'
9 – Huntsman
0 – 'Ightham White'
0 – 'Inshriach Blue'
9 – Joanita
0 – 'July Fragrance'
9 – 'Kathleen'
9 – Kiev (g.&cl.)
9 – 'Kimberly'
9 – 'Kimbeth'
0 – 'Lavendula'
0 – 'Lemon Grass'
8 – 'Leonard Messel'
0 – 'Limbatum'
0 – Linswegeanum
0 – 'Loderi Pink Diamond'
0 – 'Looking Glass'
9 – 'Lucy Lou'
8 – 'Madame Carvalho'
9 – 'Mah Jong'
9 – 'Mannheim'
0 – Margaret Findlay (g.&cl.)
0 – 'Mary Belle'
0 – 'Mayfair'
0 – 'Melpomene'
9 – 'Melville'
9 – 'Midsummer Snow'
9 – 'Mother Greer'
9 – 'Mrs Mary Ashley'
9 – 'Mrs Tom Agnew'
8 – 'Multimaculatum'
9 – 'Mum'
0 – 'Nancy Fortescue'
9 – 'Naomi Nautilus'
9 – 'Nimrod Scheherezade'
9 – 'Oporto'
9 – Orestes
0 – 'Ostbo's Low Yellow'
0 – 'Overstreet'
8 – 'Parsons' Gloriosum'
0 – 'Party Pink'
9 – 'Peekaboo'
0 – 'Pematit Cambridge'
0 – 'Pink Beauty'
9 – 'Platinum Pearl'

9 – 'Polly Clarke'
8 – 'Prinses Marijke'
0 – 'Prosti'
7 – 'Puncta'
8 – 'Purple Lace'
9 – 'Purpureum Grandiflorum'
9 – Quaker Girl
9 – 'Raoul Millais'
9 – 'Red Bells'
0 – 'Red Rum'
9 – 'Robert Seleger'
9 – Rouge (g.&cl.)
0 – 'Royal Windsor'
0 – 'Schneebukett'
0 – 'Schneewolke'
0 – 'Serena'
0 – 'Souvenir de D A Koster'
8 – 'Spring Dawn'
9 – 'Spring Glory'
0 – 'Spring Song'
7 – Stonehurst hybrids
9 – 'Suave'
9 – 'Susan Everett'
0 – 'Too Bee'
0 – 'Travis L'
7 – 'Violette'
0 – 'Virgo'
0 – 'Viscount Powerscourt'
9 – 'Vivacious'
0 – 'Wavertree'
0 – 'William Fortescue'
9 – 'Windle Brook'
9 – 'Woodchat'
9 ***irroratum pogonostylum***
9 ***kaempferi*** 'Hall's Red'
9 – ***latisepalum***
9 – 'Troll'
9 ***keiskei*** 'Cordifolium'
9 – 'Ebino'
0 ***kiusianum*** 'Chidori'
9 ***kongboense***
9 ***lapponicum***
0 – Japanese
0 ***lepidotum*** Obovatum group
0 ***ludlowii***
9 ***macrosepalum***
9 ***megeratum*** 'Bodnant'
9 ***minus minus Carolinianum group*** 'Album'
9 ***mollicomum***
0 ***mucronulatum*** best form
0 ***nakaharae*** 'Benenden'
9 ***oreotrephes*** 'Davidian's Favourite'
0 ***parmulatum*** 'Palma' ex KW 5875
9 ***pingianum***
9 ***pronum***
0 ***pseudochrysanthum*** dwarf form
9 ***russatum*** 'Hill of Tarvit'
9 – 'Keillour'
9 ***sargentianum*** 'Maricee'
0 ***serpyllifolium albiflorum***
0 ***sinogrande*** Trewithen form
0 ***tapetiforme***
0 ***telmateium*** Drumonium group
8 ***temenium***
9 ***thomsonii*** 'Balnurnie'
9 ***thymifolium***
8 ***virgatum oleifolium*** 'Penheale Pink'
9 ***viscidifolium***
9 ***williamsianum*** 'Special'
0 ***yedoense poukhanense***
0 – ***poukhanense album***
0 ***yungningense*** Glomerulatum group
9 ***yunnanense*** pale pink

RHODOHYPOXIS

0 'Bety's Carmine'
0 'Margaret Rose'
0 'Monty'

RHOICISSUS

0 ***capensis***

RIBES

0 ***alpinum*** 'Pumilum'
9 ***leptanthum***
7 ***magellanicum***
F ***nigrum*** 'Tsema'
9 ***sanguineum*** 'Atrorubens'
9 – 'Carneum'

RIGIDELLA

0 ***orthantha***

ROBINIA

9 ***boyntonii***
9 ***hispida*** 'Monument'
0 ***pseudoacacia*** 'Sandraudiga'

ROMULEA

9 ***bulbocodium*** white form

ROSA

0 'Aglaia' (Ra)
9 'Alamein' (F)
0 'Amarillo' (HT)
0 'Amorette' (Patio)
0 'Andrew's Rose' (F)
0 'Appreciation' (HT)
0 'Apricot Wine' (F)
0 'Artistic' (F)
9 'Ascot' (F)
0 Baronne Edmond de Rothchild ® (HT)
9 'Berlin' (S)
9 Blue Peter, Climbing ® (Min/ Cl)
0 'Bountiful' (F)
0 'Brandy Butter' (HT)
0 'Capistrano' (HT)
9 'Cologne Carnival' (HT)
0 'Culverbrae' (Ru)
9 'Dekorat' (HT)
9 'Doctor F L Skinner'
9 Duke Meillandina ® (Min)
0 'Eleanor' (Min)
9 'Else Poulsen' (Poly)
9 'Eve Allen' (HT)
9 ***fedtschenkoana*** 'Flore Pleno'
0 'Firecrest' (F)
0 'Firecrest, Climbing' (F/ Cl)
9 'Flashlight' (F)
9 'Frost Fire' (Min)
0 'Golden Autumn' (HT)
9 'Golden Penny' (Min)
0 'Golden Treasure' (F)
9 'Grace Kimmins' (F)
0 'Hadspen Arthur'
0 'Hadspen Eleanor'
0 x ***hardyi***
0 ***hemsleyana***
9 'Incense' (HT)
0 Indian Song ® (HT)
9 Jardins de Bagatelle ® (HT)
9 Jennie Robinson ® (Min/ Patio)
9 'Junior Miss' (F)
0 'K of K' (HT)
9 'Kumbaya' (F)
0 'Lady Hamilton' (HScB)
0 Lakeland Princess ® (HT)
9 'Madame Caroline Testout' (HT)
9 'Midget' (Min)
0 'Mood Music' (Min)
0 ***moyesii*** 'Nassau'
0 'Mrs Reynolds Hole' (T)
0 'Mrs Wakefield Christie-Miller' (HT)
0 'Mrs Wemyss Quin' (HT)
9 'Nymph'
0 'Ohio' (S)
0 Orange Minimo ® (Min)
0 'Orange Mother's Day' (F)
9 'Petula Clarke' (HT)
0 ***pimpinellifolia*** 'Variegata'
9 'Pink Cloud' (HT/ Cl)
9 Playboy ® (F)
0 'Poulbright' (F)
0 'Queenie' (F)
0 'Red Planet' (HT)
0 'Royal Conquest' (F)
0 'Sandra Marie' (HT)
0 'Santa Catalina' (FCl)
0 Shalom ® (F)
9 'Spica Red'
9 'Sunny Queen'
9 'Sylvian Dot'
9 The Coxswain ® (HT)
9 'Toddler' (F)
9 'Tzigane' (HT)
9 'Una' (Ra)
9 'White Dick Koster'
9 'Wisbech Gold' (HT)
9 With Love ® (HT)

ROSMARINUS

9 ***creticus***
7 ***officinalis angustissimus***
7 – 'Pat Vlasto'
9 – 'Suffolk Blue'

ROSULARIA

0 ***libanotica*** from Kaypak
0 ***platyphylla*** from Murat Dag
0 ***radiciflora glabra*** from Beyas Dag
0 – ***radiciflora*** from Bitlis
0 ***stylaris***

RUBUS

9 ***lasiostylus***
0 ***ulmifolius***

RUMEX

9 ***arifolius*** 'Ruber'

RUTA

9 ***montana***

SALIX

8 ***alba*** 'Dart's Snake'
0 ***arctica petrea***
0 x ***dasyclados***
0 x ***ehrhartiana***
0 x ***erdingeri***
0 ***eriocephala*** 'American Mackay'
0 x ***gillotii***
0 ***glabra***
0 ***gooddingii***
7 'Harlequin'
0 ***kitaibeliana***
0 ***mackenzieana***
9 x ***meyeriana***
9 ***microgosa***
8 ***nivalis***
9 ***pendulina blanda***
0 ***reinii***
0 ***repens*** 'Pygmaea'
0 ***retusoides***
0 ***schwerinii***
8 x ***sericans***
0 x ***sirakawensis***
0 ***syrticola***
7 ***thibetica***

SALVIA

9 ***apiana***
8 ***barrelieri***
0 ***chamaedryoides***
9 ***columbariae***
8 ***deserta***
0 ***fallax***
9 ***fruticosa***
0 ***huberi***
0 ***iodantha***
9 ***jurisicii***
0 ***officinalis*** 'Robin Hill'
0 x ***sylvestris*** 'Viola Klose'
8 ***tiliifolia***

SALVINIA

9 ***auriculata***

SAMBUCUS

9 ***caerulea***
F ***canadensis*** 'Hidden Springs'
F – 'John's'

SAPONARIA

7 ***ocymoides*** 'Splendens'

SARCOPOTERIUM

9 ***spinosum***

SARRACENIA

9 ***alata*** x minor
9 x ***courtii***
9 ***excellens***
9 ***flava*** x alata

9 x ***formosa***
9 x ***gilpinii***
9 ***psittacina*** x alata
8 x ***wrigleyana***

SASA
8 ***chrysantha***

SAUSSUREA
0 ***alpina***

SAXIFRAGA
8 'Albida' (***callosa***) (7)
0 'Armida' (***x boeckeleri***) (8)
0 'Becky Foster' (***x borisii***) (8)
0 'Bellisant' (***x hornibrookii***) (8)
8 'Big MD' (***andersonii***) (8)
0 'Buster' (***x hardingii***) (8)
9 ***cespitosa*** (12)
0 'Chelsea Pink' (***x urbium***) (3)
0 'Corona' (***x boydii***) (8)
9 'Dawn' (8)
7 ***diversifolia*** (2)
0 'Dulcimer' (***x petraschii***) (8)
0 'Duncan Lowe' (***stolitzkae***) (8)
0 'Edith' (***x edithae***)
9 ***erioblasta*** (12)
0 'Felicity' (***x anglica***) (8)
7 'Forsteriana' (***petraea***)
0 ***georgei*** (8)
0 ***grisebachii montenegrina*** (8)
8 ***hirsuta paucicrenata***
0 ***hypostoma*** (8)
0 'Intermedia' (***marginata***) (8)
0 'Jubilee' (***x edithae***) (8)
0 'Kestoniensis' (***x salmonica***) (8)
0 ***lolaensis***
0 'London Cerise' (***x urbium***) (3)
0 'Magna' (***burseriana***) (8)
0 'Marshall Joffre' (12)
8 ***michauxii*** (1)
0 'Miss Chambers' (***x urbium***) (3)
7 ***mucronulata*** (2)
9 'Nana' (***bronchialis***) (5)
7 ***nipponica*** (4)
7 ***oppositifolia grandiflora*** (9)
0 – Iceland form (9)
8 ***pedemontana*** (12)
0 – ***cervicornis*** (12)
0 'Perle Rose' (***x anglica***) (8)
7 'Pike's Primrose' (12)
7 'Pike's White' (12)
0 ***pulvinaria*** (8)
0 'Speciosa' (***burseriana***) (8)
0 ***sp.*** AGS/ES 566
0 ***sp.*** McB 1377
0 ***sp.*** McB 1379
8 'Subluteiviridis' (***x gusmusii***) (8)
0 'Theoden' (***oppositifolia***) (9)
7 'Theresia' (***x mariae-theresiae***)
0 'Timmy Foster' (***x irvingii***) (8)
9 'Valerie Keevil' (***x anglica***) (8)
8 ***vandellii*** (8)
7 'Wargrave Rose' (12)
8 'Waterperry' (***sempervivum***) (8)
0 'White Spire' (12)
9 'Zita' (8)

SCABIOSA
9 ***caucasica*** 'Backhouse'
0 – 'Mount Cook'
9 ***pseudograminifolia***

SCHEFFLERA
0 'Starshine'

SCHIMA
9 ***yunnanensis***

SCHINUS
0 ***molle***
0 ***patagonicus***

SCHIVERECKIA
9 ***doerfleri***

SCHIZOSTYLIS
8 ***coccinea*** 'Rosalie'
8 – 'Rose Glow'

SCILLA
0 ***bifolia danubialis***
8 ***nivalis***

SCINDAPSUS
0 ***pictus argyraeus***

SCOPOLIA
0 ***carniolica podolica***

SCUTELLARIA
0 ***albida***

SEDUM
0 ***cauticola*** 'Robustum'
9 ***lineare*** 'Major'
9 ***ochroleucum*** decumbent form
9 ***oreganum boreale***
9 ***pluricaule*** 'Rosenteppich' ('Rose Carpet')
9 ***reflexum albescens***
8 – 'Major'
8 – 'Minor'
9 ***sediforme*** 'Gran Canaria'
9 ***tschernokolevii***
0 ***yabeanum***

SEMIARUNDINARIA
9 ***okuboi***

SEMPERVIVUM
0 ***arachnoideum*** 'Form No 2'
9 'Big Red'
0 ***calcareum*** 'Benz'
0 'Caliph's Hat'
0 ***cantabricum*** from Someido
0 ***ciliosum galicicum*** from Ochrid
8 – x leucanthum
8 'Clara Noyes'
8 'Clipper'
0 ***davisii***
0 'Dunstan'
0 ***globiferum***
9 'Granby'
9 'Jubilation'
9 'Jungle Shadows'
8 'Kolagas Mayfair'
9 'Kristina'
0 ***leucanthum***
0 'Madame Arsac'
8 ***marmoreum*** x dinaricum from Karawanken
0 ***minus***
0 ***montanum carpaticum*** 'Cmiral's Yellow'
9 'Mors'
8 'Mount Usher'
0 'Mrs Elliott'
7 ***pumilum*** x arachnoideum
0 'Purdy's 90-1'
9 'Red Planet'
0 'Red Rum'
9 'Roosemaryn'
9 'Rubra Ray'
8 'Ruby'
8 'Samba'
9 'Sponnier'
9 'Syston Flame'
8 ***tectorum cantalicum***
0 x ***versicolor***
9 'Wega'
9 'Witchery'
0 ***zeleborii*** x kosaninii from Koprivnik

SENECIO
0 ***(See also*** LIGULARIA)
0 ***adonidifolius***
8 ***doronicum***
0 ***hypochionaeus argaeus***
9 ***littoralis***
0 ***sp.*** P&W 6553

SERENOA
0 ***repens***

SHORTIA
0 ***galacifolia***
0 – ***brevistyla***
9 x ***interdexta*** 'Wimborne'
0 ***soldanelloides magna***
0 – ***minima***
9 ***uniflora kantoensis***

SIBBALDIA
9 ***procumbens***

SIDALCEA
0 'Rose Bouquet'

SILENE
9 ***acaulis*** 'Flore Pleno'
0 – ***variegata***
0 ***burchellii***
0 ***dioica*** 'Minikin'
0 – 'Tresevern Gold'
9 ***hookeri bolanderi***
0 ***laciniata***
8 'Pink Bells'
9 ***saxifraga***
8 ***schafta*** 'Robusta'

SINARUNDINARIA
9 ***nitida*** 'Chenevieres'
9 – 'Eisenach'
9 – 'Nymphenburg'

SISYMBRIUM
9 ***officinale***

SISYRINCHIUM
0 ***convolutum***

SKIMMIA
0 ***japonica*** 'Fragrantissima' (m)
0 – 'Keessen'
9 – 'Oblata'
$ – 'Ruby King'
9 – 'Stoneham Red'
0 ***multinervia***

SMYRNIUM
9 ***perfoliatum rotundifolium***

SOLANUM
0 ***aviculare***
0 ***capsicastrum*** 'Variegatum'
0 ***elaeagnifolium***
0 ***valdiviense***

SOLIDAGO
9 'Goldenplume'
7 'Goldstrahl'
9 'Ledsham'
8 'Leraft'
0 ***multiradiata***
0 ***spathulata***
0 ***ulmifolia***

SOPHORA
9 ***japonica*** 'Violacea'

SORBUS
8 ***aucuparia*** 'Pendula'
9 ***decora***
8 'Lowndes'
8 ***minima***
0 ***mougeotii***
0 ***setchuenensis***

SPATHICARPA
0 ***sagittifolia***

SPATHIPHYLLUM
0 ***cannifolium***
0 ***cochlearispathum***
0 ***cuspidatum***
0 ***floribundum***
0 'Mauna Loa'
0 'McCoy'
0 ***patinii***

SPIRAEA
9 ***japonica*** 'Atrosanguinea'
0 'Summersnow'
8 ***trichocarpa***

SPIRODELA
9 ***polyrhiza***

STACHYS
7 ***corsica***
9 ***monieri***

0 *sp.* B&L 12325

STACHYURUS
9 *himalaicus*
9 *spinosus*

STANLEYA
0 *pinnata*
8 *pinnatifida*

STENANTHIUM
9 *robustum*

STREPTOPUS
0 *axillaris*

STROMANTHE
0 *porteana*

STYRAX
9 *americana*
0 *officinalis*

SUCCISA
9 *pratensis rosea*

SWERTIA
0 *longifolia*

SYMPHYTUM
0 *officinale ochroleucum*

SYNGONIUM
0 *podophyllum*

SYNTHYRIS
0 *pinnatifida lanuginosa*

SYRINGA
9 x *chinensis*
0 x *diversifolia* 'William H Judd'
7 x *hyacinthiflora* 'Alice Eastwood'
8 – 'Buffon'
0 'Minuet'
0 'Miss Canada'
9 *oblata*
9 x *persica* 'Gigantea'
9 x *prestoniae* 'Desdemona'
9 – 'Hiawatha'
9 x *swegiflexa*
9 *vulgaris* 'Alphonse Lavallée' (d)
9 – 'Ambassadeur'
9 – 'Charles X'
9 – 'Etna'
9 – 'General John Pershing' (d)
7 – 'Lavaliensis'
9 – 'Maréchal de Bassompierre' (d)
9 – 'Maréchal Foch' (d)
0 – 'Marie Legraye'
7 – 'Monique Lemoine' (d)
7 – 'Night'
0 – 'Paul Deschanel' (d)
7 – 'Réaumur'
9 – 'Ruhm von Horstenstein'
9 – 'Souvenir d'Alice Harding' (d)
0 – 'William Robinson' (d)
0 *wolfii*

TANACETUM
9 *bipinnatum*
7 *coccineum* 'Avalanche'
9 – 'Bees' Pink Delight'
0 – 'Kelway's Glorious'
9 – 'Langport Scarlet'
0 – 'Marjorie Robinson'
8 – 'Red King'
9 – 'Salmon Beauty'
7 – 'Silver Challenger'
9 *dolichophyllum*
0 *parthenium* 'Golden Ball'

TAXUS
0 *baccata* 'Cavendishii'
8 – 'Drinkstone'
0 – 'Erecta'
7 – 'Nana'
9 – 'Prostrata'
0 – 'Pyramidalis'
9 – 'Washingtonii'
0 *brevifolia*
9 *cuspidata*
7 – 'Densa'
0 x *hunnewelliana* 'Richard Horsey'
0 x *media* 'Halloran'

TELLIMA
0 *grandiflora* 'Pinky'

TETRADIUM
7 *velutinum*

TEUCRIUM
9 *polium pii-fontii*
8 *subspinosum roseum*

THALICTRUM
8 *delavayi* 'Amethystine'
8 *occidentale*
8 *petaloides*

THELYPTERIS
9 *dentata*

THLASPI
0 *bulbosum*
0 *montanum*

THRINAX
0 *parviflora*

THUJA
7 *occidentalis* 'Cloth of Gold'
8 – 'Columbia'
0 – 'Mastersii'
0 – 'Robusta'
8 – 'Semperaurea'
9 – 'Sudworth Pumila'
9 *orientalis* 'Flame'
9 – 'Hillieri'
I *plicata* 'Extra Gold'
8 – 'Savill Gardens'

THYMUS
0 *corsicus*
7 *pannonicus*
7 *serpyllum* 'Little Heath'
8 – 'Winter Beauty'
7 'Southcombe Spreader'
9 *striatus*
9 'Widecombe'
8 'Wintergold'

TIARELLA
0 *polyphylla* 'Moorgrün'

TILLANDSIA
9 *festucoides*
9 *recurvata*
9 *tricolor*
0 *usneoides*

TORREYA
0 *grandis*
0 *nucifera* 'Spreadeagle'

TOWNSENDIA
0 *hirsuta*
9 *jonesii tumulosa*
0 *mensana*

TRACHYMENE
0 *humilis*

TRADESCANTIA
0 x *andersoniana* 'Lilacina Plena'
8 – 'Purple Glow'
9 – 'Taplow Crimson'
8 – 'Valour'
7 *brevicaulis caerulea*
0 *spathacea*
0 *zebrina*

TRAGOPOGON
0 *ruber*

TREVESIA
9 *palmata* 'Micholitzii'

TRICYRTIS
9 *formosana* 'Variegata'
0 *hirta* dwarf form

TRILLIUM
9 *flexipes*

TROLLIUS
8 x *cultorum* 'Byrne's Giant'
0 – 'Commander in Chief'
0 – 'Empire Day'
0 – 'Glory of Leiden'
0 – 'Meteor'
0 – 'Orange Crest'
0 – 'Orange Glow'
0 – 'Orangekönig'
0 – 'Oranje Nassau'
0 – 'T Smith'
0 – 'Yellow Beauty'
0 *stenopetalus*

TSUGA
9 *canadensis* 'Aurea'
7 – 'Dawsonia'
7 – 'Essex'
7 – 'Gentsch Variegated'
7 – 'Greenwood Lake'
7 *chinensis tchekiangensis*
7 *dumosa*
0 *sieboldii*
9 *yunnanensis*

TUBERARIA
9 *globulariifolia*

TULIPA
9 'Aga Khan'
9 'Annie Salomons' (14)
9 'Blushing Beauty' (S)
9 'Blushing Bride' (5)
9 'Chatham' (5)
9 'Compostella' (14)
8 *cretica*
9 'Dante' (2)
9 'Demeter' (5)
9 'Dreamboat' (14)
9 'Dutch Princess' (3)
9 'Ellen Willmott' (6)
9 'Gold Coin'
8 *goulimyi*
9 'Hocus Pocus' (5)
9 'Lutea Major' (10)
9 'Musical' (3)
9 'Niphetos' (5)
8 'Orange Boy' (12)
0 *orphanidea* 'Splendens'
9 Peacock strain (*greigii* x kaufmanniana)
9 'Pink Emperor' (13)
0 *planifolia*
9 'Primrose (12)
9 'Prince Charles' (3)
9 'Show Girl' (5)
9 'Tambour Maître' (3)
9 'Tarakan' (5)
9 'Timay'
8 *vvedenskyi* 'Josef Marks'
0 – 'Orange Sunset'
9 'Wallflower' (5)
9 'Water Lily'
9 'Yellow River'
9 'Zomerschoon' (5)

UGNI
0 *molinae* 'Variegata'

ULEX
0 *europaeus* 'Strictus'

ULMUS
9 *glabra* 'Exoniensis'
9 – 'Lutescens'
7 *minor* 'Cornubiensis'
0 – 'Sarniensis'

UNCINIA
9 *clavata*

UNGNADIA
7 *speciosa*

UTRICULARIA
9 *sandersonii*

VACCINIUM
0 *consanguineum*
9 *corymbosum* 'Tifblue'
9 – 'Woodward'
9 *ovalifolium*

VERATRUM
0 *viride*

VERBASCUM
9 'Golden Bush'
9 *pestalozzae*
8 *wiedemannianum*

VERONICA
7 *armena rosea*
0 *austriaca*
8 *cusickii*
7 x *cynarium*
0 'Green Mound'
0 *kiusiana*
0 *kotschyana*
0 *nipponica*
0 *pinnata* 'Blue Eyes'
9 *spicata* 'Alba'

0 *tauricola* Ala Dag
0 *thymoides thymoides*
8 *virgata*

VIBURNUM
7 'Aldenhamensis'
9 *dilatatum* 'Erie'
0 – *xanthocarpum*
0 *erosum*
9 *opulus* 'Wentworth'

VICIA
9 *bithynica*
0 *orobus*
9 *sylvatica*

VICTORIA
0 *amazonica*
0 *cruziana*

VIOLA
0 'Adam's Gold' (V)
9 'Arlington' (C)
9 *arvensis*
9 'Avalanche' (V)
9 'Baby Lucia' (V)
0 'Barbara Swan' (ExV)
0 'Beth'
0 *betonicifolia* white flowered form
9 *blanda*
0 'Blue Perfection' (V)
0 'Blue Waves'
7 'Bob's Bedder'
9 *camschatalorum*
9 *canina montana*
9 'Captivation'
9 *cenisia*
9 'Chandler's Glory'
0 'Cheekie Chappie'
0 *cornuta* pale blue
9 *crassiuscula*
0 'Double Blue' (DVt)
8 'Elsie Coombs' (Vt)
0 'Fairy Tales' (V)
9 *gracilis* x cornuta
0 'Haze' (V)
8 'Jane' (V)
0 'Jenny Wren' (V)
8 'Joanna' (V)
0 'Kathleen Williams' (ExV)
0 *keiskii*
8 'Lady May'
0 'Lady Saville'
9 'Lianne'
9 'Magic Lantern'
7 'Major'
0 *mandschurica triangularis bicolor*
0 'Mandy Miller' (V)
9 'Moonshadow'
0 'Mrs Alex Forrest' (ExV)
7 'Nickie's Blue' (C)
0 *odorata* blue double
0 – 'Caerulea Plena'
9 'Old Blue'
8 'Old Jordans'
0 'Peggy Brookes' (FP)
9 'Princess Alexandra' (Vt)
0 'Roem van Aalsmeer'
9 'Royal Picotee'
9 *tricolor subalpina*
9 'Triumph' (Vt)
0 'Wendy' (SP)

VITEX
7 *agnus-castus* 'Albus'
0 – 'Silver Spire'

VITIS
8 *flexuosa*
8 'Isabella' (*vinifera*)
8 *piasezkii*
F 'Wabetta' (*vinifera*)

VRIESEA
0 *fenestralis*
0 *fosteriana*
0 – 'Red Chestnut'
0 *gigantea*
0 *platynema*
0 – 'Variegata'

WACHENDORFIA
9 *paniculata*

WAHLENBERGIA
7 *cartilaginea*
0 *ceracea*
0 *matthewsii*

WALDHEIMIA
0 *tomentosa*

WASHINGTONIA
0 *lindenii*

WATSONIA
8 *aletroides*
0 *fourcadei*
0 *species*
7 'Starspike'

WEIGELA
9 'Conquête'
8 *japonica*
7 'Kosteriana Variegata'
0 'Stelzneri'
9 *subsessilis*
9 'Van Houttei'

WISTERIA
9 *floribunda* 'Kuchi-beni'
9 – 'Reindeer'

WOODWARDIA
0 *orientalis*

XANTHOSOMA
0 *violaceum*

YUCCA
0 *aloifolia* 'Purpurea'
9 *brevifolia*
9 *gloriosa* 'Albovariegata'

ZAMIOCULCAS
0 *zamiifolia*

ZELKOVA
9 x *verschaffeltii*

ZENOBIA
7 *pulverulenta nitida*

ZIERIA
8 *arborescens*

ZIGADENUS
9 *glaberrimus*

THE NATIONAL COUNCIL FOR THE CONSERVATION OF PLANTS & GARDENS (NCCPG) COLLECTIONS

All or part of the following Genera are represented by a National Collection. Full details of these collections are contained in the *National Plant Collection Directory 1991* available from:-

R A W Lowe
NCCPG General Secretary
The Pines
c/o Wisley Gardens
Woking
Surrey GU23 6QB

Price £2.00 including post & packing.

ABELIA
ABIES
ABUTILON
ACACIA
ACANTHUS
ACER
ACHILLEA
ACTINIDIA
ADIANTUM
AECHMEA
AESCULUS
AGAPANTHUS
AJUGA
ALCHEMILLA
ALLIUM
ALNUS
AMELANCHIER
AMPELOPSIS
ANEMONE
ANTHERICUM
AQUILEGIA
ARABIS
ARBUTUS
ARGYRANTHEMUM
ARISAEMA
ARTEMISIA
ARUNDINARIA
ASPHODELINE
ASPHODELUS
ASPLENIUM
ASTER
ASTILBE
ASTRANTIA
ATHYRIUM
AUBRIETA
AZARA
BAMBUSA
BEGONIA
BELLIS
BERBERIS
BERGENIA
BETULA
BORAGO
BUDDLEJA
BUXUS
CALAMINTHA
CALATHEA
CALCEOLARIA
CALLISTEMON
CALLUNA
CALTHA
CAMASSIA
CAMELLIA
CAMPANULA
CANNA
CARPINUS
CARYA
CARYOPTERIS
CASSIOPE
CASTANEA
CATALPA
CAUTLEYA
CEANOTHUS
CERATOSTIGMA
CERCIDIPHYLLUM
CHAMAECYPARIS
CHIONODOXA
CHUSQUEA
CIMICIFUGA
CISTUS
CITRUS
CLEISTOCACTINAE
CLEMATIS
COLCHICUM
COLUTEA
CONVALLARIA
COPROSMA
CORDYLINE
COREOPSIS
CORNUS
CORTADERIA
CORYLOPSIS
CORYLUS
COTINUS
COTONEASTER
CRATAEGUS
CROCOSMIA
CROCUS
CYCLAMEN
CYSTOPTERIS
CYTISUS
DABOECIA
DAHLIA
DAPHNE
DELPHINIUM
DENDRANTHEMA
DENDROBIUM
DEUTZIA
DIANELLA
DIANTHUS
DICENTRA
DICKSONIACEAE
DIERVILLA
DIGITALIS
DODECATHEON
DORONICUM
DRYOPTERIS
ECHEVERIA
ECHINOCERUS
ECHINOPS
ELAEAGNUS
EMBOTHRIUM
ENKIANTHUS
EPIMEDIUM
ERICA
ERIGERON
ERODIUM
ERYNGIUM
ERYSIMUM
ERYTHRONIUM
ESCALLONIA
EUCALYPTUS
EUCRYPHIA
EUONYMUS
EUPHORBIA
FAGUS
FALLOPIA
FICUS
FORSYTHIA
FRAGARIA
FRAXINUS
FRITILLARIA
FUCHSIA
GALANTHUS
GARRYA
GAULTHERIA
GENISTA
GENTIANA
GERANIUM
GEUM

GLADIOLUS
GREVILLEA
HAMAMELIS
HEBE
HEDERA
HELENIUM
HELIANTHEMUM
HELIANTHUS
HELICHRYSUM
HELIOPSIS
HELLEBORUS
HEMEROCALLIS
HEPATICA
HESPERIS
HEUCHERA
HIBISCUS
HOHERIA
HOSTA
HOYA
HYACINTHUS
HYDRANGEA
HYPERICUM
ILEX
IRIS
JASMINUM
JUGLANS
JUNIPERUS
KALMIA
KNIPHOFIA
LABURNUM
LAMIUM
LARIX
LAVANDULA
LEPTOSPERMUM
LEUCANTHEMUM
LEUCOJUM
LEWISIA
LIBERTIA
LIGULARIA
LIGUSTRUM
LINUM
LIRIODENDRON
LIRIOPE
LITHOCARPUS
LOBELIA
LONICERA
LUPINUS
LYCASTE
LYCHNIS
LYSIMACHIA
MAGNOLIA
MAHONIA
MALUS
MECONOPSIS
MENTHA
MONARDA
MUSCARI
NARCISSUS
NEPETA
NERINE
NERIUM
NOTHOFAGUS
NYMPHAEA
OENOTHERA
OLEARIA
OPHIOPOGON
ORIGANUM
OSMUNDA
OSTEOSPERMUM
OURISIA
OZOTHAMNUS
PAEONIA
PAPAVER
PARADISEA
PARAHEBE
PARTHENOCISSUS
PASSIFLORA
PELARGONIUM
PENSTEMON
PERNETTYA
PERSICARIA
PHILADELPHUS
PHLOMIS
PHLOX
PHORMIUM
PHOTINIA
PHYLLODOCE
PHYLLOSTACHYS
PICEA
PIERIS
PINGUICULA
PINUS
PITTOSPORUM
PLAIBLASTUS
PLATANUS
PLATYCODON
PLEIONE
POLYGONATUM
POLYGONUM
POLYPODIUM
POLYSTICHUM
POPULUS
POTENTILLA
PRIMULA
PRUNUS
PSEUDOPANAX
PTERIDOPHYTA
PULMONARIA
PYRACANTHA
PYRUS
QUERCUS
RANUNCULUS
RHEUM
RHODODENDRON
RHUS
RIBES
ROBINIA
RODGERSIA
ROHDEA
ROSA
ROSCOEA
ROSMARINUS
RUBUS
RUSCUS
SALIX
SALVIA
SAMBUCUS
SANTOLINA
SARCOCOCCA
SARRACENIA
SASA
SAXIFRAGA
SCABIOSA
SCHIZOSTYLIS
SEDUM
SEMIAQUILEGIA
SEMIARUNIDNARIA
SEMPERVIVUM
SENECIO
SHIBATAEA
SIDALCEA
SINARUNDINARIA
SISYRINCHIUM
SKIMMIA
SLIEVE DONARD
SORBARIA
SORBUS
SPIRAEA
Sir F Stern
STEWARTIA
SYMPHYTUM
SYRINGA
TANACETUM
TAXUS
THALICTRUM
THEYPTEROID
THYMUS
TILIA
TILLANDSIA
TRICYRTIS
TRILLIUM
TROLLIUS
TROPAEOLUM
TULBAGHIA
TULIPA
VARIEGATED
VERATRUM
VERBASCUM
VERBENA
VERONICA
VIBURNUM
VINCA
VIOLA
VITIS
WATSONIA
WEIGELA
WISTERIA
WOODWARDIA
YUCCA
ZANTEDESCHIA
ZELKOVA
ZINGIBERACEAE

BIBLIOGRAPHY

INTERNATIONAL PLANT FINDERS

USA

The Andersen's Horticultural Library's Source List of Plants and Seeds. Andersen Horticultural Library, Minnesota Landscape Arboretum, 3675 Arboretum Drive, Box 39, Chanhassen, MN 55317 USA. Compiled by Richard Isaacson. Approx. 40,000 plants and seeds from 400 retail & wholesale outlets in the US & Canada. All are prepared to ship interstate. Does not include Orchids, Cacti or Succulents.

Combined Rose List. Beverly R Dobson, 215 Harriman Road, Irvington, NY 10533. Lists over 7,000 roses from about 150 nurseries mainly in US and Canada. Published annually.

The Complete Vegetable Gardener's Sourcebook. Duane & Karen Newcomb. Prentice Hall.

Fruit, Berry and Nut Inventory. Ed. Kent Whealy. Seed Saver Publications, Route 3, Box 239, Decorah, Iowa 52101.

The Garden Seed Inventory. Ed. Kent Whealy. Seed Saver Publications, Route 3, Box 239, Decorah, Iowa 52101.

Herb Resource Directory. Ed. Paula Oliver. Northwind Farm Publications, Route 2, Box 246, Shevlin, Minn. 56676.

Nursery Sources, Native Plants and Wild Flowers. New England Wild Flower Society, Garden in the Woods, Hemenway Road, Framingham, Mass. 01701. Over 200 native North American wild flowers, ferns, grasses and shrubs. Details of over 100 nurseries

Perennials: A Nursery Source Manual (1989). ed. Barbara Pesch. Brooklyn Botanic Garden, 1000 Washington Avenue, Brooklyn, NY 11225-1099. ISBN 0 945352 48 4. List 320 nurseries and some 4000 perennials.

PlantFinder ®. Betrock Information Systems, 10400 Griffin Road, Suite 301 Cooper City, Florida, USA. (305) 434-4440. *PlantFinder* ® is a monthly publication for wholesale buyers and landscape architects listing availability and price. *PlantQuest* ®: Plant availability on diskettes. *PlantTech* ®: Florida plant scientific data on diskettes. *PlantSearch* ®: On-line plant information database service world-wide.

Sources of Shade Trees in the United States. T Davis Sydnor & J R Holman. Ohio Agricultural Research and Development Centre, Wooster, Ohio 44691.

Gardening by Mail 3rd ed. Barbara J Barton. (Houghton Miffin). Available Gollanz Services UK. ISBN 0 395 52280 3.

CANADA

The Canadian Plant Source Book. Anne Ashley, 93 Fentiman Avenue, Ottawa, ON, CANADA K1S OT7. $13 + $3 p&p (Canadian). About 11,000 hardy plants from Canadian nurseries including those willing to ship to US. English names & English & French cross-indexes.

GERMANY

Pflanzen Einkaufsführer. Eugen Ulmer GmbH & Co. ISBN 3-8001-6393-4. Some 14,000 plants from German nurseries.

GENERAL

The following list of bibliographic sources and references is by no means exhaustive, but lists some of the more useful and available works used in the preparation of **THE PLANT FINDER.**

The Plantsman is published regularly by The Royal Horticultural Society, Vincent Square, London SW1P 2PE

Allan, H H et al. 1961. *Flora of New Zealand* (Vol I). Wellington, New Zealand.

Bailey, L H Bailey, E Z et al. 1976. *Hortus Third.* Macmillan, New York.

Bean, W J. 1970-1980. *Trees and Shrubs Hardy in the British Isles* (8th ed. edited Sir George Taylor & D L Clarke). John Murray, London.

Bean, W J, 1988. (Supp. to 8th ed. edited D L Clarke).

Beckett, K A. 1987. *The RHS Encyclopaedia of House Plants.* Century Hutchinson, London.

Bond, P & Goldblatt, P. 1984. *Plants of the Cape Flora.* Journal of South African Botany. (Sup. Vol. No 13). Kirstenbosch.

Bramwell, D & Z. 1974. *Wild Flowers of the Canary Islands.* Stanley Thomas, London, 1974.

Brickell, C D (ed.) et al. 1980. *International Code of Nomenclature for Cultivated Plants.* Utrecht.

Brickell, C D (ed.) 1989. *Gardeners' Encyclopaedia of Plants and Flowers.* Dorling Lindersley, London.

Bryan, J E 1989. *Bulbs* (Vols I & II). Christopher Helm, Bromley, Kent.

Chittenden, F J (ed.). 1965. *The Royal Horticultural Society Dictionary of Gardening* (2nd ed.). Oxford University Press.

Clayton, W D & Renvoize, S A. 1986. *Genera Graminum.* HMSO, London

Cribb, P & Bailes, C. 1989. *Hardy Orchids.* Christopher Helm, Bromley, Kent.

Davies, R A & Lloyd, K M (compilers). 1987-1989. *Kew Index for 1986, 1987, 1988 & 1989.* Clarendon Press, Oxford.

Davis, P H et al. (ed.). 1965-1988. *Flora of Turkey* (Vols 1-10). University Press, Edinburgh.

Forrest, M. (ed. Nelson, E C.) 1985. *Trees and Shrubs Cultivated in Ireland.* Boethius Press for An Taisce, Dublin.

Galbraith, J. 1977. *Field Guide to the Wild Flowers of South-East Australia.* Collins, London.

Graf, A B. 1981. *Tropica* (2nd ed.). Roehrs, New Jersey.

Harkness, M G & D'Angelo, D. 1986. *The Bernard E Harkness Seedlist Handbook.* Timber Press, Portland, Oregon.

Healy, A J & Edgar, E. 1980. *Flora of New Zealand* (Vol III). Wellington, New Zealand.

Heath, R E. 1981. *Collectors Alpines.* Collinridge, Twickenham.

Hilliers' Manual of Trees and Shrubs. 1972. David & Charles, Newton Abbot.

Hogg, R. 1884. *The Fruit Manual.* (5th ed.). Journal of Horticulture Office, London.

Jacobsen, H. 1973. *Lexicon of Succulent Plants.* Blandford, London.

Jones, D L. 1987. *Encyclopaedia of Ferns.* Lothian, Melbourne, Australia.

Krussmann, G. (English ed. trans. M E Epp). 1984-1986. *Manual of Cultivated Broadleaved Trees & Shrubs* (Vol I-III). Batsford, London.

Laar, H J van de. 1989. *Naamlijst van Houtige Gewassen.* Proefstation voor de Boomteelt en het Stedelijk Groen, Boskoop, Holland.

Laar, H J van de & Fortgens, Ing. G. 1988. *Naamlijst van Vaste Planten.* Proefstation voor de Boomkwekerij, Boskoop, Holland.

Lewis, J ed. Leslie, A C. 1987 & 1989. *The International Conifer Register.* Pt.I (*Abies* to *Austrotaxus*) and Pt.II (*Belis* to *Pherosphaera* excluding Cypresses and Junipers). Royal Horticultural Society, London.

Mabberley, D J. 1987. *The Plant-Book.* Cambridge University Press.

Ohwi, J. (ed F G Meyer & E H Walker). 1965. *Flora of Japan.* Smithsonian Institute, Washington.

Phillips, R. & Rix, M. *Shrubs.* 1989. Pan Books, London.

Pinner, J L M et al. (compilers) & Davies, R A (ed.). 1987. *Index Kewensis* (Supplements XVII & XVIII). Clarendon Press, Oxford.

The Plantsman. The Royal Horticultural Society, London.

Polunin, O & Stainton, A. 1984. *Flowers of the Himalaya.* Oxford University Press.

Rehder, R. 1940. *Manual of Cultivated Trees & Shrubs Hardy in North America* (2nd ed.) Macmillan, New York.

Stafleu, F A et al. 1978. *International Code of Botanical Nomenclature.* Bohn, Scheltema & Holkema, Utrecht.

Stearn, Prof. W T. *Botanical Latin* David & Charles. Newton Abbot, England.

Thomas, G S. 1990. *Perennial Garden Plants.* (3rd ed.) J M Dent & Sons, London.

Trehane, R P. 1989. *Index Hortensis.* Quarterjack Publishing, Wimborne, Dorset.

Tutin, T G. 1964-1980. *Flora Europaea* (Vols I-V). Cambridge University Press.

Walters, S M (ed.) et al. 1984 & 1986. *The European Garden Flora* (Vols I & II). Cambridge University Press.

Willis, J C. 1973. *A Dictionary of the Flowering Plants and Ferns* (8th ed. revised H K Airy Shaw, Cambridge University Press.

Wilson, H D. 1978. *Wild Plants of Mount Cook National Park.* Christchurch, New Zealand.

GENERA

ACER

Harris, J G S. 1983. *The Plantsman.* (Vol 5 Pt I).

Vertrees, J D. 1978. *Japanese Maples.* Timber Press, Oregon.

ADIANTUM

Goudry, C J. 1985. *Maidenhair Ferns in Cultivation.* Lothian, Melbourne, Australia.

AESCULUS

Wright, D. 1985. *The Plantsman.* (Vol 7 Pt IV).

AGAPETES

Argent, G C G & Woods, P J B. 1988. *The Plantsman.* (Vol 8 Pt II).

AJUGA

Adam, C G. *Alpine Garden Society Bulletin.* (Vol 50 Pt I).

ALNUS

Ashburner, K. *The Plantsman.* (Vol 8 Pt III).

ANDROSACE

Smith, G F & Lowe, D B. 1977. *Androsaces.* Alpine Garden Society.

ANEMONE, Japanese

McKendrick, M. 1990. *The Plantsman.* (Vol 12 Pt III).

ANEMONE nemorosa

Toubol, U. 1981. *The Plantsman.* (Vol 3 Pt III).

AQUILEGIA

Munz, P A. 1946. *Aquilegia: The Cultivated and Wild Columbines. Gentes Herbarum* (Vol VII Fasc I). Bailey Hortorium, New York.

ARACEAE

Bown, D. 1988. *Aroids.* Century Hutchinson, London.

ARGYRANTHEMUM

Humphries, C J. 1976. *A Revision of the Macaronesian Genus Argyranthemum.* The Bulletin of the British Museum (Natural History) Botany Vol. 5 No. 4, London.

ARISAEMA

Mayo, J J. 1982. *The Plantsman.* (Vol 3 Pt IV).

ASTER

Ranson, E R. 1947. *Michaelmas Daisies*. Garden Book Club.

AUBRIETA

International Registration Authority Checklist. Weihenstephan.

BEGONIA

Ingles, J. 1990. *American Begonia Society Listing of Begonia Cultivars (Revised Edition Buxton Checklist)*.

Wall, B. 1989. *The Plantsman*. (Vol 11 Pt I).

Thompson, M L. & Thompson, E J. 1981. *Begonias: The Complete Reference Guide*. Times Books, New York.

BETULA

Ashburner, K. 1980. *The Plantsman*. (Vol 2 Pt I).

Ashburner, K & Schilling, A D. 1985. *The Plantsman*. (Vol 7 Pt II).

BOUGAINVILLEA

Bor, N L. & Raizada, M B. 1982. *Some Beautiful Indian Climbers and Shrubs*. (2nd ed.) pp 291-304. Bombay Natural History Society.

Gillis, W T. 1976 *Bougainvilleas of Cultivation. Baileya*. Vol 20(1) pp34-41. New York.

MacDaniels, L H. 1981. *A Study of Cultivars in Bougainvillea. Baileya*. Vol 21(2) pp77-100. New York.

BROMELIACEAE

Rauh, W. 1979. *Bromeliads*. Blandford Press, Dorset.

BUDDLEJA

Tait, W A. 1988 *The Plantsman*. (Vol 10 Pt I).

BULBS

Grey-Wilson, C & Matthew, B. 1981. *Bulbs*. Collins, London.

Innes, C. 1985. *The World of Iridaceae*. Hollygate International, Sussex.

Rix, M & Phillips, R. 1981. *The Bulb Book*. Pan Books, London.

BUXUS

Batdorf, L R. 1989. *Checklist of Buxus*. American Boxwood Society.

CAMELLIA

Macoboy, S. 1981. *Colour Dictionary of Camellias*. Lansdowne, Sydney, Australia.

Treseder, N & Hyams, E. 1975. *Growing Camellias*. Nelson, London.

Woodroof, W E (ed.). 1987. *Camellia Nomenclature*. (19th ed.). Southern California Camellia Society, Pasadena.

CAMPANULA

Lewis, P & Lynch, M. 1989. *Campanulas*. Christopher Helm, Bromley, Kent.

CARNIVEROUS PLANTS

Slack, A. 1988. *Carniverous PLants*. (rev. ed.). Alphabooks, Sherbourne, Dorset.

CARPINUS

Rushforth, K. 1986. *The Plantsman* (Vol 7 Pts III & IV).

CARYOPTERIS

Pattison, G. 1989. *The Plantsman* (Vol 11 Pt I.)

CASSIOPE

Blake, F S. *Alpine Garden Society Bulletin*. (Vol 53 Pt I).

Starling, B. 1989. *The Plantsman*. (Vol 11 Pt II).

CESTRUM

Beckett, K A. 1987. *The Plantsman*. (Vol 9 Pt III).

CHRYSANTHEMUM

British National Register of Chrysanthemums. National Chrysanthemum Society. 1964-1989.

CHAENOMELES

Weber, C. 1963. *Cultivars in the Genus Chaenomeles*. Arnoldia. (Vol 23 No 3) Arnold Arboretum, Harvard, Massachusetts.

CLEMATIS

Fisk, J. 1989. *Clematis, the Queen of Climbers*. Cassell, London.

Fretwell, B. 1989. *Clematis*. Collins, London.

Grey-Wilson, C. 1986. *The Plantsman*. (Vol 7 Pt IIII).

Hutchins, G. 1990. *The Plantsman*. (Vol 11 Pt IV).

Lloyd, C & Bennett, T H. 1989. *Clematis*. Viking, London.

CODONOPSIS

Alpine Garden Society Bulletin. (Vol 48 Pt 2).

Grey-Wilson, C. 1990. *The Plantsman*. (Vol 12 Pt II).

CONIFERS

Krussmann, G. (English trans. M E Epp). 1985. *Manual of Cultivated Conifers*. Batsford, London.

Ouden, P. den & Boom, B K. 1965. *Manual of Cultivated Conifers*. Martinus Nijhorff, The Haque, Netherlands.

Welch, H J. 1979. *Manual of Dwarf Conifers*. Theophrastus, New York.

CORNUS

Howard, R A. 1961. Registration Lists of Cultivar Names in *Cornus* L., Arnoldia. (Vol 21 No 2). Arnold Arboretum, Harvard, Massachusetts.

CORYLOPSIS

Wright, D. 1982. *The Plantsman*. (Vol 4 Pt I).

CROCOSMIA

Kostelijk, P J. 1984. *The Plantsman*. (Vol 5 Pt IIII).

CYCLAMEN

Grey-Wilson, C. 1988. *The Genus Cyclamen*. Christopher Helm, Bromley, Kent.

CYRTANTHUS

Holford, F. 1989. *The Plantsman*. (Vol 11 Pt III).

DAPHNE

Brickell, C D & Mathew, B. 1976. *Daphne*. Alpine Garden Society.

DEUTZIA

Taylor, J. 1990. *The Plantsman*. (Vol 11 Pt II).

DIANTHUS

Leslie, A C. 1983. *The International Dianthus Register*. (2nd ed. & supps. 1-5). Royal Horticultural Society, London.

DIASCIA

Benham, S. 1987. *The Plantsman*. (Vol 9 Pt I).

DIERAMA

Hilliard, O M. & Burtt, B L. 1990. *The Plantsman*. (Vol 12 Pt II).

ERODIUM

Bacon, L. 1990. *A.G.S. Bulletin*. (Vol 85 No 1).

EUCOMIS

Compton, J. 1990. *The Plantsman*. (Vol 12 Pt III).

EUCRYPHIA

Wright, D. 1983. *The Plantsman*. (Vol 5 Pt 3).

EUONYMUS

Lancaster, R. 1981. *The Plantsman.* (Vol 3 Pt III).

EUPHORBIA

Turner, R & Radcliffe-Smith, A. 1983. *The Plantsman.* (Vol 5 Pt 6 III).

FAGUS

Wyman, D. 1964. Registration List of Cultivar Names of *Fagus* L., Arnoldia. (Vol 24 No 1). Arnold Arboretum, Harvard, Massachusetts.

FERNS

Kaye, R. 1968. *Hardy Ferns.* Faber & Faber, London.

Rush, R. 1984. *A Guide to Hardy Ferns.* The British Pteridological Society, London.

FRITILLARIA

Turrill, W B & Seely, J R. 1980. *Studies in the Genus Fritillaria.* Hooker's Icones Plantarum, (Vol XXXIX Pts I & II), Royal Botanic Gardens, Kew.

FUCHSIA

Boullemier, L B. 1985. *The Checklist of Species, Hybrids & Cultivars of the Genus Fuchsia.* Blandford Press, Dorset.

GAULTHERIA (inc. Pernettya)

Middleton, D. 1990. *The Plantsman.* (Vol 12 Pt III)

GENTIANA

Bartlett, M. 1975. *Gentians.* Blandford Press, Dorset.

Wilkie, D. 1950. *Gentians.* (2nd ed.) Country Life, London.

GERANIUM

Yeo, P F. 1985. *Hardy Geraniums.* Croom Helm, London.

GLADIOLUS

Lewis, G J & Obermeyer, A A & Barnard, T T. 1972. *A Revision of the South African Species of Gladiolus.* (Sup. Vol. 10). Journal of South African Botany, Purnell, Cape Town.

List of Gladiolus Cultivars. The British Gladiolus Society.

GLEDITSIA triacanthos

Santamour, F S Jr & McArdle, A J. 198?. *Checklist of Cultivars of Honeylocust.* USA.

GRAMINEAE (BAMBUSEAE)

Wang Dajun & Shen Shap-Jin. 1987. *Bamboos of China.* Timber Press, Portland, Oregon.

GRASSES

Grounds, R. 1979. *Ornamental Grasses.* Pelham Books, London.

HAEMANTHUS

Snijman, D. 1984. *A Revision of the Genus Heamanthus. Journal of South African Botany.* Supplementary Vol 12. National Botanic Gardens, Kirestenbosch.

HAMAMELIDACEAE

Wright, D. 1982. *The Plantsman.* (Vol 4 Pt I).

HEATHERS

Yates, G. 1983. *A Pocket Guide to Heather Gardening.* Aura Books, Middlesex.

HEBE

Hutchins, G. 1979. *Hebe and Parahebe Species in Cultivation.* County Park Nursery, Essex.

Chalk, D. 1988. *Hebes and Parahebes.* Christopher Helm, London.

HEDERA

Rose, P Q. 1980. *Ivies.* Blandford Press, Dorset.

McAllister, H. 1988. *The Plantsman.* (Vol10 Pt I).

HEDYCHIUM

Schilling, A D. 1982. *The Plantsman.* (Vol 4 Pt III).

HELICHRYSUM

Hilliard, O M & Burtt, B L. 1987. *The Garden.* (Vol 112 Pt VI). Royal Horticultural Society, London.

HELLEBORUS

Mathew, B. 1981. *The Plantsman.* (Vol 3 Pt I).

HEMEROCALLIS

Kitchingman, R M. 1985. *The Plantsman.* (Vol 7 Pt II).

HIBISCUS

Beers, L. & Howie, J. 1990. *Growing Hibiscus.* (2nd ed.). Kangaroo Press, Kenthurst, Australia.

HIPPEASTRUM

Alfabetische Lisjt van de in Nederland in cultuur zijnde Amaryllis (Hippeastrum) Cultivars. 1980. Koninklijke Algemeene Veereniging voor Bloembollencultur, Hillegom, Netherlands.

HOSTA

Grenfell, D. 1985. *The Plantsman.* (Vol 7 Pt IV).

Grenfell, D. 1990. *Hosta.* Batsford, London.

Hensen, K J W. 1985. *The Plantsman.* (Vol 7 Pt I).

HYDRANGEA

Haworth-Booth, M. 1975. *The Hydrangeas.* Garden Book Club, London.

HYPERICUM

Robson, N K B. 1980. *The Plantsman.* (Vol 1 Pt IIII).

ILEX

Andrews, S. 1983. *The Plantsman.* (Vol 5 Pt II).

Andrews, S. 1984. *The Plantsman.* (Vol 6 Pt III).

Andrews, S. *The Garden.* (Vol 110 p11). Royal Horticultural Society, London.

IMPATIENS

Grey-Wilson, C. 1983. *The Plantsman.* (Vol 5 Pt II).

IRIS

Hoog, M H. 1980. *The Plantsman.* (Vol 2 Pt III).

Mathew, B. 1981. *The Iris.* Batsford, London.

IRIS (Series Unguiculares)

Service, N. 1990. *The Plantsman.* (Vol 12 Pt I).

KNIPHOFIA

Taylor, J. 1985. *The Plantsman.* (Vol 7 Pt III).

LACHENALIA

Duncan, G D. 1988. *The Lachenalis Handbook. Annals of Kirstenbosch Botanic Gardens.* Vol 17. Republic of South Africa.

LANTANA

Howard, R A. 1969. A Check List of Cultivar Names used in the Genus *Lantana Arnoldia.* (Vol 29 No 11). Arnold Arboretum, Harvard, Massachusetts.

LARIX

Horsman, J. 1988 *The Plantsman.* (Vol 10 Pt I).

LAVANDULA

Tucker, A O. & Hensen, K J W. 1985. *The Cultivars of Lavender and Lavandin. Baileya.* Vol 22(4) pp168-177. New York.

LEPTOSPERMUM

Nomenclature Committee of the Royal New Zealand Institute of Horticulture. 1963. Check List of *Leptospermum Cultivars*. Journal of the Royal New Zealand Institute of Horticulture. (Vol V No V).

LEWISIA

Elliott, R. 1978. *Lewisias*. Alpine Garden Society, Woking.

Mathew, B. 1989. *The Genus Lewisia*. Christopher Helm, Bromley, Kent.

LILIACEAE

Mathew, B. 1989. *The Plantsman*. (Vol 11 Pt II).

LILIUM

Leslie, A C. 1982. *The International Lily Register* (3rd ed. & supps. 1-7). Royal Horticultural Society, London.

MAGNOLIA

Holman, N. 1979. *The Plantsman*. (Vol 7 Pt I).

Treseder, N G. 1978. *Magnolias*. Faber & Faber, London.

MALUS

Parfitt, B. 1965. *Index of the Apple Collection at the National Fruit Trials*. Ministry of Agriculture, Fisheries and Food, Faversham, Kent.

Taylor, H V. 1948. *The Apples of England*. Crosby Lockwood, London.

MECONOPSIS

Cobb, J L S. 1989. *Meconopsis*. Christopher Helm, Bromley, Kent.

MORAEA

Goldblatt, P. 1986. *The Moraeaes of Southern Africa*. National Botanic Gardens of South Africa.

NARCISSUS

Blanchard, J W. 1990. *Narcissus*. Alpine Garden Society, Woking, Surrey.

Kington, S. 1989. *The International Daffodil Checklist*. (2nd ed. & 14th supp.). Royal Horticultural Society, London.

Throckmorton, T D (ed.). 1985. *Daffodils to Show & Grow and Abridged Classified List of Daffodil Names*. Royal Horticultural Society and American Daffodil Society, Hernando, Mississippi.

NOTHOFAGUS

Hill, R S. & Read, J. 1991. *Botanical Journal of the Linnean Society*. (Vol 105 No 1).

NYMPHAEA

Swindells, P. 1983. *Waterlilies*. Croom Helm, London.

OSTRYA

Rushforth, K. 1986. *The Plantsman*. (Vol 7 Pts III & IV).

PAEONIA

Haworth-Booth, M. 1963. *The Moutan or Tree Peony*. Garden Book Club, London.

Kessenich, G M. 1976. *Peonies*. (Variety Check List, Pts 1-3). American Peony Society.

PELARGONIUM

Baggust, H. 1988. *Miniature and Dwarf Geraniums*. Christopher Helm, Bromley, Kent.

A Checklist and Register of Pelargonium Cultivar Names. Part 1 (1978) and Part 2 (unpublished). Australian Geranium Society, Sydney.

Clifford, D. 1958 *Pelargoniums*. Blandford Press, London.

Complete Copy of the Spalding Pelargonium Checklist. Unpublished. USA.

Van der Walt, J J A et al. 1977-88. *Pelargoniums of South Africa*. (Vols I-III). National Botanic Gradens, Kirstenbosch, Republic of South Africa.

PHILADELPHUS

Taylor, J. 1990. *The Plantsman.* (Vol 11 Pt IV).

Wright, D. 1980. *The Plantsman.* (Vol 2 Pt II).

PHLOX

Wherry, E T. 1955. *The Genus Phlox.* Morris Arboretum Monographs III, Philadelphia, Penn.

PHYGELIUS

Coombes, A J. 1988. *The Plantsman.* (Vol 9 Pt IV).

PIERIS

Bond, J. 1982. *The Plantsman.* (Vol 4 Pt II).

Wagenknecht, B L. 1961. Registration List of Names in the Genus *Pieris.* D. Don, Arnoldia Vol 21 No 8. Arnold Arboretum, Harvard, Massachusetts.

POTENTILLA

Davidson, C G. & Lenz, L M. 1989. *Experimental Taxonony of Potentilla fruticosa. Canadian Journal of Botany.* Vol 67 No 12) pp3520-3528.

POTENTILLA (Shrubby)

Brearley, C. 1987. *The Plantsman.* (Vol 9 Pt II)

PRIMULA

Fenderson, G K. 1986. *A Synoptic Guide to the Genus Primula.* Allen Press, Lawrence, Kansa.

Green, R. 1976. *Asiatic Primulas.* The Alpine Garden Society,Woking.

Hecker, W R. 1971. *Auriculas & Primroses.* Batsford, London.

Smith, G F, Burrow, B & Lowe, D B. 1984. *Primulas of Europe and America.* The Alpine Garden Society, Woking.

Wemyss-Cooke, T J. 1986. *Primulas Old and New.* David & Charles, Newton Abbot.

PRUNUS

Bultitude, J. *Index of the Plum Collection at the National Fruit Trials.* Ministry of Agriculture, Fisheries & Food, Faversham, Kent.

Grubb, N H. 1949. *Cherries.* Crosby Lockwood, London.

Index of the Cherry Collection at the National Fruit Trials. 1986. Ministry of Agriculture, Fisheris & Food, Faversham, Kent.

Jefferson, R M & Wain, K K. 1984. *The Nomenclature of Cultivated Flowering Cherries (Prunus): The Sato-zakura Group.* U S D A.

Smith, M W G. 1978. *Catalogue of the Plums at the National Fruit Trials.* Ministry of Agriculture, Fisheries & Food, Faversham, Kent.

Taylor, H V. 1949. *The Plums of England.* Crosby Lockwood, London.

PULMONARIA

Mathew, B. 1982. *The Plantsman.* (Vol 4 Pt II).

PYRUS

Parfitt, B. 1981. *Index of the Pear Collection at the National Fruit Trials.* Ministry of Agriculture, Fisheries & Food, Faversham, Kent.

Smith, M W G. 1976. *Catalogue of the British Pears.* Ministry of Agriculture, Fisheries & Food, Faversham, Kent

RAOULIA

Hutchins, G. 1980. *The Plantsman.* (Vol 2 Pt II).

RHODODENDRONS

Chamberlain, D F. 1982. *Notes from the Royal Botanic Garden Edinburgh.* (Vol 39 No 2). H M S O, Edinburgh.

Cox, P A & Cox, K N E. 1988 *Encyclopaedia of Rhododendron Hybrids.* Batsford, London.

Cullen, J. 1980. *Notes from the Royal Botanic Garden Edinburgh.* (Vol 39 No 1). H M S O, Edinburgh.

Davidian, H H. 1982 & 1989. *The Rhododendron Species.* (Vol I & II). Batsford, London.

Galle, F C. 1987. *Azaleas.* Timber Press, Portland, Oregon.

Lee, F P. 1958. *The Azalea Book.* D Van Nostrand, New York.

Leslie, A C. (compiler). 1980. *The Rhododendron Handbook.* Royal Horticultural Society, London.

Leslie, A C. 1989 *The International Rhododendron Register: Checklist of Rhododendron Names registered 1959-1987.* Royal Horticultural Society, London.

Salley, H E & Greer, H E. 1986. *Rhododendron Hybrids.* Batsford, London.

RIBES

Index of the Bush Fruit Collection at the National Fruit Trials. 1987. Ministry of Agriculture, Fisheries & Food, Faversham, Kent.

ROMNEYA

McMillan Browse, P. 1989. *The Plantsman.* (Vol 11 Pt II)

ROSA

AUSTIN, D. 1988. *The Heritage of the Rose.* Antique Collectors' Club, Woodbridge, Suffolk.

Beales, P. 1985. *Classic Roses.* Collins Harvill

Beales, P. 1988. *Twentieth Century Roses.* Collins Harvill, London.

Bean, W J. 1900-1988 (rev. D L Clarke & G S Thomas) *Rosa* in *Trees and Shrubs Hardy in the British Isles* 8th ed. (Vol IV & Supp.)

McCann, S. 1985. *Miniature Roses.* David & Charles, Newton Abbot, Devon.

Pawson, A. 1989. *Find That Rose (7th ed).* Rosegrowers' Association, Colchester, Essex.

Phillips, R & Rix, M. 1988. *Roses.* Macmillan, London.

Thomas, G S. 1955 (rev. 1983). *The Old Shrub Roses.* Dent, London.

Thomas, G S. 1962. *Shrub Roses of Today.* Dent, London.

Thomas, G S. (rev. ed 1978). *Climbing Roses Old and New.* Dent, London.

SALIX

Warren-Wren, S C. 1972. *Willows.* David & Charles, Newton Abbot.

SAXIFRAGA

Kohlein, F. 1984. *Saxifrages and Related Genera.* Batsford, London.

Webb, D A & Cornell, R J. 1989. *Saxifrages of Europe.* Christopher Helm, Bromley, Kent.

SEDUM

EVANS, R L. 1983. *Handbook of Cultivated Sedums.* Ivory Head Press Motcombe, Dorset.

Hensen, K J W & Groendijk-Wilders, N. 1986. *The Plantsman.* (Vol 8 Pt I).

SEMPERVIVUM

Mitchell, P J. 1985. *International Cultivar Register for Jovibarba, Rosularia, Sempervivum.* The Sempervivum Society, W Sussex.

SHORTIA

Barnes, P G. 1990 *The Plantsman.* (Vol 12 Pt I).

SKIMMIA

Brown, P D. 1980. *The Plantsman.* (Vol 1 Pt IV).

SOLENOSTEMON

Pedley, W K. & Pedley, R. 1974. *Coleus - A Guide to Cultivation and Identification.* Bartholemew, Edinburgh.

SORBUS

McAllister, H. 1985. *The Plantsman.* (Vol 6 Pt IV).

Wright, D. 1981. *The Plantsman.* (Vol 3 Pt II).

SYRINGA

Fiala, Fr J L. 1988. *Lilacs.* Christopher Helm, Bromley, Kent.

Rogers, O M. 1976. *Tentative International Register of Cultivar Names in the Genus Syringa.* University of New Hampshire.

Taylor, J. 1990. *The Plantsman.* (Vol 11 Pt IV).

Vrugtman, F. 1976-83. *Bulletin of the American Association of Botanical Gardens and Arboreta.*

TILIA

Muir, N. 1984. *The Plantsman.* (Vol 5 Pt IV).

Muir, N. 1988. *The Plantsman.* (Vol 10 PtII).

TRILLIUM

Mitchell, R J. 1989. *The Plantsman.* (Vol 10 Pt IV, Vol 11 Pts II & III, Vol 12 Pt I).

TULIPA

Classified List and International Register of Tulip Names. 1987. Royal General Bulbgrowers' Association, Hillegom, Holland.

ULMUS

Green, P S. 1964. Registration of the Cultivar Names in *Ulmus.* Arnoldia, Vol 24 Nos 608, Arnold Arboretum, Harvard, Massachusetts.

VERATRUM

Mathew, B. 1989. *The Plantsman.* (Vol 11 Pt I).

VIOLA

Coombs, R E. 1981 *Violets.* Croom Helm, London.

Farrar, E. 1989. *Pansies, Violas & Sweet Violets.* Hurst Village Publishing, Reading.

Fuller, R. 1990. *Pansies, Violas & Violettas* Crowood Press, Marlborough, Wiltshire.

VITIS

Pearkes, G. 1989. *Vine Growing in Britain.* Dent, London.

Robinson, J. 1986. *Vines, Grapes and Wines* Mitchell Beazley, London.

WATSONIA

Goldblatt, P. 1989. *The Genus Watsonia.* National Botanic Gardens, Republic of South Africa.

WEIGELA

Howard, R A. 1965. A Check-list of Cultivar Names in *Weigela.* Arnoldia, Vol 25 Nos 9-11. Arnold Arboretum, Harvard, Massachusetts.

Taylor, J. 1990. *The Plantsman.* (Vol 12 Pt IV).

WISTERIA

McMillan-Browse, P. 1984. *The Plantsman* (Vol 6 Pt II).

ZAUSCHNERIA (now EPILOBIUM)

Raven, P H. 1976. *Annals of the Missouri Botanic Garden.* (Vol 63 pp326-340).

ZELKOVA

Ainsworth, P. 1989. *The Plantsman.* (Vol 11 Pt II)

INDEX MAP

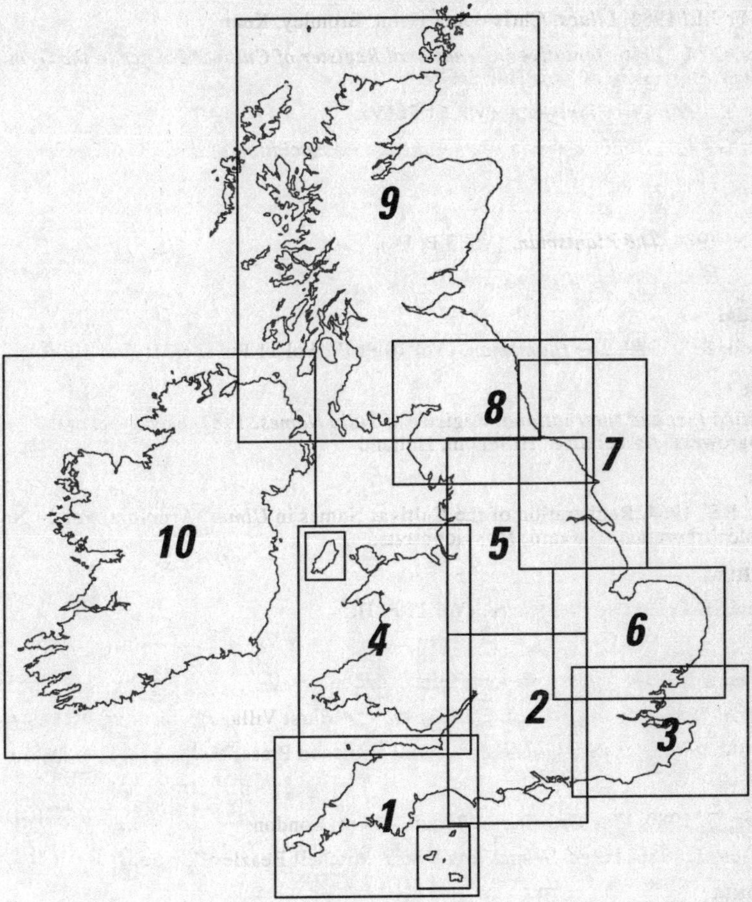

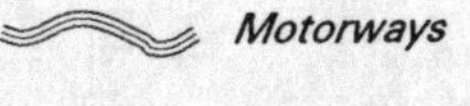
Motorways

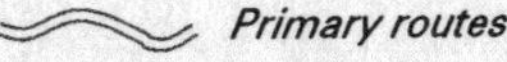
Primary routes

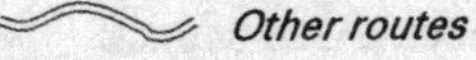
Other routes

The maps on the following pages show the *approximate* location of the nurseries whose details are listed in this directory.

Details of nurseries with letter Codes in boxes 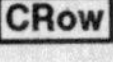

are given in the CODE-NURSERY Index.

Details of nurseries with number Codes in circles (20) are given in the ADDITIONAL NURSERY Index.

Maps prepared by à la carte

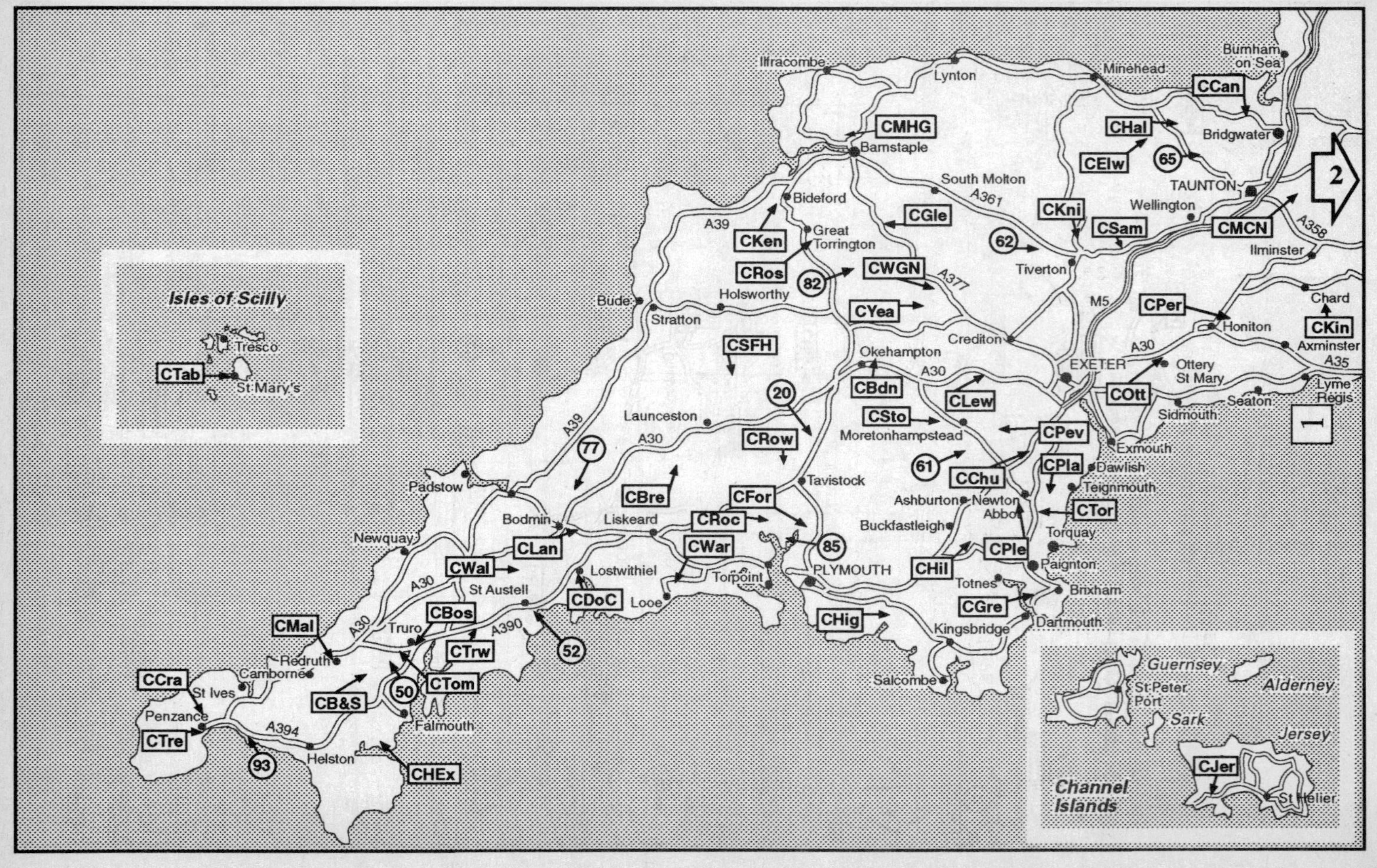

Isles of Scilly
Tresco
St Mary's
CTab
Ilfracombe
Lynton
Minehead
Burnham on Sea
CCan
CMHG
CHal
Bridgwater
Barnstaple
CElw
65
South Molton
A361
TAUNTON
2
Bideford
CGle
CKni
Wellington
A39
Great Torrington
CSam
CMCN
A358
CKen
62
Ilminster
CRos
CWGN
A377
Tiverton
82
Holsworthy
Bude
M5
CPer
Chard
Stratton
CYea
Honiton
CKin
CSFH
Crediton
A30
Axminster
Okehampton
EXETER
Ottery St Mary
A35
A30
CBdn
CLew
COtt
Lyme Regis
20
Seaton
Launceston
CSto
Sidmouth
1
A39
77
A30
CRow
Moretonhampstead
CPev
Exmouth
CPla
Dawlish
61
CChu
Padstow
Tavistock
Teignmouth
CBre
CFor
Ashburton
Newton Abbot
CTor
Bodmin
Liskeard
CRoc
Buckfastleigh
Torquay
Newquay
CLan
CWar
85
CPle
CWal
Lostwithiel
PLYMOUTH
CHil
Paignton
A30
Torpoint
Totnes
St Austell
Brixham
CDoC
Looe
CGre
CBos
Dartmouth
CMal
A30
Truro
A390
CHig
Kingsbridge
CTrw
52
Redruth
Guernsey
Camborne
CTom
St Peter Port
Alderney
CCra
Salcombe
St Ives
CB&S
50
Sark
Penzance
Falmouth
Jersey
A394
CTre
Helston
CJer
93
CHEx
St Helier
Channel Islands

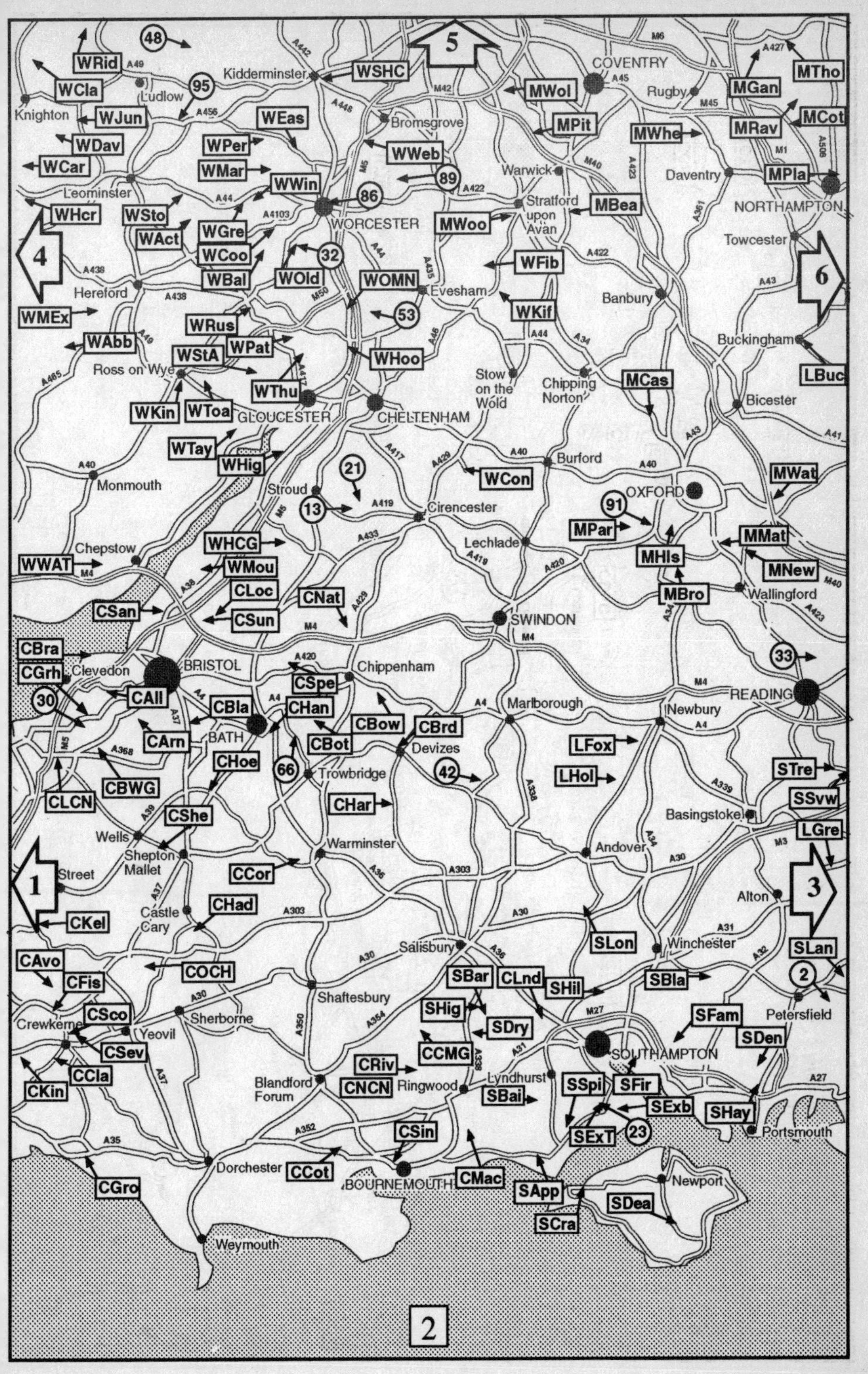

48
WRid
WCla
Knighton
Ludlow
95
WJun
WDav
WCar
Kidderminster
WSHC
5
COVENTRY
Rugby
MGan
MTho
MWol
MPit
MWhe
MRav
MCot
WEas
Bromsgrove
WPer
WWeb
WMar
89
Warwick
Daventry
MPla
WWin
86
Leominster
WHcr
WSto
WORCESTER
Stratford upon Avan
MBea
NORTHAMPTON
WMoo
WAct
WGre
WCoo
32
Towcester
4
WFib
WBal
WOld
WOMN
Evesham
6
Hereford
Banbury
WMEx
53
WKif
WRus
WAbb
WPat
WStA
WHoo
Buckingham
Ross on Wye
Stow on the Wold
Chipping Norton
MCas
LBuc
WThu
WKin
WToa
GLOUCESTER
CHELTENHAM
Bicester
WTay
WHig
21
Burford
MWat
Monmouth
WCon
Stroud
OXFORD
13
Cirencester
91
MPar
Chepstow
WHCG
Lechlade
MMat
WWAT
WMou
MHls
MNew
CLoc
CNat
MBro
Wallingford
CSan
CSun
SWINDON
CBra
33
CGrh
Clevedon
BRISTOL
Chippenham
CSpe
30
CAll
READING
CBla
CHan
Marlborough
Newbury
CArn
BATH
CBow
CBrd
CBot
Devizes
LFox
CHoe
66
Trowbridge
42
LHol
STre
CBWG
CLCN
CHar
SSvw
Basingstoke
CShe
Wells
Shepton Mallet
Warminster
Andover
LGre
1
Street
CCor
3
Castle Cary
CHad
Alton
CKel
SLon
Salisbury
Winchester
SLan
CAvo
COCH
2
CFis
SBar
CLnd
SHil
SBla
Shaftesbury
Petersfield
CSco
SHig
SFam
Crewkerne
Sherborne
Yeovil
SDry
CSev
SDen
CCMG
SOUTHAMPTON
CCla
CRiv
Lyndhurst
Blandford Forum
CNCN
Ringwood
SBai
SSpi
SFir
CKin
SExb
SHay
23
SExT
Portsmouth
CSin
Dorchester
CCot
BOURNEMOUTH
CMac
SApp
Newport
CGro
SDea
SCra
Weymouth
M6
A427
A45
M45
M1
A508
A49
A456
A442
A448
M42
M5
A44
A422
M40
A423
A361
A4103
A435
A46
A438
M50
A465
A417
A429
A40
A419
A433
A420
A34
A43
A41
M4
A38
A4
A37
A368
A39
A338
A339
A303
A36
A30
M3
A31
A32
A350
A354
A35
A352
M27
A27
2

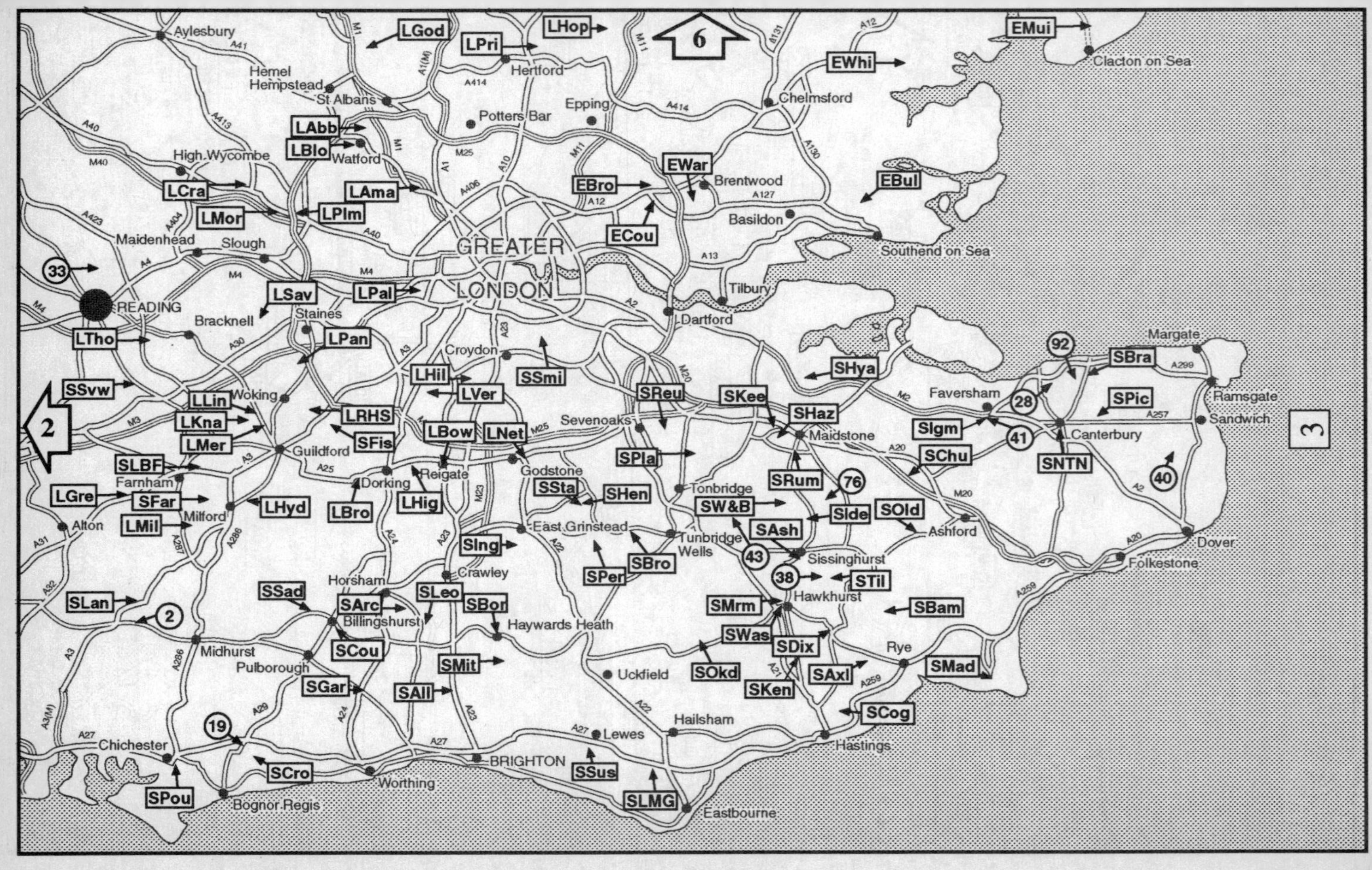

6
2
3
GREATER LONDON
Aylesbury
Hemel Hempstead
St Albans
Hertford
Potters Bar
Epping
Chelmsford
Clacton on Sea
High Wycombe
Watford
Brentwood
Basildon
Southend on Sea
Maidenhead
Slough
Tilbury
READING
Bracknell
Staines
Dartford
Woking
Croydon
Guildford
Sevenoaks
Maidstone
Faversham
Margate
Ramsgate
Sandwich
Canterbury
Farnham
Dorking
Reigate
Godstone
Tonbridge
Alton
Milford
East Grinstead
Tunbridge Wells
Ashford
Dover
Folkestone
Sissinghurst
Crawley
Horsham
Hawkhurst
Billingshurst
Haywards Heath
Midhurst
Pulborough
Rye
Uckfield
Hailsham
Lewes
Hastings
Chichester
BRIGHTON
Worthing
Bognor Regis
Eastbourne
LGod
LPri
LHop
EMui
EWhi
LAbb
LBlo
EWar
EBro
EBul
LCra
LAma
LMor
LPlm
ECou
33
LSav
LPal
LTho
LPan
SSmi
SHya
SBra
92
SSvw
LLin
LHil
LVer
SReu
SKee
SPic
LKna
LRHS
SHaz
28
LMer
SFis
LBow
LNet
SIgm
41
SLBF
SPla
SChu
SNTN
SRum
76
40
LGre
SFar
LHyd
LBro
LHig
SSta
SHen
SW&B
SIde
SOld
LMil
SAsh
SIng
SPer
SBro
43
38
STil
SLan
SSad
SArc
SLeo
SBor
SMrm
SBam
2
SWas
SDix
SCou
SMit
SMad
SOkd
SAxl
SGar
SAll
SKen
SCog
19
SCro
SSus
SPou
SLMG
M1
M4
M40
M25
M3
M23
M20
M2
M11
A1(M)
A1
A10
A12
A13
A127
A130
A131
A414
A41
A413
A40
A404
A423
A4
A406
A30
A3
A2
A20
A25
A23
A24
A22
A21
A259
A27
A29
A286
A287
A31
A32
A3(M)
A257
A299

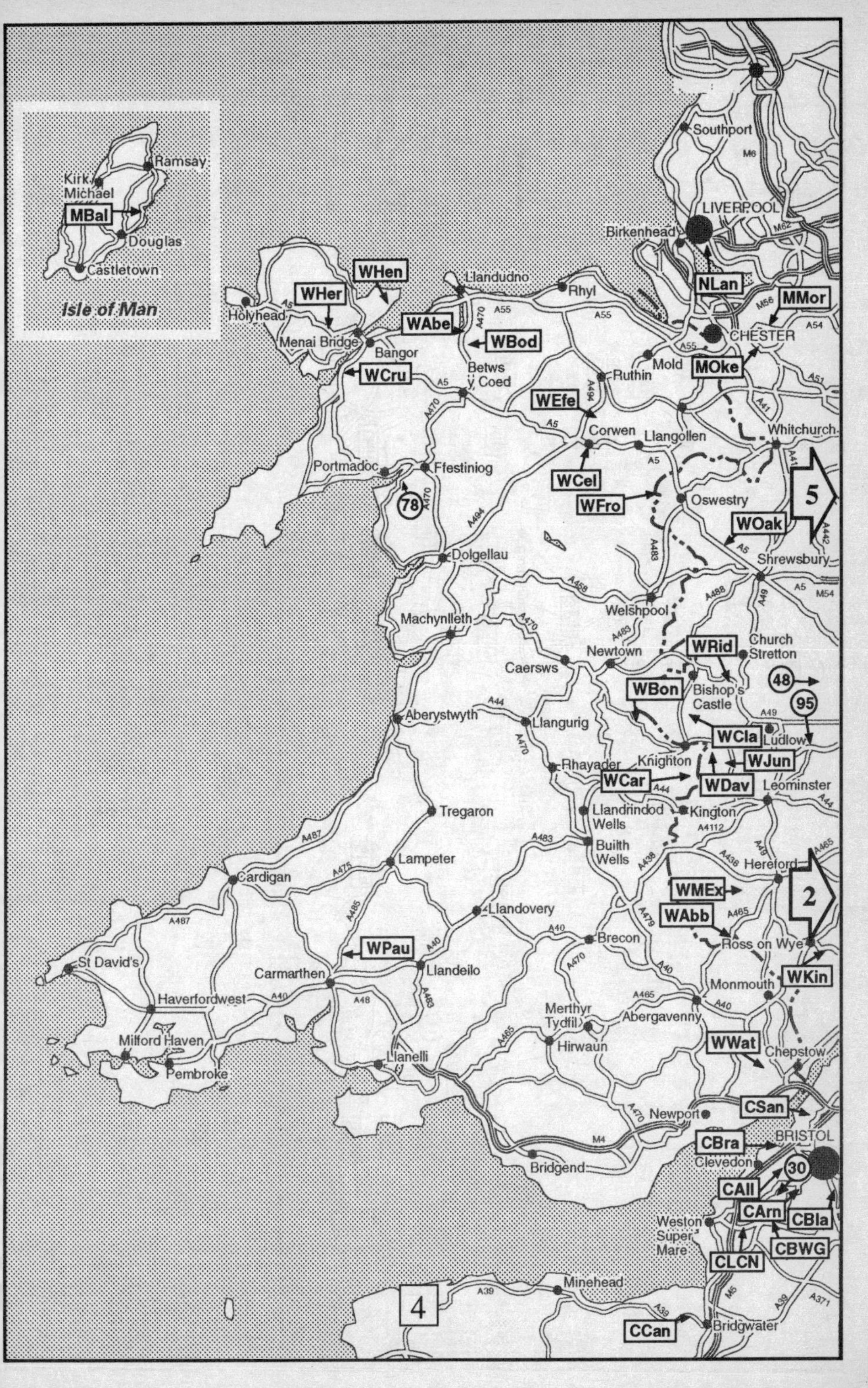

Ramsay
Kirk Michael
MBal
Douglas
Castletown
Isle of Man
Southport
LIVERPOOL
Birkenhead
NLan
MMor
CHESTER
MOke
Mold
Ruthin
Rhyl
Llandudno
WHen
WHer
Holyhead
Menai Bridge
Bangor
WAbe
WBod
WCru
Betws y Coed
WEfe
Corwen
Llangollen
Whitchurch
WCel
WFro
Oswestry
WOak
Shrewsbury
5
Portmadoc
Ffestiniog
78
Dolgellau
Welshpool
Machynlleth
Newtown
Caersws
WRid
Church Stretton
48
95
WBon
Bishop's Castle
Aberystwyth
Llangurig
WCla
Ludlow
Rhayader
Knighton
WJun
WCar
WDav
Leominster
Llandrindod Wells
Kington
Tregaron
Builth Wells
Lampeter
Hereford
Cardigan
WMEx
2
WAbb
Llandovery
Brecon
Ross on Wye
WPau
St David's
Carmarthen
Llandeilo
Monmouth
WKin
Haverfordwest
Merthyr Tydfil
Abergavenny
Hirwaun
WWat
Milford Haven
Chepstow
Pembroke
Llanelli
Newport
CSan
CBra
BRISTOL
Clevedon
30
Bridgend
CAll
CArn
CBla
Weston Super Mare
CBWG
CLCN
Minehead
4
CCan
Bridgwater

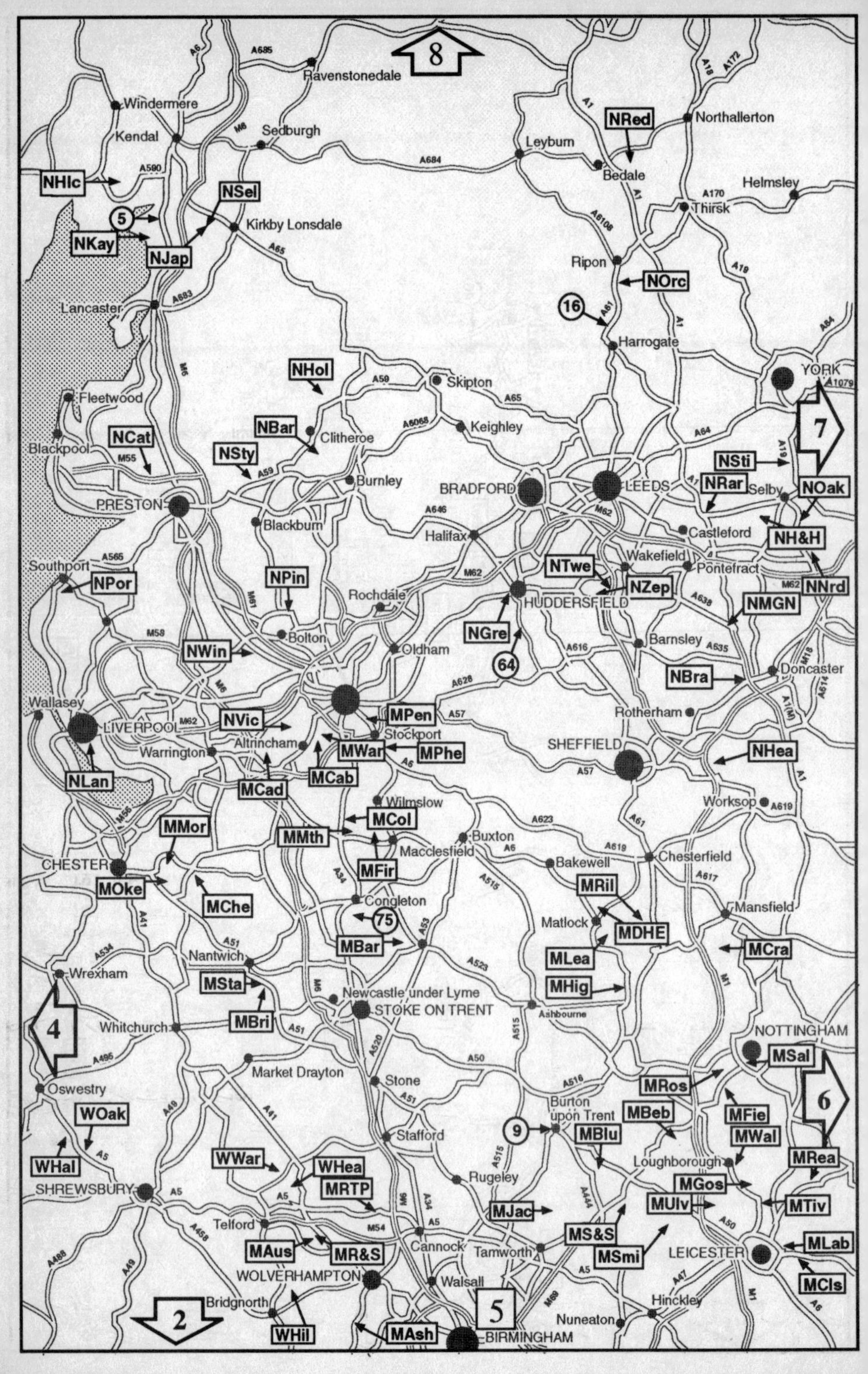

8
Ravenstonedale
Windermere
Kendal
Sedburgh
Leyburn
Northallerton
NRed
Bedale
Helmsley
Thirsk
NHlc
NSel
5
NKay
NJap
Kirkby Lonsdale
Ripon
NOrc
16
Lancaster
Harrogate
YORK
NHol
Skipton
Fleetwood
Keighley
7
NBar
Clitheroe
Blackpool
NCat
NSty
NSti
Burnley
BRADFORD
LEEDS
NRar
Selby
NOak
PRESTON
Blackburn
Halifax
Castleford
NH&H
Southport
NPor
NPin
Wakefield
Pontefract
NTwe
NZep
NNrd
Rochdale
HUDDERSFIELD
NMGN
Bolton
NGre
Barnsley
NWin
Oldham
64
Doncaster
NBra
Wallasey
MPen
Rotherham
LIVERPOOL
NVic
Stockport
Warrington
Altrincham
MWar
MPhe
SHEFFIELD
NHea
NLan
MCab
MCad
Wilmslow
Worksop
MCol
MMor
MMth
Buxton
Macclesfield
Bakewell
Chesterfield
CHESTER
MFir
MRil
MOke
MChe
Congleton
Matlock
Mansfield
75
MDHE
MBar
MCra
Nantwich
MLea
Wrexham
MSta
MHig
Newcastle under Lyme
4
STOKE ON TRENT
Whitchurch
MBri
Ashbourne
NOTTINGHAM
MSal
Market Drayton
Stone
MRos
Oswestry
6
Burton upon Trent
MBeb
MFie
WOak
MWal
9
Stafford
MBlu
WHal
WWar
WHea
Loughborough
MRea
SHREWSBURY
MRTP
Rugeley
MGos
MJac
MUlv
MTiv
Telford
MS&S
MAus
MR&S
Cannock
Tamworth
LEICESTER
MLab
MSmi
WOLVERHAMPTON
Walsall
MCls
Bridgnorth
5
Hinckley
2
Nuneaton
WHil
MAsh
BIRMINGHAM

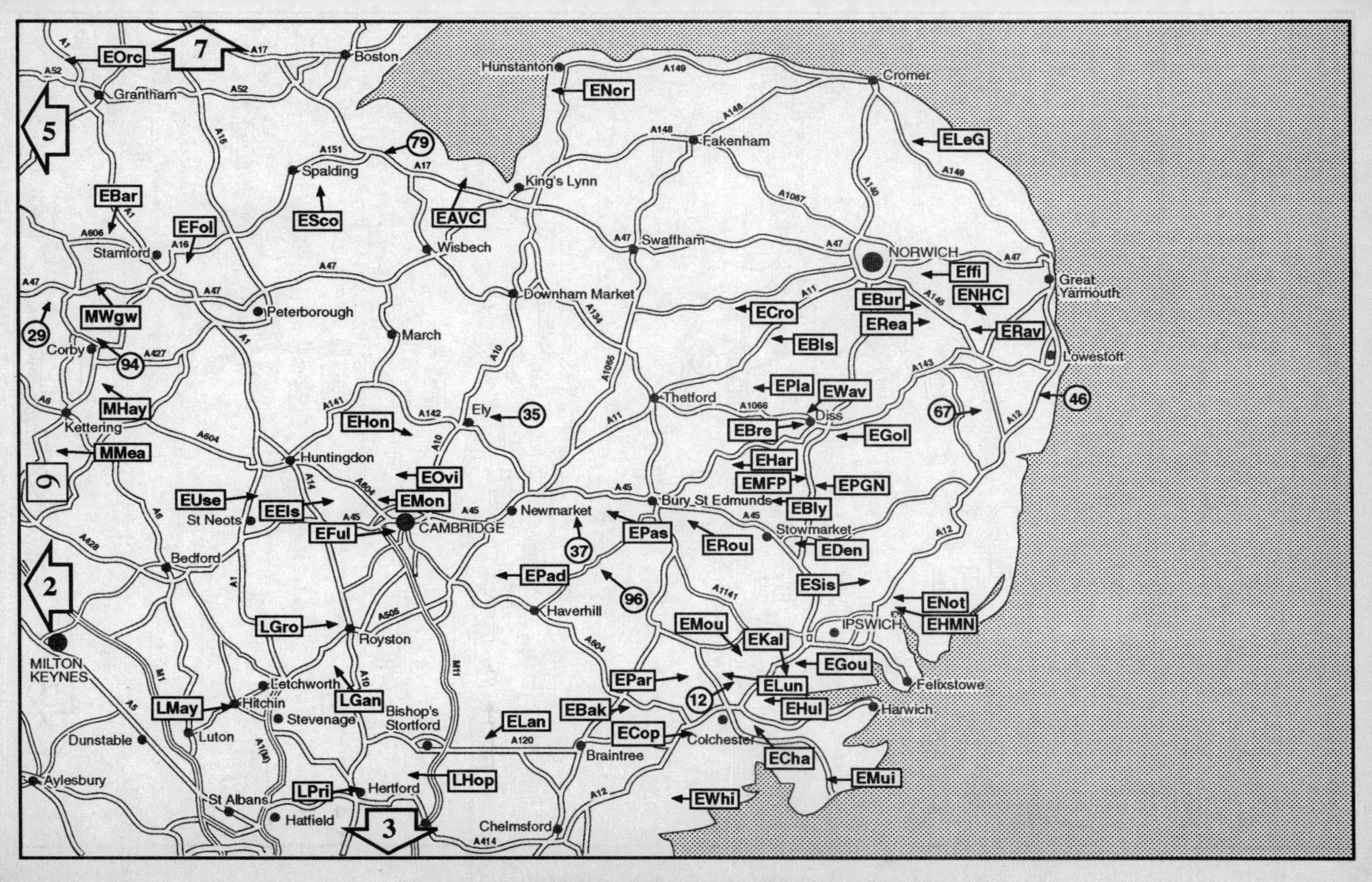

EOrc
7
Boston
Hunstanton
ENor
Cromer
Grantham
5
79
Fakenham
ELeG
Spalding
King's Lynn
EBar
ESco
EAVC
EFol
Wisbech
Swaffham
Stamford
NORWICH
Effi
Great Yarmouth
Downham Market
ENHC
EBur
MWgw
Peterborough
ECro
ERea
ERav
29
March
EBls
Corby
94
Lowestoft
EPla
EWav
Thetford
46
MHay
67
Ely
35
Diss
Kettering
EHon
EBre
EGol
MMea
Huntingdon
EHar
EOvi
EMFP
EPGN
6
EUse
EMon
Bury St Edmunds
EEls
EBly
St Neots
Newmarket
CAMBRIDGE
EFul
EPas
Stowmarket
ERou
EDen
37
Bedford
EPad
2
96
ESis
ENot
Haverhill
IPSWICH
EHMN
LGro
EMou
MILTON KEYNES
Royston
EKal
EGou
Letchworth
EPar
ELun
Felixstowe
LMay
Hitchin
LGan
12
EHul
Harwich
Stevenage
Bishop's Stortford
EBak
ELan
Dunstable
Luton
ECop
Colchester
Braintree
ECha
Aylesbury
LHop
EMui
LPri
Hertford
EWhi
St Albans
Hatfield
3
Chelmsford
A1
A17
A52
A15
A151
A149
A148
A1067
A140
A606
A16
A47
A146
A11
A134
A427
A6
A143
A1065
A10
A141
A142
A1066
A12
A604
A14
A45
A428
A505
A1141
M1
M11
A5
A1(M)
A120
A414

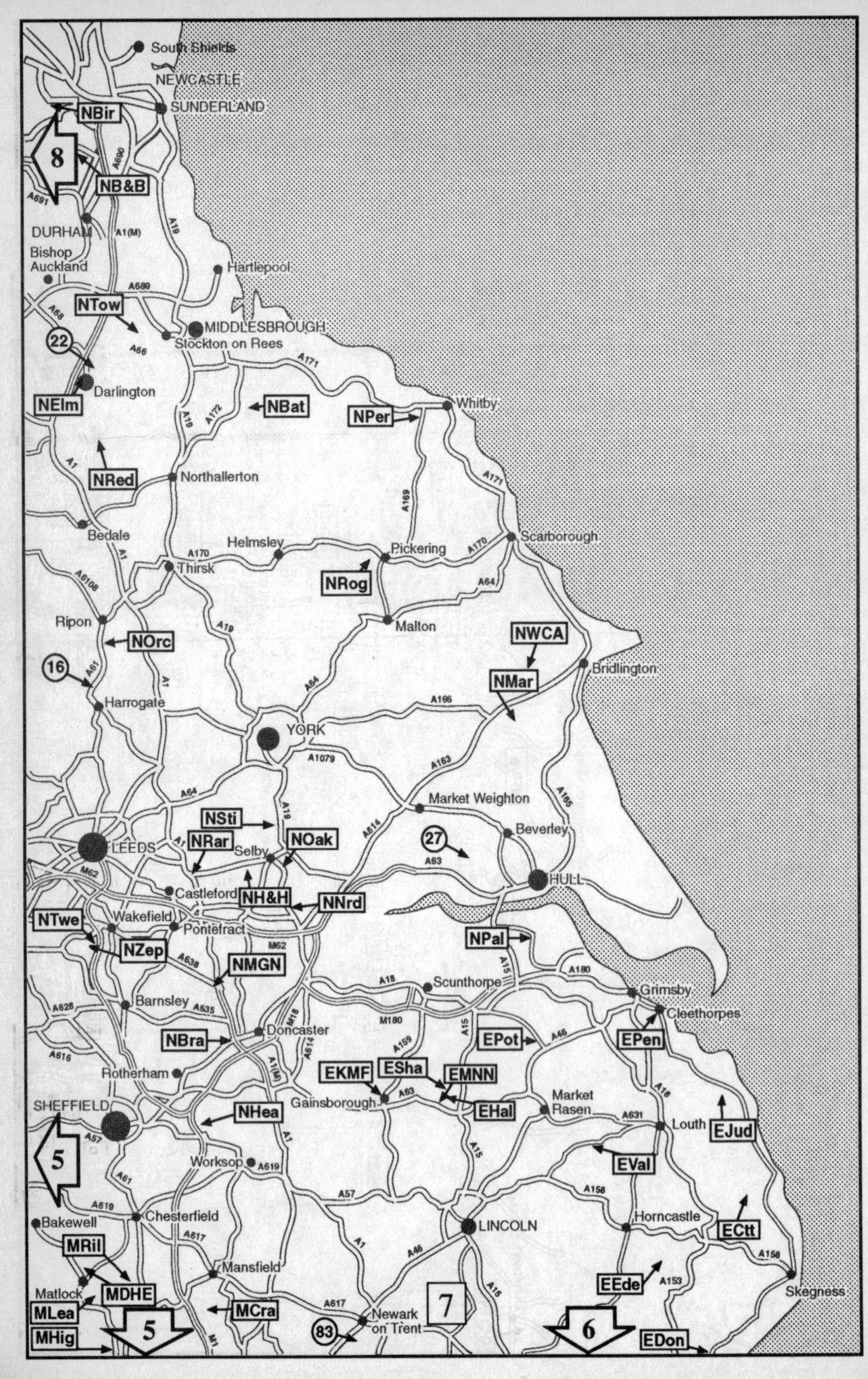

South Shields
NEWCASTLE
SUNDERLAND
NBir
8
NB&B
DURHAM
Bishop Auckland
Hartlepool
NTow
22
MIDDLESBROUGH
Stockton on Rees
Darlington
NElm
NBat
NPer
Whitby
NRed
Northallerton
Bedale
Helmsley
Pickering
Scarborough
Thirsk
NRog
Ripon
NOrc
Malton
NWCA
16
Harrogate
NMar
Bridlington
YORK
Market Weighton
NSti
LEEDS
NRar
Selby
NOak
27
Beverley
HULL
Castleford
NH&H
NNrd
NTwe
Wakefield
Pontefract
NZep
NPal
NMGN
Scunthorpe
Grimsby
Barnsley
Cleethorpes
NBra
Doncaster
EPot
EPen
EKMF
ESha
EMNN
Rotherham
Gainsborough
EHal
Market Rasen
SHEFFIELD
NHea
Louth
EJud
5
Worksop
EVal
Chesterfield
Bakewell
LINCOLN
Horncastle
ECtt
MRil
Mansfield
EEde
Matlock
MDHE
Skegness
MLea
MCra
7
MHig
5
83
Newark on Trent
6
EDon

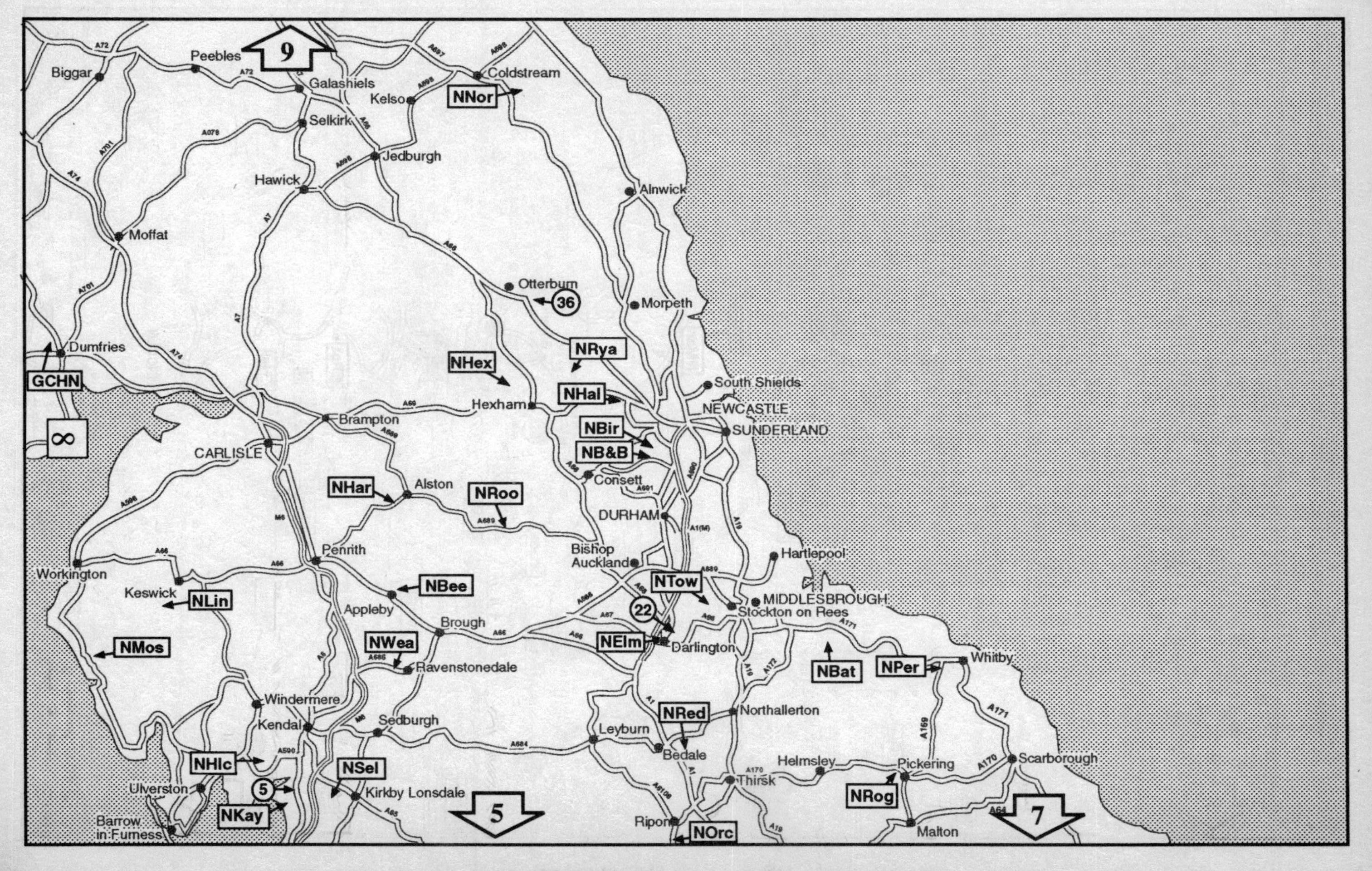

9
Peebles
Biggar
Galashiels
Kelso
Coldstream
NNor
Selkirk
Jedburgh
Hawick
Alnwick
Moffat
Otterburn
36
Morpeth
Dumfries
GCHN
8
NRya
NHex
South Shields
NHal
Hexham
NEWCASTLE
Brampton
SUNDERLAND
NBir
NB&B
CARLISLE
Consett
NHar
Alston
NRoo
DURHAM
Penrith
Bishop Auckland
Hartlepool
Workington
NTow
Keswick
NLin
NBee
MIDDLESBROUGH
Stockton on Rees
Appleby
22
Brough
NMos
NWea
NElm
Darlington
Ravenstonedale
NBat
NPer
Whitby
Windermere
Northallerton
Kendal
Sedburgh
NRed
Leyburn
Bedale
NHlc
Helmsley
Pickering
Scarborough
NSel
Thirsk
Ulverston
5
Kirkby Lonsdale
NRog
NKay
5
Barrow in Furness
Ripon
NOrc
Malton
7

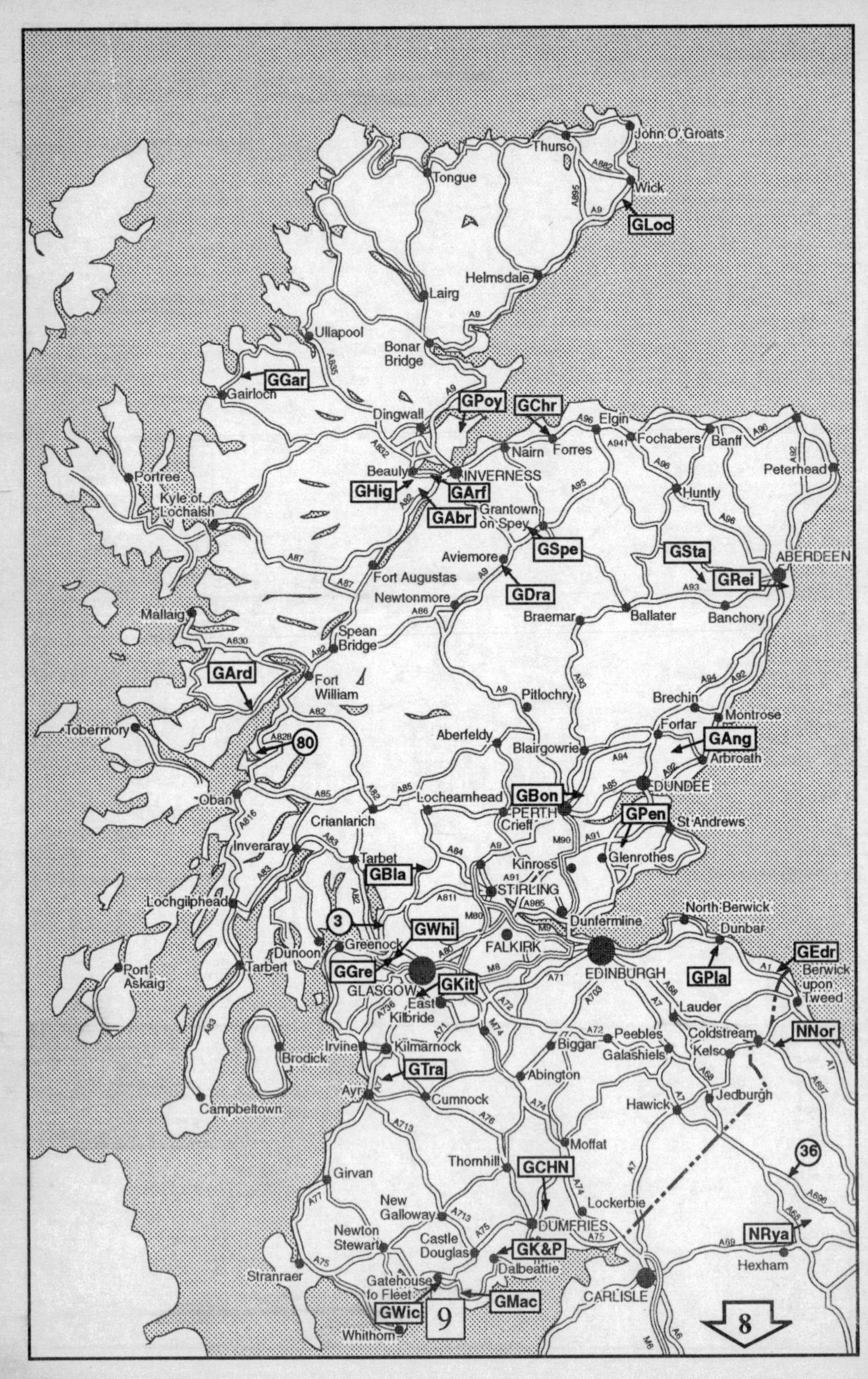

John O' Groats
Thurso
Tongue
A882
A895
Wick
A9
GLoc
Helmsdale
Lairg
A9
Ullapool
Bonar Bridge
A835
GGar
Gairloch
A9
GPoy
GChr
Dingwall
A96
Elgin
Fochabers
Banff
A96
A92
A941
A832
Nairn
Forres
A96
Peterhead
Beauly
INVERNESS
Portree
GHig
GArf
Huntly
Kyle of Lochalsh
A82
GAbr
Grantown on Spey
A95
A96
GSpe
GSta
A87
Aviemore
ABERDEEN
Fort Augustas
A9
GRei
A87
GDra
A93
Newtonmore
A86
Braemar
Ballater
Banchory
Mallaig
Spean Bridge
A830
A82
A93
A94
A92
GArd
Fort William
A9
Pitlochry
Brechin
A82
Montrose
Tobermory
Forfar
Aberfeldy
GAng
A828
80
Blairgowrie
A94
Arbroath
A92
A85
DUNDEE
Oban
A85
A82
A85
Locheamhead
GBon
PERTH
GPen
A816
Crianlarich
Crieff
St Andrews
A83
M90
A91
Inveraray
A9
Tarbet
A84
Kinross
Glenrothes
GBla
A83
A91
STIRLING
A82
A985
Lochgilphead
A811
M80
Dunfermline
North Berwick
M9
3
GWhi
Dunbar
Dunoon
Greenock
FALKIRK
GEdr
Port Askaig
Tarbert
A80
GGre
M8
EDINBURGH
GPla
A1
Berwick upon Tweed
GKit
A71
GLASGOW
East Kilbride
A72
A703
A68
A7
Lauder
A736
A71
M74
A72
Peebles
Coldstream
NNor
A83
Irvine
Kilmarnock
Biggar
Galashiels
Kelso
Brodick
A1
GTra
Abington
A68
A697
A77
Ayr
Cumnock
A7
Jedburgh
A74
Hawick
Campbeltown
A76
A713
Moffat
36
A7
Girvan
Thornhill
GCHN
A74
A77
New Galloway
Lockerbie
A696
A713
A68
A75
DUMFRIES
Newton Stewart
Castle Douglas
A75
NRya
GK&P
A69
A75
Hexham
Stranraer
Dalbeattie
Gatehouse to Fleet
CARLISLE
GMac
GWic
9
8
Whithorn
M6
A6

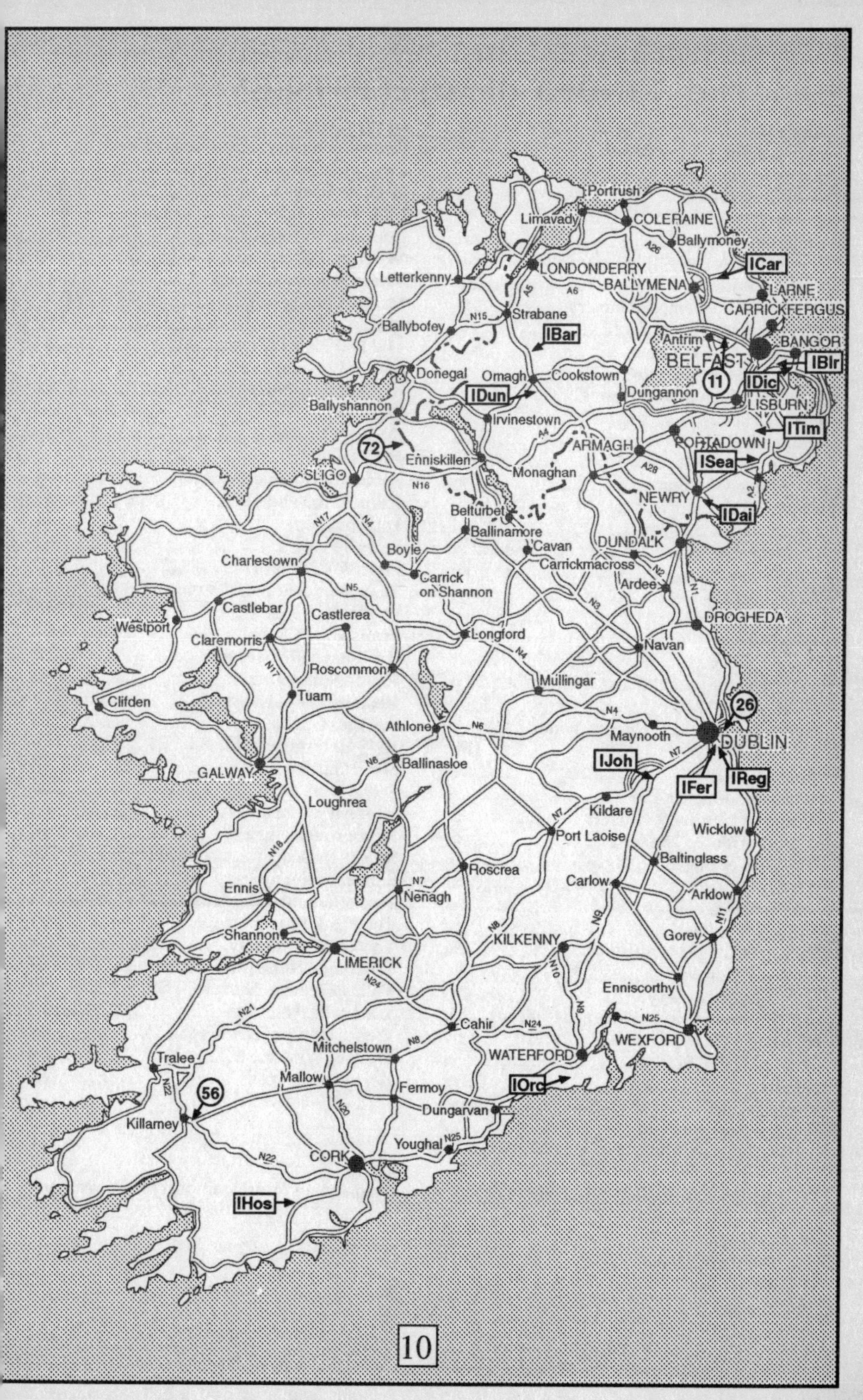
Portrush
COLERAINE
Limavady
Ballymoney
A26
ICar
LONDONDERRY
BALLYMENA
LARNE
A6
Letterkenny
N15
Strabane
CARRICKFERGUS
Ballybofey
IBar
Antrim
BANGOR
BELFAST
IBlr
Donegal
Omagh
Cookstown
11
IDic
IDun
Dungannon
LISBURN
Ballyshannon
Irvinestown
ITim
A4
ARMAGH
PORTADOWN
72
Enniskillen
ISea
SLIGO
Monaghan
A28
N16
NEWRY
A2
Belturbet
IDai
N17
N4
Ballinamore
Cavan
DUNDALK
Boyle
Charlestown
Carrickmacross
Carrick on Shannon
N2
N5
Ardee
N1
Castlebar
N3
DROGHEDA
Castlerea
Westport
Claremorris
Longford
Navan
N4
N17
Roscommon
Mullingar
Clifden
Tuam
26
N4
Athlone
N6
Maynooth
DUBLIN
IJoh
N7
N6
Ballinasloe
GALWAY
IFer
IReg
Loughrea
Kildare
N7
Wicklow
Port Laoise
N18
Baltinglass
Roscrea
Carlow
N7
Arklow
Ennis
Nenagh
N9
N11
N8
Gorey
Shannon
KILKENNY
LIMERICK
N10
N24
Enniscorthy
N9
N21
N25
Cahir
N24
WEXFORD
Mitchelstown
N8
WATERFORD
Tralee
N22
Mallow
IOrc
Fermoy
56
N20
Dungarvan
Killarney
N25
Youghal
N22
CORK
IHos

INDEX OF ADVERTISERS

For further information concerning Display Advertisements in future editions, please write to:

Leslie Morris
c/o The Plant Finder
Lakeside
Whitbourne
Worcester WR6 5RD

CHURCHILLS
GARDEN NURSERY

A nursery with an extensive and interesting range of gardenworthy trees, shrubs, climbers and herbaceous plants, many of which are unusual or hard to find.

SEE CODE C Chu

SCOTTS NURSERIES

Merriott, Somerset
Tel. 0460 72306
Fax. 77433

We are specialist growers of an extensive range of shrubs, perennials, climbers, trees and conifers.

We deliver virtually nationwide and send plants mail order.

Send for our unique and comprehensive catalogue £1.50 post free

---

CONTAINER GROWN SHRUBS & ALPINES

NO
MAIL ORDER

Brookend,
Pendock,
Glos. GL19 3PL

CHRIS PATTISON
nurseryman

RARE & CHOICE VARIETIES

Three 1st class stamps for list

Tel. (0531) 650480

JUNGLE FRESH

BAMBOOS

By mail order
Information pack £1.00 (refundable against order)
Plough Farm, Brisbane,
Herefordshire HR6 9UW
Tel: 056 886 332

JUNGLE *Giants*

Hannays of Bath

PLANTS FOR THE PLANTSMAN

We provide large size plants in a wide range of uncommon species. The Nursery in Bath (access from Sydney Mews) is on the A4 ring road between Sydney Place and the bottom of Bathwick Hill.

DESCRIPTIVE LIST £1.40
including postage

Open: Wed, Fri, Sat, Sun 10-5 and Bank Holiday Monday
or by appointment

SYDNEY WHARF NURSERY

BATHWICK, BATH BA2 4ES
TEL: (0225) 462230

ORCHARD NURSERIES

A cottage garden nursery specialising in unusual herbaceous plants

OPEN DAILY
10.00 – 18.00
MARCH – NOVEMBER

Descriptive Catalogue
3 x 1st Class Stamps

Foston, Nr. Grantham,
Lincs NG32 2LE

Tel: 0400 81354

ASHWOOD

WATER – BREAK – IT'S – NECK

See this lovely natural waterfall in the heart of the Radnor Forest amidst breathtaking scenery just a short distance from The Fforest Inn.

The Fforest Inn is a 16th Century Country Inn, set in the heart of the Radnor Forest amongst the unspoilt scenery of Mid Wales.

Guests at The Fforest Inn can enjoy comfortable rooms with showers en suite and colour TV.

Our restaurant offers good home-cooked food using local produce when possible.

Our cosy bar with log fire offers bar meals and snacks at all times.

Dogs welcome

Brochure available from

The Fforest Inn,
Llanfihangel-Nant-Melan,
New Radnor,
Powys LD8 2TN
Tel. (0544) 21246

MILLAIS NURSERIES
RHODODENDRONS
AZALEAS

VISIT THE SPECIALISTS WITH THE UNIQUE COLLECTION OF RARE SPECIES AND NEW HYBRIDS. EXCELLENT QUALITY AND VALUE

DESCRIPTIVE CATALOGUE LISTING 500 VARIETIES £1.00

TUESDAY - SATURDAY
10.00 am - 1.00 pm. 2.00 pm - 5.00 pm.
Crosswater Lane, Churt,
Farnham, Surrey, GU10 2JN
Telephone: Frensham (025 125) 2698

PATRICIA DALE R.M.S., F.S.B.A.
ORIGINAL BOTANICAL WATERCOLOUR DRAWINGS
Paintings on view and for sale. Associated stationery goods also available. Visitors to studio and garden welcome.
Please ring to check I am in.
COURT LODGE, WEST MEON, PETERSFIELD, HANTS
West Meon (073 086) 473

FRUIT FOR THE CONNOISSEUR
In wide variety: Trained tree specialists, also ornamental trees and old roses. Free catalogue (and Nursery location) from
FAMILY TREES
PO Box 3, Botley, Hampshire SO3 2EA
Tel. (0489) 895674

DAVID AUSTIN ROSES
(22) Bowling Green Lane, Albrighton
Wolverhampton WV7 3HB
Plant Centre specialising in Roses, Herbaceous Perennials. List available. Mail Order Handbooks, Roses (Free). Peonies, Irises, Daylilies (Free).
Telephone: 0902 373931

HOECROFT PLANTS
400 VARIEGATED and COLOURED-LEAVED plants and 125 ORNAMENTAL GRASSES – by far the largest selection available in this country.
Catalogue (with colour photos) £1.10.
Helpful booklets with ideas and planting plans: "Colour Gardening with Foliage" and "Colour Gardening with Grasses", 85p each.
See 'CHoe' classification for details.

Hunters Oak Nursery
Specialist in Alpines, Herbs and Perennials

Open April to October weekdays 11am to 6pm except Wednesday. Weekends 10am to 6pm

Bere Alston, Yelverton, Devon. Tel. 0822 840289

NOTES

NOTES

NOTES

NOTES

NOTES

NOTES

NOTES

NOTES